THE KITTREDGE-PLAYERS EDITION
of the Complete Works of

WILLIAM SHAKESPEARE

Edited by

George Lyman Kittredge
Gurney Professor of English Literature
in Harvard University

Illustrated with photographs of actual productions of the Old Vic Company in London, the Memorial Theatre at Stratford-upon-Avon, and other theatres throughout England

Grolier
INCORPORATED
NEW YORK

Individual plays from this collection are available
from Ginn and Company, Boston, U.S.A.

PRINTED IN THE UNITED STATES OF AMERICA

PREFACE

THE present edition of SHAKESPEARE'S COMPLETE WORKS includes all the plays and poems that are ascribed to him, in whole or in part, on satisfactory evidence.

The text has been determined by a fresh collation of the original editions. To the First Folio (1623), even in those cases in which some Quarto is more authoritative, such respect is due as attaches to a volume sponsored by Shakespeare's literary executors. So-called 'bad Quartos' often preserve correct readings. The later Folios, especially the Second (1632), though they have no claim to be authoritative, serve, at least, to correct a considerable number of old misprints. Most of these corrections, to be sure, are not beyond the powers of a modern critic, but it is comforting, at times, to know how a corrupt passage looked to a proofreader of the early seventeenth century. For *Pericles* and *The Two Noble Kinsmen* we must depend on a Quarto text—bad in the first case, excellent in the second.

In accepting the conjectural emendations of modern scholars caution is manifestly necessary. Yet conservatism may be carried too far. One should not canonize the heedless type-setters of the Elizabethan printing house. That an old reading 'makes sense' of a sort is not in and for itself a sufficient guaranty. Thus Upton's 'Adam Cupid' (*Romeo and Juliet*, ii, 1, 13) must be right, though 'Abraham' is not absolutely unintelligible; Farmer's 'holy-ales' (*Pericles*, i, Gower, 6) is better than 'holy days'; Theobald's 'a babbled' (*Henry V*, ii, 3, 17) for 'a table' is a stroke of genius. An editor should never forget Bacon's inspired epigram: 'A froward retention of custom is as turbulent a thing as an innovation.'

Care has been taken to indicate elisions and contractions in accordance with what seems to have been Shakespeare's intent in each case. To substitute *the* for the old *th'*, *to* for *t'*, *on* or *of* for *o'*, *in* for *i'*, and so forth, frequently gives a wrong impression of the author's metrical scheme. This is especially noteworthy, for example, in *Coriolanus*, where the verses abound in such clipped forms. In the case of *-ed*, the apostrophe is used when elision is intended; full spelling indicates full pronunciation. In such words as *followed*, *borrowed*, *withered*, and the like, the full spelling is retained when the old texts justify it. Uniformity is not to be expected. The metrical problems involved cannot be settled beyond question; but there is no reason why *followed* (in full) should not satisfy the metre whenever such a form as *follower* would not violate it. In prose passages a common practice of editors has been to ignore many of the distinctions between full and clipped forms which the Quartos and Folios make. To maintain the euphony of the prose, this edition preserves such indications of the sort as the texts of Shakespeare's time supply.

Careful attention has been paid to the stage directions. No liberties are taken with the old texts in this regard. Additions are often imperative, but in such cases whatever is added is enclosed within square brackets. Thus the reader is in no danger of confusing the opinions of modern editors with the testimony of Shakespeare's own time. The same policy has been adopted in dividing the plays into Acts and Scenes and in designating the place of action. In most cases, the lists of *Dramatis Personæ* are bracketed for the same reason. When (as in *The Tempest*) the Folio prints *Names of the Actors*, these have been treated in the same way as the stage directions.

In a text that adopts modern spelling, logical procedure calls for modern punctuation. Hence the present edition has been repunctuated in strict accordance with the rules that Shakespeare would presumably observe if he were writing to-day. Theorists have dallied with the idea that what is called 'dramatic punctuation' may be discovered in the old texts; but this theory has had its day.

The Introductions which preface each play undertake to give, in brief, the pertinent facts. They discuss the basis of the text, the date of composition, the source of the plot, the dramatic method, and such other significant matters as space permits.

The Glossary is unusually full. In many cases where the usage is peculiar, or where there has been much discussion about the exact meaning, references are given to the place where the word or phrase occurs in the text.

The numbering of lines has been made to accord so far as possible with that commonly used in citing the plays. This method is preferred to a new counting in order to facilitate reference to such standard works as Bartlett's *Concordance* and Schmidt's *Shakespeare-Lexicon*.

G. L. K.

CAMBRIDGE, JULY 21, 1936

contents

plays

poems

publisher's preface

A popular pastime of some years ago, known as "Desert Island," was the compilation of lists of indispensable books which would constitute the sole reading of a castaway. Needless to say, the Bible and the works of Shakespeare were initial items on all such lists. They are regarded as the noblest of our cultural legacies, the *sine qua non* of the "well-stored mind."

Unfortunately, the standard editions of Shakespeare—the musty tomes of "the complete works" which gather dust on the family bookshelf—while they contain a fund of matchless poetry, cannot convey any impression of the color and atmosphere of the plays as Shakespeare intended them to be produced. And the hypothetical castaway, like the average reader, would receive from the plain text no more than a faint notion of what the plays are like when effectively staged.

The Kittredge-Players edition is designed to supply—as well as anything less than the actual productions can hope to—those elements which are consistently lacking in the usual editions of the plays. It supplements the best available modern text with over seven hundred photographs of the plays and players, illustrating the productions of the world's finest Shakespearean repertory theaters.

The text of this edition, the result of a lifetime of Shakespeare study by the late George Lyman Kittredge, Gurney Professor of English Literature at Harvard University, presents the plays in their most readable form, with modern spelling and punctuation.

Introductions to the individual plays provide the essential literary data and historical background and concisely discuss the sources of the play and its relation to other works of the dramatist. A compendious glossary explains some five thousand archaic and unusual terms used in the plays.

The illustrations are photographs of the most magnificently staged productions in the history of the Shakespearean theater, and include hundreds of scenes from gala performances of the Old Vic Company of London and the Memorial Theatre at Stratford-upon-Avon, world famous for their distinguished casts and the originality and richness of settings and costumes. Introducing the folio of photographs that accompanies each play are portrait studies of the principals, the most noted contemporary Shakespeareans pictured in the roles in which they have been most successful.

Mr. Michael Benthall, director of the Old Vic Theatre, has contributed an informative discussion on the problems of the actor and director in the staging of the plays of Shakespeare; and a biographical essay by Edwin E. Willoughby, chief bibliographer of the Folger Shakespeare Library, affords a view of Shakespeare and his works in relation to the political and cultural developments of the Elizabethan age.

The publisher gratefully acknowledges the co-operation of the directors of the Old Vic Theatre and the Memorial Theatre and the brilliant contribution of the photographers whose work illustrates this edition. Special thanks are also due to Miss Anne Bolton for her assistance in collecting and titling the photographs.

Chicago, 1958 LEONARD S. DAVIDOW

the living shakespeare

One of the really interesting phenomena in the theater of our time is that actors and managements everywhere are rediscovering Shakespeare as a living force. That scholars have never forgotten him is beside the point: poets and pedants can exhume and honor his dry bones, but it takes actors to breathe life into them. Tourists may regard Stratford as the shrine and gape at a few relics, but what really matters is the performances in the Memorial Theatre. It may well be that the performances in the giant marquee at Stratford, Ontario, or in the pinewood reconstruction of the Globe Theatre at Stratford, Connecticut, will in the long run matter just as much. Enterprise on that scale can scarcely be dismissed as one more fashionable trend in the theater; nor can the unfailing appearance of Shakespeare's name on the program of every Drama Festival which dares to style itself "international."

We don't have to dig deep to find out why the larger public today recognizes the performance of Shakespeare's plays as a prime theatrical attraction. The first reason is simply that higher standards of performance and of presentation have revealed the sheer entertainment value of the plays when they are properly done. The second reason is the reappearance of the less familiar plays, enabling audiences to reassess their worth by more reliable standards of comparison. We used to be told the difference between the good and the bad plays in the canon; later it became the difference between the best and the next best. Nowadays we are taught to distinguish between what is good and what is better. The public is becoming familiar with a larger part of Shakespeare; and though the public rarely knows what it likes, it usually likes what it knows.

To rebut any charge of oversimplification there is the curious parallel of Beethoven, whose music has gained enormously in popular favor during the last quarter of a century. Toscanini had demonstrated—simply by playing the music as it was written instead of "interpreting" it—that Beethoven was not meant to be revered so much as enjoyed. New standards of performance were set and Beethoven found an even larger audience than Tchaikovsky because so much more of Beethoven was found to be worth a permanent place in the concert repertory. It is vitally important to try to see a creative artist as a whole.

It was a grasp of this truth, more than the advent of the new Elizabethan Age, which inspired the London Old Vic to plan the production during five years of all the Shakespeare plays in the First Folio. The need was felt to provide the ordinary theater-goer with a more direct approach to Shakespeare, and such a plan, being the kind of long-term project which the "commercial" theater could hardly contemplate, seemed the right policy for a theater receiving part of its revenue from public funds. A keen schoolboy might thus see all the plays before graduation. This might not make it any easier for him to negotiate his paper in English Literature, but he would come to regard a visit to a performance of Shakespeare as an exciting theatrical experience instead of another excuse for getting out of algebra.

Clearly there is a new generation of audiences avid for Shakespeare. Can the demand be met by the new generation of actors?

Modern audiences will no longer tolerate Shakespeare played by actors with no classical training. Drawing room comedy is no preparation for an actor in the classics; nor is any kind of technique involving the use of a microphone or of any other meretricious aid. The young actor must be prepared to serve a long and rigorous apprenticeship before he can hope to mesmerize the informed public with his Hamlet. Yet there will always be plenty of intrepid young men ready to take up the challenge, perhaps because they so rarely see the size of the obstacles ahead. For although a would-be instrumentalist knows exactly what he must learn before he can qualify for membership in a great orchestra, paradoxically there is no accepted syllabus of teaching for acting in the classical drama, the art with the greatest of all English traditional associations. Whether the answer is bigger and better schools of drama or the opportunity to carry a spear in a classical company as a means of contact with experienced actors, the fact remains that there are no short cuts to playing or directing Shakespeare. An actor relying on an imposing profile and a talent for verse-speaking will soon be put in his place by an audience content with nothing less than a vibrant personality and a capacity for verse-*acting;* a director preoccupied with handsomely mounted production and adroit choreography will quickly be decried by a public insisting on being given the sense of the play and demanding a splendid vocal line to communicate it.

Probably a judicious mixture of academic training and practical experience is the right solution for the aspiring classical actor, but it takes a great deal to deter the young artist with the instinct and the will to succeed, and if he has talent plus a magnetic personality, nothing can prevent the public from making him a star. A young artist of this kind learns automatically that an enormously wide variety of Shakespearean roles can be rewarding in terms of themselves. With Shakespeare, as much as any playwright, it is the part which makes the actor; and for a good actor there is no such thing as a small part. Attention to the somewhat derogatory term, "star-quality," is important, because it cannot be denied that such a quality contributes just as much to the popularity of Shakespeare as the teamwork and sense of style which are prerequisites of any Shakespearean company. In fact, it is the business of managements to see that the professional careers of their actors are fully developed and that each artist is given the best possible presentation in terms of parts. Planning the order of the parts played has a lot to do with an artist's ultimate success, for when he reaches the major character parts, his admirers like to remember the romantic behind the whiskers. In any case, talent in the classical theater is not so plentiful that we can afford to let any of it wither away because of lack of proper attention and the right kind of encouragement.

This very edition of Shakespeare is in itself a form of encouragement. What distinguishes this edition from all others is that it is embellished with photographs of *living* artists. In that sense it also helps to keep Shakespeare alive. It shows, too, that the major Shakespearean roles can still be really well played by quite young artists.

One much cherished illusion is that some Shakespeare roles are unplayable. What we really mean is that we don't happen to have seen an entirely satisfactory performance of this or that part; the fact that different people cite different parts effectively disposes of that particular myth. In this context, too, it is worth remembering that the female parts most often called "unactable"—*Cleopatra*, *Lady Macbeth* and *Juliet*—were originally played by boys well enough to convince an Elizabethan audience. We may be reasonably sure that the accomplishments of

Dame Sybil Thorndike, Dame Edith Evans, Miss Peggy Ashcroft, and Miss Katherine Cornell can stand comparison with anything produced by those talented boy players. It is the same with the perennial claim that the major roles are never played today so well as they used to be. The only evidence we have of the truth of this is the sentimental memories of aging critics. (Not all critics mellow with the years, and it may well be self-disillusionment that induces some of them to sneer at failure and resent success.) But in the not too distant future it may be possible to demolish this defeatist attitude. The phonograph record companies are already experimenting with full-length recordings of classical plays, and they may yet provide at least some aural evidence that the new generation of actors can measure up to the old. Film producers, too, will find a way of presenting classical acting companies in a manner which records their best achievements and communicates their individual style. Meanwhile, such distinguished artists as Sir Laurence Olivier and Sir John Gielgud have provided us with film performances of Shakespeare which will long be treasured. On the other hand, there is nothing so far to suggest that film versions of Shakespeare will ever be anything more than a celluloid substitute for the living theater. Historians have it that Shakespeare owed much to the contact between actors and audience in the theater of his day, and even contemporary methods of staging allow an audience to enjoy a sense of participation entirely absent in motion pictures. The vitality of a live performance springs from the slight insecurity which exists in a theater until contact between players and audience has been established. Everyone knows that performances of the same play by the same company vary with different audiences; what is sometimes overlooked is that the disparities between one theatrical performance and another can be just as entertaining as the similarities.

Photographs of contemporary actors in well-known classical roles, such as are to be found in this book, evoke memories not only of the part played but of the whole play. It is extraordinary how the memory of an individual performance can color one's recollected impressions of the whole, and remarkable that the first performance seen is usually the one which remains longest in the memory. In the case of the classical drama it is, therefore, all the more important that the first impressions should be the right ones, lest the interest of younger audiences is dissipated forever. One makeshift performance of a Shakespeare play by an inadequate touring company is enough to form a prejudice in a child's mind against Shakespeare as lasting as any initiated in a schoolroom; the notion that the greatest of Shakespeare's plays are indestructible and proof against demonstrably bad performance is pitifully inept and must be ruthlessly exposed wherever it is met. Where Shakespeare is concerned, say the theorists, we can't have too much of a good thing. Audiences reply (through the box office) that it depends on what you mean by "a good thing." For them the best is just good enough.

It follows that if the new popularity of Shakespeare is to be consolidated into something more permanent, enough directors will have to be found who are capable of presenting the plays properly. The shortage of directors well-versed in the classics is acute, and the services of those available have to be spread out among more and more theater organizations. Shortages usually act as a spur to newcomers, and when talented young directors are found they will continue to disagree between themselves—just as their predecessors have always done—about the right way to set about presenting the plays. The disagreements will be stimulating. There will always be convinced geniuses determined to experiment with every play from *King Lear* to *The Comedy of Errors* and to treat all known methods of production as a point of departure; there will always be plenty of charlatans resorting to every trick of the theater to "improve" Shakespeare—or at least to divert attention from the poverty of their own invention. Then there will also be the very few with an instinctive feeling for the truth of a play—and it is they who will always win the arguments in the end. The decision will be made, not by the critics nor by the acting profession, but by the audience.

The director's function during the production of a play should be to take the place of the audience. Whether he is considered a good director or not depends on whether the performance for which he is responsible gives the maximum amount of satisfaction to the largest number of people. He has to work on his own instinct and to have the confidence to believe that the audience will like what he likes. The director's "instinct" however can often so dominate a production that he directs the audience's attention from the real truth of the play; to take a broad example, he can turn a tragedy scene to comedy or vice versa, either because his instinct is awry or because he wishes to show off his own invention powers instead of relying on those of his author. Sometimes there is good reason for tampering with the text itself and a director of discretion should have the confidence to cut or rearrange a script as if the author were there himself for discussion; but, on the whole, if the play is acted and spoken with true understanding and a sense of the rhythm of the lines and scenes, no audience will fail to rise to it. A lot of nonsense is written and talked about the speaking of the verse, but it must be remembered that Shakespeare was an actor and wrote his plays to be acted, and there is one basic rule, with which Sir John Gielgud, our greatest verse speaker, concurs, which is that if you make sense of the lines and pay attention to Shakespeare's punctuation, the verse will take care of itself.

Technical problems—of staging or decor, accent or incidental music—are quite a different matter and of relatively less importance. These are the aspects most susceptible to the fashionable trends in the theater, which are mercifully short-lived and which occur among amateur societies as well as professional organizations—but most of all among the paid amateurs working in the professional theater. Directors will continue to struggle with variations of the platform theater while most theaters have a proscenium arch and most audiences are demanding the maximum illusion that the theater has to give. From time to time we shall be favored with "authentic" Elizabethan pronunciation for the delight of audiences reared on radio announcers' English. That kind of thing is always enlivening and every *enfant terrible* may at least be a catalyst for ideas.

The fundamental problems remain: the problems relating to the structure of the plays and to the poetical language that transfigures every plot and situation. These are the problems that eternally fascinate actor and director alike. Their success in solving them will make something permanent of the renewed interest in the living Shakespeare. It will help us toward a fuller appreciation of Shakespeare's greatness as a poet, his towering genius as a playwright. Above all it will teach us once again to marvel at his infinite knowledge of human nature.

September 1, 1955.

MICHAEL BENTHALL
Director,
The Old Vic Theatre

Note: Mr. Benthall wishes to acknowledge the assistance of his colleague, Alfred Francis, administrative director of the Old Vic Theatre, in compiling and coordinating his views.

the man and the playwright

WILLIAM Shakespeare was born in Stratford-upon-Avon. He was baptized in the Stratford church on April 25, 1564. As children then were usually baptized about three days after birth, it is probable that April 23, 1564, the traditional date of Shakespeare's birth is the correct one. This day, dedicated to St. George, the patron saint of England, has long been celebrated as the birthday of Shakespeare.

Shakespeare was a middle-class, small-town man. In Stratford he spent his childhood and youth. While he was away from it, he still maintained his family there. After he had become a successful dramatist and a wealthy business man, he retired to it.

Stratford, even in the 16th century, was an old historic town. It is in Warwickshire, 110 miles northwest of London. One road from Stratford to London goes through Oxford, 50 miles away—past the gray towers of the university, which was as famous then as it is now as a seat of learning.

Youth

John Shakespeare, the poet's father, came to Stratford about 1552, 12 years before the birth of his famous son. With the same enterprise which later was to characterize his son, John Shakespeare married Mary Arden, the daughter of his father's landlord, soon after he left his father's farm. He went into business as a glover and whittawer; that is, he tanned and whitened skins, then made from them gloves and other articles. Prospering in his business, John Shakespeare was elected in 1561 and in 1562 one of the two chamberlains who managed the financial affairs of Stratford. In 1568, he was chosen high bailiff or mayor of Stratford and in 1571, chief alderman. As the bailiff and the chief alderman of Stratford, John Shakespeare held the office of justice of the peace. It is not unlikely that Shakespeare's love of depicting comic country constables and solemn courtroom scenes had its origin in watching his father preside over a justice's court.

Education

As Shakespeare grew into childhood, he probably was sent to an elementary school for a short time and then at about the age of seven, as almost every boy of Stratford did, he entered the King's New School at Stratford-upon-Avon, a school which unfortunately has none of its early attendance records. The curriculum of the school was by modern standards narrow. Latin was the most emphasized subject. Taught for long hours each day, a graduate was able not only to read Latin authors but to write the language—an accomplishment necessary for success in law, medicine, the church, and the government service, and which was often of value in business. Stratford Grammar School was an excellent school. The three masters who taught there during Shakespeare's youth were Oxford graduates. Two of these Stratford teachers had been fellows of colleges.

After Shakespeare left school, according to tradition, he began to learn his father's trade, the trade of a glover. This is probable; his plays and poems show an intimate knowledge of the terms of the glover's craft. Shakespeare, according to another tradition, became for a time a country school teacher—not an impossible attainment for a young man educated at the Stratford Grammar School. Other traditions about Shakespeare's early life have resulted from misunderstanding. A favorite variety act, for instance, was for an actor to pretend to kill a calf (cf. *Hamlet* III, 2, 100). From the tradition that Shakespeare would perform this entertainment in "a high style and make a speech," early biographers concluded that in his youth he was a butcher.

Marriage

Soon after he left school, Shakespeare married hastily, with a bishop's special license, Anne Hathaway, the daughter, in all probability, of one of his father's friends. He was 18; she was 25 or 26. The wedding took place about Dec. 1, 1582 (the records of it were possibly stolen by a souvenir hunter), and a daughter was baptized on May 26, 1583. These dates, plus a little arithmetic, have produced the appearance of a scandal. But marriages then were often entered into by precontract which preceded the formal wedding ceremony.

Before their father had reached the age of 21, twins, Hamnet (or Hamlet) and Judith Shakespeare, were born. Shortly after this Shakespeare left Stratford and for about 10 years—the so-called "10 lost years in London"—Shakespeare's name disappears from the records. When it reappears, Shakespeare had become a trained professional actor and dramatist.

London

A legend long circulated that Shakespeare fled because he was persecuted by the local magnate of Stratford, Sir Thomas Lucy, for killing his deer and for writing a satirical poem about him. But Lucy had no deer park and the poem, which was later produced, is clearly a forgery.

The natural explanation of Shakespeare's coming to London is that Stratford, like other small towns, offered few opportunities to ambitious young men. Like his fellow townsman Richard Field, later the printer of his first poems, Shakespeare probably went to London to seek his fortune, managed to get a minor job in the theater, then learned the art of acting. Which company of players he joined is not known—he may have connected with more than one—but the most probable company was that which had as its patron the Earl of Pembroke.

Shakespeare became a competent actor. A contemporary witness tells us that he played the parts of kings. Good tradition assigns to him the role of Adam in *As You Like It* and of the ghost in *Hamlet*.

Shakespeare also learned to write plays. By 1592, he was attracting so much attention that a contemporary poet, Robert Greene, as he was dying in poverty, wrote a bitter attack upon him, because he, a mere actor, was by his writings taking work away from Greene and his fellow university wits who had been supplying the players with their plays. He called Shakespeare "an upstart crow beautified with our feathers . . . the only Shake-scene in a country" and parodied a line from his *Henry VI, Part 2*.

The Early Plays

These plays of Shakespeare, the success of which aroused the wrath of Greene, were varied, for Shakespeare began by experimenting with different types of plays. And unfortunately it is difficult to fix their dates. Six plays—a comedy, a tragedy, and four histories—however, can reasonably be assigned to this early period.

The Comedy of Errors is based upon a comedy by the Latin poet, Plautus, which Shakespeare may well have read in the Stratford Grammar School. It concerns the misadventures of two pairs of twins.

In contrast with this comedy stands *Titus Andronicus*. Shakespeare saw the success that Thomas Kyd was scoring in *The Spanish Tragedy*, a play filled with blood and violence. With the true showman's desire to meet the public demand, he decided to write a tragedy like it. He may have adapted a play by Kyd which is now lost, or more probably, he may have imitated those elements of Kyd's style which he believed made his play successful. *Titus Andronicus* has its scene in Rome; it is a play of revenge, crammed full of murders, rape, and mutilation.

The histories were called forth by the wave of patriotic enthusiasm which swept England at the time when Shakespeare began writing. In 1588, England scored a glorious victory by defeating the Spanish Armada. The theatergoers demanded plays which would dramatize their country's history. But they feared rebellion within their country for unrest was pervading the land. The change of the national religion grieved and angered those who remained loyal to the old faith. And the changes in the national economy brought wealth to some but desperation to others. Shakespeare, no doubt with these conditions in mind, wrote three plays, *Henry VI, Parts 1, 2*, and *3*, which depicted the sufferings caused by civil war by rebellion against a weak king, so unlike England's strong queen, Elizabeth. The theme of the value of a strong stable government is a theme also of *Richard III*. Here a tyrant is seen cunningly usurping the throne and killing many of his nobles until he finally is slain by Elizabeth's grandfather, Henry VII, who brought peace to England.

Poems

Beginning with the summer of 1592, the theaters were closed almost continuously for two years because of the bubonic plague. Shakespeare turned his attention to narrative poetry, which was considered by his fellow Elizabethans as serious literature in contrast with the drama which they esteemed mere popular entertainment. Again, he went back to a book which he had probably read in the Stratford Grammar School, the *Metamorphoses* of the Latin poet Ovid. Shakespeare took the manuscript of his *Venus and Adonis* to his Stratford friend, Richard Field, who in 1593 printed and published the volume. Shakespeare dedicated this poem to a young nobleman, Henry Wriothesley, the Earl of Southampton, then aged 20, who probably, as was customary, rewarded the author with a gift.

Venus and Adonis met with an immediate success, so great indeed that Shakespeare next year followed it with another long poem, *The Rape of Lucrece*. Again he went back to Ovid for a story, this time to his *Fasti*. This poem was also printed by Field in 1594, but it was published by John Harrison. Again Shakespeare dedicated the poem to the young Earl of Southampton but in terms which showed that a greater intimacy had grown up between the poet and the nobleman.

Sonnets

About this time also Shakespeare began writing a series of 154 poems, all but three of them 14-line sonnets. The composition of these sonnets was spread over a number of years. Possibly some even go back to 1588, the year of the attempted invasion of England by the Armada. Two were included in 1599 by William Jaggard in a collection, *The Passionate Pilgrim*, but the entire series of sonnets was not published until 1609, and then probably without the knowledge of Shakespeare. In that year Thomas Thorp by some means obtained possession of a manuscript of Shakespeare's *Sonnets* and had them published. He prefixed to them—it is not known by what authority—a dedication to a "Mr. W. H." Who "Mr. W. H." was is unknown. There have been many guesses, most of them ridiculous. "W. H." could be a reversal of the initials of Henry Wriothesley, Earl of Southampton, who is the favored candidate, and some of the sonnets fit Southampton well. But the initials and some of the other sonnets fit other candidates also.

In the *Sonnets* Shakespeare urges his patron to marry. He then speaks of a love affair between the author and a married woman, "the Dark Lady," whom his patron later takes away from him. Nevertheless he forgives his friend. Other episodes follow.

These *Sonnets* may be autobiographical or they may not be. If they describe incidents in the life of Shakespeare, it is easy to see why he did not desire to have them printed. But it is almost as unlikely, were they autobiographical, that he should be willing to have "his sugared *Sonnets*" circulated "among his private friends," as they were circulating in or before 1598. It is likely, therefore, that few, if any, of the episodes of Shakespeare's *Sonnets* were from real life. Certainly the episodes in the sonnets of Shakespeare's contemporaries were largely imaginary and those of his may well be also.

Member of Chamberlain's Company

When the plague ended late in 1594, Shakespeare is found in a new company, the Chamberlain's Men, which had as its patron, Henry Carey, Lord Hunsdon, the cousin and the closest living relative of the queen, and as the Lord Chamberlain, the master of her household. Shakespeare now had the great advantage not only of playing with the best actors of England but, even more important, of having his plays produced by a company which challenged his best efforts. This superior acting encouraged him to write better and better plays. He averaged now two plays a year.

Period of the Comedies

For his new company Shakespeare began by writing comedies, a type of play which has always appealed to English theatergoers. From about 1594 to 1603, roughly from his 30th until his 39th year, Shakespeare produced 11 comedies.

The earliest of these comedies was probably *The Taming of the Shrew*, a rollicking story of how a young husband changed his nagging, domineering bride into a sweet-tempered and dutiful wife.

Less successful was a comedy on the conflict of love and friendship, *Two Gentlemen of Verona*, and a satire on pedantry and affectation, *Love's Labour's Lost*. But in *A Midsummer-Night's Dream*, a more successful play, Shakespeare first made use of the supernatural element which he later employed so successfully in *Macbeth*, *Hamlet*, *The Tempest*, and other plays. In this comedy mortal love affairs are interrupted by a quarrel between the king and queen of fairies. In the course of this quarrel Oberon, the king, causes his wife Titania to fall madly in love with a weaver whose head he changes temporarily into that of an ass.

The next comedy, *The Merchant of Venice*, has the powerful character of the Jew, Shylock, the only major character of Shakespeare who is a business man. Its climax is the courtroom scene in which the heroine, Portia, disguised as a lawyer, successfully defends the life of her husband's friend.

Much Ado About Nothing, a play about a plot to blast the reputation of a woman, which is frustrated by a stupid constable and his watchmen, stands in contrast with *As You Like It*, probably written in the same year (1599 or 1600), a comedy with the idyllic background of the forest of Arden. Perhaps the most hilarious of Shakespeare's comedies is *Twelfth Night* in which the puritanical and officious manager of the household of a beautiful young woman is persuaded that his mistress is secretly in love with him. Consequently, he acts so strangely that he is confined as insane.

But Shakespeare did not restrict himself during this period entirely to comedies. Indeed, Shakespeare's comic art probably reached its greatest height in two of the from Scotland her successor, King James I, a lover of plays and a lavish, even extravagant, supporter of the stage. On May 19, 1603, a few weeks after his accession to the throne, he became the patron of Shakespeare's company, who became known as the King's Men. James appointed the major players to places in his household as Grooms of the Chamber. As such, Shakespeare and his fellows attended the king on various state functions. And they continued to perform at the Globe and at the court. Probably to please the king, Shakespeare wrote, about 1606, *Macbeth*, a play with a Scotch background which echoed James's political philosophy and paid the king a number of compliments.

From 1599 to the end of his residence in London (about 1610), Shakespeare lived comfortably, much of the time in the house of a Frenchman, Mountjoy, a maker of hair ornaments. He was on intimate terms with this family. Many of his evenings he spent with a group of prominent authors at the Mermaid Tavern.

Great Tragedies

It is strange to find Shakespeare, at the height of his success, changing from the comedies which he had been writing for about seven years to tragedies and to darkly serious comedies. About 1599, Shakespeare wrote his greatest drama, probably the greatest tragedy ever written, *Hamlet, Prince of Denmark*. In this play his father's ghost reveals to Hamlet that it is his duty to revenge his murder; that he had been poisoned by his brother, who desired his throne and his queen. But Hamlet hesitates to kill his own uncle, and by delaying brings death upon his beloved Ophelia, her family, his mother, and himself.

Other tragedies followed. *Othello, the Moor of Venice*, has as its hero a middle-aged general whom a subtle liar so excites with jealousy that he murders his young and innocent wife. *King Lear* is the story of an old king who is induced by flattery to disinherit a loving daughter in favor of two ungrateful older ones; they bring death to him, to their younger sister, and themselves. *Macbeth*, another tragedy of a political murder, has already been noticed. *Antony and Cleopatra* was the last of Shakespeare's great tragedies. This is the tragedy of a queen and a general who become enmeshed in an unchaste love affair which finally leads them both to disgrace and suicide. The last two tragedies which Shakespeare wrote alone are both, like *Lear*, on the theme of ingratitude. *Coriolanus* tells of the ingratitude of a commonwealth, Rome, to a general who had saved it; *Timon of Athens*, of the ingratitude of friends toward a lavish bestower of favors.

Shakespeare's turning from comedies to tragedies has called forth many explanations. Some scholars have professed to find explanations deep in the mind and philosophy of Shakespeare. Others have suggested some grief, such as the death of his son, Hamnet, in 1596, as the cause. Any of these are possible. A simpler explanation can also be advanced: *Hamlet* proved to be an outstanding box-office success. Shakespeare, a practical dramatist, might well have tried to gratify a public demand by writing more plays of this same type.

Somber Comedies

This explanation, however, only partially accounts for the comedies written at the time of these tragedies. *Troilus and Cressida*, the earliest of these, was probably written as a satirical answer to attacks by other dramatists on Shakespeare's company in the so-called "war of the theaters." The plot is a medievalized version of an episode in the Trojan war.

All's Well that Ends Well is the story of how a young woman after obtaining a husband by royal command pursues him when he flees from her and finally, disguised and in an ambiguous situation, wins his love. *Measure for Measure* is a histories. In *Henry IV*, *Part 1*, Shakespeare created Sir John Falstaff, one of his greatest characters. This fat, drunken old braggart, who is a clever, witty, and penetrating judge of men, proved so popular that Shakespeare immediately wrote *Part 2* so that he might continue his adventures. He described the death of the intriguing old rascal in *Henry V*, perhaps the greatest of his historical plays. This story of the conquest of France by England's hero-king appealed to the patriotic feelings of his audience with scenes of the battle of Agincourt. Shakespeare brought Falstaff back to life to become the hero of *The Merry Wives of Windsor*, Shakespeare's only picture of contemporary English middle-class life. In this comedy Falstaff assails the virtue of two middle-aged small-town women with disastrous consequence to himself.

During this period, Shakespeare also wrote *Richard II*, the story of a weakling who lost his throne. *King John* was a less successful play. The king who was forced to grant the Magna Carta did not appeal to a dramatist who admired the semi-absolutism of Elizabeth.

Shakespeare also wrote two tragedies during this period: one at the beginning of it, the other at its end. *Romeo and Juliet*, written about 1594, is the story of two "star-crossed lovers," the son and daughter of two quarreling families whose enmity brings death to their young children. *Julius Caesar*, written about 1599, is the story of a political assassination and the national disaster of civil war which followed it.

Landed Gentleman

While he was writing these comedies, histories, and tragedies, Shakespeare was achieving success as an actor and was growing in wealth. He desired, like many other middle-class men of his time, to be granted a coat of arms. This would entitle him to be styled "gentleman" and to occupy the rank in society next below a knight. On October 20, 1596, heralds granted to John Shakespeare and his children a coat of arms, the chief element of which is a falcon shaking a spear. The next year, 1597, Shakespeare purchased New Place, one of the largest houses in Stratford.

Globe Theatre

In 1599 he joined with four fellow-actors and with the brother of one of them to build a theater in Southwark, on the bank of the Thames. With a capacity of about 1,500 people, it was the largest theater in England. It was named "The Globe" from the sign painted above its door, a picture of Atlas holding the world on his shoulders. Shakespeare now was part owner of a theater in which he acted, and he sometimes appeared there in plays which he himself had written.

Near the end of the reign of Elizabeth occurred an event which could have ruined the dramatist. The Earl of Essex, a friend of Shakespeare's patron, Southampton, feeling aggrieved at the queen's counselors, determined to revolt against the government. He and his friends persuaded the Chamberlain's Men to present Shakespeare's *Richard II* at the Globe, hoping that the scene of the deposing of a king would inspire the people to revolt. They played it on the afternoon of February 7, 1601, the day before the attempted insurrection. But the revolt failed completely; Essex and Southampton were arrested. Fortunately the players were able to convince the authorities that they were ignorant of the intentions of the conspirators. Otherwise Shakespeare, who in *Henry V* had praised Essex, might even have been tried for treason.

Groom of the Court

Shakespeare's good fortune continued. The death of Elizabeth brought down problem play. A hypocritical official attempts to force a girl to save the life of her brother by yielding her virtue to him, but he is thwarted in this attempt by the duke, his sovereign, and is forgiven by the heroine.

Blackfriars Theatre

The King's Men were prospering under James I. But the Globe was an open air theater not suitable for winter performances. Some of the leading men of the company, Shakespeare among them, late in 1608 leased a theater situated in the old monastery of Blackfriars, which had become a fashionable residential section. With this completely roofed playhouse inside the city the King's Men could perform in both winter and summer. A wealthier group of theater-goers came to the Blackfriars Theatre, and as part lessee of this theater, Shakespeare enjoyed a considerable income.

The death, in 1607, of his youngest brother, Edmund, who had become an actor in London, at the age of 28 no doubt brought sorrow to the poet. William buried his brother in the chancel of what is now Southwark Cathedral, close to the Globe.

Late Tragi-comedies

After 1607, Shakespeare wrote on an average of but one play a year. Realizing the popularity of the tragi-comedies which Beaumont and Fletcher were producing, he turned his hand to this type of play. (Beaumont and Fletcher, in turn, may have patterned their own plays upon a romance, *Pericles, Prince of Tyre*, of which Shakespeare wrote but a part.) Alone Shakespeare wrote three romances. All of them are placed outside the bounds of definite time and space. All have improbable plots in keeping with their storyland settings. And all three voice a theme brought out before in *Measure for Measure*, the value of forgiveness on the part of the injured party, so strongly that it has even been conjectured that Shakespeare may have undergone an experience akin to a religious conversion about 1604. *Cymbeline*, the first of these tragi-comedies, has as its scene ancient Britain. Its plot concerns an attempt to slander a woman's honor. *The Winter's Tale*, the next of these, is a story of intense and causeless jealousy enacted in a land on "the sea coasts of Bohemia" and in Sicily in a time when the Greek gods were worshiped. Shakespeare's last play of his sole authorship, *The Tempest*, has as its scene an enchanted island where an exiled duke by magic power overcomes the usurper of his throne, effects a change in his moral nature, forgives him, and arranges a marriage between the usurper's son and his own daughter.

Retirement to Stratford

Shakespeare always seems to have planned to retire to Stratford. He continued investing in land in its vicinity and about 1610 he settled with his family in New Place. He was regarded by his fellow-townsmen as one of Stratford's leading citizens.

But he continued his interest in London. He leased the gate house, an old building in the Blackfriars' estate, on March 10, 1613. And he continued to write for the King's Men; in 1613, he completed two plays written in collaboration with the dramatist John Fletcher: *The Two Noble Kinsmen* and *King Henry VIII.* The first production of the latter play, on June 29, 1613, brought misfortune to its players. Guns fired during the play ignited the thatch on the roof of the Globe and set it on fire. The Globe was soon rebuilt, but the fire involved loss to the poet.

Death

Shakespeare was ill when a month before his death he made his will. He left token bequests to his fellow-players and Stratford friends, provided for his daughters, and in an interlined addition gave his wife his second-best bed. Anne Shakespeare was entitled to one-third of her husband's real estate and to other properties by her dower right; so there was no reason to mention them in the will. The second-best bed was probably that which she and her husband regularly occupied and she probably desired to possess it for sentimental reasons.

William Shakespeare died at New Place, Stratford, on April 23, 1616, and was buried in a place of honor by the high altar in the Stratford church. An expensive monument bearing his bust was placed above his grave.

Publication of Plays

Shakespeare wrote in all 39 plays, including those in which he collaborated. He probably revised a few more. Of these, 17 were published before his death, in small pamphlets (called from their size, quartos) each containing a single play. But Shakespeare's fellow-players to honor his memory collected his plays into a single large volume, now called from its size the First Folio. This, *The Comedies, Histories & Tragedies of Mr. William Shakespeare*, published in 1623, is considered the most important single volume in English literature. On its title page appears the best-known portrait of the poet.

Shakespeare lived quietly in Stratford during the last years of his life. Quite probably he was not well. His parents and probably all his brothers died before him. His eldest daughter, married in 1607 to a successful physician, John Hall, lived with him. His youngest daughter, Judith, also lived in New Place until she was 32. Then long past the usual age for marriage, she, like her mother before her, married a man six years younger than herself, Thomas Quiney, on February 10, 1616, without obtaining a required license. This caused her excommunication, which no doubt brought sorrow to her father in his last days.

Shakespeare's Unceasing Appeal

Shakespeare's plays have continued to be printed and performed for over three and a half centuries. Since the middle of the 17th century there probably has never been a decade in which Shakespeare's plays were not performed more than those of any other dramatist. For more than a century he has been a favorite dramatist in Germany. He has had an especial appeal to the Russians and the Italians. Even in the crowded cities of India adaptations of his plays are frequently performed.

Shakespeare more than any dramatist of the past has retained his hold on the ordinary man and woman of today. What is the secret of this appeal? Dr. Samuel Johnson has supplied the answer when he said, "This therefore is the praise of Shakespeare, that his drama is the mirror of life." The modern man when he sees or reads Shakespeare's plays recognizes himself in them. He sees problems growing out of faults and weaknesses like his own. He finds these problems resolved with great wisdom expressed in language of surpassing beauty. Because the problems presented in the plays of Shakespeare are fundamental ones and so essentially those of today, the appeal of Shakespeare still remains and may well remain for centuries to come.

EDWIN E. WILLOUGHBY
Folger Shakespeare Library
Washington, D. C.

THE COMPLETE WORKS

OF

SHAKESPEARE

The Tempest

The Tempest was first printed in the Folio of 1623, which affords an excellent text with unusually elaborate stage directions (see, for example, iii, 3; iv, 1; v, 1). It was acted at court by the King's Players (Shakespeare's company) sometime in the winter of 1612–1613 (or in the late autumn of 1612) during the festivities incident to the visit of Frederick the Elector Palatine, who arrived at London on October 18, 1612, was betrothed to the King's daughter Elizabeth on December 27, and married her on February 14. There is evidence, however, that The Tempest had already been presented before the King on Hallowmas (November 1), 1611. This fixes one limit for the date of composition. The other limit is fixed as the autumn of 1610 by the fact that for details of the storm, as well as for the description of Prospero's island, Shakespeare got suggestions from the Bermudan adventures and discoveries of Sir George Somers, no report of which reached England until September, 1610. The most probable date for The Tempest, then, is 1611. It may well be the latest of all Shakespeare's plays, except for his share in *Henry VIII* and in *The Two Noble Kinsmen*. The passage, however, in which Prospero speaks of "breaking his staff" and "drowning his book" (v, 1, 54–57), though it sounds like a presentiment, can hardly be interpreted as a farewell to the stage. The Folio doubtless represents the play as it was acted at court in the winter. Some scholars believe that the masque in act iv was written or enlarged expressly for that occasion; others conjecture that the masque, in whole or in part, is not Shakespeare's own work. Probably there was some adaptation of the original text for court performance, but there is no good reason for supposing that The Tempest is not all Shakespeare's or that it ever existed in an earlier form that differed, except for a touch here and there, from the text as we have it.

No source for the plot has been discovered. *Die Schöne Sidea*, a comedy by Jakob Ayrer, who died in 1605, bears some resemblance to The Tempest in outline and agrees with it in several details; but the differences are more significant than the agreements. *Die Schöne Sidea* reproduces, in a rationalized form, the ancient and widespread folk-tale of 'The Forgotten Bride.' Like the ninth story of the fifth day in Basile's *Pentamerone*, it belongs to that group of versions which include the romantic incidents (foreign to Shakespeare) of the maiden in the tree and the face mirrored in the spring. There is no forgotten bride in The Tempest. Shakespeare's plot may be remotely akin to the ancient *märchen*, but he owes nothing to the German drama, of which, indeed, he had probably never heard. Certain Italian *scenari* that resemble Shakespeare's plot may likewise be disregarded as sources. The incidents in question were the common property of novelists and playwrights.

That Shakespeare owes something to narratives of Somers's adventures is certain. In 1608 and the following years the Virginia Company and its designs were in the forefront of public interest. On June 2, 1609, a fleet of seven ships and two small vessels sailed from Plymouth for Virginia. The flagship, the Sea Adventure, carried the new Governor (Sir Thomas Gates), the Admiral (Sir George Somers), and Captain Christopher Newport. On July 24 a terrible storm scattered the fleet. It arrived at Jamestown in August, but the Sea Adventure was missing. She had run ashore on the Bermudas on July 28, but without loss of life. Gates, Somers, and the rest — some hundred and fifty in all — remained in the islands for about nine months. On May 10, 1610, they sailed away in two small pinnaces which they had built, arriving at Jamestown on the 23d. In the following July Gates and Newport sailed for England. They arrived in September, and thus the first news of the adventures of Gates and Somers in Bermuda reached the mother country.

In 1610, soon after their arrival, three narratives of these adventures were published: (1) *Newes from Virginia*, a ballad by Richard Rich; (2) *A Discovery of the Bermudas, otherwise called the Ile of Divels*, by Silvester Jourdan; and (3) *A True Declaration of the estate of the Colonie in Virginia*. Both Rich and Jourdan had been with Somers in the Sea Adventure when she was wrecked. The ballad has no Shakespearean significance. The other two narratives coincide with THE TEMPEST in some details which, though slight, warrant the inference that Shakespeare had read them, as, indeed, he was very likely to do if he felt any interest in the news of the day. More important, however, is a long letter from William Strachey, another of Somers's companions. This seems to be dated July 15, 1610, and doubtless came over with Gates in September. It was not printed until 1625, when Purchas included it in the fourth volume of his *Pilgrimes*; but it must have circulated in manuscript and we may be reasonably sure that Shakespeare read it.

These three narratives, however, are in no sense to be regarded as sources of THE TEMPEST. At most they furnished Shakespeare with a few items of information or with miscellaneous suggestions which he has followed after his own fashion. Strachey's account of the wreck, for instance, is in striking contrast to what we find in THE TEMPEST. The Sea Adventure has sprung a leak and is in imminent danger of foundering. Crew and passengers, exhausted by four days' desperate toil at the pumps, are in raptures when they sight Bermuda, which, by good fortune, is on their weather. They lay their course for the shore, run the ship aground, and make a safe landing — a hundred and fifty of them — in their boats. The situation in THE TEMPEST is utterly different. There is, in fact, no wreck at all. The sailors make every effort to weather Prospero's island, which is on their lee, for they can defy the storm if they have "room enough." They do not succeed, but by the help of Ariel the ship is not dashed to pieces upon the rocks, but makes her way into a "deep nook" or cove, where she rides in safety. Shakespeare's handling of the vessel shows an accurate knowledge of seamanship which he cannot have learned from the Bermuda narratives. Unquestionably he had talked with sailors in his time and he owes quite as much to such conversation as to anything that he read in the three narratives.

Setebos is several times mentioned as the "great devil" of the Patagonian giants by Pigafetta in his account of Magellan's circumnavigation, an English version of which Shakespeare could have seen in Richard Eden's well-known volume *The History of Trauayle in the West and East Indies* (1577). Caliban is more likely to have derived his name from 'cannibal' than from the Gypsy word *cauliban*, 'blackness.' For Gonzalo's ideal commonwealth (ii, 1, 147 ff.) Shakespeare is indebted to Florio's Montaigne (1603). Prospero and some of the other names he could have found in Thomas's *History of Italye* (1549).

THE TEMPEST

Names of the Actors.

Alonso, King of Naples.
Sebastian, his brother.
Prospero, the right Duke of Milan.
Antonio, his brother, the usurping Duke of Milan.
Ferdinand, son to the King of Naples.
Gonzalo, an honest old councillor.
Adrian and *Francisco*, lords.
Caliban, a salvage and deformed slave.
Trinculo, a jester.
Stephano, a drunken butler.

Master of a ship, Boatswain, Mariners.

Miranda, daughter to *Prospero*.
Ariel, an airy spirit.
Iris, *Ceres*, *Juno*, *Nymphs*, *Reapers*, [presented by] spirits.
[Other Spirits attending on *Prospero*.]

THE SCENE. — [*On board a ship at sea; afterwards*] *an uninhabited island.*

ACT I. Scene I. [*On board a ship at sea.*]

A tempestuous noise of thunder and lightning heard. Enter a *Shipmaster* and a *Boatswain.*

Mast. Boatswain!

Boats. Here, master. What cheer?

Mast. Good, speak to th' mariners! Fall to't — yarely, or we run ourselves aground! Bestir, bestir! *Exit.*

Enter *Mariners.*

Boats. Heigh, my hearts! Cheerly, cheerly, my hearts! Yare, yare! Take in the topsail! Tend to th' master's whistle! Blow till thou burst thy wind, if room enough!

Enter *Alonso, Sebastian, Antonio, Ferdinand, Gonzalo,* and others.

Alon. Good boatswain, have care. Where's the master? Play the men.

Boats. I pray now, keep below.

Ant. Where is the master, bos'n?

Boats. Do you not hear him? You mar our labour. Keep your cabins! You do assist the storm.

Gon. Nay, good, be patient.

Boats. When the sea is. Hence! What cares these roarers for the name of king? To cabin! Silence! Trouble us not!

Gon. Good, yet remember whom thou hast aboard.

Boats. None that I more love than myself. You are a Councillor. If you can command these elements to silence and work the peace of the present, we will not hand a rope more; use your authority. If you cannot, give thanks you have liv'd so long, and make yourself ready in your cabin for the mischance of the hour, if it so hap. — Cheerly, good hearts! — Out of our way, I say. *Exit.*

Gon. I have great comfort from this fellow. Methinks he hath no drowning mark upon him; his complexion is perfect gallows. Stand fast, good Fate, to his hanging! Make the rope of his destiny our cable, for our own doth little advantage. If he be not born to be hang'd, our case is miserable. *Exeunt.*

Enter *Boatswain.*

Boats. Down with the topmast! Yare! Lower, lower! Bring her to try with main-course! (*A cry within.*) A plague upon this howling! They are louder than the weather or our office.

Enter *Sebastian, Antonio,* and *Gonzalo.*

Yet again? What do you here? Shall we give o'er and drown? Have you a mind to sink?

Seb. A pox o' your throat, you bawling, blasphemous, incharitable dog!

Boats. Work you then.

Ant. Hang, cur, hang, you whoreson, insolent noisemaker! We are less afraid to be drown'd than thou art.

Gon. I'll warrant him for drowning, though the ship were no stronger than a nutshell and as leaky as an unstanched wench.

Boats. Lay her ahold, ahold! Set her two courses! Off to sea again! Lay her off!

Enter *Mariners* wet.

Mariners. All lost! To prayers, to prayers! All lost! [*Exeunt.*]

Boats. What, must our mouths be cold?

Gon. The King and Prince at prayers! Let's assist them,
For our case is as theirs.

Seb. I am out of patience.

Ant. We are merely cheated of our lives by drunkards.
This wide-chopp'd rascal — would thou mightst lie drowning
The washing of ten tides!

Gon. He'll be hang'd yet,
Though every drop of water swear against it
And gape at wid'st to glut him.

A confused noise within: 'Mercy on us! —
We split, we split! — Farewell, my wife and children! —
Farewell, brother! — We split, we split, we split!'

[*Exit Boatswain.*]

Ant. Let's all sink with th' King.

Seb. Let's take leave of him.

Exeunt [*Antonio and Sebastian*].

Gon. Now would I give a thousand furlongs of sea for an acre of barren ground — long heath, brown furze, anything. The wills above be done! but I would fain die a dry death. *Exit.*

Scene II. [*The island. Before Prospero's cell.*]

Enter *Prospero* and *Miranda.*

Mir. If by your art, my dearest father, you have
Put the wild waters in this roar, allay them.
The sky, it seems, would pour down stinking pitch
But that the sea, mounting to th' welkin's cheek,
Dashes the fire out. O, I have suffered
With those that I saw suffer! a brave vessel
(Who had no doubt some noble creature in her)
Dash'd all to pieces! O, the cry did knock
Against my very heart! Poor souls, they perish'd!
Had I been any god of power, I would
Have sunk the sea within the earth or ere
It should the good ship so have swallow'd and
The fraughting souls within her.

Pros. Be collected.
No more amazement. Tell your piteous heart
There's no harm done.

Mir. O, woe the day!

Pros. No harm.
I have done nothing but in care of thee,
Of thee my dear one, thee my daughter, who
Art ignorant of what thou art, naught knowing
Of whence I am; nor that I am more better
Than Prospero, master of a full poor cell,
And thy no greater father.

Mir. More to know
Did never meddle with my thoughts.

Pros. 'Tis time
I should inform thee farther. Lend thy hand
And pluck my magic garment from me. So,
[*Lays down his robe.*]
Lie there, my art. Wipe thou thine eyes; have comfort.
The direful spectacle of the wrack, which touch'd
The very virtue of compassion in thee,
I have with such provision in mine art
So safely ordered that there is no soul —
No, not so much perdition as an hair
Betid to any creature in the vessel
Which thou heard'st cry, which thou saw'st sink. Sit down;
For thou must now know farther.

Mir. You have often
Begun to tell me what I am; but stopp'd
And left me to a bootless inquisition,
Concluding, 'Stay! Not yet.'

Pros. The hour's now come;
The very minute bids thee ope thine ear.
Obey, and be attentive. Canst thou remember
A time before we came unto this cell?
I do not think thou canst, for then thou wast not
Out three years old.

Mir. Certainly, sir, I can.

Pros. By what? By any other house or person?
Of any thing the image tell me that
Hath kept with thy remembrance.

Mir. 'Tis far off,
And rather like a dream than an assurance
That my remembrance warrants. Had I not
Four or five women once that tended me?

Pros. Thou hadst, and more, Miranda. But how is it
That this lives in thy mind? What seest thou else

In the dark backward and abysm of time?
If thou remembʼrest aught ere thou camʼst here,
How thou camʼst here thou mayst.
Mir. But that I do not.
Pros. Twelve year since, Miranda, twelve year since,
Thy father was the Duke of Milan and
A prince of power.
Mir. Sir, are not you my father?
Pros. Thy mother was a piece of virtue, and
She said thou wast my daughter; and thy father
Was Duke of Milan; and his only heir
A princess — no worse issued.
Mir. O the heavens!
What foul play had we that we came from thence?
Or blessed wasʼt we did?
Pros. Both, both, my girl!
By foul play, as thou sayʼst, were we heavʼd thence,
But blessedly holp hither.
Mir. O, my heart bleeds
To think oʼ thʼ teen that I have turnʼd you to,
Which is from my remembrance! Please you, farther.
Pros. My brother, and thy uncle, callʼd Antonio —
I pray thee mark me — that a brother should
Be so perfidious! — he whom next thyself
Of all the world I lovʼd, and to him put
The manage of my state, as at that time
Through all the signories it was the first,
And Prospero the prime duke, being so reputed
In dignity, and for the liberal arts
Without a parallel; those being all my study,
The government I cast upon my brother
And to my state grew stranger, being transported
And rapt in secret studies — thy false uncle —
Dost thou attend me?
Mir. Sir, most heedfully.
Pros. Being once perfected how to grant suits,
How to deny them, who tʼ advance, and who
To trash for over-topping, new-created
The creatures that were mine, I say, or changʼd ʼem,
Or else new-formʼd ʼem; having both the key
Of officer and office, set all hearts iʼ thʼ state
To what tune pleasʼd his ear, that now he was
The ivy which had hid my princely trunk
And suckʼd my verdure out onʼt. Thou attendʼst not!
Mir. O, good sir, I do
Pros. I pray thee mark me.
I thus neglecting worldly ends, all dedicated
To closeness, and the bettering of my mind
With that which, but by being so retirʼd,
Oʼer-prizʼd all popular rate, in my false brother
Awakʼd an evil nature, and my trust,
Like a good parent, did beget of him
A falsehood in its contrary as great
As my trust was, which had indeed no limit,
A confidence sans bound. He being thus lorded,
Not only with what my revenue yielded
But what my power might else exact, like one
Who having unto truth, by telling of it,
Made such a sinner of his memory
To credit his own lie, he did believe
He was indeed the Duke, out oʼ thʼ substitution
And executing thʼ outward face of royalty
With all prerogative. Hence his ambition growing —
Dost thou hear?
Mir. Your tale, sir, would cure deafness.
Pros. To have no screen between this part he playʼd
And him he playʼd it for, he needs will be
Absolute Milan. Me (poor man) my library
Was dukedom large enough! Of temporal royalties
He thinks me now incapable; confederates
(So dry he was for sway) with thʼ King of Naples
To give him annual tribute, do him homage,
Subject his coronet to his crown, and bend
The dukedom yet unbowʼd (alas, poor Milan!)
To most ignoble stooping.
Mir. O the heavens!
Pros. Mark his condition, and thʼ event; then tell me
If this might be a brother.
Mir. I should sin
To think but nobly of my grandmother.
Good wombs have borne bad sons.
Pros. Now the condition.
This King of Naples, being an enemy
To me inveterate, hearkens my brotherʼs suit;
Which was, that he, in lieu oʼ thʼ premises,
Of homage and I know not how much tribute,
Should presently extirpate me and mine
Out of the dukedom and confer fair Milan,
With all the honours, on my brother. Whereon,
A treacherous army levied, one midnight
Fated to thʼ purpose, did Antonio open
The gates of Milan; and, iʼ thʼ dead of darkness,
The ministers for thʼ purpose hurried thence
Me and thy crying self.

Mir. Alack, for pity!
I, not rememb'ring how I cried out then,
Will cry it o'er again. It is a hint
That wrings mine eyes to't.
Pros. Hear a little further,
And then I'll bring thee to the present business
Which now 's upon 's; without the which this story
Were most impertinent.
Mir. Wherefore did they not
That hour destroy us?
Pros. Well demanded, wench.
My tale provokes that question. Dear, they durst not,
So dear the love my people bore me; nor set
A mark so bloody on the business; but
With colours fairer painted their foul ends.
In few, they hurried us aboard a bark,
Bore us some leagues to sea; where they prepar'd
A rotten carcass of a butt, not rigg'd,
Nor tackle, sail, nor mast; the very rats
Instinctively have quit it. There they hoist us,
To cry to th' sea, that roar'd to us; to sigh
To th' winds, whose pity, sighing back again,
Did us but loving wrong.
Mir. Alack, what trouble
Was I then to you!
Pros. O, a cherubin
Thou wast that did preserve me! Thou didst smile,
Infused with a fortitude from heaven,
When I have deck'd the sea with drops full salt,
Under my burthen groan'd; which rais'd in me
An undergoing stomach, to bear up
Against what should ensue.
Mir. How came we ashore?
Pros. By providence divine.
Some food we had, and some fresh water, that
A noble Neapolitan, Gonzalo,
Out of his charity, who being then appointed
Master of this design, did give us, with
Rich garments, linens, stuffs, and necessaries
Which since have steaded much. So, of his gentleness,
Knowing I lov'd my books, he furnish'd me
From mine own library with volumes that
I prize above my dukedom.
Mir. Would I might
But ever see that man!
Pros. Now I arise.
Sit still, and hear the last of our sea-sorrow.
Here in this island we arriv'd; and here
Have I, thy schoolmaster, made thee more profit
Than other princess can, that have more time
For vainer hours, and tutors not so careful.
Mir. Heavens thank you for't! And now I pray you, sir, —
For still 'tis beating in my mind, — your reason
For raising this sea-storm?
Pros. Know thus far forth.
By accident most strange, bountiful Fortune
(Now my dear lady) hath mine enemies
Brought to this shore; and by my prescience
I find my zenith doth depend upon
A most auspicious star, whose influence
If now I court not, but omit, my fortunes
Will ever after droop. Here cease more questions.
Thou art inclin'd to sleep. 'Tis a good dulness,
And give it way. I know thou canst not choose.
[*Miranda sleeps.*]
Come away, servant, come! I am ready now.
Approach, my Ariel. Come!

Enter *Ariel.*

Ari. All hail, great master! Grave sir, hail! I come
To answer thy best pleasure; be't to fly,
To swim, to dive into the fire, to ride
On the curl'd clouds. To thy strong bidding task
Ariel and all his quality.
Pros. Hast thou, spirit,
Perform'd to point the tempest that I bade thee?
Ari. To every article.
I boarded the King's ship. Now on the beak,
Now in the waist, the deck, in every cabin,
I flam'd amazement. Sometime I'ld divide
And burn in many places; on the topmast,
The yards, and boresprit would I flame distinctly,
Then meet and join. Jove's lightnings, the precursors
O' th' dreadful thunderclaps, more momentary
And sight-outrunning were not. The fire and cracks
Of sulphurous roaring the most mighty Neptune
Seem to besiege and make his bold waves tremble;
Yea, his dread trident shake.
Pros. My brave spirit!
Who was so firm, so constant, that this coil
Would not infect his reason?
Ari. Not a soul
But felt a fever of the mad and play'd
Some tricks of desperation. All but mariners
Plung'd in the foaming brine and quit the vessel,

Then all afire with me. The King's son Ferdinand,
With hair up-staring (then like reeds, not hair),
Was the first man that leapt; cried 'Hell is empty,
And all the devils are here!'

Pros. Why, that's my spirit!
But was not this nigh shore?

Ari. Close by, my master.

Pros. But are they, Ariel, safe?

Ari. Not a hair perish'd.
On their sustaining garments not a blemish,
But fresher than before; and as thou bad'st me,
In troops I have dispers'd them 'bout the isle.
The King's son have I landed by himself,
Whom I left cooling of the air with sighs
In an odd angle of the isle, and sitting,
His arms in this sad knot.

Pros. Of the King's ship
The mariners say how thou hast dispos'd,
And all the rest o' th' fleet.

Ari. Safely in harbour
Is the King's ship; in the deep nook where once
Thou call'dst me up at midnight to fetch dew
From the still-vex'd Bermoothes, there she's hid;
The mariners all under hatches stow'd,
Who, with a charm join'd to their suff'red labour,
I have left asleep; and for the rest o' th' fleet,
Which I dispers'd, they all have met again,
And are upon the Mediterranean flote
Bound sadly home for Naples,
Supposing that they saw the King's ship wrack'd
And his great person perish.

Pros. Ariel, thy charge
Exactly is perform'd; but there's more work.
What is the time o' th' day?

Ari. Past the mid season.

Pros. At least two glasses. The time 'twixt six and now
Must by us both be spent most preciously.

Ari. Is there more toil? Since thou dost give me pains,
Let me remember thee what thou hast promis'd,
Which is not yet perform'd me.

Pros. How now? moody?
What is't thou canst demand?

Ari. My liberty.

Pros. Before the time be out? No more!

Ari. I prithee,
Remember I have done thee worthy service,
Told thee no lies, made no mistakings, serv'd
Without or grudge or grumblings. Thou didst promise
To bate me a full year.

Pros. Dost thou forget
From what a torment I did free thee?

Ari. No.

Pros. Thou dost; and think'st it much t tread the ooze
Of the salt deep,
To run upon the sharp wind of the North,
To do me business in the veins o' th' earth
When it is bak'd with frost.

Ari. I do not, sir.

Pros. Thou liest, malignant thing! Hast thou forgot
The foul witch Sycorax, who with age and envy
Was grown into a hoop? Hast thou forgot her?

Ari. No, sir.

Pros. Thou hast. Where was she born? Speak! Tell me!

Ari. Sir, in Argier.

Pros. O, was she so? I must
Once in a month recount what thou hast been,
Which thou forget'st. This damn'd witch Sycorax,
For mischiefs manifold, and sorceries terrible
To enter human hearing, from Argier
Thou know'st was banish'd. For one thing she did
They would not take her life. Is not this true?

Ari. Ay, sir.

Pros. This blue-ey'd hag was hither brought with child
And here was left by th' sailors. Thou, my slave,
As thou report'st thyself, wast then her servant;
And, for thou wast a spirit too delicate
To act her earthy and abhorr'd commands,
Refusing her grand hests, she did confine thee,
By help of her more potent ministers,
And in her most unmitigable rage,
Into a cloven pine; within which rift
Imprison'd thou didst painfully remain
A dozen years; within which space she died
And left thee there; where thou didst vent thy groans
As fast as millwheels strike. Then was this island
(Save for the son that she did litter here,
A freckled whelp, hag-born) not honour'd with
A human shape.

Ari. Yes, Caliban her son.

Pros. Dull thing, I say so! he, that Caliban
Whom now I keep in service. Thou best know'st
What torment I did find thee in. Thy groans

Did make wolves howl and penetrate the breasts
Of ever-angry bears. It was a torment
To lay upon the damn'd, which Sycorax
Could not again undo. It was mine art,
When I arriv'd and heard thee, that made gape
The pine, and let thee out.

Ari. I thank thee, master.

Pros. If thou more murmur'st, I will rend an oak
And peg thee in his knotty entrails till
Thou hast howl'd away twelve winters.

Ari. Pardon, master.
I will be correspondent to command
And do my spriting gently.

Pros. Do so; and after two days
I will discharge thee.

Ari. That's my noble master!
What shall I do? Say what! What shall I do?

Pros. Go make thyself like a nymph o' th' sea. Be subject
To no sight but thine and mine; invisible
To every eyeball else. Go take this shape
And hither come in't. Go! Hence with diligence! *Exit* [*Ariel*].
Awake, dear heart, awake! Thou hast slept well.
Awake!

Mir. The strangeness of your story put
Heaviness in me.

Pros. Shake it off. Come on.
We'll visit Caliban, my slave, who never
Yields us kind answer.

Mir. 'Tis a villain, sir,
I do not love to look on.

Pros. But as 'tis,
We cannot miss him. He does make our fire,
Fetch in our wood, and serves in offices
That profit us. What, ho! slave! Caliban!
Thou earth, thou! Speak!

Cal. (*within*) There's wood enough within.

Pros. Come forth, I say! There's other business for thee.
Come, thou tortoise! When?

Enter *Ariel* like a water nymph.

Fine apparition! My quaint Ariel,
Hark in thine ear.

Ari. My lord, it shall be done. *Exit.*

Pros. Thou poisonous slave, got by the devil himself
Upon thy wicked dam, come forth!

Enter *Caliban.*

Cal. As wicked dew as e'er my mother brush'd
With raven's feather from unwholesome fen
Drop on you both! A south-west blow on ye
And blister you all o'er!

Pros. For this, be sure, to-night thou shalt have cramps,
Side-stitches that shall pen thy breath up; urchins
Shall, for that vast of night that they may work,
All exercise on thee; thou shalt be pinch'd
As thick as honeycomb, each pinch more stinging
Than bees that made 'em.

Cal. I must eat my dinner.
This island 's mine by Sycorax my mother,
Which thou tak'st from me. When thou camest first,
Thou strok'dst me and mad'st much of me; wouldst give me
Water with berries in't; and teach me how
To name the bigger light, and how the less,
That burn by day, and night; and then I lov'd thee
And show'd thee all the qualities o' th' isle,
The fresh springs, brine-pits, barren place and fertile.
Cursed be I that did so! All the charms
Of Sycorax — toads, beetles, bats light on you!
For I am all the subjects that you have,
Which first was mine own king; and here you sty me
In this hard rock, whiles you do keep from me
The rest o' th' island.

Pros. Thou most lying slave,
Whom stripes may move, not kindness! I have us'd thee,
(Filth as thou art) with humane care, and lodg'd thee
In mine own cell till thou didst seek to violate
The honour of my child.

Cal. O ho, O ho! Would 't had been done!
Thou didst prevent me; I had peopled else
This isle with Calibans.

Pros. Abhorred slave,
Which any print of goodness wilt not take,
Being capable of all ill! I pitied thee,
Took pains to make thee speak, taught thee each hour
One thing or other. When thou didst not, savage,
Know thine own meaning, but wouldst gabble like

A thing most brutish, I endow'd thy purposes
With words that made them known. But thy vile race,
Though thou didst learn, had that in't which good natures
Could not abide to be with. Therefore wast thou
Deservedly confin'd into this rock, who hadst
Deserv'd more than a prison.

Cal. You taught me language, and my profit on't
Is, I know how to curse. The red plague rid you
For learning me your language!

Pros. Hag-seed, hence!
Fetch us in fuel; and be quick, thou'rt best,
To answer other business. Shrug'st thou, malice?
If thou neglect'st or dost unwillingly
What I command, I'll rack thee with old cramps,
Fill all thy bones with achës, make thee roar
That beasts shall tremble at thy din.

Cal. No, pray thee.
[*Aside*] I must obey. His art is of such pow'r
It would control my dam's god, Setebos,
And make a vassal of him.

Pros. So, slave; hence! *Exit Caliban.*

Enter *Ferdinand*; and *Ariel* (invisible), playing and singing.

Ariel's song.

Come unto these yellow sands,
And then take hands.
Curtsied when you have and kiss'd,
The wild waves whist,
Foot it featly here and there;
And, sweet sprites, the burthen bear.
Hark, hark!
Burthen, dispersedly. Bowgh, wawgh!
The watchdogs bark.
Burthen, dispersedly. Bowgh, wawgh.
Hark, hark! I hear
The strain of strutting chanticleer
Cry, cock-a-diddle-dowe.

Fer. Where should this music be? I' th' air, or th' earth?
It sounds no more; and sure it waits upon
Some god o' th' island. Sitting on a bank,
Weeping again the King my father's wrack,
This music crept by me upon the waters,
Allaying both their fury and my passion
With its sweet air. Thence I have follow'd it,
Or it hath drawn me rather; but 'tis gone.
No, it begins again.

Ariel's song.

Full fadom five thy father lies;
Of his bones are coral made;
Those are pearls that were his eyes;
Nothing of him that doth fade
But doth suffer a sea-change
Into something rich and strange.
Sea nymphs hourly ring his knell:
Burthen. Ding-dong.
Hark! now I hear them — Ding-dong bell.

Fer. The ditty does remember my drown'd father.
This is no mortal business, nor no sound
That the earth owes. I hear it now above me.

Pros. The fringed curtains of thine eye advance
And say what thou seest yond.

Mir. What is't? a spirit?
Lord, how it looks about! Believe me, sir,
It carries a brave form. But 'tis a spirit.

Pros. No, wench. It eats, and sleeps, and hath such senses
As we have, such. This gallant which thou seest
Was in the wrack; and, but he's something stain'd
With grief (that's beauty's canker), thou mightst call him
A goodly person. He hath lost his fellows
And strays about to find 'em.

Mir. I might call him
A thing divine; for nothing natural
I ever saw so noble.

Pros. [*aside*] It goes on, I see,
As my soul prompts it. Spirit, fine spirit! I'll free thee
Within two days for this.

Fer. Most sure, the goddess
On whom these airs attend! Vouchsafe my pray'r
May know if you remain upon this island,
And that you will some good instruction give
How I may bear me here. My prime request,
Which I do last pronounce, is (O you wonder!)
If you be maid or no?

Mir. No wonder, sir,
But certainly a maid.

Fer. My language? Heavens!
I am the best of them that speak this speech,
Were I but where 'tis spoken.

Pros. How? the best?
What wert thou if the King of Naples heard thee?

Fer. A single thing, as I am now, that wonders

To hear thee speak of Naples. He does hear me;
And that he does I weep. Myself am Naples,
Who with mine eyes, never since at ebb, beheld
The King my father wrack'd.

Mir. Alack, for mercy!

Fer. Yes, faith, and all his lords, the Duke of Milan
And his brave son being twain.

Pros. [*aside*] The Duke of Milan
And his more braver daughter could control thee,
If now 'twere fit to do't. At the first sight
They have chang'd eyes. Delicate Ariel,
I'll set thee free for this! — A word, good sir.
I fear you have done yourself some wrong. A word!

Mir. Why speaks my father so ungently? This
Is the third man that e'er I saw; the first
That e'er I sigh'd for. Pity move my father
To be inclin'd my way!

Fer. O, if a virgin,
And your affection not gone forth, I'll make you
The Queen of Naples.

Pros. Soft, sir! one word more.
[*Aside*] They are both in either's pow'rs. But this swift business
I must uneasy make, lest too light winning
Make the prize light. — One word more! I charge thee
That thou attend me. Thou dost here usurp
The name thou ow'st not, and hast put thyself
Upon this island as a spy, to win it
From me, the lord on't.

Fer. No, as I am a man!

Mir. There's nothing ill can dwell in such a temple.
If the ill spirit have so fair a house,
Good things will strive to dwell with't.

Pros. Follow me. —
Speak not you for him; he's a traitor. — Come!
I'll manacle thy neck and feet together;
Sea water shalt thou drink; thy food shall be
The fresh-brook mussels, wither'd roots, and husks
Wherein the acorn cradled. Follow.

Fer. No.
I will resist such entertainment till
Mine enemy has more power.

He draws, and is charmed from moving.

Mir. O dear father,
Make not too rash a trial of him, for
He's gentle, and not fearful.

Pros. What, I say,
My foot my tutor? — Put thy sword up, traitor!
Who mak'st a show but dar'st not strike, thy conscience
Is so possess'd with guilt. Come, from thy ward!
For I can here disarm thee with this stick
And make thy weapon drop.

Mir. Beseech you, father!

Pros. Hence! Hang not on my garments.

Mir. Sir, have pity.
I'll be his surety.

Pros. Silence! One word more
Shall make me chide thee, if not hate thee. What,
An advocate for an impostor? Hush!
Thou think'st there is no more such shapes as he,
Having seen but him and Caliban. Foolish wench!
To th' most of men this is a Caliban,
And they to him are angels.

Mir. My affections
Are then most humble. I have no ambition
To see a goodlier man.

Pros. Come on, obey!
Thy nerves are in their infancy again
And have no vigour in them.

Fer. So they are.
My spirits, as in a dream, are all bound up.
My father's loss, the weakness which I feel,
The wrack of all my friends, nor this man's threats
To whom I am subdu'd, are but light to me,
Might I but through my prison once a day
Behold this maid. All corners else o' th' earth
Let liberty make use of. Space enough
Have I in such a prison.

Pros. [*aside*] It works. [*To Ferdinand*] Come on. —
Thou hast done well, fine Ariel! [*To Ferdinand*] Follow me. —
[*To Ariel*] Hark what thou else shalt do me.

Mir. Be of comfort.
My father 's of a better nature, sir,
Than he appears by speech. This is unwonted
Which now came from him.

Pros. Thou shalt be as free
As mountain winds; but then exactly do
All points of my command.

Ari. To th' syllable.

Pros. Come, follow. — Speak not for him.

Exeunt.

THE TEMPEST

Above: "Your swords are now too massy for your strengths, and will not be uplifted." The fairy Ariel (Alan Badel), in the form of a harpy, disarms Alonso (Jack Gwillim) and his companions by casting a spell on them. At the right, Michael Redgrave as Prospero (*Act III, Scene III*)

Left: Prospero lays his commands upon the inhabitants of the haunted island

PHOTOGRAPHS BY ANGUS MCBEAN
PRODUCED BY THE MEMORIAL THEATRE COMPANY
STRATFORD-UPON-AVON

"Fall to 't yarely, or we run ourselves a-ground." The opening scene, in which the ship is wrecked on the mysterious isle

Right: "Dost thou forget from what a torment I did free thee?" Prospero rebukes the restless Ariel, whom he bound to a period of servitude after freeing him from the witch's spell (*Act I, Scene II*)

Below: "A cherubim thou wast, that did preserve me!" Prospero tells his daughter Miranda (Hazel Penwarden) how her company consoled him during the first lonely years of their isolation (*Act I, Scene II*)

Above: "You taught me language; and my profit on't is, I know how to curse: the red plague rid you, for learning me your language." The monster Caliban (Hugh Griffith) rebels against the domination of Prospero, his master (*Act I, Scene II*)

Right: Evil Caliban, monstrous offspring of the witch Sycorax, was once the ruler of the island and regards Prospero as a usurper of his power

"Beseech you, sir, be merry: you have cause." Gonzalo (Geoffrey Bayldon) reminds the king that he should be grateful that he has escaped death in the shipwreck (*Act II, Scene I*)

"Then let us both be sudden." Finding King Alonso and his followers asleep, under the spell of Ariel, Sebastian (William Squire) and Antonio (William Fox) decide to kill him (*Act II, Scene I*)

"If in Naples I should report this now, would they believe me?" Alonso and his retinue are amazed at the banquet set before them through the magical powers of Prospero (*Act III, Scene III*)

"Open your mouth; here is that which will give language to you." The drunken butler, Trinculo (Michael Gwynn), and the jester (Alexander Gauge) give Caliban liquor (*Act II, Scene II*)

"I am your wife, if you will marry me." Miranda and Ferdinand (Richard Burton), Alonso's son, plight their troth (*Act III, Scene I*)

Right: "If I have too austerely punish'd you, your compensation makes amends." Having tried Ferdinand's mettle by assigning him menial tasks to perform, Prospero consents to his marriage with Miranda (*Act IV, Scene I*)

Below: "Juno sings her blessings on you." The goddess Juno (Barbara Jefford) is summoned to give her blessing at the formal betrothal of Miranda and Ferdinand (*Act IV, Scene I*)

Above: "There stand, for you are spell-stopp'd." Prospero addresses Alonso and his followers as they stand in the magic circle drawn before his cell (*Act V, Scene I*)

Right: "Sweet lord, you play me false." Miranda and Ferdinand are discovered playing chess in Prospero's cell (*Act V, Scene I*)

Below: "Give me your hands: let grief and sorrow still embrace his heart that doth not wish you joy!" Alonso blesses Miranda and his son, Ferdinand (*Act V, Scene I*)

"The best news is that we have safely found our king and company." The boatswain (Duncan Lamont) and master (David Orr) rejoice on discovering that King Alonso is alive (*Act V, Scene I*)

Left: "How beauteous mankind is! O brave new world, that has such people in 't!" Miranda is amazed at man's variety (*Act V, Scene I*)

Below: Prospero the magician. Always obsessed with the supernatural, he came to the island equipped with a whole library of necromancy

Above: "I'll break my staff, bury it certain fathoms in the earth." As he prepares a last spell, Prospero announces he is going to abjure practicing magic (*Act V, Scene I*)

Right: Light and swift, Ariel is Prospero's messenger and chief of the virtuous spirits which inhabit the magic isle

Act II. Scene I. [*Another part of the island.*]

Enter *Alonso, Sebastian, Antonio, Gonzalo, Adrian, Francisco*, and others.

Gon. Beseech you, sir, be merry. You have cause
(So have we all) of joy; for our escape
Is much beyond our loss. Our hint of woe
Is common. Every day some sailor's wife,
The master of some merchant, and the merchant,
Have just our theme of woe; but for the miracle,
I mean our preservation, few in millions
Can speak like us. Then wisely, good sir, weigh
Our sorrow with our comfort.

Alon. Prithee peace.

Seb. He receives comfort like cold porridge.

Ant. The visitor will not give him o'er so.

Seb. Look, he's winding up the watch of his wit; by-and-by it will strike.

Gon. Sir —

Seb. One. Tell.

Gon. When every grief is entertain'd that's offer'd,
Comes to th' entertainer —

Seb. A dollar.

Gon. Dolour comes to him, indeed. You have spoken truer than you purpos'd.

Seb. You have taken it wiselier than I meant you should.

Gon. Therefore, my lord —

Ant. Fie, what a spendthrift is he of his tongue!

Alon. I prithee spare.

Gon. Well, I have done. But yet —

Seb. He will be talking.

Ant. Which, of he or Adrian, for a good wager, first begins to crow?

Seb. The old cock.

Ant. The cock'rel.

Seb. Done! The wager?

Ant. A laughter.

Seb. A match!

Adr. Though this island seem to be desert —

Ant. Ha, ha, ha!

Seb. So, you're paid.

Adr. Uninhabitable and almost inaccessible—

Seb. Yet —

Adr. Yet —

Ant. He could not miss't.

Adr. It must needs be of subtle, tender, and delicate temperance.

Ant. Temperance was a delicate wench.

Seb. Ay, and a subtle, as he most learnedly deliver'd.

Adr. The air breathes upon us here most sweetly.

Seb. As if it had lungs, and rotten ones.

Ant. Or as 'twere perfum'd by a fen.

Gon. Here is everything advantageous to life.

Ant. True; save means to live.

Seb. Of that there's none, or little.

Gon. How lush and lusty the grass looks! how green!

Ant. The ground indeed is tawny.

Seb. With an eye of green in't.

Ant. He misses not much.

Seb. No; he doth but mistake the truth totally.

Gon. But the rarity of it is — which is indeed almost beyond credit —

Seb. As many vouch'd rarities are.

Gon. That our garments, being, as they were, drench'd in the sea, hold, notwithstanding, their freshness and gloss, being rather new-dy'd than stain'd with salt water.

Ant. If but one of his pockets could speak, would it not say he lies?

Seb. Ay, or very falsely pocket up his report.

Gon. Methinks our garments are now as fresh as when we put them on first in Afric, at the marriage of the King's fair daughter Claribel to the King of Tunis.

Seb. 'Twas a sweet marriage, and we prosper well in our return.

Adr. Tunis was never grac'd before with such a paragon to their queen.

Gon. Not since widow Dido's time.

Ant. Widow? A pox o' that! How came that 'widow' in? Widow Dido!

Seb. What if he had said 'widower Æneas' too? Good Lord, how you take it!

Adr. 'Widow Dido,' said you? You make me study of that. She was of Carthage, not of Tunis.

Gon. This Tunis, sir, was Carthage.

Adr. Carthage?

Gon. I assure you, Carthage.

Ant. His word is more than the miraculous harp.

Seb. He hath rais'd the wall, and houses too.

Ant. What impossible matter will he make easy next?

Seb. I think he will carry this island home in his pocket and give it his son for an apple.

Ant. And, sowing the kernels of it in the sea, bring forth more islands.

Gon. Ay!

Ant. Why, in good time!

Gon. Sir, we were talking that our garments seem now as fresh as when we were at Tunis at the marriage of your daughter, who is now Queen.

Ant. And the rarest that e'er came there.

Seb. Bate, I beseech you, widow Dido.

Ant. O, widow Dido? Ay, widow Dido!

Gon. Is not, sir, my doublet as fresh as the first day I wore it? I mean, in a sort.

Ant. That 'sort' was well fish'd for.

Gon. When I wore it at your daughter's marriage.

Alon. You cram these words into mine ears against
The stomach of my sense. Would I had never
Married my daughter there! for, coming thence,
My son is lost; and, in my rate, she too,
Who is so far from Italy remov'd
I ne'er again shall see her. O thou mine heir
Of Naples and of Milan, what strange fish
Hath made his meal on thee?

Fran. Sir, he may live.
I saw him beat the surges under him
And ride upon their backs. He trod the water,
Whose enmity he flung aside, and breasted
The surge most swol'n that met him. His bold head
'Bove the contentious waves he kept, and oar'd
Himself with his good arms in lusty stroke
To th' shore, that o'er his wave-worn basis bow'd,
As stooping to relieve him. I not doubt
He came alive to land.

Alon. No, no, he's gone.

Seb. Sir, you may thank yourself for this great loss,
That would not bless our Europe with your daughter,
But rather lose her to an African,
Where she, at least, is banish'd from your eye
Who hath cause to wet the grief on't.

Alon. Prithee peace.

Seb. You were kneel'd to and importun'd otherwise
By all of us; and the fair soul herself
Weigh'd, between loathness and obedience, at
Which end o' th' beam should bow. We have lost your son,
I fear, for ever. Milan and Naples have
Moe widows in them of this business' making
Than we bring men to comfort them.
The fault 's your own.

Alon. So is the dear'st o' th' loss.

Gon. My Lord Sebastian,
The truth you speak doth lack some gentleness,
And time to speak it in. You rub the sore
When you should bring the plaster.

Seb. Very well.

Ant. And most chirurgeonly.

Gon. It is foul weather in us all, good sir,
When you are cloudy.

Seb. Foul weather?

Ant. Very foul.

Gon. Had I plantation of this isle, my lord —

Ant. He'd sow't with nettle seed.

Seb. Or docks, or mallows.

Gon. And were the king on't, what would I do?

Seb. Scape being drunk, for want of wine.

Gon. I' th' commonwealth I would by contraries
Execute all things; for no kind of traffic
Would I admit; no name of magistrate;
Letters should not be known; riches, poverty,
And use of service, none; contract, succession,
Bourn, bound of land, tilth, vineyard, none;
No use of metal, corn, or wine, or oil;
No occupation; all men idle, all;
And women too, but innocent and pure;
No sovereignty.

Seb. Yet he would be king on't.

Ant. The latter end of his commonwealth forgets the beginning.

Gon. All things in common nature should produce
Without sweat or endeavour. Treason, felony,
Sword, pike, knife, gun, or need of any engine
Would I not have; but nature should bring forth,
Of it own kind, all foison, all abundance,
To feed my innocent people.

Seb. No marrying 'mong his subjects?

Ant. None, man! All idle — whores and knaves.

Gon. I would with such perfection govern, sir,
T' excel the golden age.

Seb. Save his Majesty!

Ant. Long live Gonzalo!

Gon. And — do you mark me, sir?

Alon. Prithee no more. Thou dost talk nothing to me.

Gon. I do well believe your Highness; and did it to minister occasion to these gentlemen, who are of such sensible and nimble lungs that they always use to laugh at nothing.

Ant. 'Twas you we laugh'd at.

Gon. Who in this kind of merry fooling am nothing to you. So you may continue, and laugh at nothing still.

Ant. What a blow was there given!

Seb. An it had not fall'n flatlong.

Gon. You are gentlemen of brave metal. You would lift the moon out of her sphere if she would continue in it five weeks without changing.

Enter *Ariel,* [invisible,] playing solemn music.

Seb. We would so, and then go a-batfowling.

Ant. Nay, good my lord, be not angry.

Gon. No, I warrant you. I will not adventure my discretion so weakly. Will you laugh me asleep, for I am very heavy?

Ant. Go sleep, and hear us.

[*All sleep except Alonso, Sebastian, and Antonio.*]

Alon. What, all so soon asleep? I wish mine eyes
Would, with themselves, shut up my thoughts. I find
They are inclin'd to do so.

Seb. Please you, sir,
Do not omit the heavy offer of it.
It seldom visits sorrow; when it doth,
It is a comforter.

Ant. We two, my lord,
Will guard your person while you take your rest,
And watch your safety.

Alon. Thank you. Wondrous heavy.

[*Alonso sleeps. Exit Ariel.*]

Seb. What a strange drowsiness possesses them!

Ant. It is the quality o' th' climate.

Seb. Why
Doth it not then our eyelids sink? I find not
Myself dispos'd to sleep.

Ant. Nor I. My spirits are nimble.
They fell together all, as by consent.
They dropp'd as by a thunder-stroke. What might,
Worthy Sebastian — O, what might? — No more!
And yet methinks I see it in thy face,
What thou shouldst be. Th' occasion speaks thee, and
My strong imagination sees a crown
Dropping upon thy head.

Seb. What? Art thou waking?

Ant. Do you not hear me speak?

Seb. I do; and surely
It is a sleepy language, and thou speak'st
Out of thy sleep. What is it thou didst say?
This is a strange repose, to be asleep
With eyes wide open; standing, speaking, moving —
And yet so fast asleep.

Ant. Noble Sebastian,
Thou let'st thy fortune sleep — die, rather; wink'st
Whiles thou art waking.

Seb. Thou dost snore distinctly;
There's meaning in thy snores.

Ant. I am more serious than my custom. You
Must be so too, if heed me; which to do
Trebles thee o'er.

Seb. Well, I am standing water.

Ant. I'll teach you how to flow.

Seb. Do so. To ebb
Hereditary sloth instructs me.

Ant. O,
If you but knew how you the purpose cherish
Whiles thus you mock it! how, in stripping it,
You more invest it! Ebbing men indeed
(Most often) do so near the bottom run
By their own fear or sloth.

Seb. Prithee say on.
The setting of thine eye and cheek proclaim
A matter from thee; and a birth, indeed,
Which throes thee much to yield.

Ant. Thus, sir:
Although this lord of weak remembrance, this
Who shall be of as little memory
When he is earth'd, hath here almost persuaded
(For he's a spirit of persuasion, only
Professes to persuade) the King his son's alive,
'Tis as impossible that he's undrown'd
As he that sleeps here swims.

Seb. I have no hope
That he's undrown'd.

Ant. O, out of that no hope
What great hope have you! No hope that way is
Another way so high a hope that even
Ambition cannot pierce a wink beyond,
But doubts discovery there. Will you grant with me
That Ferdinand is drown'd?

Seb. He's gone.

Ant. Then tell me,
Who's the next heir of Naples?

Seb. Claribel.

Ant. She that is Queen of Tunis; she that dwells

Ten leagues beyond man's life; she that from Naples
Can have no note, unless the sun were post —
The man i' th' moon 's too slow — till new-born chins
Be rough and razorable; she that from whom
We all were sea-swallow'd, though some cast again,
And, by that destiny, to perform an act
Whereof what's past is prologue, what to come,
In yours and my discharge.

Seb. What stuff is this? How say you?
'Tis true my brother's daughter 's Queen of Tunis;
So is she heir of Naples; 'twixt which regions
There is some space.

Ant. A space whose ev'ry cubit
Seems to cry out 'How shall that Claribel
Measure us back to Naples? Keep in Tunis,
And let Sebastian wake!' Say this were death
That now hath seiz'd them, why, they were no worse
Than now they are. There be that can rule Naples
As well as he that sleeps; lords that can prate
As amply and unnecessarily
As this Gonzalo. I myself could make
A chough of as deep chat. O, that you bore
The mind that I do! What a sleep were this
For your advancement! Do you understand me?

Seb. Methinks I do.

Ant. And how does your content
Tender your own good fortune?

Seb. I remember
You did supplant your brother Prospero.

Ant. True.
And look how well my garments sit upon me,
Much feater than before! My brother's servants
Were then my fellows; now they are my men.

Seb. But, for your conscience —

Ant. Ay, sir! Where lies that? If 'twere a kibe,
'Twould put me to my slipper; but I feel not
This deity in my bosom. Twenty consciences
That stand 'twixt me and Milan, candied be they
And melt, ere they molest! Here lies your brother,
No better than the earth he lies upon
If he were that which now he's like — that's dead;
Whom I with this obedient steel (three inches of it)
Can lay to bed for ever; whiles you, doing thus,
To the perpetual wink for aye might put
This ancient morsel, this Sir Prudence, who
Should not upbraid our course. For all the rest,
They'll take suggestion as a cat laps milk;
They'll tell the clock to any business that
We say befits the hour.

Seb. Thy case, dear friend,
Shall be my precedent. As thou got'st Milan,
I'll come by Naples. Draw thy sword. One stroke
Shall free thee from the tribute which thou payest,
And I the King shall love thee.

Ant. Draw together;
And when I rear my hand, do you the like,
To fall it on Gonzalo. [*They draw.*]

Seb. O, but one word!
[*They converse apart.*]

Enter *Ariel*, [invisible,] with music and song.

Ari. My master through his art foresees the danger
That you, his friend, are in, and sends me forth
(For else his project dies) to keep them living.
Sings in Gonzalo's ear.

While you here do snoring lie,
Open-ey'd conspiracy
  His time doth take.
If of life you keep a care,
Shake off slumber and beware.
  Awake, Awake!

Ant. Then let us both be sudden.

Gon. [*wakes*] Now good angels
Preserve the King!
Why, how now? — [*Shakes Alonso.*] Ho, awake! — Why are you drawn?
Wherefore this ghastly looking?

Alon. [*wakes*] What's the matter?

Seb. Whiles we stood here securing your repose,
Even now, we heard a hollow burst of bellowing
Like bulls, or rather lions. Did't not wake you?
It struck mine ear most terribly.

Alon. I heard nothing.

Ant. O, 'twas a din to fright a monster's ear,
To make an earthquake! Sure it was the roar
Of a whole herd of lions.

Alon. Heard you this, Gonzalo?

Gon. Upon mine honour, sir, I heard a humming,
And that a strange one too, which did awake me.

I shak'd you, sir, and cried. As mine eyes open'd,
I saw their weapons drawn. There was a noise;
That's verily. 'Tis best we stand upon our guard,
Or that we quit this place. Let's draw our weapons.

Alon. Lead off this ground, and let's make further search
For my poor son.

Gon. Heavens keep him from these beasts!
For he is sure i' th' island.

Alon. Lead away.

Ari. Prospero my lord shall know what I have done.
So, King, go safely on to seek thy son. *Exeunt.*

Scene II. [*Another part of the island.*]

Enter *Caliban* with a burthen of wood. A noise of thunder heard.

Cal. All the infections that the sun sucks up
From bogs, fens, flats, on Prosper fall and make him
By inchmeal a disease! His spirits hear me,
And yet I needs must curse. But they'll nor pinch,
Fright me with urchin-shows, pitch me i' th' mire,
Nor lead me, like a firebrand, in the dark
Out of my way, unless he bid 'em; but
For every trifle are they set upon me;
Sometime like apes that mow and chatter at me,
And after bite me; then like hedgehogs which
Lie tumbling in my barefoot way and mount
Their pricks at my footfall; sometime am I
All wound with adders, who with cloven tongues
Do hiss me into madness.

Enter *Trinculo.*

Lo, now, lo!
Here comes a spirit of his, and to torment me
For bringing wood in slowly. I'll fall flat.
Perchance he will not mind me. [*Lies down.*]

Trin. Here's neither bush nor shrub to bear off any weather at all, and another storm brewing. I hear it sing i' th' wind. Yond same black cloud, yond huge one, looks like a foul bombard that would shed his liquor. If it should thunder as it did before, I know not where to hide my head. Yond same cloud cannot choose but fall by pailfuls. What have we here? a man or a fish? dead or alive? A fish: he smells like a fish; a very ancient and fishlike smell; a kind of, not of the newest, poor-John. A strange fish! Were I in England now, as once I was, and had but this fish painted, not a holiday fool there but would give a piece of silver. There would this monster make a man. Any strange beast there makes a man. When they will not give a doit to relieve a lame beggar, they will lay out ten to see a dead Indian. Legg'd like a man! and his fins like arms! Warm, o' my troth! I do now let loose my opinion, hold it no longer: this is no fish, but an islander, that hath lately suffered by a thunderbolt. [*Thunder.*] Alas, the storm is come again! My best way is to creep under his gaberdine. There is no other shelter hereabout. Misery acquaints a man with strange bedfellows. I will here shroud till the dregs of the storm be past. [*Creeps under Caliban's garment.*]

Enter *Stephano,* singing; [a bottle in his hand].

Ste. I shall no more to sea, to sea;
Here shall I die ashore.

This is a very scurvy tune to sing at a man's funeral. Well, here's my comfort. *Drinks.*

The master, the swabber, the boatswain, and I,
The gunner, and his mate,
Lov'd Mall, Meg, and Marian, and Margery,
But none of us car'd for Kate.
For she had a tongue with a tang,
Would cry to a sailor 'Go hang!'
She lov'd not the savour of tar nor of pitch;
Yet a tailor might scratch her where'er she did itch.
Then to sea, boys, and let her go hang!

This is a scurvy tune too; but here's my comfort. *Drinks.*

Cal. Do not torment me! O!

Ste. What's the matter? Have we devils here? Do you put tricks upon 's with salvages and men of Inde, ha? I have not scap'd drowning to be afeard now of your four legs; for it hath been said, 'As proper a man as ever went on four legs cannot make him give ground'; and it shall be said so again, while Stephano breathes at' nostrils.

Cal. The spirit torments me. O!

Ste. This is some monster of the isle, with four legs, who hath got, as I take it, an ague. Where the devil should he learn our language? I will give him some relief, if it be but for that. If I can recover him, and keep him tame, and get to Naples with him, he's a present for any emperor that ever trod on neat's leather.

Cal. Do not torment me prithee! I'll bring my wood home faster.

Ste. He's in his fit now and does not talk after the wisest. He shall taste of my bottle. If he have never drunk wine afore, it will go near to remove his fit. If I can recover him and keep him tame, I will not take too much for him; he shall pay for him that hath him, and that soundly.

Cal. Thou dost me yet but little hurt.
Thou wilt anon; I know it by thy trembling.
Now Prosper works upon thee.

Ste. Come on your ways. Open your mouth. Here is that which will give language to you, cat. Open your mouth. This will shake your shaking, I can tell you, and that soundly. [*Gives Caliban drink.*] You cannot tell who's your friend. Open your chaps again.

Trin. I should know that voice. It should be — but he is drown'd; and these are devils. O, defend me!

Ste. Four legs and two voices — a most delicate monster! His forward voice now is to speak well of his friend; his backward voice is to utter foul speeches and to detract. If all the wine in my bottle will recover him, I will help his ague. Come! [*Gives drink.*] Amen! I will pour some in thy other mouth.

Trin. Stephano!

Ste. Doth thy other mouth call me? Mercy, mercy! This is a devil, and no monster. I will leave him; I have no long spoon.

Trin. Stephano! If thou beest Stephano, touch me and speak to me; for I am Trinculo — be not afeard — thy good friend Trinculo.

Ste. If thou beest Trinculo, come forth. I'll pull thee by the lesser legs. If any be Trinculo's legs, these are they. [*Draws him out from under Caliban's garment.*] Thou art very Trinculo indeed! How cam'st thou to be the siege of this mooncalf? Can he vent Trinculos?

Trin. I took him to be kill'd with a thunderstroke. But art thou not drown'd, Stephano? I hope now thou art not drown'd. Is the storm overblown? I hid me under the dead mooncalf's gaberdine for fear of the storm. And art thou living, Stephano? O Stephano, two Neapolitans scap'd?

Ste Prithee do not turn me about. My stomach is not constant.

Cal. [*aside*] These be fine things, an if they be not sprites.
That's a brave god and bears celestial liquor.
I will kneel to him.

Ste. How didst thou scape? How cam'st thou hither? Swear by this bottle how thou cam'st hither. I escap'd upon a butt of sack which the sailors heaved o'erboard, by this bottle! which I made of the bark of a tree with mine own hands since I was cast ashore.

Cal. I'll swear upon that bottle to be thy true subject, for the liquor is not earthly.

Ste. Here! Swear then how thou escap'dst.

Trin. Swum ashore, man, like a duck. I can swim like a duck, I ll be sworn.

Ste. Here, kiss the book. [*Gives him drink.*] Though thou canst swim like a duck, thou art made like a goose.

Trin. O Stephano, hast any more of this?

Ste. The whole butt, man. My cellar is in a rock by th' seaside, where my wine is hid. How now, mooncalf? How does thine ague?

Cal. Hast thou not dropp'd from heaven?

Ste. Out o' th' moon, I do assure thee. I was the Man i' th' Moon when time was.

Cal. I have seen thee in her, and I do adore thee.
My mistress show'd me thee, and thy dog, and thy bush.

Ste. Come, swear to that; kiss the book. I will furnish it anon with new contents. Swear. [*Caliban drinks.*]

Trin. By this good light, this is a very shallow monster! I afeard of him? A very weak monster! The Man i' th' Moon? A most poor credulous monster! Well drawn, monster, in good sooth.

Cal. I'll show thee every fertile inch o' th' island;
And I will kiss thy foot. I prithee be my god.

Trin. By this light, a most perfidious and drunken monster! When 's god 's asleep he'll rob his bottle.

Cal. I'll kiss thy foot. I'll swear myself thy subject.

Ste. Come on then. Down, and swear!

Trin. I shall laugh myself to death at this puppy-headed monster. A most scurvy monster! I could find in my heart to beat him —

Ste. Come, kiss.

Trin. But that the poor monster 's in drink. An abominable monster!

Cal. I'll show thee the best springs; I'll pluck thee berries;
I'll fish for thee, and get thee wood enough.
A plague upon the tyrant that I serve!
I'll bear him no more sticks, but follow thee,
Thou wondrous man.

Trin. A most ridiculous monster, to make a wonder of a poor drunkard!

Cal. I prithee let me bring thee where crabs grow;
And I with my long nails will dig thee pig-nuts,
Show thee a jay's nest, and instruct thee how
To snare the nimble marmoset; I'll bring thee
To clust'ring filberts, and sometimes I'll get thee
Young scamels from the rock. Wilt thou go with me?

Ste. I prithee now lead the way without any more talking. Trinculo, the King and all our company else being drown'd, we will inherit here. Here, bear my bottle. Fellow Trinculo, we'll fill him by-and-by again.

Caliban sings drunkenly.

Cal. Farewell, master; farewell, farewell!

Trin. A howling monster! a drunken monster!

Cal. No more dams I'll make for fish,
Nor fetch in firing
At requiring,
Nor scrape trenchering, nor wash dish.
'Ban, 'Ban, Ca — Caliban
Has a new master. Get a new man.

Freedom, high-day! high-day, freedom! freedom, high-day, freedom!

Ste. O brave monster! lead the way.

Exeunt.

Act III. Scene I. [*Before* Prospero's *cell.*]

Enter *Ferdinand,* bearing a log.

Fer. There be some sports are painful, and their labour
Delight in them sets off; some kinds of baseness
Are nobly undergone, and most poor matters
Point to rich ends. This my mean task
Would be as heavy to me as odious, but
The mistress which I serve quickens what's dead
And makes my labours pleasures. O, she is
Ten times more gentle than her father's crabbed;
And he's compos'd of harshness! I must remove
Some thousands of these logs and pile them up,
Upon a sore injunction. My sweet mistress
Weeps when she sees me work, and says such baseness
Had never like executor. I forget;
But these sweet thoughts do even refresh my labours
Most busiest when I do it.

Enter *Miranda*; and *Prospero* [behind, *unseen*].

Mir. Alas, now pray you
Work not so hard! I would the lightning had
Burnt up those logs that you are enjoin'd to pile!
Pray set it down and rest you. When this burns,
'Twill weep for having wearied you. My father
Is hard at study. Pray now rest yourself.
He's safe for these three hours.

Fer. O most dear mistress,
The sun will set before I shall discharge
What I must strive to do.

Mir. If you'll sit down,
I'll bear your logs the while. Pray give me that.
I'll carry it to the pile.

Fer. No, precious creature.
I had rather crack my sinews, break my back,
Than you should such dishonour undergo
While I sit lazy by.

Mir. It would become me
As well as it does you; and I should do it
With much more ease; for my good will is to it,
And yours it is against.

Pros. [*aside*] Poor worm, thou art infected!
This visitation shows it.

Mir. You look wearily.

Fer. No, noble mistress. 'Tis fresh morning with me
When you are by at night. I do beseech you,
Chiefly that I might set it in my prayers,
What is your name?

Mir. Miranda. O my father,
I have broke your hest to say so!

Fer. Admir'd Miranda!
Indeed the top of admiration, worth
What's dearest to the world! Full many a lady
I have ey'd with best regard, and many a time
Th' harmony of their tongues hath into bondage
Brought my too diligent ear; for several virtues
Have I lik'd several women; never any
With so full soul but some defect in her
Did quarrel with the noblest grace she ow'd,

And put it to the foil; but you, O you,
So perfect and so peerless, are created
Of every creature's best!
Mir. I do not know
One of my sex; no woman's face remember,
Save, from my glass, mine own; nor have I seen
More that I may call men than you, good friend,
And my dear father. How features are abroad
I am skilless of; but, by my modesty
(The jewel in my dower), I would not wish
Any companion in the world but you;
Nor can imagination form a shape,
Besides yourself, to like of. But I prattle
Something too wildly, and my father's precepts
I therein do forget.
Fer. I am, in my condition,
A prince, Miranda; I do think, a king
(I would not so!), and would no more endure
This wooden slavery than to suffer
The fleshfly blow my mouth. Hear my soul speak!
The very instant that I saw you, did
My heart fly to your service; there resides,
To make me slave to it; and for your sake
Am I this patient log-man.
Mir. Do you love me?
Fer. O heaven, O earth, bear witness to this sound,
And crown what I profess with kind event
If I speak true! if hollowly, invert
What best is boded me to mischief! I,
Beyond all limit of what else i' th' world,
Do love, prize, honour you.
Mir. I am a fool
To weep at what I am glad of.
Pros. [*aside*] Fair encounter
Of two most rare affections! Heavens rain grace
On that which breeds between 'em!
Fer. Wherefore weep you?
Mir. At mine unworthiness, that dare not offer
What I desire to give, and much less take
What I shall die to want. But this is trifling;
And all the more it seeks to hide itself,
The bigger bulk it shows. Hence, bashful cunning!
And prompt me plain and holy innocence!
I am your wife, if you will marry me;
If not, I'll die your maid. To be your fellow
You may deny me; but I'll be your servant,
Whether you will or no.
Fer. My mistress, dearest!
And I thus humble ever.
Mir. My husband then?
Fer. Ay, with a heart as willing
As bondage e'er of freedom. Here's my hand.
Mir. And mine, with my heart in't; and now farewell
Till half an hour hence.
Fer. A thousand thousand!
Exeunt [*Ferdinand and Miranda severally*].
Pros. So glad of this as they I cannot be,
Who are surpris'd withal; but my rejoicing
At nothing can be more. I'll to my book;
For yet ere supper time must I perform
Much business appertaining. *Exit.*

Scene II. [*Another part of the island.*]

Enter *Caliban*, *Stephano*, and *Trinculo*.

Ste. Tell not me! When the butt is out, we will drink water; not a drop before. Therefore bear up and board 'em! Servant monster, drink to me.

Trin. Servant monster? The folly of this island! They say there's but five upon this isle. We are three of them. If th' other two be brain'd like us, the state totters.

Ste. Drink, servant monster, when I bid thee. Thy eyes are almost set in thy head.

Trin. Where should they be set else? He were a brave monster indeed if they were set in his tail.

Ste. My man-monster hath drown'd his tongue in sack. For my part, the sea cannot drown me. I swam, ere I could recover the shore, five-and-thirty leagues off and on, by this light. Thou shalt be my lieutenant, monster, or my standard.

Trin. Your lieutenant, if you list; he's no standard.

Ste. We'll not run, Monsieur Monster.

Trin. Nor go neither; but you'll lie like dogs, and yet say nothing neither.

Ste. Mooncalf, speak once in thy life, if thou beest a good mooncalf.

Cal. How does thy honour? Let me lick thy shoe.
I'll not serve him; he is not valiant.

Trin. Thou liest, most ignorant monster! I am in case to justle a constable. Why, thou debosh'd fish thou, was there ever man a coward that hath drunk so much sack as I to-day? Wilt thou tell a monstrous lie, being but half a fish and half a monster?

Cal. Lo, how he mocks me! Wilt thou let him, my lord?

Trin. 'Lord' quoth he? That a monster should be such a natural!

Cal. Lo, lo, again! Bite him to death I prithee.

Ste. Trinculo, keep a good tongue in your head. If you prove a mutineer — the next tree! The poor monster's my subject, and he shall not suffer indignity.

Cal. I thank my noble lord. Wilt thou be pleas'd
To hearken once again to the suit I made to thee?

Ste. Marry, will I. Kneel and repeat it; I will stand, and so shall Trinculo.

Enter *Ariel*, invisible.

Cal. As I told thee before, I am subject to a tyrant,
A sorcerer, that by his cunning hath
Cheated me of the island.

Ari. Thou liest.

Cal. Thou liest, thou jesting monkey thou!
I would my valiant master would destroy thee.
I do not lie.

Ste. Trinculo, if you trouble him any more in 's tale, by this hand, I will supplant some of your teeth.

Trin. Why, I said nothing.

Ste. Mum then, and no more. — Proceed.

Cal. I say by sorcery he got this isle;
From me he got it. If thy greatness will
Revenge it on him — for I know thou dar'st,
But this thing dare not —

Ste. That's most certain.

Cal. Thou shalt be lord of it, and I'll serve thee.

Ste. How now shall this be compass'd? Canst thou bring me to the party?

Cal. Yea, yea, my lord! I'll yield him thee asleep,
Where thou mayst knock a nail into his head.

Ari. Thou liest; thou canst not.

Cal. What a pied ninny's this! Thou scurvy patch!
I do beseech thy greatness give him blows
And take his bottle from him. When that's gone,
He shall drink naught but brine, for I'll not show him
Where the quick freshes are.

Ste. Trinculo, run into no further danger. Interrupt the monster one word further and, by this hand, I'll turn my mercy out o' doors and make a stockfish of thee.

Trin. Why, what did I? I did nothing. I'll go farther off.

Ste. Didst thou not say he lied?

Ari. Thou liest.

Ste. Do I so? Take thou that! [*Strikes Trinculo.*] As you like this, give me the lie another time.

Trin. I did not give thee the lie. Out o' your wits, and hearing too? A pox o' your bottle! This can sack and drinking do. A murrain on your monster, and the devil take your fingers!

Cal. Ha, ha, ha!

Ste. Now forward with your tale. — Prithee stand further off.

Cal. Beat him enough. After a little time
I'll beat him too.

Ste. Stand farther. — Come, proceed.

Cal. Why, as I told thee, 'tis a custom with him
I' th' afternoon to sleep. There thou mayst brain him,
Having first seiz'd his books, or with a log
Batter his skull, or paunch him with a stake,
Or cut his wesand with thy knife. Remember
First to possess his books; for without them
He's but a sot, as I am, nor hath not
One spirit to command. They all do hate him
As rootedly as I. Burn but his books.
He has brave utensils (for so he calls them)
Which, when he has a house, he'll deck withal.
And that most deeply to consider is
The beauty of his daughter. He himself
Calls her a nonpareil. I never saw a woman
But only Sycorax my dam and she;
But she as far surpasseth Sycorax
As great'st does least.

Ste. Is it so brave a lass?

Cal. Ay, lord. She will become thy bed, I warrant,
And bring thee forth brave brood.

Ste. Monster, I will kill this man. His daughter and I will be king and queen, save our Graces! and Trinculo and thyself shall be viceroys. Dost thou like the plot, Trinculo?

Trin. Excellent.

Ste. Give me thy hand. I am sorry I beat thee; but while thou liv'st, keep a good tongue in thy head.

Cal. Within this half hour will he be asleep.
Wilt thou destroy him then?

Ste. Ay, on mine honour.

Ari. This will I tell my master.

Cal. Thou mak'st me merry; I am full of pleasure.

Let us be jocund. Will you troll the catch
You taught me but whilere?

Ste. At thy request, monster, I will do reason, any reason. Come on, Trinculo, let us sing. *Sings.*

Flout 'em and scout 'em
And scout 'em and flout 'em!
Thought is free.

Cal. That's not the tune.

Ariel plays the tune on a tabor and pipe.

Ste. What is this same?

Trin. This is the tune of our catch, play'd by the picture of No-body.

Ste. If thou beest a man, show thyself in thy likeness. If thou beest a devil, take't as thou list.

Trin. O, forgive me my sins!

Ste. He that dies pays all debts. I defy thee. Mercy upon us!

Cal. Art thou afeard?

Ste. No, monster, not I.

Cal. Be not afeard. The isle is full of noises,
Sounds and sweet airs that give delight and hurt not.
Sometimes a thousand twangling instruments
Will hum about mine ears; and sometime voices
That, if I then had wak'd after long sleep,
Will make me sleep again; and then, in dreaming,
The clouds methought would open and show riches
Ready to drop upon me, that, when I wak'd,
I cried to dream again.

Ste. This will prove a brave kingdom to me, where I shall have my music for nothing.

Cal. When Prospero is destroy'd.

Ste. That shall be by-and-by. I remember the story.

Trin. The sound is going away. Let's follow it, and after do our work.

Ste. Lead, monster; we'll follow. I would I could see this taborer! He lays it on. Wilt come?

Trin. I'll follow, Stephano. *Exeunt.*

Scene III. [*Another part of the island.*]

Enter *Alonso, Sebastian, Antonio, Gonzalo, Adrian, Francisco, &c.*

Gon. By'r Lakin, I can go no further, sir!
My old bones ache. Here's a maze trod indeed
Through forthrights and meanders. By your patience,
I needs must rest me.

Alon. Old lord, I cannot blame thee,
Who am myself attach'd with weariness
To th' dulling of my spirits. Sit down and rest.
Even here I will put off my hope, and keep it
No longer for my flatterer. He is drown'd
Whom thus we stray to find; and the sea mocks
Our frustrate search on land. Well, let him go.

Ant. [*aside to Sebastian*] I am right glad that he's so out of hope.
Do not for one repulse forgo the purpose
That you resolv'd t' effect.

Seb. [*aside to Antonio*] The next advantage
Will we take throughly.

Ant. [*aside to Sebastian*] Let it be to-night;
For, now they are oppress'd with travel, they
Will not nor cannot use such vigilance
As when they are fresh.

Seb. [*aside to Antonio*] I say to-night. No more.

Solemn and strange music; and *Prospero* on the top (invisible).

Alon. What harmony is this? My good friends, hark!

Gon. Marvellous sweet music!

Enter several *strange Shapes*, bringing in a banquet; and dance about it with gentle actions of salutations; and, inviting the *King &c.* to eat, they depart.

Alon. Give us kind keepers, heavens! What were these?

Seb. A living drollery. Now I will believe
That there are unicorns; that in Arabia
There is one tree, the phœnix' throne; one phœnix
At this hour reigning there.

Ant. I'll believe both;
And what does else want credit, come to me,
And I'll be sworn 'tis true. Travellers ne'er did lie,
Though fools at home condemn 'em.

Gon. If in Naples
I should report this now, would they believe me?
If I should say, I saw such islanders
(For certes these are people of the island),
Who, though they are of monstrous shape, yet, note,

Their manners are more gentle, kind, than of
Our human generation you shall find
Many — nay, almost any.
Pros. [*aside*] Honest lord,
Thou hast said well; for some of you there present
Are worse than devils.
Alon. I cannot too much muse
Such shapes, such gesture, and such sound, expressing
(Although they want the use of tongue) a kind
Of excellent dumb discourse.
Pros. [*aside*] Praise in departing.
Fran. They vanish'd strangely.
Seb. No matter, since
They have left their viands behind; for we have stomachs.
Will't please you taste of what is here?
Alon. Not I.
Gon. Faith, sir, you need not fear. When we were boys,
Who would believe that there were mountaineers
Dewlapp'd like bulls, whose throats had hanging at 'em
Wallets of flesh? or that there were such men
Whose heads stood in their breasts? which now we find
Each putter-out of five for one will bring us
Good warrant of.
Alon. I will stand to, and feed;
Although my last, no matter, since I feel
The best is past. Brother, my lord the Duke,
Stand to, and do as we.

Thunder and lightning. Enter *Ariel, like a harpy*; claps his wings upon the table; and with a quaint device *the banquet vanishes.*

Ari. You are three men of sin, whom destiny —
That hath to instrument this lower world
And what is in't — the never-surfeited sea
Hath caus'd to belch up you, and on this island,
Where man doth not inhabit — you 'mongst men
Being most unfit to live. I have made you mad;
And even with such-like valour men hang and drown
Their proper selves.
[*Alonso, Sebastian, &c. draw their swords.*]
You fools! I and my fellows
Are ministers of Fate. The elements,
Of whom your swords are temper'd, may as well
Wound the loud winds, or with bemock'd-at stabs
Kill the still-closing waters, as diminish
One dowle that's in my plume. My fellow ministers
Are like invulnerable. If you could hurt,
Your swords are now too massy for your strengths
And will not be uplifted. But remember
(For that's my business to you) that you three
From Milan did supplant good Prospero;
Expos'd unto the sea, which hath requit it,
Him and his innocent child; for which foul deed
The powers, delaying (not forgetting), have
Incens'd the seas and shores, yea, all the creatures,
Against your peace. Thee of thy son, Alonso,
They have bereft; and do pronounce by me
Ling'ring perdition (worse than any death
Can be at once) shall step by step attend
You and your ways; whose wraths to guard you from,
Which here, in this most desolate isle, else falls
Upon your heads, is nothing but heart's sorrow
And a clear life ensuing.

He vanishes in thunder; then, to soft music, enter the *Shapes* again, and dance, with mocks and mows, and carrying out the table.

Pros. [*aside*] Bravely the figure of this harpy hast thou
Perform'd, my Ariel; a grace it had, devouring.
Of my instruction hast thou nothing bated
In what thou hadst to say. So, with good life
And observation strange, my meaner ministers
Their several kinds have done. My high charms work,
And these, mine enemies, are all knit up
In their distractions. They now are in my pow'r;
And in these fits I leave them, while I visit
Young Ferdinand, whom they suppose is drown'd,
And his and mine lov'd darling. [*Exit above.*]
Gon. I' th' name of something holy, sir, why stand you
In this strange stare?
Alon. O, it is monstrous, monstrous!
Methought the billows spoke and told me of it;
The winds did sing it to me; and the thunder,
That deep and dreadful organ pipe, pronounc'd
The name of Prosper. It did bass my trespass.
Therefore my son i' th' ooze is bedded; and

I'll seek him deeper than e'er plummet sounded
And with him there lie mudded. *Exit.*
Seb. But one fiend at a time,
I'll fight their legions o'er!
Ant. I'll be thy second.
Exeunt [Sebastian and Antonio].
Gon. All three of them are desperate. Their great guilt,
Like poison given to work a great time after,
Now gins to bite the spirits. I do beseech you,
That are of suppler joints, follow them swiftly
And hinder them from what this ecstasy
May now provoke them to.
Adr. Follow, I pray you.
Exeunt omnes.

ACT IV. Scene I. [*Before* Prospero's *cell.*]

Enter *Prospero, Ferdinand,* and *Miranda.*

Pros. If I have too austerely punish'd you,
Your compensation makes amends; for I
Have given you here a third of mine own life,
Or that for which I live; who once again
I tender to thy hand. All thy vexations
Were but my trials of thy love, and thou
Hast strangely stood the test. Here, afore heaven,
I ratify this my rich gift. O Ferdinand,
Do not smile at me that I boast her off,
For thou shalt find she will outstrip all praise
And make it halt behind her.
Fer. I do believe it
Against an oracle.
Pros. Then, as my gift, and thine own acquisition
Worthily purchas'd, take my daughter. But
If thou dost break her virgin-knot before
All sanctimonious ceremonies may
With full and holy rite be minist'red,
No sweet aspersion shall the heavens let fall
To make this contract grow; but barren hate,
Sour-ey'd disdain, and discord shall bestrew
The union of your bed with weeds so loathly
That you shall hate it both. Therefore take heed,
As Hymen's lamp shall light you!
Fer. As I hope
For quiet days, fair issue, and long life,
With such love as 'tis now, the murkiest den,
The most opportune place, the strong'st suggestion
Our worser genius can, shall never melt
Mine honour into lust, to take away
The edge of that day's celebration
When I shall think or Phœbus' steeds are founder'd
Or Night kept chain'd below.
Pros. Fairly spoke.
Sit then and talk with her; she is thine own.
What, Ariel! my industrious servant, Ariel!

Enter *Ariel.*

Ari. What would my potent master? Here I am.
Pros. Thou and thy meaner fellows your last service
Did worthily perform; and I must use you
In such another trick. Go bring the rabble,
O'er whom I give thee pow'r, here to this place.
Incite them to quick motion; for I must
Bestow upon the eyes of this young couple
Some vanity of mine art. It is my promise,
And they expect it from me.
Ari. Presently?
Pros. Ay, with a twink.
Ari. Before you can say 'Come' and 'Go,'
And breathe twice and cry, 'So, so,'
Each one, tripping on his toe,
Will be here with mop and mow.
Do you love me, master? No?
Pros. Dearly, my delicate Ariel. Do not approach
Till thou dost hear me call.
Ari. Well! I conceive.
Exit.
Pros. Look thou be true. Do not give dalliance
Too much the rein. The strongest oaths are straw
To th' fire i' th' blood. Be more abstemious,
Or else good night your vow!
Fer. I warrant you, sir.
The white cold virgin snow upon my heart
Abates the ardour of my liver.
Pros. Well.
Now come, my Ariel! Bring a corollary
Rather than want a spirit. Appear, and pertly!
No tongue! All eyes! Be silent. *Soft music.*

Enter *Iris.*

Iris. Ceres, most bounteous lady, thy rich leas
Of wheat, rye, barley, fetches, oats, and pease;

Thy turfy mountains, where live nibbling sheep,
And flat meads thatch'd with stover, them to keep;
Thy banks with pioned and twilled brims,
Which spongy April at thy hest betrims
To make cold nymphs chaste crowns; and thy broom groves,
Whose shadow the dismissed bachelor loves,
Being lasslorn; thy pole-clipt vineyard;
And thy sea-marge, sterile and rocky-hard,
Where thou thyself dost air — the queen o' th' sky,
Whose wat'ry arch and messenger am I,
Bids thee leave these, and with her sovereign grace,
Here on this grass-plot, in this very place,
To come and sport. Her peacocks fly amain.
Approach, rich Ceres, her to entertain.

Enter *Ceres.*

Cer. Hail, many-coloured messenger, that ne'er
Dost disobey the wife of Jupiter,
Who, with thy saffron wings, upon my flow'rs
Diffusest honey drops, refreshing show'rs,
And with each end of thy blue bow dost crown
My bosky acres and my unshrubb'd down,
Rich scarf to my proud earth — why hath thy queen
Summon'd me hither to this short-grass'd green?

Iris. A contract of true love to celebrate
And some donation freely to estate
On the bless'd lovers.

Cer. Tell me, heavenly bow,
If Venus or her son, as thou dost know,
Do now attend the Queen. Since they did plot
The means that dusky Dis my daughter got,
Her and her blind boy's scandal'd company
I have forsworn.

Iris. Of her society
Be not afraid. I met her Deity
Cutting the clouds towards Paphos, and her son
Dove-drawn with her. Here thought they to have done
Some wanton charm upon this man and maid,
Whose vows are, that no bed-right shall be paid
Till Hymen's torch be lighted; but in vain.
Mars's hot minion is return'd again;
Her waspish-headed son has broke his arrows,
Swears he will shoot no more, but play with sparrows
And be a boy right out.

[Enter *Juno.*]

Cer. Highest queen of state,
Great Juno, comes; I know her by her gait.

Juno. How does my bounteous sister? Go with me
To bless this twain, that they may prosperous be
And honour'd in their issue.

They sing.

Juno. Honour, riches, marriage blessing,
Long continuance, and increasing,
Hourly joys be still upon you!
Juno sings her blessings on you.

Cer. Earth's increase, foison plenty,
Barns and garners never empty,
Vines with clust'ring bunches growing,
Plants with goodly burthen bowing;
Spring come to you at the farthest
In the very end of harvest!
Scarcity and want shall shun you,
Ceres' blessing so is on you.

Fer. This is a most majestic vision, and
Harmonious charmingly. May I be bold
To think these spirits?

Pros. Spirits, which by mine art
I have from their confines call'd to enact
My present fancies.

Fer. Let me live here ever!
So rare a wond'red father and a wise
Makes this place Paradise.

Juno and Ceres whisper, and send Iris on employment.

Pros. Sweet now, silence!
Juno and Ceres whisper seriously.
There's something else to do. Hush and be mute,
Or else our spell is marr'd.

Iris. You nymphs, call'd Naiades, of the wand'ring brooks,
With your sedg'd crowns and ever-harmless looks,
Leave your crisp channels, and on this green land
Answer your summons. Juno does command.
Come, temperate nymphs, and help to celebrate
A contract of true love. Be not too late.

Enter certain *Nymphs.*

You sunburn'd sicklemen, of August weary,
Come hither from the furrow and be merry.
Make holiday. Your rye-straw hats put on,
And these fresh nymphs encounter every one
In country footing.

Enter certain *Reapers*, properly habited. They join with the *Nymphs* in a graceful dance; towards the end whereof *Prospero* starts suddenly and speaks; after which, to a strange, hollow, and confused noise, *they heavily vanish.*

Pros. [*aside*] I had forgot that foul conspiracy
Of the beast Caliban and his confederates
Against my life. The minute of their plot
Is almost come. — [*To the Spirits*] Well done! Avoid! No more!
Fer. This is strange. Your father's in some passion
That works him strongly.
Mir. Never till this day
Saw I him touch'd with anger so distemper'd.
Pros. You do look, my son, in a mov'd sort,
As if you were dismay'd. Be cheerful, sir.
Our revels now are ended. These our actors,
As I foretold you, were all spirits and
Are melted into air, into thin air;
And, like the baseless fabric of this vision,
The cloud-capp'd towers, the gorgeous palaces,
The solemn temples, the great globe itself,
Yea, all which it inherit, shall dissolve,
And, like this insubstantial pageant faded,
Leave not a rack behind. We are such stuff
As dreams are made on, and our little life
Is rounded with a sleep. Sir, I am vex'd.
Bear with my weakness. My old brain is troubled.
Be not disturb'd with my infirmity.
If you be pleas'd, retire into my cell
And there repose. A turn or two I'll walk
To still my beating mind.
Fer., Mir. We wish your peace. *Exeunt.*

Enter *Ariel.*

Pros. Come with a thought! I thank thee, Ariel. Come.
Ari. Thy thoughts I cleave to. What's thy pleasure?
Pros. Spirit,
We must prepare to meet with Caliban.
Ari. Ay, my commander. When I presented Ceres,
I thought to have told thee of it, but I fear'd
Lest I might anger thee.
Pros. Say again, where didst thou leave these varlets?
Ari. I told you, sir, they were redhot with drinking;
So full of valour that they smote the air
For breathing in their faces, beat the ground
For kissing of their feet; yet always bending
Towards their project. Then I beat my tabor;
At which like unback'd colts they prick'd their ears,
Advanc'd their eyelids, lifted up their noses
As they smelt music. So I charm'd their ears
That calf-like they my lowing follow'd through
Tooth'd briers, sharp furzes, pricking goss, and thorns,
Which ent'red their frail shins. At last I left them
I' th' filthy mantled pool beyond your cell,
There dancing up to th' chins, that the foul lake
O'erstunk their feet.
Pros. This was well done, my bird.
Thy shape invisible retain thou still.
The trumpery in my house, go bring it hither
For stale to catch these thieves.
Ari. I go, I go. *Exit.*
Pros. A devil, a born devil, on whose nature
Nurture can never stick! on whom my pains,
Humanely taken, all, all lost, quite lost!
And as with age his body uglier grows,
So his mind cankers. I will plague them all,
Even to roaring.

Enter *Ariel*, loaden with glistering apparel, etc.

Come, hang them on this line.

[*Prospero* and *Ariel* remain, invisible.] Enter *Caliban*, *Stephano*, and *Trinculo*, all wet.

Cal. Pray you tread softly, that the blind mole may not
Hear a foot fall. We now are near his cell.
Ste. Monster, your fairy, which you say is a harmless fairy, has done little better than play'd the Jack with us.
Trin. Monster, I do smell all horse-piss, at which my nose is in great indignation.
Ste. So is mine. Do you hear, monster? If I should take a displeasure against you, look you —
Trin. Thou wert but a lost monster.
Cal. Good my lord, give me thy favour still.
Be patient, for the prize I'll bring thee to
Shall hoodwink this mischance. Therefore speak softly.
All's hush'd as midnight yet.
Trin. Ay, but to lose our bottles in the pool —
Ste. There is not only disgrace and dishonour in that, monster, but an infinite loss.
Trin. That's more to me than my wetting. Yet this is your harmless fairy, monster.

Ste. I will fetch off my bottle, though I be o'er ears for my labour.

Cal. Prithee, my king, be quiet. Seest thou here?
This is the mouth o' th' cell. No noise, and enter.
Do that good mischief which may make this island
Thine own for ever, and I, thy Caliban,
For aye thy foot-licker.

Ste. Give me thy hand. I do begin to have bloody thoughts.

Trin. O King Stephano! O peer! O worthy Stephano, look what a wardrobe here is for thee!

Cal. Let it alone, thou fool! It is but trash.

Trin. O, ho, monster! we know what belongs to a frippery. O King Stephano!

Ste. Put off that gown, Trinculo. By this hand, I'll have that gown!

Trin. Thy Grace shall have it.

Cal. The dropsy drown this fool! What do you mean
To dote thus on such luggage? Let't alone,
And do the murther first. If he awake,
From toe to crown he'll fill our skins with pinches,
Make us strange stuff.

Ste. Be you quiet, monster. Mistress line, is not this my jerkin? [*Takes it down.*] Now is the jerkin under the line. Now, jerkin, you are like to lose your hair and prove a bald jerkin.

Trin. Do, do! We steal by line and level, an 't like your Grace.

Ste. I thank thee for that jest. Here's a garment for't. Wit shall not go unrewarded while I am king of this country. 'Steal by line and level' is an excellent pass of pate. There's another garment for't.

Trin. Monster, come put some lime upon your fingers, and away with the rest!

Cal. I will have none on't. We shall lose our time
And all be turn'd to barnacles, or to apes
With foreheads villanous low.

Ste. Monster, lay-to your fingers. Help to bear this away where my hogshead of wine is, or I'll turn you out of my kingdom. Go to, carry this.

Trin. And this.

Ste. Ay, and this.

A noise of hunters heard. Enter divers *Spirits* in shape of dogs and hounds, hunting them about, *Prospero* and *Ariel setting them on.*

Pros. Hey, Mountain, hey!

Ari. Silver! there it goes, Silver!

Pros. Fury, Fury! There, Tyrant, there! Hark, hark!

[*Caliban, Stephano, and Trinculo are driven out.*]

Go, charge my goblins that they grind their joints
With dry convulsions, shorten up their sinews
With aged cramps, and more pinch-spotted make them
Than pard or cat o' mountain.

Ari. Hark, they roar.

Pros. Let them be hunted soundly. At this hour
Lie at my mercy all mine enemies.
Shortly shall all my labours end, and thou
Shalt have the air at freedom. For a little
Follow, and do me service. *Exeunt.*

ACT V. Scene I. [*Before the cell of* Prospero.]

Enter *Prospero* in his magic robes, and *Ariel.*

Pros. Now does my project gather to a head.
My charms crack not, my spirits obey, and time
Goes upright with his carriage. How's the day?

Ari. On the sixth hour, at which time, my lord,
You said our work should cease.

Pros. I did say so
When first I rais'd the tempest. Say, my spirit,
How fares the King and 's followers?

Ari. Confin'd together
In the same fashion as you gave in charge,
Just as you left them — all prisoners, sir,
In the line grove which weather-fends your cell.
They cannot budge till your release. The King,
His brother, and yours abide all three distracted,
And the remainder mourning over them,
Brimful of sorrow and dismay; but chiefly
Him that you term'd, sir, the good old Lord Gonzalo.
His tears run down his beard like winter's drops
From eaves of reeds. Your charm so strongly works 'em,
That if you now beheld them, your affections
Would become tender.

Pros. Dost thou think so, spirit?

Ari. Mine would, sir, were I human.

Pros. And mine shall.
Hast thou, which art but air, a touch, a feeling
Of their afflictions, and shall not myself,
One of their kind, that relish all as sharply
Passion as they, be kindlier mov'd than thou art?
Though with their high wrongs I am struck to th' quick,
Yet with my nobler reason 'gainst my fury
Do I take part. The rarer action is
In virtue than in vengeance. They being penitent,
The sole drift of my purpose doth extend
Not a frown further. Go, release them, Ariel.
My charms I'll break, their senses I'll restore,
And they shall be themselves.

Ari. I'll fetch them, sir. *Exit.*

Pros. [*makes a magic circle with his staff*] Ye elves of hills, brooks, standing lakes, and groves,
And ye that on the sands with printless foot
Do chase the ebbing Neptune, and do fly him
When he comes back; you demi-puppets that
By moonshine do the green sour ringlets make,
Whereof the ewe not bites; and you whose pastime
Is to make midnight mushrumps, that rejoice
To hear the solemn curfew; by whose aid
(Weak masters though ye be) I have bedimm'd
The noontide sun, call'd forth the mutinous winds,
And 'twixt the green sea and the azur'd vault
Set roaring war; to the dread rattling thunder
Have I given fire and rifted Jove's stout oak
With his own bolt; the strong-bas'd promontory
Have I made shake and by the spurs pluck'd up
The pine and cedar; graves at my command
Have wak'd their sleepers, op'd, and let 'em forth
By my so potent art. But this rough magic
I here abjure; and when I have requir'd
Some heavenly music (which even now I do)
To work mine end upon their senses that
This airy charm is for, I'll break my staff,
Bury it certain fadoms in the earth,
And deeper than did ever plummet sound
I'll drown my book. *Solemn music.*

Here enters *Ariel* before; then *Alonso*, with a frantic gesture, attended by *Gonzalo*; *Sebastian* and *Antonio* in like manner, attended by *Adrian* and *Francisco*. They all enter the circle which *Prospero* had made, and there stand charm'd; which *Prospero* observing, speaks.

A solemn air, and the best comforter
To an unsettled fancy, cure thy brains
Now useless, boil'd within thy skull! There stand,
For you are spell-stopp'd.
Holy Gonzalo, honourable man,
Mine eyes, ev'n sociable to the show of thine,
Fall fellowly drops. The charm dissolves apace;
And as the morning steals upon the night,
Melting the darkness, so their rising senses
Begin to chase the ignorant fumes that mantle
Their clearer reason. O good Gonzalo,
My true preserver, and a loyal sir
To him thou follow'st! I will pay thy graces
Home both in word and deed. Most cruelly
Didst thou, Alonso, use me and my daughter.
Thy brother was a furtherer in the act.
Thou art pinch'd for't now, Sebastian. Flesh and blood,
You, brother mine, that entertain'd ambition,
Expell'd remorse and nature; who, with Sebastian
(Whose inward pinches therefore are most strong),
Would here have kill'd your king, I do forgive thee,
Unnatural though thou art. Their understanding
Begins to swell, and the approaching tide
Will shortly fill the reasonable shore,
That now lies foul and muddy. Not one of them
That yet looks on me or would know me. Ariel,
Fetch me the hat and rapier in my cell.
I will discase me, and myself present
As I was sometime Milan. Quickly, spirit!
Thou shalt ere long be free.

[Exit *Ariel* and returns immediately.]

Ariel sings and helps to attire him.

Where the bee sucks, there suck I;
In a cowslip's bell I lie;
There I couch when owls do cry.
On the bat's back I do fly
After summer merrily.
Merrily, merrily shall I live now
Under the blossom that hangs on the bough.

Pros. Why, that's my dainty Ariel! I shall miss thee,
But yet thou shalt have freedom. So, so, so.
To the King's ship, invisible as thou art!
There shalt thou find the mariners asleep
Under the hatches. The master and the boatswain
Being awake, enforce them to this place,
And presently, I prithee.

Ari. I drink the air before me, and return
Or ere your pulse twice beat. *Exit.*

Gon. All torment, trouble, wonder, and amazement
Inhabits here. Some heavenly power guide us
Out of this fearful country!
Pros. Behold, sir King,
The wronged Duke of Milan, Prospero.
For more assurance that a living prince
Does now speak to thee, I embrace thy body,
And to thee and thy company I bid
A hearty welcome.
Alon. Whe'r thou be'st he or no,
Or some enchanted trifle to abuse me,
As late I have been, I not know. Thy pulse
Beats, as of flesh and blood; and, since I saw thee,
Th' affliction of my mind amends, with which,
I fear, a madness held me. This must crave
(An if this be at all) a most strange story.
Thy dukedom I resign and do entreat
Thou pardon me my wrongs. But how should Prospero
Be living and be here?
Pros. First, noble friend,
Let me embrace thine age, whose honour cannot
Be measur'd or confin'd.
Gon. Whether this be
Or be not, I'll not swear.
Pros. You do yet taste
Some subtleties o' th' isle, that will not let you
Believe things certain. Welcome, my friends all.
[*Aside to Sebastian and Antonio*] But you, my brace of lords, were I so minded,
I here could pluck his Highness' frown upon you,
And justify you traitors. At this time
I will tell no tales.
Seb. [*aside*] The devil speaks in him.
Pros. No.
For you, most wicked sir, whom to call brother
Would even infect my mouth, I do forgive
Thy rankest fault — all of them; and require
My dukedom of thee, which perforce I know
Thou must restore.
Alon. If thou beest Prospero,
Give us particulars of thy preservation;
How thou hast met us here, who three hours since
Were wrack'd upon this shore; where I have lost
(How sharp the point of this remembrance is!)
My dear son Ferdinand.
Pros. I am woe for't, sir.
Alon. Irreparable is the loss, and patience
Says it is past her cure.
Pros. I rather think
You have not sought her help, of whose soft grace
For the like loss I have her sovereign aid
And rest myself content.
Alon. You the like loss?
Pros. As great to me as late; and, supportable
To make the dear loss, have I means much weaker
Than you may call to comfort you; for I
Have lost my daughter.
Alon. A daughter?
O heavens, that they were living both in Naples,
The King and Queen there! That they were, I wish
Myself were mudded in that oozy bed
Where my son lies. When did you lose your daughter?
Pros. In this last tempest. I perceive these lords
At this encounter do so much admire
That they devour their reason, and scarce think
Their eyes do offices of truth, their words
Are natural breath. But, howsoev'r you have
Been justled from your senses, know for certain
That I am Prospero, and that very duke
Which was thrust forth of Milan, who most strangely
Upon this shore, where you were wrack'd, was landed
To be the lord on't. No more yet of this;
For 'tis a chronicle of day by day,
Not a relation for a breakfast, nor
Befitting this first meeting. Welcome, sir.
This cell's my court. Here have I few attendants,
And subjects none abroad. Pray you look in.
My dukedom since you have given me again,
I will requite you with as good a thing,
At least bring forth a wonder to content ye
As much as me my dukedom.

Here Prospero discovers Ferdinand and Miranda playing at chess.

Mir. Sweet lord, you play me false.
Fer. No, my dearest love,
I would not for the world.
Mir. Yes, for a score of kingdoms you should wrangle,
And I would call it fair play.
Alon. If this prove
A vision of the island, one dear son
Shall I twice lose.
Seb. A most high miracle!
Fer. Though the seas threaten, they are merciful.
I have curs'd them without cause. [*Kneels.*]

Alon. Now all the blessings
Of a glad father compass thee about!
Arise, and say how thou cam'st here.
Mir. O, wonder!
How many goodly creatures are there here!
How beauteous mankind is! O brave new world
That has such people in't!
Pros. 'Tis new to thee.
Alon. What is this maid with whom thou wast at play?
Your eld'st acquaintance cannot be three hours.
Is she the goddess that hath sever'd us
And brought us thus together?
Fer. Sir, she is mortal;
But by immortal providence she's mine.
I chose her when I could not ask my father
For his advice, nor thought I had one. She
Is daughter to this famous Duke of Milan,
Of whom so often I have heard renown
But never saw before; of whom I have
Receiv'd a second life; and second father
This lady makes him to me.
Alon. I am hers.
But, O, how oddly will it sound that I
Must ask my child forgiveness!
Pros. There, sir, stop.
Let us not burthen our remembrance with
A heaviness that's gone.
Gon. I have inly wept,
Or should have spoke ere this. Look down, you gods,
And on this couple drop a blessed crown!
For it is you that have chalk'd forth the way
Which brought us hither.
Alon. I say amen, Gonzalo.
Gon. Was Milan thrust from Milan that his issue
Should become kings of Naples? O, rejoice
Beyond a common joy, and set it down
With gold on lasting pillars: In one voyage
Did Claribel her husband find at Tunis,
And Ferdinand her brother found a wife
Where he himself was lost; Prospero his dukedom
In a poor isle; and all of us ourselves
When no man was his own.
Alon. [*to Ferdinand and Miranda*] Give me your hands.
Let grief and sorrow still embrace his heart
That doth not wish you joy.
Gon. Be it so! Amen!

Enter *Ariel*, with the *Master* and *Boatswain* amazedly following.

O, look, sir; look, sir! Here is more of us!
I prophesied, if a gallows were on land,
This fellow could not drown. Now, blasphemy,
That swear'st grace o'erboard, not an oath on shore?
Hast thou no mouth by land? What is the news?
Boats. The best news is that we have safely found
Our king and company; the next, our ship,
Which, but three glasses since, we gave out split,
Is tight and yare and bravely rigg'd as when
We first put out to sea.
Ari. [*aside to Prospero*] Sir, all this service
Have I done since I went.
Pros. [*aside to Ariel*] My tricksy spirit!
Alon. These are not natural events; they strengthen
From strange to stranger. Say, how came you hither?
Boats. If I did think, sir, I were well awake,
I'ld strive to tell you. We were dead of sleep
And (how we know not) all clapp'd under hatches;
Where, but even now, with strange and several noises
Of roaring, shrieking, howling, jingling chains,
And moe diversity of sounds, all horrible,
We were awak'd; straightway at liberty;
Where we, in all her trim, freshly beheld
Our royal, good, and gallant ship; our master
Cap'ring to eye her. On a trice, so please you,
Even in a dream, were we divided from them
And were brought moping hither.
Ari. [*aside to Prospero*] Was't well done?
Pros. [*aside to Ariel*] Bravely, my diligence. Thou shalt be free.
Alon. This is as strange a maze as e'er men trod,
And there is in this business more than nature
Was ever conduct of. Some oracle
Must rectify our knowledge.
Pros. Sir, my liege,
Do not infest your mind with beating on
The strangeness of this business. At pick'd leisure,
Which shall be shortly, single I'll resolve you
(Which to you shall seem probable) of every
These happen'd accidents; till when, be cheerful
And think of each thing well. [*Aside to Ariel*] Come hither, spirit.
Set Caliban and his companions free.
Untie the spell. [*Exit Ariel.*] How fares my gracious sir?
There are yet missing of your company
Some few odd lads that you remember not.

Enter *Ariel,* driving in *Caliban, Stephano,* and *Trinculo,* in their stol'n apparel.

Ste. Every man shift for all the rest, and let no man take care for himself; for all is but fortune. Coragio, bully-monster, coragio!

Trin. If these be true spies which I wear in my head, here's a goodly sight.

Cal. O Setebos, these be brave spirits indeed!
How fine my master is! I am afraid
He will chastise me.

Seb. Ha, ha!
What things are these, my Lord Antonio?
Will money buy 'em?

Ant. Very like. One of them
Is a plain fish and no doubt marketable.

Pros. Mark but the badges of these men, my lords,
Then say if they be true. This misshapen knave,
His mother was a witch, and one so strong
That could control the moon, make flows and ebbs,
And deal in her command without her power.
These three have robb'd me, and this demi-devil
(For he's a bastard one) had plotted with them
To take my life. Two of these fellows you
Must know and own; this thing of darkness I
Acknowledge mine.

Cal. I shall be pinch'd to death.

Alon. Is not this Stephano, my drunken butler?

Seb. He is drunk now. Where had he wine?

Alon. And Trinculo is reeling ripe. Where should they
Find this grand liquor that hath gilded 'em?
How cam'st thou in this pickle?

Trin. I have been in such a pickle, since I saw you last, that I fear me will never out of my bones. I shall not fear fly-blowing.

Seb. Why, how now, Stephano?

Ste. O, touch me not! I am not Stephano, but a cramp.

Pros. You'ld be king o' the isle, sirrah?

Ste. I should have been a sore one then.

Alon. This is as strange a thing as e'er I look'd on.

Pros. He is as disproportion'd in his manners
As in his shape. Go, sirrah, to my cell;
Take with you your companions. As you look
To have my pardon, trim it handsomely.

Cal. Ay, that I will! and I'll be wise hereafter,
And seek for grace. What a thrice-double ass
Was I to take this drunkard for a god
And worship this dull fool!

Pros. Go to! Away!

Alon. Hence, and bestow your luggage where you found it.

Seb. Or stole it rather.

[*Exeunt Caliban, Stephano, and Trinculo.*]

Pros. Sir, I invite your Highness and your train
To my poor cell, where you shall take your rest
For this one night; which, part of it, I'll waste
With such discourse as, I not doubt, shall make it
Go quick away — the story of my life,
And the particular accidents gone by
Since I came to this isle; and in the morn
I'll bring you to your ship, and so to Naples,
Where I have hope to see the nuptial
Of these our dear-belov'd solemnized;
And thence retire me to my Milan, where
Every third thought shall be my grave.

Alon. I long
To hear the story of your life, which must
Take the ear strangely.

Pros. I'll deliver all;
And promise you calm seas, auspicious gales,
And sail so expeditious that shall catch
Your royal fleet far off. — My Ariel, chick,
That is thy charge. Then to the elements
Be free, and fare thou well — Please you draw near. *Exeunt omnes.*

EPILOGUE.

SPOKEN BY *Prospero.*

Now my charms are all o'erthrown,
And what strength I have's mine own,
Which is most faint. Now 'tis true
I must be here confin'd by you,
Or sent to Naples. Let me not,
Since I have my dukedom got
And pardon'd the deceiver, dwell
In this bare island by your spell;
But release me from my bands
With the help of your good hands.
Gentle breath of yours my sails
Must fill, or else my project fails,
Which was to please. Now I want
Spirits to enforce, art to enchant;
And my ending is despair
Unless I be reliev'd by prayer,
Which pierces so that it assaults
Mercy itself and frees all faults.
As you from crimes would pardon'd be,
Let your indulgence set me free.

Exit.

The Two Gentlemen of Verona

The sole authority for the text of The Two Gentlemen is the First Folio (1623), in which the stage directions are limited to exits and entrances. In each scene the entrances are indicated at the outset by a single collective stage direction which enumerates the characters, once for all, in substantially the order of their appearance. No entrances and very few exits are marked within the scene, but the scene generally ends with *exeunt* or *exit*. The same plan is followed in *The Merry Wives of Windsor* and, to a limited extent, in *The Winter's Tale*. What this collective method signifies is by no means clear. Some critics regard it as evidence that The Two Gentlemen was printed from what is called an 'assembled' copy. The prompter's copy, they think, had been lost or destroyed, and a text was reconstructed by bringing together the manuscript 'parts' of the several actors and utilizing a so-called 'plot,' that is, an outline indicating the order of scenes and specifying the characters in each. This complicated and laborious process is no doubt possible, but there is no likelihood that the Folio owes its excellent text of The Two Gentlemen to any such hazardous patchwork. In modern editions the stage directions are regulated in accordance with Shakespeare's usual practice.

The date of the play is uncertain, but it is clearly one of Shakespeare's earliest comedies. This is indicated by the style and metre, and by lack of maturity in both characterization and management of the plot. The final scene, though it opens with a fine poetic soliloquy, sacrifices everything to crude sensationalism and leaves us at odds with both Valentine and Proteus. The comic element also suggests an early stage of Shakespeare's art. The quibbling dialogues, which remind one of *Love's Labour's Lost* and *The Comedy of Errors*, are good of their kind, but not extraordinary. They show the influence of Lyly and follow a classical convention to which Shakespeare was, of course, obedient at the outset of his career. More distinguished are Launce's comic monologues, which have never been surpassed. Launce in The Two Gentlemen looks forward to Launcelot Gobbo in *The Merchant of Venice*. There are other forecasts. Compare, for instance, the scene in which Julia asks Lucetta's opinion of 'the fair resort of gentlemen that every day with parle encounter me' (i, 2) with the conversation between Portia and Nerissa in *The Merchant of Venice* (i, 2). The disguised Julia's rôle in the service of Proteus is like Viola's in *Twelfth Night*. The only bit of direct evidence as to date is the passage in which Francis Meres pays tribute to Shakespeare in his *Palladis Tamia: Wits Treasury* (1598):

> As *Plautus* and *Seneca* are accounted the best for Comedy and Tragedy among the Latines: so *Shakespeare* among the English is the most excellent in both kinds for the stage; for Comedy, witnes his *Gentlemen of Verona*, his *Errors*, his *Loue labors lost*, his *Loue labours wonne*, his *Midsummers night dreame*, & his *Merchant of Venice*: for Tragedy his *Richard the* 2. *Richard the* 3. *Henry the* 4. *King Iohn*, *Titus Andronicus* and his *Romeo and Iuliet*.

A probable date for the play is 1594.

There is no likelihood that The Two Gentlemen as we have it is a revision of an earlier form, though there may be some cuts in the Folio text; nor is there any foundation for the theory that Shakespeare had a collaborator. The merits and the defects are Shakespeare's own. That he wrote rapidly we know. This accounts well enough for some confusions of place, though these may be due to a copyist. Such slips of the pen or the mind need cause no surprise.

The main plot of THE TWO GENTLEMEN is based upon the episode of Felix and Felismena in the *Diana*, a Spanish pastoral romance by Jorge de Montemayor. The *Diana* was immensely popular. Several editions appeared before 1590. Bartholomew Yong's English translation, though finished by 1582, was not published until 1598. Shakespeare may have seen it in manuscript, though this seems unlikely, for Yong in his Preface indicates that he sent to the printer the only copy he had, which was 'verie darke and enterlined.' A French version by Nicolas Colin (1578, 1582, 1587) is also a possible intermediary. A play entitled *The History of Felix and Philiomena* was acted at court by the Queen's Players in 1585. Perhaps this was the link between Montemayor's romance and Shakespeare's comedy.

The story in the *Diana* runs as follows in Yong's translation:

Felix (Shakespeare's Proteus) is in love with Felismena (Shakespeare's Julia). When he has 'by sundrie signes, as by Tylt and Tourneyes, and by prauncing vp and down upone his proude Iennet before [her] windowes' made his devotion manifest, he ventures to send her a letter by her maid, Rosina (Shakespeare's Lucetta). She declines to receive it and upbraids Rosina, who carries the letter away. Next morning, however, the sly Rosina drops it in her mistress's chamber, and Felismena, who is in fact eager to read the letter, pretends to believe that it is addressed to Rosina by some lover and bids her pick it up and let her see it. [Shakespeare (i, 2) follows the *Diana* rather closely in these incidents.] Felismena's reply to Felix's letter, though coy, is encouraging, and for 'almost a whole year' there is a constant exchange of 'amorous letters and verses.' But Felix's father, fearing a hasty marriage, sends him to the court of the Princess Augusta Cæsarina, telling him that 'it was not meet that a young gentleman, and of so noble a house as he was, should spend his youth idly at home' (cf. i, 3). Julia follows, disguised in male attire, and lodges at an inn. Shortly after midnight, the host suggests that she should open her window if she cares for music. Thus she hears the faithless Felix serenading his new love, Celia — Shakespeare's Sylvia (iv, 2). Felismena becomes Felix's page and wins his confidence. He tells her that Celia had shown him favour at first, but that she has turned against him because of a rumour that he loves a lady in his own country and is only amusing himself. He even shows Felismena Celia's reproachful letter and reads to her the reply which she is to carry to Celia.

The disguised Julia's conversation with Proteus (iv, 4), in which she describes her own feelings, and her soliloquy immediately after are strongly reminiscent of Felismena's story. The same is true of Julia's interview with Sylvia in the same scene. One notes particularly Sylvia's emphasis on the fickleness of Proteus and Julia's description of her own faded beauty. Verbal agreement, however, between the *Diana* and THE TWO GENTLEMEN is very slight. If Shakespeare had used the extant English version, such agreement would probably be conspicuous. Contrast, in this regard, the use he makes of Greene's *Pandosto* in *The Winter's Tale*. The remainder of Felismena's story is quite different from Shakespeare's plot. There is no Valentine in the *Diana*, and therefore no conflict between love and friendship. Celia falls in love with the supposed page and wooes her passionately (cf. *Twelfth Night*). Meeting with no response, she threatens to kill herself, falls in a swoon, and dies. Felix, in despair, wanders away and all trace of him is lost. Felismena assumes the habit of a shepherdess and seeks him in many countries. At last she comes to a little island where a knight is defending himself against three assailants. One of them he kills; the other two are shot to death by Felismena's arrows. When the knight takes off his helmet to thank his rescuer, she recognizes the faithless Felix. He is repentant; she forgives him, and they are happily married.

THE TWO GENTLEMEN OF VERONA

The Names of all the Actors.

Duke [*of Milan*], father to *Silvia.*
Valentine, } the Two Gentlemen.
Proteus, }
Antonio, father to *Proteus.*
Thurio, a foolish rival to *Valentine.*
Eglamour, agent for *Silvia* in her escape.
Host, where *Julia* lodges.
Outlaws, with *Valentine.*
Speed, a clownish servant to *Valentine.*
Launce, the like to *Proteus.*
Panthino, servant to *Antonio.*

Julia, beloved of *Proteus.*
Silvia, beloved of *Valentine.*
Lucetta, waiting woman to *Julia.*

[Servants, Musicians.]

[SCENE. — *Verona; Milan; and a forest on the Milan frontier.*]

ACT I. [Scene I. *Verona. An open place.*]

Enter *Valentine* and *Proteus.*

Val. Cease to persuade, my loving Proteus:
Home-keeping youth have ever homely wits.
Were't not affection chains thy tender days
To the sweet glances of thy honour'd love,
I rather would entreat thy company
To see the wonders of the world abroad
Than (living dully sluggardiz'd at home)
Wear out thy youth with shapeless idleness.
But since thou lov'st, love still, and thrive therein,
Even as I would when I to love begin.
Pro. Wilt thou be gone? Sweet Valentine, adieu!
Think on thy Proteus when thou (haply) seest
Some rare noteworthy object in thy travel.
Wish me partaker in thy happiness
When thou dost meet good hap; and in thy danger,
If ever danger do environ thee,
Commend thy grievance to my holy prayers,
For I will be thy beadsman, Valentine.
Val. And on a love-book pray for my success?
Pro. Upon some book I love I'll pray for thee.
Val. That's on some shallow story of deep love —
How young Leander cross'd the Hellespont.
Pro. That's a deep story of a deeper love,
For he was more than over shoes in love.
Val. 'Tis true; for you are over boots in love,
And yet you never swum the Hellespont.
Pro. Over the boots? Nay, give me not the boots!
Val. No, I will not; for it boots thee not.
Pro. What?
Val. To be in love, where scorn is bought with groans;
Coy looks with heart-sore sighs; one fading moment's mirth
With twenty watchful, weary, tedious nights:
If haply won, perhaps a hapless gain;
If lost, why then a grievous labour won;
However — but a folly bought with wit,
Or else a wit by folly vanquished.
Pro. So, by your circumstance, you call me fool.
Val. So, by your circumstance, I fear you'll prove.
Pro. 'Tis love you cavil at. I am not Love.
Val. Love is your master, for he masters you;
And he that is so yoked by a fool,
Methinks should not be chronicled for wise.
Pro. Yet writers say, as in the sweetest bud
The eating canker dwells, so eating love
Inhabits in the finest wits of all.
Val. And writers say, as the most forward bud
Is eaten by the canker ere it blow,
Even so by love the young and tender wit
Is turn'd to folly, blasting in the bud,
Losing his verdure, even in the prime,
And all the fair effects of future hopes.
But wherefore waste I time to counsel thee
That art a votary to fond desire?

Once more adieu! My father at the road
Expects my coming, there to see me shipp'd.

Pro. And thither will I bring thee, Valentine.

Val. Sweet Proteus, no. Now let us take our leave.
To Milan let me hear from thee by letters
Of thy success in love, and what news else
Betideth here in absence of thy friend;
And I likewise will visit thee with mine.

Pro. All happiness bechance to thee in Milan!

Val. As much to you at home! And so farewell. *Exit.*

Pro. He after honour hunts, I after love.
He leaves his friends to dignify them more;
I leave myself, my friends, and all, for love.
Thou, Julia, thou, hast metamorphis'd me,
Made me neglect my studies, lose my time,
War with good counsel, set the world at naught;
Made wit with musing weak, heart sick with thought.

[Enter *Speed*.]

Speed. Sir Proteus, save you! Saw you my master?

Pro. But now he parted hence to embark for Milan.

Speed. Twenty to one then he is shipp'd already,
And I have play'd the sheep in losing him.

Pro. Indeed a sheep doth very often stray
An if the shepherd be awhile away.

Speed. You conclude that my master is a shepherd then, and I a sheep?

Pro. I do.

Speed. Why then, my horns are his horns, whether I wake or sleep.

Pro. A silly answer, and fitting well a sheep.

Speed. This proves me still a sheep.

Pro. True, and thy master a shepherd.

Speed. Nay, that I can deny by a circumstance.

Pro. It shall go hard but I'll prove it by another.

Speed. The shepherd seeks the sheep, and not the sheep the shepherd; but I seek my master, and my master seeks not me. Therefore I am no sheep.

Pro. The sheep for fodder follow the shepherd; the shepherd for food follows not the sheep. Thou for wages followest thy master; thy master for wages follows not thee. Therefore thou art a sheep.

Speed. Such another proof will make me cry 'baa.'

Pro. But dost thou hear? Gav'st thou my letter to Julia?

Speed. Ay, sir. I (a lost mutton) gave your letter to her (a lac'd mutton), and she (a lac'd mutton) gave me (a lost mutton) nothing for my labour.

Pro. Here's too small a pasture for such store of muttons.

Speed. If the ground be overcharg'd, you were best stick her.

Pro. Nay; in that you are astray: 'twere best pound you.

Speed. Nay, sir. Less than a pound shall serve me for carrying your letter.

Pro. You mistake. I mean the pound — a pinfold.

Speed. From a pound to a pin? Fold it over and over,
'Tis threefold too little for carrying a letter to your lover.

Pro. But what said she?

Speed. [*nods*] Ay.

Pro. Nod-ay? Why, that's noddy.

Speed. You mistook, sir. I say she did nod; and you ask me if she did nod; and I say 'Ay.'

Pro. And that set together is 'noddy.'

Speed. Now you have taken the pains to set it together, take it for your pains.

Pro. No, no! You shall have it for bearing the letter.

Speed. Well, I perceive I must be fain to bear with you.

Pro. Why, sir, how do you bear with me?

Speed. Marry, sir, the letter very orderly, having nothing but the word 'noddy' for my pains.

Pro. Beshrew me, but you have a quick wit!

Speed. And yet it cannot overtake your slow purse.

Pro. Come, come, open the matter in brief. What said she?

Speed. Open your purse, that the money and the matter may be both at once delivered.

Pro. Well, sir, here is for your pains. [*Gives him money.*] What said she?

Speed. Truly, sir, I think you'll hardly win her.

Pro. Why? Couldst thou perceive so much from her?

Speed. Sir, I could perceive nothing at all from her; no, not so much as a ducat for delivering your letter; and being so hard to me that brought your mind, I fear she'll prove as hard to you in telling your mind. Give her no token but stones, for she's as hard as steel.

Pro. What said she? nothing?

Speed. No, not so much as 'Take this for thy pains.' To testify your bounty, I thank you, you have testern'd me; in requital whereof, henceforth carry your letters yourself. And so, sir, I'll commend you to my master.

Pro. Go, go, be gone, to save your ship from wrack,
Which cannot perish, having thee aboard,
Being destin'd to a drier death on shore.
[*Exit Speed.*]
I must go send some better messenger;
I fear my Julia would not deign my lines,
Receiving them from such a worthless post.
Exit.

Scene II. [*Verona. The garden of* Julia's *house.*]

Enter *Julia* and *Lucetta.*

Jul. But say, Lucetta, now we are alone,
Wouldst thou then counsel me to fall in love?

Luc. Ay, madam, so you stumble not unheedfully.

Jul. Of all the fair resort of gentlemen
That every day with parle encounter me,
In thy opinion which is worthiest love?

Luc. Please you repeat their names, I'll show my mind
According to my shallow simple skill.

Jul. What think'st thou of the fair Sir Eglamour?

Luc. As of a knight well-spoken, neat, and fine;
But, were I you, he never should be mine.

Jul. What think'st thou of the rich Mercatio?

Luc. Well of his wealth; but of himself, so so.

Jul. What think'st thou of the gentle Proteus?

Luc. Lord, Lord! to see what folly reigns in us!

Jul. How now? What means this passion at his name?

Luc. Pardon, dear madam. 'Tis a passing shame
That I, unworthy body as I am,
Should censure thus on lovely gentlemen.

Jul. Why not on Proteus, as of all the rest?

Luc. Then thus: of many good I think him best.

Jul. Your reason?

Luc. I have no other but a woman's reason:
I think him so because I think him so.

Jul. And wouldst thou have me cast my love on him?

Luc. Ay, if you thought your love not cast away.

Jul. Why, he, of all the rest, hath never mov'd me.

Luc. Yet he, of all the rest, I think best loves ye.

Jul. His little speaking shows his love but small.

Luc. Fire that's closest kept burns most of all.

Jul. They do not love that do not show their love.

Luc. O, they love least that let men know their love.

Jul. I would I knew his mind.

Luc. Peruse this paper, madam.
[*Gives a letter.*]

Jul. 'To Julia.' Say, from whom?

Luc. That the contents will show.

Jul. Say, say! Who gave it thee?

Luc. Sir Valentine's page; and sent, I think, from Proteus.
He would have given it you; but I, being in the way,
Did in your name receive it. Pardon the fault, I pray.

Jul. Now, by my modesty, a goodly broker!
Dare you presume to harbour wanton lines?
To whisper, and conspire against my youth?
Now trust me, 'tis an office of great worth
And you an officer fit for the place.
There, take the paper. See it be return'd,
Or else return no more into my sight.

Luc. To plead for love deserves more fee than hate.

Jul. Will ye be gone?

Luc. That you may ruminate.
Exit.

Jul. And yet I would I had o'erlook'd the letter.
It were a shame to call her back again
And pray her to a fault for which I chid her.
What fool is she, that knows I am a maid
And would not force the letter to my view,
Since maids, in modesty, say 'no' to that
Which they would have the profferer construe 'ay'!
Fie, fie! how wayward is this foolish love,
That, like a testy babe, will scratch the nurse
And presently, all humbled, kiss the rod!
How churlishly I chid Lucetta hence

When willingly I would have had her here!
How angerly I taught my brow to frown
When inward joy enforc'd my heart to smile!
My penance is, to call Lucetta back
And ask remission for my folly past.
What ho! Lucetta!

[Enter *Lucetta*.]

Luc. What would your ladyship?
Jul. Is it near dinner time?
Luc. I would it were,
That you might kill your stomach on your meat
And not upon your maid.
Jul. What is't that you took up so gingerly?
Luc. Nothing.
Jul. Why didst thou stoop then?
Luc. To take a paper up that I let fall.
Jul. And is that paper nothing?
Luc. Nothing concerning me.
Jul. Then let it lie, for those that it concerns.
Luc. Madam, it will not lie where it concerns
Unless it have a false interpreter.
Jul. Some love of yours hath writ to you in rhyme.
Luc. That I might sing it, madam, to a tune.
Give me a note; your ladyship can set.
Jul. As little by such toys as may be possible.
Best sing it to the tune of 'Light o' love.'
Luc. It is too heavy for so light a tune.
Jul. Heavy? Belike it hath some burden then?
Luc. Ay! and melodious were it, would you sing it.
Jul. And why not you?
Luc. I cannot reach so high.
Jul. Let's see your song. [*Takes the letter.*]
How now, minion?
Luc. Keep tune there still, so you will sing it out.
And yet methinks I do not like this tune.
Jul. You do not?
Luc. No, madam. 'Tis too sharp.
Jul. You, minion, are too saucy.
Luc. Nay, now you are too flat
And mar the concord with too harsh a descant.
There wanteth but a mean to fill your song.
Jul. The mean is drown'd with your unruly bass.
Luc. Indeed I bid the base for Proteus.
Jul. This babble shall not henceforth trouble me.
Here is a coil with protestation! [*Tears the letter.*]
Go, get you gone; and let the papers lie.
You would be fing'ring them to anger me.
Luc. She makes it strange, but she would be best pleas'd
To be so ang'red with another letter. [*Exit.*]
Jul. Nay, would I were so ang'red with the same!
O hateful hands, to tear such loving words!
Injurious wasps, to feed on such sweet honey
And kill the bees that yield it with your stings!
I'll kiss each several paper for amends.
Look, here is writ 'kind Julia.' Unkind Julia,
As in revenge of thy ingratitude,
I throw thy name against the bruising stones,
Trampling contemptuously on thy disdain.
And here is writ 'love-wounded Proteus.'
Poor wounded name! My bosom, as a bed,
Shall lodge thee till thy wound be throughly heal'd;
And thus I search it with a sovereign kiss.
But twice or thrice was 'Proteus' written down.
Be calm, good wind, blow not a word away
Till I have found each letter in the letter,
Except mine own name. That some whirlwind bear
Unto a ragged, fearful, hanging rock
And throw it thence into the raging sea!
Lo, here in one line is his name twice writ:
'Poor forlorn Proteus, passionate Proteus,
To the sweet Julia.' That I'll tear away;
And yet I will not, sith so prettily
He couples it to his complaining names.
Thus will I fold them one upon another.
Now kiss, embrace, contend, do what you will.

[Enter *Lucetta*.]

Luc. Madam,
Dinner is ready, and your father stays.
Jul. Well, let us go.
Luc. What, shall these papers lie like tell-tales here?
Jul. If you respect them, best to take them up.
Luc. Nay, I was taken up for laying them down.
Yet here they shall not lie, for catching cold.
Jul. I see you have a month's mind to them.
Luc. Ay, madam, you may say what sights you see.
I see things too, although you judge I wink.
Jul. Come, come! Will't please you go?
Exeunt.

Scene III. [*Verona.* Antonio's *house.*]

Enter *Antonio* and *Panthino.*

Ant. Tell me, Panthino, what sad talk was that
Wherewith my brother held you in the cloister?

Pan. 'Twas of his nephew Proteus, your son.

Ant. Why, what of him?

Pan. He wond'red that your lordship
Would suffer him to spend his youth at home
While other men, of slender reputation,
Put forth their sons to seek preferment out:
Some to the wars, to try their fortune there;
Some to discover islands far away;
Some to the studious universities.
For any or for all these exercises
He said that Proteus your son was meet;
And did request me to importune you
To let him spend his time no more at home,
Which would be great impeachment to his age,
In having known no travel in his youth.

Ant. Nor need'st thou much importune me to that
Whereon this month I have been hammering.
I have consider'd well his loss of time,
And how he cannot be a perfect man,
Not being tried and tutor'd in the world.
Experience is by industry achiev'd
And perfected by the swift course of time.
Then tell me, whither were I best to send him?

Pan. I think your lordship is not ignorant
How his companion, youthful Valentine,
Attends the Emperor in his royal court.

Ant. I know it well.

Pan. 'Twere good, I think, your lordship sent him thither.
There shall he practise tilts and tournaments,
Hear sweet discourse, converse with noblemen,
And be in eye of every exercise
Worthy his youth and nobleness of birth.

Ant. I like thy counsel; well hast thou advis'd.
And that thou mayst perceive how well I like it,
The execution of it shall make known.
Even with the speediest expedition
I will dispatch him to the Emperor's court.

Pan. To-morrow, may it please you, Don Alphonso,
With other gentlemen of good esteem,
Are journeying to salute the Emperor
And to commend their service to his will.

Ant. Good company. With them shall Proteus go.

[Enter *Proteus* with a letter.]

And in good time! Now will we break with him.

Pro. Sweet love, sweet lines, sweet life!
Here is her hand, the agent of her heart;
Here is her oath for love, her honour's pawn.
O that our fathers would applaud our loves,
To seal our happiness with their consents!
O heavenly Julia!

Ant. How now? What letter are you reading there?

Pro. May't please your lordship, 'tis a word or two
Of commendations sent from Valentine,
Deliver'd by a friend that came from him.

Ant. Lend me the letter. Let me see what news.

Pro. There is no news, my lord, but that he writes
How happily he lives, how well belov'd,
And daily graced by the Emperor;
Wishing me with him, partner of his fortune.

Ant. And how stand you affected to his wish?

Pro. As one relying on your lordship's will
And not depending on his friendly wish.

Ant. My will is something sorted with his wish.
Muse not that I thus suddenly proceed;
For what I will, I will, and there an end.
I am resolv'd that thou shalt spend some time
With Valentinus in the Emperor's court.
What maintenance he from his friends receives,
Like exhibition thou shalt have from me.
To-morrow be in readiness to go.
Excuse it not, for I am peremptory.

Pro. My lord, I cannot be so soon provided.
Please you deliberate a day or two.

Ant. Look, what thou want'st shall be sent after thee.
No more of stay! To-morrow thou must go.
Come on, Panthino. You shall be employ'd
To hasten on his expedition.

[*Exeunt Antonio and Panthino.*]

Pro. Thus have I shunn'd the fire for fear of burning
And drench'd me in the sea, where I am drown'd.

I fear'd to show my father Julia's letter,
Lest he should take exceptions to my love;
And with the vantage of mine own excuse
Hath he excepted most against my love.
O, how this spring of love resembleth
The uncertain glory of an April day,
Which now shows all the beauty of the sun,
And by-and-by a cloud takes all away!

[Enter *Panthino*.]

Pan. Sir Proteus, your father calls for you.
He is in haste; therefore I pray you go.
Pro. Why, this it is! My heart accords thereto,
And yet a thousand times it answers 'no.'
Exeunt.

ACT II. Scene I. [*Milan. The* Duke's *Palace*.]

Enter *Valentine, Speed.*

Speed. Sir, your glove.
Val. Not mine. My gloves are on.
Speed. Why then, this may be yours, for this is but one.
Val. Ha, let me see! Ay, give it me; it's mine.
Sweet ornament that decks a thing divine!
Ah, Silvia, Silvia!

Speed. [*shouts*] Madam Silvia, Madam Silvia!

Val. How now, sirrah?

Speed. She is not within hearing, sir.

Val. Why, sir, who bade you call her?

Speed. Your worship, sir, or else I mistook.

Val. Well, you'll still be too forward.

Speed. And yet I was last chidden for being too slow.

Val. Go to, sir. Tell me, do you know Madam Silvia?

Speed. She that your worship loves?

Val. Why, how know you that I am in love?

Speed. Marry, by these special marks: first, you have learn'd, like Sir Proteus, to wreathe your arms like a malecontent; to relish a love song like a robin redbreast; to walk alone like one that had the pestilence; to sigh like a schoolboy that had lost his A B C; to weep like a young wench that had buried her grandam; to fast like one that takes diet; to watch like one that fears robbing; to speak puling like a beggar at Hallowmas. You were wont, when you laughed, to crow like a cock; when you walk'd, to walk like one of the lions; when you fasted, it was presently after dinner; when you look'd sadly, it was for want of money. And now you are metamorphis'd with a mistress, that, when I look on you, I can hardly think you my master.

Val. Are all these things perceiv'd in me?

Speed. They are all perceiv'd without ye.

Val. Without me? They cannot.

Speed. Without you? Nay, that's certain, for, without you were so simple, none else would. But you are so without these follies that these follies are within you and shine through you like the water in an urinal, that not an eye that sees you but is a physician to comment on your malady.

Val. But tell me, dost thou know my lady Silvia?

Speed. She that you gaze on so as she sits at supper?

Val. Hast thou observ'd that? Even she I mean.

Speed. Why, sir, I know her not.

Val. Dost thou know her by my gazing on her, and yet know'st her not?

Speed. Is she not hard-favour'd, sir?

Val. Not so fair, boy, as well-favour'd.

Speed. Sir, I know that well enough.

Val. What dost thou know?

Speed. That she is not so fair as (of you) well favour'd.

Val. I mean that her beauty is exquisite, but her favour infinite.

Speed. That's because the one is painted, and the other out of all count.

Val. How painted? and how out of count?

Speed. Marry, sir, so painted, to make her fair, that no man counts of her beauty.

Val. How esteem'st thou me? I account of her beauty.

Speed. You never saw her since she was deform'd.

Val. How long hath she been deform'd?

Speed. Ever since you lov'd her.

Val. I have lov'd her ever since I saw her, and still I see her beautiful.

Speed. If you love her, you cannot see her.

Val. Why?

Speed. Because Love is blind. O, that you had mine eyes! or your own eyes had the lights they were wont to have when you chid at Sir Proteus for going ungarter'd!

Val. What should I see then?

Speed. Your own present folly and her passing deformity; for he, being in love, could not see to garter his hose; and you, being in love, cannot see to put on your hose.

Val. Belike, boy, then you are in love; for last morning you could not see to wipe my shoes.

Speed. True, sir; I was in love with my bed. I thank you, you swing'd me for my love, which makes me the bolder to chide you for yours.

Val. In conclusion, I stand affected to her.

Speed. I would you were set; so your affection would cease.

Val. Last night she enjoin'd me to write some lines to one she loves.

Speed. And have you?

Val. I have.

Speed. Are they not lamely writ?

Val. No, boy, but as well as I can do them.

[Enter *Silvia.*]

Peace! here she comes.

Speed. [*aside*] O excellent motion! O exceeding puppet! Now will he interpret to her.

Val. Madam and mistress, a thousand good-morrows!

Speed. [*aside*] O, give ye good ev'n! Here's a million of manners.

Sil. Sir Valentine and servant, to you two thousand.

Speed. [*aside*] He should give her interest, and she gives it him.

Val. As you enjoin'd me, I have writ your letter
Unto the secret nameless friend of yours;
Which I was much unwilling to proceed in,
But for my duty to your ladyship. [*Gives a letter.*]

Sil. I thank you, gentle servant. 'Tis very clerkly done.

Val. Now trust me, madam, it came hardly off;
For, being ignorant to whom it goes,
I writ at random, very doubtfully.

Sil. Perchance you think too much of so much pains?

Val. No, madam. So it stead you, I will write
(Please you command) a thousand times as much;
And yet —

Sil. A pretty period! Well, I guess the sequel.
And yet I will not name it — and yet I care not —
And yet take this again — and yet I thank you —
Meaning henceforth to trouble you no more.

Speed. [*aside*] And yet you will; and yet, another 'yet.'

Val. What means your ladyship? Do you not like it?

Sil. Yes, yes. The lines are very quaintly writ;
But, since unwillingly, take them again.
Nay, take them! [*Gives back the letter.*]

Val. Madam, they are for you.

Sil. Ay, ay! you writ them, sir, at my request;
But I will none of them: they are for you.
I would have had them writ more movingly.

Val. Please you, I'll write your ladyship another.

Sil. And when it's writ, for my sake read it over;
And if it please you, so; if not, why, so!

Val. If it please me, madam, what then?

Sil. Why, if it please you, take it for your labour;
And so good morrow, servant. *Exit.*

Speed. [*aside*] O jest unseen, inscrutable, invisible,
As a nose on a man's face or a weathercock on a steeple!
My master sues to her; and she hath taught her suitor,
He being her pupil, to become her tutor.
O, excellent device! Was there ever heard a better,
That my master, being scribe, to himself should write the letter?

Val. How now, sir? What are you reasoning with yourself?

Speed. Nay, I was rhyming; 'tis you that have the reason.

Val. To do what?

Speed. To be a spokesman from Madam Silvia.

Val. To whom?

Speed. To yourself. Why, she wooes you by a figure.

Val. What figure?

Speed. By a letter, I should say.

Val. Why, she hath not writ to me!

Speed. What need she, when she hath made you write to yourself? Why, do you not perceive the jest?

Val. No, believe me.

Speed. No believing you indeed, sir! But did you perceive her earnest?

Val. She gave me none, except an angry word.

Speed. Why, she hath given you a letter.

Val. That's the letter I writ to her friend.

Speed. And that letter hath she deliver'd, and there an end.

Val. I would it were no worse.

Speed. I'll warrant you 'tis as well;
For often have you writ to her; and she, in modesty,
Or else for want of idle time, could not again reply;
Or fearing else some messenger that might her mind discover,
Herself hath taught her love himself to write unto her lover.
All this I speak in print, for in print I found it.
Why muse you, sir? 'Tis dinner time.

Val. I have din'd.

Speed. Ay, but hearken, sir. Though the chameleon Love can feed on the air, I am one that am nourish'd by my victuals, and would fain have meat. O, be not like your mistress. Be moved, be moved. *Exeunt.*

Scene II. [*Verona.* Julia's *house.*]

Enter *Proteus, Julia.*

Pro. Have patience, gentle Julia.

Jul. I must, where is no remedy.

Pro. When possibly I can, I will return.

Jul. If you turn not, you will return the sooner.
Keep this remembrance for thy Julia's sake. [*Gives a ring.*]

Pro. Why then, we'll make exchange. Here take you this. [*Gives her another.*]

Jul. And seal the bargain with a holy kiss.

Pro. Here is my hand for my true constancy;
And when that hour o'erslips me in the day
Wherein I sigh not, Julia, for thy sake,
The next ensuing hour some foul mischance
Torment me for my love's forgetfulness!
My father stays my coming. Answer not.
The tide is now. Nay, not thy tide of tears!
That tide will stay me longer than I should.
Julia, farewell! [*Exit Julia.*]
What, gone without a word?
Ay, so true love should do. It cannot speak,
For truth hath better deeds than words to grace it.

[Enter *Panthino.*]

Pan. Sir Proteus, you are stay'd for.

Pro. Go. I come, I come!
Alas, this parting strikes poor lovers dumb!
Exeunt.

Scene III. [*Verona. A street.*]

Enter *Launce,* [leading a dog].

Launce. Nay, 'twill be this hour ere I have done weeping; all the kind of the Launces have this very fault. I have receiv'd my proportion, like the Prodigious Son, and am going with Sir Proteus to the Imperial's court. I think Crab my dog be the sourest-natured dog that lives. My mother weeping; my father wailing; my sister crying; our maid howling; our cat wringing her hands, and all our house in a great perplexity — yet did not this cruel-hearted cur shed one tear. He is a stone, a very pebble stone, and has no more pity in him than a dog. A Jew would have wept to have seen our parting. Why, my grandam, having no eyes, look you, wept herself blind at my parting! Nay, I'll show you the manner of it. This shoe is my father. No, this left shoe is my father. No, no, this left shoe is my mother. Nay, that cannot be so neither. Yes, it is so, it is so! — it hath the worser sole. This shoe with the hole in it is my mother, and this my father. A vengeance on't! there 'tis! Now, sir, this staff is my sister; for, look you, she is as white as a lily and as small as a wand. This hat is Nan, our maid. I am the dog. No, the dog is himself, and I am the dog. O, the dog is me, and I am myself. Ay, so, so! Now come I to my father: 'Father, your blessing!' Now should not the shoe speak a word for weeping. Now should I kiss my father; well, he weeps on. Now come I to my mother. O that she could speak now like a wood woman! Well, I kiss her. Why, there 'tis! here's my mother's breath up and down. Now come I to my sister; mark the moan she makes. Now the dog all this while sheds not a tear, nor speaks a word; but see how I lay the dust with my tears.

[Enter *Panthino.*]

Pan. Launce, away, away! aboard! Thy master is shipp'd, and thou art to post after with oars. What's the matter? Why weep'st thou, man? Away, ass! You'll lose the tide if you tarry any longer.

Launce. It is no matter if the tied were lost, for it is the unkindest tied that ever any man tied.

Pan. What's the unkindest tide?

Launce. Why, he that's tied here! Crab, my dog.

Pan. Tut, man! I mean thou'lt lose the flood, and in losing the flood, lose thy voyage, and in losing thy voyage, lose thy master, and in losing thy master, lose thy service, and in losing thy service — Why dost thou stop my mouth?

Launce. For fear thou shouldst lose thy tongue.

Pan. Where should I lose my tongue?

Launce. In thy tale.

Pan. In my tail?

Launce. Lose the tide, and the voyage, and the master, and the service, and the tied! Why, man, if the river were dry, I am able to fill it with my tears; if the wind were down, I could drive the boat with my sighs.

Pan. Come! come away, man! I was sent to call thee.

Launce. Sir, call me what thou dar'st.

Pan. Wilt thou go?

Launce. Well, I will go. *Exeunt.*

Scene IV. [*Milan. The* Duke's *Palace.*]

Enter *Valentine, Silvia, Thurio, Speed.*

Sil. Servant!

Val. Mistress?

Speed. Master, Sir Thurio frowns on you.

Val. Ay, boy; it's for love.

Speed. Not of you.

Val. Of my mistress then.

Speed. 'Twere good you knock'd him. [*Exit.*]

Sil. Servant, you are sad.

Val. Indeed, madam, I seem so.

Thu. Seem you that you are not?

Val. Haply I do.

Thu. So do counterfeits.

Val. So do you.

Thu. What seem I that I am not?

Val. Wise.

Thu. What instance of the contrary?

Val. Your folly.

Thu. And how quote you my folly?

Val. I quote it in your jerkin.

Thu. My jerkin is a doublet.

Val. Well then, I'll double your folly.

Thu. How?

Sil. What, angry, Sir Thurio? Do you change colour?

Val. Give him leave, madam; he is a kind of chameleon.

Thu. That hath more mind to feed on your blood than live in your air.

Val. You have said, sir.

Thu. Ay, sir, and done too, for this time.

Val. I know it well, sir. You always end ere you begin.

Sil. A fine volley of words, gentlemen, and quickly shot off.

Val. 'Tis indeed, madam. We thank the giver.

Sil. Who is that, servant?

Val. Yourself, sweet lady; for you gave the fire. Sir Thurio borrows his wit from your ladyship's looks, and spends what he borrows kindly in your company.

Thu. Sir, if you spend word for word with me, I shall make your wit bankrupt.

Val. I know it well, sir. You have an exchequer of words and, I think, no other treasure to give your followers; for it appears by their bare liveries that they live by your bare words.

[Enter *Duke.*]

Sil. No more, gentlemen, no more! Here comes my father.

Duke. Now, daughter Silvia, you are hard beset.
Sir Valentine, your father is in good health.
What say you to a letter from your friends
Of much good news?

Val. My lord, I will be thankful
To any happy messenger from thence.

Duke. Know ye Don Antonio, your countryman?

Val. Ay, my good lord, I know the gentleman
To be of worth and worthy estimation,
And not without desert so well reputed.

Duke. Hath he not a son?

Val. Ay, my good lord; a son that well deserves
The honour and regard of such a father.

Duke. You know him well?

Val. I know him as myself; for from our infancy
We have convers'd, and spent our hours together;
And though myself have been an idle truant,

Omitting the sweet benefit of time
To clothe mine age with angel-like perfection,
Yet hath Sir Proteus (for that's his name)
Made use and fair advantage of his days —
His years but young, but his experience old;
His head unmellowed, but his judgment ripe;
And in a word (for far behind his worth
Comes all the praises that I now bestow)
He is complete in feature and in mind
With all good grace to grace a gentleman.
Duke. Beshrew me, sir, but if he make this good,
He is as worthy for an empress' love
As meet to be an emperor's counsellor.
Well, sir, this gentleman is come to me
With commendation from great potentates,
And here he means to spend his time awhile.
I think 'tis no unwelcome news to you.
Val. Should I have wish'd a thing, it had been he.
Duke. Welcome him then according to his worth.
Silvia, I speak to you; and you, Sir Thurio;
For Valentine, I need not cite him to it.
I will send him hither to you presently. [*Exit.*]
Val. This is the gentleman I told your ladyship
Had come along with me, but that his mistress
Did hold his eyes lock'd in her crystal looks.
Sil. Belike that now she hath enfranchis'd them
Upon some other pawn for fealty.
Val. Nay, sure, I think she holds them prisoners still.
Sil. Nay, then he should be blind, and being blind,
How could he see his way to seek out you?
Val. Why, lady, love hath twenty pair of eyes.
Thu. They say that Love hath not an eye at all.
Val. To see such lovers, Thurio, as yourself.
Upon a homely object Love can wink.

[Enter *Proteus.*]

Sil. Have done, have done! Here comes the gentleman.
Val. Welcome, dear Proteus! Mistress, I beseech you
Confirm his welcome with some special favour.
Sil. His worth is warrant for his welcome hither,
If this be he you oft have wish'd to hear from.
Val. Mistress, it is. Sweet lady, entertain him
To be my fellow servant to your ladyship.
Sil. Too low a mistress for so high a servant.
Pro. Not so, sweet lady, but too mean a servant
To have a look of such a worthy mistress.
Val. Leave off discourse of disability.
Sweet lady, entertain him for your servant.
Pro. My duty will I boast of, nothing else.
Sil. And duty never yet did want his meed.
Servant, you are welcome to a worthless mistress.
Pro. I'll die on him that says so but yourself.
Sil. That you are welcome?
Pro. That you are worthless.

[Enter a *Servant.*]

Serv. Madam, my lord your father would speak with you.
Sil. I wait upon his pleasure. [*Exit Servant.*]
Come, Sir Thurio,
Go with me. Once more, new servant, welcome.
I'll leave you to confer of home affairs;
When you have done, we look to hear from you.
Pro. We'll both attend upon your ladyship.
[*Exeunt Silvia and Thurio.*]
Val. Now tell me, how do all from whence you came?
Pro. Your friends are well and have them much commended.
Val. And how do yours?
Pro. I left them all in health.
Val. How does your lady, and how thrives your love?
Pro. My tales of love were wont to weary you;
I know you joy not in a love discourse.
Val. Ay, Proteus, but that life is alter'd now.
I have done penance for contemning Love,
Whose high imperious thoughts have punish'd me
With bitter fasts, with penitential groans,
With nightly tears, and daily heartsore sighs;
For, in revenge of my contempt of love,
Love hath chas'd sleep from my enthralled eyes
And made them watchers of mine own heart's sorrow.
O gentle Proteus, Love's a mighty lord,
And hath so humbled me as I confess
There is no woe to his correction,
Nor to his service no such joy on earth.
Now no discourse, except it be of love!
Now can I break my fast, dine, sup, and sleep
Upon the very naked name of love.
Pro. Enough! I read your fortune in your eye.
Was this the idol that you worship so?

John Neville in the role of the restless Valentine, who leaves home for adventure in Milan

Laurence Payne as the other gentleman, the fickle, perfidious Proteus, villain of the piece

THE TWO GENTLEMEN OF VERONA

PHOTOGRAPHS BY DESMOND TRIPP
PRODUCED BY THE BRISTOL OLD VIC COMPANY

Above: With her maid, Lucetta (Patricia Blyton), Julia (Pamela Alan) plans her journey to rejoin Proteus *(Act II, Scene VII)*

Left: "What think'st thou of the gentle Proteus?" Julia seeks Lucetta's approval of Proteus *(Act I, Scene II)*

Below left: Newton Blick in the comic role of Speed, servant of Valentine.

Below right: Launce (Michael Aldridge), servant of Proteus, delivers a comic monologue which is patiently received by his dog *(Act II, Scene III)*

"I am resolv'd that thou shalt spend some time with Valentinus in the emperor's court." Proteus is dismayed as his father, Antonio (Peter Howell), advised by his old steward, Panthino (Norman Tyrrell), tells him he is to leave Verona for Milan *(Act I, Scene III)*

"Here is my hand for my true constancy." Proteus' farewell to Julia *(Act II, Scene II)*

Speed haggles with Proteus over his fee for giving information about Julia *(Act I, Scene I)*

Having learned through Proteus that Valentine is planning to elope with his daughter Silvia, the Duke of Milan (William Squire) banishes him from Milan *(Act III, Scene I)*

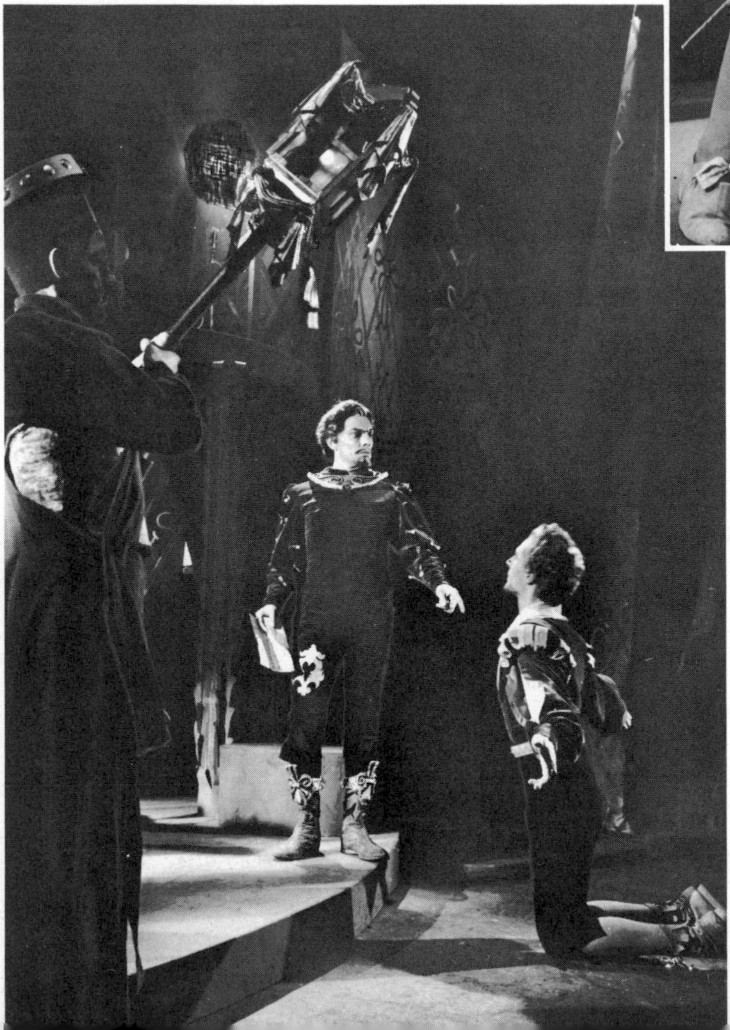

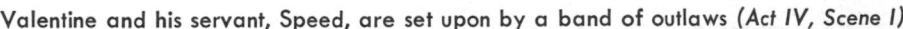

Valentine and Silvia (Gudrun Ure) are interrupted in a romantic scene by the jealous Thurio (John Warner), a favorite of the duke *(Act II, Scene IV)*

Valentine and his servant, Speed, are set upon by a band of outlaws *(Act IV, Scene I)*

Above: Disguised as a boy, Julia has taken service with Proteus. Here she punctuates the queries of the foppish Thurio with sarcastic asides *(Act V, Scene II)*

Left: Julia in her disguise as Sebastian

Below: At the bidding of Proteus, a band of musicians serenades Silvia in the courtyard of the duke's palace *(Act IV, Scene II)*

The duke assures his minion Thurio that Silvia's love will return to him now that Valentine is banished *(Act III, Scene II)*

Valentine comes to the defense of Silvia when Proteus seeks to force his attentions on her *(Act V, Scene IV)*

"Thou hast prevailed; I pardon them, and thee." The play's final scene: the lovers are united and the duke forgives both Valentine and the group of outlaws whom he joined in the forest after his banishment *(Act V, Scene IV)*

Val. Even she; and is she not a heavenly saint?
Pro. No; but she is an earthly paragon.
Val. Call her divine.
Pro. I will not flatter her.
Val. O, flatter me! for love delights in praises.
Pro. When I was sick you gave me bitter pills,
And I must minister the like to you.
Val. Then speak the truth by her. If not divine,
Yet let her be a principality,
Sovereign to all the creatures on the earth.
Pro. Except my mistress.
Val. Sweet, except not any,
Except thou wilt except against my love.
Pro. Have I not reason to prefer mine own?
Val. And I will help thee to prefer her too.
She shall be dignified with this high honour,
To bear my lady's train, lest the base earth
Should from her vesture chance to steal a kiss
And, of so great a favour growing proud,
Disdain to root the summer-swelling flow'r
And make rough winter everlastingly.
Pro. Why, Valentine! what braggardism is this?
Val. Pardon me, Proteus. All I can is nothing
To her, whose worth makes other worthies nothing.
She is alone.
Pro. Then let her alone.
Val. Not for the world! Why, man, she is mine own,
And I as rich in having such a jewel
As twenty seas, if all their sand were pearl,
The water nectar, and the rocks pure gold.
Forgive me that I do not dream on thee,
Because thou seest me dote upon my love.
My foolish rival, that her father likes
(Only for his possessions are so huge),
Is gone with her along; and I must after,
For love, thou know'st, is full of jealousy.
Pro. But she loves you?
Val. Ay, and we are betroth'd; nay more, our marriage hour,
With all the cunning manner of our flight,
Determin'd of: how I must climb her window,
The ladder made of cords, and all the means
Plotted and 'greed on for my happiness.
Good Proteus, go with me to my chamber,
In these affairs to aid me with thy counsel.
Pro. Go on before; I shall enquire you forth.
I must unto the road, to disembark
Some necessaries that I needs must use,
And then I'll presently attend you.
Val. Will you make haste?
Pro. I will. *Exit* [*Valentine*].
Even as one heat another heat expels
Or as one nail by strength drives out another,
So the remembrance of my former love
Is by a newer object quite forgotten.
Is it mine eye, or Valentinus' praise,
Her true perfection, or my false transgression,
That makes me reasonless, to reason thus?
She is fair; and so is Julia that I love —
That I did love, for now my love is thaw'd,
Which, like a waxen image 'gainst a fire,
Bears no impression of the thing it was.
Methinks my zeal to Valentine is cold
And that I love him not as I was wont.
O, but I love his lady too too much,
And that's the reason I love him so little.
How shall I dote on her with more advice
That thus without advice begin to love her!
'Tis but her picture I have yet beheld,
And that hath dazzled my reason's light;
But when I look on her perfections,
There is no reason but I shall be blind.
If I can check my erring love, I will;
If not, to compass her I'll use my skill. *Exit*

Scene V. [*Milan. A street.*]

Enter *Speed* and *Launce*, [meeting].

Speed. Launce! by mine honesty, welcome to Milan!

Launce. Forswear not thyself, sweet youth, for I am not welcome. I reckon this always: that a man is never undone till he be hang'd, nor never welcome to a place till some certain shot be paid and the hostess say 'Welcome.'

Speed. Come on, you madcap. I'll to the alehouse with you presently, where for one shot of five pence thou shalt have five thousand welcomes. But, sirrah, how did thy master part with Madam Julia?

Launce. Marry, after they clos'd in earnest, they parted very fairly in jest.

Speed. But shall she marry him?

Launce. No.

Speed. How then? Shall he marry her?

Launce. No, neither.

Speed. What, are they broken?

Launce. No, they are both as whole as a fish.

Speed. Why then, how stands the matter with them?

Launce. Marry, thus: when it stands well with him, it stands well with her.

Speed. What an ass art thou! I understand thee not.

Launce. What a block art thou that thou canst not! My staff understands me.

Speed. What thou say'st?

Launce. Ay, and what I do too. Look thee, I'll but lean, and my staff understands me.

Speed. It stands under thee indeed.

Launce. Why, stand-under and under-stand is all one.

Speed. But tell me true, will't be a match?

Launce. Ask my dog. If he say ay, it will; if he say no, it will; if he shake his tail and say nothing, it will.

Speed. The conclusion is, then, that it will.

Launce. Thou shalt never get such a secret from me but by a parable.

Speed. 'Tis well that I get it so. But, Launce, how say'st thou that my master is become a notable lover?

Launce. I never knew him otherwise.

Speed. Than how?

Launce. A notable lubber, as thou reportest him to be.

Speed. Why, thou whoreson ass, thou mistak'st me.

Launce. Why, fool, I meant not thee; I meant thy master.

Speed. I tell thee my master is become a hot lover.

Launce. Why, I tell thee I care not though he burn himself in love. If thou wilt, go with me to the alehouse; if not, thou art an Hebrew, a Jew, and not worth the name of a Christian.

Speed. Why?

Launce. Because thou hast not so much charity in thee as to go to the ale with a Christian. Wilt thou go?

Speed. At thy service. *Exeunt.*

Scene VI. [*Milan. The* Duke's *Palace.*]

Enter *Proteus* solus.

Pro. To leave my Julia, shall I be forsworn;
To love fair Silvia, shall I be forsworn;
To wrong my friend, I shall be much forsworn;
And ev'n that pow'r which gave me first my oath
Provokes me to this threefold perjury.
Love bade me swear, and Love bids me forswear.
O sweet-suggesting Love, if thou hast sinn'd,
Teach me, thy tempted subject, to excuse it!
At first I did adore a twinkling star,
But now I worship a celestial sun.
Unheedful vows may heedfully be broken,
And he wants wit that wants resolved will
To learn his wit t' exchange the bad for better.
Fie, fie, unreverend tongue, to call her bad
Whose sovereignty so oft thou hast preferr'd
With twenty thousand soul-confirming oaths!
I cannot leave to love, and yet I do;
But there I leave to love where I should love.
Julia I lose, and Valentine I lose.
If I keep them, I needs must lose myself;
If I lose them, thus find I by their loss —
For Valentine, myself; for Julia, Silvia.
I to myself am dearer than a friend,
For love is still most precious in itself;
And Silvia (witness heaven, that made her fair!)
Shows Julia but a swarthy Ethiope.
I will forget that Julia is alive,
Rememb'ring that my love to her is dead;
And Valentine I'll hold an enemy,
Aiming at Silvia as a sweeter friend.
I cannot now prove constant to myself
Without some treachery us'd to Valentine.
This night he meaneth with a corded ladder
To climb celestial Silvia's chamber window,
Myself in counsel his competitor.
Now presently I'll give her father notice
Of their disguising and pretended flight;
Who, all enrag'd, will banish Valentine,
For Thurio he intends shall wed his daughter;
But, Valentine being gone, I'll quickly cross
By some sly trick blunt Thurio's dull proceeding.
Love, lend me wings to make my purpose swift,
As thou hast lent me wit to plot this drift!
Exit.

Scene VII. [*Verona.* Julia's *house.*]

Enter *Julia* and *Lucetta.*

Jul. Counsel, Lucetta! gentle girl, assist me!
And ev'n in kind love I do conjure thee,

Who art the table wherein all my thoughts
Are visibly character'd and engrav'd,
To lesson me, and tell me some good mean
How with my honour I may undertake
A journey to my loving Proteus.

Luc. Alas, the way is wearisome and long!

Jul. A true-devoted pilgrim is not weary
To measure kingdoms with his feeble steps;
Much less shall she that hath Love's wings to fly,
And when the flight is made to one so dear,
Of such divine perfection as Sir Proteus.

Luc. Better forbear till Proteus make return.

Jul. O, know'st thou not his looks are my soul's food?
Pity the dearth that I have pined in
By longing for that food so long a time.
Didst thou but know the inly touch of love,
Thou wouldst as soon go kindle fire with snow
As seek to quench the fire of love with words.

Luc. I do not seek to quench your love's hot fire,
But qualify the fire's extreme rage,
Lest it should burn above the bounds of reason.

Jul. The more thou dam'st it up, the more it burns.
The current that with gentle murmur glides,
Thou know'st, being stopp'd, impatiently doth rage;
But when his fair course is not hindered,
He makes sweet music with th' enamell'd stones,
Giving a gentle kiss to every sedge
He overtaketh in his pilgrimage;
And so by many winding nooks he strays
With willing sport to the wide ocean.
Then let me go, and hinder not my course.
I'll be as patient as a gentle stream,
And make a pastime of each weary step
Till the last step have brought me to my love,
And there I'll rest, as after much turmoil
A blessed soul doth in Elysium.

Luc. But in what habit will you go along?

Jul. Not like a woman, for I would prevent
The loose encounters of lascivious men.
Gentle Lucetta, fit me with such weeds
As may beseem some well-reputed page.

Luc. Why then, your ladyship must cut your hair.

Jul. No, girl; I'll knit it up in silken strings
With twenty odd-conceited true-love knots.
To be fantastic may become a youth
Of greater time than I shall show to be.

Luc. What fashion, madam, shall I make your breeches?

Jul. That fits as well as 'Tell me, good my lord,
What compass will you wear your farthingale?'
Why, ev'n what fashion thou best lik'st, Lucetta.

Luc. You must needs have them with a codpiece, madam.

Jul. Out, out, Lucetta! that will be ill-favour'd.

Luc. A round hose, madam, now's not worth a pin
Unless you have a codpiece to stick pins on.

Jul. Lucetta, as thou lov'st me, let me have
What thou think'st meet, and is most mannerly.
But tell me, wench, how will the world repute me
For undertaking so unstaid a journey?
I fear me it will make me scandaliz'd.

Luc. If you think so, then stay at home and go not.

Jul. Nay, that I will not.

Luc. Then never dream on infamy, but go.
If Proteus like your journey when you come,
No matter who's displeas'd when you are gone.
I fear me he will scarce be pleas'd withal.

Jul. That is the least, Lucetta, of my fear.
A thousand oaths, an ocean of his tears,
And instances of infinite of love
Warrant me welcome to my Proteus.

Luc. All these are servants to deceitful men.

Jul. Base men that use them to so base effect!
But truer stars did govern Proteus' birth.
His words are bonds, his oaths are oracles,
His love sincere, his thoughts immaculate,
His tears pure messengers sent from his heart,
His heart as far from fraud as heaven from earth.

Luc. Pray heav'n he prove so when you come to him!

Jul. Now, as thou lov'st me, do him not that wrong
To bear a hard opinion of his truth!
Only deserve my love by loving him.
And presently go with me to my chamber
To take a note of what I stand in need of
To furnish me upon my longing journey.
All that is mine I leave at thy dispose,
My goods, my lands, my reputation;
Only, in lieu thereof, dispatch me hence.
Come, answer not, but to it presently!
I am impatient of my tarriance. *Exeunt.*

ACT III. Scene I. [*Milan. An anteroom in the* Duke's *Palace.*]

Enter *Duke, Thurio, Proteus.*

Duke. Sir Thurio, give us leave, I pray, awhile;
We have some secrets to confer about.
[*Exit Thurio.*]
Now, tell me, Proteus, what's your will with me?
Pro. My gracious lord, that which I would discover
The law of friendship bids me to conceal;
But when I call to mind your gracious favours
Done to me (undeserving as I am),
My duty pricks me on to utter that
Which else no worldly good should draw from me.
Know, worthy prince, Sir Valentine, my friend,
This night intends to steal away your daughter.
Myself am one made privy to the plot.
I know you have determin'd to bestow her
On Thurio, whom your gentle daughter hates;
And should she thus be stol'n away from you,
It would be much vexation to your age.
Thus, for my duty's sake, I rather chose
To cross my friend in his intended drift
Than, by concealing it, heap on your head
A pack of sorrows which would press you down,
Being unprevented, to your timeless grave.
Duke. Proteus, I thank thee for thine honest care,
Which to requite, command me while I live.
This love of theirs myself have often seen,
Haply when they have judg'd me fast asleep,
And oftentimes have purpos'd to forbid
Sir Valentine her company and my court;
But, fearing lest my jealous aim might err
And so (unworthily) disgrace the man
(A rashness that I ever yet have shunn'd),
I gave him gentle looks, thereby to find
That which thyself hast now disclos'd to me.
And, that thou mayst perceive my fear of this,
Knowing that tender youth is soon suggested,
I nightly lodge her in an upper tow'r,
The key whereof myself have ever kept,
And thence she cannot be convey'd away.
Pro. Know, noble lord, they have devis'd a mean
How he her chamber window will ascend
And with a corded ladder fetch her down;
For which the youthful lover now is gone,
And this way comes he with it presently,
Where, if it please you, you may intercept him.
But, good my lord, do it so cunningly
That my discovery be not aimed at;
For love of you, not hate unto my friend,
Hath made me publisher of this pretence.
Duke. Upon mine honour, he shall never know
That I had any light from thee of this.
Pro. Adieu, my lord. Sir Valentine is coming. [*Exit.*]

[Enter *Valentine.*]

Duke. Sir Valentine, whither away so fast?
Val. Please it your Grace, there is a messenger
That stays to bear my letters to my friends,
And I am going to deliver them.
Duke. Be they of much import?
Val. The tenure of them doth but signify
My health, and happy being at your court.
Duke. Nay then, no matter. Stay with me awhile.
I am to break with thee of some affairs
That touch me near; wherein thou must be secret.
'Tis not unknown to thee that I have sought
To match my friend Sir Thurio to my daughter.
Val. I know it well, my lord; and sure the match
Were rich and honourable. Besides, the gentleman
Is full of virtue, bounty. worth, and qualities
Beseeming such a wife as your fair daughter.
Cannot your Grace win her to fancy him?
Duke. No, trust me. She is peevish, sullen, froward,
Proud, disobedient, stubborn, lacking duty;
Neither regarding that she is my child
Nor fearing me as if I were her father.
And may I say to thee this pride of hers,
Upon advice, hath drawn my love from her,
And where I thought the remnant of mine age
Should have been cherish'd by her childlike duty,
I now am full resolv'd to take a wife
And turn her out to who will take her in.
Then let her beauty be her wedding dow'r;
For me and my possessions she esteems not.
Val. What would your Grace have me to do in this?

Duke. There is a lady in Milano here
Whom I affect; but she is nice and coy
And naught esteems my aged eloquence.
Now therefore would I have thee to my tutor
(For long agone I have forgot to court;
Besides, the fashion of the time is chang'd)
How and which way I may bestow myself
To be regarded in her sun-bright eye.
Val. Win her with gifts, if she respect not words.
Dumb jewels often in their silent kind
More than quick words do move a woman's mind.
Duke. But she did scorn a present that I sent her.
Val. A woman sometime scorns what best contents her.
Send her another! Never give her o'er,
For scorn at first makes after-love the more.
If she do frown, 'tis not in hate of you,
But rather to beget more love in you.
If she do chide, 'tis not to have you gone,
For why, the fools are mad if left alone.
Take no repulse, whatever she doth say;
For 'Get you gone!' she doth not mean 'Away!'
Flatter and praise, commend, extol their graces;
Though ne'er so black, say they have angels' faces.
That man that hath a tongue, I say is no man
If with his tongue he cannot win a woman.
Duke. But she I mean is promis'd by her friends
Unto a youthful gentleman of worth,
And kept severely from resort of men,
That no man hath access by day to her.
Val. Why then, I would resort to her by night.
Duke. Ay, but the doors be lock'd and keys kept safe,
That no man hath recourse to her by night.
Val. What lets but one may enter at her window?
Duke. Her chamber is aloft, far from the ground,
And built so shelving that one cannot climb it
Without apparent hazard of his life.
Val. Why then, a ladder quaintly made of cords,
To cast up, with a pair of anchoring hooks,
Would serve to scale another Hero's tow'r,
So bold Leander would adventure it.
Duke. Now, as thou art a gentleman of blood,
Advise me where I may have such a ladder.
Val. When would you use it? Pray, sir, tell me that.
Duke. This very night; for Love is like a child,
That longs for everything that he can come by.
Val. By seven o'clock I'll get you such a ladder.
Duke. But hark thee! I will go to her alone.
How shall I best convey the ladder thither?
Val. It will be light, my lord, that you may bear it
Under a cloak that is of any length.
Duke. A cloak as long as thine will serve the turn?
Val. Ay, my good lord.
Duke. Then let me see thy cloak.
I'll get me one of such another length.
Val. Why, any cloak will serve the turn, my lord.
Duke. How shall I fashion me to wear a cloak?
I pray thee let me feel thy cloak upon me.
[*Takes the cloak.*]
What letter is this same? What's here? 'To Silvia'?
And here an engine fit for my proceeding!
I'll be so bold to break the seal for once. [*Reads.*]

'My thoughts do harbour with my Silvia nightly,
And slaves they are to me, that send them flying.
O, could their master come and go as lightly,
Himself would lodge where (senseless) they are lying!
My herald thoughts in thy pure bosom rest them,
While I, their king, that thither them importune,
Do curse the grace that with such grace hath blest them,
Because myself do want my servants' fortune,
I curse myself, for they are sent by me,
That they should harbour where their lord would be.'

What's here?
'Silvia, this night I will enfranchise thee.'
'Tis so! and here's the ladder for the purpose.
Why, Phaëton (for thou art Merops' son),
Wilt thou aspire to guide the heavenly car
And with thy daring folly burn the world?
Wilt thou reach stars, because they shine on thee?
Go, base intruder, overweening slave!
Bestow thy fawning smiles on equal mates,
And think my patience, more than thy desert,
Is privilege for thy departure hence.
Thank me for this more than for all the favours
Which (all too much) I have bestow'd on thee.

But if thou linger in my territories
Longer than swiftest expedition
Will give thee time to leave our royal court,
By heaven, my wrath shall far exceed the love
I ever bore my daughter or thyself.
Be gone! I will not hear thy vain excuse,
But, as thou lov'st thy life, make speed from hence. [*Exit.*]

Val. And why not death rather than living torment?
To die is to be banish'd from myself;
And Silvia is myself. Banish'd from her
Is self from self — a deadly banishment!
What light is light, if Silvia be not seen?
What joy is joy, if Silvia be not by?
Unless it be to think that she is by
And feed upon the shadow of perfection.
Except I be by Silvia in the night,
There is no music in the nightingale.
Unless I look on Silvia in the day,
There is no day for me to look upon.
She is my essence, and I leave to be
If I be not by her fair influence
Foster'd, illumin'd, cherish'd, kept alive.
I fly not death, to fly his deadly doom:
Tarry I here, I but attend on death;
But fly I hence, I fly away from life.

[Enter *Proteus* and *Launce*.]

Pro. Run, boy, run, run, and seek him out!

Launce. So-hough, so-hough!

Pro. What seest thou?

Launce. Him we go to find. There's not a hair on 's head but 'tis a Valentine.

Pro. Valentine?

Val. No.

Pro. Who then? his spirit?

Val. Neither.

Pro. What then?

Val. Nothing.

Launce. Can nothing speak? Master, shall I strike?

Pro. Who wouldst thou strike?

Launce. Nothing.

Pro. Villain, forbear!

Launce. Why, sir, I'll strike nothing. I pray you —

Pro. Sirrah, I say forbear! — Friend Valentine, a word.

Val. My ears are stopp'd and cannot hear good news,
So much of bad already hath possess'd them.

Pro. Then in dumb silence will I bury mine,
For they are harsh, untuneable, and bad.

Val. Is Silvia dead?

Pro. No, Valentine.

Val. No Valentine indeed for sacred Silvia!
Hath she forsworn me?

Pro. No, Valentine.

Val. No Valentine, if Silvia have forsworn me!
What is your news?

Launce. Sir, there is a proclamation that you are vanished.

Pro. That thou art banished — O, that's the news! —
From hence, from Silvia, and from me thy friend.

Val. O, I have fed upon this woe already,
And now excess of it will make me surfeit.
Doth Silvia know that I am banished?

Pro. Ay, ay! and she hath offered to the doom
(Which, unrevers'd, stands in effectual force)
A sea of melting pearl, which some call tears.
Those at her father's churlish feet she tender'd;
With them, upon her knees, her humble self,
Wringing her hands, whose whiteness so became them
As if but now they waxed pale for woe.
But neither bended knees, pure hands held up,
Sad sighs, deep groans, nor silver-shedding tears
Could penetrate her uncompassionate sire;
But Valentine, if he be ta'en, must die.
Besides, her intercession chaf'd him so,
When she for thy repeal was suppliant,
That to close prison he commanded her,
With many bitter threats of biding there.

Val. No more! unless the next word that thou speak'st
Have some malignant power upon my life.
If so, I pray thee breathe it in mine ear,
As ending anthem of my endless dolour.

Pro. Cease to lament for that thou canst not help,
And study help for that which thou lament'st.
Time is the nurse and breeder of all good.
Here if thou stay, thou canst not see thy love;
Besides, thy staying will abridge thy life.
Hope is a lover's staff; walk hence with that
And manage it against despairing thoughts.
Thy letters may be here, though thou art hence,
Which, being writ to me, shall be deliver'd
Even in the milk-white bosom of thy love.
The time now serves not to expostulate.
Come, I'll convey thee through the city gate,
And, ere I part with thee, confer at large
Of all that may concern thy love affairs.
As thou lov'st Silvia (though not for thyself),
Regard thy danger, and along with me!

Val. I pray thee, Launce, an if thou seest my boy,
Bid him make haste and meet me at the North-gate.

Pro. Go, sirrah, find him out. Come, Valentine.

Val. O my dear Silvia! Hapless Valentine!
[*Exeunt Valentine and Proteus.*]

Launce. I am but a fool, look you, and yet I have the wit to think my master is a kind of a knave. But that's all one, if he be but one knave. He lives not now that knows me to be in love; yet I am in love. But a team of horse shall not pluck that from me, nor who 'tis I love. And yet 'tis a woman; but what woman, I will not tell myself. And yet 'tis a milkmaid. Yet 'tis not a maid, for she hath had gossips. Yet 'tis a maid, for she is her master's maid and serves for wages. She hath more qualities than a water spaniel, which is much in a bare Christian. [*Pulls out a paper.*] Here is the cate-log of her condition. 'Inprimis. She can fetch and carry.' Why, a horse can do no more. Nay, a horse cannot fetch, but only carry; therefore is she better than a jade. 'Item. She can milk.' Look you, a sweet virtue in a maid with clean hands.

[Enter *Speed.*]

Speed. How now, Signior Launce? What news with your mastership?

Launce. With my master's ship? Why, it is at sea.

Speed. Well, your old vice still — mistake the word. What news then in your paper?

Launce. The black'st news that ever thou heard'st.

Speed. Why, man? how black?

Launce. Why, as black as ink.

Speed. Let me read them.

Launce. Fie on thee, jolthead! Thou canst not read.

Speed. Thou liest! I can.

Launce. I will try thee. Tell me this: who begot thee?

Speed. Marry, the son of my grandfather.

Launce. O illiterate loiterer! It was the son of thy grandmother. This proves that thou canst not read.

Speed. Come, fool, come! try me in thy paper.

Launce. There! and Saint Nicholas be thy speed!

Speed. [*reads*] 'Inprimis. She can milk.'

Launce. Ay, that she can.

Speed. 'Item. She brews good ale.'

Launce. And thereof comes the proverb, 'Blessing of your heart, you brew good ale.'

Speed. 'Item. She can sew.'

Launce. That's as much as to say 'Can she so?'

Speed. 'Item. She can knit.'

Launce. What need a man care for a stock with a wench, when she can knit him a stock?

Speed. 'Item. She can wash and scour.'

Launce. A special virtue; for then she need not be wash'd and scour'd.

Speed. 'Item. She can spin.'

Launce. Then may I set the world on wheels, when she can spin for her living.

Speed. 'Item. She hath many nameless virtues.'

Launce. That's as much as to say 'bastard virtues'; that indeed know not their fathers, and therefore have no names.

Speed. Here follow her vices.

Launce. Close at the heels of her virtues.

Speed. 'Item. She is not to be kiss'd fasting, in respect of her breath.'

Launce. Well, that fault may be mended with a breakfast. Read on.

Speed. 'Item. She hath a sweet mouth.'

Launce. That makes amends for her sour breath.

Speed. 'Item. She doth talk in her sleep.'

Launce. It's no matter for that, so she sleep not in her talk.

Speed. 'Item. She is slow in words.'

Launce. O villain, that set this down among her vices! To be slow in words is a woman's only virtue. I pray thee, out with't, and place it for her chief virtue.

Speed. 'Item. She is proud.'

Launce. Out with that too! It was Eve's legacy and cannot be ta'en from her.

Speed. 'Item. She hath no teeth.'

Launce. I care not for that neither, because I love crusts.

Speed. 'Item. She is curst.'

Launce. Well, the best is, she hath no teeth to bite.

Speed. 'Item. She will often praise her liquor.'

Launce. If her liquor be good, she shall. If she will not, I will; for good things should be praised.

Speed. 'Item. She is too liberal.'

Launce. Of her tongue she cannot, for that's writ down she is slow of; of her purse she shall not, for that I'll keep shut. Now of another thing she may, and that cannot I help. Well, proceed.

Speed. 'Item. She hath more hair than wit, and more faults than hairs, and more wealth than faults.'

Launce. Stop there! I'll have her! She was mine, and not mine, twice or thrice in that last article. Rehearse that once more.

Speed. 'Item. She hath more hair than wit'—

Launce. More hair than wit. It may be. I'll prove it. The cover of the salt hides the salt, and therefore it is more than the salt; the hair that covers the wit is more than the wit, for the greater hides the less. What's next?

Speed. 'And more faults than hairs'—

Launce. That's monstrous! O that that were out!

Speed. 'And more wealth than faults.'

Launce. Why, that word makes the faults gracious. Well, I'll have her. And if it be a match, as nothing is impossible —

Speed. What then?

Launce. Why, then will I tell thee — that thy master stays for thee at the North-gate.

Speed. For me?

Launce. For thee? Ay. Who art thou? He hath stay'd for a better man than thee.

Speed. And must I go to him?

Launce. Thou must run to him, for thou hast stay'd so long that going will scarce serve the turn.

Speed. Why didst not tell me sooner? Pox of your love letters! [*Exit.*]

Launce. Now will he be swing'd for reading my letter. An unmannerly slave, that will thrust himself into secrets! I'll after, to rejoice in the boy's correction. *Exit.*

Scene II. [*Milan. The* Duke's *Palace.*]

Enter *Duke, Thurio.*

Duke. Sir Thurio, fear not but that she will love you
Now Valentine is banish'd from her sight.

Thu. Since his exile she hath despis'd me most,
Forsworn my company, and rail'd at me,
That I am desperate of obtaining her.

Duke. This weak impress of love is as a figure
Trenched in ice, which with an hour's heat
Dissolves to water and doth lose his form.
A little time will melt her frozen thoughts,
And worthless Valentine shall be forgot.

[Enter *Proteus.*]

How now, Sir Proteus? Is your countryman,
According to our proclamation, gone?

Pro. Gone, my good lord.

Duke. My daughter takes his going grievously.

Pro. A little time, my lord, will kill that grief.

Duke. So I believe, but Thurio thinks not so.
Proteus, the good conceit I hold of thee
(For thou hast shown some sign of good desert)
Makes me the better to confer with thee.

Pro. Longer than I prove loyal to your Grace
Let me not live to look upon your Grace.

Duke. Thou know'st how willingly I would effect
The match between Sir Thurio and my daughter?

Pro. I do, my lord.

Duke. And also, I think, thou art not ignorant
How she opposes her against my will?

Pro. She did, my lord, when Valentine was here.

Duke. Ay, and perversely she persevers so.
What might we do to make the girl forget
The love of Valentine and love Sir Thurio?

Pro. The best way is to slander Valentine
With falsehood, cowardice, and poor descent:
Three things that women highly hold in hate.

Duke. Ay, but she'll think that it is spoke in hate.

Pro. Ay, if his enemy deliver it.
Therefore it must with circumstance be spoken
By one whom she esteemeth as his friend.

Duke. Then you must undertake to slander him.

Pro. And that, my lord, I shall be loath to do.
'Tis an ill office for a gentleman,
Especially against his very friend.

Duke. Where your good word cannot advantage him,
Your slander never can endamage him.
Therefore the office is indifferent,
Being entreated to it by your friend.

Pro. You have prevail'd, my lord. If I can do it
By aught that I can speak in his dispraise,
She shall not long continue love to him.
But say this weed her love from Valentine,
It follows not that she will love Sir Thurio.

Thu. Therefore, as you unwind her love from him,

Lest it should ravel and be good to none,
You must provide to bottom it on me;
Which must be done by praising me as much
As you in worth dispraise Sir Valentine.

Duke. And, Proteus, we dare trust you in this kind,
Because we know, on Valentine's report,
You are already Love's firm votary
And cannot soon revolt and change your mind.
Upon this warrant shall you have access
Where you with Silvia may confer at large —
For she is lumpish, heavy, melancholy,
And, for your friend's sake, will be glad of you —
Where you may temper her by your persuasion
To hate young Valentine and love my friend.

Pro. As much as I can do, I will effect.
But you, Sir Thurio, are not sharp enough.
You must lay lime to tangle her desires
By wailful sonnets, whose composed rhymes
Should be full fraught with serviceable vows.

Duke. Ay!
Much is the force of heaven-bred poesy.

Pro. Say that upon the altar of her beauty
You sacrifice your tears, your sighs, your heart.
Write till your ink be dry, and with your tears
Moist it again; and frame some feeling line
That may discover such integrity.
For Orpheus' lute was strung with poets' sinews,
Whose golden touch could soften steel and stones,
Make tigers tame, and huge leviathans
Forsake unsounded deeps to dance on sands.
After your dire-lamenting elegies,
Visit by night your lady's chamber window
With some sweet consort. To their instruments
Tune a deploring dump. The night's dead silence
Will well become such sweet-complaining grievance.
This, or else nothing, will inherit her.

Duke. This discipline shows thou hast been in love.

Thu. And thy advice this night I'll put in practice.
Therefore, sweet Proteus, my direction-giver,
Let us into the city presently
To sort some gentlemen well skill'd in music.
I have a sonnet that will serve the turn
To give the onset to thy good advice.

Duke. About it, gentlemen!

Pro. We'll wait upon your Grace till after supper
And afterward determine our proceedings.

Duke. Even now about it! I will pardon you.
Exeunt.

ACT IV. Scene I. [*A road in a forest on the Milan frontier.*]

Enter certain *Outlaws.*

1. Out. Fellows, stand fast! I see a passenger.

2. Out. If there be ten, shrink not, but down with 'em!

Enter *Valentine* and *Speed.*

3. Out. Stand, sir, and throw us that you have about ye!
If not, we'll make you sit, and rifle you.

Speed. Sir, we are undone! These are the villains
That all the travellers do fear so much.

Val. My friends —

1. Out. That's not so, sir! We are your enemies.

2. Out. Peace! we'll hear him.

3. Out. Ay, by my beard, will we! for he is a proper man.

Val. Then know that I have little wealth to lose.
A man I am cross'd with adversity.
My riches are these poor habiliments,
Of which if you should here disfurnish me,
You take the sum and substance that I have.

2. Out. Whither travel you?

Val. To Verona.

1. Out. Whence came you?

Val. From Milan.

3. Out. Have you long sojourn'd there?

Val. Some sixteen months, and longer might have stay'd
If crooked fortune had not thwarted me.

1. Out. What, were you banish'd thence?

Val. I was.

2. Out. For what offence?

Val. For that which now torments me to rehearse.
I kill'd a man, whose death I much repent;
But yet I slew him manfully, in fight,
Without false vantage or base treachery.

1. Out. Why, ne'er repent it if it were done so.
But were you banish'd for so small a fault?

Val. I was, and held me glad of such a doom.
2. Out. Have you the tongues?
Val. My youthful travel therein made me happy,
Or else I often had been miserable.
3. Out. By the bare scalp of Robin Hood's fat friar,
This fellow were a king for our wild faction!
1. Out. We'll have him! Sirs, a word!

Speed. Master, be one of them. It's an honourable kind of thievery.

Val. Peace, villain!

2. Out. Tell us this: have you anything to take to?

Val. Nothing but my fortune.
3. Out. Know then that some of us are gentlemen,
Such as the fury of ungovern'd youth
Thrust from the company of awful men.
Myself was from Verona banished
For practising to steal away a lady,
An heir, and near allied unto the Duke.
2. Out. And I from Mantua, for a gentleman
Who, in my mood, I stabb'd unto the heart.
1. Out. And I for such-like petty crimes as these.
But to the purpose! for we cite our faults
That they may hold excus'd our lawless lives;
And partly, seeing you are beautified
With goodly shape, and by your own report
A linguist, and a man of such perfection
As we do in our quality much want —
2. Out. Indeed, because you are a banish'd man,
Therefore, above the rest, we parley to you.
Are you content to be our general?
To make a virtue of necessity
And live as we do in this wilderness?
3. Out. What say'st thou? Wilt thou be of our consort?
Say ay, and be the captain of us all!
We'll do thee homage and be rul'd by thee,
Love thee as our commander and our king.
1. Out. But if thou scorn our courtesy, thou diest.
2. Out. Thou shalt not live to brag what we have offer'd.
Val. I take your offer and will live with you,
Provided that you do no outrages
On silly women or poor passengers.
3. Out. No, we detest such vile base practises.
Come, go with us; we'll bring thee to our crew
And show thee all the treasure we have got,
Which, with ourselves, all rest at thy dispose.
Exeunt.

Scene II. [*Milan. Without the* Duke's *Palace, under* Silvia's *window.*]

Enter *Proteus.*

Pro. Already have I been false to Valentine,
And now I must be as unjust to Thurio.
Under the colour of commending him
I have access my own love to prefer.
But Silvia is too fair, too true, too holy,
To be corrupted with my worthless gifts.
When I protest true loyalty to her,
She twits me with my falsehood to my friend;
When to her beauty I commend my vows,
She bids me think how I have been forsworn
In breaking faith with Julia, whom I lov'd;
And notwithstanding all her sudden quips,
The least whereof would quell a lover's hope,
Yet, spaniel-like, the more she spurns my love,
The more it grows, and fawneth on her still.

[Enter *Thurio* and *Musicians.*]

But here comes Thurio. Now must we to her window
And give some evening music to her ear.
Thu. How now, Sir Proteus? Are you crept before us?
Pro. Ay, gentle Thurio; for you know that love
Will creep in service where it cannot go.
Thu. Ay, but I hope, sir, that you love not here.
Pro. Sir, but I do; or else I would be hence.
Thu. Who? Silvia?
Pro. Ay, Silvia — for your sake.
Thu. I thank you for your own. Now, gentlemen,
Let's tune; and to it lustily awhile.

[Enter, at a distance, *Host,* and *Julia* in boy's clothes.]

Host. Now, my young guest — methinks you're allycholly. I pray you, why is it?

Jul. Marry, mine host, because I cannot be merry.

Host. Come, we'll have you merry! I'll bring you where you shall hear music and see the gentleman that you ask'd for.

Jul. But shall I hear him speak?

Host. Ay, that you shall.

Jul. That will be music. [*Music plays.*]

Host. Hark, hark!

Jul. Is he among these?

Host. Ay; but, peace! let's hear 'em.

Song.

Who is Silvia? What is she,
That all our swains commend her?
Holy, fair, and wise is she:
The heaven such grace did lend her,
That she might admired be.

Is she kind as she is fair?
For beauty lives with kindness.
Love doth to her eyes repair
To help him of his blindness,
And being help'd, inhabits there.

Then to Silvia let us sing
That Silvia is excelling;
She excels each mortal thing
Upon the dull earth dwelling.
To her let us garlands bring.

Host. How now? Are you sadder than you were before? How do you, man? The music likes you not.

Jul. You mistake. The musician likes me not.

Host. Why, my pretty youth?

Jul. He plays false, father.

Host. How? Out of tune on the strings?

Jul. Not so; but yet so false that he grieves my very heartstrings.

Host. You have a quick ear.

Jul. Ay, I would I were deaf! It makes me have a slow heart.

Host. I perceive you delight not in music.

Jul. Not a whit, when it jars so.

Host. Hark, what fine change is in the music!

Jul. Ay, that change is the spite.

Host. You would have them always play but one thing?

Jul. I would always have one play but one thing.
But, host, doth this Sir Proteus that we talk on
Often resort unto this gentlewoman?

Host. I tell you what Launce, his man, told me: he lov'd her out of all nick.

Jul. Where is Launce?

Host. Gone to seek his dog, which to-morrow, by his master's command, he must carry for a present to his lady.

Jul. Peace, stand aside! The company parts. [*They hide.*]

Pro. Sir Thurio, fear not you. I will so plead
That you shall say my cunning drift excels.

Thu. Where meet we?

Pro. At Saint Gregory's Well.

Thu. Farewell.

[*Exeunt Thurio and Musicians.*]

[Enter *Silvia* above, at her window.]

Pro. Madam, good ev'n to your ladyship.

Sil. I thank you for your music, gentlemen.
Who is that that spake?

Pro. One, lady, if you knew his pure heart's truth,
You would quickly learn to know him by his voice.

Sil. Sir Proteus, as I take it.

Pro. Sir Proteus, gentle lady, and your servant.

Sil. What is your will?

Pro. That I may compass yours.

Sil. You have your wish. My will is even this,
That presently you hie you home to bed.
Thou subtile, perjur'd, false, disloyal man!
Think'st thou I am so shallow, so conceitless,
To be seduced by thy flattery
That hast deceiv'd so many with thy vows?
Return, return, and make thy love amends!
For me (by this pale queen of night I swear),
I am so far from granting thy request
That I despise thee for thy wrongful suit,
And by-and-by intend to chide myself
Even for this time I spend in talking to thee.

Pro. I grant, sweet love, that I did love a lady;
But she is dead.

Jul. [*aside*] 'Twere false, if I should speak it;
For I am sure she is not buried.

Sil. Say that she be, yet Valentine, thy friend,
Survives; to whom (thyself art witness)
I am betroth'd; and art thou not asham'd
To wrong him with thy importunacy?

Pro. I likewise hear that Valentine is dead.

Sil. And so suppose am I; for in his grave
Assure thyself my love is buried.

Pro. Sweet lady, let me rake it from the earth.

Sil. Go to thy lady's grave, and call hers thence,
Or, at the least, in hers sepulcher thine.

Jul. [*aside*] He heard not that.

Pro. Madam, if your heart be so obdurate,
Vouchsafe me yet your picture for my love,
The picture that is hanging in your chamber.
To that I'll speak, to that I'll sigh and weep;
For since the substance of your perfect self
Is else devoted, I am but a shadow,
And to your shadow will I make true love.

Jul. [*aside*] If 'twere a substance, you would sure deceive it
And make it but a shadow, as I am.

Sil. I am very loath to be your idol, sir;
But since your falsehood shall become you well
To worship shadows and adore false shapes,
Send to me in the morning, and I'll send it.
And so, good rest!
Pro. As wretches have o'ernight
That wait for execution in the morn.
[*Exeunt Silvia and Proteus.*]
Jul. Host, will you go?
Host. By my halidome, I was fast asleep.
Jul. Pray you, where lies Sir Proteus?
Host. Marry, at my house. Trust me, I think 'tis almost day.
Jul. Not so; but it hath been the longest night
That e'er I watch'd, and the most heaviest.
[*Exeunt.*]

Scene III. [*The same.*]

Enter *Eglamour.*

Egl. This is the hour that Madam Silvia
Entreated me to call and know her mind.
There's some great matter she'ld employ me in.
Madam, madam!

[Enter *Silvia* above, at her window.]

Sil. Who calls?
Egl. Your servant, and your friend;
One that attends your ladyship's command.
Sil. Sir Eglamour, a thousand times good morrow!
Egl. As many, worthy lady, to yourself!
According to your ladyship's impose,
I am thus early come to know what service
It is your pleasure to command me in.
Sil. O Eglamour, thou art a gentleman —
Think not I flatter, for I swear I do not —
Valiant, wise, remorseful, well-accomplish'd.
Thou art not ignorant what dear good will
I bear unto the banish'd Valentine;
Nor how my father would enforce me marry
Vain Thurio, whom my very soul abhors.
Thyself hast lov'd; and I have heard thee say
No grief did ever come so near thy heart
As when thy lady and thy true-love died,
Upon whose grave thou vow'dst pure chastity.
Sir Eglamour, I would to Valentine,
To Mantua, where I hear he makes abode;
And, for the ways are dangerous to pass,
I do desire thy worthy company,
Upon whose faith and honour I repose.
Urge not my father's anger, Eglamour,
But think upon my grief (a lady's grief)
And on the justice of my flying hence
To keep me from a most unholy match,
Which heaven and fortune still rewards with plagues.
I do desire thee, even from a heart
As full of sorrows as the sea of sands,
To bear me company and go with me;
If not, to hide what I have said to thee,
That I may venture to depart alone.
Egl. Madam, I pity much your grievances,
Which since I know they virtuously are plac'd,
I give consent to go along with you,
Recking as little what betideth me
As much I wish all good befortune you.
When will you go?
Sil. This evening coming.
Egl. Where shall I meet you?
Sil. At Friar Patrick's cell,
Where I intend holy confession.
Egl. I will not fail your ladyship. Good morrow, gentle lady.
Sil. Good morrow, kind Sir Eglamour.
Exeunt.

Scene IV. [*The same.*]

Enter *Launce* [with his dog].

Launce. When a man's servant shall play the cur with him, look you, it goes hard — one that I brought up of a puppy; one that I sav'd from drowning when three or four of his blind brothers and sisters went to it. I have taught him even as one would say precisely 'Thus I would teach a dog.' I was sent to deliver him as a present to Mistress Silvia from my master; and I came no sooner into the dining chamber but he steps me to her trencher and steals her capon's leg. O, 'tis a foul thing when a cur cannot keep himself in all companies! I would have (as one should say) one that takes upon him to be a dog indeed; to be, as it were, a dog at all things. If I had not had more wit than he, to take a fault upon me that he did, I think verily he had been hang'd for't. Sure as I live, he had suffer'd for't! You shall judge. He thrusts me himself into the company of three or four gentlemanlike dogs, under the Duke's table. He had not been there (bless the mark!) a pissing while but all the chamber smelt him. 'Out with the dog!' says one. 'What cur is that?' says another. 'Whip him out!' says the third. 'Hang him up!' says the Duke.

I, having been acquainted with the smell before, knew it was Crab, and goes me to the fellow that whips the dogs. 'Friend,' quoth I, 'you mean to whip the dog?' 'Ay, marry, do I!' quoth he. 'You do him the more wrong,' quoth I. ''Twas I did the thing you wot of.' He makes me no more ado, but whips me out of the chamber. How many masters would do this for his servant? Nay, I'll be sworn I have sat in the stocks for puddings he hath stol'n, otherwise he had been executed; I have stood on the pillory for geese he hath kill'd, otherwise he had suffer'd for't. Thou think'st not of this now! Nay, I remember the trick you serv'd me when I took my leave of Madam Silvia! Did not I bid thee still mark me and do as I do? When didst thou see me heave up my leg and make water against a gentlewoman's farthingale? Didst thou ever see me do such a trick?

[Enter *Proteus*, and *Julia* in boy's clothes.]

Pro. Sebastian is thy name? I like thee well
And will employ thee in some service presently.

Jul. In what you please. I'll do what I can.

Pro. I hope thou wilt. [*To Launce*] How now, you whoreson peasant?
Where have you been these two days loitering?

Launce. Marry, sir, I carried Mistress Silvia the dog you bade me.

Pro. And what says she to my little jewel?

Launce. Marry, she says your dog was a cur, and tells you currish thanks is good enough for such a present.

Pro. But she receiv'd my dog?

Launce. No indeed did she not! Here have I brought him back again.

Pro. What, didst thou offer her this from me?

Launce. Ay, sir. The other squirrel was stol'n from me by the hangman boys in the market place; and then I offer'd her mine own, who is a dog as big as ten of yours, and therefore the gift the greater.

Pro. Go, get thee hence, and find my dog again
Or ne'er return again into my sight.
Away, I say! Stayest thou to vex me here?
A slave that still an end turns me to shame!
[*Exit Launce.*]
Sebastian, I have entertained thee,
Partly that I have need of such a youth
That can with some discretion do my business,
For 'tis no trusting to yond foolish lout;
But chiefly for thy face and thy behaviour,
Which (if my augury deceive me not)
Witness good bringing up, fortune, and truth.
Therefore know thou, for this I entertain thee.
Go presently, and take this ring with thee;
Deliver it to Madam Silvia.
She lov'd me well deliver'd it to me.

Jul. It seems you lov'd not her, to leave her token.
She is dead belike?

Pro. Not so. I think she lives.

Jul. Alas!

Pro. Why dost thou cry 'Alas'?

Jul. I cannot choose
But pity her.

Pro. Wherefore shouldst thou pity her?

Jul. Because methinks that she lov'd you as well
As you do love your lady Silvia.
She dreams on him that has forgot her love;
You dote on her that cares not for your love.
'Tis pity love should be so contrary;
And thinking on it makes me cry 'Alas!'

Pro. Well, give her that ring, and therewithal
This letter. That's her chamber. Tell my lady
I claim the promise for her heavenly picture.
Your message done, hie home unto my chamber,
Where thou shalt find me sad and solitary.
[*Exit.*]

Jul. How many women would do such a message?
Alas, poor Proteus! thou hast entertain'd
A fox to be the shepherd of thy lambs.
Alas, poor fool! Why do I pity him
That with his very heart despiseth me?
Because he loves her, he despiseth me;
Because I love him, I must pity him.
This ring I gave him when he parted from me,
To bind him to remember my good will;
And now am I (unhappy messenger!)
To plead for that which I would not obtain,
To carry that which I would have refus'd,
To praise his faith which I would have disprais'd.
I am my master's true confirmed love,
But cannot be true servant to my master
Unless I prove false traitor to myself.
Yet will I woo for him; but yet so coldly
As (heaven it knows) I would not have him speed.

[Enter *Silvia*, attended.]

Gentlewoman, good day! I pray you be my mean
To bring me where to speak with Madam Silvia.

Sil. What would you with her, if that I be she?
Jul. If you be she, I do entreat your patience
To hear me speak the message I am sent on.
Sil. From whom?
Jul. From my master, Sir Proteus, madam.
Sil. O, he sends you for a picture?
Jul. Ay, madam.
Sil. Ursula, bring my picture there.
[*Picture brought.*]
Go give your master this. Tell him from me,
One Julia, that his changing thoughts forget,
Would better fit his chamber than this shadow.
Jul. Madam, please you peruse this letter.
[*Gives a letter.*]
Pardon me, madam! I have unadvis'd
Deliver'd you a paper that I should not.
This is the letter to your ladyship.
[*Gives another.*]
Sil. I pray thee let me look on that again.
Jul. It may not be. Good madam, pardon me!
Sil. There, hold! [*Gives back the first letter.*]
I will not look upon your master's lines.
I know they are stuff'd with protestations
And full of new-found oaths, which he will break
As easily as I do tear his paper.
[*Tears the second letter.*]
Jul. Madam, he sends your ladyship this ring.
Sil. The more shame for him that he sends it me!
For I have heard him say a thousand times
His Julia gave it him at his departure.
Though his false finger have profan'd the ring,
Mine shall not do his Julia so much wrong.
Jul. She thanks you.
Sil. What say'st thou?
Jul. I thank you, madam, that you tender her.
Poor gentlewoman! my master wrongs her much.
Sil. Dost thou know her?
Jul. Almost as well as I do know myself.
To think upon her woes, I do protest
That I have wept a hundred several times.
Sil. Belike she thinks that Proteus hath forsook her?
Jul. I think she doth; and that's her cause of sorrow.
Sil. Is she not passing fair?
Jul. She hath been fairer, madam, than she is.
When she did think my master lov'd her well,
She, in my judgment, was as fair as you;
But since she did neglect her looking glass
And threw her sun-expelling mask away,
The air hath starv'd the roses in her cheeks
And pinch'd the lily-tincture of her face,
That now she is become as black as I.
Sil. How tall was she?
Jul. About my stature; for at Pentecost,
When all our pageants of delight were play'd,
Our youth got me to play the woman's part,
And I was trimm'd in Madam Julia's gown,
Which served me as fit, by all men's judgments,
As if the garment had been made for me.
Therefore I know she is about my height.
And at that time I made her weep a good,
For I did play a lamentable part.
Madam, 'twas Ariadne, passioning
For Theseus' perjury and unjust flight;
Which I so lively acted with my tears
That my poor mistress, moved therewithal,
Wept bitterly; and would I might be dead
If I in thought felt not her very sorrow!
Sil. She is beholding to thee, gentle youth.
Alas, poor lady, desolate and left!
I weep myself to think upon thy words.
Here, youth, there is my purse. I give thee this
For thy sweet mistress' sake, because thou lov'st her.
Farewell. [*Exit Silvia with Attendants.*]
Jul. And she shall thank you for't, if e'er you know her.
A virtuous gentlewoman, mild and beautiful!
I hope my master's suit will be but cold,
Since she respects my mistress' love so much.
Alas, how love can trifle with itself!
Here is her picture. Let me see. I think,
If I had such a tire, this face of mine
Were full as lovely as is this of hers;
And yet the painter flatter'd her a little,
Unless I flatter with myself too much.
Her hair is auburn, mine is perfect yellow.
If that be all the difference in his love,
I'll get me such a colour'd periwig.
Her eyes are grey as glass, and so are mine.
Ay, but her forehead 's low, and mine's as high.
What should it be that he respects in her
But I can make respective in myself
If this fond Love were not a blinded god?
Come, shadow, come, and take this shadow up,
For 'tis thy rival. O thou senseless form,
Thou shalt be worshipp'd, kiss'd, lov'd, and ador'd!
And, were there sense in his idolatry,
My substance should be statue in thy stead.
I'll use thee kindly for thy mistress' sake
That us'd me so; or else, by Jove I vow,
I should have scratch'd out your unseeing eyes
To make my master out of love with thee!
Exit.

Act V. Scene I. [*Milan. An abbey.*]

Enter *Eglamour.*

Egl. The sun begins to gild the western sky,
And now it is about the very hour
That Silvia at Friar Patrick's cell should meet me.
She will not fail; for lovers break not hours
Unless it be to come before their time,
So much they spur their expedition.

Enter *Silvia.*

See where she comes. Lady, a happy evening!
Sil. Amen, amen! Go on, good Eglamour,
Out at the postern by the abbey wall.
I fear I am attended by some spies.
Egl. Fear not. The forest is not three leagues off.
If we recover that, we are sure enough.
Exeunt.

Scene II. [*Milan. The* Duke's *Palace.*]

Enter *Thurio, Proteus, Julia* [as *Sebastian*].

Thu. Sir Proteus, what says Silvia to my suit?
Pro. O, sir, I find her milder than she was,
And yet she takes exceptions at your person.
Thu. What? that my leg is too long?
Pro. No; that it is too little.
Thu. I'll wear a boot to make it somewhat rounder.
Jul. [*aside*] But love will not be spurr'd to what it loathes.
Thu. What says she to my face?
Pro. She says it is a fair one.
Thu. Nay then, the wanton lies! My face is black.
Pro. But pearls are fair; and the old saying is,
'Black men are pearls in beauteous ladies' eyes.'
Jul. [*aside*] 'Tis true! such pearls as put out ladies' eyes,
For I had rather wink than look on them.
Thu. How likes she my discourse?
Pro. Ill when you talk of war.
Thu. But well when I discourse of love and peace?
Jul. [*aside*] But better indeed when you hold your peace.
Thu. What says she to my valour?
Pro. O, sir, she makes
No doubt of that.
Jul. [*aside*] She needs not, when she knows it cowardice.
Thu. What says she to my birth?
Pro. That you are well deriv'd.
Jul. [*aside*] True! from a gentleman to a fool.
Thu. Considers she my possessions?
Pro. O, ay! and pities them.
Thu. Wherefore?
Jul. [*aside*] That such an ass should owe them.
Pro. That they are out by lease.
Jul. Here comes the Duke.

[Enter *Duke.*]

Duke. How now, Sir Proteus? How now, Thurio?
Which of you saw Sir Eglamour of late?
Thu. Not I.
Pro. Nor I.
Duke. Saw you my daughter?
Pro. Neither.
Duke. Why then,
She's fled unto that peasant Valentine,
And Eglamour is in her company.
'Tis true; for Friar Laurence met them both
As he in penance wander'd through the forest.
Him he knew well, and guess'd that it was she,
But, being mask'd, he was not sure of it.
Besides, she did intend confession
At Patrick's cell this even, and there she was not.
These likelihoods confirm her flight from hence.
Therefore, I pray you, stand not to discourse,
But mount you presently, and meet with me
Upon the rising of the mountain foot
That leads toward Mantua, whither they are fled.
Dispatch, sweet gentlemen, and follow me.
[*Exit.*]
Thu. Why, this it is to be a peevish girl
That flies her fortune when it follows her!
I'll after, more to be reveng'd on Eglamour
Than for the love of reckless Silvia. [*Exit.*]
Pro. And I will follow, more for Silvia's love
Than hate of Eglamour, that goes with her.
[*Exit.*]
Jul. And I will follow, more to cross that love
Than hate for Silvia, that is gone for love. *Exit.*

Scene III. [*The forest.*]

[Enter] *Silvia, Outlaws.*

1. Out. Come, come,
Be patient! We must bring you to our captain.
Sil. A thousand more mischances than this one
Have learn'd me how to brook this patiently.
2. Out. Come, bring her away!
1. Out. Where is the gentleman that was with her?
3. Out. Being nimble-footed, he hath outrun us,
But Moyses and Valerius follow him.
Go thou with her to the west end of the wood.
There is our captain. We'll follow him that's fled.
The thicket is beset; he cannot scape.
1. Out. Come, I must bring you to our captain's cave.
Fear not. He bears an honourable mind
And will not use a woman lawlessly.
Sil. O Valentine, this I endure for thee!
Exeunt.

Scene IV. [*Another part of the forest.*]

Enter *Valentine.*

Val. How use doth breed a habit in a man!
This shadowy desert, unfrequented woods,
I better brook than flourishing peopled towns.
Here can I sit alone, unseen of any,
And to the nightingale's complaining notes
Tune my distresses and record my woes.
O thou that dost inhabit in my breast,
Leave not the mansion so long tenantless,
Lest, growing ruinous, the building fall
And leave no memory of what it was!
Repair me with thy presence, Silvia.
Thou gentle nymph, cherish thy forlorn swain!
[*Noise within.*]
What halloaing and what stir is this to-day?
These are my mates, that make their wills their law,
Have some unhappy passenger in chase.
They love me well; yet I have much to do
To keep them from uncivil outrages.
Withdraw thee, Valentine. Who's this comes here? [*Retires.*]

[Enter *Proteus, Silvia,* and *Julia* as *Sebastian.*]

Pro. Madam, this service I have done for you
(Though you respect not aught your servant doth),
To hazard life, and rescue you from him
That would have forc'd your honour and your love.
Vouchsafe me, for my meed, but one fair look!
A smaller boon than this I cannot beg,
And less than this, I am sure you cannot give.
Val. [*aside*] How like a dream is this I see and hear!
Love, lend me patience to forbear awhile.
Sil. O miserable, unhappy that I am!
Pro. Unhappy were you, madam, ere I came;
But by my coming I have made you happy.
Sil. By thy approach thou mak'st me most unhappy.
Jul. [*aside*] And me, when he approacheth to your presence.
Sil. Had I been seized by a hungry lion,
I would have been a breakfast to the beast
Rather than have false Proteus rescue me.
O, heaven be judge how I love Valentine,
Whose life's as tender to me as my soul!
And full as much (for more there cannot be)
I do detest false perjur'd Proteus.
Therefore be gone! solicit me no more!
Pro. What dangerous action, stood it next to death,
Would I not undergo for one calm look?
O, 'tis the curse in love, and still approv'd,
When women cannot love where they're belov'd!
Sil. When Proteus cannot love where he's belov'd!
Read over Julia's heart, thy first best love,
For whose dear sake thou didst then rend thy faith
Into a thousand oaths; and all those oaths
Descended into perjury, to love me.
Thou hast no faith left now, unless thou'dst two;
And that's far worse than none. Better have none
Than plural faith, which is too much by one.
Thou counterfeit to thy true friend!
Pro. In love
Who respects friend?
Sil. All men but Proteus.
Pro. Nay, if the gentle spirit of moving words
Can no way change you to a milder form,
I'll woo you like a soldier, at arms' end,
And love you 'gainst the nature of love — force ye.
Sil. O heaven!
Pro. I'll force thee yield to my desire.

Val. Ruffian! let go that rude uncivil touch
Thou friend of an ill fashion!
Pro. Valentine!
Val. Thou common friend, that's without faith or love —
For such is a friend now! — Treacherous man,
Thou hast beguil'd my hopes. Naught but mine eye
Could have persuaded me. Now I dare not say
I have one friend alive: thou wouldst disprove me.
Who should be trusted when one's own right hand
Is perjured to the bosom? Proteus,
I am sorry I must never trust thee more
But count the world a stranger for thy sake.
The private wound is deepest. O time accurst,
'Mongst all foes that a friend should be the worst!
Pro. My shame and guilt confounds me.
Forgive me, Valentine. If hearty sorrow
Be a sufficient ransom for offence,
I tender't here. I do as truly suffer
As e'er I did commit.
Val. Then I am paid;
And once again I do receive thee honest.
Who by repentance is not satisfied
Is nor of heaven nor earth; for these are pleas'd;
By penitence th' Eternal's wrath 's appeas'd.
And, that my love may appear plain and free,
All that was mine in Silvia I give thee.
Jul. O me unhappy! [*Swoons.*]
Pro. Look to the boy!
Val. Why, boy! why, wag! How now? What is the matter?
Look up! speak!
Jul. O good sir, my master charg'd me
To deliver a ring to Madam Silvia,
Which, out of my neglect, was never done.
Pro. Where is that ring, boy?
Jul. Here 'tis; this is it. [*Gives a ring.*]
Pro. How? Let me see.
Why, this is the ring I gave to Julia!
Jul. O, cry you mercy, sir! I have mistook.
This is the ring you sent to Silvia.
[*Shows another ring.*]
Pro. But how cam'st thou by this ring?
At my depart I gave this unto Julia.
Jul. And Julia herself did give it me,
And Julia herself hath brought it hither.
Pro. How? Julia?
Jul. Behold her that gave aim to all thy oaths
And entertain'd 'em deeply in her heart.
How oft hast thou with perjury cleft the root!
O Proteus, let this habit make thee blush!
Be thou asham'd that I have took upon me
Such an immodest raiment — if shame live
In a disguise of love!
It is the lesser blot, modesty finds,
Women to change their shapes than men their minds.
Pro. Than men their minds? 'Tis true. O heaven, were man
But constant, he were perfect! That one error
Fills him with faults, makes him run through all th' sins.
Inconstancy falls off ere it begins.
What is in Silvia's face but I may spy
More fresh in Julia's with a constant eye?
Val. Come, come, a hand from either!
Let me be blest to make this happy close.
'Twere pity two such friends should be long foes.
Pro. Bear witness, heaven, I have my wish for ever!
Jul. And I mine.

[Enter *Outlaws*, with *Duke* and *Thurio.*]

Outlaws. A prize, a prize, a prize!
Val. Forbear!
Forbear, I say! It is my lord the Duke.
Your Grace is welcome to a man disgrac'd,
Banished Valentine.
Duke. Sir Valentine?
Thu. Yonder is Silvia; and Silvia 's mine!
Val. Thurio, give back, or else embrace thy death!
Come not within the measure of my wrath.
Do not name Silvia thine! If once again,
Milano shall not hold thee. Here she stands.
Take but possession of her with a touch!
I dare thee but to breathe upon my love.
Thu. Sir Valentine, I care not for her, I.
I hold him but a fool that will endanger
His body for a girl that loves him not.
I claim her not, and therefore she is thine.
Duke. The more degenerate and base art thou
To make such means for her as thou hast done
And leave her on such slight conditions.
Now, by the honour of my ancestry,
I do applaud thy spirit, Valentine,
And think thee worthy of an empress' love.
Know then, I here forget all former griefs,
Cancel all grudge, repeal thee home again.
Plead a new state in thy unrivall'd merit,

To which I thus subscribe: Sir Valentine,
Thou art a gentleman and well deriv'd;
Take thou thy Silvia, for thou hast deserv'd her.

Val. I thank your Grace. The gift hath made me happy.
I now beseech you, for your daughter's sake,
To grant one boon that I shall ask of you.

Duke. I grant it, for thine own, whate'er it be.

Val. These banish'd men that I have kept withal
Are men endu'd with worthy qualities.
Forgive them what they have committed here
And let them be recall'd from their exile.
They are reformed, civil, full of good,
And fit for great employment, worthy lord.

Duke. Thou hast prevail'd. I pardon them and thee.
Dispose of them as thou know'st their deserts.
Come, let us go. We will include all jars
With triumphs, mirth, and rare solemnity.

Val. And as we walk along, I dare be bold
With our discourse to make your Grace to smile.
What think you of this page, my lord?

Duke. I think the boy hath grace in him; he blushes.

Val. I warrant you, my lord — more grace than boy.

Duke. What mean you by that saying?

Val. Please you, I'll tell you as we pass along,
That you will wonder what hath fortuned.
Come, Proteus. 'Tis your penance but to hear
The story of your loves discovered.
That done, our day of marriage shall be yours;
One feast, one house, one mutual happiness.

Exeunt.

The Merry Wives of Windsor

'An excellent and pleasant conceited commedie of Sir John Faulstof and the merry wyves of Windesor' was entered in the Stationers' Register on January 18, 1602, and the First Quarto appeared in the same year. The Second Quarto (1619) is a mere reprint of the First. The Quartos afford a badly mangled form of the play — manifestly 'reported' by one of the actors, chiefly from memory, though possibly to some extent from fragments of manuscript. The reporter is thought to have been the player who represented the Host. The First Folio, on the other hand, was printed from an authoritative manuscript and may be accepted as a substantially correct copy of what Shakespeare wrote, though there are traces of adaptation in some details. The stage directions, however, are arranged in the annoying fashion described in the introduction to *The Two Gentlemen of Verona* (p. 33, above). The First Quarto, bad as it is, gives some assistance in this matter and now and then in the text. Ingenious attempts have been made to trace a process of revision between Shakespeare's original text and the Folio version, but without any substantial result. Perhaps the horse-stealing episode (iv, 3; iv, 5, 64–95; iv, 6, 1–5) has been cut down, but there is no proof that it ever had more than a rather casual place in the plot.

One line in the Quarto version of iv, 2 ('What is the reason that you use me thus?') is word for word the same as a line in *Hamlet* (v, 1, 312). This suggests that the play is later than *Hamlet* and would fix the date as 1600 or 1601; but the expression is so natural and commonplace that it need not be regarded as a quotation. The earliest possible date is 1598, since there can be no question that The Merry Wives is later than *Henry IV*. Whether it is later than *Henry V* is not quite certain. The appearance of Nym with his title of 'Corporal' indicates an affirmative answer. Sentimentally one may be disposed to a negative, on the ground that Shakespeare would not have revived Falstaff as a wildly comic character after the marvellously pathetic description of his death in *Henry V*. But this is no very substantial argument. At all events, the incidents in The Merry Wives fit the biographical interval between his repudiation by the King at the end of *2 Henry IV* and the onset of the 'burning quotidian tertian' that the Hostess describes in *Henry V*. If later than *Henry V*, the play would have to be assigned to 1599 at the earliest. On the whole, we must accept 1600 as a reasonable date, with 1601 as a possibility.

There is a tradition that Shakespeare wrote The Merry Wives by order of Queen Elizabeth. Its earliest recorder is John Dennis, who, in 1702, in the Epistle prefixed to *The Comicall Gallant*, remarks: 'I knew very well, that it had pleas'd one of the greatest Queens that ever was in the World. . . . This Comedy was written at her Command, and by her direction, and she was so eager to see it Acted, that she commanded it to be finished in fourteen days.' Rowe, in his *Life of Shakespeare* (1709), adds an amusing detail. The Queen, he tells us, 'was so well pleas'd with that admirable Character of *Falstaff*, in the two Parts of *Henry* the Fourth, that she commanded him to continue it for one Play more, and to shew him in Love.' The tradition may well be true in substance, though one is not bound to accept the fourteen days.

In Tarlton's *Newes out of Purgatorie*, 1590 (*The Tale of the Two Lovers of Pisa*), Margaret hides her lover successively in 'a great driefatte [tub or cask] full of Feathers,' in a secret place 'between two seelings,' and in 'an olde rotten chest full of writinges,' covering him 'with old papers and euidences.' Tarlton is adapting a story in *Le Tredeci Piacevoli Notti* of Straparola (iv, 4: 1550–1553), in which the concealment is behind bed curtains, in a chest which the lady covered with garments, and in a chest which, she says, contains documents concerning her dowry. In *Il Pecorone* of Giovanni Fiorentino (1558), the lady hides her lover 'under a great pile of clothes washed but not yet dried.' These are all versions of an old and widely current popular tale, in which the lady's object is to conceal her intrigue, not to play a trick on a despised suitor. In another group of stories, common in both Orient and Occident, the wife is loyal to her husband and wishes to discomfit her would-be seducer. One English specimen of this class is *The Wright's Chaste Wife* by Adam of Cobsam; another is the ballad of *The Friar in the Well* (Child, No. 276), which is mentioned (either as tale or ballad) by Anthony Munday in his play entitled *The Downfall of Robert Earl of Huntington* (1598), iv, 2, and by Skelton in his *Colyn Cloute* (before 1522), vv. 879–881. No definite source for Shakespeare's plot can be determined, since tales of these two groups were manifestly in oral as well as written and printed circulation in England and elsewhere throughout the Elizabethan period.

The episode of the German horse-thieves may be topical. It is thought to have been suggested by the visit of Frederick Count of Mömpelgart to England in 1592. The Count did not steal any horses, but he had posthorses furnished him without payment; and in 1595 one Breuning von Buchenbach, an ambassador of his, had some disagreeable experiences, not discreditable to him, with English horse-dealers. In the Quarto version Sir Hugh Evans, apropos of the horse-trick, warns the Host of the Garter Inn:

> Now my Host, I would desire you looke you now,
> To haue a care of your entertainments,
> For there is three sorts of cosen garmombles,
> Is cosen all the Host of Maidenhead & Readings.

This passage appears in the Folio text (iv, 5, 77–81) as follows:

> Have a care of your entertainments. There is a friend of mine come to town, tells me there is three cozen-germans that has cozen'd all the hosts of Readins, of Maidenhead, of Colebrook, of horses and money.

'Garmombles' certainly sounds like a distortion of 'Mömpelgart.'

That Nym with his favourite jargon about humours was intended as a caricature of Ben Jonson is very improbable.

THE MERRY WIVES OF WINDSOR

[Dramatis Personæ.

Sir John Falstaff.
Fenton, a young gentleman.
Shallow, a country justice.
Slender, cousin to *Shallow*.
Ford, } gentlemen of Windsor.
Page, }
William Page, a boy, son to *Page*.
Sir Hugh Evans, a Welsh parson.
Doctor Caius, a French physician.
Host of the Garter Inn.
Bardolph, }
Pistol, } followers of *Falstaff*.
Nym, }

Robin, page to *Falstaff*.
Simple, servant to *Slender*.
John Rugby, servant to *Doctor Caius*.

Mistress Ford.
Mistress Page.
Anne Page, her daughter.
Mistress Quickly, servant to *Doctor Caius*.

Servants to *Page, Ford*, &c.

THE SCENE. — *Windsor, and the neighbourhood*.]

ACT I. Scene I. [*Windsor. Before* Master Page's *house*.]

Enter *Justice Shallow, Slender, Sir Hugh Evans*.

Shal. Sir Hugh, persuade me not. I will make a Star Chamber matter of it. If he were twenty Sir John Falstaffs, he shall not abuse Robert Shallow, Esquire.

Slen. In the county of Gloucester, Justice of Peace and Coram.

Shal. Ay, cousin Slender, and Cust-alorum.

Slen. Ay, and Rato-lorum too; and a gentleman born, Master Parson, who writes himself 'Armigero' — in any bill, warrant, quittance, or obligation, 'Armigero.'

Shal. Ay, that I do, and have done any time these three hundred years.

Slen. All his successors (gone before him) hath done't; and all his ancestors (that come after him) may. They may give the dozen white luces in their coat.

Shal. It is an old coat.

Evans. The dozen white louses do become an old coat well. It agrees well passant. It is a familiar beast to man and signifies love.

Shal. The luce is the fresh fish. The salt fish is an old coat.

Slen. I may quarter, coz.

Shal. You may, by marrying.

Evans. It is marring indeed, if he quarter it.

Shal. Not a whit.

Evans. Yes, py'r lady! If he has a quarter of your coat, there is but three skirts for yourself, in my simple conjectures. But that is all one. If Sir John Falstaff have committed disparagements unto you, I am of the Church and will be glad to do my benevolence to make atonements and compremises between you.

Shal. The Council shall hear it. It is a riot.

Evans. It is not meet the Council hear a riot. There is no fear of Got in a riot. The Council, look you, shall desire to hear the fear of Got, and not to hear a riot. Take your vizaments in that.

Shal. Ha! o' my life, if I were young again, the sword should end it.

Evans. It is petter that friends is the sword and end it. And there is also another device in my prain, which peradventure prings goot discretions with it. There is Anne Page, which is daughter to Master George Page, which is pretty virginity.

Slen. Mistress Anne Page? She has brown hair and speaks small like a woman.

Evans. It is that fery person for all the orld, as just as you will desire; and seven hundred pounds of moneys, and gold, and silver, is her grandsire upon his death's-bed (Got deliver to a joyful resurrections!) give when she is able to overtake seventeen years old.

It were a goot motion if we leave our pribbles and prabbles and desire a marriage between Master Abraham and Mistress Anne Page.

Shal. Did her grandsire leave her seven hundred pound?

Evans. Ay, and her father is make her a petter penny.

Shal. I know the young gentlewoman. She has good gifts.

Evans. Seven hundred pounds, and possibilities, is goot gifts.

Shal. Well, let us see honest Master Page. Is Falstaff there?

Evans. Shall I tell you a lie? I do despise a liar as I do despise one that is false, or as I despise one that is not true. The knight Sir John is there; and I beseech you be ruled by your well-willers. I will peat the door for Master Page. [*Knocks.*] What, ho! Got pless your house here!

Page. [*within*] Who's there?

[Enter *Master Page.*]

Evans. Here is Got's plessing, and your friend, and Justice Shallow, and here young Master Slender, that peradventures shall tell you another tale, if matters grow to your likings.

Page. I am glad to see your worships well. I thank you for my venison, Master Shallow.

Shal. Master Page, I am glad to see you. Much good do it your good heart! I wish'd your venison better; it was ill kill'd. How doth good Mistress Page? And I thank you always with my heart, la; with my heart.

Page. Sir, I thank you.

Shal. Sir, I thank you; by yea and no, I do.

Page. I am glad to see you, good Master Slender.

Slen. How does your fallow greyhound, sir? I heard say he was outrun on Cotsall.

Page. It could not be judg'd, sir.

Slen. You'll not confess! you'll not confess!

Shal. That he will not. 'Tis your fault! 'tis your fault! 'Tis a good dog.

Page. A cur, sir.

Shal. Sir, he's a good dog and a fair dog. Can there be more said? He is good and fair. Is Sir John Falstaff here?

Page. Sir, he is within; and I would I could do a good office between you.

Evans. It is spoke as a Christians ought to speak.

Shal. He hath wrong'd me, Master Page.

Page. Sir, he doth in some sort confess it.

Shal. If it be confessed, it is not redressed. Is not that so, Master Page? He hath wrong'd me; indeed he hath; at a word, he hath. Believe me! Robert Shallow, Esquire, saith he is wronged.

Page. Here comes Sir John.

[Enter *Sir John Falstaff, Bardolph, Nym,* and *Pistol.*]

Fal. Now, Master Shallow, you'll complain of me to the King?

Shal. Knight, you have beaten my men, kill'd my deer, and broke open my lodge.

Fal. But not kiss'd your keeper's daughter?

Shal. Tut, a pin! This shall be answer'd.

Fal. I will answer it straight. I have done all this. That is now answer'd.

Shal. The Council shall know this.

Fal. 'Twere better for you if it were known in counsel. You'll be laugh'd at.

Evans. Pauca verba, Sir John; goot worts.

Fal. Good worts? Good cabbage! Slender, I broke your head. What matter have you against me?

Slen. Marry, sir, I have matter in my head against you, and against your cony-catching rascals, Bardolph, Nym, and Pistol. They carried me to the tavern and made me drunk, and afterward picked my pocket.

Bard. You Banbury cheese!

Slen. Ay, it is no matter.

Pist. How now, Mephostophilus?

Slen. Ay, it is no matter.

Nym. Slice, I say! Pauca, pauca! Slice! That's my humour.

Slen. Where's Simple, my man? Can you tell, cousin?

Evans. Peace, I pray you. Now let us understand. There is three umpires in this matter, as I understand: that is, Master Page (fidelicet Master Page) and there is myself (fidelicet myself) and the three party is (lastly and finally) mine host of the Garter.

Page. We three to hear it and end it between them.

Evans. Fery goot. I will make a prief of it in my notebook, and we will afterwards ork upon the cause with as great discreetly as we can.

Fal. Pistol!

Pist. He hears with ears.

Evans. The tevil and his tam! What phrase is this? 'He hears with ear'? Why, it is affectations.

Fal. Pistol, did you pick Master Slender's purse?

Slen. Ay, by these gloves, did he, or I would I might never come in mine own great chamber again else! of seven groats in mill-sixpences, and two Edward shovelboards that cost me two shilling and two pence apiece of Yead Miller, by these gloves!

Fal. Is this true, Pistol?

Evans. No; it is false, if it is a pickpurse.

Pist. Ha, thou mountain foreigner! Sir John and master mine,
I combat challenge of this latten bilbo.
Word of denial in thy labras here!
Word of denial! Froth and scum, thou liest!

Slen. By these gloves, then 'twas he.

Nym. Be avis'd, sir, and pass good humours. I will say 'marry trap' with you if you run the nuthook's humour on me. That is the very note of it.

Slen. By this hat, then he in the red face had it; for though I cannot remember what I did when you made me drunk, yet I am not altogether an ass.

Fal. What say you, Scarlet and John?

Bard. Why, sir, for my part, I say the gentleman had drunk himself out of his five sentences —

Evans. It is his five senses. Fie, what the ignorance is!

Bard. And being fap, sir, was, as they say, cashier'd.

Nym. And so conclusions pass'd the careers.

Slen. Ay, you spake in Latin then too. But 'tis no matter. I'll ne'er be drunk whilst I live again but in honest, civil, godly company, for this trick. If I be drunk, I'll be drunk with those that have the fear of God, and not with drunken knaves.

Evans. So Got udge me, that is a virtuous mind.

Fal. You hear all these matters denied, gentlemen; you hear it.

[Enter *Anne Page*, with wine; *Mistress Ford* and *Mistress Page*.]

Page. Nay, daughter, carry the wine in; we'll drink within. [*Exit Anne Page.*]

Slen. O heaven! this is Mistress Anne Page.

Page. How now, Mistress Ford?

Fal. Mistress Ford, by my troth, you are very well met. By your leave, good mistress. [*Kisses her.*]

Page. Wife, bid these gentlemen welcome. Come, we have a hot venison pasty to dinner. Come, gentlemen; I hope we shall drink down all unkindness.

[*Exeunt all but Shallow, Slender, and Evans.*]

Slen. I had rather than forty shillings I had my Book of Songs and Sonnets here.

[Enter *Simple.*]

How now, Simple? Where have you been? I must wait on myself, must I? You have not the Book of Riddles about you, have you?

Sim. Book of Riddles? Why, did you not lend it to Alice Shortcake upon Allhallowmas last, a fortnight afore Michaelmas?

Shal. Come, coz; come, coz! We stay for you. A word with you, coz; marry, this, coz: there is, as 'twere, a tender, a kind of tender, made afar off by Sir Hugh here. Do you understand me?

Slen. Ay, sir, you shall find me reasonable. If it be so, I shall do that that is reason.

Shal. Nay, but understand me.

Slen. So I do, sir.

Evans. Give ear to his motions, Master Slender. I will description the matter to you, if you be capacity of it.

Slen. Nay, I will do as my cousin Shallow says. I pray you pardon me; he's a justice of peace in his country, simple though I stand here.

Evans. But that is not the question. The question is concerning your marriage.

Shal. Ay, there's the point, sir.

Evans. Marry is it; the very point of it! to Mistress Anne Page.

Slen. Why, if it be so, I will marry her upon any reasonable demands.

Evans. But can you affection the oman? Let us command to know that of your mouth, or of your lips; for divers philosophers hold that the lips is parcel of the mouth. Therefore, precisely, can you carry your goot will to the maid?

Shal. Cousin Abraham Slender, can you love her?

Slen. I hope, sir, I will do as it shall become one that would do reason.

Evans. Nay, Got's lords and his ladies! you must speak possitable, if you can carry her your desires towards her.

Shal. That you must. Will you, upon good dowry, marry her?

Slen. I will do a greater thing than that upon your request, cousin, in any reason.

Shal. Nay, conceive me, conceive me, sweet coz! What I do is to pleasure you, coz. Can you love the maid?

Slen. I will marry her, sir, at your request; but if there be no great love in the beginning, yet heaven may decrease it upon better acquaintance, when we are married and have more occasion to know one another. I hope upon familiarity will grow more content. But if you say, 'Marry her,' I will marry her. That I am freely dissolved, and dissolutely.

Evans. It is a fery discretion answer, save the fall is in the ord 'dissolutely.' The ort is, according to our meaning, 'resolutely.' His meaning is good.

Shal. Ay, I think my cousin meant well.

Slen. Ay, or else I would I might be hang'd, la.

[Enter *Anne Page.*]

Shal. Here comes fair Mistress Anne. Would I were young for your sake, Mistress Anne!

Anne. The dinner is on the table. My father desires your worships' company.

Shal. I will wait on him, fair Mistress Anne.

Evans. Od's plessed will! I will not be absence at the grace.

[*Exeunt Shallow and Evans.*]

Anne. Will't please your worship to come in, sir?

Slen. No, I thank you, forsooth, heartily. I am very well.

Anne. The dinner attends you, sir.

Slen. I am not ahungry, I thank you, forsooth. — Go, sirrah! For all you are my man, go wait upon my cousin Shallow. [*Exit Simple.*] A justice of peace sometime may be beholding to his friend for a man. I keep but three men and a boy yet, till my mother be dead; but what though? Yet I live like a poor gentleman born.

Anne. I may not go in without your worship. They will not sit till you come.

Slen. I' faith, I'll eat nothing. I thank you as much as though I did.

Anne. I pray you, sir, walk in.

Slen. I had rather walk here, I thank you. I bruis'd my shin th' other day with playing at sword and dagger with a master of fence (three veneys for a dish of stew'd prunes) and, by my troth, I cannot abide the smell of hot meat since. Why do your dogs bark so? Be there bears i' th' town?

Anne. I think there are, sir. I heard them talk'd of.

Slen. I love the sport well, but I shall as soon quarrel at it as any man in England. You are afraid if you see the bear loose, are you not?

Anne. Ay indeed, sir.

Slen. That's meat and drink to me now. I have seen Sackerson loose twenty times, and have taken him by the chain; but, I warrant you, the women have so cried and shriek'd at it that it pass'd. But women, indeed, cannot abide 'em. They are very ill-favour'd rough things.

[Enter *Master Page.*]

Page. Come, gentle Master Slender, come. We stay for you.

Slen. I'll eat nothing, I thank you, sir.

Page. By cock and pie, you shall not choose, sir! Come, come.

Slen. Nay, pray you lead the way.

Page. Come on, sir.

Slen. Mistress Anne, yourself shall go first.

Anne. Not I, sir! Pray you keep on.

Slen. Truly I will not go first; truly, la! I will not do you that wrong.

Anne. I pray you, sir.

Slen. I'll rather be unmannerly than troublesome. You do yourself wrong indeed, la!

Exeunt.

Scene II. [*Before* Master Page's *house.*]

Enter *Evans* and *Simple.*

Evans. Go your ways, and ask of Doctor Caius' house which is the way; and there dwells one Mistress Quickly, which is in the manner of his nurse, or his try nurse, or his cook, or his laundry, his washer and his wringer.

Sim. Well, sir.

Evans. Nay, it is petter yet. Give her this letter; for it is a oman that altogethers acquaintance with Mistress Anne Page; and the letter is to desire and require her to solicit your master's desires to Mistress Anne Page. I pray you be gone. I will make an end of my dinner. There's pippins and cheese to come. *Exeunt.*

Scene III. [*The Garter Inn.*]

Enter *Falstaff, Host, Bardolph, Nym, Pistol,* [*Robin* (*Falstaff's*] *Page*).

Fal. Mine host of the Garter!

Host. What says my bully rook? Speak scholarly and wisely.

Fal. Truly, mine host, I must turn away some of my followers.

Host. Discard, bully Hercules! cashier! Let them wag! trot, trot!

Fal. I sit at ten pounds a week.

Host. Thou'rt an emperor — Cæsar, Keiser, and Pheazar. I will entertain Bardolph: he shall draw, he shall tap. Said I well, bully Hector?

Fal. Do so, good mine host.

Host. I have spoke. Let him follow. [*To Bardolph*] Let me see thee froth and lime. I am at a word! Follow. *Exit.*

Fal. Bardolph, follow him. A tapster is a good trade. An old cloak makes a new jerkin; a wither'd servingman a fresh tapster. Go, adieu.

Bard. It is a life that I have desir'd. I will thrive.

Pist. O base Hungarian wight! wilt thou the spigot wield? [*Exit Bardolph.*]

Nym. He was gotten in drink. Is not the humour conceited?

Fal. I am glad I am so acquit of this tinder box. His thefts were too open; his filching was like an unskilful singer — he kept not time.

Nym. The good humour is to steal at a minim's rest.

Pist. 'Convey' the wise it call. 'Steal'? foh! a fico for the phrase!

Fal. Well, sirs, I am almost out at heels.

Pist. Why then, let kibes ensue!

Fal. There is no remedy; I must cony-catch, I must shift.

Pist. Young ravens must have food.

Fal. Which of you know Ford of this town?

Pist. I ken the wight. He is of substance good.

Fal. My honest lads, I will tell you what I am about.

Pist. Two yards, and more.

Fal. No quips now, Pistol! Indeed I am in the waist two yards about; but I am now about no waste: I am about thrift. Briefly, I do mean to make love to Ford's wife. I spy entertainment in her: she discourses, she carves, she gives the leer of invitation. I can construe the action of her familiar style, and the hardest voice of her behaviour (to be English'd rightly) is 'I am Sir John Falstaff's.'

Pist. He hath studied her well and translated her will — out of honesty into English.

Nym. The anchor is deep. Will that humour pass?

Fal. Now the report goes she has all the rule of her husband's purse. He hath a legion of angels.

Pist. As many devils entertain! and 'To her, boy!' say I.

Nym. The humour rises. It is good. Humour me the angels.

Fal. I have writ me here a letter to her; and here another to Page's wife, who even now gave me good eyes too, examin'd my parts with most judicious illiads. Sometimes the beam of her view gilded my foot, sometimes my portly belly.

Pist. [*aside*] Then did the sun on dunghill shine.

Nym. [*aside*] I thank thee for that humour.

Fal. O, she did so course o'er my exteriors with such a greedy intention that the appetite of her eye did seem to scorch me up like a burning glass! Here's another letter to her. She bears the purse too. She is a region in Guiana, all gold and bounty. I will be cheaters to them both, and they shall be exchequers to me. They shall be my East and West Indies, and I will trade to them both. [*To Pistol*] Go bear thou this letter to Mistress Page; [*to Nym*] and thou this to Mistress Ford. We will thrive, lads, we will thrive.

Pist. Shall I Sir Pandarus of Troy become,
And by my side wear steel? Then Lucifer take all!

Nym. I will run no base humour. Here, take the humour-letter. I will keep the haviour of reputation.

Fal. [*to Robin*] Hold, sirrah, bear you these letters tightly.
Sail like my pinnace to these golden shores.
[*Exit Robin.*]
Rogues, hence, avaunt! vanish like hailstones, go!
Trudge, plod away o' th' hoof! seek shelter, pack!
Falstaff will learn the humour of the age,
French thrift, you rogues — myself and skirted page. [*Exit.*]

Pist. Let vultures gripe thy guts! for gourd and fullam holds,
And high and low beguiles the rich and poor.
Tester I'll have in pouch when thou shalt lack,
Base Phrygian Turk!

Nym. I have operations in my head which be humours of revenge.

Pist. Wilt thou revenge?

Nym. By welkin and her star!

Pist. With wit or steel?

Nym. With both the humours, I!
I will discuss the humour of this love to Page.

Pist. And I to Ford shall eke unfold
How Falstaff, varlet vile,
His dove will prove, his gold will hold,
And his soft couch defile.

Nym. My humour shall not cool. I will incense Page to deal with poison. I will possess him with yellowness, for this revolt of mine is dangerous. That is my true humour.

Pist. Thou art the Mars of malecontents. I second thee. Troop on! *Exeunt.*

Scene IV. [Doctor Caius's *house*.]

Enter *Mistress Quickly, Simple, John Rugby.*

Quick. What, John Rugby! I pray thee go to the casement and see if you can see my master, Master Doctor Caius, coming. If he do, i' faith, and find anybody in the house, here will be an old abusing of God's patience and the king's English.

Rug. I'll go watch.

Quick. Go, and we'll have a posset for't soon at night, in faith, at the latter end of a sea-coal fire. [*Exit Rugby.*] An honest, willing, kind fellow as ever servant shall come in house withal; and, I warrant you, no telltale nor no breedbate. His worst fault is that he is given to prayer; he is something peevish that way. But nobody but has his fault. But let that pass. Peter Simple you say your name is?

Sim. Ay, for fault of a better.

Quick. And Master Slender's your master?

Sim. Ay, forsooth.

Quick. Does he not wear a great round beard, like a glover's paring knife?

Sim. No, forsooth. He hath but a little wee face, with a little yellow beard, a Cain-colour'd beard.

Quick. A softly-sprighted man, is he not?

Sim. Ay, forsooth; but he is as tall a man of his hands as any is between this and his head. He hath fought with a warrener.

Quick. How say you? O, I should remember him! Does he not hold up his head, as it were, and strut in his gait?

Sim. Yes indeed does he.

Quick. Well, heaven send Anne Page no worse fortune! Tell Master Parson Evans I will do what I can for your master. Anne is a good girl, and I wish —

[Enter *Rugby.*]

Rug. Out alas! here comes my master.

Quick. We shall all be shent. Run in here, good young man. Go into this closet. He will not stay long. [*Shuts Simple in the closet.*] What, John Rugby! John! what, John, I say! Go, John, go enquire for my master. I doubt he be not well that he comes not home. [*Sings.*]

And down, down, adown-a, &c.

[Enter *Doctor Caius.*]

Caius. Vat is you sing? I do not like des toys. Pray you go and vetch me in my closset un boitier vert — a box, a green-a box. Do intend vat I speak? A green-a box.

Quick. Ay, forsooth, I'll fetch it you. [*Aside*] I am glad he went not in himself. If he had found the young man, he would have been horn-mad.

Caius. Fe, fe, fe, fe! ma foi, il fait fort chaud. Je m'en vais à la cour — la grande affaire.

Quick. Is it this, sir?

Caius. Oui. Mette le au mon pocket: depeech quickly. Vere is dat knave Rugby?

Quick. What, John Rugby! John!

Rug. Here, sir.

Caius. You are John Rugby, and you are Jack Rugby. Come, take-a your rapier and come after my heel to de court.

Rug. 'Tis ready, sir, here in the porch.

Caius. By my trot, I tarry too long. Od's me! Qu'ai-j'oublié! Dere is some simples in my closset dat I vill not for de varld I shall leave behind.

Quick. Ay me! he'll find the young man there and be mad.

Caius. O diable, diable! Vat is in my closset? Villany! larron! [*Pulls Simple out.*] Rugby, my rapier!

Quick. Good master, be content.

Caius. Verefore shall I be content-a?

Quick. The young man is an honest man.

Caius. Vat shall de honest man do in my closset? Dere is no honest man dat shall come in my closset.

Quick. I beseech you be not so phlegmatic. Hear the truth of it. He came of an errand to me from Parson Hugh.

Caius. Vell.

Sim. Ay, forsooth! to desire her to —

Quick. Peace, I pray you.

Caius. Peace-a your tongue. Speak-a your tale.

Sim. To desire this honest gentlewoman, your maid, to speak a good word to Mistress Anne Page for my master in the way of marriage.

Quick. This is all, indeed, la! but I'll ne'er put my finger in the fire, and need not.

Caius. Sir Hugh send-a you? Rugby, baille me some paper. Tarry you a littel-a-while. [*Writes.*]

Quick. I am glad he is so quiet. If he had been throughly moved, you should have heard him so loud and so melancholy! But notwithstanding, man, I'll do your master what good I can; and the very yea and the no is, the French doctor, my master — I may call him my master, look you, for I keep his house; and I wash, wring, brew, bake, scour, dress meat and drink, make the beds, and do all myself —

Sim. 'Tis a great charge to come under one body's hand.

Quick. Are you avis'd o' that? You shall find it a great charge. And to be up early and down late! But notwithstanding (to tell you in your ear; I would have no words of it) my master himself is in love with Mistress Anne Page — but notwithstanding that, I know Anne's mind. That's neither here nor there.

Caius. You, jack'nape! give-a dis letter to Sir Hugh. By gar, it is a shallenge! I vill cut his troat in de Park; and I vill teach a scurvy jack-a-nape priest to meddle or make! You may be gone; it is not good you tarry here. [*Exit Simple.*] By gar, I vill cut all his two stones. By gar, he shall not have a stone to trow at his dog.

Quick. Alas, he speaks but for his friend.

Caius. It is no matter-a ver dat. Do not you tell-a me dat I shall have Anne Page for myself? By gar, I vill kill de Jack priest; and I have appointed mine host of de Jarteer to measure our weapon. By gar, I vill myself have Anne Page.

Quick. Sir, the maid loves you, and all shall be well. We must give folks leave to prate. What the good-jer!

Caius. Rugby, come to de court vit me. By gar, if I have not Anne Page, I shall turn your head out of my door. Follow my heels, Rugby.

[*Exeunt Caius and Rugby.*]

Quick. You shall have An fool's-head of your own! No, I know Anne's mind for that. Never a woman in Windsor knows more of Anne's mind than I do, nor can do more than I do with her, I thank heaven.

Fen. [*within*] Who's within there, ho?

Quick. Who's there, I trow? Come near the house, I pray you.

[Enter *Fenton.*]

Fen. How now, good woman? How dost thou?

Quick. The better that it pleases your good worship to ask.

Fen. What news? How does pretty Mistress Anne?

Quick. In truth, sir, and she is pretty, and honest, and gentle, and one that is your friend. I can tell you that by the way, I praise heaven for it.

Fen. Shall I do any good, think'st thou? Shall I not lose my suit?

Quick. Troth, sir, all is in his hands above. But notwithstanding, Master Fenton, I'll be sworn on a book she loves you. Have not your worship a wart above your eye?

Fen. Yes, marry, have I. What of that?

Quick. Well, thereby hangs a tale. Good faith, it is such another Nan! but, I detest, an honest maid as ever broke bread. We had an hour's talk of that wart. I shall never laugh but in that maid's company! But, indeed, she is given too much to allicholy and musing. But for you — well — go to.

Fen. Well, I shall see her to-day. Hold, there's money for thee. Let me have thy voice in my behalf. If thou seest her before me, commend me.

Quick. Will I? I' faith, that we will! and I will tell your worship more of the wart the next time we have confidence, and of other wooers.

Fen. Well, farewell. I am in great haste now.

Quick. Farewell to your worship. [*Exit Fenton.*] Truly, an honest gentleman; but Anne loves him not, for I know Anne's mind as well as another does. Out upon't! What have I forgot? *Exit.*

ACT II. Scene I. [*Before* Master Page's *house.*]

Enter *Mistress Page* [with a letter].

Mrs. Page. What, have I scap'd love letters in the holiday time of my beauty, and am I now a subject for them? Let me see. [*Reads.*]

'Ask me no reason why I love you; for, though Love use Reason for his physician, he admits him not for his counsellor. You are not young, no more am I. Go to then, there's sympathy. You are merry, so am I. Ha, ha! then there's more sympathy. You love sack, and so do I. Would you desire better sympathy? Let it suffice thee, Mistress Page — at the least, if the love of soldier can suffice — that I love thee. I will not say, pity me, — 'tis not a soldier-like phrase; but I say, love me. By me,

Thine own true knight,
By day or night,
Or any kind of light,
With all his might
For thee to fight, John Falstaff.'

What a Herod of Jewry is this! O wicked. wicked world! One that is well-nigh worn to pieces with age to show himself a young gallant! What unweighed behaviour hath this Flemish drunkard pick'd (with the devil's name!) out of my conversation that he dares in this manner assay me? Why, he hath not been thrice in my company! What should I say to him? I was then frugal of my mirth. Heaven forgive me! Why, I'll exhibit a bill in the parliament for the putting down of men! How shall I be reveng'd on him? for reveng'd I will be, as sure as his guts are made of puddings.

[Enter *Mistress Ford*.]

Mrs. Ford. Mistress Page, trust me, I was going to your house.

Mrs. Page. And trust me, I was coming to you. You look very ill.

Mrs. Ford. Nay, I'll ne'er believe that. I have to show to the contrary.

Mrs. Page. Faith, but you do, in my mind.

Mrs. Ford. Well, I do then. Yet I say I could show you to the contrary. O Mistress Page, give me some counsel!

Mrs. Page. What's the matter, woman?

Mrs. Ford. O woman! if it were not for one trifling respect, I could come to such honour!

Mrs. Page. Hang the trifle, woman; take the honour! What is it? Dispense with trifles. What is it?

Mrs. Ford. If I would but go to hell for an eternal moment or so, I could be knighted.

Mrs. Page. What? Thou liest! Sir Alice Ford? These knights will hack, and so thou shouldst not alter the article of thy gentry.

Mrs. Ford. We burn daylight. Here, read, read! Perceive how I might be knighted. I shall think the worse of fat men as long as I have an eye to make difference of men's liking. And yet he would not swear; prais'd women's modesty, and gave such orderly and well-behaved reproof to all uncomeliness that I would have sworn his disposition would have gone to the truth of his words. But they do no more adhere and keep place together than the Hundred Psalm to the tune of 'Greensleeves.' What tempest, I trow, threw this whale, with so many tuns of oil in his belly, ashore at Windsor? How shall I be revenged on him? I think the best way were to entertain him with hope till the wicked fire of lust have melted him in his own grease. Did you ever hear the like?

Mrs. Page. Letter for letter, but that the name of Page and Ford differs! To thy great comfort in this mystery of ill opinions, here's the twin brother of thy letter. But let thine inherit first, for I protest mine never shall. I warrant he hath a thousand of these letters, writ with blank space for different names — sure, more! — and these are of the second edition. He will print them, out of doubt; for he cares not what he puts into the press, when he would put us two. I had rather be a giantess and lie under Mount Pelion. Well, I will find you twenty lascivious turtles ere one chaste man.

Mrs. Ford. Why, this is the very same! the very hand! the very words! What doth he think of us?

Mrs. Page. Nay, I know not. It makes me almost ready to wrangle with mine own honesty. I'll entertain myself like one that I am not acquainted withal; for sure, unless he know some strain in me that I know not myself, he would never have boarded me in this fury.

Mrs. Ford. Boarding call you it? I'll be sure to keep him above deck.

Mrs. Page. So will I. If he come under my hatches, I'll never to sea again. Let's be reveng'd on him. Let's appoint him a meeting, give him a show of comfort in his suit, and lead him on with a fine-baited delay till he hath pawn'd his horses to mine host of the Garter.

Mrs. Ford. Nay, I will consent to act any villany against him that may not sully the chariness of our honesty. O that my husband saw this letter! It would give eternal food to his jealousy.

Mrs. Page. Why, look where he comes! and my good man too! He's as far from jealousy as I am from giving him cause, and that, I hope, is an unmeasurable distance.

Mrs. Ford. You are the happier woman.

Mrs. Page. Let's consult together against this greasy knight. Come hither. [*They retire*.]

[Enter *Ford*, with *Pistol*; and *Page*, with *Nym*.]

Ford. Well, I hope it be not so.

Pist. Hope is a curtal dog in some affairs.
Sir John affects thy wife.

Ford. Why, sir, my wife is not young.

Pist. He wooes both high and low, both rich and poor,
Both young and old, one with another, Ford.
He loves the gallimaufry. Ford, perpend.

Ford. Love my wife?

Pist. With liver burning hot. Prevent; or go thou,
Like Sir Actæon he, with Ringwood at thy heels.
O, odious is the name!

Ford. What name, sir?

Pist. The horn, I say. Farewell.
Take heed, have open eye; for thieves do foot by night.
Take heed, ere summer comes or cuckoo birds do sing.
Away, Sir Corporal Nym!
Believe it, Page; he speaks sense. [*Exit.*]

Ford. [*aside*] I will be patient; I will find out this.

Nym. [*to Page*] And this is true. I like not the humour of lying. He hath wronged me in some humours. I should have borne the humour'd letter to her. But I have a sword; and it shall bite upon my necessity. He loves your wife: there's the short and the long.
My name is Corporal Nym; I speak, and I avouch;
'Tis true. My name is Nym, and Falstaff loves your wife.
Adieu. I love not the humour of bread and cheese; and there's the humour of it. Adieu. *Exit.*

Page. [*aside*] 'The humour of it,' quoth 'a? Here's a fellow frights English out of his wits.

Ford. [*aside*] I will seek out Falstaff.

Page. [*aside*] I never heard such a drawling, affecting rogue.

Ford. [*aside*] If I do find it — well!

Page. [*aside*] I will not believe such a Cataian, though the priest o' th' town commended him for a true man.

Ford. [*aside*] 'Twas a good sensible fellow. Well!

[*Mistress Page and Mistress Ford come forward.*]

Page. How now, Meg?

Mrs. Page. Whither go you, George? Hark you.

Mrs. Ford. How now, sweet Frank? Why art thou melancholy?

Ford. I melancholy? I am not melancholy. Get you home, go.

Mrs. Ford. Faith, thou hast some crotchets in thy head now. Will you go, Mistress Page?

Mrs. Page. Have with you. — You'll come to dinner, George?

[Enter *Mistress Quickly.*]

[*Aside to Mrs. Ford*] Look who comes yonder. She shall be our messenger to this paltry knight.

Mrs. Ford. [*aside to Mrs. Page*] Trust me, I thought on her. She'll fit it.

Mrs. Page. You are come to see my daughter Anne?

Quick. Ay, forsooth; and I pray, how does good Mistress Anne?

Mrs. Page. Go in with us and see. We have an hour's talk with you.

[*Exeunt Mistress Page, Mistress Ford, and Mistress Quickly.*]

Page. How now, Master Ford?

Ford. You heard what this knave told me, did you not?

Page. Yes, and you heard what the other told me?

Ford. Do you think there is truth in them?

Page. Hang 'em, slaves! I do not think the knight would offer it. But these that accuse him in his intent towards our wives are a yoke of his discarded men; very rogues, now they be out of service.

Ford. Were they his men?

Page. Marry were they.

Ford. I like it never the better for that. Does he lie at the Garter?

Page. Ay, marry does he. If he should intend this voyage toward my wife, I would turn her loose to him; and what he gets more of her than sharp words, let it lie on my head.

Ford. I do not misdoubt my wife; but I would be loath to turn them together. A man may be too confident. I would have nothing lie on my head. I cannot be thus satisfied.

[Enter *Host.*]

Page. Look where my ranting host of the Garter comes. There is either liquor in his pate or money in his purse when he looks so merrily. How now, mine host?

Host. How now, bully rook? Thou'rt a gentleman. Cavaleiro Justice, I say!

[Enter *Shallow.*]

Shal. I follow, mine host, I follow. Good even and twenty, good Master Page! Master Page, will you go with us? We have sport in hand.

Host. Tell him, Cavaleiro Justice! Tell him, bully rook.

Shal. Sir, there is a fray to be fought between Sir Hugh the Welsh priest and Caius the French doctor.

Ford. Good mine host o' th' Garter, a word with you.

Host. What say'st thou, my bully rook? [*They go aside.*]

Shal. [*to Page*] Will you go with us to behold it? My merry host hath had the measuring of their weapons and, I think, hath appointed them contrary places; for, believe me, I hear the parson is no jester. Hark, I will tell you what our sport shall be. [*They go aside.*]

Host. Hast thou no suit against my knight, my guest-cavaleiro?

Ford. None, I protest. But I'll give you a pottle of burnt sack to give me recourse to him and tell him my name is Brook — only for a jest.

Host. My hand, bully! Thou shalt have egress and regress (said I well?) and thy name shall be Brook. It is a merry knight. Will you go, cavaleiros?

Shal. Have with you, mine host.

Page. I have heard the Frenchman hath good skill in his rapier.

Shal. Tut, sir! I could have told you more. In these times you stand on distance: your passes, stoccadoes, and I know not what. 'Tis the heart, Master Page; 'tis here, 'tis here! I have seen the time with my long sword I would have made you four tall fellows skip like rats.

Host. Here, boys! here, here! Shall we wag?

Page. Have with you. I had rather hear them scold than fight.

[*Exeunt Host, Shallow, and Page.*]

Ford. Though Page be a secure fool and stands so firmly on his wife's frailty, yet I cannot put off my opinion so easily. She was in his company at Page's house, and what they made there I know not. Well, I will look further into't, and I have a disguise to sound Falstaff. If I find her honest, I lose not my labour; if she be otherwise, 'tis labour well bestowed. *Exit.*

Scene II. [*The Garter Inn.*]

Enter *Falstaff, Pistol.*

Pist. I will retort the sum in equipage.

Fal. I will not lend thee a penny.

Pist. Why, then the world's mine oyster,
Which I with sword will open.

Fal. Not a penny. I have been content, sir, you should lay my countenance to pawn. I have grated upon my good friends for three reprieves for you and your coach-fellow Nym; or else you had look'd through the grate, like a geminy of baboons. I am damn'd in hell for swearing to gentlemen my friends you were good soldiers and tall fellows; and when Mistress Bridget lost the handle of her fan, I took't upon mine honour thou hadst it not.

Pist. Didst not thou share? Hadst thou not fifteen pence?

Fal. Reason, you rogue, reason! Think'st thou I'll endanger my soul gratis? At a word, hang no more about me; I am no gibbet for you. Go! a short knife and a throng! To your manor of Pickt-hatch! Go. You'll not bear a letter for me, you rogue? You stand upon your honour! Why, thou unconfinable baseness, it is as much as I can do to keep the terms of my honour precise. I, I, I myself sometimes, leaving the fear of God on the left hand and hiding mine honour in my necessity, am fain to shuffle, to hedge, and to lurch; and yet you, rogue, will ensconce your rags, your cat-a-mountain looks, your red-lattice phrases, and your bold-beating oaths under the shelter of your honour? You will not do it? you?

Pist. I do relent. What would thou more of man?

[Enter *Robin.*]

Robin. Sir, here's a woman would speak with you.

Fal. Let her approach.

[Enter *Mistress Quickly.*]

Quick. Give your worship good morrow.

Fal. Good morrow, goodwife.

Quick. Not so, an't please your worship.

Fal. Good maid then.

Quick. I'll be sworn,
As my mother was the first hour I was born.

Fal. I do believe the swearer. What with me?

Quick. Shall I vouchsafe your worship a word or two?

Fal. Two thousand, fair woman, and I'll vouchsafe thee the hearing.

Quick. There is one Mistress Ford, sir — I pray come a little nearer this ways. I myself dwell with Master Doctor Caius —

Fal. Well, on! Mistress Ford, you say —

Quick. Your worship says very true. I pray your worship come a little nearer this ways.

Fal. I warrant thee, nobody hears. Mine own people, mine own people.

Quick. Are they so? God bless them and make them his servants!

Fal. Well, Mistress Ford — what of her?

Quick. Why, sir, she's a good creature. Lord, Lord! your worship 's a wanton! Well, heaven forgive you, and all of us, I pray!

Fal. Mistress Ford — come, Mistress Ford —

Quick. Marry, this is the short and the long of it. You have brought her into such a canaries as 'tis wonderful. The best courtier of them all, when the court lay at Windsor, could never have brought her to such a canary. Yet there has been knights, and lords, and gentlemen, with their coaches; I warrant you coach after coach, letter after letter, gift after gift; smelling so sweetly — all musk — and so rushling, I warrant you, in silk and gold; and in such alligant terms; and in such wine and sugar of the best, and the fairest, that would have won any woman's heart; and I warrant you they could never get an eye-wink of her. I had myself twenty angels given me this morning; but I defy all angels (in any such sort, as they say) but in the way of honesty; and I warrant you they could never get her so much as sip on a cup with the proudest of them all; and yet there has been earls — nay (which is more) pensioners; but I warrant you all is one with her.

Fal. But what says she to me? Be brief, my good she-Mercury.

Quick. Marry, she hath receiv'd your letter; for the which she thanks you a thousand times; and she gives you to notify that her husband will be absence from his house between ten and eleven.

Fal. Ten and eleven.

Quick. Ay, forsooth; and then you may come and see the picture, she says, that you wot of. Master Ford her husband will be from home. Alas, the sweet woman leads an ill life with him! He's a very jealousy man. She leads a very frampold life with him, good heart!

Fal. Ten and eleven. Woman, commend me to her. I will not fail her.

Quick. Why, you say well. But I have another messenger to your worship. Mistress Page hath her hearty commendations to you, too; and let me tell you in your ear, she's as fartuous a civil modest wife, and one (I tell you) that will not miss you morning nor evening prayer, as any is in Windsor, whoe'er be the other; and she bade me tell your worship that her husband is seldom from home, but she hopes there will come a time. I never knew a woman so dote upon a man. Surely I think you have charms, la! Yes, in truth.

Fal. Not I, I assure thee. Setting the attraction of my good parts aside, I have no other charms.

Quick. Blessing on your heart for't!

Fal. But I pray thee tell me this: has Ford's wife and Page's wife acquainted each other how they love me?

Quick. That were a jest indeed! They have not so little grace, I hope. That were a trick indeed! But Mistress Page would desire you to send her your little page, of all loves. Her husband has a marvellous infection to the little page. And truly Master Page is an honest man. Never a wife in Windsor leads a better life than she does. Do what she will, say what she will, take all, pay all, go to bed when she list, rise when she list, all is as she will. And truly she deserves it; for if there be a kind woman in Windsor, she is one. You must send her your page; no remedy.

Fal. Why, I will.

Quick. Nay, but do so then; and look you, he may come and go between you both; and in any case have a nay-word, that you may know one another's mind, and the boy never need to understand anything; for 'tis not good that children should know any wickedness. Old folks, you know, have discretion, as they say, and know the world.

Fal. Fare thee well. Commend me to them both. There's my purse. I am yet thy debtor. Boy, go along with this woman. [*Exeunt Mistress Quickly and Robin.*] This news distracts me!

Pist. [*aside*] This punk is one of Cupid's carriers.
Clap on more sails! pursue! up with your fights!
Give fire! She is my prize, or ocean whelm them all! [*Exit.*]

Fal. Say'st thou so, old Jack? Go thy ways. I'll make more of thy old body than I have done. Will they yet look after thee? Wilt thou, after the expense of so much money, be now a gainer? Good body, I thank thee. Let them say 'tis grossly done; so it be fairly done, no matter.

[Enter *Bardolph* with a cup of sack.]

Bard. Sir John, there's one Master Brook below would fain speak with you and be acquainted with you; and hath sent your worship a morning's draught of sack.

Fal. Brook is his name?

Bard. Ay, sir.

Fal. Call him in. [*Exit Bardolph.*] Such Brooks are welcome to me, that o'erflow such liquor. Aha! Mistress Ford and Mistress Page, have I encompass'd you? Go to! via!

[Enter *Bardolph*, with *Ford* disguised.]

Ford. Bless you, sir!

Fal. And you, sir! Would you speak with me?

Ford. I make bold to press with so little preparation upon you.

Fal. You're welcome. What's your will? — Give us leave, drawer. [*Exit Bardolph.*]

Ford. Sir, I am a gentleman that have spent much. My name is Brook.

Fal. Good Master Brook, I desire more acquaintance of you.

Ford. Good Sir John, I sue for yours: not to charge you, for I must let you understand I think myself in better plight for a lender than you are; the which hath something embold'ned me to this unseason'd intrusion; for they say, if money go before, all ways do lie open.

Fal. Money is a good soldier, sir, and will on.

Ford. Troth, and I have a bag of money here troubles me. If you will help to bear it, Sir John, take all, or half, for easing me of the carriage.

Fal. Sir, I know not how I may deserve to be your porter.

Ford. I will tell you, sir, if you will give me the hearing.

Fal. Speak, good Master Brook. I shall be glad to be your servant.

Ford. Sir, I hear you are a scholar (I will be brief with you) and you have been a man long known to me, though I had never so good means as desire to make myself acquainted with you. I shall discover a thing to you wherein I must very much lay open mine own imperfection; but, good Sir John, as you have one eye upon my follies, as you hear them unfolded, turn another into the register of your own, that I may pass with a reproof the easier, sith you yourself know how easy it is to be such an offender.

Fal. Very well, sir; proceed.

Ford. There is a gentlewoman in this town, her husband's name is Ford.

Fal. Well, sir.

Ford. I have long lov'd her and, I protest to you, bestowed much on her, followed her with a doting observance, engross'd opportunities to meet her, feed every slight occasion that could but niggardly give me sight of her; not only bought many presents to give her, but have given largely to many to know what she would have given. Briefly, I have pursu'd her as love hath pursued me, which hath been on the wing of all occasions. But whatsoever I have merited, either in my mind or in my means, meed, I am sure, I have received none, unless experience be a jewel. That I have purchased at an infinite rate, and that hath taught me to say this:

'Love like a shadow flies when substance love
pursues,
Pursuing that that flies, and flying what pursues.'

Fal. Have you receiv'd no promise of satisfaction at her hands?

Ford. Never.

Fal. Have you importun'd her to such a purpose?

Ford. Never.

Fal. Of what quality was your love then?

Ford. Like a fair house built on another man's ground, so that I have lost my edifice by mistaking the place where I erected it.

Fal. To what purpose have you unfolded this to me?

Ford. When I have told you that, I have told you all. Some say that, though she appear honest to me, yet in other places she enlargeth her mirth so far that there is shrewd construction made of her. Now, Sir John, here is the heart of my purpose: you are a gentleman of excellent breeding, admirable discourse, of great admittance, authentic in your place and person, generally allow'd for your many warlike, court-like, and learned preparations.

Fal. O, sir!

Ford. Believe it, for you know it. There is money. Spend it, spend it! spend more! spend all I have! Only give me so much of your time in exchange of it as to lay an amiable siege to the honesty of this Ford's wife. Use your art of wooing; win her to consent to you. If any man may, you may as soon as any.

Fal. Would it apply well to the vehemency of your affection that I should win what you would enjoy? Methinks you prescribe to yourself very preposterously.

Ford. O, understand my drift. She dwells so securely on the excellency of her honour that the folly of my soul dares not present itself. She is too bright to be look'd against. Now, could I come to her with any detection in my hand, my desires had instance and argument to commend themselves. I could drive her then from the ward of her purity, her reputation, her marriage vow, and a thousand other her defences, which now are too too strongly embattled against me. What say you to't, Sir John?

Fal. Master Brook, I will first make bold with your money; next, give me your hand; and last, as I am a gentleman, you shall, if you will, enjoy Ford's wife.

Ford. O good sir!

Fal. I say you shall.

Ford. Want no money, Sir John. You shall want none.

Fal. Want no Mistress Ford, Master Brook. You shall want none. I shall be with her (I may

The merry wives: Peggy Ashcroft as Mistress Page and Ursula Jeans as Mistress Ford

THE MERRY WIVES OF WINDSOR

PHOTOGRAPHS BY JOHN VICKERS
PRODUCED BY THE OLD VIC COMPANY

The sprightly Mistress Page, unwilling object of Falstaff's redoubtable affection

Alec Clunes as Ford, troubled by Falstaff's allegations against his wife's integrity

Nuna Davey as Mistress Quickley, housekeeper of Caius, comic French physician

Roger Livesey in the role of Sir John Falstaff, tavern knight and would-be amorist

The flighty Slender (Robert Eddison) is interrogated by Justice Shallow (William Devlin) and Sir Hugh Evans (Mark Dignam) regarding his proposed marriage with Anne Page *(Act I, Scene I)*

Left: "Mistress Anne, my cousin loves you." Justice Shallow speaks for his bashful protégé, Slender, as the boy presents Anne Page (Dorothy Tutin) with a nosegay *(Act III, Scene IV)*

Below: " 'tis the very riches of thyself that now I aim at." Fenton (Paul Hansard), the favored suitor, avows his love *(Act III, Scene IV)*

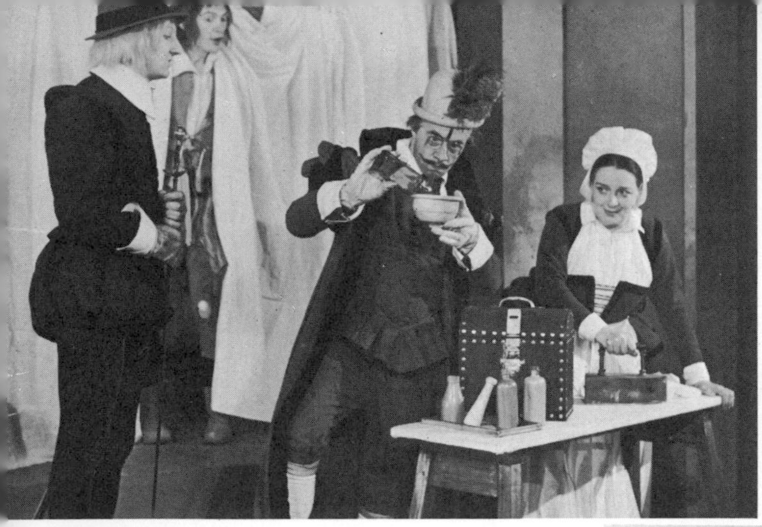

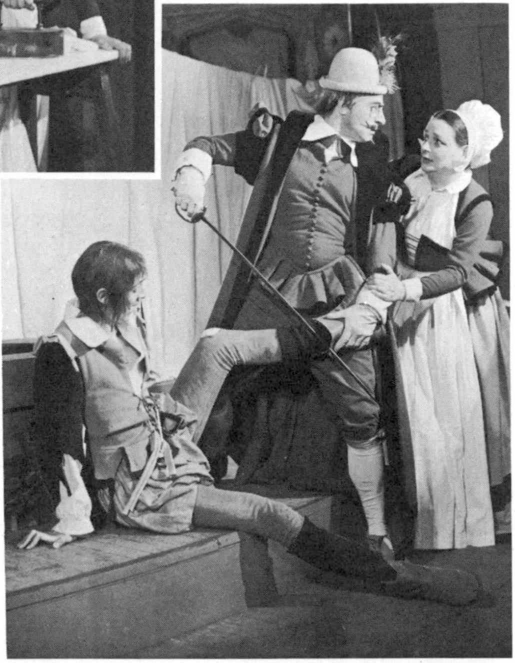

Above: Doctor Caius (Paul Rogers) prepares a potion while Mistress Quickly looks on apprehensively, fearing he will discover Simple (Richard Pasco), with whom she is conspiring to aid Slender's suit *(Act I, Scene IV)*

Right: Mistress Quickly attempts to soothe Doctor Caius, who is enraged to find Simple concealed in his house *(Act I, Scene IV)*

Below: "I warrant thee, nobody hears: mine own people." Falstaff vouches for the discretion of his followers as Mistress Quickly brings him a confidential message from Mistress Ford *(Act II, Scene II)*

Caius has challenged Sir Hugh Evans because of the parson's meddling in the affair of Anne Page and Slender. Here he berates the parson for not meeting him for the duel *(Act III, Scene I)*

"You shall have her, Master Brook." Falstaff promises to arrange a romance with Mistress Ford, not knowing that he is dealing with the husband himself
(Act II, Scene I)

"What made me love thee? let that persuade thee there's something extraordinary in thee." Falstaff's brusque, vigorous wooing of Mistress Ford
(Act III, Scene III)

"This 'tis to be married: this 'tis to have linen and buck-baskets!" Ford has just heard from the rogue knight that he escaped from his clandestine rendezvous by hiding himself in a basket of soiled linen. His anger is no whit appeased by the discomfort suffered by Falstaff *(Act III, Scene V)*

"I cannot find him: may be the knave bragged of that he could not compass." Ford is furious to find that Falstaff has escaped him *(Act III, Scene III)*

"Go fetch me a quart of sack; put a toast in't." Having escaped from Ford at the cost of a ducking in the Thames, Falstaff resorts to the consolations of the bottle and calls for sack to warm him *(Act III, Scene V)*

Disguised as Mother Prat, the Fat Woman of Brainford, Falstaff makes his second escape from Ford, suffering this time only a minor cudgeling *(Act IV, Scene II)*

"My belly's as cold as if I had swallowed snowballs for pills to cool the rains." The aftermath of Falstaff's chilly ducking *(Act III, Scene V)*

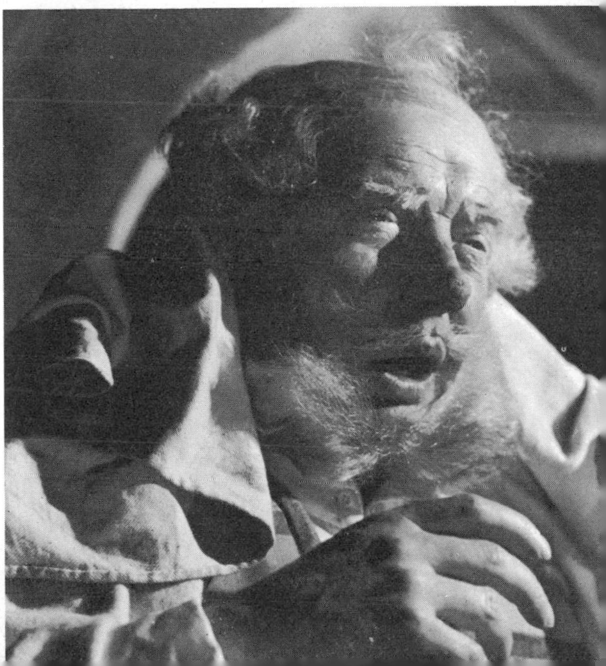

The merry wives devise a final plan for the discomfiture of Falstaff *(Act IV, Scene IV)*

Mistress Page and Mistress Ford celebrating the success of their ruse against the conniving Falstaff *(Act III, Scene III)*

tell you) by her own appointment. Even as you came in to me, her assistant or go-between parted from me. I say I shall be with her between ten and eleven; for at that time the jealious rascally knave her husband will be forth. Come you to me at night; you shall know how I speed.

Ford. I am blest in your acquaintance. Do you know Ford, sir?

Fal. Hang him, poor cuckoldly knave! I know him not. Yet I wrong him to call him poor. They say the jealous wittolly knave hath masses of money, for the which his wife seems to me well-favour'd. I will use her as the key of the cuckoldly rogue's coffer, and there's my harvest home.

Ford. I would you knew Ford, sir, that you might avoid him if you saw him.

Fal. Hang him, mechanical salt-butter rogue! I will stare him out of his wits. I will awe him with my cudgel. It shall hang like a meteor o'er the cuckold's horns. Master Brook, thou shalt know I will predominate over the peasant, and thou shalt lie with his wife. Come to me soon at night. Ford 's a knave, and I will aggravate his style. Thou, Master Brook, shalt know him for knave and cuckold. Come to me soon at night. *Exit.*

Ford. What a damn'd Epicurian rascal is this! My heart is ready to crack with impatience. Who says this is improvident jealousy? My wife hath sent to him, the hour is fix'd, the match is made. Would any man have thought this? See the hell of having a false woman! My bed shall be abus'd, my coffers ransack'd, my reputation gnawn at; and I shall not only receive this villanous wrong, but stand under the adoption of abominable terms, and by him that does me this wrong. Terms! names! Amaimon sounds well; Lucifer, well; Barbason, well; yet they are devils' additions, the names of fiends. But cuckold! wittol! Cuckold! the devil himself hath not such a name. Page is an ass, a secure ass. He will trust his wife; he will not be jealous. I will rather trust a Fleming with my butter, Parson Hugh the Welshman with my cheese, an Irishman with my aqua-vitæ bottle, or a thief to walk my ambling gelding, than my wife with herself. Then she plots, then she ruminates, then she devises; and what they think in their hearts they may effect, they will break their hearts but they will effect. God be prais'd for my jealousy! Eleven o'clock the hour. I will prevent this, detect my wife, be reveng'd on Falstaff, and laugh at Page. I will about it. Better three hours too soon than a minute too late. Fie, fie, fie! Cuckold, cuckold, cuckold! *Exit.*

Scene III. [*A field near Windsor.*]

Enter *Caius, Rugby.*

Caius. Jack Rugby!

Rug. Sir?

Caius. Vat is de clock, Jack?

Rug. 'Tis past the hour, sir, that Sir Hugh promis'd to meet.

Caius. By gar, he has save his soul dat he is no-come; he has pray his Pible vell dat he is no-come. By gar, Jack Rugby, he is dead already if he be come.

Rug. He is wise, sir. He knew your worship would kill him if he came.

Caius. By gar, de herring is no dead so as I vill kill him. Take your rapier, Jack, I vill tell you how I vill kill him.

Rug. Alas, sir, I cannot fence.

Caius. Villany, take your rapier!

Rug. Forbear! Here's company.

[Enter *Host, Shallow, Slender,* and *Page.*]

Host. Bless thee, bully Doctor!

Shal. Save you, Master Doctor Caius!

Page. Now, good Master Doctor!

Slen. Give you good morrow, sir.

Caius. Vat be all you, one, two, tree, four, come for?

Host. To see thee fight, to see thee foin, to see thee traverse; to see thee here, to see thee there; to see thee pass thy punto, thy stock, thy reverse, thy distance, thy montant. Is he dead, my Ethiopian? Is he dead, my Francisco? Ha, bully! What says my Æsculapius? my Galien? my heart of elder? Ha! is he dead, bully Stale? is he dead?

Caius. By gar, he is de coward-Jack-priest of de vorld. He is not show his face.

Host. Thou art a Castalion-King-Urinal! Hector of Greece, my boy!

Caius. I pray you bear vitness dat me have stay six or seven, two tree hours for him, and he is no-come.

Shal. He is the wiser man, Master Doctor. He is a curer of souls, and you a curer of bodies. If you should fight, you go against the hair of your professions. Is it not true, Master Page?

Page. Master Shallow, you have yourself been a great fighter, though now a man of peace.

Shal. Bodykins, Master Page, though I now be old, and of the peace, if I see a sword out, my finger itches to make one. Though we are justices, and doctors, and churchmen, Master Page, we have some salt of our youth in us; we are the sons of women, Master Page.

Page. 'Tis true, Master Shallow.

Shal. It will be found so, Master Page. Master Doctor Caius, I am come to fetch you home. I am sworn of the peace. You have show'd yourself a wise physician, and Sir Hugh hath shown himself a wise and patient churchman. You must go with me, Master Doctor.

Host. Pardon, Guest Justice. A word, Mounseur Mock-water.

Caius. Mock-vater? Vat is dat?

Host. Mock-water in our English tongue is valour, bully.

Caius. By gar, den I have as much mock-vater as de Englishman. Scurvy jack-dog-priest! By gar, me vill cut his ears.

Host. He will clapperclaw thee tightly, bully.

Caius. Clapper-de-claw? Vat is dat?

Host. That is, he will make thee amends.

Caius. By gar, me do look he shall clapper-de-claw me; for, by gar, me vill have it.

Host. And I will provoke him to't, or let him wag.

Caius. Me tanck you vor dat.

Host. And moreover, bully — But first, Master Guest, and Master Page, and eke Cavaleiro Slender, go you through the town to Frogmore. [*Aside to them.*]

Page. Sir Hugh is there, is he?

Host. He is there. See what humour he is in. And I will bring the doctor about by the fields. Will it do well?

Shal. We will do it.

All. Adieu, good Master Doctor.

[*Exeunt Page, Shallow, and Slender.*]

Caius. By gar, me vill kill de priest, for he speak for a jack-an-ape to Anne Page.

Host. Let him die. But first sheathe thy impatience; throw cold water on thy choler. Go about the fields with me through Frogmore. I will bring thee where Mistress Anne Page is, at a farmhouse a-feasting; and thou shalt woo her. Cried I aim? Said I well?

Caius. By gar, me danck you vor dat. By gar, I love you; and I shall procure-a you de good guest — de earl, de knight, de lords, de gentlemen, my patients.

Host. For the which I will be thy adversary toward Anne Page. Said I well?

Caius. By gar, 'tis good. Vell said!

Host. Let us wag then.

Caius. Come at my heels, Jack Rugby.

Exeunt.

ACT III. Scene I. [*A field near Frogmore.*]

Enter *Evans, Simple.*

Evans. I pray you now, good Master Slender's servingman, and friend Simple by your name, which way have you look'd for Master Caius, that calls himself Doctor of Physic?

Sim. Marry, sir, the pittie-ward, the Park-ward; every way; old Windsor way, and every way but the town way.

Evans. I most fehemently desire you you will also look that way.

Sim. I will, sir. [*Exit.*]

Evans. Pless my soul, how full of chollors I am, and trempling of mind! I shall be glad if he have deceived me. How melancholies I am! I will knog his urinals about his knave's costard when I have good oportunities for the ork. Pless my soul! [*Sings.*]

To shallow rivers, to whose falls
Melodious birds sings madrigals;
There will we make our peds of roses
And a thousand fragrant posies.
To shallow —

Mercy on me! I have a great dispositions to cry. [*Sings.*]

Melodious birds sing madrigals —
When as I sat in Pabylon —
And a thousand vagram posies.
To shallow, &c.

[Enter *Simple.*]

Sim. Yonder he is coming, this way, Sir Hugh.

Evans. He's welcome. [*Sings.*]

To shallow rivers, to whose falls —

Heaven prosper the right! What weapons is he?

Sim. No weapons, sir. There comes my master, Master Shallow, and another gentleman, from Frogmore, over the stile, this way.

Evans. Pray you give me my gown, or else keep it in your arms. [*Reads in a book.*]

Enter *Page, Shallow,* and *Slender.*

Shal. How now, Master Parson? Good morrow, good Sir Hugh. Keep a gamester from the dice and a good studient from his book, and it is wonderful.

Slen. [*aside*] Ah, sweet Anne Page!

Page. Save you, good Sir Hugh!

Evans. Pless you from his mercy sake, all of you!

Shal. What, the sword and the word? Do you study them both, Master Parson?

Page. And youthful still, in your doublet and hose this raw rheumatic day?

Evans. There is reasons and causes for it.

Page. We are come to you to do a good office, Master Parson.

Evans. Fery well. What is it?

Page. Yonder is a most reverend gentleman who, belike having received wrong by some person, is at most odds with his own gravity and patience that ever you saw.

Shal. I have lived fourscore years and upward. I never heard a man of his place, gravity, and learning so wide of his own respect.

Evans. What is he?

Page. I think you know him — Master Doctor Caius, the renowned French physician.

Evans. Got's will and his passion of my heart! I had as lief you would tell me of a mess of porridge.

Page. Why?

Evans. He has no more knowledge in Hibocrates and Galen, and he is a knave besides — a cowardly knave as you would desires to be acquainted withal.

Page. I warrant you he's the man should fight with him.

Slen. [*aside*] O sweet Anne Page!

Shal. It appears so by his weapons.

[Enter *Host, Caius,* and *Rugby.*]

Keep them asunder! Here comes Doctor Caius.

Page. Nay, good Master Parson, keep in your weapon.

Shal. So do you, good Master Doctor.

Host. Disarm them and let them question. Let them keep their limbs whole and hack our English.

Caius. I pray you let-a me speak a vord vit your ear. Verefore vill you not meet-a me?

Evans. [*aside to Caius*] Pray you use your patience. In goot time.

Caius. By gar, you are de coward, de Jack dog, John ape!

Evans. [*aside to Caius*] Pray you let us not be laughing-stogs to other men's humours. I desire you in friendship, and I will one way or other make you amends. [*Aloud*] I will knog your urinals about your knave's cogscomb for missing your meetings and appointments.

Caius. Diable! Jack Rugby! Mine host de Jarteer! Have I not stay for him to kill him? Have I not, at de place I did appoint?

Evans. As I am a Christians soul now, look you, this is the place appointed. I'll be judgment by mine host of the Garter.

Host. Peace, I say, Gallia and Gawlia, French and Welsh, soul-curer and body-curer!

Caius. Ay, dat is very good, excellant!

Host. Peace, I say! Hear mine host of the Garter. Am I politic? Am I subtle? Am I a Machivel? Shall I lose my doctor? No! he gives me the potions and the motions. Shall I lose my parson, my priest, my Sir Hugh? No! he gives me the proverbs and the no-verbs. Give me thy hand, terrestrial! so. Give me thy hand, celestial! so. Boys of art, I have deceiv'd you both; I have directed you to wrong places. Your hearts are mighty, your skins are whole, and let burnt sack be the issue. Come, lay their swords to pawn. Follow me, lads of peace; follow, follow, follow!

Shal. Trust me, a mad host. Follow, gentlemen, follow.

Slen. [*aside*] O sweet Anne Page!

[*Exeunt all but Caius and Evans.*]

Caius. Ha, do I perceive dat? Have you make-a de sot of us, ha, ha?

Evans. This is well. He has made us his vlouting-stog. I desire you that we may be friends; and let us knog our prains together to be revenge on this same scall scurvy cogging companion, the host of the Garter.

Caius. By gar, vit all my heart! He promise to bring me vere is Anne Page. By gar, he deceive me too.

Evans. Well, I will smite his noddles. Pray you follow. [*Exeunt.*]

Scene II. [*Windsor. The street.*]

Enter *Mistress Page, Robin.*

Mrs. Page. Nay, keep your way, little gallant. You were wont to be a follower, but now you are a leader. Whether had you rather lead mine eyes, or eye your master's heels?

Rob. I had rather, forsooth, go before you like a man than follow him like a dwarf.

Mrs. Page. O, you are a flattering boy! Now I see you'll be a courtier.

[Enter *Ford.*]

Ford. Well met, Mistress Page. Whither go you?

Mrs. Page. Truly, sir, to see your wife. Is she at home?

Ford. Ay, and as idle as she may hang together, for want of company. I think, if your husbands were dead, you two would marry.

Mrs. Page. Be sure of that — two other husbands.

Ford. Where had you this pretty weathercock?

Mrs. Page. I cannot tell what the dickens his name is my husband had him of. — What do you call your knight's name, sirrah?

Rob. Sir John Falstaff.

Ford. Sir John Falstaff?

Mrs. Page. He, he! I can never hit on's name. There is such a league between my goodman and he! Is your wife at home indeed?

Ford. Indeed she is.

Mrs. Page. By your leave, sir. I am sick till I see her. [*Exeunt Mrs. Page and Robin.*]

Ford. Has Page any brains? Hath he any eyes? Hath he any thinking? Sure they sleep; he hath no use of them. Why, this boy will carry a letter twenty mile as easy as a cannon will shoot point-blank twelve score. He pieces out his wive's inclination; he gives her folly motion and advantage; and now she's going to my wife, and Falstaff's boy with her. A man may hear this show'r sing in the wind! And Falstaff's boy with her! Good plots! They are laid, and our revolted wives share damnation together. Well, I will take him, then torture my wife, pluck the borrowed veil of modesty from the so-seeming Mistress Page, divulge Page himself for a secure and wilful Actæon, and to these violent proceedings all my neighbours shall cry aim. [*Clock strikes.*] The clock gives me my cue, and my assurance bids me search. There I shall find Falstaff. I shall be rather prais'd for this than mock'd; for it is as positive as the earth is firm that Falstaff is there. I will go.

[Enter *Page, Shallow, Slender, Host, Evans, Caius,* and *Rugby.*]

Shal., Page, &c. Well met, Master Ford.

Ford. Trust me, a good knot! I have good cheer at home, and I pray you all go with me.

Shal. I must excuse myself, Master Ford.

Slen. And so must I, sir. We have appointed to dine with Mistress Anne, and I would not break with her for more money than I'll speak of.

Shal. We have linger'd about a match between Anne Page and my cousin Slender, and this day we shall have our answer.

Slen. I hope I have your good will, father Page.

Page. You have, Master Slender. I stand wholly for you. But my wife, Master Doctor, is for you altogether.

Caius. Ay, be gar! and de maid is love-a me. My nursh-a Quickly tell me so mush.

Host. What say you to young Master Fenton? He capers, he dances, he has eyes of youth; he writes verses, he speaks holiday, he smells April and May. He will carry't, he will carry't! 'Tis in his buttons; he will carry't!

Page. Not by my consent, I promise you. The gentleman is of no having. He kept company with the wild Prince and Poins. He is of too high a region; he knows too much. No, he shall not knit a knot in his fortunes with the finger of my substance. If he take her, let him take her simply. The wealth I have waits on my consent, and my consent goes not that way.

Ford. I beseech you heartily, some of you go home with me to dinner. Besides your cheer, you shall have sport; I will show you a monster. Master Doctor, you shall go. So shall you, Master Page, and you, Sir Hugh.

Shal. Well, fare you well. We shall have the freer wooing at Master Page's.

Exeunt Shallow and Slender.

Caius. Go home, John Rugby; I come anon. [*Exit Rugby.*]

Host. Farewell, my hearts. I will to my honest knight Falstaff and drink canary with him. *Exit.*

Ford. [*aside*] I think I shall drink in pipe-wine first with him; I'll make him dance. — Will you go, gentles?

All. Have with you to see this monster. *Exeunt.*

Scene III. [Ford's *house.*]

Enter *Mistress Ford, Mistress Page.*

Mrs. Ford. What, John! What, Robert!

Mrs. Page. Quickly, quickly! Is the buck-basket —

Mrs. Ford. I warrant. What, Robin, I say!

[Enter two *Servants*] with a great buck-basket.

Mrs. Page. Come, come, come!

Mrs. Ford. Here, set it down.

Mrs. Page. Give your men the charge. We must be brief.

Mrs. Ford. Marry, as I told you before, John and Robert, be ready here hard by in the brew-house; and when I suddenly call you, come forth and, without any pause or staggering, take this basket on your shoulders. That done, trudge with it in all haste and carry it among the whitsters in Datchet Mead, and there empty it in the muddy ditch close by the Thames side.

Mrs. Page. You will do it?

Mrs. Ford. I ha' told them over and over; they lack no direction. Be gone, and come when you are call'd. [*Exeunt Servants.*]

[Enter *Robin.*]

Mrs. Page. Here comes little Robin.

Mrs. Ford. How now, my eyas-musket? What news with you?

Rob. My master, Sir John, is come in at your back door, Mistress Ford, and requests your company.

Mrs. Page. You little Jack-a-Lent, have you been true to us?

Rob. Ay, I'll be sworn. My master knows not of your being here, and hath threat'ned to put me into everlasting liberty if I tell you of it; for he swears he'll turn me away.

Mrs. Page. Thou'rt a good boy. This secrecy of thine shall be a tailor to thee and shall make thee a new doublet and hose. I'll go hide me.

Mrs. Ford. Do so. — Go tell thy master I am alone. [*Exit Robin.*] Mistress Page, remember you your cue.

Mrs. Page. I warrant thee. If I do not act it, hiss me. [*Exit.*]

Mrs. Ford. Go to, then! We'll use this unwholesome humidity, this gross wat'ry pumpion; we'll teach him to know turtles from jays.

[Enter *Falstaff.*]

Fal. 'Have I caught my heavenly jewel?' Why, now let me die, for I have liv'd long enough. This is the period of my ambition. O this blessed hour!

Mrs. Ford. O sweet Sir John!

Fal. Mistress Ford, I cannot cog, I cannot prate, Mistress Ford. Now shall I sin in my wish. I would thy husband were dead. I'll speak it before the best lord, I would make thee my lady.

Mrs. Ford. I your lady, Sir John? Alas, I should be a pitiful lady!

Fal. Let the court of France show me such another! I see how thine eye would emulate the diamond. Thou hast the right arched beauty of the brow that becomes the ship-tire, the tire-valiant, or any tire of Venetian admittance.

Mrs. Ford. A plain kerchief, Sir John. My brows become nothing else, nor that well neither.

Fal. By the Lord, thou art a tyrant to say so! Thou wouldst make an absolute courtier, and the firm fixture of thy foot would give an excellent motion to thy gait in a semicircled farthingale. I see what thou wert, if Fortune thy foe were not, Nature thy friend. Come, thou canst not hide it.

Mrs. Ford. Believe me, there's no such thing in me.

Fal. What made me love thee? Let that persuade thee. There's something extraordinary in thee. Come, I cannot cog, and say thou art this and that, like a many of these lisping hawthorn buds that come like women in men's apparel and smell like Bucklersbury in simple-time. I cannot. But I love thee, none but thee; and thou deserv'st it.

Mrs. Ford. Do not betray me, sir. I fear you love Mistress Page.

Fal. Thou mightst as well say I love to walk by the Counter gate, which is as hateful to me as the reek of a limekiln.

Mrs. Ford. Well, heaven knows how I love you, and you shall one day find it.

Fal. Keep in that mind. I'll deserve it.

Mrs. Ford. Nay, I must tell you, so you do; or else I could not be in that mind.

[Enter *Robin.*]

Rob. Mistress Ford, Mistress Ford! here's Mistress Page at the door sweating and blowing and looking wildly, and would needs speak with you presently.

Fal. She shall not see me; I will ensconce me behind the arras.

Mrs. Ford. Pray you, do so! She's a very tattling woman.

Falstaff stands behind the arras.

[Enter *Mistress Page.*]

What's the matter? How now?

Mrs. Page. O Mistress Ford, what have you done? You're sham'd, y'are overthrown, y'are undone for ever!

Mrs. Ford. What's the matter, good Mistress Page?

Mrs. Page. O well-a-day, Mistress Ford, having an honest man to your husband, to give him such cause of suspicion!

Mrs. Ford. What cause of suspicion?

Mrs. Page. What cause of suspicion? Out upon you! How am I mistook in you!

Mrs. Ford. Why, alas! what's the matter?

Mrs. Page. Your husband's coming hither, woman, with all the officers in Windsor, to search for a gentleman that he says is here now in the house by your consent to take an ill advantage of his absence. You are undone!

Mrs. Ford. 'Tis not so, I hope.

Mrs. Page. Pray heaven it be not so that you have such a man here! But 'tis most certain your husband's coming, with half Windsor at his heels, to search for such a one. I come before to tell you. If you know yourself clear, why, I am glad of it; but if you have a friend here, convey, convey him out! Be not amaz'd, call all your senses to you, defend your reputation — or bid farewell to your good life for ever.

Mrs. Ford. What shall I do? There is a gentleman, my dear friend; and I fear not mine own shame so much as his peril. I had rather than a thousand pound he were out of the house.

Mrs. Page. For shame! Never stand 'you had rather' and 'you had rather'! Your husband's here at hand; bethink you of some conveyance. In the house you cannot hide him. O, how have you deceiv'd me! Look, here is a basket. If he be of any reasonable stature, he may creep in here; and throw foul linen upon him, as if it were going to bucking; or it is whiting time — send him by your two men to Datchet Mead.

Mrs. Ford. He's too big to go in there. What shall I do?

[*Falstaff* comes from behind the arras.]

Fal. Let me see't, let me see't, O, let me see't! — I'll in, I'll in! Follow your friend's counsel. — I'll in!

Mrs. Page. What, Sir John Falstaff? Are these your letters, knight?

Fal. I love thee and none but thee. Help me away! Let me creep in here. I'll never —

Goes into the basket. They put clothes over him.

Mrs. Page. Help to cover your master, boy. Call your men, Mistress Ford. You dissembling knight!

Mrs. Ford. What, John! Robert! John!

[*Exit Robin.*]

[Enter *Servants.*]

Go take up these clothes here, quickly. Where's the cowl-staff? Look how you drumble! Carry them to the laundress in Datchet Mead. Quickly, come.

[Enter *Ford, Page, Caius,* and *Evans.*]

Ford. Pray you come near. If I suspect without cause, why then make sport at me, then let me be your jest; I deserve it. — How now? Whither bear you this?

Servant. To the laundress forsooth.

Mrs. Ford. Why, what have you to do whither they bear it? You were best meddle with buck-washing!

Ford. Buck? I would I could wash myself of the buck! Buck, buck, buck! Ay, buck! I warrant you, buck! and of the season too. It shall appear. [*Exeunt Servants with the basket.*] Gentlemen, I have dream'd to-night; I'll tell you my dream. Here, here, here be my keys. Ascend my chambers; search, seek, find out! I'll warrant we'll unkennel the fox. Let me stop this way first. [*Locks the door.*] So, now uncape.

Page. Good Master Ford, be contented. You wrong yourself too much.

Ford. True, Master Page. Up, gentlemen; you shall see sport anon. Follow me, gentlemen.

[*Exit.*]

Evans. This is fery fantastical humours and jealousies.

Caius. By gar, 'tis no de fashion of France. It is not jealous in France.

Page. Nay, follow him, gentlemen. See the issue of his search.

[*Exeunt Page, Caius, and Evans.*]

Mrs. Page. Is there not a double excellency in this?

Mrs. Ford. I know not which pleases me better, that my husband is deceived, or Sir John.

Mrs. Page. What a taking was he in when your husband ask'd what was in the basket!

Mrs. Ford. I am half afraid he will have need of washing; so throwing him into the water will do him a benefit.

Mrs. Page. Hang him, dishonest rascal! I would all of the same strain were in the same distress.

Mrs. Ford. I think my husband hath some special suspicion of Falstaff's being here; for I never saw him so gross in his jealousy till now.

Mrs. Page. I will lay a plot to try that, and we will yet have more tricks with Falstaff. His dissolute disease will scarce obey this medicine.

Mrs. Ford. Shall we send that foolish carrion, Mistress Quickly, to him and excuse his throwing into the water, and give him another hope, to betray him to another punishment?

Mrs. Page. We will do it. Let him be sent for to-morrow eight o'clock to have amends.

Enter [*Ford, Page, Caius,* and *Evans*].

Ford. I cannot find him. May be the knave bragg'd of that he could not compass.

Mrs. Page. [*aside to Mrs. Ford*] Heard you that?

Mrs. Ford. [*aside to Mrs. Page*] Ay, ay, peace. — You use me well, Master Ford, do you?

Ford. Ay, I do so.

Mrs. Ford. Heaven make you better than your thoughts!

Ford. Amen.

Mrs. Page. You do yourself mighty wrong, Master Ford.

Ford. Ay, ay! I must bear it.

Evans. If there be anypody in the house, and in the chambers, and in the coffers, and in the presses, heaven forgive my sins at the day of judgment!

Caius. Be gar, nor I too! Dere is nobodies.

Page. Fie, fie, Master Ford! are you not asham'd? What spirit, what devil suggests this imagination? I would not ha' your distemper in this kind for the wealth of Windsor Castle.

Ford. 'Tis my fault, Master Page. I suffer for it.

Evans. You suffer for a pad conscience. Your wife is as honest a omans as I will desires among five thousand, and five hundred too.

Caius. By gar, I see 'tis an honest woman.

Ford. Well, I promis'd you a dinner. Come, come, walk in the Park. I pray you pardon me. I will hereafter make known to you why I have done this. — Come, wife. Come, Mistress Page. — I pray you pardon me. Pray heartly pardon me.

Page. Let's go in, gentlemen; but, trust me, we'll mock him. I do invite you to-morrow morning to my house to breakfast. After, we'll a-birding together; I have a fine hawk for the bush. Shall it be so?

Ford. Anything.

Evans. If there is one, I shall make two in the company.

Caius. If dere be one or two, I shall make-a de turd.

Ford. Pray you go, Master Page.

Evans. I pray you now, remembrance to-morrow on the lousy knave, mine host.

Caius. Dat is good, by gar, vit all my heart.

Evans. A lousy knave, to have his gibes and his mockeries! *Exeunt.*

Scene IV. [*Before Page's house.*]

Enter *Fenton, Anne Page.*

Fen. I see I cannot get thy father's love.
Therefore no more turn me to him, sweet Nan.
Anne. Alas, how then?
Fen. Why, thou must be thyself.
He doth object I am too great of birth,
And that, my state being gall'd with my expense,
I seek to heal it only by his wealth.
Besides these, other bars he lays before me,
My riots past, my wild societies,
And tells me 'tis a thing impossible
I should love thee, but as a property.
Anne. May be he tells you true.
Fen. No, heaven so speed me in my time to come!
Albeit I will confess thy father's wealth
Was the first motive that I woo'd thee, Anne;
Yet, wooing thee, I found thee of more value
Than stamps in gold or sums in sealed bags;
And 'tis the very riches of thyself
That now I aim at.
Anne. Gentle Master Fenton,
Yet seek my father's love; still seek it, sir.
If opportunity and humblest suit
Cannot attain it, why then, hark you hither.
[*They converse apart.*]

[Enter *Shallow, Slender,* and *Mistress Quickly.*]

Shal. Break their talk, Mistress Quickly. My kinsman shall speak for himself.

Slen. I'll make a shaft or a bolt on't. 'Slid, 'tis but venturing!

Shal. Be not dismay'd.

Slen. No, she shall not dismay me. I care not for that, but that I am afeard.

Quick. Hark ye, Master Slender would speak a word with you.

Anne. I come to him. [*Aside*] This is my father's choice.
O, what a world of vile ill-favour'd faults
Looks handsome in three hundred pounds a year!

Quick. And how does good Master Fenton? Pray you a word with you.

Shal. She's coming. To her, coz. O boy, thou hadst a father!

Slen. I had a father, Mistress Anne. My uncle can tell you good jests of him. Pray you, uncle, tell Mistress Anne the jest how my father stole two geese out of a pen, good uncle.

Shal. Mistress Anne, my cousin loves you.

Slen. Ay, that I do, as well as I love any woman in Gloucestershire!

Shal. He will maintain you like a gentlewoman.

Slen. Ay, that I will, come cut and long-tail, under the degree of a squire!

Shal. He will make you a hundred and fifty pounds jointure.

Anne. Good Master Shallow, let him woo for himself.

Shal. Marry, I thank you for it. I thank you for that good comfort. She calls you, coz. I'll leave you.

Anne. Now, Master Slender —

Slen. Now, good Mistress Anne —

Anne. What is your will?

Slen. My will? Od's heartlings, that's a pretty jest indeed! I ne'er made my will yet, I thank heaven. I am not such a sickly creature, I give heaven praise.

Anne. I mean, Master Slender, what would you with me?

Slen. Truly, for mine own part, I would little or nothing with you. Your father and my uncle hath made motions. If it be my luck, so; if not, happy man be his dole! They can tell you how things go better than I can. You may ask your father; here he comes.

[Enter *Page* and *Mistress Page.*]

Page. Now, Master Slender. Love him, daughter Anne.
Why, how now? What does Master Fenton here?
You wrong me, sir, thus still to haunt my house.
I told you, sir, my daughter is dispos'd of.

Fen. Nay, Master Page, be not impatient.

Mrs. Page. Good Master Fenton, come not to my child.

Page. She is no match for you.

Fen. Sir, will you hear me?

Page. No, good Master Fenton.
Come, Master Shallow; come, son Slender; in.
Knowing my mind, you wrong me, Master Fenton.

[*Exeunt Page, Shallow, and Slender.*]

Quick. Speak to Mistress Page.

Fen. Good Mistress Page, for that I love your daughter
In such a righteous fashion as I do,
Perforce, against all checks, rebukes, and manners,
I must advance the colours of my love
And not retire. Let me have your good will.

Anne. Good mother, do not marry me to yond fool.

Mrs. Page. I mean it not; I seek you a better husband.

Quick. That's my master, Master Doctor.

Anne. Alas, I had rather be set quick i' th' earth
And bowl'd to death with turnips!

Mrs. Page. Come, trouble not yourself. Good Master Fenton,
I will not be your friend nor enemy.
My daughter will I question how she loves you,
And as I find her, so am I affected.
Till then farewell, sir; she must needs go in,
Her father will be angry.

Fen. Farewell, gentle mistress. — Farewell, Nan.

[*Exeunt Mrs. Page and Anne.*]

Quick. This is my doing now. 'Nay,' said I, 'will you cast away your child on a fool and a physician? Look on Master Fenton.' This is my doing.

Fen. I thank thee; and I pray thee, once to-night
Give my sweet Nan this ring. There's for thy pains.

Quick. Now heaven send thee good fortune! [*Exit Fenton.*] A kind heart he hath. A woman would run through fire and water for such a kind heart. But yet I would my master had Mistress Anne; or I would Master Slender had her; or, in sooth, I would Master Fenton had her. I will do what I can for them all three; for so I have promis'd, and I'll be as good as my word; but speciously for Master Fenton. Well, I must of another errand to Sir John Falstaff from my two mistresses. What a beast am I to slack it! *Exit.*

Scene V. [*The Garter Inn.*]

Enter *Falstaff.*

Fal. Bardolph, I say!

Enter *Bardolph.*

Bard. Here, sir.

Fal. Go fetch me a quart of sack; put a toast in't. [*Exit Bardolph.*] Have I liv'd to be carried in a basket like a barrow of butcher's offal? and to be thrown in the Thames? Well, if I be serv'd such another trick, I'll have my brains ta'en out and butter'd, and give them to a dog for a new-year's gift. 'Sblood! The rogues slighted me into the river with as little remorse as they would have drown'd a blind bitch's puppies, fifteen i' th' litter. And you may know by my size that I have a kind of alacrity in sinking. If the bottom were as deep as hell, I should down. I had been drown'd but that the shore was shelvy and shallow — a death that I abhor; for the water swells a man, and what a thing should I have been when I had been swell'd! I should have been a mountain of mummy.

[Enter *Bardolph* with sack.]

Bard. Here's Mistress Quickly, sir, to speak with you.

Fal. Come, let me pour in some sack to the Thames water; for my belly's as cold as if I had swallow'd snowballs for pills to cool the reins. Call her in.

Bard. Come in, woman.

[Enter *Mistress Quickly.*]

Quick. By your leave. I cry you mercy. Give your worship good morrow.

Fal. Take away these chalices. Go, brew me a pottle of sack finely.

Bard. With eggs, sir?

Fal. Simple of itself. I'll no pullet-sperm in my brewage. [*Exit Bardolph.*] How now?

Quick. Marry, sir, I come to your worship from Mistress Ford.

Fal. Mistress Ford? I have had ford enough. I was thrown into the ford; I have my belly full of ford.

Quick. Alas the day! Good heart, that was not her fault. She does so take on with her men! They mistook their erection.

Fal. So did I mine, to build upon a foolish woman's promise.

Quick. Well, she laments, sir, for it, that it would yearn your heart to see it. Her husband goes this morning a-birding. She desires you once more to come to her, between eight and nine. I must carry her word quickly. She'll make you amends, I warrant you.

Fal. Well, I will visit her; tell her so. And bid her think what a man is. Let her consider his frailty, and then judge of my merit.

Quick. I will tell her.

Fal. Do so. Between nine and ten, say'st thou?

Quick. Eight and nine, sir.

Fal. Well, be gone. I will not miss her.

Quick. Peace be with you, sir! *Exit.*

Fal. I marvel I hear not of Master Brook. He sent me word to stay within. I like his money well.

[Enter *Ford* disguised.]

O, here he comes.

Ford. Bless you, sir!

Fal. Now, Master Brook, you come to know what hath pass'd between me and Ford's wife.

Ford. That indeed, Sir John, is my business.

Fal. Master Brook, I will not lie to you; I was at her house the hour she appointed me.

Ford. And sped you, sir?

Fal. Very ill-favouredly, Master Brook.

Ford. How so, sir? Did she change her determination?

Fal. No, Master Brook; but the peaking cornuto her husband, Master Brook, dwelling in a continual 'larum of jealousy, comes me in the instant of our encounter, after we had embrac'd, kiss'd, protested, and (as it were) spoke the prologue of our comedy; and at his heels a rabble of his companions, thither provoked and instigated by his distemper, and (forsooth) to search his house for his wive's love.

Ford. What, while you were there?

Fal. While I was there.

Ford. And did he search for you and could not find you?

Fal. You shall hear. As good luck would have it, comes in one Mistress Page, gives intelligence of Ford's approach, and, in her invention and Ford's wive's distraction, they convey'd me into a buck-basket.

Ford. A buck-basket?

Fal. By the Lord, a buck-basket! — ramm'd me in with foul shirts and smocks, socks, foul stockings, greasy napkins, that, Master Brook, there was the rankest compound of villanous smell that ever offended nostril.

Ford. And how long lay you there?

Fal. Nay, you shall hear, Master Brook, what I have suffer'd to bring this woman to evil for your good. Being thus cramm'd in the basket, a couple of Ford's knaves, his hinds, were call'd forth by their mistress to carry me in the name of foul clothes to Datchet Lane. They took me on their shoulders; met the jealous knave their master in the door, who ask'd them once or twice what they had in their basket. I quak'd for fear lest the lunatic knave would have search'd it; but fate, ordaining he should be a cuckold, held his hand. Well, on went he for a search, and away went I for foul clothes. But mark the sequel, Master Brook. I suffered the pangs of three several deaths: first, an intolerable fright, to be detected with a jealious rotten bell-wether; next, to be compass'd like a good bilbo in the circumference of a peck, hilt to point, heel to head; and then, to be stopp'd in, like a strong distillation, with stinking clothes that fretted in their own grease. Think of that — a man of my kidney! — think of that! — that am as subject to heat as butter; a man of continual dissolution and thaw. It was a miracle to scape suffocation. And in the height of this bath, when I was more than half stew'd in grease (like a Dutch dish), to be thrown into the Thames and cool'd, glowing hot, in that surge, like a horseshoe! Think of that! hissing hot! Think of that, Master Brook!

Ford. In good sadness, sir, I am sorry that for my sake you have suffer'd all this. My suit then is desperate. You'll undertake her no more?

Fal. Master Brook, I will be thrown into Ætna, as I have been into Thames, ere I will leave her thus. Her husband is this morning gone a-birding. I have received from her another embassy of meeting. 'Twixt eight and nine is the hour, Master Brook.

Ford. 'Tis past eight already, sir.

Fal. Is it? I will then address me to my appointment. Come to me at your convenient leisure, and you shall know how I speed; and the conclusion shall be crowned with your enjoying her. Adieu. You shall have her, Master Brook. Master Brook, you shall cuckold Ford. [*Exit.*]

Ford. Hum, ha! Is this a vision? Is this a dream? Do I sleep? Master Ford, awake! Awake, Master Ford! There's a hole made in your best coat, Master Ford. This 'tis to be married! This 'tis to have linen and buck-baskets! Well, I will proclaim myself what I am. I will now take the lecher. He is at my house. He cannot scape me. 'Tis impossible he should. He cannot creep into a halfpenny purse nor into a pepperbox: but, lest the devil that guides him should aid him, I will search impossible places. Though what I am I cannot avoid, yet to be what I would not shall not make me tame. If I have horns to make one mad, let the proverb go with me — I'll be horn-mad. *Exit.*

ACT IV. Scene I. [*Windsor. The street.*]

Enter *Mistress Page, Quickly, William.*

Mrs. Page. Is he at Master Ford's already, think'st thou?

Quick. Sure he is by this, or will be presently. But truly he is very courageous mad about his throwing into the water. Mistress Ford desires you to come suddenly.

Mrs. Page. I'll be with her by-and-by. I'll but bring my young man here to school. Look where his master comes; 'tis a playing day, I see.

[Enter *Evans.*]

How now, Sir Hugh? No school to-day?

Evans. No. Master Slender is let the boys leave to play.

Quick. Blessing of his heart!

Mrs. Page. Sir Hugh, my husband says my son profits nothing in the world at his book. I pray you ask him some questions in his accidence.

Evans. Come hither, William; hold up your head; come.

Mrs. Page. Come on, sirrah; hold up your head; answer your master, be not afraid.

Evans. William, how many numbers is in nouns?

Will. Two.

Quick. Truly, I thought there had been one number more, because they say 'Od's nouns.'

Evans. Peace your tattlings. What is 'fair,' William?

Will. *Pulcher.*

Quick. Polecats? There are fairer things than polecats, sure.

Evans. You are a very simplicity oman. I pray you peace. What is *lapis,* William?

Will. A stone.

Evans. And what is 'a stone,' William?

Will. A pebble.

Evans. No, it is *lapis.* I pray you remember in your prain.

Will. *Lapis.*

Evans. That is a good William. What is he, William, that does lend articles?

Will. Articles are borrowed of the pronoun, and be thus declined: *Singulariter, nominativo, hic, haec, hoc.*

Evans. *Nominativo, hig, hag, hog.* Pray you mark: *genitivo, huius.* Well, what is your accusative case?

Will. *Accusativo, hinc.*

Evans. I pray you have your remembrance, child. *Accusativo, hung, hang, hog.*

Quick. *Hang-hog* is Latin for bacon, I warrant you.

Evans. Leave your prabbles, oman. What is the focative case, William?

Will. *O, vocativo, O.*

Evans. Remember, William: focative is *caret.*

Quick. And that's a good root.

Evans. Oman, forbear.

Mrs. Page. Peace!

Evans. What is your genitive case plural, William?

Will. Genitive case?

Evans. Ay.

Will. *Genitivo, horum, harum, horum.*

Quick. Vengeance of Jinny's case! Fie on her! Never name her, child, if she be a whore.

Evans. For shame, oman!

Quick. You do ill to teach the child such words. He teaches him to hick and to hack, which they'll do fast enough of themselves, and to call *horum.* Fie upon you!

Evans. Oman, art thou lunatics? Hast thou no understandings for thy cases, and the numbers of the genders? Thou art as foolish Christian creatures as I would desires.

Mrs. Page. Prithee hold thy peace.

Evans. Show me now, William, some declensions of your pronouns.

Will. Forsooth, I have forgot.

Evans. It is *qui, quae, quod.* If you forget your *qui's*, your *quae's*, and your *quod's*, you must be preeches. Go your ways and play, go.

Mrs. Page. He is a better scholar than I thought he was.

Evans. He is a good sprag memory. Farewell, Mistress Page.

Mrs. Page. Adieu, good Sir Hugh. [*Exit Sir Hugh.*] Get you home, boy. — Come, we stay too long. *Exeunt.*

Scene II. [Ford's *house.*]

Enter *Falstaff, Mistress Ford.*

Fal. Mistress Ford, your sorrow hath eaten up my sufferance. I see you are obsequious in your love, and I profess requital to a hair's breadth, not only, Mistress Ford, in the simple office of love, but in all the accustrement, complement, and ceremony of it. But are you sure of your husband now?

Mrs. Ford. He's a-birding, sweet Sir John.

Mrs. Page. [*within*] What ho, gossip Ford! what ho!

Mrs. Ford. Step into th' chamber, Sir John. [*Exit Falstaff.*]

[Enter *Mistress Page.*]

Mrs. Page. How now, sweetheart? Who's at home besides yourself?

Mrs. Ford. Why, none but mine own people.

Mrs. Page. Indeed?

Mrs. Ford. No, certainly. [*Aside to her*] Speak louder.

Mrs. Page. Truly, I am so glad you have nobody here.

Mrs. Ford. Why?

Mrs. Page. Why, woman, your husband is in his old lunes again. He so takes on yonder with my husband, so rails against all married mankind, so curses all Eve's daughters, of what complexion soever, and so buffets himself on the forehead, crying 'Peer out, peer out!' that any madness I ever yet beheld seem'd but tameness, civility, and patience to this his distemper he is in now. I am glad the fat knight is not here.

Mrs. Ford. Why, does he talk of him?

Mrs. Page. Of none but him; and swears he was carried out, the last time he search'd for him, in a basket; protests to my husband he is now here, and hath drawn him and the rest of their company from their sport to make another experiment of his suspicion. But I am glad the knight is not here. Now he shall see his own foolery.

Mrs. Ford. How near is he, Mistress Page?

Mrs. Page. Hard by, at street end; he will be here anon.

Mrs. Ford. I am undone! The knight is here.

Mrs. Page. Why then, you are utterly sham'd, and he's but a dead man. What a woman are you! Away with him, away with him! Better shame than murther.

Mrs. Ford. Which way should he go? How should I bestow him? Shall I put him into the basket again?

[Enter *Falstaff.*]

Fal. No, I'll come no more i' th' basket. May I not go out ere he come?

Mrs. Page. Alas! three of Master Ford's brothers watch the door with pistols, that none shall issue out; otherwise you might slip away ere he came. But what make you here?

Fal. What shall I do? I'll creep up into the chimney.

Mrs. Ford. There they always use to discharge their birding pieces.

Mrs. Page. Creep into the kiln-hole.

Fal. Where is it?

Mrs. Ford. He will seek there, on my word. Neither press, coffer, chest, trunk, well, vault, but he hath an abstract for the remembrance of such places and goes to them by his note. There is no hiding you in the house.

Fal. I'll go out then.

Mrs. Page. If you go out in your own semblance, you die, Sir John. Unless you go out disguis'd —

Mrs. Ford. How might we disguise him?

Mrs. Page. Alas the day, I know not! There is no woman's gown big enough for him. Otherwise he might put on a hat, a muffler, and a kerchief, and so escape.

Fal. Good hearts, devise something. Any extremity rather than a mischief!

Mrs. Ford. My maid's aunt, the fat woman of Brainford, has a gown above.

Mrs. Page. On my word, it will serve him. She's as big as he is. And there's her thrumm'd hat, and her muffler too! Run up, Sir John.

Mrs. Ford. Go, go, sweet Sir John! Mistress Page and I will look some linen for your head.

Mrs. Page. Quick, quick! We'll come dress you straight. Put on the gown the while.

[*Exit Falstaff.*]

Mrs. Ford. I would my husband would meet him in this shape. He cannot abide the old woman of Brainford; he swears she's a witch, forbade her my house, and hath threat'ned to beat her.

Mrs. Page. Heaven guide him to thy husband's cudgel! and the devil guide his cudgel afterwards!

Mrs. Ford. But is my husband coming?

Mrs. Page. Ay, in good sadness is he, and talks of the basket too, howsoever he hath had intelligence.

Mrs. Ford. We'll try that; for I'll appoint my men to carry the basket again, to meet him at the door with it, as they did last time.

Mrs. Page. Nay, but he'll be here presently. Let's go dress him like the witch of Brainford.

Mrs. Ford. I'll first direct my men what they shall do with the basket. Go up; I'll bring linen for him straight. [*Exit.*]

Mrs. Page. Hang him, dishonest varlet! We cannot misuse him enough.
We'll leave a proof by that which we will do,
Wives may be merry, and yet honest too.
We do not act that often jest and laugh;
'Tis old but true: Still swine eats all the draff.

[*Exit.*]

[Enter *Mistress Ford* with two *Servants.*]

Mrs. Ford. Go, sirs, take the basket again on your shoulders. Your master is hard at door. If he bid you set it down, obey him. Quickly, dispatch! [*Exit.*]

1. Serv. Come, come, take it up.

2. Serv. Pray heaven it be not full of knight again.

1. Serv. I hope not; I had as lief bear so much lead.

[Enter *Ford, Page, Shallow, Caius,* and *Evans.*]

Ford. Ay, but if it prove true, Master Page, have you any way then to unfool me again? Set down the basket, villains! Somebody call my wife. Youth in a basket! O you panderly rascals! There's a knot, a ging, a pack, a conspiracy against me! Now shall the devil be sham'd. What, wife, I say! Come, come forth! Behold what honest clothes you send forth to bleaching!

Page. Why, this passes, Master Ford! You are not to go loose any longer; you must be pinion'd.

Evans. Why, this is lunatics! This is mad as a mad dog!

Shal. Indeed, Master Ford, this is not well, indeed.

Ford. So say I too, sir.

[Enter *Mistress Ford.*]

Come hither, Mistress Ford! Mistress Ford, the honest woman, the modest wife, the virtuous creature, that hath the jealious fool to her husband! I suspect without cause, mistress, do I?

Mrs. Ford. Heaven be my witness you do, if you suspect me in any dishonesty.

Ford. Well said, brazen-face! hold it out. — Come forth, sirrah!

[*Pulls clothes out of the basket.*]

Page. This passes!

Mrs. Ford. Are you not asham'd? Let the clothes alone.

Ford. I shall find you anon.

Evans. 'Tis unreasonable. Will you take up your wive's clothes? Come away!

Ford. Empty the basket, I say!

Mrs. Ford. Why, man, why?

Ford. Master Page, as I am a man, there was one convey'd out of my house yesterday in this basket. Why may not he be there again? In my house I am sure he is. My intelligence is true, my jealousy is reasonable. Pluck me out all the linen.

Mrs. Ford. If you find a man there, he shall die a flea's death.

Page. Here's no man.

Shal. By my fidelity, this is not well, Master Ford. This wrongs you.

Evans. Master Ford, you must pray, and not follow the imaginations of your own heart. This is jealousies.

Ford. Well, he's not here I seek for.

Page. No, nor nowhere else but in your brain.

Ford. Help to search my house this one time. If I find not what I seek, show no colour for my extremity. Let me for ever be your table sport. Let them say of me, 'As jealous as Ford, that search'd a hollow walnut for his wive's leman.' Satisfy me once more; once more search with me.

Mrs. Ford. What, ho, Mistress Page! Come you and the old woman down. My husband will come into the chamber.

Ford. Old woman? What old woman's that?

Mrs. Ford. Why, it is my maid's aunt of Brainford.

Ford. A witch, a quean, an old cozening quean! Have I not forbid her my house? She comes of errands, does she? We are simple men; we do not know what's brought to pass under the profession of fortune-telling. She works by charms, by spells, by th' figure, and such daub'ry as this is, beyond our element: we know nothing. Come down, you witch, you hag you! come down, I say!

Mrs. Ford. Nay, good sweet husband! Good gentlemen, let him not strike the old woman.

Enter *Falstaff* disguised like an old woman, and *Mistress Page* with him.

Mrs. Page. Come, Mother Prat. Come, give me your hand.

Ford. I'll prat her! (*Beats him.*) Out of my door, you witch, you hag, you baggage, you polecat, you runnion! out, out! I'll conjure you, I'll fortune-tell you!

Falstaff runs away.

Mrs. Page. Are you not asham'd? I think you have kill'd the poor woman.

Mrs. Ford. Nay, he will do it. 'Tis a goodly credit for you.

Ford. Hang her, witch!

Evans. By Jeshu, I think the oman is a witch indeed. I like not when a oman has a great peard. I spy a great peard under his muffler.

Ford. Will you follow, gentlemen? I beseech you follow. See but the issue of my jealousy. If I cry out thus upon no trail, never trust me when I open again.

Page. Let's obey his humour a little further. Come, gentlemen.

[*Exeunt all but Mrs. Page and Mrs. Ford.*]

Mrs. Page. Trust me, he beat him most pitifully.

Mrs. Ford. Nay, by th' mass, that he did not! He beat him most unpitifully, methought.

Mrs. Page. I'll have the cudgel hallow'd and hung o'er the altar. It hath done meritorious service.

Mrs. Ford. What think you? May we with the warrant of womanhood and the witness of a good conscience pursue him with any further revenge?

Mrs. Page. The spirit of wantonness is sure scar'd out of him. If the devil have him not in fee simple, with fine and recovery, he will never, I think, in the way of waste, attempt us again.

Mrs. Ford. Shall we tell our husbands how we have serv'd him?

Mrs. Page. Yes, by all means; if it be but to scrape the figures out of your husband's brains. If they can find in their hearts the poor unvirtuous fat knight shall be any further afflicted, we two will still be the ministers.

Mrs. Ford. I'll warrant they'll have him publicly sham'd; and methinks there would be no period to the jest, should he not be publicly sham'd.

Mrs. Page. Come, to the forge with it then; shape it. I would not have things cool.

Exeunt.

Scene III. [*The Garter Inn.*]

Enter *Host* and *Bardolph.*

Bard. Sir, the Germans desire to have three of your horses. The Duke himself will be to-morrow at court, and they are going to meet him.

Host. What duke should that be comes so secretly? I hear not of him in the court. Let me speak with the gentlemen. They speak English?

Bard. Ay, sir. I'll call them to you.

Host. They shall have my horses; but I'll make them pay, I'll sauce them. They have had my house a week at command. I have turn'd away my other guests. They must come off; I'll sauce them! Come. *Exeunt.*

Scene IV. [*Ford's house.*]

Enter *Page, Ford, Mistress Page, Mistress Ford,* and *Evans.*

Evans. 'Tis one of the pest discretions of a oman as ever I did look upon.

Page. And did he send you both these letters at an instant?

Mrs. Page. Within a quarter of an hour.

Ford. Pardon me, wife. Henceforth do what thou wilt.
I rather will suspect the sun with cold
Than thee with wantonness. Now doth thy honour stand,
In him that was of late an heretic,
As firm as faith.

Page. 'Tis well, 'tis well; no more!
Be not as extreme in submission as in offence.
But let our plot go forward. Let our wives
Yet once again, to make us public sport,
Appoint a meeting with this old fat fellow
Where we may take him and disgrace him for it.

Ford. There is no better way than that they spoke of.

Page. How? to send him word they'll meet him in the Park at midnight? Fie, fie! he'll never come.

Evans. You say he has bin thrown in the rivers, and has bin grievously peaten as an old oman. Methinks there should be terrors in him, that he should not come. Methinks his flesh is punish'd; he shall have no desires.

Page. So think I too.

Mrs. Ford. Devise but how you'll use him when he comes,
And let us two devise to bring him thither.

Mrs. Page. There is an old tale goes that Herne the Hunter,
Sometime a keeper here in Windsor Forest,
Doth all the winter time, at still midnight,
Walk round about an oak, with great ragg'd horns;
And there he blasts the trees, and takes the cattle,
And makes milch kine yield blood, and shakes a chain
In a most hideous and dreadful manner.
You have heard of such a spirit, and well you know
The superstitious idle-headed eld
Receiv'd and did deliver to our age
This tale of Herne the Hunter for a truth.

Page. Why, yet there want not many that do fear
In deep of night to walk by this Herne's Oak.
But what of this?

Mrs. Ford. Marry, this is our device,
That Falstaff at that oak shall meet with us,
Disguis'd like Herne, with huge horns on his head.

Page. Well, let it not be doubted but he'll come;
And in this shape when you have brought him thither,
What shall be done with him? What is your plot?

Mrs. Page. That likewise have we thought upon, and thus:
Nan Page (my daughter) and my little son
And three or four more of their growth we'll dress
Like urchins, ouphs, and fairies, green and white,
With rounds of waxen tapers on their heads
And rattles in their hands. Upon a sudden,
As Falstaff, she, and I are newly met,
Let them from forth a sawpit rush at once
With some diffused song. Upon their sight,
We two in great amazedness will fly.
Then let them all encircle him about
And fairy-like to pinch the unclean knight,
And ask him why, that hour of fairy revel,
In their so sacred paths he dares to tread
In shape profane.

Mrs. Ford. And till he tell the truth
Let the supposed fairies pinch him, sound,
And burn him with their tapers.

Mrs. Page. The truth being known,
We'll all present ourselves, dis-horn the spirit,
And mock him home to Windsor.

Ford. The children must
Be practis'd well to this, or they'll nev'r do't.

Evans. I will teach the children their behaviours; and I will be like a jack-an-apes also, to burn the knight with my taber.

Ford. That will be excellent. I'll go buy them vizards.

Mrs. Page. My Nan shall be the Queen of all the Fairies,
Finely attired in a robe of white.

Page. That silk will I go buy, [*aside*] and in that tire
Shall Master Slender steal my Nan away
And marry her at Eton. — Go, send to Falstaff straight.

Ford. Nay, I'll to him again in name of Brook.
He'll tell me all his purpose. Sure he'll come.

Mrs. Page. Fear not you that. Go get us properties
And tricking for our fairies.

Evans. Let us about it. It is admirable pleasures and fery honest knaveries.

[*Exeunt Page, Ford, and Evans.*]

Mrs. Page. Go, Mistress Ford,
Send Quickly to Sir John to know his mind.
[*Exit Mrs. Ford.*]
I'll to the doctor. He hath my good will,
And none but he, to marry with Nan Page.
That Slender, though well landed, is an idiot;
And he my husband best of all affects.
The doctor is well money'd, and his friends
Potent at court. He, none but he, shall have her,
Though twenty thousand worthier come to crave her. [*Exit.*]

Scene V. [*The Garter Inn.*]

Enter *Host, Simple.*

Host. What wouldst thou have, boor? what, thick-skin? Speak, breathe, discuss; brief, short, quick, snap!

Sim. Marry, sir, I come to speak with Sir John Falstaff from Master Slender.

Host. There's his chamber, his house, his castle, his standing bed and truckle-bed. 'Tis painted about with the story of the Prodigal, fresh and new. Go, knock and call. He'll speak like an Anthropophaginian unto thee. Knock, I say!

Sim. There's an old woman, a fat woman, gone up into his chamber. I'll be so bold as stay, sir, till she come down. I come to speak with her indeed.

Host. Ha? a fat woman? The knight may be robb'd. I'll call. Bully knight! bully Sir John! speak from thy lungs military. Art thou there? It is thine host, thine Ephesian, calls.

Fal. [*above*] How now, mine host?

Host. Here's a Bohemian Tartar tarries the coming down of thy fat woman. Let her descend, bully, let her descend. My chambers are honourable. Fie! privacy? fie!

[Enter *Falstaff.*]

Fal. There was, mine host, an old fat woman even now with me, but she's gone.

Sim. Pray you, sir, was't not the wise woman of Brainford?

Fal. Ay, marry was it, mussel-shell. What would you with her?

Sim. My master, sir, Master Slender, sent to her, seeing her go thorough the streets, to know, sir, whether one Nym, sir, that beguil'd him of a chain, had the chain or no.

Fal. I spake with the old woman about it.

Sim. And what says she, I pray, sir?

Fal. Marry, she says that the very same man that beguil'd Master Slender of his chain cozen'd him of it.

Sim. I would I could have spoken with the woman herself. I had other things to have spoken with her too from him.

Fal. What are they? Let us know.

Host. Ay, come! quick!

Sim. I may not conceal them, sir.

Host. Conceal them, or thou diest.

Sim. Why, sir, they were nothing but about Mistress Anne Page, to know if it were my master's fortune to have her, or no.

Fal. 'Tis; 'tis his fortune.

Sim. What, sir?

Fal. To have her, or no. Go; say the woman told me so.

Sim. May I be bold to say so, sir?

Fal. Ay, Sir Tyke. Who more bold?

Sim. I thank your worship. I shall make my master glad with these tidings. [*Exit.*]

Host. Thou art clerkly, thou art clerkly, Sir John. Was there a wise woman with thee?

Fal. Ay, that there was, mine host; one that hath taught me more wit than ever I learn'd before in my life; and I paid nothing for it neither, but was paid for my learning.

Enter *Bardolph.*

Bard. Out, alas, sir! cozenage, mere cozenage!

Host. Where be my horses? Speak well of them, varletto.

Bard. Run away with the cozeners; for so soon as I came beyond Eton, they threw me off, from behind one of them, in a slough of mire; and set spurs and away, like three German devils, three Doctor Faustuses.

Host. They are gone but to meet the Duke, villain. Do not say they be fled. Germans are honest men.

[Enter *Evans.*]

Evans. Where is mine host?

Host. What is the matter, sir?

Evans. Have a care of your entertainments. There is a friend of mine come to town, tells me there is three cozen-germans that has cozen'd all the hosts of Readins, of Maidenhead, of Colebrook, of horses and money. I tell you for good will, look you. You are wise, and full of gibes and vlouting-stogs, and 'tis not convenient you should be cozened. Fare you well.
Exit

[Enter *Caius.*]

Caius. Vere is mine host de Jarteer?

Host. Here, Master Doctor, in perplexity and doubtful dilemma.

Caius. I cannot tell vat is dat; but it is tell-a me dat you make grand preparation for a Duke de Jarmanie. By my trot, dere is no duke dat de court is know to come. I tell you for good vill. Adieu. *Exit.*

Host. Hue and cry, villain, go! — Assist me, knight. — I am undone! — Fly, run! hue and cry, villain! — I am undone!

Exeunt [*Host and Bardolph*].

Fal. I would all the world might be cozen'd, for I have been cozen'd and beaten too. If it should come to the ear of the court how I have been transformed, and how my transformation hath been wash'd and cudgell'd, they would melt me out of my fat drop by drop and liquor fishermen's boots with me. I warrant they would whip me with their fine wits till I were as crestfall'n as a dried pear. I never prosper'd since I forswore myself at primero. Well, if my wind were but long enough to say my prayers, I would repent.

Enter *Mistress Quickly.*

Now? Whence come you?

Quick. From the two parties forsooth.

Fal. The devil take one party and his dam the other! and so they shall be both bestowed. I have suffer'd more for their sakes, more than the villanous inconstancy of man's disposition is able to bear.

Quick And have not they suffer'd? Yes, I warrant; speciously one of them. Mistress Ford, good heart, is beaten black and blue, that you cannot see a white spot about her.

Fal. What tell'st thou me of black and blue? I was beaten myself into all the colours of the rainbow; and I was like to be apprehended for the witch of Brainford. But that my admirable dexterity of wit, my counterfeiting the action of an old woman, deliver'd me, the knave constable had set me i' th' stocks, i' th' common stocks, for a witch.

Quick. Sir, let me speak with you in your chamber. You shall hear how things go, and (I warrant) to your content. Here is a letter will say somewhat. Good hearts, what ado here is to bring you together! Sure, one of you does not serve heaven well, that you are so cross'd.

Fal. Come up into my chamber. *Exeunt.*

Scene VI. [*Another room in the Garter Inn.*]

Enter *Fenton, Host.*

Host. Master Fenton, talk not to me; my mind is heavy. I will give over all.

Fen. Yet hear me speak. Assist me in my purpose,
And, as I am a gentleman, I'll give thee
A hundred pound in gold more than your loss.

Host. I will hear you, Master Fenton, and I will at the least keep your counsel.

Fen. From time to time I have acquainted you
With the dear love I bear to fair Anne Page,
Who, mutually, hath answer'd my affection
(So far forth as herself might be her chooser)
Even to my wish. I have a letter from her
Of such contents as you will wonder at;
The mirth whereof so larded with my matter
That neither, singly, can be manifested
Without the show of both; wherein fat Falstaff
Hath a great scene. The image of the jest
I'll show you here at large. Hark, good mine host.
To-night at Herne's Oak, just 'twixt twelve and one,
Must my sweet Nan present the Fairy Queen —
The purpose why, is here — [*Shows a letter.*] in which disguise,
While other jests are something rank on foot,
Her father hath commanded her to slip
Away with Slender, and with him at Eton
Immediately to marry. She hath consented.
Now, sir,
Her mother (even strong against that match
And firm for Doctor Caius) hath appointed
That he shall likewise shuffle her away
While other sports are tasking of their minds,
And at the dean'ry, where a priest attends,
Straight marry her. To this her mother's plot
She seemingly obedient likewise hath
Made promise to the doctor. Now thus it rests:
Her father means she shall be all in white,
And in that habit, when Slender sees his time
To take her by the hand and bid her go,
She shall go with him. Her mother hath intended
(The better to denote her to the doctor,
For they must all be mask'd and vizarded)
That quaint in green she shall be loose enrob'd,
With ribands-pendent flaring 'bout her head;
And when the doctor spies his vantage ripe,
To pinch her by the hand, and on that token
The maid hath given consent to go with him.

Host. Which means she to deceive, father or mother?

Fen. Both, my good host, to go along with me.
And here it rests, that you'll procure the vicar
To stay for me at church 'twixt twelve and one,
And in the lawful name of marrying
To give our hearts united ceremony.

Host. Well, husband your device. I'll to the vicar.
Bring you the maid, you shall not lack a priest.

Fen. So shall I evermore be bound to thee.
Besides, I'll make a present recompense.

Exeunt.

ACT V. Scene I. [*The Garter Inn.*]

Enter *Falstaff, Quickly.*

Fal. Prithee no more prattling! Go; I'll hold. This is the third time; I hope good luck lies in odd numbers. Away, go! They say there is divinity in odd numbers, either in nativity, chance, or death. Away!

Quick. I'll provide you a chain, and I'll do what I can to get you a pair of horns.

Fal. Away, I say! time wears. Hold up your head and mince. [*Exit Mrs. Quickly.*]

[Enter *Ford* disguised.]

How now, Master Brook? Master Brook, the matter will be known to-night, or never. Be you in the Park about midnight at Herne's Oak and you shall see wonders.

Ford. Went you not to her yesterday, sir, as you told me you had appointed?

Fal. I went to her, Master Brook, as you see, like a poor old man; but I came from her, Master Brook, like a poor old woman. That same knave (Ford, her husband) hath the finest mad devil of jealousy in him, Master Brook, that ever govern'd frenzy. I will tell you, he beat me grievously in the shape of a woman; for in the shape of man, Master Brook, I fear not Goliah with a weaver's beam, because I know also life is a shuttle. I am in haste. Go along with me; I'll tell you all, Master Brook. Since I pluck'd geese, play'd truant, and whipp'd top, I knew not what 'twas to be beaten till lately. Follow me. I'll tell you strange things of this knave Ford, on whom to-night I will be revenged, and I will deliver his wife into your hand. Follow! Strange things in hand, Master Brook! Follow. *Exeunt.*

Scene II. [*Windsor Park.*]

Enter *Page, Shallow, Slender.*

Page. Come, come! We'll couch i' th' Castle ditch till we see the light of our fairies. Remember, son Slender, my daughter.

Slen. Ay, forsooth. I have spoke with her, and we have a nay-word how to know one another. I come to her in white and cry 'mum'; she cries 'budget'; and by that we know one another.

Shal. That's good too. But what needs either your 'mum' or her 'budget'? The white will decipher her well enough. It hath struck ten o'clock.

Page. The night is dark. Light and spirits will become it well. Heaven prosper our sport! No man means evil but the devil, and we shall know him by his horns. Let's away. Follow me. *Exeunt.*

Scene III. [*Near the Park.*]

Enter *Mistress Page, Mistress Ford, Caius.*

Mrs. Page. Master Doctor, my daughter is in green. When you see your time, take her by the hand, away with her to the deanery, and dispatch it quickly. Go before into the Park. We two must go together.

Caius. I know vat I have to do. Adieu.

Mrs. Page. Fare you well, sir. [*Exit Caius.*] My husband will not rejoice so much at the abuse of Falstaff as he will chafe at the doctor's marrying my daughter. But 'tis no matter. Better a little chiding than a great deal of heartbreak.

Mrs. Ford. Where is Nan now? and her troop of fairies? and the Welsh devil Hugh?

Mrs. Page. They are all couch'd in a pit hard by Herne's Oak, with obscur'd lights, which at the very instant of Falstaff's and our meeting they will at once display to the night.

Mrs. Ford. That cannot choose but amaze him.

Mrs. Page. If he be not amaz'd, he will be mock'd. If he be amaz'd, he will every way be mock'd.

Mrs. Ford. We'll betray him finely.

Mrs. Page. Against such lewdsters and their lechery
Those that betray them do no treachery.

Mrs. Ford. The hour draws on. To the oak, to the oak! *Exeunt.*

Scene IV. [*Windsor Park.*]

Enter *Evans* [like a *Satyr*] and [others as] *Fairies.*

Evans. Trib, trib, fairies. Come, and remember your parts. Be pold, I pray you. Follow me into the pit; and when I give the watch-ords, do as I pid you. Come, come; trib, trib.

Exeunt.

Scene V. [*Another part of Windsor Park.*]

Enter *Falstaff* [disguised as *Herne,*] with a buck's head upon him.

Fal. The Windsor bell hath stroke twelve; the minute draws on. Now the hot-blooded gods assist me! Remember, Jove, thou wast a bull for thy Europa; love set on thy horns. O powerful love, that in some respects makes a beast a man; in some other, a man a beast! You were also, Jupiter, a swan for the love of Leda. O omnipotent love! how near the god drew to the complexion of a goose! A fault done first in the form of a beast (O Jove, a beastly fault!) and then another fault in the semblance of a fowl — think on't, Jove; a foul fault! When gods have hot backs, what shall poor men do? For me, I am here a Windsor stag, and the fattest, I think, i' th' forest. Send me a cool rut-time, Jove, or who can blame me to piss my tallow? Who comes here? my doe?

[Enter *Mistress Ford* and *Mistress Page.*]

Mrs. Ford. Sir John! art thou there, my deer, my male deer?

Fal. My doe with the black scut! Let the sky rain potatoes; let it thunder to the tune of 'Greensleeves,' hail kissing comfits, and snow eringoes. Let there come a tempest of provocation, I will shelter me here. [*Embraces her.*]

Mrs. Ford. Mistress Page is come with me, sweetheart.

Fal. Divide me like a brib'd buck, each a haunch. I will keep my sides to myself, my shoulders for the fellow of this walk, and my horns I bequeath your husbands. Am I a woodman, ha? Speak I like Herne the Hunter? Why, now is Cupid a child of conscience; he makes restitution. As I am a true spirit, welcome! *A noise of horns.*

Mrs. Page. Alas, what noise?

Mrs. Ford. Heaven forgive our sins!

Fal. What should this be?

Mrs. Ford, Mrs. Page. Away, away!

They run away.

Fal. I think the devil will not have me damn'd, lest the oil that's in me should set hell on fire. He would never else cross me thus.

Enter [*Evans* like a *Satyr*; *Pistol* like *Hobgoblin*; *Anne Page* (the *Fairy Queen*), and others, as] *Fairies.*

Queen. Fairies black, gray, green, and white,
You moonshine revellers and shades of night,
You orphan heirs of fixed destiny,
Attend your office and your quality.
Crier Hobgoblin, make the fairy oyes.

Pist. Elves, list your names. Silence, you airy toys.
Cricket, to Windsor chimneys shalt thou leap.
Where fires thou find'st unrak'd and hearths unswept,
There pinch the maids as blue as bilberry.
Our radiant queen hates sluts and sluttery.

Fal. They are fairies. He that speaks to them shall die.
I'll wink and couch. No man their works must eye. [*Lies down upon his face.*]

Evans. Where's Bead? Go you, and where you find a maid
That ere she sleep has thrice her prayers said,
Raise up the organs of her fantasy,
Sleep she as sound as careless infancy;
But those as sleep and think not on their sins,
Pinch them, arms, legs, backs, shoulders, sides, and shins.

Queen. About, about!
Search Windsor Castle, elves, within and out,
Strew good luck, ouphs, on every sacred room;
That it may stand till the perpetual doom
In state as wholesome as in state 'tis fit,
Worthy the owner, and the owner it.
The several chairs of order look you scour
With juice of balm and every precious flow'r.
Each fair instalment, coat, and sev'ral crest,
With loyal blazon, evermore be blest!
And nightly meadow-fairies, look you sing,
Like to the Garter's compass, in a ring.
Th' expressure that it bears, green let it be,
More fertile-fresh than all the field to see;
And *Honi soit qui mal y pense* write
In em'rald tufts, flow'rs purple, blue, and white,
Like sapphire, pearl, and rich embroidery,
Buckled below fair knighthood's bending knee.
Fairies use flow'rs for their charactery.
Away, disperse! But till 'tis one o'clock,
Our dance of custom round about the Oak
Of Herne the Hunter let us not forget.

Evans. Pray you lock hand in hand; yourselves in order set;
And twenty glowworms shall our lanthorns be
To guide our measure round about the tree.
But, stay! I smell a man of middle earth.

Fal. Heavens defend me from that Welsh fairy, lest he transform me to a piece of cheese!

Pist. Vile worm, thou wast o'erlook'd even in thy birth.

Queen. With trial-fire touch me his finger end.
If he be chaste, the flame will back descend
And turn him to no pain; but if he start,
It is the flesh of a corrupted heart.

Pist. A trial, come!

Evans. Come! Will this wood take fire?

They put the tapers to his fingers, and he starts.

Fal. O, O, O!

Queen. Corrupt, corrupt, and tainted in desire!
About him, fairies; sing a scornful rhyme;
And as you trip, still pinch him to your time.

The Song.

Fie on sinful fantasy!
Fie on lust and luxury!
Lust is but a bloody fire,
Kindled with unchaste desire,
Fed in heart, whose flames aspire
As thoughts do blow them, higher and higher.
Pinch him, fairies, mutually;
Pinch him for his villany;
Pinch him and burn him and turn him about
Till candles and starlight and moonshine be out.

[*During this song*] *they pinch him; and the Doctor comes one way and steals away a Fairy in green, and Slender another way, and takes a Fairy in white; and Fenton steals Mistress Anne Page. And a noise of hunting is made within; and all the Fairies run away. Falstaff pulls off his buck's head and rises up.*

[Enter *Page, Ford, Mistress Page,* and *Mistress Ford.*]

Page. Nay, do not fly. I think we have watch'd you now.
Will none but Herne the Hunter serve your turn?

Mrs. Page. I pray you, come; hold up the jest no higher.
Now, good Sir John, how like you Windsor wives?
See you these, husband? Do not these fair yokes
Become the forest better than the town?

Ford. Now, sir, who's a cuckold now? Master Brook, Falstaff's a knave, a cuckoldly knave; here are his horns, Master Brook. And, Master Brook, he hath enjoyed nothing of Ford's but his buck-basket, his cudgel, and twenty pounds of money, which must be paid to Master Brook. His horses are arrested for it, Master Brook.

Mrs. Ford. Sir John, we have had ill luck; we could never meet. I will never take you for my love again, but I will always count you my deer.

Fal. I do begin to perceive that I am made an ass.

Ford. Ay, and an ox too. Both the proofs are extant.

Fal. And these are not fairies? I was three or four times in the thought they were not fairies; and yet the guiltiness of my mind, the sudden surprise of my powers, drove the grossness of the foppery into a receiv'd belief, in despite of the teeth of all rhyme and reason, that they were fairies. See now how wit may be made a Jack-a-Lent, when 'tis upon ill employment!

Evans. Sir John Falstaff, serve Got and leave your desires, and fairies will not pinse you.

Ford. Well said, fairy Hugh.

Evans. And leave you your jealousies too, I pray you.

Ford. I will never mistrust my wife again till thou art able to woo her in good English.

Fal. Have I laid my brain in the sun, and dried it, that it wants matter to prevent so gross o'erreaching as this? Am I ridden with a Welsh goat too? Shall I have a coxcomb of frize? 'Tis time I were chok'd with a piece of toasted cheese.

Evans. Seese is not goot to give putter. Your pelly is all putter.

Fal. 'Seese,' and 'putter'? Have I liv'd to stand at the taunt of one that makes fritters of English? This is enough to be the decay of lust and late-walking through the realm.

Mrs. Page. Why, Sir John, do you think, though we would have thrust virtue out of our hearts by the head and shoulders and have given ourselves without scruple to hell, that ever the devil could have made you our delight?

Ford. What, a hodge-pudding? a bag of flax?

Mrs. Page. A puff'd man?

Page. Old, cold, wither'd, and of intolerable entrails?

Ford. And one that is as slanderous as Satan?

Page. And as poor as Job?

Ford. And as wicked as his wife?

Evans. And given to fornications and to taverns and sack and wine and metheglins, and to drinkings and swearings and starings, pribbles and prabbles?

Fal. Well, I am your theme. You have the start of me; I am dejected. I am not able to answer the Welsh flannel. Ignorance itself is a plummet o'er me. Use me as you will.

Ford. Marry, sir, we'll bring you to Windsor to one Master Brook that you have cozen'd of money, to whom you should have been a pander. Over and above that you have suffer'd, I think to repay that money will be a biting affliction.

Page. Yet be cheerful, knight. Thou shalt eat a posset to-night at my house, where I will desire thee to laugh at my wife, that now laughs at thee. Tell her Master Slender hath married her daughter.

Mrs. Page. [*aside*] Doctors doubt that. If Anne Page be my daughter, she is, by this, Doctor Caius' wife.

[Enter *Slender.*]

Slen. Whoa, ho, ho, father Page!

Page. Son, how now? How now, son? Have you dispatch'd?

Slen. Dispatch'd? I'll make the best in Gloucestershire know on't. Would I were hang'd, la, else!

Page. Of what, son?

Slen. I came yonder at Eton to marry Mistress Anne Page, and she's a great lubberly boy. If it had not been i' th' church, I would have swing'd him or he should have swing'd me. If I did not think it had been Anne Page, would I might never stir! and 'tis a postmaster's boy.

Page. Upon my life, then, you took the wrong.

Slen. What need you tell me that? I think so, when I took a boy for a girl. If I had been married to him, for all he was in woman's apparel, I would not have had him.

Page. Why, this is your own folly. Did not I tell you how you should know my daughter by her garments?

Slen. I went to her in white, and cried 'mum,' and she cried 'budget,' as Anne and I had appointed; and yet it was not Anne, but a postmaster's boy.

Mrs. Page. Good George, be not angry. I knew of your purpose, turn'd my daughter into green, and indeed she is now with the doctor at the dean'ry, and there married.

[Enter *Caius.*]

Caius. Vere is Mistress Page? By gar, I am cozened! I ha' married oon garsoon, a boy; oon pesant, by gar. A boy! It is not Anne Page. By gar, I am cozened.

Mrs. Page. Why, did you take her in green?

Caius. Ay, be gar, and 'tis a boy! Be gar, I'll raise all Windsor! [*Exit.*]

Ford. This is strange. Who hath got the right Anne?

Page. My heart misgives me. Here comes Master Fenton.

[Enter *Fenton* and *Anne Page.*]

How now, Master Fenton?

Anne. Pardon, good father! Good my mother, pardon!

Page. Now, mistress! How chance you went not with Master Slender?

Mrs. Page. Why went you not with Master Doctor, maid?

Fen. You do amaze her. Hear the truth of it.
You would have married her most shamefully,
Where there was no proportion held in love.
The truth is, she and I (long since contracted)
Are now so sure that nothing can dissolve us.
Th' offence is holy that she hath committed,
And this deceit loses the name of craft,
Of disobedience, or unduteous title,
Since therein she doth evitate and shun
A thousand irreligious cursed hours
Which forced marriage would have brought upon her.

Ford. Stand not amaz'd. Here is no remedy.
In love the heavens themselves do guide the state;
Money buys lands, and wives are sold by fate.

Fal. I am glad, though you have ta'en a special stand to strike at me, that your arrow hath glanc'd.

Page. Well, what remedy? Fenton, heaven give thee joy!
What cannot be eschew'd must be embrac'd.

Fal. When night-dogs run, all sorts of deer are chas'd.

Mrs. Page. Well, I will muse no further. Master Fenton,
Heaven give you many, many merry days!
Good husband, let us every one go home
And laugh this sport o'er by a country fire,
Sir John and all.

Ford. Let it be so. Sir John,
To Master Brook you yet shall hold your word,
For he to-night shall lie with Mistress Ford.

Exeunt.

Measure for Measure

Measure for Measure appears to have been presented at court by Shakespeare's company on St. Stephen's night (December 26), 1604. Probably it was a new play, for it accords in style and temper with Shakespeare's other work at about this time. At all events, 1604 is a reasonable date for its composition. Our only authority for the text is the First Folio, which must have been set up from a rather confused copy, certainly not from an autograph manuscript.

Here and there one may detect possible cuts in the Folio text, but there is no good reason for ascribing any part of the play to another hand than Shakespeare's, except, perhaps, the Duke's rhyming speech at the end of Act iii, and this hardly deserves the harsh language which some critics have bestowed upon it. As marking the interval between two strongly contrasted scenes and introducing, prologue-like, the business of the Moated Grange, this moralizing chorus is neither out of place nor structurally inappropriate. It emphasizes the principle of 'measure for measure' and, at the end, justifies (to the audience) the Duke's use of 'craft against vice,' and it sums up his plan. The style is good enough for the purpose — better, indeed, from that point of view, than if it were better poetically.

The plot of Measure for Measure is mainly derived from George Whetstone's two-part play *Promos and Cassandra*, published in 1578, which, in turn, is founded on the fifth novel in the eighth decade of the *Hecatommithi* of Giovanni Battista Giraldi (surnamed Cinthio or Cintio), first printed in 1565. Whetstone cannot have known Cinthio's *Epitia*, a tragicomedy on the same theme as the novel. He remarks that he 'deuided the whole history into two Commedies for that, *Decorum* vsed, it would not be conuayde in one.' He repeated his plot, as a narrative, in a story book entitled *An Heptameron of Civill Discourses* (1582), noting incidentally that his play had never been acted. The substance of the tale was current on the Continent in several variants before Cinthio wrote and was reported in 1547 as a recent occurrence. Something similar is told by Saint Augustine in his *De Sermone Domini in Monte* (i, 16, 50).

In Cinthio's novel, Juriste the Governor (Shakespeare's Angelo) promises Epitia (Shakespeare's Isabella) to release her brother, who is under sentence of death, and assures her of his own hand in marriage, though without a definite promise. On these terms she yields. Juriste has the brother beheaded and sends the body to her, with the head at its feet. In Cinthio's drama, however, the keeper of the prison, without the Governor's knowledge, substitutes a condemned criminal for the brother; and this important modification of the plot is also made by Whetstone. In both Cinthio and Whetstone the sovereign decrees that the Governor shall marry the heroine and then shall be executed, but after the marriage he spares his life at her entreaty.

Neither Cinthio nor Whetstone has any character that corresponds to Mariana. By bringing her into the story Shakespeare has transformed the plot and rescued Isabella from a really intolerable situation. She does not yield to Angelo, and it is the new character, Mariana, whom he must marry. Thus Isabella's honour is preserved and she is relieved of the necessity of marrying her worst enemy. The concluding speech shows that the Duke means to reward her with his own hand, if she 'a willing ear incline.' This arrangement, which comes as something of a shock to modern readers, was doubtless quite acceptable to the Elizabethans, always eager for Jack to have his Jill. We may infer that Isabella gives up her purpose of becoming a votaress of Saint Clare (i, 4), but this is not stated, and the conclusion of the play leaves the audience guessing — as was doubtless Shakespeare's intent.

In *Promos and Cassandra* Whetstone has sought to enliven the scene and make a strange plot more real by bringing in a good deal of low comedy. His object was also, in part, to illustrate the corruption of society in the city over which Promos rules. Thus we have Lamia, a lively courtesan, and her servant Rosko. Gripax and Rapax are two 'promoters,' whose function is to act as informers in the service of Promos's corrupt officer, Phallax. They attempt to arrest a rustic called John Adroynes. In the fight that ensues, John gets the better. Phallax stops the fray and informs John that he must die for an affair with a maidservant, but lets him off for a bribe — 'ten shillings and thirteen pence.' In one scene, a Hangman enters 'with a great many ropes about his neck.' He is followed by six prisoners on the way to execution, accompanied by a Preacher. Two of them are 'hacksters,' one is a woman, one a Gypsy fortune-teller, the rest are 'poor rogues,' one of whom says pitifully, 'Jesus save me! I am cast for a purse with three halfpence.' All this is poor stuff, no doubt; but it is not without life, and one may profitably consider it in its relation to Shakespeare's low characters in this and other plays.

Rosko is certainly a foreshadowing of Pompey in MEASURE FOR MEASURE; and there is an odd suggestion of this title in one of his moral reflections:

Who others doth deceive
Deserves himself like measure to receive.

The rôle of the Duke is much enlarged in Shakespeare. In Whetstone and Cinthio the sovereign (in Whetstone, the King; in Cinthio, the Emperor) is active only at the outset (to appoint and instruct the Governor) and at the end (to pass judgment). In MEASURE FOR MEASURE he keeps constant watch over Angelo's proceedings, prevents the execution of Claudio, and arranges the final solution of all the problems in advance.

What sounds like a prophecy of Shakespeare's play may be read in *3 Henry VI* (ii, 6, 52 ff.):

From off the gates of York fetch down the head,
Your father's head, which Clifford placed there;
Instead whereof let this supply the room.
Measure for measure must be answered.

MEASURE FOR MEASURE

The Names of all the Actors.

Vincentio, the Duke [of Vienna].
Angelo, the Deputy.
Escalus, an ancient Lord.
Claudio, a young gentleman.
Lucio, a fantastic.
Two other like Gentlemen.
Provost.
Thomas, } two friars.
Peter, }
[A Justice.]
[*Varrius.*]
Elbow, a simple constable.
Froth, a foolish gentleman.
[*Pompey*, a] clown, [servant to *Mistress Overdone*].
Abhorson, an executioner.
Barnardine, a dissolute prisoner.

Isabella, sister to *Claudio*.
Mariana, betrothed to *Angelo*.
Juliet, beloved of *Claudio*.
Francisca, a nun.
Mistress Overdone, a bawd.

[Lords, Officers, Citizens, Boy, and Attendants.]

THE SCENE. — *Vienna.*

ACT I. Scene I. [*Vienna. The* Duke's *Palace.*]

Enter *Duke, Escalus, Lords,* [and *Attendants*].

Duke. Escalus.
Escal. My lord.
Duke. Of government the properties to unfold
Would seem in me t' affect speech and discourse,
Since I am put to know that your own science
Exceeds, in that, the lists of all advice
My strength can give you. Then no more remains
But that to your sufficiency, as your worth is able,
. . . .
And let them work. The nature of our people,
Our city's institutions, and the terms
For common justice, y'are as pregnant in
As art and practice hath enriched any
That we remember. There is our commission, [*Gives it.*]
From which we would not have you warp. Call hither,
I say, bid come before us Angelo. [*Exit an Attendant.*]
What figure of us think you he will bear?
For you must know we have with special soul
Elected him our absence to supply,
Lent him our terror, dress'd him with our love,
And given his deputation all the organs
Of our own power. What think you of it?
Escal. If any in Vienna be of worth
To undergo such ample grace and honour,
It is Lord Angelo.

Enter *Angelo.*

Duke. Look where he comes.
Ang. Always obedient to your Grace's will,
I come to know your pleasure.
Duke. Angelo,
There is a kind of character in thy life
That to th' observer doth thy history
Fully unfold. Thyself and thy belongings
Are not thine own so proper as to waste
Thyself upon thy virtues, they on thee.
Heaven doth with us as we with torches do,
Not light them for themselves; for if our virtues
Did not go forth of us, 'twere all alike
As if we had them not. Spirits are not finely touch'd
But to fine issues; nor Nature never lends
The smallest scruple of her excellence
But, like a thrifty goddess, she determines
Herself the glory of a creditor,
Both thanks and use. But I do bend my speech
To one that can my part in him advertise.
Hold, therefore, Angelo.
In our remove be thou at full ourself.
Mortality and mercy in Vienna
Live in thy tongue and heart. Old Escalus,
Though first in question, is thy secondary.
Take thy commission.
Ang. Now, good my lord,
Let there be some more test made of my metal
Before so noble and so great a figure
Be stamp'd upon it.

Duke. No more evasion!
We have with a leaven'd and prepared choice
Proceeded to you. Therefore take your honours. [*Gives the commission.*]
Our haste from hence is of so quick condition
That it prefers itself, and leaves unquestion'd
Matters of needful value. We shall write to you,
As time and our concernings shall importune,
How it goes with us, and do look to know
What doth befall you here. So fare you well!
To th' hopeful execution do I leave you
Of your commissions.

Ang. Yet give leave, my lord,
That we may bring you something on the way.

Duke. My haste may not admit it;
Nor need you, on mine honour, have to do
With any scruple: your scope is as mine own,
So to enforce or qualify the laws
As to your soul seems good. Give me your hand.
I'll privily away. I love the people,
But do not like to stage me to their eyes.
Though it do well, I do not relish well
Their loud applause and ave's vehement;
Nor do I think the man of safe discretion
That does affect it. Once more fare you well.

Ang. The heavens give safety to your purposes!

Escal. Lead forth and bring you back in happiness!

Duke. I thank you. Fare you well. *Exit.*

Escal. I shall desire you, sir, to give me leave
To have free speech with you; and it concerns me
To look into the bottom of my place.
A pow'r I have, but of what strength and nature
I am not yet instructed.

Ang. 'Tis so with me. Let us withdraw together,
And we may soon our satisfaction have
Touching that point.

Escal. I'll wait upon your honour.
Exeunt.

Scene II. [*A street in Vienna.*]

Enter *Lucio* and two other *Gentlemen.*

Lucio. If the Duke, with the other dukes, come not to composition with the King of Hungary, why then, all the dukes fall upon the King.

1. Gent. Heaven grant us its peace, but not the King of Hungary's!

2. Gent. Amen.

Lucio. Thou conclud'st like the sanctimonious pirate, that went to sea with the Ten Commandments, but scrap'd one out of the table.

2. Gent. 'Thou shalt not steal'?

Lucio. Ay, that he raz'd.

1. Gent. Why, 'twas a commandment to command the captain and all the rest from their functions: they put forth to steal. There's not a soldier of us all that, in the thanksgiving before meat, do relish the petition well that prays for peace.

2. Gent. I never heard any soldier dislike it.

Lucio. I believe thee; for I think thou never wast where grace was said.

2. Gent. No? A dozen times at least.

1. Gent. What? in metre?

Lucio. In any proportion or in any language.

1. Gent. I think, or in any religion.

Lucio. Ay, why not? Grace is grace, despite of all controversy: as, for example, thou thyself art a wicked villain, despite of all grace.

1. Gent. Well, there went but a pair of shears between us.

Lucio. I grant; as there may between the lists and the velvet. Thou art the list.

1. Gent. And thou the velvet. Thou art good velvet; thou'rt a three-pil'd piece, I warrant thee. I had as lief be a list of an English kersey as be pil'd, as thou art pil'd, for a French velvet. Do I speak feelingly now?

Lucio. I think thou dost, and indeed with most painful feeling of thy speech. I will, out of thine own confession, learn to begin thy health, but, whilst I live, forget to drink after thee.

1. Gent. I think I have done myself wrong, have I not?

2. Gent. Yes, that thou hast, whether thou art tainted or free.

Enter [*Mistress Overdone, the*] *Bawd.*

Lucio. Behold, behold, where Madam Mitigation comes!

1. Gent. I have purchas'd as many diseases under her roof as come to —

2. Gent. To what, I pray?

Lucio. Judge.

2. Gent. To three thousand dolours a year.

1. Gent. Ay, and more.

Lucio. A French crown more.

1. Gent. Thou art always figuring diseases in me; but thou art full of error — I am sound.

Lucio. Nay, not (as one would say) healthy, but so sound as things that are hollow. Thy bones are hollow; impiety has made a feast of thee.

1. Gent. [*to Bawd*] How now? Which of your hips has the most profound sciatica?

Bawd. Well, well! there's one yonder arrested and carried to prison was worth five thousand of you all.

2. Gent. Who's that, I pray thee?

Bawd. Marry, sir, that's Claudio, Signior Claudio.

1. Gent. Claudio to prison? 'Tis not so.

Bawd. Nay, but I know 'tis so. I saw him arrested; saw him carried away; and, which is more, within these three days his head to be chopp'd off.

Lucio. But, after all this fooling, I would not have it so. Art thou sure of this?

Bawd. I am too sure of it; and it is for getting Madam Julietta with child.

Lucio. Believe me, this may be. He promis'd to meet me two hours since, and he was ever precise in promise-keeping.

2. Gent. Besides, you know, it draws something near to the speech we had to such a purpose.

1. Gent. But most of all, agreeing with the proclamation.

Lucio. Away! let's go learn the truth of it.

Exeunt [*Lucio and Gentlemen*].

Bawd. Thus, what with the war, what with the sweat, what with the gallows, and what with poverty, I am custom-shrunk.

Enter [*Pompey, the*] *Clown.*

How now? What's the news with you?

Pom. Yonder man is carried to prison.

Bawd. Well, what has he done?

Pom. A woman.

Bawd. But what's his offence?

Pom. Groping for trouts in a peculiar river.

Bawd. What, is there a maid with child by him?

Pom. No, but there's a woman with maid by him. You have not heard of the proclamation, have you?

Bawd. What proclamation, man?

Pom. All houses in the suburbs of Vienna must be pluck'd down.

Bawd. And what shall become of those in the city?

Pom. They shall stand for seed. They had gone down too but that a wise burgher put in for them.

Bawd. But shall all our houses of resort in the suburbs be pull'd down?

Pom. To the ground, mistress.

Bawd. Why, here's a change indeed in the commonwealth! What shall become of me?

Pom. Come, fear not you! Good counsellors lack no clients. Though you change your place, you need not change your trade. I'll be your tapster still. Courage! there will be pity taken on you. You that have worn your eyes almost out in the service, you will be considered.

Bawd. What's to do here, Thomas Tapster? Let's withdraw.

Pom. Here comes Signior Claudio, led by the provost to prison; and there's Madam Juliet.

Exeunt.

Enter *Provost, Claudio, Juliet,* and *Officers.*
Lucio and two *Gentlemen* [follow].

Claud. Fellow, why dost thou show me thus to th' world?
Bear me to prison, where I am committed.

Prov. I do it not in evil disposition,
But from Lord Angelo by special charge.

Claud. Thus can the demigod, Authority,
Make us pay down for our offence by weight
The words of heaven, on whom it will, it will;
On whom it will not, so; yet still 'tis just.

Lucio. Why, how now, Claudio? Whence comes this restraint?

Claud. From too much liberty, my Lucio, liberty.
As surfeit is the father of much fast,
So every scope by the immoderate use
Turns to restraint. Our natures do pursue,
Like rats that ravin down their proper bane,
A thirsty evil, and when we drink we die.

Lucio. If I could speak so wisely under an arrest, I would send for certain of my creditors. And yet, to say the truth, I had as lief have the foppery of freedom as the morality of imprisonment. What's thy offence, Claudio?

Claud. What but to speak of would offend again.

Lucio. What, is't murder?

Claud. No.

Lucio. Lechery?

Claud. Call it so.

Prov. Away, sir! you must go.

Claud. One word, good friend. — Lucio, a word with you.

Lucio. A hundred, if they'll do you any good.
Is lechery so look'd after?

Claud. Thus stands it with me: upon a true contract
I got possession of Julietta's bed.
You know the lady. She is fast my wife,
Save that we do the denunciation lack

Of outward order. This we came not to,
Only for propagation of a dow'r
Remaining in the coffer of her friends,
From whom we thought it meet to hide our love
Till time had made them for us. But it chances
The stealth of our most mutual entertainment
With character too gross is writ on Juliet.

Lucio. With child, perhaps?

Claud. Unhappily, even so.
And the new deputy now for the Duke —
Whether it be the fault and glimpse of newness,
Or whether that the body public be
A horse whereon the governor doth ride,
Who, newly in the seat, that it may know
He can command, lets it straight feel the spur;
Whether the tyranny be in his place
Or in his eminence that fills it up,
I stagger in — but this new governor
Awakes me all the enrolled penalties
Which have, like unscour'd armour, hung by th' wall
So long that nineteen zodiacs have gone round
And none of them been worn; and for a name
Now puts the drowsy and neglected act
Freshly on me. 'Tis surely for a name.

Lucio. I warrant it is! and thy head stands so tickle on thy shoulders that a milkmaid, if she be in love, may sigh it off. Send after the Duke and appeal to him.

Claud. I have done so, but he's not to be found.
I prithee, Lucio, do me this kind service:
This day my sister should the cloister enter
And there receive her approbation;
Acquaint her with the danger of my state;
Implore her, in my voice, that she make friends
To the strict deputy; bid herself assay him.
I have great hope in that; for in her youth
There is a prone and speechless dialect,
Such as move men. Beside, she hath prosperous art
When she will play with reason and discourse,
And well she can persuade.

Lucio. I pray she may; as well for the encouragement of the like, which else would stand under grievous imposition, as for the enjoying of thy life, who I would be sorry should be thus foolishly lost at a game of tick-tack. I'll to her.

Claud. I thank you, good friend Lucio.

Lucio. Within two hours.

Claud. Come, officer, away!

Exeunt.

Scene III. [*A monastery.*]

Enter *Duke* and *Friar Thomas.*

Duke. No, holy father! throw away that thought.
Believe not that the dribbling dart of love
Can pierce a complete bosom. Why I desire thee
To give me secret harbour hath a purpose
More grave and wrinkled than the aims and ends
Of burning youth.

Friar. May your Grace speak of it?

Duke. My holy sir, none better knows than you
How I have ever lov'd the life removed
And held in idle price to haunt assemblies
Where youth and cost and witless bravery keeps.
I have deliver'd to Lord Angelo
(A man of stricture and firm abstinence)
My absolute power and place here in Vienna,
And he supposes me travell'd to Poland;
For so I have strew'd it in the common ear
And so it is receiv'd. Now, pious sir,
You will demand of me why I do this.

Friar. Gladly, my lord.

Duke. We have strict statutes and most biting laws
(The needful bits and curbs to headstrong steeds),
Which for this fourteen years we have let sleep,
Even like an o'ergrown lion in a cave,
That goes not out to prey. Now, as fond fathers,
Having bound up the threat'ning twigs of birch,
Only to stick it in their children's sight
For terror, not to use, in time the rod
Becomes more mock'd than fear'd; so our decrees,
Dead to infliction, to themselves are dead,
And liberty plucks justice by the nose;
The baby beats the nurse, and quite athwart
Goes all decorum.

Friar. It rested in your Grace
To unloose this tied-up justice when you pleas'd;
And it in you more dreadful would have seem'd
Than in Lord Angelo.

Duke. I do fear, too dreadful.
Sith 'twas my fault to give the people scope,
'Twould be my tyranny to strike and gall them
For what I bid them do. For we bid this be done
When evil deeds have their permissive pass

And not the punishment. Therefore, indeed, my father,
I have on Angelo impos'd the office,
Who may in th' ambush of my name strike home,
And yet my nature never in the fight
To do it slander. And to behold his sway,
I will, as 'twere a brother of your order,
Visit both prince and people. Therefore I prithee
Supply me with the habit, and instruct me
How I may formally in person bear
Like a true friar. Moe reasons for this action
At our more leisure shall I render you;
Only, this one: Lord Angelo is precise,
Stands at a guard with envy, scarce confesses
That his blood flows or that his appetite
Is more to bread than stone; hence shall we see,
If power change purpose, what our seemers be.
Exeunt.

Scene IV. [*A nunnery.*]

Enter *Isabella* and *Francisca* (a *Nun*).

Isab. And have you nuns no farther privileges?
Nun. Are not these large enough?
Isab. Yes, truly; I speak not as desiring more,
But rather wishing a more strict restraint
Upon the sisterhood, the votarists of Saint Clare.
Lucio. (*within*) Ho! Peace be in this place!
Isab. Who's that which calls?
Nun. It is a man's voice. Gentle Isabella,
Turn you the key and know his business of him.
You may; I may not. You are yet unsworn.
When you have vow'd, you must not speak with men
But in the presence of the prioress;
Then if you speak, you must not show your face,
Or if you show your face, you must not speak.
He calls again. I pray you answer him. [*Exit.*]
Isab. Peace and prosperity! Who is't that calls?

[Enter *Lucio.*]

Lucio. Hail, virgin, if you be — as those cheek-roses
Proclaim you are no less. Can you so stead me
As bring me to the sight of Isabella,
A novice of this place, and the fair sister
To her unhappy brother Claudio?
Isab. Why 'her unhappy brother'? Let me ask,
The rather for I now must make you know
I am that Isabella, and his sister.
Lucio. Gentle and fair, your brother kindly greets you.
Not to be weary with you, he's in prison.
Isab. Woe me! for what?
Lucio. For that which, if myself might be his judge,
He should receive his punishment in thanks.
He hath got his friend with child.
Isab. Sir, make me not your story.
Lucio. It is true.
I would not — though 'tis my familiar sin
With maids to seem the lapwing, and to jest,
Tongue far from heart — play with all virgins so.
I hold you as a thing enskied and sainted
By your renouncement, an immortal spirit,
And to be talk'd with in sincerity,
As with a saint.
Isab. You do blaspheme the good in mocking me.
Lucio. Do not believe it. Fewness and truth, 'tis thus:
Your brother and his lover have embrac'd.
As those that feed grow full; as blossoming time,
That from the seedness the bare fallow brings
To teeming foison — even so her plenteous womb
Expresseth his full tilth and husbandry.
Isab. Some one with child by him? my cousin Juliet?
Lucio. Is she your cousin?
Isab. Adoptedly, as school-maids change their names
By vain though apt affection.
Lucio. She it is.
Isab. O, let him marry her!
Lucio. This is the point.
The Duke is very strangely gone from hence;
Bore many gentlemen (myself being one)
In hand, and hope of action; but we do learn
By those that know the very nerves of state,
His givings-out were of an infinite distance
From his true-meant design. Upon his place,
And with full line of his authority,
Governs Lord Angelo — a man whose blood
Is very snow-broth; one who never feels
The wanton stings and motions of the sense,
But doth rebate and blunt his natural edge
With profits of the mind, study and fast.
He (to give fear to use and liberty,
Which have for long run by the hideous law,
As mice by lions) hath pick'd out an act

Under whose heavy sense your brother's life
Falls into forfeit. He arrests him on it,
And follows close the rigour of the statute
To make him an example. All hope is gone,
Unless you have the grace by your fair prayer
To soften Angelo. And that's my pith of business
'Twixt you and your poor brother.
Isab. Doth he so seek his life?
Lucio. Has censur'd him
Already, and, as I hear, the provost hath
A warrant for his execution.
Isab. Alas, what poor ability 's in me
To do him good?
Lucio. Assay the pow'r you have.
Isab. My power? Alas, I doubt —
Lucio. Our doubts are traitors
And make us lose the good we oft might win
By fearing to attempt. Go to Lord Angelo
And let him learn to know, when maidens sue
Men give like gods; but when they weep and kneel,
All their petitions are as freely theirs
As they themselves would owe them.
Isab. I'll see what I can do.
Lucio. But speedily!
Isab. I will about it straight,
No longer staying but to give the Mother
Notice of my affair. I humbly thank you.
Commend me to my brother. Soon at night
I'll send him certain word of my success.
Lucio. I take my leave of you.
Isab. Good sir, adieu. *Exeunt.*

ACT II. Scene I. [*A hall in* Angelo's *house.*]

Enter *Angelo, Escalus,* and *Servants*; *Justice.*

Ang. We must not make a scarecrow of the law,
Setting it up to fear the birds of prey,
And let it keep one shape till custom make it
Their perch, and not their terror.
Escal. Ay, but yet
Let us be keen, and rather cut a little
Than fall and bruise to death. Alas, this gentleman
Whom I would save had a most noble father!
Let but your honour know
(Whom I believe to be most strait in virtue)
That, in the working of your own affections —
Had time coher'd with place, or place with wishing,
Or that the resolute acting of your blood
Could have attain'd th' effect of your own purpose,
Whether you had not sometime in your life
Err'd in this point which now you censure him
And pull'd the law upon you.
Ang. 'Tis one thing to be tempted, Escalus,
Another thing to fall. I not deny
The jury, passing on the prisoner's life,
May in the sworn twelve have a thief or two
Guiltier than him they try. What's open made to justice,
That justice seizes. What knows the law
That thieves do pass on thieves? 'Tis very pregnant,
The jewel that we find, we stoop and take't,
Because we see it; but what we do not see
We tread upon and never think of it.
You may not so extenuate his offence
For I have had such faults; but rather tell me,
When I that censure him do so offend,
Let mine own judgment pattern out my death,
And nothing come in partial. Sir, he must die.
Escal. Be it as your wisdom will.

Enter *Provost.*

Ang. Where is the provost?
Prov. Here, if it like your honour.
Ang. See that Claudio
Be executed by nine to-morrow morning.
Bring him his confessor, let him be prepar'd;
For that's the utmost of his pilgrimage.
[*Exit Provost.*]
Escal. Well, heaven forgive him! and forgive us all!
Some rise by sin, and some by virtue fall.
Some run from brakes of vice, and answer none;
And some condemned for a fault alone.

Enter *Elbow, Froth,* [*Pompey, the*] *Clown, Officers.*

Elb. Come, bring them away. If these be good people in a commonweal that do nothing but use their abuses in common houses, I know no law. Bring them away.

Ang. How now, sir! What's your name? and what's the matter?

Elb. If it please your honour, I am the poor Duke's constable, and my name is Elbow. I do lean upon justice, sir, and do bring in here before your good honour two notorious benefactors.

Ang. Benefactors? Well, what benefactors are they? Are they not malefactors?

Elb. If it please your honour, I know not well what they are; but precise villains they are, that I am sure of, and void of all profanation in the world that good Christians ought to have.

Escal. This comes off well. Here's a wise officer.

Ang. Go to. What quality are they of? Elbow is your name? Why dost thou not speak, Elbow?

Pom. He cannot, sir. He's out at elbow.

Ang. What are you, sir?

Elb. He, sir? A tapster, sir; parcel-bawd; one that serves a bad woman, whose house, sir, was, as they say, pluck'd down in the suburbs; and now she professes a hothouse, which, I think, is a very ill house too.

Escal. How know you that?

Elb. My wife, sir, whom I detest before heaven and your honour —

Escal. How? thy wife?

Elb. Ay, sir; whom I thank heaven is an honest woman.

Escal. Dost thou detest her therefore?

Elb. I say, sir, I will detest myself also, as well as she, that this house, if it be not a bawd's house, it is pity of her life, for it is a naughty house.

Escal. How dost thou know that, constable?

Elb. Marry, sir, by my wife, who, if she had been a woman cardinally given, might have been accus'd in fornication, adultery, and all uncleanliness there.

Escal. By the woman's means?

Elb. Ay, sir, by Mistress Overdone's means. But as she spit in his face, so she defied him.

Pom. Sir, if it please your honour, this is not so.

Elb. Prove it before these varlets here, thou honourable man; prove it.

Escal. [*to Angelo*] Do you hear how he misplaces?

Pom. Sir, she came in great with child; and longing (saving your honour's reverence) for stew'd prunes. Sir, we had but two in the house, which at that very distant time stood, as it were, in a fruit dish — a dish of some threepence. Your honours have seen such dishes; they are not China dishes, but very good dishes.

Escal. Go to, go to! No matter for the dish, sir.

Pom. No, indeed, sir, not of a pin! You are therein in the right. But to the point. As I say, this Mistress Elbow, being (as I say) with child, and being great-bellied, and longing (as I said) for prunes; and having but two in the dish (as I said), Master Froth here, this very man, having eaten the rest (as I said) and (as I say) paying for them very honestly; for, as you know, Master Froth, I could not give you threepence again —

Froth. No indeed.

Pom. Very well. You being then (if you be remembr'red) cracking the stones of the foresaid prunes —

Froth. Ay, so I did indeed.

Pom. Why, very well. I telling you then (if you be remembr'red) that such a one and such a one were past cure of the thing you wot of, unless they kept very good diet, as I told you —

Froth. All this is true.

Pom. Why, very well, then.

Escal. Come, you are a tedious fool. To the purpose! What was done to Elbow's wife that he hath cause to complain of? Come me to what was done to her.

Pom. Sir, your honour cannot come to that yet.

Escal. No, sir, nor I mean it not.

Pom. Sir, but you shall come to it, by your honour's leave. And I beseech you, look into Master Froth here, sir, a man of fourscore pound a year, whose father died at Hallowmas. Was't not at Hallowmas, Master Froth?

Froth. All-hallond eve.

Pom. Why, very well. I hope here be truths. He, sir, sitting (as I say) in a lower chair, sir — 'twas in the Bunch of Grapes, where, indeed, you have a delight to sit, have you not?

Froth. I have so, because it is an open room, and good for winter.

Pom. Why, very well then. I hope here be truths.

Ang. This will last out a night in Russia
When nights are longest there. I'll take my leave
And leave you to the hearing of the cause,
Hoping you'll find good cause to whip them all.

Escal. I think no less. Good morrow to your lordship. *Exit* [*Angelo*].
Now, sir, come on. What was done to Elbow's wife, once more?

Pom. Once, sir? There was nothing done to her once.

Elb. I beseech you, sir, ask him what this man did to my wife.

Pom. I beseech your honour, ask me.

Escal. Well, sir, what did this gentleman to her?

Pom. I beseech you, sir, look in this gentleman's face. Good Master Froth, look upon his honour; 'tis for a good purpose. Doth your honour mark his face?

Escal. Ay, sir, very well.

Pom. Nay, I beseech you mark it well.

Escal. Well, I do so.

Pom. Doth your honour see any harm in his face?

Escal. Why, no.

Pom. I'll be suppos'd upon a book his face is the worst thing about him. Good then. If his face be the worst thing about him, how could Master Froth do the constable's wife any harm? I would know that of your honour.

Escal. He's in the right, constable. What say you to it?

Elb. First, an it like you, the house is a respected house; next, this is a respected fellow; and his mistress is a respected woman.

Pom. By this hand, sir, his wife is a more respected person than any of us all.

Elb. Varlet, thou liest! Thou liest, wicked varlet! The time is yet to come that she was ever respected with man, woman, or child.

Pom. Sir, she was respected with him before he married with her.

Escal. Which is the wiser here, Justice or Iniquity? Is this true?

Elb. O thou caitiff! O thou varlet! O thou wicked Hannibal! I respected with her before I was married to her? If ever I was respected with her, or she with me, let not your worship think me the poor Duke's officer. Prove this, thou wicked Hannibal, or I'll have mine action of batt'ry on thee.

Escal. If he took you a box o' th' ear, you might have your action of slander too.

Elb. Marry, I thank your good worship for it. What is't your worship's pleasure I shall do with this wicked caitiff?

Escal. Truly, officer, because he hath some offences in him that thou wouldst discover if thou couldst, let him continue in his courses till thou know'st what they are.

Elb. Marry, I thank your worship for it. Thou seest, thou wicked varlet now, what's come upon thee! Thou art to continue now, thou varlet; thou art to continue.

Escal. [*to Froth*] Where were you born, friend?

Froth. Here in Vienna, sir.

Escal. Are you of fourscore pounds a year?

Froth. Yes, an't please you, sir.

Escal. So. — [*To Pompey*] What trade are you of, sir?

Pom. A tapster, a poor widow's tapster.

Escal. Your mistress' name?

Pom. Mistress Overdone.

Escal. Hath she had any more than one husband?

Pom. Nine, sir. Overdone by the last.

Escal. Nine? Come hither to me, Master Froth. Master Froth, I would not have you acquainted with tapsters. They will draw you, Master Froth, and you will hang them. Get you gone, and let me hear no more of you.

Froth. I thank your worship. For mine own part, I never come into any room in a taphouse but I am drawn in.

Escal. Well, no more of it, Master Froth! Farewell. [*Exit Froth.*] Come you hither to me, Master Tapster. What's your name, Master Tapster?

Pom. Pompey.

Escal. What else?

Pom. Bum, sir.

Escal. Troth, and your bum is the greatest thing about you, so that, in the beastliest sense, you are Pompey the Great. Pompey, you are partly a bawd, Pompey, howsoever you colour it in being a tapster, are you not? Come, tell me true; it shall be the better for you.

Pom. Truly, sir, I am a poor fellow that would live.

Escal. How would you live, Pompey? By being a bawd? What do you think of the trade, Pompey? Is it a lawful trade?

Pom. If the law would allow it, sir.

Escal. But the law will not allow it, Pompey; nor it shall not be allowed in Vienna.

Pom. Does your worship mean to geld and splay all the youth of the city?

Escal. No, Pompey.

Pom. Truly, sir, in my poor opinion, they will to't then. If your worship will take order for the drabs and the knaves, you need not to fear the bawds.

Escal. There is pretty orders beginning, I can tell you. It is but heading and hanging.

Pom. If you head and hang all that offend that way but for ten year together, you'll be glad to give out a commission for more heads. If this law hold in Vienna ten year, I'll rent the fairest house in it after threepence a bay. If you live to see this come to pass, say Pompey told you so.

Escal. Thank you, good Pompey; and in requital of your prophecy, hark you: I advise you let me not find you before me again upon any complaint whatsoever; no, not for dwelling where you do. If I do, Pompey, I shall beat you to your tent and prove a shrewd Cæsar to you: in plain dealing, Pompey, I shall have you whipt. So, for this time, Pompey, fare you well.

Pom. I thank your worship for your good counsel. [*Aside*] But I shall follow it as the flesh and fortune shall better determine.
Whip me? No, no! Let carman whip his jade;
The valiant heart's not whipt out of his trade.
Exit.

Escal. Come hither to me, Master Elbow. Come hither, Master Constable. How long have you been in this place of constable?

Elb. Seven year and a half, sir.

Escal. I thought, by your readiness in the office, you had continued in it some time. You say seven years together?

Elb. And a half, sir.

Escal. Alas, it hath been great pains to you! They do you wrong to put you so oft upon't. Are there not men in your ward sufficient to serve it?

Elb. Faith, sir, few of any wit in such matters. As they are chosen, they are glad to choose me for them. I do it for some piece of money, and go through with all.

Escal. Look you bring me in the names of some six or seven, the most sufficient of your parish.

Elb. To your worship's house, sir?

Escal. To my house. Fare you well.
[*Exit Elbow.*]
What's o'clock, think you?

Justice. Eleven, sir.

Escal. I pray you home to dinner with me.

Justice. I humbly thank you.

Escal. It grieves me for the death of Claudio;
But there's no remedy.

Justice. Lord Angelo is severe.

Escal. It is but needful.
Mercy is not itself that oft looks so.
Pardon is still the nurse of second woe.
But yet — poor Claudio! There is no remedy.
Come, sir. *Exeunt.*

Scene II. [*Another room in* Angelo's *house.*]

Enter *Provost, Servant.*

Serv. He's hearing of a cause. He will come straight.
I'll tell him of you.

Prov. Pray you do. [*Exit Servant.*]
I'll know
His pleasure. May be he will relent. Alas,
He hath but as offended in a dream!
All sects, all ages smack of this vice — and he
To die for't!

Enter *Angelo.*

Ang. Now, what's the matter, provost?

Prov. Is it your will Claudio shall die tomorrow?

Ang. Did not I tell thee yea? Hadst thou not order?
Why dost thou ask again?

Prov. Lest I might be too rash.
Under your good correction, I have seen
When, after execution, judgment hath
Repented o'er his doom.

Ang. Go to! let that be mine.
Do you your office, or give up your place,
And you shall well be spar'd.

Prov. I crave your honour's pardon.
What shall be done, sir, with the groaning Juliet?
She's very near her hour.

Ang. Dispose of her
To some more fitter place, and that with speed.

[Enter *Servant.*]

Serv. Here is the sister of the man condemn'd
Desires access to you.

Ang. Hath he a sister?

Prov. Ay, my good lord, a very virtuous maid,
And to be shortly of a sisterhood,
If not already.

Ang. Well, let her be admitted.
[*Exit Servant.*]
See you the fornicatress be remov'd.
Let her have needful but not lavish means;
There shall be order for't.

Enter *Lucio* and *Isabella.*

Prov. God save your honour!
[*Going.*]

Ang. Stay a little while. — [*To Isabella*] Y'are welcome. What's your will?

Isab. I am a woful suitor to your honour,
Please but your honour hear me.

Ang. Well, what's your suit?

Isab. There is a vice that most I do abhor
And most desire should meet the blow of justice;
For which I would not plead, but that I must;
For which I must not plead, but that I am
At war 'twixt will and will not.

Ang. Well, the matter?

Isab. I have a brother is condemn'd to die.
I do beseech you, let it be his fault,
And not my brother.
Prov. [*aside*] Heaven give thee moving graces!
Ang. Condemn the fault, and not the actor of it?
Why, every fault's condemn'd ere it be done.
Mine were the very cipher of a function,
To fine the faults whose fine stands in record,
And let go by the actor.
Isab. O just but severe law!
I had a brother, then. — Heaven keep your honour! [*Going.*]
Lucio. [*aside to Isabella*] Give't not o'er so. To him again! entreat him,
Kneel down before him, hang upon his gown!
You are too cold. If you should need a pin,
You could not with more tame a tongue desire it.
To him, I say!
Isab. Must he needs die?
Ang. Maiden, no remedy.
Isab. Yes; I do think that you might pardon him
And neither heaven nor man grieve at the mercy.
Ang. I will not do't.
Isab. But can you, if you would?
Ang. Look, what I will not, that I cannot do.
Isab. But might you do't, and do the world no wrong,
If so your heart were touch'd with that remorse
As mine is to him?
Ang. He's sentenc'd; 'tis too late.
Lucio. [*aside to Isabella*] You are too cold.
Isab. Too late? Why, no! I, that do speak a word,
May call it back again. Well, believe this:
No ceremony that to great ones 'longs,
Not the king's crown nor the deputed sword,
The marshal's truncheon nor the judge's robe,
Become them with one half so good a grace
As mercy does.
If he had been as you, and you as he,
You would have slipp'd like him, but he like you
Would not have been so stern.
Ang. Pray you be gone.
Isab. I would to heaven I had your potency
And you were Isabel! Should it then be thus?
No! I would tell what 'twere to be a judge,
And what a prisoner.
Lucio. [*aside to Isabella*] Ay, touch him! There's the vein.
Ang. Your brother is a forfeit of the law,
And you but waste your words.
Isab. Alas, alas!
Why, all the souls that were were forfeit once,
And he that might the vantage best have took
Found out the remedy. How would you be
If he which is the top of judgment should
But judge you as you are? O, think on that!
And mercy then will breathe within your lips
Like man new made.
Ang. Be you content, fair maid.
It is the law, not I, condemn your brother.
Were he my kinsman, brother, or my son,
It should be thus with him. He must die to-morrow.
Isab. To-morrow? O, that's sudden! Spare him, spare him!
He's not prepar'd for death. Even for our kitchens
We kill the fowl of season. Shall we serve heaven
With less respect than we do minister
To our gross selves? Good, good my lord, bethink you!
Who is it that hath died for this offence?
There's many have committed it.
Lucio. [*aside*] Ay, well said.
Ang. The law hath not been dead, though it hath slept.
Those many had not dar'd to do that evil
If that the first that did th' edict infringe
Had answer'd for his deed. Now 'tis awake,
Takes note of what is done, and like a prophet
Looks in a glass that shows what future evils —
Either new, or by remissness new conceiv'd,
And so in progress to be hatch'd and born —
Are now to have no successive degrees,
But, ere they live, to end.
Isab. Yet show some pity.
Ang. I show it most of all when I show justice;
For then I pity those I do not know,
Which a dismiss'd offence would after gall,
And do him right that, answering one foul wrong,
Lives not to act another. Be satisfied.
Your brother dies to-morrow. Be content.
Isab. So you must be the first that gives this sentence,
And he, that suffers. O, it is excellent
To have a giant's strength; but it is tyrannous
To use it like a giant.
Lucio. [*aside*] That's well said.
Isab. Could great men thunder
As Jove himself does, Jove would ne'er be quiet,

Vincentio (Harry Andrews), the eccentric duke of Vienna, in his disguise as a monk

MEASURE FOR MEASURE

John Gielgud as the duke's lieutenant, Angelo, who learns that justice must be meted out with mercy—"measure for measure"

PHOTOGRAPHS BY ANGUS MC BEAN
PRODUCED BY MEMORIAL THEATRE COMPANY
STRATFORD-UPON-AVON

"In our remove be thou at full ourself." Supposedly about to absent himself from Vienna, the duke empowers Angelo to serve as his agent (*Act I, Scene I*)

"Most dangerous is that temptation that doth goad us on to sin in loving virtue." Angelo's soliloquy on his motives in dealing with Isabella (*Act II, Scene II*)

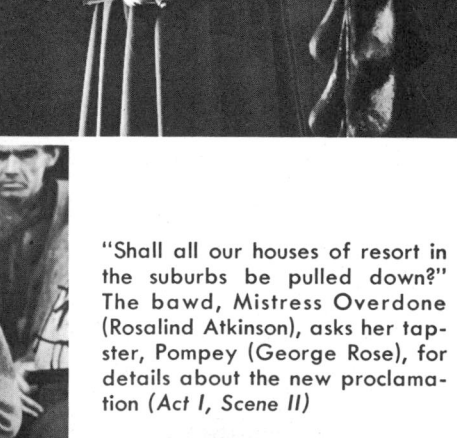

"Shall all our houses of resort in the suburbs be pulled down?" The bawd, Mistress Overdone (Rosalind Atkinson), asks her tapster, Pompey (George Rose), for details about the new proclamation (*Act I, Scene II*)

"I am the poor duke's constable." Elbow (Michael Bates), a simple-minded arm of the law, calls his prisoners Froth (Geoffrey Bayldon) and Pompey "notorious benefactors" *(Act II, Scene I)*

Left: "Why, very well: I hope here be truths." Affecting candor, Pompey delays the interrogation by Escalus (Harold Kasket), who shares power with Angelo as the duke's deputy *(Act II, Scene I)*

Below: Juliet (Hazel Penwarden) and her lover, Claudio (Alan Badel), both charged with immorality, meet before the prison *(Act I, Scene II)*

"Supply me with the habit, and instruct me how I may formally in person bear me like a true friar." Wishing to look into Angelo's ways, the duke asks Friar Thomas (Cyril Conway) to disguise him *(Act I, Scene III)*

Disguised, the duke visits the prison *(Act II, Scene III)*

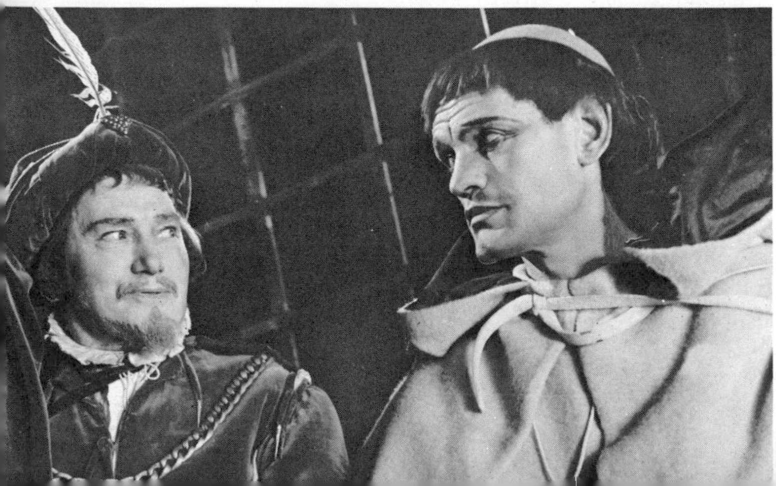

"A very superficial, ignorant, unweighing fellow." Not recognizing Vincentio in his disguise, Lucio (Leon Quartermaine) pretends to be on intimate terms with the duke and proceeds to pick his character to pieces *(Act III, Scene II)*

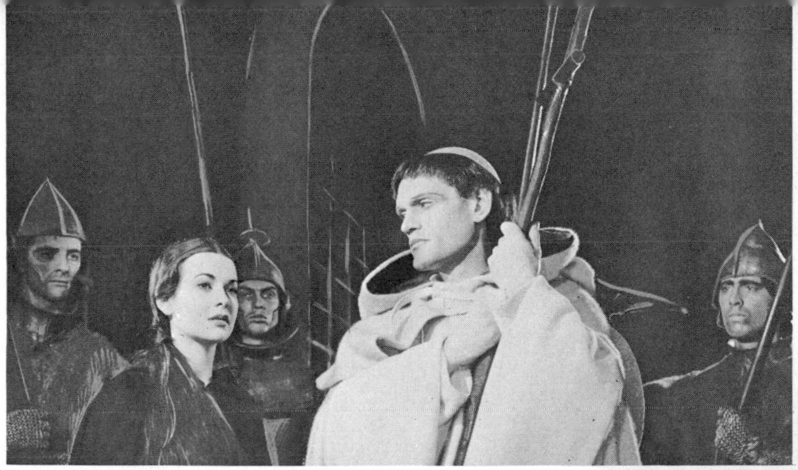

"Love you the man that wrong'd you?" On his way to visit Claudio in his cell, Vincentio meets the youth's mistress, the lovely Juliet *(Act II, Scene III)*

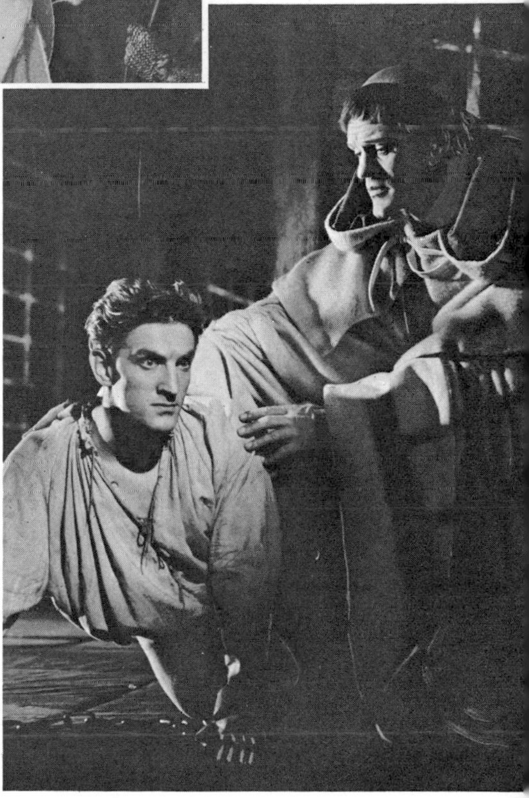

"Be absolute for death; either death or life shall thereby be the sweeter." The duke tries to persuade Claudio to accept his fate and to expect the worst *(Act III, Scene I)*

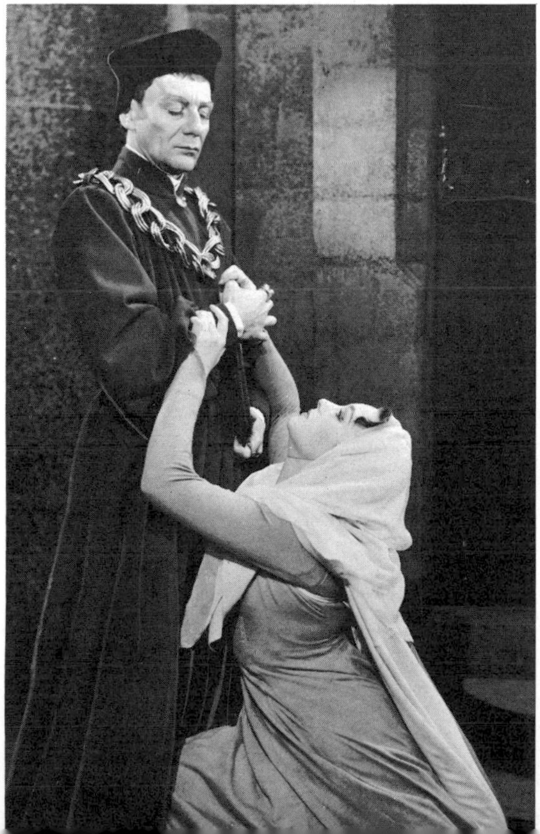

"Spare him, spare him! He's not prepar'd for death." Isabella (Barbara Jefford) begs Angelo for her brother's life *(Act II, Scene II)*

Above: "Be ready, Claudio, for your death to-morrow." Isabella tells her brother that his life would cost her her virtue, a condition she cannot accept. The duke listens undetected *(Act III, Scene I)*

"His head is off and sent to Angelo." To intensify the dénouement, the duke lets Isabella believe that Claudio is dead *(Act IV, Scene III)*

The duke comes upon Mariana (Maxine Audley), the woman whom Angelo abandoned long ago *(Act IV, Scene I)*

"This other doth command a little door which from the vineyard to the garden leads." Isabella instructs Mariana on her rendezvous with the fickle Angelo, her former lover *(Act IV, Scene I)*

"I will not consent to die this day, that's certain." Barnardine (Paul Hardwick), an extraordinary tosspot, declares he is still too drunk to be hanged *(Act IV, Scene III)*

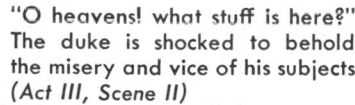

"O heavens! what stuff is here?" The duke is shocked to behold the misery and vice of his subjects *(Act III, Scene II)*

"O my dear lord! I crave no other, nor no better man." Mariana will accept no substitute for Angelo, though he once abandoned her because her dowry was too small
(Act V, Scene I)

Through the efforts of the duke, Mariana and Angelo are reconciled
(Act V, Scene I)

For every pelting petty officer
Would use his heaven for thunder — nothing but thunder!
Merciful heaven,
Thou rather with thy sharp and sulphurous bolt
Split'st the unwedgeable and gnarled oak
Than the soft myrtle. But man, proud man,
Drest in a little brief authority,
Most ignorant of what he's most assur'd
(His glassy essence), like an angry ape,
Plays such fantastic tricks before high heaven
As make the angels weep; who, with our spleens,
Would all themselves laugh mortal.

Lucio. [*aside to Isabella*] O, to him, to him, wench! He will relent;
He's coming. I perceive't.

Prov. [*aside*] Pray heaven she win him

Isab. We cannot weigh our brother with ourself.
Great men may jest with saints. 'Tis wit in them,
But in the less, foul profanation.

Lucio. [*aside to Isabella*] Thou'rt i' th' right, girl. More o' that!

Isab. That in the captain's but a choleric word
Which in the soldier is flat blasphemy.

Lucio. [*aside to Isabella*] Art avis'd o' that? More on't!

Ang. Why do you put these sayings upon me?

Isab. Because authority, though it err like others,
Hath yet a kind of medicine in itself
That skins the vice o' th' top. Go to your bosom,
Knock there, and ask your heart what it doth know
That's like my brother's fault. If it confess
A natural guiltiness such as is his,
Let it not sound a thought upon your tongue
Against my brother's life.

Ang. [*aside*] She speaks, and 'tis
Such sense that my sense breeds with it. — Fare you well.

Isab. Gentle my lord, turn back.

Ang. I will bethink me. Come again to-morrow.

Isab. Hark how I'll bribe you! Good my lord, turn back.

Ang. How? bribe me?

Isab. Ay, with such gifts that heaven shall share with you.

Lucio. [*aside to Isabella*] You had marr'd all else.

Isab. Not with fond sicles of the tested gold,
Or stones whose rates are either rich or poor
As fancy values them; but with true prayers,
That shall be up at heaven and enter there
Ere sunrise — prayers from preserved souls,
From fasting maids whose minds are dedicate
To nothing temporal.

Ang. Well, come to me to-morrow.

Lucio. [*aside to Isabella*] Go to! 'Tis well; away!

Isab. Heaven keep your honour safe!

Ang. [*aside*] Amen; for I
Am that way going to temptation
Where prayers cross.

Isab. At what hour to-morrow
Shall I attend your lordship?

Ang. At any time fore noon.

Isab. God save your honour!

[*Exeunt all but Angelo.*]

Ang. From thee! even from thy virtue!
What's this? what's this? Is this her fault, or mine?
The tempter, or the tempted, who sins most, ha?
Not she. Nor doth she tempt. But it is I
That, lying by the violet in the sun,
Do as the carrion does, not as the flow'r,
Corrupt with virtuous season. Can it be
That modesty may more betray our sense
Than woman's lightness? Having waste ground enough,
Shall we desire to raze the sanctuary,
And pitch our evils there? O, fie, fie, fie!
What dost thou? or what art thou, Angelo?
Dost thou desire her foully for those things
That make her good? O, let her brother live!
Thieves for their robbery have authority
When judges steal themselves. What, do I love her,
That I desire to hear her speak again?
And feast upon her eyes? What is't I dream on?
O cunning enemy, that, to catch a saint,
With saints dost bait thy hook! Most dangerous
Is that temptation that doth goad us on
To sin in loving virtue. Never could the strumpet,
With all her double vigour — art and nature —
Once stir my temper; but this virtuous maid
Subdues me quite. Ever till now,
When men were fond, I smil'd, and wond'red how.

Exit.

Scene III. [*A prison.*]

Enter *Duke* [disguised as a *friar,*] and *Provost.*

Duke. Hail to you, provost! So I think you are.
Prov. I am the provost. What's your will, good friar?
Duke. Bound by my charity and my blest order,
I come to visit the afflicted spirits
Here in the prison. Do me the common right
To let me see them, and to make me know
The nature of their crimes, that I may minister
To them accordingly.
Prov. I would do more than that, if more were needful.

Enter *Juliet.*

Look, here comes one — a gentlewoman of mine,
Who, falling in the flaws of her own youth,
Hath blister'd her report. She is with child,
And he that got it, sentenc'd — a young man
More fit to do another such offence
Than die for this.
Duke. When must he die?
Prov. As I do think, to-morrow.
[*To Juliet*] I have provided for you. Stay awhile,
And you shall be conducted.
Duke. Repent you, fair one, of the sin you carry?
Jul. I do, and bear the shame most patiently.
Duke. I'll teach you how you shall arraign your conscience,
And try your penitence, if it be sound
Or hollowly put on.
Jul. I'll gladly learn.
Duke. Love you the man that wrong'd you?
Jul. Yes, as I love the woman that wrong'd him.
Duke. So then it seems your most offenceful act
Was mutually committed.
Jul. Mutually.
Duke. Then was your sin of heavier kind than his.
Jul. I do confess it and repent it, father.
Duke. 'Tis meet so, daughter; but lest you do repent
As that the sin hath brought you to this shame —
Which sorrow is always toward ourselves, not heaven,
Showing we would not spare heaven as we love it,
But as we stand in fear —
Jul. I do repent me as it is an evil,
And take the shame with joy.
Duke. There rest.
Your partner, as I hear, must die to-morrow,
And I am going with instruction to him.
Grace go with you! Benedicite! *Exit.*
Jul. Must die to-morrow? O injurious law,
That respites me a life whose very comfort
Is still a dying horror!
Prov. 'Tis pity of him. *Exeunt.*

Scene IV. [Angelo's *house.*]

Enter *Angelo.*

Ang. When I would pray and think, I think and pray
To several subjects. Heaven hath my empty words,
Whilst my invention, hearing not my tongue,
Anchors on Isabel. Heaven in my mouth,
As if I did but only chew his name,
And in my heart the strong and swelling evil
Of my conception! The state, whereon I studied,
Is, like a good thing being often read,
Grown sere and tedious. Yea, my gravity,
Wherein (let no man hear me) I take pride,
Could I, with boot, change for an idle plume
Which the air beats for vain. O place, O form,
How often dost thou with thy case, thy habit,
Wrench awe from fools, and tie the wiser souls
To thy false seeming! Blood, thou art blood!
Let's write 'good angel' on the devil's horn,
'Tis not the devil's crest.

Enter *Servant.*

How now? Who's there?
Serv. One Isabel, a sister, desires access to you.
Ang. Teach her the way. [*Exit Servant.*]
O heavens!
Why does my blood thus muster to my heart,
Making both it unable for itself
And dispossessing all my other parts
Of necessary fitness?
So play the foolish throngs with one that swounds —
Come all to help him, and so stop the air
By which he should revive; and even so
The general, subject to a well-wish'd king,
Quit their own part, and in obsequious fondness
Crowd to his presence, where their untaught love
Must needs appear offence.

Enter *Isabella*.

How now, fair maid?

Isab. I am come to know your pleasure.

Ang. That you might know it, would much better please me
Than to demand what 'tis. Your brother cannot live.

Isab. Even so. — Heaven keep your honour! [*Going.*]

Ang. Yet may he live awhile; and, it may be,
As long as you or I. Yet he must die.

Isab. Under your sentence?

Ang. Yea.

Isab. When, I beseech you? that in his reprieve,
Longer or shorter, he may be so fitted
That his soul sicken not.

Ang. Ha! fie, these filthy vices! It were as good
To pardon him that hath from nature stol'n
A man already made, as to remit
Their saucy sweetness that do coin heaven's image
In stamps that are forbid. 'Tis all as easy
Falsely to take away a life true made
As to put metal in restrained means
To make a false one.

Isab. 'Tis set down so in heaven, but not in earth.

Ang. Say you so? Then I shall pose you quickly.
Which had you rather — that the most just law
Now took your brother's life or, to redeem him,
Give up your body to such sweet uncleanness
As she that he hath stain'd?

Isab. Sir, believe this:
I had rather give my body than my soul.

Ang. I talk not of your soul. Our compell'd sins
Stand more for number than for accompt.

Isab. How say you?

Ang. Nay, I'll not warrant that; for I can speak
Against the thing I say. Answer to this:
I (now the voice of the recorded law)
Pronounce a sentence on your brother's life:
Might there not be a charity in sin
To save this brother's life?

Isab. Please you to do't,
I'll take it as a peril to my soul,
It is no sin at all, but charity.

Ang. Pleas'd you to do't at peril of your soul,
Were equal poise of sin and charity.

Isab. That I do beg his life, if it be sin,
Heaven let me bear it! You granting of my suit,
If that be sin, I'll make it my morn prayer
To have it added to the faults of mine
And nothing of your answer.

Ang. Nay, but hear me.
Your sense pursues not mine. Either you are ignorant,
Or seem so, craftily; and that's not good.

Isab. Let me be ignorant, and in nothing good
But graciously to know I am no better.

Ang. Thus wisdom wishes to appear most bright
When it doth tax itself; as these black masks
Proclaim enshielded beauty ten times louder
Than beauty could, display'd. But mark me:
To be received plain, I'll speak more gross.
Your brother is to die.

Isab. So.

Ang. And his offence is so as it appears
Accountant to the law upon that pain.

Isab. True.

Ang. Admit no other way to save his life
(As I subscribe not that, nor any other,
But in the loose of question) that you, his sister,
Finding yourself desir'd of such a person
Whose credit with the judge, or own great place,
Could fetch your brother from the manacles
Of the all-binding law, and that there were
No earthly mean to save him but that either
You must lay down the treasures of your body
To this suppos'd, or else to let him suffer:
What would you do?

Isab. As much for my poor brother as myself.
That is, were I under the terms of death,
Th' impression of keen whips I'ld wear as rubies,
And strip myself to death as to a bed
That longings have been sick for, ere I'ld yield
My body up to shame.

Ang. Then must
Your brother die.

Isab. And 'twere the cheaper way.
Better it were a brother died at once
Than that a sister, by redeeming him,
Should die for ever.

Ang. Were not you then as cruel as the sentence
That you have slander'd so?

Isab. Ignomy in ransom and free pardon
Are of two houses. Lawful mercy
Is nothing kin to foul redemption.

Ang. You seem'd of late to make the law a tyrant,

And rather prov'd the sliding of your brother
A merriment than a vice.

Isab. O, pardon me, my lord! It oft falls out
To have what we would have, we speak not what we mean.
I something do excuse the thing I hate
For his advantage that I dearly love.

Ang. We are all frail.

Isab. Else let my brother die,
If not a fedary but only he
Owe and succeed thy weakness.

Ang. Nay, women are frail too.

Isab. Ay, as the glasses where they view themselves,
Which are as easy broke as they make forms.
Women? Help heaven! Men their creation mar
In profiting by them. Nay, call us ten times frail;
For we are soft as our complexions are,
And credulous to false prints.

Ang. I think it well;
And from this testimony of your own sex
(Since I suppose we are made to be no stronger
Than faults may shake our frames) let me be bold.
I do arrest your words. Be that you are;
That is, a woman. If you be more, you're none.
If you be one (as you are well express'd
By all external warrants), show it now
By putting on the destin'd livery.

Isab. I have no tongue but one. Gentle my lord,
Let me entreat you speak the former language.

Ang. Plainly conceive I love you.

Isab. My brother did love Juliet, and you tell me
That he shall die for't.

Ang. He shall not, Isabel, if you give me love.

Isab. I know your virtue hath a license in't,
Which seems a little fouler than it is
To pluck on others.

Ang. Believe me on mine honour;
My words express my purpose.

Isab. Ha! little honour to be much believ'd,
And most pernicious purpose! Seeming, seeming!
I will proclaim thee, Angelo; look for't.
Sign me a present pardon for my brother,
Or with an outstretch'd throat I'll tell the world aloud
What man thou art.

Ang. Who will believe thee, Isabel?
My unsoil'd name, th' austereness of my life,
My vouch against you, and my place i' th' state
Will so your accusation overweigh
That you shall stifle in your own report
And smell of calumny. I have begun,
And now I give my sensual race the rein.
Fit thy consent to my sharp appetite;
Lay by all nicety and prolixious blushes
That banish what they sue for. Redeem thy brother
By yielding up thy body to my will,
Or else he must not only die the death,
But thy unkindness shall his death draw out
To ling'ring sufferance. Answer me to-morrow,
Or, by the affection that now guides me most,
I'll prove a tyrant to him! As for you,
Say what you can; my false o'erweighs your true. *Exit.*

Isab. To whom should I complain? Did I tell this,
Who would believe me? O perilous mouths
That bear in them one and the selfsame tongue,
Either of condemnation or approof,
Bidding the law make curtsy to their will,
Hooking both right and wrong to th' appetite,
To follow as it draws! I'll to my brother.
Though he hath fall'n by prompture of the blood,
Yet hath he in him such a mind of honour
That, had he twenty heads to tender down
On twenty bloody blocks, he'ld yield them up
Before his sister should her body stoop
To such abhorr'd pollution.
Then, Isabel, live chaste; and, brother, die!
More than our brother is our chastity.
I'll tell him yet of Angelo's request,
And fit his mind to death for his soul's rest. *Exit.*

ACT III. Scene I. [*The prison.*]

Enter *Duke,* [disguised as a *friar,*] *Claudio,* and *Provost.*

Duke. So then, you hope of pardon from Lord Angelo?

Claud. The miserable have no other medicine
But only hope.
I have hope to live, and am prepar'd to die.

Duke. Be absolute for death. Either death or life
Shall thereby be the sweeter. Reason thus with life:
If I do lose thee, I do lose a thing
That none but fools would keep. A breath thou art,
Servile to all the skyey influences

That do this habitation where thou keep'st
Hourly afflict. Merely thou art death's fool;
For him thou labour'st by thy flight to shun,
And yet runn'st toward him still. Thou art not noble;
For all th' accommodations that thou bear'st
Are nurs'd by baseness. Thou'rt by no means valiant;
For thou dost fear the soft and tender fork
Of a poor worm. Thy best of rest is sleep,
And that thou oft provok'st; yet grossly fear'st
Thy death, which is no more. Thou art not thyself;
For thou exist'st on many a thousand grains
That issue out of dust. Happy thou art not;
For what thou hast not, still thou striv'st to get,
And what thou hast, forget'st. Thou art not certain;
For thy complexion shifts to strange effects,
After the moon. If thou art rich, thou'rt poor;
For, like an ass whose back with ingots bows,
Thou bear'st thy heavy riches but a journey,
And death unloads thee. Friend hast thou none;
For thine own bowels which do call thee sire,
The mere effusion of thy proper loins,
Do curse the gout, serpigo, and the rheum
For ending thee no sooner. Thou hast nor youth nor age,
But as it were an after-dinner's sleep,
Dreaming on both; for all thy blessed youth
Becomes as aged, and doth beg the alms
Of palsied eld; and when thou art old and rich,
Thou hast neither heat, affection, limb, nor beauty
To make thy riches pleasant. What's yet in this
That bears the name of life? Yet in this life
Lie hid moe thousand deaths; yet death we fear,
That makes these odds all even.

Claud. I humbly thank you.
To sue to live, I find I seek to die;
And seeking death, find life. Let it come on.

Enter *Isabella*.

Isab. What, ho! Peace here! Grace and good company!

Prov. Who's there? Come in! the wish deserves a welcome.

Duke. Dear son, ere long I'll visit you again.

Claud. Most holy sir, I thank you.

Isab. My business is a word or two with Claudio.

Prov. And very welcome. Look, signior, here's your sister.

Duke. Provost, a word with you.

Prov. As many as you please.

Duke. Bring me to hear them speak, where I may be conceal'd.

[*Exeunt Duke and Provost.*]

Claud. Now, sister, what's the comfort?

Isab. Why,
As all comforts are; most good, most good indeed.
Lord Angelo, having affairs to heaven,
Intends you for his swift ambassador,
Where you shall be an everlasting leiger.
Therefore your best appointment make with speed;
To-morrow you set on.

Claud. Is there no remedy?

Isab. None, but such remedy as, to save a head,
To cleave a heart in twain.

Claud. But is there any?

Isab. Yes, brother, you may live.
There is a devilish mercy in the judge,
If you'll implore it, that will free your life,
But fetter you till death.

Claud. Perpetual durance?

Isab. Ay, just! perpetual durance — a restraint,
Though all the world's vastidity you had,
To a determin'd scope.

Claud. But in what nature?

Isab. In such a one as, you consenting to't,
Would bark your honour from that trunk you bear
And leave you naked.

Claud. Let me know the point.

Isab. O, I do fear thee, Claudio, and I quake,
Lest thou a feverous life shouldst entertain,
And six or seven winters more respect
Than a perpetual honour. Dar'st thou die?
The sense of death is most in apprehension,
And the poor beetle that we tread upon,
In corporal sufferance finds a pang as great
As when a giant dies.

Claud. Why give you me this shame?
Think you I can a resolution fetch
From flow'ry tenderness? If I must die,
I will encounter darkness as a bride
And hug it in mine arms.

Isab. There spake my brother! There my father's grave
Did utter forth a voice! Yes, thou must die.
Thou art too noble to conserve a life
In base appliances. This outward-sainted deputy —
Whose settled visage and deliberate word
Nips youth i' th' head, and follies doth enew

As falcon doth the fowl — is yet a devil.
His filth within being cast, he would appear
A pond as deep as hell.
Claud. The prenzie Angelo?
Isab. O, 'tis the cunning livery of hell
The damned'st body to invest and cover
In prenzie guards! Dost thou think, Claudio?
If I would yield him my virginity,
Thou mightst be freed!
Claud. O heavens! it cannot be!
Isab. Yes, he would give't thee, from this rank offence,
So to offend him still. This night 's the time
That I should do what I abhor to name,
Or else thou diest to-morrow.
Claud. Thou shalt not do't.
Isab. O, were it but my life,
I'd throw it down for your deliverance
As frankly as a pin.
Claud. Thanks, dear Isabel.
Isab. Be ready, Claudio, for your death to-morrow.
Claud. Yes. Has he affections in him
That thus can make him bite the law by th' nose
When he would force it? Sure it is no sin,
Or of the deadly seven it is the least.
Isab. Which is the least?
Claud. If it were damnable, he being so wise,
Why would he for the momentary trick
Be perdurably fin'd? O Isabel!
Isab. What says my brother?
Claud. Death is a fearful thing.
Isab. And shamed life a hateful.
Claud. Ay, but to die, and go we know not where;
To lie in cold obstruction and to rot;
This sensible warm motion to become
A kneaded clod; and the delighted spirit
To bathe in fiery floods, or to reside
In thrilling region of thick-ribbed ice,
To be imprison'd in the viewless winds
And blown with restless violence round about
The pendent world; or to be worse than worst
Of those that lawless and incertain thought
Imagines howling! 'Tis too horrible!
The weariest and most loathed worldly life
That age, ache, penury, and imprisonment
Can lay on nature is a paradise
To what we fear of death.
Isab. Alas, alas!
Claud. Sweet sister, let me live!
What sin you do to save a brother's life,
Nature dispenses with the deed so far
That it becomes a virtue.
Isab. O you beast!
O faithless coward! O dishonest wretch!
Wilt thou be made a man out of my vice?
Is't not a kind of incest to take life
From thine own sister's shame? What should I think?
Heaven shield my mother play'd my father fair!
For such a warped slip of wilderness
Ne'er issu'd from his blood. Take my defiance!
Die, perish! Might but my bending down
Reprieve thee from thy fate, it should proceed.
I'll pray a thousand prayers for thy death,
No word to save thee.
Claud. Nay, hear me, Isabel.
Isab. O, fie, fie, fie!
Thy sin 's not accidental, but a trade.
Mercy to thee would prove itself a bawd.
'Tis best that thou diest quickly.
Claud. O, hear me, Isabella!

[Enter *Duke.*]

Duke. Vouchsafe a word, young sister, but one word.
Isab. What is your will?
Duke. Might you dispense with your leisure, I would by-and-by have some speech with you. The satisfaction I would require is likewise your own benefit.

Isab. I have no superfluous leisure; my stay must be stolen out of other affairs; but I will attend you awhile. [*Walks aside.*]

Duke. Son, I have overheard what hath pass'd between you and your sister. Angelo had never the purpose to corrupt her; only he hath made an assay of her virtue to practise his judgment with the disposition of natures. She, having the truth of honour in her, hath made him that gracious denial which he is most glad to receive. I am confessor to Angelo and I know this to be true. Therefore prepare yourself to death. Do not satisfy your resolution with hopes that are fallible. To-morrow you must die. Go to your knees and make ready.

Claud. Let me ask my sister pardon. I am so out of love with life that I will sue to be rid of it.

Duke. Hold you there. Farewell. [*Exit Claudio.*]
Provost, a word with you!

[Enter *Provost.*]

Prov. What's your will, father?

Duke. That now you are come, you will be gone. Leave me awhile with the maid. My mind promises with my habit no loss shall touch her by my company.

Prov. In good time. *Exit.*

Duke. The hand that hath made you fair hath made you good. The goodness that is cheap in beauty makes beauty brief in goodness; but grace, being the soul of your complexion, shall keep the body of it ever fair. The assault that Angelo hath made to you, fortune hath convey'd to my understanding; and, but that frailty hath examples for his falling, I should wonder at Angelo. How will you do to content this substitute and to save your brother?

Isab. I am now going to resolve him. I had rather my brother die by the law than my son should be unlawfully born. But, O, how much is the good Duke deceiv'd in Angelo! If ever he return and I can speak to him, I will open my lips in vain, or discover his government.

Duke. That shall not be much amiss. Yet, as the matter now stands, he will avoid your accusation: he made trial of you only. Therefore fasten your ear on my advisings. To the love I have in doing good a remedy presents itself. I do make myself believe that you may most uprighteously do a poor wronged lady a merited benefit; redeem your brother from the angry law; do no stain to your own gracious person; and much please the absent Duke, if peradventure he shall ever return to have hearing of this business.

Isab. Let me hear you speak farther. I have spirit to do anything that appears not foul in the truth of my spirit.

Duke. Virtue is bold, and goodness never fearful. Have you not heard speak of Mariana, the sister of Frederick, the great soldier who miscarried at sea?

Isab. I have heard of the lady and good words went with her name.

Duke. She should this Angelo have married; was affianced to her by oath, and the nuptial appointed; between which time of the contract and limit of the solemnity, her brother Frederick was wrack'd at sea, having in that perished vessel the dowry of his sister. But mark how heavily this befell to the poor gentlewoman. There she lost a noble and renowned brother, in his love toward her ever most kind and natural; with him the portion and sinew of her fortune, her marriage dowry; with both, her combinate husband, this well-seeming Angelo.

Isab. Can this be so? Did Angelo so leave her?

Duke. Left her in her tears and dried not one of them with his comfort; swallowed his vows whole, pretending in her discoveries of dishonour; in few, bestow'd her on her own lamentation, which she yet wears for his sake; and he, a marble to her tears, is washed with them but relents not.

Isab. What a merit were it in death to take this poor maid from the world! What corruption in this life, that it will let this man live! But how out of this can she avail?

Duke. It is a rupture that you may easily heal; and the cure of it not only saves your brother but keeps you from dishonour in doing it.

Isab. Show me how, good father.

Duke. This forenamed maid hath yet in her the continuance of her first affection. His unjust unkindness, that in all reason should have quenched her love, hath, like an impediment in the current, made it more violent and unruly. Go you to Angelo; answer his requiring with a plausible obedience; agree with his demands to the point: only refer yourself to this advantage — first, that your stay with him may not be long; that the time may have all shadow and silence in it, and the place answer to convenience. This being granted in course, and now follows all: we shall advise this wronged maid to stead up your appointment, go in your place. If the encounter acknowledge itself hereafter, it may compel him to her recompense; and here, by this, is your brother saved, your honour untainted, the poor Mariana advantaged, and the corrupt deputy scaled. The maid will I frame, and make fit for his attempt. If you think well to carry this as you may, the doubleness of the benefit defends the deceit from reproof. What think you of it?

Isab. The image of it gives me content already, and I trust it will grow to a most prosperous perfection.

Duke. It lies much in your holding up. Haste you speedily to Angelo. If for this night he entreat you to his bed, give him promise of satisfaction. I will presently to Saint Luke's. There at the moated grange resides this dejected Mariana. At that place call upon me; and dispatch with Angelo, that it may be quickly.

Isab. I thank you for this comfort. Fare you well, good father.

Exeunt [*severally*].

[Scene II. *The street before the prison.*]

Enter, [at one door, *Duke*, disguised as before; at the other,] *Elbow*, [*Pompey the*] *Clown*, *Officers*.

Elb. Nay, if there be no remedy for it, but that you will needs buy and sell men and women like beasts, we shall have all the world drink brown and white bastard.

Duke. O heavens! what stuff is here?

Pom. 'Twas never merry world since, of two usuries, the merriest was put down and the worser allow'd by order of law a furr'd gown to keep him warm — and furr'd with fox on lamb-skins too, to signify that craft, being richer than innocency, stands for the facing.

Elb. Come your way, sir. — Bless you, good father friar.

Duke. And you, good brother father. What offence
Hath this man made you, sir?

Elb. Marry, sir, he hath offended the law; and, sir, we take him to be a thief too, sir; for we have found upon him, sir, a strange picklock, which we have sent to the deputy.

Duke. Fie, sirrah! a bawd, a wicked bawd!
The evil that thou causest to be done,
That is thy means to live. Do thou but think
What 'tis to cram a maw or clothe a back
From such a filthy vice. Say to thyself,
'From their abominable and beastly touches
I drink, I eat, array myself, and live.'
Canst thou believe thy living is a life,
So stinkingly depending? Go mend, go mend!

Pom. Indeed, it does stink in some sort, sir. But yet, sir, I would prove —

Duke. Nay, if the devil have given thee proofs for sin,
Thou wilt prove his. Take him to prison, officer.
Correction and instruction must both work
Ere this rude beast will profit.

Elb. He must before the deputy, sir; he has given him warning. The deputy cannot abide a whoremaster. If he be a whoremonger, and comes before him, he were as good go a mile on his errand.

Duke. That we were all, as some would seem to be,
Free from our faults, as from faults seeming free!

Enter *Lucio*.

Elb. His neck will come to your waist — a cord, sir.

Pom. I spy comfort; I cry bail! Here's a gentleman and a friend of mine.

Lucio. How now, noble Pompey? What, at the wheels of Cæsar? Art thou led in triumph? What, is there none of Pygmalion's images newly made woman to be had now for putting the hand in the pocket and extracting it clutch'd? What reply? Ha? What say'st thou to this tune, matter, and method? Is't not drown'd i' th' last rain? Ha? What say'st thou, trot? Is the world as it was, man? Which is the way? Is it sad, and few words? Or how? The trick of it?

Duke. Still thus, and thus! still worse!

Lucio. How doth my dear morsel, thy mistress? Procures she still? Ha?

Pom. Troth, sir, she hath eaten up all her beef, and she is herself in the tub.

Lucio. Why, 'tis good. It is the right of it. It must be so. Ever your fresh whore and your powder'd bawd! An unshunn'd consequence; it must be so. Art going to prison, Pompey?

Pom. Yes, faith, sir.

Lucio. Why, 'tis not amiss, Pompey. Farewell. Go, say I sent thee thither. For debt, Pompey? or how?

Elb. For being a bawd; for being a bawd.

Lucio. Well, then imprison him. If imprisonment be the due of a bawd, why, 'tis his right. Bawd is he doubtless, and of antiquity too; bawd-born. Farewell, good Pompey. Commend me to the prison, Pompey. You will turn good husband now, Pompey; you will keep the house.

Pom. I hope, sir, your good worship will be my bail?

Lucio. No indeed will I not, Pompey; it is not the wear. I will pray, Pompey, to increase your bondage. If you take it not patiently, why, your mettle is the more! Adieu, trusty Pompey. Bless you, friar.

Duke. And you.

Lucio. Does Bridget paint still, Pompey? Ha?

Elb. Come your ways, sir, come.

Pom. You will not bail me then, sir?

Lucio. Then, Pompey, nor now. — What news abroad, friar? what news?

Elb. Come your ways, sir; come.

Lucio. Go to kennel, Pompey, go. [*Exeunt Elbow and Officers with Pompey.*] What news, friar, of the Duke?

Duke. I know none. Can you tell me of any?

Lucio. Some say he is with the Emperor of Russia; other some, he is in Rome. But where is he, think you?

Duke. I know not where; but wheresoever, I wish him well.

Lucio. It was a mad fantastical trick of him to steal from the state and usurp the beggary he was never born to. Lord Angelo dukes it well in his absence; he puts transgression to't.

Duke. He does well in't.

Lucio. A little more lenity to lechery would do no harm in him. Something too crabbed that way, friar.

Duke. It is too general a vice, and severity must cure it.

Lucio. Yes, in good sooth, the vice is of a great kindred — it is well allied; but it is impossible to extirp it quite, friar, till eating and drinking be put down. They say this Angelo was not made by man and woman after the downright way of creation. Is it true, think you?

Duke. How should he be made then?

Lucio. Some report a sea-maid spawn'd him; some, that he was begot between two stockfishes. But it is certain that, when he makes water, his urine is congeal'd ice; that I know to be true. And he is a motion generative; that's infallible.

Duke. You are pleasant, sir, and speak apace.

Lucio. Why, what a ruthless thing is this in him, for the rebellion of a codpiece to take away the life of a man! Would the Duke that is absent have done this? Ere he would have hang'd a man for the getting a hundred bastards, he would have paid for the nursing a thousand. He had some feeling of the sport; he knew the service, and that instructed him to mercy.

Duke. I never heard the absent Duke much detected for women. He was not inclin'd that way.

Lucio. O, sir, you are deceiv'd.

Duke. 'Tis not possible.

Lucio. Who? not the Duke? Yes, your beggar of fifty! and his use was to put a ducat in her clack-dish. The Duke had crotchets in him. He would be drunk too; that let me inform you.

Duke. You do him wrong, surely.

Lucio. Sir, I was an inward of his. A shy fellow was the Duke; and I believe I know the cause of his withdrawing.

Duke. What, I prithee, might be the cause?

Lucio. No, pardon! 'Tis a secret must be lock'd within the teeth and the lips. But this I can let you understand — the greater file of the subject held the Duke to be wise.

Duke. Wise? Why, no question but he was.

Lucio. A very superficial, ignorant, unweighing fellow.

Duke. Either this is envy in you, folly, or mistaking. The very stream of his life and the business he hath helmed must, upon a warranted need, give him a better proclamation. Let him be but testimonied in his own bringings-forth, and he shall appear to the envious a scholar, a statesman, and a soldier. Therefore you speak unskilfully; or, if your knowledge be more, it is much dark'ned in your malice.

Lucio. Sir, I know him and I love him.

Duke. Love talks with better knowledge, and knowledge with dearer love.

Lucio. Come, sir, I know what I know.

Duke. I can hardly believe that, since you know not what you speak. But if ever the Duke return, as our prayers are he may, let me desire you to make your answer before him. If it be honest you have spoke, you have courage to maintain it. I am bound to call upon you, and I pray you your name?

Lucio. Sir, my name is Lucio, well known to the Duke.

Duke. He shall know you better, sir, if I may live to report you.

Lucio. I fear you not.

Duke. O, you hope the Duke will return no more; or you imagine me too unhurtful an opposite. But indeed I can do you little harm. You'll forswear this again.

Lucio. I'll be hang'd first. Thou art deceiv'd in me, friar. But no more of this. Canst thou tell if Claudio die to-morrow or no?

Duke. Why should he die, sir?

Lucio. Why? For filling a bottle with a tundish. I would the Duke we talk of were return'd again. This ungenitur'd agent will unpeople the province with continency. Sparrows must not build in his house-eaves, because they are lecherous. The Duke yet would have dark deeds darkly answered; he would never bring them to light. Would he were return'd! Marry, this Claudio is condemned for untrussing. Farewell, good friar; I prithee pray for me. The Duke, I say to thee again, would eat mutton on Fridays. He's not past it yet; and I say to thee, he would mouth with a beggar, though she smelt brown bread and garlic. Say that I said so. Farewell. *Exit.*

Duke. No might nor greatness in mortality
Can censure scape. Back-wounding calumny
The whitest virtue strikes. What king so strong
Can tie the gall up in the slanderous tongue?
But who comes here?

Enter *Escalus, Provost,* and [*Mistress Overdone, the*] *Bawd,* [with *Officers*].

Escal. Go, away with her to prison!

Bawd. Good my lord, be good to me! Your honour is accounted a merciful man. Good my lord!

Escal. Double and treble admonition, and still forfeit in the same kind? This would make mercy swear and play the tyrant.

Prov. A bawd of eleven years' continuance, may it please your honour.

Bawd. My lord, this is one Lucio's information against me. Mistress Kate Keepdown was with child by him in the Duke's time; he promis'd her marriage. His child is a year and a quarter old, come Philip and Jacob. I have kept it myself; and see how he goes about to abuse me!

Escal. That fellow is a fellow of much license. Let him be call'd before us. Away with her to prison! Go to, no more words! [*Exeunt Officers with Mistress Overdone.*] Provost, my brother Angelo will not be alter'd; Claudio must die to-morrow. Let him be furnish'd with divines and have all charitable preparation. If my brother wrought by my pity, it should not be so with him.

Prov. So please you, this friar hath been with him and advis'd him for th' entertainment of death.

Escal. Good even, good father.

Duke. Bliss and goodness on you!

Escal. Of whence are you?

Duke. Not of this country, though my chance is now
To use it for my time. I am a brother
Of gracious order, late come from the See
In special business from his Holiness.

Escal. What news abroad i' th' world?

Duke. None, but that there is so great a fever on goodness that the dissolution of it must cure it. Novelty is only in request, and it is as dangerous to be aged in any kind of course as it is virtuous to be constant in any undertaking. There is scarce truth enough alive to make societies secure, but security enough to make fellowships accurst. Much upon this riddle runs the wisdom of the world. This news is old enough, yet it is every day's news. I pray you, sir, of what disposition was the Duke?

Escal. One that, above all other strifes, contended especially to know himself.

Duke. What pleasure was he given to?

Escal. Rather rejoicing to see another merry than merry at anything which profess'd to make him rejoice; a gentleman of all temperance. But leave we him to his events, with a prayer they may prove prosperous, and let me desire to know how you find Claudio prepar'd. I am made to understand that you have lent him visitation.

Duke. He professes to have received no sinister measure from his judge, but most willingly humbles himself to the determination of justice. Yet had he framed to himself, by the instruction of his frailty, many deceiving promises of life, which I, by my good leisure, have discredited to him, and now is he resolv'd to die.

Escal. You have paid the heavens your function and the prisoner the very debt of your calling. I have labour'd for the poor gentleman to the extremest shore of my modesty; but my brother justice have I found so severe that he hath forc'd me to tell him he is indeed Justice.

Duke. If his own life answer the straitness of his proceeding, it shall become him well; wherein if he chance to fail, he hath sentenc'd himself.

Escal. I am going to visit the prisoner. Fare you well.

Duke. Peace be with you!

[*Exeunt Escalus and Provost.*]

He who the sword of heaven will bear
Should be as holy as severe;
Pattern in himself to know,
Grace to stand, and virtue go;
More nor less to others paying
Than by self-offences weighing.
Shame to him whose cruel striking
Kills for faults of his own liking!
Twice treble shame on Angelo
To weed my vice and let his grow!
O, what may man within him hide,
Though angel on the outward side!
How may likeness made in crimes,
Mocking, practice on the times
To draw with idle spiders' strings
Most ponderous and substantial things!
Craft against vice I must apply.
With Angelo to-night shall lie
His old betrothed (but despised).
So disguise shall, by th' disguised,
Pay with falsehood false exacting
And perform an old contracting. *Exit.*

ACT IV. Scene I. [*The Moated Grange at Saint Luke's.*]

Enter *Mariana*; and *Boy* singing.

Song.

Take, O, take those lips away
That so sweetly were forsworn;
And those eyes, the break of day,
Lights that do mislead the morn;
But my kisses bring again, bring again;
Seals of love, but seal'd in vain, seal'd in vain.

Enter *Duke,* [disguised as before].

Mar. Break off thy song and haste thee quick away. [*Exit Boy.*]
Here comes a man of comfort, whose advice
Hath often still'd my brawling discontent.
I cry you mercy, sir, and well could wish
You had not found me here so musical.
Let me excuse me, and believe me so,
My mirth it much displeas'd, but pleas'd my woe.

Duke. 'Tis good; though music oft hath such a charm
To make bad good, and good provoke to harm.
I pray you tell me, hath anybody enquir'd for me here to-day? Much upon this time have I promis'd here to meet.

Mar. You have not been enquir'd after. I have sat here all day.

Enter *Isabella.*

Duke. I do constantly believe you. The time is come even now. I shall crave your forbearance a little. May be I will call upon you anon for some advantage to yourself.

Mar. I am always bound to you. *Exit.*

Duke. Very well met, and well come!
What is the news from this good deputy?

Isab. He hath a garden circummur'd with brick,
Whose western side is with a vineyard back'd;
And to that vineyard is a planched gate
That makes his opening with this bigger key.
This other doth command a little door
Which from the vineyard to the garden leads.
There have I made my promise
Upon the heavy middle of the night
To call upon him.

Duke. But shall you on your knowledge find this way?

Isab. I have ta'en a due and wary note upon't.
With whispering and most guilty diligence,
In action all of precept, he did show me
The way twice o'er.

Duke. Are there no other tokens
Between you 'greed concerning her observance?

Isab. No; none but only a repair i' th' dark,
And that I have possess'd him my most stay
Can be but brief; for I have made him know
I have a servant comes with me along
That stays upon me, whose persuasion is
I come about my brother.

Duke. 'Tis well borne up.
I have not yet made known to Mariana
A word of this. — What, ho, within! Come forth!

Enter *Mariana.*

I pray you be acquainted with this maid.
She comes to do you good.

Isab. I do desire the like.

Duke. Do you persuade yourself that I respect you?

Mar. Good friar, I know you do, and I have found it.

Duke. Take then this your companion by the hand,
Who hath a story ready for your ear.
I shall attend your leisure; but make haste;
The vaporous night approaches.

Mar. Will't please you walk aside?
Exeunt [*Mariana and Isabella*].

Duke. O place and greatness! millions of false eyes
Are stuck upon thee; volumes of report
Run with these false and most contrarious quests
Upon thy doings; thousand escapes of wit
Make thee the father of their idle dreams
And rack thee in their fancies.

Enter *Mariana* and *Isabella.*

Welcome! How agreed?

Isab. She'll take the enterprise upon her, father,
If you advise it.

Duke. It is not my consent,
But my entreaty too.

Isab. Little have you to say
When you depart from him but, soft and low,
'Remember now my brother.'

Mar. Fear me not.

Duke. Nor, gentle daughter, fear you not at all.
He is your husband on a precontract.
To bring you thus together 'tis no sin,

Sith that the justice of your title to him
Doth flourish the deceit. Come, let us go.
Our corn 's to reap, for yet our tithe 's to sow.
Exeunt.

Scene II. [*The prison.*]

Enter *Provost* and [*Pompey the*] *Clown.*

Prov. Come hither, sirrah. Can you cut off a man's head?

Pom. If the man be a bachelor, sir, I can; but if he be a married man, he's his wive's head, and I can never cut off a woman's head.

Prov. Come, sir, leave me your snatches and yield me a direct answer. To-morrow morning are to die Claudio and Barnardine. Here is in our prison a common executioner, who in his office lacks a helper. If you will take it on you to assist him, it shall redeem you from your gyves. If not, you shall have your full time of imprisonment, and your deliverance with an unpitied whipping, for you have been a notorious bawd.

Pom. Sir, I have been an unlawful bawd time out of mind, but yet I will be content to be a lawful hangman. I would be glad to receive some instruction from my fellow partner.

Prov. What, ho, Abhorson! Where's Abhorson there?

Enter *Abhorson.*

Abhor. Do you call, sir?

Prov. Sirrah, here's a fellow will help you to-morrow in your execution. If you think it meet, compound with him by the year, and let him abide here with you. If not, use him for the present and dismiss him. He cannot plead his estimation with you; he hath been a bawd.

Abhor. A bawd, sir? Fie upon him! he will discredit our mystery.

Prov. Go to, sir! You weigh equally; a feather will turn the scale. *Exit.*

Pom. Pray, sir, by your good favour — for surely, sir, a good favour you have but that you have a hanging look — do you call, sir, your occupation a mystery?

Abhor. Ay, sir, a mystery.

Pom. Painting, sir, I have heard say, is a mystery; and your whores, sir, being members of my occupation, using painting, do prove my occupation a mystery; but what mystery there should be in hanging, if I should be hang'd I cannot imagine.

Abhor. Sir, it is a mystery.

Pom. Proof.

Abhor. Every true man's apparel fits your thief. If it be too little for your thief, your true man thinks it big enough. If it be too big for your thief, your thief thinks it little enough. So every true man's apparel fits your thief.

Enter *Provost.*

Prov. Are you agreed?

Pom. Sir, I will serve him. For I do find your hangman is a more penitent trade than your bawd; he doth oftener ask forgiveness.

Prov. You, sirrah, provide your block and your axe to-morrow, four o'clock.

Abhor. Come on, bawd. I will instruct thee in my trade; follow.

Pom. I do desire to learn, sir; and I hope, if you have occasion to use me for your own turn, you shall find me yare; for truly, sir, for your kindness I owe you a good turn.

Prov. Call hither Barnardine and Claudio.
Exeunt [*Pompey and Abhorson*].
Th' one has my pity; not a jot the other,
Being a murtherer, though he were my brother.

Enter *Claudio.*

Look, here's the warrant, Claudio, for thy death.
'Tis now dead midnight, and by eight to-morrow
Thou must be made immortal. Where's Barnardine?

Claud. As fast lock'd up in sleep as guiltless labour
When it lies starkly in the traveller's bones.
He will not wake.

Prov. Who can do good on him?
Well, go, prepare yourself. [*Knocking within.*] But hark! What noise?
Heaven give your spirits comfort! [*Exit Claudio. Knocking continues.*] By-and-by!
I hope it is some pardon or reprieve
For the most gentle Claudio.

Enter *Duke,* [disguised as before].

Welcome, father.

Duke. The best and wholesom'st spirits of the night
Envelop you, good provost! Who call'd here of late?

Prov. None since the curfew rung.

Duke. Not Isabel?

Prov. No.

Duke. They will then, ere't be long.

Prov. What comfort is for Claudio?

Duke. There's some in hope.
Prov. It is a bitter deputy.
Duke. Not so, not so! His life is parallel'd
Even with the stroke and line of his great justice.
He doth with holy abstinence subdue
That in himself which he spurs on his pow'r
To qualify in others. Were he meal'd with that
Which he corrects, then were he tyrannous;
But this being so, he's just. [*Knocking within.*]
Now are they come.
[*Exit Provost.*]
This is a gentle provost. Seldom when
The steeled jailer is the friend of men.
[*Knocking within.*]
How now? What noise? That spirit 's possess'd with haste
That wounds th' unsisting postern with these strokes.

[Enter *Provost.*]

Prov. There he must stay until the officer
Arise to let him in. He is call'd up.
Duke. Have you no countermand for Claudio yet
But he must die to-morrow?
Prov. None, sir, none.
Duke. As near the dawning, provost, as it is,
You shall hear more ere morning.
Prov. Happily
You something know. Yet I believe there comes
No countermand. No such example have we.
Besides, upon the very siege of justice
Lord Angelo hath to the public ear
Profess'd the contrary.

Enter a *Messenger.*

This is his lordship's man.
Duke. And here comes Claudio's pardon.

Mes. [*gives a paper*] My lord hath sent you this note, and by me this further charge — that you swerve not from the smallest article of it, neither in time, matter, or other circumstance. Good morrow; for, as I take it, it is almost day.

Prov. I shall obey him. [*Exit Messenger.*]
Duke. [*aside*] This is his pardon, purchas'd by such sin
For which the pardoner himself is in.
Hence hath offence his quick celerity,
When it is borne in high authority.
When vice makes mercy, mercy 's so extended
That for the fault's love is th' offender friended.
Now, sir, what news?

Prov. I told you. Lord Angelo, belike thinking me remiss in mine office, awakens me with this unwonted putting-on; methinks strangely, for he hath not us'd it before.

Duke. Pray you let's hear.

Prov. [*reads*] *the letter.*

'Whatsoever you may hear to the contrary, let Claudio be executed by four of the clock, and in the afternoon Barnardine. For my better satisfaction, let me have Claudio's head sent me by five. Let this be duly performed, with a thought that more depends on it than we must yet deliver. Thus fail not to do your office, as you will answer it at your peril.'

What say you to this, sir?

Duke. What is that Barnardine who is to be executed in th' afternoon?

Prov. A Bohemian born, but here nurs'd up and bred; one that is a prisoner nine years old.

Duke. How came it that the absent Duke had not either deliver'd him to his liberty or executed him? I have heard it was ever his manner to do so.

Prov. His friends still wrought reprieves for him; and indeed his fact, till now in the government of Lord Angelo, came not to an undoubtful proof.

Duke. It is now apparent?

Prov. Most manifest, and not denied by himself.

Duke. Hath he borne himself penitently in prison? How seems he to be touch'd?

Prov. A man that apprehends death no more dreadfully but as a drunken sleep; careless, reckless, and fearless of what's past, present, or to come; insensible of mortality and desperately mortal.

Duke. He wants advice.

Prov. He will hear none. He hath evermore had the liberty of the prison. Give him leave to escape hence, he would not. Drunk many times a day, if not many days entirely drunk. We have very oft awak'd him, as if to carry him to execution, and show'd him a seeming warrant for it. It hath not moved him at all.

Duke. More of him anon. There is written in your brow, provost, honesty and constancy. If I read it not truly, my ancient skill beguiles me; but in the boldness of my cunning I will lay myself in hazard. Claudio, whom here you have warrant to execute, is no greater forfeit to the law than Angelo who hath sentenc'd him. To make you understand this in a manifested effect I crave but four days' respite, for the which you are to do me both a present and a dangerous courtesy.

Prov. Pray, sir, in what?

Duke. In the delaying death.

Prov. Alack, how may I do it, having the hour limited and an express command, under penalty, to deliver his head in the view of Angelo? I may make my case as Claudio's, to cross this in the smallest.

Duke. By the vow of mine order I warrant you, if my instructions may be your guide. Let this Barnardine be this morning executed and his head borne to Angelo.

Prov. Angelo hath seen them both and will discover the favour.

Duke. O, death 's a great disguiser, and you may add to it. Shave the head and trim the beard, and say it was the desire of the penitent to be so bar'd before his death. You know the course is common. If anything fall to you upon this more than thanks and good fortune, by the Saint whom I profess, I will plead against it with my life.

Prov. Pardon me, good father, it is against my oath.

Duke. Were you sworn to the Duke or to the deputy?

Prov. To him and to his substitutes.

Duke. You will think you have made no offence if the Duke avouch the justice of your dealing?

Prov. But what likelihood is in that?

Duke. Not a resemblance, but a certainty. Yet since I see you fearful, that neither my coat, integrity, nor persuasion can with ease attempt you, I will go further than I meant, to pluck all fears out of you. Look you, sir, here is the hand and seal of the Duke. You know the character, I doubt not, and the signet is not strange to you?

Prov. I know them both.

Duke. The contents of this is the return of the Duke. You shall anon overread it at your pleasure, where you shall find within these two days he will be here. This is a thing that Angelo knows not; for he this very day receives letters of strange tenour, perchance of the Duke's death, perchance entering into some monastery, but by chance nothing of what is writ. Look, th' unfolding star calls up the shepherd. Put not yourself into amazement how these things should be. All difficulties are but easy when they are known. Call your executioner, and off with Barnardine's head. I will give him a present shrift and advise him for a better place. Yet you are amaz'd, but this shall absolutely resolve you. Come away; it is almost clear dawn. *Exeunt.*

Scene III. [*Another room in the prison.*]

Enter [*Pompey the*] *Clown.*

Pom. I am as well acquainted here as I was in our house of profession. One would think it were Mistress Overdone's own house, for here be many of her old customers. First, here's young Master Rash: he's in for a commodity of brown paper and old ginger, ninescore and seventeen pounds, of which he made five marks ready money. Marry, then ginger was not much in request, for the old women were all dead. Then is there here one Master Caper, at the suit of Master Threepile the mercer, for some four suits of peach-colour'd satin, which now peaches him a beggar. Then have we here young Dizie, and young Master Deepvow, and Master Copperspur, and Master Starvelackey the rapier-and-dagger man, and young Dropheir that kill'd lusty Pudding, and Master Forthright the tilter, and brave Master Shoetie the great traveller, and wild Halfcan that stabb'd Pots, and I think forty more — all great doers in our trade, and are now 'for the Lord's sake.'

Enter *Abhorson.*

Abhor. Sirrah, bring Barnardine hither.

Pom. Master Barnardine, you must rise and be hang'd! Master Barnardine!

Abhor. What ho, Barnardine!

Bar. (*within*) A pox o' your throats! Who makes that noise there? What are you?

Pom. Your friends, sir; the hangman. You must be so good, sir, to rise and be put to death.

Bar. (*within*) Away, you rogue, away! I am sleepy.

Abhor. Tell him he must awake, and that quickly too.

Pom. Pray, Master Barnardine, awake till you are executed, and sleep afterwards.

Abhor. Go in to him and fetch him out.

Pom. He is coming, sir, he is coming. I hear his straw rustle.

Enter *Barnardine.*

Abhor. Is the axe upon the block, sirrah?

Pom. Very ready, sir.

Bar. How now, Abhorson? What's the news with you?

Abhor. Truly, sir, I would desire you to clap into your prayers; for look you, the warrant 's come.

Bar. You rogue, I have been drinking all night. I am not fitted for't.

Pom. O, the better, sir! for he that drinks all night, and is hanged betimes in the morning, may sleep the sounder all the next day.

Enter *Duke*, [disguised as before].

Abhor. Look you, sir, here comes your ghostly father. Do we jest now, think you?

Duke. Sir, induced by my charity, and hearing how hastily you are to depart, I am come to advise you, comfort you, and pray with you.

Bar. Friar, not I! I have been drinking hard all night, and I will have more time to prepare me, or they shall beat out my brains with billets. I will not consent to die this day, that's certain.

Duke. O, sir, you must! and therefore I beseech you
Look forward on the journey you shall go.

Bar. I swear I will not die to-day for any man's persuasion.

Duke. But hear you —

Bar. Not a word! If you have anything to say to me, come to my ward; for thence will not I to-day. *Exit.*

Enter *Provost.*

Duke. Unfit to live or die! O gravel heart!
After him, fellows! bring him to the block.
[*Exeunt Abhorson and Pompey.*]

Prov. Now, sir, how do you find the prisoner?

Duke. A creature unprepar'd, unmeet for death;
And to transport him in the mind he is
Were damnable.

Prov. Here in the prison, father,
There died this morning of a cruel fever
One Ragozine, a most notorious pirate,
A man of Claudio's years; his beard and head
Just of his colour. What if we do omit
This reprobate till he were well inclin'd,
And satisfy the deputy with the visage
Of Ragozine, more like to Claudio?

Duke. O, 'tis an accident that heaven provides!
Dispatch it presently; the hour draws on
Prefix'd by Angelo. See this be done,
And sent according to command, whiles I
Persuade this rude wretch willingly to die.

Prov. This shall be done, good father, presently.
But Barnardine must die this afternoon;
And how shall we continue Claudio,
To save me from the danger that might come
If he were known alive?

Duke. Let this be done.
Put them in secret holds, both Barnardine and Claudio.
Ere twice the sun hath made his journal greeting
To th' under generation, you shall find
Your safety manifested.

Prov. I am your free dependant.

Duke. Quick, dispatch,
And send the head to Angelo. *Exit* [*Provost*].
Now will I write letters to Angelo
(The provost, he shall bear them) whose contents
Shall witness to him I am near at home,
And that by great injunctions I am bound
To enter publicly. Him I'll desire
To meet me at the consecrated fount,
A league below the city; and from thence,
By cold gradation and well balanc'd form,
We shall proceed with Angelo.

Enter *Provost*, [with *Ragozine's* head].

Prov. Here is the head. I'll carry it myself.

Duke. Convenient is it. Make a swift return;
For I would commune with you of such things
That want no ear but yours.

Prov. I'll make all speed. *Exit.*

Isab. (*within*) Peace, ho, be here!

Duke. The tongue of Isabel. She's come to know
If yet her brother's pardon be come hither;
But I will keep her ignorant of her good,
To make her heavenly comforts of despair
When it is least expected.

Enter *Isabella.*

Isab. Ho, by your leave!

Duke. Good morning to you, fair and gracious daughter.

Isab. The better, given me by so holy a man.
Hath yet the deputy sent my brother's pardon?

Duke. He hath releas'd him, Isabel, from the world.
His head is off, and sent to Angelo.

Isab. Nay, but it is not so!

Duke. It is no other. Show your wisdom, daughter,
In your close patience.

Isab. O, I will to him and pluck out his eyes!

Duke. You shall not be admitted to his sight.

Isab. Unhappy Claudio! wretched Isabel!
Injurious world! most damned Angelo!

Duke. This nor hurts him nor profits you a jot;
Forbear it therefore; give your cause to heaven.
Mark what I say, which you shall find
By every syllable a faithful verity.

The Duke comes home to-morrow — Nay, dry your eyes!
One of our covent, and his confessor,
Gives me this instance. Already he hath carried
Notice to Escalus and Angelo,
Who do prepare to meet him at the gates,
There to give up their pow'r. If you can, pace your wisdom
In that good path that I would wish it go;
And you shall have your bosom on this wretch,
Grace of the Duke, revenges to your heart,
And general honour.

Isab. I am directed by you.

Duke. This letter, then, to Friar Peter give.
'Tis that he sent me of the Duke's return.
Say, by this token I desire his company
At Mariana's house to-night. Her cause and yours
I'll perfect him withal, and he shall bring you
Before the Duke; and to the head of Angelo
Accuse him home and home. For my poor self,
I am combined by a sacred vow
And shall be absent. Wend you with this letter.
Command these fretting waters from your eyes
With a light heart. Trust not my holy order
If I pervert your course. — Who's here?

Enter *Lucio.*

Lucio. Good even. Friar, where's the provost?

Duke. Not within, sir.

Lucio. O pretty Isabella, I am pale at mine heart to see thine eyes so red! Thou must be patient. I am fain to dine and sup with water and bran; I dare not for my head fill my belly; one fruitful meal would set me to't. But they say the Duke will be here to-morrow. By my troth, Isabel, I lov'd thy brother. If the old fantastical Duke of dark corners had been at home, he had lived. [*Exit Isabella.*]

Duke. Sir, the Duke is marvellous little beholding to your reports; but the best is, he lives not in them.

Lucio. Friar, thou knowest not the Duke so well as I do. He's a better woodman than thou tak'st him for.

Duke. Well, you'll answer this one day. Fare ye well.

Lucio. Nay, tarry; I'll go along with thee. I can tell thee pretty tales of the Duke.

Duke. You have told me too many of him already, sir, if they be true; if not true, none were enough.

Lucio. I was once before him for getting a wench with child.

Duke. Did you such a thing?

Lucio. Yes, marry, did I; but I was fain to forswear it. They would else have married me to the rotten medlar.

Duke. Sir, your company is fairer than honest. Rest you well.

Lucio. By my troth, I'll go with thee to the lane's end. If bawdy talk offend you, we'll have very little of it. Nay, friar, I am a kind of burr; I shall stick. *Exeunt.*

Scene IV. [Angelo's *house.*]

Enter *Angelo* and *Escalus.*

Escal. Every letter he hath writ hath disvouch'd other.

Ang. In most uneven and distracted manner. His actions show much like to madness; pray heaven his wisdom be not tainted! And why meet him at the gates and redeliver our authorities there?

Escal. I guess not.

Ang. And why should we proclaim it in an hour before his ent'ring, that if any crave redress of injustice, they should exhibit their petitions in the street?

Escal. He shows his reason for that: to have a dispatch of complaints, and to deliver us from devices hereafter, which shall then have no power to stand against us.

Ang. Well, I beseech you let it be proclaim'd.
Betimes i' th' morn I'll call you at your house.
Give notice to such men of sort and suit
As are to meet him.

Escal. I shall, sir. Fare you well.

Ang. Good night. *Exit* [*Escalus*].
This deed unshapes me quite, makes me unpregnant
And dull to all proceedings. A deflow'red maid!
And by an eminent body that enforc'd
The law against it! But that her tender shame
Will not proclaim against her maiden loss,
How might she tongue me! Yet reason dares her no;
For my authority bears so credent bulk
That no particular scandal once can touch
But it confounds the breather. He should have liv'd,
Save that his riotous youth, with dangerous sense,
Might in the times to come have ta'en revenge
By so receiving a dishonour'd life
With ransom of such shame. Would yet he had liv'd!
Alack, when once our grace we have forgot,

Nothing goes right! we would, and we would not! *Exit.*

Scene V. [*Fields without the City.*]

Enter *Duke*, [in his own habit,] and *Friar Peter.*

Duke. These letters at fit time deliver me. [*Gives letters.*]
The provost knows our purpose and our plot.
The matter being afoot, keep your instruction
And hold you ever to our special drift,
Though sometimes you do blench from this to that,
As cause doth minister. Go call at Flavius' house
And tell him where I stay. Give the like notice
To Valentinus, Rowland, and to Crassus,
And bid them bring the trumpets to the gate.
But send me Flavius first.
Peter. It shall be speeded well. [*Exit.*]

Enter *Varrius.*

Duke. I thank thee, Varrius; thou hast made good haste.
Come, we will walk. There's other of our friends
Will greet us here anon. My gentle Varrius! *Exeunt.*

Scene VI. [*Street near the City gate.*]

Enter *Isabella* and *Mariana.*

Isab. To speak so indirectly I am loath.
I would say the truth; but to accuse him so,
That is your part; yet I am advis'd to do it;
He says, to veil full purpose.
Mar. Be rul'd by him.
Isab. Besides, he tells me that, if peradventure
He speak against me on the adverse side,
I should not think it strange, for 'tis a physic
That's bitter to sweet end.

Enter [*Friar*] *Peter.*

Mar. I would Friar Peter —
Isab. O, peace! the friar is come.
Peter. Come, I have found you out a stand most fit,
Where you may have such vantage on the Duke
He shall not pass you. Twice have the trumpets sounded.
The generous and gravest citizens
Have hent the gates, and very near upon
The Duke is ent'ring. Therefore, hence, away! *Exeunt.*

Act V. Scene I. [*The City gate.*]

Enter *Duke* [in his own habit], *Varrius, Lords*; *Angelo, Escalus, Lucio,* [*Provost, Officers,* and] *Citizens*: at several doors.

Duke. My very worthy cousin, fairly met.
Our old and faithful friend, we are glad to see you.
Ang., Escal. Happy return be to your royal Grace!
Duke. Many and hearty thankings to you both!
We have made enquiry of you, and we hear
Such goodness of your justice that our soul
Cannot but yield you forth to public thanks,
Forerunning more requital.
Ang. You make my bonds still greater.
Duke. O, your desert speaks loud, and I should wrong it
To lock it in the wards of covert bosom
When it deserves, with characters of brass,
A forted residence 'gainst the tooth of time
And razure of oblivion. Give me your hand,
And let the subject see, to make them know
That outward courtesies would fain proclaim
Favours that keep within. Come, Escalus,
You must walk by us on our other hand;
And good supporters are you.

Enter *Peter* and *Isabella.*

Peter. Now is your time. Speak loud, and kneel before him.
Isab. Justice, O royal Duke! Vail your regard
Upon a wrong'd — I would fain have said, a maid!
O worthy prince, dishonour not your eye
By throwing it on any other object
Till you have heard me in my true complaint
And given me justice, justice, justice, justice!
Duke. Relate your wrongs. In what? by whom? Be brief.
Here is Lord Angelo shall give you justice.
Reveal yourself to him.
Isab. O worthy Duke,
You bid me seek redemption of the devil!
Hear me yourself; for that which I must speak
Must either punish me, not being believ'd,
Or wring redress from you. Hear me! O, hear me, hear!

Ang. My lord, her wits I fear me are not firm.
She hath been a suitor to me for her brother
Cut off by course of justice —

Isab. By course of justice!

Ang. And she will speak most bitterly and strange.

Isab. Most strange! but yet most truly will I speak.
That Angelo's forsworn, is it not strange?
That Angelo's a murtherer, is't not strange?
That Angelo is an adulterous thief,
An hypocrite, a virgin-violator —
Is it not strange? and strange?

Duke. Nay, it is ten times strange!

Isab. It is not truer he is Angelo
Than this is all as true as it is strange.
Nay, it is ten times true, for truth is truth
To th' end of reck'ning.

Duke. Away with her! Poor soul!
She speaks this in th' infirmity of sense.

Isab. O prince, I conjure thee, as thou believ'st
There is another comfort than this world,
That thou neglect me not with that opinion
That I am touch'd with madness! Make not impossible
That which but seems unlike. 'Tis not impossible
But one, the wicked'st caitiff on the ground,
May seem as shy, as grave, as just, as absolute
As Angelo. Even so may Angelo,
In all his dressings, characts, titles, forms,
Be an arch-villain. Believe it, royal prince!
If he be less, he's nothing; but he's more,
Had I more name for badness.

Duke. By mine honesty,
If she be mad, as I believe no other,
Her madness hath the oddest frame of sense,
Such a dependency of thing on thing,
As e'er I heard in madness.

Isab. O gracious Duke,
Harp not on that! nor do not banish reason
For inequality, but let your reason serve
To make the truth appear where it seems hid
And hide the false seems true!

Duke. Many that are not mad
Have sure more lack of reason. What would you say?

Isab. I am the sister of one Claudio,
Condemn'd upon the act of fornication
To lose his head, condemn'd by Angelo.
I, in probation of a sisterhood,
Was sent to by my brother, one Lucio
As then the messenger.

Lucio. That's I, an't like your Grace.
I came to her from Claudio and desir'd her
To try her gracious fortune with Lord Angelo
For her poor brother's pardon.

Isab. That's he indeed.

Duke. You were not bid to speak.

Lucio. No, my good lord,
Nor wish'd to hold my peace.

Duke. I wish you now then.
Pray you take note of it. And when you have
A business for yourself, pray heaven you then
Be perfect.

Lucio. I warrant your honour.

Duke. The warrant 's for yourself. Take heed to it.

Isab. This gentleman told somewhat of my tale.

Lucio. Right.

Duke. It may be right, but you are i' the wrong
To speak before your time. — Proceed.

Isab. I went
To this pernicious caitiff deputy.

Duke. That's somewhat madly spoken.

Isab. Pardon it.
The phrase is to the matter.

Duke. Mended again. The matter! Proceed.

Isab. In brief — to set the needless process by,
How I persuaded, how I pray'd and kneel'd,
How he refell'd me and how I replied
(For this was of much length) — the vile conclusion
I now begin with grief and shame to utter.
He would not, but by gift of my chaste body
To his concupiscible intemperate lust,
Release my brother; and after much debatement,
My sisterly remorse confutes mine honour,
And I did yield to him. But the next morn betimes,
His purpose surfeiting, he sends a warrant
For my poor brother's head.

Duke. This is most likely!

Isab. O that it were as like as it is true!

Duke. By heaven, fond wretch, thou know'st not what thou speak'st,
Or else thou art suborn'd against his honour
In hateful practice. First, his integrity
Stands without blemish. Next, it imports no reason
That with such vehemency he should pursue
Faults proper to himself. If he had so offended,
He would have weigh'd thy brother by himself
And not have cut him off. Some one hath set you on.

Confess the truth, and say by whose advice
Thou cam'st here to complain.
Isab. And is this all?
Then, O you blessed ministers above,
Keep me in patience, and with ripened time
Unfold the evil which is here wrapt up
In countenance! Heaven shield your Grace from woe,
As I, thus wrong'd, hence unbelieved go!
Duke. I know you'ld fain be gone. — An officer!
To prison with her! Shall we thus permit
A blasting and a scandalous breath to fall
On him so near us? This needs must be a practice.
Who knew of your intent and coming hither?
Isab. One that I would were here, Friar Lodowick.
Duke. A ghostly father, belike. Who knows that Lodowick?
Lucio. My lord, I know him. 'Tis a meddling friar.
I do not like the man. Had he been lay, my lord,
For certain words he spake against your Grace
In your retirement, I had swing'd him soundly.
Duke. Words against me! This' a good friar belike!
And to set on this wretched woman here
Against our substitute! Let this friar be found.
Lucio. But yesternight, my lord, she and that friar,
I saw them at the prison — a saucy friar,
A very scurvy fellow.
Peter. Blessed be your royal Grace!
I have stood by, my lord, and I have heard
Your royal ear abus'd. First, hath this woman
Most wrongfully accus'd your substitute,
Who is as free from touch or soil with her
As she from one ungot.
Duke. We did believe no less.
Know you that Friar Lodowick that she speaks of?
Peter. I know him for a man divine and holy;
Not scurvy, nor a temporary meddler,
As he's reported by this gentleman;
And, on my trust, a man that never yet
Did, as he vouches, misreport your Grace.
Lucio. My lord, most villanously! Believe it!
Peter. Well, he in time may come to clear himself;
But at this instant he is sick, my lord,
Of a strange fever. Upon his mere request,
Being come to knowledge that there was complaint
Intended 'gainst Lord Angelo, came I hither
To speak, as from his mouth, what he doth know
Is true and false; and what he with his oath
And all probation will make up full clear,
Whensoever he's convented. First, for this woman —
To justify this worthy nobleman,
So vulgarly and personally accus'd,
Her shall you hear disproved to her eyes
Till she herself confess it.
Duke. Good friar, let's hear it.
[*Exit Isabella, guarded.*]
Do you not smile at this, Lord Angelo?
O heaven, the vanity of wretched fools!
Give us some seats. Come, cousin Angelo;
In this I'll be impartial; be you judge
Of your own cause.

Enter *Mariana*, [veiled].

Is this the witness, friar?
First let her show her face, and after speak.
Mar. Pardon, my lord. I will not show my face
Until my husband bid me.
Duke. What, are you married?
Mar. No, my lord.
Duke. Are you a maid?
Mar. No, my lord.
Duke. A widow then?
Mar. Neither, my lord.
Duke. Why, you are nothing then — neither maid, widow, nor wife?
Lucio. My lord, she may be a punk; for many of them are neither maid, widow, nor wife.
Duke. Silence that fellow! I would he had some cause
To prattle for himself.
Lucio. Well, my lord.
Mar. My lord, I do confess I ne'er was married,
And I confess, besides, I am no maid.
I have known my husband; yet my husband knows not
That ever he knew me.
Lucio. He was drunk then, my lord. It can be no better.
Duke. For the benefit of silence, would thou wert so too!
Lucio. Well, my lord.
Duke. This is no witness for Lord Angelo.
Mar. Now I come to't, my lord.
She that accuses him of fornication,
In selfsame manner doth accuse my husband,
And charges him, my lord, with such a time
When I'll depose I had him in mine arms
With all th' effect of love.
Ang. Charges she moe than me?

Mar. Not that I know.
Duke. No? You say your husband.
Mar. Why, just, my lord, and that is Angelo,
Who thinks he knows that he ne'er knew my body,
But knows he thinks that he knows Isabel's.
Ang. This is a strange abuse. Let's see thy face.
Mar. My husband bids me; now I will unmask. [*Unveils.*]
This is that face, thou cruel Angelo,
Which once thou swor'st was worth the looking on.
This is the hand which with a vow'd contract
Was fast belock'd in thine. This is the body
That took away the match from Isabel
And did supply thee at thy garden house
In her imagin'd person.
Duke. Know you this woman?
Lucio. Carnally, she says.
Duke. Sirrah, no more!
Lucio. Enough, my lord.
Ang. My lord, I must confess I know this woman,
And five years since there was some speech of marriage
Betwixt myself and her; which was broke off,
Partly for that her promised proportions
Came short of composition, but in chief
For that her reputation was disvalued
In levity; since which time of five years
I never spake with her, saw her, nor heard from her,
Upon my faith and honour.
Mar. Noble prince,
As there comes light from heaven and words from breath,
As there is sense in truth and truth in virtue,
I am affianc'd this man's wife as strongly
As words could make up vows; and, my good lord,
But Tuesday night last gone, in's garden house,
He knew me as a wife. As this is true,
Let me in safety raise me from my knees,
Or else for ever be confixed here
A marble monument!
Ang. I did but smile till now.
Now, good my lord, give me the scope of justice;
My patience here is touch'd. I do perceive
These poor informal women are no more
But instruments of some more mightier member
That sets them on. Let me have way, my lord,
To find this practice out.
Duke. Ay, with my heart,
And punish them unto your height of pleasure.
Thou foolish friar, and thou pernicious woman,
Compact with her that's gone, think'st thou thy oaths,
Though they would swear down each particular saint,
Were testimonies 'gainst his worth and credit
That's seal'd in approbation? You, Lord Escalus,
Sit with my cousin. Lend him your kind pains
To find out this abuse, whence 'tis deriv'd.
There is another friar that set them on.
Let him be sent for.
Peter. Would he were here, my lord! for he indeed
Hath set the women on to this complaint.
Your provost knows the place where he abides,
And he may fetch him.
Duke. Go, do it instantly.
[*Exit Provost.*]
And you, my noble and well-warranted cousin,
Whom it concerns to hear this matter forth,
Do with your injuries as seems you best
In any chastisement. I for a while will leave you;
But stir not you till you have well determin'd
Upon these slanderers.
Escal. My lord, we'll do it throughly.
Exit [*Duke*].
Signior Lucio, did not you say you knew that Friar Lodowick to be a dishonest person?

Lucio. 'Cucullus non facit monachum.' Honest in nothing but in his clothes, and one that hath spoke most villanous speeches of the Duke.

Escal. We shall entreat you to abide here till he come, and enforce them against him. We shall find this friar a notable fellow.

Lucio. As any in Vienna, on my word.

Escal. Call that same Isabel here once again.
I would speak with her. [*Exit an Attendant.*]
Pray you, my lord, give me leave to question.
You shall see how I'll handle her.

Lucio. Not better than he, by her own report.

Escal. Say you?

Lucio. Marry, sir, I think, if you handled her privately, she would sooner confess; perchance, publicly, she'll be asham'd.

Enter *Duke* [in his Friar's habit], *Provost*; [*Officers* with] *Isabella.*

Escal. I will go darkly to work with her.

Lucio. That's the way: for women are light at midnight.

Escal. [*to Isabella*] Come on, mistress. Here's a gentlewoman denies all that you have said.

Lucio. My lord, here comes the rascal I spoke of — here, with the provost.

Escal. In very good time. Speak not you to him till we call upon you.

Lucio. Mum.

Escal. Come, sir, did you set these women on to slander Lord Angelo? They have confess'd you did.

Duke. 'Tis false.

Escal. How! Know you where you are?

Duke. Respect to your great place! and let the devil
Be sometime honour'd for his burning throne!
Where is the Duke? 'Tis he should hear me speak.

Escal. The Duke's in us, and we will hear you speak.
Look you speak justly.

Duke. Boldly, at least. But, O, poor souls,
Come you to seek the lamb here of the fox?
Good night to your redress! Is the Duke gone?
Then is your cause gone too. The Duke's unjust
Thus to retort your manifest appeal
And put your trial in the villain's mouth
Which here you come to accuse.

Lucio. This is the rascal. This is he I spoke of.

Escal. Why, thou unreverend and unhallowed friar,
Is't not enough thou hast suborn'd these women
To accuse this worthy man, but, in foul mouth,
And in the witness of his proper ear,
To call him villain? and then to glance from him
To th' Duke himself, to tax him with injustice?
Take him hence! To th' rack with him! We'll touse you
Joint by joint but we will know his purpose.
What? 'unjust'?

Duke. Be not so hot. The Duke
Dare no more stretch this finger of mine than he
Dare rack his own. His subject am I not,
Nor here provincial. My business in this state
Made me a looker-on here in Vienna,
Where I have seen corruption boil and bubble
Till it o'errun the stew; laws for all faults,
But faults so countenanc'd that the strong statutes
Stand like the forfeits in a barber's shop,
As much in mock as mark.

Escal. Slander to th' state! Away with him to prison!

Ang. What can you vouch against him, Signior Lucio?
Is this the man that you did tell us of?

Lucio. 'Tis he, my lord. Come hither, goodman baldpate. Do you know me?

Duke. I remember you, sir, by the sound of your voice. I met you at the prison in the absence of the Duke.

Lucio. O, did you so? And do you remember what you said of the Duke?

Duke. Most notedly, sir.

Lucio. Do you so, sir? And was the Duke a fleshmonger, a fool, and a coward, as you then reported him to be?

Duke. You must, sir, change persons with me ere you make that my report. You indeed spoke so of him, and much more, much worse.

Lucio. O thou damnable fellow! Did not I pluck thee by the nose for thy speeches?

Duke. I protest I love the Duke as I love myself.

Ang. Hark how the villain would close now, after his treasonable abuses!

Escal. Such a fellow is not to be talk'd withal. Away with him to prison! Where is the provost? Away with him to prison! Lay bolts enough upon him. Let him speak no more. Away with those giglets too, and with the other confederate companion!

Duke. [*to Provost*] Stay, sir; stay awhile.

Ang. What, resists he? Help him, Lucio.

Lucio. Come, sir; come, sir; come, sir! Foh, sir! Why, you bald-pated lying rascal, you must be hooded, must you? Show your knave's visage, with a pox to you! Show your sheep-biting face and be hang'd an hour! Will't not off?

[*Plucks off the friar's hood and discovers the Duke.*]

Duke. Thou art the first knave that e'er mad'st a duke.
First, provost, let me bail these gentle three.
[*To Lucio*] Sneak not away, sir; for the friar and you
Must have a word anon. — Lay hold on him!

Lucio. This may prove worse than hanging.

Duke. [*to Escalus*] What you have spoke I pardon. Sit you down.
We'll borrow place of him. [*To Angelo*] Sir, by your leave.
Hast thou or word, or wit, or impudence
That yet can do thee office? If thou hast,
Rely upon it till my tale be heard
And hold no longer out.

Ang. O my dread lord,
I should be guiltier than my guiltiness
To think I can be undiscernible
When I perceive your Grace, like pow'r divine,
Hath look'd upon my passes! Then, good prince,
No longer session hold upon my shame,
But let my trial be mine own confession.
Immediate sentence then, and sequent death,
Is all the grace I beg.

Duke. Come hither, Mariana.
Say, wast thou e'er contracted to this woman?
Ang. I was, my lord.
Duke. Go take her hence and marry her instantly.
Do you the office, friar; which consummate,
Return him here again. Go with him, provost.
Exeunt [Angelo, Mariana, Friar Peter, and Provost].
Escal. My lord, I am more amaz'd at his dishonour
Than at the strangeness of it.
Duke. Come hither, Isabel.
Your friar is now your prince. As I was then
Advertising and holy to your business,
Not changing heart with habit, I am still
Attorney'd at your service.
Isab. O, give me pardon
That I, your vassal, have employ'd and pain'd
Your unknown sovereignty!
Duke. You are pardon'd, Isabel;
And now, dear maid, be you as free to us.
Your brother's death I know sits at your heart;
And you may marvel why I obscur'd myself,
Labouring to save his life, and would not rather
Make rash remonstrance of my hidden pow'r
Than let him so be lost. O most kind maid,
It was the swift celerity of his death,
Which I did think with slower foot came on,
That brain'd my purpose. But peace be with him!
That life is better life, past fearing death,
Than that which lives to fear. Make it your comfort,
So happy is your brother.
Isab. I do, my lord.

Enter *Angelo, Mariana, [Friar] Peter, Provost.*

Duke. For this new-married man approaching here,
Whose salt imagination yet hath wrong'd
Your well-defended honour, you must pardon
For Mariana's sake. But as he adjudg'd your brother —
Being criminal in double violation
Of sacred chastity, and of promise-breach
Thereon dependent for your brother's life —
The very mercy of the law cries out
Most audible, even from his proper tongue,
'An Angelo for Claudio! death for death!'
Haste still pays haste, and leisure answers leisure;
Like doth quit like, and Measure still for Measure.
Then, Angelo, thy fault's thus manifested,
Which, though thou wouldst deny, denies thee vantage.
We do condemn thee to the very block
Where Claudio stoop'd to death, and with like haste.
Away with him!
Mar. O my most gracious lord,
I hope you will not mock me with a husband!
Duke. It is your husband mock'd you with a husband.
Consenting to the safeguard of your honour,
I thought your marriage fit. Else imputation,
For that he knew you, might reproach your life
And choke your good to come. For his possessions,
Although by confiscation they are ours,
We do enstate and widow you withal,
To buy you a better husband.
Mar. O my dear lord!
I crave no other, nor no better man.
Duke. Never crave him. We are definitive.
Mar. Gentle my liege — [*Kneels.*]
Duke. You do but lose your labour.
Away with him to death! — [*To Lucio*] Now, sir, to you!
Mar. O my good lord! Sweet Isabel, take my part;
Lend me your knees, and all my life to come
I'll lend you all my life to do you service.
Duke. Against all sense you do importune her.
Should she kneel down in mercy of this fact,
Her brother's ghost his paved bed would break
And take her hence in horror.
Mar. Isabel!
Sweet Isabel, do yet but kneel by me,
Hold up your hands, say nothing! I'll speak all.
They say best men are moulded out of faults,
And, for the most, become much more the better
For being a little bad. So may my husband.
O Isabel, will you not lend a knee?
Duke. He dies for Claudio's death.
Isab. Most bounteous sir, [*Kneels.*]
Look, if it please you, on this man condemn'd
As if my brother liv'd. I partly think
A due sincerity governed his deeds
Till he did look on me. Since it is so,
Let him not die. My brother had but justice
In that he did the thing for which he died.
For Angelo,
His act did not o'ertake his bad intent,
And must be buried but as an intent
That perish'd by the way. Thoughts are no subjects,
Intents but merely thoughts.
Mar. Merely, my lord.

Duke. Your suit 's unprofitable. Stand up, I say. [*They rise.*]
I have bethought me of another fault.
Provost, how came it Claudio was beheaded
At an unusual hour?
Prov. It was commanded so.
Duke. Had you a special warrant for the deed?
Prov. No, my good lord. It was by private message.
Duke. For which I do discharge you of your office.
Give up your keys.
Prov. Pardon me, noble lord.
I thought it was a fault, but knew it not;
Yet did repent me after more advice;
For testimony whereof, one in the prison,
That should by private order else have died,
I have reserv'd alive.
Duke. What's he?
Prov. His name is Barnardine.
Duke. I would thou hadst done so by Claudio.
Go fetch him hither; let me look upon him.
[*Exit Provost.*]
Escal. I am sorry one so learned and so wise
As you, Lord Angelo, have still appear'd,
Should slip so grossly, both in the heat of blood
And lack of temper'd judgment afterward.
Ang. I am sorry that such sorrow I procure;
And so deep sticks it in my penitent heart
That I crave death more willingly than mercy.
'Tis my deserving, and I do entreat it.

Enter *Barnardine* and *Provost, Claudio* [muffled], *Juliet.*

Duke. Which is that Barnardine?
Prov. This, my lord.
Duke. There was a friar told me of this man.
Sirrah, thou art said to have a stubborn soul
That apprehends no further than this world,
And squar'st thy life according. Thou'rt condemn'd.
But, for those earthly faults, I quit them all,
And pray thee take this mercy to provide
For better times to come. Friar, advise him;
I leave him to your hand. What muffled fellow 's that?
Prov. This is another prisoner that I sav'd,
Who should have died when Claudio lost his head,
As like almost to Claudio as himself.
[*Unmuffles Claudio.*]
Duke. [*to Isabella*] If he be like your brother, for his sake
Is he pardoned; and, for your lovely sake,
Give me your hand and say you will be mine,
He is my brother too. But fitter time for that!
By this Lord Angelo perceives he's safe;
Methinks I see a quick'ning in his eye.
Well, Angelo, your evil quits you well.
Look that you love your wife, her worth worth yours.
I find an apt remission in myself;
And yet here's one in place I cannot pardon.
[*To Lucio*] You, sirrah, that knew me for a fool, a coward,
One all of luxury, an ass, a madman!
Wherein have I deserved so of you
That you extol me thus?
Lucio. Faith, my lord, I spoke it but according to the trick. If you will hang me for it, you may; but I had rather it would please you I might be whipt.
Duke. Whipt first, sir, and hang'd after.
Proclaim it, provost, round about the city,
If any woman 's wrong'd by this lewd fellow
(As I have heard him swear himself there's one
Whom he begot with child) let her appear,
And he shall marry her. The nuptial finish'd,
Let him be whipt and hang'd.
Lucio. I beseech your Highness do not marry me to a whore! Your Highness said even now I made you a duke. Good my lord, do not recompense me in making me a cuckold.
Duke. Upon mine honour, thou shalt marry her.
Thy slanders I forgive, and therewithal
Remit thy other forfeits. Take him to prison,
And see our pleasure herein executed.
Lucio. Marrying a punk, my lord, is pressing to death, whipping, and hanging.
Duke. Slandering a prince deserves it.
[*Exeunt Officers with Lucio.*]
She, Claudio, that you wrong'd, look you restore.
Joy to you, Mariana! Love her, Angelo.
I have confess'd her, and I know her virtue.
Thanks, good friend Escalus, for thy much goodness;
There's more behind that is more gratulate.
Thanks, provost, for thy care and secrecy:
We shall employ thee in a worthier place.
Forgive him, Angelo, that brought you home
The head of Ragozine for Claudio's;
Th' offence pardons itself. Dear Isabel,
I have a motion much imports your good,
Whereto if you'll a willing ear incline,
What's mine is yours, and what is yours is mine.
So bring us to our palace, where we'll show
What's yet behind that's meet you all should know.
[*Exeunt.*]

The Comedy of Errors

The Comedy of Errors was first printed in the Folio of 1623, which affords a reasonably accurate text. There may be a cut here and there; but, if so, nothing of any consequence has been lost. It was performed at Gray's Inn on December 28, 1594. The punning reference to France as 'arm'd and reverted, making war against her heir' (iii, 2, 126) may carry the date of composition back to 1593, for the war in question came to an end in July of that year. But this evidence is not conclusive, for Dromio's jest would still be pertinent in 1594, when the rebellion was fresh in everybody's memory. A date as early as 1592 has been suggested on the basis of a possible quotation ('heart and good will, but neuer a ragge of money') by Nashe in his *Foure Letters Confuted*, registered on January 12, 1593. Compare Dromio of Ephesus (iv, 4, 88–89):

> Money by me? Heart and good will you might,
> But surely, master, not a rag of money.

The coincidence is striking and may be significant; but the phrase was obviously proverbial. Another parallel passage, from *Arden of Feversham* (registered on April 3, 1592, and printed in the same year), is too trivial to deserve attention. In any case, The Comedy of Errors is one of Shakespeare's earliest works. 1592 or 1593 is a reasonable date, but neither 1591 nor 1594 is out of the question.

The plot comes in the main from the *Menaechmi* of Plautus, but there is also substantial borrowing from his *Amphitruo*. This is most obvious in the first scene of the third act, but it appears in details of thought, phrase, or situation in almost every part of the play. The farcical substance of the Plautine plot is framed in a new romantic setting which dignifies it and raises the interest above the level of merely comic entertainment: the play opens with the tragic plight of the distressed Ægeon and closes with his happy reunion with his long-lost wife. For this setting Shakespeare had recourse to the old and vastly popular romance of *Apollonius of Tyre*, probably in the version which he found in Gower's *Confessio Amantis* and afterwards elaborated in his *Pericles*. Besides this tragicomical envelopment he has interwoven the romantic episode of the loves of Luciana and the Syracusan Antipholus. In thus raising the tone of the play above that of the *Menaechmi*, Shakespeare was influenced by the *Amphitruo*, which is really a tragicomedy. Thus the *Amphitruo*, besides contributing to the plot, exercised a pervasively dignifying effect, even in those scenes which are original. No English translation of the *Menaechmi* is recorded before 1594, when that of a certain W[illiam] W[arner] was registered; no English version of the *Amphitruo* is known before the late seventeenth century. That Shakespeare was familiar with both plays in the original may be taken for granted. Of course he learned to read Latin if he had any education at all. Ben Jonson's famous remark about 'small Latin and less Greek' meant something very different in those days from what it suggests to a modern reader. It should be read in its context. Jonson is exalting Shakespeare above all preceding dramatists, modern or classical. He is not describing him as an ignoramus but is emphasizing his originality by insisting that he owed little to the dramatists of Greece and Rome.

Many passages might be quoted to show that Shakespeare, though not translating, had the details of the Latin phraseology constantly in mind. The transformation is interesting. Compare the words of Antipholus of Syracuse in i, 2, 33–40, with the following speech of Messenio in the *Menaechmi* (ii, 1):

'What limit will there be to your search? This is the sixth year since we began to give our whole attention to this enterprise. We have traversed the land of the Istrians, of the Spaniards, of the Massilians, of the Illyrians, the whole Adriatic and the Ionian sea, Lower Italy and all the Italian coast. If you were hunting for a needle, I think you would have found it long ago, if it were to be found at all. We are seeking a dead man among the living; for if he were alive, we should have found him long ago.'

There is no likelihood that *The Historie of Error*, a lost play given by the St. Paul's boy actors at Hampton Court on January 1, 1577, had anything to do with Shakespeare's comedy, though scholars have dallied with the conjecture that he may have utilized it as a source. We know nothing about the contents of this *Historie*. The title suggests rather a morality (with personified abstractions for its personages) than a Plautine adaptation.

A curious question is raised by the stage directions in the Folio. Antipholus of Syracuse is styled 'Antipholis Erotes' in the first stage direction of i, 2, and 'Antipholis Errotis' in that of ii, 2; Antipholus of Ephesus is styled 'Antipholis Sereptus' in the first stage direction in Act ii. *Sereptus* is doubtless a misprint for *Surreptus* ('stolen'), which the Plautine Prologue used (as well as *surrepticius*) with reference to the twin who corresponds to the Ephesian Antipholus. *Errotis* and *Erotes* may be misprints for *Erraticus* or *Errans*, an appropriate adjective for Antipholus of Syracuse:

I to the world am like a drop of water
That in the ocean seeks another drop.
. . . .
So I, to find a mother and a brother,
In quest of them (unhappy) lose myself.

The natural inference from these terms is that Shakespeare used Plautus in the original.

The variety in metre is noteworthy. We have blank verse, decasyllabic couplets, decasyllabic verses rhyming alternately, and much rhyme doggerel in long irregular lines. This variety, which has been sometimes taken as evidence that the Comedy is an old play worked over, rather indicates Shakespeare's wish to imitate the variety that he found in Plautus. The form used by him always fits the mood, the speaker, and the situation. The alternate rhymes have a lyrical effect and are appropriate in the love scene (iii, 2), which is original. The doggerel, which has given particular offence to the fastidious, is used by the Dromios, or by others in conversing with them in farcical dialogue (as in iii, 1); and it was certainly a happy thought to make Dromio of Ephesus adopt it when he closes the play by going off the stage with his brother of Syracuse:

We came into the world like brother and brother;
And now let's go hand in hand, not one before another.

THE COMEDY OF ERRORS

[Dramatis Personæ.

Solinus, Duke of Ephesus.
Ægeon, a merchant of Syracuse.
Antipholus of Ephesus, } twin brothers, and sons
Antipholus of Syracuse, } to *Ægeon* and *Æmilia.*
Dromio of Ephesus, } twin brothers, and attendants on the two *Antipholuses.*
Dromio of Syracuse, }
Balthazar, a merchant.
Angelo, a goldsmith.
A Merchant of Ephesus, friend to *Antipholus* of Syracuse.
Another Merchant, to whom *Angelo* is a debtor.
Pinch, a schoolmaster.

Æmilia, wife to *Ægeon*, an abbess at Ephesus.
Adriana, wife to *Antipholus* of Ephesus.
Luciana, her sister.
Luce, servant to *Adriana.*
A Courtesan.
Jailer, Officers, and Attendants.

SCENE. — *Ephesus.*]

ACT I. Scene I. [*A hall of judgment in the* Duke's *Palace.*]

Enter the *Duke of Ephesus*, with the *Merchant of Syracusa*, [*Ægeon*,] *Jailer*, and other *Attendants.*

Æge. Proceed, Solinus, to procure my fall,
And by the doom of death end woes and all.
Duke. Merchant of Syracusa, plead no more;
I am not partial to infringe our laws.
The enmity and discord which of late
Sprung from the rancorous outrage of your duke
To merchants our well-dealing countrymen,
Who, wanting guilders to redeem their lives,
Have seal'd his rigorous statutes with their bloods,
Excludes all pity from our threat'ning looks.
For, since the mortal and intestine jars
'Twixt thy seditious countrymen and us,
It hath in solemn synods been decreed,
Both by the Syracusians and ourselves,
To admit no traffic to our adverse towns.
Nay more, if any born at Ephesus
Be seen at Syracusian marts and fairs —
Again, if any Syracusian born
Come to the bay of Ephesus — he dies,
His goods confiscate to the Duke's dispose,
Unless a thousand marks be levied
To quit the penalty and to ransom him.
Thy substance, valued at the highest rate,
Cannot amount unto a hundred marks.
Therefore by law thou art condemn'd to die.
Æge. Yet this my comfort: when your words are done,
My woes end likewise with the evening sun.
Duke. Well, Syracusian, say in brief the cause
Why thou departed'st from thy native home,
And for what cause thou cam'st to Ephesus.
Æge. A heavier task could not have been impos'd
Than I to speak my griefs unspeakable.
Yet, that the world may witness that my end
Was wrought by nature, not by vile offence,
I'll utter what my sorrow gives me leave.
In Syracusa was I born, and wed
Unto a woman, happy but for me,
And by me too, had not our hap been bad.
With her I liv'd in joy, our wealth increas'd
By prosperous voyages I often made
To Epidamnum, till my factor's death
And the great care of goods at randon left
Drew me from kind embracements of my spouse;
From whom my absence was not six months old
Before herself (almost at fainting under
The pleasing punishment that women bear)
Had made provision for her following me,
And soon and safe arrived where I was.
There had she not been long but she became
A joyful mother of two goodly sons,
And, which was strange, the one so like the other
As could not be distinguish'd but by names.
That very hour, and in the selfsame inn,
A meaner woman was delivered
Of such a burthen, male twins, both alike.
Those, for their parents were exceeding poor,
I bought, and brought up to attend my sons.

My wife, not meanly proud of two such boys,
Made daily motions for our home return.
Unwilling I agreed — alas, too soon!
We came aboard.
A league from Epidamnum had we sail'd
Before the always-wind-obeying deep
Gave any tragic instance of our harm.
But longer did we not retain much hope;
For what obscured light the heavens did grant
Did but convey unto our fearful minds
A doubtful warrant of immediate death;
Which though myself would gladly have embrac'd,
Yet the incessant weepings of my wife,
Weeping before for what she saw must come,
And piteous plainings of the pretty babes,
That mourn'd for fashion, ignorant what to fear,
Forc'd me to seek delays for them and me.
And this it was, for other means was none:
The sailors sought for safety by our boat
And left the ship, then sinking ripe, to us;
My wife, more careful for the latter-born,
Had fast'ned him unto a small spare mast,
Such as seafaring men provide for storms;
To him one of the other twins was bound,
Whilst I had been like heedful of the other;
The children thus dispos'd, my wife and I,
Fixing our eyes on whom our care was fix'd,
Fast'ned ourselves at either end the mast
And, floating straight, obedient to the stream,
Were carried towards Corinth, as we thought.
At length the sun, gazing upon the earth,
Dispers'd those vapours that offended us;
And by the benefit of his wished light
The seas wax'd calm, and we discovered
Two ships from far making amain to us —
Of Corinth that, of Epidaurus this.
But ere they came — O, let me say no more!
Gather the sequel by that went before.

Duke. Nay, forward, old man! do not break off so,
For we may pity though not pardon thee.

Æge. O, had the gods done so, I had not now
Worthily term'd them merciless to us!
For, ere the ships could meet by twice five leagues,
We were encount'red by a mighty rock,
Which being violently borne upon,
Our helpful ship was splitted in the midst;
So that, in this unjust divorce of us,
Fortune had left to both of us alike
What to delight in, what to sorrow for.
Her part, poor soul, seeming as burdened
With lesser weight but not with lesser woe,
Was carried with more speed before the wind,
And in our sight they three were taken up
By fishermen of Corinth, as we thought.
At length, another ship had seiz'd on us,
And, knowing whom it was their hap to save,
Gave healthful welcome to their shipwrack'd guests,
And would have reft the fishers of their prey,
Had not their bark been very slow of sail;
And therefore homeward did they bend their course.
Thus have you heard me sever'd from my bliss,
That by misfortunes was my life prolong'd
To tell sad stories of my own mishaps.

Duke. And, for the sake of them thou sorrowest for,
Do me the favour to dilate at full
What hath befall'n of them and thee till now.

Æge. My youngest boy, and yet my eldest care,
At eighteen years became inquisitive
After his brother; and importun'd me
That his attendant — so his case was like,
Reft of his brother, but retain'd his name —
Might bear him company in the quest of him;
Whom whilst I laboured of a love to see,
I hazarded the loss of whom I lov'd.
Five summers have I spent in farthest Greece,
Roaming clean through the bounds of Asia,
And, coasting homeward, came to Ephesus;
Hopeless to find, yet loath to leave unsought
Or that, or any place that harbours men.
But here must end the story of my life;
And happy were I in my timely death,
Could all my travels warrant me they live.

Duke. Hapless Ægeon, whom the fates have mark'd
To bear the extremity of dire mishap!
Now trust me, were it not against our laws,
Against my crown, my oath, my dignity,
Which princes, would they, may not disannul,
My soul should sue as advocate for thee.
But, though thou art adjudged to the death,
And passed sentence may not be recall'd
But to our honour's great disparagement,
Yet will I favour thee in what I can.
Therefore, merchant, I'll limit thee this day
To seek thy life by beneficial help.
Try all the friends thou hast in Ephesus;
Beg thou or borrow to make up the sum,
And live; if no, then thou art doom'd to die.
Jailer, take him to thy custody.

Jail. I will, my lord.

Æge. Hopeless and helpless doth Ægeon wend,
But to procrastinate his liveless end.

Exeunt.

[Scene II. *Ephesus. The Mart.*]

Enter *Antipholus Erotes* [*of Syracuse*], a *Merchant* [of Ephesus], and *Dromio* [*of Syracuse*].

Eph. Mer. Therefore give out you are of Epidamnum,
Lest that your goods too soon be confiscate.
This very day a Syracusian merchant
Is apprehended for arrival here,
And, not being able to buy out his life,
According to the statute of the town,
Dies ere the weary sun set in the west.
There is your money that I had to keep.

S. Ant. Go bear it to the Centaur, where we host,
And stay there, Dromio, till I come to thee.
Within this hour it will be dinner time;
Till that I'll view the manners of the town,
Peruse the traders, gaze upon the buildings,
And then return, and sleep within mine inn,
For with long travel I am stiff and weary.
Get thee away.

S. Dro. Many a man would take you at your word
And go indeed, having so good a mean. *Exit.*

S. Ant. A trusty villain, sir, that very oft,
When I am dull with care and melancholy,
Lightens my humour with his merry jests.
What, will you walk with me about the town,
And then go to my inn and dine with me?

Eph. Mer. I am invited, sir, to certain merchants,
Of whom I hope to make much benefit.
I crave your pardon. Soon at five o'clock,
Please you, I'll meet with you upon the mart,
And afterward consort you till bedtime.
My present business calls me from you now.

S. Ant. Farewell till then. I will go lose myself
And wander up and down to view the city.

Eph. Mer. Sir, I commend you to your own content. *Exit.*

S. Ant. He that commends me to mine own content
Commends me to the thing I cannot get.
I to the world am like a drop of water
That in the ocean seeks another drop,
Who, falling there to find his fellow forth
(Unseen, inquisitive), confounds himself.
So I, to find a mother and a brother,
In quest of them (unhappy) lose myself.

Enter *Dromio of Ephesus.*

Here comes the almanac of my true date.
What now? How chance thou art return'd so soon?

E. Dro. Return'd so soon? Rather approach'd too late!
The capon burns, the pig falls from the spit;
The clock hath strucken twelve upon the bell —
My mistress made it one upon my cheek;
She is so hot, because the meat is cold;
The meat is cold, because you come not home;
You come not home, because you have no stomach;
You have no stomach, having broke your fast;
But we, that know what 'tis to fast and pray,
Are penitent for your default to-day.

S. Ant. Stop in your wind, sir! Tell me this, I pray,
Where have you left the money that I gave you?

E. Dro. O, sixpence that I had a Wednesday last
To pay the saddler for my mistress' crupper.
The saddler had it, sir; I kept it not.

S. Ant. I am not in a sportive humour now.
Tell me, and dally not, where is the money?
We being strangers here, how dar'st thou trust
So great a charge from thine own custody?

E. Dro. I pray you jest, sir, as you sit at dinner.
I from my mistress come to you in post.
If I return, I shall be post indeed,
For she will score your fault upon my pate.
Methinks your maw, like mine, should be your clock
And strike you home without a messenger.

S. Ant. Come, Dromio, come! These jests are out of season;
Reserve them till a merrier hour than this.
Where is the gold I gave in charge to thee?

E. Dro. To me, sir? Why, you gave no gold to me!

S. Ant. Come on, sir knave! Have done your foolishness
And tell me how thou hast dispos'd thy charge.

E. Dro. My charge was but to fetch you from the mart
Home to your house, the Phœnix, sir, to dinner.
My mistress and her sister stays for you.

S. Ant. Now, as I am a Christian, answer me
In what safe place you have bestow'd my money,
Or I shall break that merry sconce of yours
That stands on tricks when I am undispos'd.
Where is the thousand marks thou hadst of me?

E. Dro. I have some marks of yours upon my pate,
Some of my mistress' marks upon my shoulders;
But not a thousand marks between you both.
If I should pay your worship those again,
Perchance you will not bear them patiently.
S. Ant. Thy mistress' marks? What mistress, slave, hast thou?
E. Dro. Your worship's wife, my mistress at the Phœnix;
She that doth fast till you come home to dinner
And prays that you will hie you home to dinner.
S. Ant. What, wilt thou flout me thus unto my face,
Being forbid? There, take you that, sir knave!
[*Beats him.*]
E. Dro. What mean you, sir? For God sake hold your hands!
Nay, an you will not, sir, I'll take my heels.
Exit.
S. Ant. Upon my life, by some device or other
The villain is o'erraught of all my money!
They say this town is full of cozenage;
As, nimble jugglers that deceive the eye,
Dark-working sorcerers that change the mind,
Soul-killing witches that deform the body,
Disguised cheaters, prating mountebanks,
And many such-like liberties of sin.
If it prove so, I will be gone the sooner.
I'll to the Centaur to go seek this slave.
I greatly fear my money is not safe. *Exit.*

ACT II. [Scene I. *The house of* Antipholus of Ephesus.]

Enter *Adriana*, Wife to *Antipholus Sereptus* [*of Ephesus*], with *Luciana*, her Sister.

Adr. Neither my husband nor the slave return'd
That in such haste I sent to seek his master?
Sure, Luciana, it is two o'clock.
Luc. Perhaps some merchant hath invited him,
And from the mart he's somewhere gone to dinner.
Good sister, let us dine, and never fret.
A man is master of his liberty.
Time is their master; and when they see time,
They'll go or come. If so, be patient, sister.
Adr. Why should their liberty than ours be more?
Luc. Because their business still lies out-o'-door.
Adr. Look, when I serve him so, he takes it ill.
Luc. O, know he is the bridle of your will.
Adr. There's none but asses will be bridled so.
Luc. Why, headstrong liberty is lash'd with woe.
There's nothing situate under heaven's eye
But hath his bound in earth, in sea, in sky.
The beasts, the fishes, and the winged fowls
Are their males' subjects and at their controls.
Men, more divine, the masters of all these,
Lords of the wide world and wild wat'ry seas,
Indu'd with intellectual sense and souls,
Of more preëminence than fish and fowls,
Are masters to their females, and their lords.
Then let your will attend on their accords.
Adr. This servitude makes you to keep unwed.
Luc. Not this, but troubles of the marriage bed.
Adr. But, were you wedded, you would bear some sway.
Luc. Ere I learn love, I'll practise to obey.
Adr. How if your husband start some otherwhere?
Luc. Till he come home again, I would forbear.
Adr. Patience unmov'd, no marvel though she pause;
They can be meek that have no other cause.
A wretched soul bruis'd with adversity
We bid be quiet when we hear it cry;
But were we burd'ned with like weight of pain,
As much, or more, we should ourselves complain.
So thou, that hast no unkind mate to grieve thee,
With urging helpless patience wouldst relieve me;
But if thou live to see like right bereft,
This fool-begg'd patience in thee will be left.
Luc. Well, I will marry one day, but to try.
Here comes your man. Now is your husband nigh.

Enter *Dromio* [*of*] *Ephesus.*

Adr. Say, is your tardy master now at hand?
E. Dro. Nay, he's at two hands with me, and that my two ears can witness.
Adr. Say, didst thou speak with him? Know'st thou his mind?

E. Dro. Ay, ay, he told his mind upon mine ear.
Beshrew his hand, I scarce could understand it!

Luc. Spake he so doubtfully thou couldst not feel his meaning?

E. Dro. Nay, he struck so plainly I could too well feel his blows; and withal so doubtfully that I could scarce understand them.

Adr. But say, I prithee, is he coming home?
It seems he hath great care to please his wife.

E. Dro. Why, mistress, sure my master is horn-mad.

Adr. Horn-mad, thou villain?

E. Dro. I mean not cuckold-mad;
But sure he is stark mad.
When I desir'd him to come home to dinner,
He ask'd me for a thousand marks in gold.
''Tis dinner time,' quoth I. 'My gold!' quoth he.
'Your meat doth burn,' quoth I. 'My gold!' quoth he.
'Will you come home?' quoth I. 'My gold!' quoth he.
'Where is the thousand marks I gave thee, villain?'
'The pig,' quoth I, 'is burn'd.' 'My gold!' quoth he.
'My mistress, sir —' quoth I. 'Hang up thy mistress!
I know not thy mistress. Out on thy mistress!'

Luc. Quoth who?

E. Dro. Quoth my master.
'I know,' quoth he, 'no house, no wife, no mistress.'
So that my arrant, due unto my tongue,
I thank him, I bare home upon my shoulders;
For, in conclusion, he did beat me there.

Adr. Go back again, thou slave, and fetch him home!

E. Dro. Go back again, and be new beaten home?
For God's sake send some other messenger.

Adr. Back, slave, or I will break thy pate across!

E. Dro. And he will bless that cross with other beating.
Between you I shall have a holy head.

Adr. Hence, prating peasant! Fetch thy master home.

E. Dro. Am I so round with you, as you with me,
That like a football you do spurn me thus?
You spurn me hence, and he will spurn me hether.
If I last in this service, you must case me in leather. [*Exit.*]

Luc. Fie, how impatience low'reth in your face!

Adr. His company must do his minions grace
Whilst I at home starve for a merry look.
Hath homely age th' alluring beauty took
From my poor cheek? Then he hath wasted it.
Are my discourses dull? barren my wit?
If voluble and sharp discourse be marr'd,
Unkindness blunts it, more than marble hard.
Do their gay vestments his affections bait?
That's not my fault — he's master of my state.
What ruins are in me that can be found
By him not ruin'd? Then is he the ground
Of my defeatures. My decayed fair
A sunny look of his would soon repair.
But, too unruly deer, he breaks the pale
And feeds from home. Poor I am but his stale.

Luc. Self-harming jealousy — fie, beat it hence!

Adr. Unfeeling fools can with such wrongs dispense.
I know his eye doth homage otherwhere,
Or else what lets it but he would be here?
Sister, you know he promis'd me a chain.
Would that alone alone he would detain,
So he would keep fair quarter with his bed!
I see the jewel best enamelled
Will lose his beauty; and though gold bides still
That others touch, yet often touching will
Wear gold; and no man that hath a name,
But falsehood and corruption doth it shame.
Since that my beauty cannot please his eye,
I'll weep what's left away, and weeping die.

Luc. How many fond fools serve mad jealousy! *Exeunt.*

[Scene II. *The Mart.*]

Enter *Antipholus Erotes* [*of Syracuse*].

S. Ant. The gold I gave to Dromio is laid up
Safe at the Centaur, and the heedful slave
Is wand'red forth in care to seek me out.
By computation and mine host's report,
I could not speak with Dromio since at first
I sent him from the mart. See, here he comes.

Enter *Dromio of Syracuse.*

How now, sir? Is your merry humour alter'd?
As you love strokes, so jest with me again.
You know no Centaur? You receiv'd no gold?

Your mistress sent to have me home to dinner?
My house was at the Phœnix? Wast thou mad
That thus so madly thou didst answer me?
S. Dro. What answer, sir? When spake I such a word?
S. Ant. Even now, even here, not half an hour since.
S. Dro. I did not see you since you sent me hence
Home to the Centaur with the gold you gave me.
S. Ant. Villain, thou didst deny the gold's receipt
And told'st me of a mistress and a dinner,
For which I hope thou felt'st I was displeas'd.
S. Dro. I am glad to see you in this merry vein.
What means this jest? I pray you, master, tell me.
S. Ant. Yea, dost thou jeer and flout me in the teeth?
Think'st thou I jest? Hold, take thou that, and that! *Beats Dromio.*
S. Dro. Hold, sir, for God's sake! Now your jest is earnest.
Upon what bargain do you give it me?
S. Ant. Because that I familiarly sometimes
Do use you for my fool and chat with you,
Your sauciness will jest upon my love
And make a common of my serious hours.
When the sun shines let foolish gnats make sport,
But creep in crannies when he hides his beams.
If you will jest with me, know my aspect
And fashion your demeanour to my looks,
Or I will beat this method in your sconce.

S. Dro. Sconce call you it? So you would leave battering, I had rather have it a head. An you use these blows long, I must get a sconce for my head, and insconce it too, or else I shall seek my wit in my shoulders. But I pray, sir, why am I beaten?

S. Ant. Dost thou not know?

S. Dro. Nothing, sir, but that I am beaten.

S. Ant. Shall I tell you why?

S. Dro. Ay, sir, and wherefore. For they say every why hath a wherefore.

S. Ant. Why first — for flouting me; and then wherefore —
For urging it the second time to me.
S. Dro. Was there ever any man thus beaten out of season,
When in the why and the wherefore is neither rhyme nor reason?
Well, sir, I thank you.
S. Ant. Thank me, sir? For what?

S. Dro. Marry, sir, for this something that you gave me for nothing.

S. Ant. I'll make you amends next, to give you nothing for something. But say, sir, is it dinner time?

S. Dro. No, sir. I think the meat wants that I have.

S. Ant. In good time, sir! What's that?

S. Dro. Basting.

S. Ant. Well, sir, then 'twill be dry.

S. Dro. If it be, sir, I pray you eat none of it.

S. Ant. Your reason?

S. Dro. Lest it make you choleric and purchase me another dry basting.

S. Ant. Well, sir, learn to jest in good time. There's a time for all things.

S. Dro. I durst have denied that before you were so choleric.

S. Ant. By what rule, sir?

S. Dro. Marry, sir, by a rule as plain as the plain bald pate of Father Time himself.

S. Ant. Let's hear it.

S. Dro. There's no time for a man to recover his hair that grows bald by nature.

S. Ant. May he not do it by fine and recovery?

S. Dro. Yes, to pay a fine for a periwig and recover the lost hair of another man.

S. Ant. Why is Time such a niggard of hair, being, as it is, so plentiful an excrement?

S. Dro. Because it is a blessing that he bestows on beasts; and what he hath scanted men in hair, he hath given them in wit.

S. Ant. Why, but there's many a man hath more hair than wit.

S. Dro. Not a man of those but he hath the wit to lose his hair.

S. Ant. Why, thou didst conclude hairy men plain dealers without wit.

S. Dro. The plainer dealer, the sooner lost. Yet he loseth it in a kind of policy.

S. Ant. For what reason?

S. Dro. For two, and sound ones too.

S. Ant. Nay, not sound, I pray you!

S. Dro. Sure ones then.

S. Ant. Nay, not sure, in a thing falsing.

S. Dro. Certain ones then.

S. Ant. Name them.

S. Dro. The one, to save the money that he spends in trimming; the other, that at dinner they should not drop in his porridge.

S. Ant. You would all this time have prov'd there is no time for all things.

S. Dro. Marry, and did, sir! namely, no time to recover hair lost by nature.

Donald Pleasance as Dromio of Syracuse and Maurice Whittaker as a citizen of Ephesus in Shakespeare's tale of the tangled affairs of two pairs of twins

THE COMEDY OF ERRORS

PHOTOGRAPHS BY LISEL HAAS
PRODUCED BY THE BIRMINGHAM REPERTORY COMPANY

Ninian Brodie as Solinus, Duke of Ephesus, who decreed that any citizen of Syracuse found in his city be sentenced to death unless he pay the state a princely ransom

Having dispatched his man Dromio to await him at an inn, Antipholus of Syracuse (Gordon Davies) asks the merchant (Tony Steedman) who befriended him to dine with him, but the merchant, with a leer at the ladies of the town, pleads prior appointments and promises to meet Antipholus later at the market of Ephesus *(Act I, Scene II)*

"What! wilt thou flout me thus unto my face, being forbid? There, take you that, sir knave." Mistaking Dromio of Ephesus (James Ottaway) for his own servant, Antipholus of Syracuse beats him when he denies knowledge of the money supposedly left in his charge *(Act I, Scene II)*

"Come, I will fasten on this sleeve of thine; thou art an elm, my husband, I a vine." Adriana (Elizabeth Clifford) mistakes Antipholus of Syracuse for her husband, to the great dismay of his servant *(Act II, Scene II)*

"If thou art chang'd to aught, 'tis to an ass." Luciana (Patricia Russell) mistakes Dromio of Syracuse for his twin and teases him when, in his bewilderment, he thinks he has been transformed *(Act II, Scene II)*

"Why call you me love? call my sister so." Believing Antipholus of Syracuse is her brother-in-law, Luciana rebukes him for making love to her *(Act III, Scene II)*

"Come, come, Antipholus; we dine too late." Mistaking the twin from Syracuse for her husband, Adriana urges Antipholus to come in with her to dinner *(Act II, Scene II)*

"What art thou that keep'st me out from the house I owe?" Antipholus of Ephesus returns home to find his door is locked against him and an armed man on watch within *(Act III, Scene I)*

"Come, where's the chain? I pray you, let me see it." Antipholus of Ephesus demands of the goldsmith Angelo (Bruce Fisk) the chain which was already given his twin *(Act IV, Scene I)*

"Is that the chain you promis'd me to-day?" The Courtezan (Betty Linton) happens to encounter Antipholus of Syracuse wearing the gold chain he has just received from Angelo. Taking him for his brother, she reminds him of his promise to give her such a chain *(Act IV, Scene III)*

"Five hundred ducats, villain, for a rope?" Antipholus of Ephesus (Eric Porter) beats his Dromio for bringing him a coil of rope whereas he had sent him (actually the other twin) for money for bail *(Act IV, Scene IV)*

"Mistress, both man and master is possess'd." The schoolmaster Pinch (Tony Steedman) tells Adriana and Luciana that Antipholus of Ephesus and his man are mad *(Act IV, Scene IV)*

"If any friend will pay the sum for him, he shall not die; so much we tender him." The duke announces he will pardon Aegeon (Peter Bentley), the father of the twins from Syracuse, if anyone will stand surety for the ransom due *(Act V, Scene I)*

"Be quiet, people. Wherefore throng you hither?" The Abbess (Barbara Cavan) inquires why Adriana and Luciana are pursuing Antipholus of Syracuse and his Dromio *(Act V, Scene I)*

S. Ant. But your reason was not substantial, why there is no time to recover.

S. Dro. Thus I mend it: Time himself is bald, and therefore to the world's end will have bald followers.

S. Ant. I knew 'twould be a bald conclusion.
But, soft! Who wafts us yonder?

Enter *Adriana* and *Luciana*.

Adr. Ay, ay, Antipholus! look strange and frown!
Some other mistress hath thy sweet aspects.
I am not Adriana nor thy wife.
The time was once when thou unurg'd wouldst vow
That never words were music to thine ear,
That never object pleasing in thine eye,
That never touch well welcome to thy hand,
That never meat sweet-savour'd in thy taste,
Unless I spake or look'd or touch'd or carv'd to thee.
How comes it now, my husband, O, how comes it,
That thou art then estranged from thyself?
Thyself I call it, being strange to me,
That, undividable incorporate,
Am better than thy dear self's better part.
Ah, do not tear away thyself from me!
For know, my love, as easy mayst thou fall
A drop of water in the breaking gulf
And take unmingled thence that drop again
Without addition or diminishing
As take from me thyself, and not me too.
How dearly would it touch thee to the quick,
Shouldst thou but hear I were licentious
And that this body, consecrate to thee,
By ruffian lust should be contaminate!
Wouldst thou not spit at me and spurn at me,
And hurl the name of husband in my face,
And tear the stain'd skin off my harlot brow,
And from my false hand cut the wedding ring
And break it with a deep-divorcing vow?
I know thou canst; and therefore see thou do it.
I am possess'd with an adulterate blot,
My blood is mingled with the crime of lust;
For, if we two be one, and thou play false,
I do digest the poison of thy flesh,
Being strumpeted by thy contagion.
Keep then fair league and truce with thy true bed,
I live unstain'd, thou undishonoured.

S. Ant. Plead you to me, fair dame? I know you not.
In Ephesus I am but two hours old,
As strange unto your town as to your talk,
Who, every word by all my wit being scann'd,
Want wit in all one word to understand.

Luc. Fie, brother! how the world is chang'd with you!
When were you wont to use my sister thus?
She sent for you by Dromio home to dinner.

S. Ant. By Dromio?

S. Dro. By me?

Adr. By thee, and this thou didst return from him:
That he did buffet thee, and in his blows
Denied my house for his, me for his wife.

S. Ant. Did you converse, sir, with this gentlewoman?
What is the course and drift of your compact?

S. Dro. I, sir? I never saw her till this time.

S. Ant. Villain, thou liest! for even her very words
Didst thou deliver to me on the mart.

S. Dro. I never spake with her in all my life.

S. Ant. How can she thus then call us by our names,
Unless it be by inspiration?

Adr. How ill agrees it with your gravity
To counterfeit thus grossly with your slave,
Abetting him to thwart me in my mood!
Be it my wrong you are from me exempt,
But wrong not that wrong with a more contempt.
Come, I will fasten on this sleeve of thine.
Thou art an elm, my husband; I a vine,
Whose weakness, married to thy stronger state,
Makes me with thy strength to communicate.
If aught possess thee from me, it is dross,
Usurping ivy, brier, or idle moss,
Who all, for want of pruning, with intrusion
Infect thy sap and live on thy confusion.

S. Ant. [*aside*] To me she speaks. She moves me for her theme.
What, was I married to her in my dream?
Or sleep I now, and think I hear all this?
What error drives our eyes and ears amiss?
Until I know this sure uncertainty,
I'll entertain the offer'd fallacy.

Luc. Dromio, go bid the servants spread for dinner.

S. Dro. O for my beads! I cross me for a sinner.
This is the fairy land. O spite of spites!
We talk with goblins, owls, and sprites.
If we obey them not, this will ensue:
They'll suck our breath or pinch us black and blue.

Luc. Why prat'st thou to thyself and answer'st not?

Dromio, thou drone, thou snail, thou slug, thou sot!
S. Dro. I am transformed, master, am not I?
S. Ant. I think thou art in mind, and so am I.
S. Dro. Nay, master, both in mind and in my shape.
S. Ant. Thou hast thine own form.
S. Dro. No, I am an ape.
Luc. If thou art chang'd to aught, 'tis to an ass.
S. Dro. 'Tis true! She rides me, and I long for grass.
'Tis so, I am an ass; else it could never be
But I should know her as well as she knows me.
Adr. Come, come, no longer will I be a fool,
To put the finger in the eye and weep
Whilst man and master laughs my woes to scorn.
Come, sir, to dinner. Dromio, keep the gate.
Husband, I'll dine above with you to-day
And shrive you of a thousand idle pranks.
Sirrah, if any ask you for your master,
Say he dines forth, and let no creature enter.
Come, sister. Dromio, play the porter well.
S. Ant. [*aside*] Am I in earth, in heaven, or in hell?
Sleeping or waking? mad or well-advis'd?
Known unto these, and to myself disguis'd!
I'll say as they say, and persever so,
And in this mist at all adventures go.
S. Dro. Master, shall I be porter at the gate?
Adr. Ay, and let none enter, lest I break your pate.
Luc. Come, come, Antipholus, we dine too late. [*Exeunt.*]

ACT III. Scene I. [*Before the house of* Antipholus of Ephesus.]

Enter *Antipholus of Ephesus*, his Man *Dromio*, *Angelo* the Goldsmith, and *Balthazar* the Merchant.

E. Ant. Good Signior Angelo, you must excuse us all.
My wife is shrewish when I keep not hours.
Say that I linger'd with you at your shop
To see the making of her carcanet,
And that to-morrow you will bring it home.
But here's a villain that would face me down
He met me on the mart, and that I beat him
And charg'd him with a thousand marks in gold,
And that I did deny my wife and house.
Thou drunkard thou! what didst thou mean by this?
E. Dro. Say what you will, sir, but I know what I know.
That you beat me at the mart, I have your hand to show.
If the skin were parchment, and the blows you gave were ink,
Your own handwriting would tell you what I think.
E. Ant. I think thou art an ass.
E. Dro. Marry, so it doth appear
By the wrongs I suffer and the blows I bear.
I should kick, being kick'd; and being at that pass,
You would keep from my heels and beware of an ass.
E. Ant. Y'are sad, Signior Balthazar. Pray God our cheer
May answer my good will and your good welcome here!
Bal. I hold your dainties cheap, sir, and your welcome dear.
E. Ant. O, Signior Balthazar, either at flesh or fish,
A table full of welcome makes scarce one dainty dish.
Bal. Good meat, sir, is common. That every churl affords.
E. Ant. And welcome more common, for that's nothing but words.
Bal. Small cheer and great welcome makes a merry feast.
E. Ant. Ay, to a niggardly host and more sparing guest.
But though my cates be mean, take them in good part;
Better cheer may you have, but not with better heart.
But, soft! my door is lock'd. — Go bid them let us in.
E. Dro. Maud, Bridget, Marian, Cisley, Gillian, Ginn!
S. Dro. [*within*] Mome, malthorse, capon, coxcomb, idiot, patch!
Either get thee from the door, or sit down at the hatch.
Dost thou conjure for wenches, that thou call'st for such store
When one is one too many? Go get thee from the door.
E. Dro. What patch is made our porter? My master stays in the street.

S. Dro. [*within*] Let him walk from whence he came, lest he catch cold on's feet.
E. Ant. Who talks within there? Ho, open the door!
S. Dro. [*within*] Right, sir! I'll tell you when, an you'll tell me wherefore.
E. Ant. Wherefore? For my dinner! I have not din'd to-day.
S. Dro. [*within*] Nor to-day here you must not, come again when you may.
E. Ant. What art thou that keep'st me out from the house I owe?
S. Dro. [*within*] The porter for this time, sir, and my name is Dromio.
E. Dro. O villain, thou hast stol'n both mine office and my name!
The one ne'er got me credit, the other mickle blame.
If thou hadst been Dromio to-day in my place,
Thou wouldst have chang'd thy face for a name, or thy name for an ass.

Enter *Luce* [above].

Luce. What a coil is there! Dromio, who are those at the gate?
E. Dro. Let my master in, Luce.
Luce. Faith, no! he comes too late;
And so tell your master.
E. Dro. O Lord, I must laugh!
Have at you with a proverb: Shall I set in my staff?
Luce. Have at you with another; that's — When? can you tell?
S. Dro. [*within*] If thy name be call'd Luce — Luce, thou hast answer'd him well.
E. Ant. Do you hear, you minion? You'll let us in, I hope?
Luce. I thought to have ask'd you.
S. Dro. [*within*] And you said no.
E. Dro. So, come help! Well struck! There was blow for blow.
E. Ant. Thou baggage, let me in.
Luce. Can you tell for whose sake?
E. Dro. Master, knock the door hard.
Luce. Let him knock till it ache.
E. Ant. You'll cry for this, minion, if I beat the door down.
Luce. What needs all that, and a pair of stocks in the town?

Enter *Adriana* [above].

Adr. Who is that at the door that keeps all this noise?
S. Dro. [*within*] By my troth, your town is troubled with unruly boys.
E. Ant. Are you there, wife? You might have come before.
Adr. Your wife, sir knave? Go get you from the door. [*Exit with Luce.*]
E. Dro. If you went in pain, master, this knave would go sore.
Ang. Here is neither cheer, sir, nor welcome. We would fain have either.
Bal. In debating which was best, we shall part with neither.
E. Dro. They stand at the door, master. Bid them welcome hither.
E. Ant. There is something in the wind, that we cannot get in.
E. Dro. You would say so, master, if your garments were thin.
Your cake is warm within; you stand here in the cold.
It would make a man mad as a buck to be so bought and sold.
E. Ant. Go fetch me something. I'll break ope the gate.
S. Dro. [*within*] Break any breaking here, and I'll break your knave's pate.
E. Dro. A man may break a word with you, sir; and words are but wind;
Ay, and break it in your face, so he break it not behind.
S. Dro. [*within*] It seems thou want'st breaking. Out upon thee, hind!
E. Dro. Here's too much 'out upon thee!' I pray thee let me in.
S. Dro. [*within*] Ay, when fowls have no feathers and fish have no fin.
E. Ant. Well, I'll break in. Go borrow me a crow.
E. Dro. A crow without feather? Master, mean you so?
For a fish without a fin there's a fowl without a feather!
If a crow help us in, sirrah, we'll pluck a crow together.
E. Ant. Go, get thee gone; fetch me an iron crow.
Bal. Have patience, sir. O, let it not be so!
Herein you war against your reputation
And draw within the compass of suspect
Th' unviolated honour of your wife.
Once this — your long experience of her wisdom,
Her sober virtue, years, and modesty,
Plead on her part some cause to you unknown;
And doubt not, sir, but she will well excuse
Why at this time the doors are made against you.
Be rul'd by me. Depart in patience,

And let us to the Tiger all to dinner,
And about evening come yourself alone
To know the reason of this strange restraint.
If by strong hand you offer to break in
Now in the stirring passage of the day,
A vulgar comment will be made of it,
And that supposed by the common rout
Against your yet ungalled estimation
That may with foul intrusion enter in
And dwell upon your grave when you are dead;
For slander lives upon succession,
For ever housed where it gets possession.

E. Ant. You have prevail'd. I will depart in quiet,
And in despite of mirth mean to be merry.
I know a wench of excellent discourse,
Pretty and witty; wild, and yet too gentle.
There will we dine. This woman that I mean,
My wife (but, I protest, without desert)
Hath oftentimes upbraided me withal.
To her will we to dinner. [*To Angelo*] Get you home
And fetch the chain; by this I know 'tis made.
Bring it, I pray you, to the Porpentine,
For there's the house. That chain will I bestow
(Be it for nothing but to spite my wife)
Upon mine hostess there. Good sir, make haste.
Since mine own doors refuse to entertain me,
I'll knock elsewhere, to see if they'll disdain me.

Ang. I'll meet you at that place some hour hence.

E. Ant. Do so. This jest shall cost me some expense. *Exeunt.*

[Scene II. *Before the house of* Antipholus of Ephesus.]

Enter, [as from the house,] *Luciana* with *Antipholus of Syracuse.*

Luc. And may it be that you have quite forgot
A husband's office? Shall, Antipholus,
Even in the spring of love, thy love-springs rot?
Shall love, in building, grow so ruinous?
If you did wed my sister for her wealth,
Then for her wealth's sake use her with more kindness.
Or, if you like elsewhere, do it by stealth,
Muffle your false love with some show of blindness:
Let not my sister read it in your eye;
Be not thy tongue thy own shame's orator:
Look sweet, speak fair, become disloyalty;
Apparel vice like virtue's harbinger;
Bear a fair presence, though your heart be tainted;
Teach sin the carriage of a holy saint;
Be secret-false. What need she be acquainted?
What simple thief brags of his own attaint?
'Tis double wrong to truant with your bed
And let her read it in thy looks at board.
Shame hath a bastard fame, well managed;
Ill deed is doubled with an evil word.
Alas, poor women! make us but believe
(Being compact of credit) that you love us;
Though others have the arm, show us the sleeve:
We in your motion turn, and you may move us.
Then, gentle brother, get you in again;
Comfort my sister, cheer her, call her wife.
'Tis holy sport to be a little vain
When the sweet breath of flattery conquers strife.

S. Ant. Sweet mistress (what your name is else, I know not,
Nor by what wonder you do hit of mine),
Less in your knowledge and your grace you show not
Than our earth's wonder, more than earth divine.
Teach me, dear creature, how to think and speak.
Lay open to my earthy gross conceit,
Smoth'red in errors, feeble, shallow, weak,
The folded meaning of your words' deceit.
Against my soul's pure truth why labour you,
To make it wander in an unknown field?
Are you a god? Would you create me new?
Transform me then, and to your pow'r I'll yield.
But if that I am I, then well I know
Your weeping sister is no wife of mine,
Nor to her bed no homage do I owe.
Far more, far more to you do I decline!
O, train me not, sweet mermaid, with thy note,
To drown me in thy sister's flood of tears.
Sing, siren, for thyself, and I will dote.
Spread o'er the silver waves thy golden hairs,
And as a bed I'll take them, and there lie
And in that glorious supposition think
He gains by death that hath such means to die.
Let Love, being light, be drowned if she sink!

Luc. What, are you mad, that you do reason so?

S. Ant. Not mad, but mated! how, I do not know.

Luc. It is a fault that springeth from your eye.

S. Ant. For gazing on your beams, fair sun, being by.

Luc. Gaze where you should, and that will clear your sight.

S. Ant. As good to wink, sweet love, as look on night.

Luc. Why call you me love? Call my sister so.

S. Ant. Thy sister's sister!

Luc. That's my sister.

S. Ant. No!
It is thyself, mine own self's better part,
Mine eye's clear eye, my dear heart's dearer heart,
My food, my fortune, and my sweet hope's aim,
My sole earth's heaven, and my heaven's claim.

Luc. All this my sister is, or else should be.

S. Ant. Call thyself sister, sweet, for I am thee.
Thee will I love and with thee lead my life;
Thou hast no husband yet, nor I no wife.
Give me thy hand.

Luc. O, soft, sir! hold you still!
I'll fetch my sister to get her good will. *Exit.*

Enter, [from the house,] *Dromio of Syracuse,* [running].

S. Ant. Why, how now, Dromio? Where run'st thou so fast?

S. Dro. Do you know me, sir? Am I Dromio? Am I your man? Am I myself?

S. Ant. Thou art Dromio; thou art my man; thou art thyself.

S. Dro. I am an ass, I am a woman's man, and besides myself.

S. Ant. What woman's man? and how besides thyself?

S. Dro. Marry, sir, besides myself, I am due to a woman — one that claims me, one that haunts me, one that will have me.

S. Ant. What claim lays she to thee?

S. Dro. Marry, sir, such claim as you would lay to your horse; and she would have me as a beast: not that, I being a beast, she would have me; but that she, being a very beastly creature, lays claim to me.

S. Ant. What is she?

S. Dro. A very reverent body. Ay, such a one as a man may not speak of without he say 'sir-reverence.' I have but lean luck in the match, and yet is she a wondrous fat marriage.

S. Ant. How dost thou mean a fat marriage?

S. Dro. Marry, sir, she's the kitchen wench, and all grease; and I know not what use to put her to but to make a lamp of her and run from her by her own light. I warrant, her rags and the tallow in them will burn a Poland winter. If she lives till doomsday, she'll burn a week longer than the whole world.

S. Ant. What complexion is she of?

S. Dro. Swart like my shoe, but her face nothing like so clean kept. For why? She sweats a man may go over shoes in the grime of it.

S. Ant. That's a fault that water will mend.

S. Dro. No, sir, 'tis in grain. Noah's flood could not do it.

S. Ant. What's her name?

S. Dro. Nell, sir. But her name and three quarters — that's an ell and three quarters — will not measure her from hip to hip.

S. Ant. Then she bears some breadth?

S. Dro. No longer from head to foot than from hip to hip. She is spherical, like a globe. I could find out countries in her.

S. Ant. In what part of her body stands Ireland?

S. Dro. Marry, sir, in her buttocks. I found it out by the bogs.

S. Ant. Where Scotland?

S. Dro. I found it by the barrenness, hard in the palm of the hand.

S. Ant. Where France?

S. Dro. In her forehead; arm'd and reverted, making war against her heir.

S. Ant. Where England?

S. Dro. I look'd for the chalky cliffs, but I could find no whiteness in them. But I guess it stood in her chin by the salt rheum that ran between France and it.

S. Ant. Where Spain?

S. Dro. Faith, I saw it not; but I felt it hot in her breath.

S. Ant. Where America, the Indies?

S. Dro. O, sir, upon her nose, all o'er embellished with rubies, carbuncles, sapphires, declining their rich aspect to the hot breath of Spain, who sent whole armadoes of carrects to be ballast at her nose.

S. Ant. Where stood Belgia, the Netherlands?

S. Dro. O, sir, I did not look so low. To conclude, this drudge or diviner laid claim to me; call'd me Dromio; swore I was assur'd to her; told me what privy marks I had about me, as, the mark of my shoulder, the mole in my neck, the great wart on my left arm, that I, amaz'd, ran from her as a witch.
And I think, if my breast had not been made of faith and my heart of steel,
She had transform'd me to a curtal dog and made me turn i' th' wheel.

S. Ant. Go hie thee presently post to the road.
An if the wind blow any way from shore,
I will not harbour in this town to-night.
If any bark put forth, come to the mart,
Where I will walk till thou return to me.
If every one knows us, and we know none,
'Tis time, I think, to trudge, pack, and be gone.
S. Dro. As from a bear a man would run for life,
So fly I from her that would be my wife.
Exit.
S. Ant. There's none but witches do inhabit here,
And therefore 'tis high time that I were hence.
She that doth call me husband, even my soul
Doth for a wife abhor. But her fair sister,
Possess'd with such a gentle sovereign grace,
Of such enchanting presence and discourse,
Hath almost made me traitor to myself.
But, lest myself be guilty to self-wrong,
I'll stop mine ears against the mermaid's song.

Enter *Angelo* with the chain.

Ang. Master Antipholus!
S. Ant. Ay, that's my name.
Ang. I know it well, sir. Lo, here is the chain.
I thought to have ta'en you at the Porpentine;
The chain unfinish'd made me stay thus long.
S. Ant. What is your will that I shall do with this?
Ang. What please yourself, sir. I have made it for you.
S. Ant. Made it for me, sir? I bespoke it not.
Ang. Not once, nor twice, but twenty times you have.
Go home with it and please your wife withal;
And soon at supper time I'll visit you
And then receive my money for the chain.
S. Ant. I pray you, sir, receive the money now,
For fear you ne'er see chain nor money more.
Ang. You are a merry man, sir. Fare you well. *Exit.*
S. Ant. What I should think of this I cannot tell;
But this I think, there's no man is so vain
That would refuse so fair an offer'd chain.
I see a man here needs not live by shifts
When in the streets he meets such golden gifts.
I'll to the mart and there for Dromio stay;
If any ship put out, then straight away! *Exit.*

ACT IV. Scene I. [*A public place.*]

Enter a *Merchant*, [*Angelo* the] Goldsmith, and an *Officer*.

Mer. You know since Pentecost the sum is due,
And since I have not much importun'd you;
Nor now I had not but that I am bound
To Persia and want guilders for my voyage.
Therefore make present satisfaction,
Or I'll attach you by this officer.
Ang. Even just the sum that I do owe to you
Is growing to me by Antipholus,
And in the instant that I met with you
He had of me a chain. At five o'clock
I shall receive the money for the same.
Pleaseth you walk with me down to his house,
I will discharge my bond and thank you too.

Enter *Antipholus* [*of*] *Ephesus* [and] *Dromio* [*of Ephesus*] from the *Courtesan's*.

Off. That labour may you save. See where he comes.
E. Ant. While I go to the goldsmith's house, go thou
And buy a rope's-end. That will I bestow
Among my wife and her confederates
For locking me out of my doors by day.
But, soft! I see the goldsmith. Get thee gone;
Buy thou a rope and bring it home to me.
E. Dro. I buy a thousand pound a year! I buy a rope! *Exit.*
E. Ant. A man is well holp up that trusts to you!
I promised your presence and the chain,
But neither chain nor goldsmith came to me.
Belike you thought our love would last too long
If it were chain'd together, and therefore came not.
Ang. Saving your merry humour, here's the note
How much your chain weighs to the utmost charect,
The fineness of the gold, and chargeful fashion,
Which doth amount to three odd ducats more
Than I stand debted to this gentleman.
I pray you see him presently discharg'd,
For he is bound to sea and stays but for it.
E. Ant. I am not furnish'd with the present money;
Besides, I have some business in the town.

Good signior, take the stranger to my house,
And with you take the chain, and bid my wife
Disburse the sum on the receipt thereof.
Perchance I will be there as soon as you.
Ang. Then you will bring the chain to her yourself?
E. Ant. No. Bear it with you, lest I come not time enough.
Ang. Well, sir, I will. Have you the chain about you?
E. Ant. An if I have not, sir, I hope you have;
Or else you may return without your money.
Ang. Nay, come, I pray you, sir, give me the chain!
Both wind and tide stays for this gentleman,
And I, to blame, have held him here too long.
E. Ant. Good Lord! you use this dalliance to excuse
Your breach of promise to the Porpentine.
I should have chid you for not bringing it,
But like a shrew you first begin to brawl.
Mer. The hour steals on. I pray you, sir, dispatch.
Ang. You hear how he importunes me. The chain!
E. Ant. Why, give it to my wife, and fetch your money.
Ang. Come, come, you know I gave it you even now!
Either send the chain or send me by some token.
E. Ant. Fie, now you run this humour out of breath!
Come, where's the chain? I pray you let me see it.
Mer. My business cannot brook this dalliance.
Good sir, say whe'r you'll answer me or no.
If not, I'll leave him to the officer.
E. Ant. I answer you? What should I answer you?
Ang. The money that you owe me for the chain.
E. Ant. I owe you none till I receive the chain.
Ang. You know I gave it you half an hour since.
E. Ant. You gave me none. You wrong me much to say so.
Ang. You wrong me more, sir, in denying it.
Consider how it stands upon my credit.
Mer. Well, officer, arrest him at my suit.
Off. I do, and charge you in the Duke's name to obey me.
Ang. This touches me in reputation.
Either consent to pay this sum for me,
Or I attach you by this officer.
E. Ant. Consent to pay thee that I never had?
Arrest me, foolish fellow, if thou dar'st.
Ang. Here is thy fee; arrest him, officer.
I would not spare my brother in this case
If he should scorn me so apparently.
Off. I do arrest you, sir. You hear the suit.
E. Ant. I do obey thee till I give thee bail.
But, sirrah, you shall buy this sport as dear
As all the metal in your shop will answer.
Ang. Sir, sir, I shall have law in Ephesus
To your notorious shame, I doubt it not.

Enter *Dromio of Syracuse* from the Bay.

S. Dro. Master, there is a bark of Epidamnum
That stays but till her owner comes aboard,
And then she bears away. Our fraughtage, sir,
I have convey'd aboard, and I have bought
The oil, the balsamum, and aqua-vitæ.
The ship is in her trim; the merry wind
Blows fair from land. They stay for naught at all
But for their owner, master, and yourself.
E. Ant. How now? a madman? Why, thou peevish sheep,
What ship of Epidamnum stays for me?
S. Dro. A ship you sent me to, to hire waftage.
E. Ant. Thou drunken slave, I sent thee for a rope,
And told thee to what purpose and what end.
S. Dro. You sent me, sir, for a rope's-end as soon!
You sent me to the bay, sir, for a bark.
E. Ant. I will debate this matter at more leisure
And teach your ears to list me with more heed.
To Adriana, villain, hie thee straight.
Give her this key, and tell her in the desk
That's cover'd o'er with Turkish tapestry
There is a purse of ducats. Let her send it.
Tell her I am arrested in the street,
And that shall bail me. Hie thee, slave, be gone!
On, officer, to prison till it come.
Exeunt [*all but Dromio*].
S. Dro. To Adriana? That is where we din'd,
Where Dowsabel did claim me for her husband.
She is too big, I hope, for me to compass.
Thither I must, although against my will,
For servants must their masters' minds fulfil.
Exit.

[Scene II. *The house of* Antipholus of Ephesus]

Enter *Adriana* and *Luciana*.

Adr. Ah, Luciana, did he tempt thee so?
Mightst thou perceive austerely in his eye
That he did plead in earnest? yea or no?
Look'd he or red or pale, or sad or merrily?
What observation mad'st thou in this case
Of his heart's meteors tilting in his face?
Luc. First he denied you had in him no right.
Adr. He meant he did me none. The more my spite!
Luc. Then swore he that he was a stranger here.
Adr. And true he swore, though yet forsworn he were.
Luc. Then pleaded I for you.
Adr. And what said he?
Luc. That love I begg'd for you he begg'd of me.
Adr. With what persuasion did he tempt thy love?
Luc. With words that in an honest suit might move.
First he did praise my beauty, then my speech.
Adr. Didst speak him fair?
Luc. Have patience, I beseech.
Adr. I cannot nor I will not hold me still;
My tongue, though not my heart, shall have his will.
He is deformed, crooked, old, and sere,
Ill-fac'd, worse bodied, shapeless everywhere;
Vicious, ungentle, foolish, blunt, unkind;
Stigmatical in making, worse in mind.
Luc. Who would be jealous then of such a one?
No evil lost is wail'd when it is gone.
Adr. Ah, but I think him better than I say,
And yet would herein others' eyes were worse.
Far from her nest the lapwing cries away;
My heart prays for him, though my tongue do curse.

Enter *Dromio of Syracuse.*

S. Dro. Here, go! the desk, the purse! Sweet now, make haste.
Luc. How hast thou lost thy breath?
S. Dro. By running fast.
Adr. Where is thy master, Dromio? Is he well?
S. Dro. No, he's in Tartar limbo, worse than hell.
A devil in an everlasting garment hath him;
One whose hard heart is button'd up with steel;
A fiend, a fury, pitiless and rough;
A wolf; nay, worse — a fellow all in buff;
A back-friend, a shoulder-clapper, one that countermands
The passages of alleys, creeks, and narrow lands;
A hound that runs counter, and yet draws dry-foot well;
One that before the Judgment carries poor souls to hell.
Adr. Why, man, what is the matter?
S. Dro. I do not know the matter. He is 'rested on the case.
Adr. What, is he arrested? Tell me at whose suit.
S. Dro. I know not at whose suit he is arrested well;
But he's in a suit of buff which 'rested him, that can I tell.
Will you send him, Mistress Redemption, the money in his desk?
Adr. Go fetch it, sister. (*Exit Luciana.*) This I wonder at,
Thus he, unknown to me, should be in debt.
Tell me, was he arrested on a band?
S. Dro. Not on a band, but on a stronger thing —
A chain, a chain! Do you not hear it ring?
Adr. What, the chain?
S. Dro. No, no, the bell! 'Tis time that I were gone.
It was two ere I left him, and now the clock strikes one.
Adr. The hours come back? That did I never hear.
S. Dro. O, yes! If any hour meet a sergeant, 'a turns back for very fear.
Adr. As if Time were in debt! How fondly dost thou reason!
S. Dro. Time is a very bankrout and owes more than he's worth to season.
Nay, he's a thief too. Have you not heard men say
That Time comes stealing on by night and day?
If he be in debt and theft, and a sergeant in the way,
Hath he not reason to turn back an hour in a day?

Enter *Luciana* [with the purse].

Adr. Go, Dromio. There's the money, bear it straight;
And bring thy master home immediately.
Come, sister. I am press'd down with conceit —
Conceit, my comfort and my injury.
Exeunt.

[Scene III. *The Mart.*]

Enter *Antipholus of Syracuse.*

S. Ant. There's not a man I meet but doth salute me
As if I were their well-acquainted friend,
And every one doth call me by my name.
Some tender money to me; some invite me;
Some other give me thanks for kindnesses;
Some offer me commodities to buy.
Even now a tailor call'd me in his shop
And show'd me silks that he had bought for me
And therewithal took measure of my body.
Sure these are but imaginary wiles,
And Lapland sorcerers inhabit here.

Enter *Dromio of Syracuse.*

S. Dro. Master, here's the gold you sent me for. What, have you got the picture of old Adam new-apparell'd?

S. Ant. What gold is this? What Adam dost thou mean?

S. Dro. Not that Adam that kept the Paradise, but that Adam that keeps the prison; he that goes in the calve's skin that was kill'd for the Prodigal; he that came behind you, sir, like an evil angel, and bid you forsake your liberty.

S. Ant. I understand thee not.

S. Dro. No? Why, 'tis a plain case. He that went, like a bass-viol, in a case of leather; the man, sir, that, when gentlemen are tired, gives them a sob and rests them; he, sir, that takes pity on decayed men and gives them suits of durance; he that sets up his rest to do more exploits with his mace than a morris-pike.

S. Ant. What, thou mean'st an officer?

S. Dro. Ay, sir, the sergeant of the band; he that brings any man to answer it that breaks his band; one that thinks a man always going to bed, and says 'God give you good rest!'

S. Ant. Well, sir, there rest in your foolery. Is there any ship puts forth to-night? May we be gone?

S. Dro. Why, sir, I brought you word an hour since that the bark Expedition put forth to-night; and then were you hind'red by the sergeant, to tarry for the hoy Delay. Here are the angels that you sent for to deliver you.

S. Ant. The fellow is distract, and so am I,
And here we wander in illusions.
Some blessed power deliver us from hence!

Enter a *Courtesan.*

Court. Well met, well met, Master Antipholus!
I see, sir, you have found the goldsmith now.
Is that the chain you promis'd me to-day?

S. Ant. Sathan, avoid! I charge thee tempt me not.

S. Dro. Master, is this Mistress Sathan?

S. Ant. It is the devil.

S. Dro. Nay, she is worse, she is the devil's dam! And here she comes in the habit of a light wench; and thereof comes that the wenches say 'God damn me!' That's as much to say, 'God make me a light wench!' It is written, 'They appear to men like angels of light.' Light is an effect of fire, and fire will burn; ergo, light wenches will burn. Come not near her!

Court. Your man and you are marvellous merry, sir.
Will you go with me? We'll mend our dinner here.

S. Dro. Master, if you do, expect spoon-meat, or bespeak a long spoon.

S. Ant. Why, Dromio?

S. Dro. Marry, he must have a long spoon that must eat with the devil.

S. Ant. Avoid, thou fiend! What tell'st thou me of supping?
Thou art, as you are all, a sorceress.
I conjure thee to leave me and be gone.

Court. Give me the ring of mine you had at dinner
Or, for my diamond, the chain you promis'd,
And I'll be gone, sir, and not trouble you.

S. Dro. Some devils ask but the parings of one's nail,
A rush, a hair, a drop of blood, a pin,
A nut, a cherry stone;
But she, more covetous, would have a chain.
Master, be wise! An if you give it her,
The devil will shake her chain and fright us with it.

Court. I pray you, sir, my ring, or else the chain.
I hope you do not mean to cheat me so.

S. Ant. Avaunt, thou witch! Come, Dromio, let us go.

S. Dro. 'Fly pride,' says the peacock. Mistress, that you know.

Exeunt [*S. Ant. and S. Dro.*].

Court. Now out of doubt Antipholus is mad,
Else would he never so demean himself.
A ring he hath of mine worth forty ducats,
And for the same he promis'd me a chain.

Both one and other he denies me now.
The reason that I gather he is mad,
Besides this present instance of his rage,
Is a mad tale he told to-day at dinner
Of his own doors being shut against his entrance.
Belike his wife, acquainted with his fits,
On purpose shut the doors against his way.
My way is now to hie home to his house
And tell his wife that, being lunatic,
He rush'd into my house and took perforce
My ring away. This course I fittest choose,
For forty ducats is too much to lose. [*Exit.*]

[Scene IV. *A street.*]

Enter *Antipholus of Ephesus* with the *Officer*.

E. Ant. Fear me not, man; I will not break away.
I'll give thee, ere I leave thee, so much money,
To warrant thee, as I am 'rested for.
My wife is in a wayward mood to-day
And will not lightly trust the messenger.
That I should be attach'd in Ephesus,
I tell you 'twill sound harshly in her ears.

Enter *Dromio of Ephesus* with a rope's-end.

Here comes my man. I think he brings the money.
How now, sir? Have you that I sent you for?

E. Dro. Here's that I warrant you will pay them all.

E. Ant. But where's the money?

E. Dro. Why, sir, I gave the money for the rope.

E. Ant. Five hundred ducats, villain, for a rope?

E. Dro. I'll serve you, sir, five hundred at the rate.

E. Ant. To what end did I bid thee hie thee home?

E. Dro. To a rope's end, sir, and to that end am I return'd.

E. Ant. And to that end, sir, I will welcome you. [*Beats him.*]

Off. Good sir, be patient.

E. Dro. Nay, 'tis for me to be patient! I am in adversity.

Off. Good now, hold thy tongue.

E. Dro. Nay, rather persuade him to hold his hands.

E. Ant. Thou whoreson senseless villain!

E. Dro. I would I were senseless, sir, that I might not feel your blows.

E. Ant. Thou art sensible in nothing but blows, and so is an ass.

E. Dro. I am an ass indeed! You may prove it by my long ears. I have served him from the hour of my nativity to this instant, and have nothing at his hands for my service but blows. When I am cold, he heats me with beating; when I am warm, he cools me with beating. I am wak'd with it when I sleep; rais'd with it when I sit; driven out of doors with it when I go from home; welcom'd home with it when I return. Nay, I bear it on my shoulders, as a beggar wont her brat; and I think, when he hath lam'd me, I shall beg with it from door to door.

Enter *Adriana*, *Luciana*, *Courtesan*, and a Schoolmaster call'd *Pinch*.

E. Ant. Come, go along! My wife is coming yonder.

E. Dro. Mistress, *respice finem*, respect your end; or rather, to prophesy like the parrot, 'beware the rope's end.'

E. Ant. Wilt thou still talk? *Beats Dromio.*

Court. How say you now? Is not your husband mad?

Adr. His incivility confirms no less.
Good Doctor Pinch, you are a conjurer;
Establish him in his true sense again,
And I will please you what you will demand.

Luc. Alas, how fiery and how sharp he looks!

Court. Mark how he trembles in his ecstasy!

Pinch. Give me your hand and let me feel your pulse.

E. Ant. There is my hand, and let it feel your ear. [*Strikes him.*]

Pinch. I charge thee, Sathan, hous'd within this man,
To yield possession to my holy prayers,
And to thy state of darkness hie thee straight.
I conjure thee by all the saints in heaven.

E. Ant. Peace, doting wizard, peace! I am not mad.

Adr. O that thou wert not, poor distressed soul!

E. Ant. You minion you, are these your customers?
Did this companion with the saffron face
Revel and feast it at my house to-day,
Whilst upon me the guilty doors were shut
And I denied to enter in my house?

Adr. O husband, God doth know you din'd at home!
Where would you had remain'd until this time,
Free from these slanders and this open shame!

E. Ant. Din'd at home? — Thou, villain, what sayest thou?

E. Dro. Sir, sooth to say, you did not dine at home.

E. Ant. Were not my doors lock'd up, and I shut out?

E. Dro. Perdie, your doors were lock'd, and you shut out.

E. Ant. And did not she herself revile me there?

E. Dro. Sans fable, she herself revil'd you there.

E. Ant. Did not her kitchen maid rail, taunt, and scorn me?

E. Dro. Certes she did. The kitchen vestal scorn'd you.

E. Ant. And did not I in rage depart from thence?

E. Dro. In verity you did. My bones bear witness,
That since have felt the vigour of his rage.

Adr. Is't good to soothe him in these contraries?

Pinch. It is no shame. The fellow finds his vein
And, yielding to him, humours well his frenzy.

E. Ant. Thou hast suborn'd the goldsmith to arrest me.

Adr. Alas, I sent you money to redeem you
By Dromio here, who came in haste for it.

E. Dro. Money by me? Heart and good will you might,
But surely, master, not a rag of money.

E. Ant. Went'st not thou to her for a purse of ducats?

Adr. He came to me, and I deliver'd it.

Luc. And I am witness with her that she did.

E. Dro. God and the rope-maker bear me witness
That I was sent for nothing but a rope!

Pinch. Mistress, both man and master is possess'd.
I know it by their pale and deadly looks.
They must be bound and laid in some dark room.

E. Ant. Say, wherefore didst thou lock me forth to-day?
And why dost thou deny the bag of gold?

Adr. I did not, gentle husband, lock thee forth.

E. Dro. And, gentle master, I receiv'd no gold;
But I confess, sir, that we were lock'd out.

Adr. Dissembling villain, thou speak'st false in both.

E. Ant. Dissembling harlot, thou art false in all,
And art confederate with a damned pack
To make a loathsome abject scorn of me;
But with these nails I'll pluck out these false eyes
That would behold in me this shameful sport.

Adr. O, bind him, bind him! Let him not come near me.

Pinch. More company! The fiend is strong within him.

Enter *three or four* and offer to bind him. He strives.

Luc. Ay me, poor man! how pale and wan he looks!

E. Ant. What, will you murther me? Thou jailer thou,
I am thy prisoner. Wilt thou suffer them
To make a rescue?

Off. Masters, let him go.
He is my prisoner, and you shall not have him.

Pinch. Go bind this man, for he is frantic too. [*Dromio is bound.*]

Adr. What wilt thou do, thou peevish officer?
Hast thou delight to see a wretched man
Do outrage and displeasure to himself?

Off. He is my prisoner. If I let him go,
The debt he owes will be requir'd of me.

Adr. I will discharge thee ere I go from thee.
Bear me forthwith unto his creditor,
And, knowing how the debt grows, I will pay it.
Good Master Doctor, see him safe convey'd
Home to my house. O most unhappy day!

E. Ant. O most unhappy strumpet!

E. Dro. Master, I am here ent'red in bond for you.

E. Ant. Out on thee, villain! Wherefore dost thou mad me?

E. Dro. Will you be bound for nothing? Be mad, good master. Cry 'The devil!'

Luc. God help poor souls! How idly do they talk!

Adr. Go bear him hence. — Sister, go you with me.

Exeunt. Manent Officer, Adriana, Luciana, Courtesan.

Say now, whose suit is he arrested at?

Off. One Angelo, a goldsmith. Do you know him?

Adr. I know the man. What is the sum he owes?

Off. Two hundred ducats.

Adr. Say, how grows it due?

Off. Due for a chain your husband had of him.

Adr. He did bespeak a chain for me, but had it not.

Court. When as your husband, all in rage, to-day
Came to my house and took away my ring —
The ring I saw upon his finger now —
Straight after did I meet him with a chain.

Adr. It may be so, but I did never see it.
Come, jailer, bring me where the goldsmith is.
I long to know the truth hereof at large.

Enter *Antipholus of Syracuse,* with his rapier drawn, and *Dromio of Syracuse.*

Luc. God for thy mercy! They are loose again.

Adr. And come with naked swords. Let's call more help
To have them bound again.

Off. Away! they'll kill us!

Exeunt omnes [except Antipholus of Syracuse and Dromio of Syracuse] as fast as may be, frighted.

S. Ant. I see these witches are afraid of swords.

S. Dro. She that would be your wife now ran from you.

S. Ant. Come to the Centaur; fetch our stuff from thence.
I long that we were safe and sound aboard.

S. Dro. Faith, stay here this night. They will surely do us no harm. You saw they speak us fair, give us gold. Methinks they are such a gentle nation that, but for the mountain of mad flesh that claims marriage of me, I could find in my heart to stay here still, and turn witch.

S. Ant. I will not stay to-night for all the town.
Therefore away, to get our stuff aboard!

Exeunt.

ACT V. Scene I. [*A street before a Priory.*]

Enter *the* [*Second*] *Merchant* and [*Angelo*] *the Goldsmith.*

Ang. I am sorry, sir, that I have hind'red you;
But I protest he had the chain of me,
Though most dishonestly he doth deny it.

Mer. How is the man esteem'd here in the city?

Ang. Of very reverent reputation, sir,
Of credit infinite, highly belov'd,
Second to none that lives here in the city.
His word might bear my wealth at any time.

Mer. Speak softly. Yonder, as I think, he walks.

Enter *Antipholus* [*of Syracuse*] and *Dromio* [*of Syracuse*] again.

Ang. 'Tis so! and that self chain about his neck
Which he forswore most monstrously to have.
Good sir, draw near with me, I'll speak to him.
Signior Antipholus, I wonder much
That you would put me to this shame and trouble,
And not without some scandal to yourself,
With circumstance and oaths so to deny
This chain which now you wear so openly.
Beside the charge, the shame, imprisonment,
You have done wrong to this my honest friend,
Who, but for staying on our controversy,
Had hoisted sail and put to sea to-day.
This chain you had of me. Can you deny it?

S. Ant. I think I had. I never did deny it.

Mer. Yes, that you did, sir, and forswore it too.

S. Ant. Who heard me to deny it or forswear it?

Mer. These ears of mine thou know'st did hear thee.
Fie on thee, wretch! 'Tis pity that thou liv'st
To walk where any honest men resort.

S. Ant. Thou art a villain to impeach me thus.
I'll prove mine honour and mine honesty
Against thee presently, if thou dar'st stand.

Mer. I dare, and do defy thee for a villain.

They draw. Enter *Adriana, Luciana, Courtesan,* and others.

Adr. Hold, hurt him not for God's sake! He is mad.
Some get within him, take his sword away.
Bind Dromio too, and bear them to my house.

S. Dro. Run, master, run! for God's sake take a house!
This is some priory. In, or we are spoil'd!

Exeunt [Antipholus of Syracuse and Dromio of Syracuse] to the Priory.

Enter *Lady Abbess.*

Abb. Be quiet, people. Wherefore throng you hither?
Adr. To fetch my poor distracted husband hence.
Let us come in, that we may bind him fast
And bear him home for his recovery.
Ang. I knew he was not in his perfect wits.
Mer. I am sorry now that I did draw on him.
Abb. How long hath this possession held the man?
Adr. This week he hath been heavy, sour, sad,
And much much different from the man he was;
But till this afternoon his passion
Ne'er brake into extremity of rage.
Abb. Hath he not lost much wealth by wrack of sea?
Buried some dear friend? Hath not else his eye
Stray'd his affection in unlawful love?
A sin prevailing much in youthful men,
Who give their eyes the liberty of gazing.
Which of these sorrows is he subject to?
Adr. To none of these, except it be the last,
Namely, some love that drew him oft from home.
Abb. You should for that have reprehended him.
Adr. Why, so I did.
Abb. Ay, but not rough enough.
Adr. As roughly as my modesty would let me.
Abb. Haply in private.
Adr. And in assemblies too.
Abb. Ay, but not enough.
Adr. It was the copy of our conference.
In bed he slept not for my urging it;
At board he fed not for my urging it;
Alone, it was the subject of my theme;
In company I often glanced it:
Still did I tell him it was vile and bad.
Abb. And thereof came it that the man was mad.
The venom clamours of a jealous woman
Poisons more deadly than a mad dog's tooth.
It seems his sleeps were hind'red by thy railing,
And thereof comes it that his head is light.
Thou say'st his meat was sauc'd with thy upbraidings:
Unquiet meals make ill digestions;
Thereof the raging fire of fever bred,
And what's a fever but a fit of madness?
Thou say'st his sports were hind'red by thy brawls:
Sweet recreation barr'd, what doth ensue
But moody and dull melancholy,
Kinsman to grim and comfortless despair,
And at her heels a huge infectious troop
Of pale distemperatures and foes to life?
In food, in sport, and life-preserving rest
To be disturb'd would mad or man or beast.
The consequence is, then, thy jealous fits
Have scar'd thy husband from the use of wits.
Luc. She never reprehended him but mildly,
When he demean'd himself rough, rude, and wildly.
Why bear you these rebukes and answer not?
Adr. She did betray me to my own reproof.
Good people, enter and lay hold on him!
Abb. No, not a creature enters in my house.
Adr. Then let your servants bring my husband forth.
Abb. Neither. He took this place for sanctuary,
And it shall privilege him from your hands
Till I have brought him to his wits again,
Or lose my labour in assaying it.
Adr. I will attend my husband, be his nurse,
Diet his sickness, for it is my office,
And will have no attorney but myself;
And therefore let me have him home with me.
Abb. Be patient; for I will not let him stir
Till I have us'd the approved means I have,
With wholesome syrups, drugs, and holy prayers
To make of him a formal man again.
It is a branch and parcel of mine oath,
A charitable duty of my order.
Therefore depart and leave him here with me.
Adr. I will not hence and leave my husband here;
And ill it doth beseem your holiness
To separate the husband and the wife.
Abb. Be quiet and depart. Thou shalt not have him. [*Exit.*]
Luc. Complain unto the Duke of this indignity.
Adr. Come, go. I will fall prostrate at his feet
And never rise until my tears and prayers
Have won his Grace to come in person hither
And take perforce my husband from the Abbess.
Mer. By this, I think, the dial points at five.
Anon I'm sure the Duke himself in person
Comes this way to the melancholy vale,
The place of death and sorry execution,
Behind the ditches of the abbey here.
Ang. Upon what cause?
Mer. To see a reverent Syracusian merchant,
Who put unluckily into this bay

Against the laws and statutes of this town,
Beheaded publicly for his offence.

Ang. See where they come. We will behold his death.

Luc. Kneel to the Duke before he pass the abbey.

Enter the *Duke of Ephesus*; and [*Ægeon*,] the *Merchant of Syracuse*, bareheaded; with the *Headsman* and other *Officers*.

Duke. Yet once again proclaim it publicly,
If any friend will pay the sum for him,
He shall not die, so much we tender him.

Adr. Justice, most sacred Duke, against the Abbess!

Duke. She is a virtuous and a reverend lady.
It cannot be that she hath done thee wrong.

Adr. May it please your Grace, Antipholus my husband —
Who I made lord of me and all I had
At your important letters — this ill day
A most outrageous fit of madness took him;
That desp'rately he hurried through the street —
With him his bondman, all as mad as he —
Doing displeasure to the citizens
By rushing in their houses, bearing thence
Rings, jewels, anything his rage did like.
Once did I get him bound and sent him home,
Whilst to take order for the wrongs I went
That here and there his fury had committed.
Anon, I wot not by what strong escape,
He broke from those that had the guard of him,
And with his mad attendant and himself,
Each one with ireful passion, with drawn swords,
Met us again and, madly bent on us,
Chas'd us away, till, raising of more aid,
We came again to bind them. Then they fled
Into this abbey, whither we pursu'd them;
And here the Abbess shuts the gates on us
And will not suffer us to fetch him out,
Nor send him forth that we may bear him hence.
Therefore, most gracious Duke, with thy command
Let him be brought forth and borne hence for help.

Duke. Long since thy husband serv'd me in my wars,
And I to thee engag'd a prince's word,
When thou didst make him master of thy bed,
To do him all the grace and good I could.
Go, some of you, knock at the abbey gate
And bid the Lady Abbess come to me.
I will determine this before I stir.

Enter a *Messenger*.

Mess. O mistress, mistress, shift and save yourself!
My master and his man are both broke loose,
Beaten the maids arow, and bound the doctor,
Whose beard they have sing'd off with brands of fire;
And ever as it blaz'd, they threw on him
Great pails of puddled mire to quench the hair.
My master preaches patience to him, and the while
His man with scissors nicks him like a fool;
And sure, unless you send some present help,
Between them they will kill the conjurer.

Adr. Peace, fool! thy master and his man are here,
And that is false thou dost report to us.

Mess. Mistress, upon my life I tell you true;
I have not breath'd almost since I did see it.
He cries for you and vows, if he can take you,
To scorch your face and to disfigure you.

Cry within.

Hark, hark! I hear him, mistress. Fly, be gone!

Duke. Come stand by me! fear nothing.— Guard with halberds!

Adr. Ay me, it is my husband! Witness you
That he is borne about invisible.
Even now we hous'd him in the abbey here,
And now he's there, past thought of human reason.

Enter *Antipholus* [*of Ephesus*] and *Dromio of Ephesus*.

E. Ant. Justice, most gracious Duke! O, grant me justice!
Even for the service that long since I did thee
When I bestrid thee in the wars and took
Deep scars to save thy life; even for the blood
That then I lost for thee, now grant me justice!

Æge. Unless the fear of death doth make me dote,
I see my son Antipholus and Dromio.

E. Ant. Justice, sweet prince, against that woman there!
She whom thou gav'st to me to be my wife,
That hath abused and dishonoured me
Even in the strength and height of injury.
Beyond imagination is the wrong
That she this day hath shameless thrown on me.

Duke. Discover how, and thou shalt find me just.

E. Ant. This day, great Duke, she shut the doors upon me,
While she with harlots feasted in my house.

Duke. A grievous fault. Say, woman, didst thou so?
Adr. No, my good lord. Myself, he, and my sister
To-day did dine together. So befall my soul
As this is false he burthens me withal!
Luc. Ne'er may I look on day nor sleep on night
But she tells to your Highness simple truth!
Ang. O perjur'd woman! They are both forsworn.
In this the madman justly chargeth them.
E. Ant. My liege, I am advised what I say,
Neither disturbed with the effect of wine
Nor heady-rash, provok'd with raging ire,
Albeit my wrongs might make one wiser mad.
This woman lock'd me out this day from dinner.
That goldsmith there, were he not pack'd with her,
Could witness it, for he was with me then,
Who parted with me to go fetch a chain,
Promising to bring it to the Porpentine,
Where Balthazar and I did dine together.
Our dinner done, and he not coming thither,
I went to seek him. In the street I met him,
And in his company that gentleman.
There did this perjur'd goldsmith swear me down
That I this day of him receiv'd the chain,
Which, God he knows, I saw not; for the which
He did arrest me with an officer.
I did obey, and sent my peasant home
For certain ducats. He with none return'd.
Then fairly I bespoke the officer
To go in person with me to my house. By th' way
We met my wife, her sister, and a rabble more
Of vile confederates. Along with them
They brought one Pinch, a hungry lean-fac'd villain,
A mere anatomy, a mountebank,
A threadbare juggler and a fortune-teller,
A needy, hollow-ey'd, sharp-looking wretch,
A living dead man. This pernicious slave
Forsooth took on him as a conjurer;
And, gazing in mine eyes, feeling my pulse,
And with no-face, as 'twere, outfacing me,
Cries out I was possess'd. Then all together
They fell upon me, bound me, bore me thence,
And in a dark and dankish vault at home
There left me and my man, both bound together,
Till, gnawing with my teeth my bonds in sunder,
I gain'd my freedom and immediately
Ran hither to your Grace. whom I beseech
To give me ample satisfaction
For these deep shames and great indignities.
Ang. My lord, in truth, thus far I witness with him,
That he din'd not at home, but was lock'd out.
Duke. But had he such a chain of thee, or no?
Ang. He had, my lord; and when he ran in here,
These people saw the chain about his neck.
Mer. Besides, I will be sworn these ears of mine
Heard you confess you had the chain of him
After you first forswore it on the mart;
And thereupon I drew my sword on you;
And then you fled into this abbey here,
From whence I think you are come by miracle.
E. Ant. I never came within these abbey walls,
Nor ever didst thou draw thy sword on me.
I never saw the chain, so help me heaven!
And this is false you burthen me withal!
Duke. Why, what an intricate impeach is this!
I think you all have drunk of Circe's cup.
If here you hous'd him, here he would have been.
If he were mad, he would not plead so coldly.
You say he din'd at home. The goldsmith here
Denies that saying. Sirrah, what say you?
E. Dro. Sir, he din'd with her there, at the Porpentine.
Court. He did, and from my finger snatch'd that ring.
E. Ant. 'Tis true, my liege. This ring I had of her.
Duke. Saw'st thou him enter at the abbey here?
Court. As sure, my liege, as I do see your Grace.
Duke. Why, this is strange. Go call the Abbess hither.
I think you are all mated or stark mad.
Exit one to the Abbess.
Æge. Most mighty Duke, vouchsafe me speak a word.
Haply I see a friend will save my life
And pay the sum that may deliver me.
Duke. Speak freely, Syracusian, what thou wilt.
Æge. Is not your name, sir, call'd Antipholus?
And is not that your bondman Dromio?
E. Dro. Within this hour I was his bondman, sir,
But he, I thank him, gnaw'd in two my cords.
Now am I Dromio, and his man unbound.

Æge. I am sure you both of you remember me.

E. Dro. Ourselves we do remember, sir, by you;
For lately we were bound as you are now.
You are not Pinch's patient, are you, sir?

Æge. Why look you strange on me? You know me well.

E. Ant. I never saw you in my life till now.

Æge. O, grief hath chang'd me since you saw me last,
And careful hours with Time's deformed hand
Have written strange defeatures in my face.
But tell me yet, dost thou not know my voice?

E. Ant. Neither.

Æge. Dromio, nor thou?

E. Dro. No, trust me, sir, nor I.

Æge. I am sure thou dost.

E. Dro. Ay, sir, but I am sure I do not; and whatsoever a man denies, you are now bound to believe him.

Æge. Not know my voice? O time's extremity,
Hast thou so crack'd and splitted my poor tongue
In seven short years that here my only son
Knows not my feeble key of untun'd cares?
Though now this grained face of mine be hid
In sap-consuming winter's drizzled snow
And all the conduits of my blood froze up,
Yet hath my night of life some memory,
My wasting lamps some fading glimmer left,
My dull deaf ears a little use to hear.
All these old witnesses I cannot err
Tell me thou art my son Antipholus.

E. Ant. I never saw my father in my life.

Æge. But seven years since, in Syracusa, boy,
Thou know'st we parted. But perhaps, my son,
Thou sham'st to acknowledge me in misery.

E. Ant. The Duke and all that know me in the city
Can witness with me that it is not so.
I ne'er saw Syracusa in my life.

Duke. I tell thee, Syracusian, twenty years
Have I been patron to Antipholus,
During which time he ne'er saw Syracusa.
I see thy age and dangers make thee dote.

Enter the *Abbess*, with *Antipholus of Syracuse* and *Dromio of Syracuse.*

Abb. Most mighty Duke, behold a man much wrong'd. *All gather to see them.*

Adr. I see two husbands, or mine eyes deceive me.

Duke. One of these men is genius to the other;
And so of these. Which is the natural man
And which the spirit? Who deciphers them?

S. Dro. I, sir, am Dromio. Command him away.

E. Dro. I, sir, am Dromio. Pray let me stay.

S. Ant. Ægeon art thou not? or else his ghost.

S. Dro. O, my old master! Who hath bound him here?

Abb. Whoever bound him, I will loose his bonds
And gain a husband by his liberty.
Speak, old Ægeon, if thou be'st the man
That hadst a wife once call'd Æmilia,
That bore thee at a burthen two fair sons.
O, if thou be'st the same Ægeon, speak,
And speak unto the same Æmilia!

Æge. If I dream not, thou art Æmilia.
If thou art she, tell me, where is that son
That floated with thee on the fatal raft?

Abb. By men of Epidamnum he and I
And the twin Dromio, all were taken up;
But by-and-by rude fishermen of Corinth
By force took Dromio and my son from them,
And me they left with those of Epidamnum.
What then became of them I cannot tell;
I to this fortune that you see me in.

Duke. Why, here begins his morning story right.
These two Antipholus', these two so like,
And these two Dromios, one in semblance —
Besides her urging of her wrack at sea —
These are the parents to these children,
Which accidentally are met together.
Antipholus, thou cam'st from Corinth first.

S. Ant. No, sir, not I! I came from Syracuse.

Duke. Stay, stand apart. I know not which is which.

E. Ant. I came from Corinth, my most gracious lord —

E. Dro. And I with him.

E. Ant. Brought to this town by that most famous warrior,
Duke Menaphon, your most renowned uncle.

Adr. Which of you two did dine with me to-day?

S. Ant. I, gentle mistress.

Adr. And are not you my husband?

E. Ant. No; I say nay to that.

S. Ant. And so do I. Yet did she call me so,
And this fair gentlewoman, her sister here,
Did call me brother. [*To Luciana*] What I told you then
I hope I shall have leisure to make good,
If this be not a dream I see and hear.

Ang. That is the chain, sir, which you had of me.

S. Ant. I think it be, sir. I deny it not.

E. Ant. And you, sir, for this chain arrested me.

Ang. I think I did, sir. I deny it not.

Adr. I sent you money, sir, to be your bail
By Dromio; but I think he brought it not.

E. Dro. No, none by me.

S. Ant. This purse of ducats I receiv'd from you,
And Dromio my man did bring them me.
I see we still did meet each other's man,
And I was ta'en for him, and he for me,
And thereupon these errors are arose.

E. Ant. These ducats pawn I for my father here.

Duke. It shall not need. Thy father hath his life.

Court. Sir, I must have that diamond from you.

E. Ant. There, take it, and much thanks for my good cheer!

Abb. Renowned Duke, vouchsafe to take the pains
To go with us into the abbey here
And hear at large discoursed all our fortunes.
And all that are assembled in this place
That by this sympathized one day's error
Have suffer'd wrong, go keep us company,
And we shall make full satisfaction.
Thirty-three years have I but gone in travail
Of you, my sons, and till this present hour
My heavy burthen ne'er delivered.
The Duke, my husband, and my children both,
And you, the calendars of their nativity,
Go to a gossips' feast, and joy with me,
After so long grief, such nativity!

Duke. With all my heart I'll gossip at this feast.

Exeunt. Manent the two Dromios and two Brothers [*Antipholus*].

S. Dro. Master, shall I fetch your stuff from shipboard?

E. Ant. Dromio, what stuff of mine hast thou embark'd?

S. Dro. Your goods that lay at host, sir, in the Centaur.

S. Ant. He speaks to me. I am your master, Dromio.
Come, go with us; we'll look to that anon.
Embrace thy brother there; rejoice with him.

Exeunt [*the two brothers Antipholus*].

S. Dro. There is a fat friend at your master's house
That kitchen'd me for you to-day at dinner.
She now shall be my sister, not my wife.

E. Dro. Methinks you are my glass, and not my brother.
I see by you I am a sweet-fac'd youth.
Will you walk in to see their gossiping?

S. Dro. Not I, sir. You are my elder.

E. Dro. That's a question. How shall we try it?

S. Dro. We'll draw cuts for the senior. Till then lead thou first.

E. Dro. Nay then, thus!
We came into the world like brother and brother;
And now let's go hand in hand, not one before another.

Exeunt.

MUCH ADO ABOUT NOTHING

On August 4, 1600, the Stationers' Register records that 'The Commedie of muche A doo about nothing' (along with 'As you like yt,' 'Henry the ffift,' and 'Euery man in his humour') is 'to be staied.' The meaning of this note is far from clear. Perhaps the actors, in accordance with their usual policy, were attempting to block publication. On August 23, however, MUCH ADO ABOUT NOTHING was regularly entered in the Register by Andrew Wyse and William Aspley. Their edition (in quarto) came out before the end of the year. On this Quarto of 1600 is based the text of the present edition. In setting up the First Folio — which is less accurate than the Quarto, but supplies a number of corrections — the printers must have used a copy of the Quarto that had served as a prompt book and contained some manuscript changes, mostly in stage directions and speech headings.

Meres,[1] in the list of Shakespeare's comedies which he gives in his *Palladis Tamia* (1598), does not mention MUCH ADO, but when the Quarto appeared, in 1600, the play had been 'sundrie times publikely acted' by the Lord Chamberlain's players, as the title-page informs us. The part of Dogberry was taken by Will Kemp. This is proved by speech headings in the Quarto (iv, 2). Kemp left the Lord Chamberlain's Company early in 1599. Thus we may confidently fix the date of the play as the winter of 1598–99. Style and metre accord with this date.

The main plot comes from the twenty-second story in Matteo Bandello's *Novelle* (1554), which Shakespeare may have read in the original or in the translation in Volume III of Belleforest's *Histoires Tragiques* (1569). Bandello goes back, somehow, to the Greek romance of *Chæreas and Callirrhoë*, by one Chariton, who lived about the late fourth or early fifth century; but all this is prehistoric, so far as Shakespeare is concerned.

Bandello's *novella* may be summarized as follows:

King Piero of Aragon, having conquered Sicily, is holding court at Messina. One of his nobles, Timbreo di Cardone, is in love with Fenicia, the daughter of Messer Lionato de' Lionati, a gentleman of that city. A marriage is arranged. A cavalier, one Girondo Olerio Valenziano, a friend of Timbreo's, also loves Fenicia, and plots with an acquaintance, a young courtier 'more fond of evil than of good' (compare Shakespeare's Don John), to break off the match and win Fenicia for himself. This accomplice informs Timbreo that Fenicia is carrying on an intrigue with a certain gentleman and offers to give him ocular proof. That night he posts Timbreo in Lionato's garden. Girondo clothes a servant in fine attire and he and his accomplice go with the servant to the garden, accompanied by an attendant with a ladder on his shoulder. The family live on the other side of the palace, so that Girondo's servant can enter the house on the garden side without disturbing them. Timbreo sees him climb the ladder and go in at a window. Convinced of Fenicia's guilt, he leaves the garden without waiting to see the supposed lover come out. He has not recognized Girondo in the darkness and has no suspicion of his perfidy.

Next day Timbreo sends word to Lionato that he refuses to marry his daughter because of her unchastity. The messenger denounces Fenicia in the presence of her father and mother. Lionato accepts the breaking off of the match, but affirms his daughter's innocence and expresses the hope that God, the just judge, will bring the truth to light. Fenicia is overcome and lies cold and lifeless. A physician pronounces her dead, but she revives. Lionato decides to conceal the fact of her recovery. Funeral rites are performed, a coffin is buried, and a tomb is built, on which is set

[1] There is no likelihood that the mysterious *Love Labour's Won*, mentioned by Meres as one of Shakespeare's comedies, is MUCH ADO. It is much more likely to be *All's Well that Ends Well*, if indeed, it is still in existence.

up an epitaph in verse declaring her innocence (compare MUCH ADO, v, 3). She is sent in secret to the country house of her uncle Girolamo. All Messina mourns her death.

Timbreo soon comes to his senses and begins to analyze the evidence, which, on consideration, he finds far from convincing. Girondo, thinking Fenicia dead, goes almost mad with remorse. He takes Timbreo to the tomb, gives him a dagger, and begs him to kill him 'as a sacrifice to the guiltless Fenicia.' He makes a full confession; but Timbreo refuses to strike: 'I should lose my friend,' he says, and 'Fenicia would not be restored to life.' They go to the house of Lionato, and Timbreo tells the whole story in the presence of Fenicia's father and mother and others of her kindred. They are forgiven, and Timbreo promises to take no wife except such a one as Lionato shall propose.

A year later Lionato tells Timbreo that he has in mind a wife he thinks suitable. They visit the villa where Fenicia (now called Lucilla) has taken refuge. She has grown so fast in the interval — she was only sixteen when the match was broken off — that she is unrecognizable; but she looks so much like Fenicia that Timbreo falls in love with her on the spot. She pardons him and they are married. That everything may be rounded off symmetrically, her sister, Belfiore, marries the repentant Girondo.

Before Bandello wrote, Ariosto had worked the ancient story into his *Orlando Furioso* (cantos iv–vi), attaching it to the adventures of Rinaldo in Scotland. He calls the lady Ginevra; her suitor is Ariodante. From Ariosto either in the original or in Sir John Harington's translation (1591), Shakespeare derived the incident of the maid's guilelessly attiring herself as her mistress at the request of her villanous lover. Spenser repeats the tale (condensed and altered) in *The Faerie Queene* (ii, 4, 17–36), adapting it from Ariosto (compare stanza 26 with *Orlando Furioso*, v, 24–25, for a significant detail in this regard). Doubtless Shakespeare knew Spenser's version, which includes the maid's disguise; but that he had his eye on Ariosto seems certain. His Claudio is challenged to mortal combat by Leonato and Antonio, and again by Benedick. There is nothing of the kind in either Bandello or Spenser, whereas in Ariosto the wager of battle (to determine the guilt or innocence of the heroine) is the very top of the narrative climax. Harington mentions a verse translation of the episode by George Turbervile, of which nothing more is known.

In 1583 *A historie of Ariodante and Geneuora* was played at court by Richard Mulcaster's pupils, the boys of the Merchant Taylors' School. Nothing more is known of it. That another lost play recorded as *Panecia* in 1574 was really *Fenicia* (and based on Bandello) is an idle guess. *Panacia* (Πανάκεια) is quite as likely, and neither is probable. Jacob Ayrer's German comedy of *Die Schöne Phänicia* and Starter's Dutch *Timbre de Cardone ende Fenicie van Messine* both go back to Bandello, but neither throws any light on Shakespeare or his sources. Bandello and Ariosto suffice. There is no sound basis for the conjecture that our MUCH ADO is a reworking of an older play.

The merry war of Benedick and Beatrice, as well as the contortions of Dogberry and Verges, is Shakespeare's own.

MUCH ADO ABOUT NOTHING

[Dramatis Personæ.

Don Pedro, Prince of Arragon.
Don John, his bastard brother.
Claudio, a young lord of Florence.
Benedick, a young lord of Padua.
Leonato, Governor of Messina.
Antonio, an old man, his brother.
Balthasar, attendant on *Don Pedro.*
Borachio, } followers of *Don John.*
Conrade, }
Friar Francis

Dogberry, a Constable.
Verges, a Headborough.
A Sexton.
A Boy.

Hero, daughter to *Leonato.*
Beatrice, niece to *Leonato.*
Margaret, } waiting gentlewomen attending on *Hero.*
Ursula, }

Messengers, Watch, Attendants, &c.

SCENE. — *Messina.*]

ACT I. Scene I. [*An orchard before* Leonato's *house.*]

Enter *Leonato* (Governor of Messina), *Hero* (his Daughter), and *Beatrice* (his Niece), with a *Messenger.*

Leon. I learn in this letter that Don Pedro of Arragon comes this night to Messina.

Mess. He is very near by this. He was not three leagues off when I left him.

Leon. How many gentlemen have you lost in this action?

Mess. But few of any sort, and none of name.

Leon. A victory is twice itself when the achiever brings home full numbers. I find here that Don Pedro hath bestowed much honour on a young Florentine called Claudio.

Mess. Much deserv'd on his part, and equally remembr'red by Don Pedro. He hath borne himself beyond the promise of his age, doing in the figure of a lamb the feats of a lion. He hath indeed better bett'red expectation than you must expect of me to tell you how.

Leon. He hath an uncle here in Messina will be very much glad of it.

Mess. I have already delivered him letters, and there appears much joy in him; even so much that joy could not show itself modest enough without a badge of bitterness.

Leon. Did he break out into tears?

Mess. In great measure.

Leon. A kind overflow of kindness. There are no faces truer than those that are so wash'd. How much better is it to weep at joy than to joy at weeping!

Beat. I pray you, is Signior Mountanto return'd from the wars or no?

Mess. I know none of that name, lady. There was none such in the army of any sort.

Leon. What is he that you ask for, niece?

Hero. My cousin means Signior Benedick of Padua.

Mess. O, he's return'd, and as pleasant as ever he was.

Beat. He set up his bills here in Messina and challeng'd Cupid at the flight, and my uncle's fool, reading the challenge, subscrib'd for Cupid and challeng'd him at the burbolt. I pray you, how many hath he kill'd and eaten in these wars? But how many hath he kill'd? For indeed I promised to eat all of his killing.

Leon. Faith, niece, you tax Signior Benedick too much; but he'll be meet with you, I doubt it not.

Mess. He hath done good service, lady, in these wars.

Beat. You had musty victual, and he hath holp to eat it. He is a very valiant trencher-man; he hath an excellent stomach.

Mess. And a good soldier too, lady.

Beat. And a good soldier to a lady; but what is he to a lord?

Mess. A lord to a lord, a man to a man; stuff'd with all honourable virtues.

Beat. It is so indeed. He is no less than a stuff'd man; but for the stuffing — well, we are all mortal.

Leon. You must not, sir, mistake my niece. There is a kind of merry war betwixt Signior Benedick and her. They never meet but there's a skirmish of wit between them.

Beat. Alas, he gets nothing by that! In our last conflict four of his five wits went halting off, and now is the whole man govern'd with one; so that if he have wit enough to keep himself warm, let him bear it for a difference between himself and his horse; for it is all the wealth that he hath left to be known a reasonable creature. Who is his companion now? He hath every month a new sworn brother.

Mess. Is't possible?

Beat. Very easily possible. He wears his faith but as the fashion of his hat; it ever changes with the next block.

Mess. I see, lady, the gentleman is not in your books.

Beat. No. An he were, I would burn my study. But I pray you, who is his companion? Is there no young squarer now that will make a voyage with him to the devil?

Mess. He is most in the company of the right noble Claudio.

Beat. O Lord, he will hang upon him like a disease! He is sooner caught than the pestilence, and the taker runs presently mad. God help the noble Claudio! If he have caught the Benedick, it will cost him a thousand pound ere 'a be cured.

Mess. I will hold friends with you, lady.

Beat. Do, good friend.

Leon. You will never run mad, niece.

Beat. No, not till a hot January.

Mess. Don Pedro is approach'd.

Enter *Don Pedro, Claudio, Benedick, Balthasar,* and *John the Bastard.*

Pedro. Good Signior Leonato, are you come to meet your trouble? The fashion of the world is to avoid cost, and you encounter it.

Leon. Never came trouble to my house in the likeness of your Grace; for trouble being gone, comfort should remain; but when you depart from me, sorrow abides and happiness takes his leave.

Pedro. You embrace your charge too willingly. I think this is your daughter.

Leon. Her mother hath many times told me so.

Bene. Were you in doubt, sir, that you ask'd her?

Leon. Signior Benedick, no; for then were you a child.

Pedro. You have it full, Benedick. We may guess by this what you are, being a man. Truly the lady fathers herself. Be happy, lady; for you are like an honourable father.

Bene. If Signior Leonato be her father, she would not have his head on her shoulders for all Messina, as like him as she is.

Beat. I wonder that you will still be talking, Signior Benedick. Nobody marks you.

Bene. What, my dear Lady Disdain! are you yet living?

Beat. Is it possible Disdain should die while she hath such meet food to feed it as Signior Benedick? Courtesy itself must convert to disdain if you come in her presence.

Bene. Then is courtesy a turncoat. But it is certain I am loved of all ladies, only you excepted; and I would I could find in my heart that I had not a hard heart, for truly I love none.

Beat. A dear happiness to women! They would else have been troubled with a pernicious suitor. I thank God and my cold blood, I am of your humour for that. I had rather hear my dog bark at a crow than a man swear he loves me.

Bene. God keep your ladyship still in that mind! So some gentleman or other shall scape a predestinate scratch'd face.

Beat. Scratching could not make it worse an 'twere such a face as yours were.

Bene. Well, you are a rare parrot-teacher.

Beat. A bird of my tongue is better than a beast of yours.

Bene. I would my horse had the speed of your tongue, and so good a continuer. But keep your way, a God's name! I have done.

Beat. You always end with a jade's trick. I know you of old.

Pedro. That is the sum of all, Leonato. Signior Claudio and Signior Benedick, my dear friend Leonato hath invited you all. I tell him we shall stay here at the least a month, and he heartily prays some occasion may detain us longer. I dare swear he is no hypocrite, but prays from his heart.

Leon. If you swear, my lord, you shall not be forsworn. [*To Don John*] Let me bid you welcome, my lord. Being reconciled to the Prince your brother, I owe you all duty.

John. I thank you. I am not of many words, but I thank you.

Leon. Please it your Grace lead on?

Pedro. Your hand, Leonato. We will go together.

Exeunt. Manent Benedick and Claudio.

Claud. Benedick, didst thou note the daughter of Signior Leonato?

Bene. I noted her not, but I look'd on her.

Claud. Is she not a modest young lady?

Bene. Do you question me, as an honest man should do, for my simple true judgment? or would you have me speak after my custom, as being a professed tyrant to their sex?

Claud. No. I pray thee speak in sober judgment.

Bene. Why, i' faith, methinks she's too low for a high praise, too brown for a fair praise, and too little for a great praise. Only this commendation I can afford her, that were she other than she is, she were unhandsome, and being no other but as she is, I do not like her.

Claud. Thou thinkest I am in sport. I pray thee tell me truly how thou lik'st her.

Bene. Would you buy her, that you enquire after her?

Claud. Can the world buy such a jewel?

Bene. Yea, and a case to put it into. But speak you this with a sad brow? or do you play the flouting Jack, to tell us Cupid is a good hare-finder and Vulcan a rare carpenter? Come, in what key shall a man take you to go in the song?

Claud. In mine eye she is the sweetest lady that ever I look'd on.

Bene. I can see yet without spectacles, and I see no such matter. There's her cousin, an she were not possess'd with a fury, exceeds her as much in beauty as the first of May doth the last of December. But I hope you have no intent to turn husband, have you?

Claud. I would scarce trust myself, though I had sworn the contrary, if Hero would be my wife.

Bene. Is't come to this? In faith, hath not the world one man but he will wear his cap with suspicion? Shall I never see a bachelor of threescore again? Go to, i' faith! An thou wilt needs thrust thy neck into a yoke, wear the print of it and sigh away Sundays.

Enter *Don Pedro.*

Look! Don Pedro is returned to seek you.

Pedro. What secret hath held you here, that you followed not to Leonato's?

Bene. I would your Grace would constrain me to tell.

Pedro. I charge thee on thy allegiance.

Bene. You hear, Count Claudio. I can be secret as a dumb man, I would have you think so; but, on my allegiance — mark you this — on my allegiance! he is in love. With who? Now that is your Grace's part. Mark how short his answer is: With Hero, Leonato's short daughter.

Claud. If this were so, so were it utt'red.

Bene. Like the old tale, my lord: 'It is not so, nor 'twas not so; but indeed, God forbid it should be so!'

Claud. If my passion change not shortly, God forbid it should be otherwise.

Pedro. Amen, if you love her; for the lady is very well worthy.

Claud. You speak this to fetch me in, my lord.

Pedro. By my troth, I speak my thought.

Claud. And, in faith, my lord, I spoke mine.

Bene. And, by my two faiths and troths, my lord, I spoke mine.

Claud. That I love her, I feel.

Pedro. That she is worthy, I know.

Bene. That I neither feel how she should be loved, nor know how she should be worthy, is the opinion that fire cannot melt out of me. I will die in it at the stake.

Pedro. Thou wast ever an obstinate heretic in the despite of beauty.

Claud. And never could maintain his part but in the force of his will.

Bene. That a woman conceived me, I thank her; that she brought me up, I likewise give her most humble thanks; but that I will have a rechate winded in my forehead, or hang my bugle in an invisible baldrick, all women shall pardon me. Because I will not do them the wrong to mistrust any, I will do myself the right to trust none; and the fine is (for the which I may go the finer), I will live a bachelor.

Pedro. I shall see thee, ere I die, look pale with love.

Bene. With anger, with sickness, or with hunger, my lord; not with love. Prove that ever I lose more blood with love than I will get again with drinking, pick out mine eyes with a ballad-maker's pen and hang me up at the door of a brothel house for the sign of blind Cupid.

Pedro. Well, if ever thou dost fall from this faith, thou wilt prove a notable argument.

Bene. If I do, hang me in a bottle like a cat and shoot at me; and he that hits me, let him be clapp'd on the shoulder and call'd Adam.

Pedro. Well, as time shall try.
'In time the savage bull doth bear the yoke.'

Bene. The savage bull may; but if ever the sensible Benedick bear it, pluck off the bull's horns and set them in my forehead, and let me be vilely painted, and in such great letters as they write 'Here is good horse to hire,' let them signify under my sign 'Here you may see Benedick the married man.'

Claud. If this should ever happen, thou wouldst be horn-mad.

Pedro. Nay, if Cupid have not spent all his quiver in Venice, thou wilt quake for this shortly.

Bene. I look for an earthquake too then.

Pedro. Well, you will temporize with the hours. In the meantime, good Signior Benedick, repair to Leonato's, commend me to him and tell him I will not fail him at supper; for indeed he hath made great preparation.

Bene. I have almost matter enough in me for such an embassage; and so I commit you —

Claud. To the tuition of God. From my house — if I had it —

Pedro. The sixth of July. Your loving friend, Benedick.

Bene. Nay, mock not, mock not. The body of your discourse is sometime guarded with fragments, and the guards are but slightly basted on neither. Ere you flout old ends any further, examine your conscience. And so I leave you. *Exit.*

Claud. My liege, your Highness now may do me good.

Pedro. My love is thine to teach. Teach it but how,
And thou shalt see how apt it is to learn
Any hard lesson that may do thee good.

Claud. Hath Leonato any son, my lord?

Pedro. No child but Hero; she's his only heir.
Dost thou affect her, Claudio?

Claud. O my lord,
When you went onward on this ended action,
I look'd upon her with a soldier's eye,
That lik'd, but had a rougher task in hand
Than to drive liking to the name of love;
But now I am return'd and that war-thoughts
Have left their places vacant, in their rooms
Come thronging soft and delicate desires,
All prompting me how fair young Hero is,
Saying I lik'd her ere I went to wars.

Pedro. Thou wilt be like a lover presently
And tire the hearer with a book of words.
If thou dost love fair Hero, cherish it,
And I will break with her and with her father,
And thou shalt have her. Was't not to this end
That thou began'st to twist so fine a story?

Claud. How sweetly you do minister to love,
That know love's grief by his complexion!
But lest my liking might too sudden seem,
I would have salv'd it with a longer treatise.

Pedro. What need the bridge much broader than the flood?
The fairest grant is the necessity.
Look, what will serve is fit. 'Tis once, thou lovest,
And I will fit thee with the remedy.
I know we shall have revelling to-night.
I will assume thy part in some disguise
And tell fair Hero I am Claudio,
And in her bosom I'll unclasp my heart
And take her hearing prisoner with the force
And strong encounter of my amorous tale.
Then after to her father will I break,
And the conclusion is, she shall be thine.
In practice let us put it presently. *Exeunt.*

[Scene II. *A room in* Leonato's *house.*]

Enter [at one door] *Leonato* and [at another door, *Antonio,*] an old man, brother to *Leonato.*

Leon. How now, brother? Where is my cousin your son? Hath he provided this music?

Ant. He is very busy about it. But, brother, I can tell you strange news that you yet dreamt not of.

Leon. Are they good?

Ant. As the event stamps them; but they have a good cover, they show well outward. The Prince and Count Claudio, walking in a thick-pleached alley in mine orchard, were thus much overheard by a man of mine: the Prince discovered to Claudio that he loved my niece your daughter and meant to acknowledge it this night in a dance, and if he found her accordant, he meant to take the present time by the top and instantly break with you of it.

Leon. Hath the fellow any wit that told you this?

Ant. A good sharp fellow. I will send for him, and question him yourself.

Leon. No, no. We will hold it as a dream till it appear itself; but I will acquaint my daughter withal, that she may be the better prepared for an answer, if peradventure this be true. Go you and tell her of it. [*Exit Antonio.*]

[Enter *Antonio's Son* with a *Musician,* and others.]

[*To the Son*] Cousin, you know what you have to do. — [*To the Musician*] O, I cry you mercy, friend. Go you with me, and I will use your skill. — Good cousin, have a care this busy time. *Exeunt.*

[Scene III. *Another room in* Leonato's *house.*]

Enter *Sir John the Bastard* and *Conrade,* his companion.

Con. What the goodyear, my lord! Why are you thus out of measure sad?

John. There is no measure in the occasion that breeds; therefore the sadness is without limit.

Con. You should hear reason.

John. And when I have heard it, what blessing brings it?

Con. If not a present remedy, at least a patient sufferance.

John. I wonder that thou (being, as thou say'st thou art, born under Saturn) goest about to apply a moral medicine to a mortifying mischief. I cannot hide what I am: I must be sad when I have cause, and smile at no man's jests; eat when I have stomach, and wait for no man's leisure; sleep when I am drowsy, and tend on no man's business; laugh when I am merry, and claw no man in his humour.

Con. Yea, but you must not make the full show of this till you may do it without controlment. You have of late stood out against your brother, and he hath ta'en you newly into his grace where it is impossible you should take true root but by the fair weather that you make yourself. It is needful that you frame the season for your own harvest.

John. I had rather be a canker in a hedge than a rose in his grace, and it better fits my blood to be disdain'd of all than to fashion a carriage to rob love from any. In this, though I cannot be said to be a flattering honest man, it must not be denied but I am a plain-dealing villain. I am trusted with a muzzle and enfranchis'd with a clog; therefore I have decreed not to sing in my cage. If I had my mouth, I would bite; if I had my liberty, I would do my liking. In the meantime let me be that I am, and seek not to alter me.

Con. Can you make no use of your discontent?

John. I make all use of it, for I use it only.

Enter *Borachio.*

Who comes here? What news, Borachio?

Bora. I came yonder from a great supper. The Prince your brother is royally entertain'd by Leonato, and I can give you intelligence of an intended marriage.

John. Will it serve for any model to build mischief on? What is he for a fool that betroths himself to unquietness?

Bora. Marry, it is your brother's right hand.

John. Who? the most exquisite Claudio?

Bora. Even he.

John. A proper squire! And who? and who? which way looks he?

Bora. Marry, on Hero, the daughter and heir of Leonato.

John. A very forward March-chick! How came you to this?

Bora. Being entertain'd for a perfumer, as I was smoking a musty room, comes me the Prince and Claudio, hand in hand in sad conference. I whipt me behind the arras and there heard it agreed upon that the Prince should woo Hero for himself, and having obtain'd her, give her to Count Claudio.

John. Come, come, let us thither. This may prove food to my displeasure. That young start-up hath all the glory of my overthrow. If I can cross him any way, I bless myself every way. You are both sure, and will assist me?

Con. To the death, my lord.

John. Let us to the great supper. Their cheer is the greater that I am subdued. Would the cook were o' my mind! Shall we go prove what's to be done?

Bora. We'll wait upon your lordship.

Exeunt.

ACT II. [Scene I. *A hall in* Leonato's *house.*]

Enter *Leonato,* [*Antonio*] his Brother, *Hero* his Daughter, and *Beatrice* his Niece, and a *Kinsman*; [also *Margaret* and *Ursula*].

Leon. Was not Count John here at supper?

Ant. I saw him not.

Beat. How tartly that gentleman looks! I never can see him but I am heart-burn'd an hour after.

Hero. He is of a very melancholy disposition.

Beat. He were an excellent man that were made just in the midway between him and Benedick. The one is too like an image and says nothing, and the other too like my lady's eldest son, evermore tattling.

Leon. Then half Signior Benedick's tongue in Count John's mouth, and half Count John's melancholy in Signior Benedick's face —

Beat. With a good leg and a good foot, uncle, and money enough in his purse, such a man would win any woman in the world — if 'a could get her good will.

Leon. By my troth, niece, thou wilt never get thee a husband if thou be so shrewd of thy tongue.

Ant. In faith, she's too curst.

Beat. Too curst is more than curst. I shall lessen God's sending that way, for it is said, 'God sends a curst cow short horns,' but to a cow too curst he sends none.

Leon. So, by being too curst, God will send you no horns.

Beat. Just, if he send me no husband; for the which blessing I am at him upon my knees every morning and evening. Lord, I could not endure a husband with a beard on his face. I had rather lie in the woollen!

Leon. You may light on a husband that hath no beard.

Beat. What should I do with him? dress him in my apparel and make him my waiting gentlewoman? He that hath a beard is more than a youth, and he that hath no beard is less than a man; and he that is more than a youth is not for me; and he that is less than a man, I am not for him. Therefore I will even take sixpence in earnest of the berrord and lead his apes into hell.

Leon. Well then, go you into hell?

Beat. No; but to the gate, and there will the devil meet me like an old cuckold with horns on his head, and say 'Get you to heaven, Beatrice, get you to heaven. Here's no place for you maids.' So deliver I up my apes, and away to Saint Peter — for the heavens. He shows me where the bachelors sit, and there live we as merry as the day is long.

Ant. [*to Hero*] Well, niece, I trust you will be rul'd by your father.

Beat. Yes faith. It is my cousin's duty to make cursy and say, 'Father, as it please you.' But yet for all that, cousin, let him be a handsome fellow, or else make another cursy, and say, 'Father, as it please me.'

Leon. Well, niece, I hope to see you one day fitted with a husband.

Beat. Not till God make men of some other metal than earth. Would it not grieve a woman to be overmaster'd with a piece of valiant dust? to make an account of her life to a clod of wayward marl? No, uncle, I'll none. Adam's sons are my brethren, and truly I hold it a sin to match in my kinred.

Leon. Daughter, remember what I told you. If the Prince do solicit you in that kind, you know your answer.

Beat. The fault will be in the music, cousin, if you be not wooed in good time. If the Prince be too important, tell him there is measure in everything, and so dance out the answer. For, hear me, Hero: wooing, wedding, and repenting is as a Scotch jig, a measure, and a cinquepace: the first suit is hot and hasty like a Scotch jig — and full as fantastical; the wedding, mannerly modest, as a measure, full of state and ancientry; and then comes Repentance and with his bad legs falls into the cinquepace faster and faster, till he sink into his grave.

Leon. Cousin, you apprehend passing shrewdly.

Beat. I have a good eye, uncle; I can see a church by daylight.

Leon. The revellers are ent'ring, brother. Make good room.

[*Exit Antonio.*]

Enter, [masked,] *Don Pedro, Claudio, Benedick,* and *Balthasar.* [With them enter *Antonio,* also masked. After them enter] *Don John* [and *Borachio* (without masks), who stand aside and look on during the dance].

Pedro. Lady, will you walk a bout with your friend?

Hero. So you walk softly and look sweetly and say nothing, I am yours for the walk; and especially when I walk away.

Pedro. With me in your company?

Hero. I may say so when I please.

Pedro. And when please you to say so?

Hero. When I like your favour, for God defend the lute should be like the case!

Pedro. My visor is Philemon's roof; within the house is Jove.

Hero. Why then, your visor should be thatch'd.

Pedro. Speak low if you speak love.

[*Takes her aside.*]

Balth. Well, I would you did like me.

Marg. So would not I for your own sake, for I have many ill qualities.

Balth. Which is one?

Marg. I say my prayers aloud.

Balth. I love you the better. The hearers may cry Amen.

Marg. God match me with a good dancer!

Balth. Amen.

Marg. And God keep him out of my sight when the dance is done! Answer, clerk.

Balth. No more words. The clerk is answered. [*Takes her aside.*]

Urs. I know you well enough. You are Signior Antonio.

Ant. At a word, I am not.

Urs. I know you by the waggling of your head.

Ant. To tell you true, I counterfeit him.

Urs. You could never do him so ill-well unless you were the very man. Here's his dry hand up and down. You are he, you are he!

Ant. At a word, I am not.

Urs. Come, come, do you think I do not know you by your excellent wit? Can virtue hide itself? Go to, mum, you are he. Graces will appear, and there's an end. [*They step aside.*]

Beat. Will you not tell me who told you so?

Bene. No, you shall pardon me.

Beat. Nor will you not tell me who you are?

Bene. Not now.

Beat. That I was disdainful, and that I had my good wit out of the 'Hundred Merry Tales.' Well, this was Signior Benedick that said so.

Bene. What's he?

Beat. I am sure you know him well enough.

Bene. Not I, believe me.

Beat. Did he never make you laugh?

Bene. I pray you, what is he?

Beat. Why, he is the Prince's jester, a very dull fool. Only his gift is in devising impossible slanders. None but libertines delight in him; and the commendation is not in his wit, but in his villany; for he both pleases men and angers them, and then they laugh at him and beat him. I am sure he is in the fleet. I would he had boarded me.

Bene. When I know the gentleman, I'll tell him what you say.

Beat. Do, do. He'll but break a comparison or two on me; which peradventure, not marked or not laugh'd at, strikes him into melancholy; and then there's a partridge wing saved, for the fool will eat no supper that night. [*Music.*] We must follow the leaders.

Bene. In every good thing.

Beat. Nay, if they lead to any ill, I will leave them at the next turning.

Dance. Exeunt [*all but Don John, Borachio, and Claudio*].

John. Sure my brother is amorous on Hero and hath withdrawn her father to break with him about it. The ladies follow her and but one visor remains.

Bora. And that is Claudio. I know him by his bearing.

John. Are you not Signior Benedick?

Claud. You know me well. I am he.

John. Signior, you are very near my brother in his love. He is enamour'd on Hero. I pray you dissuade him from her; she is no equal for his birth. You may do the part of an honest man in it.

Claud. How know you he loves her?

John. I heard him swear his affection.

Bora. So did I too, and he swore he would marry her to-night.

John. Come, let us to the banquet.

Exeunt. Manet Claudio.

Claud. Thus answer I in name of Benedick
But hear these ill news with the ears of Claudio. [*Unmasks.*]
'Tis certain so. The Prince wooes for himself.
Friendship is constant in all other things
Save in the office and affairs of love.
Therefore all hearts in love use their own tongues;
Let every eye negotiate for itself
And trust no agent; for beauty is a witch
Against whose charms faith melteth into blood.
This is an accident of hourly proof,
Which I mistrusted not. Farewell therefore Hero!

Enter *Benedick* [unmasked].

Bene. Count Claudio?

Claud. Yea, the same.

Bene. Come, will you go with me?

Claud. Whither?

Bene. Even to the next willow, about your own business, County. What fashion will you wear the garland of? about your neck, like an usurer's chain? or under your arm, like a lieutenant's scarf? You must wear it one way, for the Prince hath got your Hero.

Claud. I wish him joy of her.

Bene. Why, that's spoken like an honest drovier. So they sell bullocks. But did you think the Prince would have served you thus?

Claud. I pray you leave me.

Bene. Ho! now you strike like the blind man! 'Twas the boy that stole your meat, and you'll beat the post.

Claud. If it will not be, I'll leave you. *Exit.*

Bene. Alas, poor hurt fowl! now will he creep into sedges. But, that my Lady Beatrice should know me, and not know me! The Prince's fool! Ha! it may be I go under that title because I am merry. Yea, but so I am apt to do myself wrong. I am not so reputed. It is the base (though bitter) disposition of Beatrice that puts the world into her person and so gives me out. Well, I'll be revenged as I may.

Enter *Don Pedro*

Pedro. Now, signior, where's the Count? Did you see him?

Bene. Troth, my lord, I have played the part of Lady Fame. I found him here as melancholy as a lodge in a warren. I told him, and I think I told him true, that your Grace had got the good will of this young lady, and I off'red him my company to a willow tree, either to make him a garland, as being forsaken, or to bind him up a rod, as being worthy to be whipt.

Pedro. To be whipt? What's his fault?

Bene. The flat transgression of a schoolboy who, being overjoyed with finding a bird's nest, shows it his companion, and he steals it.

Pedro. Wilt thou make a trust a transgression? The transgression is in the stealer.

Bene. Yet it had not been amiss the rod had been made, and the garland too; for the garland he might have worn himself, and the rod he might have bestowed on you, who, as I take it, have stol'n his bird's nest.

Pedro. I will but teach them to sing and restore them to the owner.

Bene. If their singing answer your saying, by my faith you say honestly.

Pedro. The Lady Beatrice hath a quarrel to you. The gentleman that danc'd with her told her she is much wrong'd by you.

Bene. O, she misus'd me past the endurance of a block! An oak but with one green leaf on it would have answered her; my very visor began to assume life and scold with her. She told me, not thinking I had been myself, that I was the Prince's jester, that I was duller than a great thaw; huddling jest upon jest with such impossible conveyance upon me that I stood like a man at a mark, with a whole army shooting at me. She speaks poniards, and every word stabs. If her breath were as terrible as her terminations, there were no living near her; she would infect to the North Star. I would not marry her though she were endowed with all that Adam had left him before he transgress'd. She would have made Hercules have turn'd spit, yea, and have cleft his club to make the fire too. Come, talk not of her. You shall find her the infernal Ate in good apparel. I would to God some scholar would conjure her, for certainly, while she is here, a man may live as quiet in hell as in a sanctuary; and people sin upon purpose, because they would go thither; so indeed all disquiet, horror, and perturbation follows her.

Enter *Claudio* and *Beatrice, Leonato, Hero.*

Pedro. Look, here she comes.

Bene. Will your Grace command me any service to the world's end? I will go on the slightest errand now to the Antipodes that you can devise to send me on; I will fetch you a toothpicker now from the furthest inch of Asia; bring you the length of Prester John's foot; fetch you a hair off the great Cham's beard; do you any embassage to the Pygmies—rather than hold three words' conference with this harpy. You have no employment for me?

Pedro. None, but to desire your good company.

Bene. O God, sir, here's a dish I love not! I cannot endure my Lady Tongue. *Exit.*

Pedro. Come, lady, come; you have lost the heart of Signior Benedick.

Beat. Indeed, my lord, he lent it me awhile, and I gave him use for it — a double heart for his single one. Marry, once before he won it of me with false dice; therefore your Grace may well say I have lost it.

Pedro. You have put him down, lady; you have put him down.

Beat. So I would not he should do me, my lord, lest I should prove the mother of fools. I have brought Count Claudio, whom you sent me to seek.

Pedro. Why, how now, Count? Wherefore are you sad?

Claud. Not sad, my lord.

Pedro. How then? sick?

Claud. Neither, my lord.

Beat. The Count is neither sad, nor sick, nor merry, nor well; but civil count — civil as an orange, and something of that jealous complexion.

Pedro. I' faith, lady, I think your blazon to be true; though I'll be sworn, if he be so, his conceit is false. Here, Claudio, I have wooed in thy name, and fair Hero is won. I have broke with her father, and his good will obtained. Name the day of marriage, and God give thee joy!

Leon. Count, take of me my daughter, and with her my fortunes. His Grace hath made the match, and all grace say Amen to it!

Beat. Speak, Count, 'tis your cue.

Claud. Silence is the perfectest herald of joy. I were but little happy if I could say how much. Lady, as you are mine, I am yours. I give away myself for you and dote upon the exchange.

Beat. Speak, cousin; or, if you cannot, stop his mouth with a kiss and let not him speak neither.

Pedro. In faith, lady, you have a merry heart.

Beat. Yea, my lord; I thank it, poor fool, it keeps on the windy side of care. My cousin tells him in his ear that he is in her heart.

Claud. And so she doth, cousin.

Beat. Good Lord, for alliance! Thus goes every one to the world but I, and I am sunburnt. I may sit in a corner and cry 'Heigh-ho for a husband!'

Pedro. Lady Beatrice, I will get you one.

Beat. I would rather have one of your father's getting. Hath your Grace ne'er a brother like you? Your father got excellent husbands, if a maid could come by them.

Pedro. Will you have me, lady?

Beat. No, my lord, unless I might have another for working days: your Grace is too costly to wear every day. But I beseech your Grace pardon me. I was born to speak all mirth and no matter.

Pedro. Your silence most offends me, and to be merry best becomes you, for out o' question you were born in a merry hour.

Beat. No, sure, my lord, my mother cried; but then there was a star danc'd, and under that was I born. Cousins, God give you joy!

Leon. Niece, will you look to those things I told you of?

Beat. I cry you mercy, uncle. By your Grace's pardon. *Exit.*

Pedro. By my troth, a pleasant-spirited lady.

Leon. There's little of the melancholy element in her, my lord. She is never sad but when she sleeps, and not ever sad then; for I have heard my daughter say she hath often dreamt of unhappiness and wak'd herself with laughing.

Pedro. She cannot endure to hear tell of a husband.

Leon. O, by no means! She mocks all her wooers out of suit.

Pedro. She were an excellent wife for Benedick.

Leon. O Lord, my lord! if they were but a week married, they would talk themselves mad.

Pedro. County Claudio, when mean you to go to church?

Claud. To-morrow, my lord. Time goes on crutches till love have all his rites.

Leon. Not till Monday, my dear son, which is hence a just sevennight; and a time too brief too, to have all things answer my mind.

Pedro. Come, you shake the head at so long a breathing; but I warrant thee, Claudio, the time shall not go dully by us. I will in the interim undertake one of Hercules' labours, which is, to bring Signior Benedick and the Lady Beatrice into a mountain of affection th' one with th' other. I would fain have it a match, and I doubt not but to fashion it if you three will but minister such assistance as I shall give you direction.

Leon. My lord, I am for you, though it cost me ten nights' watchings.

Claud. And I, my lord.

Pedro. And you too, gentle Hero?

Hero. I will do any modest office, my lord, to help my cousin to a good husband.

Pedro. And Benedick is not the unhopefullest husband that I know. Thus far can I praise him: he is of a noble strain, of approved valour, and confirm'd honesty. I will teach you how to humour your cousin, that she shall fall in love with Benedick; and I, [*to Leonato and Claudio*] with your two helps, will so practise on Benedick that, in despite of his quick wit and his queasy stomach, he shall fall in love with Beatrice. If we can do this, Cupid is no longer an archer; his glory shall be ours, for we are the only love-gods. Go in with me, and I will tell you my drift. *Exeunt.*

[Scene II. *A hall in* Leonato's *house.*]

Enter [*Don*] *John* and *Borachio.*

John. It is so. The Count Claudio shall marry the daughter of Leonato.

Bora. Yea, my lord; but I can cross it.

John. Any bar, any cross, any impediment will be med'cinable to me. I am sick in displeasure to him, and whatsoever comes athwart his affection ranges evenly with mine. How canst thou cross this marriage?

Bora. Not honestly, my lord, but so covertly that no dishonesty shall appear in me.

John. Show me briefly how.

Bora. I think I told your lordship, a year since, how much I am in the favour of Margaret, the waiting gentlewoman to Hero.

John. I remember.

Bora. I can, at any unseasonable instant of the night, appoint her to look out at her lady's chamber window.

John. What life is in that to be the death of this marriage?

Bora. The poison of that lies in you to temper. Go you to the Prince your brother; spare not to tell him that he hath wronged his honour in marrying the renowned Claudio (whose estimation do you mightily hold up) to a contaminated stale, such a one as Hero.

John. What proof shall I make of that?

Bora. Proof enough to misuse the Prince, to vex Claudio, to undo Hero, and kill Leonato. Look you for any other issue?

John. Only to despite them I will endeavour anything.

Bora. Go then; find me a meet hour to draw Don Pedro and the Count Claudio alone; tell them that you know that Hero loves me; intend a kind of zeal both to the Prince and Claudio, as — in love of your brother's honour, who hath made this match, and his friend's reputation, who is thus like to be cozen'd with the semblance of a maid — that you have discover'd thus. They will scarcely believe this without trial. Offer them instances; which shall bear no less likelihood than to see me at her chamber window, hear me call Margaret Hero, hear Margaret term me Claudio; and bring them to see this the very night before the intended wedding (for in the meantime I will so fashion the matter that Hero shall be absent) and there shall appear such seeming truth of Hero's disloyalty that jealousy shall be call'd assurance and all the preparation overthrown.

John. Grow this to what adverse issue it can, I will put it in practice. Be cunning in the working this, and thy fee is a thousand ducats.

Bora. Be you constant in the accusation, and my cunning shall not shame me.

John. I will presently go learn their day of marriage. *Exeunt.*

[Scene III. Leonato's *orchard.*]

Enter *Benedick* alone.

Bene. Boy!

[Enter *Boy.*]

Boy. Signior?

Bene. In my chamber window lies a book. Bring it hither to me in the orchard.

Boy. I am here already, sir.

Bene. I know that, but I would have thee hence and here again. (*Exit Boy.*) I do much wonder that one man, seeing how much another man is a fool when he dedicates his behaviours to love, will, after he hath laugh'd at such shallow follies in others, become the argument of his own scorn by falling in love; and such a man is Claudio. I have known when there was no music with him but the drum and the fife; and now had he rather hear the tabor and the pipe. I have known when he would have walk'd ten mile afoot to see a good armour; and now will he lie ten nights awake carving the fashion of a new doublet. He was wont to speak plain and to the purpose, like an honest man and a soldier; and now is he turn'd orthography; his words are a very fantastical banquet — just so many strange dishes. May I be so converted and see with these eyes? I cannot tell; I think not. I will not be sworn but love may transform me to an oyster; but I'll take my oath on it, till he have made an oyster of me he shall never make me such a fool. One woman is fair, yet I am well; another is wise, yet I am well; another virtuous, yet I am well; but till all graces be in one woman, one woman shall not come in my grace. Rich she shall be, that's certain; wise, or I'll none; virtuous, or I'll never cheapen her; fair, or I'll never look on her; mild, or come not near me; noble, or not I for an angel; of good discourse, an excellent musician, and her hair shall be of what colour it please God. Ha, the Prince and Monsieur Love! I will hide me in the arbour. [*Hides.*]

Enter *Don Pedro, Leonato, Claudio.*
Music [within].

Pedro. Come, shall we hear this music?
Claud. Yea, my good lord. How still the evening is,
As hush'd on purpose to grace harmony!
Pedro. See you where Benedick hath hid himself?
Claud. O, very well, my lord. The music ended,
We'll fit the kid-fox with a pennyworth.

Enter *Balthasar* with *Music.*

Pedro. Come, Balthasar, we'll hear that song again.
Balth. O, good my lord, tax not so bad a voice
To slander music any more than once.
Pedro. It is the witness still of excellency
To put a strange face on his own perfection.
I pray thee sing, and let me woo no more.

Balth. Because you talk of wooing, I will sing,
Since many a wooer doth commence his suit
To her he thinks not worthy, yet he wooes,
Yet will he swear he loves.

Pedro. Nay, pray thee come;
Or if thou wilt hold longer argument,
Do it in notes.

Balth. Note this before my notes:
There's not a note of mine that's worth the noting.

Pedro. Why, these are very crotchets that he speaks!
Note notes, forsooth, and nothing! [*Music.*]

Bene. [*aside*] Now divine air! Now is his soul ravish'd! Is it not strange that sheep's guts should hale souls out of men's bodies? Well, a horn for my money, when all's done.

[*Balthasar sings.*]

The Song.

Sigh no more, ladies, sigh no more!
Men were deceivers ever,
One foot in sea, and one on shore;
To one thing constant never.
Then sigh not so,
But let them go,
And be you blithe and bonny,
Converting all your sounds of woe
Into Hey nonny, nonny.

Sing no more ditties, sing no moe,
Of dumps so dull and heavy!
The fraud of men was ever so,
Since summer first was leavy.
Then sigh not so, &c.

Pedro. By my troth, a good song.

Balth. And an ill singer, my lord.

Pedro. Ha, no, no, faith! Thou sing'st well enough for a shift.

Bene. [*aside*] An he had been a dog that should have howl'd thus, they would have hang'd him; and I pray God his bad voice bode no mischief. I had as live have heard the night raven, come what plague could have come after it.

Pedro. Yea, marry. Dost thou hear, Balthasar? I pray thee get us some excellent music; for to-morrow night we would have it at the Lady Hero's chamber window.

Balth. The best I can, my lord.

Pedro. Do so. Farewell.

Exit Balthasar [*with Musicians*].

Come hither, Leonato. What was it you told me of to-day? that your niece Beatrice was in love with Signior Benedick?

Claud. O, ay! — [*Aside to Pedro*] Stalk on, stalk on; the fowl sits. — I did never think that lady would have loved any man.

Leon. No, nor I neither; but most wonderful that she should so dote on Signior Benedick, whom she hath in all outward behaviours seem'd ever to abhor.

Bene. [*aside*] Is't possible? Sits the wind in that corner?

Leon. By my troth, my lord, I cannot tell what to think of it, but that she loves him with an enraged affection. It is past the infinite of thought.

Pedro. May be she doth but counterfeit.

Claud. Faith, like enough.

Leon. O God, counterfeit? There was never counterfeit of passion came so near the life of passion as she discovers it.

Pedro. Why, what effects of passion shows she?

Claud. [*aside*] Bait the hook well! This fish will bite.

Leon. What effects, my lord? She will sit you — you heard my daughter tell you how.

Claud. She did indeed.

Pedro. How, how, I pray you? You amaze me. I would have thought her spirit had been invincible against all assaults of affection.

Leon. I would have sworn it had, my lord — especially against Benedick.

Bene. [*aside*] I should think this a gull but that the white-bearded fellow speaks it. Knavery cannot, sure, hide himself in such reverence.

Claud. [*aside*] He hath ta'en th' infection. Hold it up.

Pedro. Hath she made her affection known to Benedick?

Leon. No, and swears she never will. That's her torment.

Claud. 'Tis true indeed. So your daughter says. 'Shall I,' says she, 'that have so oft encount'red him with scorn, write to him that I love him?'

Leon. This says she now when she is beginning to write to him; for she'll be up twenty times a night, and there will she sit in her smock till she have writ a sheet of paper. My daughter tells us all.

Claud. Now you talk of a sheet of paper, I remember a pretty jest your daughter told us of.

Leon. O, when she had writ it, and was reading it over, she found 'Benedick' and 'Beatrice' between the sheet?

Claud. That.

Leon. O, she tore the letter into a thousand halfpence, rail'd at herself that she should be so immodest to write to one that she knew would flout her. 'I measure him,' says she, 'by my own spirit; for I should flout him if he writ to me. Yea, though I love him, I should.'

Claud. Then down upon her knees she falls, weeps, sobs, beats her heart, tears her hair, prays, curses — 'O sweet Benedick! God give me patience!'

Leon. She doth indeed; my daughter says so. And the ecstasy hath so much overborne her that my daughter is sometime afeard she will do a desperate outrage to herself. It is very true.

Pedro. It were good that Benedick knew of it by some other, if she will not discover it.

Claud. To what end? He would make but a sport of it and torment the poor lady worse.

Pedro. An he should, it were an alms to hang him! She's an excellent sweet lady, and (out of all suspicion) she is virtuous.

Claud. And she is exceeding wise.

Pedro. In everything but in loving Benedick.

Leon. O, my lord, wisdom and blood combating in so tender a body, we have ten proofs to one that blood hath the victory. I am sorry for her, as I have just cause, being her uncle and her guardian.

Pedro. I would she had bestowed this dotage on me. I would have daff'd all other respects and made her half myself. I pray you tell Benedick of it and hear what 'a will say.

Leon. Were it good, think you?

Claud. Hero thinks surely she will die; for she says she will die if he love her not, and she will die ere she make her love known, and she will die, if he woo her, rather than she will bate one breath of her accustomed crossness.

Pedro. She doth well. If she should make tender of her love, 'tis very possible he'll scorn it; for the man (as you know all) hath a contemptible spirit.

Claud. He is a very proper man.

Pedro. He hath indeed a good outward happiness.

Claud. Before God! and in my mind, very wise.

Pedro. He doth indeed show some sparks that are like wit.

Claud. And I take him to be valiant.

Pedro. As Hector, I assure you; and in the managing of quarrels you may say he is wise, for either he avoids them with great discretion, or undertakes them with a most Christianlike fear.

Leon. If he do fear God, 'a must necessarily keep peace. If he break the peace, he ought to enter into a quarrel with fear and trembling.

Pedro. And so will he do; for the man doth fear God, howsoever it seems not in him by some large jests he will make. Well, I am sorry for your niece. Shall we go seek Benedick and tell him of her love?

Claud. Never tell him, my lord. Let her wear it out with good counsel.

Leon. Nay, that's impossible; she may wear her heart out first.

Pedro. Well, we will hear further of it by your daughter. Let it cool the while. I love Benedick well, and I could wish he would modestly examine himself to see how much he is unworthy so good a lady.

Leon. My lord, will you walk? Dinner is ready. [*They walk away.*]

Claud. If he do not dote on her upon this, I will never trust my expectation.

Pedro. Let there be the same net spread for her, and that must your daughter and her gentlewomen carry. The sport will be, when they hold one an opinion of another's dotage, and no such matter. That's the scene that I would see, which will be merely a dumb show. Let us send her to call him in to dinner.

Exeunt [*Don Pedro, Claudio, and Leonato*].

[*Benedick* advances from the arbour.]

Bene. This can be no trick. The conference was sadly borne; they have the truth of this from Hero; they seem to pity the lady. It seems her affections have their full bent. Love me? Why, it must be requited. I hear how I am censur'd. They say I will bear myself proudly if I perceive the love come from her. They say too that she will rather die than give any sign of affection. I did never think to marry. I must not seem proud. Happy are they that hear their detractions and can put them to mending. They say the lady is fair — 'tis a truth, I can bear them witness; and virtuous — 'tis so, I cannot reprove it; and wise, but for loving me — by my troth, it is no addition to her wit, nor no great argument of her folly, for I will be horribly in love with her. I may chance have some odd quirks and remnants of wit broken on me because I have railed so long against marriage. But doth not the appetite alter? A man loves the meat in his youth that he cannot endure in his age. Shall quips and sentences and these paper bullets of the brain awe a man from the career of his

Benedick and Beatrice are confronted with the documentary evidence of their love *(Act V, Scene IV)*

MUCH ADO ABOUT NOTHING

PHOTOGRAPH BY HOUSTON ROGERS
PRODUCED BY TENNENT PRODUCTIONS, LTD.

Diana Wynyard in the role of the pert and witty heroine, Beatrice

Dorothy Tutin as Hero, beloved of the foppish gallant, Claudio

Benedick, the reluctant lover of Beatrice, played by John Gielgud

Paul Scofield in the role of the meddling Don Pedro of Arragon

"I will assume thy part in some disguise, and tell fair Hero I am Claudio." Don Pedro tells Claudio (Robert Hardy) he will court Hero for him *(Act I, Scene I)*

The "plain dealing villain," Don John (Michael Goodliffe)

Left: Lewis Casson as Leonato

Right: Brewster Mason as Borachio

Left: Dogberry (George Rose)

Right: The Friar (George Howe)

Right: Leonato learns that Don Pedro has arrived in Messina *(Act I, Scene I)*

Left: "I could not endure a husband with a beard on his face." Beatrice expresses her distaste for Don John *(Act II, Scene I)*

"Hath she made her affection known to Benedick?" Don Pedro and Claudio tease Benedick by telling him Beatrice is in love with him *(Act II, Scene III)*

The revelers' masquerade in the hall of Leonato's house *(Act II, Scene I)*

Left: "Lady, will you walk about with your friend?" Don Pedro accosts Hero at the revel in her father's house *(Act II, Scene I)*

Right: "Against my will I am sent to bid you come into dinner." Beatrice's message is cold and perfunctory, but Benedick reads love into her words *(Act II, Scene III)*

Left: Hero and Ursula (Margaret Wolfit) discuss the love of Beatrice for Benedick, knowing she is listening *(Act III, Scene I)*

"You always end with a jade's trick." Beatrice and Benedick at odds *(Act I, Scene I)*

Don John plots with Borachio and Conrade (Paul Hardwick) to dupe Claudio *(Act I, Scene III)*

Constable Dogberry instructs his watchmen *(Act III, Scene III)*

Left: " 'tis almost five o'clock, cousin." Beatrice calls to Hero to prepare for her wedding *(Act III, Scene IV)*

Margaret (Penelope Munday) assists Hero in preparing for her marriage to Claudio *(Act III, Scene IV)*

Claudio interrupts his nuptials with Hero, denouncing her as unchaste *(Act IV, Scene I)*

Above: Beatrice and Friar Francis seek to revive Hero, who has fallen into a swoon after Claudio's denunciation of her *(Act IV, Scene I)*

Right: Dogberry arrests Conrade, who has been heard plotting against Claudio *(Act IV, Scene II)*

Left: "By this hand, Claudio shall render me a dear account." Benedick promises Beatrice that he will challenge Claudio *(Act IV, Scene I)*

Below: "When I liv'd, I was your other wife." Claudio and Hero reunited *(Act V, Scene IV)*

humour? No, the world must be peopled. When I said I would die a bachelor, I did not think I should live till I were married.

Enter *Beatrice.*

Here comes Beatrice. By this day, she's a fair lady! I do spy some marks of love in her.

Beat. Against my will I am sent to bid you come in to dinner.

Bene. Fair Beatrice, I thank you for your pains.

Beat. I took no more pains for those thanks than you take pains to thank me. If it had been painful, I would not have come.

Bene. You take pleasure then in the message?

Beat. Yea, just so much as you may take upon a knive's point, and choke a daw withal. You have no stomach, signior. Fare you well. *Exit.*

Bene. Ha! 'Against my will I am sent to bid you come in to dinner.' There's a double meaning in that. 'I took no more pains for those thanks than you took pains to thank me.' That's as much as to say, 'Any pains that I take for you is as easy as thanks.' If I do not take pity of her, I am a villain; if I do not love her, I am a Jew. I will go get her picture. *Exit.*

ACT III. [Scene I. Leonato's *orchard.*]

Enter *Hero* and two *Gentlewomen, Margaret* and *Ursula.*

Hero. Good Margaret, run thee to the parlour.
There shalt thou find my cousin Beatrice
Proposing with the Prince and Claudio.
Whisper her ear and tell her, I and Ursley
Walk in the orchard, and our whole discourse
Is all of her. Say that thou overheard'st us;
And bid her steal into the pleached bower,
Where honeysuckles, ripened by the sun,
Forbid the sun to enter — like favourites,
Made proud by princes, that advance their pride
Against that power that bred it. There will she hide her
To listen our propose. This is thy office.
Bear thee well in it and leave us alone.

Marg. I'll make her come, I warrant you, presently. [*Exit.*]

Hero. Now, Ursula, when Beatrice doth come,
As we do trace this alley up and down,
Our talk must only be of Benedick.
When I do name him, let it be thy part
To praise him more than ever man did merit.
My talk to thee must be how Benedick
Is sick in love with Beatrice. Of this matter
Is little Cupid's crafty arrow made,
That only wounds by hearsay.

Enter *Beatrice.*

Now begin;
For look where Beatrice like a lapwing runs
Close by the ground, to hear our conference.
[*Beatrice hides in the arbour.*]

Urs. The pleasant'st angling is to see the fish
Cut with her golden oars the silver stream
And greedily devour the treacherous bait.
So angle we for Beatrice, who even now
Is couched in the woodbine coverture.
Fear you not my part of the dialogue.

Hero. Then go we near her, that her ear lose nothing
Of the false sweet bait that we lay for it.
[*They approach the arbour.*]
No, truly, Ursula, she is too disdainful.
I know her spirits are as coy and wild
As haggards of the rock.

Urs. But are you sure
That Benedick loves Beatrice so entirely?

Hero. So says the Prince, and my new-trothed lord.

Urs. And did they bid you tell her of it, madam?

Hero. They did entreat me to acquaint her of it;
But I persuaded them, if they lov'd Benedick,
To wish him wrestle with affection
And never to let Beatrice know of it.

Urs. Why did you so? Doth not the gentleman
Deserve as full, as fortunate a bed
As ever Beatrice shall couch upon?

Hero. O god of love! I know he doth deserve
As much as may be yielded to a man;
But Nature never fram'd a woman's heart
Of prouder stuff than that of Beatrice.
Disdain and scorn ride sparkling in her eyes,
Misprizing what they look on; and her wit
Values itself so highly that to her
All matter else seems weak. She cannot love,

Nor take no shape nor project of affection,
She is so self-endeared.

Urs. Sure I think so;
And therefore certainly it were not good
She knew his love, lest she'll make sport at it.

Hero. Why, you speak truth. I never yet saw man,
How wise, how noble, young, how rarely featur'd,
But she would spell him backward. If fair-fac'd,
She would swear the gentleman should be her sister;
If black, why, Nature, drawing of an antic,
Made a foul blot; if tall, a lance ill-headed;
If low, an agate very vilely cut;
If speaking, why, a vane blown with all winds;
If silent, why, a block moved with none.
So turns she every man the wrong side out
And never gives to truth and virtue that
Which simpleness and merit purchaseth.

Urs. Sure, sure, such carping is not commendable.

Hero. No, not to be so odd, and from all fashions,
As Beatrice is, cannot be commendable.
But who dare tell her so? If I should speak,
She would mock me into air; O, she would laugh me
Out of myself, press me to death with wit!
Therefore let Benedick, like cover'd fire,
Consume away in sighs, waste inwardly.
It were a better death than die with mocks,
Which is as bad as die with tickling.

Urs. Yet tell her of it. Hear what she will say.

Hero. No; rather I will go to Benedick
And counsel him to fight against his passion.
And truly, I'll devise some honest slanders
To stain my cousin with. One doth not know
How much an ill word may empoison liking.

Urs. O, do not do your cousin such a wrong!
She cannot be so much without true judgment
(Having so swift and excellent a wit
As she is priz'd to have) as to refuse
So rare a gentleman as Signior Benedick.

Hero. He is the only man of Italy,
Always excepted my dear Claudio.

Urs. I pray you be not angry with me, madam,
Speaking my fancy: Signior Benedick,
For shape, for bearing, argument, and valour,
Goes foremost in report through Italy.

Hero. Indeed he hath an excellent good name.

Urs. His excellence did earn it ere he had it.
When are you married, madam?

Hero. Why, every day to-morrow! Come, go in.
I'll show thee some attires, and have thy counsel
Which is the best to furnish me to-morrow.
[*They walk away.*]

Urs. She's lim'd, I warrant you! We have caught her, madam.

Hero. If it prove so, then loving goes by haps;
Some Cupid kills with arrows, some with traps.
Exeunt [*Hero and Ursula*].

[*Beatrice* advances from the arbour.]

Beat. What fire is in mine ears? Can this be true?
Stand I condemn'd for pride and scorn so much?
Contempt, farewell! and maiden pride, adieu!
No glory lives behind the back of such.
And, Benedick, love on; I will requite thee,
Taming my wild heart to thy loving hand.
If thou dost love, my kindness shall incite thee
To bind our loves up in a holy band;
For others say thou dost deserve, and I
Believe it better than reportingly. *Exit.*

[Scene II. *A room in* Leonato's house.]

Enter *Don Pedro, Claudio, Benedick,* and *Leonato.*

Pedro. I do but stay till your marriage be consummate, and then go I toward Arragon.

Claud. I'll bring you thither, my lord, if you'll vouchsafe me.

Pedro. Nay, that would be as great a soil in the new gloss of your marriage as to show a child his new coat and forbid him to wear it. I will only be bold with Benedick for his company; for, from the crown of his head to the sole of his foot, he is all mirth. He hath twice or thrice cut Cupid's bowstring, and the little hangman dare not shoot at him. He hath a heart as sound as a bell; and his tongue is the clapper, for what his heart thinks, his tongue speaks.

Bene. Gallants, I am not as I have been.

Leon. So say I. Methinks you are sadder.

Claud. I hope he be in love.

Pedro. Hang him, truant! There's no true drop of blood in him to be truly touch'd with love. If he be sad, he wants money.

Bene. I have the toothache.

Pedro. Draw it.

Bene. Hang it!

Claud. You must hang it first and draw it afterwards.

Pedro. What? sigh for the toothache?

Leon. Where is but a humour or a worm.

Bene. Well, every one can master a grief but he that has it.

Claud. Yet say I he is in love.

Pedro. There is no appearance of fancy in him, unless it be a fancy that he hath to strange disguises; as to be a Dutchman to-day, a Frenchman to-morrow; or in the shape of two countries at once, as a German from the waist downward, all slops, and a Spaniard from the hip upward, no doubtlet. Unless he have a fancy to this foolery, as it appears he hath, he is no fool for fancy, as you would have it appear he is.

Claud. If he be not in love with some woman, there is no believing old signs. 'A brushes his hat o' mornings. What should that bode?

Pedro. Hath any man seen him at the barber's?

Claud. No, but the barber's man hath been seen with him, and the old ornament of his cheek hath already stuff'd tennis balls.

Leon. Indeed he looks younger than he did, by the loss of a beard.

Pedro. Nay, 'a rubs himself with civet. Can you smell him out by that?

Claud. That's as much as to say, the sweet youth's in love.

Pedro. The greatest note of it is his melancholy.

Claud. And when was he wont to wash his face?

Pedro. Yea, or to paint himself? for the which I hear what they say of him.

Claud. Nay, but his jesting spirit, which is new-crept into a lutestring, and now govern'd by stops.

Pedro. Indeed that tells a heavy tale for him. Conclude, conclude, he is in love.

Claud. Nay, but I know who loves him.

Pedro. That would I know too. I warrant, one that knows him not.

Claud. Yes, and his ill conditions; and in despite of all, dies for him.

Pedro. She shall be buried with her face upwards.

Bene. Yet is this no charm for the toothache. Old signior, walk aside with me. I have studied eight or nine wise words to speak to you, which these hobby-horses must not hear.

[*Exeunt Benedick and Leonato.*]

Pedro. For my life, to break with him about Beatrice!

Claud. 'Tis even so. Hero and Margaret have by this played their parts with Beatrice, and then the two bears will not bite one another when they meet.

Enter *John the Bastard.*

John. My lord and brother, God save you.

Pedro. Good den, brother.

John. If your leisure serv'd, I would speak with you.

Pedro. In private?

John. If it please you. Yet Count Claudio may hear, for what I would speak of concerns him.

Pedro. What's the matter?

John. [*to Claudio*] Means your lordship to be married to-morrow?

Pedro. You know he does.

John. I know not that, when he knows what I know.

Claud. If there be any impediment, I pray you discover it.

John. You may think I love you not. Let that appear hereafter, and aim better at me by that I now will manifest. For my brother, I think he holds you well and in dearness of heart hath holp to effect your ensuing marriage — surely suit ill spent and labour ill bestowed!

Pedro. Why, what's the matter?

John. I came hither to tell you, and, circumstances short'ned (for she has been too long a-talking of), the lady is disloyal.

Claud. Who? Hero?

John. Even she — Leonato's Hero, your Hero, every man's Hero.

Claud. Disloyal?

John. The word is too good to paint out her wickedness. I could say she were worse; think you of a worse title, and I will fit her to it. Wonder not till further warrant. Go but with me to-night, you shall see her chamber window ent'red, even the night before her wedding day. If you love her then, to-morrow wed her. But it would better fit your honour to change your mind.

Claud. May this be so?

Pedro. I will not think it.

John. If you dare not trust that you see, confess not that you know. If you will follow me, I will show you enough; and when you have seen more and heard more, proceed accordingly.

Claud. If I see anything to-night why I should not marry her to-morrow, in the congregation where I should wed, there will I shame her.

Pedro. And, as I wooed for thee to obtain her, I will join with thee to disgrace her.

John. I will disparage her no farther till you are my witnesses. Bear it coldly but till midnight, and let the issue show itself.

Pedro. O day untowardly turned!

Claud. O mischief strangely thwarting!

John. O plague right well prevented!
So will you say when you have seen the sequel.

Exeunt.

[Scene III. *A street.*]

Enter *Dogberry* and his *compartner* [*Verges*], with the *Watch.*

Dog. Are you good men and true?

Verg. Yea, or else it were pity but they should suffer salvation, body and soul.

Dog. Nay, that were a punishment too good for them if they should have any allegiance in them, being chosen for the Prince's watch.

Verg. Well, give them their charge, neighbour Dogberry.

Dog. First, who think you the most desartless man to be constable?

1. Watch. Hugh Oatcake, sir, or George Seacoal; for they can write and read.

Dog. Come hither, neighbour Seacoal. God hath bless'd you with a good name. To be a well-favoured man is the gift of fortune, but to write and read comes by nature.

2. Watch. Both which, Master Constable —

Dog. You have. I knew it would be your answer. Well, for your favour, sir, why, give God thanks and make no boast of it; and for your writing and reading, let that appear when there is no need of such vanity. You are thought here to be the most senseless and fit man for the constable of the watch. Therefore bear you the lanthorn. This is your charge: you shall comprehend all vagrom men; you are to bid any man stand, in the Prince's name.

2. Watch. How if 'a will not stand?

Dog. Why then, take no note of him, but let him go, and presently call the rest of the watch together and thank God you are rid of a knave.

Verg. If he will not stand when he is bidden, he is none of the Prince's subjects.

Dog. True, and they are to meddle with none but the Prince's subjects. You shall also make no noise in the streets; for for the watch to babble and to talk is most tolerable, and not to be endured.

2. Watch. We will rather sleep than talk. We know what belongs to a watch.

Dog. Why, you speak like an ancient and most quiet watchman, for I cannot see how sleeping should offend. Only have a care that your bills be not stol'n. Well, you are to call at all the alehouses and bid those that are drunk get them to bed.

2. Watch. How if they will not?

Dog. Why then, let them alone till they are sober. If they make you not then the better answer, you may say they are not the men you took them for.

2. Watch. Well, sir.

Dog. If you meet a thief, you may suspect him, by virtue of your office, to be no true man; and for such kind of men, the less you meddle or make with them, why, the more is for your honesty.

2. Watch. If we know him to be a thief, shall we not lay hands on him?

Dog. Truly, by your office you may; but I think they that touch pitch will be defil'd. The most peaceable way for you, if you do take a thief, is to let him show himself what he is, and steal out of your company.

Verg. You have been always called a merciful man, partner.

Dog. Truly, I would not hang a dog by my will, much more a man who hath any honesty in him.

Verg. If you hear a child cry in the night, you must call to the nurse and bid her still it.

2. Watch. How if the nurse be asleep and will not hear us?

Dog. Why then, depart in peace and let the child wake her with crying; for the ewe that will not hear her lamb when it baes will never answer a calf when he bleats.

Verg. 'Tis very true.

Dog. This is the end of the charge: you, constable, are to present the Prince's own person. If you meet the Prince in the night, you may stay him.

Verg. Nay, by'r lady, that I think 'a cannot.

Dog. Five shillings to one on't with any man that knows the statutes, he may stay him! Marry, not without the Prince be willing; for indeed the watch ought to offend no man, and it is an offence to stay a man against his will.

Verg. By'r lady, I think it be so.

Dog. Ha, ah, ha! Well, masters, good night. An there be any matter of weight chances, call up me. Keep your fellows' counsels and your own, and good night. Come, neighbour.

2. Watch. Well, masters, we hear our charge. Let us go sit here upon the church bench till two, and then all to bed.

Dog. One word more, honest neighbours. I pray you watch about Signior Leonato's door; for the wedding being there to-morrow, there is a great coil to-night. Adieu. Be vigitant, I beseech you. *Exeunt* [*Dogberry and Verges*].

Enter *Borachio* and *Conrade.*

Bora. What, Conrade!

2. Watch. [*aside*] Peace! stir not!

Bora. Conrade, I say!

Con. Here, man. I am at thy elbow.

Bora. Mass, and my elbow itch'd! I thought there would a scab follow.

Con. I will owe thee an answer for that; and now forward with thy tale.

Bora. Stand thee close then under this penthouse, for it drizzles rain, and I will, like a true drunkard, utter all to thee.

2. Watch. [*aside*] Some treason, masters. Yet stand close.

Bora. Therefore know I have earned of Don John a thousand ducats.

Con. Is it possible that any villany should be so dear?

Bora. Thou shouldst rather ask if it were possible any villany should be so rich; for when rich villains have need of poor ones, poor ones may make what price they will.

Con. I wonder at it.

Bora. That shows thou art unconfirm'd. Thou knowest that the fashion of a doublet, or a hat, or a cloak, is nothing to a man.

Con. Yes, it is apparel.

Bora. I mean the fashion.

Con. Yes, the fashion is the fashion.

Bora. Tush! I may as well say the fool's the fool. But seest thou not what a deformed thief this fashion is?

2. Watch. [*aside*] I know that Deformed. 'A has been a vile thief this seven year; 'a goes up and down like a gentleman. I remember his name.

Bora. Didst thou not hear somebody?

Con. No; 'twas the vane on the house.

Bora. Seest thou not, I say, what a deformed thief this fashion is? how giddily 'a turns about all the hot-bloods between fourteen and five-and-thirty? sometimes fashioning them like Pharaoh's soldiers in the reechy painting, sometime like god Bel's priests in the old church window, sometime like the shaven Hercules in the smirch'd worm-eaten tapestry, where his cod-piece seems as massy as his club?

Con. All this I see; and I see that the fashion wears out more apparel than the man. But art not thou thyself giddy with the fashion too, that thou hast shifted out of thy tale into telling me of the fashion?

Bora. Not so neither. But know that I have to-night wooed Margaret, the Lady Hero's gentlewoman, by the name of Hero. She leans me out at her mistress' chamber window, bids me a thousand times good night — I tell this tale vilely; I should first tell thee how the Prince, Claudio, and my master, planted and placed and possessed by my master Don John, saw afar off in the orchard this amiable encounter.

Con. And thought they Margaret was Hero?

Bora. Two of them did, the Prince and Claudio; but the devil my master knew she was Margaret; and partly by his oaths, which first possess'd them, partly by the dark night, which did deceive them, but chiefly by my villany, which did confirm any slander that Don John had made, away went Claudio enrag'd; swore he would meet her, as he was appointed, next morning at the temple, and there, before the whole congregation, shame her with what he saw o'ernight and send her home again without a husband.

2. Watch. We charge you in the Prince's name stand!

1. Watch. Call up the right Master Constable. We have here recover'd the most dangerous piece of lechery that ever was known in the commonwealth.

2. Watch. And one Deformed is one of them. I know him; 'a wears a lock.

Con. Masters, masters —

1. Watch. You'll be made bring Deformed forth, I warrant you.

Con. Masters —

2. Watch. Never speak, we charge you. Let us obey you to go with us.

Bora. We are like to prove a goodly commodity, being taken up of these men's bills.

Con. A commodity in question, I warrant you. Come, we'll obey you. *Exeunt.*

[Scene IV. *A room in* Leonato's *house.*]

Enter *Hero*, and *Margaret* and *Ursula*.

Hero. Good Ursula, wake my cousin Beatrice and desire her to rise.

Urs. I will, lady.

Hero. And bid her come hither.

Urs. Well. [*Exit.*]

Marg. Troth, I think your other rebato were better.

Hero. No, pray thee, good Meg, I'll wear this.

Marg. By my troth 's not so good, and I warrant your cousin will say so.

Hero. My cousin's a fool, and thou art another. I'll wear none but this.

Marg. I like the new tire within excellently, if the hair were a thought browner; and your gown's a most rare fashion, i' faith. I saw the Duchess of Milan's gown that they praise so.

Hero. O, that exceeds, they say.

Marg. By my troth, 's but a nightgown in respect of yours — cloth-o'-gold and cuts, and lac'd with silver, set with pearls down sleeves, side-sleeves, and skirts, round underborne with a bluish tinsel. But for a fine, quaint, graceful, and excellent fashion, yours is worth ten on't.

Hero. God give me joy to wear it! for my heart is exceeding heavy.

Marg. 'Twill be heavier soon by the weight of a man.

Hero. Fie upon thee! art not ashamed?

Marg. Of what, lady? of speaking honourably? Is not marriage honourable in a beggar? Is not your lord honourable without marriage? I think you would have me say, 'saving your reverence, a husband.' An bad thinking do not wrest true speaking, I'll offend nobody. Is there any harm in 'the heavier for a husband'? None, I think, an it be the right husband and the right wife. Otherwise 'tis light, and not heavy. Ask my Lady Beatrice else. Here she comes.

Enter *Beatrice.*

Hero. Good morrow, coz.

Beat. Good morrow, sweet Hero.

Hero. Why, how now? Do you speak in the sick tune?

Beat. I am out of all other tune, methinks.

Marg. Clap's into 'Light o' love.' That goes without a burden. Do you sing it, and I'll dance it.

Beat. Yea, 'Light o' love' with your heels! then, if your husband have stables enough, you'll see he shall lack no barnes.

Marg. O illegitimate construction! I scorn that with my heels.

Beat. 'Tis almost five o'clock, cousin; 'tis time you were ready. By my troth, I am exceeding ill. Hey-ho!

Marg. For a hawk, a horse, or a husband?

Beat. For the letter that begins them all, H.

Marg. Well, an you be not turn'd Turk, there's no more sailing by the star.

Beat. What means the fool, trow?

Marg. Nothing I; but God send every one their heart's desire!

Hero. These gloves the Count sent me, they are an excellent perfume.

Beat. I am stuff'd, cousin; I cannot smell.

Marg. A maid, and stuff'd! There's goodly catching of cold.

Beat. O, God help me! God help me! How long have you profess'd apprehension?

Marg. Ever since you left it. Doth not my wit become me rarely?

Beat. It is not seen enough. You should wear it in your cap. By my troth, I am sick.

Marg. Get you some of this distill'd carduus benedictus and lay it to your heart. It is the only thing for a qualm.

Hero. There thou prick'st her with a thistle.

Beat. Benedictus? why benedictus? You have some moral in this 'benedictus.'

Marg. Moral? No, by my troth, I have no moral meaning; I meant plain holy thistle. You may think perchance that I think you are in love. Nay, by'r lady, I am not such a fool to think what I list; nor I list not to think what I can; nor indeed I cannot think, if I would think my heart out of thinking, that you are in love, or that you will be in love, or that you can be in love. Yet Benedick was such another, and now is he become a man. He swore he would never marry; and yet now in despite of his heart he eats his meat without grudging; and how you may be converted I know not, but methinks you look with your eyes as other women do.

Beat. What pace is this that thy tongue keeps?

Marg. Not a false gallop.

Enter *Ursula.*

Urs. Madam, withdraw. The Prince, the Count, Signior Benedick, Don John, and all the gallants of the town are come to fetch you to church.

Hero. Help to dress me, good coz, good Meg, good Ursula. [*Exeunt.*]

[Scene V. *The hall in* Leonato's *house.*]

Enter *Leonato* and the *Constable* [*Dogberry*] and the *Headborough* [*Verges*].

Leon. What would you with me, honest neighbour?

Dog. Marry, sir, I would have some confidence with you that decerns you nearly.

Leon. Brief, I pray you; for you see it is a busy time with me.

Dog. Marry, this it is, sir.

Verg. Yes, in truth it is, sir.

Leon. What is it, my good friends?

Dog. Goodman Verges, sir, speaks a little off the matter — an old man, sir, and his wits are not so blunt as, God help, I would desire they were; but, in faith, honest as the skin between his brows.

Verg. Yes, I thank God I am as honest as any man living that is an old man and no honester than I.

Dog. Comparisons are odorous. Palabras, neighbour Verges.

Leon. Neighbours, you are tedious.

Dog. It pleases your worhsip to say so, but we are the poor Duke's officers; but truly, for mine own part, if I were as tedious as a king, I could find in my heart to bestow it all of your worship.

Leon. All thy tediousness on me, ah?

Dog. Yea, an 'twere a thousand pound more than 'tis; for I hear as good exclamation on your worship as of any man in the city; and though I be but a poor man, I am glad to hear it.

Verg. And so am I.

Leon. I would fain know what you have to say.

Verg. Marry, sir, our watch to-night, excepting your worship's presence, ha' ta'en a couple of as arrant knaves as any in Messina.

Dog. A good old man, sir; he will be talking. As they say, 'When the age is in, the wit is out.' God help us! it is a world to see! Well said, i' faith, neighbour Verges. Well, God 's a good man. An two men ride of a horse, one must ride behind. An honest soul, i' faith, sir, by my troth he is, as ever broke bread; but God is to be worshipp'd; all men are not alike, alas, good neighbour!

Leon. Indeed, neighbour, he comes too short of you.

Dog. Gifts that God gives.

Leon. I must leave you.

Dog. One word, sir. Our watch, sir, have indeed comprehended two aspicious persons, and we would have them this morning examined before your worship.

Leon. Take their examination yourself and bring it me. I am now in great haste, as it may appear unto you.

Dog. It shall be suffigance.

Leon. Drink some wine ere you go. Farc you well.

[Enter a *Messenger*.]

Mess. My lord, they stay for you to give your daughter to her husband.

Leon. I'll wait upon them. I am ready.

[*Exeunt Leonato and Messenger.*]

Dog. Go, good partner, go get you to Francis Seacoal; bid him bring his pen and inkhorn to the jail. We are now to examination these men.

Verg. And we must do it wisely.

Dog. We will spare for no wit, I warrant you. Here's that shall drive some of them to a non-come. Only get the learned writer to set down our excommunication, and meet me at the jail.

Exeunt.

ACT IV. [Scene I. *A church.*]

Enter *Don Pedro*, [*John the*] *Bastard, Leonato, Friar* [*Francis*], *Claudio, Benedick, Hero, Beatrice,* [and *Attendants*].

Leon. Come, Friar Francis, be brief. Only to the plain form of marriage, and you shall recount their particular duties afterwards.

Friar. You come hither, my lord, to marry this lady?

Claud. No.

Leon. To be married to her. Friar, you come to marry her.

Friar. Lady, you come hither to be married to this count?

Hero. I do.

Friar. If either of you know any inward impediment why you should not be conjoined, I charge you on your souls to utter it.

Claud. Know you any, Hero?

Hero. None, my lord.

Friar. Know you any, Count?

Leon. I dare make his answer — none.

Claud. O, what men dare do! what men may do! what men daily do, not knowing what they do!

Bene. How now? interjections? Why then, some be of laughing, as, ah, ha, he!

Claud. Stand thee by, friar. Father, by your leave:
Will you with free and unconstrained soul
Give me this maid your daughter?

Leon. As freely, son, as God did give her me.

Claud. And what have I to give you back whose worth
May counterpoise this rich and precious gift?
Pedro. Nothing, unless you render her again.
Claud. Sweet Prince, you learn me noble thankfulness.
There, Leonato, take her back again.
Give not this rotten orange to your friend.
She's but the sign and semblance of her honour.
Behold how like a maid she blushes here!
O, what authority and show of truth
Can cunning sin cover itself withal!
Comes not that blood as modest evidence
To witness simple virtue? Would you not swear,
All you that see her, that she were a maid
By these exterior shows? But she is none:
She knows the heat of a luxurious bed;
Her blush is guiltiness, not modesty.
Leon. What do you mean, my lord?
Claud. Not to be married,
Not to knit my soul to an approved wanton.
Leon. Dear my lord, if you, in your own proof,
Have vanquish'd the resistance of her youth
And made defeat of her virginity —
Claud. I know what you would say. If I have known her,
You will say she did embrace me as a husband,
And so extenuate the forehand sin.
No, Leonato,
I never tempted her with word too large,
But, as a brother to his sister, show'd
Bashful sincerity and comely love.
Hero. And seem'd I ever otherwise to you?
Claud. Out on the seeming! I will write against it.
You seem to me as Dian in her orb,
As chaste as is the bud ere it be blown;
But you are more intemperate in your blood
Than Venus, or those pamp'red animals
That rage in savage sensuality.
Hero. Is my lord well that he doth speak so wide?
Leon. Sweet Prince, why speak not you?
Pedro. What should I speak?
I stand dishonour'd that have gone about
To link my dear friend to a common stale.
Leon. Are these things spoken, or do I but dream?
John. Sir, they are spoken, and these things are true.
Bene. This looks not like a nuptial.
Hero. 'True!' O God!
Claud. Leonato, stand I here?
Is this the Prince? Is this the Prince's brother?
Is this face Hero's? Are our eyes our own?
Leon. All this is so; but what of this, my lord?
Claud. Let me but move one question to your daughter,
And by that fatherly and kindly power
That you have in her, bid her answer truly.
Leon. I charge thee do so, as thou art my child.
Hero. O, God defend me! How am I beset!
What kind of catechising call you this?
Claud. To make you answer truly to your name.
Hero. Is it not Hero? Who can blot that name
With any just reproach?
Claud. Marry, that can Hero!
Hero itself can blot out Hero's virtue.
What man was he talk'd with you yesternight,
Out at your window betwixt twelve and one?
Now, if you are a maid, answer to this.
Hero. I talk'd with no man at that hour, my lord.
Pedro. Why, then are you no maiden. Leonato,
I am sorry you must hear. Upon mine honour,
Myself, my brother, and this grieved Count
Did see her, hear her, at that hour last night
Talk with a ruffian at her chamber window,
Who hath indeed, most like a liberal villain,
Confess'd the vile encounters they have had
A thousand times in secret.
John. Fie, fie! they are not to be nam'd, my lord —
Not to be spoke of;
There is not chastity enough in language
Without offence to utter them. Thus, pretty lady,
I am sorry for thy much misgovernment.
Claud. O Hero! what a Hero hadst thou been
If half thy outward graces had been plac'd
About thy thoughts and counsels of thy heart!
But fare thee well, most foul, most fair! Farewell,
Thou pure impiety and impious purity!
For thee I'll lock up all the gates of love,
And on my eyelids shall conjecture hang,
To turn all beauty into thoughts of harm,
And never shall it more be gracious.
Leon. Hath no man's dagger here a point for me? [*Hero swoons.*]
Beat. Why, how now, cousin? Wherefore sink you down?

John. Come let us go. These things, come thus to light,
Smother her spirits up.
[*Exeunt Don Pedro, Don Juan, and Claudio.*]
Bene. How doth the lady?
Beat. Dead, I think. Help, uncle!
Hero! why, Hero! Uncle! Signior Benedick! Friar!
Leon. O Fate, take not away thy heavy hand!
Death is the fairest cover for her shame
That may be wish'd for.
Beat. How now, cousin Hero?
Friar. Have comfort, lady.
Leon. Dost thou look up?
Friar. Yea, wherefore should she not?
Leon. Wherefore? Why, doth not every earthly thing
Cry shame upon her? Could she here deny
The story that is printed in her blood?
Do not live, Hero; do not ope thine eyes;
For, did I think thou wouldst not quickly die,
Thought I thy spirits were stronger than thy shames,
Myself would on the rearward of reproaches
Strike at thy life. Griev'd I, I had but one?
Chid I for that at frugal nature's frame?
O, one too much by thee! Why had I one?
Why ever wast thou lovely in my eyes?
Why had I not with charitable hand
Took up a beggar's issue at my gates,
Who smirched thus and mir'd with infamy,
I might have said, 'No part of it is mine;
This shame derives itself from unknown loins'?
But mine, and mine I lov'd, and mine I prais'd,
And mine that I was proud on — mine so much
That I myself was to myself not mine,
Valuing of her — why, she, O, she is fall'n
Into a pit of ink, that the wide sea
Hath drops too few to wash her clean again,
And salt too little which may season give
To her foul tainted flesh!
Bene. Sir, sir, be patient.
For my part, I am so attir'd in wonder,
I know not what to say.
Beat. O, on my soul, my cousin is belied!
Bene. Lady, were you her bedfellow last night?
Beat. No, truly, not; although, until last night,
I have this twelvemonth been her bedfellow.
Leon. Confirm'd, confirm'd! O, that is stronger made
Which was before barr'd up with ribs of iron!
Would the two princes lie? and Claudio lie,
Who lov'd her so that, speaking of her foulness,
Wash'd it with tears? Hence from her! let her die.
Friar. Hear me a little;
For I have only been silent so long,
And given way unto this course of fortune,
By noting of the lady. I have mark'd
A thousand blushing apparitions
To start into her face, a thousand innocent shames
In angel whiteness beat away those blushes,
And in her eye there hath appear'd a fire
To burn the errors that these princes hold
Against her maiden truth. Call me a fool;
Trust not my reading nor my observation,
Which with experimental seal doth warrant
The tenure of my book; trust not my age,
My reverence, calling, nor divinity,
If this sweet lady lie not guiltless here
Under some biting error.
Leon. Friar, it cannot be.
Thou seest that all the grace that she hath left
Is that she will not add to her damnation
A sin of perjury: she not denies it.
Why seek'st thou then to cover with excuse
That which appears in proper nakedness?
Friar. Lady, what man is he you are accus'd of?
Hero. They know that do accuse me; I know none.
If I know more of any man alive
Than that which maiden modesty doth warrant,
Let all my sins lack mercy! O my father,
Prove you that any man with me convers'd
At hours unmeet, or that I yesternight
Maintain'd the change of words with any creature,
Refuse me, hate me, torture me to death!
Friar. There is some strange misprision in the princes.
Bene. Two of them have the very bent of honour;
And if their wisdoms be misled in this,
The practice of it lives in John the bastard,
Whose spirits toil in frame of villanies.
Leon. I know not. If they speak but truth of her,
These hands shall tear her. If they wrong her honour,
The proudest of them shall well hear of it.
Time hath not yet so dried this blood of mine,
Nor age so eat up my invention,
Nor fortune made such havoc of my means,

Nor my bad life reft me so much of friends,
But they shall find awak'd in such a kind
Both strength of limb and policy of mind,
Ability in means, and choice of friends,
To quit me of them throughly.

Friar. Pause awhile
And let my counsel sway you in this case.
Your daughter here the princes left for dead,
Let her awhile be secretly kept in,
And publish it that she is dead indeed;
Maintain a mourning ostentation,
And on your family's old monument
Hang mournful epitaphs, and do all rites
That appertain unto a burial.

Leon. What shall become of this? What will this do?

Friar. Marry, this well carried shall on her behalf
Change slander to remorse. That is some good.
But not for that dream I on this strange course,
But on this travail look for greater birth.
She dying, as it must be so maintain'd,
Upon the instant that she was accus'd,
Shall be lamented, pitied, and excus'd
Of every hearer; for it so falls out
That what we have we prize not to the worth
Whiles we enjoy it, but being lack'd and lost,
Why, then we rack the value, then we find
The virtue that possession would not show us
Whiles it was ours. So will it fare with Claudio.
When he shall hear she died upon his words,
Th' idea of her life shall sweetly creep
Into his study of imagination,
And every lovely organ of her life
Shall come apparell'd in more precious habit,
More moving, delicate, and full of life,
Into the eye and prospect of his soul
Than when she liv'd indeed. Then shall he mourn
(If ever love had interest in his liver)
And wish he had not so accused her —
No, though he thought his accusation true.
Let this be so, and doubt not but success
Will fashion the event in better shape
Than I can lay it down in likelihood.
But if all aim but this be levell'd false,
The supposition of the lady's death
Will quench the wonder of her infamy.
And if it sort not well, you may conceal her,
As best befits her wounded reputation,
In some reclusive and religious life,
Out of all eyes, tongues, minds, and injuries.

Bene. Signior Leonato, let the friar advise you;
And though you know my inwardness and love
Is very much unto the Prince and Claudio,
Yet, by mine honour, I will deal in this
As secretly and justly as your soul
Should with your body.

Leon. Being that I flow in grief,
The smallest twine may lead me.

Friar. 'Tis well consented. Presently away;
For to strange sores strangely they strain the cure.
Come, lady, die to live. This wedding day
Perhaps is but prolong'd. Have patience and endure.

Exeunt [all but Benedick and Beatrice].

Bene. Lady Beatrice, have you wept all this while?

Beat. Yea, and I will weep a while longer.

Bene. I will not desire that.

Beat. You have no reason. I do it freely.

Bene. Surely I do believe your fair cousin is wronged.

Beat. Ah, how much might the man deserve of me that would right her!

Bene. Is there any way to show such friendship?

Beat. A very even way, but no such friend.

Bene. May a man do it?

Beat. It is a man's office, but not yours.

Bene. I do love nothing in the world so well as you. Is not that strange?

Beat. As strange as the thing I know not. It were as possible for me to say I loved nothing so well as you. But believe me not; and yet I lie not. I confess nothing, nor I deny nothing. I am sorry for my cousin.

Bene. By my sword, Beatrice, thou lovest me.

Beat. Do not swear, and eat it.

Bene. I will swear by it that you love me, and I will make him eat it that says I love not you.

Beat. Will you not eat your word?

Bene. With no sauce that can be devised to it. I protest I love thee.

Beat. Why then, God forgive me!

Bene. What offence, sweet Beatrice?

Beat. You have stayed me in a happy hour. I was about to protest I loved you.

Bene. And do it with all thy heart.

Beat. I love you with so much of my heart that none is left to protest.

Bene. Come, bid me do anything for thee.

Beat. Kill Claudio.

Bene. Ha! not for the wide world!

Beat. You kill me to deny it. Farewell.

Bene. Tarry, sweet Beatrice.

Beat. I am gone, though I am here. There is no love in you. Nay, I pray you let me go.

Bene. Beatrice —

Beat. In faith, I will go.

Bene. We'll be friends first.

Beat. You dare easier be friends with me than fight with mine enemy.

Bene. Is Claudio thine enemy?

Beat. Is 'a not approved in the height a villain, that hath slandered, scorned, dishonoured my kinswoman? O that I were a man! What? bear her in hand until they come to take hands, and then with public accusation, uncover'd slander, unmitigated rancour — O God, that I were a man! I would eat his heart in the market place.

Bene. Hear me, Beatrice!

Beat. Talk with a man out at a window! — a proper saying!

Bene. Nay, but Beatrice —

Beat. Sweet Hero! she is wrong'd, she is sland'red, she is undone.

Bene. Beat —

Beat. Princes and Counties! Surely a princely testimony, a goodly count, Count Comfect, a sweet gallant surely! O that I were a man for his sake! or that I had any friend would be a man for my sake! But manhood is melted into cursies, valour into compliment, and men are only turn'd into tongue, and trim ones too. He is now as valiant as Hercules that only tells a lie, and swears it. I cannot be a man with wishing; therefore I will die a woman with grieving.

Bene. Tarry, good Beatrice. By this hand, I love thee.

Beat. Use it for my love some other way than swearing by it.

Bene. Think you in your soul the Count Claudio hath wrong'd Hero?

Beat. Yea, as sure as I have a thought or a soul.

Bene. Enough, I am engag'd, I will challenge him. I will kiss your hand, and so I leave you. By this hand, Claudio shall render me a dear account. As you hear of me, so think of me. Go comfort your cousin. I must say she is dead — and so farewell. [*Exeunt.*]

[Scene II. *A prison.*]

Enter the *Constables* [*Dogberry* and *Verges*] and the *Sexton*, in gowns, [and the *Watch*, with *Conrade* and] *Borachio*.

Dog. Is our whole dissembly appear'd?

Verg. O, a stool and a cushion for the sexton.

Sex. Which be the malefactors?

Dog. Marry, that am I and my partner.

Verg. Nay, that's certain. We have the exhibition to examine.

Sex. But which are the offenders that are to be examined? let them come before Master Constable.

Dog. Yea, marry, let them come before me. What is your name, friend?

Bora. Borachio.

Dog. Pray write down Borachio. Yours, sirrah?

Con. I am a gentleman, sir, and my name is Conrade.

Dog. Write down Master Gentleman Conrade. Masters, do you serve God?

Both. Yea, sir, we hope.

Dog. Write down that they hope they serve God; and write God first, for God defend but God should go before such villains! Masters, it is proved already that you are little better than false knaves, and it will go near to be thought so shortly. How answer you for yourselves?

Con. Marry, sir, we say we are none.

Dog. A marvellous witty fellow, I assure you; but I will go about with him. Come you hither, sirrah. A word in your ear. Sir, I say to you, it is thought you are false knaves.

Bora. Sir, I say to you we are none.

Dog. Well, stand aside. Fore God, they are both in a tale. Have you writ down that they are none?

Sex. Master Constable, you go not the way to examine. You must call forth the watch that are their accusers.

Dog. Yea, marry, that's the eftest way. Let the watch come forth. Masters, I charge you in the Prince's name accuse these men.

1. Watch. This man said, sir, that Don John the Prince's brother was a villain.

Dog. Write down Prince John a villain. Why, this is flat perjury, to call a prince's brother villain.

Bora. Master Constable —

Dog. Pray thee, fellow, peace. I do not like thy look, I promise thee.

Sex. What heard you him say else?

2. Watch. Marry, that he had received a thousand ducats of Don John for accusing the Lady Hero wrongfully.

Dog. Flat burglary as ever was committed.

Verg. Yea, by th' mass, that it is.

Sex. What else, fellow?

1. Watch. And that Count Claudio did mean, upon his words, to disgrace Hero before the whole assembly, and not marry her.

Dog. O villain! thou wilt be condemn'd into everlasting redemption for this.

Sex. What else?

Watchmen. This is all.

Sex. And this is more, masters, than you can deny. Prince John is this morning secretly stol'n away. Hero was in this manner accus'd, in this very manner refus'd, and upon the grief of this suddenly died. Master Constable, let these men be bound and brought to Leonato's. I will go before and show him their examination. [*Exit.*]

Dog. Come, let them be opinion'd.

Verg. Let them be in the hands —

Con. Off, coxcomb!

Dog. God's my life, where's the sexton? Let him write down the Prince's officer coxcomb. Come, bind them. — Thou naughty varlet!

Con. Away! you are an ass, you are an ass.

Dog. Dost thou not suspect my place? Dost thou not suspect my years? O that he were here to write me down an ass! But, masters, remember that I am an ass. Though it be not written down, yet forget not that I am an ass. No, thou villain, thou art full of piety, as shall be prov'd upon thee by good witness. I am a wise fellow; and which is more, an officer; and which is more, a householder; and which is more, as pretty a piece of flesh as any is in Messina, and one that knows the law, go to! and a rich fellow enough, go to! and a fellow that hath had losses; and one that hath two gowns and everything handsome about him. Bring him away. O that I had been writ down an ass! *Exeunt.*

ACT V. [Scene I. *The street, near* Leonato's *house.*]

Enter *Leonato* and his brother [*Antonio*].

Ant. If you go on thus, you will kill yourself,
And 'tis not wisdom thus to second grief
Against yourself.

Leon. I pray thee cease thy counsel,
Which falls into mine ears as profitless
As water in a sieve. Give not me counsel,
Nor let no comforter delight mine ear
But such a one whose wrongs do suit with mine.
Bring me a father that so lov'd his child,
Whose joy of her is overwhelm'd like mine,
And bid him speak to me of patience.
Measure his woe the length and breadth of mine,
And let it answer every strain for strain,
As thus for thus, and such a grief for such,
In every lineament, branch, shape, and form.
If such a one will smile and stroke his beard,
Bid sorrow wag, cry 'hem' when he should groan,
Patch grief with proverbs, make misfortune drunk
With candle-wasters — bring him yet to me,
And I of him will gather patience.
But there is no such man; for, brother, men
Can counsel and speak comfort to that grief
Which they themselves not feel; but, tasting it,
Their counsel turns to passion, which before
Would give preceptial medicine to rage,
Fetter strong madness in a silken thread,
Charm ache with air and agony with words.
No, no! 'Tis all men's office to speak patience
To those that wring under the load of sorrow,
But no man's virtue nor sufficiency
To be so moral when he shall endure
The like himself. Therefore give me no counsel.
My griefs cry louder than advertisement.

Ant. Therein do men from children nothing differ.

Leon. I pray thee peace. I will be flesh and blood;
For there was never yet philosopher
That could endure the toothache patiently,
However they have writ the style of gods
And made a push at chance and sufferance.

Ant. Yet bend not all the harm upon yourself.
Make those that do offend you suffer too.

Leon. There thou speak'st reason. Nay, I will do so.
My soul doth tell me Hero is belied;
And that shall Claudio know; so shall the Prince,
And all of them that thus dishonour her.

Enter *Don Pedro* and *Claudio.*

Ant. Here comes the Prince and Claudio hastily.

Pedro. Good den, good den.

Claud. Good day to both of you.

Leon. Hear you, my lords!

Pedro. We have some haste, Leonato.

Leon. Some haste, my lord! well, fare you well, my lord.
Are you so hasty now? Well, all is one.

Pedro. Nay, do not quarrel with us, good old man.
Ant. If he could right himself with quarrelling,
Some of us would lie low.
Claud. Who wrongs him?
Leon. Marry, thou dost wrong me, thou dissembler, thou!
Nay, never lay thy hand upon thy sword;
I fear thee not.
Claud. Marry, beshrew my hand
If it should give your age such cause of fear.
In faith, my hand meant nothing to my sword.
Leon. Tush, tush, man! never fleer and jest at me.
I speak not like a dotard nor a fool,
As under privilege of age to brag
What I have done being young, or what would do,
Were I not old. Know, Claudio, to thy head,
Thou hast so wrong'd mine innocent child and me
That I am forc'd to lay my reverence by
And, with grey hairs and bruise of many days,
Do challenge thee to trial of a man.
I say thou hast belied mine innocent child;
Thy slander hath gone through and through her heart,
And she lies buried with her ancestors —
O, in a tomb where never scandal slept,
Save this of hers, fram'd by thy villany!
Claud. My villany?
Leon. Thine, Claudio; thine I say.
Pedro. You say not right, old man.
Leon. My lord, my lord,
I'll prove it on his body if he dare,
Despite his nice fence and his active practice,
His May of youth and bloom of lustihood.
Claud. Away! I will not have to do with you.
Leon. Canst thou so daff me? Thou hast kill'd my child.
If thou kill'st me, boy, thou shalt kill a man.
Ant. He shall kill two of us, and men indeed.
But that's no matter; let him kill one first.
Win me and wear me! Let him answer me.
Come, follow me, boy. Come, sir boy, come follow me.
Sir boy, I'll whip you from your foining fence!
Nay, as I am a gentleman, I will.
Leon. Brother —
Ant. Content yourself. God knows I lov'd my niece,
And she is dead, slander'd to death by villains,
That dare as well answer a man indeed
As I dare take a serpent by the tongue.
Boys, apes, braggarts, Jacks, milksops!
Leon. Brother Anthony —
Ant. Hold you content. What, man! I know them, yea,
And what they weigh, even to the utmost scruple,
Scambling, outfacing, fashion-monging boys,
That lie and cog and flout, deprave and slander,
Go anticly, show outward hideousness,
And speak off half a dozen dang'rous words,
How they might hurt their enemies, if they durst;
And this is all.
Leon. But, brother Anthony —
Ant. Come, 'tis no matter.
Do not you meddle; let me deal in this.
Pedro. Gentlemen both, we will not wake your patience.
My heart is sorry for your daughter's death;
But, on my honour, she was charg'd with nothing
But what was true, and very full of proof.
Leon. My lord, my lord —
Pedro. I will not hear you.
Leon. No? Come, brother, away! — I will be heard.
Ant. And shall, or some of us will smart for it. *Exeunt ambo.*

Enter *Benedick.*

Pedro. See, see! Here comes the man we went to seek.
Claud. Now, signior, what news?
Bene. Good day, my lord.

Pedro. Welcome, signior. You are almost come to part almost a fray.

Claud. We had lik'd to have had our two noses snapp'd off with two old men without teeth.

Pedro. Leonato and his brother. What think'st thou? Had we fought, I doubt we should have been too young for them.

Bene. In a false quarrel there is no true valour. I came to seek you both.

Claud. We have been up and down to seek thee; for we are high-proof melancholy, and would fain have it beaten away. Wilt thou use thy wit?

Bene. It is in my scabbard. Shall I draw it?

Pedro. Dost thou wear thy wit by thy side?

Claud. Never any did so, though very many have been beside their wit. I will bid thee draw, as we do the minstrels — draw to pleasure us.

Pedro. As I am an honest man, he looks pale. Art thou sick or angry?

Claud. What, courage, man! What though care kill'd a cat, thou hast mettle enough in thee to kill care.

Bene. Sir, I shall meet your wit in the career an you charge it against me. I pray you choose another subject.

Claud. Nay then, give him another staff; this last was broke cross.

Pedro. By this light, he changes more and more. I think he be angry indeed.

Claud. If he be, he knows how to turn his girdle.

Bene. Shall I speak a word in your ear?

Claud. God bless me from a challenge!

Bene. [*aside to Claudio*] You are a villain. I jest not; I will make it good how you dare, with what you dare, and when you dare. Do me right, or I will protest your cowardice. You have kill'd a sweet lady, and her death shall fall heavy on you. Let me hear from you.

Claud. Well, I will meet you, so I may have good cheer.

Pedro. What, a feast? a feast?

Claud. I' faith, I thank him, he hath bid me to a calve's head and a capon, the which if I do not carve most curiously, say my knife's naught. Shall I not find a woodcock too?

Bene. Sir, your wit ambles well; it goes easily.

Pedro. I'll tell thee how Beatrice prais'd thy wit the other day. I said thou hadst a fine wit: 'True,' said she, 'a fine little one.' 'No,' said I, 'a great wit.' 'Right,' says she, 'a great gross one.' 'Nay,' said I, 'a good wit.' 'Just,' said she, 'it hurts nobody.' 'Nay,' said I, 'the gentleman is wise.' 'Certain,' said she, 'a wise gentleman.' 'Nay,' said I, 'he hath the tongues.' 'That I believe,' said she, 'for he swore a thing to me on Monday night which he forswore on Tuesday morning. There's a double tongue; there's two tongues.' Thus did she an hour together transshape thy particular virtues. Yet at last she concluded with a sigh, thou wast the proper'st man in Italy.

Claud. For the which she wept heartily and said she cared not.

Pedro. Yea, that she did; but yet, for all that, an if she did not hate him deadly, she would love him dearly. The old man's daughter told us all.

Claud. All, all! and moreover, God saw him when he was hid in the garden.

Pedro. But when shall we set the savage bull's horns on the sensible Benedick's head?

Claud. Yea, and text underneath, 'Here dwells Benedick, the married man'?

Bene. Fare you well, boy; you know my mind. I will leave you now to your gossiplike humour. You break jests as braggards do their blades, which God be thanked hurt not. My lord, for your many courtesies I thank you. I must discontinue your company. Your brother the bastard is fled from Messina. You have among you kill'd a sweet and innocent lady. For my Lord Lackbeard there, he and I shall meet; and till then peace be with him. [*Exit.*]

Pedro. He is in earnest.

Claud. In most profound earnest; and, I'll warrant you, for the love of Beatrice.

Pedro. And hath challeng'd thee.

Claud. Most sincerely.

Pedro. What a pretty thing man is when he goes in his doublet and hose and leaves off his wit!

Enter *Constables* [*Dogberry* and *Verges*, with the *Watch*, leading] *Conrade* and *Borachio*.

Claud. He is then a giant to an ape; but then is an ape a doctor to such a man.

Pedro. But, soft you, let me be! Pluck up, my heart, and be sad! Did he not say my brother was fled?

Dog. Come you, sir. If justice cannot tame you, she shall ne'er weigh more reasons in her balance. Nay, an you be a cursing hypocrite once, you must be look'd to.

Pedro. How now? two of my brother's men bound? Borachio one.

Claud. Hearken after their offence, my lord.

Pedro. Officers, what offence have these men done?

Dog. Marry, sir, they have committed false report; moreover, they have spoken untruths; secondarily, they are slanders; sixth and lastly, they have belied a lady; thirdly, they have verified unjust things; and to conclude, they are lying knaves.

Pedro. First, I ask thee what they have done; thirdly, I ask thee what's their offence; sixth and lastly, why they are committed; and to conclude, what you lay to their charge.

Claud. Rightly reasoned, and in his own division; and by my troth there's one meaning well suited.

Pedro. Who have you offended, masters, that you are thus bound to your answer? This learned constable is too cunning to be understood. What's your offence?

Bora. Sweet Prince, let me go no farther to mine answer. Do you hear me, and let this Count kill me. I have deceived even your very eyes. What your wisdoms could not discover, these shallow fools have brought to light, who in the night overheard me confessing to this man, how Don John your brother incensed me to slander the Lady Hero; how you were brought into the orchard and saw me court Margaret in Hero's garments; how you disgrac'd her when you should marry her. My villany they have upon record, which I had rather seal with my death than repeat over to my shame. The lady is dead upon mine and my master's false accusation; and briefly, I desire nothing but the reward of a villain.

Pedro. Runs not this speech like iron through your blood?

Claud. I have drunk poison whiles he utter'd it.

Pedro. But did my brother set thee on to this?

Bora. Yea, and paid me richly for the practice of it.

Pedro. He is compos'd and fram'd of treachery,
And fled he is upon this villany.

Claud. Sweet Hero, now thy image doth appear
In the rare semblance that I lov'd it first.

Dog. Come, bring away the plaintiffs. By this time our sexton hath reformed Signior Leonato of the matter. And, masters, do not forget to specify, when time and place shall serve, that I am an ass.

Verg. Here, here comes Master Signior Leonato, and the sexton too.

Enter *Leonato*, his brother [*Antonio*], and the *Sexton*.

Leon. Which is the villain? Let me see his eyes,
That, when I note another man like him,
I may avoid him. Which of these is he?

Bora. If you would know your wronger, look on me.

Leon. Art thou the slave that with thy breath hast kill'd
Mine innocent child?

Bora. Yea, even I alone.

Leon. No, not so, villain! thou beliest thyself.
Here stand a pair of honourable men —
A third is fled — that had a hand in it.
I thank you princes for my daughter's death.
Record it with your high and worthy deeds.
'Twas bravely done, if you bethink you of it.

Claud. I know not how to pray your patience;
Yet I must speak. Choose your revenge yourself;
Impose me to what penance your invention
Can lay upon my sin. Yet sinn'd I not
But in mistaking.

Pedro. By my soul, nor I!
And yet, to satisfy this good old man,
I would bend under any heavy weight
That he'll enjoin me to.

Leon. I cannot bid you bid my daughter live —
That were impossible; but I pray you both,
Possess the people in Messina here
How innocent she died; and if your love
Can labour aught in sad invention,
Hang her an epitaph upon her tomb,
And sing it to her bones — sing it to-night.
To-morrow morning come you to my house,
And since you could not be my son-in-law,
Be yet my nephew. My brother hath a daughter,
Almost the copy of my child that's dead,
And she alone is heir to both of us.
Give her the right you should have giv'n her cousin,
And so dies my revenge.

Claud. O noble sir!
Your over-kindness doth wring tears from me.
I do embrace your offer; and dispose
For henceforth of poor Claudio.

Leon. To-morrow then I will expect your coming;
To-night I take my leave. This naughty man
Shall face to face be brought to Margaret,
Who I believe was pack'd in all this wrong,
Hir'd to it by your brother.

Bora. No, by my soul, she was not;
Nor knew not what she did when she spoke to me;
But always hath been just and virtuous
In anything that I do know by her.

Dog. Moreover, sir, which indeed is not under white and black, this plaintiff here, the offender, did call me ass. I beseech you let it be rememb'red in his punishment. And also the watch heard them talk of one Deformed. They say he wears a key in his ear, and a lock hanging by it, and borrows money in God's name, the which he hath us'd so long and never paid that now men grow hard-hearted and will lend nothing for God's sake. Pray you examine him upon that point.

Leon. I thank thee for thy care and honest pains.

Dog. Your worship speaks like a most thankful and reverent youth, and I praise God for you.

Leon. There's for thy pains. [*Gives money.*]

Dog. God save the foundation!

Leon. Go, I discharge thee of thy prisoner, and I thank thee.

Dog. I leave an arrant knave with your worship, which I beseech your worship to correct yourself, for the example of others. God keep your worship! I wish your worship well. God restore you to health! I humbly give you leave to depart; and if a merry meeting may be wish'd, God prohibit it! Come, neighbour.

Exeunt [*Dogberry and Verges*].

Leon. Until to-morrow morning, lords, farewell.

Ant. Farewell, my lords. We look for you to-morrow.

Pedro. We will not fail.

Claud. To-night I'll mourn with Hero.

[*Exeunt Don Pedro and Claudio.*]

Leon. [*to the Watch*] Bring you these fellows on. — We'll talk with Margaret,
How her acquaintance grew with this lewd fellow. *Exeunt.*

[Scene II. Leonato's *orchard.*]

Enter *Benedick* and *Margaret* [meeting].

Bene. Pray thee, sweet Mistress Margaret, deserve well at my hands by helping me to the speech of Beatrice.

Marg. Will you then write me a sonnet in praise of my beauty?

Bene. In so high a style, Margaret, that no man living shall come over it; for in most comely truth thou deservest it.

Marg. To have no man come over me? Why, shall I always keep below stairs?

Bene. Thy wit is as quick as the greyhound's mouth — it catches.

Marg. And yours as blunt as the fencer's foils, which hit but hurt not.

Bene. A most manly wit, Margaret: it will not hurt a woman. And so I pray thee call Beatrice. I give thee the bucklers.

Marg. Give us the swords; we have bucklers of our own.

Bene. If you use them, Margaret, you must put in the pikes with a vice, and they are dangerous weapons for maids.

Marg. Well, I will call Beatrice to you, who I think hath legs.

Bene. And therefore will come.

Exit Margaret.

[*Sings.*] The god of love,
That sits above
And knows me, and knows me,
How pitiful I deserve —

I mean in singing; but in loving Leander the good swimmer, Troilus the first employer of panders, and a whole book full of these quondam carpet-mongers, whose names yet run smoothly in the even road of a blank verse — why, they were never so truly turn'd over and over as my poor self in love. Marry, I cannot show it in rhyme. I have tried. I can find out no rhyme to 'lady' but 'baby' — an innocent rhyme; for 'scorn,' 'horn' — a hard rhyme; for 'school,' 'fool' — a babbling rhyme: very ominous endings! No, I was not born under a rhyming planet, nor I cannot woo in festival terms.

Enter *Beatrice.*

Sweet Beatrice, wouldst thou come when I call'd thee?

Beat. Yea, signior, and depart when you bid me.

Bene. O, stay but till then!

Beat. 'Then' is spoken. Fare you well now. And yet, ere I go, let me go with that I came for, which is, with knowing what hath pass'd between you and Claudio.

Bene. Only foul words; and thereupon I will kiss thee.

Beat. Foul words is but foul wind, and foul wind is but foul breath, and foul breath is noisome. Therefore I will depart unkiss'd.

Bene. Thou hast frighted the word out of his right sense, so forcible is thy wit. But I must tell thee plainly, Claudio undergoes my challenge; and either I must shortly hear from him or I will subscribe him a coward. And I pray thee now tell me, for which of my bad parts didst thou first fall in love with me?

Beat. For them all together, which maintain'd so politic a state of evil that they will not admit any good part to intermingle with them. But for which of my good parts did you first suffer love for me?

Bene. Suffer love! — a good epithet. I do suffer love indeed, for I love thee against my will.

Beat. In spite of your heart, I think. Alas, poor heart! If you spite it for my sake, I will spite it for yours, for I will never love that which my friend hates.

Bene. Thou and I are too wise to woo peaceably.

Beat. It appears not in this confession. There's not one wise man among twenty that will praise himself.

Bene. An old, an old instance, Beatrice, that liv'd in the time of good neighbours. If a man do not erect in this age his own tomb ere he dies, he shall live no longer in monument than the bell rings and the widow weeps.

Beat. And how long is that, think you?

Bene. Question: why, an hour in clamour and a quarter in rheum. Therefore is it most expedient for the wise, if Don Worm (his conscience) find no impediment to the contrary, to be the trumpet of his own virtues, as I am to myself. So much for praising myself, who, I myself will bear witness, is praiseworthy. And now tell me, how doth your cousin?

Beat. Very ill.

Bene. And how do you?

Beat. Very ill too.

Bene. Serve God, love me, and mend. There will I leave you too, for here comes one in haste.

Enter *Ursula.*

Urs. Madam, you must come to your uncle. Yonder's old coil at home. It is proved my Lady Hero hath been falsely accus'd, the Prince and Claudio mightily abus'd, and Don John is the author of all, who is fled and gone. Will you come presently?

Beat. Will you go hear this news, signior?

Bene. I will live in thy heart, die in thy lap, and be buried in thy eyes; and moreover, I will go with thee to thy uncle's. *Exeunt.*

[Scene III. *A churchyard.*]

Enter *Claudio, Don Pedro,* and three or four with tapers, [followed by *Musicians*].

Claud. Is this the monument of Leonato?

Lord. It is, my lord.

Claud. [*reads from a scroll*]

Epitaph.

Done to death by slanderous tongues
Was the Hero that here lies.
Death, in guerdon of her wrongs,
Gives her fame which never dies.
So the life that died with shame
Lives in death with glorious fame.

Hang thou there upon the tomb,
[*Hangs up the scroll.*]
Praising her when I am dumb.
Now, music, sound, and sing your solemn hymn.

Song.

Pardon, goddess of the night,
Those that slew thy virgin knight;
For the which, with songs of woe,
Round about her tomb they go.
Midnight, assist our moan,
Help us to sigh and groan
Heavily, heavily.
Graves, yawn and yield your dead,
Till death be uttered
Heavily, heavily.

Claud. Now unto thy bones good night!
Yearly will I do this rite.

Pedro. Good morrow, masters. Put your torches out.
The wolves have prey'd, and look, the gentle day,
Before the wheels of Phœbus, round about
Dapples the drowsy east with spots of grey.
Thanks to you all, and leave us. Fare you well.

Claud. Good morrow, masters. Each his several way.

Pedro. Come, let us hence and put on other weeds,
And then to Leonato's we will go.

Claud. And Hymen now with luckier issue speeds
Than this for whom we rend'red up this woe.
Exeunt.

[Scene IV. *The hall in* Leonato's *house.*]

Enter *Leonato, Benedick,* [*Beatrice,*] *Margaret, Ursula, Antonio, Friar* [*Francis*], *Hero.*

Friar. Did I not tell you she was innocent?

Leon. So are the Prince and Claudio, who accus'd her
Upon the error that you heard debated.
But Margaret was in some fault for this,
Although against her will, as it appears
In the true course of all the question.

Ant. Well, I am glad that all things sort so well.

Bene. And so am I, being else by faith enforc'd
To call young Claudio to a reckoning for it.

Leon. Well, daughter, and you gentlewomen all,
Withdraw into a chamber by yourselves,
And when I send for you, come hither mask'd.
Exeunt Ladies.
The Prince and Claudio promis'd by this hour
To visit me. You know your office, brother:
You must be father to your brother's daughter,
And give her to young Claudio.
Ant. Which I will do with confirm'd countenance.
Bene. Friar, I must entreat your pains, I think.
Friar. To do what, signior?
Bene. To bind me, or undo me — one of them.
Signior Leonato, truth it is, good signior,
Your niece regards me with an eye of favour.
Leon. That eye my daughter lent her. 'Tis most true.
Bene. And I do with an eye of love requite her.
Leon. The sight whereof I think you had from me,
From Claudio, and the Prince; but what's your will?
Bene. Your answer, sir, is enigmatical;
But, for my will, my will is, your good will
May stand with ours, this day to be conjoin'd
In the state of honourable marriage;
In which, good friar, I shall desire your help.
Leon. My heart is with your liking.
Friar. And my help.

Enter *Don Pedro* and *Claudio* and two or three other.

Here comes the Prince and Claudio.
Pedro. Good morrow to this fair assembly.
Leon. Good morrow, Prince; good morrow, Claudio.
We here attend you. Are you yet determin'd
To-day to marry with my brother's daughter?
Claud. I'll hold my mind, were she an Ethiope.
Leon. Call her forth, brother. Here's the friar ready.
[*Exit Antonio.*]
Pedro. Good morrow, Benedick. Why, what's the matter
That you have such a February face,
So full of frost, of storm, and cloudiness?
Claud. I think he thinks upon the savage bull.
Tush, fear not, man! We'll tip thy horns with gold,
And all Europa shall rejoice at thee,
As once Europa did at lusty Jove
When he would play the noble beast in love.
Bene. Bull Jove, sir, had an amiable low,
And some such strange bull leap'd your father's cow
And got a calf in that same noble feat
Much like to you, for you have just his bleat.

Enter [*Leonato's*] brother [*Antonio*], *Hero*, *Beatrice*, *Margaret*, *Ursula*, [the ladies wearing masks].

Claud. For this I owe you. Here comes other reck'nings.
Which is the lady I must seize upon?
Ant. This same is she, and I do give you her.
Claud. Why then, she's mine. Sweet, let me see your face.
Leon. No, that you shall not till you take her hand
Before this friar and swear to marry her.
Claud. Give me your hand before this holy friar.
I am your husband if you like of me.
Hero. And when I liv'd I was your other wife; [*Unmasks.*]
And when you lov'd you were my other husband.
Claud. Another Hero!
Hero. Nothing certainer.
One Hero died defil'd; but I do live,
And surely as I live, I am a maid.
Pedro. The former Hero! Hero that is dead!
Leon. She died, my lord, but whiles her slander liv'd.
Friar. All this amazement can I qualify,
When, after that the holy rites are ended,
I'll tell you largely of fair Hero's death.
Meantime let wonder seem familiar,
And to the chapel let us presently.
Bene. Soft and fair, friar. Which is Beatrice?
Beat. [*unmasks*] I answer to that name. What is your will?
Bene. Do not you love me?
Beat. Why, no; no more than reason.
Bene. Why, then your uncle, and the Prince, and Claudio
Have been deceived; for they swore you did.
Beat. Do not you love me?
Bene. Troth, no; no more than reason.
Beat. Why, then my cousin, Margaret, and Ursula
Are much deceiv'd; for they did swear you did.
Bene. They swore that you were almost sick for me.

Beat. They swore that you were well-nigh dead for me.

Bene. 'Tis no such matter. Then you do not love me?

Beat. No, truly, but in friendly recompense.

Leon. Come, cousin, I am sure you love the gentleman.

Claud. And I'll be sworn upon't that he loves her;
For here's a paper written in his hand,
A halting sonnet of his own pure brain,
Fashion'd to Beatrice.

Hero. And here's another,
Writ in my cousin's hand, stol'n from her pocket,
Containing her affection unto Benedick.

Bene. A miracle! Here's our own hands against our hearts. Come, I will have thee; but, by this light, I take thee for pity.

Beat. I would not deny you; but, by this good day, I yield upon great persuasion, and partly to save your life, for I was told you were in a consumption.

Bene. Peace! I will stop your mouth. [*Kisses her.*]

Pedro. How dost thou, Benedick, the married man?

Bene. I'll tell thee what, Prince: a college of wit-crackers cannot flout me out of my humour. Dost thou think I care for a satire or an epigram? No. If a man will be beaten with brains, 'a shall wear nothing handsome about him. In brief, since I do purpose to marry, I will think nothing to any purpose that the world can say against it; and therefore never flout at me for what I have said against it; for man is a giddy thing, and this is my conclusion. For thy part, Claudio, I did think to have beaten thee; but in that thou art like to be my kinsman, live unbruis'd, and love my cousin.

Claud. I had well hop'd thou wouldst have denied Beatrice, that I might have cudgell'd thee out of thy single life, to make thee a double-dealer, which out of question thou wilt be if my cousin do not look exceeding narrowly to thee.

Bene. Come, come, we are friends. Let's have a dance ere we are married, that we may lighten our own hearts and our wives' heels.

Leon. We'll have dancing afterward.

Bene. First, of my word! Therefore play, music. Prince, thou art sad. Get thee a wife, get thee a wife! There is no staff more reverent than one tipp'd with horn.

Enter *Messenger.*

Mess. My lord, your brother John is ta'en in flight,
And brought with armed men back to Messina.

Bene. Think not on him till to-morrow. I'll devise thee brave punishments for him. Strike up, pipers! *Dance.* [*Exeunt.*]

Love's Labour's Lost

For the text of Love's Labour's Lost the Quarto of 1598 (carelessly printed from an autograph manuscript) is our only real authority. The Folio compositor used it as copy, correcting many obvious errors, but perpetrating many new misprints. The Quarto has no division into acts and scenes; the Folio marks the acts (misprinting *Quartus* for *Quintus*), but not the scenes.

Doubtless the play was written for performance at court or at some great house. The Quarto records that it 'was presented before her Highnes' Queen Elizabeth 'this last Christmas,' that is, apparently, in 1597. There was doubtless a considerable interval between composition and this performance at court. Meres's list (p. 33, above) shows that *A Midsummer Night's Dream* and *The Merchant of Venice* were known to him before October 19, 1598. Both of them seem later than Love's Labour's Lost. He also mentions a *Love's Labour's Won*. What this was, we do not know, possibly the first form of *All's Well* (see p. 361). In any event, it can hardly have come before Love's Labour's Lost if its title means anything. Love's Labour's Lost, then, should in all probability be put back to 1594 or 1595. There is no good reason for regarding it as the earliest of Shakespeare's comedies and dating it 1591. The plot seems to be original, though a hint for the visit of the Princess and her ladies has been detected in a picturesque incident of 1578 — the visit of Queen Catherine of France and Marguerite de Valois to the court of Navarre. Though slight, the plot suffices to keep things moving. Our interest centres not in the action but in the delightfully whimsical situation; and the eccentricities of that situation are managed with consummate skill, set forth vividly in ironic characterization, and illuminated by polished wit in dialogue and soliloquy. The farcical personages who bring this courtly fairyland into contact with the working-day world are, to be sure, conventional figures; but they are so robustly individualized that one is ready to accept them as original creations.

Meres's catalogue of Shakespeare's comedies may well coincide with chronology in mentioning *The Two Gentlemen* and *The Comedy of Errors* before Love's Labour's Lost. Style and versification accord with 1594 or 1595. The blank verse is not that of a tyro. The rhyming speeches and the interspersed lyrics show masterly skill in a variety of metres. The song at the end is one of the best in the world. The Euphuistic prose is as good of its kind as anything achieved by Lyly, whom Shakespeare was obviously emulating, and the 'tender juvenal,' Moth (that is, *Mote*), is quite as amusing as the wittiest of Lyly's clever youngsters. However, there is enough pleasant parody of Euphuism and other stylistic extravagances to show that Shakespeare was no blind disciple of any rhetorical master.

The 1598 title-page contains the words 'Newly corrected and augmented.' This may mean that the play had been printed before in a shorter form, or it may be a mere advertising formula to assure the customer that he was purchasing a complete and accurate text. Whether there was or was not an earlier issue, we cannot accept the title-page as evidence that the Quarto represents a rewriting by Shakespeare (for the Christmas performance) of a drama which he originally composed in or about 1593. Certain confusions and odd features of the Quarto text have been adduced in support of this theory, but they are otherwise explicable. The most striking is the repetition in Berowne's long oration (iv, 3, 289 ff.). To reduce this speech to order, something must be cut out. In the present edition lines 298–319 are italicized. If these are omitted, Berowne's discourse becomes orderly enough. The repetition seems to be due to the printer's carelessness in setting up a passage which stood in his copy, but with marks for deletion. Perhaps Shakespeare changed his mind while writing the speech and crossed out certain lines, but not so drastically as to render them illegible. The same explanation will account for lines 826–831 in Act v, scene 2 (also italicized in the present edition). These major errors and other cases of confusion or inconsistency in minor matters certainly do not prove that there were ever two distinct versions of Shakespeare's play. There may have been some revision for the Christmas performance, but we need not assume that this was either extensive or thoroughgoing.

The influence of the Italian *commedia dell' arte* is visible throughout the play. Several of the characters correspond to standard figures of the Italian convention: Armado to the bragging soldier (a lineal descendant of Pyrgopolynices of the *Miles Gloriosus* of Plautus); Moth to the *zanni* who regularly accompanies the braggart; Holofernes to the pedant; Nathaniel to the parasite; Costard to the rustic. Armado is styled 'Braggart' and Holofernes 'Pedant' in stage directions. But these similarities must not be pushed to the extreme. There were Costards enough in Shakespeare's England and the breed is not extinct. Armado is quite as much a pedant as a boaster: he is pedantic in his boasting and boastful in his pedantry.

It is merely whimsical to identify Holofernes with Florio, the translator of Montaigne, or with Chapman (even if Chapman was, as is very doubtful, the rival poet of the *Sonnets*), or with Gabriel Harvey, or to find the original of Armado in Philip of Spain or Sir Walter Raleigh, or the prototype of Moth in Thomas Nashe. No Elizabethan could have recognized Harvey, the eminent college don, as latent in a schoolmaster who 'teaches boys the hornbook.' Boyet describes Armado as 'a Monarcho' (iv, 1, 101). The real Monarcho was an Italian, a harmless and amusing madman who frequented the English court and was dead by 1580. His resemblance to Armado must have been merely generic.

A favourite literary exercise for Elizabethan wits was the paradox, and this too emerges in the rich abundance of LOVE'S LABOUR'S LOST. See, for example, Berowne's praise of the black-browed Rosaline (iv, 3, 248 ff.), which leads up to his argument that he and his associates are not bound by their rash vow. The King styles his defence a paradox in the same speech in which he calls black 'the school of night.'

This last phrase (though 'school' may be a misprint) has led to ingenious theorizing. Taken in connection with Chapman's *Shadow of Night* (1594), it has been held to indicate that there actually was a coterie called or nicknamed 'The School of Night,' which devoted itself to the study of the new astronomy; and this has been identified with the group of philosophical speculators patronized by Raleigh and regarded by their contemporaries as atheists. However this may be, there is no reason whatever for interpreting the 'Academe' of Shakespeare's play as a satire on these scientific innovators.

LOVE'S LABOUR'S LOST

[Dramatis Personæ.

Ferdinand, King of Navarre.
Berowne, *Longaville,* *Dumain,* — lords attending on the King.
Boyet, *Marcade,* — lords attending on the *Princess* of France.
Don Adriano de Armado, a Spaniard.
Sir Nathaniel, a curate.
Holofernes, a schoolmaster.
Dull, a constable.
Costard, a clown.
Moth, page to *Don Armado.*
A Forester.

The *Princess* of France.
Rosaline, *Maria,* *Katherine,* — ladies attending on the *Princess.*
Jaquenetta, a country wench.

Lords, Attendants, &c.

SCENE. — *Navarre.*]

ACT I. [Scene I. *Navarre. The King's Park.*]

Enter *Ferdinand, King of Navarre, Berowne, Longaville,* and *Dumain.*

Ferd. Let fame, that all hunt after in their lives,
Live regist'red upon our brazen tombs
And then grace us, in the disgrace of death,
When, spite of cormorant devouring Time,
Th' endeavour of this present breath may buy
That honour which shall bate his scythe's keen edge
And make us heirs of all eternity.
Therefore, brave conquerors — for so you are
That war against your own affections
And the huge army of the world's desires —
Our late edict shall strongly stand in force:
Navarre shall be the wonder of the world;
Our court shall be a little Academe,
Still and contemplative in living art.
You three, Berowne, Dumain, and Longaville,
Have sworn for three years' term to live with me,
My fellow scholars, and to keep those statutes
That are recorded in this schedule here.
Your oaths are pass'd; and now subscribe your names,
That his own hand may strike his honour down
That violates the smallest branch herein.
If you are arm'd to do as sworn to do,
Subscribe to your deep oaths, and keep it too.
Long. I am resolv'd. 'Tis but a three years' fast.
The mind shall banquet, though the body pine.
Fat paunches have lean pates, and dainty bits
Make rich the ribs but bankrout quite the wits.
Dum. My loving lord, Dumain is mortified.
The grosser manner of these world's delights
He throws upon the gross world's baser slaves.
To love, to wealth, to pomp, I pine and die,
With all these living in philosophy.
Ber. I can but say their protestation over,
So much, dear liege, I have already sworn,
That is, to live and study here three years.
But there are other strict observances:
As, not to see a woman in that term,
Which I hope well is not enrolled there;
And one day in a week to touch no food,
And but one meal on every day beside,
The which I hope is not enrolled there;
And then to sleep but three hours in the night
And not be seen to wink of all the day
(When I was wont to think no harm all night
And make a dark night too of half the day),
Which I hope well is not enrolled there.
O, these are barren tasks, too hard to keep —
Not to see ladies, study, fast, not sleep!
Ferd. Your oath is pass'd, to pass away from these.
Ber. Let me say no, my liege, an if you please.
I only swore to study with your Grace
And stay here in your court for three years' space.
Long. You swore to that, Berowne, and to the rest.
Ber. By yea and nay, sir, then I swore in jest.
What is the end of study? Let me know.

Ferd. Why, that to know which else we should not know.
Ber. Things hid and barr'd (you mean) from common sense.
Ferd. Ay, that is study's godlike recompense.
Ber. Com' on then! I will swear to study so,
To know the thing I am forbid to know:
As thus — to study where I well may dine
When I to feast expressly am forbid;
Or study where to meet some mistress fine
When mistresses from common sense are hid;
Or, having sworn too hard-a-keeping oath,
Study to break it and not break my troth.
If study's gain be thus, and this be so,
Study knows that which yet it doth not know.
Swear me to this, and I will ne'er say no.
Ferd. These be the stops that hinder study quite
And train our intellects to vain delight.
Ber. Why, all delights are vain, but that most vain
Which, with pain purchas'd, doth inherit pain:
As, painfully to pore upon a book
To seek the light of truth while truth the while
Doth falsely blind the eyesight of his look.
Light, seeking light, doth light of light beguile.
So, ere you find where light in darkness lies,
Your light grows dark by losing of your eyes.
Study me how to please the eye indeed
By fixing it upon a fairer eye,
Who dazzling so, that eye shall be his heed
And give him light that it was blinded by.
Study is like the heaven's glorious sun,
That will not be deep search'd with saucy looks.
Small have continual plodders ever won
Save base authority from others' books.
These earthly godfathers of heaven's lights
That give a name to every fixed star
Have no more profit of their shining nights
Than those that walk and wot not what they are.
Too much to know is to know naught but fame;
And every godfather can give a name.
Ferd. How well he's read, to reason against reading!
Dum. Proceeded well, to stop all good proceeding!
Long. He weeds the corn and still lets grow the weeding.
Ber. The spring is near when green geese are a-breeding.
Dum. How follows that?
Ber. Fit in his place and time.
Dum. In reason nothing.
Ber. Something then in rhyme.
Ferd. Berowne is like an envious sneaping frost
That bites the first-born infants of the spring.
Ber. Well, say I am! Why should proud summer boast
Before the birds have any cause to sing?
Why should I joy in any abortive birth?
At Christmas I no more desire a rose
Than wish a snow in May's newfangled shows,
But like of each thing that in season grows.
So you — to study now it is too late —
Climb o'er the house to unlock the little gate.
Ferd. Well, sit you out. Go home, Berowne. Adieu.
Ber. No, my good lord. I have sworn to stay with you;
And though I have for barbarism spoke more
Than for that angel knowledge you can say,
Yet confident I'll keep what I have swore
And bide the penance of each three years' day.
Give me the paper; let me read the same,
And to the strictest decrees I'll write my name.
Ferd. How well this yielding rescues thee from shame!
Ber. [*reads*] 'Item. That no woman shall come within a mile of my court' — Hath this been proclaimed?
Long. Four days ago.
Ber. Let's see the penalty: '— on pain of losing her tongue.' Who devis'd this penalty?
Long. Marry, that did I.
Ber. Sweet lord, and why?
Long. To fright them hence with that dread penalty.
Ber. A dangerous law against gentility!
[*Reads.*] 'Item. If any man be seen to talk with a woman within the term of three years, he shall endure such public shame as the rest of the court can possible devise.'
This article, my liege, yourself must break;
For well you know here comes in embassy
The French king's daughter with yourself to speak,
A maid of grace and complete majesty,
About surrender-up of Aquitaine
To her decrepit, sick, and bedrid father.
Therefore this article is made in vain,
Or vainly comes th' admired princess hither.
Ferd. What say you, lords? Why, this was quite forgot.
Ber. So study evermore is overshot.
While it doth study to have what it would,

It doth forget to do the thing it should;
And when it hath the thing it hunteth most,
'Tis won as towns with fire — so won, so lost.

Ferd. We must of force dispense with this decree.
She must lie here on mere necessity.

Ber. Necessity will make us all forsworn
Three thousand times within this three years' space;
For every man with his affects is born,
Not by might mast'red, but by special grace.
If I break faith, this word shall speak for me,
I am forsworn on mere necessity.
So to the laws at large I write my name; [*Subscribes.*]
And he that breaks them in the least degree
Stands in attainder of eternal shame.
Suggestions are to other as to me;
But I believe, although I seem so loath,
I am the last that will last keep his oath.
But is there no quick recreation granted?

Ferd. Ay, that there is. Our court you know is haunted
With a refined traveller of Spain,
A man in all the world's new fashion planted,
That hath a mint of phrases in his brain;
One whom the music of his own vain tongue
Doth ravish like enchanting harmony;
A man of complements, whom right and wrong
Have chose as umpire of their mutiny.
This child of fancy, that Armado hight,
For interim to our studies shall relate
In high-born words the worth of many a knight
From tawny Spain lost in the world's debate.
How you delight, my lords, I know not, I;
But I protest I love to hear him lie,
And I will use him for my minstrelsy.

Ber. Armado is a most illustrious wight,
A man of fire-new words, fashion's own knight.

Long. Costard the swain and he shall be our sport,
And so to study three years is but short.

Enter [*Dull,*] a Constable, with *Costard,* [a Clown,] with a letter.

Dull. Which is the Duke's own person?

Ber. This, fellow. What wouldst?

Dull. I myself reprehend his own person, for I am his Grace's farborough. But I would see his own person in flesh and blood.

Ber. This is he.

Dull. Signior Arme — Arme — commends you. There's villany abroad. This letter will tell you more.

Cost. Sir, the contempts thereof are as touching me.

Ferd. A letter from the magnificent Armado.

Ber. How low soever the matter, I hope in God for high words.

Long. A high hope for a low heaven. God grant us patience!

Ber. To hear? or forbear hearing?

Long. To hear meekly, sir, and to laugh moderately, or to forbear both.

Ber. Well, sir, be it as the style shall give us cause to climb in the merriness.

Cost. The matter is to me, sir, as concerning Jaquenetta. The manner of it is, I was taken with the manner.

Ber. In what manner?

Cost. In manner and form following, sir — all those three. I was seen with her in the manor house, sitting with her upon the form, and taken following her into the park; which put together is in manner and form following. Now, sir, for the manner — it is the manner of a man to speak to a woman; for the form — in some form.

Ber. For the following, sir?

Cost. As it shall follow in my correction — and God defend the right!

Ferd. Will you hear this letter with attention?

Ber. As we would hear an oracle.

Cost. Such is the simplicity of man to hearken after the flesh.

Ferd. [*reads*] 'Great deputy, the welkin's vicegerent, and sole dominator of Navarre, my soul's earth's god and body's fost'ring patron' —

Cost. Not a word of Costard yet.

Ferd. 'So it is' —

Cost. It may be so; but if he say it is so, he is, in telling true, but so.

Ferd. Peace!

Cost. Be to me, and every man that dares not fight!

Ferd. No words!

Cost. Of other men's secrets, I beseech you.

Ferd. 'So it is, besieged with sable-coloured melancholy, I did commend the black oppressing humour to the most wholesome physic of thy health-giving air; and, as I am a gentleman, betook myself to walk. The time When? About the sixth hour, when beasts most graze, birds best peck, and men sit down to that nourishment which is called supper. So much for the time When. Now for the ground Which? which, I mean, I walk'd upon. It is ycliped thy park. Then for the place Where? where, I mean, I did encounter that obscene and most prepost'rous event that draweth from my snow-white pen the ebon-coloured ink which here thou viewest, beholdest, surveyest, or seest. But to the place Where? It standeth north-north-east and by east from the west corner of thy curious-knotted garden. There did I see that low-spirited swain, that base minnow of thy mirth' —

Cost. Me!

Ferd. 'that unlettered small-knowing soul' —

Cost. Me!

Ferd. 'that shallow vassal' —

Cost. Still me!

Ferd. 'which, as I remember, hight Costard' —

Cost. O, me!

Ferd. 'sorted and consorted, contrary to thy established proclaimed edict and continent canon, with — with — O, with — but with this I passion to say wherewith' —

Cost. With a wench.

Ferd. 'with a child of our grandmother Eve, a female, or, for thy more sweet understanding, a woman. Him I (as my ever-esteemed duty pricks me on) have sent to thee, to receive the meed of punishment, by thy sweet Grace's officer, Anthony Dull, a man of good repute, carriage, bearing, and estimation.'

Dull. Me, an't shall please you. I am Anthony Dull.

Ferd. 'For Jaquenetta (so is the weaker vessel called), which I apprehended with the aforesaid swain, I keep her as a vessel of thy law's fury, and shall, at the least of thy sweet notice, bring her to trial.

'Thine, in all complements of devoted and heart-burning heat of duty,

'DON ADRIANO DE ARMADO.'

Ber. This is not so well as I looked for, but the best that ever I heard.

Ferd. Ay, the best for the worst. But, sirrah, what say you to this?

Cost. Sir, I confess the wench.

Ferd. Did you hear the proclamation?

Cost. I do confess much of the hearing it, but little of the marking of it.

Ferd. It was proclaimed a year's imprisonment to be taken with a wench.

Cost. I was taken with none, sir. I was taken with a damsel.

Ferd. Well, it was proclaimed 'damsel.'

Cost. This was no damsel neither, sir. She was a virgin.

Ferd. It is so varied too, for it was proclaimed 'virgin.'

Cost. If it were, I deny her virginity. I was taken with a maid.

Ferd. This 'maid' will not serve your turn, sir.

Cost. This maid will serve my turn, sir.

Ferd. Sir, I will pronounce your sentence: you shall fast a week with bran and water.

Cost. I had rather pray a month with mutton and porridge.

Ferd. And Don Armado shall be your keeper.
My Lord Berowne, see him delivered o'er,
And go we, lords, to put in practice that
Which each to other hath so strongly sworn.

[*Exeunt King Ferdinand, Longaville, and Dumain.*]

Ber. I'll lay my head to any good man's hat
These oaths and laws will prove an idle scorn.
Sirrah, come on.

Cost. I suffer for the truth, sir; for true it is I was taken with Jaquenetta, and Jaquenetta is a true girl, and therefore welcome the sour cup of prosperity! Affliction may one day smile again, and till then, sit thee down, sorrow!

Exeunt.

[Scene II. *The park.*]

Enter *Armado* and *Moth,* his page.

Arm. Boy, what sign is it when a man of great spirit grows melancholy?

Moth. A great sign, sir, that he will look sad.

Arm. Why, sadness is one and the selfsame thing, dear imp.

Moth. No, no! O Lord, sir, no!

Arm. How canst thou part sadness and melancholy, my tender juvenal?

Moth. By a familiar demonstration of the working, my tough signior.

Arm. Why tough signior? Why tough signior?

Moth. Why tender juvenal? Why tender juvenal?

Arm. I spoke it tender juvenal as a congruent epitheton appertaining to thy young days, which we may nominate tender.

Moth. And I tough signior as an appertinent title to your old time, which we may name tough.

Arm. Pretty and apt.

Moth. How mean you, sir? I pretty, and my saying apt? or I apt, and my saying pretty?

Arm. Thou pretty, because little.

Moth. Little pretty, because little. Wherefore apt?

Arm. And therefore apt, because quick.

Moth. Speak you this in my praise, master?

Arm. In thy condign praise.

Moth. I will praise an eel with the same praise.

Arm. What? that an eel is ingenious?

Moth. That an eel is quick.

Arm. I do say thou art quick in answers. Thou heat'st my blood.

Moth. I am answer'd, sir.

Arm. I love not to be cross'd.

Moth. [*aside*] He speaks the mere contrary — crosses love not him.

Arm. I have promised to study three years with the Duke.

Moth. You may do it in an hour, sir.

Arm. Impossible.

Moth. How many is one thrice told?

Arm. I am ill at reck'ning; it fitteth the spirit of a tapster.

Moth. You are a gentleman and a gamester, sir.

Arm. I confess both; they are both the varnish of a complete man.

Moth. Then I am sure you know how much the gross sum of deuce-ace amounts to.

Arm. It doth amount to one more than two.

Moth. Which the base vulgar do call three.

Arm. True.

Moth. Why, sir, is this such a piece of study? Now here is three studied ere ye'll thrice wink; and how easy it is to put 'years' to the word 'three,' and study three years in two words, the dancing horse will tell you.

Arm. A most fine figure!

Moth. [*aside*] To prove you a cipher.

Arm. I will hereupon confess I am in love; and as it is base for a soldier to love, so am I in love with a base wench. If drawing my sword against the humour of affection would deliver me from the reprobate thought of it, I would take Desire prisoner and ransom him to any French courtier for a new-devis'd cursy. I think scorn to sigh; methinks I should outswear Cupid. Comfort me, boy. What great men have been in love?

Moth. Hercules, master.

Arm. Most sweet Hercules! More authority, dear boy, name more; and, sweet my child, let them be men of good repute and carriage.

Moth. Samson, master. He was a man of good carriage, great carriage, for he carried the town gates on his back like a porter; and he was in love.

Arm. O well-knit Samson! strong-jointed Samson! I do excel thee in my rapier as much as thou didst me in carrying gates. I am in love too. Who was Samson's love, my dear Moth?

Moth. A woman, master.

Arm. Of what complexion?

Moth. Of all the four, or the three, or the two, or one of the four.

Arm. Tell me precisely of what complexion.

Moth. Of the sea-water green, sir.

Arm. Is that one of the four complexions?

Moth. As I have read, sir, and the best of them too.

Arm. Green indeed is the colour of lovers; but to have a love of that colour, methinks Samson had small reason for it. He surely affected her for her wit.

Moth. It was so, sir, for she had a green wit.

Arm. My love is most immaculate white and red.

Moth. Most maculate thoughts, master, are mask'd under such colours.

Arm. Define, define, well-educated infant.

Moth. My father's wit and my mother's tongue assist me!

Arm. Sweet invocation of a child! most pretty and pathetical!

Moth. If she be made of white and red,
Her faults will ne'er be known;
For blushing cheeks by faults are bred
And fears by pale white shown.
Then if she fear, or be to blame,
By this you shall not know;
For still her cheeks possess the same
Which native she doth owe.

A dangerous rhyme, master, against the reason of white and red.

Arm. Is there not a ballet, boy, of The King and the Beggar?

Moth. The world was very guilty of such a ballet some three ages since, but I think now 'tis not to be found; or if it were, it would neither serve for the writing nor the tune.

Arm. I will have that subject newly writ o'er, that I may example my digression by some mighty precedent. Boy, I do love that country girl that I took in the park with the rational hind Costard. She deserves well.

Moth. [*aside*] To be whipp'd — and yet a better love than my master.

Arm. Sing, boy. My spirit grows heavy in love.

Moth. And that's great marvel, loving a light wench.

Arm. I say sing.

Moth. Forbear till this company be past.

Enter Clown [*Costard*], Constable [*Dull*], and Wench [*Jaquenetta*.]

Dull. Sir, the Duke's pleasure is that you keep Costard safe, and you must suffer him to take no delight nor no penance, but 'a must fast three days a week. For this damsel, I must keep her at the park; she is allow'd for the day-woman. Fare you well.

Arm. I do betray myself with blushing. Maid.

Jaq. Man.

Arm. I will visit thee at the lodge.

Jaq. That's hereby.

Arm. I know where it is situate.

Jaq. Lord, how wise you are!

Arm. I will tell thee wonders.

Jaq. With that face?

Arm. I love thee.

Jaq. So I heard you say.

Arm. And so farewell.

Jaq. Fair weather after you!

Dull. Come, Jaquenetta, away!

Exeunt [*Dull and Jaquenetta*].

Arm. Villain, thou shalt fast for thy offences ere thou be pardoned.

Cost. Well, sir, I hope when I do it I shall do it on a full stomach.

Arm. Thou shalt be heavily punished.

Cost. I am more bound to you than your fellows, for they are but lightly rewarded.

Arm. Take away this villain; shut him up.

Moth. Come, you transgressing slave, away!

Cost. Let me not be pent up, sir. I will fast, being loose.

Moth. No, sir; that were fast and loose. Thou shalt to prison.

Cost. Well, if ever I do see the merry days of desolation that I have seen, some shall see.

Moth. What shall some see?

Cost. Nay, nothing, Master Moth, but what they look upon. It is not for prisoners to be too silent in their words, and therefore I will say nothing. I thank God I have as little patience as another man, and therefore I can be quiet.

Exeunt [*Moth and Costard*].

Arm. I do affect the very ground (which is base) where her shoe (which is baser) guided by her foot (which is basest) doth tread. I shall be forsworn (which is a great argument of falsehood) if I love. And how can that be true love which is falsely attempted? Love is a familiar; Love is a devil. There is no evil angel but Love. Yet was Samson so tempted, and he had an excellent strength. Yet was Salomon so seduced, and he had a very good wit. Cupid's buttshaft is too hard for Hercules' club, and therefore too much odds for a Spaniard's rapier. The first and second cause will not serve my turn; the passado he respects not, the duello he regards not. His disgrace is to be called boy, but his glory is to subdue men. Adieu, valour! rust, rapier! be still, drum! for your manager is in love; yea, he loveth. Assist me some extemporal god of rhyme, for I am sure I shall turn sonnet. Devise, wit! write, pen! for I am for whole volumes in folio. *Exit.*

ACT II. [Scene I. *The park.*]

Enter the *Princess of France* with three attending Ladies, [*Maria, Katherine, Rosaline,*] and three Lords, [one named *Boyet*].

Boyet. Now, madam, summon up your dearest spirits.
Consider who the King your father sends,
To whom he sends, and what's his embassy:
Yourself, held precious in the world's esteem,
To parley with the sole inheritor
Of all perfections that a man may owe,
Matchless Navarre; the plea of no less weight
Than Aquitaine, a dowry for a queen.
Be now as prodigal of all dear grace
As Nature was in making graces dear
When she did starve the general world beside
And prodigally gave them all to you.

Prin. Good Lord Boyet, my beauty, though but mean,
Needs not the painted flourish of your praise.
Beauty is bought by judgment of the eye,
Not utt'red by base sale of chapmen's tongues.
I am less proud to hear you tell my worth
Than you much willing to be counted wise
In spending your wit in the praise of mine.
But now to task the tasker: — good Boyet,
You are not ignorant all-telling fame
Doth noise abroad Navarre hath made a vow,
Till painful study shall outwear three years,
No woman may approach his silent court.
Therefore to 's seemeth it a needful course,
Before we enter his forbidden gates,
To know his pleasure; and in that behalf,
Bold of your worthiness, we single you
As our best-moving fair solicitor.
Tell him the daughter of the King of France
On serious business, craving quick dispatch,
Importunes personal conference with his Grace.

Haste, signify so much while we attend,
Like humble-visag'd suitors, his high will.

Boyet. Proud of employment, willingly I go.
Exit Boyet.

Prin. All pride is willing pride, and yours is so.
Who are the votaries, my loving lords,
That are vow-fellows with this virtuous duke?

Lord. Lord Longaville is one.

Prin. Know you the man?

Mar. I know him, madam. At a marriage feast,
Between Lord Perigort and the beauteous heir
Of Jaques Falconbridge solemnized,
In Normandy saw I this Longaville.
A man of sovereign parts he is esteem'd;
Well fitted in arts, glorious in arms.
Nothing becomes him ill that he would well.
The only soil of his fair virtue's gloss —
If virtue's gloss will stain with any soil —
Is a sharp wit match'd with too blunt a will,
Whose edge hath power to cut, whose will still wills
It should none spare that come within his power.

Prin. Some merry mocking lord belike — is't so?

Mar. They say so most that most his humours know.

Prin. Such short-liv'd wits do wither as they grow.
Who are the rest?

Kath. The young Dumain, a well-accomplish'd youth,
Of all that virtue love for virtue lov'd;
Most power to do most harm, least knowing ill;
For he hath wit to make an ill shape good,
And shape to win grace though he had no wit.
I saw him at the Duke Alençon's once,
And much too little of that good I saw
Is my report to his great worthiness.

Ros. Another of these students at that time
Was there with him, if I have heard a truth.
Berowne they call him; but a merrier man,
Within the limit of becoming mirth,
I never spent an hour's talk withal.
His eye begets occasion for his wit;
For every object that the one doth catch
The other turns to a mirth-moving jest,
Which his fair tongue (conceit's expositor)
Delivers in such apt and gracious words
That aged ears play truant at his tales
And younger hearings are quite ravished,
So sweet and voluble is his discourse.

Prin. God bless my ladies! Are they all in love,
That every one her own hath garnished
With such bedecking ornaments of praise?

Enter *Boyet.*

Lord. Here comes Boyet.

Prin. Now, what admittance, lord?

Boyet. Navarre had notice of your fair approach,
And he and his competitors in oath
Were all address'd to meet you, gentle lady,
Before I came. Marry, thus much I have learnt,
He rather means to lodge you in the field,
Like one that comes here to besiege his court,
Than seek a dispensation for his oath,
To let you enter his unpeopled house.
[*The Ladies mask.*]

Enter *Navarre, Longaville, Dumain,* and *Berowne,* [with *Attendants*].

Here comes Navarre.

Ferd. Fair Princess, welcome to the court of Navarre.

Prin. 'Fair' I give you back again, and welcome I have not yet. The roof of this court is too high to be yours, and welcome to the wide fields too base to be mine.

Ferd. You shall be welcome, madam, to my court.

Prin. I will be welcome, then. Conduct me thither.

Ferd. Hear me, dear lady — I have sworn an oath —

Prin. Our Lady help my lord! He'll be forsworn.

Ferd. Not for the world, fair madam, by my will.

Prin. Why, will shall break it; will, and nothing else.

Ferd. Your ladyship is ignorant what it is.

Prin. Were my lord so, his ignorance were wise,
Where now his knowledge must prove ignorance.
I hear your Grace hath sworn out housekeeping.
'Tis deadly sin to keep that oath, my lord,
And sin to break it.
But pardon me, I am too sudden-bold;
To teach a teacher ill beseemeth me.
Vouchsafe to read the purpose of my coming,
And suddenly resolve me in my suit.
[*Gives a paper.*]

Ferd. Madam, I will, if suddenly I may.

Prin. You will the sooner that I were away,
For you'll prove perjur'd if you make me stay.

Ber. Did not I dance with you in Brabant once?

Kath. Did not I dance with you in Brabant once?
Ber. I know you did.
Kath. How needless was it then to ask the question!
Ber. You must not be so quick.
Kath. 'Tis long of you that spur me with such questions.
Ber. Your wit's too hot, it speeds too fast, 'twill tire.
Kath. Not till it leave the rider in the mire.
Ber. What time o' day?
Kath. The hour that fools should ask.
Ber. Now fair befall your mask!
Kath. Fair fall the face it covers!
Ber. And send you many lovers!
Kath. Amen, so you be none.
Ber. Nay, then will I be gone.
Ferd. Madam, your father here doth intimate
The payment of a hundred thousand crowns,
Being but the one half of an entire sum
Disbursed by my father in his wars.
But say that he or we — as neither have —
Receiv'd that sum, yet there remains unpaid
A hundred thousand more, in surety of the which
One part of Aquitaine is bound to us,
Although not valued to the money's worth.
If then the King your father will restore
But that one half which is unsatisfied,
We will give up our right in Aquitaine
And hold fair friendship with his Majesty.
But that, it seems, he little purposeth;
For here he doth demand to have repaid
A hundred thousand crowns; and not demands,
On payment of a hundred thousand crowns,
To have his title live in Aquitaine;
Which we much rather had depart withal,
And have the money by our father lent,
Than Aquitaine, so gelded as it is.
Dear Princess, were not his requests so far
From reason's yielding, your fair self should make
A yielding 'gainst some reason in my breast,
And go well satisfied to France again.
Prin. You do the King my father too much wrong,
And wrong the reputation of your name,
In so unseeming to confess receipt
Of that which hath so faithfully been paid.
Ferd. I do protest I never heard of it;
And if you prove it, I'll repay it back
Or yield up Aquitaine.
Prin. We arrest your word.
Boyet, you can produce acquittances
For such a sum from special officers
Of Charles his father.
Ferd. Satisfy me so.
Boyet. So please your Grace, the packet is not come
Where that and other specialties are bound.
To-morrow you shall have a sight of them.
Ferd. It shall suffice me; at which interview
All liberal reason I will yield unto.
Meantime receive such welcome at my hand
As honour (without breach of honour) may
Make tender of to thy true worthiness.
You may not come, fair Princess, in my gates;
But here without you shall be so receiv'd
As you shall deem yourself lodg'd in my heart,
Though so denied fair harbour in my house.
Your own good thoughts excuse me, and farewell.
To-morrow shall we visit you again.
Prin. Sweet health and fair desires consort your Grace.
Ferd. Thy own wish wish I thee in every place. *Exeunt* [*King and his Train*].
Ber. Lady, I will commend you to mine own heart.
Ros. Pray you, do my commendations. I would be glad to see it.
Ber. I would you heard it groan.
Ros. Is the fool sick?
Ber. Sick at the heart.
Ros. Alack, let it blood!
Ber. Would that do it good?
Ros. My physic says ay.
Ber. Will you prick't with your eye?
Ros. No point, with my knife.
Ber. Now God save thy life!
Ros. And yours from long living!
Ber. I cannot stay thanks-giving. *Exit.*

Enter *Dumain.*

Dum. Sir, I pray you a word. What lady is that same?
Boyet. The heir of Alençon, Katherine her name.
Dum. A gallant lady. Monsieur, fare you well. *Exit.*

[Enter *Longaville.*]

Long. I beseech you a word. What is she in the white?
Boyet. A woman sometimes, an you saw her in the light.
Long. Perchance light in the light. I desire her name.
Boyet. She hath but one for herself. To desire that were a shame.
Long. Pray you, sir, whose daughter?
Boyet. Her mother's, I have heard.

Long. God's blessing on your beard!
Boyet. Good sir, be not offended.
She is an heir of Falconbridge.
Long. Nay, my choler is ended.
She is a most sweet lady.
Boyet. Not unlike, sir; that may be.
Exit Longaville.

Enter *Berowne.*

Ber. What's her name in the cap?
Boyet. Rosaline, by good hap.
Ber. Is she wedded or no?
Boyet. To her will, sir, or so.
Ber. O, you are welcome, sir! Adieu.
Boyet. Farewell to me, sir, and welcome to you.
Exit Berowne.

Mar. That last is Berowne, the merry mad-cap lord.
Not a word with him but a jest.
Boyet. And every jest but a word.
Prin. It was well done of you to take him at his word.
Boyet. I was as willing to grapple as he was to board.
Kath. Two hot sheeps, marry!
Boyet. And wherefore not ships?
No sheep, sweet lamb, unless we feed on your lips.
Kath. You sheep, and I pasture? Shall that finish the jest?
Boyet. So you grant pasture for me.
[*Offers to kiss her.*]
Kath. Not so, gentle beast.
My lips are no common, though several they be.
Boyet. Belonging to whom?
Kath. To my fortunes and me.
Prin. Good wits will be jangling; but, gentles, agree.
This civil war of wits were much better used
On Navarre and his bookmen, for here 'tis abused.
Boyet. If my observation (which very seldom lies),
By the heart's still rhetoric, disclosed with eyes,
Deceive me not now, Navarre is infected.
Prin. With what?
Boyet. With that which we lovers entitle 'affected.'
Prin. Your reason?
Boyet. Why, all his behaviours did make their retire
To the court of his eye, peeping thorough desire.
His heart, like an agate with your print impressed,
Proud with his form, in his eye pride expressed.
His tongue, all impatient to speak and not see,
Did stumble with haste in his eyesight to be;
All senses to that sense did make their repair,
To feel only looking on fairest of fair.
Methought all his senses were lock'd in his eye,
As jewels in crystal for some prince to buy,
Who, tend'ring their own worth from where they were glass'd,
Did point you to buy them along as you pass'd.
His face's own margent did quote such amazes
That all eyes saw his eyes enchanted with gazes.
I'll give you Aquitaine and all that is his
An you give him for my sake but one loving kiss.
Prin. Come, to our pavilion. Boyet is dispos'd.
Boyet. But to speak that in words which his eye hath disclos'd.
I only have made a mouth of his eye
By adding a tongue which I know will not lie.
Mar. Thou art an old love-monger and speakest skilfully.
Kath. He is Cupid's grandfather and learns news of him.
Ros. Then was Venus like her mother, for her father is but grim.
Boyet. Do you hear, my mad wenches?
Mar. No.
Boyet. What then? do you see?
Mar. Ay, our way to be gone.
Boyet. You are too hard for me.
Exeunt omnes.

ACT III. [Scene I. *The park.*]

Enter [*Armado* the] Braggart and his Boy [*Moth*].

Arm. Warble, child; make passionate my sense of hearing.

Moth. [*sings*] Concolinel.

Arm. Sweet air! Go, tenderness of years, take this key, give enlargement to the swain, bring him festinately hither. I must employ him in a letter to my love.

Moth. Master, will you win your love with a French brawl?

Arm. How meanest thou? Brawling in French?

Moth. No, my complete master; but to jig off a tune at the tongue's end, canary to it with your feet, humour it with turning up your eyelids; sigh a note and sing a note, sometime through the throat, as if you swallowed love with singing love, sometime through the nose, as if you snuff'd up love by smelling love, with your hat penthouse-like o'er the shop of your eyes, with your arms cross'd on your thin-belly doublet, like a rabbit on a spit, or your hands in your pocket, like a man after the old painting; and keep not too long in one tune, but a snip and away. These are complements; these are humours; these betray nice wenches that would be betrayed without these, and make them men of note — do you note me? — that most are affected to these.

Arm. How hast thou purchased this experience?

Moth. By my penny of observation.

Arm. But O — but O —

Moth. 'The hobby-horse is forgot.'

Arm. Call'st thou my love hobby-horse?

Moth. No, master. The hobby-horse is but a colt, [*aside*] and your love perhaps a hackney. But have you forgot your love?

Arm. Almost I had.

Moth. Negligent student! learn her by heart.

Arm. By heart and in heart, boy.

Moth. And out of heart, master. All those three I will prove.

Arm. What wilt thou prove?

Moth. A man, if I live; and this, by, in, and without, upon the instant. By heart you love her, because your heart cannot come by her; in heart you love her, because your heart is in love with her; and out of heart you love her, being out of heart that you cannot enjoy her.

Arm. I am all these three.

Moth. [*aside*] And three times as much more, and yet nothing at all.

Arm. Fetch hither the swain; he must carry me a letter.

Moth. A message well sympathiz'd — a horse to be ambassador for an ass!

Arm. Ha, ha! what sayest thou?

Moth. Marry, sir, you must send the ass upon the horse, for he is very slow-gaited. But I go.

Arm. The way is but short. Away!

Moth. As swift as lead, sir.

Arm. Thy meaning, pretty ingenious?
Is not lead a metal heavy, dull, and slow?

Moth. *Minime*, honest master; or rather, master, no.

Arm. I say lead is slow.

Moth. You are too swift, sir, to say so.
Is that lead slow which is fir'd from a gun?

Arm. Sweet smoke of rhetoric!
He reputes me a cannon; and the bullet, that's he.
I shoot thee at the swain.

Moth. Thump then, and I flee. [*Exit.*]

Arm. A most acute juvenal, voluble and free of grace!
By thy favour, sweet welkin, I must sigh in thy face.
Most rude melancholy, valour gives thee place.
My herald is return'd.

Enter Page [*Moth*] and Clown [*Costard*].

Moth. A wonder, master! Here's a costard broken in a shin.

Arm. Some enigma, some riddle. Come, thy l'envoy; begin.

Cost. No egma, no riddle, no l'envoy; no salve in the mail, sir. O sir, plantain, a plain plantain! No l'envoy, no l'envoy, no salve, sir, but a plantain!

Arm. By virtue, thou enforcest laughter; thy silly thought, my spleen; the heaving of my lungs provokes me to ridiculous smiling. O, pardon me, my stars! Doth the inconsiderate take salve for l'envoy, and the word 'l'envoy' for a salve?

Moth. Do the wise think them other? Is not l'envoy a salve?

Arm. No, page; it is an epilogue or discourse to make plain
Some obscure precedence that hath tofore been sain.
I will example it:
The fox, the ape, and the humblebee
Were still at odds, being but three.
There's the moral. Now the l'envoy.

Moth. I will add the l'envoy. Say the moral again.

Arm. The fox, the ape, and the humblebee
Were still at odds, being but three.

Moth. Until the goose came out of door
And stay'd the odds by adding four.
Now will I begin your moral, and do you follow with my l'envoy.
The fox, the ape, and the humblebee
Were still at odds, being but three.

Arm. Until the goose came out of door,
Staying the odds by adding four.

Moth. A good l'envoy, ending in the goose.
Would you desire more?

PHOTOGRAPHS BY JOHN VICKERS
PRODUCED BY THE OLD VIC COMPANY

LOVE'S LABOUR'S LOST

Above: The opening scene, in which the King of Navarre and his nobles bind themselves to live a monastic life for three years

Left: Angela Baddeley as the Princess of France and Michael Aldridge as the King of Navarre

Below left: Diana Churchill as Rosaline

Below right: Michael Redgrave as Berowne, lover of the witty and brilliant Rosaline

Above: "There's villainy abroad: this letter will tell you more." Constable Dull (Paul Rogers) brings the Clown Costard (George Benson) before the king and presents Don Armado's letter charging Costard with consorting with a woman, a violation of the king's monastic rule *(Act I, Scene I)*

Right: The "fantastical Spaniard," Don Armado (Baliol Holloway), and his page Moth (Brian Smith) discuss the symptoms of romantic melancholy *(Act I, Scene II)*

Left: "Who are the votaries, my loving lords." The Princess of France, on an embassy to Navarre, seeks information on the king's vows, which prevent all women from entering his court *(Act II, Scene I)*

Above: "You may not come, fair princess, in my gates." Holding to his vow respecting women, the king is forced to refuse entry to the princess *(Act II, Scene I)*

Left: "Did I not dance with you in Brabant once?" Berowne tries to strike up an acquaintance with Rosaline *(Act II, Scene I)*

Right: "What's her name, in the cap?" Berowne has gained little information in his repartee with Rosaline and now tries to learn her name from Boyet (Walter Hudd), one of the lords escorting the princess *(Act II, Scene I)*

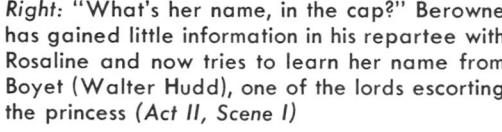

Right: "Gardon, O sweet gardon! better than remuneration; a 'levenpence farthing better. Most sweet gardon." Given a shilling by Berowne as a "guerdon" (reward) for carrying a letter, Costard esteems it above the "remuneration" Armado offered him *(Act III, Scene I)*

Left: "Thou hast no feeling of it, Moth: I will speak that l'envoy." Costard tells Moth to let him take the final lines of the pun they have been developing for the bafflement of Don Armado *(Act III, Scene I)*

The princess and her retinue hunt in the King of Navarre's park *(Act IV, Scene I)*

Left: A forester points out to the princess an advantageous stand for her to shoot from *(Act IV, Scene I)*

The king gives Berowne his love letter to Rosaline and tells him to read it aloud *(Act IV, Scene III)*

Below: "Advance your standards, and upon them, lords." Berowne rallies his companions, who have determined to renounce their vows of seclusion and are eager to begin wooing their loves *(Act IV, Scene III)*

Above: "Sir, I praise the Lord for you." Sir Nathaniel (Miles Malleson), the curate, is impressed by the spurious learning of Holofernes (Mark Dignam), the schoolmaster *(Act IV, Scene III)*

Left: Armado asks his friends to aid in presenting an entertainment for the Princess of France *(Act V, Scene I)*

Holofernes suggests a masque of the Nine Worthies (ancient heroes), with Nathaniel as Joshua and Moth, the page, as Hercules *(Act V, Scene I)*

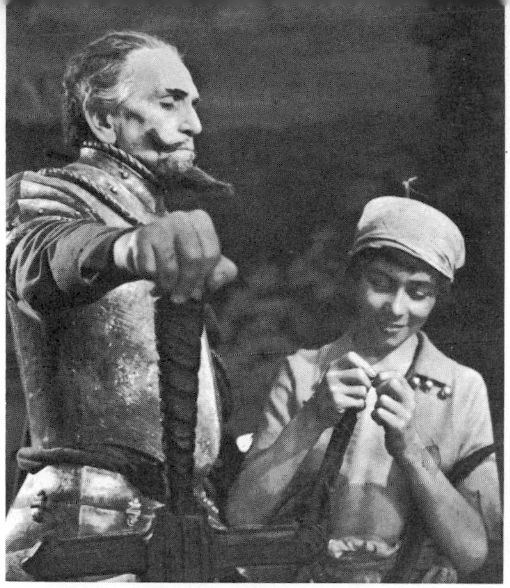

Above: In the masque, Armado represents Hector and Moth appears as the infant Hercules *(Act V, Scene II)*

Right: "We have had pastime here and pleasant game. A mess of Russians left us but of late." The princess pretends not to have recognized the king and his friends when they were disguised as Russians *(Act V, Scene II)*

Below: "When in the world I liv'd, I was the world's commander." Sir Nathaniel plays Alexander in the masque presented for the princess *(Act V, Scene II)*

"Look you what I have from the loving king." The Princess of France and her ladies admire the gifts sent to them by the King of Navarre and his companions *(Act V, Scene II)*

"I am sorry, madam; for the news I bring is heavy in my tongue." The masque is interrupted by the news that the King of France is dead *(Act V, Scene II)*

Cost. The boy hath sold him a bargain — a goose, that's flat.
Sir, your pennyworth is good an your goose be fat.
To sell a bargain well is as cunning as fast and loose.
Let me see: a fat l'envoy — ay, that's a fat goose.

Arm. Come hither, come hither. How did this argument begin?

Moth. By saying that a costard was broken in a shin.
Then call'd you for the l'envoy.

Cost. True, and I for a plantain. Thus came your argument in;
Then the boy's fat l'envoy, the goose that you bought,
And he ended the market.

Arm. But tell me! How was there a costard broken in a shin?

Moth. I will tell you sensibly.

Cost. Thou hast no feeling of it, Moth. I will speak that l'envoy:
I, Costard, running out, that was safely within,
Fell over the threshold and broke my shin.

Arm. We will talk no more of this matter.

Cost. Till there be more matter in the shin.

Arm. Sirrah Costard, I will enfranchise thee.

Cost. O, marry me to one Frances! I smell some l'envoy, some goose, in this.

Arm. By my sweet soul, I mean setting thee at liberty, enfreedoming thy person. Thou wert immured, restrained, captivated, bound.

Cost. True, true! and now you will be my purgation and let me loose.

Arm. I give thee thy liberty, set thee from durance, and, in lieu thereof, impose on thee nothing but this: bear this significant [*gives a letter*] to the country maid Jaquenetta. There is remuneration [*gives money*]; for the best ward of mine honour is rewarding my dependents. Moth, follow.

Moth. Like the sequel, I. Signior Costard, adieu.

Exit [*Armado, followed by Moth*].

Cost. My sweet ounce of man's flesh! my incony Jew! —
Now will I look to his remuneration. Remuneration — O, that's the Latin word for three farthings. Three farthings — remuneration. 'What's the price of this inkle?' 'One penny.' 'No, I'll give you a remuneration.' Why, it carries it! Remuneration. Why, it is a fairer name than French crown. I will never buy and sell out of this word.

Enter *Berowne.*

Ber. O my good knave Costard, exceedingly well met!

Cost. Pray you, sir, how much carnation ribbon may a man buy for a remuneration?

Ber. O, what is a remuneration?

Cost. Marry, sir, halfpenny farthing.

Ber. O, why then, three-farthing worth of silk.

Cost. I thank your worship. God be wi' you!

Ber. O, stay, slave; I must employ thee.
As thou wilt win my favour, good my knave,
Do one thing for me that I shall entreat.

Cost. When would you have it done, sir?

Ber. O, this afternoon.

Cost. Well, I will do it, sir. Fare you well.

Ber. O, thou knowest not what it is.

Cost. I shall know, sir, when I have done it.

Ber. Why, villain, thou must know first.

Cost. I will come to your worship to-morrow morning.

Ber. It must be done this afternoon. Hark, slave, it is but this:
The Princess comes to hunt here in the park,
And in her train there is a gentle lady.
When tongues speak sweetly, then they name her name,
And Rosaline they call her. Ask for her,
And to her white hand see thou do commend
This seal'd-up counsel. There's thy guerdon. Go. [*Gives him a shilling.*]

Cost. Gardon — O sweet gardon! better than remuneration! a 'levenpence-farthing better. Most sweet gardon! I will do it, sir, in print. Gardon — remuneration. *Exit.*

Ber. O — and I, forsooth, in love? I that have been love's whip,
A very beadle to a humorous sigh,
A critic, nay, a night-watch constable,
A domineering pedant o'er the boy,
Than whom no mortal so magnificent!
This wimpled, whining, purblind, wayward boy;
This senior junior, giant dwarf, Dan Cupid,
Regent of love-rhymes, lord of folded arms,
Th' anointed sovereign of sighs and groans,
Liege of all loiterers and malecontents,
Dread prince of plackets, king of codpieces,
Sole emperator and great general
Of trotting paritors (O my little heart!) —
And I to be a corporal of his field
And wear his colours like a tumbler's hoop!

What, I? I love? I sue? I seek a wife?
A woman, that is like a German clock,
Still a-repairing, ever out of frame,
And never going aright, being a watch,
But being watch'd that it may still go right!
Nay, to be perjur'd, which is worst of all;
And, among three, to love the worst of all,
A whitely wanton, with a velvet brow,
With two pitch-balls stuck in her face for eyes;
Ay, and, by heaven, one that will do the deed
Though Argus were her eunuch and her guard!
And I to sigh for her! to watch for her!
To pray for her! Go to! it is a plague
That Cupid will impose for my neglect
Of his almighty dreadful little might.
Well, I will love, write, sigh, pray, sue, and groan.
Some men must love my lady, and some Joan.
[*Exit.*]

ACT IV. [Scene I. *The park.*]

Enter the *Princess*, a *Forester*, her *Ladies*, and her *Lords*.

Prin. Was that the King that spurr'd his horse so hard
Against the steep uprising of the hill?
Boyet. I know not, but I think it was not he.
Prin. Whoe'er 'a was, 'a show'd a mounting mind.
Well, lords, to-day we shall have our dispatch;
On Saturday we will return to France.
Then, forester my friend, where is the bush
That we must stand and play the murtherer in?
For. Hereby upon the edge of yonder coppice,
A stand where you may make the fairest shoot.
Prin. I thank my beauty, I am fair that shoot,
And thereupon thou speak'st the fairest shoot.
For. Pardon me, madam, for I meant not so.
Prin. What, what? first praise me, and again say no?
O short-liv'd pride! Not fair? Alack for woe!
For. Yes, madam, fair.
Prin. Nay, never paint me now!
Where fair is not, praise cannot mend the brow.
Here (good my glass) take this for telling true.
[*Gives money.*]
Fair payment for foul words is more than due.
For. Nothing but fair is that which you inherit.
Prin. See, see, my beauty will be sav'd by merit!
O heresy in fair, fit for these days!
A giving hand, though foul, shall have fair praise.
But come, the bow! Now mercy goes to kill,
And shooting well is then accounted ill.
Thus will I save my credit in the shoot:
Not wounding, pity would not let me do't;
If wounding, then it was to show my skill,
That more for praise than purpose meant to kill.
And, out of question, so it is sometimes:
Glory grows guilty of detested crimes
When for fame's sake, for praise, an outward part,
We bend to that the working of the heart;
As I for praise alone now seek to spill
The poor deer's blood that my heart means no ill.
Boyet. Do not curst wives hold that self sovereignty
Only for praise sake when they strive to be
Lords o'er their lords?
Prin. Only for praise; and praise we may afford
To any lady that subdues a lord.

Enter [*Costard, the*] *Clown*.

Boyet. Here comes a member of the commonwealth.
Cost. God dig-you-den all! Pray you which is the head lady?
Prin. Thou shalt know her, fellow, by the rest that have no heads.
Cost. Which is the greatest lady, the highest?
Prin. The thickest and the tallest.
Cost. The thickest and the tallest. It is so; truth is truth.
An your waist, mistress, were as slender as my wit,
One o' these maids' girdles for your waist should be fit.
Are not you the chief woman? You are the thickest here.
Prin. What's your will, sir? What's your will?
Cost. I have a letter from Monsieur Berowne to one Lady Rosaline.
Prin. O, thy letter, thy letter! He's a good friend of mine.

Stand aside, good bearer. Boyet, you can carve;
Break up this capon.
Boyet. I am bound to serve.
This letter is mistook; it importeth none here.
It is writ to Jaquenetta.
Prin. We will read it, I swear.
Break the neck of the wax, and every one give ear.

Boyet reads. 'By heaven, that thou art fair is most infallible; true that thou art beauteous; truth itself that thou art lovely. More fairer than fair, beautiful than beauteous, truer than truth itself, have commiseration on thy heroical vassal! The magnanimous and most illustrate king Cophetua set eye upon the pernicious and indubitate beggar Zenelophon; and he it was that might rightly say, "Veni, vidi, vici"; which to annothanize in the vulgar (O base and obscure vulgar!), videlicet, He came, saw, and overcame. He came, one; saw, two; overcame, three. Who came? The king. Why did he come? To see. Why did he see? To overcome. To whom came he? To the beggar. What saw he? The beggar. Who overcame he? The beggar. The conclusion is victory. On whose side? The king's. The captive is enrich'd. On whose side? The beggar's. The catastrophe is a nuptial. On whose side? The king's. No, on both in one, or one in both. I am the king, for so stands the comparison; thou the beggar, for so witnesseth thy lowliness. Shall I command thy love? I may. Shall I enforce thy love? I could. Shall I entreat thy love? I will. What shalt thou exchange for rags? Robes. For tittles? Titles. For thyself? Me. Thus, expecting thy reply, I profane my lips on thy foot, my eyes on thy picture, and my heart on thy every part.

'Thine, in the dearest design of industry,
'DON ADRIANO DE ARMADO.'

'Thus dost thou hear the Nemean lion roar
'Gainst thee, thou lamb, that standest as his prey.
Submissive fall his princely feet before,
And he from forage will incline to play.
But if thou strive, poor soul, what art thou then?
Food for his rage, repasture for his den.'

Prin. What plume of feathers is he that indited this letter?
What vane? what weathercock? Did you ever hear better?
Boyet. I am much deceived but I remember the style.
Prin. Else your memory is bad, going o'er it erewhile.
Boyet. This Armado is a Spaniard that keeps here in court;
A phantasime, a Monarcho, and one that makes sport
To the Prince and his bookmates.
Prin. Thou fellow, a word.
Who gave thee this letter?
Cost. I told you; my lord.
Prin. To whom shouldst thou give it?
Cost. From my lord to my lady.
Prin. From which lord to which lady?
Cost. From my Lord Berowne, a good master of mine,
To a lady of France that he call'd Rosaline.
Prin. Thou hast mistaken his letter. Come, lords, away.
[*To Rosaline*] Here, sweet, put up this; 'twill be thine another day.
Exeunt [*Princess and Lords except Boyet*].
Boyet. Who is the suitor? Who is the suitor?
Ros. Shall I teach you to know?
Boyet. Ay, my continent of beauty.
Ros. Why, she that bears the bow.
Finely put off!
Boyet. My lady goes to kill horns; but if thou marry,
Hang me by the neck if horns that year miscarry.
Finely put on!
Ros. Well then, I am the shooter.
Boyet. And who is your deer?
Ros. If we choose by the horns, yourself. Come not near.
Finely put on indeed!
Mar. You still wrangle with her, Boyet, and she strikes at the brow.
Boyet. But she herself is hit lower. Have I hit her now?
Ros. Shall I come upon thee with an old saying, that was a man when King Pippen of France was a little boy, as touching the hit it?
Boyet. So I may answer thee with one as old, that was a woman when Queen Guinover of Britain was a little wench, as touching the hit it.
Ros.
'Thou canst not hit it, hit it, hit it,
Thou canst not hit it, my good man.'
Boyet.
'An I cannot, cannot, cannot,
An I cannot, another can.'
Exeunt [*Rosaline and Katherine*].
Cost. By my troth, most pleasant. How both did fit it!
Mar. A mark marvellous well shot, for they both did hit it.
Boyet. A mark! O, mark but that mark! 'A mark,' says my lady!

Let the mark have a prick in't, to mete at, if it may be.

Mar. Wide o' the bow-hand! I' faith, your hand is out.

Cost. Indeed 'a must shoot nearer, or he'll ne'er hit the clout.

Boyet. An if my hand be out, then belike your hand is in.

Cost. Then will she get the upshoot by cleaving the pin.

Mar. Come, come, you talk greasily; your lips grow foul.

Cost. She's too hard for you at pricks, sir. Challenge her to bowl.

Boyet. I fear too much rubbing. Good night, my good owl. [*Exeunt Boyet and Maria.*]

Cost. By my soul, a swain! a most simple clown!
Lord, Lord, how the ladies and I have put him down!
O' my troth, most sweet jests, most incony vulgar wit,
When it comes so smoothly off, so obscenely, as it were, so fit!
Armado o' th' t'one side — O, a most dainty man!
To see him walk before a lady and to bear her fan!
To see him kiss his hand! and how most sweetly 'a will swear!
And his page o' t'other side, that handful of wit!
Ah, heavens, it is a most pathetical nit!
Shout within.
Sowla, sowla! *Exit.*

[Scene II. *The park.*]

Enter *Dull, Holofernes the Pedant,* and *Nathaniel.*

Nath. Very reverent sport truly, and done in the testimony of a good conscience.

Hol. The deer was, as you know, *sanguis,* in blood; ripe as the pomwater, who now hangeth like a jewel in the ear of *coelo,* the sky, the welkin, the heaven, and anon falleth like a crab on the face of *terra,* the soil, the land, the earth.

Nath. Truly, Master Holofernes, the epithets are sweetly varied, like a scholar at the least; but, sir, I assure ye it was a buck of the first head.

Hol. Sir Nathaniel, haud credo.

Dull. 'Twas not a haud credo; 'twas a pricket.

Hol. Most barbarous intimation! yet a kind of insinuation, as it were, *in via,* in way, of explication; *facere,* as it were, replication, or rather, *ostentare,* to show, as it were, his inclination, after his undressed, unpolished, uneducated, unpruned, untrained, or rather, unlettered, or ratherest, unconfirmed fashion, to insert again my 'haud credo' for a deer.

Dull. I said the deer was not a haud credo, 'twas a pricket.

Hol. Twice-sod simplicity, bis coctus!
O thou monster ignorance, how deformed dost thou look!

Nath. Sir, he hath never fed of the dainties that are bred in a book.
He hath not eat paper, as it were; he hath not drunk ink. His intellect is not replenished; he is only an animal, only sensible in the duller parts;
And such barren plants are set before us that we thankful should be —
Which we of taste and feeling are — for those parts that do fructify in us more than he.
For as it would ill become me to be vain, indiscreet, or a fool,
So, were there a patch set on learning, to see him in a school.
But, omne bene, say I, being of an old father's mind —
Many can brook the weather that love not the wind.

Dull. You two are bookmen. Can you tell me by your wit
What was a month old at Cain's birth that's not five weeks old as yet?

Hol. Dictynna, goodman Dull; Dictynna, goodman Dull.

Dull. What is Dictynna?

Nath. A title to Phœbe, to Luna, to the moon.

Hol. The moon was a month old when Adam was no more,
And raught not to five weeks when he came to five-score.
Th' allusion holds in the exchange.

Dull. 'Tis true indeed; the collusion holds in the exchange.

Hol. God comfort thy capacity! I say th' allusion holds in the exchange.

Dull. And I say the polusion holds in the exchange, for the moon is never but a month old; and I say beside that, 'twas a pricket that the Princess kill'd.

Hol. Sir Nathaniel, will you hear an extemporal epitaph on the death of the deer?

And, to humour the ignorant, call I the deer the Princess kill'd a pricket.

Nath. Perge, good Master Holofernes, perge, so it shall please you to abrogate squirility.

Hol. I will something affect the letter, for it argues facility.

The preyful princess pierc'd and prick'd a pretty pleasing pricket;
Some say a sore; but not a sore till now made sore with shooting.
The dogs did yell: put el to sore, then sorel jumps from thicket,
Or pricket sore, or else sorel. The people fall a-hooting.
If sore be sore, then L to sore makes fifty sores one sorel.
Of one sore I an hundred make by adding but one more L.

Nath. A rare talent!

Dull. [*aside*] If a talent be a claw, look how he claws him with a talent.

Hol. This is a gift that I have, simple, simple; a foolish extravagant spirit, full of forms, figures, shapes, objects, ideas, apprehensions, motions, revolutions. These are begot in the ventricle of memory, nourish'd in the womb of pia mater, and delivered upon the mellowing of occasion. But the gift is good in those in whom it is acute, and I am thankful for it.

Nath. Sir, I praise the Lord for you, and so may my parishioners, for their sons are well tutor'd by you, and their daughters profit very greatly under you. You are a good member of the commonwealth.

Hol. *Mehercle*, if their sons be ingenuous, they shall want no instruction; if their daughters be capable, I will put it to them. But vir sapit qui pauca loquitur. A soul feminine saluteth us.

Enter *Jaquenetta* and [*Costard*] *the Clown.*

Jaq. God give you good morrow, Master Person.

Hol. Master Person, quasi pers-one. And if one should be pierc'd, which is the one?

Cost. Marry, Master Schoolmaster, he that is likest to a hogshead.

Hol. Of piercing a hogshead! A good lustre of conceit in a turf of earth; fire enough for a flint, pearl enough for a swine. 'Tis pretty; it is well.

Jaq. Good Master Person, be so good as read me this letter. It was given me by Costard and sent me from Don Armado. I beseech you read it.

Hol. Fauste, precor, gelida quando pecus omne sub umbra Ruminat, and so forth. Ah, good old Mantuan! I may speak of thee as the traveller doth of Venice:

Venetia, Venetia,
Chi non ti vede, non ti pretia.

Old Mantuan! old Mantuan! Who understandeth thee not, loves thee not. Ut, re, sol, la, mi, fa. Under pardon, sir, what are the contents? or rather, as Horace says in his — What, my soul, verses?

Nath. Ay, sir, and very learned.

Hol. Let me hear a staff, a stanze, a verse. Lege, domine.

Nath. [*reads*]

'If love make me forsworn, how shall I swear to love?
Ah, never faith could hold, if not to beauty vowed!
Though to myself forsworn, to thee I'll faithful prove;
Those thoughts to me were oaks, to thee like osiers bowed.
Study his bias leaves and makes his book thine eyes,
Where all those pleasures live that art would comprehend.
If knowledge be the mark, to know thee shall suffice;
Well learned is that tongue that well can thee commend,
All ignorant that soul that sees thee without wonder;
Which is to me some praise that I thy parts admire.
Thy eye Jove's lightning bears, thy voice his dreadful thunder,
Which, not to anger bent, is music and sweet fire.
Celestial as thou art, O, pardon love this wrong,
That singës heaven's praise with such an earthly tongue.'

Hol. You find not the apostrophas, and so miss the accent. Let me supervise the canzonet. Here are only numbers ratified; but for the elegancy, facility, and golden cadence of poesy, caret. Ovidius Naso was the man. And why indeed 'Naso,' but for smelling out the odoriferous flowers of fancy, the jerks of invention? Imitari is nothing. So doth the hound his master, the ape his keeper, the tired horse his rider. But, damosella virgin, was this directed to you?

Jaq. Ay, sir, from one Monsieur Berowne, one of the strange queen's lords.

Hol. I will overglance the superscript. 'To the snow-white hand of the most beauteous

Lady Rosaline.' I will look again on the intellect of the letter, for the nomination of the party writing to the person written unto. 'Your ladyship's in all desired employment, Berowne.' Sir Nathaniel, this Berowne is one of the votaries with the King; and here he hath framed a letter to a sequent of the stranger queen's, which accidentally, or by the way of progression, hath miscarried. Trip and go, my sweet; deliver this paper into the royal hand of the King; it may concern much. Stay not thy compliment; I forgive thy duty. Adieu.

Jaq. Good Costard, go with me. — Sir, God save your life!

Cost. Have with thee, my girl.

Exeunt [*Costard and Jaquenetta*].

Nath. Sir, you have done this in the fear of God, very religiously; and, as a certain father saith —

Hol. Sir, tell not me of the father; I do fear colourable colours. But to return to the verses: did they please you, Sir Nathaniel?

Nath. Marvellous well for the pen.

Hol. I do dine to-day at the father's of a certain pupil of mine, where, if (before repast) it shall please you to gratify the table with a grace, I will, on my privilege I have with the parents of the foresaid child or pupil, undertake your ben venuto, where I will prove those verses to be very unlearned, neither savouring of poetry, wit, nor invention. I beseech your society.

Nath. And thank you too; for society (saith the text) is the happiness of life.

Hol. And certes the text most infallibly concludes it. [*To Dull*] Sir, I do invite you too; you shall not say me nay. Pauca verba. Away! the gentles are at their game, and we will to our recreation. *Exeunt.*

[Scene III. *The park.*]

Enter *Berowne*, with a paper in his hand, *alone.*

Ber. The King he is hunting the deer; I am coursing myself. They have pitch'd a toil; I am toiling in a pitch — pitch that defiles. Defile! a foul word. Well, 'set thee down, sorrow!' for so they say the fool said, and so say I, and I the fool. Well proved, wit. By the Lord, this love is as mad as Ajax: it kills sheep; it kills me — I a sheep. Well proved again o' my side. I will not love; if I do, hang me. I' faith, I will not. O, but her eye! By this light, but for her eye, I would not love her; yes, for her two eyes. Well, I do nothing in the world but lie, and lie in my throat. By heaven, I do love, and it hath taught me to rhyme and to be mallicholy; and here is part of my rhyme, and here my mallicholy. Well, she hath one o' my sonnets already. The clown bore it, the fool sent it, and the lady hath it. Sweet clown, sweeter fool, sweetest lady! By the world, I would not care a pin if the other three were in. Here comes one with a paper. God give him grace to groan!

He stands aside. The *King* ent'reth [with a paper].

King. Ay me!

Ber. [*aside*] Shot, by heaven! Proceed, sweet Cupid. Thou hast thump'd him with thy birdbolt under the left pap. In faith, secrets!

King. [*reads*]

'So sweet a kiss the golden sun gives not
 To those fresh morning drops upon the rose
As thy eyebeams when their fresh rays have smot
 The night of dew that on my cheeks down flows;
Nor shines the silver moon one half so bright
 Through the transparent bosom of the deep
As doth thy face through tears of mine give light.
 Thou shin'st in every tear that I do weep;
No drop but as a coach doth carry thee.
 So ridest thou triumphing in my woe.
Do but behold the tears that swell in me,
 And they thy glory through my grief will show.
But do not love thyself; then thou wilt keep
My tears for glasses, and still make me weep.
O queen of queens, how far dost thou excel
No thought can think nor tongue of mortal tell.'

How shall she know my griefs? I'll drop the paper.
Sweet leaves, shade folly. Who is he comes here?

Enter *Longaville* [with a paper].
The *King* steps aside.

What, Longaville! and reading! Listen, ear.

Ber. [*aside*] Now, in thy likeness, one more fool appear!

Long. Ay me! I am forsworn.

Ber. [*aside*] Why, he comes in like a perjure, wearing papers.

King. [*aside*] In love, I hope — sweet fellowship in shame.

Ber. [*aside*] One drunkard loves another of the name.

Long. Am I the first that have been perjur'd so?

Ber. [*aside*] I could put thee in comfort — not by two that I know!
Thou makest the triumviry, the corner-cap of society,
The shape of Love's Tyburn, that hangs up simplicity.

Long. I fear these stubborn lines lack power to move.
O sweet Maria, empress of my love,
These numbers will I tear, and write in prose!

Ber. [*aside*] O, rhymes are guards on wanton Cupid's hose.
Disfigure not his slop.

Long. This same shall go.

He reads the Sonnet.

'Did not the heavenly rhetoric of thine eye,
'Gainst whom the world cannot hold argument,
Persuade my heart to this false perjury?
Vows for thee broke deserve not punishment.
A woman I forswore; but I will prove,
Thou being a goddess, I forswore not thee.
My vow was earthly, thou a heavenly love.
Thy grace being gain'd cures all disgrace in me.
Vows are but breath, and breath a vapour is.
Then thou, fair sun, which on my earth dost shine,
Exhal'st this vapour-vow; in thee it is.
If broken then, it is no fault of mine;
If by me broke, what fool is not so wise
To lose an oath to win a paradise?'

Ber. [*aside*] This is the liver vein, which makes flesh a deity,
A green goose a goddess — pure, pure idolatry.
God amend us, God amend! we are much out o' th' way.

Enter *Dumain* [with a paper].

Long. By whom shall I send this? — Company? Stay. [*Steps aside.*]

Ber. [*aside*] All hid, all hid — an old infant play.
Like a demigod here sit I in the sky
And wretched fools' secrets heedfully o'er-eye.
More sacks to the mill. O heavens, I have my wish!
Dumain transform'd! Four woodcocks in a dish!

Dum. O most divine Kate!

Ber. [*aside*] O most profane coxcomb!

Dum. By heaven, the wonder in a mortal eye!

Ber. [*aside*] By earth, she is not, Corporal. There you lie.

Dum. Her amber hairs for foul hath amber quoted.

Ber. [*aside*] An amber-colour'd raven was well noted.

Dum. As upright as the cedar.

Ber. [*aside*] Stoop, I say;
Her shoulder is with child.

Dum. As fair as day.

Ber. [*aside*] Ay, as some days; but then no sun must shine.

Dum. O that I had my wish!

Long. [*aside*] And I had mine!

King. [*aside*] And I mine too, good Lord!

Ber. [*aside*] Amen, so I had mine! Is not that a good word?

Dum. I would forget her, but a fever she
Reigns in my blood and will rememb'red be.

Ber. [*aside*] A fever in your blood? Why, then incision
Would let her out in saucers. Sweet misprision!

Dum. Once more I'll read the ode that I have writ.

Ber. [*aside*] Once more I'll mark how love can vary wit.

Dumain reads his Sonnet.

'On a day — alack the day! —
Love, whose month is ever May,
Spied a blossom passing fair
Playing in the wanton air.
Through the velvet leaves the wind,
All unseen, can passage find;
That the lover, sick to death,
Wish'd himself the heaven's breath.
"Air," quoth he, "thy cheeks may blow.
Air, would I might triumph so!
But, alack, my hand is sworn
Ne'er to pluck thee from thy thorn:
Vow, alack, for youth unmeet,
Youth so apt to pluck a sweet!
Do not call it sin in me
That I am forsworn for thee;
Thou for whom Jove would swear
Juno but an Æthiop were,
And deny himself for Jove,
Turning mortal for thy love."

This will I send, and something else more plain
That shall express my true love's fasting pain.
O, would the King, Berowne, and Longaville
Were lovers too! Ill, to example ill,
Would from my forehead wipe a perjur'd note;
For none offend where all alike do dote.

Long. [*advances*] Dumain, thy love is far from charity,
That in love's grief desir'st society.
You may look pale, but I should blush, I know,
To be o'erheard and taken napping so.

King. [*advances*] Come, sir, you blush! As his your case is such.

You chide at him, offending twice as much.
You do not love Maria! Longavile
Did never sonnet for her sake compile,
Nor never lay his wreathed arms athwart
His loving bosom to keep down his heart.
I have been closely shrouded in this bush,
And mark'd you both and for you both did blush.
I heard your guilty rhymes, observ'd your fashion,
Saw sighs reek from you, noted well your passion.
'Ay me!' says one. 'O Jove!' the other cries.
One, her hairs were gold; crystal the other's eyes.
You would for paradise break faith and troth, [*To Longaville.*]
And Jove for your love would infringe an oath. [*To Dumain.*]
What will Berowne say when that he shall hear
Faith infringed, which such zeal did swear?
How will he scorn! How will he spend his wit!
How will he triumph, leap, and laugh at it!
For all the wealth that ever I did see,
I would not have him know so much by me.

Ber. [*advances*] Now step I forth to whip hypocrisy.
Ah, good my liege, I pray thee pardon me!
Good heart, what grace hast thou thus to reprove
These worms for loving, that art most in love?
Your eyes do make no coaches; in your tears
There is no certain princess that appears.
You'll not be perjur'd; 'tis a hateful thing.
Tush, none but minstrels like of sonneting!
But are you not asham'd? Nay, are you not,
All three of you, to be thus much o'ershot?
You found his mote, the King your mote did see;
But I a beam do find in each of three.
O, what a scene of fool'ry have I seen —
Of sighs, of groans, of sorrow, and of teen!
O me, with what strict patience have I sat
To see a king transformed to a gnat!
To see great Hercules whipping a gig,
And profound Salomon to tune a jig,
And Nestor play at push-pin with the boys,
And critic Timon laugh at idle toys!
Where lies thy grief, O, tell me, good Dumain?
And, gentle Longaville, where lies thy pain?
And where my liege's? All about the breast.
A caudle ho!

King. Too bitter is thy jest.
Are we betray'd thus to thy over-view?

Ber. Not you to me, but I betray'd by you:
I that am honest; I that hold it sin
To break the vow I am engaged in.
I am betray'd by keeping company
With men like you, men of inconstancy.
When shall you see me write a thing in rhyme?
Or groan for love? or spend a minute's time
In pruning me? When shall you hear that I
Will praise a hand, a foot, a face, an eye,
A gait, a state, a brow, a breast, a waist,
A leg, a limb?

King. Soft! Whither away so fast?
A true man, or a thief, that gallops so?

Ber. I post from love. Good lover, let me go.

Enter *Jaquenetta* and [*Costard*] *the Clown.*

Jaq. God bless the King!

King. What present hast thou there?

Cost. Some certain treason.

King. What makes treason here?

Cost. Nay, it makes nothing, sir.

King. If it mar nothing neither,
The treason and you go in peace away together.

Jaq. I beseech your Grace let this letter be read.
Our person misdoubts it; 'twas treason, he said.

King. Berowne, read it over.

He reads the letter.

Where hadst thou it?

Jaq. Of Costard.

King. Where hadst thou it?

Cost. Of Dun Adramadio, Dun Adramadio. [*Berowne tears the letter.*]

King. How now? What is in you? Why dost thou tear it?

Ber. A toy, my liege, a toy! Your Grace needs not fear it.

Long. It did move him to passion, and therefore let's hear it.

Dum. It is Berowne's writing, and here is his name. [*Picks up the pieces.*]

Ber. [*to Costard*] Ah, you whoreson loggerhead! you were born to do me shame.
Guilty, my lord, guilty! I confess, I confess.

King. What?

Ber. That you three fools lack'd me fool to make up the mess.
He, he, and you — and you, my liege — and I
Are pickpurses in love, and we deserve to die.
O, dismiss this audience, and I shall tell you more.

Dum. Now the number is even.

Ber. True, true! We are four.
Will these turtles be gone?

King. Hence, sirs! away!
Cost. Walk aside the true folk, and let the traitors stay.
[*Exeunt Costard and Jaquenetta.*]
Ber. Sweet lords, sweet lovers, O, let us embrace!
As true we are as flesh and blood can be.
The sea will ebb and flow, heaven show his face;
Young blood doth not obey an old decree.
We cannot cross the cause why we were born;
Therefore of all hands must we be forsworn.
King. What, did these rent lines show some love of thine?
Ber. 'Did they?' quoth you? Who sees the heavenly Rosaline
That, like a rude and savage man of Inde
At the first op'ning of the gorgeous East,
Bows not his vassal head and, strucken blind,
Kisses the base ground with obedient breast?
What peremptory eagle-sighted eye
Dares look upon the heaven of her brow
That is not blinded by her majesty?
King. What zeal, what fury hath inspir'd thee now?
My love (her mistress) is a gracious moon;
She (an attending star) scarce seen a light.
Ber. My eyes are then no eyes, nor I Berowne.
O, but for my love, day would turn to night!
Of all complexions the cull'd sovereignty
Do meet, as at a fair, in her fair cheek,
Where several worthies make one dignity,
Where nothing wants that want itself doth seek.
Lend me the flourish of all gentle tongues —
Fie! painted rhetoric — O, she needs it not!
To things of sale a seller's praise belongs:
She passes praise; then praise too short doth blot.
A wither'd hermit, fivescore winters worn,
Might shake off fifty, looking in her eye.
Beauty doth varnish age, as if new-born,
And gives the crutch the cradle's infancy.
O, 'tis the sun that maketh all things shine.
King. By heaven, thy love is black as ebony!
Ber. Is ebony like her? O wood divine!
A wife of such wood were felicity.
O, who can give an oath? Where is a book?
That I may swear beauty doth beauty lack
If that she learn not of her eye to look.
No face is fair that is not full so black.
King. O paradox! Black is the badge of hell,
The hue of dungeons, and the school of night;
And beauty's crest becomes the heavens well.
Ber. Devils soonest tempt, resembling spirits of light.
O, if in black my lady's brows be deckt,
It mourns that painting and usurping hair
Should ravish doters with a false aspect;
And therefore is she born to make black fair.
Her favour turns the fashion of the days,
For native blood is counted painting now;
And therefore red that would avoid dispraise
Paints itself black to imitate her brow.
Dum. To look like her are chimney-sweepers black.
Long. And since her time are colliers counted bright.
King. And Æthiops of their sweet complexion crack.
Dum. Dark needs no candles now, for dark is light.
Ber. Your mistresses dare never come in rain
For fear their colours should be wash'd away.
King. 'Twere good yours did; for, sir, to tell you plain,
I'll find a fairer face not wash'd to-day.
Ber. I'll prove her fair, or talk till doomsday here.
King. No devil will fright thee then so much as she.
Dum. I never knew man hold vile stuff so dear.
Long. Look, here's thy love; my foot and her face see. [*Shows his shoe.*]
Ber. O, if the streets were paved with thine eyes,
Her feet were much too dainty for such tread!
Dum. O vile! Then, as she goes, what upward lies
The street should see as she walk'd overhead.
King. But what of this? Are we not all in love?
Ber. Nothing so sure, and thereby all forsworn.
King. Then leave this chat; and, good Berowne, now prove
Our loving lawful and our faith not torn.
Dum. Ay marry, there, some flattery for this evil!
Long. O, some authority how to proceed!
Some tricks, some quillets, how to cheat the devil!
Dum. Some salve for perjury.
Ber. O, 'tis more than need!
Have at you, then, affection's men-at-arms.
Consider what you first did swear unto:
To fast, to study, and to see no woman —
Flat treason 'gainst the kingly state of youth.

Say, can you fast? Your stomachs are too young,
And abstinence engenders maladies.
And where that you have vow'd to study, lords,
In that each of you have forsworn his book;
Can you still dream, and pore, and thereon look?
For when would you, my lord, or you, or you,
Have found the ground of study's excellence
Without the beauty of a woman's face?
From women's eyes this doctrine I derive:
They are the ground, the books, the academes,
From whence doth spring the true Promethean fire.
Why, universal plodding prisons up
The nimble spirits in the arteries,
As motion and long-during action tires
The sinewy vigour of the traveller.
Now for not looking on a woman's face,
You have in that forsworn the use of eyes,
And study too, the causer of your vow;
For where is any author in the world
Teaches such beauty as a woman's eye?
Learning is but an adjunct to ourself,
And where we are our learning likewise is.
Then when ourselves we see in ladies' eyes,
Do we not likewise see our learning there?
O, we have made a vow to study, lords,
And in that vow we have forsworn our books;
For when would you, my liege, or you, or you,
In leaden contemplation, have found out
Such fiery numbers as the prompting eyes
Of beauty's tutors have enrich'd you with?
Other slow arts entirely keep the brain,
And therefore finding barren practisers,
Scarce show a harvest of their heavy toil;
But love, first learned in a lady's eyes,
Lives not alone immured in the brain,
But with the motion of all elements
Courses as swift as thought in every power,
And gives to every power a double power
Above their functions and their offices.
It adds a precious seeing to the eye:
A lover's eyes will gaze an eagle blind.
A lover's ear will hear the lowest sound
When the suspicious head of theft is stopp'd.
Love's feeling is more soft and sensible
Than are the tender horns of cockled snails.
Love's tongue proves dainty Bacchus gross in taste.
For valour, is not Love a Hercules,
Still climbing trees in the Hesperides?
Subtle as Sphinx; as sweet and musical
As bright Apollo's lute, strung with his hair.
And when Love speaks, the voice of all the gods
Make heaven drowsy with the harmony.
Never durst poet touch a pen to write
Until his ink were temp'red with Love's sighs.
O, then his lines would ravish savage ears
And plant in tyrants mild humility.
From women's eyes this doctrine I derive.
They sparkle still the right Promethean fire;
They are the books, the arts, the academes,
That show, contain, and nourish all the world.
Else none at all in aught proves excellent.
Then fools you were these women to forswear;
Or keeping what is sworn, you will prove fools.
For wisdom's sake, a word that all men love;
Or for love's sake, a word that loves all men;
Or for men's sake, the authors of these women;
Or women's sake, by whom we men are men —
Let us once lose our oaths to find ourselves,
Or else we lose ourselves to keep our oaths.
It is religion to be thus forsworn;
For charity itself fulfils the law,
And who can sever love from charity?

King. Saint Cupid then! and, soldiers, to the field!

Ber. Advance your standards, and upon them, lords!
Pell-mell, down with them! But be first advis'd,
In conflict that you get the sun of them.

Long. Now to plain-dealing. Lay these glozes by.
Shall we resolve to woo these girls of France?

King. And win them too! Therefore let us devise
Some entertainment for them in their tents.

Ber. First from the park let us conduct them thither;
Then homeward every man attach the hand
Of his fair mistress. In the afternoon
We will with some strange pastime solace them,
Such as the shortness of the time can shape,
For revels, dances, masques, and merry hours
Forerun fair Love, strewing her way with flowers.

King. Away, away! No time shall be omitted
That will be time and may by us be fitted.

Ber. Allons! allons! Sow'd cockle reap'd no corn,
And justice always whirls in equal measure.
Light wenches may prove plagues to men forsworn:
If so, our copper buys no better treasure.

Exeunt.

Act V. [Scene I. *The park.*]

Enter [*Holofernes*] the Pedant, [*Sir Nathaniel*] the Curate, and *Dull*.

Hol. Satis quod sufficit.

Nath. I praise God for you, sir. Your reasons at dinner have been sharp and sententious; pleasant without scurrility, witty without affection, audacious without impudency, learned without opinion, and strange without heresy. I did converse this quondam day with a companion of the King's, who is intituled, nominated, or called Don Adriano de Armado.

Hol. Novi hominem tanquam te. His humour is lofty, his discourse peremptory, his tongue filed, his eye ambitious, his gait majestical, and his general behaviour vain, ridiculous, and thrasonical. He is too picked, too spruce, too affected, too odd, as it were, too peregrinate, as I may call it.

Nath. A most singular and choice epithet.

Draws out his table-book.

Hol. He draweth out the thread of his verbosity finer than the staple of his argument. I abhor such fanatical phantasims, such insociable and point-devise companions; such rackers of orthography as to speak 'dout' fine when he should say 'doubt,' 'det' when he should pronounce 'debt' — d, e, b, t, not d, e, t. He clepeth a calf 'cauf,' 'half' 'hauf,' neighbour vocatur 'nebour,' 'neigh' abbreviated 'ne.' This is abhominable, which he would call 'abbominable': it insinuateth me of insanie. Ne intelligis, domine? to make frantic, lunatic.

Nath. Laus Deo, bone intelligo.

Hol. 'Bone'? — 'bone' for 'bene.' Priscian a little scratch'd; 'twill serve.

Enter [*Armado* the] Braggart, [*Moth* the] Boy, [and *Costard*].

Nath. Videsne quis venit?

Hol. Video et gaudeo.

Arm. [*to Moth*] Chirrah!

Hol. Quare 'chirrah,' not 'sirrah'?

Arm. Men of peace, well encount'red.

Hol. Most military sir, salutation.

Moth. [*aside to Costard*] They have been at a great feast of languages and stol'n the scraps.

Cost. O, they have liv'd long on the alms-basket of words. I marvel thy master hath not eaten thee for a word; for thou art not so long by the head as honorificabilitudinitatibus; thou art easier swallowed than a flapdragon.

Moth. Peace! the peal begins.

Arm. [*to Holofernes*] Monsieur, are you not lett'red?

Moth. Yes, yes! he teaches boys the horn-book. What is a, b, spell'd backward with the horn on his head?

Hol. Ba, pueritia, with a horn added.

Moth. Ba, most seely sheep, with a horn! — You hear his learning.

Hol. Quis, quis, thou consonant?

Moth. The last of the five vowels, if You repeat them; or the fifth, if I.

Hol. I will repeat them: — a, e, I —

Moth. The sheep: the other two concludes it — O, U.

Arm. Now by the salt wave of the Mediterraneum, a sweet touch, a quick venew of wit! Snip, snap, quick and home! It rejoiceth my intellect. True wit!

Moth. Offer'd by a child to an old man; which is wit-old.

Hol. What is the figure? What is the figure?

Moth. Horns.

Hol. Thou disputes like an infant. Go whip thy gig.

Moth. Lend me your horn to make one, and I will whip about your infamy circum circa — a gig of a cuckold's horn.

Cost. An I had but one penny in the world, thou shouldst have it to buy gingerbread. Hold, there is the very remuneration I had of thy master, thou halfpenny purse of wit, thou pigeon egg of discretion. O, an the heavens were so pleased that thou wert but my bastard, what a joyful father wouldest thou make me! Go to; thou hast it ad dunghill, at the fingers' ends, as they say.

Hol. O, I smell false Latin! 'dunghill' for unguem.

Arm. Arts-man, preambulate. We will be singuled from the barbarous. Do you not educate youth at the charge-house on the top of the mountain?

Hol. Or mons, the hill.

Arm. At your sweet pleasure, for the mountain.

Hol. I do, sans question.

Arm. Sir, it is the King's most sweet pleasure and affection to congratulate the Princess at her pavilion in the posteriors of this day, which the rude multitude call the afternoon.

Hol. The posterior of the day, most generous sir, is liable, congruent, and measurable for the afternoon. The word is well cull'd, chose, sweet, and apt, I do assure you, sir, I do assure.

Arm. Sir, the King is a noble gentleman, and my familiar, I do assure ye, very good friend. For what is inward between us, let it pass. I do beseech thee remember thy courtesy. I beseech thee apparel thy head. And among other importunate and most serious designs, and of great import indeed, too — but let that pass; for I must tell thee it will please his Grace (by the world) sometime to lean upon my poor shoulder, and with his royal finger thus dally with my excrement, with my mustachio — but, sweet heart, let that pass. By the world, I recount no fable! Some certain special honours it pleaseth his greatness to impart to Armado, a soldier, a man of travel, that hath seen the world — but let that pass. The very all of all is — but, sweet heart, I do implore secrecy — that the King would have me present the Princess (sweet chuck) with some delightful ostentation, or show, or pageant, or antic, or firework. Now, understanding that the curate and your sweet self are good at such eruptions and sudden breaking-out of mirth, as it were, I have acquainted you withal, to the end to crave your assistance.

Hol. Sir, you shall present before her the Nine Worthies. Sir Nathaniel, as concerning some entertainment of time, some show in the posterior of this day, to be rend'red by our assistance at the King's command, and this most gallant, illustrate, and learned gentleman, before the Princess — I say none so fit as to present the Nine Worthies.

Nath. Where will you find men worthy enough to present them?

Hol. Joshua, yourself; myself, or this gallant gentleman, Judas Maccabæus; this swain, because of his great limb or joint, shall pass Pompey the Great; the page, Hercules —

Arm. Pardon, sir; error! He is not quantity enough for that Worthy's thumb; he is not so big as the end of his club.

Hol. Shall I have audience? He shall present Hercules in minority. His enter and exit shall be strangling a snake; and I will have an apology for that purpose.

Moth. An excellent device! So, if any of the audience hiss, you may cry 'Well done, Hercules! Now thou crushest the snake!' That is the way to make an offence gracious, though few have the grace to do it.

Arm. For the rest of the Worthies?

Hol. I will play three myself.

Moth. Thrice-worthy gentleman!

Arm. Shall I tell you a thing?

Hol. We attend.

Arm. We will have, if this fadge not, an antic. I beseech you follow.

Hol. Via, goodman Dull! Thou hast spoken no word all this while.

Dull. Nor understood none neither, sir.

Hol. Allons! we will employ thee.

Dull. I'll make one in a dance, or so; or I will play
On the tabor to the Worthies, and let them dance the hay.

Hol. Most dull, honest Dull! To our sport, away! *Exeunt.*

[Scene II. *The park.*]

Enter the Ladies: [the *Princess, Maria, Katherine,* and *Rosaline*].

Prin. Sweet hearts, we shall be rich ere we depart
If fairings come thus plentifully in.
A lady wall'd about with diamonds!
Look you, what I have from the loving King.

Ros. Madam, came nothing else along with that?

Prin. Nothing but this? Yes, as much love in rhyme
As would be cramm'd up in a sheet of paper
Writ o' both sides the leaf, margent and all,
That he was fain to seal on Cupid's name.

Ros. That was the way to make his godhead wax,
For he hath been five thousand years a boy.

Kath. Ay, and a shrowd unhappy gallows too.

Ros. You'll ne'er be friends with him; 'a kill'd your sister.

Kath. He made her melancholy, sad, and heavy,
And so she died. Had she been light like you,
Of such a merry, nimble, stirring spirit,
She might 'a' been a grandam ere she died.
And so may you; for a light heart lives long.

Ros. What's your dark meaning, mouse, of this light word?

Kath. A light condition in a beauty dark.

Ros. We need more light to find your meaning out.

Kath. You'll mar the light by taking it in snuff.
Therefore I'll darkly end the argument.

Ros. Look, what you do, you do it still i' th' dark.

Kath. So do not you, for you are a light wench.

Ros. Indeed I weigh not you, and therefore light.

Kath. You weigh me not? O, that's you care not for me.

Ros. Great reason; for past cure is still past care.

Prin. Well bandied both! a set of wit well play'd.
But, Rosaline, you have a favour too?
Who sent it? and what is it?

Ros. I would you knew.
An if my face were but as fair as yours,
My favour were as great. Be witness this.
Nay, I have verses too, I thank Berowne;
The numbers true; and, were the numb'ring too,
I were the fairest goddess on the ground.
I am compar'd to twenty thousand fairs.
O, he hath drawn my picture in his letter!

Prin. Anything like?

Ros. Much in the letters, nothing in the praise.

Prin. Beauteous as ink — a good conclusion.

Kath. Fair as a text B in a copy-book.

Ros. Ware pencils, ho! Let me not die your debtor,
My red dominical, my golden letter.
O, that your face were not so full of O's!

Kath. A pox of that jest, and I beshrow all shrows!

Prin. But, Katherine, what was sent to you from fair Dumain?

Kath. Madam, this glove.

Prin. Did he not send you twain?

Kath. Yes, madam; and moreover,
Some thousand verses of a faithful lover,
A huge translation of hypocrisy,
Vilely compil'd, profound simplicity.

Mar. This, and these pearl, to me sent Longavile.
The letter is too long by half a mile.

Prin. I think no less. Dost thou not wish in heart
The chain were longer and the letter short?

Mar. Ay, or I would these hands might never part.

Prin. We are wise girls to mock our lovers so.

Ros. They are worse fools to purchase mocking so.
That same Berowne I'll torture ere I go.
O that I knew he were but in by th' week!
How I would make him fawn, and beg, and seek,
And wait the season, and observe the times,
And spend his prodigal wits in bootless rhymes,
And shape his service wholly to my hests,
And make him proud to make me proud that jests!
So pertaunt-like would I o'ersway his state
That he should be my fool, and I his fate.

Prin. None are so surely caught, when they are catch'd,
As wit turn'd fool. Folly, in wisdom hatch'd,
Hath wisdom's warrant, and the help of school,
And wit's own grace to grace a learned fool.

Ros. The blood of youth burns not with such excess
As gravity's revolt to wantonness.

Mar. Folly in fools bears not so strong a note
As fool'ry in the wise when wit doth dote;
Since all the power thereof it doth apply
To prove, by wit, worth in simplicity.

Enter *Boyet.*

Prin. Here comes Boyet, and mirth is in his face.

Boyet. O, I am stabb'd with laughter! Where's her Grace?

Prin. Thy news, Boyet?

Boyet. Prepare, madam, prepare!
Arm, wenches, arm! Encounters mounted are
Against your peace; Love doth approach disguis'd,
Armed in arguments; you'll be surpris'd.
Muster your wits; stand in your own defence,
Or hide your heads like cowards and fly hence.

Prin. Saint Denis to Saint Cupid! What are they
That charge their breath against us? Say, scout, say.

Boyet. Under the cool shade of a sycamore
I thought to close mine eyes some half an hour;
When, lo! to interrupt my purpos'd rest,
Toward that shade I might behold addrest
The King and his companions! Warily
I stole into a neighbour thicket by
And overheard what you shall overhear —
That by-and-by disguis'd they will be here.
Their herald is a pretty knavish page
That well by heart hath conn'd his embassage.
Action and accent did they teach him there:
'Thus must thou speak,' and 'thus thy body bear.'
And ever and anon they made a doubt
Presence majestical would put him out;
'For,' quoth the King, 'an angel shalt thou see;
Yet fear not thou, but speak audaciously.'

The boy replied, 'An angel is not evil.
I should have fear'd her had she been a devil.'
With that all laugh'd and clapp'd him on the shoulder,
Making the bold wag by their praises bolder.
One rubb'd his elbow thus, and fleer'd, and swore
A better speech was never spoke before.
Another with his finger and his thumb
Cried, 'Via! we will do't, come what will come!'
The third he caper'd and cried 'All goes well.'
The fourth turn'd on the toe and down he fell.
With that they all did tumble on the ground
With such a zealous laughter, so profound,
That in this spleen ridiculous appears,
To check their folly, passion's solemn tears.

Prin. But what? but what? Come they to visit us?

Boyet. They do, they do! and are apparell'd thus —
Like Muscovites or Russians, as I guess.
Their purpose is, to parley, court, and dance;
And every one his love-feat will advance
Unto his several mistress; which they'll know
By favours several which they did bestow.

Prin. And will they so? The gallants shall be task'd;
For, ladies, we will every one be mask'd;
And not a man of them shall have the grace,
Despite of suit, to see a lady's face.
Hold, Rosaline, this favour thou shalt wear,
And then the King will court thee for his dear.
Hold, take thou this, my sweet, and give me thine;
So shall Berowne take me for Rosaline.
And change you favours too. So shall your loves
Woo contrary, deceiv'd by these removes.

Ros. Come on, then. Wear the favours most in sight.

Kath. But in this changing what is your intent?

Prin. The effect of my intent is to cross theirs.
They do it but in mocking merriment,
And mock for mock is only my intent.
Their several counsels they unbosom shall
To loves mistook, and so be mock'd withal
Upon the next occasion that we meet
With visages display'd to talk and greet.

Ros. But shall we dance if they desire us to't?

Prin. No, to the death we will not move a foot;
Nor to their penn'd speech render we no grace,
But while 'tis spoke each turn away her face.

Boyet. Why, that contempt will kill the speaker's heart
And quite divorce his memory from his part.

Prin. Therefore I do it; and I make no doubt
The rest will ne'er come in if he be out.
There's no such sport as sport by sport o'erthrown —
To make theirs ours, and ours none but our own.
So shall we stay, mocking intended game,
And they, well mock'd, depart away with shame. *Sound trumpet* [*within*].

Boyet. The trumpet sounds. Be mask'd; the maskers come. [*The Ladies mask.*]

Enter *Blackmoors* with music; the Boy [*Moth*] with a speech, and [the *King* and] the rest of the *Lords*, disguised [like *Russians* and masked].

Moth. 'All hail, the richest beauties on the earth!'

Boyet. Beauties no richer than rich taffeta.

Moth. 'A holy parcel of the fairest dames
The Ladies turn their backs to him.
That ever turn'd their backs to mortal views!'

Ber. 'Their eyes,' villain! 'their eyes!'

Moth. 'That ever turn'd their eyes to mortal views!
Out' —

Boyet. True! Out indeed!

Moth. 'Out of your favours, heavenly spirits, vouchsafe
Not to behold' —

Ber. 'Once to behold,' rogue!

Moth. 'Once to behold with your sun-beamed eyes,
— with your sun-beamed eyes' —

Boyet. They will not answer to that epithet.
You were best call it 'daughter-beamed eyes.'

Moth. They do not mark me, and that brings me out.

Ber. Is this your perfectness? Be gone, you rogue! [*Exit Moth.*]

Ros. What would these strangers? Know their minds, Boyet.
If they do speak our language, 'tis our will
That some plain man recount their purposes.
Know what they would.

Boyet. What would you with the Princess?

Ber. Nothing but peace and gentle visitation.

Ros. What would they, say they?

Boyet. Nothing but peace and gentle visitation.

Ros. Why, that they have, and bid them so be gone.

Boyet. She says, you have it and you may be gone.

King. Say to her we have measur'd many miles
To tread a measure with her on this grass.

Boyet. They say that they have measur'd many a mile
To tread a measure with you on this grass.

Ros. It is not so. Ask them how many inches
Is in one mile. If they have measur'd many,
The measure then of one is eas'ly told.

Boyet. If to come hither you have measur'd miles,
And many miles, the Princess bids you tell
How many inches doth fill up one mile.

Ber. Tell her we measure them by weary steps.

Boyet. She hears herself.

Ros. How many weary steps
Of many weary miles you have o'ergone
Are numb'red in the travel of one mile?

Ber. We number nothing that we spend for you.
Our duty is so rich, so infinite,
That we may do it still without accompt.
Vouchsafe to show the sunshine of your face,
That we (like savages) may worship it.

Ros. My face is but a moon, and clouded too.

King. Blessed are clouds, to do as such clouds do.
Vouchsafe, bright moon, and these thy stars, to shine
(Those clouds remov'd) upon our watery eyne.

Ros. O vain petitioner, beg a greater matter!
Thou now requests but moonshine in the water.

King. Then in our measure do but vouchsafe one change.
Thou bid'st me beg; this begging is not strange.

Ros. Play music then. Nay, you must do it soon.
Not yet? No dance! Thus change I like the moon.

King. Will you not dance? How come you thus estranged?

Ros. You took the moon at full, but now she's changed.

King. Yet still she is the Moon, and I the Man.
The music plays; vouchsafe some motion to it.

Ros. Our ears vouchsafe it.

King. But your legs should do it.

Ros. Since you are strangers, and come here by chance,
We'll not be nice. Take hands. We will not dance.

King. Why take we hands then?

Ros. Only to part friends.
Curtsy, sweet hearts — and so the measure ends.

King. More measure of this measure! Be not nice.

Ros. We can afford no more at such a price.

King. Price you yourselves. What buys your company?

Ros. Your absence only.

King. That can never be.

Ros. Then cannot we be bought; and so adieu —
Twice to your visor, and half once to you.

King. If you deny to dance, let's hold more chat.

Ros. In private then.

King. I am best pleas'd with that.
[*They converse apart.*]

Ber. White-handed mistress, one sweet word with thee.

Prin. Honey, and milk, and sugar: there is three.

Ber. Nay, then, two treys, an if you grow so nice —
Metheglin, wort, and malmsey. Well run, dice!
There's half a dozen sweets.

Prin. Seventh sweet, adieu.
Since you can cog, I'll play no more with you.

Ber. One word in secret.

Prin. Let it not be sweet.

Ber. Thou grievest my gall.

Prin. Gall! bitter.

Ber. Therefore meet.
[*They converse apart.*]

Dum. Will you vouchsafe with me to change a word?

Mar. Name it.

Dum. Fair lady —

Mar. Say you so? Fair lord.
Take that for your 'fair lady.'

Dum. Please it you,
As much in private, and I'll bid adieu.
[*They converse apart.*]

Kath. What, was your vizard made without a tongue?

Long. I know the reason, lady, why you ask.

Kath. O for your reason! Quickly, sir; I long!

Long. You have a double tongue within your mask
And would afford my speechless vizard half.

Kath. 'Veal,' quoth the Dutchman. Is not veal a calf?

Long. A calf, fair lady?

Kath. No, a fair lord calf.

Long. Let's part the word.

Kath. No, I'll not be your half.
Take all and wean it, it may prove an ox.

Long. Look how you butt yourself in these sharp mocks!
Will you give horns, chaste lady? Do not so.

Kath. Then die a calf before your horns do grow.

Long. One word in private with you ere I die.

Kath. Bleat softly then. The butcher hears you cry.

[*They converse apart.*]

Boyet. The tongues of mocking wenches are as keen
As is the razor's edge invisible,
Cutting a smaller hair than may be seen,
Above the sense of sense: so sensible
Seemeth their conference; their conceits have wings,
Fleeter than arrows, bullets, wind, thought, swifter things.

Ros. Not one word more, my maids! Break off, break off.

Ber. By heaven, all dry-beaten with pure scoff!

King. Farewell, mad wenches. You have simple wits.

Exeunt [*King, Lords, and Blackamoors*].

Prin. Twenty adieus, my frozen Muscovits.
Are these the breed of wits so wondered at?

Boyet. Tapers they are, with your sweet breaths puff'd out.

Ros. Well-liking wits they have; gross, gross; fat, fat.

Prin. O poverty in wit, kingly poor flout!
Will they not (think you) hang themselves to-night?
Or ever but in vizards show their faces?
This pert Berowne was out of count'nance quite.

Ros. O, they were all in lamentable cases.
The King was weeping-ripe for a good word.

Prin. Berowne did swear himself out of all suit.

Mar. Dumain was at my service, and his sword:
'No point,' quoth I. My servant straight was mute.

Kath. Lord Longaville said I came o'er his heart;
And trow you what he call'd me?

Prin. Qualm, perhaps.

Kath. Yes, in good faith.

Prin. Go, sickness as thou art!

Ros. Well, better wits have worn plain statute caps.
But will you hear? The King is my love sworn.

Prin. And quick Berowne hath plighted faith to me.

Kath. And Longaville was for my service born.

Mar. Dumain is mine as sure as bark on tree.

Boyet. Madam, and pretty mistresses, give ear.
Immediately they will again be here
In their own shapes; for it can never be
They will digest this harsh indignity.

Prin. Will they return?

Boyet. They will, they will, God knows,
And leap for joy, though they are lame with blows.
Therefore change favours, and when they repair,
Blow like sweet roses in this summer air.

Prin. How blow? how blow? Speak to be understood.

Boyet. Fair ladies mask'd are roses in their bud;
Dismask'd, their damask sweet commixture shown,
Are angels vailing clouds, or roses blown.

Prin. Avaunt perplexity! What shall we do
If they return in their own shapes to woo?

Ros. Good madam, if by me you'll be advis'd,
Let's mock them still, as well known as disguis'd.
Let us complain to them what fools were here,
Disguis'd like Muscovites in shapeless gear;
And wonder what they were, and to what end
Their shallow shows, and prologue vilely penn'd,
And their rough carriage so ridiculous,
Should be presented at our tent to us.

Boyet. Ladies, withdraw. The gallants are at hand.

Prin. Whip to our tents, as roes run o'er the land.

Exeunt [*Princess, Rosaline, Katherine, and Maria*].

Enter the *King* and the rest, [*Berowne, Longaville,* and *Dumain,* in their proper habits].

King. Fair sir, God save you! Where is the Princess?

Boyet. Gone to her tent. Please it your Majesty
Command me any service to her thither?

King. That she vouchsafe me audience for one word.
Boyet. I will; and so will she, I know, my lord. *Exit.*
Ber. This fellow pecks up wit as pigeons pease,
And utters it again when God doth please.
He is wit's pedlar, and retails his wares
At wakes and wassails, meetings, markets, fairs;
And we that sell by gross, the Lord doth know,
Have not the grace to grace it with such show.
This gallant pins the wenches on his sleeve.
Had he been Adam, he had tempted Eve.
'A can carve too, and lisp. Why, this is he
That kiss'd his hand away in courtesy.
This is the ape of form, Monsieur the Nice,
That, when he plays at tables, chides the dice
In honourable terms. Nay, he can sing
A mean most meanly; and in ushering
Mend him who can. The ladies call him sweet.
The stairs, as he treads on them, kiss his feet.
This is the flow'r that smiles on every one
To show his teeth as white as whalës-bone;
And consciences that will not die in debt
Pay him the due of 'honey-tongu'd Boyet.'
King. A blister on his sweet tongue with my heart,
That put Armado's page out of his part!

Enter the *Ladies* [and *Boyet*].

Ber. See where it comes! Behaviour, what wert thou
Till this man show'd thee? and what art thou now?
King. All hail, sweet madam, and fair time of day!
Prin. 'Fair' in 'all hail' is foul, as I conceive.
King. Construe my speeches better, if you may.
Prin. Then wish me better; I will give you leave.
King. We came to visit you, and purpose now
To lead you to our court. Vouchsafe it then.
Prin. This field shall hold me, and so hold your vow.
Nor God nor I delights in perjur'd men.
King. Rebuke me not for that which you provoke.
The virtue of your eye must break my oath.
Prin. You nickname virtue. 'Vice' you should have spoke;
For virtue's office never breaks men's troth.
Now, by my maiden honour, yet as pure
As the unsullied lily, I protest,
A world of torments though I should endure,
I would not yield to be your house's guest;
So much I hate a breaking cause to be
Of heavenly oaths, vow'd with integrity.
King. O, you have liv'd in desolation here,
Unseen, unvisited, much to our shame.
Prin. Not so, my lord. It is not so, I swear.
We have had pastimes here and pleasant game;
A mess of Russians left us but of late.
King. How, madam? Russians?
Prin. Ay, in truth, my lord;
Trim gallants, full of courtship and of state.
Ros. Madam, speak true. — It is not so, my lord.
My lady (to the manner of the days)
In courtesy gives undeserving praise.
We four indeed confronted were with four
In Russian habit. Here they stay'd an hour
And talk'd apace; and in that hour, my lord,
They did not bless us with one happy word.
I dare not call them fools; but this I think,
When they are thirsty, fools would fain have drink.
Ber. This jest is dry to me. Fair gentle sweet,
Your wit makes wise things foolish. When we greet,
With eyes best seeing, heaven's fiery eye,
By light we lose light. Your capacity
Is of that nature that to your huge store
Wise things seem foolish and rich things but poor.
Ros. This proves you wise and rich; for in my eye —
Ber. I am a fool, and full of poverty.
Ros. But that you take what doth to you belong,
It were a fault to snatch words from my tongue.
Ber. O, I am yours, and all that I possess!
Ros. All the fool mine?
Ber. I cannot give you less.
Ros. Which of the vizards was it that you wore?
Ber. Where? when? what vizard? Why demand you this?
Ros. There, then, that vizard; that superfluous case
That hid the worse and show'd the better face.
King. We were descried. They'll mock us now downright.
Dum. Let us confess and turn it to a jest.

Prin. Amaz'd, my lord? Why looks your Highness sad?
Ros. Help! hold his brows! He'll sound! Why look you pale?
Seasick, I think, coming from Muscovy.
Ber. Thus pour the stars down plagues for perjury.
Can any face of brass hold longer out?
Here stand I, lady. Dart thy skill at me,
Bruise me with scorn, confound me with a flout,
Thrust thy sharp wit quite through my ignorance,
Cut me to pieces with thy keen conceit;
And I will wish thee never more to dance,
Nor never more in Russian habit wait.
O, never will I trust to speeches penn'd
Nor to the motion of a schoolboy's tongue,
Nor never come in vizard to my friend,
Nor woo in rhyme like a blind harper's song!
Taffeta phrases, silken terms precise,
Three-pil'd hyperboles, spruce affectation,
Figures pedantical — these summer flies
Have blown me full of maggot ostentation.
I do forswear them; and I here protest,
By this white glove (how white the hand, God knows!),
Henceforth my wooing mind shall be express'd
In russet yea's and honest kersey no's.
And to begin: wench, so God help me, law!
My love to thee is sound, sans crack or flaw.
Ros. Sans 'sans,' I pray you!
Ber. Yet I have a trick
Of the old rage. Bear with me, I am sick.
I'll leave it by degrees. Soft, let us see!
Write 'Lord have mercy on us' on those three.
They are infected, in their hearts it lies;
They have the plague, and caught it of your eyes.
These lords are visited; you are not free,
For the Lord's tokens on you do I see.
Prin. No, they are free that gave these tokens to us.
Ber. Our states are forfeit. Seek not to undo us.
Ros. It is not so; for how can this be true,
That you stand forfeit, being those that sue?
Ber. Peace! for I will not have to do with you.
Ros. Nor shall not, if I do as I intend.
Ber. Speak for yourselves. My wit is at an end.
King. Teach us, sweet madam, for our rude transgression
Some fair excuse.
Prin. The fairest is confession.
Were not you here but even now, disguis'd?
King. Madam, I was.
Prin. And were you well advis'd?
King. I was, fair madam.
Prin. When you then were here,
What did you whisper in your lady's ear?
King. That more than all the world I did respect her.
Prin. When she shall challenge this, you will reject her.
King. Upon mine honour, no.
Prin. Peace, peace! forbear.
Your oath once broke, you force not to forswear.
King. Despise me when I break this oath of mine!
Prin. I will, and therefore keep it. — Rosaline,
What did the Russian whisper in your ear?
Ros. Madam, he swore that he did hold me dear
As precious eyesight and did value me
Above this world; adding thereto moreover,
That he would wed me or else die my lover.
Prin. God give thee joy of him! The noble lord
Most honourably doth uphold his word.
King. What mean you, madam? By my life, my troth,
I never swore this lady such an oath.
Ros. By heaven, you did! and to confirm it plain,
You gave me this; but take it, sir, again.
King. My faith and this the Princess I did give.
I knew her by this jewel on her sleeve.
Prin. Pardon me, sir, this jewel did she wear,
And Lord Berowne (I thank him) is my dear.
What? will you have me, or your pearl again?
Ber. Neither of either; I remit both twain.
I see the trick on't. Here was a consent,
Knowing aforehand of our merriment,
To dash it like a Christmas comedy.
Some carry-tale, some please-man, some slight zany,
Some mumble-news, some trencher knight, some Dick
That smiles his cheek in years and knows the trick
To make my lady laugh when she's dispos'd,
Told our intents before; which once disclos'd,
The ladies did change favours; and then we,
Following the signs, woo'd but the sign of She.
Now, to our perjury to add more terror,
We are again forsworn in will and error.

Much upon this it is. And might not you [*To Boyet.*]
Forestall our sport, to make us thus untrue?
Do not you know my lady's foot by th' squier?
And laugh upon the apple of her eye?
And stand between her back, sir, and the fire,
Holding a trencher, jesting merrily?
You put our page out. Go, you are allow'd.
Die when you will, a smock shall be your shroud.
You leer upon me, do you? There's an eye
Wounds like a leaden sword.

Boyet. Full merrily
Hath this brave manage, this career, been run.

Ber. Lo, he is tilting straight! Peace! I have done.

Enter [*Costard the*] *Clown.*

Welcome, pure wit! Thou part'st a fair fray.

Cost. O Lord, sir, they would know
Whether the three Worthies shall come in or no.

Ber. What, are there but three?

Cost. No, sir; but it is vara fine,
For every one pursents three.

Ber. And three times thrice is nine.

Cost. Not so, sir, under correction, sir; I hope it is not so.
You cannot beg us, sir, I can assure you, sir; we know what we know.
I hope, sir, three times thrice, sir —

Ber. Is not nine?

Cost. Under correction, sir, we know whereuntil it doth amount.

Ber. By Jove, I always took three threes for nine.

Cost. O Lord, sir, it were pity you should get your living by reck'ning, sir.

Ber. How much is it?

Cost. O Lord, sir, the parties themselves, the actors, sir, will show whereuntil it doth amount. For mine own part, I am, as they say, but to parfect one man in one poor man — Pompion the Great, sir.

Ber. Art thou one of the Worthies?

Cost. It pleased them to think me worthy of Pompey the Great. For mine own part, I know not the degree of the Worthy, but I am to stand for him.

Ber. Go bid them prepare.

Cost. We will turn it finely off, sir; we will take some care. *Exit.*

King. Berowne, they will shame us. Let them not approach.

Ber. We are shame-proof, my lord; and 'tis some policy
To have one show worse than the King's and his company.

King. I say they shall not come.

Prin. Nay, my good lord, let me o'errule you now.
That sport best pleases that doth least know how:
Where zeal strives to content, and the contents
Dies in the zeal of that which it presents.
Their form confounded makes most form in mirth
When great things labouring perish in their birth.

Ber. A right description of our sport, my lord.

Enter [*Armado the*] *Braggart.*

Arm. Anointed, I implore so much expense of thy royal sweet breath as will utter a brace of words.

[*Converses apart with the King and delivers a paper.*]

Prin. Doth this man serve God?

Ber. Why ask you?

Prin. 'A speaks not like a man of God his making.

Arm. That is all one, my fair, sweet, honey monarch; for, I protest, the schoolmaster is exceeding fantastical; too too vain, too too vain. But we will put it, as they say, to fortuna della guerra. I wish you the peace of mind, most royal couplement. *Exit.*

King. Here is like to be a good presence of Worthies. He presents Hector of Troy; the swain, Pompey the Great; the parish curate, Alexander; Armado's page, Hercules; the pedant, Judas Maccabæus;
And if these four Worthies in their first show thrive,
These four will change habits and present the other five.

Ber. There is five in the first show.

King. You are deceived; 'tis not so.

Ber. The pedant, the braggart, the hedge-priest, the fool, and the boy:
Abate throw at novum, and the whole world again
Cannot pick out five such, take each one in his vein.

King. The ship is under sail, and here she comes amain.

Enter [*Costard, for*] *Pompey.*

Cost. I Pompey am —

Ber. You lie! you are not he.

Cost. I Pompey am —

Boyet. With libbard's head on knee.

Ber. Well said, old mocker. I must needs be friends with thee.

Cost. I Pompey am, Pompey surnam'd the Big —

Dum. 'The Great.'

Cost. It is 'Great,' sir.
Pompey surnam'd the Great,
That oft in field with targe and shield did make my foe to sweat,
And travelling along this coast, I here am come by chance,
And lay my arms before the legs of this sweet lass of France.
If your ladyship would say 'Thanks, Pompey,' I had done.

Prin. Great thanks, great Pompey.

Cost. 'Tis not so much worth. But I hope I was perfect. I made a little fault in 'Great.'

Ber. My hat to a halfpenny, Pompey proves the best Worthy.

Enter *Curate,* [*Sir Nathaniel,*] for *Alexander.*

Nath. When in the world I liv'd, I was the world's commander;
By east, west, north, and south I spread my conquering might;
My scutcheon plain declares that I am Alisander.

Boyet. Your nose says, no, you are not; for it stands too right.

Ber. Your nose smells 'no' in this, most tender-smelling knight.

Prin. The conqueror is dismay'd. Proceed, good Alexander.

Nath. When in the world I liv'd, I was the world's commander —

Boyet. Most true, 'tis right! You were so, Alisander.

Ber. Pompey the Great!

Cost. Your servant, and Costard.

Ber. Take away the conqueror, take away Alisander.

Cost. [*to Sir Nathaniel*] O, sir, you have overthrown Alisander the conqueror! You will be scrap'd out of the painted cloth for this. Your lion that holds his poleaxe sitting on a close-stool, will be given to Ajax. He will be the ninth Worthy. A conqueror, and afeard to speak? Run away for shame, Alisander. [*Sir Nathaniel stands aside.*] There, an't shall please you! a foolish mild man; an honest man, look you, and soon dash'd. He is a marvellous good neighbour, faith, and a very good bowler; but for Alisander — alas! you see how 'tis — a little o'erparted. But there are Worthies a-coming will speak their mind in some other sort.

Prin. Stand aside, good Pompey.
[*Costard stands aside.*]

Enter [*Holofernes the*] *Pedant* for *Judas*; and *the Boy* [*Moth*] for *Hercules.*

Hol. Great Hercules is presented by this imp,
Whose club kill'd Cerberus, that three-headed canus;
And when he was a babe, a child, a shrimp,
Thus did he strangle serpents in his manus.
Quoniam he seemeth in minority,
Ergo I come with this apology.
Keep some state in thy exit, and vanish.
Boy [*stands back*].
Judas I am —

Dum. A Judas?

Hol. Not Iscariot, sir.
Judas I am, ycliped Maccabæus,

Dum. Judas Maccabæus clipt is plain Judas.

Ber. A kissing traitor. How art thou prov'd Judas?

Hol. Judas I am —

Dum. The more shame for you, Judas!

Hol. What mean you, sir?

Boyet. To make Judas hang himself.

Hol. Begin, sir; you are my elder.

Ber. Well followed: Judas was hanged on an elder.

Hol. I will not be put out of countenance.

Ber. Because thou hast no face.

Hol. What is this?

Boyet. A cittern-head.

Dum. The head of a bodkin.

Ber. A death's face in a ring.

Long. The face of an old Roman coin, scarce seen.

Boyet. The pommel of Cæsar's falchion.

Dum. The carv'd-bone face on a flask.

Ber. Saint George's half-cheek in a brooch.

Dum. Ay, and in a brooch of lead.

Ber. Ay, and worn in the cap of a tooth-drawer. And now forward, for we have put thee in countenance.

Hol. You have put me out of countenance.

Ber. False! We have given thee faces.

Hol. But you have outfac'd them all.

Ber. An thou wert a lion, we would do so.

Boyet. Therefore, as he is — an ass, let him go.
And so adieu, sweet Jude! Nay, why dost thou stay?

Dum. For the latter end of his name.

Ber. For the ass to the Jude. Give it him. Jud-as, away!

Hol. This is not generous, not gentle, not humble. [*Stands aside.*]

Boyet. A light for Monsieur Judas! It grows dark; he may stumble.

Prin. Alas, poor Maccabæus, how hath he been baited!

Enter *Braggart*, [*Armado*, for Hector].

Ber. Hide thy head, Achilles! Here comes Hector in arms.

Dum. Though my mocks come home by me, I will now be merry.

King. Hector was but a Troyan in respect of this.

Boyet. But is this Hector?

King. I think Hector was not so clean-timber'd.

Long. His leg is too big for Hector's.

Dum. More calf, certain.

Boyet. No; he is best indued in the small.

Ber. This cannot be Hector.

Dum. He's a god or a painter; for he makes faces.

Arm. The armipotent Mars, of lances the almighty,
Gave Hector a gift —

Dum. A gilt nutmeg.

Ber. A lemon.

Long. Stuck with cloves.

Dum. No, cloven.

Arm. Peace!
The armipotent Mars, of lances the almighty,
Gave Hector a gift, the heir of Ilion;
A man so breathed that certain he would fight; yea,
From morn till night out of his pavilion.
I am that flower —

Dum. That mint.

Long. That columbine.

Arm. Sweet Lord Longaville, rein thy tongue.

Long. I must rather give it the rein; for it runs against Hector.

Dum. Ay, and Hector's a greyhound.

Arm. The sweet war-man is dead and rotten. Sweet chucks, beat not the bones of the buried: when he breathed, he was a man. But I will forward with my device. [*To the Princess*] Sweet royalty, bestow on me the sense of hearing.

Berowne steps forth [*to Costard, whispers him, and returns to his place*].

Prin. Speak, brave Hector. We are much delighted.

Arm. I do adore thy sweet Grace's slipper.

Boyet. [*aside to Dumain*] Loves her by the foot.

Dum. [*aside to Boyet*] He may not by the yard.

Arm. This Hector far surmounted Hannibal —

Cost. [*suddenly comes from behind*] The party is gone. Fellow Hector, she is gone. She is two months on her way.

Arm. What meanest thou?

Cost. Faith, unless you play the honest Troyan, the poor wench is cast away. She's quick; the child brags in her belly already. 'Tis yours.

Arm. Dost thou infamonize me among potentates? Thou shalt die.

Cost. Then shall Hector be whipp'd for Jaquenetta that is quick by him, and hang'd for Pompey that is dead by him.

Dum. Most rare Pompey!

Boyet. Renowned Pompey!

Ber. Greater than Great! Great, great, great Pompey! Pompey the Huge!

Dum. Hector trembles.

Ber. Pompey is moved. More Ates, more Ates! Stir them on! stir them on!

Dum. Hector will challenge him.

Ber. Ay, if 'a have no more man's blood in his belly than will sup a flea.

Arm. By the North Pole, I do challenge thee.

Cost. I will not fight with a pole, like a Northren man. I'll slash; I'll do it by the sword. I bepray you let me borrow my arms again.

Dum. Room for the incensed Worthies!

Cost. I'll do it in my shirt.

Dum. Most resolute Pompey!

Moth. Master, let me take you a button-hole lower. Do you not see Pompey is uncasing for the combat? What mean you? You will lose your reputation.

Arm. Gentlemen and soldiers, pardon me. I will not combat in my shirt.

Dum. You may not deny it. Pompey hath made the challenge.

Arm. Sweet bloods, I both may and will.

Ber. What reason have you for't?

Arm. The naked truth of it is, I have no shirt; I go woolward for penance.

Moth. True, and it was enjoined him in Rome for want of linen, since when, I'll be sworn he wore none but a dishclout of Jaquenetta's, and that 'a wears next his heart for a favour.

Enter a Messenger, *Monsieur Marcade.*

Mar. God save you, madam!
Prin. Welcome, Marcade,
But that thou interruptest our merriment.
Mar. I am sorry, madam, for the news I bring
Is heavy in my tongue. The King your father—
Prin. Dead, for my life!
Mar. Even so. My tale is told.
Ber. Worthies, away! The scene begins to cloud.
Arm. For mine own part, I breathe free breath. I have seen the day of wrong through the little hole of discretion, and I will right myself like a soldier. *Exeunt Worthies.*
King. How fares your Majesty?
Prin. Boyet, prepare. I will away to-night.
King. Madam, not so. I do beseech you stay.
Prin. Prepare, I say. I thank you, gracious lords,
For all your fair endeavours, and entreat,
Out of a new-sad soul, that you vouchsafe
In your rich wisdom to excuse, or hide,
The liberal opposition of our spirits
If over-boldly we have borne ourselves
In the converse of breath. Your gentleness
Was guilty of it. Farewell, worthy lord.
A heavy heart bears not a nimble tongue.
Excuse me so, coming too short of thanks
For my great suit, so easily obtain'd.
King. The extreme parts of time extremely forms
All causes to the purpose of his speed;
And often at his very loose decides
That which long process could not arbitrate.
And though the mourning brow of progeny
Forbid the smiling courtesy of love
The holy suit which fain it would convince,
Yet, since love's argument was first on foot,
Let not the cloud of sorrow justle it
From what it purpos'd; since to wail friends lost
Is not by much so wholesome profitable
As to rejoice at friends but newly found.
Prin. I understand you not. My griefs are double.
Ber. Honest plain words best pierce the ear of grief,
And by these badges understand the King.
For your fair sakes have we neglected time,
Play'd foul play with our oaths. Your beauty, ladies,
Hath much deform'd us, fashioning our humours
Even to the opposed end of our intents;
And what in us hath seem'd ridiculous —
As love is full of unbefitting strains,
All wanton as a child, skipping and vain,
Form'd by the eye and therefore, like the eye,
Full of strange shapes, of habits, and of forms,
Varying in subjects as the eye doth roll
To every varied object in his glance;
Which parti-coated presence of loose love
Put on by us, if, in your heavenly eyes,
Have misbecom'd our oaths and gravities,
Those heavenly eyes that look into these faults
Suggested us to make them. Therefore, ladies,
Our love being yours, the error that love makes
Is likewise yours. We to ourselves prove false,
By being once false for ever to be true
To those that make us both — fair ladies, you;
And even that falsehood, in itself a sin,
Thus purifies itself and turns to grace.
Prin. We have receiv'd your letters, full of love;
Your favours, the ambassadors of love;
And in our maiden council rated them
At courtship, pleasant jest, and courtesy,
As bombast and as lining to the time;
But more devout than this in our respects
Have we not been, and therefore met your loves
In their own fashion, like a merriment.
Dum. Our letters, madam, show'd much more than jest.
Long. So did our looks.
Ros. We did not quote them so.
King. Now at the latest minute of the hour
Grant us your loves.
Prin. A time methinks too short
To make a world-without-end bargain in.
No, no, my lord! Your Grace is perjur'd much,
Full of dear guiltiness; and therefore this: —
If for my love (as there is no such cause)
You will do aught, this shall you do for me:
Your oath I will not trust, but go with speed
To some forlorn and naked hermitage,
Remote from all the pleasures of the world;
There stay until the twelve celestial signs
Have brought about the annual reckoning.
If this austere insociable life
Change not your offer made in heat of blood —
If frosts and fasts, hard lodging and thin weeds
Nip not the gaudy blossoms of your love,
But that it bear this trial, and last love —
Then, at the expiration of the year,
Come challenge me, challenge me by these deserts,
And, by this virgin palm now kissing thine,
I will be thine; and till that instant, shut
My woeful self up in a mourning house,

Raining the tears of lamentation
For the remembrance of my father's death.
If this thou do deny, let our hands part,
Neither intitled in the other's heart.
King. If this, or more than this, I would deny,
To flatter up these powers of mine with rest,
The sudden hand of death close up mine eye!
Hence hermit then — my heart is in thy breast.
Ber. And what to me, my love? and what to me?
Ros. You must be purged too, your sins are rack'd,
You are attaint with faults and perjury;
Therefore, if you my favour mean to get,
A twelvemonth shall you spend, and never rest,
But seek the weary beds of people sick.
Dum. But what to me, my love? but what to me?
A wife?
Kath. A beard, fair health, and honesty.
With threefold love I wish you all these three.
Dum. O, shall I say 'I thank you, gentle wife'?
Kath. Not so, my lord. A twelvemonth and a day
I'll mark no words that smooth-fac'd wooers say.
Come when the King doth to my lady come;
Then, if I have much love, I'll give you some.
Dum. I'll serve thee true and faithfully till then.
Kath. Yet swear not, lest ye be forsworn again.
Long. What says Maria?
Mar. At the twelvemonth's end
I'll change my black gown for a faithful friend.
Long. I'll stay with patience; but the time is long.
Mar. The liker you! Few taller are so young.
Ber. Studies my lady? Mistress, look on me;
Behold the window of my heart, mine eye,
What humble suit attends thy answer there.
Impose some service on me for thy love.
Ros. Oft have I heard of you, my Lord Berowne,
Before I saw you; and the world's large tongue
Proclaims you for a man replete with mocks,
Full of comparisons and wounding flouts,
Which you on all estates will execute
That lie within the mercy of your wit.
To weed this wormwood from your fructful brain,
And therewithal to win me, if you please,
Without the which I am not to be won,
You shall this twelvemonth term from day to day
Visit the speechless sick and still converse
With groaning wretches; and your task shall be,
With all the fierce endeavour of your wit
To enforce the pained impotent to smile.
Ber. To move wild laughter in the throat of death?
It cannot be; it is impossible.
Mirth cannot move a soul in agony.
Ros. Why, that's the way to choke a gibing spirit,
Whose influence is begot of that loose grace
Which shallow laughing hearers give to fools.
A jest's prosperity lies in the ear
Of him that hears it, never in the tongue
Of him that makes it. Then, if sickly ears,
Deaf'd with the clamours of their own dear groans,
Will hear your idle scorns, continue them,
And I will have you, and that fault withal;
But if they will not, throw away that spirit,
And I shall find you empty of that fault,
Right joyful of your reformation.
Ber. A twelvemonth? Well, befall what will befall,
I'll jest a twelvemonth in an hospital.
Prin. [*to the King*] Ay, sweet my lord, and so I take my leave.
King. No, madam; we will bring you on your way.
Ber. Our wooing doth not end like an old play:
Jack hath not Gill. These ladies' courtesy
Might well have made our sport a comedy.
King. Come, sir, it wants a twelvemonth and a day,
And then 'twill end.
Ber. That's too long for a play.

Enter *Braggart* [*Armado*].

Arm. Sweet Majesty, vouchsafe me.
Prin. Was not that Hector?
Dum. The worthy knight of Troy.
Arm. I will kiss thy royal finger, and take leave. I am a votary: I have vow'd to Jaquenetta to hold the plough for her sweet love three year. But, most esteemed greatness, will you hear the Dialogue that the two learned men have compiled in praise of the Owl and the Cuckoo? It should have followed in the end of our show.
King. Call them forth quickly; we will do so.
Arm. Holla! approach.

Enter *all* [*the rest*].

This side is Hiems, Winter; this Ver, the Spring: the one maintained by the Owl, th' other by the Cuckoo. Ver, begin.

The Song.

Spring. When daisies pied and violets blue
And lady-smocks all silver-white
And cuckoo-buds of yellow hue
Do paint the meadows with delight,
The cuckoo then on every tree,
Mocks married men; for thus sings he,
'Cuckoo!
Cuckoo, cuckoo!' O word of fear,
Unpleasing to a married ear!

When shepherds pipe on oaten straws,
And merry larks are ploughmen's clocks;
When turtles tread and rooks and daws,
And maidens bleach their summer smocks,
The cuckoo then on every tree,
Mocks married men; for thus sings he:
'Cuckoo!
Cuckoo, cuckoo!' O word of fear,
Unpleasing to a married ear!

Winter. When icicles hang by the wall,
And Dick the shepherd blows his nail,
And Tom bears logs into the hall,
And milk comes frozen home in pail,
When blood is nipp'd, and ways be foul,
Then nightly sings the staring owl:
'Tu-who!
Tu-whit, tu-who!' a merry note,
While greasy Joan doth keel the pot.

When all aloud the wind doth blow,
And coughing drowns the parson's saw,
And birds sit brooding in the snow,
And Marian's nose looks red and raw;
When roasted crabs hiss in the bowl,
Then nightly sings the staring owl:
'Tu-who!
Tu-whit, tu-who!' a merry note,
While greasy Joan doth keel the pot.

Arm. The words of Mercury are harsh after the songs of Apollo. You that way, we this way.

Exeunt omnes.

A MIDSUMMER NIGHT'S DREAM

A MIDSUMMER NIGHT'S DREAM was entered in the Stationers' Register on October 8, 1600, by Thomas Fisher, and the First Quarto appeared before the end of the year. Though not very carefully printed, it furnishes an authoritative text. Probably the copy used was a manuscript prompt book, which may have been in Shakespeare's own handwriting. The Second Quarto (1619, fraudulently dated 1600) reprints the First, and the text in the First Folio comes from the Second Quarto.

In the Quartos there is no division into acts and scenes. Acts, but not scenes, are marked in the Folio. At the end of Act iii, the Folio adds the stage direction 'They sleepe all the Act,' which indicates that the four lovers remain on the stage, sleeping, until they are roused by the shouts and horn-blowing after iv, 1, 141.

The date of the play cannot be exactly determined. It may have been specially composed for some wedding festivity in high life. Ingenious scholars have suggested six different marriages, ranging all the way from 1590 to 1600, as possibilities. The first of these is certainly too early; the last is certainly too late. So far as style and metre testify, the play might be dated anywhere from 1594 to 1596. An allusion to the death of Robert Greene (in 1592) has been detected in v, 1, 52–55:

> 'The thrice three Muses mourning for the death
> Of Learning, late deceas'd in beggary.'
> That is some satire keen and critical,
> Not sorting with a nuptial ceremony.

Nothing could be less likely. Not the death of any particular person, but that of Learning in general, must have been the subject of this satirical show. This consideration likewise rules out the death of Tasso (1595). Of the other topical allusions suggested the only one that has any probability is Titania's account of the horrible weather and consequent distress that Oberon's brawls have caused (ii, 1, 81–117). This fits the actual condition of things in 1594, 1595, and 1596. Titania declares that spring, summer, autumn, and winter so 'change their wonted liveries' that one cannot tell 'which is which.' This suggests that at least a year has passed since the onset of bad weather and that no relief is in sight. The best choice among the three years, then, appears to be 1595.

The plot seems to be of Shakespeare's own design. The materials he drew from his general reading. He knew Chaucer's *Knight's Tale*, of course, which summarizes the main facts about Theseus and Hippolyta and mentions 'the feast' at their wedding. Plutarch's life of Theseus was accessible to him in Sir Thomas North's translation (1579), a work which he afterwards used extensively and minutely for his Roman plays. For Pyramus and Thisbe he had only to recall the Ovid that he had read at school.

The fairy lore goes back to tales that he had heard in childhood — 'Old Wives Fables,' Ady calls them, writing forty years after Shakespeare's death, told as they sit 'chatting of many false old Stories of Witches, and Fairies, and *Robin Good-fellow*, and walking Spirits, and the Dead walking again; all of which lying fancies people are more naturally inclined to listen after than to the Scriptures.' Bishop Corbet, not yet a bishop, was lost in a forest in the North about 1620. His man William was sure that Puck was 'busy in these oakes' and, when they met a forester, thought it was 'Robin, or some sprite that walkes about.' John Gadbury, as late as 1660, found it necessary to maintain that the *ignis fatuus* is a natural phenomenon and not an imp that leads one astray. Puck, as a name, goes back to Anglo-Saxon times. Shakespeare was not obliged to consult Reginald Scot's *Discoverie of Witchcraft* (1584) for information on English folklore, though he doubtless read the book with interest if it fell into his hands.

Bottom and his ass's head need not derive from either Lukios of Patræ or Apuleius; but, anyhow, Apuleius was accessible in Adlington's translation. Oberon and Titania, to be sure, were not names known in English folklore. Titania is a name for Circe in Ovid. Oberon had already been brought upon the stage as the fairy king in Robert Greene's *James IV*. His name occurs for the first time, so far as we know, in the Old French *chanson de geste* of *Huon de Bordeaux*, in which he is a woodland dwarf with magic powers who first embarrasses the hero but afterwards befriends him. The romance was well known in Shakespeare's time in Berners's translation. In 1593 and 1594 Henslow records in his *Diary* performances of an old play on the subject: he calls it *Hewen of Burdoche* (*Burdockes*). Fairy plays and pageants had long been favourite entertainments with all ranks of society, and A MIDSUMMER NIGHT'S DREAM did nothing to lessen their popularity. In Ben Jonson's masque of *Oberon*, performed at court on New Year's Day, 1611, the fairy prince enters in a chariot drawn by two white bears (see p. 431, below).

The most famous of all tributes to Queen Elizabeth is that of Oberon (in ii, 1, 155–164) to the 'fair Vestal throned by the West.'

A MIDSUMMER NIGHT'S DREAM

[Dramatis Personæ.

Theseus, Duke of Athens.
Egeus, father to *Hermia.*
Lysander, beloved of *Hermia.*
Demetrius, suitor to *Hermia,* approved by *Egeus.*
Philostrate, Master of the Revels to *Theseus.*

Peter Quince, a carpenter; *Prologue* in the interlude.
Nick Bottom, a weaver; *Pyramus* in the same.
Francis Flute, a bellows-mender; *Thisby* in the same.
Tom Snout, a tinker; *Wall* in the same.
Snug, a joiner; *Lion* in the same.
Robin Starveling, a tailor; *Moonshine* in the same.

Hippolyta, Queen of the Amazons, betrothed to *Theseus.*
Hermia, daughter to *Egeus,* in love with *Lysander.*
Helena, in love with *Demetrius.*

Oberon, King of the Fairies.
Titania, Queen of the Fairies.
Puck, or *Robin Goodfellow.*
Peaseblossom,
Cobweb,
Moth,
Mustardseed,
} fairies.

Other Fairies attending *Oberon* and *Titania.* Attendants on *Theseus* and *Hippolyta.*

SCENE. *Athens, and a wood near by.*]

ACT I. [Scene I. *Athens. The Palace of* Theseus.]

Enter *Theseus, Hippolyta,* [*Philostrate,*] with others.

The. Now, fair Hippolyta, our nuptial hour
Draws on apace. Four happy days bring in
Another moon; but, O, methinks, how slow
This old moon wanes! She lingers my desires,
Like to a stepdame or a dowager,
Long withering out a young man's revenue.

Hip. Four days will quickly steep themselves in night;
Four nights will quickly dream away the time;
And then the moon, like to a silver bow
New-bent in heaven, shall behold the night
Of our solemnities.

The. Go, Philostrate,
Stir up the Athenian youth to merriments,
Awake the pert and nimble spirit of mirth,
Turn melancholy forth to funerals;
The pale companion is not for our pomp.
[*Exit Philostrate.*]
Hippolyta, I woo'd thee with my sword,
And won thy love doing thee injuries;
But I will wed thee in another key,
With pomp, with triumph, and with revelling.

Enter *Egeus* and his Daughter *Hermia,* and *Lysander* and *Demetrius.*

Ege. Happy be Theseus, our renowned Duke!

The. Thanks, good Egeus. What's the news with thee?

Ege. Full of vexation come I, with complaint
Against my child, my daughter Hermia.
Stand forth, Demetrius. My noble lord,
This man hath my consent to marry her.
Stand forth, Lysander. And, my gracious Duke,
This man hath bewitch'd the bosom of my child.
Thou, thou, Lysander, thou hast given her rhymes
And interchang'd love tokens with my child;
Thou hast by moonlight at her window sung
With feigning voice verses of feigning love,
And stol'n the impression of her fantasy
With bracelets of thy hair, rings, gauds, conceits,
Knacks, trifles, nosegays, sweetmeats — messengers
Of strong prevailment in unhardened youth.
With cunning hast thou filch'd my daughter's heart;
Turn'd her obedience, which is due to me,

To stubborn harshness. And, my gracious Duke,
Be it so she will not here before your Grace
Consent to marry with Demetrius,
I beg the ancient privilege of Athens —
As she is mine, I may dispose of her;
Which shall be either to this gentleman
Or to her death, according to our law
Immediately provided in that case.

The. What say you, Hermia? Be advis'd, fair maid.
To you your father should be as a god;
One that compos'd your beauties; yea, and one
To whom you are but as a form in wax,
By him imprinted, and within his power
To leave the figure, or disfigure it.
Demetrius is a worthy gentleman.

Her. So is Lysander.

The. In himself he is;
But in this kind, wanting your father's voice,
The other must be held the worthier.

Her. I would my father look'd but with my eyes.

The. Rather your eyes must with his judgment look.

Her. I do entreat your Grace to pardon me.
I know not by what power I am made bold,
Nor how it may concern my modesty
In such a presence here to plead my thoughts;
But I beseech your Grace that I may know
The worst that may befall me in this case
If I refuse to wed Demetrius.

The. Either to die the death, or to abjure
For ever the society of men.
Therefore, fair Hermia, question your desires,
Know of your youth, examine well your blood,
Whether, if you yield not to your father's choice,
You can endure the livery of a nun,
For aye to be in shady cloister mew'd,
To live a barren sister all your life,
Chaunting faint hymns to the cold fruitless moon.
Thrice blessed they that master so their blood
To undergo such maiden pilgrimage;
But earthlier happy is the rose distill'd
Than that which, withering on the virgin thorn,
Grows, lives, and dies in single blessedness.

Her. So will I grow, so live, so die, my lord,
Ere I will yield my virgin patent up
Unto his lordship whose unwished yoke
My soul consents not to give sovereignty.

The. Take time to pause; and by the next new moon —
The sealing day betwixt my love and me
For everlasting bond of fellowship —
Upon that day either prepare to die
For disobedience to your father's will,
Or else to wed Demetrius, as he would,
Or on Diana's altar to protest
For aye austerity and single life.

Dem. Relent, sweet Hermia; and, Lysander, yield
Thy crazed title to my certain right.

Lys. You have her father's love, Demetrius;
Let me have Hermia's. Do you marry him.

Ege. Scornful Lysander, true, he hath my love;
And what is mine my love shall render him;
And she is mine, and all my right of her
I do estate unto Demetrius.

Lys. I am, my lord, as well deriv'd as he,
As well possess'd; my love is more than his;
My fortunes every way as fairly rank'd
(If not with vantage) as Demetrius';
And (which is more than all these boasts can be)
I am belov'd of beauteous Hermia.
Why should not I then prosecute my right?
Demetrius, I'll avouch it to his head,
Made love to Nedar's daughter, Helena,
And won her soul; and she (sweet lady) dotes,
Devoutly dotes, dotes in idolatry,
Upon this spotted and inconstant man.

The. I must confess that I have heard so much,
And with Demetrius thought to have spoke thereof;
But, being over-full of self-affairs,
My mind did lose it. But, Demetrius, come;
And come, Egeus. You shall go with me;
I have some private schooling for you both.
For you, fair Hermia, look you arm yourself
To fit your fancies to your father's will;
Or else the law of Athens yields you up
(Which by no means we may extenuate)
To death or to a vow of single life.
Come, my Hippolyta. What cheer, my love?
Demetrius and Egeus, go along.
I must employ you in some business
Against our nuptial and confer with you
Of something nearly that concerns yourselves.

Ege. With duty and desire we follow you.

Exeunt. Manent Lysander and Hermia.

Lys. How now, my love? Why is your cheek so pale?
How chance the roses there do fade so fast?

Her. Belike for want of rain, which I could well
Beteem them from the tempest of my eyes.

Lys. Ay me! for aught that I could ever read,
Could ever hear by tale or history,

The course of true love never did run smooth;
But, either it was different in blood —
Her. O cross! too high to be enthrall'd to low!
Lys. Or else misgraffed in respect of years —
Her. O spite! too old to be engag'd to young!
Lys. Or else it stood upon the choice of friends —
Her. O hell! to choose love by another's eyes!
Lys. Or, if there were a sympathy in choice,
War, death, or sickness did lay siege to it,
Making it momentany as a sound,
Swift as a shadow, short as any dream,
Brief as the lightning in the collied night,
That, in a spleen, unfolds both heaven and earth,
And ere a man hath power to say 'Behold!'
The jaws of darkness do devour it up:
So quick bright things come to confusion.
Her. If then true lovers have been ever cross'd,
It stands as an edict in destiny.
Then let us teach cur trial patience,
Because it is a customary cross,
As due to love as thoughts and dreams and sighs,
Wishes and tears, poor Fancy's followers.
Lys. A good persuasion. Therefore hear me, Hermia.
I have a widow aunt, a dowager,
Of great revenue, and she hath no child.
From Athens is her house remote seven leagues;
And she respects me as her only son.
There, gentle Hermia, may I marry thee;
And to that place the sharp Athenian law
Cannot pursue us. If thou lovest me then,
Steal forth thy father's house to-morrow night;
And in the wood, a league without the town,
Where I did meet thee once with Helena
To do observance to a morn of May,
There will I stay for thee.
Her. My good Lysander!
I swear to thee by Cupid's strongest bow,
By his best arrow, with the golden head,
By the simplicity of Venus' doves,
By that which knitteth souls and prospers loves,
And by that fire which burn'd the Carthage queen
When the false Troyan under sail was seen,
By all the vows that ever men have broke
(In number more than ever women spoke),
In that same place thou hast appointed me
To-morrow truly will I meet with thee.
Lys. Keep promise, love. Look, here comes Helena.

Enter *Helena.*

Her. God speed fair Helena! Whither away?
Hel. Call you me fair? That fair again unsay.
Demetrius loves your fair. O happy fair!
Your eyes are lodestars, and your tongue's sweet air
More tuneable than lark to shepherd's ear
When wheat is green, when hawthorn buds appear.
Sickness is catching. O, were favour so,
Yours would I catch, fair Hermia, ere I go!
My ear should catch your voice, my eye your eye,
My tongue should catch your tongue's sweet melody.
Were the world mine, Demetrius being bated,
The rest I'ld give to be to you translated.
O, teach me how you look, and with what art
You sway the motion of Demetrius' heart!
Her. I frown upon him; yet he loves me still.
Hel. O that your frowns would teach my smiles such skill!
Her. I give him curses; yet he gives me love.
Hel. O that my prayers could such affection move!
Her. The more I hate, the more he follows me.
Hel. The more I love, the more he hateth me.
Her. His folly, Helena, is no fault of mine.
Hel. None but your beauty. Would that fault were mine!
Her. Take comfort. He no more shall see my face;
Lysander and myself will fly this place.
Before the time I did Lysander see,
Seem'd Athens as a paradise to me.
O, then, what graces in my love do dwell
That he hath turn'd a heaven unto a hell!
Lys. Helen, to you our minds we will unfold.
To-morrow night, when Phœbe doth behold
Her silver visage in the wat'ry glass,
Decking with liquid pearl the bladed grass
(A time that lovers' flights doth still conceal),
Through Athens gates have we devis'd to steal.
Her. And in the wood where often you and I
Upon faint primrose beds were wont to lie,
Emptying our bosoms of their counsel sweet,
There my Lysander and myself shall meet,
And thence from Athens turn away our eyes
To seek new friends and stranger companies.
Farewell, sweet playfellow. Pray thou for us:
And good luck grant thee thy Demetrius!

Keep word, Lysander. We must starve our sight
From lovers' food till morrow deep midnight.
Lys. I will, my Hermia. *Exit Hermia.*
Helena, adieu.
As you on him, Demetrius dote on you! *Exit.*
Hel. How happy some o'er other some can be!
Through Athens I am thought as fair as she.
But what of that? Demetrius thinks not so;
He will not know what all but he do know.
And as he errs, doting on Hermia's eyes,
So I, admiring of his qualities.
Things base and vile, holding no quantity,
Love can transpose to form and dignity.
Love looks not with the eyes, but with the mind;
And therefore is wing'd Cupid painted blind.
Nor hath Love's mind of any judgment taste;
Wings, and no eyes, figure unheedy haste.
And therefore is Love said to be a child,
Because in choice he is so oft beguil'd.
As waggish boys in game themselves forswear,
So the boy Love is perjur'd everywhere;
For ere Demetrius look'd on Hermia's eyne,
He hail'd down oaths that he was only mine;
And when this hail some heat from Hermia felt,
So he dissolv'd, and show'rs of oaths did melt.
I will go tell him of fair Hermia's flight.
Then to the wood will he to-morrow night
Pursue her; and for this intelligence
If I have thanks, it is a dear expense;
But herein mean I to enrich my pain,
To have his sight thither and back again. *Exit.*

[Scene II. *Athens.* Quince's *house.*]

Enter *Quince* the Carpenter, and *Snug* the Joiner, and *Bottom* the Weaver, and *Flute* the Bellows-mender, and *Snout* the Tinker, and *Starveling* the Tailor.

Quince. Is all our company here?

Bot. You were best to call them generally, man by man, according to the scrip.

Quince. Here is the scroll of every man's name which is thought fit, through all Athens, to play in our enterlude before the Duke and the Duchess on his wedding day at night.

Bot. First, good Peter Quince, say what the play treats on; then read the names of the actors; and so grow to a point.

Quince. Marry, our play is 'The most Lamentable Comedy and most Cruel Death of Pyramus and Thisby.'

Bot. A very good piece of work, I assure you, and a merry. Now, good Peter Quince, call forth your actors by the scroll. Masters, spread yourselves.

Quince. Answer as I call you. Nick Bottom the weaver.

Bot. Ready. Name what part I am for, and proceed.

Quince. You, Nick Bottom, are set down for Pyramus.

Bot. What is Pyramus? a lover, or a tyrant?

Quince. A lover that kills himself, most gallant, for love.

Bot. That will ask some tears in the true performing of it. If I do it, let the audience look to their eyes! I will move storms; I will condole in some measure. To the rest. Yet my chief humour is for a tyrant. I could play Ercles rarely, or a part to tear a cat in, to make all split.

'The raging rocks
And shivering shocks
Shall break the locks
Of prison gates;
And Phibbus' car
Shall shine from far
And make and mar
The foolish Fates.'

This was lofty! Now name the rest of the players. This is Ercles' vein, a tyrant's vein. A lover is more condoling.

Quince. Francis Flute the bellows-mender.

Flute. Here, Peter Quince.

Quince. Flute, you must take Thisby on you.

Flute. What is Thisby? a wand'ring knight?

Quince. It is the lady that Pyramus must love.

Flute. Nay, faith, let not me play a woman. I have a beard coming.

Quince. That's all one. You shall play it in a mask, and you may speak as small as you will.

Bot. An I may hide my face, let me play Thisby too. I'll speak in a monstrous little voice: — 'Thisne, Thisne!' 'Ah, Pyramus, my lover dear! thy Thisby dear, and lady dear!'

Quince. No, no! you must play Pyramus; and, Flute, you Thisby.

Bot. Well, proceed.

Quince. Robin Starveling the tailor.

Starv. Here, Peter Quince.

Quince. Robin Starveling, you must play Thisby's mother. Tom Snout the tinker.

Snout. Here, Peter Quince.

Quince. You, Pyramus' father; myself, Thisby's father; Snug, the joiner, you the lion's part. And I hope here is a play fitted.

Snug. Have you the lion's part written? Pray you, if it be, give it me, for I am slow of study.

Quince. You may do it extempore, for it is nothing but roaring.

Bot. Let me play the lion too. I will roar that I will do any man's heart good to hear me. I will roar that I will make the Duke say 'Let him roar again; let him roar again.'

Quince. An you should do it too terribly, you would fright the Duchess and the ladies, that they would shrike; and that were enough to hang us all.

All. That would hang us, every mother's son.

Bot. I grant you, friends, if you should fright the ladies out of their wits, they would have no more discretion but to hang us; but I will aggravate my voice so that I will roar you as gently as any sucking dove; I will roar you an 'twere any nightingale.

Quince. You can play no part but Pyramus; for Pyramus is a sweet-fac'd man; a proper man as one shall see in a summer's day; a most lovely gentlemanlike man. Therefore you must needs play Pyramus.

Bot. Well, I will undertake it. What beard were I best to play it in?

Quince. Why, what you will.

Bot. I will discharge it in either your straw-colour beard, your orange-tawny beard, your purple-in-grain beard, or your French-crown-colour beard, your perfit yellow.

Quince. Some of your French crowns have no hair at all, and then you will play barefac'd. But, masters, here are your parts; and I am to entreat you, request you, and desire you to con them by to-morrow night; and meet me in the palace wood, a mile without the town, by moonlight. There will we rehearse; for if we meet in the city, we shall be dogg'd with company, and our devices known. In the meantime I will draw a bill of properties, such as our play wants. I pray you fail me not.

Bot. We will meet; and there we may rehearse most obscenely and courageously. Take pains; be perfit. Adieu.

Quince. At the Duke's Oak we meet.

Bot. Enough. Hold, or cut bowstrings.

Exeunt.

ACT II. [Scene I. *A wood near Athens.*]

Enter a *Fairy* at one door, and *Robin Goodfellow* at another.

Rob. How now, spirit? Whither wander you?

Fai. Over hill, over dale,
Thorough bush, thorough brier,
Over park, over pale,
Thorough flood, thorough fire;
I do wander everywhere,
Swifter than the moonës sphere;
And I serve the Fairy Queen,
To dew her orbs upon the green.
The cowslips tall her pensioners be;
In their gold coats spots you see.
Those be rubies, fairy favours;
In those freckles live their savours.
I must go seek some dewdrops here,
And hang a pearl in every cowslip's ear.
Farewell, thou lob of spirits; I'll be gone.
Our Queen and all her elves come here anon.

Rob. The King doth keep his revels here to-night.
Take heed the Queen come not within his sight.
For Oberon is passing fell and wrath,
Because that she, as her attendant, hath
A lovely boy, stolen from an Indian king;
She never had so sweet a changeling.
And jealous Oberon would have the child
Knight of his train, to trace the forests wild;
But she perforce withholds the loved boy,
Crowns him with flowers, and makes him all her joy.
And now they never meet in grove or green,
By fountain clear or spangled starlight sheen,
But they do square, that all their elves, for fear,
Creep into acorn cups and hide them there.

Fai. Either I mistake your shape and making quite,
Or else you are that shrewd and knavish sprite
Call'd Robin Goodfellow. Are not you he
That frights the maidens of the villagery;
Skim milk, and sometimes labour in the quern,
And bootless make the breathless housewife churn;
And sometime make the drink to bear no barm;
Mislead night-wanderers, laughing at their harm?
Those that Hobgoblin call you, and sweet Puck,
You do their work, and they shall have good luck.
Are not you he?

Rob. Thou speakest aright;
I am that merry wanderer of the night.
I jest to Oberon, and make him smile
When I a fat and bean-fed horse beguile,
Neighing in likeness of a filly foal;
And sometime lurk I in a gossip's bowl
In very likeness of a roasted crab,
And when she drinks, against her lips I bob
And on her withered dewlap pour the ale.
The wisest aunt, telling the saddest tale,
Sometime for three-foot stool mistaketh me;
Then slip I from her bum, down topples she,
And 'tailor' cries, and falls into a cough;
And then the whole quire hold their hips and loffe,
And waxen in their mirth, and neeze, and swear
A merrier hour was never wasted there.
But room, fairy! Here comes Oberon.
Fai. And here my mistress. Would that he were gone!

Enter [*Oberon*] the *King of Fairies*, at one door, with his *Train*; and the *Queen*, [*Titania*,] at another, with hers.

Ob. Ill met by moonlight, proud Titania.
Queen. What, jealous Oberon? Fairies, skip hence.
I have forsworn his bed and company.
Ob. Tarry, rash wanton. Am not I thy lord?
Queen. Then I must be thy lady; but I know
When thou hast stolen away from fairyland,
And in the shape of Corin sat all day,
Playing on pipes of corn, and versing love
To amorous Phillida. Why art thou here,
Come from the farthest steep of India,
But that, forsooth, the bouncing Amazon,
Your buskin'd mistress and your warrior love,
To Theseus must be wedded, and you come
To give their bed joy and prosperity?
Ob. How canst thou thus, for shame, Titania,
Glance at my credit with Hippolyta,
Knowing I know thy love to Theseus?
Didst thou not lead him through the glimmering night
From Perigouna, whom he ravished?
And make him with fair Ægles break his faith,
With Ariadne, and Antiopa?
Queen. These are the forgeries of jealousy;
And never, since the middle summer's spring,
Met we on hill, in dale, forest, or mead,
By paved fountain or by rushy brook,
Or in the beached margent of the sea,
To dance our ringlets to the whistling wind,
But with thy brawls thou hast disturb'd our sport.
Therefore the winds, piping to us in vain,
As in revenge, have suck'd up from the sea
Contagious fogs; which falling in the land
Hath every pelting river made so proud
That they have overborne their continents.
The ox hath therefore stretch'd his yoke in vain,
The ploughman lost his sweat, and the green corn
Hath rotted ere his youth attain'd a beard;
The fold stands empty in the drowned field,
And crows are fatted with the murrion flock;
The nine men's morris is fill'd up with mud;
And the quaint mazes in the wanton green
For lack of tread are undistinguishable.
The human mortals want their winter cheer;
No night is now with hymn or carol blest.
Therefore the moon, the governess of floods,
Pale in her anger, washes all the air,
That rheumatic diseases do abound.
And thorough this distemperature we see
The seasons alter. Hoary-headed frosts
Fall in the fresh lap of the crimson rose;
And on old Hiems' thin and icy crown
An odorous chaplet of sweet summer buds
Is, as in mockery, set. The spring, the summer,
The childing autumn, angry winter change
Their wonted liveries; and the mazed world,
By their increase, now knows not which is which.
And this same progeny of evils comes
From our debate, from our dissension;
We are their parents and original.
Ob. Do you amend it then; it lies in you.
Why should Titania cross her Oberon?
I do but beg a little changeling boy
To be my henchman.
Queen. Set your heart at rest.
The fairyland buys not the child of me.
His mother was a vot'ress of my order;
And in the spiced Indian air, by night,
Full often hath she gossip'd by my side,
And sat with me on Neptune's yellow sands,
Marking th' embarked traders on the flood;
When we have laugh'd to see the sails conceive
And grow big-bellied with the wanton wind;
Which she, with pretty and with swimming gait
Following (her womb then rich with my young squire)
Would imitate, and sail upon the land
To fetch me trifles, and return again,
As from a voyage, rich with merchandise.
But she, being mortal, of that boy did die,
And for her sake do I rear up her boy;
And for her sake I will not part with him.
Ob. How long within this wood intend you stay?

Robert Helpmann as Oberon, king of the fairies, and Moira Shearer as his queen, Titania

A MIDSUMMER-NIGHT'S DREAM

Philip Guard as Oberon's mischievous helper, Puck, whose pranks and antics twist the fates of both human and fairy lovers on a midsummer night

PHOTOGRAPHS BY HOUSTON ROGERS
PRODUCED BY THE OLD VIC COMPANY

Right: King Oberon. At odds with his queen, Titania, over her interest in Theseus and the possession of a changeling boy, he sends Puck to fetch a magic herb whose juice, placed in the eyes of the sleeping queen, will make her love the first thing she sees on waking

Below: The fairy king surrounded by a band of henchmen

Right: Titania, Oberon's beautiful but capricious wife

Below: Titania asleep in the forest, "Lull'd in these flowers with dances and delight" *(Act II, Scene I)*

Left: Margaret Courtenay as Hippolyta, the queen of the Amazons, betrothed of Theseus

Right: Theseus, Duke of Athens, played by Anthony Nicholls

Left: Joan Benham as Helena and Patrick MacNee as Demetrius

Right: Ann Walford as Hermia and Terence Longdon as Lysander

Left: Bottom (Stanley Holloway) in his role as the lover, Pyramus

Right: Eliot Makeham as Quince, the carpenter

"And maidens call it, Love-in-idleness. Fetch me that flower: the herb I show'd thee once." Oberon sends Puck for the magic herb with which he intends to revenge himself on Titania *(Act II, Scene I)*

"What thou seest when thou dost wake do it for thy true-love take." While Titania is sleeping, Oberon drops the juice of the magic herb into her eyes, casting a spell (*Act II, Scene II*)

Puck with the fairy Pease-Blossom (Jocelyn Britton), one of the four fairies assigned by Titania as Bottom's attendants (*Act III, Scene I*)

Puck, who has made himself invisible, annoys the Athenian craftsmen as they rehearse their play in the forest. Philip Locke in the role of Flute and Norman Rossington playing Snout (*Act III, Scene I*)

The craftsmen of Athens rehearse the play they intend to give to celebrate the nuptials of Duke Theseus (*Act III, Scene I*)

"If I were fair, Thisby, I were only thine." Changed into an ass, Bottom startles Flute (*Act III, Scene I*)

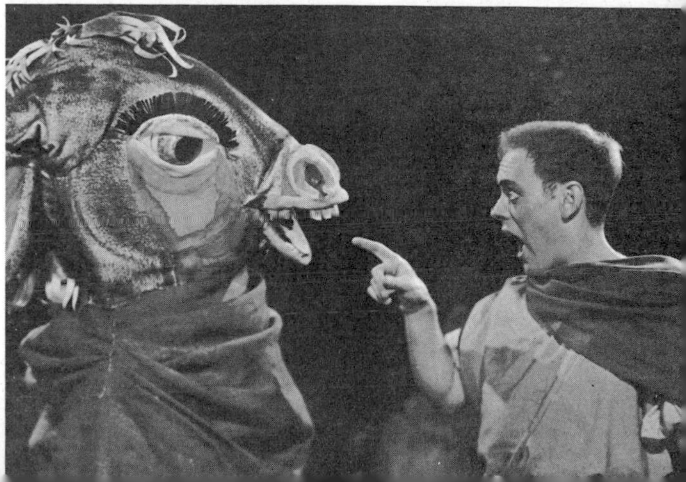

"Be kind and courteous to this gentleman." Infatuated with the donkey-headed Bottom through Oberon's spell, Titania orders her fairies to deck him in flowers (*Act III, Scene I*)

Titania dotes on the enraptured donkey head, Bottom (*Act III, Scene I*)

Lysander and Demetrius, both in love with Helena through the power of Oberon's drug, prevent Hermia from attacking her rival (*Act III, Scene II*)

Hunting in the forest, Theseus and Hippolyta find the sleeping lovers and waken them
(*Act IV, Scene I*)

Left: Bottom and his companions present their play to the duke (*Act V, Scene I*)

Below: Snug the Joiner (Michael Redington) as the Lion and Starveling the Tailor (Daniel Thorndike) as the Moon in the masque presented to celebrate the nuptials of Duke Theseus
(*Act V, Scene I*)

Below: Bottom and Flute in the nonsensical pantomime of Pyramus and Thisby. Snout portrays the wall through which the ill-fated couple whisper their love
(*Act V, Scene I*)

With the two pairs of lovers reunited before the throne, Theseus and his bride, Hippolyta watch as Bottom and his craftsmen players present the drama of Pyramus and Thisby *(Act V, Scene I)*

Like the human lovers in whose lives they have intervened, Oberon and Titania are reconciled as the enchanted night ends (*Act V, Scene II*)

Queen. Perchance till after Theseus' wedding day.
If you will patiently dance in our round
And see our moonlight revels, go with us.
If not, shun me, and I will spare your haunts.

Ob. Give me that boy, and I will go with thee.

Queen. Not for thy fairy kingdom. Fairies, away!
We shall chide downright if I longer stay.
Exeunt [Titania and her Train].

Ob. Well, go thy way. Thou shalt not from this grove
Till I torment thee for this injury.
My gentle Puck, come hither. Thou remem-b'rest
Since once I sat upon a promontory
And heard a mermaid, on a dolphin's back,
Uttering such dulcet and harmonious breath
That the rude sea grew civil at her song,
And certain stars shot madly from their spheres
To hear the sea-maid's music.

Puck. I remember.

Ob. That very time I saw (but thou couldst not)
Flying between the cold moon and the earth
Cupid, all arm'd. A certain aim he took
At a fair Vestal, throned by the West,
And loos'd his love-shaft smartly from his bow,
As it should pierce a hundred thousand hearts.
But I might see young Cupid's fiery shaft
Quench'd in the chaste beams of the wat'ry moon,
And the imperial vot'ress passed on,
In maiden meditation, fancy-free.
Yet mark'd I where the bolt of Cupid fell.
It fell upon a little Western flower,
Before milk-white, now purple with love's wound,
And maidens call it love-in-idleness.
Fetch me that flow'r; the herb I show'd thee once.
The juice of it, on sleeping eyelids laid,
Will make or man or woman madly dote
Upon the next live creature that it sees.
Fetch me this herb, and be thou here again
Ere the Leviathan can swim a league.

Puck. I'll put a girdle round about the earth
In forty minutes. [*Exit.*]

Ob. Having once this juice,
I'll watch Titania when she is asleep
And drop the liquor of it in her eyes.
The next thing then she, waking, looks upon
(Be it on lion, bear, or wolf, or bull,
On meddling monkey, or on busy ape)
She shall pursue it with the soul of love.
And ere I take this charm from off her sight
(As I can take it with another herb)
I'll make her render up her page to me.
But who comes here? I am invisible,
And I will overhear their conference.

Enter *Demetrius, Helena* following him.

Dem. I love thee not; therefore pursue me not.
Where is Lysander and fair Hermia?
The one I'll slay, the other slayeth me.
Thou told'st me they were stol'n unto this wood;
And here am I, and wood within this wood
Because I cannot meet my Hermia.
Hence, get thee gone, and follow me no more!

Hel. You draw me, you hard-hearted adamant!
But yet you draw not iron, for my heart
Is true as steel. Leave you your power to draw,
And I shall have no power to follow you.

Dem. Do I entice you? Do I speak you fair?
Or rather do I not in plainest truth
Tell you I do not nor I cannot love you?

Hel. And even for that do I love you the more.
I am your spaniel; and, Demetrius,
The more you beat me, I will fawn on you.
Use me but as your spaniel — spurn me, strike me,
Neglect me, lose me; only give me leave
(Unworthy as I am) to follow you.
What worser place can I beg in your love
(And yet a place of high respect with me)
Than to be used as you use your dog?

Dem. Tempt not too much the hatred of my spirit;
For I am sick when I do look on thee.

Hel. And I am sick when I look not on you.

Dem. You do impeach your modesty too much
To leave the city and commit yourself
Into the hands of one that loves you not;
To trust the opportunity of night
And the ill counsel of a desert place
With the rich worth of your virginity.

Hel. Your virtue is my privilege. For that
It is not night when I do see your face,
Therefore I think I am not in the night;
Nor doth this wood lack worlds of company,
For you, in my respect, are all the world.
Then how can it be said I am alone
When all the world is here to look on me?

Dem. I'll run from thee and hide me in the brakes
And leave thee to the mercy of wild beasts.
Hel. The wildest hath not such a heart as you.
Run when you will. The story shall be chang'd:
Apollo flies, and Daphne holds the chase;
The dove pursues the griffon; the mild hind
Makes speed to catch the tiger — bootless speed,
When cowardice pursues, and valour flies!
Dem. I will not stay thy questions. Let me go!
Or if thou follow me, do not believe
But I shall do thee mischief in the wood.
Hel. Ay, in the temple, in the town, the field
You do me mischief. Fie, Demetrius!
Your wrongs do set a scandal on my sex.
We cannot fight for love, as men may do;
We should be woo'd, and were not made to woo.
[*Exit Demetrius.*]
I'll follow thee, and make a heaven of hell
To die upon the hand I love so well. *Exit.*
Ob. Fare thee well, nymph. Ere he do leave this grove,
Thou shalt fly him, and he shall seek thy love.

Enter *Puck.*

Hast thou the flower there? Welcome, wanderer.
Puck. Ay, there it is.
Ob. I pray thee give it me.
I know a bank where the wild thyme blows,
Where oxlips and the nodding violet grows;
Quite over-canopied with luscious woodbine,
With sweet musk-roses, and with eglantine.
There sleeps Titania sometime of the night,
Lull'd in these flowers with dances and delight;
And there the snake throws her enamell'd skin,
Weed wide enough to wrap a fairy in;
And with the juice of this I'll streak her eyes
And make her full of hateful fantasies.
Take thou some of it and seek through this grove.
A sweet Athenian lady is in love
With a disdainful youth. Anoint his eyes;
But do it when the next thing he espies
May be the lady. Thou shalt know the man
By the Athenian garments he hath on.
Effect it with some care, that he may prove
More fond on her than she upon her love;
And look thou meet me ere the first cock crow.
Puck. Fear not, my lord; your servant shall do so. *Exeunt.*

[Scene II. *Another part of the wood.*]

Enter *Titania, Queen of Fairies,* with her *Train.*

Queen. Come, now a roundel and a fairy song;
Then, for the third part of a minute, hence —
Some to kill cankers in the musk-rose buds,
Some war with reremice for their leathren wings,
To make my small elves coats, and some keep back
The clamorous owl, that nightly hoots and wonders
At our quaint spirits. Sing me now asleep.
Then to your offices, and let me rest.

Fairies sing.

1. Fai. You spotted snakes with double tongue,
Thorny hedgehogs, be not seen;
Newts and blindworms, do no wrong,
Come not near our Fairy Queen.

[CHORUS.]

Philomele, with melody
Sing in our sweet lullaby;
Lulla, lulla, lullaby; lulla, lulla, lullaby:
Never harm
Nor spell nor charm
Come our lovely lady nigh.
So good night, with lullaby.

1. Fai. Weaving spiders, come not here;
Hence, you long-legg'd spinners, hence!
Beetles black, approach not near;
Worm nor snail, do no offence.

[CHORUS.]

Philomele, with melody, &c.
She sleeps.

2. Fai. Hence, away! Now all is well.
One aloof stand sentinel.
[*Exeunt Fairies.*]

Enter *Oberon,* [and squeezes the flower on *Titania's* eyelids].

Ob. What thou seest when thou dost wake,
Do it for thy true-love take;
Love and languish for his sake.
Be it ounce or cat or bear,
Pard, or boar with bristled hair
In thy eye that shall appear
When thou wak'st, it is thy dear.
Wake when some vile thing is near.
[*Exit.*]

Enter *Lysander* and *Hermia.*

Lys. Fair love, you faint with wand'ring in the wood;
And to speak troth, I have forgot our way.
We'll rest us, Hermia, if you think it good,
And tarry for the comfort of the day.
Her. Be it so, Lysander. Find you out a bed;
For I upon this bank will rest my head.
Lys. One turf shall serve as pillow for us both;
One heart, one bed, two bosoms, and one troth.
Her. Nay, good Lysander. For my sake, my dear,
Lie further off yet; do not lie so near.
Lys. O, take the sense, sweet, of my innocence!
Love takes the meaning in love's conference.
I mean that my heart unto yours is knit,
So that but one heart we can make of it;
Two bosoms interchained with an oath —
So then two bosoms and a single troth.
Then by your side no bed-room me deny;
For lying so, Hermia, I do not lie.
Her. Lysander riddles very prettily.
Now much beshrew my manners and my pride
If Hermia meant to say Lysander lied!
But, gentle friend, for love and courtesy
Lie further off, in humane modesty;
Such separation as may well be said
Becomes a virtuous bachelor and a maid,
So far be distant; and good night, sweet friend.
Thy love ne'er alter till thy sweet life end!
Lys. Amen, amen, to that fair prayer say I,
And then end life when I end loyalty!
Here is my bed. Sleep give thee all his rest!
Her. With half that wish the wisher's eyes be press'd! *They sleep.*

Enter *Puck.*

Puck. Through the forest have I gone,
But Athenian found I none
On whose eyes I might approve
This flower's force in stirring love.
Night and silence! Who is here?
Weeds of Athens he doth wear.
This is he (my master said)
Despised the Athenian maid;
And here the maiden, sleeping sound
On the dank and dirty ground.
Pretty soul! she durst not lie
Near this lack-love, this kill-courtesy.
Churl, upon thy eyes I throw
All the power this charm doth owe.
When thou wak'st, let love forbid
Sleep his seat on thy eyelid.
So awake when I am gone;
For I must now to Oberon. *Exit.*

Enter *Demetrius* and *Helena,* running.

Hel. Stay, though thou kill me, sweet Demetrius.
Dem. I charge thee, hence, and do not haunt me thus.
Hel. O, wilt thou darkling leave me? Do not so.
Dem. Stay, on thy peril! I alone will go. *Exit.*
Hel. O, I am out of breath in this fond chase!
The more my prayer, the lesser is my grace.
Happy is Hermia, wheresoe'er she lies;
For she hath blessed and attractive eyes.
How came her eyes so bright? Not with salt tears.
If so, my eyes are oft'ner wash'd than hers.
No, no! I am as ugly as a bear;
For beasts that meet me run away for fear.
Therefore no marvel though Demetrius
Do, as a monster, fly my presence thus.
What wicked and dissembling glass of mine
Made me compare with Hermia's sphery eyne?
But who is here? Lysander! on the ground?
Dead, or asleep? I see no blood, no wound.
Lysander, if you live, good sir, awake.
Lys. [*starts up*] And run through fire I will for thy sweet sake.
Transparent Helena! Nature shows art,
That through thy bosom makes me see thy heart.
Where is Demetrius? O, how fit a word
Is that vile name to perish on my sword!
Hel. Do not say so, Lysander; say not so.
What though he love your Hermia? Lord! what though?
Yet Hermia still loves you. Then be content.
Lys. Content with Hermia? No! I do repent
The tedious minutes I with her have spent.
Not Hermia, but Helena I love.
Who will not change a raven for a dove?
The will of man is by his reason sway'd;
And reason says you are the worthier maid.
Things growing are not ripe until their season;
So I, being young, till now ripe not to reason;
And touching now the point of human skill,
Reason becomes the marshal to my will
And leads me to your eyes; where I o'erlook
Love's stories, written in Love's richest book.
Hel. Wherefore was I to this keen mockery born?

When at your hands did I deserve this scorn?
Is't not enough, is't not enough, young man,
That I did never, no, nor never can,
Deserve a sweet look from Demetrius' eye,
But you must flout my insufficiency?
Good troth, you do me wrong! good sooth, you do!
In such disdainful manner me to woo.
But fare you well. Perforce I must confess
I thought you lord of more true gentleness.
O, that a lady, of one man refus'd,
Should of another therefore be abus'd! *Exit.*

Lys. She sees not Hermia. Hermia, sleep thou there,
And never mayst thou come Lysander near!
For, as a surfeit of the sweetest things
The deepest loathing to the stomach brings,
Or as the heresies that men do leave
Are hated most of those they did deceive,
So thou, my surfeit and my heresy,
Of all be hated, but the most of me!
And, all my powers, address your love and might
To honour Helen and to be her knight! *Exit.*

Her. [*awakes*] Help me, Lysander, help me! Do thy best
To pluck this crawling serpent from my breast!
Ay me, for pity! What a dream was here!
Lysander, look how I do quake with fear.
Methought a serpent eat my heart away,
And you sat smiling at his cruel prey.
Lysander! What, remov'd? Lysander! lord!
What, out of hearing? gone? No sound, no word?
Alack, where are you? Speak, an if you hear.
Speak, of all loves! I swoon almost with fear.
No? Then I well perceive you are not nigh.
Either death or you I'll find immediately. *Exit.*

ACT III. [Scene I. *The wood.* Titania *lying asleep.*]

Enter the Clowns — [*Quince, Snug, Bottom, Flute, Snout,* and *Starveling*].

Bot. Are we all met?

Quince. Pat, pat; and here's a marvail's convenient place for our rehearsal. This green plot shall be our stage, this hawthorn brake our tiring house, and we will do it in action as we will do it before the Duke.

Bot. Peter Quince!

Quince. What sayest thou, bully Bottom?

Bot. There are things in this Comedy of Pyramus and Thisby that will never please. First, Pyramus must draw a sword to kill himself; which the ladies cannot abide. How answer you that?

Snout. By'r lakin, a parlous fear!

Starv. I believe we must leave the killing out, when all is done.

Bot. Not a whit. I have a device to make all well. Write me a prologue; and let the prologue seem to say, we will do no harm with our swords, and that Pyramus is not kill'd indeed; and for the more better assurance, tell them that I Pyramus am not Pyramus, but Bottom the weaver. This will put them out of fear.

Quince. Well, we will have such a prologue, and it shall be written in eight and six.

Bot. No, make it two more; let it be written in eight and eight.

Snout. Will not the ladies be afeard of the lion?

Starv. I fear it, I promise you.

Bot. Masters, you ought to consider with yourselves, to bring in (God shield us!) a lion among ladies is a most dreadful thing. For there is not a more fearful wild-fowl than your lion living; and we ought to look to't.

Snout. Therefore another prologue must tell he is not a lion.

Bot. Nay, you must name his name, and half his face must be seen through the lion's neck, and he himself must speak through, saying thus, or to the same defect: 'Ladies,' — or 'Fair ladies, — I would wish you' — or 'I would request you' — or 'I would entreat you — not to fear, not to tremble. My life for yours! If you think I come hither as a lion, it were pity of my life. No! I am no such thing. I am a man as other men are.' And there, indeed, let him name his name and tell them plainly he is Snug the joiner.

Quince. Well, it shall be so. But there is two hard things: that is, to bring the moonlight into a chamber; for, you know, Pyramus and Thisby meet by moonlight.

Snout. Doth the moon shine that night we play our play?

Bot. A calendar, a calendar! Look in the almanac. Find out moonshine, find out moonshine!

Quince. Yes, it doth shine that night.

Bot. Why, then may you leave a casement of the great chamber window, where we play, open, and the moon may shine in at the casement.

Quince. Ay; or else one must come in with a bush of thorns and a lantern, and say he comes to disfigure, or to present, the person of Moonshine. Then there is another thing. We must have a wall in the great chamber; for Pyramus and Thisby, says the story, did talk through the chink of a wall.

Snout. You can never bring in a wall. What say you, Bottom?

Bot. Some man or other must present Wall; and let him have some plaster, or some loam, or some roughcast about him, to signify wall; and let him hold his fingers thus; and through that cranny shall Pyramus and Thisby whisper.

Quince. If that may be, then all is well. Come, sit down every mother's son, and rehearse your parts. Pyramus, you begin. When you have spoken your speech, enter into that brake; and so every one according to his cue.

Enter *Robin* [*Goodfellow*].

Rob. What hempen homespuns have we swagg'ring here,
So near the cradle of the Fairy Queen?
What, a play toward? I'll be an auditor;
An actor too perhaps, if I see cause.

Quince. Speak, Pyramus. Thisby, stand forth.

Pyr. Thisby, the flowers of odious savours sweet —

Quince. Odorous! odorous!

Pyr. —— odours savours sweet;
So hath thy breath, my dearest Thisby dear.
But hark, a voice! Stay thou but here awhile,
And by-and-by I will to thee appear. *Exit*.

Rob. A stranger Pyramus than e'er play'd here! [*Exit*.]

This. Must I speak now?

Quince. Ay, marry, must you; for you must understand he goes but to see a noise that he heard, and is to come again.

This. Most radiant Pyramus, most lily-white of hue,
Of colour like the red rose on triumphant brier,
Most brisky juvenal, and eke most lovely Jew,
As true as truest horse, that yet would never tire,
I'll meet thee, Pyramus, at Ninny's tomb.

Quince. 'Ninus' tomb,' man! Why, you must not speak that yet. That you answer to Pyramus. You speak all your part at once, cues and all. Pyramus, enter. Your cue is past; it is 'never tire.'

This. O — As true as truest horse, that yet would never tire.

[Enter *Robin*, and] *Pyramus* with an ass-head.

Pyr. If I were fair, Thisby, I were only thine.

Quince. O monstrous! O strange! We are haunted. Pray, masters! Fly, masters! Help!
Exeunt all the Clowns [*but Bottom*].

Rob. I'll follow you; I'll lead you about a round,
Through bog, through bush, through brake, through brier.
Sometime a horse I'll be, sometime a hound,
A hog, a headless bear, sometime a fire;
And neigh, and bark, and grunt, and roar, and burn,
Like horse, hound, hog, bear, fire, at every turn. *Exit*.

Bot. Why do they run away? This is a knavery of them to make me afeard.

Enter *Snout*.

Snout. O Bottom, thou art chang'd! What do I see on thee?

Bot. What do you see? You see an ass-head of your own, do you? [*Exit Snout*.]

Enter *Quince*.

Quince. Bless thee, Bottom! bless thee! Thou art translated. *Exit*.

Bot. I see their knavery. This is to make an ass of me; to fright me, if they could. But I will not stir from this place, do what they can. I will walk up and down here, and will sing, that they shall hear I am not afraid. [*Sings*.]

The woosel cock so black of hue,
With orange-tawny bill,
The throstle with his note so true,
The wren with little quill —

Tita. What angel wakes me from my flow'ry bed?

Bot. [*sings*]

The finch, the sparrow, and the lark,
The plain-song cuckoo gray,
Whose note full many a man doth mark,
And dares not answer nay.

For, indeed, who would set his wit to so foolish a bird? Who would give a bird the lie, though he cry 'cuckoo' never so?

Tita. I pray thee, gentle mortal, sing again.
Mine ear is much enamoured of thy note;
So is mine eye enthralled to thy shape;
And thy fair virtue's force (perforce) doth move me,
On the first view, to say, to swear, I love thee.

Bot. Methinks, mistress, you should have little reason for that. And yet, to say the truth, reason and love keep little company together now-a-days. The more the pity that some honest neighbours will not make them friends. Nay, I can gleek, upon occasion.

Tita. Thou art as wise as thou art beautiful.

Bot. Not so, neither; but if I had wit enough to get out of this wood, I have enough to serve mine own turn.

Tita. Out of this wood do not desire to go.
Thou shalt remain here, whether thou wilt or no.
I am a spirit of no common rate,
The summer still doth tend upon my state;
And I do love thee. Therefore go with me.
I'll give thee fairies to attend on thee;
And they shall fetch thee jewels from the deep,
And sing while thou on pressed flowers dost sleep;
And I will purge thy mortal grossness so
That thou shalt like an airy spirit go.
Peaseblossom! Cobweb! Moth! and Mustardseed!

Enter four *Fairies* — [*Peaseblossom, Cobweb, Moth,* and *Mustardseed*].

Peas. Ready.
Cob. And I.
Moth. And I.
Must. And I.
All. Where shall we go?

Tita. Be kind and courteous to this gentleman.
Hop in his walks and gambol in his eyes;
Feed him with apricocks and dewberries,
With purple grapes, green figs, and mulberries;
The honey-bags steal from the humblebees,
And for night tapers crop their waxen thighs,
And light them at the fiery glowworm's eyes,
To have my love to bed and to arise;
And pluck the wings from painted butterflies
To fan the moonbeams from his sleeping eyes.
Nod to him, elves, and do him courtesies.

Peas. Hail, mortal!
Cob. Hail!
Moth. Hail!
Must. Hail!

Bot. I cry your worships mercy, heartily. I beseech your worship's name.

Cob. Cobweb.

Bot. I shall desire you of more acquaintance, good Master Cobweb. If I cut my finger, I shall make bold with you. Your name, honest gentleman?

Peas. Peaseblossom.

Bot. I pray you, commend me to Mistress Squash, your mother, and to Master Peascod, your father. Good Master Peaseblossom, I shall desire you of more acquaintance too. Your name, I beseech you, sir?

Must. Mustardseed.

Bot. Good Master Mustardseed, I know your patience well. That same cowardly, giantlike ox-beef hath devour'd many a gentleman of your house. I promise you your kindred hath made my eyes water ere now. I desire you of more acquaintance, good Master Mustardseed.

Tita. Come wait upon him; lead him to my bower.
The moon, methinks, looks with a wat'ry eye;
And when she weeps, weeps every little flower,
Lamenting some enforced chastity.
Tie up my love's tongue, bring him silently.
Exeunt.

[Scene II. *Another part of the wood.*]

Enter [*Oberon,*] *King of Fairies.*

Ob. I wonder if Titania be awak'd;
Then, what it was that next came in her eye,
Which she must dote on in extremity.

Enter *Puck.*

Here comes my messenger. How now, mad spirit?
What night-rule now about this haunted grove?

Puck. My mistress with a monster is in love.
Near to her close and consecrated bower,
While she was in her dull and sleeping hour,
A crew of patches, rude mechanicals,
That work for bread upon Athenian stalls,
Were met together to rehearse a play,
Intended for great Theseus' nuptial day.
The shallowest thickskin of that barren sort,
Who Pyramus presented in their sport,
Forsook his scene and ent'red in a brake.
When I did him at this advantage take,
An ass's nole I fixed on his head.
Anon his Thisby must be answered,
And forth my mimic comes. When they him spy,
As wild geese that the creeping fowler eye,
Or russet-pated choughs, many in sort,
Rising and cawing at the gun's report,
Sever themselves and madly sweep the sky;
So at his sight away his fellows fly;
And, at a stump, here o'er and o'er one falls;
He murther cries and help from Athens calls.

Their sense thus weak, lost with their fears thus strong,
Made senseless things begin to do them wrong;
For briers and thorns at their apparel snatch;
Some, sleeves — some, hats; from yielders all things catch.
I led them on in this distracted fear
And left sweet Pyramus translated there;
When in that moment (so it came to pass)
Titania wak'd, and straightway lov'd an ass.
Ob. This falls out better than I could devise.
But hast thou yet latch'd the Athenian's eyes
With the love-juice, as I did bid thee do?
Rob. I took him sleeping (that is finish'd too)
And the Athenian woman by his side,
That, when he wak'd, of force she must be ey'd.

Enter *Demetrius* and *Hermia*.

Ob. Stand close. This is the same Athenian.
Rob. This is the woman; but not this the man.
Dem. O, why rebuke you him that loves you so?
Lay breath so bitter on your bitter foe.
Her. Now I but chide; but I should use thee worse,
For thou, I fear, hast given me cause to curse.
If thou hast slain Lysander in his sleep,
Being o'er shoes in blood, plunge in the deep,
And kill me too.
The sun was not so true unto the day
As he to me. Would he have stolen away
From sleeping Hermia? I'll believe as soon
This whole earth may be bor'd, and that the moon
May through the centre creep, and so displease
Her brother's noontide with th' Antipodes.
It cannot be but thou hast murth'red him.
So should a murtherer look — so dead, so grim.
Dem. So should the murthered look, and so should I,
Pierc'd through the heart with your stern cruelty.
Yet you, the murtherer, look as bright, as clear,
As yonder Venus in her glimmering sphere.
Her. What's this to my Lysander? Where is he?
Ah, good Demetrius, wilt thou give him me?
Dem. I had rather give his carcass to my hounds.
Her. Out, dog! out, cur! Thou driv'st me past the bounds
Of maiden's patience. Hast thou slain him then?
Henceforth be never numb'red among men!
O, once tell true! tell true, even for my sake!
Durst thou have look'd upon him, being awake?
And hast thou kill'd him sleeping? O brave touch!
Could not a worm, an adder, do so much?
An adder did it; for with doubler tongue
Than thine (thou serpent!) never adder stung.
Dem. You spend your passion on a mispris'd mood.
I am not guilty of Lysander's blood;
Nor is he dead, for aught that I can tell.
Her. I pray thee, tell me then that he is well.
Dem. An if I could, what should I get therefore?
Her. A privilege never to see me more;
And from thy hated presence part I so.
See me no more, whether he be dead or no.
Exit.
Dem. There is no following her in this fierce vein.
Here therefore for a while I will remain.
So sorrow's heaviness doth heavier grow
For debt that bankrout sleep doth sorrow owe;
Which now in some slight measure it will pay,
If for his tender here I make some stay.
Lie down [*and sleep*].
Ob. What hast thou done? Thou hast mistaken quite
And laid the love-juice on some true-love's sight.
Of thy misprision must perforce ensue
Some true-love turn'd, and not a false turn'd true.
Rob. The fate o'errules, that, one man holding troth,
A million fail, confounding oath on oath.
Ob. About the wood! Go swifter than the wind,
And Helena of Athens look thou find.
All fancy-sick she is, and pale of cheer
With sighs of love, that costs the fresh blood dear.
By some illusion see thou bring her here.
I'll charm his eyes against she do appear.
Rob. I go, I go! Look how I go!
Swifter than arrow from the Tartar's bow.
Exit.
Ob. Flower of this purple dye,
Hit with Cupid's archery,
Sink in apple of his eye!
When his love he doth espy,
Let her shine as gloriously
As the Venus of the sky.
When thou wak'st, if she be by,
Beg of her for remedy.

Enter *Puck*.

Puck. Captain of our fairy band,
Helena is here at hand,
And the youth, mistook by me,
Pleading for a lover's fee.
Shall we their fond pageant see?
Lord, what fools these mortals be!

Ob. Stand aside. The noise they make
Will cause Demetrius to awake.

Puck. Then will two at once woo one.
That must needs be sport alone;
And those things do best please me
That befall prepost'rously.

Enter *Lysander* and *Helena*.

Lys. Why should you think that I should woo in scorn?
Scorn and derision never come in tears.
Look, when I vow, I weep; and vows so born,
In their nativity all truth appears.
How can these things in me seem scorn to you,
Bearing the badge of faith to prove them true?

Hel. You do advance your cunning more and more.
When truth kills truth, O devilish-holy fray!
Those vows are Hermia's. Will you give her o'er?
Weigh oath with oath, and you will nothing weigh.
Your vows to her and me, put in two scales,
Will even weigh; and both as light as tales.

Lys. I had no judgment when to her I swore.

Hel. Nor none, in my mind, now you give her o'er.

Lys. Demetrius loves her; and he loves not you.

Dem. (*awakes*) O Helen, goddess, nymph, perfect, divine!
To what, my love, shall I compare thine eyne?
Crystal is muddy. O, how ripe in show
Thy lips, those kissing cherries, tempting grow!
That pure congealed white, high Taurus' snow,
Fann'd with the eastern wind, turns to a crow
When thou hold'st up thy hand. O, let me kiss
This princess of pure white, this seal of bliss!

Hel. O spite! O hell! I see you all are bent
To set against me for your merriment.
If you were civil and knew courtesy,
You would not do me thus much injury.
Can you not hate me, as I know you do,
But you must join in souls to mock me too?
If you were men, as men you are in show,
You would not use a gentle lady so;
To vow, and swear, and superpraise my parts,
When I am sure you hate me with your hearts.
You both are rivals, and love Hermia;
And now both rivals to mock Helena.
A trim exploit, a manly enterprise,
To conjure tears up in a poor maid's eyes
With your derision! None of noble sort
Would so offend a virgin and extort
A poor soul's patience, all to make you sport.

Lys. You are unkind, Demetrius. Be not so!
For you love Hermia. This you know I know;
And here, with all good will, with all my heart,
In Hermia's love I yield you up my part;
And yours of Helena to me bequeath,
Whom I do love, and will do to my death.

Hel. Never did mockers waste more idle breath.

Dem. Lysander, keep thy Hermia. I will none.
If e'er I lov'd her, all that love is gone.
My heart to her but as guestwise sojourn'd,
And now to Helen is it home return'd,
There to remain.

Lys. Helen, it is not so.

Dem. Disparage not the faith thou dost not know,
Lest, to thy peril, thou aby it dear.
Look where thy love comes. Yonder is thy dear.

Enter *Hermia*.

Her. Dark night, that from the eye his function takes,
The ear more quick of apprehension makes.
Wherein it doth impair the seeing sense,
It pays the hearing double recompense.
Thou art not by mine eye, Lysander, found;
Mine ear, I thank it, brought me to thy sound.
But why unkindly didst thou leave me so?

Lys. Why should he stay whom love doth press to go?

Her. What love could press Lysander from my side?

Lys. Lysander's love, that would not let him bide —
Fair Helena; who more engilds the night
Than all yon fiery oes and eyes of light.
Why seek'st thou me? Could not this make thee know,
The hate I bare thee made me leave thee so?

Her. You speak not as you think. It cannot be.

Hel. Lo, she is one of this confederacy!
Now I perceive they have conjoin'd all three
To fashion this false sport in spite of me.
Injurious Hermia! most ungrateful maid!
Have you conspir'd, have you with these contriv'd

To bait me with this foul derision?
Is all the counsel that we two have shar'd,
The sister's vows, the hours that we have spent
When we have chid the hasty-footed time
For parting us — O, is all forgot?
All schooldays friendship, childhood innocence?
We, Hermia, like two artificial gods,
Have with our needles created both one flower,
Both on one sampler, sitting on one cushion,
Both warbling of one song, both in one key;
As if our hands, our sides, voices, and minds
Had been incorporate. So we grew together,
Like to a double cherry, seeming parted,
But yet an union in partition —
Two lovely berries moulded on one stem;
So, with two seeming bodies, but one heart;
Two of the first, like coats in heraldry,
Due but to one, and crowned with one crest.
And will you rent our ancient love asunder,
To join with men in scorning your poor friend?
It is not friendly, 'tis not maidenly!
Our sex, as well as I, may chide you for it,
Though I alone do feel the injury.

Her. I am amazed at your passionate words.
I scorn you not. It seems that you scorn me.

Hel. Have you not set Lysander, as in scorn,
To follow me and praise my eyes and face?
And made your other love, Demetrius
(Who even but now did spurn me with his foot),
To call me goddess, nymph, divine, and rare,
Precious, celestial? Wherefore speaks he this
To her he hates? And wherefore doth Lysander
Deny your love (so rich within his soul)
And tender me (forsooth) affection,
But by your setting on, by your consent?
What though I be not so in grace as you,
So hung upon with love, so fortunate;
But miserable most, to love unlov'd?
This you should pity rather than despise.

Her. I understand not what you mean by this.

Hel. Ay, do! persever, counterfeit sad looks;
Make mouths upon me when I turn my back;
Wink each at other; hold the sweet jest up.
This sport, well carried, shall be chronicled.
If you have any pity, grace, or manners,
You would not make me such an argument.
But fare ye well. 'Tis partly my own fault;
Which death or absence soon shall remedy.

Lys. Stay, gentle Helena; hear my excuse,
My love, my life, my soul, fair Helena!

Hel. O excellent!

Her. Sweet, do not scorn her so.

Dem. If she cannot entreat, I can compel.

Lys. Thou canst compel no more than she entreat.
Thy threats have no more strength than her weak prayers.
Helen, I love thee; by my life, I do!
I swear by that which I will lose for thee
To prove him false that says I love thee not.

Dem. I say I love thee more than he can do.

Lys. If thou say so, withdraw and prove it too.

Dem. Quick, come!

Her. Lysander, whereto tends all this?

Lys. Away, you Ethiope!

Dem. No, no, sir! You
Seem to break loose, take on as you would follow,
But yet come not. You are a tame man, go!

Lys. Hang off, thou cat, thou burr! Vile thing, let loose,
Or I will shake thee from me like a serpent!

Her. Why are you grown so rude? What change is this,
Sweet love?

Lys. Thy love? Out, tawny Tartar, out!
Out, loathed med'cine! O hated potion, hence!

Her. Do you not jest?

Hel. Yes, sooth! and so do you.

Lys. Demetrius, I will keep my word with thee.

Dem. I would I had your bond; for I perceive
A weak bond holds you. I'll not trust your word.

Lys. What, should I hurt her, strike her, kill her dead?
Although I hate her, I'll not harm her so.

Her. What, can you do me greater harm than hate?
Hate me? Wherefore? O me! what news, my love?
Am not I Hermia? Are not you Lysander?
I am as fair now as I was erewhile.
Since night you lov'd me; yet since night you left me.
Why then, you left me (O, the gods forbid!)
In earnest, shall I say?

Lys. Ay, by my life!
And never did desire to see thee more.
Therefore be out of hope, of question, doubt;
Be certain! Nothing truer. 'Tis no jest
That I do hate thee, and love Helena.

Her. O me! you juggler! you canker blossom!
You thief of love! What, have you come by night
And stol'n my love's heart from him?

Hel. Fine, i' faith!
Have you no modesty, no maiden shame,
No touch of bashfulness? What, will you tear
Impatient answers from my gentle tongue?
Fie, fie! you counterfeit, you puppet you!
Her. Puppet? Why, so! Ay, that way goes the game.
Now I perceive that she hath made compare
Between our statures; she hath urg'd her height,
And with her personage, her tall personage,
Her height (forsooth), she hath prevail'd with him.
And are you grown so high in his esteem
Because I am so dwarfish and so low?
How low am I, thou painted maypole? Speak!
How low am I? I am not yet so low
But that my nails can reach unto thine eyes.
Hel. I pray you, though you mock me, gentlemen,
Let her not hurt me. I was never curst;
I have no gift at all in shrewishness;
I am a right maid for my cowardice.
Let her not strike me. You perhaps may think,
Because she is something lower than myself,
That I can match her.
Her. Lower? Hark again!
Hel. Good Hermia, do not be so bitter with me.
I evermore did love you, Hermia,
Did ever keep your counsels, never wrong'd you;
Save that, in love unto Demetrius,
I told him of your stealth unto this wood.
He followed you; for love I followed him;
But he hath chid me hence, and threat'ned me
To strike me, spurn me; nay, to kill me too.
And now, so you will let me quiet go,
To Athens will I bear my folly back
And follow you no further. Let me go.
You see how simple and how fond I am.
Her. Why, get you gone! Who is't that hinders you?
Hel. A foolish heart, that I leave here behind.
Her. What, with Lysander?
Hel. With Demetrius.
Lys. Be not afraid. She shall not harm thee, Helena.
Dem. No, sir, she shall not, though you take her part.
Hel. O, when she is angry, she is keen and shrewd!
She was a vixen when she went to school;
And though she be but little, she is fierce.
Her. 'Little' again? nothing but 'low' and 'little'?
Why will you suffer her to flout me thus?
Let me come to her.
Lys. Get you gone, you dwarf!
You minimus, of hind'ring knotgrass made!
You bead, you acorn!
Dem. You are too officious
In her behalf that scorns your services.
Let her alone. Speak not of Helena;
Take not her part; for if thou dost intend
Never so little show of love to her,
Thou shalt aby it.
Lys. Now she holds me not.
Now follow, if thou dar'st, to try whose right,
Of thine or mine, is most in Helena.
Dem. Follow? Nay, I'll go with thee, cheek by jowl.
Exeunt Lysander and Demetrius.
Her. You, mistress, all this coil is long of you.
Nay, go not back.
Hel. I will not trust you, I,
Nor longer stay in your curst company.
Your hands than mine are quicker for a fray;
My legs are longer though, to run away. [*Exit.*]
Her. I am amaz'd, and know not what to say.
Exit.
Ob. This is thy negligence. Still thou mistak'st,
Or else committ'st thy knaveries wilfully.
Puck. Believe me, king of shadows, I mistook.
Did not you tell me I should know the man
By the Athenian garments he had on?
And so far blameless proves my enterprise
That I have 'nointed an Athenian's eyes;
And so far am I glad it so did sort
As this their jangling I esteem a sport.
Ob. Thou seest these lovers seek a place to fight.
Hie therefore, Robin, overcast the night.
The starry welkin cover thou anon
With drooping fog as black as Acheron,
And lead these testy rivals so astray
As one come not within another's way.
Like to Lysander sometime frame thy tongue,
Then stir Demetrius up with bitter wrong;
And sometime rail thou like Demetrius.
And from each other look thou lead them thus
Till o'er their brows death-counterfeiting sleep
With leaden legs and batty wings doth creep.
Then crush this herb into Lysander's eye;
Whose liquor hath this virtuous property,
To take from thence all error with his might
And make his eyeballs roll with wonted sight.
When they next wake, all this derision
Shall seem a dream and fruitless vision;

And back to Athens shall the lovers wend
With league whose date till death shall never end.
Whiles I in this affair do thee employ,
I'll to my queen and beg her Indian boy;
And then I will her charmed eye release
From monster's view, and all things shall be peace.

Puck. My fairy lord, this must be done with haste,
For night's swift dragons cut the clouds full fast,
And yonder shines Aurora's harbinger;
At whose approach ghosts, wand'ring here and there,
Troop home to churchyards; damned spirits all,
That in crossways and floods have burial,
Already to their wormy beds are gone.
For fear lest day should look their shames upon,
They wilfully themselves exile from light,
And must for aye consort with black-brow'd night.

Ob. But we are spirits of another sort.
I with the Morning's love have oft made sport;
And, like a forester, the groves may tread
Even till the eastern gate, all fiery red,
Opening on Neptune, with fair blessed beams
Turns into yellow gold his salt green streams.
But notwithstanding, haste; make no delay.
We may effect this business yet ere day. [*Exit.*]

Puck. Up and down, up and down,
I will lead them up and down.
I am fear'd in field and town.
Goblin, lead them up and down.
Here comes one.

Enter *Lysander.*

Lys. Where art thou, proud Demetrius? Speak thou now.

Rob. Here, villain, drawn and ready. Where art thou?

Lys. I will be with thee straight.

Rob. Follow me then
To plainer ground.

[*Exit Lysander.*]

Enter *Demetrius.*

Dem. Lysander, speak again!
Thou runaway, thou coward, art thou fled?
Speak! In some bush? Where dost thou hide thy head?

Rob. Thou coward, art thou bragging to the stars,
Telling the bushes that thou look'st for wars,
And wilt not come? Come, recreant! come, thou child!
I'll whip thee with a rod. He is defil'd
That draws a sword on thee.

Dem. Yea, art thou there?

Rob. Follow my voice. We'll try no manhood here. *Exeunt.*

[Enter *Lysander.*]

Lys. He goes before me and still dares me on;
When I come where he calls, then he is gone.
The villain is much lighter-heel'd than I.
I followed fast, but faster he did fly,
That fallen am I in dark uneven way,
And here will rest me. (*Lie down.*) Come, thou gentle day!
For if but once thou show me thy grey light,
I'll find Demetrius and revenge this spite.
[*Sleeps.*]

Enter *Robin* and *Demetrius.*

Rob. Ho, ho, ho! Coward, why com'st thou not?

Dem. Abide me, if thou dar'st; for well I wot
Thou run'st before me, shifting every place,
And dar'st not stand nor look me in the face.
Where art thou now?

Rob. Come hither. I am here.

Dem. Nay then, thou mock'st me. Thou shalt buy this dear
If ever I thy face by daylight see.
Now, go thy way. Faintness constraineth me
To measure out my length on this cold bed.
By day's approach look to be visited.
[*Lies down and sleeps.*]

Enter *Helena.*

Hel. O weary night, O long and tedious night,
Abate thy hours! Shine comforts from the East,
That I may back to Athens by daylight
From these that my poor company detest;
And sleep, that sometimes shuts up sorrow's eye,
Steal me awhile from mine own company.
Sleep.

Rob. Yet but three? Come one more.
Two of both kinds makes up four.
Here she comes, curst and sad.
Cupid is a knavish lad
Thus to make poor females mad.

Enter *Hermia.*

Her. Never so weary, never so in woe;
Bedabbled with the dew, and torn with briers;
I can no further crawl, no further go;
My legs can keep no pace with my desires.
Here will I rest me till the break of day.
Heavens shield Lysander, if they mean a fray!
[*Lies down and sleeps.*]

Rob. On the ground
Sleep sound.
I'll apply
To your eye,
Gentle lover, remedy.
[*Squeezes the herb on Lysander's eyelids.*]
When thou wak'st,
Thou tak'st
True delight
In the sight
Of thy former lady's eye;
And the country proverb known,
That every man should take his own,
In your waking shall be shown:
Jack shall have Jill;
Naught shall go ill;
The man shall have his mare again, and all shall be well. [*Exit.*]

ACT IV. [Scene I. *The wood.* Lysander, Demetrius, Helena, *and* Hermia, *all lying asleep.*]

Enter [*Titania,*] *Queen of Fairies,* and [*Bottom the*] *Clown* and *Fairies,* [*Peaseblossom, Cobweb, Moth, Mustardseed,* and others]; and the *King,* [*Oberon,*] behind them.

Tita. Come, sit thee down upon this flow'ry bed,
While I thy amiable cheeks do coy,
And stick musk-roses in thy sleek smooth head,
And kiss thy fair large ears, my gentle joy.

Bot. Where's Peaseblossom?

Peas. Ready.

Bot. Scratch my head, Peaseblossom. Where's Mounsieur Cobweb?

Cob. Ready.

Bot. Mounsieur Cobweb, good mounsieur, get you your weapons in your hand, and kill me a red-hipp'd humblebee on the top of a thistle; and, good mounsieur, bring me the honey-bag. Do not fret yourself too much in the action, mounsieur; and, good mounsieur, have a care the honey-bag break not. I would be loath to have you overflowen with a honey-bag, signior. Where's Mounsieur Mustardseed?

Mus. Ready.

Bot. Give me your neaf, Mounsieur Mustardseed. Pray you, leave your curtsy, good mounsieur.

Mus. What's your will?

Bot. Nothing, good mounsieur, but to help Cavalery Peaseblossom to scratch. I must to the barber's, mounsieur; for methinks I am marvail's hairy about the face; and I am such a tender ass, if my hair do but tickle me, I must scratch.

Tita. What, wilt thou hear some music, my sweet love?

Bot. I have a reasonable good ear in music. Let's have the tongs and the bones.

Tita. Or say, sweet love, what thou desirest to eat.

Bot. Truly, a peck of provender. I could munch your good dry oats. Methinks I have a great desire to a bottle of hay. Good hay, sweet hay, hath no fellow.

Tita. I have a venturous fairy that shall seek
The squirrel's hoard, and fetch thee thence new nuts.

Bot. I had rather have a handful or two of dried pease. But I pray you, let none of your people stir me. I have an exposition of sleep come upon me.

Tita. Sleep thou, and I will wind thee in my arms.
Fairies, be gone, and be all ways away.
[*Exeunt Fairies.*]
So doth the woodbine the sweet honeysuckle
Gently entwist; the female ivy so
Enrings the barky fingers of the elm.
O, how I love thee! how I dote on thee!
[*They sleep.*]

Enter *Robin Goodfellow.*

Ob. [*advances*] Welcome, good Robin. Seest thou this sweet sight?
Her dotage now I do begin to pity;
For, meeting her of late behind the wood,
Seeking sweet favours for this hateful fool,
I did upbraid her and fall out with her.
For she his hairy temples then had rounded
With coronet of fresh and fragrant flowers;
And that same dew which sometime on the buds
Was wont to swell like round and orient pearls
Stood now within the pretty flouriets' eyes,
Like tears that did their own disgrace bewail.
When I had at my pleasure taunted her,
And she in mild terms begg'd my patience,
I then did ask of her her changeling child;
Which straight she gave me, and her fairy sent
To bear him to my bower in fairyland.
And now I have the boy, I will undo

This hateful imperfection of her eyes.
And, gentle Puck, take this transformed scalp
From off the head of this Athenian swain;
That, he awaking when the other do,
May all to Athens back again repair,
And think no more of this night's accidents
But as the fierce vexation of a dream.
But first I will release the Fairy Queen.
    Be as thou wast wont to be;
    See as thou wast wont to see.
    Dian's bud o'er Cupid's flower
    Hath such force and blessed power.
Now, my Titania! Wake you, my sweet queen.
  Tita. My Oberon, what visions have I seen!
Methought I was enamour'd of an ass.
  Ob. There lies your love.
  Tita. How came these things to pass?
O, how mine eyes do loathe his visage now!
  Ob. Silence awhile. Robin, take off this head.
Titania, music call; and strike more dead
Than common sleep of all these five the sense.
  Tita. Music, ho, music! such as charmeth sleep!
  Rob. Now, when thou wak'st, with thine own fool's eyes peep.
  Ob. Sound, music! [*Music.*]
    Come, my queen, take hands with me.
And rock the ground whereon these sleepers be.
[*Dance.*]
Now thou and I are new in amity,
And will to-morrow midnight solemnly
Dance in Duke Theseus' house triumphantly
And bless it to all fair prosperity.
There shall the pairs of faithful lovers be
Wedded, with Theseus, all in jollity.
  Rob. Fairy King, attend and mark.
    I do hear the morning lark.
  Ob. Then, my queen, in silence sad
    Trip we after night's shade.
    We the globe can compass soon,
    Swifter than the wand'ring moon.
  Tita. Come, my lord, and in our flight
    Tell me how it came this night
    That I sleeping here was found
    With these mortals on the ground.
Exeunt.

Wind horn.

Enter *Theseus* and all his *Train*; [*Hippolyta, Egeus*].

  The. Go, one of you, find out the forester;
For now our observation is perform'd;
And since we have the vaward of the day,
My love shall hear the music of my hounds.
Uncouple in the western valley; let them go.
Dispatch, I say, and find the forester.
[*Exit an Attendant.*]
We will, fair Queen, up to the mountain's top
And mark the musical confusion
Of hounds and echo in conjunction.
  Hip. I was with Hercules and Cadmus once
When in a wood of Crete they bay'd the bear
With hounds of Sparta. Never did I hear
Such gallant chiding; for, besides the groves,
The skies, the fountains, every region near
Seem'd all one mutual cry. I never heard
So musical a discord, such sweet thunder.
  The. My hounds are bred out of the Spartan kind;
So flew'd, so sanded; and their heads are hung
With ears that sweep away the morning dew;
Crook-knee'd, and dew-lapp'd like Thessalian bulls;
Slow in pursuit, but match'd in mouth like bells,
Each under each. A cry more tuneable
Was never holloa'd to nor cheer'd with horn
In Crete, in Sparta, nor in Thessaly.
Judge when you hear. But, soft! What nymphs are these?
  Ege. My lord, this is my daughter here asleep;
And this, Lysander; this Demetrius is;
This Helena, old Nedar's Helena.
I wonder of their being here together.
  The. No doubt they rose up early to observe
The rite of May; and, hearing our intent,
Came here in grace of our solemnity.
But speak, Egeus. Is not this the day
That Hermia should give answer of her choice?
  Ege. It is, my lord.
  The. Go, bid the huntsmen wake them with their horns.
[*Exit an Attendant.*] *Shout within. Wind horns. They all start up.*
Good morrow, friends. Saint Valentine is past.
Begin these woodbirds but to couple now?
  Lys. Pardon, my lord. [*They kneel.*]
  The. I pray you all, stand up.
I know you two are rival enemies.
How comes this gentle concord in the world
That hatred is so far from jealousy
To sleep by hate and fear no enmity?
  Lys. My lord, I shall reply amazedly,
Half sleep, half waking; but as yet, I swear,
I cannot truly say how I came here;
But, as I think (for truly would I speak).
And now I do bethink me, so it is —
I came with Hermia hither. Our intent
Was to be gone from Athens, where we might.
Without the peril of the Athenian law —

Ege. Enough, enough, my lord! you have enough.
I beg the law, the law, upon his head.
They would have stol'n away; they would, Demetrius!
Thereby to have defeated you and me —
You of your wife, and me of my consent,
Of my consent that she should be your wife.

Dem. My lord, fair Helen told me of their stealth,
Of this their purpose hither, to this wood;
And I in fury hither followed them,
Fair Helena in fancy following me.
But, my good lord, I wot not by what power
(But by some power it is) my love to Hermia,
Melted as the snow, seems to me now
As the remembrance of an idle gaud
Which in my childhood I did dote upon;
And all the faith, the virtue of my heart,
The object and the pleasure of mine eye,
Is only Helena. To her, my lord,
Was I betroth'd ere I saw Hermia;
But, like a sickness, did I loathe this food;
But, as in health, come to my natural taste,
Now I do wish it, love it, long for it,
And will for evermore be true to it.

The. Fair lovers, you are fortunately met.
Of this discourse we more will hear anon.
Egeus, I will overbear your will;
For in the temple, by-and-by, with us,
These couples shall eternally be knit;
And, for the morning now is something worn,
Our purpos'd hunting shall be set aside.
Away, with us to Athens! Three and three,
We'll hold a feast in great solemnity.
Come, Hippolyta.

Exeunt Duke [Theseus, Hippolyta, Egeus,] and Lords.

Dem. These things seem small and undistinguishable,
Like far-off mountains turned into clouds.

Her. Methinks I see these things with parted eye,
When everything seems double.

Hel. So methinks;
And I have found Demetrius like a jewel,
Mine own, and not mine own.

Dem. Are you sure
That we are awake? It seems to me
That yet we sleep, we dream. Do not you think
The Duke was here, and bid us follow him?

Her. Yea, and my father.

Hel. And Hippolyta.

Lys. And he did bid us follow to the temple.

Dem. Why then, we are awake. Let's follow him,
And by the way let us recount our dreams.

Exeunt.

Bot. (*wakes*) When my cue comes, call me, and I will answer. My next is 'Most fair Pyramus.' Hey-ho! Peter Quince! Flute the bellows-mender! Snout the tinker! Starveling! God's my life! Stol'n hence, and left me asleep! I have had a most rare vision. I have had a dream, past the wit of man to say what dream it was. Man is but an ass if he go about to expound this dream. Methought I was — there is no man can tell what. Methought I was, and methought I had — But man is but a patch'd fool if he will offer to say what methought I had. The eye of man hath not heard, the ear of man hath not seen, man's hand is not able to taste, his tongue to conceive, nor his heart to report what my dream was. I will get Peter Quince to write a ballet of this dream. It shall be call'd 'Bottom's Dream,' because it hath no bottom; and I will sing it in the latter end of our play, before the Duke. Peradventure, to make it the more gracious, I shall sing it at her death. *Exit.*

[Scene II. *Athens.* Quince's *house.*]

Enter *Quince, Flute, Snout,* and *Starveling.*

Quince. Have you sent to Bottom's house? Is he come home yet?

Starv. He cannot be heard of. Out of doubt he is transported.

Flute. If he come not, then the play is marr'd; it goes not forward, doth it?

Quince. It is not possible. You have not a man in all Athens able to discharge Pyramus but he.

Flute. No, he hath simply the best wit of any handicraft man in Athens.

Quince. Yea, and the best person too, and he is a very paramour for a sweet voice.

Flute. You must say 'paragon.' A paramour is (God bless us!) a thing of naught.

Enter *Snug the Joiner.*

Snug. Masters, the Duke is coming from the temple, and there is two or three lords and ladies more married. If our sport had gone forward, we had all been made men.

Flute. O sweet bully Bottom! Thus hath he lost sixpence a day during his life. He could not have scaped sixpence a day. An the Duke had not given him sixpence a day for playing Pyramus, I'll be hanged! He would have deserved it. Sixpence a day in Pyramus, or nothing!

Enter *Bottom.*

Bot. Where are these lads? Where are these hearts?

Quince. Bottom! O most courageous day! O most happy hour!

Bot. Masters, I am to discourse wonders; but ask me not what. For if I tell you, I am no true Athenian. I will tell you everything, right as it fell out.

Quince. Let us hear, sweet Bottom.

Bot. Not a word of me. All that I will tell you is, that the Duke hath dined. Get your apparel together, good strings to your beards, new ribbands to your pumps; meet presently at the palace; every man look o'er his part; for the short and the long is, our play is preferr'd. In any case, let Thisby have clean linen; and let not him that plays the lion pare his nails, for they shall hang out for the lion's claws. And, most dear actors, eat no onions nor garlic, for we are to utter sweet breath; and I do not doubt but to hear them say it is a sweet comedy. No more words. Away! go, away! *Exeunt.*

ACT V. [Scene I. *Athens. The Palace of* Theseus.]

Enter *Theseus, Hippolyta,* and *Philostrate,* [with *Lords* and *Attendants*].

Hip. 'Tis strange, my Theseus, that these lovers speak of.
The. More strange than true. I never may believe
These antique fables nor these fairy toys.
Lovers and madmen have such seething brains,
Such shaping fantasies, that apprehend
More than cool reason ever comprehends.
The lunatic, the lover, and the poet
Are of imagination all compact.
One sees more devils than vast hell can hold:
That is the madman. The lover, all as frantic,
Sees Helen's beauty in a brow of Egypt.
The poet's eye, in a fine frenzy rolling,
Doth glance from heaven to earth, from earth to heaven;
And as imagination bodies forth
The forms of things unknown, the poet's pen
Turns them to shapes, and gives to airy nothing
A local habitation and a name.
Such tricks hath strong imagination
That, if it would but apprehend some joy,
It comprehends some bringer of that joy;
Or in the night, imagining some fear,
How easy is a bush suppos'd a bear!
Hip. But all the story of the night told over,
And all their minds transfigur'd so together,
More witnesseth than fancy's images
And grows to something of great constancy;
But howsoever, strange and admirable.

Enter Lovers — *Lysander, Demetrius, Hermia,* and *Helena.*

The. Here come the lovers, full of joy and mirth.
Joy, gentle friends, joy and fresh days of love
Accompany your hearts!
Lys. More than to us
Wait in your royal walks, your board, your bed!
The. Come now, what masques, what dances shall we have,
To wear away this long age of three hours
Between our after-supper and bedtime?
Where is our usual manager of mirth?
What revels are in hand? Is there no play
To ease the anguish of a torturing hour?
Call Philostrate.
Phil. Here, mighty Theseus.
The. Say, what abridgment have you for this evening?
What masque? what music? How shall we beguile
The lazy time, if not with some delight?
Phil. There is a brief how many sports are ripe.
Make choice of which your Highness will see first. [*Gives a paper.*]
The. 'The battle with the Centaurs, to be sung
By an Athenian eunuch to the harp.'
We'll none of that. That have I told my love
In glory of my kinsman Hercules.
'The riot of the tipsy Bacchanals,
Tearing the Thracian singer in their rage.'
That is an old device; and it was play'd
When I from Thebes came last a conqueror.
'The thrice three Muses mourning for the death
Of Learning, late deceas'd in beggary.'
That is some satire keen and critical,
Not sorting with a nuptial ceremony.
'A tedious brief scene of young Pyramus
And his love Thisby; very tragical mirth.'
Merry and tragical? tedious and brief?

That is hot ice and wondrous strange snow.
How shall we find the concord of this discord?

Phil. A play there is, my lord, some ten words long,
Which is as brief as I have known a play;
But by ten words, my lord, it is too long,
Which makes it tedious; for in all the play
There is not one word apt, one player fitted.
And tragical, my noble lord, it is;
For Pyramus therein doth kill himself.
Which when I saw rehears'd, I must confess,
Made mine eyes water; but more merry tears
The passion of loud laughter never shed.

The. What are they that do play it?

Phil. Hard-handed men that work in Athens here,
Which never labour'd in their minds till now;
And now have toil'd their unbreathed memories
With this same play, against your nuptial.

The. And we will hear it.

Phil. No, my noble lord;
It is not for you. I have heard it over,
And it is nothing, nothing in the world;
Unless you can find sport in their intents,
Extremely stretch'd and conn'd with cruel pain,
To do you service.

The. I will hear that play;
For never anything can be amiss
When simpleness and duty tender it.
Go bring them in; and take your places, ladies.
[*Exit Philostrate.*]

Hip. I love not to see wretchedness o'ercharg'd,
And duty in his service perishing.

The. Why, gentle sweet, you shall see no such thing.

Hip. He says they can do nothing in this kind.

The. The kinder we, to give them thanks for nothing.
Our sport shall be to take what they mistake;
And what poor duty cannot do, noble respect
Takes it in might, not merit.
Where I have come, great clerks have purposed
To greet me with premeditated welcomes;
Where I have seen them shiver and look pale,
Make periods in the midst of sentences,
Throttle their practis'd accent in their fears,
And, in conclusion, dumbly have broke off,
Not paying me a welcome. Trust me, sweet,
Out of this silence yet I pick'd a welcome;
And in the modesty of fearful duty
I read as much as from the rattling tongue
Of saucy and audacious eloquence.
Love, therefore, and tongue-tied simplicity
In least speak most, to my capacity.

[Enter *Philostrate.*]

Phil. So please your Grace, the Prologue is address'd.

The. Let him approach.

Flourish trumpets. Enter the *Prologue* (*Quince*).

Pro. If we offend, it is with our good will.
That you should think, we come not to offend,
But with good will. To show our simple skill,
That is the true beginning of our end.
Consider then, we come but in despite.
We do not come, as minding to content you,
Our true intent is. All for your delight,
We are not here. That you should here repent you,
The actors are at hand: and, by their show,
You shall know all, that you are like to know.

The. This fellow doth not stand upon points.

Lys. He hath rid his prologue like a rough colt; he knows not the stop. A good moral, my lord: it is not enough to speak, but to speak true.

Hip. Indeed he hath play'd on his prologue like a child on a recorder — a sound, but not in government.

The. His speech was like a tangled chain; nothing impaired, but all disordered. Who is next?

Enter *Pyramus* and *Thisby*, and *Wall* and *Moonshine* and *Lion.*

Pro. Gentles, perchance you wonder at this show;
But wonder on, till truth make all things plain.
This man is Pyramus, if you would know;
This beauteous lady Thisby is certain.
This man, with lime and roughcast, doth present
Wall, that vile Wall which did these lovers sunder;
And through Wall's chink, poor souls, they are content
To whisper. At the which let no man wonder.
This man, with lantern, dog, and bush of thorn,
Presenteth Moonshine. For, if you will know,
By moonshine did these lovers think no scorn
To meet at Ninus' tomb, there, there to woo.
This grisly beast, which Lion hight by name,
The trusty Thisby, coming first by night,
Did scare away, or rather did affright;
And as she fled, her mantle she did fall,
Which Lion vile with bloody mouth did stain.
Anon comes Pyramus, sweet youth and tall,
And finds his trusty Thisby's mantle slain;
Whereat, with blade, with bloody blameful blade,
He bravely broach'd his boiling bloody breast.
And Thisby, tarrying in mulberry shade,
His dagger drew, and died. For all the rest,
Let Lion, Moonshine, Wall, and lovers twain
At large discourse while here they do remain.

The. I wonder if the lion be to speak.

Dem. No wonder, my lord. One lion may, when many asses do.

Exeunt [*Prologue, Pyramus,*] *Lion, Thisby, and Moonshine.*

Wall. In this same enterlude it doth befall
That I, one Snout by name, present a wall;
And such a wall, as I would have you think,
That had in it a crannied hole or chink;
Through which the lovers, Pyramus and Thisby,
Did whisper often, very secretly.
This loam, this roughcast, and this stone doth show
That I am that same wall. The truth is so.
And this the cranny is, right and sinister,
Through which the fearful lovers are to whisper.

The. Would you desire lime and hair to speak better?

Dem. It is the wittiest partition that ever I heard discourse, my lord.

Enter *Pyramus.*

The. Pyramus draws near the wall. Silence!

Pyr. O grim-look'd night! O night with hue so black!
O night, which ever art when day is not!
O night, O night! alack, alack, alack,
I fear my Thisby's promise is forgot!
And thou, O wall, O sweet, O lovely wall,
That stand'st between her father's ground and mine!
Thou wall, O wall, O sweet and lovely wall,
Show me thy chink, to blink through with mine eyne!

[*Wall holds up his fingers.*]

Thanks, courteous wall. Jove shield thee well for this!
But what see I? No Thisby do I see.
O wicked wall, through whom I see no bliss,
Curs'd be thy stones for thus deceiving me!

The. The wall, methinks, being sensible, should curse again.

Pyr. No, in truth, sir, he should not. 'Deceiving me' is Thisby's cue. She is to enter now, and I am to spy her through the wall. You shall see it will fall pat as I told you. Yonder she comes.

Enter *Thisby.*

This. O Wall, full often hast thou heard my moans
For parting my fair Pyramus and me!
My cherry lips have often kiss'd thy stones,
Thy stones with lime and hair knit up in thee.

Pyr. I see a voice. Now will I to the chink,
To spy an I can hear my Thisby's face.
Thisby!

This. My love! thou art my love, I think.

Pyr. Think what thou wilt, I am thy lover's grace;
And, like Limander, am I trusty still.

This. And I, like Helen, till the Fates me kill.

Pyr. Not Shafalus to Procrus was so true.

This. As Shafalus to Procrus, I to you.

Pyr. O, kiss me through the hole of this vile wall!

This. I kiss the wall's hole, not your lips at all.

Pyr. Wilt thou at Ninny's tomb meet me straightway?

This. Tide life, tide death, I come without delay.

[*Exeunt Pyramus and Thisby.*]

Wall. Thus have I, Wall, my part discharged so;
And, being done, thus Wall away doth go.

Exit.

The. Now is the mural down between the two neighbours.

Dem. No remedy, my lord, when walls are so wilful to hear without warning.

Hip. This is the silliest stuff that ever I heard.

The. The best in this kind are but shadows; and the worst are no worse, if imagination amend them.

Hip. It must be your imagination then, and not theirs.

The. If we imagine no worse of them than they of themselves, they may pass for excellent men. Here come two noble beasts in, a man and a lion.

Enter *Lion* and *Moonshine.*

Lion. You, ladies, you, whose gentle hearts do fear
The smallest monstrous mouse that creeps on floor,
May now perchance both quake and tremble here,
When lion rough in wildest rage doth roar.
Then know that I one Snug the joiner am,
A lion fell, nor else no lion's dam;
For, if I should as lion come in strife
Into this place, 'twere pity on my life.

The. A very gentle beast, and of a good conscience.

Dem. The very best at a beast, my lord, that e'er I saw.

Lys. This lion is a very fox for his valour.

The. True; and a goose for his discretion.

Dem. Not so, my lord; for his valour cannot carry his discretion, and the fox carries the goose.

The. His discretion, I am sure, cannot carry his valour; for the goose carries not the fox. It is well. Leave it to his discretion, and let us listen to the moon.

Moon. This lanthorn doth the horned moon present —

Dem. He should have worn the horns on his head.

The. He is no crescent, and his horns are invisible within the circumference.

Moon. This lanthorn doth the horned moon present.
Myself the man i' th' moon do seem to be.

The. This is the greatest error of all the rest. The man should be put into the lanthorn. How is it else the man i' th' moon?

Dem. He dares not come there for the candle; for, you see, it is already in snuff.

Hip. I am aweary of this moon. Would he would change!

The. It appears, by his small light of discretion, that he is in the wane; but yet, in courtesy, in all reason, we must stay the time.

Lys. Proceed, Moon.

Moon. All that I have to say is to tell you that the lanthorn is the moon; I, the man i' th' moon; this thornbush, my thornbush; and this dog, my dog.

Dem. Why, all these should be in the lanthorn; for all these are in the moon. But silence! Here comes Thisby.

Enter *Thisby.*

This. This is old Ninny's tomb. Where is my love?

Lion. O! *The Lion roars. Thisby runs off.*

Dem. Well roar'd, Lion!

The. Well run, Thisby!

Hip. Well shone, Moon! Truly, the moon shines with a good grace.

[*The Lion tears Thisby's mantle, and exit.*]

The. Well mous'd, Lion!

Dem. And then came Pyramus.

Lys. And so the lion vanish'd.

Enter *Pyramus.*

Pyr. Sweet moon, I thank thee for thy sunny beams;
I thank thee, moon, for shining now so bright;
For, by thy gracious, golden, glittering gleams,
I trust to take of truest Thisby sight.
But stay! O spite!
But mark, poor knight!
What dreadful dole is here?
Eyes, do you see?
How can it be?
O dainty duck! O dear!
Thy mantle good,
What, stain'd with blood?
Approach, ye Furies fell!
O Fates, come, come!
Cut thread and thrum;
Quail, crush, conclude, and quell!

The. This passion, and the death of a dear friend, would go near to make a man look sad.

Hip. Beshrew my heart but I pity the man.

Pyr. O, wherefore, Nature, didst thou lions frame?
Since lion vile hath here deflow'r'd my dear;
Which is — no, no! — which was the fairest dame
That liv'd, that lov'd, that lik'd, that look'd with cheer.
Come, tears, confound!
Out, sword, and wound
The pap of Pyramus!
Ay, that left pap
Where heart doth hop.
[*Stabs himself.*]
Thus die I, thus, thus, thus.
Now am I dead,
Now am I fled;
My soul is in the sky.
Tongue, lose thy light;
Moon, take thy flight.
[*Exit Moonshine.*]
Now die, die, die, die, die! [*Dies.*]

Dem. No die, but an ace, for him! for he is but one.

Lys. Less than an ace, man; for he is dead, he is nothing.

The. With the help of a surgeon he might yet recover, and yet prove an ass.

Hip. How chance Moonshine is gone before Thisby comes back and finds her lover?

Enter *Thisby.*

The. She will find him by starlight. Here she comes; and her passion ends the play.

Hip. Methinks she should not use a long one for such a Pyramus. I hope she will be brief.

Dem. A mote will turn the balance, which Pyramus, which Thisby, is the better; he for a man, God warr'nd us! — she for a woman, God bless us!

Lys. She hath spied him already with those sweet eyes.

Dem. And thus she means, videlicet:

This. Asleep, my love?
What, dead, my dove?
O Pyramus, arise!
Speak, speak! Quite dumb?
Dead, dead? A tomb
Must cover thy sweet eyes.
These lily lips,
This cherry nose,
These yellow cowslip cheeks,
Are gone, are gone.
Lovers, make moan!
His eyes were green as leeks.
O Sisters Three,
Come, come to me,
With hands as pale as milk;
Lay them in gore,
Since you have shore

With shears his thread of silk.
  Tongue, not a word!
  Come, trusty sword;
Come, blade, my breast imbrue!
[*Stabs herself.*]
  And farewell, friends.
  Thus Thisby ends.
Adieu, adieu, adieu! [*Dies.*]

The. Moonshine and Lion are left to bury the dead.

Dem. Ay, and Wall too.

Bot. [*starts up*] No, I assure you; the wall is down that parted their fathers. Will it please you to see the Epilogue, or to hear a Bergomask dance between two of our company?

The. No epilogue, I pray you; for your play needs no excuse. Never excuse; for when the players are all dead, there need none to be blamed. Marry, if he that writ it had played Pyramus and hang'd himself in Thisby's garter, it would have been a fine tragedy; and so it is truly, and very notably discharg'd. But, come, your Bergomask! Let your epilogue alone.
[*A dance.*]
The iron tongue of midnight hath told twelve.
Lovers, to bed; 'tis almost fairy time.
I fear we shall outsleep the coming morn
As much as we this night have overwatch'd.
This palpable gross play hath well beguil'd
The heavy gait of night. Sweet friends, to bed.
A fortnight hold we this solemnity
In nightly revels and new jollity. *Exeunt.*

Enter *Puck*, [with a broom].

Puck. Now the hungry lion roars,
  And the wolf behowls the moon;
Whilst the heavy ploughman snores,
  All with weary task fordone.
Now the wasted brands do glow,
  Whilst the screech owl, screeching loud,
Puts the wretch that lies in woe
  In remembrance of a shroud.
Now it is the time of night
  That the graves, all gaping wide,
Every one lets forth his sprite,
  In the churchway paths to glide;
And we fairies, that do run
  By the triple Hecate's team
From the presence of the sun,
  Following darkness like a dream,
Now are frolic. Not a mouse
Shall disturb this hallowed house.
I am sent, with broom, before,
To sweep the dust behind the door.

Enter *King* and *Queen of Fairies*, with all their *Train*.

Ob. Through the house give glimmering light,
  By the dead and drowsy fire;
Every elf and fairy sprite
  Hop as light as bird from brier;
And this ditty, after me,
Sing, and dance it trippingly.

Tita. First rehearse your song by rote,
To each word a warbling note.
Hand in hand, with fairy grace,
Will we sing, and bless this place.
[*Song and dance.*]

Ob. Now, until the break of day,
Through this house each fairy stray.
To the best bride-bed will we,
Which by us shall blessed be;
And the issue there create
Ever shall be fortunate.
So shall all the couples three
Ever true in loving be;
And the blots of Nature's hand
Shall not in their issue stand;
Never mole, harelip, nor scar,
Nor mark prodigious, such as are
Despised in nativity,
Shall upon their children be.
With this field-dew consecrate,
Every fairy take his gait,
And each several chamber bless,
Through this palace, with sweet peace.
And the owner of it blest
Ever shall in safety rest.
Trip away; make no stay;
Meet me all by break of day.
Exeunt [*all but Robin Goodfellow*].

Rob. If we shadows have offended,
Think but this, and all is mended —
That you have but slumb'red here
While these visions did appear.
And this weak and idle theme,
No more yielding but a dream,
Gentles, do not reprehend.
If you pardon, we will mend.
And, as I am an honest Puck,
If we have unearned luck
Now to scape the serpent's tongue,
We will make amends ere long;
Else the Puck a liar call.
So, good night unto you all.
Give me your hands, if we be friends,
And Robin shall restore amends.
[*Exit.*]

Enter King and Queen of Fairies, with all their Train.

Ob. Through the house give glimmering light,
By the dead and drowsy fire;
Every elf and fairy sprite
Hop as light as bird from brier;
And this ditty, after me,
Sing, and dance it trippingly.

Tita. First, rehearse your song by rote,
To each word a warbling note:
Hand in hand, with fairy grace,
Will we sing, and bless this place.
[*Song and dance.*

Ob. Now, until the break of day,
Through this house each fairy stray.
To the best bride-bed will we,
Which by us shall blessed be;
And the issue there create
Ever shall be fortunate.
So shall all the couples three
Ever true in loving be;
And the blots of Nature's hand
Shall not in their issue stand;
Never mole, hare lip, nor scar,
Nor mark prodigious, such as are
Despised in nativity,
Shall upon their children be.
With this field-dew consecrate,
Every fairy take his gait;
And each several chamber bless,
Through this palace, with sweet peace;
And the owner of it blest
Ever shall in safety rest.
Trip away; make no stay;
Meet me all by break of day.
[*Exeunt Oberon, Titania, and train.*

Puck. If we shadows have offended,
Think but this, and all is mended,
That you have but slumber'd here
While these visions did appear.
And this weak and idle theme,
No more yielding but a dream,
Gentles, do not reprehend:
If you pardon, we will mend:
And, as I am an honest Puck,
If we have unearned luck
Now to 'scape the serpent's tongue,
We will make amends ere long;
Else the Puck a liar call:
So, good night unto you all.
Give me your hands, if we be friends,
And Robin shall restore amends. [*Exit.*

The Merchant of Venice

The Merchant of Venice was entered in the Stationers' Register on July 22, 1598 ('a booke of the Marchaunt of Venyce, or otherwise called the Jewe of Venyce'), and again (without the alternative title) on October 28, 1600. In 1600 the First Quarto appeared. It furnishes a good text, on which the present edition is based. The Second Quarto (1619, fraudulently misdated 1600) and the First Folio go back to the First Quarto. For the composition of the play a reasonable date is 1596. Meres mentions it in 1598 (see p. 33, above).

Most of the plot comes in some fashion from the story of Giannetto, in *Il Pecorone* of Ser Giovanni Fiorentino (iv, 1), which dates from the last quarter of the fourteenth century but was not printed until 1558. Here we have the name Belmonte and the whole plot except for two features — The Choice of a Casket and the episode of Jessica. There are no caskets; to win the lady one must avoid a craftily administered sleeping potion. The twelfth-century *Dolopathos* by Joannes de Alta Silva affords a version like that in *Il Pecorone*, except for the concluding episode of the rings. Sleep is caused by an enchanted feather of an owl, laid under the suitor's pillow. From the *Dolopathos* comes the version in the Latin *Gesta Romanorum* (cap. 195; No. 40 in the English *Gesta* in the fifteenth-century Harleian MS. 7333).

The wooing story (without The Pound of Flesh) represents an ancient and wide-spread theme — The Winning of an Otherworld Wife — of which the tale of Ulysses and Circe is a variant. The ballad of *The Broomfield Hill* (Child, No. 43) and the Old French *Lai de Doon* belong in this same group.

The Pound of Flesh (without the wooing) is also old and has circulated extensively. In the Middle English *Cursor Mundi* it is worked into the legend of the discovery of the True Cross. It occurs in *Les Divers Propos Memorables* of Gilles Corrozet (1556), in the ballad of *The Crueltie of Gernutus* (earlier, probably, than 1590), and in *The Orator*, 'Englished by L. P.' (Lazarus Piot) from the *Histoires Tragiques* of Alexandre van den Busche (*alias* Sylvain) and published in 1596. There are striking resemblances between the language of Gernutus and Shylock's words in ii, 1, 139–152; and Shylock's argument in court has points in common with the Jew's oration in Piot.

The Choice of the Casket comes from the Orient. It had originally nothing to do with winning a wife but was used to illustrate the perverse judgment that prefers show to substance. From the legend of *Barlaam and Joasaph* it was taken in the thirteenth century by Vincent of Beauvais into his *Speculum Historiale* (xv, 10) and by Jacobus de Voragine into his *Legenda Aurea* (cap. 176). In several variants it found a place in mediæval collections of *exempla* (including the *Gesta Romanorum*), and Gower's *Confessio Amantis* repeats it in two forms (v, 2273–2434), neither of which agrees with that in the *Decameron* (x, 1). The *Speculum*, the *Golden Legend*, the *Decameron*, and the *Confessio Amantis* were all accessible to Shakespeare. So was at least one of the versions in the *Gesta* — that which appears in the English translation edited by Richard Robinson (1577). This is particularly interesting since the choice is applied to the winning of a husband and there are details that remind one of Shakespeare's play.

At this point we are confronted by one of those phantom plays that haunt the literary history of the Elizabethan age. Stephen Gosson, in his famous diatribe against the stage *The School of Abuse* (1579), describes a drama called *The Jew*, 'showne at the Bull,' as 'representing the greedinesse of worldly chusers, and bloody mindes of Usurers.' These phrases suggest that the plot anticipated Shakespeare in combining The Choice of the Casket with The Pound of Flesh. If he owed anything to *The Jew*, his indebtedness was doubtless limited to the substitution of the caskets for the dramatically unmanageable sleeping potion. Some scholars maintain, however, that THE MERCHANT OF VENICE is a rifacimento of *The Jew* (or of some derivative) worked up by Shakespeare in 1594 and revised by him a few years later. This is very improbable. William Wager's 'interlude of the Cruell Detter,' licensed in 1565 or 1566, is not likely to have been *The Jew*.

Anthony Munday combines the bond story with the winning of the usurer's daughter in Part III of his *Zelauto* (1580), but the episode is not very similar to that of Jessica. There is a story much like Jessica's in the 14th tale in *Le Cinquanta Novelle* (1541) of Masuccio Salernitano, who died *ca.* 1477. The girl (Charmosina) is the daughter of an avaricious old merchant (not a Jew). Perhaps no source for the Jessica episode need be sought beyond the rôle of Marlowe's Abigail in *The Jew of Malta*. That Shakespeare knew Marlowe's tragedy was a matter of course. Its influence is pervasively discernible and there are several points of special contact — in particular, the scene in which the daughter throws the treasure out of the window. But Jessica is not Abigail, and Shylock is not, like Barabas, a Machiavellian villain.

The name *Shylock* is thought to be the Hebrew *shalach*, translated by 'cormorant' in *Leviticus*, xi, 17, and *Deuteronomy*, xiv, 17. 'Away, thou moneymong'ring cormorant!' says Eutrapelus to the usurer Philargurus in the anonymous play of *Timon* (v, 5), which may date from 1590 or earlier. In *Coriolanus* (i, 1, 125) 'the cormorant belly' typifies the patricians who 'make edicts for usury, to support usurers.' *Jessica* seems to come from *Jesca* (*Iescha* in the Vulgate), a form of *Iscah*, the name of the daughter of Haran (*Genesis*, xi, 29), interpreted as 'she that looketh out.' This would fit ii, 5, 29 ff., where Shylock forbids Jessica to 'clamber up to the casements' and 'thrust her head into the public street to gaze on Christian fools,' and Launcelot prompts her to 'look out at a window, for all this.' Roderigo Lopez, Queen Elizabeth's physician, a converted Jew, was accused of plotting to poison her. Though probably innocent, he was executed for high treason on June 7, 1594. It is hard to see what this affair has to do with Shakespeare's play. *Lopez*, to be sure, resembles *lupus*, and Gratiano imagines Shylock's 'currish spirit' to be that of a wolf 'hang'd for human slaughter' since his 'desires are wolvish, bloody, starv'd and ravenous.' The character of Shylock fascinates critics and has lured them into endless mazes of debate. One thing is clear, however: THE MERCHANT OF VENICE is no anti-Semitic document; Shakespeare was not attacking the Jewish people when he gave Shylock the villain's rôle. If so, he was attacking the Moors in *Titus Andronicus*, the Spaniards in *Much Ado*, the Italians in *Cymbeline*, the Viennese in *Measure for Measure*, the Danes in *Hamlet*, the Britons in *King Lear*, the Scots in *Macbeth*, and the English in *Richard the Third*.

THE MERCHANT OF VENICE

[Dramatis Personæ.

The Duke of Venice.
The Prince of Morocco, } suitors to *Portia.*
The Prince of Arragon, }
Antonio, a Venetian merchant.
Bassanio, his friend, suitor to *Portia.*
Solanio, }
Salerio, } friends to *Antonio* and *Bassanio.*
Gratiano, }
Lorenzo, in love with *Jessica.*
Shylock, a Jew.
Tubal, a Jew, his friend.

Launcelot Gobbo, a clown, servant to *Shylock.*
Old Gobbo, father to *Launcelot.*
Leonardo, servant to *Bassanio.*
Balthasar, }
Stephano, } servants to *Portia.*

Portia, an heiress.
Nerissa, her waiting gentlewoman.
Jessica, daughter to *Shylock.*

Magnificoes, Officers, Jailer, Servants, and other Attendants.

SCENE. — *Partly at Venice and partly at Belmont, Portia's estate.*]

ACT I. [Scene I. *Venice. A street.*]

Enter *Antonio, Salerio,* and *Solanio.*

Ant. In sooth, I know not why I am so sad.
It wearies me; you say it wearies you;
But how I caught it, found it, or came by it,
What stuff 'tis made of, whereof it is born,
I am to learn;
And such a want-wit sadness makes of me
That I have much ado to know myself.
Saler. Your mind is tossing on the ocean;
There where your argosies with portly sail —
Like signiors and rich burghers on the flood,
Or, as it were, the pageants of the sea —
Do overpeer the petty traffickers,
That cursy to them, do them reverence,
As they fly by them with their woven wings.
Solan. Believe me, sir, had I such venture forth,
The better part of my affections would
Be with my hopes abroad. I should be still
Plucking the grass to know where sits the wind,
Piring in maps for ports, and piers, and roads;
And every object that might make me fear
Misfortune to my ventures, out of doubt
Would make me sad.
Saler. My wind, cooling my broth,
Would blow me to an ague when I thought
What harm a wind too great might do at sea.
I should not see the sandy hourglass run
But I should think of shallows and of flats,
And see my wealthy Andrew dock'd in sand,
Vailing her high top lower than her ribs
To kiss her burial. Should I go to church
And see the holy edifice of stone
And not bethink me straight of dangerous rocks,
Which, touching but my gentle vessel's side,
Would scatter all her spices on the stream,
Enrobe the roaring waters with my silks,
And, in a word, but even now worth this,
And now worth nothing? Shall I have the thought
To think on this, and shall I lack the thought
That such a thing bechanc'd would make me sad?
But tell not me! I know Antonio
Is sad to think upon his merchandise.
Ant. Believe me, no. I thank my fortune for it,
My ventures are not in one bottom trusted,
Nor to one place; nor is my whole estate
Upon the fortune of this present year.
Therefore my merchandise makes me not sad.
Solan. Why, then you are in love.
Ant. Fie, fie!
Solan. Not in love neither? Then let us say you are sad
Because you are not merry; and 'twere as easy
For you to laugh, and leap, and say you are merry
Because you are not sad. Now, by two-headed Janus,
Nature hath fram'd strange fellows in her time:
Some that will evermore peep through their eyes,
And laugh like parrots at a bagpiper;
And other of such vinegar aspect

That they'll not show their teeth in way of smile,
Though Nestor swear the jest be laughable.

Enter *Bassanio, Lorenzo,* and *Gratiano.*

Here comes Bassanio, your most noble kinsman,
Gratiano, and Lorenzo. Fare ye well.
We leave you now with better company.

Saler. I would have stay'd till I had made you merry,
If worthier friends had not prevented me.

Ant. Your worth is very dear in my regard.
I take it your own business calls on you,
And you embrace th' occasion to depart.

Saler. Good morrow, my good lords.

Bass. Good signiors both, when shall we laugh? Say, when?
You grow exceeding strange. Must it be so?

Saler. We'll make our leisures to attend on yours. *Exeunt Salerio and Solanio.*

Lor. My Lord Bassanio, since you have found Antonio,
We two will leave you; but at dinner time
I pray you have in mind where we must meet.

Bass. I will not fail you.

Gra. You look not well, Signior Antonio.
You have too much respect upon the world;
They lose it that do buy it with much care.
Believe me, you are marvellously chang'd.

Ant. I hold the world but as the world, Gratiano —
A stage, where every man must play a part,
And mine a sad one.

Gra. Let me play the fool.
With mirth and laughter let old wrinkles come,
And let my liver rather heat with wine
Than my heart cool with mortifying groans.
Why should a man whose blood is warm within
Sit like his grandsire cut in alablaster?
Sleep when he wakes? and creep into the jaundice
By being peevish? I tell thee what, Antonio —
I love thee, and it is my love that speaks —
There are a sort of men whose visages
Do cream and mantle like a standing pond,
And do a wilful stillness entertain
With purpose to be dress'd in an opinion
Of wisdom, gravity, profound conceit;
As who should say, 'I am Sir Oracle,
And when I ope my lips, let no dog bark!'
O my Antonio, I do know of these
That therefore only are reputed wise
For saying nothing; when, I am very sure,
If they should speak, would almost damn those ears
Which, hearing them, would call their brothers fools.
I'll tell thee more of this another time.
But fish not with this melancholy bait
For this fool gudgeon, this opinion.
Come, good Lorenzo. Fare ye well awhile.
I'll end my exhortation after dinner.

Lor. Well, we will leave you then till dinner time.
I must be one of these same dumb wise men,
For Gratiano never lets me speak.

Gra. Well, keep me company but two years moe,
Thou shalt not know the sound of thine own tongue.

Ant. Fare you well. I'll grow a talker for this gear.

Gra. Thanks, i' faith; for silence is only commendable
In a neat's tongue dried and a maid not vendible. *Exeunt [Gratiano and Lorenzo].*

Ant. Is that anything now?

Bass. Gratiano speaks an infinite deal of nothing, more than any man in all Venice. His reasons are as two grains of wheat hid in two bushels of chaff. You shall seek all day ere you find them; and when you have them, they are not worth the search.

Ant. Well, tell me now, what lady is the same
To whom you swore a secret pilgrimage
That you to-day promis'd to tell me of?

Bass. 'Tis not unknown to you, Antonio,
How much I have disabled mine estate
By something showing a more swelling port
Than my faint means would grant continuance;
Nor do I now make moan to be abridg'd
From such a noble rate; but my chief care
Is to come fairly off from the great debts
Wherein my time, something too prodigal,
Hath left me gag'd. To you, Antonio,
I owe the most, in money and in love;
And from your love I have a warranty
To unburthen all my plots and purposes
How to get clear of all the debts I owe.

Ant. I pray you, good Bassanio, let me know it;
And if it stand, as you yourself still do,
Within the eye of honour, be assur'd
My purse, my person, my extremest means
Lie all unlock'd to your occasions.

Bass. In my schooldays, when I had lost one shaft,
I shot his fellow of the selfsame flight
The selfsame way with more advised watch,
To find the other forth; and by adventuring both

I oft found both. I urge this childhood proof
Because what follows is pure innocence.
I owe you much, and, like a wilful youth,
That which I owe is lost; but if you please
To shoot another arrow that self way
Which you did shoot the first, I do not doubt,
As I will watch the aim, or to find both,
Or bring your latter hazard back again
And thankfully rest debtor for the first.

Ant. You know me well, and herein spend but time
To wind about my love with circumstance;
And out of doubt you do me now more wrong
In making question of my uttermost
Than if you had made waste of all I have.
Then do but say to me what I should do
That in your knowledge may by me be done,
And I am prest unto it. Therefore speak.

Bass. In Belmont is a lady richly left;
And she is fair, and, fairer than that word,
Of wondrous virtues. Sometimes from her eyes
I did receive fair speechless messages.
Her name is Portia — nothing undervalu'd
To Cato's daughter, Brutus' Portia.
Nor is the wide world ignorant of her worth;
For the four winds blow in from every coast
Renowned suitors, and her sunny locks
Hang on her temples like a golden fleece,
Which makes her seat of Belmont Colchos' strond,
And many Jasons come in quest of her.
O my Antonio, had I but the means
To hold a rival place with one of them,
I have a mind presages me such thrift
That I should questionless be fortunate!

Ant. Thou know'st that all my fortunes are at sea;
Neither have I money, nor commodity
To raise a present sum. Therefore go forth;
Try what my credit can in Venice do.
That shall be rack'd, even to the uttermost,
To furnish thee to Belmont to fair Portia.
Go presently enquire, and so will I,
Where money is; and I no question make
To have it of my trust, or for my sake. *Exeunt.*

[Scene II. *Belmont.* Portia's *house.*]

Enter *Portia* with her waiting woman, *Nerissa.*

Por. By my troth, Nerissa, my little body is aweary of this great world.

Ner. You would be, sweet madam, if your miseries were in the same abundance as your good fortunes are; and yet, for aught I see, they are as sick that surfeit with too much as they that starve with nothing. It is no mean happiness, therefore, to be seated in the mean. Superfluity comes sooner by white hairs, but competency lives longer.

Por. Good sentences, and well pronounc'd.

Ner. They would be better if well followed.

Por. If to do were as easy as to know what were good to do, chapels had been churches, and poor men's cottages princes' palaces. It is a good divine that follows his own instructions. I can easier teach twenty what were good to be done than be one of the twenty to follow mine own teaching. The brain may devise laws for the blood, but a hot temper leaps o'er a cold decree: such a hare is madness the youth, to skip o'er the meshes of good counsel the cripple. But this reasoning is not in the fashion to choose me a husband. O me, the word 'choose'! I may neither choose who I would nor refuse who I dislike, so is the will of a living daughter curb'd by the will of a dead father. Is it not hard, Nerissa, that I cannot choose one nor refuse none?

Ner. Your father was ever virtuous; and holy men at their death have good inspirations. Therefore the lott'ry that he hath devised in these three chests of gold, silver, and lead, whereof who chooses his meaning chooses you, will no doubt never be chosen by any rightly but one who you shall rightly love. But what warmth is there in your affection towards any of these princely suitors that are already come?

Por. I pray thee overname them; and as thou namest them, I will describe them; and according to my description level at my affection.

Ner. First, there is the Neapolitan prince.

Por. Ay, that's a colt indeed, for he doth nothing but talk of his horse; and he makes it a great appropriation to his own good parts that he can shoe him himself. I am much afeard my lady his mother play'd false with a smith.

Ner. Then is there the County Palatine.

Por. He doth nothing but frown; as who should say, 'An you will not have me, choose!' He hears merry tales and smiles not. I fear he will prove the weeping philosopher when he grows old, being so full of unmannerly sadness in his youth. I had rather be married to a death's-head with a bone in his mouth than to either of these. God defend me from these two!

Ner. How say you by the French lord, Monsieur Le Bon?

Por. God made him, and therefore let him pass for a man. In truth, I know it is a sin to be a mocker; but he — why, he hath a horse better than the Neapolitan's, a better bad habit of frowning than the Count Palatine. He is every man in no man. If a throstle sing, he falls straight a-cap'ring; he will fence with his own shadow. If I should marry him, I should marry twenty husbands. If he would despise me, I would forgive him; for if he love me to madness, I shall never requite him.

Ner. What say you then to Falconbridge, the young baron of England?

Por. You know I say nothing to him; for he understands not me, nor I him. He hath neither Latin, French, nor Italian; and you will come into the court and swear that I have a poor pennyworth in the English. He is a proper man's picture; but alas! who can converse with a dumb-show? How oddly he is suited! I think he bought his doublet in Italy, his round hose in France, his bonnet in Germany, and his behaviour everywhere.

Ner. What think you of the Scottish lord, his neighbour?

Por. That he hath a neighbourly charity in him; for he borrowed a box of the ear of the Englishman, and swore he would pay him again when he was able. I think the Frenchman became his surety and seal'd under for another.

Ner. How like you the young German, the Duke of Saxony's nephew?

Por. Very vilely in the morning, when he is sober, and most vilely in the afternoon, when he is drunk. When he is best, he is a little worse than a man; and when he is worst, he is little better than a beast. An the worst fall that ever fell, I hope I shall make shift to go without him.

Ner. If he should offer to choose, and choose the right casket, you should refuse to perform your father's will if you should refuse to accept him.

Por. Therefore, for fear of the worst, I pray thee set a deep glass of Rhenish wine on the contrary casket; for, if the devil be within and that temptation without, I know he will choose it. I will do anything, Nerissa, ere I will be married to a sponge.

Ner. You need not fear, lady, the having any of these lords. They have acquainted me with their determinations; which is indeed to return to their home, and to trouble you with no more suit, unless you may be won by some other sort than your father's imposition, depending on the caskets.

Por. If I live to be as old as Sibylla, I will die as chaste as Diana unless I be obtained by the manner of my father's will. I am glad this parcel of wooers are so reasonable, for there is not one among them but I dote on his very absence; and I pray God grant them a fair departure.

Ner. Do you not remember, lady, in your father's time, a Venetian, a scholar and a soldier, that came hither in company of the Marquis of Montferrat?

Por. Yes, yes, it was Bassanio. As I think, so was he call'd.

Ner. True, madam. He, of all the men that ever my foolish eyes look'd upon, was the best deserving a fair lady.

Por. I remember him well, and I remember him worthy of thy praise.

Enter a *Servingman.*

How now? What news?

Serv. The four strangers seek for you, madam, to take their leave; and there is a forerunner come from a fifth, the Prince of Morocco, who brings word the Prince his master will be here to-night.

Por. If I could bid the fifth welcome with so good heart as I can bid the other four farewell, I should be glad of his approach. If he have the condition of a saint and the complexion of a devil, I had rather he should shrive me than wive me.

Come, Nerissa. Sirrah, go before.
Whiles we shut the gate upon one wooer, another knocks at the door. *Exeunt.*

[Scene III. *Venice. A public place.*]

Enter *Bassanio* with *Shylock the Jew.*

Shy. Three thousand ducats — well.

Bass. Ay, sir, for three months.

Shy. For three months — well.

Bass. For the which, as I told you, Antonio shall be bound.

Shy. Antonio shall become bound — well.

Bass. May you stead me? Will you pleasure me? Shall I know your answer?

Shy. Three thousand ducats for three months, and Antonio bound.

Bass. Your answer to that.

Shy. Antonio is a good man.

Bass. Have you heard any imputation to the contrary?

Shy. Ho, no, no, no, no! My meaning in saying he is a good man is to have you understand me that he is sufficient. Yet his means are in supposition. He hath an argosy bound to

Tripolis, another to the Indies. I understand, moreover, upon the Rialto, he hath a third at Mexico, a fourth for England, and other ventures he hath, squand'red abroad. But ships are but boards, sailors but men; there be land rats and water rats, land thieves and water thieves — I mean pirates; and then there is the peril of waters, winds, and rocks. The man is, notwithstanding, sufficient. Three thousand ducats. I think I may take his bond.

Bass. Be assur'd you may.

Shy. I will be assur'd I may; and, that I may be assured, I will bethink me. May I speak with Antonio?

Bass. If it please you to dine with us.

Shy. Yes, to smell pork, to eat of the habitation which your prophet the Nazarite conjured the devil into! I will buy with you, sell with you, talk with you, walk with you, and so following; but I will not eat with you, drink with you, nor pray with you. What news on the Rialto? Who is he comes here?

Enter *Antonio.*

Bass. This is Signior Antonio.

Shy. [*aside*] How like a fawning publican he looks!
I hate him for he is a Christian;
But more for that in low simplicity
He lends out money gratis and brings down
The rate of usance here with us in Venice.
If I can catch him once upon the hip,
I will feed fat the ancient grudge I bear him.
He hates our sacred nation, and he rails,
Even there where merchants most do congregate,
On me, my bargains, and my well-won thrift,
Which he calls interest. Cursed be my tribe
If I forgive him!

Bass. Shylock, do you hear?

Shy. I am debating of my present store,
And by the near guess of my memory
I cannot instantly raise up the gross
Of full three thousand ducats. What of that?
Tubal, a wealthy Hebrew of my tribe,
Will furnish me. But soft! How many months
Do you desire? — [*To Antonio*] Rest you fair, good signior!
Your worship was the last man in our mouths.

Ant. Shylock, albeit I neither lend nor borrow
By taking nor by giving of excess,
Yet, to supply the ripe wants of my friend,
I'll break a custom. [*To Bassanio*] Is he yet possess'd
How much ye would?

Shy. Ay, ay, three thousand ducats.

Ant. And for three months.

Shy. I had forgot — three months, you told me so.
Well then, your bond. And let me see — but hear you:
Methoughts you said you neither lend nor borrow
Upon advantage.

Ant. I do never use it.

Shy. When Jacob graz'd his uncle Laban's sheep —
This Jacob from our holy Abram was
(As his wise mother wrought in his behalf)
The third possessor; ay, he was the third —

Ant. And what of him? Did he take interest?

Shy. No, not take interest; not, as you would say,
Directly int'rest. Mark what Jacob did.
When Laban and himself were compremis'd
That all the eanlings which were streak'd and pied
Should fall as Jacob's hire, the ewes, being rank,
In end of autumn turned to the rams;
And when the work of generation was
Between these woolly breeders in the act,
The skilful shepherd pill'd me certain wands,
And, in the doing of the deed of kind,
He stuck them up before the fulsome ewes,
Who then conceiving, did in eaning time
Fall parti-colour'd lambs, and those were Jacob's.
This was a way to thrive, and he was blest;
And thrift is blessing, if men steal it not.

Ant. This was a venture, sir, that Jacob serv'd for;
A thing not in his power to bring to pass,
But sway'd and fashion'd by the hand of heaven.
Was this inserted to make interest good?
Or is your gold and silver ewes and rams?

Shy. I cannot tell; I make it breed as fast.
But note me, signior.

Ant. [*aside*] Mark you this, Bassanio,
The devil can cite Scripture for his purpose.
An evil soul, producing holy witness,
Is like a villain with a smiling cheek,
A goodly apple rotten at the heart.
O, what a goodly outside falsehood hath!

Shy. Three thousand ducats — 'tis a good round sum.
Three months from twelve — then, let me see, the rate —

Ant. Well, Shylock, shall we be beholding to you?

Shy. Signior Antonio, many a time and oft
In the Rialto you have rated me
About my moneys and my usances.

Still have I borne it with a patient shrug;
For suff'rance is the badge of all our tribe.
You call me misbeliever, cutthroat dog,
And spet upon my Jewish gaberdine,
And all for use of that which is mine own.
Well then, it now appears you need my help.
Go to then, you come to me and you say,
'Shylock, we would have moneys.' You say so—
You that did void your rheum upon my beard
And foot me as you spurn a stranger cur
Over your threshold. Moneys is your suit.
What should I say to you? Should I not say
'Hath a dog money? Is it possible
A cur can lend three thousand ducats?' or
Shall I bend low, and in a bondman's key,
With bated breath and whisp'ring humbleness,
Say this:
'Fair sir, you spet on me on Wednesday last;
You spurn'd me such a day; another time
You call'd me dog; and for these courtesies
I'll lend you thus much moneys'?

Ant. I am as like to call thee so again,
To spet on thee again, to spurn thee too.
If thou wilt lend this money, lend it not
As to thy friends — for when did friendship take
A breed for barren metal of his friend?
But lend it rather to thine enemy,
Who if he break, thou mayst with better face
Exact the penalty.

Shy. Why, look you, how you storm!
I would be friends with you and have your love,
Forget the shames that you have stain'd me with,
Supply your present wants, and take no doit
Of usance for my moneys,
And you'll not hear me. This is kind I offer.

Bass. This were kindness.

Shy. This kindness will I show.
Go with me to a notary, seal me there
Your single bond; and, in a merry sport,
If you repay me not on such a day,
In such a place, such sum or sums as are
Express'd in the condition, let the forfeit
Be nominated for an equal pound
Of your fair flesh, to be cut off and taken
In what part of your body pleaseth me.

Ant. Content, in faith. I'll seal to such a bond,
And say there is much kindness in the Jew.

Bass. You shall not seal to such a bond for me!
I'll rather dwell in my necessity.

Ant. Why, fear not, man! I will not forfeit it.
Within these two months — that's a month before
This bond expires — I do expect return
Of thrice three times the value of this bond.

Shy. O father Abram, what these Christians are,
Whose own hard dealing teaches them suspect
The thoughts of others! Pray you tell me this:
If he should break his day, what should I gain
By the exaction of the forfeiture?
A pound of man's flesh taken from a man
Is not so estimable, profitable neither,
As flesh of muttons, beefs, or goats. I say,
To buy his favour I extend this friendship.
If he will take it, so; if not, adieu;
And for my love I pray you wrong me not.

Ant. Yes, Shylock, I will seal unto this bond.

Shy. Then meet me forthwith at the notary's;
Give him direction for this merry bond,
And I will go and purse the ducats straight,
See to my house, left in the fearful guard
Of an unthrifty knave, and presently
I will be with you.

Ant. Hie thee, gentle Jew. *Exit* [*Shylock*].
The Hebrew will turn Christian; he grows kind.

Bass. I like not fair terms and a villain's mind.

Ant. Come on. In this there can be no dismay;
My ships come home a month before the day.
Exeunt.

ACT II. [Scene I. *Belmont.* Portia's *house.*]

Enter [the *Prince of*] *Morocco*, a tawny Moor, all in white, and three or four *Followers* accordingly, with *Portia, Nerissa,* and their *Train.*

Mor. Mislike me not for my complexion,
The shadowed livery of the burnish'd sun,
To whom I am a neighbour and near bred.
Bring me the fairest creature northward born,
Where Phœbus' fire scarce thaws the icicles,
And let us make incision for your love
To prove whose blood is reddest, his or mine.
I tell thee, lady, this aspect of mine
Hath fear'd the valiant. By my love I swear,
The best-regarded virgins of our clime
Have lov'd it too. I would not change this hue,
Except to steal your thoughts, my gentle queen.

Por. In terms of choice I am not solely led
By nice direction of a maiden's eyes.
Besides, the lott'ry of my destiny
Bars me the right of voluntary choosing.
But, if my father had not scanted me,
And hedg'd me by his wit to yield myself
His wife who wins me by that means I told you,
Yourself, renowned Prince, then stood as fair
As any comer I have look'd on yet
For my affection.

Mor. Even for that I thank you.
Therefore I pray you lead me to the caskets
To try my fortune. By this scimitar,
That slew the Sophy and a Persian prince
That won three fields of Sultan Solyman,
I would o'erstare the sternest eyes that look,
Outbrave the heart most daring on the earth,
Pluck the young sucking cubs from the she-bear,
Yea, mock the lion when 'a roars for prey,
To win thee, lady. But, alas the while!
If Hercules and Lichas play at dice
Which is the better man, the greater throw
May turn by fortune from the weaker hand:
So is Alcides beaten by his page,
And so may I, blind Fortune leading me,
Miss that which one unworthier may attain,
And die with grieving.

Por. You must take your chance;
And either not attempt to choose at all,
Or swear before you choose, if you choose wrong,
Never to speak to lady afterward
In way of marriage. Therefore be advis'd.

Mor. Nor will not. Come, bring me unto my chance.

Por. First, forward to the temple; after dinner
Your hazard shall be made.

Mor. Good fortune then!
To make me blest or cursed'st among men.

Exeunt.

[Scene II. *Venice. A street.*]

Enter [*Launcelot*] *the Clown*, alone.

Laun. Certainly my conscience will serve me to run from this Jew my master. The fiend is at mine elbow and tempts me, saying to me, 'Gobbo, Launcelot Gobbo, good Launcelot,' or 'good Gobbo,' or 'good Launcelot Gobbo, use your legs, take the start, run away.' My conscience says, 'No. Take heed, honest Launcelot; take heed, honest Gobbo,' or, as aforesaid, 'honest Launcelot Gobbo, do not run; scorn running with thy heels.' Well, the most courageous fiend bids me pack. 'Via!' says the fiend. 'Away!' says the fiend. 'For the heavens, rouse up a brave mind,' says the fiend, 'and run.' Well, my conscience, hanging about the neck of my heart, says very wisely to me, 'My honest friend Launcelot, being an honest man's son' — or rather an honest woman's son; for indeed my father did something smack, something grow to, he had a kind of taste —Well, my conscience says, 'Launcelot, budge not.' 'Budge,' says the fiend. 'Budge not,' says my conscience. 'Conscience,' say I, 'you counsel well.' 'Fiend,' say I, 'you counsel well.' To be rul'd by my conscience, I should stay with the Jew my master, who (God bless the mark!) is a kind of devil; and, to run away from the Jew, I should be ruled by the fiend, who (saving your reverence) is the devil himself. Certainly the Jew is the very devil incarnation; and, in my conscience, my conscience is but a kind of hard conscience to offer to counsel me to stay with the Jew. The fiend gives the more friendly counsel. I will run, fiend; my heels are at your commandment; I will run.

Enter *Old Gobbo*, with a basket.

Gob. Master young man, you, I pray you, which is the way to Master Jew's?

Laun. [*aside*] O heavens, this is my true-begotten father! who, being more than sand-blind, high-gravel-blind, knows me not. I will try confusions with him.

Gob. Master young gentleman, I pray you which is the way to Master Jew's?

Laun. Turn up on your right hand at the next turning, but, at the next turning of all, on your left; marry, at the very next turning, turn of no hand, but turn down indirectly to the Jew's house.

Gob. Be God's sonties, 'twill be a hard way to hit! Can you tell me whether one Launcelot that dwells with him, dwell with him or no?

Laun. Talk you of young Master Launcelot? [*Aside*] Mark me now! Now will I raise the waters.—Talk you of young Master Launcelot?

Gob. No master, sir, but a poor man's son. His father, though I say't, is an honest exceeding poor man, and, God be thanked, well to live.

Laun. Well, let his father be what 'a will, we talk of young Master Launcelot.

Gob. Your worship's friend, and Launcelot, sir.

Laun. But, I pray you, ergo, old man, ergo, I beseech you, talk you of young Master Launcelot?

Gob. Of Launcelot, an't please your mastership.

Laun. Ergo Master Launcelot. Talk not of Master Launcelot, father; for the young gentleman, according to Fates and Destinies and such odd sayings, the Sisters Three and such branches of learning, is indeed deceased, or, as you would say in plain terms, gone to heaven.

Gob. Marry, God forbid! The boy was the very staff of my age, my very prop.

Laun. [*aside*] Do I look like a cudgel or a hovel-post, a staff, or a prop? — Do you know me, father?

Gob. Alack the day, I know you not, young gentleman! but I pray you tell me, is my boy (God rest his soul!) alive or dead?

Laun. Do you not know me, father?

Gob. Alack, sir, I am sand-blind! I know you not.

Laun. Nay, indeed, if you had your eyes, you might fail of the knowing me. It is a wise father that knows his own child. Well, old man, I will tell you news of your son. [*Kneels.*] Give me your blessing. Truth will come to light; murder cannot be hid long — a man's son may, but in the end truth will out.

Gob. Pray you, sir, stand up. I am sure you are not Launcelot, my boy.

Laun. Pray you let's have no more fooling about it, but give me your blessing. I am Launcelot — your boy that was, your son that is, your child that shall be.

Gob. I cannot think you are my son.

Laun. I know not what I shall think of that; but I am Launcelot, the Jew's man, and I am sure Margery your wife is my mother.

Gob. Her name is Margery indeed. I'll be sworn, if thou be Launcelot, thou art mine own flesh and blood. Lord worshipp'd might he be! What a beard hast thou got! Thou hast got more hair on thy chin than Dobbin my fill-horse has on his tail.

Laun. [*rises*] It should seem then that Dobbin's tail grows backward. I am sure he had more hair of his tail than I have of my face when I last saw him.

Gob. Lord, how art thou chang'd! How dost thou and thy master agree? I have brought him a present. How 'gree you now?

Laun. Well, well; but, for mine own part, as I have set up my rest to run away, so I will not rest till I have run some ground. My master's a very Jew. Give him a present? Give him a halter! I am famish'd in his service. You may tell every finger I have with my ribs. Father, I am glad you are come. Give me your present to one Master Bassanio, who indeed gives rare new liveries. If I serve not him, I will run as far as God has any ground. O rare fortune! here comes the man. To him, father; for I am a Jew if I serve the Jew any longer.

Enter *Bassanio,* with [*Leonardo* and] a *Follower* or two.

Bass. You may do so; but let it be so hasted that supper be ready at the farthest by five of the clock. See these letters delivered, put the liveries to making, and desire Gratiano to come anon to my lodging.

Exit one of his men.

Laun. To him, father.

Gob. God bless your worship!

Bass. Gramercy. Wouldst thou aught with me?

Gob. Here's my son, sir, a poor boy —

Laun. Not a poor boy, sir, but the rich Jew's man, that would, sir, as my father shall specify —

Gob. He hath a great infection, sir, as one would say, to serve —

Laun. Indeed, the short and the long is, I serve the Jew, and have a desire, as my father shall specify —

Gob. His master and he (saving your worship's reverence) are scarce cater-cousins.

Laun. To be brief, the very truth is, that the Jew having done me wrong, doth cause me, as my father, being, I hope, an old man, shall frutify unto you —

Gob. I have here a dish of doves that I would bestow upon your worship; and my suit is --

Laun. In very brief, the suit is impertinent to myself, as your worship shall know by this honest old man; and, though I say it, though old man, yet poor man, my father.

Bass. One speak for both. What would you?

Laun. Serve you, sir.

Gob. That is the very defect of the matter, sir.

Bass. I know thee well; thou hast obtain'd thy suit.
Shylock thy master spoke with me this day
And hath preferr'd thee, if it be preferment
To leave a rich Jew's service to become
The follower of so poor a gentleman.

Laun. The old proverb is very well parted between my master Shylock and you, sir. You have the grace of God, sir, and he hath enough.

Bass. Thou speak'st it well. Go, father, with thy son.
Take leave of thy old master and enquire

My lodging out. [*To a Servant*] Give him a livery
More guarded than his fellows'. See it done.

Laun. Father, in. I cannot get a service, no! I have ne'er a tongue in my head! Well, [*looks on his palm*] if any man in Italy have a fairer table which doth offer to swear upon a book —! I shall have good fortune. Go to, here's a simple line of life! Here's a small trifle of wives! Alas, fifteen wives is nothing! a 'leven widows and nine maids is a simple coming-in for one man; and then to scape drowning thrice, and to be in peril of my life with the edge of a feather-bed! Here are simple scapes. Well, if Fortune be a woman, she's a good wench for this gear. Father, come. I'll take my leave of the Jew in the twinkling. *Exit* [*with Old Gobbo*].

Bass. I pray thee, good Leonardo, think on this:
These things being bought and orderly bestow'd
Return in haste, for I do feast to-night
My best-esteem'd acquaintance. Hie thee, go.

Leon. My best endeavours shall be done herein.

Enter *Gratiano.*

Gra. Where 's your master?
Leon. Yonder, sir, he walks. *Exit.*
Gra. Signior Bassanio!
Bass. Gratiano!
Gra. I have a suit to you.
Bass. You have obtain'd it.
Gra. You must not deny me. I must go with you
To Belmont.
Bass. Why, then you must. But hear thee, Gratiano.
Thou art too wild, too rude, and bold of voice—
Parts that become thee happily enough
And in such eyes as ours appear not faults;
But where thou art not known, why, there they show
Something too liberal. Pray thee take pain
To allay with some cold drops of modesty
Thy skipping spirit, lest through thy wild behaviour
I be misconst'red in the place I go to
And lose my hopes.
Gra. Signior Bassanio, hear me.
If I do not put on a sober habit,
Talk with respect, and swear but now and then,
Wear prayer books in my pocket, look demurely,
Nay more, while grace is saying hood mine eyes
Thus with my hat, and sigh, and say amen,
Use all the observance of civility
Like one well studied in a sad ostent
To please his grandam, never trust me more.
Bass. Well, we shall see your bearing.
Gra. Nay, but I bar to-night. You shall not gauge me
By what we do to-night.
Bass. No, that were pity.
I would entreat you rather to put on
Your boldest suit of mirth, for we have friends
That purpose merriment. But fare you well.
I have some business.
Gra. And I must to Lorenzo and the rest;
But we will visit you at supper time. *Exeunt.*

[Scene III. *Venice.* Shylock's *house.*]

Enter *Jessica* and [*Launcelot*] *the Clown.*

Jes. I am sorry thou wilt leave my father so.
Our house is hell; and thou, a merry devil,
Didst rob it of some taste of tediousness.
But fare thee well. There is a ducat for thee;
And, Launcelot, soon at supper shalt thou see
Lorenzo, who is thy new master's guest.
Give him this letter; do it secretly;
And so farewell. I would not have my father
See me in talk with thee.

Laun. Adieu! Tears exhibit my tongue. Most beautiful pagan, most sweet Jew! if a Christian did not play the knave and get thee, I am much deceived. But adieu! These foolish drops do something drown my manly spirit. Adieu!

Jes. Farewell, good Launcelot.
Exit [*Launcelot*].
Alack, what heinous sin is it in me
To be asham'd to be my father's child!
But though I am a daughter to his blood,
I am not to his manners. O Lorenzo,
If thou keep promise, I shall end this strife,
Become a Christian and thy loving wife. *Exit.*

[Scene IV. *Venice. A street.*]

Enter *Gratiano, Lorenzo, Salerio,* and *Solanio.*

Lor. Nay, we will slink away in supper time,
Disguise us at my lodging, and return
All in an hour.
Gra. We have not made good preparation.
Saler. We have not spoke us yet of torch-bearers.
Solan. 'Tis vile, unless it may be quaintly ordered,
And better in my mind not undertook.

Lor. 'Tis now but four o'clock. We have two hours
To furnish us.

Enter *Launcelot,* with a letter.

Friend Launcelot, what's the news?
Laun. An it shall please you to break up this, it shall seem to signify.
Lor. I know the hand. In faith, 'tis a fair hand,
And whiter than the paper it writ on
Is the fair hand that writ.
Gra. Love-news, in faith!
Laun. By your leave, sir.
Lor. Whither goest thou?
Laun. Marry, sir, to bid my old master the Jew to sup to-night with my new master the Christian.
Lor. Hold here, take this [*gives money*]. Tell gentle Jessica
I will not fail her. Speak it privately.
Go. [*Exit Launcelot.*] Gentlemen,
Will you prepare you for this masque to-night?
I am provided of a torchbearer.
Saler. Ay, marry, I'll be gone about it straight.
Solan. And so will I.
Lor. Meet me and Gratiano
At Gratiano's lodging some hour hence.
Saler. 'Tis good we do so.

Exeunt [*Salerio and Solanio*].

Gra. Was not that letter from fair Jessica?
Lor. I must needs tell thee all. She hath directed
How I shall take her from her father's house;
What gold and jewels she is furnish'd with;
What page's suit she hath in readiness.
If e'er the Jew her father come to heaven,
It will be for his gentle daughter's sake;
And never dare misfortune cross her foot,
Unless she do it under this excuse,
That she is issue to a faithless Jew.
Come, go with me; peruse this as thou goest.
Fair Jessica shall be my torchbearer. *Exeunt.*

[Scene V. *Venice. Before* Shylock's *house.*]

Enter [*the*] *Jew* [*Shylock*] and [*Launcelot,*] his man that was the *Clown.*

Shy. Well, thou shalt see, thy eyes shall be thy judge,
The difference of old Shylock and Bassanio. —
What, Jessica! — Thou shalt not gormandize
As thou hast done with me — What, Jessica! —
And sleep, and snore, and rend apparel out. —
Why, Jessica, I say!
Laun. Why, Jessica!
Shy. Who bids thee call? I do not bid thee call.
Laun. Your worship was wont to tell me I could do nothing without bidding.

Enter *Jessica.*

Jes. Call you? What is your will?
Shy. I am bid forth to supper, Jessica.
There are my keys. But wherefore should I go?
I am not bid for love; they flatter me.
But yet I'll go in hate, to feed upon
The prodigal Christian. Jessica, my girl,
Look to my house. I am right loath to go.
There is some ill a-brewing towards my rest,
For I did dream of money bags to-night.
Laun. I beseech you, sir, go. My young master doth expect your reproach.
Shy. So do I his.
Laun. And they have conspired together. I will not say you shall see a masque; but if you do, then it was not for nothing that my nose fell a-bleeding on Black Monday last at six o'clock i' th' morning, falling out that year on Ash Wednesday was four year in th' afternoon.
Shy. What, are there masques? Hear you me, Jessica.
Lock up my doors; and when you hear the drum
And the vile squealing of the wry-neck'd fife,
Clamber not you up to the casements then,
Nor thrust your head into the public street
To gaze on Christian fools with varnish'd faces;
But stop my house's ears — I mean my casements.
Let not the sound of shallow fopp'ry enter
My sober house. By Jacob's staff I swear
I have no mind of feasting forth to-night;
But I will go. Go you before me, sirrah.
Say I will come.
Laun. I will go before, sir. Mistress, look out at window for all this.
There will come a Christian by
Will be worth a Jewess' eye. [*Exit.*]
Shy. What says that fool of Hagar's offspring? ha?
Jes. His words were 'Farewell, mistress' — nothing else.
Shy. The patch is kind enough, but a huge feeder,
Snail-slow in profit, and he sleeps by day
More than the wildcat. Drones hive not with me;

Paul Rogers in the role of the crafty, vindictive Shylock. Claire Bloom as dark-eyed Jessica, his daughter

THE MERCHANT of VENICE

Left: The lovely Portia (Irene Worth), as wise as she is beautiful

Right: Robert Urquhart in the role of Bassanio, Portia's suitor

Left: Jane Wenham as Nerissa, Portia's maid

Right: Nerissa's lover, Gratiano (William Squire)

Left: Richard Gale in the role of Lorenzo, the lover of Jessica

Right: Douglas Campbell as the Merchant of Venice, Antonio

Right: "I would have stay'd till I had made you merry, if worthier friends had not prevented me." Having vainly attempted to cheer up the dispirited Antonio, Salarino (Tony van Bridge) and Salanio (Patrick Wymark) depart as his young friends arrive *(Act I, Scene I)*

Left: "He will fence with his own shadow: if I should marry him, I should marry twenty husbands." Portia mimics one of her suitors *(Act I, Scene II)*

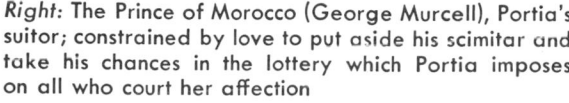

Right: The Prince of Morocco (George Murcell), Portia's suitor; constrained by love to put aside his scimitar and take his chances in the lottery which Portia imposes on all who court her affection

Left: Misguided by outward show, the Prince of Morocco chooses the golden casket and is forced to withdraw his suit for the fair Portia *(Act II, Scene VII)*

Right: The Prince of Arragon (John Warner) departs after choosing the silver casket and finding in it "the portrait of a blinking idiot" *(Act II, Scene IX)*

Below: "Master young man, you; I pray you, which is the way to Master Jew's." Not recognizing his son Launcelot (Kenneth Connor), Old Gobbo (Newton Blick) asks him the way to his master's house *(Act II, Scene II)*

Shylock's daughter Jessica, whose dusky beauty captures the heart of young Lorenzo

"Give him this letter; do it secretly." Jessica entrusts Launcelot with a letter for Lorenzo *(Act II, Scene III)*

Left: "The villainy you teach me I will execute, and it shall go hard but I will better the instruction." Shylock broods upon his vengeance *(Act III, Scene I)*

Below: Disguised as revelers, Lorenzo and his friends come to help Jessica escape from Shylock *(Act II, Scene VI)*

"Why, this bond is forfeit; and lawfully by this the Jew may claim a pound of flesh to be by him cut off nearest the merchant's heart." Disguised as a lawyer, Portia leads Shylock on by confirming the validity of his bond *(Act IV, Scene I)*

"Most learned judge! A sentence! come, prepare!" Unaware of the trap laid for him, Shylock praises the lawyer's decision *(Act IV, Scene I)*

"Tarry a little, there is something else." As Shylock prepares to collect his pound of flesh, Portia points out that his lands and goods will be forfeit if he sheds a single drop of Antonio's blood *(Act IV, Scene I)*

Left: "Well, while I live I'll fear no other thing so sore as keeping safe Nerissa's ring." Nerissa returns to Gratiano the ring which he gave her when she was disguised as a law clerk *(Act V, Scene I)*

Right: "Let us go in; and charge us there upon inter'gatories, and we will answer all things faithfully." Bassiano and Portia are united in the final scene of the play *(Act V, Scene I)*

The last scene of the play finds Antonio absolved of his debt and the six young lovers blissfully paired *(Act V, Scene I)*

Therefore I part with him, and part with him
To one that I would have him help to waste
His borrowed purse. Well, Jessica, go in.
Perhaps I will return immediately.
Do as I bid you; shut doors after you.
Fast bind, fast find —
A proverb never stale in thrifty mind. *Exit.*

Jes. Farewell; and if my fortune be not crost,
I have a father, you a daughter, lost. *Exit.*

[Scene VI. *Venice. Near* Shylock's *house.*]

Enter the Maskers, *Gratiano* and *Salerio.*

Gra. This is the penthouse under which Lorenzo
Desir'd us to make stand.
Saler. His hour is almost past.
Gra. And it is marvel he outdwells his hour,
For lovers ever run before the clock.
Saler. O, ten times faster Venus' pigeons fly
To seal love's bonds new-made than they are wont
To keep obliged faith unforfeited!
Gra. That ever holds. Who riseth from a feast
With that keen appetite that he sits down?
Where is the horse that doth untread again
His tedious measures with the unbated fire
That he did pace them first? All things that are
Are with more spirit chased than enjoy'd.
How like a younker or a prodigal
The scarfed bark puts from her native bay,
Hugg'd and embraced by the strumpet wind!
How like the Prodigal doth she return,
With over-weather'd ribs and ragged sails,
Lean, rent, and beggar'd by the strumpet wind!

Enter *Lorenzo.*

Saler. Here comes Lorenzo. More of this hereafter.
Lor. Sweet friends, your patience for my long abode.
Not I, but my affairs, have made you wait.
When you shall please to play the thieves for wives,
I'll watch as long for you then. Approach.
Here dwells my father Jew. Ho! who's within?

[Enter] *Jessica,* above, [in boy's clothes].

Jes. Who are you? Tell me for more certainty,
Albeit I'll swear that I do know your tongue.
Lor. Lorenzo, and thy love.
Jes. Lorenzo certain, and my love indeed,
For who love I so much? And now who knows
But you, Lorenzo, whether I am yours?
Lor. Heaven and thy thoughts are witness that thou art.
Jes. Here, catch this casket; it is worth the pains.
I am glad 'tis night, you do not look on me,
For I am much asham'd of my exchange.
But love is blind, and lovers cannot see
The pretty follies that themselves commit;
For if they could, Cupid himself would blush
To see me thus transformed to a boy.
Lor. Descend, for you must be my torch-bearer.
Jes. What, must I hold a candle to my shames?
They in themselves, good sooth, are too too light.
Why, 'tis an office of discovery, love,
And I should be obscur'd.
Lor. So are you, sweet,
Even in the lovely garnish of a boy.
But come at once;
For the close night doth play the runaway,
And we are stay'd for at Bassanio's feast.
Jes. I will make fast the doors, and gild myself
With some moe ducats, and be with you straight. [*Exit above.*]
Gra. Now, by my hood, a gentle, and no Jew!
Lor. Beshrow me but I love her heartily;
For she is wise, if I can judge of her;
And fair she is, if that mine eyes be true;
And true she is, as she hath prov'd herself;
And therefore, like herself, wise, fair, and true,
Shall she be placed in my constant soul.

Enter *Jessica,* [below].

What, art thou come? On, gentlemen! away!
Our masquing mates by this time for us stay.
Exit [*with Jessica and Salerio*].

Enter *Antonio.*

Ant. Who's there?
Gra. Signior Antonio?
Ant. Fie, fie, Gratiano! Where are all the rest?
'Tis nine o'clock; our friends all stay for you.
No masque to-night. The wind is come about;
Bassanio presently will go aboard.
I have sent twenty out to seek for you.
Gra. I am glad on't. I desire no more delight
Than to be under sail and gone to-night. *Exeunt.*

[Scene VII. *Belmont.* Portia's *house.*]

Enter *Portia,* with *Morocco,* and both their *Trains.*

Por. Go, draw aside the curtains and discover
The several caskets to this noble Prince.
Now make your choice.
[*The curtains are drawn aside.*]

Mor. The first, of gold, which this inscription bears,
'Who chooseth me shall gain what many men desire.'
The second, silver, which this promise carries,
'Who chooseth me shall get as much as he deserves.'
This third, dull lead, with warning all as blunt,
'Who chooseth me must give and hazard all he hath.'
How shall I know if I do choose the right?

Por. The one of them contains my picture, Prince.
If you choose that, then I am yours withal.

Mor. Some god direct my judgment! Let me see.
I will survey th' inscriptions back again.
What says this leaden casket?
'Who chooseth me must give and hazard all he hath.'
Must give — for what? for lead! hazard for lead?
This casket threatens. Men that hazard all
Do it in hope of fair advantages.
A golden mind stoops not to shows of dross.
I'll then nor give nor hazard aught for lead.
What says the silver, with her virgin hue?
'Who chooseth me shall get as much as he deserves.'
As much as he deserves? Pause there, Morocco,
And weigh thy value with an even hand.
If thou beest rated by thy estimation,
Thou dost deserve enough; and yet enough
May not extend so far as to the lady;
And yet to be afeard of my deserving
Were but a weak disabling of myself.
As much as I deserve? Why, that's the lady!
I do in birth deserve her, and in fortunes,
In graces, and in qualities of breeding;
But more than these, in love I do deserve.
What if I stray'd no farther, but chose here?
Let's see once more this saying grav'd in gold:
'Who chooseth me shall gain what many men desire.'
Why, that's the lady! All the world desires her.
From the four corners of the earth they come
To kiss this shrine, this mortal breathing saint.
The Hyrcanian deserts and the vasty wilds
Of wide Arabia are as throughfares now
For princes to come view fair Portia.
The watery kingdom, whose ambitious head
Spets in the face of heaven, is no bar
To stop the foreign spirits; but they come,
As o'er a brook, to see fair Portia.
One of these three contains her heavenly picture.
Is't like that lead contains her? 'Twere damnation
To think so base a thought. It were too gross
To rib her cerecloth in the obscure grave.
Or shall I think in silver she's immur'd,
Being ten times undervalued to tried gold?
O sinful thought! Never so rich a gem
Was set in worse than gold. They have in England
A coin that bears the figure of an angel
Stamped in gold — but that's insculp'd upon;
But here an angel in a golden bed
Lies all within. Deliver me the key.
Here do I choose, and thrive I as I may!

Por. There, take it, Prince; and if my form lie there,
Then I am yours. [*He opens the golden casket.*]

Mor. O hell! what have we here?
A carrion Death, within whose empty eye
There is a written scroll! I'll read the writing.

'All that glisters is not gold —
Often have you heard that told.
Many a man his life hath sold
But my outside to behold.
Gilded tombs do worms infold.
Had you been as wise as bold,
Young in limbs, in judgment old,
Your answer had not been inscroll'd.
Fare you well; your suit is cold.'

Cold indeed, and labour lost.
Then farewell heat, and welcome frost!
Portia, adieu. I have too griev'd a heart
To take a tedious leave. Thus losers part.
Exit [*with his Train*].

Por. A gentle riddance. Draw the curtains, go.
Let all of his complexion choose me so. *Exeunt.*

[Scene VIII. *Venice. A street.*]

Enter *Salerio* and *Solanio.*

Saler. Why, man, I saw Bassanio under sail;
With him is Gratiano gone along;
And in their ship I am sure Lorenzo is not.

Solan. The villain Jew with outcries rais'd the Duke,
Who went with him to search Bassanio's ship.
Saler. He came too late, the ship was under sail;
But there the Duke was given to understand
That in a gondilo were seen together
Lorenzo and his amorous Jessica.
Besides, Antonio certified the Duke
They were not with Bassanio in his ship.
Solan. I never heard a passion so confus'd,
So strange, outrageous, and so variable,
As the dog Jew did utter in the streets.
'My daughter! O my ducats! O my daughter!
Fled with a Christian! O my Christian ducats!
Justice! the law! My ducats, and my daughter!
A sealed bag, two sealed bags of ducats,
Of double ducats, stol'n from me by my daughter!
And jewels — two stones, two rich and precious stones,
Stol'n by my daughter! Justice! Find the girl!
She hath the stones upon her, and the ducats!'
Saler. Why, all the boys in Venice follow him,
Crying his stones, his daughter, and his ducats.
Solan. Let good Antonio look he keep his day,
Or he shall pay for this.
Saler. Marry, well remem'bred.
I reason'd with a Frenchman yesterday,
Who told me, in the narrow seas that part
The French and English there miscarried
A vessel of our country richly fraught.
I thought upon Antonio when he told me,
And wish'd in silence that it were not his.
Solan. You were best to tell Antonio what you hear.
Yet do not suddenly, for it may grieve him.
Saler. A kinder gentleman treads not the earth.
I saw Bassanio and Antonio part.
Bassanio told him he would make some speed
Of his return; he answered, 'Do not so.
Slubber not business for my sake, Bassanio,
But stay the very riping of the time;
And for the Jew's bond which he hath of me,
Let it not enter in your mind of love.
Be merry, and employ your chiefest thoughts
To courtship, and such fair ostents of love
As shall conveniently become you there.'
And even there, his eye being big with tears,
Turning his face, he put his hand behind him,
And with affection wondrous sensible
He wrung Bassanio's hand; and so they parted.
Solan. I think he only loves the world for him.
I pray thee let us go and find him out,
And quicken his embraced heaviness
With some delight or other.
Saler. Do we so. *Exeunt.*

[Scene IX. *Belmont.* Portia's *house.*]

Enter *Nerissa* and a *Servitor.*

Ner. Quick, quick, I pray thee; draw the curtain straight.
The Prince of Arragon hath ta'en his oath
And comes to his election presently.

Enter *Arragon,* his *Train,* and *Portia* [with her *Train*].

Por. Behold, there stand the caskets, noble Prince.
If you choose that wherein I am contain'd,
Straight shall our nuptial rites be solemniz'd;
But if you fail, without more speech, my lord,
You must be gone from hence immediately.
Ar. I am enjoin'd by oath to observe three things:
First, never to unfold to any one
Which casket 'twas I chose; next, if I fail
Of the right casket, never in my life
To woo a maid in way of marriage;
Lastly,
If I do fail in fortune of my choice,
Immediately to leave you and be gone.
Por. To these injunctions every one doth swear
That comes to hazard for my worthless self.
Ar. And so have I address'd me. Fortune now
To my heart's hope! Gold, silver, and base lead.
'Who chooseth me must give and hazard all he hath.'
You shall look fairer ere I give or hazard.
What says the golden chest? Ha, let me see!
'Who chooseth me shall gain what many men desire.'
What many men desire! That 'many' may be meant
By the fool multitude, that choose by show,
Not learning more than the fond eye doth teach;
Which pries not to th' interior, but, like the martlet,
Builds in the weather on the outward wall,
Even in the force and road of casualty.
I will not choose what many men desire,
Because I will not jump with common spirits

And rank me with the barbarous multitude,
Why then, to thee, thou silver treasure house!
Tell me once more what title thou dost bear.
'Who chooseth me shall get as much as he deserves.'
And well said too; for who shall go about
To cozen fortune, and be honourable
Without the stamp of merit? Let none presume
To wear an undeserved dignity.
O that estates, degrees, and offices
Were not deriv'd corruptly, and that clear honour
Were purchas'd by the merit of the wearer!
How many then should cover that stand bare!
How many be commanded that command!
How much low peasantry would then be gleaned
From the true seed of honour! and how much honour
Pick'd from the chaff and ruin of the times
To be new varnish'd! Well, but to my choice.
'Who chooseth me shall get as much as he deserves.'
I will assume desert. Give me a key for this,
And instantly unlock my fortunes here.
[*He opens the silver casket.*]

Por. [*aside*] Too long a pause for that which you find there.

Ar. What's here? The portrait of a blinking idiot,
Presenting me a schedule! I will read it.
How much unlike art thou to Portia!
How much unlike my hopes and my deservings!
'Who chooseth me shall have as much as he deserves.'
Did I deserve no more than a fool's head?
Is that my prize? Are my deserts no better?

Por. To offend and judge are distinct offices
And of opposed natures.

Ar. What is here?
'The fire seven times tried this.
Seven times tried that judgment is
That did never choose amiss.
Some there be that shadows kiss;
Such have but a shadow's bliss.
There be fools alive iwis
Silver'd o'er, and so was this.
Take what wife you will to bed,
I will ever be your head.
So be gone; you are sped.'

Still more fool I shall appear
By the time I linger here.
With one fool's head I came to woo,
But I go away with two.
Sweet, adieu. I'll keep my oath,
Patiently to bear my wroth.
[*Exit with his Train.*]

Por. Thus hath the candle sing'd the moth.
O, these deliberate fools! When they do choose,
They have the wisdom by their wit to lose.

Ner. The ancient saying is no heresy,
Hanging and wiving goes by destiny.

Por. Come draw the curtain, Nerissa.

Enter *Messenger*.

Mess. Where is my lady?

Por. Here. What would my lord?

Mess. Madam, there is alighted at your gate
A young Venetian, one that comes before
To signify th' approaching of his lord;
From whom he bringeth sensible regreets,
To wit, besides commends and courteous breath,
Gifts of rich value. Yet I have not seen
So likely an ambassador of love.
A day in April never came so sweet
To show how costly summer was at hand
As this fore-spurrer comes before his lord.

Por. No more, I pray thee. I am half afeard
Thou wilt say anon he is some kin to thee,
Thou spend'st such high-day wit in praising him.
Come, come, Nerissa; for I long to see
Quick Cupid's post that comes so mannerly.

Ner. Bassanio, Lord Love, if thy will it be!
Exeunt.

ACT III. [Scene I. *Venice. A street.*]

Enter *Solanio* and *Salerio*.

Solan. Now what news on the Rialto?

Saler. Why, yet it lives there uncheck'd that Antonio hath a ship of rich lading wrack'd on the narrow seas — the Goodwins I think they call the place — a very dangerous flat, and fatal, where the carcases of many a tall ship lie buried, as they say, if my gossip Report be an honest woman of her word.

Solan. I would she were as lying a gossip in that as ever knapp'd ginger or made her neighbours believe she wept for the death of a third husband. But it is true, without any slips of prolixity or crossing the plain highway of talk, that the good Antonio, the honest Antonio — O that I had a title good enough to keep his name company! —

Saler. Come, the full stop.

Solan. Ha, what sayest thou? Why, the end is, he hath lost a ship.

Saler. I would it might prove the end of his losses.

Solan. Let me say amen betimes, lest the devil cross my prayer, for here he comes in the likeness of a Jew.

Enter *Shylock.*

How now, Shylock? What news among the merchants?

Shy. You knew, none so well, none so well as you, of my daughter's flight.

Saler. That's certain. I, for my part, knew the tailor that made the wings she flew withal.

Solan. And Shylock, for his own part, knew the bird was fledge; and then it is the complexion of them all to leave the dam.

Shy. She is damn'd for it.

Saler. That's certain, if the devil may be her judge.

Shy. My own flesh and blood to rebel!

Solan. Out upon it, old carrion! Rebels it at these years?

Shy. I say my daughter is my flesh and my blood.

Saler. There is more difference between thy flesh and hers than between jet and ivory; more between your bloods than there is between red wine and Rhenish. But tell us, do you hear whether Antonio have had any loss at sea or no?

Shy. There I have another bad match! A bankrout, a prodigal, who dare scarce show his head on the Rialto! a beggar, that was us'd to come so smug upon the mart! Let him look to his bond. He was wont to call me usurer. Let him look to his bond. He was wont to lend money for a Christian cursy. Let him look to his bond.

Saler. Why, I am sure, if he forfeit, thou wilt not take his flesh. What's that good for?

Shy. To bait fish withal. If it will feed nothing else, it will feed my revenge. He hath disgrac'd me, and hind'red me half a million; laugh'd at my losses, mock'd at my gains, scorned my nation, thwarted my bargains, cooled my friends, heated mine enemies — and what's his reason? I am a Jew. Hath not a Jew eyes? Hath not a Jew hands, organs, dimensions, senses, affections, passions? fed with the same food, hurt with the same weapons, subject to the same diseases, healed by the same means, warmed and cooled by the same winter and summer as a Christian is? If you prick us, do we not bleed? If you tickle us, do we not laugh? If you poison us, do we not die? And if you wrong us, shall we not revenge? If we are like you in the rest, we will resemble you in that. If a Jew wrong a Christian, what is his humility? Revenge. If a Christian wrong a Jew, what should his sufferance be by Christian example? Why, revenge. The villany you teach me I will execute, and it shall go hard but I will better the instruction.

Enter a *Man* from *Antonio.*

Man. Gentlemen, my master Antonio is at his house, and desires to speak with you both.

Saler. We have been up and down to seek him.

Enter *Tubal.*

Solan. Here comes another of the tribe. A third cannot be match'd, unless the devil himself turn Jew.

Exeunt [*Solanio, Salerio, and Man*].

Shy. How now, Tubal? What news from Genoa? Hast thou found my daughter?

Tub. I often came where I did hear of her, but cannot find her.

Shy. Why, there, there, there, there! A diamond gone cost me two thousand ducats in Frankford! The curse never fell upon our nation till now; I never felt it till now. Two thousand ducats in that, and other precious, precious jewels. I would my daughter were dead at my foot, and the jewels in her ear! Would she were hears'd at my foot, and the ducats in her coffin! No news of them? Why, so — and I know not what's spent in the search. Why, thou loss upon loss! the thief gone with so much, and so much to find the thief; and no satisfaction, no revenge! nor no ill luck stirring but what lights o' my shoulders; no sighs but o' my breathing; no tears but o' my shedding.

Tub. Yes, other men have ill luck too. Antonio, as I heard in Genoa —

Shy. What, what, what? Ill luck, ill luck?

Tub. Hath an argosy cast away coming from Tripolis.

Shy. I thank God, I thank God! Is it true? is it true?

Tub. I spoke with some of the sailors that escaped the wrack.

Shy. I thank thee, good Tubal. Good news, good news! Ha, ha! Where? in Genoa?

Tub. Your daughter spent in Genoa, as I heard, one night fourscore ducats.

Shy. Thou stick'st a dagger in me. I shall never see my gold again. Fourscore ducats at a sitting! fourscore ducats!

Tub. There came divers of Antonio's creditors in my company to Venice that swear he cannot choose but break.

Shy. I am very glad of it. I'll plague him; I'll torture him. I am glad of it.

Tub. One of them showed me a ring that he had of your daughter for a monkey.

Shy. Out upon her! Thou torturest me, Tubal. It was my turquoise; I had it of Leah when I was a bachelor. I would not have given it for a wilderness of monkeys.

Tub. But Antonio is certainly undone.

Shy. Nay, that's true, that's very true. Go, Tubal, fee me an officer; bespeak him a fortnight before. I will have the heart of him if he forfeit; for, were he out of Venice, I can make what merchandise I will. Go, Tubal, and meet me at our synagogue; go, good Tubal; at our synagogue, Tubal. *Exeunt.*

[Scene II. *Belmont.* Portia's *house.*]

Enter *Bassanio, Portia, Gratiano,* and all their *Trains*; [*Nerissa*].

Por. I pray you tarry; pause a day or two
Before you hazard; for in choosing wrong
I lose your company. Therefore forbear awhile.
There's something tells me (but it is not love)
I would not lose you; and you know yourself
Hate counsels not in such a quality.
But lest you should not understand me well —
And yet a maiden hath no tongue but thought —
I would detain you here some month or two
Before you venture for me. I could teach you
How to choose right, but then I am forsworn.
So will I never be; so may you miss me;
But if you do, you'll make me wish a sin —
That I had been forsworn. Beshrow your eyes!
They have o'erlook'd me and divided me;
One half of me is yours, the other half yours —
Mine own, I would say; but if mine, then yours,
And so all yours! O, these naughty times
Puts bars between the owners and their rights!
And so, though yours, not yours. Prove it so,
Let fortune go to hell for it, not I.
I speak too long; but 'tis to peize the time,
To eche it, and to draw it out in length,
To stay you from election.

Bass. Let me choose;
For as I am, I live upon the rack.

Por. Upon the rack, Bassanio? Then confess
What treason there is mingled with your love.

Bass. None but that ugly treason of mistrust,
Which makes me fear th' enjoying of my love.
There may as well be amity and life
'Tween snow and fire as treason and my love.

Por. Ay, but I fear you speak upon the rack,
Where men enforced do speak anything.

Bass. Promise me life, and I'll confess the truth.

Por. Well then, confess and live.

Bass. 'Confess' and 'love'
Had been the very sum of my confession.
O happy torment, when my torturer
Doth teach me answers for deliverance!
But let me to my fortune and the caskets.

Por. Away then! I am lock'd in one of them.
If you do love me, you will find me out.
Nerissa and the rest, stand all aloof.
Let music sound while he doth make his choice;
Then, if he lose, he makes a swanlike end,
Fading in music. That the comparison
May stand more proper, my eye shall be the stream
And wat'ry deathbed for him. He may win;
And what is music then? Then music is
Even as the flourish when true subjects bow
To a new-crowned monarch. Such it is
As are those dulcet sounds in break of day
That creep into the dreaming bridegroom's ear
And summon him to marriage. Now he goes
With no less presence, but with much more love,
Than young Alcides when he did redeem
The virgin tribute paid by howling Troy
To the sea monster. I stand for sacrifice;
The rest aloof are the Dardanian wives,
With bleared visages come forth to view
The issue of th' exploit. Go, Hercules!
Live thou, I live. With much much more dismay
I view the fight than thou that mak'st the fray.

A Song, the whilst Bassanio comments on the caskets to himself.

Tell me, where is fancy bred,
Or in the heart, or in the head?
How begot, how nourished?
Reply, reply.
It is engend'red in the eyes,
With gazing fed; and fancy dies
In the cradle where it lies.
Let us all ring fancy's knell.
I'll begin it — Ding, dong, bell.

All. Ding, dong, bell.

Bass. So may the outward shows be least themselves;
The world is still deceiv'd with ornament.
In law, what plea so tainted and corrupt
But, being season'd with a gracious voice,
Obscures the show of evil? In religion,
What damned error but some sober brow
Will bless it, and approve it with a text,
Hiding the grossness with fair ornament?
There is no vice so simple but assumes
Some mark of virtue on his outward parts.
How many cowards, whose hearts are all as false
As stairs of sand, wear yet upon their chins
The beards of Hercules and frowning Mars;
Who, inward search'd, have livers white as milk!
And these assume but valour's excrement
To render them redoubted. Look on beauty,
And you shall see 'tis purchas'd by the weight,
Which therein works a miracle in nature,
Making them lightest that wear most of it.
So are those crisped snaky golden locks
Which make such wanton gambols with the wind
Upon supposed fairness often known
To be the dowry of a second head,
The skull that bred them in the sepulchre.
Thus ornament is but the guiled shore
To a most dangerous sea; the beauteous scarf
Veiling an Indian beauty; in a word,
The seeming truth which cunning times put on
To entrap the wisest. Therefore, thou gaudy gold,
Hard food for Midas, I will none of thee;
Nor none of thee, thou pale and common drudge
'Tween man and man: but thou, thou meagre lead,
Which rather threaten'st than dost promise aught,
Thy plainness moves me more than eloquence;
And here choose I. Joy be the consequence!

Por. [*aside*] How all the other passions fleet to air,
As doubtful thoughts, and rash-embrac'd despair,
And shudd'ring fear, and green-ey'd jealousy!
O love, be moderate; allay thy ecstasy;
In measure rain thy joy; scant this excess!
I feel too much thy blessing. Make it less
For fear I surfeit!

Bass. [*opening the leaden casket*] What find I here?
Fair Portia's counterfeit! What demigod
Hath come so near creation? Move these eyes?
Or whether, riding on the balls of mine,
Seem they in motion? Here are sever'd lips,
Parted with sugar breath. So sweet a bar
Should sunder such sweet friends. Here in her hairs
The painter plays the spider; and hath woven
A golden mesh t' entrap the hearts of men
Faster than gnats in cobwebs. But her eyes —
How could he see to do them? Having made one,
Methinks it should have power to steal both his
And leave itself unfurnish'd. Yet look, how far
The substance of my praise doth wrong this shadow
In underprizing it, so far this shadow
Doth limp behind the substance. Here's the scroll,
The continent and summary of my fortune.

'You that choose not by the view
Chance as fair and choose as true.
Since this fortune falls to you,
Be content and seek no new.
If you be well pleas'd with this
And hold your fortune for your bliss,
Turn you where your lady is
And claim her with a loving kiss.'

A gentle scroll. Fair lady, by your leave;
[*Kisses her.*]
I come by note, to give and to receive.
Like one of two contending in a prize,
That thinks he hath done well in people's eyes,
Hearing applause and universal shout,
Giddy in spirit, still gazing in a doubt
Whether those peals of praise be his or no;
So, thrice-fair lady, stand I, even so,
As doubtful whether what I see be true,
Until confirm'd, sign'd, ratified by you.

Por. You see me, Lord Bassanio, where I stand,
Such as I am. Though for myself alone
I would not be ambitious in my wish
To wish myself much better, yet for you
I would be trebled twenty times myself,
A thousand times more fair, ten thousand times more rich,
That, only to stand high in your account,
I might in virtues, beauties, livings, friends,
Exceed account. But the full sum of me
Is sum of nothing, which, to term in gross,
Is an unlesson'd girl, unschool'd, unpractis'd;
Happy in this, she is not yet so old
But she may learn; happier than this,
She is not bred so dull but she can learn;
Happiest of all is that her gentle spirit
Commits itself to yours to be directed,
As from her lord, her governor, her king.

Myself and what is mine to you and yours
Is now converted. But now I was the lord
Of this fair mansion, master of my servants,
Queen o'er myself; and even now, but now,
This house, these servants, and this same myself
Are yours, my lord's. I give them with this ring;
Which when you part from, lose, or give away,
Let it presage the ruin of your love
And be my vantage to exclaim on you.

Bass. Madam, you have bereft me of all words,
Only my blood speaks to you in my veins;
And there is such confusion in my powers
As, after some oration fairly spoke
By a beloved prince, there doth appear
Among the buzzing pleased multitude,
Where every something, being blent together,
Turns to a wild of nothing, save of joy,
Express'd and not express'd. But when this ring
Parts from this finger, then parts life from hence!
O, then be bold to say Bassanio's dead!

Ner. My lord and lady, it is now our time
That have stood by and seen our wishes prosper
To cry 'good joy.' Good joy, my lord and lady!

Gra. My Lord Bassanio, and my gentle lady,
I wish you all the joy that you can wish;
For I am sure you can wish none from me;
And when your honours mean to solemnize
The bargain of your faith, I do beseech you
Even at that time I may be married too.

Bass. With all my heart, so thou canst get a wife.

Gra. I thank your lordship, you have got me one.
My eyes, my lord, can look as swift as yours.
You saw the mistress, I beheld the maid;
You lov'd, I lov'd; for intermission
No more pertains to me, my lord, than you.
Your fortune stood upon the caskets there,
And so did mine too, as the matter falls;
For wooing here until I sweat again,
And swearing till my very roof was dry
With oaths of love, at last — if promise last —
I got a promise of this fair one here
To have her love, provided that your fortune
Achiev'd her mistress.

Por. Is this true, Nerissa?

Ner. Madam, it is, so you stand pleas'd withal.

Bass. And do you, Gratiano, mean good faith?

Gra. Yes, faith, my lord.

Bass. Our feast shall be much honoured in your marriage.

Gra. We'll play with them the first boy for a thousand ducats.

Ner. What, and stake down?

Gra. No, we shall ne'er win at that sport, and stake down.
But who comes here? Lorenzo and his infidel?
What, and my old Venetian friend Salerio?

Enter *Lorenzo, Jessica,* and *Salerio* (a *Messenger* from Venice).

Bass. Lorenzo and Salerio, welcome hither,
If that the youth of my new int'rest here
Have power to bid you welcome. By your leave,
I bid my very friends and countrymen,
Sweet Portia, welcome.

Por. So do I, my lord.
They are entirely welcome.

Lor. I thank your honour. For my part, my lord,
My purpose was not to have seen you here;
But meeting with Salerio by the way,
He did entreat me, past all saying nay,
To come with him along.

Saler. I did, my lord,
And I have reason for it. Signior Antonio
Commends him to you.

[*Gives Bassanio a letter.*]

Bass. Ere I ope his letter,
I pray you tell me how my good friend doth.

Saler. Not sick, my lord, unless it be in mind;
Nor well, unless in mind. His letter there
Will show you his estate.

Open the letter.

Gra. Nerissa, cheer yond stranger; bid her welcome.
Your hand, Salerio. What's the news from Venice?
How doth that royal merchant, good Antonio?
I know he will be glad of our success.
We are the Jasons, we have won the Fleece.

Saler. I would you had won the fleece that he hath lost!

Por. There are some shrowd contents in yond same paper
That steals the colour from Bassanio's cheek:
Some dear friend dead; else nothing in the world
Could turn so much the constitution
Of any constant man. What, worse and worse?
With leave, Bassanio — I am half yourself,
And I must freely have the half of anything
That this same paper brings you.

Bass. O sweet Portia,
Here are a few of the unpleasant'st words
That ever blotted paper! Gentle lady,
When I did first impart my love to you,
I freely told you all the wealth I had
Ran in my veins — I was a gentleman;
And then I told you true; and yet, dear lady,
Rating myself at nothing, you shall see
How much I was a braggart. When I told you
My state was nothing, I should then have told you
That I was worse than nothing; for indeed
I have engag'd myself to a dear friend,
Engag'd my friend to his mere enemy
To feed my means. Here is a letter, lady —
The paper as the body of my friend,
And every word in it a gaping wound
Issuing lifeblood. But is it true, Salerio?
Have all his ventures fail'd? What, not one hit?
From Tripolis, from Mexico, and England,
From Lisbon, Barbary, and India?
And not one vessel scape the dreadful touch
Of merchant-marring rocks?
Saler. Not one, my lord.
Besides, it should appear that, if he had
The present money to discharge the Jew,
He would not take it. Never did I know
A creature that did bear the shape of man
So keen and greedy to confound a man.
He plies the Duke at morning and at night,
And doth impeach the freedom of the state
If they deny him justice. Twenty merchants,
The Duke himself, and the magnificoes
Of greatest port have all persuaded with him;
But none can drive him from the envious plea
Of forfeiture, of justice, and his bond.
Jes. When I was with him, I have heard him swear
To Tubal and to Chus, his countrymen,
That he would rather have Antonio's flesh
Than twenty times the value of the sum
That he did owe him; and I know, my lord,
If law, authority, and power deny not,
It will go hard with poor Antonio.
Por. Is it your dear friend that is thus in trouble?
Bass. The dearest friend to me, the kindest man,
The best-condition'd and unwearied spirit
In doing courtesies, and one in whom
The ancient Roman honour more appears
Than any that draws breath in Italy.
Por. What sum owes he the Jew?
Bass. For me three thousand ducats.
Por. What, no more?
Pay him six thousand, and deface the bond.
Double six thousand and then treble that
Before a friend of this description
Shall lose a hair through Bassanio's fault.
First go with me to church and call me wife,
And then away to Venice to your friend!
For never shall you lie by Portia's side
With an unquiet soul. You shall have gold
To pay the petty debt twenty times over.
When it is paid, bring your true friend along.
My maid Nerissa and myself meantime
Will live as maids and widows. Come, away!
For you shall hence upon your wedding day.
Bid your friends welcome, show a merry cheer;
Since you are dear bought, I will love you dear.
But let me hear the letter of your friend.

Bass. 'Sweet Bassanio, my ships have all miscarried, my creditors grow cruel, my estate is very low, my bond to the Jew is forfeit; and since in paying it, it is impossible I should live, all debts are clear'd between you and I if I might but see you at my death. Notwithstanding, use your pleasure. If your love do not persuade you to come, let not my letter.'

Por. O love, dispatch all business and be gone!
Bass. Since I have your good leave to go away,
I will make haste; but till I come again,
No bed shall e'er be guilty of my stay,
Nor rest be interposer 'twixt us twain.
Exeunt.

[Scene III. *Venice. The street before* Shylock's *house.*]

Enter [*Shylock*] *the Jew* and *Solanio* and *Antonio* and the *Jailer.*

Shy. Jailer, look to him. Tell not me of mercy.
This is the fool that lent out money gratis.
Jailer, look to him.
Ant. Hear me yet, good Shylock.
Shy. I'll have my bond! Speak not against my bond!
I have sworn an oath that I will have my bond.
Thou call'dst me dog before thou hadst a cause;
But, since I am a dog, beware my fangs.
The Duke shall grant me justice. I do wonder,
Thou naughty jailer, that thou art so fond
To come abroad with him at his request.
Ant. I pray thee hear me speak.
Shy. I'll have my bond. I will not hear thee speak.

I'll have my bond, and therefore speak no more.
I'll not be made a soft and dull-ey'd fool,
To shake the head, relent, and sigh, and yield
To Christian intercessors. Follow not.
I'll have no speaking; I will have my bond.
Exit.

Solan. It is the most impenetrable cur
That ever kept with men.

Ant. Let him alone.
I'll follow him no more with bootless prayers.
He seeks my life. His reason well I know:
I oft deliver'd from his forfeitures
Many that have at times made moan to me.
Therefore he hates me.

Solan. I am sure the Duke
Will never grant this forfeiture to hold.

Ant. The Duke cannot deny the course of law;
For the commodity that strangers have
With us in Venice, if it be denied,
Will much impeach the justice of the state,
Since that the trade and profit of the city
Consisteth of all nations. Therefore go.
These griefs and losses have so bated me
That I shall hardly spare a pound of flesh
To-morrow to my bloody creditor.
Well, jailer, on. Pray God Bassanio come
To see me pay his debt, and then I care not!
Exeunt.

[Scene IV. *Belmont.* Portia's *house.*]

Enter *Portia, Nerissa, Lorenzo, Jessica,* and [*Balthasar,*] a Man of *Portia's.*

Lor. Madam, although I speak it in your presence,
You have a noble and a true conceit
Of godlike amity, which appears most strongly
In bearing thus the absence of your lord.
But if you knew to whom you show this honour,
How true a gentleman you send relief,
How dear a lover of my lord your husband,
I know you would be prouder of the work
Than customary bounty can enforce you.

Por. I never did repent for doing good,
Nor shall not now; for in companions
That do converse and waste the time together,
Whose souls do bear an egal yoke of love,
There must be needs a like proportion
Of lineaments, of manners, and of spirit;
Which makes me think that this Antonio,
Being the bosom lover of my lord,
Must needs be like my lord. If it be so,
How little is the cost I have bestow'd
In purchasing the semblance of my soul
From out the state of hellish cruelty!
This comes too near the praising of myself.
Therefore no more of it. Hear other things.
Lorenzo, I commit into your hands
The husbandry and manage of my house
Until my lord's return. For mine own part,
I have toward heaven breath'd a secret vow
To live in prayer and contemplation,
Only attended by Nerissa here,
Until her husband and my lord's return.
There is a monastery two miles off,
And there we will abide. I do desire you
Not to deny this imposition,
The which my love and some necessity
Now lays upon you.

Lor. Madam, with all my heart.
I shall obey you in all fair commands.

Por. My people do already know my mind
And will acknowledge you and Jessica
In place of Lord Bassanio and myself.
So fare you well till we shall meet again.

Lor. Fair thoughts and happy hours attend on you!

Jes. I wish your ladyship all heart's content.

Por. I thank you for your wish, and am well pleas'd
To wish it back on you. Fare you well, Jessica.
Exeunt [*Jessica and Lorenzo*].
Now, Balthasar,
As I have ever found thee honest-true,
So let me find thee still. Take this same letter,
And use thou all th' endeavour of a man
In speed to Padua. See thou render this
Into my cousin's hand, Doctor Bellario;
And look, what notes and garments he doth give thee,
Bring them, I pray thee, with imagin'd speed
Unto the Tranect, to the common ferry
Which trades to Venice. Waste no time in words
But get thee gone. I shall be there before thee.

Balth. Madam, I go with all convenient speed. *Exit.*

Por. Come on, Nerissa. I have work in hand
That you yet know not of. We'll see our husbands
Before they think of us.

Ner. Shall they see us?

Por. They shall, Nerissa, but in such a habit
That they shall think we are accomplished
With that we lack. I'll hold thee any wager,
When we are both accoutered like young men,

I'll prove the prettier fellow of the two,
And wear my dagger with the braver grace,
And speak between the change of man and boy
With a reed voice, and turn two mincing steps
Into a manly stride; and speak of frays
Like a fine bragging youth; and tell quaint lies,
How honourable ladies sought my love,
Which I denying, they fell sick and died —
I could not do withal! Then I'll repent,
And wish, for all that, that I had not kill'd them.
And twenty of these puny lies I'll tell,
That men shall swear I have discontinued school
Above a twelvemonth. I have within my mind
A thousand raw tricks of these bragging Jacks,
Which I will practise.

Ner. Why, shall we turn to men?

Por. Fie, what a question 's that,
If thou wert near a lewd interpreter!
But come, I'll tell thee all my whole device
When I am in my coach, which stays for us
At the park gate; and therefore haste away,
For we must measure twenty miles to-day.
Exeunt.

[Scene V. *Belmont. A garden.*]

Enter [*Launcelot the*] *Clown* and *Jessica.*

Laun. Yes, truly; for look you, the sins of the father are to be laid upon the children. Therefore, I promise you, I fear you. I was always plain with you, and so now I speak my agitation of the matter. Therefore be o' good cheer, for truly I think you are damn'd. There is but one hope in it that can do you any good, and that is but a kind of bastard hope neither.

Jes. And what hope is that, I pray thee?

Laun. Marry, you may partly hope that your father got you not — that you are not the Jew's daughter.

Jes. That were a kind of bastard hope indeed! So the sins of my mother should be visited upon me.

Laun. Truly then I fear you are damn'd both by father and mother. Thus when I shun Scylla, your father, I fall into Charybdis, your mother. Well, you are gone both ways.

Jes. I shall be sav'd by my husband. He hath made me a Christian.

Laun. Truly, the more to blame he! We were Christians enow before, e'en as many as could well live one by another. This making of Christians will raise the price of hogs. If we grow all to be pork-eaters, we shall not shortly have a rasher on the coals for money.

Enter *Lorenzo.*

Jes. I'll tell my husband, Launcelot, what you say. Here he comes.

Lor. I shall grow jealious of you shortly, Launcelot, if you thus get my wife into corners.

Jes. Nay, you need not fear us, Lorenzo. Launcelot and I are out. He tells me flatly there's no mercy for me in heaven because I am a Jew's daughter; and he says you are no good member of the commonwealth, for in converting Jews to Christians you raise the price of pork.

Lor. I shall answer that better to the commonwealth than you can the getting up of the Negro's belly. The Moor is with child by you, Launcelot.

Laun. It is much that the Moor should be more than reason; but if she be less than an honest woman, she is indeed more than I took her for.

Lor. How every fool can play upon the word! I think the best grace of wit will shortly turn into silence, and discourse grow commendable in none only but parrots. Go in, sirrah; bid them prepare for dinner.

Laun. That is done, sir. They have all stomachs.

Lor. Goodly Lord, what a wit-snapper are you! Then bid them prepare dinner.

Laun. That is done too, sir. Only 'cover' is the word.

Lor. Will you cover then, sir?

Laun. Not so, sir, neither! I know my duty.

Lor. Yet more quarrelling with occasion? Wilt thou show the whole wealth of thy wit in an instant? I pray thee understand a plain man in his plain meaning. Go to thy fellows, bid them cover the table, serve in the meat, and we will come in to dinner.

Laun. For the table, sir, it shall be serv'd in; for the meat, sir, it shall be cover'd; for your coming in to dinner, sir, why, let it be as humours and conceits shall govern. *Exit.*

Lor. O dear discretion, how his words are suited!
The fool hath planted in his memory
An army of good words; and I do know
A many fools, that stand in better place,
Garnish'd like him, that for a tricksy word
Defy the matter. How cheer'st thou, Jessica?
And now, good sweet, say thy opinion —
How dost thou like the Lord Bassanio's wife?

Jes. Past all expressing. It is very meet
The Lord Bassanio live an upright life;
For, having such a blessing in his lady,
He finds the joys of heaven here on earth;
And if on earth he do not merit it,
In reason he should never come to heaven.
Why, if two gods should play some heavenly match,
And on the wager lay two earthly women,
And Portia one, there must be something else
Pawn'd with the other; for the poor rude world
Hath not her fellow.
Lor. Even such a husband
Hast thou of me as she is for a wife.
Jes. Nay, but ask my opinion too of that!
Lor. I will anon. First let us go to dinner.
Jes. Nay, let me praise you while I have a stomach.
Lor. No, pray thee, let it serve for table-talk;
Then, howsome'er thou speak'st, 'mong other things
I shall disgest it.
Jes. Well, I'll set you forth.
Exeunt.

ACT IV. [Scene I. *Venice. A court of justice.*]

Enter the *Duke*, the *Magnificoes, Antonio, Bassanio, Gratiano,* [*Solanio*, and others].

Duke. What, is Antonio here?
Ant. Ready, so please your Grace.
Duke. I am sorry for thee. Thou art come to answer
A stony adversary, an inhuman wretch,
Uncapable of pity, void and empty
From any dram of mercy.
Ant. I have heard
Your Grace hath ta'en great pains to qualify
His rigorous course; but since he stands obdurate,
And that no lawful means can carry me
Out of his envy's reach, I do oppose
My patience to his fury, and am arm'd
To suffer with a quietness of spirit
The very tyranny and rage of his.
Duke. Go one, and call the Jew into the court.
Solan. He is ready at the door; he comes, my lord.

Enter *Shylock.*

Duke. Make room, and let him stand before our face.
Shylock, the world thinks, and I think so too,
That thou but leadest this fashion of thy malice
To the last hour of act; and then 'tis thought
Thou'lt show thy mercy and remorse more strange
Than is thy strange apparent cruelty;
And where thou now exacts the penalty,
Which is a pound of this poor merchant's flesh,
Thou wilt not only loose the forfeiture,
But, touch'd with humane gentleness and love,
Forgive a moiety of the principal,
Glancing an eye of pity on his losses,
That have of late so huddled on his back —
Enow to press a royal merchant down
And pluck commiseration of his state
From brassy bosoms and rough hearts of flint,
From stubborn Turks and Tartars, never train'd
To offices of tender courtesy.
We all expect a gentle answer, Jew.
Shy. I have possess'd your Grace of what I purpose,
And by our holy Sabbath have I sworn
To have the due and forfeit of my bond.
If you deny it, let the danger light
Upon your charter and your city's freedom!
You'll ask me why I rather choose to have
A weight of carrion flesh than to receive
Three thousand ducats. I'll not answer that!
But say it is my humour, is it answer'd?
What if my house be troubled with a rat,
And I be pleas'd to give ten thousand ducats
To have it ban'd? What, are you answer'd yet?
Some men there are love not a gaping pig,
Some that are mad if they behold a cat,
And others, when the bagpipe sings i' th' nose,
Cannot contain their urine; for affection,
Mistress of passion, sways it to the mood
Of what it likes or loathes. Now for your answer:
As there is no firm reason to be rend'red
Why he cannot abide a gaping pig,
Why he a harmless necessary cat,
Why he a woollen bagpipe — but of force
Must yield to such inevitable shame
As to offend himself, being offended;
So can I give no reason, nor I will not,
More than a lodg'd hate and a certain loathing
I bear Antonio, that I follow thus
A losing suit against him. Are you answer'd?
Bass. This is no answer, thou unfeeling man,
To excuse the current of thy cruelty!

Shy. I am not bound to please thee with my answers.
Bass. Do all men kill the things they do not love?
Shy. Hates any man the thing he would not kill?
Bass. Every offence is not a hate at first.
Shy. What, wouldst thou have a serpent sting thee twice?
Ant. I pray you think you question with the Jew.
You may as well go stand upon the beach
And bid the main flood bate his usual height;
You may as well use question with the wolf,
Why he hath made the ewe bleat for the lamb;
You may as well forbid the mountain pines
To wag their high tops and to make no noise
When they are fretten with the gusts of heaven;
You may as well do anything most hard
As seek to soften that — than which what's harder? —
His Jewish heart. Therefore I do beseech you
Make no moe offers, use no farther means,
But with all brief and plain conveniency
Let me have judgment, and the Jew his will.
Bass. For thy three thousand ducats here is six.
Shy. If every ducat in six thousand ducats
Were in six parts, and every part a ducat,
I would not draw them, I would have my bond.
Duke. How shalt thou hope for mercy, rend'ring none?
Shy. What judgment shall I dread, doing no wrong?
You have among you many a purchas'd slave,
Which, like your asses and your dogs and mules,
You use in abject and in slavish parts,
Because you bought them. Shall I say to you,
'Let them be free, marry them to your heirs!
Why sweat they under burthens? Let their beds
Be made as soft as yours, and let their palates
Be season'd with such viands'? You will answer,
'The slaves are ours.' So do I answer you.
The pound of flesh which I demand of him
Is dearly bought, 'tis mine, and I will have it.
If you deny me, fie upon your law!
There is no force in the decrees of Venice.
I stand for judgment. Answer. Shall I have it?
Duke. Upon my power I may dismiss this court
Unless Bellario, a learned doctor,
Whom I have sent for to determine this,
Come here to-day.
Solan. My lord, here stays without
A messenger with letters from the doctor,
New come from Padua.
Duke. Bring us the letters. Call the messenger.
Bass. Good cheer, Antonio! What, man, courage yet!
The Jew shall have my flesh, blood, bones, and all,
Ere thou shalt lose for me one drop of blood.
Ant. I am a tainted wether of the flock,
Meetest for death. The weakest kind of fruit
Drops earliest to the ground, and so let me.
You cannot better be employ'd, Bassanio,
Than to live still, and write mine epitaph.

Enter *Nerissa,* [dressed like a *Lawyer's Clerk*].

Duke. Came you from Padua from Bellario?
Ner. From both, my lord. Bellario greets your Grace. [*Presents a letter.*]
Bass. Why dost thou whet thy knife so earnestly?
Shy. To cut the forfeiture from that bankrout there.
Gra. Not on thy sole, but on thy soul, harsh Jew,
Thou mak'st thy knife keen; but no metal can—
No, not the hangman's axe — bear half the keenness
Of thy sharp envy. Can no prayers pierce thee?
Shy. No, none that thou hast wit enough to make.
Gra. O, be thou damn'd, inexorable dog,
And for thy life let justice be accus'd!
Thou almost mak'st me waver in my faith,
To hold opinion with Pythagoras,
That souls of animals infuse themselves
Into the trunks of men. Thy currish spirit
Govern'd a wolf, who, hang'd for human slaughter,
Even from the gallows did his fell soul fleet,
And, whilst thou layest in thy unhallowed dam,
Infus'd itself in thee; for thy desires
Are wolvish, bloody, starv'd, and ravenous.
Shy. Till thou canst rail the seal from off my bond,
Thou but offend'st thy lungs to speak so loud.
Repair thy wit, good youth, or it will fall
To cureless ruin. I stand here for law.
Duke. This letter from Bellario doth commend
A young and learned doctor to our court.
Where is he?
Ner. He attendeth here hard by
To know your answer whether you'll admit him.
Duke. With all my heart. Some three or four of you

Go give him courteous conduct to this place.
Meantime the court shall hear Bellario's letter.

[*Clerk reads.*] 'Your Grace shall understand that at the receipt of your letter I am very sick; but in the instant that your messenger came, in loving visitation was with me a young doctor of Rome — his name is Balthasar. I acquainted him with the cause in controversy between the Jew and Antonio the merchant. We turn'd o'er many books together. He is furnished with my opinion, which, bettered with his own learning (the greatness whereof I cannot enough commend), comes with him at my importunity to fill up your Grace's request in my stead. I beseech you let his lack of years be no impediment to let him lack a reverend estimation; for I never knew so young a body with so old a head. I leave him to your gracious acceptance, whose trial shall better publish his commendation.'

Enter *Portia* for *Balthasar*, [dressed like a *Doctor of Laws*].

Duke. You hear the learn'd Bellario what he writes;
And here, I take it, is the doctor come.
Give me your hand. Come you from old Bellario?
Por. I did, my lord.
Duke. You are welcome; take your place.
Are you acquainted with the difference
That holds this present question in the court?
Por. I am informed throughly of the cause.
Which is the merchant here? and which the Jew?
Duke. Antonio and old Shylock, both stand forth.
Por. Is your name Shylock?
Shy. Shylock is my name.
Por. Of a strange nature is the suit you follow;
Yet in such rule that the Venetian law
Cannot impugn you as you do proceed. —
You stand within his danger, do you not?
Ant. Ay, so he says.
Por. Do you confess the bond?
Ant. I do.
Por. Then must the Jew be merciful.
Shy. On what compulsion must I? Tell me that.
Por. The quality of mercy is not strain'd;
It droppeth as the gentle rain from heaven
Upon the place beneath. It is twice blest —
It blesseth him that gives, and him that takes.
'Tis mightiest in the mightiest. It becomes
The throned monarch better than his crown.
His sceptre shows the force of temporal power,
The attribute to awe and majesty,
Wherein doth sit the dread and fear of kings;
But mercy is above this sceptred sway;
It is enthroned in the hearts of kings,
It is an attribute to God himself;
And earthly power doth then show likest God's
When mercy seasons justice. Therefore, Jew,
Though justice be thy plea, consider this —
That, in the course of justice, none of us
Should see salvation. We do pray for mercy,
And that same prayer doth teach us all to render
The deeds of mercy. I have spoke thus much
To mitigate the justice of thy plea;
Which if thou follow, this strict court of Venice
Must needs give sentence 'gainst the merchant there.
Shy. My deeds upon my head! I crave the law,
The penalty and forfeit of my bond.
Por. Is he not able to discharge the money?
Bass. Yes, here I tender it for him in the court;
Yea, thrice the sum. If that will not suffice,
I will be bound to pay it ten times o'er
On forfeit of my hands, my head, my heart.
If this will not suffice, it must appear
That malice bears down truth. And I beseech you,
Wrest once the law to your authority.
To do a great right, do a little wrong,
And curb this cruel devil of his will.
Por. It must not be. There is no power in Venice
Can alter a decree established.
'Twill be recorded for a precedent;
And many an error by the same example
Will rush into the state. It cannot be.
Shy. A Daniel come to judgment! yea, a Daniel!
O wise young judge, how I do honour thee!
Por. I pray you let me look upon the bond.
Shy. Here 'tis, most reverend Doctor, here it is.
Por. Shylock, there's thrice thy money offer'd thee.
Shy. An oath, an oath, I have an oath in heaven!
Shall I lay perjury upon my soul?
No, not for Venice.
Por. Why, this bond is forfeit;
And lawfully by this the Jew may claim
A pound of flesh, to be by him cut off
Nearest the merchant's heart. Be merciful.
Take thrice thy money; bid me tear the bond.
Shy. When it is paid, according to the tenure.
It doth appear you are a worthy judge;
You know the law, your exposition
Hath been most sound. I charge you by the law,

Whereof you are a well-deserving pillar,
Proceed to judgment. By my soul I swear
There is no power in the tongue of man
To alter me. I stay here on my bond.
Ant. Most heartily I do beseech the court
To give the judgment.
Por. Why then, thus it is:
You must prepare your bosom for his knife.
Shy. O noble judge! O excellent young man!
Por. For the intent and purpose of the law
Hath full relation to the penalty,
Which here appeareth due upon the bond.
Shy. 'Tis very true. O wise and upright judge!
How much more elder art thou than thy looks!
Por. Therefore lay bare your bosom.
Shy. Ay, his breast—
So says the bond; doth it not, noble judge?
Nearest his heart. Those are the very words.
Por. It is so. Are there balance here to weigh
The flesh?
Shy. I have them ready.
Por. Have by some surgeon, Shylock, on your charge,
To stop his wounds, lest he do bleed to death.
Shy. Is it so nominated in the bond?
Por. It is not so express'd; but what of that?
'Twere good you do so much for charity.
Shy. I cannot find it; 'tis not in the bond.
Por. You, merchant, have you anything to say?
Ant. But little. I am arm'd and well prepar'd.
Give me your hand, Bassanio. Fare you well!
Grieve not that I am fall'n to this for you;
For herein Fortune shows herself more kind
Than is her custom. It is still her use
To let the wretched man outlive his wealth
To view with hollow eye and wrinkled brow
An age of poverty; from which ling'ring penance
Of such misery doth she cut me off.
Commend me to your honourable wife;
Tell her the process of Antonio's end;
Say how I lov'd you, speak me fair in death;
And when the tale is told, bid her be judge
Whether Bassanio had not once a love.
Repent but you that you shall lose your friend,
And he repents not that he pays your debt;
For if the Jew do cut but deep enough,
I'll pay it instantly with all my heart.
Bass. Antonio, I am married to a wife
Which is as dear to me as life itself;
But life itself, my wife, and all the world
Are not with me esteem'd above thy life.
I would lose all, ay, sacrifice them all
Here to this devil, to deliver you.
Por. Your wife would give you little thanks for that
If she were by to hear you make the offer.
Gra. I have a wife who I protest I love.
I would she were in heaven, so she could
Entreat some power to change this currish Jew.
Ner. 'Tis well you offer it behind her back.
The wish would make else an unquiet house.
Shy. [*aside*] These be the Christian husbands! I have a daughter—
Would any of the stock of Barrabas
Had been her husband rather than a Christian!—
We trifle time. I pray thee pursue sentence.
Por. A pound of that same merchant's flesh is thine.
The court awards it, and the law doth give it.
Shy. Most rightful judge!
Por. And you must cut this flesh from off his breast.
The law allows it, and the court awards it.
Shy. Most learned judge! A sentence! Come, prepare!
Por. Tarry a little; there is something else.
This bond doth give thee here no jot of blood;
The words expressly are 'a pound of flesh.'
Take then thy bond, take thou thy pound of flesh;
But in the cutting it if thou dost shed
One drop of Christian blood, thy lands and goods
Are, by the laws of Venice, confiscate
Unto the state of Venice.
Gra. O upright judge! Mark, Jew. O learned judge!
Shy. Is that the law?
Por. Thyself shalt see the act;
For, as thou urgest justice, be assur'd
Thou shalt have justice more than thou desir'st.
Gra. O learned judge! Mark, Jew. A learned judge!
Shy. I take this offer then. Pay the bond thrice,
And let the Christian go.
Bass. Here is the money.
Por. Soft!
The Jew shall have all justice. Soft! no haste.
He shall have nothing but the penalty.
Gra. O Jew! an upright judge! a learned judge!
Por. Therefore prepare thee to cut off the flesh.
Shed thou no blood, nor cut thou less nor more
But just a pound of flesh. If thou tak'st more

Or less than a just pound — be it but so much
As makes it light or heavy in the substance
Or the division of the twentieth part
Of one poor scruple; nay, if the scale do turn
But in the estimation of a hair —
Thou diest, and all thy goods are confiscate.
Gra. A second Daniel! a Daniel, Jew!
Now, infidel, I have you on the hip.
Por. Why doth the Jew pause? Take thy forfeiture.
Shy. Give me my principal, and let me go.
Bass. I have it ready for thee; here it is.
Por. He hath refus'd it in the open court.
He shall have merely justice and his bond.
Gra. A Daniel still say I, a second Daniel!
I thank thee, Jew, for teaching me that word.
Shy. Shall I not have barely my principal?
Por. Thou shalt have nothing but the forfeiture,
To be so taken at thy peril, Jew.
Shy. Why, then the devil give him good of it!
I'll stay no longer question.
Por. Tarry, Jew.
The law hath yet another hold on you.
It is enacted in the laws of Venice,
If it be prov'd against an alien
That by direct or indirect attempts
He seek the life of any citizen,
The party 'gainst the which he doth contrive
Shall seize one half his goods; the other half
Comes to the privy coffer of the state;
And the offender's life lies in the mercy
Of the Duke only, 'gainst all other voice.
In which predicament I say thou stand'st;
For it appears by manifest proceeding
That indirectly, and directly too,
Thou hast contriv'd against the very life
Of the defendant, and thou hast incurr'd
The danger formerly by me rehears'd.
Down, therefore, and beg mercy of the Duke.
Gra. Beg that thou mayst have leave to hang thyself!
And yet, thy wealth being forfeit to the state,
Thou hast not left the value of a cord;
Therefore thou must be hang'd at the state's charge.
Duke. That thou shalt see the difference of our spirit,
I pardon thee thy life before thou ask it.
For half thy wealth, it is Antonio's;
The other half comes to the general state,
Which humbleness may drive unto a fine.
Por. Ay, for the state, not for Antonio.
Shy. Nay, take my life and all! Pardon not that!
You take my house when you do take the prop
That doth sustain my house. You take my life
When you do take the means whereby I live.
Por. What mercy can you render him, Antonio?
Gra. A halter gratis. Nothing else, for God's sake!
Ant. So please my lord the Duke and all the court
To quit the fine for one half of his goods,
I am content; so he will let me have
The other half in use, to render it
Upon his death unto the gentleman
That lately stole his daughter —
Two things provided more: that, for this favour,
He presently become a Christian;
The other, that he do record a gift
Here in the court of all he dies possess'd
Unto his son Lorenzo and his daughter.
Duke. He shall do this, or else I do recant
The pardon that I late pronounced here.
Por. Art thou contented, Jew? What dost thou say?
Shy. I am content.
Por. Clerk, draw a deed of gift.
Shy. I pray you give me leave to go from hence.
I am not well. Send the deed after me,
And I will sign it.
Duke. Get thee gone, but do it.
Gra. In christ'ning shalt thou have two godfathers.
Had I been judge, thou shouldst have had ten more,
To bring thee to the gallows, not the font.
Exit [*Shylock*].
Duke. Sir, I entreat you home with me to dinner.
Por. I humbly do desire your Grace of pardon.
I must away this night toward Padua,
And it is meet I presently set forth.
Duke. I am sorry that your leisure serves you not.
Antonio, gratify this gentleman,
For in my mind you are much bound to him.
Exeunt Duke and his Train.
Bass. Most worthy gentleman, I and my friend
Have by your wisdom been this day acquitted
Of grievous penalties, in lieu whereof,
Three thousand ducats, due unto the Jew,
We freely cope your courteous pains withal.
Ant. And stand indebted, over and above,
In love and service to you evermore.

Por. He is well paid that is well satisfied;
And I, delivering you, am satisfied,
And therein do account myself well paid.
My mind was never yet more mercenary.
I pray you know me when we meet again.
I wish you well, and so I take my leave.
Bass. Dear sir, of force I must attempt you further.
Take some remembrance of us as a tribute,
Not as a fee. Grant me two things, I pray you—
Not to deny me, and to pardon me.
Por. You press me far, and therefore I will yield.
Give me your gloves, I'll wear them for your sake; [*Bassanio takes off his gloves.*]
And for your love I'll take this ring from you.
Do not draw back your hand. I'll take no more;
And you in love shall not deny me this.
Bass. This ring, good sir? Alas, it is a trifle!
I will not shame myself to give you this.
Por. I will have nothing else but only this;
And now methinks I have a mind to it.
Bass. There's more depends on this than on the value.
The dearest ring in Venice will I give you,
And find it out by proclamation.
Only for this, I pray you pardon me.
Por. I see, sir, you are liberal in offers.
You taught me first to beg, and now methinks
You teach me how a beggar should be answer'd.
Bass. Good sir, this ring was given me by my wife;
And when she put it on, she made me vow
That I should neither sell nor give nor lose it.
Por. That 'scuse serves many men to save their gifts.
And if your wife be not a madwoman,
And know how well I have deserv'd this ring,
She would not hold out enemy for ever
For giving it to me. Well, peace be with you!
Exeunt [*Portia and Nerissa*].
Ant. My Lord Bassanio, let him have the ring.
Let his deservings, and my love withal,
Be valued 'gainst your wive's commandëment.
Bass. Go, Gratiano, run and overtake him.
Give him the ring and bring him, if thou canst,
Unto Antonio's house. Away! make haste.
Exit Gratiano.
Come, you and I will thither presently,
And in the morning early will we both
Fly toward Belmont. Come, Antonio. *Exeunt.*

[Scene II. *Venice. A street.*]

Enter *Portia* and *Nerissa,* [disguised as before].

Por. Enquire the Jew's house out, give him this deed,
And let him sign it. We'll away to-night
And be a day before our husbands home.
This deed will be well welcome to Lorenzo.

Enter *Gratiano.*

Gra. Fair sir, you are well o'erta'en.
My Lord Bassanio, upon more advice,
Hath sent you here this ring, and doth entreat
Your company at dinner.
Por. That cannot be.
His ring I do accept most thankfully,
And so I pray you tell him. Furthermore,
I pray you show my youth old Shylock's house.
Gra. That will I do.
Ner. Sir, I would speak with you.
[*Aside to Portia*] I'll see if I can get my husband's ring,
Which I did make him swear to keep for ever.
Por. [*aside to Nerissa*] Thou mayst, I warrant. We shall have old swearing
That they did give the rings away to men;
But we'll outface them, and outswear them too.
[*Aloud*] Away! make haste. Thou know'st where I will tarry.
Ner. Come, good sir, will you show me to this house? *Exeunt.*

ACT V. [Scene I. *Belmont. Grounds of* Portia's *house.*]

Enter *Lorenzo* and *Jessica.*

Lor. The moon shines bright. In such a night as this,
When the sweet wind did gently kiss the trees
And they did make no noise — in such a night
Troilus methinks mounted the Troyan walls
And sigh'd his soul toward the Grecian tents,
Where Cressid lay that night.
Jes. In such a night
Did Thisbe fearfully o'ertrip the dew,
And saw the lion's shadow ere himself,
And ran dismay'd away.
Lor. In such a night
Stood Dido with a willow in her hand
Upon the wild sea-banks, and waft her love
To come again to Carthage.
Jes. In such a night

Medea gathered the enchanted herbs
That did renew old Æson.

Lor. In such a night
Did Jessica steal from the wealthy Jew,
And with an unthrift love did run from Venice
As far as Belmont.

Jes. In such a night
Did young Lorenzo swear he lov'd her well,
Stealing her soul with many vows of faith,
And ne'er a true one.

Lor. In such a night
Did pretty Jessica (like a little shrow)
Slander her love, and he forgave it her.

Jes. I would out-night you, did no body come;
But, hark, I hear the footing of a man.

Enter [*Stephano,*] a *Messenger.*

Lor. Who comes so fast in silence of the night?

Mess. A friend.

Lor. A friend? What friend? Your name, I pray you, friend?

Mess. Stephano is my name, and I bring word
My mistress will before the break of day
Be here at Belmont. She doth stray about
By holy crosses, where she kneels and prays
For happy wedlock hours.

Lor. Who comes with her?

Mess. None but a holy hermit and her maid.
I pray you, is my master yet return'd?

Lor. He is not, nor we have not heard from him.
But go we in, I pray thee, Jessica,
And ceremoniously let us prepare
Some welcome for the mistress of the house.

Enter [*Launcelot, the*] *Clown.*

Laun. Sola, sola! wo ha, ho! sola, sola!

Lor. Who calls?

Laun. Sola! Did you see Master Lorenzo and Mistress Lorenzo? Sola, sola!

Lor. Leave holloaing, man! Here.

Laun. Sola! Where? where?

Lor. Here!

Laun. Tell him there's a post come from my master, with his horn full of good news. My master will be here ere morning. [*Exit.*]

Lor. Sweet soul, let's in, and there expect their coming.
And yet no matter. Why should we go in?
My friend Stephano, signify, I pray you,
Within the house, your mistress is at hand
And bring your music forth into the air.
[*Exit Stephano.*]
How sweet the moonlight sleeps upon this bank!
Here will we sit and let the sounds of music
Creep in our ears. Soft stillness and the night
Become the touches of sweet harmony.
Sit, Jessica. Look how the floor of heaven
Is thick inlaid with patens of bright gold.
There's not the smallest orb which thou behold'st
But in his motion like an angel sings,
Still quiring to the young-ey'd cherubins;
Such harmony is in immortal souls;
But whilst this muddy vesture of decay
Doth grossly close it in, we cannot hear it.

[Enter *Musicians.*]

Come, ho, and wake Diana with a hymn!
With sweetest touches pierce your mistress' ear
And draw her home with music. *Play music.*

Jes. I am never merry when I hear sweet music.

Lor. The reason is, your spirits are attentive.
For do but note a wild and wanton herd,
Or race of youthful and unhandled colts,
Fetching mad bounds, bellowing and neighing loud,
Which is the hot condition of their blood:
If they but hear perchance a trumpet sound,
Or any air of music touch their ears,
You shall perceive them make a mutual stand,
Their savage eyes turn'd to a modest gaze
By the sweet power of music. Therefore the poet
Did feign that Orpheus drew trees, stones, and floods,
Since naught so stockish, hard, and full of rage
But music for the time doth change his nature.
The man that hath no music in himself,
Nor is not mov'd with concord of sweet sounds,
Is fit for treasons, stratagems, and spoils;
The motions of his spirit are dull as night,
And his affections dark as Erebus.
Let no such man be trusted. Mark the music.

Enter *Portia* and *Nerissa.*

Por. That light we see is burning in my hall.
How far that little candle throws his beams!
So shines a good deed in a naughty world.

Ner. When the moon shone, we did not see the candle.

Por. So doth the greater glory dim the less.
A substitute shines brightly as a king
Until a king be by; and then his state
Empties itself, as doth an inland brook
Into the main of waters. Music! hark!

Ner. It is your music, madam, of the house.

Por. Nothing is good, I see, without respect.
Methinks it sounds much sweeter than by day.
Ner. Silence bestows that virtue on it, madam.
Por. The crow doth sing as sweetly as the lark
When neither is attended; and I think
The nightingale, if she should sing by day
When every goose is cackling, would be thought
No better a musician than the wren.
How many things by season season'd are
To their right praise and true perfection!
Peace, ho! The moon sleeps with Endymion,
And would not be awak'd. *Music ceases.*
Lor. That is the voice,
Or I am much deceiv'd, of Portia.
Por. He knows me as the blind man knows the cuckoo,
By the bad voice.
Lor. Dear lady, welcome home.
Por. We have been praying for our husbands' welfare,
Which speed, we hope, the better for our words.
Are they return'd?
Lor. Madam, they are not yet;
But there is come a messenger before
To signify their coming.
Por. Go in, Nerissa.
Give order to my servants that they take
No note at all of our being absent hence —
Nor you, Lorenzo — Jessica, nor you.
A tucket sounds.
Lor. Your husband is at hand; I hear his trumpet.
We are no telltales, madam; fear you not.
Por. This night methinks is but the daylight sick;
It looks a little paler. 'Tis a day
Such as the day is when the sun is hid.

Enter *Bassanio, Antonio, Gratiano,* and their *Followers.*

Bass. We should hold day with the Antipodes
If you would walk in absence of the sun.
Por. Let me give light, but let me not be light;
For a light wife doth make a heavy husband,
And never be Bassanio so for me.
But God sort all! You are welcome home, my lord.
Bass. I thank you, madam. Give welcome to my friend.
This is the man, this is Antonio,
To whom I am so infinitely bound.
Por. You should in all sense be much bound to him,
For, as I hear, he was much bound for you.
Ant. No more than I am well acquitted of.
Por. Sir, you are very welcome to our house.
It must appear in other ways than words,
Therefore I scant this breathing courtesy.
Gra. [*to Nerissa*] By yonder moon I swear you do me wrong!
In faith, I gave it to the judge's clerk.
Would he were gelt that had it, for my part,
Since you do take it, love, so much at heart.
Por. A quarrel, ho, already! What's the matter?
Gra. About a hoop of gold, a paltry ring
That she did give to me, whose posy was
For all the world like cutler's poetry
Upon a knife, 'Love me, and leave me not.'
Ner. What talk you of the posy or the value?
You swore to me, when I did give it you,
That you would wear it till your hour of death,
And that it should lie with you in your grave.
Though not for me, yet for your vehement oaths,
You should have been respective and have kept it.
Gave it a judge's clerk! No, God 's my judge,
The clerk will ne'er wear hair on's face that had it.
Gra. He will, an if he live to be a man.
Ner. Ay, if a woman live to be a man.
Gra. Now, by this hand, I gave it to a youth,
A kind of boy, a little scrubbed boy,
No higher than thyself, the judge's clerk,
A prating boy that begg'd it as a fee.
I could not for my heart deny it him.
Por. You were to blame — I must be plain with you —
To part so slightly with your wive's first gift,
A thing stuck on with oaths upon your finger
And so riveted with faith unto your flesh.
I gave my love a ring, and made him swear
Never to part with it; and here he stands.
I dare be sworn for him he would not leave it
Nor pluck it from his finger for the wealth
That the world masters. Now, in faith, Gratiano,
You give your wife too unkind a cause of grief.
An 'twere to me, I should be mad at it.
Bass. [*aside*] Why, I were best to cut my left hand off
And swear I lost the ring defending it.
Gra. My Lord Bassanio gave his ring away
Unto the judge that begg'd it, and indeed
Deserv'd it too; and then the boy, his clerk,
That took some pains in writing, he begg'd mine;
And neither man nor master would take aught
But the two rings.

Por. What ring gave you, my lord?
Not that, I hope, which you receiv'd of me.
Bass. If I could add a lie unto a fault,
I would deny it; but you see my finger
Hath not the ring upon it — it is gone.
Por. Even so void is your false heart of truth.
By heaven, I will ne'er come in your bed
Until I see the ring!
Ner. Nor I in yours
Till I again see mine!
Bass. Sweet Portia,
If you did know to whom I gave the ring,
If you did know for whom I gave the ring,
And would conceive for what I gave the ring,
And how unwillingly I left the ring
When naught would be accepted but the ring,
You would abate the strength of your displeasure.
Por. If you had known the virtue of the ring,
Or half her worthiness that gave the ring,
Or your own honour to contain the ring,
You would not then have parted with the ring.
What man is there so much unreasonable,
If you had pleas'd to have defended it
With any terms of zeal, wanted the modesty
To urge the thing held as a ceremony?
Nerissa teaches me what to believe.
I'll die for't but some woman had the ring!
Bass. No, by my honour, madam, by my soul,
No woman had it, but a civil doctor,
Which did refuse three thousand ducats of me
And begg'd the ring; the which I did deny him,
And suffer'd him to go displeas'd away,
Even he that had held up the very life
Of my dear friend. What should I say, sweet lady?
I was enforc'd to send it after him.
I was beset with shame and courtesy.
My honour would not let ingratitude
So much besmear it. Pardon me, good lady;
For, by these blessed candles of the night,
Had you been there, I think you would have begg'd
The ring of me to give the worthy doctor.
Por. Let not that doctor e'er come near my house.
Since he hath got the jewel that I lov'd,
And that which you did swear to keep for me,
I will become as liberal as you;
I'll not deny him anything I have,
No, not my body, nor my husband's bed.
Know him I shall, I am well sure of it.
Lie not a night from home; watch me like Argus.
If you do not, if I be left alone,
Now, by mine honour, which is yet mine own,
I'll have that doctor for my bedfellow.
Ner. And I his clerk. Therefore be well advis'd
How you do leave me to mine own protection.
Gra. Well, do you so. Let not me take him then;
For if I do, I'll mar the young clerk's pen.
Ant. I am th' unhappy subject of these quarrels.
Por. Sir, grieve not you. You are welcome notwithstanding.
Bass. Portia, forgive me this enforced wrong,
And in the hearing of these many friends
I swear to thee, even by thine own fair eyes,
Wherein I see myself —
Por. Mark you but that?
In both my eyes he doubly sees himself;
In each eye one. Swear by your double self,
And there's an oath of credit.
Bass. Nay, but hear me.
Pardon this fault, and by my soul I swear
I never more will break an oath with thee.
Ant. I once did lend my body for his wealth,
Which, but for him that had your husband's ring,
Had quite miscarried. I dare be bound again,
My soul upon the forfeit, that your lord
Will never more break faith advisedly.
Por. Then you shall be his surety. Give him this,
And bid him keep it better than the other.
Ant. Here, Lord Bassanio. Swear to keep this ring.
Bass. By heaven, it is the same I gave the doctor!
Por. I had it of him. Pardon me, Bassanio;
For, by this ring, the doctor lay with me.
Ner. And pardon me, my gentle Gratiano;
For that same scrubbed boy, the doctor's clerk,
In lieu of this, last night did lie with me.
Gra. Why, this is like the mending of highways
In summer, where the ways are fair enough.
What, are we cuckolds ere we have deserv'd it?
Por. Speak not so grossly. You are all amaz'd.
Here is a letter, read it at your leisure;
It comes from Padua from Bellario.
There you shall find that Portia was the doctor,
Nerissa there her clerk. Lorenzo here
Shall witness I set forth as soon as you,
And even but now return'd. I have not yet

Enter'd my house. Antonio, you are welcome,
And I have better news in store for you
Than you expect. Unseal this letter soon.
There you shall find three of your argosies
Are richly come to harbour suddenly.
You shall not know by what strange accident
I chanced on this letter.

Ant. I am dumb.

Bass. Were you the doctor, and I knew you not?

Gra. Were you the clerk that is to make me cuckold?

Ner. Ay, but the clerk that never means to do it,
Unless he live until he be a man.

Bass. Sweet Doctor, you shall be my bed-fellow.
When I am absent, then lie with my wife.

Ant. Sweet lady, you have given me life and living;
For here I read for certain that my ships
Are safely come to road.

Por. How now, Lorenzo?
My clerk hath some good comforts too for you.

Ner. Ay, and I'll give them him without a fee.
There do I give to you and Jessica,
From the rich Jew, a special deed of gift,
After his death, of all he dies possess'd of.

Lor. Fair ladies, you drop manna in the way
Of starved people.

Por. It is almost morning,
And yet I am sure you are not satisfied
Of these events at full. Let us go in;
And charge us there upon inter'gatories,
And we will answer all things faithfully.

Gra. Let it be so. The first inter'gatory
That my Nerissa shall be sworn on is,
Whether till the next night she had rather stay,
Or go to bed now, being two hours to day.
But were the day come, I should wish it dark
Till I were couching with the doctor's clerk.
Well, while I live I'll fear no other thing
So sore as keeping safe Nerissa's ring. *Exeunt.*

As You Like It

As You Like It was first published, so far as we know, in the Folio of 1623, which affords a reasonably good text. For the date of composition 1599 may be confidently accepted. Meres, writing in 1598 (before October 19), does not record the play, but it is mentioned in the Stationers' Register on August 4, 1600. Marlowe's Hero and Leander, first printed in 1598, is quoted in iii, 5, 81–82:

> Dead shepherd, now I find thy saw of might:
> 'Who ever lov'd that lov'd not at first sight?'

There is no good ground for the theory that Shakespeare wrote As You Like It in 1593 and drastically revised it some years later. This conjecture depends in part on the detection of blank-verse lines embedded in prose passages. These 'fossils,' it is argued, are an indication that verse has been turned into prose. The evidence is fallacious. Such lines abound in works which certainly never existed in verse form: in North's Plutarch, for example, and Milton's *Doctrine and Discipline of Divorce*. English prose runs easily into occasional blank-verse rhythm.

The speeches of Hymen and the nuptial song (v, 4) have often been regarded as un-Shakespearean — that is, as not good enough for Shakespeare, and therefore, in all probability, an insertion by some dramatic journeyman. But Hymen is no interloper. An actual marriage could not be brought upon the stage; some kind of symbolism was needed; Hymen makes an appropriate master of ceremonies, and his speeches are every bit as good as they need be. In real life, no one expects formalities to soar.

The plot is taken from Thomas Lodge's novel *Rosalynde. Euphues golden legacie: found after his death in his Cell at Silexedra* (1590). Lodge informs us in his dedication that he 'writ this booke' to 'beguile the time' on his voyage to the islands of 'Terceras and the Canaries' with Captain Clarke. This would have been about 1588. In his address 'To the Gentlemen Readers' he says that he wrote it 'in the Ocean, when euerie line was wet with a surge, and euerie humorous passion countercheckt with a storme.'

Shakespeare follows Lodge's story closely, but softens some of the more violent incidents.

In Lodge, the quarrel with which the play begins is terrific. Saladyne (Shakespeare's Oliver) bids his servants lay hold on Rosader (Orlando) and bind him. Rosader, 'half mad' with wrath, though 'of a mild and courteous nature,' belabours them with a great rake and forces Saladyne to take refuge in a loft adjoining the garden. They make peace, Saladyne promising to reinstate Rosader in his proper rank in the family. After the wrestling match, in which the champion is killed, Rosader goes home with a troop of gentlemen. The door is shut against him, but he breaks it down, enters the hall, sword in hand, and feasts his companions royally. As soon as they are gone, Rosader draws his sword, resolved to be revenged on Saladyne, but peace is made once more, this time by the mediation of Adam Spencer. Shortly after, however, Saladyne surprises Rosader in his sleep and has him chained to a post. He is released by Adam, who tells him that Saladyne has informed their kindred and allies that he is insane and has invited them to breakfast next morning to see him chained up as a desperate madman. Adam fastens him once more to the post, but leaves the fetters unlocked. The guests are convinced that Rosader is mad indeed, and after dinner, heated with wine, they begin to rail at him. Adam gives a sign, Rosader breaks loose, and armed with poleaxes, they attack the guests, hurting many, killing some, and driving the rest out of the house. The sheriff of the county is summoned and vows to arrest Rosader. He and

Adam break through the sheriff's posse and make their way to the Forest of Arden. There is no plot on Saladyne's part (as there is in Shakespeare) to murder his brother by burning down his lodging (ii, 3).

From this point the novel proceeds like the play. In the love story Shakespeare follows Lodge closely. Le Beau, Jaques, Touchstone, Audrey, William, and Sir Oliver Martext are Shakespeare's own. All the other important characters have their representatives in Lodge. The conclusion of the play is like that of the novel, except that Lodge's usurper, instead of being 'converted both from his enterprise' against his brother (Shakespeare's Duke Senior) 'and from the world' (v, 4, 167–168), is killed in battle.

The novel is intensely Euphuistic in style and tells its tale in a leisurely fashion, but it has considerable merit. Like the play, it contains a number of love poems. The only character who is at all humorous is Coridon, and his humour is very mild indeed. The leisurely mode gives the novelist one advantage over the playwright. The sudden conversion of the wicked brother seems less precipitate in Lodge than in Shakespeare.

Lodge's source is the anonymous *Tale of Gamelyn*, which dates from about the middle of the fourteenth century. It occurs in manuscripts of *The Canterbury Tales* and once passed as Chaucer's work. Lodge must have had access to a manuscript, for *Gamelyn* was not printed until 1721, when Urry included it in his edition of Chaucer. In the violent features of his novel (summarized above), Lodge follows *Gamelyn* pretty closely. On reaching the woods, Gamelyn and Adam encounter certain banished men, who conduct them to their 'master, king of outlaws.' He makes Gamelyn second in command. Soon after, the leader has tidings that he can return home, since his peace is made, and Gamelyn is crowned as outlaw king. For the rest of the story Lodge varies considerably from the old tale. In the upshot, Gamelyn makes his peace with the king of the country and becomes Chief Justice of the royal forest. His companions are pardoned and the wicked brother is hanged. There is no love story in the old tale. All such matter in the novel is Lodge's own contribution. The poem ends with Gamelyn's marriage and death, but there are no details as to his wife. Not even her name is mentioned. The conclusion is simply:

> And siththen wedded Gamelyn a wyf both good and feyr.
> They lyueden to-gidere whil that Crist wolde,
> And sithen was Gamelyn grauen vnder molde;
> And so schal we alle; may ther no man fle.
> God bringe vs to the Ioye that euer schal be!

It is just possible that Shakespeare had recourse to the *Tale of Gamelyn* for a few details, but the balance of probabilities is against it.

The famous song 'It was a lover and his lass' (v, 3) is contained, with music, in Thomas Morley's *First Booke of Ayres* (1600). The order of stanzas in the present text follows Morley. In the Folio the fourth stanza comes second. The first line of the last stanza runs in Morley 'Then prettie louers take the time.' In line 19 Morley reads 'corne fields,' in line 25 'Countrie fooles.'

AS YOU LIKE IT

[Dramatis Personæ.

Duke Senior, living in banishment.
Duke Frederick, his brother, and usurper of his dukedom.
Amiens, } *Jaques,* } lords attending on the banished *Duke.*
Le Beau, a courtier attending on *Duke Frederick.*
Charles, wrestler to *Duke Frederick.*
Oliver, } *Jaques de Boys,* } *Orlando,* } sons of *Sir Rowland de Boys.*
Adam, } *Dennis,* } servants to *Oliver.*
Touchstone, a clown.
Sir Oliver Martext, a vicar.
Corin, } *Silvius,* } shepherds.
William, a country fellow, in love with *Audrey.*
Hymen.

Rosalind, daughter to the banished *Duke.*
Celia, daughter to *Duke Frederick.*
Phebe, a shepherdess.
Audrey, a country wench.
Lords, pages, and attendants, &c.

SCENE — *Oliver's orchard; Duke Frederick's court; the Forest of Arden.*]

ACT I. Scene I. [Oliver's *orchard.*]

Enter *Orlando* and *Adam.*

Orl. As I remember, Adam, it was upon this fashion: he bequeathed me by will but poor a thousand crowns, and, as thou say'st, charged my brother on his blessing to breed me well; and there begins my sadness. My brother Jaques he keeps at school, and report speaks goldenly of his profit. For my part, he keeps me rustically at home or, to speak more properly, stays me here at home unkept; for call you that keeping for a gentleman of my birth that differs not from the stalling of an ox? His horses are bred better; for, besides that they are fair with their feeding, they are taught their manage, and to that end riders dearly hir'd; but I, his brother, gain nothing under him but growth, for the which his animals on his dunghills are as much bound to him as I. Besides this nothing that he so plentifully gives me, the something that nature gave me his countenance seems to take from me. He lets me feed with his hinds, bars me the place of a brother, and, as much as in him lies, mines my gentility with my education. This is it, Adam, that grieves me; and the spirit of my father, which I think is within me, begins to mutiny against this servitude. I will no longer endure it, though yet I know no wise remedy how to avoid it.

Enter *Oliver.*

Adam. Yonder comes my master, your brother.

Orl. Go apart, Adam, and thou shalt hear how he will shake me up.

[*Adam retires.*]

Oli. Now, sir, what make you here?

Orl. Nothing. I am not taught to make anything.

Oli. What mar you then, sir?

Orl. Marry, sir, I am helping you to mar that which God made, a poor unworthy brother of yours, with idleness.

Oli. Marry, sir, be better employed, and be naught awhile!

Orl. Shall I keep your hogs and eat husks with them? What prodigal portion have I spent that I should come to such penury?

Oli. Know you where you are, sir?

Orl. O, sir, very well. Here in your orchard.

Oli. Know you before whom, sir?

Orl. Ay, better than him I am before knows me. I know you are my eldest brother, and in the gentle condition of blood you should so know me. The courtesy of nations allows you my better in that you are the first born; but the same tradition takes not away my blood, were there twenty brothers betwixt us. I have as much of my father in me as you, albeit I confess your coming before me is nearer to his reverence.

Oli. What, boy! [*Strikes him.*]

Orl. Come, come, elder brother, you are too young in this. [*Seizes him.*]

Oli. Wilt thou lay hands on me, villain?

Orl. I am no villain. I am the youngest son of Sir Rowland de Boys; he was my father, and he is thrice a villain that says such a father begot villains. Wert thou not my brother, I would not take this hand from thy throat till this other had pull'd out thy tongue for saying so. Thou hast rail'd on thyself.

Adam. [*comes forward*] Sweet masters, be patient! For your father's remembrance, be at accord!

Oli. Let me go, I say.

Orl. I will not till I please. You shall hear me. My father charg'd you in his will to give me good education. You have train'd me like a peasant, obscuring and hiding from me all gentlemanlike qualities. The spirit of my father grows strong in me, and I will no longer endure it. Therefore allow me such exercises as may become a gentleman, or give me the poor allottery my father left me by testament. With that I will go buy my fortunes. [*Releases him.*]

Oli. And what wilt thou do? beg when that is spent? Well, sir, get you in. I will not long be troubled with you. You shall have some part of your will. I pray you leave me.

Orl. I will no further offend you than becomes me for my good.

Oli. Get you with him, you old dog!

Adam. Is 'old dog' my reward? Most true, I have lost my teeth in your service. God be with my old master! he would not have spoke such a word.

Exeunt Orlando, Adam.

Oli. Is it even so? Begin you to grow upon me? I will physic your rankness, and yet give no thousand crowns neither. Holla, Dennis!

Enter *Dennis.*

Den. Calls your worship?

Oli. Was not Charles the Duke's wrestler here to speak with me?

Den. So please you, he is here at the door and importunes access to you.

Oli. Call him in. [*Exit Dennis.*] 'Twill be a good way; and to-morrow the wrestling is.

Enter *Charles.*

Cha. Good morrow to your worship.

Oli. Good Monsieur Charles! What's the new news at the new court?

Cha. There's no news at the court, sir, but the old news. That is, the old Duke is banished by his younger brother the new Duke, and three or four loving lords have put themselves into voluntary exile with him, whose lands and revenues enrich the new Duke; therefore he gives them good leave to wander.

Oli. Can you tell if Rosalind, the Duke's daughter, be banished with her father?

Cha. O, no! for the Duke's daughter her cousin so loves her, being ever from their cradles bred together, that she would have followed her exile, or have died to stay behind her. She is at the court, and no less beloved of her uncle than his own daughter, and never two ladies loved as they do.

Oli. Where will the old Duke live?

Cha. They say he is already in the Forest of Arden, and a many merry men with him; and there they live like the old Robin Hood of England. They say many young gentlemen flock to him every day, and fleet the time carelessly as they did in the golden world.

Oli. What, you wrestle to-morrow before the new Duke?

Cha. Marry do I, sir; and I came to acquaint you with a matter. I am given, sir, secretly to understand that your younger brother, Orlando, hath a disposition to come in disguis'd against me to try a fall. To-morrow, sir, I wrestle for my credit, and he that escapes me without some broken limb shall acquit him well. Your brother is but young and tender, and for your love I would be loath to foil him, as I must for my own honour if he come in. Therefore, out of my love to you, I came hither to acquaint you withal, that either you might stay him from his intendment, or brook such disgrace well as he shall run into, in that it is a thing of his own search and altogether against my will.

Oli. Charles, I thank thee for thy love to me, which thou shalt find I will most kindly requite. I had myself notice of my brother's purpose herein and have by underhand means laboured to dissuade him from it; but he is resolute. I'll tell thee, Charles, it is the stubbornest young fellow of France; full of ambition, an envious emulator of every man's good parts, a secret and villanous contriver against me his natural brother. Therefore use thy discretion. I had as lief thou didst break his neck as his finger. And thou wert best look to't; for if thou dost him any slight disgrace, or if he do not mightily grace himself on thee, he will practise against thee by poison, entrap thee by some treacherous device, and never leave thee till he hath ta'en thy life by some indirect means or other; for I assure thee (and almost with tears I speak it) there is not one so young and so villanous this day living. I speak but brotherly of him; but should I anatomize him to thee as he is, I must blush and weep, and thou must look pale and wonder.

Cha. I am heartily glad I came hither to you. If he come to-morrow, I'll give him his payment. If ever he go alone again, I'll never wrestle for prize more. And so God keep your worship!

Oli. Farewell, good Charles. *Exit* [*Charles*]. Now will I stir this gamester. I hope I shall see an end of him; for my soul (yet I know not why) hates nothing more than he. Yet he's gentle; never school'd and yet learned; full of noble device; of all sorts enchantingly beloved, and indeed so much in the heart of the world, and especially of my own people, who best know him, that I am altogether misprised. But it shall not be so long; this wrestler shall clear all. Nothing remains but that I kindle the boy thither, which now I'll go about. *Exit.*

Scene II. [*A lawn before* Duke Frederick's *Palace.*]

Enter *Rosalind* and *Celia.*

Cel. I pray thee, Rosalind, sweet my coz, be merry.

Ros. Dear Celia, I show more mirth than I am mistress of, and would you yet I were merrier? Unless you could teach me to forget a banished father, you must not learn me how to remember any extraordinary pleasure.

Cel. Herein I see thou lov'st me not with the full weight that I love thee. If my uncle, thy banished father, had banished thy uncle, the Duke my father, so thou hadst been still with me, I could have taught my love to take thy father for mine. So wouldst thou, if the truth of thy love to me were so righteously temper'd as mine is to thee.

Ros. Well, I will forget the condition of my estate to rejoice in yours.

Cel. You know my father hath no child but I, nor none is like to have; and truly, when he dies, thou shalt be his heir; for what he hath taken away from thy father perforce, I will render thee again in affection. By mine honour, I will! and when I break that oath, let me turn monster. Therefore, my sweet Rose, my dear Rose, be merry.

Ros. From henceforth I will, coz, and devise sports. Let me see. What think you of falling in love?

Cel. Marry, I prithee do, to make sport withal! But love no man in good earnest, nor no further in sport neither than with safety of a pure blush thou mayst in honour come off again.

Ros. What shall be our sport then?

Cel. Let us sit and mock the good housewife Fortune from her wheel, that her gifts may henceforth be bestowed equally.

Ros. I would we could do so; for her benefits are mightily misplaced, and the bountiful blind woman doth most mistake in her gifts to women.

Cel. 'Tis true; for those that she makes fair she scarce makes honest, and those that she makes honest she makes very ill-favouredly.

Ros. Nay, now thou goest from Fortune's office to Nature's. Fortune reigns in gifts of the world, not in the lineaments of Nature.

Enter [*Touchstone, the*] *Clown.*

Cel. No? When Nature hath made a fair creature, may she not by Fortune fall into the fire? Though Nature hath given us wit to flout at Fortune, hath not Fortune sent in this fool to cut off the argument?

Ros. Indeed, there is Fortune too hard for Nature when Fortune makes Nature's natural the cutter-off of Nature's wit.

Cel. Peradventure this is not Fortune's work neither, but Nature's; who perceiveth our natural wits too dull to reason of such goddesses and hath sent this natural for our whetstone, for always the dulness of the fool is the whetstone of the wits. How now, wit? Whither wander you?

Touch. Mistress, you must come away to your father.

Cel. Were you made the messenger?

Touch. No, by mine honour; but I was bid to come for you.

Ros. Where learned you that oath, fool?

Touch. Of a certain knight that swore by his honour they were good pancakes, and swore by his honour the mustard was naught. Now I'll stand to it, the pancakes were naught, and the mustard was good, and yet was not the knight forsworn.

Cel. How prove you that in the great heap of your knowledge?

Ros. Ay, marry, now unmuzzle your wisdom.

Touch. Stand you both forth now. Stroke your chins, and swear by your beards that I am a knave.

Cel. By our beards (if we had them), thou art.

Touch. By my knavery (if I had it), then I were. But if you swear by that that is not, you are not forsworn. No more was this knight, swearing by his honour, for he never had any; or if he had, he had sworn it away before ever he saw those pancakes or that mustard.

Cel. Prithee, who is't that thou mean'st?

Touch. One that old Frederick, your father, loves.

Cel. My father's love is enough to honour him. Enough! Speak no more of him. You'll be whipp'd for taxation one of these days.

Touch. The more pity that fools may not speak wisely what wise men do foolishly.

Cel. By my troth, thou sayest true; for, since the little wit that fools have was silenced, the little foolery that wise men have makes a great show. Here comes Monsieur Le Beau.

Enter *Le Beau.*

Ros. With his mouth full of news.

Cel. Which he will put on us as pigeons feed their young.

Ros. Then shall we be news-cramm'd.

Cel. All the better! We shall be the more marketable. — Bon jour, Monsieur Le Beau. What's the news?

Le Beau. Fair princess, you have lost much good sport.

Cel. Sport? of what colour?

Le Beau. What colour, madam? How shall answer you?

Ros. As wit and fortune will.

Touch. Or as the Destinies decree.

Cel. Well said! That was laid on with a trowel.

Touch. Nay, if I keep not my rank —

Ros. Thou losest thy old smell.

Le Beau. You amaze me, ladies. I would have told you of good wrestling, which you have lost the sight of.

Ros. Yet tell us the manner of the wrestling.

Le Beau. I will tell you the beginning; and if it please your ladyships, you may see the end; for the best is yet to do; and here, where you are, they are coming to perform it.

Cel. Well, the beginning that is dead and buried.

Le Beau. There comes an old man and his three sons —

Cel. I could match this beginning with an old tale.

Le Beau. Three proper young men, of excellent growth and presence.

Ros. With bills on their necks, 'Be it known unto all men by these presents' —

Le Beau. The eldest of the three wrestled with Charles, the Duke's wrestler; which Charles in a moment threw him and broke three of his ribs, that there is little hope of life in him. So he serv'd the second, and so the third. Yonder they lie, the poor old man, their father, making such pitiful dole over them that all the beholders take his part with weeping.

Ros. Alas!

Touch. But what is the sport, monsieur, that the ladies have lost?

Le Beau. Why, this that I speak of.

Touch. Thus men may grow wiser every day. It is the first time that ever I heard breaking of ribs was sport for ladies.

Cel. Or I, I promise thee.

Ros. But is there any else longs to see this broken music in his sides? Is there yet another dotes upon rib-breaking? Shall we see this wrestling, cousin?

Le Beau. You must, if you stay here; for here is the place appointed for the wrestling, and they are ready to perform it.

Cel. Yonder sure they are coming. Let us now stay and see it.

Flourish. Enter *Duke* [*Frederick*], *Lords, Orlando, Charles,* and *Attendants.*

Duke. Come on. Since the youth will not be entreated, his own peril on his forwardness!

Ros. Is yonder the man?

Le Beau. Even he, madam.

Cel. Alas, he is too young! Yet he looks successfully.

Duke. How now, daughter, and cousin! Are you crept hither to see the wrestling?

Ros. Ay, my liege, so please you give us leave.

Duke. You will take little delight in it, I can tell you, there is such odds in the men. In pity of the challenger's youth I would fain dissuade him, but he will not be entreated. Speak to him, ladies; see if you can move him.

Cel. Call him hither, good Monsieur Le Beau.

Duke. Do so. I'll not be by. [*Steps aside.*]

Le Beau. Monsieur the challenger, the princess calls for you.

Orl. I attend them with all respect and duty.

Ros. Young man, have you challeng'd Charles the wrestler?

Orl. No, fair princess. He is the general

challenger; I come but in as others do, to try with him the strength of my youth.

Cel. Young gentleman, your spirits are too bold for your years. You have seen cruel proof of this man's strength. If you saw yourself with your eyes, or knew yourself with your judgment, the fear of your adventure would counsel you to a more equal enterprise. We pray you for your own sake to embrace your own safety and give over this attempt.

Ros. Do, young sir. Your reputation shall not therefore be misprised. We will make it our suit to the Duke that the wrestling might not go forward.

Orl. I beseech you, punish me not with your hard thoughts, wherein I confess me much guilty to deny so fair and excellent ladies anything. But let your fair eyes and gentle wishes go with me to my trial; wherein if I be foil'd, there is but one sham'd that was never gracious; if kill'd, but one dead that is willing to be so. I shall do my friends no wrong, for I have none to lament me; the world no injury, for in it I have nothing. Only in the world I fill up a place, which may be better supplied when I have made it empty.

Ros. The little strength that I have, I would it were with you.

Cel. And mine, to eke out hers.

Ros. Fare you well. Pray heaven I be deceiv'd in you!

Cel. Your heart's desires be with you!

Cha. Come, where is this young gallant that is so desirous to lie with his mother earth?

Orl. Ready, sir; but his will hath in it a more modest working.

Duke. You shall try but one fall.

Cha. No, I warrant your Grace you shall not entreat him to a second that have so mightily persuaded him from a first.

Orl. You mean to mock me after. You should not have mock'd me before. But come your ways!

Ros. Now Hercules be thy speed, young man!

Cel. I would I were invisible, to catch the strong fellow by the leg. *Wrestle.*

Ros. O excellent young man!

Cel. If I had a thunderbolt in mine eye, I can tell who should down.

[*Charles is thrown.*] *Shout.*

Duke. No more, no more!

Orl. Yes, I beseech your Grace. I am not yet well breath'd.

Duke. How dost thou, Charles?

Le Beau. He cannot speak, my lord.

Duke. Bear him away. [*Charles is borne out.*]
What is thy name, young man?

Orl. Orlando, my liege, the youngest son of Sir Rowland de Boys.

Duke. I would thou hadst been son to some man else!
The world esteem'd thy father honourable,
But I did find him still mine enemy.
Thou shouldst have better pleas'd me with this deed,
Hadst thou descended from another house.
But fare thee well; thou art a gallant youth;
I would thou hadst told me of another father.

Exeunt Duke, [*Train, and Le Beau*].

Cel. Were I my father, coz, would I do this?

Orl. I am more proud to be Sir Rowland's son,
His youngest son, and would not change that calling
To be adopted heir to Frederick.

Ros. My father lov'd Sir Rowland as his soul,
And all the world was of my father's mind.
Had I before known this young man his son,
I should have given him tears unto entreaties
Ere he should thus have ventur'd.

Cel. Gentle cousin,
Let us go thank him and encourage him.
My father's rough and envious disposition
Sticks me at heart. Sir, you have well deserv'd.
If you do keep your promises in love
But justly as you have exceeded all promise,
Your mistress shall be happy.

Ros. Gentleman,
[*Gives him a chain from her neck.*]
Wear this for me, one out of suits with fortune,
That could give more but that her hand lacks means.
Shall we go, coz?

Cel. Ay. Fare you well, fair gentleman.

Orl. Can I not say 'I thank you'? My better parts
Are all thrown down, and that which here stands up
Is but a quintain, a mere liveless block.

Ros. He calls us back. My pride fell with my fortunes;
I'll ask him what he would. Did you call, sir?
Sir, you have wrestled well, and overthrown
More than your enemies.

Cel. Will you go, coz?

Ros. Have with you. Fare you well.
Exeunt [*Rosalind and Celia*].

Orl. What passion hangs these weights upon my tongue?
I cannot speak to her, yet she urg'd conference.

Enter *Le Beau.*

O poor Orlando, thou art overthrown!
Or Charles or something weaker masters thee.

Le Beau. Good sir, I do in friendship counsel you
To leave this place. Albeit you have deserv'd
High commendation, true applause, and love,
Yet such is now the Duke's condition
That he misconsters all that you have done.
The Duke is humorous. What he is, indeed,
More suits you to conceive than I to speak of.

Orl. I thank you, sir: and pray you tell me this —
Which of the two was daughter of the Duke,
That here was at the wrestling?

Le Beau. Neither his daughter, if we judge by manners;
But yet indeed the smaller is his daughter;
The other is daughter to the banish'd Duke,
And here detain'd by her usurping uncle
To keep his daughter company, whose loves
Are dearer than the natural bond of sisters.
But I can tell you that of late this Duke
Hath ta'en displeasure 'gainst his gentle niece,
Grounded upon no other argument
But that the people praise her for her virtues
And pity her for her good father's sake;
And, on my life, his malice 'gainst the lady
Will suddenly break forth. Sir, fare you well.
Hereafter, in a better world than this,
I shall desire more love and knowledge of you.

Orl. I rest much bounden to you. Fare you well.
[*Exit Le Beau.*]
Thus must I from the smoke into the smother,
From tyrant Duke unto a tyrant brother.
But heavenly Rosalind! *Exit.*

Scene III. [*A room in the* Duke's *Palace.*]

Enter *Celia* and *Rosalind.*

Cel. Why, cousin! why, Rosalind! Cupid have mercy! not a word?

Ros. Not one to throw at a dog.

Cel. No, thy words are too precious to be cast away upon curs; throw some of them at me. Come, lame me with reasons.

Ros. Then there were two cousins laid up, when the one should be lam'd with reasons, and the other mad without any.

Cel. But is all this for your father?

Ros. No, some of it is for my child's father. O, how full of briers is this working-day world!

Cel. They are but burrs, cousin, thrown upon thee in holiday foolery. If we walk not in the trodden paths, our very petticoats will catch them.

Ros. I could shake them off my coat. These burrs are in my heart.

Cel. Hem them away.

Ros. I would try, if I could cry 'hem!' and have him.

Cel. Come, come, wrestle with thy affections.

Ros. O, they take the part of a better wrestler than myself!

Cel. O, a good wish upon you! You will try in time, in despite of a fall. But, turning these jests out of service, let us talk in good earnest. Is it possible on such a sudden you should fall into so strong a liking with old Sir Rowland's youngest son?

Ros. The Duke my father lov'd his father dearly.

Cel. Doth it therefore ensue that you should love his son dearly? By this kind of chase, I should hate him, for my father hated his father dearly; yet I hate not Orlando.

Ros. No, faith, hate him not, for my sake!

Cel. Why should I not? Doth he not deserve well?

Enter *Duke* [*Frederick*], with *Lords.*

Ros. Let me love him for that; and do you love him because I do. Look, here comes the Duke.

Cel. With his eyes full of anger.

Duke. Mistress, dispatch you with your safest haste
And get you from our court!

Ros. Me, uncle?

Duke. You, cousin.
Within these ten days if that thou beest found
So near our public court as twenty miles,
Thou diest for it.

Ros. I do beseech your Grace
Let me the knowledge of my fault bear with me.
If with myself I hold intelligence
Or have acquaintance with mine own desires;
If that I do not dream or be not frantic,

As I do trust I am not — then, dear uncle,
Never so much as in a thought unborn
Did I offend your Highness.
Duke. Thus do all traitors.
If their purgation did consist in words,
They are as innocent as grace itself.
Let it suffice thee that I trust thee not.
Ros. Yet your mistrust cannot make me a traitor.
Tell me whereon the likelihood depends.
Duke. Thou art thy father's daughter. There's enough!
Ros. So was I when your Highness took his dukedom;
So was I when your Highness banish'd him.
Treason is not inherited, my lord;
Or if we did derive it from our friends,
What's that to me? My father was no traitor.
Then, good my liege, mistake me not so much
To think my poverty is treacherous.
Cel. Dear sovereign, hear me speak.
Duke. Ay, Celia. We stay'd her for your sake,
Else had she with her father rang'd along.
Cel. I did not then entreat to have her stay;
It was your pleasure and your own remorse.
I was too young that time to value her;
But now I know her. If she be a traitor,
Why, so am I! We still have slept together,
Rose at an instant, learn'd, play'd, eat together;
And wheresoe'er we went, like Juno's swans,
Still we went coupled and inseparable.
Duke. She is too subtile for thee; and her smoothness,
Her very silence and her patience,
Speak to the people, and they pity her.
Thou art a fool. She robs thee of thy name,
And thou wilt show more bright and seem more virtuous
When she is gone. Then open not thy lips.
Firm and irrevocable is my doom
Which I have pass'd upon her. She is banish'd.
Cel. Pronounce that sentence then on me, my liege!
I cannot live out of her company.
Duke. You are a fool. You, niece, provide yourself.
If you outstay the time, upon mine honour,
And in the greatness of my word, you die.
Exeunt Duke &c.
Cel. O my poor Rosalind! whither wilt thou go?
Wilt thou change fathers? I will give thee mine.
I charge thee be not thou more griev'd than I am.
Ros. I have more cause.
Cel. Thou hast not, cousin.
Prithee be cheerful. Know'st thou not the Duke
Hath banish'd me, his daughter?
Ros. That he hath not!
Cel. No? hath not? Rosalind lacks then the love
Which teacheth me that thou and I am one.
Shall we be sund'red? shall we part, sweet girl?
No! let my father seek another heir.
Therefore devise with me how we may fly,
Whither to go, and what to bear with us.
And do not seek to take your charge upon you,
To bear your griefs yourself and leave me out;
For, by this heaven, now at our sorrows pale,
Say what thou canst, I'll go along with thee!
Ros. Why, whither shall we go?
Cel. To seek my uncle in the Forest of Arden.
Ros. Alas, what danger will it be to us,
Maids as we are, to travel forth so far!
Beauty provoketh thieves sooner than gold.
Cel. I'll put myself in poor and mean attire
And with a kind of umber smirch my face;
The like do you. So shall we pass along
And never stir assailants.
Ros. Were it not better,
Because that I am more than common tall,
That I did suit me all points like a man?
A gallant curtleaxe upon my thigh,
A boar-spear in my hand, and — in my heart
Lie there what hidden woman's fear there will —
We'll have a swashing and a martial outside,
As many other mannish cowards have
That do outface it with their semblances.
Cel. What shall I call thee when thou art a man?
Ros. I'll have no worse a name than Jove's own page,
And therefore look you call me Ganymede.
But what will you be call'd?
Cel. Something that hath a reference to my state —
No longer Celia, but Aliena.
Ros. But, cousin, what if we assay'd to steal
The clownish fool out of your father's court?
Would he not be a comfort to our travel?
Cel. He'll go along o'er the wide world with me.
Leave me alone to woo him. Let's away
And get our jewels and our wealth together,
Devise the fittest time and safest way
To hide us from pursuit that will be made
After my flight. Now go we in content
To liberty, and not to banishment. *Exeunt.*

ACT II. Scene I. [*The Forest of Arden. Before* Duke Senior's *cave.*]

Enter *Duke Senior, Amiens,* and two or three *Lords,* like *Foresters.*

Duke S. Now, my co-mates and brothers in exile,
Hath not old custom made this life more sweet
Than that of painted pomp? Are not these woods
More free from peril than the envious court?
Here feel we but the penalty of Adam,
The seasons' difference; as, the icy fang
And churlish chiding of the winter's wind,
Which, when it bites and blows upon my body
Even till I shrink with cold, I smile, and say
'This is no flattery; these are counsellors
That feelingly persuade me what I am.'
Sweet are the uses of adversity,
Which, like the toad, ugly and venomous,
Wears yet a precious jewel in his head;
And this our life, exempt from public haunt,
Finds tongues in trees, books in the running brooks,
Sermons in stones, and good in everything:
I would not change it.

Ami. Happy is your Grace
That can translate the stubbornness of fortune
Into so quiet and so sweet a style.

Duke S. Come, shall we go and kill us venison?
And yet it irks me the poor dappled fools,
Being native burghers of this desert city,
Should, in their own confines, with forked heads
Have their round haunches gor'd.

1. Lord. Indeed, my lord,
The melancholy Jaques grieves at that,
And in that kind swears you do more usurp
Than doth your brother that hath banish'd you.
To-day my Lord of Amiens and myself
Did steal behind him as he lay along
Under an oak, whose antique root peeps out
Upon the brook that brawls along this wood;
To the which place a poor sequest'red stag,
That from the hunter's aim had ta'en a hurt,
Did come to languish; and indeed, my lord,
The wretched animal heav'd forth such groans
That their discharge did stretch his leathern coat
Almost to bursting, and the big round tears
Cours'd one another down his innocent nose
In piteous chase; and thus the hairy fool,
Much marked of the melancholy Jaques,
Stood on th' extremest verge of the swift brook,
Augmenting it with tears.

Duke S. But what said Jaques?
Did he not moralize this spectacle?

1. Lord. O, yes, into a thousand similes.
First, for his weeping into the needless stream:
'Poor deer,' quoth he, 'thou mak'st a testament
As worldlings do, giving thy sum of more
To that which had too much.' Then, being alone,
Left and abandoned of his velvet friends:
''Tis right!' quoth he, 'thus misery doth part
The flux of company.' Anon a careless herd,
Full of the pasture, jumps along by him
And never stays to greet him: 'Ay,' quoth Jaques,
'Sweep on, you fat and greasy citizens!
'Tis just the fashion! Wherefore do you look
Upon that poor and broken bankrupt there?'
Thus most invectively he pierceth through
The body of the country, city, court;
Yea, and of this our life, swearing that we
Are mere usurpers, tyrants, and what's worse,
To fright the animals and to kill them up
In their assign'd and native dwelling place.

Duke S. And did you leave him in this contemplation?

2. Lord. We did, my lord, weeping and commenting
Upon the sobbing deer.

Duke S. Show me the place.
I love to cope him in these sullen fits,
For then he's full of matter.

1. Lord. I'll bring you to him straight.

Exeunt.

Scene II. [*A room in* Duke Frederick's *Palace.*]

Enter *Duke* [*Frederick*], with *Lords.*

Duke. Can it be possible that no man saw them?
It cannot be. Some villains of my court
Are of consent and sufferance in this.

1. Lord. I cannot hear of any that did see her.
The ladies her attendants of her chamber
Saw her abed, and in the morning early
They found the bed untreasur'd of their mistress.

AS YOU LIKE IT

The mock marriage in the Forest of Arden (*Act IV, Scene I*). Gwen Cherrell as Celia, John Neville as Orlando, and Virginia Mc-Kenna as Rosalind, daughter of the banished duke

Paul Rogers in the role of Touchstone, the clown, master of dry, caustic humor

PHOTOGRAPHS BY HOUSTON ROGERS
PRODUCED BY THE OLD VIC COMPANY

Orlando in his wrestling bout with Charles (Kerrigan Prescott), the bully of the usurping duke. Here seen at a disadvantage, he eventually triumphs over the champion (*Act I, Scene II*)

"Wear this for me, one out of suits with fortune." Victor in the wrestling match with Charles, Orlando receives a locket from Rosalind as his reward (*Act I, Scene II*)

"I cannot live out of her company." Celia beseeches her father, Duke Frederick (Charles Gray), the usurper, not to banish her cousin Rosalind (*Act I, Scene III*)

Touchstone comforts Celia when they are lost in the forest (*Act II, Scene IV*)

Celia tells Rosalind she has found Orlando in the forest (*Act III, Scene II*)

"Forbear, and eat no more." Seeking food in the Forest of Arden, the famished Orlando comes upon the banished duke (John Woodvine) and his followers at their supper (*Act II, Scene VII*)

"Sweet are the uses of adversity." The banished duke exhorts his men (*Act II, Scene I*)

"All the world's a stage, and all the men and women merely players." Jaques (Eric Porter) delivers his celebrated monologue, developing a remark made by the duke (*Act II, Scene VII*)

"I would cure you, if you would but call me Rosalind." Disguised as a boy, Rosalind leads the unwitting Orlando to expound on the sweet anguish of his love for her (*Act III, Scene II*)

"And how like you this shepherd's life, Master Touchstone?" Corin (Paul Daneman) introduces a debate on city versus country living (*Act III, Scene II*)

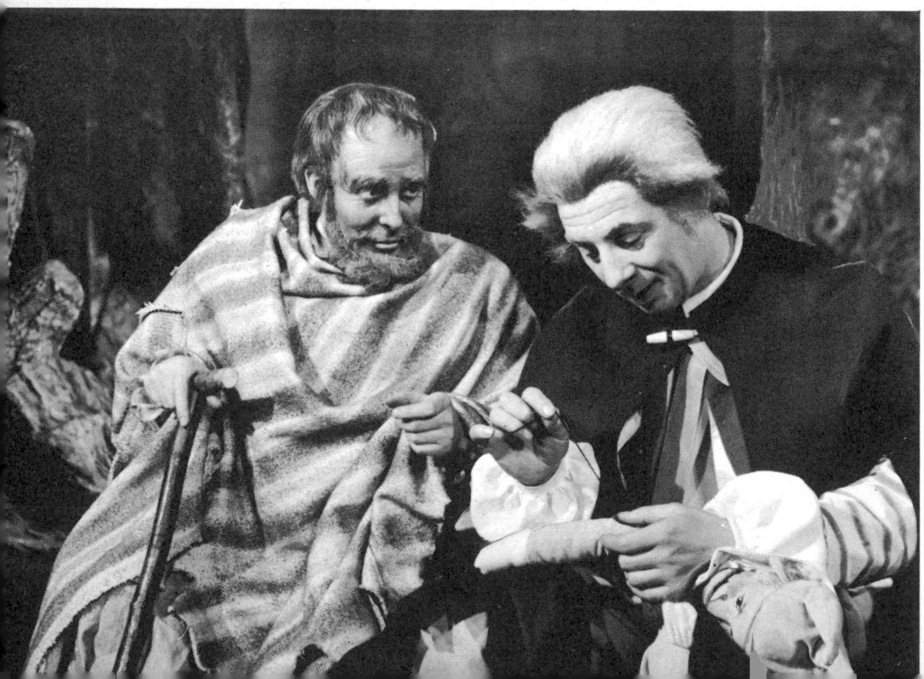

"I will kill thee a hundred and fifty ways." Touchstone disposes of his rival, William (Job Stewart), while Audrey (Rachel Roberts) watches (*Act V, Scene I*)

"Say that you love me not, but say not so in bitterness." The wooing of Phebe (Eleanore Bryan) by Silvius (Alan Dobie) becomes a model for Orlando in his courting of Rosalind (*Act III, Scene V*)

Disguised as a shepherd, Rosalind rests in the Forest of Arden and dreams of her sweetheart, Orlando

The final scene: the formal betrothal of Orlando and Rosalind (*Act. V, Scene IV*)

2. Lord. My lord, the roynish clown at whom so oft
Your Grace was wont to laugh is also missing.
Hisperia, the princess' gentlewoman,
Confesses that she secretly o'erheard
Your daughter and her cousin much commend
The parts and graces of the wrestler
That did but lately foil the sinewy Charles;
And she believes, wherever they are gone,
That youth is surely in their company.

Duke. Send to his brother, fetch that gallant hither.
If he be absent, bring his brother to me;
I'll make him find him. Do this suddenly,
And let not search and inquisition quail
To bring again these foolish runaways. *Exeunt.*

Scene III. [*Before* Oliver's *house.*]

Enter *Orlando* and *Adam,* [meeting].

Orl. Who's there?

Adam. What, my young master! O my gentle master!
O my sweet master! O you memory
Of old Sir Rowland! Why, what make you here?
Why are you virtuous? Why do people love you?
And wherefore are you gentle, strong, and valiant?
Why would you be so fond to overcome
The bonny prizer of the humorous Duke?
Your praise is come too swiftly home before you.
Know you not, master, to some kind of men
Their graces serve them but as enemies?
No more do yours. Your virtues, gentle master,
Are sanctified and holy traitors to you.
O, what a world is this, when what is comely
Envenoms him that bears it!

Orl. Why, what's the matter?

Adam. O unhappy youth,
Come not within these doors! Within this roof
The enemy of all your graces lives.
Your brother (no, no brother! yet the son —
Yet not the son — I will not call him son
Of him I was about to call his father)
Hath heard your praises, and this night he means
To burn the lodging where you use to lie
And you within it. If he fail of that,
He will have other means to cut you off.
I overheard him and his practices.
This is no place, this house is but a butchery.
Abhor it, fear it, do not enter it!

Orl. Why, whither, Adam, wouldst thou have me go?

Adam. No matter whither, so you come not here.

Orl. What, wouldst thou have me go and beg my food,
Or with a base and boist'rous sword enforce
A thievish living on the common road?
This I must do, or know not what to do.
Yet this I will not do, do how I can.
I rather will subject me to the malice
Of a diverted blood and bloody brother.

Adam. But do not so. I have five hundred crowns,
The thrifty hire I sav'd under your father,
Which I did store to be my foster nurse
When service should in my old limbs lie lame
And unregarded age in corners thrown.
Take that, and he that doth the ravens feed,
Yea, providently caters for the sparrow,
Be comfort to my age! Here is the gold;
All this I give you. Let me be your servant.
Though I look old, yet I am strong and lusty;
For in my youth I never did apply
Hot and rebellious liquors in my blood,
Nor did not with unbashful forehead woo
The means of weakness and debility;
Therefore my age is as a lusty winter,
Frosty, but kindly. Let me go with you;
I'll do the service of a younger man
In all your business and necessities.

Orl. O good old man, how well in thee appears
The constant service of the antique world,
When service sweat for duty, not for meed!
Thou art not for the fashion of these times,
Where none will sweat but for promotion,
And having that, do choke their service up
Even with the having. It is not so with thee.
But, poor old man, thou prun'st a rotten tree
That cannot so much as a blossom yield
In lieu of all thy pains and husbandry.
But come thy ways! We'll go along together,
And ere we have thy youthful wages spent,
We'll light upon some settled low content.

Adam. Master, go on, and I will follow thee
To the last gasp with truth and loyalty!
From seventeen years till now almost fourscore
Here lived I, but now live here no more.
At seventeen years many their fortunes seek,
But at fourscore it is too late a week;
Yet fortune cannot recompense me better
Than to die well and not my master's debtor.
Exeunt.

Scene IV. [*The Forest of Arden. Near a sheepcote.*]

Enter *Rosalind* for *Ganymede*, *Celia* for *Aliena*, and *Clown*, alias *Touchstone*.

Ros. O Jupiter, how weary are my spirits!

Touch. I care not for my spirits if my legs were not weary.

Ros. I could find in my heart to disgrace my man's apparel and to cry like a woman; but I must comfort the weaker vessel, as doublet and hose ought to show itself courageous to petticoat. Therefore, courage, good Aliena!

Cel. I pray you bear with me; I cannot go no further.

Touch. For my part, I had rather bear with you than bear you. Yet I should bear no cross if I did bear you, for I think you have no money in your purse.

Ros. Well, this is the Forest of Arden.

Touch. Ay, now am I in Arden, the more fool I! When I was at home, I was in a better place; but travellers must be content.

Enter *Corin* and *Silvius*.

Ros. Ay, be so, good Touchstone. — Look you, who comes here,
A young man and an old in solemn talk.

Cor. That is the way to make her scorn you still.

Sil. O Corin, that thou knew'st how I do love her!

Cor. I partly guess; for I have lov'd ere now.

Sil. No, Corin, being old, thou canst not guess,
Though in thy youth thou wast as true a lover
As ever sigh'd upon a midnight pillow.
But if thy love were ever like to mine
(As sure I think did never man love so),
How many actions most ridiculous
Hast thou been drawn to by thy fantasy!

Cor. Into a thousand that I have forgotten.

Sil. O, thou didst then never love so heartily!
If thou remembʼrest not the slightest folly
That ever love did make thee run into,
Thou hast not lov'd.
Or if thou hast not sat as I do now,
Wearing thy hearer in thy mistress' praise,
Thou hast not lov'd.
Or if thou hast not broke from company
Abruptly, as my passion now makes me,
Thou hast not lov'd. O Phebe, Phebe, Phebe!
Exit.

Ros. Alas, poor shepherd! Searching of thy wound,
I have by hard adventure found mine own.

Touch. And I mine. I remember, when I was in love I broke my sword upon a stone and bid him take that for coming a-night to Jane Smile; and I remember the kissing of her batlet, and the cow's dugs that her pretty chopt hands had milk'd; and I remember the wooing of a peascod instead of her, from whom I took two cods, and giving her them again, said with weeping tears, 'Wear these for my sake.' We that are true lovers run into strange capers; but as all is mortal in nature, so is all nature in love mortal in folly.

Ros. Thou speak'st wiser than thou art ware of.

Touch. Nay, I shall ne'er be ware of mine own wit till I break my shins against it.

Ros. Jove, Jove! this shepherd's passion
Is much upon my fashion.

Touch. And mine, but it grows something stale with me.

Cel. I pray you, one of you question yond man
If he for gold will give us any food.
I faint almost to death.

Touch. Holla, you clown!

Ros. Peace, fool! he's not thy kinsman.

Cor. Who calls?

Touch. Your betters, sir.

Cor. Else are they very wretched.

Ros. Peace, I say! — Good even to you, friend.

Cor. And to you, gentle sir, and to you all.

Ros. I prithee, shepherd, if that love or gold
Can in this desert place buy entertainment,
Bring us where we may rest ourselves and feed.
Here's a young maid with travel much oppress'd,
And faints for succour.

Cor. Fair sir, I pity her
And wish, for her sake more than for mine own,
My fortunes were more able to relieve her;
But I am shepherd to another man
And do not shear the fleeces that I graze.
My master is of churlish disposition
And little recks to find the way to heaven
By doing deeds of hospitality.
Besides, his cote, his flocks, and bounds of feed
Are now on sale, and at our sheepcote now,
By reason of his absence, there is nothing
That you will feed on; but what is, come see,
And in my voice most welcome shall you be.

Ros. What is he that shall buy his flock and pasture?

Cor. That young swain that you saw here but erewhile,
That little cares for buying anything.

Ros. I pray thee, if it stand with honesty,
Buy thou the cottage, pasture, and the flock,
And thou shalt have to pay for it of us.

Cel. And we will mend thy wages. I like this place
And willingly could waste my time in it.

Cor. Assuredly the thing is to be sold.
Go with me. If you like, upon report,
The soil, the profit, and this kind of life,
I will your very faithful feeder be
And buy it with your gold right suddenly.

Exeunt.

Scene V. [*The Forest. Before* Duke Senior's *cave.*]

Enter *Amiens, Jaques,* and others.

Song.

Ami. Under the greenwood tree
Who loves to lie with me,
And turn his merry note
Unto the sweet bird's throat,
Come hither, come hither, come hither!
Here shall he see
No enemy
But winter and rough weather.

Jaq. More, more, I prithee more!

Ami. It will make you melancholy, Monsieur Jaques.

Jaq. I thank it. More, I prithee more! I can suck melancholy out of a song as a weasel sucks eggs. More, I prithee more!

Ami. My voice is ragged. I know I cannot please you.

Jaq. I do not desire you to please me; I do desire you to sing. Come, more! another stanzo! Call you 'em stanzos?

Ami. What you will, Monsieur Jaques.

Jaq. Nay, I care not for their names; they owe me nothing. Will you sing?

Ami. More at your request than to please myself.

Jaq. Well then, if ever I thank any man, I'll thank you. But that they call compliment is like th' encounter of two dog-apes; and when a man thanks me heartily, methinks I have given him a penny, and he renders me the beggarly thanks. Come, sing! and you that will not, hold your tongues.

Ami. Well, I'll end the song. Sirs, cover the while; the Duke will drink under this tree. He hath been all this day to look you.

Jaq. And I have been all this day to avoid him. He is too disputable for my company. I think of as many matters as he; but I give heaven thanks and make no boast of them. Come, warble, come.

Song.
All together here.

Who doth ambition shun
And loves to live i' th' sun,
Seeking the food he eats,
And pleas'd with what he gets,
Come hither, come hither, come hither!
Here shall he see
No enemy
But winter and rough weather.

Jaq. I'll give you a verse to this note that I made yesterday in despite of my invention.

Ami. And I'll sing it.

Jaq. Thus it goes:

If it do come to pass
That any man turn ass,
Leaving his wealth and ease
A stubborn will to please,
Ducdame, ducdame, ducdame!
Here shall he see
Gross fools as he,
An if he will come to me.

Ami. What's that 'ducdame'?

Jaq. 'Tis a Greek invocation to call fools into a circle. I'll go sleep, if I can; if I cannot, I'll rail against all the first-born of Egypt.

Ami. And I'll go seek the Duke. His banquet is prepar'd. *Exeunt* [*severally*]

Scene VI. [*The Forest.*]

Enter *Orlando* and *Adam.*

Adam. Dear master, I can go no further. O, I die for food! Here lie I down and measure out my grave. Farewell, kind master.

Orl. Why, how now, Adam? no greater heart in thee? Live a little, comfort a little, cheer thyself a little. If this uncouth forest yield anything savage, I will either be food for it or bring it for food to thee. Thy conceit is nearer death than thy powers. For my sake be comfortable; hold death awhile at the arm's end. I will here be with thee presently; and if I bring thee not something to eat, I will give thee leave to die; but if thou diest before I come, thou art a mocker of my labour. Well said! thou look'st cheerly, and I'll be with thee quickly. Yet thou liest in the bleak air. Come, I will bear thee to some shelter, and thou shalt not die for lack of a dinner if there live anything in this desert. Cheerly, good Adam! *Exeunt.*

Scene VII. [*The Forest. Before the Cave.*]

[A table set out.] Enter *Duke Senior*, [*Amiens*,] and *Lords*, like *Outlaws*.

Duke S. I think he be transform'd into a beast,
For I can nowhere find him like a man.
1. Lord. My lord, he is but even now gone hence.
Here was he merry, hearing of a song.
Duke S. If he, compact of jars, grow musical,
We shall have shortly discord in the spheres.
Go seek him; tell him I would speak with him.

Enter *Jaques*.

1. Lord. He saves my labour by his own approach.
Duke S. Why, how now, monsieur! what a life is this,
That your poor friends must woo your company!
What, you look merrily.
Jaq. A fool, a fool! I met a fool i' th' forest,
A motley fool! — a miserable world! —
As I do live by food, I met a fool,
Who laid him down and bask'd him in the sun
And rail'd on Lady Fortune in good terms,
In good set terms — and yet a motley fool.
'Good morrow, fool,' quoth I. 'No, sir,' quoth he,
'Call me not fool till heaven hath sent me fortune.'
And then he drew a dial from his poke,
And looking on it with lack-lustre eye,
Says very wisely, 'It is ten o'clock.
Thus we may see,' quoth he, 'how the world wags.
'Tis but an hour ago since it was nine,
And after one hour more 'twill be eleven;
And so, from hour to hour, we ripe and ripe,
And then, from hour to hour, we rot and rot;
And thereby hangs a tale.' When I did hear
The motley fool thus moral on the time,
My lungs began to crow like chanticleer
That fools should be so deep contemplative;
And I did laugh sans intermission
An hour by his dial. O noble fool!
A worthy fool! Motley 's the only wear!
Duke S. What fool is this?
Jaq. O worthy fool! One that hath been a courtier,
And says, if ladies be but young and fair,
They have the gift to know it. And in his brain,
Which is as dry as the remainder biscuit
After a voyage, he hath strange places cramm'd
With observation, the which he vents
In mangled forms. O that I were a fool!
I am ambitious for a motley coat.
Duke S. Thou shalt have one.
Jaq. It is my only suit,
Provided that you weed your better judgments
Of all opinion that grows rank in them
That I am wise. I must have liberty
Withal, as large a charter as the wind,
To blow on whom I please; for so fools have.
And they that are most galled with my folly,
They most must laugh. And why, sir, must they so?
The why is plain as way to parish church:
He that a fool doth very wisely hit
Doth very foolishly, although he smart,
Not to seem senseless of the bob. If not,
The wise man's folly is anatomiz'd
Even by the squand'ring glances of the fool.
Invest me in my motley. Give me leave
To speak my mind, and I will through and through
Cleanse the foul body of th' infected world,
If they will patiently receive my medicine.
Duke S. Fie on thee! I can tell what thou wouldst do.
Jaq. What, for a counter, would I do but good?
Duke S. Most mischievous foul sin, in chiding sin.
For thou thyself hast been a libertine,
As sensual as the brutish sting itself;
And all th' embossed sores and headed evils
That thou with license of free foot hast caught,
Wouldst thou disgorge into the general world.
Jaq. Why, who cries out on pride
That can therein tax any private party?
Doth it not flow as hugely as the sea
Till that the wearer's very means do ebb?
What woman in the city do I name
When that I say the city woman bears
The cost of princes on unworthy shoulders?
Who can come in and say that I mean her,

When such a one as she, such is her neighbour?
Or what is he of basest function
That says his bravery is not on my cost,
Thinking that I mean him, but therein suits
His folly to the mettle of my speech?
There then! how then? what then? Let me see wherein
My tongue hath wrong'd him. If it do him right,
Then he hath wrong'd himself. If he be free,
Why, then my taxing like a wild goose flies,
Unclaim'd of any man. But who comes here?

Enter *Orlando* [with his sword drawn].

Orl. Forbear, and eat no more!
Jaq. Why, I have eat none yet.
Orl. Nor shalt not, till necessity be serv'd.
Jaq. Of what kind should this cock come of?
Duke S. Art thou thus bolden'd, man, by thy distress,
Or else a rude despiser of good manners,
That in civility thou seem'st so empty?
Orl. You touch'd my vein at first. The thorny point
Of bare distress hath ta'en from me the show
Of smooth civility; yet am I inland bred
And know some nurture. But forbear, I say!
He dies that touches any of this fruit
Till I and my affairs are answered.
Jaq. An you will not be answer'd with reason, I must die.
Duke S. What would you have? Your gentleness shall force
More than your force move us to gentleness.
Orl. I almost die for food, and let me have it!
Duke S. Sit down and feed, and welcome to our table.
Orl. Speak you so gently? Pardon me, I pray you.
I thought that all things had been savage here,
And therefore put I on the countenance
Of stern commandment. But whate'er you are
That in this desert inaccessible,
Under the shade of melancholy boughs,
Lose and neglect the creeping hours of time —
If ever you have look'd on better days,
If ever been where bells have knoll'd to church,
If ever sat at any good man's feast,
If ever from your eyelids wip'd a tear
And know what 'tis to pity and be pitied,
Let gentleness my strong enforcement be;
In the which hope I blush, and hide my sword.
Duke S. True is it that we have seen better days,
And have with holy bell been knoll'd to church,
And sat at good men's feasts, and wip'd our eyes
Of drops that sacred pity hath engend'red;
And therefore sit you down in gentleness,
And take upon command what help we have
That to your wanting may be minist'red.
Orl. Then but forbear your food a little while,
Whiles, like a doe, I go to find my fawn
And give it food. There is an old poor man
Who after me hath many a weary step
Limp'd in pure love. Till he be first suffic'd,
Oppress'd with two weak evils, age and hunger,
I will not touch a bit.
Duke S. Go find him out,
And we will nothing waste till you return.
Orl. I thank ye, and be blest for your good comfort! [*Exit.*]
Duke S. Thou seest we are not all alone unhappy.
This wide and universal theatre
Presents more woful pageants than the scene
Wherein we play in.
Jaq. All the world's a stage,
And all the men and women merely players.
They have their exits and their entrances,
And one man in his time plays many parts,
His acts being seven ages. At first, the infant,
Mewling and puking in the nurse's arms.
Then the whining schoolboy, with his satchel
And shining morning face, creeping like snail
Unwillingly to school. And then the lover,
Sighing like furnace, with a woful ballad
Made to his mistress' eyebrow. Then a soldier,
Full of strange oaths and bearded like the pard,
Jealous in honour, sudden and quick in quarrel,
Seeking the bubble reputation
Even in the cannon's mouth. And then the justice,
In fair round belly with good capon lin'd,
With eyes severe and beard of formal cut,
Full of wise saws and modern instances;
And so he plays his part. The sixth age shifts
Into the lean and slipper'd pantaloon,
With spectacles on nose and pouch on side;
His youthful hose, well sav'd, a world too wide
For his shrunk shank, and his big manly voice,
Turning again toward childish treble, pipes
And whistles in his sound. Last scene of all,
That ends this strange eventful history,
Is second childishness and mere oblivion,
Sans teeth, sans eyes, sans taste, sans everything.

Enter *Orlando*, with *Adam*.

Duke S. Welcome. Set down your venerable burthen
And let him feed.

Orl. I thank you most for him.
Adam. So had you need.
I scarce can speak to thank you for myself.
Duke S. Welcome, fall to. I will not trouble you,
As yet to question you about your fortunes.
Give us some music; and, good cousin, sing.

Song.

Ami. Blow, blow, thou winter wind,
Thou art not so unkind
As man's ingratitude.
Thy tooth is not so keen,
Because thou art not seen,
Although thy breath be rude.
Heigh-ho, sing heigh-ho, unto the green holly!
Most friendship is feigning, most loving mere folly:
Then, heigh-ho, the holly!
This life is most jolly.

Freeze, freeze, thou bitter sky,
That dost not bite so nigh
As benefits forgot.
Though thou the waters warp,
Thy sting is not so sharp
As friend rememb'red not.
Heigh-ho! sing, &c.

Duke S. If that you were the good Sir Rowland's son —
As you have whisper'd faithfully you were,
And as mine eye doth his effigies witness
Most truly limn'd and living in your face —
Be truly welcome hither. I am the Duke
That lov'd your father. The residue of your fortune,
Go to my cave and tell me. Good old man,
Thou art right welcome, as thy master is.
Support him by the arm. Give me your hand,
And let me all your fortunes understand.
Exeunt.

ACT III. Scene I. [*A room in the Palace.*]

Enter *Duke* [*Frederick*], *Lords*, and *Oliver*.

Duke. Not see him since? Sir, sir, that cannot be!
But were I not the better part made mercy,
I should not seek an absent argument
Of my revenge, thou present. But look to it!
Find out thy brother, wheresoe'er he is;
Seek him with candle; bring him dead or living
Within this twelvemonth, or turn thou no more
To seek a living in our territory.
Thy lands, and all things that thou dost call thine
Worth seizure, do we seize into our hands
Till thou canst quit thee by thy brother's mouth
Of what we think against thee.
Oli. O that your Highness knew my heart in this!
I never lov'd my brother in my life.
Duke. More villain thou! Well, push him out of doors,
And let my officers of such a nature
Make an extent upon his house and lands.
Do this expediently and turn him going.
Exeunt.

Scene II. [*The Forest. Near the sheepcote.*]

Enter *Orlando*, [with a paper, which he hangs on a tree].

Orl. Hang there, my verse, in witness of my love;
And thou, thrice-crowned Queen of Night, survey
With thy chaste eye, from thy pale sphere above,
Thy huntress' name that my full life doth sway.
O Rosalind! these trees shall be my books,
And in their barks my thoughts I'll character,
That every eye which in this forest looks
Shall see thy virtue witness'd everywhere.
Run, run, Orlando! carve on every tree
The fair, the chaste, and unexpressive she.
Exit.

Enter *Corin* and [*Touchstone the*] *Clown*.

Cor. And how like you this shepherd's life, Master Touchstone?

Touch. Truly, shepherd, in respect of itself, it is a good life; but in respect that it is a shepherd's life, it is naught. In respect that it is solitary, I like it very well; but in respect that it is private, it is a very vile life. Now in respect it is in the fields, it pleaseth me well; but in respect it is not in the court, it is tedious. As it is a spare life, look you, it fits my humour well; but as there is no more plenty in it, it goes much against my stomach. Hast any philosophy in thee, shepherd?

Cor. No more but that I know the more one sickens, the worse at ease he is; and that he that wants money, means, and content is without three good friends; that the property of rain is to wet and fire to burn; that good pasture makes fat sheep, and that a great cause of the night is lack of the sun; that he that hath learned no wit by nature nor art may complain of good breeding, or comes of a very dull kindred.

Touch. Such a one is a natural philosopher. Wast ever in court, shepherd?

Cor. No, truly.

Touch. Then thou art damn'd.

Cor. Nay, I hope.

Touch. Truly thou art damn'd, like an ill-roasted egg, all on one side.

Cor. For not being at court? Your reason.

Touch. Why, if thou never wast at court, thou never saw'st good manners; if thou never saw'st good manners, then thy manners must be wicked; and wickedness is sin, and sin is damnation. Thou art in a parlous state, shepherd.

Cor. Not a whit, Touchstone. Those that are good manners at the court are as ridiculous in the country as the behaviour of the country is most mockable at the court. You told me you salute not at the court but you kiss your hands. That courtesy would be uncleanly if courtiers were shepherds.

Touch. Instance, briefly. Come, instance.

Cor. Why, we are still handling our ewes, and their fells you know are greasy.

Touch. Why, do not your courtier's hands sweat? and is not the grease of a mutton as wholesome as the sweat of a man? Shallow, shallow! A better instance, I say. Come.

Cor. Besides, our hands are hard.

Touch. Your lips will feel them the sooner. Shallow again! A more sounder instance, come.

Cor. And they are often tarr'd over with the surgery of our sheep, and would you have us kiss tar? The courtier's hands are perfum'd with civet.

Touch. Most shallow man! Thou worm's meat in respect of a good piece of flesh indeed! Learn of the wise, and perpend. Civet is of a baser birth than tar — the very uncleanly flux of a cat. Mend the instance, shepherd.

Cor. You have too courtly a wit for me. I'll rest.

Touch. Wilt thou rest damn'd? God help thee, shallow man! God make incision in thee, thou art raw!

Cor. Sir, I am a true labourer; I earn that I eat, get that I wear; owe no man hate, envy no man's happiness; glad of other men's good, content with my harm; and the greatest of my pride is to see my ewes graze and my lambs suck.

Touch. That is another simple sin in you: to bring the ewes and the rams together and to offer to get your living by the copulation of cattle; to be bawd to a bell-wether, and to betray a she-lamb of a twelvemonth to a crooked-pated old cuckoldly ram, out of all reasonable match. If thou beest not damn'd for this, the devil himself will have no shepherds; I cannot see else how thou shouldst scape.

Cor. Here comes young Master Ganymede, my new mistress's brother.

Enter *Rosalind*, [reading a paper].

Ros. 'From the east to western Inde,
No jewel is like Rosalinde.
Her worth, being mounted on the wind,
Through all the world bears Rosalinde.
All the pictures fairest lin'd
Are but black to Rosalinde.
Let no face be kept in mind
But the fair of Rosalinde.'

Touch. I'll rhyme you so eight years together, dinners and suppers and sleeping hours excepted. It is the right butter-women's rank to market.

Ros. Out, fool!

Touch. For a taste:

If a hart do lack a hind,
Let him seek out Rosalinde.
If the cat will after kind,
So be sure will Rosalinde.
Winter garments must be lin'd,
So must slender Rosalinde.
They that reap must sheaf and bind,
Then to cart with Rosalinde.
Sweetest nut hath sourest rind,
Such a nut is Rosalinde.
He that sweetest rose will find
Must find love's prick, and Rosalinde.

This is the very false gallop of verses! Why do you infect yourself with them?

Ros. Peace, you dull fool! I found them on a tree.

Touch. Truly the tree yields bad fruit.

Ros. I'll graff it with you, and then I shall graff it with a medlar. Then it will be the earliest fruit i' th' country; for you'll be rotten ere you be half ripe, and that's the right virtue of the medlar.

Touch. You have said; but whether wisely or no, let the forest judge.

Enter *Celia*, with a writing.

Ros. Peace!
Here comes my sister reading. Stand aside.

Cel. 'Why should this a desert be,
For it is unpeopled? No!
Tongues I'll hang on every tree
That shall civil sayings show:
Some, how brief the life of man
Runs his erring pilgrimage,
That the stretching of a span
Buckles in his sum of age;
Some, of violated vows
'Twixt the souls of friend and friend;
But upon the fairest boughs,
Or at every sentence end,
Will I "Rosalinda" write,
Teaching all that read to know
The quintessence of every sprite
Heaven would in little show.
Therefore heaven Nature charg'd
That one body should be fill'd
With all graces wide-enlarg'd.
Nature presently distill'd
Helen's cheek, but not her heart,
Cleopatra's majesty,
Atalanta's better part,
Sad Lucretia's modesty.
Thus Rosalinde of many parts
By heavenly synod was devis'd,
Of many faces, eyes, and hearts,
To have the touches dearest priz'd.
Heaven would that she these gifts should have,
And I to live and die her slave.'

Ros. O most gentle pulpiter! what tedious homily of love have you wearied your parishioners withal, and never cried, 'Have patience, good people'!

Cel. How now? Back, friends. Shepherd, go off a little. Go with him, sirrah.

Touch. Come, shepherd, let us make an honourable retreat; though not with bag and baggage, yet with scrip and scrippage.

Exeunt [*Corin and Touchstone*].

Cel. Didst thou hear these verses?

Ros. O, yes, I heard them all, and more too; for some of them had in them more feet than the verses would bear.

Cel. That's no matter. The feet might bear the verses.

Ros. Ay, but the feet were lame, and could not bear themselves without the verse, and therefore stood lamely in the verse.

Cel. But didst thou hear without wondering how thy name should be hang'd and carved upon these trees?

Ros. I was seven of the nine days out of the wonder before you came; for look here what I found on a palm tree. I was never so berhym'd since Pythagoras' time that I was an Irish rat, which I can hardly remember.

Cel. Trow you who hath done this?

Ros. Is it a man?

Cel. And a chain that you once wore, about his neck. Change you colour?

Ros. I prithee who?

Cel. O Lord, Lord! it is a hard matter for friends to meet; but mountains may be remov'd with earthquakes, and so encounter.

Ros. Nay, but who is it?

Cel. Is it possible?

Ros. Nay, I prithee now with most petitionary vehemence, tell me who it is.

Cel. O wonderful, wonderful, and most wonderful wonderful! and yet again wonderful, and after that, out of all hooping!

Ros. Good my complexion! Dost thou think, though I am caparison'd like a man, I have a doublet and hose in my disposition? One inch of delay more is a South Sea of discovery. I prithee tell me who is it quickly, and speak apace. I would thou couldst stammer, that thou mightst pour this conceal'd man out of thy mouth as wine comes out of a narrow-mouth'd bottle — either too much at once, or none at all. I prithee take the cork out of thy mouth, that I may drink thy tidings.

Cel. So you may put a man in your belly.

Ros. Is he of God's making? What manner of man? Is his head worth a hat? or his chin worth a beard?

Cel. Nay, he hath but a little beard.

Ros. Why, God will send more, if the man will be thankful! Let me stay the growth of his beard, if thou delay me not the knowledge of his chin.

Cel. It is young Orlando, that tripp'd up the wrestler's heels and your heart both in an instant.

Ros. Nay, but the devil take mocking! Speak sad brow and true maid.

Cel. I' faith, coz, 'tis he.

Ros. Orlando?

Cel. Orlando.

Ros. Alas the day! what shall I do with my doublet and hose? What did he when thou saw'st him? What said he? How look'd he? Wherein went he? What makes he here? Did he ask for me? Where remains he? How parted he with thee? and when shalt thou see him again? Answer me in one word.

Cel. You must borrow me Gargantua's mouth first; 'tis a word too great for any mouth of this age's size. To say ay and no to these particulars is more than to answer in a catechism.

Ros. But doth he know that I am in this forest, and in man's apparel? Looks he as freshly as he did the day he wrestled?

Cel. It is as easy to count atomies as to resolve the propositions of a lover; but take a taste of my finding him, and relish it with good observance. I found him under a tree, like a dropp'd acorn.

Ros. It may well be called Jove's tree when it drops forth such fruit.

Cel. Give me audience, good madam.

Ros. Proceed.

Cel. There lay he stretch'd along like a wounded knight.

Ros. Though it be pity to see such a sight, it well becomes the ground.

Cel. Cry 'holla' to thy tongue, I prithee. It curvets unseasonably. He was furnish'd like a hunter.

Ros. O, ominous! he comes to kill my heart.

Cel. I would sing my song without a burthen. Thou bring'st me out of tune.

Ros. Do you not know I am a woman? When I think, I must speak. Sweet, say on.

Cel. You bring me out.

Enter *Orlando* and *Jaques.*

Soft! comes he not here?

Ros. 'Tis he! Slink by, and note him.

[*They step aside.*]

Jaq. I thank you for your company; but, good faith, I had as lief have been myself alone.

Orl. And so had I; but yet for fashion sake I thank you too for your society.

Jaq. God b'wi' you! Let's meet as little as we can.

Orl. I do desire we may be better strangers.

Jaq. I pray you mar no more trees with writing love songs in their barks.

Orl. I pray you mar no moe of my verses with reading them ill-favouredly.

Jaq. Rosalind is your love's name?

Orl. Yes, just.

Jaq. I do not like her name.

Orl. There was no thought of pleasing you when she was christen'd.

Jaq. What stature is she of?

Orl. Just as high as my heart.

Jaq. You are full of pretty answers. Have you not been acquainted with goldsmiths' wives, and conn'd them out of rings?

Orl. Not so; but I answer you right painted cloth, from whence you have studied your questions.

Jaq. You have a nimble wit; I think 'twas made of Atalanta's heels. Will you sit down with me? and we two will rail against our mistress the world and all our misery.

Orl. I will chide no breather in the world but myself, against whom I know most faults.

Jaq. The worst fault you have is to be in love.

Orl. 'Tis a fault I will not change for your best virtue. I am weary of you.

Jaq. By my troth, I was seeking for a fool when I found you.

Orl. He is drown'd in the brook. Look but in and you shall see him.

Jaq. There I shall see mine own figure.

Orl. Which I take to be either a fool or a cipher.

Jaq. I'll tarry no longer with you. Farewell, good Signior Love.

Orl. I am glad of your departure. Adieu, good Monsieur Melancholy.

[*Exit Jaques. Celia and Rosalind come forward.*]

Ros. [*aside to Celia*] I will speak to him like a saucy lackey, and under that habit play the knave with him.— Do you hear, forester?

Orl. Very well. What would you?

Ros. I pray you, what is't o'clock?

Orl. You should ask me, what time o' day. There's no clock in the forest.

Ros. Then there is no true lover in the forest; else sighing every minute and groaning every hour would detect the lazy foot of Time as well as a clock.

Orl. And why not the swift foot of Time? Had not that been as proper?

Ros. By no means, sir. Time travels in divers paces with divers persons. I'll tell you who Time ambles withal, who Time trots withal, who Time gallops withal, and who he stands still withal.

Orl. I prithee, who doth he trot withal?

Ros. Marry, he trots hard with a young maid between the contract of her marriage and the day it is solemniz'd. If the interim be but a se'nnight, Time's pace is so hard that it seems the length of seven year.

Orl. Who ambles Time withal?

Ros. With a priest that lacks Latin and a rich man that hath not the gout; for the one sleeps easily because he cannot study, and the other lives merrily because he feels no pain; the one lacking the burthen of lean and wasteful learning, the other knowing no burthen of heavy tedious penury. These Time ambles withal.

Orl. Who doth he gallop withal?

Ros. With a thief to the gallows; for though he go as softly as foot can fall, he thinks himself too soon there.

Orl. Who stays it still withal?

Ros. With lawyers in the vacation; for they sleep between term and term, and then they perceive not how time moves.

Orl. Where dwell you, pretty youth?

Ros. With this shepherdess, my sister; here in the skirts of the forest, like fringe upon a petticoat.

Orl. Are you native of this place?

Ros. As the cony that you see dwell where she is kindled.

Orl. Your accent is something finer than you could purchase in so removed a dwelling.

Ros. I have been told so of many. But indeed an old religious uncle of mine taught me to speak, who was in his youth an inland man; one that knew courtship too well, for there he fell in love. I have heard him read many lectures against it; and I thank God I am not a woman, to be touch'd with so many giddy offences as he hath generally tax'd their whole sex withal.

Orl. Can you remember any of the principal evils that he laid to the charge of women?

Ros. There were none principal. They were all like one another as halfpence are, every one fault seeming monstrous till his fellow-fault came to match it.

Orl. I prithee recount some of them.

Ros. No, I will not cast away my physic but on those that are sick. There is a man haunts the forest that abuses our young plants with carving 'Rosalind' on their barks; hangs odes upon hawthorns, and elegies on brambles; all, forsooth, deifying the name of Rosalind. If I could meet that fancy-monger, I would give him some good counsel, for he seems to have the quotidian of love upon him.

Orl. I am he that is so love-shak'd. I pray you tell me your remedy.

Ros. There is none of my uncle's marks upon you. He taught me how to know a man in love; in which cage of rushes I am sure you are not prisoner.

Orl. What were his marks?

Ros. A lean cheek, which you have not; a blue eye and sunken, which you have not; an unquestionable spirit, which you have not; a beard neglected, which you have not. But I pardon you for that, for simply your having in beard is a younger brother's revenue. Then your hose should be ungarter'd, your bonnet unbanded, your sleeve unbutton'd, your shoe untied, and everything about you demonstrating a careless desolation. But you are no such man: you are rather point-device in your accoustrements, as loving yourself, than seeming the lover of any other.

Orl. Fair youth, I would I could make thee believe I love.

Ros. Me believe it? You may as soon make her that you love believe it, which I warrant she is apter to do than to confess she does. That is one of the points in the which women still give the lie to their consciences. But in good sooth, are you he that hangs the verses on the trees wherein Rosalind is so admired?

Orl. I swear to thee, youth, by the white hand of Rosalind, I am that he, that unfortunate he.

Ros. But are you so much in love as your rhymes speak?

Orl. Neither rhyme nor reason can express how much.

Ros. Love is merely a madness, and, I tell you, deserves as well a dark house and a whip as madmen do; and the reason why they are not so punish'd and cured is that the lunacy is so ordinary that the whippers are in love too. Yet I profess curing it by counsel.

Orl. Did you ever cure any so?

Ros. Yes, one, and in this manner. He was to imagine me his love, his mistress; and I set him every day to woo me. At which time would I, being but a moonish youth, grieve, be effeminate, changeable, longing, and liking, proud, fantastical, apish, shallow, inconstant, full of tears, full of smiles; for every passion something and for no passion truly anything, as boys and women are for the most part cattle of this colour; would now like him, now loathe him; then entertain him, then forswear him; now weep for him, then spit at him; that I drave my suitor from his mad humour of love to a living humour of madness, which was, to forswear the full stream of the world and to live in a nook merely monastic. And thus I cur'd him; and this way will I take upon me to wash your liver as clean as a sound sheep's heart, that there shall not be one spot of love in't.

Orl. I would not be cured, youth.

Ros. I would cure you, if you would but call me Rosalind and come every day to my cote and woo me.

Orl. Now, by the faith of my love, I will! Tell me where it is.

Ros. Go with me to it, and I'll show it you; and by the way you shall tell me where in the forest you live. Will you go?

Orl. With all my heart, good youth.

Ros. Nay, you must call me Rosalind. Come, sister, will you go? *Exeunt.*

Scene III. [*The Forest. Near the sheepcote.*]

Enter [*Touchstone the*] *Clown, Audrey*; and *Jaques* [behind].

Touch. Come apace, good Audrey. I will fetch up your goats, Audrey. And how, Audrey, am I the man yet? Doth my simple feature content you?

Aud. Your features? Lord warrant us! What features?

Touch. I am here with thee and thy goats, as the most capricious poet, honest Ovid, was among the Goths.

Jaq. [*aside*] O knowledge ill-inhabited, worse than Jove in a thatch'd house!

Touch. When a man's verses cannot be understood, nor a man's good wit seconded with the forward child, understanding, it strikes a man more dead than a great reckoning in a little room. Truly, I would the gods had made thee poetical.

Aud. I do not know what poetical is. Is it honest in deed and word? Is it a true thing?

Touch. No, truly; for the truest poetry is the most feigning, and lovers are given to poetry; and what they swear in poetry may be said, as lovers, they do feign.

Aud. Do you wish then that the gods had made me poetical?

Touch. I do truly. For thou swear'st to me thou art honest. Now if thou wert a poet, I might have some hope thou didst feign.

Aud. Would you not have me honest?

Touch. No, truly, unless thou wert hard-favour'd; for honesty coupled to beauty is to have honey a sauce to sugar.

Jaq. [*aside*] A material fool!

Aud. Well, I am not fair; and therefore I pray the gods make me honest.

Touch. Truly, and to cast away honesty upon a foul slut were to put good meat into an unclean dish.

Aud. I am not a slut, though I thank the gods I am foul.

Touch. Well, praised be the gods for thy foulness! Sluttishness may come hereafter. But be it as it may be, I will marry thee; and to that end I have been with Sir Oliver Martext, the vicar of the next village, who hath promis'd to meet me in this place of the forest and to couple us.

Jaq. [*aside*] I would fain see this meeting.

Aud. Well, the gods give us joy!

Touch. Amen. A man may, if he were of a fearful heart, stagger in this attempt; for here we have no temple but the wood, no assembly but horn-beasts. But what though? Courage! As horns are odious, they are necessary. It is said, 'Many a man knows no end of his goods.' Right! Many a man has good horns and knows no end of them. Well, that is the dowry of his wife; 'tis none of his own getting. Horns? Even so. Poor men alone? No, no! the noblest deer hath them as huge as the rascal. Is the single man therefore blessed? No; as a wall'd town is more worthier than a village, so is the forehead of a married man more honourable than the bare brow of a bachelor; and by how much defence is better than no skill, by so much is a horn more precious than to want.

Enter *Sir Oliver Martext.*

Here comes Sir Oliver. Sir Oliver Martext, you are well met. Will you dispatch us here under this tree, or shall we go with you to your chapel?

Oli. Is there none here to give the woman?

Touch. I will not take her on gift of any man.

Oli. Truly, she must be given, or the marriage is not lawful.

Jaq. [*comes forward*] Proceed, proceed! I'll give her.

Touch. Good even, good Master What-ye-call't. How do you, sir? You are very well met. Goddild you for your last company. I am very glad to see you. Even a toy in hand here, sir. Nay, pray be cover'd.

Jaq. Will you be married, motley?

Touch. As the ox hath his bow, sir, the horse his curb, and the falcon her bells, so man hath his desires; and as pigeons bill, so wedlock would be nibbling.

Jaq. And will you, being a man of your breeding, be married under a bush like a beggar? Get you to church, and have a good priest that can tell you what marriage is. This fellow will but join you together as they join wainscot; then one of you will prove a shrunk panel, and like green timber warp, warp.

Touch. [*aside*] I am not in the mind but I were better to be married of him than of another; for he is not like to marry me well; and not being well married, it will be a good excuse for me hereafter to leave my wife.

Jaq. Go thou with me and let me counsel thee.

Touch. Come, sweet Audrey.
We must be married, or we must live in bawdry.
Farewell, good Master Oliver: not

O sweet Oliver,
O brave Oliver,
Leave me not behind thee!

but

Wind away,
Be gone, I say!
I will not to wedding with thee.

[*Exeunt Jaques, Touchstone, and Audrey.*]

Oli. 'Tis no matter. Ne'er a fantastical knave of them all shall flout me out of my calling. *Exit.*

Scene IV. [*The Forest. Near the sheepcote.*]

Enter *Rosalind* and *Celia*.

Ros. Never talk to me! I will weep.

Cel. Do, I prithee; but yet have the grace to consider that tears do not become a man.

Ros. But have I not cause to weep?

Cel. As good cause as one would desire. Therefore weep.

Ros. His very hair is of the dissembling colour.

Cel. Something browner than Judas's. Marry, his kisses are Judas's own children.

Ros. I' faith, his hair is of a good colour.

Cel. An excellent colour. Your chestnut was ever the only colour.

Ros. And his kissing is as full of sanctity as the touch of holy bread.

Cel. He hath bought a pair of cast lips of Diana. A nun of winter's sisterhood kisses not more religiously; the very ice of chastity is in them.

Ros. But why did he swear he would come this morning, and comes not?

Cel. Nay, certainly there is no truth in him.

Ros. Do you think so?

Cel. Yes. I think he is not a pickpurse nor a horse-stealer; but for his verity in love, I do think him as concave as a covered goblet or a worm-eaten nut.

Ros. Not true in love?

Cel. Yes, when he is in; but I think he is not in.

Ros. You have heard him swear downright he was.

Cel. 'Was' is not 'is.' Besides, the oath of a lover is no stronger than the word of a tapster: they are both the confirmer of false reckonings. He attends here in the forest on the Duke your father.

Ros. I met the Duke yesterday and had much question with him. He ask'd me of what parentage I was. I told him, of as good as he. So he laugh'd and let me go. But what talk we of fathers when there is such a man as Orlando?

Cel. O, that's a brave man! He writes brave verses, speaks brave words, swears brave oaths, and breaks them bravely — quite traverse, athwart the heart of his lover; as a puisny tilter, that spurs his horse but on one side, breaks his staff like a noble goose. But all's brave that youth mounts and folly guides. Who comes here?

Enter *Corin*.

Cor. Mistress and master, you have oft enquir'd
After the shepherd that complain'd of love,
Who you saw sitting by me on the turf,
Praising the proud disdainful shepherdess
That was his mistress.

Cel. Well, and what of him?

Cor. If you will see a pageant truly play'd
Between the pale complexion of true love
And the red glow of scorn and proud disdain,
Go hence a little, and I shall conduct you,
If you will mark it.

Ros. O, come, let us remove!
The sight of lovers feedeth those in love.
Bring us to this sight, and you shall say
I'll prove a busy actor in their play. *Exeunt.*

Scene V. [*Another part of the Forest.*]

Enter *Silvius* and *Phebe*.

Sil. Sweet Phebe, do not scorn me; do not, Phebe!
Say that you love me not, but say not so
In bitterness. The common executioner,

Whose heart th' accustom'd sight of death makes hard,
Falls not the axe upon the humbled neck
But first begs pardon. Will you sterner be
Than he that dies and lives by bloody drops?

Enter *Rosalind, Celia,* and *Corin,* [behind].

Phe. I would not be thy executioner.
I fly thee, for I would not injure thee.
Thou tell'st me there is murder in mine eye:
'Tis pretty, sure, and very probable
That eyes, that are the frail'st and softest things,
Who shut their coward gates on atomies,
Should be call'd tyrants, butchers, murtherers!
Now I do frown on thee with all my heart;
And if mine eyes can wound, now let them kill thee!
Now counterfeit to swound; why, now fall down;
Or if thou canst not, O, for shame, for shame,
Lie not, to say mine eyes are murtherers!
Now show the wound mine eye hath made in thee.
Scratch thee but with a pin, and there remains
Some scar of it; lean but upon a rush,
The cicatrice and capable impressure
Thy palm some moment keeps; but now mine eyes,
Which I have darted at thee, hurt thee not,
Nor I am sure there is no force in eyes
That can do hurt.

Sil. O dear Phebe,
If ever (as that ever may be near)
You meet in some fresh cheek the power of fancy,
Then shall you know the wounds invisible
That love's keen arrows make.

Phe. But till that time
Come not thou near me; and when that time comes,
Afflict me with thy mocks, pity me not,
As till that time I shall not pity thee.

Ros. And why, I pray you? Who might be your mother,
That you insult, exult, and all at once,
Over the wretched? What though you have no beauty —
As, by my faith, I see no more in you
Than without candle may go dark to bed! —
Must you be therefore proud and pitiless?
Why, what means this? Why do you look on me?
I see no more in you than in the ordinary
Of nature's sale-work. 'Od's my little life,
I think she means to tangle my eyes too!
No, faith, proud mistress, hope not after it.
'Tis not your inky brows, your black silk hair,
Your bugle eyeballs, nor your cheek of cream
That can entame my spirits to your worship.
You foolish shepherd, wherefore do you follow her,
Like foggy south, puffing with wind and rain?
You are a thousand times a properer man
Than she a woman. 'Tis such fools as you
That makes the world full of ill-favour'd children.
'Tis not her glass, but you, that flatters her,
And out of you she sees herself more proper
Than any of her lineaments can show her.
But, mistress, know yourself. Down on your knees,
And thank heaven, fasting, for a good man's love;
For I must tell you friendly in your ear,
Sell when you can! you are not for all markets.
Cry the man mercy, love him, take his offer.
Foul is most foul, being foul to be a scoffer.
So take her to thee, shepherd. Fare you well.

Phe. Sweet youth, I pray you chide a year together.
I had rather hear you chide than this man woo.

Ros. [*to Phebe*] He's fall'n in love with your foulness, [*to Silvius*] and she'll fall in love with my anger. If it be so, as fast as she answers thee with frowning looks, I'll sauce her with bitter words. — Why look you so upon me?

Phe. For no ill will I bear you.

Ros. I pray you do not fall in love with me,
For I am falser than vows made in wine.
Besides, I like you not. If you will know my house,
'Tis at the tuft of olives, here hard by. —
Will you go, sister? — Shepherd, ply her hard.—
Come, sister. — Shepherdess, look on him better
And be not proud. Though all the world could see,
None could be so abus'd in sight as he. —
Come, to our flock.

Exeunt [*Rosalind, Celia, and Corin*].

Phe. Dead shepherd, now I find thy saw of might,
'Who ever lov'd that lov'd not at first sight?'

Sil. Sweet Phebe —

Phe. Ha! what say'st thou, Silvius?

Sil. Sweet Phebe, pity me.

Phe. Why, I am sorry for thee, gentle Silvius.

Sil. Wherever sorrow is, relief would be.
If you do sorrow at my grief in love,
By giving love your sorrow and my grief
Were both extermin'd.

Phe. Thou hast my love. Is not that neighbourly?
Sil. I would have you.
Phe. Why, that were covetousness.
Silvius, the time was that I hated thee,
And yet it is not that I bear thee love;
But since that thou canst talk of love so well,
Thy company, which erst was irksome to me,
I will endure; and I'll employ thee too.
But do not look for further recompense
Than thine own gladness that thou art employ'd.
Sil. So holy and so perfect is my love,
And I in such a poverty of grace,
That I shall think it a most plenteous crop
To glean the broken ears after the man
That the main harvest reaps. Loose now and then
A scatt'red smile, and that I'll live upon.
Phe. Know'st thou the youth that spoke to me erewhile?
Sil. Not very well, but I have met him oft,
And he hath bought the cottage and the bounds
That the old Carlot once was master of.
Phe. Think not I love him, though I ask for him.
'Tis but a peevish boy; yet he talks well.
But what care I for words? Yet words do well
When he that speaks them pleases those that hear.
It is a pretty youth — not very pretty —
But sure he's proud; and yet his pride becomes him.
He'll make a proper man. The best thing in him
Is his complexion; and faster than his tongue
Did make offence, his eye did heal it up.
He is not very tall; yet for his years he's tall.
His leg is but so so; and yet 'tis well.
There was a pretty redness in his lip,
A little riper and more lusty red
Than that mix'd in his cheek; 'twas just the difference
Betwixt the constant red and mingled damask.
There be some women, Silvius, had they mark'd him
In parcels as I did, would have gone near
To fall in love with him; but, for my part,
I love him not nor hate him not; and yet
I have more cause to hate him than to love him;
For what had he to do to chide at me?
He said mine eyes were black and my hair black;
And, now I am remembʼred, scorn'd at me.
I marvel why I answer'd not again.
But that's all one: omittance is no quittance.
I'll write to him a very taunting letter,
And thou shalt bear it. Wilt thou, Silvius?
Sil. Phebe, with all my heart.
Phe. I'll write it straight;
The matter's in my head and in my heart.
I will be bitter with him and passing short.
Go with me, Silvius. *Exeunt.*

ACT IV. Scene I. [*The Forest. Near the sheepcote.*]

Enter *Rosalind* and *Celia* and *Jaques.*

Jaq. I prithee, pretty youth, let me be better acquainted with thee.

Ros. They say you are a melancholy fellow.

Jaq. I am so. I do love it better than laughing.

Ros. Those that are in extremity of either are abominable fellows, and betray themselves to every modern censure worse than drunkards.

Jaq. Why, 'tis good to be sad and say nothing.

Ros. Why then, 'tis good to be a post.

Jaq. I have neither the scholar's melancholy, which is emulation; nor the musician's, which is fantastical; nor the courtier's, which is proud; nor the soldier's, which is ambitious; nor the lawyer's, which is politic; nor the lady's, which is nice; nor the lover's, which is all these: but it is a melancholy of mine own, compounded of many simples, extracted from many objects, and indeed the sundry contemplation of my travels, in which my often rumination wraps me in a most humorous sadness.

Ros. A traveller! By my faith, you have great reason to be sad. I fear you have sold your own lands to see other men's. Then to have seen much and to have nothing is to have rich eyes and poor hands.

Jaq. Yes, I have gain'd my experience.

Enter *Orlando.*

Ros. And your experience makes you sad. I had rather have a fool to make me merry than experience to make me sad — and to travel for it too!

Orl. Good day and happiness, dear Rosalind!

Jaq. Nay then, God b'wi' you, an you talk in blank verse!

Ros. Farewell, Monsieur Traveller. Look you lisp and wear strange suits, disable all the benefits of your own country, be out of love with your nativity and almost chide God for making you that countenance you are; or I will scarce think you have swam in a gundello. [*Exit Jaques.*] Why, how now, Orlando? Where have you been all this while? You a lover? An you serve me such another trick, never come in my sight more.

Orl. My fair Rosalind, I come within an hour of my promise.

Ros. Break an hour's promise in love? He that will divide a minute into a thousand parts and break but a part of the thousand part of a minute in the affairs of love, it may be said of him that Cupid hath clapp'd him o' th' shoulder, but I'll warrant him heart-whole.

Orl. Pardon me, dear Rosalind.

Ros. Nay, an you be so tardy, come no more in my sight. I had as lief be woo'd of a snail.

Orl. Of a snail?

Ros. Ay, of a snail; for though he comes slowly, he carries his house on his head — a better jointure, I think, than you make a woman. Besides, he brings his destiny with him.

Orl. What's that?

Ros. Why, horns! which such as you are fain to be beholding to your wives for; but he comes armed in his fortune and prevents the slander of his wife.

Orl. Virtue is no horn-maker, and my Rosalind is virtuous.

Ros. And I am your Rosalind.

Cel. It pleases him to call you so; but he hath a Rosalind of a better leer than you.

Ros. Come, woo me, woo me! for now I am in a holiday humour and like enough to consent. What would you say to me now, an I were your very very Rosalind?

Orl. I would kiss before I spoke.

Ros. Nay, you were better speak first; and when you were gravell'd for lack of matter, you might take occasion to kiss. Very good orators, when they are out, they will spit; and for lovers, lacking (God warn us!) matter, the cleanliest shift is to kiss.

Orl. How if the kiss be denied?

Ros. Then she puts you to entreaty, and there begins new matter.

Orl. Who could be out, being before his beloved mistress?

Ros. Marry, that should you, if I were your mistress, or I should think my honesty ranker than my wit.

Orl. What, of my suit?

Ros. Not out of your apparel, and yet out of your suit. Am not I your Rosalind?

Orl. I take some joy to say you are, because I would be talking of her.

Ros. Well, in her person, I say I will not have you.

Orl. Then, in mine own person, I die.

Ros. No, faith, die by attorney. The poor world is almost six thousand years old, and in all this time there was not any man died in his own person, videlicet, in a love cause. Troilus had his brains dash'd out with a Grecian club; yet he did what he could to die before, and he is one of the patterns of love. Leander, he would have liv'd many a fair year though Hero had turn'd nun, if it had not been for a hot midsummer night; for (good youth) he went but forth to wash him in the Hellespont, and being taken with the cramp, was drown'd; and the foolish chroniclers of that age found it was 'Hero of Sestos.' But these are all lies. Men have died from time to time, and worms have eaten them, but not for love.

Orl. I would not have my right Rosalind of this mind, for I protest her frown might kill me.

Ros. By this hand, it will not kill a fly! But come, now I will be your Rosalind in a more coming-on disposition; and ask me what you will, I will grant it.

Orl. Then love me, Rosalind.

Ros. Yes, faith, will I, Fridays and Saturdays and all.

Orl. And wilt thou have me?

Ros. Ay, and twenty such.

Orl. What sayest thou?

Ros. Are you not good?

Orl. I hope so.

Ros. Why then, can one desire too much of a good thing? Come, sister, you shall be the priest and marry us. Give me your hand, Orlando. What do you say, sister?

Orl. Pray thee marry us.

Cel. I cannot say the words.

Ros. You must begin, 'Will you, Orlando' —

Cel. Go to. Will you, Orlando, have to wife this Rosalind?

Orl. I will.

Ros. Ay, but when?

Orl. Why now, as fast as she can marry us.

Ros. Then you must say, 'I take thee, Rosalind, for wife.'

Orl. I take thee, Rosalind, for wife.

Ros. I might ask you for your commission; but I do take thee, Orlando, for my husband. There's a girl goes before the priest, and certainly a woman's thought runs before her actions.

Orl. So do all thoughts; they are wing'd.

Ros. Now tell me how long you would have her after you have possess'd her.

Orl. For ever and a day.

Ros. Say 'a day,' without the 'ever.' No, no, Orlando! Men are April when they woo, December when they wed. Maids are May when they are maids, but the sky changes when they are wives. I will be more jealous of thee than a Barbary cock-pigeon over his hen, more clamorous than a parrot against rain, more newfangled than an ape, more giddy in my desires than a monkey. I will weep for nothing, like Diana in the fountain, and I will do that when you are dispos'd to be merry; I will laugh like a hyen, and that when thou art inclin'd to sleep.

Orl. But will my Rosalind do so?

Ros. By my life, she will do as I do.

Orl. O, but she is wise!

Ros. Or else she could not have the wit to do this. The wiser, the waywarder. Make the doors upon a woman's wit, and it will out at the casement; shut that, and 'twill out at the key-hole; stop that, 'twill fly with the smoke out at the chimney.

Orl. A man that had a wife with such a wit, he might say, 'Wit, whither wilt?'

Ros. Nay, you might keep that check for it till you met your wive's wit going to your neighbour's bed.

Orl. And what wit could wit have to excuse that?

Ros. Marry, to say she came to seek you there. You shall never take her without her answer unless you take her without her tongue. O, that woman that cannot make her fault her husband's occasion, let her never nurse her child herself, for she will breed it like a fool!

Orl. For these two hours, Rosalind, I will leave thee.

Ros. Alas, dear love, I cannot lack thee two hours!

Orl. I must attend the Duke at dinner. By two o'clock I will be with thee again.

Ros. Ay, go your ways, go your ways! I knew what you would prove. My friends told me as much, and I thought no less. That flattering tongue of yours won me. 'Tis but one cast away, and so, come death! Two o'clock is your hour?

Orl. Ay, sweet Rosalind.

Ros. By my troth, and in good earnest, and so God mend me, and by all pretty oaths that are not dangerous, if you break one jot of your promise or come one minute behind your hour, I will think you the most pathetical break-promise, and the most hollow lover, and the most unworthy of her you call Rosalind, that may be chosen out of the gross band of the unfaithful. Therefore beware my censure and keep your promise.

Orl. With no less religion than if thou wert indeed my Rosalind. So adieu.

Ros. Well, Time is the old justice that examines all such offenders, and let Time try. Adieu. *Exit [Orlando].*

Cel. You have simply misus'd our sex in your love-prate. We must have your doublet and hose pluck'd over your head, and show the world what the bird hath done to her own nest.

Ros. O coz, coz, coz, my pretty little coz, that thou didst know how many fathom deep I am in love! But it cannot be sounded. My affection hath an unknown bottom, like the Bay of Portugal.

Cel. Or rather, bottomless, that as fast as you pour affection in, it runs out.

Ros. No, that same wicked bastard of Venus that was begot of thought, conceiv'd of spleen, and born of madness, that blind rascally boy that abuses every one's eyes because his own are out — let him be judge how deep I am in love. I'll tell thee, Aliena, I cannot be out of the sight of Orlando. I'll go find a shadow, and sigh till he come.

Cel. And I'll sleep. *Exeunt.*

Scene II. [*The Forest. Before* Duke Senior's *cave.*]

Enter *Jaques,* and *Lords* ([like] *Foresters*) [with a dead deer].

Jaq. Which is he that killed the deer?

Lord. Sir, it was I.

Jaq. Let's present him to the Duke like a Roman conqueror; and it would do well to set the deer's horns upon his head for a branch of victory. Have you no song, forester, for this purpose?

Lord. Yes, sir.

Jaq. Sing it. 'Tis no matter how it be in tune, so it make noise enough. *Music.*

Song.

What shall he have that kill'd the deer?
His leather skin and horns to wear.
    Then sing him home.
        (*The rest shall bear this burthen.*)

Take thou no scorn to wear the horn;
It was a crest ere thou wast born:
Thy father's father wore it,
And thy father bore it.
The horn, the horn, the lusty horn,
Is not a thing to laugh to scorn.

Exeunt.

Scene III. [*The Forest. Near the sheepcote.*]

Enter *Rosalind* and *Celia*.

Ros. How say you now? Is it not past two o'clock? and here much Orlando!

Cel. I warrant you, with pure love and troubled brain, he hath ta'en his bow and arrows, and is gone forth to sleep.

Enter *Silvius*.

Look who comes here.

Sil. My errand is to you, fair youth.
My gentle Phebe bid me give you this.
[*Gives a letter.*]
I know not the contents; but, as I guess
By the stern brow and waspish action
Which she did use as she was writing of it,
It bears an angry tenure. Pardon me;
I am but as a guiltless messenger.

Ros. Patience herself would startle at this letter
And play the swaggerer. Bear this, bear all!
She says I am not fair, that I lack manners;
She calls me proud, and that she could not love me,
Were man as rare as phœnix. 'Od's my will!
Her love is not the hare that I do hunt.
Why writes she so to me? Well, shepherd, well,
This is a letter of your own device.

Sil. No, I protest, I know not the contents.
Phebe did write it.

Ros. Come, come, you are a fool,
And turn'd into the extremity of love.
I saw her hand. She has a leathern hand,
A freestone-coloured hand. I verily did think
That her old gloves were on, but 'twas her hands.
She has a housewive's hand; but that's no matter.
I say she never did invent this letter;
This is a man's invention and his hand.

Sil. Sure it is hers.

Ros. Why, 'tis a boisterous and a cruel style,
A style for challengers. Why, she defies me
Like Turk to Christian! Women's gentle brain
Could not drop forth such giant-rude invention,
Such Ethiop words, blacker in their effect
Than in their countenance. Will you hear the letter?

Sil. So please you, for I never heard it yet —
Yet heard too much of Phebe's cruelty.

Ros. She Phebes me. Mark how the tyrant writes. *Read.*

'Art thou god to shepherd turn'd,
That a maiden's heart hath burn'd?'

Can a woman rail thus?

Sil. Call you this railing?

Ros.

'Why, thy godhead laid apart, *Read.*
Warr'st thou with a woman's heart?'

Did you ever hear such railing?

'Whiles the eye of man did woo me,
That could do no vengeance to me.'

Meaning me a beast.

'If the scorn of your bright eyne
Have power to raise such love in mine,
Alack, in me what strange effect
Would they work in mild aspect!
Whiles you chid me, I did love;
How then might your prayers move!
He that brings this love to thee
Little knows this love in me;
And by him seal up thy mind,
Whether that thy youth and kind
Will the faithful offer take
Of me and all that I can make,
Or else by him my love deny,
And then I'll study how to die.'

Sil. Call you this chiding?

Cel. Alas, poor shepherd!

Ros. Do you pity him? No, he deserves no pity. Wilt thou love such a woman? What, to make thee an instrument, and play false strains upon thee? Not to be endur'd! Well, go your way to her (for I see love hath made thee a tame snake) and say this to her: that if she love me, I charge her to love thee; if she will not, I will never have her unless thou entreat for her. If you be a true lover, hence, and not a word; for here comes more company.

Exit Silvius.

Enter *Oliver*.

Oli. Good morrow, fair ones. Pray you, if you know,
Where in the purlieus of this forest stands
A sheepcote, fenc'd about with olive trees?

Cel. West of this place, down in the neighbour bottom.

The rank of osiers by the murmuring stream
Left on your right hand brings you to the place.
But at this hour the house doth keep itself;
There's none within.
Oli. If that an eye may profit by a tongue,
Then should I know you by description —
Such garments and such years: 'The boy is fair,
Of female favour, and bestows himself
Like a ripe sister; the woman low,
And browner than her brother.' Are not you
The owner of the house I did enquire for?
Cel. It is no boast, being ask'd, to say we are.
Oli. Orlando doth commend him to you both,
And to that youth he calls his Rosalind
He sends this bloody napkin. Are you he?
Ros. I am. What must we understand by this?
Oli. Some of my shame, if you will know of me
What man I am, and how, and why, and where
This handkercher was stain'd.
Cel. I pray you tell it.
Oli. When last the young Orlando parted from you,
He left a promise to return again
Within an hour; and pacing through the forest,
Chewing the food of sweet and bitter fancy,
Lo, what befell! He threw his eye aside,
And mark what object did present itself.
Under an oak, whose boughs were moss'd with age
And high top bald with dry antiquity,
A wretched ragged man, o'ergrown with hair,
Lay sleeping on his back. About his neck
A green and gilded snake had wreath'd itself,
Who with her head, nimble in threats, approach'd
The opening of his mouth; but suddenly,
Seeing Orlando, it unlink'd itself
And with indented glides did slip away
Into a bush, under which bush's shade
A lioness, with udders all drawn dry,
Lay couching, head on ground, with catlike watch
When that the sleeping man should stir; for 'tis
The royal disposition of that beast
To prey on nothing that doth seem as dead.
This seen, Orlando did approach the man
And found it was his brother, his elder brother.
Cel. O, I have heard him speak of that same brother,
And he did render him the most unnatural
That liv'd amongst men.
Oli. And well he might so do,
For well I know he was unnatural.
Ros. But, to Orlando! Did he leave him there,
Food to the suck'd and hungry lioness?
Oli. Twice did he turn his back and purpos'd so;
But kindness, nobler ever than revenge,
And nature, stronger than his just occasion,
Made him give battle to the lioness,
Who quickly fell before him; in which hurtling
From miserable slumber I awak'd.
Cel. Are you his brother?
Ros. Was it you he rescu'd?
Cel. Was't you that did so oft contrive to kill him?
Oli. 'Twas I. But 'tis not I! I do not shame
To tell you what I was, since my conversion
So sweetly tastes, being the thing I am.
Ros. But, for the bloody napkin?
Oli. By-and-by.
When from the first to last, betwixt us two,
Tears our recountments had most kindly bath'd,
As how I came into that desert place —
In brief, he led me to the gentle Duke,
Who gave me fresh array and entertainment,
Committing me unto my brother's love,
Who led me instantly unto his cave,
There stripp'd himself, and here upon his arm
The lioness had torn some flesh away,
Which all this while had bled; and now he fainted,
And cried, in fainting, upon Rosalind.
Brief, I recover'd him, bound up his wound;
And after some small space, being strong at heart,
He sent me hither, stranger as I am,
To tell this story, that you might excuse
His broken promise, and to give this napkin,
Dy'd in his blood, unto the shepherd youth
That he in sport doth call his Rosalind.
[*Rosalind swoons.*]
Cel. Why, how now, Ganymede? sweet Ganymede!
Oli. Many will swoon when they do look on blood.
Cel. There is more in it. Cousin Ganymede!
Oli. Look, he recovers.
Ros. I would I were at home.
Cel. We'll lead you thither.
I pray you, will you take him by the arm?
Oli. Be of good cheer, youth. You a man?
You lack a man's heart.
Ros. I do so, I confess it. Ah, sirrah, a body would think this was well counterfeited! I pray you tell your brother how well I counterfeited. Heigh-ho!

Oli. This was not counterfeit. There is too great testimony in your complexion that it was a passion of earnest.

Ros. Counterfeit, I assure you.

Oli. Well then, take a good heart and counterfeit to be a man.

Ros. So I do; but, i' faith, I should have been a woman by right.

Cel. Come, you look paler and paler. Pray you draw homewards. Good sir, go with us.

Oli. That will I; for I must bear answer back How you excuse my brother, Rosalind.

Ros. I shall devise something. But I pray you commend my counterfeiting to him. Will you go? *Exeunt.*

ACT V. Scene I. [*The Forest. Near the sheepcote.*]

Enter [*Touchstone the*] *Clown* and *Audrey.*

Touch. We shall find a time, Audrey. Patience, gentle Audrey.

Aud. Faith, the priest was good enough, for all the old gentleman's saying.

Touch. A most wicked Sir Oliver, Audrey, a most vile Martext! But, Audrey, there is a youth here in the forest lays claim to you.

Aud. Ay, I know who 'tis. He hath no interest in me in the world. Here comes the man you mean.

Enter *William.*

Touch. It is meat and drink to me to see a clown. By my troth, we that have good wits have much to answer for. We shall be flouting; we cannot hold.

Will. Good ev'n, Audrey.

Aud. God ye good ev'n, William.

Will. And good ev'n to you, sir.

Touch. Good ev'n, gentle friend. Cover thy head, cover thy head. Nay, prithee be cover'd. How old are you, friend?

Will. Five-and-twenty, sir.

Touch. A ripe age. Is thy name William?

Will. William, sir.

Touch. A fair name. Wast born i' th' forest here?

Will. Ay, sir, I thank God.

Touch. 'Thank God.' A good answer. Art rich?

Will. Faith, sir, so so.

Touch. 'So so' is good, very good, very excellent good; and yet it is not, it is but so so. Art thou wise?

Will. Ay, sir, I have a pretty wit.

Touch. Why, thou say'st well. I do now remember a saying, 'The fool doth think he is wise, but the wise man knows himself to be a fool.' The heathen philosopher, when he had a desire to eat a grape, would open his lips when he put it into his mouth, meaning thereby that grapes were made to eat and lips to open. You do love this maid?

Will. I do, sir.

Touch. Give me your hand. Art thou learned?

Will. No, sir.

Touch. Then learn this of me: to have is to have; for it is a figure in rhetoric that drink, being pour'd out of a cup into a glass, by filling the one doth empty the other; for all your writers do consent that *ipse* is he. Now, you are not *ipse*, for I am he.

Will. Which he, sir?

Touch. He, sir, that must marry this woman. Therefore, you clown, abandon (which is in the vulgar, leave) the society (which in the boorish is, company) of this female (which in the common is, woman); which together is, abandon the society of this female, or, clown, thou perishest; or, to thy better understanding, diest; or, to wit, I kill thee, make thee away, translate thy life into death, thy liberty into bondage. I will deal in poison with thee, or in bastinado, or in steel. I will bandy with thee in faction; I will o'errun thee with policy; I will kill thee a hundred and fifty ways. Therefore tremble and depart.

Aud. Do, good William.

Will. God rest you merry, sir. *Exit.*

Enter *Corin.*

Cor. Our master and mistress seeks you. Come away, away!

Touch. Trip, Audrey! trip, Audrey! I attend, I attend. *Exeunt.*

Scene II. [*The Forest. Near the sheepcote.*]

Enter *Orlando* and *Oliver.*

Orl. Is't possible that on so little acquaintance you should like her? that but seeing, you should love her? and loving, woo? and wooing, she should grant? And will you persever to enjoy her?

Oli. Neither call the giddiness of it in question, the poverty of her, the small acquaintance, my sudden wooing, nor her sudden consenting; but say with me, I love Aliena; say with her that she loves me; consent with both that we may enjoy each other. It shall be to your good; for my father's house, and all the revenue that was old Sir Rowland's, will I estate upon you, and here live and die a shepherd.

Enter *Rosalind.*

Orl. You have my consent. Let your wedding be to-morrow. Thither will I invite the Duke and all's contented followers. Go you and prepare Aliena; for look you, here comes my Rosalind.

Ros. God save you, brother.

Oli. And you, fair sister. [*Exit.*]

Ros. O my dear Orlando, how it grieves me to see thee wear thy heart in a scarf!

Orl. It is my arm.

Ros. I thought thy heart had been wounded with the claws of a lion.

Orl. Wounded it is, but with the eyes of a lady.

Ros. Did your brother tell you how I counterfeited to sound when he show'd me your handkercher?

Orl. Ay, and greater wonders than that.

Ros. O, I know where you are! Nay, 'tis true. There was never anything so sudden but the fight of two rams and Cæsar's thrasonical brag of 'I came, saw, and overcame.' For your brother and my sister no sooner met but they look'd; no sooner look'd but they lov'd; no sooner lov'd but they sigh'd; no sooner sigh'd but they ask'd one another the reason; no sooner knew the reason but they sought the remedy: and in these degrees have they made a pair of stairs to marriage, which they will climb incontinent, or else be incontinent before marriage. They are in the very wrath of love, and they will together. Clubs cannot part them.

Orl. They shall be married to-morrow, and I will bid the Duke to the nuptial. But, O, how bitter a thing it is to look into happiness through another man's eyes! By so much the more shall I to-morrow be at the height of heart-heaviness, by how much I shall think my brother happy in having what he wishes for.

Ros. Why then, to-morrow I cannot serve your turn for Rosalind?

Orl. I can live no longer by thinking.

Ros. I will weary you then no longer with idle talking. Know of me then (for now I speak to some purpose) that I know you are a gentleman of good conceit. I speak not this that you should bear a good opinion of my knowledge, insomuch I say I know you are; neither do I labour for a greater esteem than may in some little measure draw a belief from you, to do yourself good, and not to grace me. Believe then, if you please, that I can do strange things. I have, since I was three year old, convers'd with a magician, most profound in his art and yet not damnable. If you do love Rosalind so near the heart as your gesture cries it out, when your brother marries Aliena shall you marry her. I know into what straits of fortune she is driven; and it is not impossible to me, if it appear not inconvenient to you, to set her before your eyes to-morrow human as she is, and without any danger.

Orl. Speak'st thou in sober meanings?

Ros. By my life, I do! which I tender dearly, though I say I am a magician. Therefore put you in your best array, bid your friends; for if you will be married to-morrow, you shall; and to Rosalind, if you will.

Enter *Silvius* and *Phebe.*

Look, here comes a lover of mine and a lover of hers.

Phe. Youth, you have done me much ungentleness
To show the letter that I writ to you.

Ros. I care not if I have. It is my study
To seem despiteful and ungentle to you.
You are there followed by a faithful shepherd.
Look upon him, love him; he worships you.

Phe. Good shepherd, tell this youth what 'tis to love.

Sil. It is to be all made of sighs and tears;
And so am I for Phebe.

Phe. And I for Ganymede.

Orl. And I for Rosalind.

Ros. And I for no woman.

Sil. It is to be all made of faith and service;
And so am I for Phebe.

Phe. And I for Ganymede.

Orl. And I for Rosalind.

Ros. And I for no woman

Sil. It is to be all made of fantasy,
All made of passion, and all made of wishes,
All adoration, duty, and observance,
All humbleness, all patience, and impatience,
All purity, all trial, all obedience;
And so am I for Phebe.

Phe. And so am I for Ganymede.

Orl. And so am I for Rosalind.

Ros. And so am I for no woman.

Phe. [*to Rosalind*] If this be so, why blame you me to love you?

Sil. [*to Phebe*] If this be so, why blame you me to love you?

Orl. If this be so, why blame you me to love you?

Ros. Who do you speak to, 'Why blame you me to love you?'

Orl. To her that is not here, nor doth not hear.

Ros. Pray you, no more of this; 'tis like the howling of Irish wolves against the moon. [*To Silvius*] I will help you if I can. — [*To Phebe*] I would love you if I could. — To-morrow meet me all together. — [*To Phebe*] I will marry you if ever I marry woman, and I'll be married to-morrow. — [*To Orlando*] I will satisfy you if ever I satisfied man, and you shall be married to-morrow. — [*To Silvius*] I will content you if what pleases you contents you, and you shall be married to-morrow. — [*To Orlando*] As you love Rosalind, meet. — [*To Silvius*] As you love Phebe, meet. — And as I love no woman, I'll meet. So fare you well. I have left you commands.

Sil. I'll not fail if I live.

Phe. Nor I.

Orl. Nor I. *Exeunt.*

Scene III. [*The Forest. Near the sheepcote.*]

Enter [*Touchstone the*] *Clown* and *Audrey*.

Touch. To-morrow is the joyful day, Audrey; to-morrow will we be married.

Aud. I do desire it with all my heart; and I hope it is no dishonest desire to desire to be a woman of the world. Here come two of the banish'd Duke's pages.

Enter two *Pages*.

1. Page. Well met, honest gentleman.

Touch. By my troth, well met. Come, sit, sit, and a song!

2. Page. We are for you. Sit i' th' middle.

1. Page. Shall we clap into't roundly, without hawking or spitting or saying we are hoarse, which are the only prologues to a bad voice?

2. Page. I' faith, i' faith! and both in a tune, like two gypsies on a horse.

Song.

It was a lover and his lass —
With a hey, and a ho, and a hey nonino —
That o'er the green cornfield did pass
In springtime, the only pretty ring-time,
When birds do sing, hey ding a ding, ding.
Sweet lovers love the spring.

Between the acres of the rye —
With a hey, and a ho, and a hey nonino —
These pretty country folks would lie
In springtime, &c.

This carol they began that hour —
With a hey, and a ho, and a hey nonino —
How that a life was but a flower
In springtime, &c.

And therefore take the present time —
With a hey, and a ho, and a hey nonino —
For love is crowned with the prime
In springtime, &c.

Touch. Truly, young gentlemen, though there was no great matter in the ditty, yet the note was very untuneable.

1. Page. You are deceiv'd, sir. We kept time, we lost not our time.

Touch. By my troth, yes! I count it but time lost to hear such a foolish song. God b'wi' you, and God mend your voices! Come, Audrey. *Exeunt.*

Scene IV. [*The Forest. Near the sheepcote.*]

Enter *Duke Senior, Amiens, Jaques, Orlando, Oliver, Celia.*

Duke S. Dost thou believe, Orlando, that the boy
Can do all this that he hath promised?

Orl. I sometimes do believe, and sometimes do not,
As those that fear they hope, and know they fear.

Enter *Rosalind, Silvius,* and *Phebe.*

Ros. Patience once more, whiles our compact is urg'd.
You say, if I bring in your Rosalind,
You will bestow her on Orlando here?

Duke. S. That would I, had I kingdoms to give with her.

Ros. And you say you will have her when I bring her?

Orl. That would I, were I of all kingdoms king.

Ros. You say you'll marry me, if I be willing?

Phe. That will I, should I die the hour after.

Ros. But if you do refuse to marry me,
You'll give yourself to this most faithful shepherd?

Phe. So is the bargain.

Ros. You say that you'll have Phebe, if she will?

Sil. Though to have her and death were both one thing.

Ros. I have promis'd to make all this matter even.
Keep you your word, O Duke, to give your daughter;
You yours, Orlando, to receive his daughter;
Keep your word, Phebe, that you'll marry me,
Or else, refusing me, to wed this shepherd;
Keep your word, Silvius, that you'll marry her
If she refuse me; and from hence I go,
To make these doubts all even.

Exeunt Rosalind and Celia.

Duke S. I do remember in this shepherd boy
Some lively touches of my daughter's favour.

Orl. My lord, the first time that I ever saw him
Methought he was a brother to your daughter.
But, my good lord, this boy is forest-born,
And hath been tutor'd in the rudiments
Of many desperate studies by his uncle,
Whom he reports to be a great magician,
Obscured in the circle of this forest.

Enter [*Touchstone the*] *Clown* and *Audrey.*

Jaq. There is, sure, another flood toward, and these couples are coming to the ark. Here comes a pair of very strange beasts, which in all tongues are call'd fools.

Touch. Salutation and greeting to you all!

Jaq. Good my lord, bid him welcome. This is the motley-minded gentleman that I have so often met in the forest. He hath been a courtier, he swears.

Touch. If any man doubt that, let him put me to my purgation. I have trod a measure; I have flatt'red a lady; I have been politic with my friend, smooth with mine enemy; I have undone three tailors; I have had four quarrels, and like to have fought one.

Jaq. And how was that ta'en up?

Touch. Faith, we met, and found the quarrel was upon the seventh cause.

Jaq. How seventh cause? Good my lord, like this fellow.

Duke S. I like him very well.

Touch. God 'ild you, sir; I desire you of the like. I press in here, sir, amongst the rest of the country copulatives, to swear and to forswear, according as marriage binds and blood breaks. A poor virgin, sir, an ill-favour'd thing, sir, but mine own. A poor humour of mine, sir, to take that that no man else will. Rich honesty dwells like a miser, sir, in a poor house, as your pearl in your foul oyster.

Duke S. By my faith, he is very swift and sententious.

Touch. According to the fool's bolt, sir, and such dulcet diseases.

Jaq. But, for the seventh cause. How did you find the quarrel on the seventh cause?

Touch. Upon a lie seven times removed (bear your body more seeming, Audrey): as thus, sir. I did dislike the cut of a certain courtier's beard. He sent me word, if I said his beard was not cut well, he was in the mind it was. This is call'd the Retort Courteous. If I sent him word again it was not well cut, he would send me word he cut it to please himself. This is call'd the Quip Modest. If again, it was not well cut, he disabled my judgment. This is call'd the Reply Churlish. If again, it was not well cut, he would answer I spake not true. This is call'd the Reproof Valiant. If again, it was not well cut, he would say I lie. This is call'd the Countercheck Quarrelsome; and so to the Lie Circumstantial and the Lie Direct.

Jaq. And how oft did you say his beard was not well cut?

Touch. I durst go no further than the Lie Circumstantial, nor he durst not give me the Lie Direct; and so we measur'd swords and parted.

Jaq. Can you nominate in order now the degrees of the lie?

Touch. O sir, we quarrel in print, by the book, as you have books for good manners. I will name you the degrees. The first, the Retort Courteous; the second, the Quip Modest; the third, the Reply Churlish; the fourth, the Reproof Valiant; the fifth, the Countercheck Quarrelsome; the sixth, the Lie with Circumstance; the seventh, the Lie Direct. All these you may avoid but the Lie Direct, and you may avoid that too, with an If. I knew when seven justices could not take up a quarrel, but when the parties were met themselves, one of them thought but of an If: as, 'If you said so, then I said so'; and they shook hands and swore brothers. Your If is the only peacemaker. Much virtue in If.

Jaq. Is not this a rare fellow, my lord? He's as good at anything, and yet a fool.

Duke S. He uses his folly like a stalking horse, and under the presentation of that he shoots his wit.

Enter *Hymen, Rosalind,* and *Celia.* Still music.

Hym. Then is there mirth in heaven
When earthly things made even
Atone together.
Good Duke, receive thy daughter;
Hymen from heaven brought her,
Yea, brought her hether,
That thou mightst join her hand with his
Whose heart within his bosom is.

Ros. To you I give myself, for I am yours. [*To Duke.*]
To you I give myself, for I am yours. [*To Orlando.*]

Duke S. If there be truth in sight, you are my daughter.

Orl. If there be truth in shape, you are my Rosalind.

Phe. If sight and shape be true,
Why then, my love adieu!

Ros. I'll have no father, if you be not he. [*To Duke.*]
I'll have no husband, if you be not he. [*To Orlando.*]
Nor ne'er wed woman, if you be not she. [*To Phebe.*]

Hym. Peace ho! I bar confusion.
'Tis I must make conclusion
Of these most strange events.
Here's eight that must take hands
To join in Hymen's bands,
If truth holds true contents.
You and you no cross shall part. [*To Orlando and Rosalind.*]
You and you are heart in heart. [*To Oliver and Celia.*]
You to his love must accord, [*To Phebe.*]
Or have a woman to your lord.
You and you are sure together [*To Touchstone and Audrey.*]
As the winter to foul weather.
Whiles a wedlock hymn we sing,
Feed yourselves with questioning,
That reason wonder may diminish
How thus we met, and these things finish.

Song.

Wedding is great Juno's crown —
O blessed bond of board and bed!
'Tis Hymen peoples every town;
High wedlock then be honoured.
Honour, high honour, and renown
To Hymen, god of every town!

Duke S. O my dear niece, welcome thou art to me,
Even daughter, welcome, in no less degree!

Phe. [*to Silvius*] I will not eat my word, now thou art mine;
Thy faith my fancy to thee doth combine.

Enter *Second Brother,* [*Jaques de Boys*].

2. Bro. Let me have audience for a word or two.
I am the second son of old Sir Rowland
That bring these tidings to this fair assembly.
Duke Frederick, hearing how that every day
Men of great worth resorted to this forest,
Address'd a mighty power, which were on foot
In his own conduct, purposely to take
His brother here and put him to the sword;
And to the skirts of this wild wood he came,
Where, meeting with an old religious man,
After some question with him, was converted
Both from his enterprise and from the world,
His crown bequeathing to his banish'd brother,
And all their lands restor'd to them again
That were with him exil'd. This to be true
I do engage my life.

Duke S. Welcome, young man.
Thou offer'st fairly to thy brothers' wedding:
To one, his lands withheld; and to the other,
A land itself at large, a potent dukedom.
First, in this forest let us do those ends
That here were well begun and well begot;
And after, every of this happy number
That have endur'd shrewd days and nights with us
Shall share the good of our returned fortune,
According to the measure of their states.
Meantime forget this new-fall'n dignity
And fall into our rustic revelry.
Play, music, and you brides and bridegrooms all,
With measure heap'd in joy, to th' measures fall.

Jaq. Sir, by your patience. If I heard you rightly,
The Duke hath put on a religious life
And thrown into neglect the pompous court.

2. Bro. He hath.

Jaq. To him will I. Out of these convertites
There is much matter to be heard and learn'd.
[*To Duke*] You to your former honour I bequeath;
Your patience and your virtue well deserves it.
[*To Orlando*] You to a love that your true faith doth merit;
[*To Oliver*] You to your land and love and great allies;
[*To Silvius*] You to a long and well-deserved bed;
[*To Touchstone*] And you to wrangling, for thy loving voyage
Is but for two months victuall'd. — So, to your pleasures!
I am for other than for dancing measures.

Duke S. Stay, Jaques, stay.

Jaq. To see no pastime I! What you would have
I'll stay to know at your abandon'd cave.
Exit.

Duke S. Proceed, proceed. We will begin these rites,
As we do trust they'll end, in true delights.
[*A dance.*]

[EPILOGUE.]

Ros. It is not the fashion to see the lady the epilogue; but it is no more unhandsome than to see the lord the prologue. If it be true that good wine needs no bush, 'tis true that a good play needs no epilogue. Yet to good wine they do use good bushes, and good plays prove the better by the help of good epilogues. What a case am I in then, that am neither a good epilogue, nor cannot insinuate with you in the behalf of a good play! I am not furnish'd like a beggar; therefore to beg will not become me. My way is to conjure you, and I'll begin with the women. I charge you, O women, for the love you bear to men, to like as much of this play as please you; and I charge you, O men, for the love you bear to women (as I perceive by your simp'ring none of you hates them), that between you and the women the play may please. If I were a woman, I would kiss as many of you as had beards that pleas'd me, complexions that lik'd me, and breaths that I defied not; and I am sure, as many as have good beards, or good faces, or sweet breaths, will, for my kind offer, when I make curtsy, bid me farewell. *Exeunt.*

The Taming of the Shrew

For The Taming of the Shrew the Folio of 1623 is our sole authority. The date of the play is uncertain. The extreme possibilities appear to be 1594 (which seems too early) and 1598 (which seems rather late). It is not mentioned by Meres in 1598 (see p. 33), for surely it cannot be the mysterious *Love Labour's Won.*

The main source is *The Taming of a Shrew*, an anonymous play printed in 1594 but obviously written some years earlier. This combines the taming story with much of the plot of Ariosto's *I Suppositi*, which had been translated by George Gascoigne as *The Supposes* (1566; printed 1573, 1575).

For the taming story no exact original has been found. It handles a theme widely current in the folklore of Orient and Occident and has points of contact with a large variety of tales and proverbs. 'The tongue can no man tame,' St. James avers. 'It is an unruly evil, full of deadly poison'; and the Abbess in *The Comedy of Errors* echoes his words (v, 1, 69–70):

> The venom clamours of a jealous woman
> Poisons more deadly than a mad dog's tooth.

The tale of the Shrewish Wife who is a Terror to Demons, an ancient anecdote in the East, is well represented in English by the ballad of *The Farmer's Curst Wife* (Child, No. 278): she is carried off to hell, but the devil is glad to take her back to her husband. The cucking stool is not the only corrective for shrews. Witness a savage old story in verse (printed before 1575) — *A merry Ieste of a shrewde and curste Wyfe lapped in Morrelles skin* (see Child, No. 277). Petruchio's declaration in iii, 2, 232–234,

> She is my goods, my chattels; she is my house,
> My household stuff, my field, my barn,
> My horse, my dog, my ass, my anything!

sounds like an echo from other folk-tales. Thus in *El Conde Lucanor* by Juan Manuel (1282–1347; first printed in 1575) a bridegroom tames his shrew by killing his dog, his cat, and his horse when they disregard his call for water to wash his hands. In another tale in the same collection an obedient wife agrees with her husband that certain cows are mares (cf. iv, 5). A folk-tale from Jutland combines the two and includes a test of obedience like that at the end of the play. Perhaps the Elizabethans knew a similar complex.

In reworking the material of *A Shrew* Shakespeare is commonly thought to have had a collaborator, to whom is ascribed the subplot of Bianca and her suitors. Everybody is ready to credit the Induction and the main plot (Katherine and Petruchio) to the master's hand. However, the differences in style and metre are hardly sufficient to establish dual authorship. The technical excellence in construction is a good argument on the conservative side. The author of *A Shrew* did good work in combining two stories, but The Shrew, which increases the complexity of the Bianca plot, goes far beyond its source in ingenious unification.

When *I Suppositi* begins, Polinesta has been carrying on an intrigue for two years with Erostrato, who came to the city to study, fell in love with her, exchanged identities with his man Dulipo, and took service with her father. Cleandro, an elderly lawyer, is now suing for her hand. To thwart him, Dulipo, in the character of Erostrato, is posing as a rival suitor. In THE TAMING OF THE SHREW we have a similar situation. Lucentio, who came to the city to study, falls in love with Bianca, exchanges identities with his man Tranio, and takes service with her father as a tutor in polite letters. There are two avowed rivals for her hand — young Hortensio and old Gremio. Hortensio, disguised, is engaged by her father as instructor in music. In *The Taming of a Shrew* things are simpler, except for the fusion with the taming story. The student (Aurelius), who is a duke's son, neither exchanges identities with his man nor enters the service of the girl's father (Alfonso). He conceals his high rank, passes as the son of a merchant, and is acceptable to Alfonso as a suitor for his second daughter. Polidor, a friend of Aurelius, is equally acceptable as a suitor for the youngest daughter. The only obstacle is Alfonso's determination that his eldest daughter, the shrew, must be married before either of her sisters. There is no rival, old or young, in either case. Neither Aurelius nor Polidor disguises himself as a tutor. Aurelius does cause his man Valerio to take service with Alfonso as an instructor in music, but this is merely to enable the two younger girls to meet their lovers while the eldest is busy with her lessons on the lute, for otherwise she would keep them at work in the house. There is no Latin tutor in *A Shrew*, nor does either lover enter the father's house as a servant.

This comparison shows that Shakespeare, though utilizing the old play, has had recourse to *I Suppositi* as well. Such recourse is obvious elsewhere — in iv, 2, 59–121, for example, and in v, 1. In one passage, indeed, THE SHREW may be said to acknowledge its indebtedness to Gascoigne's translation: 'While counterfeit supposes blear'd thine eyne' (v, 1, 120).

The Induction dramatizes an old tale, best known to modern readers from 'The Sleeper Wakes' in the *Arabian Nights*, but current in Western Europe as a supposedly historical anecdote in the sixteenth and seventeenth centuries.

The Induction of *A Shrew* has been completely rewritten for THE SHREW; but the plan is retained in detail and there are many echoes of the old phrases. In THE SHREW, however, nothing is heard of Sly and the rest after i, 1, 259, whereas in *A Shrew* the Sly *motif* persists, emerging at appropriate intervals. Sly falls asleep. Stripped of his fine clothes and dressed 'in his own apparel,' he is left near the alehouse door. He tells the tapster, who rouses him, that he has had a fine dream which has taught him 'how to tame a shrew' and that he will straightway go home and tame his wife. The tapster declares that he will accompany him and hear the rest of the dream. Thus the old tale is brought to its appropriate and traditional conclusion. One suspects that the absence of this material in THE SHREW is due to a cut in the Folio text.

The names *Tranio* and *Grumio* come from the *Mostellaria* of Plautus.

Fletcher capped THE TAMING OF THE SHREW by *The Woman's Prize; or, The Tamer Tamed*. Petruchio weds Maria after his first wife's death. His friends pity her for marrying 'this dragon,' but she soon reduces him to submissive decorum.

The Taming of the Shrew

[Dramatis Personæ.

A Lord.
Christopher Sly, a tinker.
Hostess, Page, Players, Huntsmen, and Servants. } Persons in the Induction.
Baptista Minola, a gentleman of Padua.
Vincentio, a merchant of Pisa.
Lucentio, son to *Vincentio,* in love with *Bianca.*
Petruchio, a gentleman of Verona, suitor to *Katherina.*
Gremio, *Hortensio,* } suitors to *Bianca.*
Tranio, *Biondello,* } servants to *Lucentio.*
Grumio, *Curtis,* &c. } servants to *Petruchio.*
A Pedant.
Katherina, the shrew, *Bianca,* } daughters to *Baptista.*
A Widow.

Tailor, Haberdasher, and Servants.

Scene. — *Padua, and Petruchio's house in the country.*]

[Induction.] [Scene I. *Before an alehouse on a heath.*]

Enter *Beggar* (*Christopher Sly*) and *Hostess.*

Beg. I'll pheeze you, in faith!

Host. A pair of stocks, you rogue!

Beg. Y'are a baggage! The Slys are no rogues. Look in the chronicles: we came in with Richard Conqueror. Therefore paucas pallabris; let the world slide. Sessa!

Host. You will not pay for the glasses you have burst?

Beg. No, not a denier. Go by, Saint Jeronimy! Go to thy cold bed and warm thee.

Host. I know my remedy; I must go fetch the thirdborough. [*Exit.*]

Beg. Third or fourth or fifth borough, I'll answer him by law. I'll not budge an inch, boy. Let him come, and kindly.

Falls asleep [*on the ground*].

Wind horns. Enter a *Lord* from hunting, with his *Train* [of *Huntsmen* and *Servants*].

Lord. Huntsman, I charge thee, tender well my hounds:
Broach Merriman, the poor cur is emboss'd;
And couple Clowder with the deep-mouth'd brach.
Saw'st thou not, boy, how Silver made it good
At the hedge corner, in the coldest fault?
I would not lose the dog for twenty pound.

1. Hunt. Why, Belman is as good as he, my lord.
He cried upon it at the merest loss
And twice to-day pick'd out the dullest scent.
Trust me, I take him for the better dog.

Lord. Thou art a fool. If Echo were as fleet,
I would esteem him worth a dozen such.
But sup them well and look unto them all.
To-morrow I intend to hunt again.

1. Hunt. I will, my lord.

Lord. What's here? One dead, or drunk? See, doth he breathe?

2. Hunt. He breathes, my lord. Were he not warm'd with ale,
This were a bed but cold to sleep so soundly.

Lord. O monstrous beast! how like a swine he lies!
Grim death, how foul and loathsome is thine image!
Sirs, I will practise on this drunken man.
What think you? If he were convey'd to bed,
Wrapp'd in sweet clothes, rings put upon his fingers,
A most delicious banquet by his bed,
And brave attendants near him when he wakes,
Would not the beggar then forget himself?

1. Hunt. Believe me, lord, I think he cannot choose.

2. Hunt. It would seem strange unto him when he wak'd.

Lord. Even as a flatt'ring dream or worthless fancy.
Then take him up and manage well the jest.
Carry him gently to my fairest chamber
And hang it round with all my wanton pictures.
Balm his foul head in warm distilled waters
And burn sweet wood to make the lodging sweet.
Procure me music ready when he wakes
To make a dulcet and a heavenly sound;

And if he chance to speak, be ready straight
And with a low submissive reverence
Say 'What is it your honour will command?'
Let one attend him with a silver basin
Full of rosewater and bestrew'd with flowers;
Another bear the ewer, the third a diaper,
And say 'Will't please your lordship cool your hands?'
Some one be ready with a costly suit
And ask him what apparel he will wear.
Another tell him of his hounds and horse,
And that his lady mourns at his disease.
Persuade him that he hath been lunatic;
And when he says he is — say that he dreams,
For he is nothing but a mighty lord.
This do, and do it kindly, gentle sirs.
It will be pastime passing excellent,
If it be husbanded with modesty.

1. Hunt. My lord, I warrant you we will play our part
As he shall think, by our true diligence,
He is no less than what we say he is.

Lord. Take him up gently and to bed with him,
And each one to his office when he wakes.

[*Sly is borne out.*] *Sound trumpet.*

Sirrah, go see what trumpet 'tis that sounds.

[*Exit Servingman.*]

Belike some noble gentleman that means,
Travelling some journey, to repose him here.

Enter *Servingman.*

How now? Who is it?

Serv. An't please your honour, players,
That offer service to your lordship.

Lord. Bid them come near.

Enter *Players.*

Now, fellows, you are welcome.

Players. We thank your honour.

Lord. Do you intend to stay with me to-night?

Player. So please your lordship to accept our duty.

Lord. With all my heart. This fellow I remember
Since once he play'd a farmer's eldest son.
'Twas where you woo'd the gentlewoman so well.
I have forgot your name; but sure that part
Was aptly fitted and naturally perform'd.

Player. I think 'twas Soto that your honour means.

Lord. 'Tis very true. Thou didst it excellent.
Well, you are come to me in happy time,
The rather for I have some sport in hand
Wherein your cunning can assist me much.
There is a lord will hear you play to-night;
But I am doubtful of your modesties,
Lest, over-eying of his odd behaviour
(For yet his honour never heard a play),
You break into some merry passion
And so offend him; for I tell you, sirs,
If you should smile, he grows impatient.

Player. Fear not, my lord. We can contain ourselves,
Were he the veriest antic in the world.

Lord. Go, sirrah, take them to the buttery
And give them friendly welcome every one.
Let them want nothing that my house affords.

Exit one with the Players.

Sirrah, go you to Barthol'mew my page,
And see him dress'd in all suits like a lady.
That done, conduct him to the drunkard's chamber,
And call him 'madam,' do him obeisance.
Tell him from me, as he will win my love,
He bear himself with honourable action,
Such as he hath observ'd in noble ladies
Unto their lords by them accomplished.
Such duty to the drunkard let him do
With soft low tongue and lowly courtesy,
And say 'What is't your honour will command
Wherein your lady and your humble wife
May show her duty and make known her love?'
And then with kind embracements, tempting kisses,
And with declining head into his bosom,
Bid him shed tears, as being overjoy'd
To see her noble lord restor'd to health,
Who for this seven years hath esteemed him
No better than a poor and loathsome beggar.
And if the boy have not a woman's gift
To rain a shower of commanded tears,
An onion will do well for such a shift,
Which, in a napkin being close convey'd,
Shall in despite enforce a watery eye.
See this dispatch'd with all the haste thou canst.
Anon I'll give thee more instructions.

Exit a Servingman.

I know the boy will well usurp the grace,
Voice, gait, and action of a gentlewoman.
I long to hear him call the drunkard husband,
And how my men will stay themselves from laughter
When they do homage to this simple peasant.
I'll in to counsel them. Haply my presence
May well abate the over-merry spleen,
Which otherwise would grow into extremes.

[*Exeunt.*]

[Scene II. *A bedchamber in the Lord's house.*]

Enter aloft *the Drunkard,* [*Sly the Beggar,*] with *Attendants,* some with apparel, basin and ewer, and other appurtenances; and *Lord.*

Beg. For God's sake, a pot of small ale!

1. Serv. Will't please your lordship drink a cup of sack?

2. Serv. Will't please your honour taste of these conserves?

3. Serv. What raiment will your honour wear to-day?

Beg. I am Christophero Sly. Call not me 'honour' nor 'lordship.' I ne'er drank sack in my life; and if you give me any conserves, give me conserves of beef. Ne'er ask me what raiment I'll wear; for I have no more doublets than backs, no more stockings than legs, nor no more shoes than feet; nay, sometime more feet than shoes, or such shoes as my toes look through the overleather.

Lord. Heaven cease this idle humour in your honour!
O that a mighty man of such descent,
Of such possessions and so high esteem,
Should be infused with so foul a spirit!

Beg. What, would you make me mad? Am not I Christopher Sly, old Sly's son of Burton Heath; by birth a pedlar, by education a card-maker, by transmutation a bearherd, and now by present profession a tinker? Ask Marian Hacket, the fat alewife of Wincot, if she know me not. If she say I am not fourteen pence on the score for sheer ale, score me up for the lying'st knave in Christendom. What! I am not bestraught. Here's —

3. Man. O, this it is that makes your lady mourn!

2. Man. O, this is it that makes your servants droop!

Lord. Hence comes it that your kindred shuns your house,
As beaten hence by your strange lunacy.
O noble lord, bethink thee of thy birth,
Call home thy ancient thoughts from banishment
And banish hence these abject lowly dreams!
Look how thy servants do attend on thee,
Each in his office ready at thy beck.
Wilt thou have music? Hark! Apollo plays,
Music.
And twenty caged nightingales do sing.
Or wilt thou sleep? We'll have thee to a couch
Softer and sweeter than the lustful bed
On purpose trimm'd up for Semiramis.
Say thou wilt walk. We will bestrow the ground.
Or wilt thou ride? Thy horses shall be trapp'd,
Their harness studded all with gold and pearl.
Dost thou love hawking? Thou hast hawks will soar
Above the morning lark. Or wilt thou hunt?
Thy hounds shall make the welkin answer them
And fetch shrill echoes from the hollow earth.

1. Man. Say thou wilt course. Thy greyhounds are as swift
As breathed stags; ay, fleeter than the roe.

2. Man. Dost thou love pictures? We will fetch thee straight
Adonis painted by a running brook,
And Cytherea all in sedges hid,
Which seem to move and wanton with her breath,
Even as the waving sedges play with wind.

Lord. We'll show thee Io as she was a maid,
And how she was beguiled and surpris'd,
As lively painted as the deed was done.

3. Man. Or Daphne roaming through a thorny wood,
Scratching her legs that one shall swear she bleeds,
And at that sight shall sad Apollo weep,
So workmanly the blood and tears are drawn.

Lord. Thou art a lord, and nothing but a lord.
Thou hast a lady far more beautiful
Than any woman in this waning age.

1. Man. And, till the tears that she hath shed for thee
Like envious floods o'errun her lovely face,
She was the fairest creature in the world;
And yet she is inferior to none.

Beg. Am I a lord? and have I such a lady?
Or do I dream? or have I dream'd till now?
I do not sleep: I see, I hear, I speak;
I smell sweet savours and I feel soft things.
Upon my life, I am a lord indeed,
And not a tinker, nor Christophero Sly.
Well, bring our lady hither to our sight,
And once again a pot o' th' smallest ale.

2. Man. Will't please your Mightiness to wash your hands?
O, how we joy to see your wit restor'd!
O that once more you knew but what you are!
These fifteen years you have been in a dream,
Or when you wak'd, so wak'd as if you slept.

Beg. These fifteen years! by my fay, a goodly nap.
But did I never speak of all that time?

1. Man. O, yes, my lord! but very idle words;

For though you lay here in this goodly chamber,
Yet would you say ye were beaten out of door,
And rail upon the hostess of the house,
And say you would present her at the leet
Because she brought stone jugs and no seal'd quarts.
Sometimes you would call out for Cicely Hacket.

Beg. Ay, the woman's maid of the house.

3 Man. Why, sir, you know no house nor no such maid,
Nor no such men as you have reckon'd up —
As Stephen Sly, and old John Naps of Greece,
And Peter Turph, and Henry Pimpernell,
And twenty more such names and men as these,
Which never were nor no man ever saw.

Beg. Now, Lord be thanked for my good amends!

All. Amen.

Enter [*the Page* as] *Lady,* with *Attendants.*

Beg. I thank thee. Thou shalt not lose by it.

Lady. How fares my noble lord?

Beg. Marry, I fare well, for here is cheer enough.
Where is my wife?

Lady. Here, noble lord. What is thy will with her?

Beg. Are you my wife, and will not call me husband?
My men should call me 'lord'; I am your goodman.

Lady. My husband and my lord, my lord and husband,
I am your wife in all obedience.

Beg. I know it well. What must I call her?

Lord. Madam.

Beg. Al'ce madam, or Joan madam?

Lord. Madam, and nothing else. So lords call ladies.

Beg. Madam wife, they say that I have dream'd,
And slept above some fifteen year or more.

Lady. Ay, and the time seems thirty unto me,
Being all this time abandon'd from your bed.

Beg. 'Tis much. Servants, leave me and her alone. [*Exeunt Servants.*]
Madam, undress you and come now to bed.

Lady. Thrice-noble lord, let me entreat of you
To pardon me yet for a night or two,
Or if not so, until the sun be set,
For your physicians have expressly charg'd,
In peril to incur your former malady,
That I should yet absent me from your bed.
I hope this reason stands for my excuse.

Beg. Ay, it stands so that I may hardly tarry so long. But I would be loath to fall into my dreams again. I will therefore tarry in despite of the flesh and the blood.

Enter a *Messenger.*

Mess. Your honour's players, hearing your amendment,
Are come to play a pleasant comedy;
For so your doctors hold it very meet,
Seeing too much sadness hath congeal'd your blood
And melancholy is the nurse of frenzy.
Therefore they thought it good you hear a play
And frame your mind to mirth and merriment,
Which bars a thousand harms and lengthens life.

Beg. Marry, I will; let them play it. Is not a comonty a Christmas gambold or a tumbling trick?

Lady. No, my good lord; it is more pleasing stuff.

Beg. What, household stuff?

Lady. It is a kind of history.

Beg. Well, we'll see't. Come, madam wife, sit by my side and let the world slip. We shall ne'er be younger.

[Act I. Scene I. *Padua. A public place before* Baptista's *house.*]

Flourish. Enter *Lucentio* and his man *Tranio.*

Luc. Tranio, since, for the great desire I had
To see fair Padua, nursery of arts,
I am arriv'd for fruitful Lombardy,
The pleasant garden of great Italy,
And by my father's love and leave am arm'd
With his good will and thy good company,
My trusty servant, well approv'd in all —
Here let us breathe, and haply institute
A course of learning and ingenious studies.
Pisa, renowned for grave citizens,
Gave me my being and my father first,
A merchant of great traffic through the world,
Vincentio, come of the Bentivolii.
Vincentio's son, brought up in Florence,
It shall become to serve all hopes conceiv'd,
To deck his fortune with his virtuous deeds;

And therefore, Tranio, for the time I study,
Virtue and that part of philosophy
Will I apply that treats of happiness
By virtue specially to be achiev'd.
Tell me thy mind; for I have Pisa left
And am to Padua come as he that leaves
A shallow plash to plunge him in the deep,
And with satiety seeks to quench his thirst.
Tra. Mi perdonato, gentle master mine.
I am in all affected as yourself;
Glad that you thus continue your resolve
To suck the sweets of sweet philosophy.
Only, good master, while we do admire
This virtue and this moral discipline,
Let's be no Stoics nor no stocks, I pray,
Or so devote to Aristotle's checks
As Ovid be an outcast quite abjur'd.
Balk logic with acquaintance that you have,
And practise rhetoric in your common talk;
Music and poesy use to quicken you;
The mathematics and the metaphysics,
Fall to them as you find your stomach serves you.
No profit grows where is no pleasure ta'en.
In brief, sir, study what you most affect.
Luc. Gramercies, Tranio, well dost thou advise.
If, Biondello, thou wert come ashore,
We could at once put us in readiness
And take a lodging fit to entertain
Such friends as time in Padua shall beget.

Enter *Baptista*, with his two daughters *Katherina* and *Bianca*; *Gremio*, a pantaloon; *Hortensio*, suitor to *Bianca*. *Lucentio*, *Tranio* stand by.

But stay awhile. What company is this?
Tra. Master, some show to welcome us to town.
Bap. Gentlemen, importune me no farther,
For how I firmly am resolv'd you know;
That is, not to bestow my youngest daughter
Before I have a husband for the elder.
If either of you both love Katherina,
Because I know you well and love you well,
Leave shall you have to court her at your pleasure.
Gre. To cart her rather. She's too rough for me.
There, there, Hortensio, will you any wife?
Kath. [*to Baptista*] I pray you, sir, is it your will
To make a stale of me amongst these mates?
Hor. Mates, maid? How mean you that? No mates for you,
Unless you were of gentler, milder mould.
Kath. I' faith, sir, you shall never need to fear.
Iwis it is not halfway to her heart;
But if it were, doubt not her care should be
To comb your noddle with a three-legg'd stool
And paint your face and use you like a fool.
Hor. From all such devils good Lord deliver us!
Gre. And me too, good Lord!
Tra. [*aside to Lucentio*] Husht, master! Here's some good pastime toward.
That wench is stark mad or wonderful froward.
Luc. [*aside to Tranio*] But in the other's silence do I see
Maid's mild behaviour and sobriety.
Peace, Tranio!
Tra. [*aside to Lucentio*] Well said, master. Mum! and gaze your fill.
Bap. Gentlemen, that I may soon make good
What I have said — Bianca, get you in;
And let it not displease thee, good Bianca,
For I will love thee ne'er the less, my girl.
Kath. A pretty peat! it is best
Put finger in the eye, an she knew why.
Bian. Sister, content you in my discontent.
Sir, to your pleasure humbly I subscribe.
My books and instruments shall be my company,
On them to look and practise by myself.
Luc. [*aside to Tranio*] Hark, Tranio! thou mayst hear Minerva speak.
Hor. Signior Baptista, will you be so strange?
Sorry am I that our good will effects
Bianca's grief.
Gre. Why will you mew her up,
Signior Baptista, for this fiend of hell,
And make her bear the penance of her tongue?
Bap. Gentlemen, content ye. I am resolv'd.
Go in, Bianca.
[*Exit Bianca.*]
And for I know she taketh most delight
In music, instruments, and poetry,
Schoolmasters will I keep within my house
Fit to instruct her youth. If you, Hortensio —
Or, Signior Gremio, you — know any such,
Prefer them hither; for to cunning men
I will be very kind, and liberal
To mine own children in good bringing-up.
And so farewell. Katherina, you may stay,
For I have more to commune with Bianca.
Exit.
Kath. Why, and I trust I may go too, may I not?
What, shall I be appointed hours, as though, belike,

I knew not what to take, and what to leave?
Ha! *Exit.*

Gre. You may go to the devil's dam! Your gifts are so good here's none will hold you. Our love is not so great, Hortensio, but we may blow our nails together and fast it fairly out. Our cake's dough on both sides. Farewell. Yet, for the love I bear my sweet Bianca, if I can by any means light on a fit man to teach her that wherein she delights, I will wish him to her father.

Hor. So will I, Signior Gremio. But a word, I pray. Though the nature of our quarrel yet never brook'd parle, know now, upon advice, it toucheth us both — that we may yet again have access to our fair mistress, and be happy rivals in Bianca's love — to labour and effect one thing specially.

Gre. What's that, I pray?

Hor. Marry, sir, to get a husband for her sister.

Gre. A husband? a devil!

Hor. I say a husband.

Gre. I say a devil. Think'st thou, Hortensio, though her father be very rich, any man is so very a fool to be married to hell?

Hor. Tush, Gremio! Though it pass your patience and mine to endure her loud alarums, why, man, there be good fellows in the world, an a man could light on them, would take her with all faults, and money enough.

Gre. I cannot tell; but I had as lief take her dowry with this condition — to be whipp'd at the high cross every morning.

Hor. Faith, as you say, there's small choice in rotten apples. But come; since this bar in law makes us friends, it shall be so far forth friendly maintain'd till by helping Baptista's eldest daughter to a husband we set his youngest free for a husband; and then have to't afresh! Sweet Bianca! Happy man be his dole! He that runs fastest gets the ring. How say you, Signior Gremio?

Gre. I am agreed; and would I had given him the best horse in Padua to begin his wooing that would thoroughly woo her, wed her, and bed her, and rid the house of her! Come on.

Exeunt ambo. Manent Tranio and Lucentio.

Tra. I pray, sir, tell me, is it possible
That love should of a sudden take such hold?

Luc. O Tranio, till I found it to be true,
I never thought it possible or likely.
But, see! while idly I stood looking on,
I found the effect of love in idleness;
And now in plainness do confess to thee —
That art to me as secret and as dear
As Anna to the Queen of Carthage was —
Tranio, I burn, I pine; I perish, Tranio,
If I achieve not this young modest girl.
Counsel me, Tranio, for I know thou canst;
Assist me, Tranio, for I know thou wilt.

Tra. Master, it is no time to chide you now;
Affection is not rated from the heart.
If love have touch'd you, naught remains but so:
Redime te captum quam queas minimo.

Luc. Gramercies, lad. Go forward; this contents;
The rest will comfort, for thy counsel's sound.

Tra. Master, you look'd so longly on the maid
Perhaps you mark'd not what's the pith of all.

Luc. O, yes, I saw sweet beauty in her face,
Such as the daughter of Agenor had,
That made great Jove to humble him to her hand
When with his knees he kiss'd the Cretan strand.

Tra. Saw you no more? Mark'd you not how her sister
Began to scold and raise up such a storm
That mortal ears might hardly endure the din?

Luc. Tranio, I saw her coral lips to move,
And with her breath she did perfume the air.
Sacred and sweet was all I saw in her.

Tra. Nay, then 'tis time to stir him from his trance.
I pray, awake, sir. If you love the maid,
Bend thoughts and wits to achieve her. Thus it stands:
Her elder sister is so curst and shrewd
That, till the father rid his hands of her,
Master, your love must live a maid at home;
And therefore has he closely mew'd her up,
Because he will not be annoy'd with suitors.

Luc. Ah, Tranio, what a cruel father's he!
But art thou not advis'd he took some care
To get her cunning schoolmasters to instruct her?

Tra. Ay, marry, am I, sir; and now 'tis plotted.

Luc. I have it, Tranio.

Tra. Master, for my hand,
Both our inventions meet and jump in one.

Luc. Tell me thine first.

Tra. You will be schoolmaster
And undertake the teaching of the maid.
That's your device.

Luc. It is. May it be done?

Tra. Not possible; for who shall bear your part

THE TAMING OF THE SHREW

PHOTOGRAPHS BY HOUSTON ROGERS
PRODUCED BY THE OLD VIC COMPANY

Above: The hot-tempered Katharina (Ann Todd), "as curst and shrewd as Socrates' Xantippe"

Right: Paul Rogers portraying Petruchio, who tamed the shrew by killing her with kindness

Below: "I know not what to say; but give me your hands. God send you joy, Petruchio! 'tis a match." Baptista (Laurence Hardy) rejoices at Petruchio's request to marry the fiery Katharina, who revolts at the prospect (*Act II, Scene I*)

Left: Paul Rogers as the patient Petruchio

Right: Katharina demands that her sister Bianca (Gwen Cherrell) name her favored suitor
(Act II, Scene I)

Left: Tranio (Alan Dobie) outbids Gremio for Bianca's hand
(Act II, Scene I)

Right: Lucentio (Paul Daneman) and Tranio try to explain to Biondello (Job Stewart) the reasons for their exchanging identities
(Act I, Scene I)

Left: "I find you passing gentle." Petruchio defends himself against Katharina during their first meeting
(Act II, Scene I)

Right: "I am he am born to tame you, Kate." Petruchio tells Katharina of his plans for her
(Act II, Scene I)

"Come, come, you wasp; i' faith you are too angry." Petruchio drubs Katharina at the first stormy encounter (*Act II, Scene I*)

Below: "If you strike me, you are no gentleman." The shrew turns petulant as Petruchio gives her blow for blow and treats her like a stubborn young child (*Act II, Scene I*)

Below: "Master, master! news! Biondello tells the wedding guests that Petruchio is coming to his marriage wearing shabby old clothes and mounted on a spavined and staggering sway-backed nag (*Act III, Scene II*)

Petruchio takes his bride away immediately after the wedding, giving her no chance to enjoy the banquet *(Act III, Scene II)*

Petruchio infuriates his famished spouse by asking a blessing before the frugal meal *(Act IV, Scene I)*

"Where is the rascal cook?" Petruchio finds fault with all the food so that Katharina goes to bed hungry *(Act IV, Scene I)*

"Here, love; thou seest how diligent I am to dress thy meat myself." Petruchio continues his experiment in tantalizing the starving Katharina *(Act IV, Scene III)*

Gremio (Meredith Edwards) also teases his master's wife *(Act IV, Scene III)*

Tranio and Biondello arrange for an old pedant (Aubrey Morris) to pass himself off as the father of Lucentio *(Act IV, Scene IV)*

"And happily I have arriv'd at last unto the wished haven of my bliss." The arrival of his real father forces Lucentio to acknowledge his ruse and confess that he and Bianca have been married *(Act V, Scene I)*

"Why, what, i' the devil's name, tailor, call'st thou this?" Petruchio criticizes the new gown he has ordered for his wife *(Act IV, Scene III)*

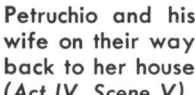

Petruchio and his wife on their way back to her house *(Act IV, Scene V)*

"Young budding virgin, fair and fresh and sweet." Accepting Petruchio's caprice, Katharina pretends to think Vincentio (John Woodvine) is a girl *(Act IV, Scene V)*

At Lucentio's wedding feast, Vincentio and Gremio witness the proof Petruchio has tamed his shrew *(Act V, Scene II)*

"I would your duty were as foolish too." Jesting with his wife at the wedding feast, Lucentio compares her obedience with that of the unquestioning Katharina *(Act V, Scene II)*

Above: "My hand is ready; may it do him ease." At the wedding feast, Petruchio wins his wager when Katharina confesses her complete submission to her husband *(Act V, Scene II)*

Right: "Why, there's a wench! Come on, and kiss me, Kate." Petruchio rewards the shrew's profession of loyalty *(Act V, Scene II)*

Below: Katharina kneels in token of her submission to Petruchio *(Act V, Scene II)*

And be in Padua here Vincentio's son;
Keep house and ply his book, welcome his friends,
Visit his countrymen and banquet them?

Luc. Basta! content thee! for I have it full.
We have not yet been seen in any house,
Nor can we be distinguish'd by our faces
For man or master. Then it follows thus:
Thou shalt be master, Tranio, in my stead,
Keep house and port and servants as I should;
I will some other be — some Florentine,
Some Neapolitan, or meaner man of Pisa.
'Tis hatch'd, and shall be so! Tranio, at once
Uncase thee; take my colour'd hat and cloak.
When Biondello comes, he waits on thee,
But I will charm him first to keep his tongue.

Tra. So had you need.
In brief, sir, sith it your pleasure is,
And I am tied to be obedient,
For so your father charg'd me at our parting:
'Be serviceable to my son,' quoth he,
Although I think 'twas in another sense —
I am content to be Lucentio,
Because so well I love Lucentio.
[*They exchange habits.*]

Luc. Tranio, be so because Lucentio loves;
And let me be a slave t' achieve that maid
Whose sudden sight hath thrall'd my wounded eye.

Enter *Biondello.*

Here comes the rogue. Sirrah, where have you been?

Bion. Where have I been? Nay, how now? where are you?
Master, has my fellow Tranio stol'n your clothes?
Or you stol'n his? or both? Pray what's the news?

Luc. Sirrah, come hither. 'Tis no time to jest,
And therefore frame your manners to the time.
Your fellow Tranio here, to save my life,
Puts my apparel and my count'nance on,
And I for my escape have put on his;
For in a quarrel since I came ashore
I kill'd a man, and fear I was descried.
Wait you on him, I charge you, as becomes,
While I make way from hence to save my life.
You understand me?

Bion. I, sir? Ne'er a whit!

Luc. And not a jot of Tranio in your mouth!
Tranio is chang'd into Lucentio.

Bion. The better for him. Would I were so too!

Tra. So could I, faith, boy, to have the next wish after,
That Lucentio indeed had Baptista's youngest daughter.
But, sirrah, not for my sake but your master's, I advise
You use your manners discreetly in all kind of companies.
When I am alone, why, then I am Tranio;
But in all places else, your master Lucentio.

Luc. Tranio, let's go.
One thing more rests, that thyself execute —
To make one among these wooers. If thou ask me why,
Sufficeth my reasons are both good and weighty.
Exeunt.

The Presenters above speak.

1. Man. My lord, you nod; you do not mind the play.

Beg. Yes, by Saint Anne, do I! A good matter, surely. Comes there any more of it?

Lady. My lord, 'tis but begun.

Beg. 'Tis a very excellent piece of work, madam lady. Would 'twere done!

They sit and mark.

[Scene II. *Padua. Before* Hortensio's *house.*]

Enter *Petruchio* and his man *Grumio.*

Pet. Verona, for a while I take my leave,
To see my friends in Padua; but of all
My best beloved and approved friend,
Hortensio; and I trow this is his house.
Here, sirrah Grumio; knock, I say.

Gru. Knock, sir? Whom should I knock?
Is there any man has rebus'd your worship?

Pet. Villain, I say knock me here soundly.

Gru. Knock you here, sir? Why, sir, what am I, sir, that I should knock you here, sir?

Pet. Villain, I say knock me at this gate,
And rap me well or I'll knock your knave's pate.

Gru. My master is grown quarrelsome. I should knock you first,
And then I know after who comes by the worst.

Pet. Will it not be?
Faith, sirrah, an you'll not knock, I'll ring it;
I'll try how you can *sol, fa,* and sing it.
He wrings him by the ears.

Gru. Help, masters, help! My master is mad.

Pet. Now knock when I bid you, sirrah villain!

Enter *Hortensio.*

Hor. How now? what's the matter? My old friend Grumio, and my good friend Petruchio? How do you all at Verona?

Pet. Signior Hortensio, come you to part the fray?
Con tutto il core ben trovato, may I say.

Hor. *Alla nostra casa ben venuto, molto honorato signor mio Petrucio.*
Rise, Grumio, rise. We will compound this quarrel.

Gru. Nay, 'tis no matter, sir, what he 'leges in Latin. If this be not a lawful cause for me to leave his service, look you, sir. He bid me knock him and rap him soundly, sir. Well, was it fit for a servant to use his master so, being perhaps (for aught I see) two-and-thirty, a peep out?
Whom would to God I had well knock'd at first!
Then had not Grumio come by the worst.

Pet. A senseless villain! Good Hortensio,
I bade the rascal knock upon your gate
And could not get him for my heart to do it.

Gru. Knock at the gate? O heavens! Spake you not these words plain, 'Sirrah, knock me here; rap me here; knock me well, and knock me soundly'? And come you now with 'knocking at the gate'?

Pet. Sirrah, be gone; or talk not, I advise you.

Hor. Petruchio, patience; I am Grumio's pledge.
Why, this' a heavy chance 'twixt him and you,
Your ancient, trusty, pleasant servant Grumio.
And tell me now, sweet friend, what happy gale
Blows you to Padua here from old Verona?

Pet. Such wind as scatters young men through the world
To seek their fortunes farther than at home,
Where small experience grows. But in a few,
Signior Hortensio, thus it stands with me:
Antonio, my father, is deceas'd,
And I have thrust myself into this maze,
Happily to wive and thrive as best I may.
Crowns in my purse I have, and goods at home,
And so am come abroad to see the world.

Hor. Petruchio, shall I then come roundly to thee
And wish thee to a shrewd ill-favour'd wife?
Thou'dst thank me but a little for my counsel;
And yet I'll promise thee she shall be rich,
And very rich. But th'art too much my friend,
And I'll not wish thee to her.

Pet. Signior Hortensio, 'twixt such friends as we
Few words suffice; and therefore, if thou know
One rich enough to be Petruchio's wife
(As wealth is burthen of my wooing dance),
Be she as foul as was Florentius' love,
As old as Sibyl, and as curst and shrowd
As Socrates' Xantippe or a worse,
She moves me not, or not removes, at least,
Affection's edge in me, were she as rough
As are the swelling Adriatic seas.
I come to wive it wealthily in Padua;
If wealthily, then happily in Padua.

Gru. Nay, look you, sir, he tells you flatly what his mind is. Why, give him gold enough and marry him to a puppet or an aglet-baby, or an old trot with ne'er a tooth in her head, though she have as many diseases as two-and-fifty horses. Why, nothing comes amiss, so money comes withal.

Hor. Petruchio, since we are stepp'd thus far in,
I will continue that I broach'd in jest.
I can, Petruchio, help thee to a wife
With wealth enough and young and beauteous,
Brought up as best becomes a gentlewoman.
Her only fault (and that is faults enough)
Is that she is intolerable curst,
And shrowd and froward so beyond all measure
That, were my state far worser than it is,
I would not wed her for a mine of gold.

Pet. Hortensio, peace! thou know'st not gold's effect.
Tell me her father's name, and 'tis enough;
For I will board her, though she chide as loud
As thunder when the clouds in autumn crack.

Hor. Her father is Baptista Minola,
An affable and courteous gentleman.
Her name is Katherina Minola,
Renown'd in Padua for her scolding tongue.

Pet. I know her father, though I know not her,
And he knew my deceased father well.
I will not sleep, Hortensio, till I see her;
And therefore let me be thus bold with you,
To give you over at this first encounter,
Unless you will accompany me thither.

Gru. I pray you, sir, let him go while the humour lasts. O' my word, an she knew him as well as I do, she would think scolding would do little good upon him. She may perhaps call him half a score knaves, or so. Why, that's nothing! An he begin once, he'll rail in his rope-tricks. I'll tell you what, sir, an she stand him but a little, he will throw a figure in her face, and so disfigure her with it that she shall have no more eyes to see withal than a cat. You know him not, sir.

Hor. Tarry, Petruchio, I must go with thee,
For in Baptista's keep my treasure is.
He hath the jewel of my life in hold,
His youngest daughter, beautiful Bianca,
And her withholds from me and other more,
Suitors to her and rivals in my love,
Supposing it a thing impossible,
For those defects I have before rehears'd,
That ever Katherina will be woo'd.
Therefore this order hath Baptista ta'en,
That none shall have access unto Bianca
Till Katherine the curst have got a husband.

Gru. Katherine the curst!
A title for a maid of all titles the worst.

Hor. Now shall my friend Petruchio do me grace,
And offer me, disguis'd in sober robes,
To old Baptista as a schoolmaster
Well seen in music, to instruct Bianca,
That so I may by this device at least
Have leave and leisure to make love to her
And unsuspected court her by herself.

Gru. [*aside*] Here's no knavery! See, to beguile the old folks, how the young folks lay their heads together!

Enter *Gremio*; and *Lucentio* disguised [as *Cambio*, with books under his arm].

Master, master, look about you! Who goes there? Ha!

Hor. Peace, Grumio! It is the rival of my love.
Petruchio, stand by awhile.

Gru. A proper stripling and an amorous!
[*They stand aside.*]

Gre. O, very well, I have perus'd the note.
Hark you, sir; I'll have them very fairly bound —
All books of love, see that at any hand;
And see you read no other lectures to her.
You understand me. Over and beside
Signior Baptista's liberality,
I'll mend it with a largess. Take your paper too;
And let me have them very well perfum'd,
For she is sweeter than perfume itself
To whom they go to. What will you read to her?

Luc. Whate'er I read to her, I'll plead for you
As for my patron — stand you so assur'd —
As firmly as yourself were still in place;
Yea, and perhaps with more successful words
Than you, unless you were a scholar, sir.

Gre. O this learning, what a thing it is!

Gru. O this woodcock, what an ass it is!

Pet. Peace, sirrah!

Hor. Grumio, mum! [*Comes forward.*] God save you, Signior Gremio!

Gre. And you are well met, Signior Hortensio.
Trow you whither I am going? To Baptista Minola.
I promis'd to enquire carefully
About a schoolmaster for the fair Bianca;
And by good fortune I have lighted well
On this young man, for learning and behaviour
Fit for her turn, well read in poetry
And other books — good ones, I warrant ye.

Hor. 'Tis well; and I have met a gentleman
Hath promis'd me to help me to another,
A fine musician to instruct our mistress.
So shall I no whit be behind in duty
To fair Bianca, so belov'd of me.

Gre. Belov'd of me, and that my deeds shall prove.

Gru. [*aside*] And that his bags shall prove.

Hor. Gremio, 'tis now no time to vent our love.
Listen to me, and if you speak me fair,
I'll tell you news indifferent good for either.
Here is a gentleman whom by chance I met,
Upon agreement from us to his liking,
Will undertake to woo curst Katherine,
Yea, and to marry her, if her dowry please.

Gre. So said, so done, is well.
Hortensio, have you told him all her faults?

Pet. I know she is an irksome brawling scold.
If that be all, masters, I hear no harm.

Gre. No, say'st me so, friend? What countryman?

Pet. Born in Verona, old Antonio's son.
My father dead, my fortune lives for me,
And I do hope good days and long to see.

Gre. O sir, such a life with such a wife were strange.
But if you have a stomach, to't a God's name!
You shall have me assisting you in all.
But will you woo this wildcat?

Pet. Will I live?

Gru. [*aside*] Will he woo her? Ay, or I'll hang her.

Pet. Why came I hither but to that intent?
Think you a little din can daunt mine ears?
Have I not in my time heard lions roar?

Have I not heard the sea, puff'd up with winds,
Rage like an angry boar chafed with sweat?
Have I not heard great ordnance in the field,
And heaven's artillery thunder in the skies?
Have I not in a pitched battle heard
Loud 'larums, neighing steeds, and trumpets' clang?
And do you tell me of a woman's tongue,
That gives not half so great a blow to th' ear
As will a chestnut in a farmer's fire?
Tush, tush! Fear boys with bugs!

Gru. [*aside*] For he fears none.

Gre. Hortensio, hark.
This gentleman is happily arriv'd,
My mind presumes, for his own good and ours.

Hor. I promis'd we would be contributors
And bear his charge of wooing, whatsoe'er.

Gre. And so we will, provided that he win her.

Gru. [*aside*] I would I were as sure of a good dinner.

Enter *Tranio* brave, [as *Lucentio*,] and *Biondello*.

Tra. Gentlemen, God save you! If I may be bold,
Tell me, I beseech you, which is the readiest way
To the house of Signior Baptista Minola?

Bion. He that has the two fair daughters, is't he you mean?

Tra. Even he, Biondello.

Gre. Hark you, sir; you mean not her too?

Tra. Perhaps him and her, sir. What have you to do?

Pet. Not her that chides, sir, at any hand, I pray.

Tra. I love no chiders, sir. Biondello, let's away.

Luc. [*aside*] Well begun, Tranio.

Hor. Sir, a word ere you go.
Are you a suitor to the maid you talk of, yea or no?

Tra. And if I be, sir, is it any offence?

Gre. No, if without more words you will get you hence.

Tra. Why, sir, I pray, are not the streets as free
For me as for you?

Gre. But so is not she.

Tra. For what reason, I beseech you?

Gre. For this reason, if you'll know,
That she's the choice love of Signior Gremio.

Hor. That she's the chosen of Signior Hortensio.

Tra. Softly, my masters! If you be gentlemen,
Do me this right — hear me with patience.
Baptista is a noble gentleman,
To whom my father is not all unknown,
And, were his daughter fairer than she is,
She may more suitors have, and me for one.
Fair Leda's daughter had a thousand wooers;
Then well one more may fair Bianca have;
And so she shall: Lucentio shall make one,
Though Paris came in hope to speed alone.

Gre. What, this gentleman will outtalk us all!

Luc. Sir, give him head; I know he'll prove a jade.

Pet. Hortensio, to what end are all these words?

Hor. Sir, let me be so bold as ask you,
Did you yet ever see Baptista's daughter?

Tra. No, sir, but hear I do that he hath two;
The one as famous for a scolding tongue
As is the other for beauteous modesty.

Pet. Sir, sir, the first's for me! let her go by.

Gre. Yea, leave that labour to great Hercules,
And let it be more than Alcides' twelve.

Pet. Sir, understand you this of me, in sooth:
The youngest daughter, whom you hearken for,
Her father keeps from all access of suitors,
And will not promise her to any man
Until the elder sister first be wed.
The younger then is free, and not before.

Tra. If it be so, sir, that you are the man
Must stead us all, and me amongst the rest;
And if you break the ice and do this feat,
Achieve the elder, set the younger free
For our access — whose hap shall be to have her
Will not so graceless be to be ingrate.

Hor. Sir, you say well, and well you do conceive;
And since you do profess to be a suitor,
You must, as we do, gratify this gentleman,
To whom we all rest generally beholding.

Tra. Sir, I shall not be slack; in sign whereof,
Please ye we may contrive this afternoon,
And quaff carouses to our mistress' health,
And do as adversaries do in law —
Strive mightily, but eat and drink as friends.

Gru., Bion. O excellent motion! Fellows, let's be gone.

Hor. The motion's good indeed, and be it so.
Petruchio, I shall be your ben venuto. *Exeunt.*

[Act II. Scene I. *Padua.* Baptista's *house.*]

Enter *Katherina,* and *Bianca* [with her hands bound].

Bian. Good sister, wrong me not, nor wrong yourself,
To make a bondmaid and a slave of me.
That I disdain; but for these other gauds,
Unbind my hands, I'll pull them off myself,
Yea, all my raiment, to my petticoat;
Or what you will command me will I do,
So well I know my duty to my elders.

Kath. Of all thy suitors here I charge thee tell
Whom thou lov'st best. See thou dissemble not.

Bian. Believe me, sister, of all the men alive
I never yet beheld that special face
Which I could fancy more than any other.

Kath. Minion, thou liest. Is't not Hortensio?

Bian. If you affect him, sister, here I swear
I'll plead for you myself but you shall have him.

Kath. O, then belike you fancy riches more;
You will have Gremio to keep you fair.

Bian. Is it for him you do envy me so?
Nay then, you jest, and now I well perceive
You have but jested with me all this while.
I prithee, sister Kate, untie my hands.

Kath. (*strikes her*) If that be jest, then all the rest was so.

Enter *Baptista.*

Bap. Why, how now, dame? Whence grows this insolence?
Bianca, stand aside. Poor girl! she weeps.
[*Unbinds her.*]
Go ply thy needle; meddle not with her.
For shame, thou hilding of a devilish spirit!
Why dost thou wrong her that did ne'er wrong thee?
When did she cross thee with a bitter word?

Kath. Her silence flouts me, and I'll be reveng'd. *Flies after Bianca.*

Bap. [*holds her back*] What, in my sight?
Bianca, get thee in.
Exit [*Bianca*].

Kath. What, will you not suffer me? Nay, now I see
She is your treasure, she must have a husband;
I must dance barefoot on her wedding day
And for your love to her lead apes in hell.
Talk not to me! I will go sit and weep
Till I can find occasion of revenge. [*Exit.*]

Bap. Was ever gentleman thus griev'd as I?
But who comes here?

Enter *Gremio*; *Lucentio* in the habit of a mean man; *Petruchio,* [with *Hortensio* as a musician]; *Tranio* [as *Lucentio*], with his boy [*Biondello*] bearing a lute and books.

Gre. Good morrow, neighbour Baptista.

Bap. Good morrow, neighbour Gremio. God save you, gentlemen.

Pet. And you, good sir. Pray have you not a daughter
Call'd Katherina, fair and virtuous?

Bap. I have a daughter, sir, call'd Katherina.

Gre. You are too blunt. Go to it orderly.

Pet. You wrong me, Signior Gremio; give me leave.
I am a gentleman of Verona, sir,
That, hearing of her beauty and her wit,
Her affability and bashful modesty,
Her wondrous qualities and mild behaviour,
Am bold to show myself a forward guest
Within your house, to make mine eye the witness
Of that report which I so oft have heard.
And for an entrance to my entertainment,
I do present you with a man of mine,
[*Presents Hortensio.*]
Cunning in music and the mathematics,
To instruct her fully in those sciences,
Whereof I know she is not ignorant.
Accept of him, or else you do me wrong.
His name is Licio, born in Mantua.

Bap. Y'are welcome, sir, and he for your good sake.
But for my daughter Katherine, this I know,
She is not for your turn, the more my grief.

Pet. I see you do not mean to part with her,
Or else you like not of my company.

Bap. Mistake me not; I speak but as I find.
Whence are you, sir? What may I call your name?

Pet. Petruchio is my name, Antonio's son,
A man well known throughout all Italy.

Bap. I know him well; you are welcome for his sake.

Gre. Saving your tale, Petruchio, I pray
Let us that are poor petitioners speak too.
Bacare! you are marvellous forward.

Pet. O, pardon me, Signior Gremio! I would fain be doing.

Gre. I doubt it not, sir, but you will curse your wooing.
Neighbour, this is a gift very grateful, I am sure of it. To express the like kindness, myself, that have been more kindly beholding to you than any, freely give unto you this young scholar [*presents Lucentio*], that hath been long studying at Rheims, as cunning in Greek, Latin, and other languages as the other in music and mathematics. His name is Cambio. Pray accept his service.

Bap. A thousand thanks, Signior Gremio! Welcome, good Cambio. [*To Tranio*] But, gentle sir, methinks you walk like a stranger. May I be so bold to know the cause of your coming?

Tra. Pardon me, sir, the boldness is mine own
That, being a stranger in this city here,
Do make myself a suitor to your daughter,
Unto Bianca, fair and virtuous.
Nor is your firm resolve unknown to me
In the preferment of the eldest sister.
This liberty is all that I request,
That, upon knowledge of my parentage,
I may have welcome 'mongst the rest that woo
And free access and favour as the rest.
And toward the education of your daughters
I here bestow a simple instrument,
[*Offers the lute.*]
And this small packet of Greek and Latin books.
If you accept them, then their worth is great.

Bap. Lucentio is your name — of whence, I pray?

Tra. Of Pisa, sir, son to Vincentio.

Bap. A mighty man of Pisa; by report
I know him well. You are very welcome, sir.
Take you [*to Hortensio*] the lute, and you [*to Lucentio*] the set of books.
You shall go see your pupils presently.
Holla, within!

Enter a *Servant.*

Sirrah, lead these gentlemen
To my two daughters, and tell them both
These are their tutors. Bid them use them well.
[*Exit Servant, with Hortensio, Lucentio, and Biondello.*]
We will go walk a little in the orchard,
And then to dinner. You are passing welcome,
And so I pray you all to think yourselves.

Pet. Signior Baptista, my business asketh haste,
And every day I cannot come to woo.
You knew my father well, and in him me,
Left solely heir to all his lands and goods,
Which I have bettered rather than decreas'd.
Then tell me, if I get your daughter's love,
What dowry shall I have with her to wife?

Bap. After my death the one half of my lands,
And in possession twenty thousand crowns.

Pet. And, for that dowry, I'll assure her of
Her widowhood, be it that she survive me,
In all my lands and leases whatsoever.
Let specialties be therefore drawn between us,
That covenants may be kept on either hand.

Bap. Ay, when the special thing is well obtain'd,
That is, her love; for that is all in all.

Pet. Why, that is nothing! for I tell you, father,
I am as peremptory as she proud-minded;
And where two raging fires meet together,
They do consume the thing that feeds their fury.
Though little fire grows great with little wind,
Yet extreme gusts will blow out fire and all.
So I to her, and so she yields to me,
For I am rough and woo not like a babe.

Bap. Well mayst thou woo and happy be thy speed!
But be thou arm'd for some unhappy words.

Pet. Ay, to the proof, as mountains are for winds,
That shake not, though they blow perpetually.

Enter *Hortensio,* with his head broke.

Bap. How now, my friend? Why dost thou look so pale?

Hor. For fear, I promise you, if I look pale.

Bap. What, will my daughter prove a good musician?

Hor. I think she'll sooner prove a soldier.
Iron may hold with her, but never lutes.

Bap. Why, then thou canst not break her to the lute?

Hor. Why, no! for she hath broke the lute to me.
I did but tell her she mistook her frets,
And bow'd her hand to teach her fingering,
When, with a most impatient devilish spirit,
'Frets call you these?' quoth she. 'I'll fume with them!'
And with that word she stroke me on the head,
And through the instrument my pate made way,
And there I stood amazed for a while,
As on a pillory, looking through the lute,
While she did call me rascal fiddler
And twangling Jack, with twenty such vile terms,
As had she studied to misuse me so.

Pet. Now, by the world, it is a lusty wench!
I love her ten times more than e'er I did.
O, how I long to have some chat with her!
Bap. Well, go with me, and be not so discomfited.
Proceed in practice with my younger daughter;
She's apt to learn and thankful for good turns.
Signior Petruchio, will you go with us,
Or shall I send my daughter Kate to you?
Pet. I pray you do; I will attend her here,
Exeunt. Manet Petruchio.
And woo her with some spirit when she comes.
Say that she rail; why, then I'll tell her plain
She sings as sweetly as a nightingale.
Say that she frown; I'll say she looks as clear
As morning roses newly wash'd with dew.
Say she be mute and will not speak a word;
Then I'll commend her volubility
And say she uttereth piercing eloquence.
If she do bid me pack, I'll give her thanks,
As though she bid me stay by her a week.
If she deny to wed, I'll crave the day
When I shall ask the banes, and when be married.
But here she comes; and now, Petruchio, speak.

Enter *Katherina.*

Good morrow, Kate; for that's your name, I hear.
Kath. Well have you heard, but something hard of hearing.
They call me Katherine that do talk of me.
Pet. You lie, in faith! for you are call'd plain Kate,
And bonny Kate, and sometimes Kate the curst;
But, Kate, the prettiest Kate in Christendom,
Kate of Kate Hall, my super-dainty Kate,
For dainties are all Kates — and therefore, Kate,
Take this of me, Kate of my consolation:
Hearing thy mildness prais'd in every town,
Thy virtues spoke of, and thy beauty sounded,
Yet not so deeply as to thee belongs,
Myself am mov'd to woo thee for my wife.
Kath. Mov'd? In good time! Let him that mov'd you hither
Remove you hence. I knew you at the first
You were a moveable.
Pet. Why, what's a moveable?
Kath. A join'd-stool.
Pet. Thou hast hit it! Come sit on me.
Kath. Asses are made to bear, and so are you.
Pet. Women are made to bear, and so are you.
Kath. No such jade as you, if me you mean.
Pet. Alas, good Kate, I will not burthen thee!
For, knowing thee to be but young and light —
Kath. Too light for such a swain as you to catch,
And yet as heavy as my weight should be.
Pet. Should be! should — buzz!
Kath. Well ta'en, and like a buzzard.
Pet. O slow-wing'd turtle! shall a buzzard take thee?
Kath. Ay, for a turtle, as he takes a buzzard.
Pet. Come, come, you wasp! i' faith, you are too angry.
Kath. If I be waspish, best beware my sting.
Pet. My remedy is then to pluck it out.
Kath. Ay, if the fool could find it where it lies.
Pet. Who knows not where a wasp does wear his sting?
In his tail.
Kath. In his tongue.
Pet. Whose tongue?
Kath. Yours, if you talk of tales. And so farewell.
Pet. What, with my tongue in your tail? Nay, come again!
Good Kate, I am a gentleman.
Kath. That I'll try.
She strikes him.
Pet. I swear I'll cuff you if you strike again.
Kath. So may you lose your arms.
If you strike me, you are no gentleman;
And if no gentleman, why then no arms.
Pet. A herald, Kate? O, put me in thy books!
Kath. What is your crest? a coxcomb?
Pet. A combless cock, so Kate will be my hen.
Kath. No cock of mine; you crow too like a craven.
Pet. Nay, come, Kate, come! you must not look so sour.
Kath. It is my fashion when I see a crab.
Pet. Why, here's no crab, and therefore look not sour.
Kath. There is, there is!
Pet. Then show it me.
Kath. Had I a glass, I would.
Pet. What, you mean my face?
Kath. Well aim'd of such a young one.
Pet. Now, by Saint George, I am too young for you.
Kath. Yet you are wither'd.
Pet. 'Tis with cares.
Kath. I care not.
Pet. Nay, hear you, Kate. In sooth you scape not so!

Kath. I chafe you if I tarry. Let me go.
Pet. No, not a whit; I find you passing gentle.
'Twas told me you were rough and coy and sullen,
And now I find report a very liar;
For thou art pleasant, gamesome, passing courteous,
But slow in speech, yet sweet as springtime flowers.
Thou canst not frown, thou canst not look askance,
Nor bite the lip, as angry wenches will,
Nor hast thou pleasure to be cross in talk;
But thou with mildness entertain'st thy wooers,
With gentle conference, soft and affable.
Why does the world report that Kate doth limp?
O sland'rous world! Kate like the hazel twig
Is straight and slender, and as brown in hue
As hazelnuts, and sweeter than the kernels.
O, let me see thee walk: thou dost not halt.
Kath. Go, fool! and whom thou keep'st command.
Pet. Did ever Dian so become a grove
As Kate this chamber with her princely gait?
O, be thou Dian, and let her be Kate;
And then let Kate be chaste, and Dian sportful!
Kath. Where did you study all this goodly speech?
Pet. It is extempore, from my mother wit.
Kath. A witty mother! witless else her son.
Pet. Am I not wise?
Kath. Yes; keep you warm.
Pet. Marry, so I mean, sweet Katherine, in thy bed.
And therefore, setting all this chat aside,
Thus in plain terms: your father hath consented
That you shall be my wife, your dowry 'greed on;
And, will you, nill you, I will marry you.
Now, Kate, I am a husband for your turn;
For, by this light, whereby I see thy beauty,
Thy beauty, that doth make me like thee well,
Thou must be married to no man but me;
For I am he am born to tame you, Kate,
And bring you from a wild Kate to a Kate
Conformable as other household Kates.

Enter *Baptista, Gremio, Tranio.*

Here comes your father. Never make denial.
I must and will have Katherine to my wife.
Bap. Now, Signior Petruchio, how speed you with my daughter?
Pet. How but well, sir? how but well?
It were impossible I should speed amiss.
Bap. Why, how now, daughter Katherine? in your dumps?
Kath. Call you me daughter? Now I promise you
You have show'd a tender fatherly regard
To wish me wed to one half lunatic,
A madcap ruffian and a swearing Jack,
That thinks with oaths to face the matter out.
Pet. Father, 'tis thus: yourself and all the world
That talk'd of her have talk'd amiss of her.
If she be curst, it is for policy,
For she's not froward, but modest as the dove;
She is not hot, but temperate as the morn;
For patience she will prove a second Grissel,
And Roman Lucrece for her chastity;
And to conclude, we have 'greed so well together
That upon Sunday is the wedding day.
Kath. I'll see thee hang'd on Sunday first.
Gre. Hark, Petruchio; she says she'll see thee hang'd first.
Tra. Is this your speeding? Nay then, good night our part!
Pet. Be patient, gentlemen; I choose her for myself.
If she and I be pleas'd, what's that to you?
'Tis bargain'd 'twixt us twain, being alone,
That she shall still be curst in company.
I tell you 'tis incredible to believe
How much she loves me. O, the kindest Kate!
She hung about my neck, and kiss on kiss
She vied so fast, protesting oath on oath,
That in a twink she won me to her love.
O, you are novices! 'Tis a world to see
How tame, when men and women are alone,
A meacock wretch can make the curstest shrew.
Give me thy hand, Kate; I will unto Venice
To buy apparel 'gainst the wedding day.
Provide the feast, father, and bid the guests;
I will be sure my Katherine shall be fine.
Bap. I know not what to say — but give me your hands;
God send you joy, Petruchio! 'tis a match.
Gre., Tra. Amen say we; we will be witnesses.
Pet. Father, and wife, and gentlemen, adieu.
I will to Venice; Sunday comes apace.
We will have rings and things and fine array;
And kiss me, Kate! We will be married a Sunday.
Exeunt Petruchio and Katherine [*severally*].
Gre. Was ever match clapp'd up so suddenly?

Bap. Faith, gentlemen, now I play a merchant's part
And venture madly on a desperate mart.
Tra. 'Twas a commodity lay fretting by you.
'Twill bring you gain, or perish on the seas.
Bap. The gain I seek is, quiet in the match.
Gre. No doubt but he hath got a quiet catch.
But now, Baptista, to your younger daughter:
Now is the day we long have looked for;
I am your neighbour and was suitor first.
Tra. And I am one that love Bianca more
Than words can witness or your thoughts can guess.
Gre. Youngling, thou canst not love so dear as I.
Tra. Greybeard, thy love doth freeze.
Gre. But thine doth fry.
Skipper, stand back! 'tis age that nourisheth.
Tra. But youth in ladies' eyes that flourisheth.
Bap. Content you, gentlemen; I will compound this strife.
'Tis deeds must win the prize, and he of both
That can assure my daughter greatest dower
Shall have my Bianca's love.
Say, Signior Gremio, what can you assure her?
Gre. First, as you know, my house within the city
Is richly furnished with plate and gold,
Basins and ewers to lave her dainty hands;
My hangings all of Tyrian tapestry;
In ivory coffers I have stuff'd my crowns;
In cypress chests my arras counterpoints,
Costly apparel, tents, and canopies,
Fine linen, Turkey cushions boss'd with pearl,
Valance of Venice gold in needlework;
Pewter and brass and all things that belong
To house or housekeeping. Then at my farm
I have a hundred milch kine to the pail,
Sixscore fat oxen standing in my stalls,
And all things answerable to this portion.
Myself am struck in years, I must confess;
And if I die to-morrow, this is hers,
If whilst I live she will be only mine.
Tra. That 'only' came well in. Sir, list to me.
I am my father's heir and only son.
If I may have your daughter to my wife,
I'll leave her houses three or four as good
Within rich Pisa walls as any one
Old Signior Gremio has in Padua;
Besides, two thousand ducats by the year
Of fruitful land, all which shall be her jointure.
What, have I pinch'd you, Signior Gremio?
Gre. [*aside*] Two thousand ducats by the year of land!
My land amounts not to so much in all. —
That she shall have, besides an argosy
That now is lying in Marseilles road.
What, have I chok'd you with an argosy?
Tra. Gremio, 'tis known my father hath no less
Than three great argosies, besides two galliasses
And twelve tight galleys. These I will assure her,
And twice as much whate'er thou off'rest next.
Gre. Nay, I have off'red all! I have no more;
And she can have no more than all I have.
If you like me, she shall have me and mine.
Tra. Why, then the maid is mine from all the world
By your firm promise; Gremio is outvied.
Bap. I must confess your offer is the best;
And, let your father make her the assurance,
She is your own; else you must pardon me.
If you should die before him, where's her dower?
Tra. That's but a cavil. He is old, I young.
Gre. And may not young men die as well as old?
Bap. Well, gentlemen,
I am thus resolv'd: on Sunday next you know
My daughter Katherine is to be married;
Now on the Sunday following shall Bianca
Be bride to you, if you make this assurance;
If not, to Signior Gremio.
And so I take my leave, and thank you both.
Exit.
Gre. Adieu, good neighbour. — Now I fear thee not.
Sirrah, young gamester, your father were a fool
To give thee all, and in his waning age
Set foot under thy table. Tut, a toy!
An old Italian fox is not so kind, my boy.
Exit.
Tra. A vengeance on your crafty withered hide!
Yet I have fac'd it with a card of ten.
'Tis in my head to do my master good.
I see no reason but suppos'd Lucentio
Must get a father, call'd suppos'd Vincentio;
And that's a wonder: fathers commonly
Do get their children; but in this case of wooing,
A child shall get a sire, if I fail not of my cunning. *Exit.*

Act III. [Scene I. *Padua.* Baptista's *house.*]

Enter *Lucentio* [as *Cambio*], *Hortensio* [as *Licio*], and *Bianca*.

Luc. Fiddler, forbear! you grow too forward, sir.
Have you so soon forgot the entertainment
Her sister Katherine welcom'd you withal?

Hor. But, wrangling pedant, this is
The patroness of heavenly harmony.
Then give me leave to have prerogative;
And when in music we have spent an hour,
Your lecture shall have leisure for as much.

Luc. Preposterous ass, that never read so far
To know the cause why music was ordain'd!
Was it not to refresh the mind of man
After his studies or his usual pain?
Then give me leave to read philosophy,
And while I pause, serve in your harmony.

Hor. Sirrah, I will not bear these braves of thine.

Bian. Why, gentlemen, you do me double wrong
To strive for that which resteth in my choice.
I am no breeching scholar in the schools;
I'll not be tied to hours, nor 'pointed times,
But learn my lessons as I please myself.
And, to cut off all strife, here sit we down:
Take you your instrument, play you the whiles;
His lecture will be done ere you have tun'd.

Hor. You'll leave his lecture when I am in tune?

Luc. That will be never. Tune your instrument. [*Hortensio steps aside.*]

Bian. Where left we last?

Luc. Here, madam: [*Reads.*]

'Hic ibat Simois, hic est Sigeia tellus,
Hic steterat Priami regia celsa senis.'

Bian. Conster them.

Luc. *Hic ibat,* as I told you before; *Simois,* I am Lucentio; *hic est,* son unto Vincentio of Pisa; *Sigeia tellus,* disguised thus to get your love; *Hic steterat,* and that Lucentio that comes a-wooing; *Priami,* is my man Tranio; *regia,* bearing my port; *celsa senis,* that we might beguile the old pantaloon.

Hor. Madam, my instrument's in tune.

Bian. Let's hear. [*He plays.*]
O, fie! the treble jars.

Luc. Spit in the hole, man,
And tune again.

Bian. Now let me see if I can conster it: *Hic ibat Simois,* I know you not; *hic est Sigeia tellus,* I trust you not; *Hic steterat Priami,* take heed he hear us not; *regia,* presume not; *celsa senis,* despair not.

Hor. Madam, 'tis now in tune. [*He plays.*]

Luc. All but the bass.

Hor. The bass is right; 'tis the base knave that jars.
[*Aside*] How fiery and forward our pedant is!
Now, for my life, the knave doth court my love.
Pedascule, I'll watch you better yet.

Bian. In time I may believe, yet I mistrust.

Luc. Mistrust it not; for, sure, Æacides
Was Ajax, call'd so from his grandfather.

Bian. I must believe my master; else, I promise you,
I should be arguing still upon that doubt;
But let it rest. Now, Licio, to you.
Good master, take it not unkindly, pray,
That I have been thus pleasant with you both.

Hor. [*to Lucentio*] You may go walk and give me leave awhile;
My lessons make no music in three parts.

Luc. Are you so formal, sir? Well, I must wait,
[*Aside*] And watch withal; for, but I be deceiv'd,
Our fine musician groweth amorous.

Hor. Madam, before you touch the instrument
To learn the order of my fingering,
I must begin with rudiments of art,
To teach you gamouth in a briefer sort,
More pleasant, pithy, and effectual,
Than hath been taught by any of my trade;
And there it is in writing fairly drawn.

Bian. Why, I am past my gamouth long ago!

Hor. Yet read the gamouth of Hortensio.

Bian. [*reads*]

'*Gamouth* I am, the ground of all accord,
A re, to plead Hortensio's passion.
B mi, Bianca, take him for thy lord,
C fa ut, that loves with all affection.
D sol re, one cliff, two notes have I;
E la mi, show pity, or I die.'

Call you this gamouth? Tut, I like it not!
Old fashions please me best; I am not so nice
To change true rules for odd inventions.

Enter a *Messenger*.

Mess. Mistress, your father prays you leave your books
And help to dress your sister's chamber up.
You know to-morrow is the wedding day.

Bian. Farewell, sweet masters both; I must be gone.

[*Exeunt Bianca and Messenger*.]

Luc. Faith, mistress, then I have no cause to stay. [*Exit.*]

Hor. But I have cause to pry into this pedant;
Methinks he looks as though he were in love.
Yet if thy thoughts, Bianca, be so humble
To cast thy wand'ring eyes on every stale,
Seize thee that list! If once I find thee ranging,
Hortensio will be quit with thee by changing.
Exit.

[Scene II. *Padua. Before* Baptista's *house.*]

Enter *Baptista, Gremio, Tranio* [(as *Lucentio*)], *Katherina, Bianca,* [*Lucentio* (as *Cambio*),] and others, *Attendants*.

Bap. [*to Tranio*] Signior Lucentio, this is the 'pointed day
That Katherine and Petruchio should be married,
And yet we hear not of our son-in-law.
What will be said? What mockery will it be
To want the bridegroom when the priest attends
To speak the ceremonial rites of marriage!
What says Lucentio to this shame of ours?

Kath. No shame but mine! I must forsooth be forc'd
To give my hand, oppos'd against my heart,
Unto a mad-brain rudesby, full of spleen,
Who woo'd in haste and means to wed at leisure.
I told you, I, he was a frantic fool,
Hiding his bitter jests in blunt behaviour;
And, to be noted for a merry man,
He'll woo a thousand, 'point the day of marriage,
Make feast, invite friends, and proclaim the banes;
Yet never means to wed where he hath woo'd.
Now must the world point at poor Katherine
And say, 'Lo, there is mad Petruchio's wife,
If it would please him come and marry her!'

Tra. Patience, good Katherine, and Baptista too!
Upon my life, Petruchio means but well,
Whatever fortune stays him from his word.
Though be he blunt, I know him passing wise;
Though he be merry, yet withal he's honest.

Kath. Would Katherine had never seen him though!

Exit weeping [*followed by Bianca and others*].

Bap. Go, girl. I cannot blame thee now to weep;
For such an injury would vex a saint,
Much more a shrew of thy impatient humour.

Enter *Biondello*.

Bion. Master, master! News! and such old news as you never heard of!

Bap. Is it new and old too? How may that be?

Bion. Why, is it not news to hear of Petruchio's coming?

Bap. Is he come?

Bion. Why, no, sir.

Bap. What then?

Bion. He is coming.

Bap. When will he be here?

Bion. When he stands where I am and sees you there.

Tra. But say, what to thine old news?

Bion. Why, Petruchio is coming — in a new hat and an old jerkin; a pair of old breeches thrice turn'd; a pair of boots that have been candle-cases, one buckled, another lac'd; an old rusty sword ta'en out of the town armoury, with a broken hilt, and chapeless; with two broken points; his horse hipp'd, with an old mothy saddle and stirrups of no kindred; besides possess'd with the glanders and like to mose in the chine, troubled with the lampass, infected with the fashions, full of windgalls, sped with spavins, rayed with the yellows, past cure of the fives, stark spoil'd with the staggers, begnawn with the bots, sway'd in the back and shoulder-shotten, near-legg'd before, and with a half-cheek'd bit, and a headstall of sheep's leather which, being restrain'd to keep him from stumbling, hath been often burst, and now repaired with knots; one girth six times piec'd, and a woman's crupper of velure, which hath two letters for her name fairly set down in studs, and here and there piec'd with packthread.

Bap. Who comes with him?

Bion. O, sir, his lackey, for all the world caparison'd like the horse — with a linen stock on one leg and a kersey boothose on the other, gart'red with a red and blue list; an old hat, and 'The Humour of Forty Fancies' prick'd in't for a feather; a monster, a very monster in apparel, and not like a Christian footboy or a gentleman's lackey.

Tra. 'Tis some odd humour pricks him to this fashion.
Yet oftentimes he goes but mean-apparell'd.

Bap. I am glad he's come, howsoe'er he comes.

Bion. Why, sir, he comes not.

Bap. Didst thou not say he comes?

Bion. Who? that Petruchio came?

Bap. Ay, that Petruchio came.

Bion. No, sir. I say his horse comes with him on his back.

Bap. Why, that's all one.

Bion. Nay, by Saint Jamy,
I hold you a penny,
A horse and a man
Is more than one,
And yet not many.

Enter *Petruchio* and *Grumio.*

Pet. Come, where be these gallants? Who's at home?

Bap. You are welcome, sir.

Pet. And yet I come not well.

Bap. And yet you halt not.

Tra. Not so well apparell'd
As I wish you were.

Pet. Were it better, I should rush in thus.
But where is Kate? Where is my lovely bride?
How does my father? Gentles, methinks you frown;
And wherefore gaze this goodly company,
As if they saw some wondrous monument,
Some comet or unusual prodigy?

Bap. Why, sir, you know this is your wedding day.
First were we sad, fearing you would not come;
Now sadder that you come so unprovided.
Fie! doff this habit, shame to your estate,
An eyesore to our solemn festival.

Tra. And tell us what occasion of import
Hath all so long detain'd you from your wife
And sent you hither so unlike yourself.

Pet. Tedious it were to tell, and harsh to hear.
Sufficeth I am come to keep my word,
Though in some part enforced to digress;
Which at more leisure I will so excuse
As you shall well be satisfied withal.
But where is Kate? I stay too long from her;
The morning wears; 'tis time we were at church.

Tra. See not your bride in these unreverent robes.
Go to my chamber; put on clothes of mine.

Pet. Not I, believe me! Thus I'll visit her.

Bap. But thus I trust you will not marry her.

Pet. Good sooth, even thus. Therefore ha' done with words!
To me she's married, not unto my clothes.
Could I repair what she will wear in me
As I can change these poor accoutrements,
'Twere well for Kate and better for myself.
But what a fool am I to chat with you
When I should bid good morrow to my bride
And seal the title with a lovely kiss!

Exit [with Grumio].

Tra. He hath some meaning in his mad attire.
We will persuade him, be it possible,
To put on better ere he go to church.

Bap. I'll after him and see the event of this.

Exeunt [Baptista, Gremio, and Attendants].

Tra. But to her love concerneth us to add
Her father's liking; which to bring to pass,
As I before imparted to your worship,
I am to get a man, whate'er he be —
It skills not much, we'll fit him to our turn —
And he shall be Vincentio of Pisa
And make assurance, here in Padua,
Of greater sums than I have promised.
So shall you quietly enjoy your hope
And marry sweet Bianca with consent.

Luc. Were it not that my fellow schoolmaster
Doth watch Bianca's steps so narrowly,
'Twere good, methinks, to steal our marriage;
Which once perform'd, let all the world say no,
I'll keep mine own despite of all the world.

Tra. That by degrees we mean to look into
And watch our vantage in this business.
We'll overreach the greybeard, Gremio,
The narrow-prying father, Minola,
The quaint musician, amorous Licio —
All for my master's sake, Lucentio.

Enter *Gremio.*

Signior Gremio, came you from the church?

Gre. As willingly as e'er I came from school.

Tra. And is the bride and bridegroom coming home?

Gre. A bridegroom say you? 'Tis a groom indeed,
A grumbling groom, and that the girl shall find.

Tra. Curster than she? Why, 'tis impossible.

Gre. Why, he's a devil, a devil, a very fiend.
Tra. Why, she's a devil, a devil, the devil's dam.
Gre. Tut, she's a lamb, a dove, a fool to him!
I'll tell you, Sir Lucentio — when the priest
Should ask if Katherine should be his wife,
'Ay, by gogs-woons!' quoth he, and swore so loud
That, all amaz'd, the priest let fall the book;
And as he stoop'd again to take it up,
This mad-brain'd bridegroom took him such a cuff
That down fell priest and book, and book and priest.
'Now take them up,' quoth he, 'if any list!'
Tra. What said the wench when he arose again?
Gre. Trembled and shook; for-why he stamp'd and swore
As if the vicar meant to cozen him.
But after many ceremonies done,
He calls for wine. 'A health!' quoth he, as if
He had been aboard, carousing to his mates
After a storm; quaff'd off the muscadel
And threw the sops all in the sexton's face;
Having no other reason
But that his beard grew thin and hungerly
And seem'd to ask him sops as he was drinking.
This done, he took the bride about the neck
And kiss'd her lips with such a clamorous smack
That at the parting all the church did echo.
And I, seeing this, came thence for very shame,
And after me I know the rout is coming.
Such a mad marriage never was before.
Hark, hark! I hear the minstrels play.
Music plays.

Enter *Petruchio, Kate, Bianca, Hortensio, Baptista,* [*Grumio,* and *Train*].

Pet. Gentlemen and friends, I thank you for your pains.
I know you think to dine with me to-day,
And have prepar'd great store of wedding cheer;
But so it is, my haste doth call me hence,
And therefore here I mean to take my leave.
Bap. Is't possible you will away to-night?
Pet. I must away to-day before night come.
Make it no wonder. If you knew my business,
You would entreat me rather go than stay.
And, honest company, I thank you all
That have beheld me give away myself
To this most patient, sweet, and virtuous wife.
Dine with my father, drink a health to me;
For I must hence — and farewell to you all.
Tra. Let us entreat you stay till after dinner.
Pet. It may not be.
Gre. Let me entreat you.
Pet. It cannot be.
Kath. Let me entreat you.
Pet. I am content.
Kath. Are you content to stay?
Pet. I am content you shall entreat me stay;
But yet not stay, entreat me how you can.
Kath. Now if you love me, stay!
Pet. Grumio, my horse!
Gru. Ay, sir, they be ready. The oats have eaten the horses.
Kath. Nay then,
Do what thou canst, I will not go to-day!
No, nor to-morrow! not till I please myself.
The door is open, sir; there lies your way;
You may be jogging whiles your boots are green.
For me, I'll not be gone till I please myself.
'Tis like you'll prove a jolly surly groom
That take it on you at the first so roundly.
Pet. O, Kate, content thee; prithee be not angry.
Kath. I will be angry. What hast thou to do?
Father, be quiet! He shall stay my leisure.
Gre. Ay, marry, sir, now it begins to work.
Kath. Gentlemen, forward to the bridal dinner.
I see a woman may be made a fool
If she had not a spirit to resist.
Pet. They shall go forward, Kate, at thy command.
Obey the bride, you that attend on her.
Go to the feast, revel and domineer,
Carouse full measure to her maidenhead,
Be mad and merry, or go hang yourselves!
But for my bonny Kate, she must with me.
Nay, look not big nor stamp nor stare nor fret!
I will be master of what is mine own.
She is my goods, my chattels; she is my house,
My household stuff, my field, my barn,
My horse, my ox, my ass, my anything!
And here she stands, touch her whoever dare.
I'll bring mine action on the proudest he
That stops my way in Padua. Grumio,
Draw forth thy weapon, we are beset with thieves!
Rescue thy mistress if thou be a man.
Fear not, sweet wench; they shall not touch thee, Kate!
I'll buckler thee against a million.
Exeunt Petruchio, Katherina. [*and Grumio*].
Bap. Nay, let them go! a couple of quiet ones.
Gre. Went they not quickly, I should die with laughing.

Tra. Of all mad matches never was the like.

Luc. Mistress, what's your opinion of your sister?

Bian. That, being mad herself, she's madly mated.

Gre. I warrant him, Petruchio is Kated.

Bap. Neighbours and friends, though bride and bridegroom wants
For to supply the places at the table,
You know there wants no junkets at the feast.
Lucentio, you shall supply the bridegroom's place,
And let Bianca take her sister's room.

Tra. Shall sweet Bianca practise how to bride it?

Bap. She shall, Lucentio. Come, gentlemen, let's go. *Exeunt.*

[ACT IV. Scene I. Petruchio's *country house.*]

Enter *Grumio.*

Gru. Fie, fie on all tired jades, on all mad masters, and all foul ways! Was ever man so beaten? Was ever man so ray'd? Was ever man so weary? I am sent before to make a fire, and they are coming after to warm them. Now were not I a little pot and soon hot, my very lips might freeze to my teeth, my tongue to the roof of my mouth, my heart in my belly, ere I should come by a fire to thaw me. But I with blowing the fire shall warm myself; for, considering the weather, a taller man than I will take cold. Holla, ho! Curtis!

Enter *Curtis.*

Curt. Who is that calls so coldly?

Gru. A piece of ice. If thou doubt it, thou mayst slide from my shoulder to my heel with no greater a run but my head and my neck. A fire, good Curtis!

Curt. Is my master and his wife coming, Grumio?

Gru. O, ay, Curtis, ay! and therefore fire, fire! Cast on no water.

Curt. Is she so hot a shrew as she's reported?

Gru. She was, good Curtis, before this frost; but thou know'st winter tames man, woman, and beast; for it hath tam'd my old master, and my new mistress, and myself, fellow Curtis.

Curt. Away, you three-inch fool! I am no beast.

Gru. Am I but three inches? Why, thy horn is a foot, and so long am I at the least. But wilt thou make a fire, or shall I complain on thee to our mistress? whose hand (she being now at hand) thou shalt soon feel, to thy cold comfort, for being slow in thy hot office.

Curt. I prithee, good Grumio, tell me, how goes the world?

Gru. A cold world, Curtis, in every office but thine; and therefore fire! Do thy duty, and have thy duty; for my master and mistress are almost frozen to death.

Curt. There's fire ready; and therefore, good Grumio, the news!

Gru. Why, 'Jack, boy! ho, boy!' and as much news as wilt thou.

Curt. Come, you are so full of cony-catching!

Gru. Why, therefore fire! for I have caught extreme cold. Where's the cook? Is supper ready, the house trimm'd, rushes strew'd, cobwebs swept, the servingmen in their new fustian, their white stockings, and every officer his wedding garment on? Be the Jacks fair within, the Gills fair without, the carpets laid, and everything in order?

Curt. All ready; and therefore, I pray thee, news!

Gru. First, know my horse is tired, my master and mistress fall'n out.

Curt. How?

Gru. Out of their saddles into the dirt, and thereby hangs a tale.

Curt. Let's ha't, good Grumio.

Gru. Lend thine ear.

Curt. Here.

Gru. There! [*Cuffs him.*]

Curt. This is to feel a tale, not to hear a tale.

Gru. And therefore 'tis call'd a sensible tale, and this cuff was but to knock at your ear and beseech list'ning. Now I begin: Inprimis, we came down a foul hill, my master riding behind my mistress —

Curt. Both of one horse?

Gru. What's that to thee?

Curt. Why, a horse!

Gru. Tell thou the tale! But hadst thou not cross'd me, thou shouldst have heard how her horse fell, and she under her horse; thou shouldst have heard in how miry a place, how she was bemoil'd, how he left her with the horse upon her, how he beat me because her horse stumbled, how she waded through the dirt to pluck him off me; how he swore, how she pray'd that never pray'd before; how I cried, how the horses ran away, how her bridle was burst; how I lost my crupper — with many things of worthy memory, which now shall die in oblivion, and thou return unexperienc'd to thy grave.

Curt. By this reck'ning, he is more shrew than she.

Gru. Ay! and that thou and the proudest of you all shall find when he comes home. But what talk I of this? Call forth Nathaniel, Joseph, Nicholas, Philip, Walter, Sugarsop, and the rest. Let their heads be slickly comb'd, their blue coats brush'd, and their garters of an indifferent knit. Let them curtsy with their left legs, and not presume to touch a hair of my master's horse-tail till they kiss their hands. Are they all ready?

Curt. They are.

Gru. Call them forth.

Curt. Do you hear, ho? You must meet my master, to countenance my mistress!

Gru. Why, she hath a face of her own.

Curt. Who knows not that?

Gru. Thou, it seems, that calls for company to countenance her.

Curt. I call them forth to credit her.

Gru. Why, she comes to borrow nothing of them.

Enter four or five *Servingmen.*

Nathaniel. Welcome home, Grumio!

Philip. How now, Grumio?

Joseph. What, Grumio?

Nick. Fellow Grumio!

Nathaniel. How now, old lad?

Gru. Welcome, you! — How now, you! — What, you! — Fellow, you! — and thus much for greeting. Now, my spruce companions, is all ready, and all things neat?

Nathaniel. All things is ready. How near is our master?

Gru. E'en at hand, alighted by this; and therefore be not — Cock's passion, silence! I hear my master.

Enter *Petruchio* and *Kate.*

Pet. Where be these knaves? What, no man at door
To hold my stirrup nor to take my horse?
Where is Nathaniel, Gregory, Philip?

All Serv. Here! here, sir! here, sir!

Pet. Here, sir! here, sir! here, sir! here, sir!
You loggerheaded and unpolish'd grooms!
What, no attendance? no regard? no duty?
Where is the foolish knave I sent before?

Gru. Here, sir, as foolish as I was before.

Pet. You peasant swain! you whoreson malt-horse drudge!
Did I not bid thee meet me in the park
And bring along these rascal knaves with thee?

Gru. Nathaniel's coat, sir, was not fully made,
And Gabriel's pumps were all unpink'd i' th' heel;
There was no link to colour Peter's hat,
And Walter's dagger was not come from sheathing.
There were none fine but Adam, Ralph, and Gregory;
The rest were ragged, old, and beggarly.
Yet, as they are, here are they come to meet you.

Pet. Go, rascals, go, and fetch my supper in.
Exeunt [*some of the*] *Servants.* [*Petruchio sings.*]

Where is the life that late I led?
Where are those —

Sit down, Kate, and welcome. Soud, soud, soud, soud!

Enter *Servants* with supper.

Why, when, I say! Nay, good sweet Kate, be merry.
Off with my boots, you rogues! you villains, when? [*Sings.*]

It was the friar of orders grey,
As he forth walked on his way.

Out, you rogue! you pluck my foot awry.
Take that, and mend the plucking off the other.
[*Strikes him.*]
Be merry, Kate. Some water, here! what, ho!

Enter *one with water.*

Where's my spaniel Troilus? Sirrah, get you hence
And bid my cousin Ferdinand come hither.
[*Exit Servant.*]
One, Kate, that you must kiss and be acquainted with.
Where are my slippers? Shall I have some water?
Come, Kate, and wash, and welcome heartily.
You whoreson villain! will you let it fall?
[*Strikes him.*]

Kath. Patience, I pray you. 'Twas a fault unwilling.

Pet. A whoreson, beetle-headed, flap-ear'd knave!
Come, Kate, sit down; I know you have a stomach.
Will you give thanks, sweet Kate, or else shall I?
What's this? mutton?
1. Serv. Ay.
Pet. Who brought it?
Peter. I.
Pet. 'Tis burnt, and so is all the meat.
What dogs are these! Where is the rascal cook?
How durst you villains bring it from the dresser
And serve it thus to me that love it not?
There, take it to you — trenchers, cups, and all.
[*Throws the meat &c. at them.*]
You heedless joltheads and unmanner'd slaves!
What, do you grumble? I'll be with you straight.
[*Exeunt Servants.*]
Kath. I pray you, husband, be not so disquiet.
The meat was well, if you were so contented.
Pet. I tell thee, Kate, 'twas burnt and dried away,
And I expressly am forbid to touch it;
For it engenders choler, planteth anger,
And better 'twere that both of us did fast,
Since, of ourselves, ourselves are choleric,
Than feed it with such over-roasted flesh.
Be patient. To-morrow 't shall be mended,
And for this night we'll fast for company.
Come, I will bring thee to thy bridal chamber.
Exeunt.

Enter *Servants* severally.

Nathaniel. Peter, didst ever see the like?
Peter. He kills her in her own humour.

Enter *Curtis, a Servant.*

Gru. Where is he?
Curt. In her chamber, making a sermon of continency to her;
And rails and swears and rates, that she, poor soul,
Knows not which way to stand, to look, to speak,
And sits as one new risen from a dream.
Away, away! for he is coming hither. [*Exeunt.*]

Enter *Petruchio.*

Pet. Thus have I politicly begun my reign,
And 'tis my hope to end successfully.
My falcon now is sharp, and passing empty,
And till she stoop she must not be full-gorg'd,
For then she never looks upon her lure.
Another way I have to man my haggard,
To make her come, and know her keeper's call:
That is, to watch her, as we watch these kites
That bate and beat and will not be obedient.
She eat no meat to-day, nor none shall eat;
Last night she slept not, nor to-night she shall not.
As with the meat, some undeserved fault
I'll find about the making of the bed;
And here I'll fling the pillow, there the bolster,
This way the coverlet, another way the sheets.
Ay, and amid this hurly I intend
That all is done in reverend care of her;
And in conclusion, she shall watch all night;
And if she chance to nod, I'll rail and brawl
And with the clamour keep her still awake.
This is a way to kill a wife with kindness,
And thus I'll curb her mad and headstrong humour.
He that knows better how to tame a shrew,
Now let him speak: 'tis charity to shew. *Exit.*

[Scene II. *Padua. Before* Baptista's *house.*]

Enter *Tranio* [as *Lucentio*] and *Hortensio* [as *Licio*].

Tra. Is't possible, friend Licio, that Mistress Bianca
Doth fancy any other but Lucentio?
I tell you, sir, she bears me fair in hand.
Hor. Sir, to satisfy you in what I have said,
Stand by and mark the manner of his teaching.
[*They stand aside.*]

Enter *Bianca* [and *Lucentio* as *Cambio*].

Luc. Now, mistress, profit you in what you read?
Bian. What, master, read you? First resolve me that.
Luc. I read that I profess, 'The Art to Love.'
Bian. And may you prove, sir, master of your art!
Luc. While you, sweet dear, prove mistress of my heart!
[*They step aside.*]
Hor. Quick proceeders, marry! Now tell me, I pray,
You that durst swear that your mistress Bianca
Lov'd none in the world so well as Lucentio!
Tra. O despiteful love! unconstant womankind!
I tell thee, Licio, this is wonderful.

Hor. Mistake no more. I am not Licio,
Nor a musician, as I seem to be,
But one that scorn to live in this disguise
For such a one as leaves a gentleman
And makes a god of such a cullion.
Know, sir, that I am call'd Hortensio.
Tra. Signior Hortensio, I have often heard
Of your entire affection to Bianca;
And since mine eyes are witness of her lightness,
I will with you, if you be so contented,
Forswear Bianca and her love for ever.
Hor. See how they kiss and court! Signior Lucentio,
Here is my hand, and here I firmly vow
Never to woo her more, but do forswear her,
As one unworthy all the former favours
That I have fondly flatter'd her withal.
Tra. And here I take the like unfeigned oath,
Never to marry with her though she would entreat.
Fie on her! See how beastly she doth court him!
Hor. Would all the world but he had quite forsworn!
For me, that I may surely keep mine oath,
I will be married to a wealthy widow,
Ere three days pass, which hath as long lov'd me
As I have lov'd this proud disdainful haggard.
And so farewell, Signior Lucentio.
Kindness in women, not their beauteous looks,
Shall win my love. And so I take my leave,
In resolution as I swore before. [*Exit.*]
Tra. Mistress Bianca, bless you with such grace
As 'longeth to a lover's blessed case!
Nay, I have ta'en you napping, gentle love,
And have forsworn you with Hortensio.
Bian. Tranio, you jest, But have you both forsworn me?
Tra. Mistress, we have.
Luc. Then we are rid of Licio.
Tra. I' faith, he'll have a lusty widow now
That shall be woo'd and wedded in a day.
Bian. God give him joy!
Tra. Ay, and he'll tame her.
Bian. He says so, Tranio.
Tra. Faith, he is gone unto the taming school.
Bian. The taming school? What, is there such a place?
Tra. Ay, mistress, and Petruchio is the master,
That teacheth tricks eleven-and-twenty long,
To tame a shrew and charm her chattering tongue.

Enter *Biondello.*

Bion. O master, master, I have watch'd so long
That I am dog-weary! but at last I spied
An ancient angel coming down the hill
Will serve the turn.
Tra. What is he, Biondello?
Bion. Master, a mercatante, or a pedant —
I know not what; but formal in apparel,
In gait and countenance surely like a father.
Luc. And what of him, Tranio?
Tra. If he be credulous and trust my tale,
I'll make him glad to seem Vincentio
And give assurance to Baptista Minola,
As if he were the right Vincentio.
Take in your love, and then let me alone.
[*Exeunt Lucentio and Bianca.*]

Enter a *Pedant.*

Ped. God save you, sir.
Tra. And you, sir. You are welcome.
Travel you far on, or are you at the farthest?
Ped. Sir, at the farthest for a week or two;
But then up farther, and as far as Rome;
And so to Tripoli, if God lend me life.
Tra. What countryman, I pray?
Ped. Of Mantua.
Tra. Of Mantua, sir? Marry, God forbid,
And come to Padua, careless of your life!
Ped. My life, sir? How, I pray? For that goes hard.
Tra. 'Tis death for any one in Mantua
To come to Padua. Know you not the cause?
Your ships are stay'd at Venice; and the Duke,
For private quarrel 'twixt your Duke and him,
Hath publish'd and proclaim'd it openly.
'Tis marvel, but that you are but newly come;
You might have heard it else proclaim'd about.
Ped. Alas, sir, it is worse for me than so!
For I have bills for money by exchange
From Florence, and must here deliver them.
Tra. Well, sir, to do you courtesy,
This will I do, and this I will advise you:
First tell me, have you ever been at Pisa?
Ped. Ay, sir, in Pisa have I often been,
Pisa, renowned for grave citizens.
Tra. Among them know you one Vincentio?
Ped. I know him not, but I have heard of him;
A merchant of incomparable wealth.
Tra. He is my father, sir; and, sooth to say,
In count'nance somewhat doth resemble you.
Bion. [*aside*] As much as an apple doth an oyster, and all one!

Tra. To save your life in this extremity,
This favour will I do you for his sake;
And think it not the worst of all your fortunes
That you are like to Sir Vincentio.
His name and credit shall you undertake,
And in my house you shall be friendly lodg'd.
Look that you take upon you as you should.
You understand me, sir. So shall you stay
Till you have done your business in the city.
If this be court'sy, sir, accept of it.

Ped. O, sir, I do! and will repute you ever
The patron of my life and liberty.

Tra. Then go with me to make the matter good.
This by the way I let you understand:
My father is here look'd for every day
To pass assurance of a dow'r in marriage
'Twixt me and one Baptista's daughter here.
In all these circumstances I'll instruct you.
Go with me, sir, to clothe you as becomes you.
Exeunt.

[Scene III. Petruchio's *house*.]

Enter *Katherina* and *Grumio*.

Gru. No, no, forsooth! I dare not for my life.

Kath. The more my wrong, the more his spite appears.
What, did he marry me to famish me?
Beggars that come unto my father's door
Upon entreaty have a present alms;
If not, elsewhere they meet with charity;
But I, who never knew how to entreat,
Nor never needed that I should entreat,
Am starv'd for meat, giddy for lack of sleep;
With oaths kept waking, and with brawling fed.
And that which spites me more than all these wants —
He does it under name of perfect love;
As who should say, if I should sleep or eat,
'Twere deadly sickness or else present death.
I prithee go and get me some repast;
I care not what, so it be wholesome food.

Gru. What say you to a neat's foot?

Kath. 'Tis passing good. I prithee let me have it.

Gru. I fear it is too choleric a meat.
How say you to a fat tripe finely broil'd?

Kath. I like it well. Good Grumio, fetch it me.

Gru. I cannot tell. I fear 'tis choleric.
What say you to a piece of beef and mustard?

Kath. A dish that I do love to feed upon.

Gru. Ay, but the mustard is too hot a little.

Kath. Why then, the beef! and let the mustard rest.

Gru. Nay then, I will not. You shall have the mustard,
Or else you get no beef of Grumio.

Kath. Then both, or one, or anything thou wilt.

Gru. Why then, the mustard without the beef.

Kath. Go, get thee gone, thou false deluding slave, *Beats him.*
That feed'st me with the very name of meat.
Sorrow on thee and all the pack of you
That triumph thus upon my misery!
Go, get thee gone, I say!

Enter *Petruchio* and *Hortensio* with meat.

Pet. How fares my Kate? What, sweeting, all amort?

Hor. Mistress, what cheer?

Kath. Faith, as cold as can be.

Pet. Pluck up thy spirits; look cheerfully upon me.
Here, love; thou seest how diligent I am,
To dress thy meat myself and bring it thee.
I am sure, sweet Kate, this kindness merits thanks.
What, not a word? Nay then, thou lov'st it not,
And all my pains is sorted to no proof.
Here, take away this dish.

Kath. I pray you let it stand.

Pet. The poorest service is repaid with thanks;
And so shall mine before you touch the meat.

Kath. I thank you, sir.

Hor. Signior Petruchio, fie! you are to blame.
Come, Mistress Kate, I'll bear you company.

Pet. [*aside to Hortensio*] Eat it up all, Hortensio, if thou lovest me.
[*To Katherine*] Much good do it unto thy gentle heart!
Kate, eat apace. And now, my honey love,
Will we return unto thy father's house,
And revel it as bravely as the best
With silken coats and caps, and golden rings,
With ruffs and cuffs and fardingales and things,
With scarfs and fans and double change of brav'ry,
With amber bracelets, beads, and all this knav'ry.
What, hast thou din'd? The tailor stays thy leisure,
To deck thy body with his ruffling treasure.

Enter *Tailor*.

Come, tailor, let us see these ornaments.
Lay forth the gown.

Enter *Haberdasher*.

What news with you, sir?

Hab. Here is the cap your worship did bespeak.

Pet. Why, this was moulded on a porringer!
A velvet dish! Fie, fie, 'tis lewd and filthy!
Why, 'tis a cockle or a walnut shell,
A knack, a toy, a trick, a baby's cap.
Away with it! Come, let me have a bigger.

Kath. I'll have no bigger. This doth fit the time,
And gentlewomen wear such caps as these.

Pet. When you are gentle, you shall have one too,
And not till then.

Hor. [*aside*] That will not be in haste.

Kath. Why, sir, I trust I may have leave to speak,
And speak I will! I am no child, no babe.
Your betters have endur'd me say my mind,
And if you cannot, best you stop your ears.
My tongue will tell the anger of my heart,
Or else my heart, concealing it, will break;
And rather than it shall, I will be free
Even to the uttermost, as I please, in words.

Pet. Why, thou say'st true. It is a paltry cap,
A custard coffin, a bauble, a silken pie.
I love thee well in that thou lik'st it not.

Kath. Love me or love me not, I like the cap;
And it I will have, or I will have none.

[*Exit Haberdasher*.]

Pet. Thy gown? Why, ay. Come, tailor, let us see't.
O mercy, God! what masquing stuff is here?
What's this? a sleeve? 'Tis like a demi-cannon!
What, up and down carv'd like an apple tart?
Here's snip and nip and cut, and slish and slash,
Like to a censer in a barber's shop.
Why, what a devil's name, tailor, call'st thou this?

Hor. [*aside*] I see she's like to have neither cap nor gown.

Tai. You bid me make it orderly and well,
According to the fashion and the time.

Pet. Marry, and did; but if you be remember'd,
I did not bid you mar it to the time.
Go hop me over every kennel home,
For you shall hop without my custom, sir.
I'll none of it. Hence! make your best of it.

Kath. I never saw a better-fashion'd gown,
More quaint, more pleasing, nor more commendable.
Belike you mean to make a puppet of me.

Pet. Why, true! he means to make a puppet of thee.

Tai. She says your worship means to make a puppet of her.

Pet. O monstrous arrogance! Thou liest, thou thread, thou thimble,
Thou yard, three-quarters, half-yard, quarter, nail!
Thou flea, thou nit, thou winter cricket thou!
Brav'd in mine own house with a skein of thread?
Away, thou rag, thou quantity, thou remnant,
Or I shall so bemete thee with thy yard
As thou shalt think on prating whilst thou liv'st!
I tell thee, I, that thou hast marr'd her gown.

Tai. Your worship is deceiv'd. The gown is made
Just as my master had direction.
Grumio gave order how it should be done.

Gru. I gave him no order. I gave him the stuff.

Tai. But how did you desire it should be made?

Gru. Marry, sir, with needle and thread.

Tai. But did you not request to have it cut?

Gru. Thou hast fac'd many things.

Tai. I have.

Gru. Face not me. Thou hast brav'd many men; brave not me. I will neither be fac'd nor brav'd. I say unto thee, I bid thy master cut out the gown, but I did not bid him cut it to pieces. Ergo, thou liest.

Tai. Why, here is the note of the fashion to testify.

Pet. Read it.

Gru. The note lies in 's throat if he say I said so.

Tai. [*reads*] 'Inprimis, a loose-bodied gown'—

Gru. Master, if ever I said loose-bodied gown, sew me in the skirts of it and beat me to death with a bottom of brown thread. I said a gown.

Pet. Proceed.

Tai. [*reads*] 'With a small compass'd cape'—

Gru. I confess the cape.

Tai. [*reads*] 'With a trunk sleeve'—

Gru. I confess two sleeves.

Tai. [*reads*] 'The sleeves curiously cut.'

Pet. Ay, there's the villany!

Gru. Error i' th' bill, sir! error i' th' bill! I commanded the sleeves should be cut out and sew'd up again; and that I'll prove upon thee, though thy little finger be armed in a thimble.

Tai. This is true that I say. An I had thee in place where, thou shouldst know it.

Gru. I am for thee straight. Take thou the bill, give me thy mete-yard, and spare not me.

Hor. God-a-mercy, Grumio! Then he shall have no odds.

Pet. Well, sir, in brief, the gown is not for me.

Gru. You are i' th' right, sir. 'Tis for my mistress.

Pet. [*to Tailor*] Go take it up unto thy master's use.

Gru. Villain, not for thy life! Take up my mistress' gown for thy master's use?

Pet. Why, sir, what's your conceit in that?

Gru. O, sir, the conceit is deeper than you think for.
Take up my mistress' gown to his master's use?
O, fie, fie, fie!

Pet. [*aside to Hortensio*] Hortensio, say thou wilt see the tailor paid.
[*To Tailor*] Go take it hence. Be gone, and say no more.

Hor. Tailor, I'll pay thee for thy gown to-morrow.
Take no unkindness of his hasty words.
Away, I say! commend me to thy master.
Exit Tailor.

Pet. Well, come, my Kate. We will unto your father's
Even in these honest mean habiliments.
Our purses shall be proud, our garments poor;
For 'tis the mind that makes the body rich;
And as the sun breaks through the darkest clouds,
So honour peereth in the meanest habit.
What, is the jay more precious than the lark
Because his feathers are more beautiful?
Or is the adder better than the eel
Because his painted skin contents the eye?
O, no, good Kate! Neither art thou the worse
For this poor furniture and mean array.
If thou account'st it shame, lay it on me.
And therefore frolic! We will hence forthwith
To feast and sport us at thy father's house.
Go call my men, and let us straight to him,
And bring our horses unto Long Lane end;
There will we mount, and thither walk on foot.
Let's see; I think 'tis now some seven o'clock,
And well we may come there by dinner time.

Kath. I dare assure you, sir, 'tis almost two,
And 'twill be supper time ere you come there.

Pet. It shall be seven ere I go to horse.
Look, what I speak, or do, or think to do,
You are still crossing it. Sirs, let 't alone.
I will not go to-day; and ere I do,
It shall be what o'clock I say it is.

Hor. Why, so! this gallant will command the sun! [*Exeunt.*]

[Scene IV. *Padua. Before* Baptista's *house.*]

Enter *Tranio* [as *Lucentio*]; and the *Pedant* dress'd like *Vincentio,* booted.

Tra. Sir, this is the house. Please it you that I call?

Ped. Ay, what else? and, but I be deceiv'd,
Signior Baptista may remember me
Near twenty years ago in Genoa,
Where we were lodgers at the Pegasus.

Tra. 'Tis well; and hold your own, in any case,
With such austerity as longeth to a father.

Enter *Biondello.*

Ped. I warrant you. But, sir, here comes your boy.
'Twere good he were school'd.

Tra. Fear you not him. Sirrah Biondello,
Now do your duty throughly, I advise you.
Imagine 'twere the right Vincentio.

Bion. Tut, fear not me.

Tra. But hast thou done thy errand to Baptista?

Bion. I told him that your father was at Venice,
And that you look'd for him this day in Padua.

Tra. Th'art a tall fellow. Hold thee that to drink. [*Gives money.*]

Enter *Baptista* and *Lucentio* [as *Cambio*].

Here comes Baptista. Set your countenance, sir.
Signior Baptista, you are happily met.
[*To the Pedant*] Sir, this is the gentleman I told you of.
I pray you stand good father to me now;
Give me Bianca for my patrimony.

Ped. Soft, son!
Sir, by your leave. Having come to Padua
To gather in some debts, my son Lucentio
Made me acquainted with a weighty cause

Of love between your daughter and himself
And, for the good report I hear of you,
And for the love he beareth to your daughter,
And she to him — to stay him not too long —
I am content, in a good father's care,
To have him match'd; and, if you please to like
No worse than I, upon some agreement
Me shall you find most ready and most willing
With one consent to have her so bestow'd;
For curious I cannot be with you,
Signior Baptista, of whom I hear so well.

Bap. Sir, pardon me in what I have to say.
Your plainness and your shortness please me well.
Right true it is your son Lucentio here
Doth love my daughter, and she loveth him,
Or both dissemble deeply their affections;
And therefore, if you say no more than this,
That like a father you will deal with him,
And pass my daughter a sufficient dower,
The match is made, and all is done:
Your son shall have my daughter with consent.

Tra. I thank you, sir. Where then do you know best
We be affied, and such assurance ta'en
As shall with either part's agreement stand?

Bap. Not in my house, Lucentio; for you know
Pitchers have ears, and I have many servants;
Besides, old Gremio is heark'ning still,
And happily we might be interrupted.

Tra. Then at my lodging, an it like you, sir.
There doth my father lie; and there this night
We'll pass the business privately and well.
Send for your daughter by your servant here;
My boy shall fetch the scrivener presently.
The worst is this, that at so slender warning
You are like to have a thin and slender pittance.

Bap. It likes me well. Cambio, hie you home,
And bid Bianca make her ready straight;
And, if you will, tell what hath happened:
Lucentio's father is arriv'd in Padua,
And how she's like to be Lucentio's wife.
[*Exit Lucentio.*]

Bion. I pray the gods she may with all my heart!

Tra. Dally not with the gods, but get thee gone.
Exit [*Biondello*].
Signior Baptista, shall I lead the way?
Welcome! One mess is like to be your cheer;
Come, sir; we will better it in Pisa.

Bap I follow you.
Exeunt [*Tranio, Pedant, and Baptista*].

Enter *Lucentio* and *Biondello.*

Bion. Cambio.

Luc. What say'st thou, Biondello?

Bion. You saw my master wink and laugh upon you?

Luc. Biondello, what of that?

Bion. Faith, nothing; but has left me here behind to expound the meaning or moral of his signs and tokens.

Luc. I pray thee moralize them.

Bion. Then thus: Baptista is safe, talking with the deceiving father of a deceitful son.

Luc. And what of him?

Bion. His daughter is to be brought by you to the supper.

Luc. And then?

Bion. The old priest at Saint Luke's Church is at your command at all hours.

Luc. And what of all this?

Bion. I cannot tell, except they are busied about a counterfeit assurance. Take you assurance of her *cum privilegio ad imprimendum solum.* To th' church! Take the priest, clerk, and some sufficient honest witnesses.
If this be not that you look for, I have no more to say,
But bid Bianca farewell for ever and a day.
[*Going.*]

Luc. Hear'st thou, Biondello?

Bion. I cannot tarry. I knew a wench married in an afternoon as she went to the garden for parsley to stuff a rabbit; and so may you, sir; and so, adieu, sir. My master hath appointed me to go to Saint Luke's to bid the priest be ready to come against you come with your appendix. *Exit.*

Luc. I may and will, if she be so contented.
She will be pleas'd; then wherefore should I doubt?
Hap what hap may, I'll roundly go about her;
It shall go hard if Cambio go without her. *Exit.*

[Scene V. *A public road.*]

Enter *Petruchio, Kate, Hortensio,* [with *Servants*].

Pet. Come on, a God's name! once more toward our father's.
Good Lord, how bright and goodly shines the moon!

Kath. The moon? the sun. It is not moonlight now.

Pet. I say it is the moon that shines so bright.

Kath. I know it is the sun that shines so bright.

Pet. Now by my mother's son, and that's myself,
It shall be moon, or star, or what I list,
Or ere I journey to your father's house.
[*To Servants*] Go on, and fetch our horses back again.—
Evermore cross'd and cross'd! nothing but cross'd!

Hor. [*aside to Katherina*] Say as he says, or we shall never go.

Kath. Forward, I pray, since we have come so far,
And be it moon, or sun, or what you please.
And if you please to call it a rush candle,
Henceforth I vow it shall be so for me.

Pet. I say it is the moon.

Kath. I know it is the moon.

Pet. Nay then, you lie! it is the blessed sun.

Kath. Then God be bless'd, it is the blessed sun!
But sun it is not when you say it is not,
And the moon changes even as your mind.
What you will have it nam'd, even that it is,
And so it shall be so for Katherine.

Hor. [*aside*] Petruchio, go thy ways; the field is won.

Pet. Well, forward, forward! thus the bowl should run,
And not unluckily against the bias.
But, soft! what company is coming here?

Enter *Vincentio.*

[*To Vincentio*] Good morrow, gentle mistress, where away?
Tell me, sweet Kate, and tell me truly too,
Hast thou beheld a fresher gentlewoman?
Such war of white and red within her cheeks!
What stars do spangle heaven with such beauty
As those two eyes become that heavenly face?
Fair lovely maid, once more good day to thee.
Sweet Kate, embrace her for her beauty's sake.

Hor. [*aside*] 'A will make the man mad to make a woman of him.

Kath. Young budding virgin, fair and fresh and sweet,
Whither away? or where is thy abode?
Happy the parents of so fair a child!
Happier the man whom favourable stars
Allot thee for his lovely bedfellow!

Pet. Why, how now, Kate? I hope thou art not mad.
This is a man, old, wrinkled, faded, withered,
And not a maiden, as thou say'st he is.

Kath. Pardon, old father, my mistaking eyes,
That have been so bedazzled with the sun
That everything I look on seemeth green.
Now I perceive thou art a reverent father.
Pardon, I pray thee, for my mad mistaking!

Pet. Do, good old grandsire, and withal make known
Which way thou travellest; if along with us,
We shall be joyful of thy company.

Vin. Fair sir, and you, my merry mistress,
That with your strange encounter much amaz'd me,
My name is call'd Vincentio, my dwelling Pisa,
And bound I am to Padua, there to visit
A son of mine, which long I have not seen.

Pet. What is his name?

Vin. Lucentio, gentle sir.

Pet. Happily met; the happier for thy son.
And now by law, as well as reverent age,
I may entitle thee my loving father:
The sister to my wife, this gentlewoman,
Thy son by this hath married. Wonder not,
Nor be not griev'd. She is of good esteem,
Her dowry wealthy, and of worthy birth;
Beside, so qualified as may beseem
The spouse of any noble gentleman.
Let me embrace with old Vincentio;
And wander we to see thy honest son,
Who will of thy arrival be full joyous.

Vin. But is this true? or is it else your pleasure,
Like pleasant travellers, to break a jest
Upon the company you overtake?

Hor. I do assure thee, father, so it is.

Pet. Come, go along, and see the truth hereof;
For our first merriment hath made thee jealous.

Exeunt [*Petruchio, Katherina, and Vincentio, with Servants*].

Hor. Well, Petruchio, this has put me in heart.
Have to my widow! and if she be froward,
Then hast thou taught Hortensio to be untoward. *Exit.*

[Act V. Scene I. *Padua. Before* Lucentio's *house.*]

Enter *Biondello, Lucentio,* and *Bianca. Gremio* is out before.

Bion. Softly and swiftly, sir, for the priest is ready.

Luc. I fly, Biondello. But they may chance to need thee at home; therefore leave us.

Bion. Nay, faith, I'll see the church a your back and then come back to my master's as soon as I can.

Exeunt [*Lucentio, Bianca, and Biondello*].

Gre. I marvel Cambio comes not all this while.

Enter *Petruchio, Kate, Vincentio, Grumio,* with *Attendants.*

Pet. Sir, here's the door; this is Lucentio's house;
My father's bears more toward the market place.
Thither must I, and here I leave you, sir.

Vin. You shall not choose but drink before you go.
I think I shall command your welcome here,
And by all likelihood some cheer is toward.

Knock.

Gre. They're busy within. You were best knock louder.

Pedant looks out of the window.

Ped. What's he that knocks as he would beat down the gate?

Vin. Is Signior Lucentio within, sir?

Ped. He's within, sir, but not to be spoken withal.

Vin. What if a man bring him a hundred pound or two to make merry withal?

Ped. Keep your hundred pounds to yourself. He shall need none so long as I live.

Pet. Nay, I told you your son was well beloved in Padua. Do you hear, sir? To leave frivolous circumstances, I pray you tell Signior Lucentio that his father is come from Pisa and is here at the door to speak with him.

Ped. Thou liest. His father is come from Padua and here looking out at the window.

Vin. Art thou his father?

Ped. Ay, sir. So his mother says, if I may believe her.

Pet. [*to Vincentio*] Why, how now, gentleman? Why, this is flat knavery to take upon you another man's name.

Ped. Lay hands on the villain. I believe 'a means to cozen somebody in this city under my countenance.

Enter *Biondello.*

Bion. I have seen them in the church together, God send 'em good shipping! But who is here? Mine old master, Vincentio! Now we are undone and brought to nothing.

Vin. Come hither, crackhemp.

Bion. I hope I may choose, sir.

Vin. Come hither, you rogue. What, have you forgot me?

Bion. Forgot you? No, sir. I could not forget you, for I never saw you before in all my life.

Vin. What, you notorious villain, didst thou never see thy master's father, Vincentio?

Bion. What, my old worshipful old master? Yes, marry, sir! See where he looks out of the window.

Vin. Is't so indeed? *He beats Biondello.*

Bion. Help, help, help! Here's a madman will murder me. [*Exit.*]

Ped. Help, son! help, Signior Baptista! [*Exit above.*]

Pet. Prithee, Kate, let's stand aside and see the end of this controversy. [*They stand aside.*]

Enter *Pedant* with *Servants*; *Baptista, Tranio.*

Tra. Sir, what are you that offer to beat my servant?

Vin. What am I, sir? Nay, what are you, sir? O immortal gods! O fine villain! A silken doublet, a velvet hose, a scarlet cloak, and a copatain hat! O, I am undone, I am undone! While I play the good husband at home, my son and my servant spend all at the university.

Tra. How now? What's the matter?

Bap. What, is the man lunatic?

Tra. Sir, you seem a sober ancient gentleman by your habit, but your words show you a madman. Why, sir, what 'cerns it you if I wear pearl and gold? I thank my good father, I am able to maintain it.

Vin. Thy father? O villain! he is a sailmaker in Bergamo.

Bap. You mistake, sir; you mistake, sir. Pray what do you think is his name?

Vin. His name? As if I knew not his name! I have brought him up ever since he was three years old, and his name is Tranio.

Ped. Away, away, mad ass! His name is Lucentio; and he is mine only son, and heir to the lands of me, Signior Vincentio.

Vin. Lucentio? O, he hath murd'red his master! Lay hold on him, I charge you in the Duke's name. O my son, my son! Tell me, thou villain, where is my son Lucentio?

Tra. Call forth an officer.

[Enter one with an *Officer*.]

Carry this mad knave to the jail. Father Baptista, I charge you see that he be forthcoming.

Vin. Carry me to the jail?

Gre. Stay, officer! He shall not go to prison.

Bap. Talk not, Signior Gremio. I say he shall go to prison.

Gre. Take heed, Signior Baptista, lest you be cony-catch'd in this business. I dare swear this is the right Vincentio.

Ped. Swear if thou dar'st!

Gre. Nay, I dare not swear it.

Tra. Then thou wert best say that I am not Lucentio.

Gre. Yes, I know thee to be Signior Lucentio.

Bap. Away with the dotard! To the jail with him!

Vin. Thus strangers may be haled and abus'd.
O monstrous villain!

Enter *Biondello, Lucentio,* and *Bianca.*

Bion. O, we are spoil'd, and yonder he is! Deny him, forswear him, or else we are all undone.

Luc. Pardon, sweet father. *Kneel.*

Vin. Lives my sweet son?

Exeunt Biondello, Tranio, and Pedant, as fast as may be.

Bian. Pardon, dear father.

Bap. How hast thou offended?
Where is Lucentio?

Luc. Here's Lucentio,
Right son unto the right Vincentio,
That have by marriage made thy daughter mine
While counterfeit supposes blear'd thine eyne.

Gre. Here's packing, with a witness, to deceive us all!

Vin. Where is that damned villain Tranio
That fac'd and brav'd me in this matter so?

Bap. Why, tell me, is not this my Cambio?

Bian. Cambio is chang'd into Lucentio.

Luc. Love wrought these miracles. Bianca's love
Made me exchange my state with Tranio,
While he did bear my countenance in the town;
And happily I have arriv'd at last
Unto the wished haven of my bliss.
What Tranio did, myself enforc'd him to.
Then pardon him, sweet father, for my sake.

Vin. I'll slit the villain's nose that would have sent me to the jail.

Bap. [*to Lucentio*] But do you hear, sir? Have you married my daughter without asking my good will?

Vin. Fear not, Baptista. We will content you; go to. But I will in, to be reveng'd for this villany. *Exit.*

Bap. And I, to sound the depth of this knavery. *Exit.*

Luc. Look not pale, Bianca. Thy father will not frown. *Exeunt* [*Lucentio and Bianca*].

Gre. My cake is dough. But I'll in among the rest,
Out of hope of all but my share of the feast.
[*Exit.*]

Kath. Husband, let's follow, to see the end of this ado.

Pet. First kiss me, Kate, and we will.

Kath. What, in the midst of the street?

Pet. What, art thou asham'd of me?

Kath. No, sir, God forbid! but asham'd to kiss.

Pet. Why then, let's home again. Come, sirrah, let's away.

Kath. Nay, I will give thee a kiss [*kisses him*]. Now pray thee, love, stay.

Pet. Is not this well? Come, my sweet Kate.
Better once than never, for never too late.
Exeunt.

[Scene II. Lucentio's *house*.]

Enter *Baptista, Vincentio, Gremio, the Pedant, Lucentio* and *Bianca,* [*Petruchio* and *Katherina, Hortensio*] and *Widow, Tranio, Biondello, Grumio*; the *Servingmen,* with *Tranio,* bringing in a banquet.

Luc. At last, though long, our jarring notes agree;
And time it is, when raging war is done,
To smile at scapes and perils overblown.
My fair Bianca, bid my father welcome,
While I with selfsame kindness welcome thine.
Brother Petruchio, sister Katherina,
And thou, Hortensio, with thy loving widow,
Feast with the best, and welcome to my house.

My banquet is to close our stomachs up
After our great good cheer. Pray you sit down;
For now we sit to chat as well as eat.

[*They sit.*]

Pet. Nothing but sit and sit, and eat and eat!

Bap. Padua affords this kindness, son Petruchio.

Pet. Padua affords nothing but what is kind.

Hor. For both our sakes I would that word were true.

Pet. Now, for my life, Hortensio fears his widow.

Wid. Then never trust me if I be afeard.

Pet. You are very sensible, and yet you miss my sense.
I mean Hortensio is afeard of you.

Wid. He that is giddy thinks the world turns round.

Pet. Roundly replied.

Kath. Mistress, how mean you that?

Wid. Thus I conceive by him.

Pet. Conceives by me? How likes Hortensio that?

Hor. My widow says, thus she conceives her tale.

Pet. Very well mended. Kiss him for that, good widow.

Kath. 'He that is giddy thinks the world turns round'—
I pray you tell me what you meant by that.

Wid. Your husband, being troubled with a shrow,
Measures my husband's sorrow by his woe.
And now you know my meaning.

Kath. A very mean meaning.

Wid. Right, I mean you.

Kath. And I am mean indeed, respecting you.

Pet. To her, Kate!

Hor. To her, widow!

Pet. A hundred marks, my Kate does put her down!

Hor. That's my office.

Pet. Spoke like an officer. Ha' to thee, lad!

Drinks to Hortensio.

Bap. How likes Gremio these quick-witted folks?

Gre. Believe me, sir, they butt together well.

Bian. Head and butt! An hasty-witted body
Would say your head and butt were head and horn.

Vin. Ay, mistress bride, hath that awakened you?

Bian. Ay, but not fiighted me; therefore I'll sleep again.

Pet. Nay, that you shall not. Since you have begun,
Have at you for a bitter jest or two!

Bian. Am I your bird? I mean to shift my bush;
And then pursue me as you draw your bow.
You are welcome all.

Exeunt Bianca, [*Katherina, and Widow*].

Pet. She hath prevented me. Here, Signior Tranio,
This bird you aim'd at, though you hit her not.
Therefore a health to all that shot and miss'd!

Tra. O sir, Lucentio slipp'd me like his greyhound,
Which runs himself, and catches for his master.

Pet. A good swift simile, but something currish.

Tra. 'Tis well, sir, that you hunted for yourself.
'Tis thought your deer does hold you at a bay.

Bap. O, O, Petruchio! Tranio hits you now.

Luc. I thank thee for that gird, good Tranio.

Hor. Confess, confess! Hath he not hit you here?

Pet. 'A has a little gall'd me, I confess;
And, as the jest did glance away from me,
'Tis ten to one it maim'd you two outright.

Bap. Now in good sadness, son Petruchio,
I think thou hast the veriest shrew of all.

Pet. Well, I say no; and therefore, for assurance,
Let's each one send unto his wife,
And he whose wife is most obedient,
To come at first when he doth send for her,
Shall win the wager which we will propose.

Hor. Content. What is the wager?

Luc. Twenty crowns.

Pet. Twenty crowns!
I'll venture so much of my hawk or hound,
But twenty times so much upon my wife.

Luc. A hundred then.

Hor. Content.

Pet. A match! 'tis done.

Hor. Who shall begin?

Luc. That will I. Go, Biondello,
Bid your mistress come to me.

Bion. I go. *Exit.*

Bap. Son, I will be your half, Bianca comes.

Luc. I'll have no halves. I'll bear it all myself.

Enter *Biondello.*

How now? what news?

Bion. Sir, my mistress sends you word
That she is busy and she cannot come.

Pet. How? She is busy, and she cannot come!
Is that an answer?
Gre. Ay, and a kind one too.
Pray God, sir, your wife send you not a worse.
Pet. I hope better.
Hor. Sirrah Biondello, go and entreat my wife
To come to me forthwith.
Exit Biondello.
Pet. O, ho! entreat her?
Nay, then she must needs come.
Hor. I am afraid, sir,
Do what you can, yours will not be entreated.

Enter *Biondello.*

Now where's my wife?
Bion. She says you have some goodly jest in hand.
She will not come; she bids you come to her.
Pet. Worse and worse! She will not come? O vile,
Intolerable, not to be endur'd!
Sirrah Grumio, go to your mistress;
Say I command her come to me.
Exit [*Grumio*].
Hor. I know her answer.
Pet. What?
Hor. She will not.
Pet. The fouler fortune mine, and there an end.

Enter *Katherina.*

Bap. Now, by my holidam, here comes Katherina!
Kath. What is your will, sir, that you send for me?
Pet. Where is your sister, and Hortensio's wife?
Kath. They sit conferring by the parlour fire.
Pet. Go fetch them hither. If they deny to come,
Swinge me them soundly forth unto their husbands.
Away, I say, and bring them hither straight.
[*Exit Katherina.*]
Luc. Here is a wonder, if you talk of a wonder.
Hor. And so it is. I wonder what it bodes.
Pet. Marry, peace it bodes, and love, and quiet life,
An awful rule, and right supremacy,
And, to be short, what not that's sweet and happy.
Bap. Now, fair befall thee, good Petruchio!
The wager thou hast won; and I will add
Unto their losses twenty thousand crowns,
Another dowry to another daughter,
For she is chang'd, as she had never been.
Pet. Nay, I will win my wager better yet
And show more sign of her obedience,
Her new-built virtue and obedience.

Enter *Kate, Bianca,* and *Widow.*

See where she comes, and brings your froward wives
As prisoners to her womanly persuasion.
Katherine, that cap of yours becomes you not.
Off with that bauble, throw it under foot!
[*She obeys.*]
Wid. Lord let me never have a cause to sigh
Till I be brought to such a silly pass!
Bian. Fie, what a foolish duty call you this?
Luc. I would your duty were as foolish too.
The wisdom of your duty, fair Bianca,
Hath cost me a hundred crowns since supper time.
Bian. The more fool you for laying on my duty!
Pet. Katherine, I charge thee tell these headstrong women
What duty they do owe their lords and husbands.
Wid. Come, come, you're mocking! We will have no telling.
Pet. Come on, I say! and first begin with her.
Wid. She shall not.
Pet. I say she shall. And first begin with her.
Kath. Fie, fie! unknit that threat'ning unkind brow,
And dart not scornful glances from those eyes
To wound thy lord, thy king, thy governor!
It blots thy beauty as frosts do bite the meads,
Confounds thy fame as whirlwinds shake fair buds,
And in no sense is meet or amiable.
A woman mov'd is like a fountain troubled,
Muddy, ill-seeming, thick, bereft of beauty;
And while it is so, none so dry or thirsty
Will deign to sip or touch one drop of it.
Thy husband is thy lord, thy life, thy keeper,
Thy head, thy sovereign; one that cares for thee
And for thy maintenance; commits his body
To painful labour both by sea and land,
To watch the night in storms, the day in cold,
Whilst thou li'st warm at home, secure and safe;
And craves no other tribute at thy hands
But love, fair looks, and true obedience —

Too little payment for so great a debt.
Such duty as the subject owes the prince,
Even such a woman oweth to her husband;
And when she is froward, peevish, sullen, sour,
And not obedient to his honest will,
What is she but a foul contending rebel
And graceless traitor to her loving lord?
I am asham'd that women are so simple
To offer war where they should kneel for peace;
Or seek for rule, supremacy, and sway
When they are bound to serve, love, and obey.
Why are our bodies soft and weak and smooth,
Unapt to toil and trouble in the world,
But that our soft conditions and our hearts
Should well agree with our external parts?
Come, come, you froward and unable worms!
My mind hath been as big as one of yours,
My heart as great, my reason haply more,
To bandy word for word and frown for frown;
But now I see our lances are but straws,
Our strength as weak, our weakness past compare,
That seeming to be most which we indeed least are.
Then vail your stomachs, for it is no boot,
And place your hands below your husband's foot;
In token of which duty, if he please,
My hand is ready, may it do him ease.

Pet. Why, there's a wench! Come on and kiss me, Kate.

Luc. Well, go thy ways, old lad; for thou shalt ha't.

Vin. 'Tis a good hearing when children are toward.

Luc. But a harsh hearing when women are froward.

Pet. Come, Kate, we'll to bed.
We three are married, but you two are sped.
[*To Lucentio*] 'Twas I won the wager, though you hit the white;
And being a winner, God give you good night!

Exit Petruchio [*with Katherina*].

Hor. Now go thy ways. Thou hast tam'd a curst shrow.

Luc. 'Tis a wonder, by your leave, she will be tam'd so. [*Exeunt.*]

ALL'S WELL THAT ENDS WELL

For the text of ALL'S WELL THAT ENDS WELL the First Folio is our only authority. The date of composition is very uncertain. Much of the blank verse suggests a time much later than one would infer from the rhyming passages. Probably Shakespeare revised, and in part rewrote, an earlier play of his own. There is slight ground for the conjecture that the earlier play was from some other hand.

In its present form the play may be safely dated about 1602. In its earlier form it may have been the *Love Labour's Won* mentioned by Meres in 1598. That would be an appropriate title for it. On the other hand, one would expect *Love Labour's Won* to be more in the tone and temper of *Love's Labour's Lost.*

External evidence as to date is almost *nil.* In *The Weakest Goeth to the Wall* (printed in 1600), there is a Dutchman whose pet ejaculation is 'lustick,' and some regard Lafew's 'Lustick! as the Dutchman says' (ii, 3, 47), as an allusion to this character. But the article 'the' is probably generic, and Shakespeare must have been personally acquainted with many Dutchmen, to say nothing of his familiarity with stage Dutch or German. The Clown's mention of an earthquake (i, 3, 91), if read in the context, does not sound like anything that must needs have been suggested by the earthquake actually felt in England on December 24, 1601. However, even if these points are of no significance, they at least do not conflict with what is in any case a reasonable date.

The plot comes in the main from the *novella* of Beltramo de Rossiglione and Giglietta di Nerbone in Boccaccio's *Decameron* (iii, 9), as translated in Painter's *Palace of Pleasure* (1566). There are important changes, however. In the source, the king disappears from the story immediately after the marriage, and the girl corresponding to Diana (nameless) drops out as soon as she has played her part in the deception of Beltramo. She remains at Rome or Florence, having received a good *dot* from Giglietta (Helena). Giglietta stays away from home until she has borne twin sons. Then she returns to Rossiglione, presents herself to Count Beltramo with the infants in her arms, and shows him the ring. The occasion is a great feast that he is giving at his palace on All Saints' Day. He recognizes the ring, acknowledges the children as his own ('they were so like him'), and accepts Giglietta as his wife without demur, though with no great enthusiasm. The king is not present. There is no imbroglio about rings and no suggestion of a second marriage. The dowager Countess, one of Shakespeare's most delightful characters, is new. So are Lafew, Parolles, and the Clown.

To the Elizabethan theatre-goer ALL'S WELL was undoubtedly a romantic play with a happy ending. To some serious-minded moderns it appears to be ironic or even cynical, for they cannot accept the ending as happy. We sometimes forget that we are just as conventional as the Elizabethans, though with a different set of conventions, and that to Shakespeare, the practical playwright, the conventions of his age were rules of the game. We are not obliged to defend Bertram — we may detest and despise him if we like — but Helena was in love with him, and to Shakespeare's audience she was doubly fortunate, in winning the man of her choice and in making a brilliant marriage. If they had bothered their minds about the further history of the couple, they would doubtless have felt confident that Bertram had learned his lesson and would behave himself in the future. We are not obliged to enjoy the plot as a plot, but we can take comfort in the character of the Countess; we can enjoy the cleverness of Lavatch, who, though he is not a philosopher (like Touchstone) or a tragic chorus individualized (like Lear's fool), is as witty as any humourist has a right to be; we can associate with a genial gentleman in the person of Lafew; we can luxuriate in the magnificent new language, a veritable esperanto, which the poet has created to satisfy his own fondness for 'words, words, words' and to take the downfall of Parolles out of the sternly moral realm into the wonderland of fantastic comedy.

Parolles is one of Shakespeare's masterpieces. He has been called a forerunner of Falstaff, but that description misses the mark. Falstaff is disinclined to underrate his own exploits, but he is not a braggart, for he is always a humourist in his boasting; in fact, he is an experienced professional soldier. Parolles is more like Pistol in high life. Like Pistol, he lacks a sense of humour. He has seen military service, but we are left dubious as to his previous record. That he is a coward is certain. He is a bit of a fop, and may pass (for analysis' sake) as a cross between the *miles gloriosus* and the parasite. When exposed and disgraced — shamed out of the army like the cudgelled Pistol in *Henry V* (v, 1, 92–94) — he resembles that 'ancient swaggerer' in refusing to be despondent. 'To England,' says Pistol,

> 'To England will I steal, and there I'll steal;
> And patches will I get unto these cudgell'd scars,
> And swear I got them in the Gallia wars.'

And note the rebound of Parolles (iv, 3, 373–375) — less spirited, but equally sanguine:

> 'Rust, sword! cool, blushes! and, Parolles, live
> Safest in shame! Being fool'd, by fool'ry thrive!
> There's place and means for every man alive.'

ALL'S WELL THAT ENDS WELL

[Dramatis Personæ.

The *King of France.*
The *Duke of Florence.*
Bertram, Count of Rossillion.
Lafew, an old lord.
Parolles, a follower of *Bertram.*
Two French Lords in the Florentine service.
Rinaldo, steward to the *Countess.*
Lavatch, a clown, servant to the *Countess.*
A Page.
The *Dowager Countess of Rossillion,* mother to *Bertram.*
Helena, a gentlewoman, protected by the *Countess.*
A Widow of Florence.
Diana, her daughter.
Violenta, } neighbours and friends to the Widow.
Mariana, }
Lords, Soldiers, etc.

SCENE. — *Rossillion; Paris; Florence; Marseilles.*]

ACT I. Scene I. [*Rossillion. The* Count's *Palace.*]

Enter young *Bertram, Count of Rossillion,* his Mother [the *Dowager Countess*], and *Helena*; *Lord Lafew* — all in black.

Countess. In delivering my son from me I bury a second husband.

Ber. And I in going, madam, weep o'er my father's death anew; but I must attend his Majesty's command, to whom I am now in ward, evermore in subjection.

Laf. You shall find of the King a husband, madam; you, sir, a father. He that so generally is at all times good must of necessity hold his virtue to you, whose worthiness would stir it up where it wanted, rather than lack it where there is such abundance.

Countess. What hope is there of his Majesty's amendment?

Laf. He hath abandon'd his physicians, madam; under whose practices he hath persecuted time with hope, and finds no other advantage in the process but only the losing of hope by time.

Countess. This young gentlewoman had a father — O, that 'had,' how sad a passage 'tis! — whose skill was almost as great as his honesty; had it stretch'd so far, would have made nature immortal, and death should have play for lack of work. Would for the King's sake he were living! I think it would be the death of the King's disease.

Laf. How call'd you the man you speak of, madam?

Countess. He was famous, sir, in his profession, and it was his great right to be so — Gerard de Narbon.

Laf. He was excellent indeed, madam. The King very lately spoke of him admiringly and mourningly. He was skilful enough to have liv'd still, if knowledge could be set up against mortality.

Ber. What is it, my good lord, the King languishes of?

Laf. A fistula, my lord.

Ber. I heard not of it before.

Laf. I would it were not notorious. Was this gentlewoman the daughter of Gerard de Narbon?

Countess. His sole child, my lord, and bequeathed to my overlooking. I have those hopes of her good that her education promises. Her dispositions she inherits, which makes fair gifts fairer; for where an unclean mind carries virtuous qualities, their commendations go with pity — they are virtues and traitors too. In her they are the better for their simpleness. She derives her honesty and achieves her goodness.

Laf. Your commendations, madam, get from her tears.

Countess. 'Tis the best brine a maiden can season her praise in. The remembrance of her father never approaches her heart but the tyranny of her sorrows takes all livelihood from her cheek. No more of this, Helena. Go to, no more! lest it be rather thought you affect a sorrow than to have.

Hel. [*aside*] I do affect a sorrow indeed, but I have it too.

Laf. Moderate lamentation is the right of the dead; excessive grief the enemy to the living.

Countess. If the living be enemy to the grief, the excess makes it soon mortal.

Laf. How understand we that?

Ber. Madam, I desire your holy wishes.

Countess. Be thou blest, Bertram, and succeed thy father
In manners, as in shape! Thy blood and virtue
Contend for empire in thee, and thy goodness
Share with thy birthright! Love all, trust a few,
Do wrong to none. Be able for thine enemy
Rather in power than use, and keep thy friend
Under thy own life's key. Be check'd for silence,
But never tax'd for speech. What heaven more will,
That thee may furnish, and my prayers pluck down,
Fall on thy head! — Farewell, my lord.
'Tis an unseason'd courtier; good my lord,
Advise him.

Laf. He cannot want the best
That shall attend his love.

Countess. Heaven bless him! Farewell, Bertram. [*Exit.*]

Ber. [*to Helena*] The best wishes that can be forg'd in your thoughts be servants to you! Be comfortable to my mother, your mistress, and make much of her.

Laf. Farewell, pretty lady. You must hold the credit of your father.

[*Exeunt Bertram and Lafew.*]

Hel. O, were that all! I think not on my father,
And these great tears grace his remembrance more
Than those I shed for him. What was he like?
I have forgot him. My imagination
Carries no favour in't but Bertram's.
I am undone! There is no living, none,
If Bertram be away. 'Twere all one
That I should love a bright particular star
And think to wed it, he is so above me.
In his bright radiance and collateral light
Must I be comforted, not in his sphere.
Th' ambition in my love thus plagues itself.
The hind that would be mated by the lion
Must die for love. 'Twas pretty, though a plague,
To see him every hour; to sit and draw
His arched brows, his hawking eye, his curls,
In our heart's table — heart too capable
Of every line and trick of his sweet favour.
But now he's gone, and my idolatrous fancy
Must sanctify his relics. Who comes here?

Enter *Parolles.*

One that goes with him. I love him for his sake;
And yet I know him a notorious liar,
Think him a great way fool, solely a coward.
Yet these fix'd evils sit so fit in him
That they take place when virtue's steely bones
Look bleak i' th' cold wind. Withal, full oft we see
Cold wisdom waiting on superfluous folly.

Par. Save you, fair queen!

Hel. And you, monarch!

Par. No.

Hel. And no.

Par. Are you meditating on virginity?

Hel. Ay. You have some stain of soldier in you: let me ask you a question. Man is enemy to virginity; how may we barricado it against him?

Par. Keep him out.

Hel. But he assails, and our virginity, though valiant in the defence, yet is weak. Unfold to us some warlike resistance.

Par. There is none. Man, setting down before you, will undermine you and blow you up.

Hel. Bless our poor virginity from underminers and blowers-up! Is there no military policy how virgins might blow up men?

Par. Virginity being blown down, man will quicklier be blown up. Marry, in blowing him down again, with the breach yourselves made you lose your city. It is not politic in the commonwealth of nature to preserve virginity. Loss of virginity is rational increase; and there was never virgin got till virginity was first lost. That you were made of, is metal to make virgins. Virginity by being once lost may be ten times found; by being ever kept it is ever lost. 'Tis too cold a companion. Away with't!

Hel. I will stand for't a little, though therefore I die a virgin.

Par. There's little can be said in't; 'tis against the rule of nature. To speak on the part of virginity is to accuse your mothers, which is most infallible disobedience. He that hangs himself is a virgin: virginity murthers itself, and should be buried in highways out of all sanctified limit, as a desperate offendress against

Joyce Redman in the role of Helena, whose quest for her errant husband is the subject of the play

ALL'S WELL THAT ENDS WELL

PHOTOGRAPHS BY ANGUS MCBEAN
PRODUCED BY MEMORIAL THEATRE COMPANY, STRATFORD-UPON-AVON

"Be thou blest, Bertram; and succeed thy father in manners, as in shape." The Countess of Rousillon (Rosalind Atkinson) bids farewell to her son Bertram (Michael Denison) as he departs for court
(Act I, Scene I)

Below left: Asking advice of Parolles (Keith Mitchell), Bertram's rakehell comrade, who is to accompany him to the French court, Helena is rewarded with a barrage of cynical, scurrilous witticisms *(Act I, Scene I)*

Below right: "Then, I confess, here on my knee, before high heaven and you, that before you, and next unto high heaven, I love your son." Helena tells the gentle countess of her affection for Bertram
(Act I, Scene III)

Above: "Youth, thou bearest thy father's face; frank nature, rather curious than in haste, hath well compos'd thee." The king (Alan Webb) welcomes Bertram de Rousillon as the youth arrives at court *(Act I, Scene II)*

Above: "An thy mind stand to 't, boy, steal away bravely." As Bertram's companions leave for the wars in Italy, Parolles suggests that he leave the court and join them *(Act II, Scene I)*

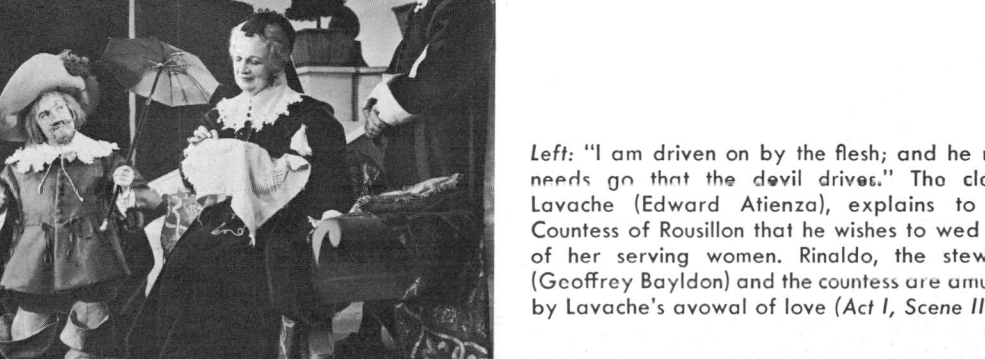

Left: "I am driven on by the flesh; and he must needs go that the devil drives." The clown, Lavache (Edward Atienza), explains to the Countess of Rousillon that he wishes to wed one of her serving women. Rinaldo, the steward (Geoffrey Bayldon) and the countess are amused by Lavache's avowal of love *(Act I, Scene III)*

"This is his Majesty, say your mind to him: a traitor you do look like; but such traitors his Majesty seldom fears." The king's confidant, Lafeu (Ralph Michael), presents Helena, who has claimed that a remedy she received from her deceased father, a physician, will cure the king's illness *(Act II, Scene I)*

Left: "But if I help, what do you promise me?" Helena makes a pact with the king whereby if she cannot cure him she will die, but if she is successful, he will give her in marriage to any man she shall choose among his courtiers *(Act II, Scene I)*

Right: "Sit, my preserver, by thy patient's side." Restored to health by Helena's remedy, the king expresses his gratitude and invites her to choose among his courtiers the husband he promised her if her medicine proved to be successful *(Act II, Scene III)*

Above: "I dare not say I take you; but I give me and my service, ever whilst I live, into your guiding power." Helena chooses Bertram from amongst the suitors assembled for her *(Act II, Scene III)*

Above: "Till I have no wife, I have nothing in France." Helena reads a bitter letter from Bertram, who has left for the wars in Italy and swears never to return while she still claims to be his wife. Lavache and the countess share her dismay *(Act III, Scene II)*

Right: "Come, pilgrim, I will bring you where you shall host." Disguised as a pilgrim, Helena has followed Bertram to Florence, where a widow (Nancye Stewart) and her daughter, Diana (Jill Dixon) offer her hospitality *(Act III, Scene IV)*

"By the hand of a soldier, I will undertake it." Eager to perform some feat of valor, Parolles promises to recover from the enemy a drum lost in battle *(Act III, Scene VI)*

To prove the cowardice of Parolles, Bertram and his companions trick him into believing that he has been captured by the enemy *(Act IV, Scene I)*

Above: Continuing their sport with Parolles, Bertram and his friends lead him to denounce his fellow officers *(Act IV, Scene III)*

Left: Lavache greets Parolles quizzically as the bedraggled warrior returns to Rousillon *(Act V, Scene II)*

Left: "This exceeding posting, day and night, must wear your spirits low." Pausing at Marseille during the trip back to France, Helena tries to cheer the weary widow, whom she is bringing back as her servant *(Act V, Scene I)*

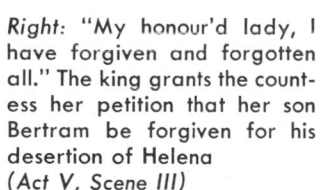

Right: "My honour'd lady, I have forgiven and forgotten all." The king grants the countess her petition that her son Bertram be forgiven for his desertion of Helena *(Act V, Scene III)*

Below: "He's guilty, and he's not guilty. He knows I am no maid, and he'll swear to 't." Diana's speech becomes cryptic as she tries to explain the romantic imbroglio to the angry monarch *(Act V, Scene III)*

"There is your ring." Helena proves that she is wife in fact as well as name *(Act V, Scene III)*

"If she, my liege, can make me know this clearly, I'll love her dearly, ever, ever dearly." All ends well as the elusive Bertram and Helena are finally united *(Act V, Scene III)*

nature. Virginity breeds mites, much like a cheese; consumes itself to the very paring, and so dies with feeding his own stomach. Besides, virginity is peevish, proud, idle, made of self-love, which is the most inhibited sin in the canon. Keep it not; you cannot choose but lose by't. Out with't! within ten year it will make itself ten, which is a goodly increase, and the principal itself not much the worse. Away with't!

Hel. How might one do, sir, to lose it to her own liking?

Par. Let me see. Marry, ill, to like him that ne'er it likes. 'Tis a commodity will lose the gloss with lying; the longer kept, the less worth. Off with't while 'tis vendible; answer the time of request. Virginity, like an old courtier, wears her cap out of fashion; richly suited, but unsuitable: just like the brooch and the toothpick, which wear not now. Your date is better in your pie and your porridge than in your cheek; and your virginity, your old virginity, is like one of our French wither'd pears: it looks ill, it eats drily. Marry, 'tis a wither'd pear; it was formerly better; marry, yet 'tis a wither'd pear! Will you anything with it?

Hel. Not my virginity yet. . . .
There shall your master have a thousand loves,
A mother, and a mistress, and a friend,
A phœnix, captain, and an enemy,
A guide, a goddess, and a sovereign,
A counsellor, a traitress, and a dear;
His humble ambition, proud humility,
His jarring concord, and his discord dulcet,
His faith, his sweet disaster; with a world
Of pretty, fond, adoptious christendoms
That blinking Cupid gossips. Now shall he —
I know not what he shall. God send him well!
The court's a learning place, and he is one —

Par. What one, i' faith?

Hel. That I wish well. 'Tis pity —

Par. What's pity?

Hel. That wishing well had not a body in't
Which might be felt; that we, the poorer born,
Whose baser stars do shut us up in wishes,
Might with effects of them follow our friends
And show what we alone must think, which never
Returns us thanks.

Enter *Page*.

Page. Monsieur Parolles, my lord calls for you. [*Exit.*]

Par. Little Helen, farewell. If I can remember thee, I will think of thee at court.

Hel. Monsieur Parolles, you were born under a charitable star.

Par. Under Mars I.

Hel. I especially think, under Mars.

Par. Why under Mars?

Hel. The wars have so kept you under that you must needs be born under Mars.

Par. When he was predominant.

Hel. When he was retrograde, I think rather.

Par. Why think you so?

Hel. You go so much backward when you fight.

Par. That's for advantage.

Hel. So is running away when fear proposes the safety. But the composition that your valour and fear makes in you is a virtue of a good wing, and I like the wear well.

Par. I am so full of businesses I cannot answer thee acutely. I will return perfect courtier; in the which my instruction shall serve to naturalize thee, so thou wilt be capable of a courtier's counsel and understand what advice shall thrust upon thee; else thou diest in thine unthankfulness, and thine ignorance makes thee away. Farewell. When thou hast leisure, say thy prayers; when thou hast none, remember thy friends. Get thee a good husband, and use him as he uses thee. So, farewell. [*Exit.*]

Hel. Our remedies oft in ourselves do lie,
Which we ascribe to heaven. The fated sky
Gives us free scope; only doth backward pull
Our slow designs when we ourselves are dull.
What power is it which mounts my love so high?
That makes me see, and cannot feed mine eye?
The mightiest space in fortune nature brings
To join like likes and kiss like native things.
Impossible be strange attempts to those
That weigh their pains in sense, and do suppose
What hath been cannot be. Who ever strove
To show her merit that did miss her love?
The King's disease — my project may deceive me,
But my intents are fix'd and will not leave me.
Exit.

[Scene II. *Paris. The* King's *Palace.*]

Flourish cornets. Enter the *King of France* with letters, and divers *Attendants*.

King. The Florentines and Senoys are by th' ears,
Have fought with equal fortune, and continue
A braving war.

1. Lord. So 'tis reported, sir.
King. Nay, 'tis most credible. We here receive it
A certainty vouch'd from our cousin Austria,
With caution, that the Florentine will move us
For speedy aid; wherein our dearest friend
Prejudicates the business, and would seem
To have us make denial.
1. Lord. His love and wisdom,
Approv'd so to your Majesty, may plead
For amplest credence.
King. He hath arm'd our answer,
And Florence is denied before he comes.
Yet for our gentlemen that mean to see
The Tuscan service, freely have they leave
To stand on either part.
2. Lord. It well may serve
A nursery to our gentry, who are sick
For breathing and exploit.
King. What's he comes here?

Enter *Bertram, Lafew,* and *Parolles.*

1. Lord. It is the Count Rossillion, my good lord,
Young Bertram.
King. Youth, thou bear'st thy father's face.
Frank nature, rather curious than in haste,
Hath well compos'd thee. Thy father's moral parts
Mayst thou inherit too! Welcome to Paris.
Ber. My thanks and duty are your Majesty's.
King. I would I had that corporal soundness now
As when thy father and myself in friendship
First tried our soldiership! He did look far
Into the service of the time, and was
Discipled of the bravest. He lasted long;
But on us both did haggish age steal on,
And wore us out of act. It much repairs me
To talk of your good father. In his youth
He had the wit which I can well observe
To-day in our young lords; but they may jest
Till their own scorn return to them unnoted
Ere they can hide their levity in honour
So like a courtier. Contempt nor bitterness
Were in his pride or sharpness. If they were,
His equal had awak'd them; and his honour,
Clock to itself, knew the true minute when
Exception bid him speak, and at this time
His tongue obey'd his hand. Who were below him
He us'd as creatures of another place;
And bow'd his eminent top to their low ranks,
Making them proud of his humility,
In their poor praise he humbled. Such a man
Might be a copy to these younger times,
Which, followed well, would demonstrate them now
But goers backward.
Ber. His good remembrance, sir,
Lies richer in your thoughts than on his tomb.
So in approof lives not his epitaph
As in your royal speech.
King. Would I were with him! He would always say —
Methinks I hear him now; his plausive words
He scatter'd not in ears, but grafted them
To grow there and to bear — 'Let me not live' —
Thus his good melancholy oft began,
On the catastrophe and heel of pastime,
When it was out — 'Let me not live,' quoth he,
'After my flame lacks oil, to be the snuff
Of younger spirits, whose apprehensive senses
All but new things disdain; whose judgments are
Mere fathers of their garments; whose constancies
Expire before their fashions.' This he wish'd.
I, after him, do after him wish too,
Since I nor wax nor honey can bring home,
I quickly were dissolved from my hive,
To give some labourers room.
2. Lord. You're loved, sir.
They that least lend it you shall lack you first.
King. I fill a place, I know't. How long is't, Count,
Since the physician at your father's died?
He was much fam'd.
Ber. Some six months since, my lord.
King. If he were living, I would try him yet.
Lend me an arm. The rest have worn me out
With several applications. Nature and sickness
Debate it at their leisure. Welcome, Count;
My son's no dearer.
Ber. Thank your Majesty.
Exeunt. Flourish.

[Scene III. *Rossillion. The* Count's *Palace.*]

Enter *Countess, Steward,* and *Clown.*

Count. I will now hear. What say you of this gentlewoman?

Stew. Madam, the care I have had to even your content I wish might be found in the calendar of my past endeavours; for then we wound our modesty, and make foul the clearness of our deservings, when of ourselves we publish them.

Count. What does this knave here? Get you gone, sirrah. The complaints I have heard of you I do not all believe. 'Tis my slowness that I do not; for I know you lack not folly to commit them and have ability enough to make such knaveries yours.

Clown. 'Tis not unknown to you, madam, I am a poor fellow.

Count. Well, sir.

Clown. No, madam. 'Tis not so well that I am poor, though many of the rich are damn'd. But, if I may have your ladyship's good will to go to the world, Isbel the woman and I will do as we may.

Count. Wilt thou needs be a beggar?

Clown. I do beg your good will in this case.

Count. In what case?

Clown. In Isbel's case and mine own. Service is no heritage; and I think I shall never have the blessing of God till I have issue o' my body; for they say barnes are blessings.

Count. Tell me thy reason why thou wilt marry.

Clown. My poor body, madam, requires it. I am driven on by the flesh; and he must needs go that the devil drives.

Count. Is this all your worship's reason?

Clown. Faith, madam, I have other holy reasons, such as they are.

Count. May the world know them?

Clown. I have been, madam, a wicked creature, as you and all flesh and blood are, and indeed I do marry that I may repent.

Count. Thy marriage, sooner than thy wickedness.

Clown. I am out o' friends, madam, and I hope to have friends for my wive's sake.

Count. Such friends are thine enemies, knave.

Clown. Y'are shallow, madam, in great friends; for the knaves come to do that for me which I am aweary of. He that ears my land spares my team and gives me leave to inn the crop. If I be his cuckold, he's my drudge. He that comforts my wife is the cherisher of my flesh and blood; he that cherishes my flesh and blood loves my flesh and blood; he that loves my flesh and blood is my friend: ergo, he that kisses my wife is my friend. If men could be contented to be what they are, there were no fear in marriage; for young Charbon the Puritan and old Poysam the Papist, howsome'er their hearts are sever'd in religion, their heads are both one — they may jowl horns together like any deer i' th' herd.

Count. Wilt thou ever be a foul-mouth'd and calumnious knave?

Clown. A prophet I, madam, and I speak the truth the next way:

For I the ballad will repeat,
  Which men full true shall find:
Your marriage comes by destiny,
  Your cuckoo sings by kind.

Count. Get you gone, sir. I'll talk with you more anon.

Stew. May it please you, madam, that he bid Helen come to you. Of her I am to speak.

Count. Sirrah, tell my gentlewoman I would speak with her; Helen I mean.

Clown. 'Was this fair face the cause,' quoth she,
  'Why the Grecians sacked Troy?
Fond done, done fond!
  Was this King Priam's joy?'
With that she sighed as she stood,
With that she sighed as she stood,
  And gave this sentence then:
'Among nine bad if one be good,
Among nine bad if one be good,
  There's yet one good in ten.'

Count. What, one good in ten? You corrupt the song, sirrah.

Clown. One good woman in ten, madam; which is a purifying o' th' song. Would God would serve the world so all the year! We'd find no fault with the tithe woman, if I were the parson. One in ten, quoth 'a? An we might have a good woman born but for every blazing star, or at an earthquake, 'twould mend the lottery well. A man may draw his heart out ere 'a pluck one.

Count. You'll be gone, sir knave, and do as I command you.

Clown. That man should be at woman's command, and yet no hurt done! Though honesty be no Puritan, yet it will do no hurt. It will wear the surplice of humility over the black gown of a big heart. I am going forsooth! The business is for Helen to come hither. *Exit.*

Count. Well now.

Stew. I know, madam, you love your gentlewoman entirely.

Count. Faith, I do. Her father bequeath'd her to me; and she herself, without other advantage, may lawfully make title to as much love as she finds. There is more owing her than is paid, and more shall be paid her than she'll demand.

Stew. Madam, I was very late more near her than I think she wish'd me. Alone she was, and did communicate to herself her own words to her own ears. She thought, I dare vow for her, they touch'd not any stranger sense. Her matter was, she loved your son. 'Fortune,' she said, 'was no goddess, that had put such difference betwixt their two estates; Love no god, that would not extend his might, only where qualities were level; Dian no queen of virgins, that would suffer her poor knight surpris'd without rescue in the first assault or ransom afterward.' This she deliver'd in the most bitter touch of sorrow that e'er I heard virgin exclaim in; which I held my duty speedily to acquaint you withal, sithence, in the loss that may happen, it concerns you something to know it.

Count. You have discharg'd this honestly. Keep it to yourself. Many likelihoods inform'd me of this before, which hung so tott'ring in the balance that I could neither believe nor misdoubt. Pray you leave me. Stall this in your bosom, and I thank you for your honest care. I will speak with you further anon.

Exit Steward.

Enter *Helen.*

Even so it was with me when I was young!
If ever we are nature's, these are ours. This thorn
Doth to our rose of youth rightly belong;
Our blood to us, this to our blood is born.
It is the show and seal of nature's truth
Where love's strong passion is impress'd in youth.
By our remembrances of days foregone,
Such were our faults, or then we thought them none.
Her eye is sick on't. I observe her now.

Hel. What is your pleasure, madam?

Count. You know, Helen,
I am a mother to you.

Hel. Mine honourable mistress.

Count. Nay, a mother.
Why not a mother? When I said 'a mother,'
Methought you saw a serpent. What's in 'mother'
That you start at it? I say I am your mother,
And put you in the catalogue of those
That were enwombed mine. 'Tis often seen
Adoption strives with nature, and choice breeds
A native slip to us from foreign seeds.
You ne'er oppress'd me with a mother's groan,
Yet I express to you a mother's care.
God's mercy, maiden! does it curd thy blood
To say I am thy mother? What's the matter,
That this distempered messenger of wet,
The many-colour'd Iris, rounds thine eye?
Why? that you are my daughter?

Hel. That I am not.

Count. I say I am your mother.

Hel. Pardon, madam.
The Count Rossillion cannot be my brother.
I am from humble, he from honoured name;
No note upon my parents, his all noble.
My master, my dear lord he is, and I
His servant live and will his vassal die.
He must not be my brother.

Count. Nor I your mother?

Hel. You are my mother, madam. Would you were
(So that my lord your son were not my brother)
Indeed my mother! or were you both our mothers,
I care no more for than I do for heaven,
So I were not his sister! Can't no other,
But, I your daughter, he must be my brother?

Count. Yes, Helen, you might be my daughter-in-law.
God shield you mean it not! 'daughter' and 'mother'
So strive upon your pulse. What, pale again?
My fear hath catch'd your fondness. Now I see
The myst'ry of your loneliness and find
Your salt tears' head. Now to all sense 'tis gross —
You love my son. Invention is asham'd,
Against the proclamation of thy passion,
To say thou dost not. Therefore tell me true!
But tell me then, 'tis so; for look! thy cheeks
Confess it, th' one to th' other; and thine eyes
See it so grossly shown in thy behaviours
That in their kind they speak it. Only sin
And hellish obstinacy tie thy tongue,
That truth should be suspected. Speak, is't so?
If it be so, you have wound a goodly clew;
If it be not, forswear 't. Howe'er, I charge thee,
As heaven shall work in me for thine avail,
To tell me truly.

Hel. Good madam, pardon me!

Count. Do you love my son?

Hel. Your pardon, noble mistress!

Count. Love you my son?

Hel. Do not you love him, madam?

Count. Go not about. My love hath in't a bond,
Whereof the world takes note. Come, come, disclose
The state of your affection, for your passions
Have to the full appeach'd.

Hel. Then I confess
Here on my knee before high heaven and you,

That before you, and next unto high heaven,
I love your son.
My friends were poor but honest; so's my love.
Be not offended, for it hurts not him
That he is lov'd of me. I follow him not
By any token of presumptuous suit;
Nor would I have him till I do deserve him,
Yet never know how that desert should be.
I know I love in vain, strive against hope;
Yet in this captious and intenible sieve
I still pour in the waters of my love
And lack not to lose still. Thus, Indian-like,
Religious in mine error, I adore
The sun, that looks upon his worshipper
But knows of him no more. My dearest madam,
Let not your hate encounter with my love
For loving where you do; but if yourself,
Whose aged honour cites a virtuous youth,
Did ever in so true a flame of liking
Wish chastely and love dearly that your Dian
Was both herself and Love, O, then give pity
To her whose state is such that cannot choose
But lend and give where she is sure to lose;
That seeks not to find that her search implies,
But, riddle-like, lives sweetly where she dies!

Count. Had you not lately an intent — speak truly —
To go to Paris?

Hel. Madam, I had.

Count. Wherefore? Tell true.

Hel. I will tell truth, by grace itself I swear!
You know my father left me some prescriptions
Of rare and prov'd effects, such as his reading
And manifest experience had collected
For general sovereignty; and that he will'd me
In heedfull'st reservation to bestow them,
As notes whose faculties inclusive were
More than they were in note. Amongst the rest
There is a remedy, approv'd, set down,
To cure the desperate languishings whereof
The King is render'd lost.

Count. This was your motive
For Paris, was it? Speak.

Hel. My lord your son made me to think of this;
Else Paris and the medicine and the King
Had from the conversation of my thoughts
Happily been absent then.

Count. But think you, Helen,
If you should tender your supposed aid,
He would receive it? He and his physicians
Are of a mind: he, that they cannot help him;
They, that they cannot help. How shall they credit
A poor unlearned virgin, when the schools,
Embowell'd of their doctrine, have left off
The danger to itself?

Hel. There's something in't
More than my father's skill, which was the great'st
Of his profession, that his good receipt
Shall for my legacy be sanctified
By th' luckiest stars in heaven: and, would your honour
But give me leave to try success, I'd venture
The well-lost life of mine on his Grace's cure
By such a day and hour.

Count. Dost thou believe 't?

Hel. Ay, madam, knowingly.

Count. Why, Helen, thou shalt have my leave and love,
Means and attendants, and my loving greetings
To those of mine in court. I'll stay at home
And pray God's blessing into thy attempt.
Be gone to-morrow; and be sure of this,
What I can help thee to, thou shalt not miss.

Exeunt.

ACT II. [Scene I. *Paris. The* King's *Palace.*]

Enter the *King* [attended], with divers young *Lords* taking leave for the Florentine war; [*Bertram*] *Count Rossillion,* and *Parolles.* Flourish cornets.

King. Farewell, young lords; these warlike principles
Do not throw from you. And you, my lords, farewell.
Share the advice betwixt you; if both gain all,
The gift doth stretch itself as 'tis receiv'd
And is enough for both.

1. Lord. 'Tis our hope, sir,
After well-ent'red soldiers, to return
And find your Grace in health.

King. No, no, it cannot be. And yet my heart
Will not confess he owes the malady
That doth my life besiege. Farewell, young lords.
Whether I live or die, be you the sons
Of worthy Frenchmen. Let higher Italy
(Those bated that inherit but the fall
Of the last monarchy) see that you come

Not to woo honour, but to wed it. When
The bravest questant shrinks, find what you seek,
That fame may cry you loud. I say, farewell.

2. Lord. Health at your bidding serve your Majesty!

King. Those girls of Italy, take heed of them.
They say our French lack language to deny
If they demand. Beware of being captives
Before you serve.

Both. Our hearts receive your warnings.

King. Farewell. [*To Attendants*] Come hither to me. [*Exit, led by Attendants.*]

1. Lord. O my sweet lord, that you will stay behind us!

Par. 'Tis not his fault, the spark.

2. Lord. O, 'tis brave wars!

Par. Most admirable. I have seen those wars.

Ber. I am commanded here and kept a coil with —
'Too young,' and 'The next year,' and ''Tis too early.'

Par. An thy mind stand to't, boy, steal away bravely.

Ber. I shall stay here the forehorse to a smock,
Creaking my shoes on the plain masonry,
Till honour be bought up, and no sword worn
But one to dance with. By heaven, I'll steal away!

1. Lord. There's honour in the theft.

Par. Commit it, Count.

2. Lord. I am your accessary; and so farewell.

Ber. I grow to you, and our parting is a tortur'd body.

1. Lord. Farewell, Captain.

2. Lord. Sweet Monsieur Parolles!

Par. Noble heroes, my sword and yours are kin. Good sparks and lustrous, a word, good metals: you shall find in the regiment of the Spinii one Captain Spurio, with his cicatrice, an emblem of war, here on his sinister cheek. It was this very sword entrench'd it. Say to him I live, and observe his reports for me.

1. Lord. We shall, noble Captain.

Par. Mars dote on you for his novices! [*Exeunt Lords.*]
What will ye do?

[Enter the *King*, led back to his chair by *Attendants.*]

Ber. Stay — the King!

Par. Use a more spacious ceremony to the noble lords. You have restrain'd yourself within the list of too cold an adieu. Be more expressive to them; for they wear themselves in the cap of the time, there do muster true gait; eat, speak, and move under the influence of the most receiv'd star; and though the devil lead the measure, such are to be followed. After them! and take a more dilated farewell.

Ber. And I will do so.

Par. Worthy fellows! and like to prove most sinewy swordmen.

Exeunt [*Bertram and Parolles*].

Enter *Lafew.*

Laf. [*kneels*] Pardon, my lord, for me and for my tidings!

King. I'll fee thee to stand up.

Laf. [*rises*] Then here's a man stands that has brought his pardon.
I would you had kneel'd, my lord, to ask me mercy,
And that at my bidding you could so stand up.

King. I would I had. So I had broke thy pate
And ask'd thee mercy for't.

Laf. Good faith, across! But, my good lord, 'tis thus:
Will you be cur'd of your infirmity?

King. No.

Laf. O, will you eat no grapes, my royal fox?
Yes, but you will my noble grapes, an if
My royal fox could reach them. I have seen a medicine
That's able to breathe life into a stone,
Quicken a rock, and make you dance canary
With sprightly fire and motion; whose simple touch
Is powerful to araise King Pepin, nay,
To give great Charlemaine a pen in's hand,
And write to her a love-line.

King. What her is this?

Laf. Why, Doctor She! My lord, there's one arriv'd,
If you will see her. Now by my faith and honour,
If seriously I may convey my thoughts
In this my light deliverance, I have spoke
With one that in her sex, her years, profession,
Wisdom and constancy, hath amaz'd me more
Than I dare blame my weakness. Will you see her,
For that is her demand, and know her business?
That done, laugh well at me.

King. Now, good Lafew,
Bring in the admiration, that we with thee
May spend our wonder too, or take off thine
By wond'ring how thou took'st it.

Laf. Nay, I'll fit you,
And not be all day neither. [*Exit.*]

King. Thus he his special nothing ever prologues.

Enter [*Lafew,* with] *Helen.*

Laf. Nay, come your ways!

King. This haste hath wings indeed.

Laf. Nay, come your ways!
This is his Majesty; say your mind to him.
A traitor you do look like, but such traitors
His Majesty seldom fears. I am Cressid's uncle,
That dare leave two together. Fare you well.
Exit.

King. Now, fair one, does your business follow us?

Hel. Ay, my good lord.
Gerard de Narbon was my father;
In what he did profess, well-found.

King. I knew him.

Hel. The rather will I spare my praises towards him;
Knowing him is enough. On 's bed of death
Many receipts he gave me; chiefly one,
Which, as the dearest issue of his practice,
And of his old experience th' only darling,
He bade me store up as a triple eye,
Safer than mine own two, more dear. I have so;
And hearing your high Majesty is touch'd
With that malignant cause wherein the honour
Of my dear father's gift stands chief in power,
I come to tender it, and my appliance,
With all bound humbleness.

King. We thank you, maiden;
But may not be so credulous of cure,
When our most learned doctors leave us, and
The congregated college have concluded
That labouring art can never ransom nature
From her inaidable estate. I say, we must not
So stain our judgment or corrupt our hope
To prostitute our past-cure malady
To empirics, or to dissever so
Our great self and our credit to esteem
A senseless help, when help past sense we deem.

Hel. My duty then shall pay me for my pains.
I will no more enforce mine office on you,
Humbly entreating from your royal thoughts
A modest one, to bear me back again.

King. I cannot give thee less, to be call'd grateful.
Thou thought'st to help me, and such thanks I give
As one near death to those that wish him live.
But what at full I know, thou know'st no part,
I knowing all my peril, thou no art.

Hel. What I can do can do no hurt to try,
Since you set up your rest 'gainst remedy.
He that of greatest works is finisher
Oft does them by the weakest minister.
So holy writ in babes hath judgment shown
When judges have been babes; great floods have flown
From simple sources, and great seas have dried
When miracles have by the greatest been denied.
Oft expectation fails, and most oft there
Where most it promises; and oft it hits
Where hope is coldest and despair most fits.

King. I must not hear thee. Fare thee well, kind maid!
Thy pains, not us'd, must by thyself be paid;
Proffers not took reap thanks for their reward.

Hel. Inspired merit so by breath is barr'd.
It is not so with him that all things knows
As 'tis with us that square our guess by shows;
But most it is presumption in us when
The help of heaven we count the act of men.
Dear sir, to my endeavours give consent;
Of heaven, not me, make an experiment.
I am not an impostor that proclaim
Myself against the level of mine aim;
But know I think, and think I know most sure,
My art is not past power, nor you past cure.

King. Art thou so confident? Within what space
Hop'st thou my cure?

Hel. The great'st grace lending grace,
Ere twice the horses of the sun shall bring
Their fiery torcher his diurnal ring,
Ere twice in murk and occidental damp
Moist Hesperus hath quench'd his sleepy lamp,
Or four-and-twenty times the pilot's glass
Hath told the thievish minutes how they pass,
What is infirm from your sound parts shall fly,
Health shall live free, and sickness freely die.

King. Upon thy certainty and confidence
What dar'st thou venture?

Hel. Tax of impudence,
A strumpet's boldness, a divulged shame
Traduc'd by odious ballads; my maiden's name
Sear'd otherwise; nay, worst of worst extended,
With vilest torture let my life be ended.

King. Methinks in thee some blessed spirit doth speak
His powerful sound within an organ weak;
And what impossibility would slay
In common sense, sense saves another way.
Thy life is dear; for all that life can rate
Worth name of life in thee hath estimate —
Youth, beauty, wisdom, courage, all

That happiness and prime can happy call:
Thou this to hazard needs must intimate
Skill infinite, or monstrous desperate.
Sweet practiser, thy physic I will try,
That ministers thine own death if I die.

Hel. If I break time or flinch in property
Of what I spoke, unpitied let me die;
And well deserv'd. Not helping, death 's my fee;
But if I help, what do you promise me?

King. Make thy demand.

Hel. But will you make it even?

King. Ay, by my sceptre and my hopes of heaven.

Hel. Then shalt thou give me with thy kingly hand
What husband in thy power I will command.
Exempted be from me the arrogance
To choose from forth the royal blood of France,
My low and humble name to propagate
With any branch or image of thy state;
But such a one, thy vassal, whom I know
Is free for me to ask, thee to bestow.

King. Here is my hand. The premises observ'd,
Thy will by my performance shall be serv'd.
So make the choice of thy own time; for I,
Thy resolv'd patient, on thee still rely.
More should I question thee, and more I must,
Though more to know could not be more to trust —
From whence thou cam'st, how tended on. But rest
Unquestion'd welcome, and undoubted blest.
Give me some help here, ho! — If thou proceed
As high as word, my deed shall match thy deed.

Flourish. Exeunt.

[Scene II. *Rossillion. The* Count's *Palace.*]

Enter *Countess* and *Clown.*

Count. Come on, sir; I shall now put you to the height of your breeding.

Clown. I will show myself highly fed and lowly taught. I know my business is but to the court.

Count. To the court? Why, what place make you special, when you put off that with such contempt? But to the court?

Clown. Truly, madam, if God have lent a man any manners, he may easily put it off at court. He that cannot make a leg, put off's cap, kiss his hand, and say nothing, has neither leg, hands, lip, nor cap; and indeed such a fellow, to say precisely, were not for the court; but for me, I have an answer will serve all men.

Count. Marry, that's a bountiful answer that fits all questions.

Clown. It is like a barber's chair, that fits all buttocks — the pin buttock, the quatch buttock, the brawn buttock, or any buttock.

Count. Will your answer serve fit to all questions?

Clown. As fit as ten groats is for the hand of an attorney, as your French crown for your taffety punk, as Tib's rush for Tom's forefinger, as a pancake for Shrove Tuesday, a morris for May Day, as the nail to his hole, the cuckold to his horn, as a scolding quean to a wrangling knave, as the nun's lip to the friar's mouth, nay, as the pudding to his skin.

Count. Have you, I say, an answer of such fitness for all questions?

Clown. From below your duke to beneath your constable, it will fit any question.

Count. It must be an answer of most monstrous size that must fit all demands.

Clown. But a trifle neither, in good faith, if the learned should speak truth of it. Here it is, and all that belongs to't. Ask me if I am a courtier. It shall do you no harm to learn.

Count. To be young again, if we could! I will be a fool in question, hoping to be the wiser by your answer. I pray you, sir, are you a courtier?

Clown. O Lord, sir! — There's a simple putting off. More, more! a hundred of them!

Count. Sir, I am a poor friend of yours, that loves you.

Clown. O Lord, sir! — Thick, thick, spare not me!

Count. I think, sir, you can eat none of this homely meat.

Clown. O Lord, sir! — Nay, put me to't, I warrant you.

Count. You were lately whipp'd, sir, as I think.

Clown. O Lord, sir! — Spare not me.

Count. Do you cry, 'O Lord, sir!' at your whipping, and 'Spare not me'? Indeed, your 'O Lord, sir!' is very sequent to your whipping. You would answer very well to a whipping, if you were but bound to't.

Clown. I ne'er had worse luck in my life in my 'O Lord, sir!' I see things may serve long, but not serve ever.

Count. I play the noble housewife with the time
To entertain it so merrily with a fool.

Clown. O Lord, sir! — Why, there't serves well again.

Count. An end, sir! To your business. Give Helen this,
And urge her to a present answer back;
Commend me to my kinsmen and my son.
This is not much.

Clown. Not much commendation to them?

Count. Not much employment for you. You understand me?

Clown. Most fruitfully. I am there before my legs.

Count. Haste you again. *Exeunt.*

[Scene III. *Paris. The* King's *Palace.*]

Enter *Count* [*Bertram*], *Lafew,* and *Parolles.*

Laf. They say miracles are past, and we have our philosophical persons, to make modern and familiar, things supernatural and causeless. Hence is it that we make trifles of terrors, ensconcing ourselves into seeming knowledge when we should submit ourselves to an unknown fear.

Par. Why, 'tis the rarest argument of wonder that hath shot out in our latter times.

Ber. And so 'tis.

Laf. To be relinquish'd of the artists —

Par. So I say.

Laf. Both of Galen and Paracelsus —

Par. So I say.

Laf. Of all the learned and authentic fellows —

Par. Right! So I say.

Laf. That gave him out incurable —

Par. Why, there 'tis! so say I too.

Laf. Not to be help'd —

Par. Right! as 'twere a man assured of a —

Laf. Uncertain life, and sure death.

Par. Just! you say well. So would I have said.

Laf. I may truly say it is a novelty to the world.

Par. It is indeed. If you will have it in showing, you shall read it in What-do-ye-call there.

Laf. A showing of a heavenly effect in an earthly actor.

Par. That's it I would have said, the very same.

Laf. Why, your dolphin is not lustier. Fore me, I speak in respect

Par. Nay, 'tis strange, 'tis very strange! that is the brief and the tedious of it; and he's of a most facinerious spirit that will not acknowledge it to be the —

Laf. Very hand of heaven —

Par. Ay, so I say.

Laf. In a most weak —

Par. And debile minister, great power, great transcendence; which should, indeed, give us a further use to be made than alone the recov'ry of the King, as to be —

Laf. Generally thankful.

Enter *King, Helen,* and *Attendants.*

Par. I would have said it! you say well. Here comes the King.

Laf. Lustick! as the Dutchman says. I'll like a maid the better whilst I have a tooth in my head. Why, he's able to lead her a coranto.

Par. Mort du vinaigre! Is not this Helen?

Laf. Fore God, I think so.

King. Go call before me all the lords in court. [*Exit an Attendant.*]
Sit, my preserver, by thy patient's side
And with this healthful hand whose banish'd sense
Thou hast repeal'd, a second time receive
The confirmation of my promis'd gift,
Which but attends thy naming.

Enter three or four *Lords.*

Fair maid, send forth thine eye. This youthful parcel
Of noble bachelors stand at my bestowing,
O'er whom both sovereign power and father's voice
I have to use. Thy frank election make.
Thou hast power to choose, and they none to forsake.

Hel. To each of you one fair and virtuous mistress
Fall, when Love please! Marry, to each but one!

Laf. [*aside*] I'd give bay Curtal and his furniture
My mouth no more were broken than these boys'
And writ as little beard.

King. Peruse them well.
Not one of those but had a noble father.

Hel. Gentlemen,
Heaven hath through me restor'd the King to health.

All. We understand it, and thank heaven for you.

Hel. I am a simple maid, and therein wealthiest

That I protest I simply am a maid.
Please it your Majesty, I have done already.
The blushes in my cheeks thus whisper me,
'We blush that thou shouldst choose; but be refus'd,
Let the white death sit on thy cheek for ever,
We'll ne'er come there again.'

King. Make choice and see —
Who shuns thy love shuns all his love in me.

Hel. Now, Dian, from thy altar do I fly,
And to imperial Love, that god most high,
Do my sighs stream.

She addresses her to a Lord.

Sir, will you hear my suit?

1. Lord. And grant it.

Hel. Thanks, sir. All the rest is mute.

Laf. [*aside*] I had rather be in this choice than throw ames-ace for my life.

Hel. [*to another*] The honour, sir, that flames in your fair eyes,
Before I speak, too threat'ningly replies.
Love make your fortunes twenty times above
Her that so wishes and her humble love!

2. Lord. No better, if you please.

Hel. My wish receive,
Which great Love grant! and so I take my leave.

Laf. [*aside*] Do all they deny her? An they were sons of mine, I'd have them whipp'd, or I would send them to th' Turk to make eunuchs of.

Hel. [*to a third*] Be not afraid that I your hand should take;
I'll never do you wrong for your own sake.
Blessing upon your vows! and in your bed
Find fairer fortune, if you ever wed!

Laf. [*aside*] These boys are boys of ice; they'll none have her. Sure they are bastards to the English; the French ne'er got 'em.

Hel. [*to a fourth*] You are too young, too happy, and too good
To make yourself a son out of my blood.

4. Lord. Fair one, I think not so.

Laf. [*aside*] There's one grape yet; I am sure thy father drunk wine. But if thou be'st not an ass, I am a youth of fourteen. I have known thee already.

Hel. [*to Bertram*] I dare not say I take you; but I give
Me and my service, ever whilst I live,
Into your guiding power. — This is the man.

King. Why then, young Bertram, take her; she's thy wife.

Ber. My wife, my liege? I shall beseech your Highness,
In such a business give me leave to use
The help of mine own eyes.

King. Know'st thou not, Bertram,
What she has done for me?

Ber. Yes, my good lord;
But never hope to know why I should marry her.

King. Thou know'st she has rais'd me from my sickly bed.

Ber. But follows it, my lord, to bring me down
Must answer for your raising? I know her well.
She had her breeding at my father's charge.
A poor physician's daughter my wife? Disdain
Rather corrupt me ever!

King. 'Tis only title thou disdain'st in her, the which
I can build up. Strange is it that our bloods,
Of colour, weight, and heat, pour'd all together,
Would quite confound distinction, yet stand off
In differences so mighty. If she be
All that is virtuous — save what thou dislik'st,
A poor physician's daughter — thou dislik'st
Of virtue for the name. But do not so.
From lowest place when virtuous things proceed,
The place is dignified by th' doer's deed.
Where great additions swell's, and virtue none,
It is a dropsied honour. Good alone
Is good without a name; vileness is so:
The property by what it is should go,
Not by the title. She is young, wise, fair;
In these to nature she's immediate heir;
And these breed honour. That is honour's scorn
Which challenges itself as honour's born
And is not like the sire. Honours thrive
When rather from our acts we them derive
Than our foregoers. The mere word's a slave,
Debosh'd on every tomb, on every grave
A lying trophy; and as oft is dumb
Where dust and damn'd oblivion is the tomb
Of honour'd bones indeed. What should be said?
If thou canst like this creature as a maid,
I can create the rest. Virtue and she
Is her own dower; honour and wealth from me.

Ber. I cannot love her, nor will strive to do't.

King. Thou wrong'st thyself if thou shouldst strive to choose.

Hel. That you are well restor'd, my lord, I'm glad.
Let the rest go.

King. My honour's at the stake; which to defeat,
I must produce my power. Here, take her hand,

Proud scornful boy, unworthy this good gift,
That dost in vile misprision shackle up
My love and her desert; that canst not dream
We, poising us in her defective scale,
Shall weigh thee to the beam; that wilt not know,
It is in us to plant thine honour where
We please to have it grow. Check thy contempt.
Obey our will, which travails in thy good.
Believe not thy disdain, but presently
Do thine own fortunes that obedient right
Which both thy duty owes and our power claims;
Or I will throw thee from my care for ever
Into the staggers and the careless lapse
Of youth and ignorance; both my revenge and hate
Loosing upon thee in the name of justice,
Without all terms of pity. Speak! thine answer!

Ber. Pardon, my gracious lord! for I submit
My fancy to your eyes. When I consider
What great creation and what dole of honour
Flies where you bid it, I find that she which late
Was in my nobler thoughts most base, is now
The praised of the King, who, so ennobled,
Is as 'twere born so.

King. Take her by the hand,
And tell her she is thine; to whom I promise
A counterpoise, if not to thy estate
A balance more replete.

Ber. I take her hand.

King. Good fortune and the favour of the King
Smile upon this contract, whose ceremony
Shall seem expedient on the now-born brief
And be perform'd to-night. The solemn feast
Shall more attend upon the coming space,
Expecting absent friends. As thou lov'st her,
Thy love's to me religious; else, does err.

Exeunt.

Parolles and Lafew stay behind, commenting of this wedding.

Laf. Do you hear, monsieur? A word with you.

Par. Your pleasure, sir?

Laf. Your lord and master did well to make his recantation.

Par. Recantation? My lord? my master?

Laf. Ay. Is it not a language I speak?

Par. A most harsh one, and not to be understood without bloody succeeding. My master?

Laf. Are you companion to the Count Rossillion?

Par. To any count! to all counts! to what is man!

Laf. To what is count's man; count's master is of another style.

Par. You are too old, sir. Let it satisfy you, you are too old.

Laf. I must tell thee, sirrah, I write Man; to which title age cannot bring thee.

Par. What I dare too well do, I dare not do.

Laf. I did think thee, for two ordinaries, to be a pretty wise fellow; thou didst make tolerable vent of thy travel, it might pass. Yet the scarfs and the bannerets about thee did manifoldly dissuade me from believing thee a vessel of too great a burthen. I have now found thee; when I lose thee again, I care not. Yet art thou good for nothing but taking up; and that thou'rt scarce worth.

Par. Hadst thou not the privilege of antiquity upon thee —

Laf. Do not plunge thyself too far in anger, lest thou hasten thy trial; which if — Lord have mercy on thee for a hen! So, my good window of lattice, fare thee well. Thy casement I need not open, for I look through thee. Give me thy hand.

Par. My lord, you give me most egregious indignity.

Laf. Ay, with all my heart! and thou art worthy of it.

Par. I have not, my lord, deserv'd it.

Laf. Yes, good faith, ev'ry dram of it, and I will not bate thee a scruple.

Par. Well, I shall be wiser.

Laf. Ev'n as soon as thou canst, for thou hast to pull at a smack o' th' contrary. If ever thou be'st bound in thy scarf and beaten, thou shalt find what it is to be proud of thy bondage. I have a desire to hold my acquaintance with thee, or rather my knowledge, that I may say in the default, 'He is a man I know.'

Par. My lord, you do me most insupportable vexation.

Laf. I would it were hell pains for thy sake, and my poor doing eternal; for doing I am past, as I will by thee, in what motion age will give me leave. *Exit.*

Par. Well, thou hast a son shall take this disgrace off me, scurvy, old, filthy, scurvy lord! Well, I must be patient; there is no fettering of authority. I'll beat him, by my life, if I can meet him with any convenience, an he were double and double a lord. I'll have no more pity of his age than I would have of — I'll beat him, an if I could but meet him again.

Enter *Lafew*.

Laf. Sirrah, your lord and master's married; there's news for you. You have a new mistress.

Par. I most unfeignedly beseech your lordship to make some reservation of your wrongs. He is my good lord; whom I serve above is my master.

Laf. Who? God?

Par. Ay, sir.

Laf. The devil it is that's thy master. Why dost thou garter up thy arms o' this fashion? Dost make hose of thy sleeves? Do other servants so? Thou wert best set thy lower part where thy nose stands. By mine honour, if I were but two hours younger, I'd beat thee. Methink'st thou art a general offence, and every man should beat thee. I think thou wast created for men to breathe themselves upon thee.

Par. This is hard and undeserved measure, my lord.

Laf. Go to, sir! You were beaten in Italy for picking a kernel out of a pomegranate. You are a vagabond, and no true traveller. You are more saucy with lords and honourable personages than the commission of your birth and virtue gives you heraldry. You are not worth another word, else I'd call you knave. I leave you. *Exit*.

Enter [*Bertram*] *Count Rossillion*.

Par. Good, very good! It is so then. Good, very good! Let it be conceal'd awhile.

Ber. Undone, and forfeited to cares for ever!

Par. What's the matter, sweetheart?

Ber. Although before the solemn priest I have sworn,
I will not bed her.

Par. What? what, sweetheart?

Ber. O my Parolles, they have married me!
I'll to the Tuscan wars, and never bed her.

Par. France is a dog-hole, and it no more merits
The tread of a man's foot. To th' wars!

Ber. There's letters from my mother. What th' import is,
I know not yet.

Par. Ay, that would be known. To th' wars, my boy, to th' wars!
He wears his honour in a box unseen
That hugs his kicky-wicky here at home,
Spending his manly marrow in her arms,
Which should sustain the bound and high curvet
Of Mars's fiery steed. To other regions!
France is a stable; we that dwell in't jades.
Therefore, to th' wars!

Ber. It shall be so. I'll send her to my house,
Acquaint my mother with my hate to her,
And wherefore I am fled; write to the King
That which I durst not speak. His present gift
Shall furnish me to those Italian fields
Where noble fellows strike. War is no strife
To the dark house and the detested wife.

Par. Will this caprichio hold in thee? art sure?

Ber. Go with me to my chamber and advise me.
I'll send her straight away. To-morrow
I'll to the wars, she to her single sorrow.

Par. Why, these balls bound! there's noise in it! 'Tis hard:
A young man married is a man that's marr'd.
Therefore away, and leave her bravely, go!
The King has done you wrong; but hush! 'tis so. *Exeunt*.

[Scene IV. *Paris*. *The* King's *Palace*.]

Enter *Helena* and *Clown*.

Hel. My mother greets me kindly. Is she well?

Clown. She is not well, but yet she has her health. She's very merry, but yet she is not well. But thanks be given, she's very well and wants nothing i' th' world. But yet she is not well.

Hel. If she be very well, what does she ail that she's not very well?

Clown. Truly she's very well indeed, but for two things.

Hel. What two things?

Clown. One, that she's not in heaven, whither God send her quickly! the other, that she's in earth, from whence God send her quickly!

Enter *Parolles*.

Par. Bless you, my fortunate lady!

Hel. I hope, sir, I have your good will to have mine own good fortunes.

Par. You had my prayers to lead them on; and to keep them on, have them still. O my knave, how does my old lady?

Clown. So that you had her wrinkles and I her money, I would she did as you say.

Par. Why, I say nothing.

Clown. Marry, you are the wiser man; for many a man's tongue shakes out his master's undoing. To say nothing, to do nothing, to know nothing, and to have nothing, is to be a great part of your title, which is within a very little of nothing.

Par. Away! th'art a knave!

Clown. You should have said, sir, 'Before a knave th'art a knave'; that's 'Before me th'art a knave.' This had been truth, sir.

Par. Go to, thou art a witty fool! I have found thee.

Clown. Did you find me in yourself, sir, or were you taught to find me? The search, sir, was profitable; and much fool may you find in you, even to the world's pleasure and the increase of laughter.

Par. A good knave, i' faith, and well fed!
Madam, my lord will go away to-night;
A very serious business calls on him.
The great prerogative and rite of love,
Which, as your due, time claims, he does acknowledge;
But puts it off to a compell'd restraint;
Whose want, and whose delay, is strew'd with sweets,
Which they distil now in the curbed time,
To make the coming hour o'erflow with joy
And pleasure drown the brim.

Hel. What's his will else?

Par. That you will take your instant leave o' th' King
And make this haste as your own good proceeding,
Strength'ned with what apology you think
May make it probable need.

Hel. What more commands he?

Par. That, having this obtain'd, you presently
Attend his further pleasure.

Hel. In everything I wait upon his will.

Par. I shall report it so.

Hel. I pray you.

Exit Parolles.

Come, sirrah.

Exeunt.

[Scene V. *Paris. The* King's *Palace.*]

Enter *Lafew* and *Bertram.*

Laf. But I hope your lordship thinks not him a soldier.

Ber. Yes, my lord, and of very valiant approof.

Laf. You have it from his own deliverance.

Ber. And by other warranted testimony.

Laf. Then my dial goes not true. I took this lark for a bunting.

Ber. I do assure you, my lord, he is very great in knowledge and accordingly valiant.

Laf. I have then sinn'd against his experience and transgress'd against his valour; and my state that way is dangerous, since I cannot yet find in my heart to repent.

Enter *Parolles.*

Here he comes. I pray you make us friends; I will pursue the amity.

Par. [*to Bertram*] These things shall be done, sir.

Laf. Pray you, sir, who's his tailor?

Par. Sir?

Laf. O, I know him well, I, sir. He, sir, 's a good workman, a very good tailor.

Ber. [*aside to Parolles*] Is she gone to the King?

Par. She is.

Ber. Will she away to-night?

Par. As you'll have her.

Ber. I have writ my letters, casketed my treasure,
Given order for our horses, and to-night,
When I should take possession of the bride,
End ere I do begin.

Laf. A good traveller is something at the latter end of a dinner; but one that lies three thirds and uses a known truth to pass a thousand nothings with, should be once heard and thrice beaten. God save you, Captain.

Ber. Is there any unkindness between my lord and you, monsieur?

Par. I know not how I have deserved to run into my lord's displeasure.

Laf. You have made shift to run into't, boots and spurs and all, like him that leapt into the custard; and out of it you'll run again rather than suffer question for your residence.

Ber. It may be you have mistaken him, my lord.

Laf. And shall do so ever, though I took him at 's prayers. Fare you well, my lord; and believe this of me, there can be no kernel in this light nut. The soul of this man is his clothes. Trust him not in matter of heavy consequence. I have kept of them tame and know their natures. — Farewell, monsieur. I have spoken better of you than you have or will to deserve at my hand; but we must do good against evil.

[*Exit.*]

Par. An idle lord, I swear.

Ber. I think so.

Par. Why, do you not know him?

Ber. Yes, I do know him well, and common speech
Gives him a worthy pass.

Enter *Helena*.

Here comes my clog.
Hel. I have, sir, as I was commanded from you,
Spoke with the King, and have procur'd his leave
For present parting. Only he desires
Some private speech with you.
Ber. I shall obey his will.
You must not marvel, Helen, at my course,
Which holds not colour with the time, nor does
The ministration and required office
On my particular. Prepar'd I was not
For such a business; therefore am I found
So much unsettled. This drives me to entreat you
That presently you take your way for home,
And rather muse than ask why I entreat you;
For my respects are better than they seem,
And my appointments have in them a need
Greater than shows itself at the first view
To you that know them not. This to my mother: [*Gives a letter.*]
'Twill be two days ere I shall see you. So
I leave you to your wisdom.
Hel. Sir, I can nothing say
But that I am your most obedient servant.
Ber. Come, come, no more of that!
Hel. And ever shall
With true observance seek to eke out that
Wherein toward me my homely stars have fail'd
To equal my great fortune.
Ber. Let that go!
My haste is very great. Farewell, hie home.
Hel. Pray, sir, your pardon.
Ber. Well, what would you say?
Hel. I am not worthy of the wealth I owe,
Nor dare I say 'tis mine; and yet it is —
But, like a timorous thief, most fain would steal
What law does vouch mine own.
Ber. What would you have?
Hel. Something, and scarce so much; nothing, indeed.
I would not tell you what I would, my lord.
Faith, yes!
Strangers and foes do sunder, and not kiss.
Ber. I pray you stay not, but in haste to horse!
Hel. I shall not break your bidding, good my lord.
Ber. Where are my other men, monsieur? Farewell.
Go thou toward home — *Exit* [*Helena*].
where I will never come
Whilst I can shake my sword or hear the drum.
Away, and for our flight!
Par. Bravely, coragio!
[*Exeunt.*]

ACT III. [Scene I. *Florence. The* Duke's *Palace.*]

Flourish. Enter the *Duke of Florence*, the two *Frenchmen*, with a *Troop of Soldiers.*

Duke. So that from point to point now have you heard
The fundamental reasons of this war,
Whose great decision hath much blood let forth,
And more thirsts after.
1. Lord. Holy seems the quarrel
Upon your Grace's part, black and fearful
On the opposer.
Duke. Therefore we marvel much our cousin France
Would in so just a business shut his bosom
Against our borrowing prayers.
2. Lord. Good my lord,
The reasons of our state I cannot yield
But like a common and an outward man
That the great figure of a council frames
By self-unable motion; therefore dare not
Say what I think of it, since I have found
Myself in my incertain grounds to fail
As often as I guess'd.
Duke. Be it his pleasure.
1. Lord. But I am sure the younger of our nature,
That surfeit on their ease, will day by day
Come here for physic.
Duke. Welcome shall they be,
And all the honours that can fly from us
Shall on them settle. You know your places well.
When better fall, for your avails they fell:
To-morrow to th' field.
Flourish. [*Exeunt.*]

[Scene II. *Rossillion. The* Count's *Palace.*]

Enter *Countess* and *Clown.*

Count. It hath happen'd all as I would have had it, save that he comes not along with her.

Clown. By my troth, I take my young lord to be a very melancholy man.

Count. By what observance, I pray you?

Clown. Why, he will look upon his boot, and sing; mend the ruff, and sing; ask questions, and sing; pick his teeth, and sing. I know a man that had this trick of melancholy sold a goodly manor for a song.

Count. Let me see what he writes, and when he means to come. [*Opens a letter.*]

Clown. I have no mind to Isbel since I was at court. Our old ling and our Isbels o' th' country are nothing like your old ling and your Isbels o' th' court. The brains of my Cupid's knock'd out, and I begin to love, as an old man loves money, with no stomach.

Count. What have we here?

Clown. E'en that you have there. *Exit.*

[*Countess reads*] *a letter.* 'I have sent you a daughter-in-law. She hath recovered the King, and undone me. I have wedded her, not bedded her; and sworn to make the "not" eternal. You shall hear I am run away. Know it before the report come. If there be breadth enough in the world, I will hold a long distance. My duty to you.

'Your unfortunate son,

'BERTRAM.'

This is not well, rash and unbridled boy,
To fly the favours of so good a king,
To pluck his indignation on thy head
By the misprizing of a maid too virtuous
For the contempt of empire.

Enter *Clown.*

Clown. O madam, yonder is heavy news within between two soldiers and my young lady!

Count. What is the matter?

Clown. Nay, there is some comfort in the news, some comfort. Your son will not be kill'd so soon as I thought he would.

Count. Why should he be kill'd?

Clown. So say I, madam, if he run away, as I hear he does. The danger is in standing to't; that's the loss of men, though it be the getting of children. Here they come will tell you more. For my part, I only hear your son was run away. [*Exit.*]

Enter *Helen* and [the] two [French] *Gentlemen.*

2. Lord. Save you, good madam.

Hel. Madam, my lord is gone, for ever gone!

1. Lord. Do not say so.

Count. Think upon patience. Pray you, gentlemen—
I have felt so many quirks of joy and grief
That the first face of neither on the start
Can woman me unto't. Where is my son, I pray you?

1. Lord. Madam, he's gone to serve the Duke of Florence.
We met him thitherward; for thence we came,
And, after some dispatch in hand at court,
Thither we bend again.

Hel. Look on his letter, madam. Here's my passport.

[*Reads*] 'When thou canst get the ring upon my finger which never shall come off, and show me a child begotten of thy body that I am father to, then call me husband; but in such a "then" I write a "never."'

This is a dreadful sentence.

Count. Brought you this letter, gentlemen?

1. Lord. Ay, madam,
And for the contents' sake are sorry for our pains.

Count. I prithee, lady, have a better cheer.
If thou engrossest all the griefs are thine,
Thou robb'st me of a moiety. He was my son;
But I do wash his name out of my blood,
And thou art all my child. Towards Florence is he?

1. Lord. Ay, madam.

Count. And to be a soldier?

1. Lord. Such is his noble purpose; and believe't,
The Duke will lay upon him all the honour
That good convenience claims.

Count. Return you thither?

2. Lord. Ay, madam, with the swiftest wing of speed.

Hel. [*reads*] 'Till I have no wife, I have nothing in France.'
'Tis bitter.

Count. Find you that there?

Hel. Ay, madam.

2. Lord. 'Tis but the boldness of his hand haply, which his heart was not consenting to.

Count. Nothing in France until he have no wife!
There's nothing here that is too good for him
But only she; and she deserves a lord
That twenty such rude boys might tend upon

And call her hourly mistress. Who was with him?
2. Lord. A servant only, and a gentleman
Which I have sometime known.
Count. Parolles, was it not?
2. Lord. Ay, my good lady, he.
Count. A very tainted fellow, and full of wickedness.
My son corrupts a well-derived nature
With his inducement.
2. Lord. Indeed, good lady,
The fellow has a deal of that too-much
Which holds him much to have.
Count. Y'are welcome, gentlemen.
I will entreat you, when you see my son,
To tell him that his sword can never win
The honour that he loses. More I'll entreat you
Written to bear along.
1. Lord. We serve you, madam,
In that and all your worthiest affairs.
Count. Not so, but as we change our courtesies.
Will you draw near?
Exit [*with the Gentlemen*].
Hel. 'Till I have no wife I have nothing in France.'
Nothing in France until he has no wife!
Thou shalt have none, Rossillion, none in France;
Then hast thou all again. Poor lord! is't I
That chase thee from thy country and expose
Those tender limbs of thine to the event
Of the none-sparing war? And is it I
That drive thee from the sportive court, where thou
Wast shot at with fair eyes, to be the mark
Of smoky muskets? O you leaden messengers
That ride upon the violent speed of fire,
Fly with false aim! move the still-piecing air,
That sings with piercing! do not touch my lord!
Whoever shoots at him, I set him there;
Whoever charges on his forward breast,
I am the caitiff that do hold him to't,
And though I kill him not, I am the cause
His death was so effected. Better 'twere
I met the ravin lion when he roar'd
With sharp constraint of hunger; better 'twere
That all the miseries which nature owes
Were mine at once. No! come thou home, Rossillion,
Whence honour but of danger wins a scar,
As oft it loses all. I will be gone.
My being here it is that holds thee hence.
Shall I stay here to do't? No, no, although
The air of paradise did fan the house
And angels offic'd all! I will be gone,
That pitiful rumour may report my flight
To consolate thine ear. Come, night! end, day!
For with the dark (poor thief) I'll steal away.
Exit.

[Scene III. *Florence. Before the* Duke's *Palace.*]

Flourish. Enter the *Duke of Florence, Bertram, Drum* and *Trumpets, Soldiers, Parolles.*

Duke. The General of our Horse thou art; and we,
Great in our hope, lay our best love and credence
Upon thy promising fortune.
Ber. Sir, it is
A charge too heavy for my strength; but yet
We'll strive to bear it for your worthy sake
To th' extreme edge of hazard.
Duke. Then go thou forth,
And Fortune play upon thy prosperous helm
As thy auspicious mistress!
Ber. This very day,
Great Mars, I put myself into thy file.
Make me but like my thoughts, and I shall prove
A lover of thy drum, hater of love.
Exeunt omnes.

[Scene IV. *Rossillion. The* Count's *Palace.*]

Enter *Countess* and *Steward.*

Count. Alas! and would you take the letter of her?
Might you not know she would do as she has done
By sending me a letter? Read it again.
[*Steward reads the*] *letter.*

'I am Saint Jaques' pilgrim, thither gone.
Ambitious love hath so in me offended
That barefoot plod I the cold ground upon
With sainted vow my faults to have amended.
Write, write, that from the bloody course of war
My dearest master, your dear son, may hie!
Bless him at home in peace, whilst I from far
His name with zealous fervour sanctify.
His taken labours bid him me forgive.
I, his despiteful Juno, sent him forth
From courtly friends, with camping foes to live,
Where death and danger dogs the heels of worth.
He is too good and fair for death and me;
Whom I myself embrace to set him free.'

Count. Ah, what sharp stings are in her mildest words!
Rinaldo, you did never lack advice so much
As letting her pass so. Had I spoke with her,
I could have well diverted her intents,
Which thus she hath prevented.
Stew. Pardon me, madam.
If I had given you this at overnight,
She might have been o'erta'en; and yet she writes
Pursuit would be but vain.
Count. What angel shall
Bless this unworthy husband? He cannot thrive
Unless her prayers, whom heaven delights to hear
And loves to grant, reprieve him from the wrath
Of greatest justice. Write, write, Rinaldo,
To this unworthy husband of his wife.
Let every word weigh heavy of her worth
That he does weigh too light. My greatest grief,
Though little he do feel it, set down sharply.
Dispatch the most convenient messenger.
When haply he shall hear that she is gone,
He will return; and hope I may that she,
Hearing so much, will speed her foot again,
Led hither by pure love. Which of them both
Is dearest to me, I have no skill in sense
To make distinction. Provide this messenger.
My heart is heavy, and mine age is weak.
Grief would have tears, and sorrow bids me speak. *Exeunt.*

[Scene V. *Without the walls of Florence.*]

A tucket afar off. Enter old *Widow* of Florence, her Daughter [*Diana*], *Violenta,* and *Mariana,* with other *Citizens.*

Wid. Nay, come; for if they do approach the city, we shall lose all the sight.

Dia. They say the French count has done most honourable service.

Wid. It is reported that he has taken their great'st commander, and that with his own hand he slew the Duke's brother. [*Tucket.*] We have lost our labour; they are gone a contrary way. Hark! you may know by their trumpets.

Mar. Come, let's return again and suffice ourselves with the report of it. Well, Diana, take heed of this French earl. The honour of a maid is her name, and no legacy is so rich as honesty.

Wid. I have told my neighbour how you have been solicited by a gentleman his companion.

Mar. I know that knave, hang him! one Parolles. A filthy officer he is in those suggestions for the young earl. Beware of them, Diana. Their promises, enticements, oaths, tokens, and all these engines of lust, are not the things they go under. Many a maid hath been seduced by them; and the misery is, example, that so terrible shows in the wrack of maidenhood, cannot for all that dissuade succession but that they are limed with the twigs that threaten them. I hope I need not to advise you further; but I hope your own grace will keep you where you are, though there were no further danger known but the modesty which is so lost.

Dia. You shall not need to fear me.

Enter *Helen,* [like a pilgrim].

Wid. I hope so. Look, here comes a pilgrim. I know she will lie at my house. Thither they send one another. I'll question her.
God save you, pilgrim! Whither are you bound?
Hel. To Saint Jaques le Grand.
Where do the palmers lodge, I do beseech you?
Wid. At the Saint Francis here, beside the port.
Hel. Is this the way?
Wid. Ay, marry, is't. *A march afar.*
Hark you! they come this way.
If you will tarry, holy pilgrim,
But till the troops come by,
I will conduct you where you shall be lodg'd,
The rather for I think I know your hostess
As ample as myself.
Hel. Is it yourself?
Wid. If you shall please so, pilgrim.
Hel. I thank you and will stay upon your leisure.
Wid. You came, I think, from France?
Hel. I did so.
Wid. Here you shall see a countryman of yours
That has done worthy service.
Hel. His name, I pray you?
Dia. The Count Rossillion. Know you such a one?
Hel. But by the ear, that hears most nobly of him;
His face I know not.
Dia. Whatsome'er he is,
He's bravely taken here. He stole from France,
As 'tis reported, for the King had married him
Against his liking. Think you it is so?

Hel. Ay, surely, mere the truth. I know his lady.
Dia. There is a gentleman that serves the Count
Reports but coarsely of her.
Hel. What's his name?
Dia. Monsieur Parolles.
Hel. O, I believe with him,
In argument of praise, or to the worth
Of the great Count himself, she is too mean
To have her name repeated. All her deserving
Is a reserved honesty, and that
I have not heard examin'd.
Dia. Alas, poor lady!
'Tis a hard bondage to become the wife
Of a detesting lord.
Wid. I write, good creature, wheresoe'er she is,
Her heart weighs sadly. This young maid might do her
A shrewd turn, if she pleas'd.
Hel. How do you mean?
May be the amorous Count solicits her
In the unlawful purpose.
Wid. He does indeed!
And brokes with all that can in such a suit
Corrupt the tender honour of a maid;
But she is arm'd for him, and keeps her guard
In honestest defence.

Drum and Colours.

Enter [*Bertram*] *Count Rossillion, Parolles,* and the whole *Army.*

Mar. The gods forbid else!
Wid. So, now they come.
That is Antonio, the Duke's eldest son;
That, Escalus.
Hel. Which is the Frenchman?
Dia. He!
That with the plume. 'Tis a most gallant fellow.
I would he lov'd his wife. If he were honester,
He were much goodlier. Is't not a handsome gentleman?
Hel. I like him well.
Dia. 'Tis pity he is not honest. Yond's that same knave
That leads him to these places. Were I his lady,
I would poison that vile rascal.
Hel. Which is he?
Dia. That jackanapes with scarfs. Why is he melancholy?
Hel. Perchance he's hurt i' th' battle.
Par. Lose our drum? well.
Mar. He's shrewdly vex'd at something. Look, he has spied us.
Wid. Marry, hang you!
Mar. And your courtesy, for a ring-carrier!
Exeunt [*Bertram, Parolles, and Army*].
Wid. The troop is past. Come, pilgrim, I will bring you
Where you shall host. Of enjoin'd penitents
There's four or five, to Great Saint Jaques bound,
Already at my house.
Hel. I humbly thank you.
Please it this matron and this gentle maid
To eat with us to-night, the charge and thanking
Shall be for me; and, to require you further,
I will bestow some precepts of this virgin
Worthy the note.
Both. We'll take your offer kindly.
Exeunt.

[Scene VI. *Camp before Florence.*]

Enter [*Bertram*] *Count Rossillion* and the *Frenchmen,* as at first.

2. Lord. Nay, good my lord, put him to't. Let him have his way.

1. Lord. If your lordship find him not a hilding, hold me no more in your respect.

2. Lord. On my life, my lord, a bubble!

Ber. Do you think I am so far deceived in him?

2. Lord. Believe it, my lord, in mine own direct knowledge, without any malice, but to speak of him as my kinsman, he's a most notable coward, an infinite and endless liar, an hourly promise-breaker, the owner of no one good quality worthy your lordship's entertainment.

1. Lord. It were fit you knew him, lest, reposing too far in his virtue, which he hath not, he might at some great and trusty business in a main danger fail you.

Ber. I would I knew in what particular action to try him.

1. Lord. None better than to let him fetch off his drum, which you hear him so confidently undertake to do.

2. Lord. I with a troop of Florentines will suddenly surprise him. Such I will have whom I am sure he knows not from the enemy. We will bind and hoodwink him so that he shall suppose no other but that he is carried into the leaguer of the adversaries when we bring him to our own tents. Be but your lordship present at his examination. If he do not, for the promise of his life and in the highest compulsion of base fear, offer to betray you and deliver all the intelligence in his power against you, and that with the divine forfeit of his soul upon oath, never trust my judgment in anything.

1. Lord. O, for the love of laughter, let him fetch his drum! He says he has a stratagem for't. When your lordship sees the bottom of his success in't, and to what metal this counterfeit lump of ore will be melted, if you give him not John Drum's entertainment, your inclining cannot be removed. Here he comes.

Enter *Parolles.*

2. Lord. O, for the love of laughter, hinder not the honour of his design! Let him fetch off his drum in any hand.

Ber. How now, monsieur? This drum sticks sorely in your disposition.

1. Lord. A pox on't, let it go! 'tis but a drum.

Par. But a drum? Is't but a drum? A drum so lost! There was excellent command — to charge in with our horse upon our own wings and to rend our own soldiers!

1. Lord. That was not to be blam'd in the command of the service. It was a disaster of war that Cæsar himself could not have prevented, if he had been there to command.

Ber. Well, we cannot greatly condemn our success. Some dishonour we had in the loss of that drum; but it is not to be recovered.

Par. It might have been recovered.

Ber. It might, but it is not now.

Par. It is to be recovered. But that the merit of service is seldom attributed to the true and exact performer, I would have that drum or another, or *hic jacet*!

Ber. Why, if you have a stomach, to't, monsieur! If you think your mystery in stratagem can bring this instrument of honour again into his native quarter, be magnanimous in the enterprise and go on. I will grace the attempt for a worthy exploit. If you speed well in it, the Duke shall both speak of it and extend to you what further becomes his greatness, even to the utmost syllable of your worthiness.

Par. By the hand of a soldier, I will undertake it.

Ber. But you must not now slumber in it.

Par. I'll about it this evening; and I will presently pen down my dilemmas, encourage myself in my certainty, put myself into my mortal preparation; and by midnight look to hear further from me.

Ber. May I be bold to acquaint his Grace you are gone about it?

Par. I know not what the success will be, my lord, but the attempt I vow.

Ber. I know th'art valiant, and to the possibility of thy soldiership will subscribe for thee. Farewell.

Par. I love not many words. *Exit.*

2. Lord. No more than a fish loves water. Is not this a strange fellow, my lord, that so confidently seems to undertake this business, which he knows is not to be done; damns himself to do, and dares better be damn'd than to do't?

1. Lord. You do not know him, my lord, as we do. Certain it is that he will steal himself into a man's favour and for a week escape a great deal of discoveries; but when you find him out, you have him ever after.

Ber. Why, do you think he will make no deed at all of this that so seriously he does address himself unto?

2. Lord. None in the world; but return with an invention, and clap upon you two or three probable lies. But we have almost emboss'd him. You shall see his fall to-night; for indeed he is not for your lordship's respect.

1. Lord. We'll make you some sport with the fox ere we case him. He was first smok'd by the old Lord Lafew. When his disguise and he is parted, tell me what a sprat you shall find him; which you shall see this very night.

2. Lord. I must go look my twigs. He shall be caught.

Ber. Your brother, he shall go along with me.

2. Lord. As 't please your lordship. I'll leave you. [*Exit.*]

Ber. Now will I lead you to the house and show you
The lass I spoke of.

1. Lord. But you say she's honest.

Ber. That's all the fault. I spoke with her but once,
And found her wondrous cold; but I sent to her,
By this same coxcomb that we have i' th' wind,
Tokens and letters, which she did resend;
And this is all I have done. She's a fair creature.
Will you go see her?

1. Lord. With all my heart, my lord.

Exeunt.

[Scene VII. *Florence. The* Widow's *house.*]

Enter *Helen* and *Widow.*

Hel. If you misdoubt me that I am not she,
I know not how I shall assure you further
But I shall lose the grounds I work upon.

Wid. Though my estate be fall'n, I was well born,
Nothing acquainted with these businesses,
And would not put my reputation now
In any staining act.

Hel. Nor would I wish you.
First give me trust the Count he is my husband,
And what to your sworn counsel I have spoken
Is so from word to word; and then you cannot,
By the good aid that I of you shall borrow,
Err in bestowing it.

Wid. I should believe you,
For you have show'd me that which well approves
Y'are great in fortune.

Hel. Take this purse of gold,
And let me buy your friendly help thus far,
Which I will overpay and pay again
When I have found it. The Count he wooes your daughter,
Lays down his wanton siege before her beauty,
Resolv'd to carry her. Let her in fine consent,
As we'll direct her how 'tis best to bear it.
Now his important blood will naught deny
That she'll demand. A ring the County wears
That downward hath succeeded in his house
From son to son some four or five descents
Since the first father wore it. This ring he holds
In most rich choice; yet in his idle fire,
To buy his will, it would not seem too dear,
Howe'er repented after.

Wid. Now I see
The bottom of your purpose.

Hel. You see it lawful then. It is no more
But that your daughter, ere she seems as won,
Desires this ring; appoints him an encounter;
In fine, delivers me to fill the time,
Herself most chastely absent. After this,
To marry her, I'll add three thousand crowns
To what is pass'd already.

Wid. I have yielded.
Instruct my daughter how she shall persever,
That time and place with this deceit so lawful
May prove coherent. Every night he comes
With musics of all sorts, and songs compos'd
To her unworthiness. It nothing steads us
To chide him from our eaves, for he persists
As if his life lay on't.

Hel. Why then, to-night
Let us assay our plot; which, if it speed,
Is wicked meaning in a lawful deed,
And lawful meaning in a wicked act,
Where both not sin, and yet a sinful fact.
But let's about it. [*Exeunt.*]

ACT IV. [Scene I. *Without the Florentine camp.*]

Enter one of the *Frenchmen,* [the *Second Lord,*] with five or six other *Soldiers,* in ambush.

2. Lord. He can come no other way but by this hedge corner. When you sally upon him, speak what terrible language you will. Though you understand it not yourselves, no matter; for we must not seem to understand him, unless some one among us, whom we must produce for an interpreter.

1. Sold. Good Captain, let me be th' interpreter.

2. Lord. Art not acquainted with him? Knows he not thy voice?

1. Sold. No, sir, I warrant you.

2. Lord. But what linsey-woolsey hast thou to speak to us again?

1. Sold. E'en such as you speak to me.

2. Lord. He must think us some band of strangers i' th' adversary's entertainment. Now he hath a smack of all neighbouring languages. Therefore we must every one be a man of his own fancy, not to know what we speak one to another. So we seem to know, is to know straight our purpose. Choughs' language — gabble enough, and good enough. As for you, interpreter, you must seem very politic. But couch, ho! Here he comes, to beguile two hours in a sleep, and then to return and swear the lies he forges. [*They hide.*]

Enter *Parolles.*

Par. Ten o'clock. Within these three hours 'twill be time enough to go home. What shall I say I have done? It must be a very plausive invention that carries it. They begin to smoke me, and disgraces have of late knock'd too often at my door. I find my tongue is too foolhardy; but my heart hath the fear of Mars before it, and of his creatures, not daring the reports of my tongue.

2. Lord. This is the first truth that e'er thine own tongue was guilty of.

Par. What the devil should move me to undertake the recovery of this drum, being not ignorant of the impossibility, and knowing I had no such purpose? I must give myself some hurts and say I got them in exploit. Yet slight ones will not carry it. They will say, 'Came you off with so little?' And great ones I dare not give. Wherefore, what's the instance? Tongue, I must put you into a butter-woman's mouth, and buy myself another of Bajazet's mule, if you prattle me into these perils.

2. Lord. Is it possible he should know what he is, and be that he is?

Par. I would the cutting of my garments would serve the turn, or the breaking of my Spanish sword.

2. Lord. We cannot afford you so.

Par. Or the baring of my beard, and to say it was in stratagem.

2. Lord. 'Twould not do.

Par. Or to drown my clothes, and say I was stripp'd.

2. Lord. Hardly serve.

Par. Though I swore I leapt from the window of the citadel —

2. Lord. How deep?

Par. Thirty fadom.

2. Lord. Three great oaths would scarce make that be believed.

Par. I would I had any drum of the enemy's. I would swear I recover'd it.

2. Lord. You shall hear one anon.

Alarum within.

Par. A drum now of the enemy's!

2. Lord. Throca movousus, cargo, cargo, cargo.

All. Cargo, cargo, cargo, villianda par corbo, cargo.

Par. O, ransom, ransom! Do not hide mine eyes. [*They hoodwink him.*]

[*1. Sold. as*] *Interpreter. Boskos thromuldo boskos.*

Par. I know you are the Muskos' regiment,
And I shall lose my life for want of language.
If there be here German, or Dane, Low Dutch,
Italian, or French, let him speak to me.
I'll discover that which shall undo the Florentine.

Interp. Boskos vauvado.
I understand thee, and can speak thy tongue.
Kerelybonto. Sir,
Betake thee to thy faith, for seventeen poniards
Are at thy bosom.

Par. O!

Interp. O, pray, pray, pray!
Manka revania dulche.

2. Lord. Oscorbidulchos volivorco.

Interp. The General is content to spare thee yet,
And, hoodwink'd as thou art, will lead thee on
To gather from thee. Haply thou mayst inform
Something to save thy life.

Par. O, let me live!
And all the secrets of our camp I'll show,
Their force, their purposes. Nay, I'll speak that
Which you will wonder at.

Interp. But wilt thou faithfully?

Par. If I do not, damn me.

Interp. Acordo linta.
Come on. Thou art granted space.

Exit [*with Parolles*]. *A short alarum within.*

2. Lord. Go tell the Count Rossillion and my brother
We have caught the woodcock and will keep him muffled
Till we do hear from them.

2. Sold. Captain, I will.

2. Lord. 'A will betray us all unto ourselves.
Inform on that.

2. Sold. So I will, sir.

2. Lord. Till then I'll keep him dark and safely lock'd. *Exeunt.*

[Scene II. *Florence. The* Widow's *house.*]

Enter *Bertram* and the Maid called *Diana.*

Ber. They told me that your name was Fontibell.

Dia. No, my good lord, Diana.

Ber. Titled goddess!
And worth it with addition! But, fair soul,
In your fine frame hath love no quality?
If the quick fire of youth light not your mind,
You are no maiden, but a monument.
When you are dead you should be such a one
As you are now; for you are cold and stern,
And now you should be as your mother was
When your sweet self was got.

Dia. She then was honest.

Ber. So should you be.

Dia. No.
My mother did but duty; such, my lord,
As you owe to your wife.

Ber. No more o' that!
I prithee do not strive against my vows.
I was compell'd to her, but I love thee
By love's own sweet constraint, and will for ever
Do thee all rights of service.
Dia. Ay, so you serve us
Till we serve you; but when you have our roses,
You barely leave our thorns to prick ourselves
And mock us with our bareness.
Ber. How have I sworn!
Dia. 'Tis not the many oaths that makes the truth,
But the plain single vow that is vow'd true.
What is not holy, that we swear not by,
But take the High'st to witness. Then pray you tell me,
If I should swear by Jove's great attributes
I lov'd you dearly, would you believe my oaths
When I did love you ill? This has no holding,
To swear by Him whom I protest to love,
That I will work against Him. Therefore your oaths
Are words and poor conditions, but unseal'd —
At least, in my opinion.
Ber. Change it, change it!
Be not so holy-cruel. Love is holy,
And my integrity ne'er knew the crafts
That you do charge men with. Stand no more off,
But give thyself unto my sick desires,
Who then recover. Say thou art mine, and ever
My love, as it begins, shall so persever.
Dia. I see that men make ropes in such a scarre,
That we'll forsake ourselves. Give me that ring.
Ber. I'll lend it thee, my dear, but have no power
To give it from me.
Dia. Will you not, my lord?
Ber. It is an honour 'longing to our house,
Bequeathed down from many ancestors,
Which were the greatest obloquy i' th' world
In me to lose.
Dia. Mine honour's such a ring;
My chastity's the jewel of our house,
Bequeathed down from many ancestors,
Which were the greatest obloquy i' th' world
In me to lose. Thus your own proper wisdom
Brings in the champion Honour on my part
Against your vain assault.
Ber. Here, take my ring!
My house, mine honour, yea, my life, be thine,
And I'll be bid by thee.
Dia. When midnight comes, knock at my chamber window.
I'll order take my mother shall not hear.
Now will I charge you in the band of truth,
When you have conquer'd my yet maiden bed,
Remain there but an hour, nor speak to me.
My reasons are most strong, and you shall know them
When back again this ring shall be deliver'd.
And on your finger in the night I'll put
Another ring, that what in time proceeds
May token to the future our past deeds.
Adieu till then! then fail not. You have won
A wife of me, though there my hope be done.
Ber. A heaven on earth I have won by wooing thee! [*Exit.*]
Dia. For which live long to thank both heaven and me!
You may so in the end.
My mother told me just how he would woo,
As if she sat in 's heart. She says all men
Have the like oaths. He has sworn to marry me
When his wife's dead. Therefore I'll lie with him
When I am buried. Since Frenchmen are so braid,
Marry that will, I live and die a maid.
Only, in this disguise I think't no sin
To cozen him that would unjustly win. *Exit.*

[Scene III. *The Florentine camp.*]

Enter the two *French Captains* and some two or three *Soldiers.*

2. Lord. You have not given him his mother's letter?

1. Lord. I have deliv'red it an hour since. There is something in't that stings his nature; for on the reading it he chang'd almost into another man.

2. Lord. He has much worthy blame laid upon him for shaking off so good a wife and so sweet a lady.

1. Lord. Especially he hath incurred the everlasting displeasure of the King, who had even tun'd his bounty to sing happiness to him. I will tell you a thing, but you shall let it dwell darkly with you.

2. Lord. When you have spoken it, 'tis dead, and I am the grave of it.

1. Lord. He hath perverted a young gentlewoman here in Florence, of a most chaste renown; and this night he fleshes his will in the spoil of her honour. He hath given her his monumental ring, and thinks himself made in the unchaste composition.

2. Lord. Now God delay our rebellion! As we are ourselves, what things are we!

1. Lord. Merely our own traitors. And as, in the common course of all treasons, we still see them reveal themselves till they attain to their abhorr'd ends, so he that in this action contrives against his own nobility, in his proper stream o'erflows himself.

2. Lord. Is it not meant damnable in us, to be trumpeters of our unlawful intents? We shall not then have his company to-night?

1. Lord. Not till after midnight, for he is dieted to his hour.

2. Lord. That approaches apace. I would gladly have him see his company anatomiz'd, that he might take a measure of his own judgments, wherein so curiously he had set this counterfeit.

1. Lord. We will not meddle with him till he come; for his presence must be the whip of the other.

2. Lord. In the meantime, what hear you of these wars?

1. Lord. I hear there is an overture of peace.

2. Lord. Nay, I assure you, a peace concluded.

1. Lord. What will Count Rossillion do then? Will he travel higher or return again into France?

2. Lord. I perceive by this demand you are not altogether of his council.

1. Lord. Let it be forbid, sir! So should I be a great deal of his act.

2. Lord. Sir, his wife some two months since fled from his house. Her pretence is a pilgrimage to Saint Jaques le Grand; which holy undertaking with most austere sanctimony she accomplish'd; and there residing, the tenderness of her nature became as a prey to her grief; in fine, made a groan of her last breath, and now she sings in heaven.

1. Lord. How is this justified?

2. Lord. The stronger part of it by her own letters, which makes her story true, even to the point of her death. Her death itself, which could not be her office to say is come, was faithfully confirm'd by the rector of the place.

1. Lord. Hath the Count all this intelligence?

2. Lord. Ay, and the particular confirmations, point from point, to the full arming of the verity.

1. Lord. I am heartily sorry that he'll be glad of this.

2. Lord. How mightily sometimes we make us comforts of our losses!

1. Lord. And how mightily some other times we drown our gain in tears! The great dignity that his valour hath here acquir'd for him shall at home be encount'red with a shame as ample.

2. Lord. The web of our life is of a mingled yarn, good and ill together. Our virtues would be proud if our faults whipp'd them not, and our crimes would despair if they were not cherish'd by our virtues.

Enter a [*Servant* as] *Messenger.*

How now? Where's your master?

Serv. He met the Duke in the street, sir, of whom he hath taken a solemn leave. His lordship will next morning for France. The Duke hath offered him letters of commendations to the King. [*Exit.*]

2. Lord. They shall be no more than needful there, if they were more than they can commend.

Enter [*Bertram*] *Count Rossillion.*

1. Lord. They cannot be too sweet for the King's tartness. Here's his lordship now. How now, my lord! Is't not after midnight?

Ber. I have to-night dispatch'd sixteen businesses, a month's length apiece, by an abstract of success. I have congied with the Duke, done my adieu with his nearest, buried a wife, mourn'd for her, writ to my lady mother I am returning, entertain'd my convoy, and between these main parcels of dispatch effected many nicer needs. The last was the greatest, but that I have not ended yet.

2. Lord. If the business be of any difficulty, and this morning your departure hence, it requires haste of your lordship.

Ber. I mean the business is not ended, as fearing to hear of it hereafter. But shall we have this dialogue between the Fool and the Soldier? Come, bring forth this counterfeit module has deceiv'd me like a double-meaning prophesier.

2. Lord. Bring him forth. [*Exeunt Soldiers.*] Has sat i' th' stocks all night, poor gallant knave.

Ber. No matter. His heels have deserv'd it, in usurping his spurs so long. How does he carry himself?

2. Lord. I have told your lordship already: the stocks carry him. But to answer you as you would be understood, he weeps like a wench that had shed her milk. He hath confess'd himself to Morgan, whom he supposes to be a friar, from the time of his remembrance to this very instant disaster of his setting i' th' stocks. And what think you he hath confess'd?

Ber. Nothing of me, has 'a?

2. Lord. His confession is taken, and it shall be read to his face. If your lordship be in't, as I believe you are, you must have the patience to hear it.

Enter *Parolles* with his *Interpreter.*

Ber. A plague upon him! muffled? He can say nothing of me.

1. Lord. Hush, hush! Hoodman comes! *Portotartarossa.*

Interp. He calls for the tortures. What will you say without 'em?

Par. I will confess what I know without constraint. If ye pinch me like a pasty, I can say no more.

Interp. Bosko chimurcho.

1. Lord. Boblibindo chicurmurco.

Interp. You are a merciful general. Our General bids you answer to what I shall ask you out of a note.

Par. And truly, as I hope to live!

Interp. [*reads*] 'First demand of him how many horse the Duke is strong.' What say you to that?

Par. Five or six thousand, but very weak and unserviceable. The troops are all scattered, and the commanders very poor rogues, upon my reputation and credit, and as I hope to live.

Interp. Shall I set down your answer so?

Par. Do. I'll take the sacrament on't, how and which way you will.

Ber. All's one to him. What a past-saving slave is this!

1. Lord. Y'are deceiv'd, my lord. This is Monsieur Parolles, the gallant militarist (that was his own phrase) that had the whole theoric of war in the knot of his scarf, and the practice in the chape of his dagger.

2. Lord. I will never trust a man again for keeping his sword clean, nor believe he can have everything in him by wearing his apparel neatly.

Interp. Well, that's set down.

Par. 'Five or six thousand horse,' I said — I will say true — 'or thereabouts' set down, for I'll speak truth.

1. Lord. He's very near the truth in this.

Ber. But I con him no thanks for't, in the nature he delivers it.

Par. 'Poor rogues,' I pray you say.

Interp. Well, that's set down.

Par. I humbly thank you, sir. A truth's a truth — the rogues are marvellous poor.

Interp. [*reads*] 'Demand of him of what strength they are afoot.' What say you to that?

Par. By my troth, sir, if I were to live this present hour, I will tell true. Let me see: Spurio, a hundred and fifty; Sebastian, so many; Corambus, so many; Jaques, so many; Guiltian, Cosmo, Lodowick, and Gratii, two hundred fifty each; mine own company, Chitopher, Vaumond, Bentii, two hundred fifty each; so that the muster file, rotten and sound, upon my life, amounts not to fifteen thousand poll, half of the which dare not shake the snow from off their cassocks, lest they shake themselves to pieces.

Ber. What shall be done to him?

1. Lord. Nothing, but let him have thanks. Demand of him my condition, and what credit I have with the Duke.

Interp. Well, that's set down. [*Reads*] 'You shall demand of him whether one Captain Dumain be i' th' camp, a Frenchman; what his reputation is with the Duke; what his valour, honesty, and expertness in wars; or whether he thinks it were not possible, with well-weighing sums of gold, to corrupt him to a revolt.' What say you to this? What do you know of it?

Par. I beseech you let me answer to the particular of the inter'gatories. Demand them singly.

Interp. Do you know this Captain Dumain?

Par. I know him. 'A was a botcher's prentice in Paris, from whence he was whipp'd for getting the shrieve's fool with child — a dumb innocent, that could not say him nay.

[*First Lord makes as if to strike him.*]

Ber. Nay, by your leave, hold your hands, though I know his brains are forfeit to the next tile that falls.

Interp. Well, is this captain in the Duke of Florence's camp?

Par. Upon my knowledge he is, and lousy.

1. Lord. Nay, look not so upon me. We shall hear of your lordship anon.

Interp. What is his reputation with the Duke?

Par. The Duke knows him for no other but a poor officer of mine, and writ to me this other day to turn him out o' th' band. I think I have his letter in my pocket.

Interp. Marry, we'll search.

Par. In good sadness, I do not know. Either it is there, or it is upon a file with the Duke's other letters in my tent.

Interp. Here 'tis; here's a paper. Shall I read it to you?

Par. I do not know if it be it or no.

Ber. Our interpreter does it well.

1. Lord. Excellently.

Interp. [*reads*]

'Dian, the Count 's a fool, and full of gold.'

Par. That is not the Duke's letter, sir. That is an advertisement to a proper maid in Florence, one Diana, to take heed of the allurement of one Count Rossillion, a foolish idle boy; but for all that very ruttish. I pray you, sir, put it up again.

Interp. Nay, I'll read it first, by your favour.

Par. My meaning in't, I protest, was very honest in the behalf of the maid; for I knew the young Count to be a dangerous and lascivious boy, who is a whale to virginity, and devours up all the fry it finds.

Ber. Damnable both-sides rogue!

Interp. [*reads*]

'When he swears oaths, bid him drop gold, and take it:
After he scores, he never pays the score.
Half won is match well made; match, and well make it;
He ne'er pays after-debts, take it before;
And say a soldier, Dian, told thee this;
Men are to mell with, boys are not to kiss:
For count of this, the Count's a fool, I know it,
Who pays before, but not when he does owe it.

'Thine, as he vow'd to thee in thine ear,
'PAROLLES.'

Ber. He shall be whipp'd through the army with this rhyme in 's forehead.

2. Lord. This is your devoted friend, sir, the manifold linguist and the armipotent soldier.

Ber. I could endure anything before but a cat, and now he's a cat to me.

Interp. I perceive, sir, by the General's looks, we shall be fain to hang you.

Par. My life, sir, in any case! Not that I am afraid to die; but that, my offences being many, I would repent out the remainder of nature. Let me live, sir, in a dungeon, i' th' stocks, or anywhere, so I may live.

Interp. We'll see what may be done, so you confess freely. Therefore, once more to this Captain Dumain! You have answer'd to his reputation with the Duke and to his valour. What is his honesty?

Par. He will steal, sir, an egg out of a cloister. For rapes and ravishments he parallels Nessus. He professes not keeping of oaths; in breaking 'em he is stronger than Hercules. He will lie, sir, with such volubility that you would think truth were a fool. Drunkenness is his best virtue, for he will be swine-drunk, and in his sleep he does little harm, save to his bedclothes about him; but they know his conditions and lay him in straw. I have but little more to say, sir, of his honesty. He has everything that an honest man should not have; what an honest man should have, he has nothing.

1. Lord. I begin to love him for this.

Ber. For this description of thine honesty? A pox upon him for me! he's more and more a cat.

Interp. What say you to his expertness in war?

Par. Faith, sir, has led the drum before the English tragedians. To belie him I will not, and more of his soldiership I know not, except in that country he had the honour to be the officer at a place there called Mile-end, to instruct for the doubling of files. I would do the man what honour I can, but of this I am not certain.

1. Lord. He hath out-villain'd villany so far that the rarity redeems him.

Ber. A pox on him! he's a cat still.

Interp. His qualities being at this poor price, I need not to ask you if gold will corrupt him to revolt.

Par. Sir, for a cardecue he will sell the fee simple of his salvation, the inheritance of it, and cut th' entail from all remainders, and a perpetual succession for it perpetually.

Interp. What's his brother, the other Captain Dumain?

2. Lord. Why does he ask him of me?

Interp. What's he?

Par. E'en a crow o' th' same nest; not altogether so great as the first in goodness, but greater a great deal in evil. He excels his brother for a coward; yet his brother is reputed one of the best that is. In a retreat he outruns any lackey; marry, in coming on he has the cramp.

Interp. If your life be saved, will you undertake to betray the Florentine?

Par. Ay, and the Captain of his Horse, Count Rossillion.

Interp. I'll whisper with the General and know his pleasure.

Par. [*aside*] I'll no more drumming; a plague of all drums! Only to seem to deserve well, and to beguile the supposition of that lascivious young boy the Count, have I run into this danger. Yet who would have suspected an ambush where I was taken?

Interp. There is no remedy, sir, but you must die. The General says, you that have so traitorously discover'd the secrets of your army, and made such pestiferous reports of men very nobly held, can serve the world for no honest use; therefore you must die. Come, headsman, off with his head!

Par. O Lord, sir, let me live, or let me see my death!

Interp. That shall you, and take your leave of all your friends. [*Unmuffles him.*]
So, look about you. Know you any here?

Ber. Good morrow, noble Captain.

2. Lord. God bless you, Captain Parolles!

1. Lord. God save you, noble Captain!

2. Lord. Captain, what greeting will you to my Lord Lafew? I am for France.

1. Lord. Good Captain, will you give me a copy of the sonnet you writ to Diana in behalf of the Count Rossillion? An I were not a very coward, I'd compel it of you. But fare you well.
Exeunt [*Bertram and Lords*].

Interp. You are undone, Captain, all but your scarf; that has a knot on't yet.

Par. Who cannot be crush'd with a plot?

Interp. If you could find out a country where but women were that had received so much shame, you might begin an impudent nation. Fare ye well, sir. I am for France too. We shall speak of you there. *Exit* [*with Soldiers*].

Par. Yet am I thankful. If my heart were great,
'Twould burst at this. Captain I'll be no more;
But I will eat, and drink, and sleep as soft
As captain shall. Simply the thing I am
Shall make me live. Who knows himself a braggart,
Let him fear this; for it will come to pass
That every braggart shall be found an ass.
Rust, sword! cool, blushes! and, Parolles, live
Safest in shame! Being fool'd, by fool'ry thrive!
There's place and means for every man alive.
I'll after them. *Exit.*

[Scene IV. *Florence. The* Widow's *house.*]

Enter *Helen, Widow,* and *Diana.*

Hel. That you may well perceive I have not wrong'd you,
One of the greatest in the Christian world
Shall be my surety; fore whose throne 'tis needful,
Ere I can perfect mine intents, to kneel.
Time was I did him a desired office,
Dear almost as his life; which gratitude
Through flinty Tartar's bosom would peep forth
And answer thanks. I duly am inform'd
His Grace is at Marseilles, to which place
We have convenient convoy. You must know
I am supposed dead. The army breaking,
My husband hies him home, where, heaven aiding,
And by the leave of my good lord the King,
We'll be before our welcome.

Wid. Gentle madam,
You never had a servant to whose trust
Your business was more welcome.

Hel. Nor you, mistress,
Ever a friend whose thoughts more truly labour
To recompense your love. Doubt not but heaven
Hath brought me up to be your daughter's dower,
As it hath fated her to be my motive
And helper to a husband. But, O strange men!
That can such sweet use make of what they hate,
When saucy trusting of the cozen'd thoughts
Defiles the pitchy night! So lust doth play
With what it loathes, for that which is away.
But more of this hereafter. You, Diana,
Under my poor instructions yet must suffer
Something in my behalf.

Dia. Let death and honesty
Go with your impositions, I am yours
Upon your will to suffer.

Hel. Yet, I pray you!
But with the word the time will bring on summer,
When briers shall have leaves as well as thorns
And be as sweet as sharp. We must away;
Our wagon is prepar'd, and time revives us.
All's well that ends well. Still the fine's the crown.
Whate'er the course, the end is the renown.
Exeunt.

[Scene V. *Rossillion. The* Count's *Palace.*]

Enter *Clown, Old Lady* [*Countess*], and *Lafew.*

Laf. No, no, no! your son was misled with a snipt-taffeta fellow there, whose villanous saffron would have made all the unbak'd and doughy youth of a nation in his colour. Your daughter-in-law had been alive at this hour, and your son here at home, more advanc'd by the King than by that red-tail'd humblebee I speak of.

Count. I would I had not known him! It was

the death of the most virtuous gentlewoman that ever nature had praise for creating. If she had partaken of my flesh and cost me the dearest groans of a mother, I could not have owed her a more rooted love.

Laf. 'Twas a good lady, 'twas a good lady. We may pick a thousand sallets ere we light on such another herb.

Clown. Indeed, sir, she was the sweet marjoram of the sallet, or rather, the herb of grace.

Laf. They are not sallet herbs, you knave; they are nose herbs.

Clown. I am no great Nebuchadnezzar, sir; I have not much skill in grass.

Laf. Whether dost thou profess thyself — a knave or a fool?

Clown. A fool, sir, at a woman's service, and a knave at a man's.

Laf. Your distinction?

Clown. I would cozen the man of his wife and do his service.

Laf. So you were a knave at his service indeed.

Clown. And I would give his wife my bauble, sir, to do her service.

Laf. I will subscribe for thee, thou art both knave and fool.

Clown. At your service.

Laf. No, no, no!

Clown. Why, sir, if I cannot serve you, I can serve as great a prince as you are.

Laf. Who's that? a Frenchman?

Clown. Faith, sir, 'a has an English name; but his fisnomy is more hotter in France than there.

Laf. What prince is that?

Clown. The Black Prince, sir, alias the Prince of Darkness, alias the devil.

Laf. Hold thee, there's my purse. I give thee not this to suggest thee from thy master thou talk'st of. Serve him still.

Clown. I am a woodland fellow, sir, that always loved a great fire; and the master I speak of ever keeps a good fire. But sure he is the prince of the world; let his nobility remain in 's court. I am for the house with the narrow gate, which I take to be too little for pomp to enter. Some that humble themselves may; but the many will be too chill and tender, and they'll be for the flow'ry way that leads to the broad gate and the great fire.

Laf. Go thy ways, I begin to be aweary of thee; and I tell thee so before, because I would not fall out with thee. Go thy ways. Let my horses be well look'd to without any tricks.

Clown. If I put any tricks upon 'em, sir, they shall be jades' tricks, which are their own right by the law of nature. *Exit.*

Laf. A shrewd knave and an unhappy.

Count. So 'a is. My lord that's gone made himself much sport out of him. By his authority he remains here, which he thinks is a patent for his sauciness; and indeed he has no pace, but runs where he will.

Laf. I like him well; 'tis not amiss. And I was about to tell you, since I heard of the good lady's death, and that my lord your son was upon his return home, I moved the King my master to speak in the behalf of my daughter; which, in the minority of them both, his Majesty out of a self-gracious remembrance did first propose. His Highness hath promis'd me to do it; and to stop up the displeasure he hath conceived against your son there is no fitter matter. How does your ladyship like it?

Count. With very much content, my lord, and I wish it happily effected.

Laf. His Highness comes post from Marseilles, of as able body as when he number'd thirty; 'a will be here to-morrow, or I am deceiv'd by him that in such intelligence hath seldom fail'd.

Count. It rejoices me that I hope I shall see him ere I die. I have letters that my son will be here to-night. I shall beseech your lordship to remain with me till they meet together.

Laf. Madam, I was thinking with what manners I might safely be admitted.

Count. You need but plead your honourable privilege.

Laf. Lady, of that I have made a bold charter; but I thank my God it holds yet.

Enter *Clown.*

Clown. O madam, yonder's my lord your son with a patch of velvet on 's face. Whether there be a scar under't or no, the velvet knows; but 'tis a goodly patch of velvet. His left cheek is a cheek of two pile and a half, but his right cheek is worn bare.

Laf. A scar nobly got, or a noble scar, is a good liv'ry of honour. So belike is that.

Clown. But it is your carbonado'd face.

Laf. Let us go see your son, I pray you. I long to talk with the young noble soldier.

Clown. Faith, there's a dozen of 'em, with delicate fine hats, and most courteous feathers, which bow the head and nod at every man.

Exeunt.

ACT V. [Scene I. *Marseilles. A street.*]

Enter *Helen, Widow,* and *Diana,* with two *Attendants.*

Hel. But this exceeding posting day and night
Must wear your spirits low; we cannot help it.
But, since you have made the days and nights as one,
To wear your gentle limbs in my affairs,
Be bold you do so grow in my requital
As nothing can unroot you.

Enter a *Gentleman,* a stranger.

In happy time
This man may help me to his Majesty's ear,
If he would spend his power. God save you, sir.
Gent. And you.
Hel. Sir, I have seen you in the court of France.
Gent. I have been sometimes there.
Hel. I do presume, sir, that you are not fall'n
From the report that goes upon your goodness;
And therefore, goaded with most sharp occasions,
Which lay nice manners by, I put you to
The use of your own virtues, for the which
I shall continue thankful.
Gent. What's your will?
Hel. That it will please you
To give this poor petition to the King,
And aid me with that store of power you have
To come into his presence.
Gent. The King's not here.
Hel. Not here, sir?
Gent. Not indeed.
He hence remov'd last night, and with more haste
Than is his use.
Wid. Lord, how we lose our pains!
Hel. All's well that ends well yet,
Though time seem so adverse and means unfit.
I do beseech you, whither is he gone?
Gent. Marry, as I take it, to Rossillion,
Whither I am going.
Hel. I do beseech you, sir,
Since you are like to see the King before me,
Commend the paper to his gracious hand,
Which I presume shall render you no blame,
But rather make you thank your pains for it.
I will come after you with what good speed
Our means will make us means.
Gent. This I'll do for you.
Hel. And you shall find yourself to be well thank'd,
Whate'er falls more. — We must to horse again.
Go, go, provide. [*Exeunt.*]

[Scene II. *Rossillion. Before the* Count's *Palace.*]

Enter *Clown* and *Parolles.*

Par. Good Monsieur Lavatch, give my Lord Lafew this letter. I have ere now, sir, been better known to you, when I have held familiarity with fresher clothes; but I am now, sir, muddied in Fortune's mood, and smell somewhat strong of her strong displeasure.

Clown. Truly, Fortune's displeasure is but sluttish if it smell so strongly as thou speak'st of. I will henceforth eat no fish of Fortune's butt'ring. Prithee allow the wind!

Par. Nay, you need not to stop your nose, sir. I spake but by a metaphor.

Clown. Indeed, sir, if your metaphor stink, I will stop my nose, or against any man's metaphor. Prithee get thee further!

Par. Pray you, sir, deliver me this paper.

Clown. Foh! prithee stand away! A paper from Fortune's close-stool to give to a nobleman! Look, here he comes himself.

Enter *Lafew.*

Here is a purr of Fortune's, sir, or of Fortune's cat, but not a musk cat, that has fall'n into the unclean fishpond of her displeasure and, as he says, is muddied withal. Pray you, sir, use the carp as you may; for he looks like a poor decayed, ingenious, foolish, rascally knave. I do pity his distress in my similes of comfort, and leave him to your lordship. [*Exit.*]

Par. My lord, I am a man whom Fortune hath cruelly scratch'd.

Laf. And what would you have me to do? 'Tis too late to pare her nails now. Wherein have you played the knave with Fortune that she should scratch you, who of herself is a good lady, and would not have knaves thrive long under her? There's a cardecue for you. Let the justices make you and Fortune friends; I am for other business.

Par. I beseech your honour to hear me one single word.

Laf. You beg a single penny more. Come, you shall ha't; save your word.

Par. My name, my good lord, is Parolles.

Laf. You beg more than word then. Cox my passion! give me your hand. How does your drum?

Par. O my good lord, you were the first that found me.

Laf. Was I, in sooth? And I was the first that lost thee.

Par. It lies in you, my lord, to bring me in some grace, for you did bring me out.

Laf. Out upon thee, knave! Dost thou put upon me at once both the office of God and the devil? One brings thee in grace, and the other brings thee out. [*Trumpets sound.*] The King's coming; I know by his trumpets. Sirrah, inquire further after me. I had talk of you last night. Though you are a fool and a knave, you shall eat. Go to, follow.

Par. I praise God for you. [*Exeunt.*]

[Scene III. *Rossillion. The* Count's *Palace.*]

Flourish. Enter *King, Old Lady* [*Countess*], *Lafew,* the two *French Lords,* with *Attendants.*

King. We lost a jewel of her, and our esteem
Was made much poorer by it; but your son,
As mad in folly, lack'd the sense to know
Her estimation home.

Count. 'Tis past, my liege,
And I beseech your Majesty to make it
Natural rebellion, done i' th' blaze of youth,
When oil and fire, too strong for reason's force,
O'erbears it and burns on.

King. My honour'd lady,
I have forgiven and forgotten all,
Though my revenges were high bent upon him
And watch'd the time to shoot.

Laf. This I must say —
But first I beg my pardon — the young lord
Did to his Majesty, his mother, and his lady,
Offence of mighty note; but to himself
The greatest wrong of all. He lost a wife
Whose beauty did astonish the survey
Of richest eyes; whose words all ears took captive;
Whose dear perfection hearts that scorn'd to serve
Humbly call'd mistress

King. Praising what is lost
Makes the remembrance dear. Well, call him hither.
We are reconcil'd, and the first view shall kill
All repetition. Let him not ask our pardon;
The nature of his great offence is dead,
And deeper than oblivion we do bury
Th' incensing relics of it. Let him approach,
A stranger, no offender; and inform him
So 'tis our will he should.

Gent. I shall, my liege. [*Exit.*]

King. What says he to your daughter? Have you spoke?

Laf. All that he is hath reference to your Highness.

King. Then shall we have a match. I have letters sent me
That sets him high in fame.

Enter *Count Bertram.*

Laf. He looks well on't.

King. I am not a day of season,
For thou mayst see a sunshine and a hail
In me at once. But to the brightest beams
Distracted clouds give way. So stand thou forth,
The time is fair again.

Ber. My high-repented blames,
Dear sovereign, pardon to me.

King. All is whole.
Not one word more of the consumed time!
Let's take the instant by the forward top;
For we are old, and on our quick'st decrees
Th' inaudible and noiseless foot of Time
Steals, ere we can effect them. You remember
The daughter of this lord?

Ber. Admiringly, my liege. At first
I stuck my choice upon her, ere my heart
Durst make too bold a herald of my tongue;
Where the impression of mine eye infixing,
Contempt his scornful perspective did lend me,
Which warp'd the line of every other favour,
Scorn'd a fair colour or express'd it stol'n,
Extended or contracted all proportions
To a most hideous object. Thence it came
That she whom all men prais'd, and whom myself,
Since I have lost, have lov'd, was in mine eye
The dust that did offend it.

King. Well excus'd!
That thou didst love her strikes some scores away
From the great compt But love that comes too late,

Like a remorseful pardon slowly carried,
To the great sender turns a sour offence,
Crying, 'That's good that's gone.' Our rash faults
Make trivial price of serious things we have,
Not knowing them until we know their grave.
Oft our displeasures, to ourselves unjust,
Destroy our friends, and after weep their dust;
Our own love, waking, cries to see what's done,
While shameful hate sleeps out the afternoon.
Be this sweet Helen's knell, and now forget her.
Send forth your amorous token for fair Maudlin.
The main consents are had, and here we'll stay
To see our widower's second marriage day.

Count. Which better than the first, O dear heaven, bless,
Or, ere they meet, in me, O nature, cesse!

Laf. Come on, my son, in whom my house's name
Must be digested. Give a favour from you
To sparkle in the spirits of my daughter,
That she may quickly come.
[*Bertram gives him a ring.*]
By my old beard
And ev'ry hair that's on't, Helen that's dead
Was a sweet creature! Such a ring as this,
The last that e'er I took her leave at court,
I saw upon her finger.

Ber. Hers it was not.

King. Now pray you let me see it; for mine eye,
While I was speaking, oft was fasten'd to't.
[*Takes the ring.*]
This ring was mine; and when I gave it Helen,
I bade her, if her fortunes ever stood
Necessitied to help, that by this token
I would relieve her. Had you that craft to reave her
Of what should stead her most?

Ber. My gracious sovereign,
Howe'er it pleases you to take it so,
The ring was never hers.

Count. Son, on my life,
I have seen her wear it, and she reckon'd it
At her live's rate.

Laf. I am sure I saw her wear it.

Ber. You are deceiv'd, my lord; she never saw it.
In Florence was it from a casement thrown me,
Wrapp'd in a paper, which contain'd the name
Of her that threw it. Noble she was, and thought
I stood engag'd; but when I had subscrib'd
To mine own fortune and inform'd her fully
I could not answer in that course of honour
As she had made the overture, she ceas'd
In heavy satisfaction, and would never
Receive the ring again.

King. Plutus himself,
That knows the tinct and multiplying med'cine,
Hath not in nature's mystery more science
Than I have in this ring. 'Twas mine, 'twas Helen's,
Whoever gave it you. Then if you know
That you are well acquainted with yourself,
Confess 'twas hers, and by what rough enforcement
You got it from her. She call'd the saints to surety
That she would never put it from her finger
Unless she gave it to yourself in bed —
Where you have never come — or sent it us
Upon her great disaster.

Ber. She never saw it.

King. Thou speak'st it falsely, as I love mine honour!
And mak'st conjectural fears to come into me
Which I would fain shut out. If it should prove
That thou art so inhuman — 'Twill not prove so!
And yet I know not — thou didst hate her deadly,
And she is dead, which nothing but to close
Her eyes myself could win me to believe
More than to see this ring. Take him away.
[*Attendants arrest Bertram.*]
My forepast proofs, howe'er the matter fall,
Shall tax my fears of little vanity,
Having vainly fear'd too little. Away with him!
We'll sift this matter further.

Ber. If you shall prove
This ring was ever hers, you shall as easy
Prove that I husbanded her bed in Florence,
Where yet she never was. [*Exit, guarded.*]

Enter a *Gentleman.*

King. I am wrapp'd in dismal thinkings.

Gent. Gracious sovereign,
Whether I have been to blame or no, I know not.
Here's a petition from a Florentine,
Who hath for four or five removes come short
To tender it herself. I undertook it,
Vanquish'd thereto by the fair grace and speech
Of the poor suppliant, who by this, I know,
Is here attending. Her business looks in her
With an importing visage, and she told me
In a sweet verbal brief it did concern
Your Highness with herself.

[*King reads*] *a letter.* 'Upon his many protestations to marry me when his wife was dead, I blush to say it, he won me. Now is the Count Rossillion a widower, his vows are forfeited to me, and my honour's paid to him. He stole from Florence, taking no leave, and I follow him to his country for justice. Grant it me, O King! in you it best lies; otherwise a seducer flourishes, and a poor maid is undone.

'DIANA CAPILET.'

Laf. I will buy me a son-in-law in a fair, and toll for this. I'll none of him.

King. The heavens have thought well on thee, Lafew,
To bring forth this discov'ry. Seek these suitors.
Go speedily and bring again the Count.
[*Exeunt Gentleman and an Attendant.*]
I am afeard the life of Helen, lady,
Was foully snatch'd.
Count. Now justice on the doers!

Enter *Bertram*, [guarded].

King. I wonder, sir, sith wives are monsters to you,
And that you fly them as you swear them lordship,
Yet you desire to marry.

Enter *Widow* [and] *Diana*.

What woman's that?
Dia. I am, my lord, a wretched Florentine,
Derived from the ancient Capilet.
My suit, as I do understand, you know,
And therefore know how far I may be pitied.
Wid. I am her mother, sir, whose age and honour
Both suffer under this complaint we bring,
And both shall cease, without your remedy.
King. Come hither, Count. Do you know these women?
Ber. My lord, I neither can nor will deny
But that I know them. Do they charge me further?
Dia. Why do you look so strange upon your wife?
Ber. She's none of mine, my lord.
Dia. If you shall marry,
You give away this hand, and that is mine;
You give away heaven's vows, and those are mine;
You give away myself, which is known mine,
For I by vow am so embodied yours
That she which marries you must marry me,
Either both or none.

Laf. Your reputation comes too short for my daughter; you are no husband for her.

Ber. My lord, this is a fond and desp'rate creature,
Whom sometime I have laugh'd with. Let your Highness
Lay a more noble thought upon mine honour
Than for to think that I would sink it here.
King. Sir, for my thoughts, you have them ill to friend
Till your deeds gain them. Fairer prove your honour
Than in my thought it lies!
Dia. Good my lord,
Ask him upon his oath if he does think
He had not my virginity.
King. What say'st thou to her?
Ber. She's impudent, my lord,
And was a common gamester to the camp.
Dia. He does me wrong, my lord. If I were so,
He might have bought me at a common price.
Do not believe him. O, behold this ring,
Whose high respect and rich validity
Did lack a parallel. Yet for all that
He gave it to a commoner o' th' camp
If I be one.
Count. He blushes, and 'tis his.
Of six preceding ancestors, that gem,
Conferr'd by testament to th' sequent issue,
Hath it been ow'd and worn. This is his wife.
That ring's a thousand proofs.
King. Methought you said
You saw one here in court could witness it.
Dia. I did, my lord, but loath am to produce
So bad an instrument. His name's Parolles.
Laf. I saw the man to-day, if man he be.
King. Find him and bring him hither.
[*Exit an Attendant.*]
Ber. What of him?
He's quoted for a most perfidious slave
With all the spots o' th' world tax'd and debosh'd,
Whose nature sickens but to speak a truth.
Am I or that or this for what he'll utter,
That will speak anything?
King. She hath that ring of yours.
Ber. I think she has. Certain it is I lik'd her,
And boarded her i' th' wanton way of youth.
She knew her distance and did angle for me,
Madding my eagerness with her restraint,
As all impediments in fancy's course
Are motives of more fancy; and, in fine,
Her infinite cunning, with her modern grace,
Subdu'd me to her rate. She got the ring,
And I had that which any inferior might
At market price have bought.

Dia. I must be patient.
You that turn'd off a first so noble wife
May justly diet me. I pray you yet
(Since you lack virtue, I will lose a husband)
Send for your ring, I will return it home,
And give me mine again.

Ber. I have it not.

King. What ring was yours, I pray you?

Dia. Sir, much like
The same upon your finger.

King. Know you this ring? This ring was his of late.

Dia. And this was it I gave him, being abed.

King. The story then goes false, you threw it him
Out of a casement?

Dia. I have spoke the truth.

Enter *Parolles.*

Ber. My lord, I do confess the ring was hers.

King. You boggle shrewdly, every feather starts you.
Is this the man you speak of?

Dia. Ay, my lord.

King. Tell me, sirrah — but tell me true I charge you,
Not fearing the displeasure of your master,
Which, on your just proceeding, I'll keep off —
By him and by this woman here what know you?

Par. So please your Majesty, my master hath been an honourable gentleman. Tricks he hath had in him, which gentlemen have.

King. Come, come, to th' purpose! Did he love this woman?

Par. Faith, sir, he did love her! but how?

King. How, I pray you?

Par. He did love her, sir, as a gentleman loves a woman.

King. How is that?

Par. He lov'd her, sir, and lov'd her not.

King. As thou art a knave, and no knave.
What an equivocal companion is this!

Par. I am a poor man, and at your Majesty's command.

Laf. He's a good drum, my lord, but a naughty orator.

Dia. Do you know he promis'd me marriage?

Par. Faith, I know more than I'll speak.

King. But wilt thou not speak all thou know'st?

Par. Yes, so please your Majesty. I did go between them as I said; but more than that, he loved her — for indeed he was mad for her, and talk'd of Sathan and of Limbo and of Furies and I know not what. Yet I was in that credit with them at that time that I knew of their going to bed, and of other motions, as promising her marriage, and things which would derive me ill will to speak of. Therefore I will not speak what I know.

King. Thou hast spoken all already, unless thou canst say they are married. But thou art too fine in thy evidence; therefore stand aside.
This ring you say was yours?

Dia. Ay, my good lord.

King. Where did you buy it? or who gave it you?

Dia. It was not given me, nor I did not buy it.

King. Who lent it you?

Dia. It was not lent me neither.

King. Where did you find it then?

Dia. I found it not.

King. If it were yours by none of all these ways,
How could you give it him?

Dia. I never gave it him.

Laf. This woman's an easy glove, my lord; she goes off and on at pleasure.

King. This ring was mine. I gave it his first wife.

Dia. It might be yours or hers for aught I know.

King. Take her away, I do not like her now;
To prison with her! and away with him!
Unless thou tell'st me where thou hadst this ring,
Thou diest within this hour.

Dia. I'll never tell you.

King. Take her away!

Dia. I'll put in bail, my liege.

King. I think thee now some common customer.

Dia. [*to Lafew*] By Jove, if ever I knew man, 'twas you!

King. Wherefore hast thou accus'd him all this while?

Dia. Because he's guilty, and he is not guilty.
He knows I am no maid, and he'll swear to't;
I'll swear I am a maid and he knows not.
Great King, I am no strumpet, by my life!
I am either maid, or else this old man's wife.
[*Points to Lafew.*]

King. She does abuse our ears. To prison with her!

Dia. Good mother, fetch my bail. Stay, royal sir:
[*Exit Widow.*]
The jeweller that owes the ring is sent for,

And he shall surety me. But for this lord,
Who hath abus'd me, as he knows himself,
Though yet he never harm'd me, here I quit him.
He knows himself my bed he hath defil'd,
And at that time he got his wife with child.
Dead though she be, she feels her young one kick.
So there's my riddle: one that's dead is quick —
And now behold the meaning.

Enter *Helen* and *Widow*.

King. Is there no exorcist
Beguiles the truer office of mine eyes?
Is't real that I see?
Hel. No, my good lord.
'Tis but the shadow of a wife you see,
The name and not the thing.
Ber. Both, both! O, pardon!
Hel. O my good lord, when I was like this maid
I found you wondrous kind. There is your ring,
And look you, here's your letter. This it says:
'When from my finger you can get this ring,
And are by me with child,' &c. This is done.
Will you be mine now you are doubly won?
Ber. If she, my liege, can make me know this clearly,
I'll love her dearly — ever, ever dearly.
Hel. If it appear not plain, and prove untrue,
Deadly divorce step between me and you!
O my dear mother, do I see you living?
Laf. Mine eyes smell onions; I shall weep anon.
[*To Parolles*] Good Tom Drum, lend me a handkercher. So,
I thank thee. Wait on me home; I'll make sport with thee.
Let thy curtsies alone! they are scurvy ones.
King. Let us from point to point this story know,
To make the even truth in pleasure flow.
[*To Diana*] If thou beest yet a fresh uncropped flower,
Choose thou thy husband, and I'll pay thy dower;
For I can guess that by thy honest aid
Thou kept'st a wife herself, thyself a maid.
Of that and all the progress more and less
Resolvedly more leisure shall express.
All yet seems well; and if it end so meet,
The bitter past, more welcome is the sweet,
Flourish.

[EPILOGUE.]

The King's a beggar, now the play is done.
All is well ended if this suit be won,
That you express content; which we will pay
With strife to please you, day exceeding day.
Ours be your patience then, and yours our parts;
Your gentle hands lend us, and take our hearts.
Exeunt omnes.

TWELFTH NIGHT

The text of TWELFTH NIGHT, as printed in the Folio of 1623, is unusually accurate. There is no earlier edition.

John Manningham of the Middle Temple saw TWELFTH NIGHT performed on February 2, 1602. 'At our feast,' he notes in his *Diary*, 'wee had a play called Twelue Night, or What You Will, much like the Commedy of Errores, or Menechmi in Plautus, but most like and neere to that in Italian called *Inganni*.' He commends particularly the trick played on Malvolio, which he calls 'a good practise' (i. e., a clever device). 'Twelue' is an old form of the ordinal; the Folio spells it 'twelfe.' Manningham's record fixes one limit for the date of composition. Obviously he had never seen the play before, but that does not prove that it was absolutely new. The title tempts inference that the first production was on the twelfth night (Epiphany) immediately preceding, that is, on January 6, 1602. Anyhow, 1601 (or 1600 at the earliest) may safely be accepted as the date of composition. No circumstantial evidence conflicts with this date. 'The new map with the augmentation of the Indies' (iii, 2, 85) was doubtless that of Emerie Molyneux (*ca.* 1599). The 'pension of thousands to be paid from the Sophy' (ii, 5, 197), that is, the Shah of Persia, may allude to Sir Robert Shirley's return from that country in 1599, with rich gifts from the Shah. Support for the accepted date (1600 or 1601) has been sought in Ben Jonson's *Poetaster* (iii, 4), where Captain Tucca describes a certain 'fat fool' called Mango. The passage has been thought to glance at Sir Toby Belch. *Poetaster* was acted in 1601. The evidence would be welcome if it were trustworthy, but Tucca's Mango never could have played Sir Toby.

The source for the main plot of TWELFTH NIGHT is Barnabe Riche's tale *Of Apolonius and Silla*, the second 'historie' in *Riche his Farewell to Militarie Profession* (1581).

Shakespeare's Viola is Riche's Silla. Viola's romance begins with a shipwreck, which separated her from her brother Sebastian and cast her up on Duke Orsino's Illyrian coast. Silla is likewise shipwrecked, but the first chapter of her love story is staged in Cyprus, at her father's court, where she fell in love with Duke Apolonius, her father's guest, and sought to win him, but in vain. Apolonius returns to his home in Constantinople and Silla determines to follow him. The shipwreck is the end of her journey. Her brother Silvio is not with her, but she is accompanied by a trusty servant (Pedro) who passes for her brother during the voyage. The shipwreck is fortunate, for, though it separates her from Pedro, it saves her from the violent attentions of the shipmaster. She is washed ashore on a chest that contains good store of coin and sundry suits of the captain's clothes. Under the name of her brother Silvio (Shakespeare's Sebastian) she takes service with Apolonius, who of course does not recognize her. He, in the meantime, has succumbed to the charms of an obdurate young widow, Julina (Shakespeare's Olivia), and he employs Silla as his messenger with letters and gifts. Julina falls in love with her while she is pleading her master's cause and interrupts: 'Silvio, it is enough that you have said for your maister; from henceforthe, either speake for your self, or saie nothyng at all.' Shakespeare's Olivia is less blunt, but equally frank (iii, 1, 117–121):

> 'O, by your leave, I pray you!
> I bade you never speak again of him;
> But, would you undertake another suit,
> I had rather hear you to solicit that
> Than music from the spheres.'

In the interval, Silvio has arrived at Constantinople, after wandering through many cities in search of his sister, who he supposes has eloped with Pedro. Julina falls in love with him as he is walking about the city, mistakes him for Silla, whom he resembles closely, and reproves him in gentle terms for his coldness. He apologizes and they are secretly betrothed; but he soon decamps, to continue his quest, leaving Julina with child.

Apolonius calls upon Julina for a final answer. She replies that she is already betrothed. Somewhat later he learns from the gossip of servants that she has received Silvio (Silla) at her house. He infers that it is his own man who has 'thrust his nose so farre out of joynte' and shuts Silla up in a dungeon. She tries every means, except that of revealing her sex, to induce him to suspend judgment, but to no purpose.

Julina visits Apolonius and begs him to show mercy to her betrothed husband. He draws his rapier and swears that he will kill Silla if she does not consent to marry Julina (cf. v, 1, 128 ff.). Silla takes Julina aside, confesses that she is a woman, and explains how she had come to Constantinople because of her love for Apolonius. Julina repeats the story to Apolonius and goes home in despair.

Apolonius, enraptured, transfers his affections to Silla on the spot, and they are married. The romantic tale of Silla's adventurous love quest spreads throughout Greece and reaches the ears of the wandering Silvio. He hastens back to Constantinople and is joyfully received by his sister and her husband. Apolonius tells him, as a matter of curious interest, how Silla had been claimed by Julina as her betrothed husband. Silvio explains the circumstances and Apolonius escorts him to Julina's house. She recognizes him and they are married. Both couples live happily forever after.

Riche's tale is based on the thirty-sixth story in Part II of Bandello's *Novelle*, which he may have known either directly or through the translation in Belleforest's *Histoires Tragiques*. Bandello seems to have taken his story from *Gl' Ingannati*, a comedy written about 1531 by some member of the Sienese academy of the Intronati, perhaps Alessandro Piccolomini. This is doubtless the play which Manningham miscalls *Inganni*. A Latin version, *Lælia*, was acted at Queen's College, Cambridge, in 1595.

In adapting Bandello's *novella* Riche has made significant changes.

There is no shipwreck in Bandello. The twins have been separated in infancy at the sack of Rome. The boy (Paolo) was captured by a German who took him to Naples and treated him as his son and, at his death, left him all his property. The girl (Nicuola) fell into the hands of two Spaniards. They treated her well and she was recovered by her father (Ambrogio), who bought her for five hundred ducats. He could get no trace of Paolo. The rest of the story takes place at Esi, Ambrogio's native town. Nicuola puts on man's attire, takes the name Romulo, and acts as page and messenger for Lattantio, her own lover, who has transferred his affections to Catella, the daughter of one Gerardo, an elderly citizen of Esi and himself a suitor for Nicuola's hand. Catella falls in love with the disguised messenger. Paolo comes to Esi; she mistakes him for Romulo, and they are betrothed. Meantime Nicuola has revealed her identity to Lattantio and he has repented of his fickleness. They also pledge their troth. The *finale* is at Ambrogio's house. He is overjoyed at the sudden appearance of his long-lost son and accepts Lattantio as son-in-law. Gerardo consents to the match between Catella and Paolo. All are happy except Gerardo, who has lost his chance of winning Nicuola.

The significance of a study of sources lies in the opportunity it gives to see Shakespeare at work. The most casual comparison of Riche's novel with TWELFTH NIGHT reveals what Shakespeare has done in the mere matter of plot. Characterization one does not expect of an Elizabethan writer of short stories. That Riche's men and women are puppets is no discredit to Riche; for that is all they need be: he is telling a tale: he is not bringing men and women before us (on the stage) in their habits as they lived. Viola and Olivia and Duke Orsino have their prototypes in Riche, but are Shakespeare's own delightful creations. Sebastian is lightly sketched, but is quite worthy to be Viola's brother. No plausible suggestion has ever been made as to a source for the underplot; nor is it profitable to identify its characters with other characters in Shakespeare. Sir Toby is not Falstaff, nor is Sir Andrew our good friend Slender. Somehow, one thinks that poor Yorick must have resembled Feste — the merriest of all Shakespeare's fools.

TWELFTH NIGHT;

OR, WHAT YOU WILL

[Dramatis Personæ.

Orsino, Duke of Illyria.
Sebastian, a young gentleman, brother to *Viola.*
Antonio, a sea captain, friend to *Sebastian.*
A Sea Captain, friend to *Viola.*
Valentine,
Curio, } gentlemen attending on the *Duke.*
Sir Toby Belch, uncle to *Olivia.*
Sir Andrew Aguecheek.
Malvolio, steward to *Olivia.*

Fabian,
Feste, a Clown, } servants to *Olivia.*

Olivia, a countess.
Viola, sister to *Sebastian.*
Maria, Olivia's woman.

Lords, a Priest, Sailors, Officers, Musicians, and Attendants.

SCENE. — *A city in Illyria, and the seacoast near by.*]

ACT I. Scene I. [*The* Duke's *Palace.*]

Enter *Orsino* (*Duke of Illyria*), *Curio,* and other *Lords*; [with *Musicians*].

Duke. If music be the food of love, play on,
Give me excess of it, that, surfeiting,
The appetite may sicken, and so die.
That strain again! It had a dying fall;
O, it came o'er my ear like the sweet sound
That breathes upon a bank of violets,
Stealing and giving odour! Enough, no more!
'Tis not so sweet now as it was before.
O spirit of love, how quick and fresh art thou!
That, notwithstanding thy capacity
Receiveth as the sea, naught enters there,
Of what validity and pitch soe'er,
But falls into abatement and low price
Even in a minute! So full of shapes is fancy
That it alone is high fantastical.
Cur. Will you go hunt, my lord?
Duke. What, Curio?
Cur. The hart.
Duke. Why, so I do, the noblest that I have.
O, when mine eyes did see Olivia first,
Methought she purg'd the air of pestilence!
That instant was I turn'd into a hart,
And my desires, like fell and cruel hounds,
E'er since pursue me.

Enter *Valentine.*

How now? What news from her?
Val. So please my lord, I might not be admitted,
But from her handmaid do return this answer:
The element itself, till seven years' heat,
Shall not behold her face at ample view;
But like a cloistress she will veiled walk,
And water once a day her chamber round
With eye-offending brine: all this to season
A brother's dead love, which she would keep fresh
And lasting in her sad remembrance.
Duke. O, she that hath a heart of that fine frame
To pay this debt of love but to a brother,
How will she love when the rich golden shaft
Hath kill'd the flock of all affections else
That live in her; when liver, brain, and heart,
These sovereign thrones, are all supplied and fill'd,
Her sweet perfections, with one self king!
Away before me to sweet beds of flow'rs!
Love-thoughts lie rich when canopied with bow'rs. *Exeunt.*

Scene II. [*The seacoast.*]

Enter *Viola,* a *Captain,* and *Sailors.*

Vio. What country, friends, is this?
Capt. This is Illyria, lady.
Vio. And what should I do in Illyria?
My brother he is in Elysium.
Perchance he is not drown'd. What think you, sailors?

Capt. It is perchance that you yourself were sav'd.
Vio. O my poor brother! and so perchance may he be.
Capt. True, madam; and, to comfort you with chance,
Assure yourself, after our ship did split,
When you, and those poor number sav'd with you,
Hung on our driving boat, I saw your brother,
Most provident in peril, bind himself
(Courage and hope both teaching him the practice)
To a strong mast that liv'd upon the sea;
Where, like Arion on the dolphin's back,
I saw him hold acquaintance with the waves
So long as I could see.
Vio. For saying so, there's gold.
Mine own escape unfoldeth to my hope,
Whereto thy speech serves for authority,
The like of him. Know'st thou this country?
Capt. Ay, madam, well, for I was bred and born
Not three hours' travel from this very place.
Vio. Who governs here?
Capt. A noble duke, in nature as in name.
Vio. What is his name?
Capt. Orsino.
Vio. Orsino! I have heard my father name him.
He was a bachelor then.
Capt. And so is now, or was so very late;
For but a month ago I went from hence,
And then 'twas fresh in murmur (as you know
What great ones do, the less will prattle of)
That he did seek the love of fair Olivia.
Vio. What's she?
Capt. A virtuous maid, the daughter of a count
That died some twelvemonth since; then leaving her
In the protection of his son, her brother,
Who shortly also died; for whose dear love,
They say, she hath abjur'd the company
And sight of men.
Vio. O that I serv'd that lady,
And might not be delivered to the world,
Till I had made mine own occasion mellow,
What my estate is!
Capt. That were hard to compass,
Because she will admit no kind of suit;
No, not the Duke's.
Vio. There is a fair behaviour in thee, Captain;
And though that nature with a beauteous wall
Doth oft close in pollution, yet of thee
I will believe thou hast a mind that suits
With this thy fair and outward character.
I prithee (and I'll pay thee bounteously)
Conceal me what I am, and be my aid
For such disguise as haply shall become
The form of my intent. I'll serve this duke,
Thou shalt present me as an eunuch to him;
It may be worth thy pains. For I can sing,
And speak to him in many sorts of music
That will allow me very worth his service.
What else may hap, to time I will commit;
Only shape thou thy silence to my wit.
Capt. Be you his eunuch, and your mute I'll be.
When my tongue blabs, then let mine eyes not see.
Vio. I thank thee. Lead me on. *Exeunt.*

Scene III. [Olivia's *house.*]

Enter *Sir Toby* and *Maria.*

To. What a plague means my niece to take the death of her brother thus? I am sure care's an enemy to life.

Mar. By my troth, Sir Toby, you must come in earlier o' nights. Your cousin, my lady, takes great exceptions to your ill hours. 6

To. Why, let her except before excepted!

Mar. Ay, but you must confine yourself within the modest limits of order. 9

To. Confine? I'll confine myself no finer than I am. These clothes are good enough to drink in, and so be these boots too. An they be not, let them hang themselves in their own straps.

Mar. That quaffing and drinking will undo you. I heard my lady talk of it yesterday; and of a foolish knight that you brought in one night here to be her wooer. 17

To. Who? Sir Andrew Aguecheek?

Mar. Ay, he.

To. He's as tall a man as any's in Illyria.

Mar. What's that to th' purpose? 21

To. Why, he has three thousand ducats a year.

Mar. Ay, but he'll have but a year in all these ducats. He's a very fool and a prodigal.

To. Fie that you'll say so! He plays o' th' viol-de-gamboys, and speaks three or four languages word for word without book, and hath all the good gifts of nature. 29

Mar. He hath, indeed, almost natural! for, besides that he's a fool, he's a great quarreller; and but that he hath the gift of a coward to allay the gust he hath in quarrelling, 'tis thought among the prudent he would quickly have the gift of a grave.

To. By this hand, they are scoundrels and substractors that say so of him. Who are they?

Mar. They that add, moreover, he's drunk nightly in your company.

To. With drinking healths to my niece. I'll drink to her as long as there is a passage in my throat and drink in Illyria. He's a coward and a coystrill that will not drink to my niece till his brains turn o' th' toe like a parish top. What, wench! *Castiliano vulgo!* for here comes Sir Andrew Agueface.

Enter *Sir Andrew.*

And. Sir Toby Belch! How now, Sir Toby Belch?

To. Sweet Sir Andrew!

And. Bless you, fair shrew.

Mar. And you too, sir.

To. Accost, Sir Andrew, accost.

And. What's that?

To. My niece's chambermaid.

And. Good Mistress Accost, I desire better acquaintance.

Mar. My name is Mary, sir.

And. Good Mistress Mary Accost —

To. You mistake, knight. 'Accost' is front her, board her, woo her, assail her.

And. By my troth, I would not undertake her in this company. Is that the meaning of 'accost'?

Mar. Fare you well, gentlemen.

To. An thou let part so, Sir Andrew, would thou mightst never draw sword again!

And. An you part so, mistress, I would I might never draw sword again! Fair lady, do you think you have fools in hand?

Mar. Sir, I have not you by th' hand.

And. Marry, but you shall have! and here's my hand.

Mar. Now, sir, thought is free. I pray you, bring your hand to th' butt'ry bar and let it drink.

And. Wherefore, sweetheart? What's your metaphor?

Mar. It's dry, sir.

And. Why, I think so. I am not such an ass but I can keep my hand dry. But what's your jest?

Mar. A dry jest, sir.

And. Are you full of them?

Mar. Ay, sir, I have them at my fingers' ends. Marry, now I let go your hand, I am barren. *Exit.*

To. O knight, thou lack'st a cup of canary! When did I see thee so put down?

And. Never in your life, I think, unless you see canary put me down. Methinks sometimes I have no more wit than a Christian or an ordinary man has. But I am a great eater of beef, and I believe that does harm to my wit.

To. No question.

And. An I thought that, I'd forswear it. I'll ride home to-morrow, Sir Toby.

To. Pourquoi, my dear knight?

And. What is 'pourquoi'? Do, or not do? I would I had bestowed that time in the tongues that I have in fencing, dancing, and bear-baiting. O, had I but followed the arts!

To. Then hadst thou had an excellent head of hair.

And. Why, would that have mended my hair?

To. Past question, for thou seest it will not curl by nature.

And. But it becomes me well enough, does't not?

To. Excellent. It hangs like flax on a distaff; and I hope to see a housewife take thee between her legs and spin it off.

And. Faith, I'll home to-morrow, Sir Toby. Your niece will not be seen; or if she be, it's four to one she'll none of me. The Count himself here hard by wooes her.

To. She'll none o' th' Count. She'll not match above her degree, neither in estate, years, nor wit; I have heard her swear't. Tut, there's life in't, man.

And. I'll stay a month longer. I am a fellow o' th' strangest mind i' th' world. I delight in masques and revels sometimes altogether.

To. Art thou good at these kickshawses, knight?

And. As any man in Illyria, whatsoever he be, under the degree of my betters; and yet I will not compare with an old man.

To. What is thy excellence in a galliard, knight?

And. Faith, I can cut a caper.

To. And I can cut the mutton to't.

And. And I think I have the back-trick simply as strong as any man in Illyria.

To. Wherefore are these things hid? Wherefore have these gifts a curtain before 'em? Are they like to take dust, like Mistress Mall's picture? Why dost thou not go to church in a galliard and come home in a coranto? My very walk should be a jig. I would not so much as make water but in a sink-a-pace. What dost thou mean? Is it a world to hide virtues in? I did think, by the excellent constitution of thy leg, it was form'd under the star of a galliard.

And. Ay, 'tis strong, and it does indifferent well in a flame-colour'd stock. Shall we set about some revels?

To. What shall we do else? Were we not born under Taurus?

And. Taurus? That's sides and heart.

To. No, sir; it is legs and thighs. Let me see thee caper. [*Sir Andrew dances.*] Ha, higher! Ha, ha, excellent! *Exeunt.*

Scene IV. [*The* Duke's *Palace.*]

Enter *Valentine*, and *Viola* in man's attire.

Val. If the Duke continue these favours towards you, Cesario, you are like to be much advanc'd. He hath known you but three days, and already you are no stranger.

Vio. You either fear his humour or my negligence, that you call in question the continuance of his love. Is he inconstant, sir, in his favours?

Val. No, believe me.

Enter *Duke, Curio,* and *Attendants.*

Vio. I thank you. Here comes the Count.

Duke. Who saw Cesario, ho?

Vio. On your attendance, my lord, here.

Duke. Stand you awhile aloof. — Cesario,
Thou know'st no less but all. I have unclasp'd
To thee the book even of my secret soul.
Therefore, good youth, address thy gait unto her;
Be not denied access, stand at her doors,
And tell them there thy fixed foot shall grow
Till thou have audience.

Vio. Sure, my noble lord,
If she be so abandon'd to her sorrow
As it is spoke, she never will admit me.

Duke. Be clamorous and leap all civil bounds
Rather than make unprofited return.

Vio. Say I do speak with her, my lord, what then?

Duke. O, then unfold the passion of my love;
Surprise her with discourse of my dear faith!
It shall become thee well to act my woes.
She will attend it better in thy youth
Than in a nuncio's of more grave aspect.

Vio. I think not so, my lord.

Duke. Dear lad, believe it;
For they shall yet belie thy happy years
That say thou art a man. Diana's lip
Is not more smooth and rubious; thy small pipe
Is as the maiden's organ, shrill and sound,
And all is semblative a woman's part.
I know thy constellation is right apt
For this affair. Some four or five attend him —
All, if you will; for I myself am best
When least in company. Prosper well in this,
And thou shalt live as freely as thy lord
To call his fortunes thine.

Vio. I'll do my best
To woo your lady. [*Aside*] Yet a barful strife!
Whoe'er I woo, myself would be his wife.
Exeunt.

Scene V. [Olivia's *house.*]

Enter *Maria* and *Clown.*

Mar. Nay, either tell me where thou hast been, or I will not open my lips so wide as a bristle may enter in way of thy excuse. My lady will hang thee for thy absence.

Clown. Let her hang me! He that is well hang'd in this world needs to fear no colours.

Mar. Make that good.

Clown. He shall see none to fear.

Mar. A good lenten answer. I can tell thee where that saying was born, of 'I fear no colours.'

Clown. Where, good Mistress Mary?

Mar. In the wars; and that may you be bold to say in your foolery.

Clown. Well, God give them wisdom that have it; and those that are fools, let them use their talents.

Mar. Yet you will be hang'd for being so long absent, or to be turn'd away — is not that as good as a hanging to you?

Clown. Many a good hanging prevents a bad marriage; and for turning away, let summer bear it out.

Mar. You are resolute then?

Clown. Not so, neither; but I am resolv'd on two points.

Mar. That if one break, the other will hold; or if both break, your gaskins fall.

Clown. Apt, in good faith; very apt. Well, go thy way! If Sir Toby would leave drinking, thou wert as witty a piece of Eve's flesh as any in Illyria.

Mar. Peace, you rogue; no more o' that. Here comes my lady. Make your excuse wisely, you were best. [*Exit*

Enter *Lady Olivia* with *Malvolio.*

Clown. Wit, an't be thy will, put me into good fooling! Those wits that think they have thee do very oft prove fools; and I that am sure I lack thee may pass for a wise man. For what says Quinapalus? 'Better a witty fool than a foolish wit.' — God bless thee, lady!

Oli. Take the fool away.

Clown. Do you not hear, fellows? Take away the lady.

Oli. Go to, y'are a dry fool! I'll no more of you. Besides, you grow dishonest.

Clown. Two faults, madonna, that drink and good counsel will amend. For give the dry fool drink, then is the fool not dry. Bid the dishonest man mend himself: if he mend, he is no longer dishonest; if he cannot, let the botcher mend him. Anything that's mended is but patch'd; virtue that transgresses is but patch'd with sin, and sin that amends is but patch'd with virtue. If that this simple syllogism will serve, so; if it will not, what remedy? As there is no true cuckold but calamity, so beauty's a flower. The lady bade take away the fool; therefore, I say again, take her away.

Oli. Sir, I bade them take away you.

Clown. Misprision in the highest degree! Lady, cucullus non facit monachum. That's as much to say as, I wear not motley in my brain. Good madonna, give me leave to prove you a fool.

Oli. Can you do it?

Clown. Dexteriously, good madonna.

Oli. Make your proof.

Clown. I must catechize you for it, madonna. Good my mouse of virtue, answer me.

Oli. Well, sir, for want of other idleness, I'll bide your proof.

Clown. Good madonna, why mourn'st thou?

Oli. Good fool, for my brother's death.

Clown. I think his soul is in hell, madonna.

Oli. I know his soul is in heaven, fool.

Clown. The more fool, madonna, to mourn for your brother's soul, being in heaven. Take away the fool, gentlemen.

Oli. What think you of this fool, Malvolio? Doth he not mend?

Mal. Yes, and shall do till the pangs of death shake him. Infirmity, that decays the wise, doth ever make the better fool.

Clown. God send you, sir, a speedy infirmity, for the better increasing your folly! Sir Toby will be sworn that I am no fox; but he will not pass his word for twopence that you are no fool.

Oli. How say you to that, Malvolio?

Mal. I marvel your ladyship takes delight in such a barren rascal. I saw him put down the other day with an ordinary fool that has no more brain than a stone. Look you now, he's out of his guard already. Unless you laugh and minister occasion to him, he is gagg'd. I protest I take these wise men that crow so at these set kind of fools no better than the fools' zanies.

Oli. O, you are sick of self-love, Malvolio, and taste with a distemper'd appetite. To be generous, guiltless, and of free disposition, is to take those things for birdbolts that you deem cannon bullets. There is no slander in an allow'd fool, though he do nothing but rail; nor no railing in a known discreet man, though he do nothing but reprove.

Clown. Now Mercury indue thee with leasing, for thou speak'st well of fools!

Enter *Maria.*

Mar. Madam, there is at the gate a young gentleman much desires to speak with you.

Oli. From the Count Orsino, is it?

Mar. I know not, madam. 'Tis a fair young man, and well attended.

Oli. Who of my people hold him in delay?

Mar. Sir Toby, madam, your kinsman.

Oli. Fetch him off, I pray you. He speaks nothing but madman. Fie on him! [*Exit Maria.*] Go you, Malvolio. If it be a suit from the Count, I am sick, or not at home. What you will, to dismiss it. (*Exit Malvolio.*) Now you see, sir, how your fooling grows old, and people dislike it.

Clown. Thou hast spoke for us, madonna, as if thy eldest son should be a fool; whose skull Jove cram with brains!

Enter *Sir Toby.*

for — here he comes — one of thy kin has a most weak pia mater.

Oli. By mine honour, half drunk! What is he at the gate, cousin?

To. A gentleman.

Oli. A gentleman? What gentleman?

To. 'Tis a gentleman here. A plague o' these pickle-herring! How now, sot?

Clown. Good Sir Toby!

Oli. Cousin, cousin, how have you come so early by this lethargy?

To. Lechery? I defy lechery. There's one at the gate.

Oli. Ay, marry, what is he?

To. Let him be the devil an he will, I care not! Give me faith, say I. Well, it's all one. *Exit.*

Oli. What's a drunken man like, fool?

Clown. Like a drown'd man, a fool, and a madman. One draught above heat makes him a fool, the second mads him, and a third drowns him.

Oli. Go thou and seek the crowner, and let him sit o' my coz; for he's in the third degree of drink — he's drown'd. Go look after him.

Clown. He is but mad yet, madonna, and the fool shall look to the madman. [*Exit.*]

Enter *Malvolio.*

Mal. Madam, yond young fellow swears he will speak with you. I told him you were sick: he takes on him to understand so much, and therefore comes to speak with you. I told him you were asleep: he seems to have a foreknowledge of that too, and therefore comes to speak with you. What is to be said to him, lady? He's fortified against any denial.

Oli. Tell him he shall not speak with me.

Mal. Has been told so; and he says he'll stand at your door like a sheriff's post, and be the supporter to a bench, but he'll speak with you.

Oli. What kind o' man is he?

Mal. Why, of mankind.

Oli. What manner of man?

Mal. Of very ill manner. He'll speak with you, will you or no.

Oli. Of what personage and years is he?

Mal. Not yet old enough for a man nor young enough for a boy; as a squash is before 'tis a peascod, or a codling when 'tis almost an apple. 'Tis with him in standing water, between boy and man. He is very well-favour'd and he speaks very shrewishly. One would think his mother's milk were scarce out of him.

Oli. Let him approach. Call in my gentlewoman.

Mal. Gentlewoman, my lady calls. *Exit.*

Enter *Maria.*

Oli. Give me my veil; come, throw it o'er my face.
We'll once more hear Orsino's embassy.

Enter *Viola.*

Vio. The honourable lady of the house, which is she?

Oli. Speak to me; I shall answer for her. Your will?

Vio. Most radiant, exquisite, and unmatchable beauty — I pray you tell me if this be the lady of the house, for I never saw her. I would be loath to cast away my speech; for, besides that it is excellently well penn'd, I have taken great pains to con it. Good beauties, let me sustain no scorn. I am very comptible, even to the least sinister usage.

Oli. Whence came you, sir?

Vio. I can say little more than I have studied, and that question's out of my part. Good gentle one, give me modest assurance if you be the lady of the house, that I may proceed in my speech.

Oli. Are you a comedian?

Vio. No, my profound heart; and yet (by the very fangs of malice I swear) I am not that I play. Are you the lady of the house?

Oli. If I do not usurp myself, I am.

Vio. Most certain, if you are she, you do usurp yourself; for what is yours to bestow is not yours to reserve. But this is from my commission. I will on with my speech in your praise and then show you the heart of my message.

Oli. Come to what is important in't. I forgive you the praise.

Vio. Alas, I took great pains to study it, and 'tis poetical.

Oli. It is the more like to be feigned; I pray you keep it in. I heard you were saucy at my gates; and allow'd your approach rather to wonder at you than to hear you. If you be not mad, be gone; if you have reason, be brief. 'Tis not that time of moon with me to make one in so skipping a dialogue.

Mar. Will you hoist sail, sir? Here lies your way.

Vio. No, good swabber; I am to hull here a little longer. Some mollification for your giant, sweet lady!

Oli. Tell me your mind.

Vio. I am a messenger.

Oli. Sure you have some hideous matter to deliver, when the courtesy of it is so fearful. Speak your office.

Vio. It alone concerns your ear. I bring no overture of war, no taxation of homage. I hold the olive in my hand. My words are as full of peace as matter.

Oli. Yet you began rudely. What are you? What would you?

Vio. The rudeness that hath appear'd in me have I learn'd from my entertainment. What I am, and what I would, are as secret as maidenhead: to your ears, divinity; to any other's, profanation.

Oli. Give us the place alone; we will hear this divinity. [*Exit Maria.*] Now, sir, what is your text?

Vio. Most sweet lady —

Oli. A comfortable doctrine, and much may be said of it. Where lies your text?

Vio. In Orsino's bosom.

Oli. In his bosom? In what chapter of his bosom?

Vio. To answer by the method, in the first of his heart.

Oli. O, I have read it! it is heresy. Have you no more to say?

Vio. Good madam, let me see your face.

Oli. Have you any commission from your lord to negotiate with my face? You are now out of your text. But we will draw the curtain and show you the picture. [*Unveils.*] Look you, sir, such a one I was this present. Is't not well done?

Vio. Excellently done, if God did all.

Oli. 'Tis in grain, sir; 'twill endure wind and weather.

Vio. 'Tis beauty truly blent, whose red and white
Nature's own sweet and cunning hand laid on.
Lady, you are the cruell'st she alive
If you will lead these graces to the grave,
And leave the world no copy.

Oli. O, sir, I will not be so hard-hearted. I will give out divers schedules of my beauty. It shall be inventoried, and every particle and utensil labell'd to my will: — as, item, two lips, indifferent red; item, two grey eyes, with lids to them; item, one neck, one chin, and so forth. Were you sent hither to praise me?

Vio. I see you what you are — you are too proud;
But if you were the devil, you are fair.
My lord and master loves you. O, such love
Could be but recompens'd though you were crown'd
The nonpareil of beauty!

Oli. How does he love me?

Vio. With adorations, with fertile tears,
With groans that thunder love, with sighs of fire.

Oli. Your lord does know my mind; I cannot love him.
Yet I suppose him virtuous, know him noble,
Of great estate, of fresh and stainless youth;
In voices well divulg'd, free, learn'd, and valiant,
And in dimension and the shape of nature
A gracious person. But yet I cannot love him.
He might have took his answer long ago.

Vio. If I did love you in my master's flame,
With such a suff'ring, such a deadly life,
In your denial I would find no sense;
I would not understand it.

Oli. Why, what would you?

Vio. Make me a willow cabin at your gate
And call upon my soul within the house;
Write loyal cantons of contemned love
And sing them loud even in the dead of night;
Halloa your name to the reverberate hills
And make the babbling gossip of the air
Cry out 'Olivia!' O, you should not rest
Between the elements of air and earth
But you should pity me!

Oli. You might do much. What is your parentage?

Vio. Above my fortunes, yet my state is well.
I am a gentleman.

Oli. Get you to your lord.
I cannot love him. Let him send no more,
Unless, perchance, you come to me again
To tell me how he takes it. Fare you well.
I thank you for your pains. Spend this for me.

Vio. I am no fee'd post, lady; keep your purse;
My master, not myself, lacks recompense.
Love make his heart of flint that you shall love;
And let your fervour, like my master's, be
Plac'd in contempt! Farewell, fair cruelty.
Exit.

Oli. 'What is your parentage?'
'Above my fortunes, yet my state is well.
I am a gentleman.' I'll be sworn thou art.
Thy tongue, thy face, thy limbs, actions, and spirit
Do give thee fivefold blazon. Not too fast! soft, soft!
Unless the master were the man. How now?
Even so quickly may one catch the plague?
Methinks I feel this youth's perfections
With an invisible and subtle stealth
To creep in at mine eyes. Well, let it be.
What ho, Malvolio!

Enter *Malvolio.*

Mal. Here, madam, at your service.

Oli. Run after that same peevish messenger,
The County's man. He left this ring behind him,
Would I or not. Tell him I'll none of it.
Desire him not to flatter with his lord
Nor hold him up with hopes. I am not for him.
If that the youth will come this way to-morrow,
I'll give him reasons for't. Hie thee, Malvolio.

Mal. Madam, I will. *Exit.*

Oli. I do I know not what, and fear to find
Mine eye too great a flatterer for my mind.
Fate, show thy force! Ourselves we do not owe.
What is decreed must be — and be this so!
[*Exit.*]

Act II. Scene I. [*The seacoast.*]

Enter *Antonio* and *Sebastian*.

Ant. Will you stay no longer? nor will you not that I go with you?

Seb. By your patience, no. My stars shine darkly over me; the malignancy of my fate might perhaps distemper yours. Therefore I shall crave of you your leave, that I may bear my evils alone. It were a bad recompense for your love to lay any of them on you.

Ant. Let me yet know of you whither you are bound.

Seb. No, sooth, sir. My determinate voyage is mere extravagancy. But I perceive in you so excellent a touch of modesty that you will not extort from me what I am willing to keep in; therefore it charges me in manners the rather to express myself. You must know of me then, Antonio, my name is Sebastian, which I call'd Roderigo. My father was that Sebastian of Messaline whom I know you have heard of. He left behind him myself and a sister, both born in an hour. If the heavens had been pleas'd, would we had so ended! But you, sir, alter'd that, for some hour before you took me from the breach of the sea was my sister drown'd.

Ant. Alas the day!

Seb. A lady, sir, though it was said she much resembled me, was yet of many accounted beautiful. But though I could not with such estimable wonder overfar believe that, yet thus far I will boldly publish her: she bore a mind that envy could not but call fair. She is drown'd already, sir, with salt water, though I seem to drown her remembrance again with more.

Ant. Pardon me, sir, your bad entertainment.

Seb. O good Antonio, forgive me your trouble!

Ant. If you will not murther me for my love, let me be your servant.

Seb. If you will not undo what you have done, that is, kill him whom you have recover'd, desire it not. Fare ye well at once. My bosom is full of kindness; and I am yet so near the manners of my mother that, upon the least occasion more, mine eyes will tell tales of me. I am bound to the Count Orsino's court. Farewell. *Exit.*

Ant. The gentleness of all the gods go with thee!
I have many enemies in Orsino's court,
Else would I very shortly see thee there.
But come what may, I do adore thee so
That danger shall seem sport, and I will go.
Exit.

Scene II. [*A street.*]

Enter *Viola* and *Malvolio* at several doors.

Mal. Were not you ev'n now with the Countess Olivia?

Vio. Even now, sir. On a moderate pace I have since arriv'd but hither.

Mal. She returns this ring to you, sir. You might have saved me my pains, to have taken it away yourself. She adds, moreover, that you should put your lord into a desperate assurance she will none of him. And one thing more, that you be never so hardy to come again in his affairs, unless it be to report your lord's taking of this. Receive it so.

Vio. She took the ring of me. I'll none of it.

Mal. Come, sir, you peevishly threw it to her; and her will is, it should be so return'd. If it be worth stooping for, there it lies, in your eye; if not, be it his that finds it. *Exit.*

Vio. I left no ring with her. What means this lady?
Fortune forbid my outside have not charm'd her!
She made good view of me; indeed, so much
That, as methought, her eyes had lost her tongue,
For she did speak in starts distractedly.
She loves me sure; the cunning of her passion
Invites me in this churlish messenger.
None of my lord's ring? Why, he sent her none!
I am the man. If it be so — as 'tis —
Poor lady, she were better love a dream!
Disguise, I see thou art a wickedness
Wherein the pregnant enemy does much.
How easy is it for the proper false
In women's waxen hearts to set their forms!
Alas, our frailty is the cause, not we!
For such as we are made of, such we be.
How will this fadge? My master loves her dearly;
And I (poor monster) fond as much on him;
And she (mistaken) seems to dote on me.

What will become of this? As I am man,
My state is desperate for my master's love.
As I am woman (now alas the day!),
What thriftless sighs shall poor Olivia breathe!
O Time, thou must untangle this, not I;
It is too hard a knot for me t' untie! [*Exit.*]

Scene III. [Olivia's *house.*]

Enter *Sir Toby* and *Sir Andrew.*

To. Approach, Sir Andrew. Not to be abed after midnight is to be up betimes; and 'diluculo surgere,' thou know'st —

And. Nay, by my troth, I know not; but I know to be up late is to be up late.

To. A false conclusion! I hate it as an unfill'd can. To be up after midnight, and to go to bed then, is early; so that to go to bed after midnight is to go to bed betimes. Does not our life consist of the four elements?

And. Faith, so they say; but I think it rather consists of eating and drinking.

To. Th'art a scholar! Let us therefore eat and drink. Marian I say! a stoup of wine!

Enter *Clown.*

And. Here comes the fool, i' faith.

Clown. How now, my hearts? Did you never see the picture of We Three?

To. Welcome, ass. Now let's have a catch.

And. By my troth, the fool has an excellent breast. I had rather than forty shillings I had such a leg, and so sweet a breath to sing, as the fool has. In sooth, thou wast in very gracious fooling last night, when thou spok'st of Pigrogromitus, of the Vapians passing the equinoctial of Queubus. 'Twas very good, i' faith. I sent thee sixpence for thy leman. Hadst it?

Clown. I did impeticos thy gratillity; for Malvolio's nose is no whipstock. My lady has a white hand, and the Myrmidons are no bottle-ale houses.

And. Excellent! Why, this is the best fooling, when all is done. Now a song!

To. Come on! there is sixpence for you. Let's have a song.

And. There's a testril of me too. If one knight give a —

Clown. Would you have a love song, or a song of good life?

To. A love song, a love song

And. Ay, ay! I care not for good life.

Clown sings.

O mistress mine, where are you roaming?
O, stay and hear! your true-love 's coming,
  That can sing both high and low.
Trip no further, pretty sweeting;
Journeys end in lovers meeting,
  Every wise man's son doth know.

And. Excellent good, i' faith!

To. Good, good!

Clown [*sings*].

What is love? 'Tis not hereafter;
Present mirth hath present laughter;
  What's to come is still unsure:
In delay there lies no plenty;
Then come kiss me, sweet and twenty!
  Youth's a stuff will not endure.

And. A mellifluous voice, as I am true knight.

To. A contagious breath.

And. Very sweet and contagious, i' faith.

To. To hear by the nose, it is dulcet in contagion. But shall we make the welkin dance indeed? Shall we rouse the night owl in a catch that will draw three souls out of one weaver? Shall we do that?

And. An you love me, let's do't! I am dog at a catch.

Clown. By'r Lady, sir, and some dogs will catch well.

And. Most certain. Let our catch be 'Thou knave.'

Clown. 'Hold thy peace, thou knave,' knight? I shall be constrain'd in't to call thee knave, knight.

And. 'Tis not the first time I have constrained one to call me knave. Begin, fool. It begins, 'Hold thy peace.'

Clown. I shall never begin if I hold my peace.

And. Good, i' faith! Come, begin.

Catch sung. Enter *Maria.*

Mar. What a caterwauling do you keep here! If my lady have not call'd up her steward Malvolio and bid him turn you out of doors, never trust me.

To. My lady 's a Catayan, we are politicians, Malvolio 's a Peg-a-Ramsey, and [*sings*] 'Three merry men be we.' Am not I consanguineous? Am I not of her blood? Tilly-vally, lady! [*sings*] 'There dwelt a man in Babylon, lady, lady!'

Clown. Beshrew me, the knight 's in admirable fooling.

And. Ay, he does well enough if he be dispos'd, and so do I too. He does it with a better grace, but I do it more natural.

To. [*sings*] 'O' the twelf day of December'—

Mar. For the love o' God, peace!

Enter *Malvolio.*

Mal. My masters, are you mad? or what are you? Have you no wit, manners, nor honesty, but to gabble like tinkers at this time of night? Do ye make an alehouse of my lady's house, that ye squeak out your coziers' catches without any mitigation or remorse of voice? Is there no respect of place, persons, nor time in you?

To. We did keep time, sir, in our catches. Sneck up!

Mal. Sir Toby, I must be round with you. My lady bade me tell you that, though she harbours you as her kinsman, she's nothing allied to your disorders. If you can separate yourself and your misdemeanours, you are welcome to the house. If not, and it would please you to take leave of her, she is very willing to bid you farewell.

To. [*sings*] 'Farewell, dear heart since I must needs be gone.'

Mar. Nay, good Sir Toby!

Clown. [*sings*] 'His eyes do show his days are almost done.'

Mal. Is't even so?

To. 'But I will never die.'

Clown. Sir Toby, there you lie.

Mal. This is much credit to you!

To. 'Shall I bid him go?'

Clown. 'What an if you do?'

To. 'Shall I bid him go, and spare not?'

Clown. 'O, no, no, no, no, you dare not!'

To. Out o' tune, sir? Ye lie. Art any more than a steward? Dost thou think, because thou art virtuous, there shall be no more cakes and ale?

Clown. Yes, by Saint Anne! and ginger shall be hot i' th' mouth too.

To. Th'art i' th' right. — Go, sir, rub your chain with crumbs. A stoup of wine, Maria!

Mal. Mistress Mary, if you priz'd my lady's favour at anything more than contempt, you would not give means for this uncivil rule. She shall know of it, by this hand. *Exit.*

Mar. Go shake your ears!

And. 'Twere as good a deed as to drink when a man's ahungry, to challenge him the field, and then to break promise with him and make a fool of him.

To. Do't, knight. I'll write thee a challenge; or I'll deliver thy indignation to him by word of mouth.

Mar. Sweet Sir Toby, be patient for to-night. Since the youth of the Count's was to-day with my lady, she is much out of quiet. For Monsieur Malvolio, let me alone with him. If I do not gull him into a nayword, and make him a common recreation, do not think I have wit enough to lie straight in my bed. I know I can do it.

To. Possess us, possess us! Tell us something of him.

Mar. Marry, sir, sometimes he is a kind of Puritan.

And. O, if I thought that, I'd beat him like a dog!

To. What, for being a Puritan? Thy exquisite reason, dear knight?

And. I have no exquisite reason for't, but I have reason good enough.

Mar. The devil a Puritan that he is, or anything constantly but a time-pleaser; an affection'd ass, that cons state without book and utters it by great swarths; the best persuaded of himself; so cramm'd, as he thinks, with excellencies that it is his grounds of faith that all that look on him love him; and on that vice in him will my revenge find notable cause to work.

To. What wilt thou do?

Mar. I will drop in his way some obscure epistles of love, wherein by the colour of his beard, the shape of his leg, the manner of his gait, the expressure of his eye, forehead, and complexion, he shall find himself most feelingly personated. I can write very like my lady your niece; on a forgotten matter we can hardly make distinction of our hands.

To. Excellent! I smell a device.

And. I have't in my nose too.

To. He shall think by the letters that thou wilt drop that they come from my niece, and that she's in love with him.

Mar. My purpose is indeed a horse of that colour.

And. And your horse now would make him an ass.

Mar. Ass, I doubt not.

And. O, 'twill be admirable!

Mar. Sport royal, I warrant you. I know my physic will work with him. I will plant you two, and let the fool make a third, where he shall find the letter. Observe his construction of it. For this night, to bed, and dream on the event. Farewell. *Exit.*

To. Good night, Penthesilea.

And. Before me, she's a good wench.

To. She's a beagle true-bred, and one that adores me. What o' that?

And. I was ador'd once too.

To. Let's to bed, knight. Thou hadst need send for more money.

And. If I cannot recover your niece, I am a foul way out.

To. Send for money, knight. If thou hast her not i' th' end, call me Cut.

And. If I do not, never trust me, take it how you will.

To. Come, come; I'll go burn some sack. 'Tis too late to go to bed now. Come, knight; come, knight. *Exeunt.*

Scene IV. [*The* Duke's *Palace.*]

Enter *Duke, Viola, Curio,* and others.

Duke. Give me some music. Now good morrow, friends.
Now, good Cesario, but that piece of song,
That old and antique song we heard last night.
Methought it did relieve my passion much,
More than light airs and recollected terms
Of these most brisk and giddy-paced times.
Come, but one verse.

Cur. He is not here, so please your lordship, that should sing it.

Duke. Who was it?

Cur. Feste the jester, my lord, a fool that the Lady Olivia's father took much delight in. He is about the house.

Duke. Seek him out. [*Exit Curio.*] And play the tune the while. *Music plays.*
Come hither, boy. If ever thou shalt love,
In the sweet pangs of it remember me;
For such as I am all true lovers are,
Unstaid and skittish in all motions else
Save in the constant image of the creature
That is belov'd. How dost thou like this tune?

Vio. It gives a very echo to the seat
Where Love is thron'd.

Duke. Thou dost speak masterly.
My life upon't, young though thou art, thine eye
Hath stay'd upon some favour that it loves.
Hath it not, boy?

Vio. A little, by your favour.

Duke. What kind of woman is't?

Vio. Of your complexion.

Duke. She is not worth thee then. What years, i' faith?

Vio. About your years, my lord.

Duke. Too old, by heaven! Let still the woman take
An elder than herself: so wears she to him,
So sways she level in her husband's heart;
For, boy, however we do praise ourselves,
Our fancies are more giddy and unfirm,
More longing, wavering, sooner lost and won,
Than women's are.

Vio. I think it well, my lord.

Duke. Then let thy love be younger than thyself,
Or thy affection cannot hold the bent;
For women are as roses, whose fair flow'r,
Being once display'd, doth fall that very hour.

Vio. And so they are; alas, that they are so!
To die, even when they to perfection grow!

Enter *Curio* and *Clown.*

Duke. O, fellow, come, the song we had last night.
Mark it, Cesario; it is old and plain.
The spinsters and the knitters in the sun,
And the free maids that weave their thread with bones,
Do use to chant it. It is silly sooth,
And dallies with the innocence of love
Like the old age.

Clown. Are you ready, sir?

Duke. Ay; prithee sing. *Music.*

The [*Clown's*] *Song.*

Come away, come away, death,
And in sad cypress let me be laid.
Fly away, fly away, breath;
I am slain by a fair cruel maid.
My shroud of white, stuck all with yew,
O, prepare it!
My part of death, no one so true
Did share it.

Not a flower, not a flower sweet,
On my black coffin let there be strown;
Not a friend, not a friend greet
My poor corpse, where my bones shall be thrown.
A thousand thousand sighs to save,
Lay me, O, where
Sad true lover never find my grave,
To weep there!

Duke. There's for thy pains.

Clown. No pains, sir. I take pleasure in singing, sir.

Duke. I'll pay thy pleasure then.

Clown. Truly, sir, and pleasure will be paid one time or another.

Duke. Give me now leave to leave thee.

Clown. Now the melancholy god protect thee, and the tailor make thy doublet of changeable taffeta, for thy mind is a very opal! I would have men of such constancy put to sea, that their business might be everything, and their intent everywhere; for that's it that always makes a good voyage of nothing. Farewell. *Exit.*

Duke. Let all the rest give place.
[*Exeunt Curio and Attendants.*]
Once more, Cesario,
Get thee to yond same sovereign cruelty.
Tell her, my love, more noble than the world,
Prizes not quantity of dirty lands.
The parts that fortune hath bestow'd upon her,
Tell her I hold as giddily as fortune;
But 'tis that miracle and queen of gems
That nature pranks her in, attracts my soul.

Vio. But if she cannot love you, sir —

Duke. I cannot be so answer'd.

Vio. Sooth, but you must.
Say that some lady, as perhaps there is,
Hath for your love as great a pang of heart
As you have for Olivia. You cannot love her.
You tell her so. Must she not then be answer'd?

Duke. There is no woman's sides
Can bide the beating of so strong a passion
As love doth give my heart; no woman's heart
So big to hold so much; they lack retention.
Alas, their love may be call'd appetite —
No motion of the liver, but the palate —
That suffers surfeit, cloyment, and revolt;
But mine is all as hungry as the sea
And can digest as much. Make no compare
Between that love a woman can bear me
And that I owe Olivia.

Vio. Ay, but I know —

Duke. What dost thou know?

Vio. Too well what love women to men may owe.
In faith, they are as true of heart as we.
My father had a daughter lov'd a man
As it might be perhaps, were I a woman,
I should your lordship.

Duke. And what's her history?

Vio. A blank, my lord. She never told her love,
But let concealment, like a worm i' th' bud,
Feed on her damask cheek. She pin'd in thought;
And, with a green and yellow melancholy,
She sat like Patience on a monument,
Smiling at grief. Was not this love indeed?
We men may say more, swear more; but indeed
Our shows are more than will; for still we prove
Much in our vows but little in our love.

Duke. But died thy sister of her love, my boy?

Vio. I am all the daughters of my father's house,
And all the brothers too — and yet I know not.
Sir, shall I to this lady?

Duke. Ay, that's the theme.
To her in haste! Give her this jewel. Say
My love can give no place, bide no denay.
Exeunt.

Scene V. [Olivia's *orchard.*]

Enter *Sir Toby, Sir Andrew,* and *Fabian.*

To. Come thy ways, Signior Fabian.

Fab. Nay, I'll come. If I lose a scruple of this sport, let me be boil'd to death with melancholy.

To. Wouldst thou not be glad to have the niggardly rascally sheep-biter come by some notable shame?

Fab. I would exult, man. You know he brought me out o' favour with my lady about a bear-baiting here.

To. To anger him we'll have the bear again; and we will fool him black and blue. Shall we not, Sir Andrew?

And. An we do not, it is pity of our lives.

Enter *Maria.*

To. Here comes the little villain. How now, my metal of India?

Mar. Get ye all three into the box tree. Malvolio's coming down this walk. He has been yonder i' the sun practising behaviour to his own shadow this half hour. Observe him, for the love of mockery; for I know this letter will make a contemplative idiot of him. Close, in the name of jesting! [*The others hide.*] Lie thou there [*Throws down a letter*]; for here comes the trout that must be caught with tickling. *Exit.*

Enter *Malvolio.*

Mal. 'Tis but fortune; all is fortune. Maria once told me she did affect me; and I have heard herself come thus near, that, should she fancy, it should be one of my complexion. Besides, she uses me with a more exalted respect than any one else that follows her. What should I think on't?

To. Here's an overweening rogue!

Fab. O, peace! Contemplation makes a rare turkey cock of him. How he jets under his advanc'd plumes!

And. 'Slight, I could so beat the rogue!

Fab. Peace, I say.

Mal. To be Count Malvolio!

To. Ah, rogue!

And. Pistol him, pistol him!

Fab. Peace, peace!

Mal. There is example for't. The Lady of the Strachy married the yeoman of the wardrobe.

And. Fie on him, Jezebel!

Fab. O, peace! Now he's deeply in. Look how imagination blows him.

Mal. Having been three months married to her, sitting in my state —

To. O for a stone-bow, to hit him in the eye!

Mal. Calling my officers about me, in my branch'd velvet gown; having come from a day-bed, where I have left Olivia sleeping —

To. Fire and brimstone!

Fab. O, peace, peace!

Mal. And then to have the humour of state; and after a demure travel of regard — telling them I know my place, as I would they should do theirs — to ask for my kinsman Toby —

To. Bolts and shackles!

Fab. O, peace, peace, peace! Now, now.

Mal. Seven of my people, with an obedient start, make out for him. I frown the while, and perchance wind up my watch, or play with my — some rich jewel. Toby approaches; curtsies there to me —

To. Shall this fellow live?

Fab. Though our silence be drawn from us by th' ears, yet peace!

Mal. I extend my hand to him thus, quenching my familiar smile with an austere regard of control —

To. And does not Toby take you a blow o' the lips then?

Mal. Saying, 'Cousin Toby, my fortunes having cast me on your niece, give me this prerogative of speech.'

To. What, what?

Mal. 'You must amend your drunkenness.'

To. Out, scab!

Fab. Nay, patience, or we break the sinews of our plot.

Mal. 'Besides, you waste the treasure of your time with a foolish knight' —

And. That's me, I warrant you.

Mal. 'One Sir Andrew' —

And. I knew 'twas I, for many do call me fool.

Mal. What employment have we here?

[*Takes up the letter.*]

Fab. Now is the woodcock near the gin.

To. O, peace! and the spirit of humours intimate reading aloud to him!

Mal. By my life, this is my lady's hand! These be her very C's, her U's, and her T's; and thus makes she her great P's. It is, in contempt of question, her hand.

And. Her C's, her U's, and her T's? Why that?

Mal. [*reads*] 'To the unknown belov'd, this, and my good wishes.' Her very phrases! By your leave, wax. Soft! and the impressure her Lucrece, with which she uses to seal! 'Tis my lady. To whom should this be?

Fab. This wins him, liver and all.

Mal. [*reads*]

'Jove knows I love —
But who?
Lips, do not move;
No man must know.'

'No man must know.' What follows? The numbers alter'd! 'No man must know.' If this should be thee, Malvolio?

To. Marry, hang thee, brock!

Mal. [*reads*]

'I may command where I adore;
But silence, like a Lucrece knife,
With bloodless stroke my heart doth gore.
M. O. A. I. doth sway my life.'

Fab. A fustian riddle!

To. Excellent wench, say I.

Mal. 'M. O. A. I. doth sway my life.' Nay, but first, let me see, let me see, let me see.

Fab. What dish o' poison has she dress'd him!

To. And with what wing the staniel checks at it!

Mal. 'I may command where I adore.' Why, she may command me: I serve her; she is my lady. Why, this is evident to any formal capacity. There is no obstruction in this. And the end — what should that alphabetical position portend? If I could make that resemble something in me! Softly! M. O. A. I.

To. O, ay, make up that! He is now at a cold scent.

Fab. Sowter will cry upon't for all this, though it be as rank as a fox.

Mal. M. — Malvolio. M. — Why, that begins my name!

Fab. Did not I say he would work it out? The cur is excellent at faults.

Mal. M. — But then there is no consonancy in the sequel. That suffers under probation. A should follow, but O does.

Fab. And O shall end, I hope.

To. Ay, or I'll cudgel him, and make him cry O!

Mal. And then I comes behind.

Fab. Ay, an you had any eye behind you, you might see more detraction at your heels than fortunes before you.

Mal. M, O, A, I. This simulation is not as the former; and yet, to crush this a little, it would bow to me, for every one of these letters are in my name. Soft! here follows prose.

[*Reads*] 'If this fall into thy hand, revolve. In my stars I am above thee; but be not afraid of greatness. Some are born great, some achieve greatness, and some have greatness thrust upon 'em. Thy Fates open their hands; let thy blood and spirit embrace them; and to inure thyself to what thou art like to be, cast thy humble slough and appear fresh. Be opposite with a kinsman, surly with servants. Let thy tongue tang arguments of state; put thyself into the trick of singularity. She thus advises thee that sighs for thee. Remember who commended thy yellow stockings and wish'd to see thee ever cross-garter'd. I say, remember. Go to, thou art made, if thou desir'st to be so. If not, let me see thee a steward still, the fellow of servants, and not worthy to touch Fortune's fingers. Farewell. She that would alter services with thee,

'The Fortunate Unhappy.'

Daylight and champian discovers not more. This is open. I will be proud, I will read politic authors, I will baffle Sir Toby, I will wash off gross acquaintance, I will be point-devise, the very man. I do not now fool myself, to let imagination jade me; for every reason excites to this, that my lady loves me. She did commend my yellow stockings of late, she did praise my leg being cross-garter'd; and in this she manifests herself to my love, and with a kind of injunction drives me to these habits of her liking. I thank my stars, I am happy. I will be strange, stout, in yellow stockings, and cross-garter'd, even with the swiftness of putting on. Jove and my stars be praised! Here is yet a postscript.

'Thou canst not choose but know who I am. If thou entertain'st my love, let it appear in thy smiling. Thy smiles become thee well. Therefore in my presence still smile, dear my sweet, I prithee.'

Jove, I thank thee. I will smile; I will do everything that thou wilt have me. *Exit.*

Fab. I will not give my part of this sport for a pension of thousands to be paid from the Sophy.

To. I could marry this wench for this device —

And. So could I too.

To. And ask no other dowry with her but such another jest.

Enter *Maria.*

And. Nor I neither.

Fab. Here comes my noble gull-catcher.

To. Wilt thou set thy foot o' my neck?

And. Or o' mine either?

To. Shall I play my freedom at tray-trip and become thy bondslave?

And. I' faith, or I either?

To. Why, thou hast put him in such a dream that, when the image of it leaves him, he must run mad.

Mar. Nay, but say true, does it work upon him?

To. Like aqua-vitæ with a midwife.

Mar. If you will, then, see the fruits of the sport, mark his first approach before my lady. He will come to her in yellow stockings, and 'tis a colour she abhors, and cross-garter'd, a fashion she detests; and he will smile upon her, which will now be so unsuitable to her disposition, being addicted to a melancholy as she is, that it cannot but turn him into a notable contempt. If you will see it, follow me.

To. To the gates of Tartar, thou most excellent devil of wit!

And. I'll make one too. *Exeunt.*

Act III. Scene I. [Olivia's *orchard.*]

Enter *Viola,* and *Clown* [with a tabor and pipe].

Vio. Save thee, friend, and thy music! Dost thou live by thy tabor?

Clown. No, sir, I live by the church.

Vio. Art thou a churchman?

Clown. No such matter, sir. I do live by the church; for I do live at my house, and my house doth stand by the church.

Vio. So thou mayst say, the king lies by a beggar, if a beggar dwell near him; or, the church stands by thy tabor, if thy tabor stand by the church.

Clown. You have said, sir. To see this age! A sentence is but a chev'ril glove to a good wit. How quickly the wrong side may be turn'd outward!

Vio. Nay, that's certain. They that dally nicely with words may quickly make them wanton.

Clown. I would therefore my sister had had no name, sir.

Vio. Why, man?

Clown. Why, sir, her name's a word, and to dally with that word might make my sister wanton. But indeed words are very rascals since bonds disgrac'd them.

Vio. Thy reason, man?

Clown. Troth, sir, I can yield you none without words, and words are grown so false I am loath to prove reason with them.

Vio. I warrant thou art a merry fellow and car'st for nothing.

Clown. Not so, sir; I do care for something; but in my conscience, sir, I do not care for you. If that be to care for nothing, sir, I would it would make you invisible.

Vio. Art not thou the Lady Olivia's fool?

Clown. No, indeed, sir. The Lady Olivia has no folly. She will keep no fool, sir, till she be married; and fools are as like husbands as pilchers are to herrings — the husband's the bigger. I am indeed not her fool, but her corrupter of words.

Vio. I saw thee late at the Count Orsino's.

Clown. Foolery, sir, does walk about the orb like the sun; it shines everywhere. I would be sorry, sir, but the fool should be as oft with your master as with my mistress. I think I saw your wisdom there.

Vio. Nay, an thou pass upon me, I'll no more with thee. Hold, there's expenses for thee. [*Gives a piece of money.*]

Clown. Now Jove, in his next commodity of hair, send thee a beard!

Vio. By my troth, I'll tell thee, I am almost sick for one, though I would not have it grow on my chin. Is thy lady within?

Clown. Would not a pair of these have bred, sir?

Vio. Yes, being kept together and put to use.

Clown. I would play Lord Pandarus of Phrygia, sir, to bring a Cressida to this Troilus.

Vio. I understand you, sir. 'Tis well begg'd. [*Gives another piece.*]

Clown. The matter, I hope, is not great, sir, begging but a beggar: Cressida was a beggar. My lady is within, sir. I will conster to them whence you come. Who you are and what you would are out of my welkin — I might say 'element,' but the word is over-worn. *Exit.*

Vio. This fellow is wise enough to play the fool,
And to do that well craves a kind of wit.
He must observe their mood on whom he jests,
The quality of persons, and the time;
Not, like the haggard, check at every feather
That comes before his eye. This is a practice
As full of labour as a wise man's art;
For folly that he wisely shows, is fit;
But wise men, folly-fall'n, quite taint their wit.

Enter *Sir Toby* and [*Sir*] *Andrew.*

To. Save you, gentleman!

Vio. And you, sir.

And. Dieu vous garde, monsieur.

Vio. Et vous aussi; vostre serviteur.

And. I hope, sir, you are, and I am yours.

To. Will you encounter the house? My niece is desirous you should enter, if your trade be to her.

Vio. I am bound to your niece, sir. I mean, she is the list of my voyage.

To. Taste your legs, sir; put them to motion.

Vio. My legs do better understand me, sir, than I understand what you mean by bidding me taste my legs.

To. I mean, to go, sir, to enter.

Vio. I will answer you with gait and entrance. But we are prevented.

Enter *Olivia* and *Gentlewoman,* [*Maria*].

Most excellent accomplish'd lady, the heavens rain odours on you!

And. [*aside*] That youth's a rare courtier. 'Rain odours' — well!

Vio. My matter hath no voice, lady, but to your own most pregnant and vouchsafed ear.

And. [*aside*] 'Odours,' 'pregnant,' and 'vouchsafed' — I'll get 'em all three all ready.

Oli. Let the garden door be shut, and leave me to my hearing. [*Exeunt Sir Toby, Sir Andrew, and Maria.*] Give me your hand, sir.

Vio. My duty, madam, and most humble service.

Oli. What is your name?

Vio. Cesario is your servant's name, fair princess.

Oli. My servant, sir? 'Twas never merry world
Since lowly feigning was call'd compliment.
Y'are servant to the Count Orsino, youth.

Vio. And he is yours, and his must needs be yours.
Your servant's servant is your servant, madam.

Oli. For him, I think not on him; for his thoughts,
Would they were blanks, rather than fill'd with me!

Vio. Madam, I come to whet your gentle thoughts
On his behalf.
Oli. O, by your leave, I pray you!
I bade you never speak again of him;
But, would you undertake another suit,
I had rather hear you to solicit that
Than music from the spheres.
Vio. Dear lady —
Oli. Give me leave, beseech you. I did send,
After the last enchantment you did here,
A ring in chase of you. So did I abuse
Myself, my servant, and, I fear me, you.
Under your hard construction must I sit,
To force that on you in a shameful cunning
Which you knew none of yours. What might you think?
Have you not set mine honour at the stake
And baited it with all th' unmuzzled thoughts
That tyrannous heart can think? To one of your receiving
Enough is shown; a cypress, not a bosom,
Hides my heart. So, let me hear you speak.
Vio. I pity you.
Oli. That's a degree to love.
Vio. No, not a grize; for 'tis a vulgar proof
That very oft we pity enemies.
Oli. Why then, methinks 'tis time to smile again.
O world, how apt the poor are to be proud!
If one should be a prey, how much the better
To fall before the lion than the wolf!
Clock strikes.
The clock upbraids me with the waste of time.
Be not afraid, good youth, I will not have you;
And yet, when wit and youth is come to harvest,
Your wife is like to reap a proper man.
There lies your way, due west.
Vio. Then westward ho!
Grace and good disposition attend your ladyship!
You'll nothing, madam, to my lord by me?
Oli. Stay.
I prithee tell me what thou think'st of me.
Vio. That you do think you are not what you are.
Oli. If I think so, I think the same of you.
Vio. Then think you right. I am not what I am.
Oli. I would you were as I would have you be!
Vio. Would it be better, madam, than I am?
I wish it might; for now I am your fool.
Oli. O, what a deal of scorn looks beautiful
In the contempt and anger of his lip!
A murd'rous guilt shows not itself more soon
Than love that would seem hid: love's night is noon.
Cesario, by the roses of the spring,
By maidhood, honour, truth, and everything,
I love thee so that, maugre all thy pride,
Nor wit nor reason can my passion hide.
Do not extort thy reasons from this clause,
For that I woo, thou therefore hast no cause;
But rather reason thus with reason fetter:
Love sought is good, but given unsought is better.
Vio. By innocence I swear, and by my youth,
I have one heart, one bosom, and one truth,
And that no woman has; nor never none
Shall mistress be of it, save I alone.
And so adieu, good madam. Never more
Will I my master's tears to you deplore.
Oli. Yet come again; for thou perhaps mayst move
That heart which now abhors to like his love.
Exeunt.

Scene II. [Olivia's *house.*]

Enter *Sir Toby, Sir Andrew,* and *Fabian.*

And. No, faith, I'll not stay a jot longer.

To. Thy reason, dear venom; give thy reason.

Fab. You must needs yield your reason, Sir Andrew.

And. Marry, I saw your niece do more favours to the Count's servingman than ever she bestow'd upon me. I saw't i' th' orchard.

To. Did she see thee the while, old boy? Tell me that.

And. As plain as I see you now.

Fab. This was a great argument of love in her toward you.

And. 'Slight! will you make an ass o' me?

Fab. I will prove it legitimate, sir, upon the oaths of judgment and reason.

To. And they have been grand-jurymen since before Noah was a sailor.

Fab. She did show favour to the youth in your sight only to exasperate you, to awake your dormouse valour, to put fire in your heart and brimstone in your liver. You should then have accosted her; and with some excellent jests, fire-new from the mint, you should have bang'd the youth into dumbness. This was look'd for at your hand, and this was balk'd. The double gilt of this opportunity you let time wash off, and you are now sail'd into the North of my lady's opinion, where you will hang like an icicle on a Dutchman's beard unless you do redeem it by some laudable attempt either of valour or policy.

And. An't be any way, it must be with valour; for policy I hate. I had as lief be a Brownist as a politician.

To. Why then, build me thy fortunes upon the basis of valour. Challenge me the Count's youth to fight with him; hurt him in eleven places. My niece shall take note of it; and assure thyself there is no love-broker in the world can more prevail in man's commendation with woman than report of valour.

Fab. There is no way but this, Sir Andrew.

And. Will either of you bear me a challenge to him?

To. Go, write it in a martial hand. Be curst and brief; it is no matter how witty, so it be eloquent and full of invention. Taunt him with the license of ink. If thou thou'st him some thrice, it shall not be amiss; and as many lies as will lie in thy sheet of paper, although the sheet were big enough for the bed of Ware in England, set 'em down. Go, about it! Let there be gall enough in thy ink, though thou write with a goose-pen, no matter. About it!

And. Where shall I find you?

To. We'll call thee at the cubiculo. Go.

Exit Sir Andrew.

Fab. This is a dear manikin to you, Sir Toby.

To. I have been dear to him, lad — some two thousand strong, or so.

Fab. We shall have a rare letter from him — but you'll not deliver 't?

To. Never trust me then; and by all means stir on the youth to an answer. I think oxen and wainropes cannot hale them together. For Andrew, if he were open'd, and you find so much blood in his liver as will clog the foot of a flea, I'll eat the rest of th' anatomy.

Fab. And his opposite, the youth, bears in his visage no great presage of cruelty.

Enter *Maria.*

To. Look where the youngest wren of nine comes.

Mar. If you desire the spleen, and will laugh yourselves into stitches, follow me. Yond gull Malvolio is turned heathen, a very renegado; for there is no Christian that means to be saved by believing rightly can ever believe such impossible passages of grossness. He's in yellow stockings!

To. And cross-garter'd?

Mar. Most villanously; like a pedant that keeps a school i' th' church. I have dogg'd him like his murtherer. He does obey every point of the letter that I dropp'd to betray him. He does smile his face into more lines than is in the new map with the augmentation of the Indies. You have not seen such a thing as 'tis. I can hardly forbear hurling things at him. I know my lady will strike him. If she do, he'll smile, and take't for a great favour.

To. Come bring us, bring us where he is!

Exeunt omnes.

Scene III. [*A street.*]

Enter *Sebastian* and *Antonio.*

Seb. I would not by my will have troubled you;
But since you make your pleasure of your pains,
I will no further chide you.

Ant. I could not stay behind you. My desire,
More sharp than filed steel, did spur me forth;
And not all love to see you (though so much
As might have drawn one to a longer voyage)
But jealousy what might befall your travel,
Being skilless in these parts; which to a stranger,
Unguided and unfriended, often prove
Rough and unhospitable. My willing love,
The rather by these arguments of fear,
Set forth in your pursuit.

Seb. My kind Antonio,
I can no other answer make but thanks,
And thanks, and ever thanks; and oft good turns
Are shuffled off with such uncurrent pay.
But, were my worth as is my conscience firm,
You should find better dealing. What's to do?
Shall we go see the relics of this town?

Ant. To-morrow, sir; best first go see your lodging.

Seb. I am not weary, and 'tis long to night.
I pray you let us satisfy our eyes
With the memorials and the things of fame
That do renown this city.

Ant. Would you'd pardon me.
I do not without danger walk these streets.
Once in a sea-fight 'gainst the Count his galleys
I did some service; of such note indeed
That, were I ta'en here, it would scarce be answer'd.

Seb. Belike you slew great number of his people?

Ant. Th' offence is not of such a bloody nature,
Albeit the quality of the time and quarrel
Might well have given us bloody argument.
It might have since been answer'd in repaying
What we took from them, which for traffic's sake
Most of our city did. Only myself stood out;
For which, if I be lapsed in this place,
I shall pay dear.
Seb. Do not then walk too open.
Ant. It doth not fit me. Hold, sir, here's my purse.
In the south suburbs at the Elephant
Is best to lodge. I will bespeak our diet,
Whiles you beguile the time and feed your knowledge
With viewing of the town. There shall you have me.
Seb. Why I your purse?
Ant. Haply your eye shall light upon some toy
You have desire to purchase; and your store
I think is not for idle markets, sir.
Seb. I'll be your purse-bearer, and leave you for
An hour.
Ant. To th' Elephant.
Seb. I do remember.
Exeunt.

Scene IV. [Olivia's *orchard.*]

Enter *Olivia* and *Maria.*

Oli. I have sent after him; he says he'll come.
How shall I feast him? what bestow of him?
For youth is bought more oft than begg'd or borrow'd.
I speak too loud.
Where is Malvolio? He is sad and civil,
And suits well for a servant with my fortunes.
Where is Malvolio?

Mar. He's coming, madam; but in very strange manner. He is sure possess'd, madam.

Oli. Why, what's the matter? Does he rave?

Mar. No, madam, he does nothing but smile. Your ladyship were best to have some guard about you if he come, for sure the man is tainted in 's wits.

Oli. Go call him hither. [*Exit Maria.*] I am as mad as he,
If sad and merry madness equal be.

Enter [*Maria,* with] *Malvolio.*

How now, Malvolio?

Mal. Sweet lady, ho, ho!

Oli. Smil'st thou?
I sent for thee upon a sad occasion.

Mal. Sad, lady? I could be sad. This does make some obstruction in the blood, this cross-gartering; but what of that? If it please the eye of one, it is with me as the very true sonnet is, 'Please one, and please all.'

Oli. Why, how dost thou, man? What is the matter with thee?

Mal. Not black in my mind, though yellow in my legs. It did come to his hands, and commands shall be executed. I think we do know the sweet Roman hand.

Oli. Wilt thou go to bed, Malvolio?

Mal. To bed? Ay, sweetheart; and I'll come to thee.

Oli. God comfort thee! Why dost thou smile so, and kiss thy hand so oft?

Mar. How do you, Malvolio?

Mal. At your request? Yes, nightingales answer daws!

Mar. Why appear you with this ridiculous boldness before my lady?

Mal. 'Be not afraid of greatness.' 'Twas well writ.

Oli. What mean'st thou by that, Malvolio?

Mal. 'Some are born great' —

Oli. Ha?

Mal. 'Some achieve greatness' —

Oli. What say'st thou?

Mal. 'And some have greatness thrust upon them.'

Oli. Heaven restore thee!

Mal. 'Remember who commended thy yellow stockings' —

Oli. My yellow stockings?

Mal. 'And wish'd to see thee cross-garter'd.'

Oli. Cross-garter'd?

Mal. 'Go to, thou art made, if thou desir'st to be so' —

Oli. Am I made?

Mal. 'If not, let me see thee a servant still.'

Oli. Why, this is very midsummer madness.

Enter *Servant.*

Ser. Madam, the young gentleman of the Count Orsino's is return'd. I could hardly entreat him back. He attends your ladyship's pleasure.

Oli. I'll come to him. [*Exit Servant.*] Good Maria, let this fellow be look'd to. Where's my cousin Toby? Let some of my people have a special care of him. I would not have him miscarry for the half of my dowry.

Exit [*Olivia; then Maria*].

Mal. O ho! do you come near me now? No worse man than Sir Toby to look to me! This concurs directly with the letter. She sends him on purpose, that I may appear stubborn to him; for she incites me to that in the letter. 'Cast thy humble slough,' says she; 'be opposite with a kinsman, surly with servants; let thy tongue tang with arguments of state; put thyself into the trick of singularity'; — and consequently sets down the manner how: as, a sad face, a reverend carriage, a slow tongue, in the habit of some sir of note, and so forth. I have lim'd her; but it is Jove's doing, and Jove make me thankful! And when she went away now, 'Let this fellow be look'd to.' 'Fellow!' not 'Malvolio,' nor after my degree, but 'fellow.' Why, everything adheres together, that no dram of a scruple, no scruple of a scruple, no obstacle, no incredulous or unsafe circumstance — What can be said? Nothing that can be can come between me and the full prospect of my hopes. Well, Jove, not I, is the doer of this, and he is to be thanked.

Enter [*Sir*] *Toby, Fabian,* and *Maria.*

To. Which way is he, in the name of sanctity? If all the devils of hell be drawn in little, and Legion himself possess'd him, yet I'll speak to him.

Fab. Here he is, here he is! How is't with you, sir?

To. How is't with you, man?

Mal. Go off; I discard you. Let me enjoy my private. Go off.

Mar. Lo, how hollow the fiend speaks within him! Did not I tell you? Sir Toby, my lady prays you to have a care of him.

Mal. Aha! does she so?

To. Go to, go to; peace, peace! We must deal gently with him. Let me alone. How do you, Malvolio? How is't with you? What, man! defy the devil! Consider, he's an enemy to mankind.

Mal. Do you know what you say?

Mar. La you, an you speak ill of the devil, how he takes it at heart! Pray God he be not bewitch'd!

Fab. Carry his water to th' wise woman.

Mar. Marry, and it shall be done to-morrow morning if I live. My lady would not lose him for more than I'll say.

Mal. How now, mistress?

Mar. O Lord!

To. Prithee hold thy peace. This is not the way. Do you not see you move him? Let me alone with him.

Fab. No way but gentleness; gently, gently. The fiend is rough and will not be roughly us'd.

To. Why, how now, my bawcock? How dost thou, chuck?

Mal. Sir!

To. Ay, biddy, come with me. What, man! 'tis not for gravity to play at cherry-pit with Satan. Hang him, foul collier!

Mar. Get him to say his prayers. Good Sir Toby, get him to pray.

Mal. My prayers, minx?

Mar. No, I warrant you, he will not hear of godliness.

Mal. Go hang yourselves all! You are idle shallow things; I am not of your element. You shall know more hereafter. *Exit.*

To. Is't possible?

Fab. If this were play'd upon a stage now, I could condemn it as an improbable fiction.

To. His very genius hath taken the infection of the device, man.

Mar. Nay, pursue him now, lest the device take air and taint.

Fab. Why, we shall make him mad indeed.

Mar. The house will be the quieter.

To. Come, we'll have him in a dark room and bound. My niece is already in the belief that he's mad. We may carry it thus, for our pleasure and his penance, till our very pastime, tired out of breath, prompt us to have mercy on him; at which time we will bring the device to the bar and crown thee for a finder of madmen. But see, but see!

Enter *Sir Andrew.*

Fab. More matter for a May morning.

And. Here's the challenge; read it. I warrant there's vinegar and pepper in't.

Fab. Is't so saucy?

And. Ay, is't, I warrant him. Do but read.

To. Give me. [*Reads*] 'Youth, whatsoever thou art, thou art but a scurvy fellow.'

Fab. Good, and valiant.

To. [*reads*] 'Wonder not nor admire not in thy mind why I do call thee so, for I will show thee no reason for't.'

Fab. A good note! That keeps you from the blow of the law.

To. [*reads*] 'Thou com'st to the Lady Olivia, and in my sight she uses thee kindly. But thou liest in thy throat; that is not the matter I challenge thee for.'

Fab. Very brief, and to exceeding good sense — less.

To. [*reads*] 'I will waylay thee going home; where if it be thy chance to kill me' —

Fab. Good.

To. [*reads*] 'Thou kill'st me like a rogue and a villain.'

Fab. Still you keep o' th' windy side of the law. Good.

To. [*reads*] 'Fare thee well, and God have mercy upon one of our souls! He may have mercy upon mine, but my hope is better; and so look to thyself. Thy friend, as thou usest him, and thy sworn enemy,

'ANDREW AGUECHEEK.'

If this letter move him not, his legs cannot. I'll give't him.

Mar. You may have very fit occasion for't. He is now in some commerce with my lady and will by-and-by depart.

To. Go, Sir Andrew! Scout me for him at the corner of the orchard like a bum-baily. So soon as ever thou seest him, draw; and as thou draw'st, swear horrible; for it comes to pass oft that a terrible oath, with a swaggering accent sharply twang'd off, gives manhood more approbation than ever proof itself would have earn'd him. Away!

And. Nay, let me alone for swearing. *Exit.*

To. Now will not I deliver his letter; for the behaviour of the young gentleman gives him out to be of good capacity and breeding; his employment between his lord and my niece confirms no less. Therefore this letter, being so excellently ignorant, will breed no terror in the youth. He will find it comes from a clodpoll. But, sir, I will deliver his challenge by word of mouth, set upon Aguecheek a notable report of valour, and drive the gentleman (as I know his youth will aptly receive it) into a most hideous opinion of his rage, skill, fury, and impetuosity. This will so fright them both that they will kill one another by the look, like cockatrices.

Enter *Olivia* and *Viola.*

Fab. Here he comes with your niece. Give them way till he take leave, and presently after him.

To. I will meditate the while upon some horrid message for a challenge.

[*Exeunt Sir Toby, Fabian, and Maria.*]

Oli. I have said too much unto a heart of stone
And laid mine honour too unchary out.
There's something in me that reproves my fault;
But such a headstrong potent fault it is
That it but mocks reproof.

Vio. With the same haviour that your passion bears
Goes on my master's grief.

Oli. Here, wear this jewel for me; 'tis my picture.
Refuse it not; it hath no tongue to vex you.
And I beseech you come again to-morrow.
What shall you ask of me that I'll deny,
That honour, sav'd, may upon asking give?

Vio. Nothing but this — your true love for my master.

Oli. How with mine honour may I give him that
Which I have given to you?

Vio. I will acquit you.

Oli. Well, come again to-morrow. Fare thee well.
A fiend like thee might bear my soul to hell.

[*Exit.*]

Enter [*Sir*] *Toby* and *Fabian.*

To. Gentleman, God save thee!

Vio. And you, sir.

To. That defence thou hast, betake thee to't. Of what nature the wrongs are thou hast done him, I know not; but thy intercepter, full of despite, bloody as the hunter, attends thee at the orchard end. Dismount thy tuck, be yare in thy preparation; for thy assailant is quick, skilful, and deadly.

Vio. You mistake, sir. I am sure no man hath any quarrel to me. My remembrance is very free and clear from any image of offence done to any man.

To. You'll find it otherwise, I assure you. Therefore, if you hold your life at any price, betake you to your guard; for your opposite hath in him what youth, strength, skill, and wrath can furnish man withal.

Vio. I pray you, sir, what is he?

To. He is knight, dubb'd with unhatch'd rapier and on carpet consideration; but he is a devil in private brawl. Souls and bodies hath he divorc'd three; and his incensement at this moment is so implacable that satisfaction can be none but by pangs of death and sepulchre. 'Hob, nob' is his word; 'give't or take't.'

Vio. I will return again into the house and desire some conduct of the lady. I am no fighter. I have heard of some kind of men that put quarrels purposely on others to taste their valour. Belike this is a man of that quirk.

To. Sir, no. His indignation derives itself out of a very competent injury; therefore get you on and give him his desire. Back you shall not to the house, unless you undertake that with me which with as much safety you might answer him. Therefore on! or strip your sword stark naked; for meddle you must, that's certain, or forswear to wear iron about you.

Vio. This is as uncivil as strange. I beseech you do me this courteous office, as to know of the knight what my offence to him is. It is something of my negligence, nothing of my purpose.

To. I will do so. Signior Fabian, stay you by this gentleman till my return. *Exit.*

Vio. Pray you, sir, do you know of this matter?

Fab. I know the knight is incens'd against you, even to a mortal arbitrement; but nothing of the circumstance more.

Vio. I beseech you, what manner of man is he?

Fab. Nothing of that wonderful promise, to read him by his form, as you are like to find him in the proof of his valour. He is indeed, sir, the most skilful, bloody, and fatal opposite that you could possibly have found in any part of Illyria. Will you walk towards him? I will make your peace with him if I can.

Vio. I shall be much bound to you for't. I am one that had rather go with sir priest than sir knight. I care not who knows so much of my mettle. *Exeunt.*

Enter [*Sir*] *Toby* and [*Sir*] *Andrew* [at the orchard end].

To. Why, man, he's a very devil; I have not seen such a firago. I had a pass with him, rapier, scabbard, and all, and he gives me the stuck-in with such a mortal motion that it is inevitable; and on the answer he pays you as surely as your feet hit the ground they step on. They say he has been fencer to the Sophy.

And. Pox on't, I'll not meddle with him.

To. Ay, but he will not now be pacified. Fabian can scarce hold him yonder.

And. Plague on't, an I thought he had been valiant, and so cunning in fence, I'd have seen him damn'd ere I'd have challeng'd him. Let him let the matter slip, and I'll give him my horse, grey Capilet.

To. I'll make the motion. Stand here; make a good show on't. This shall end without the perdition of souls. [*Aside*] Marry, I'll ride your horse as well as I ride you.

Enter *Fabian* and *Viola*.

I have his horse to take up the quarrel. I have persuaded him the youth 's a devil.

Fab. He is as horribly conceited of him; and pants and looks pale, as if a bear were at his heels.

To. There's no remedy, sir; he will fight with you for 's oath sake. Marry, he hath better bethought him of his quarrel, and he finds that now scarce to be worth talking of. Therefore draw for the supportance of his vow. He protests he will not hurt you.

Vio. [*aside*] Pray God defend me! A little thing would make me tell them how much I lack of a man.

Fab. Give ground if you see him furious.

To. Come, Sir Andrew, there's no remedy. The gentleman will for his honour's sake have one bout with you; he cannot by the duello avoid it; but he has promised me, as he is a gentleman and a soldier, he will not hurt you. Come on, to't!

And. Pray God he keep his oath! [*Draws.*]

Enter *Antonio*.

Vio. I do assure you 'tis against my will. [*Draws.*]

Ant. Put up your sword. If this young gentleman
Have done offence, I take the fault on me;
If you offend him, I for him defy you.

To. You, sir? Why, what are you?

Ant. [*draws*] One, sir, that for his love dares yet do more
Than you have heard him brag to you he will.

To. Nay, if you be an undertaker, I am for you. [*Draws.*]

Enter *Officers*.

Fab. O good Sir Toby, hold! Here come the officers.

To. [*to Antonio*] I'll be with you anon.

Vio. [*to Sir Andrew*] Pray, sir, put your sword up, if you please.

And. Marry, will I, sir; and for that I promis'd you, I'll be as good as my word. He will bear you easily, and reins well.

1. Off. This is the man; do thy office.

2. Off. Antonio, I arrest thee at the suit
Of Count Orsino.

Ant. You do mistake me, sir.

1. Off. No, sir, no jot. I know your favour well,

Though now you have no sea-cap on your head.
Take him away. He knows I know him well.

Ant. I must obey. [*To Viola*] This comes with seeking you.
But there's no remedy; I shall answer it.
What will you do, now my necessity
Makes me to ask you for my purse? It grieves me
Much more for what I cannot do for you
Than what befalls myself. You stand amaz'd,
But be of comfort.

2. Off. Come, sir, away.

Ant. I must entreat of you some of that money.

Vio. What money, sir?
For the fair kindness you have show'd me here,
And part being prompted by your present trouble,
Out of my lean and low ability
I'll lend you something. My having is not much.
I'll make division of my present with you.
Hold, there's half my coffer.

Ant. Will you deny me now?
Is't possible that my deserts to you
Can lack persuasion? Do not tempt my misery,
Lest that it make me so unsound a man
As to upbraid you with those kindnesses
That I have done for you.

Vio. I know of none,
Nor know I you by voice or any feature.
I hate ingratitude more in a man
Than lying, vainness, babbling, drunkenness,
Or any taint of vice whose strong corruption
Inhabits our frail blood.

Ant. O heavens themselves!

2. Off. Come, sir, I pray you go.

Ant. Let me speak a little. This youth that you see here
I snatch'd one half out of the jaws of death;
Reliev'd him with such sanctity of love,
And to his image, which methought did promise
Most venerable worth, did I devotion.

1. Off. What's that to us? The time goes by. Away!

Ant. But, O, how vile an idol proves this god!
Thou hast, Sebastian, done good feature shame.
In nature there's no blemish but the mind;
None can be call'd deform'd but the unkind.
Virtue is beauty; but the beauteous evil
Are empty trunks, o'erflourish'd by the devil.

1. Off. The man grows mad. Away with him! Come, come, sir.

Ant. Lead me on. *Exit* [*with Officers*].

Vio. Methinks his words do from such passion fly
That he believes himself; so do not I.
Prove true, imagination, O, prove true,
That I, dear brother, be now ta'en for you!

To. Come hither, knight; come hither, Fabian. We'll whisper o'er a couplet or two of most sage saws.

Vio. He nam'd Sebastian. I my brother know
Yet living in my glass. Even such and so
In favour was my brother, and he went
Still in this fashion, colour, ornament,
For him I imitate. O, if it prove,
Tempests are kind, and salt waves fresh in love! [*Exit.*]

To. A very dishonest paltry boy, and more a coward than a hare. His dishonesty appears in leaving his friend here in necessity and denying him; and for his cowardship, ask Fabian.

Fab. A coward, a most devout coward; religious in it.

And. 'Slid, I'll after him again and beat him!

To. Do; cuff him soundly, but never draw thy sword.

And. An I do not — [*Exit.*]

Fab. Come, let's see the event.

To. I dare lay any money 'twill be nothing yet. *Exeunt.*

ACT IV. Scene I. [*Before* Olivia's *house.*]

Enter *Sebastian* and *Clown.*

Clown. Will you make me believe that I am not sent for you?

Seb. Go to, go to, thou art a foolish fellow. Let me be clear of thee.

Clown. Well held out, i' faith! No, I do not know you; nor I am not sent to you by my lady, to bid you come speak with her; nor your name is not Master Cesario; nor this is not my nose neither. Nothing that is so is so.

Seb. I prithee vent thy folly somewhere else. Thou know'st not me.

Clown. Vent my folly! He has heard that word of some great man, and now applies it to a fool. Vent my folly! I am afraid this great lubber, the world, will prove a cockney. I prithee now, ungird thy strangeness, and tell me what I shall vent to my lady. Shall I vent to her that thou art coming?

Seb. I prithee, foolish Greek, depart from me.
There's money for thee. If you tarry longer,
I shall give worse payment.

Clown. By my troth, thou hast an open hand. These wise men that give fools money get themselves a good report — after fourteen years' purchase.

Enter [*Sir*] *Andrew*, [*Sir*] *Toby*, and *Fabian*.

And. Now, sir, have I met you again? There's for you! [*Strikes Sebastian.*]

Seb. Why, there's for thee, and there, and there! [*Strikes Sir Andrew.*]
Are all the people mad?

To. Hold, sir, or I'll throw your dagger o'er the house. [*Seizes Sebastian.*]

Clown. This will I tell my lady straight. I would not be in some of your coats for two-pence. [*Exit.*]

To. Come on, sir; hold!

And. Nay, let him alone. I'll go another way to work with him. I'll have an action of battery against him, if there be any law in Illyria. Though I stroke him first, yet it's no matter for that.

Seb. Let go thy hand.

To. Come, sir, I will not let you go. Come, my young soldier, put up your iron. You are well flesh'd. Come on.

Seb. I will be free from thee. [*Disengages himself.*] What wouldst thou now?
If thou dar'st tempt me further, draw thy sword. [*Draws.*]

To. What, what? Nay then, I must have an ounce or two of this malapert blood from you. [*Draws.*]

Enter *Olivia*.

Oli. Hold, Toby! On thy life I charge thee hold!

To. Madam!

Oli. Will it be ever thus? Ungracious wretch,
Fit for the mountains and the barbarous caves,
Where manners ne'er were preach'd! Out of my sight!
Be not offended, dear Cesario.
Rudesby, be gone!
[*Exeunt Sir Toby, Sir Andrew, and Fabian.*]
I prithee, gentle friend,
Let thy fair wisdom, not thy passion, sway
In this uncivil and unjust extent
Against thy peace. Go with me to my house,
And hear thou there how many fruitless pranks
This ruffian hath botch'd up, that thou thereby
Mayst smile at this. Thou shalt not choose but go;
Do not deny. Beshrew his soul for me!
He started one poor heart of mine, in thee.

Seb. What relish is in this? How runs the stream?
Or I am mad, or else this is a dream.
Let fancy still my sense in Lethe steep;
If it be thus to dream, still let me sleep!

Oli. Nay, come, I prithee. Would thou'dst be rul'd by me!

Seb. Madam, I will.

Oli. O, say so, and so be!
Exeunt.

Scene II. [Olivia's *house.*]

Enter *Maria* and *Clown*.

Mar. Nay, I prithee put on this gown and this beard; make him believe thou art Sir Topas the curate; do it quickly. I'll call Sir Toby the whilst. [*Exit.*]

Clown. Well, I'll put it on, and I will dissemble myself in't, and I would I were the first that ever dissembled in such a gown. I am not tall enough to become the function well, nor lean enough to be thought a good studient; but to be said an honest man and a good housekeeper goes as fairly as to say a careful man and a great scholar. The competitors enter.

Enter [*Sir*] *Toby* [and *Maria*].

To. Jove bless thee, Master Parson.

Clown. Bonos dies, Sir Toby; for, as the old hermit of Prague, that never saw pen and ink, very wittily said to a niece of King Gorboduc, 'That that is is'; so I, being Master Parson, am Master Parson; for what is 'that' but that, and 'is' but is?

To. To him, Sir Topas.

Clown. What ho, I say. Peace in this prison!

To. The knave counterfeits well; a good knave.

Malvolio within.

Mal. Who calls there?

Clown. Sir Topas the curate, who comes to visit Malvolio the lunatic.

Mal. Sir Topas, Sir Topas, good Sir Topas, go to my lady.

Clown. Out, hyperbolical fiend! How vexest thou this man! Talkest thou nothing but of ladies?

To. Well said, Master Parson.

Mal. Sir Topas, never was man thus wronged. Good Sir Topas, do not think I am mad. They have laid me here in hideous darkness.

Clown. Fie, thou dishonest Satan! I call thee by the most modest terms; for I am one of those gentle ones that will use the devil himself with courtesy. Say'st thou that house is dark?

Mal. As hell, Sir Topas.

Clown. Why, it hath bay windows transparent as barricadoes, and the clerestories toward the south north are as lustrous as ebony; and yet complainest thou of obstruction?

Mal. I am not mad, Sir Topas. I say to you this house is dark.

Clown. Madman, thou errest. I say there is no darkness but ignorance, in which thou art more puzzled than the Egyptians in their fog.

Mal. I say this house is as dark as ignorance, though ignorance were as dark as hell; and I say there was never man thus abus'd. I am no more mad than you are. Make the trial of it in any constant question.

Clown. What is the opinion of Pythagoras concerning wild fowl?

Mal. That the soul of our grandam might happily inhabit a bird.

Clown. What think'st thou of his opinion?

Mal. I think nobly of the soul and no way approve his opinion.

Clown. Fare thee well. Remain thou still in darkness. Thou shalt hold th' opinion of Pythagoras ere I will allow of thy wits, and fear to kill a woodcock, lest thou dispossess the soul of thy grandam. Fare thee well.

Mal. Sir Topas, Sir Topas!

To. My most exquisite Sir Topas!

Clown. Nay, I am for all waters.

Mar. Thou mightst have done this without thy beard and gown. He sees thee not.

To. To him in thine own voice, and bring me word how thou find'st him. — [*To Maria*] I would we were well rid of this knavery. If he may be conveniently deliver'd, I would he were; for I am now so far in offence with my niece that I cannot pursue with any safety this sport to the upshot. — [*To the Clown*] Come by-and-by to my chamber.

Exit [*with Maria*].

Clown. [*sings*] 'Hey, Robin, jolly Robin,
Tell me how thy lady does.'

Mal. Fool!

Clown. 'My lady is unkind, perdie!'

Mal. Fool!

Clown. 'Alas, why is she so?'

Mal. Fool, I say!

Clown. 'She loves another' — Who calls, ha?

Mal. Good fool, as ever thou wilt deserve well at my hand, help me to a candle, and pen, ink, and paper. As I am a gentleman, I will live to be thankful to thee for't.

Clown. Master Malvolio?

Mal. Ay, good fool.

Clown. Alas, sir, how fell you besides your five wits?

Mal. Fool, there was never man so notoriously abus'd. I am as well in my wits, fool, as thou art.

Clown. But as well? Then you are mad indeed, if you be no better in your wits than a fool.

Mal. They have here propertied me; keep me in darkness, send ministers to me, asses, and do all they can to face me out of my wits.

Clown. Advise you what you say. The minister is here. — Malvolio, Malvolio, thy wits the heavens restore! Endeavour thyself to sleep and leave thy vain bibble babble.

Mal. Sir Topas!

Clown. Maintain no words with him, good fellow. — Who, I, sir? Not I, sir. God b' wi' you, good Sir Topas! — Marry, amen. — I will, sir, I will.

Mal. Fool, fool, fool, I say!

Clown. Alas, sir, be patient. What say you, sir? I am shent for speaking to you.

Mal. Good fool, help me to some light and some paper. I tell thee, I am as well in my wits as any man in Illyria.

Clown. Well-a-day that you were, sir!

Mal. By this hand, I am. Good fool, some ink, paper, and light; and convey what I will set down to my lady. It shall advantage thee more than ever the bearing of letter did.

Clown. I will help you to't. But tell me true, are you not mad indeed? or do you but counterfeit?

Mal. Believe me, I am not. I tell thee true.

Clown. Nay, I'll ne'er believe a madman till I see his brains. I will fetch you light and paper and ink.

Mal. Fool, I'll requite it in the highest degree. I prithee be gone.

Clown. [*sings*] I am gone, sir;
And anon, sir,
I'll be with you again,
In a trice,
Like to the old Vice,
Your need to sustain;

Who, with dagger of lath,
In his rage and his wrath,
Cries 'aha!' to the devil.
Like a mad lad,
'Pare thy nails, dad.'
Adieu, goodman devil. *Exit.*

Scene III. [Olivia's *orchard.*]

Enter *Sebastian.*

Seb. This is the air; that is the glorious sun;
This pearl she gave me, I do feel't and see't;
And though 'tis wonder that enwraps me thus,
Yet 'tis not madness. Where's Antonio then?
I could not find him at the Elephant;
Yet there he was; and there I found this credit,
That he did range the town to seek me out.
His counsel now might do me golden service;
For though my soul disputes well with my sense
That this may be some error, but no madness,
Yet doth this accident and flood of fortune
So far exceed all instance, all discourse,
That I am ready to distrust mine eyes
And wrangle with my reason, that persuades me
To any other trust but that I am mad,
Or else the lady's mad. Yet, if 'twere so,
She could not sway her house, command her followers,
Take and give back affairs and their dispatch
With such a smooth, discreet, and stable bearing
As I perceive she does. There's something in't
That is deceivable. But here the lady comes.

Enter *Olivia* and *Priest.*

Oli. Blame not this haste of mine. If you mean well,
Now go with me and with this holy man
Into the chantry by. There, before him,
And underneath that consecrated roof,
Plight me the full assurance of your faith,
That my most jealious and too doubtful soul
May live at peace. He shall conceal it
Whiles you are willing it shall come to note,
What time we will our celebration keep
According to my birth. What do you say?

Seb. I'll follow this good man and go with you
And having sworn truth, ever will be true.

Oli. Then lead the way, good father; and heavens so shine
That they may fairly note this act of mine! *Exeunt.*

Act V. Scene I. [*Before* Olivia's *house.*]

Enter *Clown* and *Fabian.*

Fab. Now as thou lov'st me, let me see his letter.

Clown. Good Master Fabian, grant me another request.

Fab. Anything.

Clown. Do not desire to see this letter.

Fab. This is to give a dog, and in recompense desire my dog again.

Enter *Duke, Viola, Curio,* and *Lords.*

Duke. Belong you to the Lady Olivia, friends?

Clown. Ay, sir, we are some of her trappings.

Duke. I know thee well. How dost thou, my good fellow?

Clown. Truly, sir, the better for my foes, and the worse for my friends.

Duke. Just the contrary: the better for thy friends.

Clown. No, sir, the worse.

Duke. How can that be?

Clown. Marry, sir, they praise me and make an ass of me. Now my foes tell me plainly I am an ass; so that by my foes, sir, I profit in the knowledge of myself, and by my friends I am abused; so that, conclusions to be as kisses, if your four negatives make your two affirmatives, why then, the worse for my friends and the better for my foes.

Duke. Why, this is excellent.

Clown. By my troth, sir, no; though it please you to be one of my friends.

Duke. Thou shalt not be the worse for me. There's gold.

Clown. But that it would be double-dealing, sir, I would you could make it another.

Duke. O, you give me ill counsel.

Clown. Put your grace in your pocket, sir, for this once, and let your flesh and blood obey it.

Duke. Well, I will be so much a sinner to be a double-dealer. There's another.

Clown. Primo, secundo, tertio is a good play; and the old saying is 'The third pays for all.' The triplex, sir, is a good tripping measure; or the bells of Saint Bennet, sir, may put you in mind — one, two, three.

Duke. You can fool no more money out of me at this throw. If you will let your lady know I am here to speak with her, and bring her along with you, it may awake my bounty further.

Clown. Marry, sir, lullaby to your bounty till I come again! I go, sir; but I would not have you to think that my desire of having is the sin of covetousness. But, as you say, sir, let your bounty take a nap; I will awake it anon. *Exit.*

Enter *Antonio* and *Officers.*

Vio. Here comes the man, sir, that did rescue me.
Duke. That face of his I do remember well;
Yet when I saw it last, it was besmear'd
As black as Vulcan in the smoke of war.
A baubling vessel was he captain of,
For shallow draught and bulk unprizable,
With which such scathful grapple did he make
With the most noble bottom of our fleet
That very envy and the tongue of loss
Cried fame and honour on him. What's the matter?
1. Off. Orsino, this is that Antonio
That took the Phœnix and her fraught from Candy;
And this is he that did the Tiger board
When your young nephew Titus lost his leg.
Here in the streets, desperate of shame and state,
In private brabble did we apprehend him.
Vio. He did me kindness, sir; drew on my side;
But in conclusion put strange speech upon me.
I know not what 'twas but distraction.
Duke. Notable pirate, thou salt-water thief!
What foolish boldness brought thee to their mercies
Whom thou in terms so bloody and so dear
Hast made thine enemies?
Ant. Orsino, noble sir,
Be pleas'd that I shake off these names you give me.
Antonio never yet was thief or pirate,
Though I confess, on base and ground enough,
Orsino's enemy. A witchcraft drew me hither.
That most ingrateful boy there by your side
From the rude sea's enrag'd and foamy mouth
Did I redeem. A wrack past hope he was.
His life I gave him, and did thereto add
My love without retention or restraint,
All his in dedication. For his sake
Did I expose myself (pure for his love)
Into the danger of this adverse town;
Drew to defend him when he was beset;
Where being apprehended, his false cunning
(Not meaning to partake with me in danger)
Taught him to face me out of his acquaintance,
And grew a twenty years removed thing
While one would wink; denied me mine own purse,
Which I had recommended to his use
Not half an hour before.
Vio. How can this be?
Duke. When came he to this town?
Ant. To-day, my lord; and for three months before,
No int'rim, not a minute's vacancy,
Both day and night did we keep company.

Enter *Olivia* and *Attendants.*

Duke. Here comes the Countess; now heaven walks on earth.
But for thee, fellow — fellow, thy words are madness.
Three months this youth hath tended upon me;
But more of that anon. Take him aside.
Oli. What would my lord, but that he may not have,
Wherein Olivia may seem serviceable?
Cesario, you do not keep promise with me.
Vio. Madam!
Duke. Gracious Olivia —
Oli. What do you say, Cesario? — Good my lord —
Vio. My lord would speak; my duty hushes me.
Oli. If it be aught to the old tune, my lord,
It is as fat and fulsome to mine ear
As howling after music.
Duke. Still so cruel?
Oli. Still so constant, lord.
Duke. What, to perverseness? You uncivil lady,
To whose ingrate and unauspicious altars
My soul the faithfull'st off'rings hath breath'd out
That e'er devotion tender'd! What shall I do?
Oli. Even what it please my lord, that shall become him.
Duke. Why should I not, had I the heart to do it,
Like to th' Egyptian thief at point of death,
Kill what I love? — a savage jealousy
That sometime savours nobly. But hear me this:
Since you to non-regardance cast my faith,
And that I partly know the instrument
That screws me from my true place in your favour,

Live you the marble-breasted tyrant still.
But this your minion, whom I know you love,
And whom, by heaven I swear, I tender dearly,
Him will I tear out of that cruel eye
Where he sits crowned in his master's spite.
Come, boy, with me. My thoughts are ripe in mischief.
I'll sacrifice the lamb that I do love
To spite a raven's heart within a dove. [*Going.*]

Vio. And I, most jocund, apt, and willingly,
To do you rest a thousand deaths would die. [*Following.*]

Oli. Where goes Cesario?

Vio. After him I love
More than I love these eyes, more than my life,
More, by all mores, than e'er I shall love wife.
If I do feign, you witnesses above
Punish my life for tainting of my love!

Oli. Ay me detested! how am I beguil'd!

Vio. Who does beguile you? Who does do you wrong?

Oli. Hast thou forgot thyself? Is it so long?
Call forth the holy father. [*Exit an Attendant.*]

Duke. [*to Viola*] Come, away!

Oli. Whither, my lord? Cesario, husband, stay.

Duke. Husband?

Oli. Ay, husband. Can he that deny?

Duke. Her husband, sirrah?

Vio. No, my lord, not I.

Oli. Alas, it is the baseness of thy fear
That makes thee strangle thy propriety.
Fear not, Cesario; take thy fortunes up;
Be that thou know'st thou art, and then thou art
As great as that thou fear'st.

Enter *Priest.*

O, welcome, father!
Father, I charge thee by thy reverence
Here to unfold — though lately we intended
To keep in darkness what occasion now
Reveals before 'tis ripe — what thou dost know
Hath newly pass'd between this youth and me.

Priest. A contract of eternal bond of love,
Confirm'd by mutual joinder of your hands,
Attested by the holy close of lips,
Strength'ned by interchangement of your rings;
And all the ceremony of this compact
Seal'd in my function, by my testimony;
Since when, my watch hath told me, toward my grave
I have travell'd but two hours.

Duke. O thou dissembling cub! What wilt thou be
When time hath sow'd a grizzle on thy case?
Or will not else thy craft so quickly grow
That thine own trip shall be thine overthrow?
Farewell, and take her; but direct thy feet
Where thou and I, henceforth, may never meet.

Vio. My lord, I do protest —

Oli. O, do not swear!
Hold little faith, though thou hast too much fear.

Enter *Sir Andrew.*

And. For the love of God, a surgeon! Send one presently to Sir Toby.

Oli. What's the matter?

And. Has broke my head across, and has given Sir Toby a bloody coxcomb too. For the love of God, your help! I had rather than forty pound I were at home.

Oli. Who has done this, Sir Andrew?

And. The Count's gentleman, one Cesario. We took him for a coward, but he's the very devil incardinate.

Duke. My gentleman Cesario?

And. Od's lifelings, here he is! You broke my head for nothing; and that that I did, I was set on to do't by Sir Toby.

Vio. Why do you speak to me? I never hurt you.
You drew your sword upon me without cause,
But I bespake you fair and hurt you not.

Enter [*Sir*] *Toby* and *Clown.*

And. If a bloody coxcomb be a hurt, you have hurt me. I think you set nothing by a bloody coxcomb. Here comes Sir Toby halting — you shall hear more. But if he had not been in drink, he would have tickled you othergates than he did.

Duke. How now, gentleman? How is't with you?

To. That's all one! Has hurt me, and there's th' end on't. — Sot, didst see Dick Surgeon, sot?

Clown. O, he's drunk, Sir Toby, an hour agone. His eyes were set at eight i' th' morning.

To. Then he's a rogue and a passy measures pavin. I hate a drunken rogue.

Oli. Away with him! Who hath made this havoc with them?

And. I'll help you, Sir Toby, because we'll be dress'd together.

To. Will you help — an ass-head and a coxcomb and a knave — a thin-fac'd knave, a gull?

Oli. Get him to bed, and let his hurt be look'd to.
[*Exeunt Clown, Fabian, Sir Toby, and Sir Andrew.*]

Enter *Sebastian.*

Seb. I am sorry, madam, I have hurt your kinsman;
But had it been the brother of my blood,
I must have done no less with wit and safety.
You throw a strange regard upon me, and by that
I do perceive it hath offended you.
Pardon me, sweet one, even for the vows
We made each other but so late ago.
Duke. One face, one voice, one habit, and two persons!
A natural perspective, that is and is not!
Seb. Antonio! O my dear Antonio!
How have the hours rack'd and tortur'd me
Since I have lost thee!
Ant. Sebastian are you?
Seb. Fear'st thou that, Antonio?
Ant. How have you made division of yourself?
An apple cleft in two is not more twin
Than these two creatures. Which is Sebastian?
Oli. Most wonderful!
Seb. Do I stand there? I never had a brother;
Nor can there be that deity in my nature
Of here and everywhere. I had a sister,
Whom the blind waves and surges have devour'd.
Of charity, what kin are you to me?
What countryman? what name? what parentage?
Vio. Of Messaline; Sebastian was my father —
Such a Sebastian was my brother too;
So went he suited to his watery tomb.
If spirits can assume both form and suit,
You come to fright us.
Seb. A spirit I am indeed,
But am in that dimension grossly clad
Which from the womb I did participate.
Were you a woman, as the rest goes even,
I should my tears let fall upon your cheek
And say, 'Thrice welcome, drowned Viola!'
Vio. My father had a mole upon his brow —
Seb. And so had mine.
Vio. And died that day when Viola from her birth
Had numb'red thirteen years.
Seb. O, that record is lively in my soul!
He finished indeed his mortal act
That day that made my sister thirteen years.
Vio. If nothing lets to make us happy both
But this my masculine usurp'd attire,
Do not embrace me till each circumstance
Of place, time, fortune do cohere and jump
That I am Viola; which to confirm,
I'll bring you to a captain in this town,
Where lie my maiden weeds; by whose gentle help
I was preserv'd to serve this noble Count.
All the occurrence of my fortune since
Hath been between this lady and this lord.
Seb. [*to Olivia*] So comes it, lady, you have been mistook.
But nature to her bias drew in that.
You would have been contracted to a maid;
Nor are you therein, by my life, deceiv'd:
You are betroth'd both to a maid and man.
Duke. Be not amaz'd; right noble is his blood.
If this be so, as yet the glass seems true,
I shall have share in this most happy wrack.
[*To Viola*] Boy, thou hast said to me a thousand times
Thou never shouldst love woman like to me.
Vio. And all those sayings will I over swear,
And all those swearings keep as true in soul
As doth that orbed continent the fire
That severs day from night.
Duke. Give me thy hand,
And let me see thee in thy woman's weeds.
Vio. The captain that did bring me first on shore
Hath my maid's garments. He upon some action
Is now in durance, at Malvolio's suit,
A gentleman, and follower of my lady's.
Oli. He shall enlarge him. Fetch Malvolio hither.
And yet alas! now I remember me,
They say, poor gentleman, he's much distract.

Enter *Clown* with a letter, and *Fabian.*

A most extracting frenzy of mine own
From my remembrance clearly banish'd his.
How does he, sirrah?
Clown. Truly, madam, he holds Belzebub at the stave's end as well as a man in his case may do. Has here writ a letter to you; I should have given't you to-day morning. [*Offers the letter.*] But as a madman's epistles are no gos-

Vivien Leigh as the winsome heroine, Viola, enamored of Duke Orsino

TWELFTH NIGHT

Attired in her brother's clothes, Viola enters Orsino's service as a page

PHOTOGRAPHS BY ANGUS MCBEAN
PRODUCED BY THE MEMORIAL THEATRE COMPANY
STRATFORD-UPON-AVON

"What country, friends, is this?" Voyaging with her brother, Viola is shipwrecked on the coast of Illyria, in the realm of the melancholy Duke Orsino (*Act I, Scene II*)

"I prithee,—and I'll pay thee bounteously,—conceal me what I am, and be my aid." Viola persuades the captain (Mervyn Blake) to aid her in entering the duke's service and in disguising herself as a man (*Act I, Scene II*)

"So please my lord, I might not be admitted." An attendant, Valentine (Gabriel Woolf), reports to Orsino (Keith Michell) that the Countess Olivia receives his wooing coldly (*Act I, Scene I*)

"Give us the place alone: we will hear this divinity." Olivia (Maxine Audley) is attracted by the handsome page, who comes to her with a love letter from Orsino (*Act I, Scene V*)

"Holla your name to the reverberate hills, and make the babbling gossip of the air cry out, 'Olivia!'" Romantic rhetoric marks Viola's vicarious wooing of the countess (*Act I, Scene V*)

Seeking to ingratiate herself with Orsino's page, Olivia sends her man Malvolio (Laurence Olivier) after Viola to present her with a ring (*Act II, Scene II*)

Alan Webb as the uncle of Olivia, Sir Toby Belch, capricious, light-headed winebibber

Feste (Edward Atienza), the jester of the duke, gives vent to a melancholy madrigal

Right: Michael Denison in the role of Sir Andrew Aguecheek, the senile suitor of Countess Olivia

Below: "My masters, are you mad?" Malvolio interrupts the reveling of Sir Toby (*Act II, Scene III*)

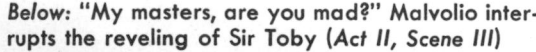

"Come away, come away, death." The jester Feste sings an old love song before the duke and his court (*Act II, Scene IV*)

"My father had a daughter lov'd a man, as it might be, perhaps, were I a woman, I should your lordship." Viola hints at her affection for the duke (*Act II, Scene IV*)

"By my life, this is my lady's hand!" Malvolio finds the letter which the conspirators have forged to lead him to believe that Countess Olivia is in love with him (*Act II, Scene V*)

Above: "How do you, Malvolio? How is 't with you?" Sir Toby baits Malvolio (*Act III, Scene IV*)

Left: Certified as mad by Sir Toby, the lovesick Malvolio is confined in a dark room in the house of the Countess Olivia (*Act IV, Scene II*)

"What is the opinion of Pythagoras concerning wild fowl?" Disguised as Sir Topas, the curate, Feste brings Malvolio cold consolation from an ancient Greek philosopher (*Act IV, Scene II*)

Viola engages in a duel with Sir Andrew Aguecheek, who thinks she is his rival for the love of the countess (*Act III, Scene IV*)

"Put up your sword. If this young gentleman have done offence, I take the fault on me." Mistaking Viola for her brother, Antonio (William Devlin) interrupts the duel and crosses swords with Sir Toby Belch (*Act III, Scene IV*)

Viola and her brother Sebastian (Trader Faulkner) are reunited (*Act V, Scene I*)

Sir Andrew Aguecheek is soundly beaten by Viola's brother (*Act IV, Scene I*)

"One face, one voice, one habit, and two persons." The duke is astonished at the resemblance between Viola and Sebastian (*Act V, Scene I*)

"Is this the madman?" Malvolio is released from his confinement (*Act V, Scene I*)

"With hey, ho, the wind and the rain." Feste sings an idle ditty as Viola and the duke embrace in the last scene of the play pels, so it skills not much when they are deliver'd.

Oli. Open't and read it.

Clown. Look then to be well edified, when the fool delivers the madman. [*Reads in a loud voice*] 'By the Lord, madam' —

Oli. How now? Art thou mad?

Clown. No, madam, I do but read madness. An your ladyship will have it as it ought to be, you must allow vox.

Oli. Prithee read i' thy right wits.

Clown. So I do, madonna; but to read his right wits is to read thus. Therefore perpend, my princess, and give ear.

Oli. [*to Fabian*] Read it you, sirrah.

Fab. (*reads*) 'By the Lord, madam, you wrong me, and the world shall know it. Though you have put me into darkness, and given your drunken cousin rule over me, yet have I the benefit of my senses as well as your ladyship. I have your own letter that induced me to the semblance I put on; with the which I doubt not but to do myself much right, or you much shame. Think of me as you please. I leave my duty a little unthought of, and speak out of my injury.

'THE MADLY US'D MALVOLIO.'

Oli. Did he write this?

Clown. Ay, madam.

Duke. This savours not much of distraction.

Oli. See him deliver'd, Fabian; bring him hither.

[*Exit Fabian.*]

My lord, so please you, these things further thought on,
To think me as well a sister as a wife,
One day shall crown th' alliance on't, so please you,
Here at my house and at my proper cost.

Duke. Madam, I am most apt t' embrace your offer.
[*To Viola*] Your master quits you; and for your service done him,
So much against the mettle of your sex,
So far beneath your soft and tender breeding,
And since you call'd me master, for so long,
Here is my hand: you shall from this time be
Your master's mistress.

Oli. A sister! you are she.

Enter [*Fabian*, with] *Malvolio*.

Duke. Is this the madman?

Oli. Ay, my lord, this same.
How now, Malvolio?

Mal. Madam, you have done me wrong,
Notorious wrong.

Oli. Have I, Malvolio? No.

Mal. Lady, you have. Pray you peruse that letter.
You must not now deny it is your hand.
Write from it if you can, in hand or phrase,
Or say 'tis not your seal, not your invention.
You can say none of this. Well, grant it then,
And tell me, in the modesty of honour,
Why you have given me such clear lights of favour,
Bade me come smiling and cross-garter'd to you,
To put on yellow stockings, and to frown
Upon Sir Toby and the lighter people;
And, acting this in an obedient hope,
Why have you suffer'd me to be imprison'd,
Kept in a dark house, visited by the priest,
And made the most notorious geck and gull
That e'er invention play'd on? Tell me why.

Oli. Alas, Malvolio, this is not my writing,
Though I confess much like the character;
But, out of question, 'tis Maria's hand.
And now I do bethink me, it was she
First told me thou wast mad. Thou cam'st in smiling,
And in such forms which here were presuppos'd
Upon thee in the letter. Prithee be content.
This practice hath most shrewdly pass'd upon thee;
But when we know the grounds and authors of it,
Thou shalt be both the plaintiff and the judge
Of thine own cause.

Fab. Good madam, hear me speak,
And let no quarrel, nor no brawl to come,
Taint the condition of this present hour,
Which I have wond'red at. In hope it shall not,
Most freely I confess myself and Toby
Set this device against Malvolio here,
Upon some stubborn and uncourteous parts
We had conceiv'd against him. Maria writ
The letter, at Sir Toby's great importance,
In recompense whereof he hath married her.
How with a sportful malice it was follow'd
May rather pluck on laughter than revenge,
If that the injuries be justly weigh'd
That have on both sides pass'd.

Oli. Alas poor fool, how have they baffled thee!

Clown. Why, 'some are born great, some achieve greatness, and some have greatness thrown upon them.' I was one, sir, in this interlude — one Sir Topas, sir; but that's all one. 'By the Lord, fool, I am not mad!' But do you remember — 'Madam, why laugh you at such a barren rascal? An you smile not, he's gagg'd'? And thus the whirligig of time brings in his revenges.

Mal. I'll be reveng'd on the whole pack of you! [*Exit.*]

Oli. He hath been most notoriously abus'd.

Duke. Pursue him and entreat him to a peace.
He hath not told us of the captain yet.
When that is known, and golden time convents,
A solemn combination shall be made
Of our dear souls. Meantime, sweet sister,
We will not part from hence. Cesario, come —
For so you shall be while you are a man;
But when in other habits you are seen,
Orsino's mistress and his fancy's queen.
Exeunt [*all but the Clown*].

Clown sings.

When that I was and a little tiny boy,
With hey, ho, the wind and the rain,
A foolish thing was but a toy,
For the rain it raineth every day.

But when I came to man's estate,
With hey, ho, the wind and the rain,
'Gainst knaves and thieves men shut their gate,
For the rain it raineth every day.

But when I came, alas! to wive,
With hey, ho, the wind and the rain,
By swaggering could I never thrive,
For the rain it raineth every day.

But when I came unto my beds,
With hey, ho, the wind and the rain,
With tosspots still had drunken heads,
For the rain it raineth every day.

A great while ago the world begun,
With hey, ho, the wind and the rain;
But that's all one, our play is done,
And we'll strive to please you every day.
[*Exit.*]

THE WINTER'S TALE

For the text of THE WINTER'S TALE our sole authority is the First Folio. In style and metre, tone and dramatic method, the play reveals itself as one of Shakespeare's latest works. Perhaps it followed *Cymbeline* and preceded *The Tempest*.

On May 15, 1611, Simon Forman, astrologer and physician, saw THE WINTER'S TALE at the Globe. His summary of the plot, in his own handwriting, is preserved in Ashmole MS. 208. If either the bear (iii, 3, 58) or the dance of satyrs (iv, 4, 352) was suggested by Ben Jonson's masque of *Oberon*, which was exhibited at court on the first day of that same year, the limits of composition are fixed with almost uncanny precision. The bear, however, is not a very trustworthy witness, even if Oberon's chariot is drawn by two white bears. The evidence of the satyrs is more satisfactory, for three of Shakespeare's 'saltiers' had 'danced before the king.' At all events, 1611 is a satisfactory date for THE WINTER'S TALE.

The source of the main plot is Robert Greene's novel *Pandosto. The Triumph of Time*, printed in 1588 and reprinted in 1607 under the title of *Dorastus and Fawnia* (the subtitle in the original edition). Pandosto, King of Bohemia, is Shakespeare's Leontes; his wife Bellaria is his Hermione; their son (Mamillius in the play) is named Garinter. Egistus, King of Sicilia, is Shakespeare's Polixenes. Shakespeare has exchanged the kingdoms.

Greene takes pains to describe the jealousy of Pandosto as to all intents and purposes insane. 'A certaine melancholy passion entring the minde of Pandosto drave him into sundry and doubtfull [i.e. suspicious] thoughts.' These, 'a long time smoothering in his stomacke, beganne at last to kindle in his minde a secret mistrust, which increased by suspition, grewe at last to be a flaming Iealousie, that so tormented him as he could take no rest.' These phrases accord with Shakespeare's account of Leontes. He is not, as a modern critic has called him, 'an irritable, suspicious, jealous-natured tyrant.' The whole atmosphere of the court — which is like a happy family — shows that he is no tyrant, and the perplexity of Hermione and Polixenes proves that he has never shown jealousy before. His paroxysm of jealous fury is virtually a fit of madness. It seizes him in a moment, and it releases him with equal suddenness.

The seacoast of Bohemia, which Shakespeare took from Greene, called forth some remarks from Ben Jonson in his conversations with William Drummond of Hawthornden (1619). All we know of the matter is Drummond's jotting: 'Shakspear in a play brought in a number of men saying they had suffered Shipwrack in Bohemia, wher ther is no Sea neer by some 100 Miles.' Ben's remark has been repeated, in substance, by multitudes who, but for this supposed geographical blunder, would not have known whether Bohemia has, or ever had, a seacoast. With equal persistence for more than a hundred years others have defended Shakespeare by arguing that once upon a time (in the thirteenth century) Bohemian sovereignty actually extended to the ports of Aquileia and Trieste. But it is very prosy to equate Shakespeare's Bohemia with any actual Bohemia. Had Bohemia a seacoast? Yes. When? At some indeterminate date B.C., when Leontes was king of Sicilia — that

Leontes who married a daughter of the Emperor of Russia and was a boyhood friend of Polixenes, King of Bohemia.

The Chorus at the beginning of the Fourth Act has for almost two hundred years been under suspicion as the work of an interpolator, but for no good reason. Somebody who knows things must hold forth at this juncture, for the audience needs information and there are no printed programmes. Father Time meets the exigency with admirable precision. He tells us that sixteen years have elapsed; that Leontes is a penitent hermit; that the scene shifts from Sicilia to Bohemia; that the son of Polixenes is named Florizel; that Perdita (who has 'grown in grace equal with wond'ring') passes for the old shepherd's daughter, and that our next concern is with her. And how is Father Time to speak? Shall it be in Shakespeare's best style — with the tragic passion of Lear, the philosophy of Hamlet, the gaiety of Beatrice, the cynicism of Apemantus, the warlike parade of Coriolanus? Of course not. He should speak in character. And that is precisely how he does speak — as old Father Time — a doddering, toothless ancient, halting but fluent, senile but self-assured, ridiculous but triumphant. His verse, his dialect, his jests, his truisms, all are in character. The stumbling emptiness of which the critics complain is Time's own. If the speech were better, it would not be so good.

Shakespeare follows Greene's story for the most part, except at the end, nor does he hesitate to borrow ideas or striking turns of phrase. Perdita's

> I think affliction may subdue the cheek,
> But not take in the mind (iv, 4, 587–588)

is transmuted from Fawnia's 'The body is subiect to victories, but the minde not to be subdued by conquest.' Hermione's ''Tis rigour, and not law' (iii, 2, 115) comes word for word from Greene. Her whole defensive argument, indeed, is Greene's prose turned into poetry.

Some significant variations may be noted.

Apollo is consulted at the request of the queen. The king does not blaspheme when the oracle is read in court; he repents instantly and is making public confession when word is brought that his son is dead. This news is fatal to the queen: 'she fell down presently dead, and could never be revived.' The baby is not left on the shore; it is abandoned at sea (like Prospero and Miranda in *The Tempest*) in a boat without sail or rudder, which comes safe to land by good fortune after a mighty storm. Antigonus and Paulina have no prototypes in the novel and Shakespeare's Camillo combines the rôles of two of Greene's characters.

The old shepherd comes from the novel, but his son and Dorcas and Mopsa and Autolycus are all new characters. Rustic revels are mentioned in the tale, but not described. The trick by which Autolycus picks the young shepherd's pocket agrees well enough with that in an anecdote told for a fact in Greene's *Second Part of Conny-catching* (1592).

The novel has a happy ending, so far as the young people are concerned, but Pandosto (Leontes) is a tragic personage throughout. After years of mourning for his dead wife, he falls in love with Fawnia (Perdita), whom of course he supposes to be the shepherd's daughter. When he learns that she is his own child 'whome he sent to floate in the sea,' he is overjoyed; but after her marriage he is smitten with remorse for all his sins, falls once more 'into a melancholie fit,' and kills himself.

The recognition scene which Shakespeare has substituted for this dismal conclusion, however improbable in fact, has proved superbly effective on the stage. For the suggestion of the statue that comes to life one need not have recourse to Lyly's *Woman in the Moon* (1597) or to Marston's *Pygmalion's Image* (1598). A poet who wrote *Venus and Adonis* in 1593 (or earlier) did not need to ask Lyly or Marston in 1611 to lead him to the story of Pygmalion in Ovid's *Metamorphoses* (x, 243 ff.).

THE WINTER'S TALE

The Names of the Actors.

Leontes, King of Sicilia.
Mamillius, [his son,] young Prince of Sicilia.
Camillo, *Antigonus*, *Cleomenes*, *Dion*, — Four Lords of Sicilia.
Polixenes, King of Bohemia.
Florizel, [his son,] Prince of Bohemia.
Archidamus, a Lord of Bohemia.
Old Shepherd, reputed father of *Perdita*.
Clown, his son.
Autolycus, a rogue.
[A Mariner.]
[A Jailer.]

Hermione, queen to *Leontes*.
Perdita, daughter to *Leontes* and *Hermione*.
Paulina, wife to *Antigonus*.
Emilia, a lady, [Other Ladies,] — [attending on the Queen].
[*Mopsa*, *Dorcas*, — Shepherdesses.]
Other Lords and Gentlemen, [Ladies, Officers,] and Servants, Shepherds and Shepherdesses.
[*Time*, as Chorus.]

[SCENE. — *Sicilia; Bohemia.*]

ACT I. Scene I. [*Sicilia. The Palace of* Leontes.]

Enter *Camillo* and *Archidamus*.

Arch. If you shall chance, Camillo, to visit Bohemia, on the like occasion whereon my services are now on foot, you shall see, as I have said, great difference betwixt our Bohemia and your Sicilia.

Cam. I think this coming summer the King of Sicilia means to pay Bohemia the visitation which he justly owes him.

Arch. Wherein our entertainment shall shame us we will be justified in our loves; for indeed —

Cam. Beseech you —

Arch. Verily I speak it in the freedom of my knowledge: we cannot with such magnificence — in so rare — I know not what to say. We will give you sleepy drinks, that your senses (unintelligent of our insufficience) may, though they cannot praise us, as little accuse us.

Cam. You pay a great deal too dear for what's given freely.

Arch. Believe me, I speak as my understanding instructs me and as mine honesty puts it to utterance.

Cam. Sicilia cannot show himself over-kind to Bohemia. They were train'd together in their childhoods; and there rooted betwixt them then such an affection which cannot choose but branch now. Since their more mature dignities and royal necessities made separation of their society, their encounters (though not personal) have been royally attorneyed with interchange of gifts, letters, loving embassies; that they have seem'd to be together, though absent; shook hands, as over a vast; and embrac'd as it were from the ends of opposed winds. The heavens continue their love!

Arch. I think there is not in the world either malice or matter to alter it. You have an unspeakable comfort of your young Prince Mamillius. It is a gentleman of the greatest promise that ever came into my note.

Cam. I very well agree with you in the hopes of him. It is a gallant child; one that, indeed, physics the subject, makes old hearts fresh. They that went on crutches ere he was born desire yet their life, to see him a man.

Arch. Would they else be content to die?

Cam. Yes; if there were no other excuse why they should desire to live.

Arch. If the King had no son, they would desire to live on crutches till he had one.

Exeunt.

Scene II. [*Sicilia. The Palace of* Leontes.]

Enter *Leontes*, *Hermione*, *Mamillius*, *Polixenes*, *Camillo*, [and *Attendants*].

Pol. Nine changes of the wat'ry star hath been
The shepherd's note since we have left our throne

Without a burthen. Time as long again
Would be fill'd up, my brother, with our thanks,
And yet we should, for perpetuity,
Go hence in debt. And therefore, like a cipher,
Yet standing in rich place, I multiply
With one 'We thank you' many thousands moe
That go before it.

Leon. Stay your thanks a while,
And pay them when you part.

Pol. Sir, that's to-morrow.
I am question'd by my fears, of what may chance,
Or breed upon our absence. That may blow
No sneaping winds at home, to make us say
'This is put forth too truly'! Besides, I have stay'd
To tire your royalty.

Leon. We are tougher, brother,
Than you can put us to't.

Pol. No longer stay.

Leon. One sev'nnight longer.

Pol. Very sooth, to-morrow.

Leon. We'll part the time between 's then; and in that
I'll no gainsaying.

Pol. Press me not, beseech you, so.
There is no tongue that moves, none, none i' th' world,
So soon as yours could win me. So it should now,
Were there necessity in your request, although
'Twere needful I denied it. My affairs
Do even drag me homeward; which to hinder,
Were, in your love, a whip to me; my stay
To you a charge and trouble: to save both,
Farewell, our brother.

Leon. Tongue-tied our queen? Speak you.

Her. I had thought, sir, to have held my peace until
You had drawn oaths from him not to stay. You, sir,
Charge him too coldly. Tell him you are sure
All in Bohemia's well; this satisfaction
The bygone day proclaim'd. Say this to him,
He's beat from his best ward.

Leon. Well said, Hermione.

Her. To tell he longs to see his son, were strong.
But let him say so then, and let him go;
But let him swear so, and he shall not stay,
We'll thwack him hence with distaffs.
[*To Polixenes*] Yet of your royal presence I'll adventure
The borrow of a week. When at Bohemia
You take my lord, I'll give him my commission
To let him there a month behind the gest
Prefix'd for 's parting.—Yet, good-deed, Leontes,
I love thee not a jar o' th' clock behind
What lady she her lord. — You'll stay?

Pol. No, madam.

Her. Nay, but you will?

Pol. I may not, verily.

Her. Verily?
You put me off with limber vows; but I,
Though you would seek t' unsphere the stars with oaths,
Should yet say, 'Sir, no going.' Verily
You shall not go! a lady's 'verily' is
As potent as a lord's. Will you go yet?
Force me to keep you as a prisoner,
Not like a guest: so you shall pay your fees
When you depart, and save your thanks. How say you?
My prisoner? or my guest? By your dread 'verily,'
One of them you shall be.

Pol. Your guest then, madam.
To be your prisoner should import offending;
Which is for me less easy to commit
Than you to punish.

Her. Not your jailer then,
But your kind hostess. Come, I'll question you
Of my lord's tricks and yours when you were boys.
You were pretty lordings then?

Pol. We were, fair queen,
Two lads that thought there was no more behind
But such a day to-morrow as to-day,
And to be boy eternal.

Her. Was not my lord
The verier wag o' th' two?

Pol. We were as twinn'd lambs that did frisk i' th' sun
And bleat the one at th' other. What we chang'd
Was innocence for innocence; we knew not
The doctrine of ill-doing, nor dream'd
That any did. Had we pursu'd that life,
And our weak spirits ne'er been higher rear'd
With stronger blood, we should have answer'd heaven
Boldly, 'Not guilty,' the imposition clear'd
Hereditary ours.

Her. By this we gather
You have tripp'd since.

Pol. O my most sacred lady,
Temptations have since then been born to 's; for
In those unfledg'd days was my wife a girl;
Your precious self had then not cross'd the eyes
Of my young playfellow.

Her. Grace to boot!
Of this make no conclusion, lest you say
Your queen and I are devils. Yet go on.
Th' offences we have made you do, we'll answer,
If you first sinn'd with us, and that with us
You did continue fault, and that you slipp'd not
With any but with us.
Leon. Is he won yet?
Her. He'll stay, my lord.
Leon. At my request he would not.
Hermione, my dearest, thou never spok'st
To better purpose.
Her. Never?
Leon. Never, but once.
Her. What? have I twice said well? When was't before?
I prithee tell me. Cram 's with praise, and make 's
As fat as tame things. One good deed dying tongueless
Slaughters a thousand waiting upon that.
Our praises are our wages. You may ride 's
With one soft kiss a thousand furlongs ere
With spur we heat an acre. But to th' goal!
My last good deed was to entreat his stay.
What was my first? It has an elder sister,
Or I mistake you. O, would her name were Grace!
But once before I spoke to th' purpose? When?
Nay, let me have't! I long.
Leon. Why, that was when
Three crabbed months had sour'd themselves to death
Ere I could make thee open thy white hand
And clap thyself my love. Then didst thou utter,
'I am yours for ever.'
Her. 'Tis Grace indeed.
Why, lo you now! I have spoke to th' purpose twice.
The one for ever earn'd a royal husband;
Th' other for some while a friend.
[*Gives her hand to Polixenes.*]
Leon. [*aside*] Too hot, too hot!
To mingle friendship far, is mingling bloods.
I have tremor cordis on me; my heart dances,
But not for joy; not joy. This entertainment
May a free face put on; derive a liberty
From heartiness, from bounty's fertile bosom,
And well become the agent. 'T may, I grant.
But to be paddling palms and pinching fingers,
As now they are, and making practis'd smiles
As in a looking glass; and then to sigh, as 'twere
The mort o' th' deer — O, that is entertainment
My bosom likes not, nor my brows. — Mamillius,
Art thou my boy?
Mam. Ay, my good lord.
Leon. I' fecks!
Why, that's my bawcock! What? hast smutch'd thy nose?
They say it is a copy out of mine. Come, captain,
We must be neat — not neat, but cleanly, captain.
And yet the steer, the heifer, and the calf
Are all call'd neat. — Still virginalling
Upon his palm? — How now, you wanton calf?
Art thou my calf?
Mam. Yes, if you will, my lord.
Leon. Thou want'st a rough pash and the shoots that I have,
To be full like me. Yet they say we are
Almost as like as eggs. Women say so —
That will say anything! But were they false
As o'er-dy'd blacks, as wind, as waters — false
As dice are to be wish'd by one that fixes
No bourn 'twixt his and mine; yet were it true
To say this boy were like me. Come, sir page,
Look on me with your welkin eye. Sweet villain!
Most dear'st! my collop! Can thy dam — may't be?
Affection! thy intention stabs the centre.
Thou dost make possible things not so held,
Communicat'st with dreams! How can this be?
With what's unreal thou coactive art,
And fellow'st nothing. Then 'tis very credent
Thou mayst cojoin with something; and thou dost —
And that beyond commission; and I find it,
And that to the infection of my brains
And hard'ning of my brows.
Pol. What means Sicilia?
Her. He something seems unsettled.
Pol. How, my lord?
What cheer? How is't with you, best brother?
Her. You look
As if you held a brow of much distraction.
Are you mov'd, my lord?
Leon. No, in good earnest.
How sometimes nature will betray its folly,
Its tenderness, and make itself a pastime
To harder bosoms! Looking on the lines
Of my boy's face, methoughts I did recoil
Twenty-three years, and saw myself unbreech'd,
In my green velvet coat, my dagger muzzled,
Lest it should bite its master and so prove
(As ornaments oft do) too dangerous.
How like, methought, I then was to this kernel.

This squash, this gentleman. Mine honest friend,
Will you take eggs for money?
Mam. No, my lord, I'll fight.
Leon. You will? Why, happy man be 's dole! My brother,
Are you so fond of your young prince as we
Do seem to be of ours?
Pol. If at home, sir,
He's all my exercise, my mirth, my matter;
Now my sworn friend, and then mine enemy;
My parasite, my soldier, statesman — all.
He makes a July's day short as December,
And with his varying childness cures in me
Thoughts that would thick my blood.
Leon. So stands this squire
Offic'd with me. We two will walk, my lord,
And leave you to your graver steps. Hermione,
How thou lov'st us, show in our brother's welcome.
Let what is dear in Sicily be cheap.
Next to thyself and my young rover, he's
Apparent to my heart.
Her. If you would seek us,
We are yours i' th' garden. Shall 's attend you there?
Leon. To your own bents dispose you. You'll be found,
Be you beneath the sky. [*Aside*] I am angling now,
Though you perceive me not how I give line.
Go to, go to!
How she holds up the neb, the bill to him!
And arms her with the boldness of a wife
To her allowing husband!
[*Exeunt Polixenes, Hermione, and Attendants.*]
Gone already!
Inch-thick, knee-deep, o'er head and ears a fork'd one!
Go play, boy, play. Thy mother plays, and I
Play too; but so disgrac'd a part whose issue
Will hiss me to my grave. Contempt and clamour
Will be my knell. — Go play, boy, play. — There have been
(Or I am much deceiv'd) cuckolds ere now;
And many a man there is (even at this present,
Now, while I speak this) holds his wife by th' arm
That little thinks she has been sluic'd in 's absence
And his pond fish'd by his next neighbour — by
Sir Smile, his neighbour. Nay, there's comfort in't
Whiles other men have gates, and those gates open'd
(As mine) against their will. Should all despair
That have revolted wives, the tenth of mankind
Would hang themselves. Physic for't there's none.
It is a bawdy planet, that will strike
Where 'tis predominant; and 'tis pow'rful, think it,
From east, west, north, and south. Be it concluded,
No barricado for a belly! Know't,
It will let in and out the enemy
With bag and baggage. Many thousand on 's
Have the disease, and feel't not. How now, boy?
Mam. I am like you, they say.
Leon. Why, that's some comfort.
What? Camillo there?
Cam. Ay, my good lord.
Leon. Go play, Mamillius. Thou'rt an honest man.
[*Exit Mamillius.*]
Camillo, this great sir will yet stay longer.
Cam. You had much ado to make his anchor hold;
When you cast out, it still came home.
Leon. Didst note it?
Cam. He would not stay at your petitions, made
His business more material.
Leon. Didst perceive it?
[*Aside*] They're here with me already; whisp'ring, rounding,
'Sicilia is a so-forth!' 'Tis far gone
When I shall gust it last. — How came't, Camillo,
That he did stay?
Cam. At the good Queen's entreaty.
Leon. 'At the Queen's' be't. 'Good' should be pertinent;
But so it is, it is not. Was this taken
By any understanding pate but thine?
For thy conceit is soaking, will draw in
More than the common blocks. Not noted, is't,
But of the finer natures? by some severals
Of headpiece extraordinary? Lower messes
Perchance are to this business purblind? Say.
Cam. Business, my lord? I think most understand
Bohemia stays here longer.
Leon. Ha?
Cam. Stays here longer.
Leon. Ay, but why?

Cam. To satisfy your Highness, and the entreaties
Of our most gracious mistress.
Leon. Satisfy?
Th' entreaties of your mistress? Satisfy?
Let that suffice. I have trusted thee, Camillo,
With all the nearest things to my heart, as well
My chamber-councils, wherein (priest-like) thou
Hast cleans'd my bosom, I from thee departed
Thy penitent reform'd. But we have been
Deceiv'd in thy integrity, deceiv'd
In that which seems so.
Cam. Be it forbid, my lord!
Leon. To bide upon't: thou art not honest; or,
If thou inclin'st that way, thou art a coward,
Which hoxes honesty behind, restraining
From course requir'd; or else thou must be counted
A servant grafted in my serious trust
And therein negligent; or else a fool
That seest a game play'd home, the rich stake drawn,
And tak'st it all for jest.
Cam. My gracious lord,
I may be negligent, foolish, and fearful:
In every one of these no man is free,
But that his negligence, his folly, fear,
Among the infinite doings of the world,
Sometime puts forth. In your affairs, my lord,
If ever I were wilful-negligent,
It was my folly; if industriously
I play'd the fool, it was my negligence,
Not weighing well the end; if ever fearful
To do a thing where I the issue doubted,
Whereof the execution did cry out
Against the non-performance, 'twas a fear
Which oft infects the wisest. These, my lord,
Are such allow'd infirmities that honesty
Is never free of. But beseech your Grace
Be plainer with me; let me know my trespass
By its own visage. If I then deny it
'Tis none of mine.
Leon. Ha' not you seen, Camillo
(But that's past doubt; you have, or your eye-glass
Is thicker than a cuckold's horn), or heard
(For to a vision so apparent rumour
Cannot be mute) or thought (for cogitation
Resides not in that man that does not think)
My wife is slippery? If thou wilt confess —
Or else be impudently negative
To have nor eyes nor ears nor thought — then say
My wife 's a hobby-horse, deserves a name
As rank as any flax-wench that puts to
Before her troth-plight. Say't, and justify't.
Cam. I would not be a stander-by to hear
My sovereign mistress clouded so, without
My present vengeance taken. Shrew my heart!
You never spoke what did become you less
Than this; which to reiterate were sin
As deep as that, though true.
Leon. Is whispering nothing?
Is leaning cheek to cheek? Is meeting noses?
Kissing with inside lip? stopping the career
Of laughter with a sigh? — a note infallible
Of breaking honesty! — horsing foot on foot?
Skulking in corners? wishing clocks more swift?
Hours, minutes? noon, midnight? and all eyes
Blind with the pin and web but theirs — theirs only,
That would unseen be wicked? Is this nothing?
Why, then the world and all that's in't is nothing;
The covering sky is nothing; Bohemia nothing;
My wife is nothing; nor nothing have these nothings,
If this be nothing.
Cam. Good my lord, be cur'd
Of this diseas'd opinion, and betimes;
For 'tis most dangerous.
Leon. Say it be, 'tis true.
Cam. No, no, my lord.
Leon. It is! You lie, you lie!
I say thou liest, Camillo, and I hate thee,
Pronounce thee a gross lout, a mindless slave,
Or else a hovering temporizer that
Canst with thine eyes at once see good and evil,
Inclining to them both. Were my wive's liver
Infected as her life, she would not live
The running of one glass.
Cam. Who does infect her?
Leon. Why, he that wears her like her medal, hanging
About his neck — Bohemia; who — if I
Had servants true about me, that bare eyes
To see alike mine honour as their profits,
Their own particular thrifts, they would do that
Which should undo more doing. Ay, and thou,
His cupbearer — whom I from meaner form
Have bench'd, and rear'd to worship; who mayst see,
Plainly as heaven sees earth and earth sees heaven,
How I am gall'd — thou mightst bespice a cup
To give mine enemy a lasting wink;
Which draught to me were cordial.

Cam. Sir, my lord,
I could do this, and that with no rash potion,
But with a ling'ring dram that should not work
Maliciously, like poison. But I cannot
Believe this crack to be in my dread mistress,
So sovereignly being honourable.
I have lov'd thee —

Leon. Make that thy question, and go rot!
Dost think I am so muddy, so unsettled,
To appoint myself in this vexation, sully
The purity and whiteness of my sheets
(Which to preserve is sleep; which being spotted
Is goads, thorns, nettles, tails of wasps),
Give scandal to the blood o' th' Prince, my son
(Who I do think is mine, and love as mine),
Without ripe moving to't? Would I do this?
Could man so blench?

Cam. I must believe you, sir.
I do, and will fetch off Bohemia for't;
Provided that, when he's remov'd, your Highness
Will take again your queen as yours at first,
Even for your son's sake, and thereby for sealing
The injury of tongues in courts and kingdoms
Known and allied to yours.

Leon. Thou dost advise me
Even so as I mine own course have set down.
I'll give no blemish to her honour, none.

Cam. My lord,
Go then; and with a countenance as clear
As friendship wears at feasts, keep with Bohemia
And with your queen. I am his cupbearer;
If from me he have wholesome beverage,
Account me not your servant.

Leon. This is all:
Do't, and thou hast the one half of my heart;
Do't not, thou splitt'st thine own.

Cam. I'll do't, my lord.

Leon. I will seem friendly, as thou hast advis'd me. *Exit.*

Cam. O miserable lady! But, for me,
What case stand I in? I must be the poisoner
Of good Polixenes; and my ground to do't
Is the obedience to a master — one
Who, in rebellion with himself, will have
All that are his so too. To do this deed,
Promotion follows. If I could find example
Of thousands that had struck anointed kings
And flourish'd after, I'ld not do't. But since
Nor brass nor stone nor parchment bears not one,
Let villany itself forswear't. I must
Forsake the court. To do't, or no, is certain
To me a break-neck. Happy star reign now!
Here comes Bohemia.

Enter *Polixenes.*

Pol. This is strange. Methinks
My favour here begins to warp. Not speak?
Good day, Camillo.

Cam. Hail, most royal sir.

Pol. What is the news i' th' court?

Cam. None rare, my lord.

Pol. The King hath on him such a countenance
As he had lost some province, and a region
Lov'd as he loves himself. Even now I met him
With customary compliment, when he,
Wafting his eyes to th' contrary and falling
A lip of much contempt, speeds from me, and
So leaves me to consider what is breeding
That changes thus his manners.

Cam. I dare not know, my lord.

Pol. How? dare not? do not? Do you know, and dare not
Be intelligent to me? 'Tis thereabouts;
For, to yourself, what you do know, you must,
And cannot say you dare not. Good Camillo,
Your chang'd complexions are to me a mirror,
Which shows me mine chang'd too; for I must be
A party in this alteration, finding
Myself thus alter'd with't.

Cam. There is a sickness
Which puts some of us in distemper, but
I cannot name the disease; and it is caught
Of you, that yet are well.

Pol. How? caught of me?
Make me not sighted like the basilisk.
I have look'd on thousands who have sped the better
By my regard, but kill'd none so. Camillo —
As you are certainly a gentleman; thereto
Clerk-like experienc'd, which no less adorns
Our gentry than our parents' noble names,
In whose success we are gentle — I beseech you,
If you know aught which does behove my knowledge
Thereof to be inform'd, imprison't not
In ignorant concealment.

Cam. I may not answer.

Pol. A sickness caught of me, and yet I well?
I must be answer'd. Dost thou hear, Camillo?
I conjure thee, by all the parts of man
Which honour does acknowledge, whereof the least
Is not this suit of mine, that thou declare
What incidency thou dost guess of harm

Is creeping toward me; how far off, how near;
Which way to be prevented, if to be;
If not, how best to bear it.
Cam. Sir, I will tell you,
Since I am charg'd in honour, and by him
That I think honourable. Therefore mark my counsel,
Which must be ev'n as swiftly followed as
I mean to utter it; or both yourself and me
Cry lost, and so good night!
Pol. On, good Camillo.
Cam. I am appointed him to murther you.
Pol. By whom, Camillo?
Cam. By the King.
Pol. For what?
Cam. He thinks — nay, with all confidence he swears,
As he had seen't, or been an instrument
To vice you to't — that you have touch'd his queen
Forbiddenly.
Pol. O, then my best blood turn
To an infected jelly, and my name
Be yok'd with his that did betray the Best!
Turn then my freshest reputation to
A savour that may strike the dullest nostril
Where I arrive, and my approach be shunn'd,
Nay, hated too, worse than the great'st infection
That e'er was heard or read!
Cam. Swear his thought over
By each particular star in heaven and
By all their influences, you may as well
Forbid the sea for to obey the moon
As or by oath remove or counsel shake
The fabric of his folly, whose foundation
Is pil'd upon his faith and will continue
The standing of his body.
Pol. How should this grow?
Cam. I know not; but I am sure 'tis safer to
Avoid what's grown than question how 'tis born.
If therefore you dare trust my honesty,
That lies enclosed in this trunk, which you
Shall bear along impawn'd, away to-night!
Your followers I will whisper to the business,
And will, by twos and threes, at several posterns,
Clear them o' th' city. For myself, I'll put
My fortunes to your service, which are here
By this discovery lost. Be not uncertain,
For, by the honour of my parents, I
Have utt'red truth; which if you seek to prove,
I dare not stand by; nor shall you be safer
Than one condemn'd by the King's own mouth — thereon
His execution sworn.
Pol. I do believe thee.
I saw his heart in 's face. Give me thy hand.
Be pilot to me, and thy places shall
Still neighbour mine. My ships are ready, and
My people did expect my hence departure
Two days ago. This jealousy
Is for a precious creature. As she's rare,
Must it be great; and as his person's mighty,
Must it be violent; and as he does conceive
He is dishonour'd by a man which ever
Profess'd to him, why, his revenges must
In that be made more bitter. Fear o'ershades me.
Good expedition be my friend, and comfort
The gracious Queen, part of his theme, but nothing
Of his ill-ta'en suspicion! Come, Camillo.
I will respect thee as a father if
Thou bear'st my life off. Hence! Let us avoid.
Cam. It is in mine authority to command
The keys of all the posterns. Please your Highness
To take the urgent hour. Come, sir, away!
Exeunt.

ACT II. Scene I. [*Sicilia. The Palace of* Leontes.]

Enter *Hermione, Mamillius, Ladies.*

Her. Take the boy to you. He so troubles me
'Tis past enduring.
1. Lady. Come, my gracious lord,
Shall I be your playfellow?
Mam. No, I'll none of you.
1. Lady. Why, my sweet lord?
Mam. You'll kiss me hard, and speak to me as if
I were a baby still. I love you better.
2. Lady. And why so, my lord?
Mam. Not for because
Your brows are blacker. Yet black brows, they say,
Become some women best, so that there be not
Too much hair there, but in a semicircle
Or a half-moon made with a pen.
2. Lady. Who taught you this?
Mam. I learn'd it out of women's faces. Pray now,
What colour are your eyebrows?

1. Lady. Blue, my lord.

Mam. Nay, that's a mock. I have seen a lady's nose
That has been blue, but not her eyebrows.

1. Lady. Hark ye!
The Queen your mother rounds apace. We shall
Present our services to a fine new prince
One of these days, and then you'ld wanton with us
If we would have you.

2. Lady. She is spread of late
Into a goodly bulk. Good time encounter her!

Her. What wisdom stirs amongst you? Come, sir, now
I am for you again. Pray you sit by us
And tell 's a tale.

Mam. Merry, or sad, shall't be?

Her. As merry as you will.

Mam. A sad tale's best for winter. I have one
Of sprites and goblins.

Her. Let's have that, good sir.
Come on, sit down; come on, and do your best
To fright me with your sprites; you're pow'rful at it.

Mam. There was a man —

Her. Nay, come sit down; then on.

Mam. Dwelt by a churchyard. I will tell it softly;
Yond crickets shall not hear it.

Her. Come on then,
And give't me in mine ear.

Enter *Leontes, Antigonus, Lords,* [and others].

Leon. Was he met there? his train? Camillo with him?

Lord. Behind the tuft of pines I met them. Never
Saw I men scour so on their way. I ey'd them
Even to their ships.

Leon. How blest am I
In my just censure, in my true opinion!
Alack for lesser knowledge! how accurs'd
In being so blest! There may be in the cup
A spider steep'd, and one may drink, depart,
And yet partake no venom, for his knowledge
Is not infected; but if one present
Th' abhorr'd ingredient to his eye, make known
How he hath drunk, he cracks his gorge, his sides,
With violent hefts. I have drunk, and seen the spider.
Camillo was his help in this, his pander;
There is a plot against my life, my crown;
All's true that is mistrusted. That false villain
Whom I employ'd was pre-employ'd by him.
He has discover'd my design, and I
Remain a pinch'd thing; yea, a very trick
For them to play at will. How came the posterns
So easily open?

Lord. By his great authority,
Which often hath no less prevail'd than so
On your command.

Leon. I know't too well.
Give me the boy. I am glad you did not nurse him.
Though he does bear some signs of me, yet you
Have too much blood in him.

Her. What is this? sport?

Leon. Bear the boy hence; he shall not come about her.
Away with him! and let her sport herself
[*Mamillius is carried out.*]
With that she's big with — for 'tis Polixenes
Has made thee swell thus.

Her. But I'ld say he had not,
And I'll be sworn you would believe my saying,
Howe'er you lean to th' nayward.

Leon. You, my lords,
Look on her, mark her well. Be but about
To say 'She is a goodly lady,' and
The justice of your hearts will thereto add
''Tis pity she's not honest — honourable!'
Praise her but for this her without-door form
(Which on my faith deserves high speech) and straight
The shrug, the 'hum!' or 'ha!' — these petty brands
That calumny doth use — O, I am out!
That mercy does; for calumny will sear
Virtue itself — these shrugs, these hum's and ha's,
When you have said she's goodly, come between,
Ere you can say she's honest. But be't known
(From him that has most cause to grieve it should be)
She's an adultress.

Her. Should a villain say so,
The most replenish'd villain in the world,
He were as much more villain. You, my lord,
Do but mistake.

Leon. You have mistook, my lady,
Polixenes for Leontes. O thou thing!
Which I'll not call a creature of thy place,
Lest barbarism, making me the precedent,
Should a like language use to all degrees
And mannerly distinguishment leave out
Betwixt the prince and beggar. I have said

She's an adultress; I have said with whom.
More, she's a traitor, and Camillo is
A federary with her, and one that knows
What she should shame to know herself
But with her most vile principal — that she's
A bed-swerver, even as bad as those
That vulgars give bold'st titles; ay, and privy
To this their late escape.

Her. No, by my life,
Privy to none of this! How will this grieve you,
When you shall come to clearer knowledge, that
You thus have publish'd me! Gentle my lord,
You scarce can right me throughly then to say
You did mistake.

Leon. No! If I mistake
In those foundations which I build upon,
The centre is not big enough to bear
A schoolboy's top. Away with her to prison!
He who shall speak for her is afar off guilty
But that he speaks.

Her. There's some ill planet reigns.
I must be patient till the heavens look
With an aspect more favourable. Good my lords,
I am not prone to weeping, as our sex
Commonly are; the want of which vain dew
Perchance shall dry your pities; but I have
That honourable grief lodg'd here which burns
Worse than tears drown. Beseech you all, my lords,
With thoughts so qualified as your charities
Shall best instruct you, measure me; and so
The King's will be perform'd!

Leon. Shall I be heard?

Her. Who is't that goes with me? Beseech your Highness
My women may be with me; for you see
My plight requires it. Do not weep, good fools;
There is no cause. When you shall know your mistress
Has deserv'd prison, then abound in tears
As I come out. This action I now go on
Is for my better grace. Adieu, my lord.
I never wish'd to see you sorry; now
I trust I shall. My women, come; you have leave.

Leon. Go, do our bidding! hence!

[*Exeunt Hermione, guarded, with Ladies.*]

Lord. Beseech your Highness call the Queen again!

Ant. Be certain what you do, sir, lest your justice
Prove violence, in the which three great ones suffer,
Yourself, your queen, your son.

Lord. For her, my lord,
I dare my life lay down, and will do't, sir,
Please you t' accept it, that the Queen is spotless
I' th' eyes of heaven and to you — I mean,
In this which you accuse her.

Ant. If it prove
She's otherwise, I'll keep my stables where
I lodge my wife; I'll go in couples with her;
Than when I feel and see her no farther trust her;
For every inch of woman in the world,
Ay, every dram of woman's flesh is false,
If she be.

Leon. Hold your peaces!

Lord. Good my lord —

Ant. It is for you we speak, not for ourselves.
You are abus'd, and by some putter-on
That will be damn'd for't. Would I knew the villain!
I would land-damn him! Be she honour-flaw'd,
I have three daughters: the eldest is eleven;
The second and the third, nine and some five —
If this prove true, they'll pay for't! By mine honour,
I'll geld 'em all. Fourteen they shall not see
To bring false generations. They are co-heirs,
And I had rather glib myself than they
Should not produce fair issue.

Leon. Cease! no more!
You smell this business with a sense as cold
As is a dead man's nose; but I do see't and feel't,
As you feel doing thus — [*Seizes his arm.*]
and see withal
The instruments that feel.

Ant. If it be so,
We need no grave to bury honesty.
There's not a grain of it the face to sweeten
Of the whole dungy earth.

Leon. What? lack I credit?

Lord. I had rather you did lack than I, my lord,
Upon this ground; and more it would content me
To have her honour true than your suspicion,
Be blam'd for't how you might.

Leon. Why, what need we
Commune with you of this, but rather follow
Our forceful instigation? Our prerogative
Calls not your counsels, but our natural goodness
Imparts this; which, if you (or stupefied,
Or seeming so in skill) cannot or will not
Relish a truth like us, inform yourselves
We need no more of your advice. The matter,

The loss, the gain, the ord'ring on't, is all
Properly ours.
Ant. And I wish, my liege,
You had only in your silent judgment tried it,
Without more overture.
Leon. How could that be?
Either thou art most ignorant by age
Or thou wert born a fool. Camillo's flight,
Added to their familiarity
(Which was as gross as ever touch'd conjecture,
That lack'd sight only, naught for approbation
But only seeing; all other circumstances
Made up to th' deed), doth push on this proceeding.
Yet, for a greater confirmation
(For in an act of this importance 'twere
Most piteous to be wild) I have dispatch'd in post
To sacred Delphos, to Apollo's temple,
Cleomenes and Dion, whom you know
Of stuff'd sufficiency. Now from the oracle
They will bring all, whose spiritual counsel had,
Shall stop or spur me. Have I done well?
Lord. Well done, my lord.
Leon. Though I am satisfied and need no more
Than what I know, yet shall the oracle
Give rest to th' minds of others, such as he
Whose ignorant credulity will not
Come up to th' truth. So have we thought it good
From our free person she should be confin'd,
Lest that the treachery of the two fled hence
Be left her to perform. Come follow us.
We are to speak in public; for this business
Will raise us all.
Ant. [*aside*] To laughter, as I take it,
If the good truth were known. *Exeunt.*

Scene II. [*Sicilia. A prison.*]

Enter *Paulina*, a *Gentleman*, [and *Attendants*].

Paul. The keeper of the prison — call to him;
Let him have knowledge who I am.
[*Exit Gentleman.*]
Good lady!
No court in Europe is too good for thee.
What dost thou then in prison?

Enter *Jailer.*

Now, good sir,
You know me, do you not?
Jail. For a worthy lady,
And one who much I honour.
Paul. Pray you then,
Conduct me to the Queen.
Jail. I may not, madam; to the contrary
I have express commandment.
Paul. Here's ado
To lock up honesty and honour from
Th' access of gentle visitors! Is't lawful, pray you,
To see her women? any of them? Emilia?
Jail. So please you, madam,
To put apart these your attendants, I
Shall bring Emilia forth.
Paul. I pray now call her.
Withdraw yourselves. [*Exeunt Attendants.*]
Jail. And, madam,
I must be present at your conference.
Paul. Well, be't so. Prithee.
[*Exit Jailer.*]
Here's such ado to make no stain a stain
As passes colouring.

[Enter *Jailer*, with] *Emilia.*

Dear gentlewoman,
How fares our gracious lady?
Emil. As well as one so great and so forlorn
May hold together. On her frights and griefs
(Which never tender lady hath borne greater)
She is, something before her time, deliver'd.
Paul. A boy?
Emil. A daughter, and a goodly babe,
Lusty, and like to live. The Queen receives
Much comfort in't; says 'My poor prisoner,
I am innocent as you.'
Paul. I dare be sworn.
These dangerous unsafe lunes i' th' King, beshrew them!
He must be told on't, and he shall. The office
Becomes a woman best; I'll take't upon me.
If I prove honey-mouth'd, let my tongue blister,
And never to my red-look'd anger be
The trumpet any more. Pray you, Emilia,
Commend my best obedience to the Queen.
If she dares trust me with her little babe,
I'll show't the King and undertake to be
Her advocate to th' loud'st. We do not know
How he may soften at the sight o' th' child.
The silence often of pure innocence
Persuades when speaking fails.
Emil. Most worthy madam,
Your honour and your goodness is so evident
That your free undertaking cannot miss
A thriving issue. There is no lady living
So meet for this great errand. Please your ladyship
To visit the next room, I'll presently

Acquaint the Queen of your most noble offer,
Who but to-day hammered of this design,
But durst not tempt a minister of honour,
Lest she should be denied.

Paul. Tell her, Emilia,
I'll use that tongue I have. If wit flow from't
As boldness from my bosom, let't not be doubted
I shall do good.

Emil. Now be you blest for it!
I'll to the Queen. Please you come something nearer.

Jail. Madam, if't please the Queen to send the babe,
I know not what I shall incur to pass it,
Having no warrant.

Paul. You need not fear it, sir.
This child was prisoner to the womb, and is
By law and process of great Nature thence
Freed and enfranchis'd — not a party to
The anger of the King, nor guilty of
(If any be) the trespass of the Queen.

Jail. I do believe it.

Paul. Do not you fear. Upon mine honour, I
Will stand betwixt you and danger. *Exeunt.*

Scene III. [*Sicilia. The Palace.*]

Enter *Leontes, Servants, Antigonus,* and *Lords.*

Leon. Nor night nor day no rest! It is but weakness
To bear the matter thus — mere weakness. If
The cause were not in being — part o' th' cause,
She, the adultress; for the harlot king
Is quite beyond mine arm, out of the blank
And level of my brain, plot-proof; but she
I can hook to me — say that she were gone,
Given to the fire, a moiety of my rest
Might come to me again. Who's there?

Serv. My lord?

Leon. How does the boy?

Serv. He took good rest to-night.
'Tis hop'd his sickness is discharg'd.

Leon. To see his nobleness!
Conceiving the dishonour of his mother,
He straight declin'd, droop'd, took it deeply,
Fasten'd and fix'd the shame on't in himself,
Threw off his spirit, his appetite, his sleep,
And downright languish'd. Leave me solely. Go,
See how he fares. [*Exit Servant.*] Fie, fie, no thought of him!
The very thought of my revenges that way
Recoil upon me — in himself too mighty,
And in his parties, his alliance. Let him be
Until a time may serve. For present vengeance,
Take it on her. Camillo and Polixenes
Laugh at me, make their pastime at my sorrow.
They should not laugh if I could reach them; nor
Shall she, within my pow'r.

Enter *Paulina,* [with a Child].

Lord. You must not enter.

Paul. Nay, rather, good my lords, be second to me.
Fear you his tyrannous passion more, alas!
Than the Queen's life? a gracious innocent soul,
More free than he is jealous.

Ant. That's enough.

Serv. Madam, he hath not slept to-night, commanded
None should come at him.

Paul. Not so hot, good sir!
I come to bring him sleep. 'Tis such as you,
That creep like shadows by him and do sigh
At each his needless heavings — such as you
Nourish the cause of his awaking. I
Do come with words as medicinal as true,
Honest as either, to purge him of that humour
That presses him from sleep.

Leon. What noise there, ho?

Paul. No noise, my lord, but needful conference
About some gossips for your Highness.

Leon. How?
Away with that audacious lady! Antigonus,
I charg'd thee that she should not come about me.
I knew she would.

Ant. I told her so, my lord,
On your displeasure's peril and on mine,
She should not visit you.

Leon. What? canst not rule her?

Paul. From all dishonesty he can. In this,
Unless he take the course that you have done,
Commit me for committing honour, trust it,
He shall not rule me.

Ant. La you now, you hear!
When she will take the rein, I let her run;
But she'll not stumble.

Paul. Good my liege, I come;
And I beseech you hear me, who professes
Myself your loyal servant, your physician,
Your most obedient counsellor; yet that dares
Less appear so, in comforting your evils,
Than such as most seem yours. I say, I come
From your good queen.

Leon. Good queen?
Paul. Good queen, my lord, good queen; I say, good queen,
And would by combat make her good, so were I
A man, the worst about you.
Leon. Force her hence.
Paul. Let him that makes but trifles of his eyes
First hand me. On mine own accord I'll off;
But first I'll do my errand. The good queen
(For she is good) hath brought you forth a daughter;
Here 'tis — commends it to your blessing.
[*Lays down the child.*]
Leon. Out!
A mankind witch! Hence with her, out o' door!
A most intelligencing bawd!
Paul. Not so.
I am as ignorant in that as you
In so entitling me; and no less honest
Than you are mad; which is enough, I'll warrant,
As this world goes, to pass for honest.
Leon. Traitors!
Will you not push her out? [*To Antigonus*] Give her the bastard.
Thou dotard, thou art woman-tir'd; unroosted
By thy Dame Partlet here. Take up the bastard.
Take't up, I say! give't to thy crone.
Paul. For ever
Unvenerable be thy hands if thou
Tak'st up the Princess by that forced baseness
Which he has put upon't!
Leon. He dreads his wife.
Paul. So I would you did. Then 'twere past all doubt
You'ld call your children yours.
Leon. A nest of traitors!
Ant. I am none, by this good light.
Paul. Nor I; nor any,
But one, that's here, and that's himself; for he
The sacred honour of himself, his queen's,
His hopeful son's, his babe's, betrays to slander,
Whose sting is sharper than the sword's; and will not
(For, as the case now stands, it is a curse
He cannot be compell'd to't) once remove
The root of his opinion, which is rotten
As ever oak or stone was sound.
Leon. A callat
Of boundless tongue, who late hath beat her husband
And now baits me! This brat is none of mine;
It is the issue of Polixenes.
Hence with it, and together with the dam
Commit them to the fire!
Paul. It is yours;
And, might we lay th' old proverb to your charge,
So like you 'tis the worse. Behold, my lords,
Although the print be little, the whole matter
And copy of the father — eye, nose, lip,
The trick of 's frown, his forehead; nay, the valley,
The pretty dimples of his chin and cheek; his smiles;
The very mould and frame of hand, nail, finger.
And thou, good goddess Nature, which hast made it
So like to him that got it, if thou hast
The ordering of the mind too, 'mongst all colours
No yellow in't, lest she suspect, as he does,
Her children not her husband's!
Leon. A gross hag!
And, lozel, thou art worthy to be hang'd
That wilt not stay her tongue.
Ant. Hang all the husbands
That cannot do that feat, you'll leave yourself
Hardly one subject.
Leon. Once more, take her hence.
Paul. A most unworthy and unnatural lord
Can do no more.
Leon. I'll ha' thee burnt.
Paul. I care not.
It is an heretic that makes the fire,
Not she which burns in't. I'll not call you tyrant;
But this most cruel usage of your queen
(Not able to produce more accusation
Than your own weak-hing'd fancy) something savours
Of tyranny, and will ignoble make you,
Yea, scandalous to the world.
Leon. On your allegiance,
Out of the chamber with her! Were I a tyrant,
Where were her life? She durst not call me so
If she did know me one. Away with her!
Paul. I pray you do not push me; I'll be gone.
Look to your babe, my lord; 'tis yours. Jove send her
A better guiding spirit! What needs these hands?
You that are thus so tender o'er his follies
Will never do him good, not one of you.
So, so. Farewell, we are gone. *Exit.*
Leon. Thou, traitor, hast set on thy wife to this.

My child? Away with't! Even thou, that hast
A heart so tender o'er it, take it hence
And see it instantly consum'd with fire.
Even thou, and none but thou. Take it up straight!
Within this hour bring me word 'tis done,
And by good testimony, or I'll seize thy life,
With what thou else call'st thine. If thou refuse
And wilt encounter with my wrath, say so:
The bastard brains with these my proper hands
Shall I dash out. Go, take it to the fire!
For thou set'st on thy wife.

Ant. I did not, sir.
These lords, my noble fellows, if they please,
Can clear me in't.

Lords. We can. My royal liege,
He is not guilty of her coming hither.

Leon. You're liars all.

Lord. Beseech your Highness, give us better credit.
We have always truly serv'd you, and beseech
So to esteem of us; and on our knees we beg
(As recompense of our dear services
Past and to come) that you do change this purpose,
Which being so horrible, so bloody, must
Lead on to some foul issue. We all kneel.

Leon. I am a feather for each wind that blows.
Shall I live on to see this bastard kneel
And call me father? Better burn it now
Than curse it then. But be it; let it live.
It shall not neither! [*To Antigonus*] You, sir, come you hither.
You that have been so tenderly officious,
With Lady Margery, your midwife there,
To save this bastard's life — for 'tis a bastard,
So sure as this beard's grey — what will you adventure
To save this brat's life?

Ant. Anything, my lord,
That my ability may undergo
And nobleness impose. At least, thus much —
I'll pawn the little blood which I have left
To save the innocent. Anything possible.

Leon. It shall be possible. Swear by this sword
Thou wilt perform my bidding.

Ant. I will, my lord.

Leon. Mark, and perform it — seest thou? for the fail
Of any point in't shall not only be
Death to thyself, but to thy lewd-tongu'd wife,
Whom for this time we pardon. We enjoin thee,
As thou art liegeman to us, that thou carry
This female bastard hence; and that thou bear it
To some remote and desert place, quite out
Of our dominions; and that there thou leave it
(Without more mercy) to it own protection
And favour of the climate. As by strange fortune
It came to us, I do in justice charge thee,
On thy soul's peril and thy body's torture,
That thou commend it strangely to some place
Where chance may nurse or end it. Take it up.

Ant. I swear to do this; though a present death
Had been more merciful. Come on, poor babe!
Some powerful spirit instruct the kites and ravens
To be thy nurses! Wolves and bears, they say,
Casting their savageness aside, have done
Like offices of pity. Sir, be prosperous
In more than this deed does require! And blessing
Against this cruelty fight on thy side,
Poor thing, condemn'd to loss!

Exit [*with the child*].

Leon. No, I'll not rear
Another's issue.

Enter a *Servant*.

Serv. Please your Highness, posts
From those you sent to th' oracle are come
An hour since. Cleomenes and Dion,
Being well arriv'd from Delphos, are both landed,
Hasting to th' court.

Lord. So please you, sir, their speed
Hath been beyond accompt.

Leon. Twenty-three days
They have been absent. 'Tis good speed, foretells
The great Apollo suddenly will have
The truth of this appear. Prepare you, lords;
Summon a session, that we may arraign
Our most disloyal lady; for, as she hath
Been publicly accus'd, so shall she have
A just and open trial. While she lives,
My heart will be a burthen to me. Leave me,
And think upon my bidding. *Exeunt.*

Act III. Scene I. [*Sicilia. On the road.*]

Enter *Cleomenes* and *Dion*.

Cleo. The climate's delicate, the air most sweet;
Fertile the isle, the temple much surpassing
The common praise it bears.
Dion. I shall report,
For most it caught me, the celestial habits
(Methinks I so should term them) and the reverence
Of the grave wearers. O, the sacrifice!
How ceremonious, solemn, and unearthly
It was i' th' off'ring!
Cleo. But of all, the burst
And the ear-deaf'ning voice o' th' oracle,
Kin to Jove's thunder, so surpris'd my sense
That I was nothing.
Dion. If th' event o' th' journey
Prove as successful to the Queen (O, be't so!)
As it hath been to us rare, pleasant, speedy,
The time is worth the use on't.
Cleo. Great Apollo
Turn all to th' best! These proclamations,
So forcing faults upon Hermione,
I little like.
Dion. The violent carriage of it
Will clear or end the business. When the oracle
(Thus by Apollo's great divine seal'd up)
Shall the contents discover, something rare
Even then will rush to knowledge. Go; fresh horses!
And gracious be the issue! *Exeunt.*

Scene II. [*Sicilia. A court of justice.*]

Enter *Leontes, Lords, Officers.*

Leon. This sessions (to our great grief we pronounce)
Even pushes 'gainst our heart — the party tried
The daughter of a king, our wife, and one
Of us too much belov'd. Let us be clear'd
Of being tyrannous, since we so openly
Proceed in justice, which shall have due course,
Even to the guilt or the purgation.
Produce the prisoner.
Officer. It is his Highness' pleasure that the Queen
Appear in person here in court. Silence!

Enter *Hermione*, as to her trial, [*Paulina*, and] *Ladies.*

Leon. Read the indictment.

Officer. [*reads*] 'Hermione, Queen to the worthy Leontes, King of Sicilia, thou art here accused and arraigned of high treason, in committing adultery with Polixenes, King of Bohemia, and conspiring with Camillo to take away the life of our sovereign lord the King, thy royal husband; the pretence whereof being by circumstances partly laid open, thou, Hermione, contrary to the faith and allegiance of a true subject, didst counsel and aid them, for their better safety, to fly away by night.'

Her. Since what I am to say must be but that
Which contradicts my accusation, and
The testimony on my part no other
But what comes from myself, it shall scarce boot me
To say 'Not guilty.' Mine integrity,
Being counted falsehood, shall, as I express it,
Be so receiv'd. But thus: — if pow'rs divine
Behold our human actions (as they do),
I doubt not then but innocence shall make
False accusation blush and tyranny
Tremble at patience. You, my lord, best know
(Who least will seem to do so) my past life
Hath been as continent, as chaste, as true,
As I am now unhappy; which is more
Than history can pattern, though devis'd
And play'd to take spectators. For behold me —
A fellow of the royal bed, which owe
A moiety of the throne, a great king's daughter,
The mother to a hopeful prince — here standing
To prate and talk for life and honour fore
Who please to come and hear. For life, I prize it
As I weigh grief, which I would spare. For honour,
'Tis a derivative from me to mine,
And only that I stand for. I appeal
To your own conscience, sir, before Polixenes
Came to your court, how I was in your grace,
How merited to be so; since he came,
With what encounter so uncurrent I
Have strain'd t' appear thus; if one jot beyond
The bound of honour, or in act or will
That way inclining, hard'ned be the hearts
Of all that hear me, and my near'st of kin
Cry fie upon my grave!
Leon. I ne'er heard yet
That any of these bolder vices wanted

Less impudence to gainsay what they did
Than to perform it first.

Her. That's true enough;
Though 'tis a saying, sir, not due to me.

Leon. You will not own it.

Her. More than mistress of
Which comes to me in name of fault, I must not
At all acknowledge. For Polixenes,
With whom I am accus'd, I do confess
I lov'd him as in honour he requir'd;
With such a kind of love as might become
A lady like me; with a love even such,
So and no other, as yourself commanded;
Which not to have done, I think had been in me
Both disobedience and ingratitude
To you and toward your friend, whose love had spoke,
Even since it could speak, from an infant, freely,
That it was yours. Now for conspiracy,
I know not how it tastes, though it be dish'd
For me to try how. All I know of it
Is, that Camillo was an honest man;
And why he left your court, the gods themselves
(Wotting no more than I) are ignorant.

Leon. You knew of his departure, as you know
What you have underta'en to do in 's absence.

Her. Sir,
You speak a language that I understand not.
My life stands in the level of your dreams,
Which I'll lay down.

Leon. Your actions are my dreams.
You had a bastard by Polixenes,
And I but dream'd it. As you were past all shame
(Those of your fact are so), so past all truth;
Which to deny concerns more than avails; for as
Thy brat hath been cast out, like to itself,
No father owning it (which is indeed
More criminal in thee than it), so thou
Shalt feel our justice; in whose easiest passage
Look for no less than death.

Her. Sir, spare your threats.
The bug which you would fright me with I seek.
To me can life be no commodity.
The crown and comfort of my life, your favour,
I do give lost, for I do feel it gone,
But know not how it went. My second joy
And first fruits of my body, from his presence
I am barr'd, like one infectious. My third comfort,
Starr'd most unluckily, is from my breast
(The innocent milk in it most innocent mouth)
Hal'd out to murther. Myself on every post
Proclaim'd a strumpet. With immodest hatred
The childbed privilege denied, which 'longs
To women of all fashion. Lastly, hurried
Here to this place, i' th' open air, before
I have got strength of limit. Now, my liege,
Tell me what blessings I have here alive
That I should fear to die. Therefore proceed.
But yet hear this — mistake me not: for life,
I prize it not a straw; but for mine honour,
Which I would free — if I shall be condemn'd
Upon surmises (all proofs sleeping else,
But what your jealousies awake), I tell you,
'Tis rigour, and not law. Your honours all,
I do refer me to the oracle.
Apollo be my judge!

Lord. This your request
Is altogether just. Therefore bring forth,
And in Apollo's name, his oracle.
[*Exeunt certain Officers.*]

Her. The Emperor of Russia was my father.
O that he were alive, and here beholding
His daughter's trial! that he did but see
The flatness of my misery! yet with eyes
Of pity, not revenge.

[Enter *Officers,* with] *Cleomenes* [and] *Dion.*

Officer. You here shall swear upon this sword of justice
That you, Cleomenes and Dion, have
Been both at Delphos, and from thence have brought
This seal'd-up oracle, by the hand deliver'd
Of great Apollo's priest; and that since then
You have not dar'd to break the holy seal
Nor read the secrets in't.

Cleo., Dion. All this we swear.

Leon. Break up the seals and read.

Officer. [*reads*] 'Hermione is chaste; Polixenes blameless; Camillo a true subject; Leontes a jealous tyrant; his innocent babe truly begotten; and the King shall live without an heir, if that which is lost be not found.'

Lords. Now blessed be the great Apollo!

Her. Praised!

Leon. Hast thou read truth?

Officer. Ay, my lord; even so
As it is here set down.

Leon. There is no truth at all i' th' oracle!
The sessions shall proceed. This is mere falsehood!

[Enter a *Servant.*]

Serv. My lord the King! the King!

Leon. What is the business?

Serv. O sir, I shall be hated to report it.
The Prince your son, with mere conceit and fear
Of the Queen's speed, is gone.
Leon. How? gone?
Serv. Is dead.
Leon. Apollo 's angry, and the heavens themselves
Do strike at my injustice. [*Hermione swoons.*] How now there?
Paul. This news is mortal to the Queen. Look down
And see what death is doing.
Leon. Take her hence.
Her heart is but o'ercharg'd; she will recover.
I have too much believ'd mine own suspicion.
Beseech you tenderly apply to her
Some remedies for life.
[*Exeunt Paulina and Ladies, with Hermione.*]
Apollo, pardon
My great profaneness 'gainst thine oracle!
I'll reconcile me to Polixenes,
New woo my queen, recall the good Camillo,
Whom I proclaim a man of truth, of mercy;
For, being transported by my jealousies
To bloody thoughts and to revenge, I chose
Camillo for the minister to poison
My friend Polixenes; which had been done
But that the good mind of Camillo tardied
My swift command, though I with death and with
Reward did threaten and encourage him,
Not doing it and being done. He (most humane,
And fill'd with honour) to my kingly guest
Unclasp'd my practice, quit his fortunes here,
Which you knew great, and to the certain hazard
Of all incertainties himself commended,
No richer than his honour. How he glisters
Thorough my rust! and how his piety
Does my deeds make the blacker!

[Enter *Paulina.*]

Paul. Woe the while!
O, cut my lace, lest my heart, cracking it,
Break too!
Lord. What fit is this, good lady?
Paul. What studied torments, tyrant, hast for me?
What wheels? racks? fires? what flaying? boiling
In leads or oils? What old or newer torture
Must I receive, whose every word deserves
To taste of thy most worst? Thy tyranny
Together working with thy jealousies
Fancies too weak for boys, too green and idle
For girls of nine) — O, think what they have done,
And then run mad indeed, stark mad! for all
Thy bygone fooleries were but spices of it.
That thou betray'dst Polixenes, 'twas nothing:
That did but show thee, of a fool, inconstant,
And damnable ingrateful. Nor was't much
Thou wouldst have poison'd good Camillo's honour,
To have him kill a king — poor trespasses,
More monstrous standing by; whereof I reckon
The casting forth to crows thy baby daughter
To be or none or little, though a devil
Would have shed water out of fire ere done't;
Nor is't directly laid to thee, the death
Of the young Prince, whose honourable thoughts
(Thoughts high for one so tender) cleft the heart
That could conceive a gross and foolish sire
Blemish'd his gracious dam. This is not, no,
Laid to thy answer; but the last — O lords,
When I have said, cry 'woe!' — the Queen, the Queen,
The sweet'st, dear'st creature 's dead; and vengeance for't
Not dropp'd down yet.
Lord. The higher pow'rs forbid!
Paul. I say she's dead; I'll swear't. If word nor oath
Prevail not, go and see. If you can bring
Tincture or lustre in her lip, her eye,
Heat outwardly or breath within, I'll serve you
As I would do the gods. But, O thou tyrant!
Do not repent these things; for they are heavier
Than all thy woes can stir. Therefore betake thee
To nothing but despair. A thousand knees,
Ten thousand years together, naked, fasting,
Upon a barren mountain, and still winter
In storm perpetual, could not move the gods
To look that way thou wert!
Leon. Go on, go on.
Thou canst not speak too much. I have deserv'd
All tongues to talk their bitt'rest.
Lord. Say no more.
Howe'er the business goes, you have made fault
I' th' boldness of your speech.
Paul. I am sorry for't.
All faults I make, when I shall come to know them,
I do repent. Alas, I have show'd too much
The rashness of a woman! He is touch'd
To th' noble heart. What's gone and what's past help

Should be past grief. Do not receive affliction
At my petition. I beseech you, rather
Let me be punish'd that have minded you
Of what you should forget. Now, good my liege,
Sir, royal sir, forgive a foolish woman.
The love I bore your queen — lo, fool again!
I'll speak of her no more, nor of your children;
I'll not remember you of my own lord,
Who is lost too. Take you your patience to you,
And I'll say nothing.

Leon. Thou didst speak but well
When most the truth; which I receive much better
Than to be pitied of thee. Prithee bring me
To the dead bodies of my queen and son.
One grave shall be for both. Upon them shall
The causes of their death appear, unto
Our shame perpetual. Once a day I'll visit
The chapel where they lie, and tears shed there
Shall be my recreation. So long as nature
Will bear up with this exercise, so long
I daily vow to use it. Come, and lead me
To these sorrows. *Exeunt.*

Scene III. [*Bohemia. The seacoast.*]

Enter *Antigonus* [with the] *Babe*, a *Mariner*.

Ant. Thou art perfect then our ship hath touch'd upon
The deserts of Bohemia?

Mar. Ay, my lord, and fear
We have landed in ill time. The skies look grimly
And threaten present blusters. In my conscience
The heavens with that we have in hand are angry
And frown upon 's.

Ant. Their sacred wills be done! Go get aboard;
Look to thy bark. I'll not be long before
I call upon thee.

Mar. Make your best haste, and go not
Too far i' th' land. 'Tis like to be loud weather.
Besides, this place is famous for the creatures
Of prey that keep upon't.

Ant. Go thou away;
I'll follow instantly.

Mar. I am glad at heart
To be so rid o' th' business. *Exit.*

Ant. Come, poor babe.
I have heard, but not believ'd, the spirits o' th' dead
May walk again. If such thing be, thy mother
Appear'd to me last night; for ne'er was dream
So like a waking. To me comes a creature,
Sometimes her head on one side, some another;
I never saw a vessel of like sorrow,
So fill'd and so becoming. In pure white robes,
Like very sanctity, she did approach
My cabin where I lay; thrice bow'd before me;
And, gasping to begin some speech, her eyes
Became two spouts. The fury spent, anon
Did this break from her: 'Good Antigonus,
Since fate, against thy better disposition,
Hath made thy person for the thrower-out
Of my poor babe, according to thine oath,
Places remote enough are in Bohemia,
There weep, and leave it crying; and, for the babe
Is counted lost for ever, Perdita
I prithee call't. For this ungentle business,
Put on thee by my lord, thou ne'er shalt see
Thy wife Paulina more.' And so, with shrieks
She melted into air. Affrighted much,
I did in time collect myself, and thought
This was so and no slumber. Dreams are toys;
Yet for this once, yea, superstitiously,
I will be squar'd by this. I do believe
Hermione hath suffer'd death, and that
Apollo would (this being indeed the issue
Of King Polixenes) it should here be laid,
Either for life or death, upon the earth
Of its right father. Blossom, speed thee well!
[*Lays down the Child, with a scroll.*]
There lie, and there thy character; there these,
[*Lays down a bundle.*]
Which may, if fortune please, both breed thee, pretty,
And still rest thine. [*Thunder.*] The storm begins. Poor wretch,
That for thy mother's fault art thus expos'd
To loss and what may follow! Weep I cannot,
But my heart bleeds; and most accurs'd am I
To be by oath enjoin'd to this. Farewell!
The day frowns more and more. Thou'rt like to have
A lullaby too rough. I never saw
The heavens so dim by day.
[*Noise of hunters and dogs within.*]
A savage clamour!
Well may I get aboard. — This is the chase.
I am gone for ever. *Exit, pursued by a bear.*

Enter *Shepherd*.

Shep. I would there were no age between ten and three-and-twenty, or that youth would sleep out the rest; for there is nothing in the between but getting wenches with child, wronging the ancientry, stealing, fighting — Hark you now! Would any but these boil'd-brains of nineteen and two-and-twenty hunt this weather? They have scar'd away two of my best sheep, which I fear the wolf will sooner find than the master. If anywhere I have them, 'tis by the seaside, browsing of ivy. [*Sees the child.*] Good luck, an't be thy will! What have we here? Mercy on 's, a barne! a very pretty barne! A boy or a child, I wonder? A pretty one; a very pretty one. Sure, some scape! Though I am not bookish, yet I can read waiting gentlewoman in the scape. This has been some stair-work, some trunk-work, some behind-door-work. They were warmer that got this than the poor thing is here. I'll take it up for pity. Yet I'll tarry till my son come. He halloa'd but even now. Whoa-ho-hoa!

Enter *Clown.*

Clown. Hilloa, loa!

Shep. What? art so near? If thou'lt see a thing to talk on when thou art dead and rotten, come hither. What ail'st thou, man?

Clown. I have seen two such sights, by sea and by land! But I am not to say it is a sea, for it is now the sky; betwixt the firmament and it you cannot thrust a bodkin's point.

Shep. Why, boy, how is it?

Clown. I would you did but see how it chafes, how it rages, how it takes up the shore! But that's not to the point. O, the most piteous cry of the poor souls! Sometimes to see 'em, and not to see 'em! Now the ship boring the moon with her mainmast, and anon swallowed with yeast and froth, as you'ld thrust a cork into a hogshead. And then for the land service — to see how the bear tore out his shoulder bone; how he cried to me for help and said his name was Antigonus, a nobleman! But to make an end of the ship — to see how the sea flap-dragon'd it; but first, how the poor souls roared, and the sea mock'd them; and how the poor gentleman roared, and the bear mock'd him, both roaring louder than the sea or weather.

Shep. Name of mercy, when was this, boy?

Clown. Now, now! I have not wink'd since I saw these sights. The men are not yet cold under water, nor the bear half din'd on the gentleman — he's at it now.

Shep. Would I had been by, to have help'd the old man!

Clown. I would you had been by the ship side, to have help'd her! There your charity would have lack'd footing.

Shep. Heavy matters, heavy matters! But look thee here, boy. Now bless thyself! thou met'st with things dying, I with things new-born. Here's a sight for thee. Look thee a bearing cloth for a squire's child! Look thee here; take up, take up, boy; open't. So, let's see. It was told me I should be rich by the fairies. This is some changeling. Open't. What's within, boy?

Clown. You're a made old man. If the sins of your youth are forgiven you, you're well to live. Gold! all gold!

Shep. This is fairy gold, boy, and 'twill prove so. Up with't, keep it close. Home, home, the next way! We are lucky, boy, and to be so still requires nothing but secrecy. Let my sheep go. Come, good boy, the next way home!

Clown. Go you the next way with your findings. I'll go see if the bear be gone from the gentleman, and how much he hath eaten. They are never curst but when they are hungry. If there be any of him left, I'll bury it.

Shep. That's a good deed. If thou mayest discern by that which is left of him what he is, fetch me to th' sight of him.

Clown. Marry, will I; and you shall help to put him i' th' ground.

Shep. 'Tis a lucky day, boy, and we'll do good deeds on't. *Exeunt.*

ACT IV. Scene I.

Enter *Time, the Chorus.*

Time. I, that please some, try all, both joy and terror
Of good and bad, that makes and unfolds error,
Now take upon me, in the name of Time,
To use my wings. Impute it not a crime
To me or my swift passage that I slide
O'er sixteen years and leave the growth untried
Of that wide gap, since it is in my pow'r
To o'erthrow law, and in one self born hour
To plant and o'erwhelm custom. Let me pass
The same I am, ere ancient'st order was
Or what is now receiv'd. I witness to
The times that brought them in; so shall I do

To th' freshest things now reigning, and make stale
The glistering of this present, as my tale
Now seems to it. Your patience this allowing,
I turn my glass, and give my scene such growing
As you had slept between. Leontes leaving
Th' effects of his fond jealousies so grieving
That he shuts up himself, imagine me,
Gentle spectators, that I now may be
In fair Bohemia; and remember well
I mention'd a son o' th' King's, which Florizel
I now name to you; and with speed so pace
To speak of Perdita, now grown in grace
Equal with wond'ring. What of her ensues
I list not prophesy; but let Time's news
Be known when 'tis brought forth. A shepherd's daughter
And what to her adheres, which follows after,
Is th' argument of Time. Of this allow,
If ever you have spent time worse ere now;
If never, yet that Time himself doth say
He wishes earnestly you never may. *Exit.*

Scene II. [*Bohemia. The Palace of* Polixenes.]

Enter *Polixenes* and *Camillo.*

Pol. I pray thee, good Camillo, be no more importunate. 'Tis a sickness denying thee anything; a death to grant this.

Cam. It is fifteen years since I saw my country. Though I have for the most part been aired abroad, I desire to lay my bones there. Besides, the penitent King, my master, hath sent for me, to whose feeling sorrows I might be some allay, or I o'erween to think so, which is another spur to my departure.

Pol. As thou lov'st me, Camillo, wipe not out the rest of thy services by leaving me now. The need I have of thee thine own goodness hath made. Better not to have had thee than thus to want thee. Thou, having made me businesses which none without thee can sufficiently manage, must either stay to execute them thyself or take away with thee the very services thou hast done; which if I have not enough considered (as too much I cannot), to be more thankful to thee shall be my study, and my profit therein the heaping friendships. Of that fatal country Sicilia prithee speak no more, whose very naming punishes me with the remembrance of that penitent (as thou call'st him) and reconciled king, my brother, whose loss of his most precious queen and children are even now to be afresh lamented. Say to me, when saw'st thou the Prince Florizel, my son? Kings are no less unhappy, their issue not being gracious, than they are in losing them when they have approved their virtues.

Cam. Sir, it is three days since I saw the Prince. What his happier affairs may be, are to me unknown; but I have (missingly) noted he is of late much retired from court, and is less frequent to his princely exercises than formerly he hath appeared.

Pol. I have considered so much, Camillo, and with some care, so far that I have eyes under my service which look upon his removedness; from whom I have this intelligence, that he is seldom from the house of a most homely shepherd; a man, they say, that from very nothing, and beyond the imagination of his neighbours, is grown into an unspeakable estate.

Cam. I have heard, sir, of such a man, who hath a daughter of most rare note. The report of her is extended more than can be thought to begin from such a cottage.

Pol. That's likewise part of my intelligence; but, I fear, the angle that plucks our son thither. Thou shalt accompany us to the place, where we will (not appearing what we are) have some question with the shepherd; from whose simplicity I think it not uneasy to get the cause of my son's resort thither. Prithee be my present partner in this business and lay aside the thoughts of Sicilia.

Cam. I willingly obey your command.

Pol. My best Camillo! We must disguise ourselves. *Exeunt.*

Scene III. [*Bohemia. A highway near the* Shepherd's *house.*

Enter *Autolycus,* singing.

When daffodils begin to peer,
With heigh! the doxy over the dale —
Why, then comes in the sweet o' the year,
For the red blood reigns in the winter's pale.

The white sheet bleaching on the hedge —
With heigh! the sweet birds, O, how they sing!
Doth set my pugging tooth on edge,
For a quart of ale is a dish for a king.

The lark, that tirra-lyra chants, —
With heigh! with heigh! the thrush and the jay —
Are summer songs for me and my aunts,
While we lie tumbling in the hay.

I have serv'd Prince Florizel and in my time wore three-pile, but now I am out of service.

> But shall I go mourn for that, my dear?
> The pale moon shines by night;
> And when I wander here and there,
> I then do most go right.
>
> If tinkers may have leave to live
> And bear the sow-skin budget,
> Then my account I well may give,
> And in the stocks avouch it.

My traffic is sheets. When the kite builds, look to lesser linen. My father nam'd me Autolycus, who being, as I am, litter'd under Mercury, was likewise a snapper-up of unconsidered trifles. With die and drab I purchas'd this caparison, and my revenue is the silly cheat. Gallows and knock are too powerful on the highway. Beating and hanging are terrors to me. For the life to come, I sleep out the thought of it. A prize! a prize!

Enter *Clown.*

Clown. Let me see: every 'leven wether tods; every tod yields pound and odd shilling; fifteen hundred shorn, what comes the wool to?

Aut. [*aside*] If the springe hold, the cock's mine.

Clown. I cannot do't without compters. Let me see: what am I to buy for our sheep-shearing feast? Three pound of sugar, five pound of currants, rice — What will this sister of mine do with rice? But my father hath made her mistress of the feast, and she lays it on. She hath made me four-and-twenty nosegays for the shearers — three-man songmen all, and very good ones; but they are most of them means and basses; but one Puritan amongst them, and he sings psalms to hornpipes. I must have saffron to colour the warden pies, mace; dates — none, that's out of my note; nutmegs, seven; a race or two of ginger, but that I may beg; four pound of prunes, and as many of raisins o' th' sun.

Aut. O, that ever I was born!

[*Grovels on the ground.*]

Clown. I' th' name of me!

Aut. O, help me, help me! Pluck but off these rags; and then, death, death!

Clown. Alack, poor soul! thou hast need of more rags to lay on thee, rather than have these off.

Aut. O sir, the loathsomeness of them offends me more than the stripes I have received, which are mighty ones and millions.

Clown. Alas, poor man! A million of beating may come to a great matter.

Aut. I am robb'd, sir, and beaten; my money and apparel ta'en from me, and these detestable things put upon me.

Clown. What, by a horseman or a footman?

Aut. A footman, sweet sir, a footman.

Clown. Indeed, he should be a footman by the garments he has left with thee. If this be a horseman's coat, it hath seen very hot service. Lend me thy hand, I'll help thee. Come, lend me thy hand. [*Helps him up.*]

Aut. O, good sir, tenderly, O!

Clown. Alas, poor soul!

Aut. O, good sir, softly, good sir! I fear, sir, my shoulder blade is out.

Clown. How now? Canst stand?

Aut. Softly, dear sir! good sir, softly! [*Picks his pocket.*] You ha' done me a charitable office.

Clown. Dost lack any money? I have a little money for thee.

Aut. No, good sweet sir; no, I beseech you, sir. I have a kinsman not past three quarters of a mile hence, unto whom I was going. I shall there have money or anything I want. Offer me no money, I pray you; that kills my heart.

Clown. What manner of fellow was he that robb'd you?

Aut. A fellow, sir, that I have known to go about with troll-my-dames. I knew him once a servant of the Prince. I cannot tell, good sir, for which of his virtues it was, but he was certainly whipp'd out of the court.

Clown. His vices, you would say. There's no virtue whipp'd out of the court. They cherish it to make it stay there; and yet it will no more but abide.

Aut. Vices I would say, sir. I know this man well. He hath been since an ape-bearer; then a process-server, a bailiff; then he compass'd a motion of the Prodigal Son, and married a tinker's wife within a mile where my land and living lies; and, having flown over many knavish professions, he settled only in rogue. Some call him Autolycus.

Clown. Out upon him! prig, for my life, prig! He haunts wakes, fairs, and bear-baitings.

Aut. Very true, sir; he, sir, he. That's the rogue that put me into this apparel.

Clown. Not a more cowardly rogue in all Bohemia. If you had but look'd big and spit at him, he'ld have run.

Aut. I must confess to you, sir, I am no fighter. I am false of heart that way; and that he knew, I warrant him.

Clown. How do you now?

Aut. Sweet sir, much better than I was. I can stand and walk. I will even take my leave of you and pace softly towards my kinsman's.

Clown. Shall I bring thee on the way?

Aut. No, good-fac'd sir; no, sweet sir.

Clown. Then fare thee well. I must go buy spices for our sheep-shearing.

Aut. Prosper you, sweet sir! *Exit* [*Clown*]. Your purse is not hot enough to purchase your spice. I'll be with you at your sheep-shearing too. If I make not this cheat bring out another and the shearers prove sheep, let me be unroll'd and my name put in the book of virtue!

Song.

Jog on, jog on the footpath way,
And merrily hent the stile-a.
A merry heart goes all the day,
Your sad tires in a mile-a. *Exit.*

Scene IV. [*Bohemia. A green before the* Shepherd's *house.*]

Enter *Florizel* [and] *Perdita.*

Flo. These your unusual weeds to each part of you
Do give a life — no shepherdess, but Flora
Peering in April's front! This your sheep-shearing
Is as a meeting of the petty gods,
And you the queen on't.

Per. Sir, my gracious lord,
To chide at your extremes it not becomes me;
O, pardon that I name them! Your high self,
The gracious mark o' th' land, you have obscur'd
With a swain's wearing; and me, poor lowly maid,
Most goddess-like prank'd up. But that our feasts
In every mess have folly, and the feeders
Digest it with a custom, I should blush
To see you so attir'd — sworn, I think,
To show myself a glass.

Flo. I bless the time
When my good falcon made her flight across
Thy father's ground.

Per. Now Jove afford you cause!
To me the difference forges dread; your greatness
Hath not been us'd to fear. Even now I tremble
To think your father, by some accident,
Should pass this way, as you did. O, the Fates!
How would he look to see his work, so noble,
Vilely bound up? What would he say? Or how
Should I, in these my borrowed flaunts, behold
The sternness of his presence?

Flo. Apprehend
Nothing but jollity. The gods themselves,
Humbling their deities to love, have taken
The shapes of beasts upon them. Jupiter
Became a bull, and bellow'd; the green Neptune
A ram, and bleated; and the fire-rob'd god,
Golden Apollo, a poor humble swain,
As I seem now. Their transformations
Were never for a piece of beauty rarer,
Nor in a way so chaste, since my desires
Run not before mine honour, nor my lusts
Burn hotter than my faith.

Per. O, but, sir,
Your resolution cannot hold when 'tis
Oppos'd, as it must be, by th' pow'r of the King!
One of these two must be necessities,
Which then will speak — that you must change this purpose,
Or I my life.

Flo. Thou dearest Perdita,
With these forc'd thoughts I prithee darken not
The mirth o' th' feast. Or I'll be thine, my fair,
Or not my father's; for I cannot be
Mine own, nor anything to any, if
I be not thine. To this I am most constant,
Though destiny say no. Be merry, gentle!
Strangle such thoughts as these with anything
That you behold the while. Your guests are coming.
Lift up your countenance, as it were the day
Of celebration of that nuptial which
We two have sworn shall come.

Per. O Lady Fortune,
Stand you auspicious!

Flo. See, your guests approach.
Address yourself to entertain them sprightly,
And let's be red with mirth.

Enter *Shepherd, Clown, Polixenes* [and] *Camillo* [disguised], *Mopsa, Dorcas,* [and others].

Shep. Fie, daughter! When my old wife liv'd, upon
This day she was both pantler, butler, cook,
Both dame and servant; welcom'd all; serv'd all;
Would sing her song and dance her turn; now here
At upper end o' th' table, now i' th' middle;

On his shoulder, and his; her face o' fire
With labour, and the thing she took to quench it
She would to each one sip. You are retir'd,
As if you were a feasted one, and not
The hostess of the meeting. Pray you bid
These unknown friends to 's welcome, for it is
A way to make us better friends, more known.
Come, quench your blushes and present yourself
That which you are, mistress o' th' feast. Come on,
And bid us welcome to your sheep-shearing,
As your good flock shall prosper.

Per. [*to Polixenes*] Sir, welcome.
It is my father's will I should take on me
The hostessship o' th' day. [*To Camillo*] You're welcome, sir.
Give me those flow'rs there, Dorcas. Reverend sirs,
For you there's rosemary and rue; these keep
Seeming and savour all the winter long.
Grace and remembrance be to you both,
And welcome to our shearing!

Pol. Shepherdess
(A fair one are you), well you fit our ages
With flow'rs of winter.

Per. Sir, the year growing ancient,
Not yet on summer's death nor on the birth
Of trembling winter, the fairest flow'rs o' th' season
Are our carnations and streak'd gillyvors,
Which some call nature's bastards. Of that kind
Our rustic garden 's barren, and I care not
To get slips of them.

Pol. Wherefore, gentle maiden,
Do you neglect them?

Per. For I have heard it said
There is an art which in their piedness shares
With great creating nature.

Pol. Say there be.
Yet nature is made better by no mean
But nature makes that mean. So, over that art
Which you say adds to nature, is an art
That nature makes. You see, sweet maid, we marry
A gentler scion to the wildest stock
And make conceive a bark of baser kind
By bud of nobler race. This is an art
Which does mend nature — change it rather; but
The art itself is nature.

Per. So it is.

Pol. Then make your garden rich in gillyvors,
And do not call them bastards.

Per. I'll not put
The dibble in earth to set one slip of them;
No more than, were I painted, I would wish
This youth should say 'twere well, and only therefore
Desire to breed by me. Here's flow'rs for you:
Hot lavender, mints, savory, marjoram;
The marigold, that goes to bed wi' th' sun
And with him rises weeping. These are flow'rs
Of middle summer, and I think they are given
To men of middle age. Y'are very welcome.

Cam. I should leave grazing, were I of your flock,
And only live by gazing.

Per. Out, alas!
You'ld be so lean that blasts of January
Would blow you through and through. [*To Florizel*] Now, my fair'st friend,
I would I had some flow'rs o' th' spring that might
Become your time of day; [*to the Girls*] and yours, and yours,
That wear upon your virgin branches yet
Your maidenheads growing. O Proserpina,
For the flowers now that, frighted, thou let'st fall
From Dis's wagon! daffodils,
That come before the swallow dares and take
The winds of March with beauty; violets — dim,
But sweeter than the lids of Juno's eyes
Or Cytherea's breath; pale primeroses,
That die unmarried ere they can behold
Bright Phœbus in his strength (a malady
Most incident to maids); bold oxlips and
The crown imperial; lilies of all kinds,
The flow'r-de-luce being one! O, these I lack
To make you garlands of; and my sweet friend,
To strew him o'er and o'er!

Flo. What, like a corse?

Per. No, like a bank for love to lie and play on;
Not like a corse; or if — not to be buried,
But quick, and in mine arms. Come, take your flow'rs.
Methinks I play as I have seen them do
In Whitsun pastorals. Sure this robe of mine
Does change my disposition.

Flo. What you do
Still betters what is done. When you speak, sweet,
I'ld have you do it ever. When you sing,
I'ld have you buy and sell so; so give alms;
Pray so; and for the ord'ring your affairs,
To sing them too. When you do dance, I wish you
A wave o' th' sea. that you might ever do

Nothing but that; move still, still so,
And own no other function. Each your doing,
So singular in each particular,
Crowns what you are doing in the present deed,
That all your acts are queens.

Per. O Doricles,
Your praises are too large. But that your youth,
And the true blood which peeps so fairly through't,
Do plainly give you out an unstain'd shepherd,
With wisdom I might fear, my Doricles,
You woo'd me the false way.

Flo. I think you have
As little skill to fear as I have purpose
To put you to't. But come; our dance, I pray!
Your hand, my Perdita. So turtles pair,
That never mean to part.

Per. I'll swear for 'em.

Pol. This is the prettiest low-born lass that ever
Ran on the greensward. Nothing she does or seems
But smacks of something greater than herself,
Too noble for this place.

Cam. He tells her something
That makes her blood look out. Good sooth, she is
The queen of curds and cream.

Clown. Come on, strike up!

Dor. Mopsa must be your mistress! Marry, garlic,
To mend her kissing with!

Mop. Now in good time!

Clown. Not a word, a word! We stand upon our manners.
Come, strike up!

[*Music.*] *Here a dance of Shepherds and Shepherdesses.*

Pol. Pray, good shepherd, what fair swain is this
Which dances with your daughter?

Shep. They call him Doricles, and boasts himself
To have a worthy feeding; but I have it
Upon his own report, and I believe it:
He looks like sooth. He says he loves my daughter.
I think so too; for never gaz'd the moon
Upon the water as he'll stand and read,
As 'twere, my daughter's eyes; and to be plain,
I think there is not half a kiss to choose
Who loves another best.

Pol. She dances featly.

Shep. So she does anything, though I report it
That should be silent. If young Doricles
Do light upon her, she shall bring him that
Which he not dreams of.

Enter *Servant.*

Serv. O master! if you did but hear the pedlar at the door, you would never dance again after a tabor and pipe; no, the bagpipe could not move you! He sings several tunes faster than you'll tell money; he utters them as he had eaten ballads, and all men's ears grow to his tunes.

Clown. He could never come better. He shall come in. I love a ballad but even too well, if it be doleful matter merrily set down, or a very pleasant thing indeed and sung lamentably.

Serv. He hath songs for man or woman, of all sizes. No milliner can so fit his customers with gloves. He has the prettiest love songs for maids; so without bawdry, which is strange; with such delicate burthens of dildo's and fading's, 'jump her and thump her'! and where some stretch-mouth'd rascal would, as it were, mean mischief, and break a foul gap into the matter, he makes the maid to answer 'Whoop, do me no harm, good man!' puts him off, slights him, with 'Whoop, do me no harm, good man!'

Pol. This is a brave fellow.

Clown. Believe me, thou talkest of an admirable conceited fellow. Has he any unbraided wares?

Serv. He hath ribbons of all the colours i' th' rainbow; points, more than all the lawyers in Bohemia can learnedly handle, though they come to him by th' gross; inkles, caddisses, cambrics, lawns. Why, he sings 'em over as they were gods or goddesses. You would think a smock were a she-angel, he so chants to the sleeve-hand and the work about the square on't.

Clown. Prithee bring him in, and let him approach singing.

Per. Forewarn him that he use no scurrilous words in 's tunes. [*Exit Servant.*]

Clown. You have of these pedlars that have more in them than you'ld think, sister.

Per. Ay, good brother, or go about to think.

Enter *Autolycus*, singing.

Lawn as white as driven snow;
Cypress black as e'er was crow;
Gloves as sweet as damask roses;
Masks for faces and for noses;
Bugle bracelet, necklace amber,
Perfume for a lady's chamber;

Golden quoifs and stomachers
For my lads to give their dears;
Pins, and poking sticks of steel:
What maids lack from head to heel.
Come buy of me, come! come buy, come buy!
Buy, lads, or else your lasses cry. Come buy!

Clown. If I were not in love with Mopsa, thou shouldst take no money of me; but being enthrall'd as I am, it will also be the bondage of certain ribbons and gloves.

Mop. I was promis'd them against the feast, but they come not too late now.

Dor. He hath promis'd you more than that, or there be liars.

Mop. He hath paid you all he promis'd you. May be he has paid you more, which will shame you to give him again.

Clown. Is there no manners left among maids? Will they wear their plackets where they should bear their faces? Is there not milking time, when you are going to bed, or kilnhole, to whistle off these secrets, but you must be tittle-tattling before all our guests? 'Tis well they are whisp'ring. Charm your tongues, and not a word more!

Mop. I have done. Come, you promis'd me a tawdry-lace and a pair of sweet gloves.

Clown. Have I not told thee how I was cozen'd by the way and lost all my money?

Aut. And indeed, sir, there are cozeners abroad. Therefore it behooves men to be wary.

Clown. Fear not thou, man; thou shalt lose nothing here.

Aut. I hope so, sir, for I have about me many parcels of charge.

Clown. What hast here? ballads?

Mop. Pray now buy some. I love a ballet in print a-life, for then we are sure they are true.

Aut. Here's one, to a very doleful tune, how a usurer's wife was brought to bed of twenty money bags at a burthen, and how she long'd to eat adders' heads, and toads carbonado'd.

Mop. Is it true, think you?

Aut. Very true, and but a month old.

Dor. Bless me from marrying a usurer!

Aut. Here's the midwive's name to't, one Mistress Taleporter, and five or six honest wives that were present. Why should I carry lies abroad?

Mop. Pray you now buy it.

Clown. Come on, lay it by; and let's first see moe ballads. We'll buy the other things anon.

Aut. Here's another ballad, of a fish that appeared upon the coast on Wednesday the fourscore of April, forty thousand fadom above water and sung this ballad against the hard hearts of maids. It was thought she was a woman, and was turn'd into a cold fish for she would not exchange flesh with one that lov'd her. The ballad is very pitiful, and as true.

Dor. Is it true too, think you?

Aut. Five justices' hands at it, and witnesses more than my pack will hold.

Clown. Lay it by too. Another.

Aut. This is a merry ballad, but a very pretty one.

Mop. Let's have some merry ones.

Aut. Why, this is a passing merry one, and goes to the tune of 'Two maids wooing a man.' There's scarce a maid westward but she sings it. 'Tis in request, I can tell you.

Mop. We can both sing it. If thou'lt bear a part, thou shalt hear; 'tis in three parts.

Dor. We had the tune on't a month ago.

Aut. I can bear my part; you must know 'tis my occupation. Have at it with you!

Song.

Aut. Get you hence, for I must go
Where it fits not you to know.
Dor. Whither? *Mop.* O, whither?
Dor. Whither?
Mop. It becomes thy oath full well
Thou to me thy secrets tell.
Dor. Me too! Let me go thither.

Mop. Or thou goest to th' grange or mill.
Dor. If to either, thou dost ill.
Aut. Neither. *Dor.* What, neither?
Aut. Neither.
Dor. Thou hast sworn my love to be.
Mop. Thou hast sworn it more to me.
Then whither goest? Say, whither?

Clown. We'll have this song out anon by ourselves. My father and the gentlemen are in sad talk, and we'll not trouble them. Come, bring away thy pack after me. Wenches, I'll buy for you both. Pedlar, let's have the first choice. Follow me, girls. [*Exit with Dorcas and Mopsa.*]

Aut. And you shall pay well for 'em.

Song.

Will you buy any tape,
Or lace for your cape,
My dainty duck, my dear-a?
Any silk, any thread,
Any toys for your head
Of the new'st and fin'st, fin'st wear-a?
Come to the pedlar.
Money 's a meddler
That doth utter all men's ware-a.

Exit.

[Enter *Servant.*]

Serv. Master, there is three carters, three shepherds, three neatherds, three swineherds, that have made themselves all men of hair. They call themselves Saltiers; and they have a dance which the wenches say is a gallimaufry of gambols, because they are not in't; but they themselves are o' th' mind (if it be not too rough for some that know little but bowling) it will please plentifully.

Shep. Away! We'll none on't. Here has been too much homely foolery already. I know, sir, we weary you.

Pol. You weary those that refresh us. Pray let's see these four threes of herdsmen.

Serv. One three of them, by their own report, sir, hath danc'd before the King; and not the worst of the three but jumps twelve foot and a half by th' squire.

Shep. Leave your prating. Since these good men are pleas'd, let them come in; but quickly now.

Serv. Why, they stay at door, sir.

Here a Dance of twelve Satyrs.

Pol. [*to Shepherd*] O, father, you'll know more of that hereafter.
[*To Camillo*] Is it not too far gone? 'Tis time to part them.
He's simple and tells much. [*To Florizel*] How now, fair shepherd?
Your heart is full of something that does take
Your mind from feasting. Sooth, when I was young,
And handed love as you do, I was wont
To load my she with knacks. I would have ransack'd
The pedlar's silken treasury and have pour'd it
To her acceptance. You have let him go
And nothing marted with him. If your lass
Interpretation should abuse and call this
Your lack of love or bounty, you were straited
For a reply, at least if you make a care
Of happy holding her.

Flo. Old sir, I know
She prizes not such trifles as these are.
The gifts she looks from me are pack'd and lock'd
Up in my heart, which I have given already,
But not deliver'd. O, hear me breathe my life
Before this ancient sir, who, it should seem,
Hath sometime lov'd! I take thy hand — this hand,
As soft as dove's down and as white as it,
Or Ethiopian's tooth, or the fann'd snow that's bolted
By th' northern blasts twice o'er.

Pol. What follows this?
How prettily the young swain seems to wash
The hand was fair before! I have put you out;
But to your protestation! Let me hear
What you profess.

Flo. Do, and be witness to't.

Pol. And this my neighbour too?

Flo. And he, and more
Than he, and men — the earth, the heavens, and all!
That, were I crown'd the most imperial monarch —
Thereof most worthy — were I the fairest youth
That ever made eye swerve, had force and knowledge
More than was ever man's, I would not prize them
Without her love; for her employ them all;
Commend them and condemn them to her service
Or to their own perdition.

Pol. Fairly offer'd.

Cam. This shows a sound affection.

Shep. But, my daughter,
Say you the like to him?

Per. I cannot speak
So well, nothing so well; no, nor mean better.
By th' pattern of mine own thoughts I cut out
The purity of his.

Shep. Take hands, a bargain!
And, friends unknown, you shall bear witness to't:
I give my daughter to him, and will make
Her portion equal his.

Flo. O, that must be
I' th' virtue of your daughter. One being dead,
I shall have more than you can dream of yet;
Enough then for your wonder. But come on,
Contract us fore these witnesses.

Shep. Come, your hand;
And, daughter, yours.

Pol. Soft, swain, awhile, beseech you.
Have you a father?

Flo. I have; but what of him?

Pol. Knows he of this?

Flo. He neither does nor shall.

Pol. Methinks a father
Is at the nuptial of his son a guest
That best becomes the table. Pray you once more,
Is not your father grown incapable
Of reasonable affairs? Is he not stupid

With age and alt'ring rheums? Can he speak? hear?
Know man from man? dispute his own estate?
Lies he not bedrid? and again does nothing
But what he did being childish?
Flo. No, good sir;
He has his health, and ampler strength indeed
Than most have of his age.
Pol. By my white beard,
You offer him, if this be so, a wrong
Something unfilial. Reason my son
Should choose himself a wife; but as good reason
The father (all whose joy is nothing else
But fair posterity) should hold some counsel
In such a business.
Flo. I yield all this;
But for some other reasons, my grave sir,
Which 'tis not fit you know, I not acquaint
My father of this business.
Pol. Let him know't.
Flo. He shall not.
Pol. Prithee let him.
Flo. No, he must not.
Shep. Let him, my son. He shall not need to grieve
At knowing of thy choice.
Flo. Come, come, he must not.
Mark our contract.
Pol. [*Discovers himself.*] Mark your divorce, young sir!
Whom son I dare not call. Thou art too base
To be acknowledg'd. Thou a sceptre's heir,
That thus affects a sheephook? — Thou, old traitor,
I am sorry that by hanging thee I can but
Shorten thy life one week. — And thou, fresh piece
Of excellent witchcraft, who of force must know
The royal fool thou cop'st with —
Shep. O, my heart!
Pol. I'll have thy beauty scratch'd with briers and made
More homely than thy state. — For thee, fond boy,
If I may ever know thou dost but sigh
That thou no more shalt see this knack (as never
I mean thou shalt), we'll bar thee from succession;
Not hold thee of our blood, no, not our kin,
Farre than Deucalion off! Mark thou my words.
Follow us to the court. — Thou churl, for this time,
Though full of our displeasure, yet we free thee
From the dead blow of it. — And you, enchantment,
Worthy enough a herdsman; yea, him too
That makes himself (but for our honour therein)
Unworthy thee — if ever henceforth thou
These rural latches to his entrance open,
Or hoop his body more with thy embraces,
I will devise a death as cruel for thee
As thou art tender to't. *Exit.*
Per. Even here undone!
I was not much afeard; for once or twice
I was about to speak, and tell him plainly
The selfsame sun that shines upon his court
Hides not his visage from our cottage, but
Looks on alike. [*To Florizel*] Will't please you, sir, be gone?
I told you what would come of this. Beseech you
Of your own state take care. This dream of mine —
Being now awake, I'll queen it no inch farther,
But milk my ewes and weep.
Cam. Why, how now, father?
Speak ere thou diest.
Shep. I cannot speak nor think,
Nor dare to know that which I know. [*To Florizel*] O sir,
You have undone a man of fourscore three,
That thought to fill his grave in quiet; yea,
To die upon the bed my father died,
To lie close by his honest bones; but now
Some hangman must put on my shroud and lay me
Where no priest shovels-in dust. [*To Perdita*] O cursed wretch,
That knew'st this was the Prince and wouldst adventure
To mingle faith with him! — Undone! undone!
If I might die within this hour, I have liv'd
To die when I desire. *Exit.*
Flo. Why look you so upon me?
I am but sorry, not afeard; delay'd,
But nothing alt'red. What I was, I am;
More straining on for plucking back; not following
My leash unwillingly.
Cam. Gracious my lord,
You know your father's temper. At this time
He will allow no speech (which I do guess
You do not purpose to him) and as hardly
Will he endure your sight as yet, I fear.
Then, till the fury of his highness settle,
Come not before him.
Flo. I not purpose it.
I think Camillo?

Cam. Even he, my lord.
Per. How often have I told you 'twould be thus!
How often said my dignity would last
But till 'twere known!
Flo. It cannot fail but by
The violation of my faith; and then
Let nature crush the sides o' th' earth together
And mar the seeds within! Lift up thy looks.
From my succession wipe me, father! I
Am heir to my affection.
Cam. Be advis'd.
Flo. I am, and by my fancy. If my reason
Will thereto be obedient, I have reason;
If not, my senses, better pleas'd with madness,
Do bid it welcome.
Cam. This is desperate, sir.
Flo. So call it; but it does fulfil my vow;
I needs must think it honesty. Camillo,
Not for Bohemia nor the pomp that may
Be thereat glean'd, for all the sun sees or
The close earth wombs or the profound sea hides
In unknown fadoms, will I break my oath
To this my fair belov'd. Therefore, I pray you,
As you have ever been my father's honour'd friend,
When he shall miss me (as, in faith, I mean not
To see him any more), cast your good counsels
Upon his passion. Let myself and Fortune
Tug for the time to come. This you may know,
And so deliver: I am put to sea
With her who here I cannot hold on shore;
And most opportune to our need, I have
A vessel rides fast by, but not prepar'd
For this design. What course I mean to hold
Shall nothing benefit your knowledge nor
Concern me the reporting.
Cam. O my lord,
I would your spirit were easier for advice
Or stronger for your need!
Flo. Hark, Perdita.
[*Takes her aside.*]
[*To Camillo*] I'll hear you by-and-by.
Cam. He's irremovable,
Resolv'd for flight. Now were I happy if
His going I could frame to serve my turn,
Save him from danger, do him love and honour,
Purchase the sight again of dear Sicilia
And that unhappy king my master, whom
I so much thirst to see.
Flo. Now, good Camillo,
I am so fraught with curious business that
I leave out ceremony.
Cam. Sir, I think
You have heard of my poor services i' th' love
That I have borne your father?
Flo. Very nobly
Have you deserv'd. It is my father's music
To speak your deeds; not little of his care
To have them recompens'd as thought on.
Cam. Well, my lord,
If you may please to think I love the King
And, through him, what is nearest to him, which is
Your gracious self, embrace but my direction,
If your more ponderous and settled project
May suffer alteration. On mine honour,
I'll point you where you shall have such receiving
As shall become your Highness, where you may
Enjoy your mistress, — from the whom I see
There's no disjunction to be made but by
(As heavens forfend!) your ruin,—marry her;
And with my best endeavours, in your absence,
Your discontenting father strive to qualify
And bring him up to liking.
Flo. How, Camillo,
May this (almost a miracle) be done?
That I may call thee something more than man,
And after that trust to thee.
Cam. Have you thought on
A place whereto you'll go?
Flo. Not any yet;
But as th' unthought-on accident is guilty
To what we wildly do, so we profess
Ourselves to be the slaves of chance and flies
Of every wind that blows.
Cam. Then list to me.
This follows, if you will not change your purpose,
But undergo this flight: make for Sicilia,
And there present yourself and your fair princess
(For so I see she must be) fore Leontes.
She shall be habited as it becomes
The partner of your bed. Methinks I see
Leontes opening his free arms and weeping
His welcomes forth; asks thee, the son, forgiveness,
As 'twere i' th' father's person; kisses the hands
Of your fresh princess; o'er and o'er divides him
'Twixt his unkindness and his kindness: th' one
He chides to hell, and bids the other grow
Faster than thought or time.
Flo. Worthy Camillo,
What colour for my visitation shall I
Hold up before him?

Cam. Sent by the King your father
To greet him and to give him comforts. Sir,
The manner of your bearing towards him, with
What you (as from your father) shall deliver,
Things known betwixt us three, I'll write you down,
The which shall point you forth at every sitting
What you must say; that he shall not perceive
But that you have your father's bosom there
And speak his very heart.

Flo. I am bound to you.
There is some sap in this!

Cam. A course more promising
Than a wild dedication of yourselves
To unpath'd waters, undream'd shores, most certain
To miseries enough; no hope to help you,
But, as you shake off one, to take another;
Nothing so certain as your anchors, who
Do their best office if they can but stay you
Where you'll be loath to be. Besides, you know
Prosperity's the very bond of love,
Whose fresh complexion and whose heart together
Affliction alters.

Per. One of these is true.
I think affliction may subdue the cheek,
But not take in the mind.

Cam. Yea? say you so?
There shall not at your father's house these seven years
Be born another such.

Flo. My good Camillo,
She is as forward of her breeding as
She is i' th' rear 'our birth.

Cam. I cannot say 'tis pity
She lacks instructions, for she seems a mistress
To most that teach.

Per. Your pardon, sir! For this
I'll blush you thanks.

Flo. My prettiest Perdita!
But, O, the thorns we stand upon! Camillo —
Preserver of my father, now of me,
The medicine of our house — how shall we do?
We are not furnish'd like Bohemia's son,
Nor shall appear in Sicilia.

Cam. My lord,
Fear none of this. I think you know my fortunes
Do all lie there. It shall be so my care
To have you royally appointed as if
The scene you play were mine. For instance, sir,
That you may know you shall not want — one word.

[*They talk aside.*]

Enter *Autolycus.*

Aut. Ha, ha! what a fool Honesty is! and Trust, his sworn brother, a very simple gentleman! I have sold all my trumpery. Not a counterfeit stone, not a ribbon, glass, pomander, brooch, table book, ballad, knife, tape, glove, shoe-tie, bracelet, horn ring, to keep my pack from fasting! They throng who should buy first, as if my trinkets had been hallowed and brought a benediction to the buyer; by which means I saw whose purse was best in picture; and what I saw, to my good use I rememb'red. My clown (who wants but something to be a reasonable man) grew so in love with the wenches' song that he would not stir his pettitoes till he had both tune and words, which so drew the rest of the herd to me that all their other senses stuck in ears. You might have pinch'd a placket, it was senseless; 'twas nothing to geld a codpiece of a purse; I would have fil'd keys off that hung in chains. No hearing, no feeling, but my sir's song, and admiring the nothing of it! So that, in this time of lethargy, I pick'd and cut most of their festival purses; and had not the old man come in with a whoobub against his daughter and the King's son and scar'd my choughs from the chaff, I had not left a purse alive in the whole army.

[*Camillo, Florizel, and Perdita come forward.*]

Cam. Nay, but my letters, by this means being there
So soon as you arrive, shall clear that doubt.

Flo. And those that you'll procure from King Leontes?

Cam. Shall satisfy your father.

Per. Happy be you!
All that you speak shows fair.

Cam. [*sees Autolycus*] Who have we here?
We'll make an instrument of this; omit
Nothing may give us aid.

Aut. [*aside*] If they have overheard me now — why, hanging!

Cam. How now, good fellow? Why shak'st thou so? Fear not, man. Here's no harm intended to thee.

Aut. I am a poor fellow, sir.

Cam. Why, be so still. Here's nobody will steal that from thee. Yet, for the outside of thy poverty, we must make an exchange. Therefore discase thee instantly (thou must think there's a necessity in't) and change garments with this gentleman. Though the pennyworth (on his

The song of Autolycus (George Rose), a "snapper-up of unconsidered trifles," introduces the first joyful note in the somber winter's tale *(Act IV, Scene II)*

THE WINTER'S TALE

PHOTOGRAPHS BY ANGUS MCBEAN
PRODUCED BY TENNENT PRODUCTIONS, LTD.

"Verily, you shall not go." At the request of Leontes (John Gielgud), her husband, Hermione (Diana Wynyard) invites Polixenes (Brewster Mason) to extend his already long visit
(Act I, Scene II)

Polixenes' innocent conversation with Hermione wakens her husband's jealousy *(Act I, Scene II)*

Above: Temporizing with Leontes, whom he sees to be mad with jealousy, Lord Camillo (Michael Goodliffe) tells him he will poison Polixenes *(Act I, Scene II)*

Left: "You, sir, charge him too coldly." Leontes is suspicious of Hermione's warmth in pressing Polixenes to extend his stay as their guest *(Act I, Scene II)*

John Gielgud as King Leontes of Sicilia, sick with jealousy of his innocent wife, Hermione

"Let us be clear'd of being tyrannous, since we so openly proceed in justice." Leontes himself opens the trial of his wife, Hermione, who is accused of adultery
(Act III, Scene II)

Left: Paulina (Flora Robson) promises to bring Hermione's child to its father *(Act II, Scene II)*

Below: Leontes completely disowns the child born to Hermione while in prison *(Act II, Scene III)*

The old shepherd (George Howe) and his son (Philip Guard) discover the gold which Leontes left for the care of Hermione's infant *(Act III, Scene III)*

Virginia McKenna as Hermione's child, Perdita, who has been brought up by the shepherd who found her on the seashore

"I cannot be mine own, nor any thing to any, if I be not thine." Polixenes' son, Prince Florizel (Richard Gale), plights his troth to Perdita at the sheep-shearing festival *(Act IV, Scene III)*

Florizel greets Perdita at the sheep-shearing festival *(Act IV, Scene III)*

Below: "Reverend sirs, for you there's rosemary and rue; these keep seeming and savour all the winter long." Perdita offers herbs to Polixenes and Camillo, who have disguised themselves as curates and have come to the festival to look for Prince Florizel *(Act IV, Scene III)*

Autolycus directs the ballad singing at the festival *(Act IV, Scene III)*

Having eloped with Perdita to Sicilia, Prince Florizel is welcomed by Leontes, who promises to attempt to reconcile Polixenes to the prince's marriage *(Act V, Scene I)*

Paulina, Antigonus' wife and the confidant of Hermione, devises a strange ruse to reunite the remorseful Leontes and his wife, whom he supposes to have died many years before

Autolycus meets the shepherds on their way to the court of Leontes *(Act IV, Scene III)*

Asking help of the shepherd, Autolycus skillfully picks his pocket *(Act IV, Scene II)*

Above: "No longer shall you gaze on't, lest your fancy may think anon it moves." Paulina reveals to Leontes what he thinks is a statue of Hermione by an Italian artist, but is, in fact, Hermione herself *(Act V, Scene III)*

Above: "Tell me, mine own, where hast thou been preserved?" Hermione is reunited with her lost daughter, Perdita *(Act V, Scene III)*

Left: John Gielgud as Leontes, who paid with years of bitter loneliness for his cruel suspicion and persecution of Hermione

Hermione gently forgives Leontes for his cruelty to her *(Act V, Scene III)*

side) be the worst, yet hold thee, there's some boot. [*Gives money.*]

Aut. I am a poor fellow, sir. [*Aside*] I know ye well enough.

Cam. Nay, prithee dispatch! The gentleman is half flay'd already.

Aut. Are you in earnest, sir? [*Aside*] I smell the trick on't.

Flo. Dispatch, I prithee.

Aut. Indeed I have had earnest, but I cannot with conscience take it.

Cam. Unbuckle, unbuckle.

[*Florizel and Autolycus exchange garments.*]

Fortunate mistress (let my prophecy
Come home to ye!), you must retire yourself
Into some covert; take your sweetheart's hat
And pluck it o'er your brows; muffle your face;
Dismantle you; and (as you can) disliken
The truth of your own seeming, that you may
(For I do fear eyes over) to shipboard
Get undescried.

Per. I see the play so lies
That I must bear a part.

Cam. No remedy.
Have you done there?

Flo. Should I now meet my father,
He would not call me son.

Cam. Nay, you shall have no hat.
[*Gives it to Perdita.*]
Come, lady, come. Farewell, my friend.

Aut. Adieu, sir.

Flo. O Perdita, what have we twain forgot!
Pray you a word. [*They converse apart.*]

Cam. [*aside*] What I do next shall be to tell the King
Of this escape and whither they are bound;
Wherein, my hope is, I shall so prevail
To force him after; in whose company
I shall review Sicilia, for whose sight
I have a woman's longing.

Flo. Fortune speed us!
Thus we set on, Camillo, to the seaside.

Cam. The swifter speed the better.

Exit [*with Florizel and Perdita*].

Aut. I understand the business, I hear it. To have an open ear, a quick eye, and a nimble hand is necessary for a cutpurse; a good nose is requisite also, to smell out work for th' other senses. I see this is the time that the unjust man doth thrive. What an exchange had this been without boot! What a boot is here with this exchange! Sure the gods do this year connive at us, and we may do anything extempore. The Prince himself is about a piece of iniquity — stealing away from his father with his clog at his heels. If I thought it were a piece of honesty to acquaint the King withal, I would not do't. I hold it the more knavery to conceal it; and therein am I constant to my profession.

Enter *Clown* and *Shepherd.*

Aside, aside! Here is more matter for a hot brain. Every lane's end, every shop, church, session, hanging, yields a careful man work.

Clown. See, see! What a man you are now! There is no other way but to tell the King she's a changeling and none of your flesh and blood.

Shep. Nay, but hear me.

Clown. Nay, but hear me.

Shep. Go to, then.

Clown. She being none of your flesh and blood, your flesh and blood has not offended the King, and so your flesh and blood is not to be punish'd by him. Show those things you found about her — those secret things, all but what she has with her. This being done, let the law go whistle; I warrant you.

Shep. I will tell the King all, every word! yea, and his son's pranks too; who, I may say, is no honest man, neither to his father nor to me, to go about to make me the King's brother-in-law.

Clown. Indeed, brother-in-law was the farthest off you could have been to him, and then your blood had been the dearer by I know not how much an ounce.

Aut. [*aside*] Very wisely, puppies!

Shep. Well, let us to the King. There is that in this farthel will make him scratch his beard.

Aut. [*aside*] I know not what impediment this complaint may be to the flight of my master.

Clown. Pray heartily he be at' palace.

Aut. [*aside*] Though I am not naturally honest, I am so sometimes by chance. Let me pocket up my pedlar's excrement. *Takes off his false beard.*] How now, rustics? Whither are you bound?

Shep. To th' palace, an it like your worship.

Aut. Your affairs there? what? with whom? the condition of that farthel? the place of your dwelling? your names? your ages? of what having? breeding? and anything that is fitting to be known, discover.

Clown. We are but plain fellows, sir.

Aut. A lie! You are rough and hairy. Let me have no lying. It becomes none but tradesmen, and they often give us soldiers the lie; but we pay them for it with stamped coin, not stabbing steel; therefore they do not give us the lie.

Clown. Your worship had like to have given us one, if you had not taken yourself with the manner.

Shep. Are you a courtier, an't like you, sir?

Aut. Whether it like me or no, I am a courtier. Seest thou not the air of the court in these enfoldings? Hath not my gait in it the measure of the court? Receives not thy nose court odour from me? Reflect I not on thy baseness court contempt? Think'st thou, for that I insinuate, or toaze from thee thy business, I am therefore no courtier? I am courtier cap-a-pe; and one that will either push on or pluck back thy business there. Whereupon I command thee to open thy affair.

Shep. My business, sir, is to the King.

Aut. What advocate hast thou to him?

Shep. I know not, an't like you.

Clown. [*aside to Shepherd*] Advocate's the court word for a pheasant. Say you have none.

Shep. None, sir. I have no pheasant, cock nor hen.

Aut. How blessed are we that are not simple men!
Yet Nature might have made me as these are;
Therefore I will not disdain.

Clown. [*aside to Shepherd*] This cannot be but a great courtier.

Shep. [*aside to Clown*] His garments are rich, but he wears them not handsomely.

Clown. [*aside to Shepherd*] He seems to be the more noble in being fantastical. A great man, I'll warrant; I know by the picking on 's teeth.

Aut. The farthel there? What's i' th' farthel? Wherefore that box?

Shep. Sir, there lies such secrets in this farthel and box which none must know but the King, and which he shall know within this hour if I may come to th' speech of him.

Aut. Age, thou hast lost thy labour.

Shep. Why, sir?

Aut. The King is not at the palace. He is gone aboard a new ship to purge melancholy and air himself; for, if thou be'st capable of things serious, thou must know the King is full of grief.

Shep. So 'tis said, sir — about his son, that should have married a shepherd's daughter.

Aut. If that shepherd be not in handfast, let him fly! The curses he shall have, the tortures he shall feel, will break the back of man, the heart of monster.

Clown. Think you so, sir?

Aut. Not he alone shall suffer what wit can make heavy and vengeance bitter; but those that are germane to him, though remov'd fifty times, shall all come under the hangman; which, though it be great pity, yet it is necessary. An old sheep-whistling rogue, a ram-tender, to offer to have his daughter come into grace? Some say he shall be ston'd; but that death is too soft for him, say I. Draw our throne into a sheepcote? All deaths are too few, the sharpest too easy.

Clown. Has the old man e'er a son, sir, do you hear, an't like you, sir?

Aut. He has a son — who shall be flay'd alive; then, 'nointed over with honey, set on the head of a wasps' nest; then stand till he be three quarters and a dram dead; then recover'd again with aqua-vitæ or some other hot infusion; then, raw as he is, and in the hottest day prognostication proclaims, shall he be set against a brick wall, the sun looking with a southward eye upon him, where he is to behold him with flies blown to death. But what talk we of these traitorly rascals, whose miseries are to be smil'd at, their offences being so capital? Tell me (for you seem to be honest plain men) what you have to the King. Being something gently consider'd, I'll bring you where he is aboard, tender your persons to his presence, whisper him in your behalfs; and if it be in man, besides the King, to effect your suits, here is man shall do it.

Clown. [*aside to Shepherd*] He seems to be of great authority. Close with him, give him gold; and though Authority be a stubborn bear, yet he is oft led by the nose with gold. Show the inside of your purse to the outside of his hand, and no more ado. Remember — ston'd, and flay'd alive.

Shep. An't please you, sir, to undertake the business for us, here is that gold I have. I'll make it as much more, and leave this young man in pawn till I bring it you.

Aut. After I have done what I promised?

Shep. Ay, sir.

Aut. Well, give me the moiety. Are you a party in this business?

Clown. In some sort, sir; but though my case be a pitiful one, I hope I shall not be flay'd out of it.

Aut. O, that's the case of the shepherd's son! Hang him, he'll be made an example.

Clown. [*aside to Shepherd*] Comfort, good comfort! We must to the King and show our strange sights. He must know 'tis none of your daughter nor my sister: we are gone else. — Sir, I will give you as much as this old man does when the business is performed, and remain, as he says, your pawn till it be brought you.

Aut. I will trust you. Walk before toward the seaside; go on the right hand. I will but look upon the hedge, and follow you.

[*Steps aside.*]

Clown. We are bless'd in this man, as I may say; even bless'd.

Shep. Let's before, as he bids us. He was provided to do us good.

[*Exeunt Shepherd and Clown.*]

Aut. If I had a mind to be honest, I see Fortune would not suffer me; she drops booties in my mouth. I am courted now with a double occasion — gold, and a means to do the Prince my master good; which who knows how that may turn back to my advancement? I will bring these two moles, these blind ones, aboard him. If he think it fit to shore them again, and that the complaint they have to the King concerns him nothing, let him call me rogue for being so far officious; for I am proof against that title and what shame else belongs to't. To him will I present them; there may be matter in it. *Exit.*

ACT V. Scene I. [*Sicilia. The Palace of* Leontes.]

Enter *Leontes, Cleomenes, Dion, Paulina.*

Cleo. Sir, you have done enough, and have perform'd
A saintlike sorrow. No fault could you make
Which you have not redeem'd; indeed, paid down
More penitence than done trespass. At the last,
Do as the heavens have done: forget your evil;
With them, forgive yourself.

Leon. Whilst I remember
Her and her virtues, I cannot forget
My blemishes in them, and so still think of
The wrong I did myself; which was so much
That heirless it hath made my kingdom and
Destroy'd the sweet'st companion that e'er man
Bred his hopes out of.

Paul. True, too true, my lord!
If, one by one, you wedded all the world,
Or from the all that are took something good
To make a perfect woman, she you kill'd
Would be unparallel'd.

Leon. I think so. Kill'd?
She I kill'd? I did so; but thou strik'st me
Sorely to say I did. It is as bitter
Upon thy tongue as in my thought. Now, good now,
Say so but seldom.

Cleo. Not at all, good lady.
You might have spoken a thousand things that would
Have done the time more benefit and grac'd
Your kindness better.

Paul. You are one of those
Would have him wed again.

Dion. If you would not so,
You pity not the state nor the remembrance
Of his most sovereign name; consider little
What dangers, by his Highness' fail of issue,
May drop upon his kingdom and devour
Incertain lookers-on. What were more holy
Than to rejoice the former queen is well?
What holier than, for royalty's repair,
For present comfort and for future good,
To bless the bed of majesty again
With a sweet fellow to't?

Paul. There is none worthy,
Respecting her that's gone. Besides, the gods
Will have fulfill'd their secret purposes;
For has not the divine Apollo said,
Is't not the tenour of his oracle,
That King Leontes shall not have an heir
Till his lost child be found? Which that it shall
Is all as monstrous to our human reason
As my Antigonus to break his grave
And come again to me; who, on my life,
Did perish with the infant. 'Tis your counsel
My lord should to the heavens be contrary,
Oppose against their wills. [*To Leontes*] Care not for issue;
The crown will find an heir. Great Alexander
Left his to th' worthiest; so his successor
Was like to be the best.

Leon. Good Paulina,
Who hast the memory of Hermione,
I know, in honour, O that ever I
Had squar'd me to thy counsel! Then, even now,
I might have look'd upon my queen's full eyes,
Have taken treasure from her lips —

Paul. And left them
More rich for what they yielded.

Leon. Thou speak'st truth.
No more such wives; therefore no wife! One worse,

And better us'd, would make her sainted spirit
Again possess her corpse, and on this stage
Where we offenders now, appear soul-vex'd,
And begin, 'Why to me —?'

Paul. Had she such power,
She had just cause.

Leon. She had, and would incense me
To murther her I married.

Paul. I should so.
Were I the ghost that walk'd, I'ld bid you mark
Her eye, and tell me for what dull part in't
You chose her; then I'ld shriek, that even your ears
Should rift to hear me, and the words that follow'd
Should be, 'Remember mine!'

Leon. Stars, stars!
And all eyes else dead coals. Fear thou no wife;
I'll have no wife, Paulina.

Paul. Will you swear
Never to marry but by my free leave?

Leon. Never, Paulina, so be bless'd my spirit!

Paul. Then, good my lords, bear witness to his oath.

Cleo. You tempt him over-much.

Paul. Unless another,
As like Hermione as is her picture,
Affront his eye.

Cleo. Good madam —

Paul. I have done.
Yet, if my lord will marry — if you will, sir,
No remedy but you will — give me the office
To choose you a queen. She shall not be so young
As was your former; but she shall be such
As, walk'd your first queen's ghost, it should take joy
To see her in your arms.

Leon. My true Paulina,
We shall not marry till thou bid'st us.

Paul. That
Shall be when your first queen's again in breath;
Never till then.

Enter a *Servant.*

Serv. One that gives out himself Prince Florizel,
Son of Polixenes, with his princess (she
The fairest I have yet beheld) desires access
To your high presence.

Leon. What with him? He comes not
Like to his father's greatness. His approach,
So out of circumstance and sudden, tells us
'Tis not a visitation fram'd, but forc'd
By need and accident. What train?

Serv. But few,
And those but mean.

Leon. His princess, say you, with him?

Serv. Ay, the most peerless piece of earth, I think,
That e'er the sun shone bright on.

Paul. O Hermione,
As every present time doth boast itself
Above a better, gone, so must thy grave
Give way to what's seen now! Sir, you yourself
Have said and writ so, but your writing now
Is colder than that theme: 'She had not been
Nor was not to be equall'd.' Thus your verse
Flow'd with her beauty once. 'Tis shrewdly ebb'd
To say you have seen a better.

Serv. Pardon, madam.
The one I have almost forgot — your pardon.
The other, when she has obtain'd your eye,
Will have your tongue too. This is a creature,
Would she begin a sect, might quench the zeal
Of all professors else, make proselytes
Of who she but bid follow.

Paul. How? not women?

Serv. Women will love her that she is a woman
More worth than any man; men, that she is
The rarest of all women.

Leon. Go, Cleomenes;
Yourself, assisted with your honour'd friends,
Bring them to our embracement.

Exit [*Cleomenes*].

Still, 'tis strange
He thus should steal upon us.

Paul. Had our Prince,
Jewel of children, seen this hour, he had pair'd
Well with this lord. There was not full a month
Between their births.

Leon. Prithee, no more! cease! Thou know'st
He dies to me again when talk'd of. Sure,
When I shall see this gentleman, thy speeches
Will bring me to consider that which may
Unfurnish me of reason.

Enter *Florizel, Perdita, Cleomenes,* and others.

They are come.
Your mother was most true to wedlock, Prince,
For she did print your royal father off,
Conceiving you. Were I but twenty-one,
Your father's image is so hit in you,

His very air, that I should call you brother,
As I did him, and speak of something wildly
By us perform'd before. Most dearly welcome!
And your fair princess — goddess! O, alas,
I lost a couple that 'twixt heaven and earth
Might thus have stood begetting wonder, as
You, gracious couple, do! and then I lost
(All mine own folly) the society,
Amity too, of your brave father, whom,
Though bearing misery, I desire my life
Once more to look on him.

Flo. By his command
Have I here touch'd Sicilia, and from him
Give you all greetings that a king, at friend,
Can send his brother; and, but infirmity,
Which waits upon worn times, hath something seiz'd
His wish'd ability, he had himself
The lands and waters 'twixt your throne and his
Measur'd to look upon you; whom he loves
(He bade me say so) more than all the sceptres
And those that bear them living.

Leon. O my brother,
Good gentleman, the wrongs I have done thee stir
Afresh within me; and these thy offices,
So rarely kind, are as interpreters
Of my behindhand slackness! Welcome hither
As is the spring to th' earth. And hath he too
Expos'd this paragon to th' fearful usage
(At least ungentle) of the dreadful Neptune,
To greet a man not worth her pains, much less
Th' adventure of her person?

Flo. Good my lord,
She came from Libya.

Leon. Where the warlike Smalus,
That noble honour'd lord, is fear'd and lov'd?

Flo. Most royal sir, from thence; from him, whose daughter
His tears proclaim'd his, parting with her. Thence
(A prosperous south wind friendly) we have cross'd,
To execute the charge my father gave me
For visiting your Highness. My best train
I have from your Sicilian shores dismiss'd;
Who for Bohemia bend, to signify
Not only my success in Libya, sir,
But my arrival and my wife's in safety
Here where we are.

Leon. The blessed gods
Purge all infection from our air whilst you
Do climate here! You have a holy father,
A graceful gentleman, against whose person,
So sacred as it is, I have done sin,
For which the heavens, taking angry note,
Have left me issueless; and your father's bless'd,
As he from heaven merits it, with you,
Worthy his goodness. What might I have been,
Might I a son and daughter now have look'd on,
Such goodly things as you!

Enter a *Lord*.

Lord. Most noble sir,
That which I shall report will bear no credit,
Were not the proof so nigh. Please you, great sir,
Bohemia greets you from himself by me;
Desires you to attach his son, who has
(His dignity and duty both cast off)
Fled from his father, from his hopes, and with
A shepherd's daughter.

Leon. Where's Bohemia? Speak.

Lord. Here in your city. I now came from him.
I speak amazedly, and it becomes
My marvel and my message. To your court
Whiles he was hast'ning (in the chase, it seems,
Of this fair couple), meets he on the way
The father of this seeming lady and
Her brother, having both their country quitted
With this young prince.

Flo. Camillo has betray'd me,
Whose honour and whose honesty till now
Endur'd all weathers.

Lord. Lay't so to his charge.
He's with the King your father.

Leon. Who? Camillo?

Lord. Camillo, sir. I spake with him; who now
Has these poor men in question. Never saw I
Wretches so quake. They kneel, they kiss the earth;
Forswear themselves as often as they speak.
Bohemia stops his ears, and threatens them
With divers deaths in death.

Per. O my poor father!
The heaven sets spies upon us, will not have
Our contract celebrated.

Leon. You are married?

Flo. We are not, sir, nor are we like to be.
The stars, I see, will kiss the valleys first.
The odds for high and low's alike.

Leon. My lord,
Is this the daughter of a king?

Flo. She is,
When once she is my wife.

Leon. That 'once,' I see, by your good father's speed,
Will come on very slowly. I am sorry,
Most sorry, you have broken from his liking
Where you were tied in duty; and as sorry
Your choice is not so rich in worth as beauty,
That you might well enjoy her.

Flo. Dear, look up.
Though Fortune, visible an enemy,
Should chase us, with my father, pow'r no jot
Hath she to change our loves. Beseech you, sir,
Remember since you ow'd no more to time
Than I do now. With thought of such affections,
Step forth mine advocate. At your request
My father will grant precious things as trifles.

Leon. Would he do so, I'ld beg your precious mistress,
Which he counts but a trifle.

Paul. Sir, my liege,
Your eye hath too much youth in't. Not a month
Fore your queen died, she was more worth such gazes
Than what you look on now.

Leon. I thought of her
Even in these looks I made. [*To Florizel*] But your petition
Is yet unanswer'd. I will to your father.
Your honour not o'erthrown by your desires,
I am friend to them and you. Upon which errand
I now go toward him; therefore follow me,
And mark what way I make. Come, good my lord. *Exeunt.*

Scene II. [*Sicilia. Before the Palace of* Leontes.]

Enter *Autolycus* and a *Gentleman.*

Aut. Beseech you, sir, were you present at this relation?

1. Gent. I was by at the opening of the farthel, heard the old shepherd deliver the manner how he found it; whereupon, after a little amazedness, we were all commanded out of the chamber. Only this, methought, I heard the shepherd say — he found the child.

Aut. I would most gladly know the issue of it.

1. Gent. I make a broken delivery of the business; but the changes I perceived in the King and Camillo were very notes of admiration. They seem'd almost, with staring on one another, to tear the cases of their eyes. There was speech in their dumbness, language in their very gesture. They look'd as they had heard of a world ransom'd, or one destroyed. A notable passion of wonder appeared in them; but the wisest beholder that knew no more but seeing, could not say if th' importance were joy or sorrow; but in the extremity of the one it must needs be.

Enter another *Gentleman.*

Here comes a gentleman that happily knows more. The news, Rogero?

2. Gent. Nothing but bonfires. The oracle is fulfill'd; the King's daughter is found. Such a deal of wonder is broken out within this hour that ballad-makers cannot be able to express it.

Enter another *Gentleman.*

Here comes the Lady Paulina's steward; he can deliver you more. How goes it now, sir? This news, which is call'd true, is so like an old tale that the verity of it is in strong suspicion. Has the King found his heir?

3. Gent. Most true, if ever truth were pregnant by circumstance. That which you hear you'll swear you see, there is such unity in the proofs. The mantle of Queen Hermione's; her jewel about the neck of it; the letters of Antigonus found with it, which they know to be his character; the majesty of the creature, in resemblance of the mother; the affection of nobleness which nature shows above her breeding, and many other evidences — proclaim her with all certainty to be the King's daughter. Did you see the meeting of the two kings?

2. Gent. No.

3. Gent. Then have you lost a sight which was to be seen, cannot be spoken of. There might you have beheld one joy crown another, so and in such manner that it seem'd sorrow wept to take leave of them; for their joy waded in tears. There was casting up of eyes, holding up of hands, with countenance of such distraction that they were to be known by garment, not by favour. Our king, being ready to leap out of himself for joy of his found daughter, as if that joy were now become a loss, cries, 'O, thy mother, thy mother!' then asks Bohemia forgiveness; then embraces his son-in-law; then again worries he his daughter with clipping her. Now he thanks the old shepherd, which stands by like a weather-bitten conduit of many kings' reigns. I never heard of such another encounter, which lames report to follow it and undoes description to do it.

2. Gent. What, pray you, became of Antigonus, that carried hence the child?

3. Gent. Like an old tale still, which will have matter to rehearse, though credit be asleep and not an ear open. He was torn to pieces with a bear! This avouches the shepherd's son, who has not only his innocence (which seems much) to justify him, but a handkerchief and rings of his that Paulina knows.

1. Gent. What became of his bark and his followers?

3. Gent. Wrack'd the same instant of their master's death, and in the view of the shepherd; so that all the instruments which aided to expose the child were even then lost when it was found. But, O, the noble combat that 'twixt joy and sorrow was fought in Paulina! She had one eye declin'd for the loss of her husband, another elevated that the oracle was fulfill'd. She lifted the Princess from the earth, and so locks her in embracing as if she would pin her to her heart, that she might no more be in danger of losing.

1. Gent. The dignity of this act was worth the audience of kings and princes, for by such was it acted.

3. Gent. One of the prettiest touches of all, and that which angled for mine eyes (caught the water, though not the fish) was when, at the relation of the Queen's death (with the manner how she came to't bravely confess'd and lamented by the King), how attentiveness wounded his daughter, till, from one sign of dolour to another, she did (with an 'Alas!'), I would fain say, bleed tears; for I am sure my heart wept blood. Who was most marble there changed colour; some swounded, all sorrowed. If all the world could have seen't, the woe had been universal.

1. Gent. Are they returned to the court?

3. Gent. No. The Princess hearing of her mother's statue, which is in the keeping of Paulina — a piece many years in doing, and now newly perform'd, by that rare Italian master, Julio Romano, who, had he himself eternity and could put breath into his work, would beguile Nature of her custom, so perfectly he is her ape — he so near to Hermione hath done Hermione that they say one would speak to her and stand in hope of answer. Thither with all greediness of affection are they gone, and there they intend to sup.

2. Gent. I thought she had some great matter there in hand; for she hath privately twice or thrice a day, ever since the death of Hermione, visited that removed house. Shall we thither, and with our company piece the rejoicing?

1. Gent. Who would be thence that has the benefit of access? Every wink of an eye, some new grace will be born. Our absence makes us unthrifty to our knowledge. Let's along.

Exeunt [*Gentlemen*].

Aut. Now, had I not the dash of my former life in me, would preferment drop on my head. I brought the old man and his son aboard the Prince; told him I heard them talk of a farthel and I know not what; but he at that time over-fond of the shepherd's daughter (so he then took her to be), who began to be much seasick, and himself little better, extremity of weather continuing, this mystery remained undiscover'd. But 'tis all one to me; for had I been the finder-out of this secret, it would not have relish'd among my other discredits.

Enter *Shepherd* and *Clown,* [richly dressed].

Here come those I have done good to against my will, and already appearing in the blossoms of their fortune.

Shep. Come, boy. I am past moe children, but thy sons and daughters will be all gentlemen born.

Clown. You are well met, sir. You denied to fight with me this other day, because I was no gentleman born. See you these clothes? Say you see them not and think me still no gentleman born. You were best say these robes are not gentlemen born. Give me the lie, do; and try whether I am not now a gentleman born.

Aut. I know you are now, sir, a gentleman born.

Clown. Ay, and have been so any time these four hours.

Shep. And so have I, boy.

Clown. So you have. But I was a gentleman born before my father; for the King's son took me by the hand and call'd me brother; and then the two kings call'd my father brother; and then the Prince, my brother, and the Princess, my sister, call'd my father father; and so we wept — and there was the first gentlemanlike tears that ever we shed.

Shep. We may live, son, to shed many more.

Clown. Ay! or else 'twere hard luck, being in so preposterous estate as we are.

Aut. I humbly beseech you, sir, to pardon me all the faults I have committed to your worship, and to give me your good report to the Prince my master.

Shep. Prithee, son, do; for we must be gentle, now we are gentlemen.

Clown. Thou wilt amend thy life?

Aut. Ay, an it like your good worship.

Clown. Give me thy hand. I will swear to the Prince thou art as honest a true fellow as any is in Bohemia.

Shep. You may say it, but not swear it.

Clown. Not swear it, now I am a gentleman? Let boors and franklins say it; I'll swear it.

Shep. How if it be false, son?

Clown. If it be ne'er so false, a true gentleman may swear it in the behalf of his friend. And I'll swear to the Prince thou art a tall fellow of thy hands, and that thou wilt not be drunk; but I know thou art no tall fellow of thy hands, and that thou wilt be drunk. But I'll swear it; and I would thou wouldst be a tall fellow of thy hands.

Aut. I will prove so, sir, to my power.

Clown. Ay, by any means prove a tall fellow. If I do not wonder how thou dar'st venture to be drunk, not being a tall fellow, trust me not. Hark! the kings and the princes, our kindred, are going to see the Queen's picture. Come, follow us. We'll be thy good masters. *Exeunt.*

Scene III. [*Sicilia. A chapel in* Paulina's *house.*]

Enter *Leontes, Polixenes, Florizel, Perdita, Camillo, Paulina, Lords,* &c.

Leon. O grave and good Paulina, the great comfort
That I have had of thee!
Paul. What, sovereign sir,
I did not well, I meant well. All my services
You have paid home. But that you have vouchsaf'd,
With your crown'd brother and these your contracted
Heirs of your kingdoms, my poor house to visit,
It is a surplus of your grace, which never
My life may last to answer.
Leon. O Paulina,
We honour you with trouble. But we came
To see the statue of our queen. Your gallery
Have we pass'd through, not without much content
In many singularities; but we saw not
That which my daughter came to look upon,
The statue of her mother.
Paul. As she liv'd peerless,
So her dead likeness I do well believe
Excels whatever yet you look'd upon,
Or hand of man hath done. Therefore I keep it
Lonely, apart. But here it is. Prepare
To see the life as lively mock'd as ever
Still sleep mock'd death. Behold, and say 'tis well.

[*Paulina draws a curtain and discovers Hermione standing like a statue.*]

I like your silence; it the more shows off
Your wonder. But yet speak; first you, my liege.
Comes it not something near?
Leon. Her natural posture!
Chide me, dear stone, that I may say indeed
Thou art Hermione; or rather, thou art she
In thy not chiding; for she was as tender
As infancy and grace. But yet, Paulina,
Hermione was not so much wrinkled, nothing
So aged as this seems.
Pol. O, not by much!
Paul. So much the more our carver's excellence,
Which lets go by some sixteen years and makes her
As she liv'd now.
Leon. As now she might have done,
So much to my good comfort as it is
Now piercing to my soul. O, thus she stood,
Even with such life of majesty (warm life,
As now it coldly stands), when first I woo'd her!
I am asham'd. Does not the stone rebuke me
For being more stone than it? O royal piece,
There's magic in thy majesty, which has
My evils conjur'd to remembrance, and
From thy admiring daughter took the spirits,
Standing like stone with thee!
Per. And give me leave,
And do not say 'tis superstition that
I kneel, and then implore her blessing. Lady,
Dear queen, that ended when I but began,
Give me that hand of yours to kiss.
Paul. O, patience!
The statue is but newly fix'd; the colour's
Not dry.
Cam. My lord, your sorrow was too sore laid on,
Which sixteen winters cannot blow away,
So many summers dry. Scarce any joy
Did ever so long live; no sorrow
But kill'd itself much sooner.
Pol. Dear my brother,
Let him that was the cause of this have pow'r

To take off so much grief from you as he
Will piece up in himself.
Paul. Indeed, my lord,
If I had thought the sight of my poor image
Would thus have wrought you — for the stone is mine —
I'ld not have show'd it.
Leon. Do not draw the curtain.
Paul. No longer shall you gaze on't, lest your fancy
May think anon it moves.
Leon. Let be, let be!
Would I were dead, but that methinks already —
What was he that did make it? See, my lord,
Would you not deem it breath'd? and that those veins
Did verily bear blood?
Pol. Masterly done!
The very life seems warm upon her lip.
Leon. The fixure of her eye has motion in't,
As we are mock'd with art.
Paul. I'll draw the curtain.
My lord's almost so far transported that
He'll think anon it lives.
Leon. O sweet Paulina,
Make me to think so twenty years together!
No settled senses of the world can match
The pleasure of that madness. Let't alone.
Paul. I am sorry, sir, I have thus far stirr'd you; but
I could afflict you farther.
Leon. Do, Paulina!
For this affliction has a taste as sweet
As any cordial comfort. Still methinks
There is an air comes from her. What fine chisel
Could ever yet cut breath? Let no man mock me,
For I will kiss her.
Paul. Good my lord, forbear!
The ruddiness upon her lip is wet.
You'll mar it if you kiss it; stain your own
With oily painting. Shall I draw the curtain?
Leon. No, not these twenty years!
Per. So long could I
Stand by, a looker-on.
Paul. Either forbear,
Quit presently the chapel, or resolve you
For more amazement. If you can behold it,
I'll make the statue move indeed, descend,
And take you by the hand. But then you'll think
(Which I protest against) I am assisted
By wicked powers.
Leon. What you can make her do,
I am content to look on; what to speak,
I am content to hear; for 'tis as easy
To make her speak as move.
Paul. It is requir'd
You do awake your faith. Then all stand still;
Or those that think it is unlawful business
I am about, let them depart.
Leon. Proceed.
No foot shall stir.
Paul. Music! awake her! strike! [*Music.*]
'Tis time; descend; be stone no more; approach;
Strike all that look upon with marvel. Come;
I'll fill your grave up! Stir; nay, come away!
Bequeath to death your numbness, for from him
Dear life redeems you. You perceive she stirs:
[*Hermione comes down from the pedestal.*]
Start not! Her actions shall be holy as
You hear my spell is lawful. Do not shun her
Until you see her die again; for then
You kill her double. Nay, present your hand.
When she was young, you woo'd her; now, in age,
Is she become the suitor?
Leon. O, she's warm!
If this be magic, let it be an art
Lawful as eating.
Pol. She embraces him.
Cam. She hangs about his neck.
If she pertain to life, let her speak too.
Pol. Ay, and make it manifest where she has liv'd,
Or how stol'n from the dead.
Paul. That she is living,
Were it but told you, should be hooted at
Like an old tale; but it appears she lives,
Though yet she speak not. Mark a little while.
Please you to interpose, fair madam; kneel,
And pray your mother's blessing. — Turn, good lady;
Our Perdita is found.
[*Perdita kneels.*]
Her. You gods, look down,
And from your sacred vials pour your graces
Upon my daughter's head! Tell me, mine own,
Where hast thou been preserv'd? where liv'd? how found
Thy father's court? For thou shalt hear that I,
Knowing by Paulina that the oracle
Gave hope thou wast in being, have preserv'd
Myself to see the issue.

Paul. There's time enough for that,
Lest they desire, upon this push, to trouble
Your joys with like relation. Go together,
You precious winners all; your exultation
Partake to every one. I, an old turtle,
Will wing me to some wither'd bough, and there
My mate, that's never to be found again,
Lament till I am lost.

Leon. O, peace, Paulina!
Thou shouldst a husband take by my consent,
As I by thine a wife. This is a match,
And made between's by vows. Thou hast found mine;
But how, is to be question'd; for I saw her,
As I thought, dead; and have (in vain) said many
A prayer upon her grave. I'll not seek far
(For him, I partly know his mind) to find thee
An honourable husband. — Come, Camillo,
And take her by the hand; whose worth and honesty
Is richly noted, and here justified
By us, a pair of kings. — Let's from this place. —
What! look upon my brother. Both your pardons,
That e'er I put between your holy looks
My ill suspicion. This' your son-in-law,
And son unto the King, whom heavens directing,
Is troth-plight to your daughter. — Good Paulina,
Lead us from hence where we may leisurely
Each one demand, and answer to his part
Perform'd in this wide gap of time since first
We were dissever'd. Hastily lead away.

Exeunt.

King John

'The Troublesome Raigne of Iohn King of England. . . . As it was (sundry times) publikely acted by the Queenes Maiesties Players' and 'The Second part of the troublesome Raigne of King Iohn. . . . As it was (sundry times) publikely acted by' the same were both published in 1591 as distinct quartos and republished together in 1611 and 1622. The title page of 1611 asserts that the whole was 'Written by W. Sh.' and that of 1622 spells the surname at full length. This ascription is unquestionably false. The author must remain anonymous. George Peele is a possible candidate, but the evidence in his favour is purely internal and not very impressive. The date of composition may be conjecturally put back two or three years before the publication in 1591. The short address in verse 'To the Gentlemen Readers,' prefixed to Part I, mentions *Tamburlaine* as having been received with applause. It sounds like a prologue, but may or may not have been written at the same time as the play. *Tamburlaine* dates from about 1587.

Shakespeare's play, THE LIFE AND DEATH OF KING JOHN, was first printed in the Folio of 1623, which is therefore our only authority for the text. Meres mentions it in 1598 among Shakespeare's tragedies (see p. 33, above). How much earlier it was written cannot be exactly determined. Shakespeare's son Hamnet died in August, 1596, and biographers are tempted to read his father's own grief in the passionate laments of Constance for Arthur. But that is reasoning in a circle, for nobody doubts that the greatest of all dramatists could have written these passages if he had never had a son. Still, 1596 is a reasonable date for KING JOHN. In any case, it is more likely to have preceded *Richard II* than to have followed it.

For his material Shakespeare went to *The Troublesome Reign* instead of working up a plot from Holinshed's *Chronicle*; but KING JOHN is a new play, not a revision. Like its predecessor it covers the whole of John's reign (1199–1216), and the order of events is the same, with a modicum of readjustment. That order quite warrantably sacrifices historical preciseness to dramatic effect. Chatillon's embassy is the invention of the older playwright. So is the episode of the Faulconbridge brothers, for which he may have taken a hint from the case of Dunois, the famous Bastard of Orleans, as recorded by Holinshed. Austria (in both plays) is a fusion (accidental or deliberate) of Duke Leopold, Richard Cœur-de-Lion's captor, who died in 1195, with Widomar Viscount of Limoges, killed, Holinshed says, by a bastard son of Richard to avenge his father, who met his death while besieging the viscount's castle.

Many incidents or whole episodes of *The Troublesome Reign* are dropped by Shakespeare. His omissions are: — Philip Faulconbridge's fruitless attempt to arrange for a duel with the Duke of Austria; his tearing the lion's skin from Austria's shoulders; his killing Austria in battle *coram populo*; the long scene in which he ransacks the chests of monk and nun and arrests Peter the prophet; the interview between Peter and King John in which the prophet interprets the omen of the five moons and tells the king that he shall lose his crown before high noon on Ascension Day; the very long scene on Ascension Day in which the king hears Peter reiterate his prophecy, is informed by

Hubert of Arthur's fatal fall, orders him to hang Peter forthwith, is told by Faulconbridge that the sentence has been carried out and also that Lewis (having been elected King of England by the peers) is expected to land at any moment, submits to Pandulph, and learns that the French fleet has actually been sighted off the coast of Kent; the scene at St. Edmondsbury, in which the English peers, despite the efforts of Faulconbridge, swear fealty to Lewis, and Lewis and the French nobles take an oath to put their English allies to death when the victory is won; the soliloquy of Thomas, a monk of Swinstead, in which he resolves to murder King John, and the interview between him and the Abbot, in which he discloses his purpose and is absolved; the poisoning of the king in a wassail cup and the death of the monk, who must, as 'taster,' drink first from the cup which he offers; the coronation of Henry III.

In most instances nothing is lost by these omissions, for the facts are made known to the audience in the course of the dialogue. Shakespeare has been censured, however, for nowhere revealing the poisoner's motive. Surely no such explanation was requisite. We have King John's orders to Faulconbridge (iii, 3, 7–11):

> See thou shake the bags
> Of hoarding abbots; set at liberty
> Imprison'd angels. The fat ribs of peace
> Must by the hungry now be fed upon.
> Use our commission in his utmost force.

And Faulconbridge has duly rendered his account (iv, 2, 141–142):

> How I have sped among the clergymen
> The sums I have collected shall express.

After that, the monk's motive might reasonably be taken for granted.

Most of the old play is in sonorous blank verse with occasional bits of competent prose. One scene exhibits a riotous mingle-mangle of rhyming measures — fourteeners, octosyllabics, and Skeltonical short lines — as well as a bit of prose dialogue. This is the comic scene (omitted by Shakespeare) in which Faulconbridge plunders the clergy.

In King John the language is Shakespeare's throughout, with occasional slight echoes of the older phraseology. He rewrites completely even those passages of which he keeps the substance. Compare with Faulconbridge's concluding speech in King John the similar valediction in the old play, which runs as follows:

> Thus England's peace begins in Henry's reign,
> And bloody wars are clos'd with happy league.
> Let England live but true within itself,
> And all the world can never wrong her state;
> Lewis, thou shalt be bravely shipp'd to France,
> For never Frenchman got of English ground
> The twentieth part that thou hast conquered.
> Dauphin, thy hand! To Worcester we will march.
> Lords all, lay hands to bear your sovereign
> With obsequies of honour to his grave.
> If England's peers and people join in one,
> Nor Pope, nor France, nor Spain can do them wrong.

THE LIFE AND DEATH OF
KING JOHN

[Dramatis Personæ.

King John.
Prince Henry, his son.
Arthur, Duke of Britain (Bretagne), son of the *King's* elder brother, Geffrey.
The Earl of Pembroke.
The Earl of Essex.
The Earl of Salisbury.
The Lord Bigot.
Hubert de Burgh.
Robert Faulconbridge, son to Sir Robert Faulconbridge.
Philip the Bastard, his half-brother.
James Gurney, servant to *Lady Faulconbridge.*
Peter of Pomfret, a prophet.
Philip, King of France.
Lewis, the Dauphin.
The Duke of Austria.
Cardinal Pandulph, the Pope's legate.
Melun, a French lord.
Chatillon, ambassador from France.

Queen Elinor, widow of King Henry II, and mother to *King John.*
Constance, mother to *Arthur.*
Blanch of Spain, daughter to the King of Castile and niece to *King John.*
Lady Faulconbridge, widow of Sir Robert Faulconbridge.

Lords, Citizens of Angiers, Sheriff, Heralds, Officers, Soldiers, Executioners, Messengers, Attendants.

SCENE. — *Sometimes in England, sometimes in France.*]

ACT I. Scene I. [King John's *Palace.*]

Enter *King John, Queen Elinor, Pembroke, Essex,* and *Salisbury,* [and others,] with *Chatillon* of France.

K. John. Now say, Chatillon, what would France with us?
Chat. Thus, after greeting, speaks the King of France
In my behaviour to the majesty,
The borrowed majesty, of England here.
Eli. A strange beginning! 'Borrowed majesty'?
K. John. Silence, good mother; hear the embassy.
Chat. Philip of France, in right and true behalf
Of thy deceased brother Geffrey's son,
Arthur Plantagenet, lays most lawful claim
To this fair island and the territories,
To Ireland, Poictiers, Anjou, Touraine, Maine,
Desiring thee to lay aside the sword
Which sways usurpingly these several titles
And put the same into young Arthur's hand,
Thy nephew and right royal sovereign.
K. John. What follows if we disallow of this?
Chat. The proud control of fierce and bloody war,
To enforce these rights so forcibly withheld.
K. John. Here have we war for war and blood for blood,
Controlment for controlment. So answer France.
Chat. Then take my king's defiance from my mouth,
The farthest limit of my embassy.
K. John. Bear mine to him, and so depart in peace.
Be thou as lightning in the eyes of France;
For ere thou canst report I will be there,
The thunder of my cannon shall be heard.
So hence! Be thou the trumpet of our wrath
And sullen presage of your own decay.
An honourable conduct let him have;
Pembroke, look to't. Farewell, Chatillon.
Exeunt Chatillon and Pembroke.
Eli. What now, my son? Have I not ever said
How that ambitious Constance would not cease
Till she had kindled France and all the world
Upon the right and party of her son?
This might have been prevented and made whole
With very easy arguments of love,

Which now the manage of two kingdoms must
With fearful bloody issue arbitrate.

K. John. Our strong possession and our right for us!

Eli. [*aside to K. John*] Your strong possession much more than your right,
Or else it must go wrong with you and me.
So much my conscience whispers in your ear,
Which none but heaven and you and I shall hear.

Enter a *Sheriff*.

Essex. My liege, here is the strangest controversy
Come from the country to be judg'd by you
That e'er I heard. Shall I produce the men?

K. John. Let them approach. [*Exit Sheriff*.]
Our abbeys and our priories shall pay
This expedition's charge.

Enter *Robert Faulconbridge* and *Philip* [his bastard brother].

What men are you?

Phil. Your faithful subject I, a gentleman,
Born in Northamptonshire, and eldest son, 51
As I suppose, to Robert Faulconbridge,
A soldier by the honour-giving hand
Of Cœur-de-lion knighted in the field.

K. John. What art thou?

Rob. The son and heir to that same Faulconbridge.

K. John. Is that the elder, and art thou the heir?
You came not of one mother then, it seems.

Phil. Most certain of one mother, mighty king —
That is well known — and, as I think, one father;
But for the certain knowledge of that truth
I put you o'er to heaven and to my mother.
Of that I doubt, as all men's children may.

Eli. Out on thee, rude man! Thou dost shame thy mother
And wound her honour with this diffidence.

Phil. I, madam? No, I have no reason for it.
That is my brother's plea, and none of mine;
The which if he can prove, 'a pops me out
At least from fair five hundred pound a year.
Heaven guard my mother's honour and my land!

K. John. A good blunt fellow. Why, being younger born,
Doth he lay claim to thine inheritance?

Phil. I know not why, except to get the land;
But once he slander'd me with bastardy.
But whe'r I be as true begot or no,
That still I lay upon my mother's head;
But that I am as well begot, my liege
(Fair fall the bones that took the pains for me!),
Compare our faces and be judge yourself.
If old Sir Robert did beget us both
And were our father, and this son like him —
O old Sir Robert, father, on my knee
I give heaven thanks I was not like to thee!

K. John. Why, what a madcap hath heaven lent us here! 84

Eli. He hath a trick of Cœur-de-lion's face;
The accent of his tongue affecteth him.
Do you not read some tokens of my son
In the large composition of this man?

K. John. Mine eye hath well examined his parts 89
And finds them perfect Richard. Sirrah, speak,
What doth move you to claim your brother's land?

Phil. Because he hath a half-face, like my father.
With half that face would he have all my land.
A half-fac'd groat, five hundred pound a year!

Rob. My gracious liege, when that my father liv'd,
Your brother did employ my father much —

Phil. Well, sir, by this you cannot get my land.
Your tale must be how he employ'd my mother.

Rob. And once dispatch'd him in an embassy
To Germany, there with the Emperor
To treat of high affairs touching that time.
Th' advantage of his absence took the King
And in the meantime sojourn'd at my father's;
Where how he did prevail I shame to speak,
But truth is truth. Large lengths of seas and shores
Between my father and my mother lay,
As I have heard my father speak himself,
When this same lusty gentleman was got.
Upon his deathbed he by will bequeath'd
His lands to me, and took it on his death
That this, my mother's son, was none of his;
And if he were, he came into the world
Full fourteen weeks before the course of time.
Then, good my liege, let me have what is mine,
My father's land, as was my father's will.

K. John. Sirrah, your brother is legitimate.
Your father's wife did after wedlock bear him,
And if she did play false, the fault was hers;
Which fault lies on the hazards of all husbands
That marry wives. Tell me, how if my brother,

Who, as you say, took pains to get this son,
Had of your father claim'd this son for his?
In sooth, good friend, your father might have kept
This calf, bred from his cow, from all the world.
In sooth he might. Then, if he were my brother's,
My brother might not claim him; nor your father,
Being none of his, refuse him. This concludes:
My mother's son did get your father's heir;
Your father's heir must have your father's land.
Rob. Shall then my father's will be of no force
To dispossess that child which is not his?
Phil. Of no more force to dispossess me, sir,
Than was his will to get me, as I think.
Eli. Whether hadst thou rather be a Faulconbridge,
And like thy brother, to enjoy thy land,
Or the reputed son of Cœur-de-lion,
Lord of thy presence and no land beside?
Bast. Madam, an if my brother had my shape,
And I had his, Sir Robert his, like him;
And if my legs were two such riding rods,
My arms such eel-skins stuff'd, my face so thin
That in mine ear I durst not stick a rose
Lest men should say 'Look where three-farthings goes!'
And, to his shape, were heir to all this land —
Would I might never stir from off this place,
I would give it every foot to have this face!
I would not be Sir Nob in any case.
Eli. I like thee well. Wilt thou forsake thy fortune,
Bequeath thy land to him, and follow me?
I am a soldier, and now bound to France.
Bast. Brother, take you my land, I'll take my chance.
Your face hath got five hundred pound a year;
Yet sell your face for fivepence, and 'tis dear.
Madam, I'll follow you unto the death.
Eli. Nay, I would have you go before me thither.
Bast. Our country manners give our betters way.
K. John. What is thy name?
Bast. Philip, my liege, so is my name begun —
Philip, good old Sir Robert's wive's eldest son.
K. John. From henceforth bear his name whose form thou bearest.
Kneel thou down Philip, but arise more great;
Arise Sir Richard and Plantagenet.
Bast. Brother by th' mother's side, give me your hand!
My father gave me honour, yours gave land.
Now blessed be the hour, by night or day,
When I was got, Sir Robert was away!
Eli. The very spirit of Plantagenet!
I am thy grandam, Richard. Call me so.
Bast. Madam, by chance, but not by truth. What though?
Something about, a little from the right,
In at the window, or else o'er the hatch.
Who dares not stir by day must walk by night;
And have is have, however men do catch.
Near or far off, well won is still well shot,
And I am I, howe'er I was begot.
K. John. Go, Faulconbridge; now hast thou thy desire:
A landless knight makes thee a landed squire.
Come, madam, and come, Richard; we must speed
For France, for France, for it is more than need.
Bast. Brother, adieu. Good fortune come to thee!
For thou wast got i' th' way of honesty.
Exeunt all but Bastard.
A foot of honour better than I was,
But many a many foot of land the worse!
Well, now can I make any Joan a lady.
'Good den, Sir Richard!' 'God-a-mercy, fellow!'
And if his name be George, I'll call him Peter;
For new-made honour doth forget men's names:
'Tis too respective and too sociable
For your conversion. Now your traveller,
He and his toothpick at my worship's mess:
And when my knightly stomach is suffic'd,
Why, then I suck my teeth and catechize
My picked man of countries. 'My dear sir,'
Thus, leaning on mine elbow, I begin,
'I shall beseech you.' That is question now,
And then comes answer like an Absey-book:
'O sir,' says answer, 'at your best command,
At your employment, at your service, sir!'
'No, sir,' says question. 'I, sweet sir, at yours!'
And so, ere answer knows what question would —
Saving in dialogue of compliment,
And talking of the Alps and Apennines,
The Pyrenean and the river Po —
It draws toward supper in conclusion so.
But this is worshipful society
And fits the mounting spirit like myself;
For he is but a bastard to the time
That doth not smack of observation —
And so am I, whether I smack or no;

And not alone in habit and device,
Exterior form, outward accoutrement,
But from the inward motion to deliver
Sweet, sweet, sweet poison for the age's tooth;
Which, though I will not practise to deceive,
Yet, to avoid deceit, I mean to learn;
For it shall strew the footsteps of my rising.
But who comes in such haste in riding robes?
What woman post is this? Hath she no husband
That will take pains to blow a horn before her?

Enter *Lady Faulconbridge* and *James Gurney.*

O me! it is my mother. How now, good lady?
What brings you here to court so hastily?

Lady. Where is that slave, thy brother? Where is he,
That holds in chase mine honour up and down?

Bast. My brother Robert? old Sir Robert's son?
Colbrand the giant, that same mighty man?
Is it Sir Robert's son that you seek so?

Lady. Sir Robert's son? Ay, thou unreverend boy,
Sir Robert's son. Why scorn'st thou at Sir Robert?
He is Sir Robert's son, and so art thou.

Bast. James Gurney, wilt thou give us leave awhile?

Gur. Good leave, good Philip.

Bast. Philip? — sparrow! — James,
There's toys abroad. Anon I'll tell thee more.
Exit James.
Madam, I was not old Sir Robert's son;
Sir Robert might have eat his part in me
Upon Good Friday and ne'er broke his fast.
Sir Robert could do well: marry, to confess,
Could he get me? Sir Robert could not do it;
We know his handiwork. Therefore, good mother,
To whom am I beholding for these limbs?
Sir Robert never holp to make this leg.

Lady. Hast thou conspired with thy brother too,
That for thine own gain shouldst defend mine honour?
What means this scorn, thou most untoward knave?

Bast. Knight, knight, good mother, Basilisco-like!
What! I am dubb'd; I have it on my shoulder.
But, mother, I am not Sir Robert's son;
I have disclaim'd Sir Robert and my land;
Legitimation, name, and all is gone.
Then, good my mother, let me know my father!
Some proper man, I hope. Who was it, mother?

Lady. Hast thou denied thyself a Faulconbridge?

Bast. As faithfully as I deny the devil.

Lady. King Richard Cœur-de-lion was thy father.
By long and vehement suit I was seduc'd
To make room for him in my husband's bed.
Heaven lay not my transgression to my charge!
Thou art the issue of my dear offence,
Which was so strongly urg'd past my defence.

Bast. Now, by this light, were I to get again,
Madam, I would not wish a better father.
Some sins do bear their privilege on earth,
And so doth yours. Your fault was not your folly.
Needs must you lay your heart at his dispose,
Subjected tribute to commanding love,
Against whose fury and unmatched force
The awless lion could not wage the fight
Nor keep his princely heart from Richard's hand.
He that perforce robs lions of their hearts
May easily win a woman's. Ay, my mother,
With all my heart I thank thee for my father!
Who lives and dares but say thou didst not well
When I was got, I'll send his soul to hell.
Come, lady, I will show thee to my kin;
And they shall say, when Richard me begot,
If thou hadst said him nay, it had been sin.
Who says it was, he lies; I say 'twas not.
Exeunt.

[ACT II. Scene I. *France. Before Angiers.*]

Enter, before Angiers, *Philip King of France, Lewis* [*the*] *Dauphin, Constance, Arthur,* [with *Forces,* at one door; at the other,] *Austria* [with *Forces*].

France. Before Angiers well met, brave Austria.
Arthur, that great forerunner of thy blood,
Richard, that robb'd the lion of his heart
And fought the holy wars in Palestine,
By this brave duke came early to his grave;
And, for amends to his posterity,
At our importance hither is he come
To spread his colours, boy, in thy behalf,
And to rebuke the usurpation
Of thy unnatural uncle, English John.

Embrace him, love him, give him welcome hither.

Arth. God shall forgive you Cœur-de-lion's death
The rather that you give his offspring life,
Shadowing their right under your wings of war.
I give you welcome with a powerless hand,
But with a heart full of unstained love.
Welcome before the gates of Angiers, Duke.

France. A noble boy! Who would not do thee right?

Aust. Upon thy cheek lay I this zealous kiss
As seal to this indenture of my love:
That to my home I will no more return
Till Angiers and the right thou hast in France,
Together with that pale, that white-fac'd shore
Whose foot spurns back the ocean's roaring tides
And coops from other lands her islanders —
Even till that England, hedg'd in with the main,
That water-walled bulwark, still secure
And confident from foreign purposes —
Even till that utmost corner of the West
Salute thee for her king. Till then, fair boy,
Will I not think of home, but follow arms.

Const. O, take his mother's thanks, a widow's thanks,
Till your strong hand shall help to give him strength
To make a more requital to your love!

Aust. The peace of heaven is theirs that lift their swords
In such a just and charitable war.

France. Well then, to work! Our cannon shall be bent
Against the brows of this resisting town.
Call for our chiefest men of discipline,
To cull the plots of best advantages.
We'll lay before this town our royal bones,
Wade to the market place in Frenchmen's blood,
But we will make it subject to this boy.

Const. Stay for an answer to your embassy,
Lest unadvis'd you stain your swords with blood.
My Lord Chatillon may from England bring
That right in peace which here we urge in war,
And then we shall repent each drop of blood
That hot rash haste so indirectly shed.

Enter *Chatillon.*

France. A wonder, lady! Lo, upon thy wish
Our messenger Chatillon is arriv'd!
What England says, say briefly, gentle lord.
We coldly pause for thee; Chatillon, speak.

Chat. Then turn your forces from this paltry siege
And stir them up against a mightier task.
England, impatient of your just demands,
Hath put himself in arms. The adverse winds,
Whose leisure I have stay'd, have given him time
To land his legions all as soon as I.
His marches are expedient to this town,
His forces strong, his soldiers confident.
With him along is come the mother queen,
An Ate stirring him to blood and strife;
With her her niece, the Lady Blanch of Spain;
With them a bastard of the King's deceas'd;
And all th' unsettled humours of the land,
Rash, inconsiderate, fiery voluntaries,
With ladies' faces and fierce dragons' spleens,
Have sold their fortunes at their native homes,
Bearing their birthrights proudly on their backs,
To make a hazard of new fortunes here.
In brief, a braver choice of dauntless spirits
Than now the English bottoms have waft o'er
Did never float upon the swelling tide
To do offence and scathe in Christendom.

Drum beats.

The interruption of their churlish drums
Cuts off more circumstance. They are at hand,
To parley or to fight; therefore prepare.

France. How much unlook'd for is this expedition!

Aust. By how much unexpected, by so much
We must awake endeavour for defence;
For courage mounteth with occasion.
Let them be welcome then; we are prepar'd.

Enter *King of England, Bastard, Queen* [*Elinor*], *Blanch, Pembroke,* and others.

K. John. Peace be to France, if France in peace permit
Our just and lineal entrance to our own!
If not, bleed France, and peace ascend to heaven,
Whiles we, God's wrathful agent, do correct
Their proud contempt that beats his peace to heaven!

France. Peace be to England, if that war return
From France to England, there to live in peace!
England we love, and for that England's sake
With burden of our armour here we sweat.
This toil of ours should be a work of thine;
But thou from loving England art so far
That thou hast underwrought his lawful king,
Cut off the sequence of posterity,
Outfaced infant state, and done a rape

Upon the maiden virtue of the crown.
Look here upon thy brother Geffrey's face!
These eyes, these brows, were moulded out of his;
This little abstract doth contain that large
Which died in Geffrey, and the hand of time
Shall draw this brief into as huge a volume.
That Geffrey was thy elder brother born,
And this his son. England was Geffrey's right,
And this is Geffrey's. In the name of God,
How comes it then that thou art call'd a king
When living blood doth in these temples beat
Which owe the crown that thou o'ermasterest?

K. John. From whom hast thou this great commission, France,
To draw my answer from thy articles?

France. From that supernal judge that stirs good thoughts
In any breast of strong authority
To look into the blots and stains of right.
That judge hath made me guardian to this boy;
Under whose warrant I impeach thy wrong,
And by whose help I mean to chastise it.

K. John. Alack! thou dost usurp authority.

France. Excuse — it is to beat usurping down.

Eli. Who is it thou dost call usurper, France?

Const. Let me make answer: thy usurping son.

Eli. Out, insolent! Thy bastard shall be King,
That thou mayst be a queen and check the world!

Const. My bed was ever to thy son as true
As thine was to thy husband; and this boy
Liker in feature to his father Geffrey
Than thou and John in manners, being as like
As rain to water or devil to his dam.
My boy a bastard? By my soul, I think
His father never was so true begot!
It cannot be, an if thou wert his mother.

Eli. There's a good mother, boy, that blots thy father!

Const. There's a good grandam, boy, that would blot thee!

Aust. Peace!

Bast. Hear the crier.

Aust. What the devil art thou?

Bast. One that will play the devil, sir, with you
An 'a may catch your hide and you alone.
You are the hare of whom the proverb goes,
Whose valour plucks dead lions by the beard.
I'll smoke your skin-coat an I catch you right.
Sirrah, look to't! I' faith I will, i' faith!

Blanch. O, well did he become that lion's robe
That did disrobe the lion of that robe!

Bast. It lies as sightly on the back of him
As great Alcides' shows upon an ass.
But, ass, I'll take that burthen from your back
Or lay on that shall make your shoulders crack.

Aust. What cracker is this same that deafs our ears
With this abundance of superfluous breath?
King Philip, determine what we shall do straight.

France. Women and fools, break off your conference.
King John, this is the very sum of all:
England and Ireland, Anjou, Touraine, Maine,
In right of Arthur do I claim of thee.
Wilt thou resign them and lay down thy arms?

K. John. My life as soon. I do defy thee, France.
Arthur of Britain, yield thee to my hand,
And out of my dear love I'll give thee more
Than e'er the coward hand of France can win.
Submit thee, boy.

Eli. Come to thy grandam, child.

Const. Do, child! go to it grandam, child!
Give grandam kingdom, and it grandam will
Give it a plum, a cherry, and a fig.
There's a good grandam!

Arth. Good my mother, peace!
I would that I were low laid in my grave.
I am not worth this coil that's made for me.

Eli. His mother shames him so, poor boy he weeps.

Const. Now shame upon you, whe'r she does or no!
His grandam's wrongs, and not his mother's shames,
Draws those heaven-moving pearls from his poor eyes,
Which heaven shall take in nature of a fee.
Ay, with these crystal beads heaven shall be brib'd
To do him justice and revenge on you.

Eli. Thou monstrous slanderer of heaven and earth!

Const. Thou monstrous injurer of heaven and earth,
Call not me slanderer! Thou and thine usurp
The dominations, royalties, and rights
Of this oppressed boy. This is thy eldest son's son,
Infortunate in nothing but in thee.
Thy sins are visited in this poor child;
The canon of the law is laid on him,

Being but the second generation
Removed from thy sin-conceiving womb.
K. John. Bedlam, have done!
Const. I have but this to say,
That he is not only plagued for her sin,
But God hath made her sin and her the plague
On this removed issue, plagu'd for her
And with her plague; her sin his injury,
Her injury the beadle to her sin;
All punish'd in the person of this child,
And all for her — a plague upon her!
Eli. Thou unadvised scold, I can produce
A will that bars the title of thy son.
Const. Ay, who doubts that? A will! a wicked will;
A woman's will; a cank'red grandam's will!
France. Peace, lady! pause, or be more temperate.
It ill beseems this presence to cry aim
To these ill-tuned repetitions.
Some trumpet summon hither to the walls
These men of Angiers. Let us hear them speak
Whose title they admit, Arthur's or John's.

Trumpet sounds. Enter *Citizens* upon the walls.

Citizen. Who is it that hath warn'd us to the walls?
France. 'Tis France, for England.
K. John. England for itself.
You men of Angiers, and my loving subjects —
France. You loving men of Angiers, Arthur's subjects,
Our trumpet call'd you to this gentle parle —
K. John. For our advantage; therefore hear us first.
These flags of France that are advanced here
Before the eye and prospect of your town
Have hither march'd to your endamagement.
The cannons have their bowels full of wrath,
And ready mounted are they to spit forth
Their iron indignation 'gainst your walls.
All preparation for a bloody siege
And merciless proceeding by these French
Confronts your city's eyes, your winking gates;
And but for our approach, those sleeping stones
That as a waist doth girdle you about,
By the compulsion of their ordinance
By this time from their fixed beds of lime
Had been dishabited, and wide havoc made
For bloody power to rush upon your peace.
But on the sight of us your lawful king,
Who painfully with much expedient march
Have brought a countercheck before your gates,
To save unscratch'd your city's threat'ned cheeks —
Behold, the French amaz'd vouchsafe a parle;
And now, instead of bullets wrapp'd in fire
To make a shaking fever in your walls,
They shoot but calm words folded up in smoke,
To make a faithless error in your ears;
Which trust accordingly, kind citizens,
And let us in, your king, whose labour'd spirits,
Forwearied in this action of swift speed,
Crave harbourage within your city walls.
France. When I have said, make answer to us both.
Lo, in this right hand, whose protection
Is most divinely vow'd upon the right
Of him it holds, stands young Plantagenet,
Son to the elder brother of this man,
And king o'er him and all that he enjoys.
For this downtrodden equity we tread
In warlike march these greens before your town,
Being no further enemy to you
Than the constraint of hospitable zeal
In the relief of this oppressed child
Religiously provokes. Be pleased then
To pay that duty which you truly owe
To him that owes it, namely, this young prince;
And then our arms, like to a muzzled bear,
Save in aspect, hath all offence seal'd up;
Our cannons' malice vainly shall be spent
Against th' invulnerable clouds of heaven;
And with a blessed and unvex'd retire,
With unhack'd swords and helmets all unbruis'd,
We will bear home that lusty blood again
Which here we came to spout against your town,
And leave your children, wives, and you in peace.
But if you fondly pass our proffer'd offer,
'Tis not the roundure of your old-fac'd walls
Can hide you from our messengers of war,
Though all these English and their discipline
Were harbour'd in their rude circumference.
Then tell us, shall your city call us lord
In that behalf which we have challeng'd it?
Or shall we give the signal to our rage
And stalk in blood to our possession?
Citizen. In brief, we are the King of England's subjects.
For him, and in his right, we hold this town.
K. John. Acknowledge then the King, and let me in.
Citizen. That can we not; but he that proves the King,
To him will we prove loyal. Till that time
Have we ramm'd up our gates against the world.

K. John. Doth not the crown of England prove the King?
And if not that, I bring you witnesses,
Twice fifteen thousand hearts of England's breed —

Bast. Bastards and else.

K. John. To verify our title with their lives.

France. As many and as well-born bloods as those —

Bast. Some bastards too.

France. Stand in his face to contradict his claim.

Citizen. Till you compound whose right is worthiest,
We for the worthiest hold the right from both.

K. John. Then God forgive the sin of all those souls
That to their everlasting residence,
Before the dew of evening fall, shall fleet
In dreadful trial of our kingdom's king!

France. Amen, amen! Mount, chevaliers! to arms!

Bast. Saint George that swing'd the dragon, and e'er since
Sits on his horseback at mine hostess' door,
Teach us some fence! [*To Austria*] Sirrah, were I at home,
At your den, sirrah, with your lioness,
I would set an ox-head to your lion's hide
And make a monster of you.

Aust. Peace, no more!

Bast. O, tremble! for you hear the lion roar.

K. John. Up higher to the plain, where we'll set forth
In best appointment all our regiments.

Bast. Speed then to take advantage of the field.

France. It shall be so; and at the other hill
Command the rest to stand. God and our right!
Exeunt.

Here, after excursions, enter the *Herald of France*, with *Trumpets*, to the gates.

F. Her. You men of Angiers, open wide your gates
And let young Arthur, Duke of Britain, in,
Who by the hand of France this day hath made
Much work for tears in many an English mother
Whose sons lie scattered on the bleeding ground.
Many a widow's husband grovelling lies,
Coldly embracing the discoloured earth;
And victory with little loss doth play
Upon the dancing banners of the French,
Who are at hand, triumphantly display'd,
To enter conquerors and to proclaim
Arthur of Britain England's King and yours.

Enter *English Herald*, with *Trumpet*.

E. Her. Rejoice, you men of Angiers, ring your bells!
King John, your king and England's, doth approach,
Commander of this hot malicious day.
Their armours that march'd hence so silver-bright
Hither return all gilt with Frenchmen's blood.
There stuck no plume in any English crest
That is removed by a staff of France.
Our colours do return in those same hands
That did display them when we first march'd forth;
And like a jolly troop of huntsmen come
Our lusty English, all with purpled hands,
Dy'd in the dying slaughter of their foes.
Open your gates, and give the victors way!

Citizen. Heralds, from off our tow'rs we might behold
From first to last the onset and retire
Of both your armies, whose equality
By our best eyes cannot be censured.
Blood hath bought blood, and blows have answer'd blows;
Strength match'd with strength, and power confronted power.
Both are alike, and both alike we like.
One must prove greatest. While they weigh so even,
We hold our town for neither; yet for both.

Enter the two *Kings*, with their *Powers*, at several doors.

K. John. France, hast thou yet more blood to cast away?
Say, shall the current of our right run on?
Whose passage, vex'd with thy impediment,
Shall leave his native channel and o'erswell
With course disturb'd even thy confining shores,
Unless thou let his silver water keep
A peaceful progress to the ocean.

France. England, thou hast not sav'd one drop of blood
In this hot trial more than we of France;
Rather, lost more. And by this hand I swear,
That sways the earth this climate overlooks,
Before we will lay down our just-borne arms,
We'll put thee down, 'gainst whom these arms we bear,
Or add a royal number to the dead,

Gracing the scroll that tells of this war's loss
With slaughter coupled to the name of kings.

Bast. Ha, majesty! how high thy glory tow'rs
When the rich blood of kings is set on fire!
O, now doth Death line his dead chaps with steel;
The swords of soldiers are his teeth, his fangs;
And now he feasts, mousing the flesh of men,
In undetermin'd differences of kings.
Why stand these royal fronts amazed thus?
Cry 'havoc,' kings. Back to the stained field,
You equal potents, fiery kindled spirits!
Then let confusion of one part confirm
The other's peace. Till then, blows, blood, and death!

K. John. Whose party do the townsmen yet admit?

France. Speak, citizens, for England. Who's your king?

Citizen. The King of England, when we know the King.

France. Know him in us that here hold up his right.

K. John. In us that are our own great deputy
And bear possession of our person here,
Lord of our presence, Angiers, and of you.

Citizen. A greater pow'r than we denies all this;
And till it be undoubted, we do lock
Our former scruple in our strong-barr'd gates;
King'd of our fears, until our fears, resolv'd,
Be by some certain king purg'd and depos'd.

Bast. By heaven, these scroyles of Angiers flout you, kings,
And stand securely on their battlements,
As in a theatre, whence they gape and point
At your industrious scenes and acts of death.
Your royal presences be rul'd by me:
Do like the mutines of Jerusalem,
Be friends awhile, and both conjointly bend
Your sharpest deeds of malice on this town.
By east and west let France and England mount
Their battering cannon, charged to the mouths,
Till their soul-fearing clamours have brawl'd down
The flinty ribs of this contemptuous city.
I'd play incessantly upon these jades,
Even till unfenced desolation
Leave them as naked as the vulgar air.
That done, dissever your united strengths
And part your mingled colours once again,
Turn face to face and bloody point to point.
Then in a moment Fortune shall cull forth
Out of one side her happy minion,
To whom in favour she shall give the day
And kiss him with a glorious victory.
How like you this wild counsel, mighty states?
Smacks it not something of the policy?

K. John. Now, by the sky that hangs above our heads,
I like it well. France, shall we knit our pow'rs
And lay this Angiers even with the ground;
Then after fight who shall be king of it?

Bast. An if thou hast the mettle of a king,
Being wrong'd as we are by this peevish town,
Turn thou the mouth of thy artillery,
As we will ours, against these saucy walls;
And when that we have dash'd them to the ground,
Why, then defy each other, and pell-mell
Make work upon ourselves, for heaven or hell.

France. Let it be so. Say, where will you assault?

K. John. We from the west will send destruction
Into this city's bosom.

Aust. I from the north.

France. Our thunder from the south
Shall rain their drift of bullets on this town.

Bast. [*aside*] O prudent discipline! From north to south!
Austria and France shoot in each other's mouth.
I'll stir them to it. — Come, away, away!

Citizen. Hear us, great kings. Vouchsafe awhile to stay,
And I shall show you peace and fair-fac'd league,
Win you this city without stroke or wound,
Rescue those breathing lives to die in beds
That here come sacrifices for the field.
Persever not, but hear me, mighty kings!

K. John. Speak on with favour; we are bent to hear.

Citizen. That daughter there of Spain, the Lady Blanch,
Is niece to England. Look upon the years
Of Lewis the Dauphin and that lovely maid.
If lusty love should go in quest of beauty,
Where should he find it fairer than in Blanch?
If zealous love should go in search of virtue,
Where should he find it purer than in Blanch?
If love ambitious sought a match of birth,
Whose veins bound richer blood than Lady Blanch?
Such as she is, in beauty, virtue, birth,
Is the young Dauphin every way complete:
If not complete, I say, he is not she;
And she again wants nothing to name want,

If want it be not that she is not he.
He is the half part of a blessed man,
Left to be finished by such as she;
And she a fair divided excellence,
Whose fulness of perfection lies in him.
O, two such silver currents, when they join,
Do glorify the banks that bound them in;
And two such shores to two such streams made one,
Two such controlling bounds, shall you be, kings,
To these two princes, if you marry them.
This union shall do more than battery can
To our fast-closed gates; for at this match,
With swifter spleen than powder can enforce,
The mouth of passage shall we fling wide ope
And give you entrance; but without this match,
The sea enraged is not half so deaf,
Lions more confident, mountains and rocks
More free from motion — no, not Death himself
In mortal fury half so peremptory
As we to keep this city.

Bast. Here's a 'Stay!'
That shakes the rotten carcass of old Death
Out of his rags! Here's a large mouth indeed,
That spits forth death, and mountains, rocks and seas;
Talks as familiarly of roaring lions
As maids of thirteen do of puppy-dogs!
What cannoneer begot this lusty blood?
He speaks plain cannon-fire and smoke and bounce;
He gives the bastinado with his tongue.
Our ears are cudgell'd; not a word of his
But buffets better than a fist of France.
Zounds! I was never so bethump'd with words
Since I first call'd my brother's father dad.

Eli. Son, list to this conjunction, make this match,
Give with our niece a dowry large enough;
For by this knot thou shalt so surely tie
Thy now-unsur'd assurance to the crown
That yon green boy shall have no sun to ripe
The bloom that promiseth a mighty fruit.
I see a yielding in the looks of France.
Mark how they whisper. Urge them while their souls
Are capable of this ambition,
Lest zeal, now melted by the windy breath
Of soft petitions, pity, and remorse,
Cool and congeal again to what it was.

Citizen. Why answer not the double Majesties
This friendly treaty of our threat'ned town?

France. Speak England first, that hath been forward first
To speak unto this city. What say you?

K. John. If that the Dauphin there, thy princely son,
Can in this book of beauty read 'I love,'
Her dowry shall weigh equal with a queen;
For Anjou, and fair Touraine, Maine, Poictiers,
And all that we upon this side the sea
(Except this city now by us besieg'd)
Find liable to our crown and dignity,
Shall gild her bridal bed and make her rich
In titles, honours, and promotions,
As she in beauty, education, blood,
Holds hand with any princess of the world.

France. What say'st thou, boy? Look in the lady's face.

Dau. I do, my lord, and in her eye I find
A wonder, or a wondrous miracle —
The shadow of myself form'd in her eye;
Which, being but the shadow of your son,
Becomes a sun and makes your son a shadow.
I do protest I never lov'd myself
Till now infixed I beheld myself
Drawn in the flattering table of her eye.
Whispers with Blanch.

Bast. [*aside*] Drawn in the flattering table of her eye,
Hang'd in the frowning wrinkle of her brow,
And quarter'd in her heart! He doth espy
Himself love's traitor. This is pity now!
That hang'd and drawn and quarter'd there should be
In such a love so vile a lout as he.

Blanch. My uncle's will in this respect is mine.
If he see aught in you that makes him like,
That anything he sees which moves his liking,
I can with ease translate it to my will;
Or if you will, to speak more properly,
I will enforce it eas'ly to my love.
Further I will not flatter you, my lord,
That all I see in you is worthy love
Than this — that nothing do I see in you,
Though churlish thoughts themselves should be your judge,
That I can find should merit any hate.

K. John. What say these young ones? What say you, my niece?

Blanch. That she is bound in honour still to do
What you in wisdom still vouchsafe to say.

K. John. Speak then, Prince Dauphin. Can you love this lady?

Dau. Nay, ask me if I can refrain from love,
For I do love her most unfeignedly.

K. John. Then do I give Volquessen, Touraine, Maine,
Poictiers, and Anjou, these five provinces,
With her to thee; and this addition more,
Full thirty thousand marks of English coin.
Philip of France, if thou be pleas'd withal,
Command thy son and daughter to join hands.

France. It likes us well. Young princes, close your hands.

Aust. And your lips too; for I am well assur'd
That I did so when I was first assur'd.

France. Now, citizens of Angiers, ope your gates,
Let in that amity which you have made;
For at Saint Mary's Chapel presently
The rites of marriage shall be solemniz'd.
Is not the Lady Constance in this troop?
I know she is not; for this match made up
Her presence would have interrupted much.
Where is she and her son? Tell me, who knows.

Dau. She is sad and passionate at your Highness' tent.

France. And, by my faith, this league that we have made
Will give her sadness very little cure.
Brother of England, how may we content
This widow lady? In her right we came,
Which we, God knows, have turn'd another way,
To our own vantage.

K. John. We will heal up all;
For we'll create young Arthur Duke of Britain
And Earl of Richmond, and this rich fair town
We make him lord of. Call the Lady Constance.
Some speedy messenger bid her repair
To our solemnity. I trust we shall,
If not fill up the measure of her will,
Yet in some measure satisfy her so
That we shall stop her exclamation.
Go we as well as haste will suffer us
To this unlook'd-for, unprepared pomp.

Exeunt [all but the Bastard].

Bast. Mad world! mad kings! mad composition!
John, to stop Arthur's title in the whole,
Hath willingly departed with a part;
And France — whose armour conscience buckled on,
Whom zeal and charity brought to the field
As God's own soldier — rounded in the ear
With that same purpose-changer, that sly devil,
That broker that still breaks the pate of faith,
That daily break-vow, he that wins of all,
Of kings, of beggars, old men, young men, maids,
Who, having no external thing to lose
But the word 'maid,' cheats the poor maid of that —
That smooth-fac'd gentleman, tickling Commodity,
Commodity, the bias of the world —
The world, who of itself is peised well,
Made to run even upon even ground
Till this advantage, this vile drawing bias,
This sway of motion, this Commodity,
Makes it take head from all indifferency,
From all direction, purpose, course, intent —
And this same bias, this Commodity,
This bawd, this broker, this all-changing word,
Clapp'd on the outward eye of fickle France,
Hath drawn him from his own determin'd aid,
From a resolv'd and honourable war,
To a most base and vile-concluded peace.
And why rail I on this Commodity?
But for because he hath not woo'd me yet:
Not that I have the power to clutch my hand
When his fair angels would salute my palm,
But for my hand, as unattempted yet,
Like a poor beggar, raileth on the rich.
Well, whiles I am a beggar, I will rail
And say there is no sin but to be rich;
And being rich, my virtue then shall be
To say there is no vice but beggary.
Since kings break faith upon commodity,
Gain, be my lord, for I will worship thee!

Exit.

[ACT III. Scene I. *France.* *The* French King's *tent.*]

Enter *Constance, Arthur,* and *Salisbury.*

Const. Gone to be married? Gone to swear a peace?
False blood to false blood join'd! Gone to be friends?
Shall Lewis have Blanch, and Blanch those provinces?
It is not so! thou hast misspoke, misheard.
Be well advis'd, tell o'er thy tale again.
It cannot be; thou dost but say 'tis so.
I trust I may not trust thee, for thy word]
Is but the vain breath of a common man.
Believe me, I do not believe thee, man;
I have a king's oath to the contrary.
Thou shalt be punish'd for thus frighting me,

For I am sick, and capable of fears;
Oppress'd with wrongs, and therefore full of fears;
A widow, husbandless, subject to fears;
A woman, naturally born to fears;
And though thou now confess thou didst but jest,
With my vex'd spirits I cannot take a truce,
But they will quake and tremble all this day.
What dost thou mean by shaking of thy head?
Why dost thou look so sadly on my son?
What means that hand upon that breast of thine?
Why holds thine eye that lamentable rheum,
Like a proud river peering o'er his bounds?
Be these sad signs confirmers of thy words?
Then speak again — not all thy former tale,
But this one word, whether thy tale be true.

Sal. As true as I believe you think them false
That give you cause to prove my saying true.

Const. O, if thou teach me to believe this sorrow,
Teach thou this sorrow how to make me die;
And let belief and life encounter so
As doth the fury of two desperate men
Which in the very meeting fall and die!
Lewis marry Blanch? O boy, then where art thou?
France friend with England? What becomes of me?
Fellow, be gone. I cannot brook thy sight;
This news hath made thee a most ugly man.

Sal. What other harm have I, good lady, done
But spoke the harm that is by others done?

Const. Which harm within itself so heinous is
As it makes harmful all that speak of it.

Arth. I do beseech you, madam, be content.

Const. If thou that bid'st me be content wert grim,
Ugly, and sland'rous to thy mother's womb,
Full of unpleasing blots and sightless stains,
Lame, foolish, crooked, swart, prodigious,
Patch'd with foul moles and eye-offending marks,
I would not care, I then would be content,
For then I should not love thee — no, nor thou
Become thy great birth nor deserve a crown.
But thou art fair, and at thy birth, dear boy,
Nature and Fortune join'd to make thee great.
Of Nature's gifts thou mayst with lilies boast
And with the half-blown rose. But Fortune, O,
She is corrupted, chang'd, and won from thee!
Sh' adulterates hourly with thine uncle John,
And with her golden hand hath pluck'd on France
To tread down fair respect of sovereignty,
And made his majesty the bawd to theirs.
France is a bawd to Fortune and King John —
That strumpet Fortune! that usurping John!
Tell me, thou fellow, is not France forsworn?
Envenom him with words; or get thee gone
And leave those woes alone which I alone
Am bound to underbear.

Sal. Pardon me, madam,
I may not go without you to the kings.

Const. Thou mayst! thou shalt! I will not go with thee.
I will instruct my sorrows to be proud;
For grief is proud, and makes his owner stoop
To me, and to the state of my great grief,
Let kings assemble; for my grief 's so great
That no supporter but the huge firm earth
Can hold it up. [*Seats herself on the ground.*]
Here I and sorrows sit;
Here is my throne, bid kings come bow to it.

Enter *King John, France, Dauphin, Blanch, Elinor, Philip* [*the Bastard*], *Austria*, [and *Attendants*].

France. 'Tis true, fair daughter, and this blessed day
Ever in France shall be kept festival.
To solemnize this day the glorious sun
Stays in his course and plays the alchymist,
Turning with splendour of his precious eye
The meagre cloddy earth to glittering gold.
The yearly course that brings this day about
Shall never see it but a holiday.

Const. [*rises*] A wicked day, and not a holy day!
What hath this day deserv'd? what hath it done
That it in golden letters should be set
Among the high tides in the calendar?
Nay, rather turn this day out of the week,
This day of shame, oppression, perjury.
Or, if it must stand still, let wives with child
Pray that their burthens may not fall this day,
Lest that their hopes prodigiously be cross'd;
But on this day, let seamen fear no wrack;
No bargains break that are not this day made;
This day all things begun, come to ill end,
Yea, faith itself to hollow falsehood change!

France. By heaven, lady, you shall have no cause
To curse the fair proceedings of this day.
Have I not pawn'd to you my majesty?

Const. You have beguil'd me with a counterfeit
Resembling majesty, which, being touch'd and tried,

Proves valueless. You are forsworn, forsworn!
You came in arms to spill mine enemies' blood,
But now in arms you strengthen it with yours.
The grappling vigour and rough frown of war
Is cold in amity and painted peace,
And our oppression hath made up this league.
Arm, arm, you heavens, against these perjur'd kings!
A widow cries; be husband to me, heavens!
Let not the hours of this ungodly day
Wear out the day in peace; but ere sunset
Set armed discord 'twixt these perjur'd kings!
Hear me, O, hear me!

Aust. Lady Constance, peace!

Const. War! war! no peace! Peace is to me a war.
O Limoges! O Austria! thou dost shame
That bloody spoil. Thou slave, thou wretch, thou coward!
Thou little valiant, great in villany!
Thou ever strong upon the stronger side!
Thou Fortune's champion, that dost never fight
But when her humorous ladyship is by
To teach thee safety! Thou art perjur'd too,
And sooth'st up greatness. What a fool art thou,
A ramping fool, to brag and stamp and swear
Upon my party! Thou cold-blooded slave,
Hast thou not spoke like thunder on my side?
Been sworn my soldier, bidding me depend
Upon thy stars, thy fortune, and thy strength?
And dost thou now fall over to my foes?
Thou wear a lion's hide? Doff it for shame,
And hang a calve's-skin on those recreant limbs.

Aust. O, that a man should speak those words to me!

Bast. And hang a calve's-skin on those recreant limbs.

Aust. Thou dar'st not say so, villain, for thy life.

Bast. And hang a calve's-skin on those recreant limbs.

K. John. We like not this; thou dost forget thyself.

Enter *Pandulph.*

France. Here comes the holy legate of the Pope.

Pand. Hail, you anointed deputies of heaven!
To thee, King John, my holy errand is.
I Pandulph, of fair Milan Cardinal,
And from Pope Innocent the legate here,
Do in his name religiously demand
Why thou against the Church, our holy mother,
So wilfully dost spurn, and force perforce
Keep Stephen Langton, chosen Archbishop
Of Canterbury, from that holy see.
This, in our foresaid holy father's name,
Pope Innocent, I do demand of thee.

K. John. What earthly name to interrogatories
Can task the free breath of a sacred king?
Thou canst not, Cardinal, devise a name
So slight, unworthy, and ridiculous
To charge me to an answer, as the Pope.
Tell him this tale, and from the mouth of England
Add thus much more, that no Italian priest
Shall tithe or toll in our dominions;
But as we, under heaven, are supreme head,
So, under Him that great supremacy,
Where we do reign, we will alone uphold,
Without th' assistance of a mortal hand.
So tell the Pope, all reverence set apart
To him and his usurp'd authority.

France. Brother of England, you blaspheme in this.

K. John. Though you and all the kings of Christendom
Are led so grossly by this meddling priest,
Dreading the curse that money may buy out,
And by the merit of vile gold, dross, dust,
Purchase corrupted pardon of a man,
Who in that sale sells pardon from himself—
Though you, and all the rest so grossly led,
This juggling witchcraft with revenue cherish,
Yet I alone, alone do me oppose
Against the Pope and count his friends my foes.

Pand. Then by the lawful power that I have
Thou shalt stand curs'd and excommunicate,
And blessed shall he be that doth revolt
From his allegiance to an heretic,
And meritorious shall that hand be call'd,
Canonized, and worshipp'd as a saint,
That takes away by any secret course
Thy hateful life.

Const. O, lawful let it be
That I have room with Rome to curse awhile!
Good father Cardinal, cry thou amen
To my keen curses; for without my wrong
There is no tongue hath power to curse him right.

Pand. There's law and warrant, lady, for my curse.

Const. And for mine too! When law can do no right,
Let it be lawful that law bar no wrong.
Law cannot give my child his kingdom here,
For he that holds his kingdom holds the law.
Therefore, since law itself is perfect wrong,
How can the law forbid my tongue to curse?

Pand. Philip of France, on peril of a curse,
Let go the hand of that arch-heretic,
And raise the power of France upon his head
Unless he do submit himself to Rome.
Eli. Look'st thou pale, France? Do not let go thy hand.
Const. Look to that, devil! lest that France repent,
And by disjoining hands hell lose a soul.
Aust. King Philip, listen to the Cardinal.
Bast. And hang a calve's-skin on his recreant limbs.
Aust. Well, ruffian, I must pocket up these wrongs,
Because —
Bast. Your breeches best may carry them.
K. John. Philip, what say'st thou to the Cardinal?
Const. What should he say, but as the Cardinal?
Dau. Bethink you, father; for the difference
Is purchase of a heavy curse from Rome
Or the light loss of England for a friend.
Forgo the easier.
Blanch. That's the curse of Rome.
Const. O Lewis, stand fast! The devil tempts thee here
In likeness of a new untrimmed bride.
Blanch. The Lady Constance speaks not from her faith,
But from her need.
Const. O, if thou grant my need,
Which only lives but by the death of faith,
That need must needs infer this principle —
That faith would live again by death of need!
O, then tread down my need, and faith mounts up;
Keep my need up, and faith is trodden down!
K. John. The King is mov'd and answers not to this.
Const. O, be remov'd from him, and answer well!
Aust. Do so, King Philip; hang no more in doubt.
Bast. Hang nothing but a calve's-skin, most sweet lout.
France. I am perplex'd and know not what to say.
Pand. What canst thou say but will perplex thee more,
If thou stand excommunicate and curs'd?
France. Good reverend father, make my person yours
And tell me how you would bestow yourself.
This royal hand and mine are newly knit,
And the conjunction of our inward souls
Married in league, coupled, and link'd together
With all religious strength of sacred vows.
The latest breath that gave the sound of words
Was deep-sworn faith, peace, amity, true love
Between our kingdoms and our royal selves;
And even before this truce, but new before,
No longer than we well could wash our hands
To clap this royal bargain up of peace,
Heaven knows they were besmear'd and over-stain'd
With slaughter's pencil, where revenge did paint
The fearful difference of incensed kings.
And shall these hands so lately purg'd of blood,
So newly join'd in love, so strong in both,
Unyoke this seizure and this kind regreet?
Play fast and loose with faith? so jest with heaven,
Make such unconstant children of ourselves,
As now again to snatch our palm from palm,
Unswear faith sworn, and on the marriage bed
Of smiling peace to march a bloody host
And make a riot on the gentle brow
Of true sincerity? O holy sir,
My reverend father, let it not be so!
Out of your grace, devise, ordain, impose
Some gentle order, and then we shall be blest
To do your pleasure and continue friends.
Pand. All form is formless, order orderless,
Save what is opposite to England's love.
Therefore, to arms! be champion of our Church!
Or let the Church our mother breathe her curse,
A mother's curse, on her revolting son.
France, thou mayst hold a serpent by the tongue,
A chafed lion by the mortal paw,
A fasting tiger safer by the tooth,
Than keep in peace that hand which thou dost hold.
France. I may disjoin my hand, but not my faith.
Pand. So mak'st thou faith an enemy to faith,
And like a civil war set'st oath to oath,
Thy tongue against thy tongue. O, let thy vow
First made to heaven, first be to heaven perform'd,
That is, to be the champion of our Church!
What since thou swor'st is sworn against thyself
And may not be performed by thyself;
For that which thou hast sworn to do amiss
Is not amiss when it is truly done;
And being not done where doing tends to ill,
The truth is then most done, not doing it.

The better act of purposes mistook
Is to mistake again. Though indirect,
Yet indirection thereby grows direct,
And falsehood falsehood cures, as fire cools fire
Within the scorched veins of one new burn'd.
It is religion that doth make vows kept;
But thou hast sworn against religion,
By what thou swear'st against the thing thou swear'st,
And mak'st an oath the surety for thy truth
Against an oath. The truth thou art unsure
To swear, swears only not to be forsworn;
Else what a mockery should it be to swear!
But thou dost swear, only to be forsworn,
And most forsworn to keep what thou dost swear.
Therefore thy later vows against thy first
Is in thyself rebellion to thyself;
And better conquest never canst thou make
Than arm thy constant and thy nobler parts
Against these giddy loose suggestions;
Upon which better part our pray'rs come in,
If thou vouchsafe them. But if not, then know
The peril of our curses light on thee
So heavy as thou shalt not shake them off,
But in despair die under their black weight.

Aust. Rebellion, flat rebellion!

Bast. Will't not be?
Will not a calve's-skin stop that mouth of thine?

Dau. Father, to arms!

Blanch. Upon thy wedding day?
Against the blood that thou hast married?
What, shall our feast be kept with slaughtered men?
Shall braying trumpets and loud churlish drums,
Clamours of hell, be measures to our pomp?
O husband, hear me (ay, alack, how new
Is husband in my mouth!) even for that name
Which till this time my tongue did ne'er pronounce!
Upon my knee I beg, go not to arms
Against mine uncle.

Const. O, upon my knee,
Made hard with kneeling, I do pray to thee,
Thou virtuous Dauphin, alter not the doom
Forethought by heaven!

Blanch. Now shall I see thy love. What motive may
Be stronger with thee than the name of wife?

Const. That which upholdeth him that thee upholds,
His honour. O, thine honour, Lewis, thine honour!

Dau. I muse your Majesty doth seem so cold
When such profound respects do pull you on.

Pand. I will denounce a curse upon his head.

France. Thou shalt not need. England, I will fall from thee.

Const. O fair return of banish'd majesty!

Eli. O foul revolt of French inconstancy!

K. John. France, thou shalt rue this hour within this hour.

Bast. Old Time the clock-setter, that bald sexton Time—
Is it as he will? Well then, France shall rue.

Blanch. The sun's o'ercast with blood. Fair day, adieu!
Which is the side that I must go withal?
I am with both; each army hath a hand,
And in their rage, I having hold of both,
They whirl asunder and dismember me.
Husband, I cannot pray that thou mayst win;
Uncle, I needs must pray that thou mayst lose;
Father, I may not wish the fortune thine;
Grandam, I will not wish thy wishes thrive.
Whoever wins, on that side shall I lose:
Assured loss before the match be play'd!

Dau. Lady, with me! With me thy fortune lies.

Blanch. There where my fortune lives, there my life dies.

K. John. Cousin, go draw our puissance together.
[*Exit Bastard.*]
France, I am burn'd up with inflaming wrath,
A rage whose heat hath this condition,
That nothing can allay—nothing but blood,
The blood, and dearest-valued blood, of France.

France. Thy rage shall burn thee up, and thou shalt turn
To ashes, ere our blood shall quench that fire.
Look to thyself; thou art in jeopardy.

K. John. No more than he that threats. To arms let's hie!
Exeunt.

Scene II. [*France. Plains near Angiers.*]

Alarums, excursions. Enter *Bastard,* with *Austria's* head.

Bast. Now, by my life, this day grows wondrous hot!
Some airy devil hovers in the sky
And pours down mischief. Austria's head lie there
While Philip breathes.

Enter [*King*] *John, Arthur, Hubert.*

K. John. Hubert, keep this boy. Philip, make up!
My mother is assailed in our tent,
And ta'en, I fear.
Bast. My lord, I rescued her.
Her Highness is in safety, fear you not.
But on, my liege! for very little pains
Will bring this labour to an happy end.
Exeunt.

[Scene III. *France. Another part of the plains.*]

Alarums, excursions, retreat. Enter [*King*] *John, Elinor, Arthur, Bastard, Hubert, Lords.*

K. John. [*to Elinor*] So shall it be. Your Grace shall stay behind,
So strongly guarded. [*To Arthur*] Cousin, look not sad.
Thy grandam loves thee, and thy uncle will
As dear be to thee as thy father was.
Arth. O, this will make my mother die with grief!
K. John. [*to Bastard*] Cousin, away for England! Haste before;
And ere our coming see thou shake the bags
Of hoarding abbots; set at liberty
Imprison'd angels. The fat ribs of peace
Must by the hungry now be fed upon.
Use our commission in his utmost force.
Bast. Bell, book, and candle shall not drive me back
When gold and silver becks me to come on.
I leave your Highness. Grandam, I will pray
(If ever I remember to be holy)
For your fair safety. So I kiss your hand.
Eli. Farewell, gentle cousin.
K. John. Coz, farewell.
[*Exit Bastard.*]
Eli. Come hither, little kinsman. Hark, a word. [*Takes Arthur aside.*]
K. John. Come hither, Hubert. O my gentle Hubert,
We owe thee much! Within this wall of flesh
There is a soul counts thee her creditor
And with advantage means to pay thy love;
And, my good friend, thy voluntary oath
Lives in this bosom, dearly cherished.
Give me thy hand. I had a thing to say,
But I will fit it with some better time.
By heaven, Hubert, I am almost asham'd
To say what good respect I have of thee.
Hub. I am much bounden to your Majesty.
K. John. Good friend, thou hast no cause to say so yet,
But thou shalt have; and, creep time ne'er so slow,
Yet it shall come for me to do thee good.
I had a thing to say; but let it go.
The sun is in the heaven, and the proud day,
Attended with the pleasures of the world,
Is all too wanton and too full of gauds
To give me audience. If the midnight bell
Did with his iron tongue and brazen mouth
Sound on into the drowsy ear of night;
If this same were a churchyard where we stand,
And thou possessed with a thousand wrongs;
Or if that surly spirit, melancholy,
Had bak'd thy blood and made it heavy, thick,
Which else runs tickling up and down the veins,
Making that idiot, laughter, keep men's eyes
And strain their cheeks to idle merriment,
A passion hateful to my purposes;
Or if that thou couldst see me without eyes,
Hear me without thine ears, and make reply
Without a tongue, using conceit alone,
Without eyes, ears, and harmful sound of words:
Then, in despite of brooded watchful day,
I would into thy bosom pour my thoughts.
But, ah, I will not! Yet I love thee well,
And, by my troth, I think thou lov'st me well.
Hub. So well that what you bid me undertake,
Though that my death were adjunct to my act,
By heaven, I would do it!
K. John. Do not I know thou wouldst?
Good Hubert, Hubert, Hubert, throw thine eye
On yon young boy. I'll tell thee what, my friend,
He is a very serpent in my way;
And wheresoe'er this foot of mine doth tread,
He lies before me. Dost thou understand me?
Thou art his keeper.
Hub. And I'll keep him so
That he shall not offend your Majesty.
K. John. Death.
Hub. My lord?
K. John. A grave.
Hub. He shall not live.
K. John. Enough.
I could be merry now. Hubert, I love thee.
Well, I'll not say what I intend for thee.
Remember. — Madam, fare you well.
I'll send those powers o'er to your Majesty.
Eli. My blessing go with thee!

K. John. [*To Arthur*] For England, cousin! go.
Hubert shall be your man, attend on you
With all true duty. — On toward Calais, ho!
Exeunt.

Scene IV. [*France. The* French King's *tent.*]

Enter *France, Dauphin, Pandulph, Attendants.*

France. So by a roaring tempest on the flood
A whole armado of convicted sail
Is scattered and disjoin'd from fellowship.
Pand. Courage and comfort! All shall yet go well.
France. What can go well when we have run so ill?
Are we not beaten? Is not Angiers lost?
Arthur ta'en prisoner? divers dear friends slain?
And bloody England into England gone,
O'erbearing interruption, spite of France?
Dau. What he hath won, that hath he fortified.
So hot a speed with such advice dispos'd,
Such temperate order in so fierce a course,
Doth want example. Who hath read or heard
Of any kindred action like to this?
France. Well could I bear that England had this praise,
So we could find some pattern of our shame.

Enter *Constance.*

Look who comes here! a grave unto a soul,
Holding th' eternal spirit against her will
In the vile prison of afflicted breath.
I prithee, lady, go away with me.
Const. Lo now! now see the issue of your peace!
France. Patience, good lady! comfort, gentle Constance!
Const. No, I defy all counsel, all redress,
But that which ends all counsel, true redress.
Death, death, O amiable lovely death!
Thou odoriferous stench! sound rottenness!
Arise forth from the couch of lasting night,
Thou hate and terror to prosperity,
And I will kiss thy detestable bones,
And put my eyeballs in thy vaulty brows,
And ring these fingers with thy household worms,
And stop this gap of breath with fulsome dust,
And be a carrion monster like thyself.
Come, grin on me, and I will think thou smil'st
And buss thee as thy wife. Misery's love,
O, come to me!
France. O fair affliction, peace!
Const. No, no, I will not, having breath to cry.
O that my tongue were in the thunder's mouth!
Then with a passion would I shake the world
And rouse from sleep that fell anatomy
Which cannot hear a lady's feeble voice,
Which scorns a modern invocation.
Pand. Lady, you utter madness and not sorrow.
Const. Thou art not holy to belie me so.
I am not mad. This hair I tear is mine;
My name is Constance; I was Geffrey's wife;
Young Arthur is my son, and he is lost.
I am not mad. I would to heaven I were!
For then 'tis like I should forget myself.
O, if I could, what grief should I forget!
Preach some philosophy to make me mad,
And thou shalt be canoniz'd, Cardinal;
For, being not mad, but sensible of grief,
My reasonable part produces reason
How I may be deliver'd of these woes
And teaches me to kill or hang myself.
If I were mad, I should forget my son,
Or madly think a babe of clouts were he.
I am not mad. Too well, too well I feel
The different plague of each calamity.
France. Bind up those tresses. O, what love I note
In the fair multitude of those her hairs!
Where but by chance a silver drop hath fall'n,
Even to that drop ten thousand wiry friends
Do glue themselves in sociable grief,
Like true, inseparable, faithful loves,
Sticking together in calamity.
Const. To England, if you will.
France. Bind up your hairs.
Const. Yes, that I will! and wherefore will I do it? 69
I tore them from their bonds and cried aloud
'O that these hands could so redeem my son
As they have given these hairs their liberty!'
But now I envy at their liberty
And will again commit them to their bonds,
Because my poor child is a prisoner.
And, father Cardinal, I have heard you say
That we shall see and know our friends in heaven.
If that be true, I shall see my boy again;
For since the birth of Cain, the first male child,
To him that did but yesterday suspire,
There was not such a gracious creature born.

But now will canker-sorrow eat my bud
And chase the native beauty from his cheek,
And he will look as hollow as a ghost,
As dim and meagre as an ague's fit;
And so he'll die; and rising so again,
When I shall meet him in the court of heaven
I shall not know him. Therefore never, never
Must I behold my pretty Arthur more!

Pand. You hold too heinous a respect of grief.

Const. He talks to me that never had a son.

France. You are as fond of grief as of your child.

Const. Grief fills the room up of my absent child:
Lies in his bed, walks up and down with me,
Puts on his pretty looks, repeats his words,
Remembers me of all his gracious parts,
Stuffs out his vacant garments with his form.
Then have I reason to be fond of grief?
Fare you well. Had you such a loss as I,
I could give better comfort than you do.
I will not keep this form upon my head
[*Tears her hair.*]
When there is such disorder in my wit.
O Lord! my boy, my Arthur, my fair son!
My life, my joy, my food, my all the world!
My widow-comfort, and my sorrows' cure!
Exit.

France. I fear some outrage, and I'll follow her. *Exit.*

Dau. There's nothing in this world can make me joy.
Life is as tedious as a twice-told tale
Vexing the dull ear of a drowsy man;
And bitter shame hath spoil'd the sweet world's taste,
That it yields naught but shame and bitterness.

Pand. Before the curing of a strong disease,
Even in the instant of repair and health,
The fit is strongest. Evils that take leave
On their departure most of all show evil.
What have you lost by losing of this day?

Dau. All days of glory, joy, and happiness.

Pand. If you had won it, certainly you had.
No, no! When Fortune means to men most good,
She looks upon them with a threat'ning eye.
'Tis strange to think how much King John hath lost
In this which he accounts so clearly won.
Are not you griev'd that Arthur is his prisoner?

Dau. As heartily as he is glad he hath him.

Pand. Your mind is all as youthful as your blood.
Now hear me speak with a prophetic spirit;
For even the breath of what I mean to speak
Shall blow each dust, each straw, each little rub,
Out of the path which shall directly lead
Thy foot to England's throne; and therefore mark.
John hath seiz'd Arthur; and it cannot be
That, whiles warm life plays in that infant's veins,
The misplac'd John should entertain an hour,
One minute, nay, one quiet breath of rest.
A sceptre snatch'd with an unruly hand
Must be as boisterously maintain'd as gain'd;
And he that stands upon a slipp'ry place
Makes nice of no vile hold to stay him up.
That John may stand, then Arthur needs must fall.
So be it, for it cannot be but so.

Dau. But what shall I gain by young Arthur's fall?

Pand. You, in the right of Lady Blanch your wife,
May then make all the claim that Arthur did.

Dau. And lose it, life and all, as Arthur did.

Pand. How green you are and fresh in this old world!
John lays you plots; the times conspire with you;
For he that steeps his safety in true blood
Shall find but bloody safety and untrue.
This act so evilly borne shall cool the hearts
Of all his people and freeze up their zeal,
That none so small advantage shall step forth
To check his reign but they will cherish it;
No natural exhalation in the sky,
No scope of nature, no distemper'd day,
No common wind, no customed event,
But they will pluck away his natural cause
And call them meteors, prodigies, and signs,
Abortives, presages, and tongues of heaven,
Plainly denouncing vengeance upon John.

Dau. May be he will not touch young Arthur's life,
But hold himself safe in his prisonment.

Pand. O, sir, when he shall hear of your approach,
If that young Arthur be not gone already,
Even at that news he dies; and then the hearts
Of all his people shall revolt from him,
And kiss the lips of unacquainted change,
And pick strong matter of revolt and wrath
Out of the bloody fingers' ends of John.
Methinks I see this hurly all on foot.
And O, what better matter breeds for you
Than I have nam'd! The bastard Faulconbridge

Is now in England ransacking the Church,
Offending charity. If but a dozen French
Were there in arms, they would be as a call
To train ten thousand English to their side,
Or as a little snow, tumbled about,
Anon becomes a mountain. O noble Dauphin,
Go with me to the King. 'Tis wonderful
What may be wrought out of their discontent
Now that their souls are topful of offence.
For England go! I will whet on the King.

Dau. Strong reasons make strange actions. Let us go.
If you say ay, the King will not say no.

Exeunt.

ACT IV. Scene I. [*England. A room in a castle.*]

Enter *Hubert* and *Executioners.*

Hub. Heat me these irons hot, and look you stand
Within the arras. When I strike my foot
Upon the bosom of the ground, rush forth
And bind the boy which you shall find with me
Fast to the chair. Be heedful. Hence, and watch.

Exec. I hope your warrant will bear out the deed.

Hub. Uncleanly scruples! Fear not you. Look to't.

[*Exeunt Executioners.*]

Young lad, come forth; I have to say with you.

Enter *Arthur.*

Arth. Good morrow, Hubert.

Hub. Good morrow, little Prince.

Arth. As little Prince, having so great a title
To be more prince, as may be. You are sad.

Hub. Indeed I have been merrier.

Arth. Mercy on me!
Methinks nobody should be sad but I.
Yet I remember, when I was in France,
Young gentlemen would be as sad as night
Only for wantonness. By my christendom,
So I were out of prison and kept sheep,
I should be as merry as the day is long!
And so I would be here but that I doubt
My uncle practises more harm to me.
He is afraid of me, and I of him.
Is it my fault that I was Geffrey's son?
No indeed is't not! and I would to heaven
I were your son, so you would love me, Hubert.

Hub. [*aside*] If I talk to him, with his innocent prate
He will awake my mercy, which lies dead.
Therefore I will be sudden and dispatch.

Arth. Are you sick, Hubert? You look pale to-day.
In sooth I would you were a little sick,
That I might sit all night and watch with you.
I warrant I love you more than you do me.

Hub. [*aside*] His words do take possession of my bosom. —
Read here, young Arthur. [*Shows a paper.*]
[*Aside*] How now, foolish rheum?
Turning dispiteous torture out of door?
I must be brief, lest resolution drop
Out at mine eyes in tender womanish tears. —
Can you not read it? Is it not fair writ?

Arth. Too fairly, Hubert, for so foul effect!
Must you with hot irons burn out both mine eyes?

Hub. Young boy, I must.

Arth. And will you?

Hub. And I will.

Arth. Have you the heart? When your head did but ache,
I knit my handkercher about your brows
(The best I had; a princess wrought it me)
And I did never ask it you again;
And with my hand at midnight held your head;
And like the watchful minutes to the hour
Still and anon cheer'd up the heavy time,
Saying 'What lack you?' and 'Where lies your grief?'
Or 'What good love may I perform for you?'
Many a poor man's son would have lien still
And ne'er have spoke a loving word to you;
But you at your sick service had a prince.
Nay, you may think my love was crafty love
And call it cunning. Do, an if you will.
If heaven be pleas'd that you must use me ill,
Why, then you must. Will you put out mine eyes?
These eyes that never did nor never shall
So much as frown on you?

Hub. I have sworn to do it;
And with hot irons must I burn them out.

Arth. Ah, none but in this iron age would do it!
The iron of itself, though heat redhot,
Approaching near these eyes, would drink my tears
And quench his fiery indignation
Even in the water of mine innocence;

Nay, after that, consume away in rust
But for containing fire to harm mine eyes.
Are you more stubborn-hard than hammer'd iron?
An if an angel should have come to me
And told me Hubert should put out mine eyes,
I would not have believ'd him — no tongue but Hubert's.

Hub. [*stamps*] Come forth!

[Enter *Executioners*, with cord, irons, &c.]

Do as I bid you do.

Arth. O, save me, Hubert, save me! My eyes are out
Even with the fierce looks of these bloody men.

Hub. Give me the iron, I say, and bind him here.

Arth. Alas, what need you be so boist'rous-rough?
I will not struggle, I will stand stone-still.
For heaven sake, Hubert, let me not be bound!
Nay, hear me, Hubert! Drive these men away,
And I will sit as quiet as a lamb;
I will not stir nor winch nor speak a word,
Nor look upon the iron angerly.
Thrust but these men away, and I'll forgive you,
Whatever torment you do put me to.

Hub. Go stand within; let me alone with him.

Exec. I am best pleas'd to be from such a deed. [*Exeunt Executioners.*]

Arth. Alas, I then have chid away my friend!
He hath a stern look, but a gentle heart.
Let him come back, that his compassion may
Give life to yours.

Hub. Come, boy, prepare yourself.

Arth. Is there no remedy?

Hub. None, but to lose your eyes.

Arth. O heaven! that there were but a mote in yours,
A grain, a dust, a gnat, a wandering hair,
Any annoyance in that precious sense!
Then, feeling what small things are boisterous there,
Your vile intent must needs seem horrible.

Hub. Is this your promise? Go to, hold your tongue.

Arth. Hubert, the utterance of a brace of tongues
Must needs want pleading for a pair of eyes.
Let me not hold my tongue; let me not, Hubert!
Or, Hubert, if you will, cut out my tongue,
So I may keep mine eyes. O, spare mine eyes,
Though to no use but still to look on you!
Lo, by my troth, the instrument is cold
And would not harm me.

Hub. I can heat it, boy.

Arth. No, in good sooth! The fire is dead with grief,
Being create for comfort, to be us'd
In undeserv'd extremes. See else yourself!
There is no malice in this burning coal;
The breath of heaven hath blown his spirit out
And strew'd repentant ashes on his head.

Hub. But with my breath I can revive it, boy.

Arth. And if you do, you will but make it blush
And glow with shame of your proceedings, Hubert.
Nay, it perchance will sparkle in your eyes,
And, like a dog that is compell'd to fight,
Snatch at his master that doth tarre him on.
All things that you should use to do me wrong
Deny their office. Only you do lack
That mercy which fierce fire and iron extends,
Creatures of note for mercy-lacking uses.

Hub. Well, see to live! I will not touch thine eyes
For all the treasure that thine uncle owes.
Yet am I sworn, and I did purpose, boy,
With this same very iron to burn them out.

Arth. O, now you look like Hubert! All this while
You were disguised.

Hub. Peace! no more! Adieu.
Your uncle must not know but you are dead.
I'll fill these dogged spies with false reports;
And, pretty child, sleep doubtless and secure
That Hubert, for the wealth of all the world,
Will not offend thee.

Arth. O heaven! I thank you, Hubert.

Hub. Silence! no more! Go closely in with me.
Much danger do I undergo for thee. *Exeunt.*

Scene II. [King John's *Palace*.]

Enter [*King*] *John*, *Pembroke*, *Salisbury*, and other *Lords*. [The *King* takes his state.]

K. John. Here once again we sit, once again crown'd,
And look'd upon, I hope, with cheerful eyes.

Pem. This once again, but that your Highness pleas'd,
Was once superfluous. You were crown'd before,
And that high royalty was ne'er pluck'd off,

Michael Hordern in the sinister role of King John, usurper and murderer

THE LIFE AND DEATH OF KING JOHN

PHOTOGRAPHS BY ANGUS MCBEAN
PRODUCED BY THE OLD VIC COMPANY

Constance (Fay Compton), mother of Arthur

"But thou art fair; and at thy birth, dear boy, Nature and Fortune join'd to make thee great." Constance takes pride in her son Arthur (Nicky Edmett), rightful heir to King Richard *(Act III, Scene I)*

Richard Burton as Philip the Bastard, King John's adjutant and adviser

"Now, say, Chatillon, what would France with us?" In the play's opening scene, King John *(above)* receives Chatillon (David William), the French ambassador *(Act I, Scene I)*

"Why, being younger born, doth he lay claim to thine inheritance?" King John questions the Bastard. Because of Philip's illegitimacy, his younger brother, Robert Faulconbridge (Timothy Bateson), claimed the succession to his father's estate *(Act I, Scene I)*

Before the gates of Angiers, Arthur, accompanied by King Philip of France (William Squire) and the Dauphin (John Neville), greets the duke of Austria (Laurence Hardy), another of his allies *(Act II, Scene I)*

"Peace be to France." The French and English leaders meet before the gates of Angiers *(Act II, Scene I)*

"Thou unadvised scold, I can produce a will that bars the title of thy son." Queen Elinor (Viola Lyel) threatens to bar Constance's son from the throne *(Act II, Scene I)*

"Philip of France, on peril of a curse, let go the hand of that arch-heretic." Pandulph (Paul Daneman) announces the excommunication of King John and forbids the French king to support him *(Act III, Scene I)*

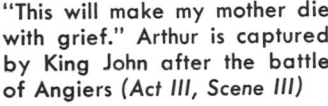

"Hang a calf's-skin on his recreant limbs." The Bastard provokes the duke of Austria by repeating the taunting remark of Constance *(Act III, Scene I)*

"This will make my mother die with grief." Arthur is captured by King John after the battle of Angiers *(Act III, Scene III)*

"He talks to me, that never had a son." The outburst of Constance when Pandulph rebukes her for excessive grief *(Act III, Scene IV)*

"I am much bounden to your Majesty." Assured of the loyalty of Hubert (Edgar Wreford), King John proceeds to give him the task of murdering Arthur *(Act III, Scene III)*

"Will you put out mine eyes?" Prince Arthur pleads for Hubert to be merciful *(Act IV, Scene I)*

"It is a damned and a bloody work." The Bastard comes upon the body of Arthur who has fallen to his death from the castle where he was imprisoned *(Act IV, Scene III)*

"According to the fair play of the world, let me have audience." The Bastard asks Pandulph for news of his intervention *(Act V, Scene II)*

"Strike up our drums, to find this danger out." The Dauphin and Philip the Bastard challenge each other on the eve of the battle of St. Edmundsbury *(Act V, Scene II)*

"I will not keep this form upon my head when there is such disorder in my wit." The terrible grief of Constance on being separated from her son Arthur *(Act III, Scene IV)*

"O cousin! thou art come to set mine eye." Poisoned by a monk, King John dies at Swinstead Abbey. The Bastard and Prince Henry (John Greenwood) attend upon the king in his last hours *(Act V, Scene VII)*

The faiths of men ne'er stained with revolt;
Fresh expectation troubled not the land
With any long'd-for change or better state.

Sal. Therefore, to be possess'd with double pomp,
To guard a title that was rich before,
To gild refined gold, to paint the lily,
To throw a perfume on the violet,
To smooth the ice, or add another hue
Unto the rainbow, or with taper light
To seek the beauteous eye of heaven to garnish,
Is wasteful and ridiculous excess.

Pem. But that your royal pleasure must be done,
This act is as an ancient tale new told
And, in the last repeating, troublesome,
Being urged at a time unseasonable.

Sal. In this the antique and well-noted face
Of plain old form is much disfigured,
And, like a shifted wind unto a sail,
It makes the course of thoughts to fetch about,
Startles and frights consideration,
Makes sound opinion sick, and truth suspected
For putting on so new a fashion'd robe.

Pem. When workmen strive to do better than well,
They do confound their skill in covetousness;
And oftentimes excusing of a fault
Doth make the fault the worse by the excuse,
As patches set upon a little breach
Discredit more in hiding of the fault
Than did the fault before it was so patch'd.

Sal. To this effect, before you were new crown'd,
We breath'd our counsel; but it pleas'd your Highness
To overbear it, and we are all well pleas'd,
Since all and every part of what we would
Doth make a stand at what your Highness will.

K. John. Some reasons of this double coronation
I have possess'd you with, and think them strong;
And more, more strong (then lesser is my fear),
I shall indue you with. Meantime but ask
What you would have reform'd that is not well,
And well shall you perceive how willingly
I will both hear and grant you your requests.

Pem. Then I — as one that am the tongue of these
To sound the purposes of all their hearts,
Both for myself and them, but chief of all,
Your safety, for the which myself and them
Bend their best studies — heartily request
Th' enfranchisement of Arthur, whose restraint
Doth move the murmuring lips of discontent
To break into this dangerous argument: —
If what in rest you have in right you hold,
Why then your fears, which (as they say) attend
The steps of wrong, should move you to mew up
Your tender kinsman, and to choke his days
With barbarous ignorance and deny his youth
The rich advantage of good exercise.
That the time's enemies may not have this
To grace occasions, let it be our suit
That you have bid us ask his liberty;
Which for our goods we do no further ask
Than whereupon our weal, on you depending,
Counts it your weal he have his liberty.

Enter *Hubert.*

K. John. Let it be so. I do commit his youth
To your direction. [*Talks with Hubert aside.*]
Hubert, what news with you?

Pem. This is the man should do the bloody deed;
He show'd his warrant to a friend of mine.
The image of a wicked heinous fault
Lives in his eye; that close aspect of his
Does show the mood of a much-troubled breast;
And I do fearfully believe 'tis done,
What we so fear'd he had a charge to do.

Sal. The colour of the King doth come and go
Between his purpose and his conscience,
Like heralds 'twixt two dreadful battles set.
His passion is so ripe it needs must break.

Pem. And when it breaks, I fear will issue thence
The foul corruption of a sweet child's death.

K. John. We cannot hold mortality's strong hand.
Good lords, although my will to give is living,
The suit which you demand is gone and dead.
He tells us Arthur is deceas'd to-night.

Sal. Indeed we fear'd his sickness was past cure.

Pem. Indeed we heard how near his death he was
Before the child himself felt he was sick.
This must be answer'd, either here or hence.

K. John. Why do you bend such solemn brows on me?
Think you I bear the shears of destiny?
Have I commandment on the pulse of life?

Sal. It is apparent foul play, and 'tis shame
That greatness should so grossly offer it.
So thrive it in your game! and so farewell.

Pem. Stay yet, Lord Salisbury. I'll go with thee

And find th' inheritance of this poor child,
His little kingdom of a forced grave.
That blood which ow'd the breadth of all this isle
Three foot of it doth hold — bad world the while!
This must not be thus borne; this will break out
To all our sorrows, and ere long I doubt.
Exeunt [*Lords*].

K. John. They burn in indignation. I repent.

Enter *Messenger*.

There is no sure foundation set on blood,
No certain life achiev'd by others' death. —
A fearful eye thou hast. Where is that blood,
That I have seen inhabit in those cheeks?
So foul a sky clears not without a storm.
Pour down thy weather. How goes all in France?

Mess. From France to England. Never such a pow'r
For any foreign preparation
Was levied in the body of a land.
The copy of your speed is learn'd by them;
For when you should be told they do prepare,
The tidings comes that they are all arriv'd.

K. John. O, where hath our intelligence been drunk?
Where hath it slept? Where is my mother's care,
That such an army could be drawn in France
And she not hear of it?

Mess. My liege, her ear
Is stopp'd with dust. The first of April died
Your noble mother; and, as I hear, my lord,
The Lady Constance in a frenzy died
Three days before. But this from rumour's tongue
I idly heard; if true or false I know not.

K. John. Withhold thy speed, dreadful Occasion!
O, make a league with me, till I have pleas'd
My discontented peers! What? mother dead?
How wildly then walks my estate in France!
Under whose conduct came those pow'rs of France
That thou for truth giv'st out are landed here?

Mess. Under the Dauphin.

Enter *Bastard* and *Peter of Pomfret*.

K. John. Thou hast made me giddy
With these ill tidings. — Now? What says the world
To your proceedings? Do not seek to stuff
My head with more ill news; for it is full.

Bast. But if you be afeard to hear the worst,
Then let the worst, unheard, fall on your head!

K. John. Bear with me, cousin, for I was amaz'd
Under the tide; but now I breathe again
Aloft the flood, and can give audience
To any tongue, speak it of what it will.

Bast. How I have sped among the clergymen
The sums I have collected shall express.
But as I travell'd hither through the land,
I find the people strangely fantasied,
Possess'd with rumours, full of idle dreams,
Not knowing what they fear, but full of fear.
And here's a prophet that I brought with me
From forth the streets of Pomfret, whom I found
With many hundreds treading on his heels;
To whom he sung in rude harsh-sounding rhymes
That, ere the next Ascension Day at noon,
Your Highness should deliver up your crown.

K. John. Thou idle dreamer, wherefore didst thou so?

Peter. Foreknowing that the truth will fall out so.

K. John. Hubert, away with him! imprison him,
And on that day at noon whereon he says
I shall yield up my crown, let him be hang'd.
Deliver him to safety, and return,
For I must use thee.
[*Exit Hubert with Peter.*]
O my gentle cousin,
Hear'st thou the news abroad, who are arriv'd?

Bast. The French, my lord. Men's mouths are full of it.
Besides, I met Lord Bigot and Lord Salisbury
With eyes as red as new-enkindled fire,
And others more, going to seek the grave
Of Arthur, whom they say is kill'd to-night
On your suggestion.

K. John. Gentle kinsman, go
And thrust thyself into their companies.
I have a way to win their loves again.
Bring them before me.

Bast. I will seek them out.

K. John. Nay, but make haste! the better foot before.
O, let me have no subject enemies
When adverse foreigners affright my towns
With dreadful pomp of stout invasion!
Be Mercury, set feathers to thy heels,
And fly (like thought) from them to me again.

Bast. The spirit of the time shall teach me speed. *Exit.*

K. John. Spoke like a sprightful noble gentleman.

Go after him; for he perhaps shall need
Some messenger betwixt me and the peers,
And be thou he.

Mess. With all my heart, my liege. [*Exit.*]

K. John. My mother dead?

Enter *Hubert.*

Hub. My lord, they say five moons were seen to-night;
Four fixed, and the fifth did whirl about
The other four in wondrous motion.

K. John. Five moons?

Hub. Old men and beldames in the streets
Do prophesy upon it dangerously.
Young Arthur's death is common in their mouths;
And when they talk of him, they shake their heads
And whisper one another in the ear;
And he that speaks doth gripe the hearer's wrist,
Whilst he that hears makes fearful action
With wrinkled brows, with nods, with rolling eyes.
I saw a smith stand with his hammer, thus,
The whilst his iron did on the anvil cool,
With open mouth swallowing a tailor's news,
Who, with his shears and measure in his hand,
Standing on slippers, which his nimble haste
Had falsely thrust upon contrary feet,
Told of a many thousand warlike French
That were embattailed and rank'd in Kent.
Another lean unwash'd artificer
Cuts off his tale and talks of Arthur's death.

K. John. Why seek'st thou to possess me with these fears?
Why urgest thou so oft young Arthur's death?
Thy hand hath murd'red him. I had a mighty cause
To wish him dead, but thou hadst none to kill him.

Hub. No had, my lord? Why, did you not provoke me?

K. John. It is the curse of kings to be attended
By slaves that take their humours for a warrant
To break within the bloody house of life,
And on the winking of authority
To understand a law; to know the meaning
Of dangerous majesty when perchance it frowns
More upon humour than advis'd respect.

Hub. Here is your hand and seal for what I did.

K. John. O, when the last accompt 'twixt heaven and earth
Is to be made, then shall this hand and seal
Witness against us to damnation!
How oft the sight of means to do ill deeds
Make deeds ill done! Hadst not thou been by,
A fellow by the hand of nature mark'd,
Quoted, and sign'd to do a deed of shame,
This murther had not come into my mind;
But, taking note of thy abhorr'd aspect,
Finding thee fit for bloody villany,
Apt, liable to be employ'd in danger,
I faintly broke with thee of Arthur's death;
And thou, to be endeared to a king,
Made it no conscience to destroy a prince.

Hub. My lord —

K. John. Hadst thou but shook thy head or made a pause
When I spake darkly what I purposed,
Or turn'd an eye of doubt upon my face,
As bid me tell my tale in express words,
Deep shame had struck me dumb, made me break off,
And those thy fears might have wrought fears in me.
But thou didst understand me by my signs
And didst in signs again parley with sin;
Yea, without stop, didst let thy heart consent,
And consequently thy rude hand to act
The deed which both our tongues held vile to name.
Out of my sight, and never see me more!
My nobles leave me, and my state is brav'd,
Even at my gates, with ranks of foreign pow'rs.
Nay, in the body of this fleshly land,
This kingdom, this confine of blood and breath,
Hostility and civil tumult reigns
Between my conscience and my cousin's death.

Hub. Arm you against your other enemies;
I'll make a peace between your soul and you.
Young Arthur is alive. This hand of mine
Is yet a maiden and an innocent hand,
Not painted with the crimson spots of blood.
Within this bosom never ent'red yet
The dreadful motion of a murderous thought;
And you have slander'd nature in my form,
Which, howsoever rude exteriorly,
Is yet the cover of a fairer mind
Than to be butcher of an innocent child.

K. John. Doth Arthur live? O, haste thee to the peers!
Throw this report on their incensed rage
And make them tame to their obedience!
Forgive the comment that my passion made
Upon thy feature; for my rage was blind,
And foul imaginary eyes of blood
Presented thee more hideous than thou art.

O, answer not! but to my closet bring
The angry lords with all expedient haste!
I conjure thee but slowly; run more fast.
Exeunt.

Scene III. [*Before the castle.*]

Enter *Arthur* on the walls, [disguised as a shipboy].

Arth. The wall is high, and yet will I leap down.
Good ground, be pitiful and hurt me not!
There's few or none do know me; if they did,
This shipboy's semblance hath disguis'd me quite.
I am afraid, and yet I'll venture it.
If I get down and do not break my limbs,
I'll find a thousand shifts to get away.
As good to die and go, as die and stay.
[*Leaps down.*]
O me! my uncle's spirit is in these stones.
Heaven take my soul, and England keep my bones! *Dies.*

Enter *Pembroke, Salisbury,* and *Bigot.*

Sal. Lords, I will meet him at Saint Edmundsbury.
It is our safety, and we must embrace
This gentle offer of the perilous time.
Pem. Who brought that letter from the Cardinal?
Sal. The Count Melun, a noble lord of France,
Whose private with me of the Dauphin's love
Is much more general than these lines import.
Big. To-morrow morning let us meet him then.
Sal. Or rather then set forward; for 'twill be
Two long days' journey, lords, or ere we meet.

Enter *Bastard.*

Bast. Once more to-day well met, distemper'd lords!
The King by me requests your presence straight.
Sal. The King hath dispossess'd himself of us.
We will not line his thin bestained cloak
With our pure honours, nor attend the foot
That leaves the print of blood where'er it walks.
Return and tell him so. We know the worst.
Bast. Whate'er you think, good words I think were best.
Sal. Our griefs, and not our manners, reason now.
Bast. But there is little reason in your grief.
Therefore 'twere reason you had manners now.
Pem. Sir, sir, impatience hath his privilege.
Bast. 'Tis true — to hurt his master, no man else.
Sal. This is the prison. What is he lies here?
Pem. O death, made proud with pure and princely beauty!
The earth had not a hole to hide this deed.
Sal. Murther, as hating what himself hath done,
Doth lay it open to urge on revenge.
Big. Or, when he doom'd this beauty to a grave,
Found it too precious-princely for a grave.
Sal. Sir Richard, what think you? Have you beheld,
Or have you read or heard, or could you think?
Or do you almost think, although you see,
That you do see? Could thought, without this object,
Form such another? This is the very top,
The heighth, the crest, or crest unto the crest,
Of murther's arms. This is the bloodiest shame,
The wildest savagery, the vilest stroke
That ever wall-ey'd wrath or staring rage
Presented to the tears of soft remorse.
Pem. All murthers past do stand excus'd in this;
And this, so sole and so unmatchable,
Shall give a holiness, a purity,
To the yet unbegotten sin of times,
And prove a deadly bloodshed but a jest,
Exampled by this heinous spectacle.
Bast. It is a damned and a bloody work,
The graceless action of a heavy hand,
If that it be the work of any hand.
Sal. If that it be the work of any hand?
We had a kind of light what would ensue.
It is the shameful work of Hubert's hand,
The practice and the purpose of the King;
From whose obedience I forbid my soul,
Kneeling before this ruin of sweet life,
And breathing to his breathless excellence
The incense of a vow, a holy vow,
Never to taste the pleasures of the world,
Never to be infected with delight
Nor conversant with ease and idleness,
Till I have set a glory to this hand
By giving it the worship of revenge.
Pem., Big. Our souls religiously confirm thy words.

Enter *Hubert.*

Hub. Lords, I am hot with haste in seeking you.
Arthur doth live; the King hath sent for you.

Sal. O, he is bold, and blushes not at death.
Avaunt, thou hateful villain, get thee gone!
Hub. I am no villain.
Sal. Must I rob the law?
[*Draws.*]
Bast. Your sword is bright, sir; put it up again.
Sal. Not till I sheathe it in a murtherer's skin.
Hub. Stand back, Lord Salisbury! stand back, I say!
By heaven, I think my sword's as sharp as yours. [*Draws.*]
I would not have you, lord, forget yourself
Nor tempt the danger of my true defence,
Lest I, by marking of your rage, forget
Your worth, your greatness, and nobility.
Big. Out, dunghill! Dar'st thou brave a nobleman?
Hub. Not for my life; but yet I dare defend
My innocent life against an emperor.
Sal. Thou art a murtherer.
Hub. Do not prove me so.
Yet I am none! Whose tongue soe'er speaks false,
Not truly speaks; who speaks not truly, lies.
Pem. Cut him to pieces!
Bast. Keep the peace, I say.
Sal. Stand by, or I shall gall you, Faulconbridge.
Bast. Thou wert better gall the devil, Salisbury.
If thou but frown on me, or stir thy foot,
Or teach thy hasty spleen to do me shame,
I'll strike thee dead. Put up thy sword betime,
Or I'll so maul you and your toasting iron
That you shall think the devil is come from hell.
Big. What wilt thou do, renowned Faulconbridge?
Second a villain and a murtherer?
Hub. Lord Bigot, I am none.
Big. Who kill'd this prince?
Hub. 'Tis not an hour since I left him well.
I honour'd him, I lov'd him, and will weep
My date of life out for his sweet live's loss.
Sal. Trust not those cunning waters of his eyes,
For villany is not without such rheum;
And he, long traded in it, makes it seem
Like rivers of remorse and innocency.
Away with me, all you whose souls abhor
Th' uncleanly savours of a slaughterhouse,
For I am stifled with this smell of sin.
Big. Away toward Bury, to the Dauphin there!
Pem. There, tell the King, he may inquire us out.
Exeunt Lords.
Bast. Here's a good world! Knew you of this fair work?
Beyond the infinite and boundless reach
Of mercy, if thou didst this deed of death,
Art thou damn'd, Hubert.
Hub. Do but hear me, sir!
Bast. Ha! I'll tell thee what.
Thou'rt damn'd as black — nay, nothing is so black!
Thou art more deep damn'd than Prince Lucifer.
There is not yet so ugly a fiend of hell
As thou shalt be, if thou didst kill this child.
Hub. Upon my soul —
Bast. If thou didst but consent
To this most cruel act, do but despair;
And if thou want'st a cord, the smallest thread
That ever spider twisted from her womb
Will serve to strangle thee; a rush will be a beam
To hang thee on. Or wouldst thou drown thyself,
Put but a little water in a spoon,
And it shall be as all the ocean,
Enough to stifle such a villain up.
I do suspect thee very grievously.
Hub. If I in act, consent, or sin of thought
Be guilty of the stealing that sweet breath
Which was embounded in this beauteous clay,
Let hell want pains enough to torture me!
I left him well.
Bast. Go, bear him in thine arms.
I am amaz'd, methinks, and lose my way
Among the thorns and dangers of this world.
How easy dost thou take all England up!
From forth this morsel of dead royalty
The life, the right, and truth of all this realm
Is fled to heaven; and England now is left
To tug and scamble, and to part by th' teeth
The unowed interest of proud-swelling state.
Now for the bare-pick'd bone of majesty
Doth dogged war bristle his angry crest
And snarleth in the gentle eyes of peace.
Now powers from home and discontents at home
Meet in one line; and vast confusion waits,
As doth a raven on a sick-fall'n beast,
The imminent decay of wrested pomp.
Now happy he whose cloak and cincture can
Hold out this tempest! Bear away that child
And follow me with speed. I'll to the King.
A thousand businesses are brief in hand,
And heaven itself doth frown upon the land.
Exeunt.

Act V. Scene I. [King John's *Palace*.]

Enter *King John* and *Pandulph, Attendants.*

K. John. [*Gives the crown*] Thus have I yielded up into your hand
The circle of my glory.
Pand. Take again
From this my hand, as holding of the Pope
Your sovereign greatness and authority.
[*Gives back the crown.*]
K. John. Now keep your holy word: go meet the French,
And from his Holiness use all your power
To stop their marches fore we are inflam'd.
Our discontented counties do revolt;
Our people quarrel with obedience,
Swearing allegiance and the love of soul
To stranger blood, to foreign royalty.
This inundation of mistemp'red humour
Rests by you only to be qualified.
Then pause not; for the present time's so sick
That present med'cine must be minist'red
Or overthrow incurable ensues.
Pand. It was my breath that blew this tempest up,
Upon your stubborn usage of the Pope;
But since you are a gentle convertite,
My tongue shall hush again this storm of war
And make fair weather in your blust'ring land.
On this Ascension Day, remember well,
Upon your oath of service to the Pope,
Go I to make the French lay down their arms.
Exit.
K. John. Is this Ascension Day? Did not the prophet
Say that before Ascension Day at noon
My crown I should give off? Even so I have.
I did suppose it should be on constraint;
But (heav'n be thank'd!) it is but voluntary.

Enter *Bastard.*

Bast. All Kent hath yielded; nothing there holds out
But Dover Castle. London hath receiv'd,
Like a kind host, the Dauphin and his powers.
Your nobles will not hear you, but are gone
To offer service to your enemy;
And wild amazement hurries up and down
The little number of your doubtful friends.
K. John. Would not my lords return to me again
After they heard young Arthur was alive?
Bast. They found him dead and cast into the streets —
An empty casket where the jewel of life
By some damn'd hand was robb'd and ta'en away.
K. John. That villain Hubert told me he did live.
Bast. So, on my soul, he did, for aught he knew.
But wherefore do you droop? Why look you sad?
Be great in act, as you have been in thought.
Let not the world see fear and sad distrust
Govern the motion of a kingly eye.
Be stirring as the time; be fire with fire;
Threaten the threat'ner and outface the brow
Of bragging horror. So shall inferior eyes,
That borrow their behaviours from the great,
Grow great by your example and put on
The dauntless spirit of resolution.
Away, and glister like the god of war
When he intendeth to become the field.
Show boldness and aspiring confidence.
What, shall they seek the lion in his den,
And fright him there? and make him tremble there?
O, let it not be said! Forage, and run
To meet displeasure farther from the doors
And grapple with him ere he come so nigh.
K. John. The legate of the Pope hath been with me,
And I have made a happy peace with him,
And he hath promis'd to dismiss the powers
Led by the Dauphin.
Bast. O inglorious league!
Shall we, upon the footing of our land,
Send fair-play orders and make compremise,
Insinuation, parley, and base truce
To arms invasive? Shall a beardless boy,
A cock'red silken wanton, brave our fields
And flesh his spirit in a warlike soil,
Mocking the air with colours idly spread,
And find no check? Let us, my liege, to arms.
Perchance the Cardinal cannot make your peace;
Or if he do, let it at least be said
They saw we had a purpose of defence.
K. John. Have thou the ordering of this present time.
Bast. Away, then, with good courage! Yet I know
Our party may well meet a prouder foe. *Exeunt.*

Scene II. [*Near St. Edmundsbury. The* Dauphin's *camp.*]

Enter, in arms, *Dauphin, Salisbury, Melun, Pembroke, Bigot, Soldiers.*

Dau. My Lord Melun, let this be copied out
And keep it safe for our remembrance.
Return the precedent to these lords again,
That, having our fair order written down,
Both they and we, perusing o'er these notes,
May know wherefore we took the sacrament
And keep our faiths firm and inviolable.

Sal. Upon our sides it never shall be broken.
And, noble Dauphin, albeit we swear
A voluntary zeal, an unurg'd faith,
To your proceedings, yet believe me, Prince,
I am not glad that such a sore of time
Should seek a plaster by contemn'd revolt
And heal the inveterate canker of one wound
By making many. O, it grieves my soul
That I must draw this metal from my side
To be a widow-maker! O, and there
Where honourable rescue and defence
Cries out upon the name of Salisbury!
But such is the infection of the time
That, for the health and physic of our right,
We cannot deal but with the very hand
Of stern injustice and confused wrong.
And is't not pity, O my grieved friends,
That we, the sons and children of this isle,
Were born to see so sad an hour as this,
Wherein we step after a stranger, march
Upon her gentle bosom, and fill up
Her enemies' ranks (I must withdraw and weep
Upon the spot of this enforced cause)
To grace the gentry of a land remote
And follow unacquainted colours here?
What, here? O nation, that thou couldst remove!
That Neptune's arms, who clippeth thee about,
Would bear thee from the knowledge of thyself
And gripple thee unto a pagan shore,
Where these two Christian armies might combine
The blood of malice in a vein of league,
And not to spend it so unneighbourly!

Dau. A noble temper dost thou show in this,
And great affections wrestling in thy bosom
Doth make an earthquake of nobility.
O, what a noble combat hast thou fought
Between compulsion and a brave respect!
Let me wipe off this honourable dew
That silverly doth progress on thy cheeks.
My heart hath melted at a lady's tears,
Being an ordinary inundation;
But this effusion of such manly drops,
This show'r, blown up by tempest of the soul,
Startles mine eyes and makes me more amaz'd
Than had I seen the vaulty top of heaven
Figur'd quite o'er with burning meteors.
Lift up thy brow, renowned Salisbury,
And with a great heart heave away this storm.
Commend these waters to those baby eyes
That never saw the giant world enrag'd,
Nor met with fortune other than at feasts,
Full of warm blood, of mirth, of gossipping.
Come, come! for thou shalt thrust thy hand as deep
Into the purse of rich prosperity
As Lewis himself. So, nobles, shall you all
That knit your sinews to the strength of mine.

Enter *Pundulph.*

And even there, methinks an angel spake.
Look where the holy legate comes apace,
To give us warrant from the hand of heaven
And on our actions set the name of right
With holy breath.

Pand. Hail, noble Prince of France!
The next is this: King John hath reconcil'd
Himself to Rome; his spirit is come in,
That so stood out against the holy Church,
The great metropolis and see of Rome.
Therefore thy threat'ning colours now wind up
And tame the savage spirit of wild war,
That, like a lion fostered up at hand,
It may lie gently at the foot of peace
And be no further harmful than in show.

Dau. Your Grace shall pardon me, I will not back.
I am too high-born to be propertied,
To be a secondary at control,
Or useful servingman and instrument
To any sovereign state throughout the world.
Your breath first kindled the dead coal of wars
Between this chastis'd kingdom and myself
And brought in matter that should feed this fire;
And now 'tis far too huge to be blown out
With that same weak wind which enkindled it.
You taught me how to know the face of right,
Acquainted me with interest to this land,
Yea, thrust this enterprise into my heart;
And come ye now to tell me John hath made
His peace with Rome? What is that peace to me?

I, by the honour of my marriage bed,
After young Arthur claim this land for mine;
And, now it is half conquer'd, must I back
Because that John hath made his peace with Rome?
Am I Rome's slave? What penny hath Rome borne,
What men provided, what munition sent
To underprop this action? Is't not I
That undergo this charge? Who else but I,
And such as to my claim are liable,
Sweat in this business and maintain this war?
Have I not heard these islanders shout out
'Vive le roi!' as I have bank'd their towns?
Have I not here the best cards for the game
To win this easy match, play'd for a crown?
And shall I now give o'er the yielded set?
No, no! on my soul, it never shall be said!

Pand. You look but on the outside of this work.

Dau. Outside or inside, I will not return
Till my attempt so much be glorified
As to my ample hope was promised
Before I drew this gallant head of war,
And cull'd these fiery spirits from the world
To outlook conquest, and to win renown
Even in the jaws of danger and of death.
[*Trumpet sounds.*]
What lusty trumpet thus doth summon us?

Enter *Bastard*, [attended].

Bast. According to the fair play of the world,
Let me have audience. I am sent to speak.
My holy Lord of Milan, from the King
I come to learn how you have dealt for him;
And as you answer, I do know the scope
And warrant limited unto my tongue.

Pand. The Dauphin is too wilful-opposite
And will not temporize with my entreaties.
He flatly says he'll not lay down his arms.

Bast. By all the blood that ever fury breath'd,
The youth says well! Now hear our English King,
For thus his royalty doth speak in me:
He is prepar'd — and reason too he should;
This apish and unmannerly approach,
This harness'd masque and unadvised revel,
This unhair'd sauciness and boyish troop,
The King doth smile at, and is well prepar'd
To whip this dwarfish war, these pygmy arms,
From out the circle of his territories.
That hand which had the strength, even at your door,
To cudgel you and make you take the hatch,
To dive like buckets in concealed wells,
To crouch in litter of your stable planks,
To lie like pawns lock'd up in chests and trunks,
To hug with swine, to seek sweet safety out
In vaults and prisons, and to thrill and shake
Even at the crying of your nation's crow,
Thinking his voice an armed Englishman —
Shall that victorious hand be feebled here
That in your chambers gave you chastisement?
No! Know the gallant monarch is in arms
And like an eagle o'er his aery tow'rs
To souse annoyance that comes near his nest.
And you degenerate, you ingrate revolts,
You bloody Neroes, ripping up the womb
Of your dear Mother England, blush for shame!
For your own ladies, and pale-visag'd maids,
Like Amazons, come tripping after drums,
Their thimbles into armed gauntlets change,
Their neelds to lances, and their gentle hearts
To fierce and bloody inclination.

Dau. There end thy brave, and turn thy face in peace.
We grant thou canst outscold us. Fare thee well.
We hold our time too precious to be spent
With such a brabbler.

Pand. Give me leave to speak.

Bast. No, I will speak.

Dau. We will attend to neither.
Strike up the drums, and let the tongue of war
Plead for our interest and our being here.

Bast. Indeed, your drums, being beaten, will cry out;
And so shall you, being beaten. Do but start
An echo with the clamour of thy drum,
And even at hand a drum is ready brac'd
That shall reverberate all, as loud as thine.
Sound but another, and another shall,
As loud as thine, rattle the welkin's ear
And mock the deep-mouth'd thunder; for at hand
(Not trusting to this halting legate here,
Whom he hath us'd rather for sport than need)
Is warlike John; and in his forehead sits
A bare-ribb'd death, whose office is this day
To feast upon whole thousands of the French.

Dau. Strike up our drums to find this danger out.

Bast. And thou shalt find it, Dauphin; do not doubt. *Exeunt.*

Scene III. [*Near Saint Edmundsbury. A field of battle.*]

Alarums. Enter [*King*] *John* and *Hubert.*

K. John. How goes the day with us? O, tell me, Hubert.
Hub. Badly, I fear. How fares your Majesty?
K. John. This fever that hath troubled me so long
Lies heavy on me. O, my heart is sick!

Enter a *Messenger.*

Mess. My lord, your valiant kinsman, Faulconbridge,
Desires your Majesty to leave the field
And send him word by me which way you go.
K. John. Tell him toward Swinstead, to the abbey there.
Mess. Be of good comfort; for the great supply
That was expected by the Dauphin here
Are wrack'd three nights ago on Goodwin Sands.
This news was brought to Richard but even now.
The French fight coldly, and retire themselves.
K. John. Ay me, this tyrant fever burns me up
And will not let me welcome this good news!
Set on toward Swinstead. To my litter straight.
Weakness possesseth me, and I am faint.
Exeunt.

Scene IV. [*Another part of the field.*]

Enter *Salisbury, Pembroke,* and *Bigot.*

Sal. I did not think the King so stor'd with friends.
Pem. Up once again! put spirit in the French.
If they miscarry, we miscarry too.
Sal. That misbegotten devil, Faulconbridge,
In spite of spite, alone upholds the day.
Pem. They say King John, sore sick, hath left the field.

Enter *Melun* wounded.

Mel. Lead me to the revolts of England here.
Sal. When we were happy we had other names.
Pem. It is the Count Melun.
Sal. Wounded to death.
Mel. Fly, noble English; you are bought and sold!
Unthread the rude eye of rebellion
And welcome home again discarded faith.
Seek out King John, and fall before his feet;
For if the French be lords of this loud day,
He means to recompense the pains you take
By cutting off your heads. Thus hath he sworn,
And I with him, and many moe with me,
Upon the altar at Saint Edmundsbury,
Even on that altar where we swore to you
Dear amity and everlasting love.
Sal. May this be possible? May this be true?
Mel. Have I not hideous death within my view,
Retaining but a quantity of life,
Which bleeds away, even as a form of wax
Resolveth from his figure 'gainst the fire?
What in the world should make me now deceive,
Since I must lose the use of all deceit?
Why should I then be false, since it is true
That I must die here, and live hence, by truth?
I say again, if Lewis do win the day,
He is forsworn if e'er those eyes of yours
Behold another day break in the East;
But even this night, whose black contagious breath
Already smokes about the burning crest
Of the old, feeble, and day-wearied sun —
Even this ill night, your breathing shall expire,
Paying the fine of rated treachery
Even with a treacherous fine of all your lives,
If Lewis by your assistance win the day.
Commend me to one Hubert, with your king.
The love of him, and this respect besides,
For that my grandsire was an Englishman,
Awakes my conscience to confess all this.
In lieu whereof I pray you bear me hence
From forth the noise and rumour of the field,
Where I may think the remnant of my thoughts
In peace, and part this body and my soul
With contemplation and devout desires.
Sal. We do believe thee; and beshrew my soul
But I do love the favour and the form
Of this most fair occasion, by the which
We will untread the steps of damned flight
And, like a bated and retired flood,
Leaving our rankness and irregular course,
Stoop low within those bounds we have o'erlook'd
And calmly run on in obedience
Even to our ocean, to our great King John.
My arm shall give thee help to bear thee hence,
For I do see the cruel pangs of death
Right in thine eye. Away, my friends! New flight!
And happy newness, that intends old right!
Exeunt, [*leading off Melun*].

Scene V. [*The French camp.*]

Enter *Dauphin* and his *Train.*

Dau. The sun of heaven, methought, was loath to set,
But stay'd and made the western welkin blush,
When English measure backward their own ground
In faint retire. O, bravely came we off
When with a volley of our needless shot,
After such bloody toil, we bid good night
And wound our tott'ring colours clearly up,
Last in the field and almost lords of it!

Enter a *Messenger.*

Mess. Where is my prince, the Dauphin?
Dau. Here. What news?
Mess. The Count Melun is slain. The English lords
By his persuasion are again fall'n off,
And your supply, which you have wish'd so long,
Are cast away and sunk on Goodwin Sands.
Dau. Ah, foul shrewd news! Beshrew thy very heart!
I did not think to be so sad to-night
As this hath made me. Who was he that said
King John did fly an hour or two before
The stumbling night did part our weary pow'rs?
Mess. Whoever spoke it, it is true, my lord.
Dau. Well; keep good quarter and good care to-night.
The day shall not be up so soon as I
To try the fair adventure of to-morrow. *Exeunt.*

Scene VI. [*An open place near Swinstead Abbey.*]

Enter *Bastard* and *Hubert,* severally.

Hub. Who's there? Speak, ho! speak quickly, or I shoot!
Bast. A friend. What art thou?
Hub. Of the part of England.
Bast. Whither dost thou go?
Hub. What's that to thee? Why may not I demand
Of thine affairs as well as thou of mine?
Bast. Hubert, I think.
Hub. Thou hast a perfect thought.
I will upon all hazards well believe
Thou art my friend that know'st my tongue so well.
Who art thou?
Bast. Who thou wilt; and if thou please,
Thou mayst befriend me so much as to think
I come one way of the Plantagenets.
Hub. Unkind remembrance! thou and eyeless night
Have done me shame. Brave soldier, pardon me
That any accent breaking from thy tongue
Should scape the true acquaintance of mine ear.
Bast. Come, come! Sans compliment, what news abroad?
Hub. Why, here walk I in the black brow of night
To find you out.
Bast. Brief then! and what's the news?
Hub. O my sweet sir, news fitting to the night,
Black, fearful, comfortless, and horrible.
Bast. Show me the very wound of this ill news.
I am no woman; I'll not swound at it.
Hub. The King, I fear, is poison'd by a monk.
I left him almost speechless, and broke out
To acquaint you with this evil, that you might
The better arm you to the sudden time
Than if you had at leisure known of this.
Bast. How did he take it? Who did taste to him?
Hub. A monk, I tell you, a resolved villain,
Whose bowels suddenly burst out. The King
Yet speaks and peradventure may recover.
Bast. Who didst thou leave to tend his Majesty?
Hub. Why, know you not? The lords are all come back,
And brought Prince Henry in their company,
At whose request the King hath pardon'd them,
And they are all about his Majesty.
Bast. Withhold thine indignation, mighty heaven,
And tempt us not to bear above our power!
I'll tell thee, Hubert, half my power this night,
Passing these flats, are taken by the tide;
These Lincoln Washes have devoured them;
Myself, well mounted, hardly have escap'd.
Away before! conduct me to the King;
I doubt he will be dead or ere I come. *Exeunt.*

Scene VII. [*The orchard of Swinstead Abbey.*]

Enter *Prince Henry*, *Salisbury*, and *Bigot*.

Hen. It is too late. The life of all his blood
Is touch'd corruptibly; and his pure brain
(Which some suppose the soul's frail dwelling house)
Doth, by the idle comments that it makes,
Foretell the ending of mortality.

Enter *Pembroke*.

Pem. His Highness yet doth speak, and holds belief
That, being brought into the open air,
It would allay the burning quality
Of that fell poison which assaileth him.
Hen. Let him be brought into the orchard here.
[*Exit Bigot.*]
Doth he still rage?
Pem. He is more patient
Than when you left him. Even now he sung.
Hen. O vanity of sickness! Fierce extremes
In their continuance will not feel themselves.
Death, having prey'd upon the outward parts,
Leaves them insensible; and his siege is now
Against the mind, the which he pricks and wounds
With many legions of strange fantasies,
Which, in their throng and press to that last hold,
Confound themselves. 'Tis strange that death should sing!
I am the cygnet to this pale faint swan
Who chants a doleful hymn to his own death
And from the organ-pipe of frailty sings
His soul and body to their lasting rest.
Sal. Be of good comfort, Prince; for you are born
To set a form upon that indigest
Which he hath left so shapeless and so rude.

[*King*] *John* brought in [by *Attendants*, *Bigot* accompanying him].

K. John. Ay, marry, now my soul hath elbow room.
It would not out at windows nor at doors.
There is so hot a summer in my bosom
That all my bowels crumble up to dust.
I am a scribbled form drawn with a pen
Upon a parchment, and against this fire
Do I shrink up.
Hen. How fares your Majesty?
K. John. Poison'd, ill fare! dead, forsook, cast off!
And none of you will bid the winter come
To thrust his icy fingers in my maw,
Nor let my kingdom's rivers take their course
Through my burn'd bosom, nor entreat the North
To make his bleak winds kiss my parched lips
And comfort me with cold. I do not ask you much;
I beg cold comfort; and you are so strait
And so ingrateful you deny me that.
Hen. O that there were some virtue in my tears
That might relieve you!
K. John. The salt in them is hot.
Within me is a hell, and there the poison
Is, as a fiend, confin'd to tyrannize
On unreprievable condemned blood.

Enter *Bastard*.

Bast. O, I am scalded with my violent motion
And spleen of speed to see your Majesty!
K. John. O cousin, thou art come to set mine eye!
The tackle of my heart is crack'd and burnt,
And all the shrouds wherewith my life should sail
Are turned to one thread, one little hair.
My heart hath one poor string to stay it by,
Which holds but till thy news be uttered;
And then all this thou seest is but a clod,
And module of confounded royalty.
Bast. The Dauphin is preparing hitherward,
Where God he knows how we shall answer him;
For in a night the best part of my pow'r,
As I upon advantage did remove,
Were in the Washes all unwarily
Devoured by the unexpected flood.
[*King John dies.*]
Sal. You breathe these dead news in as dead an ear.
My liege! my lord! But now a king, now thus!
Hen. Even so must I run on, and even so stop.
What surety of the world, what hope, what stay,
When this was now a king, and now is clay?
Bast. Art thou gone so? I do but stay behind
To do the office for thee of revenge,
And then my soul shall wait on thee to heaven,
As it on earth hath been thy servant still.
Now, now, you stars that move in your right spheres,

Where be your pow'rs? Show now your mended faiths,
And instantly return with me again
To push destruction and perpetual shame
Out of the weak door of our fainting land.
Straight let us seek, or straight we shall be sought.
The Dauphin rages at our very heels.

Sal. It seems you know not, then, so much as we.
The Cardinal Pandulph is within at rest,
Who half an hour since came from the Dauphin,
And brings from him such offers of our peace
As we with honour and respect may take,
With purpose presently to leave this war.

Bast. He will the rather do it when he sees
Ourselves well sinewed to our defence.

Sal. Nay, it is in a manner done already;
For many carriages he hath dispatch'd
To the seaside, and put his cause and quarrel
To the disposing of the Cardinal;
With whom yourself, myself, and other lords,
If you think meet, this afternoon will post
To consummate this business happily.

Bast. Let it be so; and you, my noble Prince,
With other princes that may best be spar'd,
Shall wait upon your father's funeral.

Hen. At Worcester must his body be interr'd,
For so he will'd it.

Bast. Thither shall it then;
And happily may your sweet self put on
The lineal state and glory of the land!
To whom with all submission, on my knee,
I do bequeath my faithful services
And true subjection everlastingly.

Sal. And the like tender of our love we make,
To rest without a spot for evermore.

Hen. I have a kind soul that would give you thanks,
And knows not how to do it but with tears.

Bast. O, let us pay the time but needful woe,
Since it hath been beforehand with our griefs.
This England never did, nor never shall,
Lie at the proud foot of a conqueror
But when it first did help to wound itself.
Now these her princes are come home again,
Come the three corners of the world in arms,
And we shall shock them. Naught shall make us rue
If England to itself do rest but true. *Exeunt.*

Richard the Second

For Richard the Second the First Quarto (1597) furnishes a good text, which, except for the abdication scene (iv, 1, 154–318), is the basis of the present edition. Later quartos date from 1598 (two), 1608, and 1615, each being set up from its immediate predecessor. For the First Folio a copy of the Fifth Quarto (1615) seems to have been used. The abdication scene was published for the first time in the Fourth Quarto (1608). Its omission from the earlier Quartos was probably due to official censorship or to the publishers' fear of prosecution. At all events, it was manifestly present in the drama as originally written. The Quarto text is defective and corrupt in the abdication scene, but the Folio affords most of the necessary corrections.

Style and blank verse put Richard the Second close to the time of *King John*. Which came first is doubtful, but *King John* is probably the older; for it would have been more natural for Shakespeare to pass on to *Henry IV* after writing Richard the Second than to turn back two hundred years for his next historical subject. This consideration outweighs the argument that, since Richard the Second belongs to the so-called 'lyrical group' and *King John* does not, Richard the Second must be the earlier, inasmuch as Shakespeare would never have returned to his lyrical manner after he had once abandoned it. But Shakespeare was surely capable of lyricism at any period, and, though he dropped this manner in *King John*, there is no reason why he should not have resumed it under the compulsion of a theme so essentially lyrical as the character and misfortunes of King Richard. If, as is possible, he had written *A Midsummer Night's Dream* in the interval, the lyric manner of Richard the Second may well have been influenced thereby. Reasonable dates, then, are 1594 for *King John*, early in 1595 for *A Midsummer Night's Dream*, and late in 1595 or early in 1596 for Richard the Second.

Parallels between Richard the Second and Samuel Daniel's poem on *The Civil Wars* have been cited as evidence for 1595 as a date for the play, but these prove nothing. Quite as elusive is the testimony of a letter written by Sir Edward Hoby on December 7, 1595, to invite Sir Robert Cecil to his house in Canon Row, Westminster, on the 9th, 'where as late as it shal please you a gate for your supper shal be open: & K. Richard present him selfe to your vewe.' If Hoby was referring to a dramatic entertainment (as may or may not be the case), nothing proves that he had Shakespeare's play in mind, for there were other dramas in existence dealing with the same reign; nor is it certain that some *Richard the Third* was not the piece in question.

For his historical materials Shakespeare used the second edition of Holinshed's *Chronicle* (1587). Perhaps he took a hint now and then from other easily accessible books. The pretty story about 'roan Barbary,' for instance (v, 5, 76 ff.), may have been suggested by what is told about the king's greyhound by Froissart, whom Shakespeare doubtless knew in Berners's translation. Froissart is mentioned in *1 Henry VI*, i, 2, 29. The garden scene (iii, 4) and the parting of Richard and his queen (v, 1) are Shakespeare's own. The time covered by the action is so short that no such chronological vagaries are to be expected as we have noted in *King John* (p. 471). The play opens on April 29, 1398; on September 16, Bolingbroke and Mowbray met in the lists at Coventry and were banished; Bolingbroke landed at Ravenspurgh in June or July, 1399; King Richard was deposed on September 30 in the same year and was murdered at Pomfret Castle in January, 1400.

The connection of RICHARD THE SECOND with Essex's rebellion in 1601 is a matter of curious interest but has no literary significance, except as showing the popularity of the play. When Essex was tried in 1600 for his acts in Ireland, his fondness for this play was part of the evidence against him; and RICHARD THE SECOND was played at the Globe, at the instance of his partisans, on the day before the outbreak.

Because RICHARD THE SECOND does not maintain an absolutely uniform standard of excellence in style and metre, critics have suspected that Shakespeare utilized some lost play on the subject and kept fragments of the old text without change. There is not much to be said in favour of any such theory.

Though RICHARD THE SECOND is not Marlowesque in style, Shakespeare was undoubtedly influenced by Marlowe's *Edward II* in his choice of a subject; and there is more or less resemblance between his Richard and Marlowe's Edward. Both are weak, impulsive, and self-willed, and both are governed by unworthy favourites. But Marlowe's king is worse than frivolous; he is frankly despicable. He has neither the poetic nature nor the imaginative intensity of Shakespeare's Richard. There is no comparison between the plays in the matter of pathos and emotional sway.

THE TRAGEDY OF
KING RICHARD THE SECOND

[Dramatis Personæ.

King Richard II.
John of Gaunt, Duke of Lancaster, } uncles to the King.
Edmund of Langley, Duke of York, } uncles to the King.
Henry, surnamed *Bolingbroke,* Duke of Hereford, son to *John of Gaunt*; afterwards *King Henry IV.*
Duke of Aumerle, son to the *Duke of York.*
Thomas Mowbray, Duke of Norfolk.
Duke of Surrey.
Earl of Salisbury.
Lord Berkeley.
Bushy, } servants to *King Richard.*
Bagot, } servants to *King Richard.*
Green, } servants to *King Richard.*
Earl of Northumberland.
Henry Percy, surnamed *Hotspur,* his son.
Lord Ross.
Lord Willoughby.
Lord Fitzwater.
Bishop of Carlisle.
Abbot of Westminster.
Lord Marshal.
Sir Stephen Scroop.
Sir Pierce of Exton.
Captain of a band of Welshmen.
Two Gardeners.

Queen to King Richard.
Duchess of York.
Duchess of Gloucester.
Ladies attending on the *Queen.*
Lords, Heralds, Officers, Soldiers, Keeper, Messenger, Groom, and other Attendants.

SCENE. — *England and Wales.*]

ACT I. Scene I. [*London. The Palace.*]

Enter *King Richard, John of Gaunt,* with other *Nobles* and *Attendants.*

King. Old John of Gaunt, time-honoured Lancaster,
Hast thou, according to thy oath and band,
Brought hither Henry Hereford, thy bold son,
Here to make good the boist'rous late appeal,
Which then our leisure would not let us hear,
Against the Duke of Norfolk, Thomas Mowbray?
Gaunt. I have, my liege.
King. Tell me, moreover, hast thou sounded him
If he appeal the Duke on ancient malice,
Or worthily, as a good subject should,
On some known ground of treachery in him?
Gaunt. As near as I could sift him on that argument,
On some apparent danger seen in him
Aim'd at your Highness, no inveterate malice.
King. Then call them to our presence.
[*Exit Attendant.*]
Face to face,
And frowning brow to brow, ourselves will hear
The accuser and the accused freely speak.
High-stomach'd are they both and full of ire,
In rage deaf as the sea, hasty as fire.

Enter *Bolingbroke* and *Mowbray.*

Boling. Many years of happy days befall
My gracious sovereign, my most loving liege!
Mowb. Each day still better other's happiness
Until the heavens, envying earth's good hap,
Add an immortal title to your crown!
King. We thank you both. Yet one but flatters us,
As well appeareth by the cause you come —
Namely, to appeal each other of high treason.
Cousin of Hereford, what dost thou object
Against the Duke of Norfolk, Thomas Mowbray?
Boling. First — heaven be the record to my speech! —
In the devotion of a subject's love,
Tend'ring the precious safety of my prince
And free from other misbegotten hate,
Come I appellant to this princely presence.
Now, Thomas Mowbray, do I turn to thee,
And mark my greeting well; for what I speak
My body shall make good upon this earth

Or my divine soul answer it in heaven.
Thou art a traitor and a miscreant,
Too good to be so, and too bad to live,
Since the more fair and crystal is the sky,
The uglier seem the clouds that in it fly.
Once more, the more to aggravate the note,
With a foul traitor's name stuff I thy throat
And wish (so please my sovereign), ere I move,
What my tongue speaks my right-drawn sword may prove.

Mowb. Let not my cold words here accuse my zeal.
'Tis not the trial of a woman's war,
The bitter clamour of two eager tongues,
Can arbitrate this cause betwixt us twain;
The blood is hot that must be cool'd for this.
Yet can I not of such tame patience boast
As to be hush'd and naught at all to say.
First, the fair reverence of your Highness curbs me
From giving reins and spurs to my free speech,
Which else would post until it had return'd
These terms of treason doubled down his throat.
Setting aside his high blood's royalty,
And let him be no kinsman to my liege,
I do defy him and I spit at him,
Call him a slanderous coward and a villain;
Which to maintain, I would allow him odds
And meet him, were I tied to run afoot
Even to the frozen ridges of the Alps,
Or any other ground inhabitable
Where ever Englishman durst set his foot.
Meantime let this defend my loyalty —
By all my hopes, most falsely doth he lie.

Boling. Pale trembling coward, there I throw my gage,
Disclaiming here the kinred of the King,
And lay aside my high blood's royalty,
Which fear, not reverence, makes thee to except.
If guilty dread have left thee so much strength
As to take up mine honour's pawn, then stoop.
By that and all the rites of knighthood else,
Will I make good against thee, arm to arm,
What I have spoke or thou canst worse devise.

Mowb. I take it up; and by that sword I swear
Which gently laid my knighthood on my shoulder,
I'll answer thee in any fair degree
Or chivalrous design of knightly trial;
And when I mount, alive may I not light
If I be traitor or unjustly fight!

King. What doth our cousin lay to Mowbray's charge?
It must be great that can inherit us
So much as of a thought of ill in him.

Boling. Look, what I speak, my life shall prove it true —
That Mowbray hath receiv'd eight thousand nobles
In name of lendings for your Highness' soldiers,
The which he hath detain'd for lewd employments,
Like a false traitor and injurious villain.
Besides I say, and will in battle prove —
Or here, or elsewhere to the furthest verge
That ever was survey'd by English eye —
That all the treasons for these eighteen years
Complotted and contrived in this land
Fetch from false Mowbray their first head and spring.
Further I say, and further will maintain
Upon his bad life to make all this good,
That he did plot the Duke of Gloucester's death,
Suggest his soon-believing adversaries,
And consequently, like a traitor coward,
Sluic'd out his innocent soul through streams of blood;
Which blood, like sacrificing Abel's, cries,
Even from the tongueless caverns of the earth,
To me for justice and rough chastisement;
And, by the glorious worth of my descent,
This arm shall do it, or this life be spent.

King. How high a pitch his resolution soars!
Thomas of Norfolk, what say'st thou to this?

Mowb. O, let my sovereign turn away his face
And bid his ears a little while be deaf,
Till I have told this slander of his blood
How God and good men hate so foul a liar!

King. Mowbray, impartial are our eyes and ears.
Were he my brother, nay, my kingdom's heir,
As he is but my father's brother's son,
Now by my sceptre's awe I make a vow,
Such neighbour nearness to our sacred blood
Should nothing privilege him nor partialize
The unstooping firmness of my upright soul.
He is our subject, Mowbray; so art thou:
Free speech and fearless I to thee allow.

Mowb. Then, Bolingbroke, as low as to thy heart
Through the false passage of thy throat, thou liest!
Three parts of that receipt I had for Calais
Disburs'd I duly to his Highness' soldiers.
The other part reserv'd I by consent,
For that my sovereign liege was in my debt

Upon remainder of a dear account
Since last I went to France to fetch his queen.
Now swallow down that lie! For Gloucester's death,
I slew him not, but, to my own disgrace,
Neglected my sworn duty in that case.
For you, my noble Lord of Lancaster,
The honourable father to my foe,
Once did I lay an ambush for your life —
A trespass that doth vex my grieved soul;
But ere I last receiv'd the sacrament,
I did confess it and exactly begg'd
Your Grace's pardon, and I hope I had it.
This is my fault. As for the rest appeal'd,
It issues from the rancour of a villain,
A recreant and most degenerate traitor;
Which in myself I boldly will defend,
And interchangeably hurl down my gage
Upon this overweening traitor's foot
To prove myself a loyal gentleman
Even in the best blood chamber'd in his bosom.
In haste whereof most heartily I pray
Your Highness to assign our trial day.

King. Wrath-kindled gentlemen, be rul'd by me;
Let's purge this choler without letting blood.
This we prescribe, though no physician;
Deep malice makes too deep incision.
Forget, forgive; conclude and be agreed;
Our doctors say this is no month to bleed.
Good uncle, let this end where it begun;
We'll calm the Duke of Norfolk, you your son.

Gaunt. To be a make-peace shall become my age.
Throw down, my son, the Duke of Norfolk's gage.

King. And, Norfolk, throw down his.

Gaunt. When, Harry? when?
Obedience bids I should not bid again.

King. Norfolk, throw down, we bid. There is no boot.

Mowb. Myself I throw, dread sovereign, at thy foot.
My life thou shalt command, but not my shame.
The one my duty owes; but my fair name,
Despite of death that lives upon my grave,
To dark dishonour's use thou shalt not have.
I am disgrac'd, impeach'd, and baffled here;
Pierc'd to the soul with slander's venom'd spear,
The which no balm can cure but his heart-blood
Which breath'd this poison.

King. Rage must be withstood.
Give me his gage. Lions make leopards tame.

Mowb. Yea, but not change his spots! Take but my shame,
And I resign my gage. My dear dear lord,
The purest treasure mortal times afford
Is spotless reputation. That away,
Men are but gilded loam or painted clay.
A jewel in a ten times barr'd-up chest
Is a bold spirit in a loyal breast.
Mine honour is my life. Both grow in one;
Take honour from me, and my life is done.
Then, dear my liege, mine honour let me try;
In that I live, and for that will I die.

King. Cousin, throw up your gage. Do you begin.

Boling. O, God defend my soul from such deep sin!
Shall I seem crestfallen in my father's sight?
Or with pale beggar-fear impeach my height
Before this outdar'd dastard? Ere my tongue
Shall wound my honour with such feeble wrong
Or sound so base a parle, my teeth shall tear
The slavish motive of recanting fear
And spit it bleeding in his high disgrace,
Where shame doth harbour, even in Mowbray's face. *Exit Gaunt.*

King. We were not born to sue, but to command;
Which since we cannot do to make you friends,
Be ready, as your lives shall answer it,
At Coventry upon Saint Lambert's day.
There shall your swords and lances arbitrate
The swelling difference of your settled hate:
Since we cannot atone you, we shall see
Justice design the victor's chivalry.
Lord Marshal, command our officers-at-arms
Be ready to direct these home alarms. *Exeunt.*

Scene II. [*London. The* Duke of Lancaster's *Palace.*]

Enter *John of Gaunt* with the *Duchess of Gloucester.*

Gaunt. Alas, the part I had in Woodstock's blood
Doth more solicit me than your exclaims
To stir against the butchers of his life!
But since correction lieth in those hands
Which made the fault that we cannot correct,
Put we our quarrel to the will of heaven,
Who, when they see the hours ripe on earth,
Will rain hot vengeance on offenders' heads.

Duch. Finds brotherhood in thee no sharper spur?

Hath love in thy old blood no living fire?
Edward's seven sons, whereof thyself art one,
Were as seven vials of his sacred blood,
Or seven fair branches springing from one root.
Some of those seven are dried by nature's course,
Some of those branches by the Destinies cut;
But Thomas, my dear lord, my life, my Gloucester,
One vial full of Edward's sacred blood,
One flourishing branch of his most royal root,
Is crack'd, and all the precious liquor spilt,
Is hack'd down, and his summer leaves all faded,
By envy's hand and murder's bloody axe.
Ah, Gaunt, his blood was thine! That bed, that womb,
That metal, that self mould that fashioned thee,
Made him a man; and though thou livest and breathest,
Yet art thou slain in him. Thou dost consent
In some large measure to thy father's death
In that thou seest thy wretched brother die,
Who was the model of thy father's life.
Call it not patience, Gaunt; it is despair.
In suff'ring thus thy brother to be slaught'red
Thou showest the naked pathway to thy life,
Teaching stern murder how to butcher thee.
That which in mean men we entitle patience
Is pale cold cowardice in noble breasts.
What shall I say? To safeguard thine own life
The best way is to venge my Gloucester's death.

Gaunt. God's is the quarrel; for God's substitute,
His deputy anointed in his sight,
Hath caus'd his death; the which if wrongfully,
Let heaven revenge; for I may never lift
An angry arm against his minister.

Duch. Where then, alas, may I complain myself?

Gaunt. To God, the widow's champion and defence.

Duch. Why then, I will. Farewell, old Gaunt.
Thou goest to Coventry, there to behold
Our cousin Hereford and fell Mowbray fight.
O, sit my husband's wrongs on Hereford's spear,
That it may enter butcher Mowbray's breast!
Or, if misfortune miss the first career,
Be Mowbray's sins so heavy in his bosom
That they may break his foaming courser's back
And throw the rider headlong in the lists,
A caitiff recreant to my cousin Hereford!
Farewell, old Gaunt. Thy sometimes brother's wife
With her companion, Grief, must end her life.

Gaunt. Sister, farewell; I must to Coventry.
As much good stay with thee as go with me!

Duch. Yet one word more! Grief boundeth where it falls,
Not with the empty hollowness, but weight.
I take my leave before I have begun,
For sorrow ends not when it seemeth done.
Commend me to thy brother, Edmund York.
Lo, this is all. Nay, yet depart not so!
Though this be all, do not so quickly go.
I shall remember more. Bid him—ah, what?—
With all good speed at Plashy visit me.
Alack, and what shall good old York there see
But empty lodgings and unfurnish'd walls,
Unpeopled offices, untrodden stones?
And what hear there for welcome but my groans?
Therefore commend me — let him not come there
To seek out sorrow that dwells everywhere.
Desolate, desolate will I hence and die!
The last leave of thee takes my weeping eye.
Exeunt.

Scene III. [*The lists at Coventry.*]

Enter *Lord Marshal* and the *Duke Aumerle.*

Mar. My Lord Aumerle, is Harry Hereford arm'd?

Aum. Yea, at all points, and longs to enter in.

Mar. The Duke of Norfolk, sprightfully and bold,
Stays but the summons of the appellant's trumpet.

Aum. Why, then the champions are prepar'd, and stay
For nothing but his Majesty's approach.

The trumpets sound and the *King* enters with his Nobles, *Gaunt, Bushy, Bagot, Green,* and others. When they are set, enter *Mowbray the Duke of Norfolk* in arms, defendant, and *Herald.*

King. Marshal, demand of yonder champion
The cause of his arrival here in arms.
Ask him his name and orderly proceed
To swear him in the justice of his cause.

Mar. In God's name and the King's, say who thou art,

And why thou comest thus knightly clad in arms;
Against what man thou com'st, and what thy quarrel.
Speak truly on thy knighthood and thy oath,
As so defend thee heaven and thy valour!

Mowb. My name is Thomas Mowbray, Duke of Norfolk,
Who hither come engaged by my oath
(Which God defend a knight should violate!)
Both to defend my loyalty and truth
To God, my King, and his succeeding issue
Against the Duke of Hereford that appeals me;
And, by the grace of God and this mine arm,
To prove him, in defending of myself,
A traitor to my God, my King, and me;
And as I truly fight, defend me heaven!

The trumpets sound. Enter [*Bolingbroke*], *Duke of Hereford*, appellant, in armour, and *Herald.*

King. Marshal, ask yonder knight in arms
Both who he is and why he cometh hither
Thus plated in habiliments of war;
And formally, according to our law,
Depose him in the justice of his cause.

Mar. What is thy name? and wherefore com'st thou hither,
Before King Richard in his royal lists?
Against whom comest thou? and what's thy quarrel?
Speak like a true knight, so defend thee heaven!

Boling. Harry of Hereford, Lancaster, and Derby
Am I, who ready here do stand in arms
To prove, by God's grace and my body's valour
In lists on Thomas Mowbray, Duke of Norfolk,
That he is a traitor, foul and dangerous,
To God of heaven, King Richard, and to me;
And as I truly fight, defend me heaven!

Mar. On pain of death, no person be so bold
Or daring-hardy as to touch the lists,
Except the Marshal and such officers
Appointed to direct these fair designs.

Boling. Lord Marshal, let me kiss my sovereign's hand
And bow my knee before his Majesty;
For Mowbray and myself are like two men
That vow a long and weary pilgrimage.
Then let us take a ceremonious leave
And loving farewell of our several friends.

Mar. The appellant in all duty greets your Highness
And craves to kiss your hand and take his leave.

King. We will descend and fold him in our arms.
Cousin of Hereford, as thy cause is right,
So be thy fortune in this royal fight!
Farewell, my blood; which if to-day thou shed,
Lament we may, but not revenge thee dead.

Boling. O, let no noble eye profane a tear
For me, if I be gor'd with Mowbray's spear.
As confident as is the falcon's flight
Against a bird, do I with Mowbray fight.
My loving lord, I take my leave of you;
Of you, my noble cousin, Lord Aumerle;
Not sick, although I have to do with death,
But lusty, young, and cheerly drawing breath.
Lo, as at English feasts, so I regreet
The daintiest last, to make the end most sweet.
O thou, the earthly author of my blood,
Whose youthful spirit, in me regenerate,
Doth with a twofold vigour lift me up
To reach at victory above my head,
Add proof unto mine armour with thy prayers,
And with thy blessings steel my lance's point,
That it may enter Mowbray's waxen coat
And furbish new the name of John o' Gaunt
Even in the lusty haviour of his son.

Gaunt. God in thy good cause make thee prosperous!
Be swift like lightning in the execution
And let thy blows, doubly redoubled,
Fall like amazing thunder on the casque
Of thy adverse pernicious enemy.
Rouse up thy youthful blood; be valiant and live.

Boling. Mine innocency and Saint George to thrive!

Mowb. However God or fortune cast my lot,
There lives or dies, true to King Richard's throne,
A loyal, just, and upright gentleman.
Never did captive with a freer heart
Cast off his chains of bondage and embrace
His golden uncontroll'd enfranchisement,
More than my dancing soul doth celebrate
This feast of battle with mine adversary.
Most mighty liege, and my companion peers,
Take from my mouth the wish of happy years.
As gentle and as jocund as to jest
Go I to fight. Truth hath a quiet breast.

King. Farewell, my lord. Securely I espy
Virtue with valour couched in thine eye.
Order the trial, Marshal, and begin.

Mar. Harry of Hereford, Lancaster, and Derby,
Receive thy lance, and God defend the right!

Boling. Strong as a tower in hope, I cry amen.

Mar. [*to an Officer*] Go bear this lance to Thomas, Duke of Norfolk.

1. Herald. Harry of Hereford, Lancaster, and Derby
Stands here for God, his sovereign, and himself,
On pain to be found false and recreant,
To prove the Duke of Norfolk, Thomas Mowbray,
A traitor to his God, his King, and him,
And dares him to set forward to the fight.

2. Herald. Here standeth Thomas Mowbray, Duke of Norfolk,
On pain to be found false and recreant,
Both to defend himself and to approve
Henry of Hereford, Lancaster, and Derby
To God, his sovereign, and to him disloyal,
Courageously and with a free desire
Attending but the signal to begin.

Mar. Sound trumpets, and set forward combatants.

A charge sounded.

Stay! The King hath thrown his warder down.

King. Let them lay by their helmets and their spears
And both return back to their chairs again.
Withdraw with us; and let the trumpets sound
While we return these dukes what we decree.

A long flourish.

Draw near,
And list what with our Council we have done.
For that our kingdom's earth should not be soil'd
With that dear blood which it hath fostered;
And for our eyes do hate the dire aspect
Of civil wounds plough'd up with neighbours' sword;
And for we think the eagle-winged pride
Of sky-aspiring and ambitious thoughts
With rival-hating envy set on you
To wake our peace, which in our country's cradle
Draws the sweet infant breath of gentle sleep;
Which so rous'd up with boist'rous untun'd drums,
With harsh-resounding trumpets' dreadful bray
And grating shock of wrathful iron arms,
Might from our quiet confines fright fair peace
And make us wade even in our kinred's blood:
Therefore we banish you our territories.
You, cousin Hereford, upon pain of life,
Till twice five summers have enrich'd our fields
Shall not regreet our fair dominions
But tread the stranger paths of banishment.

Boling. Your will be done. This must my comfort be —
That sun that warms you here shall shine on me,
And those his golden beams to you here lent
Shall point on me and gild my banishment.

King. Norfolk, for thee remains a heavier doom,
Which I with some unwillingness pronounce·
The sly-slow hours shall not determinate
The dateless limit of thy dear exile.
The hopeless word of 'never to return'
Breathe I against thee, upon pain of life.

Mowb. A heavy sentence, my most sovereign liege,
And all unlook'd for from your Highness' mouth.
A dearer merit, not so deep a maim
As to be cast forth in the common air,
Have I deserved at your Highness' hands.
The language I have learnt these forty years,
My native English, now I must forgo;
And now my tongue's use is to me no more
Than an unstringed viol or a harp,
Or like a cunning instrument cas'd up
Or, being open, put into his hands
That knows no touch to tune the harmony.
Within my mouth you have enjail'd my tongue,
Doubly portcullis'd with my teeth and lips;
And dull, unfeeling, barren ignorance
Is made my jailer to attend on me.
I am too old to fawn upon a nurse,
Too far in years to be a pupil now.
What is thy sentence then but speechless death,
Which robs my tongue from breathing native breath?

King. It boots thee not to be compassionate.
After our sentence plaining comes too late.

Mowb. Then thus I turn me from my country's light
To dwell in solemn shades of endless night.

King. Return again and take an oath with thee.
Lay on our royal sword your banish'd hands;
Swear by the duty that you owe to God
(Our part therein we banish with yourselves)
To keep the oath that we administer:
You never shall, so help you truth and God,
Embrace each other's love in banishment;
Nor never look upon each other's face:
Nor never write, regreet, nor reconcile
This low'ring tempest of your home-bred hate;
Nor never by advised purpose meet
To plot, contrive, or complot any ill
'Gainst us, our state, our subjects, or our land.

Boling. I swear.

Mowb. And I, to keep all this.
Boling. Norfolk, so far as to mine enemy:
By this time, had the King permitted us,
One of our souls had wand'red in the air,
Banish'd this frail sepulchre of our flesh,
As now our flesh is banish'd from this land.
Confess thy treasons ere thou fly the realm.
Since thou hast far to go, bear not along
The clogging burthen of a guilty soul.
Mowb. No, Bolingbroke. If ever I were traitor,
My name be blotted from the book of life
And I from heaven banish'd as from hence!
But what thou art, God, thou, and I do know;
And all too soon, I fear, the King shall rue.
Farewell, my liege. Now no way can I stray.
Save back to England, all the world 's my way.
Exit.
King. Uncle, even in the glasses of thine eyes
I see thy grieved heart. Thy sad aspect
Hath from the number of his banish'd years
Pluck'd four away. [*To Bolingbroke*] Six frozen winters spent,
Return with welcome home from banishment.
Boling. How long a time lies in one little word!
Four lagging winters and four wanton springs
End in a word, such is the breath of kings.
Gaunt. I thank my liege that in regard of me
He shortens four years of my son's exile.
But little vantage shall I reap thereby;
For ere the six years that he hath to spend
Can change their moons and bring their times about,
My oil-dried lamp and time-bewasted light
Shall be extinct with age and endless night,
My inch of taper will be burnt and done,
And blindfold death not let me see my son.
King. Why, uncle, thou hast many years to live.
Gaunt. But not a minute, King, that thou canst give.
Shorten my days thou canst with sullen sorrow
And pluck nights from me, but not lend a morrow.
Thou canst help time to furrow me with age,
But stop no wrinkle in his pilgrimage.
Thy word is current with him for my death,
But dead, thy kingdom cannot buy my breath.
King. Thy son is banish'd upon good advice,
Whereto thy tongue a party-verdict gave.
Why at our justice seem'st thou then to low'r?
Gaunt. Things sweet to taste prove in digestion sour.
You urg'd me as a judge; but I had rather
You would have bid me argue like a father.
O, had it been a stranger, not my child,
To smooth his fault I should have been more mild.
A partial slander sought I to avoid,
And in the sentence my own life destroy'd.
Alas, I look'd when some of you should say
I was too strict to make mine own away;
But you gave leave to my unwilling tongue
Against my will to do myself this wrong.
King. Cousin, farewell; and, uncle, bid him so.
Six years we banish him, and he shall go.
Flourish. Exit [*King with his Train*].
Aum. Cousin, farewell. What presence must not know,
From where you do remain let paper show.
Mar. My lord, no leave take I; for I will ride,
As far as land will let me, by your side.
Gaunt. O, to what purpose dost thou hoard thy words
That thou returnest no greeting to thy friends?
Boling. I have too few to take my leave of you,
When the tongue's office should be prodigal
To breathe the abundant dolour of the heart.
Gaunt. Thy grief is but thy absence for a time.
Boling. Joy absent, grief is present for that time.
Gaunt. What is six winters? They are quickly gone.
Boling. To men in joy; but grief makes one hour ten.
Gaunt. Call it a travel that thou tak'st for pleasure.
Boling. My heart will sigh when I miscall it so,
Which finds it an enforced pilgrimage.
Gaunt. The sullen passage of thy weary steps
Esteem as foil wherein thou art to set
The precious jewel of thy home return.
Boling. Nay, rather every tedious stride I make
Will but remember me what a deal of world
I wander from the jewels that I love.
Must I not serve a long apprenticehood
To foreign passages and, in the end,
Having my freedom, boast of nothing else
But that I was a journeyman to grief?
Gaunt. All places that the eye of heaven visits
Are to a wise man ports and happy havens.
Teach thy necessity to reason thus:

There is no virtue like necessity.
Think not the King did banish thee,
But thou the King. Woe doth the heavier sit
Where it perceives it is but faintly borne.
Go, say I sent thee forth to purchase honour,
And not, the King exil'd thee; or suppose
Devouring pestilence hangs in our air
And thou art flying to a fresher clime.
Look, what thy soul holds dear, imagine it
To lie that way thou goest, not whence thou com'st.
Suppose the singing birds musicians,
The grass whereon thou tread'st the presence strow'd,
The flowers fair ladies, and thy steps no more
Than a delightful measure or a dance;
For gnarling sorrow hath less power to bite
The man that mocks at it and sets it light.
Boling. O, who can hold a fire in his hand
By thinking on the frosty Caucasus?
Or cloy the hungry edge of appetite
By bare imagination of a feast?
Or wallow naked in December snow
By thinking on fantastic summer's heat?
O, no! The apprehension of the good
Gives but the greater feeling to the worse.
Fell sorrow's tooth doth never rankle more
Than when he bites, but lanceth not the sore.
Gaunt. Come, come, my son, I'll bring thee on thy way.
Had I thy youth and cause, I would not stay.
Boling. Then, England's ground, farewell; sweet soil, adieu,
My mother, and my nurse, that bears me yet!
Where'er I wander, boast of this I can,
Though banish'd, yet a trueborn English man.
Exeunt.

Scene IV. [*London. The court*.]

Enter the *King*, with *Green* and *Bagot*, at one door, and the *Lord Aumerle* at another.

King. We did observe. Cousin Aumerle,
How far brought you high Hereford on his way?
Aum. I brought high Hereford, if you call him so,
But to the next high way, and there I left him.
King. And say, what store of parting tears were shed?
Aum. Faith, none for me; except the north-east wind,
Which then blew bitterly against our faces,
Awak'd the sleeping rheum, and so by chance
Did grace our hollow parting with a tear.
King. What said our cousin when you parted with him?
Aum. 'Farewell!'
And, for my heart disdained that my tongue
Should so profane the word, that taught me craft
To counterfeit oppression of such grief
That words seem'd buried in my sorrow's grave.
Marry, would the word 'farewell' have length-'ned hours
And added years to his short banishment,
He should have had a volume of farewells;
But since it would not, he had none of me.
King. He is our cousin, cousin; but 'tis doubt,
When time shall call him home from banish-ment,
Whether our kinsman come to see his friends.
Ourself and Bushy, Bagot here, and Green
Observ'd his courtship to the common people;
How he did seem to dive into their hearts
With humble and familiar courtesy;
What reverence he did throw away on slaves,
Wooing poor craftsmen with the craft of smiles
And patient underbearing of his fortune,
As 'twere to banish their affects with him.
Off goes his bonnet to an oyster-wench;
A brace of draymen bid God speed him well
And had the tribute of his supple knee,
With 'Thanks, my countrymen, my loving friends';
As were our England in reversion his,
And he our subjects' next degree in hope.
Green. Well, he is gone, and with him go these thoughts!
Now for the rebels which stand out in Ireland,
Expedient manage must be made, my liege,
Ere further leisure yield them further means
For their advantage and your Highness' loss.
King. We will ourself in person to this war;
And, for our coffers, with too great a court
And liberal largess, are grown somewhat light,
We are enforc'd to farm our royal realm,
The revenue whereof shall furnish us
For our affairs in hand. If that come short,
Our substitutes at home shall have blank charters,
Whereto, when they shall know what men are rich,
They shall subscribe them for large sums of gold
And send them after to supply our wants,
For we will make for Ireland presently.

Enter *Bushy*.

Bushy, what news?

Bushy. Old John of Gaunt is grievous sick, my lord,
Suddenly taken, and hath sent post-haste
To entreat your Majesty to visit him.

King. Where lies he?

Bushy. At Ely House.

King. Now put it, God, in the physician's mind
To help him to his grave immediately!
The lining of his coffers shall make coats
To deck our soldiers for these Irish wars.
Come, gentlemen, let's all go visit him.
Pray God we may make haste, and come too late!

All. Amen. *Exeunt*.

ACT II. Scene I. [*London. Ely House.*]

Enter *John of Gaunt*, sick, with the *Duke of York* &c.

Gaunt. Will the King come, that I may breathe my last
In wholesome counsel to his unstaid youth?

York. Vex not yourself nor strive not with your breath,
For all in vain comes counsel to his ear.

Gaunt. O, but they say the tongues of dying men
Enforce attention like deep harmony.
Where words are scarce, they are seldom spent in vain,
For they breathe truth that breathe their words in pain.
He that no more must say is listened more
Than they whom youth and ease have taught to glose.
More are men's ends mark'd than their lives before.
The setting sun, and music at the close,
As the last taste of sweets, is sweetest last,
Writ in remembrance more than things long past.
Though Richard my live's counsel would not hear,
My death's sad tale may yet undeaf his ear.

York. No; it is stopp'd with other flattering sounds,
As praises, of whose taste the wise are fond,
Lascivious metres, to whose venom sound
The open ear of youth doth always listen;
Report of fashions in proud Italy,
Whose manners still our tardy apish nation
Limps after in base imitation.
Where doth the world thrust forth a vanity
(So it be new, there's no respect how vile)
That is not quickly buzz'd into his ears?
Then all too late comes counsel to be heard
Where will doth mutiny with wit's regard.
Direct not him whose way himself will choose.
'Tis breath thou lack'st, and that breath wilt thou lose.

Gaunt. Methinks I am a prophet new inspir'd
And thus, expiring, do foretell of him:
His rash fierce blaze of riot cannot last,
For violent fires soon burn out themselves;
Small show'rs last long, but sudden storms are short;
He tires betimes that spurs too fast betimes;
With eager feeding food doth choke the feeder;
Light vanity, insatiate cormorant,
Consuming means, soon preys upon itself.
This royal throne of kings, this scept'red isle,
This earth of majesty, this seat of Mars,
This other Eden, demi-paradise,
This fortress built by Nature for herself
Against infection and the hand of war,
This happy breed of men, this little world,
This precious stone set in the silver sea,
Which serves it in the office of a wall,
Or as a moat defensive to a house,
Against the envy of less happier lands;
This blessed plot, this earth, this realm, this England,
This nurse, this teeming womb of royal kings,
Fear'd by their breed and famous by their birth,
Renowned for their deeds as far from home,
For Christian service and true chivalry,
As is the sepulchre in stubborn Jewry
Of the world's ransom, blessed Mary's son;
This land of such dear souls, this dear dear land,
Dear for her reputation through the world,
Is now leas'd out (I die pronouncing it)
Like to a tenement or pelting farm.
England, bound in with the triumphant sea,
Whose rocky shore beats back the envious siege
Of wat'ry Neptune, is now bound in with shame,
With inky blots and rotten parchment bonds.
That England that was wont to conquer others
Hath made a shameful conquest of itself.

Ah, would the scandal vanish with my life,
How happy then were my ensuing death!

Enter *King, Queen, Aumerle, Bushy, Green, Bagot, Ross,* and *Willoughby.*

York. The King is come. Deal mildly with his youth;
For young hot colts, being rag'd, do rage the more.

Queen. How fares our noble uncle Lancaster?

King. What comfort, man? How is't with aged Gaunt?

Gaunt. O, how that name befits my composition!
Old Gaunt indeed, and gaunt in being old.
Within me grief hath kept a tedious fast;
And who abstains from meat that is not gaunt?
For sleeping England long time have I watch'd;
Watching breeds leanness, leanness is all gaunt.
The pleasure that some fathers feed upon
Is my strict fast—I mean my children's looks—
And therein fasting hast thou made me gaunt.
Gaunt am I for the grave, gaunt as a grave,
Whose hollow womb inherits naught but bones.

King. Can sick men play so nicely with their names?

Gaunt. No, misery makes sport to mock itself.
Since thou dost seek to kill my name in me,
I mock my name, great King, to flatter thee.

King. Should dying men flatter with those that live?

Gaunt. No, no! men living flatter those that die.

King. Thou, now a-dying, say'st thou flatterest me.

Gaunt. O, no! thou diest, though I the sicker be.

King. I am in health, I breathe, and see thee ill.

Gaunt. Now, he that made me knows I see thee ill;
Ill in myself to see, and in thee seeing ill.
Thy deathbed is no lesser than thy land,
Wherein thou liest in reputation sick;
And thou, too careless patient as thou art,
Committ'st thy anointed body to the cure
Of those physicians that first wounded thee.
A thousand flatterers sit within thy crown,
Whose compass is no bigger than thy head;
And yet, incaged in so small a verge,
The waste is no whit lesser than thy land.
O, had thy grandsire, with a prophet's eye,
Seen how his son's son should destroy his sons,
From forth thy reach he would have laid thy shame,
Deposing thee before thou wert possess'd,
Which art possess'd now to depose thyself.
Why, cousin, wert thou regent of the world,
It were a shame to let this land by lease;
But, for thy world enjoying but this land,
Is it not more than shame to shame it so?
Landlord of England art thou now, not King.
Thy state of law is bondslave to the law,
And thou —

King. A lunatic lean-witted fool,
Presuming on an ague's privilege,
Dar'st with thy frozen admonition
Make pale our cheek, chasing the royal blood
With fury from his native residence.
Now, by my seat's right royal majesty,
Wert thou not brother to great Edward's son,
This tongue that runs so roundly in thy head
Should run thy head from thy unreverent shoulders.

Gaunt. O, spare me not, my brother Edward's son,
For that I was his father Edward's son!
That blood already, like the pelican,
Hast thou tapp'd out and drunkenly carous'd.
My brother Gloucester, plain well-meaning soul
(Whom fair befall in heaven 'mongst happy souls!),
May be a precedent and witness good
That thou respect'st not spilling Edward's blood.
Join with the present sickness that I have,
And thy unkindness be like crooked age,
To crop at once a too long withered flower.
Live in thy shame, but die not shame with thee!
These words hereafter thy tormenters be!
Convey me to my bed, then to my grave.
Love they to live that love and honour have.
Exit [*borne off by Attendants*].

King. And let them die that age and sullens have;
For both hast thou, and both become the grave.

York. I do beseech your Majesty, impute his words
To wayward sickliness and age in him.
He loves you, on my life, and holds you dear
As Harry Duke of Hereford, were he here.

King. Right, you say true! As Hereford's love, so his;
As theirs, so mine; and all be as it is!

Enter *Northumberland.*

North. My liege, old Gaunt commends him to your Majesty.

King. What says he?
North. Nay, nothing; all is said.
His tongue is now a stringless instrument;
Words, life, and all, old Lancaster hath spent.
York. Be York the next that must be bankrout so!
Though death be poor, it ends a mortal woe.
King. The ripest fruit first falls, and so doth he;
His time is spent, our pilgrimage must be.
So much for that. Now for our Irish wars.
We must supplant those rough rug-headed kerns,
Which live like venom where no venom else
But only they have privilege to live.
And, for these great affairs do ask some charge,
Towards our assistance we do seize to us
The plate, coin, revenues, and moveables
Whereof our uncle Gaunt did stand possess'd.
York. How long shall I be patient? Ah, how long
Shall tender duty make me suffer wrong?
Not Gloucester's death, nor Hereford's banishment,
Nor Gaunt's rebukes, nor England's private wrongs,
Nor the prevention of poor Bolingbroke
About his marriage, nor my own disgrace,
Have ever made me sour my patient cheek
Or bend one wrinkle on my sovereign's face.
I am the last of noble Edward's sons,
Of whom thy father, Prince of Wales, was first.
In war was never lion rag'd more fierce,
In peace was never gentle lamb more mild,
Than was that young and princely gentleman.
His face thou hast, for even so look'd he,
Accomplish'd with the number of thy hours;
But when he frown'd, it was against the French
And not against his friends. His noble hand
Did win what he did spend, and spent not that
Which his triumphant father's hand had won.
His hands were guilty of no kinred blood,
But bloody with the enemies of his kin.
O Richard! York is too far gone with grief,
Or else he never would compare between.
King. Why, uncle, what's the matter?
York. O my liege,
Pardon me, if you please; if not, I, pleas'd
Not to be pardoned, am content withal.
Seek you to seize and gripe into your hands
The royalties and rights of banish'd Hereford?
Is not Gaunt dead? and doth not Hereford live?
Was not Gaunt just? and is not Harry true?
Did not the one deserve to have an heir?
Is not his heir a well-deserving son?
Take Hereford's rights away, and take from Time
His charters and his customary rights;
Let not to-morrow then ensue to-day;
Be not thyself — for how art thou a king
But by fair sequence and succession?
Now, afore God (God forbid I say true!),
If you do wrongfully seize Hereford's rights,
Call in the letters patents that he hath
By his attorneys general to sue
His livery, and deny his off'red homage,
You pluck a thousand dangers on your head,
You lose a thousand well-disposed hearts,
And prick my tender patience to those thoughts
Which honour and allegiance cannot think.
King. Think what you will, we seize into our hands
His plate, his goods, his money, and his lands.
York. I'll not be by the while. My liege, farewell.
What will ensue hereof there's none can tell;
But by bad courses may be understood
That their events can never fall out good. *Exit.*
King. Go, Bushy, to the Earl of Wiltshire straight.
Bid him repair to us to Ely House
To see this business. To-morrow next
We will for Ireland; and 'tis time, I trow.
And we create, in absence of ourself,
Our uncle York Lord Governor of England;
For he is just and always lov'd us well.
Come on, our queen. To-morrow must we part.
Be merry, for our time of stay is short.
Flourish. Exeunt. Manent Northumberland, Willoughby, and Ross.
North. Well, lords, the Duke of Lancaster is dead.
Ross. And living too; for now his son is Duke.
Wil. Barely in title, not in revenues.
North. Richly in both, if justice had her right.
Ross. My heart is great; but it must break with silence,
Ere 't be disburdened with a liberal tongue.
North. Nay, speak thy mind; and let him ne'er speak more
That speaks thy words again to do thee harm!
Wil. Tends that thou wouldst speak to the Duke of Hereford?
If it be so, out with it boldly, man!
Quick is mine ear to hear of good towards him.
Ross. No good at all that I can do for him;
Unless you call it good to pity him,
Bereft and gelded of his patrimony.

North. Now, afore God, 'tis shame such wrongs are borne
In him a royal prince and many moe
Of noble blood in this declining land.
The King is not himself, but basely led
By flatterers; and what they will inform,
Merely in hate, 'gainst any of us all,
That will the King severely prosecute
'Gainst us, our lives, our children, and our heirs.
Ross. The commons hath he pill'd with grievous taxes
And quite lost their hearts; the nobles hath he fin'd
For ancient quarrels and quite lost their hearts.
Wil. And daily new exactions are devis'd,
As blanks, benevolences, and I wot not what;
But what, a God's name, doth become of this?
North. Wars have not wasted it, for warr'd he hath not,
But basely yielded upon compromise
That which his noble ancestors achiev'd with blows.
More hath he spent in peace than they in wars.
Ross. The Earl of Wiltshire hath the realm in farm.
Wil. The King's grown bankrout, like a broken man.
North. Reproach and dissolution hangeth over him.
Ross. He hath not money for these Irish wars,
His burthenous taxations notwithstanding,
But by the robbing of the banish'd Duke.
North. His noble kinsman. Most degenerate king!
But, lords, we hear this fearful tempest sing,
Yet seek no shelter to avoid the storm.
We see the wind sit sore upon our sails,
And yet we strike not, but securely perish.
Ross. We see the very wrack that we must suffer,
And unavoided is the danger now
For suffering so the causes of our wrack.
North. Not so. Even through the hollow eyes of death
I spy life peering; but I dare not say
How near the tidings of our comfort is.
Wil. Nay, let us share thy thoughts as thou dost ours.
Ross. Be confident to speak, Northumberland.
We three are but thyself, and speaking so,
Thy words are but as thoughts. Therefore be bold.
North. Then thus: I have from Le Port Blanc, a bay
In Britain, receiv'd intelligence
That Harry Duke of Hereford, Rainold Lord Cobham,
. . . .
That late broke from the Duke of Exeter,
His brother, Archbishop late of Canterbury,
Sir Thomas Erpingham, Sir John Ramston,
Sir John Norbery, Sir Robert Waterton, and Francis Quoint,
All these well furnish'd by the Duke of Britain
With eight tall ships, three thousand men of war,
Are making hither with all due expedience
And shortly mean to touch our northern shore.
Perhaps they had ere this, but that they stay
The first departing of the King for Ireland.
If then we shall shake off our slavish yoke,
Imp out our drooping country's broken wing,
Redeem from broking pawn the blemish'd crown,
Wipe off the dust that hides our sceptre's gilt,
And make high majesty look like itself,
Away with me in post to Ravenspurgh;
But if you faint, as fearing to do so,
Stay and be secret, and myself will go.
Ross. To horse, to horse! Urge doubts to them that fear.
Wil. Hold out my horse, and I will first be there.
Exeunt.

Scene II. [*Windsor Castle.*]

Enter the *Queen, Bushy, Bagot.*

Bushy. Madam, your Majesty is too much sad.
You promis'd, when you parted with the King,
To lay aside life-harming heaviness
And entertain a cheerful disposition.
Queen. To please the King, I did; to please myself,
I cannot do it. Yet I know no cause
Why I should welcome such a guest as grief
Save bidding farewell to so sweet a guest
As my sweet Richard. Yet again, methinks,
Some unborn sorrow, ripe in fortune's womb,
Is coming towards me, and my inward soul
With nothing trembles. At something it grieves
More than with parting from my lord the King.
Bushy. Each substance of a grief hath twenty shadows,

Which shows like grief itself, but is not so;
For sorrow's eye, glazed with blinding tears,
Divides one thing entire to many objects,
Like perspectives, which rightly gaz'd upon,
Show nothing but confusion — ey'd awry,
Distinguish form. So your sweet Majesty,
Looking awry upon your lord's departure,
Find shapes of grief more than himself to wail,
Which, look'd on as it is, is naught but shadows
Of what it is not. Then, thrice-gracious Queen,
More than your lord's departure weep not. More's not seen;
Or if it be, 'tis with false sorrow's eye,
Which for things true weeps things imaginary.

Queen. It may be so; but yet my inward soul
Persuades me it is otherwise. Howe'er it be,
I cannot but be sad — so heavy sad
As, though in thinking on no thought I think,
Makes me with heavy nothing faint and shrink.

Bushy. 'Tis nothing but conceit, my gracious lady.

Queen. 'Tis nothing less. Conceit is still deriv'd
From some forefather grief. Mine is not so,
For nothing hath begot my something grief,
Or something hath the nothing that I grieve.
'Tis in reversion that I do possess;
But what it is that is not yet known what,
I cannot name. 'Tis nameless woe, I wot.

Enter *Green.*

Green. God save your Majesty! and well met, gentlemen.
I hope the King is not yet shipp'd for Ireland.

Queen. Why hopest thou so? 'Tis better hope he is;
For his designs crave haste, his haste good hope.
Then wherefore dost thou hope he is not shipp'd?

Green. That he, our hope, might have retir'd his power
And driven into despair an enemy's hope
Who strongly hath set footing in this land.
The banish'd Bolingbroke repeals himself
And with uplifted arms is safe arriv'd
At Ravenspurgh.

Queen. Now God in heaven forbid!

Green. Ah, madam, 'tis too true; and that is worse,
The Lord Northumberland, his son young Henry Percy,
The Lords of Ross, Beaumond, and Willoughby,
With all their powerful friends, are fled to him.

Bushy. Why have you not proclaim'd Northumberland
And all the rest revolted faction traitors?

Green. We have; whereupon the Earl of Worcester
Hath broken his staff, resign'd his stewardship,
And all the household servants fled with him to Bolingbroke.

Queen. So, Green, thou art the midwife to my woe,
And Bolingbroke my sorrow's dismal heir.
Now hath my soul brought forth her prodigy;
And I, a gasping new-deliver'd mother,
Have woe to woe, sorrow to sorrow join'd.

Bushy. Despair not, madam.

Queen. Who shall hinder me?
I will despair, and be at enmity
With cozening Hope. He is a flatterer,
A parasite, a keeper-back of Death,
Who gently would dissolve the bands of life,
Which false hope lingers in extremity.

Enter *York.*

Green. Here comes the Duke of York.

Queen. With signs of war about his aged neck.
O, full of careful business are his looks.
Uncle, for God's sake, speak comfortable words!

York. Should I do so, I should belie my thoughts.
Comfort's in heaven, and we are on the earth,
Where nothing lives but crosses, cares, and grief.
Your husband, he is gone to save far off,
Whilst others come to make him lose at home.
Here am I left to underprop his land,
Who, weak with age, cannot support myself.
Now comes the sick hour that his surfeit made;
Now shall he try his friends that flatter'd him.

Enter a *Servingman.*

Serv. My lord, your son was gone before I came.

York. He was? Why, so! Go all which way it will!
The nobles they are fled, the commons they are cold
And will, I fear, revolt on Hereford's side.
Sirrah, get thee to Plashy to my sister Gloucester;
Bid her send me presently a thousand pound.
Hold, take my ring.

Serv. My lord, I had forgot to tell your lordship
To-day, as I came by, I called there —
But I shall grieve you to report the rest.

York. What is't, knave?

Serv. An hour before I came the Duchess died.

York. God for his mercy! what a tide of woes
Comes rushing on this woful land at once!
I know not what to do. I would to God
(So my untruth had not provok'd him to it)
The King had cut off my head with my brother's.
What, are there no posts dispatch'd for Ireland?
How shall we do for money for these wars?
Come, sister — cousin I would say — pray pardon me. —
Go, fellow, get thee home, provide some carts
And bring away the armour that is there.
[*Exit Servingman.*]
Gentlemen, will you go muster men? If I
Know how or which way to order these affairs,
Thus thrust disorderly into my hands,
Never believe me. Both are my kinsmen.
Th' one is my sovereign, whom both my oath
And duty bids defend; t' other again
Is my kinsman, whom the King hath wrong'd,
Whom conscience and my kinred bids to right.
Well, somewhat we must do. Come, cousin, I'll
Dispose of you.
Gentlemen, go muster up your men,
And meet me presently at Berkeley Castle.
I should to Plashy too,
But time will not permit. All is uneven,
And everything is left at six and seven.
Exeunt Duke, Queen.

Bushy. The wind sits fair for news to go for Ireland,
But none returns. For us to levy power
Proportionable to the enemy
Is all unpossible.

Green. Besides, our nearness to the King in love
Is near the hate of those love not the King.

Bagot. And that's the wavering commons; for their love
Lies in their purses, and whoso empties them,
By so much fills their hearts with deadly hate.

Bushy. Wherein the King stands generally condemn'd.

Bagot. If judgment lie in them, then so do we,
Because we ever have been near the King.

Green. Well, I will for refuge straight to Bristow Castle.
The Earl of Wiltshire is already there.

Bushy. Thither will I with you; for little office
The hateful commons will perform for us,
Except like curs to tear us all to pieces.
Will you go along with us?

Bagot. No; I will to Ireland to his Majesty.
Farewell. If heart's presages be not vain,
We three here part that ne'er shall meet again.

Bushy. That's as York thrives to beat back Bolingbroke.

Green. Alas, poor Duke! The task he undertakes
Is numb'ring sands and drinking oceans dry.
Where one on his side fights, thousands will fly.

Bagot. Farewell at once — for once, for all, and ever.

Bushy. Well, we may meet again.

Bagot. I fear me, never.
Exeunt.

Scene III. [*The wilds in Gloucestershire.*]

Enter [*Bolingbroke*] *the Duke of Hereford,* and *Northumberland.*

Boling. How far is it, my lord, to Berkeley now?

North. Believe me, noble lord,
I am a stranger here in Gloucestershire.
These high wild hills and rough uneven ways
Draws out our miles and makes them wearisome;
And yet your fair discourse hath been as sugar,
Making the hard way sweet and delectable.
But I bethink me what a weary way
From Ravenspurgh to Cotshall will be found
In Ross and Willoughby, wanting your company,
Which, I protest, hath very much beguil'd
The tediousness and process of my travel;
But theirs is sweet'ned with the hope to have
The present benefit which I possess;
And hope to joy is little less in joy
Than hope enjoy'd. By this the weary lords
Shall make their way seem short, as mine hath done
By sight of what I have, your noble company.

Boling. Of much less value is my company
Than your good words. But who comes here?

Enter *Harry Percy.*

North. It is my son, young Harry Percy,
Sent from my brother Worcester, whencesoever.
Harry, how fares your uncle?

Percy. I had thought, my lord, to have learn'd his health of you.

North. Why, is he not with the Queen?

Percy. No, my good lord; he hath forsook the court,
Broken his staff of office, and dispers'd
The household of the King.

North. What was his reason?
He was not so resolv'd when last we spake together.

Percy. Because your lordship was proclaimed traitor.
But he, my lord, is gone to Ravenspurgh
To offer service to the Duke of Hereford;
And sent me over by Berkeley to discover
What power the Duke of York had levied there;
Then with directions to repair to Ravenspurgh.

North. Have you forgot the Duke of Hereford, boy?

Percy. No, my good lord, for that is not forgot
Which ne'er I did remember. To my knowledge,
I never in my life did look on him.

North. Then learn to know him now. This is the Duke.

Percy. My gracious lord, I tender you my service,
Such as it is, being tender, raw, and young;
Which elder days shall ripen and confirm
To more approved service and desert.

Boling. I thank thee, gentle Percy; and be sure
I count myself in nothing else so happy
As in a soul rememb'ring my good friends;
And, as my fortune ripens with thy love,
It shall be still thy true love's recompense.
My heart this covenant makes, my hand thus seals it.

North. How far is it to Berkeley? and what stir
Keeps good old York there with his men of war?

Percy. There stands the castle by yon tuft of trees,
Mann'd with three hundred men, as I have heard;
And in it are the Lords of York, Berkeley, and Seymour,
None else of name and noble estimate.

Enter *Ross* and *Willoughby.*

North. Here come the Lords of Ross and Willoughby,
Bloody with spurring, fiery red with haste.

Boling. Welcome, my lords. I wot your love pursues
A banish'd traitor. All my treasury
Is yet but unfelt thanks, which, more enrich'd,
Shall be your love and labour's recompense.

Ross. Your presence makes us rich, most noble lord.

Wil. And far surmounts our labour to attain it.

Boling. Evermore thanks, the exchequer of the poor,
Which, till my infant fortune comes to years,
Stands for my bounty. But who comes here?

Enter *Berkeley.*

North. It is my Lord of Berkeley, as I guess.

Berk. My Lord of Hereford, my message is to you.

Boling. My lord, my answer is — 'to Lancaster';
And I am come to seek that name in England;
And I must find that title in your tongue
Before I make reply to aught you say.

Berk. Mistake me not, my lord. 'Tis not my meaning
To rase one title of your honour out.
To you, my lord, I come (what lord you will)
From the most gracious Regent of this land,
The Duke of York, to know what pricks you on
To take advantage of the absent time
And fright our native peace with self-born arms.

Enter *York* [attended].

Boling. I shall not need transport my words by you;
Here comes his Grace in person. My noble uncle! [*Kneels.*]

York. Show me thy humble heart, and not thy knee,
Whose duty is deceivable and false.

Boling. My gracious uncle!

York. Tut, tut!
Grace me no grace, nor uncle me no uncle.
I am no traitor's uncle, and that word 'grace'
In an ungracious mouth is but profane.
Why have those banish'd and forbidden legs
Dar'd once to touch a dust of England's ground?
But then more why? — why have they dar'd to march
So many miles upon her peaceful bosom,
Frighting her pale-fac'd villages with war
And ostentation of despised arms?
Com'st thou because the anointed King is hence?
Why, foolish boy, the King is left behind,
And in my loyal bosom lies his power.
Were I but now lord of such hot youth
As when brave Gaunt thy father and myself
Rescued the Black Prince, that young Mars of men,
From forth the ranks of many thousand French,
O, then how quickly should this arm of mine,
Now prisoner to the palsy, chastise thee
And minister correction to thy fault!

Boling. My gracious uncle, let me know my fault;
On what condition stands it and wherein?
York. Even in condition of the worst degree,
In gross rebellion and detested treason.
Thou art a banish'd man; and here art come,
Before the expiration of thy time,
In braving arms against thy sovereign.
Boling. As I was banish'd, I was banish'd Hereford;
But as I come, I come for Lancaster.
And, noble uncle, I beseech your Grace
Look on my wrongs with an indifferent eye.
You are my father, for methinks in you
I see old Gaunt alive. O, then, my father,
Will you permit that I shall stand condemn'd
A wandering vagabond, my rights and royalties
Pluck'd from my arms perforce, and given away
To upstart unthrifts? Wherefore was I born?
If that my cousin king be King of England,
It must be granted I am Duke of Lancaster.
You have a son, Aumerle, my noble cousin.
Had you first died, and he been thus trod down,
He should have found his uncle Gaunt a father
To rouse his wrongs and chase them to the bay.
I am denied to sue my livery here,
And yet my letters patents give me leave.
My father's goods are all distrain'd and sold;
And these, and all, are all amiss employ'd.
What would you have me do? I am a subject,
And I challenge law. Attorneys are denied me,
And therefore personally I lay my claim
To my inheritance of free descent.
North. The noble Duke hath been too much abus'd.
Ross. It stands your Grace upon to do him right.
Wil. Base men by his endowments are made great.
York. My lords of England, let me tell you this:
I have had feeling of my cousin's wrongs,
And labour'd all I could to do him right;
But in this kind to come, in braving arms,
Be his own carver and cut out his way
To find out right with wrong — it may not be;
And you that do abet him in this kind
Cherish rebellion and are rebels all.
North. The noble Duke hath sworn his coming is
But for his own; and for the right of that
We all have strongly sworn to give him aid;
And let him never see joy that breaks that oath!
York. Well, well, I see the issue of these arms.
I cannot mend it, I must needs confess,
Because my power is weak and all ill left;
But if I could, by him that gave me life,
I would attach you all and make you stoop
Unto the sovereign mercy of the King;
But since I cannot, be it known to you
I do remain as neuter. So fare you well —
Unless you please to enter in the castle
And there repose you for this night.
Boling. An offer, uncle, that we will accept;
But we must win your Grace to go with us
To Bristow Castle, which they say is held
By Bushy, Bagot, and their complices,
The caterpillars of the commonwealth,
Which I have sworn to weed and pluck away.
York. It may be I will go with you; but yet I'll pause,
For I am loath to break our country's laws.
Nor friends nor foes, to me welcome you are.
Things past redress are now with me past care.
Exeunt.

Scene IV. [*A camp in Wales.*]

Enter *Earl of Salisbury* and a *Welsh Captain.*

Welsh. My Lord of Salisbury, we have stay'd ten days
And hardly kept our countrymen together,
And yet we hear no tidings from the King.
Therefore we will disperse ourselves. Farewell.
Sal. Stay yet another day, thou trusty Welshman.
The King reposeth all his confidence in thee.
Welsh. 'Tis thought the King is dead. We will not stay.
The bay trees in our country all are wither'd,
And meteors fright the fixed stars of heaven;
The pale-fac'd moon looks bloody on the earth,
And lean-look'd prophets whisper fearful change;
Rich men look sad, and ruffians dance and leap —
The one in fear to lose what they enjoy,
The other to enjoy by rage and war.
These signs forerun the death or fall of kings.
Farewell. Our countrymen are gone and fled,
As well assur'd Richard their king is dead.
Exit.
Sal. Ah, Richard! with the eyes of heavy mind,
I see thy glory, like a shooting star,
Fall to the base earth from the firmament.
Thy sun sets weeping in the lowly West,
Witnessing storms to come, woe, and unrest;
Thy friends are fled to wait upon thy foes,
And crossly to thy good all fortune goes. *Exit.*

Act III. Scene I. [Bolingbroke's *camp at Bristol.*]

Enter *Bolingbroke Duke of Hereford, York, Northumberland, Ross, Percy, Willoughby,* with *Bushy* and *Green* prisoners.

Boling. Bring forth these men.
Bushy and Green, I will not vex your souls
(Since presently your souls must part your bodies)
With too much urging your pernicious lives,
For 'twere no charity; yet, to wash your blood
From off my hands, here in the view of men
I will unfold some causes of your deaths.
You have misled a prince, a royal king,
A happy gentleman in blood and lineaments,
By you unhappied and disfigured clean.
You have in manner with your sinful hours
Made a divorce betwixt his queen and him,
Broke the possession of a royal bed,
And stain'd the beauty of a fair queen's cheeks
With tears drawn from her eyes by your foul wrongs.
Myself — a prince by fortune of my birth,
Near to the King in blood, and near in love
Till you did make him misinterpret me —
Have stoop'd my neck under your injuries
And sigh'd my English breath in foreign clouds,
Eating the bitter bread of banishment,
Whilst you have fed upon my signories,
Dispark'd my parks and fell'd my forest woods,
From my own windows torn my household coat,
Ras'd out my imprese, leaving me no sign,
Save men's opinions and my living blood,
To show the world I am a gentleman.
This and much more, much more than twice all this,
Condemns you to the death. See them delivered over
To execution and the hand of death.

Bushy. More welcome is the stroke of death to me
Than Bolingbroke to England. Lords, farewell.

Green. My comfort is that heaven will take our souls
And plague injustice with the pains of hell.

Boling. My Lord Northumberland, see them dispatch'd.
[*Exeunt Northumberland and others, with the prisoners.*]
Uncle, you say the Queen is at your house.
For God's sake, fairly let her be entreated.
Tell her I send to her my kind commends;
Take special care my greetings be delivered.

York. A gentleman of mine I have dispatch'd
With letters of your love to her at large.

Boling. Thanks, gentle uncle. Come, lords, away,
To fight with Glendower and his complices.
Awhile to work, and after holiday. *Exeunt.*

Scene II. [*The coast of Wales. A castle in view.*]

Drums. Flourish and Colours. Enter *the King, Aumerle,* [*the Bishop of*] *Carlisle,* and *Soldiers.*

King. Barkloughly Castle call they this at hand?

Aum. Yea, my lord. How brooks your Grace the air
After your late tossing on the breaking seas?

King. Needs must I like it well. I weep for joy
To stand upon my kingdom once again.
Dear earth, I do salute thee with my hand,
Though rebels wound thee with their horses' hoofs.
As a long-parted mother with her child
Plays fondly with her tears and smiles in meeting,
So weeping, smiling, greet I thee, my earth,
And do thee favours with my royal hands.
Feed not thy sovereign's foe, my gentle earth,
Nor with thy sweets comfort his ravenous sense;
But let thy spiders that suck up thy venom,
And heavy-gaited toads, lie in their way,
Doing annoyance to the treacherous feet
Which with usurping steps do trample thee.
Yield stinging nettles to mine enemies;
And when they from thy bosom pluck a flower,
Guard it, I pray thee, with a lurking adder
Whose double tongue may with a mortal touch
Throw death upon thy sovereign's enemies.
Mock not my senseless conjuration, lords.
This earth shall have a feeling, and these stones
Prove armed soldiers ere her native king
Shall falter under foul rebellion's arms.

Car. Fear not, my lord. That Power that made you king
Hath power to keep you king in spite of all.

The means that heaven yields must be embrac'd,
And not neglected; else, if heaven would,
And we will not, heaven's offer we refuse,
The proffered means of succour and redress.
Aum. He means, my lord, that we are too remiss,
Whilst Bolingbroke, through our security,
Grows strong and great in substance and in power.
King. Discomfortable cousin! know'st thou not
That when the searching eye of heaven is hid
Behind the globe, that lights the lower world,
Then thieves and robbers range abroad unseen
In murthers and in outrage boldly here;
But when from under this terrestrial ball
He fires the proud tops of the Eastern pines
And darts his light through every guilty hole,
Then murthers, treasons, and detested sins,
The cloak of night being pluck'd from off their backs,
Stand bare and naked, trembling at themselves?
So when this thief, this traitor Bolingbroke,
Who all this while hath revell'd in the night
Whilst we were wand'ring with the Antipodes,
Shall see us rising in our throne, the East,
His treasons will sit blushing in his face,
Not able to endure the sight of day,
But self-affrighted tremble at his sin.
Not all the water in the rough rude sea
Can wash the balm off from an anointed king.
The breath of worldly men cannot depose
The deputy elected by the Lord.
For every man that Bolingbroke hath press'd
To lift shrewd steel against our golden crown,
God for his Richard hath in heavenly pay
A glorious angel. Then, if angels fight,
Weak men must fall; for heaven still guards the right.

Enter *Salisbury.*

Welcome, my lord. How far off lies your power?
Sal. Nor near nor farther off, my gracious lord,
Than this weak arm. Discomfort guides my tongue
And bids me speak of nothing but despair.
One day too late, I fear me, noble lord,
Hath clouded all thy happy days on earth.
O, call back yesterday, bid time return,
And thou shalt have twelve thousand fighting men!
To-day, to-day, unhappy day too late,
O'erthrows thy joys, friends, fortune, and thy state;
For all the Welshmen, hearing thou wert dead,
Are gone to Bolingbroke, dispers'd, and fled.
Aum. Comfort, my liege. Why looks your Grace so pale?
King. But now the blood of twenty thousand men
Did triumph in my face, and they are fled;
And, till so much blood thither come again,
Have I not reason to look pale and dead?
All souls that will be safe, fly from my side;
For time hath set a blot upon my pride.
Aum. Comfort, my liege. Remember who you are.
King. I had forgot myself. Am I not King?
Awake, thou coward majesty! thou sleepest.
Is not the King's name twenty thousand names?
Arm, arm, my name! A puny subject strikes
At thy great glory. Look not to the ground,
Ye favourites of a king. Are we not high?
High be our thoughts. I know my uncle York
Hath power enough to serve our turn. But who comes here?

Enter *Scroop.*

Scroop. More health and happiness betide my liege
Than can my care-tun'd tongue deliver him!
King. Mine ear is open and my heart prepar'd.
The worst is worldly loss thou canst unfold.
Say, is my kingdom lost? Why, 'twas my care;
And what loss is it to be rid of care?
Strives Bolingbroke to be as great as we?
Greater he shall not be; if he serve God,
We'll serve him too, and be his fellow so.
Revolt our subjects? That we cannot mend;
They break their faith to God as well as us.
Cry woe, destruction, ruin, and decay:
The worst is death, and death will have his day.
Scroop. Glad am I that your Highness is so arm'd
To bear the tidings of calamity.
Like an unseasonable stormy day
Which makes the silver rivers drown their shores
As if the world were all dissolv'd to tears,
So high above his limits swells the rage
Of Bolingbroke, covering your fearful land
With hard bright steel, and hearts harder than steel.
White-beards have arm'd their thin and hairless scalps

THE TRAGEDY OF KING RICHARD II

PHOTOGRAPHS BY ANGUS McBEAN
PRODUCED BY TENNENT PRODUCTIONS LTD.

Paul Scofield as the weak and tragic Richard II

Queen to Richard II, played by Joy Parker

The king surrounded by his favorites. *Left:* Bushy, played by Basil Henson; seated right: Green, Nicholas Amer; standing: Bagot, Edward Mulhare

"Look, what I speak, my life shall prove it true." Richard's cousin Henry Bolingbroke (Eric Porter) points accusingly at Mowbray, the Duke of Norfolk (Paul Daneman) *(Act I, Scene I)*

Before fhe lists near Coventry—where there is to be a trial by combat between Bolingbroke and Mowbray—Richard speaks to his cousin: "As thy cause is right, so be thy fortune in this royal fight!" *(Act I, Scene III)*

An instant before the adversaries cross lances, Richard halts the trial. He then banishes Mowbray from his territories for life; his cousin for ten years *(Act I, Scene III)*

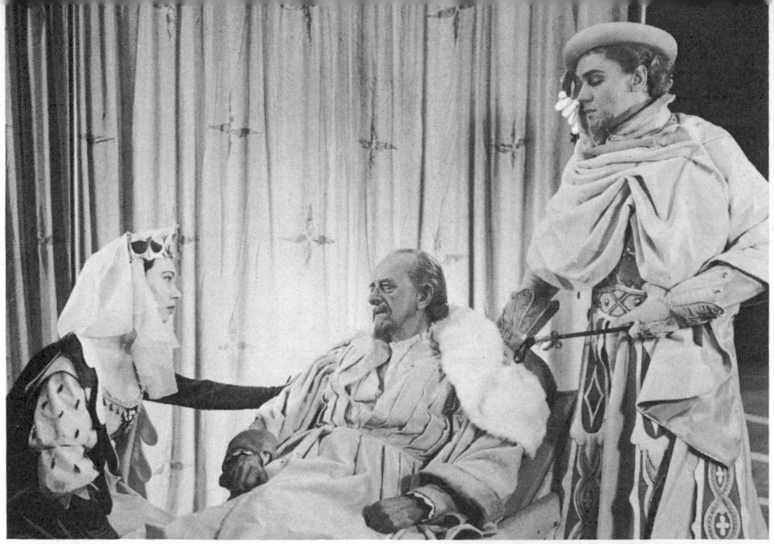

"This happy breed of men, this little world, this precious stone set in the silver sea." So had the aged John of Gaunt (Herbert Lomas) apostrophized on England. Dying, he is visited by the King and Queen *(Act II, Scene I)*

Bagot, Green, and Bushy attempt to cheer a woeful Queen *(Act II, Scene II)*. The King—having seized the dead Gaunt's property, claiming need of the revenue for wars—has gone to Ireland

"For God's sake, let us sit upon the ground and tell sad stories of the death of kings." Aumerle (Leo Ciceri) and the Bishop of Carlisle (Paul Daneman) look on as the King pities himself *(Act III, Scene II)*. Bolingbroke, Gaunt's rightful heir, has broken exile

Returned from Ireland to Wales, Richard takes refuge from Bolingbroke's forces in Flint Castle *(Act III, Scene III)*

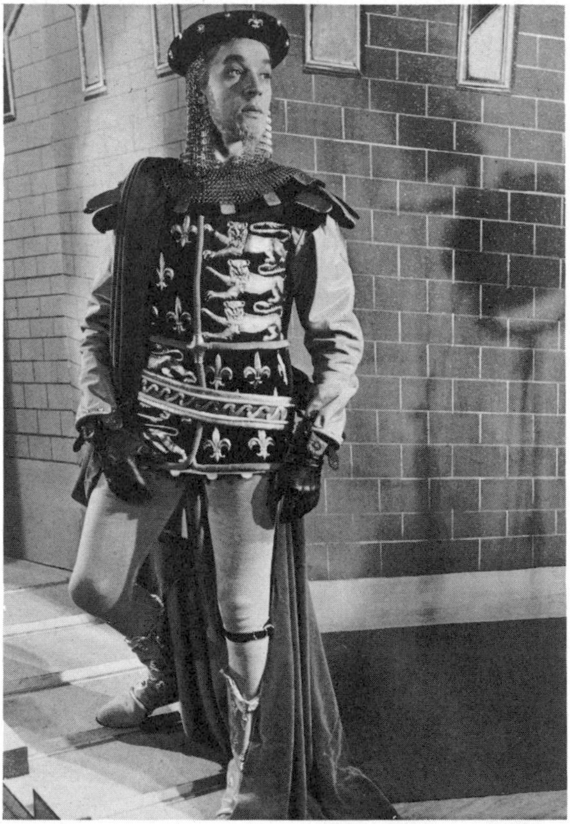

"Tell Bolingbroke . . . that every stride he makes upon my land is dangerous treason"
(Act III, Scene III)

Richard surrenders his sword to the Earl of Northumberland (Brewster Mason), who has joined Bolingbroke's army *(Act III, Scene III)*

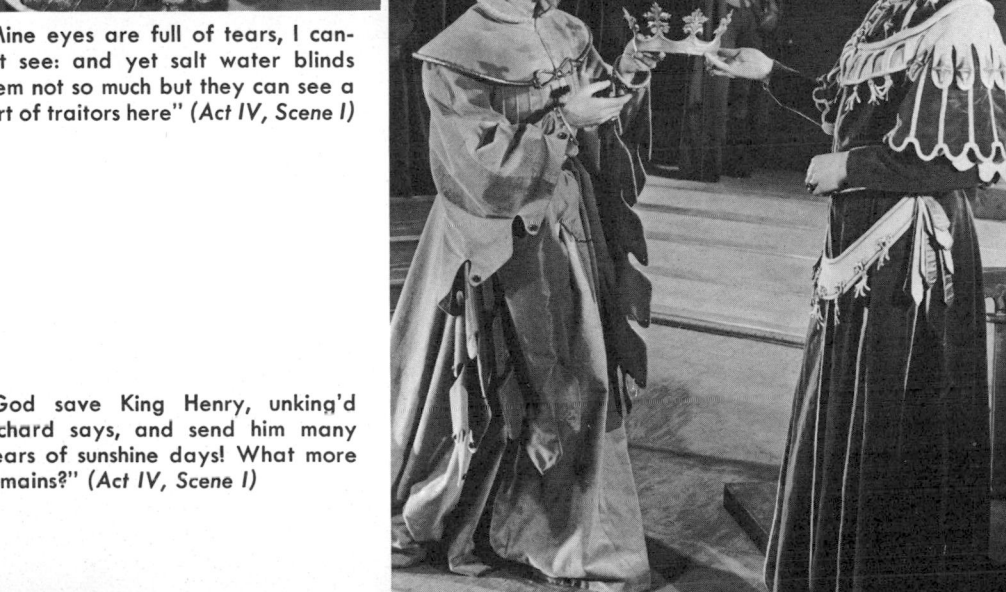

"I give this heavy weight from off my head." In Westminster Hall, London, Richard resigns his crown to Bolingbroke *(Act IV, Scene I)*

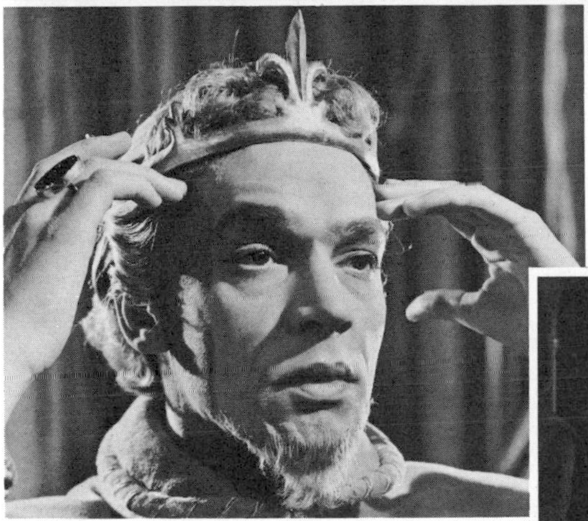

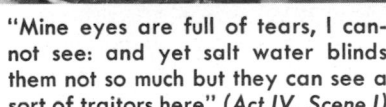

"Mine eyes are full of tears, I cannot see: and yet salt water blinds them not so much but they can see a sort of traitors here" *(Act IV, Scene I)*

"God save King Henry, unking'd Richard says, and send him many years of sunshine days! What more remains?" *(Act IV, Scene I)*

"And must we be divided? must we part?" Under Northumberland's watchful gaze, Richard bids farewell to his Queen. "Ay, hand from hand, my love, and heart from heart" *(Act V, Scene I)*

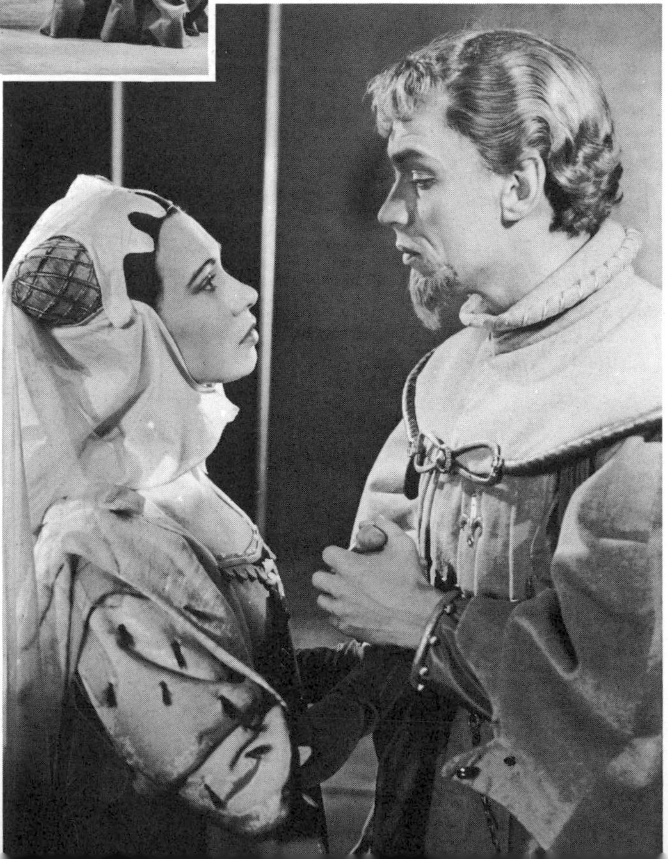

"We make woe wanton with this fond delay: once more, adieu; the rest let sorrow say" *(Act V, Scene I)*

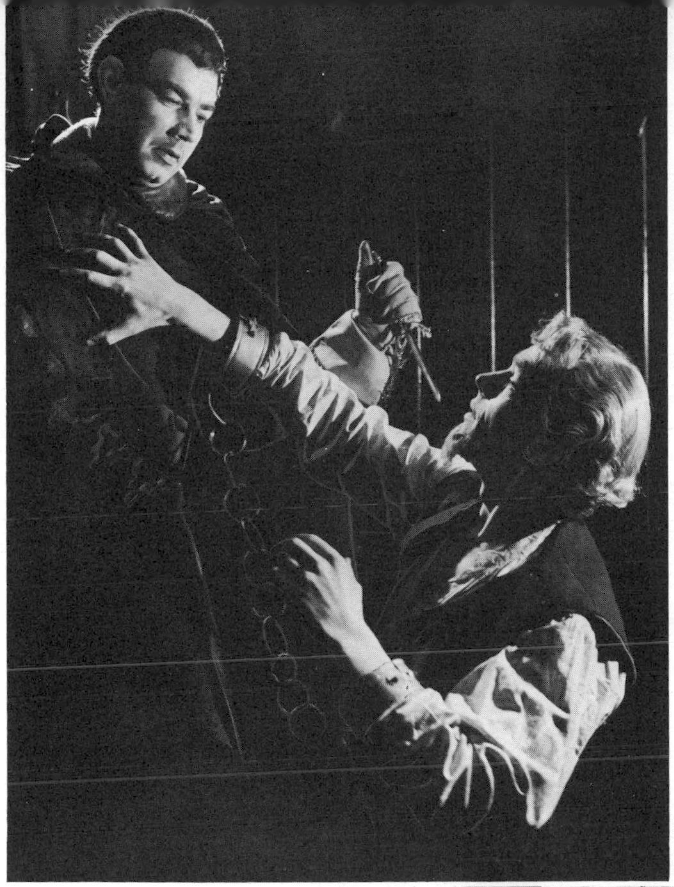

Sir Pierce of Exton (Paul Hardwick), on a hint from the new king, murders the deposed and imprisoned Richard II *(Act V, Scene V)*

Exton is repudiated by the new king: "Though I did wish him dead, I hate the murderer" *(Act V, Scene VI)*

Henry, surnamed Bolingbroke, son to John of Gaunt, now Henry IV

Against thy majesty. Boys with women's voices
Strive to speak big, and clap their female joints
In stiff unwieldy arms against thy crown.
Thy very beadsmen learn to bend their bows
Of double-fatal yew against thy state.
Yea, distaff-women manage rusty bills
Against thy seat. Both young and old rebel,
And all goes worse than I have power to tell.

King. Too well, too well thou tell'st a tale so ill.
Where is the Earl of Wiltshire? Where is Bagot?
What is become of Bushy? Where is Green?
That they have let the dangerous enemy
Measure our confines with such peaceful steps?
If we prevail, their heads shall pay for it.
I warrant they have made peace with Bolingbroke.

Scroop. Peace have they made with him indeed, my lord.

King. O villains, vipers, damn'd without redemption!
Dogs easily won to fawn on any man!
Snakes in my heart-blood warm'd that sting my heart!
Three Judases, each one thrice worse than Judas!
Would they make peace? Terrible hell make war
Upon their spotted souls for this offence!

Scroop. Sweet love, I see, changing his property,
Turns to the sourest and most deadly hate.
Again uncurse their souls. Their peace is made
With heads, and not with hands. Those whom you curse
Have felt the worst of death's destroying wound
And lie full low, grav'd in the hollow ground.

Aum. Is Bushy, Green, and the Earl of Wiltshire dead?

Scroop. Ay, all of them at Bristow lost their heads.

Aum. Where is the Duke my father with his power?

King. No matter where. Of comfort no man speak!
Let's talk of graves, of worms, and epitaphs,
Make dust our paper, and with rainy eyes
Write sorrow on the bosom of the earth.
Let's choose executors and talk of wills.
And yet not so — for what can we bequeath,
Save our deposed bodies to the ground?
Our lands, our lives, and all are Bolingbroke's,
And nothing can we call our own but death
And that small model of the barren earth
Which serves as paste and cover to our bones.
For God's sake let us sit upon the ground
And tell sad stories of the death of kings!
How some have been depos'd, some slain in war,
Some haunted by the ghosts they have depos'd,
Some poisoned by their wives, some sleeping kill'd —
All murthered; for within the hollow crown
That rounds the mortal temples of a king
Keeps Death his court; and there the antic sits,
Scoffing his state and grinning at his pomp;
Allowing him a breath, a little scene,
To monarchize, be fear'd, and kill with looks;
Infusing him with self and vain conceit,
As if this flesh which walls about our life
Were brass impregnable; and humour'd thus,
Comes at the last, and with a little pin
Bores through his castle wall, and farewell king!
Cover your heads, and mock not flesh and blood
With solemn reverence. Throw away respect,
Tradition, form, and ceremonious duty;
For you have but mistook me all this while.
I live with bread like you, feel want, taste grief,
Need friends. Subjected thus,
How can you say to me I am a king?

Car. My lord, wise men ne'er sit and wail their woes,
But presently prevent the ways to wail.
To fear the foe, since fear oppresseth strength,
Gives, in your weakness, strength unto your foe,
And so your follies fight against yourself.
Fear, and be slain — no worse can come to fight;
And fight and die is death destroying death,
Where fearing dying pays death servile breath.

Aum. My father hath a power. Inquire of him,
And learn to make a body of a limb.

King. Thou chid'st me well. Proud Bolingbroke, I come
To change blows with thee for our day of doom.
This ague fit of fear is overblown.
An easy task it is to win our own.
Say, Scroop, where lies our uncle with his power?
Speak sweetly, man, although thy looks be sour.

Scroop. Men judge by the complexion of the sky
The state and inclination of the day;
So may you by my dull and heavy eye:
My tongue hath but a heavier tale to say.
I play the torturer, by small and small
To lengthen out the worst that must be spoken.
Your uncle York is join'd with Bolingbroke,
And all your Northern castles yielded up,

And all your Southern gentlemen in arms
Upon his party.

King. Thou hast said enough.
[*To Aumerle*] Beshrew thee, cousin, which didst lead me forth
Of that sweet way I was in to despair!
What say you now? What comfort have we now?
By heaven, I'll hate him everlastingly
That bids me be of comfort any more.
Go to Flint Castle. There I'll pine away;
A king, woe's slave, shall kingly woe obey.
That power I have, discharge; and let them go
To ear the land that hath some hope to grow,
For I have none. Let no man speak again
To alter this, for counsel is but vain.

Aum. My liege, one word.

King. He does me double wrong
That wounds me with the flatteries of his tongue.
Discharge my followers. Let them hence away,
From Richard's night to Bolingbroke's fair day.
Exeunt.

Scene III. [*Wales. Before Flint Castle.*]

Enter, with *Drum* and *Colours, Bolingbroke, York, Northumberland, Attendants,* [and *Soldiers*].

Boling. So that by this intelligence we learn
The Welshmen are dispers'd, and Salisbury
Is gone to meet the King, who lately landed
With some few private friends upon this coast.

North. The news is very fair and good, my lord.
Richard not far from hence hath hid his head.

York. It would beseem the Lord Northumberland
To say 'King Richard.' Alack the heavy day
When such a sacred king should hide his head!

North. Your Grace mistakes. Only to be brief,
Left I his title out.

York. The time hath been,
Would you have been so brief with him, he would
Have been so brief with you to shorten you,
For taking so the head, your whole head's length.

Boling. Mistake not, uncle, further than you should.

York. Take not, good cousin, further than you should,
Lest you mistake. The heavens are over our heads.

Boling. I know it, uncle, and oppose not myself
Against their will. But who comes here?

Enter *Percy.*

Welcome, Harry. What, will not this castle yield?

Percy. The castle royally is mann'd, my lord,
Against thy entrance.

Boling. Royally?
Why, it contains no king?

Percy. Yes, my good lord,
It doth contain a king. King Richard lies
Within the limits of yon lime and stone;
And with him are the Lord Aumerle, Lord Salisbury,
Sir Stephen Scroop, besides a clergyman
Of holy reverence — who, I cannot learn.

North. O, belike it is the Bishop of Carlisle.

Boling. Noble lords,
Go to the rude ribs of that ancient castle;
Through brazen trumpet send the breath of parley
Into his ruin'd ears, and thus deliver:
Henry Bolingbroke
On both his knees doth kiss King Richard's hand
And sends allegiance and true faith of heart
To his most royal person; hither come
Even at his feet to lay my arms and power,
Provided that my banishment repeal'd
And lands restor'd again be freely granted.
If not, I'll use the advantage of my power,
And lay the summer's dust with show'rs of blood
Rain'd from the wounds of slaughtered Englishmen;
The which, how far off from the mind of Bolingbroke
It is, such crimson tempest should bedrench
The fresh green lap of fair King Richard's land,
My stooping duty tenderly shall show.
Go signify as much, while here we march
Upon the grassy carpet of this plain.
Let's march without the noise of threat'ning drum,
That from this castle's tattered battlements
Our fair appointments may be well perus'd.
Methinks King Richard and myself should meet
With no less terror than the elements
Of fire and water when their thund'ring shock
At meeting tears the cloudy cheeks of heaven.

Be he the fire, I'll be the yielding water;
The rage be his, whilst on the earth I rain
My waters — on the earth, and not on him.
March on, and mark King Richard how he looks.

Parle without, and answer within; then a flourish.
Enter, on the walls, [*King*] *Richard*, [the *Bishop of*] *Carlisle, Aumerle, Scroop, Salisbury.*

See, see, King Richard doth himself appear,
As doth the blushing discontented sun
From out the fiery portal of the East
When he perceives the envious clouds are bent
To dim his glory and to stain the track
Of his bright passage to the Occident.

York. Yet looks he like a king. Behold, his eye,
As bright as is the eagle's, lightens forth
Controlling majesty. Alack, alack, for woe,
That any harm should stain so fair a show!

King. [*to Northumberland*] We are amaz'd; and thus long have we stood
To watch the fearful bending of thy knee,
Because we thought ourself thy lawful king.
And if we be, how dare thy joints forget
To pay their awful duty to our presence?
If we be not, show us the hand of God
That hath dismiss'd us from our stewardship;
For well we know no hand of blood and bone
Can gripe the sacred handle of our sceptre,
Unless he do profane, steal, or usurp.
And though you think that all, as you have done,
Have torn their souls by turning them from us
And we are barren and bereft of friends,
Yet know, my master, God omnipotent,
Is mustering in his clouds on our behalf
Armies of pestilence, and they shall strike
Your children yet unborn and unbegot
That lift your vassal hands against my head
And threat the glory of my precious crown.
Tell Bolingbroke, for yon methinks he stands,
That every stride he makes upon my land
Is dangerous treason. He is come to open
The purple testament of bleeding war.
But ere the crown he looks for live in peace,
Ten thousand bloody crowns of mothers' sons
Shall ill become the flower of England's face,
Change the complexion of her maid-pale peace
To scarlet indignation, and bedew
Her pastures' grass with faithful English blood.

North. The King of Heaven forbid our lord the King
Should so with civil and uncivil arms
Be rush'd upon! Thy thrice-noble cousin
Harry Bolingbroke doth humbly kiss thy hand;
And by the honourable tomb he swears
That stands upon your royal grandsire's bones,
And by the royalties of both your bloods
(Currents that spring from one most gracious head),
And by the buried hand of warlike Gaunt,
And by the worth and honour of himself,
Comprising all that may be sworn or said,
His coming hither hath no further scope
Than for his lineal royalties, and to beg
Enfranchisement immediate on his knees;
Which on thy royal party granted once,
His glittering arms he will commend to rust,
His barbed steeds to stables, and his heart
To faithful service of your Majesty.
This swears he, as he is a prince, is just;
And as I am a gentleman, I credit him.

King. Northumberland, say thus the King returns:
His noble cousin is right welcome hither;
And all the number of his fair demands
Shall be accomplish'd without contradiction.
With all the gracious utterance thou hast
Speak to his gentle hearing kind commends.
[*To Aumerle*] We do debase ourselves, cousin, do we not,
To look so poorly and to speak so fair?
Shall we call back Northumberland and send
Defiance to the traitor, and so die?

Aum. No, good my lord. Let's fight with gentle words
Till time lend friends, and friends their helpful swords.

King. O God, O God! that e'er this tongue of mine
That laid the sentence of dread banishment
On yon proud man, should take it off again
With words of sooth! O that I were as great
As is my grief, or lesser than my name!
Or that I could forget what I have been!
Or not remember what I must be now!
Swell'st thou, proud heart? I'll give thee scope to beat,
Since foes have scope to beat both thee and me.

Aum. Northumberland comes back from Bolingbroke.

King. What must the King do now? Must he submit?
The King shall do it. Must he be depos'd?
The King shall be contented. Must he lose
The name of king? A God's name, let it go!
I'll give my jewels for a set of beads,
My gorgeous palace for a hermitage,
My gay apparel for an almsman's gown,
My figur'd goblets for a dish of wood,

My sceptre for a palmer's walking staff,
My subjects for a pair of carved saints,
And my large kingdom for a little grave,
A little little grave, an obscure grave;
Or I'll be buried in the king's highway,
Some way of common trade, where subjects' feet
May hourly trample on their sovereign's head;
For on my heart they tread now whilst I live,
And buried once, why not upon my head?
Aumerle, thou weep'st, my tender-hearted cousin!
We'll make foul weather with despised tears;
Our sighs and they shall lodge the summer corn
And make a dearth in this revolting land.
Or shall we play the wantons with our woes
And make some pretty match with shedding tears?
As thus — to drop them still upon one place
Till they have fretted us a pair of graves
Within the earth; and therein laid — there lies
Two kinsmen digg'd their graves with weeping eyes.
Would not this ill do well? Well, well, I see
I talk but idly, and you laugh at me.
Most mighty prince, my Lord Northumberland,
What says King Bolingbroke? Will his Majesty
Give Richard leave to live till Richard die?
You make a leg, and Bolingbroke says ay.

North. My lord, in the base court he doth attend
To speak with you, may it please you to come down.

King. Down, down I come, like glist'ring Phaëton,
Wanting the manage of unruly jades.
In the base court? Base court, where kings grow base,
To come at traitors' calls and do them grace!
In the base court? Come down? Down court! down king!
For night owls shriek where mounting larks should sing. [*Exeunt from above.*]

Boling. What says his Majesty?

North. Sorrow and grief of heart
Makes him speak fondly, like a frantic man.
Yet he is come.

[Enter *King Richard* attended, below.]

Boling. Stand all apart
And show fair duty to his Majesty.
He kneels down.
My gracious lord —

King. Fair cousin, you debase your princely knee
To make the base earth proud with kissing it.
Me rather had my heart might feel your love
Than my unpleas'd eye see your courtesy.
Up, cousin, up! Your heart is up, I know,
Thus high at least [*touches his own head*], although your knee be low.

Boling. [*rises*] My gracious lord, I come but for mine own.

King. Your own is yours, and I am yours, and all.

Boling. So far be mine, my most redoubted lord,
As my true service shall deserve your love.

King. Well you deserve. They well deserve to have
That know the strong'st and surest way to get.
Uncle, give me your hand. Nay, dry your eyes.
Tears show their love, but want their remedies.
Cousin, I am too young to be your father,
Though you are old enough to be my heir.
What you will have, I'll give, and willing too;
For do we must what force will have us do.
Set on towards London. Cousin, is it so?

Boling. Yea, my good lord.

King. Then I must not say no.
Flourish. Exeunt.

Scene IV. [*Langley. The* Duke of York's *garden.*]

Enter the *Queen* with two *Ladies*, her *Attendants*.

Queen. What sport shall we devise here in this garden
To drive away the heavy thought of care?

Lady. Madam, we'll play at bowls.

Queen. 'Twill make me think the world is full of rubs
And that my fortune runs against the bias.

Lady. Madam, we'll dance.

Queen. My legs can keep no measure in delight
When my poor heart no measure keeps in grief.
Therefore no dancing, girl; some other sport.

Lady. Madam, we'll tell tales.

Queen. Of sorrow or of joy?

Lady. Of either, madam.

Queen. Of neither, girl;
For if of joy, being altogether wanting,
It doth remember me the more of sorrow;
Or if of grief, being altogether had,

It adds more sorrow to my want of joy;
For what I have I need not to repeat,
And what I want it boots not to complain.

Lady. Madam, I'll sing.

Queen. 'Tis well that thou hast cause;
But thou shouldst please me better, wouldst thou weep.

Lady. I could weep, madam, would it do you good.

Queen. And I could sing, would weeping do me good,
And never borrow any tear of thee.

Enter a *Gardener* and two *Servants.*

But stay, here come the gardeners.
Let's step into the shadow of these trees.
My wretchedness unto a row of pins,
They will talk of state, for every one doth so
Against a change: woe is forerun with woe.
[*Queen and Ladies step aside.*]

Gard. Go bind thou up yon dangling apricocks,
Which, like unruly children, make their sire
Stoop with oppression of their prodigal weight.
Give some supportance to the bending twigs.
Go thou and, like an executioner,
Cut off the heads of too fast growing sprays
That look too lofty in our commonwealth.
All must be even in our government.
You thus employ'd, I will go root away
The noisome weeds which without profit suck
The soil's fertility from wholesome flowers.

Man. Why should we, in the compass of a pale,
Keep law and form and due proportion,
Showing, as in a model, our firm estate,
When our sea-walled garden, the whole land,
Is full of weeds, her fairest flowers chok'd up,
Her fruit trees all unprun'd, her hedges ruin'd,
Her knots disordered, and her wholesome herbs
Swarming with caterpillars?

Gard. Hold thy peace.
He that hath suffer'd this disordered spring
Hath now himself met with the fall of leaf.
The weeds which his broad-spreading leaves did shelter,
That seem'd in eating him to hold him up,
Are pluck'd up root and all by Bolingbroke —
I mean the Earl of Wiltshire, Bushy, Green.

Man. What, are they dead?

Gard. They are; and Bolingbroke
Hath seiz'd the wasteful King. O, what pity is it
That he had not so trimm'd and dress'd his land
As we this garden! We at time of year
Do wound the bark, the skin of our fruit trees,
Lest, being over-proud in sap and blood,
With too much riches it confound itself.
Had he done so to great and growing men,
They might have liv'd to bear, and he to taste
Their fruits of duty. Superfluous branches
We lop away, that bearing boughs may live.
Had he done so, himself had borne the crown,
Which waste of idle hours hath quite thrown down.

Man. What, think you the King shall be depos'd?

Gard. Depress'd he is already, and depos'd
'Tis doubt he will be. Letters came last night
To a dear friend of the good Duke of York's
That tell black tidings.

Queen. O, I am press'd to death through want of speaking! [*Comes forward.*]
Thou old Adam's likeness, set to dress this garden,
How dares thy harsh rude tongue sound this unpleasing news?
What Eve, what serpent, hath suggested thee
To make a second fall of cursed man?
Why dost thou say King Richard is depos'd?
Dar'st thou, thou little better thing than earth,
Divine his downfall? Say, where, when, and how
Cam'st thou by this ill tidings? Speak, thou wretch!

Gard. Pardon me, madam. Little joy have I
To breathe this news; yet what I say is true.
King Richard, he is in the mighty hold
Of Bolingbroke. Their fortunes both are weigh'd.
In your lord's scale is nothing but himself,
And some few vanities that make him light;
But in the balance of great Bolingbroke,
Besides himself, are all the English peers,
And with that odds he weighs King Richard down.
Post you to London, and you will find it so.
I speak no more than every one doth know.

Queen. Nimble mischance, that art so light of foot,
Doth not thy embassage belong to me,
And am I last that knows it? O, thou thinkest
To serve me last, that I may longest keep
Thy sorrow in my breast. Come, ladies, go
To meet at London London's king in woe.
What, was I born to this, that my sad look

Should grace the triumph of great Bolingbroke?
Gard'ner, for telling me these news of woe,
Pray God the plants thou graft'st may never grow. *Exit* [*with Ladies*].

Gard. Poor Queen, so that thy state might be no worse,
I would my skill were subject to thy curse!
Here did she fall a tear; here in this place
I'll set a bank of rue, sour herb of grace.
Rue, even for ruth, here shortly shall be seen,
In the remembrance of a weeping queen.
Exeunt.

ACT IV. Scene I. [*Westminster Hall.*]

Enter, as to the Parliament, *Bolingbroke, Aumerle, Northumberland, Percy, Fitzwater, Surrey,* [and another *Lord, the Bishop of*] *Carlisle, Abbot of Westminster, Herald*; *Officers* and *Bagot.*

Boling. Call forth Bagot.
[*Officers bring him forward.*]
Now, Bagot, freely speak thy mind,
What thou dost know of noble Gloucester's death;
Who wrought it with the King, and who perform'd
The bloody office of his timeless end.

Bagot. Then set before my face the Lord Aumerle.

Boling. Cousin, stand forth, and look upon that man.

Bagot. My Lord Aumerle, I know your daring tongue
Scorns to unsay what once it hath deliver'd.
In that dead time when Gloucester's death was plotted,
I heard you say, 'Is not my arm of length,
That reacheth from the restful English court
As far as Calais to mine uncle's head?'
Amongst much other talk that very time
I heard you say that you had rather refuse
The offer of an hundred thousand crowns
Than Bolingbroke's return to England;
Adding withal, how blest this land would be
In this your cousin's death.

Aum. Princes and noble lords,
What answer shall I make to this base man?
Shall I so much dishonour my fair stars
On equal terms to give him chastisement?
Either I must, or have mine honour soil'd
With the attainder of his slanderous lips.
There is my gage, the manual seal of death
That marks thee out for hell. I say thou liest,
And will maintain what thou hast said is false
In thy heart-blood, though being all too base
To stain the temper of my knightly sword.

Boling. Bagot, forbear; thou shalt not take it up.

Aum. Excepting one, I would he were the best
In all this presence that hath mov'd me so.

Fitz. If that thy valour stand on sympathy,
There is my gage, Aumerle, in gage to thine.
By that fair sun which shows me where thou stand'st,
I heard thee say, and vauntingly thou spak'st it,
That thou wert cause of noble Gloucester's death.
If thou deniest it twenty times, thou liest,
And I will turn thy falsehood to thy heart,
Where it was forged, with my rapier's point.

Aum. Thou dar'st not, coward, live to see that day.

Fitz. Now, by my soul, I would it were this hour.

Aum. Fitzwater, thou art damn'd to hell for this.

Percy. Aumerle, thou liest. His honour is as true
In this appeal as thou art all unjust;
And that thou art so, there I throw my gage
To prove it on thee to the extremest point
Of mortal breathing. Seize it if thou dar'st.

Aum. And if I do not, may my hands rot off
And never brandish more revengeful steel
Over the glittering helmet of my foe!

Another Lord. I task thee to the like, forsworn Aumerle;
And spur thee on with full as many lies
As may be holloa'd in thy treacherous ear
From sun to sun. There is my honour's pawn.
Engage it to the trial, if thou dar'st.

Aum. Who sets me else? By heaven, I'll throw at all!
I have a thousand spirits in one breast
To answer twenty thousand such as you.

Surrey. My Lord Fitzwater, I do remember well
The very time Aumerle and you did talk.

Fitz. 'Tis very true. You were in presence then,
And you can witness with me this is true.

Surrey. As false, by heaven, as heaven itself is true!
Fitz. Surrey, thou liest.
Surrey. Dishonourable boy!
That lie shall lie so heavy on my sword
That it shall render vengeance and revenge
Till thou the lie-giver and that lie do lie
In earth as quiet as thy father's skull.
In proof whereof there is my honour's pawn.
Engage it to the trial if thou dar'st.
Fitz. How fondly dost thou spur a forward horse!
If I dare eat, or drink, or breathe, or live,
I dare meet Surrey in a wilderness,
And spit upon him whilst I say he lies,
And lies, and lies. There is my bond of faith
To tie thee to my strong correction.
As I intend to thrive in this new world,
Aumerle is guilty of my true appeal.
Besides, I heard the banish'd Norfolk say
That thou, Aumerle, didst send two of thy men
To execute the noble Duke at Calais.
Aum. Some honest Christian trust me with a gage
That Norfolk lies. Here do I throw down this,
If he may be repeal'd to try his honour.
Boling. These differences shall all rest under gage
Till Norfolk be repeal'd. Repeal'd he shall be
And, though mine enemy, restor'd again
To all his lands and signories. When he's return'd,
Against Aumerle we will enforce his trial.
Car. That honourable day shall ne'er be seen.
Many a time hath banish'd Norfolk fought
For Jesu Christ in glorious Christian field,
Streaming the ensign of the Christian cross
Against black pagans, Turks, and Saracens;
And, toil'd with works of war, retir'd himself
To Italy; and there, at Venice, gave
His body to that pleasant country's earth
And his pure soul unto his captain, Christ,
Under whose colours he had fought so long.
Boling. Why, Bishop, is Norfolk dead?
Car. As surely as I live, my lord.
Boling. Sweet peace conduct his sweet soul to the bosom
Of good old Abraham! Lords appellants,
Your differences shall all rest under gage
Till we assign you to your days of trial.

Enter *York* [attended].

York. Great Duke of Lancaster, I come to thee
From plume-pluck'd Richard, who with willing soul
Adopts thee heir and his high sceptre yields
To the possession of thy royal hand.
Ascend his throne, descending now from him,
And long live Henry, fourth of that name!
Boling. In God's name I'll ascend the regal throne.
Car. Marry, God forbid!
Worst in this royal presence may I speak,
Yet best beseeming me to speak the truth.
Would God that any in this noble presence
Were enough noble to be upright judge
Of noble Richard! then true noblesse would
Learn him forbearance from so foul a wrong.
What subject can give sentence on his king?
And who sits here that is not Richard's subject?
Thieves are not judg'd but they are by to hear,
Although apparent guilt be seen in them;
And shall the figure of God's majesty,
His captain, steward, deputy elect,
Anointed, crowned, planted many years,
Be judg'd by subject and inferior breath,
And he himself not present? O, forfend it God
That, in a Christian climate, souls refin'd
Should show so heinous, black, obscene a deed!
I speak to subjects, and a subject speaks,
Stirr'd up by God, thus boldly for his king.
My Lord of Hereford here, whom you call king,
Is a foul traitor to proud Hereford's king;
And if you crown him, let me prophesy,
The blood of English shall manure the ground
And future ages groan for this foul act;
Peace shall go sleep with Turks and infidels,
And in this seat of peace tumultuous wars
Shall kin with kin and kind with kind confound;
Disorder, horror, fear, and mutiny
Shall here inhabit, and this land be call'd
The field of Golgotha and dead men's skulls.
O, if you raise this house against this house,
It will the wofullest division prove
That ever fell upon this cursed earth.
Prevent it, resist it, let it not be so,
Lest child, child's children cry against you woe!
North. Well have you argued, sir; and for your pains
Of capital treason we arrest you here.
My Lord of Westminster, be it your charge
To keep him safely till his day of trial.
May it please you, lords, to grant the commons' suit.
Boling. Fetch hither Richard, that in common view
He may surrender. So we shall proceed
Without suspicion.

York. I will be his conduct. *Exit.*
Boling. Lords, you that here are under our arrest,
Procure your sureties for your days of answer.
Little are we beholding to your love,
And little look'd for at your helping hands.

Enter *Richard* and *York*, [with *Officers* bearing the crown, &c.].

Rich. Alack, why am I sent for to a king
Before I have shook off the regal thoughts
Wherewith I reign'd? I hardly yet have learn'd
To insinuate, flatter, bow, and bend my limbs.
Give sorrow leave awhile to tutor me
To this submission. Yet I well remember
The favours of these men. Were they not mine?
Did they not sometime cry 'All hail!' to me?
So Judas did to Christ; but he, in twelve,
Found truth in all but one; I, in twelve thousand none.
God save the King! Will no man say amen?
Am I both priest and clerk? Well then, amen!
God save the King! although I be not he;
And yet amen, if heaven do think him me.
To do what service am I sent for hither?
York. To do that office of thine own good will
Which tired majesty did make thee offer —
The resignation of thy state and crown
To Henry Bolingbroke.
Rich. Give me the crown. Here, cousin, seize the crown.
Here, cousin,
On this side my hand, and on that side yours.
Now is this golden crown like a deep well
That owes two buckets, filling one another,
The emptier ever dancing in the air,
The other down, unseen, and full of water.
That bucket down and full of tears am I,
Drinking my griefs whilst you mount up on high.
Boling. I thought you had been willing to resign.
Rich. My crown I am, but still my griefs are mine.
You may my glories and my state depose,
But not my griefs. Still am I king of those.
Boling. Part of your cares you give me with your crown.
Rich. Your cares set up do not pluck my cares down.
My care is loss of care, by old care done;
Your care is gain of care, by new care won.
The cares I give I have, though given away;
They tend the crown, yet still with me they stay.
Boling. Are you contented to resign the crown?
Rich. Ay, no; no, ay; for I must nothing be;
Therefore no no, for I resign to thee.
Now mark me how I will undo myself.
I give this heavy weight from off my head
And this unwieldy sceptre from my hand,
The pride of kingly sway from out my heart.
With mine own tears I wash away my balm,
With mine own hands I give away my crown,
With mine own tongue deny my sacred state,
With mine own breath release all duty's rites.
All pomp and majesty I do forswear;
My manors, rents, revenues I forgo;
My acts, decrees, and statutes I deny.
God pardon all oaths that are broke to me!
God keep all vows unbroke that swear to thee!
Make me, that nothing have, with nothing griev'd,
And thou with all pleas'd, that hast all achiev'd!
Long mayst thou live in Richard's seat to sit,
And soon lie Richard in an earthy pit!
God save King Harry, unking'd Richard says,
And send him many years of sunshine days!
What more remains?
North. No more, but that you read
These accusations and these grievous crimes
Committed by your person and your followers
Against the state and profit of this land,
That, by confessing them, the souls of men
May deem that you are worthily depos'd.
Rich. Must I do so? and must I ravel out
My weav'd-up folly? Gentle Northumberland,
If thy offences were upon record,
Would it not shame thee in so fair a troop
To read a lecture of them? If thou wouldst,
There shouldst thou find one heinous article,
Containing the deposing of a king
And cracking the strong warrant of an oath,
Mark'd with a blot, damn'd in the book of heaven.
Nay, all of you that stand and look upon
Whilst that my wretchedness doth bait myself,
Though some of you, with Pilate, wash your hands,
Showing an outward pity, yet you Pilates
Have here deliver'd me to my sour cross,
And water cannot wash away your sin.
North. My lord, dispatch. Read o'er these articles.
Rich. Mine eyes are full of tears; I cannot see.
And yet salt water blinds them not so much
But they can see a sort of traitors here.
Nay, if I turn mine eyes upon myself,

I find myself a traitor with the rest;
For I have given here my soul's consent
To undeck the pompous body of a king;
Made glory base, and sovereignty a slave,
Proud majesty a subject, state a peasant.

North. My lord —

Rich. No lord of thine, thou haught insulting man,
Nor no man's lord. I have no name, no title —
No, not that name was given me at the font —
But 'tis usurp'd. Alack the heavy day,
That I have worn so many winters out
And know not now what name to call myself!
O that I were a mockery king of snow,
Standing before the sun of Bolingbroke
To melt myself away in water drops!
Good king, great king, and yet not greatly good,
An if my word be sterling yet in England,
Let it command a mirror hither straight,
That it may show me what a face I have
Since it is bankrout of his majesty.

Boling. Go some of you and fetch a looking glass. [*Exit an Attendant.*]

North. Read o'er this paper while the glass doth come.

Rich. Fiend, thou torments me ere I come to hell!

Boling. Urge it no more, my Lord Northumberland.

North. The commons will not then be satisfied.

Rich. They shall be satisfied. I'll read enough
When I do see the very book indeed
Where all my sins are writ, and that's myself.

Enter *one with a glass.*

Give me the glass, and therein will I read.
No deeper wrinkles yet? Hath sorrow struck
So many blows upon this face of mine
And made no deeper wounds? O flattering glass,
Like to my followers in prosperity,
Thou dost beguile me! Was this face the face
That every day under his household roof
Did keep ten thousand men? Was this the face
That like the sun did make beholders wink?
Was this the face that fac'd so many follies
And was at last outfac'd by Bolingbroke?
A brittle glory shineth in this face.
As brittle as the glory is the face,
[*Dashes the glass to the floor.*]
For there it is, crack'd in a hundred shivers.
Mark, silent king, the moral of this sport —
How soon my sorrow hath destroy'd my face.

Boling. The shadow of your sorrow hath destroy'd
The shadow of your face.

Rich. Say that again.
The shadow of my sorrow? Ha! let's see!
'Tis very true: my grief lies all within;
And these external manners of laments
Are merely shadows to the unseen grief
That swells with silence in the tortured soul.
There lies the substance; and I thank thee, king,
For thy great bounty that not only giv'st
Me cause to wail, but teachest me the way
How to lament the cause. I'll beg one boon,
And then be gone and trouble you no more.
Shall I obtain it?

Boling. Name it, fair cousin.

Rich. Fair cousin? I am greater than a king;
For when I was a king, my flatterers
Were then but subjects; being now a subject,
I have a king here to my flatterer.
Being so great, I have no need to beg.

Boling. Yet ask.

Rich. And shall I have?

Boling. You shall.

Rich. Then give me leave to go.

Boling. Whither?

Rich. Whither you will, so I were from your sights.

Boling. Go some of you, convey him to the Tower.

Rich. O, good! Convey? Conveyers are you all,
That rise thus nimbly by a true king's fall.
[*Exit Richard, with some Lords and a Guard.*]

Boling. On Wednesday next we solemnly set down
Our coronation. Lords, prepare yourselves.
Exeunt. Manent [*the Abbot of*] *Westminster,* [*the Bishop of*] *Carlisle, Aumerle.*

Abbot. A woful pageant have we here beheld.

Car. The woe's to come. The children yet unborn
Shall feel this day as sharp to them as thorn.

Aum. You holy clergymen, is there no plot
To rid the realm of this pernicious blot?

Abbot. My lord,
Before I freely speak my mind herein,
You shall not only take the sacrament
To bury mine intents, but also to effect
Whatever I shall happen to devise.
I see your brows are full of discontent,
Your hearts of sorrow, and your eyes of tears.
Come home with me to supper. I will lay
A plot shall show us all a merry day. *Exeunt.*

ACT V. Scene I. [*London. A street leading to the Tower.*]

Enter the *Queen* with *Ladies*, her *Attendants*.

Queen. This way the King will come. This is the way
To Julius Cæsar's ill-erected tower,
To whose flint bosom my condemned lord
Is doom'd a prisoner by proud Bolingbroke.
Here let us rest, if this rebellious earth
Have any resting for her true king's queen.

Enter *Richard* and *Guard*.

But soft, but see, or rather do not see,
My fair rose wither. Yet look up, behold,
That you in pity may dissolve to dew
And wash him fresh again with true-love tears.
Ah, thou the model where old Troy did stand,
Thou map of honour, thou King Richard's tomb,
And not King Richard! Thou most beauteous inn,
Why should hard-favour'd grief be lodg'd in thee
When triumph is become an alehouse guest?

Rich. Join not with grief, fair woman, do not so,
To make my end too sudden. Learn, good soul,
To think our former state a happy dream;
From which awak'd, the truth of what we are
Shows us but this. I am sworn brother, sweet,
To grim Necessity, and he and I
Will keep a league till death. Hie thee to France
And cloister thee in some religious house.
Our holy lives must win a new world's crown,
Which our profane hours here have stricken down.

Queen. What, is my Richard both in shape and mind
Transform'd and weak'ned? Hath Bolingbroke depos'd
Thine intellect? Hath he been in thy heart?
The lion dying thrusteth forth his paw
And wounds the earth, if nothing else, with rage
To be o'erpow'r'd; and wilt thou pupil-like
Take thy correction, mildly kiss the rod,
And fawn on rage with base humility,
Which art a lion and the king of beasts?

Rich. A king of beasts indeed! If aught but beasts,
I had been still a happy king of men.
Good sometime queen, prepare thee hence for France.
Think I am dead, and that even here thou takest,
As from my deathbed, thy last living leave.
In winter's tedious nights sit by the fire
With good old folks, and let them tell thee tales
Of woful ages long ago betid;
And ere thou bid good-night, to quite their griefs
Tell thou the lamentable tale of me,
And send the hearers weeping to their beds.
For why, the senseless brands will sympathize
The heavy accent of thy moving tongue
And in compassion weep the fire out;
And some will mourn in ashes, some coal-black,
For the deposing of a rightful king.

Enter *Northumberland* [attended].

North. My lord, the mind of Bolingbroke is chang'd.
You must to Pomfret, not unto the Tower.
And, madam, there is order ta'en for you:
With all swift speed you must away to France.

Rich. Northumberland, thou ladder wherewithal
The mounting Bolingbroke ascends my throne,
The time shall not be many hours of age
More than it is, ere foul sin gathering head
Shall break into corruption. Thou shalt think,
Though he divide the realm and give thee half,
It is too little, helping him to all.
And he shall think that thou, which know'st the way
To plant unrightful kings, wilt know again,
Being ne'er so little urg'd, another way,
To pluck him headlong from the usurped throne.
The love of wicked men converts to fear;
That fear to hate, and hate turns one or both
To worthy danger and deserved death.

North. My guilt be on my head, and there an end!
Take leave and part, for you must part forthwith.

Rich. Doubly divorc'd! Bad men, you violate
A twofold marriage — 'twixt my crown and me,
And then betwixt me and my married wife.
Let me unkiss the oath 'twixt thee and me;
And yet not so, for with a kiss 'twas made.
Part us, Northumberland — I towards the North,

Where shivering cold and sickness pines the clime;
My wife to France, from whence, set forth in pomp,
She came adorned hither like sweet May,
Sent back like Hallowmas or short'st of day.

Queen. And must we be divided? Must we part?

Rich. Ay, hand from hand, my love, and heart from heart.

Queen. Banish us both, and send the King with me.

North. That were some love, but little policy.

Queen. Then whither he goes, thither let me go.

Rich. So two, together weeping, make one woe.
Weep thou for me in France, I for thee here.
Better far off than near be ne'er the near.
Go, count thy way with sighs; I mine with groans.

Queen. So longest way shall have the longest moans.

Rich. Twice for one step I'll groan, the way being short,
And piece the way out with a heavy heart.
Come, come, in wooing sorrow let's be brief,
Since, wedding it, there is such length in grief.
One kiss shall stop our mouths, and dumbly part.
Thus give I mine, and thus take I thy heart.

Queen. Give me mine own again. 'Twere no good part
To take on me to keep and kill thy heart.
So, now I have mine own again, be gone,
That I may strive to kill it with a groan.

Rich. We make woe wanton with this fond delay.
Once more adieu! The rest let sorrow say.
Exeunt.

Scene II. [*London. The* Duke of York's *Palace.*]

Enter *Duke of York* and the *Duchess.*

Duch. My lord, you told me you would tell the rest,
When weeping made you break the story off
Of our two cousins' coming into London.

York. Where did I leave?

Duch. At that sad stop, my lord,
Where rude misgoverned hands from windows' tops
Threw dust and rubbish on King Richard's head.

York. Then, as I said, the Duke, great Bolingbroke,
Mounted upon a hot and fiery steed
Which his aspiring rider seem'd to know,
With slow but stately pace kept on his course,
Whilst all tongues cried 'God save thee, Bolingbroke!'
You would have thought the very windows spake,
So many greedy looks of young and old
Through casements darted their desiring eyes
Upon his visage; and that all the walls
With painted imagery had said at once
'Jesu preserve thee! Welcome, Bolingbroke!'
Whilst he, from the one side to the other turning,
Bareheaded, lower than his proud steed's neck,
Bespake them thus, 'I thank you, countrymen.'
And thus still doing, thus he pass'd along.

Duch. Alack, poor Richard! Where rode he the whilst?

York. As in a theatre the eyes of men,
After a well-grac'd actor leaves the stage,
Are idly bent on him that enters next,
Thinking his prattle to be tedious,
Even so, or with much more contempt, men's eyes
Did scowl on gentle Richard. No man cried 'God save him!'
No joyful tongue gave him his welcome home,
But dust was thrown upon his sacred head;
Which with such gentle sorrow he shook off,
His face still combating with tears and smiles
(The badges of his grief and patience),
That, had not God for some strong purpose steel'd
The hearts of men, they must perforce have melted
And barbarism itself have pitied him.
But heaven hath a hand in these events,
To whose high will we bound our calm contents.
To Bolingbroke are we sworn subjects now,
Whose state and honour I for aye allow.

Enter *Aumerle.*

Duch. Here comes my son Aumerle.

York. Aumerle that was;
But that is lost for being Richard's friend,
And, madam, you must call him Rutland now.
I am in parliament pledge for his truth
And lasting fealty to the new-made king.

Duch. Welcome, my son. Who are the violets now

That strew the green lap of the new-come spring?
Aum. Madam, I know not, nor I greatly care not.
God knows I had as lief be none as one.
York. Well, bear you well in this new spring of time,
Lest you be cropp'd before you come to prime.
What news from Oxford? Do these justs and triumphs hold?
Aum. For aught I know, my lord, they do.
York. You will be there, I know.
Aum. If God prevent not, I purpose so.
York. What seal is that that hangs without thy bosom?
Yea, look'st thou pale? Let me see the writing.
Aum. My lord, 'tis nothing.
York. No matter then who see it.
I will be satisfied; let me see the writing.
Aum. I do beseech your Grace to pardon me.
It is a matter of small consequence
Which for some reasons I would not have seen.
York. Which for some reasons, sir, I mean to see.
I fear, I fear —
Duch. What should you fear?
'Tis nothing but some bond that he is ent'red into
For gay apparel 'gainst the triumph day.
York. Bound to himself? What doth he with a bond
That he is bound to? Wife, thou art a fool.
Boy, let me see the writing.
Aum. I do beseech you pardon me. I may not show it.
York. I will be satisfied. Let me see it, I say.

He plucks it out of his bosom and reads it.

Treason, foul treason! Villain! traitor! slave!
Duch. What is the matter, my lord?
York. Ho! who is within there?

[Enter a *Servant.*]

Saddle my horse.
God for his mercy, what treachery is here!
Duch. Why, what is it, my lord?
York. Give me my boots, I say. Saddle my horse.

[*Exit Servant.*]

Now, by mine honour, by my life, by my troth,
I will appeach the villain.
Duch. What is the matter?
York. Peace, foolish woman.
Duch. I will not peace. What is the matter, Aumerle?
Aum. Good mother, be content. It is no more
Than my poor life must answer.
Duch. Thy life answer?
York. Bring me my boots! I will unto the King.

His *Man* enters with his boots.

Duch. Strike him, Aumerle. Poor boy, thou art amaz'd. —
Hence, villain! Never more come in my sight.
York. Give me my boots, I say!

[*Servant does so and exit.*]

Duch. Why, York, what wilt thou do?
Wilt thou not hide the trespass of thine own?
Have we more sons? or are we like to have?
Is not my teeming date drunk up with time?
And wilt thou pluck my fair son from mine age
And rob me of a happy mother's name?
Is he not like thee? Is he not thine own?
York. Thou fond mad woman,
Wilt thou conceal this dark conspiracy?
A dozen of them here have ta'en the sacrament,
And interchangeably set down their hands,
To kill the King at Oxford.
Duch. He shall be none;
We'll keep him here. Then what is that to him?
York. Away, fond woman! Were he twenty times
My son, I would appeach him.
Duch. Hadst thou groan'd for him
As I have done, thou wouldst be more pitiful.
But now I know thy mind. Thou dost suspect
That I have been disloyal to thy bed
And that he is a bastard, not thy son.
Sweet York, sweet husband, be not of that mind!
He is as like thee as a man may be,
Not like to me, or any of my kin,
And yet I love him.
York. Make way, unruly woman!
Exit.
Duch. After, Aumerle! Mount thee upon his horse,
Spur post and get before him to the King,
And beg thy pardon ere he do accuse thee.
I'll not be long behind. Though I be old,
I doubt not but to ride as fast as York;
And never will I rise up from the ground
Till Bolingbroke have pardon'd thee. Away, be gone! *Exeunt.*

Scene III. [*Windsor Castle.*]

Enter *King* [*Henry*], *Percy*, and other *Lords*.

King H. Can no man tell me of my unthrifty son?
'Tis full three months since I did see him last.
If any plague hang over us, 'tis he.
I would to God, my lords, he might be found.
Inquire at London, 'mongst the taverns there,
For there, they say, he daily doth frequent,
With unrestrained loose companions,
Even such, they say, as stand in narrow lanes
And beat our watch and rob our passengers,
Which he, young wanton and effeminate boy,
Takes on the point of honour to support
So dissolute a crew.

Percy. My lord, some two days since I saw the Prince
And told him of those triumphs held at Oxford.

King H. And what said the gallant?

Percy. His answer was, he would unto the stews,
And from the common'st creature pluck a glove
And wear it as a favour, and with that
He would unhorse the lustiest challenger.

King H. As dissolute as desperate! Yet through both
I see some sparks of better hope, which elder years
May happily bring forth. But who comes here?

Enter *Aumerle*, amazed.

Aum. Where is the King?

King H. What means our cousin, that he stares and looks
So wildly?

Aum. God save your Grace! I do beseech your Majesty
To have some conference with your Grace alone.

King H. Withdraw yourselves and leave us here alone.

[*Exeunt Percy and Lords.*]

What is the matter with our cousin now?

Aum. For ever may my knees grow to the earth, [*Kneels.*]
My tongue cleave to the roof within my mouth,
Unless a pardon ere I rise or speak.

King H. Intended, or committed, was this fault?
If on the first, how heinous e'er it be,
To win thy after-love I pardon thee.

Aum. Then give me leave that I may turn the key,
That no man enter till my tale be done.

King H. Have thy desire.

[*Aumerle locks the door.*] *The Duke of York knocks at the door and crieth.*

York. (*within*) My liege, beware! look to thyself!
Thou hast a traitor in thy presence there.

King H. Villain, I'll make thee safe. [*Draws.*]

Aum. Stay thy revengeful hand; thou hast no cause to fear.

York. (*within*) Open the door, secure foolhardy king!
Shall I for love speak treason to thy face?
Open the door, or I will break it open!

Enter *York*.

King H. What is the matter, uncle? Speak.
Recover breath; tell us how near is danger,
That we may arm us to encounter it.

York. Peruse this writing here, and thou shalt know
The treason that my haste forbids me show.

Aum. Remember, as thou read'st, thy promise pass'd.
I do repent me. Read not my name there.
My heart is not confederate with my hand.

York. It was, villain, ere thy hand did set it down.
I tore it from the traitor's bosom, King.
Fear, and not love, begets his penitence.
Forget to pity him, lest thy pity prove
A serpent that will sting thee to the heart.

King H. O heinous, strong, and bold conspiracy!
O loyal father of a treacherous son!
Thou sheer, immaculate, and silver fountain,
From whence this stream through muddy passages
Hath held his current and defil'd himself!
Thy overflow of good converts to bad,
And thy abundant goodness shall excuse
This deadly blot in thy digressing son.

York. So shall my virtue be his vice's bawd,
And he shall spend mine honour with his shame,
As thriftless sons their scraping father's gold.
Mine honour lives when his dishonour dies,
Or my sham'd life in his dishonour lies.
Thou kill'st me in his life; giving him breath,
The traitor lives, the true man's put to death.

Duch. (*within*) What ho, my liege! For God's sake let me in!
King H. What shrill-voic'd suppliant makes this eager cry?
Duch. (*within*) A woman, and thy aunt, great King. 'Tis I.
Speak with me, pity me, open the door!
A beggar begs that never begg'd before.
King H. Our scene is alt'red from a serious thing,
And now chang'd to 'The Beggar and the King.'
My dangerous cousin, let your mother in.
I know she is come to pray for your foul sin.
York. If thou do pardon, whosoever pray,
More sins for this forgiveness prosper may.
This fest'red joint cut off, the rest rest sound;
This let alone will all the rest confound.

Enter *Duchess.*

Duch. O King, believe not this hard-hearted man!
Love loving not itself, none other can.
York. Thou frantic woman, what dost thou make here?
Shall thy old dugs once more a traitor rear?
Duch. Sweet York, be patient. Hear me, gentle liege. [*Kneels.*]
King H. Rise up, good aunt.
Duch. Not yet, I thee beseech.
For ever will I walk upon my knees,
And never see day that the happy sees,
Till thou give joy, until thou bid me joy
By pardoning Rutland, my transgressing boy.
Aum. Unto my mother's prayers I bend my knee. [*Kneels.*]
York. Against them both my true joints bended be. [*Kneels.*]
Ill mayst thou thrive if thou grant any grace!
Duch. Pleads he in earnest? Look upon his face.
His eyes do drop no tears, his prayers are in jest;
His words come from his mouth, ours from our breast.
He prays but faintly and would be denied;
We pray with heart and soul and all beside:
His weary joints would gladly rise, I know;
Our knees shall kneel till to the ground they grow.
His prayers are full of false hypocrisy;
Ours of true zeal and deep integrity.
Our prayers do outpray his; then let them have
That mercy which true prayer ought to have.
King H. Good aunt, stand up.
Duch. Nay, do not say 'stand up.'
Say 'pardon' first, and afterwards 'stand up.'
An if I were thy nurse, thy tongue to teach,
'Pardon' should be the first word of thy speech.
I never long'd to hear a word till now.
Say 'pardon,' King; let pity teach thee how.
The word is short, but not so short as sweet;
No word like 'pardon' for kings' mouths so meet.
York. Speak it in French, King. Say 'Pardonne moi.'
Duch. Dost thou teach pardon pardon to destroy?
Ah, my sour husband, my hard-hearted lord,
That sets the word itself against the word!
Speak 'pardon' as 'tis current in our land;
The chopping French we do not understand.
Thine eye begins to speak, set thy tongue there;
Or in thy piteous heart plant thou thine ear,
That hearing how our plaints and prayers do pierce,
Pity may move thee 'pardon' to rehearse.
King H. Good aunt, stand up.
Duch. I do not sue to stand.
Pardon is all the suit I have in hand.
King H. I pardon him as God shall pardon me.
Duch. O happy vantage of a kneeling knee!
Yet am I sick for fear. Speak it again.
Twice saying 'pardon' doth not pardon twain,
But makes one pardon strong.
King H. With all my heart
I pardon him.
Duch. A god on earth thou art. [*Rises.*]
King H. But for our trusty brother-in-law and the Abbot,
With all the rest of that consorted crew,
Destruction straight shall dog them at the heels.
Good uncle, help to order several powers,
To Oxford, or where'er these traitors are.
They shall not live within this world, I swear,
But I will have them, if I once know where.
Uncle, farewell; and, cousin, adieu.
Your mother well hath pray'd, and prove you true.
Duch. Come, my old son. I pray God make thee new. *Exeunt.*

[Scene IV. *Windsor Castle.*]

Enter *Sir Pierce Exton* and *Servant.*

Exton. Didst thou not mark the King, what words he spake?
'Have I no friend will rid me of this living fear?'
Was it not so?

Man. These were his very words.
Exton. 'Have I no friend?' quoth he. He spake it twice
And urg'd it twice together, did he not?
Man. He did.
Exton. And speaking it, he wishtly look'd on me,
As who should say, 'I would thou wert the man
That would divorce this terror from my heart!'
Meaning the king at Pomfret. Come, let's go.
I am the King's friend, and will rid his foe.
Exeunt.

Scene V. [*Pomfret Castle.*]

Enter *Richard*, alone.

Rich. I have been studying how I may compare
This prison where I live unto the world;
And, for because the world is populous,
And here is not a creature but myself,
I cannot do it. Yet I'll hammer it out.
My brain I'll prove the female to my soul,
My soul the father; and these two beget
A generation of still-breeding thoughts;
And these same thoughts people this little world,
In humours like the people of this world,
For no thought is contented. The better sort,
As thoughts of things divine, are intermix'd
With scruples, and do set the word itself
Against the word:
As thus, 'Come, little ones,' and then again,
'It is as hard to come as for a camel
To thread the postern of a small needle's eye.'
Thoughts tending to ambition, they do plot
Unlikely wonders — how these vain weak nails
May tear a passage through the flinty ribs
Of this hard world, my ragged prison walls;
And, for they cannot, die in their own pride.
Thoughts tending to content flatter themselves
That they are not the first of fortune's slaves,
Nor shall not be the last; like seely beggars
Who, sitting in the stocks, refuge their shame,
That many have, and others must sit there.
And in this thought they find a kind of ease,
Bearing their own misfortunes on the back
Of such as have before endur'd the like.
Thus play I in one person many people,
And none contented. Sometimes am I king:
Then treasons make me wish myself a beggar,
And so I am. Then crushing penury
Persuades me I was better when a king;
Then am I king'd again; and by-and-by
Think that I am unking'd by Bolingbroke,
And straight am nothing. But whate'er I be,
Nor I, nor any man that but man is,
With nothing shall be pleas'd till he be eas'd
With being nothing. *The music plays.*
Music do I hear?
Ha, ha! keep time. How sour sweet music is
When time is broke and no proportion kept!
So is it in the music of men's lives.
And here have I the daintiness of ear
To check time broke in a disordered string;
But, for the concord of my state and time,
Had not an ear to hear my true time broke.
I wasted time, and now doth time waste me;
For now hath time made me his numb'ring clock:
My thoughts are minutes; and with sighs they jar
Their watches on unto mine eyes, the outward watch,
Whereto my finger, like a dial's point,
Is pointing still, in cleansing them from tears.
Now, sir, the sounds that tell what hour it is
Are clamorous groans, that strike upon my heart,
Which is the bell. So sighs and tears and groans
Show minutes, times, and hours. But my time
Runs posting on in Bolingbroke's proud joy,
While I stand fooling here, his Jack o' th' clock.
This music mads me. Let it sound no more;
For though it have holp madmen to their wits,
In me it seems it will make wise men mad.
Yet blessing on his heart that gives it me!
For 'tis a sign of love, and love to Richard
Is a strange brooch in this all-hating world.

Enter a *Groom* of the stable.

Groom. Hail, royal prince!
Rich. Thanks, noble peer.
The cheapest of us is ten groats too dear.
What art thou? and how comest thou hither,
Where no man never comes but that sad dog
That brings me food to make misfortune live?
Groom. I was a poor groom of thy stable, King,
When thou wert king; who, travelling towards York,
With much ado, at length, have gotten leave
To look upon my sometimes royal master's face.
O, how it ern'd my heart when I beheld,
In London streets, that coronation day,
When Bolingbroke rode on roan Barbary,

That horse that thou so often hast bestrid,
That horse that I so carefully have dress'd!
Rich. Rode he on Barbary? Tell me, gentle friend,
How went he under him?
Groom. So proudly as if he had disdain'd the ground.
Rich. So proud that Bolingbroke was on his back!
That jade hath eat bread from my royal hand;
This hand hath made him proud with clapping him.
Would he not stumble? would he not fall down
(Since pride must have a fall) and break the neck
Of that proud man that did usurp his back?
Forgiveness, horse! Why do I rail on thee,
Since thou, created to be aw'd by man,
Wast born to bear? I was not made a horse;
And yet I bear a burthen like an ass,
Spurr'd, gall'd and tir'd by jauncing Bolingbroke.

Enter *Keeper*, with a dish.

Keeper. Fellow, give place. Here is no longer stay.
Rich. If thou love me, 'tis time thou wert away.
Groom. What my tongue dares not, that my heart shall say. *Exit.*
Keeper. My lord, will't please you to fall to?
Rich. Taste of it first, as thou art wont to do.
Keeper. My lord, I dare not. Sir Pierce of Exton,
Who lately came from the King, commands the contrary.
Rich. The devil take Henry of Lancaster, and thee!
Patience is stale, and I am weary of it.
[*Beats the Keeper.*]
Keeper. Help, help, help!

Exton and *Servants*, the Murderers, rush in.

Rich. How now! What means death in this rude assault?
Villain, thy own hand yields thy death's instrument.
[*Snatches a weapon from a Servant and kills him.*]
Go thou and fill another room in hell.
[*Kills another.*] *Here Exton strikes him down.*
That hand shall burn in never-quenching fire
That staggers thus my person. Exton, thy fierce hand
Hath with the King's blood stain'd the King's own land.
Mount, mount, my soul! thy seat is up on high;
Whilst my gross flesh sinks downward, here to die. [*Dies.*]
Exton. As full of valour as of royal blood.
Both have I spill'd. O, would the deed were good!
For now the devil, that told me I did well,
Says that this deed is chronicled in hell.
This dead king to the living king I'll bear.
Take hence the rest, and give them burial here.
Exeunt.

Scene VI. [*Windsor Castle.*]

Flourish. Enter *Bolingbroke* [as *King*], the *Duke of York*, with other *Lords*, and *Attendants.*

King. Kind uncle York, the latest news we hear
Is that the rebels have consum'd with fire
Our town of Ciceter in Gloucestershire;
But whether they be ta'en or slain we hear not.

Enter *Northumberland.*

Welcome, my lord. What is the news?
North. First, to thy sacred state wish I all happiness.
The next news is, I have to London sent
The heads of Oxford, Salisbury, Blunt, and Kent.
The manner of their taking may appear
At large discoursed in this paper here.
King. We thank thee, gentle Percy, for thy pains
And to thy worth will add right worthy gains.

Enter *Lord Fitzwater.*

Fitz. My lord, I have from Oxford sent to London
The heads of Brocas and Sir Bennet Seely,
Two of the dangerous consorted traitors
That sought at Oxford thy dire overthrow.
King. Thy pains, Fitzwater, shall not be forgot.
Right noble is thy merit, well I wot.

Enter *Henry Percy* and [the *Bishop of*] *Carlisle.*

Percy. The grand conspirator, Abbot of Westminster,
With clog of conscience and sour melancholy

Hath yielded up his body to the grave;
But here is Carlisle living, to abide
Thy kingly doom and sentence of his pride.
King. Carlisle, this is your doom:
Choose out some secret place, some reverend room,
More than thou hast, and with it joy thy life.
So, as thou liv'st in peace, die free from strife;
For though mine enemy thou hast ever been,
High sparks of honour in thee have I seen.

Enter *Exton*, with [*Attendants* bearing] a coffin.

Exton. Great King, within this coffin I present
Thy buried fear. Herein all breathless lies
The mightiest of thy greatest enemies,
Richard of Bordeaux, by me hither brought.
King. Exton, I thank thee not; for thou hast wrought
A deed of slander, with thy fatal hand,
Upon my head and all this famous land.
Exton. From your own mouth, my lord, did I this deed.
King. They love not poison that do poison need,
Nor do I thee. Though I did wish him dead,
I hate the murtherer, love him murthered.
The guilt of conscience take thou for thy labour,
But neither my good word nor princely favour.
With Cain go wander thorough shades of night,
And never show thy head by day nor light.
Lords, I protest my soul is full of woe
That blood should sprinkle me to make me grow.
Come, mourn with me for what I do lament,
And put on sullen black incontinent.
I'll make a voyage to the Holy Land
To wash this blood off from my guilty hand.
March sadly after. Grace my mournings here
In weeping after this untimely bier.

Exeunt.

THE FIRST PART OF KING HENRY THE FOURTH

PART I OF HENRY THE FOURTH was entered in the Stationers' Register on February 25, 1598, as 'The historye of Henry the IIIIth . . . with the conceipted mirthe of Sir John Falstoff,' and the First Quarto (our authority for the text) came out in the same year. Meres, before October 19, 1598, mentions 'Henry the 4' among Shakespeare's excellent tragedies. Perhaps he means to include both Parts under that title; but his evidence is ambiguous. The Second Part must have followed the First rather promptly, and doubtless with no other drama intervening. For *Part I* we may fix upon 1597, and for *Part II* upon 1598, without risk of serious error. Jonson mentions Justice Silence in his *Every Man out of his Humour*, which was acted in 1599.

PART I is manifestly later than *Richard the Second.* The connection between them is close. Bolingbroke's character, well intimated in *Richard the Second*, is so developed in the later play that he becomes, as King Henry, one of the most baffling of all Shakespeare's complex creatures. He is genuinely patriotic. He had the good of his country at heart, and not merely personal advantage, when he deposed King Richard. His anxiety about his dissolute son is not paternal only: it is largely due to his fear of what will happen to England if another Harry shows himself another Richard in instability and tyrannical license. And so, profound dissembler as he is, he actually lays bare his own dissimulation in admonishing his son (iii, 2):

> And then I stole all courtesy from heaven
> And dress'd myself in such humility
> That I did pluck allegiance from men's hearts,
> Loud shouts and salutations from their mouths,
> Even in the presence of the crowned king.

This whole speech would be almost cynical, were it not for the passionate intensity which submerges the cynicism of its outspokenness. It looks back to King Richard's account of Bolingbroke's 'courtship of the common people' (i, 4, 20 ff.) and to York's description of his triumphal progress after his return from banishment (v, 2).

Prince Hal does not appear in *Richard the Second*, but his riotous conduct and his companionship with highwaymen are deplored by his father in v, 3, where Hotspur's scorn of him, so hotly uttered in 1 HENRY IV (i, 3, 230 ff.), comes out by implication in his answer to King Henry's question. Before he began PART I, Shakespeare had somewhat modified his former conception of the Prince's character. In *Richard the Second* he is called 'as dissolute as desperate.' In 1 HENRY IV, on the contrary, he is neither desperate nor, in the full sense of the word, dissolute. His riots are mere frolics. He does not get drunk and is never involved in any scandal with a woman. Shakespeare, indeed, is so much concerned to guard against misconception on the part of the audience, that he deliberately renounces dramatic propriety in the famous soliloquy at the end of i, 2. This is, in effect, the author's explanation — a kind of chorus — and should be so understood. It is not the expression of the Prince's actual motive in upholding 'the unyoked humour' of his riotous comrades. It amounts to a mere statement of the fact in the third person:

'When this Prince turns over a new leaf, he will be all the more admired for the contrast.'

For historical materials in HENRY THE FOURTH, as in *Richard the Second*, Shakespeare went to the second edition of Holinshed (1587). The events in PART I all come within the limits of almost exactly a year. Sir Edmund Mortimer (whom Shakespeare, like Holinshed, confuses with the Earl of March) was taken prisoner by Glendower on June 22, 1402; the defeat of the Scots at Homildon followed on September 14; on July 21, 1403, Hotspur was killed in the Battle of Shrewsbury — no one knows by whom; Worcester and Vernon were executed two days later. Henry IV was born in 1367; Prince Hal in 1387. Hotspur was quite as old as the King — indeed, a little older. Shakespeare has so reduced his age that he is 'not more in debt to years' than the Prince. Thus the contrast is made dramatically possible.

Shakespeare owes much to Holinshed for facts and ideas; little for phraseology. A typical instance is Hotspur's famous speech before the battle (v, 2, 82 ff.): 'O, gentlemen, the time of life is short!' Holinshed reports it thus:

> This daie shall either bring vs all to aduauncement & honor, or else, if it shall chance vs to be ouercome, shall deliuer vs from the kings spitefull malice and cruell disdaine: for plaieng the men (as we ought to doo), better it is to die in battell for the commonwealths cause, than through cowardlike feare to prolong life which after shall be taken from vs, by sentence of the enimie.

For the riotous behaviour of Hal and his companions Shakespeare found suggestions in Holinshed and Stow; but more noteworthy are the curious details that he derived from the old play of *The Famous Victories of Henry the Fifth*. This he used for both Parts of HENRY THE FOURTH. In the old play, for instance, when the Prince promises Ned that he shall be Chief Justice, Ned replies, 'By gogs wounds, ile be the brauest Lord chiefe Iustice That euer was in England' (cf. I, i, 2, 72); Derick tickles his nose with a straw to make it bleed (cf. I, ii, 4, 340); the Prince's resort is 'the olde Tauerne in Eastcheape'; there is a comic scene of conscription (cf. II, iii, 2), and so on.

When Shakespeare wrote the FIRST PART OF HENRY THE FOURTH he gave to the character whom we know as Falstaff the name of Sir John Oldcastle, which he took from *The Famous Victories of Henry the Fifth*. This he changed to Falstaff before the play was printed. Traces of the change appear in the text of both parts. In *Part I*, the Prince calls him 'my old lad of the castle' (i, 2, 47); and one line (ii, 2, 115), though not unmetrical as it stands, would be more regular if 'Oldcastle' were read instead of 'Falstaff.' In *Part II*, a speech of Falstaff's (i, 2, 137) is still marked *Old.* in the Quarto of 1600; the Epilogue expressly declares that 'Oldcastle died a martyr, and this is not the man.' The historical Sir John Oldcastle (called Lord Cobham in his wife's right) was executed for heresy in 1417. The Cobham family was powerful in Shakespeare's time and no doubt protested against the profanation of what to them was a sacred name. For a substitute, Shakespeare went back to *1 Henry VI*, in which one Sir John Fastolfe plays a coward's part, and borrowed the name, with a shift of letters. Perhaps this choice of name suggested itself because the Prince accuses Oldcastle-Falstaff of cowardice in ii, 4, after the robbers have been robbed; but Falstaff is not a coward in fact, though traditional interpretation has heedlessly taken the Prince's practical joke as if it justified the accusation.

THE FIRST PART OF
KING HENRY THE FOURTH

[Dramatis Personæ.

King Henry the Fourth.
Henry, Prince of Wales, } sons to the *King.*
Prince John of Lancaster, } sons to the *King.*
Earl of Westmoreland.
Sir Walter Blunt.
Thomas Percy, Earl of Worcester.
Henry Percy, Earl of Northumberland.
Henry Percy, surnamed *Hotspur,* his son.
Edmund Mortimer, Earl of March.
Richard Scroop. Archbishop of York.
Archibald, Earl of Douglas.
Owen Glendower.
Sir Richard Vernon.
Sir John Falstaff.
Sir Michael, a friend to the *Archbishop of York.*
Poins.
Gadshill.
Peto.
Bardolph.

Lady Percy, wife to *Hotspur,* and sister to *Mortimer.*
Lady Mortimer, daughter to *Glendower,* and wife to *Mortimer.*
Mistress Quickly, hostess of the Boar's Head in Eastcheap.

Lords, Officers, Sheriff, Vintner, Chamberlain, Drawers, two Carriers, Travellers, and Attendants.

SCENE. — *England and Wales.*]

ACT I. Scene I. [*London. The Palace.*]

Enter the *King, Lord John of Lancaster, Earl of Westmoreland,* [*Sir Walter Blunt,*] with others.

King. So shaken as we are, so wan with care,
Find we a time for frighted peace to pant
And breathe short-winded accents of new broils
To be commenc'd in stronds afar remote.
No more the thirsty entrance of this soil
Shall daub her lips with her own children's blood.
No more shall trenching war channel her fields,
Nor bruise her flow'rets with the armed hoofs
Of hostile paces. Those opposed eyes
Which, like the meteors of a troubled heaven,
All of one nature, of one substance bred,
Did lately meet in the intestine shock
And furious close of civil butchery,
Shall now in mutual well-beseeming ranks
March all one way and be no more oppos'd
Against acquaintance, kindred, and allies.
The edge of war, like an ill-sheathed knife,
No more shall cut his master. Therefore, friends,
As far as to the sepulchre of Christ —
Whose soldier now, under whose blessed cross
We are impressed and engag'd to fight —
Forthwith a power of English shall we levy,
Whose arms were moulded in their mother's womb
To chase these pagans in those holy fields
Over whose acres walk'd those blessed feet
Which fourteen hundred years ago were nail'd
For our advantage on the bitter cross.
But this our purpose now is twelvemonth old,
And bootless 'tis to tell you we will go.
Therefore we meet not now. Then let me hear
Of you, my gentle cousin Westmoreland,
What yesternight our Council did decree
In forwarding this dear expedience.

West. My liege, this haste was hot in question
And many limits of the charge set down
But yesternight; when all athwart there came
A post from Wales, loaden with heavy news;
Whose worst was that the noble Mortimer,
Leading the men of Herefordshire to fight
Against the irregular and wild Glendower,
Was by the rude hands of that Welshman taken,
A thousand of his people butchered;
Upon whose dead corpse there was such misuse,
Such beastly shameless transformation,
By those Welshwomen done as may not be
Without much shame retold or spoken of.

King. It seems then that the tidings of this broil
Brake off our business for the Holy Land.
West. This, match'd with other, did, my gracious lord;
For more uneven and unwelcome news
Came from the North, and thus it did import:
On Holy-rood Day the gallant Hotspur there,
Young Harry Percy, and brave Archibald,
That ever-valiant and approved Scot,
At Holmedon met,
Where they did spend a sad and bloody hour;
As by discharge of their artillery
And shape of likelihood the news was told;
For he that brought them, in the very heat
And pride of their contention did take horse,
Uncertain of the issue any way.
King. Here is a dear, a true-industrious friend,
Sir Walter Blunt, new lighted from his horse,
Stain'd with the variation of each soil
Betwixt that Holmedon and this seat of ours,
And he hath brought us smooth and welcome news.
The Earl of Douglas is discomfited;
Ten thousand bold Scots, two-and-twenty knights,
Balk'd in their own blood did Sir Walter see
On Holmedon's plains. Of prisoners, Hotspur took
Mordake Earl of Fife and eldest son
To beaten Douglas, and the Earl of Athol,
Of Murray, Angus, and Menteith.
And is not this an honourable spoil?
A gallant prize? Ha, cousin, is it not?
West. In faith,
It is a conquest for a prince to boast of.
King. Yea, there thou mak'st me sad, and mak'st me sin
In envy that my Lord Northumberland
Should be the father to so blest a son —
A son who is the theme of honour's tongue,
Amongst a grove the very straightest plant;
Who is sweet Fortune's minion and her pride;
Whilst I, by looking on the praise of him,
See riot and dishonour stain the brow
Of my young Harry. O that it could be prov'd
That some night-tripping fairy had exchang'd
In cradle clothes our children where they lay,
And call'd mine Percy, his Plantagenet!
Then would I have his Harry, and he mine.
But let him from my thoughts. What think you, coz,
Of this young Percy's pride? The prisoners
Which he in this adventure hath surpris'd
To his own use he keeps, and sends me word
I shall have none but Mordake Earl of Fife.
West. This is his uncle's teaching, this is Worcester,
Malevolent to you in all aspects,
Which makes him prune himself and bristle up
The crest of youth against your dignity.
King. But I have sent for him to answer this;
And for this cause awhile we must neglect
Our holy purpose to Jerusalem.
Cousin, on Wednesday next our council we
Will hold at Windsor. So inform the lords;
But come yourself with speed to us again;
For more is to be said and to be done
Than out of anger can be uttered.
West. I will, my liege. *Exeunt.*

Scene II. [*London. An apartment of the* Prince's.]

Enter *Prince of Wales* and *Sir John Falstaff.*

Fal. Now, Hal, what time of day is it, lad?

Prince. Thou art so fat-witted with drinking of old sack, and unbuttoning thee after supper, and sleeping upon benches after noon, that thou hast forgotten to demand that truly which thou wouldest truly know. What a devil hast thou to do with the time of the day? Unless hours were cups of sack, and minutes capons, and clocks the tongues of bawds, and dials the signs of leaping houses, and the blessed sun himself a fair hot wench in flame-coloured taffeta, I see no reason why thou shouldst be so superfluous to demand the time of the day.

Fal. Indeed you come near me now, Hal; for we that take purses go by the moon and the seven stars, and not by Phœbus, he, that wand'ring knight so fair. And I prithee, sweet wag, when thou art king, as, God save thy Grace — Majesty I should say, for grace thou wilt have none —

Prince. What, none?

Fal. No, by my troth; not so much as will serve to be prologue to an egg and butter.

Prince. Well, how then? Come, roundly, roundly.

Fal. Marry, then, sweet wag, when thou art king, let not us that are squires of the night's body be called thieves of the day's beauty. Let us be Diana's Foresters, Gentlemen of the Shade, Minions of the Moon; and let men say we be men of good government, being governed as the sea is, by our noble and chaste mistress the moon, under whose countenance we steal.

Prince. Thou sayest well, and it holds well too; for the fortune of us that are the moon's men doth ebb and flow like the sea, being governed, as the sea is, by the moon. As, for proof now: a purse of gold most resolutely snatch'd on Monday night and most dissolutely spent on Tuesday morning; got with swearing 'Lay by,' and spent with crying 'Bring in'; now in as low an ebb as the foot of the ladder, and by-and-by in as high a flow as the ridge of the gallows.

Fal. By the Lord, thou say'st true, lad — and is not my hostess of the tavern a most sweet wench?

Prince. As the honey of Hybla, my old lad of the castle — and is not a buff jerkin a most sweet robe of durance?

Fal. How now, how now, mad wag? What, in thy quips and thy quiddities? What a plague have I to do with a buff jerkin?

Prince. Why, what a pox have I to do with my hostess of the tavern?

Fal. Well, thou hast call'd her to a reckoning many a time and oft.

Prince. Did I ever call for thee to pay thy part?

Fal. No; I'll give thee thy due, thou hast paid all there.

Prince. Yea, and elsewhere, so far as my coin would stretch; and where it would not, I have used my credit.

Fal. Yea, and so us'd it that, were it not here apparent that thou art heir apparent — But I prithee, sweet wag, shall there be gallows standing in England when thou art king? and resolution thus fubb'd as it is with the rusty curb of old father antic the law? Do not thou, when thou art king, hang a thief.

Prince. No; thou shalt.

Fal. Shall I? O rare! By the Lord, I'll be a brave judge.

Prince. Thou judgest false already. I mean, thou shalt have the hanging of the thieves and so become a rare hangman.

Fal. Well, Hal, well; and in some sort it jumps with my humour as well as waiting in the court, I can tell you.

Prince. For obtaining of suits?

Fal. Yea, for obtaining of suits, whereof the hangman hath no lean wardrobe. 'Sblood, I am as melancholy as a gib-cat or a lugg'd bear.

Prince. Or an old lion, or a lover's lute.

Fal. Yea, or the drone of a Lincolnshire bagpipe.

Prince. What sayest thou to a hare, or the melancholy of Moor Ditch?

Fal. Thou hast the most unsavoury similes, and art indeed the most comparative, rascalliest, sweet young prince. But, Hal, I prithee trouble me no more with vanity. I would to God thou and I knew where a commodity of good names were to be bought. An old lord of the Council rated me the other day in the street about you, sir, but I mark'd him not; and yet he talk'd very wisely, but I regarded him not; and yet he talk'd wisely, and in the street too.

Prince. Thou didst well; for wisdom cries out in the streets, and no man regards it.

Fal. O, thou hast damnable iteration, and art indeed able to corrupt a saint. Thou hast done much harm upon me, Hal — God forgive thee for it! Before I knew thee, Hal, I knew nothing; and now am I, if a man should speak truly, little better than one of the wicked. I must give over this life, and I will give it over! By the Lord, an I do not, I am a villain! I'll be damn'd for never a king's son in Christendom.

Prince. Where shall we take a purse tomorrow, Jack?

Fal. Zounds, where thou wilt, lad! I'll make one. An I do not, call me villain and baffle me.

Prince. I see a good amendment of life in thee — from praying to purse-taking.

Fal. Why, Hal, 'tis my vocation, Hal. 'Tis no sin for a man to labour in his vocation.

Enter *Poins.*

Poins! Now shall we know if Gadshill have set a match. O, if men were to be saved by merit, what hole in hell were hot enough for him? This is the most omnipotent villain that ever cried 'Stand!' to a true man.

Prince. Good morrow, Ned.

Poins. Good morrow, sweet Hal. What says Monsieur Remorse? What says Sir John Sack and Sugar? Jack, how agrees the devil and thee about thy soul, that thou soldest him on Good Friday last for a cup of Madeira and a cold capon's leg?

Prince. Sir John stands to his word, the devil shall have his bargain; for he was never yet a breaker of proverbs. He will give the devil his due.

Poins. Then art thou damn'd for keeping thy word with the devil.

Prince. Else he had been damn'd for cozening the devil.

Poins. But, my lads, my lads, to-morrow morning, by four o'clock early, at Gadshill! There are pilgrims going to Canterbury with rich offerings, and traders riding to London with fat purses. I have vizards for you all; you have horses for yourselves. Gadshill lies to-night in Rochester. I have bespoke supper to-morrow night in Eastcheap. We may do it as secure as sleep. If you will go, I will stuff your purses full of crowns; if you will not, tarry at home and be hang'd!

Fal. Hear ye, Yedward: if I tarry at home and go not, I'll hang you for going.

Poins. You will, chops?

Fal. Hal, wilt thou make one?

Prince. Who, I rob? I a thief? Not I, by my faith.

Fal. There's neither honesty, manhood, nor good fellowship in thee, nor thou cam'st not of the blood royal if thou darest not stand for ten shillings.

Prince. Well then, once in my days I'll be a madcap.

Fal. Why, that's well said.

Prince. Well, come what will, I'll tarry at home.

Fal. By the Lord, I'll be a traitor then, when thou art king.

Prince. I care not.

Poins. Sir John, I prithee, leave the Prince and me alone. I will lay him down such reasons for this adventure that he shall go.

Fal. Well, God give thee the spirit of persuasion and him the ears of profiting, that what thou speakest may move and what he hears may be believed, that the true prince may (for recreation sake) prove a false thief; for the poor abuses of the time want countenance. Farewell; you shall find me in Eastcheap.

Prince. Farewell, thou latter spring! farewell, All-hallown summer!

[*Exit Falstaff.*]

Poins. Now, my good sweet honey lord, ride with us to-morrow. I have a jest to execute that I cannot manage alone. Falstaff, Bardolph, Peto, and Gadshill shall rob those men that we have already waylaid; yourself and I will not be there; and when they have the booty, if you and I do not rob them, cut this head off from my shoulders.

Prince. How shall we part with them in setting forth?

Poins. Why, we will set forth before or after them and appoint them a place of meeting, wherein it is at our pleasure to fail; and then will they adventure upon the exploit themselves; which they shall have no sooner achieved, but we'll set upon them.

Prince. Yea, but 'tis like that they will know us by our horses, by our habits, and by every other appointment, to be ourselves.

Poins. Tut! our horses they shall not see — I'll tie them in the wood; our vizards we will change after we leave them; and, sirrah, I have cases of buckram for the nonce, to immask our noted outward garments.

Prince. Yea, but I doubt they will be too hard for us.

Poins. Well, for two of them, I know them to be as true-bred cowards as ever turn'd back; and for the third, if he fight longer than he sees reason, I'll forswear arms. The virtue of this jest will be the incomprehensible lies that this same fat rogue will tell us when we meet at supper: how thirty, at least, he fought with; what wards, what blows, what extremities he endured; and in the reproof of this lies the jest.

Prince. Well, I'll go with thee. Provide us all things necessary and meet me to-night in Eastcheap. There I'll sup. Farewell.

Poins. Farewell, my lord. *Exit.*

Prince. I know you all, and will awhile uphold
The unyok'd humour of your idleness.
Yet herein will I imitate the sun,
Who doth permit the base contagious clouds
To smother up his beauty from the world,
That, when he please again to be himself,
Being wanted, he may be more wond'red at
By breaking through the foul and ugly mists
Of vapours that did seem to strangle him.
If all the year were playing holidays,
To sport would be as tedious as to work;
But when they seldom come, they wish'd-for come,
And nothing pleaseth but rare accidents.
So, when this loose behaviour I throw off
And pay the debt I never promised,
By how much better than my word I am,
By so much shall I falsify men's hopes;
And, like bright metal on a sullen ground,
My reformation, glitt'ring o'er my fault,
Shall show more goodly and attract more eyes
Than that which hath no foil to set it off.
I'll so offend to make offence a skill,
Redeeming time when men think least I will.
Exit.

Scene III. [*London. The Palace.*]

Enter the *King, Northumberland, Worcester, Hotspur, Sir Walter Blunt,* with others.

King. My blood hath been too cold and temperate,
Unapt to stir at these indignities,
And you have found me, for accordingly
You tread upon my patience; but be sure
I will from henceforth rather be myself,
Mighty and to be fear'd, than my condition,
Which hath been smooth as oil, soft as young down,
And therefore lost that title of respect
Which the proud soul ne'er pays but to the proud.

Wor. Our house, my sovereign liege, little deserves
The scourge of greatness to be us'd on it —
And that same greatness too which our own hands
Have holp to make so portly.

North. My lord —

King. Worcester, get thee gone; for I do see
Danger and disobedience in thine eye.
O, sir, your presence is too bold and peremptory,
And majesty might never yet endure
The moody frontier of a servant brow.
You have good leave to leave us. When we need
Your use and counsel, we shall send for you.
Exit Worcester.
You were about to speak.

North. Yea, my good lord.
Those prisoners in your Highness' name demanded
Which Harry Percy here at Holmedon took,
Were, as he says, not with such strength denied
As is delivered to your Majesty.
Either envy, therefore, or misprision
Is guilty of this fault, and not my son.

Hot. My liege, I did deny no prisoners.
But I remember, when the fight was done,
When I was dry with rage and extreme toil,
Breathless and faint, leaning upon my sword,
Came there a certain lord, neat and trimly dress'd,
Fresh as a bridegroom; and his chin new reap'd
Show'd like a stubble land at harvest home.
He was perfumed like a milliner,
And 'twixt his finger and his thumb he held
A pouncet box, which ever and anon
He gave his nose, and took't away again;
Who therewith angry, when it next came there,
Took it in snuff; and still he smil'd and talk'd;
And as the soldiers bore dead bodies by,
He call'd them untaught knaves, unmannerly,
To bring a slovenly unhandsome corse
Betwixt the wind and his nobility.
With many holiday and lady terms
He questioned me, amongst the rest demanded
My prisoners in your Majesty's behalf.
I then, all smarting with my wounds being cold,
To be so pest'red with a popingay,
Out of my grief and my impatience
Answer'd neglectingly, I know not what —
He should, or he should not; for he made me mad
To see him shine so brisk, and smell so sweet,
And talk so like a waiting gentlewoman
Of guns and drums and wounds — God save the mark! —
And telling me the sovereignest thing on earth
Was parmacity for an inward bruise;
And that it was great pity, so it was,
This villanous saltpetre should be digg'd
Out of the bowels of the harmless earth,
Which many a good tall fellow had destroy'd
So cowardly; and but for these vile guns,
He would himself have been a soldier.
This bald unjointed chat of his, my lord,
I answered indirectly, as I said,
And I beseech you, let not his report
Come current for an accusation
Betwixt my love and your high majesty.

Blunt. The circumstance considered, good my lord,
Whate'er Lord Harry Percy then had said
To such a person, and in such a place,
At such a time, with all the rest retold,
May reasonably die, and never rise
To do him wrong, or any way impeach
What then he said, so he unsay it now.

King. Why, yet he doth deny his prisoners,
But with proviso and exception,
That we at our own charge shall ransom straight
His brother-in-law, the foolish Mortimer;
Who, on my soul, hath wilfully betray'd
The lives of those that he did lead to fight
Against that great magician, damn'd Glendower,
Whose daughter, as we hear, the Earl of March
Hath lately married. Shall our coffers, then,
Be emptied to redeem a traitor home?
Shall we buy treason? and indent with fears
When they have lost and forfeited themselves?
No, on the barren mountains let him starve!
For I shall never hold that man my friend

Whose tongue shall ask me for one penny cost
To ransom home revolted Mortimer.

Hot. Revolted Mortimer?
He never did fall off, my sovereign liege,
But by the chance of war. To prove that true
Needs no more but one tongue for all those wounds,
Those mouthed wounds, which valiantly he took
When on the gentle Severn's sedgy bank,
In single opposition hand to hand,
He did confound the best part of an hour
In changing hardiment with great Glendower.
Three times they breath'd, and three times did they drink,
Upon agreement, of swift Severn's flood;
Who then, affrighted with their bloody looks,
Ran fearfully among the trembling reeds
And hid his crisp head in the hollow bank,
Bloodstained with these valiant combatants.
Never did base and rotten policy
Colour her working with such deadly wounds;
Nor never could the noble Mortimer
Receive so many, and all willingly.
Then let not him be slandered with revolt.

King. Thou dost belie him, Percy, thou dost belie him!
He never did encounter with Glendower.
I tell thee
He durst as well have met the devil alone
As Owen Glendower for an enemy.
Art thou not asham'd? But, sirrah, henceforth
Let me not hear you speak of Mortimer.
Send me your prisoners with the speediest means,
Or you shall hear in such a kind from me
As will displease you. My Lord Northumberland,
We license your departure with your son. —
Send us your prisoners, or you will hear of it.

Exeunt King, [Blunt, and Train].

Hot. An if the devil come and roar for them,
I will not send them. I will after straight
And tell him so; for I will ease my heart,
Albeit I make a hazard of my head.

North. What, drunk with choler? Stay, and pause awhile.
Here comes your uncle.

Enter *Worcester*.

Hot. Speak of Mortimer?
Zounds, I will speak of him, and let my soul
Want mercy if I do not join with him!
Yea, on his part I'll empty all these veins,
And shed my dear blood drop by drop in the dust,
But I will lift the downtrod Mortimer
As high in the air as this unthankful king,
As this ingrate and cank'red Bolingbroke.

North. Brother, the King hath made your nephew mad.

Wor. Who struck this heat up after I was gone?

Hot. He will (forsooth) have all my prisoners;
And when I urg'd the ransom once again
Of my wive's brother, then his cheek look'd pale,
And on my face he turn'd an eye of death,
Trembling even at the name of Mortimer.

Wor. I cannot blame him. Was not he proclaim'd
By Richard that dead is, the next of blood?

North. He was; I heard the proclamation.
And then it was when the unhappy King
(Whose wrongs in us God pardon!) did set forth
Upon his Irish expedition;
From whence he intercepted did return
To be depos'd, and shortly murdered.

Wor. And for whose death we in the world's wide mouth
Live scandaliz'd and foully spoken of.

Hot. But soft, I pray you. Did King Richard then
Proclaim my brother Edmund Mortimer
Heir to the crown?

North. He did; myself did hear it.

Hot. Nay, then I cannot blame his cousin king,
That wish'd him on the barren mountains starve.
But shall it be that you, that set the crown
Upon the head of this forgetful man,
And for his sake wear the detested blot
Of murtherous subornation — shall it be
That you a world of curses undergo,
Being the agents or base second means,
The cords, the ladder, or the hangman rather?
O, pardon me that I descend so low
To show the line and the predicament
Wherein you range under this subtile king!
Shall it for shame be spoken in these days,
Or fill up chronicles in time to come,
That men of your nobility and power
Did gage them both in an unjust behalf
(As both of you, God pardon it! have done)
To put down Richard, that sweet lovely rose,
And plant this thorn, this canker, Bolingbroke?
And shall it in more shame be further spoken
That you are fool'd, discarded, and shook off
By him for whom these shames ye underwent?
No! yet time serves wherein you may redeem

Your banish'd honours and restore yourselves
Into the good thoughts of the world again;
Revenge the jeering and disdain'd contempt
Of this proud king, who studies day and night
To answer all the debt he owes to you
Even with the bloody payment of your deaths.
Therefore I say —
Wor. Peace, cousin, say no more;
And now I will unclasp a secret book,
And to your quick-conceiving discontents
I'll read you matter deep and dangerous,
As full of peril and adventurous spirit
As to o'erwalk a current roaring loud
On the unsteadfast footing of a spear.
Hot. If he fall in, good night, or sink or swim!
Send danger from the east unto the west,
So honour cross it from the north to south,
And let them grapple. O, the blood more stirs
To rouse a lion than to start a hare!
North. Imagination of some great exploit
Drives him beyond the bounds of patience.
Hot. By heaven, methinks it were an easy leap
To pluck bright honour from the pale-fac'd moon,
Or dive into the bottom of the deep,
Where fadom line could never touch the ground,
And pluck up drowned honour by the locks,
So he that doth redeem her thence might wear
Without corrival all her dignities;
But out upon this half-fac'd fellowship!
Wor. He apprehends a world of figures here,
But not the form of what he should attend.
Good cousin, give me audience for a while.
Hot. I cry you mercy.
Wor. Those same noble Scots
That are your prisoners —
Hot. I'll keep them all.
By God, he shall not have a Scot of them!
No, if a Scot would save his soul, he shall not.
I'll keep them, by this hand!
Wor. You start away.
And lend no ear unto my purposes.
Those prisoners you shall keep.
Hot. Nay, I will! That's flat!
He said he would not ransom Mortimer,
Forbade my tongue to speak of Mortimer,
But I will find him when he lies asleep,
And in his ear I'll holloa 'Mortimer.'
Nay;
I'll have a starling shall be taught to speak
Nothing but 'Mortimer,' and give it him
To keep his anger still in motion.
Wor. Hear you, cousin, a word.
Hot. All studies here I solemnly defy
Save how to gall and pinch this Bolingbroke;
And that same sword-and-buckler Prince of Wales —
But that I think his father loves him not
And would be glad he met with some mischance,
I would have him poisoned with a pot of ale.
Wor. Farewell, kinsman. I will talk to you
When you are better temper'd to attend.
North. Why, what a wasp-stung and impatient fool
Art thou to break into this woman's mood,
Tying thine ear to no tongue but thine own!
Hot. Why, look you, I am whipp'd and scourg'd with rods,
Nettled, and stung with pismires when I hear
Of this vile politician, Bolingbroke.
In Richard's time — what do you call the place? —
A plague upon it! it is in Gloucestershire —
'Twas where the madcap Duke his uncle kept —
His uncle York — where I first bow'd my knee
Unto this king of smiles, this Bolingbroke —
'Sblood!
When you and he came back from Ravenspurgh —
North. At Berkeley Castle.
Hot. You say true.
Why, what a candy deal of courtesy
This fawning greyhound then did proffer me!
Look, 'when his infant fortune came to age,'
And 'gentle Harry Percy,' and 'kind cousin' —
O, the devil take such cozeners! — God forgive me!
Good uncle, tell your tale, for I have done.
Wor. Nay, if you have not, to it again.
We will stay your leisure.
Hot. I have done, i' faith.
Wor. Then once more to your Scottish prisoners.
Deliver them up without their ransom straight,
And make the Douglas' son your only mean
For powers in Scotland; which, for divers reasons
Which I shall send you written, be assur'd
Will easily be granted. [*To Northumberland*] You, my lord,
Your son in Scotland being thus employ'd,
Shall secretly into the bosom creep
Of that same noble prelate well-belov'd,
The Archbishop.
Hot. Of York, is it not?
Wor. True; who bears hard
His brother's death at Bristow, the Lord Scroop.
I speak not this in estimation,

As what I think might be, but what I know
Is ruminated, plotted, and set down,
And only stays but to behold the face
Of that occasion that shall bring it on.

Hot. I smell it. Upon my life, it will do well.

North. Before the game is afoot thou still let'st slip.

Hot. Why, it cannot choose but be a noble plot.
And then the power of Scotland and of York
To join with Mortimer, ha?

Wor. And so they shall.

Hot. In faith, it is exceedingly well aim'd.

Wor. And 'tis no little reason bids us speed,
To save our heads by raising of a head;
For, bear ourselves as even as we can,
The King will always think him in our debt,
And think we think ourselves unsatisfied,
Till he hath found a time to pay us home.
And see already how he doth begin
To make us strangers to his looks of love.

Hot. He does, he does! We'll be reveng'd on him.

Wor. Cousin, farewell. No further go in this
Than I by letters shall direct your course.
When time is ripe, which will be suddenly,
I'll steal to Glendower and Lord Mortimer,
Where you and Douglas, and our pow'rs at once,
As I will fashion it, shall happily meet,
To bear our fortunes in our own strong arms,
Which now we hold at much uncertainty.

North. Farewell, good brother. We shall thrive, I trust.

Hot. Uncle, adieu. O, let the hours be short
Till fields and blows and groans applaud our sport! *Exeunt.*

ACT II. Scene I. [*Rochester. An inn yard.*]

Enter a *Carrier* with a lantern in his hand.

1. Car. Heigh-ho! an it be not four by the day, I'll be hang'd. Charles' wain is over the new chimney, and yet our horse not pack'd. — What, ostler!

Ost. [*within*] Anon, anon.

1. Car. I prithee, Tom, beat Cut's saddle, put a few flocks in the point. Poor jade is wrung in the withers out of all cess.

Enter another *Carrier*.

2. Car. Peas and beans are as dank here as a dog, and that is the next way to give poor jades the bots. This house is turned upside down since Robin Ostler died.

1. Car. Poor fellow never joyed since the price of oats rose. It was the death of him.

2. Car. I think this be the most villanous house in all London road for fleas. I am stung like a tench.

1. Car. Like a tench? By the mass, there is ne'er a king christen could be better bit than I have been since the first cock.

2. Car. Why, they will allow us ne'er a jordan, and then we leak in your chimney, and your chamber-lye breeds fleas like a loach.

1. Car. What, ostler! come away and be hang'd! come away!

2. Car. I have a gammon of bacon and two razes of ginger, to be delivered as far as Charing Cross.

1. Car. God's body! the turkeys in my pannier are quite starved. What, ostler! A plague on thee! hast thou never an eye in thy head? Canst not hear? An 'twere not as good deed as drink to break the pate on thee, I am a very villain. Come, and be hang'd! Hast no faith in thee?

Enter *Gadshill.*

Gads. Good morrow, carriers. What's o'clock?

1. Car. I think it be two o'clock.

Gads. I prithee lend me thy lantern to see my gelding in the stable.

1. Car. Nay, by God, soft! I know a trick worth two of that, i' faith.

Gads. I pray thee lend me thine.

2. Car. Ay, when? canst tell? Lend me thy lantern, quoth he? Marry, I'll see thee hang'd first!

Gads. Sirrah carrier, what time do you mean to come to London?

2. Car. Time enough to go to bed with a candle, I warrant thee. Come, neighbour Mugs, we'll call up the gentlemen. They will along with company, for they have great charge. *Exeunt* [*Carriers*].

Gads. What, ho! chamberlain!

Enter *Chamberlain.*

Cham. At hand, quoth pickpurse.

Gads. That's even as fair as — 'at hand, quoth the chamberlain'; for thou variest no more from picking of purses than giving direction doth from labouring: thou layest the plot how.

Cham. Good morrow, Master Gadshill. It holds current that I told you yesternight. There's a franklin in the Wild of Kent hath brought three hundred marks with him in gold. I heard him tell it to one of his company last night at supper — a kind of auditor; one that hath abundance of charge too, God knows what. They are up already and call for eggs and butter. They will away presently.

Gads. Sirrah, if they meet not with Saint Nicholas' clerks, I'll give thee this neck.

Cham. No, I'll none of it. I pray thee keep that for the hangman; for I know thou worshippest Saint Nicholas as truly as a man of falsehood may.

Gads. What talkest thou to me of the hangman? If I hang, I'll make a fat pair of gallows; for if I hang, old Sir John hangs with me, and thou knowest he is no starveling. Tut! there are other Troyans that thou dream'st not of, the which for sport sake are content to do the profession some grace; that would (if matters should be look'd into) for their own credit sake make all whole. I am joined with no foot landrakers, no long-staff sixpenny strikers, none of these mad mustachio purple-hued maltworms; but with nobility and tranquillity, burgomasters and great oneyers, such as can hold in, such as will strike sooner than speak, and speak sooner than drink, and drink sooner than pray; and yet, zounds, I lie; for they pray continually to their saint, the commonwealth, or rather, not pray to her, but prey on her, for they ride up and down on her and make her their boots.

Cham. What, the commonwealth their boots? Will she hold out water in foul way?

Gads. She will, she will! Justice hath liquor'd her. We steal as in a castle, cocksure. We have the receipt of fernseed, we walk invisible.

Cham. Nay, by my faith, I think you are more beholding to the night than to fernseed for your walking invisible.

Gads. Give me thy hand. Thou shalt have a share in our purchase, as I am a true man.

Cham. Nay, rather let me have it, as you are a false thief.

Gads. Go to; 'homo' is a common name to all men. Bid the ostler bring my gelding out of the stable. Farewell, you muddy knave.

Exeunt.

Scene II. [*The highway near Gadshill.*]

Enter *Prince* and *Poins.*

Poins. Come, shelter, shelter! I have remov'd Falstaff's horse, and he frets like a gumm'd velvet.

Prince. Stand close. [*They step aside.*]

Enter *Falstaff.*

Fal. Poins! Poins, and be hang'd! Poins!

Prince. [*comes forward*] Peace, ye fat-kidney'd rascal! What a brawling dost thou keep!

Fal. Where's Poins, Hal?

Prince. He is walk'd up to the top of the hill. I'll go seek him. [*Steps aside.*]

Fal. I am accurs'd to rob in that thief's company. The rascal hath removed my horse and tied him I know not where. If I travel but four foot by the squire further afoot, I shall break my wind. Well, I doubt not but to die a fair death for all this, if I scape hanging for killing that rogue. I have forsworn his company hourly any time this two-and-twenty years, and yet I am bewitch'd with the rogue's company. If the rascal have not given me medicines to make me love him, I'll be hang'd. It could not be else. I have drunk medicines. Poins! Hal! A plague upon you both! Bardolph! Peto! I'll starve ere I'll rob a foot further. An 'twere not as good a deed as drink to turn true man and to leave these rogues, I am the veriest varlet that ever chewed with a tooth. Eight yards of uneven ground is threescore and ten miles afoot with me, and the stony-hearted villains know it well enough. A plague upon it when thieves cannot be true one to another! (*They whistle.*) Whew! A plague upon you all! Give me my horse, you rogues! give me my horse and be hang'd!

Prince. [*comes forward*] Peace, ye fat-guts! Lie down, lay thine ear close to the ground, and list if thou canst hear the tread of travellers.

Fal. Have you any levers to lift me up again, being down? 'Sblood, I'll not bear mine own flesh so far afoot again for all the coin in thy father's exchequer. What a plague mean ye to colt me thus?

Prince. Thou liest; thou art not colted, thou art uncolted.

Fal. I prithee, good Prince Hal, help me to my horse, good king's son.

Prince. Out, ye rogue! Shall I be your ostler?

Fal. Go hang thyself in thine own heir-apparent garters! If I be ta'en, I'll peach for this. An I have not ballads made on you all, and sung to filthy tunes, let a cup of sack be my poison. When a jest is so forward — and afoot too — I hate it.

Enter *Gadshill*, [*Bardolph* and *Peto* with him].

Gads. Stand!

Fal. So I do, against my will.

Poins. [*comes forward*] O, 'tis our setter. I know his voice. Bardolph, what news?

Bar. Case ye, case ye! On with your vizards! There's money of the King's coming down the hill; 'tis going to the King's exchequer.

Fal. You lie, ye rogue! 'Tis going to the King's tavern.

Gads. There's enough to make us all.

Fal. To be hang'd.

Prince. Sirs, you four shall front them in the narrow lane; Ned Poins and I will walk lower. If they scape from your encounter, then they light on us.

Peto. How many be there of them?

Gads. Some eight or ten.

Fal. Zounds, will they not rob us?

Prince. What, a coward, Sir John Paunch?

Fal. Indeed, I am not John of Gaunt, your grandfather; but yet no coward, Hal.

Prince. Well, we leave that to the proof.

Poins. Sirrah Jack, thy horse stands behind the hedge. When thou need'st him, there thou shalt find him. Farewell and stand fast.

Fal. Now cannot I strike him, if I should be hang'd.

Prince. [*aside to Poins*] Ned, where are our disguises?

Poins. [*aside to Prince*] Here, hard by. Stand close. [*Exeunt Prince and Poins.*]

Fal. Now, my masters, happy man be his dole, say I. Every man to his business.

Enter the *Travellers*.

Traveller. Come, neighbour.
The boy shall lead our horses down the hill;
We'll walk afoot awhile and ease our legs.

Thieves. Stand!

Traveller. Jesus bless us!

Fal. Strike! down with them! cut the villains' throats! Ah, whoreson caterpillars! bacon-fed knaves! they hate us youth. Down with them! fleece them!

Traveller. O, we are undone, both we and ours for ever!

Fal. Hang ye, gorbellied knaves, are ye undone? No, ye fat chuffs; I would your store were here! On, bacons, on! What, ye knaves! young men must live. You are grandjurors, are ye? We'll jure ye, faith!

Here they rob and bind them. Exeunt.

Enter the *Prince* and *Poins* [in buckram suits].

Prince. The thieves have bound the true men. Now could thou and I rob the thieves and go merrily to London, it would be argument for a week, laughter for a month, and a good jest for ever.

Poins. Stand close! I hear them coming. [*They stand aside.*]

Enter the *Thieves* again.

Fal. Come, my masters, let us share, and then to horse before day. An the Prince and Poins be not two arrant cowards, there's no equity stirring. There's no more valour in that Poins than in a wild duck.

Prince. Your money!

Poins. Villains!

As they are sharing, the Prince and Poins set upon them. They all run away, and Falstaff, after a blow or two, runs away too, leaving the booty behind them.

Prince. Got with much ease. Now merrily to horse.
The thieves are scattered, and possess'd with fear
So strongly that they dare not meet each other.
Each takes his fellow for an officer.
Away, good Ned. Falstaff sweats to death
And lards the lean earth as he walks along.
Were't not for laughing, I should pity him.

Poins. How the rogue roar'd! *Exeunt.*

Scene III. [*Warkworth Castle.*]

Enter *Hotspur* solus, reading a letter.

Hot. 'But, for mine own part, my lord, I could be well contented to be there, in respect of the love I bear your house.' He could be contented — why is he not then? In respect of the love he bears our house! He shows in this he loves his own barn better than he loves our house. Let me see some more. 'The purpose you undertake is dangerous' — Why, that's certain! 'Tis dangerous to take a cold, to sleep, to drink; but I tell you, my lord fool, out of this nettle, danger, we pluck this flower, safety. 'The purpose you undertake is dangerous, the friends you have named uncertain, the time itself unsorted, and your whole plot too light for the counterpoise of so great an opposition.' Say you so, say you so? I say unto you again, you are a shallow, cowardly hind, and you lie. What a lack-brain is this! By the Lord, our plot is a good plot as ever was laid; our friends true and constant: a good plot, good friends, and full of expectation; an excellent plot, very good friends. What a frosty-spirited rogue is this! Why, my Lord of York commends the plot and the general course of the action. Zounds, an I were now by this rascal, I could brain him with his lady's fan. Is there not my father, my uncle, and myself; Lord Edmund Mortimer, my Lord of York, and Owen Glendower? Is there not, besides, the Douglas? Have I not all their letters to meet me in arms by the ninth of the next month, and are they not some of them set forward already? What a pagan rascal is this! an infidel! Ha! you shall see now, in very sincerity of fear and cold heart will he to the King and lay open all our proceedings. O, I could divide myself and go to buffets for moving such a dish of skim milk with so honourable an action! Hang him, let him tell the King! we are prepared. I will set forward to-night.

Enter his *Lady*.

How now, Kate? I must leave you within these two hours.
Lady. O my good lord, why are you thus alone?
For what offence have I this fortnight been
A banish'd woman from my Harry's bed?
Tell me, sweet lord, what is't that takes from thee
Thy stomach, pleasure, and thy golden sleep?
Why dost thou bend thine eyes upon the earth,
And start so often when thou sit'st alone?
Why hast thou lost the fresh blood in thy cheeks
And given my treasures and my rights of thee
To thick-ey'd musing and curs'd melancholy?
In thy faint slumbers I by thee have watch'd,
And heard thee murmur tales of iron wars,
Speak terms of manage to thy bounding steed,
Cry 'Courage! to the field!' And thou hast talk'd
Of sallies and retires, of trenches, tents,
Of palisadoes, frontiers, parapets,
Of basilisks, of cannon, culverin,
Of prisoners' ransom, and of soldiers slain,
And all the currents of a heady fight.
Thy spirit within thee hath been so at war,
And thus hath so bestirr'd thee in thy sleep,
That beads of sweat have stood upon thy brow
Like bubbles in a late-disturbed stream,
And in thy face strange motions have appear'd,
Such as we see when men restrain their breath
On some great sudden hest. O, what portents are these?
Some heavy business hath my lord in hand,
And I must know it, else he loves me not.
Hot. What, ho!

[Enter a *Servant*.]

Is Gilliams with the packet gone?
Serv. He is, my lord, an hour ago.
Hot. Hath Butler brought those horses from the sheriff?
Serv. One horse, my lord, he brought even now.
Hot. What horse? A roan, a crop-ear, is it not?
Serv. It is, my lord.
Hot. That roan shall be my throne.
Well, I will back him straight. O esperance!
Bid Butler lead him forth into the park.
[*Exit Servant*.]
Lady. But hear you, my lord.
Hot. What say'st thou, my lady?
Lady. What is it carries you away?
Hot. Why, my horse, my love — my horse!
Lady. Out, you mad-headed ape!
A weasel hath not such a deal of spleen
As you are toss'd with. In faith,
I'll know your business, Harry; that I will!
I fear my brother Mortimer doth stir
About his title and hath sent for you
To line his enterprise; but if you go —
Hot. So far afoot, I shall be weary, love.
Lady. Come, come, you paraquito, answer me
Directly unto this question that I ask.
In faith, I'll break thy little finger, Harry,
An if thou wilt not tell me all things true.
Hot. Away,
Away, you trifler! Love? I love thee not;
I care not for thee, Kate. This is no world
To play with mammets and to tilt with lips.
We must have bloody noses and crack'd crowns,
And pass them current too. Gods me, my horse!
What say'st thou, Kate? What wouldst thou have with me?
Lady. Do you not love me? do you not indeed?
Well, do not then; for since you love me not,
I will not love myself. Do you not love me?
Nay, tell me if you speak in jest or no.

Hot. Come, wilt thou see me ride?
And when I am a-horseback, I will swear
I love thee infinitely. But hark you, Kate:
I must not have you henceforth question me
Whither I go, nor reason whereabout.
Whither I must, I must; and to conclude,
This evening must I leave you, gentle Kate.
I know you wise; but yet no farther wise
Than Harry Percy's wife; constant you are,
But yet a woman; and for secrecy,
No lady closer, for I well believe
Thou wilt not utter what thou dost not know,
And so far will I trust thee, gentle Kate.
Lady. How? so far?
Hot. Not an inch further. But hark you, Kate:
Whither I go, thither shall you go too;
To-day will I set forth, to-morrow you.
Will this content you, Kate?
Lady. It must of force. *Exeunt.*

Scene IV. [*Eastcheap. The Boar's Head Tavern.*]

Enter *Prince* and *Poins.*

Prince. Ned, prithee come out of that fat-room and lend me thy hand to laugh a little.

Poins. Where hast been, Hal?

Prince. With three or four loggerheads amongst three or fourscore hogsheads. I have sounded the very bass-string of humility. Sirrah, I am sworn brother to a leash of drawers and can call them all by their christen names, as Tom, Dick, and Francis. They take it already upon their salvation that, though I be but Prince of Wales, yet I am the king of courtesy; and tell me flatly I am no proud Jack like Falstaff, but a Corinthian, a lad of mettle, a good boy (by the Lord, so they call me!), and when I am King of England I shall command all the good lads in Eastcheap. They call drinking deep, dying scarlet; and when you breathe in your watering, they cry 'hem!' and bid you play it off. To conclude, I am so good a proficient in one quarter of an hour that I can drink with any tinker in his own language during my life. I tell thee, Ned, thou hast lost much honour that thou wert not with me in this action. But, sweet Ned — to sweeten which name of Ned, I give thee this pennyworth of sugar, clapp'd even now into my hand by an under-skinker, one that never spake other English in his life than 'Eight shillings and sixpence,' and 'You are welcome,' with this shrill addition, 'Anon, anon, sir! Score a pint of bastard in the Half-moon,' or so — but, Ned, to drive away the time till Falstaff come, I prithee do thou stand in some by-room while I question my puny drawer to what end he gave me the sugar; and do thou never leave calling 'Francis!' that his tale to me may be nothing but 'Anon!' Step aside, and I'll show thee a precedent.

Poins. Francis!

Prince. Thou art perfect.

Poins. Francis! [*Exit Poins.*]

Enter [*Francis,* a] Drawer.

Fran. Anon, anon, sir. — Look down into the Pomgarnet, Ralph.

Prince. Come hither, Francis.

Fran. My lord?

Prince. How long hast thou to serve, Francis?

Fran. Forsooth, five years, and as much as to —

Poins. [*within*] Francis!

Fran. Anon, anon, sir.

Prince. Five year! by'r Lady, a long lease for the clinking of pewter. But, Francis, darest thou be so valiant as to play the coward with thy indenture and show it a fair pair of heels and run from it?

Fran. O Lord, sir, I'll be sworn upon all the books in England I could find in my heart —

Poins. [*within*] Francis!

Fran. Anon, sir.

Prince. How old art thou, Francis?

Fran. Let me see. About Michaelmas next I shall be —

Poins. [*within*] Francis!

Fran. Anon, sir. Pray stay a little, my lord.

Prince. Nay, but hark you, Francis. For the sugar thou gavest me — 'twas a pennyworth, was't not?

Fran. O Lord! I would it had been two!

Prince. I will give thee for it a thousand pound. Ask me when thou wilt, and thou shalt have it.

Poins. [*within*] Francis!

Fran. Anon, anon.

Prince. Anon, Francis? No, Francis; but to-morrow, Francis; or, Francis, a Thursday; or indeed, Francis, when thou wilt. But Francis —

Fran. My lord?

Prince. Wilt thou rob this leathern-jerkin, crystal-button, not-pated, agate-ring, puke-

Falstaff (Paul Rogers), enthroned, chides Prince Hal (Robert Hardy) for his antics

HENRY IV

PART ONE

PHOTOGRAPHS BY HOUSTON ROGERS
PRODUCED BY THE OLD VIC COMPANY

Henry Percy, surnamed Hotspur, son to the Earl of Northumberland. Outspoken, manly, easily provoked, and eager "To pluck bright honour from the pale-fac'd moon" *(Act I, Scene III)*. His rebuke from Henry IV leads him to think of war

Hotspur (John Neville), rebuked for not surrendering prisoners *(Act I, Scene III). Left to right:* Hotspur; Northumberland (Laurence Hardy); the king; Blunt (Daniel Thorndike)

Engaged in banter, Falstaff justifies purse-taking to an attentive Prince. "Why, Hal, 'tis my vocation, Hal; 'tis no sin for a man to labour in his vocation"
(Act I, Scene II)

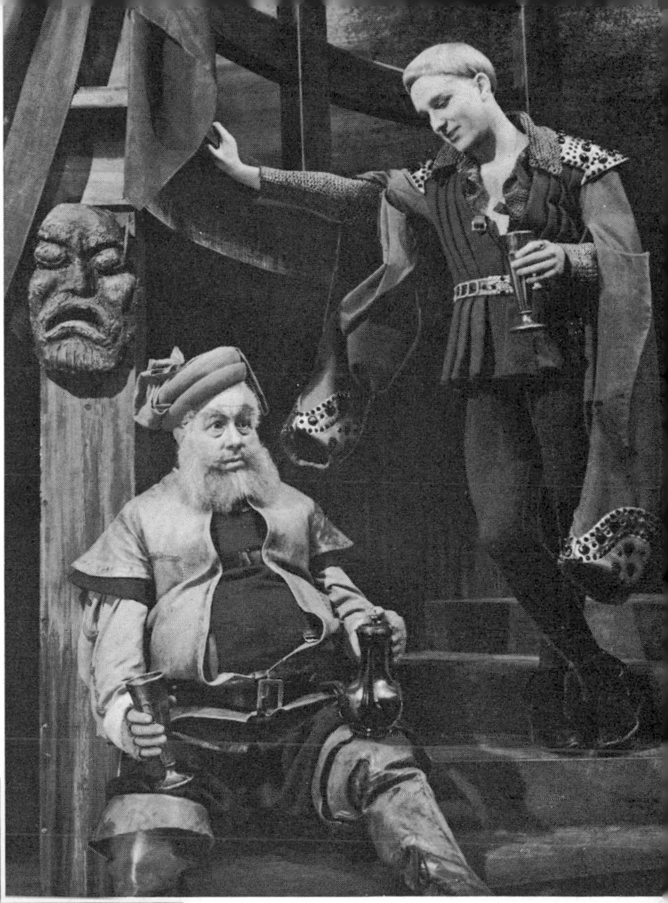

Hotspur's wife (Ann Todd), unaware of his plans for rebellion, seeks to discover the cause of her husband's unrest. "I must know it, else he loves me not"
(Act II, Scene III)

Amoral, irrepressible, cunning, crafty, witty, and fat, Falstaff is jestingly characterized by his friend, Prince Hal, as "That villanous abominable misleader of youth" *(Act II, Scene IV)*

Lady Mortimer (Virginia McKenna), the wife of Edmund Mortimer, brother-in-law to Hotspur. An additional injury was felt by Hotspur in his interview with the king when Mortimer was accused of treason *(Act I, Scene III)*

"The hope and expectation of thy time is ruin'd, and the soul of every man prophetically do fore-think thy fall." Henry IV (Eric Porter) to his son *(Act III, Scene II)*

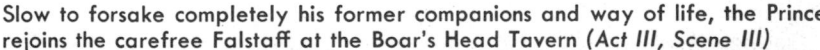

Slow to forsake completely his former companions and way of life, the Prince rejoins the carefree Falstaff at the Boar's Head Tavern *(Act III, Scene III)*

The Welsh rebel and dreamer, Owen Glendower, calls on the musicians to accompany his daughter, Lady Mortimer, as she sings a Welsh song *(Act III, Scene I)*

The rebels, Worcester (Paul Daneman), Mortimer (Anthony White), Hotspur, and Glendower (Meredith Edwards), plot to divide a country they have not yet won (*Act III, Scene I*)

The king's camp near Shrewsbury before the battle with the rebels (*Act V, Scene I*). The king, his sons—Prince Hal at his right, John of Lancaster (Alan Dobie) at his left—and his followers in an act of dedication

"Two stars keep not their motion in one sphere." Prince Henry slays Hotspur *(Act V, Scene IV)*

Henry, Prince of Wales, reformed. "So, when this loose behaviour throw off . . . my reformation, glittering o'er my fault, shall show more goodly" *(Act I, Scene II)*

stocking, caddis-garter, smooth-tongue, Spanish-pouch —

Fran. O Lord, sir, who do you mean?

Prince. Why then, your brown bastard is your only drink; for look you, Francis, your white canvas doublet will sully. In Barbary, sir, it cannot come to so much.

Fran. What, sir?

Poins. [*within*] Francis!

Prince. Away, you rogue! Dost thou not hear them call?

Here they both call him. The Drawer stands amazed, not knowing which way to go.

Enter *Vintner.*

Vint. What, stand'st thou still, and hear'st such a calling? Look to the guests within. [*Exit Francis.*] My lord, old Sir John, with half-a-dozen more, are at the door. Shall I let them in?

Prince. Let them alone awhile, and then open the door. [*Exit Vintner.*] Poins!

Poins. [*within*] Anon, anon, sir.

Enter *Poins.*

Prince. Sirrah, Falstaff and the rest of the thieves are at the door. Shall we be merry?

Poins. As merry as crickets, my lad. But hark ye; what cunning match have you made with this jest of the drawer? Come, what's the issue?

Prince. I am now of all humours that have showed themselves humours since the old days of goodman Adam to the pupil age of this present twelve o'clock at midnight.

[Enter *Francis.*]

What's o'clock, Francis?

Fran. Anon, anon, sir. [*Exit.*]

Prince. That ever this fellow should have fewer words than a parrot, and yet the son of a woman! His industry is upstairs and downstairs, his eloquence the parcel of a reckoning. I am not yet of Percy's mind, the Hotspur of the North; he that kills me some six or seven dozen of Scots at a breakfast, washes his hands, and says to his wife, 'Fie upon this quiet life! I want work.' 'O my sweet Harry,' says she, 'how many hast thou kill'd to-day?' 'Give my roan horse a drench,' says he, and answers 'Some fourteen,' an hour after, 'a trifle, a trifle.' I prithee call in Falstaff. I'll play Percy, and that damn'd brawn shall play Dame Mortimer his wife. 'Rivo!' says the drunkard. Call in ribs, call in tallow.

Enter *Falstaff,* [*Gadshill, Bardolph,* and *Peto; Francis* follows with wine].

Poins. Welcome, Jack. Where hast thou been?

Fal. A plague of all cowards, I say, and a vengeance too! Marry and amen! Give me a cup of sack, boy. Ere I lead this life long, I'll sew nether-stocks, and mend them and foot them too. A plague of all cowards! Give me a cup of sack, rogue. Is there no virtue extant? *He drinketh.*

Prince. Didst thou never see Titan kiss a dish of butter? Pitiful-hearted butter, that melted at the sweet tale of the sun! If thou didst, then behold that compound.

Fal. You rogue, here's lime in this sack too! There is nothing but roguery to be found in villanous man. Yet a coward is worse than a cup of sack with lime in it — a villanous coward! Go thy ways, old Jack, die when thou wilt; if manhood, good manhood, be not forgot upon the face of the earth, then am I a shotten herring. There lives not three good men unhang'd in England; and one of them is fat, and grows old. God help the while! A bad world, I say. I would I were a weaver; I could sing psalms or anything. A plague of all cowards I say still!

Prince. How now, woolsack? What mutter you?

Fal. A king's son! If I do not beat thee out of thy kingdom with a dagger of lath and drive all thy subjects afore thee like a flock of wild geese, I'll never wear hair on my face more. You Prince of Wales?

Prince. Why, you whoreson round man, what's the matter?

Fal. Are not you a coward? Answer me to that — and Poins there?

Poins. Zounds, ye fat paunch, an ye call me coward, by the Lord, I'll stab thee.

Fal. I call thee coward? I'll see thee damn'd ere I call thee coward, but I would give a thousand pound I could run as fast as thou canst. You are straight enough in the shoulders; you care not who sees your back. Call you that backing of your friends? A plague upon such backing! Give me them that will face me. Give me a cup of sack. I am a rogue if I drunk to-day.

Prince. O villain! thy lips are scarce wip'd since thou drunk'st last.

Fal. All is one for that. (*He drinketh.*) A plague of all cowards still say I.

Prince. What's the matter?

Fal. What's the matter? There be four of us here have ta'en a thousand pound this day morning.

Prince. Where is it, Jack? Where is it?

Fal. Where is it? Taken from us it is. A hundred upon poor four of us!

Prince. What, a hundred, man?

Fal. I am a rogue if I were not at half-sword with a dozen of them two hours together. I have scap'd by miracle. I am eight times thrust through the doublet, four through the hose; my buckler cut through and through; my sword hack'd like a handsaw — ecce signum! I never dealt better since I was a man. All would not do. A plague of all cowards! Let them speak. If they speak more or less than truth, they are villains and the sons of darkness.

Prince. Speak, sirs. How was it?

Gads. We four set upon some dozen —

Fal. Sixteen at least, my lord.

Gads. And bound them.

Peto. No, no, they were not bound.

Fal. You rogue, they were bound, every man of them, or I am a Jew else — an Ebrew Jew.

Gads. As we were sharing, some six or seven fresh men set upon us —

Fal. And unbound the rest, and then come in the other.

Prince. What, fought you with them all?

Fal. All? I know not what you call all, but if I fought not with fifty of them, I am a bunch of radish! If there were not two or three and fifty upon poor old Jack, then am I no two-legg'd creature.

Prince. Pray God you have not murd'red some of them.

Fal. Nay, that's past praying for. I have pepper'd two of them. Two I am sure I have paid, two rogues in buckram suits. I tell thee what, Hal — if I tell thee a lie, spit in my face, call me horse. Thou knowest my old ward. Here I lay, and thus I bore my point. Four rogues in buckram let drive at me.

Prince. What, four? Thou saidst but two even now.

Fal. Four, Hal. I told thee four.

Poins. Ay, ay, he said four.

Fal. These four came all afront and mainly thrust at me. I made me no more ado but took all their seven points in my target, thus.

Prince. Seven? Why, there were but four even now.

Fal. In buckram?

Poins. Ay, four, in buckram suits.

Fal. Seven, by these hilts, or I am a villain else.

Prince. [*aside to Poins*] Prithee let him alone. We shall have more anon.

Fal. Dost thou hear me, Hal?

Prince. Ay, and mark thee too, Jack.

Fal. Do so, for it is worth the list'ning to. These nine in buckram that I told thee of —

Prince. So, two more already.

Fal. Their points being broken —

Poins. Down fell their hose.

Fal. Began to give me ground; but I followed me close, came in, foot and hand, and with a thought seven of the eleven I paid.

Prince. O monstrous! Eleven buckram men grown out of two!

Fal. But, as the devil would have it, three misbegotten knaves in Kendal green came at my back and let drive at me; for it was so dark, Hal, that thou couldst not see thy hand.

Prince. These lies are like their father that begets them — gross as a mountain, open, palpable. Why, thou clay-brain'd guts, thou knotty-pated fool, thou whoreson obscene greasy tallow-catch —

Fal. What, art thou mad? art thou mad? Is not the truth the truth?

Prince. Why, how couldst thou know these men in Kendal green when it was so dark thou couldst not see thy hand? Come, tell us your reason. What sayest thou to this?

Poins. Come, your reason, Jack, your reason.

Fal. What, upon compulsion? Zounds, an I were at the strappado or all the racks in the world, I would not tell you on compulsion. Give you a reason on compulsion? If reasons were as plentiful as blackberries, I would give no man a reason upon compulsion, I.

Prince. I'll be no longer guilty of this sin; this sanguine coward, this bed-presser, this horseback-breaker, this huge hill of flesh —

Fal. 'Sblood, you starveling, you elf-skin, you dried neat's-tongue, you bull's pizzle, you stockfish — O for breath to utter what is like thee! — you tailor's yard, you sheath, you bow-case, you vile standing tuck!

Prince. Well, breathe awhile, and then to it again; and when thou hast tired thyself in base comparisons, hear me speak but this.

Poins. Mark, Jack.

Prince. We two saw you four set on four, and bound them and were masters of their wealth. Mark now how a plain tale shall put you down. Then did we two set on you four and, with a word, outfac'd you from your prize, and have it;

yea, and can show it you here in the house. And, Falstaff, you carried your guts away as nimbly, with as quick dexterity, and roar'd for mercy, and still run and roar'd, as ever I heard bullcalf. What a slave art thou to hack thy sword as thou hast done, and then say it was in fight! What trick, what device, what starting hole canst thou now find out to hide thee from this open and apparent shame?

Poins. Come, let's hear, Jack. What trick hast thou now?

Fal. By the Lord, I knew ye as well as he that made ye. Why, hear you, my masters. Was it for me to kill the heir apparent? Should I turn upon the true prince? Why, thou knowest I am as valiant as Hercules; but beware instinct. The lion will not touch the true prince. Instinct is a great matter. I was now a coward on instinct. I shall think the better of myself, and thee, during my life — I for a valiant lion, and thou for a true prince. But, by the Lord, lads, I am glad you have the money. Hostess, clap to the doors. Watch to-night, pray to-morrow. Gallants, lads, boys, hearts of gold, all the titles of good fellowship come to you! What, shall we be merry? Shall we have a play extempore?

Prince. Content — and the argument shall be thy running away.

Fal. Ah, no more of that, Hal, an thou lovest me!

Enter *Hostess.*

Host. O Jesu, my lord the Prince!

Prince. How now, my lady the hostess? What say'st thou to me?

Host. Marry, my lord, there is a nobleman of the court at door would speak with you. He says he comes from your father.

Prince. Give him as much as will make him a royal man, and send him back again to my mother.

Fal. What manner of man is he?

Host. An old man.

Fal. What doth gravity out of his bed at midnight? Shall I give him his answer?

Prince. Prithee do, Jack.

Fal. Faith, and I'll send him packing.

Exit.

Prince. Now, sirs. By'r lady, you fought fair; so did you, Peto; so did you, Bardolph. You are lions too, you ran away upon instinct, you will not touch the true prince; no — fie!

Bard. Faith, I ran when I saw others run.

Prince. Tell me now in earnest, how came Falstaff's sword so hack'd?

Peto. Why, he hack'd it with his dagger, and said he would swear truth out of England but he would make you believe it was done in fight, and persuaded us to do the like.

Bard. Yea, and to tickle our noses with spear-grass to make them bleed, and then to beslubber our garments with it and swear it was the blood of true men. I did that I did not this seven year before — I blush'd to hear his monstrous devices.

Prince. O villain! thou stolest a cup of sack eighteen years ago and wert taken with the manner, and ever since thou hast blush'd extempore. Thou hadst fire and sword on thy side, and yet thou ran'st away. What instinct hadst thou for it?

Bard. My lord, do you see these meteors? Do you behold these exhalations?

Prince. I do.

Bard. What think you they portend?

Prince. Hot livers and cold purses.

Bard. Choler, my lord, if rightly taken.

Prince. No, if rightly taken, halter.

Enter *Falstaff.*

Here comes lean Jack; here comes bare-bone. How now, my sweet creature of bombast? How long is't ago, Jack, since thou sawest thine own knee?

Fal. My own knee? When I was about thy years, Hal, I was not an eagle's talent in the waist; I could have crept into any alderman's thumb-ring. A plague of sighing and grief! It blows a man up like a bladder. There's villanous news abroad. Here was Sir John Bracy from your father. You must to the court in the morning. That same mad fellow of the North, Percy, and he of Wales that gave Amamon the bastinado, and made Lucifer cuckold, and swore the devil his true liegeman upon the cross of a Welsh hook — what a plague call you him?

Poins. O, Glendower.

Fal. Owen, Owen — the same; and his son-in-law Mortimer, and old Northumberland, and that sprightly Scot of Scots, Douglas, that runs a-horseback up a hill perpendicular —

Prince. He that rides at high speed and with his pistol kills a sparrow flying.

Fal. You have hit it.

Prince. So did he never the sparrow.

Fal. Well, that rascal hath good metal in him; he will not run.

Prince. Why, what a rascal art thou then, to praise him so for running!

Fal. A-horseback, ye cuckoo! but afoot he will not budge a foot.

Prince. Yes, Jack, upon instinct.

Fal. I grant ye, upon instinct. Well, he is there too, and one Mordake, and a thousand bluecaps more. Worcester is stol'n away to-night; thy father's beard is turn'd white with the news; you may buy land now as cheap as stinking mack'rel.

Prince. Why then, it is like, if there come a hot June, and this civil buffeting hold, we shall buy maidenheads as they buy hobnails, by the hundreds.

Fal. By the mass, lad, thou sayest true; it is like we shall have good trading that way. But tell me, Hal, art not thou horrible afeard? Thou being heir apparent, could the world pick thee out three such enemies again as that fiend Douglas, that spirit Percy, and that devil Glendower? Art thou not horribly afraid? Doth not thy blood thrill at it?

Prince. Not a whit, i' faith. I lack some of thy instinct.

Fal. Well, thou wilt be horribly chid to-morrow when thou comest to thy father. If thou love me, practise an answer.

Prince. Do thou stand for my father and examine me upon the particulars of my life.

Fal. Shall I? Content. This chair shall be my state, this dagger my sceptre, and this cushion my crown.

Prince. Thy state is taken for a join'd-stool, thy golden sceptre for a leaden dagger, and thy precious rich crown for a pitiful bald crown.

Fal. Well, an the fire of grace be not quite out of thee, now shalt thou be moved. Give me a cup of sack to make my eyes look red, that it may be thought I have wept; for I must speak in passion, and I will do it in King Cambyses' vein.

Prince. Well, here is my leg.

Fal. And here is my speech. Stand aside, nobility.

Host. O Jesu, this is excellent sport, i' faith!

Fal. Weep not, sweet queen, for trickling
tears are vain.

Host. O, the Father, how he holds his countenance!

Fal. For God's sake, lords, convey my tristful queen!
For tears do stop the floodgates of her eyes.

Host. O Jesu, he doth it as like one of these harlotry players as ever I see!

Fal. Peace, good pintpot. Peace, good tickle-brain. — Harry, I do not only marvel where thou spendest thy time, but also how thou art accompanied. For though the camomile, the more it is trodden on, the faster it grows, yet youth, the more it is wasted, the sooner it wears. That thou art my son I have partly thy mother's word, partly my own opinion, but chiefly a villanous trick of thine eye and a foolish hanging of thy nether lip that doth warrant me. If then thou be son to me, here lies the point: why, being son to me, art thou so pointed at? Shall the blessed sun of heaven prove a micher and eat blackberries? A question not to be ask'd. Shall the son of England prove a thief and take purses? A question to be ask'd. There is a thing, Harry, which thou hast often heard of, and it is known to many in our land by the name of pitch. This pitch, as ancient writers do report, doth defile; so doth the company thou keepest. For, Harry, now I do not speak to thee in drink, but in tears; not in pleasure, but in passion; not in words only, but in woes also: and yet there is a virtuous man whom I have often noted in thy company, but I know not his name.

Prince. What manner of man, an it like your Majesty?

Fal. A goodly portly man, i' faith, and a corpulent; of a cheerful look, a pleasing eye, and a most noble carriage; and, as I think, his age some fifty, or, by'r Lady, inclining to threescore; and now I remember me, his name is Falstaff. If that man should be lewdly given, he deceiveth me; for, Harry, I see virtue in his looks. If then the tree may be known by the fruit, as the fruit by the tree, then, peremptorily I speak it, there is virtue in that Falstaff. Him keep with, the rest banish. And tell me now, thou naughty varlet, tell me where hast thou been this month?

Prince. Dost thou speak like a king? Do thou stand for me, and I'll play my father.

Fal. Depose me? If thou dost it half so gravely, so majestically, both in word and matter, hang me up by the heels for a rabbit-sucker or a poulter's hare.

Prince. Well, here I am set.

Fal. And here I stand. Judge, my masters.

Prince. Now, Harry, whence come you?

Fal. My noble lord, from Eastcheap.

Prince. The complaints I hear of thee are grievous.

Fal. 'Sblood, my lord, they are false! Nay, I'll tickle ye for a young prince, i' faith.

Prince. Swearest thou, ungracious boy? Henceforth ne'er look on me. Thou art violently carried away from grace. There is a devil haunts thee in the likeness of an old fat man; a tun of man is thy companion. Why dost thou converse with that trunk of humours, that bolting hutch of beastliness, that swoll'n parcel of dropsies, that huge bombard of sack, that stuff'd cloakbag of guts, that roasted Manningtree ox with the pudding in his belly, that reverend vice, that grey iniquity, that father ruffian, that vanity in years? Wherein is he good, but to taste sack and drink it? wherein neat and cleanly, but to carve a capon and eat it? wherein cunning, but in craft? wherein crafty, but in villany? wherein villanous, but in all things? wherein worthy, but in nothing?

Fal. I would your Grace would take me with you. Whom means your Grace?

Prince. That villanous abominable misleader of youth, Falstaff, that old white-bearded Satan.

Fal. My lord, the man I know.

Prince. I know thou dost.

Fal. But to say I know more harm in him than in myself were to say more than I know. That he is old (the more the pity) his white hairs do witness it; but that he is (saving your reverence) a whoremaster, that I utterly deny. If sack and sugar be a fault, God help the wicked! If to be old and merry be a sin, then many an old host that I know is damn'd. If to be fat be to be hated, then Pharaoh's lean kine are to be loved. No, my good lord. Banish Peto, banish Bardolph, banish Poins; but for sweet Jack Falstaff, kind Jack Falstaff, true Jack Falstaff, valiant Jack Falstaff, and therefore more valiant being, as he is, old Jack Falstaff, banish not him thy Harry's company, banish not him thy Harry's company. Banish plump Jack, and banish all the world!

Prince. I do, I will. [*A knocking heard.*]
[*Exeunt Hostess, Francis, and Bardolph.*]

Enter *Bardolph*, running.

Bard. O, my lord, my lord! the sheriff with a most monstrous watch is at the door.

Fal. Out, ye rogue! Play out the play. I have much to say in the behalf of that Falstaff.

Enter the *Hostess.*

Host. O Jesu, my lord, my lord!

Prince. Heigh, heigh, the devil rides upon a fiddlestick! What's the matter?

Host. The sheriff and all the watch are at the door. They are come to search the house. Shall I let them in?

Fal. Dost thou hear, Hal? Never call a true piece of gold a counterfeit. Thou art essentially mad without seeming so.

Prince. And thou a natural coward without instinct.

Fal. I deny your major. If you will deny the sheriff, so; if not, let him enter. If I become not a cart as well as another man, a plague on my bringing up! I hope I shall as soon be strangled with a halter as another.

Prince. Go hide thee behind the arras. The rest walk up above. Now, my masters, for a true face and good conscience.

Fal. Both which I have had; but their date is out, and therefore I'll hide me. *Exit.*

Prince. Call in the sheriff.
[*Exeunt. Manent the Prince and Peto.*]

Enter *Sheriff* and the *Carrier.*

Now, Master Sheriff, what is your will with me?

Sher. First, pardon me, my lord. A hue and cry
Hath followed certain men unto this house.

Prince. What men?

Sher. One of them is well known, my gracious lord —
A gross fat man.

Carrier. As fat as butter.

Prince. The man, I do assure you, is not here,
For I myself at this time have employ'd him.
And, sheriff, I will engage my word to thee
That I will by to-morrow dinner time
Send him to answer thee, or any man,
For anything he shall be charg'd withal;
And so let me entreat you leave the house.

Sher. I will, my lord. There are two gentlemen
Have in this robbery lost three hundred marks.

Prince. It may be so. If he have robb'd these men,
He shall be answerable; and so farewell.

Sher. Good night, my noble lord.

Prince. I think it is good morrow, is it not?

Sher. Indeed, my lord, I think it be two o'clock. *Exit* [*with Carrier*].

Prince. This oily rascal is known as well as Paul's. Go call him forth.

Peto. Falstaff! Fast asleep behind the arras, and snorting like a horse.

Prince. Hark how hard he fetches breath. Search his pockets.

He searcheth his pockets and findeth certain papers.

What hast thou found?

Peto. Nothing but papers, my lord.

Prince. Let's see what they be. Read them.

Peto. [*reads*] 'Item, A capon . . ii s. ii d.
Item, Sauce . . . iiii d.
Item, Sack two gallons v s. viii d.
Item, Anchovies and Sack after supper . ii s. vi d.
Item, Bread . . ob.'

Prince. O monstrous! but one halfpennyworth of bread to this intolerable deal of sack! What there is else, keep close; we'll read it at more advantage. There let him sleep till day. I'll to the court in the morning. We must all to the wars, and thy place shall be honourable. I'll procure this fat rogue a charge of foot; and I know his death will be a march of twelve score. The money shall be paid back again with advantage. Be with me betimes in the morning, and so good morrow, Peto.

Peto. Good morrow, good my lord.

Exeunt.

ACT III. Scene I. [*Bangor. The Archdeacon's house.*]

Enter *Hotspur, Worcester, Lord Mortimer, Owen Glendower.*

Mort. These promises are fair, the parties sure,
And our induction full of prosperous hope.

Hot. Lord Mortimer, and cousin Glendower,
Will you sit down?
And uncle Worcester. A plague upon it!
I have forgot the map.

Glend. No, here it is.
Sit, cousin Percy; sit, good cousin Hotspur,
For by that name as oft as Lancaster
Doth speak of you, his cheek looks pale, and with
A rising sigh he wisheth you in heaven.

Hot. And you in hell, as oft as he hears
Owen Glendower spoke of.

Glend. I cannot blame him. At my nativity
The front of heaven was full of fiery shapes
Of burning cressets, and at my birth
The frame and huge foundation of the earth
Shak'd like a coward.

Hot. Why, so it would have done at the same season, if your mother's cat had but kitten'd, though yourself had never been born.

Glend. I say the earth did shake when I was born.

Hot. And I say the earth was not of my mind,
If you suppose as fearing you it shook.

Glend. The heavens were all on fire, the earth did tremble.

Hot. O, then the earth shook to see the heavens on fire,
And not in fear of your nativity.
Diseased nature oftentimes breaks forth
In strange eruptions; oft the teeming earth
Is with a kind of colic pinch'd and vex'd
By the imprisoning of unruly wind
Within her womb, which, for enlargement striving,
Shakes the old beldame earth and topples down
Steeples and mossgrown towers. At your birth
Our grandam earth, having this distemp'rature,
In passion shook.

Glend. Cousin, of many men
I do not bear these crossings. Give me leave
To tell you once again that at my birth
The front of heaven was full of fiery shapes,
The goats ran from the mountains, and the herds
Were strangely clamorous to the frighted fields.
These signs have mark'd me extraordinary,
And all the courses of my life do show
I am not in the roll of common men.
Where is he living, clipp'd in with the sea
That chides the banks of England, Scotland, Wales,
Which calls me pupil or hath read to me?
And bring him out that is but woman's son
Can trace me in the tedious ways of art
And hold me pace in deep experiments.

Hot. I think there's no man speaks better Welsh. I'll to dinner.

Mort. Peace, cousin Percy; you will make him mad.

Glend. I can call spirits from the vasty deep.

Hot. Why, so can I, or so can any man;
But will they come when you do call for them?

Glend. Why, I can teach you, cousin, to command
The devil.

Hot. And I can teach thee, coz, to shame the devil —

By telling truth. Tell truth and shame the devil.
If thou have power to raise him, bring him hither,
And I'll be sworn I have power to shame him hence.
O, while you live, tell truth and shame the devil!

Mort. Come, come, no more of this unprofitable chat.

Glend. Three times hath Henry Bolingbroke made head
Against my power; thrice from the banks of Wye
And sandy-bottom'd Severn have I sent him
Bootless home and weather-beaten back.

Hot. Home without boots, and in foul weather too?
How scapes he agues, in the devil's name?

Glend. Come, here's the map. Shall we divide our right
According to our threefold order ta'en?

Mort. The Archdeacon hath divided it
Into three limits very equally.
England, from Trent and Severn hitherto,
By south and east is to my part assign'd;
All westward, Wales beyond the Severn shore,
And all the fertile land within that bound,
To Owen Glendower; and, dear coz, to you
The remnant northward lying off from Trent.
And our indentures tripartite are drawn;
Which being sealed interchangeably
(A business that this night may execute),
To-morrow, cousin Percy, you and I
And my good Lord of Worcester will set forth
To meet your father and the Scottish power,
As is appointed us, at Shrewsbury.
My father Glendower is not ready yet,
Nor shall we need his help these fourteen days.
[*To Glend.*] Within that space you may have drawn together
Your tenants, friends, and neighbouring gentlemen.

Glend. A shorter time shall send me to you, lords;
And in my conduct shall your ladies come,
From whom you now must steal and take no leave,
For there will be a world of water shed
Upon the parting of your wives and you.

Hot. Methinks my moiety, north from Burton here,
In quantity equals not one of yours.
See how this river comes me cranking in
And cuts me from the best of all my land
A huge half-moon, a monstrous cantle out.
I'll have the current in this place damm'd up,
And here the smug and silver Trent shall run
In a new channel fair and evenly.
It shall not wind with such a deep indent
To rob me of so rich a bottom here.

Glend. Not wind? It shall, it must! You see it doth.

Mort. Yea, but
Mark how he bears his course, and runs me up
With like advantage on the other side,
Gelding the opposed continent as much
As on the other side it takes from you.

Wor. Yea, but a little charge will trench him here
And on this north side win this cape of land;
And then he runs straight and even.

Hot. I'll have it so. A little charge will do it.

Glend. I will not have it alt'red.

Hot. Will not you?

Glend. No, nor you shall not.

Hot. Who shall say me nay?

Glend. Why, that will I.

Hot. Let me not understand you then; speak it in Welsh.

Glend. I can speak English, lord, as well as you;
For I was train'd up in the English court,
Where, being but young, I framed to the harp
Many an English ditty lovely well,
And gave the tongue a helpful ornament —
A virtue that was never seen in you.

Hot. Marry,
And I am glad of it with all my heart!
I had rather be a kitten and cry mew
Than one of these same metre ballet-mongers.
I had rather hear a brazen canstick turn'd
Or a dry wheel grate on the axletree,
And that would set my teeth nothing on edge,
Nothing so much as mincing poetry.
'Tis like the forc'd gait of a shuffling nag.

Glend. Come, you shall have Trent turn'd.

Hot. I do not care. I'll give thrice so much land
To any well-deserving friend;
But in the way of bargain, mark ye me,
I'll cavil on the ninth part of a hair.
Are the indentures drawn? Shall we be gone?

Glend. The moon shines fair; you may away by night.
I'll haste the writer, and withal
Break with your wives of your departure hence.
I am afraid my daughter will run mad,
So much she doteth on her Mortimer. *Exit*

Mort. Fie, cousin Percy! how you cross my father!

Hot. I cannot choose. Sometime he angers me
With telling me of the moldwarp and the ant,
Of the dreamer Merlin and his prophecies,
And of a dragon and a finless fish,
A clip-wing'd griffin and a moulten raven,
A couching lion and a ramping cat,
And such a deal of skimble-skamble stuff
As puts me from my faith. I tell you what —
He held me last night at least nine hours
In reckoning up the several devils' names
That were his lackeys. I cried 'hum,' and 'Well, go to!'
But mark'd him not a word. O, he is as tedious
As a tired horse, a railing wife;
Worse than a smoky house. I had rather live
With cheese and garlic in a windmill far
Than feed on cates and have him talk to me
In any summer house in Christendom.
Mort. In faith, he is a worthy gentleman,
Exceedingly well read, and profited
In strange concealments, valiant as a lion,
And wondrous affable, and as bountiful
As mines of India. Shall I tell you, cousin?
He holds your temper in a high respect
And curbs himself even of his natural scope
When you come 'cross his humour. Faith, he does.
I warrant you that man is not alive
Might so have tempted him as you have done
Without the taste of danger and reproof.
But do not use it oft, let me entreat you.
Wor. In faith, my lord, you are too wilful-blame,
And since your coming hither have done enough
To put him quite besides his patience.
You must needs learn, lord, to amend this fault.
Though sometimes it show greatness, courage, blood —
And that's the dearest grace it renders you —
Yet oftentimes it doth present harsh rage,
Defect of manners, want of government,
Pride, haughtiness, opinion, and disdain;
The least of which haunting a nobleman
Loseth men's hearts, and leaves behind a stain
Upon the beauty of all parts besides,
Beguiling them of commendation.
Hot. Well, I am school'd. Good manners be your speed!
Here come our wives, and let us take our leave.

Enter *Glendower* with the *Ladies.*

Mort. This is the deadly spite that angers me —
My wife can speak no English, I no Welsh.
Glend. My daughter weeps; she will not part with you;
She'll be a soldier too, she'll to the wars.
Mort. Good father, tell her that she and my aunt Percy
Shall follow in your conduct speedily.

Glendower speaks to her in Welsh, and she answers him in the same.

Glend. She is desperate here. A peevish self-will'd harlotry,
One that no persuasion can do good upon.

The Lady speaks in Welsh.

Mort. I understand thy looks. That pretty Welsh
Which thou pourest down from these swelling heavens
I am too perfect in; and, but for shame,
In such a parley should I answer thee.

The Lady again in Welsh.

I understand thy kisses, and thou mine,
And that's a feeling disputation.
But I will never be a truant, love,
Till I have learnt thy language; for thy tongue
Makes Welsh as sweet as ditties highly penn'd,
Sung by a fair queen in a summer's bow'r,
With ravishing division, to her lute.
Glend. Nay, if you melt, then will she run mad.

The Lady speaks again in Welsh.

Mort. O, I am ignorance itself in this!
Glend. She bids you on the wanton rushes lay you down
And rest your gentle head upon her lap,
And she will sing the song that pleaseth you
And on your eyelids crown the god of sleep,
Charming your blood with pleasing heaviness,
Making such difference 'twixt wake and sleep
As is the difference betwixt day and night
The hour before the heavenly-harness'd team
Begins his golden progress in the East.
Mort. With all my heart I'll sit and hear her sing.
By that time will our book, I think, be drawn.
Glend. Do so,
And those musicians that shall play to you
Hang in the air a thousand leagues from hence,
And straight they shall be here. Sit, and attend.
Hot. Come, Kate, thou art perfect in lying down. Come, quick, quick, that I may lay my head in thy lap.
Lady. Go, ye giddy goose.

The music plays.

Hot. Now I perceive the devil understands Welsh;

And 'tis no marvel, he is so humorous.
By'r Lady, he is a good musician.

Lady P. Then should you be nothing but musical; for you are altogether govern'd by humours. Lie still, ye thief, and hear the lady sing in Welsh.

Hot. I had rather hear Lady, my brach, howl in Irish.

Lady P. Wouldst thou have thy head broken?

Hot. No.

Lady P. Then be still.

Hot. Neither! 'Tis a woman's fault.

Lady P. Now God help thee!

Hot. To the Welsh lady's bed.

Lady P. What's that?

Hot. Peace! she sings.

Here the Lady sings a Welsh song.

Come, Kate, I'll have your song too.

Lady P. Not mine, in good sooth.

Hot. Not yours, in good sooth? Heart! you swear like a comfit-maker's wife. 'Not you, in good sooth!' and 'as true as I live!' and 'as God shall mend me!' and 'as sure as day!'
And givest such sarcenet surety for thy oaths
As if thou ne'er walk'st further than Finsbury.
Swear me, Kate, like a lady as thou art,
A good mouth-filling oath; and leave 'in sooth'
And such protest of pepper gingerbread
To velvet guards and Sunday citizens.
Come, sing.

Lady P. I will not sing.

Hot. 'Tis the next way to turn tailor or be redbreast-teacher. An the indentures be drawn, I'll away within these two hours; and so come in when ye will. *Exit.*

Glend. Come, come, Lord Mortimer. You are as slow
As hot Lord Percy is on fire to go.
By this our book is drawn; we'll but seal,
And then to horse immediately.

Mort. With all my heart.

Exeunt.

Scene II. [*London. The Palace.*]

Enter the *King, Prince of Wales,* and others.

King. Lords, give us leave. The Prince of Wales and I
Must have some private conference; but be near at hand,
For we shall presently have need of you.

Exeunt Lords.

I know not whether God will have it so,
For some displeasing service I have done,
That, in his secret doom, out of my blood
He'll breed revengement and a scourge for me;
But thou dost in thy passages of life
Make me believe that thou art only mark'd
For the hot vengeance and the rod of heaven
To punish my mistreadings. Tell me else,
Could such inordinate and low desires,
Such poor, such bare, such lewd, such mean attempts,
Such barren pleasures, rude society,
As thou art match'd withal and grafted to,
Accompany the greatness of thy blood
And hold their level with thy princely heart?

Prince. So please your Majesty, I would I could
Quit all offences with as clear excuse
As well as I am doubtless I can purge
Myself of many I am charg'd withal.
Yet such extenuation let me beg
As, in reproof of many tales devis'd,
Which oft the ear of greatness needs must hear
By smiling pickthanks and base newsmongers,
I may, for some things true wherein my youth
Hath faulty wand'red and irregular,
Find pardon on my true submission.

King. God pardon thee! Yet let me wonder, Harry,
At thy affections, which do hold a wing
Quite from the flight of all thy ancestors.
Thy place in Council thou hast rudely lost,
Which by thy younger brother is supplied,
And art almost an alien to the hearts
Of all the court and princes of my blood.
The hope and expectation of thy time
Is ruin'd, and the soul of every man
Prophetically do forethink thy fall.
Had I so lavish of my presence been,
So common-hackney'd in the eyes of men,
So stale and cheap to vulgar company,
Opinion, that did help me to the crown,
Had still kept loyal to possession
And left me in reputeless banishment,
A fellow of no mark nor likelihood.
By being seldom seen, I could not stir
But, like a comet, I was wond'red at;
That men would tell their children, 'This is he!'
Others would say, 'Where? Which is Bolingbroke?'
And then I stole all courtesy from heaven,
And dress'd myself in such humility
That I did pluck allegiance from men's hearts,
Loud shouts and salutations from their mouths
Even in the presence of the crowned King.

Thus did I keep my person fresh and new,
My presence, like a robe pontifical,
Ne'er seen but wond'red at; and so my state,
Seldom but sumptuous, show'd like a feast
And won by rareness such solemnity.
The skipping King, he ambled up and down
With shallow jesters and rash bavin wits,
Soon kindled and soon burnt; carded his state;
Mingled his royalty with cap'ring fools;
Had his great name profaned with their scorns
And gave his countenance, against his name,
To laugh at gibing boys and stand the push
Of every beardless vain comparative;
Grew a companion to the common streets,
Enfeoff'd himself to popularity;
That, being daily swallowed by men's eyes,
They surfeited with honey and began
To loathe the taste of sweetness, whereof a little
More than a little is by much too much.
So, when he had occasion to be seen,
He was but as the cuckoo is in June,
Heard, not regarded — seen, but with such eyes
As, sick and blunted with community,
Afford no extraordinary gaze,
Such as is bent on sunlike majesty
When it shines seldom in admiring eyes;
But rather drows'd and hung their eyelids down,
Slept in his face, and rend'red such aspect
As cloudy men use to their adversaries,
Being with his presence glutted, gorg'd, and full.
And in that very line, Harry, standest thou;
For thou hast lost thy princely privilege
With vile participation. Not an eye
But is aweary of thy common sight,
Save mine, which hath desir'd to see thee more;
Which now doth that I would not have it do —
Make blind itself with foolish tenderness.

Prince. I shall hereafter, my thrice-gracious lord,
Be more myself.

King. For all the world,
As thou art to this hour, was Richard then
When I from France set foot at Ravenspurgh;
And even as I was then is Percy now.
Now, by my sceptre, and my soul to boot,
He hath more worthy interest to the state
Than thou, the shadow of succession;
For of no right, nor colour like to right,
He doth fill fields with harness in the realm,
Turns head against the lion's armed jaws,
And, being no more in debt to years than thou,
Leads ancient lords and reverend bishops on
To bloody battles and to bruising arms.
What never-dying honour hath he got
Against renowmed Douglas! whose high deeds,
Whose hot incursions and great name in arms
Holds from all soldiers chief majority
And military title capital
Through all the kingdoms that acknowledge Christ.
Thrice hath this Hotspur, Mars in swathling clothes,
This infant warrior, in his enterprises
Discomfited great Douglas; ta'en him once,
Enlarged him, and made a friend of him,
To fill the mouth of deep defiance up
And shake the peace and safety of our throne.
And what say you to this? Percy, Northumberland,
The Archbishop's Grace of York, Douglas, Mortimer
Capitulate against us and are up.
But wherefore do I tell these news to thee?
Why, Harry, do I tell thee of my foes,
Which art my nearest and dearest enemy?
Thou that art like enough, through vassal fear,
Base inclination, and the start of spleen,
To fight against me under Percy's pay,
To dog his heels and curtsy at his frowns,
To show how much thou art degenerate.

Prince. Do not think so. You shall not find it so.
And God forgive them that so much have sway'd
Your Majesty's good thoughts away from me!
I will redeem all this on Percy's head
And, in the closing of some glorious day,
Be bold to tell you that I am your son,
When I will wear a garment all of blood,
And stain my favours in a bloody mask,
Which, wash'd away, shall scour my shame with it.
And that shall be the day, whene'er it lights,
That this same child of honour and renown,
This gallant Hotspur, this all-praised knight,
And your unthought-of Harry chance to meet.
For every honour sitting on his helm,
Would they were multitudes, and on my head
My shames redoubled! For the time will come
That I shall make this Northern youth exchange
His glorious deeds for my indignities.
Percy is but my factor, good my lord,
To engross up glorious deeds on my behalf;
And I will call him to so strict account
That he shall render every glory up,
Yea, even the slightest worship of his time,
Or I will tear the reckoning from his heart.
This in the name of God I promise here;

The which if he be pleas'd I shall perform,
I do beseech your Majesty may salve
The long-grown wounds of my intemperance.
If not, the end of life cancels all bands,
And I will die a hundred thousand deaths
Ere break the smallest parcel of this vow.

King. A hundred thousand rebels die in this!
Thou shalt have charge and sovereign trust herein.

Enter *Blunt.*

How now, good Blunt? Thy looks are full of speed.

Blunt. So hath the business that I come to speak of.
Lord Mortimer of Scotland hath sent word
That Douglas and the English rebels met
The eleventh of this month at Shrewsbury.
A mighty and a fearful head they are,
If promises be kept on every hand,
As ever off'red foul play in a state.

King. The Earl of Westmoreland set forth to-day;
With him my son, Lord John of Lancaster;
For this advertisement is five days old.
On Wednesday next, Harry, you shall set forward;
On Thursday we ourselves will march. Our meeting
Is Bridgenorth; and, Harry, you shall march
Through Gloucestershire; by which account,
Our business valued, some twelve days hence
Our general forces at Bridgenorth shall meet.
Our hands are full of business. Let's away.
Advantage feeds him fat while men delay.
Exeunt.

Scene III. [*Eastcheap. The Boar's Head Tavern.*]

Enter *Falstaff* and *Bardolph.*

Fal. Bardolph, am I not fall'n away vilely since this last action? Do I not bate? Do I not dwindle? Why, my skin hangs about me like an old lady's loose gown! I am withered like an old apple John. Well, I'll repent, and that suddenly, while I am in some liking. I shall be out of heart shortly, and then I shall have no strength to repent. An I have not forgotten what the inside of a church is made of, I am a peppercorn, a brewer's horse. The inside of a church! Company, villanous company, hath been the spoil of me.

Bard. Sir John, you are so fretful you cannot live long.

Fal. Why, there is it! Come, sing me a bawdy song; make me merry. I was as virtuously given as a gentleman need to be, virtuous enough: swore little, dic'd not above seven times a week, went to a bawdy house not above once in a quarter — of an hour, paid money that I borrowed — three or four times, lived well, and in good compass; and now I live out of all order, out of all compass.

Bard. Why, you are so fat, Sir John, that you must needs be out of all compass — out of all reasonable compass, Sir John.

Fal. Do thou amend thy face, and I'll amend my life. Thou art our admiral, thou bearest the lantern in the poop — but 'tis in the nose of thee. Thou art the Knight of the Burning Lamp.

Bard. Why, Sir John, my face does you no harm.

Fal. No, I'll be sworn. I make as good use of it as many a man doth of a death's-head or a memento mori. I never see thy face but I think upon hellfire and Dives that lived in purple; for there he is in his robes, burning, burning. If thou wert any way given to virtue, I would swear by thy face; my oath should be 'By this fire, that's God's angel.' But thou art altogether given over, and wert indeed, but for the light in thy face, the son of utter darkness. When thou ran'st up Gadshill in the night to catch my horse, if I did not think thou hadst been an ignis fatuus or a ball of wildfire, there's no purchase in money. O, thou art a perpetual triumph, an everlasting bonfire-light! Thou hast saved me a thousand marks in links and torches, walking with thee in the night betwixt tavern and tavern; but the sack that thou hast drunk me would have bought me lights as good cheap at the dearest chandler's in Europe. I have maintained that salamander of yours with fire any time this two-and-thirty years. God reward me for it!

Bard. 'Sblood, I would my face were in your belly!

Fal. God-a-mercy! so should I be sure to be heart-burn'd.

Enter *Hostess.*

How now, Dame Partlet the hen? Have you enquir'd yet who pick'd my pocket?

Host. Why, Sir John, what do you think, Sir John? Do you think I keep thieves in my house? I have search'd, I have enquired, so has my husband, man by man, boy by boy, servant by servant. The tithe of a hair was never lost in my house before.

Fal. Ye lie, hostess. Bardolph was shav'd and lost many a hair, and I'll be sworn my pocket was pick'd. Go to, you are a woman, go!

Host. Who, I? No; I defy thee! God's light, I was never call'd so in mine own house before!

Fal. Go to, I know you well enough.

Host. No, Sir John; you do not know me, Sir John. I know you, Sir John. You owe me money, Sir John, and now you pick a quarrel to beguile me of it. I bought you a dozen of shirts to your back.

Fal. Dowlas, filthy dowlas! I have given them away to bakers' wives; they have made bolters of them.

Host. Now, as I am a true woman, holland of eight shillings an ell. You owe money here besides, Sir John, for your diet and by-drinkings, and money lent you, four-and-twenty pound.

Fal. He had his part of it; let him pay.

Host. He? Alas, he is poor; he hath nothing.

Fal. How? Poor? Look upon his face. What call you rich? Let them coin his nose, let them coin his cheeks. I'll not pay a denier. What, will you make a younker of me? Shall I not take mine ease in mine inn but I shall have my pocket pick'd? I have lost a seal-ring of my grandfather's worth forty mark.

Host. O Jesu, I have heard the Prince tell him, I know not how oft, that that ring was copper!

Fal. How? the Prince is a Jack, a sneak-cup. 'Sblood, an he were here, I would cudgel him like a dog if he would say so.

Enter the *Prince* [and *Poins*], marching; and *Falstaff* meets them, playing upon his truncheon like a fife.

How now, lad? Is the wind in that door, i' faith? Must we all march?

Bard. Yea, two and two, Newgate fashion.

Host. My lord, I pray you hear me.

Prince. What say'st thou, Mistress Quickly? How doth thy husband? I love him well; he is an honest man.

Host. Good my lord, hear me.

Fal. Prithee let her alone and list to me.

Prince. What say'st thou, Jack?

Fal. The other night I fell asleep here behind the arras and had my pocket pick'd. This house is turn'd bawdy house; they pick pockets.

Prince. What didst thou lose, Jack?

Fal. Wilt thou believe me, Hal? Three or four bonds of forty pound apiece and a seal-ring of my grandfather's.

Prince. A trifle, some eightpenny matter.

Host. So I told him, my lord, and I said I heard your Grace say so; and, my lord, he speaks most vilely of you, like a foul-mouth'd man as he is, and said he would cudgel you.

Prince. What! he did not?

Host. There's neither faith, truth, nor womanhood in me else.

Fal. There's no more faith in thee than in a stewed prune, nor no more truth in thee than in a drawn fox; and for womanhood, Maid Marian may be the deputy's wife of the ward to thee. Go, you thing, go!

Host. Say, what thing? what thing?

Fal. What thing? Why, a thing to thank God on.

Host. I am no thing to thank God on, I would thou shouldst know it! I am an honest man's wife, and, setting thy knighthood aside, thou art a knave to call me so.

Fal. Setting thy womanhood aside, thou art a beast to say otherwise.

Host. Say, what beast, thou knave, thou?

Fal. What beast? Why, an otter.

Prince. An otter, Sir John? Why an otter?

Fal. Why, she's neither fish nor flesh; a man knows not where to have her.

Host. Thou art an unjust man in saying so. Thou or any man knows where to have me, thou knave, thou!

Prince. Thou say'st true, hostess, and he slanders thee most grossly.

Host. So he doth you, my lord, and said this other day you ought him a thousand pound.

Prince. Sirrah, do I owe you a thousand pound?

Fal. A thousand pound, Hal? A million! Thy love is worth a million; thou owest me thy love.

Host. Nay, my lord, he call'd you Jack and said he would cudgel you.

Fal. Did I, Bardolph?

Bard. Indeed, Sir John, you said so.

Fal. Yea, if he said my ring was copper.

Prince. I say 'tis copper. Darest thou be as good as thy word now?

Fal. Why, Hal, thou knowest, as thou art but man, I dare; but as thou art Prince, I fear thee as I fear the roaring of the lion's whelp.

Prince. And why not as the lion?

Fal. The King himself is to be feared as the lion. Dost thou think I'll fear thee as I fear thy father? Nay, an I do, I pray God my girdle break.

Prince. O, if it should, how would thy guts fall about thy knees! But, sirrah, there's no room for faith, truth, nor honesty in this bosom of thine. It is all fill'd up with guts and midriff. Charge an honest woman with picking thy pocket? Why, thou whoreson, impudent, emboss'd rascal, if there were anything in thy pocket but tavern reckonings, memorandums of bawdy houses, and one poor pennyworth of sugar candy to make thee long-winded — if thy pocket were enrich'd with any other injuries but these, I am a villain. And yet you will stand to it; you will not pocket up wrong. Art thou not ashamed?

Fal. Dost thou hear, Hal? Thou knowest in the state of innocency Adam fell; and what should poor Jack Falstaff do in the days of villany? Thou seest I have more flesh than another man, and therefore more frailty. You confess then, you pick'd my pocket?

Prince. It appears so by the story.

Fal. Hostess, I forgive thee. Go make ready breakfast. Love thy husband, look to thy servants, cherish thy guests. Thou shalt find me tractable to any honest reason. Thou seest I am pacified. — Still? — Nay, prithee be gone. (*Exit Hostess.*) Now, Hal, to the news at court. For the robbery, lad — how is that answered?

Prince. O my sweet beef, I must still be good angel to thee. The money is paid back again.

Fal. O, I do not like that paying back! 'Tis a double labour.

Prince. I am good friends with my father, and may do anything.

Fal. Rob me the exchequer the first thing thou doest, and do it with unwash'd hands too.

Bard. Do, my lord.

Prince. I have procured thee, Jack, a charge of foot.

Fal. I would it had been of horse. Where shall I find one that can steal well? O for a fine thief of the age of two-and-twenty or thereabouts! I am heinously unprovided. Well, God be thanked for these rebels. They offend none but the virtuous. I laud them, I praise them.

Prince. Bardolph!

Bard. My lord?

Prince. Go bear this letter to Lord John of Lancaster,
To my brother John; this to my Lord of Westmoreland.
[*Exit Bardolph.*]
Go, Poins, to horse, to horse; for thou and I
Have thirty miles to ride yet ere dinner time.
[*Exit Poins.*]
Jack, meet me to-morrow in the Temple Hall
At two o'clock in the afternoon.
There shalt thou know thy charge, and there receive
Money and order for their furniture.
The land is burning; Percy stands on high;
And either they or we must lower lie. [*Exit.*]

Fal. Rare words! brave world! Hostess, my breakfast, come.
O, I could wish this tavern were my drum!
Exit.

ACT IV. Scene I. [*The rebel camp near Shrewsbury.*]

Enter *Harry Hotspur, Worcester,* and *Douglas.*

Hot. Well said, my noble Scot. If speaking truth
In this fine age were not thought flattery,
Such attribution should the Douglas have
As not a soldier of this season's stamp
Should go so general current through the world.
By God, I cannot flatter, I defy
The tongues of soothers! but a braver place
In my heart's love hath no man than yourself.
Nay, task me to my word; approve me, lord.

Doug. Thou art the king of honour.
No man so potent breathes upon the ground
But I will beard him.

Enter *one with letters.*

Hot. Do so, and 'tis well.—
What letters hast thou there? — I can but thank you.

Messenger. These letters come from your father.

Hot. Letters from him? Why comes he not himself?

Mess. He cannot come, my lord; he is grievous sick.

Hot. Zounds! how has he the leisure to be sick
In such a justling time? Who leads his power?
Under whose government come they along?

Mess. His letters bears his mind, not I, my lord.
Wor. I prithee tell me, doth he keep his bed?
Mess. He did, my lord, four days ere I set forth,
And at the time of my departure thence
He was much fear'd by his physicians.
Wor. I would the state of time had first been whole
Ere he by sickness had been visited.
His health was never better worth than now.
Hot. Sick now? droop now? This sickness doth infect
The very lifeblood of our enterprise.
'Tis catching hither, even to our camp.
He writes me here that inward sickness —
And that his friends by deputation could not
So soon be drawn; nor did he think it meet
To lay so dangerous and dear a trust
On any soul remov'd but on his own.
Yet doth he give us bold advertisement,
That with our small conjunction we should on,
To see how fortune is dispos'd to us;
For, as he writes, there is no quailing now,
Because the King is certainly possess'd
Of all our purposes. What say you to it?
Wor. Your father's sickness is a maim to us.
Hot. A perilous gash, a very limb lopp'd off.
And yet, in faith, it is not! His present want
Seems more than we shall find it. Were it good
To set the exact wealth of all our states
All at one cast? to set so rich a main
On the nice hazard of one doubtful hour?
It were not good; for therein should we read
The very bottom and the soul of hope,
The very list, the very utmost bound
Of all our fortunes.
Doug. Faith, and so we should;
Where now remains a sweet reversion.
We may boldly spend upon the hope of what
Is to come in.
A comfort of retirement lives in this.
Hot. A rendezvous, a home to fly unto,
If that the devil and mischance look big
Upon the maidenhead of our affairs.
Wor. But yet I would your father had been here.
The quality and hair of our attempt
Brooks no division. It will be thought
By some that know not why he is away,
That wisdom, loyalty, and mere dislike
Of our proceedings kept the Earl from hence.
And think how such an apprehension
May turn the tide of fearful faction
And breed a kind of question in our cause.
For well you know we of the off'ring side
Must keep aloof from strict arbitrement,
And stop all sight-holes, every loop from whence
The eye of reason may pry in upon us.
This absence of your father's draws a curtain
That shows the ignorant a kind of fear
Before not dreamt of.
Hot. You strain too far.
I rather of his absence make this use:
It lends a lustre and more great opinion,
A larger dare to our great enterprise,
Than if the Earl were here; for men must think,
If we, without his help, can make a head
To push against a kingdom, with his help
We shall o'erturn it topsy-turvy down.
Yet all goes well; yet all our joints are whole.
Doug. As heart can think. There is not such a word
Spoke of in Scotland as this term of fear.

Enter *Sir Richard Vernon.*

Hot. My cousin Vernon! welcome, by my soul.
Ver. Pray God my news be worth a welcome, lord.
The Earl of Westmoreland, seven thousand strong,
Is marching hitherwards; with him Prince John.
Hot. No harm. What more?
Ver. And further, I have learn'd
The King himself in person is set forth,
Or hitherwards intended speedily,
With strong and mighty preparation.
Hot. He shall be welcome too. Where is his son,
The nimble-footed madcap Prince of Wales,
And his comrades, that daff'd the world aside
And bid it pass?
Ver. All furnish'd, all in arms;
All plum'd like estridges that with the wind
Bated like eagles having lately bath'd;
Glittering in golden coats like images;
As full of spirit as the month of May
And gorgeous as the sun at midsummer;
Wanton as youthful goats, wild as young bulls.
I saw young Harry with his beaver on,
His cushes on his thighs, gallantly arm'd,
Rise from the ground like feathered Mercury,
And vaulted with such ease into his seat
As if an angel dropp'd down from the clouds
To turn and wind a fiery Pegasus
And witch the world with noble horsemanship.
Hot. No more, no more! Worse than the sun in March,

This praise doth nourish agues. Let them come.
They come like sacrifices in their trim,
And to the fire-ey'd maid of smoky war
All hot and bleeding will we offer them.
The mailed Mars shall on his altar sit
Up to the ears in blood. I am on fire
To hear this rich reprisal is so nigh,
And yet not ours. Come, let me taste my horse,
Who is to bear me like a thunderbolt
Against the bosom of the Prince of Wales.
Harry to Harry shall, hot horse to horse,
Meet, and ne'er part till one drop down a corse.
O that Glendower were come!

Ver. There is more news.
I learn'd in Worcester, as I rode along,
He cannot draw his power this fourteen days.

Doug. That's the worst tidings that I hear of yet.

Wor. Ay, by my faith, that bears a frosty sound.

Hot. What may the King's whole battle reach unto?

Ver. To thirty thousand.

Hot. Forty let it be.
My father and Glendower being both away,
The powers of us may serve so great a day.
Come, let us take a muster speedily.
Doomsday is near. Die all, die merrily.

Doug. Talk not of dying. I am out of fear
Of death or death's hand for this one half-year.
Exeunt.

Scene II. [*A public road near Coventry.*]

Enter *Falstaff* and *Bardolph.*

Fal. Bardolph, get thee before to Coventry; fill me a bottle of sack. Our soldiers shall march through. We'll to Sutton Co'fil' to-night.

Bard. Will you give me money, Captain?

Fal. Lay out, lay out.

Bard. This bottle makes an angel.

Fal. An if it do, take it for thy labour; an if it make twenty, take them all; I'll answer the coinage. Bid my lieutenant Peto meet me at town's end.

Bard. I will, Captain. Farewell. *Exit.*

Fal. If I be not ashamed of my soldiers, I am a sous'd gurnet. I have misused the King's press damnably. I have got, in exchange of a hundred and fifty soldiers, three hundred and odd pounds. I press me none but good householders, yeomen's sons; inquire me out contracted bachelors, such as had been ask'd twice on the banes — such a commodity of warm slaves as had as lieve hear the devil as a drum; such as fear the report of a caliver worse than a struck fowl or a hurt wild duck. I press'd me none but such toasts-and-butter, with hearts in their bellies no bigger than pins' heads, and they have bought out their services; and now my whole charge consists of ancients, corporals, lieutenants, gentlemen of companies — slaves as ragged as Lazarus in the painted cloth, where the glutton's dogs licked his sores; and such as indeed were never soldiers, but discarded unjust servingmen, younger sons to younger brothers, revolted tapsters, and ostlers trade-fall'n; the cankers of a calm world and a long peace; ten times more dishonourable ragged than an old fac'd ancient; and such have I to fill up the rooms of them that have bought out their services that you would think that I had a hundred and fifty tattered Prodigals lately come from swine-keeping, from eating draff and husks. A mad fellow met me on the way, and told me I had unloaded all the gibbets and press'd the dead bodies. No eye hath seen such scarecrows. I'll not march through Coventry with them, that's flat. Nay, and the villains march wide betwixt the legs, as if they had gyves on; for indeed I had the most of them out of prison. There's but a shirt and a half in all my company; and the half-shirt is two napkins tack'd together and thrown over the shoulders like a herald's coat without sleeves; and the shirt, to say the truth, stol'n from my host at Saint Alban's, or the red-nose innkeeper of Daventry. But that's all one; they'll find linen enough on every hedge.

Enter the *Prince* and the *Lord of Westmoreland.*

Prince. How now, blown Jack? How now, quilt?

Fal. What, Hal? How now, mad wag? What a devil dost thou in Warwickshire? My good Lord of Westmoreland, I cry you mercy. I thought your honour had already been at Shrewsbury.

West. Faith, Sir John, 'tis more than time that I were there, and you too; but my powers are there already. The King, I can tell you, looks for us all. We must away all, to-night.

Fal. Tut, never fear me. I am as vigilant as a cat to steal cream.

Prince. I think, to steal cream indeed, for thy theft hath already made thee butter. But tell me, Jack, whose fellows are these that come after?

Fal. Mine, Hal, mine.

Prince. I did never see such pitiful rascals.

Fal. Tut, tut! good enough to toss; food for powder, food for powder. They'll fill a pit as well as better. Tush, man, mortal men, mortal men.

West. Ay, but, Sir John, methinks they are exceeding poor and bare — too beggarly.

Fal. Faith, for their poverty, I know not where they had that; and for their bareness, I am sure they never learn'd that of me.

Prince. No, I'll be sworn, unless you call three fingers on the ribs bare. But, sirrah, make haste. Percy is already in the field. *Exit.*

Fal. What, is the King encamp'd?
West. He is, Sir John. I fear we shall stay too long. [*Exit.*]
Fal. Well,
To the latter end of a fray and the beginning of a feast
Fits a dull fighter and a keen guest. *Exit.*

Scene III. [*The rebel camp near Shrewsbury.*]

Enter *Hotspur, Worcester, Douglas, Vernon.*

Hot. We'll fight with him to-night.
Wor. It may not be.
Doug. You give him then advantage.
Ver. Not a whit.
Hot. Why say you so? Looks he not for supply?
Ver. So do we.
Hot. His is certain, ours is doubtful.
Wor. Good cousin, be advis'd; stir not to-night.
Ver. Do not, my lord.
Doug. You do not counsel well.
You speak it out of fear and cold heart.
Ver. Do me no slander, Douglas. By my life —
And I dare well maintain it with my life —
If well-respected honour bid me on,
I hold as little counsel with weak fear
As you, my lord, or any Scot that this day lives.
Let it be seen to-morrow in the battle
Which of us fears.
Doug. Yea, or to-night.
Ver. Content.
Hot. To-night, say I.
Ver. Come, come, it may not be. I wonder much,
Being men of such great leading as you are,
That you foresee not what impediments
Drag back our expedition. Certain horse
Of my cousin Vernon's are not yet come up.
Your uncle Worcester's horse came but to-day;
And now their pride and mettle is asleep,
Their courage with hard labour tame and dull,
That not a horse is half the half of himself.
Hot. So are the horses of the enemy,
In general journey-bated and brought low.
The better part of ours are full of rest.
Wor. The number of the King exceedeth ours.
For God's sake, cousin, stay till all come in.

The trumpet sounds a parley.

Enter *Sir Walter Blunt.*

Blunt. I come with gracious offers from the King,
If you vouchsafe me hearing and respect.
Hot. Welcome, Sir Walter Blunt, and would to God
You were of our determination!
Some of us love you well; and even those some
Envy your great deservings and good name,
Because you are not of our quality,
But stand against us like an enemy.
Blunt. And God defend but still I should stand so,
So long as out of limit and true rule
You stand against anointed majesty!
But to my charge. The King hath sent to know
The nature of your griefs; and whereupon
You conjure from the breast of civil peace
Such bold hostility, teaching his duteous land
Audacious cruelty. If that the King
Have any way your good deserts forgot,
Which he confesseth to be manifold,
He bids you name your griefs, and with all speed
You shall have your desires with interest,
And pardon absolute for yourself and these
Herein misled by your suggestion.
Hot. The King is kind; and well we know the King
Knows at what time to promise, when to pay.
My father and my uncle and myself
Did give him that same royalty he wears;
And when he was not six-and-twenty strong,
Sick in the world's regard, wretched and low,
A poor unminded outlaw sneaking home,
My father gave him welcome to the shore;
And when he heard him swear and vow to God
He came but to be Duke of Lancaster,
To sue his livery and beg his peace,
With tears of innocency and terms of zeal,
My father, in kind heart and pity mov'd,

Swore him assistance, and perform'd it too.
Now when the lords and barons of the realm
Perceiv'd Northumberland did lean to him,
The more and less came in with cap and knee;
Met him in boroughs, cities, villages,
Attended him on bridges, stood in lanes,
Laid gifts before him, proffer'd him their oaths,
Gave him their heirs as pages, followed him
Even at the heels in golden multitudes.
He presently, as greatness knows itself,
Steps me a little higher than his vow
Made to my father, while his blood was poor,
Upon the naked shore at Ravenspurgh;
And now, forsooth, takes on him to reform
Some certain edicts and some strait decrees
That lie too heavy on the commonwealth;
Cries out upon abuses, seems to weep
Over his country's wrongs; and by this face,
This seeming brow of justice, did he win
The hearts of all that he did angle for;
Proceeded further — cut me off the heads
Of all the favourites that the absent King
In deputation left behind him here
When he was personal in the Irish war.
Blunt. Tut! I came not to hear this.
Hot. Then to the point.
In short time after he depos'd the King;
Soon after that depriv'd him of his life;
And in the neck of that task'd the whole state;
To make that worse, suff'red his kinsman March
(Who is, if every owner were well plac'd,
Indeed his king) to be engag'd in Wales,
There without ransom to lie forfeited;
Disgrac'd me in my happy victories,
Sought to entrap me by intelligence;
Rated mine uncle from the Council board;
In rage dismiss'd my father from the court;
Broke oath on oath, committed wrong on wrong;
And in conclusion drove us to seek out
This head of safety, and withal to pry
Into his title, the which we find
Too indirect for long continuance.
Blunt. Shall I return this answer to the King?
Hot. Not so, Sir Walter. We'll withdraw awhile.
Go to the King; and let there be impawn'd
Some surety for a safe return again,
And in the morning early shall mine uncle
Bring him our purposes; and so farewell.
Blunt. I would you would accept of grace and love.
Hot. And may be so we shall.
Blunt. Pray God you do.
Exeunt.

Scene IV. [*York. The* Archbishop's *Palace.*]

Enter the *Archbishop of York* and *Sir Michael.*

Arch. Hie, good Sir Michael; bear this sealed brief
With winged haste to the Lord Marshal;
This to my cousin Scroop; and all the rest
To whom they are directed. If you knew
How much they do import, you would make haste.
Sir M. My good lord,
I guess their tenour.
Arch. Like enough you do.
To-morrow, good Sir Michael, is a day
Wherein the fortune of ten thousand men
Must bide the touch; for, sir, at Shrewsbury,
As I am truly given to understand,
The King with mighty and quick-raised power
Meets with Lord Harry; and I fear, Sir Michael,
What with the sickness of Northumberland,
Whose power was in the first proportion,
And what with Owen Glendower's absence thence,
Who with them was a rated sinew too
And comes not in, overrul'd by prophecies —
I fear the power of Percy is too weak
To wage an instant trial with the King.
Sir M. Why, my good lord, you need not fear;
There is Douglas and Lord Mortimer.
Arch. No, Mortimer is not there.
Sir M. But there is Mordake, Vernon, Lord Harry Percy,
And there is my Lord of Worcester, and a head
Of gallant warriors, noble gentlemen.
Arch. And so there is; but yet the King hath drawn
The special head of all the land together —
The Prince of Wales, Lord John of Lancaster,
The noble Westmoreland and warlike Blunt,
And many moe corrivals and dear men
Of estimation and command in arms.
Sir M. Doubt not, my lord, they shall be well oppos'd.
Arch. I hope no less, yet needful 'tis to fear;
And, to prevent the worst, Sir Michael, speed.
For if Lord Percy thrive not, ere the King
Dismiss his power, he means to visit us,
For he hath heard of our confederacy,
And 'tis but wisdom to make strong against him.
Therefore make haste. I must go write again
To other friends; and so farewell, Sir Michael.
Exeunt.

Act V. Scene I. [*The* King's *camp near Shrewsbury.*]

Enter the *King, Prince of Wales, Lord John of Lancaster, Sir Walter Blunt, Falstaff.*

King. How bloodily the sun begins to peer
Above yon busky hill! The day looks pale
At his distemp'rature.
Prince. The southern wind
Doth play the trumpet to his purposes
And by his hollow whistling in the leaves
Foretells a tempest and a blust'ring day.
King. Then with the losers let it sympathize,
For nothing can seem foul to those that win.

The trumpet sounds. Enter *Worcester* [and *Vernon*].

How now, my Lord of Worcester? 'Tis not well
That you and I should meet upon such terms
As now we meet. You have deceiv'd our trust
And made us doff our easy robes of peace
To crush our old limbs in ungentle steel.
This is not well, my lord; this is not well.
What say you to it? Will you again unknit
This churlish knot of all-abhorred war,
And move in that obedient orb again
Where you did give a fair and natural light,
And be no more an exhal'd meteor,
A prodigy of fear, and a portent
Of broached mischief to the unborn times?
Wor. Hear me, my liege.
For mine own part, I could be well content
To entertain the lag-end of my life
With quiet hours; for I do protest
I have not sought the day of this dislike.
King. You have not sought it! How comes it then?
Fal. Rebellion lay in his way, and he found it.
Prince. Peace, chewet, peace!
Wor. It pleas'd your Majesty to turn your looks
Of favour from myself and all our house;
And yet I must remember you, my lord,
We were the first and dearest of your friends.
For you my staff of office did I break
In Richard's time, and posted day and night
To meet you on the way and kiss your hand
When yet you were in place and in account
Nothing so strong and fortunate as I.
It was myself, my brother, and his son
That brought you home and boldly did outdare
The dangers of the time. You swore to us,
And you did swear that oath at Doncaster,
That you did nothing purpose 'gainst the state,
Nor claim no further than your new-fall'n right,
The seat of Gaunt, dukedom of Lancaster.
To this we swore our aid. But in short space
It rain'd down fortune show'ring on your head,
And such a flood of greatness fell on you —
What with our help, what with the absent King,
What with the injuries of a wanton time,
The seeming sufferances that you had borne,
And the contrarious winds that held the King
So long in his unlucky Irish wars
That all in England did repute him dead —
And from this swarm of fair advantages
You took occasion to be quickly woo'd
To gripe the general sway into your hand;
Forgot your oath to us at Doncaster;
And, being fed by us, you us'd us so
As that ungentle gull, the cuckoo's bird,
Useth the sparrow — did oppress our nest;
Grew by our feeding to so great a bulk
That even our love durst not come near your sight
For fear of swallowing; but with nimble wing
We were enforc'd for safety sake to fly
Out of your sight and raise this present head;
Whereby we stand opposed by such means
As you yourself have forg'd against yourself
By unkind usage, dangerous countenance,
And violation of all faith and troth
Sworn to us in your younger enterprise.
King. These things, indeed, you have articulate,
Proclaim'd at market crosses, read in churches,
To face the garment of rebellion
With some fine colour that may please the eye
Of fickle changelings and poor discontents,
Which gape and rub the elbow at the news
Of hurlyburly innovation.
And never yet did insurrection want
Such water colours to impaint his cause,
Nor moody beggars, starving for a time
Of pell-mell havoc and confusion.
Prince. In both our armies there is many a soul
Shall pay full dearly for this encounter,
If once they join in trial. Tell your nephew
The Prince of Wales doth join with all the world
In praise of Henry Percy. By my hopes,
This present enterprise set off his head,
I do not think a braver gentleman,
More active-valiant or more valiant-young,

More daring or more bold, is now alive
To grace this latter age with noble deeds.
For my part, I may speak it to my shame,
I have a truant been to chivalry;
And so I hear he doth account me too.
Yet this before my father's Majesty —
I am content that he shall take the odds
Of his great name and estimation,
And will, to save the blood on either side,
Try fortune with him in a single fight.

King. And, Prince of Wales, so dare we venture thee,
Albeit considerations infinite
Do make against it. No, good Worcester, no!
We love our people well; even those we love
That are misled upon your cousin's part;
And, will they take the offer of our grace,
Both he, and they, and you, yea, every man
Shall be my friend again, and I'll be his.
So tell your cousin, and bring me word
What he will do. But if he will not yield,
Rebuke and dread correction wait on us,
And they shall do their office. So be gone.
We will not now be troubled with reply.
We offer fair; take it advisedly.

Exit Worcester [*with Vernon*].

Prince. It will not be accepted, on my life.
The Douglas and the Hotspur both together
Are confident against the world in arms.

King. Hence, therefore, every leader to his charge;
For, on their answer, will we set on them,
And God befriend us as our cause is just!

Exeunt. Manent Prince, Falstaff.

Fal. Hal, if thou see me down in the battle and bestride me, so! 'Tis a point of friendship.

Prince. Nothing but a Colossus can do thee that friendship. Say thy prayers, and farewell.

Fal. I would 'twere bedtime, Hal, and all well.

Prince. Why, thou owest God a death.

[*Exit.*]

Fal. 'Tis not due yet. I would be loath to pay him before his day. What need I be so forward with him that calls not on me? Well, 'tis no matter; honour pricks me on. Yea, but how if honour prick me off when I come on? How then? Can honour set to a leg? No. Or an arm? No. Or take away the grief of a wound? No. Honour hath no skill in surgery then? No. What is honour? A word. What is that word honour? Air. A trim reckoning! Who hath it? He that died a Wednesday. Doth he feel it? No. Doth he hear it? No. 'Tis insensible then? Yea, to the dead. But will it not live with the living? No. Why? Detraction will not suffer it. Therefore I'll none of it. Honour is a mere scutcheon — and so ends my catechism. *Exit.*

Scene II. [*The rebel camp.*]

Enter *Worcester* and *Sir Richard Vernon.*

Wor. O no, my nephew must not know, Sir Richard,
The liberal and kind offer of the King.

Ver. 'Twere best he did.

Wor. Then are we all undone.
It is not possible, it cannot be,
The King should keep his word in loving us.
He will suspect us still and find a time
To punish this offence in other faults.
Suspicion all our lives shall be stuck full of eyes;
For treason is but trusted like the fox,
Who, ne'er so tame, so cherish'd and lock'd up,
Will have a wild trick of his ancestors.
Look how we can, or sad or merrily,
Interpretation will misquote our looks,
And we shall feed like oxen at a stall,
The better cherish'd, still the nearer death.
My nephew's trespass may be well forgot;
It hath the excuse of youth and heat of blood,
And an adopted name of privilege —
A hare-brain'd Hotspur, govern'd by a spleen.
All his offences live upon my head
And on his father's. We did train him on;
And, his corruption being ta'en from us,
We, as the spring of all, shall pay for all.
Therefore, good cousin, let not Harry know,
In any case, the offer of the King.

Enter *Hotspur* [and *Douglas*].

Ver. Deliver what you will, I'll say 'tis so.
Here comes your cousin.

Hot. My uncle is return'd.
Deliver up my Lord of Westmoreland.
Uncle, what news?

Wor. The King will bid you battle presently.

Doug. Defy him by the Lord of Westmoreland.

Hot. Lord Douglas, go you and tell him so.

Doug. Marry, and shall, and very willingly.

Exit.

Wor. There is no seeming mercy in the King.

Hot. Did you beg any? God forbid!

Wor. I told him gently of our grievances,
Of his oath-breaking; which he mended thus,
By now forswearing that he is forsworn.

He calls us rebels, traitors, and will scourge
With haughty arms this hateful name in us.

Enter *Douglas.*

Doug. Arm, gentlemen! to arms! for I have thrown
A brave defiance in King Henry's teeth,
And Westmoreland, that was engag'd, did bear it;
Which cannot choose but bring him quickly on.

Wor. The Prince of Wales stepp'd forth before the King
And, nephew, challeng'd you to single fight.

Hot. O, would the quarrel lay upon our heads,
And that no man might draw short breath to-day
But I and Harry Monmouth! Tell me, tell me,
How show'd his tasking? Seem'd it in contempt?

Ver. No, by my soul. I never in my life
Did hear a challenge urg'd more modestly,
Unless a brother should a brother dare
To gentle exercise and proof of arms.
He gave you all the duties of a man;
Trimm'd up your praises with a princely tongue;
Spoke your deservings like a chronicle;
Making you ever better than his praise
By still dispraising praise valued with you;
And, which became him like a prince indeed,
He made a blushing cital of himself,
And chid his truant youth with such a grace
As if he mast'red there a double spirit
Of teaching and of learning instantly.
There did he pause; but let me tell the world,
If he outlive the envy of this day,
England did never owe so sweet a hope,
So much misconstrued in his wantonness.

Hot. Cousin, I think thou art enamoured
Upon his follies. Never did I hear
Of any prince so wild a libertine.
But be he as he will, yet once ere night
I will embrace him with a soldier's arm,
That he shall shrink under my courtesy.
Arm, arm with speed! and, fellows, soldiers, friends,
Better consider what you have to do
Than I, that have not well the gift of tongue,
Can lift your blood up with persuasion.

Enter a *Messenger.*

Mess. My lord, here are letters for you.

Hot. I cannot read them now. —
O gentlemen, the time of life is short!
To spend that shortness basely were too long
If life did ride upon a dial's point,
Still ending at the arrival of an hour.
An if we live, we live to tread on kings;
If die, brave death, when princes die with us!
Now for our consciences, the arms are fair,
When the intent of bearing them is just.

Enter another *Messenger.*

Mess. My lord, prepare. The King comes on apace.

Hot. I thank him that he cuts me from my tale,
For I profess not talking. Only this —
Let each man do his best; and here draw I
A sword whose temper I intend to stain
With the best blood that I can meet withal
In the adventure of this perilous day.
Now, Esperance! Percy! and set on.
Sound all the lofty instruments of war,
And by that music let us all embrace;
For, heaven to earth, some of us never shall
A second time do such a courtesy.

Here they embrace. The trumpets sound. [*Exeunt.*]

[Scene III. *Plain between the camps.*]

The *King* enters with his *Power.* Alarum to the battle. Then enter *Douglas* and *Sir Walter Blunt.*

Blunt. What is thy name, that in the battle thus
Thou crossest me? What honour dost thou seek
Upon my head?

Doug. Know then my name is Douglas,
And I do haunt thee in the battle thus
Because some tell me that thou art a king.

Blunt. They tell thee true.

Doug. The Lord of Stafford dear to-day hath bought
Thy likeness; for instead of thee, King Harry,
This sword hath ended him. So shall it thee,
Unless thou yield thee as my prisoner.

Blunt. I was not born a yielder, thou proud Scot;
And thou shalt find a king that will revenge
Lord Stafford's death.

They fight. Douglas kills Blunt. Then enter *Hotspur.*

Hot. O Douglas, hadst thou fought at Holmedon thus,
I never had triumph'd upon a Scot.

Doug. All's done, all's won. Here breathless lies the King.

Hot. Where?

Doug. Here.

Hot. This, Douglas? No. I know this face full well.
A gallant knight he was, his name was Blunt;
Semblably furnish'd like the King himself.

Doug. A fool go with thy soul, whither it goes!
A borrowed title hast thou bought too dear:
Why didst thou tell me that thou wert a king?

Hot. The King hath many marching in his coats.

Doug. Now, by my sword, I will kill all his coats;
I'll murder all his wardrop, piece by piece,
Until I meet the King.

Hot. Up and away!
Our soldiers stand full fairly for the day.

Exeunt.

Alarum. Enter *Falstaff* solus.

Fal. Though I could scape shot-free at London, I fear the shot here. Here's no scoring but upon the pate. Soft! who are you? Sir Walter Blunt. There's honour for you! Here's no vanity! I am as hot as molten lead, and as heavy too. God keep lead out of me! I need no more weight than mine own bowels. I have led my rag-of-muffins where they are pepper'd. There's not three of my hundred and fifty left alive; and they are for the town's end, to beg during life. But who comes here?

Enter the *Prince.*

Prince. What, stand'st thou idle here? Lend me thy sword.
Many a nobleman lies stark and stiff
Under the hoofs of vaunting enemies,
Whose deaths are yet unreveng'd. I prithee
Lend me thy sword.

Fal. O Hal, I prithee give me leave to breathe awhile. Turk Gregory never did such deeds in arms as I have done this day. I have paid Percy; I have made him sure.

Prince. He is indeed, and living to kill thee.
I prithee lend me thy sword.

Fal. Nay, before God, Hal, if Percy be alive, thou get'st not my sword; but take my pistol, if thou wilt.

Prince. Give it me. What, is it in the case?

Fal. Ay, Hal. 'Tis hot, 'tis hot. There's that will sack a city.

The Prince draws it out and finds it to be a bottle of sack.

Prince. What, is it a time to jest and dally now? *He throws the bottle at him. Exit.*

Fal. Well, if Percy be alive, I'll pierce him. If he do come in my way, so; if he do not, if I come in his willingly, let him make a carbonado of me. I like not such grinning honour as Sir Walter hath. Give me life; which if I can save, so; if not, honour comes unlook'd for, and there's an end. *Exit.*

Scene IV. [*Another part of the field.*]

Alarum. Excursions. Enter the *King*, the *Prince, Lord John of Lancaster, Earl of Westmoreland.*

King. I prithee,
Harry, withdraw thyself; thou bleedest too much.
Lord John of Lancaster, go you with him.

John. Not I, my lord, unless I did bleed too.

Prince. I do beseech your Majesty make up,
Lest your retirement do amaze your friends.

King. I will do so.
My Lord of Westmoreland, lead him to his tent.

West. Come, my lord, I'll lead you to your tent.

Prince. Lead me, my lord? I do not need your help;
And God forbid a shallow scratch should drive
The Prince of Wales from such a field as this,
Where stain'd nobility lies trodden on,
And rebels' arms triumph in massacres!

John. We breathe too long. Come, cousin Westmoreland,
Our duty this way lies. For God's sake, come.

[*Exeunt Prince John and Westmoreland.*]

Prince. By God, thou hast deceiv'd me, Lancaster!
I did not think thee lord of such a spirit.
Before, I lov'd thee as a brother, John;
But now, I do respect thee as my soul.

King. I saw him hold Lord Percy at the point
With lustier maintenance than I did look for
Of such an ungrown warrior.

Prince. O, this boy
Lends mettle to us all! *Exit.*

Enter *Douglas.*

Doug. Another king? They grow like Hydra's heads.
I am the Douglas, fatal to all those
That wear those colours on them. What art thou
That counterfeit'st the person of a king?

King. The King himself, who, Douglas, grieves at heart
So many of his shadows thou hast met,
And not the very King. I have two boys
Seek Percy and thyself about the field;
But, seeing thou fall'st on me so luckily,
I will assay thee. So defend thyself.
Doug. I fear thou art another counterfeit;
And yet, in faith, thou bearest thee like a king.
But mine I am sure thou art, whoe'er thou be,
And thus I win thee.

They fight. The King being in danger, enter *Prince of Wales.*

Prince. Hold up thy head, vile Scot, or thou art like
Never to hold it up again! The spirits
Of valiant Shirley, Stafford, Blunt are in my arms.
It is the Prince of Wales that threatens thee,
Who never promiseth but he means to pay.
They fight. Douglas flieth.
Cheerly, my lord. How fares your Grace?
Sir Nicholas Gawsey hath for succour sent,
And so hath Clifton. I'll to Clifton straight.
King. Stay and breathe awhile.
Thou hast redeem'd thy lost opinion,
And show'd thou mak'st some tender of my life,
In this fair rescue thou hast brought to me.
Prince. O God! they did me too much injury
That ever said I heark'ned for your death.
If it were so, I might have let alone
The insulting hand of Douglas over you,
Which would have been as speedy in your end
As all the poisonous potions in the world,
And sav'd the treacherous labour of your son.
King. Make up to Clifton; I'll to Sir Nicholas Gawsey. *Exit.*

Enter *Hotspur.*

Hot. If I mistake not, thou art Harry Monmouth.
Prince. Thou speak'st as if I would deny my name.
Hot. My name is Harry Percy.
Prince. Why, then I see
A very valiant rebel of the name.
I am the Prince of Wales; and think not, Percy,
To share with me in glory any more.
Two stars keep not their motion in one sphere,
Nor can one England brook a double reign
Of Harry Percy and the Prince of Wales.
Hot. Nor shall it, Harry; for the hour is come
To end the one of us; and would to God
Thy name in arms were now as great as mine!
Prince. I'll make it greater ere I part from thee,
And all the budding honours on thy crest
I'll crop to make a garland for my head.
Hot. I can no longer brook thy vanities.
They fight.

Enter *Falstaff.*

Fal. Well said, Hal! to it, Hal! Nay, you shall find no boy's play here, I can tell you.

Enter *Douglas.* He fighteth with *Falstaff,* who falls down as if he were dead. [*Exit Douglas.*]
The *Prince* killeth *Percy.*

Hot. O Harry, thou hast robb'd me of my youth!
I better brook the loss of brittle life
Than those proud titles thou hast won of me.
They wound my thoughts worse than thy sword my flesh.
But thoughts the slaves of life, and life time's fool,
And time, that takes survey of all the world,
Must have a stop. O, I could prophesy,
But that the earthy and cold hand of death
Lies on my tongue. No, Percy, thou art dust,
And food for [*Dies.*]
Prince. For worms, brave Percy. Fare thee well, great heart!
Ill-weav'd ambition, how much art thou shrunk!
When that this body did contain a spirit,
A kingdom for it was too small a bound;
But now two paces of the vilest earth
Is room enough. This earth that bears thee dead
Bears not alive so stout a gentleman.
If thou wert sensible of courtesy,
I should not make so dear a show of zeal.
But let my favours hide thy mangled face;
And, even in thy behalf, I'll thank myself
For doing these fair rites of tenderness.
Adieu, and take thy praise with thee to heaven!
Thy ignominy sleep with thee in the grave,
But not remember'd in thy epitaph!
He spieth Falstaff on the ground.
What, old acquaintance? Could not all this flesh
Keep in a little life? Poor Jack, farewell!
I could have better spar'd a better man.
O, I should have a heavy miss of thee
If I were much in love with vanity!

Death hath not struck so fat a deer to-day,
Though many dearer, in this bloody fray.
Embowell'd will I see thee by-and-by;
Till then in blood by noble Percy lie. *Exit.*

Falstaff riseth up.

Fal. Embowell'd? If thou embowel me to-day, I'll give you leave to powder me and eat me too to-morrow. 'Sblood, 'twas time to counterfeit, or that hot termagant Scot had paid me scot and lot too. Counterfeit? I lie; I am no counterfeit. To die is to be a counterfeit; for he is but the counterfeit of a man who hath not the life of a man; but to counterfeit dying when a man thereby liveth, is to be no counterfeit, but the true and perfect image of life indeed. The better part of valour is discretion; in the which better part I have saved my life. Zounds, I am afraid of this gunpowder Percy, though he be dead. How if he should counterfeit too, and rise? By my faith, I am afraid he would prove the better counterfeit. Therefore I'll make him sure; yea, and I'll swear I kill'd him. Why may not he rise as well as I? Nothing confutes me but eyes, and nobody sees me. Therefore, sirrah [*stabs him*], with a new wound in your thigh, come you along with me.

He takes up Hotspur on his back. Enter *Prince*, and *John of Lancaster*.

Prince. Come, brother John; full bravely hast thou flesh'd
Thy maiden sword.
John. But, soft! whom have we here?
Did you not tell me this fat man was dead?
Prince. I did; I saw him dead,
Breathless and bleeding on the ground. Art thou alive,
Or is it fantasy that plays upon our eye-sight?
I prithee speak. We will not trust our eyes
Without our ears. Thou art not what thou seem'st.

Fal. No, that's certain! I am not a double man; but if I be not Jack Falstaff, then am I a Jack. There is Percy. If your father will do me any honour, so; if not, let him kill the next Percy himself. I look to be either earl or duke, I can assure you.

Prince. Why, Percy I kill'd myself, and saw thee dead!

Fal. Didst thou? Lord, Lord, how this world is given to lying! I grant you I was down, and out of breath, and so was he; but we rose both at an instant and fought a long hour by Shrewsbury clock. If I may be believ'd, so; if not, let them that should reward valour bear the sin upon their own heads. I'll take it upon my death, I gave him this wound in the thigh. If the man were alive and would deny it, zounds! I would make him eat a piece of my sword.

John. This is the strangest tale that ever I heard.
Prince. This is the strangest fellow, brother John.
Come, bring your luggage nobly on your back.
For my part, if a lie may do thee grace,
I'll gild it with the happiest terms I have.
A retreat is sounded.
The trumpet sounds retreat; the day is ours.
Come, brother, let's to the highest of the field,
To see what friends are living, who are dead.
Exeunt [Prince Henry and Prince John].

Fal. I'll follow, as they say, for reward. He that rewards me, God reward him! If I do grow great, I'll grow less; for I'll purge, and leave sack, and live cleanly, as a nobleman should do. *Exit [bearing off the body].*

Scene V. [*Another part of the field.*]

The trumpets sound. Enter the *King*, *Prince of Wales*, *Lord John of Lancaster*, *Earl of Westmoreland*, with *Worcester* and *Vernon* prisoners.

King. Thus ever did rebellion find rebuke.
Ill-spirited Worcester! did not we send grace,
Pardon, and terms of love to all of you?
And wouldst thou turn our offers contrary?
Misuse the tenour of thy kinsman's trust?
Three knights upon our party slain to-day,
A noble earl, and many a creature else
Had been alive this hour,
If like a Christian thou hadst truly borne
Betwixt our armies true intelligence.
Wor. What I have done my safety urg'd me to;
And I embrace this fortune patiently,
Since not to be avoided it falls on me.
King. Bear Worcester to the death, and Vernon too;
Other offenders we will pause upon.
Exeunt Worcester and Vernon, [guarded].
How goes the field?
Prince. The noble Scot, Lord Douglas, when he saw

The fortune of the day quite turn'd from him,
The noble Percy slain, and all his men
Upon the foot of fear, fled with the rest;
And falling from a hill, he was so bruis'd
That the pursuers took him. At my tent
The Douglas is, and I beseech your Grace
I may dispose of him.

King. With all my heart.

Prince. Then, brother John of Lancaster, to you
This honourable bounty shall belong.
Go to the Douglas and deliver him
Up to his pleasure, ransomless and free.
His valour shown upon our crests to-day
Hath taught us how to cherish such high deeds,
Even in the bosom of our adversaries.

John. I thank your Grace for this high courtesy,
Which I shall give away immediately.

King. Then this remains, that we divide our power.
You, son John, and my cousin Westmoreland,
Towards York shall bend you with your dearest speed
To meet Northumberland and the prelate Scroop,
Who, as we hear, are busily in arms.
Myself and you, son Harry, will towards Wales
To fight with Glendower and the Earl of March.
Rebellion in this land shall lose his sway,
Meeting the check of such another day;
And since this business so fair is done,
Let us not leave till all our own be won.

Exeunt.

The Second Part of King Henry the Fourth

The Second Part of King Henry the Fourth was entered in the Stationers' Register on August 23, 1600, and the Quarto appeared in the same year.

The title page reads like a table of contents: 'The Second part of Henrie the fourth, continuing to his death, and coronation of Henrie the fift. With the humours of sir Iohn Falstaffe, and swaggering Pistoll. As it hath been sundrie times publikely acted by the right honourable, the Lord Chamberlaine his seruants. Written by William Shakespeare.'

Part I ends with the King's victory over Hotspur at Shrewsbury (July 21, 1403) and the closing speech is to all intents and purposes an announcement that a continuation may be expected. Doubtless Shakespeare began to write the Second Part soon after he finished the First. As dates, 1597 for *Part I* and 1598 for *Part II* are probable.

Between the two plays there is only the interval needed to carry the news to Hotspur's father, the Earl of Northumberland. In the first scene of Part II the tidings reach the Earl's castle at Warkworth. In the same scene we learn that the Archbishop of York has raised an army against the King and that 'more and less do flock to follow him.' In fact, the Archbishop's rebellion occurred in May and June, 1405, almost two years after the Battle of Shrewsbury. Part II ends with the coronation of Henry V, which took place on April 9, 1413.

For most of the text the Quarto is the basis, but the Folio supplies several passages that the Quarto lacks. Important omissions in the Quarto are i, 1, 166–179, 189–209; i, 3, 21–24, 36–55, 85 (second part)–108; ii, 3, 23–45 (first part); iv, 1, 55–79, 103 (second part)–139. All these passages undoubtedly stood in the original text.

Some of the cuts were heedlessly made. Thus, when Morton's speech (i, 1, 187–209) is reduced to the first two lines (187–188), it has no meaning and Northumberland's reply becomes unintelligible. In such cases the printer may have misunderstood deletions in his copy. Sometimes the cut seems to have a special reason. Thus the omission of i, 1, 166–179, spares Northumberland reproaches that sound rather unfeeling. Cf. also lines 32–45, a part of the cut (ii, 3, 23–45) in Lady Percy's long speech. The excision of iv, 1, 55–79, may be due to a feeling (perhaps on the censor's part) that these lines sounded too much like a justification of Essex. His trial took place in June, 1600, and he was not completely set at liberty until August, the very month in which the First Quarto was entered in the Register. The Folio omits a few short passages, amounting in the aggregate to about forty lines.

Oldcastle, not Falstaff, was in the original text, as the accidental retention of *Old.* by the Quarto in one speech heading (i, 2, 137) proves. This is corrected to *Fal.* in the Folio. The Epilogue, in announcing *Henry V* as in prospect, calls attention to the change of name: 'If you be not too much cloy'd with fat meat, our humble author will continue the story, with Sir John in it, and make you merry with fair Katherine of France; where for anything I know, Falstaff shall die of a sweat, unless already 'a be kill'd with your hard opinions; for Oldcastle died a martyr, and this is not the man.' See p. 544, above.

For material Shakespeare drew upon Holinshed, as heretofore, and seems to have consulted Stow. He also made liberal use of *The Famous Victories* (see p. 544). The anecdote of the attack upon the Chief Justice illustrates his procedure. Holinshed says that the Prince struck the Chief Justice with his fist; in *The Famous Victories* he gives him a box on the ear; in Sir Thomas Elyot's *Governour* (1531), copied by Stow, he threatens violence but commits no assault. In the old play the scene is dramatized. Shakespeare, suppressing the action, has the Justice describe the affair in defending his own conduct (v, 2): '[You] struck me in my very seat of judgment.' His speech echoes a phrase of the old play; but neither the old play nor Holinshed records the words that King Henry used in praising the sternness of the judge and the obedience of his son. These are found in Elyot (whom Stow copies). Shakespeare makes Henry V quote them (v, 2, 107–112):

> So shall I live to speak my father's words:
> 'Happy am I that have a man so bold
> That dares do justice on my proper son;
> And not less happy, having such a son
> That would deliver up his greatness so
> Into the hands of justice.'

In Elyot, Henry IV exclaims:

> O mercifull god, how moche am I, aboue all other men, bounde to your infinite goodnes! specially for that ye haue gyuen me a iuge who feareth nat to ministre iustice, and also a sonne who can suffre semblably and obey iustice!

The conscription scene (iii, 2) takes a hint or two from *The Famous Victories*.

The scene of Falstaff's humiliation (v, 5) was also suggested by the old play. Jockey and Ned and Tom, the Prince's roistering companions, have been present at the coronation and accost the king in the street as he comes out 'with the Archbishop and the Lord of Oxford.' He repulses them and speaks their sentence: 'Not vpon pain of death to approach my presence by ten miles space, then if I heare wel of you, it may be I wil do somewhat for you.' There is no such incident in Holinshed, who simply records the fact that, 'whereas aforetime he had made himselfe a companion vnto misrulie mates of dissolute order and life, he now banished them all from his presence (but not vnrewarded, or else vnpreferred); inhibiting them vpon a great paine, not once to approch, lodge, or soiourne within ten miles of his court or presence.' As Shakespeare has adjusted the situation, the young king's severity, which sentimentalists deplore, is stern necessity. There stands Falstaff, stained with travel and sweating with eagerness — a tun of man. Behind him is Pistol, that 'roaring devil i' th' old play' — tall, stalwart, and long-haired, with the ferocious swagger of the professional bully. By Falstaff's side is Bardolph, with his face 'all bubukles and whelks and knobs and flames o' fire.' And there too is Justice Shallow — a starveling figure of comic dignity, like a hermit's staff with a head. 'God save thy Grace, King Hal, my royal Hal!' Falstaff, infatuated, has doomed himself. There is no answer possible but King Henry's:

> 'I know thee not, old man. Fall to thy prayers.
> How ill white hairs become a fool and jester!'

THE SECOND PART OF
KING HENRY THE FOURTH

The Actors' Names.

Rumour, the Presenter.

King Henry the Fourth.
Prince Henry, afterwards crowned *King Henry the Fifth.*

Prince John of Lancaster, *Humphrey of Gloucester*, *Thomas of Clarence*, — sons to *Henry IV* and brethren to *Henry V.*

[*Earl of*] *Northumberland*, [*Richard Scroop*,] the Archbishop of York, [*Lord*] *Mowbray*, [*Lord*] *Hastings*, *Lord Bardolph*, *Travers*, *Morton*, [retainers of Northumberland,] [*Sir John*] *Colevile*, — opposites against *King Henry the Fourth.*

[*Earl of*] *Warwick*, [*Earl of*] *Westmoreland*, [*Earl of*] *Surrey*, *Gower*, *Harcourt*, [*Blunt*,] *Lord Chief Justice*, — of the *King's* party.

[A servant of the *Chief Justice.*]

[*Sir John*] *Falstaff*, *Poins*, *Bardolph*, *Pistol*, *Peto*, *Page* [to *Falstaff*], — irregular humourists.

[*Robert*] *Shallow*, *Silence*, — both country Justices.

Davy, servant to *Shallow.*
Fang and *Snare*, two Sergeants.

[*Ralph*] *Mouldy*, [*Simon*] *Shadow*, [*Thomas*] *Wart*, [*Francis*] *Feeble*, [*Peter*] *Bullcalf*, — country soldiers [or recruits].

Northumberland's Wife.
[*Lady Percy*,] Percy's widow.
Hostess Quickly, [of the Boar's Head tavern, Eastcheap].
Doll Tearsheet.

[Lords and Attendants; a Porter;] Drawers, Beadles, Grooms, [Servants; a Dancer as] Epilogue.

[Scene. — *England.*]

INDUCTION. [*Warkworth. Before* Northumberland's *Castle.*]

Enter *Rumour*, painted full of tongues.

Open your ears, for which of you will stop
The vent of hearing when loud Rumour speaks?
I from the Orient to the drooping West,
Making the wind my posthorse, still unfold
The acts commenced on this ball of earth.
Upon my tongues continual slanders ride,
The which in every language I pronounce,
Stuffing the ears of men with false reports.
I speak of peace while covert enmity,
Under the smile of safety, wounds the world.
And who but Rumour, who but only I,
Make fearful musters and prepar'd defence,
Whiles the big year, swol'n with some other grief,
Is thought with child by the stern tyrant War,
And no such matter? Rumour is a pipe
Blown by surmises, jealousies, conjectures;
And of so easy and so plain a stop
That the blunt monster with uncounted heads,
The still-discordant wav'ring multitude,
Can play upon it. But what need I thus
My well-known body to anatomize
Among my household? Why is Rumour here?
I run before King Harry's victory,
Who, in a bloody field by Shrewsbury,
Hath beaten down young Hotspur and his troops,
Quenching the flame of bold rebellion
Even with the rebels' blood. But what mean I
To speak so true at first? My office is
To noise abroad that Harry Monmouth fell
Under the wrath of noble Hotspur's sword,
And that the King before the Douglas' rage
Stoop'd his anointed head as low as death.
This have I rumour'd through the peasant towns

Between that royal field of Shrewsbury
And this worm-eaten hold of ragged stone,
Where Hotspur's father, old Northumberland,
Lies crafty-sick. The posts come tiring on,
And not a man of them brings other news
Than they have learnt of me. From Rumour's tongues
They bring smooth comforts false, worse than true wrongs. *Exit.*

ACT I. Scene I. [*Warkworth. Before* Northumberland's *Castle.*]

Enter the *Lord Bardolph.*

L. Bard. Who keeps the gate here, ho?

Enter the *Porter.*

Where is the Earl?
Port. What shall I say you are?
L. Bard. Tell thou the Earl
That the Lord Bardolph doth attend him here.
Port. His lordship is walk'd forth into the orchard.
Please it your honour knock but at the gate,
And he himself will answer.

Enter the *Earl of Northumberland.*

L. Bard. Here comes the Earl. [*Exit Porter.*]
North. What news, Lord Bardolph? Every minute now
Should be the father of some stratagem.
The times are wild. Contention, like a horse
Full of high feeding, madly hath broke loose
And bears down all before him.
L. Bard. Noble Earl,
I bring you certain news from Shrewsbury.
North. Good, an God will!
L. Bard. As good as heart can wish.
The King is almost wounded to the death;
And, in the fortune of my lord your son,
Prince Harry slain outright; and both the Blunts
Kill'd by the hand of Douglas; young Prince John
And Westmoreland and Stafford fled the field;
And Harry Monmouth's brawn, the hulk Sir John,
Is prisoner to your son. O, such a day,
So fought, so followed, and so fairly won,
Came not till now to dignify the times,
Since Cæsar's fortunes!
North. How is this deriv'd?
Saw you the field? Came you from Shrewsbury?
L. Bard. I spake with one, my lord, that came from thence,
A gentleman well bred and of good name,
That freely rend'red me these news for true.

Enter *Travers.*

North. Here comes my servant Travers, whom I sent
On Tuesday last to listen after news.
L. Bard. My lord, I overrode him on the way,
And he is furnish'd with no certainties
More than he haply may retail from me.
North. Now, Travers, what good tidings comes with you?
Tra. My lord, Sir John Umfrevile turn'd me back
With joyful tidings and, being better hors'd,
Outrode me. After him came spurring hard
A gentleman, almost forspent with speed,
That stopp'd by me to breathe his bloodied horse.
He ask'd the way to Chester, and of him
I did demand what news from Shrewsbury.
He told me that rebellion had bad luck
And that young Harry Percy's spur was cold.
With that he gave his able horse the head
And, bending forward, struck his armed heels
Against the panting sides of his poor jade
Up to the rowel-head; and starting so,
He seem'd in running to devour the way,
Staying no longer question.
North. Ha! Again.
Said he young Harry Percy's spur was cold?
Of Hotspur, Coldspur? that rebellion
Had met ill luck?
L. Bard. My lord, I'll tell you what:
If my young lord your son have not the day,
Upon mine honour, for a silken point
I'll give my barony. Never talk of it.
North. Why should that gentleman that rode by Travers
Give then such instances of loss?
L. Bard. Who? he?
He was some hilding fellow that had stol'n
The horse he rode on and, upon my life,
Spoke at a venture. Look, here comes more news.

Enter *Morton.*

North. Yea, this man's brow, like to a title-leaf,

Foretells the nature of a tragic volume.
So looks the strond whereon the imperious flood
Hath left a witness'd usurpation.
Say, Morton, didst thou come from Shrewsbury?

Mor. I ran from Shrewsbury, my noble lord,
Where hateful death put on his ugliest mask
To fright our party.

North. How doth my son and brother?
Thou tremblest, and the whiteness in thy cheek
Is apter than thy tongue to tell thy errand.
Even such a man, so faint, so spiritless,
So dull, so dead in look, so woe-begone,
Drew Priam's curtain in the dead of night
And would have told him half his Troy was burnt;
But Priam found the fire ere he his tongue,
And I my Percy's death ere thou report'st it.
This thou wouldst say, 'Your son did thus and thus;
Your brother thus; so fought the noble Douglas' —
Stopping my greedy ear with their bold deeds;
But in the end, to stop my ear indeed,
Thou hast a sigh to blow away this praise,
Ending with 'Brother, son, and all are dead.'

Mor. Douglas is living, and your brother yet;
But for my lord your son —

North. Why, he is dead!
See what a ready tongue suspicion hath!
He that but fears the thing he would not know
Hath by instinct knowledge from others' eyes
That what he fear'd is chanced. Yet speak, Morton.
Tell thou an earl his divination lies,
And I will take it as a sweet disgrace
And make thee rich for doing me such wrong.

Mor. You are too great to be by me gainsaid.
Your spirit is too true, your fears too certain.

North. Yet for all this, say not that Percy 's dead.
I see a strange confession in thine eye.
Thou shak'st thy head and hold'st it fear or sin
To speak a truth. If he be slain, say so.
The tongue offends not that reports his death;
And he doth sin that doth belie the dead,
Not he which says the dead is not alive.
Yet the first bringer of unwelcome news
Hath but a losing office, and his tongue
Sounds ever after as a sullen bell,
Rememb'red tolling a departing friend.

L. Bard. I cannot think, my lord, your son is dead.

Mor. I am sorry I should force you to believe
That which I would to God I had not seen!
But these mine eyes saw him in bloody state,
Rend'ring faint quittance, wearied and out-breath'd,
To Harry Monmouth; whose swift wrath beat down
The never-daunted Percy to the earth,
From whence with life he never more sprung up.
In few, his death (whose spirit lent a fire
Even to the dullest peasant in his camp)
Being bruited once, took fire and heat away
From the best-temper'd courage in his troops;
For from his metal was his party steel'd,
Which once in him abated, all the rest
Turn'd on themselves, like dull and heavy lead;
And as the thing that's heavy in itself
Upon enforcement flies with greatest speed,
So did our men, heavy in Hotspur's loss,
Lend to this weight such lightness with their fear
That arrows fled not swifter toward their aim
Than did our soldiers, aiming at their safety,
Fly from the field. Then was the noble Worcester
Too soon ta'en prisoner, and that furious Scot,
The bloody Douglas, whose well-labouring sword
Had three times slain th' appearance of the King,
Gan vail his stomach and did grace the shame
Of those that turn'd their backs, and in his flight,
Stumbling in fear, was took. The sum of all
Is that the King hath won, and hath sent out
A speedy power to encounter you, my lord,
Under the conduct of young Lancaster
And Westmoreland. This is the news at full.

North. For this I shall have time enough to mourn.
In poison there is physic, and these news,
Having been well, that would have made me sick,
Being sick, have in some measure made me well;
And as the wretch whose fever-weak'ned joints,
Like strengthless hinges, buckle under life,
Impatient of his fit, breaks like a fire
Out of his keeper's arms, even so my limbs,
Weakened with grief, being now enrag'd with grief,
Are thrice themselves. Hence, therefore, thou nice crutch!
A scaly gauntlet now, with joints of steel,
Must glove this hand; and hence, thou sickly coif!
Thou art a guard too wanton for the head

Which princes, flesh'd with conquest, aim to hit.
Now bind my brows with iron, and approach
The ragged'st hour that time and spite dare bring
To frown upon th' enrag'd Northumberland!
Let heaven kiss earth! Now let not Nature's hand
Keep the wild flood confin'd! Let order die!
And let this world no longer be a stage
To feed contention in a ling'ring act;
But let one spirit of the first-born Cain
Reign in all bosoms, that, each heart being set
On bloody courses, the rude scene may end,
And darkness be the burier of the dead!

Tra. This strained passion doth you wrong, my lord.

L. Bard. Sweet Earl, divorce not wisdom from your honour.

Mor. The lives of all your loving complices
Lean on your health; the which, if you give o'er
To stormy passion, must perforce decay.
You cast th' event of war, my noble lord,
And summ'd the accompt of chance before you said,
'Let us make head.' It was your presurmise
That, in the dole of blows, your son might drop.
You knew he walk'd o'er perils on an edge,
More likely to fall in than to get o'er.
You were advis'd his flesh was capable
Of wounds and scars, and that his forward spirit
Would lift him where most trade of danger rang'd.
Yet did you say 'Go forth,' and none of this,
Though strongly apprehended, could restrain
The stiff-borne action. What hath, then, befall'n,
Or what hath this bold enterprise brought forth,
More than that being which was like to be?

L. Bard. We all that are engaged to this loss
Knew that we ventured on such dangerous seas
That if we wrought out life, 'twas ten to one;
And yet we ventur'd, for the gain propos'd
Chok'd the respect of likely peril fear'd;
And since we are o'erset, venture again.
Come, we will all put forth, body and goods.

Mor. 'Tis more than time. And, my most noble lord,
I hear for certain, and dare speak the truth:
The gentle Archbishop of York is up
With well-appointed pow'rs. He is a man
Who with a double surety binds his followers.
My lord your son had only but the corpse,
But shadows and the shows of men, to fight;
For that same word 'rebellion' did divide
The action of their bodies from their souls;
And they did fight with queasiness, constrain'd,
As men drink potions; that their weapons only
Seem'd on our side, but for their spirits and souls,
This word 'rebellion' it had froze them up,
As fish are in a pond. But now the Bishop
Turns insurrection to religion.
Suppos'd sincere, and holy in his thoughts,
He's follow'd both with body and with mind;
And doth enlarge his rising with the blood
Of fair King Richard, scrap'd from Pomfret stones;
Derives from heaven his quarrel and his cause;
Tells them he doth bestride a bleeding land,
Gasping for life under great Bolingbroke;
And more and less do flock to follow him.

North. I knew of this before; but, to speak truth,
This present grief had wip'd it from my mind.
Go in with me; and counsel every man
The aptest way for safety and revenge.
Get posts and letters, and make friends with speed —
Never so few, and never yet more need. *Exeunt.*

Scene II. [*London. A street.*]

Enter *Sir John Falstaff*, with his *Page* bearing his sword and buckler.

Fal. Sirrah, you giant, what says the doctor to my water?

Page. He said, sir, the water itself was a good healthy water; but, for the party that owed it, he might have moe diseases than he knew for.

Fal. Men of all sorts take a pride to gird at me. The brain of this foolish-compounded clay, man, is not able to invent anything that intends to laughter, more than I invent or is invented on me. I am not only witty in myself, but the cause that wit is in other men. I do here walk before thee like a sow that hath overwhelm'd all her litter but one. If the Prince put thee into my service for any other reason than to set me off, why then I have no judgment. Thou whoreson mandrake, thou art fitter to be worn in my cap than to wait at my heels. I was never manned with an agate till now; but I will inset you neither in gold nor silver, but in vile apparel, and send you back again to your master for a jewel — the juvenal, the Prince your master, whose chin is not yet fledge. I will sooner have a beard grow in the palm of my hand than he shall get one off his cheek; and yet he will not stick to say his face is a face-royal! God may finish it when he will; 'tis not a hair amiss yet. He may keep it still at a face-royal, for a barber shall never earn sixpence out of it; and yet he'll be crowing as if he had writ man ever since his father was a bachelor. He may keep his own grace, but he's almost out of mine, I can assure him. What said Master Dommelton about the satin for my short cloak and my slops?

Page. He said, sir, you should procure him better assurance than Bardolph. He would not take his band and yours. He liked not the security.

Fal. Let him be damn'd like the glutton! Pray God his tongue be hotter! A whoreson Achitophel! a rascally yea-forsooth knave! to bear a gentleman in hand, and then stand upon security! The whoreson smooth-pates do now wear nothing but high shoes, and bunches of keys at their girdles; and if a man is through with them in honest taking-up, then they must stand upon security. I had as live they would put ratsbane in my mouth as offer to stop it with security. I look'd 'a should have sent me two-and-twenty yards of satin, as I am a true knight, and he sends me security. Well, he may sleep in security; for he hath the horn of abundance, and the lightness of his wife shines through it; and yet cannot he see, though he have his own lanthorn to light him. Where's Bardolph?

Page. He's gone into Smithfield to buy your worship a horse.

Fal. I bought him in Paul's, and he'll buy me a horse in Smithfield. An I could get me but a wife in the stews, I were mann'd, hors'd, and wiv'd.

Enter *Lord Chief Justice* and *Servant.*

Page. Sir, here comes the nobleman that committed the Prince for striking him about Bardolph.

Fal. Wait close. I will not see him.

Just. What's he that goes there?

Serv. Falstaff, an't please your lordship.

Just. He that was in question for the robb'ry?

Serv. He, my lord; but he hath since done good service at Shrewsbury, and, as I hear, is now going with some charge to the Lord John of Lancaster.

Just. What, to York? Call him back again.

Serv. Sir John Falstaff!

Fal. Boy, tell him I am deaf.

Page. You must speak louder. My master is deaf.

Just. I am sure he is, to the hearing of anything good. Go pluck him by the elbow. I must speak with him.

Serv. Sir John!

Fal. What? A young knave, and begging? Is there not wars? Is there not employment? Doth not the King lack subjects? Do not the rebels need soldiers? Though it be a shame to be on any side but one, it is worse shame to beg than to be on the worst side, were it worse than the name of rebellion can tell how to make it.

Serv. You mistake me, sir.

Fal. Why, sir, did I say you were an honest man? Setting my knighthood and my soldiership aside, I had lied in my throat if I had said so.

Serv. I pray you, sir, then set your knighthood and your soldiership aside, and give me leave to tell you you lie in your throat if you say I am any other than an honest man.

Fal. I give thee leave to tell me so? I lay aside that which grows to me? If thou get'st any leave of me, hang me; if thou tak'st leave, thou wert better be hang'd. You hunt counter. Hence! avaunt!

Serv. Sir, my lord would speak with you.

Just. Sir John Falstaff, a word with you.

Fal. My good lord! God give your lordship good time of day! I am glad to see your lordship abroad. I heard say your lordship was sick. I hope your lordship goes abroad by advice. Your lordship, though not clean past your youth, hath yet some smack of age in you, some relish of the saltness of time; and I most humbly beseech your lordship to have a reverend care of your health.

Just. Sir John, I sent for you before your expedition to Shrewsbury.

Fal. An't please your lordship, I hear his Majesty is return'd with some discomfort from Wales.

Just. I talk not of his Majesty. You would not come when I sent for you.

Fal. And I hear, moreover, his Highness is fall'n into this same whoreson apoplexy.

Just. Well, God mend him! I pray you let me speak with you.

Fal. This apoplexy, as I take it, is a kind of lethargy, an't please your lordship; a kind of sleeping in the blood, a whoreson tingling.

Just. What tell you me of it? Be it as it is.

Fal. It hath it original from much grief, from study and perturbation of the brain. I have read the cause of his effects in Galen. It is a kind of deafness.

Just. I think you are fall'n into the disease, for you hear not what I say to you.

Fal. Very well, my lord, very well. Rather, an't please you, it is the disease of not list'ning, the malady of not marking, that I am troubled withal.

Just. To punish you by the heels would amend the attention of your ears, and I care not if I do become your physician.

Fal. I am as poor as Job, my lord, but not so patient. Your lordship may minister the potion of imprisonment to me in respect of poverty; but how I should be your patient to follow your prescriptions, the wise may make some dram of a scruple, or indeed a scruple itself.

Just. I sent for you when there were matters against you for your life, to come speak with me.

Fal. As I was then advis'd by my learned counsel in the laws of this land service, I did not come.

Just. Well, the truth is, Sir John, you live in great infamy.

Fal. He that buckles himself in my belt cannot live in less.

Just. Your means are very slender, and your waste is great.

Fal. I would it were otherwise. I would my means were greater and my waist slenderer.

Just. You have misled the youthful prince.

Fal. The young prince hath misled me. I am the fellow with the great belly, and he my dog.

Just. Well, I am loath to gall a new-heal'd wound. Your day's service at Shrewsbury hath a little gilded over your night's exploit on Gadshill. You may thank th' unquiet time for your quiet o'erposting that action.

Fal. My lord —

Just. But since all is well, keep it so. Wake not a sleeping wolf.

Fal. To wake a wolf is as bad as smell a fox.

Just. What! you are as a candle, the better part burnt out.

Fal. A wassail candle, my lord; all tallow. If I did say of wax, my growth would approve the truth.

Just. There is not a white hair on your face but should have his effect of gravity.

Fal. His effect of gravy, gravy, gravy.

Just. You follow the young prince up and down, like his ill angel.

Fal. Not so, my lord. Your ill angel is light, but I hope he that looks upon me will take me without weighing. And yet, in some respects, I grant, I cannot go. I cannot tell. Virtue is of so little regard in these costermonger's times that true valour is turn'd berod; pregnancy is made a tapster, and his quick wit wasted in giving reckonings. All the other gifts appertinent to man, as the malice of this age shapes them, are not worth a gooseberry. You that are old consider not the capacities of us that are young. You do measure the heat of our livers with the bitterness of your galls; and we that are in the vaward of our youth, I must confess, are wags too.

Just. Do you set down your name in the scroll of youth, that are written down old with all the characters of age? Have you not a moist eye, a dry hand, a yellow cheek, a white beard, a decreasing leg, an increasing belly? Is not your voice broken, your wind short, your chin double, your wit single, and every part about you blasted with antiquity? And will you yet call yourself young? Fie, fie, fie, Sir John!

Fal. My lord, I was born about three of the clock in the afternoon, with a white head and something a round belly. For my voice, I have lost it with halloaing, and singing of anthems. To approve my youth further, I will not. The truth is, I am only old in judgment and understanding; and he that will caper with me for a thousand marks, let him lend me the money, and have at him. For the box of the ear that the Prince gave you, he gave it like a rude prince, and you took it like a sensible lord. I have check'd him for it, and the young lion repents — marry, not in ashes and sackcloth, but in new silk and old sack.

Just. Well, God send the Prince a better companion!

Fal. God send the companion a better Prince! I cannot rid my hands of him.

Just. Well, the King hath sever'd you and Prince Harry. I hear you are going with Lord John of Lancaster against the Archbishop and the Earl of Northumberland.

Fal. Yea, I thank your pretty sweet wit for it! But look you pray, all you that kiss my Lady Peace at home, that our armies join not in a hot day; for, by the Lord, I take but two shirts out with me, and I mean not to sweat extraordinarily. If it be a hot day, and I brandish anything but a bottle, I would I might never spit white again! There is not a dangerous

Henry, Prince of Wales (Robert Hardy), and a companion, Poins (Michael Bates)

HENRY IV

PART TWO

PHOTOGRAPHS BY HOUSTON ROGERS
PRODUCED BY THE OLD VIC COMPANY

Pistol (John Neville), Justice Shallow (Paul Daneman), and Sir John Falstaff (Paul Rogers)

Falstaff's toast: "I would to God my name were not so terrible to the enemy" *(Act I, Scene II)*

A forgetful Falstaff is reproached by Mistress Quickly (Rachel Roberts) *(Act II, Scene I)*

Pistol shocks Mistress Quickly, hostess at the Boar's Head Tavern *(Act II, Scene IV)*

"Saturn and Venus this year in conjunction! What says the almanack to that?" Doll Tearsheet (Gwen Cherrell) grants the aging Falstaff a kiss *(Act II, Scene IV)*

Doll suits action to her words: "Thou abominable damned cheater, art thou not ashamed to be called captain?" *(Act II, Scene IV)*

The braggadocio, Pistol. "Fear we broadsides? no, let the fiend give fire" *(Act II, Scene IV)*

With Silence (Meredith Edwards), Bardolph (Ronald Fraser), and Falstaff looking on, Justice Shallow demonstrates the handling of the musket to Falstaff's motley, ragged band of new recruits for King Henry's army *(Act III, Scene III)*

Left: John of Lancaster (Alan Dobie, center), by an act of treachery overcomes the rebels *(Act IV, Scene II)*. To Lancaster's left stands the Archbishop of York (Daniel Thorndike)

Right: Lady Percy (Ann Todd), widow of Hotspur. "... And never shall have length of life enough to rain upon remembrance with mine eyes ... for recordation of my noble husband" *(Act II, Scene III)*

Westmoreland (John Wood), Warwick (Donald Moffat), Prince Hal, and Clarence (Clifford

"I know thee not, old man: fall to thy prayers." Prince Hal, now Henry V, shuns Falstaff *(Act V, Scene V)*

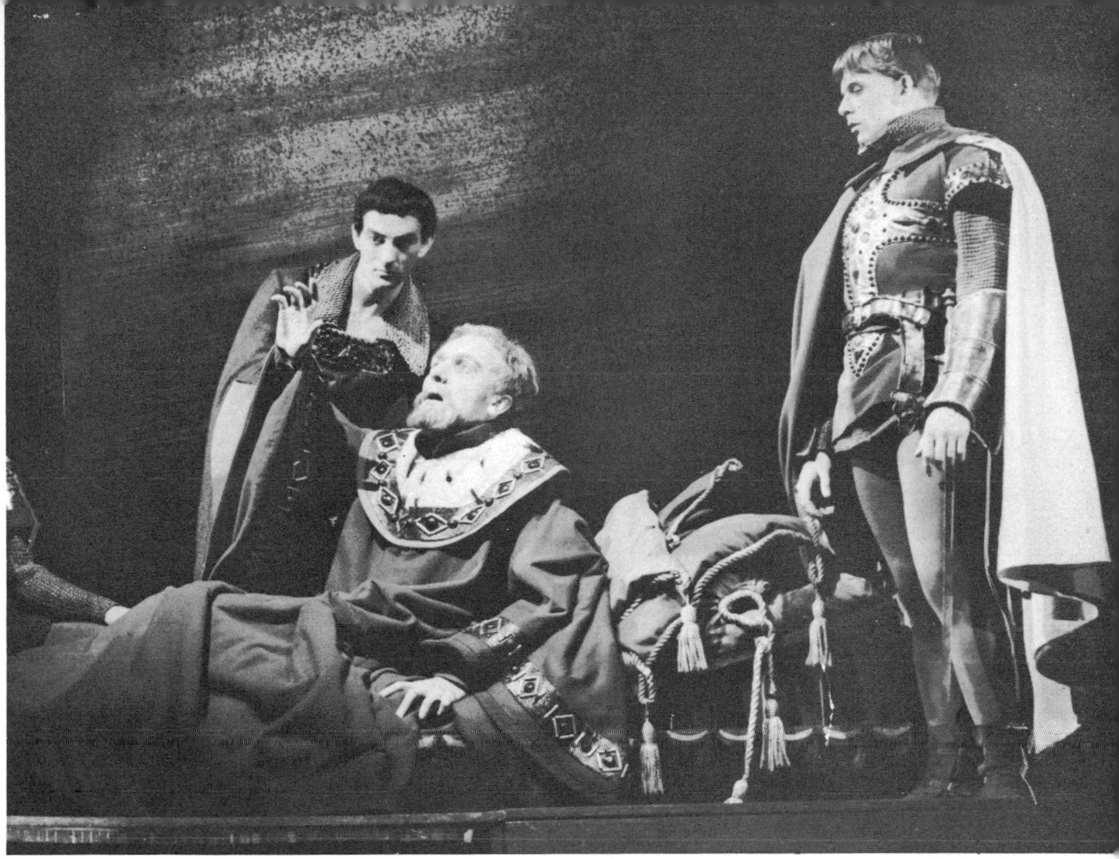

Williams) before the stricken King (Eric Porter). Behind the King, Gloucester (Nicholas Amer); right, Lancaster *(Act IV, Scene V)*

"How ill white hairs become a fool and jester! I have long dream'd of such a man, so surfeit-swell'd, so old and so profane; but, being awak'd, I do despise my dream." Thus does Henry V reject the friend of his immaturity *(Act V, Scene V)*

The King to the King-to-be: "Therefore, my Harry, be it thy course to busy giddy minds with foreign quarrels" *(Act IV, Scene III)*

action can peep out his head but I am thrust upon it. Well, I cannot last ever; but it was alway yet the trick of our English nation, if they have a good thing, to make it too common. If ye will needs say I am an old man, you should give me rest. I would to God my name were not so terrible to the enemy as it is. I were better to be eaten to death with a rust than to be scoured to nothing with perpetual motion.

Just. Well, be honest, be honest; and God bless your expedition!

Fal. Will your lordship lend me a thousand pound to furnish me forth?

Just. Not a penny, not a penny! You are too impatient to bear crosses. Fare you well. Commend me to my cousin Westmoreland.

[*Exeunt Chief Justice and Servant.*]

Fal. If I do, fillip me with a three-man beetle! A man can no more separate age and covetousness than 'a can part young limbs and lechery; but the gout galls the one, and the pox pinches the other; and so both the degrees prevent my curses. Boy!

Page. Sir?

Fal. What money is in my purse?

Page. Seven groats and twopence.

Fal. I can get no remedy against this consumption of the purse. Borrowing only lingers and lingers it out, but the disease is incurable. Go bear this letter to my Lord of Lancaster; this to the Prince; this to the Earl of Westmoreland; and this to old Mistress Ursula, whom I have weekly sworn to marry since I perceiv'd the first white hair on my chin. About it! You know where to find me. [*Exit Page.*] A pox of this gout! or, a gout of this pox! for the one or the other plays the rogue with my great toe. 'Tis no matter if I do halt. I have the wars for my colour, and my pension shall seem the more reasonable. A good wit will make use of anything. I will turn diseases to commodity. *Exit.*

Scene III. [*York. The* Archbishop's *Palace.*]

Enter the *Archbishop, Thomas Mowbray* (*Earl Marshal*), the *Lords Hastings* and *Bardolph.*

Arch. Thus have you heard our cause and known our means;
And, my most noble friends, I pray you all
Speak plainly your opinions of our hopes.
And first, Lord Marshal, what say you to it?
Mowb. I well allow the occasion of our arms,
But gladly would be better satisfied
How in our means we should advance ourselves
To look with forehead bold and big enough
Upon the power and puissance of the King.
Hast. Our present musters grow upon the file
To five-and-twenty thousand men of choice;
And our supplies live largely in the hope
Of great Northumberland, whose bosom burns
With an incensed fire of injuries.
L. Bard. The question then, Lord Hastings, standeth thus:
Whether our present five-and-twenty thousand
May hold up head without Northumberland.
Hast. With him, we may.
L. Bard. Yea, marry, there's the point!
But if without him we be thought too feeble,
My judgment is we should not step too far
Till we had his assistance by the hand;
For, in a theme so bloody-fac'd as this,
Conjecture, expectation, and surmise
Of aids incertain should not be admitted.
Arch. 'Tis very true, Lord Bardolph; for indeed
It was young Hotspur's case at Shrewsbury.
L. Bard. It was, my lord; who lin'd himself with hope,
Eating the air on promise of supply,
Flatt'ring himself in project of a power
Much smaller than the smallest of his thoughts,
And so, with great imagination,
Proper to madmen, led his powers to death
And, winking, leapt into destruction.
Hast. But, by your leave, it never yet did hurt
To lay down likelihoods and forms of hope.
L. Bard. Yes, in this present quality of war,
Indeed, the instant action. A cause on foot
Lives so in hope as in an early spring
We see th' appearing buds, which to prove fruit
Hope gives not so much warrant as despair
That frosts will bite them. When we mean to build,
We first survey the plot, then draw the model;
And when we see the figure of the house,
Then must we rate the cost of the erection,
Which if we find outweighs ability,
What do we then but draw anew the model
In fewer offices, or at least desist
To build at all? Much more, in this great work —
Which is (almost) to pluck a kingdom down
And set another up — should we survey
The plot of situation and the model,
Consent upon a sure foundation,
Question surveyors, know our own estate,
How able such a work to undergo.

To weigh against his opposite; or else
We fortify in paper and in figures,
Using the names of men instead of men,
Like one that draws the model of a house
Beyond his power to build it, who (half through)
Gives o'er, and leaves his part-created cost
A naked subject to the weeping clouds
And waste for churlish winter's tyranny.

Hast. Grant that our hopes (yet likely of fair birth)
Should be stillborn, and that we now possess'd
The utmost man of expectation,
I think we are so a body strong enough,
Even as we are, to equal with the King.

L. Bard. What, is the King but five-and-twenty thousand?

Hast. To us no more; nay, not so much, Lord Bardolph.
For his divisions, as the times do brawl,
Are in three heads: one power against the French
And one against Glendower; perforce a third
Must take up us. So is the unfirm King
In three divided, and his coffers sound
With hollow poverty and emptiness.

Arch. That he should draw his several strengths together
And come against us in full puissance
Need not be dreaded.

Hast. If he should do so,
To French and Welsh he leaves his back unarm'd,
They baying him at the heels. Never fear that.

L. Bard. Who is it like should lead his forces hither?

Hast. The Duke of Lancaster and Westmoreland;
Against the Welsh, himself and Harry Monmouth;
But who is substituted 'gainst the French,
I have no certain notice.

Arch. Let us on,
And publish the occasion of our arms.
The commonwealth is sick of their own choice;
Their over-greedy love hath surfeited.
An habitation giddy and unsure
Hath he that buildeth on the vulgar heart.
O thou fond Many! with what loud applause
Didst thou beat heaven with blessing Bolingbroke
Before he was what thou wouldst have him be!
And being now trimm'd in thine own desires,
Thou (beastly feeder) art so full of him
That thou provok'st thyself to cast him up.
So, so (thou common dog) didst thou disgorge
Thy glutton bosom of the royal Richard;
And now thou wouldst eat thy dead vomit up,
And howl'st to find it. What trust is in these times?
They that, when Richard liv'd, would have him die
Are now become enamour'd on his grave.
Thou that threw'st dust upon his goodly head
When through proud London he came sighing on
After th' admired heels of Bolingbroke,
Criest now, 'O earth, yield us that king again,
And take thou this!' O thoughts of men accurs'd!
Past, and to come, seems best; things present, worst.

Mowb. Shall we go draw our numbers and set on?

Hast. We are time's subjects, and time bids be gone.
Exeunt.

ACT II. Scene I. [*London. A street.*]

Enter *Hostess* of the Tavern, with two *Officers* (*Fang* and *Snare*) [and *Fang's Boy*].

Host. Master Fang, have you ent'red the action?

Fang. It is ent'red.

Host. Where's your yeoman? Is't a lusty yeoman? Will 'a stand to't?

Fang. Sirrah, where's Snare?

Host. O Lord, ay! good Master Snare.

Snare. Here, here.

Fang. Snare, we must arrest Sir John Falstaff.

Host. Yea, good Master Snare. I have ent'red him and all.

Snare. It may chance cost some of us our lives, for he will stab.

Host. Alas the day! take heed of him. He stabb'd me in mine own house most beastly, in good faith! 'A cares not what mischief he does, if his weapon be out. He will foin like any devil; he will spare neither man, woman, nor child.

Fang. If I can close with him, I care not for his thrust.

Host. No, nor I neither. I'll be at your elbow.

Fang. An I but fist him once! An 'a come but within my vice!

Host. I am undone by his going. I warrant you he's an infinitive thing upon my score. Good Master Fang, hold him sure. Good Master Snare, let him not scape. 'A comes continuantly to Pie Corner (saving your manhoods) to buy a saddle, and he is indited to dinner to the Lubber's Head in Lumbert Street, to Master Smooth's the silkman. I pray you, since my exion is ent'red, and my case so openly known to the world, let him be brought in to his answer. A hundred mark is a long one for a poor lone woman to bear; and I have borne, and borne, and borne; and have been fubb'd off, and fubb'd off, and fubb'd off, from this day to that day, that it is a shame to be thought on. There is no honesty in such dealing, unless a woman should be made an ass and a beast, to bear every knave's wrong.

Enter *Sir John* [*Falstaff*] and *Bardolph* and the *Boy.*

Yonder he comes! and that arrant malmsey-nose knave Bardolph with him! Do your offices, do your offices! Master Fang and Master Snare, do me, do me, do me your offices!

Fal. How now? Whose mare's dead? What's the matter?

Fang. Sir John, I arrest you at the suit of Mistress Quickly.

Fal. Away, varlets! Draw, Bardolph! Cut me off the villain's head! Throw the quean in the channel.

Host. Throw me in the channel? I'll throw thee in the channel! Wilt thou? wilt thou, thou bastardly rogue? Murder, murder! Ah, thou honeysuckle villain! wilt thou kill God's officers and the King's? Ah, thou honeyseed rogue! thou art a honeyseed, a man-queller and a woman-queller.

Fal. Keep them off, Bardolph.

Fang. A rescue! a rescue!

Host. Good people, bring a rescue or two. Thou wo't, wo't thou? Thou wo't, wo't ta? Do, do, thou rogue! do, thou hempseed!

Fal. Away, you scullion! you rampallian! you fustilarian! I'll tickle your catastrophe.

Enter *Lord Chief Justice* and his *men.*

Just. What is the matter? Keep the peace here, ho!

Host. Good my lord, be good to me! I beseech you stand to me!

Just. How now, Sir John? What are you brawling here?
Doth this become your place, your time, and business?
You should have been well on your way to York.
Stand from him, fellow. Wherefore hang'st upon him?

Host. O my most worshipful lord! an't please your Grace, I am a poor widow of Eastcheap, and he is arrested at my suit.

Just. For what sum?

Host. It is more than for some, my lord; it is for all — all I have. He hath eaten me out of house and home; he hath put all my substance into that fat belly of his. But I will have some of it out again, or I will ride thee a-nights like the mare.

Fal. I think I am as like to ride the mare, if I have any vantage of ground to get up.

Just. How comes this, Sir John? Fie! what man of good temper would endure this tempest of exclamation? Are you not ashamed to enforce a poor widow to so rough a course to come by her own?

Fal. What is the gross sum that I owe thee?

Host. Marry, if thou wert an honest man, thyself and the money too! Thou didst swear to me upon a parcel-gilt goblet, sitting in my Dolphin chamber, at the round table by a sea-coal fire, upon Wednesday in Wheeson week, when the Prince broke thy head for liking his father to a singing man of Windsor — thou didst swear to me then, as I was washing thy wound, to marry me and make me my lady thy wife. Canst thou deny it? Did not goodwife Keech, the butcher's wife, come in then and call me gossip Quickly? coming in to borrow a mess of vinegar, telling us she had a good dish of prawns, whereby thou didst desire to eat some, whereby I told thee they were ill for a green wound? And didst thou not, when she was gone down stairs, desire me to be no more so familiarity with such poor people, saying that ere long they should call me madam? And didst thou not kiss me, and bid me fetch thee thirty shillings? I put thee now to thy book-oath. Deny it if thou canst.

Fal. My lord, this is a poor mad soul; and she says, up and down the town, that her eldest son is like you. She hath been in good case, and the truth is, poverty hath distracted her. But for these foolish officers, I beseech you I may have redress against them.

Just. Sir John, Sir John, I am well acquainted with your manner of wrenching the true cause the false way. It is not a confident brow, nor the throng of words that come with such more than impudent sauciness from you, can thrust me from a level consideration. You have, as it appears to me, practis'd upon the easy-yielding spirit of this woman, and made her serve your uses both in purse and in person.

Host. Yea, in truth, my lord.

Just. Pray thee peace. Pay her the debt you owe her, and unpay the villany you have done her. The one you may do with sterling money, and the other with current repentance.

Fal. My lord, I will not undergo this sneap without reply. You call honourable boldness impudent sauciness. If a man will make curtsy and say nothing, he is virtuous. No, my lord, my humble duty remembʼred, I will not be your suitor. I say to you I do desire deliverance from these officers, being upon hasty employment in the King's affairs.

Just. You speak as having power to do wrong. But answer in th' effect of your reputation, and satisfy the poor woman.

Fal. Come hither, hostess.

[*Takes her aside.*]

Enter *Master Gower* (a Messenger).

Just. Now, Master Gower, what news?

Gow. The King, my lord, and Harry Prince of Wales
Are near at hand. The rest the paper tells.

[*Gives a letter.*]

Fal. As I am a gentleman!

Host. Faith, you said so before.

Fal. As I am a gentleman! Come, no more words of it.

Host. By this heav'nly ground I tread on, I must be fain to pawn both my plate and the tapestry of my dining chambers.

Fal. Glasses, glasses is the only drinking; and for thy walls, a pretty slight drollery, or the story of the Prodigal, or the German Hunting in waterwork, is worth a thousand of these bed-hangers and these fly-bitten tapestries. Let it be ten pound, if thou canst. Come, an 'twere not for thy humours, there's not a better wench in England. Go wash thy face and draw the action. Come, thou must not be in this humour with me. Dost not know me? Come, come, I know thou wast set on to this.

Host. Pray thee, Sir John, let it be but twenty nobles. I' faith, I am loath to pawn my plate, so God save me, la!

Fal. Let it alone. I'll make other shift. You'll be a fool still.

Host. Well, you shall have it, though I pawn my gown. I hope you'll come to supper. You'll pay me all together?

Fal. Will I live? [*To Bardolph*] Go with her, with her! Hook on, hook on.

Host. Will you have Doll Tearsheet meet you at supper?

Fal. No more words. Let's have her.

Exeunt Hostess, [*Bardolph,*] *Officers,* [*and Boy*].

Just. I have heard better news.

Fal. What's the news, my lord?

Just. Where lay the King to-night?

Gow. At Basingstoke, my lord.

Fal. I hope, my lord, all's well. What is the news, my lord?

Just. Come all his forces back?

Gow. No; fifteen hundred foot, five hundred horse
Are march'd up to my Lord of Lancaster
Against Northumberland and the Archbishop.

Fal. Comes the King back from Wales, my noble lord?

Just. You shall have letters of me presently.
Come, go along with me, good Master Gower.

Fal. My lord!

Just. What's the matter?

Fal. Master Gower, shall I entreat you with me to dinner?

Gow. I must wait upon my good lord here, I thank you, good Sir John.

Just. Sir John, you loiter here too long, being you are to take soldiers up in counties as you go.

Fal. Will you sup with me, Master Gower?

Just. What foolish master taught you these manners, Sir John?

Fal. Master Gower, if they become me not, he was a fool that taught them me. This is the right fencing grace, my lord — tap for tap, and so part fair.

Just. Now, the Lord lighten thee! thou art a great fool. *Exeunt.*

Scene II. [*London. Another street.*]

Enter *Prince Henry* and *Poins.*

Prince. Before God, I am exceeding weary.

Poins. Is't come to that? I had thought weariness durst not have attach'd one of so high blood.

Prince. Faith, it does me, though it discolours the complexion of my greatness to acknowledge it. Doth it not show vilely in me to desire small beer?

Poins. Why, a prince should not be so loosely studied as to remember so weak a composition.

Prince. Belike then my appetite was not princely got; for, by my troth, I do now remember the poor creature, small beer. But indeed these humble considerations make me out of love with my greatness. What a disgrace is it to me to remember thy name! or to know thy face to-morrow! or to take note how many pair of silk stockings thou hast, — viz., these, and those that were thy peach-colour'd ones! or to bear the inventory of thy shirts — as, one for superfluity and another for use! But that the tennis-court-keeper knows better than I; for it is a low ebb of linen with thee when thou keepest not racket there; as thou hast not done a great while, because the rest of thy low countries have made a shift to eat up thy holland; and God knows whether those that bawl out the ruins of thy linen shall inherit his kingdom; but the midwives say the children are not in the fault; whereupon the world increases, and kinreds are mightily strengthened.

Poins. How ill it follows, after you have laboured so hard, you should talk so idly! Tell me, how many good young princes would do so, their fathers being so sick as yours at this time is?

Prince. Shall I tell thee one thing, Poins?

Poins. Yes, faith; and let it be an excellent good thing.

Prince. It shall serve among wits of no higher breeding than thine.

Poins. Go to! I stand the push of your one thing that you will tell.

Prince. Marry, I tell thee it is not meet that I should be sad now my father is sick; albeit I could tell to thee (as to one it pleases me, for fault of a better, to call my friend) I could be sad, and sad indeed too.

Poins. Very hardly, upon such a subject.

Prince. By this hand, thou thinkest me as far in the devil's book as thou and Falstaff for obduracy and persistency. Let the end try the man. But I tell thee, my heart bleeds inwardly that my father is so sick; and keeping such vile company as thou art hath in reason taken from me all ostentation of sorrow.

Poins. The reason?

Prince. What wouldst thou think of me if I should weep?

Poins. I would think thee a most princely hypocrite.

Prince. It would be every man's thought, and thou art a blessed fellow to think as every man thinks. Never a man's thought in the world keeps the roadway better than thine. Every man would think me an hypocrite indeed. And what accites your most worshipful thought to think so?

Poins. Why, because you have been so lewd and so much engraffed to Falstaff.

Prince. And to thee.

Poins. By this light, I am well spoke on; I can hear it with mine own ears. The worst that they can say of me is, that I am a second brother, and that I am a proper fellow of my hands; and those two things I confess I cannot help. By the mass, here comes Bardolph.

Enter *Bardolph* and *Page.*

Prince. And the boy that I gave Falstaff. 'A had him from me Christian, and look if the fat villain have not transform'd him ape.

Bard. God save your Grace!

Prince. And yours, most noble Bardolph!

Bard. [*to the Page*] Come, you virtuous ass, you bashful fool, must you be blushing? Wherefore blush you now? What a maidenly man-at-arms are you become! Is't such a matter to get a pottle-pot's maidenhead?

Page. 'A calls me e'en now, my lord, through a red lattice, and I could discern no part of his face from the window. At last I spied his eyes, and methought he had made two holes in the alewive's new petticoat, and so peep'd through.

Prince. Has not the boy profited?

Bard. Away, you whoreson upright rabbit, away!

Page. Away, you rascally Althæa's dream, away!

Prince. Instruct us, boy. What dream, boy?

Page. Marry, my lord, Althæa dreamt she was delivered of a firebrand, and therefore I call him her dream.

Prince. A crown's worth of good interpretation. There 'tis, boy.

Poins. O that this good blossom could be kept from cankers! Well, there is sixpence to preserve thee.

Bard. An you do not make him be hang'd among you, the gallows shall have wrong.

Prince. And how doth thy master, Bardolph?

Bard. Well, my lord. He heard of your Grace's coming to town. There's a letter for you.

Poins. Deliver'd with good respect! And how doth the Martlemas, your master?

Bard. In bodily health, sir.

Poins. Marry, the immortal part needs a physician. But that moves not him; though that be sick, it dies not.

Prince. I do allow this wen to be as familiar with me as my dog; and he holds his place, for look you how he writes.

Poins. [*reads*] 'John Falstaff, knight'— Every man must know that as oft as he has occasion to name himself; even like those that are kin to the King; for they never prick their finger but they say, 'There's some of the King's blood spilt.' 'How comes that?' says he that takes upon him not to conceive. The answer is as ready as a borrower's cap: 'I am the King's poor cousin, sir.'

Prince. Nay, they will be kin to us, or they will fetch it from Japhet. But to the letter!

Poins. [*reads*] 'Sir John Falstaff, knight, to the son of the King, nearest his father, Harry Prince of Wales, greeting.' Why, this is a certificate.

Prince. Peace!

Poins. [*reads*] 'I will imitate the honourable Romans in brevity.' He sure means brevity in breath — short-winded. 'I commend me to thee, I commend thee, and I leave thee. Be not too familiar with Poins, for he misuses thy favours so much that he swears thou art to marry his sister Nell. Repent at idle times as thou mayst; and so farewell.

'Thine, by yea and no (which is as much as to say, as thou usest him), JACK FALSTAFF with my familiars, JOHN with my brothers and sisters, and SIR JOHN with all Europe.'

My lord, I'll steep this letter in sack and make him eat it.

Prince. That's to make him eat twenty of his words. But do you use me thus, Ned? Must I marry your sister?

Poins. God send the wench no worse fortune! but I never said so.

Prince. Well, thus we play the fools with the time, and the spirits of the wise sit in the clouds and mock us. Is your master here in London?

Bard. Yea, my lord.

Prince. Where sups he? Doth the old boar feed in the old frank?

Bard. At the old place, my lord, in Eastcheap.

Prince. What company?

Page. Ephesians, my lord, of the old church.

Prince. Sup any women with him?

Page. None, my lord, but old Mistress Quickly and Mistress Doll Tearsheet.

Prince. What pagan may that be?

Page. A proper gentlewoman, sir, and a kinswoman of my master's.

Prince. Even such kin as the parish heifers are to the town bull. Shall we steal upon them, Ned, at supper?

Poins. I am your shadow, my lord; I'll follow you.

Prince. Sirrah, you boy, and Bardolph, no word to your master that I am yet come to town. There's for your silence. [*Gives money.*]

Bard. I have no tongue, sir.

Page. And for mine, sir, I will govern it.

Prince. Fare you well, go. [*Exeunt Bardolph and Boy.*] This Doll Tearsheet should be some road.

Poins. I warrant you, as common as the way between Saint Alban's and London.

Prince. How might we see Falstaff bestow himself to-night in his true colours, and not ourselves be seen?

Poins. Put on two leathern jerkins and aprons and wait upon him at his table as drawers.

Prince. From a god to a bull? A heavy descension! It was Jove's case. From a prince to a prentice? A low transformation! That shall be mine; for in everything the purpose must weigh with the folly. Follow me, Ned. *Exeunt.*

Scene III. [*Warkworth. Before the Castle.*]

Enter *Northumberland,* his *Wife,* and the *Wife* to *Harry Percy.*

North. I pray thee, loving wife, and gentle daughter,
Give even way unto my rough affairs.
Put not you on the visage of the times
And be, like them, to Percy troublesome.

Wife. I have given over, I will speak no more.
Do what you will; your wisdom be your guide.

North. Alas, sweet wife, my honour is at pawn;
And but my going, nothing can redeem it.

Lady Percy. O, yet, for God's sake, go not to these wars!

The time was, father, that you broke your word
When you were more endear'd to it than now;
When your own Percy, when my heart's dear Harry
Threw many a northward look to see his father
Bring up his powers; but he did long in vain.
Who then persuaded you to stay at home?
There were two honours lost, yours and your son's.
For yours, the God of heaven brighten it!
For his, it stuck upon him as the sun
In the grey vault of heaven, and by his light
Did all the chivalry of England move
To do brave acts. He was indeed the glass
Wherein the noble youth did dress themselves.
He had no legs that practis'd not his gait;
And speaking thick (which nature made his blemish)
Became the accents of the valiant;
For those that could speak low and tardily
Would turn their own perfection to abuse
To seem like him; so that in speech, in gait,
In diet, in affections of delight,
In military rules, humours of blood,
He was the mark and glass, copy and book,
That fashion'd others. And him — O wondrous him!
O miracle of men! — him did you leave —
Second to none, unseconded by you —
To look upon the hideous god of war
In disadvantage, to abide a field
Where nothing but the sound of Hotspur's name
Did seem defensible. So you left him.
Never, O never, do his ghost the wrong
To hold your honour more precise and nice
With others than with him! Let them alone.
The Marshal and the Archbishop are strong.
Had my sweet Harry had but half their numbers,
To-day might I, hanging on Hotspur's neck,
Have talk'd of Monmouth's grave.

North. Beshrew your heart,
Fair daughter! you do draw my spirits from me
With new lamenting ancient oversights.
But I must go and meet with danger there,
Or it will seek me in another place
And find me worse provided.

Wife. O, fly to Scotland,
Till that the nobles and the armed commons
Have of their puissance made a little taste.

Lady Percy. If they get ground and vantage of the King,
Then join you with them like a rib of steel,
To make strength stronger; but, for all our loves,
First let them try themselves. So did your son;
He was so suff'red; so came I a widow,
And never shall have length of life enough
To rain upon remembrance with mine eyes,
That it may grow and sprout as high as heaven,
For recordation to my noble husband.

North. Come, come, go in with me. 'Tis with my mind
As with the tide swell'd up unto his height,
That makes a still-stand, running neither way.
Fain would I go to meet the Archbishop,
But many thousand reasons hold me back.
I will resolve for Scotland. There am I,
Till time and vantage crave my company.

Exeunt.

Scene IV. [*London. The Boar's Head Tavern in Eastcheap.*]

Enter two *Drawers.*

1. Draw. What the devil hast thou brought there? apple Johns? Thou knowest Sir John cannot endure an apple John.

2. Draw. Mass, thou say'st true. The Prince once set a dish of apple Johns before him and told him there were five more Sir Johns, and, putting off his hat, said, 'I will now take my leave of these six dry, round, old, withered knights.' It ang'red him to the heart. But he hath forgot that.

1. Draw. Why then, cover and set them down; and see if thou canst find out Sneak's noise. Mistress Tearsheet would fain hear some music. Dispatch! The room where they supp'd is too hot; they'll come in straight.

2. Draw. Sirrah, here will be the Prince and Master Poins anon; and they will put on two of our jerkins and aprons, and Sir John must not know of it. Bardolph hath brought word.

1. Draw. By the mass, here will be old utis! It will be an excellent stratagem.]

2. Draw. I'll see if I can find out Sneak.

Exit.

Enter *Mistress Quickly* (*Hostess*) and *Doll Tearsheet.*

Host. I' faith, sweetheart, methinks now you are in an excellent good temperality. Your pulsidge beats as extraordinarily as heart would desire; and your colour, I warrant you, is as red as any rose, in good truth, la. But, i' faith, you have drunk too much canaries; and that's a marvellous searching wine, and it perfumes the blood ere one can say 'What's this?' How do you now?

Doll. Better than I was. Hem.

Host. Why, that's well said! A good heart's worth gold. Lo, here comes Sir John.

Enter *Sir John Falstaff.*

Fal. [*sings*] 'When Arthur first in court'— Empty the jordan. [*Exit First Drawer.*]—[*Sings*] 'And was a worthy king.'— How now, Mistress Doll?

Host. Sick of a calm; yea, good faith.

Fal. So is all her sect. An they be once in a calm, they are sick.

Doll. A pox damn you, you muddy rascal! Is that all the comfort you give me?

Fal. You make fat rascals, Mistress Doll.

Doll. I make them? Gluttony and diseases make them. I make them not.

Fal. If the cook help to make the gluttony, you help to make the diseases, Doll. We catch of you, Doll; we catch of you. Grant that, my poor virtue, grant that.

Doll. Yea, joy — our chains and our jewels.

Fal. 'Your brooches, pearls, and ouches.' For to serve bravely is to come halting off: you know, to come off the breach with his pike bent bravely, and to surgery bravely; to venture upon the charg'd chambers bravely —

Doll. Hang yourself, you muddy conger, hang yourself!

Host. By my troth, this is the old fashion! You two never meet but you fall to some discord. You are both, i' good truth, as rheumatic as two dry toasts. You cannot one bear with another's confirmities. What the goodyere! One must bear, and that must be you. You are the weaker vessel, as they say, the emptier vessel.

Doll. Can a weak empty vessel bear such a huge full hogshead? There's a whole merchant's venture of Bordeaux stuff in him. You have not seen a hulk better stuff'd in the hold. Come, I'll be friends with thee, Jack. Thou art going to the wars; and whether I shall ever see thee again or no, there is nobody cares.

Enter *Drawer.*

Draw. Sir, Ancient Pistol 's below, and would speak with you.

Doll. Hang him, swaggering rascal! let him not come hither. It is the foul-mouth'dst rogue in England.

Host. If he swagger, let him not come here. No, by my faith! I must live among my neighbours. I'll no swaggerers. I am in good name and fame with the very best. Shut the door! There comes no swaggerers here. I have not liv'd all this while to have swaggering now. Shut the door, I pray you.

Fal. Dost thou hear, hostess?

Host. Pray ye pacify yourself, Sir John. There comes no swaggerers here.

Fal . Dost thou hear? It is mine ancient.

Host. Tilly-fally, Sir John, ne'er tell me! Your ancient swagg'rer comes not in my doors. I was before Master Tisick, the debuty, t'other day; and, as he said to me — 'twas no longer ago than Wednesday last i' good faith — 'Neighbour Quickly,' says he—Master Dumbe, our minister, was by then — 'Neighbour Quickly,' says he, 'receive those that are civil, for,' said he, 'you are in an ill name.' Now 'a said so, I can tell whereupon. 'For,' says he, 'you are an honest woman, and well thought on; therefore take heed what guests you receive. Receive,' says he, 'no swaggering companions.' There comes none here! You would bless you to hear what he said. No! I'll no swagg'rers.

Fal. He's no swagg'rer, hostess — a tame cheater, i' faith. You may stroke him as gently as a puppy greyhound. He'll not swagger with a Barbary hen if her feathers turn back in any show of resistance. Call him up, drawer.

[*Exit Drawer.*]

Host. Cheater call you him? I will bar no honest man my house, nor no cheater; but I do not love swaggering. By my troth, I am the worse when one says 'swagger.' Feel, masters, how I shake. Look you, I warrant you.

Doll. So you do, hostess.

Host. Do I? Yea, in very truth, do I, an 'twere an aspen leaf. I cannot abide swagg'rers.

Enter *Ancient Pistol* and *Bardolph* and *Boy.*

Pist. God save you, Sir John!

Fal. Welcome, Ancient Pistol. Here, Pistol, I charge you with a cup of sack. Do you discharge upon mine hostess.

Pist. I will discharge upon her, Sir John, with two bullets.

Fal. She is pistol-proof, sir. You shall hardly offend her.

Host. Come, I'll drink no proofs nor no bullets. I'll drink no more than will do me good, for no man's pleasure, I.

Pist. Then to you, Mistress Dorothy! I will charge you.

Doll. Charge me? I scorn you, scurvy companion. What! you poor, base, rascally, cheating, lack-linen mate! Away, you mouldy rogue, away! I am meat for your master.

Pist. I know you, Mistress Dorothy.

Doll. Away, you cutpurse rascal! You filthy bung, away! By this wine, I'll thrust my knife in your mouldy chaps an you play the saucy cuttle with me. Away, you bottle-ale rascal! you basket-hilt stale juggler, you! Since when, I pray you, sir? God's light, with two points on your shoulder? Much!

Pist. God let me not live but I will murther your ruff for this.

Fal. No more, Pistol. I would not have you go off here. Discharge yourself of our company, Pistol.

Host. No, good Captain Pistol! not here, sweet Captain.

Doll. Captain? Thou abominable damn'd cheater, art thou not ashamed to be called Captain? An captains were of my mind, they would truncheon you out for taking their names upon you before you have earn'd them. You a captain? You slave, for what? For tearing a poor whore's ruff in a bawdy house! He a captain? Hang him, rogue! he lives upon mouldy stew'd prunes and dried cakes. A captain? God's light! these villains will make the word as odious as the word 'occupy,' which was an excellent good word before it was ill sorted. Therefore captains had need look to't.

Bard. Pray thee go down, good Ancient.

Fal. Hark thee hither, Mistress Doll.

Pist. Not I! I tell thee what, Corporal Bardolph, I could tear her. I'll be reveng'd of her.

Boy. Pray thee go down.

Pist. I'll see her damn'd first! to Pluto's damned lake, by this hand, to th' infernal deep, with Erebus and tortures vile also! Hold hook and line, say I. Down! down, dogs! down, faitors! Have we not Hiren here?

Host. Good Captain Peesell, be quiet. 'Tis very late, i' faith. I beseek you now, aggravate your choler.

Pist. These be good humours indeed. Shall packhorses,
And hollow pamper'd jades of Asia,
Which cannot go but thirty mile a day,
Compare with Cæsars, and with Cannibals,
And Troyan Greeks? Nay, rather damn them with
King Cerberus and let the welkin roar!
Shall we fall foul for toys?

Host. By my troth, Captain, these are very bitter words.

Bard. Be gone, good Ancient. This will grow to a brawl anon.

Pist. Die men like dogs! Give crowns like pins! Have we not Hiren here?

Host. O' my word, Captain, there's none such here. What the goodyere! Do you think I would deny her? For God's sake, be quiet.

Pist. Then feed, and be fat, my fair Calipolis.
Come, give 's some sack.
'Si fortune me tormente, sperato me contento.'
Fear we broadsides? No, let the fiend give fire!
Give me some sack; and, sweetheart, lie thou there. [*Lays down his sword.*]
Come we to full points here, and are et-ceteras nothing?

Fal. Pistol, I would be quiet.

Pist. Sweet knight, I kiss thy neaf. What! we have seen the Seven Stars.

Doll. For God's sake, thrust him down stairs! I cannot endure such a fustian rascal.

Pist. Thrust him down stairs? Know we not Galloway nags?

Fal. Quoit him down, Bardolph, like a shove-groat shilling. Nay, an 'a do nothing but speak nothing, 'a shall be nothing here.

Bard. Come, get you down stairs.

Pist. What? shall we have incision? Shall we imbrue? [*Snatches up his sword.*]
Then death rock me asleep, abridge my doleful days!
Why then, let grievous, ghastly, gaping wounds
Untwine the Sisters Three! Come, Atropos, I say!

Host. Here's goodly stuff toward!

Fal. Give me my rapier, boy.

Doll. I pray thee, Jack, I pray thee do not draw.

Fal. Get you down stairs.

[*Draws and drives Pistol out.*]

Host. Here's a goodly tumult! I'll forswear keeping house afore I'll be in these tirrits and frights. So! Murder, I warrant now. Alas, alas! Put up your naked weapons, put up your naked weapons.

[*Exeunt Pistol and Bardolph.*]

Doll. I pray thee, Jack, be quiet; the rascal's gone. Ah, you whoreson little valiant villain, you!

Host. Are you not hurt i' th' groin? Methought 'a made a shrewd thrust at your belly.

[Enter *Bardolph*.]

Fal. Have you turn'd him out o' doors?

Bard. Yea, sir. The rascal's drunk. You have hurt him, sir, i' th' shoulder.

Fal. A rascal! to brave me?

Doll. Ah, you sweet little rogue, you! Alas, poor ape, how thou sweat'st! Come, let me wipe thy face. Come on, you whoreson chops. Ah, rogue! i' faith, I love thee. Thou art as valorous as Hector of Troy, worth five of Agamemnon, and ten times better than the Nine Worthies. Ah, villain!

Fal. A rascally slave! I will toss the rogue in a blanket.

Doll. Do, an thou dar'st for thy heart. An thou dost, I'll canvass thee between a pair of sheets.

Enter *Music*.

Page. The music is come, sir.

Fal. Let them play. Play, sirs. Sit on my knee, Doll. A rascal bragging slave! The rogue fled from me like quicksilver.

Doll. I' faith, and thou follow'dst him like a church. Thou whoreson little tidy Bartholomew boar-pig, when wilt thou leave fighting a-days and foining a-nights, and begin to patch up thine old body for heaven?

Enter, [behind,] *Prince* and *Poins* disguis'd [as *Drawers*].

Fal. Peace, good Doll! Do not speak like a death's-head. Do not bid me remember mine end.

Doll. Sirrah, what humour's the Prince of?

Fal. A good shallow young fellow. 'A would have made a good pantler; 'a would 'a' chipp'd bread well.

Doll. They say Poins has a good wit.

Fal. He a good wit? Hang him, baboon! His wit's as thick as Tewksbury mustard. There's no more conceit in him than is in a mallet.

Doll. Why does the Prince love him so then?

Fal. Because their legs are both of a bigness, and 'a plays at quoits well, and eats conger and fennel, and drinks off candles' ends for flapdragons, and rides the wild mare with the boys, and jumps upon join'd-stools, and swears with a good grace, and wears his boots very smooth like unto the sign of the Leg, and breeds no bate with telling of discreet stories, and such other gambol faculties 'a has that show a weak mind and an able body, for the which the Prince admits him; for the Prince himself is such another. The weight of a hair will turn scales between their avoirdupois.

Prince. Would not this nave of a wheel have his ears cut off?

Poins. Let's beat him before his whore.

Prince. Look, whe'r the wither'd elder hath not his poll claw'd like a parrot.

Poins. Is it not strange that desire should so many years outlive performance?

Fal. Kiss me, Doll.

Prince. Saturn and Venus this year in conjunction? What says th' almanac to that?

Poins. And look whether the fiery Trigon, his man, be not lisping to his master's old tables, his notebook, his counsel-keeper.

Fal. Thou dost give me flattering busses.

Doll. By my troth, I kiss thee with a most constant heart.

Fal. I am old, I am old.

Doll. I love thee better than I love e'er a scurvy young boy of them all.

Fal. What stuff wilt have a kirtle of? I shall receive money a Thursday. Shalt have a cap to-morrow. A merry song, come. It grows late; we'll to bed. Thou't forget me when I am gone.

Doll. By my troth, thou't set me a-weeping an thou say'st so. Prove that ever I dress myself handsome till thy return. Well, hearken o' th' end.

Fal. Some sack, Francis.

Prince, Poins. Anon, anon, sir.

Fal. Ha! a bastard son of the King's? And art not thou Poins his brother?

Prince. Why, thou globe of sinful continents, what a life dost thou lead!

Fal. A better than thou. I am a gentleman; thou art a drawer.

Prince. Very true, sir; and I come to draw you out by the ears.

Host. O, the Lord preserve thy good Grace! By my troth, welcome to London. Now the Lord bless that sweet face of thine! O Jesu, are you come from Wales?

Fal. Thou whoreson mad compound of majesty, by this light flesh and corrupt blood, thou art welcome. [*Lays his hand upon Doll.*]

Doll. How, you fat fool? I scorn you.

Poins. My lord, he will drive you out of your revenge, and turn all to a merriment, if you take not the heat.

Prince. You whoreson candle-mine, you, how vilely did you speak of me even now before this honest, virtuous, civil gentlewoman!

Host. God's blessing of your good heart! and so she is, by my troth.

Fal. Didst thou hear me?

Prince. Yea; and you knew me, as you did when you ran away by Gadshill. You knew I was at your back, and spoke it on purpose to try my patience.

Fal. No, no, no! not so. I did not think thou wast within hearing.

Prince. I shall drive you then to confess the wilful abuse, and then I know how to handle you.

Fal. No abuse, Hal, o' mine honour! no abuse.

Prince. Not — to dispraise me, and call me pantler, and bread-chipper, and I know not what?

Fal. No abuse, Hal.

Poins. No abuse?

Fal. No abuse, Ned, i' th' world! honest Ned, none. I disprais'd him before the wicked, that the wicked might not fall in love with him; in which doing, I have done the part of a careful friend and a true subject, and thy father is to give me thanks for it. No abuse, Hal. None, Ned, none. No, faith, boys, none.

Prince. See now whether pure fear and entire cowardice doth not make thee wrong this virtuous gentlewoman to close with us? Is she of the wicked? Is thine hostess here of the wicked? or is thy boy of the wicked? or honest Bardolph, whose zeal burns in his nose, of the wicked?

Poins. Answer, thou dead elm, answer.

Fal. The fiend hath prick'd down Bardolph irrecoverable; and his face is Lucifer's privy kitchen, where he doth nothing but roast maltworms. For the boy, there is a good angel about him; but the devil outbids him too.

Prince. For the women?

Fal. For one of them, she's in hell already, and burns poor souls. For th' other, I owe her money; and whether she be damn'd for that, I know not.

Host. No, I warrant you.

Fal. No, I think thou art not; I think thou art quit for that. Marry, there is another indictment upon thee, for suffering flesh to be eaten in thy house contrary to the law, for the which I think thou wilt howl.

Host. All vict'lers do so. What's a joint of mutton or two in a whole Lent?

Prince. You, gentlewoman —

Doll. What says your Grace?

Fal. His grace says that which his flesh rebels against.

Peto knocks at door.

Host. Who knocks so loud at door? Look to th' door there, Francis.

Enter *Peto.*

Prince. Peto, how now? What news?

Peto. The King your father is at Westminster;
And there are twenty weak and wearied posts
Come from the North; and as I came along,
I met and overtook a dozen captains,
Bareheaded, sweating, knocking at the taverns,
And asking every one for Sir John Falstaff.

Prince. By heaven, Poins, I feel me much to blame
So idly to profane the precious time,
When tempest of commotion, like the South,
Borne with black vapour, doth begin to melt
And drop upon our bare unarmed heads.
Give me my sword and cloak. Falstaff, good night.

Exeunt Prince, Poins, [*Peto, and Bardolph*].

Fal. Now comes in the sweetest morsel of the night, and we must hence and leave it unpick'd. [*Knocking within.*] More knocking at the door?

[Enter *Bardolph.*]

How now? What's the matter?

Bard. You must away to court, sir, presently.
A dozen captains stay at door for you.

Fal. [*to the Page*] Pay the musicians, sirrah. — Farewell, hostess; farewell, Doll. You see, my good wenches, how men of merit are sought after. The undeserver may sleep, when the man of action is call'd on. Farewell, good wenches. If I be not sent away post, I will see you again ere I go.

Doll. I cannot speak. If my heart be not ready to burst! — Well, sweet Jack, have a care of thyself.

Fal. Farewell, farewell.

Exit [*with Bardolph*].

Host. Well, fare thee well. I have known thee these twenty-nine years, come peascod-time; but an honester and truer-hearted man — Well, fare thee well.

Bard. [*within*] Mistress Tearsheet!

Host. What's the matter?

Bard. [*within*] Bid Mistress Tearsheet come to my master.

Host. O, run, Doll, run! run, good Doll! come. (*She comes blubber'd.*) Yea, will you come, Doll? *Exeunt.*

Act III. Scene I. [*Westminster. The Palace.*]

Enter the *King* in his nightgown, with a *Page.*

King. Go call the Earls of Surrey and of Warwick;
But ere they come, bid them o'erread these letters
And well consider of them. Make good speed.
Exit [*Page*].
How many thousand of my poorest subjects
Are at this hour asleep! O sleep, O gentle sleep!
Nature's soft nurse, how have I frighted thee,
That thou no more wilt weigh my eyelids down
And steep my senses in forgetfulness?
Why rather, sleep, liest thou in smoky cribs,
Upon uneasy pallets stretching thee,
And hush'd with buzzing night-flies to thy slumber,
Than in the perfum'd chambers of the great,
Under the canopies of costly state,
And lull'd with sound of sweetest melody?
O thou dull god, why liest thou with the vile
In loathsome beds, and leav'st the kingly couch
A watchcase or a common 'larum-bell?
Wilt thou upon the high and giddy mast
Seel up the shipboy's eyes, and rock his brains
In cradle of the rude imperious surge,
And in the visitation of the winds,
Who take the ruffian billows by the top,
Curling their monstrous heads, and hanging them
With deaf'ning clamour in the slippery clouds,
That with the hurly death itself awakes?
Canst thou, O partial sleep, give thy repose
To the wet seaboy in an hour so rude,
And in the calmest and most stillest night,
With all appliances and means to boot,
Deny it to a king? Then, happy low, lie down!
Uneasy lies the head that wears a crown.

Enter *Warwick* and *Surrey.*

War. Many good morrows to your Majesty!
King. Is it good morrow, lords?
War. 'Tis one o'clock, and past.
King. Why then, good morrow to you all, my lords.
Have you read o'er the letters that I sent you?
War. We have, my liege.
King. Then you perceive the body of our kingdom,
How foul it is; what rank diseases grow,
And with what danger, near the heart of it.
War. It is but as a body yet distempered,
Which to his former strength may be restor'd
With good advice and little medicine.
My Lord Northumberland will soon be cool'd.
King. O God, that one might read the book of fate,
And see the revolution of the times
Make mountains level, and the continent,
Weary of solid firmness, melt itself
Into the sea! and other times to see
The beachy girdle of the ocean
Too wide for Neptune's hips; how chances mock,
And changes fill the cup of alteration
With divers liquors! O, if this were seen,
The happiest youth, viewing his progress through,
What perils past, what crosses to ensue,
Would shut the book and sit him down and die
'Tis not ten years gone
Since Richard and Northumberland, great friends,
Did feast together, and in two years after
Were they at wars. It is but eight years since
This Percy was the man nearest my soul,
Who like a brother toil'd in my affairs
And laid his love and life under my foot;
Yea, for my sake, even to the eyes of Richard
Gave him defiance. But which of you was by —
[*To Warwick*] You, cousin Nevil, as I may remember —
When Richard, with his eye brimful of tears,
Then check'd and rated by Northumberland,
Did speak these words, now prov'd a prophecy?
'Northumberland, thou ladder by the which
My cousin Bolingbroke ascends my throne —'
Though then, God knows, I had no such intent,
But that necessity so bow'd the state
That I and greatness were compell'd to kiss —
'The time shall come,' thus did he follow it,
'The time will come that foul sin, gathering head,
Shall break into corruption': so went on,
Foretelling this same time's condition
And the division of our amity.
War. There is a history in all men's lives,
Figuring the nature of the times deceas'd;
The which observ'd, a man may prophesy,
With a near aim, of the main chance of things
As yet not come to life, which in their seeds
And weak beginnings lie intreasured.

Such things become the hatch and brood of time.
And by the necessary form of this
King Richard might create a perfect guess
That great Northumberland, then false to him,
Would of that seed grow to a greater falseness,
Which should not find a ground to root upon
Unless on you.

King. Are these things then necessities?
Then let us meet them like necessities!
And that same word even now cries out on us.
They say the Bishop and Northumberland
Are fifty thousand strong.

War. It cannot be, my lord.
Rumour doth double, like the voice and echo,
The numbers of the fear'd. Please it your Grace
To go to bed. Upon my soul, my lord,
The powers that you already have sent forth
Shall bring this prize in very easily.
To comfort you the more, I have receiv'd
A certain instance that Glendower is dead.
Your Majesty hath been this fortnight ill,
And these unseasoned hours perforce must add
Unto your sickness.

King. I will take your counsel.
And were these inward wars once out of hand.
We would, dear lords, unto the Holy Land.

Exeunt.

Scene II. [*Before* Justice Shallow's *house in Gloucestershire.*]

Enter *Justice Shallow* and *Justice Silence* [meeting]; *Mouldy, Shadow, Wart, Feeble, Bullcalf,* [and *Servants,* behind].

Shal. Come on, come on, come on, sir. Give me your hand, sir; give me your hand, sir. An early stirrer, by the rood. And how doth my good cousin Silence?

Sil. Good morrow, good cousin Shallow.

Shal. And how doth my cousin your bedfellow? and your fairest daughter and mine, my goddaughter Ellen?

Sil. Alas, a black woosel, cousin Shallow!

Shal. By yea and no, sir, I dare say my cousin William is become a good scholar. He is at Oxford still, is he not?

Sil. Indeed, sir, to my cost.

Shal. 'A must, then, to the Inns o' Court shortly. I was once of Clement's Inn, where I think they will talk of mad Shallow yet.

Sil. You were call'd 'lusty Shallow' then, cousin.

Shal. By the mass, I was call'd anything! and I would have done anything indeed too, and roundly too. There was I, and little John Doit of Staffordshire, and black George Barnes, and Francis Pickbone, and Will Squele, a Cotsole man — you had not four such swinge-bucklers in all the Inns o' Court again. And I may say to you, we knew where the bona robas were and had the best of them all at commandment. Then was Jack Falstaff, now Sir John, a boy, and page to Thomas Mowbray, Duke of Norfolk.

Sil. This Sir John, cousin, that comes hither anon about soldiers?

Shal. The same Sir John, the very same. I see him break Skogan's head at the court gate when 'a was a crack not thus high; and the very same day did I fight with one Samson Stockfish, a fruiterer, behind Gray's Inn. Jesu, Jesu, the mad days that I have spent! And to see how many of my old acquaintance are dead!

Sil. We shall all follow, cousin.

Shal. Certain, 'tis certain; very sure, very sure. Death, as the Psalmist saith, is certain to all; all shall die. How a good yoke of bullocks at Stamford fair?

Sil. By my troth, I was not there.

Shal. Death is certain. Is old Dooble of your town living yet?

Sil. Dead, sir.

Shal. Jesu, Jesu, dead! 'A drew a good bow — and dead! 'A shot a fine shoot. John o' Gaunt loved him well and betted much money on his head. Dead! 'A would have clapp'd i' th' clout at twelve score, and carried you a forehand shaft a fourteen and fourteen and a half, that it would have done a man's heart good to see. How a score of ewes now?

Sil. Thereafter as they be. A score of good ewes may be worth ten pounds.

Shal. And is old Dooble dead?

Sil. Here come two of Sir John Falstaff's men, as I think.

Enter *Bardolph,* and *one with him.*

Bard. Good morrow, honest gentlemen. I beseech you, which is Justice Shallow?

Shal. I am Robert Shallow, sir, a poor esquire of this county, and one of the King's justices of the peace. What is your good pleasure with me?

Bard. My captain, sir, commends him to you — my captain, Sir John Falstaff, a tall gentleman, by heaven, and a most gallant leader.

Shal. He greets me well, sir. I knew him a good backsword man. How doth the good knight? May I ask how my lady his wife doth?

Bard. Sir, pardon; a soldier is better accommodated than with a wife.

Shal. It is well said, in faith, sir; and it is well said indeed too. 'Better accommodated!' It is good; yea indeed is it. Good phrases are surely, and ever were, very commendable. 'Accommodated!' It comes of *accommodo*. Very good; a good phrase.

Bard. Pardon me, sir; I have heard the word. 'Phrase' call you it? By this good day, I know not the phrase; but I will maintain the word with my sword to be a soldier-like word and a word of exceeding good command, by heaven. Accommodated: that is, when a man is, as they say, accommodated; or when a man is, being, whereby 'a may be thought to be accommodated — which is an excellent thing.

Enter *Sir John Falstaff*.

Shal. It is very just. Look, here comes good Sir John. Give me your good hand, give me your worship's good hand. By my troth, you like well, and bear your years very well. Welcome, good Sir John.

Fal. I am glad to see you well, good Master Robert Shallow. Master Surecard, as I think?

Shal. No, Sir John. It is my cousin Silence, in commission with me.

Fal. Good Master Silence, it well befits you should be of the peace.

Sil. Your good worship is welcome.

Fal. Fie! this is hot weather. Gentlemen, have you provided me here half a dozen sufficient men?

Shal. Marry have we, sir. Will you sit?

Fal. Let me see them, I beseech you.

Shal. Where's the roll? Where's the roll? Where's the roll? Let me see, let me see, let me see. So, so, so, so, so — so, so. Yea, marry, sir. Ralph Mouldy! Let them appear as I call; let them do so, let them do so. Let me see. Where is Mouldy?

Moul. Here, an it please you.

Shal. What think you, Sir John? A good-limb'd fellow, young, strong, and of good friends.

Fal. Is thy name Mouldy?

Moul. Yea, an't please you.

Fal. 'Tis the more time thou wert us'd.

Shal. Ha, ha, ha! Most excellent, i' faith! Things that are mouldy lack use. Very singular good! In faith, well said, Sir John, very well said.

Fal. Prick him.

Moul. I was prick'd well enough before, an you could have let me alone. My old dame will be undone now for one to do her husbandry and her drudgery. You need not to have prick'd me. There are other men fitter to go out than I.

Fal. Go to! peace, Mouldy; you shall go. Mouldy, it is time you were spent.

Moul. Spent?

Shal. Peace, fellow, peace; stand aside. Know you where you are? For th' other, Sir John. Let me see. Simon Shadow!

Fal. Yea, marry, let me have him to sit under. He's like to be a cold soldier.

Shal. Where's Shadow?

Shad. Here, sir.

Fal. Shadow, whose son art thou?

Shad. My mother's son, sir.

Fal. Thy mother's son! Like enough; and thy father's shadow. So the son of the female is the shadow of the male. It is often so indeed; but much of the father's substance!

Shal. Do you like him, Sir John?

Fal. Shadow will serve for summer. Prick him; for we have a number of shadows to fill up the muster book.

Shal. Thomas Wart!

Fal. Where's he?

Wart. Here, sir.

Fal. Is thy name Wart?

Wart. Yea, sir.

Fal. Thou art a very ragged wart.

Shal. Shall I prick him, Sir John?

Fal. It were superfluous; for his apparel is built upon his back, and the whole frame stands upon pins. Prick him no more.

Shal. Ha, ha, ha! You can do it, sir; you can do it! I commend you well. Francis Feeble!

Fee. Here, sir.

Fal. What trade art thou, Feeble?

Fee. A woman's tailor, sir.

Shal. Shall I prick him, sir?

Fal. You may; but if he had been a man's tailor, he'd 'a' prick'd you. Wilt thou make as many holes in an enemy's battle as thou hast done in a woman's petticoat?

Fee. I will do my good will, sir. You can have no more.

Fal. Well said, good woman's tailor! Well said, courageous Feeble! Thou wilt be as valiant as the wrathful dove or most magnanimous mouse. Prick the woman's tailor well, Master Shallow; deep, Master Shallow.

Fee. I would Wart might have gone, sir.

Fal. I would thou wert a man's tailor, that thou mightst mend him and make him fit to go. I cannot put him to a private soldier that is the leader of so many thousands. Let that suffice, most forcible Feeble.

Fee. It shall suffice, sir.

Fal. I am bound to thee, reverend Feeble. Who is next?

Shal. Peter Bullcalf o' th' green!

Fal. Yea, marry, let's see Bullcalf.

Bull. Here, sir.

Fal. Fore God, a likely fellow! Come, prick me Bullcalf till he roar again.

Bull. O Lord! good my Lord Captain —

Fal. What, dost thou roar before thou art prick'd?

Bull. O Lord, sir! I am a diseased man.

Fal. What disease hast thou?

Bull. A whoreson cold, sir, a cough, sir, which I caught with ringing in the King's affairs upon his coronation day, sir.

Fal. Come, thou shalt go to the wars in a gown. We will have away thy cold; and I will take such order that thy friends shall ring for thee. Is here all?

Shal. Here is two more call'd than your number. You must have but four here, sir; and so I pray you go in with me to dinner.

Fal. Come, I will go drink with you, but I cannot tarry dinner. I am glad to see you, by my troth, Master Shallow.

Shal. O Sir John, do you remember since we lay all night in the windmill in Saint George's Field?

Fal. No more of that, good Master Shallow! No more of that!

Shal. Ha, 'twas a merry night. And is Jane Nightwork alive?

Fal. She lives, Master Shallow.

Shal. She never could away with me.

Fal. Never, never. She would always say she could not abide Master Shallow.

Shal. By the mass, I could anger her to th' heart. She was then a bona roba. Doth she hold her own well?

Fal. Old, old, Master Shallow.

Shal. Nay, she must be old; she cannot choose but be old; certain she's old; and had Robin Nightwork by old Nightwork before I came to Clement's Inn.

Sil. That's fifty-five year ago.

Shal. Ha, cousin Silence, that thou hadst seen that that this knight and I have seen! Ha, Sir John, said I well?

Fal. We have heard the chimes at midnight, Master Shallow.

Shal. That we have, that we have, that we have! In faith, Sir John, we have. Our watchword was 'Hem, boys!' Come, let's to dinner; come, let's to dinner. Jesus, the days that we have seen! Come, come.

Exeunt [*Falstaff and the Justices*].

Bull. Good Master Corporate Bardolph, stand my friend, and here's four Harry tenshillings in French crowns for you. In very truth, sir, I had as live be hang'd, sir, as go. And yet, for mine own part, sir, I do not care; but rather because I am unwilling and, for mine own part, have a desire to stay with my friends. Else, sir, I did not care, for mine own part, so much.

Bard. Go to; stand aside.

Moul. And, good Master Corporal Captain, for my dame's sake stand my friend. She has nobody to do anything about her when I am gone, and she is old and cannot help herself. You shall have forty, sir.

Bard. Go to; stand aside.

Fee. By my troth, I care not. A man can die but once; we owe God a death. I'll ne'er bear a base mind. An't be my destiny, so; an't be not, so. No man 's too good to serve 's prince; and let it go which way it will, he that dies this year is quit for the next.

Bard. Well said. Th'art a good fellow.

Fee. Faith, I'll bear no base mind.

Enter *Falstaff* and the *Justices*.

Fal. Come, sir, which men shall I have?

Shal. Four of which you please.

Bard. Sir, a word with you. I have three pound to free Mouldy and Bullcalf.

Fal. Go to; well.

Shal. Come, Sir John, which four will you have?

Fal. Do you choose for me.

Shal. Marry, then, Mouldy, Bullcalf, Feeble, and Shadow.

Fal. Mouldy and Bullcalf: for you, Mouldy, stay at home till you are past service; and for your part, Bullcalf, grow till you come unto it. I will none of you.

Shal. Sir John, Sir John, do not yourself wrong. They are your likeliest men, and I would have you serv'd with the best.

Fal. Will you tell me, Master Shallow, how to choose a man? Care I for the limb, the thews, the stature, bulk, and big assemblance of a man? Give me the spirit, Master Shallow.

Here's Wart. You see what a ragged appearance it is. 'A shall charge you and discharge you with the motion of a pewterer's hammer, come off and on swifter than he that gibbets on the brewer's bucket. And this same half-fac'd fellow, Shadow — give me this man. He presents no mark to the enemy; the foeman may with as great aim level at the edge of a penknife. And for a retreat — how swiftly will this Feeble, the woman's tailor, run off! O, give me the spare men and spare me the great ones. Put me a caliver into Wart's hand, Bardolph.

Bard. Hold, Wart, traverse. Thas, thas, thas!

Fal. Come, manage me your caliver. So; very well! go to; very good, exceeding good. O, give me always a little, lean, old, chopt, bald shot. Well said, i' faith, Wart. Th'art a good scab. Hold, there's a tester for thee.

Shal. He is not his craft's master; he doth not do it right. I remember at Mile-end Green, when I lay at Clement's Inn, — I was then Sir Dagonet in Arthur's Show, — there was a little quiver fellow, and 'a would manage you his piece thus; and 'a would about and about, and come you in and come you in. 'Rah, tah, tah!' would 'a say; 'Bounce!' would 'a say; and away again would 'a go, and again would 'a come. I shall ne'er see such a fellow.

Fal. These fellows will do well, Master Shallow. God keep you, Master Silence. I will not use many words with you. Fare you well, gentlemen both. I thank you. I must a dozen mile to-night. Bardolph, give the soldiers coats.

Shal. Sir John, the Lord bless you! God prosper your affairs! God send us peace! At your return visit our house; let our old acquaintance be renewed. Peradventure I will with ye to the court.

Fal. Fore God, I would you would, Master Shallow.

Shal. Go to; I have spoke at a word. God keep you!

Fal. Fare you well, gentle gentlemen. (*Exeunt* [*Shallow and Silence*].) On, Bardolph; lead the men away. [*Exeunt all but Falstaff.*] As I return, I will fetch off these justices. I do see the bottom of Justice Shallow. Lord, Lord, how subject we old men are to this vice of lying! This same starv'd justice hath done nothing but prate to me of the wildness of his youth and the feats he hath done about Turnbull Street; and every third word a lie, duer paid to the hearer than the Turk's tribute. I do remember him at Clement's Inn, like a man made after supper of a cheese paring. When 'a was naked, he was for all the world like a fork'd radish, with a head fantastically carved upon it with a knife; 'a was so forlorn that his dimensions to any thick sight were invincible. 'A was the very genius of famine; yet lecherous as a monkey, and the whores call'd him 'mandrake.' 'A came ever in the rearward of the fashion, and sung those tunes to the overscutch'd huswives that he heard the carmen whistle, and sware they were his Fancies or his Good-nights. And now is this Vice's dagger become a squire, and talks as familiarly of John o' Gaunt as if he had been sworn brother to him; and I'll be sworn 'a ne'er saw him but once in the Tilt Yard, and then he burst his head for crowding among the marshal's men. I saw it, and told John o' Gaunt he beat his own name; for you might have thrust him and all his apparel into an eel-skin; the case of a treble hautboy was a mansion for him, a court; and now has he land and beeves. Well, I'll be acquainted with him, if I return; and 't shall go hard but I'll make him a philosopher's two stones to me. If the young dace be a bait for the old pike, I see no reason in the law of nature but I may snap at him. Let time shape, and there an end. *Exit.*

ACT IV. Scene I. [*Gaultree Forest in Yorkshire.*]

Enter the *Archbishop* [*of York*], *Mowbray*, [*Lord*] *Bardolph, Hastings*, within the Forest of Gaultree.

Arch. What is this forest call'd?
Hast. 'Tis Gaultree Forest, an't shall please your Grace.
Arch. Here stand, my lords, and send discoverers forth
To know the numbers of our enemies.
Hast. We have sent forth already.
Arch. 'Tis well done.
My friends, and brethren in these great affairs,
I must acquaint you that I have receiv'd
New-dated letters from Northumberland,
Their cold intent, tenure, and substance thus:
Here doth he wish his person, with such powers
As might hold sortance with his quality,
The which he could not levy; whereupon
He is retir'd, to ripe his growing fortunes,

To Scotland; and concludes in hearty prayers
That your attempts may overlive the hazard
And fearful meeting of their opposite.
Mowb. Thus do the hopes we have in him touch ground
And dash themselves to pieces.

Enter *Messenger.*

Hast. Now, what news?
Mess. West of this forest, scarcely off a mile,
In goodly form comes on the enemy;
And by the ground they hide, I judge their number
Upon or near the rate of thirty thousand.
Mowb. The just proportion that we gave them out.
Let us sway on and face them in the field.

Enter *Westmoreland.*

Arch. What well-appointed leader fronts us here?
Mowb. I think it is my Lord of Westmoreland.
West. Health and fair greeting from our general,
The prince, Lord John and Duke of Lancaster.
Arch. Say on, my Lord of Westmoreland, in peace.
What doth concern your coming?
West. Then, my lord,
Unto your Grace do I in chief address
The substance of my speech. If that rebellion
Came like itself, in base and abject routs,
Led on by bloody youth, guarded with rags,
And countenanc'd by boys and beggary —
I say, if damn'd commotion so appear'd,
In his true, native, and most proper shape,
You, reverend Father, and these noble lords
Had not been here to dress the ugly form
Of base and bloody insurrection
With your fair honours. You, Lord Archbishop,
Whose see is by a civil peace maintain'd,
Whose beard the silver hand of peace hath touch'd,
Whose learning and good letters peace hath tutor'd,
Whose white investments figure innocence,
The dove and very blessed spirit of peace —
Wherefore do you so ill translate yourself
Out of the speech of peace, that bears such grace,
Into the harsh and boist'rous tongue of war;
Turning your books to graves, your ink to blood,
Your pens to lances, and your tongue divine
To a loud trumpet and a point of war?
Arch. Wherefore do I this? So the question stands.
Briefly to this end: we are all diseas'd
And with our surfeiting and wanton hours
Have brought ourselves into a burning fever,
And we must bleed for it; of which disease
Our late King, Richard, being infected, died.
But, my most noble Lord of Westmoreland,
I take not on me here as a physician;
Nor do I, as an enemy to peace,
Troop in the throngs of military men;
But rather show awhile like fearful war
To diet rank minds, sick of happiness,
And purge th' obstructions which begin to stop
Our very veins of life. Hear me more plainly.
I have in equal balance justly weigh'd
What wrongs our arms may do, what wrongs we suffer,
And find our griefs heavier than our offences.
We see which way the stream of time doth run,
And are enforc'd from our most quiet there
By the rough torrent of occasion;
And have the summary of all our griefs,
When time shall serve, to show in articles,
Which long ere this we offer'd to the King
And might by no suit gain our audience.
When we are wrong'd, and would unfold our griefs,
We are denied access unto his person
Even by those men that most have done us wrong.
The dangers of the days but newly gone,
Whose memory is written on the earth
With yet-appearing blood, and the examples
Of every minute's instance (present now)
Hath put us in these ill-beseeming arms;
Not to break peace, or any branch of it,
But to establish here a peace indeed,
Concurring both in name and quality.
West. When ever yet was your appeal denied?
Wherein have you been galled by the King?
What peer hath been suborn'd to grate on you?
That you should seal this lawless bloody book
Of forg'd rebellion with a seal divine
And consecrate commotion's bitter edge?
Arch. My brother general, the commonwealth,
To brother born an household cruelty,
I make my quarrel in particular.
West. There is no need of any such redress;
Or if there were, it not belongs to you.

Mowb. Why not to him in part, and to us all
That feel the bruises of the days before
And suffer the condition of these times
To lay a heavy and unequal hand
Upon our honours?
West. O, my good Lord Mowbray,
Construe the times to their necessities,
And you shall say, indeed, it is the time,
And not the King, that doth you injuries.
Yet, for your part, it not appears to me,
Either from the King, or in the present time,
That you should have an inch of any ground
To build a grief on. Were you not restor'd
To all the Duke of Norfolk's signiories,
Your noble and right well-rememb'red father's?
Mowb. What thing, in honour, had my father lost
That need to be reviv'd and breath'd in me?
The King that lov'd him, as the state stood then,
Was force perforce compell'd to banish him;
And when that Henry Bolingbroke and he —
Being mounted and both roused in their seats,
Their neighing coursers daring of the spur,
Their armed staves in charge, their beavers down,
Their eyes of fire sparkling through sights of steel,
And the loud trumpet blowing them together —
Then, then, when there was nothing could have stay'd
My father from the breast of Bolingbroke,
O, when the King did throw his warder down,
His own life hung upon the staff he threw.
Then threw he down himself, and all their lives
That by indictment and by dint of sword
Have since miscarried under Bolingbroke.
West. You speak, Lord Mowbray, now you know not what.
The Earl of Hereford was reputed then
In England the most valiant gentleman.
Who knows on whom fortune would then have smil'd?
But if your father had been victor there,
He ne'er had borne it out of Coventry;
For all the country, in a general voice,
Cried hate upon him; and all their prayers and love
Were set on Hereford, whom they doted on,
And bless'd and grac'd, indeed, more than the King.
But this is mere digression from my purpose.
Here come I from our princely general
To know your griefs; to tell you from his Grace
That he will give you audience, and wherein
It shall appear that your demands are just,
You shall enjoy them, everything set off
That might so much as think you enemies.
Mowb. But he hath forc'd us to compel this offer;
And it proceeds from policy, not love.
West. Mowbray, you overween to take it so.
This offer comes from mercy, not from fear;
For, lo! within a ken our army lies —
Upon mine honour, all too confident
To give admittance to a thought of fear.
Our battle is more full of names than yours,
Our men more perfect in the use of arms,
Our armour all as strong, our cause the best:
Then reason will our hearts should be as good.
Say you not, then, our offer is compell'd.
Mowb. Well, by my will we shall admit no parley.
West. That argues but the shame of your offence.
A rotten case abides no handling.
Hast. Hath the Prince John a full commission,
In very ample virtue of his father,
To hear and absolutely to determine
Of what conditions we shall stand upon?
West. That is intended in the general's name.
I muse you make so slight a question.
Arch. Then take, my Lord of Westmoreland, this schedule,
For this contains our general grievances.
Each several article herein redress'd,
All members of our cause, both here and hence,
That are ensinewed to this action
Acquitted by a true substantial form,
And present execution of our wills
To us and to our purposes confin'd —
We come within our awful banks again
And knit our powers to the arm of peace.
West. This will I show the general. Please you, lords,
In sight of both our battles we may meet;
And either end in peace (which God so frame!)
Or to the place of diff'rence call the swords
Which must decide it.
Arch. My lord, we will do so.
Exit Westmoreland.
Mowb. There is a thing within my bosom tells me
That no conditions of our peace can stand.
Hast. Fear you not that. If we can make our peace

Upon such large terms and so absolute
As our conditions shall consist upon,
Our peace shall stand as firm as rocky mountains.
Mowb. Yea, but our valuation shall be such
That every slight and false-derived cause,
Yea, every idle, nice, and wanton reason,
Shall to the King taste of this action;
That, were our royal faiths martyrs in love,
We shall be winnow'd with so rough a wind
That even our corn shall seem as light as chaff,
And good from bad find no partition.
Arch. No, no, my lord. Note this: the King is weary
Of dainty and such picking grievances;
For he hath found, to end one doubt by death
Revives two greater in the heirs of life;
And therefore will he wipe his tables clean,
And keep no telltale to his memory
That may repeat and history his loss
To new remembrance. For full well he knows
He cannot so precisely weed this land
As his misdoubts present occasion.
His foes are so enrooted with his friends
That, plucking to unfix an enemy,
He doth unfasten so and shake a friend;
So that this land, like an offensive wife
That hath enrag'd him on to offer strokes,
As he is striking, holds his infant up,
And hangs resolv'd correction in the arm
That was uprear'd to execution.
Hast. Besides, the King hath wasted all his rods
On late offenders, that he now doth lack
The very instruments of chastisement;
So that his power, like to a fangless lion,
May offer, but not hold.
Arch. 'Tis very true;
And therefore be assur'd, my good Lord Marshal,
If we do now make our atonement well,
Our peace will, like a broken limb united,
Grow stronger for the breaking.
Mowb. Be it so.
Here is return'd my Lord of Westmoreland.

Enter *Westmoreland.*

West. The Prince is here at hand. Pleaseth your lordship
To meet his Grace just distance 'tween our armies.
Mowb. Your Grace of York, in God's name, then, set forward.
Arch. Before, and greet his Grace. My lord, we come. [*Exeunt.*]

[Scene II. *Another part of Gaultree Forest.*]

Enter *Prince John* [*of Lancaster*] and his *Army,* [with *Westmoreland*; meeting the *Archbishop, Mowbray, Hastings,* and *Officers*].

John. You are well encount'red here, my cousin Mowbray.
Good day to you, gentle Lord Archbishop;
And so to you, Lord Hastings, and to all.
My Lord of York, it better show'd with you
When that your flock, assembled by the bell,
Encircled you to hear with reverence
Your exposition on the holy text
Than now to see you here an iron man,
Cheering a rout of rebels with your drum,
Turning the word to sword, and life to death.
That man that sits within a monarch's heart
And ripens in the sunshine of his favour,
Would he abuse the countenance of the king,
Alack, what mischiefs might be set abroach
In shadow of such greatness! With you, Lord Bishop,
It is even so. Who hath not heard it spoken
How deep you were within the books of God?
To us the speaker in his parliament;
To us th' imagin'd voice of God himself;
The very opener and intelligencer
Between the grace, the sanctities of heaven
And our dull workings. O, who shall believe
But you misuse the reverence of your place,
Employ the countenance and grace of heav'n,
As a false favourite doth his prince's name,
In deeds dishonourable? You have ta'en up,
Under the counterfeited zeal of God,
The subjects of his substitute, my father,
And both against the peace of heaven and him
Have here upswarm'd them.
Arch. Good my Lord of Lancaster,
I am not here against your father's peace;
But, as I told my Lord of Westmoreland,
The time misord'red doth, in common sense,
Crowd us and crush us to this monstrous form
To hold our safety up. I sent your Grace
The parcels and particulars of our grief,
The which hath been with scorn shov'd from the court,
Whereon this Hydra son of war is born;
Whose dangerous eyes may well be charm'd asleep
With grant of our most just and right desires,
And true obedience, of this madness cur'd,
Stoop tamely to the foot of majesty.

Mowb. If not, we ready are to try our fortunes
To the last man.
Hast. And though we here fall down,
We have supplies to second our attempt.
If they miscarry, theirs shall second them;
And so success of mischief shall be born,
And heir from heir shall hold this quarrel up
Whiles England shall have generation.
John. You are too shallow, Hastings, much too shallow
To sound the bottom of the after-times.
West. Pleaseth your Grace to answer them directly,
How far forth you do like their articles.
John. I like them all and do allow them well,
And swear here, by the honour of my blood,
My father's purposes have been mistook,
And some about him have too lavishly
Wrested his meaning and authority.
My lord, these griefs shall be with speed redress'd;
Upon my soul, they shall. If this may please you,
Discharge your powers unto their several counties,
As we will ours; and here. between the armies,
Let's drink together friendly and embrace,
That all their eyes may bear those tokens home
Of our restored love and amity.
Arch. I take your princely word for these redresses.
John. I give it you and will maintain my word;
And thereupon I drink unto your Grace.
[*Drinks.*]
Hast. [*to an Officer*] Go, Captain, and deliver to the army
This news of peace. Let them have pay, and part.
I know it will well please them. Hie thee, Captain.
Exit [*Officer*].
Arch. To you, my noble Lord of Westmoreland. [*Drinks.*]
West. I pledge your Grace [*drinks*]; and, if you knew what pains
I have bestowed to breed this present peace,
You would drink freely; but my love to ye
Shall show itself more openly hereafter.
Arch. I do not doubt you.
West. I am glad of it.
Health to my lord and gentle cousin Mowbray.
[*Drinks.*]
Mowb. You wish me health in very happy season,
For I am on the sudden something ill.
Arch. Against ill chances men are ever merry,
But heaviness foreruns the good event.
West. Therefore be merry, coz; since sudden sorrow
Serves to say thus, 'Some good thing comes tomorrow.'
Arch. Believe me, I am passing light in spirit.
Mowb. So much the worse, if your own rule be true.
Shout [*within*].
John. The word of peace is rend'red. Hark how they shout!
Mowb. This had been cheerful after victory.
Arch. A peace is of the nature of a conquest;
For then both parties nobly are subdu'd,
And neither party loser.
John. Go, my lord,
And let our army be discharged too.
Exit [*Westmoreland*].
And, good my lord, so please you, let our trains
March by us, that we may peruse the men
We should have cop'd withal.
Arch. Go, good Lord Hastings,
And ere they be dismiss'd, let them march by.
Exit [*Hastings*].
John. I trust, lords, we shall lie to-night together.

Enter *Westmoreland.*

Now, cousin, wherefore stands our army still?
West. The leaders, having charge from you to stand,
Will not go off until they hear you speak.
John. They know their duties.

Enter *Hastings.*

Hast. My lord, our army is dispers'd already.
Like youthful steers unyok'd, they take their courses
East, west, north, south; or, like a school broke up,
Each hurries toward his home and sporting place.
West. Good tidings, my Lord Hastings; for the which
I do arrest thee, traitor, of high treason;
And you, Lord Archbishop; and you, Lord Mowbray,
Of capital treason I attach you both.
Mowb. Is this proceeding just and honourable?
West. Is your assembly so?

Arch. Will you thus break your faith?
John. I pawn'd thee none:
I promis'd you redress of these same grievances
Whereof you did complain; which, by mine honour,
I will perform with a most Christian care.
But for you rebels — look to taste the due
Meet for rebellion and such acts as yours.
Most shallowly did you these arms commence,
Fondly brought here, and foolishly sent hence.
Strike up our drums, pursue the scatt'red stray.
God, and not we, hath safely fought to-day.
Some guard these traitors to the block of death,
Treason's true bed and yielder-up of breath.
Exeunt.

[Scene III. *Another part of the Gaultree Forest.*]

Alarum; excursions. Enter *Falstaff* and *Colevile,* [meeting].

Fal. What's your name, sir? Of what condition are you and of what place, I pray?

Cole. I am a knight, sir, and my name is Colevile of the Dale.

Fal. Well then, Colevile is your name, a knight is your degree, and your place the Dale. Colevile shall be still your name, a traitor your degree, and the dungeon your place — a place deep enough. So shall you be still Colevile of the Dale.

Cole. Are you not Sir John Falstaff?

Fal. As good a man as he, sir, whoe'er I am. Do ye yield, sir, or shall I sweat for you? If I do sweat, they are the drops of thy lovers, and they weep for thy death. Therefore rouse up fear and trembling and do observance to my mercy.

Cole. I think you are Sir John Falstaff, and in that thought yield me.

Fal. I have a whole school of tongues in this belly of mine, and not a tongue of them all speaks any other word but my name. An I had but a belly of any indifferency, I were simply the most active fellow in Europe. My womb, my womb, my womb undoes me! Here comes our general.

Enter *Prince John, Westmoreland,* [*Blunt,*] and the rest.

John. The heat is past; follow no further now.
Call in the powers, good cousin Westmoreland.
[*Exit Westmoreland.*]
Now, Falstaff, where have you been all this while?
When everything is ended, then you come.
These tardy tricks of yours will, on my life,
One time or other break some gallows' back.

Fal. I would be sorry, my lord, but it should be thus. I never knew yet but rebuke and check was the reward of valour. Do you think me a swallow, an arrow, or a bullet? Have I in my poor and old motion the expedition of thought? I have speeded hither with the very extremest inch of possibility; I have found'red ninescore and odd posts; and here, travel-tainted as I am, have, in my pure and immaculate valour, taken Sir John Colevile of the Dale, a most furious knight and valorous enemy. But what of that? He saw me, and yielded; that I may justly say with the hook-nos'd fellow of Rome — I came, saw, and overcame.

John. It was more of his courtesy than your deserving.

Fal. I know not. Here he is, and here I yield him. And I beseech your Grace let it be book'd with the rest of this day's deeds; or, by the Lord, I will have it in a particular ballad else, with mine own picture on the top on't, Colevile kissing my foot; to the which course if I be enforc'd, if you do not all show like gilt twopences to me, and I in the clear sky of fame o'ershine you as much as the full moon doth the cinders of the element, which show like pins' heads to her, believe not the word of the noble. Therefore let me have right, and let desert mount.

John. Thine's too heavy to mount.

Fal. Let it shine then.

John. Thine's too thick to shine.

Fal. Let it do something, my good lord, that may do me good, and call it what you will.

John. Is thy name Colevile?

Cole. It is, my lord.

John. A famous rebel art thou, Colevile.

Fal. And a famous true subject took him.

Cole. I am, my lord, but as my betters are,
That led me hither. Had they been rul'd by me,
You should have won them dearer than you have.

Fal. I know not how they sold themselves; but thou, like a kind fellow, gavest thyself away gratis, and I thank thee for thee.

Enter *Westmoreland.*

John. Now, have you left pursuit?

West. Retreat is made and execution stay'd.

John. Send Colevile, with his confederates,
To York, to present execution.

Blunt, lead him hence and see you guard him sure. *Exit [Blunt] with Colevile.*
And now dispatch we toward the court, my lords.
I hear the King my father is sore sick.
Our news shall go before us to his Majesty,
Which, cousin, you shall bear to comfort him,
And we with sober speed will follow you.

Fal. My lord, I beseech you give me leave to go
Through Gloucestershire; and when you come to court,
Stand my good lord, pray, in your good report.

John. Fare you well, Falstaff. I, in my condition,
Shall better speak of you than you deserve.
Exeunt [all but Falstaff].

Fal. I would you had but the wit. 'Twere better than your dukedom. Good faith, this same young sober-blooded boy doth not love me; nor a man cannot make him laugh. But that's no marvel; he drinks no wine. There's never none of these demure boys come to any proof; for thin drink doth so over-cool their blood, and making many fish-meals, that they fall into a kind of male greensickness; and then, when they marry, they get wenches. They are generally fools and cowards — which some of us should be too, but for inflammation. A good sherris sack hath a twofold operation in it. It ascends me into the brain; dries me there all the foolish and dull and crudy vapours which environ it; makes it apprehensive, quick, forgetive, full of nimble, fiery, and delectable shapes; which delivered o'er to the voice, the tongue, which is the birth, becomes excellent wit. The second property of your excellent sherris is the warming of the blood; which before (cold and settled) left the liver white and pale, which is the badge of pusillanimity and cowardice; but the sherris warms it and makes it course from the inwards to the parts extremes. It illumineth the face, which, as a beacon, gives warning to all the rest of this little kingdom, man, to arm; and then the vital commoners and inland petty spirits muster me all to their captain, the heart; who, great and puff'd up with this retinue, doth any deed of courage. And this valour comes of sherris: so that skill in the weapon is nothing without sack, for that sets it awork; and learning a mere hoard of gold kept by a devil, till sack commences it and sets it in act and use. Hereof comes it that Prince Harry is valiant; for the cold blood he did naturally inherit of his father, he hath, like lean, sterile, and bare land, manured, husbanded, and till'd with excellent endeavour of drinking good and good store of fertile sherris, that he is become very hot and valiant. If I had a thousand sons, the first humane principle I would teach them should be to forswear thin potations and to addict themselves to sack.

Enter *Bardolph.*

How now, Bardolph?

Bard. The army is discharged all and gone.

Fal. Let them go. I'll through Gloucestershire, and there will I visit Master Robert Shallow, Esquire. I have him already temp'ring between my finger and my thumb, and shortly will I seal with him. Come away. *Exeunt.*

Scene IV. [*Westminster. The Jerusalem Chamber.*]

Enter the *King, Warwick, Thomas Duke of Clarence, Humphrey of Gloucester,* [and others].

King. Now, lords, if God doth give successful end
To this debate that bleedeth at our doors,
We will our youth lead on to higher fields
And draw no swords but what are sanctified.
Our navy is address'd, our power collected,
Our substitutes in absence well invested,
And everything lies level to our wish.
Only we want a little personal strength;
And pause us till these rebels, now afoot,
Come underneath the yoke of government.

War. Both which we doubt not but your Majesty
Shall soon enjoy.

King. Humphrey, my son of Gloucester,
Where is the Prince your brother?

Glouc. I think he's gone to hunt, my lord, at Windsor.

King. And how accompanied?

Glouc. I do not know, my lord.

King. Is not his brother Thomas of Clarence with him?

Glouc. No, my good lord; he is in presence here.

Clar. What would my lord and father?

King. Nothing but well to thee, Thomas of Clarence.
How chance thou art not with the Prince thy brother?
He loves thee, and thou dost neglect him, Thomas.

Thou hast a better place in his affection
Than all thy brothers. Cherish it, my boy,
And noble offices thou mayst effect
Of mediation, after I am dead,
Between his greatness and thy other brethren.
Therefore omit him not; blunt not his love,
Nor lose the good advantage of his grace
By seeming cold, or careless of his will;
For he is gracious, if he be observ'd;
He hath a tear for pity, and a hand
Open as day for melting charity.
Yet notwithstanding, being incens'd, he's flint;
As humorous as winter, and as sudden
As flaws congealed in the spring of day.
His temper, therefore, must be well observ'd.
Chide him for faults, and do it reverently,
When you perceive his blood inclin'd to mirth;
But being moody, give him line and scope
Till that his passions, like a whale on ground,
Confound themselves with working. Learn this, Thomas,
And thou shalt prove a shelter to thy friends;
A hoop of gold to bind thy brothers in,
That the united vessel of their blood,
Mingled with venom of suggestion
(As, force perforce, the age will pour it in),
Shall never leak, though it do work as strong
As aconitum or rash gunpowder.

Clar. I shall observe him with all care and love.

King. Why art thou not at Windsor with him, Thomas?

Clar. He is not there to-day; he dines in London.

King. And how accompanied? Canst thou tell that?

Clar. With Poins and other his continual followers.

King. Most subject is the fattest soil to weeds;
And he, the noble image of my youth,
Is overspread with them. Therefore my grief
Stretches itself beyond the hour of death.
The blood weeps from my heart when I do shape,
In forms imaginary, th' unguided days
And rotten times that you shall look upon
When I am sleeping with my ancestors.
For when his headstrong riot hath no curb,
When rage and hot blood are his counsellors,
When means and lavish manners meet together,
O, with what wings shall his affections fly
Towards fronting peril and oppos'd decay!

War. My gracious lord, you look beyond him quite.
The Prince but studies his companions
Like a strange tongue, wherein, to gain the language,
'Tis needful that the most immodest word
Be look'd upon and learnt; which once attain'd,
Your Highness knows, comes to no further use
But to be known and hated. So, like gross terms,
The Prince will, in the perfectness of time,
Cast off his followers; and their memory
Shall as a pattern or a measure live
By which his Grace must mete the lives of others,
Turning past evils to advantages.

King. 'Tis seldom when the bee doth leave her comb
In the dead carrion.

Enter *Westmoreland.*

Who's here? Westmoreland?

West. Health to my sovereign, and new happiness
Added to that that I am to deliver!
Prince John, your son, doth kiss your Grace's hand.
Mowbray, the Bishop Scroop, Hastings, and all
Are brought to the correction of your law.
There is not now a rebel's sword unsheath'd,
But Peace puts forth her olive everywhere.
The manner how this action hath been borne
Here at more leisure may your Highness read,
With every course in his particular.

King. O Westmoreland, thou art a summer bird,
Which ever in the haunch of winter sings
The lifting-up of day.

Enter *Harcourt.*

Look, here's more news.

Har. From enemies heaven keep your Majesty;
And when they stand against you, may they fall
As those that I am come to tell you of!
The Earl Northumberland and the Lord Bardolph,
With a great power of English and of Scots,
Are by the shrieve of Yorkshire overthrown.
The manner and true order of the fight
This packet, please it you, contains at large.

King. And wherefore should these good news make me sick?
Will Fortune never come with both hands full,
But write her fair words still in foulest letters?
She either gives a stomach, and no food
(Such are the poor, in health), or else a feast,

And takes away the stomach — such are the rich
That have abundance and enjoy it not.
I should rejoice now at this happy news;
And now my sight fails and my brain is giddy.
O me! come near me. Now I am much ill.

Glouc. Comfort your Majesty!

Clar. O my royal father!

West. My sovereign lord, cheer up yourself, look up.

War. Be patient, Princes. You do know these fits
Are with his Highness very ordinary.
Stand from him, give him air; he'll straight be well.

Clar. No, no! he cannot long hold out these pangs.
Th' incessant care and labour of his mind
Hath wrought the mure that should confine it in
So thin that life looks through, and will break out.

Glouc. The people fear me, for they do observe
Unfather'd heirs and loathly births of nature.
The seasons change their manners, as the year
Had found some months asleep, and leapt them over.

Clar. The river hath thrice flow'd, no ebb between;
And the old folk, Time's doting chronicles,
Say it did so a little time before
That our great-grandsire, Edward, sick'd and died.

War. Speak lower, Princes, for the King recovers.

Glouc. This apoplexy will certain be his end.

King. I pray you take me up, and bear me hence
Into some other chamber. Softly, pray.
[*Exeunt.*]

[Scene V. *Westminster. Another chamber in the Palace.*]

[The *King* on a bed, *Clarence, Gloucester, Warwick,* and others attending.]

King. Let there be no noise made, my gentle friends,
Unless some dull and favourable hand
Will whisper music to my weary spirit.

War. Call for the music in the other room.

King. Set me the crown upon my pillow here.

Clar. His eye is hollow, and he changes much.

War. Less noise, less noise!

Enter *Prince Henry.*

Prince. Who saw the Duke of Clarence?

Clar. I am here, brother, full of heaviness.

Prince. How now? Rain within doors, and none abroad?
How doth the King?

Glouc. Exceeding ill.

Prince. Heard he the good news yet?
Tell it him.

Glouc. He alter'd much upon the hearing it.

Prince. If he be sick
With joy, he'll recover without physic.

War. Not so much noise, my lords. Sweet Prince, speak low.
The King your father is dispos'd to sleep.

Clar. Let us withdraw into the other room.

War. Will't please your Grace to go along with us?

Prince. No, I will sit and watch here by the King. [*Exeunt all but the Prince.*]
Why doth the crown lie there upon his pillow,
Being so troublesome a bedfellow?
O polish'd perturbation! golden care!
That keep'st the ports of slumber open wide
To many a watchful night! Sleep with it now!
Yet not so sound and half so deeply sweet
As he whose brow, with homely biggen bound,
Snores out the watch of night. O majesty!
When thou dost pinch thy bearer, thou dost sit
Like a rich armour worn in heat of day,
That scalds with safety. By his gates of breath
There lies a dowlny feather which stirs not.
Did he suspire, that light and weightless dowln
Perforce must move. My gracious lord! my father!
This sleep is sound indeed. This is a sleep
That from this golden rigoll hath divorc'd
So many English kings. Thy due from me
Is tears and heavy sorrows of the blood,
Which nature, love, and filial tenderness
Shall, O dear father, pay thee plenteously.
My due from thee is this imperial crown,
Which, as immediate from thy place and blood,
Derives itself to me. Lo, where it sits —
[*Puts it on.*]
Which God shall guard; and put the world's whole strength
Into one giant arm, it shall not force
This lineal honour from me. This from thee
Will I to mine leave, as 'tis left to me. *Exit.*

King. Warwick! Gloucester! Clarence!

Enter *Warwick, Gloucester, Clarence*.

Clar. Doth the King call?

War. What would your Majesty? How fares your Grace?

King. Why did you leave me here alone, my lords?

Clar. We left the Prince my brother here, my liege,
Who undertook to sit and watch by you.

King. The Prince of Wales? Where is he? Let me see him.
He is not here.

War. This door is open; he is gone this way.

Glouc. He came not through the chamber where we stay'd.

King. Where is the crown? Who took it from my pillow?

War. When we withdrew, my liege, we left it here.

King. The Prince hath ta'en it hence. Go seek him out.
Is he so hasty that he doth suppose
My sleep my death?
Find him, my Lord of Warwick; chide him hither.

[*Exit Warwick*.]

This part of his conjoins with my disease
And helps to end me. See, sons, what things you are!
How quickly nature falls into revolt
When gold becomes her object!
For this the foolish over-careful fathers
Have broke their sleep with thoughts, their brains with care,
Their bones with industry;
For this they have engrossed and pil'd up
The cank'red heaps of strange-achieved gold;
For this they have been thoughtful to invest
Their sons with arts and martial exercises:
When, like the bee, tolling from every flower
The virtuous sweets,
Our thighs pack'd with wax, our mouths with honey,
We bring it to the hive, and, like the bees,
Are murd'red for our pains. This bitter taste
Yields his engrossments to the ending father.

Enter *Warwick*.

Now where is he that will not stay so long
Till his friend sickness hath determin'd me?

War. My lord, I found the Prince in the next room,
Washing with kindly tears his gentle cheeks,
With such a deep demeanour in great sorrow
That tyranny, which never quaff'd but blood
Would, by beholding him, have wash'd his knife
With gentle eye-drops. He is coming hither.

King. But wherefore did he take away the crown?

Enter *Prince Henry*.

Lo where he comes. Come hither to me, Harry.
Depart the chamber, leave us here alone.

Exeunt [*all but the King and the Prince*].

Prince. I never thought to hear you speak again.

King. Thy wish was father, Harry, to that thought.
I stay too long by thee, I weary thee.
Dost thou so hunger for mine empty chair
That thou wilt needs invest thee with my honours
Before thy hour be ripe? O foolish youth!
Thou seek'st the greatness that will overwhelm thee.
Stay but a little; for my cloud of dignity
Is held from falling with so weak a wind
That it will quickly drop; my day is dim.
Thou hast stol'n that which, after some few hours,
Were thine without offence; and at my death
Thou hast seal'd up my expectation.
Thy life did manifest thou lov'dst me not,
And thou wilt have me die assur'd of it.
Thou hid'st a thousand daggers in thy thoughts,
Which thou hast whetted on thy stony heart
To stab at half an hour of my life.
What, canst thou not forbear me half an hour?
Then get thee gone and dig my grave thyself,
And bid the merry bells ring to thine ear,
That thou art crowned, not that I am dead.
Let all the tears that should bedew my hearse
Be drops of balm to sanctify thy head.
Only compound me with forgotten dust;
Give that which gave thee life unto the worms.
Pluck down my officers, break my decrees;
For now a time is come to mock at form.
Harry the Fifth is crown'd. Up, vanity!
Down, royal state! All you sage counsellors, hence!
And to the English court assemble now,
From every region, apes of idleness!
Now, neighbour confines, purge you of your scum.
Have you a ruffian that will swear, drink, dance,
Revel the night, rob, murder, and commit
The oldest sins the newest kind of ways?
Be happy, he will trouble you no more!
England shall double gild his treble guilt;

England shall give him office, honour, might;
For the Fifth Harry from curb'd license plucks
The muzzle of restraint, and the wild dog
Shall flesh his tooth on every innocent.
O my poor kingdom, sick with civil blows!
When that my care could not withhold thy riots,
What wilt thou do when riot is thy care?
O, thou wilt be a wilderness again,
Peopled with wolves, thy old inhabitants!

Prince. O, pardon me, my liege! But for my tears,
The moist impediments unto my speech,
I had forestall'd this dear and deep rebuke,
Ere you with grief had spoke and I had heard
The course of it so far. There is your crown;
And he that wears the crown immortally
Long guard it yours! [*Kneels.*] If I affect it more
Than as your honour and as your renown,
Let me no more from this obedience rise
Which my most inward true and duteous spirit
Teacheth — this prostrate and exterior bending!
[*Rises.*] God witness with me, when I here came in,
And found no course of breath within your Majesty,
How cold it struck my heart! If I do feign,
O, let me in my present wildness die,
And never live to show th' incredulous world
The noble change that I have purposed!
Coming to look on you, thinking you dead —
And dead almost, my liege, to think you were —
I spake unto this crown as having sense,
And thus upbraided it: 'The care on thee depending
Hath fed upon the body of my father.
Therefore thou best of gold art worst of gold.
Other, less fine in carat, is more precious,
Preserving life in med'cine potable;
But thou, most fine, most honour'd, most renown'd,
Hast eat thy bearer up.' Thus, my most royal liege,
Accusing it, I put it on my head,
To try with it (as with an enemy
That had before my face murdered my father)
The quarrel of a true inheritor.
But if it did infect my blood with joy
Or swell my thoughts to any strain of pride,
If any rebel or vain spirit of mine
Did with the least affection of a welcome
Give entertainment to the might of it,
Let God for ever keep it from my head
And make me as the poorest vassal is
That doth with awe and terror kneel to it!

King. O my son,
God put it in thy mind to take it hence,
That thou mightst win the more thy father's love,
Pleading so wisely in excuse of it!
Come hither, Harry, sit thou by my bed,
And hear, I think, the very latest counsel
That ever I shall breathe. God knows, my son,
By what bypaths and indirect crook'd ways
I met this crown; and I myself know well
How troublesome it sat upon my head.
To thee it shall descend with better quiet,
Better opinion, better confirmation;
For all the soil of the achievement goes
With me into the earth. It seem'd in me
But as an honour snatch'd with boist'rous hand;
And I had many living to upbraid
My gain of it by their assistances;
Which daily grew to quarrel and to bloodshed,
Wounding supposed peace. All these bold fears
Thou seest with peril I have answered;
For all my reign hath been but as a scene
Acting that argument. And now my death
Changes the mood; for what in me was purchas'd,
Falls upon thee in a more fairer sort;
So thou the garland wear'st successively.
Yet, though thou stand'st more sure than I could do,
Thou art not firm enough, since griefs are green;
And all my friends, which thou must make thy friends,
Have but their stings and teeth newly ta'en out;
By whose fell working I was first advanc'd,
And by whose power I well might lodge a fear
To be again displac'd; which to avoid,
I cut them off, and had a purpose now
To lead out many to the Holy Land,
Lest rest and lying still might make them look
Too near unto my state. Therefore, my Harry,
Be it thy course to busy giddy minds
With foreign quarrels, that action, hence borne out,
May waste the memory of the former days.
More would I, but my lungs are wasted so
That strength of speech is utterly denied me.
How I came by the crown, O God forgive,
And grant it may with thee in true peace live!

Prince. My gracious liege,
You won it, wore it, kept it, gave it me;

Then plain and right must my possession be;
Which I with more than with a common pain
'Gainst all the world will rightfully maintain.

Enter *Lord John of Lancaster* and *Warwick*.

King. Look, look, here comes my John of Lancaster.
John. Health, peace, and happiness to my royal father!
King. Thou bring'st me happiness and peace, son John;
But health, alack, with youthful wings is flown
From this bare wither'd trunk. Upon thy sight,
My worldly business makes a period.
Where is my Lord of Warwick?
Prince. My Lord of Warwick!
King. Doth any name particular belong
Unto the lodging where I first did swound?
War. 'Tis call'd Jerusalem, my noble lord.
King. Laud be to God! Even there my life must end.
It hath been prophesied to me many years,
I should not die but in Jerusalem;
Which vainly I suppos'd the Holy Land.
But bear me to that chamber; there I'll lie.
In that Jerusalem shall Harry die. *Exeunt*.

ACT V. Scene I. [*Gloucestershire*. Shallow's *house*.]

Enter *Shallow*, *Falstaff*, *Bardolph*, and *Page*.

Shal. By cock and pie, sir, you shall not away to-night. What, Davy, I say!

Fal. You must excuse me, Master Robert Shallow.

Shal. I will not excuse you; you shall not be excus'd; excuses shall not be admitted; there is no excuse shall serve; you shall not be excus'd. Why, Davy!

Enter *Davy*.

Davy. Here, sir.

Shal. Davy, Davy, Davy, Davy; let me see, Davy; let me see, Davy; let me see — Yea, marry, William Cook! bid him come hither. Sir John, you shall not be excus'd.

Davy. Marry, sir, thus: those precepts cannot be served. And again, sir — shall we sow the headland with wheat?

Shal. With red wheat, Davy. But for William Cook — Are there no young pigeons?

Davy. Yes, sir. Here is now the smith's note for shoeing and plough-irons.

Shal. Let it be cast and paid. Sir John, you shall not be excus'd.

Davy. Now, sir, a new link to the bucket must needs be had; and, sir, do you mean to stop any of William's wages about the sack he lost the other day at Hinckley fair?

Shal. 'A shall answer it. Some pigeons, Davy, a couple of short-legg'd hens, a joint of mutton, and any pretty little tiny kickshaws, tell William Cook.

Davy. Doth the man of war stay all night, sir?

Shal. Yea, Davy, I will use him well. A friend i' th' court is better than a penny in purse. Use his men well, Davy; for they are arrant knaves and will backbite.

Davy. No worse than they are backbitten, sir; for they have marvail's foul linen.

Shal. Well conceited, Davy. About thy business, Davy.

Davy. I beseech you, sir, to countenance William Visor of Woncot against Clement Perkes o' th' hill.

Shal. There is many complaints, Davy, against that Visor. That Visor is an arrant knave, on my knowledge.

Davy. I grant your worship that he is a knave, sir; but yet God forbid, sir, but a knave should have some countenance at his friend's request! An honest man, sir, is able to speak for himself when a knave is not. I have serv'd your worship truly, sir, this eight years; and if I cannot once or twice in a quarter bear out a knave against an honest man, I have but a very little credit with your worship. The knave is mine honest friend, sir. Therefore, I beseech you, let him be countenanc'd.

Shal. Go to. I say he shall have no wrong. Look about, Davy. [*Exit Davy*.] Where are you, Sir John? Come, come, come, off with your boots. Give me your hand, Master Bardolph.

Bard. I am glad to see your worship.

Shal. I thank thee with all my heart, kind Master Bardolph. [*To the Page*] And welcome, my tall fellow. — Come, Sir John.

Fal. I'll follow you, good Master Robert Shallow. [*Exit Shallow*.] Bardolph, look to our horses. [*Exeunt Bardolph and Page*.] If I were sawed into quantities, I should make four dozen of such bearded hermits' staves as Master Shallow. It is a wonderful thing to see the semblable coherence of his men's spirits and his. They, by observing of him, do bear themselves like foolish justices; he, by conversing with them, is turned into a justice-like servingman. Their spirits are so married in conjunction with the participation of society that they flock together in consent, like so many wild geese. If I had a suit to Master Shallow, I would humour his men with the imputation of being near their master; if to his men, I would curry with Master Shallow that no man could better command his servants. It is certain that either wise bearing or ignorant carriage is caught, as men take diseases, one of another. Therefore let men take heed of their company. I will devise matter enough out of this Shallow to keep Prince Harry in continual laughter the wearing-out of six fashions, which is four terms, or two actions; and 'a shall laugh without intervallums. O, it is much that a lie with a slight oath, and a jest with a sad brow, will do with a fellow that never had the ache in his shoulders! O, you shall see him laugh till his face be like a wet cloak ill laid up!

Shal. [*within*] Sir John!

Fal. I come, Master Shallow. I come, Master Shallow. *Exit.*

Scene II. [*Westminster. The Palace.*]

Enter *Warwick* and the *Lord Chief Justice*, [meeting].

War. How now, my Lord Chief Justice? Whither away?

Just. How doth the King?

War. Exceeding well; his cares are now all ended.

Just. I hope, not dead.

War. He's walk'd the way of nature,
And, to our purposes, he lives no more.

Just. I would his Majesty had call'd me with him.
The service that I truly did his life
Hath left me open to all injuries.

War. Indeed I think the young King loves you not.

Just. I know he doth not, and do arm myself
To welcome the condition of the time,
Which cannot look more hideously upon me
Than I have drawn it in my fantasy.

Enter *John of Lancaster, Thomas* [*of Clarence*], and *Humphrey* [*of Gloucester*, with *Westmoreland* and others].

War. Here come the heavy issue of dead Harry.
O that the living Harry had the temper
Of him, the worst of these three gentlemen!
How many nobles then should hold their places
That must strike sail to spirits of vile sort!

Just. O God, I fear all will be overturn'd!

John. Good morrow, cousin Warwick, good morrow.

Glouc., Clar. Good morrow, cousin.

John. We meet like men that had forgot to speak.

War. We do remember; but our argument
Is all too heavy to admit much talk.

John. Well, peace be with him that hath made us heavy!

Just. Peace be with us, lest we be heavier!

Glouc. O, good my lord, you have lost a friend indeed!
And I dare swear you borrow not that face
Of seeming sorrow — it is sure your own.

John. Though no man be assur'd what grace to find,
You stand in coldest expectation.
I am the sorrier. Would 'twere otherwise.

Clar. Well, you must now speak Sir John Falstaff fair;
Which swims against your stream of quality.

Just. Sweet Princes, what I did, I did in honour,
Led by th' impartial conduct of my soul;
And never shall you see that I will beg
A ragged and forestall'd remission.
If truth and upright innocency fail me,
I'll to the King my master that is dead
And tell him who hath sent me after him.

Enter the *Prince*, [now *King Henry the Fifth*, attended].

War. Here comes the Prince.

Just. Good morrow, and God save your Majesty!

Prince. This new and gorgeous garment, majesty,
Sits not so easy on me as you think.
Brothers, you mix your sadness with some fear.
This is the English, not the Turkish court;
Not Amurath an Amurath succeeds,
But Harry Harry. Yet be sad, good brothers,
For, by my faith, it very well becomes you.

Sorrow so royally in you appears
That I will deeply put the fashion on
And wear it in my heart. Why then, be sad;
But entertain no more of it, good brothers,
Than a joint burden laid upon us all.
For me, by heaven, I bid you be assur'd
I'll be your father and your brother too.
Let me but bear your love, I'll bear your cares.
Yet weep that Harry 's dead, and so will I;
But Harry lives, that shall convert those tears,
By number, into hours of happiness.
Brothers. We hope no otherwise from your Majesty.
Prince. You all look strangely on me; and you most.
You are, I think, assur'd I love you not.
Just. I am assur'd, if I be measur'd rightly,
Your Majesty hath no just cause to hate me.
Prince. No?
How might a prince of my great hopes forget
So great indignities you laid upon me?
What? rate, rebuke, and roughly send to prison
Th' immediate heir of England! Was this easy?
May this be wash'd in Lethe and forgotten?
Just. I then did use the person of your father;
The image of his power lay then in me;
And in th' administration of his law,
Whiles I was busy for the commonwealth,
Your Highness pleased to forget my place,
The majesty and power of law and justice,
The image of the King whom I presented,
And struck me in my very seat of judgment;
Whereon, as an offender to your father,
I gave bold way to my authority
And did commit you. If the deed were ill,
Be you contented, wearing now the garland,
To have a son set your decrees at naught,
To pluck down justice from your awful bench,
To trip the course of law, and blunt the sword
That guards the peace and safety of your person;
Nay, more, to spurn at your most royal image
And mock your workings in a second body.
Question your royal thoughts, make the case yours;
Be now the father, and propose a son;
Hear your own dignity so much profan'd,
See your most dreadful laws so loosely slighted,
Behold yourself so by a son disdain'd;
And then imagine me taking your part
And, in your power, so silencing your son.
After this cold considerance, sentence me;
And, as you are a king, speak in your state
What I have done that misbecame my place,
My person, or my liege's sovereignty.
Prince. You are right, Justice, and you weigh this well.
Therefore still bear the balance and the sword;
And I do wish your honours may increase
Till you do live to see a son of mine
Offend you, and obey you, as I did.
So shall I live to speak my father's words:
'Happy am I that have a man so bold
That dares do justice on my proper son;
And not less happy, having such a son
That would deliver up his greatness so
Into the hands of justice.' You did commit me;
For which I do commit into your hand
Th' unstained sword that you have us'd to bear,
With this remembrance, that you use the same
With the like bold, just, and impartial spirit
As you have done 'gainst me. There is my hand.
You shall be as a father to my youth;
My voice shall sound as you do prompt mine ear,
And I will stoop and humble my intents
To your well-practis'd wise directions.
And, Princes all, believe me, I beseech you:
My father is gone wild into his grave;
For in his tomb lie my affections,
And with his spirit sadly I survive,
To mock the expectation of the world,
To frustrate prophecies, and to rase out
Rotten opinion, who hath writ me down
After my seeming. The tide of blood in me
Hath proudly flow'd in vanity till now.
Now doth it turn and ebb back to the sea,
Where it shall mingle with the state of floods
And flow henceforth in formal majesty.
Now call we our high court of parliament;
And let us choose such limbs of noble counsel
That the great body of our state may go
In equal rank with the best-govern'd nation;
That war, or peace, or both at once, may be
As things acquainted and familiar to us;
In which you, father, shall have foremost hand.
Our coronation done, we will accite,
As I before remem'bred, all our state;
And (God consigning to my good intents)
No prince nor peer shall have just cause to say,
'God shorten Harry's happy life one day!'
Exeunt.

Scene III. [*Gloucestershire. Shallow's garden.*]

Enter *Sir John Falstaff, Shallow, Silence, Davy, Bardolph, Page.*

Shal. Nay, you shall see my orchard, where, in an arbour, we will eat a last year's pippin of mine own graffing, with a dish of caraways and so forth. Come, cousin Silence. And then to bed.

Fal. Fore God, you have here a goodly dwelling and a rich.

Shal. Barren, barren, barren! beggars all, beggars all, Sir John! Marry, good air. Spread, Davy; spread, Davy. Well said, Davy.

Fal. This Davy serves you for good uses. He is your servingman and your husband.

Shal. A good varlet, a good varlet, a very good varlet, Sir John. By the mass, I have drunk too much sack at supper. A good varlet. Now sit down, now sit down. Come, cousin.

Sil. Ah, sirrah! quoth-a — we shall

[*Sings.*]

Do nothing but eat and make good cheer
And praise God for the merry year,
When flesh is cheap and females dear,
And lusty lads roam here and there
So merrily,
And ever among so merrily.

Fal. There's a merry heart! Good Master Silence, I'll give you a health for that anon.

Shal. Give Master Bardolph some wine, Davy.

Davy. Sweet sir, sit; I'll be with you anon. Most sweet sir, sit. Master page, good master page, sit. Proface! What you want in meat, we'll have in drink. But you must bear; the heart 's all. [*Exit.*]

Shal. Be merry, Master Bardolph; and, my little soldier there, be merry.

Sil. [*sings*]

Be merry, be merry, my wife has all,
For women are shrows, both short and tall.
'Tis merry in hall when beards wag all,
And welcome merry Shrovetide!
Be merry, be merry.

Fal. I did not think Master Silence had been a man of this metal.

Sil. Who, I? I have been merry twice and once ere now.

Enter *Davy.*

Davy. [*To Bardolph*] There's a dish of leather-coats for you.

Shal. Davy!

Davy. Your worship? [*To Bardolph*] I'll be with you straight. — A cup of wine, sir?

Sil. [*sings*]

A cup of wine that's brisk and fine,
And drink unto the leman mine,
And a merry heart lives long-a.

Fal. Well said, Master Silence.

Sil. An we shall be merry, now comes in the sweet o' th' night.

Fal. Health and long life to you, Master Silence!

Sil. [*sings*]

Fill the cup, and let it come!
I'll pledge you a mile to th' bottom.

Shal. Honest Bardolph, welcome! If thou want'st anything and wilt not call, beshrew thy heart. [*To the Page*] Welcome, my little tiny thief, and welcome indeed too!—I'll drink to Master Bardolph, and to all the cabileros about London.

Davy. I hope to see London once ere I die.

Bard. An I might see you there, Davy!

Shal. By the mass, you'll crack a quart together. Ha, will you not, Master Bardolph?

Bard. Yea, sir, in a pottle-pot.

Shal. By God's liggens, I thank thee. The knave will stick by thee, I can assure thee that. 'A will not out; 'a is true-bred.

Bard. And I'll stick by him, sir.

Shal. Why, there spoke a king! Lack nothing; be merry. (*One knocks at door.*) Look who's at door there, ho! Who knocks? [*Exit Davy.*]

Fal. Why, now you have done me right. [*To Silence, who has just drunk a bumper.*]

Sil. [*sings*] Do me right
And dub me knight.
Samingo!

Is't not so?

Fal. 'Tis so.

Sil. Is't so? Why then, say an old man can do somewhat.

[Enter *Davy.*]

Davy. An't please your worship, there's one Pistol come from the court with news.

Fal. From the court? Let him come in.

Enter *Pistol.*

How now, Pistol?

Pist. Sir John, God save you!

Fal. What wind blew you hither, Pistol?

Pist. Not the ill wind which blows no man to good.
Sweet knight, thou art now one of the greatest men in this realm.

Sil. By'r Lady, I think 'a be, but goodman Puff of Barson.

Pist. Puff?
Puff i' thy teeth, most recreant coward base!
Sir John, I am thy Pistol and thy friend,
And helter-skelter have I rode to thee;
And tidings do I bring, and lucky joys,
And golden times, and happy news of price.

Fal. I pray thee now deliver them like a man of this world.

Pist. A foutra for the world and worldlings base!
I speak of Africa and golden joys.

Fal. O base Assyrian knight, what is thy news?
Let King Cophetua know the truth thereof.

Sil. [*sings*] And Robin Hood, Scarlet, and John.

Pist. Shall dunghill curs confront the Helicons?
And shall good news be baffled?
Then, Pistol, lay thy head in Furies' lap.

Shal. Honest, gentleman I know not your breeding.

Pist. Why then, lament therefore.

Shal. Give me pardon, sir. If, sir, you come with news from the court, I take it there's but two ways — either to utter them, or conceal them. I am, sir, under the King, in some authority.

Pist. Under which king, Besonian? Speak, or die!

Shal. Under King Harry.

Pist. Harry the Fourth — or Fifth?

Shal. Harry the Fourth.

Pist. A foutra for thine office!
Sir John, thy tender lambkin now is King.
Harry the Fifth's the man. I speak the truth.
When Pistol lies, do this, and fig me, like
The bragging Spaniard.

Fal. What, is the old king dead?

Pist. As nail in door. The things I speak are just.

Fal. Away, Bardolph! saddle my horse. Master Robert Shallow, choose what office thou wilt in the land, 'tis thine. Pistol, I will double-charge thee with dignities.

Bard. O joyful day!
I would not take a knighthood for my fortune.

Pist. What, I do bring good news?

Fal. Carry Master Silence to bed. Master Shallow, my Lord Shallow, be what thou wilt: I am Fortune's steward. Get on thy boots; we'll ride all night. O sweet Pistol! Away, Bardolph! [*Exit Bardolph.*] Come, Pistol, utter more to me; and withal devise something to do thyself good. Boot, boot, Master Shallow! I know the young king is sick for me. Let us take any man's horses; the laws of England are at my commandment. Blessed are they that have been my friends, and woe to my Lord Chief Justice!

Pist. Let vultures vile seize on his lungs also!
'Where is the life that late I led?' say they.
Why, here it is! welcome these pleasant days!
Exeunt.

Scene IV. [*London. A street.*]

Enter *Hostess Quickly, Doll Tearsheet,* and *Beadles.*

Host. No, thou arrant knave! I would to God that I might die, that I might have thee hang'd. Thou hast drawn my shoulder out of joint.

Officer. The constables have delivered her over to me; and she shall have whipping cheer enough, I warrant her. There hath been a man or two lately kill'd about her.

Doll. Nuthook, nuthook, you lie! Come on! I'll tell thee what, thou damn'd tripe-visag'd rascal, an the child I now go with do miscarry, thou wert better thou hadst struck thy mother, thou paper-fac'd villain.

Host. O the Lord, that Sir John were come! He would make this a bloody day to somebody! But I pray God the fruit of her womb miscarry!

Officer. If it do, you shall have a dozen of cushions again; you have but eleven now. Come, I charge you both go with me; for the man is dead that you and Pistol beat amongst you.

Doll. I'll tell you what, you thin man in a censer, I will have you as soundly swing'd for this! You blue-bottle rogue, you filthy famish'd correctioner, if you be not swing'd, I'll forswear half-kirtles.

Officer. Come, come, you she knight-errant, come.

Host. O God, that right should thus overcome might! Well, of sufferance comes ease.

Doll. Come, you rogue, come! Bring me to a justice.

Host. Ay, come, you starv'd bloodhound!

Doll. Goodman Death, goodman Bones!

Host. Thou atomy thou!

Doll. Come, you thin thing! Come, you rascal!

Officer. Very well. *Exeunt.*

Scene V. [*A public place near Westminster Abbey.*]

Enter three *Grooms*, strewers of rushes.

1. Groom. More rushes, more rushes!

2. Groom. The trumpets have sounded twice.

3. Groom. 'Twill be two o'clock ere they come from the coronation. Dispatch, dispatch. *Exeunt.*

Trumpets sound and the King and his Train pass over the stage. After them enter *Falstaff, Shallow, Pistol, Bardolph,* and the *Boy.*

Fal. Stand here by me, Master Robert Shallow. I will make the King do you grace. I will leer upon him as 'a comes by; and do but mark the countenance that he will give me.

Pist. God bless thy lungs, good knight.

Fal. Come here, Pistol, stand behind me! [*To Shallow*] O, if I had had time to have made new liveries, I would have bestowed the thousand pound I borrowed of you. But 'tis no matter. This poor show doth better; this doth infer the zeal I had to see him.

Shal. It doth so.

Fal. It shows my earnestness of affection —

Shal. It doth so.

Fal. My devotion —

Shal. It doth, it doth, it doth.

Fal. As it were, to ride day and night; and not to deliberate, not to remember, not to have patience to shift me —

Shal. It is best, certain.

Fal. But to stand stained with travel and sweating with desire to see him, thinking of nothing else, putting all affairs else in oblivion, as if there were nothing else to be done but to see him.

Pist. 'Tis 'semper idem,' for 'absque hoc nihil est.' 'Tis all in every part.

Shal. 'Tis so indeed.

Pist. My knight, I will inflame thy noble liver
And make thee rage.
Thy Doll, and Helen of thy noble thoughts,
Is in base durance and contagious prison,
Hal'd thither
By most mechanical and dirty hand.
Rouse up revenge from ebon den with fell Alecto's snake,
For Doll is in. Pistol speaks naught but truth.

Fal. I will deliver her.

[*Shouts within.*] *The trumpets sound.*

Pist. There roar'd the sea, and trumpet clangor sounds.

Enter the *King* and his *Train, Lord Chief Justice* [among them].

Fal. God save thy Grace, King Hal, my royal Hal!

Pist. The heavens thee guard and keep, most royal imp of fame!

Fal. God save thee, my sweet boy!

King. My Lord Chief Justice, speak to that vain man.

Just. Have you your wits? Know you what 'tis you speak?

Fal. My king! my Jove! I speak to thee, my heart!

King. I know thee not, old man. Fall to thy prayers.
How ill white hairs become a fool and jester!
I have long dreamt of such a kind of man,
So surfeit-swell'd, so old, and so profane;
But being awak'd, I do despise my dream.
Make less thy body, hence, and more thy grace;
Leave gormandizing. Know the grave doth gape
For thee thrice wider than for other men.
Reply not to me with a fool-born jest.
Presume not that I am the thing I was;
For God doth know (so shall the world perceive)
That I have turn'd away my former self;
So will I those that kept me company.
When thou dost hear I am as I have been,
Approach me, and thou shalt be as thou wast,
The tutor and the feeder of my riots.
Till then I banish thee, on pain of death,
As I have done the rest of my misleaders,
Not to come near our person by ten mile.
For competence of life I will allow you,
That lack of means enforce you not to evil;
And, as we hear you do reform yourselves,
We will, according to your strengths and qualities,

Give you advancement. Be it your charge, my lord,
To see perform'd the tenure of our word.
Set on. *Exit King* [*with his Train*].

Fal. Master Shallow, I owe you a thousand pound.

Shal. Yea, marry, Sir John; which I beseech you to let me have home with me.

Fal. That can hardly be, Master Shallow. Do not you grieve at this. I shall be sent for in private to him. Look you, he must seem thus to the world. Fear not your advancements. I will be the man yet that shall make you great.

Shal. I cannot well perceive how, unless you should give me your doublet and stuff me out with straw. I beseech you, good Sir John, let me have five hundred of my thousand.

Fal. Sir, I will be as good as my word. This that you heard was but a colour.

Shal. A colour that I fear you will die in, Sir John.

Fal. Fear no colours! Go with me to dinner. Come, Lieutenant Pistol; come, Bardolph. I shall be sent for soon at night.

Enter [*Chief*] *Justice* and *Prince John,* [with *Officers*].

Just. Go carry Sir John Falstaff to the Fleet.
Take all his company along with him.

Fal. My lord, my lord —

Just. I cannot now speak; I will hear you soon.
Take them away.

Pist. 'Si fortuna me tormenta, spero contenta.'

Exeunt. Manent Lancaster and Chief Justice.

John. I like this fair proceeding of the King's.
He hath intent his wonted followers
Shall all be very well provided for;
But all are banish'd till their conversations
Appear more wise and modest to the world.

Just. And so they are.

John. The King hath call'd his parliament, my lord.

Just. He hath.

John. I will lay odds that, ere this year expire,
We bear our civil swords and native fire
As far as France. I heard a bird so sing,
Whose music, to my thinking, pleas'd the King.
Come, will you hence? *Exeunt.*

EPILOGUE.

[SPOKEN BY A *Dancer*.]

First my fear; then my cursy; last my speech. My fear, is your displeasure; my cursy, my duty; and my speech, to beg your pardons. If you look for a good speech now, you undo me; for what I have to say is of mine own making; and what indeed I should say will, I doubt, prove mine own marring. But to the purpose, and so to the venture. Be it known to you (as it is very well) I was lately here in the end of a displeasing play, to pray your patience for it and to promise you a better. I meant indeed to pay you with this; which, if like an ill venture it come unluckily home, I break, and you my gentle creditors lose. Here I promis'd you I would be, and here I commit my body to your mercies. Bate me some, and I will pay you some, and, as most debtors do, promise you infinitely.

If my tongue cannot entreat you to acquit me, will you command me to use my legs? And yet that were but light payment — to dance out of your debt. But a good conscience will make any possible satisfaction, and so would I. All the gentlewomen here have forgiven me. If the gentlemen will not, then the gentlemen do not agree with the gentlewomen, which was never seen before in such an assembly.

One word more, I beseech you. If you be not too much cloy'd with fat meat, our humble author will continue the story, with Sir John in it, and make you merry with fair Katherine of France; where, for anything I know, Falstaff shall die of a sweat, unless already 'a be kill'd with your hard opinions; for Oldcastle died a martyr, and this is not the man. My tongue is weary. When my legs are too, I will bid you good night; and so kneel down before you — but, indeed, to pray for the Queen.

King Henry the Fifth

Henry the Fifth is mentioned in the Stationers' Register on August 4, 1600, and the formal entry, by Thomas Pavyer, comes ten days later. The First Quarto (1600) offers a garbled text of a drastically cut-down version. The Second Quarto (1602) was printed from the First; and so, apparently, was the Third, which, though dated 1608, was in fact published in 1619. The First Folio contains the play in its full and authentic form. Bad as it is, the First Quarto enables one to correct a good many of the Folio's misprints. Three lines not found in the Folio appear to be genuine and are supplied from the Quarto in the present text (ii, 1, 110–111; iv, 3, 48). The most famous of all Shakespearean emendations is Theobald's correction of the Folio reading 'and a Table of greene fields' (ii, 3, 17), which makes no sense, to 'and 'a babbled of green fields.' The Quartos omit the words.

The proper division into acts is shown by the Chorus in each case. In the Quarto (which omits the speeches of the Chorus) there is no division. The Folio marks the acts, but in some instances erroneously.

The date of Henry the Fifth is fixed with unusual exactness by the reference to Essex in the Chorus to Act V:

> Were now the general of our gracious Empress
> (As in good time he may) from Ireland coming,
> Bringing rebellion broached on his sword,
> How many would the peaceful city quit
> To welcome him!

Essex left London on March 27, 1599, reached Dublin in April, and, returning from a campaign which was a complete fiasco, arrived at London on September 28 in the same year. Meres, in his *Palladis Tamia*, published in the autumn of 1598, mentions *Henry the Fourth*, but not Henry the Fifth. The play is promised in the Epilogue to *Henry the Fourth, Part II*.

For history Shakespeare relies for the most part on Holinshed's *Chronicle*. *The Famous Victories of Henry the Fifth* includes most of the reign, ending with the betrothal to Katherine of France, which took place on May 21, 1420. From this old play Shakespeare took hints for the action and he sometimes echoes its phrases. Thus, in the famous anecdote of the tennis balls (i, 2, 234 ff.), the king's eloquent reply to the Dauphin's insulting message is quite original; but there are traces of both Holinshed and the old play. In the play we have: 'My lord prince Dolphin is very pleasant with me: but tel him, that in steed of balles of leather, we wil tosse him balles of brasse and yron, yea such balles as neuer were tost in France, the proudest tennis court shall rue it. . . . Therfore get thee hence, and tel him thy message quickly, least I be there before thee: away priest, be gone.' In Holinshed: 'The K[ing] wrote to him, [the Dauphin,] that yer ought long, he would tosse him some London balles that perchance should shake the walles of the best court in France.'

The French nobles are not well treated by Shakespeare. Their rather vulgar frivolity is distasteful to the modern reader, who looks at the situation impartially, and not with the eyes of a patriotic Elizabethan. Holinshed tells us simply that the French, confident of victory, 'made great triumph; for the capteins had determined before how to diuide the spoile, and the soldiers the night before had plaid the Englishmen at dice.' The old play dramatizes Holinshed. It brings in three soldiers and a drummer playing at dice and speaking broken English; also a captain who has 'set three or foure chaire makers a worke, to make a new disguised chaire to set that womanly King of England in, that all the people may laugh and scoffe at him.' Yet he pities the 'poore English scabs': 'Why, take an English man out of his warme bed and his stale drinke, but one moneth, and alas what wil become of him? But giue the Frenchman a Reddish roote, and he wil liue with it all the dayes of his life.' (Cf. iii, 7, 93, 158 ff.; iv, Chorus, 17–22.) Alençon is of much the same opinion in *1 Henry VI*, i, 2, 9–12:

> They want their porridge and their fat bull-beeves.
> Either they must be dieted like mules
> And have their provender tied to their mouths,
> Or piteous they will look, like drowned mice.

The way in which Shakespeare picked up phrases is well illustrated in the Prologue:

> Then should the warlike Harry, like himself,
> Assume the port of Mars, and at his heels
> (Leash'd in, like hounds) should famine, sword, and fire
> Crouch for employment.

In Holinshed King Henry uses a similar figure in reply to an ambassador from the besieged citizens of Rouen: 'He declared that the goddesse of battell, called *Bellona*, had three handmaidens, euer of necessitie attending vpon her, as blood, fire, and famine.' Cf. also the exhortation of the Archbishop of Canterbury (i, 2, 131): 'With blood and sword and fire to win your right.' Canterbury's long address in explanation of King Henry's title to the crown of France (i, 2, 35–100) is simply versified from Holinshed, with only such slight changes as are needed to transfer prose into blank verse. Indeed, Shakespeare found in Holinshed's prose four or five lines which he could take over as verse without the change of a word. This illustrates the fallacy of any argument based on the discovery of so-called 'verse fossils' in prose passages.

The Quarto omits the Prologue and all other speeches of the Chorus. Some of these furnish historical information that the audience cannot do without. Incidentally, they are interesting documents in the history of dramatic criticism. They express, over and over again, the doctrine of the voluntary subjection of our minds to the illusion of the stage (as opposed to dramatic deception) — a principle which a succession of eminent critics arrived at by a long course of study and debate, and which Schlegel and Coleridge are often thought to have finally worked out.

The character of Henry V in this play is inconsistent with the character of the Prince in *Henry the Fourth*. The difference is not moral, but mental. The Prince has a brilliant intellect that works with flashing rapidity; King Henry's mind is not inferior, but it is of another order: it is strong and sure, but does not scintillate. No such mental transformation could result from a reform in manners and morals. The inconsistency is, of course, in no sense a fault in Shakespeare's portrayal. He was quite at liberty to give different accounts of the same personage in different plays. For the intensely religious nature of King Henry, Shakespeare had ample justification in Holinshed, and he has emphasized it throughout, so that the conquest of France becomes to all intents and purposes a holy war.

THE LIFE OF
KING HENRY THE FIFTH

[Dramatis Personæ.

Chorus.

King Henry the Fifth.
Duke of Gloucester,
Duke of Bedford, } brothers to the *King.*
Duke of Exeter, uncle to the *King.*
Duke of York, cousin to the *King.*
Earl of Salisbury.
Earl of Westmoreland.
Earl of Warwick.
Archbishop of Canterbury.
Bishop of Ely.
Earl of Cambridge.
Lord Scroop.
Sir Thomas Grey.
Sir Thomas Erpingham,
Gower, an English captain,
Fluellen, a Welsh captain,
Macmorris, an Irish captain,
Jamy, a Scottish captain, } officers in *King Henry's* army.
John Bates,
Alexander Court,
Michael Williams, } soldiers in the same.
Pistol.
Nym.
Bardolph.
Boy.
A Herald.

Charles the Sixth, King of France.
Lewis, the Dauphin.
Duke of Burgundy.
Duke of Orleans.
Duke of Bourbon.
The Constable of France.
Rambures,
Grandpré,
Beaumont, } French lords.
Governor of Harfleur.
Montjoy, a French herald.
Ambassadors to the *King of England.*

Isabel, Queen of France.
Katherine, daughter to *Charles* and *Isabel.*
Alice, a lady attending on her.
Hostess of the Boar's Head tavern in Eastcheap (formerly *Mistress Quickly,* now married to *Pistol*).

Lords, Ladies, Officers, Soldiers, Citizens, Messengers, and Attendants.

SCENE. — *England and France.*]

Enter *Prologue.*

O for a Muse of fire, that would ascend
The brightest heaven of invention,
A kingdom for a stage, princes to act,
And monarchs to behold the swelling scene!
Then should the warlike Harry, like himself,
Assume the port of Mars, and at his heels
(Leash'd in, like hounds) should famine, sword, and fire
Crouch for employment. But pardon, gentles all,
The flat unraised spirits that have dar'd
On this unworthy scaffold to bring forth
So great an object. Can this cockpit hold
The vasty fields of France? Or may we cram
Within this wooden O the very casques
That did affright the air at Agincourt?
O, pardon! since a crooked figure may
Attest in little place a million,
And let us, ciphers to this great accompt,
On your imaginary forces work.
Suppose within the girdle of these walls
Are now confin'd two mighty monarchies,
Whose high-upreared and abutting fronts
The perilous narrow ocean parts asunder.
Piece out our imperfections with your thoughts:
Into a thousand parts divide one man
And make imaginary puissance.
Think, when we talk of horses, that you see them
Printing their proud hoofs i' th' receiving earth.
For 'tis your thoughts that now must deck our kings,
Carry them here and there, jumping o'er times,
Turning th' accomplishment of many years
Into an hourglass; for the which supply,
Admit me Chorus to this history,
Who, Prologue-like, your humble patience pray,
Gently to hear, kindly to judge our play. *Exit.*

ACT I. Scene I. [*London. An antechamber in the* King's *Palace.*]

Enter the two *Bishops* — [*the Archbishop*] *of Canterbury* and [*the Bishop of*] *Ely*.

Cant. My lord, I'll tell you, that self bill is urg'd
Which in th' eleventh year of the last king's reign
Was like, and had indeed against us pass'd
But that the scambling and unquiet time
Did push it out of farther question.

Ely. But how, my lord, shall we resist it now?

Cant. It must be thought on. If it pass against us,
We lose the better half of our possession;
For all the temporal lands which men devout
By testament have given to the Church
Would they strip from us; being valu'd thus —
As much as would maintain, to the King's honour,
Full fifteen earls and fifteen hundred knights,
Six thousand and two hundred good esquires,
And, to relief of lazars and weak age,
Of indigent faint souls, past corporal toil,
A hundred almshouses right well supplied;
And to the coffers of the King beside,
A thousand pounds by th' year. Thus runs the bill.

Ely. This would drink deep.

Cant. 'Twould drink the cup and all.

Ely. But what prevention?

Cant. The King is full of grace and fair regard.

Ely. And a true lover of the holy Church.

Cant. The courses of his youth promis'd it not.
The breath no sooner left his father's body
But that his wildness, mortified in him,
Seem'd to die too. Yea, at that very moment
Consideration like an angel came
And whipp'd th' offending Adam out of him,
Leaving his body as a paradise
T' envelop and contain celestial spirits.
Never was such a sudden scholar made;
Never came reformation in a flood
With such a heady currance scouring faults;
Nor never hydra-headed wilfulness
So soon did lose his seat, and all at once,
As in this king.

Ely. We are blessed in the change.

Cant. Hear him but reason in divinity,
And, all-admiring, with an inward wish
You would desire the King were made a prelate;
Hear him debate of commonwealth affairs,
You would say it hath been all in all his study;
List his discourse of war, and you shall hear
A fearful battle rend'red you in music;
Turn him to any cause of policy,
The Gordian knot of it he will unloose,
Familiar as his garter; that, when he speaks,
The air, a charter'd libertine, is still,
And the mute wonder lurketh in men's ears
To steal his sweet and honey'd sentences;
So that the art and practic part of life
Must be the mistress to this theoric;
Which is a wonder how his Grace should glean it,
Since his addiction was to courses vain,
His companies unletter'd, rude, and shallow,
His hours fill'd up with riots, banquets, sports;
And never noted in him any study,
Any retirement, any sequestration
From open haunts and popularity.

Ely. The strawberry grows underneath the nettle,
And wholesome berries thrive and ripen best
Neighbour'd by fruit of baser quality;
And so the Prince obscur'd his contemplation
Under the veil of wildness, which (no doubt)
Grew like the summer grass, fastest by night,
Unseen, yet crescive in his faculty.

Cant. It must be so; for miracles are ceas'd,
And therefore we must needs admit the means
How things are perfected.

Ely. But, my good lord,
How now for mitigation of this bill
Urg'd by the commons? Doth his Majesty
Incline to it, or no?

Cant. He seems indifferent;
Or rather swaying more upon our part
Than cherishing th' exhibiters against us;
For I have made an offer to his Majesty —
Upon our spiritual Convocation,
And in regard of causes now in hand,
Which I have open'd to his Grace at large,
As touching France — to give a greater sum
Than ever at one time the clergy yet
Did to his predecessors part withal.

Ely. How did this offer seem receiv'd, my lord?

Cant. With good acceptance of his Majesty;
Save that there was not time enough to hear,

As I perceiv'd his Grace would fain have done,
The severals and unhidden passages
Of his true titles to some certain dukedoms,
And generally to the crown and seat of France,
Deriv'd from Edward, his great-grandfather.
Ely. What was th' impediment that broke this off?
Cant. The French ambassador upon that instant
Crav'd audience; and the hour I think is come
To give him hearing. Is it four o'clock?
Ely. It is.
Cant. Then go we in to know his embassy,
Which I could with a ready guess declare
Before the Frenchman speak a word of it.
Ely. I'll wait upon you, and I long to hear it.
Exeunt.

[Scene II. *London. The presence chamber in the Palace.*]

Enter the *King, Humphrey* [*Duke of Gloucester*], *Bedford, Clarence, Warwick, Westmoreland,* and *Exeter,* [with *Attendants*].

King. Where is my gracious Lord of Canterbury?
Exe. Not here in presence.
King. Send for him, good uncle.
West. Shall we call in th' ambassador, my liege?
King. Not yet, my cousin. We would be resolv'd,
Before we hear him, of some things of weight,
That task our thoughts, concerning us and France.

Enter two *Bishops* — [the *Archbishop of Canterbury* and the *Bishop of Ely*].

Cant. God and his angels guard your sacred throne
And make you long become it!
King. Sure we thank you.
My learned lord, we pray you to proceed
And justly and religiously unfold
Why the Law Salique, that they have in France,
Or should or should not bar us in our claim.
And God forbid, my dear and faithful lord,
That you should fashion, wrest, or bow your reading,
Or nicely charge your understanding soul
With opening titles miscreate whose right
Suits not in native colours with the truth;
For God doth know how many, now in health,
Shall drop their blood in approbation
Of what your reverence shall incite us to.
Therefore take heed how you impawn our person,
How you awake our sleeping sword of war.
We charge you in the name of God, take heed;
For never two such kingdoms did contend
Without much fall of blood, whose guiltless drops
Are every one a woe, a sore complaint
'Gainst him whose wrong gives edge unto the swords
That make such waste in brief mortality.
Under this conjuration speak, my lord;
For we will hear, note, and believe in heart
That what you speak is in your conscience wash'd
As pure as sin with baptism.
Cant. Then hear me, gracious sovereign, and you peers,
That owe yourselves, your lives, and services
To this imperial throne. There is no bar
To make against your Highness' claim to France
But this which they produce from Pharamond:
'In terram Salicam mulieres ne succedant';
'No woman shall succeed in Salique land.'
Which Salique land the French unjustly gloze
To be the realm of France, and Pharamond
The founder of this law and female bar.
Yet their own authors faithfully affirm
That the land Salique is in Germany,
Between the floods of Sala and of Elbe;
Where Charles the Great, having subdu'd the Saxons,
There left behind and settled certain French;
Who, holding in disdain the German women
For some dishonest manners of their life,
Establish'd then this law: to wit, no female
Should be inheritrix in Salique land;
Which Salique (as I said) 'twixt Elbe and Sala
Is at this day in Germany call'd Meisen.
Then doth it well appear the Salique Law
Was not devised for the realm of France;
Nor did the French possess the Salique land
Until four hundred one and twenty years
After defunction of King Pharamond,
Idly suppos'd the founder of this law,
Who died within the year of our redemption
Four hundred twenty-six; and Charles the Great
Subdu'd the Saxons, and did seat the French
Beyond the river Sala, in the year
Eight hundred five. Besides, their writers say,
King Pepin, which deposed Childeric,

Did, as heir general, being descended
Of Blithild, which was daughter to King Clothair,
Make claim and title to the crown of France.
Hugh Capet also — who usurp'd the crown
Of Charles the Duke of Lorraine, sole heir male
Of the true line and stock of Charles the Great —
To fine his title with some shows of truth,
Though in pure truth it was corrupt and naught,
Convey'd himself as heir to th' Lady Lingare,
Daughter to Charlemain, who was the son
To Lewis the Emperor, and Lewis the son
Of Charles the Great. Also King Lewis the Tenth,
Who was sole heir to the usurper Capet,
Could not keep quiet in his conscience,
Wearing the crown of France, till satisfied
That fair Queen Isabel, his grandmother,
Was lineal of the Lady Ermengare,
Daughter to Charles the foresaid Duke of Lorraine;
By the which marriage the line of Charles the Great
Was reunited to the crown of France.
So that, as clear as is the summer's sun,
King Pepin's title and Hugh Capet's claim,
King Lewis his satisfaction, all appear
To hold in right and title of the female.
So do the kings of France unto this day,
Howbeit they would hold up this Salique Law
To bar your Highness claiming from the female,
And rather choose to hide them in a net
Than amply to imbare their crooked titles
Usurp'd from you and your progenitors.

King. May I with right and conscience make this claim?

Cant. The sin upon my head, dread sovereign!
For in the Book of Numbers is it writ:
When the man dies, let the inheritance
Descend unto the daughter. Gracious lord,
Stand for your own, unwind your bloody flag,
Look back into your mighty ancestors;
Go, my dread lord, to your great-grandsire's tomb,
From whom you claim; invoke his warlike spirit,
And your great-uncle's, Edward the Black Prince,
Who on the French ground play'd a tragedy,
Making defeat on the full power of France,
Whiles his most mighty father on a hill
Stood smiling to behold his lion's whelp
Forage in blood of French nobility.
O noble English, that could entertain
With half their forces the full pride of France
And let another half stand laughing by,
All out of work and cold for action!

Ely. Awake remembrance of these valiant dead
And with your puissant arm renew their feats.
You are their heir; you sit upon their throne;
The blood and courage that renowned them
Runs in your veins; and my thrice-puissant liege
Is in the very May-morn of his youth,
Ripe for exploits and mighty enterprises.

Exe. Your brother kings and monarchs of the earth
Do all expect that you should rouse yourself,
As did the former lions of your blood.

West. They know your Grace hath cause and means and might;
So hath your Highness. Never king of England
Had nobles richer and more loyal subjects,
Whose hearts have left their bodies here in England
And lie pavilion'd in the fields of France.

Cant. O, let their bodies follow, my dear liege,
With blood and sword and fire, to win your right!
In aid whereof we of the spiritualty
Will raise your Highness such a mighty sum
As never did the clergy at one time
Bring in to any of your ancestors.

King. We must not only arm t' invade the French,
But lay down our proportions to defend
Against the Scot, who will make road upon us
With all advantages.

Cant. They of those marches, gracious sovereign,
Shall be a wall sufficient to defend
Our inland from the pilfering borderers.

King. We do not mean the coursing snatchers only,
But fear the main intendment of the Scot,
Who hath been still a giddy neighbour to us;
For you shall read that my great-grandfather
Never went with his forces into France
But that the Scot on his unfurnish'd kingdom
Came pouring like the tide into a breach,
With ample and brim fulness of his force,
Galling the gleaned land with hot assays,
Girding with grievous siege castles and towns;
That England, being empty of defence,
Hath shook and trembled at th' ill neighbourhood.

Cant. She hath been then more fear'd than harm'd, my liege;
For hear her but exampled by herself:
When all her chivalry hath been in France,
And she a mourning widow of her nobles,
She hath herself not only well defended
But taken and impounded as a stray
The King of Scots; whom she did send to France
To fill King Edward's fame with prisoner kings,
And make her chronicle as rich with praise
As is the ooze and bottom of the sea
With sunken wrack and sumless treasuries.

West. But there's a saying very old and true—
'If that you will France win,
Then with Scotland first begin.'
For once the eagle (England) being in prey,
To her unguarded nest the weasel (Scot)
Comes sneaking, and so sucks her princely eggs,
Playing the mouse in absence of the cat,
To spoil and havoc more than she can eat.

Exe. It follows then, the cat must stay at home.
Yet that is but a curst necessity,
Since we have locks to safeguard necessaries,
And pretty traps to catch the petty thieves.
While that the armed hand doth fight abroad,
Th' advised head defends itself at home;
For government, though high, and low, and lower,
Put into parts, doth keep in one consent,
Congreeing in a full and natural close,
Like music.

Cant. True! Therefore doth heaven divide
The state of man in divers functions,
Setting endeavour in continual motion;
To which is fixed as an aim or butt
Obedience; for so work the honeybees,
Creatures that by a rule in nature teach
The act of order to a peopled kingdom.
They have a king, and officers of sorts,
Where some like magistrates correct at home,
Others like merchants venture trade abroad,
Others like soldiers armed in their stings
Make boot upon the summer's velvet buds,
Which pillage they with merry march bring home
To the tent-royal of their emperor,
Who, busied in his majesty, surveys
The singing masons building roofs of gold,
The civil citizens kneading up the honey,
The poor mechanic porters crowding in
Their heavy burthens at his narrow gate,
The sad-ey'd justice, with his surly hum,
Delivering o'er to executors pale
The lazy yawning drone. I this infer,
That many things having full reference
To one consent may work contrariously,
As many arrows loosed several ways
Come to one mark, as many ways meet in one town,
As many fresh streams meet in one salt sea,
As many lines close in the dial's centre;
So may a thousand actions, once afoot,
End in one purpose, and be all well borne
Without defeat. Therefore to France, my liege!
Divide your happy England into four,
Whereof take you one quarter into France,
And you withal shall make all Gallia shake.
If we, with thrice such powers left at home,
Cannot defend our own doors from the dog,
Let us be worried, and our nation lose
The name of hardiness and policy.

King. Call in the messengers sent from the Dauphin.
[*Exeunt some Attendants.*]
Now are we well resolv'd, and by God's help
And yours, the noble sinews of our power,
France being ours, we'll bend it to our awe,
Or break it all to pieces. Or there we'll sit,
Ruling in large and ample empery
O'er France and all her (almost) kingly dukedoms,
Or lay these bones in an unworthy urn,
Tombless, with no remembrance over them.
Either our history shall with full mouth
Speak freely of our acts, or else our grave,
Like Turkish mute, shall have a tongueless mouth,
Not worshipp'd with a waxen epitaph.

Enter *Ambassadors* of France, [attended].

Now are we well prepar'd to know the pleasure
Of our fair cousin Dauphin; for we hear
Your greeting is from him, not from the King.

Ambassador. May't please your Majesty to give us leave
Freely to render what we have in charge;
Or shall we sparingly show you far off
The Dauphin's meaning, and our embassy?

King. We are no tyrant, but a Christian king,
Unto whose grace our passion is as subject
As are our wretches fett'red in our prisons.
Therefore with frank and with uncurbed plainness
Tell us the Dauphin's mind.

Ambassador. Thus then, in few:
Your Highness, lately sending into France,

Did claim some certain dukedoms, in the right
Of your great predecessor, King Edward the Third.
In answer of which claim, the Prince our master
Says that you savour too much of your youth,
And bids you be advis'd. There's naught in France
That can be with a nimble galliard won;
You cannot revel into dukedoms there.
He therefore sends you, meeter for your spirit,
This tun of treasure; and, in lieu of this,
Desires you let the dukedoms that you claim
Hear no more of you. This the Dauphin speaks.

King. What treasure, uncle?

Exe. Tennis balls, my liege.

King. We are glad the Dauphin is so pleasant with us.
His present and your pains we thank you for.
When we have match'd our rackets to these balls,
We will in France (by God's grace) play a set
Shall strike his father's crown into the hazard.
Tell him he hath made a match with such a wrangler
That all the courts of France will be disturb'd
With chases. And we understand him well,
How he comes o'er us with our wilder days,
Not measuring what use we made of them.
We never valu'd this poor seat of England,
And therefore, living hence, did give ourself
To barbarous license; as 'tis ever common
That men are merriest when they are from home.
But tell the Dauphin I will keep my state,
Be like a king, and show my sail of greatness,
When I do rouse me in my throne of France.
For that I have laid by my majesty
And plodded like a man for working days.
But I will rise there with so full a glory
That I will dazzle all the eyes of France,
Yea, strike the Dauphin blind to look on us.
And tell the pleasant Prince this mock of his
Hath turn'd his balls to gunstones, and his soul
Shall stand sore charged for the wasteful vengeance
That shall fly with them; for many a thousand widows
Shall this his mock mock out of their dear husbands,
Mock mothers from their sons, mock castles down;
And some are yet ungotten and unborn
That shall have cause to curse the Dauphin's scorn.
But this lies all within the will of God,
To whom I do appeal, and in whose name,
Tell you the Dauphin, I am coming on,
To venge me as I may and to put forth
My rightful hand in a well-hallow'd cause.
So get you hence in peace. And tell the Dauphin
His jest will savour but of shallow wit
When thousands weep more than did laugh at it.
Convey them with safe conduct. Fare you well.

Exeunt Ambassadors.

Exe. This was a merry message.

King. We hope to make the sender blush at it.
Therefore, my lords, omit no happy hour
That may give furth'rance to our expedition;
For we have now no thought in us but France,
Save those to God, that run before our business.
Therefore let our proportions for these wars
Be soon collected, and all things thought upon
That may with reasonable swiftness add
More feathers to our wings; for, God before,
We'll chide this Dauphin at his father's door.
Therefore let every man now task his thought
That this fair action may on foot be brought.

Exeunt.

[ACT II.]

Flourish. Enter *Chorus.*

Now all the youth of England are on fire,
And silken dalliance in the wardrobe lies.
Now thrive the armourers, and honour's thought
Reigns solely in the breast of every man.
They sell the pasture now to buy the horse,
Following the mirror of all Christian kings
With winged heels, as English Mercuries.
For now sits Expectation in the air
And hides a sword, from hilts unto the point,
With crowns imperial, crowns, and coronets
Promis'd to Harry and his followers.
The French, advis'd by good intelligence
Of this most dreadful preparation,
Shake in their fear and with pale policy
Seek to divert the English purposes.
O England! model to thy inward greatness,
Like little body with a mighty heart,
What mightst thou do that honour would thee do,
Were all thy children kind and natural!

But see thy fault! France hath in thee found out
A nest of hollow bosoms, which he fills
With treacherous crowns; and three corrupted men —
One, Richard Earl of Cambridge, and the second,
Henry Lord Scroop of Masham, and the third,
Sir Thomas Grey, knight, of Northumberland—
Have, for the gilt of France (O guilt indeed!)
Confirm'd conspiracy with fearful France,
And by their hands this grace of kings must die,
If hell and treason hold their promises,
Ere he take ship for France, and in Southampton.
Linger your patience on, and well digest
Th' abuse of distance. Force a play!
The sum is paid, the traitors are agreed,
The King is set from London, and the scene
Is now transported, gentles, to Southampton.
There is the playhouse now, there must you sit,
And thence to France shall we convey you safe
And bring you back, charming the narrow seas
To give you gentle pass; for, if we may,
We'll not offend one stomach with our play.
But, till the King come forth, and not till then,
Unto Southampton do we shift our scene. *Exit.*

[Scene I. *London. A street.*]

Enter *Corporal Nym* and *Lieutenant Bardolph.*

Bard. Well met, Corporal Nym.

Nym. Good morrow, Lieutenant Bardolph.

Bard. What, are Ancient Pistol and you friends yet?

Nym. For my part, I care not. I say little; but when time shall serve, there shall be smiles — but that shall be as it may. I dare not fight; but I will wink and hold out mine iron. It is a simple one; but what though? It will toast cheese, and it will endure cold as another man's sword will — and there's an end.

Bard. I will bestow a breakfast to make you friends, and we'll be all three sworn brothers to France. Let't be so, good Corporal Nym.

Nym. Faith, I will live so long as I may, that's the certain of it; and when I cannot live any longer, I will do as I may. That is my rest, that is the rendezvous of it.

Bard. It is certain, Corporal, that he is married to Nell Quickly, and certainly she did you wrong, for you were troth-plight to her.

Nym. I cannot tell. Things must be as they may. Men may sleep, and they may have their throats about them at that time, and some say knives have edges. It must be as it may. Though patience be a tired mare, yet she will plod. There must be conclusions. Well, I cannot tell.

Enter *Pistol* and *Hostess Quickly.*

Bard. Here comes Ancient Pistol and his wife. Good Corporal, be patient here. How now, mine host Pistol?

Pist. Base tyke, call'st thou me host?
Now by this hand I swear I scorn the term;
Nor shall my Nell keep lodgers!

Host. No, by my troth, not long; for we cannot lodge and board a dozen or fourteen gentlewomen that live honestly by the prick of their needles but it will be thought we keep a bawdy house straight. [*Nym and Pistol draw.*] O well-a-day, Lady, if he be not drawn now! We shall see wilful adultery and murther committed.

Bard. Good Lieutenant — good Corporal — offer nothing here.

Nym. Pish!

Pist. Pish for thee, Iceland dog! thou prick-ear'd cur of Iceland!

Host. Good Corporal Nym, show thy valour, and put up your sword.

Nym. Will you shog off? I would have you solus.

Pist. 'Solus,' egregrious dog? O viper vile!
The 'solus' in thy most mervailous face!
The 'solus' in thy teeth, and in thy throat,
And in thy hateful lungs, yea, in thy maw, perdy!
And, which is worse, within thy nasty mouth!
I do retort the 'solus' in thy bowels;
For I can take, and Pistol's cock is up,
And flashing fire will follow.

Nym. I am not Barbason; you cannot conjure me. I have an humour to knock you indifferently well. If you grow foul with me, Pistol, I will scour you with my rapier, as I may, in fair terms. If you would walk off, I would prick your guts a little in good terms, as I may, and that's the humour of it.

Pist. O braggard vile, and damned furious wight,
The grave doth gape, and doting death is near.
Therefore exhale!

Bard. Hear me, hear me what I say! He that strikes the first stroke, I'll run him up to the hilts, as I am a soldier. [*Draws.*]

Pist. An oath of mickle might, and fury shall abate.
[*Pistol and Nym sheathe their swords.*]
Give me thy fist, thy forefoot to me give.
Thy spirits are most tall.

Nym. I will cut thy throat one time or other in fair terms. That is the humour of it.

Pist. Couple a gorge!
That is the word. I thee defy again.
O hound of Crete, think'st thou my spouse to get?
No; to the spital go,
And from the powd'ring tub of infamy
Fetch forth the lazar kite of Cressid's kind,
Doll Tearsheet, she by name, and her espouse.
I have, and I will hold, the quondam Quickly
For the only she; and — pauca, there's enough.
Go to!

Enter the *Boy*.

Boy. Mine host Pistol, you must come to my master — and you, hostess. He is very sick and would to bed. Good Bardolph, put thy face between his sheets and do the office of a warming pan. Faith, he's very ill.

Bard. Away, you rogue!

Host. By my troth, he'll yield the crow a pudding one of these days. The King has kill'd his heart. Good husband, come home presently.
Exit [*with Boy*].

Bard. Come, shall I make you two friends? We must to France together. Why the devil should we keep knives to cut one another's throats?

Pist. Let floods o'erswell, and fiends for food howl on!

Nym. You'll pay me the eight shillings I won of you at betting?

Pist. Base is the slave that pays.

Nym. That now I will have. That's the humour of it.

Pist. As manhood shall compound. Push home. *They draw.*

Bard. By this sword, he that makes the first thrust, I'll kill him! By this sword, I will.
[*Draws.*]

Pist. 'Sword' is an oath, and oaths must have their course. [*Sheathes his sword.*]

Bard. Corporal Nym, an thou wilt be friends, be friends; an thou wilt not, why then be enemies with me too. Prithee put up.

Nym. I shall have my eight shillings I won of you at betting?

Pist. A noble shalt thou have, and present pay;
And liquor likewise will I give to thee,
And friendship shall combine, and brotherhood.
I'll live by Nym, and Nym shall live by me.
Is not this just? For I shall sutler be
Unto the camp, and profits will accrue.
Give me thy hand.
[*Nym sheathes his sword.*]

Nym. I shall have my noble?

Pist. In cash, most justly paid.

Nym. Well then, that's the humour of't.
[*They shake hands.*]

Enter *Hostess.*

Host. As ever you came of women, come in quickly to Sir John. Ah, poor heart! he is so shak'd of a burning quotidian tertian that it is most lamentable to behold. Sweet men, come to him.

Nym. The King hath run bad humours on the knight; that's the even of it.

Pist. Nym, thou hast spoke the right.
His heart is fracted and corroborate.

Nym. The King is a good king, but it must be as it may. He passes some humours and careers.

Pist. Let us condole the knight; for, lambkins, we will live. *Exeunt.*

[Scene II. *Southampton. A council chamber.*]

Enter *Exeter*, *Bedford*, and *Westmoreland*.

Bed. Fore God, his Grace is bold to trust these traitors.

Exe. They shall be apprehended by-and-by.

West. How smooth and even they do bear themselves,
As if allegiance in their bosoms sat,
Crowned with faith and constant loyalty!

Bed. The King hath note of all that they intend,
By interception which they dream not of.

Exe. Nay, but the man that was his bedfellow,
Whom he hath dull'd and cloy'd with gracious favours —
That he should, for a foreign purse, so sell
His sovereign's life to death and treachery!

Sound trumpets. Enter the *King*, *Scroop*, *Cambridge*, and *Grey*, [*Lords*, and *Attendants*].

King. Now sits the wind fair, and we will aboard.

My Lord of Cambridge, and my kind Lord of Masham,
And you, my gentle knight, give me your thoughts.
Think you not that the pow'rs we bear with us
Will cut their passage through the force of France,
Doing the execution and the act
For which we have in head assembled them?
Scroop. No doubt, my liege, if each man do his best.
King. I doubt not that, since we are well persuaded
We carry not a heart with us from hence
That grows not in a fair consent with ours,
Nor leave not one behind that doth not wish
Success and conquest to attend on us.
Cam. Never was monarch better fear'd and lov'd
Than is your Majesty. There's not, I think, a subject
That sits in heart-grief and uneasiness
Under the sweet shade of your government.
Grey. True. Those that were your father's enemies
Have steep'd their galls in honey and do serve you
With hearts create of duty and of zeal.
King. We therefore have great cause of thankfulness,
And shall forget the office of our hand
Sooner than quittance of desert and merit
According to the weight and worthiness.
Scroop. So service shall with steeled sinews toil,
And labour shall refresh itself with hope,
To do your Grace incessant services.
King. We judge no less. Uncle of Exeter,
Enlarge the man committed yesterday
That rail'd against our person. We consider
It was excess of wine that set him on,
And on his more advice, we pardon him.
Scroop. That's mercy, but too much security.
Let him be punish'd, sovereign, lest example
Breed (by his sufferance) more of such a kind.
King. O, let us yet be merciful!
Cam. So may your Highness, and yet punish too.
Grey. Sir,
You show great mercy if you give him life
After the taste of much correction.
King. Alas, your too much love and care of me
Are heavy orisons 'gainst this poor wretch!
If little faults proceeding on distemper
Shall not be wink'd at, how shall we stretch our eye
When capital crimes, chew'd, swallow'd, and digested,
Appear before us? We'll yet enlarge that man,
Though Cambridge, Scroop, and Grey, in their dear care
And tender preservation of our person,
Would have him punish'd. And now to our French causes.
Who are the late commissioners?
Cam. I one, my lord.
Your Highness bade me ask for it to-day.
Scroop. So did you me, my liege.
Grey. And I, my royal sovereign.
King. Then, Richard Earl of Cambridge, there is yours;
There yours, Lord Scroop of Masham; and, Sir Knight,
Grey of Northumberland, this same is yours.
Read them, and know I know your worthiness.
My Lord of Westmoreland, and uncle Exeter,
We will aboard to-night. — Why how now, gentlemen?
What see you in those papers that you lose
So much complexion? — Look ye, how they change!
Their cheeks are paper. — Why, what read you there
That hath so cowarded and chas'd your blood
Out of appearance?
Cam. I do confess my fault,
And do submit me to your Highness' mercy.
Grey, Scroop. To which we all appeal.
King. The mercy that was quick in us but late,
By your own counsel is suppress'd and kill'd.
You must not dare (for shame) to talk of mercy;
For your own reasons turn into your bosoms
As dogs upon their masters, worrying you.
See you, my princes and my noble peers,
These English monsters! My Lord of Cambridge here —
You know how apt our love was to accord
To furnish him with all appertinents
Belonging to his honour; and this man
Hath, for a few light crowns, lightly conspir'd
And sworn unto the practices of France
To kill us here in Hampton; to the which
This knight, no less for bounty bound to us
Than Cambridge is, hath likewise sworn. But O,
What shall I say to thee, Lord Scroop, thou cruel,
Ingrateful, savage, and inhuman creature?

Thou that didst bear the key of all my counsels,
That knew'st the very bottom of my soul,
That (almost) mightst have coin'd me into gold,
Wouldst thou have practis'd on me for thy use —
May it be possible that foreign hire
Could out of thee extract one spark of evil
That might annoy my finger? 'Tis so strange
That, though the truth of it stands off as gross
As black and white, my eye will scarcely see it.
Treason and murther ever kept together,
As two yoke-devils sworn to either's purpose,
Working so grossly in a natural cause
That admiration did not whoop at them;
But thou ('gainst all proportion) didst bring in
Wonder to wait on treason and on murther;
And whatsoever cunning fiend it was
That wrought upon thee so preposterously
Hath got the voice in hell for excellence.
All other devils that suggest by treasons
Do botch and bungle up damnation
With patches, colours, and with forms being fetch'd
From glist'ring semblances of piety;
But he that temper'd thee bade thee stand up,
Gave thee no instance why thou shouldst do treason,
Unless to dub thee with the name of traitor.
If that same demon that hath gull'd thee thus
Should with his lion gait walk the whole world,
He might return to vasty Tartar back
And tell the legions, 'I can never win
A soul so easy as that Englishman's.'
O, how hast thou with jealousy infected
The sweetness of affiance! Show men dutiful?
Why, so didst thou. Seem they grave and learned?
Why, so didst thou. Come they of noble family?
Why, so didst thou. Seem they religious?
Why, so didst thou. Or are they spare in diet,
Free from gross passion or of mirth or anger,
Constant in spirit, not swerving with the blood,
Garnish'd and deck'd in modest complement,
Not working with the eye without the ear,
And but in purged judgment trusting neither?
Such and so finely bolted didst thou seem;
And thus thy fall hath left a kind of blot
To mark the full-fraught man and best indu'd
With some suspicion. I will weep for thee;
For this revolt of thine, methinks, is like
Another fall of man. Their faults are open.
Arrest them to the answer of the law;
And God acquit them of their practices!

Exe. I arrest thee of high treason by the name of Richard Earl of Cambridge.
I arrest thee of high treason by the name of Henry Lord Scroop of Masham.
I arrest thee of high treason by the name of Thomas Grey, knight, of Northumberland.

Scroop. Our purposes God justly hath discover'd,
And I repent my fault more than my death,
Which I beseech your Highness to forgive,
Although my body pay the price of it.

Cam. For me, the gold of France did not seduce,
Although I did admit it as a motive
The sooner to effect what I intended.
But God be thanked for prevention,
Which I in sufferance heartily will rejoice,
Beseeching God, and you, to pardon me.

Grey. Never did faithful subject more rejoice
At the discovery of most dangerous treason
Than I do at this hour joy o'er myself,
Prevented from a damned enterprise.
My fault, but not my body, pardon, sovereign.

King. God quit you in his mercy! Hear your sentence.
You have conspir'd against our royal person,
Join'd with an enemy proclaim'd, and from his coffers
Receiv'd the golden earnest of our death;
Wherein you would have sold your king to slaughter,
His princes and his peers to servitude,
His subjects to oppression and contempt,
And his whole kingdom into desolation.
Touching our person, seek we no revenge,
But we our kingdom's safety must so tender,
Whose ruin you have sought, that to her laws
We do deliver you. Get you therefore hence
(Poor miserable wretches) to your death;
The taste whereof God of his mercy give
You patience to endure, and true repentance
Of all your dear offences! Bear them hence.

Exeunt [Cambridge, Scroop, and Grey, guarded].

Now, lords, for France; the enterprise whereof
Shall be to you as us, like glorious.
We doubt not of a fair and lucky war,
Since God so graciously hath brought to light
This dangerous treason, lurking in our way
To hinder our beginnings. We doubt not now
But every rub is smoothed on our way.
Then, forth, dear countrymen. Let us deliver
Our puissance into the hand of God,
Putting it straight in expedition.
Cheerly to sea; the signs of war advance.
No king of England, if not King of France!

Flourish. Exeunt.

[Scene III. *London. Before the Boar's Head Tavern, Eastcheap.*]

Enter *Pistol, Nym, Bardolph, Boy,* and *Hostess.*

Host. Prithee, honey-sweet husband, let me bring thee to Staines.

Pist. No; for my manly heart doth ern.
Bardolph, be blithe; Nym, rouse thy vaunting veins;
Boy, bristle thy courage up; for Falstaff he is dead,
And we must ern therefore.

Bard. Would I were with him, wheresome'er he is, either in heaven or in hell!

Host. Nay sure, he's not in hell! He's in Arthur's bosom, if ever man went to Arthur's bosom. 'A made a finer end, and went away an it had been any christom child. 'A parted ev'n just between twelve and one, ev'n at the turning o' th' tide. For after I saw him fumble with the sheets, and play with flowers, and smile upon his fingers' ends, I knew there was but one way; for his nose was as sharp as a pen, and 'a babbled of green fields. 'How now, Sir John?' quoth I. 'What, man? be o' good cheer.' So 'a cried out 'God, God, God!' three or four times. Now I, to comfort him, bid him 'a should not think of God; I hop'd there was no need to trouble himself with any such thoughts yet. So 'a bade me lay more clothes on his feet. I put my hand into the bed and felt them, and they were as cold as any stone. Then I felt to his knees, and so upward and upward, and all was as cold as any stone.

Nym. They say he cried out of sack.

Host. Ay, that 'a did.

Bard. And of women.

Host. Nay, that 'a did not.

Boy. Yes, that 'a did, and said they were devils incarnate.

Host. 'A could never abide carnation; 'twas a colour he never lik'd.

Boy. 'A said once the devil would have him about women.

Host. 'A did in some sort, indeed, handle women; but then he was rheumatic, and talk'd of the Whore of Babylon.

Boy. Do you not remember 'a saw a flea stick upon Bardolph's nose, and 'a said it was a black soul burning in hellfire?

Bard. Well, the fuel is gone that maintain'd that fire. That's all the riches I got in his service.

Nym. Shall we shog? The King will be gone from Southampton.

Pist. Come, let's away. My love, give me thy lips.
Look to my chattels and my moveables.
Let senses rule. The word is 'Pitch and pay.'
Trust none;
For oaths are straws, men's faiths are wafer-cakes,
And Hold-fast is the only dog, my duck.
Therefore Caveto be thy counsellor.
Go, clear thy crystals. Yoke-fellows in arms,
Let us to France, like horse-leeches, my boys,
To suck, to suck, the very blood to suck!

Boy. And that's but unwholesome food, they say.

Pist. Touch her soft mouth, and march.

Bard. Farewell, hostess. [*Kisses her.*]

Nym. I cannot kiss, that is the humour of it; but adieu!

Pist. Let housewifery appear. Keep close, I thee command.

Host. Farewell! adieu! *Exeunt.*

[Scene IV. *France. The* French King's *Palace.*]

Flourish. Enter the *French King,* the *Dauphin,* the *Dukes of Berri* and *Britain,* [the *Constable,* and others].

King. Thus comes the English with full power upon us,
And more than carefully it us concerns
To answer royally in our defences.
Therefore the Dukes of Berri and Britain,
Of Brabant and of Orleans, shall make forth,
And you, Prince Dauphin, with all swift dispatch,
To line and new repair our towns of war
With men of courage and with means defendant;
For England his approaches makes as fierce
As waters to the sucking of a gulf.
It fits us then to be as provident
As fear may teach us out of late examples
Left by the fatal and neglected English
Upon our fields.

Dau. My most redoubted father,
It is most meet we arm us 'gainst the foe;
For peace itself should not so dull a kingdom
(Though war nor no known quarrel were in question)
But that defences, musters, preparations

Should be maintain'd, assembled, and collected,
As were a war in expectation.
Therefore I say 'tis meet we all go forth
To view the sick and feeble parts of France;
And let us do it with no show of fear —
No, with no more than if we heard that England
Were busied with a Whitsun morris dance;
For, my good liege, she is so idly king'd,
Her sceptre so fantastically borne,
By a vain, giddy, shallow, humorous youth,
That fear attends her not.

Con. O peace, Prince Dauphin!
You are too much mistaken in this king.
Question your Grace the late ambassadors,
With what great state he heard their embassy,
How well supplied with noble counsellors,
How modest in exception, and withal
How terrible in constant resolution,
And you shall find his vanities forespent
Were but the outside of the Roman Brutus,
Covering discretion with a coat of folly;
As gardeners do with ordure hide those roots
That shall first spring and be most delicate.

Dau. Well, 'tis not so, my Lord High Constable!
But though we think it so, it is no matter.
In cases of defence 'tis best to weigh
The enemy more mighty than he seems.
So the proportions of defence are fill'd;
Which of a weak and niggardly projection
Doth, like a miser, spoil his coat with scanting
A little cloth.

King. Think we King Harry strong;
And, princes, look you strongly arm to meet him.
The kindred of him hath been flesh'd upon us;
And he is bred out of that bloody strain
That haunted us in our familiar paths.
Witness our too much memorable shame
When Cressy battle fatally was struck,
And all our princes captiv'd, by the hand
Of that black name, Edward, Black Prince of Wales;
Whiles that his mountain sire — on mountain standing,
Up in the air, crown'd with the golden sun —
Saw his heroical seed, and smil'd to see him,
Mangle the work of nature, and deface
The patterns that by God and by French fathers
Had twenty years been made. This is a stem
Of that victorious stock; and let us fear
The native mightiness and fate of him.

Enter a *Messenger.*

Mess. Ambassadors from Harry King of England
Do crave admittance to your Majesty.

King. We'll give them present audience. Go, and bring them.
[*Exeunt Messenger and certain Lords.*]
You see this chase is hotly followed, friends.

Dau. Turn head, and stop pursuit; for coward dogs
Most spend their mouths when what they seem to threaten
Runs far before them. Good my sovereign,
Take up the English short, and let them know
Of what a monarchy you are the head.
Self-love, my liege, is not so vile a sin
As self-neglecting.

Enter [*Lords,* with] *Exeter* [and *Train*].

King. From our brother England?

Exe. From him, and thus he greets your Majesty:
He wills you, in the name of God Almighty,
That you devest yourself, and lay apart
The borrowed glories that by gift of heaven,
By law of nature and of nations, 'longs
To him and to his heirs — namely, the crown
And all wide-stretched honours that pertain
By custom, and the ordinance of times,
Unto the crown of France. That you may know
'Tis no sinister nor no awkward claim,
Pick'd from the wormholes of long-vanish'd days,
Nor from the dust of old oblivion rak'd,
He sends you this most memorable line,
[*Gives a paper.*]
In every branch truly demonstrative;
Willing you overlook this pedigree;
And when you find him evenly deriv'd
From his most fam'd of famous ancestors,
Edward the Third, he bids you then resign
Your crown and kingdom, indirectly held
From him, the native and true challenger.

King. Or else what follows?

Exe. Bloody constraint; for if you hide the crown
Even in your hearts, there will he rake for it.
Therefore in fiery tempest is he coming,
In thunder and in earthquake, like a Jove;
That, if requiring fail, he will compel;
And bids you, in the bowels of the Lord,
Deliver up the crown, and to take mercy
On the poor souls for whom this hungry war
Opens his vasty jaws; and on your head

Turns he the widows' tears, the orphans' cries,
The dead men's blood, the pining maidens' groans,
For husbands, fathers, and betrothed lovers
That shall be swallowed in this controversy.
This is his claim, his threat'ning, and my message;
Unless the Dauphin be in presence here,
To whom expressly I bring greeting too.

King. For us, we will consider of this further.
To-morrow shall you bear our full intent
Back to our brother England.

Dau. For the Dauphin,
I stand here for him. What to him from England?

Exe. Scorn and defiance, slight regard, contempt,
And anything that may not misbecome
The mighty sender, doth he prize you at.
Thus says my king: An if your father's Highness
Do not, in grant of all demands at large,
Sweeten the bitter mock you sent his Majesty,
He'll call you to so hot an answer of it
That caves and womby vaultages of France
Shall chide your trespass, and return your mock
In second accent of his ordinance.

Dau. Say, if my father render fair return,
It is against my will; for I desire
Nothing but odds with England. To that end,
As matching to his youth and vanity,
I did present him with the Paris balls.

Exe. He'll make your Paris Louvre shake for it,
Were it the mistress court of mighty Europe;
And be assur'd you'll find a difference,
As we his subjects have in wonder found,
Between the promise of his greener days
And these he masters now. Now he weighs time
Even to the utmost grain. That you shall read
In your own losses, if he stay in France.

King. To-morrow shall you know our mind at full.

Exe. Dispatch us with all speed, lest that our king
Come here himself to question our delay;
For he is footed in this land already.

King. You shall be soon dispatch'd with fair conditions.
A night is but small breath and little pause
To answer matters of this consequence.

Flourish. Exeunt.

ACT III.

Enter *Chorus.*

Thus with imagin'd wing our swift scene flies,
In motion of no less celerity
Than that of thought. Suppose that you have seen
The well-appointed King at Hampton pier
Embark his royalty; and his brave fleet
With silken streamers the young Phœbus fanning.
Play with your fancies; and in them behold
Upon the hempen tackle shipboys climbing;
Hear the shrill whistle, which doth order give
To sounds confus'd; behold the threaden sails,
Borne with th' invisible and creeping wind,
Draw the huge bottoms through the furrowed sea,
Breasting the lofty surge. O, do but think
You stand upon the rivage and behold
A city on th' inconstant billows dancing;
For so appears this fleet majestical,
Holding due course to Harflew. Follow, follow!
Grapple your minds to sternage of this navy,
And leave your England as dead midnight still,
Guarded with grandsires, babies, and old women,
Either past or not arriv'd to pith and puissance;
For who is he whose chin is but enrich'd
With one appearing hair that will not follow
These cull'd and choice-drawn cavaliers to France?
Work, work your thoughts, and therein see a siege.
Behold the ordinance on their carriages,
With fatal mouths gaping on girded Harflew.
Suppose th' ambassador from the French comes back;
Tells Harry that the King doth offer him
Katherine his daughter, and with her to dowry
Some petty and unprofitable dukedoms.
The offer likes not; and the nimble gunner
With linstock now the devilish cannon touches.

Alarum, and chambers go off.

And down goes all before them. Still be kind,
And eke out our performance with your mind.

Exit.

[Scene I. *France. Before Harfleur.*]

Alarum. Enter the *King, Exeter, Bedford,* and *Gloucester,* [with *Soldiers* carrying] scaling ladders at Harflew.

King. Once more unto the breach, dear friends, once more;
Or close the wall up with our English dead!
In peace there's nothing so becomes a man
As modest stillness and humility;
But when the blast of war blows in our ears,
Then imitate the action of the tiger:
Stiffen the sinews, summon up the blood,
Disguise fair nature with hard-favour'd rage;
Then lend the eye a terrible aspect;
Let it pry through the portage of the head
Like the brass cannon; let the brow o'erwhelm it
As fearfully as doth a galled rock
O'erhang and jutty his confounded base,
Swill'd with the wild and wasteful ocean.
Now set the teeth and stretch the nostril wide,
Hold hard the breath and bend up every spirit
To his full height! On, on, you noble English,
Whose blood is fet from fathers of war-proof!
Fathers that like so many Alexanders
Have in these parts from morn till even fought,
And sheath'd their swords for lack of argument.
Dishonour not your mothers; now attest
That those whom you call'd fathers did beget you!
Be copy now to men of grosser blood
And teach them how to war! And you, good yeomen,
Whose limbs were made in England, show us here
The mettle of your pasture. Let us swear
That you are worth your breeding; which I doubt not,
For there is none of you so mean and base
That hath not noble lustre in your eyes.
I see you stand like greyhounds in the slips,
Straining upon the start. The game's afoot!
Follow your spirit; and upon this charge
Cry 'God for Harry! England and Saint George!'

[*Exeunt.*] *Alarum, and chambers go off.*

[Scene II. *Before Harfleur.*]

Enter *Nym, Bardolph, Pistol,* and *Boy.*

Bard. On, on, on, on. on! to the breach, to the breach!

Nym. Pray thee, Corporal, stay. The knocks are too hot; and, for mine own part, I have not a case of lives. The humour of it is too hot; that is the very plain-song of it.

Pist. The plain-song is most just; for humours do abound.

Knocks go and come; God's vassals drop and die;
And sword and shield
In bloody field
Doth win immortal fame.

Boy. Would I were in an alehouse in London! I would give all my fame for a pot of ale and safety.

Pist. And I:

If wishes would prevail with me,
My purpose should not fail with me,
But thither would I hie.

Boy. As duly, but not as truly,
As bird doth sing on bough.

Enter *Fluellen.*

Flu. Up to the breach, you dogs! Avaunt, you cullions! [*Drives them forward.*]

Pist. Be merciful, great duke, to men of mould!
Abate thy rage, abate thy manly rage,
Abate thy rage, great duke!
Good bawcock, bate thy rage! Use lenity, sweet chuck!

Nym. These be good humours. Your honour wins bad humours.

Exeunt [*all but Boy*].

Boy. As young as I am, I have observ'd these three swashers. I am boy to them all three; but all they three, though they would serve me, could not be man to me; for indeed three such antics do not amount to a man. For Bardolph, he is white-liver'd and red-fac'd; by the means whereof 'a faces it out, but fights not. For Pistol, he hath a killing tongue and a quiet sword; by the means whereof 'a breaks words and keeps whole weapons. For Nym, he hath heard that men of few words are the best men, and therefore he scorns to say his prayers, lest 'a should be thought a coward; but his few bad words are match'd with as few good deeds, for 'a never broke any man's head but his own, and that was against a post when he was drunk. They will steal anything, and call it purchase. Bardolph stole a lute-case, bore it twelve leagues, and sold it for three halfpence. Nym and Bardolph are sworn brothers in filching, and in Calais they stole a fire-shovel. I knew by that piece of service the men would carry coals. They would have me as familiar with men's pockets as their gloves or their handkerchers; which makes much against my manhood, if I should take from another's pocket to put into mine; for it is plain pocketing up of wrongs. I must leave them and seek some better service. Their villany goes against my weak stomach, and therefore I must cast it up. *Exit.*

Enter *Gower* [and *Fluellen*].

Gow. Captain Fluellen, you must come presently to the mines. The Duke of Gloucester would speak with you.

Flu. To the mines? Tell you the Duke, it is not so good to come to the mines; for look you, the mines is not according to the disciplines of the war. The concavities of it is not sufficient; for look you, th' athversary, you may discuss unto the Duke, look you, is digt himself four yard under the countermines. By Cheshu, I think 'a will plow up all, if there is not better directions.

Gow. The Duke of Gloucester, to whom the order of the siege is given, is altogether directed by an Irishman, a very valiant gentleman, i' faith.

Flu. It is Captain Macmorris, is it not?

Gow. I think it be.

Flu. By Cheshu, he is an ass, as in the world! I will verify as much in his beard. He has no more directions in the true disciplines of the wars, look you, of the Roman disciplines, than is a puppy-dog.

Enter *Macmorris* and *Captain Jamy.*

Gow. Here 'a comes, and the Scots captain, Captain Jamy, with him.

Flu. Captain Jamy is a marvellous falorous gentleman, that is certain, and of great expedition and knowledge in th' aunchiant wars, upon my particular knowledge of his directions. By Cheshu, he will maintain his argument as well as any military man in the world in the disciplines of the pristine wars of the Romans.

Jamy. I say gud day, Captain Fluellen.

Flu. God-den to your worship, good Captain James.

Gow. How now, Captain Macmorris? Have you quit the mines? Have the pioners given o'er?

Mac. By Chrish, la, tish ill done! The work ish give over, the trompet sound the retreat. By my hand I swear, and my father's soul, the work ish ill done! It ish give over. I would have blowed up the town, so Chrish save me la! in an hour. O, tish ill done! tish ill done! By my hand, tish ill done!

Flu. Captain Macmorris, I beseech you now, will you voutsafe me, look you, a few disputations with you, as partly touching or concerning the disciplines of the war, the Roman wars? In the way of argument, look you, and friendly communication; partly to satisfy my opinion, and partly for the satisfaction, look you, of my mind — as touching the direction of the military discipline, that is the point.

Jamy. It sall be vary gud, gud feith, gud Captens bath, and I sall quit you with gud leve, as I may pick occasion. That sall I, mary.

Mac. It is no time to discourse, so Chrish save me! The day is hot, and the weather, and the wars, and the King, and the Dukes. It is no time to discourse. The town is beseech'd, and the trompet call us to the breach, and we talk, and, be Chrish, do nothing. 'Tis shame for us all. So God sa' me, 'tis shame to stand still, it is shame, by my hand! and there is throats to be cut, and works to be done, and there ish nothing done, so Chrish sa' me, la!

Jamy. By the mess, ere theise eyes of mine take themselves to slomber, ay'll de gud service, or ay'll lig i' th' grund for it! ay, or go to death! And ay'll pay't as valorously as I may, that sall I suerly do, that is the breff and the long. Mary, I wad full fain heard some question 'tween you tway.

Flu. Captain Macmorris, I think, look you, under your correction, there is not many of your nation —

Mac. Of my nation? What ish my nation? Ish a villain, and a basterd, and a knave, and a rascal. What ish my nation? Who talks of my nation?

Flu. Look you, if you take the matter otherwise than is meant, Captain Macmorris, peradventure I shall think you do not use me with that affability as in discretion you ought to use me, look you, being as good a man as yourself, both in the disciplines of war, and in the derivation of my birth, and in other particularities.

Mac. I do not know you so good a man as myself. So Chrish save me, I will cut off your head!

Gow. Gentlemen both, you will mistake each other.

Jamy. Ah, that's a foul fault!

A parley [*sounded*].

Gow. The town sounds a parley.

Flu. Captain Macmorris, when there is more better oportunity to be required, look you, I will be so bold as to tell you I know the disciplines of war; and there is an end. *Exeunt.*

[Scene III. *Before the gates of Harfleur.*]

[Enter the *Governor* and some *Citizens* on the walls.] Enter *King* [*Henry*] and all his *Train* before the gates.

King. How yet resolves the Governor of the town?
This is the latest parle we will admit.
Therefore to our best mercy give yourselves,
Or, like to men proud of destruction,
Defy us to our worst; for, as I am a soldier,
A name that in my thoughts becomes me best,
If I begin the batt'ry once again,
I will not leave the half-achieved Harflew
Till in her ashes she lie buried.
The gates of mercy shall be all shut up,
And the flesh'd soldier, rough and hard of heart,
In liberty of bloody hand shall range
With conscience wide as hell, mowing like grass
Your fresh fair virgins and your flow'ring infants.
What is it then to me if impious war,
Array'd in flames like to the prince of fiends,
Do with his smirch'd complexion all fell feats
Enlink'd to waste and desolation?
What is't to me, when you yourselves are cause,
If your pure maidens fall into the hand
Of hot and forcing violation?
What rein can hold licentious wickedness
When down the hill he holds his fierce career?
We may as bootless spend our vain command
Upon th' enraged soldiers in their spoil
As send precepts to the Leviathan
To come ashore. Therefore, you men of Harflew,
Take pity of your town and of your people
Whiles yet my soldiers are in my command,
Whiles yet the cool and temperate wind of grace
O'erblows the filthy and contagious clouds
Of heady murther, spoil, and villany.
If not — why, in a moment look to see
The blind and bloody soldier with foul hand
Defile the locks of your shrill-shrieking daughters;
Your fathers taken by the silver beards,
And their most reverend heads dash'd to the walls;
Your naked infants spitted upon pikes,
Whiles the mad mothers with their howls confus'd
Do break the clouds, as did the wives of Jewry
At Herod's bloody-hunting slaughtermen.
What say you? Will you yield, and this avoid?
Or, guilty in defence, be thus destroy'd?

Gov. Our expectation hath this day an end.
The Dauphin, whom of succours we entreated,
Returns us that his powers are yet not ready
To raise so great a siege. Therefore, dread king,
We yield our town and lives to thy soft mercy.
Enter our gates, dispose of us and ours,
For we no longer are defensible.

King. Open your gates. [*Exit Governor.*] Come, uncle Exeter,
Go you and enter Harflew; there remain
And fortify it strongly 'gainst the French.
Use mercy to them all. For us, dear uncle,
The winter coming on, and sickness growing
Upon our soldiers, we will retire to Calais.
To-night in Harflew will we be your guest;
To-morrow for the march are we addrest.

Flourish, and enter the town.

[Scene IV. *Rouen. The* French King's *Palace.*]

Enter *Katherine* and [*Alice,*] an old *Gentlewoman.*

Kath. Alice, tu as esté en Angleterre, et tu parles bien le langage.

Alice. Un peu, madame.

Kath. Je te prie m'enseignez; il faut que j'apprenne à parler. Comment appelez-vous la main en Anglois?

Alice. La main? Elle est appelée 'de hand.'

Kath. 'De hand.' Et les doigts?

Alice. Les doigts? Ma foi, j'oublie les doigts; mais je me souviendrai. Les doigts? Je pense qu'ils sont appelés 'de fingres'; oui, 'de fingres.'

Kath. La main, 'de hand'; les doigts, 'de fingres.' Je pense que je suis le bon escolier; j'ai gagné deux mots d'Anglois vistement. Comment appelez-vous les ongles?

Alice. Les ongles? Nous les appelons 'de nails.'

Kath. 'De nails.' Escoutez; dites-moi, si je parle bien: 'de hand, de fingres,' et 'de nails.'

Alice. C'est bien dict, madame; il est fort bon Anglois.

Kath. Dites-moi l'Anglois pour le bras.

Alice. 'De arm,' madame.

Kath. Et le coude.

Alice. 'D' elbow.'

Kath. 'D' elbow.' Je m'en fais la répétition de tous les mots que vous m'avez appris dès à présent.

Alice. Il est trop difficile, madame, comme je pense.

Kath. Excusez-moi, Alice; escoutez: 'd' hand, de fingres, de nails, d' arma, de bilbow.'

Alice. 'D' elbow,' madame.

Kath. O Seigneur Dieu, je m'en oublie! 'D' elbow.' Comment appelez-vous le col?

Alice. 'De nick,' madame.

Kath. 'De nick.' Et le menton?

Alice. 'De chin.'

Kath. 'De sin.' Le col, 'de nick'; le menton, 'de sin.'

Alice. Oui. Sauf vostre honneur, en vérité, vous prononcez les mots aussi droict que les natifs d'Angleterre.

Kath. Je ne doute point d'apprendre, par la grace de Dieu, et en peu de temps.

Alice. N'avez-vous pas déjà oublié ce que je vous ai enseigné?

Kath. Non, je réciterai à vous promptement: 'd' hand, de fingres, de mails' —

Alice. 'De nails,' madame.

Kath. 'De nails, de arm, de ilbow.'

Alice. Sauf vostre honneur, 'd' elbow.'

Kath. Ainsi dis-je; 'd' elbow, de nick,' et 'de sin.' Comment appelez-vous le pied et la robe?

Alice. 'De foot,' madame; et 'de coun.'

Kath. 'De foot et de coun!' O Seigneur Dieu! ce sont mots de son mauvais, corruptible, gros, et impudique, et non pour les dames d'honneur d'user: je ne voudrois prononcer ces mots devant les seigneurs de France pour tout le monde. Foh! 'le foot' et 'le coun'! Néantmoins, je réciterai une autre fois ma leçon ensemble: 'd' hand, de fingres, de nails, d' arm, d' elbow, de nick, de sin, de foot, de coun.'

Alice. Excellent, madame!

Kath. C'est assez pour une fois: allons-nous à dîner. *Exeunt.*

[Scene V. *Rouen. The Palace.*]

Enter the *King of France,* the *Dauphin, Bourbon,* the *Constable of France,* and others.

King. 'Tis certain he hath pass'd the river Somme.

Con. And if he be not fought withal, my lord,
Let us not live in France; let us quit all
And give our vineyards to a barbarous people.

Dau. O Dieu vivant! Shall a few sprays of us,
The emptying of our fathers' luxury,
Our scions, put in wild and savage stock,
Spirt up so suddenly into the clouds
And overlook their grafters?

Bour. Normans, but bastard Normans, Norman bastards!
Mort de ma vie! if they march along
Unfought withal, but I will sell my dukedom
To buy a slobb'ry and a dirty farm
In that nook-shotten isle of Albion.

Con. Dieu de batailles! whence have they this mettle?
Is not their climate foggy, raw, and dull,
On whom, as in despite, the sun looks pale,
Killing their fruit with frowns? Can sodden water,
A drench for sur-rein'd jades, their barley broth,
Decoct their cold blood to such valiant heat?
And shall our quick blood, spirited with wine,
Seem frosty? O, for honour of our land,
Let us not hang like roping icicles
Upon our houses' thatch, whiles a more frosty people
Sweat drops of gallant youth in our rich fields —
'Poor' we may call them in their native lords!

Dau. By faith and honour,
Our madams mock at us and plainly say
Our mettle is bred out, and they will give
Their bodies to the lust of English youth
To new-store France with bastard warriors.

Bour. They bid us to the English dancing schools
And teach lavoltas high and swift corantos,
Saying our grace is only in our heels
And that we are most lofty runaways.

King. Where is Montjoy the herald? Speed him hence;
Let him greet England with our sharp defiance.
Up, princes! and, with spirit of honour edged,
More sharper than your swords, hie to the field.
Charles Delabreth, High Constable of France,
You Dukes of Orleans, Bourbon, and of Berri,
Alençon, Brabant, Bar, and Burgundy;
Jaques Chatillon, Rambures, Vaudemont,
Beaumont, Grandpré, Roussi, and Fauconberg,
Foix, Lestrale, Bouciqualt, and Charolois,
High dukes, great princes, barons, lords, and knights,
For your great seats now quit you of great shames.
Bar Harry England, that sweeps through our land
With pennons painted in the blood of Harflew.

Rush on his host as doth the melted snow
Upon the valleys whose low vassal seat
The Alps doth spit and void his rheum upon.
Go down upon him — you have power enough—
And in a captive chariot into Roan
Bring him our prisoner.

Con. This becomes the great.
Sorry am I his numbers are so few,
His soldiers sick and famish'd in their march;
For I am sure, when he shall see our army,
He'll drop his heart into the sink of fear
And, for achievement, offer us his ransom.

King. Therefore, Lord Constable, haste on Montjoy,
And let him say to England that we send
To know what willing ransom he will give.
Prince Dauphin, you shall stay with us in Roan.

Dau. Not so, I do beseech your Majesty.

King. Be patient, for you shall remain with us.
Now forth, Lord Constable and princes all,
And quickly bring us word of England's fall.
Exeunt.

[Scene VI. *The English camp in Picardy.*]

Enter *Captains*, English and Welsh — *Gower* and *Fluellen.*

Gow. How now, Captain Fluellen? Come you from the bridge?

Flu. I assure you there is very excellent services committed at the bridge.

Gow. Is the Duke of Exeter safe?

Flu. The Duke of Exeter is as magnanimous as Agamemnon, and a man that I love and honour with my soul, and my heart, and my duty, and my live, and my living, and my uttermost power. He is not — God be praised and plessed! — any hurt in the world, but keeps the pridge most valiantly, with excellent discipline. There is an aunchient lieutenant there at the pridge, I think in my very conscience he is as valiant a man as Mark Anthony, and he is a man of no estimation in the world, but I did see him do as gallant service.

Gow. What do you call him?

Flu. He is call'd Aunchient Pistol.

Gow. I know him not.

Enter *Pistol.*

Flu. Here is the man.

Pist. Captain, I thee beseech to do me favours.
The Duke of Exeter doth love thee well.

Flu. Ay, I praise God; and I have merited some love at his hands.

Pist. Bardolph, a soldier firm and sound of heart,
And of buxom valour, hath by cruel fate,
And giddy Fortune's furious fickle wheel —
That goddess blind,
That stands upon the rolling restless stone —

Flu. By your patience, Aunchient Pistol. Fortune is painted plind, with a muffler afore her eyes, to signify to you that Fortune is plind; and she is painted also with a wheel, to signify to you, which is the moral of it, that she is turning and inconstant, and mutability, and variation; and her foot, look you, is fixed upon a spherical stone, which rolls, and rolls, and rolls. In good truth, the poet makes a most excellent description of it. Fortune is an excellent moral.

Pist. Fortune is Bardolph's foe, and frowns on him;
For he hath stol'n a pax, and hanged must 'a be —
A damned death!
Let gallows gape for dog; let man go free,
And let not hemp his windpipe suffocate.
But Exeter hath given the doom of death
For pax of little price.
Therefore, go speak — the Duke will hear thy voice;
And let not Bardolph's vital thread be cut
With edge of penny cord and vile reproach.
Speak, Captain, for his life, and I will thee requite.

Flu. Aunchient Pistol, I do partly understand your meaning.

Pist. Why then, rejoice therefore!

Flu. Certainly, aunchient, it is not a thing to rejoice at; for if, look you, he were my brother, I would desire the Duke to use his good pleasure and put him to execution; for discipline ought to be used.

Pist. Die and be damn'd! and figo for thy friendship!

Flu. It is well.

Pist. The fig of Spain! *Exit.*

Flu. Very good.

Gow. Why, this is an arrant counterfeit rascal! I remember him now — a bawd, a cutpurse.

Flu. I'll assure you, 'a utt'red as prave words at the pridge as you shall see in a summer's day. But it is very well. What he has spoke to me, that is well, I warrant you, when time is serve.

Gow. Why, 'tis a gull, a fool, a rogue, that now and then goes to the wars to grace himself, at his return into London, under the form of a soldier. And such fellows are perfect in the great commanders' names, and they will learn you by rote where services were done: — at such and such a sconce, at such a breach, at such a convoy; who came off bravely, who was shot, who disgrac'd, what terms the enemy stood on; and this they con perfectly in the phrase of war, which they trick up with new-tuned oaths; and what a beard of the General's cut and a horrid suit of the camp will do among foaming bottles and ale-wash'd wits is wonderful to be thought on. But you must learn to know such slanders of the age, or else you may be marvellously mistook.

Flu. I tell you what, Captain Gower, I do perceive he is not the man that he would gladly make show to the world he is. If I find a hole in his coat, I will tell him my mind. [*Drum within.*] Hark you, the King is coming, and I must speak with him from the pridge.

Drum and colours. Enter the *King* and his poor *Soldiers,* [and *Gloucester*].

God pless your Majesty!

King. How now, Fluellen? Cam'st thou from the bridge?

Flu. Ay, so please your Majesty. The Duke of Exeter has very gallantly maintain'd the pridge; the French is gone off, look you, and there is gallant and most prave passages. Marry, th' athversary was have possession of the pridge, but he is enforced to retire, and the Duke of Exeter is master of the pridge. I can tell your Majesty, the Duke is a prave man.

King. What men have you lost, Fluellen?

Flu. The perdition of th' athversary hath been very great, reasonable great. Marry, for my part, I think the Duke hath lost never a man but one that is like to be executed for robbing a church — one Bardolph, if your Majesty know the man. His face is all bubukles and whelks, and knobs, and flames o' fire, and his lips blows at his nose, and it is like a coal of fire, sometimes plue and sometimes red; but his nose is executed, and his fire's out.

King. We would have all such offenders so cut off. And we give express charge that in our marches through the country there be nothing compell'd from the villages, nothing taken but paid for; none of the French upbraided or abused in disdainful language; for when lenity and cruelty play for a kingdom, the gentler gamester is the soonest winner.

Tucket. Enter *Montjoy.*

Mont. You know me by my habit.

King. Well then, I know thee. What shall I know of thee?

Mont. My master's mind.

King. Unfold it.

Mont. Thus says my king: — Say thou to Harry of England: Though we seem'd dead, we did but sleep. Advantage is a better soldier than rashness. Tell him we could have rebuk'd him at Harflew, but that we thought not good to bruise an injury till it were full ripe. Now we speak upon our cue, and our voice is imperial. England shall repent his folly, see his weakness, and admire our sufferance. Bid him therefore consider of his ransom, which must proportion the losses we have borne, the subjects we have lost, the disgrace we have digested; which in weight to re-answer, his pettiness would bow under. For our losses, his exchequer is too poor; for th' effusion of our blood, the muster of his kingdom too faint a number; and for our disgrace, his own person kneeling at our feet but a weak and worthless satisfaction. To this add defiance; and tell him for conclusion, he hath betrayed his followers, whose condemnation is pronounc'd. So far my king and master; so much my office.

King. What is thy name? I know thy quality.

Mont. Montjoy.

King. Thou dost thy office fairly. Turn thee back,
And tell thy king I do not seek him now,
But could be willing to march on to Calais
Without impeachment: for, to say the sooth,
Though 'tis no wisdom to confess so much
Unto an enemy of craft and vantage,
My people are with sickness much enfeebled,
My numbers lessen'd, and those few I have,
Almost no better than so many French;
Who when they were in health, I tell thee, herald,
I thought upon one pair of English legs
Did march three Frenchmen. Yet forgive me, God,
That I do brag thus! This your air of France
Hath blown that vice in me. I must repent.
Go therefore tell thy master here I am;
My ransom is this frail and worthless trunk;
My army but a weak and sickly guard;

Yet, God before, tell him we will come on,
Though France himself and such another neighbour
Stand in our way. There's for thy labour, Montjoy. [*Gives a purse.*]
Go bid thy master well advise himself:
If we may pass, we will; if we be hind'red,
We shall your tawny ground with your red blood
Discolour; and so, Montjoy, fare you well.
The sum of all our answer is but this:
We would not seek a battle, as we are,
Nor, as we are, we say we will not shun it.
So tell your master.

Mont. I shall deliver so. Thanks to your Highness. [*Exit.*]

Glouc. I hope they will not come upon us now.

King. We are in God's hand, brother, not in theirs.
March to the bridge. It now draws toward night.
Beyond the river we'll encamp ourselves,
And on to-morrow bid them march away.
Exeunt.

[Scene VII. *The French camp, near Agincourt.*]

Enter the *Constable of France*, the *Lord Rambures, Orleans, Dauphin,* with others.

Con. Tut! I have the best armour of the world. Would it were day!

Orl. You have an excellent armour; but let my horse have his due.

Con. It is the best horse of Europe.

Orl. Will it never be morning?

Dau. My Lord of Orleans, and my Lord High Constable, you talk of horse and armour?

Orl. You are as well provided of both as any prince in the world.

Dau. What a long night is this! I will not change my horse with any that treads but on four pasterns. Ça, ha! he bounds from the earth, as if his entrails were hairs; le cheval volant, the Pegasus, avec les narines de feu! When I bestride him, I soar, I am a hawk. He trots the air. The earth sings when he touches it. The basest horn of his hoof is more musical than the pipe of Hermes.

Orl. He's of the colour of the nutmeg.

Dau. And of the heat of the ginger. It is a beast for Perseus: he is pure air and fire; and the dull elements of earth and water never appear in him, but only in patient stillness while his rider mounts him. He is indeed a horse, and all other jades you may call beasts.

Con. Indeed, my lord, it is a most absolute and excellent horse.

Dau. It is the prince of palfreys. His neigh is like the bidding of a monarch, and his countenance enforces homage.

Orl. No more, cousin.

Dau. Nay, the man hath no wit that cannot, from the rising of the lark to the lodging of the lamb, vary deserved praise on my palfrey. It is a theme as fluent as the sea. Turn the sands into eloquent tongues, and my horse is argument for them all. 'Tis a subject for a sovereign to reason on, and for a sovereign's sovereign to ride on; and for the world, familiar to us and unknown, to lay apart their particular functions and wonder at him. I once writ a sonnet in his praise and began thus, 'Wonder of nature!'

Orl. I have heard a sonnet begin so to one's mistress.

Dau. Then did they imitate that which I compos'd to my courser, for my horse is my mistress.

Orl. Your mistress bears well.

Dau. Me well, which is the prescript praise and perfection of a good and particular mistress.

Con. Nay, for methought yesterday your mistress shrewdly shook your back.

Dau. So perhaps did yours.

Con. Mine was not bridled.

Dau. O, then belike she was old and gentle, and you rode like a kern of Ireland, your French hose off, and in your strait strossers.

Con. You have good judgment in horsemanship.

Dau. Be warn'd by me then. They that ride so, and ride not warily, fall into foul bogs. I had rather have my horse to my mistress.

Con. I had as live have my mistress a jade.

Dau. I tell thee, Constable, my mistress wears his own hair.

Con. I could make as true a boast as that, if I had a sow to my mistress.

Dau. 'Le chien est retourné à son propre vomissement, et la truie lavée au bourbier.' Thou mak'st use of anything.

Con. Yet do I not use my horse for my mistress, or any such proverb so little kin to the purpose.

Ram. My Lord Constable, the armour that I saw in your tent to-night — are those stars or suns upon it?

Con. Stars, my lord.

Dau. Some of them will fall to-morrow, I hope.

Con. And yet my sky shall not want.

Dau. That may be, for you bear a many superfluously, and 'twere more honour some were away.

Con. Ev'n as your horse bears your praises, who would trot as well, were some of your brags dismounted.

Dau. Would I were able to load him with his desert! Will it never be day? I will trot to-morrow a mile, and my way shall be paved with English faces.

Con. I will not say so, for fear I should be fac'd out of my way; but I would it were morning, for I would fain be about the ears of the English.

Ram. Who will go to hazard with me for twenty prisoners?

Con. You must first go yourself to hazard ere you have them.

Dau. 'Tis midnight; I'll go arm myself. *Exit.*

Orl. The Dauphin longs for morning.

Ram. He longs to eat the English.

Con. I think he will eat all he kills.

Orl. By the white hand of my lady, he's a gallant prince.

Con. Swear by her foot, that she may tread out the oath

Orl. He is simply the most active gentleman of France.

Con. Doing is activity, and he will still be doing.

Orl. He never did harm, that I heard of.

Con. Nor will do none to-morrow. He will keep that good name still.

Orl. I know him to be valiant.

Con. I was told that by one that knows him better than you.

Orl. What's he?

Con. Marry, he told me so himself, and he said he car'd not who knew it.

Orl. He needs not; it is no hidden virtue in him.

Con. By my faith, sir, but it is! Never anybody saw it but his lackey. 'Tis a hooded valour; and when it appears, it will bate.

Orl. Ill will never said well.

Con. I will cap that proverb with 'There is flattery in friendship.'

Orl. And I will take up that with 'Give the devil his due.'

Con. Well plac'd! There stands your friend for the devil. Have at the very eye of that proverb with 'A pox of the devil!'

Orl. You are the better at proverbs, by how much 'a fool's bolt is soon shot.'

Con. You have shot over.

Orl. 'Tis not the first time you were overshot.

Enter a *Messenger.*

Mess. My Lord High Constable, the English lie within fifteen hundred paces of your tents.

Con. Who hath measur'd the ground?

Mess. The Lord Grandpré.

Con. A valiant and most expert gentleman. Would it were day! Alas, poor Harry of England! He longs not for the dawning, as we do.

Orl. What a wretched and peevish fellow is this King of England, to mope with his fat-brain'd followers so far out of his knowledge!

Con. If the English had any apprehension, they would run away.

Orl. That they lack; for if their heads had any intellectual armour, they could never wear such heavy headpieces.

Ram. That island of England breeds very valiant creatures. Their mastiffs are of unmatchable courage.

Orl. Foolish curs, that run winking into the mouth of a Russian bear and have their heads crush'd like rotten apples! You may as well say that's a valiant flea that dare eat his breakfast on the lip of a lion.

Con. Just, just! and the men do sympathize with the mastiffs in robustious and rough coming on, leaving their wits with their wives; and then give them great meals of beef and iron and steel, they will eat like wolves and fight like devils.

Orl. Ay, but these English are shrowdly out of beef.

Con. Then shall we find to-morrow they have only stomachs to eat and none to fight. Now is it time to arm. Come, shall we about it?

Orl. It is now two o'clock; but let me see — by ten
We shall have each a hundred Englishmen.

Exeunt.

Act [IV].

Chorus.

Now entertain conjecture of a time
When creeping murmur and the poring dark
Fills the wide vessel of the universe.
From camp to camp, through the foul womb of night,
The hum of either army stilly sounds,
That the fix'd sentinels almost receive
The secret whispers of each other's watch.
Fire answers fire, and through their paly flames
Each battle sees the other's umber'd face.
Steed threatens steed, in high and boastful neighs
Piercing the night's dull ear; and from the tents
The armourers accomplishing the knights,
With busy hammers closing rivets up,
Give dreadful note of preparation.
The country cocks do crow, the clocks do toll
And the third hour of drowsy morning name.
Proud of their numbers and secure in soul,
The confident and over-lusty French
Do the low-rated English play at dice;
And chide the cripple tardy-gaited night
Who like a foul and ugly witch doth limp
So tediously away. The poor condemned English,
Like sacrifices, by their watchful fires
Sit patiently and inly ruminate
The morning's danger; and their gesture sad,
Investing lank-lean cheeks and war-worn coats,
Presenteth them unto the gazing moon
So many horrid ghosts. O, now, who will behold
The royal captain of this ruin'd band
Walking from watch to watch, from tent to tent,
Let him cry 'Praise and glory on his head!'
For forth he goes and visits all his host,
Bids them good morrow with a modest smile
And calls them brothers, friends, and countrymen.
Upon his royal face there is no note
How dread an army hath enrounded him;
Nor doth he dedicate one jot of colour
Unto the weary and all-watched night,
But freshly looks, and overbears attaint
With cheerful semblance and sweet majesty;
That every wretch, pining and pale before,
Beholding him, plucks comfort from his looks.
A largess universal, like the sun,
His liberal eye doth give to every one,
Thawing cold fear. Then, mean and gentle all,
Behold, as may unworthiness define,
A little touch of Harry in the night.
And so our scene must to the battle fly;
Where (O for pity!) we shall much disgrace
With four or five most vile and ragged foils,
Right ill-dispos'd in brawl ridiculous,
The name of Agincourt. Yet sit and see,
Minding true things by what their mock'ries be.
Exit.

[Scene I. *France. The English camp at Agincourt.*]

Enter the *King*, *Bedford*, and *Gloucester*.

King. Gloucester, 'tis true that we are in great danger;
The greater therefore should our courage be.
Good morrow, brother Bedford. God Almighty!
There is some soul of goodness in things evil,
Would men observingly distil it out;
For our bad neighbour makes us early stirrers,
Which is both healthful, and good husbandry.
Besides, they are our outward consciences,
And preachers to us all, admonishing
That we should dress us fairly for our end.
Thus may we gather honey from the weed
And make a moral of the devil himself.

Enter *Erpingham.*

Good morrow, old Sir Thomas Erpingham.
A good soft pillow for that good white head
Were better than a churlish turf of France.
Erp. Not so, my liege. This lodging likes me better,
Since I may say 'Now lie I like a king.'
King. 'Tis good for men to love their present pains
Upon example: so the spirit is eas'd;
And when the mind is quick'ned, out of doubt
The organs, though defunct and dead before,
Break up their drowsy grave and newly move
With casted slough and fresh legerity.
Lend me thy cloak, Sir Thomas. Brothers both,

Commend me to the princes in our camp;
Do my good morrow to them, and anon
Desire them all to my pavilion.

Glouc. We shall, my liege.

Erp. Shall I attend your Grace?

King. No, my good knight.
Go with my brothers to my lords of England.
I and my bosom must debate awhile,
And then I would no other company.

Erp. The Lord in heaven bless thee, noble Harry!

Exeunt [*all but the King*].

King. God-a-mercy, old heart! thou speak'st cheerfully.

Enter *Pistol.*

Pist. Qui va là?

King. A friend.

Pist. Discuss unto me, art thou officer;
Or art thou base, common, and popular?

King. I am a gentleman of a company.

Pist. Trail'st thou the puissant pike?

King. Even so. What are you?

Pist. As good a gentleman as the Emperor.

King. Then you are a better than the King.

Pist. The King's a bawcock, and a heart of gold,
A lad of life, an imp of fame,
Of parents good, of fist most valiant.
I kiss his dirty shoe, and from heartstring
I love the lovely bully. What is thy name?

King. Harry le Roy.

Pist. Le Roy? A Cornish name. Art thou of Cornish crew?

King. No, I am a Welshman.

Pist. Know'st thou Fluellen?

King. Yes.

Pist. Tell him I'll knock his leek about his pate
Upon Saint Davy's day.

King. Do not you wear your dagger in your cap that day, lest he knock that about yours.

Pist. Art thou his friend?

King. And his kinsman too.

Pist. The figo for thee then!

King. I thank you. God be with you!

Pist. My name is Pistol call'd.

Exit. Manet King.

King. It sorts well with your fierceness.

Enter *Fluellen* and *Gower.*

Gow. Captain Fluellen!

Flu. So! in the name of Jesu Christ, speak lower. It is the greatest admiration in the universal world, when the true and aunchient prerogatifes and laws of the wars is not kept. If you would take the pains but to examine the wars of Pompey the Great, you shall find, I warrant you, that there is no tiddle taddle nor pibble pabble in Pompey's camp. I warrant you, you shall find the ceremonies of the wars, and the cares of it, and the forms of it, and the sobriety of it, and the modesty of it, to be otherwise.

Gow. Why, the enemy is loud; you hear him all night.

Flu. If the enemy is an ass and a fool and a prating coxcomb, is it meet, think you, that we should also, look you, be an ass and a fool and a prating coxcomb? In your own conscience now?

Gow. I will speak lower.

Flu. I pray you and beseech you that you will.

Exeunt [*Gower and Fluellen*].

King. Though it appear a little out of fashion,
There is much care and valour in this Welshman.

Enter three Soldiers, *John Bates, Alexander Court,* and *Michael Williams.*

Court. Brother John Bates, is not that the morning which breaks yonder?

Bates. I think it be; but we have no great cause to desire the approach of day.

Will. We see yonder the beginning of the day, but I think we shall never see the end of it. Who goes there?

King. A friend.

Will. Under what captain serve you?

King. Under Sir Thomas Erpingham.

Will. A good old commander and a most kind gentleman. I pray you, what thinks he of our estate?

King. Even as men wrack'd upon a sand, that look to be wash'd off the next tide.

Bates. He hath not told his thought to the King?

King. No; nor is it not meet he should. For though I speak it to you, I think the King is but a man, as I am. The violet smells to him as it doth to me; the element shows to him as it doth to me; all his senses have but human conditions. His ceremonies laid by, in his nakedness he appears but a man; and though his affections are higher mounted than ours, yet, when they stoop, they stoop with the like wing. Therefore, when he sees reason of fears, as we do, his fears, out of doubt, be of the same relish as ours are. Yet, in reason, no man should possess him with any appearance of fear, lest he, by showing it, should dishearten his army.

Bates. He may show what outward courage he will; but I believe, as cold a night as 'tis, he could wish himself in Thames up to the neck; and so I would he were, and I by him, at all adventures, so we were quit here.

King. By my troth, I will speak my conscience of the King: I think he would not wish himself anywhere but where he is.

Bates. Then I would he were here alone. So should he be sure to be ransomed, and a many poor men's lives saved.

King. I dare say you love him not so ill to wish him here alone, howsoever you speak this to feel other men's minds. Methinks I could not die anywhere so contented as in the King's company, his cause being just and his quarrel honourable.

Will. That's more than we know.

Bates. Ay, or more than we should seek after; for we know enough if we know we are the King's subjects. If his cause be wrong, our obedience to the King wipes the crime of it out of us.

Will. But if the cause be not good, the King himself hath a heavy reckoning to make when all those legs and arms and heads, chopp'd off in a battle, shall join together at the latter day and cry all 'We died at such a place!' some swearing, some crying for a surgeon, some upon their wives left poor behind them, some upon the debts they owe, some upon their children rawly left. I am afeard there are few die well that die in a battle; for how can they charitably dispose of anything when blood is their argument? Now, if these men do not die well, it will be a black matter for the King that led them to it; who to disobey were against all proportion of subjection.

King. So, if a son that is by his father sent about merchandise do sinfully miscarry upon the sea, the imputation of his wickedness, by your rule, should be imposed upon his father that sent him; or if a servant, under his master's command transporting a sum of money, be assailed by robbers and die in many irreconcil'd iniquities, you may call the business of the master the author of the servant's damnation. But this is not so. The King is not bound to answer the particular endings of his soldiers, the father of his son, nor the master of his servant; for they purpose not their death when they purpose their services. Besides, there is no king, be his cause never so spotless, if it come to the arbitrement of swords, can try it out with all unspotted soldiers. Some (peradventure) have on them the guilt of premeditated and contrived murther; some, of beguiling virgins with the broken seals of perjury; some, making the wars their bulwark, that have before gored the gentle bosom of peace with pillage and robbery. Now, if these men have defeated the law and outrun native punishment, though they can outstrip men, they have no wings to fly from God. War is his beadle, war is his vengeance; so that here men are punish'd for before-breach of the King's laws in now the King's quarrel. Where they feared the death, they have borne life away; and where they would be safe, they perish. Then if they die unprovided, no more is the King guilty of their damnation than he was before guilty of those impieties for the which they are now visited. Every subject's duty is the King's, but every subject's soul is his own. Therefore should every soldier in the wars do as every sick man in his bed — wash every mote out of his conscience; and dying so, death is to him advantage; or not dying, the time was blessedly lost wherein such preparation was gained; and in him that escapes, it were not sin to think that, making God so free an offer, he let him outlive that day to see his greatness and to teach others how they should prepare.

Will. 'Tis certain, every man that dies ill, the ill upon his own head — the King is not to answer it.

Bates. I do not desire he should answer for me, and yet I determine to fight lustily for him.

King. I myself heard the King say he would not be ransom'd.

Will. Ay, he said so, to make us fight cheerfully; but when our throats are cut, he may be ransom'd, and we ne'er the wiser.

King. If I live to see it, I will never trust his word after.

Will. You pay him then! That's a perilous shot out of an elder-gun that a poor and a private displeasure can do against a monarch! You may as well go about to turn the sun to ice with fanning in his face with a peacock's feather. You'll never trust his word after! Come, 'tis a foolish saying.

King. Your reproof is something too round. I should be angry with you if the time were convenient.

Will. Let it be a quarrel between us if you live.

King. I embrace it.

Will. How shall I know thee again?

King. Give me any gage of thine, and I will wear it in my bonnet. Then, if ever thou dar'st acknowledge it, I will make it my quarrel.

Will. Here's my glove. Give me another of thine.

King. There.

Will. This will I also wear in my cap. If ever thou come to me and say, after to-morrow, 'This is my glove,' by this hand, I will take thee a box on the ear.

King. If ever I live to see it, I will challenge it.

Will. Thou dar'st as well be hang'd.

King. Well, I will do it, though I take thee in the King's company.

Will. Keep thy word. Fare thee well.

Bates. Be friends, you English fools, be friends! We have French quarrels enow, if you could tell how to reckon.

King. Indeed the French may lay twenty French crowns to one they will beat us, for they bear them on their shoulders; but it is no English treason to cut French crowns, and to-morrow the King himself will be a clipper.

Exeunt Soldiers.

Upon the King! Let us our lives, our souls,
Our debts, our careful wives,
Our children, and our sins, lay on the King!
We must bear all. O hard condition,
Twin-born with greatness, subject to the breath
Of every fool, whose sense no more can feel
But his own wringing! What infinite heart's-ease
Must kings neglect that private men enjoy!
And what have kings that privates have not too,
Save ceremony, save general ceremony?
And what art thou, thou idol Ceremony?
What kind of god art thou, that suffer'st more
Of mortal griefs than do thy worshippers?
What are thy rents? What are thy comings-in?
O Ceremony, show me but thy worth!
What is thy soul of adoration?
Art thou aught else but place, degree, and form,
Creating awe and fear in other men?
Wherein thou art less happy being fear'd
Than they in fearing.
What drink'st thou oft, instead of homage sweet,
But poison'd flattery? O, be sick, great greatness,
And bid thy ceremony give thee cure!
Think'st thou the fiery fever will go out
With titles blown from adulation?
Will it give place to flexure and low bending?
Canst thou, when thou command'st the beggar's knee,
Command the health of it? No, thou proud dream,
That play'st so subtilly with a king's repose.
I am a king that find thee; and I know
'Tis not the balm, the sceptre, and the ball,
The sword, the mace, the crown imperial,
The intertissued robe of gold and pearl,
The farced title running fore the king,
The throne he sits on, nor the tide of pomp
That beats upon the high shore of this world —
No, not all these, thrice-gorgeous ceremony,
Not all these, laid in bed majestical,
Can sleep so soundly as the wretched slave,
Who, with a body fill'd, and vacant mind,
Gets him to rest, cramm'd with distressful bread;
Never sees horrid night, the child of hell;
But like a lackey, from the rise to set,
Sweats in the eye of Phœbus, and all night
Sleeps in Elysium; next day after dawn,
Doth rise and help Hyperion to his horse;
And follows so the ever-running year
With profitable labour to his grave;
And but for ceremony, such a wretch,
Winding up days with toil and nights with sleep,
Had the forehand and vantage of a king.
The slave, a member of the country's peace,
Enjoys it; but in gross brain little wots
What watch the king keeps to maintain the peace,
Whose hours the peasant best advantages.

Enter *Erpingham.*

Erp. My lord, your nobles, jealous of your absence,
Seek through your camp to find you.
King. Good old knight,
Collect them all together at my tent.
I'll be before thee.
Erp. I shall do't, my lord. *Exit.*

King. O God of battles, steel my soldiers' hearts,
Possess them not with fear! Take from them now
The sense of reck'ning, if th' opposed numbers
Pluck their hearts from them. Not to day, O Lord,
O, not to-day, think not upon the fault

My father made in compassing the crown!
I Richard's body have interred new;
And on it have bestowed more contrite tears
Than from it issued forced drops of blood.
Five hundred poor I have in yearly pay,
Who twice a day their wither'd hands hold up
Toward heaven, to pardon blood; and I have built
Two chantries, where the sad and solemn priests
Sing still for Richard's soul. More will I do!
Though all that I can do is nothing worth,
Since that my penitence comes after all,
Imploring pardon.

Enter *Gloucester.*

Glouc. My liege!
King. My brother Gloucester's voice? Ay.
I know thy errand; I will go with thee.
The day, my friends, and all things stay for me.
Exeunt.

[Scene II. *The French camp.*]

Enter the *Dauphin, Orleans, Rambures,* and *Beaumont.*

Orl. The sun doth gild our armour. Up, my lords!
Dau. Montez à cheval! My horse! Varlet, laquais! Ha!
Orl. O brave spirit!
Dau. Via! les eaux et la terre—
Orl. Rien puis? L'air et le feu.
Dau. Ciel! cousin Orleans.

Enter *Constable.*

Now, my Lord Constable?
Con. Hark how our steeds for present service neigh!
Dau. Mount them and make incision in their hides,
That their hot blood may spin in English eyes
And dout them with superfluous courage, ha!
Ram. What, will you have them weep our horses' blood?
How shall we then behold their natural tears?

Enter *Messenger.*

Mess. The English are embattail'd, you French peers.
Con. To horse, you gallant princes! straight to horse!
Do but behold yond poor and starved band,
And your fair show shall suck away their souls,
Leaving them but the shales and husks of men.
There is not work enough for all our hands,
Scarce blood enough in all their sickly veins
To give each naked curtleaxe a stain
That our French gallants shall to-day draw out
And sheathe for lack of sport. Let us but blow on them,
The vapour of our valour will o'erturn them.
'Tis positive 'gainst all exceptions, lords,
That our superfluous lackeys and our peasants,
Who in unnecessary action swarm
About our squares of battle, were enow
To purge this field of such a hilding foe,
Though we upon this mountain's basis by
Took stand for idle speculation:
But that our honours must not. What's to say?
A very little little let us do,
And all is done. Then let the trumpets sound
The tucket sonance and the note to mount;
For our approach shall so much dare the field
That England shall couch down in fear and yield.

Enter *Grandpré.*

Grand. Why do you stay so long, my lords of France?
Yond island carrions, desperate of their bones,
Ill-favouredly become the morning field.
Their ragged curtains poorly are let loose,
And our air shakes them passing scornfully.
Big Mars seems bankrout in their beggar'd host
And faintly through a rusty beaver peeps.
The horsemen sit like fixed candlesticks
With torch-staves in their hand; and their poor jades
Lob down their heads, dropping the hides and hips,
The gum down roping from their pale-dead eyes,
And in their pale dull mouths the gimmal'd bit
Lies foul with chaw'd grass, still and motionless;
And their executors, the knavish crows,
Fly o'er them, all impatient for their hour.
Description cannot suit itself in words
To demonstrate the life of such a battle
In life so liveless as it shows itself.
Con. They have said their prayers, and they stay for death.
Dau. Shall we go send them dinners and fresh suits
And give their fasting horses provender,
And after fight with them?

Con. I stay but for my guidon. To the field!
I will the banner from a trumpet take
And use it for my haste. Come, come away!
The sun is high, and we outwear the day.
Exeunt.

[Scene III. *The English camp.*]

Enter *Gloucester, Bedford, Exeter, Erpingham* with all his host, *Salisbury,* and *Westmoreland.*

Glouc. Where is the King?
Bed. The King himself is rode to view their battle.
West. Of fighting men they have full three-score thousand.
Exe. There's five to one; besides, they all are fresh.
Sal. God's arm strike with us! 'Tis a fearful odds.
God b' wi' you, princes all; I'll to my charge.
If we no more meet till we meet in heaven,
Then joyfully, my noble Lord of Bedford,
My dear Lord Gloucester, and my good Lord Exeter,
And my kind kinsman, warriors all, adieu!
Bed. Farewell, good Salisbury, and good luck go with thee!
Exe. Farewell, kind lord. Fight valiantly to-day;
And yet I do thee wrong to mind thee of it,
For thou art fram'd of the firm truth of valour.
[*Exit Salisbury.*]
Bed. He is as full of valour as of kindness,
Princely in both.

Enter the *King.*

West. O that we now had here
But one ten thousand of those men in England
That do no work to-day!
King. What's he that wishes so?
My cousin Westmoreland? No, my fair cousin.
If we are mark'd to die, we are enow
To do our country loss; and if to live,
The fewer men, the greater share of honour.
God's will! I pray thee wish not one man more.
By Jove, I am not covetous for gold,
Nor care I who doth feed upon my cost;
It yearns me not if men my garments wear;
Such outward things dwell not in my desires:
But if it be a sin to covet honour,
I am the most offending soul alive.
No, faith, my coz, wish not a man from England.
God's peace! I would not lose so great an honour
As one man more methinks would share from me
For the best hope I have. O, do not wish one more!
Rather proclaim it, Westmoreland, through my host,
That he which hath no stomach to this fight,
Let him depart; his passport shall be made,
And crowns for convoy put into his purse.
We would not die in that man's company
That fears his fellowship to die with us.
This day is call'd the Feast of Crispian.
He that outlives this day, and comes safe home,
Will stand a-tiptoe when this day is nam'd
And rouse him at the name of Crispian.
He that shall live this day, and see old age,
Will yearly on the vigil feast his neighbours
And say 'To morrow is Saint Crispian.'
Then will he strip his sleeve and show his scars,
And say 'These wounds I had on Crispin's day.'
Old men forget; yet all shall be forgot,
But he'll remember, with advantages,
What feats he did that day. Then shall our names,
Familiar in his mouth as household words —
Harry the King, Bedford and Exeter,
Warwick and Talbot, Salisbury and Gloucester —
Be in their flowing cups freshly remember'd.
This story shall the good man teach his son;
And Crispin Crispian shall ne'er go by,
From this day to the ending of the world,
But we in it shall be remembered —
We few, we happy few, we band of brothers;
For he to-day that sheds his blood with me
Shall be my brother. Be he ne'er so vile,
This day shall gentle his condition;
And gentlemen in England now abed
Shall think themselves accurs'd they were not here,
And hold their manhoods cheap whiles any speaks
That fought with us upon Saint Crispin's day.

Enter *Salisbury.*

Sal. My sovereign lord, bestow yourself with speed.
The French are bravely in their battles set
And will with all expedience charge on us.
King. All things are ready, if our minds be so.
West. Perish the man whose mind is backward now!
King. Thou dost not wish more help from England, coz?

West. God's will, my liege! would you and I alone,
Without more help, could fight this royal battle!
King. Why, now thou hast unwish'd five thousand men!
Which likes me better than to wish us one.
You know your places. God be with you all!

Tucket. Enter *Montjoy.*

Mont. Once more I come to know of thee, King Harry,
If for thy ransom thou wilt now compound,
Before thy most assured overthrow;
For certainly thou art so near the gulf
Thou needs must be englutted. Besides, in mercy,
The Constable desires thee thou wilt mind
Thy followers of repentance, that their souls
May make a peaceful and a sweet retire
From all these fields, where (wretches!) their poor bodies
Must lie and fester.
King. Who hath sent thee now?
Mont. The Constable of France.
King. I pray thee bear my former answer back:
Bid them achieve me, and then sell my bones.
Good God! why should they mock poor fellows thus?
The man that once did sell the lion's skin
While the beast liv'd, was kill'd with hunting him.
A many of our bodies shall no doubt
Find native graves; upon the which, I trust,
Shall witness live in brass of this day's work;
And those that leave their valiant bones in France,
Dying like men, though buried in your dunghills,
They shall be fam'd; for there the sun shall greet them
And draw their honours reeking up to heaven,
Leaving their earthly parts to choke your clime,
The smell whereof shall breed a plague in France.
Mark then abounding valour in our English,
That, being dead, like to the bullet's grazing,
Break out into a second course of mischief,
Killing in relapse of mortality.
Let me speak proudly. Tell the Constable
We are but warriors for the working day.
Our gayness and our gilt are all besmirch'd
With rainy marching in the painful field.
There's not a piece of feather in our host —
Good argument, I hope, we will not fly —
And time hath worn us into slovenry.
But, by the mass, our hearts are in the trim;
And my poor soldiers tell me, yet ere night
They'll be in fresher robes, or they will pluck
The gay new coats o'er the French soldiers' heads
And turn them out of service. If they do this
(As, if God please, they shall), my ransom then
Will soon be levied. Herald, save thou thy labour.
Come thou no more for ransom, gentle herald.
They shall have none, I swear, but these my joints;
Which if they have as I will leave 'em them,
Shall yield them little, tell the Constable.
Mont. I shall, King Harry. And so fare thee well.
Thou never shalt hear herald any more. *Exit.*
King. I fear thou wilt once more come again for ransom.

Enter *York.*

York. My lord, most humbly on my knee I beg
The leading of the vaward.
King. Take it, brave York. Now, soldiers, march away;
And how thou pleasest, God, dispose the day!
Exeunt.

[Scene IV. *The field of battle.*]

Alarum. Excursions. Enter *Pistol, French Soldier, Boy.*

Pist. Yield, cur!

French. Je pense que vous estes le gentilhomme de bonne qualité.

Pist. Quality! Callino custore me! Art thou a gentleman? What is thy name? Discuss.

French. O Seigneur Dieu!

Pist. O Signieur Dew should be a gentleman.
Perpend my words, O Signieur Dew, and mark.
O Signieur Dew, thou diest on point of fox,
Except, O signieur, thou do give to me
Egregious ransom.

French. O, prenez miséricorde! ayez pitié de moi!

Pist. Moy shall not serve. I will have forty moys;
Or I will fetch thy rim out at thy throat
In drops of crimson blood.

French. Est-il impossible d'eschapper la force de ton bras?

THE LIFE OF KING HENRY V

Alec Clunes in the role of Henry V, bluff, valorous king of England

PHOTOGRAPHS BY JOHN VICKERS
PRODUCED BY THE OLD VIC COMPANY

"O God! thy arm was here." Henry gives thanks after his victory at Agincourt (*Act IV, Scene VIII*)

Dorothy Tutin as Katharine of France

Henry V, Katharine's English suitor

Exeter (Mark Dignam), King Henry's uncle

Paul Rogers as the Dauphin, the French prince

Right: William Devlin playing Fluellen, an officer in Henry's army

Below: The comic Pistol (Robert Eddison), Nell Quickly's husband

Above: Henry V, valiant leader of the English

Right: Chorus (Roger Livesey) sets the scenes

The French ambassador (Douglas Campbell) delivers his taunt to King Henry *(Act I, Scene II)*

"His nose was as sharp as a pen, and a' babbled of green fields." Mistress Quickly (Nuna Davey) describes the death of Falstaff to his followers *(Act II, Scene III)*

"Come, let's away. My love, give me thy lips." Pistol kisses his wife as he leaves for the army *(Act II, Scene III)*

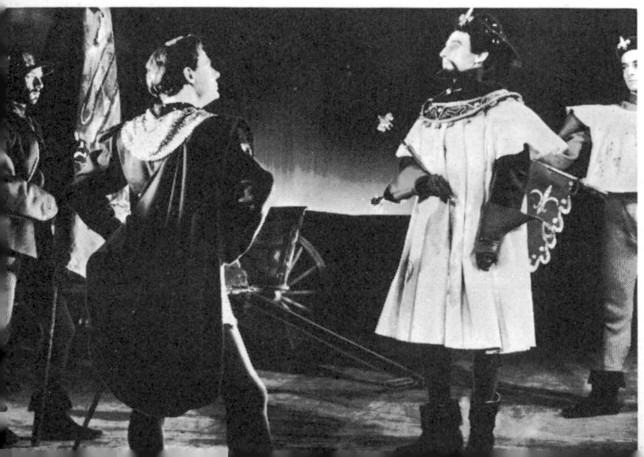

"Com'st thou again for ransom?" The English king jokingly challenges Montjoy (James Wellman), the French herald *(Act IV, Scene VII)*

Henry has Exeter arrest three of his lords for treason *(Act II, Scene II)*

"So Chrish save me, I will cut off your head." The Irish captain, Macmorris (Anthony van Bridge), threatens the Welshman, Fluellen *(Act III, Scene II)*

Below: "Once more unto the breach." Henry exhorts his men before Harfleur *(Act III, Scene I)*

"I think the king is but a man, as I am." His men fail to recognize Henry as he goes among them in disguise on the eve of battle *(Act IV, Scene I)*

"We few, we happy few, we band of brothers." Henry speaks to his followers before Agincourt *(Act IV, Scene III)*

"I was not angry since I came to France." The king is outraged to find the French have murdered the scullions in the English camp *(Act IV, Scene VII)*

Exeter delivers Henry's ultimatum to the king of France *(Act II, Scene IV)*

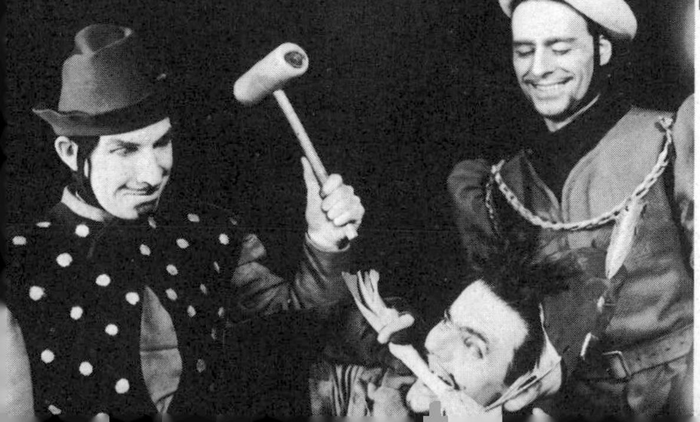

"I pray you, fall to." The Welshman Fluellen turns on the mocking Pistol and forces him to eat a leek, emblem of Saint David, patron of Wales *(Act V, Scene I)*

The Dauphin boasts of his horse's prowess *(Act III, Scene VII)*

Katharine of France with her ladies. *Right Center:* Pauline Jameson as her attendant Alice

"God, the best maker of all marriages, combine your hearts in one." Isabel (Dorothy Green) blesses the union of Katharine and Henry *(Act V, Scene II)*

"By mine honour, in true English I love thee, Kate." Henry finally abandons his attempts to woo the Princess Katharine in her tongue *(Act V, Scene II)*

"You have witchcraft in your lips, Kate." Henry's wooing becomes eloquent and poetic *(Act V, Scene II)*

"You and I cannot be confined within the weak list of a country's fashion." Henry kisses Katharine in spite of protests *(Act V, Scene II)*

Pist. Brass, cur?
Thou damned and luxurious mountain goat,
Offer'st me brass?

French. O, pardonnez-moi!

Pist. Say'st thou me so? Is that a ton of moys?
Come hither, boy; ask me this slave in French
What is his name.

Boy. Escoutez. Comment estes-vous appelé?

French. Monsieur le Fer.

Boy. He says his name is Master Fer.

Pist. Master Fer? I'll fer him, and firk him, and ferret him! Discuss the same in French unto him.

Boy. I do not know the French for 'fer,' and 'ferret,' and 'firk.'

Pist. Bid him prepare, for I will cut his throat.

French. Que dit-il, monsieur?

Boy. Il me commande à vous dire que vous faites vous prest; car ce soldat ici est disposé tout à cette heure de couper vostre gorge.

Pist. Owy, cuppele gorge, permafoy!
Peasant, unless thou give me crowns, brave crowns;
Or mangled shalt thou be by this my sword.

French. O, je vous supplie, pour l'amour de Dieu, me pardonner! Je suis gentilhomme de bonne maison. Gardez ma vie, et je vous donnerai deux cents escus.

Pist. What are his words?

Boy. He prays you to save his life. He is a gentleman of a good house, and for his ransom he will give you two hundred crowns.

Pist. Tell him my fury shall abate, and I
The crowns will take.

French. Petit monsieur, que dit-il?

Boy. Encore qu'il est contre son jurement de pardonner aucun prisonnier, néantmoins, pour les escus que vous l'avez promis, il est content de vous donner la liberté, le franchisement.

French. Sur mes genoux je vous donne mille remercîmens; et je m'estime heureux que je suis tombé entre les mains d'un chevalier, je pense, le plus brave, vaillant, et très-distingué seigneur d'Angleterre.

Pist. Expound unto me, boy.

Boy. He gives you, upon his knees, a thousand thanks; and he esteems himself happy that he hath fall'n into the hands of one (as he thinks) the most brave, valorous, and thrice-worthy signieur of England.

Pist. As I suck blood, I will some mercy show!
Follow me, cur. [*Exit.*]

Boy. Suivez-vous le grand Capitaine. [*Exit French Soldier.*] I did never know so full a voice issue from so empty a heart; but the saying is true, 'The empty vessel makes the greatest sound.' Bardolph and Nym had ten times more valour than this roaring devil i' th' old play that every one may pare his nails with a wooden dagger; and they are both hang'd; and so would this be, if he durst steal anything adventurously. I must stay with the lackeys with the luggage of our camp. The French might have a good prey of us, if he knew of it; for there is none to guard it but boys. *Exit.*

[Scene V. *Another part of the field of battle.*]

Enter *Constable, Orleans, Bourbon, Dauphin,* and *Rambures.*

Con. O diable!

Orl. O Seigneur! le jour est perdu, tout est perdu!

Dau. Mort de ma vie! all is confounded, all!
Reproach and everlasting shame
Sits mocking in our plumes.
A short alarum.
O méchante fortune! Do not run away.

Con. Why, all our ranks are broke.

Dau. O perdurable shame! Let's stab ourselves.
Be these the wretches that we play'd at dice for?

Orl. Is this the king we sent to for his ransom?

Bour. Shame, and eternal shame! nothing but shame!
Let's die in honour. Once more back again!
And he that will not follow Bourbon now,
Let him go hence, and with his cap in hand
Like a base pander hold the chamber door
Whilst by a slave, no gentler than my dog,
His fairest daughter is contaminated.

Con. Disorder, that hath spoil'd us, friend us now!
Let us on heaps go offer up our lives.

Orl. We are enow yet living in the field
To smother up the English in our throngs,
If any order might be thought upon.

Bour. The devil take order now! I'll to the throng.
Let life be short; else shame will be too long.
Exeunt.

[Scene VI. *Another part of the field.*]

Alarum. Enter the *King* and his *Train*, [*Exeter*, and others,] with *Prisoners*.

King. Well have we done, thrice-valiant countrymen;
But all's not done, yet keep the French the field.

Exe. The Duke of York commends him to your Majesty.

King. Lives he, good uncle? Thrice within this hour
I saw him down; thrice up again and fighting.
From helmet to the spur all blood he was.

Exe. In which array, brave soldier, doth he lie,
Larding the plain; and by his bloody side,
Yoke-fellow to his honour-owing wounds,
The noble Earl of Suffolk also lies.
Suffolk first died; and York, all haggled over,
Comes to him, where in gore he lay insteep'd,
And takes him by the beard, kisses the gashes
That bloodily did yawn upon his face,
And cries aloud, 'Tarry, dear cousin Suffolk!
My soul shall thine keep company to heaven.
Tarry, sweet soul, for mine, then fly abreast;
As in this glorious and well-foughten field
We kept together in our chivalry!'
Upon these words I came and cheer'd him up.
He smil'd me in the face, raught me his hand,
And, with a feeble gripe, says 'Dear my lord,
Commend my service to my sovereign.'
So did he turn, and over Suffolk's neck
He threw his wounded arm and kiss'd his lips;
And so, espous'd to death, with blood he seal'd
A testament of noble-ending love.
The pretty and sweet manner of it forc'd
Those waters from me which I would have stopp'd;
But I had not so much of man in me,
And all my mother came into mine eyes
And gave me up to tears.

King. I blame you not;
For, hearing this, I must perforce compound
With mistful eyes, or they will issue too.
Alarum.
But hark! what new alarum is this same?
The French have reinforc'd their scatter'd men.
Then every soldier kill his prisoners!
Give the word through. *Exeunt.*

[Scene VII. *Another part of the field.*]

Enter *Fluellen* and *Gower*.

Flu. Kill the poys and the luggage? 'Tis expressly against the law of arms. 'Tis as arrant a piece of knavery, mark you now, as can be offert. In your conscience, now, is it not?

Gow. 'Tis certain there's not a boy left alive; and the cowardly rascals that ran from the battle ha' done this slaughter. Besides, they have burned and carried away all that was in the King's tent; wherefore the King most worthily hath caus'd every soldier to cut his prisoner's throat. O, 'tis a gallant king!

Flu. Ay, he was porn at Monmouth, Captain Gower. What call you the town's name where Alexander the Pig was born?

Gow. Alexander the Great.

Flu. Why, I pray you, is not 'pig' great? The pig, or the great, or the mighty, or the huge, or the magnanimous are all one reckonings, save the phrase is a little variations.

Gow. I think Alexander the Great was born in Macedon. His father was called Philip of Macedon, as I take it.

Flu. I think it is in Macedon where Alexander is porn. I tell you, Captain, if you look in the maps of the orld, I warrant you sall find, in the comparisons between Macedon and Monmouth, that the situations, look you, is both alike. There is a river in Macedon, and there is also moreover a river at Monmouth. It is call'd Wye at Monmouth; but it is out of my prains what is the name of the other river. But 'tis all one; 'tis alike as my fingers is to my fingers, and there is salmons in both. If you mark Alexander's life well, Harry of Monmouth's life is come after it indifferent well; for there is figures in all things. Alexander, God knows and you know, in his rages, and his furies, and his wraths, and his cholers, and his moods, and his displeasures, and his indignations, and also being a little intoxicates in his prains, did, in his ales and his angers, look you, kill his best friend, Cleitus.

Gow. Our King is not like him in that. He never kill'd any of his friends.

Flu. It is not well done, mark you now, to take the tales out of my mouth ere it is made and finished. I speak but in the figures and comparisons of it. As Alexander kill'd his friend Cleitus, being in his ales and his cups, so also Harry Monmouth, being in his right wits and his good judgments, turn'd away the fat knight with the great belly doublet. He was full of jests, and gipes, and knaveries, and mocks. I have forgot his name.

Gow. Sir John Falstaff.

Flu. That is he. I'll tell you there is good men porn at Monmouth.

Gow. Here comes his Majesty.

Alarum. Enter *King Harry,* [*Warwick, Gloucester, Exeter,* and others,] with *Prisoners. Flourish.*

King. I was not angry since I came to France
Until this instant. Take a trumpet, herald;
Ride thou unto the horsemen on yond hill.
If they will fight with us, bid them come down,
Or void the field. They do offend our sight.
If they'll do neither, we will come to them
And make them skirr away as swift as stones
Enforced from the old Assyrian slings.
Besides, we'll cut the throats of those we have;
And not a man of them that we shall take
Shall taste our mercy. Go and tell them so.

Enter *Montjoy* [the *Herald*].

Exe. Here comes the herald of the French, my liege.

Glouc. His eyes are humbler than they us'd to be.

King. How now? What means this, herald? Know'st thou not
That I have fin'd these bones of mine for ransom?
Com'st thou again for ransom?

Herald. No, great King.
I come to thee for charitable license
That we may wander o'er this bloody field
To look our dead, and then to bury them;
To sort our nobles from our common men;
For many of our princes (woe the while!)
Lie drown'd and soak'd in mercenary blood;
So do our vulgar drench their peasant limbs
In blood of princes; and the wounded steeds
Fret fetlock deep in gore and with wild rage
Yerk out their armed heels at their dead masters,
Killing them twice. O, give us leave, great King,
To view the field in safety and dispose
Of their dead bodies!

King. I tell thee truly, herald,
I know not if the day be ours or no;
For yet a many of your horsemen peer
And gallop o'er the field.

Herald. The day is yours.

King. Praised be God and not our strength for it!
What is this castle call'd that stands hard by?

Herald. They call it Agincourt.

King. Then call we this the field of Agincourt,
Fought on the day of Crispin Crispianus.

Flu. Your grandfather of famous memory, an't please your Majesty, and your great-uncle Edward the Plack Prince of Wales, as I have read in the chronicles, fought a most prave pattle here in France.

King. They did, Fluellen.

Flu. Your Majesty says very true. If your Majesties is remem'bred of it, the Welshmen did good service in a garden where leeks did grow, wearing leeks in their Monmouth caps; which your Majesty know to this hour is an honourable badge of the service; and I do believe your Majesty takes no scorn to wear the leek upon Saint Tavy's day.

King. I wear it for a memorable honour;
For I am Welsh, you know, good countryman.

Flu. All the water in Wye cannot wash your Majesty's Welsh plood out of your pody, I can tell you that. God pless it and preserve it, as long as it pleases his grace, and his majesty too!

King. Thanks, good my countryman.

Flu. By Jeshu, I am your Majesty's countryman, I care not who know it! I will confess it to all the orld. I need not to be ashamed of your Majesty, praised be God, so long as your Majesty is an honest man.

King. God keep me so!

Enter *Williams.*

Our heralds go with him.
Bring me just notice of the numbers dead
On both our parts.

[*Exeunt Heralds with Montjoy.*]

Call yonder fellow hither.

Exe. Soldier, you must come to the King.

King. Soldier, why wear'st thou that glove in thy cap?

Will. An't please your Majesty, 'tis the gage of one that I should fight withal, if he be alive.

King. An Englishman?

Will. An't please your Majesty, a rascal that swagger'd with me last night; who, if 'a live and ever dare to challenge this glove, I have sworn to take him a box o' th' ear; or if I can see my glove in his cap, which he swore, as he was a soldier, he would wear (if alive), I will strike it out soundly.

King. What think you, Captain Fluellen? Is it fit this soldier keep his oath?

Flu. He is a craven and a villain else, an't please your Majesty, in my conscience.

King. It may be his enemy is a gentleman of great sort, quite from the answer of his degree.

Flu. Though he be as good a gentleman as the devil is, as Lucifer and Belzebub himself, it is necessary, look your Grace, that he keep his vow and his oath. If he be perjur'd, see you now, his reputation is as arrant a villain and a Jacksauce as ever his black shoe trod upon God's ground and his earth, in my conscience, la!

King. Then keep thy vow, sirrah, when thou meet'st the fellow.

Will. So I will, my liege, as I live.

King. Who serv'st thou under?

Will. Under Captain Gower, my liege.

Flu. Gower is a good captain and is good knowledge and literatured in the wars.

King. Call him hither to me, soldier.

Will. I will, my liege. *Exit.*

King. Here, Fluellen; wear thou this favour for me and stick it in thy cap. When Alençon and myself were down together, I pluck'd this glove from his helm. If any man challenge this, he is a friend to Alençon and an enemy to our person. If thou encounter any such, apprehend him, an thou dost me love.

Flu. Your Grace doo's me as great honours as can be desir'd in the hearts of his subjects. I would fain see the man, that has but two legs, that shall find himself aggrief'd at this glove, that is all. But I would fain see it once, an please God of his grace that I might see.

King. Know'st thou Gower?

Flu. He is my dear friend, an please you.

King. Pray thee go seek him and bring him to my tent.

Flu. I will fetch him. *Exit.*

King. My Lord of Warwick, and my brother Gloucester,
Follow Fluellen closely at the heels.
The glove which I have given him for a favour
May haply purchase him a box o' th' ear;
It is the soldier's. I by bargain should
Wear it myself. Follow, good cousin Warwick.
If that the soldier strike him — as I judge
By his blunt bearing, he will keep his word —
Some sudden mischief may arise of it;
For I do know Fluellen valiant,
And, touch'd with choler, hot as gunpowder,
And quickly will return an injury.
Follow, and see there be no harm between them.
Go you with me, uncle of Exeter. *Exeunt.*

[Scene VIII. *Before* King Henry's *pavilion.*]

Enter *Gower* and *Williams.*

Will. I warrant it is to knight you, Captain.

Enter *Fluellen.*

Flu. God's will and his pleasure, Captain, I beseech you now, come apace to the King. There is more good toward you peradventure than is in your knowledge to dream of.

Will. Sir, know you this glove?

Flu. Know the glove? I know the glove is a glove.

Will. I know this; and thus I challenge it. *Strikes him.*

Flu. 'Sblood! an arrant traitor as any's in the universal world, or in France, or in England!

Gow. How now, sir? You villain!

Will. Do you think I'll be forsworn?

Flu. Stand away, Captain Gower. I will give treason his payment into plows, I warrant you.

Will. I am no traitor.

Flu. That's a lie in thy throat. I charge you in his Majesty's name apprehend him. He's a friend of the Duke Alençon's.

Enter *Warwick* and *Gloucester.*

War. How now, how now? What's the matter?

Flu. My Lord of Warwick, here is (praised be God for it!) a most contagious treason come to light, look you, as you shall desire in a summer's day. Here is his Majesty.

Enter *King* and *Exeter.*

King. How now? What's the matter?

Flu. My liege, here is a villain and a traitor that, look your Grace, has struck the glove which your Majesty is take out of the helmet of Alençon.

Will. My liege, this was my glove, here is the fellow of it; and he that I gave it to in change promis'd to wear it in his cap. I promis'd to strike him if he did. I met this man with my glove in his cap, and I have been as good as my word.

Flu. Your Majesty hear now, saving your Majesty's manhood, what an arrant, rascally, beggarly, lousy knave it is! I hope your Majesty is pear me testimony and witness, and will avouchment, that this is the glove of Alençon that your Majesty is give me, in your conscience, now.

King. Give me thy glove, soldier. Look, here is the fellow of it.
'Twas I indeed thou promised'st to strike;
And thou hast given me most bitter terms.

Flu. An please your Majesty, let his neck answer for it, if there is any martial law in the world.

King. How canst thou make me satisfaction?

Will. All offences, my lord, come from the heart. Never came any from mine that might offend your Majesty.

King. It was ourself thou didst abuse.

Will. Your Majesty came not like yourself. You appear'd to me but as a common man; witness the night, your garments, your lowliness. And what your Highness suffer'd under that shape, I beseech you take it for your own fault, and not mine; for had you been as I took you for, I made no offence. Therefore I beseech your Highness pardon me.

King. Here, uncle Exeter, fill this glove with crowns
And give it to this fellow. Keep it, fellow,
And wear it for an honour in thy cap
Till I do challenge it. Give him the crowns;
And, Captain, you must needs be friends with him.

Flu. By this day and this light, the fellow has mettle enough in his belly. Hold, there is twelve pence for you; and I pray you to serve God, and keep you out of prawls, and prabbles, and quarrels, and dissensions, and, I warrant you it is the better for you.

Will. I will none of your money.

Flu. It is with a good will. I can tell you it will serve you to mend your shoes. Come, wherefore should you be so pashful? Your shoes is not so good. 'Tis a good silling, I warrant you, or I will change it.

Enter [an English] *Herald.*

King. Now, herald, are the dead numb'red?

Her. Here is the number of the slaught'red French. [*Gives a paper.*]

King. What prisoners of good sort are taken, uncle?

Exe. Charles Duke of Orleans, nephew to the King;
John Duke of Bourbon and Lord Bouciqualt:
Of other lords and barons, knights and squires,
Full fifteen hundred, besides common men.

King. This note doth tell me of ten thousand French
That in the field lie slain. Of princes, in this number,
And nobles bearing banners, there lie dead
One hundred twenty-six; added to these,
Of knights, esquires, and gallant gentlemen,
Eight thousand and four hundred; of the which,
Five hundred were but yesterday dubb'd knights;
So that in these ten thousand they have lost
There are but sixteen hundred mercenaries;
The rest are princes, barons, lords, knights, squires,
And gentlemen of blood and quality.
The names of those their nobles that lie dead:
Charles Delabreth, High Constable of France;
Jaques of Chatillon, Admiral of France;
The master of the crossbows, Lord Rambures;
Great Master of France, the brave Sir Guichard Dauphin;
John Duke of Alençon; Anthony Duke of Brabant,
The brother to the Duke of Burgundy;
And Edward Duke of Bar; of lusty earls,
Grandpré and Roussi, Fauconberg and Foix,
Beaumont and Marle, Vaudemont and Lestrale.
Here was a royal fellowship of death!
Where is the number of our English dead?
[*Herald gives another paper.*]
Edward the Duke of York, the Earl of Suffolk,
Sir Richard Ketly, Davy Gam, Esquire;
None else of name; and of all other men
But five-and-twenty. O God, thy arm was here!
And not to us, but to thy arm alone,
Ascribe we all! When, without stratagem,
But in plain shock and even play of battle,
Was ever known so great and little loss
On one part and on th' other? Take it, God,
For it is only thine!

Exe. 'Tis wonderful!

King. Come, go we in procession to the village;
And be it death proclaimed through our host
To boast of this, or take that praise from God
Which is his only.

Flu. Is it not lawful, an please your Majesty, to tell how many is kill'd?

King. Yes, Captain; but with this acknowledgment,
That God fought for us.

Flu. Yes, my conscience, he did us great good.

King. Do we all holy rites.
Let there be sung 'Non nobis' and 'Te Deum,'
The dead with charity enclos'd in clay,
And then to Calais; and to England then;
Where ne'er from France arriv'd more happy men. *Exeunt.*

Act V.

Enter *Chorus.*

Vouchsafe to those that have not read the story
That I may prompt them; and of such as have,
I humbly pray them to admit th' excuse
Of time, of numbers, and due course of things
Which cannot in their huge and proper life
Be here presented. Now we bear the King
Toward Calais. Grant him there. There seen,
Heave him away upon your winged thoughts
Athwart the sea. Behold, the English beach
Pales in the flood with men, with wives and boys,
Whose shouts and claps outvoice the deep-mouth'd sea,
Which, like a mighty whiffler fore the King,
Seems to prepare his way. So let him land,
And solemnly see him set on to London.
So swift a pace hath thought that even now
You may imagine him upon Blackheath;
Where that his lords desire him to have borne
His bruised helmet and his bended sword
Before him through the city. He forbids it,
Being free from vainness and self-glorious pride;
Giving full trophy, signal, and ostent
Quite from himself to God. But now behold,
In the quick forge and working house of thought,
How London doth pour out her citizens!
The Mayor and all his brethren in best sort —
Like to the senators of th' antique Rome,
With the plebeians swarming at their heels —
Go forth and fetch their conqu'ring Cæsar in;
As, by a lower but loving likelihood,
Were now the general of our gracious Empress
(As in good time he may) from Ireland coming,
Bringing rebellion broached on his sword,
How many would the peaceful city quit
To welcome him! Much more, and much more cause,
Did they this Harry. Now in London place him;
As yet the lamentation of the French
Invites the King of England's stay at home;
The Emperor's coming in behalf of France
To order peace between them; and omit
All the occurrences, whatever chanc'd,
Till Harry's back-return again to France.
There must we bring him; and myself have play'd
The interim, by rememb'ring you 'tis past.
Then brook abridgment; and your eyes advance,
After your thoughts, straight back again to France. *Exit.*

[Scene I. *France. The English camp.*]

Enter *Fluellen* and *Gower.*

Gow. Nay, that's right. But why wear you your leek to-day? Saint Davy's day is past.

Flu. There is occasions and causes why and wherefore in all things. I will tell you ass my friend, Captain Gower. The rascally, scauld, beggarly, lousy, pragging knave, Pistol — which you and yourself and all the world know to be no petter than a fellow, look you now, of no merits — he is come to me and prings me pread and salt yesterday, look you, and bid me eat my leek. It was in a place where I could not breed no contention with him; but I will be so bold as to wear it in my cap till I see him once again, and then I will tell him a little piece of my desires.

Enter *Pistol.*

Gow. Why, here he comes, swelling like a turkey cock.

Flu. 'Tis no matter for his swellings nor his turkey cocks. God pless you, Aunchient Pistol! you scurvy, lousy knave, God pless you!

Pist. Ha! art thou bedlam? Dost thou thirst, base Troyan,
To have me fold up Parca's fatal web?
Hence! I am qualmish at the smell of leek.

Flu. I peseech you heartily, scurvy, lousy knave, at my desires, and my requests, and my petitions, to eat, look you, this leek. Because, look you, you do not love it, nor your affections and your appetites and your disgestions doo's not agree with it, I would desire you to eat it.

Pist. Not for Cadwallader and all his goats.

Flu. There is one goat for you. (*Strikes him.*) Will you be so good, scauld knave, as eat it?

Pist. Base Troyan, thou shalt die!

Flu. You say very true, scauld knave, when God's will is. I will desire you to live in the meantime, and eat your victuals. Come, there is sauce for it. [*Strikes him.*] You call'd me yesterday mountain-squire; but I will make you to-day a squire of low degree. I pray you fall to. If you can mock a leek, you can eat a leek.

Gow. Enough, Captain. You have astonish'd him.

Flu. I say I will make him eat some part of my leek, or I will peat his pate four days. — Bite, I pray you. It is good for your green wound and your ploody coxcomb.

Pist. Must I bite?

Flu. Yes, certainly, and out of doubt, and out of question too, and ambiguities.

Pist. By this leek, I will most horribly revenge! I eat, and yet, I swear —

Flu. Eat, I pray you. Will you have some more sauce to your leek? There is not enough leek to swear by.

Pist. Quiet thy cudgel. Thou dost see I eat.

Flu. Much good do you, scauld knave, heartily. Nay, pray you throw none away. The skin is good for your broken coxcomb. When you take occasions to see leeks hereafter, I pray you mock at 'em; that is all.

Pist. Good.

Flu. Ay, leeks is good. Hold you, there is a groat to heal your pate.

Pist. Me a groat?

Flu. Yes, verily and in truth, you shall take it; or I have another leek in my pocket, which you shall eat.

Pist. I take thy groat in earnest of revenge.

Flu. If I owe you anything, I will pay you in cudgels. You shall be a woodmonger and buy nothing of me but cudgels. God b' wi' you, and keep you, and heal your pate. *Exit.*

Pist. All hell shall stir for this!

Gow. Go, go. You are a counterfeit cowardly knave. Will you mock at an ancient tradition, begun upon an honourable respect and worn as a memorable trophy of predeceased valour, and dare not avouch in your deeds any of your words? I have seen you gleeking and galling at this gentleman twice or thrice. You thought, because he could not speak English in the native garb, he could not therefore handle an English cudgel. You find it otherwise; and henceforth let a Welsh correction teach you a good English condition. Fare ye well. *Exit.*

Pist. Doth Fortune play the huswife with me now?
News have I, that my Nell is dead i' th' spital
Of malady of France;
And there my rendezvous is quite cut off.
Old I do wax, and from my weary limbs
Honour is cudgell'd. Well, bawd will I turn,
And something lean to cutpurse of quick hand.
To England will I steal, and there I'll steal;
And patches will I get unto these cudgell'd scars
And swear I got them in the Gallia wars. *Exit.*

[Scene II. *France. The* French King's *Palace.*]

Enter, at one door, *King Henry, Exeter, Bedford,* [*Gloucester,*] *Warwick,* [*Westmoreland,*] and other *Lords*; at another, *Queen Isabel,* the [*French*] *King,* the *Duke of Burgundy,* [the *Princess Katherine, Alice,*] and other *French.*

King H. Peace to this meeting, wherefore we are met!
Unto our brother France and to our sister
Health and fair time of day. Joy and good wishes
To our most fair and princely cousin Katherine.
And as a branch and member of this royalty,
By whom this great assembly is contriv'd,
We do salute you, Duke of Burgundy.
And, princes French, and peers, health to you all!

France. Right joyous are we to behold your face,
Most worthy brother England. Fairly met.
So are you, princes English, every one.

Queen. So happy be the issue, brother England,
Of this good day and of this gracious meeting
As we are now glad to behold your eyes —
Your eyes which hitherto have borne in them,
Against the French that met them in their bent,
The fatal balls of murthering basilisks.
The venom of such looks, we fairly hope,
Have lost their quality, and that this day
Shall change all griefs and quarrels into love.

King H. To cry amen to that, thus we appear.

Queen. You English princes all, I do salute you.

Burg. My duty to you both, on equal love,
Great Kings of France and England! That I have labour'd
With all my wits, my pains, and strong endeavours
To bring your most imperial Majesties
Unto this bar and royal interview,
Your mightiness on both parts best can witness.
Since, then, my office hath so far prevail'd

That, face to face and royal eye to eye,
You have congreeted, let it not disgrace me
If I demand, before this royal view,
What rub or what impediment there is
Why that the naked, poor, and mangled Peace,
Dear nurse of arts, plenty, and joyful births,
Should not, in this best garden of the world,
Our fertile France, put up her lovely visage.
Alas, she hath from France too long been chas'd!
And all her husbandry doth lie on heaps,
Corrupting in it own fertility.
Her vine, the merry cheerer of the heart,
Unpruned dies; her hedges even-pleach'd,
Like prisoners wildly overgrown with hair,
Put forth disorder'd twigs; her fallow leas
The darnel, hemlock, and rank fumitory
Doth root upon, while that the coulter rusts
That should deracinate such savagery.
The even mead, that erst brought sweetly forth
The freckled cowslip, burnet, and green clover,
Wanting the scythe, all uncorrected, rank,
Conceives by idleness and nothing teems
But hateful docks, rough thistles, kecksies, burrs,
Losing both beauty and utility.
And as our vineyards, fallows, meads, and hedges,
Defective in their natures, grow to wildness,
Even so our houses and ourselves and children
Have lost, or do not learn for want of time,
The sciences that should become our country;
But grow like savages — as soldiers will,
That nothing do but meditate on blood —
To swearing and stern looks, defus'd attire,
And everything that seems unnatural.
Which to reduce into our former favour
You are assembled; and my speech entreats
That I may know the let why gentle Peace
Should not expel these inconveniences
And bless us with her former qualities.

King H. If, Duke of Burgundy, you would the peace
Whose want gives growth to th' imperfections
Which you have cited, you must buy that peace
With full accord to all our just demands;
Whose tenures and particular effects
You have, enschedul'd briefly, in your hands.

Burg. The King hath heard them; to the which as yet
There is no answer made.

King H. Well then, the peace,
Which you before so urg'd, lies in his answer.

France. I have but with a cursorary eye
O'erglanc'd the articles. Pleaseth your Grace
To appoint some of your Council presently
To sit with us once more, with better heed
To resurvey them, we will suddenly
Pass our accept and peremptory answer.

King H. Brother, we shall. Go, uncle Exeter,
And brother Clarence, and you, brother Gloucester,
Warwick, and Huntingdon — go with the King;
And take with you free power to ratify,
Augment, or alter, as your wisdoms best
Shall see advantageable for our dignity,
Anything in or out of our demands;
And we'll consign thereto. Will you, fair sister,
Go with the princes or stay here with us?

Queen. Our gracious brother, I will go with them.
Happily a woman's voice may do some good
When articles too nicely urg'd be stood on.

King H. Yet leave our cousin Katherine here with us.
She is our capital demand, compris'd
Within the fore-rank of our articles.

Queen. She hath good leave.

Exeunt. Manent King Henry, Katherine, and the Gentlewoman [*Alice*].

King H. Fair Katherine, and most fair!
Will you vouchsafe to teach a soldier terms
Such as will enter at a lady's ear
And plead his love suit to her gentle heart?

Kath. Your Majesty shall mock at me. I cannot speak your England.

King H. O fair Katherine, if you will love me soundly with your French heart, I will be glad to hear you confess it brokenly with your English tongue. Do you like me, Kate?

Kath. Pardonnez-moi, I cannot tell vat is 'like me.'

King H. An angel is like you, Kate, and you are like an angel.

Kath. Que dit-il? Que je suis semblable à les anges?

Alice. Oui, vraiment, sauf vostre grâce, ainsi dit-il.

King H. I said so, dear Katherine, and I must not blush to affirm it.

Kath. O bon Dieu! les langues des hommes sont pleines de tromperies.

King H. What says she, fair one? that the tongues of men are full of deceits?

Alice. Oui, dat de tongues of de mans is be full of deceits. Dat is de Princesse.

King H. The Princess is the better Englishwoman. I' faith, Kate, my wooing is fit for thy understanding. I am glad thou canst speak no better English; for if thou couldst, thou wouldst find me such a plain king that thou wouldst think I had sold my farm to buy my crown. I know no ways to mince it in love but directly to say 'I love you.' Then, if you urge me farther than to say, 'Do you in faith?' I wear out my suit. Give me your answer; i' faith, do! and so clap hands and a bargain. How say you, lady?

Kath. Sauf vostre honneur, me understand well.

King H. Marry, if you would put me to verses or to dance for your sake, Kate, why, you undid me. For the one I have neither words nor measure; and for the other I have no strength in measure, yet a reasonable measure in strength. If I could win a lady at leapfrog, or by vaulting into my saddle with my armour on my back, under the correction of bragging be it spoken, I should quickly leap into a wife. Or if I might buffet for my love, or bound my horse for her favours, I could lay on like a butcher and sit like a jackanapes, never off. But, before God, Kate, I cannot look greenly nor gasp out my eloquence, nor I have no cunning in protestation; only downright oaths, which I never use till urg'd, nor never break for urging. If thou canst love a fellow of this temper, Kate, whose face is not worth sunburning, that never looks in his glass for love of anything he sees there, let thine eye be thy cook. I speak to thee plain soldier. If thou canst love me for this, take me; if not, to say to thee that I shall die, is true — but for thy love, by the Lord, no; yet I love thee too. And while thou liv'st, dear Kate, take a fellow of plain and uncoined constancy; for he perforce must do thee right, because he hath not the gift to woo in other places. For these fellows of infinite tongue that can rhyme themselves into ladies' favours, they do always reason themselves out again. What! A speaker is but a prater; a rhyme is but a ballad. A good leg will fall, a straight back will stoop, a black beard will turn white, a curl'd pate will grow bald, a fair face will wither, a full eye will wax hollow; but a good heart, Kate, is the sun and the moon; or rather, the sun, and not the moon, for it shines bright and never changes, but keeps his course truly. If thou would have such a one, take me; and take me, take a soldier; take a soldier, take a king. And what say'st thou then to my love? Speak, my fair — and fairly, I pray thee.

Kath. Is it possible dat I sould love de ennemie of France?

King H. No, it is not possible you should love the enemy of France, Kate; but in loving me you should love the friend of France; for I love France so well that I will not part with a village of it — I will have it all mine. And, Kate, when France is mine and I am yours, then yours is France and you are mine.

Kath. I cannot tell vat is dat.

King H. No, Kate? I will tell thee in French; which I am sure will hang upon my tongue like a new-married wife about her husband's neck, hardly to be shook off. Quand j'ai la possession de France, et quand vous avez la possession de moi (Let me see, what then? Saint Denis be my speed!), donc vostre est France et vous estes mienne. It is as easy for me, Kate, to conquer the kingdom as to speak so much more French. I shall never move thee in French, unless it be to laugh at me.

Kath. Sauf vostre honneur, le François que vous parlez, il est meilleur que l'Anglois lequel je parle.

King H. No, faith, is't not, Kate. But thy speaking of my tongue, and I thine, most truly-falsely, must needs be granted to be much at one. But, Kate, dost thou understand thus much English? Canst thou love me?

Kath. I cannot tell.

King H. Can any of your neighbours tell, Kate? I'll ask them. Come, I know thou lovest me; and at night when you come into your closet, you'll question this gentlewoman about me; and I know, Kate, you will to her dispraise those parts in me that you love with your heart; but, good Kate, mock me mercifully; the rather, gentle Princess, because I love thee cruelly. If ever thou beest mine, Kate — as I have a saving faith within me tells me thou shalt — I get thee with scambling, and thou must therefore needs prove a good soldier-breeder. Shall not thou and I, between Saint Denis and Saint George, compound a boy, half French, half English, that shall go to Constantinople and take the Turk by the beard? Shall we not? What say'st thou, my fair flower-de-luce?

Kath. I do not know dat.

King H. No; 'tis hereafter to know, but now to promise. Do but now promise, Kate, you will endeavour for your French part of such a boy; and for my English moiety take the word of a king and a bachelor. How answer you, la plus belle Katherine du monde, mon très-cher et devin déesse?

Kath. Your Majestee ave fausse French enough to deceive de most sage damoisell dat is en France.

King H. Now, fie upon my false French! By mine honour in true English, I love thee, Kate; by which honour I dare not swear thou lovest me; yet my blood begins to flatter me that thou dost, notwithstanding the poor and untempering effect of my visage. Now beshrew my father's ambition! He was thinking of civil wars when he got me; therefore was I created with a stubborn outside, with an aspect of iron, that, when I come to woo ladies, I fright them. But in faith, Kate, the elder I wax, the better I shall appear. My comfort is, that old age, that ill layer-up of beauty, can do no more spoil upon my face. Thou hast me, if thou hast me, at the worst; and thou shalt wear me, if thou wear me, better and better; and therefore tell me, most fair Katherine, will you have me? Put off your maiden blushes; avouch the thoughts of your heart with the looks of an empress; take me by the hand, and say 'Harry of England, I am thine!' which word thou shalt no sooner bless mine ear withal but I will tell thee aloud 'England is thine, Ireland is thine, France is thine, and Henry Plantagenet is thine'; who, though I speak it before his face, if he be not fellow with the best king, thou shalt find the best king of good fellows. Come, your answer in broken music! for thy voice is music and thy English broken; therefore, queen of all Katherines, break thy mind to me in broken English. Wilt thou have me?

Kath. Dat is as it sall please de roi mon père.

King H. Nay, it will please him well, Kate. It shall please him, Kate.

Kath. Den it sall also content me.

King H. Upon that I kiss your hand and I call you my queen.

Kath. Laissez, mon seigneur, laissez, laissez! Ma foi, je ne veux point que vous abaissiez vostre grandeur en baisant la main d'une de vostre Seigneurie indigne serviteur. Excusez-moi, je vous supplie, mon très-puissant seigneur.

King H. Then I will kiss your lips, Kate.

Kath. Les dames et demoiselles pour estre baisées devant leur noces, il n'est pas la coutume de France.

King H. Madam my interpreter, what says she?

Alice. Dat it is not be de fashon pour de ladies of France — I cannot tell vat is 'baiser' en Anglish.

King H. To kiss.

Alice. Your Majestee entendre bettre que moi.

King H. It is not a fashion for the maids in France to kiss before they are married, would she say?

Alice. Oui, vraiment.

King H. O Kate, nice customs cursy to great kings. Dear Kate, you and I cannot be confin'd within the weak list of a country's fashion. We are the makers of manners, Kate; and the liberty that follows our places stops the mouth of all find-faults, as I will do yours for upholding the nice fashion of your country in denying me a kiss. Therefore patiently, and yielding. [*Kisses her.*] You have witchcraft in your lips, Kate. There is more eloquence in a sugar touch of them than in the tongues of the French Council, and they should sooner persuade Harry of England than a general petition of monarchs. Here comes your father.

Enter the *French Power* and the *English Lords.*

Burg. God save your Majesty! My royal cousin,
Teach you our princess English?

King H. I would have her learn, my fair cousin, how perfectly I love her, and that is good English.

Burg. Is she not apt?

King H. Our tongue is rough, coz, and my condition is not smooth; so that, having neither the voice nor the heart of flattery about me, I cannot so conjure up the spirit of love in her that he will appear in his true likeness.

Burg. Pardon the frankness of my mirth if I answer you for that. If you would conjure in her, you must make a circle; if conjure up love in her in his true likeness, he must appear naked and blind. Can you blame her then, being a maid yet ros'd over with the virgin crimson of modesty, if she deny the appearance of a naked blind boy in her naked seeing self? It were, my lord, a hard condition for a maid to consign to.

King H. Yet they do wink and yield, as love is blind and enforces.

Burg. They are then excus'd, my lord, when they see not what they do.

King H. Then, good my lord, teach your cousin to consent winking.

Burg. I will wink on her to consent, my lord, if you will teach her to know my meaning; for maids well summer'd and warm kept are like flies at Bartholomew-tide, blind, though they have their eyes; and then they will endure handling which before would not abide looking on.

King H. This moral ties me over to time and a hot summer; and so I shall catch the fly, your cousin, in the latter end, and she must be blind too.

Burg. As love is, my lord, before it loves.

King H. It is so; and you may, some of you, thank love for my blindness, who cannot see many a fair French city for one fair French maid that stands in my way.

France. Yes, my lord, you see them perspectively — the cities turn'd into a maid; for they are all girdled with maiden walls that war hath never ent'red.

King H. Shall Kate be my wife?

France. So please you.

King H. I am content, so the maiden cities you talk of may wait on her. So the maid that stood in the way for my wish shall show me the way to my will.

France. We have consented to all terms of reason.

King H. Is't so, my lords of England?

West. The King hath granted every article:
His daughter first; and in sequel, all,
According to their firm proposed natures.

Exe. Only he hath not yet subscribed this:
Where your Majesty demands that the King of France, having any occasion to write for matter of grant, shall name your Highness in this form and with this addition, in French, 'Nostre très-cher fils Henri, Roi d'Angleterre, héritier de France'; and thus in Latin, 'Praecarissimus filius noster Henricus, Rex Angliae et haeres Franciae.'

France. Nor this I have not, brother, so denied
But your request shall make me let it pass.

King H. I pray you then, in love and dear alliance,
Let that one article rank with the rest,
And thereupon give me your daughter.

France. Take her, fair son, and from her blood raise up
Issue to me, that the contending kingdoms
Of France and England, whose very shores look pale
With envy of each other's happiness,
May cease their hatred; and this dear conjunction
Plant neighbourhood and Christianlike accord
In their sweet bosoms, that never war advance
His bleeding sword 'twixt England and fair France.

Lords. Amen!

King H. Now, welcome, Kate; and bear me witness all
That here I kiss her as my sovereign queen.
Flourish.

Queen. God, the best maker of all marriages,
Combine your hearts in one, your realms in one!
As man and wife, being two, are one in love,
So be there 'twixt your kingdoms such a spousal
That never may ill office, or fell jealousy,
Which troubles oft the bed of blessed marriage,
Thrust in between the paction of these kingdoms
To make divorce of their incorporate league;
That English may as French, French Englishmen,
Receive each other! God speak this Amen!

All. Amen!

King H. Prepare we for our marriage: on which day,
My Lord of Burgundy, we'll take your oath,
And all the peers', for surety of our leagues.
Then shall I swear to Kate, and you to me,
And may our oaths well kept and prosp'rous be!
Sennet. Exeunt.

[EPILOGUE.]

Enter *Chorus.*

Thus far, with rough and all-unable pen,
Our bending author hath pursu'd the story,
In little room confining mighty men,
Mangling by starts the full course of their glory.
Small time; but in that small, most greatly lived
This Star of England. Fortune made his sword;
By which the world's best garden he achieved,
And of it left his son imperial lord.
Henry the Sixth, in infant bands crown'd King
Of France and England, did this king succeed;
Whose state so many had the managing
That they lost France and made his England bleed;
Which oft our stage hath shown; and for their sake
In your fair minds let this acceptance take.
[*Exit.*]

The First Part of King Henry the Sixth

For The First Part of King Henry the Sixth the Folio of 1623 is our only authority. The play shows great variety in style and manner, as well as in metre. There is no agreement as to the authorship, but the usual opinion is that Shakespeare's share was small. It seems to be a reworking of one or more older plays. In such a process some scenes might be kept and others replaced by fresh matter covering the same ground, while still others were merely revised. That there were more stages than one in the process is also possible.

In its present form the play might well be called the Tragedy of Talbot. His career is the framework of the structure. The scheme is the struggle of Talbot and Joan, in which he represents the forces of England and righteousness; she the forces of France and demonic malice. Their first encounter is at Orleans, where they fight hand-to-hand (i, 5). A second encounter is at Rouen, where Joan is on the walls and Talbot below (iii, 2). After the battle in which Talbot and his son are killed, Joan exults over their bodies (iv, 7). Finally, Joan is captured by York and condemned to death (v, 3–4). On all but one of these occasions Joan's dealing with devils is emphasized by the English, and immediately before her capture her fiends are actually brought upon the stage and desert her. All these incidents are set forth in a style which marks them as the work of a single author. The scenes in which they occur, and other scenes intimately connected, are by some regarded as too poor to be Shakespeare's and as probably survivals of the old play. One theory is that this play (including almost everything in the Folio text except the undoubtedly Shakespearean scenes) was put together in 1592. If so, it must be the drama mentioned by Nashe in *Pierce Penilesse* (1592): 'How would it have ioyed braue Talbot (the terror of the French) to thinke that after he had lyne two hundred yeares in his Tombe, hee should triumphe againe on the Stage, and haue his bones newe embalmed with the teares of ten thousand spectators at least (at seuerall times) who, in the Tragedian that represents his person, imagine they behold him fresh bleeding.' Nashe seems to be referring to the 'Harey the VI' which Henslowe records as a new play produced on March 3, 1592.

The 1592 play must have included all or most of the Talbot scenes, either in substantially their present form or in some form which that supersedes. How far it drew from lost predecessors is debatable. It is also uncertain whether or not Shakespeare had a hand in its composition. Much of the material that deals with affairs in England is good enough to be his work in 1592, when he was still under the influence of Marlowe, to whom, indeed, a good deal of the Folio text is often ascribed. Greene and Peele have also been suggested as authors in part.

Undoubtedly Shakespearean are the Temple Garden scene (ii, 4) and that in which Talbot summons Bordeaux (iv, 2). One theory is that these were written by Shakespeare in 1594, or later, for a revival of the three plays on Henry VI. Such a revival is probable enough. It may be plausibly inferred from the language of the Epilogue to *Henry the Fifth*. Meres, in 1598, mentions neither *Henry V* nor Henry VI. Perhaps the revival took place in that year, but later than the date on which he wrote (before October 19). The Mortimer scene (ii, 5) and the rhyming Talbot scenes (in Act iv) may also be

Shakespeare's work. The last act of the 1592 play must have ended with the fourth scene, which makes a good formal conclusion. The fifth scene was obviously added to lead up to the *Second Part*. Who wrote it we cannot tell, but it may well enough be Shakespeare's.

For most of the facts the author or authors went to Holinshed or Halle. The play begins with the funeral of Henry V in 1422 and ends in 1444 with the arrangements for the marriage of Henry VI. Chronology is handled with the utmost freedom. For instance, Joan, who was put to death in 1431, takes part in the battle in which Talbot lost his life in 1453.

Much of the play is unhistorical. Purely fictitious are Talbot's capture of Orleans after Joan had forced the English to raise the siege (ii, 1); the romantic episode of Talbot and the Duchess of Auvergne (ii, 2, 34–60; ii, 3); the scene in the Temple Garden (ii, 4); the interview between Richard Plantagenet and Mortimer in the Tower, followed by Mortimer's death (ii, 5); Joan's capture of Rouen and Talbot's recovery of the town on the same day (iii, 2); Fastolfe's cowardice on this occasion (iii, 2); Joan's persuading Burgundy to abandon his English allegiance (iii, 3); Talbot's interview with the French general at Bordeaux (iv, 2); the whole imbroglio between York and Somerset as to the relief of Talbot (iv, 3–4); the wooing of Margaret by Suffolk (v, 3, 45 ff.).

The episode of Talbot and the Duchess is somehow related to an ancient and very popular romance of which Solomon, Don Ramiro II of Leon, and the Bastard of Bouillon appear as the hero in different versions. The substance of the romance was doubtless known to the Elizabethans as an anecdote which might attach itself to any favourite hero. At all events, the tale was current in Scotland in the eighteenth century as the ballad of *John Thomson and the Turk* (Child, No. 266).

On the whole, it seems likely that Shakespeare was the author, at one time or other, of much more of the text than critics admit. Reluctance to make him responsible for the offensive passages concerning Joan of Arc has tempted skepticism, perhaps unduly. The Duke of Bedford, in 1434, termed Joan 'a disciple and limb of the fiend . . . that used false enchantments and sorcery.' She was believed to have been trained by hags of her neighbourhood, which (so the articles of accusation aver) was infamous of old for such practices. The opinion of Shakespeare's day is well illustrated by Cotta, an enlightened physician, skeptical about witchcraft, who refers to her, in 1616, as 'that infamous woman.' Holinshed tells of her association with wicked spirits, says she was 'fullie possest of the feend,' and approves her execution. He likewise repeats the slanderous tale of her attempt to prolong her life by pleading pregnancy. Cauchon, the Bishop of Beauvais, was her judge, and it was not until 1456, twenty-five years after her death, that the proceedings were annulled. In 1909 Joan was beatified, and canonized in 1919. Shakespeare, or whoever it was that wrote the scenes that we find so shocking, could not be expected to criticize the historians whom he consulted. It is enough that he made the Dauphin prophesy: 'Joan la Pucelle shall be France's saint.'

THE FIRST PART OF KING HENRY THE SIXTH

[Dramatis Personæ.

King Henry the Sixth.
Duke of Gloucester, uncle to the *King,* and Protector.
Duke of Bedford, uncle to the *King,* and Regent of France.
Thomas Beaufort, Duke of Exeter, great-uncle to the *King.*
Henry Beaufort, great-uncle to the *King,* Bishop of Winchester, and afterwards Cardinal.
John Beaufort, Earl of Somerset, afterwards Duke.
Richard Plantagenet, son of Richard late Earl of Cambridge, afterwards Duke of York.
Earl of Warwick.
Earl of Salisbury.
Earl of Suffolk.
Lord Talbot, afterwards Earl of Shrewsbury.
John Talbot, his son.
Edmund Mortimer, Earl of March.
Sir John Fastolfe.
Sir William Lucy.
Sir William Glansdale.
Sir Thomas Gargrave.
Mayor of London.
Woodvile, Lieutenant of the Tower.
Vernon, of the White Rose or York faction.
Basset, of the Red Rose or Lancaster faction.
A Lawyer.
Mortimer's Keepers.

Charles, Dauphin, and afterwards King, of France.
Reignier, Duke of Anjou, and titular King of Naples.
Duke of Burgundy.
Duke of Alençon.
Bastard of Orleans.
Governor of Paris.
Master Gunner of Orleans, and his Son.
General of the French forces in Bordeaux.
A French Sergeant.
A Porter.
An old Shepherd, father to *Joan la Pucelle.*

Margaret, daughter to *Reignier,* afterwards married to *King Henry.*
Countess of Auvergne.
Joan la Pucelle, commonly called *Joan of Arc.*

Fiends appearing to *La Pucelle.*

Lords, Warders of the Tower, Heralds, Officers, Soldiers, Messengers, and several Attendants both on the English and the French.

SCENE. — *Partly in England, partly in France.*]

ACT I. Scene I. [*Westminster Abbey.*]

Dead march. Enter the *Funeral of King Henry the Fifth,* attended on by the *Duke of Bedford* (Regent of France), the *Duke of Gloucester* (Protector), the *Duke of Exeter,* [the *Earl of*] *Warwick,* the *Bishop of Winchester,* and the *Duke of Somerset,* [with *Heralds,* etc.].

Bed. Hung be the heavens with black, yield day to night!
Comets, importing change of times and states,
Brandish your crystal tresses in the sky
And with them scourge the bad revolting stars
That have consented unto Henry's death —
King Henry the Fifth, too famous to live long!
England ne'er lost a king of so much worth.

Glou. England ne'er had a king until his time.
Virtue he had, deserving to command;
His brandish'd sword did blind men with his beams;
His arms spread wider than a dragon's wings;
His sparkling eyes, replete with wrathful fire,
More dazzled and drove back his enemies
Than midday sun fierce bent against their faces.
What should I say? His deeds exceed all speech.
He ne'er lift up his hand but conquered.

Exe. We mourn in black. Why mourn we not in blood?
Henry is dead and never shall revive.
Upon a wooden coffin we attend,
And death's dishonourable victory
We with our stately presence glorify,
Like captives bound to a triumphant car.
What? Shall we curse the planets of mishap
That plotted thus our glory's overthrow?
Or shall we think the subtile-witted French
Conjurers and sorcerers, that, afraid of him,
By magic verses have contriv'd his end?

Win. He was a king bless'd of the King of Kings.
Unto the French the dreadful judgment day
So dreadful will not be as was his sight.
The battles of the Lord of Hosts he fought;
The church's prayers made him so prosperous.
Glou. The Church? Where is it? Had not churchmen pray'd,
His thread of life had not so soon decay'd.
None do you like but an effeminate prince
Whom like a schoolboy you may overawe.
Win. Gloucester, whate'er we like, thou art Protector
And lookest to command the prince and realm.
Thy wife is proud. She holdeth thee in awe
More than God or religious churchmen may.
Glou. Name not religion, for thou lov'st the flesh,
And ne'er throughout the year to church thou go'st,
Except it be to pray against thy foes.
Bed. Cease, cease these jars, and rest your minds in peace!
Let's to the altar. Heralds, wait on us.
Instead of gold we'll offer up our arms,
Since arms avail not, now that Henry 's dead.
Posterity, await for wretched years,
When at their mothers' moist eyes babes shall suck,
Our isle be made a marish of salt tears,
And none but women left to wail the dead.
Henry the Fifth, thy ghost I invocate:
Prosper this realm, keep it from civil broils!
Combat with adverse planets in the heavens!
A far more glorious star thy soul will make
Than Julius Cæsar or bright —

Enter a *Messenger.*

Mess. My honourable lords, health to you all!
Sad tidings bring I to you out of France,
Of loss, of slaughter, and discomfiture.
Guyenne, Champagne, Rheims, Orleans,
Paris, Guysors, Poictiers, are all quite lost.
Bed. What say'st thou, man, before dead Henry's corse?
Speak softly, or the loss of those great towns
Will make him burst his lead and rise from death.
Glou. Is Paris lost? Is Roan yielded up?
If Henry were recall'd to life again,
These news would cause him once more yield the ghost.
Exe. How were they lost? What treachery was us'd?
Mess. No treachery, but want of men and money.
Amongst the soldiers this is muttered,
That here you maintain several factions,
And whilst a field should be dispatch'd and fought,
You are disputing of your generals.
One would have ling'ring wars, with little cost;
Another would fly swift, but wanteth wings;
A third thinks, without expense at all,
By guileful fair words peace may be obtain'd.
Awake, awake, English nobility!
Let not sloth dim your honours new begot.
Cropp'd are the flower-de-luces in your arms;
Of England's coat one half is cut away. [*Exit.*]
Exe. Were our tears wanting to this funeral,
These tidings would call forth their flowing tides.
Bed. Me they concern; Regent I am of France.
Give me my steeled coat! I'll fight for France.
Away with these disgraceful wailing robes!
Wounds will I lend the French, instead of eyes,
To weep their intermissive miseries.

Enter to them another *Messenger.*

Mess. Lords, view these letters, full of bad mischance.
France is revolted from the English quite,
Except some petty towns of no import.
The Dauphin Charles is crowned king in Rheims;
The Bastard of Orleans with him is join'd;
Reignier, Duke of Anjou, doth take his part;
The Duke of Alençon flieth to his side. *Exit.*
Exe. The Dauphin crowned king? All fly to him?
O, whither shall we fly from this reproach?
Glou. We will not fly, but to our enemies' throats!
Bedford, if thou be slack, I'll fight it out.
Bed. Gloucester, why doubt'st thou of my forwardness?
An army have I muster'd in my thoughts,
Wherewith already France is overrun.

Enter another *Messenger.*

Mess. My gracious lords, to add to your laments,
Wherewith you now bedew King Henry's hearse,
I must inform you of a dismal fight
Betwixt the stout Lord Talbot and the French.
Win. What? Wherein Talbot overcame, is't so?

Mess. O, no! wherein Lord Talbot was o'erthrown.
The circumstance I'll tell you more at large.
The tenth of August last this dreadful lord,
Retiring from the siege of Orleans,
Having full scarce six thousand in his troop,
By three-and-twenty thousand of the French
Was round encompassed and set upon.
No leisure had he to enrank his men;
He wanted pikes to set before his archers;
Instead whereof, sharp stakes pluck'd out of hedges
They pitched in the ground confusedly
To keep the horsemen off from breaking in.
More than three hours the fight continued,
Where valiant Talbot above human thought
Enacted wonders with his sword and lance.
Hundreds he sent to hell, and none durst stand him;
Here, there, and everywhere enrag'd he slew.
The French exclaim'd the devil was in arms;
All the whole army stood agaz'd on him.
His soldiers, spying his undaunted spirit,
'A Talbot! a Talbot!' cried out amain
And rush'd into the bowels of the battle.
Here had the conquest fully been seal'd up
If Sir John Fastolfe had not play'd the coward.
He, being in the vaward, plac'd behind
With purpose to relieve and follow them,
Cowardly fled, not having struck one stroke.
Hence grew the general wrack and massacre.
Enclosed were they with their enemies.
A base Walloon, to win the Dauphin's grace,
Thrust Talbot with a spear into the back,
Whom all France with their chief assembled strength
Durst not presume to look once in the face.
Bed. Is Talbot slain? Then I will slay myself
For living idly here in pomp and ease
Whilst such a worthy leader, wanting aid,
Unto his dastard foemen is betray'd.
Mess. O, no, he lives, but is took prisoner,
And Lord Scales with him, and Lord Hungerford;
Most of the rest slaughter'd or took likewise.
Bed. His ransom there is none but I shall pay.
I'll hale the Dauphin headlong from his throne;
His crown shall be the ransom of my friend.
Four of their lords I'll change for one of ours.
Farewell, my masters; to my task will I.
Bonfires in France forthwith I am to make
To keep our great Saint George's feast withal.
Ten thousand soldiers with me I will take,
Whose bloody deeds shall make all Europe quake.
Mess. So you had need; for Orleans is besieg'd;
The English army is grown weak and faint;
The Earl of Salisbury craveth supply
And hardly keeps his men from mutiny,
Since they, so few, watch such a multitude.
[*Exit.*]
Exe. Remember, lords, your oaths to Henry sworn,
Either to quell the Dauphin utterly
Or bring him in obedience to your yoke.
Bed. I do remember it, and here take my leave
To go about my preparation. *Exit.*
Glou. I'll to the Tower with all the haste I can
To view th' artillery and munition,
And then I will proclaim young Henry king.
Exit.
Exe. To Eltham will I, where the young King is,
Being ordain'd his special governor,
And for his safety there I'll best devise. *Exit.*
Win. Each hath his place and function to attend:
I am left out; for me nothing remains.
But long I will not be Jack out of office!
The King from Eltham I intend to steal
And sit at chiefest stern of public weal. *Exit.*
[*Curtain drawn to shut off the bier and Attendants.*]

[Scene II. *France. Before Orleans.*]

Sound a flourish. Enter *Charles* [*the Dauphin*], *Alençon,* and *Reignier,* marching with *Drum* and *Soldiers.*

Char. Mars his true moving, even as in the heavens
So in the earth, to this day is not known.
Late did he shine upon the English side;
Now we are victors, upon us he smiles.
What towns of any moment but we have?
At pleasure here we lie, near Orleans;
Otherwhiles the famish'd English, like pale ghosts,
Faintly besiege us one hour in a month.
Alen. They want their porridge and their fat bull-beeves.
Either they must be dieted like mules
And have their provender tied to their mouths
Or piteous they will look, like drowned mice.

Reig. Let's raise the siege. Why live we idly here?
Talbot is taken, whom we wont to fear.
Remaineth none but mad-brain'd Salisbury,
And he may well in fretting spend his gall;
Nor men nor money hath he to make war.

Char. Sound, sound alarum! We will rush on them.
Now for the honour of the forlorn French!
Him I forgive my death that killeth me
When he sees me go back one foot or fly.
Exeunt.

Here alarum. They are beaten back by the English with great loss. Enter *Charles, Alençon,* and *Reignier.*

Char. Who ever saw the like? What men have I!
Dogs! cowards! dastards! I would ne'er have fled
But that they left me 'midst my enemies.

Reig. Salisbury is a desperate homicide;
He fighteth as one weary of his life.
The other lords, like lions wanting food,
Do rush upon us as their hungry prey.

Alen. Froissart, a countryman of ours, records
England all Olivers and Rowlands bred
During the time Edward the Third did reign.
More truly now may this be verified;
For none but Samsons and Goliases
It sendeth forth to skirmish. One to ten?
Lean raw-bon'd rascals — who would e'er suppose
They had such courage and audacity?

Char. Let's leave this town; for they are harebrain'd slaves,
And hunger will enforce them to be more eager.
Of old I know them. Rather with their teeth
The walls they'll tear down than forsake the siege.

Reig. I think by some odd gimmors or device
Their arms are set, like clocks, still to strike on.
Else ne'er could they hold out so as they do.
By my consent, we'll even let them alone.

Alen. Be it so.

Enter the *Bastard of Orleans.*

Bast. Where's the Prince Dauphin? I have news for him.

Dauph. Bastard of Orleans, thrice welcome to us.

Bast. Methinks your looks are sad, your cheer appall'd.
Hath the late overthrow wrought this offence?
Be not dismay'd, for succour is at hand.
A holy maid hither with me I bring
Which by a vision sent to her from heaven
Ordained is to raise this tedious siege
And drive the English forth the bounds of France.
The spirit of deep prophecy she hath,
Exceeding the nine Sibyls of old Rome:
What's past and what's to come she can descry.
Speak, shall I call her in? Believe my words,
For they are certain and unfallible.

Dauph. Go, call her in. [*Exit Bastard.*] But first, to try her skill,
Reignier, stand thou as Dauphin in my place:
Question her proudly; let thy looks be stern.
By this means shall we sound what skill she hath. [*Steps back.*]

Enter *Joan Pucelle* [and *Bastard*].

Reig. Fair maid, is't thou wilt do these wondrous feats?

Puc. Reignier, is't thou that thinkest to beguile me?
Where is the Dauphin? Come, come from behind.
I know thee well, though never seen before.
Be not amaz'd; there's nothing hid from me.
In private will I talk with thee apart.
Stand back, you lords, and give us leave awhile.

Reig. She takes upon her bravely at first dash.

Puc. Dauphin, I am by birth a shepherd's daughter,
My wit untrain'd in any kind of art.
Heaven and our Lady gracious hath it pleas'd
To shine on my contemptible estate.
Lo, whilst I waited on my tender lambs
And to sun's parching heat display'd my cheeks,
God's Mother deigned to appear to me,
And in a vision full of majesty
Will'd me to leave my base vocation
And free my country from calamity;
Her aid she promis'd and assur'd success.
In complete glory she reveal'd herself;
And whereas I was black and swart before,
With those clear rays which she infus'd on me
That beauty am I blest with which you see.
Ask me what question thou canst possible,
And I will answer unpremeditated.
My courage try by combat, if thou dar'st,
And thou shalt find that I exceed my sex.
Resolve on this: thou shalt be fortunate
If thou receive me for thy warlike mate.

Dauph. Thou hast astonish'd me with thy high terms.

Only this proof I'll of thy valour make:
In single combat thou shalt buckle with me,
And if thou vanquishest, thy words are true;
Otherwise I renounce all confidence.
Puc. I am prepar'd. Here is my keen-edg'd sword,
Deck'd with five flower-de-luces on each side,
The which at Touraine in Saint Katherine's churchyard
Out of a great deal of old iron I chose forth.
Dauph. Then come, a God's name! I fear no woman.
Puc. And while I live, I'll ne'er fly from a man.

Here they fight, and Joan la Pucelle overcomes.

Dauph. Stay, stay thy hands! Thou art an Amazon
And fightest with the sword of Deborah.
Puc. Christ's Mother helps me, else I were too weak.
Dauph. Whoe'er helps thee, 'tis thou that must help me!
Impatiently I burn with thy desire;
My heart and hands thou hast at once subdu'd.
Excellent Pucelle, if thy name be so,
Let me thy servant and not sovereign be.
'Tis the French Dauphin sueth to thee thus.
Puc. I must not yield to any rites of love,
For my profession's sacred from above.
When I have chased all thy foes from hence,
Then will I think upon a recompense.
Dauph. Meantime look gracious on thy prostrate thrall.
Reig. My lord, methinks, is very long in talk.
Alen. Doubtless he shrives this woman to her smock;
Else ne'er could he so long protract his speech.
Reig. Shall we disturb him, since he keeps no mean?
Alen. He may mean more than we poor men do know.
These women are shrewd tempters with their tongues.
Reig. My lord, where are you? What devise you on?
Shall we give o'er Orleans, or no?
Puc. Why, no, I say! Distrustful recreants,
Fight till the last gasp. I will be your guard.
Dauph. What she says, I'll confirm. We'll fight it out.
Puc. Assign'd am I to be the English scourge.
This night the siege assuredly I'll raise.
Expect Saint Martin's summer, halcyon days,
Since I have entered into these wars.
Glory is like a circle in the water,
Which never ceaseth to enlarge itself
Till by broad spreading it disperse to naught.
With Henry's death the English circle ends;
Dispersed are the glories it included.
Now am I like that proud insulting ship
Which Cæsar and his fortune bare at once.
Dauph. Was Mahomet inspired with a dove?
Thou with an eagle art inspired then!
Helen, the mother of great Constantine,
Nor yet Saint Philip's daughters, were like thee.
Bright star of Venus, fall'n down on the earth,
How may I reverently worship thee enough?
Alen. Leave off delays and let us raise the siege.
Reig. Woman, do what thou canst to save our honours.
Drive them from Orleans and be immortaliz'd.
Dauph. Presently we'll try. Come, let's away about it.
No prophet will I trust if she prove false.
Exeunt.

[Scene III. *London. Before the Tower gates.*]

Enter *Gloucester*, with his *Servingmen* [in blue coats].

Glou. I am come to survey the Tower this day.
Since Henry's death I fear there is conveyance.
Where be these warders that they wait not here?
Open the gates! 'Tis Gloucester that calls.
[*Servingmen knock.*]
1. Warder. [*within*] Who's there that knocks so imperiously?
Glouc.'s 1. Man. It is the noble Duke of Gloucester.
2. Warder. [*within*] Whoe'er he be, you may not be let in.
1. Man. Villains, answer you so the Lord Protector?
1. Warder. [*within*] The Lord protect him! So we answer him.
We do no otherwise than we are will'd.
Glou. Who willed you? or whose will stands but mine?
There's none Protector of the realm but I.
Break up the gates! I'll be your warrantize.
Shall I be flouted thus by dunghill grooms?

Gloucester's men rush at the Tower gates, and Woodvile the Lieutenant speaks within.

Wood. What noise is this? What traitors have we here?
Glou. Lieutenant, is it you whose voice I hear?
Open the gates. Here's Gloucester that would enter.
Wood. Have patience, noble Duke. I may not open;
The Cardinal of Winchester forbids.
From him I have express commandëment
That thou nor none of thine shall be let in.
Glou. Faint-hearted Woodvile, prizest him fore me?
Arrogant Winchester, that haughty prelate,
Whom Henry, our late sovereign, ne'er could brook?
Thou art no friend to God or to the King.
Open the gates, or I'll shut thee out shortly.
Servingmen. Open the gates unto the Lord Protector!
Or we'll burst them open if that you come not quickly.

Enter to the *Protector* at the Tower gates *Winchester*, and his *Men* in tawny coats.

Win. How now, ambitious Humphrey? What means this?
Glou. Peel'd priest, dost thou command me to be shut out?
Win. I do, thou most usurping Proditor,
And not Protector of the King or realm.
Glou. Stand back, thou manifest conspirator,
Thou that contrivedst to murther our dead lord,
Thou that giv'st whores indulgences to sin.
I'll canvass thee in thy broad cardinal's hat
If thou proceed in this thy insolence.
Win. Nay, stand thou back! I will not budge a foot.
This be Damascus, be thou cursed Cain,
To slay thy brother Abel, if thou wilt.
Glou. I will not slay thee, but I'll drive thee back.
Thy scarlet robes as a child's bearing cloth
I'll use to carry thee out of this place.
Win. Do what thou dar'st! I beard thee to thy face.
Glou. What? Am I dar'd, and bearded to my face?
Draw, men, for all this privileged place.
Blue-coats to tawny-coats! Priest, beware your beard.
I mean to tug it and to cuff you soundly
Under my feet I stamp thy cardinal's hat.
In spite of Pope or dignities of Church,
Here by the cheeks I'll drag thee up and down.
Win. Gloucester, thou wilt answer this before the Pope.
Glou. Winchester goose! I cry a rope! a rope!
Now beat them hence. Why do you let them stay?
Thee I'll chase hence, thou wolf in sheep's array.
Out, tawny-coats! Out, scarlet hypocrite!

Here *Gloucester's Men* beat out the *Cardinal's Men*; and enter in the hurly-burly the *Mayor of London* and his *Officers*.

May. Fie, lords, that you, being supreme magistrates,
Thus contumeliously should break the peace!
Glou. Peace, Mayor! Thou know'st little of my wrongs.
Here's Beaufort, that regards nor God nor king,
Hath here distrain'd the Tower to his use.
Win. Here's Gloucester, a foe to citizens;
One that still motions war and never peace,
O'ercharging your free purses with large fines,
That seeks to overthrow religion
Because he is Protector of the realm,
And would have armour here out of the Tower
To crown himself king and suppress the Prince.
Glou. I will not answer thee with words, but blows. *Here they skirmish again.*
May. Naught rests for me in this tumultuous strife
But to make open proclamation.
Come, officer; as loud as e'er thou canst.

[*The Officer*] *cries* [*out, reading the proclamation*]:

All manner of men assembled here in arms this day against God's peace and the King's, we charge and command you, in his Highness' name, to repair to your several dwelling places, and not to wear, handle, or use any sword, weapon, or dagger henceforward, upon pain of death.

Glou. Cardinal, I'll be no breaker of the law;
But we shall meet and break our minds at large.
Win. Gloucester, we'll meet to thy cost, be sure:
Thy heart-blood I will have for this day's work.
May. I'll call for clubs if you will not away.
This cardinal 's more haughty than the devil.
Glou. Mayor, farewell. Thou dost but what thou mayst.
Win. Abominable Gloucester, guard thy head;
For I intend to have it ere long.
Exeunt [*Gloucester and Winchester with their Servingmen*].

May. See the coast clear'd, and then we will depart.
Good God, these nobles should such stomachs bear!
I myself fight not once in forty year. *Exeunt.*

[Scene IV. *Orleans.*]

Enter [on the walls] the *Master Gunner* of Orleans and his *Boy.*

M. Gun. Sirrah, thou know'st how Orleans is besieg'd
And how the English have the suburbs won.
Boy. Father, I know, and oft have shot at them,
Howe'er unfortunate I miss'd my aim.
M. Gun. But now thou shalt not. Be thou rul'd by me.
Chief master gunner am I of this town;
Something I must do to procure me grace.
The Prince's espials have informed me
How the English, in the suburbs close intrench'd,
Wont through a secret grate of iron bars
In yonder tower to overpeer the city,
And thence discover how with most advantage
They may vex us with shot or with assault.
To intercept this inconvenience
A piece of ordnance 'gainst it I have plac'd,
And even these three days have I watch'd,
If I could see them.
Now do thou watch, for I can stay no longer.
If thou spy'st any, run and bring me word,
And thou shalt find me at the Governor's.
Exit.
Boy. Father, I warrant you; take you no care.
I'll never trouble you if I may spy them. *Exit.*

Enter *Salisbury* and *Talbot* on the turrets, with [*Sir William Glandsdale, Sir Thomas Gargrave,* and] others.

Sal. Talbot, my life, my joy, again return'd?
How wert thou handled being prisoner,
Or by what means got'st thou to be releas'd?
Discourse, I prithee, on this turret's top.
Tal. The Duke of Bedford had a prisoner
Call'd the brave Lord Ponton de Santrailles;
For him was I exchang'd and ransomed.
But with a baser man-of-arms by far
Once in contempt they would have barter'd me;
Which I disdaining scorn'd, and craved death
Rather than I would be so vile esteem'd.
In fine, redeem'd I was as I desir'd.
But, O, the treacherous Fastolfe wounds my heart!
Whom with my bare fists I would execute
If I now had him brought into my power.
Sal. Yet tell'st thou not how thou wert entertain'd.
Tal. With scoffs and scorns and contumelious taunts
In open market place produc'd they me
To be a public spectacle to all.
'Here,' said they, 'is the terror of the French,
The scarecrow that affrights our children so.'
Then broke I from the officers that led me
And with my nails digg'd stones out of the ground
To hurl at the beholders of my shame.
My grisly countenance made others fly;
None durst come near for fear of sudden death.
In iron walls they deem'd me not secure;
So great fear of my name 'mongst them was spread
That they suppos'd I could rend bars of steel
And spurn in pieces posts of adamant.
Wherefore a guard of chosen shot I had
That walk'd about me every minute while;
And if I did but stir out of my bed,
Ready they were to shoot me to the heart.

Enter the *Boy* with a linstock.

Sal. I grieve to hear what torments you endur'd,
But we will be reveng'd sufficiently.
Now it is supper time in Orleans.
Here, through this secret grate, I count each one
And view the Frenchmen how they fortify.
Let us look in; the sight will much delight thee.
Sir Thomas Gargrave and Sir William Glansdale,
Let me have your express opinions
Where is best place to make our batt'ry next.
Gar. I think at the north gate, for there stand lords.
Glan. And I here, at the bulwark of the bridge.
Tal. For aught I see, this city must be famish'd
Or with light skirmishes enfeebled.
Here they shoot, and Salisbury [*and Gargrave*] *fall down.*
Sal. O Lord have mercy on us, wretched sinners!
Gar. O Lord have mercy on me, woful man!
Tal. What chance is this that suddenly hath cross'd us?

Speak, Salisbury; at least, if thou canst speak.
How far'st thou, mirror of all martial men?
One of thy eyes and thy cheek's side struck off?
Accursed tower! Accursed fatal hand
That hath contriv'd this woful tragedy!
In thirteen battles Salisbury o'ercame;
Henry the Fifth he first train'd to the wars;
Whilst any trump did sound or drum struck up
His sword did ne'er leave striking in the field.
Yet liv'st thou, Salisbury? Though thy speech doth fail,
One eye thou hast to look to heaven for grace.
The sun with one eye vieweth all the world.
Heaven, be thou gracious to none alive
If Salisbury wants mercy at thy hands!
Bear hence his body; I will help to bury it.
Sir Thomas Gargrave, hast thou any life?
Speak unto Talbot. Nay, look up to him.
Salisbury, cheer thy spirit with this comfort,
Thou shalt not die whiles —
He beckons with his hand and smiles on me,
As who should say 'When I am dead and gone,
Remember to avenge me on the French.'
Plantagenet, I will, and like thee, Nero,
Play on the lute, beholding the towns burn.
Wretched shall France be only in my name.

Here an alarum, and it thunders and lightens.

What stir is this? What tumult's in the heavens?
Whence cometh this alarum and the noise?

Enter a *Messenger*.

Mess. My lord, my lord, the French have gather'd head!
The Dauphin, with one Joan la Pucelle join'd,
A holy prophetess new risen up,
Is come with a great power to raise the siege.

Here Salisbury lifteth himself up and groans.

Tal. Hear, hear, how dying Salisbury doth groan!
It irks his heart he cannot be reveng'd.
Frenchmen, I'll be a Salisbury to you.
Pucelle or Pussel, Dolphin or Dogfish,
Your hearts I'll stamp out with my horse's heels
And make a quagmire of your mingled brains.
Convey me Salisbury into his tent,
And then we'll try what these dastard Frenchmen dare.

Alarum. Exeunt [*with the bodies*].

[Scene V. *Before Orleans.*]

Here an alarum again, and Talbot pursueth the Dauphin and driveth him. Then enter *Joan la Pucelle,* driving Englishmen before her [and exit]. Then enter *Talbot.*

Tal. Where is my strength, my valour, and my force?
Our English troops retire, I cannot stay them;
A woman clad in armour chaseth them.

Enter *Pucelle.*

Here, here she comes. I'll have a bout with thee.
Devil or devil's dam, I'll conjure thee.
Blood will I draw on thee — thou art a witch —
And straightway give thy soul to him thou serv'st.

Puc. Come, come, 'tis only I that must disgrace thee. *Here they fight.*

Tal. Heavens, can you suffer hell so to prevail?
My breast I'll burst with straining of my courage
And from my shoulders crack my arms asunder
But I will chastise this high-minded strumpet.

They fight again.

Puc. Talbot, farewell; thy hour is not yet come.
I must go victual Orleans forthwith.

A short alarum. Then enter the town with *Soldiers.*

O'ertake me if thou canst! I scorn thy strength.
Go, go, cheer up thy hungry starved men.
Help Salisbury to make his testament.
This day is ours, as many more shall be. *Exit.*

Tal. My thoughts are whirled like a potter's wheel;
I know not where I am nor what I do.
A witch by fear, not force, like Hannibal,
Drives back our troops and conquers as she lists.
So bees with smoke and doves with noisome stench
Are from their hives and houses driven away.
They call'd us, for our fierceness, English dogs;
Now, like to whelps, we crying run away.

A short alarum.

Hark, countrymen! Either renew the fight
Or tear the lions out of England's coat,
Renounce your soil, give sheep in lions' stead.
Sheep run not half so treacherous from the wolf,
Or horse or oxen from the leopard,

As you fly from your oft-subdued slaves.
Alarum. Here another skirmish.
It will not be. Retire into your trenches.
You all consented unto Salisbury's death,
For none would strike a stroke in his revenge.
Pucelle is ent'red into Orleans
In spite of us or aught that we could do.
O, would I were to die with Salisbury!
The shame hereof will make me hide my head.
Exit.
Alarum. Retreat.

[Scene VI. *Orleans.*]

Flourish. Enter, on the walls, *Pucelle, Dauphin, Reignier, Alençon,* and *Soldiers.*

Puc. Advance our waving colours on the walls;
Rescu'd is Orleans from the English.
Thus Joan la Pucelle hath perform'd her word.
Dauph. Divinest creature, Astræa's daughter,
How shall I honour thee for this success?
Thy promises are like Adonis' gardens,
That one day bloom'd and fruitful were the next.
France, triumph in thy glorious prophetess!
Recover'd is the town of Orleans.
More blessed hap did ne'er befall our state.
Reig. Why ring not out the bells aloud throughout the town?
Dauphin, command the citizens make bonfires
And feast and banquet in the open streets
To celebrate the joy that God hath given us.
Alen. All France will be replete with mirth and joy
When they shall hear how we have play'd the men.
Dauph. 'Tis Joan, not we, by whom the day is won;
For which I will divide my crown with her,
And all the priests and friars in my realm
Shall in procession sing her endless praise.
A statelier pyramis to her I'll rear
Than Rhodope's of Memphis ever was.
In memory of her, when she is dead,
Her ashes, in an urn more precious
Than the rich-jewell'd coffer of Darius,
Transported shall be at high festivals
Before the kings and queens of France.
No longer on Saint Denis will we cry,
But Joan la Pucelle shall be France's saint.
Come in, and let us banquet royally
After this golden day of victory.
Flourish. Exeunt.

ACT II. Scene I. [*Orleans.*]

Enter a [*French*] *Sergeant of a Band,* with two *Sentinels.*

Serg. Sirs, take your places and be vigilant.
If any noise or soldier you perceive
Near to the walls, by some apparent sign
Let us have knowledge at the court of guard.
Sentinel. Sergeant, you shall. [*Exit Sergeant.*] Thus are poor servitors,
When others sleep upon their quiet beds,
Constrain'd to watch in darkness, rain, and cold.

Enter *Talbot, Bedford,* and *Burgundy,* [and *Forces,*] with scaling ladders, their *Drums* beating a dead march.

Tal. Lord Regent, and redoubted Burgundy,
By whose approach the regions of Artois,
Wallon, and Picardy are friends to us,
This happy night the Frenchmen are secure,
Having all day carous'd and banqueted.
Embrace we then this opportunity,
As fitting best to quittance their deceit,
Contriv'd by art and baleful sorcery.
Bed. Coward of France! How much he wrongs his fame,
Despairing of his own arm's fortitude,
To join with witches and the help of hell!
Bur. Traitors have never other company.
But what's that Pucelle whom they term so pure?
Tal. A maid, they say.
Bed. A maid? and be so martial?
Bur. Pray God she prove not masculine ere long,
If underneath the standard of the French
She carry armour as she hath begun.
Tal. Well, let them practise and converse with spirits.
God is our fortress, in whose conquering name
Let us resolve to scale their flinty bulwarks.
Bed. Ascend, brave Talbot. We will follow thee.
Tal. Not all together. Better far, I guess,
That we do make our entrance several ways;
That, if it chance the one of us do fail,
The other yet may rise against their force.

Bed. Agreed. I'll to yond corner.
Bur. And I to this.
Tal. And here will Talbot mount, or make his grave.
Now, Salisbury, for thee, and for the right
Of English Henry! Shall this night appear
How much in duty I am bound to both.
Sentinel. Arm! arm! The enemy doth make assault!

[*The English scale the walls.*] *Cry:* 'Saint George! a Talbot!'

The French leap o'er the walls in their shirts. Enter, several ways, *Bastard* [*of Orleans*], *Alençon, Reignier,* half ready and half unready.

Alen. How now, my lords? What, all unready so?
Bast. Unready? Ay, and glad we scap'd so well.
Reig. 'Twas time, I trow, to wake and leave our beds,
Hearing alarums at our chamber doors.
Alen. Of all exploits since first I follow'd arms
Ne'er heard I of a warlike enterprise
More venturous or desperate than this.
Bast. I think this Talbot be a fiend of hell.
Reig. If not of hell, the heavens sure favour him.
Alen. Here cometh Charles. I marvel how he sped.

Enter *Charles* [the *Dauphin*] and *Joan.*

Bast. Tut! holy Joan was his defensive guard.
Char. Is this thy cunning, thou deceitful dame?
Didst thou at first, to flatter us withal,
Make us partakers of a little gain
That now our loss might be ten times so much?
Joan. Wherefore is Charles impatient with his friend?
At all times will you have my power alike?
Sleeping or waking must I still prevail,
Or will you blame and lay the fault on me?
Improvident soldiers, had your watch been good,
This sudden mischief never could have fall'n!
Char. Duke of Alençon, this was your default
That, being captain of the watch to-night,
Did look no better to that weighty charge
Alen. Had all your quarters been as safely kept
As that whereof I had the government,
We had not been thus shamefully surpris'd.
Bast. Mine was secure.
Reig. And so was mine, my lord.
Char. And for myself, most part of all this night
Within her quarter and mine own precinct
I was employ'd in passing to and fro
About relieving of the sentinels.
Then how or which way should they first break in?
Joan. Question, my lords, no further of the case,
How or which way. 'Tis sure they found some place
But weakly guarded, where the breach was made.
And now there rests no other shift but this —
To gather our soldiers, scatter'd and dispers'd,
And lay new platforms to endamage them.

Alarum. Enter a *Soldier,* crying 'A Talbot! a Talbot!' *They fly, leaving their clothes behind.*

Sold. I'll be so bold to take what they have left.
The cry of 'Talbot' serves me for a sword;
For I have loaden me with many spoils,
Using no other weapon but his name. *Exit.*

[Scene II. *Orleans. Within the town.*]

Enter *Talbot, Bedford, Burgundy,* [a *Captain,* and others].

Bed. The day begins to break and night is fled,
Whose pitchy mantle overveil'd the earth.
Here sound retreat and cease our hot pursuit.
Retreat [*sounded*].
Tal. Bring forth the body of old Salisbury
And here advance it in the market place,
The middle centre of this cursed town.
Now have I paid my vow unto his soul:
For every drop of blood was drawn from him
There hath at least five Frenchmen died to-night.
And that hereafter ages may behold
What ruin happened in revenge of him,
Within their chiefest temple I'll erect
A tomb, wherein his corpse shall be interr'd;
Upon the which, that every one may read,
Shall be engrav'd the sack of Orleans,
The treacherous manner of his mournful death,
And what a terror he had been to France.

But, lords, in all our bloody massacre,
I muse we met not with the Dauphin's Grace,
His new-come champion, virtuous Joan of Arc,
Nor any of his false confederates.

Bed. 'Tis thought, Lord Talbot, when the fight began,
Rous'd on the sudden from their drowsy beds,
They did amongst the troops of armed men
Leap o'er the walls for refuge in the field.

Bur. Myself, as far as I could well discern
For smoke and dusky vapours of the night,
Am sure I scar'd the Dauphin and his trull,
When arm in arm they both came swifty running,
Like to a pair of loving turtledoves
That could not live asunder day or night.
After that things are set in order here,
We'll follow them with all the power we have.

Enter a *Messenger*.

Mess. All hail, my lords! Which of this princely train
Call ye the warlike Talbot, for his acts
So much applauded through the realm of France?

Tal. Here is the Talbot. Who would speak with him?

Mess. The virtuous lady, Countess of Auvergne,
With modesty admiring thy renown,
By me entreats, great lord, thou wouldst vouchsafe
To visit her poor castle where she lies,
That she may boast she hath beheld the man
Whose glory fills the world with loud report.

Bur. Is it even so? Nay, then I see our wars
Will turn unto a peaceful comic sport,
When ladies crave to be encount'red with.
You may not, my lord, despise her gentle suit.

Tal. Ne'er trust me then; for when a world of men
Could not prevail with all their oratory,
Yet hath a woman's kindness overrul'd;
And therefore tell her I return great thanks
And in submission will attend on her.
Will not your honours bear me company?

Bed. No, truly! 'tis more than manners will;
And I have heard it said, unbidden guests
Are often welcomest when they are gone.

Tal. Well then, alone (since there's no remedy)
I mean to prove this lady's courtesy.
Come hither, Captain. (*Whispers.*) You perceive my mind?

Capt. I do, my lord, and mean accordingly.
Exeunt.

[Scene III. *Auvergne. The Castle of the* Countess.]

Enter *Countess* [and her *Porter*].

Count. Porter, remember what I gave in charge,
And when you have done so, bring the keys to me.

Port. Madam, I will. *Exit.*

Count. The plot is laid. If all things fall out right,
I shall as famous be by this exploit
As Scythian Tomyris by Cyrus' death.
Great is the rumour of this dreadful knight,
And his achievements of no less account.
Fain would mine eyes be witness with mine ears,
To give their censure of these rare reports.

Enter *Messenger* and *Talbot.*

Mess. Madam,
According as your ladyship desir'd,
By message crav'd, so is Lord Talbot come.

Count. And he is welcome. What? Is this the man?

Mess. Madam, it is.

Count. Is this the scourge of France?
Is this the Talbot, so much fear'd abroad
That with his name the mothers still their babes?
I see report is fabulous and false.
I thought I should have seen some Hercules,
A second Hector, for his grim aspect
And large proportion of his strong-knit limbs.
Alas, this is a child, a silly dwarf!
It cannot be this weak and writhled shrimp
Should strike such terror to his enemies.

Tal. Madam, I have been bold to trouble you;
But since your ladyship is not at leisure,
I'll sort some other time to visit you. [*Going.*]

Count. What means he now? Go ask him whither he goes.

Mess. Stay, my Lord Talbot; for my lady craves
To know the cause of your abrupt departure.

Tal. Marry, for that she's in a wrong belief,
I go to certify her Talbot's here.

Enter *Porter* with keys.

Count. If thou be he, then art thou prisoner.

Tal. Prisoner? to whom?

Count. To me, bloodthirsty lord!
And for that cause I train'd thee to my house.
Long time thy shadow hath been thrall to me,

For in my gallery thy picture hangs;
But now the substance shall endure the like,
And I will chain these legs and arms of thine
That hast by tyranny these many years
Wasted our country, slain our citizens,
And sent our sons and husbands captivate.

Tal. Ha, ha, ha!

Count. Laughest thou, wretch? Thy mirth shall turn to moan.

Tal. I laugh to see your ladyship so fond
To think that you have aught but Talbot's shadow
Whereon to practise your severity.

Count. Why? Art not thou the man?

Tal. I am indeed.

Count. Then have I substance too.

Tal. No, no! I am but shadow of myself.
You are deceiv'd, my substance is not here;
For what you see is but the smallest part
And least proportion of humanity.
I tell you, madam, were the whole frame here,
It is of such a spacious lofty pitch
Your roof were not sufficient to contain't.

Count. This is a riddling merchant for the nonce!
He will be here, and yet he is not here.
How can these contrarieties agree?

Tal. That will I show you presently.

Winds his horn. Drums strike up. A peal of ordinance. Enter *Soldiers.*

How say you, madam? Are you now persuaded
That Talbot is but shadow of himself?
These are his substance, sinews, arms, and strength,
With which he yoketh your rebellious necks,
Razeth your cities, and subverts your towns
And in a moment makes them desolate.

Count. Victorious Talbot, pardon my abuse!
I find thou art no less than fame hath bruited,
And more than may be gathered by thy shape.
Let my presumption not provoke thy wrath,
For I am sorry that with reverence
I did not entertain thee as thou art.

Tal. Be not dismay'd, fair lady, nor misconster
The mind of Talbot as you did mistake
The outward composition of his body.
What you have done hath not offended me;
Nor other satisfaction do I crave
But only, with your patience, that we may
Taste of your wine and see what cates you have;
For soldiers' stomachs always serve them well.

Count. With all my heart, and think me honoured
To feast so great a warrior in my house.

Exeunt.

[Scene IV. *London. The Temple Garden.*]

Enter *Richard Plantagenet, Warwick, Somerset, Pole* [*Earl of Suffolk, Vernon,*] and others.

Rich. Great lords and gentlemen, what means this silence?
Dare no man answer in a case of truth?

Suf. Within the Temple Hall we were too loud.
The Garden here is more convenient.

Rich. Then say at once if I maintain'd the truth;
Or else was wrangling Somerset in th' error?

Suf. Faith, I have been a truant in the law
And never yet could frame my will to it,
And therefore frame the law unto my will.

Som. Judge you, my Lord of Warwick, then between us.

War. Between two hawks, which flies the higher pitch —
Between two dogs, which hath the deeper mouth —
Between two blades, which bears the better temper —
Between two horses, which doth bear him best —
Between two girls, which hath the merriest eye —
I have perhaps some shallow spirit of judgment;
But in these nice sharp quillets of the law,
Good faith, I am no wiser than a daw.

Rich. Tut, tut! here is a mannerly forbearance.
The truth appears so naked on my side
That any purblind eye may find it out.

Som. And on my side it is so well apparell'd,
So clear, so shining, and so evident,
That it will glimmer through a blind man's eye.

Rich. Since you are tongue-tied and so loath to speak,
In dumb significants proclaim your thoughts.
Let him that is a true-born gentleman
And stands upon the honour of his birth,
If he suppose that I have pleaded truth,
From off this brier pluck a white rose with me.

Som. Let him that is no coward nor no flatterer.

But dare maintain the party of the truth,
Pluck a red rose from off this thorn with me.
War. I love no colours, and without all colour
Of base insinuating flattery
I pluck this white rose with Plantagenet.
Suf. I pluck this red rose with young Somerset,
And say withal I think he held the right.
Ver. Stay, lords and gentlemen, and pluck no more
Till you conclude that he upon whose side
The fewest roses are cropp'd from the tree
Shall yield the other in the right opinion.
Som. Good Master Vernon, it is well objected.
If I have fewest, I subscribe in silence.
Rich. And I.
Ver. Then for the truth and plainness of the case
I pluck this pale and maiden blossom here,
Giving my verdict on the white rose side.
Som. Prick not your finger as you pluck it off,
Lest, bleeding, you do paint the white rose red
And fall on my side so against your will.
Ver. If I, my lord, for my opinion bleed,
Opinion shall be surgeon to my hurt
And keep me on the side where still I am.
Som. Well, well, come on! Who else?
Lawyer. [*to Somerset*] Unless my study and my books be false,
The argument you held was wrong in you;
In sign whereof I pluck a white rose too.
Rich. Now, Somerset, where is your argument?
Som. Here in my scabbard, meditating that
Shall dye your white rose in a bloody red.
Rich. Meantime your cheeks do counterfeit our roses;
For pale they look with fear, as witnessing
The truth on our side.
Som. No, Plantagenet!
'Tis not for fear, but anger, that thy cheeks
Blush for pure shame to counterfeit our roses,
And yet thy tongue will not confess thy error.
Rich. Hath not thy rose a canker, Somerset?
Som. Hath not thy rose a thorn, Plantagenet?
Rich. Ay, sharp and piercing, to maintain his truth,
Whiles thy consuming canker eats his falsehood.
Som. Well, I'll find friends to wear my bleeding roses,
That shall maintain what I have said is true
Where false Plantagenet dare not be seen.
Rich. Now by this maiden blossom in my hand,
I scorn thee and thy faction, peevish boy!
Suf. Turn not thy scorns this way, Plantagenet.
Rich. Proud Pole, I will, and scorn both him and thee.
Suf. I'll turn my part thereof into thy throat.
Som. Away, away, good William de la Pole!
We grace the yeoman by conversing with him.
War. Now, by God's will, thou wrong'st him, Somerset!
His grandfather was Lionel Duke of Clarence,
Third son to the third Edward, King of England.
Spring crestless yeomen from so deep a root?
Rich. He bears him on the place's privilege,
Or durst not for his craven heart say thus.
Som. By him that made me, I'll maintain my words
On any plot of ground in Christendom!
Was not thy father, Richard Earl of Cambridge,
For treason executed in our late king's days?
And by his treason stand'st not thou attainted,
Corrupted, and exempt from ancient gentry?
His trespass yet lives guilty in thy blood,
And till thou be restor'd thou art a yeoman.
Rich. My father was attached, not attainted;
Condemn'd to die for treason, but no traitor;
And that I'll prove on better men than Somerset,
Were growing time once ripened to my will.
For your partaker Pole, and you yourself,
I'll note you in my book of memory
To scourge you for this apprehension.
Look to it well and say you are well warn'd.
Som. Ah, thou shalt find us ready for thee still;
And know us by these colours for thy foes,
For these my friends in spite of thee shall wear.
Rich. And, by my soul, this pale and angry rose,
As cognizance of my blood-drinking hate,
Will I for ever, and my faction, wear
Until it wither with me to my grave
Or flourish to the height of my degree.
Suf. Go forward, and be chok'd with thy ambition!
And so farewell until I meet thee next. *Exit*
Som. Have with thee, Pole. Farewell, ambitious Richard. *Exit.*
Rich. How I am brav'd and must perforce endure it!
War. This blot that they object against your house

Shall be wip'd out in the next parliament,
Call'd for the truce of Winchester and Gloucester;
And if thou be not then created York,
I will not live to be accounted Warwick.
Meantime, in signal of my love to thee,
Against proud Somerset and William Pole
Will I upon thy party wear this rose;
And here I prophesy: this brawl to-day
Grown to this faction in the Temple Garden
Shall send, between the Red Rose and the White,
A thousand souls to death and deadly night.

Rich. Good Master Vernon, I am bound to you
That you on my behalf would pluck a flower.

Ver. In your behalf still will I wear the same.

Lawyer. And so will I.

Rich. Thanks, gentle sir.
Come, let us four to dinner. I dare say
This quarrel will drink blood another day.
Exeunt.

[Scene V. *The Tower of London.*]

Enter *Mortimer*, brought in a chair, and *Jailers.*

Mor. Kind keepers of my weak decaying age,
Let dying Mortimer here rest himself.
Even like a man new haled from the rack,
So fare my limbs with long imprisonment;
And these grey locks, the pursuivants of death,
Nestor-like aged in an age of care,
Argue the end of Edmund Mortimer.
These eyes, like lamps whose wasting oil is spent,
Wax dim, as drawing to their exigent;
Weak shoulders, overborne with burthening grief,
And pithless arms, like to a withered vine
That droops his sapless branches to the ground.
Yet are these feet (whose strengthless stay is numb,
Unable to support this lump of clay)
Swift-winged with desire to get a grave,
As witting I no other comfort have.
But tell me, keeper, will my nephew come?

Keeper. Richard Plantagenet, my lord, will come.
We sent unto the Temple, unto his chamber,
And answer was return'd that he will come.

Mor. Enough. My soul shall then be satisfied.
Poor gentleman! his wrong doth equal mine.
Since Henry Monmouth first began to reign
Before whose glory I was great in arms,
This loathsome sequestration have I had;
And even since then hath Richard been obscur'd,
Depriv'd of honour and inheritance.
But now the arbitrator of despairs,
Just Death, kind umpire of men's miseries,
With sweet enlargement doth dismiss me hence.
I would his troubles likewise were expir'd,
That so he might recover what was lost.

Enter *Richard* [*Plantagenet*].

Keeper. My lord, your loving nephew now is come.

Mor. Richard Plantagenet, friend, is he come?

Rich. Ay, noble uncle, thus ignobly us'd,
Your nephew, late despised Richard, comes.

Mor. Direct mine arms I may embrace his neck
And in his bosom spend my latter gasp.
O, tell me when my lips do touch his cheeks,
That I may kindly give one fainting kiss!
And now declare, sweet stem from York's great stock,
Why didst thou say of late thou wert despis'd?

Rich. First lean thine aged back against mine arm,
And in that ease I'll tell thee my disease.
This day in argument upon a case
Some words there grew 'twixt Somerset and me;
Among which terms he us'd his lavish tongue
And did upbraid me with my father's death;
Which obloquy set bars before my tongue,
Else with the like I had requited him.
Therefore, good uncle, for my father's sake,
In honour of a true Plantagenet,
And for alliance sake, declare the cause
My father, Earl of Cambridge, lost his head.

Mor. That cause, fair nephew, that imprison'd me
And hath detain'd me all my flow'ring youth
Within a loathsome dungeon, there to pine,
Was cursed instrument of his decease.

Rich. Discover more at large what cause that was,
For I am ignorant and cannot guess.

Mor. I will, if that my fading breath permit
And death approach not ere my tale be done.
Henry the Fourth, grandfather to this king,
Depos'd his nephew Richard, Edward's son.
The first-begotten and the lawful heir
Of Edward king, the third of that descent;
During whose reign, the Percies of the North,

Finding his usurpation most unjust,
Endeavour'd my advancement to the throne.
The reason mov'd these warlike lords to this
Was for that (young King Richard thus remov'd,
Leaving no heir begotten of his body)
I was the next by birth and parentage;
For by my mother I derived am
From Lionel Duke of Clarence, third son
To King Edward the Third; whereas he
From John of Gaunt doth bring his pedigree,
Being but fourth of that heroic line.
But mark! As in this haughty great attempt
They laboured to plant the rightful heir,
I lost my liberty, and they their lives.
Long after this, when Henry the Fifth
(Succeeding his father Bolingbroke) did reign,
Thy father, Earl of Cambridge, then deriv'd
From famous Edmund Langley, Duke of York,
Marrying my sister that thy mother was,
Again, in pity of my hard distress,
Levied an army, weening to redeem
And have install'd me in the diadem;
But, as the rest, so fell that noble earl,
And was beheaded. Thus the Mortimers,
In whom the title rested, were suppress'd.

Rich. Of which, my lord, your Honour is the last.

Mor. True, and thou seest that I no issue have,
And that my fainting words do warrant death.
Thou art my heir. The rest I wish thee gather;
But yet be wary in thy studious care.

Rich. Thy grave admonishments prevail with me.
But yet methinks my father's execution
Was nothing less than bloody tyranny.

Mor. With silence, nephew, be thou politic.
Strong fixed is the house of Lancaster
And like a mountain, not to be remov'd.
But now thy uncle is removing hence,
As princes do their courts when they are cloy'd
With long continuance in a settled place.

Rich. O uncle, would some part of my young years
Might but redeem the passage of your age!

Mor. Thou dost then wrong me, as that slaughterer doth
Which giveth many wounds when one will kill.
Mourn not, except thou sorrow for my good;
Only give order for my funeral.
And so farewell, and fair be all thy hopes,
And prosperous be thy life in peace and war! *Dies.*

Rich. And peace, no war, befall thy parting soul!
In prison hast thou spent a pilgrimage
And like a hermit overpass'd thy days.
Well, I will lock his counsel in my breast,
And what I do imagine, let that rest.
Keepers, convey him hence, and I myself
Will see his burial better than his life.
Exeunt [*Jailers, with Mortimer's body*].
Here dies the dusky torch of Mortimer,
Chok'd with ambition of the meaner sort.
And for those wrongs, those bitter injuries,
Which Somerset hath offer'd to my house
I doubt not but with honour to redress;
And therefore haste I to the parliament,
Either to be restored to my blood
Or make my ill th' advantage of my good. *Exit.*

ACT III. Scene I. [*London. The Parliament House.*]

Flourish. Enter *King, Exeter, Gloucester, Winchester, Warwick, Somerset, Suffolk, Richard Plantagenet,* [and others]. *Gloucester* offers to put up a bill. *Winchester* snatches it, tears it.

Win. Com'st thou with deep premeditated lines?
With written pamphlets studiously devis'd?
Humphrey of Gloucester, if thou canst accuse
Or aught intend'st to lay unto my charge,
Do it without invention, suddenly,
As I with sudden and extemporal speech
Purpose to answer what thou canst object.

Glou. Presumptuous priest, this place commands my patience,
Or thou shouldst find thou hast dishonour'd me.
Think not, although in writing I preferr'd
The manner of thy vile outrageous crimes,
That therefore I have forg'd, or am not able
Verbatim to rehearse the method of my pen.
No, prelate! Such is thy audacious wickedness,
Thy lewd, pestiferous, and dissentious pranks,
As very infants prattle of thy pride.
Thou art a most pernicious usurer;
Froward by nature, enemy to peace,
Lascivious, wanton, more than well beseems
A man of thy profession and degree.
And for thy treachery, what's more manifest?
In that thou laid'st a trap to take my life
As well at London Bridge as at the Tower.

Beside, I fear me, if thy thoughts were sifted,
The King thy sovereign is not quite exempt
From envious malice of thy swelling heart.
Win. Gloucester, I do defy thee. Lords, vouchsafe
To give me hearing what I shall reply.
If I were covetous, ambitious, or perverse,
As he will have me — how am I so poor?
Or how haps it I seek not to advance
Or raise myself, but keep my wonted calling?
And for dissension, who preferreth peace
More than I do, except I be provok'd?
No, my good lords, it is not that offends;
It is not that that hath incens'd the Duke.
It is because no one should sway but he,
No one but he should be about the King;
And that engenders thunder in his breast
And makes him roar these accusations forth.
But he shall know I am as good —
Glou. As good?
Thou bastard of my grandfather!
Win. Ay, lordly sir! For what are you, I pray,
But one imperious in another's throne?
Glou. Am I not Protector, saucy priest?
Win. And am not I a prelate of the Church?
Glou. Yes, as an outlaw in a castle keeps
And useth it to patronage his theft.
Win. Unreverent Gloucester.
Glou. Thou art reverent
Touching thy spiritual function, not thy life.
Win. Rome shall remedy this.
War. Roam thither then!
Som. My lord, it were your duty to forbear.
War. Ay, see the Bishop be not overborne.
Som. Methinks my lord should be religious
And know the office that belongs to such.
War. Methinks his lordship should be humbler.
It fitteth not a prelate so to plead.
Som. Yes, when his holy state is touch'd so near.
War. State holy, or unhallow'd, what of that?
Is not his Grace Protector to the King?
Rich. [*aside*] Plantagenet, I see, must hold his tongue,
Lest it be said 'Speak, sirrah, when you should!
Must your bold verdict enter talk with lords?'
Else would I have a fling at Winchester.
King. Uncles of Gloucester and of Winchester,
The special watchmen of our English weal,
I would prevail, if prayers might prevail,
To join your hearts in love and amity.
O, what a scandal is it to our crown
That two such noble peers as ye should jar!
Believe me, lords, my tender years can tell
Civil dissension is a viperous worm
That gnaws the bowels of the commonwealth.

A noise within, 'Down with the Tawny Coats!'

King. What tumult 's this?
War. An uproar, I dare warrant,
Begun through malice of the Bishop's men.

A noise again [*within*], 'Stones! stones!'

Enter *Mayor* [*of London*, attended].

May. O my good lords, and virtuous Henry,
Pity the city of London, pity us!
The Bishop and the Duke of Gloucester's men,
Forbidden late to carry any weapon,
Have fill'd their pockets full of pebble stones
And, banding themselves in contrary parts,
Do pelt so fast at one another's pate
That many have their giddy brains knock'd out.
Our windows are broke down in every street
And we, for fear, compell'd to shut our shops.

Enter in skirmish [*Servingmen* of *Gloucester* and *Winchester*] with bloody pates.

King. We charge you, on allegiance to ourself,
To hold your slaught'ring hands and keep the peace.
Pray, uncle Gloucester, mitigate this strife.
1. Serv. Nay, if we be forbidden stones, we'll fall to it with our teeth.
2. Serv. Do what ye dare, we are as resolute.
Skirmish again.
Glou. You of my household, leave this peevish broil
And set this unaccustom'd fight aside.
3. Serv. My lord, we know your Grace to be a man
Just and upright, and for your royal birth
Inferior to none but to his Majesty;
And ere that we will suffer such a prince,
So kind a father of the commonweal,
To be disgraced by an inkhorn mate,
We and our wives and children all will fight
And have our bodies slaught'red by thy foes.
1. Serv. Ay, and the very parings of our nails
Shall pitch a field when we are dead.
Begin again.
Glou. Stay, stay, I say!
And if you love me, as you say you do,
Let me persuade you to forbear awhile.
King. O, how this discord doth afflict my soul!
Can you, my Lord of Winchester, behold

My sighs and tears and will not once relent?
Who should be pitiful if you be not?
Or who should study to prefer a peace
If holy churchmen take delight in broils?

War. Yield, my Lord Protector! yield, Winchester!
Except you mean with obstinate repulse
To slay your sovereign and destroy the realm.
You see what mischief, and what murther too,
Hath been enacted through your enmity.
Then be at peace, except ye thirst for blood.

Win. He shall submit, or I will never yield.

Glou. Compassion on the King commands me stoop,
Or I would see his heart out ere the priest
Should ever get that privilege of me.

War. Behold, my Lord of Winchester, the Duke
Hath banish'd moody discontented fury,
As by his smoothed brows it doth appear.
Why look you still so stern and tragical?

Glou. Here, Winchester, I offer thee my hand.

King. Fie, uncle Beaufort! I have heard you preach
That malice was a great and grievous sin;
And will not you maintain the thing you teach,
But prove a chief offender in the same?

War. [*aside*] Sweet King! The Bishop hath a kindly gird.—
For shame, my Lord of Winchester, relent!
What, shall a child instruct you what to do?

Win. Well, Duke of Gloucester, I will yield to thee.
Love for thy love and hand for hand I give.

Glou. [*aside*] Ay, but I fear me with a hollow heart!—
See here, my friends and loving countrymen:
This token serveth for a flag of truce
Betwixt ourselves and all our followers.
So help me God as I dissemble not!

Win. [*aside*] So help me God as I intend it not!

King. O loving uncle, kind Duke of Gloucester,
How joyful am I made by this contract!
Away, my masters! Trouble us no more,
But join in friendship, as your lords have done.

1. Serv. Content. I'll to the surgeon's.

2. Serv. And so will I.

3. Serv. And I will see what physic the tavern affords.

Exeunt [*Servingmen, Mayor, &c.*].

War. Accept this scroll, most gracious sovereign,
Which in the right of Richard Plantagenet
We do exhibit to your Majesty.

Glou. Well urg'd, my Lord of Warwick; for, sweet prince,
An if your Grace mark every circumstance,
You have great reason to do Richard right,
Especially for those occasions
At Eltham Place I told your Majesty.

King. And those occasions, uncle, were of force.
Therefore, my loving lords, our pleasure is
That Richard be restored to his blood.

War. Let Richard be restored to his blood.
So shall his father's wrongs be recompens'd.

Win. As will the rest, so willeth Winchester.

King. If Richard will be true, not that alone
But all the whole inheritance I give
That doth belong unto the house of York,
From whence you spring by lineal descent.

Rich. Thy humble servant vows obedience
And humble service till the point of death.

King. Stoop then and set your knee against my foot,
And in reguerdon of that duty done
I girt thee with the valiant sword of York.
Rise, Richard, like a true Plantagenet,
And rise created princely Duke of York.

Rich. And so thrive Richard as thy foes may fall!
And as my duty springs, so perish they
That grudge one thought against your Majesty!

All. Welcome, high prince, the mighty Duke of York!

Som. [*aside*] Perish, base prince, ignoble Duke of York!

Glou. Now will it best avail your Majesty
To cross the seas and to be crown'd in France.
The presence of a king engenders love
Amongst his subjects and his loyal friends,
As it disanimates his enemies.

King. When Gloucester says the word, King Henry goes,
For friendly counsel cuts off many foes.

Glou. Your ships already are in readiness.

Sennet. Flourish. Exeunt. Manet Exeter.

Exe. Ay, we may march in England or in France,
Not seeing what is likely to ensue.
This late dissension grown betwixt the peers
Burns under feigned ashes of forg'd love
And will at last break out into a flame.
As fest'red members rot but by degree
Till bones and flesh and sinews fall away,
So will this base and envious discord breed.
And now I fear that fatal prophecy

Which in the time of Henry nam'd the Fifth
Was in the mouth of every sucking babe:
That Henry born at Monmouth should win all
And Henry born at Windsor should lose all;
Which is so plain that Exeter doth wish
His days may finish ere that hapless time.
Exit.

Scene II. [*Before Rouen.*]

Enter *Pucelle* disguis'd, with four *Soldiers* [dressed like *Countrymen*] with sacks upon their backs.

Puc. These are the city gates, the gates of Roan,
Through which our policy must make a breach.
Take heed, be wary how you place your words;
Talk like the vulgar sort of marketmen
That come to gather money for their corn.
If we have entrance, as I hope we shall,
And that we find the slothful watch but weak,
I'll by a sign give notice to our friends,
That Charles the Dauphin may encounter them.

Soldier. Our sacks shall be a mean to sack the city,
And we be lords and rulers over Roan.
Therefore we'll knock. *Knock.*

Watch. [*within*] Qui est là?

Puc. Paysans, pauvres gens de France,
Poor market folks that come to sell their corn.

Watch. Enter, go in; the market bell is rung.

Puc. Now, Roan, I'll shake thy bulwarks to the ground. *Exeunt.*

Enter *Charles, Bastard, Alençon,* [*Reignier,* and *Soldiers*].

Char. Saint Denis bless this happy stratagem,
And once again we'll sleep secure in Roan.

Bast. Here ent'red Pucelle and her practisants.
Now she is there, how will she specify
Where is the best and safest passage in?

Reig. By thrusting out a torch from yonder tower,
Which, once discern'd, shows that her meaning is,
No way to that (for weakness) which she ent'red.

Enter *Pucelle* on the top, thrusting out a torch burning.

Puc. Behold, this is the happy wedding torch
That joineth Roan unto her countrymen,
But burning fatal to the Talbonites.

Bast. See, noble Charles, the beacon of our friend.
The burning torch in yonder turret stands.

Char. Now shine it like a comet of revenge,
A prophet to the fall of all our foes!

Reig. Defer no time; delays have dangerous ends.
Enter and cry 'The Dauphin!' presently,
And then do execution on the watch.

Alarum. [*They enter the town. Exit Pucelle above.*]

An Alarum. [Enter, from the town,] *Talbot* [and *English Soldiers*] in an excursion.

Tal. France, thou shalt rue this treason with thy tears
If Talbot but survive thy treachery.
Pucelle, that witch, that damned sorceress,
Hath wrought this hellish mischief unawares,
That hardly we escap'd the pride of France.
Exeunt.

An Alarum. Excursions. Bedford brought in sick in a chair. Enter *Talbot* and *Burgundy* without; within, *Pucelle, Charles, Bastard,* [*Alençon,*] and *Reignier* on the walls.

Puc. Good morrow, gallants! Want ye corn for bread?
I think the Duke of Burgundy will fast
Before he'll buy again at such a rate.
'Twas full of darnel. Do you like the taste?

Bur. Scoff on, vile fiend and shameless courtesan!
I trust ere long to choke thee with thine own
And make thee curse the harvest of that corn.

Char. Your Grace may starve, perhaps, before that time.

Bed. O, let no words, but deeds, revenge this treason!

Puc. What will you do, good greybeard? break a lance
And run a-tilt at death within a chair?

Tal. Foul fiend of France and hag of all despite,
Encompass'd with thy lustful paramours,
Becomes it thee to taunt his valiant age
And twit with cowardice a man half dead?
Damsel, I'll have a bout with you again,
Or else let Talbot perish with this shame.

Puc. Are ye so hot, sir? Yet, Pucelle, hold thy peace.
If Talbot do but thunder, rain will follow.

They [*i.e. Talbot, Bedford, and Burgundy*] *whisper together in counsel.*

God speed the parliament! Who shall be the Speaker?
Tal. Dare ye come forth and meet us in the field?
Puc. Belike your lordship takes us then for fools,
To try if that our own be ours or no.
Tal. I speak not to that railing Hecate,
But unto thee, Alençon, and the rest.
Will ye, like soldiers, come and fight it out?
Alen. Signior, no.
Tal. Signior, hang! Base muleters of France!
Like peasant footboys do they keep the walls
And dare not take up arms like gentlemen.
Puc. Away, captains! Let's get us from the walls,
For Talbot means no goodness by his looks.
God b'uy, my lord! We came but to tell you
That we are here.

Exeunt [Pucelle and the French] from the walls.

Tal. And there will we be too ere it be long,
Or else reproach be Talbot's greatest fame!
Vow, Burgundy, by honour of thy house,
Prick'd on by public wrongs sustain'd in France,
Either to get the town again or die;
And I, as sure as English Henry lives
And as his father here was conqueror,
As sure as in this late betrayed town
Great Cœur-de-lion's heart was buried —
So sure I swear to get the town or die.
Bur. My vows are equal partners with thy vows.
Tal. But, ere we go, regard this dying prince,
The valiant Duke of Bedford. Come, my lord,
We will bestow you in some better place,
Fitter for sickness and for crazy age.
Bed. Lord Talbot, do not so dishonour me.
Here will I sit, before the walls of Roan,
And will be partner of your weal or woe.
Bur. Courageous Bedford, let us now persuade you.
Bed. Not to be gone from hence; for once I read
That stout Pendragon in his litter sick
Came to the field and vanquished his foes.
Methinks I should revive the soldiers' hearts,
Because I ever found them as myself.
Tal. Undaunted spirit in a dying breast!
Then be it so. Heavens keep old Bedford safe!
And now no more ado, brave Burgundy,
But gather we our forces out of hand
And set upon our boasting enemy.

Exeunt [to the assault all but Bedford and Attendants].

An Alarum. Excursions. Enter *Sir John Fastolfe* and a *Captain.*

Capt. Whither away, Sir John Fastolfe, in such haste?
Fast. Whither away? To save myself by flight.
We are like to have the overthrow again.
Capt. What? Will you fly and leave Lord Talbot?
Fast. Ay!
All the Talbots in the world, to save my life. *Exit.*
Capt. Cowardly knight, ill fortune follow thee! *Exit.*

Retreat. Excursions. Pucelle, Alençon, and Charles fly.

Bed. Now, quiet soul, depart when heaven please,
For I have seen our enemies' overthrow.
What is the trust or strength of foolish man?
They that of late were daring with their scoffs
Are glad and fain by flight to save themselves.

Bedford dies and is carried in by two in his chair.

An Alarum. Enter *Talbot, Burgundy,* and the rest.

Tal. Lost and recovered in a day again!
This is a double honour, Burgundy.
Yet heavens have glory for this victory!
Bur. Warlike and martial Talbot, Burgundy
Enshrines thee in his heart and there erects
Thy noble deeds as valour's monuments.
Tal. Thanks, gentle Duke. But where is Pucelle now?
I think her old familiar is asleep.
Now where's the Bastard's braves and Charles his glikes?
What, all amort? Roan hangs her head for grief
That such a valiant company are fled.
Now will we take some order in the town,
Placing therein some expert officers,
And then depart to Paris to the King,
For there young Henry with his nobles lie.
Bur. What wills Lord Talbot pleaseth Burgundy.
Tal. But yet, before we go, let's not forget
The noble Duke of Bedford, late deceas'd,
But see his exequies fulfill'd in Roan.
A braver soldier never couched lance,
A gentler heart did never sway in court.
But kings and mightiest potentates must die,
For that's the end of human misery. *Exeunt.*

Scene III. [*The plains near Rouen.*]

Enter *Charles, Bastard, Alençon, Pucelle,* [and *Soldiers*].

Puc. Dismay not, princes, at this accident,
Nor grieve that Roan is so recovered.
Care is no cure, but rather corrosive,
For things that are not to be remedied.
Let frantic Talbot triumph for a while
And like a peacock sweep along his tail;
We'll pull his plumes and take away his train,
If Dauphin and the rest will be but rul'd.

Char. We have been guided by thee hitherto
And of thy cunning had no diffidence.
One sudden foil shall never breed distrust.

Bast. Search out thy wit for secret policies,
And we will make thee famous through the world.

Alen. We'll set thy statue in some holy place
And have thee reverenc'd like a blessed saint.
Employ thee then, sweet virgin, for our good.

Puc. Then thus it must be; this doth Joan devise:
By fair persuasions, mix'd with sug'red words,
We will entice the Duke of Burgundy
To leave the Talbot and to follow us.

Char. Ay, marry, sweeting, if we could do that,
France were no place for Henry's warriors,
Nor should that nation boast it so with us,
But be extirped from our provinces.

Alen. For ever should they be expuls'd from France
And not have title of an earldom here.

Puc. Your Honours shall perceive how I will work
To bring this matter to the wished end.
Drum sounds afar off.
Hark! by the sound of drum you may perceive
Their powers are marching unto Paris-ward.

Here sound an English march. [Enter, and pass over at a distance, *Talbot* and his *Troops.*]

There goes the Talbot, with his colours spread,
And all the troops of English after him.

French march. [Enter the *Duke of Burgundy* and his *Troops.*]

Now in the rearward comes the Duke and his.
Fortune in favour makes him lag behind.
Summon a parley; we will talk with him.
Trumpets sound a parley.

Char. A parley with the Duke of Burgundy!

Bur. Who craves a parley with the Burgundy?

Puc. The princely Charles of France, thy countryman.

Bur. What say'st thou, Charles? for I am marching hence.

Char. Speak, Pucelle, and enchant him with thy words.

Puc. Brave Burgundy, undoubted hope of France,
Stay, let thy humble handmaid speak to thee!

Bur. Speak on; but be not over-tedious.

Puc. Look on thy country, look on fertile France,
And see the cities and the towns defac'd
By wasting ruin of the cruel foe,
As looks the mother on her lowly babe
When death doth close his tender dying eyes.
See, see the pining malady of France!
Behold the wounds, the most unnatural wounds,
Which thou thyself hast given her woful breast!
O, turn thy edged sword another way;
Strike those that hurt, and hurt not those that help!
One drop of blood drawn from thy country's bosom
Should grieve thee more than streams of foreign gore.
Return thee therefore with a flood of tears
And wash away thy country's stained spots.

Bur. [*aside*] Either she hath bewitch'd me with her words,
Or nature makes me suddenly relent.

Puc. Besides, all French and France exclaims on thee,
Doubting thy birth and lawful progeny.
Who join'st thou with but with a lordly nation
That will not trust thee but for profit's sake?
When Talbot hath set footing once in France
And fashion'd thee that instrument of ill,
Who then but English Henry will be lord,
And thou be thrust out like a fugitive?
Call we to mind — and mark but this for proof:
Was not the Duke of Orleans thy foe?
And was he not in England prisoner?
But when they heard he was thine enemy,
They set him free without his ransom paid,
In spite of Burgundy and all his friends.
See then, thou fight'st against thy countrymen
And join'st with them will be thy slaughtermen.
Come, come, return! Return, thou wandering lord!
Charles and the rest will take thee in their arms.

Bur. [*aside*] I am vanquished! These haughty words of hers

Have batt'red me like roaring cannon-shot
And made me almost yield upon my knees.—
Forgive me, country, and sweet countrymen!
And, lords, accept this hearty kind embrace.
My forces and my power of men are yours.
So farewell, Talbot! I'll no longer trust thee.

Puc. Done like a Frenchman — [*aside*] turn and turn again!

Char. Welcome, brave Duke! Thy friendship makes us fresh.

Bast. And doth beget new courage in our breasts.

Alen. Pucelle hath bravely play'd her part in this
And doth deserve a coronet of gold.

Char. Now let us on, my lords, and join our powers,
And seek how we may prejudice the foe.

Exeunt.

Scene IV. [*Paris. The Palace.*]

Enter the *King, Gloucester, Winchester,* [*Richard Duke of*] *York, Suffolk, Somerset, Warwick, Exeter,* [*Vernon, Basset,* and others]. To them, with his *Soldiers, Talbot.*

Tal. My gracious prince, and honourable peers,
Hearing of your arrival in this realm,
I have awhile given truce unto my wars
To do my duty to my sovereign;
In sign whereof this arm that hath reclaim'd
To your obedience fifty fortresses,
Twelve cities, and seven walled towns of strength,
Beside five hundred prisoners of esteem,
Lets fall his sword before your Highness' feet
[*Kneels.*]
And with submissive loyalty of heart
Ascribes the glory of his conquest got
First to my God and next unto your Grace.

King. Is this the Lord Talbot, uncle Gloucester,
That hath so long been resident in France?

Glou. Yes, if it please your Majesty, my liege.

King. Welcome, brave captain and victorious lord!
When I was young (as yet I am not old)
I do remember how my father said
A stouter champion never handled sword.
Long since we were resolved of your truth,
Your faithful service, and your toil in war;
Yet never have you tasted our reward
Or been reguerdon'd with so much as thanks,
Because till now we never saw your face.
Therefore stand up, and for these good deserts
We here create you Earl of Shrewsbury,
And in our coronation take your place.

Sennet. Flourish. Exeunt. Manent Vernon and Basset.

Ver. Now, sir, to you, that were so hot at sea,
Disgracing of these colours that I wear
In honour of my noble Lord of York —
Dar'st thou maintain the former words thou spak'st?

Bas. Yes, sir, as well as you dare patronage
The envious barking of your saucy tongue
Against my lord the Duke of Somerset.

Ver. Sirrah, thy lord I honour as he is.

Bas. Why, what is he? As good a man as York.

Ver. Hark ye! Not so. In witness take ye that.
Strikes him.

Bas. Villain, thou knowest the law of arms is such
That whoso draws a sword, 'tis present death,
Or else this blow should broach thy dearest blood.
But I'll unto his Majesty and crave
I may have liberty to venge this wrong,
When thou shalt see I'll meet thee to thy cost.

Ver. Well, miscreant, I'll be there as soon as you,
And after meet you, sooner than you would.

Exeunt.

ACT IV. Scene I. [*Paris. A room of state in the Palace.*]

Enter *King, Gloucester, Winchester, York, Suffolk, Somerset, Warwick, Talbot, Exeter,* and *Governor* [*of Paris*].

Glou. Lord Bishop, set the crown upon his head.

Win. God save King Henry, of that name the Sixth!

Glou. Now, Governor of Paris, take your oath, [*Governor kneels.*]
That you elect no other king but him,
Esteem none friends but such as are his friends,
And none your foes but such as shall pretend
Malicious practices against his state.
This shall ye do, so help you righteous God!
[*Governor rises and retires.*]

Enter *Fastolfe.*

Fast. My gracious sovereign, as I rode from Calais
To haste unto your coronation,
A letter was deliver'd to my hands,
Writ to your Grace from th' Duke of Burgundy.
[*Presents it.*]

Tal. Shame to the Duke of Burgundy and thee!
I vow'd, base knight, when I did meet thee next
To tear the Garter from thy craven's leg,
[*Plucks it off.*]
Which I have done, because, unworthily,
Thou wast installed in that high degree.
Pardon me, princely Henry, and the rest.
This dastard, at the battle of Patay,
When, but in all, I was six thousand strong
And that the French were almost ten to one,
Before we met or that a stroke was given,
Like to a trusty squire did run away;
In which assault we lost twelve hundred men.
Myself and divers gentlemen beside
Were there surpris'd and taken prisoners.
Then judge, great lords, if I have done amiss,
Or whether that such cowards ought to wear
This ornament of knighthood — yea or no?

Glou. To say the truth, this fact was infamous,
And ill beseeming any common man;
Much more a knight, a captain, and a leader.

Tal. When first this order was ordain'd, my lords,
Knights of the Garter were of noble birth,
Valiant and virtuous, full of haughty courage,
Such as were grown to credit by the wars;
Not fearing death nor shrinking for distress,
But always resolute in most extremes.
He then that is not furnish'd in this sort
Doth but usurp the sacred name of knight,
Profaning this most honourable order,
And should (if I were worthy to be judge)
Be quite degraded, like a hedge-born swain
That doth presume to boast of gentle blood.

King. Stain to thy countrymen, thou hear'st thy doom!
Be packing therefore, thou that wast a knight.
Henceforth we banish thee on pain of death.
[*Exit Fastolfe.*]
And now, my Lord Protector, view the letter
Sent from our uncle Duke of Burgundy.

Glou. What means his Grace that he hath chang'd his style?
[*Views the superscription.*]
No more but plain and bluntly 'To the King'?
Hath he forgot he is his sovereign?
Or doth this churlish superscription
Pretend some alteration in good will?
What's here? [*Reads*] 'I have, upon especial cause,
Mov'd with compassion of my country's wrack
Together with the pitiful complaints
Of such as your oppression feeds upon,
Forsaken your pernicious faction
And join'd with Charles, the rightful King of France.'
O monstrous treachery! Can this be so?
That in alliance, amity, and oaths
There should be found such false dissembling guile?

King. What? Doth my uncle Burgundy revolt?

Glou. He doth, my lord, and is become your foe.

King. Is that the worst this letter doth contain?

Glou. It is the worst, and all, my lord, he writes.

King. Why, then Lord Talbot there shall talk with him
And give him chastisement for this abuse.
How say you, my lord? Are you not content?

Tal. Content, my liege? Yes. But that I am prevented,
I should have begg'd I might have been employ'd.

King. Then gather strength and march unto him straight.
Let him perceive how ill we brook his treason
And what offence it is to flout his friends.

Tal. I go, my lord, in heart desiring still
You may behold confusion of your foes.
[*Exit.*]

Enter *Vernon* and *Basset.*

Ver. Grant me the combat, gracious sovereign!

Bas. And me, my lord — grant me the combat too!

York. This is my servant. Hear him, noble prince!

Som. And this is mine. Sweet Henry, favour him!

King. Be patient, lords, and give them leave to speak.
Say, gentlemen, what makes you thus exclaim?
And wherefore crave you combat? or with whom?

Ver. With him, my lord, for he hath done me wrong.

Bas. And I with him, for he hath done me wrong.
King. What is that wrong whereof you both complain?
First let me know, and then I'll answer you.
Bas. Crossing the sea from England into France,
This fellow here with envious carping tongue
Upbraided me about the rose I wear,
Saying the sanguine colour of the leaves
Did represent my master's blushing cheeks
When stubbornly he did repugn the truth
About a certain question in the law
Argu'd betwixt the Duke of York and him —
With other vile and ignominious terms;
In confutation of which rude reproach,
And in defence of my lord's worthiness,
I crave the benefit of law of arms.
Ver. And that is my petition, noble lord.
For though he seem with forged quaint conceit
To set a gloss upon his bold intent,
Yet know, my lord, I was provok'd by him,
And he first took exceptions at this badge,
Pronouncing that the paleness of this flower
Bewray'd the faintness of my master's heart.
York. Will not this malice, Somerset, be left?
Som. Your private grudge, my Lord of York, will out,
Though ne'er so cunningly you smother it.
King. Good Lord, what madness rules in brainsick men
When for so slight and frivolous a cause
Such factious emulations shall arise!
Good cousins both, of York and Somerset,
Quiet yourselves, I pray, and be at peace.
York. Let this dissension first be tried by fight,
And then your Highness shall command a peace.
Som. The quarrel toucheth none but us alone.
Betwixt ourselves let us decide it then.
York. There is my pledge. Accept it, Somerset.
Ver. Nay, let it rest where it began at first.
Bas. Confirm it so, mine honourable lord.
Glou. Confirm it so? Confounded be your strife!
And perish ye with your audacious prate!
Presumptuous vassals, are you not asham'd
With this immodest clamorous outrage
To trouble and disturb the King and us?
And you, my lords, methinks you do not well
To bear with their perverse objections;
Much less to take occasion from their mouths
To raise a mutiny betwixt yourselves.
Let me persuade you take a better course.
Exe. It grieves his Highness. Good my lords, be friends.
King. Come hither you that would be combatants.
Henceforth I charge you, as you love our favour,
Quite to forget this quarrel and the cause.
And you, my lords — remember where we are,
In France, amongst a fickle wavering nation.
If they perceive dissension in our looks
And that within ourselves we disagree,
How will their grudging stomachs be provok'd
To wilful disobedience, and rebel!
Beside, what infamy will there arise
When foreign princes shall be certified
That for a toy, a thing of no regard,
King Henry's peers and chief nobility
Destroy'd themselves and lost the realm of France!
O, think upon the conquest of my father,
My tender years, and let us not forgo
That for a trifle that was bought with blood!
Let me be umpire in this doubtful strife.
I see no reason, if I wear this rose,
[*Puts on a red rose.*]
That any one should therefore be suspicious
I more incline to Somerset than York.
Both are my kinsmen, and I love them both.
As well they may upbraid me with my crown
Because (forsooth) the King of Scots is crown'd!
But your discretions better can persuade
Than I am able to instruct or teach;
And therefore, as we hither came in peace,
So let us still continue peace and love.
Cousin of York, we institute your Grace
To be our Regent in these parts of France;
And, good my Lord of Somerset, unite
Your troops of horsemen with his bands of foot;
And like true subjects, sons of your progenitors,
Go cheerfully together and digest
Your angry choler on your enemies.
Ourself, my Lord Protector, and the rest,
After some respite will return to Calais;
From thence to England, where I hope ere long
To be presented, by your victories,
With Charles, Alençon, and that traitorous rout.
Flourish. Exeunt. Manent York, Warwick, Exeter, Vernon.
War. My Lord of York, I promise you, the King
Prettily, methought, did play the orator.

York. And so he did; but yet I like it not,
In that he wears the badge of Somerset.
War. Tush, that was but his fancy. Blame him not!
I dare presume, sweet prince, he thought no harm.
York. An if I wist he did — But let it rest;
Other affairs must now be managed.
Exeunt. Manet Exeter.
Exe. Well didst thou, Richard, to suppress thy voice;
For, had the passions of thy heart burst out,
I fear we should have seen decipher'd there
More rancorous spite, more furious raging broils,
Than yet can be imagin'd or suppos'd.
But howsoe'er, no simple man that sees
This jarring discord of nobility,
This shouldering of each other in the court,
This factious bandying of their favourites,
But that it doth presage some ill event.
'Tis much when sceptres are in children's hands,
But more when envy breeds unkind division.
There comes the ruin, there begins confusion.
Exit.

[Scene II.]

Enter *Talbot,* with *Trump* and *Drum* before Bordeaux.

Tal. Go to the gates of Bordeaux, trumpeter.
Summon their general unto the wall.

[*Trumpet*] *sounds* [*a parley*]. Enter [the *Captain*] *General* [*of the French,* and others], aloft.

English John Talbot, Captains, calls you forth,
Servant in arms to Harry King of England;
And thus he would: Open your city gates,
Be humble to us, call my sovereign yours
And do him homage as obedient subjects,
And I'll withdraw me and my bloody power;
But if you frown upon this proffer'd peace,
You tempt the fury of my three attendants,
Lean famine, quartering steel, and climbing fire,
Who in a moment even with the earth
Shall lay your stately and air-braving towers,
If you forsake the offer of their love.
Capt. Thou ominous and fearful owl of death,
Our nation's terror and their bloody scourge,
The period of thy tyranny approacheth!
On us thou canst not enter but by death;
For I protest we are well fortified
And strong enough to issue out and fight.
If thou retire, the Dauphin, well appointed,
Stands with the snares of war to tangle thee.
On either hand thee there are squadrons pitch'd,
To wall thee from the liberty of flight;
And no way canst thou turn thee for redress
But death doth front thee with apparent spoil
And pale destruction meets thee in the face.
Ten thousand French have ta'en the sacrament
To rive their dangerous artillery
Upon no Christian soul but English Talbot.
Lo, there thou stand'st, a breathing valiant man
Of an invincible unconquer'd spirit!
This is the latest glory of thy praise
That I thy enemy due thee withal;
For ere the glass that now begins to run
Finish the process of his sandy hour,
These eyes that see thee now well-coloured
Shall see thee withered, bloody, pale, and dead.
Drum afar off.
Hark! hark! The Dauphin's drum, a warning bell,
Sings heavy music to thy timorous soul;
And mine shall ring thy dire departure out.
Exit [*with his men*].
Tal. He fables not; I hear the enemy.
Out, some light horsemen, and peruse their wings.
O, negligent and heedless discipline!
How are we park'd and bounded in a pale,
A little herd of England's timorous deer,
Maz'd with a yelping kennel of French curs!
If we be English deer, be then in blood;
Not rascal-like, to fall down with a pinch,
But rather, moody-mad and desperate stags,
Turn on the bloody hounds with heads of steel
And make the cowards stand aloof at bay.
Sell every man his life as dear as mine,
And they shall find dear deer of us, my friends.
God and Saint George, Talbot and England's right,
Prosper our colours in this dangerous fight!
[*Exeunt.*]

[Scene III. *Plains in Gascony.*]

Enter a *Messenger* that meets *York.* Enter *York,* with *Trumpet* and many *Soldiers.*

York. Are not the speedy scouts return'd again
That dogg'd the mighty army of the Dauphin?

Mess. They are return'd, my lord, and give it out
That he is march'd to Bordeaux with his power
To fight with Talbot. As he march'd along,
By your espials were discovered
Two mightier troops than that the Dauphin led,
Which join'd with him and made their march for Bordeaux.

York. A plague upon that villain Somerset
That thus delays my promised supply
Of horsemen that were levied for this siege!
Renowned Talbot doth expect my aid,
And I am louted by a traitor villain
And cannot help the noble chevalier.
God comfort him in this necessity!
If he miscarry, farewell wars in France.

Enter [*Sir William Lucy,*] another *Messenger.*

Lucy. Thou princely leader of our English strength,
Never so needful on the earth of France,
Spur to the rescue of the noble Talbot,
Who now is girdled with a waist of iron
And hemm'd about with grim destruction.
To Bordeaux, warlike Duke! to Bordeaux, York!
Else farewell Talbot, France, and England's honour.

York. O God, that Somerset, who in proud heart
Doth stop my cornets, were in Talbot's place!
So should we save a valiant gentleman
By forfeiting a traitor and a coward.
Mad ire and wrathful fury makes me weep
That thus we die while remiss traitors sleep.

Lucy. O, send some succour to the distress'd lord!

York. He dies, we lose; I break my warlike word;
We mourn, France smiles; we lose, they daily get:
All long of this vile traitor Somerset.

Lucy. Then God take mercy on brave Talbot's soul
And on his son, young John, who two hours since
I met in travel toward his warlike father!
This seven years did not Talbot see his son,
And now they meet where both their lives are done.

York. Alas, what joy shall noble Talbot have
To bid his young son welcome to his grave?
Away! Vexation almost stops my breath
That sund'red friends greet in the hour of death.
Lucy, farewell. No more my fortune can
But curse the cause I cannot aid the man.
Maine, Blois, Poictiers, and Tours are won away,
Long all of Somerset and his delay.

Exit [*with Soldiers*].

Lucy. Thus, while the vulture of sedition
Feeds in the bosom of such great commanders,
Sleeping neglection doth betray to loss
The conquest of our scarce-cold conqueror,
That ever-living man of memory,
Henry the Fifth. Whiles they each other cross,
Lives, honours, lands, and all hurry to loss.

[*Exit.*]

[Scene IV. *Other plains in Gascony.*]

Enter *Somerset,* with his *Army,* [a *Captain* of *Talbot's* with him].

Som. It is too late; I cannot send them now.
This expedition was by York and Talbot
Too rashly plotted. All our general force
Might with a sally of the very town
Be buckled with. The over-daring Talbot
Hath sullied all his gloss of former honour
By this unheedful, desperate, wild adventure.
York set him on to fight, and die in shame,
That, Talbot dead, great York might bear the name.

[Enter *Sir William Lucy.*]

Capt. Here is Sir William Lucy, who with me
Set from our o'ermatch'd forces forth for aid.

Som. How now, Sir William? Whither were you sent?

Lucy. Whither, my lord? From bought and sold Lord Talbot,
Who, ring'd about with bold adversity,
Cries out for noble York and Somerset
To beat assailing death from his weak legions;
And whiles the honourable captain there
Drops bloody sweat from his war-wearied limbs,
And, in advantage ling'ring, looks for rescue,
You, his false hopes, the trust of England's honour,
Keep off aloof with worthless emulation.
Let not your private discord keep away
The levied succours that should lend him aid,
While he, renowned noble gentleman,
Yield up his life unto a world of odds.
Orleans the Bastard, Charles, Burgundy,
Alençon, Reignier compass him about,
And Talbot perisheth by your default.

Som. York set him on; York should have sent him aid.

Lucy. And York as fast upon your Grace exclaims,
Swearing that you withhold his levied host,
Collected for this expedition.

Som. York lies. He might have sent and had the horse.
I owe him little duty, and less love,
And take foul scorn to fawn on him by sending.

Lucy. The fraud of England, not the force of France,
Hath now entrapp'd the noble-minded Talbot.
Never to England shall he bear his life,
But dies betray'd to fortune by your strife.

Som. Come, go! I will dispatch the horsemen straight;
Within six hours they will be at his aid.

Lucy. Too late comes rescue. He is ta'en or slain;
For fly he could not, if he would have fled;
And fly would Talbot never, though he might.

Som. If he be dead, brave Talbot, then adieu!

Lucy. His fame lives in the world, his shame in you. *Exeunt.*

[Scene V. *The English camp near Bordeaux.*]

Enter *Talbot* and [*John*] his son.

Tal. O young John Talbot, I did send for thee
To tutor thee in stratagems of war,
That Talbot's name might be in thee reviv'd
When sapless age and weak unable limbs
Should bring thy father to his drooping chair.
But O malignant and ill-boding stars!
Now thou art come unto a feast of death,
A terrible and unavoided danger.
Therefore, dear boy, mount on my swiftest horse,
And I'll direct thee how thou shalt escape
By sudden flight. Come, dally not, be gone!

John. Is my name Talbot? and am I your son?
And shall I fly? O, if you love my mother,
Dishonour not her honourable name
To make a bastard and a slave of me!
The world will say he is not Talbot's blood
That basely fled when noble Talbot stood.

Tal. Fly, to revenge my death if I be slain.

John. He that flies so will ne'er return again.

Tal. If we both stay, we both are sure to die.

John. Then let me stay, and, father, do you fly.
Your loss is great, so your regard should be;
My worth unknown, no loss is known in me.
Upon my death the French can little boast;
In yours they will, in you all hopes are lost.
Flight cannot stain the honour you have won;
But mine it will, that no exploit have done.
You fled for vantage, every one will swear;
But if I bow, they'll say it was for fear.
There is no hope that ever I will stay
If the first hour I shrink and run away.
Here on my knee I beg mortality
Rather than life preserv'd with infamy.

Tal. Shall all thy mother's hopes lie in one tomb?

John. Ay, rather than I'll shame my mother's womb.

Tal. Upon my blessing I command thee go.

John. To fight I will, but not to fly the foe.

Tal. Part of thy father may be sav'd in thee.

John. No part of him but will be shame in me.

Tal. Thou never hadst renown, nor canst not lose it.

John. Yes, your renowned name. Shall flight abuse it?

Tal. Thy father's charge shall clear thee from that stain.

John. You cannot witness for me, being slain.
If death be so apparent, then both fly.

Tal. And leave my followers here to fight and die?
My age was never tainted with such shame.

John. And shall my youth be guilty of such blame?
No more can I be severed from your side
Than can yourself yourself in twain divide.
Stay, go, do what you will — the like do I;
For live I will not if my father die.

Tal. Then here I take my leave of thee, fair son,
Born to eclipse thy life this afternoon.
Come, side by side together live and die,
And soul with soul from France to heaven fly! *Exeunt.*

[Scene VI. *A field of battle.*]

Alarum. Excursions, wherein Talbot's Son is hemm'd about and Talbot rescues him.

Tal. Saint George and victory! Fight, soldiers, fight!
The Regent hath with Talbot broke his word
And left us to the rage of France his sword.
Where is John Talbot? Pause, and take thy breath.
I gave thee life and rescu'd thee from death.

John. O twice my father, twice am I thy son!
The life thou gav'st me first was lost and done
Till with thy warlike sword, despite of fate,
To my determin'd time thou gav'st new date.

Tal. When from the Dauphin's crest thy sword struck fire,
It warm'd thy father's heart with proud desire
Of bold-fac'd victory. Then leaden age,
Quicken'd with youthful spleen and warlike rage,
Beat down Alençon, Orleans, Burgundy,
And from the pride of Gallia rescued thee.
The ireful Bastard Orleans, that drew blood
From thee, my boy, and had the maidenhood
Of thy first fight, I soon encountered,
And interchanging blows, I quickly shed
Some of his bastard blood; and in disgrace
Bespoke him thus: 'Contaminated, base,
And misbegotten blood I spill of thine,
Mean and right poor, for that pure blood of mine
Which thou didst force from Talbot, my brave boy.
Here, purposing the Bastard to destroy,
Came in strong rescue. Speak, thy father's care.
Art thou not weary, John? How dost thou fare?
Wilt thou yet leave the battle, boy, and fly,
Now thou art seal'd the son of chivalry?
Fly, to revenge my death when I am dead.
The help of one stands me in little stead.
O, too much folly is it, well I wot,
To hazard all our lives in one small boat!
If I to-day die not with Frenchmen's rage,
To-morrow I shall die with mickle age.
By me they nothing gain an if I stay;
'Tis but the short'ning of my life one day.
In thee thy mother dies, our household's name,
My death's revenge, thy youth, and England's fame.
All these, and more, we hazard by thy stay;
All these are sav'd if thou wilt fly away.

John. The sword of Orleans hath not made me smart;
These words of yours draw lifeblood from my heart.
On that advantage, bought with such a shame,
To save a paltry life and slay bright fame,
Before young Talbot from old Talbot fly,
The coward horse that bears me fall and die!
And like me to the peasant boys of France,
To be shame's scorn and subject of mischance!
Surely, by all the glory you have won,
An if I fly, I am not Talbot's son.
Then talk no more of flight! It is no boot.
If son to Talbot, die at Talbot's foot.

Tal. Then follow thou thy desp'rate sire of Crete,
Thou Icarus. Thy life to me is sweet.
If thou wilt fight, fight by thy father's side;
And, commendable prov'd, let's die in pride.
Exeunt.

[Scene VII. *Another part of the field.*]

Alarum. Excursions. Enter old *Talbot,* led.

Tal. Where is my other life? Mine own is gone.
O, where's young Talbot? Where is valiant John?
Triumphant death, smear'd with captivity,
Young Talbot's valour makes me smile at thee.
When he perceiv'd me shrink and on my knee,
His bloody sword he brandish'd over me
And like a hungry lion did commence
Rough deeds of rage and stern impatience;
But when my angry guardant stood alone,
Tend'ring my ruin and assail'd of none,
Dizzy-ey'd fury and great rage of heart
Suddenly made him from my side to start
Into the clust'ring battle of the French;
And in that sea of blood my boy did drench
His over-mounting spirit; and there died
My Icarus, my blossom, in his pride.

Enter [*Soldiers*] with *John Talbot,* borne.

Servant. O my dear lord, lo where your son is borne!

Tal. Thou antic Death, which laugh'st us here to scorn,
Anon, from thy insulting tyranny,
Coupled in bonds of perpetuity,
Two Talbots, winged through the lither sky,

In thy despite shall scape mortality.
O thou whose wounds become hard-favoured death,
Speak to thy father ere thou yield thy breath!
Brave Death by speaking, whether he will or no.
Imagine him a Frenchman, and thy foe.
Poor boy! he smiles, methinks, as who should say,
'Had Death been French, then Death had died to-day.'
Come, come, and lay him in his father's arms!
My spirit can no longer bear these harms.
Soldiers, adieu! I have what I would have,
Now my old arms are young John Talbot's grave. *Dies.*

Enter *Charles, Alençon, Burgundy, Bastard,* and *Pucelle.*

Char. Had York and Somerset brought rescue in,
We should have found a bloody day of this.

Bast. How the young whelp of Talbot's, raging wood,
Did flesh his puny sword in Frenchmen's blood!

Puc. Once I encount'red him and thus I said,
'Thou maiden youth, be vanquish'd by a maid.'
But with a proud majestical high scorn
He answer'd thus, 'Young Talbot was not born
To be the pillage of a giglot wench.'
So, rushing in the bowels of the French,
He left me proudly, as unworthy fight.

Bur. Doubtless he would have made a noble knight.
See where he lies inhearsed in the arms
Of the most bloody nurser of his harms.

Bast. Hew them to pieces! hack their bones asunder
Whose life was England's glory, Gallia's wonder!

Char. O, no, forbear! For that which we have fled
During the life, let us not wrong it dead.

Enter *Lucy,* [attended; a *French Herald* preceding].

Lucy. Herald, conduct me to the Dauphin's tent,
To know who hath obtain'd the glory of the day.

Char. On what submissive message art thou sent?

Lucy. Submission, Dauphin? 'Tis a mere French word.
We English warriors wot not what it means.
I come to know what prisoners thou hast ta'en
And to survey the bodies of the dead.

Char. For prisoners ask'st thou? Hell our prison is.
But tell me whom thou seek'st.

Lucy. Where is the great Alcides of the field,
Valiant Lord Talbot, Earl of Shrewsbury,
Created for his rare success in arms
Great Earl of Washford, Waterford, and Valence,
Lord Talbot of Goodrig and Urchinfield,
Lord Strange of Blackmere, Lord Verdun of Alton,
Lord Cromwell of Wingfield, Lord Furnival of Sheffield,
The thrice-victorious Lord of Falconbridge,
Knight of the noble order of Saint George,
Worthy Saint Michael, and the Golden Fleece,
Great Marshal to Henry the Sixth
Of all his wars within the realm of France?

Puc. Here is a silly-stately style indeed!
The Turk, that two-and-fifty kingdoms hath,
Writes not so tedious a style as this.
Him that thou magnifi'st with all these titles,
Stinking and flyblown lies here at our feet.

Lucy. Is Talbot slain, the Frenchmen's only scourge,
Your kingdom's terror and black Nemesis?
O, were mine eyeballs into bullets turn'd,
That I in rage might shoot them at your faces!
O that I could but call these dead to life!
It were enough to fright the realm of France.
Were but his picture left amongst you here,
It would amaze the proudest of you all.
Give me their bodies, that I may bear them hence
And give them burial as beseems their worth.

Puc. I think this upstart is old Talbot's ghost,
He speaks with such a proud commanding spirit.
For God's sake, let him have them! To keep them here,
They would but stink and putrefy the air.

Char. Go take their bodies hence.

Lucy. I'll bear them hence; but from their ashes shall be rear'd
A phœnix that shall make all France afeard.

Char. So we be rid of them, do with them what thou wilt.
And now to Paris in this conquering vein!
All will be ours, now bloody Talbot's slain.
Exeunt.

[Act V.] Scene [I. *London. The Palace.*]

Sennet. Enter *King, Gloucester,* and *Exeter.*

King. Have you perus'd the letters from the Pope,
The Emperor, and the Earl of Armagnac?

Glou. I have, my lord, and their intent is this:
They humbly sue unto your Excellence
To have a godly peace concluded of
Between the realms of England and of France.

King. How doth your Grace affect their motion?

Glou. Well, my good lord, and as the only means
To stop effusion of our Christian blood
And stablish quietness on every side.

King. Ay, marry, uncle; for I always thought
It was both impious and unnatural
That such immanity and bloody strife
Should reign among professors of one faith.

Glou. Beside, my lord, the sooner to effect
And surer bind this knot of amity,
The Earl of Armagnac, near knit to Charles,
A man of great authority in France,
Proffers his only daughter to your Grace
In marriage, with a large and sumptuous dowry.

King. Marriage, uncle? Alas! my years are young,
And fitter is my study and my books
Than wanton dalliance with a paramour.
Yet, call th' ambassadors; and as you please,
So let them have their answers every one.
I shall be well content with any choice
Tends to God's glory and my country's weal.

Enter *Winchester* [in Cardinal's habit] and three *Ambassadors,* [one a *Papal Legate*].

Exe. [*aside*] What, is my Lord of Winchester install'd,
And call'd unto a cardinal's degree?
Then I perceive that will be verified
Henry the Fifth did sometime prophesy—
'If once he come to be a cardinal,
He'll make his cap coequal with the crown.'

King. My Lords Ambassadors, your several suits
Have been consider'd and debated on.
Your purpose is both good and reasonable,
And therefore are we certainly resolv'd
To draw conditions of a friendly peace,
Which by my Lord of Winchester we mean
Shall be transported presently to France.

Glou. And for the proffer of my lord your master,
I have inform'd his Highness so at large
As, liking of the lady's virtuous gifts,
Her beauty, and the value of her dower,
He doth intend she shall be England's Queen.

King. In argument and proof of which contract
Bear her this jewel, pledge of my affection.
And so, my Lord Protector, see them guarded
And safely brought to Dover, where inshipp'd
Commit them to the fortune of the sea.

Exeunt [*all but Winchester and the Legate*].

Win. Stay, my Lord Legate. You shall first receive
The sum of money which I promised
Should be delivered to his Holiness
For clothing me in these grave ornaments.

Legate. I will attend upon your lordship's leisure. [*Steps aside.*]

Win. Now Winchester will not submit, I trow,
Or be inferior to the proudest peer.
Humphrey of Gloucester, thou shalt well perceive
That neither in birth or for authority
The Bishop will be overborne by thee.
I'll either make thee stoop and bend thy knee
Or sack this country with a mutiny. *Exeunt.*

Scene [II. *France. Plains in Anjou.*]

Enter *Charles, Burgundy, Alençon, Bastard, Reignier,* and *Joan.*

Char. These news, my lords, may cheer our drooping spirits:
'Tis said the stout Parisians do revolt
And turn again unto the warlike French.

Alen. Then march to Paris, royal Charles of France,
And keep not back your powers in dalliance.

Puc. Peace be amongst them if they turn to us;
Else ruin combat with their palaces!

Enter *Scout.*

Scout. Success unto our valiant general
And happiness to his accomplices!

Char. What tidings send our scouts? I prithee speak.

Scout. The English army, that divided was
Into two parties, is now conjoin'd in one
And means to give you battle presently.
Char. Somewhat too sudden, sirs, the warning is,
But we will presently provide for them.
Bur. I trust the ghost of Talbot is not there.
Now he is gone, my lord, you need not fear.
Puc. Of all base passions fear is most accurs'd.
Command the conquest, Charles, it shall be thine,
Let Henry fret and all the world repine.
Char. Then on, my lords; and France be fortunate! *Exeunt.*

[Scene III. *Before Angiers.*]

Alarum. Excursions. Enter *Joan la Pucelle.*

Puc. The Regent conquers and the Frenchmen fly.
Now help, ye charming spells and periapts;
And ye choice spirits that admonish me,
And give me signs of future accidents. *Thunder.*
You speedy helpers that are substitutes
Under the lordly Monarch of the North,
Appear and aid me in this enterprise!

Enter *Fiends.*

This speedy and quick appearance argues proof
Of your accustom'd diligence to me.
Now, ye familiar spirits that are cull'd
Out of the powerful legions under earth,
Help me this once, that France may get the field. *They walk, and speak not.*
O, hold me not with silence over-long!
Where I was wont to feed you with my blood,
I'll lop a member off and give it you
In earnest of a further benefit,
So you do condescend to help me now. *They hang their heads.*
No hope to have redress? My body shall
Pay recompense if you will grant my suit. *They shake their heads.*
Cannot my body nor blood-sacrifice
Entreat you to your wonted furtherance?
Then take my soul — my body, soul, and all,
Before that England give the French the foil. *They depart.*
See, they forsake me! Now the time is come
That France must vail her lofty-plumed crest
And let her head fall into England's lap.
My ancient incantations are too weak,
And hell too strong for me to buckle with.
Now, France, thy glory droopeth to the dust. *Exit.*

Excursions. [Enter *French* and *English,* fighting.] *Burgundy* and *York* fight hand to hand. French fly. [*La Pucelle* is taken.]

York. Damsel of France, I think I have you fast.
Unchain your spirits now with spelling charms
And try if they can gain your liberty.
A goodly prize, fit for the devil's grace!
See how the ugly witch doth bend her brows
As if, with Circe, she would change my shape!
Puc. Chang'd to a worser shape thou canst not be.
York. O, Charles the Dauphin is a proper man!
No shape but his can please your dainty eye.
Puc. A plaguing mischief light on Charles and thee!
And may ye both be suddenly surpris'd
By bloody hands in sleeping on your beds!
York. Fell banning hag, enchantress, hold thy tongue!
Puc. I prithee give me leave to curse awhile.
York. Curse, miscreant, when thou comest to the stake. *Exeunt.*

Alarum. Enter *Suffolk,* with *Margaret* in his hand.

Suf. Be what thou wilt, thou art my prisoner. *Gazes on her.*
O fairest beauty, do not fear nor fly!
For I will touch thee but with reverent hands;
I kiss these fingers for eternal peace
And lay them gently on thy tender side.
Who art thou? Say, that I may honour thee.
Mar. Margaret my name, and daughter to a king,
The King of Naples, whosoe'er thou art.
Suf. An earl I am and Suffolk am I call'd.
Be not offended, nature's miracle,
Thou art allotted to be ta'en by me.
So doth the swan her downy cygnets save,
Keeping them prisoner underneath her wings.
Yet, if this servile usage once offend,
Go and be free again as Suffolk's friend. *She is going.*
O, stay! [*Aside*] I have no power to let her pass;
My hand would free her, but my heart says no.
As plays the sun upon the glassy streams,
Twinkling another counterfeited beam,
So seems this gorgeous beauty to mine eyes.
Fain would I woo her, yet I dare not speak.

I'll call for pen and ink and write my mind.
Fie, de la Pole! disable not thyself.
Hast not a tongue? Is she not here thy prisoner?
Wilt thou be daunted at a woman's sight?
Ay, beauty's princely majesty is such
Confounds the tongue and makes the senses rough.

Mar. Say, Earl of Suffolk, if thy name be so,
What ransom must I pay before I pass?
For I perceive I am thy prisoner.

Suf. How canst thou tell she will deny thy suit
Before thou make a trial of her love?

Mar. Why speak'st thou not? What ransom must I pay?

Suf. She's beautiful, and therefore to be woo'd;
She is a woman, therefore to be won.

Mar. Wilt thou accept of ransom — yea or no?

Suf. Fond man, remember that thou hast a wife.
Then how can Margaret be thy paramour?

Mar. I were best to leave him, for he will not hear.

Suf. There all is marr'd; there lies a cooling card.

Mar. He talks at randon. Sure the man is mad.

Suf. And yet a dispensation may be had.

Mar. And yet I would that you would answer me.

Suf. I'll win this Lady Margaret. For whom?
Why, for my king. Tush, that's a wooden thing!

Mar. He talks of wood. It is some carpenter.

Suf. Yet so my fancy may be satisfied
And peace established between these realms.
But there remains a scruple in that too;
For though her father be the King of Naples,
Duke of Anjou and Maine, yet is he poor,
And our nobility will scorn the match.

Mar. Hear ye, Captain? Are you not at leisure?

Suf. It shall be so, disdain they ne'er so much.
Henry is youthful and will quickly yield. —
Madam, I have a secret to reveal.

Mar. What though I be enthrall'd? He seems a knight
And will not any way dishonour me.

Suf. Lady, vouchsafe to listen what I say.

Mar. Perhaps I shall be rescu'd by the French,
And then I need not crave his courtesy.

Suf. Sweet madam, give me hearing in a cause —

Mar. Tush, women have been captivate ere now.

Suf. Lady, wherefore talk you so?

Mar. I cry you mercy, 'tis but Quid for Quo.

Suf. Say, gentle Princess, would you not suppose
Your bondage happy, to be made a queen?

Mar. To be a queen in bondage is more vile
Than is a slave in base servility;
For princes should be free.

Suf. And so shall you,
If happy England's royal king be free.

Mar. Why, what concerns his freedom unto me?

Suf. I'll undertake to make thee Henry's queen,
To put a golden sceptre in thy hand
And set a precious crown upon thy head,
If thou wilt condescend to be my —

Mar. What?

Suf. His love.

Mar. I am unworthy to be Henry's wife.

Suf. No, gentle madam. I unworthy am
To woo so fair a dame to be his wife
And have no portion in the choice myself.
How say you, madam? Are ye so content?

Mar. An if my father please, I am content.

Suf. Then call our captains and our colours forth!
And, madam, at your father's castle walls
We'll crave a parley to confer with him.

Sound [a parley]. Enter Reignier on the walls.

See, Reignier, see, thy daughter prisoner!

Reig. To whom?

Suf. To me.

Reig. Suffolk, what remedy?
I am a soldier, and unapt to weep
Or to exclaim on fortune's fickleness.

Suf. Yes, there is remedy enough, my lord.
Consent, and for thy honour give consent,
Thy daughter shall be wedded to my king,
Whom I with pain have woo'd and won thereto;
And this her easy-held imprisonment
Hath gain'd thy daughter princely liberty.

Reig. Speaks Suffolk as he thinks?

Suf. Fair Margaret knows
That Suffolk doth not flatter, face, or feign.

Reig. Upon thy princely warrant I descend
To give thee answer of thy just demand.

Suf. And here I will expect thy coming.

[*Exit Reignier.*]

Trumpets sound. Enter *Reignier* [below].

Reig. Welcome, brave Earl, into our territories.
Command in Anjou what your Honour pleases.
Suf. Thanks, Reignier, happy for so sweet a child,
Fit to be made companion with a king.
What answer makes your Grace unto my suit?
Reig. Since thou dost deign to woo her little worth
To be the princely bride of such a lord,
Upon condition I may quietly
Enjoy mine own, the counties Maine and Anjou,
Free from oppression or the stroke of war,
My daughter shall be Henry's, if he please.
Suf. That is her ransom. I deliver her,
And those two counties I will undertake
Your Grace shall well and quietly enjoy.
Reig. And I again, in Henry's royal name,
As deputy unto that gracious king,
Give thee her hand for sign of plighted faith.
Suf. Reignier of France, I give thee kingly thanks,
Because this is in traffic of a king.
[*Aside*] And yet methinks I could be well content
To be mine own attorney in this case. —
I'll over then to England with this news
And make this marriage to be solemniz'd.
So, farewell, Reignier. Set this diamond safe
In golden palaces, as it becomes.
Reig. I do embrace thee as I would embrace
The Christian prince King Henry, were he here.
Mar. Farewell, my lord. Good wishes, praise, and prayers
Shall Suffolk ever have of Margaret.
She is going.
Suf. Farewell, sweet madam. But hark you, Margaret —
No princely commendations to my king?
Mar. Such commendations as becomes a maid,
A virgin, and his servant, say to him.
Suf. Words sweetly plac'd and modestly directed.
But, madam, I must trouble you again —
No loving token to his Majesty?
Mar. Yes, my good lord: a pure unspotted heart,
Never yet taint with love, I send the King.
Suf. And this withal. *Kiss her.*
Mar. That for thyself. I will not so presume
To send such peevish tokens to a king.
[*Exeunt Reignier and Margaret.*]
Suf. O, wert thou for myself! But, Suffolk, stay.
Thou mayst not wander in that labyrinth;
There Minotaurs and ugly treasons lurk.
Solicit Henry with her wondrous praise.
Bethink thee on her virtues that surmount,
And natural graces that extinguish art;
Repeat their semblance often on the seas,
That, when thou com'st to kneel at Henry's feet,
Thou mayst bereave him of his wits with wonder. *Exit.*

[Scene IV. *Camp of the* Duke of York *in Anjou.*]

Enter *York, Warwick, Shepherd, Pucelle* [guarded].

York. Bring forth that sorceress condemn'd to burn.
Shep. Ah, Joan, this kills thy father's heart outright!
Have I sought every country far and near,
And, now it is my chance to find thee out,
Must I behold thy timeless cruel death?
Ah, Joan, sweet daughter Joan, I'll die with thee!
Puc. Decrepit miser! base ignoble wretch!
I am descended of a gentler blood.
Thou art no father nor no friend of mine.
Shep. Out, out! My lords, an please you, 'tis not so.
I did beget her, all the parish knows.
Her mother liveth yet, can testify
She was the first fruit of my bach'lorship.
War. Graceless! wilt thou deny thy parentage?
York. This argues what her kind of life hath been,
Wicked and vile; and so her death concludes.
Shep. Fie, Joan, that thou wilt be so obstacle!
God knows thou art a collop of my flesh,
And for thy sake have I shed many a tear.
Deny me not, I prithee, gentle Joan.
Puc. Peasant, avaunt! You have suborn'd this man,
Of purpose to obscure my noble birth.
Shep. 'Tis true, I gave a noble to the priest
The morn that I was wedded to her mother.
Kneel down and take my blessing, good my girl.
Wilt thou not stoop? Now cursed be the time
Of thy nativity! I would the milk

Thy mother gave thee when thou suck'dst her breast
Had been a little ratsbane for thy sake!
Or else, when thou didst keep my lambs afield,
I wish some ravenous wolf had eaten thee!
Dost thou deny thy father, cursed drab?
O, burn her, burn her! Hanging is too good.
Exit.

York. Take her away; for she hath liv'd too long,
To fill the world with vicious qualities.

Puc. First let me tell you whom you have condemn'd:
Not one begotten of a shepherd swain,
But issued from the progeny of kings,
Virtuous and holy, chosen from above
By inspiration of celestial grace
To work exceeding miracles on earth.
I never had to do with wicked spirits;
But you, that are polluted with your lusts,
Stain'd with the guiltless blood of innocents,
Corrupt and tainted with a thousand vices —
Because you want the grace that others have,
You judge it straight a thing impossible
To compass wonders but by help of devils.
No, misconceived! Joan of Arc hath been
A virgin from her tender infancy,
Chaste and immaculate in very thought,
Whose maiden blood, thus rigorously effus'd,
Will cry for vengeance at the gates of heaven.

York. Ay, ay. Away with her to execution!

War. And hark ye, sirs. Because she is a maid,
Spare for no fagots, let there be enow.
Place barrels of pitch upon the fatal stake,
That so her torture may be shortened.

Puc. Will nothing turn your unrelenting hearts?
Then, Joan, discover thine infirmity,
That warranteth by law to be thy privilege.
I am with child, ye bloody homicides.
Murther not then the fruit within my womb,
Although ye hale me to a violent death.

York. Now heaven forfend! The holy maid with child?

War. The greatest miracle that e'er ye wrought.
Is all your strict preciseness come to this?

York. She and the Dauphin have been juggling.
I did imagine what would be her refuge.

War. Well, go to! We'll have no bastards live,
Especially since Charles must father it.

Puc. You are deceiv'd. My child is none of his.
It was Alençon that enjoy'd my love.

York. Alençon! that notorious Machiavel?
It dies, an if it had a thousand lives.

Puc. O, give me leave! I have deluded you.
'Twas neither Charles nor yet the duke I nam'd,
But Reignier, King of Naples, that prevail'd.

War. A married man! That's most intolerable.

York. Why, here's a girl! I think she knows not well
(There were so many) whom she may accuse.

War. It's sign she hath been liberal and free.

York. And yet, forsooth, she is a virgin pure!
Strumpet, thy words condemn thy brat and thee.
Use no entreaty, for it is in vain.

Puc. Then lead me hence; with whom I leave my curse.
May never glorious sun reflex his beams
Upon the country where you make abode;
But darkness and the gloomy shade of death
Environ you, till mischief and despair
Drive you to break your necks or hang yourselves!
Exit [guarded].

York. Break thou in pieces and consume to ashes,
Thou foul accursed minister of hell!

Enter *Cardinal* [*Beaufort,* attended].

Car. Lord Regent, I do greet your Excellence
With letters of commission from the King.
For know, my lords, the states of Christendom,
Mov'd with remorse of these outrageous broils,
Have earnestly implor'd a general peace
Betwixt our nation and the aspiring French;
And here at hand the Dauphin and his train
Approacheth, to confer about some matter.

York. Is all our travail turn'd to this effect?
After the slaughter of so many peers,
So many captains, gentlemen, and soldiers,
That in this quarrel have been overthrown
And sold their bodies for their country's benefit,
Shall we at last conclude effeminate peace?
Have we not lost most part of all the towns
By treason, falsehood, and by treachery
Our great progenitors had conquered?
O, Warwick, Warwick! I foresee with grief
The utter loss of all the realm of France.

War. Be patient, York. If we conclude a peace,
It shall be with such strict and severe covenants
As little shall the Frenchmen gain thereby.

Enter *Charles, Alençon, Bastard, Reignier,* [and others].

Char. Since, lords of England, it is thus agreed
That peaceful truce shall be proclaim'd in France,
We come to be informed by yourselves
What the conditions of that league must be.
York. Speak, Winchester; for boiling choler chokes
The hollow passage of my poison'd voice
By sight of these our baleful enemies.
Car. Charles, and the rest, it is enacted thus:
That, in regard King Henry gives consent,
Of mere compassion and of lenity,
To ease your country of distressful war
And suffer you to breathe in fruitful peace,
You shall become true liegemen to his crown;
And, Charles, upon condition thou wilt swear
To pay him tribute and submit thyself,
Thou shalt be plac'd as viceroy under him
And still enjoy thy regal dignity.
Alen. Must he be then as shadow of himself?
Adorn his temples with a coronet,
And yet, in substance and authority,
Retain but privilege of a private man?
This proffer is absurd and reasonless.
Char. 'Tis known already that I am possess'd
With more than half the Gallian territories
And therein reverenc'd for their lawful king.
Shall I, for lucre of the rest unvanquish'd,
Detract so much from that prerogative
As to be call'd but viceroy of the whole?
No, Lord Ambassador. I'll rather keep
That which I have than, coveting for more,
Be cast from possibility of all.
York. Insulting Charles, hast thou by secret means
Us'd intercession to obtain a league,
And, now the matter grows to compremise,
Stand'st thou aloof upon comparison?
Either accept the title thou usurp'st,
Of benefit proceeding from our king
And not of any challenge of desert,
Or we will plague thee with incessant wars.
Reig. [*aside to Charles*] My lord, you do not well in obstinacy
To cavil in the course of this contract.
If once it be neglected, ten to one
We shall not find like opportunity.
Alen. [*aside to Charles*] To say the truth, it is your policy
To save your subjects from such massacre
And ruthless slaughters as are daily seen
By our proceeding in hostility;
And therefore take this compact of a truce,
Although you break it when your pleasure serves.
War. How say'st thou, Charles? Shall our condition stand?
Char. It shall;
Only reserv'd, you claim no interest
In any of our towns of garrison.
York. Then swear allegiance to his Majesty:
As thou art knight, never to disobey
Nor be rebellious to the crown of England —
Thou, nor thy nobles, to the crown of England.
[*Charles and the rest give tokens of fealty.*]
So, now dismiss your army when ye please,
Hang up your ensigns, let your drums be still,
For here we entertain a solemn peace.
Exeunt.

[Scene V. *London. The Palace.*]

Enter *Suffolk,* in conference with the *King*; *Gloucester* and *Exeter.*

King. Your wondrous rare description, noble Earl,
Of beauteous Margaret hath astonish'd me.
Her virtues, graced with external gifts,
Do breed love's settled passions in my heart;
And like as rigour of tempestuous gusts
Provokes the mightiest hulk against the tide,
So am I driven by breath of her renown
Either to suffer shipwrack or arrive
Where I may have fruition of her love.
Suf. Tush, my good lord! This superficial tale
Is but a preface of her worthy praise.
The chief perfections of that lovely dame
(Had I sufficient skill to utter them)
Would make a volume of enticing lines
Able to ravish any dull conceit;
And, which is more, she is not so divine,
So full replete with choice of all delights,
But with as humble lowliness of mind
She is content to be at your command;
Command, I mean, of virtuous chaste intents,
To love and honour Henry as her lord.
King. And otherwise will Henry ne'er presume.
Therefore, my Lord Protector, give consent
That Marg'ret may be England's royal Queen.
Glou. So should I give consent to flatter sin.
You know, my lord, your Highness is betroth'd

HENRY VI

PART ONE

"God save King Henry, of that name the sixth." In Paris, Henry Beaufort, Bishop of Winchester (Alfred Burke), sets the crown upon the head of Henry (Jack May)
(Act IV, Scene I)

PHOTOGRAPHS BY LISEL HAAS
PRODUCED BY THE BIRMINGHAM
REPERTORY THEATRE

"Henry the Sixth, in infant bands crown'd King of France and England . . . whose state so many had the managing, that they lost France and made his England bleed"
(Henry the Fifth: Act V, Scene II)

Gloucester (Edgar Wreford), the king's uncle and protector, withdraws from Henry's presence to leave for France. His long-time rival, Winchester, through bribery now a Cardinal, glares balefully at right *(Act V, Scene I)*

The leader of the English, Lord Talbot (Alan Bridges), taunts the shepherd maid of France, Joan la Pucelle (Nancie Jackson), before one of the gates of Orleans: "Blood will I draw on thee, thou art a witch" *(Act I, Scene V)*

Once rescued by his father, Talbot's son (John Greenwood) later leaves his father's side and is killed by the French. "Come, come, and lay him in his father's arms: my spirit can no longer bear these harms. Soldiers, adieu! I have what I would have" *(Act IV, Scene VII)*

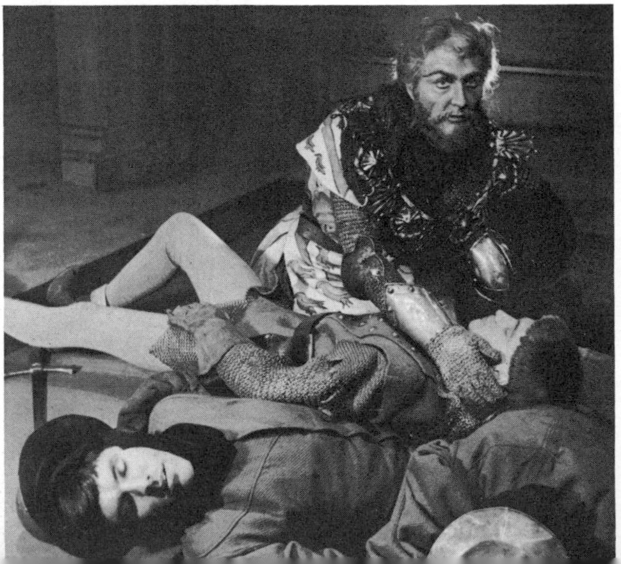

The French, led by Joan la Pucelle, famous as Joan of Arc, arrive in time to hear Talbot's last words over the body of his son: "Now my old arms are young John Talbot's grave." Then he too dies *(Act IV, Scene VII)*

"Fond man! remember that thou hast a wife; then how can Margaret be thy paramour?" In an aside, Suffolk (Richard Pasco) reasons with himself after taking captive Margaret of Anjou (Rosalind Boxall) *(Act V, Scene III)*

"My ancient incantations are too weak, and hell too strong for me to buckle with: now, France, thy glory droopeth to the dust." Deserted by the "familiars" who had appeared to her, Joan is captured by the English under York *(Act V, Scene III)*

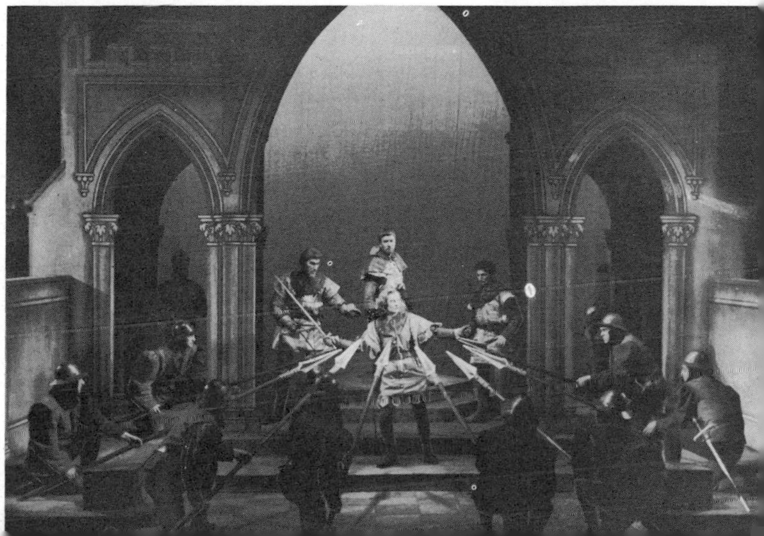

Richard Plantagenet, Duke of York (John Arnatt), addresses his captive: "Damsel of France, I think I have you fast: unchain your spirits now with spelling charms, and try if they can gain your liberty"
(Act V, Scene III)

"First, let me tell you whom you have condemn'd: not me begotten of a shepherd swain, but issu'd from the progeny of kings; virtuous and holy; chosen from above, by inspiration of celestial grace, to work exceeding miracles on earth." Joan's futile plea *(Act V, Scene IV)*

Unto another lady of esteem.
How shall we then dispense with that contract
And not deface your honour with reproach?

Suf. As doth a ruler with unlawful oaths,
Or one that at a triumph, having vow'd
To try his strength, forsaketh yet the lists
By reason of his adversary's odds.
A poor earl's daughter is unequal odds,
And therefore may be broke without offence.

Glou. Why, what, I pray, is Margaret more than that?
Her father is no better than an earl,
Although in glorious titles he excel.

Suf. Yes, my lord, her father is a king,
The King of Naples and Jerusalem,
And of such great authority in France
As his alliance will confirm our peace
And keep the Frenchmen in allegiance.

Glou. And so the Earl of Armagnac may do,
Because he is near kinsman unto Charles.

Exe. Beside, his wealth doth warrant a liberal dower,
Where Reignier sooner will receive than give.

Suf. A dow'r, my lords? Disgrace not so your king
That he should be so abject, base, and poor
To choose for wealth and not for perfect love!
Henry is able to enrich his queen,
And not to seek a queen to make him rich.
So worthless peasants bargain for their wives,
As marketmen for oxen, sheep, or horse.
Marriage is a matter of more worth
Than to be dealt in by attorneyship.
Not whom we will, but whom his Grace affects,
Must be companion of his nuptial bed.
And therefore, lords, since he affects her most,
It most of all these reasons bindeth us
In our opinions she should be preferr'd;
For what is wedlock forced but a hell,
An age of discord and continual strife?
Whereas the contrary bringeth bliss
And is a pattern of celestial peace.
Whom should we match with Henry, being a king,
But Margaret, that is daughter to a king?
Her peerless feature, joined with her birth,
Approves her fit for none but for a king.
Her valiant courage and undaunted spirit
(More than in women commonly is seen)
Will answer our hope in issue of a king;
For Henry, son unto a conqueror,
Is likely to beget more conquerors
If with a lady of so high resolve
As is fair Margaret he be link'd in love.
Then yield, my lords, and here conclude with me
That Margaret shall be Queen, and none but she.

King. Whether it be through force of your report,
My noble Lord of Suffolk, or for that
My tender youth was never yet attaint
With any passion of inflaming love,
I cannot tell; but this I am assur'd,
I feel such sharp dissension in my breast,
Such fierce alarums both of hope and fear,
As I am sick with working of my thoughts.
Take, therefore, shipping; post, my lord, to France;
Agree to any covenants, and procure
That Lady Margaret do vouchsafe to come
To cross the seas to England and be crown'd
King Henry's faithful and anointed queen.
For your expenses and sufficient charge,
Among the people gather up a tenth.
Be gone, I say; for till you do return
I rest perplexed with a thousand cares.
And you, good uncle, banish all offence.
If you do censure me by what you were,
Not what you are, I know it will excuse
This sudden execution of my will.
And so conduct me where, from company,
I may revolve and ruminate my grief. *Exit.*

Glou. Ay, grief, I fear me, both at first and last! *Exit Gloucester [with Exeter].*

Suf. Thus Suffolk hath prevail'd; and thus he goes,
As did the youthful Paris once to Greece,
With hope to find the like event in love
But prosper better than the Troyan did.
Margaret shall now be Queen, and rule the King;
But I will rule both her, the King, and realm.
Exit.

The Second Part of King Henry the Sixth

'The First part of the Contention betwixt the two famous Houses of Yorke and Lancaster, with the death of the good Duke Humphrey: And the banishment and death of the Duke of Suffolke, and the Tragicall end of the proud Cardinall of Winchester, with the notable Rebellion of Iacke Cade' was published as a quarto in 1594 and again in 1600. This is an imperfect form of The Second Part of King Henry the Sixth. In 1595 appeared 'The true Tragedie of Richard Duke of Yorke,' which is an imperfect form of *Part III.* In 1619 *The First Part of the Contention* and *The True Tragedie* came out together as 'The Whole Contention betweene the two Famous Houses, Lancaster and Yorke . . . Diuided into two Parts. . . . Written by William Shakespeare, Gent.' For the text of The Second Part of King Henry the Sixth our only authority is the Folio of 1623. The relation of this Part II to *The First Part of the Contention* is a matter of debate. There are three possibilities: *The First Part of the Contention* may be Shakespeare's own work in an earlier form than Henry the Sixth, Part II; it may be the work of some other dramatist which Shakespeare rewrote with extensive additions; it may be merely an abbreviated and garbled text of Shakespeare's Part II. On the whole, this third hypothesis seems to explain the phenomena most satisfactorily. Demonstration is impossible, but we may tentatively accept the Folio text of Part II as Shakespeare's in its entirety. Many scholars, however, maintain that *The First Part of the Contention* is Marlowe's, except for the Cade scenes, which show a comic spirit quite foreign to his genius and are sometimes credited to Greene. These, even in the form that they have in *The Contention*, are often ascribed to Shakespeare. For the rest, Shakespeare's work in his Part II (except for minutiæ in revision) would, on this hypothesis, be limited to those portions of Part II that are lacking in *The Contention.*

The text of *The First Part of the Contention* is in a deplorable state. Not to speak of other corruptions, the blank verse limps continually and sometimes lapses into prose, or into a halting mixture of prose and metre. A flagrant instance is the pedigree which York expounds to support his claim to the throne (cf. *2 Henry VI*, ii, 2), in which facts and metre are equally disordered. The Quarto of 1619 amends the genealogy but makes no attempt to restore the verse. Many differences between *The Contention* and Part II are due to omissions in the Quarto text that may well be cuts made to shorten the play for acting.

The Second Part of King Henry VI contains all the material of *The First Part of the Contention*, arranged in substantially the same order. Most of the lines in *The Contention* appear also in 2 Henry VI in some shape or other, — rarely word for word, often with but slight variation, frequently in what looks like paraphrase. An instance of close verbal agreement, line for line, may be seen in iii, 2, 188–229. Instances of considerable variation are the conjuring scene (i, 4, 1–43) and the last two scenes of Act v. In none of them, however, is there any inconsistency in substance. The concluding speech is identical in *The First Part of the Contention* and in Shakespeare's Part II. His Part II is longer than *The First Part of the Contention* by about a third, and the additional passages are among the best in the play. See, for examples, iii, 1, 15–27, 199–220, 241–281, 360–373; iii, 2, 76–81, 87–121, 254–269 (cf. *As You Like It*, iv, 3, 105–114), 360–366; iv, 1, 1–7, 77–105; v, 1, 6–11, 149–191; v, 2, 19–61. The Cade scenes are much better in PART II than in *The Contention* and are credited to Shakespeare by an almost unanimous vote.

With due allowance for the badness of the Quarto text, the style and metre of *The First Part of the Contention*, as well as the dramatic method and the characters of the *dramatis personæ*, undoubtedly accord with what we know of Marlowe's work. But Marlowe exercised a strong influence upon Shakespeare in the period to which KING HENRY THE SIXTH belongs, and some of the admittedly Shakespearean portions of PART II are quite as much like Marlowe as anything in *The Contention*. That Shakespeare actually collaborated with Marlowe and Greene, or with either of them, is altogether unlikely.

For PART II OF HENRY THE SIXTH a probable date is 1590 or 1591. It is, at all events, earlier than PART I. If there was a revival in 1594 or later (see p. 665), the Folio text may be the result of some slight revision by the author.

For facts Shakespeare relied upon Holinshed or Halle, whom for this period Holinshed paraphrases. The episode of the feigned miracle, with Simpcox's discomfiture, is worked up from a story that Sir Thomas More had heard his father tell. More records it in his *Dialogue of the Worship of Images*, and Richard Grafton copied it from More. Of course Shakespeare knew Grafton's *Chronicle*. The action of the play begins in 1445 with Margaret's arrival from France and closes with York's victory at St. Albans ten years later. Chronology is adjusted to suit the dramatist's convenience. Thus young Richard (afterwards Richard III) distinguishes himself in the battle, though in fact he was then less than three years old.

THE SECOND PART OF
KING HENRY THE SIXTH

[Dramatis Personæ.

King Henry the Sixth.
Humphrey, Duke of Gloucester, his uncle.
Cardinal Beaufort, Bishop of Winchester, great-uncle to the *King*.
Richard Plantagenet, Duke of York.
Edward and *Richard*, his sons.
Duke of Somerset.
Duke of Suffolk.
Duke of Buckingham.
Lord Clifford.
Young Clifford, his son.
Earl of Salisbury.
Earl of Warwick.
Lord Scales.
Lord Say.
Sir Humphrey Stafford.
William Stafford, his brother.
Sir John Stanley.
Vaux.
Matthew Goffe.
A Lieutenant, a Shipmaster, a Master's Mate, and *Walter Whitmore.*
Two Gentlemen, prisoners with *Suffolk.*
Alexander Iden, a Kentish gentleman.
John Hume and *John Southwell*, two priests.
Roger Bolingbroke, a conjurer.
Thomas Horner, an armourer.
Peter, his man.
Clerk of Chatham.
Mayor of Saint Alban's.
Saunder Simpcox, an impostor.
Jack Cade, a rebel.
George Bevis, John Holland, Dick the butcher, *Smith* the weaver, *Michael, &c.*, his followers.
Two Murderers.

Margaret, Queen to *King Henry*.
Eleanor, Duchess of Gloucester.
Margery Jourdain, a witch.
Wife to *Simpcox*.

Lords, Ladies, and Attendants, Petitioners, Aldermen, a Herald, a Beadle, a Sheriff, Officers, Citizens, Prentices, Falconers, Guards, Soldiers, Messengers, &c.

A Spirit.

SCENE. — *England.*]

ACT I. Scene I. [*London. The Palace.*]

Flourish of trumpets; then hautboys. Enter *King, Duke Humphrey of Gloucester, Salisbury, Warwick,* and *Cardinal Beaufort* on the one side; *the Queen, Suffolk, York, Somerset,* and *Buckingham,* on the other.

Suf. As by your high imperial Majesty
I had in charge at my depart for France,
As procurator to your Excellence,
To marry Princess Margaret for your Grace,
So, in the famous ancient city Tours,
In presence of the Kings of France and Sicil,
The Dukes of Orleans, Calaber, Bretagne, and Alençon,
Seven earls, twelve barons, and twenty reverend bishops,
I have perform'd my task and was espous'd;
And humbly now upon my bended knee,
In sight of England and her lordly peers,
Deliver up my title in the Queen
To your most gracious hands, that are the substance
Of that great shadow I did represent:
The happiest gift that ever marquess gave,
The fairest queen that ever king receiv'd.

King. Suffolk, arise. Welcome, Queen Margaret.
I can express no kinder sign of love
Than this kind kiss. O Lord, that lends me life,
Lend me a heart replete with thankfulness!
For thou hast given me in this beauteous face
A world of earthly blessings to my soul,
If sympathy of love unite our thoughts.

Queen. Great King of England and my gracious lord,
The mutual conference that my mind hath had,
By day, by night, waking and in my dreams,
In courtly company or at my beads,
With you, mine alderliefest sovereign,
Makes me the bolder to salute my king

With ruder terms, such as my wit affords
And over-joy of heart doth minister.

King. Her sight did ravish, but her grace in speech,
Her words yclad with wisdom's majesty,
Makes me from wond'ring fall to weeping joys,
Such is the fulness of my heart's content.
Lords, with one cheerful voice welcome my love.

All. (*kneel*) Long live Queen Margaret, England's happiness!

Queen. We thank you all. *Flourish.*

Suf. My Lord Protector, so it please your Grace,
Here are the articles of contracted peace
Between our sovereign and the French king Charles,
For eighteen months concluded by consent.

Glou. (*reads*) '*Inprimis,* It is agreed between the French king Charles and William de la Pole, Marquess of Suffolk, ambassador for Henry King of England, that the said Henry shall espouse the Lady Margaret, daughter unto Reignier King of Naples, Sicilia, and Jerusalem, and crown her Queen of England ere the thirtieth of May next ensuing.

Item, that the duchy of Anjou and the county of Maine shall be released and delivered to the King her father' —

Duke Humphrey lets it fall.

King. Uncle, how now?

Glou. Pardon me, gracious lord.
Some sudden qualm hath struck me at the heart,
And dimm'd mine eyes that I can read no further.

King. Uncle of Winchester, I pray read on.

Car. [*reads*] '*Item,* It is further agreed between them that the duchies of Anjou and Maine shall be released and delivered over to the King her father, and she sent over of the King of England's own proper cost and charges, without having any dowry.'

King. They please us well. Lord Marquess, kneel down.
We here create thee the first Duke of Suffolk
And girt thee with the sword. Cousin of York.
We here discharge your Grace from being Regent
I' th' parts of France till term of eighteen months
Be full expir'd. Thanks, uncle Winchester,
Gloucester, York, Buckingham, Somerset,
Salisbury, and Warwick.
We thank you all for this great favour done
In entertainment to my princely queen.
Come, let us in, and with all speed provide
To see her coronation be perform'd.

Exeunt King, Queen, and Suffolk. Manent the rest.

Glou. Brave peers of England, pillars of the state,
To you Duke Humphrey must unload his grief —
Your grief, the common grief of all the land.
What? Did my brother Henry spend his youth,
His valour, coin, and people in the wars?
Did he so often lodge in open field,
In winter's cold and summer's parching heat,
To conquer France, his true inheritance?
And did my brother Bedford toil his wits
To keep by policy what Henry got?
Have you yourselves, Somerset, Buckingham,
Brave York, Salisbury, and victorious Warwick,
Receiv'd deep scars in France and Normandy?
Or hath mine uncle Beaufort and myself,
With all the learned Council of the realm,
Studied so long, sat in the Council House
Early and late, debating to and fro
How France and Frenchmen might be kept in awe?
And was his Highness in his infancy
Crowned in Paris in despite of foes?
And shall these labours and these honours die?
Shall Henry's conquest, Bedford's vigilance,
Your deeds of war, and all our counsel die?
O peers of England, shameful is this league!
Fatal this marriage, cancelling your fame,
Blotting your names from books of memory,
Rasing the characters of your renown,
Defacing monuments of conquer'd France,
Undoing all as all had never been!

Car. Nephew, what means this passionate discourse,
This peroration with such circumstance?
For France, 'tis ours; and we will keep it still.

Glou. Ay, uncle, we will keep it if we can;
But now it is impossible we should.
Suffolk, the new-made duke that rules the roast,
Hath given the duchy of Anjou, and Maine
Unto the poor King Reignier, whose large style
Agrees not with the leanness of his purse.

Sal. Now, by the death of him that died for all,
These counties were the keys of Normandy!
But wherefore weeps Warwick, my valiant son?

War. For grief that they are past recovery;
For, were there hope to conquer them again,
My sword should shed hot blood, mine eyes no tears.
Anjou and Maine? Myself did win them both;

Those provinces these arms of mine did conquer;
And are the cities that I got with wounds
Deliver'd up again with peaceful words?
Mort Dieu!

York. For Suffolk's duke, may he be suffocate,
That dims the honour of this warlike isle!
France should have torn and rent my very heart
Before I would have yielded to this league.
I never read but England's kings have had
Large sums of gold and dowries with their wives,
And our King Henry gives away his own
To match with her that brings no vantages.

Hum. A proper jest, and never heard before,
That Suffolk should demand a whole fifteenth
For costs and charges in transporting her!
She should have stay'd in France, and starv'd in France,
Before —

Car. My Lord of Gloucester, now ye grow too hot.
It was the pleasure of my lord the King.

Hum. My Lord of Winchester, I know your mind.
'Tis not my speeches that you do mislike,
But 'tis my presence that doth trouble ye.
Rancour will out. Proud prelate, in thy face
I see thy fury. If I longer stay,
We shall begin our ancient bickerings.
Lordings, farewell; and say, when I am gone,
I prophesied, France will be lost ere long. *Exit.*

Car. So, there goes our Protector in a rage.
'Tis known to you he is mine enemy;
Nay more, an enemy unto you all,
And no great friend, I fear me, to the King.
Consider, lords, he is the next of blood
And heir apparent to the English crown.
Had Henry got an empire by his marriage
And all the wealthy kingdoms of the West,
There's reason he should be displeas'd at it.
Look to it, lords. Let not his smoothing words
Bewitch your hearts; be wise and circumspect.
What though the common people favour him,
Calling him 'Humphrey, the good Duke of Gloucester,'
Clapping their hands and crying with loud voice
'Jesu maintain your royal Excellence!'
With 'God preserve the good Duke Humphrey!'
I fear me, lords, for all this flattering gloss,
He will be found a dangerous Protector.

Buck. Why should he then protect our sovereign,
He being of age to govern of himself?
Cousin of Somerset, join you with me,
And all together with the Duke of Suffolk,
We'll quickly hoise Duke Humphrey from his seat.

Car. This weighty business will not brook delay.
I'll to the Duke of Suffolk presently. *Exit.*

Som. Cousin of Buckingham, though Humphrey's pride
And greatness of his place be grief to us,
Yet let us watch the haughty Cardinal.
His insolence is more intolerable
Than all the princes in the land beside.
If Gloucester be displac'd, he'll be Protector.

Buck. Or thou or I, Somerset, will be Protector
Despite Duke Humphrey or the Cardinal.

Exeunt Buckingham and Somerset.

Sal. Pride went before, ambition follows him.
While these do labour for their own preferment,
Behooves it us to labour for the realm.
I never saw but Humphrey Duke of Gloucester
Did bear him like a noble gentleman.
Oft have I seen the haughty Cardinal,
More like a soldier than a man o' th' church,
As stout and proud as he were lord of all,
Swear like a ruffian and demean himself
Unlike the ruler of a commonweal.
Warwick my son, the comfort of my age,
Thy deeds, thy plainness, and thy housekeeping
Hath won the greatest favour of the commons,
Excepting none but good Duke Humphrey.
And, brother York, thy acts in Ireland
In bringing them to civil discipline,
Thy late exploits done in the heart of France
When thou wert Regent for our sovereign,
Have made thee fear'd and honour'd of the people.
Join we together for the public good,
In what we can to bridle and suppress
The pride of Suffolk and the Cardinal
With Somerset's and Buckingham's ambition;
And, as we may, cherish Duke Humphrey's deeds
While they do tend the profit of the land.

War. So God help Warwick as he loves the land
And common profit of his country!

York. [*aside*] And so says York, for he hath greatest cause.

Sal. Then let's make haste away, and look unto the main.

War. Unto the main? O father, Maine is lost!
That Maine which by main force Warwick did win,

And would have kept so long as breath did last.
Main chance, father, you meant; but I meant Maine,
Which I will win from France, or else be slain.
Exeunt Warwick and Salisbury. Manet York.

York. Anjou and Maine are given to the French,
Paris is lost, the state of Normandy
Stands on a tickle point now they are gone.
Suffolk concluded on the articles,
The peers agreed, and Henry was well pleas'd
To change two dukedoms for a duke's fair daughter.
I cannot blame them all. What is't to them?
'Tis thine they give away, and not their own.
Pirates may make cheap pennyworths of their pillage,
And purchase friends, and give to courtesans,
Still revelling like lords till all be gone,
While as the silly owner of the goods
Weeps over them and wrings his hapless hands
And shakes his head and trembling stands aloof
While all is shar'd and all is borne away,
Ready to starve and dare not touch his own.
So York must sit and fret and bite his tongue
While his own lands are bargain'd for and sold.
Methinks the realms of England, France, and Ireland
Bear that proportion to my flesh and blood
As did the fatal brand Althæa burnt
Unto the prince's heart of Calydon.
Anjou and Maine both given unto the French?
Cold news for me! for I had hope of France,
Even as I have of fertile England's soil.
A day will come when York shall claim his own;
And therefore I will take the Nevils' parts,
And make a show of love to proud Duke Humphrey,
And when I spy advantage, claim the crown,
For that's the golden mark I seek to hit.
Nor shall proud Lancaster usurp my right,
Nor hold the sceptre in his childish fist,
Nor wear the diadem upon his head,
Whose churchlike humours fits not for a crown.
Then, York, be still awhile, till time do serve.
Watch thou and wake when others be asleep,
To pry into the secrets of the state,
Till Henry, surfeiting in joys of love,
With his new bride and England's dear-bought queen,
And Humphrey with the peers be fall'n at jars.
Then will I raise aloft the milk-white rose,
With whose sweet smell the air shall be perfum'd,
And in my standard bear the arms of York
To grapple with the house of Lancaster;
And force perforce I'll make him yield the crown
Whose bookish rule hath pull'd fair England down. *Exit.*

[Scene II. *London. The* Duke of Gloucester's *house.*]

Enter *Duke Humphrey* and his wife *Eleanor.*

Elean. Why droops my lord, like over-ripen'd corn
Hanging the head at Ceres' plenteous load?
Why doth the great Duke Humphrey knit his brows,
As frowning at the favours of the world?
Why are thine eyes fix'd to the sullen earth,
Gazing on that which seems to dim thy sight?
What seest thou there? King Henry's diadem,
Enchas'd with all the honours of the world?
If so, gaze on, and grovel on thy face,
Until thy head be circled with the same.
Put forth thy hand, reach at the glorious gold.
What, is't too short? I'll lengthen it with mine;
And having both together heav'd it up,
We'll both together lift our heads to heaven
And never more abase our sight so low
As to vouchsafe one glance unto the ground.

Hum. O Nell, sweet Nell, if thou dost love thy lord,
Banish the canker of ambitious thoughts!
And may that thought, when I imagine ill
Against my king and nephew, virtuous Henry,
Be my last breathing in this mortal world!
My troublous dream this night doth make me sad.

Elean. What dream'd my lord? Tell me, and I'll requite it
With sweet rehearsal of my morning's dream.

Hum. Methought this staff, mine office-badge in court,
Was broke in twain; by whom I have forgot,
But as I think, it was by th' Cardinal;
And on the pieces of the broken wand
Were plac'd the heads of Edmund Duke of Somerset
And William de la Pole, first Duke of Suffolk.
This was my dream. What it doth bode, God knows.

Elean. Tut, this was nothing but an argument
That he that breaks a stick of Gloucester's grove

Shall lose his head for his presumption.
But list to me, my Humphrey, my sweet duke.
Methought I sat in seat of majesty
In the cathedral church of Westminster
And in that chair where kings and queens are crown'd;
Where Henry and Dame Margaret kneel'd to me
And on my head did set the diadem.

Hum. Nay, Eleanor, then must I chide outright.
Presumptuous dame, ill-nurtur'd Eleanor!
Art thou not second woman in the realm,
And the Protector's wife, belov'd of him?
Hast thou not worldly pleasure at command
Above the reach or compass of thy thought?
And wilt thou still be hammering treachery
To tumble down thy husband and thyself
From top of honour to disgrace's feet?
Away from me, and let me hear no more!

Elean. What, what, my lord? Are you so choleric
With Eleanor for telling but her dream?
Next time I'll keep my dreams unto myself
And not be check'd.

Hum. Nay, be not angry. I am pleas'd again.

Enter *Messenger.*

Mess. My Lord Protector, 'tis his Highness' pleasure
You do prepare to ride unto Saint Alban's,
Where as the King and Queen do mean to hawk.

Hum. I go. Come, Nell — thou wilt ride with us?

Elean. Yes, my good lord, I'll follow presently.

Exit Humphrey [*with Messenger*].

Follow I must; I cannot go before
While Gloucester bears this base and humble mind.
Were I a man, a duke, and next of blood,
I would remove these tedious stumbling blocks
And smooth my way upon their headless necks;
And being a woman, I will not be slack
To play my part in Fortune's pageant.
Where are you there? Sir John! Nay, fear not, man.
We are alone; here's none but thee and I.

Enter *Hume.*

Hume. Jesus preserve your Royal Majesty!

Elean. What say'st thou? Majesty? I am but Grace.

Hume. But by the grace of God and Hume's advice
Your Grace's title shall be multiplied.

Elean. What say'st thou, man? Hast thou as yet conferr'd
With Margery Jourdain, the cunning witch,
With Roger Bolingbroke, the conjurer?
And will they undertake to do me good?

Hume. This they have promised, to show your Highness
A spirit rais'd from depth of underground
That shall make answer to such questions
As by your Grace shall be propounded him.

Elean. It is enough. I'll think upon the questions.
When from Saint Alban's we do make return
We'll see these things effected to the full.
Here, Hume, take this reward. Make merry, man,
With thy confederates in this weighty cause.

Exit.

Hume. Hume must make merry with the Duchess' gold.
Marry, and shall! But, how now, Sir John Hume?
Seal up your lips and give no words but mum;
The business asketh silent secrecy.
Dame Eleanor gives gold to bring the witch;
Gold cannot come amiss, were she a devil.
Yet have I gold flies from another coast:
I dare not say, from the rich Cardinal
And from the great and new-made Duke of Suffolk;
Yet I do find it so; for, to be plain,
They (knowing Dame Eleanor's aspiring humour)
Have hired me to undermine the Duchess
And buzz these conjurations in her brain.
They say, 'A crafty knave does need no broker';
Yet am I Suffolk and the Cardinal's broker.
Hume, if you take not heed, you shall go near
To call them both a pair of crafty knaves.
Well, so it stands; and thus, I fear, at last
Hume's knavery will be the Duchess' wrack
And her attainture will be Humphrey's fall.
Sort how it will, I shall have gold for all. *Exit.*

[Scene III. *London. The Palace.*]

Enter three or four *Petitioners*, the *Armourer's Man* (*Peter*) being one.

1. Petit. My masters, let's stand close. My Lord Protector will come this way by-and-by, and then we may deliver our supplications in the quill.

2. Petit. Marry, the Lord protect him, for he's a good man, Jesu bless him!

Enter *Suffolk* and *Queen.*

1. Petit. Here 'a comes, methinks, and the Queen with him. I'll be the first, sure.

2. Petit. Come back, fool. This is the Duke of Suffolk and not my Lord Protector.

Suf. How now, fellow? Wouldst anything with me?

1. Petit. I pray, my lord, pardon me. I took ye for my Lord Protector.

Queen. [*reads*] 'To my Lord Protector'? Are your supplications to his lordship? Let me see them. What is thine?

1. Petit. Mine is, an't please your Grace, against John Goodman, my Lord Cardinal's man, for keeping my house and lands, and wife and all, from me.

Suf. Thy wife too? That's some wrong indeed. What's yours? What's here? [*Reads*] Against the Duke of Suffolk, for enclosing the commons of Melford.' How now, sir knave?

2. Petit. Alas, sir, I am but a poor petitioner of our whole township.

Peter. [*presents his petition*] Against my master, Thomas Horner, for saying that the Duke of York was rightful heir to the crown.

Queen. What say'st thou? Did the Duke of York say he was rightful heir to the crown?

Peter. That my master was? No, forsooth! My master said that he was, and that the King was an usurper.

Suf. Who is there?

Enter *Servant.*

Take this fellow in and send for his master with a pursuivant presently. We'll hear more of your matter before the King.

Exit [*Servant with Peter*].

Queen. And as for you that love to be protected
Under the wings of our Protector's grace,
Begin your suits anew and sue to him.

Tear the supplication.

Away, base cullions! Suffolk, let them go.

All. Come, let's be gone. *Exeunt.*

Queen. My Lord of Suffolk, say, is this the guise,
Is this the fashion in the court of England?
Is this the government of Britain's isle,
And this the royalty of Albion's king?
What, shall King Henry be a pupil still,
Under the surly Gloucester's governance?
Am I a queen in title and in style
And must be made a subject to a duke?
I tell thee, Pole, when in the city Tours
Thou ran'st a-tilt in honour of my love
And stol'st away the ladies' hearts of France,
I thought King Henry had resembled thee
In courage, courtship, and proportion;
But all his mind is bent to holiness,
To number Ave-Maries on his beads;
His champions are the prophets and apostles,
His weapons holy saws of sacred writ;
His study is his tiltyard, and his loves
Are brazen images of canonized saints.
I would the college of the Cardinals
Would choose him Pope and carry him to Rome
And set the triple crown upon his head!
That were a state fit for his holiness.

Suf. Madam, be patient. As I was cause
Your Highness came to England, so will I
In England work your Grace's full content.

Queen. Beside the haughty Protector, have we Beaufort
The imperious churchman, Somerset, Buckingham,
And grumbling York; and not the least of these
But can do more in England than the King.

Suf. And he of these that can do most of all
Cannot do more in England than the Nevils.
Salisbury and Warwick are no simple peers.

Queen. Not all these lords do vex me half so much
As that proud dame, the Lord Protector's wife.
She sweeps it through the court with troops of ladies,
More like an empress than Duke Humphrey's wife.
Strangers in court do take her for the Queen.
She bears a duke's revenues on her back,
And in her heart she scorns our poverty.
Shall I not live to be aveng'd on her?
Contemptuous base-born callot as she is,
She vaunted 'mongst her minions t'other day,
The very train of her worst wearing gown
Was better worth than all my father's lands
Till Suffolk gave two dukedoms for his daughter.

Suf. Madam, myself have lim'd a bush for her,
And plac'd a choir of such enticing birds
That she will light to listen to their lays
And never mount to trouble you again.
So let her rest. And, madam, list to me,
For I am bold to counsel you in this:
Although we fancy not the Cardinal,
Yet must we join with him and with the lords
Till we have brought Duke Humphrey in disgrace.

As for the Duke of York, this late complaint
Will make but little for his benefit.
So one by one we'll weed them all at last,
And you yourself shall steer the happy helm.

Sound a sennet. Enter the *King, Duke Humphrey, Cardinal* [*Beaufort*], *Buckingham, York, Somerset, Salisbury, Warwick,* and the *Duchess* [*of Gloucester*].

King. For my part, noble lords, I care not which:
Or Somerset or York, all 's one to me.
York. If York have ill demean'd himself in France,
Then let him be denay'd the regentship.
Som. If Somerset be unworthy of the place,
Let York be Regent; I will yield to him.
War. Whether your Grace be worthy, yea or no,
Dispute not that. York is the worthier.
Car. Ambitious Warwick, let thy betters speak!
War. The Cardinal's not my better in the field.
Buck. All in this presence are thy betters, Warwick.
War. Warwick may live to be the best of all.
Sal. Peace, son! and show some reason, Buckingham,
Why Somerset should be preferr'd in this.
Queen. Because the King forsooth will have it so.
Hum. Madam, the King is old enough himself
To give his censure. These are no women's matters.
Queen. If he be old enough, what needs your Grace
To be Protector of his Excellence?
Hum. Madam, I am Protector of the realm,
And at his pleasure will resign my place.
Suf. Resign it then and leave thine insolence.
Since thou wert king (as who is king but thou?)
The commonwealth hath daily run to wrack,
The Dauphin hath prevail'd beyond the seas,
And all the peers and nobles of the realm
Have been as bondmen to thy sovereignty.
Car. The commons hast thou rack'd; the clergy's bags
Are lank and lean with thy extortions.
Som. Thy sumptuous buildings and thy wive's attire
Have cost a mass of public treasury.
Buck. Thy cruelty in execution
Upon offenders hath exceeded law,
And left thee to the mercy of the law.
Queen. Thy sale of offices and towns in France —
If they were known, as the suspect is great —
Would make thee quickly hop without thy head.
Exit Humphrey. [*The Queen drops her fan.*]
Give me my fan! What, minion, can ye not?
She gives the Duchess a box on the ear.
I cry you mercy, madam. Was it you?
Duch. Was't I? Yea, I it was, proud Frenchwoman!
Could I come near your beauty with my nails,
I would set my ten commandments in your face.
King. Sweet aunt, be quiet. 'Twas against her will.
Duch. Against her will, good King? Look to't in time!
She'll hamper thee and dandle thee like a baby.
Though in this place most master wear no breeches,
She shall not strike Dame Eleanor unreveng'd.
Exit.
Buck. Lord Cardinal, I will follow Eleanor,
And listen after Humphrey, how he proceeds.
She's tickled now; her fume needs no spurs,
She'll gallop far enough to her destruction.
Exit.

Enter [*Duke*] *Humphrey.*

Hum. Now, lords, my choler being overblown
With walking once about the quadrangle,
I come to talk of commonwealth affairs.
As for your spiteful false objections,
Prove them, and I lie open to the law;
But God in mercy so deal with my soul
As I in duty love my king and country!
But to the matter that we have in hand:
I say, my sovereign, York is meetest man
To be your Regent in the realm of France.
Suf. Before we make election, give me leave
To show some reason, of no little force,
That York is most unmeet of any man.
York. I'll tell thee, Suffolk, why I am unmeet:
First, for I cannot flatter thee in pride;
Next, if I be appointed for the place,
My Lord of Somerset will keep me here
Without discharge, money, or furniture
Till France be won into the Dauphin's hands.
Last time I danc'd attendance on his will
Till Paris was besieg'd, famish'd, and lost.
War. That can I witness; and a fouler fact
Did never traitor in the land commit.
Suf. Peace, headstrong Warwick!

War. Image of pride, why should I hold my peace?

Enter [*Horner*] *the Armourer*, and his *Man* [*Peter*, guarded].

Suf. Because here is a man accus'd of treason.
Pray God the Duke of York excuse himself!

York. Doth any one accuse York for a traitor?

King. What mean'st thou, Suffolk? Tell me, what are these?

Suf. Please it your Majesty, this is the man
That doth accuse his master of high treason.
His words were these: that Richard Duke of York
Was rightful heir unto the English crown
And that your Majesty was an usurper.

King. Say, man, were these thy words?

Arm. An't shall please your Majesty, I never said nor thought any such matter. God is my witness, I am falsely accus'd by the villain.

Peter. By these ten bones, my lords, he did speak them to me in the garret one night, as we were scouring my Lord of York's armour.

York. Base dunghill villain and mechanical,
I'll have thy head for this thy traitor's speech.
I do beseech your royal Majesty,
Let him have all the rigour of the law.

Arm. Alas, my lord, hang me if ever I spake the words! My accuser is my prentice; and when I did correct him for his fault the other day, he did vow upon his knees he would be even with me. I have good witness of this. Therefore I beseech your Majesty, do not cast away an honest man for a villain's accusation.

King. Uncle, what shall we say to this in law?

Hum. This is my doom, my lord, if I may judge:
Let Somerset be Regent o'er the French,
Because in York this breeds suspicion;
And let these have a day appointed them
For single combat in convenient place,
For he hath witness of his servant's malice.
This is the law, and this Duke Humphrey's doom.

King. Then be it so. My Lord of Somerset,
We make your Grace Regent over the French.

Som. I humbly thank your royal Majesty.

Arm. And I accept the combat willingly.

Peter. Alas, my lord, I cannot fight! For God's sake pity my case! The spite of man prevaileth against me. O Lord have mercy upon me! I shall never be able to fight a blow. O Lord, my heart!

Hum. Sirrah, or you must fight or else be hang'd.

King. Away with them to prison! and the day
Of combat shall be the last of the next month.
Come, Somerset, we'll see thee sent away.

Flourish. Exeunt.

[Scene IV. *London.* Gloucester's *garden.*]

Enter *Margery Jourdain* the *Witch*, the two *Priests* [*Hume* and *Southwell*], and *Bolingbroke.*

Hume. Come, my masters. The Duchess, I tell you, expects performance of your promises.

Boling. Master Hume, we are therefore provided. Will her ladyship behold and hear our exorcisms?

Hume. Ay, what else? Fear you not her courage.

Boling. I have heard her reported to be a woman of an invincible spirit. But it shall be convenient, Master Hume, that you be by her aloft while we be busy below; and so I pray you go in God's name, and leave us. (*Exit Hume.*) Mother Jourdain, be you prostrate and grovel on the earth. John Southwell, read you, and let us to our work.

Enter [*Duchess*] *Eleanor* aloft, [followed by *Hume*].

Elean. Well said, my masters, and welcome all. To this gear, the sooner the better.

Boling. Patience, good lady; wizards know their times.
Deep night, dark night, the silent of the night,
The time of night when Troy was set on fire;
The time when screech owls cry and bandogs howl
And spirits walk and ghosts break up their graves —
That time best fits the work we have in hand.
Madam, sit you and fear not. Whom we raise,
We will make fast within a hallow'd verge.

Here do the ceremonies belonging, and make the circle. Bolingbroke or Southwell reads: 'Coniuro te,' &c. *It thunders and lightens terribly; then the Spirit riseth.*

Spirit. Adsum.

Witch. Asmath,
By the eternal God, whose name and power
Thou tremblest at, answer that I shall ask;

For till thou speak thou shalt not pass from hence.

Spirit. Ask what thou wilt. That I had said and done!

Boling. [*reads*] 'First of the King: what shall of him become?'

Spirit. The duke yet lives that Henry shall depose;
But him outlive, and die a violent death.

[*As the Spirit speaks, Southwell writes the answer.*]

Boling. 'What fates await the Duke of Suffolk?'

Spirit. By water shall he die and take his end.

Boling. 'What shall befall the Duke of Somerset?'

Spirit. Let him shun castles.
Safer shall he be upon the sandy plains
Than where castles mounted stand.
Have done, for more I hardly can endure.

Boling. Descend to darkness and the burning lake!
False fiend, avoid!

Thunder and lightning. Exit Spirit.

Enter the *Duke of York* and the *Duke of Buckingham,* with their *Guard,* and break in.

York. Lay hands upon these traitors and their trash.
Beldam, I think we watch'd you at an inch.
What, madam, are you there? The King and commonweal
Are deeply indebted for this piece of pains.
My Lord Protector will, I doubt it not,
See you well guerdon'd for these good deserts.

Elean. Not half so bad as thine to England's king,
Injurious Duke, that threatest where's no cause.

Buck. True, madam, none at all. What call you this? [*Shows her the paper.*]
Away with them! Let them be clapp'd up close
And kept asunder. You, madam, shall with us.
Stafford, take her to thee.
We'll see your trinkets here all forthcoming.
All away!

Exeunt [*above, Duchess and Hume, guarded; below, Witch, Southwell, and Bolingbroke, guarded*].

York. Lord Buckingham, methinks you watch'd her well.
A pretty plot, well chosen to build upon!
Now pray, my lord, let's see the devil's writ.
What have we here? *Reads.*
'The duke yet lives that Henry shall depose;
But him outlive, and die a violent death.'
Why, this is just
'Aio te, Aeacida, Romanos vincere posse.'
Well, to the rest:
'Tell me, what fate awaits the Duke of Suffolk?
By water shall he die and take his end.
What shall betide the Duke of Somerset?
Let him shun castles.
Safer shall he be upon the sandy plains
Than where castles mounted stand.'
Come, come, my lords! These oracles
Are hardly attain'd and hardly understood.
The King is now in progress towards Saint Alban's,
With him the husband of this lovely lady.
Thither goes these news as fast as horse can carry them —
A sorry breakfast for my Lord Protector.

Buck. Your Grace shall give me leave, my Lord of York,
To be the post, in hope of his reward.

York. At your pleasure, my good lord.
Who's within there, ho?

Enter a *Servingman.*

Invite my Lords of Salisbury and Warwick
To sup with me to-morrow night. Away!

Exeunt.

[ACT II. Scene I. *Saint Alban's.*]

Enter the *King, Queen, Protector* [*Gloucester*], *Cardinal,* and *Suffolk,* with *Falconers* halloaing.

Queen. Believe me, lords, for flying at the brook
I saw not better sport these seven years' day.
Yet, by your leave, the wind was very high,
And, ten to one, old Joan had not gone out.

King. But what a point, my lord, your falcon made,
And what a pitch she flew above the rest!
To see how God in all his creatures works!
Yea, man and birds are fain of climbing high.

Suf. No marvel, an it like your Majesty,
My Lord Protector's hawks do tow'r so well.
They know their master loves to be aloft
And bears his thoughts above his falcon's pitch.

Glouc. My lord, 'tis but a base ignoble mind
That mounts no higher than a bird can soar.

Car. I thought as much. He would be above the clouds.

Glou. Ay, my Lord Cardinal, how think you by that?
Were it not good your Grace could fly to heaven?

King. The treasury of everlasting joy.

Car. Thy heaven is on earth; thine eyes and thoughts
Beat on a crown, the treasure of thy heart,
Pernicious Protector, dangerous peer,
That smooth'st it so with King and commonweal!

Glou. What, Cardinal, is your priesthood grown peremptory?
'Tantaene animis coelestibus irae?'
Churchmen so hot? Good uncle, hide such malice;
For with such holiness well can you do it.

Suf. No malice, sir; no more than well becomes
So good a quarrel and so bad a peer.

Glou. As who, my lord?

Suf. Why, as you, my lord,
An't like your lordly Lord's Protectorship.

Glou. Why, Suffolk, England knows thine insolence.

Queen. And thy ambition, Gloucester.

King. I prithee, peace,
Good Queen, and whet not on these furious peers;
For blessed are the peacemakers on earth.

Car. Let me be blessed for the peace I make
Against this proud Protector with my sword!

Glou. [*aside to Cardinal*] Faith, holy uncle, would 'twere come to that!

Car. [*aside to Gloucester*] Marry, when thou dar'st.

Glou. [*aside to Cardinal*] Make up no factious numbers for the matter;
In thine own person answer thy abuse.

Car. [*aside to Gloucester*] Ay, where thou dar'st not peep; and if thou dar'st,
This evening on the east side of the grove.

King. How now, my lords?

Car. Believe me, cousin Gloucester,
Had not your man put up the fowl so suddenly,
We had had more sport — [*Aside to Gloucester*] Come with thy two-hand sword. 46

Glou. True, uncle.

Car. [*aside to Gloucester*] Are ye advis'd? The east side of the grove.

Glou. [*aside to Cardinal*] Cardinal, I am with you.

King. Why, how now, uncle Gloucester?

Glou. Talking of hawking; nothing else, my lord.
[*Aside to Cardinal*] Now, by God's Mother, priest, I'll shave your crown for this,
Or all my fence shall fail.

Car. [*aside to Gloucester*] Medice, teipsum.
Protector, see to't well; protect yourself.

King. The winds grow high; so do your stomachs, lords.
How irksome is this music to my heart!
When such strings jar, what hope of harmony?
I pray, my lords, let me compound this strife.

Enter *one crying* 'A miracle!'

Glou. What means this noise?
Fellow, what miracle dost thou proclaim?

One. A miracle! a miracle!

Suf. Come to the King and tell him what miracle.

One. Forsooth, a blind man at Saint Alban's shrine
Within this half hour hath receiv'd his sight —
A man that ne'er saw in his life before.

King. Now God be prais'd that to believing souls
Gives light in darkness, comfort in despair!

Enter the *Mayor of Saint Alban's* and his *Brethren*, bearing the man, [*Simpcox*,] between two in a chair, [*Simpcox's Wife* and a *crowd of Townsmen* following].

Car. Here comes the townsmen on procession
To present your Highness with the man.

King. Great is his comfort in this earthly vale,
Although by his sight his sin be multiplied.

Glou. Stand by, my masters. Bring him near the King;
His Highness' pleasure is to talk with him.

King. Good fellow, tell us here the circumstance,
That we for thee may glorify the Lord.
What, hast thou been long blind, and now restor'd?

Simp. Born blind, an't please your Grace.

Wife. Ay indeed was he.

Suf. What woman is this?

Wife. His wife, an't like your worship.

Glou. Hadst thou been his mother, thou couldst have better told.

King. Where wert thou born?

Simp. At Berwick in the North, an't like your Grace.

King. Poor soul, God's goodness hath been great to thee!

Let never day nor night unhallowed pass,
But still remember what the Lord hath done.

Queen. Tell me, good fellow, cam'st thou here by chance,
Or of devotion, to this holy shrine?

Simp. God knows, of pure devotion, being call'd
A hundred times and oft'ner in my sleep
By good Saint Alban, who said 'Simpcox, come;
Come offer at my shrine and I will help thee.'

Wife. Most true, forsooth! and many time and oft
Myself have heard a voice to call him so.

Car. What, art thou lame?

Simp. Ay, God Almighty help me!

Suf. How cam'st thou so?

Simp. A fall off of a tree.

Wife. A plum tree, master.

Glou. How long hast thou been blind?

Simp. O, born so, master!

Glou. What, and wouldst climb a tree?

Simp. But that in all my life, when I was a youth.

Wife. Too true, and bought his climbing very dear.

Glou. Mass, thou lov'dst plums well, that wouldst venture so.

Simp. Alas, good master, my wife desir'd some damsons
And made me climb, with danger of my life.

Glou. A subtile knave! But yet it shall not serve.
Let me see thine eyes. Wink now. Now open them.
In my opinion yet thou seest not well.

Simp. Yes, master, clear as day, I thank God and Saint Alban.

Glou. Say'st thou me so? What colour is this cloak of?

Simp. Red, master; red as blood.

Glou. Why, that's well said. What colour is my gown of?

Simp. Black, forsooth; coal-black, as jet.

King. Why then, thou know'st what colour jet is of?

Suf. And yet, I think, jet did he never see.

Glou. But cloaks and gowns before this day a many.

Wife. Never before this day in all his life.

Glou. Tell me, sirrah, what's my name?

Simp. Alas, master, I know not.

Glou. What's his name?

Simp. I know not.

Glou. Nor his?

Simp. No indeed, master.

Glou. What's thine own name?

Simp. Saunder Simpcox, an if it please you, master.

Glou. Then, Saunder, sit there, the lying'st knave in Christendom. If thou hadst been born blind, thou mightst as well have known all our names as thus to name the several colours we do wear. Sight may distinguish of colours; but suddenly to nominate them all, it is impossible. My lords, Saint Alban here hath done a miracle; and would ye not think his cunning to be great that could restore this cripple to his legs again?

Simp. O master, that you could!

Glou. My masters of Saint Alban's, have you not beadles in your town, and things call'd whips?

Mayor. Yes, my lord, if it please your Grace.

Glou. Then send for one presently.

Mayor. Sirrah, go fetch the beadle hither straight. *Exit [an Attendant]*.

Glou. Now fetch me a stool hither by-and-by. [*A stool brought*.] Now, sirrah, if you mean to save yourself from whipping, leap me over this stool and run away.

Simp. Alas, master, I am not able to stand alone!
You go about to torture me in vain.

Enter a *Beadle* with whips.

Glou. Well, sir, we must have you find your legs. Sirrah beadle, whip him till he leap over that same stool.

Bead. I will, my lord. Come on, sirrah. Off with your doublet quickly.

Simp. Alas, master, what shall I do? I am not able to stand.

After the Beadle hath hit him once, he leaps over the stool and runs away; and they follow and cry 'A miracle!'

King. O God, seest thou this, and bearest so long?

Queen. It made me laugh to see the villain run.

Glou. Follow the knave, and take this drab away.

Wife. Alas, sir, we did it for pure need!

Glou. Let them be whipp'd through every market town till they come to Berwick, from whence they came.

Exeunt Mayor, [*Beadle, Wife, &c.*].

Car. Duke Humphrey has done a miracle to-day.

Suf. True; made the lame to leap and fly away.

Glou. But you have done more miracles than I;
You made in a day, my lord, whole towns to fly.

Enter *Buckingham.*

King. What tidings with our cousin Buckingham?
Buck. Such as my heart doth tremble to unfold.
A sort of naughty persons, lewdly bent,
Under the countenance and confederacy
Of Lady Eleanor, the Protector's wife,
The ringleader and head of all this rout,
Have practis'd dangerously against your state,
Dealing with witches and with conjurers,
Whom we have apprehended in the fact,
Raising up wicked spirits from underground,
Demanding of King Henry's life and death
And other of your Highness' Privy Council,
As more at large your Grace shall understand.
Car. And so, my Lord Protector, by this means
Your lady is forthcoming yet at London.
This news, I think, hath turn'd your weapon's edge.
'Tis like, my lord, you will not keep your hour.
Glou. Ambitious churchman, leave to afflict my heart.
Sorrow and grief have vanquish'd all my powers;
And, vanquish'd as I am, I yield to thee
Or to the meanest groom.
King. O God, what mischiefs work the wicked ones,
Heaping confusion on their own heads thereby!
Queen. Gloucester, see here the taincture of thy nest;
And look thyself be faultless, thou wert best.
Glou. Madam, for myself, to heaven I do appeal,
How I have lov'd my king and commonweal;
And for my wife, I know not how it stands.
Sorry I am to hear what I have heard.
Noble she is; but if she have forgot
Honour and virtue and convers'd with such
As, like to pitch, defile nobility,
I banish her my bed and company
And give her as a prey to law and shame
That hath dishonoured Gloucester's honest name.
King. Well, for this night we will repose us here.
To-morrow toward London back again
To look into this business thoroughly
And call these foul offenders to their answers
And poise the cause in justice' equal scales,
Whose beam stands sure, whose rightful cause prevails. *Flourish. Exeunt.*

[Scene II. *London. The* Duke of York's *garden.*]

Enter *York, Salisbury,* and *Warwick.*

York. Now, my good Lords of Salisbury and Warwick,
Our simple supper ended, give me leave
In this close walk to satisfy myself
In craving your opinion of my title,
Which is infallible, to England's crown.
Sal. My lord, I long to hear it at full.
War. Sweet York, begin; and if thy claim be good,
The Nevils are thy subjects to command.
York. Then thus:
Edward the Third, my lords, had seven sons:
The first, Edward the Black Prince, Prince of Wales;
The second, William of Hatfield; and the third,
Lionel Duke of Clarence; next to whom
Was John of Gaunt, the Duke of Lancaster;
The fifth was Edmund Langley, Duke of York;
The sixth was Thomas of Woodstock, Duke of Gloucester;
William of Windsor was the seventh and last.
Edward the Black Prince died before his father
And left behind him Richard, his only son,
Who after Edward the Third's death reign'd as king
Till Henry Bolingbroke, Duke of Lancaster,
The eldest son and heir of John of Gaunt,
Crown'd by the name of Henry the Fourth,
Seiz'd on the realm, depos'd the rightful king,
Sent his poor queen to France, from whence she came,
And him to Pomfret, where, as all you know,
Harmless Richard was murthered traitorously.
War. Father, the Duke hath told the truth.
Thus got the house of Lancaster the crown.
York. Which now they hold by force, and not by right;
For Richard, the first son's heir, being dead,
The issue of the next son should have reign'd.
Sal. But William of Hatfield died without an heir.
York. The third son, Duke of Clarence, from whose line
I claim the crown, had issue, Philip, a daughter,

Who married Edmund Mortimer, Earl of March.
Edmund had issue, Roger Earl of March;
Roger had issue, Edmund, Anne, and Eleanor.
Sal. This Edmund in the reign of Bolingbroke,
As I have read, laid claim unto the crown;
And, but for Owen Glendower, had been king,
Who kept him in captivity till he died.
But to the rest.
York. His eldest sister, Anne,
My mother, being heir unto the crown,
Married Richard Earl of Cambridge, who was son
To Edmund Langley, Edward the Third's fifth son.
By her I claim the kingdom. She was heir
To Roger Earl of March, who was the son
Of Edmund Mortimer, who married Philip,
Sole daughter unto Lionel Duke of Clarence.
So, if the issue of the elder son
Succeed before the younger, I am King.
War. What plain proceeding is more plain than this?
Henry doth claim the crown from John of Gaunt,
The fourth son; York claims it from the third.
Till Lionel's issue fails, his should not reign.
It fails not yet, but flourishes in thee
And in thy sons, fair slips of such a stock.
Then, father Salisbury, kneel we together,
And in this private plot be we the first
That shall salute our rightful sovereign
With honour of his birthright to the crown.
Both. Long live our sovereign Richard, England's King!
York. We thank you, lords. But I am not your king
Till I be crown'd and that my sword be stain'd
With heart-blood of the house of Lancaster.
And that's not suddenly to be perform'd,
But with advice and silent secrecy.
Do you as I do in these dangerous days:
Wink at the Duke of Suffolk's insolence,
At Beaufort's pride, at Somerset's ambition,
At Buckingham and all the crew of them,
Till they have snar'd the shepherd of the flock
That virtuous prince, the good Duke Humphrey.
'Tis that they seek; and they in seeking that
Shall find their deaths, if York can prophesy.
Sal. My lord, break we off. We know your mind at full.
War. My heart assures me that the Earl of Warwick
Shall one day make the Duke of York a king.
York. And, Nevil, this I do assure myself,
Richard shall live to make the Earl of Warwick
The greatest man in England but the King.
Exeunt.

[Scene III. *London. A hall of justice.*]

Sound trumpets. Enter the *King* and *State,* [i.e. the *Queen, Gloucester, York, Suffolk,* and *Salisbury,*] with *Guard,* to banish the *Duchess.* [Enter, guarded, the *Duchess of Gloucester, Margery Jourdain, Hume, Southwell,* and *Bolingbroke.*]

King. Stand forth, Dame Eleanor Cobham, Gloucester's wife.
In sight of God and us your guilt is great.
Receive the sentence of the law for sins
Such as by God's book are adjudg'd to death.
[*To Jourdain and the others*] You four, from hence to prison back again;
From thence unto the place of execution. —
The witch in Smithfield shall be burn'd to ashes,
And you three shall be strangled on the gallows. —
[*To the Duchess*] You, madam, for you are more nobly born,
Despoiled of your honour in your life,
Shall, after three days' open penance done,
Live in your country here in banishment
With Sir John Stanley in the Isle of Man.
Elean. Welcome is banishment! Welcome were my death!
Glou. Eleanor, the law, thou seest, hath judged thee.
I cannot justify whom the law condemns.
Exeunt [*the Duchess and the other prisoners, guarded*].
Mine eyes are full of tears, my heart of grief.
Ah, Humphrey, this dishonour in thine age
Will bring thy head with sorrow to the ground!
I beseech your Majesty give me leave to go.
Sorrow would solace, and mine age would ease.
King. Stay, Humphrey Duke of Gloucester. Ere thou go,
Give up thy staff. Henry will to himself
Protector be; and God shall be my hope,
My stay, my guide, and lanthorn to my feet.
And go in peace, Humphrey, no less belov'd
Than when thou wert Protector to thy king.
Queen. I see no reason why a king of years
Should be to be protected like a child.

God and King Henry govern England's helm!
Give up your staff, sir, and the King his realm.

Glou. My staff? Here, noble Henry, is my staff.
As willingly do I the same resign
As e'er thy father Henry made it mine;
And even as willingly at thy feet I leave it
As others would ambitiously receive it.
Farewell, good King. When I am dead and gone,
May honourable peace attend thy throne!
Exit.

Queen. Why, now is Henry king, and Margaret queen,
And Humphrey Duke of Gloucester scarce himself,
That bears so shrewd a maim: two pulls at once —
His lady banish'd, and a limb lopp'd off.
This staff of honour raught, there let it stand
Where it best fits to be, in Henry's hand.

Suf. Thus droops this lofty pine and hangs his sprays;
Thus Eleanor's pride dies in her youngest days.

York. Lords, let him go. Please it your Majesty,
This is the day appointed for the combat;
And ready are the appellant and defendant,
The armourer and his man, to enter the lists,
So please your Highness to behold the fight.

Queen. Ay, good my lord; for purposely therefore
Left I the court, to see this quarrel tried.

King. A God's name see the lists and all things fit.
Here let them end it, and God defend the right!

York. I never saw a fellow worse bestead
Or more afraid to fight than is the appellant,
The servant of this armourer, my lords.

Enter at one door, the *Armourer* [*Horner*] and his *Neighbours*, drinking to him so much that he is drunk; and he enters with a *Drum* before him, and his staff with a sandbag fastened to it; and, at the other door, his *Man* [*Peter*], with a *Drum* and sandbag, and *Prentices* *drinking to him.*

1. Neigh. Here, neighbour Horner, I drink to you in a cup of sack; and fear not, neighbour, you shall do well enough.

2. Neigh. And here, neighbour, here's a cup of charneco.

3. Neigh. And here's a pot of good double-beer, neighbour. Drink, and fear not your man.

Arm. Let it come, i' faith, and I'll pledge you all; and a fig for Peter!

1. Pren. Here, Peter, I drink to thee; and be not afraid.

2 Pren. Be merry, Peter, and fear not thy master. Fight for credit of the prentices.

Peter. I thank you all. Drink, and pray for me, I pray you; for I think I have taken my last draught in this world. Here, Robin, an if I die, I give thee my apron: and, Will, thou shalt have my hammer; and here, Tom, take all the money that I have. O Lord bless me, I pray God! for I am never able to deal with my master, he hath learnt so much fence already.

Sal. Come, leave your drinking and fall to blows. Sirrah, what's thy name?

Peter. Peter, forsooth.

Sal. Peter? What more?

Peter. Thump.

Sal. Thump? Then see thou thump thy master well.

Arm. Masters, I am come hither, as it were, upon my man's instigation, to prove him a knave and myself an honest man; and touching the Duke of York, I will take my death I never meant him any ill, nor the King, nor the Queen; and therefore, Peter, have at thee with a downright blow!

York. Dispatch. This knave's tongue begins to double.
Sound, trumpets, alarum to the combatants!

Alarum. They fight, and Peter strikes him down.

Arm. Hold, Peter, hold! I confess, I confess treason. *Dies.*

York. Take away his weapon. Fellow, thank God, and the good wine in thy master's way.

Peter. O God, have I overcome mine enemies in this presence? O Peter, thou hast prevail'd in right!

King. Go, take hence that traitor from our sight,
For by his death we do perceive his guilt,
And God in justice hath reveal'd to us
The truth and innocence of this poor fellow,
Which he had thought to have murther'd wrongfully.
Come, fellow, follow us for thy reward.

Sound a flourish. Exeunt.

[Scene IV. *London. A street.*]

Enter *Duke Humphrey* [*of Gloucester*] and his *Men* in mourning cloaks.

Glou. Thus sometimes hath the brightest day a cloud,
And after summer evermore succeeds
Barren winter with his wrathful nipping cold.
So cares and joys abound, as seasons fleet.
Sirs, what's o'clock?

Servant. Ten, my lord.

Glou. Ten is the hour that was appointed me
To watch the coming of my punish'd duchess.
Uneath may she endure the flinty streets
To tread them with her tender-feeling feet.
Sweet Nell, ill can thy noble mind abrook
The abject people gazing on thy face,
With envious looks laughing at thy shame,
That erst did follow thy proud chariot wheels
When thou didst ride in triumph through the streets.
But, soft! I think she comes, and I'll prepare
My tear-stain'd eyes to see her miseries. 16

Enter the *Duchess* barefoot in a white sheet, [with papers pinned upon her back] and a taper burning in her hand; with the *Sheriff* and *Officers*; *Sir John Stanley.*

Servant. So please your Grace, we'll take her from the sheriff.

Glou. No, stir not for your lives! Let her pass by.

Elean. Come you, my lord, to see my open shame?
Now thou dost penance too. Look how they gaze!
See how the giddy multitude do point
And nod their heads and throw their eyes on thee!
Ah, Gloucester, hide thee from their hateful looks,
And in thy closet pent up, rue my shame 24
And ban thine enemies, both mine and thine!

Glou. Be patient, gentle Nell; forget this grief.

Elean. Ah, Gloucester, teach me to forget myself!
For, whilst I think I am thy married wife
And thou a prince, Protector of this land,
Methinks I should not thus be led along,
Mail'd up in shame, with papers on my back,
And follow'd with a rabble that rejoice
To see my tears and hear my deep-fet groans.
The ruthless flint doth cut my tender feet;
And when I start, the envious people laugh
And bid me be advised how I tread.
Ah, Humphrey, can I bear this shameful yoke?
Trowest thou that e'er I'll look upon the world
Or count them happy that enjoy the sun?
No! Dark shall be my light, and night my day;
To think upon my pomp shall be my hell. 41
Sometime I'll say, I am Duke Humphrey's wife,
And he a prince, and ruler of the land;
Yet so he rul'd, and such a prince he was,
As he stood by whilst I, his forlorn duchess,
Was made a wonder and a pointing stock
To every idle rascal follower.
But be thou mild and blush not at my shame,
Nor stir at nothing till the axe of death
Hang over thee, as sure it shortly will.
For Suffolk — he that can do all in all
With her that hateth thee and hates us all —
And York and impious Beaufort, that false priest,
Have all lim'd bushes to betray thy wings,
And, fly thou how thou canst, they'll tangle thee.
But fear not thou until thy foot be snar'd,
Nor never seek prevention of thy foes.

Glou. Ah, Nell, forbear! Thou aimest all awry.
I must offend before I be attainted;
And had I twenty times so many foes,
And each of them had twenty times their power,
All these could not procure me any scathe
So long as I am loyal, true, and crimeless.
Wouldst have me rescue thee from this reproach?
Why, yet thy scandal were not wip'd away,
But I in danger for the breach of law!
Thy greatest help is quiet, gentle Nell.
I pray thee sort thy heart to patience;
These few days' wonder will be quickly worn.

Enter a *Herald.*

Her. I summon your Grace to his Majesty's parliament,
Holden at Bury the first of this next month.

Glou. And my consent ne'er ask'd herein before?
This is close dealing. Well, I will be there.

Exit Herald.

My Nell, I take my leave. And, Master Sheriff,
Let not her penance exceed the King's commission.

Sheriff. An't please your Grace, here my commission stays,
And Sir John Stanley is appointed now
To take her with him to the Isle of Man.

Glou. Must you, Sir John, protect my lady here?

Stanley. So am I given in charge, may't please your Grace.

Glou. Entreat her not the worse in that I pray
You use her well. The world may laugh again,
And I may live to do you kindness if
You do it her; and so, Sir John, farewell.

Elean. What, gone, my lord, and bid me not farewell?

Glou. Witness my tears, I cannot stay to speak.

Exeunt Gloucester and his Men.

Elean. Art thou gone too? All comfort go with thee!
For none abides with me. My joy is death —
Death, at whose name I oft have been afeard,
Because I wish'd this world's eternity.
Stanley, I prithee go, and take me hence;
I care not whither, for I beg no favour.
Only convey me where thou art commanded.

Stanley. Why, madam, that is to the Isle of Man,
There to be us'd according to your state.

Elean. That's bad enough, for I am but reproach!
And shall I then be us'd reproachfully?

Stanley. Like to a duchess and Duke Humphrey's lady —
According to that state you shall be us'd.

Elean. Sheriff, farewell, and better than I fare,
Although thou hast been conduct of my shame.

Sheriff. It is my office; and, madam, pardon me.

Elean. Ay, ay, farewell; thy office is discharg'd.
Come, Stanley, shall we go?

Stanley. Madam, your penance done, throw off this sheet,
And go we to attire you for our journey.

Elean. My shame will not be shifted with my sheet.
No! it will hang upon my richest robes
And show itself, attire me how I can.
Go, lead the way; I long to see my prison.

Exeunt.

[ACT III. Scene I. *The Abbey at Bury St. Edmund's.*]

Sound a sennet. Enter *King, Queen, Cardinal, Suffolk, York, Buckingham, Salisbury,* and *Warwick,* to the Parliament.

King. I muse my Lord of Gloucester is not come.
'Tis not his wont to be the hindmost man,
Whate'er occasion keeps him from us now.

Queen. Can you not see? or will ye not observe
The strangeness of his alter'd countenance —
With what a majesty he bears himself;
How insolent of late he is become,
How proud, how peremptory, and unlike himself?
We know the time since he was mild and affable,
And if we did but glance a far-off look,
Immediately he was upon his knee,
That all the court admir'd him for submission;
But meet him now and, be it in the morn,
When every one will give the time of day,
He knits his brow and shows an angry eye
And passeth by with stiff unbowed knee,
Disdaining duty that to us belongs.
Small curs are not regarded when they grin,
But great men tremble when the lion roars,
And Humphrey is no little man in England.
First note that he is near you in descent,
And should you fall, he is the next will mount.
Me seemeth then it is no policy,
Respecting what a rancorous mind he bears
And his advantage following your decease,
That he should come about your royal person
Or be admitted to your Highness' Council.
By flattery hath he won the commons' hearts;
And when he please to make commotion,
'Tis to be fear'd they all will follow him.
Now 'tis the spring, and weeds are shallow-rooted.
Suffer them now, and they'll o'ergrow the garden
And choke the herbs for want of husbandry.
The reverent care I bear unto my lord
Made me collect these dangers in the Duke.
If it be fond, call it a woman's fear;
Which fear if better reasons can supplant,
I will subscribe and say I wrong'd the Duke.
My Lords of Suffolk, Buckingham, and York,
Reprove my allegation if you can,
Or else conclude my words effectual.

Suf. Well hath your Highness seen into this duke;

And, had I first been put to speak my mind,
I think I should have told your Grace's tale.
The Duchess by his subornation,
Upon my life, began her devilish practices;
Or if he were not privy to those faults,
Yet by reputing of his high descent —
As next the King he was successive heir,
And such high vaunts of his nobility—
Did instigate the bedlam brainsick Duchess
By wicked means to frame our sovereign's fall.
Smooth runs the water where the brook is deep,
And in his simple show he harbours treason.
The fox barks not when he would steal the lamb.
No, no, my sovereign! Gloucester is a man
Unsounded yet and full of deep deceit.

Car. Did he not, contrary to form of law,
Devise strange deaths for small offences done?

York. And did he not in his protectorship
Levy great sums of money through the realm
For soldiers' pay in France, and never sent it?
By means whereof the towns each day revolted.

Buck. Tut, these are petty faults to faults unknown
Which time will bring to light in smooth Duke Humphrey.

King. My lords at once, the care you have of us,
To mow down thorns that would annoy our foot,
Is worthy praise; but, shall I speak my conscience,
Our kinsman Gloucester is as innocent
From meaning treason to our royal person
As is the sucking lamb or harmless dove.
The Duke is virtuous, mild, and too well-given
To dream on evil or to work my downfall.

Queen. Ah, what's more dangerous than this fond affiance?
Seems he a dove? His feathers are but borrow'd,
For he's disposed as the hateful raven.
Is he a lamb? His skin is surely lent him,
For he's inclin'd as is the ravenous wolf.
Who cannot steal a shape that means deceit?
Take heed, my lord. The welfare of us all
Hangs on the cutting short that fraudful man.

Enter *Somerset.*

Som. All health unto my gracious sovereign!

King. Welcome, Lord Somerset. What news from France?

Som. That all your interest in those territories
Is utterly bereft you. All is lost.

King. Cold news, Lord Somerset! but God's will be done.

York. [*aside*] Cold news for me! for I had hope of France
As firmly as I hope for fertile England.
Thus are my blossoms blasted in the bud,
And caterpillars eat my leaves away;
But I will remedy this gear ere long
Or sell my title for a glorious grave.

Enter *Gloucester.*

Glou. All happiness unto my lord the King!
Pardon, my liege, that I have stay'd so long.

Suf. Nay, Gloucester, know that thou art come too soon
Unless thou wert more loyal than thou art.
I do arrest thee of high treason here.

Glou. Well, Suffolk, thou shalt not see me blush
Nor change my countenance for this arrest.
A heart unspotted is not easily daunted.
The purest spring is not so free from mud
As I am clear from treason to my sovereign.
Who can accuse me? Wherein am I guilty?

York. 'Tis thought, my lord, that you took bribes of France
And, being Protector, stay'd the soldiers' pay,
By means whereof his Highness hath lost France.

Glou. Is it but thought so? What are they that think it?
I never robb'd the soldiers of their pay
Nor ever had one penny bribe from France.
So help me God as I have watch'd the night —
Ay, night by night — in studying good for England!
That doit that e'er I wrested from the King,
Or any groat I hoarded to my use,
Be brought against me at my trial day!
No! Many a pound of mine own proper store,
Because I would not tax the needy commons,
Have I dispursed to the garrisons,
And never ask'd for restitution.

Car. It serves you well, my lord, to say so much.

Glou. I say no more than truth, so help me God!

York. In your protectorship you did devise
Strange tortures for offenders, never heard of,
That England was defam'd by tyranny.

Glou. Why, 'tis well known that, whiles I was Protector,
Pity was all the fault that was in me;
For I should melt at an offender's tears
And lowly words were ransom for their fault.

Unless it were a bloody murtherer,
Or foul felonious thief that fleec'd poor passengers,
I never gave them condign punishment.
Murther indeed, that bloody sin, I tortur'd
Above the felon or what trespass else.

Suf. My lord, these faults are easy, quickly answer'd;
But mightier crimes are laid unto your charge,
Whereof you cannot easily purge yourself.
I do arrest you in his Highness' name
And here commit you to my Lord Cardinal
To keep until your further time of trial.

King. My Lord of Gloucester, 'tis my special hope
That you will clear yourself from all suspect.
My conscience tells me you are innocent.

Glou. Ah, gracious lord, these days are dangerous!
Virtue is chok'd with foul ambition
And charity chas'd hence by rancour's hand;
Foul subornation is predominant
And equity exil'd your Highness' land.
I know their complot is to have my life;
And if my death might make this island happy
And prove the period of their tyranny,
I would expend it with all willingness.
But mine is made the prologue to their play;
For thousands more, that yet suspect no peril,
Will not conclude their plotted tragedy.
Beaufort's red sparkling eyes blab his heart's malice
And Suffolk's cloudy brow his stormy hate;
Sharp Buckingham unburthens with his tongue
The envious load that lies upon his heart;
And dogged York, that reaches at the moon,
Whose overweening arm I have pluck'd back,
By false accuse doth level at my life;
And you, my sovereign lady, with the rest,
Causeless have laid disgraces on my head
And with your best endeavour have stirr'd up
My liefest liege to be mine enemy.
Ay, all of you have laid your heads together —
Myself had notice of your conventicles —
And all to make away my guiltless life.
I shall not want false witness to condemn me
Nor store of treasons to augment my guilt.
The ancient proverb will be well effected —
'A staff is quickly found to beat a dog.'

Car. My liege, his railing is intolerable.
If those that care to keep your royal person
From treason's secret knife and traitor's rage
Be thus upbraided, chid, and rated at,
And the offender granted scope of speech,
'Twill make them cool in zeal unto your Grace.

Suf. Hath he not twit our sovereign lady here
With ignominious words, though clerkly couch'd,
As if she had suborned some to swear
False allegations to o'erthrow his state?

Queen. But I can give the loser leave to chide.

Glou. Far truer spoke than meant! I lose indeed.
Beshrew the winners, for they play'd me false!
And well such losers may have leave to speak.

Buck. He'll wrest the sense and hold us here all day.
Lord Cardinal, he is your prisoner.

Car. Sirs, take away the Duke and guard him sure.

Glou. Ah, thus King Henry throws away his crutch
Before his legs be firm to bear his body.
Thus is the shepherd beaten from thy side,
And wolves are gnarling who shall gnaw thee first.
Ah that my fear were false! ah that it were!
For, good King Henry, thy decay I fear.
Exit [guarded].

King. My lords, what to your wisdoms seemeth best
Do or undo, as if ourself were here.

Queen. What, will your Highness leave the parliament?

King. Ay, Margaret. My heart is drown'd with grief,
Whose flood begins to flow within mine eyes;
My body round engirt with misery —
For what's more miserable than discontent?
Ah, uncle Humphrey, in thy face I see
The map of honour, truth, and loyalty;
And yet, good Humphrey, is the hour to come
That e'er I prov'd thee false or fear'd thy faith.
What low'ring star now envies thy estate
That these great lords and Margaret our queen
Do seek subversion of thy harmless life?
Thou never didst them wrong nor no man wrong!
And as the butcher takes away the calf
And binds the wretch and beats it when it strays,
Bearing it to the bloody slaughterhouse,
Even so remorseless have they borne him hence;
And as the dam runs lowing up and down,
Looking the way her harmless young one went,
And can do naught but wail her darling's loss,
Even so myself bewails good Gloucester's case
With sad unhelpful tears, and with dimm'd eyes
Look after him and cannot do him good,

So mighty are his vowed enemies.
His fortunes I will weep, and 'twixt each groan
Say 'Who's a traitor? Gloucester he is none.'
Exeunt [all but Queen, Cardinal, Suffolk, York, and Somerset].

Queen. Free lords, cold snow melts with the sun's hot beams.
Henry my lord is cold in great affairs,
Too full of foolish pity; and Gloucester's show
Beguiles him as the mournful crocodile
With sorrow snares relenting passengers,
Or as the snake, roll'd in a flow'ring bank,
With shining checker'd slough, doth sting a child
That for the beauty thinks it excellent.
Believe me, lords, were none more wise than I —
And yet herein I judge mine own wit good —
This Gloucester should be quickly rid the world,
To rid us from the fear we have of him.

Car. That he should die is worthy policy;
But yet we want a colour for his death.
'Tis meet he be condemn'd by course of law.

Suf. But, in my mind, that were no policy.
The King will labour still to save his life,
The commons haply rise to save his life;
And yet we have but trivial argument,
More than mistrust, that shows him worthy death.

York. So that, by this, you would not have him die.

Suf. Ah, York, no man alive so fain as I!

York. 'Tis York that hath more reason for his death.
But, my Lord Cardinal, and you, my Lord of Suffolk,
Say as you think and speak it from your souls:
Were't not all one an empty eagle were set
To guard the chicken from a hungry kite
As place Duke Humphrey for the King's Protector?

Queen. So the poor chicken should be sure of death.

Suf. Madam, 'tis true; and were't not madness then
To make the fox surveyor of the fold?
Who being accus'd a crafty murtherer,
His guilt should be but idly posted over
Because his purpose is not executed.
No! Let him die in that he is a fox,
By nature prov'd an enemy to the flock,
Before his chaps be stain'd with crimson blood,
As Humphrey, prov'd by reasons, to my liege.
And do not stand on quillets how to slay him.
Be it by gins, by snares, by subtlety,
Sleeping or waking, 'tis no matter how,
So he be dead; for that is good deceit
Which mates him first that first intends deceit.

Queen. Thrice-noble Suffolk, 'tis resolutely spoke.

Suf. Not resolute, except so much were done,
For things are often spoke and seldom meant;
But that my heart accordeth with my tongue,
Seeing the deed is meritorious,
And to preserve my sovereign from his foe,
Say but the word, and I will be his priest.

Car. But I would have him dead, my Lord of Suffolk,
Ere you can take due orders for a priest.
Say you consent and censure well the deed,
And I'll provide his executioner,
I tender so the safety of my liege.

Suf. Here is my hand, the deed is worthy doing.

Queen. And so say I.

York. And I. And now we three have spoken it,
It skills not greatly who impugns our doom.

Enter a *Post.*

Post. Great lords, from Ireland am I come amain
To signify that rebels there are up
And put the Englishmen unto the sword.
Send succours, lords, and stop the rage betime,
Before the wound do grow uncurable;
For, being green, there is great hope of help.

Car. A breach that craves a quick expedient stop!
What counsel give you in this weighty cause?

York. That Somerset be sent as Regent thither.
'Tis meet that lucky ruler be employ'd;
Witness the fortune he hath had in France.

Som. If York with all his far-fet policy
Had been the Regent there instead of me,
He never would have stay'd in France so long.

York. No, not to lose it all, as thou hast done.
I rather would have lost my life betimes
Than bring a burthen of dishonour home
By staying there so long till all were lost.
Show me one scar character'd on thy skin.
Men's flesh preserv'd so whole do seldom win.

Queen. Nay then, this spark will prove a raging fire
If wind and fuel be brought to feed it with
No more, good York! Sweet Somerset, be still!
Thy fortune, York, hadst thou been Regent there,
Might happily have prov'd far worse than his.

York. What, worse than naught? Nay, then a shame take all!
Som. And, in the number, thee that wishest shame!
Car. My Lord of York, try what your fortune is.
Th' uncivil kerns of Ireland are in arms
And temper clay with blood of Englishmen.
To Ireland will you lead a band of men,
Collected choicely, from each county some,
And try your hap against the Irishmen?
York. I will, my lord, so please his Majesty.
Suf. Why, our authority is his consent,
And what we do establish he confirms.
Then, noble York, take thou this task in hand.
York. I am content. Provide me soldiers, lords,
Whiles I take order for mine own affairs.
Suf. A charge, Lord York, that I will see perform'd.
But now return we to the false Duke Humphrey.
Car. No more of him; for I will deal with him
That henceforth he shall trouble us no more.
And so break off; the day is almost spent.
Lord Suffolk, you and I must talk of that event.
York. My Lord of Suffolk, within fourteen days
At Bristow I expect my soldiers,
For there I'll ship them all for Ireland.
Suf. I'll see it truly done, my Lord of York.
Exeunt. Manet York.
York. Now, York, or never, steel thy fearful thoughts
And change misdoubt to resolution.
Be that thou hop'st to be; or what thou art
Resign to death: it is not worth th' enjoying.
Let pale-fac'd fear keep with the mean-born man
And find no harbour in a royal heart.
Faster than springtime show'rs comes thought on thought,
And not a thought but thinks on dignity.
My brain, more busy than the labouring spider,
Weaves tedious snares to trap mine enemies.
Well, nobles, well! 'tis politicly done
To send me packing with an host of men.
I fear me you but warm the starved snake,
Who, cherish'd in your breasts, will sting your hearts.
'Twas men I lack'd, and you will give them me.
I take it kindly. Yet be well assur'd
You put sharp weapons in a madman's hands.
Whiles I in Ireland nourish a mighty band,
I will stir up in England some black storm
Shall blow ten thousand souls to heaven or hell;
And this fell tempest shall not cease to rage
Until the golden circuit on my head,
Like to the glorious sun's transparent beams,
Do calm the fury of this mad-bred flaw.
And for a minister of my intent
I have seduc'd a headstrong Kentishman,
John Cade of Ashford,
To make commotion, as full well he can,
Under the title of John Mortimer.
In Ireland have I seen this stubborn Cade
Oppose himself against a troop of kerns,
And fought so long till that his thighs with darts
Were almost like a sharp-quill'd porpentine;
And in the end being rescued, I have seen
Him caper upright like a wild Morisco,
Shaking the bloody darts as he his bells.
Full often, like a shag-hair'd crafty kern,
Hath he conversed with the enemy
And undiscover'd come to me again
And given me notice of their villanies.
This devil here shall be my substitute;
For that John Mortimer which now is dead
In face, in gait, in speech, he doth resemble.
By this I shall perceive the commons' mind,
How they affect the house and claim of York.
Say he be taken, rack'd, and tortured;
I know no pain they can inflict upon him
Will make him say I mov'd him to those arms.
Say that he thrive, as 'tis great like he will;
Why, then from Ireland come I with my strength
And reap the harvest which that rascal sow'd;
For, Humphrey being dead, as he shall be,
And Henry put apart, the next for me! *Exit.*

[Scene II. *Bury St. Edmund's. A room of state.*]

Enter *two or three* running over the stage, from the murther of *Duke Humphrey.*

1. Mur. Run to my Lord of Suffolk. Let him know
We have dispatch'd the Duke, as he commanded.
2. Mur. O that it were to do! What have we done?
Didst ever hear a man so penitent?

Enter *Suffolk.*

1. Mur. Here comes my lord.
Suf. Now, sirs, have you dispatch'd this thing?

1. Mur. Ay, my good lord; he's dead.
Suf. Why, that's well said. Go, get you to my house.
I will reward you for this venturous deed.
The King and all the peers are here at hand.
Have you laid fair the bed? Is all things well,
According as I gave directions?
1. Mur. 'Tis, my good lord.
Suf. Away! be gone!
Exeunt Murtherers.

Sound trumpets. Enter the *King*, the *Queen*, *Cardinal*, *Somerset*, with *Attendants.*

King. Go call our uncle to our presence straight.
Say we intend to try his Grace to-day,
If he be guilty, as 'tis published.
Suf. I'll call him presently, my noble lord.
Exit.
King. Lords, take your places; and I pray you all
Proceed no straiter 'gainst our uncle Gloucester
Than from true evidence, of good esteem,
He be approv'd in practice culpable.
Queen. God forbid any malice should prevail
That faultless may condemn a nobleman!
Pray God he may acquit him of suspicion.
King. I thank thee, Meg. These words content me much.

Enter *Suffolk.*

How now? Why look'st thou pale? Why tremblest thou?
Where is our uncle? What's the matter, Suffolk?
Suf. Dead in his bed, my lord! Gloucester is dead.
Queen. Marry, God forfend!
Car. God's secret judgment! I did dream to-night
The Duke was dumb and could not speak a word.
King sounds.
Queen. How fares my lord? Help, lords! The King is dead.
Som. Rear up his body; wring him by the nose.
Queen. Run, go! help, help! O Henry, ope thine eyes!
Suf. He doth revive again. Madam, be patient.
King. O heavenly God!
Queen. How fares my gracious lord?
Suf. Comfort, my sovereign! Gracious Henry, comfort!
King. What, doth my Lord of Suffolk comfort me?
Came he right now to sing a raven's note
Whose dismal tune bereft my vital pow'rs,
And thinks he that the chirping of a wren,
By crying comfort from a hollow breast,
Can chase away the first-conceived sound?
Hide not thy poison with such sug'red words.
Lay not thy hands on me. Forbear, I say!
Their touch affrights me as a serpent's sting.
Thou baleful messenger, out of my sight!
Upon thy eyeballs murderous tyranny
Sits in grim majesty, to fright the world.
Look not upon me, for thine eyes are wounding.
Yet do not go away. Come, basilisk,
And kill the innocent gazer with thy sight;
For in the shade of death I shall find joy —
In life but double death, now Gloucester's dead.
Queen. Why do you rate my Lord of Suffolk thus?
Although the Duke was enemy to him,
Yet he most Christianlike laments his death;
And for myself, foe as he was to me,
Might liquid tears or heart-offending groans
Or blood-consuming sighs recall his life,
I would be blind with weeping, sick with groans,
Look pale as primrose with blood-drinking sighs,
And all to have the noble Duke alive.
What know I how the world may deem of me?
For it is known we were but hollow friends.
It may be judg'd I made the Duke away;
So shall my name with slander's tongue be wounded
And princes' courts be fill'd with my reproach.
This get I by his death. Ay me unhappy,
To be a queen, and crown'd with infamy!
King. Ah, woe is me for Gloucester, wretched man!
Queen. Be woe for me, more wretched than he is!
What, dost thou turn away, and hide thy face?
I am no loathsome leper. Look on me.
What? Art thou like the adder waxen deaf?
Be poisonous too, and kill thy forlorn queen.
Is all thy comfort shut in Gloucester's tomb?
Why, then Dame Margaret was ne'er thy joy.
Erect his statuë and worship it,
And make my image but an alehouse sign.
Was I for this nigh wrack'd upon the sea
And twice by awkward wind from England's bank
Drove back again unto my native clime?
What boded this but well-forewarning wind
Did seem to say 'Seek not a scorpion's nest

Nor set no footing on this unkind shore'?
What did I then but curs'd the gentle gusts
And he that loos'd them forth their brazen caves,
And bid them blow towards England's blessed shore
Or turn our stern upon a dreadful rock?
Yet Æolus would not be a murtherer,
But left that hateful office unto thee.
The pretty vaulting sea refus'd to drown me,
Knowing that thou wouldst have me drown'd on shore
With tears as salt as sea through thy unkindness.
The splitting rocks cow'r'd in the sinking sands
And would not dash me with their ragged sides,
Because thy flinty heart, more hard than they,
Might in thy palace perish Margaret.
As far as I could ken thy chalky cliffs,
When from thy shore the tempest beat us back,
I stood upon the hatches in the storm;
And when the dusky sky began to rob
My earnest-gaping sight of thy land's view,
I took a costly jewel from my neck,
A heart it was, bound in with diamonds,
And threw it towards thy land. The sea receiv'd it,
And so I wish'd thy body might my heart;
And even with this I lost fair England's view,
And bid mine eyes be packing with my heart,
And call'd them blind and dusky spectacles
For losing ken of Albion's wished coast.
How often have I tempted Suffolk's tongue
(The agent of thy foul inconstancy)
To sit and witch me as Ascanius did
When he to madding Dido would unfold
His father's acts commenc'd in burning Troy!
Am I not witch'd like her? or thou not false like him?
Ay me, I can no more! Die, Margaret!
For Henry weeps that thou dost live so long.

Noise within. Enter *Warwick, Salisbury,* and many *Commons.*

War. It is reported, mighty sovereign,
That good Duke Humphrey traitorously is murd'red
By Suffolk and the Cardinal Beaufort's means.
The commons, like an angry hive of bees
That want their leader, scatter up and down
And care not who they sting in his revenge.
Myself have calm'd their spleenful mutiny
Until they hear the order of his death.

King. That he is dead, good Warwick, 'tis too true;
But how he died God knows, not Henry.
Enter his chamber, view his breathless corpse,
And comment then upon his sudden death.

War. That shall I do, my liege. Stay, Salisbury,
With the rude multitude till I return.

[*Exit.*] *Exit Salisbury* [*with the Commons*].

King. O thou that judgest all things, stay my thoughts —
My thoughts, that labour to persuade my soul
Some violent hands were laid on Humphrey's life!
If my suspect be false, forgive me, God;
For judgment only doth belong to thee.
Fain would I go to chafe his paly lips
With twenty thousand kisses and to drain
Upon his face an ocean of salt tears,
To tell my love unto his dumb deaf trunk,
And with my fingers feel his hand unfeeling.
But all in vain are these mean obsequies;

Bed put forth [*with the body.* Enter *Warwick*].

And to survey his dead and earthy image,
What were it but to make my sorrow greater?

War. Come hither, gracious sovereign, view this body.

King. That is to see how deep my grave is made;
For with his soul fled all my worldly solace,
And seeing him, I see my life in death.

War. As surely as my soul intends to live
With that dread King that took our state upon him
To free us from his Father's wrathful curse,
I do believe that violent hands were laid
Upon the life of this thrice-famed duke.

Suf. A dreadful oath, sworn with a solemn tongue!
What instance gives Lord Warwick for his vow?

War. See how the blood is settled in his face.
Oft have I seen a timely-parted ghost,
Of ashy semblance, meagre, pale, and bloodless,
Being all descended to the labouring heart,
Who, in the conflict that it holds with death,
Attracts the same for aidance 'gainst the enemy,
Which with the heart there cools, and ne'er returneth
To blush and beautify the cheek again.
But see, his face is black and full of blood;
His eyeballs further out than when he liv'd,
Staring full ghastly, like a strangled man;
His hair uprear'd, his nostrils stretch'd with struggling;
His hands abroad display'd, as one that grasp'd
And tugg'd for life and was by strength subdu'd.

Look, on the sheets his hair, you see, is sticking;
His well-proportion'd beard made rough and rugged,
Like to the summer's corn by tempest lodg'd.
It cannot be but he was murd'red here.
The least of all these signs were probable.

Suf. Why, Warwick, who should do the Duke to death?
Myself and Beaufort had him in protection,
And we, I hope, sir, are no murtherers.

War. But both of you were vow'd Duke Humphrey's foes,
And you (forsooth) had the good Duke to keep.
'Tis like you would not feast him like a friend,
And 'tis well seen he found an enemy.

Queen. Then you belike suspect these noblemen
As guilty of Duke Humphrey's timeless death.

War. Who finds the heifer dead, and bleeding fresh,
And sees fast-by a butcher with an axe,
But will suspect 'twas he that made the slaughter?
Who finds the partridge in the puttock's nest
But may imagine how the bird was dead,
Although the kite soar with unbloodied beak?
Even so suspicious is this tragedy.

Queen. Are you the butcher, Suffolk? Where's your knife?
Is Beaufort term'd a kite? Where are his talons?

Suf. I wear no knife to slaughter sleeping men;
But here's a vengeful sword, rusted with ease,
That shall be scoured in his rancorous heart
That slanders me with murther's crimson badge.
Say, if thou dar'st, proud Lord of Warwickshire,
That I am faulty in Duke Humphrey's death.

Exeunt Cardinal, [*Somerset, and others*].

War. What dares not Warwick, if false Suffolk dare him?

Queen. He dares not calm his contumelious spirit,
Nor cease to be an arrogant controller,
Though Suffolk dare him twenty thousand times.

War. Madam, be still. With reverence may I say;
For every word you speak in his behalf
Is slander to your royal dignity.

Suf. Blunt-witted lord, ignoble in demeanour!
If ever lady wrong'd her lord so much,
Thy mother took into her blameful bed
Some stern untutor'd churl, and noble stock
Was graft with crab-tree slip, whose fruit thou art,
And never of the Nevils' noble race.

War. But that the guilt of murther bucklers thee,
And I should rob the deathsman of his fee,
Quitting thee thereby of ten thousand shames,
And that my sovereign's presence makes me mild,
I would, false murd'rous coward, on thy knee
Make thee beg pardon for thy passed speech
And say it was thy mother that thou meant'st,
That thou thyself wast born in bastardy;
And after all this fearful homage done,
Give thee thy hire, and send thy soul to hell,
Pernicious bloodsucker of sleeping men!

Suf. Thou shalt be waking while I shed thy blood,
If from this presence thou dar'st go with me.

War. Away even now, or I will drag thee hence!
Unworthy though thou art, I'll cope with thee
And do some service to Duke Humphrey's ghost. *Exeunt Suffolk and Warwick.*

King. What stronger breastplate than a heart untainted?
Thrice is he arm'd that hath his quarrel just,
And he but naked, though lock'd up in steel,
Whose conscience with injustice is corrupted.

A noise within.

Queen. What noise is this?

Enter *Suffolk* and *Warwick,* with their weapons drawn.

King. Why, how now, lords? your wrathful weapons drawn
Here in our presence? Dare you be so bold?
Why, what tumultuous clamour have we here?

Suf. The trait'rous Warwick, with the men of Bury,
Set all upon me, mighty sovereign.

Enter *Salisbury.*

Sal. [*to the Commons, who are within*] Sirs, stand apart. The King shall know your mind.—
Dread lord, the commons send you word by me,
Unless false Suffolk straight be done to death
Or banished fair England's territories,
They will by violence tear him from your palace
And torture him with grievous ling'ring death.
They say, by him the good Duke Humphrey died;

They say, in him they fear your Highness' death;
And mere instinct of love and loyalty —
Free from a stubborn opposite intent,
As being thought to contradict your liking —
Makes them thus forward in his banishment.
They say, in care of your most royal person,
That if your Highness should intend to sleep
And charge that no man should disturb your rest
In pain of your dislike or pain of death,
Yet, notwithstanding such a strait edict,
Were there a serpent seen with forked tongue
That slily glided towards your Majesty,
It were but necessary you were wak'd,
Lest, being suffer'd in that harmful slumber,
The mortal worm might make the sleep eternal.
And therefore do they cry, though you forbid,
That they will guard you, whe'r you will or no,
From such fell serpents as false Suffolk is;
With whose envenomed and fatal sting
Your loving uncle, twenty times his worth,
They say is shamefully bereft of life.

Commons. (*within*) An answer from the King, my Lord of Salisbury!

Suf. 'Tis like the commons, rude unpolish'd hinds,
Could send such message to their sovereign!
But you, my lord, were glad to be employ'd,
To show how quaint an orator you are.
But all the honour Salisbury hath won
Is, that he was the lord ambassador
Sent from a sort of tinkers to the King.

Commons. (*within*) An answer from the King, or we will all break in!

King. Go, Salisbury, and tell them all from me
I thank them for their tender loving care;
And had I not been cited so by them,
Yet did I purpose as they do entreat.
For sure my thoughts do hourly prophesy
Mischance unto my state by Suffolk's means;
And therefore by his majesty I swear
Whose far unworthy deputy I am,
He shall not breathe infection in this air
But three days longer, on the pain of death.
Exit Salisbury.

Queen. O Henry, let me plead for gentle Suffolk!

King. Ungentle queen, to call him gentle Suffolk!
No more, I say. If thou dost plead for him,
Thou wilt but add increase unto my wrath.
Had I but said, I would have kept my word;
But when I swear, it is irrevocable. —
If after three days' space thou here be'st found
On any ground that I am ruler of,
The world shall not be ransom for thy life. —
Come, Warwick, come, good Warwick, go with me;
I have great matters to impart to thee.
Exeunt all but Queen and Suffolk.

Queen. Mischance and sorrow go along with you!
Heart's discontent and sour affliction
Be playfellows to keep you company!
There's two of you; the devil make a third,
And threefold vengeance tend upon your steps!

Suf. Cease, gentle queen, these execrations
And let thy Suffolk take his heavy leave.

Queen. Fie, coward woman and soft-hearted wretch!
Hast thou not spirit to curse thine enemy?

Suf. A plague upon them! Wherefore should I curse them?
Would curses kill as doth the mandrake's groan,
I would invent as bitter searching terms,
As curst, as harsh, and horrible to hear,
Deliver'd strongly through my fixed teeth,
With full as many signs of deadly hate,
As lean-fac'd Envy in her loathsome cave.
My tongue should stumble in mine earnest words,
Mine eyes should sparkle like the beaten flint,
Mine hair be fix'd an end, as one distract;
Ay, every joint should seem to curse and ban;
And even now my burthen'd heart would break
Should I not curse them. Poison be their drink!
Gall, worse than gall, the daintiest that they taste!
Their sweetest shade a grove of cypress trees!
Their chiefest prospect murd'ring basilisks!
Their softest touch as smart as lizards' stings!
Their music frightful as the serpent's hiss,
And boding screech owls make the consort full!
All the foul terrors in dark-seated hell —

Queen. Enough, sweet Suffolk. Thou torment'st thyself;
And these dread curses, like the sun 'gainst glass,
Or like an overcharged gun, recoil
And turn the force of them upon thyself.

Suf. You bade me ban, and will you bid me leave?
Now by the ground that I am banish'd from,
Well could I curse away a winter's night,
Though standing naked on a mountain top
Where biting cold would never let grass grow,
And think it but a minute spent in sport.

Queen. O, let me entreat thee cease! Give me thy hand,
That I may dew it with my mournful tears;
Nor let the rain of heaven wet this place
To wash away my woful monuments.
O, could this kiss be printed in thy hand, [*Kisses his hand.*]
That thou mightst think upon these by the seal
Through whom a thousand sighs are breath'd for thee!
So get thee gone, that I may know my grief!
'Tis but surmis'd whiles thou art standing by,
As one that surfeits, thinking on a want.
I will repeal thee or, be well assur'd,
Adventure to be banished myself;
And banished I am, if but from thee.
Go, speak not to me. Even now be gone!
O, go not yet! Even thus two friends condemn'd
Embrace, and kiss, and take ten thousand leaves,
Loather a hundred times to part than die.
Yet now farewell, and farewell life with thee!
Suf. Thus is poor Suffolk ten times banished,
Once by the King and three times thrice by thee.
'Tis not the land I care for, wert thou thence.
A wilderness is populous enough,
So Suffolk had thy heavenly company;
For where thou art, there is the world itself
With every several pleasure in the world;
And where thou art not, desolation.
I can no more. Live thou to joy thy life;
Myself no joy in naught, but that thou liv'st.

Enter *Vaux.*

Queen. Whither goes Vaux so fast? What news, I prithee?
Vaux. To signify unto his Majesty
That Cardinal Beaufort is at point of death;
For suddenly a grievous sickness took him
That makes him gasp and stare and catch the air,
Blaspheming God and cursing men on earth.
Sometime he talks as if Duke Humphrey's ghost
Were by his side; sometime he calls the King
And whispers to his pillow, as to him,
The secrets of his overcharged soul;
And I am sent to tell his Majesty
That even now he cries aloud for him.
Queen. Go tell this heavy message to the King. *Exit Vaux.*
Ay me! What is this world? What news are these!
But wherefore grieve I at an hour's poor loss,
Omitting Suffolk's exile, my soul's treasure?
Why only, Suffolk, mourn I not for thee,
And with the southern clouds contend in tears—
Theirs for the earth's increase, mine for my sorrows?
Now get thee hence. The King thou know'st is coming.
If thou be found by me, thou art but dead.
Suf. If I depart from thee, I cannot live;
And in thy sight to die, what were it else
But like a pleasant slumber in thy lap?
Here could I breathe my soul into the air,
As mild and gentle as the cradle-babe
Dying with mother's dug between its lips;
Where, from thy sight, I should be raging mad
And cry out for thee to close up mine eyes,
To have thee with thy lips to stop my mouth.
So shouldst thou either turn my flying soul,
Or I should breathe it so into thy body,
And then it liv'd in sweet Elysium.
To die by thee were but to die in jest;
From thee to die were torture more than death.
O, let me stay, befall what may befall!
Queen. Away! Though parting be a fretful corrosive,
It is applied to a deathful wound.
To France, sweet Suffolk! Let me hear from thee;
For wheresoe'er thou art in this world's globe,
I'll have an Iris that shall find thee out.
Suf. I go.
Queen. And take my heart with thee.
Suf. A jewel, lock'd into the wofull'st cask
That ever did contain a thing of worth.
Even as a splitted bark, so sunder we.
This way fall I to death.
Queen. This way for me.
Exeunt [*severally*].

[Scene III. *London.* Cardinal Beaufort's *bedchamber.*]

Enter the *King, Salisbury,* and *Warwick,* to the *Cardinal* in bed.

King. How fares my lord? Speak, Beaufort, to thy sovereign.
Car. If thou be'st Death, I'll give thee England's treasure,
Enough to purchase such another island,
So thou wilt let me live and feel no pain.

King. Ah, what a sign it is of evil life
Where death's approach is seen so terrible!
War. Beaufort, it is thy sovereign speaks to thee.
Car. Bring me unto my trial when you will.
Died he not in his bed? Where should he die?
Can I make men live, whe'r they will or no?
O, torture me no more! I will confess.
Alive again? Then show me where he is.
I'll give a thousand pound to look upon him.
He hath no eyes; the dust hath blinded them.
Comb down his hair. Look, look! it stands upright,
Like lime-twigs set to catch my winged soul!
Give me some drink, and bid the apothecary
Bring the strong poison that I bought of him.
King. O thou eternal Mover of the heavens,
Look with a gentle eye upon this wretch!
O, beat away the busy meddling fiend
That lays strong siege unto this wretch's soul,
And from his bosom purge this black despair!
War. See how the pangs of death do make him grin!
Sal. Disturb him not; let him pass peaceably.
King. Peace to his soul, if God's good pleasure be!
Lord Card'nal, if thou think'st on heaven's bliss,
Hold up thy hand, make signal of thy hope.
He dies and makes no sign. O God, forgive him!
War. So bad a death argues a monstrous life.
King. Forbear to judge, for we are sinners all.
Close up his eyes and draw the curtain close,
And let us all to meditation. *Exeunt.*

[ACT IV. Scene I. *Kent, the seashore.*]

Alarum. Fight at sea. Ordnance goes off.

Enter *Lieutenant*, a *Shipmaster* and his *Mate*, and *Walter Whitmore*, [with *Sailors*]; *Suffolk* and others [as prisoners].

Lieut. The gaudy, blabbing, and remorseful day
Is crept into the bosom of the sea;
And now loud-howling wolves arouse the jades
That drag the tragic melancholy night,
Who with their drowsy, slow, and flagging wings
Cleep dead men's graves, and from their misty jaws
Breathe foul contagious darkness in the air.
Therefore bring forth the soldiers of our prize;
For, whilst our pinnace anchors in the Downs,
Here shall they make their ransom on the sand
Or with their blood stain this discoloured shore.
Master, this prisoner freely give I thee;
And thou that art his mate, make boot of this;
The other, Walter Whitmore, is thy share.
1. Gent. What is my ransom, master? Let me know.
Mast. A thousand crowns, or else lay down your head.
Mate. And so much shall you give, or off goes yours.
Lieut. What, think you much to pay two thousand crowns,
And bear the name and port of gentlemen?
Cut both the villains' throats; for die you shall!
The lives of those which we have lost in fight
Be counterpois'd with such a petty sum!
1. Gent. I'll give it, sir; and therefore spare my life.
2. Gent. And so will I, and write home for it straight.
Whit. I lost mine eye in laying the prize aboard,
[*To Suffolk*] And therefore to revenge it shalt thou die;
And so should these, if I might have my will.
Lieut. Be not so rash. Take ransom, let him live.
Suf. Look on my George; I am a gentleman.
Rate me at what thou wilt, thou shalt be paid.
Whit. And so am I. My name is Walter Whitmore.
How now? Why starts thou? What, doth death affright?
Suf. Thy name affrights me, in whose sound is death.
A cunning man did calculate my birth
And told me that by Water I should die.
Yet let not this make thee be bloody-minded.
Thy name is Gaultier, being rightly sounded.
Whit. Gaultier or Walter, which it is I care not.
Never yet did base dishonour blur our name
But with our sword we wip'd away the blot;
Therefore, when merchantlike I sell revenge,
Broke be my sword, my arms torn and defac'd,
And I proclaim'd a coward through the world!

Suf. Stay, Whitmore; for thy prisoner is a prince,
The Duke of Suffolk, William de la Pole.
Whit. The Duke of Suffolk muffled up in rags?
Suf. Ay, but these rags are no part of the Duke.
Jove sometime went disguis'd, and why not I?
Lieut. But Jove was never slain, as thou shalt be.
Suf. Obscure and lowly swain, King Henry's blood,
The honourable blood of Lancaster,
Must not be shed by such a jaded groom.
Hast thou not kiss'd thy hand and held my stirrup?
Bare-headed plodded by my footcloth mule,
And thought thee happy when I shook my head?
How often hast thou waited at my cup,
Fed from my trencher, kneel'd down at the board,
When I have feasted with Queen Margaret!
Remember it, and let it make thee crestfall'n,
Ay, and allay this thy abortive pride.
How in our voiding lobby hast thou stood
And duly waited for my coming forth!
This hand of mine hath writ in thy behalf,
And therefore shall it charm thy riotous tongue.
Whit. Speak, Captain, shall I stab the forlorn swain?
Lieut. First let my words stab him, as he hath me.
Suf. Base slave, thy words are blunt, and so art thou.
Lieut. Convey him hence, and on our longboat's side
Strike off his head.
Suf. Thou dar'st not, for thy own!
Lieut. Yes, Pole.
Suf. Pole?
Lieut. Pool? Sir Pool? Lord!
Ay, kennel, puddle, sink! whose filth and dirt
Troubles the silver spring where England drinks.
Now will I dam up this thy yawning mouth
For swallowing the treasure of the realm.
Thy lips that kiss'd the Queen shall sweep the ground;
And thou that smil'dst at good Duke Humphrey's death
Against the senseless winds shalt grin in vain,
Who in contempt shall hiss at thee again.
And wedded be thou to the hags of hell
For daring to affy a mighty lord
Unto the daughter of a worthless king,
Having neither subject, wealth, nor diadem.
By devilish policy art thou grown great,
And, like ambitious Sylla, overgorg'd
With gobbets of thy mother's bleeding heart.
By thee Anjou and Maine were sold to France;
The false revolting Normans thorough thee
Disdain to call us lord, and Picardy
Hath slain their governors, surpris'd our forts,
And sent the ragged soldiers wounded home.
The princely Warwick and the Nevils all,
Whose dreadful swords were never drawn in vain,
As hating thee, are rising up in arms;
And now the house of York, thrust from the crown
By shameful murther of a guiltless king
And lofty, proud, encroaching tyranny,
Burns with revenging fire, whose hopeful colours
Advance our half-fac'd sun, striving to shine,
Under the which is writ 'Invitis nubibus.'
The commons here in Kent are up in arms,
And to conclude, reproach and beggary
Is crept into the palace of our king,
And all by thee. Away! convey him hence.
Suf. O that I were a god, to shoot forth thunder
Upon these paltry, servile, abject drudges!
Small things make base men proud. This villain here,
Being captain of a pinnace, threatens more
Than Bargulus, the strong Illyrian pirate.
Drones suck not eagles' blood but rob beehives.
It is impossible that I should die
By such a lowly vassal as thyself.
Thy words move rage and not remorse in me.
I go of message from the Queen to France.
I charge thee waft me safely 'cross the Channel.
Lieut. Walter!
Whit. Come, Suffolk, I must waft thee to thy death.
Suf. Gelidus timor occupat artus. It is thee I fear.
Whit. Thou shalt have cause to fear before I leave thee.
What, are ye daunted now? Now will ye stoop?
1. Gent. My gracious lord, entreat him, speak him fair.
Suf. Suffolk's imperial tongue is stern and rough,
Us'd to command, untaught to plead for favour.
Far be it we should honour such as these
With humble suit. No, rather let my head
Stoop to the block than these knees bow to any

Save to the God of heaven and to my king;
And sooner dance upon a bloody pole
Than stand uncover'd to the vulgar groom.
True nobility is exempt from fear.
More can I bear than you dare execute.

Lieut. Hale him away and let him talk no more.

Suf. Come, soldiers, show what cruelty ye can,
That this my death may never be forgot!
Great men oft die by vile bezonians.
A Roman sworder and banditto slave
Murder'd sweet Tully; Brutus' bastard hand
Stabb'd Julius Cæsar; savage islanders
Pompey the Great; and Suffolk dies by pirates.
Exit Walter [*Whitmore*] *with Suffolk.*

Lieut. And as for these whose ransom we have set,
It is our pleasure one of them depart.
Therefore come you with us, and let him go.
Exeunt Lieutenant and the rest. Manet the First Gentleman.

Enter *Walter* [*Whitmore*] with the body [of *Suffolk*].

Whit. There let his head and liveless body lie
Until the Queen his mistress bury it. *Exit.*

1. Gent. O barbarous and bloody spectacle!
His body will I bear unto the King.
If he revenge it not, yet will his friends;
So will the Queen, that living held him dear.
[*Exit with the body.*]

[Scene II. *Blackheath.*]

Enter [*George*] *Bevis* and *John Holland.*

Bevis. Come and get thee a sword, though made of a lath. They have been up these two days.

Hol. They have the more need to sleep now then.

Bevis. I tell thee Jack Cade the clothier means to dress the commonwealth and turn it and set a new nap upon it.

Hol. So he had need, for 'tis threadbare. Well, I say it was never merry world in England since gentlemen came up.

Bevis. O miserable age! Virtue is not regarded in handicraftsmen.

Hol. The nobility think scorn to go in leather aprons.

Bevis. Nay, more, the King's Council are no good workmen.

Hol. True; and yet it is said, 'Labour in thy vocation'; which is as much to say as 'Let the magistrates be labouring men'; and therefore should we be magistrates.

Bevis. Thou hast hit it; for there's no better sign of a brave mind than a hard hand.

Hol. I see them! I see them! There's Best's son, the tanner of Wingham —

Bevis. He shall have the skins of our enemies to make dog's leather of.

Hol. And Dick the butcher —

Bevis. Then is sin struck down like an ox and iniquity's throat cut like a calf.

Hol. And Smith the weaver.

Bevis. Argo, their thread of life is spun.

Hol. Come, come, let's fall in with them.

Drum. Enter *Cade, Dick Butcher, Smith* the *Weaver*, and a *Sawyer*, with *infinite numbers.*

Cade. We, John Cade, so term'd of our supposed father —

Butch. [*aside*] Or rather, of stealing a cade of herrings.

Cade. For our enemies shall fall before us — inspired with the spirit of putting down kings and princes — Command silence.

Butch. Silence!

Cade. My father was a Mortimer —

Butch. [*aside*] He was an honest man and a good bricklayer.

Cade. My mother a Plantagenet —

Butch. [*aside*] I knew her well. She was a midwife.

Cade. My wife descended of the Lacies.

Butch. [*aside*] She was indeed a pedlar's daughter and sold many laces.

Weav. [*aside*] But now of late, not able to travel with her furr'd pack, she washes bucks here at home.

Cade. Therefore am I of an honourable house.

Butch. [*aside*] Ay, by my faith, the field is honourable and there was he born, under a hedge; for his father had never a house but the cage.

Cade. Valiant I am.

Weav. [*aside*] 'A must needs, for beggary is valiant.

Cade. I am able to endure much.

Butch. [*aside*] No question of that; for I have seen him whipp'd three market days together.

Cade. I fear neither sword nor fire.

Unable to wed her for himself, Suffolk acts as procurator and delivers Margaret of Anjou to the court as queen to Henry. In dismay, Gloucester reads the marriage-treaty *(Act I, Scene I)*

HENRY VI
PART TWO

Suspecting treachery, the commons demand Suffolk's death *(Act III, Scene II)*

The Duchess of Gloucester (Hazel Hughes) is cautioned by her husband to "banish the canker of ambitious thoughts" *(Act I, Scene II)*

Sword in hand, the Duke of York (Peter Neil) tells the Earls of Warwick (John York) and Salisbury (Robert Webber; seated) of his claim to the crown of England and gains their support *(Act II, Scene II)*

In a hall of justice—the king present—an apprentice and his master settle their dispute by single combat *(Act II, Scene III)*

Desiring to be queen, the Duchess of Gloucester resorts to sorcery. She is arrested and made to do public penance *(Act II, Scene IV)*

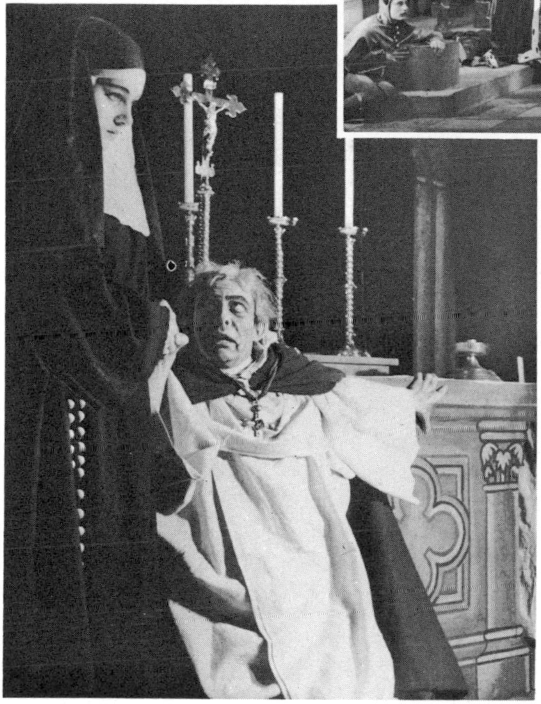

"So bad a death argues a monstrous life." The evil Cardinal (Paul Daneman), taken suddenly ill, dies *(Act III, Scene III)*

The Queen bids farewell to Suffolk (Alfred Burke) after Henry, at the insistence of the commons, has banished him *(Act III, Scene II)*

Sir Humphrey Stafford (Frederick Treves) defies the rabble of Jack Cade (Paul Daneman) *(Act IV, Scene II)*. Cade has been encouraged by the rebellious Duke of York to provoke trouble in England

"Thou hast most traitorously corrupted the youth of the realm in erecting a grammar-school." Cade baits Lord Say (Eric Jones) before having him beheaded *(Act IV, Scene VII)*

"Thy hand is made to grasp a palmer's staff, and not to grace an awful princely sceptre." York openly defies the king *(Act V, Scene I)*

Lord Clifford (Philip Whibley), leader of the king's forces, is slain by York *(Act V, Scene II)*

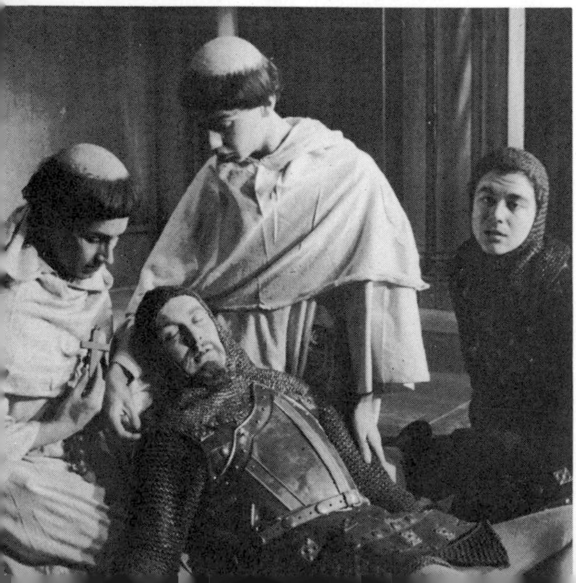

A victorious York rejoices: "The king is fled to London . . . Let us pursue" *(Act V, Scene III)*

Weav. [*aside*] He need not fear the sword, for his coat is of proof.

Butch. [*aside*] But methinks he should stand in fear of fire, being burnt i' th' hand for stealing of sheep.

Cade. Be brave then, for your captain is brave and vows reformation. There shall be in England seven halfpenny loaves sold for a penny; the three-hoop'd pot shall have ten hoops, and I will make it felony to drink small beer. All the realm shall be in common, and in Cheapside shall my palfrey go to grass; and when I am king, as king I will be —

All. God save your Majesty!

Cade. I thank you, good people. There shall be no money; all shall eat and drink on my score; and I will apparel them all in one livery, that they may agree like brothers and worship me their lord.

Butch. The first thing we do, let's kill all the lawyers.

Cade. Nay, that I mean to do. Is not this a lamentable thing, that of the skin of an innocent lamb should be made parchment? that parchment, being scribbled o'er, should undo a man? Some say the bee stings; but I say 'tis the bee's wax; for I did but seal once to a thing, and I was never mine own man since. How now? Who's there?

Enter a *Clerk* [as prisoner].

Weav. The clerk of Chatham. He can write and read and cast accompt.

Cade. O monstrous!

Weav. We took him setting of boys' copies.

Cade. Here's a villain!

Weav. Has a book in his pocket with red letters in't.

Cade. Nay, then he is a conjurer.

Butch. Nay, he can make obligations and write court-hand.

Cade. I am sorry for't. The man is a proper man, of mine honour. Unless I find him guilty, he shall not die. Come hither, sirrah, I must examine thee. What is thy name?

Clerk. Emanuel.

Butch. They use to write it on the top of letters. 'Twill go hard with you.

Cade. Let me alone. Dost thou use to write thy name? or hast thou a mark to thyself, like an honest plain-dealing man?

Clerk. Sir, I thank God, I have been so well brought up that I can write my name.

All. He hath confess'd! Away with him! He's a villain and a traitor!

Cade. Away with him, I say! Hang him with his pen and inkhorn about his neck.

Exit one with the Clerk.

Enter *Michael.*

Mich. Where's our general?

Cade. Here I am, thou particular fellow.

Mich. Fly, fly, fly! Sir Humphrey Stafford and his brother are hard by, with the King's forces.

Cade. Stand, villain, stand, or I'll fell thee down! He shall be encount'red with a man as good as himself. He is but a knight, is 'a?

Mich. No.

Cade. To equal him, I will make myself a knight presently. [*Kneels.*] Rise up Sir John Mortimer. [*Rises.*] Now have at him!

Enter *Sir Humphrey Stafford* and his brother [*William*], with *Drum* and *Soldiers.*

Staf. Rebellious hinds, the filth and scum of Kent,
Mark'd for the gallows! Lay your weapons down;
Home to your cottages; forsake this groom.
The King is merciful, if you revolt.

Bro. But angry, wrathful, and inclin'd to blood,
If you go forward. Therefore yield or die.

Cade. As for these silken-coated slaves, I pass not.
It is to you, good people, that I speak,
O'er whom (in time to come) I hope to reign;
For I am rightful heir unto the crown.

Staf. Villain, thy father was a plasterer,
And thou thyself a shearman, art thou not?

Cade. And Adam was a gardener.

Bro. And what of that?

Cade. Marry, this: Edmund Mortimer, Earl of March,
Married the Duke of Clarence' daughter, did he not?

Staf. Ay, sir.

Cade. By her he had two children at one birth.

Bro. That's false.

Cade. Ay, there's the question. But I say 'tis true.
The elder of them, being put to nurse,
Was by a beggar woman stol'n away
And, ignorant of his birth and parentage,
Became a bricklayer when he came to age.
His son am I. Deny it if you can.

Butch. Nay, 'tis too true. Therefore he shall be king.

Weav. Sir, he made a chimney in my father's house, and the bricks are alive at this day to testify it. Therefore deny it not.

Staf. And will you credit this base drudge's words
That speaks he knows not what?

All. Ay, marry, will we. Therefore get ye gone.

Bro. Jack Cade, the Duke of York hath taught you this.

Cade. [*aside*] He lies, for I invented it myself. — Go to, sirrah, tell the King from me that, for his father's sake, Henry the Fifth (in whose time boys went to span-counter for French crowns), I am content he shall reign, but I'll be Protector over him.

Butch. And furthermore we'll have the Lord Say's head for selling the dukedom of Maine.

Cade. And good reason; for thereby is England main'd and fain to go with a staff, but that my puissance holds it up. Fellow kings, I tell you that that Lord Say hath gelded the commonwealth and made it an eunuch; and more than that, he can speak French, and therefore he is a traitor.

Staf. O gross and miserable ignorance!

Cade. Nay, answer, if you can. The Frenchmen are our enemies. Go to then, I ask but this: Can he that speaks with the tongue of an enemy be a good counsellor, or no?

All. No, no! and therefore we'll have his head.

Bro. Well, seeing gentle words will not prevail,
Assail them with the army of the King.

Staf. Herald, away; and throughout every town
Proclaim them traitors that are up with Cade;
That those which fly before the battle ends
May, even in their wives' and children's sight,
Be hang'd up for example at their doors;
And you that be the King's friends, follow me.

Exeunt [*the two Staffords and Soldiers*].

Cade. And you that love the commons, follow me.
Now show yourselves men! 'Tis for liberty.
We will not leave one lord, one gentleman.
Spare none but such as go in clouted shoon,
For they are thrifty honest men and such
As would (but that they dare not) take our parts.

Butch. They are all in order and march toward us.

Cade. But then are we in order when we are most out of order. Come, march forward!

Exeunt.

[Scene III. *Another part of Blackheath.*]

Alarums to the fight, wherein both the Staffords are slain. Enter *Cade* and the rest.

Cade. Where's Dick, the butcher of Ashford?

Butch. Here, sir.

Cade. They fell before thee like sheep and oxen, and thou behavedst thyself as if thou hadst been in thine own slaughterhouse. Therefore thus will I reward thee: the Lent shall be as long again as it is, and thou shalt have a license to kill for a hundred lacking one a week.

Butch. I desire no more.

Cade. And, to speak truth, thou deserv'st no less. This monument of the victory will I bear [*puts on Sir Humphrey's brigandine*]; and the bodies shall be dragg'd at my horse heels till I do come to London, where we will have the mayor's sword borne before us.

Butch. If we mean to thrive and do good, break open the jails and let out the prisoners.

Cade. Fear not that, I warrant thee. Come, let's march towards London. *Exeunt.*

[Scene IV. *London. The Palace.*]

Enter the *King*, with a supplication, and the *Queen* with *Suffolk's* head; the *Duke of Buckingham* and the *Lord Say.*

Queen. Oft have I heard that grief softens the mind
And makes it fearful and degenerate.
Think therefore on revenge and cease to weep.
But who can cease to weep, and look on this?
Here may his head lie on my throbbing breast;
But where's the body that I should embrace?

Buck. What answer makes your Grace to the rebels' supplication?

King. I'll send some holy bishop to entreat;
For God forbid so many simple souls
Should perish by the sword! And I myself,
Rather than bloody war shall cut them short,
Will parley with Jack Cade their general.
But stay, I'll read it over once again.

Queen. Ah, barbarous villains! Hath this lovely face
Rul'd like a wandering planet over me,
And could it not enforce them to relent
That were unworthy to behold the same?

King. Lord Say, Jack Cade hath sworn to have thy head.

Say. Ay, but I hope your Highness shall have his.

King. How now, madam?
Still lamenting and mourning for Suffolk's death?
I fear me, love, if that I had been dead,
Thou wouldest not have mourn'd so much for me.

Queen. No, my love, I should not mourn, but die for thee.

Enter a *Messenger*.

King. How now? What news? Why com'st thou in such haste?

Mess. The rebels are in Southwark. Fly, my lord!
Jack Cade proclaims himself Lord Mortimer,
Descended from the Duke of Clarence' house,
And calls your Grace usurper openly
And vows to crown himself in Westminster.
His army is a ragged multitude
Of hinds and peasants, rude and merciless.
Sir Humphrey Stafford and his brother's death
Hath given them heart and courage to proceed.
All scholars, lawyers, courtiers, gentlemen,
They call false caterpillars and intend their death.

King. O graceless men! they know not what they do.

Buck. My gracious lord, retire to Killingworth
Until a power be rais'd to put them down.

Queen. Ah, were the Duke of Suffolk now alive,
These Kentish rebels would be soon appeas'd.

King. Lord Say, the traitors hate thee;
Therefore away with us to Killingworth.

Say. So might your Grace's person be in danger.
The sight of me is odious in their eyes;
And therefore in this city will I stay
And live alone as secret as I may.

Enter another *Messenger*.

Mess. Jack Cade hath gotten London Bridge;
The citizens fly and forsake their houses;
The rascal people, thirsting after prey,
Join with the traitor, and they jointly swear
To spoil the city and your royal court.

Buck. Then linger not, my lord. Away, take horse!

King. Come, Margaret. God, our hope, will succour us.

Queen. My hope is gone now Suffolk is deceas'd.

King. [*to Lord Say*] Farewell, my lord. Trust not the Kentish rebels.

Buck. Trust nobody, for fear you be betray'd.

Say. The trust I have is in mine innocence,
And therefore am I bold and resolute.

Exeunt.

[Scene V. *London. The Tower.*]

Enter *Lord Scales* upon the Tower, walking. Then enter *two or three Citizens* below.

Scales. How now? Is Jack Cade slain?

1. Cit. No, my lord, nor likely to be slain; for they have won the Bridge, killing all those that withstand them. The Lord Mayor craves aid of your honour from the Tower to defend the city from the rebels.

Scales. Such aid as I can spare you shall command,
But I am troubled here with them myself;
The rebels have assay'd to win the Tower.
But get you to Smithfield and gather head,
And thither I will send you Matthew Goffe.
Fight for your king, your country, and your lives;
And so farewell, for I must hence again.

Exeunt.

[Scene VI. *London. Cannon Street.*]

Enter *Jack Cade* and the rest, and strikes his staff on London Stone.

Cade. Now is Mortimer lord of this city. And here, sitting upon London Stone, I charge and command that, of the city's cost, the pissing conduit run nothing but claret wine this first year of our reign. And now henceforward it shall be treason for any that calls me other than Lord Mortimer.

Enter a *Soldier*, running.

Sold. Jack Cade! Jack Cade!

Cade. Knock him down there.

They kill him.

Weav. If this fellow be wise, he'll never call ye Jack Cade more. I think he hath a very fair warning.

Butch. My lord, there's an army gathered together in Smithfield.

Cade. Come then, let's go fight with them. But first go and set London Bridge on fire, and, if you can, burn down the Tower too. Come, let's away. *Exeunt omnes.*

[Scene VII. *London. Smithfield.*]

Alarums. Matthew Goffe is slain, and all the rest [of the loyal forces]. Then enter *Jack Cade* with his *Company.*

Cade. So, sirs. Now go some and pull down the Savoy; others to th' Inns of Court. Down with them all!

Butch. I have a suit unto your lordship.

Cade. Be it a lordship, thou shalt have it for that word.

Butch. Only that the laws of England may come out of your mouth.

Hol. [*aside*] Mass, 'twill be sore law then; for he was thrust in the mouth with a spear, and 'tis not whole yet.

Weav. [*aside*] Nay, John, it will be stinking law; for his breath stinks with eating toasted cheese.

Cade. I have thought upon it; it shall be so. Away, burn all the records of the realm! My mouth shall be the parliament of England.

Hol. [*aside*] Then we are like to have biting statutes, unless his teeth be pull'd out.

Cade. And henceforward all things shall be in common.

Enter a *Messenger.*

Mess. My lord, a prize, a prize! Here's the Lord Say, which sold the towns in France; he that made us pay one-and-twenty fifteens, and one shilling to the pound, the last subsidy.

Enter *George* [*Bevis*], with the *Lord Say.*

Cade. Well, he shall be beheaded for it ten times. Ah, thou say, thou serge, nay, thou buckram lord! now art thou within point-blank of our jurisdiction regal. What canst thou answer to my Majesty for giving up of Normandy unto Mounsieur Basimecu, the Dauphin of France? Be it known unto thee by these presence, even the presence of Lord Mortimer, that I am the besom that must sweep the court clean of such filth as thou art. Thou hast most traitorously corrupted the youth of the realm in erecting a grammar school; and whereas, before, our forefathers had no other books but the score and the tally, thou hast caused printing to be us'd, and, contrary to the King, his crown and dignity, thou hast built a paper mill. It will be proved to thy face that thou hast men about thee that usually talk of a noun and a verb and such abominable words as no Christian ear can endure to hear. Thou hast appointed justices of peace, to call poor men before them about matters they were not able to answer. Moreover, thou hast put them in prison, and because they could not read, thou hast hang'd them, when, indeed, only for that cause they have been most worthy to live. Thou dost ride in a footcloth, dost thou not?

Say. What of that?

Cade. Marry, thou ought'st not to let thy horse wear a cloak when honester men than thou go in their hose and doublets.

Butch. And work in their shirt too; as myself, for example, that am a butcher.

Say. You men of Kent —

Butch. What say you of Kent?

Say. Nothing but this — 'tis 'bona terra, mala gens.'

Cade. Away with him, away with him! He speaks Latin.

Say. Hear me but speak, and bear me where you will.
Kent, in the Commentaries Cæsar writ,
Is term'd the civil'st place of all this isle.
Sweet is the country, because full of riches;
The people liberal, valiant, active, wealthy,
Which makes me hope you are not void of pity.
I sold not Maine, I lost not Normandy;
Yet to recover them would lose my life.
Justice with favour have I always done;
Prayers and tears have mov'd me, gifts could never.
When have I aught exacted at your hands
But to maintain the King, the realm, and you?
Large gifts have I bestow'd on learned clerks,
Because my book preferr'd me to the King;
And, seeing ignorance is the curse of God,
Knowledge the wing wherewith we fly to heaven,
Unless you be possess'd with devilish spirits,
You cannot but forbear to murther me.
This tongue hath parley'd unto foreign kings
For your behoof.

Cade. Tut! when struck'st thou one blow in the field?

Say. Great men have reaching hands. Oft have I struck
Those that I never saw, and struck them dead.

Bevis. O monstrous coward! What, to come behind folks?

Say. These cheeks are pale for watching for your good.

Cade. Give him a box o' th' ear, and that will make 'em red again.

Say. Long sitting to determine poor men's causes
Hath made me full of sickness and diseases.

Cade. Ye shall have a hempen caudle then, and the help of hatchet.

Butch. Why dost thou quiver, man?

Say. It is the palsy, and not fear, provokes me.

Cade. Nay, he nods at us, as who should say, 'I'll be even with you.' I'll see if his head will stand steadier on a pole or no. Take him away and behead him.

Say. Tell me: wherein have I offended most?
Have I affected wealth or honour? Speak.
Are my chests fill'd up with extorted gold?
Is my apparel sumptuous to behold?
Whom have I injur'd, that ye seek my death?
These hands are free from guiltless bloodshedding,
This breast from harbouring foul deceitful thoughts.
O, let me live!

Cade. [*aside*] I feel remorse in myself with his words; but I'll bridle it. He shall die, an it be but for pleading so well for his life.— Away with him! he has a familiar under his tongue; he speaks not a God's name. Go, take him away, I say, and strike off his head presently; and then break into his son-in-law's house, Sir James Cromer, and strike off his head, and bring them both upon two poles hither.

All. It shall be done.

Say. Ah, countrymen! If when you make your pray'rs,
God should be so obdurate as yourselves,
How would it fare with your departed souls?
And therefore yet relent, and save my life.

Cade. Away with him, and do as I command ye! *Exeunt some with Lord Say.* The proudest peer in the realm shall not wear a head on his shoulders unless he pay me tribute. There shall not a maid be married but she shall pay to me her maidenhead ere they have it. Men shall hold of me *in capite*; and we charge and command that their wives be as free as heart can wish or tongue can tell.

Butch. My lord, when shall we go to Cheapside and take up commodities upon our bills?

Cade. Marry, presently.

All. O brave!

Enter *one, with the heads.*

Cade. But is not this braver? Let them kiss one another, for they lov'd well when they were alive. Now part them again, lest they consult about the giving up of some more towns in France. Soldiers, defer the spoil of the city until night; for with these borne before us instead of maces will we ride through the streets, and at every corner have them kiss. Away!

Exeunt.

[Scene VIII. *Southwark.*]

Alarum and Retreat. Enter again *Cade* and all his *rabblement.*

Cade. Up Fish Street! down Saint Magnus Corner! Kill and knock down! Throw them into Thames! (*Sound a parley.*) What noise is this I hear? Dare any be so bold to sound retreat or parley when I command them kill?

Enter *Buckingham* and *Old Clifford.*

Buck. Ay, here they be that dare and will disturb thee.
Know, Cade, we come ambassadors from the King
Unto the commons, whom thou hast misled;
And here pronounce free pardon to them all
That will forsake thee and go home in peace.

Clif. What say ye, countrymen? Will ye relent
And yield to mercy whilst 'tis offered you,
Or let a rebel lead you to your deaths?
Who loves the King, and will embrace his pardon,
Fling up his cap and say 'God save his Majesty!'
Who hateth him and honours not his father,
Henry the Fifth, that made all France to quake,
Shake he his weapon at us and pass by.

All. God save the King! God save the King!

Cade. What, Buckingham and Clifford, are ye so brave? And you, base peasants, do ye believe them? Will you needs be hang'd with your pardons about your necks? Hath my sword therefore broke through London gates, that you should leave me at the White Hart in Southwark? I thought ye would never have given out these arms till you had recovered your ancient freedom. But you are all recreants and dastards and delight to live in slavery to the nobility. Let them break your backs with burthens, take your houses over your heads, ravish your wives and daughters before your faces. For me, I will make shift for one; and so God's curse light upon you all!

All. We'll follow Cade! We'll follow Cade!

Clif. Is Cade the son of Henry the Fifth
That thus you do exclaim you'll go with him?
Will he conduct you through the heart of France
And make the meanest of you earls and dukes?
Alas, he hath no home, no place to fly to;
Nor knows he how to live but by the spoil,
Unless by robbing of your friends and us.
Were't not a shame that whilst you live at jar
The fearful French, whom you late vanquished,
Should make a start o'er seas and vanquish you?
Methinks already in this civil broil
I see them lording it in London streets,
Crying 'Villiago!' unto all they meet.
Better ten thousand base-born Cades miscarry
Than you should stoop unto a Frenchman's mercy.
To France, to France, and get what you have lost!
Spare England, for it is your native coast.
Henry hath money, you are strong and manly;
God on our side, doubt not of victory.

All. A Clifford! a Clifford! We'll follow the King and Clifford.

Cade. Was ever feather so lightly blown to and fro as this multitude? The name of Henry the Fifth hales them to an hundred mischiefs and makes them leave me desolate. I see them lay their heads together to surprise me. My sword make way for me, for here is no staying. In despite of the devils and hell, have through the very middest of you! and heavens and honour be witness that no want of resolution in me, but only my followers' base and ignominious treasons, makes me betake me to my heels.

Exit.

Buck. What, is he fled? Go some, and follow him;
And he that brings his head unto the King
Shall have a thousand crowns for his reward.

Exeunt some of them.

Follow me, soldiers. We'll devise a mean
To reconcile you all unto the King.

Exeunt omnes.

[Scene IX. *Killingworth Castle.*]

Sound trumpets. Enter *King, Queen,* and *Somerset,* on the terrace.

King. Was ever king that joy'd an earthly throne
And could command no more content than I?
No sooner was I crept out of my cradle
But I was made a king, at nine months old.
Was never subject long'd to be a king
As I do long and wish to be a subject.

Enter *Buckingham* and [*Old*] *Clifford.*

Buck. Health and glad tidings to your Majesty!

King. Why, Buckingham, is the traitor Cade surpris'd?
Or is he but retir'd to make him strong?

Enter [below] *Multitudes,* with halters about their necks.

Clif. He is fled, my lord, and all his powers do yield,
And humbly thus, with halters on their necks,
Expect your Highness' doom of life or death.

King. Then, heaven, set ope thy everlasting gates
To entertain my vows of thanks and praise!
Soldiers, this day have you redeem'd your lives
And show'd how well you love your prince and country.
Continue still in this so good a mind,
And Henry, though he be infortunate,
Assure yourselves, will never be unkind.
And so, with thanks, and pardon to you all,
I do dismiss you to your several countries.

All. God save the King! God save the King!

Enter a *Messenger.*

Mess. Please it your Grace to be advertised
The Duke of York is newly come from Ireland
And with a puissant and a mighty power
Of gallowglasses and stout kerns
Is marching hitherward in proud array,
And still proclaimeth, as he comes along,
His arms are only to remove from thee
The Duke of Somerset, whom he terms a traitor.

King. Thus stands my state, 'twixt Cade and York distress'd;
Like to a ship that, having scap'd a tempest,
Is straightway calm'd, and boarded with a pirate.
But now is Cade driven back, his men dispers'd,

And now is York in arms to second him.
I pray thee, Buckingham, go and meet him,
And ask him what's the reason of these arms.
Tell him I'll send Duke Edmund to the Tower;
And, Somerset, we will commit thee thither
Until his army be dismiss'd from him.

Som. My lord,
I'll yield myself to prison willingly,
Or unto death, to do my country good.

King. In any case, be not too rough in terms,
For he is fierce and cannot brook hard language.

Buck. I will, my lord, and doubt not so to deal
As all things shall redound unto your good.

King. Come, wife, let's in, and learn to govern better;
For yet may England curse my wretched reign.

Flourish. Exeunt.

[Scene X. *Kent.* Iden's *garden.*]

Enter *Cade.*

Cade. Fie on ambitions! Fie on myself, that have a sword and yet am ready to famish! These five days have I hid me in these woods and durst not peep out, for all the country is laid for me; but now am I so hungry that, if I might have a lease of my life for a thousand years, I could stay no longer. Wherefore, on a brick wall have I climb'd into this garden, to see if I can eat grass, or pick a sallet another while, which is not amiss to cool a man's stomach this hot weather. And I think this word 'sallet' was born to do me good; for many a time, but for a sallet, my brainpan had been cleft with a brown bill; and many a time, when I have been dry, and bravely marching, it hath serv'd me instead of a quart pot to drink in; and now the word 'sallet' must serve me to feed on.

Enter *Iden.*

Iden. Lord, who would live turmoiled in the court
And may enjoy such quiet walks as these?
This small inheritance my father left me
Contenteth me, and worth a monarchy.
I seek not to wax great by others' waning,
Or gather wealth, I care not with what envy.
Sufficeth that I have maintains my state
And sends the poor well pleased from my gate.

Cade. Here's the lord of the soil come to seize me for a stray, for entering his fee simple without leave. Ah, villain, thou wilt betray me and get a thousand crowns of the King by carrying my head to him; but I'll make thee eat iron like an ostridge and swallow my sword like a great pin ere thou and I part.

Iden. Why, rude companion, whatsoe'er thou be,
I know thee not. Why then should I betray thee?
Is't not enough to break into my garden
And like a thief to come to rob my grounds,
Climbing my walls in spite of me the owner,
But thou wilt brave me with these saucy terms?

Cade. Brave thee? Ay, by the best blood that ever was broach'd, and beard thee too! Look on me well. I have eat no meat these five days; yet, come thou and thy five men, and if I do not leave you all as dead as a doornail, I pray God I may never eat grass more.

Iden. Nay, it shall ne'er be said, while England stands,
That Alexander Iden, an esquire of Kent,
Took odds to combat a poor famish'd man.
Oppose thy steadfast-gazing eyes to mine;
See if thou canst outface me with thy looks.
Set limb to limb, and thou art far the lesser;
Thy hand is but a finger to my fist,
Thy leg a stick compared with this truncheon;
My foot shall fight with all the strength thou hast;
And if mine arm be heaved in the air,
Thy grave is digg'd already in the earth.
As for words, whose greatness answers words,
Let this my sword report what speech forbears.

Cade. By my valour, the most complete champion that ever I heard! Steel, if thou turn the edge, or cut not out the burly-bon'd clown in chines of beef ere thou sleep in thy sheath, I beseech God on my knees thou mayst be turn'd to hobnails. (*Here they fight. Cade falls.*) O, I am slain! Famine and no other hath slain me. Let ten thousand devils come against me, and give me but the ten meals I have lost, and I'd defy them all. Wither, garden, and be henceforth a burying place to all that do dwell in this house, because the unconquered soul of Cade is fled.

Iden. Is't Cade that I have slain, that monstrous traitor?
Sword, I will hallow thee for this thy deed
And hang thee o'er my tomb when I am dead.
Ne'er shall this blood be wiped from thy point,
But thou shalt wear it as a herald's coat,
To emblaze the honour that thy master got.

Cade. Iden, farewell, and be proud of thy victory. Tell Kent from me, she hath lost her best man, and exhort all the world to be cowards; for I, that never feared any, am vanquished by famine, not by valour. *Dies.*

Iden. How much thou wrong'st me, heaven be my judge.
Die, damned wretch, the curse of her that bare thee!
And as I thrust thy body in with my sword,
So wish I, I might thrust thy soul to hell!
Hence will I drag thee headlong by the heels
Unto a dunghill, which shall be thy grave,
And there cut off thy most ungracious head,
Which I will bear in triumph to the King,
Leaving thy trunk for crows to feed upon.
Exit.

[ACT V. Scene I. *Fields between Dartford and Blackheath.*]

Enter *York* and his army of *Irish,* with *Drum* and *Colours.*

York. From Ireland thus comes York to claim his right
And pluck the crown from feeble Henry's head.
Ring bells aloud, burn bonfires clear and bright,
To entertain great England's lawful king.
Ah, Sancta Maiestas! who would not buy thee dear?
Let them obey that know not how to rule;
This hand was made to handle naught but gold.
I cannot give due action to my words
Except a sword or sceptre balance it.
A sceptre shall it have, have I a soul,
On which I'll toss the fleur-de-luce of France.

Enter *Buckingham.*

[*Aside*] Whom have we here? Buckingham, to disturb me?
The King hath sent him sure. I must dissemble.

Buck. York, if thou meanest well, I greet thee well.

York. Humphrey of Buckingham, I accept thy greeting.
Art thou a messenger or come of pleasure?

Buck. A messenger from Henry, our dread liege,
To know the reason of these arms in peace;
Or why thou, being a subject as I am,
Against thy oath and true allegiance sworn
Should raise so great a power without his leave,
Or dare to bring thy force so near the court.

York. [*aside*] Scarce can I speak, my choler is so great.
O, I could hew up rocks and fight with flint,
I am so angry at these abject terms;
And now, like Ajax Telamonius,
On sheep or oxen could I spend my fury!
I am far better born than is the King,
More like a king, more kingly in my thoughts.
But I must make fair weather yet a while,
Till Henry be more weak, and I more strong.—
Buckingham, I prithee pardon me
That I have given no answer all this while.
My mind was troubled with deep melancholy.
The cause why I have brought this army hither
Is to remove proud Somerset from the King,
Seditious to his Grace and to the state.

Buck. That is too much presumption on thy part.
But if thy arms be to no other end,
The King hath yielded unto thy demand.
The Duke of Somerset is in the Tower.

York. Upon thine honour, is he prisoner?

Buck. Upon mine honour, he is prisoner.

York. Then, Buckingham, I do dismiss my pow'rs.
Soldiers, I thank you all. Disperse yourselves.
Meet me to-morrow in Saint George's Field,
You shall have pay and everything you wish.
And let my sovereign, virtuous Henry,
Command my eldest son, nay, all my sons,
As pledges of my fealty and love.
I'll send them all as willing as I live.
Lands, goods, horse, armour, anything I have
Is his to use, so Somerset may die.
Exeunt Soldiers.

Buck. York, I commend this kind submission.
We twain will go into his Highness' tent.

Enter *King* and *Attendants.*

King. Buckingham, doth York intend no harm to us
That thus he marcheth with thee arm in arm?

York. In all submission and humility
York doth present himself unto your Highness.

King. Then what intends these forces thou dost bring?

York. To heave the traitor Somerset from hence
And fight against that monstrous rebel Cade,
Who since I heard to be discomfited.

Enter *Iden,* with *Cade's* head.

Iden. If one so rude and of so mean condition
May pass into the presence of a king,

Lo, I present your Grace a traitor's head,
The head of Cade, whom I in combat slew.

King. The head of Cade? Great God, how just art thou!
O, let me view his visage, being dead,
That living wrought me such exceeding trouble.
Tell me, my friend, art thou the man that slew him?

Iden. I was, an 't like your Majesty.

King. How art thou call'd, and what is thy degree?

Iden. Alexander Iden, that's my name;
A poor esquire of Kent that loves his king.

Buck. So please it you, my lord, 'twere not amiss
He were created knight for his good service.

King. Iden, kneel down. [*He kneels.*] Rise up a knight. [*He rises.*]
We give thee for reward a thousand marks,
And will that thou henceforth attend on us.

Iden. May Iden live to merit such a bounty,
And never live but true unto his liege!

Enter *Queen* and *Somerset.*

King. See, Buckingham! Somerset comes with th' Queen.
Go bid her hide him quickly from the Duke.

Queen. For thousand Yorks he shall not hide his head,
But boldly stand and front him to his face.

York. How now? Is Somerset at liberty?
Then, York, unloose thy long-imprisoned thoughts
And let thy tongue be equal with thy heart.
Shall I endure the sight of Somerset?
False king, why hast thou broken faith with me,
Knowing how hardly I can brook abuse?
King did I call thee? No! thou art not King,
Not fit to govern and rule multitudes,
Which dar'st not, no, nor canst not rule a traitor.
That head of thine doth not become a crown;
Thy hand is made to grasp a palmer's staff
And not to grace an awful princely sceptre.
That gold must round engirt these brows of mine,
Whose smile and frown, like to Achilles' spear,
Is able with the change to kill and cure.
Here is a hand to hold a sceptre up
And with the same to act controlling laws.
Give place. By heaven, thou shalt rule no more
O'er him whom heaven created for thy ruler.

Som. O monstrous traitor! I arrest thee, York,
Of capital treason 'gainst the King and crown.
Obey, audacious traitor; kneel for grace.

York. Wouldst have me kneel? First let me ask of these
If they can brook I bow a knee to man.
Sirrah, call in my sons to be my bail. [*Exit an Attendant.*]
I know, ere they will have me go to ward,
They'll pawn their swords for my enfranchisement.

Queen. Call hither Clifford. Bid him come amain
To say if that the bastard boys of York
Shall be the surety for their traitor father. [*Exit Buckingham.*]

York. O blood-bespotted Neapolitan,
Outcast of Naples, England's bloody scourge!
The sons of York, thy betters in their birth,
Shall be their father's bail; and bane to those
That for my surety will refuse the boys!

Enter *Edward* and *Richard* [*Plantagenet*].

See where they come. I'll warrant they'll make it good.

Enter *Clifford* and his *Son.*

Queen. And here comes Clifford to deny their bail.

Clif. Health and all happiness to my lord the King! *Kneels.*

York. I thank thee, Clifford. Say, what news with thee?
Nay, do not fright us with an angry look.
We are thy sovereign, Clifford, kneel again.
For thy mistaking so, we pardon thee.

Clif. This is my king, York, I do not mistake;
But thou mistak'st me much to think I do.
To Bedlam with him! Is the man grown mad?

King. Ay, Clifford. A bedlam and ambitious humour
Makes him oppose himself against his king.

Clif. He is a traitor; let him to the Tower,
And chop away that factious pate of his.

Queen. He is arrested, but will not obey.
His sons, he says, shall give their words for him.

York. Will you not, sons?

Edw. Ay, noble father, if our words will serve.

Rich. And if words will not, then our weapons shall.

Clif. Why, what a brood of traitors have we here!

York. Look in a glass and call thy image so.
I am thy king, and thou a false-heart traitor.
Call hither to the stake my two brave bears,

That with the very shaking of their chains
They may astonish these fell-lurking curs.
Bid Salisbury and Warwick come to me.
[*Exit an Attendant.*]

Enter the *Earls of Warwick* and *Salisbury.*

Clif. Are these thy bears? We'll bait thy bears to death
And manacle the berard in their chains
If thou dar'st bring them to the baiting place.
Rich. Oft have I seen a hot o'erweening cur
Run back and bite because he was withheld,
Who, being suffer'd, with the bear's fell paw
Hath clapp'd his tail between his legs and cried;
And such a piece of service will you do
If you oppose yourselves to match Lord Warwick.
Clif. Hence, heap of wrath, foul indigested lump,
As crooked in thy manners as thy shape!
York. Nay, we shall heat you thoroughly anon.
Clif. Take heed lest by your heat you burn yourselves.
King. Why Warwick, hath thy knee forgot to bow?
Old Salisbury, shame to thy silver hair,
Thou mad misleader of thy brainsick son!
What, wilt thou on thy deathbed play the ruffian
And seek for sorrow with thy spectacles?
O, where is faith? O, where is loyalty?
If it be banish'd from the frosty head,
Where shall it find a harbour in the earth?
Wilt thou go dig a grave to find out war,
And stain thine honourable age with blood?
Why art thou old, and want'st experience?
Or wherefore dost abuse it if thou hast it?
For shame! In duty bend thy knee to me,
That bows unto the grave with mickle age.
Sal. My lord, I have considered with myself
The title of this most renowned duke
And, in my conscience, do repute his Grace
The rightful heir to England's royal seat.
King. Hast thou not sworn allegiance unto me?
Sal. I have.
King. Canst thou dispense with heaven for such an oath?
Sal. It is great sin to swear unto a sin,
But greater sin to keep a sinful oath.
Who can be bound by any solemn vow
To do a murd'rous deed, to rob a man,
To force a spotless virgin's chastity,
To reave the orphan of his patrimony,
To wring the widow from her custom'd right,
And have no other reason for this wrong
But that he was bound by a solemn oath?
Queen. A subtle traitor needs no sophister.
King. Call Buckingham and bid him arm himself.
York. Call Buckingham and all the friends thou hast,
I am resolv'd for death or dignity.
Clif. The first I warrant thee, if dreams prove true.
War. You were best to go to bed and dream again
To keep thee from the tempest of the field.
Clif. I am resolv'd to bear a greater storm
Than any thou canst conjure up to-day;
And that I'll write upon thy burgonet,
Might I but know thee by thy household badge.
War. Now, by my father's badge, old Nevil's crest,
The rampant bear chain'd to the ragged staff,
This day I'll wear aloft my burgonet,
As on a mountain top the cedar shows,
That keeps his leaves in spite of any storm,
Even to affright thee with the view thereof.
Clif. And from thy burgonet I'll rend thy bear
And tread it under foot with all contempt,
Despite the berard that protects the bear.
Young Clif. And so to arms, victorious father,
To quell the rebels and their complices!
Rich. Fie! charity, for shame! Speak not in spite,
For you shall sup with Jesu Christ to-night.
Young Clif. Foul stigmatic, that's more than thou canst tell.
Rich. If not in heaven, you'll surely sup in hell. *Exeunt* [*severally*].

[Scene II. *Saint Alban's.*]

Alarums to the battle. Enter *Warwick.*

War. Clifford of Cumberland, 'tis Warwick calls!
And if thou dost not hide thee from the bear,
Now, when the angry trumpet sounds alarum
And dead men's cries do fill the empty air,
Clifford, I say, come forth and fight with me!
Proud Northern lord, Clifford of Cumberland,
Warwick is hoarse with calling thee to arms.

Enter *York.*

How now, my noble lord? What, all afoot?
York. The deadly-handed Clifford slew my steed;

But match to match I have encount'red him
And made a prey for carrion kites and crows
Even of the bonny beast he lov'd so well.

Enter [*Old*] *Clifford.*

War. Of one or both of us the time is come.
York. Hold, Warwick, seek thee out some other chase,
For I myself must hunt this deer to death.
War. Then nobly, York! 'Tis for a crown thou fight'st.
As I intend, Clifford, to thrive to-day,
It grieves my soul to leave thee unassail'd.
Exit.
Clif. What seest thou in me, York? Why dost thou pause?
York. With thy brave bearing should I be in love
But that thou art so fast mine enemy.
Clif. Nor should thy prowess want praise and esteem
But that 'tis shown ignobly and in treason.
York. So let it help me now against thy sword
As I in justice and true right express it!
Clif. My soul and body on the action both!
York. A dreadful lay! Address thee instantly. *They fight, and York kills Clifford.*
Clif. La fin couronne les œuvres. [*Dies.*]
York. Thus war hath given thee peace, for thou art still.
Peace with his soul, heaven, if it be thy will!
Exit.

Enter *Young Clifford.*

Clif. Shame and confusion! All is on the rout.
Fear frames disorder, and disorder wounds
Where it should guard. O war, thou son of hell,
Whom angry heavens do make their minister,
Throw in the frozen bosoms of our part
Hot coals of vengeance! Let no soldier fly.
He that is truly dedicate to war
Hath no self-love; nor he that loves himself
Hath not essentially, but by circumstance,
The name of valour. [*Sees his father's body.*]
O, let the vile world end
And the premised flames of the last day
Knit earth and heaven together!
Now let the general trumpet blow his blast,
Particularities and petty sounds
To cease! Wast thou ordain'd, dear father,
To lose thy youth in peace and to achieve
The silver livery of advised age,
And in thy reverence and thy chair-days thus
To die in ruffian battle? Even at this sight
My heart is turn'd to stone; and while 'tis mine,
It shall be stony. York not our old men spares;
No more will I their babes. Tears virginal
Shall be to me even as the dew to fire;
And beauty, that the tyrant oft reclaims,
Shall to my flaming wrath be oil and flax.
Henceforth I will not have to do with pity.
Meet I an infant of the house of York,
Into as many gobbets will I cut it
As wild Medea young Absyrtus did.
In cruelty will I seek out my fame.
Come, thou new ruin of old Clifford's house.
As did Æneas old Anchises bear,
So bear I thee upon my manly shoulders;
But then Æneas bare a living load,
Nothing so heavy as these woes of mine.
[*Exit with the body.*]

Enter *Richard* and *Somerset* to fight. [*Somerset is killed.*]

Rich. So lie thou there!
For underneath an alehouse' paltry sign,
The Castle in Saint Alban's, Somerset
Hath made the wizard famous in his death.
Sword, hold thy temper. Heart, be wrathful still.
Priests pray for enemies, but princes kill.
Exit.

Fight. Excursions. Enter *King, Queen,* and others.

Queen. Away, my lord! You are slow. For shame, away!
King. Can we outrun the heavens? Good Margaret, stay.
Queen. What are you made of? You'll nor fight nor fly.
Now is it manhood, wisdom, and defence
To give the enemy way, and to secure us
By what we can, which can no more but fly.
Alarum afar off.
If you be ta'en, we then should see the bottom
Of all our fortunes; but if we haply scape
(As well we may, if not through your neglect),
We shall to London get, where you are lov'd,
And where this breach now in our fortunes made
May readily be stopp'd.

Enter [*Young*] *Clifford.*

Clif. But that my heart's on future mischief set,
I would speak blasphemy ere bid you fly!
But fly you must. Uncurable discomfite

Reigns in the hearts of all our present parts.
Away, for your relief! and we will live
To see their day and them our fortune give.
Away, my lord, away! *Exeunt.*

[Scene III. *Field near Saint Alban's.*]

Alarum. Retreat. Enter *York, Richard, Warwick,* and *Soldiers,* with *Drum* and *Colours.*

York. Old Salisbury, who can report of him,
That winter lion, who in rage forgets
Aged contusions and all brush of time
And, like a gallant in the brow of youth,
Repairs him with occasion? This happy day
Is not itself, nor have we won one foot,
If Salisbury be lost.
Rich. My noble father,
Three times to-day I holp him to his horse,
Three times bestrid him, thrice I led him off,
Persuaded him from any further act;
But still where danger was, still there I met him;
And like rich hangings in a homely house,
So was his will in his old feeble body.
But, noble as he is, look where he comes.

Enter *Salisbury.*

Sal. Now, by my sword, well hast thou fought to-day!
By th' mass, so did we all! I thank you, Richard.
God knows how long it is I have to live;
And it hath pleas'd him that three times to-day
You have defended me from imminent death.
Well, lords, we have not got that which we have.
'Tis not enough our foes are this time fled,
Being opposites of such repairing nature.
York. I know our safety is to follow them;
For, as I hear, the King is fled to London
To call a present court of parliament.
Let us pursue him ere the writs go forth.
What says Lord Warwick? Shall we after them?
War. After them? Nay, before them, if we can!
Now, by my faith, lords, 'twas a glorious day.
Saint Alban's battle, won by famous York,
Shall be eterniz'd in all age to come.
Sound drums and trumpets, and to London all;
And more such days as these to us befall!
Exeunt.

THE THIRD PART OF KING HENRY THE SIXTH

THE THIRD PART OF KING HENRY THE SIXTH bears the same relation to *The True Tragedie of Richard Duke of Yorke* that the *Second Part* bears to *The First Part of the Contention*, and the theories discussed in the Introduction to *Part II* are all applicable to the present play (see p. 703). As before, we may accept the Folio version, which is the sole authority for the text, as entirely Shakespeare's work. The Quarto of *The True Tragedie* is, then, a reduced and imperfect form of Shakespeare's play, and not an older drama from which Shakespeare elaborated his PART III.

The so-called First Quarto of *The True Tragedie* (really an octavo) appeared in 1595, the Second Quarto in 1600, and the Quarto of 1619 (*The Whole Contention*) includes both *The First Part of the Contention* and *The True Tragedie*.

The True Tragedie covers the same ground as Shakespeare's PART III, but is only two-thirds as long. Material and arrangement are substantially identical, and differences in phraseology are less striking than in the case of PART II and *The Contention*. In the opening scene the text is almost literally identical, verse for verse and word for word, until Queen Margaret enters — that is, for about two hundred lines. Both texts close with a typical concluding speech in which they disagree in only a single word.

For specimens of the additional matter in PART III compare i, 1, 215–229; i, 2, 28–34; ii, 5, 20–54; iii, 1, 72–96; iii, 2, 164–181; iii, 3, 4–43; iv, 3, 1–22; iv, 6, 3–36, 77–102; v, 4, 1–43. In some instances, the lack of the passage in *The True Tragedie* is manifestly due to a cut; in some, the Quarto shows slight traces of the Folio text; in others, it partly fills the gap with other lines.

PART III plunges *in medias res*. Abundant expository matter follows at once. The Battle of St. Albans (May 22, 1455) is fused with the Yorkist victory at Northampton (July 10, 1460), and the opening scene in the Parliament House (October, 1460) is made to follow the battle with only the interval required to reach London. The crown is assured to Henry for life, but the title is to pass to Richard of York and his heirs. Civil war follows, and the Battle of Wakefield is won by the King's party (December 30). As a matter of history, York fell in the battle; but Halle (copied by Holinshed) relates an alternative story, according to which he was taken alive and 'in derision caused to stand upon a molehill.' This is dramatized in i, 4.

Act ii takes us through the Battle of Towton (March, 1461). The famous scene (ii, 5) in which a son who has killed his father appears, and a father who has killed his son, was suggested by a sentence in Halle: 'This conflict was in maner vnnaturall, for in it the sonne fought agaynst the father, the brother agaynst the brother, the nephew against the uncle, and the tenaunt agaynst his lord.' King Henry flees to Scotland. The coronation of Edward IV (June 28, 1461) is assumed to take place between the acts.

In the first scene of Act iii, Henry, having returned in disguise, is arrested (1465). An interlude is now provided by King Edward's wooing of Lady Grey (iii, 2). The marriage took place on May Day, 1464. Scene iii condenses history in defiance of dates: Queen Margaret's reception by the French king (1462), Warwick's negotiations for Edward's marriage with the

Lady Bona (1464) — frustrated by the marriage of Edward and Lady Grey — and his return with French forces (1470) to reinstate Henry, are brought together.

Act iv dramatizes Warwick's military operations of 1470 and the restoration of King Henry. The capture of Edward (iv, 3) actually took place in the campaign of 1469, and he escaped in October of that year. In 1470 he was not captured but fled to the Continent (iv, 6, 78 ff.) on hearing of Warwick's approach. Henry's release from the Tower (October, 1470) is dramatized in scene 6. King Henry's prophecy about young Richmond (iv, 6, 68–76) was suggested by a passage in Halle-Holinshed.

From Act iv, scene 7, to the end the order of events agrees well enough with the historical record. Edward's return (March 14, 1471) and the Battle of Barnet (April 14), in which Warwick is killed, decide the fate of the Lancastrians (iv, 7–8; v, 1–5). Henry has been captured in the interval (iv, 8) and sent to the Tower. The Battle of Tewkesbury (May 4) results in the capture of Queen Margaret and young Prince Edward (v, 4–5). The murder of the Prince follows immediately. Holinshed writes (on Halle's authority) that, on being asked by the king 'how he durst so presumptuouslie enter into his realme with banner displaied,' he replied boldly: 'To recouer my father's kingdome and heritage, from his father and grandfather to him, and from him after him to me, lineallie descended' (v, 5, 14 ff.), whereupon he was 'suddenlie murthered' by Clarence, Richard, Dorset, and Hastings. King Henry died in the Tower soon after — no one knows under what circumstances; but Shakespeare is justified by 'constant fame' in making Richard of Gloucester his murderer (v, 6). The closing scene of the play is imaginary. It is supposed to occur soon after King Henry's death.

From this review it appears that THE THIRD PART OF KING HENRY THE SIXTH is quite intelligible in and for itself. It required no *Part I* or *Part II* to make it clear to any audience.

The association of Marlowe and Greene with the three plays on Henry VI seems to owe its origin to a misunderstanding of a passage in Robert Greene's *Groatsworth of Wit*. Addressing three playwrights of his acquaintance, Greene bids them put no trust in actors — 'painted monsters' — 'puppets that spake from our mouths' — 'anticks garnisht in our colours.' 'Trust them not: for there is an vpstart Crow, beautified with our feathers, that with his *Tygers hart wrapt in a Players hyde*, supposes he is as well able to bombast out a blanke verse as the best of you: and beeing an absolute *Iohannes fac totum*, is in his owne conceit the onely Shake-scene in a countrey.' He adjures the three to abandon play-writing for 'more profitable courses.' One of the persons addressed was undoubtedly Marlowe. 'Shake-scene' is obviously Shakespeare. All this has been taken as an assertion that Shakespeare had stolen literary matter from Marlowe and Greene to use in his HENRY THE SIXTH. But no charge of plagiarism is involved. Greene despises those speaking puppets, the actors, because they owe their fame to the mere declamation of other men's verses; and one of these puppets has even presumed to write plays of his own, and thinks he can make as good blank verse as the best of us.

Greene was writing shortly before September, 1592. The italicized line parodies 3 HENRY VI, i, 4, 137. His evidence suffices to put PART III as early as that year. A reasonable date is 1591.

THE THIRD PART OF
KING HENRY THE SIXTH

[Dramatis Personae.

King Henry the Sixth.
Edward, Prince of Wales, his son.
Lewis XI, King of France.
Duke of Somerset.
Duke of Exeter.
Earl of Oxford.
Earl of Northumberland.
Earl of Westmoreland.
Lord Clifford.
Richard Plantagenet, Duke of York.
Edward, Earl of March, afterwards *King Edward IV,* } his sons.
Edmund, Earl of Rutland, } his sons.
George, afterwards *Duke of Clarence,* } his sons.
Richard, afterwards *Duke of Gloucester,* } his sons.
Duke of Norfolk.
Marquess of Montague.
Earl of Warwick.
Earl of Pembroke.
Lord Hastings.
Lord Stafford.
Sir John Mortimer, } uncles to *Richard,* Duke of York.
Sir Hugh Mortimer, } uncles to *Richard,* Duke of York.
Henry, young Earl of Richmond.
Lord Rivers, brother to *Lady Grey.*
Sir William Stanley.
Sir John Montgomery.
Sir John Somervile.
Tutor to *Rutland.*
Mayor of York and Aldermen.
Mayor of Coventry.
Lieutenant of the Tower.
A Nobleman.
Two Keepers (*Sinklo* and *Humphrey*).
A Son that has killed his father.
A Father that has killed his son.
The French Admiral.

Queen Margaret.
Lady Grey, a widow, afterwards Queen to *Edward IV.*
Bona, sister to the French Queen.

Soldiers, Attendants, Messengers, Watchmen, a Huntsman.

SCENE. — *England and France.*]

ACT I. Scene I. [*London. The Parliament House.*]

Alarum. Enter *Plantagenet Duke of York, Edward, Richard, Norfolk, Montague, Warwick,* and *Soldiers.*

War. I wonder how the King escap'd our hands.
York. While we pursu'd the horsemen of the North,
He slily stole away and left his men;
Whereat the great Lord of Northumberland,
Whose warlike ears could never brook retreat,
Cheer'd up the drooping army, and himself,
Lord Clifford, and Lord Stafford, all abreast,
Charg'd our main battle's front and, breaking in,
Were by the swords of common soldiers slain.
Edw. Lord Stafford's father, Duke of Buckingham,
Is either slain or wounded dangerous;
I cleft his beaver with a downright blow.
That this is true, father, behold his blood.
[*Shows his bloody sword.*]
Mont. And, brother, here's the Earl of Wiltshire's blood,
Whom I encount'red as the battles join'd.
Rich. Speak thou for me, and tell them what I did. [*Throws down Somerset's head.*]
York. Richard hath best deserv'd of all my sons.
But is your Grace dead, my Lord of Somerset?
Norf. Such hap have all the line of John of Gaunt!
Rich. Thus do I hope to shake King Henry's head.
War. And so do I. Victorious Prince of York,
Before I see thee seated in that throne
Which now the house of Lancaster usurps,
I vow by heaven these eyes shall never close.

This is the palace of the fearful King
And this the regal seat. Possess it, York;
For this is thine, and not King Henry's heirs'.

York. Assist me then, sweet Warwick, and I will;
For hither we have broken in by force.

Norf. We'll all assist you. He that flies shall die.

York. Thanks, gentle Norfolk. Stay by me, my lords;
And, soldiers, stay, and lodge by me this night.
They go up.

War. And when the King comes, offer him no violence
Unless he seek to thrust you out perforce.
[*The Soldiers stand back.*]

York. The Queen this day here holds her parliament,
But little thinks we shall be of her council.
By words or blows here let us win our right.

Rich. Arm'd as we are, let's stay within this house.

War. The bloody parliament shall this be call'd
Unless Plantagenet, Duke of York, be King
And bashful Henry depos'd, whose cowardice
Hath made us bywords to our enemies.

York. Then leave me not, my lords. Be resolute.
I mean to take possession of my right.

War. Neither the King, nor he that loves him best,
The proudest he that holds up Lancaster,
Dares stir a wing if Warwick shake his bells.
I'll plant Plantagenet, root him up who dares.
Resolve thee, Richard; claim the English crown. [*York seats himself in the throne.*]

Flourish. Enter *King Henry, Clifford, Northumberland, Westmoreland, Exeter,* and the rest.

K. Hen. My lords, look where the sturdy rebel sits,
Even in the chair of state! Belike he means,
Back'd by the power of Warwick, that false peer,
To aspire unto the crown and reign as king.
Earl of Northumberland, he slew thy father,
And thine, Lord Clifford, and you both have vow'd revenge
On him, his sons, his favourites, and his friends.

North. If I be not, heavens be reveng'd on me!

Clif. The hope thereof makes Clifford mourn in steel.

West. What, shall we suffer this? Let's pluck him down.
My heart for anger burns. I cannot brook it.

K. Hen. Be patient, gentle Earl of Westmoreland.

Clif. Patience is for poltroons, such as he.
He durst not sit there, had your father liv'd.
My gracious lord, here in the parliament
Let us assail the family of York.

North. Well hast thou spoken, cousin. Be it so.

K. Hen. Ah, know you not the city favours them
And they have troops of soldiers at their beck?

Exe. But when the Duke is slain, they'll quickly fly.

K. Hen. Far be the thought of this from Henry's heart,
To make a shambles of the Parliament House!
Cousin of Exeter, frowns, words, and threats
Shall be the war that Henry means to use.
Thou factious Duke of York, descend my throne
And kneel for grace and mercy at my feet.
I am thy sovereign.

York. Thou art deceiv'd. I am thine.

Exe. For shame! come down. He made thee Duke of York.

York. It was my inheritance, as the earldom was.

Exe. Thy father was a traitor to the crown.

War. Exeter, thou art a traitor to the crown
In following this usurping Henry.

Clif. Whom should he follow but his natural king?

War. True, Clifford; and that's Richard Duke of York.

K. Hen. And shall I stand, and thou sit in my throne?

York. It must and shall be so. Content thyself.

War. Be Duke of Lancaster; let him be King.

West. He is both King and Duke of Lancaster,
And that the Lord of Westmoreland shall maintain.

War. And Warwick shall disprove it. You forget
That we are those which chas'd you from the field
And slew your fathers and with colours spread
March'd through the city to the palace gates.

North. Yes, Warwick, I remember it to my grief;

HENRY VI

PART THREE

PHOTOGRAPHS BY LISEL HAAS
PRODUCED BY THE BIRMINGHAM REPERTORY THEATRE

Henry VI (Jack May). Wishing to live a simple, peaceful life, he weakly promises the throne to the Duke of York when he shall die on condition "that here thou take an oath to cease this civil war" *(Act I, Scene I)*

The remorseless Margaret, Queen to Henry VI (Rosalind Boxall). "Ah! timorous wretch; thou hast undone thyself, thy son, and me . . . And yet shalt thou be safe? such safety finds the trembling lamb environed with wolves" *(Act I, Scene I)*

The widowed Lady Grey as played by Christine Finn

The proud-hearted kingmaker, Warwick (Edgar Wreford)

Richard (Paul Daneman), son of the Duke of York, later the Duke of Gloucester: "I'll make my heaven to dream upon the crown"

York rises to answer the king's charge of usurpation. "Henry ot Lancaster, resign thy crown. What mutter you, or what conspire you, lords?" *(Act I, Scene I)*

Backed by his sons and Warwick, York listens from the throne as King Henry speaks: "My lords, look where the sturdy rebel sits, even in the chair of state!" *(Act I, Scene I)*

Warwick joins in the pledge to honor Henry as King, yet has already prophetically observed that "Neither the king, nor he that loves him best . . . dares stir a wing if Warwick shake his bells" *(Act I, Scene I)*

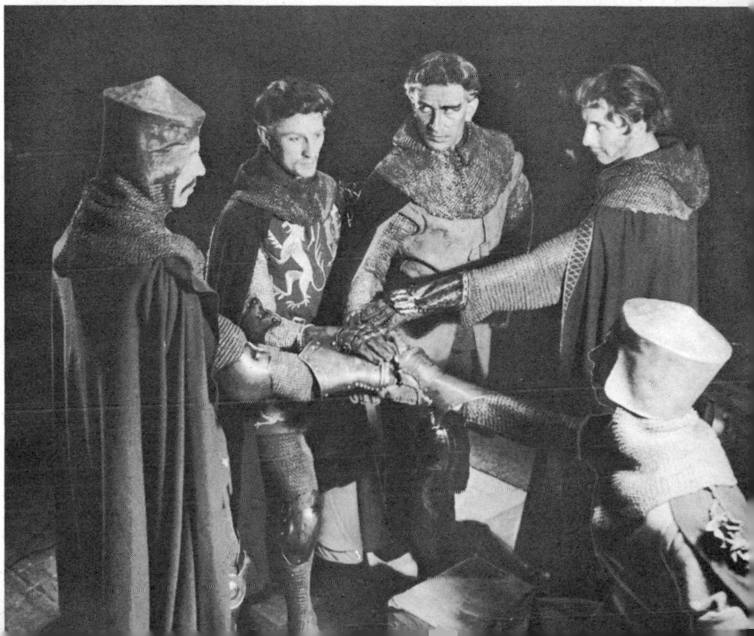

Richard to his father: "For a kingdom any oath may be broken; I would break a thousand oaths to reign one year" *(Act I, Scene II)*

Captured in a battle near Wakefield, York is taunted by the queen as she places a paper crown upon his head. "A crown for York! and, lords, bow low to him." Moments later he is slain and then beheaded *(Act I, Scene IV)*

The murdered York's son, Edward (Basil Henson), hurls a challenge: "Now, perjud'd Henry, wilt thou kneel for grace, and set thy diadem upon my head; or bide the mortal fortune of the field?" *(Act II, Scene II)*

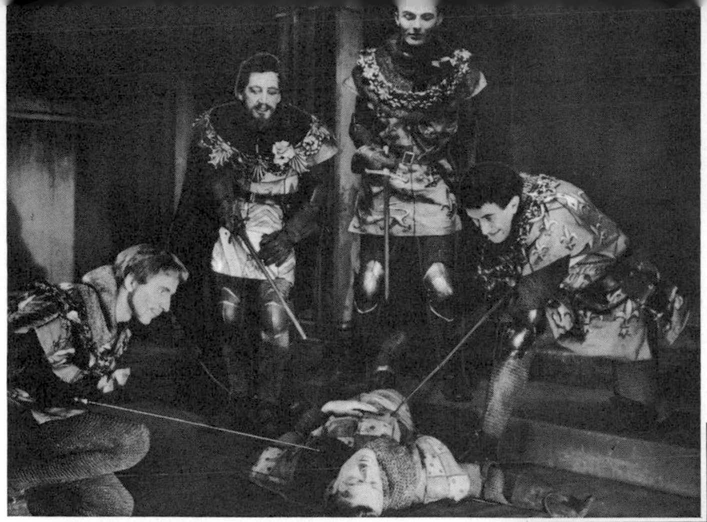

Crook-back Richard exults over the body of the man who killed his father
(Act II, Scene VI)

With Henry deposed, the widowed Lady Grey comes to the palace to beg the new king, Edward IV, to restore her husband's estates to her. Edward, in turn, advances a proposal of his own: "To tell thee plain, I aim to lie with thee"
(Act III, Scene II)

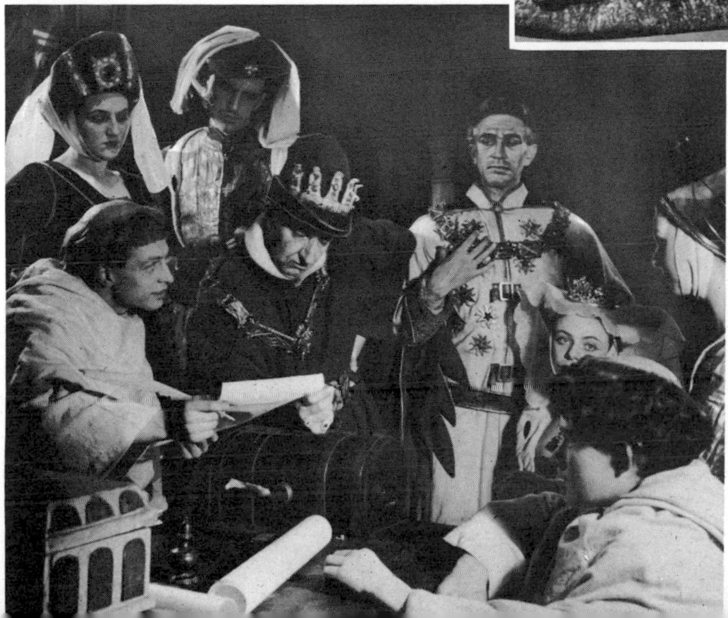

At the French court, Margaret and Warwick press conflicting petitions on Lewis XI (Redmond Phillips). Warwick's request is about to be granted when word arrives that Edward has married Lady Grey. This news prompts Warwick to denounce Edward and reconcile himself with Margaret
(Act III, Scene III)

The king of France, alluding to forces which he is sending with Warwick and Margaret, bids a messenger "Tell false Edward . . . that Lewis of France is sending over masquers to revel it with him and his new bride" *(Act III, Scene III)*

The invading forces surprise Edward in his camp *(Act IV, Scene III)*

Warwick tells Edward that "Henry now shall wear the English crown, and be true king indeed, thou but the shadow" *(Act IV, Scene III)*

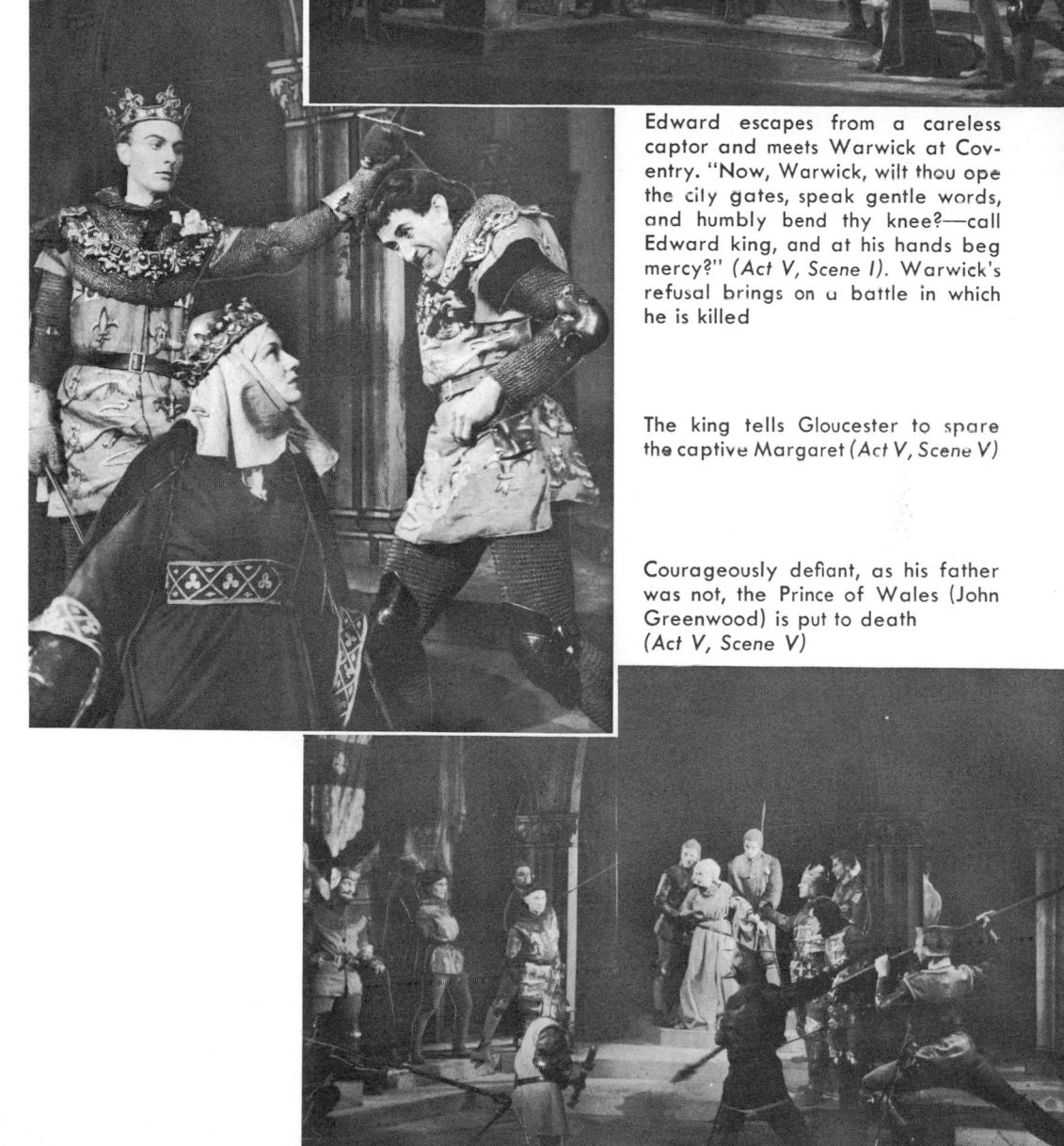

Edward escapes from a careless captor and meets Warwick at Coventry. "Now, Warwick, wilt thou ope the city gates, speak gentle words, and humbly bend thy knee?—call Edward king, and at his hands beg mercy?" *(Act V, Scene I)*. Warwick's refusal brings on a battle in which he is killed

The king tells Gloucester to spare the captive Margaret *(Act V, Scene V)*

Courageously defiant, as his father was not, the Prince of Wales (John Greenwood) is put to death *(Act V, Scene V)*

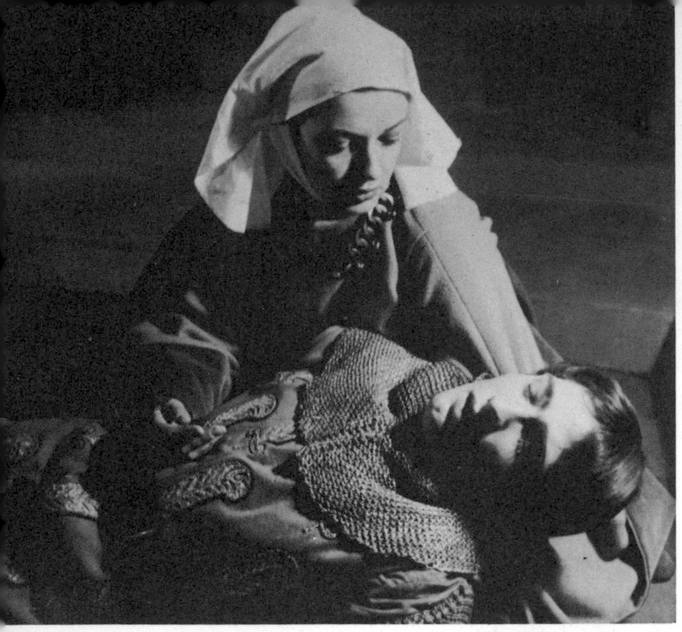

Margaret, the prince's mother, mourns his death. "No, no, my heart will burst, an if I speak: and I will speak, that so my heart may burst" *(Act V, Scene V)*

Having murdered Henry VI and thus made his brother Edward's claim to the throne secure, Richard bides his time. "This shoulder was ordain'd so thick to heave; and heave it shall some weight, or break my back" *(Act V, Scene VII)*

And, by his soul, thou and thy house shall rue it.
West. Plantagenet, of thee and these thy sons,
Thy kinsmen, and thy friends, I'll have more lives
Than drops of blood were in my father's veins.
Clif. Urge it no more; lest that instead of words
I send thee, Warwick, such a messenger
As shall revenge his death before I stir.
War. Poor Clifford! how I scorn his worthless threats!
York. Will you we show our title to the crown?
If not, our swords shall plead it in the field.
K. Hen. What title hast thou, traitor, to the crown?
Thy father was, as thou art, Duke of York;
Thy grandfather, Roger Mortimer, Earl of March.
I am the son of Henry the Fifth,
Who made the Dauphin and the French to stoop
And seiz'd upon their towns and provinces.
War. Talk not of France, sith thou hast lost it all.
K. Hen. The Lord Protector lost it, and not I.
When I was crown'd I was but nine months old.
Rich. You are old enough now, and yet methinks you lose.
Father, tear the crown from the usurper's head.
Edw. Sweet father, do so. Set it on your head.
Mont. [*to York*] Good brother, as thou lov'st and honourest arms,
Let's fight it out and not stand cavilling thus.
Rich. Sound drums and trumpets, and the King will fly.
York. Sons, peace!
K. Hen. Peace thou! and give King Henry leave to speak.
War. Plantagenet shall speak first. Hear him, lords,
And be you silent and attentive too,
For he that interrupts him shall not live.
K. Hen. Think'st thou that I will leave my kingly throne,
Wherein my grandsire and my father sat?
No! First shall war unpeople this my realm;
Ay, and their colours, often borne in France,
And now in England to our heart's great sorrow,
Shall be my winding sheet. Why faint you, lords?
My title's good, and better far than his.
War. Prove it, Henry, and thou shalt be King.
K. Hen. Henry the Fourth by conquest got the crown.
York. 'Twas by rebellion against his king.
K. Hen. [*aside*] I know not what to say; my title's weak. —
Tell me, may not a king adopt an heir?
York. What then?
K. Hen. An if he may, then am I lawful king;
For Richard, in the view of many lords,
Resign'd the crown to Henry the Fourth,
Whose heir my father was, and I am his.
York. He rose against him, being his sovereign,
And made him to resign his crown perforce.
War. Suppose, my lords, he did it unconstrain'd,
Think you 'twere prejudicial to his crown?
Exe. No, for he could not so resign his crown
But that the next heir should succeed and reign.
K. Hen. Art thou against us, Duke of Exeter?
Exe. His is the right, and therefore pardon me.
York. Why whisper you, my lords, and answer not?
Exe. My conscience tells me he is lawful king.
K. Hen. [*aside*] All will revolt from me and turn to him.
North. Plantagenet, for all the claim thou lay'st,
Think not that Henry shall be so depos'd.
War. Depos'd he shall be, in despite of all.
North. Thou art deceiv'd. 'Tis not thy Southern power
Of Essex, Norfolk, Suffolk, nor of Kent,
Which makes thee thus presumptuous and proud,
Can set the Duke up in despite of me.
Clif. King Henry, be thy title right or wrong,
Lord Clifford vows to fight in thy defence.
May that ground gape and swallow me alive
Where I shall kneel to him that slew my father!
K. Hen. O Clifford, how thy words revive my heart!
York. Henry of Lancaster, resign thy crown.
What mutter you or what conspire you, lords?

War. Do right unto this princely Duke of York,
Or I will fill the house with armed men
And over the chair of state, where now he sits,
Write up his title with usurping blood.

He stamps with his foot, and the Soldiers show themselves.

K. Hen. My Lord of Warwick, hear me but one word.
Let me for this my lifetime reign as king.

York. Confirm the crown to me and to mine heirs
And thou shalt reign in quiet while thou liv'st.

K. Hen. I am content. Richard Plantagenet,
Enjoy the kingdom after my decease.

Clif. What wrong is this unto the Prince your son!

War. What good is this to England and himself!

West. Base, fearful, and despairing Henry!

Clif. How hast thou injur'd both thyself and us!

West. I cannot stay to hear these articles.

North. Nor I.

Clif. Come, cousin, let us tell the Queen these news.

West. Farewell, faint-hearted and degenerate king,
In whose cold blood no spark of honour bides.

North. Be thou a prey unto the house of York
And die in bands for this unmanly deed!

Clif. In dreadful war mayst thou be overcome
Or live in peace abandon'd and despis'd!

[*Exeunt Northumberland, Clifford, and Westmoreland.*]

War. Turn this way, Henry, and regard them not.

Exe. They seek revenge and therefore will not yield.

K. Hen. Ah, Exeter!

War. Why should you sigh, my lord?

K. Hen. Not for myself, Lord Warwick, but my son,
Whom I unnaturally shall disinherit.
But be it as it may. [*To York.*] I here entail
The crown to thee and to thine heirs for ever,
Conditionally that here thou take an oath
To cease this civil war, and whilst I live
To honour me as thy king and sovereign,
And neither by treason nor hostility
To seek to put me down and reign thyself.

York. This oath I willingly take, and will perform. [*Comes from the throne.*]

War. Long live King Henry! Plantagenet, embrace him.

K. Hen. And long live thou, and these thy forward sons!

York. Now York and Lancaster are reconcil'd.

Exe. Accurs'd be he that seeks to make them foes!

Sennet. Here they come down.

York. Farewell, my gracious lord. I'll to my castle.

War. And I'll keep London with my soldiers.

Norf. And I to Norfolk with my followers.

Mont. And I unto the sea, from whence I came.

Exeunt York and his Sons, [*Warwick, Norfolk, Montague, with their Soldiers, and Attendants*].

K. Hen. And I with grief and sorrow to the court.

Enter the *Queen* [*Margaret*] and [*Edward*] *Prince* [*of Wales*].

Exe. Here comes the Queen, whose looks bewray her anger.
I'll steal away.

K. Hen. Exeter, so will I.

Queen. Nay, go not from me. I will follow thee.

K. Hen. Be patient, gentle queen, and I will stay.

Queen. Who can be patient in such extremes?
Ah, wretched man! Would I had died a maid
And never seen thee, never borne thee son,
Seeing thou hast prov'd so unnatural a father!
Hath he deserv'd to lose his birthright thus?
Hadst thou but lov'd him half so well as I,
Or felt that pain which I did for him once,
Or nourish'd him as I did with my blood,
Thou wouldst have left thy dearest heart-blood there
Rather than have made that savage duke thine heir
And disinherited thine only son.

Prince. Father, you cannot disinherit me.
If you be King, why should not I succeed?

K. Hen. Pardon me, Margaret. Pardon me, sweet son.
The Earl of Warwick and the Duke enforc'd me.

Queen. Enforc'd thee? Art thou King, and wilt be forc'd?
I shame to hear thee speak. Ah, timorous wretch!

Thou hast undone thyself, thy son, and me,
And giv'n unto the house of York such head
As thou shalt reign but by their sufferance.
To entail him and his heirs unto the crown,
What is it but to make thy sepulchre
And creep into it far before thy time?
Warwick is Chancellor and the lord of Calais;
Stern Falconbridge commands the narrow seas;
The Duke is made Protector of the realm;
And yet shalt thou be safe? Such safety finds
The trembling lamb environed with wolves.
Had I been there, which am a silly woman,
The soldiers should have toss'd me on their pikes
Before I would have granted to that act.
But thou preferr'st thy life before thine honour;
And seeing thou dost, I here divorce myself
Both from thy table, Henry, and thy bed
Until that act of parliament be repeal'd
Whereby my son is disinherited.
The Northern lords, that have forsworn thy colours,
Will follow mine, if once they see them spread;
And spread they shall be, to thy foul disgrace
And utter ruin of the house of York.
Thus do I leave thee. Come, son, let's away.
Our army is ready. Come, we'll after them.

K. Hen. Stay, gentle Margaret, and hear me speak.

Queen. Thou hast spoke too much already. Get thee gone.

K. Hen. Gentle son Edward, thou wilt stay with me?

Queen. Ay, to be murther'd by his enemies!

Prince. When I return with victory from the field
I'll see your Grace. Till then I'll follow her.

Queen. Come, son, away. We may not linger thus.

[*Exeunt Queen Margaret and the Prince.*]

K. Hen. Poor queen! How love to me and to her son
Hath made her break out into terms of rage!
Reveng'd may she be on that hateful duke,
Whose haughty spirit, winged with desire,
Will cost my crown and like an empty eagle
Tire on the flesh of me and of my son!
The loss of those three lords torments my heart.
I'll write unto them and entreat them fair.
Come, cousin, you shall be the messenger.

Exe. And I, I hope, shall reconcile them all.

Exeunt.

[Scene II. *Sandal Castle, near Wakefield, in Yorkshire.*]

Enter *Richard, Edward,* and *Montague.*

Rich. Brother, though I be youngest, give me leave.

Edw. No, I can better play the orator.

Mont. But I have reasons strong and forcible.

Enter the *Duke of York.*

York. Why, how now, sons and brother? at a strife?
What is your quarrel? How began it first?

Edw. No quarrel, but a slight contention.

York. About what?

Rich. About that which concerns your Grace and us —
The crown of England, father, which is yours.

York. Mine, boy? Not till King Henry be dead.

Rich. Your right depends not on his life or death.

Edw. Now you are heir; therefore enjoy it now.
By giving the house of Lancaster leave to breathe,
It will outrun you, father, in the end.

York. I took an oath that he should quietly reign.

Edw. But for a kingdom any oath may be broken.
I would break a thousand oaths to reign one year.

Rich. No. God forbid your Grace should be forsworn!

York. I shall be, if I claim by open war.

Rich. I'll prove the contrary if you'll hear me speak.

York. Thou canst not, son. It is impossible.

Rich. An oath is of no moment, being not took
Before a true and lawful magistrate
That hath authority over him that swears.
Henry had none, but did usurp the place.
Then, seeing 'twas he that made you to depose,
Your oath, my lord, is vain and frivolous.
Therefore, to arms! And, father, do but think
How sweet a thing it is to wear a crown,
Within whose circuit is Elysium
And all that poets feign of bliss and joy.
Why do we linger thus? I cannot rest
Until the white rose that I wear be dy'd
Even in the lukewarm blood of Henry's heart.

York. Richard, enough. I will be King or die!
Brother, thou shalt to London presently
And whet on Warwick to this enterprise.
Thou, Richard, shalt to the Duke of Norfolk
And tell him privily of our intent.
You, Edward, shall unto my Lord Cobham,
With whom the Kentishmen will willingly rise.
In them I trust; for they are soldiers,
Witty, courteous, liberal, full of spirit.
While you are thus employ'd, what resteth more
But that I seek occasion how to rise,
And yet the King not privy to my drift,
Nor any of the house of Lancaster?

Enter *Gabriel* (a *Messenger*).

But stay! What news? Why com'st thou in such post?

Gabr. The Queen with all the Northern earls and lords
Intend here to besiege you in your castle.
She is hard by with twenty thousand men;
And therefore fortify your hold, my lord.

York. Ay, with my sword! What? Think'st thou that we fear them?
Edward and Richard, you shall stay with me;
My brother Montague shall post to London.
Let noble Warwick, Cobham, and the rest,
Whom we have left protectors of the King,
With pow'rful policy strengthen themselves
And trust not simple Henry nor his oaths.

Mont. Brother, I go. I'll win them; fear it not;
And thus most humbly I do take my leave.
Exit.

Enter *Sir John Mortimer* and *Sir Hugh*, his *Brother*.

York. Sir John and Sir Hugh Mortimer, mine uncles!
You are come to Sandal in a happy hour.
The army of the Queen mean to besiege us.

John. She shall not need; we'll meet her in the field.

York. What, with five thousand men?

Rich. Ay, with five hundred, father, for a need!
A woman's general. What should we fear?
A march afar off.

Edw. I hear their drums. Let's set our men in order
And issue forth and bid them battle straight.

York. Five men to twenty! Though the odds be great,
I doubt not, uncle, of our victory.
Many a battle have I won in France
When as the enemy hath been ten to one.
Why should I not now have the like success?
Alarum. Exeunt.

[Scene III. *Field of battle between Sandal Castle and Wakefield.*]

Alarums. Enter *Rutland* and his *Tutor.*

Rut. Ah, whither shall I fly to scape their hands?
Ah, tutor, look where bloody Clifford comes!

Enter *Clifford* [and *Soldiers*].

Clif. Chaplain, away! Thy priesthood saves thy life.
As for the brat of this accursed duke,
Whose father slew my father, he shall die.

Tutor. And I, my lord, will bear him company.

Clif. Soldiers, away with him!

Tutor. Ah, Clifford, murther not this innocent child,
Lest thou be hated both of God and man!
Exit [*dragged off by Soldiers*].

Clif. How now? Is he dead already? Or is it fear
That makes him close his eyes? I'll open them.

Rut. So looks the pent-up lion o'er the wretch
That trembles under his devouring paws;
And so he walks, insulting o'er his prey,
And so he comes, to rend his limbs asunder.
Ah, gentle Clifford, kill me with thy sword
And not with such a cruel threat'ning look!
Sweet Clifford, hear me speak before I die!
I am too mean a subject for thy wrath.
Be thou reveng'd on men and let me live.

Clif. In vain thou speak'st, poor boy! My father's blood
Hath stopp'd the passage where thy words should enter.

Rut. Then let my father's blood open it again.
He is a man, and, Clifford, cope with him.

Clif. Had I thy brethren here, their lives and thine
Were not revenge sufficient for me.
No, if I digg'd up thy forefathers' graves
And hung their rotten coffins up in chains,
It could not slake mine ire nor ease my heart.
The sight of any of the house of York
Is as a Fury to torment my soul;
And till I root out their accursed line

And leave not one alive, I live in hell.
Therefore —

Rut. O, let me pray before I take my death!
To thee I pray. Sweet Clifford, pity me!

Clif. Such pity as my rapier's point affords.

Rut. I never did thee harm. Why wilt thou slay me?

Clif. Thy father hath.

Rut. But 'twas ere I was born.
Thou hast one son. For his sake pity me!
Lest in revenge thereof, sith God is just,
He be as miserably slain as I.
Ah, let me live in prison all my days;
And when I give occasion of offence,
Then let me die, for now thou hast no cause.

Clif. No cause?
Thy father slew my father. Therefore die.
[*Stabs him.*]

Rut. Di faciant laudis summa sit ista tuae!
[*Dies.*]

Clif. Plantagenet, I come, Plantagenet!
And this thy son's blood cleaving to my blade
Shall rust upon my weapon till thy blood,
Congeal'd with this, do make me wipe off both.
Exit.

[Scene IV. *Another part of the field.*]

Alarum. Enter *Richard Duke of York.*

York. The army of the Queen hath got the field.
My uncles both are slain in rescuing me,
And all my followers to the eager foe
Turn back and fly, like ships before the wind
Or lambs pursu'd by hunger-starved wolves.
My sons — God knows what hath bechanced them;
But this I know, they have demean'd themselves
Like men born to renown by life or death.
Three times did Richard make a lane to me
And thrice cried 'Courage, father! fight it out!'
And full as oft came Edward to my side
With purple falchion, painted to the hilt
In blood of those that had encount'red him.
And when the hardiest warriors did retire,
Richard cried 'Charge! and give no foot of ground!'
And cried 'A crown, or else a glorious tomb!
A sceptre, or an earthly sepulchre!'
With this we charg'd again; but out alas!
We bodg'd again, as I have seen a swan
With bootless labour swim against the tide
And spend her strength with overmatching waves. *A short alarum within.*
Ah, hark! The fatal followers do pursue,
And I am faint and cannot fly their fury;
And were I strong, I would not shun their fury.
The sands are numb'red that makes up my life.
Here must I stay and here my life must end.

Enter the *Queen* [*Margaret*], *Clifford, Northumberland,* the young *Prince,* and *Soldiers.*

Come, bloody Clifford, rough Northumberland,
I dare your quenchless fury to more rage.
I am your butt and I abide your shot.

North. Yield to our mercy, proud Plantagenet.

Clif. Ay, to such mercy as his ruthless arm
With downright payment show'd unto my father.
Now Phaëton hath tumbled from his car
And made an evening at the noontide prick.

York. My ashes, as the phœnix, may bring forth
A bird that will revenge upon you all;
And in that hope I throw mine eyes to heaven,
Scorning whate'er you can afflict me with.
Why come you not? What? multitudes, and fear?

Clif. So cowards fight when they can fly no further;
So doves do peck the falcon's piercing talons;
So desperate thieves, all hopeless of their lives,
Breathe out invectives 'gainst the officers.

York. O Clifford, but bethink thee once again,
And in thy thought o'errun my former time;
And, if thou canst for blushing, view this face,
And bite thy tongue that slanders him with cowardice
Whose frown hath made thee faint and fly ere this.

Clif. I will not bandy with thee word for word,
But buckle with thee blows, twice two for one.

Queen. Hold, valiant Clifford! For a thousand causes
I would prolong awhile the traitor's life.
Wrath makes him deaf. Speak thou, Northumberland.

North. Hold, Clifford! Do not honour him so much
To prick thy finger, though to wound his heart.
What valour were it, when a cur doth grin,
For one to thrust his hand between his teeth
When he might spurn him with his foot away?
It is war's prize to take all vantages;
And ten to one is no impeach of valour.
[*They lay hands on York, who struggles.*]

Clif. Ay, ay, so strives the woodcock with the gin.
North. So doth the cony struggle in the net.
York. So triumph thieves upon their conquer'd booty;
So true men yield, with robbers so o'ermatch'd.
North. What would your Grace have done unto him now?
Queen. Brave warriors, Clifford and Northumberland,
Come, make him stand upon this molehill here
That raught at mountains with outstretched arms,
Yet parted but the shadow with his hand.
What, was it you that would be England's king?
Was't you that revell'd in our parliament
And made a preachment of your high descent?
Where are your mess of sons to back you now?
The wanton Edward, and the lusty George?
And where's that valiant crookback prodigy,
Dicky your boy, that with his grumbling voice
Was wont to cheer his dad in mutinies?
Or, with the rest, where is your darling Rutland?
Look, York! I stain'd this napkin with the blood
That valiant Clifford with his rapier's point
Made issue from the bosom of the boy;
And if thine eyes can water for his death,
I give thee this to dry thy cheeks withal.
Alas, poor York! but that I hate thee deadly,
I should lament thy miserable state.
I prithee grieve, to make me merry, York.
What? hath thy fiery heart so parch'd thine entrails
That not a tear can fall for Rutland's death?
Why art thou patient, man? Thou shouldst be mad;
And I to make thee mad do mock thee thus.
Stamp, rave, and fret, that I may sing and dance.
Thou wouldst be fee'd, I see, to make me sport.
York cannot speak unless he wear a crown.
A crown for York! and, lords, bow low to him.
Hold you his hands whilst I do set it on.
[*Puts a paper crown on his head.*]
Ay, marry, sir, now looks he like a king!
Ay, this is he that took King Henry's chair
And this is he was his adopted heir.
But how is it that great Plantagenet
Is crown'd so soon, and broke his solemn oath?
As I bethink me, you should not be King
Till our King Henry had shook hands with death.
And will you pale your head in Henry's glory
And rob his temples of the diadem
Now in his life, against your holy oath?
O, 'tis a fault too too unpardonable!
Off with the crown, and with the crown his head!
And whilst we breathe, take time to do him dead.
Clif. That is my office, for my father's sake.
Queen. Nay, stay. Let's hear the orisons he makes.
York. She-wolf of France, but worse than wolves of France,
Whose tongue more poisons than the adder's tooth!
How ill-beseeming is it in thy sex
To triumph like an Amazonian trull
Upon their woes whom fortune captivates!
But that thy face is vizard-like, unchanging,
Made impudent with use of evil deeds,
I would assay, proud queen, to make thee blush.
To tell thee whence thou cam'st, of whom deriv'd,
Were shame enough to shame thee, wert thou not shameless.
Thy father bears the type of King of Naples,
Of both the Sicils and Jerusalem,
Yet not so wealthy as an English yeoman.
Hath that poor monarch taught thee to insult?
It needs not nor it boots thee not, proud queen,
Unless the adage must be verified,
That beggars mounted run their horse to death.
'Tis beauty that doth oft make women proud;
But God he knows thy share thereof is small.
'Tis virtue that doth make them most admir'd;
The contrary doth make thee wond'red at.
'Tis government that makes them seem divine;
The want thereof makes thee abominable.
Thou art as opposite to every good
As the Antipodes are unto us
Or as the South to the Septentrion.
O tiger's heart wrapp'd in a woman's hide!
How couldst thou drain the lifeblood of the child,
To bid the father wipe his eyes withal,
And yet be seen to bear a woman's face?
Women are soft, mild, pitiful, and flexible;
Thou stern, obdurate, flinty, rough, remorseless.
Bid'st thou me rage? Why, now thou hast thy wish.
Wouldst have me weep? Why, now thou hast thy will.
For raging wind blows up incessant showers,
And when the rage allays the rain begins.
These tears are my sweet Rutland's obsequies,

And every drop cries vengeance for his death
'Gainst thee, fell Clifford, and thee, false Frenchwoman.

North. Beshrew me but his passion moves me so
That hardly can I check my eyes from tears.

York. That face of his the hungry cannibals
Would not have touch'd, would not have stain'd with blood;
But you are more inhuman, more inexorable —
O, ten times more! — than tigers of Hyrcania.
See, ruthless queen, a hapless father's tears.
This cloth thou dipp'dst in blood of my sweet boy,
And I with tears do wash the blood away.
Keep thou the napkin and go boast of this;
And if thou tell'st the heavy story right,
Upon my soul, the hearers will shed tears.
Yea, even my foes will shed fast-falling tears
And say 'Alas, it was a piteous deed!'
There, take the crown, and with the crown my curse;
And in thy need such comfort come to thee
As now I reap at thy too cruel hand!
Hard-hearted Clifford, take me from the world.
My soul to heaven, my blood upon your heads!

North. Had he been slaughterman to all my kin,
I should not for my life but weep with him
To see how inly sorrow gripes his soul.

Queen. What, weeping-ripe, my Lord Northumberland?
Think but upon the wrong he did us all
And that will quickly dry thy melting tears.

Clif. Here's for my oath! here's for my father's death! [*Stabs him.*]

Queen. And here's to right our gentle-hearted king! [*Stabs him.*]

York. Open thy gate of mercy, gracious God!
My soul flies through these wounds to seek out thee. [*Dies.*]

Queen. Off with his head and set it on York gates!
So York may overlook the town of York.

Flourish. Exeunt.

[ACT II. Scene I. *A plain near Mortimer's Cross in Herefordshire.*]

A march. Enter *Edward, Richard,* and their *Power.*

Edw. I wonder how our princely father scap'd,
Or whether he be scap'd away or no
From Clifford's and Northumberland's pursuit.
Had he been ta'en, we should have heard the news;
Had he been slain, we should have heard the news;
Or had he scap'd, methinks we should have heard
The happy tidings of his good escape.
How fares my brother? Why is he so sad?

Rich. I cannot joy until I be resolv'd
Where our right valiant father is become.
I saw him in the battle range about
And watch'd him how he singled Clifford forth.
Methought he bore him in the thickest troop
As doth a lion in a herd of neat,
Or as a bear encompass'd round with dogs,
Who having pinch'd a few and made them cry,
The rest stand all aloof and bark at him.
So far'd our father with his enemies;
So fled his enemies my warlike father.
Methinks 'tis prize enough to be his son.
See how the morning opes her golden gates
And takes her farewell of the glorious sun!
How well resembles it the prime of youth,
Trimm'd like a younker prancing to his love!

Edw. Dazzle mine eyes, or do I see three suns?

Rich. Three glorious suns, each one a perfect sun,
Not separated with the racking clouds,
But sever'd in a pale clear-shining sky.
See, see! They join, embrace, and seem to kiss,
As if they vow'd some league inviolable.
Now are they but one lamp, one light, one sun.
In this the heaven figures some event.

Edw. 'Tis wondrous strange, the like yet never heard of.
I think it cites us, brother, to the field,
That we, the sons of brave Plantagenet,
Each one already blazing by our meeds,
Should notwithstanding join our lights together
And overshine the earth, as this the world.
Whate'er it bodes, henceforward will I bear
Upon my target three fair-shining suns.

Rich. Nay, bear three daughters. By your leave I speak it,
You love the breeder better than the male.

Enter *one blowing.*

But what art thou whose heavy looks foretell
Some dreadful story hanging on thy tongue?
Messenger. Ah, one that was a woful looker-on
When as the noble Duke of York was slain,
Your princely father and my loving lord!
Edw. O, speak no more, for I have heard too much!
Rich. Say how he died, for I will hear it all.
Messenger. Environed he was with many foes,
And stood against them as the hope of Troy
Against the Greeks that would have ent'red Troy.
But Hercules himself must yield to odds;
And many strokes, though with a little axe,
Hews down and fells the hardest-timber'd oak.
By many hands your father was subdu'd,
But only slaught'red by the ireful arm
Of unrelenting Clifford and the Queen,
Who crown'd the gracious Duke in high despite,
Laugh'd in his face, and when with grief he wept,
The ruthless Queen gave him, to dry his cheeks,
A napkin steeped in the harmless blood
Of sweet young Rutland, by rough Clifford slain;
And after many scorns, many foul taunts,
They took his head and on the gates of York
They set the same; and there it doth remain,
The saddest spectacle that e'er I view'd.
Edw. Sweet Duke of York, our prop to lean upon,
Now thou art gone, we have no staff, no stay!
O Clifford, boist'rous Clifford, thou hast slain
The flow'r of Europe for his chivalry;
And treacherously hast thou vanquish'd him,
For hand to hand he would have vanquish'd thee!
Now my soul's palace is become a prison.
Ah, would she break from hence, that this my body
Might in the ground be closed up in rest!
For never henceforth shall I joy again;
Never, O never, shall I see more joy.
Rich. I cannot weep, for all my body's moisture
Scarce serves to quench my furnace-burning heart;
Nor can my tongue unload my heart's great burthen,
For selfsame wind that I should speak withal
Is kindling coals that fires all my breast
And burns me up with flames that tears would quench.
To weep is to make less the depth of grief.
Tears, then, for babes; blows and revenge for me!
Richard, I bear thy name; I'll venge thy death
Or die renowned by attempting it.
Edw. His name that valiant duke hath left with thee;
His dukedom and his chair with me is left.
Rich. Nay, if thou be that princely eagle's bird,
Show thy descent by gazing 'gainst the sun;
For chair and dukedom, throne and kingdom say,
Either that is thine, or else thou wert not his.

March. Enter *Warwick, Marquess Montague,* and their *Army.*

War. How now, fair lords! What fare? What news abroad?
Rich. Great Lord of Warwick, if we should recompt
Our baleful news and at each word's deliverance
Stab poniards in our flesh till all were told,
The words would add more anguish than the wounds.
O valiant lord, the Duke of York is slain!
Edw. O Warwick, Warwick! that Plantagenet
Which held thee dearly as his soul's redemption
Is by the stern Lord Clifford done to death.
War. Ten days ago I drown'd these news in tears;
And now, to add more measure to your woes,
I come to tell you things sith then befall'n.
After the bloody fray at Wakefield fought,
Where your brave father breath'd his latest gasp,
Tidings, as swiftly as the posts could run,
Were brought me of your loss and his depart.
I, then in London, keeper of the King,
Muster'd my soldiers, gathered flocks of friends,
And very well appointed, as I thought,
March'd toward Saint Alban's to intercept the Queen,
Bearing the King in my behalf along;
For by my scouts I was advertised
That she was coming with a full intent
To dash our late decree in parliament
Touching King Henry's oath and your succession.
Short tale to make, we at Saint Alban's met,
Our battles join'd, and both sides fiercely fought;

But whether 'twas the coldness of the King,
Who look'd full gently on his warlike queen,
That robb'd my soldiers of their heated spleen,
Or whether 'twas report of her success,
Or more than common fear of Clifford's rigour,
Who thunders to his captives blood and death,
I cannot judge; but to conclude with truth,
Their weapons like to lightning came and went;
Our soldiers', like the night owl's lazy flight
Or like an idle thresher with a flail,
Fell gently down, as if they struck their friends.
I cheer'd them up with justice of our cause,
With promise of high pay and great rewards;
But all in vain; they had no heart to fight,
And we (in them) no hope to win the day;
So that we fled: the King unto the Queen;
Lord George your brother, Norfolk, and myself,
In haste, post-haste, are come to join with you;
For in the marches here we heard you were,
Making another head to fight again.

Edw. Where is the Duke of Norfolk, gentle Warwick?
And when came George from Burgundy to England?

War. Some six miles off the Duke is with his power;
And for your brother, he was lately sent
From your kind aunt, Duchess of Burgundy,
With aid of soldiers to this needful war.

Rich. 'Twas odds belike when valiant Warwick fled.
Oft have I heard his praises in pursuit,
But ne'er till now his scandal of retire.

War. Nor now my scandal, Richard, dost thou hear;
For thou shalt know this strong right hand of mine
Can pluck the diadem from faint Henry's head
And wring the awful sceptre from his fist,
Were he as famous and as bold in war
As he is fam'd for mildness, peace, and prayer.

Rich. I know it well, Lord Warwick. Blame me not.
'Tis love I bear thy glories makes me speak.
But in this troublous time what's to be done?
Shall we go throw away our coats of steel
And wrap our bodies in black mourning gowns,
Numb'ring our Ave-Maries with our beads?
Or shall we on the helmets of our foes
Tell our devotion with revengeful arms?
If for the last, say 'Ay,' and to it, lords!

War. Why, therefore Warwick came to seek you out,
And therefore comes my brother Montague.
Attend me, lords. The proud insulting Queen,
With Clifford and the haught Northumberland,
And of their feather many moe proud birds,
Have wrought the easy-melting King like wax.
He swore consent to your succession,
His oath enrolled in the parliament;
And now to London all the crew are gone,
To frustrate both his oath, and what beside
May make against the house of Lancaster.
Their power, I think, is thirty thousand strong.
Now if the help of Norfolk and myself
With all the friends that thou, brave Earl of March,
Amongst the loving Welshmen canst procure,
Will but amount to five-and-twenty thousand,
Why, via! to London will we march amain,
And once again bestride our foaming steeds,
And once again cry 'Charge!' upon our foes,
But never once again turn back and fly.

Rich. Ay, now methinks I hear great Warwick speak.
Ne'er may he live to see a sunshine day
That cries, 'Retire!' if Warwick bid him stay.

Edw. Lord Warwick, on thy shoulder will I lean,
And when thou fail'st (as God forbid the hour!)
Must Edward fall, which peril heaven forfend!

War. No longer Earl of March, but Duke of York.
The next degree is England's royal throne;
For King of England shalt thou be proclaim'd
In every borough as we pass along;
And he that throws not up his cap for joy
Shall for the fault make forfeit of his head.
King Edward, valiant Richard, Montague,
Stay we no longer, dreaming of renown,
But sound the trumpets and about our task!

Rich. Then, Clifford, were thy heart as hard as steel,
As thou hast shown it flinty by thy deeds,
I come to pierce it or to give thee mine.

Edw. Then strike up drums. God and Saint George for us!

Enter a *Messenger.*

War. How now? What news?

Mess. The Duke of Norfolk sends you word by me
The Queen is coming with a puissant host,
And craves your company for speedy counsel.

War. Why, then it sorts. Brave warriors, let's away. *Exeunt omnes.*

[Scene II. *Before York.*]

Flourish. Enter the *King*, the *Queen* [*Margaret*], *Clifford*, *Northumberland*, and *young Prince*, with *Drum* and *Trumpets*.

Queen. Welcome, my lord, to this brave town of York.
Yonder's the head of that arch-enemy
That sought to be encompass'd with your crown.
Doth not the object cheer your heart, my lord?

K. Hen. Ay, as the rocks cheer them that fear their wrack.
To see this sight it irks my very soul.
Withhold revenge, dear God! 'Tis not my fault,
Nor wittingly have I infring'd my vow.

Clif. My gracious liege, this too much lenity
And harmful pity must be laid aside.
To whom do lions cast their gentle looks?
Not to the beast that would usurp their den.
Whose hand is that the forest bear doth lick?
Not his that spoils her young before her face.
Who scapes the lurking serpent's mortal sting?
Not he that sets his foot upon her back.
The smallest worm will turn, being trodden on,
And doves will peck in safeguard of their brood.
Ambitious York did level at thy crown,
Thou smiling while he knit his angry brows.
He, but a duke, would have his son a king
And raise his issue like a loving sire;
Thou, being a king, blest with a goodly son,
Didst yield consent to disinherit him,
Which argued thee a most unloving father.
Unreasonable creatures feed their young;
And though man's face be fearful to their eyes,
Yet, in protection of their tender ones,
Who hath not seen them, even with those wings
Which sometime they have us'd in fearful flight,
Make war with him that climb'd unto their nest,
Offering their own lives in their young's defence?
For shame, my liege! Make them your precedent!
Were it not pity that this goodly boy
Should lose his birthright by his father's fault
And long hereafter say unto his child,
'What my great-grandfather and grandsire got
My careless father fondly gave away'?
Ah, what a shame were this! Look on the boy,
And let his manly face, which promiseth
Successful fortune, steel thy melting heart
To hold thine own and leave thine own with him.

K. Hen. Full well hath Clifford play'd the orator,
Inferring arguments of mighty force.
But, Clifford, tell me, didst thou never hear
That things ill got had ever bad success?
And happy always was it for that son
Whose father for his hoarding went to hell?
I'll leave my son my virtuous deeds behind,
And would my father had left me no more!
For all the rest is held at such a rate
As brings a thousandfold more care to keep
Than in possession any jot of pleasure.
Ah, cousin York, would thy best friends did know
How it doth grieve me that thy head is here!

Queen. My lord, cheer up your spirits. Our foes are nigh,
And this soft courage makes your followers faint.
You promis'd knighthood to our forward son.
Unsheathe your sword and dub him presently.
Edward, kneel down.

K. Hen. Edward Plantagenet, arise a knight,
And learn this lesson: Draw thy sword in right.

Prince. My gracious father, by your kingly leave,
I'll draw it as apparent to the crown
And in that quarrel use it to the death.

Clif. Why, that is spoken like a toward prince.

Enter a *Messenger*.

Mess. Royal commanders, be in readiness;
For with a band of thirty thousand men
Comes Warwick, backing of the Duke of York,
And in the towns, as they do march along,
Proclaims him King, and many fly to him.
Darraign your battle, for they are at hand.

Clif. I would your Highness would depart the field.
The Queen hath best success when you are absent.

Queen. Ay, good my lord, and leave us to our fortune.

K. Hen. Why, that's my fortune too. Therefore I'll stay.

North. Be it with resolution, then, to fight.

Prince. My royal father, cheer these noble lords
And hearten those that fight in your defence.
Unsheathe your sword, good father. Cry 'Saint George!'

March. Enter *Edward, Warwick, Richard, Clarence, Norfolk, Montague,* and *Soldiers.*

Edw. Now, perjur'd Henry, wilt thou kneel for grace
And set thy diadem upon my head,
Or bide the mortal fortune of the field?

Queen. Go rate thy minions, proud insulting boy!
Becomes it thee to be thus bold in terms
Before thy sovereign and thy lawful king?

Edw. I am his king, and he should bow his knee.
I was adopted heir by his consent;
Since when, his oath is broke; for, as I hear,
You that are King, though he do wear the crown,
Have caus'd him by new act of parliament
To blot out me and put his own son in.

Clif. And reason too!
Who should succeed the father but the son?

Rich. Are you there, butcher? O, I cannot speak!

Clif. Ay, Crookback, here I stand to answer thee,
Or any he, the proudest of thy sort.

Rich. 'Twas you that kill'd young Rutland, was it not?

Clif. Ay, and old York, and yet not satisfied.

Rich. For God's sake, lords, give signal to the fight.

War. What say'st thou, Henry? Wilt thou yield the crown?

Queen. Why, how now, long-tongu'd Warwick? Dare you speak?
When you and I met at Saint Alban's last,
Your legs did better service than your hands.

War. Then 'twas my turn to fly, and now 'tis thine.

Clif. You said so much before, and yet you fled.

War. 'Twas not your valour, Clifford, drove me thence.

North. No, nor your manhood that durst make you stay.

Rich. Northumberland, I hold thee reverently.
Break off the parley, for scarce I can refrain
The execution of my big-swol'n heart
Upon that Clifford, that cruel child-killer.

Clif. I slew thy father. Call'st thou him a child?

Rich. Ay, like a dastard and a treacherous coward,
As thou didst kill our tender brother Rutland!
But ere sun set I'll make thee curse the deed.

K. Hen. Have done with words, my lords, and hear me speak.

Queen. Defy them then, or else hold close thy lips.

K. Hen. I prithee give no limits to my tongue.
I am a king, and privileg'd to speak.

Clif. My liege, the wound that bred this meeting here
Cannot be cur'd by words. Therefore be still.

Rich. Then, executioner, unsheathe thy sword.
By him that made us all, I am resolv'd
That Clifford's manhood lies upon his tongue.

Edw. Say, Henry, shall I have my right, or no?
A thousand men have broke their fasts to-day
That ne'er shall dine unless thou yield the crown.

War. If thou deny, their blood upon thy head!
For York in justice puts his armour on.

Prince. If that be right which Warwick says is right,
There is no wrong, but everything is right.

Rich. Whoever got thee, there thy mother stands;
For well I wot thou hast thy mother's tongue.

Queen. But thou art neither like thy sire nor dam,
But like a foul misshapen stigmatic,
Mark'd by the Destinies to be avoided,
As venom toads or lizards' dreadful stings.

Rich. Iron of Naples, hid with English gilt,
Whose father bears the title of a king
(As if a channel should be call'd the sea),
Sham'st thou not, knowing whence thou art extraught,
To let thy tongue detect thy base-born heart?

Edw. A wisp of straw were worth a thousand crowns,
To make this shameless callet know herself.
Helen of Greece was fairer far than thou,
Although thy husband may be Menelaus;
And ne'er was Agamemnon's brother wrong'd
By that false woman as this king by thee.
His father revell'd in the heart of France,
And tam'd the King, and made the Dauphin stoop;
And had he match'd according to his state,
He might have kept that glory to this day;
But when he took a beggar to his bed
And grac'd thy poor sire with his bridal day,

Even then that sunshine brew'd a show'r for him
That wash'd his father's fortunes forth of France
And heap'd sedition on his crown at home.
For what hath broach'd this tumult but thy pride?
Hadst thou been meek, our title still had slept,
And we, in pity of the gentle King,
Had slipp'd our claim until another age.
Clar. But when we saw our sunshine made thy spring
And that thy summer bred us no increase,
We set the axe to thy usurping root;
And though the edge hath something hit ourselves,
Yet know thou, since we have begun to strike,
We'll never leave till we have hewn thee down
Or bath'd thy growing with our heated bloods.
Edw. And in this resolution I defy thee,
Not willing any longer conference,
Since thou deniest the gentle King to speak.
Sound trumpets! Let our bloody colours wave!
And either victory, or else a grave!
Queen. Stay, Edward.
Edw. No, wrangling woman, we'll no longer stay.
These words will cost ten thousand lives this day. *Exeunt omnes.*

[Scene III. *A field of battle between Towton and Saxton, in Yorkshire.*]

Alarum. Excursions. Enter *Warwick.*

War. Forspent with toil, as runners with a race,
I lay me down a little while to breathe;
For strokes receiv'd and many blows repaid
Have robb'd my strong-knit sinews of their strength,
And spite of spite needs must I rest awhile.

Enter *Edward,* running.

Edw. Smile, gentle heaven! or strike, ungentle death!
For this world frowns, and Edward's sun is clouded.
War. How now, my lord? What hap? What hope of good?

Enter *Clarence.*

Clar. Our hap is loss, our hope but sad despair!
Our ranks are broke and ruin follows us.
What counsel give you? Whither shall we fly?
Edw. Bootless is flight. They follow us with wings,
And weak we are and cannot shun pursuit.

Enter *Richard.*

Rich. Ah, Warwick, why hast thou withdrawn thyself?
Thy brother's blood the thirsty earth hath drunk,
Broach'd with the steely point of Clifford's lance;
And in the very pangs of death he cried,
Like to a dismal clangor heard from far,
'Warwick, revenge! Brother, revenge my death!'
So, underneath the belly of their steeds,
That stain'd their fetlocks in his smoking blood,
The noble gentleman gave up the ghost.
War. Then let the earth be drunken with our blood!
I'll kill my horse, because I will not fly.
Why stand we like soft-hearted women here,
Wailing our losses, whiles the foe doth rage,
And look upon, as if the tragedy
Were play'd in jest by counterfeiting actors?
Here on my knee I vow to God above
I'll never pause again, never stand still,
Till either death hath clos'd these eyes of mine
Or fortune given me measure of revenge.
Edw. O Warwick, I do bend my knee with thine
And in this vow do chain my soul to thine!
And ere my knee rise from the earth's cold face,
I throw my hands, mine eyes, my heart to thee,
Thou setter up and plucker down of kings,
Beseeching thee (if with thy will it stands)
That to my foes this body must be prey,
Yet that thy brazen gates of heaven may ope
And give sweet passage to my sinful soul!
Now, lords, take leave until we meet again,
Where'er it be, in heaven or in earth.
Rich. Brother, give me thy hand; and, gentle Warwick,
Let me embrace thee in my weary arms.
I, that did never weep, now melt with woe
That winter should cut off our springtime so.
War. Away, away! Once more, sweet lords, farewell.
Clar. Yet let us all together to our troops,
And give them leave to fly that will not stay,
And call them pillars that will stand to us;
And, if we thrive, promise them such rewards
As victors wear at the Olympian games.

This may plant courage in their quailing breasts;
For yet is hope of life and victory.
Forslow no longer! Make we hence amain!
Exeunt.

[Scene IV. *Another part of the field.*]

Excursions. Enter *Richard* and *Clifford.*

Rich. Now, Clifford, I have singled thee alone.
Suppose this arm is for the Duke of York,
And this for Rutland — both bound to revenge,
Wert thou environ'd with a brazen wall.

Clif. Now, Richard, I am with thee here alone.
This is the hand that stabb'd thy father York,
And this the hand that slew thy brother Rutland;
And here's the heart that triumphs in their death
And cheers these hands that slew thy sire and brother
To execute the like upon thyself.
And so have at thee!

They fight. Warwick comes. Clifford flies.

Rich. Nay, Warwick, single out some other chase,
For I myself will hunt this wolf to death.
Exeunt.

[Scene V. *Another part of the field.*]

Alarum. Enter *King Henry* alone.

K. Hen. This battle fares like to the morning's war,
When dying clouds contend with growing light,
What time the shepherd, blowing of his nails,
Can neither call it perfect day nor night.
Now sways it this way, like a mighty sea
Forc'd by the tide to combat with the wind;
Now sways it that way, like the selfsame sea
Forc'd to retire by fury of the wind.
Sometime the flood prevails, and then the wind;
Now one the better, then another best;
Both tugging to be victors, breast to breast,
Yet neither conqueror nor conquered.
So is the equal poise of this fell war.
Here on this molehill will I sit me down.
To whom God will, there be the victory!
For Margaret my queen, and Clifford too,
Have chid me from the battle, swearing both
They prosper best of all when I am thence.
Would I were dead, if God's good will were so!
For what is in this world but grief and woe?
O God! methinks it were a happy life
To be no better than a homely swain;
To sit upon a hill, as I do now,
To carve out dials quaintly, point by point,
Thereby to see the minutes how they run —
How many makes the hour full complete,
How many hours brings about the day,
How many days will finish up the year,
How many years a mortal man may live;
When this is known, then to divide the times —
So many hours must I tend my flock,
So many hours must I take my rest,
So many hours must I contemplate,
So many hours must I sport myself;
So many days my ewes have been with young,
So many weeks ere the poor fools will ean,
So many months ere I shall shear the fleece.
So minutes, hours, days, weeks, months, and years,
Pass'd over to the end they were created,
Would bring white hairs unto a quiet grave.
Ah, what a life were this! how sweet! how lovely!
Gives not the hawthorn bush a sweeter shade
To shepherds looking on their silly sheep
Than doth a rich embroider'd canopy
To kings that fear their subjects' treachery?
O yes, it doth! a thousandfold it doth!
And to conclude, the shepherd's homely curds,
His cold thin drink out of his leather bottle,
His wonted sleep under a fresh tree's shade,
All which secure and sweetly he enjoys,
Is far beyond a prince's delicates,
His viands sparkling in a golden cup,
His body couched in a curious bed,
When care, mistrust, and treason waits on him.

Alarum. Enter a *Son* that hath kill'd his Father, at one door, [dragging in the body].

Son. Ill blows the wind that profits nobody.
This man whom hand to hand I slew in fight
May be possessed with some store of crowns;
And I that, haply, take them from him now
May yet, ere night, yield both my life and them
To some man else, as this dead man doth me.
Who's this? O God! It is my father's face,
Whom in this conflict I, unawares, have kill'd.
O heavy times, begetting such events!
From London by the King was I press'd forth;
My father, being the Earl of Warwick's man,

Came on the part of York, press'd by his master;
And I, who at his hands receiv'd my life,
Have by my hands of life bereaved him.
Pardon me, God! I knew not what I did.
And pardon, father, for I knew not thee!
My tears shall wipe away these bloody marks;
And no more words till they have flow'd their fill.

K. Hen. O piteous spectacle! O bloody times!
Whiles lions war and battle for their dens,
Poor harmless lambs abide their enmity.
Weep, wretched man! I'll aid thee tear for tear;
And let our hearts and eyes, like civil war,
Be blind with tears and break o'ercharg'd with grief.

Enter, at another door, a *Father* that hath kill'd his Son, bearing of his Son['s body].

Father. Thou that so stoutly hast resisted me,
Give me thy gold, if thou hast any gold;
For I have bought it with an hundred blows.
But let me see. Is this our foeman's face?
Ah, no, no, no! It is mine only son!
Ah, boy, if any life be left in thee,
Throw up thine eye! See, see what show'rs arise,
Blown with the windy tempest of my heart
Upon thy wounds, that kills mine eye and heart!
O, pity, God, this miserable age!
What stratagems, how fell, how butcherly,
Erroneous, mutinous, and unnatural,
This deadly quarrel daily doth beget!
O boy! thy father gave thee life too soon,
And hath bereft thee of thy life too late.

K. Hen. Woe above woe! grief more than common grief!
O that my death would stay these ruthful deeds!
O, pity, pity, gentle heaven, pity!
The red rose and the white are on his face,
The fatal colours of our striving houses.
The one his purple blood right well resembles;
The other his pale cheeks, methinks, presenteth.
Wither one rose, and let the other flourish!
If you contend, a thousand lives must wither.

Son. How will my mother for a father's death
Take on with me, and ne'er be satisfied!

Father. How will my wife for slaughter of my son
Shed seas of tears, and ne'er be satisfied!

K. Hen. How will the country for these woful chances
Misthink the King, and not be satisfied!

Son. Was ever son so ru'd a father's death?

Father. Was ever father so bemoan'd his son?

K. Hen. Was ever king so griev'd for subject's woe?
Much is your sorrow; mine ten times so much.

Son. I'll bear thee hence, where I may weep my fill. *Exit [with the body].*

Father. These arms of mine shall be thy winding sheet;
My heart, sweet boy, shall be thy sepulchre,
For from my heart thine image ne'er shall go.
My sighing breast shall be thy funeral bell;
And so obsequious will thy father be,
Even for the loss of thee, having no more,
As Priam was for all his valiant sons.
I'll bear thee hence, and let them fight that will,
For I have murthered where I should not kill.
Exit [with the body].

K. Hen. Sad-hearted men, much overgone with care,
Here sits a king more woful than you are.

Alarums. Excursions. Enter the *Queen* [*Margaret*], the *Prince*, and *Exeter*.

Prince. Fly, father, fly! for all your friends are fled
And Warwick rages like a chafed bull.
Away! for death doth hold us in pursuit.

Queen. Mount you, my lord. Towards Berwick post amain.
Edward and Richard, like a brace of greyhounds
Having the fearful flying hare in sight,
With fiery eyes, sparkling for very wrath,
And bloody steel grasp'd in their ireful hands,
Are at our backs; and therefore hence amain!

Exe. Away! for vengeance comes along with them.
Nay, stay not to expostulate; make speed!
Or else come after. I'll away before.

K. Hen. Nay, take me with thee, good sweet Exeter.
Not that I fear to stay, but love to go
Whither the Queen intends. Forward, away!
Exeunt.

[Scene VI. *Another part of the field.*]

A loud alarum. Enter *Clifford*, wounded.

Clif. Here burns my candle out; ay, here it dies,
Which, whiles it lasted, gave King Henry light.

O Lancaster! I fear thy overthrow
More than my body's parting with my soul.
My love and fear glu'd many friends to thee,
And now I fall, the tough commixture melts,
Impairing Henry, strength'ning misproud York.
The common people swarm like summer flies;
And whither fly the gnats but to the sun?
And who shines now but Henry's enemies?
O Phœbus, hadst thou never given consent
That Phaëton should check thy fiery steeds,
Thy burning car never had scorch'd the earth!
And, Henry, hadst thou sway'd as kings should do,
Or as thy father and his father did,
Giving no ground unto the house of York,
They never then had sprung like summer flies;
I and ten thousand in this luckless realm
Had left no mourning widows for our death,
And thou this day hadst kept thy chair in peace.
For what doth cherish weeds but gentle air?
And what makes robbers bold but too much lenity?
Bootless are plaints and cureless are my wounds;
No way to fly, nor strength to hold out flight;
The foe is merciless and will not pity,
For at their hands I have deserv'd no pity.
The air hath got into my deadly wounds
And much effuse of blood doth make me faint.
Come, York and Richard, Warwick and the rest.
I stabb'd your fathers' bosoms; split my breast. [*Faints.*]

Alarum and retreat. Enter *Edward, Warwick, Richard, Montague,* and *Clarence,* and *Soldiers.*

Edw. Now breathe we, lords. Good fortune bids us pause
And smooth the frowns of war with peaceful looks.
Some troops pursue the bloody-minded Queen
That led calm Henry, though he were a king,
As doth a sail, fill'd with a fretting gust,
Command an argosy to stem the waves.
But think you, lords, that Clifford fled with them?

War. No, 'tis impossible he should escape;
For, though before his face I speak the words,
Your brother Richard mark'd him for the grave;
And wheresoe'er he is, he's surely dead.

Clifford groans and dies.

Edw. Whose soul is that which takes her heavy leave?

Rich. A deadly groan, like life and death's departing.

Edw. See who it is; and now the battle's ended,
If friend or foe, let him be gently us'd.

Rich. Revoke that doom of mercy, for 'tis Clifford,
Who not contented that he lopp'd the branch
In hewing Rutland when his leaves put forth,
But set his murth'ring knife unto the root
From whence that tender spray did sweetly spring:
I mean our princely father, Duke of York.

War. From off the gates of York fetch down the head,
Your father's head, which Clifford placed there;
Instead whereof let this supply the room.
Measure for measure must be answered.

Edw. Bring forth that fatal screech owl to our house,
That nothing sung but death to us and ours.
Now death shall stop his dismal threat'ning sound
And his ill-boding tongue no more shall speak.

War. I think his understanding is bereft.
Speak, Clifford, dost thou know who speaks to thee?
Dark cloudy death o'ershades his beams of life,
And he nor sees, nor hears us what we say.

Rich. O, would he did! and so, perhaps, he doth.
'Tis but his policy to counterfeit,
Because he would avoid such bitter taunts
Which in the time of death he gave our father.

Clar. If so thou think'st, vex him with eager words.

Rich. Clifford, ask mercy, and obtain no grace.

Edw. Clifford, repent in bootless penitence.

War. Clifford, devise excuses for thy faults.

Clar. While we devise fell tortures for thy faults.

Rich. Thou didst love York, and I am son to York.

Edw. Thou pitied'st Rutland; I will pity thee.

Clar. Where's Captain Margaret, to fence you now?

War. They mock thee, Clifford. Swear as thou wast wont.

Rich. What, not an oath? Nay, then the world goes hard
When Clifford cannot spare his friends an oath.
I know by that he's dead; and, by my soul,

If this right hand would buy two hours' life,
That I (in all despite) might rail at him,
This hand should chop it off, and with the issuing blood
Stifle the villain whose unstanched thirst
York and young Rutland could not satisfy.

War. Ay, but he's dead. Off with the traitor's head
And rear it in the place your father's stands.
And now to London with triumphant march,
There to be crowned England's royal King;
From whence shall Warwick cut the sea to France
And ask the Lady Bona for thy queen.
So shalt thou sinew both these lands together;
And, having France thy friend, thou shalt not dread
The scatt'red foe that hopes to rise again;
For though they cannot greatly sting to hurt,
Yet look to have them buzz to offend thine ears.
First will I see the coronation,
And then to Brittany I'll cross the sea
To effect this marriage, so it please my lord.

Edw. Even as thou wilt, sweet Warwick, let it be;
For in thy shoulder do I build my seat,
And never will I undertake the thing
Wherein thy counsel and consent is wanting.
Richard, I will create thee Duke of Gloucester;
And George, of Clarence. Warwick, as ourself,
Shall do and undo as him pleaseth best.

Rich. Let me be Duke of Clarence, George of Gloucester;
For Gloucester's dukedom is too ominous.

War. Tut, that's a foolish observation!
Richard, be Duke of Gloucester. Now to London
To see these honours in possession. *Exeunt.*

[ACT III. Scene I. *A forest in the North of England.*]

Enter *Sinklo* and *Humfrey* (two *Keepers*) with crossbows in their hands.

Sink. Under this thick-grown brake we'll shroud ourselves,
For through this laund anon the deer will come,
And in this covert will we make our stand,
Culling the principal of all the deer.

Hum. I'll stay above the hill, so both may shoot.

Sink. That cannot be; the noise of thy crossbow
Will scare the herd, and so my shoot is lost.
Here stand we both and aim we at the best;
And, for the time shall not seem tedious,
I'll tell thee what befell me on a day
In this self place where now we mean to stand.

Hum. Here comes a man. Let's stay till he be past.

Enter *King Henry*, disguis'd, with a prayer book.

K. Hen. From Scotland am I stol'n, even of pure love,
To greet mine own land with my wishful sight.
No, Harry, Harry, 'tis no land of thine!
Thy place is fill'd, thy sceptre wrung from thee,
Thy balm wash'd off wherewith thou wast anointed.
No bending knee will call thee Cæsar now,
No humble suitors press to speak for right:
No, not a man comes for redress of thee;
For how can I help them, and not myself?

Sink. Ay, here's a deer whose skin's a keeper's fee!
This is the quondam king. Let's seize upon him.

K. Hen. Let me embrace thee, sour adversity,
For wise men say it is the wisest course.

Hum. Why linger we? Let us lay hands upon him.

Sink. Forbear awhile. We'll hear a little more.

K. Hen. My queen and son are gone to France for aid;
And, as I hear, the great commanding Warwick
Is thither gone to crave the French king's sister
To wife for Edward. If this news be true,
Poor queen and son, your labour is but lost;
For Warwick is a subtle orator
And Lewis a prince soon won with moving words.
By this account, then, Margaret may win him;
For she's a woman to be pitied much.
Her sighs will make a batt'ry in his breast;
Her tears will pierce into a marble heart;
The tiger will be mild whiles she doth mourn,
And Nero will be tainted with remorse
To hear and see her plaints, her brinish tears.
Ay, but she's come to beg; Warwick, to give;
She on his left side, craving aid for Henry;
He on his right, asking a wife for Edward.
She weeps, and says her Henry is depos'd;
He smiles, and says his Edward is install'd;

That she (poor wretch) for grief can speak no more,
Whiles Warwick tells his title, smooths the wrong,
Inferreth arguments of mighty strength,
And in conclusion wins the king from her
With promise of his sister, and what else,
To strengthen and support King Edward's place.
O Margaret, thus 'twill be! and thou (poor soul)
Art then forsaken, as thou went'st forlorn!

Hum. Say, what art thou that talk'st of kings and queens?

K. Hen. More than I seem, and less than I was born to:
A man at least, for less I should not be;
And men may talk of kings, and why not I?

Hum. Ay, but thou talk'st as if thou wert a king.

K. Hen. Why, so I am (in mind), and that's enough.

Hum. But if thou be a king, where is thy crown?

K. Hen. My crown is in my heart, not on my head;
Not deck'd with diamonds and Indian stones,
Nor to be seen. My crown is call'd content;
A crown it is that seldom kings enjoy.

Hum. Well, if you be a king crown'd with content,
Your crown content and you must be contented
To go along with us; for, as we think,
You are the king King Edward hath depos'd;
And we his subjects, sworn in all allegiance,
Will apprehend you as his enemy.

K. Hen. But did you never swear, and break an oath?

Hum. No, never such an oath; nor will not now.

K. Hen. Where did you dwell when I was King of England?

Hum. Here in this country where we now remain.

K. Hen. I was anointed king at nine months old;
My father and my grandfather were kings;
And you were sworn true subjects unto me;
And tell me then, have you not broke your oaths?

Sink. No;
For we were subjects but while you were king.

K. Hen. Why, am I dead? Do I not breathe a man?
Ah, simple men, you know not what you swear!
Look, as I blow this feather from my face
And as the air blows it to me again,
Obeying with my wind when I do blow
And yielding to another when it blows,
Commanded always by the greater gust —
Such is the lightness of you common men.
But do not break your oaths; for of that sin
My mild entreaty shall not make you guilty.
Go where you will, the King shall be commanded;
And be you kings. Command, and I'll obey.

Sink. We are true subjects to the king, King Edward.

K. Hen. So would you be again to Henry
If he were seated as King Edward is.

Sink. We charge you, in God's name and the King's,
To go with us unto the officers.

K. Hen. In God's name, lead. Your king's name be obey'd;
And what God will, that let your king perform;
And what he will, I humbly yield unto.

Exeunt.

[Scene II. *London. The Palace.*]

Enter *King Edward,* [*Richard of*] *Gloucester, Clarence, Lady Grey* [*a widow*].

K. Edw. Brother of Gloucester, at Saint Alban's field
This lady's husband, Sir Richard Grey, was slain,
His lands then seiz'd on by the conqueror.
Her suit is now to repossess those lands;
Which we in justice cannot well deny,
Because in quarrel of the house of York
The worthy gentleman did lose his life.

Rich. Your Highness shall do well to grant her suit.
It were dishonour to deny it her.

K. Edw. It were no less; but yet I'll make a pause.

Rich. [*aside to Clarence*] Yea, is it so?
I see the lady hath a thing to grant
Before the King will grant her humble suit.

Clar. [*aside to Richard*] He knows the game. How true he keeps the wind!

Rich. [*aside to Clarence*] Silence!

K. Edw. Widow, we will consider of your suit;
And come some other time to know our mind.

Widow. Right gracious lord, I cannot brook delay.

May it please your Highness to resolve me now,
And what your pleasure is shall satisfy me.

Rich. [*aside*] Ay, widow? Then I'll warrant you all your lands
An if what pleases him shall pleasure you.
Fight closer or, good faith, you'll catch a blow.

Clar. [*aside to Richard*] I fear her not, unless she chance to fall.

Rich. [*aside to Clarence*] God forbid that! for he'll take vantages.

K. Edw. How many children hast thou, widow? Tell me.

Clar. [*aside to Richard*] I think he means to beg a child of her.

Rich. [*aside to Clarence*] Nay, whip me then! He'll rather give her two.

Widow. Three, my most gracious lord.

Rich. [*aside*] You shall have four if you'll be rul'd by him.

K. Edw. 'Twere pity they should lose their father's lands.

Widow. Be pitiful, dread lord, and grant it then.

K. Edw. Lords, give us leave. I'll try this widow's wit.

Rich. [*aside*] Ay, good leave have you; for you will have leave
Till youth take leave and leave you to the crutch. [*Retires with Clarence.*]

K. Edw. Now tell me, madam, do you love your children?

Widow. Ay, full as dearly as I love myself.

K. Edw. And would you not do much to do them good?

Widow. To do them good I would sustain some harm.

K. Edw. Then get your husband's lands, to do them good.

Widow. Therefore I came unto your Majesty.

K. Edw. I'll tell you how these lands are to be got.

Widow. So shall you bind me to your Highness' service.

K. Edw. What service wilt thou do me if I give them?

Widow. What you command that rests in me to do.

K. Edw. But you will take exceptions to my boon.

Widow. No, gracious lord, except I cannot do it.

K. Edw. Ay, but thou canst do what I mean to ask.

Widow. Why, then I will do what your Grace commands.

Rich. [*aside to Clarence*] He plies her hard, and much rain wears the marble.

Clar. [*aside to Richard*] As red as fire? Nay then, her wax must melt.

Widow. Why stops my lord? Shall I not hear my task?

K. Edw. An easy task. 'Tis but to love a king.

Widow. That's soon perform'd, because I am a subject.

K. Edw. Why then, thy husband's lands I freely give thee.

Widow. I take my leave with many thousand thanks.

Rich. [*aside to Clarence*] The match is made. She seals it with a cursy.

K. Edw. But stay thee. 'Tis the fruits of love I mean.

Widow. The fruits of love I mean, my loving liege.

K. Edw. Ay, but, I fear me, in another sense.
What love, think'st thou, I sue so much to get?

Widow. My love till death, my humble thanks, my prayers;
That love which virtue begs and virtue grants.

K. Edw. No, by my troth, I did not mean such love.

Widow. Why, then you mean not as I thought you did.

K. Edw. But now you partly may perceive my mind.

Widow. My mind will never grant what I perceive
Your Highness aims at, if I aim aright.

K. Edw. To tell thee plain, I aim to lie with thee.

Widow. To tell you plain, I had rather lie in prison.

K. Edw. Why, then thou shalt not have thy husband's lands.

Widow. Why, then mine honesty shall be my dower;
For by that loss I will not purchase them.

K. Edw. Therein thou wrong'st thy children mightily.

Widow. Herein your Highness wrongs both them and me.
But, mighty lord, this merry inclination
Accords not with the sadness of my suit.
Please you dismiss me, either with ay or no.

K. Edw. Ay, if thou wilt say ay to my request;
No, if thou dost say no to my demand.

Widow. Then, no, my lord. My suit is at an end.

Rich. [*aside to Clarence*] The widow likes him not; she knits her brows.
Clar. [*aside to Richard*] He is the bluntest wooer in Christendom.
K. Edw. [*aside*] Her looks do argue her replete with modesty;
Her words do show her wit incomparable;
All her perfections challenge sovereignty.
One way or other, she is for a king;
And she shall be my love, or else my queen. —
Say that King Edward take thee for his queen?
Widow. 'Tis better said than done, my gracious lord.
I am a subject fit to jest withal,
But far unfit to be a sovereign.
K. Edw. Sweet widow, by my state I swear to thee
I speak no more than what my soul intends;
And that is, to enjoy thee for my love.
Widow. And that is more than I will yield unto.
I know I am too mean to be your queen,
And yet too good to be your concubine.
K. Edw. You cavil, widow. I did mean my queen.
Widow. 'Twill grieve your Grace my sons should call you father.
K. Edw. No more than when my daughters call thee mother.
Thou art a widow, and thou hast some children;
And, by God's Mother, I, being but a bachelor,
Have other some. Why, 'tis a happy thing
To be the father unto many sons.
Answer no more, for thou shalt be my queen.
Rich. [*aside to Clarence*] The ghostly father now hath done his shrift.
Clar. [*aside to Richard*] When he was made a shriver, 'twas for shift.
K. Edw. Brothers, you muse what chat we two have had.
Rich. The widow likes it not, for she looks very sad.
K. Edw. You'ld think it strange if I should marry her.
Clar. To who, my lord?
K. Edw. Why, Clarence, to myself.
Rich. That would be ten days' wonder at the least.
Clar. That's a day longer than a wonder lasts.
Rich. By so much is the wonder in extremes.
K. Edw. Well, jest on, brothers. I can tell you both
Her suit is granted for her husband's lands.

Enter a *Nobleman.*

Nob. My gracious lord, Henry your foe is taken
And brought as prisoner to your palace gate.
K. Edw. See that he be convey'd unto the Tower.
And go we, brothers, to the man that took him
To question of his apprehension.
Widow, go you along. Lords, use her honourably. *Exeunt. Manet Richard.*
Rich. Ay, Edward will use women honourably!
Would he were wasted, marrow, bones, and all,
That from his loins no hopeful branch may spring
To cross me from the golden time I look for!
And yet, between my soul's desire and me —
The lustful Edward's title buried —
Is Clarence, Henry, and his son young Edward,
And all the unlook'd-for issue of their bodies,
To take their rooms ere I can place myself.
A cold premeditation for my purpose!
Why, then I do but dream on sovereignty,
Like one that stands upon a promontory
And spies a far-off shore where he would tread,
Wishing his foot were equal with his eye,
And chides the sea that sunders him from thence,
Saying he'll lade it dry to have his way:
So do I wish the crown, being so far off;
And so I chide the means that keeps me from it,
And so, I say, I'll cut the causes off,
Flattering me with impossibilities.
My eye's too quick, my heart o'erweens too much,
Unless my hand and strength could equal them.
Well, say there is no kingdom then for Richard:
What other pleasure can the world afford?
I'll make my heaven in a lady's lap
And deck my body in gay ornaments
And witch sweet ladies with my words and looks.
O miserable thought! and more unlikely
Than to accomplish twenty golden crowns!
Why, love forswore me in my mother's womb;
And, for I should not deal in her soft laws,
She did corrupt frail nature with some bribe
To shrink mine arm up like a wither'd shrub;
To make an envious mountain on my back,
Where sits deformity to mock my body;
To shape my legs of an unequal size;
To disproportion me in every part,
Like to a chaos, or an unlick'd bear-whelp,
That carries no impression like the dam.

And am I then a man to be belov'd?
O monstrous fault to harbour such a thought!
Then, since this earth affords no joy to me
But to command, to check, to o'erbear such
As are of better person than myself,
I'll make my heaven to dream upon the crown
And, whiles I live, t' account this world but hell
Until my misshap'd trunk that bears this head
Be round impaled with a glorious crown.
And yet I know not how to get the crown,
For many lives stand between me and home;
And I — like one lost in a thorny wood,
That rents the thorns and is rent with the thorns,
Seeking a way and straying from the way,
Not knowing how to find the open air
But toiling desperately to find it out —
Torment myself to catch the English crown;
And from that torment I will free myself
Or hew my way out with a bloody axe.
Why, I can smile, and murther whiles I smile,
And cry 'Content!' to that which grieves my heart,
And wet my cheeks with artificial tears,
And frame my face to all occasions.
I'll drown more sailors than the mermaid shall;
I'll slay more gazers than the basilisk;
I'll play the orator as well as Nestor,
Deceive more slily than Ulysses could,
And, like a Sinon, take another Troy.
I can add colours to the chameleon,
Change shapes with Proteus for advantages,
And set the murtherous Machiavel to school.
Can I do this, and cannot get a crown?
Tut, were it farther off, I'll pluck it down.
Exit.

[Scene III. *France. The* King's *Palace.*]

Flourish. Enter *Lewis* the *French King,* his sister *Bona,* his *Admiral,* call'd *Bourbon*; *Prince Edward, Queen Margaret,* and the *Earl of Oxford. Lewis* sits, and riseth up again.

Lewis. Fair Queen of England, worthy Margaret,
Sit down with us. It ill befits thy state
And birth that thou shouldst stand while Lewis doth sit.

Marg. No, mighty King of France. Now Margaret
Must strike her sail, and learn awhile to serve
Where kings command. I was, I must confess,
Great Albion's Queen in former golden days;
But now mischance hath trod my title down
And with dishonour laid me on the ground,
Where I must take like seat unto my fortune
And to my humble seat conform myself.

Lewis. Why, say, fair queen, whence springs this deep despair?

Marg. From such a cause as fills mine eyes with tears
And stops my tongue, while heart is drown'd in cares.

Lewis. Whate'er it be, be thou still like thyself,
And sit thee by our side. (*Seats her by him.*) Yield not thy neck
To fortune's yoke, but let thy dauntless mind
Still ride in triumph over all mischance.
Be plain, Queen Margaret, and tell thy grief.
It shall be eas'd if France can yield relief.

Marg. Those gracious words revive my drooping thoughts
And give my tongue-tied sorrows leave to speak.
Now therefore be it known to noble Lewis
That Henry, sole possessor of my love,
Is, of a king, become a banish'd man
And forc'd to live in Scotland a forlorn;
While proud ambitious Edward Duke of York
Usurps the regal title and the seat
Of England's true anointed lawful King.
This is the cause that I, poor Margaret,
With this my son, Prince Edward, Henry's heir,
Am come to crave thy just and lawful aid;
And if thou fail us, all our hope is done.
Scotland hath will to help, but cannot help;
Our people and our peers are both misled,
Our treasure seiz'd, our soldiers put to flight,
And (as thou seest) ourselves in heavy plight.

Lewis. Renowned queen, with patience calm the storm
While we bethink a means to break it off.

Marg. The more we stay, the stronger grows our foe.

Lewis. The more I stay, the more I'll succour thee.

Marg. O, but impatience waiteth on true sorrow.
And see where comes the breeder of my sorrow!

Enter *Warwick.*

Lewis. What's he approacheth boldly to our presence?

Marg. Our Earl of Warwick, Edward's greatest friend.

Lewis. Welcome, brave Warwick! What brings thee to France?
He descends. She ariseth.

Marg. [*aside*] Ay, now begins a second storm to rise;
For this is he that moves both wind and tide.
War. From worthy Edward, King of Albion,
My lord and sovereign and thy vowed friend,
I come, in kindness and unfeigned love,
First to do greetings to thy royal person,
And then to crave a league of amity,
And lastly to confirm that amity
With nuptial knot, if thou vouchsafe to grant
That virtuous Lady Bona, thy fair sister,
To England's King in lawful marriage.
Marg. [*aside*] If that go forward, Henry's hope is done.
War. (*speaking to Bona*) And, gracious madam, in our king's behalf,
I am commanded, with your leave and favour,
Humbly to kiss your hand, and with my tongue
To tell the passion of my sovereign's heart;
Where fame, late ent'ring at his heedful ears,
Hath plac'd thy beauty's image and thy virtue.
Marg. King Lewis, and Lady Bona, hear me speak
Before you answer Warwick. His demand
Springs not from Edward's well-meant honest love,
But from deceit, bred by necessity;
For how can tyrants safely govern home
Unless abroad they purchase great alliance?
To prove him tyrant this reason may suffice,
That Henry liveth still; but were he dead,
Yet here Prince Edward stands, King Henry's son.
Look, therefore, Lewis, that by this league and marriage
Thou draw not on thy danger and dishonour;
For though usurpers sway the rule awhile,
Yet heav'ns are just and time suppresseth wrongs.
War. Injurious Margaret!
Prince Edw. And why not Queen?
War. Because thy father Henry did usurp,
And thou no more art Prince than she is Queen.
Oxf. Then Warwick disannuls great John of Gaunt,
Which did subdue the greatest part of Spain;
And after John of Gaunt, Henry the Fourth,
Whose wisdom was a mirror to the wisest;
And after that wise prince, Henry the Fifth,
Who by his prowess conquered all France.
From these our Henry lineally descends.
War. Oxford, how haps it in this smooth discourse
You told not how Henry the Sixth hath lost
All that which Henry the Fifth had gotten?
Methinks these peers of France should smile at that.
But for the rest: you tell a pedigree
Of threescore and two years — a silly time
To make prescription for a kingdom's worth.
Oxf. Why, Warwick, canst thou speak against thy liege,
Whom thou obeyed'st thirty and six years,
And not bewray thy treason with a blush?
War. Can Oxford, that did ever fence the right,
Now buckler falsehood with a pedigree?
For shame! Leave Henry and call Edward king.
Oxf. Call him my king by whose injurious doom
My elder brother, the Lord Aubrey Vere,
Was done to death? and more than so, my father,
Even in the downfall of his mellow'd years,
When nature brought him to the door of death?
No, Warwick, no! While life upholds this arm,
This arm upholds the house of Lancaster.
War. And I the house of York.
Lewis. Queen Margaret, Prince Edward, and Oxford,
Vouchsafe at our request to stand aside
While I use further conference with Warwick.
They stand aloof.
Marg. Heavens grant that Warwick's words bewitch him not!
Lewis. Now, Warwick, tell me, even upon thy conscience,
Is Edward your true king? For I were loath
To link with him that were not lawful chosen.
War. Thereon I pawn my credit and mine honour.
Lewis. But is he gracious in the people's eye?
War. The more that Henry was unfortunate.
Lewis. Then further: all dissembling set aside,
Tell me for truth the measure of his love
Unto our sister Bona.
War. Such it seems
As may beseem a monarch like himself.
Myself have often heard him say and swear
That this his love was an eternal plant,
Whereof the root was fix'd in virtue's ground,
The leaves and fruit maintain'd with beauty's sun,
Exempt from envy, but not from disdain,
Unless the Lady Bona quit his pain.
Lewis. Now, sister, let us hear your firm resolve.

Bona. Your grant, or your denial, shall be mine.
(*Speaks to Warwick.*) Yet I confess that often ere this day,
When I have heard your king's desert recounted,
Mine ear hath tempted judgment to desire.

Lewis. Then, Warwick, thus: our sister shall be Edward's,
And now forthwith shall articles be drawn
Touching the jointure that your king must make,
Which with her dowry shall be counterpois'd.
Draw near, Queen Margaret, and be a witness
That Bona shall be wife to the English king.

Prince Edw. To Edward, but not to the English king.

Marg. Deceitful Warwick, it was thy device
By this alliance to make void my suit!
Before thy coming Lewis was Henry's friend.

Lewis. And still is friend to him, and Margaret.
But if your title to the crown be weak,
As may appear by Edward's good success,
Then 'tis but reason that I be releas'd
From giving aid which late I promised.
Yet shall you have all kindness at my hand
That your estate requires and mine can yield.

War. Henry now lives in Scotland at his ease,
Where having nothing, nothing can he lose.
And as for you yourself, our quondam queen,
You have a father able to maintain you,
And better 'twere you troubled him than France.

Marg. Peace, impudent and shameless Warwick! peace,
Proud setter up and puller down of kings!
I will not hence till with my talk and tears
(Both full of truth) I make King Lewis behold
Thy sly conveyance and thy lord's false love;
For both of you are birds of selfsame feather.

Post blowing a horn within.

Lewis. Warwick, this is some post to us or thee.

Enter the *Post.*

Post. (*speaks to Warwick*) My Lord Ambassador, these letters are for you,
Sent from your brother, Marquess Montague;
(*To Lewis*) These from our king unto your Majesty;
(*To Margaret*) And, madam, these for you: from whom I know not.

They all read their letters.

Oxf. I like it well that our fair queen and mistress
Smiles at her news, while Warwick frowns at his.

Prince Edw. Nay, mark how Lewis stamps as he were nettled.
I hope all's for the best.

Lewis. Warwick, what are thy news? and yours, fair queen?

Marg. Mine such as fill my heart with unhop'd joys.

War. Mine full of sorrow and heart's discontent.

Lewis. What? Has your king married the Lady Grey?
And now, to soothe your forgery and his,
Sends me a paper to persuade me patience?
Is this th' alliance that he seeks with France?
Dare he presume to scorn us in this manner?

Marg. I told your Majesty as much before.
This proveth Edward's love and Warwick's honesty.

War. King Lewis, I here protest in sight of heaven
And by the hope I have of heavenly bliss
That I am clear from this misdeed of Edward's —
No more my king, for he dishonours me,
But most himself, if he could see his shame.
Did I forget that by the House of York
My father came untimely to his death?
Did I let pass th' abuse done to my niece?
Did I impale him with the regal crown?
Did I put Henry from his native right?
And am I guerdon'd at the last with shame?
Shame on himself! for my desert is honour;
And to repair my honour, lost for him,
I here renounce him and return to Henry.
My noble queen, let former grudges pass,
And henceforth I am thy true servitor.
I will revenge his wrong to Lady Bona
And replant Henry in his former state.

Marg. Warwick, these words have turn'd my hate to love,
And I forgive and quite forget old faults
And joy that thou becom'st King Henry's friend.

War. So much his friend, ay, his unfeigned friend,
That, if King Lewis vouchsafe to furnish us
With some few bands of chosen soldiers,
I'll undertake to land them on our coast
And force the tyrant from his seat by war.
'Tis not his new-made bride shall succour him!
And as for Clarence, as my letters tell me,

He's very likely now to fall from him
For matching more for wanton lust than honour
Or than for strength and safety of our country.

Bona. Dear brother, how shall Bona be reveng'd
But by thy help to this distressed queen?

Marg. Renowned prince, how shall poor Henry live
Unless thou rescue him from foul despair?

Bona. My quarrel and this English queen's are one.

War. And mine, fair Lady Bona, joins with yours.

Lewis. And mine with hers and thine and Margaret's.
Therefore, at last, I firmly am resolv'd
You shall have aid.

Marg. Let me give humble thanks for all at once.

Lewis. Then, England's messenger, return in post
And tell false Edward, thy supposed king,
That Lewis of France is sending over masquers
To revel it with him and his new bride.
Thou seest what's past. Go fear thy king withal.

Bona. Tell him, in hope he'll prove a widower shortly,
I'll wear the willow garland for his sake.

Marg. Tell him my mourning weeds are laid aside
And I am ready to put armour on.

War. Tell him from me that he hath done me wrong
And therefore I'll uncrown him ere't be long.
There's thy reward. [*Gives a purse.*] Be gone.

Exit Post.

Lewis. But, Warwick,
Thou and Oxford, with five thousand men,
Shall cross the seas and bid false Edward battle;
And as occasion serves, this noble queen
And prince shall follow with a fresh supply.
Yet, ere thou go, but answer me one doubt:
What pledge have we of thy firm loyalty?

War. This shall assure my constant loyalty,
That if our queen and this young prince agree,
I'll join mine eldest daughter, and my joy,
To him forthwith in holy wedlock bands.

Marg. Yes, I agree, and thank you for your motion.
Son Edward, she is fair and virtuous.
Therefore delay not; give thy hand to Warwick
And, with thy hand, thy faith irrevocable
That only Warwick's daughter shall be thine.

Prince Edw. Yes, I accept her, for she well deserves it,
And here to pledge my vow I give my hand.

He gives his hand to Warwick.

Lewis. Why stay we now? These soldiers shall be levied,
And thou, Lord Bourbon, our High Admiral,
Shalt waft them over with our royal fleet.
I long till Edward fall by war's mischance
For mocking marriage with a dame of France.

Exeunt. Manet Warwick.

War. I came from Edward as ambassador,
But I return his sworn and mortal foe.
Matter of marriage was the charge he gave me,
But dreadful war shall answer his demand.
Had he none else to make a stale but me?
Then none but I shall turn his jest to sorrow.
I was the chief that rais'd him to the crown
And I'll be chief to bring him down again;
Not that I pity Henry's misery,
But seek revenge on Edward's mockery. *Exit.*

[ACT IV. Scene I. *London. The Palace.*]

Enter *Richard, Clarence, Somerset, and Montague.*

Rich. Now tell me, brother Clarence, what think you
Of this new marriage with the Lady Grey?
Hath not our brother made a worthy choice?

Clar. Alas, you know 'tis far from hence to France!
How could he stay till Warwick made return?

Som. My lords, forbear this talk. Here comes the King.

Flourish. Enter *King Edward,* [attended,] *Lady Grey* [as *Queen*], *Pembroke, Stafford, Hastings. Four stand on one side and four on the other.*

Rich. And his well-chosen bride.

Clar. I mind to tell him plainly what I think.

K. Edw. Now, brother of Clarence, how like you our choice,
That you stand pensive, as half malecontent?

Clar. As well as Lewis of France or the Earl of Warwick,

Which are so weak of courage and in judgment
That they'll take no offence at our abuse.
K. Edw. Suppose they take offence without a cause:
They are but Lewis and Warwick; I am Edward,
Your king and Warwick's, and must have my will.
Rich. And you shall have your will, because our king.
Yet hasty marriage seldom proveth well.
K. Edw. Yea, brother Richard, are you offended too?
Rich. Not I.
No, God forbid that I should wish them sever'd
Whom God hath join'd together! Ay, and 'twere pity
To sunder them that yoke so well together.
K. Edw. Setting your scorns and your mislike aside,
Tell me some reason why the Lady Grey
Should not become my wife and England's Queen.
And you too, Somerset, and Montague,
Speak freely what you think.
Clar. Then this is mine opinion, that King Lewis
Becomes your enemy for mocking him
About the marriage of the Lady Bona.
Rich. And Warwick, doing what you gave in charge,
Is now dishonoured by this new marriage.
K. Edw. What if both Lewis and Warwick be appeas'd
By such invention as I can devise?
Mont. Yet, to have join'd with France in such alliance
Would more have strength'ned this our commonwealth
'Gainst foreign storms than any home-bred marriage.
Hast. Why, knows not Montague that of itself
England is safe, if true within itself?
Mont. Yes, but the safer when 'tis back'd with France.
Hast. 'Tis better using France than trusting France.
Let us be back'd with God, and with the seas,
Which he hath giv'n for fence impregnable,
And with their helps only defend ourselves.
In them and in ourselves our safety lies.
Clar. For this one speech Lord Hastings well deserves
To have the heir of the Lord Hungerford.
K. Edw. Ay, what of that? It was my will and grant,
And for this once my will shall stand for law.
Rich. And yet methinks your Grace hath not done well
To give the heir and daughter of Lord Scales
Unto the brother of your loving bride.
She better would have fitted me or Clarence;
But in your bride you bury brotherhood.
Clar. Or else you would not have bestow'd the heir
Of the Lord Bonville on your new wive's son
And leave your brothers to go speed elsewhere.
K. Edw. Alas, poor Clarence! Is it for a wife
That thou are malecontent? I will provide thee.
Clar. In choosing for yourself you show'd your judgment,
Which being shallow, you shall give me leave
To play the broker in mine own behalf;
And to that end I shortly mind to leave you.
K. Edw. Leave me or tarry, Edward will be King
And not be tied unto his brother's will.
Lady Grey. My lords, before it pleas'd his Majesty
To raise my state to title of a queen,
Do me but right, and you must all confess
That I was not ignoble of descent,
And meaner than myself have had like fortune.
But as this title honours me and mine,
So your dislikes, to whom I would be pleasing,
Doth cloud my joys with danger and with sorrow.
K. Edw. My love, forbear to fawn upon their frowns.
What danger or what sorrow can befall thee
So long as Edward is thy constant friend
And their true sovereign, whom they must obey?
Nay, whom they shall obey, and love thee too,
Unless they seek for hatred at my hands;
Which if they do, yet will I keep thee safe,
And they shall feel the vengeance of my wrath.
Rich. [*aside*] I hear; yet say not much, but think the more.

Enter a *Post.*

K. Edw. Now, messenger, what letters or what news
From France?
Post. My sovereign liege, no letters, and few words,
But such as I, without your special pardon,
Dare not relate.

K. Edw. Go to, we pardon thee. Therefore, in brief,
Tell me their words as near as thou canst guess them.
What answer makes King Lewis unto our letters?

Post. At my depart these were his very words:
'Go tell false Edward, thy supposed king,
That Lewis of France is sending over masquers
To revel it with him and his new bride.'

K. Edw. Is Lewis so brave? Belike he thinks me Henry.
But what said Lady Bona to my marriage?

Post. These were her words, utt'red with mild disdain:
'Tell him, in hope he'll prove a widower shortly,
I'll wear the willow garland for his sake.'

K. Edw. I blame not her. She could say little less.
She had the wrong. But what said Henry's queen?
For I have heard that she was there in place.

Post. 'Tell him,' quoth she, 'my mourning weeds are done
And I am ready to put armour on.'

K. Edw. Belike she minds to play the Amazon.
But what said Warwick to these injuries?

Post. He, more incens'd against your Majesty
Than all the rest, discharg'd me with these words:
'Tell him from me that he hath done me wrong,
And therefore I'll uncrown him ere't be long.'

K. Edw. Ha! durst the traitor breathe out so proud words?
Well, I will arm me, being thus forewarn'd.
They shall have wars and pay for their presumption.
But say, is Warwick friends with Margaret?

Post. Ay, gracious sovereign. They are so link'd in friendship
That young Prince Edward marries Warwick's daughter.

Clar. Belike the elder; Clarence will have the younger.
Now, brother king, farewell, and sit you fast;
For I will hence to Warwick's other daughter,
That, though I want a kingdom, yet in marriage
I may not prove inferior to yourself.
You that love me and Warwick, follow me.

Exit Clarence, and Somerset follows.

Rich. [*aside*] Not I.
My thoughts aim at a further matter. I
Stay not for the love of Edward but the crown.

K. Edw. Clarence and Somerset both gone to Warwick?
Yet am I arm'd against the worst can happen;
And haste is needful in this desp'rate case.
Pembroke and Stafford, you in our behalf
Go levy men and make prepare for war.
They are already, or quickly will be landed.
Myself in person will straight follow you.

Exeunt Pembroke and Stafford.

But ere I go, Hastings and Montague,
Resolve my doubt. You twain, of all the rest,
Are near to Warwick by blood and by alliance.
Tell me if you love Warwick more than me.
If it be so, then both depart to him;
I rather wish you foes than hollow friends.
But if you mind to hold your true obedience,
Give me assurance with some friendly vow,
That I may never have you in suspect.

Mont. So God help Montague as he proves true!

Hast. And Hastings as he favours Edward's cause!

K. Edw. Now, brother Richard, will you stand by us?

Rich. Ay, in despite of all that shall withstand you.

K. Edw. Why, so! then am I sure of victory.
Now therefore let us hence, and lose no hour
Till we meet Warwick with his foreign pow'r.

Exeunt.

[Scene II. *A plain in Warwickshire.*]

Enter *Warwick* and *Oxford* in England with *French Soldiers.*

War. Trust me, my lord, all hitherto goes well.
The common people by numbers swarm to us.

Enter *Clarence* and *Somerset.*

But see where Somerset and Clarence comes!
Speak suddenly, my lords, are we all friends?

Clar. Fear not that, my lord.

War. Then, gentle Clarence, welcome unto Warwick;
And welcome, Somerset. I hold it cowardice
To rest mistrustful where a noble heart
Hath pawn'd an open hand in sign of love.
Else might I think that Clarence, Edward's brother.

Were but a feigned friend to our proceedings.
But welcome, sweet Clarence. My daughter shall be thine.
And now what rests but, in night's coverture,
Thy brother being carelessly encamp'd,
His soldiers lurking in the towns about,
And but attended by a simple guard,
We may surprise and take him at our pleasure?
Our scouts have found the adventure very easy;
That as Ulysses and stout Diomede
With sleight and manhood stole to Rhesus' tents
And brought from thence the Thracian fatal steeds,
So we, well cover'd with the night's black mantle,
At unawares may beat down Edward's guard
And seize himself. I say not, slaughter him,
For I intend but only to surprise him.
You that will follow me to this attempt,
Applaud the name of Henry with your leader.
They all cry 'Henry!'
Why then, let's on our way in silent sort.
For Warwick and his friends, God and Saint George! *Exeunt.*

[Scene III. Edward's *camp, near Warwick.*]

Enter three *Watchmen,* to guard the *King's* tent.

1. Watch. Come on, my masters. Each man take his stand.
The King by this is set him down to sleep.
2. Watch. What, will he not to bed?
1. Watch. Why, no; for he hath made a solemn vow
Never to lie and take his natural rest
Till Warwick or himself be quite suppress'd.
2. Watch. To-morrow then belike shall be the day,
If Warwick be so near as men report.
3. Watch. But say, I pray, what nobleman is that
That with the King here resteth in his tent?
1. Watch. 'Tis the Lord Hastings, the King's chiefest friend.
3. Watch. O, is it so? But why commands the King
That his chief followers lodge in towns about him,
While he himself keeps in the cold field?
2. Watch. 'Tis the more honour, because more dangerous.
3. Watch. Ay, but give me worship and quietness.
I like it better than a dangerous honour.
If Warwick knew in what estate he stands,
'Tis to be doubted he would waken him.
1. Watch. Unless our halberds did shut up his passage.
2. Watch. Ay! wherefore else guard we his royal tent
But to defend his person from night-foes?

Enter *Warwick, Clarence, Oxford, Somerset,* and *French Soldiers,* silent all.

War. This is his tent; and see where stand his guard.
Courage, my masters! Honour now or never!
But follow me, and Edward shall be ours.
1. Watch. Who goes there?
2. Watch. Stay, or thou diest!
Warwick and the rest cry all 'Warwick! Warwick!' *and set upon the Guard, who fly, crying* 'Arm! arm!' *Warwick and the rest following them.*

The *Drum* playing and *Trumpet* sounding, enter *Warwick, Somerset,* and the rest, bringing the *King* out in his gown, sitting in a chair. *Richard* and *Hastings* fly over the stage.

Som. What are they that fly there?
War. Richard and Hastings. Let them go. Here is the Duke.
K. Edw. The Duke? Why, Warwick, when we parted last
Thou call'dst me King.
War. Ay, but the case is alter'd.
When you disgrac'd me in my embassade,
Then I degraded you from being King,
And come now to create you Duke of York.
Alas, how should you govern any kingdom
That know not how to use ambassadors,
Nor how to be contented with one wife,
Nor how to use your brothers brotherly,
Nor how to study for the people's welfare,
Nor how to shroud yourself from enemies?
K. Edw. Yea, brother of Clarence, art thou here too?
Nay, then I see that Edward needs must down.
Yet, Warwick, in despite of all mischance,
Of thee thyself, and all thy complices,
Edward will always bear himself as King.
Though Fortune's malice overthrow my state,
My mind exceeds the compass of her wheel.
War. Then, for his mind, be Edward England's King; *Takes off his crown.*
But Henry now shall wear the English crown
And be true king indeed, thou but the shadow.
My Lord of Somerset, at my request

See that forthwith Duke Edward be convey'd
Unto my brother, Archbishop of York.
When I have fought with Pembroke and his fellows,
I'll follow you and tell what answer
Lewis and the Lady Bona send to him.
Now for a while farewell, good Duke of York.

They lead him out forcibly.

K. Edw. What fates impose, that men must needs abide;
It boots not to resist both wind and tide.

Exeunt [*King Edward, guarded, and Somerset*].

Oxf. What now remains, my lords, for us to do
But march to London with our soldiers?

War. Ay, that's the first thing that we have to do,
To free King Henry from imprisonment
And see him seated in the regal throne.

Exeunt.

[Scene IV. *London. The Palace.*]

[Enter *Rivers* and *Lady Grey* [as *Queen*].

Riv. Madam, what makes you in this sudden change?

Grey. Why, brother Rivers, are you yet to learn
What late misfortune is befall'n King Edward?

Riv. What? loss of some pitch'd battle against Warwick?

Grey. No, but the loss of his own royal person.

Riv. Then is my sovereign slain?

Grey. Ay, almost slain, for he is taken prisoner,
Either betray'd by falsehood of his guard
Or by his foe surpris'd at unawares;
And, as I further have to understand,
Is new committed to the Bishop of York,
Fell Warwick's brother, and by that our foe.

Riv. These news, I must confess, are full of grief.
Yet, gracious madam, bear it as you may;
Warwick may lose, that now hath won the day.

Grey. Till then fair hope must hinder live's decay.
And I the rather wean me from despair
For love of Edward's offspring in my womb.
This is it that makes me bridle passion
And bear with mildness my misfortune's cross.
Ay, ay, for this I draw in many a tear
And stop the rising of bloodsucking sighs,
Lest with my sighs or tears I blast or drown
King Edward's fruit, true heir to th' English crown.

Riv. But, madam, where is Warwick then become?

Grey. I am inform'd that he comes towards London
To set the crown once more on Henry's head.
Guess thou the rest. King Edward's friends must down.
But, to prevent the tyrant's violence
(For trust not him that hath once broken faith)
I'll hence forthwith unto the sanctuary,
To save, at least, the heir of Edward's right.
There shall I rest secure from force and fraud.
Come, therefore, let us fly while we may fly.
If Warwick take us, we are sure to die.

Exeunt.

[Scene V. *A park near Middleham Castle in Yorkshire.*]

Enter *Richard, Lord Hastings,* and *Sir William Stanley.*

Rich. Now, my Lord Hastings and Sir William Stanley,
Leave off to wonder why I drew you hither
Into this chiefest thicket of the park.
Thus stands the case: you know our king, my brother,
Is prisoner to the Bishop here, at whose hands
He hath good usage and great liberty;
And often, but attended with weak guard,
Comes hunting this way to disport himself.
I have advertis'd him by secret means
That if about this hour he make this way
Under the colour of his usual game,
He shall here find his friends with horse and men
To set him free from his captivity.

Enter *King Edward* and a *Huntsman* with him.

Hunt. This way, my lord, for this way lies the game.

K. Edw. Nay, this way, man! See where the huntsmen stand.
Now, brother of Gloucester, Lord Hastings, and the rest,
Stand you thus close to steal the Bishop's deer?

Rich. Brother, the time and case requireth haste.
Your horse stands ready at the park corner.

K. Edw. But whither shall we then?

Hast. To Lynn, my lord, and ship from thence to Flanders.
Rich. Well guess'd, believe me; for that was my meaning.
K. Edw. Stanley, I will requite thy forwardness.
Rich. But wherefore stay we? 'Tis no time to talk.
K. Edw. Huntsman, what say'st thou? Wilt thou go along?
Hunt. Better do so than tarry and be hang'd.
Rich. Come then, away. Let's ha' no more ado.
K. Edw. Bishop, farewell. Shield thee from Warwick's frown
And pray that I may repossess the crown.
Exeunt.

[Scene VI. *London. The Tower.*]

Flourish. Enter *King Henry the Sixth, Clarence, Warwick, Somerset,* young *Henry Earl of Richmond, Oxford, Montague,* and *Lieutenant* [*of the Tower*].

K. Hen. Master Lieutenant, now that God and friends
Have shaken Edward from the regal seat
And turn'd my captive state to liberty,
My fear to hope, my sorrows unto joys,
At our enlargement what are thy due fees?
Lieut. Subjects may challenge nothing of their sov'reigns;
But if an humble prayer may prevail,
I then crave pardon of your Majesty.
K. Hen. For what, Lieutenant? for well using me?
Nay, be thou sure I'll well requite thy kindness
For that it made my imprisonment a pleasure;
Ay, such a pleasure as incaged birds
Conceive when, after many moody thoughts,
At last by notes of household harmony
They quite forget their loss of liberty.
But, Warwick, after God, thou set'st me free,
And chiefly therefore I thank God and thee;
He was the author, thou the instrument.
Therefore, that I may conquer fortune's spite
By living low, where fortune cannot hurt me,
And that the people of this blessed land
May not be punish'd with my thwarting stars,
Warwick, although my head still wear the crown,
I here resign my government to thee,
For thou art fortunate in all thy deeds.
War. Your Grace hath still been fam'd for virtuous,
And now may seem as wise as virtuous
By spying and avoiding fortune's malice,
For few men rightly temper with the stars.
Yet in this one thing let me blame your Grace,
For choosing me when Clarence is in place.
Clar. No, Warwick, thou art worthy of the sway,
To whom the heav'ns in thy nativity
Adjudg'd an olive branch and laurel crown,
As likely to be blest in peace and war;
And therefore I yield thee my free consent.
War. And I choose Clarence only for Protector.
K. Hen. Warwick and Clarence, give me both your hands.
Now join your hands, and with your hands your hearts,
That no dissension hinder government.
I make you both Protectors of this land,
While I myself will lead a private life
And in devotion spend my latter days,
To sin's rebuke and my Creator's praise.
War. What answers Clarence to his sovereign's will?
Clar. That he consents, if Warwick yield consent,
For on thy fortune I repose myself.
War. Why then, though loath, yet must I be content.
We'll yoke together, like a double shadow
To Henry's body, and supply his place;
I mean, in bearing weight of government,
While he enjoys the honour and his ease.
And, Clarence, now then it is more than needful
Forthwith that Edward be pronounc'd a traitor
And all his lands and goods be confiscate.
Clar. What else? And that succession be determin'd.
War. Ay, therein Clarence shall not want his part.
K. Hen. But with the first of all your chief affairs,
Let me entreat (for I command no more)
That Margaret your queen and my son Edward
Be sent for, to return from France with speed;
For till I see them here, by doubtful fear
My joy of liberty is half eclips'd.
Clar. It shall be done, my sovereign, with all speed.

K. Hen. My Lord of Somerset, what youth is that
Of whom you seem to have so tender care?
Som. My liege, it is young Henry, Earl of Richmond.
K. Hen. Come hither, England's hope.
Lays his hand on his head.
If secret powers
Suggest but truth to my divining thoughts,
This pretty lad will prove our country's bliss.
His looks are full of peaceful majesty,
His head by nature fram'd to wear a crown,
His hand to wield a sceptre, and himself
Likely in time to bless a regal throne.
Make much of him, my lords; for this is he
Must help you more than you are hurt by me.

Enter a *Post.*

War. What news, my friend?
Post. That Edward is escaped from your brother
And fled, as he hears since, to Burgundy.
War. Unsavoury news! But how made he escape?
Post. He was convey'd by Richard Duke of Gloucester
And the Lord Hastings, who attended him
In secret ambush on the forest side
And from the Bishop's huntsmen rescu'd him;
For hunting was his daily exercise.
War. My brother was too careless of his charge.
But let us hence, my sovereign, to provide
A salve for any sore that may betide.
Exeunt. Manent Somerset, Richmond, and Oxford.
Som. My lord, I like not of this flight of Edward's,
For doubtless Burgundy will yield him help
And we shall have more wars before 't be long.
As Henry's late presaging prophecy
Did glad my heart with hope of this young Richmond,
So doth my heart misgive me, in these conflicts
What may befall him, to his harm and ours.
Therefore, Lord Oxford, to prevent the worst,
Forthwith we'll send him hence to Brittany
Till storms be past of civil enmity.
Oxf. Ay, for if Edward repossess the crown,
'Tis like that Richmond with the rest shall down.
Som. It shall be so; he shall to Brittany.
Come therefore, let's about it speedily.
Exeunt.

[Scene VII. *Before York.*]

Flourish. Enter [*King*] *Edward, Richard, Hastings,* and *Soldiers.*

K. Edw. Now, brother Richard, Lord Hastings, and the rest,
Yet thus far Fortune maketh us amends
And says that once more I shall interchange
My waned state for Henry's regal crown.
Well have we pass'd and now repass'd the seas
And brought desired help from Burgundy.
What then remains, we being thus arriv'd
From Ravenspurgh haven before the gates of York,
But that we enter, as into our dukedom?
Rich. The gates made fast? Brother, I like not this!
For many men that stumble at the threshold
Are well foretold that danger lurks within.
K. Edw. Tush, man, abodements must not now affright us!
By fair or foul means we must enter in,
For hither will our friends repair to us.
Hast. My liege, I'll knock once more to summon them.

Enter, on the walls, the *Mayor of York* and his *Brethren.*

May. My lords, we were forewarned of your coming
And shut the gates for safety of ourselves;
For now we owe allegiance unto Henry.
K. Edw. But, Master Mayor, if Henry be your king,
Yet Edward at the least is Duke of York.
May. True, my good lord. I know you for no less.
K. Edw. Why, and I challenge nothing but my dukedom,
As being well content with that alone.
Rich. [*aside*] But when the fox hath once got in his nose,
He'll soon find means to make the body follow.
Hast. Why, Master Mayor, why stand you in a doubt?
Open the gates. We are King Henry's friends.
May. Ay, say you so? The gates shall then be opened.
He descends [*with the Aldermen*].
Rich. A wise stout captain, and soon persuaded!
Hast. The good old man would fain that all were well,
So 'twere not long of him; but being ent'red,

I doubt not, I, but we shall soon persuade
Both him and all his brothers unto reason.

Enter the *Mayor* and two *Aldermen* [below].

K. Edw. So, Master Mayor. These gates must not be shut
But in the night or in the time of war.
What, fear not, man, but yield me up the keys;
Takes his keys.
For Edward will defend the town and thee
And all those friends that deign to follow me.

March. Enter *Montgomery* with *Drum* and *Soldiers.*

Rich. Brother, this is Sir John Montgomery,
Our trusty friend, unless I be deceiv'd.
K. Edw. Welcome, Sir John! But why come you in arms?
Mont. To help King Edward in his time of storm,
As every loyal subject ought to do.
K. Edw. Thanks, good Montgomery. But we now forget
Our title to the crown and only claim
Our dukedom till God please to send the rest.
Mont. Then fare you well, for I will hence again.
I came to serve a king and not a duke.
Drummer, strike up, and let us march away.
The Drum begins to march.
K. Edw. Nay, stay, Sir John, awhile, and we'll debate
By what safe means the crown may be recover'd.
Mont. What talk you of debating? In few words,
If you'll not here proclaim yourself our king,
I'll leave you to your fortune and be gone
To keep them back that come to succour you.
Why shall we fight, if you pretend no title?
Rich. Why, brother, wherefore stand you on nice points?
K. Edw. When we grow stronger, then we'll make our claim;
Till then 'tis wisdom to conceal our meaning.
Hast. Away with scrupulous wit! Now arms must rule.
Rich. And fearless minds climb soonest unto crowns.
Brother, we will proclaim you out of hand;
The bruit thereof will bring you many friends.
K. Edw. Then be it as you will; for 'tis my right,
And Henry but usurps the diadem.
Mont. Ay, now my sovereign speaketh like himself
And now will I be Edward's champion.
Hast. Sound trumpet. Edward shall be here proclaim'd.
Come, fellow soldier, make thou proclamation.
[*Gives him a paper.*] *Flourish. Sound.*
Soldier. [*reads*] 'Edward the Fourth, by the grace of God, King of England and France, and Lord of Ireland, &c.'
Mont. And whosoe'er gainsays King Edward's right,
By this I challenge him to single fight.
Throws down his gauntlet.
All. Long live Edward the Fourth!
K. Edw. Thanks, brave Montgomery, and thanks unto you all.
If fortune serve me, I'll requite this kindness.
Now for this night let's harbour here in York,
And when the morning sun shall raise his car
Above the border of this horizon,
We'll forward towards Warwick and his mates;
For well I wot that Henry is no soldier.
Ah, froward Clarence, how evil it beseems thee
To flatter Henry and forsake thy brother!
Yet, as we may, we'll meet both thee and Warwick.
Come on, brave soldiers. Doubt not of the day,
And that once gotten, doubt not of large pay.
Exeunt.

[Scene VIII. *London. The* Bishop of London's *Palace.*]

Flourish. Enter the *King* [*Henry*], *Warwick, Montague, Clarence, Oxford,* [and *Exeter*].

War. What counsel, lords? Edward from Belgia,
With hasty Germans and blunt Hollanders,
Hath pass'd in safety through the narrow seas
And with his troops doth march amain to London,
And many giddy people flock to him.
Oxf. Let's levy men and beat him back again.
Clar. A little fire is quickly trodden out,
Which, being suffer'd, rivers cannot quench.
War. In Warwickshire I have true-hearted friends,
Not mutinous in peace, yet bold in war.
Those will I muster up; and thou, son Clarence,
Shalt stir up in Suffolk, Norfolk, and in Kent
The knights and gentlemen to come with thee.

Thou, brother Montague, in Buckingham,
Northampton, and in Leicestershire shalt find
Men well inclin'd to hear what thou command'st.
And thou, brave Oxford, wondrous well belov'd,
In Oxfordshire shalt muster up thy friends.
My sovereign, with the loving citizens,
Like to his island girt in with the ocean
Or modest Dian circled with her nymphs,
Shall rest in London till we come to him.
Fair lords, take leave and stand not to reply.
Farewell, my sovereign.

K. Hen. Farewell, my Hector and my Troy's true hope.

Clar. In sign of truth I kiss your Highness' hand.

K. Hen. Well-minded Clarence, be thou fortunate!

Mont. Comfort, my lord! and so I take my leave.

Oxf. [*kisses Henry's hand*] And thus I seal my truth and bid adieu.

K. Hen. Sweet Oxford, and my loving Montague,
And all at once, once more a happy farewell!

War. Farewell, sweet lords. Let's meet at Coventry.

Exeunt [*all but King Henry and Exeter*].

K. Hen. Here at the palace will I rest awhile.
Cousin of Exeter, what thinks your lordship?
Methinks the power that Edward hath in field
Should not be able to encounter mine.

Exe. The doubt is that he will seduce the rest.

K. Hen. That's not my fear. My meed hath got me fame.
I have not stopp'd mine ears to their demands
Nor posted off their suits with slow delays.
My pity hath been balm to heal their wounds,
My mildness hath allay'd their swelling griefs,
My mercy dried their water-flowing tears.
I have not been desirous of their wealth
Nor much oppress'd them with great subsidies,
Nor forward of revenge, though they much err'd.
Then why should they love Edward more than me?
No, Exeter, these graces challenge grace;
And when the lion fawns upon the lamb,
The lamb will never cease to follow him.

Shout within, 'A Lancaster! A Lancaster!'

Exe. Hark, hark, my lord! what shouts are these?

Enter [*King*] *Edward* and his *Soldiers,* [with *Richard*].

K. Edw. Seize on the shamefac'd Henry, bear him hence,
And once again proclaim us King of England.
You are the fount that makes small brooks to flow,
Now stops thy spring; my sea shall suck them dry
And swell so much the higher by their ebb.
Hence with him to the Tower. Let him not speak.

Exeunt [*some*] *with King Henry.*

And, lords, towards Coventry bend we our course,
Where peremptory Warwick now remains.
The sun shines hot, and if we use delay,
Cold biting winter mars our hop'd-for hay.

Rich. Away betimes, before his forces join,
And take the great-grown traitor unawares.
Brave warriors, march amain towards Coventry. *Exeunt.*

[ACT V. Scene I. *Coventry.*]

Enter *Warwick,* the *Mayor of Coventry,* two *Messengers,* and others, upon the walls.

War. Where is the post that came from valiant Oxford?
How far hence is thy lord, mine honest fellow?

1. Mess. By this at Dunsmore, marching hitherward.

War. How far off is our brother Montague?
Where is the post that came from Montague?

2. Mess. By this at Daintry, with a puissant troop.

Enter [*Sir John*] *Somervile.*

War. Say, Somervile, what says my loving son?
And by thy guess how nigh is Clarence now?

Som. At Southam I did leave him with his forces
And do expect him here some two hours hence.

[*Drum heard.*]

War. Then Clarence is at hand. I hear his drum.

Som. It is not his, my lord. Here Southam lies.

The drum your Honour hears marcheth from Warwick.

War. Who should that be? Belike unlook'd-for friends.

Som. They are at hand, and you shall quickly know.

March. Flourish. Enter [*King*] *Edward, Richard,* and *Soldiers.*

K. Edw. Go, trumpet, to the walls, and sound a parle.

Rich. See how the surly Warwick mans the wall!

War. O unbid spite! Is sportful Edward come?
Where slept our scouts or how are they seduc'd
That we could hear no news of his repair?

K. Edw. Now, Warwick, wilt thou ope the city gates,
Speak gentle words, and humbly bend thy knee,
Call Edward king, and at his hands beg mercy?
And he shall pardon thee these outrages.

War. Nay rather, wilt thou draw thy forces hence,
Confess who set thee up and pluck'd thee down,
Call Warwick patron, and be penitent?
And thou shalt still remain the Duke of York.

Rich. I thought at least he would have said 'the King';
Or did he make the jest against his will?

War. Is not a dukedom, sir, a goodly gift?

Rich. Ay, by my faith, for a poor earl to give!
I'll do thee service for so good a gift.

War. 'Twas I that gave the kingdom to thy brother.

K. Edw. Why, then 'tis mine, if but by Warwick's gift.

War. Thou art no Atlas for so great a weight;
And, weakling, Warwick takes his gift again,
And Henry is my king, Warwick his subject.

K. Edw. But Warwick's king is Edward's prisoner;
And, gallant Warwick, do but answer this:
What is the body when the head is off?

Rich. Alas that Warwick had no more forecast,
But, whiles he thought to steal the single ten,
The king was slily finger'd from the deck!
You left poor Henry at the Bishop's palace
And ten to one you'll meet him in the Tower.

K. Edw. 'Tis even so. Yet you are Warwick still.

Rich. Come, Warwick, take the time. Kneel down, kneel down!
Nay, when? Strike now, or else the iron cools.

War. I had rather chop this hand off at a blow
And with the other fling it at thy face
Than bear so low a sail to strike to thee.

K. Edw. Sail how thou canst, have wind and tide thy friend,
This hand, fast wound about thy coal-black hair,
Shall, whiles thy head is warm and new cut off,
Write in the dust this sentence with thy blood:
'Wind-changing Warwick now can change no more.'

Enter *Oxford,* with *Drum* and *Colours.*

War. O cheerful colours! See where Oxford comes!

Oxf. Oxford, Oxford, for Lancaster!
[*He and his Forces enter the city.*]

Rich. The gates are open; let us enter too.

K. Edw. So other foes may set upon our backs.
Stand we in good array, for they no doubt
Will issue out again and bid us battle.
If not, the city being but of small defence,
We'll quickly rouse the traitors in the same.

War. O, welcome, Oxford! for we want thy help.

Enter *Montague,* with *Drum* and *Colours.*

Mont. Montague, Montague, for Lancaster!
[*He and his Forces enter the city.*]

Rich. Thou and thy brother both shall buy this treason
Even with the dearest blood your bodies bear.

K. Edw. The harder match'd, the greater victory!
My mind presageth happy gain and conquest.

Enter *Somerset,* with *Drum* and *Colours.*

Som. Somerset, Somerset, for Lancaster!
[*He and his Forces enter the city.*]

Rich. Two of thy name, both Dukes of Somerset,
Have sold their lives unto the house of York;
And thou shalt be the third, if this sword hold.

Enter *Clarence,* with *Drum* and *Colours.*

War. And lo where George of Clarence sweeps along,
Of force enough to bid his brother battle;
With whom an upright zeal to right prevails
More than the nature of a brother's love!
Come, Clarence, come! Thou wilt, if Warwick call.

Clar. Father of Warwick, know you what this means?
Takes his red rose out of his hat.
Look here, I throw my infamy at thee.
I will not ruinate my father's house,
Who gave his blood to lime the stones together,
And set up Lancaster. Why, trowest thou, Warwick,
That Clarence is so harsh, so blunt, unnatural,
To bend the fatal instruments of war
Against his brother and his lawful king?
Perhaps thou wilt object my holy oath.
To keep that oath were more impiety
Than Jephtha when he sacrific'd his daughter.
I am so sorry for my trespass made
That, to deserve well at my brother's hands,
I here proclaim myself thy mortal foe;
With resolution, wheresoe'er I meet thee
(As I will meet thee if thou stir abroad),
To plague thee for thy foul misleading me.
And so, proud-hearted Warwick, I defy thee
And to my brother turn my blushing cheeks.
Pardon me, Edward! I will make amends;
And, Richard, do not frown upon my faults,
For I will henceforth be no more unconstant.
K. Edw. Now welcome more, and ten times more belov'd,
Than if thou never hadst deserv'd our hate.
Rich. Welcome, good Clarence! This is brotherlike.
War. O passing traitor, perjur'd and unjust!
K. Edw. What, Warwick, wilt thou leave the town and fight?
Or shall we beat the stones about thine ears?
War. Alas, I am not coop'd here for defence!
I will away towards Barnet presently
And bid thee battle, Edward, if thou dar'st.
K. Edw. Yes, Warwick, Edward dares and leads the way.
Lords, to the field. Saint George and victory!
Exeunt [King Edward and his Company]. March. Warwick and his Company follows.

[Scene II. *A field of battle near Barnet.*]

Alarum and excursions. Enter [*King*] *Edward*, bringing forth *Warwick* wounded.

K. Edw. So, lie thou there! Die thou, and die our fear!
For Warwick was a bug that fear'd us all.
Now, Montague, sit fast. I seek for thee,
That Warwick's bones may keep thine company. *Exit.*
War. Ah, who is nigh? Come to me, friend or foe,
And tell me who is victor, York or Warwick.
Why ask I that? My mangled body shows,
My blood, my want of strength, my sick heart shows,
That I must yield my body to the earth
And, by my fall, the conquest to my foe.
Thus yields the cedar to the axe's edge,
Whose arms gave shelter to the princely eagle,
Under whose shade the ramping lion slept,
Whose top-branch overpeer'd Jove's spreading tree
And kept low shrubs from winter's pow'rful wind.
These eyes, that now are dimm'd with death's black veil,
Have been as piercing as the midday sun
To search the secret treasons of the world.
The wrinkles in my brows, now fill'd with blood,
Were lik'ned oft to kingly sepulchres;
For who liv'd king but I could dig his grave?
And who durst smile when Warwick bent his brow?
Lo now my glory smear'd in dust and blood!
My parks, my walks, my manors that I had,
Even now forsake me; and of all my lands
Is nothing left me but my body's length!
Why, what is pomp, rule, reign, but earth and dust?
And, live we how we can, yet die we must.

Enter *Oxford* and *Somerset.*

Som. Ah, Warwick, Warwick, wert thou as we are,
We might recover all our loss again!
The Queen from France hath brought a puissant power.
Even now we heard the news. Ah, couldst thou fly!
War. Why, then I would not fly. Ah, Montague,
If thou be there, sweet brother, take my hand
And with thy lips keep in my soul awhile!
Thou lov'st me not; for, brother, if thou didst,
Thy tears would wash this cold congealed blood
That glues my lips and will not let me speak.
Come quickly, Montague, or I am dead.
Som. Ah, Warwick! Montague hath breath'd his last,

And to the latest gasp cried out for Warwick
And said 'Commend me to my valiant brother.'
And more he would have said, and more he spoke,
Which sounded like a clamour in a vault,
That mought not be distinguish'd; but at last
I well might hear, delivered with a groan,
'O, farewell, Warwick!'

War. Sweet rest his soul! Fly, lords, and save yourselves;
For Warwick bids you all farewell, to meet in heaven. *Dies.*

Oxf. Away, away, to meet the Queen's great power!

Here they bear away his body. Exeunt.

[Scene III. *Another part of the field.*]

Flourish. Enter *King Edward* in triumph; with *Richard, Clarence,* and the rest.

K. Edw. Thus far our fortune keeps an upward course
And we are grac'd with wreaths of victory;
But in the midst of this bright-shining day
I spy a black, suspicious, threat'ning cloud
That will encounter with our glorious sun
Ere he attain his easeful western bed.
I mean, my lords, those powers that the Queen
Hath rais'd in Gallia have arriv'd our coast
And, as we hear, march on to fight with us.

Clar. A little gale will soon disperse that cloud
And blow it to the source from whence it came.
Thy very beams will dry those vapours up,
For every cloud engenders not a storm.

Rich. The Queen is valued thirty thousand strong,
And Somerset, with Oxford, fled to her.
If she have time to breathe, be well assur'd
Her faction will be full as strong as ours.

K. Edw. We are advertis'd by our loving friends
That they do hold their course toward Tewksbury.
We, having now the best at Barnet field,
Will thither straight, for willingness rids way;
And as we march our strength will be augmented
In every county as we go along.
Strike up the drum. Cry 'Courage!' and away. *Exeunt.*

[Scene IV. *Plains near Tewksbury.*]

Flourish. March. Enter the *Queen* [*Margaret*], *young Prince Edward, Somerset, Oxford,* and *Soldiers.*

Queen. Great lords, wise men ne'er sit and wail their loss
But cheerly seek how to redress their harms.
What though the mast be now blown overboard,
The cable broke, the holding anchor lost,
And half our sailors swallow'd in the flood?
Yet lives our pilot still. Is't meet that he
Should leave the helm and, like a fearful lad,
With tearful eyes add water to the sea
And give more strength to that which hath too much,
Whiles, in his moan, the ship splits on the rock,
Which industry and courage might have sav'd?
Ah, what a shame! ah, what a fault were this
Say Warwick was our anchor. What of that?
And Montague our topmast. What of him?
Our slaught'red friends the tackles. What of these?
Why, is not Oxford here, another anchor?
And Somerset, another goodly mast?
The friends of France our shrouds and tacklings?
And, though unskilful, why not Ned and I
For once allow'd the skilful pilot's charge?
We will not from the helm, to sit and weep,
But keep our course (though the rough wind say no)
From shelves and rocks that threaten us with wrack.
As good to chide the waves as speak them fair.
And what is Edward but a ruthless sea?
What Clarence but a quicksand of deceit?
And Richard but a ragged fatal rock?
All these the enemies to our poor bark.
Say you can swim — alas, 'tis but a while!
Tread on the sand — why, there you quickly sink!
Bestride the rock — the tide will wash you off,
Or else you famish: that's a threefold death.
This speak I, lords, to let you understand,
If case some one of you would fly from us,
That there's no hop'd-for mercy with the brothers
More than with ruthless waves, with sands and rocks.
Why, courage then! What cannot be avoided
'Twere childish weakness to lament or fear.

Prince. Methinks a woman of this valiant spirit

Should, if a coward heard her speak these words,
Infuse his breast with magnanimity
And make him, naked, foil a man-at-arms.
I speak not this as doubting any here;
For did I but suspect a fearful man,
He should have leave to go away betimes,
Lest in our need he might infect another
And make him of like spirit to himself.
If any such be here (as God forbid!),
Let him depart before we need his help.

Oxf. Women and children of so high a courage,
And warriors faint? Why, 'twere perpetual shame.
O brave young Prince! Thy famous grandfather
Doth live again in thee. Long mayst thou live
To bear his image and renew his glories!

Som. And he that will not fight for such a hope,
Go home to bed, and, like the owl by day,
If he arise, be mock'd and wond'red at.

Queen. Thanks, gentle Somerset. Sweet Oxford, thanks.

Prince. And take his thanks that yet hath nothing else.

Enter a *Messenger*.

Mess. Prepare you, lords; for Edward is at hand,
Ready to fight. Therefore be resolute.

Oxf. I thought no less. It is his policy
To haste thus fast, to find us unprovided.

Som. But he's deceiv'd; we are in readiness.

Queen. This cheers my heart, to see your forwardness.

Oxf. Here pitch our battle; hence we will not budge.

Flourish and march. Enter, *King Edward, Richard, Clarence*, and *Soldiers*.

K. Edw. Brave followers, yonder stands the thorny wood
Which, by the heavens' assistance and your strength,
Must by the roots be hewn up yet ere night.
I need not add more fuel to your fire,
For well I wot ye blaze to burn them out.
Give signal to the fight, and to it, lords!

Queen. Lords, knights, and gentlemen, what I should say
My tears gainsay; for every word I speak,
Ye see I drink the water of mine eyes.
Therefore, no more but this: Henry, your sovereign,
Is prisoner to the foe, his state usurp'd,
His realm a slaughterhouse, his subjects slain,
His statutes cancell'd, and his treasure spent;
And yonder is the wolf that makes this spoil.
You fight in justice. Then, in God's name, lords, 81
Be valiant and give signal to the fight.

Alarum. Retreat. Excursions. Exeunt.

[Scene V. *Another part of the field.*]

Flourish. Enter [*King*] *Edward, Richard, Clarence*, [*Soldiers*; with] *Queen* [*Margaret*], *Oxford, Somerset* [as prisoners].

K. Edw. Now here a period of tumultuous broils!
Away with Oxford to Hames Castle straight.
For Somerset, off with his guilty head!
Go bear them hence. I will not hear them speak.

Oxf. For my part, I'll not trouble thee with words.

Som. Nor I, but stoop with patience to my fortune.

Exeunt [*Oxford and Somerset, guarded*].

Queen. So part we sadly in this troublous world
To meet with joy in sweet Jerusalem.

K. Edw. Is proclamation made that who finds Edward
Shall have a high reward, and he his life?

Rich. It is. And lo where youthful Edward comes!

Enter [*Soldiers*, with] the *Prince* [*Edward*].

K. Edw. Bring forth the gallant; let us hear him speak.
What? Can so young a thorn begin to prick?
Edward, what satisfaction canst thou make 14
For bearing arms, for stirring up my subjects,
And all the trouble thou hast turn'd me to?

Prince. Speak like a subject, proud ambitious York!
Suppose that I am now my father's mouth;
Resign thy chair, and where I stand kneel thou,
Whilst I propose the selfsame words to thee
Which, traitor, thou wouldst have me answer to.

Queen. Ah, that thy father had been so resolv'd!

Rich. That you might still have worn the petticoat

And ne'er have stol'n the breech from Lancaster.

Prince. Let Æsop fable in a winter's night.
His currish riddles sorts not with this place.

Rich. By heaven, brat, I'll plague ye for that word.

Queen. Ay, thou wast born to be a plague to men.

Rich. For God's sake take away this captive scold!

Prince. Nay, take away this scolding crookback rather.

K. Edw. Peace, wilful boy, or I will charm your tongue.

Clar. Untutor'd lad, thou art too malapert.

Prince. I know my duty; you are all undutiful.
Lascivious Edward, and thou perjur'd George,
And thou misshapen Dick, I tell ye all
I am your better, traitors as ye are,
And thou usurp'st my father's right and mine.

K. Edw. Take that, the likeness of this railer here! *Stabs him.*

Rich. Sprawl'st thou? Take that, to end thy agony. *Richard stabs him.*

Clar. And there's for twitting me with perjury! *Clarence stabs him.*

Queen. O, kill me too!

Rich. Marry, and shall! *Offers to kill her.*

K. Edw. Hold, Richard, hold; for we have done too much.

Rich. Why should she live to fill the world with words?

K. Edw. What? Doth she swoon? Use means for her recovery.

Rich. Clarence, excuse me to the King my brother.
I'll hence to London on a serious matter;
Ere ye come there, be sure to hear some news.

Clar. What? what?

Rich. The Tower, the Tower! *Exit.*

Queen. O Ned, sweet Ned, speak to thy mother, boy!
Canst thou not speak? O traitors! murtherers!
They that stabb'd Cæsar shed no blood at all,
Did not offend, nor were not worthy blame,
If this foul deed were by, to equal it.
He was a man; this (in respect) a child,
And men ne'er spend their fury on a child.
What's worse than murtherer, that I may name it?
No, no, my heart will burst an if I speak!
And I will speak, that so my heart may burst.
Butchers and villains, bloody cannibals,
How sweet a plant have you untimely cropp'd!
You have no children, butchers! If you had,
The thought of them would have stirr'd up remorse;
But if you ever chance to have a child,
Look in his youth to have him so cut off
As, deathsmen, you have rid this sweet young prince!

K. Edw. Away with her! Go bear her hence perforce!

Queen. Nay, never bear me hence! Dispatch me here.
Here sheathe thy sword, I'll pardon thee my death.
What, wilt thou not? Then, Clarence, do it thou.

Clar. By heaven, I will not do thee so much ease.

Queen. Good Clarence, do! Sweet Clarence, do thou do it!

Clar. Didst thou not hear me swear I would not do it?

Queen. Ay, but thou usest to forswear thyself.
'Twas sin before, but now 'tis charity.
What, wilt thou not? Where is that devil's butcher,
Hard-favour'd Richard? Richard, where art thou?
Thou art not here. Murther is thy almsdeed.
Petitioners for blood thou ne'er put'st back.

K. Edw. Away, I say. I charge ye bear her hence.

Queen. So come to you and yours as to this prince! *Exit [led out].*

K. Edw. Where's Richard gone?

Clar. To London, all in post; and, as I guess,
To make a bloody supper in the Tower.

K. Edw. He's sudden if a thing comes in his head.
Now march we hence, discharge the common sort
With pay and thanks, and let's away to London
And see our gentle queen how well she fares.
By this, I hope, she hath a son for me.
Exeunt.

[Scene VI. *London. The Tower.*]

Enter *Henry the Sixth* and *Richard,* with the *Lieutenant,* on the walls.

Rich. Good day, my lord. What, at your book so hard?

K. Hen. Ay, my good lord — 'my lord' I should say rather.

'Tis sin to flatter. 'Good' was little better.
'Good Gloucester' and 'good devil' were alike,
And both preposterous. Therefore, not 'good lord.'

Rich. Sirrah, leave us to ourselves; we must confer.

[*Exit Lieutenant.*]

K. Hen. So flies the reckless shepherd from the wolf;
So first the harmless sheep doth yield his fleece,
And next his throat unto the butcher's knife.
What scene of death hath Roscius now to act?

Rich. Suspicion always haunts the guilty mind;
The thief doth fear each bush an officer.

K. Hen. The bird that hath been limed in a bush
With trembling wings misdoubteth every bush;
And I, the hapless male to one sweet bird,
Have now the fatal object in my eye
Where my poor young was lim'd, was caught, and kill'd.

Rich. Why, what a peevish fool was that of Crete
That taught his son the office of a fowl!
And yet, for all his wings, the fool was drown'd.

K. Hen. I, Dædalus; my poor boy, Icarus;
Thy father, Minos, that denied our course;
The sun that sear'd the wings of my sweet boy,
Thy brother Edward; and thyself, the sea
Whose envious gulf did swallow up his life.
Ah, kill me with thy weapon, not with words!
My breast can better brook thy dagger's point
Than can my ears that tragic history.
But wherefore dost thou come? Is't for my life?

Rich. Think'st thou I am an executioner?

K. Hen. A persecutor I am sure thou art.
If murthering innocents be executing,
Why, then thou art an executioner.

Rich. Thy son I kill'd for his presumption.

K. Hen. Hadst thou been kill'd when first thou didst presume,
Thou hadst not liv'd to kill a son of mine.
And thus I prophesy, that many a thousand
Which now mistrust no parcel of my fear,
And many an old man's sigh and many a widow's,
And many an orphan's water-standing eye —
Men for their sons, wives for their husbands,
And orphans for their parents' timeless death —
Shall rue the hour that ever thou wast born.
The owl shriek'd at thy birth, an evil sign;
The night crow cried, aboding luckless time;
Dogs howl'd and hideous tempest shook down trees;
The raven rook'd her on the chimney's top,
And chatt'ring pies in dismal discord sung.
Thy mother felt more than a mother's pain,
And yet brought forth less than a mother's hope,
To wit, an indigested and deformed lump,
Not like the fruit of such a goodly tree.
Teeth hadst thou in thy head when thou wast born,
To signify thou cam'st to bite the world;
And, if the rest be true which I have heard,
Thou cam'st —

Rich. I'll hear no more. Die, prophet, in thy speech. *Stabs him.*
For this (amongst the rest) was I ordain'd.

K. Hen. Ay, and for much more slaughter after this.
O, God forgive my sins and pardon thee! *Dies.*

Rich. What? Will the aspiring blood of Lancaster
Sink in the ground? I thought it would have mounted.
See how my sword weeps for the poor King's death!
O may such purple tears be alway shed
From those that wish the downfall of our house!
If any spark of life be yet remaining,
Down, down to hell, and say I sent thee thither! *Stabs him again.*
I, that have neither pity, love, nor fear.
Indeed 'tis true that Henry told me of;
For I have often heard my mother say
I came into the world with my legs forward.
Had I not reason, think ye, to make haste
And seek their ruin that usurp'd our right?
The midwife wonder'd, and the women cried
'O, Jesus bless us! He is born with teeth!'
And so I was; which plainly signified
That I should snarl and bite and play the dog.
Then, since the heavens have shap'd my body so,
Let hell make crook'd my mind to answer it.
I have no brother, I am like no brother;
And this word 'love,' which greybeards call divine,
Be resident in men like one another,
And not in me! I am myself alone.
Clarence, beware. Thou keep'st me from the light;
But I will sort a pitchy day for thee;
For I will buzz abroad such prophecies

That Edward shall be fearful of his life;
And then, to purge his fear, I'll be thy death.
King Henry and the Prince his son are gone.
Clarence, thy turn is next, and then the rest,
Counting myself but bad till I be best.
I'll throw thy body in another room
And triumph, Henry, in thy day of doom.
Exit [*with the body*].

[Scene VII. *London. The Palace.*]

Flourish. Enter *King Edward, Queen Elizabeth, Clarence, Richard, Hastings, Nurse* (with the *young Prince*), and *Attendants.*

K. Edw. Once more we sit in England's royal throne,
Repurchas'd with the blood of enemies.
What valiant foemen, like to autumn's corn,
Have we mow'd down in tops of all their pride!
Three Dukes of Somerset, threefold renown'd
For hardly and undoubted champions;
Two Cliffords, as the father and the son;
And two Northumberlands — two braver men
Ne'er spurr'd their coursers at the trumpet's sound;
With them, the two brave bears, Warwick and Montague,
That in their chains fetter'd the kingly lion
And made the forest tremble when they roar'd.
Thus have we swept suspicion from our seat
And made our footstool of security.
Come hither, Bess, and let me kiss my boy.
Young Ned, for thee thine uncles and myself
Have in our armours watch'd the winter's night,
Went all afoot in summer's scalding heat,
That thou mightst repossess the crown in peace;
And of our labours thou shalt reap the gain.

Rich. [*aside*] I'll blast his harvest, if your head were laid;
For yet I am not look'd on in the world.
This shoulder was ordain'd so thick to heave,
And heave it shall some weight or break my back.
Work thou the way, and thou shalt execute.

K. Edw. Clarence and Gloucester, love my lovely queen,
And kiss your princely nephew, brothers both.

Clar. The duty that I owe unto your Majesty
I seal upon the lips of this sweet babe.

Queen. Thanks, noble Clarence; worthy brother, thanks.

Rich. And that I love the tree from whence thou sprang'st
Witness the loving kiss I give the fruit.
[*Aside*] To say the truth, so Judas kiss'd his master
And cried 'All hail!' when as he meant all harm.

K. Edw. Now am I seated as my soul delights,
Having my country's peace and brothers' loves.

Clar. What will your Grace have done with Margaret?
Reignier, her father, to the King of France
Hath pawn'd the Sicils and Jerusalem,
And hither have they sent it for her ransom.

K. Edw. Away with her, and waft her hence to France!
And now what rests but that we spend the time
With stately triumphs, mirthful comic shows,
Such as befits the pleasure of the court?
Sound drums and trumpets! Farewell sour annoy!
For here I hope begins our lasting joy.
Exeunt omnes.

King Richard the Third

Richard the Third was entered in the Stationers' Register on October 20, 1597, and the First Quarto came out in that year: 'The Tragedy of King Richard the third. . . . As it hath beene lately Acted by the Right honourable the Lord Chamberlaine his seruants' — Shakespeare's company. No author's name is mentioned in the title page or elsewhere. Five other quartos were published (1598, 1602, 1605, 1612, 1622) before the Folio of 1623, and all of them ascribe the play to 'William Shake-speare' or 'William Shakespeare.' The textual differences among the quartos are of no moment. In contents, the First Quarto and the Folio agree in the main; but the Quarto has about forty lines that the Folio lacks, and the Folio has about two hundred and thirty that are not found in the Quarto. For the text, the Folio is the authority, but most of the missing lines are undoubtedly genuine and are supplied from the Quarto. The only considerable omission in the Folio consists of lines 101–118 in iv, 2.

Apart from misprints, the Quarto text differs from that of the Folio in an infinity of little matters of expression. Many of the differences consist in the mere substitution of a synonym: as, for example, 'spie' (Quarto) for 'see' (i, 1, 26), 'holes' for 'wounds' (i, 2, 11), 'euils' for 'Crimes' (76), 'bloudy' for 'murd'rous' (94), 'slew' (137) for 'kill'd.' In some cases the Quarto reading has been adopted in many modern editions and has become so consecrated by usage that one finds it hard to be conscientious and accept the Folio text. Thus, in Clarence's dream, 'that grim ferriman' may seem better than 'that sowre Ferry-man' (i, 4, 46), but 'sowre' is probably what Shakespeare wrote. The connotation of words — what we may call their atmosphere — changes from age to age; and 'sour' was a more poetical adjective in Shakespeare's time than it is to-day.

Some critics regard the Quarto text as Shakespeare's first draft and take the Folio text for his (or another's) revision; but there is little to be said for such a theory. The First Quarto may have been printed from a carelessly made copy of Shakespeare's manuscript. In general, its readings are not authoritative when they disagree with the Folio, though now and then they enable us to correct a Folio misprint.

In *The Second Part of King Henry the Sixth* Richard fights valiantly at the Battle of St. Albans (May 22, 1455), though in fact he was less than three years old at the time (v, 2, 66 ff.; v, 3). His character is worked out with care in the *Third Part of King Henry the Sixth.* His main characteristics appear when he urges his father to repudiate his oath (i, 2, 18 ff.). His words express not alone his conscious delight in the arts of the sophist and his restless ferocity, but that imperious spirit which makes him a Marlovian character — his passionate love of sovereign power:

> And, father, do but think
> How sweet a thing it is to wear a crown,
> Within whose circuit is Elysium
> And all that poets feign of bliss and joy.
> Why do we linger thus? I cannot rest
> Until the white rose that I wear be dy'd
> Even in the lukewarm blood of Henry's heart.

His valour is emphasized from the outset, even by Queen Margaret (i, 4, 75 ff.):

> That valiant crookback prodigy,
> Dicky your boy, that with his grumbling voice
> Was wont to cheer his dad in mutinies.

Two fine soliloquies (iii, 2, 124 ff.; v, 6, 68 ff.), in which Shakespeare out-Marlowes Marlowe, develop the hints already given. They look forward to the tragedy of RICHARD THE THIRD, and indeed may almost be said to announce it as in preparation. Their connection with the soliloquy with which the play begins is obvious. 'I am determined to prove a villain' echoes Richard's self-analysis in *Part III*, in which he declares that he can 'set the murtherous Machiavel to school' (iii, 2, 193).

Richard, then, may be termed Shakespeare's dramatic interpretation of the Machiavellian villain — a type whose general features were already well settled in the Elizabethan mind. Comparison with Marlowe's *Jew of Malta* is inevitable. There Machiavel speaks the Prologue and registers Barabas as a disciple of his school. That Shakespeare was strongly influenced by Marlowe in this period is certain; and that is enough to account for those features of the present play and its immediate predecessors that have tempted critics, with no sound arguments to support them, to contend that Marlowe had some hand in *Henry the Sixth* and RICHARD THE THIRD.

As to date, the close connection with *3 Henry VI* suggests that RICHARD THE THIRD followed that play almost immediately. If we refer *Part III* to 1591, RICHARD THE THIRD may well be dated 1592. There is no direct evidence to the contrary.

For material, Shakespeare went to Holinshed, who for this reign uses Sir Thomas More's life of Richard III and Halle's *Chronicle*. The play covers the period from the funeral of Henry VI (1471) to the defeat and death of Richard on Bosworth field (August 22, 1485). Historical time is condensed. The murder of Clarence, which in Shakespeare comes soon after the funeral, took place in 1478. King Edward's death (ii, 2) occurred on April 9, 1483. The coronation of Richard followed on July 6. The wooing of Lady Anne, which interrupts King Henry's funeral procession (i, 2), is imaginary.

Richardus Tertius, a Latin drama by Thomas Legge, was performed at Cambridge in 1580. The anonymous *True Tragedie of Richard the Third*, printed in 1594, may or may not be older than Shakespeare's play. Neither can be regarded as a source for his KING RICHARD THE THIRD.

Colley Cibber's adaptation of RICHARD THE THIRD was first acted in 1700 at Drury Lane and held the stage for more than a hundred and fifty years. At least two of Richard's lines in Cibber's play have become proverbial and are often quoted as Shakespeare's: — 'Off with his head — so much for Buckingham!' (iv, 3) and 'Conscience avaunt, Richard's himself again!' (v, 3).

THE TRAGEDY OF
KING RICHARD THE THIRD

[Dramatis Personæ.

King Edward the Fourth.
Edward, Prince of Wales, afterwards *King Edward V*, } sons to the *King*.
Richard, Duke of York, } sons to the *King*.
George, Duke of Clarence, } brothers to the *King*.
Richard, Duke of Gloucester, afterwards *King Richard III*, } brothers to the *King*.
A young *Son of Clarence.*
Henry, Earl of Richmond, afterwards *King Henry VII.*
Cardinal Bourchier, Archbishop of Canterbury.
Thomas Rotherham, Archbishop of York.
John Morton, Bishop of Ely.
Duke of Buckingham.
Duke of Norfolk.
Earl of Surrey, his son.
Earl Rivers, brother to *Queen Elizabeth*.
Marquess of Dorset and *Lord Grey*, her sons.
Earl of Oxford.
Lord Hastings.
Lord Stanley (also styled *Earl of Derby*).
Lord Lovel.
Sir Thomas Vaughan.
Sir Richard Ratcliff.
Sir William Catesby.
Sir James Tyrrel.
Sir James Blunt.
Sir Walter Herbert.
Sir Robert Brakenbury, Lieutenant of the Tower.
Keeper in the Tower.
Sir William Brandon.
Christopher Urswick, a priest.
Lord Mayor of London.
Sheriff of Wiltshire.
Tressel and *Berkeley*, gentlemen attending on *Lady Anne*.

Elizabeth, Queen to *King Edward IV.*
Margaret, widow of *King Henry VI.*
Duchess of York, mother to *King Edward IV.*
Lady Anne, widow of *Edward*, Prince of Wales, son to *King Henry VI*; afterwards married to *Richard*, Duke of Gloucester.
A young *Daughter of Clarence* (*Lady Margaret Plantagenet*).

Ghosts of *Richard's* victims.

Lords, Gentlemen, and other Attendants; a Pursuivant, a Page, a Scrivener, a Priest, Bishops, Citizens, Aldermen, Councillors, Murderers, Messengers, Soldiers, &c.

SCENE. — *England*.]

ACT I. Scene I. [*London. A street.*]

Enter *Richard Duke of Gloucester* solus.

Rich. Now is the winter of our discontent
Made glorious summer by this sun of York,
And all the clouds that low'rd upon our house
In the deep bosom of the ocean buried.
Now are our brows bound with victorious wreaths,
Our bruised arms hung up for monuments,
Our stern alarums chang'd to merry meetings,
Our dreadful marches to delightful measures.
Grim-visag'd War hath smooth'd his wrinkled front,
And now, instead of mounting barbed steeds
To fright the souls of fearful adversaries,
He capers nimbly in a lady's chamber
To the lascivious pleasing of a lute.
But I, that am not shap'd for sportive tricks
Nor made to court an amorous looking glass;
I, that am rudely stamp'd, and want love's majesty
To strut before a wanton ambling nymph;
I, that am curtail'd of this fair proportion,
Cheated of feature by dissembling Nature,
Deform'd, unfinish'd, sent before my time
Into this breathing world, scarce half made up,
And that so lamely and unfashionable
That dogs bark at me as I halt by them —
Why, I, in this weak piping time of peace,
Have no delight to pass away the time,
Unless to see my shadow in the sun
And descant on mine own deformity.
And therefore, since I cannot prove a lover
To entertain these fair well-spoken days,
I am determined to prove a villain
And hate the idle pleasures of these days.

Plots have I laid, inductions dangerous.
By drunken prophecies, libels, and dreams,
To set my brother Clarence and the King
In deadly hate the one against the other;
And if King Edward be as true and just
As I am subtle, false, and treacherous,
This day should Clarence closely be mew'd up
About a prophecy which says that G
Of Edward's heirs the murtherer shall be.
Dive, thoughts, down to my soul! Here Clarence comes.

Enter *Clarence* guarded, and *Brakenbury.*

Brother, good day. What means this armed guard
That waits upon your Grace?
Clar. His Majesty,
Tend'ring my person's safety, hath appointed
This conduct to convey me to the Tower.
Rich. Upon what cause?
Clar. Because my name is George.
Rich. Alack, my lord, that fault is none of yours!
He should for that commit your godfathers.
O, belike his Majesty hath some intent
That you should be new christ'ned in the Tower.
But what's the matter, Clarence? May I know?
Clar. Yea, Richard, when I know; for I protest
As yet I do not. But, as I can learn,
He hearkens after prophecies and dreams,
And from the cross-row plucks the letter G,
And says a wizard told him that by G
His issue disinherited should be;
And, for my name of George begins with G,
It follows in his thought that I am he.
These (as I learn) and such-like toys as these
Have mov'd his Highness to commit me now.
Rich. Why, this it is when men are rul'd by women!
'Tis not the King that sends you to the Tower;
My Lady Grey his wife, Clarence, 'tis she
That tempts him to this harsh extremity.
Was it not she, and that good man of worship,
Anthony Woodville, her brother there,
That made him send Lord Hastings to the Tower,
From whence this present day he is deliver'd?
We are not safe, Clarence; we are not safe.
Clar. By heaven, I think there is no man secure
But the Queen's kindred, and night-walking heralds
That trudge betwixt the King and Mistress Shore.
Heard you not what an humble suppliant
Lord Hastings was to her for his delivery?
Rich. Humbly complaining to her deity
Got my Lord Chamberlain his liberty.
I'll tell you what —I think it is our way,
If we will keep in favour with the King,
To be her men and wear her livery.
The jealous o'erworn widow and herself,
Since that our brother dubb'd them gentlewomen,
Are mighty gossips in our monarchy.
Brak. I beseech your Graces both to pardon me.
His Majesty hath straitly given in charge
That no man shall have private conference
(Of what degree soever) with your brother.
Rich. Even so, an't please your worship. Brakenbury,
You may partake of anything we say.
We speak no treason, man. We say the King
Is wise and virtuous, and his noble queen
Well struck in years, fair, and not jealious.
We say that Shore's wife hath a pretty foot,
A cherry lip, a bonny eye, a passing pleasing tongue;
And that the Queen's kindred are made gentlefolks.
How say you, sir? Can you deny all this?
Brak. With this, my lord, myself have naught to do.
Rich. Naught to do with Mistress Shore? I tell thee, fellow,
He that doth naught with her (excepting one)
Were best to do it secretly alone.
Brak. What one, my lord?
Rich. Her husband, knave. Wouldst thou betray me?
Brak. I beseech your Grace to pardon me, and withal
Forbear your conference with the noble Duke.
Clar. We know thy charge, Brakenbury, and will obey.
Rich. We are the Queen's abjects, and must obey.
Brother, farewell. I will unto the King;
And whatsoe'er you will employ me in,
Were it to call King Edward's widow sister,
I will perform it to enfranchise you.
Meantime, this deep disgrace in brotherhood
Touches me deeper than you can imagine.
Clar. I know it pleaseth neither of us well.
Rich. Well, your imprisonment shall not be long:
I will deliver you, or else lie for you.
Meantime, have patience.

Clar. I must perforce. Farewell.
Exit Clarence, [with Brakenbury and Guard].
Rich. Go tread the path that thou shalt ne'er return,
Simple plain Clarence! I do love thee so
That I will shortly send thy soul to heaven,
If heaven will take the present at our hands.
But who comes here? The new-delivered Hastings?

Enter *Lord Hastings.*

Hast. Good time of day unto my gracious lord.
Rich. As much unto my good Lord Chamberlain.
Well are you welcome to this open air.
How hath your lordship brook'd imprisonment?
Hast. With patience, noble lord, as prisoners must;
But I shall live, my lord, to give them thanks
That were the cause of my imprisonment.
Rich. No doubt, no doubt; and so shall Clarence too,
For they that were your enemies are his
And have prevail'd as much on him as you.
Hast. More pity that the eagle should be mew'd,
While kites and buzzards prey at liberty.
Rich. What news abroad?
Hast. No news so bad abroad as this at home:
The King is sickly, weak, and melancholy,
And his physicians fear him mightily.
Rich. Now, by Saint Paul, that news is bad indeed!
O, he hath kept an evil diet long
And overmuch consum'd his royal person.
'Tis very grievous to be thought upon.
Where is he? In his bed?
Hast. He is.
Rich. Go you before, and I will follow you.
Exit Hastings.
He cannot live, I hope, and must not die
Till George be pack'd with posthorse up to heaven.
I'll in, to urge his hatred more to Clarence
With lies well steel'd with weighty arguments;
And, if I fail not in my deep intent,
Clarence hath not another day to live.
Which done, God take King Edward to his mercy
And leave the world for me to bustle in!
For then I'll marry Warwick's youngest daughter.
What though I kill'd her husband and her father?
The readiest way to make the wench amends
Is to become her husband and her father;
The which will I — not all so much for love
As for another secret close intent
By marrying her which I must reach unto.
But yet I run before my horse to market:
Clarence still breathes; Edward still lives and reigns;
When they are gone, then must I count my gains.
Exit.

Scene II. [*London. Another street.*]

Enter the corse of *Henry the Sixth,* with *Halberds* to guard it, [with them *Tressel* and *Berkeley*]; *Lady Anne* being the mourner.

Anne. Set down, set down your honourable load,
If honour may be shrouded in a hearse,
Whilst I awhile obsequiously lament
Th' untimely fall of virtuous Lancaster.
[*The Bearers set down the coffin.*]
Poor key-cold figure of a holy king,
Pale ashes of the house of Lancaster,
Thou bloodless remnant of that royal blood,
Be it lawful that I invocate thy ghost
To hear the lamentations of poor Anne,
Wife to thy Edward, to thy slaught'red son
Stabb'd by the selfsame hand that made these wounds!
Lo, in these windows that let forth thy life
I pour the helpless balm of my poor eyes.
O, cursed be the hand that made these holes!
Cursed the heart that had the heart to do it!
Cursed the blood that let this blood from hence!
More direful hap betide that hated wretch
That makes us wretched by the death of thee
Than I can wish to wolves — to spiders, toads,
Or any creeping venom'd thing that lives!
If ever he have child, abortive be it,
Prodigious, and untimely brought to light,
Whose ugly and unnatural aspect
May fright the hopeful mother at the view,
And that be heir to his unhappiness!
If ever he have wife, let her be made
More miserable by the death of him
Than I am made by my young lord and thee!
Come, now towards Chertsey with your holy load,
Taken from Paul's to be interred there;
And still as you are weary of this weight,
Rest you whiles I lament King Henry's corse.
[*The Bearers take up the coffin.*]

Enter *Richard Duke of Gloucester.*

Rich. Stay, you that bear the corse, and set it down.
Anne. What black magician conjures up this fiend
To stop devoted charitable deeds?
Rich. Villains, set down the corse, or, by Saint Paul,
I'll make a corse of him that disobeys!
Gent. My lord, stand back, and let the coffin pass.
Rich. Unmanner'd dog, stand thou when I command!
Advance thy halberd higher than my breast,
Or, by Saint Paul, I'll strike thee to my foot
And spurn upon thee, beggar, for thy boldness.
[*The Bearers set down the coffin.*]
Anne. What, do you tremble? Are you all afraid?
Alas, I blame you not, for you are mortal,
And mortal eyes cannot endure the devil.
Avaunt, thou dreadful minister of hell!
Thou hadst but power over his mortal body;
His soul thou canst not have. Therefore, be gone.
Rich. Sweet saint, for charity, be not so curst.
Anne. Foul devil, for God's sake hence, and trouble us not!
For thou hast made the happy earth thy hell,
Fill'd it with cursing cries and deep exclaims.
If thou delight to view thy heinous deeds,
Behold this pattern of thy butcheries.
O gentlemen, see, see! Dead Henry's wounds
Open their congeal'd mouths and bleed afresh!
Blush, blush, thou lump of foul deformity;
For 'tis thy presence that exhales this blood
From cold and empty veins where no blood dwells.
Thy deed inhuman and unnatural
Provokes this deluge most unnatural.
O God, which this blood mad'st, revenge his death!
O earth, which this blood drink'st, revenge his death!
Either, heav'n, with lightning strike the mur-th'rer dead;
Or, earth, gape open wide and eat him quick,
As thou dost swallow up this good king's blood
Which his hell-govern'd arm hath butchered!
Rich. Lady, you know no rules of charity,
Which renders good for bad, blessings for curses.
Anne. Villain, thou know'st no law of God nor man.
No beast so fierce but knows some touch of pity.
Rich. But I know none, and therefore am no beast.
Anne. O wonderful, when devils tell the truth!
Rich. More wonderful, when angels are so angry.
Vouchsafe, divine perfection of a woman,
Of these supposed crimes to give me leave
By circumstance but to acquit myself.
Anne. Vouchsafe, defus'd infection of a man,
For these known evils, but to give me leave
By circumstance to curse thy cursed self.
Rich. Fairer than tongue can name thee, let me have
Some patient leisure to excuse myself.
Anne. Fouler than heart can think thee, thou canst make
No excuse current but to hang thyself.
Rich. By such despair I should accuse myself.
Anne. And by despairing shalt thou stand excus'd
For doing worthy vengeance on thyself
That didst unworthy slaughter upon others.
Rich. Say that I slew them not?
Anne. Then say they were not slain.
But dead they are, and, devilish slave, by thee.
Rich. I did not kill your husband.
Anne. Why, then he is alive.
Rich. Nay, he is dead, and slain by Edward's hand.
Anne. In thy foul throat thou liest! Queen Margaret saw
Thy murd'rous falchion smoking in his blood;
The which thou once didst bend against her breast,
But that thy brothers beat aside the point.
Rich. I was provoked by her sland'rous tongue
That laid their guilt upon my guiltless shoulders.
Anne. Thou wast provoked by thy bloody mind
That never dream'st on aught but butcheries.
Didst thou not kill this king?
Rich. I grant ye.
Anne. Dost grant me, hedgehog? Then God grant me too
Thou mayst be damned for that wicked deed!
O, he was gentle, mild, and virtuous!
Rich. The better for the King of Heaven, that hath him.
Anne. He is in heaven, where thou shalt never come.

Rich. Let him thank me, that holp to send him thither;
For he was fitter for that place than earth.
Anne. And thou unfit for any place, but hell.
Rich. Yes, one place else, if you will hear me name it.
Anne. Some dungeon.
Rich. Your bedchamber.
Anne. Ill rest betide the chamber where thou liest!
Rich. So will it, madam, till I lie with you.
Anne. I hope so.
Rich. I know so. But, gentle Lady Anne,
To leave this keen encounter of our wits
And fall something into a slower method —
Is not the causer of the timeless deaths
Of these Plantagenets, Henry and Edward,
As blameful as the executioner?
Anne. Thou wast the cause and most accurs'd effect.
Rich. Your beauty was the cause of that effect —
Your beauty, that did haunt me in my sleep
To undertake the death of all the world,
So I might live one hour in your sweet bosom.
Anne. If I thought that, I tell thee, homicide,
These nails should rent that beauty from my cheeks.
Rich. These eyes could not endure that beauty's wrack;
You should not blemish it, if I stood by.
As all the world is cheered by the sun,
So I by that. It is my day, my life.
Anne. Black night o'ershade thy day, and death thy life!
Rich. Curse not thyself, fair creature! Thou art both.
Anne. I would I were, to be reveng'd on thee.
Rich. It is a quarrel most unnatural,
To be reveng'd on him that loveth thee.
Anne. It is a quarrel just and reasonable,
To be reveng'd on him that kill'd my husband.
Rich. He that bereft thee, lady, of thy husband,
Did it to help thee to a better husband.
Anne. His better doth not breathe upon the earth.
Rich. He lives that loves thee better than he could.
Anne. Name him.
Rich. Plantagenet.
Anne. Why, that was he.
Rich. The selfsame name, but one of better nature.
Anne. Where is he?
Rich. Here. (*She spitteth at him.*) Why dost thou spit at me?
Anne. Would it were mortal poison for thy sake!
Rich. Never came poison from so sweet a place.
Anne. Never hung poison on a fouler toad.
Out of my sight! Thou dost infect mine eyes.
Rich. Thine eyes, sweet lady, have infected mine.
Anne. Would they were basilisks, to strike thee dead!
Rich. I would they were, that I might die at once;
For now they kill me with a living death.
Those eyes of thine from mine have drawn salt tears,
Sham'd their aspects with store of childish drops —
These eyes, which never shed remorseful tear.
No, when my father York and Edward wept
To hear the piteous moan that Rutland made
When black-fac'd Clifford shook his sword at him;
Nor when thy warlike father, like a child,
Told the sad story of my father's death
And twenty times made pause to sob and weep,
That all the standers-by had wet their cheeks
Like trees bedash'd with rain in that sad time
My manly eyes did scorn an humble tear;
And what these sorrows could not thence exhale,
Thy beauty hath, and made them blind with weeping.
I never sued to friend nor enemy;
My tongue could never learn sweet smoothing word;
But, now thy beauty is propos'd my fee,
My proud heart sues, and prompts my tongue to speak.
She looks scornfully at him.
Teach not thy lip such scorn; for it was made
For kissing, lady, not for such contempt.
If thy revengeful heart cannot forgive,
Lo, here I lend thee this sharp-pointed sword,
Which if thou please to hide in this true breast
And let the soul forth that adoreth thee,
I lay it naked to the deadly stroke
And humbly beg the death upon my knee.
He [kneels and] lays his breast open. She offers at it with his sword.
Nay, do not pause; for I did kill King Henry —
But 'twas thy beauty that provoked me.
Nay, now dispatch. 'Twas I that stabb'd young Edward —

But 'twas thy heavenly face that set me on.
She falls the sword.
Take up the sword again, or take up me.
Anne. Arise, dissembler. Though I wish thy death,
I will not be thy executioner.
Rich. Then bid me kill myself, and I will do it. [*Rises, and takes up his sword.*]
Anne. I have already.
Rich. That was in thy rage.
Speak it again, and even with the word
This hand, which for thy love did kill thy love,
Shall for thy love kill a far truer love.
To both their deaths shalt thou be accessary.
Anne. I would I knew thy heart.
Rich. 'Tis figur'd in my tongue.
Anne. I fear me both are false.
Rich. Then never man was true.
Anne. Well, well, put up your sword.
Rich. Say then my peace is made.
Anne. That shalt thou know hereafter.
Rich. But shall I live in hope?
Anne. All men, I hope, live so.
Rich. Vouchsafe to wear this ring.
Anne. To take is not to give.
[*Puts on the ring.*]
Rich. Look how my ring encompasseth thy finger,
Even so thy breast encloseth my poor heart.
Wear both of them, for both of them are thine.
And if thy poor devoted servant may
But beg one favour at thy gracious hand,
Thou dost confirm his happiness for ever.
Anne. What is it?
Rich. That it may please you leave these sad designs
To him that hath most cause to be a mourner,
And presently repair to Crosby House;
Where — after I have solemnly interr'd
At Chertsey monast'ry this noble king
And wet his grave with my repentant tears
I will with all expedient duty see you.
For divers unknown reasons I beseech you,
Grant me this boon.
Anne. With all my heart; and much it joys me too
To see you are become so penitent.
Tressel and Berkeley, go along with me.
Rich. Bid me farewell.
Anne. 'Tis more than you deserve;
But since you teach me how to flatter you,
Imagine I have said farewell already.
Exeunt two, [*Tressel and Berkeley,*] *with Anne.*
Rich. Sirs, take up the corse.
Gent. Towards Chertsey, noble lord?
Rich. No, to White Friars. There attend my coming. *Exeunt. Manet Gloucester.*
Was ever woman in this humour woo'd?
Was ever woman in this humour won?
I'll have her, but I will not keep her long.
What? I that kill'd her husband and his father
To take her in her heart's extremest hate,
With curses in her mouth, tears in her eyes,
The bleeding witness of my hatred by,
Having God, her conscience, and these bars against me,
And I no friends to back my suit withal
But the plain devil and dissembling looks?
And yet to win her — all the world to nothing?
Ha!
Hath she forgot already that brave prince,
Edward, her lord, whom I, some three months since,
Stabb'd in my angry mood at Tewksbury?
A sweeter and a lovelier gentleman —
Fram'd in the prodigality of nature,
Young, valiant, wise, and (no doubt) right royal —
The spacious world cannot again afford;
And will she yet abase her eyes on me,
That cropp'd the golden prime of this sweet prince
And made her widow to a woful bed?
On me, whose all not equals Edward's moiety?
On me, that halt and am misshapen thus?
My dukedom to a beggarly denier,
I do mistake my person all this while!
Upon my life, she finds (although I cannot)
Myself to be a marv'llous proper man.
I'll be at charges for a looking glass
And entertain a score or two of tailors
To study fashions to adorn my body.
Since I am crept in favour with myself,
I will maintain it with some little cost.
But first I'll turn yon fellow in his grave,
And then return lamenting to my love.
Shine out, fair sun, till I have bought a glass,
That I may see my shadow as I pass. *Exit.*

Scene III. [*London. The Palace.*]

Enter *Queen* [*Elizabeth*], *Lord Rivers,* and *Lord Grey.*

Riv. Have patience, madam. There's no doubt his Majesty
Will soon recover his accustom'd health.
Grey. In that you brook it ill, it makes him worse.

Therefore for God's sake entertain good comfort
And cheer his Grace with quick and merry eyes.
Queen. If he were dead, what would betide on me?
Grey. No other harm but loss of such a lord.
Queen. The loss of such a lord includes all harms.
Grey. The heavens have bless'd you with a goodly son
To be your comforter when he is gone.
Queen. Ah, he is young; and his minority
Is put unto the trust of Richard Gloucester,
A man that loves not me, nor none of you.
Riv. Is it concluded he shall be Protector?
Queen. It is determin'd, not concluded yet;
But so it must be if the King miscarry.

Enter *Buckingham* and *Derby*.

Grey. Here come the lords of Buckingham and Derby.
Buck. Good time of day unto your royal Grace!
Der. God make your Majesty joyful, as you have been!
Queen. The Countess Richmond, good my Lord of Derby,
To your good prayer will scarcely say amen.
Yet, Derby, notwithstanding she's your wife
And loves not me, be you, good lord, assur'd
I hate not you for her proud arrogance.
Der. I do beseech you, either not believe
The envious slanders of her false accusers;
Or, if she be accus'd on true report,
Bear with her weakness, which I think proceeds
From wayward sickness, and no grounded malice.
Queen. Saw you the King to-day, my Lord of Derby?
Der. But now the Duke of Buckingham and I
Are come from visiting his Majesty.
Queen. What likelihood of his amendment, lords?
Buck. Madam, good hope. His Grace speaks cheerfully.
Queen. God grant him health! Did you confer with him?
Buck. Ay, madam. He desires to make atonement
Between the Duke of Gloucester and your brothers,
And between them and my Lord Chamberlain,
And sent to warn them to his royal presence.
Queen. Would all were well! but that will never be.
I fear our happiness is at the height.

Enter *Richard*, [*Hastings*, and *Dorset*].

Rich. They do me wrong, and I will not endure it!
Who is it that complains unto the King
That I (forsooth) am stern, and love them not?
By holy Paul, they love his Grace but lightly
That fill his ears with such dissentious rumours.
Because I cannot flatter and look fair,
Smile in men's faces, smooth, deceive, and cog,
Duck with French nods and apish courtesy,
I must be held a rancorous enemy.
Cannot a plain man live and think no harm
But thus his simple truth must be abus'd
With silken, sly, insinuating Jacks?
Grey. To whom in all this presence speaks your Grace?
Rich. To thee, that hast nor honesty nor grace.
When have I injur'd thee? when done thee wrong?
Or thee? or thee? or any of your faction?
A plague upon you all! His royal Grace
(Whom God preserve better than you would wish!)
Cannot be quiet scarce a breathing while
But you must trouble him with lewd complaints.
Queen. Brother of Gloucester, you mistake the matter.
The King, on his own royal disposition,
And not provok'd by any suitor else,
Aiming (belike) at your interior hatred,
That in your outward action shows itself
Against my children, brothers, and myself,
Makes him to send, that thereby he may gather
The ground of your ill will and so remove it.
Rich. I cannot tell. The world is grown so bad
That wrens make prey where eagles dare not perch.
Since every Jack became a gentleman,
There's many a gentle person made a Jack.
Queen. Come, come, we know your meaning, brother Gloucester:
You envy my advancement and my friends'.
God grant we never may have need of you!
Rich. Meantime, God grants that I have need of you.
Our brother is imprison'd by your means,
Myself disgrac'd, and the nobility
Held in contempt, while great promotions
Are daily given to ennoble those

That scarce, some two days since, were worth a noble.
Queen. By Him that rais'd me to this careful height
From that contented hap which I enjoy'd,
I never did incense his Majesty
Against the Duke of Clarence, but have been
An earnest advocate to plead for him.
My lord, you do me shameful injury
Falsely to draw me in these vile suspects.
Rich. You may deny that you were not the mean
Of my Lord Hastings' late imprisonment.
Riv. She may, my lord, for —
Rich. She may, Lord Rivers? Why, who knows not so?
She may do more, sir, than denying that:
She may help you to many fair preferments,
And then deny her aiding hand therein
And lay those honours on your high desert.
What may she not? She may — ay marry may she —
Riv. What marry may she?
Rich. What marry may she? Marry with a king,
A bachelor and a handsome stripling too.
Iwis your grandam had a worser match.
Queen. My Lord of Gloucester, I have too long borne
Your blunt upbraidings and your bitter scoffs.
By heaven, I will acquaint his Majesty
Of those gross taunts that oft I have endur'd.
I had rather be a country servant maid
Than a great queen with this condition,
To be so baited, scorn'd, and stormed at.

Enter old *Queen Margaret,* [behind].

Small joy have I in being England's Queen.
Q. Marg. [*aside*] And less'ned be that small, God I beseech him!
Thy honour, state, and seat is due to me.
Rich. What? Threat you me with telling of the King?
Tell him, and spare not. Look, what I have said
I will avouch't in presence of the King.
I dare adventure to be sent to th' Tower.
'Tis time to speak: my pains are quite forgot.
Q. Marg. [*aside*] Out, devil! I do remember them too well.
Thou kill'dst my husband Henry in the Tower,
And Edward, my poor son, at Tewksbury.
Rich. Ere you were Queen, ay, or your husband King,
I was a packhorse in his great affairs;
A weeder-out of his proud adversaries,
A liberal rewarder of his friends.
To royalize his blood I spent mine own.
Q. Marg. [*aside*] Ay, and much better blood than his or thine.
Rich. In all which time you and your husband Grey
Were factious for the house of Lancaster.
And, Rivers, so were you. Was not your husband
In Margaret's battle at Saint Alban's slain?
Let me put in your minds, if you forget,
What you have been ere this, and what you are;
Withal, what I have been, and what I am.
Q. Marg. [*aside*] A murth'rous villain, and so still thou art.
Rich. Poor Clarence did forsake his father Warwick;
Ay, and forswore himself (which Jesu pardon!) —
Q. Marg. [*aside*] Which God revenge!
Rich. To fight on Edward's party for the crown;
And for his meed, poor lord, he is mewed up.
I would to God my heart were flint like Edward's,
Or Edward's soft and pitiful like mine.
I am too childish-foolish for this world.
Q. Marg. [*aside*] Hie thee to hell for shame, and leave this world,
Thou cacodemon! There thy kingdom is.
Riv. My Lord of Gloucester, in those busy days
Which here you urge to prove us enemies,
We follow'd then our lord, our sovereign king.
So should we you, if you should be our king.
Rich. If I should be? I had rather be a pedlar.
Far be it from my heart, the thought thereof!
Queen. As little joy, my lord, as you suppose
You should enjoy, were you this country's king —
As little joy may you suppose in me
That I enjoy, being the queen thereof.
Q. Marg. [*aside*] As little joy enjoys the queen thereof;
For I am she, and altogether joyless.
I can no longer hold me patient. [*Comes forward.*]
Hear me, you wrangling pirates, that fall out
In sharing that which you have pill'd from me!
Which of you trembles not that looks on me?
If not that I am Queen, you bow like subjects,
Yet that, by you depos'd, you quake like rebels?
Ah, gentle villain, do not turn away!

Rich. Foul wrinkled witch, what mak'st thou in my sight?
Q. Marg. But repetition of what thou hast marr'd.
That will I make before I let thee go.
Rich. Wert thou not banished on pain of death?
Q. Marg. I was; but I do find more pain in banishment
Than death can yield me here by my abode.
A husband and a son thou ow'st to me —
And thou a kingdom — all of you allegiance.
This sorrow that I have, by right is yours,
And all the pleasures you usurp are mine.
Rich. The curse my noble father laid on thee
When thou didst crown his warlike brows with paper
And with thy scorns drew'st rivers from his eyes
And then, to dry them, gav'st the Duke a clout
Steep'd in the faultless blood of pretty Rutland —
His curses then, from bitterness of soul
Denounc'd against thee, are all fall'n upon thee;
And God, not we, hath plagu'd thy bloody deed.
Queen. So just is God, to right the innocent.
Hast. O, 'twas the foulest deed to slay that babe
And the most merciless that e'er was heard of!
Riv. Tyrants themselves wept when it was reported.
Dor. No man but prophesied revenge for it.
Buck. Northumberland, then present, wept to see it.
Q. Marg. What? Were you snarling all before I came,
Ready to catch each other by the throat,
And turn you all your hatred now on me?
Did York's dread curse prevail so much with heaven
That Henry's death, my lovely Edward's death,
Their kingdom's loss, my woful banishment,
Should all but answer for that peevish brat?
Can curses pierce the clouds and enter heaven?
Why then, give way, dull clouds, to my quick curses!
Though not by war, by surfeit die your king,
As ours by murther to make him a king!
Edward thy son, that now is Prince of Wales,
For Edward our son, that was Prince of Wales,
Die in his youth by like untimely violence!
Thyself a queen, for me that was a queen,
Outlive thy glory, like my wretched self!
Long mayst thou live to wail thy children's death
And see another, as I see thee now,
Deck'd in thy rights as thou art stall'd in mine!
Long die thy happy days before thy death,
And, after many length'ned hours of grief,
Die neither mother, wife, nor England's Queen!
Rivers and Dorset, you were standers-by,
And so wast thou, Lord Hastings, when my son
Was stabb'd with bloody daggers. God I pray him
That none of you may live his natural age,
But by some unlook'd accident cut off!
Rich. Have done thy charm, thou hateful wither'd hag!
Q. Marg. And leave out thee? Stay, dog, for thou shalt hear me.
If heaven have any grievous plague in store
Exceeding those that I can wish upon thee,
O let them keep it till thy sins be ripe,
And then hurl down their indignation
On thee, the troubler of the poor world's peace!
The worm of conscience still begnaw thy soul!
Thy friends suspect for traitors while thou liv'st,
And take deep traitors for thy dearest friends!
No sleep close up that deadly eye of thine,
Unless it be while some tormenting dream
Affrights thee with a hell of ugly devils!
Thou elvish-mark'd, abortive, rooting hog!
Thou that wast seal'd in thy nativity
The slave of nature and the son of hell!
Thou slander of thy heavy mother's womb!
Thou loathed issue of thy father's loins!
Thou rag of honour! thou detested —
Rich. Margaret.
Q. Marg. Richard!
Rich. Ha!
Q. Marg. I call thee not.
Rich. I cry thee mercy then; for I did think
That thou hadst call'd me all these bitter names.
Q. Marg. Why, so I did, but look'd for no reply.
O, let me make the period to my curse!
Rich. 'Tis done by me, and ends in 'Margaret.'
Queen. Thus have you breath'd your curse against yourself.
Q. Marg. Poor painted queen, vain flourish of my fortune!
Why strew'st thou sugar on that bottled spider
Whose deadly web ensnareth thee about?
Fool, fool! thou whet'st a knife to kill thyself.
The day will come that thou shalt wish for me
To help thee curse this poisonous bunch-back'd toad.
Hast. False-boding woman, end thy frantic curse,
Lest to thy harm thou move our patience.

Q. Marg. Foul shame upon you! You have all mov'd mine.

Riv. Were you well serv'd, you would be taught your duty.

Q. Marg. To serve me well, you all should do me duty,
Teach me to be your queen, and you my subjects.
O, serve me well, and teach yourselves that duty!

Dor. Dispute not with her; she is lunatic.

Q. Marg. Peace, Master Marquess, you are malapert.
Your fire-new stamp of honour is scarce current.
O that your young nobility could judge
What 'twere to lose it and be miserable!
They that stand high have many blasts to shake them,
And if they fall, they dash themselves to pieces.

Rich. Good counsel, marry! Learn it, learn it, Marquess.

Dor. It touches you, my lord, as much as me.

Rich. Ay, and much more; but I was born so high:
Our aëry buildeth in the cedar's top
And dallies with the wind and scorns the sun.

Q. Marg. And turns the sun to shade — alas! alas!
Witness my son, now in the shade of death,
Whose bright outshining beams thy cloudy wrath
Hath in eternal darkness folded up.
Your aëry buildeth in our aëry's nest.
O God, that seest it, do not suffer it!
As it is won with blood, lost be it so!

Buck. Peace, peace, for shame, if not for charity.

Q. Marg. Urge neither charity nor shame to me.
Uncharitably with me have you dealt,
And shamefully my hopes by you are butcher'd.
My charity is outrage, life my shame,
And in that shame still live my sorrow's rage!

Buck. Have done, have done.

Q. Marg. O princely Buckingham, I'll kiss thy hand
In sign of league and amity with thee.
Now fair befall thee and thy noble house!
Thy garments are not spotted with our blood,
Nor thou within the compass of my curse.

Buck. Nor no one here; for curses never pass
The lips of those that breathe them in the air.

Q. Marg. I will not think but they ascend the sky
And there awake God's gentle-sleeping peace.
O Buckingham, take heed of yonder dog!
Look, when he fawns he bites; and when he bites,
His venom tooth will rankle to the death.
Have not to do with him, beware of him;
Sin, death, and hell have set their marks on him,
And all their ministers attend on him.

Rich. What doth she say, my Lord of Buckingham?

Buck. Nothing that I respect, my gracious lord.

Q. Marg. What, dost thou scorn me for my gentle counsel
And soothe the devil that I warn thee from?
O, but remember this another day,
When he shall split thy very heart with sorrow,
And say poor Margaret was a prophetess!
Live each of you the subjects to his hate,
And he to yours, and all of you to God's!

Exit.

Hast. My hair doth stand an end to hear her curses.

Riv. And so doth mine. I muse why she's at liberty.

Rich. I cannot blame her. By God's holy Mother,
She hath had too much wrong, and I repent
My part thereof that I have done to her.

Queen. I never did her any to my knowledge.

Rich. Yet you have all the vantage of her wrong.
I was too hot to do somebody good
That is too cold in thinking of it now.
Marry, as for Clarence, he is well repaid;
He is frank'd up to fatting for his pains —
God pardon them that are the cause thereof!

Riv. A virtuous and a Christianlike conclusion —
To pray for them that have done scath to us.

Rich. So do I ever — (*speaks to himself*) being well advis'd;
For had I curs'd now, I had curs'd myself.

Enter *Catesby.*

Cates. Madam, his Majesty doth call for you;
And for your Grace; and you, my noble lords.

Queen. Catesby, I come. Lords, will you go with me?

Riv. We wait upon your Grace.

Exeunt all but Gloucester.

Rich. I do the wrong, and first begin to brawl.
The secret mischiefs that I set abroach
I lay unto the grievous charge of others.

Clarence, whom I indeed have cast in darkness,
I do beweep to many simple gulls —
Namely, to Derby, Hastings, Buckingham —
And tell them 'tis the Queen and her allies
That stir the King against the Duke my brother.
Now they believe it, and withal whet me
To be reveng'd on Rivers, Dorset, Grey.
But then I sigh, and, with a piece of Scripture,
Tell them that God bids us do good for evil;
And thus I clothe my naked villany
With odd old ends stol'n forth of holy writ,
And seem a saint when most I play the devil.

Enter two *Murtherers.*

But soft! Here come my executioners.
How now, my hardy, stout, resolved mates?
Are you now going to dispatch this thing?

Villain. We are, my lord, and come to have the warrant,
That we may be admitted where he is.

Rich. Well thought upon. I have it here about me: [*Gives the warrant.*]
When you have done, repair to Crosby Place.
But, sirs, be sudden in the execution;
Withal obdurate, do not hear him plead;
For Clarence is well-spoken, and perhaps
May move your hearts to pity if you mark him.

Villain. Tut, tut, my lord! we will not stand to prate;
Talkers are no good doers. Be assur'd
We go to use our hands, and not our tongues.

Rich. Your eyes drop millstones when fools' eyes fall tears.
I like you, lads. About your business straight.
Go, go, dispatch.

Villain. We will, my noble lord.

Exeunt.

Scene IV. [*London. The Tower.*]

Enter *Clarence* and *Keeper.*

Keep. Why looks your Grace so heavily to-day?

Clar. O, I have pass'd a miserable night,
So full of fearful dreams, of ugly sights,
That, as I am a Christian faithful man,
I would not spend another such a night
Though 'twere to buy a world of happy days —
So full of dismal terror was the time.

Keep. What was your dream, my lord? I pray you tell me.

Clar. Methoughts that I had broken from the Tower
And was embark'd to cross to Burgundy,
And in my company my brother Gloucester,
Who from my cabin tempted me to walk
Upon the hatches. Thence we look'd toward England
And cited up a thousand heavy times,
During the wars of York and Lancaster,
That had befall'n us. As we pac'd along
Upon the giddy footing of the hatches,
Methought that Gloucester stumbled, and in falling
Struck me (that thought to stay him) overboard
Into the tumbling billows of the main.
O Lord! methought what pain it was to drown!
What dreadful noise of water in mine ears!
What sights of ugly death within mine eyes!
Methoughts I saw a thousand fearful wracks;
A thousand men that fishes gnaw'd upon;
Wedges of gold, great anchors, heaps of pearl,
Inestimable stones, unvalued jewels,
All scatt'red in the bottom of the sea.
Some lay in dead men's skulls, and in the holes
Where eyes did once inhabit, there were crept
(As 'twere in scorn of eyes) reflecting gems,
That woo'd the slimy bottom of the deep
And mock'd the dead bones that lay scatt'red by.

Keep. Had you such leisure in the time of death
To gaze upon these secrets of the deep?

Clar. Methought I had; and often did I strive
To yield the ghost; but still the envious flood
Stopp'd in my soul, and would not let it forth
To find the empty, vast, and wand'ring air,
But smother'd it within my panting bulk,
Which almost burst to belch it in the sea.

Keep. Awak'd you not in this sore agony?

Clar. No, no, my dream was lengthen'd after life.
O, then began the tempest to my soul!
I pass'd (methought) the melancholy flood,
With that sour ferryman which poets write of,
Unto the kingdom of perpetual night.
The first that there did greet my stranger soul
Was my great father-in-law, renowned Warwick,
Who spake aloud 'What scourge for perjury
Can this dark monarchy afford false Clarence?'
And so he vanish'd. Then came wand'ring by
A shadow like an angel, with bright hair
Dabbled in blood, and he shriek'd out aloud
'Clarence is come — false, fleeting, perjur'd Clarence,
That stabb'd me in the field by Tewksbury.
Seize on him, Furies, take him unto torment!'

With that (methought) a legion of foul fiends
Environ'd me, and howled in mine ears
Such hideous cries that with the very noise
I trembling wak'd, and for a season after
Could not believe but that I was in hell,
Such terrible impression made my dream.

Keep. No marvel, lord, though it affrighted you.
I am afraid (methinks) to hear you tell it.

Clar. Ah, keeper, keeper, I have done these things
(That now give evidence against my soul)
For Edward's sake, and see how he requites me!
O God! if my deep pray'rs cannot appease thee,
But thou wilt be aveng'd on my misdeeds,
Yet execute thy wrath in me alone.
O, spare my guiltless wife and my poor children!
Keeper, I prithee sit by me awhile.
My soul is heavy, and I fain would sleep.

Keep. I will, my lord. God give your Grace good rest!

[*Clarence sleeps.*]

Enter *Brakenbury*, the *Lieutenant.*

Brak. Sorrow breaks seasons and reposing hours,
Makes the night morning and the noontide night.
Princes have but their titles for their glories,
An outward honour for an inward toil;
And for unfelt imaginations
They often feel a world of restless cares;
So that between their titles and low name
There's nothing differs but the outward fame.

Enter two *Murtherers.*

1. Murd. Ho! who's here?

Brak. What wouldst thou, fellow? and how cam'st thou hither?

1. Murd. I would speak with Clarence, and I came hither on my legs.

Brak. What, so brief?

2. Murd. 'Tis better, sir, than to be tedious.
Let him see our commission; and talk no more.

[*Brakenbury*] *reads it.*

Brak. I am, in this, commanded to deliver
The noble Duke of Clarence to your hands.
I will not reason what is meant hereby,
Because I will be guiltless from the meaning.
There lies the Duke asleep, and there the keys.
I'll to the King and signify to him
That thus I have resign'd to you my charge.

1. Murd. You may, sir; 'tis a point of wisdom. Fare you well.

Exit [*Brakenbury with Keeper*].

2. Murd. What? Shall we stab him as he sleeps?

1. Murd. No. He'll say 'twas done cowardly when he wakes.

2. Murd. When he wakes? Why, fool, he shall never wake until the great Judgment Day.

1. Murd. Why, then he'll say we stabb'd him sleeping.

2. Murd. The urging of that word 'judgment' hath bred a kind of remorse in me.

1. Murd. What? Art thou afraid?

2. Murd. Not to kill him, having a warrant; but to be damn'd for killing him, from the which no warrant can defend me.

1. Murd. I thought thou hadst been resolute.

2. Murd. So I am, to let him live.

1. Murd. I'll back to the Duke of Gloucester and tell him so.

2. Murd. Nay, I prithee stay a little. I hope this passionate humour of mine will change. It was wont to hold me but while one tells twenty.

1. Murd. How dost thou feel thyself now?

2. Murd. Faith, some certain dregs of conscience are yet within me.

1. Murd. Remember our reward when the deed's done.

2. Murd. Zounds, he dies! I had forgot the reward.

1. Murd. Where's thy conscience now?

2. Murd. O, in the Duke of Gloucester's purse.

1. Murd. So, when he opens his purse to give us our reward, thy conscience flies out.

2. Murd. 'Tis no matter; let it go. There's few or none will entertain it.

1. Murd. What if it come to thee again?

2. Murd. I'll not meddle with it; it makes a man a coward. A man cannot steal, but it accuseth him; a man cannot swear, but it checks him; a man cannot lie with his neighbour's wife, but it detects him. 'Tis a blushing shamefac'd spirit that mutinies in a man's bosom. It fills a man full of obstacles. It made me once restore a purse of gold that (by chance) I found. It beggars any man that keeps it. It is turn'd out of towns and cities for a dangerous thing, and every man that means to live well endeavours to trust to himself and live without it.

1. Murd. Zounds, it is even now at my elbow, persuading me not to kill the Duke.

2. Murd. Take the devil in thy mind, and believe him not. He would insinuate with thee but to make thee sigh.

1. Murd. I am strong-fram'd; he cannot prevail with me.

2. Murd. Spoke like a tall man that respects thy reputation. Come, shall we fall to work?

1. Murd. Take him on the costard with the hilts of thy sword, and then throw him into the malmsey butt in the next room.

2. Murd. O excellent device! and make a sop of him.

1. Murd. Soft! he wakes.

2. Murd. Strike!

1. Murd. No, we'll reason with him.

Clar. Where art thou, keeper? Give me a cup of wine.

1. Murd. You shall have wine enough, my lord, anon.

Clar. In God's name, what art thou?

1. Murd. A man, as you are.

Clar. But not as I am, royal.

1. Murd. Nor you as we are, loyal.

Clar. Thy voice is thunder, but thy looks are humble.

1. Murd. My voice is now the King's, my looks mine own.

Clar. How darkly and how deadly dost thou speak!
Your eyes do menace me. Why look you pale?
Who sent you hither? Wherefore do you come?

Both. To, to, to —

Clar. To murther me?

Both. Ay, ay.

Clar. You scarcely have the hearts to tell me so,
And therefore cannot have the hearts to do it.
Wherein, my friends, have I offended you?

1. Murd. Offended us you have not, but the King.

Clar. I shall be reconcil'd to him again.

2. Murd. Never, my lord; therefore prepare to die.

Clar. Are you drawn forth among a world of men
To slay the innocent? What is my offence?
Where is the evidence that doth accuse me?
What lawful quest have given their verdict up
Unto the frowning judge? or who pronounc'd
The bitter sentence of poor Clarence' death?
Before I be convict by course of law
To threaten me with death is most unlawful.
I charge you, as you hope to have redemption
By Christ's dear blood shed for our grievous sins,
That you depart, and lay no hands on me.
The deed you undertake is damnable.

1. Murd. What we will do, we do upon command.

2. Murd. And he that hath commanded is our king.

Clar. Erroneous vassals! the great King of Kings
Hath in the table of his law commanded
That thou shalt do no murther. Will you then
Spurn at his edict, and fulfil a man's?
Take heed; for he holds vengeance in his hand
To hurl upon their heads that break his law.

2. Murd. And that same vengeance doth he hurl on thee
For false forswearing and for murther too.
Thou didst receive the sacrament to fight
In quarrel of the house of Lancaster.

1. Murd. And like a traitor to the name of God
Didst break that vow, and with thy treacherous blade
Unrip'dst the bowels of thy sov'reign's son.

2. Murd. Whom thou wast sworn to cherish and defend.

1. Murd. How canst thou urge God's dreadful law to us
When thou hast broke it in such dear degree?

Clar. Alas! for whose sake did I that ill deed?
For Edward, for my brother, for his sake.
He sends you not to murther me for this,
For in that sin he is as deep as I.
If God will be avenged for the deed,
O, know you yet he doth it publicly!
Take not the quarrel from his pow'rful arm.
He needs no indirect or lawless course
To cut off those that have offended him.

1. Murd. Who made thee then a bloody minister
When gallant-springing brave Plantagenet,
That princely novice, was struck dead by thee?

Clar. My brother's love, the devil, and my rage.

1. Murd. Thy brother's love, our duty, and thy faults
Provoke us hither now to slaughter thee.

Clar. If you do love my brother, hate not me;
I am his brother, and I love him well.
If you are hir'd for meed, go back again,
And I will send you to my brother Gloucester,
Who shall reward you better for my life
Than Edward will for tidings of my death.

2. Murd. You are deceiv'd. Your brother Gloucester hates you.

Clar. O, no, he loves me and he holds me dear.
Go you to him from me.

1. Murd. Ay, so we will.

Clar. Tell him, when that our princely father York
Bless'd his three sons with his victorious arm
And charg'd us from his soul to love each other,
He little thought of this divided friendship.
Bid Gloucester think on this, and he will weep.
1. Murd. Ay, millstones, as he lessoned us to weep.
Clar. O, do not slander him, for he is kind.
1. Murd. Right,
As snow in harvest. Come, you deceive yourself.
'Tis he that sends us to destroy you here.
Clar. It cannot be, for he bewept my fortune,
And hugg'd me in his arms, and swore with sobs
That he would labour my delivery.
1. Murd. Why, so he doth when he delivers you
From this earth's thraldom to the joys of heaven.
2. Murd. Make peace with God, for you must die, my lord.
Clar. Have you that holy feeling in your souls
To counsel me to make my peace with God,
And are you yet to your own souls so blind
That you will war with God by murd'ring me?
O sirs, consider, they that set you on
To do this deed will hate you for the deed.
2. Murd. What shall we do?
Clar. Relent, and save your souls.
1. Murd. Relent? 'tis cowardly and womanish.
Clar. Not to relent is beastly, savage, devilish.
Which of you, if you were a prince's son,
Being pent from liberty, as I am now,
If two such murtherers as yourselves came to you,
Would not entreat for life?
My friend, I spy some pity in thy looks.
O, if thine eye be not a flatterer,
Come thou on my side, and entreat for me
As you would beg, were you in my distress.
A begging prince what beggar pities not?
2. Murd. Look behind you, my lord!
1. Murd. Take that! and that! (*Stabs him.*)
If all this will not do,
I'll drown you in the malmsey butt within.
Exit [*with the body*].
2. Murd. A bloody deed, and desperately dispatch'd!
How fain (like Pilate) would I wash my hands
Of this most grievous guilty murther!

Enter *First Murtherer.*

1. Murd. How now? What mean'st thou that thou help'st me not?
By heaven, the Duke shall know how slack you have been.
2. Murd. I would he knew that I had sav'd his brother!
Take thou the fee and tell him what I say,
For I repent me that the Duke is slain. *Exit.*
1. Murd. So do not I. Go, coward as thou art.
Well, I'll go hide the body in some hole
Till that the Duke give order for his burial;
And when I have my meed, I will away,
For this will out, and then I must not stay.
Exit.

ACT II. Scene I. [*London. The Palace.*]

Flourish. Enter the *King*, [*Edward*,] sick, the *Queen, Lord Marquess Dorset, Rivers, Hastings, Catesby, Buckingham*, [*Grey*, and others].

King. Why, so! Now have I done a good day's work.
You peers, continue this united league.
I every day expect an embassage
From my Redeemer to redeem me hence;
And more in peace my soul shall part to heaven,
Since I have made my friends at peace on earth.
Rivers and Hastings, take each other's hand;
Dissemble not your hatred, swear your love.
Riv. By heaven, my soul is purg'd from grudging hate,
And with my hand I seal my true heart's love.
Hast. So thrive I as I truly swear the like!
King. Take heed you dally not before your king,
Lest he that is the supreme King of Kings
Confound your hidden falsehood and award
Either of you to be the other's end.
Hast. So prosper I as I swear perfect love!
Riv. And I as I love Hastings with my heart!
King. Madam, yourself are not exempt from this;
Nor you, son Dorset; Buckingham, nor you:
You have been factious one against the other.
Wife, love Lord Hastings, let him kiss your hand,
And what you do, do it unfeignedly.

Queen. There, Hastings. I will never more remember
Our former hatred, so thrive I and mine!
King. Dorset, embrace him; Hastings, love Lord Marquess.
Dor. This interchange of love, I here protest,
Upon my part shall be inviolable.
Hast. And so swear I.
[*They embrace*.]
King. Now, princely Buckingham, seal thou this league
With thy embracements to my wive's allies,
And make me happy in your unity.
Buck. [*to the Queen*] Whenever Buckingham doth turn his hate
Upon your Grace, but with all duteous love
Doth cherish you and yours, God punish me
With hate in those where I expect most love!
When I have most need to employ a friend,
And most assured that he is a friend,
Deep, hollow, treacherous, and full of guile
Be he unto me! This do I beg of heaven,
When I am cold in love to you or yours.
Embrace.
King. A pleasing cordial, princely Buckingham,
Is this thy vow unto my sickly heart.
There wanteth now our brother Gloucester here
To make the blessed period of this peace.

Enter *Gloucester*.

Buck. And in good time here comes the noble Duke.
Rich. Good morrow to my sovereign King and Queen
And princely peers. A happy time of day!
King. Happy indeed, as we have spent the day.
Gloucester, we have done deeds of charity,
Made peace of enmity, fair love of hate,
Between these swelling wrong-incensed peers.
Rich. A blessed labour, my most sovereign lord.
Among this princely heap, if any here
By false intelligence or wrong surmise
Hold me a foe —
If I unwittingly, or in my rage,
Have aught committed that is hardly borne
By any in this presence, I desire
To reconcile me to his friendly peace.
'Tis death to me to be at enmity:
I hate it, and desire all good men's love.
First, madam, I entreat true peace of you,
Which I will purchase with my duteous service;
Of you, my noble cousin Buckingham,
If ever any grudge were lodg'd between us;
Of you, Lord Rivers, and, Lord Grey, of you,
That all without desert have frown'd on me;
Dukes, earls, lords, gentlemen — indeed, of all.
I do not know that Englishman alive
With whom my soul is any jot at odds
More than the infant that is born to-night.
I thank my God for my humility.
Queen. A holy day shall this be kept hereafter.
I would to God all strifes were well compounded.
My sovereign lord, I do beseech your Highness
To take our brother Clarence to your grace.
Rich. Why, madam, have I off'red love for this,
To be so flouted in this royal presence?
Who knows not that the gentle duke is dead?
They all start.
You do him injury to scorn his corse.
King. Who knows not he is dead? Who knows he is?
Queen. All-seeing heaven, what a world is this!
Buck. Look I so pale, Lord Dorset, as the rest?
Dor. Ay, my good lord; and no man in the presence
But his red colour hath forsook his cheeks.
King. Is Clarence dead? The order was revers'd.
Rich. But he (poor soul) by your first order died,
And that a winged Mercury did bear.
Some tardy cripple bore the countermand,
That came too lag to see him buried.
God grant that some, less noble and less loyal,
Nearer in bloody thoughts, but not in blood,
Deserve not worse than wretched Clarence did.
And yet go current from suspicion!

Enter *Derby*.

Der. A boon, my sovereign, for my service done!
[*Kneels*.]
King. I prithee peace. My soul is full of sorrow.
Der. I will not rise unless your Highness hear me.
King. Then say at once what is it thou requests.
Der. The forfeit, sovereign, of my servant's life,
Who slew to-day a riotous gentleman
Lately attendant on the Duke of Norfolk.
King. Have I a tongue to doom my brother's death

And shall that tongue give pardon to a slave?
My brother kill'd no man: his fault was thought,
And yet his punishment was bitter death.
Who sued to me for him? Who (in my wrath)
Kneel'd at my feet and bid me be advis'd?
Who spoke of brotherhood? Who spoke of love?
Who told me how the poor soul did forsake
The mighty Warwick and did fight for me?
Who told me, in the field at Tewksbury,
When Oxford had me down, he rescued me
And said, 'Dear brother, live, and be a king'?
Who told me, when we both lay in the field
Frozen (almost) to death, how he did lap me
Even in his garments, and did give himself
(All thin and naked) to the numb cold night?
All this from my remembrance brutish wrath
Sinfully pluck'd, and not a man of you
Had so much grace to put it in my mind.
But when your carters or your waiting vassals
Have done a drunken slaughter and defac'd
The precious image of our dear Redeemer,
You straight are on your knees for pardon, pardon;
And I (unjustly too) must grant it you.
[*Derby rises.*]
But for my brother not a man would speak,
Nor I (ungracious) speak unto myself
For him, poor soul! The proudest of you all
Have been beholding to him in his life;
Yet none of you would once beg for his life.
O God, I fear thy justice will take hold
On me and you, and mine and yours, for this!
Come, Hastings, help me to my closet. Ah, poor Clarence!
Exeunt some with King and Queen.

Rich. This is the fruit of rashness! Mark'd you not
How that the guilty kindred of the Queen
Look'd pale when they did hear of Clarence' death?
O, they did urge it still unto the King!
God will revenge it. Come, lords, will you go
To comfort Edward with our company?

Buck. We wait upon your Grace. *Exeunt.*

Scene II. [*London. The Palace.*]

Enter the old *Duchess of York,* with the two Children of *Clarence.*

Boy. Good grandam, tell us, is our father dead?

Duch. No, boy.

Daughter. Why do you weep so oft, and beat your breast,
And cry 'O Clarence, my unhappy son'?

Boy. Why do you look on us, and shake your head,
And call us orphans, wretches, castaways,
If that our noble father were alive?

Duch. My pretty cousins, you mistake me both.
I do lament the sickness of the King,
As loath to lose him, not your father's death.
It were lost sorrow to wail one that's lost.

Boy. Then you conclude, my grandam, he is dead.
The King mine uncle is to blame for this.
God will revenge it, whom I will importune
With earnest prayers all to that effect.

Daughter. And so will I.

Duch. Peace, children, peace! The King doth love you well.
Incapable and shallow innocents,
You cannot guess who caus'd your father's death.

Boy. Grandam, we can; for my good uncle Gloucester
Told me the King, provok'd to it by the Queen,
Devis'd impeachments to imprison him;
And when my uncle told me so, he wept,
And pitied me, and kindly kiss'd my cheek;
Bade me rely on him as on my father,
And he would love me dearly as a child.

Duch. Ah, that deceit should steal such gentle shape
And with a virtuous visor hide deep vice!
He is my son — ay, and therein my shame;
Yet from my dugs he drew not this deceit.

Boy. Think you my uncle did dissemble, grandam?

Duch. Ay, boy.

Boy. I cannot think it. Hark! What noise is this?

Enter *Queen* [*Elizabeth*] with her hair about her ears, *Rivers* and *Dorset* after her.

Queen. Ah, who shall hinder me to wail and weep,
To chide my fortune, and torment myself?
I'll join with black despair against my soul
And to myself become an enemy.

Duch. What means this scene of rude impatience?

Queen. To make an act of tragic violence.
Edward, my lord, thy son, our king, is dead!
Why grow the branches when the root is gone?
Why wither not the leaves that want their sap?

If you will live, lament; if die, be brief,
That our swift-winged souls may catch the King's,
Or like obedient subjects follow him
To his new kingdom of ne'er-changing night.
Duch. Ah, so much interest have I in thy sorrow
As I had title in thy noble husband.
I have bewept a worthy husband's death,
And liv'd with looking on his images;
But now two mirrors of his princely semblance
Are crack'd in pieces by malignant death,
And I for comfort have but one false glass
That grieves me when I see my shame in him.
Thou art a widow; yet thou art a mother
And hast the comfort of thy children left;
But death hath snatch'd my husband from mine arms
And pluck'd two crutches from my feeble hands,
Clarence and Edward. O, what cause have I
(Thine being but a moiety of my moan)
To overgo thy woes and drown thy cries!
Boy. Good aunt, you wept not for our father's death.
How can we aid you with our kindred tears?
Daughter. Our fatherless distress was left unmoan'd.
Your widow-dolour likewise be unwept!
Queen. Give me no help in lamentation;
I am not barren to bring forth complaints.
All springs reduce their currents to mine eyes,
That I, being govern'd by the watery moon,
May send forth plenteous tears to drown the world.
Ah for my husband, for my dear lord Edward!
Children. Ah for our father, for our dear lord Clarence!
Duch. Alas for both, both mine, Edward and Clarence!
Queen. What stay had I but Edward? and he's gone.
Children. What stay had we but Clarence? and he's gone.
Duch. What stays had I but they? and they are gone.
Queen. Was never widow had so dear a loss.
Children. Were never orphans had so dear a loss.
Duch. Was never mother had so dear a loss.
Alas, I am the mother of these griefs!
Their woes are parcell'd, mine is general.
She for an Edward weeps, and so do I;
I for a Clarence weep, so doth not she:
These babes for Clarence weep, and so do I;
I for an Edward weep, so do not they.
Alas, you three on me, threefold distress'd,
Pour all your tears! I am your sorrow's nurse,
And I will pamper it with lamentation.
Dor. Comfort, dear mother. God is much displeas'd
That you take with unthankfulness his doing.
In common worldly things 'tis call'd ungrateful
With dull unwillingness to repay a debt
Which with a bounteous hand was kindly lent;
Much more to be thus opposite with heaven
For it requires the royal debt it lent you.
Riv. Madam, bethink you like a careful mother
Of the young Prince your son. Send straight for him;
Let him be crown'd; in him your comfort lives.
Drown desperate sorrow in dead Edward's grave
And plant your joys in living Edward's throne.

Enter *Richard, Buckingham, Derby, Hastings,* and *Ratcliff.*

Rich. Sister, have comfort. All of us have cause
To wail the dimming of our shining star;
But none can help our harms by wailing them.
Madam, my mother, I do cry you mercy;
I did not see your Grace. Humbly on my knee
I crave your blessing.
Duch. God bless thee, and put meekness in thy breast,
Love, charity, obedience, and true duty!
Rich. Amen! — [*aside*] and make me die a good old man!
That is the butt end of a mother's blessing.
I marvel that her Grace did leave it out.
Buck. You cloudy princes and heart-sorrowing peers
That bear this heavy mutual load of moan,
Now cheer each other in each other's love.
Though we have spent our harvest of this king,
We are to reap the harvest of his son.
The broken rancour of your high-swol'n hates,
But lately splinter'd, knit, and join'd together,
Must gently be preserv'd, cherish'd, and kept.
Me seemeth good that with some little train
Forthwith from Ludlow the young Prince be fet
Hither to London, to be crown'd our king.
Riv. Why with some little train, my Lord of Buckingham?
Buck. Marry, my lord, lest by a multitude
The new-heal'd wound of malice should break out,
Which would be so much the more dangerous

By how much the estate is green and yet ungovern'd.
Where every horse bears his commanding rein
And may direct his course as please himself,
As well the fear of harm as harm apparent,
In my opinion, ought to be prevented.

Rich. I hope the King made peace with all of us;
And the compact is firm and true in me.

Riv. And so in me; and so (I think) in all.
Yet, since it is but green, it should be put
To no apparent likelihood of breach,
Which haply by much company might be urg'd.
Therefore I say with noble Buckingham
That it is meet so few should fetch the Prince.

Hast. And so say I.

Rich. Then be it so; and go we to determine
Who they shall be that straight shall post to Ludlow.
Madam, and you, my sister, will you go
To give your censures in this business?

Both. With all our hearts.

Exeunt. Manent Buckingham and Richard.

Buck. My lord, whoever journeys to the Prince,
For God's sake let not us two stay at home;
For by the way I'll sort occasion,
As index to the story we late talk'd of,
To part the Queen's proud kindred from the Prince.

Rich. My other self, my counsel's consistory,
My oracle, my prophet, my dear cousin,
I, as a child, will go by thy direction.
Toward Ludlow then, for we'll not stay behind.

Exeunt.

Scene III. [*London. A street.*]

Enter one *Citizen* at one door and another at the other.

1. Cit. Good morrow, neighbour. Whither away so fast?

2. Cit. I promise you I scarcely know myself.
Hear you the news abroad?

1. Cit. Yes, that the King is dead.

2. Cit. Ill news, by'r Lady. Seldom comes the better.
I fear, I fear 'twill prove a giddy world.

Enter another *Citizen.*

3. Cit. Neighbours, God speed!

1. Cit. Give you good morrow, sir.

3. Cit. Doth the news hold of good King Edward's death?

2. Cit. Ay, sir, it is too true. God help the while!

3. Cit. Then, masters, look to see a troublous world.

1. Cit. No, no! By God's good grace his son shall reign.

3. Cit. Woe to that land that's govern'd by a child!

2. Cit. In him there is a hope of government,
That, in his nonage, council under him,
And, in his full and ripened years, himself,
No doubt shall then, and till then, govern well.

1. Cit. So stood the state when Henry the Sixth
Was crown'd in Paris but at nine months old.

3. Cit. Stood the state so? No, no, good friends, God wot!
For then this land was famously enrich'd
With politic grave counsel; then the King
Had virtuous uncles to protect his Grace.

1. Cit. Why, so hath this, both by his father and mother.

3. Cit. Better it were they all came by his father,
Or by his father there were none at all;
For emulation who shall now be nearest
Will touch us all too near, if God prevent not.
O, full of danger is the Duke of Gloucester,
And the Queen's sons and brothers haught and proud;
And were they to be rul'd, and not to rule,
This sickly land might solace as before.

1. Cit. Come, come, we fear the worst. All will be well.

3. Cit. When clouds are seen, wise men put on their cloaks;
When great leaves fall, then winter is at hand;
When the sun sets, who doth not look for night?
Untimely storms make men expect a dearth.
All may be well; but if God sort it so,
'Tis more than we deserve or I expect.

2. Cit. Truly, the hearts of men are full of fear.
You cannot reason (almost) with a man
That looks not heavily and full of dread.

3. Cit. Before the days of change, still is it so.
By a divine instinct men's minds mistrust
Ensuing danger; as by proof we see
The water swell before a boist'rous storm.
But leave it all to God. Whither away?

2. Cit. Marry, we were sent for to the justices.

3. Cit. And so was I. I'll bear you company.

Exeunt.

Scene IV. [*London. The Palace.*]

Enter [the] *Archbishop* [*of York*], [the] young [*Duke of*] *York*, *Queen* [*Elizabeth*], and the *Duchess of York*.

Arch. Last night, I hear, they lay at Northampton;
At Stony Stratford they do rest to-night;
To-morrow or next day they will be here.
Duch. I long with all my heart to see the Prince.
I hope he is much grown since last I saw him.
Queen. But I hear no. They say my son of York
Has almost overta'en him in his growth.
York. Ay, mother; but I would not have it so.
Duch. Why, my young cousin, it is good to grow.
York. Grandam, one night as we did sit at supper,
My uncle Rivers talk'd how I did grow
More than my brother. 'Ay,' quoth my uncle Gloucester,
'Small herbs have grace; great weeds do grow apace.'
And since, methinks, I would not grow so fast,
Because sweet flow'rs are slow and weeds make haste.
Duch. Good faith, good faith, the saying did not hold
In him that did object the same to thee.
He was the wretched'st thing when he was young,
So long a-growing and so leisurely
That, if his rule were true, he should be gracious.
Arch. And so no doubt he is, my gracious madam.
Duch. I hope he is; but yet let mothers doubt.
York. Now, by my troth, if I had been rememb'red,
I could have given my uncle's Grace a flout
To touch his growth nearer than he touch'd mine.
Duch. How, my young York? I prithee let me hear it.
York. Marry, they say my uncle grew so fast
That he could gnaw a crust at two hours old.
'Twas full two years ere I could get a tooth.
Grandam, this would have been a biting jest.
Duch. I prithee, pretty York, who told thee this?
York. Grandam, his nurse.
Duch. His nurse? Why, she was dead ere thou wast born.
York. If 'twere not she, I cannot tell who told me.
Queen. A parlous boy! Go to, you are too shrewd.
Duch. Good madam, be not angry with the child.
Queen. Pitchers have ears.

Enter a *Messenger*.

Arch. Here comes a messenger. What news?
Mess. Such news, my lord, as grieves me to report.
Queen. How doth the Prince?
Mess. Well, madam, and in health.
Duch. What is thy news then?
Mess. Lord Rivers and Lord Grey are sent to Pomfret,
With them Sir Thomas Vaughan, prisoners.
Duch. Who hath committed them?
Mess. The mighty Dukes,
Gloucester and Buckingham.
Arch. For what offence?
Mess. The sum of all I can I have disclos'd.
Why or for what the nobles were committed
Is all unknown to me, my gracious lord.
Queen. Ay me! I see the ruin of our house.
The tiger now hath seiz'd the gentle hind;
Insulting tyranny begins to jut
Upon the innocent and aweless throne.
Welcome destruction, blood, and massacre!
I see (as in a map) the end of all.
Duch. Accursed and unquiet wrangling days,
How many of you have mine eyes beheld!
My husband lost his life to get the crown,
And often up and down my sons were toss'd
For me to joy and weep their gain and loss;
And being seated, and domestic broils
Clean overblown, themselves the conquerors
Make war upon themselves, brother to brother,
Blood to blood, self against self. O preposterous
And frantic outrage, end thy damned spleen,
Or let me die, to look on death no more!
Queen. Come, come, my boy; we will to sanctuary.
Madam, farewell.
Duch. Stay, I will go with you.
Queen. You have no cause.
Arch. [*to the Queen*] My gracious lady, go,
And thither bear your treasure and your goods.
For my part, I'll resign unto your Grace
The seal I keep; and so betide to me
As well I tender you and all of yours!
Go, I'll conduct you to the sanctuary. *Exeunt.*

Act III. Scene I. [*London. A street.*]

The trumpets sound. Enter young *Prince,* the *Dukes of Gloucester* and *Buckingham, Lord Cardinal* [*Bourchier, Catesby,*] with others.

Buck. Welcome, sweet Prince, to London, to your chamber.
Rich. Welcome, dear cousin, my thoughts' sovereign.
The weary way hath made you melancholy.
Prince. No, uncle; but our crosses on the way
Have made it tedious, wearisome, and heavy.
I want more uncles here to welcome me.
Rich. Sweet Prince, the untainted virtue of your years
Hath not yet div'd into the world's deceit.
No more can you distinguish of a man
Than of his outward show; which, God he knows,
Seldom or never jumpeth with the heart.
Those uncles which you want were dangerous.
Your Grace attended to their sug'red words
But look'd not on the poison of their hearts:
God keep you from them, and from such false friends!
Prince. God keep me from false friends! But they were none.
Rich. My lord, the Mayor of London comes to greet you.

Enter *Lord Mayor* [and his *Train*].

L. May. God bless your Grace with health and happy days!
Prince. I thank you, good my lord, and thank you all.
[*Mayor and his Train retire.*]
I thought my mother and my brother York
Would long ere this have met us on the way.
Fie, what a slug is Hastings that he comes not
To tell us whether they will come or no!

Enter *Lord Hastings.*

Buck. And, in good time, here comes the sweating lord.
Prince. Welcome, my lord. What, will our mother come?
Hast. On what occasion God he knows, not I,
The Queen your mother and your brother York
Have taken sanctuary. The tender Prince
Would fain have come with me to meet your Grace,
But by his mother was perforce withheld.
Buck. Fie, what an indirect and peevish course
Is this of hers! Lord Cardinal, will your Grace
Persuade the Queen to send the Duke of York
Unto his princely brother presently?
If she deny, Lord Hastings, go with him
And from her jealous arms pluck him perforce.
Card. My Lord of Buckingham, if my weak oratory
Can from his mother win the Duke of York,
Anon expect him here; but if she be obdurate
To mild entreaties, God in heaven forbid
We should infringe the holy privilege
Of blessed sanctuary! Not for all this land
Would I be guilty of so great a sin.
Buck. You are too senseless-obstinate, my lord,
Too ceremonious and traditional.
Weigh it but with the grossness of his age,
You break not sanctuary in seizing him.
The benefit thereof is always granted
To those whose dealings have deserv'd the place
And those who have the wit to claim the place.
This prince hath neither claim'd it nor deserv'd it,
And therefore, in mine opinion, cannot have it.
Then, taking him from thence that is not there,
You break no privilege nor charter there.
Oft have I heard of sanctuary men,
But sanctuary children ne'er till now.
Card. My lord, you shall o'errule my mind for once.
Come on, Lord Hastings, will you go with me?
Hast. I go, my lord.
Prince. Good lords, make all the speedy haste you may.
Exeunt Cardinal and Hastings.
Say, uncle Gloucester, if our brother come,
Where shall we sojourn till our coronation?
Rich. Where it think'st best unto your royal self.
If I may counsel you, some day or two
Your Highness shall repose you at the Tower;
Then where you please, and shall be thought most fit
For your best health and recreation.
Prince. I do not like the Tower, of any place.
Did Julius Cæsar build that place, my lord?
Buck. He did, my gracious lord, begin that place,
Which, since, succeeding ages have re-edified.

Prince. Is it upon record, or else reported
Successively from age to age, he built it?
Buck. Upon record, my gracious lord.
Prince. But say, my lord, it were not regis- t'red,
Methinks the truth should live from age to age,
As 'twere retail'd to all posterity,
Even to the general all-ending day.
Rich. [*aside*] So wise so young, they say do never live long.
Prince. What say you, uncle?
Rich. I say, without characters fame lives long.
[*Aside*] Thus, like the formal vice, Iniquity,
I moralize two meanings in one word.
Prince. That Julius Cæsar was a famous man.
With what his valour did enrich his wit,
His wit set down to make his valour live.
Death makes no conquest of this conqueror,
For now he lives in fame, though not in life.
I'll tell you what, my cousin Buckingham —
Buck. What, my gracious lord?
Prince. An if I live until I be a man,
I'll win our ancient right in France again
Or die a soldier as I liv'd a king.
Rich. [*aside*] Short summers lightly have a forward spring.

Enter young *York, Hastings,* and *Cardinal.*

Buck. Now in good time, here comes the Duke of York.
Prince. Richard of York, how fares our noble brother?
York. Well, my dread lord — so must I call you now.
Prince. Ay, brother — to our grief, as it is yours.
Too late he died that might have kept that title,
Which by his death hath lost much majesty.
Rich. How fares our cousin, noble Lord of York?
York. I thank you, gentle uncle. O, my lord,
You said that idle weeds are fast in growth.
The Prince my brother hath outgrown me far.
Rich. He hath, my lord.
York. And therefore is he idle?
Rich. O my fair cousin, I must not say so.
York. Then he is more beholding to you than I.
Rich. He may command me as my sovereign,
But you have power in me as in a kinsman.
York. I pray you, uncle, give me this dagger.
Rich. My dagger, little cousin? With all my heart.
Prince. A beggar, brother?
York. Of my kind uncle, that I know will give,
And being but a toy, which is no grief to give.
Rich. A greater gift than that I'll give my cousin.
York. A greater gift? O, that's the sword to it.
Rich. Ay, gentle cousin, were it light enough.
York. O, then I see you will part but with light gifts!
In weightier things you'll say a beggar nay.
Rich. It is too weighty for your Grace to wear.
York. I weigh it lightly, were it heavier.
Rich. What, would you have my weapon, little lord?
York. I would, that I might thank you as you call me.
Rich. How?
York. Little.
Prince. My Lord of York will still be cross in talk.
Uncle, your Grace knows how to bear with him.
York. You mean, to bear me, not to bear with me.
Uncle, my brother mocks both you and me:
Because that I am little, like an ape,
He thinks that you should bear me on your shoulders.
Buck. [*aside to Hastings*] With what a sharp-provided wit he reasons!
To mitigate the scorn he gives his uncle,
He prettily and aptly taunts himself.
So cunning, and so young, is wonderful.
Rich. My lord, will 't please you pass along?
Myself and my good cousin Buckingham
Will to your mother, to entreat of her
To meet you at the Tower and welcome you.
York. What, will you go unto the Tower, my lord?
Prince. My Lord Protector needs will have it so.
York. I shall not sleep in quiet at the Tower.
Rich. Why, what should you fear?
York. Marry, my uncle Clarence' angry ghost.
My grandam told me he was murther'd there.
Prince. I fear no uncles dead.
Rich. Nor none that live, I hope.
Prince. An if they live, I hope I need not fear.

But come, my lord; and with a heavy heart,
Thinking on them, go I unto the Tower.

A sennet. Exeunt Prince, York, Hastings, [Cardinal, and others]. Manent Richard, Buckingham, and Catesby.

Buck. Think you, my lord, this little prating York
Was not incensed by his subtile mother
To taunt and scorn you thus opprobriously?

Rich. No doubt, no doubt. O, 'tis a parlous boy,
Bold, quick, ingenious, forward, capable.
He is all the mother's, from the top to toe.

Buck. Well, let them rest. Come hither, Catesby.
Thou art sworn as deeply to effect what we intend
As closely to conceal what we impart.
Thou know'st our reasons urg'd upon the way.
What think'st thou? Is it not an easy matter
To make William Lord Hastings of our mind
For the instalment of this noble Duke
In the seat royal of this famous isle?

Cates. He for his father's sake so loves the Prince
That he will not be won to aught against him.

Buck. What think'st thou then of Stanley? Will not he?

Cates. He will do all in all as Hastings doth.

Buck. Well then, no more but this: go, gentle Catesby,
And, as it were far off, sound thou Lord Hastings
How he doth stand affected to our purpose,
And summon him to-morrow to the Tower
To sit about the coronation.
If thou dost find him tractable to us,
Encourage him, and tell him all our reasons:
If he be leaden, icy, cold, unwilling,
Be thou so too, and so break off the talk,
And give us notice of his inclination;
For we to-morrow hold divided councils,
Wherein thyself shalt highly be employ'd.

Rich. Commend me to Lord William. Tell him, Catesby,
His ancient knot of dangerous adversaries
To-morrow are let blood at Pomfret Castle,
And bid my lord, for joy of this good news,
Give Mistress Shore one gentle kiss the more.

Buck. Good Catesby, go effect this business soundly.

Cates. My good lords both, with all the heed I can.

Rich. Shall we hear from you, Catesby, ere we sleep?

Cates. You shall, my lord.

Rich. At Crosby House, there shall you find us both.

Exit Catesby.

Buck. Now, my lord, what shall we do if we perceive
Lord Hastings will not yield to our complots?

Rich. Chop off his head! Something we will determine.
And look, when I am King, claim thou of me
The earldom of Hereford and all the moveables
Whereof the King my brother was possess'd.

Buck. I'll claim that promise at your Grace's hand.

Rich. And look to have it yielded with all kindness.
Come, let us sup betimes, that afterwards
We may digest our complots in some form.

Exeunt.

Scene II. [*Before the house of* Lord Hastings.]

Enter a *Messenger* to the door of *Hastings.*

Mess. My lord! my lord!

Hast. [*within*] Who knocks?

Mess. One from the Lord Stanley.

Hast. [*within*] What is't o'clock?

Mess. Upon the stroke of four.

Enter *Lord Hastings.*

Hast. Cannot my Lord Stanley sleep these tedious nights?

Mess. So it appears by that I have to say.
First, he commends him to your noble self.

Hast. What then?

Mess. Then certifies your lordship that this night
He dreamt the boar had rased off his helm.
Besides, he says there are two councils kept;
And that may be determin'd at the one
Which may make you and him to rue at th' other.
Therefore he sends to know your lordship's pleasure,
If you will presently take horse with him
And with all speed post with him toward the North
To shun the danger that his soul divines.

Hast. Go, fellow, go, return unto thy lord;
Bid him not fear the separated councils.
His Honour and myself are at the one,
And at the other is my good friend Catesby;

Where nothing can proceed that toucheth us
Whereof I shall not have intelligence.
Tell him his fears are shallow, without instance;
And for his dreams, I wonder he's so simple
To trust the mock'ry of unquiet slumbers.
To fly the boar before the boar pursues
Were to incense the boar to follow us
And make pursuit where he did mean no chase.
Go, bid thy master rise and come to me,
And we will both together to the Tower,
Where he shall see the boar will use us kindly.

Mess. I'll go, my lord, and tell him what you say. *Exit.*

Enter *Catesby.*

Cates. Many good morrows to my noble lord!

Hast. Good morrow, Catesby; you are early stirring.
What news, what news, in this our tott'ring state?

Cates. It is a reeling world indeed, my lord,
And I believe will never stand upright
Till Richard wear the garland of the realm.

Hast. How? wear the garland? Dost thou mean the crown?

Cates. Ay, my good lord.

Hast. I'll have this crown of mine cut from my shoulders
Before I'll see the crown so foul misplac'd.
But canst thou guess that he doth aim at it?

Cates. Ay, on my life; and hopes to find you forward
Upon his party for the gain thereof;
And thereupon he sends you this good news,
That this same very day your enemies,
The kindred of the Queen, must die at Pomfret.

Hast. Indeed I am no mourner for that news,
Because they have been still my adversaries;
But that I'll give my voice on Richard's side
To bar my master's heirs in true descent —
God knows I will not do it, to the death!

Cates. God keep your lordship in that gracious mind!

Hast. But I shall laugh at this a twelvemonth hence,
That they which brought me in my master's hate,
I live to look upon their tragedy.
Well, Catesby, ere a fortnight make me older,
I'll send some packing that yet think not on't.

Cates. 'Tis a vile thing to die, my gracious lord,
When men are unprepar'd and look not for it.

Hast. O monstrous, monstrous! and so falls it out
With Rivers, Vaughan, Grey; and so 'twill do
With some men else, that think themselves as safe
As thou and I, who (as thou know'st) are dear
To princely Richard and to Buckingham.

Cates. The Princes both make high account of you —
[*Aside*] For they account his head upon the bridge.

Hast. I know they do, and I have well deserv'd it.

Enter *Lord Stanley.*

Come on, come on! Where is your boar-spear, man?
Fear you the boar, and go so unprovided?

Stan. My lord, good morrow. Good morrow, Catesby.
You may jest on, but, by the Holy Rood,
I do not like these several councils, I.

Hast. My lord,
I hold my life as dear as you do yours,
And never in my days, I do protest,
Was it so precious to me as 'tis now.
Think you, but that I know our state secure,
I would be so triumphant as I am?

Stan. The lords at Pomfret, when they rode from London,
Were jocund and suppos'd their states were sure,
And they indeed had no cause to mistrust;
But yet you see how soon the day o'ercast.
This sudden stab of rancour I misdoubt.
Pray God, I say, I prove a needless coward!
What, shall we toward the Tower? The day is spent.

Hast. Come, come, have with you. Wot you what, my lord?
To-day the lords you talk of are beheaded.

Stan. They, for their truth, might better wear their heads
Than some that have accus'd them wear their hats.
But come, my lord, let us away.

Enter a *Pursuivant.*

Hast. Go on before. I'll talk with this good fellow.

Exeunt Lord Stanley and Catesby.

How now, sirrah? How goes the world with thee?

Purs. The better that your lordship please to ask.

Hast. I tell thee, man, 'tis better with me now
Than when thou met'st me last where now we meet.
Then was I going prisoner to the Tower
By the suggestion of the Queen's allies;
But now I tell thee (keep it to thyself)
This day those enemies are put to death,
And I in better state than e'er I was.

Purs. God hold it, to your Honour's good content!

Hast. Gramercy, fellow. There, drink that for me. *Throws him his purse.*

Purs. God save your lordship! *Exit.*

Enter a *Priest.*

Priest. Well met, my lord. I am glad to see your Honour.

Hast. I thank thee, good Sir John, with all my heart.
I am in your debt for your last exercise;
Come the next Sabbath, and I will content you.
He whispers in his ear.

Enter *Buckingham.*

Buck. What, talking with a priest, Lord Chamberlain?
Your friends at Pomfret, they do need the priest;
Your Honour hath no shriving work in hand.

Hast. Good faith, and when I met this holy man,
The men you talk of came into my mind.
What, go you toward the Tower?

Buck. I do, my lord, but long I cannot stay there.
I shall return before your lordship thence.

Hast. Nay, like enough, for I stay dinner there.

Buck. [*aside*] And supper too, although thou know'st it not.—
Come, will you go?

Hast. I'll wait upon your lordship. *Exeunt.*

Scene III. [*Pomfret Castle.*]

Enter *Sir Richard Ratcliff*, with *Halberds*, carrying the *Nobles, Rivers, Grey,* and *Vaughan,* to death at Pomfret.

Riv. Sir Richard Ratcliff, let me tell thee this:
To-day shalt thou behold a subject die
For truth, for duty, and for loyalty.

Grey. God bless the Prince from all the pack of you!
A knot you are of damned bloodsuckers.

Vaugh. You live that shall cry woe for this hereafter.

Rat. Dispatch! The limit of your lives is out.

Riv. O Pomfret, Pomfret! O thou bloody prison,
Fatal and ominous to noble peers!
Within the guilty closure of thy walls
Richard the Second here was hack'd to death;
And, for more slander to thy dismal seat,
We give to thee our guiltless blood to drink.

Grey. Now Margaret's curse is fall'n upon our heads,
When she exclaim'd on Hastings, you, and I,
For standing by when Richard stabb'd her son.

Riv. Then curs'd she Richard, then curs'd she Buckingham,
Then curs'd she Hastings. O, remember, God,
To hear her prayer for them, as now for us!
And for my sister and her princely sons,
Be satisfied, dear God, with our true blood,
Which, as thou know'st, unjustly must be spilt.

Rat. Make haste. The hour of death is expiate.

Riv. Come, Grey; come, Vaughan; let us here embrace.
Farewell, until we meet again in heaven.
Exeunt.

Scene IV. [*London. The Tower.*]

Enter *Buckingham, Derby, Hastings, Bishop of Ely, Norfolk, Ratcliff, Lovel,* with others, at a table; [*Officers of the Council* attending].

Hast. Now, noble peers, the cause why we are met
Is to determine of the coronation.
In God's name, speak. When is the royal day?

Buck. Is all things ready for that royal time?

Der. It is, and wants but nomination.

Ely. To-morrow then I judge a happy day.

Buck. Who knows the Lord Protector's mind herein?
Who is most inward with the noble Duke?

Ely. Your Grace, we think, should soonest know his mind.

Buck. We know each other's faces; for our hearts,
He knows no more of mine than I of yours;
Nor I of his, my lord, than you of mine.
Lord Hastings, you and he are near in love.

THE TRAGEDY OF KING RICHARD III

PHOTOGRAPHS BY JOHN VICKERS
PRODUCED BY THE OLD VIC COMPANY

Laurence Olivier in the role of the villainous monster, King Richard III

Though hunch-backed, Richard is a valiant warrior, and is skilled in the use of arms

"Anointed let me be with deadly venom; and die, ere men can say 'God save the queen!' " Anne (Joyce Redman) regrets her destiny as Richard's queen *(Act IV, Scene I)*

"And if thy poor devoted servant may but beg one favour at thy gracious hand, thou dost confirm his happiness for ever." Richard's wooing of Anne *(Act I, Scene II)*

Queen Margaret (Sybil Thorndike) prophesies against Elizabeth (Margaret Leighton) *(Act I, Scene III)*

"Our brother is imprison'd by your means, myself disgrac'd, and the nobility held in contempt." Richard accuses Elizabeth of working against him and his brother *(Act I, Scene III)*

Above: "And he shriek'd out aloud, ' . . . false, fleeting, perjur'd Clarence.' " Clarence (George Relph) tells Brakenbury (Humphrey Heathcote) of his tormented dream *(Act I, Scene IV)*

Left: "Come, Hastings, help me to my closet." In his last hours, King Edward (Harcourt Williams) is aided by Hastings (Michael Warre) and Queen Elizabeth *(Act II, Scene I)*

"My other self . . my oracle, my prophet!" Richard welcomes the support of Buckingham (Nicholas Hannen) *(Act II, Scene II)*

"Richard of York! how fares our loving brother?" The two young princes meet after the death of their father *(Act III, Scene I)*

"I pray you, uncle, give me this dagger." The young duke asks Richard for an ominous gift *(Act III, Scene I)*

"Look how I am bewitch'd; behold mine arm is like a blasted sapling, wither'd up." In order to destroy Hastings, Richard blames him for bewitching and deforming him *(Act III, Scene IV)*

"So dear I lov'd the man, that I must weep." Richard affects distress after having Hastings executed *(Act III, Scene V)*

"O Margaret, Margaret! now thy heavy curse is lighted on poor Hastings' wretched head." On his way to his death, Hastings recalls Margaret's prophecy *(Act III, Scene IV)*

"See, a book of prayer in his hand; true ornament to know a holy man." Richard assumes a pious pose while Buckingham lauds him to the people *(Act III, Scene VII)*

"Then I salute you with this royal title: Long live King Richard, England's worthy king!" Buckingham salutes the new king *(Act III, Scene VII)*

"Poor heart, adieu! I pity thy complaining." On her way to visit her two sons, imprisoned by Richard, Elizabeth commiserates with Queen Anne, whom Richard has widowed *(Act IV, Scene I)*

Laurence Olivier as Richard, "that bottled spider, that foul bunch-backed toad"

"I am not in the giving vein to-day." Richard is irritated by Buckingham's reminder that he has been promised an earldom *(Act IV, Scene II)*

Richmond (Ralph Richardson) and King Richard III meet on Bosworth Field *(Act V, Scene IV)*

"God and your arms be prais'd, victorious friends; the day is ours, the bloody dog is dead."
Richmond announces Richard's death *(Act V, Scene IV)*

Hast. I thank his Grace, I know he loves me well;
But, for his purpose in the coronation,
I have not sounded him, nor he deliver'd
His gracious pleasure any way therein;
But you, my honourable lords, may name the time,
And in the Duke's behalf I'll give my voice,
Which, I presume, he'll take in gentle part.

Enter [*Richard, Duke of*] *Gloucester.*

Ely. In happy time, here comes the Duke himself.
Rich. My noble lords and cousins all, good morrow.
I have been long a sleeper; but I trust
My absence doth neglect no great design
Which by my presence might have been concluded.
Buck. Had you not come upon your cue, my lord,
William Lord Hastings had pronounc'd your part —
I mean, your voice for crowning of the King.
Rich. Than my Lord Hastings no man might be bolder.
His lordship knows me well, and loves me well.
My Lord of Ely, when I was last in Holborn
I saw good strawberries in your garden there.
I do beseech you send for some of them.
Ely. Marry and will, my lord, with all my heart. *Exit.*
Rich. Cousin of Buckingham, a word with you. [*Takes him aside.*]
Catesby hath sounded Hastings in our business
And finds the testy gentleman so hot
That he will lose his head ere give consent
His master's child, as worshipfully he terms it,
Shall lose the royalty of England's throne.
Buck. Withdraw yourself awhile. I'll go with you.
Exeunt Gloucester [*and Buckingham*].
Der. We have not yet set down this day of triumph.
To-morrow, in my judgment, is too sudden;
For I myself am not so well provided
As else I would be, were the day prolong'd.

Enter the *Bishop of Ely.*

Ely. Where is my lord the Duke of Gloucester? I have sent for these strawberries.
Hast. His Grace looks cheerfully and smooth this morning;
There's some conceit or other likes him well
When that he bids good morrow with such spirit.
I think there's never a man in Christendom
Can lesser hide his love or hate than he,
For by his face straight shall you know his heart.
Der. What of his heart perceive you in his face
By any likelihood he show'd to-day?
Hast. Marry, that with no man here he is offended;
For were he, he had shown it in his looks.

Enter *Richard* and *Buckingham.*

Rich. I pray you all, tell me what they deserve
That do conspire my death with devilish plots
Of damned witchcraft, and that have prevail'd
Upon my body with their hellish charms.
Hast. The tender love I bear your Grace, my lord,
Makes me most forward in this princely presence
To doom th' offenders, whosoe'er they be.
I say, my lord, they have deserved death.
Rich. Then be your eyes the witness of their evil.
Look how I am bewitch'd. Behold, mine arm
Is like a blasted sapling, wither'd up;
And this is Edward's wife, that monstrous witch,
Consorted with that harlot strumpet Shore,
That by their witchcraft thus have marked me.
Hast. If they have done this deed, my noble lord —
Rich. If? Thou protector of this damned strumpet,
Talk'st thou to me of if's? Thou art a traitor.
Off with his head! Now by Saint Paul I swear
I will not dine until I see the same.
Lovel and Ratcliff, look that it be done.
The rest that love me, rise and follow me.
Exeunt. Manent Lovel and Ratcliff, with the Lord Hastings.
Hast. Woe, woe for England, not a whit for me!
For I, too fond, might have prevented this.
Stanley did dream the boar did rase his helm;
But I did scorn it, and disdain to fly.
Three times to-day my footcloth horse did stumble,
And startled when he look'd upon the Tower,
As loath to bear me to the slaughterhouse.
O, now I need the priest that spake to me!
I now repent I told the pursuivant,
As too triumphing, how mine enemies

To-day at Pomfret bloodily were butcher'd,
And I myself secure, in grace and favour.
O Margaret, Margaret, now thy heavy curse
Is lighted on poor Hastings' wretched head!

Rat. Come, come, dispatch! The Duke would be at dinner.
Make a short shrift; he longs to see your head.

Hast. O momentary grace of mortal men,
Which we more hunt for than the grace of God!
Who builds his hope in air of your good looks
Lives like a drunken sailor on a mast,
Ready with every nod to tumble down
Into the fatal bowels of the deep.

Lov. Come, come, dispatch! 'Tis bootless to exclaim.

Hast. O bloody Richard! Miserable England,
I prophesy the fearfull'st time to thee
That ever wretched age hath look'd upon.
Come, lead me to the block; bear him my head.
They smile at me who shortly shall be dead.
Exeunt.

[Scene V. *London. The Tower walls.*]

Enter *Richard* and *Buckingham,* in rotten armour, marvellous ill-favoured.

Rich. Come, cousin, canst thou quake and change thy colour,
Murther thy breath in middle of a word,
And then again begin, and stop again,
As if thou wert distraught and mad with terror?

Buck. Tut, I can counterfeit the deep tragedian,
Speak and look back, and pry on every side,
Tremble and start at wagging of a straw,
Intending deep suspicion. Ghastly looks
Are at my service, like enforced smiles;
And both are ready in their offices,
At any time to grace my stratagems.
But what, is Catesby gone?

Rich. He is; and see, he brings the Mayor along.

Enter the [*Lord*] *Mayor* and *Catesby.*

Buck. Lord Mayor —

Rich. Look to the drawbridge there!

Buck. Hark! a drum.

Rich. Catesby, o'erlook the walls.

Buck. Lord Mayor, the reason we have sent —

Rich. Look back! defend thee! Here are enemies!

Buck. God and our innocency defend and guard us!

Enter *Lovel* and *Ratcliff,* with *Hastings'* head.

Rich. Be patient, they are friends — Ratcliff and Lovel.

Lov. Here is the head of that ignoble traitor,
The dangerous and unsuspected Hastings.

Rich. So dear I lov'd the man that I must weep.
I took him for the plainest harmless creature
That breath'd upon the earth a Christian;
Made him my book, wherein my soul recorded
The history of all her secret thoughts.
So smooth he daub'd his vice with show of virtue
That, his apparent open guilt omitted —
I mean, his conversation with Shore's wife —
He liv'd from all attainder of suspect.

Buck. Well, well, he was the covert'st shelt'red traitor
That ever lived. Look ye, my Lord Mayor.
Would you imagine, or almost believe,
Were't not that by great preservation
We live to tell it, that the subtile traitor
This day had plotted, in the Council House
To murther me and my good Lord of Gloucester?

May. Had he done so?

Rich. What? Think you we are Turks or infidels?
Or that we would, against the form of law,
Proceed thus rashly in the villain's death
But that the extreme peril of the case,
The peace of England, and our persons' safety
Enforc'd us to this execution?

May. Now fair befall you! He deserv'd his death,
And your good Graces both have well proceeded
To warn false traitors from the like attempts.
I never look'd for better at his hands
After he once fell in with Mistress Shore.

Buck. Yet had we not determin'd he should die
Until your lordship came to see his end,
Which now the loving haste of these our friends,
Something against our meanings, have prevented;
Because, my lord, we would have had you heard
The traitor speak, and timorously confess
The manner and the purpose of his treasons,
That you might well have signified the same
Unto the citizens, who haply may
Misconster us in him and wail his death.

May. But, my good lord, your Grace's word shall serve,

As well as I had seen, and heard him speak;
And do not doubt, right noble princes both,
But I'll acquaint our duteous citizens
With all your just proceedings in this case.

Rich. And to that end we wish'd your lordship here,
T' avoid the censures of the carping world.

Buck. But since you come too late of our intent,
Yet witness what you hear we did intend.
And so, my good Lord Mayor, we bid farewell.

Exit Mayor.

Rich. Go after, after, cousin Buckingham.
The Mayor towards Guildhall hies him in all post.
There, at your meetest vantage of the time,
Infer the bastardy of Edward's children.
Tell them how Edward put to death a citizen
Only for saying he would make his son
Heir to the Crown, meaning indeed his house,
Which by the sign thereof was termed so.
Moreover, urge his hateful luxury
And bestial appetite in change of lust,
Which stretch'd unto their servants, daughters, wives,
Even where his raging eye or savage heart,
Without control, lusted to make a prey.
Nay, for a need, thus far come near my person:
Tell them, when that my mother went with child
Of that insatiate Edward, noble York,
My princely father, then had wars in France,
And by true computation of the time
Found that the issue was not his begot;
Which well appeared in his lineaments,
Being nothing like the noble Duke my father.
Yet touch this sparingly, as 'twere far off,
Because, my lord, you know my mother lives.

Buck. Doubt not, my lord, I'll play the orator
As if the golden fee for which I plead
Were for myself — and so, my lord, adieu.

Rich. If you thrive well, bring them to Baynard's Castle,
Where you shall find me well accompanied
With reverend fathers and well-learned bishops.

Buck. I go; and towards three or four o'clock
Look for the news that the Guildhall affords.

Exit.

Rich. Go, Lovel, with all speed to Doctor Shaw —
[*To Catesby*] Go thou to Friar Penker. — Bid them both
Meet me within this hour at Baynard's Castle.

Exeunt [*Lovel, Catesby, and Ratcliff*].

Now will I go, to take some privy order
To draw the brats of Clarence out of sight,
And to give order that no manner person
Have any time recourse unto the Princes.

Exit.

[Scene VI. *London. A street.*]

Enter a *Scrivener* with a paper in his hand.

Scriv. Here is the indictment of the good Lord Hastings,
Which in a set hand fairly is engross'd
That it may be to-day read o'er in Paul's.
And mark how well the sequel hangs together:
Eleven hours I have spent to write it over,
For yesternight by Catesby was it sent me;
The precedent was full as long a-doing;
And yet within these five hours Hastings liv'd,
Untainted, unexamin'd, free, at liberty.
Here's a good world the while! Who is so gross
That cannot see this palpable device?
Yet who so bold but says he sees it not?
Bad is the world, and all will come to naught
When such ill dealing must be seen in thought.

Exit.

[Scene VII. *London. Baynard's Castle.*]

Enter *Richard* and *Buckingham* at several doors.

Rich. How now, how now? What say the citizens?

Buck. Now, by the holy Mother of our Lord,
The citizens are mum, say not a word.

Rich. Touch'd you the bastardy of Edward's children?

Buck. I did, with his contract with Lady Lucy
And his contract by deputy in France;
Th' insatiate greediness of his desire
And his enforcement of the city wives;
His tyranny for trifles; his own bastardy,
As being got, your father then in France,
And his resemblance, being not like the Duke.
Withal I did infer your lineaments,
Being the right idea of your father
Both in your form and nobleness of mind;
Laid open all your victories in Scotland,
Your discipline in war, wisdom in peace,
Your bounty, virtue, fair humility;
Indeed, left nothing fitting for your purpose
Untouch'd, or slightly handled in discourse;

And when my oratory drew toward end,
I bid them that did love their country's good
Cry, 'God save Richard, England's royal King!'
Rich. And did they so?
Buck. No, so God help me, they spake not a word,
But, like dumb statuës or breathing stones,
Star'd each on other, and look'd deadly pale.
Which when I saw, I reprehended them
And ask'd the Mayor what meant this wilful silence.
His answer was, the people were not us'd
To be spoke to but by the Recorder.
Then he was urg'd to tell my tale again:
'Thus saith the Duke, thus hath the Duke inferr'd,' —
But nothing spake in warrant from himself.
When he had done, some followers of mine own,
At lower end of the hall, hurl'd up their caps,
And some ten voices cried 'God save King Richard!'
And thus I took the vantage of those few: —
'Thanks, gentle citizens and friends,' quoth I.
'This general applause and cheerful shout
Argues your wisdom and your love to Richard,'
And even here brake off and came away.
Rich. What tongueless blocks were they! Would they not speak?
Buck. No, by my troth, my lord.
Rich. Will not the Mayor then and his brethren come?
Buck. The Mayor is here at hand. Intend some fear;
Be not you spoke with but by mighty suit;
And look you get a prayer book in your hand
And stand between two churchmen, good my lord,
For on that ground I'll make a holy descant;
And be not easily won to our requests.
Play the maid's part: still answer nay, and take it.
Rich. I go; and if you plead as well for them
As I can say nay to thee for myself,
No doubt we bring it to a happy issue.
Buck. Go, go up to the leads! The Lord Mayor knocks.
Exit [*Richard*].

Enter the [*Lord*] *Mayor*, [*Aldermen*,] and *Citizens*.

Welcome, my lord. I dance attendance here.
I think the Duke will not be spoke withal.

Enter *Catesby*.

Now, Catesby, what says your lord to my request?
Cates. He doth entreat your Grace, my noble lord,
To visit him to-morrow or next day.
He is within, with two right reverend fathers,
Divinely bent to meditation,
And in no worldly suits would he be mov'd
To draw him from his holy exercise.
Buck. Return, good Catesby, to the gracious Duke.
Tell him, myself, the Mayor and Aldermen,
In deep designs, in matter of great moment,
No less importing than our general good,
Are come to have some conference with his Grace.
Cates. I'll signify so much unto him straight. *Exit.*
Buck. Aha, my lord! this prince is not an Edward.
He is not lulling on a lewd love-bed,
But on his knees at meditation;
Not dallying with a brace of courtesans,
But meditating with two deep divines;
Not sleeping, to engross his idle body,
But praying, to enrich his watchful soul.
Happy were England, would this virtuous prince
Take on his Grace the sovereignty thereof;
But sure I fear we shall not win him to it.
May. Marry, God defend his Grace should say us nay!
Buck. I fear he will. Here Catesby comes again.

Enter *Catesby*.

Now, Catesby, what says his Grace?
Cates. My lord
He wonders to what end you have assembled
Such troops of citizens to come to him,
His Grace not being warn'd thereof before.
He fears, my lord, you mean no good to him.
Buck. Sorry I am my noble cousin should
Suspect me that I mean no good to him.
By heaven, we come to him in perfect love;
And so once more return and tell his Grace.
Exit Catesby.
When holy and devout religious men
Are at their beads, 'tis much to draw them thence,
So sweet is zealous contemplation.

Enter *Richard* aloft, between two *Bishops*. [*Catesby* returns.]

May. See where his Grace stands, 'tween two clergymen.
Buck. Two props of virtue for a Christian prince,
To stay him from the fall of vanity;
And see, a book of prayer in his hand,
True ornaments to know a holy man.
Famous Plantagenet, most gracious prince,
Lend favourable ear to our requests,
And pardon us the interruption
Of thy devotion and right Christian zeal.
Rich. My lord, there needs no such apology.
I do beseech your Grace to pardon me,
Who, earnest in the service of my God,
Deferr'd the visitation of my friends.
But, leaving this, what is your Grace's pleasure?
Buck. Even that (I hope) which pleaseth God above
And all good men of this ungovern'd isle.
Rich. I do suspect I have done some offence
That seems disgracious in the city's eye,
And that you come to reprehend my ignorance.
Buck. You have, my lord. Would it might please your Grace,
On our entreaties, to amend your fault!
Rich. Else wherefore breathe I in a Christian land?
Buck. Know then it is your fault that you resign
The supreme seat, the throne majestical,
The scept'red office of your ancestors,
Your state of fortune and your due of birth,
The lineal glory of your royal house,
To the corruption of a blemish'd stock;
Whiles, in the mildness of your sleepy thoughts,
Which here we waken to our country's good,
The noble isle doth want his proper limbs;
His face defac'd with scars of infamy,
His royal stock graft with ignoble plants,
And almost should'red in the swallowing gulf
Of dark forgetfulness and deep oblivion.
Which to recure, we heartily solicit
Your gracious self to take on you the charge
And kingly government of this your land;
Not as Protector, steward, substitute,
Or lowly factor for another's gain;
But as successively, from blood to blood,
Your right of birth, your empery, your own.
For this, consorted with the citizens,
Your very worshipful and loving friends,
And by their vehement instigation,
In this just cause come I to move your Grace.
Rich. I cannot tell if to depart in silence,
Or bitterly to speak in your reproof,
Best fitteth my degree or your condition.
If not to answer, you might haply think
Tongue-tied ambition, not replying, yielded
To bear the golden yoke of sovereignty
Which fondly you would here impose on me.
If to reprove you for this suit of yours,
So season'd with your faithful love to me,
Then, on the other side, I check'd my friends.
Therefore — to speak, and to avoid the first,
And then, in speaking, not to incur the last —
Definitively thus I answer you.
Your love deserves my thanks, but my desert
Unmeritable shuns your high request.
First, if all obstacles were cut away,
And that my path were even to the crown
As the ripe revenue and due of birth,
Yet so much is my poverty of spirit,
So mighty and so many my defects,
That I would rather hide me from my greatness,
Being a bark to brook no mighty sea,
Than in my greatness covet to be hid
And in the vapour of my glory smother'd.
But, God be thank'd, there is no need of me,
And much I need to help you, were there need.
The royal tree hath left us royal fruit,
Which, mellow'd by the stealing hours of time,
Will well become the seat of majesty
And make (no doubt) us happy by his reign.
On him I lay that you would lay on me,
The right and fortune of his happy stars,
Which God defend that I should wring from him!
Buck. My lord, this argues conscience in your Grace,
But the respects thereof are nice and trivial,
All circumstances well considered.
You say that Edward is your brother's son.
So say we too, but not by Edward's wife;
For first was he contract to Lady Lucy —
Your mother lives a witness to his vow —
And afterward by substitute betroth'd
To Bona, sister to the King of France.
These both put off, a poor petitioner,
A care-craz'd mother to a many sons,
A beauty-waning and distressed widow,
Even in the afternoon of her best days,
Made prize and purchase of his wanton eye,
Seduc'd the pitch and height of his degree
To base declension and loath'd bigamy.
By her, in his unlawful bed, he got
This Edward, whom our manners call the Prince.
More bitterly could I expostulate

Save that, for reverence to some alive,
I give a sparing limit to my tongue.
Then, good my lord, take to your royal self
This proffer'd benefit of dignity;
If not to bless us and the land withal,
Yet to draw forth your noble ancestry
From the corruption of abusing times
Unto a lineal true-derived course.

May. Do, good my lord. Your citizens entreat you.

Buck. Refuse not, mighty lord, this proffer'd love.

Cates. O, make them joyful, grant their lawful suit!

Rich. Alas, why would you heap this care on me?
I am unfit for state and majesty.
I do beseech you take it not amiss,
I cannot nor I will not yield to you.

Buck. If you refuse it — as, in love and zeal,
Loath to depose the child, your brother's son;
As well we know your tenderness of heart
And gentle, kind, effeminate remorse,
Which we have noted in you to your kindred
And egally indeed to all estates —
Yet know, whe'r you accept our suit or no,
Your brother's son shall never reign our king,
But we will plant some other in the throne
To the disgrace and downfall of your house;
And in this resolution here we leave you.
Come, citizens. Zounds, I'll entreat no more!

Rich. O, do not swear, my lord of Buckingham.

Exeunt [Buckingham, Mayor, Aldermen, and Citizens].

Cates. Call him again, sweet prince, accept their suit.
If you deny them, all the land will rue it.

Rich. Will you enforce me to a world of cares?
Call them again. I am not made of stone,
But penetrable to your kind entreaties,
Albeit against my conscience and my soul.

Enter *Buckingham* and the rest.

Cousin of Buckingham, and sage grave men,
Since you will buckle fortune on my back,
To bear her burthen, whe'r I will or no,
I must have patience to endure the load;
But if black scandal or foul-fac'd reproach
Attend the sequel of your imposition,
Your mere enforcement shall acquittance me
From all the impure blots and stains thereof;
For God doth know, and you may partly see,
How far I am from the desire of this.

May. God bless your Grace! We see it and will say it.

Rich. In saying so you shall but say the truth.

Buck. Then I salute you with this royal title —
Long live King Richard, England's worthy King!

All. Amen.

Buck. To-morrow may it please you to be crown'd?

Rich. Even when you please, for you will have it so.

Buck. To-morrow then we will attend your Grace,
And so most joyfully we take our leave.

Rich. [*to the Bishops*] Come, let us to our holy work again. —
Farewell, my cousin; farewell, gentle friends.

Exeunt.

ACT IV. Scene I. [*London. Before the Tower.*]

Enter the *Queen* [*Elizabeth*], *Duchess of York*, and *Marquess Dorset*, at one door; *Anne Duchess of Gloucester*, [leading *Lady Margaret Plantagenet, Clarence's* young daughter,] at another door.

Duch. York. Who meets us here? My niece Plantagenet,
Led in the hand of her kind aunt of Gloucester?
Now, for my life, she's wand'ring to the Tower,
On pure heart's love, to greet the tender Prince.
Daughter, well met.

Anne. God give your Graces both
A happy and a joyful time of day!

Queen. As much to you, good sister. Whither away?

Anne. No farther than the Tower, and, as I guess,
Upon the like devotion as yourselves,
To gratulate the gentle Princes there.

Queen. Kind sister, thanks. We'll enter all together;

Enter the *Lieutenant* [*Brakenbury*].

And in good time, here the Lieutenant comes.
Master Lieutenant, pray you, by your leave,
How doth the Prince, and my young son of York?

Lieut. Right well, dear madam. By your patience,
I may not suffer you to visit them;
The King hath strictly charg'd the contrary.

Queen. The King? Who's that?

Lieut. I cry you mercy! I mean the Lord Protector.

Queen. The Lord protect him from that kingly title!
Hath he set bounds between their love and me?
I am their mother. Who shall bar me from them?

Duch. York. I am their father's mother. I will see them.

Anne. Their aunt I am in law, in love their mother.
Then bring me to their sights. I'll bear thy blame
And take thy office from thee on my peril.

Lieut. No, madam, no! I may not leave it so.
I am bound by oath, and therefore pardon me.
Exit.

Enter *Stanley*.

Stan. Let me but meet you, ladies, one hour hence,
And I'll salute your Grace of York as mother
And reverend looker-on of two fair queens.
[*To Anne*] Come, madam, you must straight to Westminster,
There to be crowned Richard's royal queen.

Queen. Ah, cut my lace asunder,
That my pent heart may have some scope to beat,
Or else I swoon with this dead-killing news!

Anne. Despiteful tidings! O unpleasing news!

Dor. Be of good cheer. Mother, how fares your Grace?

Queen. O Dorset, speak not to me, get thee gone!
Death and destruction dogs thee at thy heels;
Thy mother's name is ominous to children.
If thou wilt outstrip death, go cross the seas,
And live with Richmond, from the reach of hell.
Go hie thee, hie thee from this slaughterhouse,
Lest thou increase the number of the dead
And make me die the thrall of Margaret's curse,
Nor mother, wife, nor England's counted Queen.

Stan. Full of wise care is this your counsel, madam.
Take all the swift advantage of the hours.
You shall have letters from me to my son
In your behalf, to meet you on the way.
Be not ta'en tardy by unwise delay.

Duch. York. O ill-dispersing wind of misery!
O my accursed womb, the bed of death!
A cockatrice hast thou hatch'd to the world,
Whose unavoided eye is murtherous.

Stan. Come, madam, come! I in all haste was sent.

Anne. And I with all unwillingness will go.
O, would to God that the inclusive verge
Of golden metal that must round my brow
Were redhot steel, to scar me to the brains!
Anointed let me be with deadly venom,
And die ere men can say 'God save the Queen!'

Queen. Go, go, poor soul! I envy not thy glory.
To feed my humour wish thyself no harm.

Anne. No? Why! when he that is my husband now
Came to me as I follow'd Henry's corse,
When scarce the blood was well wash'd from his hands
Which issued from my other angel husband
And that dear saint which then I weeping follow'd —
O, when, I say, I look'd on Richard's face,
This was my wish: 'Be thou,' quoth I, 'accurs'd
For making me, so young, so old a widow!
And when thou wed'st, let sorrow haunt thy bed;
And be thy wife, if any be so mad,
More miserable by the life of thee
Than thou hast made me by my dear lord's death!'
Lo, ere I can repeat this curse again,
Within so small a time, my woman's heart
Grossly grew captive to his honey words
And prov'd the subject of mine own soul's curse,
Which hitherto hath held mine eyes from rest;
For never yet one hour in his bed
Did I enjoy the golden dew of sleep,
But with his timorous dreams was still awak'd.
Besides, he hates me for my father Warwick,
And will (no doubt) shortly be rid of me.

Queen. Poor heart, adieu! I pity thy complaining.

Anne. No more than with my soul I mourn for yours.

Queen. Farewell, thou woful welcomer of glory.

Anne. Adieu, poor soul, that tak'st thy leave of it.

Duch. York. [*to Dorset*] Go thou to Richmond, and good fortune guide thee!
[*To Anne*] Go thou to Richard, and good angels tend thee!
[*To Queen Elizabeth*] Go thou to sanctuary, and good thoughts possess thee!
I to my grave, where peace and rest lie with me!
Eighty odd years of sorrow have I seen,
And each hour's joy wrack'd with a week of teen.

Queen. Stay, yet look back with me unto the Tower.
Pity, you ancient stones, those tender babes
Whom envy hath immur'd within your walls —
Rough cradle for such little pretty ones!
Rude ragged nurse, old sullen playfellow
For tender princes — use my babies well!
So foolish sorrow bids your stones farewell.
Exeunt.

Scene II. [*London. The Palace.*]

Sound a sennet. Enter *Richard*, in pomp, *Buckingham, Catesby, Ratcliff, Lovel,* [a *Page*, and others].

Rich. Stand all apart. Cousin of Buckingham —

Buck. My gracious sovereign?

Rich. Give me thy hand.

Sound. Here he ascendeth the throne.

Thus high, by thy advice
And thy assistance, is King Richard seated.
But shall we wear these glories for a day?
Or shall they last, and we rejoice in them?

Buck. Still live they, and for ever let them last!

Rich. Ah, Buckingham, now do I play the touch,
To try if thou be current gold indeed.
Young Edward lives. Think now what I would speak.

Buck. Say on, my loving lord.

Rich. Why, Buckingham, I say I would be king.

Buck. Why, so you are, my thrice-renowned liege.

Rich. Ha! Am I king? 'Tis so. But Edward lives.

Buck. True, noble prince.

Rich. O bitter consequence,
That Edward still should live true noble prince!
Cousin, thou wast not wont to be so dull.
Shall I be plain? I wish the bastards dead,
And I would have it suddenly perform'd.
What say'st thou now? Speak suddenly, be brief.

Buck. Your Grace may do your pleasure.

Rich. Tut, tut, thou art all ice; thy kindness freezes.
Say, have I thy consent that they shall die?

Buck. Give me some little breath, some pause, dear lord,
Before I positively speak in this.
I will resolve you herein presently. *Exit.*

Cates. [*aside to another*] The King is angry. See, he gnaws his lip.

Rich. I will converse with iron-witted fools
[*Descends from the throne.*]
And unrespective boys. None are for me
That look into me with considerate eyes.
High-reaching Buckingham grows circumspect.
Boy!

Page. My lord?

Rich. Know'st thou not any whom corrupting gold
Will tempt unto a close exploit of death?

Page. I know a discontented gentleman
Whose humble means match not his haughty spirit.
Gold were as good as twenty orators,
And will, no doubt, tempt him to anything.

Rich. What is his name?

Page. His name, my lord, is Tyrrel.

Rich. I partly know the man. Go call him hither.
Exit [*Page*].
The deep-revolving witty Buckingham
No more shall be the neighbour to my counsels.
Hath he so long held out with me, untir'd,
And stops he now for breath? Well, be it so.

Enter *Stanley*.

How now, Lord Stanley? What's the news with you?

Stan. My lord, I hear the Marquess Dorset's fled
To Richmond, in those parts beyond the seas
Where he abides. [*Stands aside.*]

Rich. Come hither, Catesby. Rumour it abroad
That Anne my wife is very grievous sick.
I will take order for her keeping close.
Inquire me out some mean poor gentleman,
Whom I will marry straight to Clarence' daughter.
The boy is foolish, and I fear not him.
Look how thou dream'st! I say again, give out

That Anne, my queen, is sick and like to die.
About it! for it stands me much upon
To stop all hopes whose growth may damage me.
[*Exit Catesby.*]
I must be married to my brother's daughter,
Or else my kingdom stands on brittle glass.
Murther her brothers, and then marry her —
Uncertain way of gain! But I am in
So far in blood that sin will pluck on sin.
Tear-falling pity dwells not in this eye.

Enter [*Page,* with] *Tyrrel.*

Is thy name Tyrrel?

Tyr. James Tyrrel, and your most obedient subject.

Rich. Art thou indeed?

Tyr. Prove me, my gracious lord.

Rich. Dar'st thou resolve to kill a friend of mine?

Tyr. Please you;
But I had rather kill two enemies.

Rich. Why, there thou hast it! Two deep enemies,
Foes to my rest and my sweet sleep's disturbers,
Are they that I would have thee deal upon.
Tyrrel, I mean those bastards in the Tower.

Tyr. Let me have open means to come to them,
And soon I'll rid you from the fear of them.

Rich. Thou sing'st sweet music. Hark, come hither, Tyrrel.
Go, by this token. Rise, and lend thine ear.
Whispers.
There is no more but so: say it is done,
And I will love thee and prefer thee for it.

Tyr. I will dispatch it straight.

Rich. Shall we hear from thee, Tyrrel, ere we sleep?

Tyr. Ye shall, my lord. *Exit.*

Enter *Buckingham.*

Buck. My lord, I have consider'd in my mind
The late request that you did sound me in. 86

Rich. Well, let that rest. Dorset is fled to Richmond.

Buck. I hear the news, my lord.

Rich. Stanley, he is your wive's son. Well, look unto it.

Buck. My lord, I claim the gift, my due by promise,
For which your honour and your faith is pawn'd:
Th' earldom of Hereford and the moveables
Which you have promised I shall possess.

Rich. Stanley, look to your wife. If she convey
Letters to Richmond, you shall answer it.

Buck. What says your Highness to my just request?

Rich. I do remember me Henry the Sixth
Did prophesy that Richmond should be King
When Richmond was a little peevish boy.
A king! — perhaps — perhaps —

Buck. My lord —

Rich. How chance the prophet could not at that time
Have told me, I being by, that I should kill him?

Buck. My lord, your promise for the earldom!

Rich. Richmond! When last I was at Exeter,
The Mayor in courtesy show'd me the castle,
And call'd it Rouge-mount; at which name I started,
Because a bard of Ireland told me once
I should not live long after I saw Richmond.

Buck. My lord —

Rich. Ay, what's o'clock?

Buck. I am thus bold to put your Grace in mind
Of what you promis'd me.

Rich. Well, but what's o'clock?

Buck. Upon the stroke of ten.

Rich. Well, let it strike.

Buck. Why let it strike?

Rich. Because that like a Jack thou keep'st the stroke
Betwixt thy begging and my meditation.
I am not in the giving vein to-day.

Buck. May it please you to resolve me in my suit.

Rich. Thou troublest me; I am not in the vein.
Exeunt [*all but Buckingham*].

Buck. And is it thus? Repays he my deep service
With such contempt? Made I him King for this?
O, let me think on Hastings, and be gone
To Brecknock while my fearful head is on!
Exit.

[Scene III. *London. The Palace.*]

Enter *Tyrrel.*

Tyr. The tyrannous and bloody act is done,
The most arch deed of piteous massacre
That ever yet this land was guilty of.
Dighton and Forrest, whom I did suborn

To do this piece of ruthful butchery,
Albeit they were flesh'd villains, bloody dogs,
Melted with tenderness and mild compassion,
Wept like two children in their death's sad story.
'Lo, thus,' quoth Dighton, 'lay the gentle babes.'
'Thus, thus,' quoth Forrest, 'girdling one another
Within their alablaster innocent arms.
Their lips were four red roses on a stalk,
And in their summer beauty kiss'd each other.
A book of prayers on their pillow lay,
Which once,' quoth Forrest, 'almost chang'd my mind;
But O! the devil' — there the villain stopp'd;
When Dighton thus told on — 'We smothered
The most replenished sweet work of nature
That from the prime creation e'er she fram'd.'
Hence both are gone with conscience and remorse
They could not speak; and so I left them both,
To bear this tidings to the bloody King.

Enter *Richard*.

And here he comes. All health, my sovereign lord!

Rich. Kind Tyrrel, am I happy in thy news?

Tyr. If to have done the thing you gave in charge
Beget your happiness, be happy then,
For it is done.

Rich. But didst thou see them dead?

Tyr. I did, my lord.

Rich. And buried, gentle Tyrrel?

Tyr. The chaplain of the Tower hath buried them;
But where (to say the truth) I do not know.

Rich. Come to me, Tyrrel, soon at after supper,
When thou shalt tell the process of their death.
Meantime, but think how I may do thee good,
And be inheritor of thy desire.
Farewell till then.

Tyr. I humbly take my leave. *Exit.*

Rich. The son of Clarence have I pent up close,
His daughter meanly have I match'd in marriage,
The sons of Edward sleep in Abraham's bosom,
And Anne my wife hath bid this world good night.
Now, for I know the Britain Richmond aims
At young Elizabeth, my brother's daughter,
And by that knot looks proudly on the crown,
To her go I, a jolly thriving wooer.

Enter *Ratcliff*.

Rat. My lord —

Rich. Good or bad news, that thou com'st in so bluntly?

Rat. Bad news, my lord. Morton is fled to Richmond,
And Buckingham, back'd with the hardy Welshmen,
Is in the field, and still his power increaseth.

Rich. Ely with Richmond troubles me more near
Than Buckingham and his rash-levied strength.
Come! I have learn'd that fearful commenting
Is leaden servitor to dull delay;
Delay leads impotent and snail-pac'd beggary.
Then fiery expedition be my wing,
Jove's Mercury, and herald for a king!
Go muster men. My counsel is my shield.
We must be brief when traitors brave the field.
Exeunt.

Scene [IV. *London. Before the Palace.*]

Enter old *Queen Margaret*.

Q. Marg. So now prosperity begins to mellow
And drop into the rotten mouth of death.
Here in these confines slily have I lurk'd
To watch the waning of mine enemies.
A dire induction am I witness to,
And will to France, hoping the consequence
Will prove as bitter, black, and tragical.
Withdraw thee, wretched Margaret! Who comes here? [*Retires.*]

Enter *Duchess of York* and *Queen* [*Elizabeth*].

Queen. Ah, my poor princes! ah, my tender babes!
My unblown flowers, new-appearing sweets!
If yet your gentle souls fly in the air
And be not fix'd in doom perpetual,
Hover about me with your airy wings
And hear your mother's lamentation!

Q. Marg. [*aside*] Hover about her. Say that right for right
Hath dimm'd your infant morn to aged night.

Duch. So many miseries have craz'd my voice
That my woe-wearied tongue is still and mute.
Edward Plantagenet, why art thou dead?

Q. Marg. [*aside*] Plantagenet doth quit Plantagenet;
Edward for Edward pays a dying debt.

Queen. Wilt thou, O God, fly from such gentle lambs
And throw them in the entrails of the wolf?
When didst thou sleep when such a deed was done?
Q. Marg. [*aside*] When holy Harry died, and my sweet son.
Duch. Dead life, blind sight, poor mortal living ghost,
Woe's scene, world's shame, grave's due by life usurp'd,
Brief abstract and record of tedious days,
Rest thy unrest on England's lawful earth, [*Sits down.*]
Unlawfully made drunk with innocent blood!
Queen. Ah that thou wouldst as soon afford a grave
As thou canst yield a melancholy seat!
Then would I hide my bones, not rest them here.
Ah, who hath any cause to mourn but we? [*Sits down by her.*]
Q. Marg. [*comes forward*] If ancient sorrow be most reverent,
Give mine the benefit of seignory
And let my griefs frown on the upper hand.
If sorrow can admit society, [*Sits down with them.*]
Tell o'er your woes again by viewing mine.
I had an Edward, till a Richard kill'd him;
I had a Harry, till a Richard kill'd him:
Thou hadst an Edward, till a Richard kill'd him;
Thou hadst a Richard, till a Richard kill'd him.
Duch. I had a Richard too, and thou didst kill him;
I had a Rutland too, thou holp'st to kill him.
Q. Marg. Thou hadst a Clarence too, and Richard kill'd him.
From forth the kennel of thy womb hath crept
A hellhound that doth hunt us all to death.
That dog, that had his teeth before his eyes,
To worry lambs and lap their gentle blood,
That foul defacer of God's handiwork,
That excellent grand tyrant of the earth
That reigns in galled eyes of weeping souls,
Thy womb let loose to chase us to our graves.
O upright, just, and true-disposing God,
How do I thank thee that this carnal cur
Preys on the issue of his mother's body
And makes her pew-fellow with others' moan!
Duch. O Harry's wife, triumph not in my woes!
God witness with me I have wept for thine.
Q. Marg. Bear with me! I am hungry for revenge
And now I cloy me with beholding it.
Thy Edward he is dead, that kill'd my Edward;
Thy other Edward dead, to quit my Edward;
Young York he is but boot, because both they
Match'd not the high perfection of my loss.
Thy Clarence he is dead that stabb'd my Edward,
And the beholders of this frantic play,
Th' adulterate Hastings, Rivers, Vaughan, Grey,
Untimely smother'd in their dusky graves.
Richard yet lives, hell's black intelligencer;
Only reserv'd their factor to buy souls
And send them thither. But at hand, at hand,
Ensues his piteous and unpitied end.
Earth gapes, hell burns, fiends roar, saints pray,
To have him suddenly convey'd from hence.
Cancel his bond of life, dear God, I pray,
That I may live to say, 'The dog is dead.'
Queen. O, thou didst prophesy the time would come
That I should wish for thee to help me curse
That bottled spider, that foul bunch-back'd toad!
Q. Marg. I call'd thee then vain flourish of my fortune;
I call'd thee then poor shadow, painted queen,
The presentation of but what I was,
The flattering index of a direful pageant,
One heav'd a-high to be hurl'd down below,
A mother only mock'd with two fair babes,
A dream of what thou wast, a garish flag,
To be the aim of every dangerous shot;
A sign of dignity, a breath, a bubble,
A queen in jest, only to fill the scene.
Where is thy husband now? Where be thy brothers?
Where be thy two sons? Wherein dost thou joy?
Who sues and kneels and says 'God save the Queen'?
Where be the bending peers that flattered thee?
Where be the thronging troops that followed thee?
Decline all this, and see what now thou art:
For happy wife, a most distressed widow;
For joyful mother, one that wails the name;
For queen, a very caitiff crown'd with care;
For one being su'd to, one that humbly sues;
For she that scorn'd at me, now scorn'd of me;
For she being fear'd of all, now fearing one;
For she commanding all, obey'd of none.
Thus hath the course of justice whirl'd about
And left thee but a very prey to time,
Having no more but thought of what thou wast,

To torture thee the more, being what thou art.
Thou didst usurp my place, and dost thou not
Usurp the just proportion of my sorrow?
Now thy proud neck bears half my burthen'd yoke,
From which even here I slip my wearied head
And leave the burthen of it all on thee.
Farewell, York's wife and queen of sad mischance!
These English woes shall make me smile in France.

Queen. O thou well skill'd in curses, stay awhile
And teach me how to curse mine enemies!

Q. Marg. Forbear to sleep the night, and fast the day;
Compare dead happiness with living woe;
Think that thy babes were sweeter than they were
And he that slew them fouler than he is.
Bett'ring thy loss makes the bad causer worse;
Revolving this will teach thee how to curse.

Queen. My words are dull. O, quicken them with thine!

Q. Marg. Thy woes will make them sharp and pierce like mine. *Exit.*

Duch. Why should calamity be full of words?

Queen. Windy attorneys to their client woes,
Airy succeeders of intestate joys,
Poor breathing orators of miseries,
Let them have scope! Though what they will impart
Help nothing else, yet do they ease the heart.

Duch. If so, then be not tongue-tied. Go with me,
And in the breath of bitter words let's smother
My damned son that thy two sweet sons smother'd.
[*Trumpet within.*]
The trumpet sounds. Be copious in exclaims.

Enter *King Richard* and his *Train*, marching, with *Drums* and *Trumpets.*

Rich. Who intercepts me in my expedition?

Duch. O, she that might have intercepted thee,
By strangling thee in her accursed womb,
From all the slaughters (wretch!) that thou hast done!

Queen. Hid'st thou that forehead with a golden crown
Where should be branded, if that right were right,
The slaughter of the prince that ow'd that crown
And the dire death of my poor sons and brothers?
Tell me, thou villain-slave, where are my children?

Duch. Thou toad, thou toad, where is thy brother Clarence?
And little Ned Plantagenet, his son?

Queen. Where is the gentle Rivers, Vaughan, Grey?

Duch. Where is kind Hastings?

Rich. A flourish, trumpets! Strike alarum, drums!
Let not the heavens hear these telltale women
Rail on the Lord's anointed. Strike, I say!
Flourish. Alarums.
Either be patient and entreat me fair,
Or with the clamorous report of war
Thus will I drown your exclamations.

Duch. Art thou my son?

Rich. Ay, I thank God, my father, and yourself.

Duch. Then patiently hear my impatience.

Rich. Madam, I have a touch of your condition
That cannot brook the accent of reproof.

Duch. O, let me speak!

Rich. Do then, but I'll not hear.

Duch. I will be mild and gentle in my words.

Rich. And brief, good mother, for I am in haste.

Duch. Art thou so hasty? I have stay'd for thee
(God knows) in torment and in agony.

Rich. And came I not at last to comfort you?

Duch. No, by the holy rood, thou know'st it well,
Thou cam'st on earth to make the earth my hell.
A grievous burthen was thy birth to me;
Tetchy and wayward was thy infancy;
Thy schooldays frightful, desp'rate, wild, and furious;
Thy prime of manhood daring, bold, and venturous;
Thy age confirm'd, proud, subtle, sly, and bloody,
More mild, but yet more harmful — kind in hatred.
What comfortable hour canst thou name
That ever grac'd me with thy company?

Rich. Faith, none, but Humphrey Hour, that call'd your Grace
To breakfast once, forth of my company.
If I be so disgracious in your eye,

Let me march on and not offend you, madam.
Strike up the drum.
Duch. I prithee hear me speak.
Rich. You speak too bitterly.
Duch. Hear me a word;
For I shall never speak to thee again.
Rich. So.
Duch. Either thou wilt die by God's just ordinance
Ere from this war thou turn a conqueror,
Or I with grief and extreme age shall perish
And never more behold thy face again.
Therefore take with thee my most grievous curse,
Which in the day of battle tire thee more
Than all the complete armour that thou wear'st!
My prayers on the adverse party fight,
And there the little souls of Edward's children
Whisper the spirits of thine enemies
And promise them success and victory!
Bloody thou art, bloody will be thy end;
Shame serves thy life and doth thy death attend. *Exit.*
Queen. Though far more cause, yet much less spirit to curse
Abides in me. I say amen to her.
Rich. Stay, madam. I must talk a word with you.
Queen. I have no more sons of the royal blood
For thee to slaughter. For my daughters, Richard,
They shall be praying nuns, not weeping queens;
And therefore level not to hit their lives.
Rich. You have a daughter call'd Elizabeth,
Virtuous and fair, royal and gracious.
Queen. And must she die for this? O, let her live,
And I'll corrupt her manners, stain her beauty,
Slander myself as false to Edward's bed,
Throw over her the veil of infamy.
So she may live unscarr'd of bleeding slaughter,
I will confess she was not Edward's daughter.
Rich. Wrong not her birth. She is a royal princess.
Queen. To save her life, I'll say she is not so.
Rich. Her life is safest only in her birth.
Queen. And only in that safety died her brothers.
Rich. Lo, at their birth good stars were opposite.
Queen. No, to their lives ill friends were contrary.
Rich. All unavoided is the doom of destiny.
Queen. True, when avoided grace makes destiny.
My babes were destin'd to a fairer death
If grace had bless'd thee with a fairer life.
Rich. You speak as if that I had slain my cousins.
Queen. Cousins indeed, and by their uncle cozen'd
Of comfort, kingdom, kindred, freedom, life.
Whose hand soever lanch'd their tender hearts,
Thy head (all indirectly) gave direction.
No doubt the murd'rous knife was dull and blunt
Till it was whetted on thy stone-hard heart
To revel in the entrails of my lambs.
But that still use of grief makes wild grief tame,
My tongue should to thy ears not name my boys
Till that my nails were anchor'd in thine eyes;
And I, in such a desp'rate bay of death,
Like a poor bark of sails and tackling reft,
Rush all to pieces on thy rocky bosom.
Rich. Madam, so thrive I in my enterprise
And dangerous success of bloody wars
As I intend more good to you and yours
Than ever you and yours by me were harm'd!
Queen. What good is cover'd with the face of heaven,
To be discovered, that can do me good?
Rich. Th' advancement of your children, gentle lady.
Queen. Up to some scaffold, there to lose their heads!
Rich. Unto the dignity and height of fortune,
The high imperial type of this earth's glory.
Queen. Flatter my sorrow with report of it.
Tell me, what state, what dignity, what honour
Canst thou demise to any child of mine?
Rich. Even all I have — ay, and myself and all —
Will I withal endow a child of thine,
So in the Lethe of thy angry soul
Thou drown the sad remembrance of those wrongs
Which thou supposest I have done to thee.
Queen. Be brief, lest that the process of thy kindness
Last longer telling than thy kindness' date.
Rich. Then know that from my soul I love thy daughter.
Queen. My daughter's mother thinks it with her soul.
Rich. What do you think?

Queen. That thou dost love my daughter from thy soul.
So from thy soul's love didst thou love her brothers,
And from my heart's love I do thank thee for it.
Rich. Be not so hasty to confound my meaning.
I mean that with my soul I love thy daughter
And do intend to make her Queen of England.
Queen. Well then, who dost thou mean shall be her king?
Rich. Even he that makes her Queen. Who else should be?
Queen. What, thou?
Rich. Even so. How think you of it, madam?
Queen. How canst thou woo her?
Rich. That I would learn of you,
As one being best acquainted with her humour.
Queen. And wilt thou learn of me?
Rich. Madam, with all my heart.
Queen. Send to her by the man that slew her brothers
A pair of bleeding hearts; thereon engrave
'Edward' and 'York.' Then haply will she weep.
Therefore present to her — as sometime Margaret
Did to thy father, steep'd in Rutland's blood —
A handkerchief, which say to her did drain
The purple sap from her sweet brother's body,
And bid her wipe her weeping eyes withal.
If this inducement move her not to love,
Send her a letter of thy noble deeds:
Tell her thou mad'st away her uncle Clarence,
Her uncle Rivers; ay (and for her sake!),
Mad'st quick conveyance with her good aunt Anne.
Rich. You mock me, madam. This is not the way
To win your daughter.
Queen. There is no other way,
Unless thou couldst put on some other shape,
And not be Richard that hath done all this.
Rich. Say that I did all this for love of her.
Queen. Nay, then indeed she cannot choose but hate thee,
Having bought love with such a bloody spoil.
Rich. Look, what is done cannot be now amended.
Men shall deal unadvisedly sometimes,
Which after-hours gives leisure to repent.
If I did take the kingdom from your sons,
To make amends I'll give it to your daughter.
If I have kill'd the issue of your womb,
To quicken your increase I will beget
Mine issue of your blood upon your daughter.
A grandam's name is little less in love
Than is the doting title of a mother.
They are as children but one step below,
Even of your metal, of your very blood,
Of all one pain, save for a night of groans
Endur'd of her for whom you bid like sorrow.
Your children were vexation to your youth,
But mine shall be a comfort to your age.
The loss you have is but a son being king,
And by that loss your daughter is made queen.
I cannot make you what amends I would;
Therefore accept such kindness as I can.
Dorset your son, that with a fearful soul
Leads discontented steps in foreign soil,
This fair alliance quickly shall call home
To high promotions and great dignity.
The King, that calls your beauteous daughter wife,
Familiarly shall call thy Dorset brother.
Again shall you be mother to a king,
And all the ruins of distressful times
Repair'd with double riches of content.
What, we have many goodly days to see.
The liquid drops of tears that you have shed
Shall come again, transform'd to orient pearl,
Advantaging their loan with interest
Of ten times double gain of happiness.
Go then, my mother; to thy daughter go;
Make bold her bashful years with your experience;
Prepare her ears to hear a wooer's tale;
Put in her tender heart th' aspiring flame
Of golden sovereignty; acquaint the princess
With the sweet silent hours of marriage joys;
And when this arm of mine hath chastised
The petty rebel, dull-brain'd Buckingham,
Bound with triumphant garlands will I come
And lead thy daughter to a conqueror's bed;
To whom I will retail my conquest won,
And she shall be sole victoress, Cæsar's Cæsar.
Queen. What were I best to say? Her father's brother
Would be her lord? Or shall I say her uncle?
Or he that slew her brothers and her uncles?
Under what title shall I woo for thee
That God, the law, my honour, and her love
Can make seem pleasing to her tender years?
Rich. Infer fair England's peace by this alliance.
Queen. Which she shall purchase with still-lasting war.
Rich. Tell her the King, that may command, entreats.

Queen. That at her hands which the King's King forbids.
Rich. Say she shall be a high and mighty queen.
Queen. To wail the title, as her mother doth.
Rich. Say I will love her everlastingly.
Queen. But how long shall that title 'ever' last?
Rich. Sweetly in force unto her fair live's end.
Queen. But how long fairly shall her sweet life last?
Rich. As long as heaven and nature lengthens it.
Queen. As long as hell and Richard likes of it.
Rich. Say I, her sovereign, am her subject low.
Queen. But she, your subject, loathes such sovereignty.
Rich. Be eloquent in my behalf to her.
Queen. An honest tale speeds best being plainly told.
Rich. Then plainly to her tell my loving tale.
Queen. Plain and not honest is too harsh a style.
Rich. Your reasons are too shallow and too quick.
Queen. O no, my reasons are too deep and dead —
Too deep and dead (poor infants) in their graves.
Rich. Harp not on that string, madam; that is past.
Queen. Harp on it still shall I till heart-strings break.
Rich. Now, by my George, my garter, and my crown —
Queen. Profan'd, dishonour'd, and the third usurp'd.
Rich. I swear —
Queen. By nothing, for this is no oath.
Thy George, profan'd, hath lost his lordly honour;
Thy garter, blemish'd, pawn'd his knightly virtue;
Thy crown, usurp'd, disgrac'd his kingly glory.
If something thou wouldst swear to be believ'd,
Swear then by something that thou hast not wrong'd.
Rich. Now by the world —
Queen. 'Tis full of thy foul wrongs.
Rich. My father's death —
Queen. Thy life hath that dishonour'd.
Rich. Then by myself —
Queen. Thyself is self-misus'd.
Rich. Why then, by God, —
Queen. God's wrong is most of all.
If thou didst fear to break an oath by him,
The unity the King my husband made
Thou hadst not broken, nor my brothers died.
If thou hadst fear'd to break an oath by him,
Th' imperial metal, circling now thy head,
Had grac'd the tender temples of my child,
And both the Princes had been breathing here,
Which now, two tender bedfellows for dust,
Thy broken faith hath made the prey for worms.
What canst thou swear by now?
Rich. The time to come.
Queen. That thou hast wronged in the time o'erpast;
For I myself have many tears to wash
Hereafter time, for time past wrong'd by thee.
The children live whose fathers thou hast slaughter'd,
Ungovern'd youth, to wail it with their age;
The parents live whose children thou hast butcher'd,
Old barren plants, to wail it with their age.
Swear not by time to come, for that thou hast
Misus'd ere us'd, by times ill-us'd o'erpast.
Rich. As I intend to prosper and repent,
So thrive I in my dangerous affairs
Of hostile arms! Myself myself confound!
Heaven and fortune bar me happy hours!
Day, yield me not thy light, nor, night, thy rest!
Be opposite all planets of good luck
To my proceeding if, with dear heart's love,
Immaculate devotion, holy thoughts,
I tender not thy beauteous princely daughter!
In her consists my happiness and thine;
Without her, follows to myself and thee,
Herself, the land, and many a Christian soul,
Death, desolation, ruin, and decay.
It cannot be avoided but by this;
It will not be avoided but by this.
Therefore, dear mother (I must call you so),
Be the attorney of my love to her.
Plead what I will be, not what I have been;
Not my deserts, but what I will deserve.
Urge the necessity and state of times,
And be not peevish-fond in great designs.
Queen. Shall I be tempted of the devil thus?
Rich. Ay, if the devil tempt you to do good.
Queen. Shall I forget myself to be myself?

Rich. Ay, if yourself's remembrance wrong yourself.
Queen. Yet thou didst kill my children.
Rich. But in your daughter's womb I bury them,
Where, in that nest of spicery, they will breed
Selves of themselves, to your recomforture.
Queen. Shall I go win my daughter to thy will?
Rich. And be a happy mother by the deed.
Queen. I go. Write to me very shortly,
And you shall understand from me her mind.
Rich. Bear her my true love's kiss; and so farewell —
Exit Queen [*Elizabeth*].
Relenting fool, and shallow, changing woman!

Enter *Ratcliff*, [*Catesby* following].

How now? What news?
Rat. Most mighty sovereign, on the western coast
Rideth a puissant navy; to our shores
Throng many doubtful hollow-hearted friends,
Unarm'd, and unresolv'd to beat them back.
'Tis thought that Richmond is their admiral;
And there they hull, expecting but the aid
Of Buckingham to welcome them ashore.
Rich. Some light-foot friend post to the Duke of Norfolk.
Ratcliff, thyself — or Catesby — where is he?
Cates. Here, my good lord.
Rich. Catesby, fly to the Duke.
Cates. I will, my lord, with all convenient haste.
Rich. Ratcliff, come hither. Post to Salisbury.
When thou com'st thither — [*To Catesby*] Dull unmindful villain,
Why stay'st thou here and go'st not to the Duke?
Cates. First, mighty liege, tell me your Highness' pleasure,
What from your Grace I shall deliver to him.
Rich. O, true, good Catesby. Bid him levy straight
The greatest strength and power that he can make
And meet me suddenly at Salisbury.
Cates. I go. *Exit.*
Rat. What, may it please you, shall I do at Salisbury?
Rich. Why, what wouldst thou do there before I go?
Rat. Your Highness told me I should post before.
Rich. My mind is chang'd.

Enter *Lord Stanley*.

Stanley, what news with you?
Stan. None good, my liege, to please you with the hearing,
Nor none so bad but well may be reported.
Rich. Hoyday, a riddle! Neither good nor bad!
What need'st thou run so many miles about
When thou mayst tell thy tale the nearest way?
Once more, what news?
Stan. Richmond is on the seas.
Rich. There let him sink, and be the seas on him!
White-liver'd runagate! what doth he there?
Stan. I know not, mighty sovereign, but by guess.
Rich. Well, as you guess?
Stan. Stirr'd up by Dorset, Buckingham, and Morton,
He makes for England, here to claim the crown.
Rich. Is the chair empty? Is the sword unsway'd?
Is the King dead? the empire unpossess'd?
What heir of York is there alive but we?
And who is England's king but great York's heir?
Then tell me, what makes he upon the seas?
Stan. Unless for that, my liege, I cannot guess.
Rich. Unless for that he comes to be your liege
You cannot guess wherefore the Welshman comes.
Thou wilt revolt and fly to him, I fear.
Stan. No, my good lord. Therefore mistrust me not.
Rich. Where is thy power then to beat him back?
Where be thy tenants and thy followers?
Are they not now upon the western shore,
Safe-conducting the rebels from their ships?
Stan. No, my good lord, my friends are in the North.
Rich. Cold friends to me! What do they in the North
When they should serve their sovereign in the West?
Stan. They have not been commanded, mighty king.
Pleaseth your Majesty to give me leave,
I'll muster up my friends and meet your Grace
Where and what time your Majesty shall please.
Rich. Ay, ay, thou wouldst be gone to join with Richmond.
But I'll not trust you, sir.

Stan. Most mighty sovereign,
You have no cause to hold my friendship doubtful.
I never was nor never will be false.
Rich. Go then and muster men. But leave behind
Your son, George Stanley. Look your heart be firm,
Or else his head's assurance is but frail.
Stan. So deal with him as I prove true to you. *Exit.*

Enter a *Messenger.*

Mess. My gracious sovereign, now in Devonshire,
As I by friends am well advertised,
Sir Edward Courtney and the haughty prelate,
Bishop of Exeter, his elder brother,
With many moe confederates, are in arms.

Enter another *Messenger.*

Mess. In Kent, my liege, the Guildfords are in arms,
And every hour more competitors
Flock to the rebels, and their power grows strong.

Enter another *Messenger.*

Mess. My lord, the army of great Buckingham —
Rich. Out on ye, owls! Nothing but songs of death? *He striketh him.*
There, take thou that, till thou bring better news.
Mess. The news I have to tell your Majesty
Is that by sudden floods and fall of waters
Buckingham's army is dispers'd and scatter'd,
And he himself wand'red away alone,
No man knows whither.
Rich. I cry thee mercy.
There is my purse to cure that blow of thine.
Hath any well-advised friend proclaim'd
Reward to him that brings the traitor in?
Mess. Such proclamation hath been made, my lord.

Enter another *Messenger.*

Mess. Sir Thomas Lovel and Lord Marquess Dorset,
'Tis said, my liege, in Yorkshire are in arms.
But this good comfort bring I to your Highness:
The Britain navy is dispers'd by tempest.
Richmond in Dorsetshire sent out a boat
Unto the shore to ask those on the banks
If they were his assistants, yea or no;
Who answer'd him they came from Buckingham
Upon his party. He, mistrusting them,
Hois'd sail, and made his course again for Britain.
Rich. March on, march on, since we are up in arms;
If not to fight with foreign enemies,
Yet to beat down these rebels here at home.

Enter *Catesby.*

Cates. My liege, the Duke of Buckingham is taken.
That is the best news. That the Earl of Richmond
Is with a mighty power landed at Milford
Is colder news, but yet they must be told.
Rich. Away towards Salisbury! While we reason here,
A royal battle might be won and lost.
Some one take order Buckingham be brought
To Salisbury; the rest march on with me.
Flourish. Exeunt.

Scene [V. Lord Derby's *house.*]

Enter *Derby* and *Sir Christopher* [*Urswick*].

Der. Sir Christopher, tell Richmond this from me:
That in the sty of the most deadly boar
My son George Stanley is frank'd up in hold;
If I revolt, off goes young George's head;
The fear of that holds off my present aid.
So get thee gone. Commend me to thy lord.
Withal say that the Queen hath heartily consented
He should espouse Elizabeth her daughter.
But tell me, where is princely Richmond now?
Chris. At Pembroke, or at Ha'rford-West in Wales.
Der. What men of name resort to him?
Chris. Sir Walter Herbert, a renowned soldier,
Sir Gilbert Talbot, Sir William Stanley,
Oxford, redoubted Pembroke, Sir James Blunt,
And Rice ap Thomas, with a valiant crew,
And many other of great name and worth;
And towards London do they bend their power,
If by the way they be not fought withal.
Der. Well, hie thee to thy lord. I kiss his hand.
My letter will resolve him of my mind.
[*Gives letter.*]
Farewell. *Exeunt.*

ACT V. Scene I. [*Salisbury. An open place.*]

Enter *Buckingham* with *Halberds* [and the *Sheriff*], led to execution.

Buck. Will not King Richard let me speak with him?

Sher. No, my good lord. Therefore be patient.

Buck. Hastings, and Edward's children, Grey and Rivers,
Holy King Henry and thy fair son Edward,
Vaughan and all that have miscarried
By underhand corrupted foul injustice,
If that your moody discontented souls
Do through the clouds behold this present hour,
Even for revenge mock my destruction!
This is All Souls' day, fellow, is it not?

Sher. It is, my lord.

Buck. Why, then All Souls' day is my body's doomsday.
This is the day which in King Edward's time
I wish'd might fall on me when I was found
False to his children and his wive's allies.
This is the day wherein I wish'd to fall
By the false faith of him whom most I trusted.
This, this All Souls' day to my fearful soul
Is the determin'd respite of my wrongs.
That high All-seer which I dallied with
Hath turn'd my feigned prayer on my head
And given in earnest what I begg'd in jest.
Thus doth he force the swords of wicked men
To turn their own points in their masters' bosoms.
Thus Margaret's curse falls heavy on my neck.
'When he,' quoth she, 'shall split thy heart with sorrow,
Remember Margaret was a prophetess.' —
Come lead me, officers, to the block of shame.
Wrong hath but wrong, and blame the due of blame. *Exit with officers.*

Scene II. [*Camp near Tamworth.*]

Enter *Richmond, Oxford,* [*Sir James*] *Blunt,* [*Sir Walter*] *Herbert,* and others, with *Drum* and *Colours.*

Richm. Fellows in arms, and my most loving friends,
Bruis'd underneath the yoke of tyranny,
Thus far into the bowels of the land
Have we march'd on without impediment;
And here receive we from our father Stanley
Lines of fair comfort and encouragement.
The wretched, bloody, and usurping boar,
That spoil'd your summer fields and fruitful vines,
Swills your warm blood like wash, and makes his trough
In your embowell'd bosoms — this foul swine
Lies now even in the centre of this isle,
Near to the town of Leicester, as we learn.
From Tamworth thither is but one day's march.
In God's name cheerly on, courageous friends,
To reap the harvest of perpetual peace
By this one bloody trial of sharp war.

Oxf. Every man's conscience is a thousand men,
To fight against this guilty homicide.

Herb. I doubt not but his friends will turn to us.

Blunt. He hath no friends but what are friends for fear,
Which in his dearest need will fly from him.

Richm. All for our vantage. Then in God's name march!
True hope is swift and flies with swallow's wings;
Kings it makes gods, and meaner creatures kings. *Exeunt.*

[Scene III. *Bosworth Field.*]

Enter *King Richard* in arms, with *Norfolk, Ratcliff,* the *Earl of Surrey,* [and *Soldiers*].

Rich. Here pitch our tent, even here in Bosworth field.
My Lord of Surrey, why look you so sad?

Sur. My heart is ten times lighter than my looks.

Rich. My Lord of Norfolk —

Nor. Here, most gracious liege.

Rich. Norfolk, we must have knocks. Ha! must we not?

Nor. We must both give and take, my loving lord.

Rich. Up with my tent! Here will I lie to-night;

[*Soldiers begin to set up the King's tent.*]

But where to-morrow? Well, all's one for that.
Who hath descried the number of the traitors?
Nor. Six or seven thousand is their utmost power.
Rich. Why, our battalia trebles that account.
Besides, the King's name is a tower of strength,
Which they upon the adverse faction want.
Up with the tent! Come, noble gentlemen,
Let us survey the vantage of the ground.
Call for some men of sound direction.
Let's lack no discipline, make no delay,
For, lords, to-morrow is a busy day. *Exeunt.*

Enter *Richmond, Sir William Brandon, Oxford, Dorset, Herbert, and Blunt.* [Some of the *Soldiers* pitch *Richmond's* tent.]

Richm. The weary sun hath made a golden set
And by the bright tract of his fiery car
Gives token of a goodly day to-morrow.
Sir William Brandon, you shall bear my standard.
Give me some ink and paper in my tent.
I'll draw the form and model of our battle,
Limit each leader to his several charge,
And part in just proportion our small power.
My Lord of Oxford, — you, Sir William Brandon, —
And you, Sir Walter Herbert — stay with me.
The Earl of Pembroke keeps his regiment.
Good Captain Blunt, bear my good-night to him,
And by the second hour in the morning
Desire the Earl to see me in my tent.
Yet one thing more, good Captain, do for me.
Where is Lord Stanley quarter'd, do you know?
Blunt. Unless I have mista'en his colours much
(Which well I am assur'd I have not done),
His regiment lies half a mile at least
South from the mighty power of the King.
Richm. If without peril it be possible,
Sweet Blunt, make some good means to speak with him
And give him from me this most needful note.
Blunt. Upon my life, my lord, I'll undertake it;
And so God give you quiet rest to-night!
Richm. Good night, good Captain Blunt. [*Exit Blunt.*] Come, gentlemen,
Let us consult upon to-morrow's business.
Into my tent; the dew is raw and cold.
They withdraw into the tent.

Enter, [to his tent,] *Richard, Ratcliff, Norfolk,* and *Catesby.*

Rich. What is't o'clock?
Cates. It's supper time, my lord;
It's nine o'clock.
Rich. I will not sup to-night.
Give me some ink and paper.
What, is my beaver easier than it was,
And all my armour laid into my tent?
Cates. It is, my liege; and all things are in readiness.
Rich. Good Norfolk, hie thee to thy charge;
Use careful watch, choose trusty sentinels.
Nor. I go, my lord.
Rich. Stir with the lark to-morrow, gentle Norfolk.
Nor. I warrant you, my lord. *Exit.*
Rich. Catesby!
Cates. My lord?
Rich. Send out a pursuivant-at-arms
To Stanley's regiment. Bid him bring his power
Before sunrising, lest his son George fall
Into the blind cave of eternal night.
[*Exit Catesby.*]
Fill me a bowl of wine. Give me a watch.
Saddle white Surrey for the field to-morrow.
Look that my staves be sound and not too heavy.
Ratcliff!
Rat. My lord?
Rich. Saw'st thou the melancholy Lord Northumberland?
Rat. Thomas the Earl of Surrey and himself,
Much about cockshut time, from troop to troop
Went through the army, cheering up the soldiers.
Rich. So, I am satisfied. Give me a bowl of wine.
I have not that alacrity of spirit
Nor cheer of mind that I was wont to have.
[*Wine brought.*]
Set it down. Is ink and paper ready?
Rat. It is, my lord.
Rich. Bid my guard watch. Leave me. Ratcliff,
About the mid of night come to my tent
And help to arm me. Leave me, I say.
Exit Ratcliff [*with others*].
[*King Richard retires into his tent, and sleeps.*]

Enter *Derby* to *Richmond* in his tent.

Der. Fortune and victory sit on thy helm!

Richm. All comfort that the dark night can afford
Be to thy person, noble father-in-law!
Tell me, how fares our loving mother?

Der. I, by attorney, bless thee from thy mother,
Who prays continually for Richmond's good.
So much for that. The silent hours steal on
And flaky darkness breaks within the east.
In brief, for so the season bids us be,
Prepare thy battle early in the morning
And put thy fortune to th' arbitrement
Of bloody strokes and mortal-staring war.
I, as I may, — that which I would I cannot, —
With best advantage will deceive the time
And aid thee in this doubtful shock of arms.
But on thy side I may not be too forward,
Lest, being seen, thy brother, tender George,
Be executed in his father's sight.
Farewell. The leisure and the fearful time
Cuts off the ceremonious vows of love
And ample interchange of sweet discourse
Which so long sund'red friends should dwell upon.
God give us leisure for these rites of love!
Once more adieu. Be valiant, and speed well!

Richm. Good lords, conduct him to his regiment.
I'll strive with troubled noise, to take a nap,
Lest leaden slumber peise me down to-morrow
When I should mount with wings of victory.
Once more, good night, kind lords and gentlemen.

Exeunt. Manet Richmond.

O thou whose captain I account myself,
Look on my forces with a gracious eye.
Put in their hands thy bruising irons of wrath,
That they may crush down with a heavy fall
Th' usurping helmets of our adversaries.
Make us thy ministers of chastisement,
That we may praise thee in thy victory.
To thee I do commend my watchful soul
Ere I let fall the windows of mine eyes.
Sleeping and waking, O defend me still!

Sleeps.

Enter the *Ghost of Prince Edward,* son to *Henry the Sixth.*

Ghost. (*to Richard*) Let me sit heavy in thy soul to-morrow!
Think how thou stab'dst me in my prime of youth
At Tewksbury. Despair, therefore, and die!
(*To Richmond*) Be cheerful, Richmond; for the wronged souls
Of butcher'd princes fight in thy behalf.
King Henry's issue, Richmond, comforts thee.

Enter the *Ghost of Henry the Sixth.*

Ghost. (*to Richard*) When I was mortal, my anointed body
By thee was punched full of deadly holes.
Think on the Tower, and me. Despair and die!
Harry the Sixth bids thee despair and die!
(*To Richmond*) Virtuous and holy, be thou conqueror!
Harry, that prophesied thou shouldst be King,
Doth comfort thee in sleep. Live and flourish!

Enter the *Ghost of Clarence.*

Ghost. [*to Richard*] Let me sit heavy in thy soul to-morrow —
I that was wash'd to death with fulsome wine,
Poor Clarence by thy guile betray'd to death!
To-morrow in the battle think on me,
And fall thy edgeless sword. Despair and die!
(*To Richmond*) Thou offspring of the house of Lancaster,
The wronged heirs of York do pray for thee.
Good angels guard thy battle! Live and flourish!

Enter the *Ghosts* of *Rivers, Grey,* and *Vaughan.*

Riv. [*to Richard*] Let me sit heavy in thy soul to-morrow,
Rivers, that died at Pomfret! Despair and die!

Grey. Think upon Grey, and let thy soul despair!

Vaugh. Think upon Vaughan and with guilty fear
Let fall thy lance. Despair and die!

All. (*to Richmond*) Awake, and think our wrongs in Richard's bosom
Will conquer him! Awake and win the day!

Enter the *Ghost* of *Lord Hastings.*

Ghost. [*to Richard*] Bloody and guilty, guiltily awake
And in a bloody battle end thy days!
Think on Lord Hastings. Despair and die!
(*To Richmond*) Quiet untroubled soul, awake, awake!
Arm, fight, and conquer, for fair England's sake!

Enter the *Ghosts* of the two young *Princes.*

Ghosts. (*to Richard*) Dream on thy cousins smothered in the Tower.
Let us be lead within thy bosom, Richard,

And weigh thee down to ruin, shame, and death!
Thy nephews' souls bid thee despair and die!
(*To Richmond*) Sleep, Richmond, sleep in peace and wake in joy.
Good angels guard thee from the boar's annoy!
Live, and beget a happy race of kings!
Edward's unhappy sons do bid thee flourish.

Enter the *Ghost* of *Anne*, his wife.

Ghost. (*to Richard*) Richard, thy wife, that wretched Anne thy wife,
That never slept a quiet hour with thee,
Now fills thy sleep with perturbations.
To-morrow in the battle think on me,
And fall thy edgeless sword. Despair and die!
(*To Richmond*) Thou quiet soul, sleep thou a quiet sleep.
Dream of success and happy victory!
Thy adversary's wife doth pray for thee.

Enter the *Ghost* of *Buckingham.*

Ghost. (*to Richard*) The first was I that help'd thee to the crown;
The last was I that felt thy tyranny.
O, in the battle think on Buckingham,
And die in terror of thy guiltiness!
Dream on, dream on, of bloody deeds and death.
Fainting, despair; despairing, yield thy breath!
(*To Richmond*) I died for hope ere I could lend thee aid.
But cheer thy heart and be thou not dismay'd.
God and good angels fight on Richmond's side,
And Richard fall in height of all his pride!

[*The Ghosts vanish.*] *Richard starts out of his dream.*

Rich. Give me another horse! Bind up my wounds!
Have mercy, Jesu! Soft! I did but dream.
O coward conscience, how dost thou afflict me!
The lights burn blue. It is now dead midnight.
Cold fearful drops stand on my trembling flesh.
What do I fear? Myself? There's none else by.
Richard loves Richard: that is, I am I.
Is there a murtherer here? No. Yes, I am.
Then fly. What, from myself? Great reason why —
Lest I revenge myself upon myself?
Alack, I love myself. Wherefore? For any good
That I myself have done unto myself?
O no! Alas, I rather hate myself
For hateful deeds committed by myself.
I am a villain. Yet I lie, I am not.
Fool, of thyself speak well. Fool, do not flatter.
My conscience hath a thousand several tongues,
And every tongue brings in a several tale,
And every tale condemns me for a villain.
Perjury, perjury, in the high'st degree,
Murther, stern murther, in the dir'st degree,
All several sins, all us'd in each degree,
Throng to the bar, crying all 'Guilty! guilty!'
I shall despair. There is no creature loves me;
And if I die, no soul shall pity me.
Nay, wherefore should they, since that I myself
Find in myself no pity to myself?
Methought the souls of all that I had murther'd
Came to my tent, and every one did threat
To-morrow's vengeance on the head of Richard.

Enter *Ratcliff.*

Rat. My lord!
Rich. Zounds, who's there?
Rat. My lord, 'tis I. The early village cock
Hath twice done salutation to the morn.
Your friends are up and buckle on their armour.
Rich. O Ratcliff, I have dream'd a fearful dream!
What thinkest thou? Will our friends prove all true?
Rat. No doubt, my lord.
Rich. O Ratcliff, I fear, I fear!
Rat. Nay, good my lord, be not afraid of shadows.
Rich. By the apostle Paul, shadows to-night
Have struck more terror to the soul of Richard
Than can the substance of ten thousand soldiers
Armed in proof and led by shallow Richmond.
It is not yet near day. Come, go with me.
Under our tents I'll play the easedropper,
To hear if any mean to shrink from me.
Exeunt Richard and Ratcliff.

Enter the *Lords,* to *Richmond* sitting in his tent.

Lords. Good morrow, Richmond.
Richm. Cry mercy, lords and watchful gentlemen,
That you have ta'en a tardy sluggard here.
Lords. How have you slept, my lord?
Richm. The sweetest sleep, and fairest-boding dreams
That ever ent'red in a drowsy head
Have I since your departure had, my lords.

Methought their souls whose bodies Richard murther'd
Came to my tent and cried on 'Victory.'
I promise you my heart is very jocund
In the remembrance of so fair a dream.
How far into the morning is it, lords?

Lords. Upon the stroke of four.

Richm. Why, then 'tis time to arm and give direction.

His Oration to his Soldiers.

More than I have said, loving countrymen,
The leisure and enforcement of the time
Forbids to dwell upon. Yet remember this:
God and our good cause fight upon our side;
The prayers of holy saints and wronged souls,
Like high-rear'd bulwarks, stand before our faces.
Richard except, those whom we fight against
Had rather have us win than him they follow.
For what is he they follow? Truly, gentlemen,
A bloody tyrant and a homicide;
One rais'd in blood and one in blood establish'd;
One that made means to come by what he hath,
And slaughter'd those that were the means to help him;
A base foul stone, made precious by the foil
Of England's chair, where he is falsely set;
One that hath ever been God's enemy.
Then if you fight against God's enemy,
God will in justice ward you as his soldiers.
If you do sweat to put a tyrant down,
You sleep in peace, the tyrant being slain.
If you do fight against your country's foes,
Your country's fat shall pay your pains the hire.
If you do fight in safeguard of your wives,
Your wives shall welcome home the conquerors.
If you do free your children from the sword,
Your children's children quit it in your age.
Then in the name of God and all these rights,
Advance your standards, draw your willing swords.
For me, the ransom of my bold attempt
Shall be this cold corpse on the earth's cold face.
But if I thrive, the gain of my attempt
The least of you shall share his part thereof.
Sound drums and trumpets boldly and cheerfully.
God and Saint George! Richmond and victory!
[*Exeunt.*]

Enter *King Richard, Ratcliff,* etc.

Rich. What said Northumberland as touching Richmond?

Rat. That he was never trained up in arms.

Rich. He said the truth. And what said Surrey then?

Rat. He smil'd and said, 'The better for our purpose.'

Rich. He was in the right, and so indeed it is.
Clock strikes.
Tell the clock there. Give me a calendar.
Who saw the sun to-day?

Rat. Not I, my lord.

Rich. Then he disdains to shine; for by the book
He should have brav'd the East an hour ago.
A black day will it be to somebody.
Ratcliff!

Rat. My lord?

Rich. The sun will not be seen to-day;
The sky doth frown and low'r upon our army.
I would these dewy tears were from the ground.
Not shine to-day? Why, what is that to me
More than to Richmond? For the selfsame heaven
That frowns on me looks sadly upon him.

Enter *Norfolk.*

Nor. Arm, arm, my lord! The foe vaunts in the field.

Rich. Come, bustle, bustle! Caparison my horse!
Call up Lord Stanley, bid him bring his power.
I will lead forth my soldiers to the plain,
And thus my battle shall be ordered:
My foreward shall be drawn out all in length,
Consisting equally of horse and foot;
Our archers shall be placed in the midst;
John Duke of Norfolk, Thomas Earl of Surrey,
Shall have the leading of the foot and horse.
They thus directed, we ourself will follow
In the main battle, whose puissance on either side
Shall be well-winged with our chiefest horse.
This, and Saint George to boot! What think'st thou, Norfolk?

Nor. A good direction, warlike sovereign.
This found I on my tent this morning.
He showeth him a paper.

Jockey of Norfolk, be not so bold,
For Dickon thy master is bought and sold.

Rich. A thing devised by the enemy.
Go, gentlemen, every man to his charge.
Let not our babbling dreams affright our souls;
For conscience is a word that cowards use,
Devis'd at first to keep the strong in awe.
Our strong arms be our conscience, swords our law!

March on, join bravely, let us to't pell-mell,
If not to heaven, then hand in hand to hell.

His Oration to his Army.

What shall I say more than I have inferr'd?
Remember whom you are to cope withal —
A sort of vagabonds, rascals, and runaways,
A scum of Britons and base lackey peasants,
Whom their o'ercloyed country vomits forth
To desperate adventures and assur'd destruction.
You sleeping safe, they bring to you unrest;
You having lands, and bless'd with beauteous wives,
They would restrain the one, distain the other.
And who doth lead them but a paltry fellow,
Long kept in Britain at our mother's cost,
A milksop, one that never in his life
Felt so much cold as over shoes in snow?
Let's whip these stragglers o'er the seas again,
Lash hence these overweening rags of France,
These famish'd beggars, weary of their lives,
Who (but for dreaming on this fond exploit)
For want of means (poor rats) had hang'd themselves.
If we be conquered, let men conquer us,
And not these bastard Britons, whom our fathers
Have in their own land beaten, bobb'd, and thump'd,
And, on record, left them the heirs of shame.
Shall these enjoy our lands? lie with our wives?
Ravish our daughters? (*Drum afar off.*) Hark! I hear their drum.
Fight, gentlemen of England! Fight, bold yeomen!
Draw, archers, draw your arrows to the head!
Spur your proud horses hard, and ride in blood!
Amaze the welkin with your broken staves!

Enter a *Messenger.*

What says Lord Stanley? Will he bring his power?

Mess. My lord, he doth deny to come.

Rich. Off with his son George's head!

Nor. My lord, the enemy is past the marsh.
After the battle let George Stanley die.

Rich. A thousand hearts are great within my bosom.
Advance our standards, set upon our foes.
Our ancient word of courage, fair Saint George,
Inspire us with the spleen of fiery dragons!
Upon them! Victory sits on our helms.

Exeunt.

[Scene IV. *Another part of the field.*]

Alarum; excursions. Enter [*Norfolk* and *Forces*; to him] *Catesby.*

Cates. Rescue, my Lord of Norfolk, rescue, rescue!
The King enacts more wonders than a man,
Daring an opposite to every danger.
His horse is slain, and all on foot he fights,
Seeking for Richmond in the throat of death.
Rescue, fair lord, or else the day is lost!

Alarums. Enter *Richard.*

Rich. A horse! a horse! my kingdom for a horse!

Cates. Withdraw, my lord. I'll help you to a horse.

Rich. Slave, I have set my life upon a cast
And I will stand the hazard of the die.
I think there be six Richmonds in the field;
Five have I slain to-day instead of him.
A horse! a horse! my kingdom for a horse!

[*Exeunt.*]

[Scene V. *Another part of the field.*]

Alarum. Enter *Richard* and *Richmond*; they fight; *Richard* is slain.

Retreat and flourish. Enter *Richmond, Derby* bearing the crown, with *divers other Lords.*

Richm. God and your arms be prais'd, victorious friends!
The day is ours; the bloody dog is dead.

Der. Courageous Richmond, well hast thou acquit thee.
Lo, here these long usurped royalties
From the dead temples of this bloody wretch
Have I pluck'd off, to grace thy brows withal.
Wear it, enjoy it, and make much of it.

Richm. Great God of heaven, say amen to all!
But tell me, is young George Stanley living?

Der. He is, my lord, and safe in Leicester town,
Whither, if it please you, we may now withdraw us.

Richm. What men of name are slain on either side?

Der. John Duke of Norfolk, Walter Lord Ferrers,
Sir Robert Brakenbury, and Sir William Brandon.

Richm. Inter their bodies as become their births.
Proclaim a pardon to the soldiers fled
That in submission will return to us;
And then, as we have ta'en the sacrament,
We will unite the White Rose and the Red.
Smile heaven upon this fair conjunction,
That long have frown'd upon their enmity!
What traitor hears me, and says not amen?
England hath long been mad and scarr'd herself;
The brother blindly shed the brother's blood;
The father rashly slaughtered his own son;
The son, compell'd, been butcher to the sire.
All this divided York and Lancaster,
Divided in their dire division,
O, now let Richmond and Elizabeth,
The true succeeders of each royal house,
By God's fair ordinance conjoin together!
And let their heirs (God, if thy will be so)
Enrich the time to come with smooth-fac'd peace,
With smiling plenty, and fair prosperous days!
Abate the edge of traitors, gracious Lord,
That would reduce these bloody days again
And make poor England weep in streams of blood!
Let them not live to taste this land's increase
That would with treason wound this fair land's peace!
Now civil wounds are stopp'd, peace lives again:
That she may long live here, God say amen!
Exeunt.

KING HENRY THE EIGHTH

KING HENRY THE EIGHTH was first printed in the Folio of 1623, which is therefore the sole authority for the text.

The date of composition must be shortly before June 29, 1613, for on that day, during a performance of KING HENRY THE EIGHTH, then a new play, the Globe theatre caught fire from the cannon salute that marks the king's approach (i, 4, 49) and was burned down. Sir Henry Wotton gave a lively account of the accident in a letter to his nephew Sir Edmund Bacon written a few days later (July 2):

> Now, to let matters of state sleep, I will entertain you at the present with what has happened this week at the Bank's side. The King's players had a new play, called *All is True*, representing some principal pieces of the reign of Henry VIII, which was set forth with many extraordinary circumstances of pomp and majesty, even to the matting of the stage; the Knights of the Order with their Georges and garters, the Guards with their embroidered coats, and the like: sufficient in truth within a while to make greatness very familiar, if not ridiculous. Now, King Henry making a masque at the Cardinal Wolsey's house, and certain chambers being shot off at his entry, some of the paper, or other stuff, wherewith one of them was stopped, did light on the thatch, where being thought at first but an idle smoke, and their eyes more attentive to the show, it kindled inwardly, and ran round like a train, consuming within less than an hour the whole house to the very grounds. This was the fatal period of that virtuous fabric, wherein yet nothing did perish but wood and straw, and a few forsaken cloaks; only one man had his breeches set on fire, that would perhaps have broiled him, if he had not by the benefit of a provident wit put it out with bottle ale.

That the 'new play' that Wotton mentions was HENRY VIII — though he gives it a different title — is certain, not only from his description but from other testimony. Thus Thomas Lorkin, in a letter written on June 30, says that the fire occurred 'yesterday, while Burbage's company were acting at the Globe the play of HENRY VIII, and there shooting off certain chambers [i.e. short cannon, standing upright] in way of triumph.' *All is True* was doubtless an alternative title. The Prologue of KING HENRY THE EIGHTH insists that the play is 'our chosen truth,' and a contemporary ballad 'upon the pittifal burneing of the Globe playhowse' has 'all this is true' in the refrain. The style and metre of the Shakespearean part of the drama accord with a late date.

That the greater part of KING HENRY THE EIGHTH is not Shakespeare's is certain. His share, except for a possible touch now and then, seems to comprise only scenes 1 and 2 of Act i, scenes 3 and 4 of Act ii, the first 203 lines of scene 2 in Act iii, and scene 1 in Act v. The rest is proved — to all intents and purposes — by style and manner, and especially by metre, to be the work of John Fletcher, though no direct evidence connects his name with the play. Such evidence, however, does exist for his association with Shakespeare in *The Two Noble Kinsmen*, which must be of about the same date (see p. 1409). The allotment gives Fletcher the two most famous passages in the drama — Wolsey's farewell to greatness and his advice to Cromwell (iii, 2, 351–372, 428–457). But Shakespeare can spare them, and they are not beyond Fletcher's powers. There is no reason to detect a third hand (Beaumont or another) in the play or to ascribe the Shakespearean scenes to Massinger.

That some of Shakespeare's scenes (v, 1, for instance) have been touched up by Fletcher is of course possible. Whether there was intimate collaboration, or whether Fletcher completed an unfinished Shakespearean play, cannot be determined by any tests beyond those of editorial imagination. What Fletcher did, however, he must have done by Shakespeare's authority, for HENRY THE EIGHTH was prepared for Shakespeare's company, and it was accepted by his partners — Heminge and Condell — as sufficiently his to be included in their edition, the Folio of 1623.

For history, the authors went to Holinshed's *Chronicle*. For the Cranmer episode (v, 1–3), however, both Shakespeare and Fletcher, whether they worked in concert or not, had recourse to Foxe's *Book of Martyrs*, phrases from which appear frequently in the text of both. Henry's remark in v, 3, 174–6, for example, simply versifies Foxe's words: 'It came into a common prouerbe: "Do vnto my Lord of Canterbury displeasure or a shrewed turne, and then you may be sure to haue him your frend whiles he lyueth."' Queen Katherine's speech at the Blackfriar's trial (ii, 4, 13–57) is versified from Holinshed with very little change. At least two lines of the blank verse are taken word for word from the prose chronicle. The whole may be compared with Hermione's defence in *The Winter's Tale* (iii, 2).

Chronology is sacrificed, as usual, to dramatic convenience, but without doing violence to the title *All is True*. Thus Queen Katherine's petition in behalf of the commons overwhelmed by the sixth-part tax (i, 2) comes immediately after the arrest of Buckingham (i, 1) and before his trial and conviction (ii, 1). In fact, he was arrested in April, 1521, and convicted on May 13, 1521; whereas the exaction of 'the sixth part of every man's substance' was not decreed until 1525. Wolsey died in 1530; Elizabeth was born in 1533; Queen Katherine died in 1536. In the play, Queen Katherine's death precedes Elizabeth's birth, and Wolsey's death is told the Queen just before her own takes place. The accusation of Cranmer before the Council (v, 3) was not until after 1540 (probably in 1544). In the play, however, it precedes the christening of Elizabeth (1533).

In 1605 was published a play by Samuel Rowley entitled 'When you see me, You know me. Or the famous Chronicle Historie of King Henry the eight, with the birth and vertuous life of Edward Prince of Wales.' It was probably known to the authors of HENRY THE EIGHTH, but they owe it nothing. Had they borrowed from this random-roaming play, their procedure would have merited what Rowley makes Patch, the Cardinal's fool, say to Will Sommers: 'Wee haue but little wit betweene vs already, and so we should haue none at all!'

THE FAMOUS HISTORY OF THE LIFE OF
KING HENRY THE EIGHTH

[Dramatis Personæ.

King Henry the Eighth.
Cardinal Wolsey.
Cardinal Campeius.
Capucius, Ambassador from the Emperor Charles V.
Cranmer, Archbishop of Canterbury.
Duke of Norfolk.
Duke of Buckingham.
Duke of Suffolk.
Earl of Surrey.
Lord Chamberlain.
Lord Chancellor.
Gardiner, King's Secretary, afterwards Bishop of Winchester.
Bishop of Lincoln.
Lord Abergavenny.
Lord Sandys (also styled *Sir William Sandys*).
Sir Henry Guildford.
Sir Thomas Lovell.
Sir Anthony Denny.
Sir Nicholas Vaux.
Cromwell, servant to *Wolsey.*
Secretaries to *Wolsey.*
Griffith, Gentleman Usher to *Queen Katherine.*
Three Gentlemen.
Doctor Butts, Physician to the *King.*
Garter King-at-Arms.
Surveyor to the *Duke of Buckingham.*
Brandon, and a Sergeant-at-Arms.
Doorkeeper of the Council Chamber.
Porter, and his Man.
Page to *Gardiner.*
A Crier.

Queen Katherine, wife to *King Henry,* afterwards divorced.
Anne Bullen, her Maid of Honour, afterwards Queen.
An old Lady, friend to *Anne Bullen.*
Patience, woman to *Queen Katherine.*

Spirits.

Several Bishops, Lords, and Ladies in the Dumb Shows; Women attending upon the Queen; Scribes, Officers, Guards, and other Attendants.

SCENE. — *London; Westminster; Kimbolton.*]

THE PROLOGUE.

I come no more to make you laugh. Things now
That bear a weighty and a serious brow,
Sad, high, and working, full of state and woe,
Such noble scenes as draw the eye to flow,
We now present. Those that can pity, here
May (if they think it well) let fall a tear:
The subject will deserve it. Such as give
Their money out of hope they may believe,
May here find truth too. Those that come to see
Only a show or two and so agree
The play may pass — if they be still and willing,
I'll undertake may see away their shilling
Richly in two short hours. Only they
That come to hear a merry bawdy play,
A noise of targets, or to see a fellow
In a long motley coat guarded with yellow,
Will be deceiv'd. For, gentle hearers, know,
To rank our chosen truth with such a show
As fool and fight is, beside forfeiting
Our own brains and the opinion that we bring
To make that only true we now intend,
Will leave us never an understanding friend.
Therefore, for goodness sake, and as you are known
The first and happiest hearers of the town,
Be sad, as we would make ye. Think ye see
The very persons of our noble story
As they were living. Think you see them great,
And follow'd with the general throng, and sweat
Of thousand friends. Then, in a moment, see
How soon this mightiness meets misery.
And if you can be merry then, I'll say
A man may weep upon his wedding day.

Act I. Scene I. [*London. An antechamber in the Palace.*]

Enter the *Duke of Norfolk* at one door; at the other, the *Duke of Buckingham* and the *Lord Abergavenny.*

Buck. Good morrow and well met. How have ye done
Since last we saw in France?
Nor. I thank your Grace:
Healthful, and ever since a fresh admirer
Of what I saw there.
Buck. An untimely ague
Stay'd me a prisoner in my chamber when
Those suns of glory, those two lights of men,
Met in the vale of Andren.
Nor. 'Twixt Guynes and Arde.
I was then present, saw them salute on horseback;
Beheld them when they lighted, how they clung
In their embracement, as they grew together;
Which had they, what four thron'd ones could have weigh'd
Such a compounded one?
Buck. All the whole time
I was my chamber's prisoner.
Nor. Then you lost
The view of earthly glory. Men might say,
Till this time pomp was single, but now married
To one above itself. Each following day
Became the next day's master, till the last
Made former wonders its. To-day the French,
All clinquant, all in gold, like heathen gods,
Shone down the English; and to-morrow they
Made Britain India — every man that stood
Show'd like a mine. Their dwarfish pages were
As cherubins, all gilt. The madams too,
Not us'd to toil, did almost sweat to bear
The pride upon them, that their very labour
Was to them as a painting. Now this masque
Was cried incomparable; and th' ensuing night
Made it a fool and beggar. The two kings,
Equal in lustre, were now best, now worst,
As presence did present them — him in eye
Still him in praise; and being present both,
'Twas said they saw but one, and no discerner
Durst wag his tongue in censure. When these suns
(For so they phrase 'em) by their heralds challeng'd
The noble spirits to arms, they did perform
Beyond thought's compass, that former fabulous story,
Being now seen possible enough, got credit,
That Bevis was believ'd.
Buck. O, you go far!
Nor. As I belong to worship and affect
In honour honesty, the tract of ev'ry thing
Would by a good discourser lose some life
Which action's self was tongue to. All was royal.
To the disposing of it naught rebell'd;
Order gave each thing view. The office did
Distinctly his full function.
Buck. Who did guide —
I mean, who set the body and the limbs
Of this great sport together, as you guess?
Nor. One, certes, that promises no element
In such a business.
Buck. I pray you, who, my lord?
Nor. All this was ord'red by the good discretion
Of the right reverend Cardinal of York.
Buck. The devil speed him! No man's pie is freed
From his ambitious finger. What had he
To do in these fierce vanities? I wonder
That such a keech can with his very bulk
Take up the rays o' th' beneficial sun
And keep it from the earth.
Nor. Surely, sir,
There's in him stuff that puts him to these ends;
For, being not propp'd by ancestry, whose grace
Chalks successors their way, nor call'd upon
For high feats done to th' crown, neither allied
To eminent assistants, but spiderlike
Out of his self-drawing web, 'a gives us note
The force of his own merit makes his way —
A gift that heaven gives for him, which buys
A place next to the King.
Aber. I cannot tell
What heaven hath given him. Let some graver eye
Pierce into that; but I can see his pride
Peep through each part of him. Whence has he that?
If not from hell, the devil is a niggard,
Or has given all before and he begins
A new hell in himself.
Buck. Why the devil,
Upon this French going out, took he upon him
(Without the privity o' th' King) t' appoint
Who should attend on him? He makes up the file

Of all the gentry; for the most part such
To whom as great a charge as little honour
He meant to lay upon; and his own letter,
The Honourable Board of Council out,
Must fetch him in he papers.

Aber. I do know
Kinsmen of mine, three at the least, that have
By this so sicken'd their estates that never
They shall abound as formerly.

Buck. O, many
Have broke their backs with laying manors on 'em
For this great journey. What did this vanity
But minister communication of
A most poor issue?

Nor. Grievingly I think
The peace between the French and us not values
The cost that did conclude it.

Buck. Every man,
After the hideous storm that follow'd, was
A thing inspir'd, and, not consulting, broke
Into a general prophecy — that this tempest,
Dashing the garment of this peace, aboded
The sudden breach on't.

Nor. Which is budded out;
For France hath flaw'd the league and hath attach'd
Our merchants' goods at Bordeaux.

Aber. Is it therefore
Th' ambassador is silenc'd?

Nor. Marry is't!

Aber. A proper title of a peace, and purchas'd
At a superfluous rate!

Buck. Why, all this business
Our reverend Cardinal carried.

Nor. Like it your Grace,
The state takes notice of the private difference
Betwixt you and the Cardinal. I advise you
(And take it from a heart that wishes towards you
Honour and plenteous safety) that you read
The Cardinal's malice and his potency
Together; to consider further, that
What his high hatred would effect wants not
A minister in his power. You know his nature,
That he's revengeful; and I know his sword
Hath a sharp edge; it's long, and 't may be said
It reaches far, and where 'twill not extend,
Thither he darts it. Bosom up my counsel;
You'll find it wholesome. Lo, where comes that rock
That I advise your shunning.

Enter *Cardinal Wolsey*, the purse borne before him, certain of the *Guard*, and two *Secretaries* with papers. The *Cardinal* in his passage fixeth his eye on *Buckingham*, and *Buckingham* on him, both full of disdain.

Car. The Duke of Buckingham's surveyor? Ha!
Where's his examination?

Secr. Here, so please you.

Car. Is he in person ready?

Secr. Ay, please your Grace.

Car. Well, we shall then know more, and Buckingham
Shall lessen this big look.

Exeunt Cardinal and his Train.

Buck. This butcher's cur is venom-mouth'd, and I
Have not the power to muzzle him; therefore best
Not wake him in his slumber. A beggar's book
Outworths a noble's blood.

Nor. What, are you chaf'd?
Ask God for temp'rance. That's th' appliance only
Which your disease requires.

Buck. I read in's looks
Matter against me, and his eye revil'd
Me as his abject object. At this instant
He bores me with some trick. He's gone to th' King.
I'll follow and outstare him.

Nor. Stay, my lord,
And let your reason with your choler question
What 'tis you go about. To climb steep hills
Requires slow pace at first. Anger is like
A full hot horse, who being allow'd his way,
Self-mettle tires him. Not a man in England
Can advise me like you. Be to yourself
As you would to your friend.

Buck. I'll to the King
And from a mouth of honour quite cry down
This Ipswich fellow's insolence, or proclaim
There's difference in no persons.

Nor. Be advis'd.
Heat not a furnace for your foe so hot
That it do singe yourself. We may outrun
By violent swiftness that which we run at,
And lose by overrunning. Know you not
The fire that mounts the liquor till 't run o'er
In seeming to augment it wastes it? Be advis'd.
I say again there is no English soul
More stronger to direct you than yourself,
If with the sap of reason you would quench,
Or but allay, the fire of passion.

Buck. Sir,
I am thankful to you, and I'll go along
By your prescription. But this top-proud fellow —
Whom from the flow of gall I name not, but
From sincere motions, by intelligence,
And proofs as clear as founts in July when
We see each grain of gravel — I do know
To be corrupt and treasonous.
Nor. Say not treasonous.
Buck. To th' King I'll say't and make my vouch as strong
As shore of rock. Attend. This holy fox,
Or wolf, or both (for he is equal rav'nous
As he is subtile, and as prone to mischief
As able to perform't, his mind and place
Infecting one another, yea, reciprocally),
Only to show his pomp as well in France
As here at home, suggests the King our master
To this last costly treaty, th' interview
That swallowed so much treasure and like a glass
Did break i' th' wrenching.
Nor. Faith, and so it did.
Buck. Pray give me favour, sir. This cunning Cardinal
The articles o' th' combination drew
As himself pleas'd; and they were ratified
As he cried 'Thus let be!' to as much end
As give a crutch to th' dead. But our Count-Cardinal
Has done this, and 'tis well; for worthy Wolsey
(Who cannot err) he did it. Now this follows
(Which, as I take it, is a kind of puppy
To th' old dam, treason), Charles the Emperor,
Under pretence to see the Queen his aunt
(For 'twas indeed his colour, but he came
To whisper Wolsey), here makes visitation.
His fears were that the interview betwixt
England and France might through their amity
Breed him some prejudice; for from this league
Peep'd harms that menac'd him. He privily
Deals with our Cardinal; and, as I trow —
Which I do well, for I am sure the Emperor
Paid ere he promis'd; whereby his suit was granted
Ere it was ask'd — but when the way was made,
And pav'd with gold, the Emperor thus desir'd,
That he would please to alter the King's course
And break the foresaid peace. Let the King know
(As soon he shall by me) that thus the Cardinal
Does buy and sell his honour as he pleases,
And for his own advantage.
Nor. I am sorry
To hear this of him, and could wish he were
Something mistaken in't.
Buck. No, not a syllable.
I do pronounce him in that very shape
He shall appear in proof.

Enter *Brandon*, a *Sergeant-at-arms* before him, and two or three of the *Guard*.

Bran. Your office, sergeant; execute it.
Serg. Sir,
My lord the Duke of Buckingham and Earl
Of Hereford, Stafford, and Northampton, I
Arrest thee of high treason, in the name
Of our most sovereign King.
Buck. Lo you, my lord,
The net has fall'n upon me! I shall perish
Under device and practice.
Bran. I am sorry
To see you ta'en from liberty, to look on
The business present. 'Tis his Highness' pleasure
You shall to th' Tower.
Buck. It will help me nothing
To plead mine innocence, for that dye is on me
Which makes my whit'st part black. The will of heav'n
Be done in this and all things! I obey.
O my Lord Aberga'ny, fare you well!
Bran. Nay, he must bear you company. [*To Abergavenny*] The King
Is pleas'd you shall to th' Tower till you know
How he determines further.
Aber. As the Duke said,
The will of heaven be done, and the King's pleasure
By me obey'd!
Bran. Here is a warrant from
The King t' attach Lord Montacute and the bodies
Of the Duke's confessor, John de la Car,
One Gilbert Peck, his chancellor —
Buck. So, so!
These are the limbs o' th' plot. No more, I hope.
Bran. A monk o' th' Chartreux.
Buck. O, Nicholas Hopkins?
Bran. He.
Buck. My surveyor is false. The o'er-great Cardinal
Hath show'd him gold; my life is spann'd already.
I am the shadow of poor Buckingham,
Whose figure even this instant cloud puts on
By dark'ning my clear sun. My lord, farewell.
Exeunt.

Scene II. [*London. The Council Chamber.*]

Cornets. Enter *King Henry,* leaning on the *Cardinal's* shoulder, the *Nobles,* and *Sir Thomas Lovell* [with others]. The *Cardinal* places himself under the *King's* feet on his right side.

King. My life itself, and the best heart of it,
Thanks you for this great care. I stood i' th' level
Of a full-charg'd confederacy, and give thanks
To you that chok'd it. Let be call'd before us
That gentleman of Buckingham's. In person
I'll hear him his confessions justify,
And point by point the treasons of his master
He shall again relate.

A noise within, crying 'Room for the Queen!' Enter the *Queen* [*Katherine*], usher'd by the *Dukes of Norfolk* and *Suffolk.* She kneels. The *King* riseth from his state, takes her up, kisses and placeth her by him.

Queen. Nay, we must longer kneel. I am a suitor.
King. Arise and take place by us. Half your suit
Never name to us; you have half our power.
The other moiety ere you ask is given.
Repeat your will, and take it.
Queen. Thank your Majesty.
That you would love yourself, and in that love
Not unconsidered leave your honour nor
The dignity of your office, is the point
Of my petition.
King. Lady mine, proceed.
Queen. I am solicited, not by a few,
And those of true condition, that your subjects
Are in great grievance. There have been commissions
Sent down among 'em, which hath flaw'd the heart
Of all their loyalties; wherein, although,
My good Lord Cardinal, they vent reproaches
Most bitterly on you as putter-on
Of these exactions, yet the King our master,
Whose honour heaven shield from soil! — even he escapes not
Language unmannerly; yea, such which breaks
The sides of loyalty and almost appears
In loud rebellion.
Nor. Not almost appears —
It doth appear! for, upon these taxations,
The clothiers all, not able to maintain
The many to them 'longing, have put off
The spinsters, carders, fullers, weavers, who,
Unfit for other life, compell'd by hunger
And lack of other means, in desperate manner
Daring th' event to th' teeth, are all in uproar,
And danger serves among them.
King. Taxation?
Wherein? and what taxation? My Lord Cardinal,
You that are blam'd for it alike with us,
Know you of this taxation?
Card. Please you, sir,
I know but of a single part in aught
Pertains to th' state, and front but in that file
Where others tell steps with me.
Queen. No, my lord;
You know no more than others! But you frame
Things that are known alike, which are not wholesome
To those which would not know them and yet must
Perforce be their acquaintance. These exactions
(Whereof my sovereign would have note) — they are
Most pestilent to th' hearing; and, to bear 'em,
The back is sacrifice to th' load. They say
They are devis'd by you, or else you suffer
Too hard an exclamation.
King. Still exaction!
The nature of it? In what kind, let's know,
Is this exaction?
Queen. I am much too venturous
In tempting of your patience, but am bold'ned
Under your promis'd pardon. The subject's grief
Comes through commissions, which compels from each
The sixth part of his substance, to be levied
Without delay; and the pretence for this
Is nam'd, your wars in France. This makes bold mouths.
Tongues spit their duties out, and cold hearts freeze
Allegiance in them. Their curses now
Live where their prayers did; and it's come to pass
This tractable obedience is a slave
To each incensed will. I would your Highness
Would give it quick consideration, for
There is no primer business.
King. By my life,
This is against our pleasure.
Card. And for me,
I have no further gone in this than by
A single voice, and that not pass'd me but
By learned approbation of the judges. If I am

Traduc'd by ignorant tongues, which neither know
My faculties nor person yet will be
The chronicles of my doing, let me say
'Tis but the fate of place and the rough brake
That virtue must go through. We must not stint
Our necessary actions in the fear
To cope malicious censurers, which ever,
As rav'nous fishes, do a vessel follow
That is new-trimm'd, but benefit no further
Than vainly longing. What we oft do best,
By sick interpreters (once weak ones) is
Not ours, or not allow'd; what worst, as oft,
Hitting a grosser quality, is cried up
For our best action. If we shall stand still,
In fear our motion will be mock'd or carp'd at,
We should take root here where we sit, or sit
State-statues only.

King. Things done well
And with a care exempt themselves from fear;
Things done without example, in their issue
Are to be fear'd. Have you a precedent
Of this commission? I believe, not any.
We must not rend our subjects from our laws
And stick them in our will. Sixth part of each?
A trembling contribution! Why, we take
From every tree lop, bark, and part o' th' timber;
And though we leave it with a root, thus hack'd,
The air will drink the sap. To every county
Where this is question'd send our letters with
Free pardon to each man that has denied
The force of this commission. Pray look to't.
I put it to your care.

Card. [*aside to the Secretary*] A word with you.
Let there be letters writ to every shire
Of the King's grace and pardon. The grieved commons
Hardly conceive of me. Let it be nois'd
That through our intercession this revokement
And pardon comes. I shall anon advise you
Further in the proceeding.

Exit Secretary.

Enter *Surveyor.*

Queen. I am sorry that the Duke of Buckingham
Is run in your displeasure.

King. It grieves many.
The gentleman is learn'd and a most rare speaker,
To nature none more bound; his training such
That he may furnish and instruct great teachers
And never seek for aid out of himself. Yet see,
When these so noble benefits shall prove
Not well dispos'd, the mind growing once corrupt,
They turn to vicious forms, ten times more ugly
Than ever they were fair. This man so complete,
Who was enroll'd 'mongst wonders, and when we,
Almost with ravish'd list'ning, could not find
His hour of speech a minute — he, my lady,
Hath into monstrous habits put the graces
That once were his and is become as black
As if besmear'd in hell. Sit by us; you shall hear
(This was his gentleman in trust) of him
Things to strike honour sad. Bid him recount
The fore-recited practices, whereof
We cannot feel too little, hear too much.

Card. Stand forth and with bold spirit relate what you,
Most like a careful subject, have collected
Out of the Duke of Buckingham.

King. Speak freely.

Surv. First, it was usual with him — every day
It would infect his speech — that if the King
Should without issue die, he'll carry it so
To make the sceptre his. These very words
I've heard him utter to his son-in-law,
Lord Aberga'ny, to whom by oath he menac'd
Revenge upon the Cardinal.

Card. Please your Highness note
His dangerous conception in this point.
Not friended by his wish, to your high person
His will is most malignant, and it stretches
Beyond you to your friends.

Queen. My learn'd Lord Cardinal,
Deliver all with charity.

King. Speak on.
How grounded he his title to the crown
Upon our fail? To this point hast thou heard him
At any time speak aught?

Surv. He was brought to this
By a vain prophecy of Nicholas Hopkins.

King. What was that Hopkins?

Surv. Sir, a Chartreux friar,
His confessor, who fed him every minute
With words of sovereignty.

King. How know'st thou this?

Surv. Not long before your Highness sped to France,
The Duke being at the Rose, within the parish
Saint Lawrence Poultney, did of me demand

Paul Rogers playing the part of the portly, uxorious English sovereign, Henry VIII

THE FAMOUS STORY OF THE LIFE OF KING HENRY VIII

PHOTOGRAPHS BY HOUSTON ROGERS
PRODUCED BY THE OLD VIC COMPANY

"Lo you, my lord, the net has fall'n upon me." Arrested on a charge of treason, Buckingham despairs of escaping *(Act I, Scene I)*

Leo Genn as the ill-fated Buckingham, victim of the intrigues of Cardinal Wolsey

At the order of Wolsey (Alexander Fox), the Duke of Buckingham's surveyor (Wolfe Morris) testifies against him before Henry and Katharine (Gwen Ffrangcon Davies) *(Act I, Scene II)*

Gwen Ffrangcon Davies as Henry's queen, Katharine, divorced by Henry on the grounds she had been married to his brother

Alexander Knox as Wolsey, who destroys Buckingham, but is himself overturned through his double dealings with Henry.

Henry drinks a toast to Anne Bullen at the masque *(Act I, Scene IV)*

Below: Lord Sands (James Ottaway) in dalliance with Anne Bullen (Jeannette Sterke) and another woman of the court

An old woman (Wynne Clarke) jests with Anne Bullen about King Henry's interest *(Act II, Scene III)*

The ecclesiastical hearing on the marriage of Henry and Katharine *(Act II, Scene IV)*

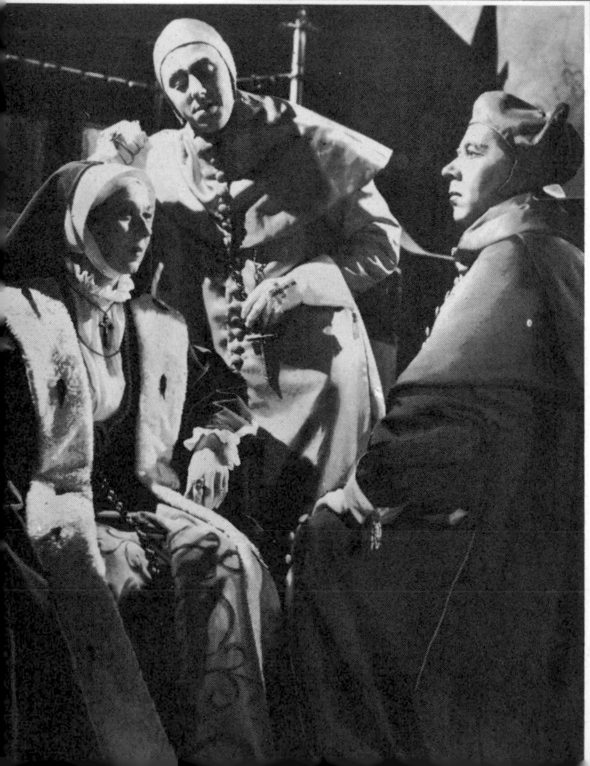

Campeius and Wolsey seek to persuade Queen Katharine to accept an annulment of her marriage with Henry *(Act III, Scene I)*

The King dismisses Wolsey and Campeius, the hearing having been adjourned *(Act II, Scene IV)*

"Read o'er this; and after, this: and then to breakfast with what appetite you have." The king presents Wolsey with the evidence of his malfeasance *(Act III, Scene II)*

Wolsey bids his secretary Cromwell (Timothy Bateson) to profit by his example. "Had I but served my God with half the zeal I served my king, he would not in mine age have left me naked to mine enemies" *(Act III, Scene II)*

"Be of good cheer; they shall no more prevail than we give way to." Henry assures Cranmer (William Squire) that he will support him against the unfriendly primates *(Act V, Scene I)*

King Henry honours Cranmer, Archbishop of Canterbury, in the Council *(Act V, Scene III)*

While Katharine lies ill at Kimbolton, her steward Griffith (Wolfe Morris) tells of the fall of Wolsey *(Act IV, Scene II)*

A porter (Newton Blick) and his man making preparations for the christening of Elizabeth *(Act V, Scene IV)*

Below: James Ottaway, Robert Hardy, and Newton Blick as three gentlemen watching the coronation *(Act IV, Scene I)*

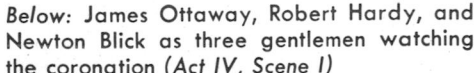

Cranmer presides at the christening of the infant Princess Elizabeth (*Act V, Scene V*)

What was the speech among the Londoners
Concerning the French journey. I replied
Men fear'd the French would prove perfidious,
To the King's danger. Presently the Duke
Said 'twas the fear indeed, and that he doubted
'Twould prove the verity of certain words
Spoke by a holy monk 'that oft,' says he,
'Hath sent to me, wishing me to permit
John de la Car, my chaplain, a choice hour
To hear from him a matter of some moment;
Whom after under the confession's seal
He solemnly had sworn that what he spoke
My chaplain to no creature living but
To me should utter, with demure confidence
This pausingly ensu'd: "Neither the King nor 's heirs
(Tell you the Duke) shall prosper. Bid him strive
To gain the love o' th' commonalty. The Duke
Shall govern England."'

Queen. If I know you well,
You were the Duke's surveyor and lost your office
On the complaint o' th' tenants. Take good heed
You charge not in your spleen a noble person
And spoil your nobler soul. I say, take heed;
Yes, heartily beseech you.

King. Let him on.
Go forward.

Surv. On my soul, I'll speak but truth.
I told my lord the Duke, by th' devil's illusions
The monk might be deceiv'd; and that 'twas dangerous for him
To ruminate on this so far until
It forg'd him some design, which, being believ'd,
It was much like to do. He answer'd 'Tush,
It can do me no damage!' adding further
That, had the King in his last sickness fail'd,
The Cardinal's and Sir Thomas Lovell's heads
Should have gone off.

King. Ha! What? so rank? Aha!
There's mischief in this man. Canst thou say further?

Surv. I can, my liege.

King. Proceed.

Surv. Being at Greenwich,
After your Highness had reprov'd the Duke
About Sir William Bulmer —

King. I remember
Of such a time. Being my sworn servant,
The Duke retain'd him his. But on! What hence?

Surv. 'If,' quoth he, 'I for this had been committed,
As to the Tower I thought, I would have play'd
The part my father meant to act upon
Th' usurper Richard, who, being at Salisbury,
Made suit to come in's presence, which if granted,
As he made semblance of his duty, would
Have put his knife into him.'

King. A giant traitor!

Card. Now, madam, may his Highness live in freedom,
And this man out of prison?

Queen. God mend all!

King. There's something more would out of thee. What say'st?

Surv. After 'the Duke his father,' with the 'knife,'
He stretch'd him, and, with one hand on his dagger,
Another spread on 's breast, mounting his eyes,
He did discharge a horrible oath, whose tenour
Was, were he evil us'd, he would outgo
His father by as much as a performance
Does an irresolute purpose.

King. There's his period,
To sheathe his knife in us. He is attach'd.
Call him to present trial. If he may
Find mercy in the law, 'tis his; if none,
Let him not seek't of us. By day and night,
He's traitor to the height! *Exeunt.*

Scene III. [*London. An antechamber in the Palace.*]

Enter *Lord Chamberlain* and *Lord Sandys*.

L. Cham. Is't possible the spells of France should juggle
Men into such strange mysteries?

L. Sandys. New customs,
Though they be never so ridiculous
(Nay, let 'em be unmanly), yet are follow'd.

L. Cham. As far as I see, all the good our English
Have got by the late voyage is but merely
A fit or two o' th' face; but they are shrewd ones;
For when they hold 'em, you would swear directly
Their very noses had been councillors
To Pepin or Clotharius, they keep state so.

L. Sandys. They have all new legs, and lame ones. One would take it,
That never saw 'em pace before, the spavin
Or springhalt reign'd among 'em.

L. Cham. Death, my lord!
Their clothes are after such a pagan cut to't
That sure th' have worn out Christendom.

Enter *Sir Thomas Lovell.*

How now?
What news, Sir Thomas Lovell?

Lov. Faith, my lord,
I hear of none but the new proclamation
That's clapp'd upon the court gate.

L. Cham. What is't for?

Lov. The reformation of our travell'd gallants
That fill the court with quarrels, talk, and tailors.

L. Cham. I'm glad 'tis there. Now I would pray our monsieurs
To think an English courtier may be wise
And never see the Louvre.

Lov. They must either
(For so run the conditions) leave those remnants
Of fool and feather that they got in France,
With all their honourable points of ignorance
Pertaining thereunto, — as fights and fireworks;
Abusing better men than they can be,
Out of a foreign wisdom, — renouncing clean
The faith they have in tennis and tall stockings,
Short blist'red breeches, and those types of travel,
And understand again like honest men,
Or pack to their old playfellows. There, I take it,
They may *cum privilegio* wear away
The lag-end of their lewdness and be laugh'd at.

L. Sandys. 'Tis time to give 'em physic, their diseases
Are grown so catching.

L. Cham. What a loss our ladies
Will have of these trim vanities!

Lov. Ay, marry,
There will be woe indeed, lords. The sly whoresons
Have got a speeding trick to lay down ladies.
A French song and a fiddle has no fellow.

L. Sandys. The devil fiddle 'em! I am glad they are going,
For sure there's no converting of 'em. Now
An honest country lord, as I am, beaten
A long time out of play, may bring his plain-song
And have an hour of hearing, and, by'r Lady,
Held current music too.

L. Cham. Well said, Lord Sandys.
Your colt's tooth is not cast yet.

L. Sandys. No, my lord,
Nor shall not while I have a stump.

L. Cham. Sir Thomas,
Whither were you a-going?

Lov. To the Cardinal's.
Your lordship is a guest too.

L. Cham. O, 'tis true.
This night he makes a supper, and a great one,
To many lords and ladies. There will be
The beauty of this kingdom, I'll assure you.

Lov. That churchman bears a bounteous mind indeed,
A hand as fruitful as the land that feeds us;
His dews fall everywhere.

L. Cham. No doubt he's noble.
He had a black mouth that said other of him.

L. Sandys. He may, my lord; has wherewithal. In him
Sparing would show a worse sin than ill doctrine.
Men of his way should be most liberal;
They are set here for examples.

L. Cham. True, they are so;
But few now give so great ones. My barge stays;
Your lordship shall along. Come, good Sir Thomas,
We shall be late else; which I would not be,
For I was spoke to, with Sir Henry Guildford,
This night to be comptrollers.

L. Sandys. I am your lordship's.
Exeunt.

Scene IV. [*Westminster. The presence chamber in York Place.*]

Hautboys. A small table under a state for the Cardinal, a longer table for the guests. Then enter *Anne Bullen* and divers other *Ladies* and *Gentlemen,* as guests at one door; at another door enter *Sir Henry Guildford.*

Sir H. Guild. Ladies, a general welcome from his Grace
Salutes ye all. This night he dedicates
To fair content and you. None here, he hopes,
In all this noble bevy, has brought with her
One care abroad. He would have all as merry

As, first, good company, good wine, good welcome
Can make good people.

Enter *Lord Chamberlain, Lord Sandys,* and [*Sir Thomas*] *Lovell.*

O my lord, y'are tardy!
The very thought of this fair company
Clapp'd wings to me.
Cham. You are young, Sir Harry Guildford.
Sandys. Sir Thomas Lovell, had the Cardinal
But half my lay thoughts in him, some of these
Should find a running banquet ere they rested
I think would better please 'em. By my life,
They are a sweet society of fair ones.
Lov. O that your lordship were but now confessor
To one or two of these!
Sandys. I would I were.
They should find easy penance.
Lov. Faith, how easy?
Sandys. As easy as a down bed would afford it.
Cham. Sweet ladies, will it please you sit? Sir Harry,
Place you that side; I'll take the charge of this.
His Grace is ent'ring. Nay, you must not freeze!
Two women plac'd together makes cold weather.
My Lord Sandys, you are one will keep 'em waking.
Pray sit between these ladies.
Sandys. By my faith,
And thank your lordship. By your leave, sweet ladies.

[*Seats himself between Anne Bullen and another Lady.*]

If I chance to talk a little wild, forgive me.
I had it from my father.
Anne B. Was he mad, sir?
Sandys. O, very mad, exceeding mad, in love too.
But he would bite none. Just as I do now,
He would kiss you twenty with a breath.
[*Kisses her.*]
Cham. Well said, my lord.
So, now y'are fairly seated. Gentlemen,
The penance lies on you if these fair ladies
Pass away frowning.
Sandys. For my little cure,
Let me alone.

Hautboys. Enter *Cardinal Wolsey,* [attended] and takes his state.

Card. Y'are welcome, my fair guests. That noble lady
Or gentleman that is not freely merry
Is not my friend. This to confirm my welcome;
And to you all, good health. [*Drinks.*]
Sandys. Your Grace is noble.
Let me have such a bowl may hold my thanks
And save me so much talking.
Card. My Lord Sandys,
I am beholding to you. Cheer your neighbours.
Ladies, you are not merry. Gentlemen,
Whose fault is this?
Sandys. The red wine first must rise
In their fair cheeks, my lord; then we shall have 'em
Talk us to silence.
Anne B. You are a merry gamester,
My Lord Sandys.
Sandys. Yes, if I make my play.
Here's to your ladyship; and pledge it, madam,
For 'tis to such a thing —
Anne B. You cannot show me.
Sandys. I told your Grace they would talk anon.
Drum and trumpet. Chambers discharg'd.
Card. What's that?
Cham. Look out there, some of ye.
[*Exit a Servant.*]
Card. What warlike voice,
And to what end, is this? Nay, ladies, fear not.
By all the laws of war y'are privileg'd.

Enter a *Servant.*

Cham. How now? What is't?
Serv. A noble troop of strangers,
For so they seem. Th' have left their barge and landed,
And hither make, as great ambassadors
From foreign princes.
Card. Good Lord Chamberlain,
Go, give 'em welcome; you can speak the French tongue;
And pray receive 'em nobly and conduct 'em
Into our presence, where this heaven of beauty
Shall shine at full upon them. Some attend him.
[*Exit Chamberlain, attended.*] *All rise, and tables remov'd.*
You have now a broken banquet; but we'll mend it.
A good digestion to you all! and once more
I show'r a welcome on ye. Welcome all.

Hautboys. Enter *King* and others, as Maskers, habited like shepherds, usher'd by the *Lord Chamberlain.* They pass directly before the *Cardinal* and gracefully salute him.

A noble company! What are their pleasures?

Cham. Because they speak no English, thus they pray'd
To tell your Grace: that, having heard by fame
Of this so noble and so fair assembly
This night to meet here, they could do no less
(Out of the great respect they bear to beauty)
But leave their flocks and, under your fair conduct,
Crave leave to view these ladies and entreat
An hour of revels with 'em.

Card. Say, Lord Chamberlain,
They have done my poor house grace; for which I pay 'em
A thousand thanks and pray 'em take their pleasures.

Choose ladies. King and Anne Bullen.

King. The fairest hand I ever touch'd! O beauty,
Till now I never knew thee!

Music. Dance.

Card. My lord!

Cham. Your Grace?

Card. Pray tell 'em thus much from me:
There should be one amongst 'em, by his person,
More worthy this place than myself; to whom,
If I but knew him, with my love and duty
I would surrender it.

Cham. I will, my lord.

Whisper [*with the Maskers*].

Card. What say they?

Cham. Such a one they all confess
There is indeed, which they would have your Grace
Find out, and he will take it.

Card. Let me see then.

[*Comes from his state.*]

By all your good leaves, gentlemen, here I'll make
My royal choice.

King. [*unmasks*] Ye have found him, Cardinal.
You hold a fair assembly. You do well, lord.
You are a churchman, or, I'll tell you, Cardinal,
I should judge now unhappily.

Card. I am glad
Your Grace is grown so pleasant.

King. My Lord Chamberlain,
Prithee come hither. What fair lady's that?

Cham. An't please your Grace, Sir Thomas Bullen's daughter,
The Viscount Rochford, one of her Highness' women.

King. By heaven, she is a dainty one! Sweetheart,
I were unmannerly to take you out
And not to kiss you. [*Kisses her.*] A health, gentlemen!
Let it go round.

Card. Sir Thomas Lovell, is the banquet ready
I' th' privy chamber?

Lov. Yes, my lord.

Card. Your Grace,
I fear, with dancing is a little heated.

King. I fear, too much.

Card. There's fresher air, my lord,
In the next chamber.

King. Lead in your ladies, ev'ry one. Sweet partner,
I must not yet forsake you. Let's be merry.
Good my Lord Cardinal, I have half a dozen healths
To drink to these fair ladies and a measure
To lead 'em once again; and then let's dream
Who's best in favour. Let the music knock it.

Exeunt with Trumpets.

ACT II. Scene I. [*Westminster. A street.*]

Enter two *Gentlemen* at several doors.

1. Gent. Whither away so fast?

2. Gent. O, God save ye!
Ev'n to the Hall, to hear what shall become
Of the great Duke of Buckingham.

1. Gent. I'll save you
That labour, sir. All's now done but the ceremony
Of bringing back the prisoner.

2. Gent. Were you there?

1. Gent. Yes indeed was I.

2. Gent. Pray speak what has happen'd.

1. Gent. You may guess quickly what.

2. Gent. Is he found guilty?

1. Gent. Yes, truly is he, and condemn'd upon't.

2. Gent. I am sorry for't.

1. Gent. So are a number more.

2. Gent. But pray how pass'd it?

1. Gent. I'll tell you in a little. The great Duke
Came to the bar; where to his accusations
He pleaded still not guilty and alleg'd
Many sharp reasons to defeat the law.
The King's Attorney, on the contrary,
Urg'd on the examinations, proofs, confessions
Of divers witnesses, which the Duke desir'd
To have brought *viva voce* to his face;
At which appear'd against him his surveyor,
Sir Gilbert Peck his chancellor, and John Car,
Confessor to him, with that devil monk,
Hopkins, that made this mischief.
2. Gent. That was he
That fed him with his prophecies.
1. Gent. The same.
All these accus'd him strongly, which he fain
Would have flung from him, but indeed he could not;
And so his peers upon this evidence
Have found him guilty of high treason. Much
He spoke, and learnedly, for life, but all
Was either pitied in him or forgotten.
2. Gent. After all this how did he bear himself?
1. Gent. When he was brought again to th' bar to hear
His knell rung out, his judgment, he was stirr'd
With such an agony he sweat extremely
And something spoke in choler, ill and hasty;
But he fell to himself again and sweetly
In all the rest show'd a most noble patience.
2. Gent. I do not think he fears death.
1. Gent. Sure he does not;
He never was so womanish. The cause
He may a little grieve at.
2. Gent. Certainly
The Cardinal is the end of this.
1. Gent. 'Tis likely
By all conjectures: first, Kildare's attainder,
Then Deputy of Ireland, who remov'd,
Earl Surrey was sent thither, and in haste too,
Lest he should help his father.
2. Gent. That trick of state
Was a deep envious one.
1. Gent. At his return
No doubt he will requite it. This is noted
(And generally), whoever the King favours
The Cardinal instantly will find employment,
And far enough from court too.
2. Gent. All the commons
Hate him perniciously and, o' my conscience,
Wish him ten fadom deep. This duke as much
They love and dote on, call him bounteous Buckingham,
The mirror of all courtesy —

Enter *Buckingham* from his arraignment; *Tipstaves* before him; the axe with the edge towards him; *Halberds* on each side; accompanied with *Sir Thomas Lovell, Sir Nicholas Vaux, Sir William Sandys,* and *common people,* &c.

1. Gent. Stay there, sir,
And see the noble ruin'd man you speak of.
2. Gent. Let's stand close and behold him.
Buck. All good people,
You that thus far have come to pity me,
Hear what I say and then go home and lose me.
I have this day receiv'd a traitor's judgment
And by that name must die. Yet heaven bear witness,
And if I have a conscience, let it sink me
Even as the axe falls, if I be not faithful!
The law I bear no malice for my death:
'T has done, upon the premises, but justice.
But those that sought it I could wish more Christians.
Be what they will, I heartily forgive 'em.
Yet let 'em look they glory not in mischief
Nor build their evils on the graves of great men;
For then my guiltless blood must cry against 'em.
For further life in this world I ne'er hope,
Nor will I sue, although the King have mercies
More than I dare make faults. You few that lov'd me
And dare be bold to weep for Buckingham,
His noble friends and fellows, whom to leave
Is only bitter to him, only dying,
Go with me like good angels to my end;
And, as the long divorce of steel falls on me,
Make of your prayers one sweet sacrifice
And lift my soul to heaven. Lead on, a God's name!
Lov. I do beseech your Grace, for charity,
If ever any malice in your heart
Were hid against me, now to forgive me frankly.
Buck. Sir Thomas Lovell, I as free forgive you
As I would be forgiven. I forgive all.
There cannot be those numberless offences
'Gainst me that I cannot take peace with. No black envy
Shall mark my grave. Commend me to his Grace;
And if he speak of Buckingham, pray tell him

You met him half in heaven. My vows and prayers
Yet are the King's and, till my soul forsake me,
Shall cry for blessings on him. May he live
Longer than I have time to tell his years!
Ever belov'd and loving may his rule be!
And when old time shall lead him to his end,
Goodness and he fill up one monument!

Lov. To th' waterside I must conduct your Grace;
Then give my charge up to Sir Nicholas Vaux,
Who undertakes you to your end.

Vaux. Prepare there;
The Duke is coming. See the barge be ready
And fit it with such furniture as suits
The greatness of his person.

Buck. Nay, Sir Nicholas,
Let it alone. My state now will but mock me.
When I came hither, I was Lord High Constable
And Duke of Buckingham; now, poor Edward Bohun.
Yet I am richer than my base accusers,
That never knew what truth meant. I now seal it;
And with that blood will make 'em one day groan for't.
My noble father, Henry of Buckingham,
Who first rais'd head against usurping Richard,
Flying for succour to his servant Banister,
Being distress'd, was by that wretch betray'd
And without trial fell. God's peace be with him!
Henry the Seventh succeeding, truly pitying
My father's loss, like a most royal prince
Restor'd me to my honours and out of ruins
Made my name once more noble. Now his son,
Henry the Eighth, life, honour, name, and all
That made me happy, at one stroke has taken
For ever from the world. I had my trial,
And must needs say a noble one; which makes me
A little happier than my wretched father.
Yet thus far we are one in fortunes: both
Fell by our servants, by those men we lov'd most —
A most unnatural and faithless service!
Heaven has an end in all. Yet, you that hear me,
This from a dying man receive as certain:
Where you are liberal of your loves and counsels
Be sure you be not loose; for those you make friends
And give your hearts to, when they once perceive
The least rub in your fortunes, fall away
Like water from ye, never found again
But where they mean to sink ye. All good people,
Pray for me! I must now forsake ye. The last hour
Of my long weary life is come upon me.
Farewell!
And when you would say something that is sad,
Speak how I fell. I have done; and God forgive me! *Exeunt Duke and Train.*

1. Gent. O, this is full of pity! Sir, it calls,
I fear, too many curses on their heads
That were the authors.

2. Gent. If the Duke be guiltless,
'Tis full of woe. Yet I can give you inkling
Of an ensuing evil, if it fall,
Greater than this.

1. Gent. Good angels keep it from us!
What may it be? You do not doubt my faith, sir?

2. Gent. This secret is so weighty 'twill require
A strong faith to conceal it.

1. Gent. Let me have it.
I do not talk much.

2. Gent. I am confident.
You shall, sir. Did you not of late days hear
A buzzing of a separation
Between the King and Katherine?

1. Gent. Yes, but it held not;
For when the King once heard it, out of anger
He sent command to the Lord Mayor straight
To stop the rumour and allay those tongues
That durst disperse it.

2. Gent. But that slander, sir,
Is found a truth now; for it grows again
Fresher than e'er it was, and held for certain
The King will venture at it. Either the Cardinal,
Or some about him near, have out of malice
To the good Queen possess'd him with a scruple
That will undo her. To confirm this too,
Cardinal Campeius is arriv'd, and lately;
As all think, for this business.

1. Gent. 'Tis the Cardinal;
And merely to revenge him on the Emperor
For not bestowing on him at his asking
The archbishopric of Toledo, this is purpos'd.

2. Gent. I think you have hit the mark. But is't not cruel
That she should feel the smart of this? The Cardinal
Will have his will, and she must fall.

1. Gent. 'Tis woful.
We are too open here to argue this.
Let's think in private more. *Exeunt.*

Scene II. [*London. An antechamber in the Palace.*]

Enter *Lord Chamberlain,* reading this letter.

Cham. 'My Lord, — The horses your lordship sent for, with all the care I had, I saw well chosen, ridden, and furnish'd. They were young and handsome and of the best breed in the North. When they were ready to set out for London, a man of my Lord Cardinal's by commission and main power took 'em from me, with this reason — his master would be serv'd before a subject, if not before the King; which stopp'd our mouths, sir.'

I fear he will indeed. Well, let him have them.
He will have all, I think.

Enter to the *Lord Chamberlain* the *Dukes of Norfolk* and *Suffolk.*

Nor. Well met, my Lord Chamberlain.
Cham. Good day to both your Graces.
Suf. How is the King employ'd?
Cham. I left him private,
Full of sad thoughts and troubles.
Nor. What's the cause?
Cham. It seems the marriage with his brother's wife
Has crept too near his conscience.
Suf. No, his conscience
Has crept too near another lady.
Nor. 'Tis so.
This is the Cardinal's doing, the King-Cardinal!
That blind priest, like the eldest son of Fortune,
Turns what he list. The King will know him one day.
Suf. Pray God he do! He'll never know himself else.
Nor. How holily he works in all his business
And with what zeal! for, now he has crack'd the league
Between us and the Emperor, the Queen's great nephew,
He dives into the King's soul, and there scatters
Dangers, doubts, wringing of the conscience,
Fears, and despairs — and all these for his marriage.
And out of all these to restore the King,
He counsels a divorce, a loss of her
That like a jewel has hung twenty years
About his neck, yet never lost her lustre;
Of her that loves him with that excellence
That angels love good men with; even of her
That, when the greatest stroke of fortune falls,
Will bless the King: — and is not this course pious?
Cham. Heaven keep me from such counsel! 'Tis most true
These news are everywhere, every tongue speaks 'em,
And every true heart weeps for't. All that dare
Look into these affairs see this main end —
The French King's sister. Heaven will one day open
The King's eyes that so long have slept upon
This bold bad man.
Suf. And free us from his slavery.
Nor. We had need pray,
And heartily, for our deliverance,
Or this imperious man will work us all
From princes into pages. All men's honours
Lie like one lump before him, to be fashion'd
Into what pitch he please.
Suf. For me, my lords,
I love him not, nor fear him. There's my creed.
As I am made without him, so I'll stand,
If the King please. His curses and his blessings
Touch me alike; th' are breath I not believe in.
I knew him, and I know him; so I leave him
To him that made him proud, the Pope.
Nor. Let's in
And with some other business put the King
From these sad thoughts that work too much upon him.
My lord, you'll bear us company?
Cham. Excuse me.
The King has sent me otherwhere. Besides,
You'll find a most unfit time to disturb him.
Health to your lordships!
Nor. Thanks, my good Lord Chamberlain.
Exit Lord Chamberlain; and the King draws the curtain and sits reading pensively.
Suf. How sad he looks! Sure he is much afflicted.
King. Who's there, ha?
Nor. Pray God he be not angry.
King. Who's there, I say? How dare you thrust yourselves
Into my private meditations?
Who am I? ha?
Nor. A gracious king, that pardons all offences
Malice ne'er meant. Our breach of duty this way
Is business of estate; in which we come
To know your royal pleasure.

King. Ye are too bold.
Go to! I'll make ye know your times of business.
Is this an hour for temporal affairs? ha?

Enter [*Cardinals*] *Wolsey* and *Campeius* with a commission.

Who's there? My good Lord Cardinal? O my Wolsey,
The quiet of my wounded conscience!
Thou art a cure fit for a king. [*To Campeius*] You're welcome,
Most learned reverend sir, into our kingdom.
Use us and it. [*To Wolsey*] My good lord, have great care
I be not found a talker.

Wol. Sir, you cannot.
I would your Grace would give us but an hour
Of private conference.

King. [*to Norfolk and Suffolk*] We are busy. Go.

Nor. [*aside to Suffolk*] This priest has no pride in him!

Suf. [*aside to Norfolk*] Not to speak of.
I would not be so sick though for his place.
But this cannot continue.

Nor. [*aside to Suffolk*] If it do,
I'll venture one have-at-him.

Suf. [*aside to Norfolk*] I another.

Exeunt Norfolk and Suffolk.

Wol. Your Grace has given a precedent of wisdom
Above all princes in committing freely
Your scruple to the voice of Christendom.
Who can be angry now? what envy reach you?
The Spaniard, tied by blood and favour to her
Must now confess, if they have any goodness,
The trial just and noble. All the clerks
(I mean the learned ones) in Christian kingdoms
Have their free voices. Rome, the nurse of judgment,
Invited by your noble self, hath sent
One general tongue unto us, this good man,
This just and learned priest, Cardinal Campeius,
Whom once more I present unto your Highness.

King. And once more in mine arms I bid him welcome
And thank the holy conclave for their loves.
They have sent me such a man I would have wish'd for.

Camp. Your Grace must needs deserve all strangers' loves,
You are so noble. To your Highness' hand
I tender my commission; by whose virtue,
The Court of Rome commanding, you, my Lord
Cardinal of York, are join'd with me their servant
In the unpartial judging of this business.

King. Two equal men. The Queen shall be acquainted
Forthwith for what you come. Where's Gardiner?

Wol. I know your Majesty has always lov'd her
So dear in heart not to deny her that
A woman of less place might ask by law —
Scholars allow'd freely to argue for her.

King. Ay, and the best she shall have; and my favour
To him that does best. God forbid else. Cardinal,
Prithee call Gardiner to me, my new Secretary.
I find him a fit fellow.

[*Exit Wolsey.*]

Enter [*Wolsey*, with] *Gardiner.*

Wol. [*aside to Gardiner*] Give me your hand. Much joy and favour to you!
You are the King's now.

Gard. [*aside to Wolsey*] But to be commanded
For ever by your Grace, whose hand has rais'd me.

King. Come hither, Gardiner.

Walks and whispers.

Camp. My Lord of York, was not one Doctor Pace
In this man's place before him?

Wol. Yes, he was.

Camp. Was he not held a learned man?

Wol. Yes, surely.

Camp. Believe me, there's an ill opinion spread then,
Even of yourself, Lord Cardinal.

Wol. How? of me?

Camp. They will not stick to say you envied him,
And fearing he would rise (he was so virtuous),
Kept him a foreign man still, which so griev'd him
That he ran mad and died.

Wol. Heav'n's peace be with him!
That's Christian care enough. For living murmurers
There's places of rebuke. He was a fool,
For he would needs be virtuous. That good fellow,
If I command him, follows my appointment.

I will have none so near else. Learn this, brother,
We live not to be grip'd by meaner persons.
King. Deliver this with modesty to th' Queen.
Exit Gardiner.
The most convenient place that I can think of
For such receipt of learning is Blackfriars.
There ye shall meet about this weighty business.
My Wolsey, see it furnish'd. O my lord,
Would it not grieve an able man to leave
So sweet a bedfellow? But, conscience, conscience!
O, 'tis a tender place! and I must leave her.
Exeunt.

Scene III. [*London. An antechamber in the* Queen's *apartments.*]

Enter *Anne Bullen* and an *Old Lady.*

Anne. Not for that neither! Here's the pang that pinches:
His Highness having liv'd so long with her, and she
So good a lady that no tongue could ever
Pronounce dishonour of her — by my life,
She never knew harm-doing! — O, now, after
So many courses of the sun enthroned,
Still growing in a majesty and pomp, the which
To leave a thousandfold more bitter than
'Tis sweet at first t' acquire — after this process
To give her the avaunt, it is a pity
Would move a monster.
Old L. Hearts of most hard temper
Melt and lament for her.
Anne. O, God's will! much better
She ne'er had known pomp. Though't be temporal,
Yet, if that quarrel, fortune, do divorce
It from the bearer, 'tis a sufferance panging
As soul and body's severing.
Old. L. Alas, poor lady!
She's a stranger now again.
Anne. So much the more
Must pity drop upon her. Verily
I swear 'tis better to be lowly born
And range with humble livers in content
Than to be perk'd up in a glist'ring grief
And wear a golden sorrow.
Old L. Our content
Is our best having.
Anne. By my troth and maidenhead,
I would not be a queen.
Old L. Beshrew me, I would,
And venture maidenhead for't! and so would you,
For all this spice of your hypocrisy.
You that have so fair parts of woman on you
Have, too, a woman's heart, which ever yet
Affected eminence, wealth, sovereignty;
Which, to say sooth, are blessings, and which gifts
(Saving your mincing) the capacity
Of your soft chiverel conscience would receive,
If you might please to stretch it.
Anne. Nay, good troth!
Old L. Yes, troth, and troth! You would not be a queen?
Anne. No, not for all the riches under heaven.
Old L. 'Tis strange! A threepence bow'd would hire me,
Old as I am, to queen it. But I pray you,
What think you of a duchess? Have you limbs
To bear that load of title?
Anne. No, in truth.
Old L. Then you are weakly made. Pluck off a little.
I would not be a young count in your way
For more than blushing comes to. If your back
Cannot vouchsafe this burthen, 'tis too weak
Ever to get a boy.
Anne. How you do talk!
I swear again, I would not be a queen
For all the world.
Old L. In faith, for little England
You'ld venture an emballing. I myself
Would for Carnarvonshire, although there 'long'd
No more to th' crown but that. Lo, who comes here?

Enter *Lord Chamberlain.*

Cham. Good morrow, ladies. What were't worth to know
The secret of your conference?
Anne. My good lord,
Not your demand; it values not your asking.
Our mistress' sorrows we were pitying.
Cham. It was a gentle business and becoming
The action of good women. There is hope
All will be well.
Anne. Now I pray God, amen!
Cham. You bear a gentle mind, and heav'nly blessings
Follow such creatures. That you may, fair lady,
Perceive I speak sincerely and high note's
Ta'en of your many virtues, the King's Majesty
Commends his good opinion of you, and

Does purpose honour to you no less flowing
Than Marchioness of Pembroke; to which title
A thousand pound a year, annual support,
Out of his grace he adds.
Anne. I do not know
What kind of my obedience I should tender.
More than my all is nothing; nor my prayers
Are not words duly hallowed, nor my wishes
More worth than empty vanities. Yet prayers and wishes
Are all I can return. Beseech your lordship,
Vouchsafe to speak my thanks and my obedience,
As from a blushing handmaid, to his Highness;
Whose health and royalty I pray for.
Cham. Lady,
I shall not fail t' approve the fair conceit
The King hath of you. [*Aside*] I have perus'd her well.
Beauty and honour in her are so mingled
That they have caught the King; and who knows yet
But from this lady may proceed a gem
To lighten all this isle? — I'll to the King
And say I spoke with you.
Anne. My honour'd lord!
Exit Lord Chamberlain.
Old L. Why, this it is! See, see!
I have been begging sixteen years in court
(Am yet a courtier beggarly) nor could
Come pat betwixt too early and too late
For any suit of pounds; and you (O fate!),
A very fresh fish here — fie, fie, fie upon
This compell'd fortune! — have your mouth fill'd up
Before you open it.
Anne. This is strange to me.
Old L. How tastes it? Is it bitter? Forty pence, no.
There was a lady once ('tis an old story)
That would not be a queen, that would she not,
For all the mud in Egypt. Have you heard it?
Anne. Come, you are pleasant.
Old L. With your theme I could
O'ermount the lark. The Marchioness of Pembroke?
A thousand pounds a year, for pure respect?
No other obligation? By my life,
That promises moe thousands! Honour's train
Is longer than his foreskirt. By this time
I know your back will bear a duchess. Say,
Are you not stronger than you were?
Anne. Good lady,
Make yourself mirth with your particular fancy
And leave me out on't. Would I had no being
If this salute my blood a jot! It faints me
To think what follows.
The Queen is comfortless, and we forgetful
In our long absence. Pray do not deliver
What here y'have heard to her.
Old L. What do you think me?
Exeunt.

Scene IV. [*London. A hall in Blackfriars.*]

Trumpets, sennet, and cornets. Enter two *Vergers,* with short silver wands; next them, two *Scribes,* in the habit of Doctors; after them, the [*Arch*]*bishop of Canterbury* alone; after him, the *Bishops of Lincoln, Ely, Rochester,* and *Saint Asaph*; next them, with some small distance, follows a *Gentleman* bearing the purse, with the great seal, and a Cardinal's hat; then two *Priests,* bearing each a silver cross; then a *Gentleman Usher* bareheaded, accompanied with a *Sergeant-at-arms* bearing a silver mace; then two *Gentlemen* bearing two great silver pillars; after them, side by side, the two *Cardinals,* [*Wolsey* and *Campeius,*] two *Noblemen* with the sword and mace. The *King* takes place under the cloth of state; the two *Cardinals* sit under him as Judges. The *Queen* takes place some distance from the *King.* The *Bishops* place themselves on each side the court, in manner of a consistory; below them, the *Scribes.* The *Lords* sit next the *Bishops.* *The rest of the Attendants stand in convenient order about the stage*

Wol. Whilst our commission from Rome is read,
Let silence be commanded.
King. What's the need?
It hath already publicly been read,
And on all sides th' authority allow'd.
You may then spare that time.
Wol. Be't so. Proceed.
Scribe. Say, 'Henry King of England, come into the court.'
Crier. Henry King of England, &c.
King. Here.
Scribe. Say, 'Katherine Queen of England come into the court.'
Crier. Katherine Queen of England, &c.
The Queen makes no answer, rises out of her chair, goes about the court, comes to the King, and kneels at his feet; then speaks.
Queen. Sir, I desire you do me right and justice

And to bestow your pity on me; for
I am a most poor woman and a stranger,
Born out of your dominions, having here
No judge indifferent, nor no more assurance
Of equal friendship and proceeding. Alas, sir,
In what have I offended you? What cause
Hath my behaviour given to your displeasure
That thus you should proceed to put me off
And take your good grace from me? Heaven witness
I have been to you a true and humble wife,
At all times to your will conformable,
Ever in fear to kindle your dislike,
Yea, subject to your countenance — glad or sorry
As I saw it inclin'd. When was the hour
I ever contradicted your desire
Or made it not mine too? Or which of your friends
Have I not strove to love, although I knew
He were mine enemy? What friend of mine
That had to him deriv'd your anger did I
Continue in my liking? nay, gave notice
He was from thence discharg'd? Sir, call to mind
That I have been your wife in this obedience
Upward of twenty years and have been blest
With many children by you. If in the course
And process of this time you can report,
And prove it too, against mine honour aught,
My bond to wedlock, or my love and duty,
Against your sacred person, in God's name
Turn me away, and let the foul'st contempt
Shut door upon me, and so give me up
To the sharp'st kind of justice. Please you, sir,
The King your father was reputed for
A prince most prudent, of an excellent
And unmatch'd wit and judgment. Ferdinand,
My father, King of Spain, was reckon'd one
The wisest prince that there had reign'd by many
A year before. It is not to be question'd
That they had gather'd a wise council to them
Of every realm, that did debate this business,
Who deem'd our marriage lawful. Wherefore I humbly
Beseech you, sir, to spare me till I may
Be by my friends in Spain advis'd, whose counsel
I will implore. If not, i' th' name of God,
Your pleasure be fulfill'd!

Wol. You have here, lady
(And of your choice), these reverend fathers, men
Of singular integrity and learning,
Yea, the elect o' th' land, who are assembled
To plead your cause. It shall be therefore bootless
That longer you defer the court, as well
For your own quiet as to rectify
What is unsettled in the King.

Camp. His Grace
Hath spoken well and justly. Therefore, madam,
It's fit this royal session do proceed
And that (without delay) their arguments
Be now produc'd and heard.

Queen. Lord Cardinal,
To you I speak.

Wol. Your pleasure, madam?

Queen. Sir,
I am about to weep; but, thinking that
We are a queen (or long have dream'd so), certain
The daughter of a king, my drops of tears
I'll turn to sparks of fire.

Wol. Be patient yet.

Queen. I will, when you are humble; nay, before,
Or God will punish me. I do believe
(Induc'd by potent circumstances) that
You are mine enemy; and make my challenge
You shall not be my judge; for it is you
Have blown this coal betwixt my lord and me —
Which God's dew quench! Therefore I say again
I utterly abhor, yea, from my soul
Refuse you for my judge, whom yet once more
I hold my most malicious foe and think not
At all a friend to truth.

Wol. I do profess
You speak not like yourself, who ever yet
Have stood to charity and display'd th' effects
Of disposition gentle and of wisdom
O'ertopping woman's pow'r. Madam, you do me wrong.
I have no spleen against you, nor injustice
For you or any. How far I have proceeded,
Or how far further shall, is warranted
By a commission from the Consistory,
Yea, the whole Consistory of Rome. You charge me
That I have blown this coal. I do deny it.
The King is present. If it be known to him
That I gainsay my deed, how may he wound,
And worthily, my falsehood! Yea, as much
As you have done my truth. If he know
That I am free of your report, he knows
I am not of your wrong. Therefore in him
It lies to cure me, and the cure is to

Remove these thoughts from you; the which before
His Highness shall speak in, I do beseech
You, gracious madam, to unthink your speaking
And to say so no more.

Queen. My lord, my lord,
I am a simple woman, much too weak
T' oppose your cunning. Y'are meek and humble-mouth'd;
You sign your place and calling, in full seeming,
With meekness and humility; but your heart
Is cramm'd with arrogancy, spleen, and pride.
You have, by fortune and his Highness' favours,
Gone slightly o'er low steps and now are mounted
Where pow'rs are your retainers and your words
(Domestics to you) serve your will as't please
Yourself pronounce their office. I must tell you
You tender more your person's honour than
Your high profession spiritual; that again
I do refuse you for my judge and here,
Before you all, appeal unto the Pope,
To bring my whole cause fore his Holiness
And to be judg'd by him.

She curtsies to the King and offers to depart.

Camp. The Queen is obstinate,
Stubborn to justice, apt to accuse it, and
Disdainful to be tried by't. 'Tis not well.
She's going away.

King. Call her again.

Crier. Katherine Queen of England, come into the court.

Gent. Usher. Madam, you are call'd back.

Queen. What need you note it? Pray you keep your way.
When you are call'd, return. Now the Lord help!
They vex me past my patience. Pray you pass on.
I will not tarry; no, nor ever more
Upon this business my appearance make
In any of their courts.

Exeunt Queen and her Attendants.

King. Go thy ways, Kate.
That man i' th' world who shall report he has
A better wife, let him in naught be trusted
For speaking false in that. Thou art, alone
(If thy rare qualities, sweet gentleness,
Thy meekness saintlike, wifelike government,
Obeying in commanding, and thy parts
Sovereign and pious else, could speak thee out)
The queen of earthly queens. She's noble born,
And like her true nobility she has
Carried herself towards me.

Wol. Most gracious sir,
In humblest manner I require your Highness
That it shall please you to declare in hearing
Of all these ears (for where I am robb'd and bound,
There must I be unloos'd, although not there
At once and fully satisfied) whether ever I
Did broach this business to your Highness, or
Laid any scruple in your way which might
Induce you to the question on't, or ever
Have to you, but with thanks to God for such
A royal lady, spake one the least word that might
Be to the prejudice of her present state
Or touch of her good person.

King. My Lord Cardinal,
I do excuse you; yea, upon mine honour,
I free you from't. You are not to be taught
That you have many enemies that know not
Why they are so, but, like to village curs,
Bark when their fellows do. By some of these
The Queen is put in anger. Y'are excus'd.
But will you be more justified? You ever
Have wish'd the sleeping of this business; never
Desir'd it to be stirr'd; but oft have hind'red, oft,
The passages made toward it. On my honour,
I speak my good Lord Cardinal to this point,
And thus far clear him. Now, what mov'd me to't,
I will be bold with time and your attention.
Then mark th' inducement. Thus it came; give heed to't.
My conscience first receiv'd a tenderness,
Scruple, and prick on certain speeches utter'd
By th' Bishop of Bayonne, then French ambassador,
Who had been hither sent on the debating
A marriage 'twixt the Duke of Orleans and
Our daughter Mary. I' th' progress of this business,
Ere a determinate resolution, he
(I mean the Bishop) did require a respite
Wherein he might the King his lord advertise
Whether our daughter were legitimate,
Respecting this our marriage with the dowager,
Sometimes our brother's wife. This respite shook
The bottom of my conscience, enter'd me,
Yea, with a splitting power and made to tremble
The region of my breast, which forc'd such way
That many maz'd considerings did throng
And press'd in with this caution. First, methought
I stood not in the smile of heaven, who had

Commanded nature that my lady's womb,
If it conceiv'd a male child by me, should
Do no more offices of life to't than
The grave does to th' dead; for her male issue
Or died where they were made or shortly after
This world had air'd them. Hence I took a thought
This was a judgment on me, that my kingdom
(Well worthy the best heir o' th' world) should not
Be gladded in't by me. Then follows that
I weigh'd the danger which my realms stood in
By this my issue's fail, and that gave to me
Many a groaning throe. Thus hulling in
The wild sea of my conscience, I did steer
Toward this remedy whereupon we are
Now present here together. That's to say
I meant to rectify my conscience, which
I then did feel full sick, and yet not well,
By all the reverend fathers of the land
And doctors learn'd. First I began in private
With you, my Lord of Lincoln. You remember
How under my oppression I did reek
When I first mov'd you.
B. Linc. Very well, my liege.
King. I have spoke long. Be pleas'd yourself to say
How far you satisfied me.
B. Linc. So please your Highness,
The question did at first so stagger me,
Bearing a state of mighty moment in't
And consequence of dread, that I committed
The daring'st counsel which I had to doubt
And did entreat your Highness to this course
Which you are running here.
King. I then mov'd you,
My Lord of Canterbury, and got your leave
To make this present summons. Unsolicited
I left no reverend person in this court,
But by particular consent proceeded
Under your hands and seals. Therefore go on;
For no dislike i' th' world against the person
Of the good Queen, but the sharp thorny points
Of my alleged reasons, drives this forward.
Prove but our marriage lawful, by my life
And kingly dignity, we are contented
To wear our mortal state to come with her,
Katherine our queen, before the primest creature
That's paragon'd o' th' world.
Camp. So please your Highness,
The Queen being absent, 'tis a needful fitness
That we adjourn this court till further day.
Meanwhile must be an earnest motion
Made to the Queen to call back her appeal
She intends unto his Holiness.
King. [*aside*] I may perceive
These Cardinals trifle with me. I abhor
This dilatory sloth and tricks of Rome.
My learn'd and well-beloved servant Cranmer,
Prithee return. With thy approach I know
My comfort comes along. — Break up the court.
I say, set on. *Exeunt in manner as they enter'd.*

ACT III. Scene I. [*London. A room in the* Queen's *apartments.*]

Enter the *Queen* and her *Women,* as at work.

Queen. Take thy lute, wench. My soul grows sad with troubles.
Sing, and disperse 'em if thou canst. Leave working.

Song.

Orpheus with his lute made trees
And the mountain tops that freeze
Bow themselves when he did sing.
To his music plants and flowers
Ever sprung, as sun and showers
There had made a lasting spring.

Everything that heard him play,
Even the billows of the sea,
Hung their heads, and then lay by.
In sweet music is such art
Killing care and grief of heart
Fall asleep, or hearing, die.

Enter a *Gentleman.*

Queen. How now?
Gent. An't please your Grace, the two great Cardinals
Wait in the presence.
Queen. Would they speak with me?
Gent. They will'd me say so, madam.
Queen. Pray their Graces
To come near. [*Exit Gent.*] What can be their business
With me, a poor weak woman, fall'n from favour?
I do not like their coming. Now I think on't,
They should be good men, their affairs as righteous;
But all hoods make not monks.

Enter the two *Cardinals, Wolsey* and *Campeius.*

Wol. Peace to your Highness!
Queen. Your Graces find me here part of a housewife
(I would be all) against the worst may happen.
What are your pleasures with me, reverend lords?
Wol. May it please you, noble madam, to withdraw
Into your private chamber, we shall give you
The full cause of our coming.
Queen. Speak it here.
There's nothing I have done yet, o' my conscience,
Deserves a corner. Would all other women
Could speak this with as free a soul as I do!
My lords, I care not (so much I am happy
Above a number) if my actions
Were tried by ev'ry tongue, ev'ry eye saw 'em,
Envy and base opinion set against 'em,
I know my life so even. If your business
Seek me out, and that way I am wife in,
Out with it boldly. Truth loves open dealing.
Wol. Tanta est erga te mentis integritas, regina serenissima —
Queen. O, good my lord, no Latin!
I am not such a truant since my coming
As not to know the language I have liv'd in.
A strange tongue makes my cause more strange, suspicious.
Pray speak in English. Here are some will thank you,
If you speak truth, for their poor mistress' sake.
Believe me, she has had much wrong. Lord Cardinal,
The willing'st sin I ever yet committed
May be absolv'd in English.
Wol. Noble lady,
I am sorry my integrity should breed
(And service to his Majesty and you)
So deep suspicion where all faith was meant.
We come not by the way of accusation
To taint that honour every good tongue blesses,
Nor to betray you any way to sorrow —
You have too much, good lady — but to know
How you stand minded in the weighty difference
Between the King and you, and to deliver
(Like free and honest men) our just opinions
And comforts to your cause.
Camp. Most honour'd madam,
My Lord of York, out of his noble nature,
Zeal and obedience he still bore your Grace,
Forgetting (like a good man) your late censure
Both of his truth and him (which was too far),
Offers, as I do, in a sign of peace,
His service and his counsel.
Queen. [*aside*] To betray me. —
My lords, I thank you both for your good wills.
Ye speak like honest men (pray God ye prove so!).
But how to make ye suddenly an answer
In such a point of weight, so near mine honour
(More near my life, I fear), with my weak wit,
And to such men of gravity and learning,
In truth I know not. I was set at work
Among my maids, full little (God knows) looking
Either for such men or such business.
For her sake that I have been — for I feel
The last fit of my greatness — good your Graces,
Let me have time and counsel for my cause.
Alas, I am a woman friendless, hopeless!
Wol. Madam, you wrong the King's love with these fears.
Your hopes and friends are infinite.
Queen. In England
But little for my profit. Can you think, lords,
That any Englishman dare give me counsel?
Or be a known friend 'gainst his highness' pleasure
(Though he be grown so desperate to be honest)
And live a subject? Nay forsooth, my friends,
They that must weigh out my afflictions,
They that my trust must grow to, live not here.
They are (as all my other comforts) far hence,
In mine own country, lords.
Camp. I would your Grace
Would leave your griefs and take my counsel.
Queen. How, sir?
Camp. Put your main cause into the King's protection.
He's loving and most gracious. 'Twill be much
Both for your honour better and your cause;
For if the trial of the law o'ertake ye,
You'll part away disgrac'd.
Wol. He tells you rightly.
Queen. Ye tell me what ye wish for both — my ruin.
Is this your Christian counsel? Out upon ye!
Heaven is above all yet. There sits a judge
That no king can corrupt.
Camp. Your rage mistakes us.
Queen. The more shame for ye! Holy men I thought ye,
Upon my soul, two reverend cardinal virtues;
But cardinal sins and hollow hearts I fear ye.

Mend 'em for shame, my lords! Is this your comfort?
The cordial that ye bring a wretched lady?
A woman lost among ye, laugh'd at, scorn'd?
I will not wish ye half my miseries;
I have more charity. But say I warn'd ye.
Take heed, for heaven's sake take heed, lest at once
The burthen of my sorrows fall upon ye.
Wol. Madam, this is a mere distraction.
You turn the good we offer into envy.
Queen. Ye turn me into nothing. Woe upon ye
And all such false professors! Would you have me
(If you have any justice, any pity,
If ye be anything but churchmen's habits)
Put my sick cause into his hands that hates me?
Alas, has banish'd me his bed already,
His love, too long ago! I am old, my lords,
And all the fellowship I hold now with him
Is only my obedience. What can happen
To me above this wretchedness? All your studies
Make me a curse like this!
Camp. Your fears are worse.
Queen. Have I liv'd thus long (let me speak myself,
Since virtue finds no friends) a wife, a true one?
A woman (I dare say, without vainglory)
Never yet branded with suspicion?
Have I with all my full affections
Still met the King? lov'd him next heav'n? obey'd him?
Been (out of fondness) superstitious to him?
Almost forgot my prayers to content him?
And am I thus rewarded? 'Tis not well, lords.
Bring me a constant woman to her husband,
One that ne'er dream'd a joy beyond his pleasure,
And to that woman (when she has done most)
Yet will I add an honour — a great patience.
Wol. Madam, you wander from the good we aim at.
Queen. My lord, I dare not make myself so guilty
To give up willingly that noble title
Your master wed me to. Nothing but death
Shall e'er divorce my dignities.
Wol. Pray hear me.
Queen. Would I had never trod this English earth
Or felt the flatteries that grow upon it!
Ye have angels' faces, but heaven knows your hearts.
What will become of me now, wretched lady?
I am the most unhappy woman living.
[*To her Women*] Alas, poor wenches, where are now your fortunes?
Shipwrack'd upon a kingdom where no pity,
No friends, no hope, no kindred weep for me,
Almost no grave allow'd me! Like the lily
That once was mistress of the field and flourish'd,
I'll hang my head and perish.
Wol. If your Grace
Could but be brought to know our ends are honest,
You'ld feel more comfort. Why should we, good lady,
Upon what cause, wrong you? Alas, our places,
The way of our profession is against it.
We are to cure such sorrows, not to sow 'em.
For goodness sake, consider what you do;
How you may hurt yourself, ay, utterly
Grow from the King's acquaintance, by this carriage.
The hearts of princes kiss obedience,
So much they love it; but to stubborn spirits
They swell and grow as terrible as storms.
I know you have a gentle, noble temper,
A soul as even as a calm. Pray think us
Those we profess — peacemakers, friends, and servants.
Camp. Madam, you'll find it so. You wrong your virtues
With these weak women's fears. A noble spirit,
As yours was put into you, ever casts
Such doubts as false coin from it. The King loves you.
Beware you lose it not. For us, if you please
To trust us in your business, we are ready
To use our utmost studies in your service.
Queen. Do what ye will, my lords; and pray forgive me
If I have us'd myself unmannerly.
You know I am a woman, lacking wit
To make a seemly answer to such persons.
Pray do my service to his Majesty.
He has my heart yet and shall have my prayers
While I shall have my life. Come, reverend fathers,
Bestow your counsels on me. She now begs
That little thought, when she set footing here,
She should have bought her dignities so dear.
Exeunt.

Scene II. [*London. Antechamber to the* King's *apartment.*]

Enter the *Duke of Norfolk, Duke of Suffolk, Lord Surrey,* and *Lord Chamberlain.*

Nor. If you will now unite in your complaints
And force them with a constancy, the Cardinal
Cannot stand under them. If you omit
The offer of this time, I cannot promise
But that you shall sustain moe new disgraces
With these you bear already.
Sur. I am joyful
To meet the least occasion that may give me
Remembrance of my father-in-law, the Duke,
To be reveng'd on him.
Suf. Which of the peers
Have uncontemn'd gone by him, or at least
Strangely neglected? When did he regard
The stamp of nobleness in any person
Out of himself?
Cham. My lords, you speak your pleasures.
What he deserves of you and me I know.
What we can do to him (though now the time
Gives way to us) I much fear. If you cannot
Bar his access to th' King, never attempt
Anything on him; for he hath a witchcraft
Over the King in's tongue.
Nor. O, fear him not!
His spell in that is out. The King hath found
Matter against him that for ever mars
The honey of his language. No, he's settled
(Not to come off) in his displeasure.
Sur. Sir,
I should be glad to hear such news as this
Once every hour.
Nor. Believe it, this is true.
In the divorce his contrary proceedings
Are all unfolded; wherein he appears
As I would wish mine enemy.
Sur. How came
His practices to light?
Suf. Most strangely.
Sur. O, how? how?
Suf. The Cardinal's letters to the Pope miscarried
And came to th' eye o' th' King, wherein was read
How that the Cardinal did entreat his Holiness
To stay the judgment o' th' divorce; for if
It did take place, 'I do,' quoth he, 'perceive
My king is tangled in affection to
A creature of the Queen's, Lady Anne Bullen.'
Sur. Has the King this?
Suf. Believe it.
Sur. Will this work?
Cham. The King in this perceives him, how he coasts
And hedges his own way. But in this point
All his tricks founder and he brings his physic
After his patient's death: the King already
Hath married the fair lady.
Sur. Would he had!
Suf. May you be happy in your wish, my lord!
For I profess you have it.
Sur. Now all my joy
Trace the conjunction!
Suf. My amen to't!
Nor. All men's!
Suf. There's order given for her coronation.
Marry, this is yet but young and may be left
To some ears unrecounted. But, my lords,
She is a gallant creature and complete
In mind and feature. I persuade me, from her
Will fall some blessing to this land which shall
In it be memoriz'd.
Sur. But will the King
Digest this letter of the Cardinal's?
The Lord forbid!
Nor. Marry amen!
Suf. No, no!
There be moe wasps that buzz about his nose
Will make this sting the sooner. Cardinal Campeius
Is stol'n away to Rome, hath ta'en no leave,
Has left the cause o' th' King unhandled, and
Is posted as the agent of our Cardinal
To second all his plot. I do assure you
The King cried 'Ha!' at this.
Cham. Now God incense him
And let him cry 'Ha!' louder!
Nor. But, my lord,
When returns Cranmer?
Suf. He is return'd in his opinions, which
Have satisfied the King for his divorce,
Together with all famous colleges
Almost in Christendom. Shortly, I believe,
His second marriage shall be publish'd and
Her coronation. Katherine no more
Shall be call'd Queen, but Princess Dowager
And widow to Prince Arthur.
Nor. This same Cranmer's
A worthy fellow and hath ta'en much pain
In the King's business.
Suf. He has, and we shall see him
For it an archbishop.
Nor. So I hear.
Suf. 'Tis so.

Enter [*Cardinal*] *Wolsey* and *Cromwell.*

The Cardinal!
Nor. Observe, observe! He's moody.
Card. The packet, Cromwell,
Gave't you the King?
Crom. To his own hand, in's bedchamber.
Card. Look'd he o' th' inside of the papers?
Crom. Presently
He did unseal them; and the first he view'd,
He did it with a serious mind; a heed
Was in his countenance. You he bade
Attend him here this morning.
Card. Is he ready
To come abroad?
Crom. I think by this he is.
Wol. Leave me awhile.
Exit Cromwell.
[*Aside*] It shall be to the Duchess of Alençon,
The French king's sister. He shall marry her.
Anne Bullen? No! I'll no Anne Bullens for him.
There's more in't than fair visage. Bullen?
No, we'll no Bullens! Speedily I wish
To hear from Rome. The Marchioness of Pembroke?
Nor. He's discontented.
Suf. May be he hears the King
Does whet his anger to him.
Sur. Sharp enough,
Lord, for thy justice!
Wol. [*aside*] The late Queen's gentlewoman, a knight's daughter,
To be her mistress' mistress? the Queen's queen?
This candle burns not clear. 'Tis I must snuff it.
Then out it goes! What though I know her virtuous
And well deserving? Yet I know her for
A spleeny Lutheran, and not wholesome to
Our cause that she should lie i' th' bosom of
Our hard-rul'd king. Again, there is sprung up
An heretic, an arch one — Cranmer, one
Hath crawl'd into the favour of the King
And is his oracle.
Nor. He is vex'd at something.

Enter *King*, reading of a schedule, [and *Lovell*].

Sur. I would 'twere something that would fret the string,
The master-cord on's heart!
Suf. The King, the King!
King. What piles of wealth hath he accumulated
To his own portion! and what expense by th' hour
Seems to flow from him! How i' th' name of thrift
Does he rake this together? — Now, my lords,
Saw you the Cardinal?
Nor. My lord, we have
Stood here observing him. Some strange commotion
Is in his brain. He bites his lip and starts,
Stops on a sudden, looks upon the ground,
Then lays his finger on his temple; straight
Springs out into fast gait, then stops again,
Strikes his breast hard, and anon he casts
His eye against the moon. In most strange postures
We have seen him set himself.
King. It may well be;
There is a mutiny in's mind. This morning
Papers of state he sent me to peruse,
As I requir'd; and wot you what I found
There — on my conscience, put unwittingly?
Forsooth, an inventory, thus importing,
The several parcels of his plate, his treasure,
Rich stuffs and ornaments of household; which
I find at such proud rate that it outspeaks
Possession of a subject.
Nor. It's heaven's will.
Some spirit put this paper in the packet
To bless your eye withal.
King. If we did think
His contemplation were above the earth
And fix'd on spiritual object, he should still
Dwell in his musings; but I am afraid
His thinkings are below the moon, not worth
His serious considering.
King takes his seat; whispers Lovell, who goes to the Cardinal.
Card. Heaven forgive me!
Ever God bless your Highness!
King. Good my lord,
You are full of heavenly stuff and bear the inventory
Of your best graces in your mind; the which
You were now running o'er. You have scarce time
To steal from spiritual leisure a brief span
To keep your earthly audit. Sure, in that
I deem you an ill husband, and am glad
To have you therein my companion.
Card. Sir,
For holy offices I have a time; a time
To think upon the part of business which
I bear i' th' state; and nature does require
Her times of preservation, which perforce

I, her frail son, amongst my brethren mortal,
Must give my tendance to.
King. You have said well.
Card. And ever may your Highness yoke together
(As I will lend you cause) my doing well
With my well saying!
King. 'Tis well said again,
And 'tis a kind of good deed to say well;
And yet words are no deeds. My father lov'd you;
He said he did, and with his deed did crown
His word upon you. Since I had my office,
I have kept you next my heart; have not alone
Employ'd you where high profits might come home,
But par'd my present havings to bestow
My bounties upon you.
Card. [*aside*] What should this mean?
Sur. [*aside*] The Lord increase this business!
King. Have I not made you
The prime man of the state? I pray you tell me
If what I now pronounce you have found true;
And if you may confess it, say withal
If you are bound to us or no. What say you?
Card. My sovereign, I confess your royal graces,
Show'r'd on me daily, have been more than could
My studied purposes requite, which went
Beyond all man's endeavours. My endeavours
Have ever come too short of my desires,
Yet fil'd with my abilities. Mine own ends
Have been mine so that evermore they pointed
To th' good of your most sacred person and
The profit of the state. For your great graces
Heap'd upon me (poor undeserver) I
Can nothing render but allegiant thanks,
My pray'rs to heaven for you, my loyalty,
Which ever has and ever shall be growing
Till death (that winter) kill it.
King. Fairly answer'd!
A loyal and obedient subject is
Therein illustrated. The honour of it
Does pay the act of it, as, i' th' contrary,
The foulness is the punishment. I presume
That, as my hand has open'd bounty to you,
My heart dropp'd love, my pow'r rain'd honour, more
On you than any, so your hand and heart,
Your brain, and every function of your power
Should, notwithstanding that your bond of duty,
As 'twere in love's particular, be more
To me, your friend, than any.
Card. I do profess
That for your Highness' good I ever labour'd
More than mine own; that am, have, and will be —
Though all the world should crack their duty to you
And throw it from their soul; though perils did
Abound as thick as thought could make 'em and
Appear in forms more horrid — yet my duty,
As doth a rock against the chiding flood,
Should the approach of this wild river break
And stand unshaken yours.
King. 'Tis nobly spoken.
Take notice, lords, he has a loyal breast,
For you have seen him open't. Read o'er this;
[*Gives him papers.*]
And after, this; and then to breakfast with
What appetite you have.
Exit King frowning upon the Cardinal. The Nobles throng after him, smiling and whispering.
Card. What should this mean?
What sudden anger's this? How have I reap'd it?
He parted frowning from me, as if ruin
Leap'd from his eyes. So looks the chafed lion
Upon the daring huntsman that has gall'd him;
Then makes him nothing. I must read this paper;
I fear, the story of his anger. 'Tis so!
This paper has undone me. 'Tis th' accompt
Of all that world of wealth I have drawn together
For mine own ends; indeed, to gain the popedom
And fee my friends in Rome. O negligence
Fit for a fool to fall by! What cross devil
Made me put this main secret in the packet
I sent the King? Is there no way to cure this?
No new device to beat this from his brains?
I know 'twill stir him strongly; yet I know
A way, if it take right, in spite of fortune,
Will bring me off again. What's this? 'To th' Pope'?
The letter (as I live!) with all the business
I writ to's Holiness! Nay then, farewell!
I have touch'd the highest point of all my greatness,
And from that full meridian of my glory
I haste now to my setting. I shall fall
Like a bright exhalation in the evening,
And no man see me more.

Enter to *Wolsey* the *Dukes of Norfolk* and *Suffolk,* the *Earl of Surrey,* and the *Lord Chamberlain.*

Nor. Hear the King's pleasure, Cardinal, who commands you
To render up the great seal presently
Into our hands and to confine yourself
To Asher House, my Lord of Winchester's,
Till you hear further from his Highness.
Card. Stay.
Where's your commission, lords? Words cannot carry
Authority so weighty.
Suf. Who dares cross 'em,
Bearing the King's will from his mouth expressly?
Card. Till I find more than will or words to do it
(I mean your malice), know, officious lords,
I dare and must deny it. Now I feel
Of what coarse metal ye are moulded — envy;
How eagerly ye follow my disgraces,
As if it fed ye! and how sleek and wanton
Ye appear in everything may bring my ruin!
Follow your envious courses, men of malice.
You have Christian warrant for 'em, and no doubt
In time will find their fit rewards. That seal
You ask with such a violence, the King
(Mine and your master) with his own hand gave me;
Bade me enjoy it, with the place and honours,
During my life, and to confirm his goodness
Tied it by letters patents. Now who'll take it?
Sur. The King, that gave it.
Card. It must be himself then.
Sur. Thou art a proud traitor, priest.
Card. Proud lord, thou liest!
Within these forty hours Surrey durst better
Have burnt that tongue than said so.
Sur. Thy ambition
(Thou scarlet sin) robb'd this bewailing land
Of noble Buckingham, my father-in-law.
The heads of all thy brother cardinals
(With thee and all thy best parts bound together)
Weigh'd not a hair of his. Plague of your policy!
You sent me Deputy for Ireland;
Far from his succour, from the King, from all
That might have mercy on the fault thou gav'st him;
Whilst your great goodness, out of holy pity,
Absolv'd him with an axe.
Wol. This, and all else
This talking lord can lay upon my credit,
I answer is most false. The Duke by law
Found his deserts. How innocent I was
From any private malice in his end,
His noble jury and foul cause can witness.
If I lov'd many words, lord, I should tell you
You have as little honesty as honour,
That in the way of loyalty and truth
Toward the King, my ever royal master,
Dare mate a sounder man than Surrey can be
And all that love his follies.
Sur. By my soul,
Your long coat, priest, protects you! Thou shouldst feel
My sword i' th' lifeblood of thee else. My lords,
Can ye endure to hear this arrogance?
And from this fellow? If we live thus tamely,
To be thus jaded by a piece of scarlet,
Farewell nobility! let his Grace go forward
And dare us with his cap, like larks!
Card. All goodness
Is poison to thy stomach.
Sur. Yes, that goodness
Of gleaning all the land's wealth into one,
Into your own hands, Cardinal, by extortion;
The goodness of your intercepted packets
You writ to th' Pope against the King. Your goodness,
Since you provoke me, shall be most notorious.
My Lord of Norfolk, — as you are truly noble,
As you respect the common good, the state
Of our despis'd nobility, our issues
(Who, if he live, will scarce be gentlemen), —
Produce the grand sum of his sins, the articles
Collected from his life. I'll startle you
Worse than the sacring bell when the brown wench
Lay kissing in your arms, Lord Cardinal.
Card. How much, methinks, I could despise this man
But that I am bound in charity against it!
Nor. Those articles, my lord, are in the King's hand;
But thus much — they are foul ones.
Wol. So much fairer
And spotless shall mine innocence arise
When the King knows my truth.
Sur. This cannot save you.
I thank my memory, I yet remember

Some of these articles, and out they shall!
Now if you can blush and cry guilty, Cardinal,
You'll show a little honesty.
Wol. Speak on, sir.
I dare your worst objections. If I blush,
It is to see a nobleman want manners.
Sur. I had rather want those than my head. Have at you!
First, that without the King's assent or knowledge
You wrought to be a legate, by which power
You maim'd the jurisdiction of all bishops.
Nor. Then, that in all you writ to Rome, or else
To foreign princes, 'Ego et Rex meus'
Was still inscrib'd; in which you brought the King
To be your servant.
Suf. Then, that without the knowledge
Either of King or Council, when you went
Ambassador to the Emperor, you made bold
To carry into Flanders the great seal.
Sur. Item, you sent a large commission
To Gregory de Cassado to conclude,
Without the King's will or the state's allowance,
A league between his Highness and Ferrara.
Suf. That out of mere ambition you have caus'd
Your holy hat to be stamp'd on the King's coin.
Sur. Then, that you have sent innumerable substance
(By what means got, I leave to your own conscience)
To furnish Rome and to prepare the ways
You have for dignities, to the mere undoing
Of all the kingdom. Many more there are,
Which, since they are of you, and odious,
I will not taint my mouth with.
Cham. O my lord,
Press not a falling man too far! 'Tis virtue.
His faults lie open to the laws; let them,
Not you, correct him. My heart weeps to see him
So little of his great self.
Sur. I forgive him.
Suf. Lord Cardinal, the King's further pleasure is —
Because all those things you have done of late
By your power legatine within this kingdom
Fall into th' compass of a præmunire —
That therefore such a writ be sued against you,
To forfeit all your goods, lands, tenements,
Chattels, and whatsoever, and to be
Out of the King's protection. This is my charge.
Nor. And so we'll leave you to your meditations
How to live better. For your stubborn answer
About the giving back the great seal to us,
The King shall know it, and (no doubt) shall thank you.
So fare you well, my little good Lord Cardinal.
Exeunt all but Wolsey.
Wol. So farewell to the little good you bear me!
Farewell, a long farewell, to all my greatness!
This is the state of man: to-day he puts forth
The tender leaves of hopes; to-morrow blossoms
And bears his blushing honours thick upon him;
The third day comes a frost, a killing frost,
And when he thinks, good easy man, full surely
His greatness is a-ripening, nips his root,
And then he falls, as I do. I have ventur'd,
Like little wanton boys that swim on bladders,
This many summers in a sea of glory;
But far beyond my depth. My high-blown pride
At length broke under me, and now has left me,
Weary and old with service, to the mercy
Of a rude stream that must for ever hide me.
Vain pomp and glory of this world, I hate ye!
I feel my heart new open'd. O, how wretched
Is that poor man that hangs on princes' favours!
There is betwixt that smile we would aspire to,
That sweet aspect of princes, and their ruin
More pangs and fears than wars or women have;
And when he falls, he falls like Lucifer,
Never to hope again.

Enter *Cromwell*, standing amazed.

Why, how now, Cromwell!
Crom. I have no power to speak, sir.
Card. What, amaz'd
At my misfortunes? Can thy spirit wonder
A great man should decline? Nay, an you weep,
I am fall'n indeed.
Crom. How does your Grace?
Card. Why, well;
Never so truly happy, my good Cromwell.
I know myself now, and I feel within me
A peace above all earthly dignities,
A still and quiet conscience. The King has cur'd me —
I humbly thank his Grace — and from these shoulders,

These ruin'd pillars, out of pity taken
A load would sink a navy — too much honour.
O 'tis a burden, Cromwell, 'tis a burden
Too heavy for a man that hopes for heaven!
Crom. I am glad your Grace has made that right use of it.
Card. I hope I have. I am able now, methinks,
Out of a fortitude of soul I feel,
To endure more miseries and greater far
Than my weak-hearted enemies dare offer.
What news abroad?
Crom. The heaviest and the worst
Is your displeasure with the King.
Card. God bless him!
Crom. The next is that Sir Thomas More is chosen
Lord Chancellor in your place.
Card. That's somewhat sudden.
But he's a learned man. May he continue
Long in his Highness' favour and do justice
For truth's sake and his conscience; that his bones,
When he has run his course and sleeps in blessings,
May have a tomb of orphans' tears wept on him!
What more?
Crom. That Cranmer is return'd with welcome,
Install'd Lord Archbishop of Canterbury.
Card. That's news indeed.
Crom. Last, that the Lady Anne,
Whom the King hath in secrecy long married,
This day was view'd in open as his queen,
Going to chapel; and the voice is now
Only about her coronation.
Card. There was the weight that pull'd me down. O Cromwell,
The King has gone beyond me! All my glories
In that one woman I have lost for ever.
No sun shall ever usher forth mine honours
Or gild again the noble troops that waited
Upon my smiles. Go get thee from me, Cromwell!
I am a poor fall'n man, unworthy now
To be thy lord and master. Seek the King.
That sun, I pray, may never set! I have told him
What and how true thou art. He will advance thee.
Some little memory of me will stir him
(I know his noble nature) not to let
Thy hopeful service perish too. Good Cromwell,
Neglect him not; make use now, and provide
For thine own future safety.
Crom. O my lord,
Must I then leave you? Must I needs forgo
So good, so noble, and so true a master?
Bear witness, all that have not hearts of iron,
With what a sorrow Cromwell leaves his lord.
The King shall have my service, but my pray'rs
For ever and for ever shall be yours.
Card. Cromwell, I did not think to shed a tear
In all my miseries; but thou hast forc'd me
(Out of thy honest truth) to play the woman.
Let's dry our eyes; and thus far hear me, Cromwell,
And when I am forgotten, as I shall be,
And sleep in dull cold marble, where no mention
Of me more must be heard of, say I taught thee —
Say Wolsey, that once trod the ways of glory
And sounded all the depths and shoals of honour,
Found thee a way (out of his wrack) to rise in —
A sure and safe one, though thy master miss'd it.
Mark but my fall and that that ruin'd me.
Cromwell, I charge thee, fling away ambition!
By that sin fell the angels. How can man then
(The image of his Maker) hope to win by it?
Love thyself last. Cherish those hearts that hate thee;
Corruption wins not more than honesty.
Still in thy right hand carry gentle peace
To silence envious tongues. Be just, and fear not.
Let all the ends thou aim'st at be thy country's,
Thy God's, and truth's. Then if thou fall'st, O Cromwell,
Thou fall'st a blessed martyr. Serve the King.
And prithee lead me in.
There take an inventory of all I have
To the last penny. 'Tis the King's. My robe,
And my integrity to heaven, is all
I dare now call mine own. O Cromwell, Cromwell!
Had I but serv'd my God with half the zeal
I serv'd my king, he would not in mine age
Have left me naked to mine enemies.
Crom. Good sir, have patience.
Card. So I have. Farewell
The hopes of court! My hopes in heaven do dwell. *Exeunt.*

Act IV. Scene I. [*A street in Westminster.*]

Enter two *Gentlemen*, meeting one another.

1. Gent. Y'are well met once again.
2. Gent. So are you.
1. Gent. You come to take your stand here and behold
The Lady Anne pass from her coronation?
2. Gent. 'Tis all my business. At our last encounter
The Duke of Buckingham came from his trial.
1. Gent. 'Tis very true; but that time offer'd sorrow;
This, general joy.
2. Gent. 'Tis well. The citizens
I am sure have shown at full their royal minds—
As, let 'em have their rights, they are ever forward—
In celebration of this day with shows,
Pageants, and sights of honour.
1. Gent. Never greater,
Nor, I'll assure you, better taken, sir.
2. Gent. May I be bold to ask what that contains,
That paper in your hand?
1. Gent. Yes. 'Tis the list
Of those that claim their offices this day
By custom of the coronation.
The Duke of Suffolk is the first, and claims
To be High Steward; next, the Duke of Norfolk,
He to be Earl Marshal. You may read the rest.
2. Gent. I thank you, sir. Had I not known those customs,
I should have been beholding to your paper.
But, I beseech you, what's become of Katherine,
The Princess Dowager? How goes her business?
1. Gent. That I can tell you too. The Archbishop
Of Canterbury, accompanied with other
Learned and reverend fathers of his order,
Held a late court at Dunstable, six miles off
From Ampthill, where the Princess lay, to which
She was often cited by them, but appear'd not;
And, to be short, for not appearance and
The King's late scruple, by the main assent
Of all these learned men she was divorc'd
And the late marriage made of none effect;
Since which she was remov'd to Kimbolton,
Where she remains now sick.
2. Gent. Alas, good lady!
[*Trumpets.*]
The trumpets sound. Stand close! The Queen is coming. *Hautboys.*

THE ORDER OF THE CORONATION.

1. A lively flourish of trumpets.
2. Then two *Judges*.
3. *Lord Chancellor*, with purse and mace before him.
4. *Choristers* singing. *Music.*
5. *Mayor of London*, bearing the mace. Then *Garter*, in his coat of arms, and on his head he wore a gilt copper crown.
6. *Marquess Dorset*, bearing a sceptre of gold, on his head a demi-coronal of gold. With him the *Earl of Surrey*, bearing the rod of silver with the dove, crowned with an earl's coronet. Collars of Esses.
7. *Duke of Suffolk*, in his robe of estate, his coronet on his head, bearing a long white wand, as High Steward. With him the *Duke of Norfolk*, with the rod of marshalship, a coronet on his head. Collars of Esses.
8. A canopy borne by four of the *Cinque Ports*; under it, the *Queen* in her robe, in her hair, richly adorned with pearl, crowned. On each side her the *Bishops of London* and *Winchester*.
9. The old *Duchess of Norfolk*, in a coronal of gold, wrought with flowers, bearing the *Queen's* train.
10. Certain *Ladies* or *Countesses*, with plain circlets of gold without flowers.

Exeunt, first passing over the stage in order and state, and then a great flourish of trumpets.

2. Gent. A royal train, believe me. These I know.
Who's that that bears the sceptre?
1. Gent. Marquess Dorset;
And that the Earl of Surrey with the rod.
2. Gent. A bold brave gentleman. That should be
The Duke of Suffolk.
1. Gent. 'Tis the same: High Steward.
2. Gent. And that my Lord of Norfolk?
1. Gent. Yes.

2. Gent. [*looks on the Queen*] Heaven bless thee!
Thou hast the sweetest face I ever look'd on.
Sir, as I have a soul, she is an angel!
Our king has all the Indies in his arms,
And more, and richer, when he strains that lady.
I cannot blame his conscience.
1. Gent. They that bear
The cloth of honour over her are four Barons
Of the Cinque Ports.
2. Gent. Those men are happy, and so are all are near her.
I take it, she that carries up the train
Is that old noble lady, Duchess of Norfolk.
1. Gent. It is, and all the rest are countesses.
2. Gent. Their coronets say so. These are stars indeed,
And sometimes falling ones.
1. Gent. No more of that.
[*Exit procession.*]

Enter a third *Gentleman.*

God save you, sir! Where have you been broiling?
3. Gent. Among the crowd i' th' Abbey, where a finger
Could not be wedg'd in more. I am stifled
With the mere rankness of their joy.
2. Gent. You saw
The ceremony?
3. Gent. That I did.
1. Gent. How was it?
3. Gent. Well worth the seeing.
2. Gent. Good sir, speak it to us.
3. Gent. As well as I am able. The rich stream
Of lords and ladies, having brought the Queen
To a prepar'd place in the choir, fell off
A distance from her, while her Grace sat down
To rest awhile, some half an hour or so,
In a rich chair of state, opposing freely
The beauty of her person to the people.
Believe me, sir, she is the goodliest woman
That ever lay by man; which when the people
Had the full view of, such a noise arose
As the shrouds make at sea in a stiff tempest,
As loud, and to as many tunes. Hats, cloaks
(Doublets, I think) flew up; and had their faces
Been loose, this day they had been lost. Such joy
I never saw before. Great-bellied women
That had not half a week to go, like rams
In the old time of war, would shake the press
And make 'em reel before 'em. No man living
Could say 'This is my wife' there, all were woven
So strangely in one piece.
2. Gent. But what follow'd?
3. Gent. At length her Grace rose and with modest paces
Came to the altar, where she kneel'd and saintlike
Cast her fair eyes to heaven and pray'd devoutly;
Then rose again and bow'd her to the people;
When by the Archbishop of Canterbury
She had all the royal makings of a queen;
As holy oil, Edward Confessor's crown,
The rod, and bird of peace, and all such emblems,
Laid nobly on her; which perform'd, the choir
With all the choicest music of the kingdom
Together sung 'Te Deum.' So she parted
And with the same full state pac'd back again
To York Place, where the feast is held.
1. Gent. Sir,
You must no more call it York Place. That's past;
For since the Cardinal fell that title's lost.
'Tis now the King's, and call'd Whitehall.
3. Gent. I know it;
But 'tis so lately alter'd that the old name
Is fresh about me.
2. Gent. What two reverend bishops
Were those that went on each side of the Queen?
3. Gent. Stokesly and Gardiner; the one of Winchester,
Newly preferr'd from the King's Secretary,
The other, London.
2. Gent. He of Winchester
Is held no great good lover of the Archbishop's,
The virtuous Cranmer.
3. Gent. All the land knows that.
However, yet there is no great breach. When it comes,
Cranmer will find a friend will not shrink from him.
2. Gent. Who may that be, I pray you?
3. Gent. Thomas Cromwell,
A man in much esteem with th' King, and truly
A worthy friend. The King has made him Master
O' th' Jewel House
And one, already, of the Privy Council.
2. Gent. He will deserve more.
3. Gent. Yes, without all doubt.
Come, gentlemen, ye shall go my way, which
Is to th' court, and there ye shall be my guests.
Something I can command. As I walk thither,
I'll tell ye more.
Both. You may command us, sir.
Exeunt.

Scene II. [*Kimbolton.*]

Enter *Katherine,* Dowager, sick; led between *Griffith* (her *Gentleman Usher*) and *Patience* (her *Woman*).

Grif. How does your Grace?
Kath. O Griffith, sick to death!
My legs like loaden branches bow to th' earth,
Willing to leave their burthen. Reach a chair.
So. Now, methinks, I feel a little ease.
Didst thou not tell me, Griffith, as thou led'st me,
That the great child of honour, Cardinal Wolsey,
Was dead?
Grif. Yes, madam; but I think your Grace,
Out of the pain you suffer'd, gave no ear to't.
Kath. Prithee, good Griffith, tell me how he died.
If well, he stepp'd before me happily
For my example.
Grif. Well, the voice goes, madam;
For after the stout Earl Northumberland
Arrested him at York and brought him forward,
As a man sorely tainted, to his answer,
He fell sick suddenly and grew so ill
He could not sit his mule.
Kath. Alas, poor man!
Grif. At last, with easy roads, he came to Leicester,
Lodg'd in the abbey; where the reverend Abbot,
With all his covent, honourably receiv'd him;
To whom he gave these words: 'O Father Abbot,
An old man, broken with the storms of state,
Is come to lay his weary bones among ye.
Give him a little earth for charity!'
So went to bed; where eagerly his sickness
Pursu'd him still; and three nights after this,
After the hour of eight, which he himself
Foretold should be his last, full of repentance,
Continual meditations, tears, and sorrows,
He gave his honours to the world again,
His blessed part to heaven, and slept in peace.
Kath. So may he rest! His faults lie gently on him!
Yet thus far, Griffith, give me leave to speak him,
And yet with charity. He was a man
Of an unbounded stomach, ever ranking
Himself with princes; one that by suggestion
Tied all the kingdom. Simony was fair play;
His own opinion was his law. I' th' presence
He would say untruths, and be ever double
Both in his words and meaning. He was never
(But where he meant to ruin) pitiful.
His promises were, as he then was, mighty;
But his performance, as he is now, nothing.
Of his own body he was ill, and gave
The clergy ill example.
Grif. Noble madam,
Men's evil manners live in brass; their virtues
We write in water. May it please your Highness
To hear me speak his good now?
Kath. Yes, good Griffith.
I were malicious else.
Grif. This Cardinal,
Though from an humble stock, undoubtedly
Was fashion'd to much honour from his cradle.
He was a scholar, and a ripe and good one;
Exceeding wise, fair-spoken, and persuading;
Lofty and sour to them that lov'd him not,
But to those men that sought him sweet as summer.
And though he were unsatisfied in getting
(Which was a sin), yet in bestowing, madam,
He was most princely. Ever witness for him
Those twins of learning that he rais'd in you,
Ipswich and Oxford; one of which fell with him,
Unwilling to outlive the good that did it;
The other, though unfinish'd, yet so famous,
So excellent in art, and still so rising,
That Christendom shall ever speak his virtue.
His overthrow heap'd happiness upon him;
For then, and not till then, he felt himself
And found the blessedness of being little.
And, to add greater honours to his age
Than man could give him, he died fearing God.
Kath. After my death I wish no other herald,
No other speaker of my living actions
To keep mine honour from corruption,
But such an honest chronicler as Griffith.
Whom I most hated living, thou hast made me,
With thy religious truth and modesty,
Now, in his ashes, honour. Peace be with him!
Patience, be near me still, and set me lower.
I have not long to trouble thee. Good Griffith,
Cause the musicians play me that sad note
I nam'd my knell, whilst I sit meditating.
On that celestial harmony I go to.
Sad and solemn music.
Grif. She is asleep. Good wench, let's sit down quiet
For fear we wake her. Softly, gentle Patience.

The Vision.

Enter, solemnly tripping one after another, six personages clad in white robes, wearing on their heads garlands of bays, and golden vizards on their faces; branches of bays or palm in their hands. They first congee unto her, then dance; and, at certain changes, the first two hold a spare garland over her head; at which the other four make reverent curtsies. Then the two that held the garland deliver the same to the other next two, who observe the same order in their changes and holding the garland over her head; which done, they deliver the same garland to the last two, who likewise observe the same order; at which (as it were by inspiration) she makes (in her sleep) signs of rejoicing and holdeth up her hands to heaven. And so in their dancing vanish, carrying the garland with them. *The music continues.*

Kath. Spirits of peace, where are ye? Are ye all gone
And leave me here in wretchedness behind ye?
Grif. Madam, we are here.
Kath. It is not you I call for.
Saw ye none enter since I slept?
Grif. None, madam.
Kath. No? Saw you not even now a blessed troop
Invite me to a banquet, whose bright faces
Cast thousand beams upon me like the sun?
They promis'd me eternal happiness
And brought me garlands, Griffith, which I feel
I am not worthy yet to wear. I shall, assuredly.
Grif. I am most joyful, madam, such good dreams
Possess your fancy.
Kath. Bid the music leave.
They are harsh and heavy to me.
Music ceases.
Pat. Do you note
How much her Grace is alter'd on the sudden?
How long her face is drawn? how pale she looks,
And of an earthy colour? Mark her eyes!
Grif. She is going, wench. Pray, pray!
Pat. Heaven comfort her!

Enter a *Messenger.*

Mess. An't like your Grace —
Kath. You are a saucy fellow.
Deserve we no more reverence?
Grif. You are to blame,
Knowing she will not lose her wonted greatness,
To use so rude behaviour. Go to, kneel!
Mess. I humbly do entreat your Highness' pardon.
My haste made me unmannerly. There is staying
A gentleman, sent from the King, to see you.
Kath. Admit him entrance, Griffith. But this fellow
Let me ne'er see again.
Exit Messenger.

Enter *Lord Capucius.*

If my sight fail not,
You should be Lord Ambassador from the Emperor,
My royal nephew, and your name Capucius.
Cap. Madam, the same — your servant.
Kath. O my lord,
The times and titles now are alter'd strangely
With me since first you knew me. But I pray you,
What is your pleasure with me?
Cap. Noble lady,
First mine own service to your Grace; the next,
The King's request that I would visit you,
Who grieves much for your weakness and by me
Sends you his princely commendations
And heartily entreats you take good comfort.
Kath. O my good lord, that comfort comes too late!
'Tis like a pardon after execution.
That gentle physic, given in time, had cur'd me;
But now I am past all comforts here but prayers.
How does his Highness?
Cap. Madam, in good health.
Kath. So may he ever do! and ever flourish
When I shall dwell with worms, and my poor name
Banish'd the kingdom! Patience, is that letter
I caus'd you write yet sent away?
Pat. No, madam.
[*Gives it to Katherine.*]
Kath. Sir, I most humbly pray you to deliver
This to my lord the King.
Cap. Most willing, madam.
Kath. In which I have commended to his goodness
The model of our chaste loves, his young daughter —
The dews of heaven fall thick in blessings on her! —
Beseeching him to give her virtuous breeding —
She is young and of a noble modest nature;
I hope she will deserve well — and a little

To love her for her mother's sake, that lov'd him,
Heaven knows how dearly. My next poor petition
Is that his noble Grace would have some pity
Upon my wretched women, that so long
Have follow'd both my fortunes faithfully;
Of which there is not one, I dare avow
(And now I should not lie), but will deserve,
For virtue and true beauty of the soul,
For honesty and decent carriage,
A right good husband — let him be a noble;
And sure those men are happy that shall have 'em.
The last is for my men — they are the poorest
(But poverty could never draw 'em from me) —
That they may have their wages duly paid 'em,
And something over to remember me by.
If heaven had pleas'd to have given me longer life
And able means, we had not parted thus.
These are the whole contents; and, good my lord,
By that you love the dearest in this world,
As you wish Christian peace to souls departed,
Stand these poor people's friend and urge the King
To do me this last right.

Cap. By heaven, I will,
Or let me lose the fashion of a man!

Kath. I thank you, honest lord. Remember me
In all humility unto his Highness.
Say his long trouble now is passing
Out of this world. Tell him in death I bless'd him,
For so I will. Mine eyes grow dim. Farewell,
My lord. Griffith, farewell. Nay, Patience,
You must not leave me yet. I must to bed;
Call in more women. When I am dead, good wench,
Let me be us'd with honour. Strew me over
With maiden flowers, that all the world may know
I was a chaste wife to my grave. Embalm me,
Then lay me forth. Although unqueen'd, yet like
A queen, and daughter to a king, inter me.
I can no more. *Exeunt, leading Katherine.*

ACT V. Scene I. [*London. A gallery in the Palace.*]

Enter *Gardiner, Bishop of Winchester,* a *Page* with a torch before him, met by *Sir Thomas Lovell.*

Gard. It's one o'clock, boy, is't not?

Boy. It hath struck.

Gard. These should be hours for necessities,
Not for delights; times to repair our nature
With comforting repose, and not for us
To waste these times. Good hour of night, Sir Thomas!
Whither so late?

Lov. Came you from the King, my lord?

Gard. I did, Sir Thomas, and left him at primero
With the Duke of Suffolk.

Lov. I must to him too,
Before he go to bed. I'll take my leave.

Gard. Not yet, Sir Thomas Lovell. What's the matter?
It seems you are in haste. An if there be
No great offence belongs to't, give your friend
Some touch of your late business. Affairs that walk
(As they say spirits do) at midnight have
In them a wilder nature than the business
That seeks dispatch by day.

Lov. My lord, I love you,
And durst commend a secret to your ear
Much weightier than this work. The Queen's in labour,
They say in great extremity, and fear'd
She'll with the labour end.

Gard. The fruit she goes with
I pray for heartily, that it may find
Good time, and live; but for the stock, Sir Thomas,
I wish it grubb'd up now.

Lov. Methinks I could
Cry the amen; and yet my conscience says
She's a good creature, and, sweet lady, does
Deserve our better wishes.

Gard. But, sir, sir!
Hear me, Sir Thomas! Y'are a gentleman
Of mine own way. I know you wise, religious;
And let me tell you it will ne'er be well —
'Twill not, Sir Thomas Lovell, take't of me —
Till Cranmer, Cromwell, her two hands, and she
Sleep in their graves.

Lov. Now, sir, you speak of two
The most remark'd i' th' kingdom. As for Cromwell,
Beside that of the Jewel House, is made Master

O' th' Rolls and the King's Secretary; further, sir,
Stands in the gap and trade of moe preferments,
With which the time will load him. Th' Archbishop
Is the King's hand and tongue; and who dare speak
One syllable against him?
Gard. Yes, yes, Sir Thomas,
There are that dare, and I myself have ventur'd
To speak my mind of him; and indeed this day
(Sir I may tell it you, I think) I have
Incens'd the lords o' th' Council that he is
(For so I know he is, they know he is)
A most arch-heretic, a pestilence
That does infect the land; with which they mov'd
Have broken with the King, who hath so far
Given ear to our complaint — of his great grace
And princely care, foreseeing those fell mischiefs
Our reasons laid before him — hath commanded
To-morrow morning to the Council board
He be convented. He's a rank weed, Sir Thomas,
And we must root him out. From your affairs
I hinder you too long. Good night, Sir Thomas.
Lov. Many good nights, my lord! I rest your servant.
Exeunt Gardiner and Page.

Enter *King* and *Suffolk.*

King. Charles, I will play no more to-night;
My mind's not on't; you are too hard for me.
Suf. Sir, I did never win of you before.
King. But little, Charles,
Nor shall not when my fancy's on my play.
Now, Lovell, from the Queen what is the news?
Lov. I could not personally deliver to her
What you commanded me, but by her woman
I sent your message, who return'd her thanks
In the great'st humbleness and desir'd your Highness
Most heartily to pray for her.
King. What say'st thou? Ha?
To pray for her? What, is she crying out?
Lov. So said her woman, and that her suff'rance made
Almost each pang a death.
King. Alas, good lady!
Suf. God safely quit her of her burthen and
With gentle travail, to the gladding of
Your Highness with an heir!
King. 'Tis midnight, Charles.
Prithee to bed, and in thy pray'rs remember
Th' estate of my poor queen. Leave me alone,
For I must think of that which company
Would not be friendly to.
Suf. I wish your Highness
A quiet night and my good mistress will
Remember in my prayers.
King. Charles, good night.
Exit Suffolk.

Enter *Sir Anthony Denny.*

Well, sir, what follows?
Den. Sir, I have brought my lord the Archbishop,
As you commanded me.
King. Ha? Canterbury?
Den. Ay, my good lord.
King. 'Tis true. Where is he, Denny?
Den. He attends your Highness' pleasure.
King. Bring him to us.
[*Exit Denny.*]
Lov. [*aside*] This is about that which the Bishop spake.
I am happily come hither.

Enter *Cranmer* and *Denny.*

King. Avoid the gallery. (*Lovell seems to stay.*) Ha! I have said. Be gone.
What!
Exeunt Lovell and Denny.
Cran. [*aside*] I am fearful. Wherefore frowns he thus?
'Tis his aspect of terror. All's not well.
King. How now, my lord? You do desire to know
Wherefore I sent for you?
Cran. [*kneels*] It is my duty
T' attend your Highness' pleasure.
King. Pray you arise,
My good and gracious Lord of Canterbury.
Come, you and I must walk a turn together.
I have news to tell you. Come, come, give me your hand.
Ah, my good lord, I grieve at what I speak
And am right sorry to repeat what follows.
I have, and most unwillingly, of late
Heard many grievous — I do say, my lord,
Grievous complaints of you; which, being consider'd,
Have mov'd us and our Council that you shall
This morning come before us; where I know
You cannot with such freedom purge yourself
But that, till further trial in those charges
Which will require your answer, you must take

Your patience to you and be well contented
To make your house our Tow'r. You a brother of us,
It fits we thus proceed, or else no witness
Would come against you.

Cran. I humbly thank your Highness,
And am right glad to catch this good occasion
Most throughly to be winnowed where my chaff
And corn shall fly asunder; for I know
There's none stands under more calumnious tongues
Than I myself, poor man.

King. Stand up, good Canterbury.
Thy truth and thy integrity is rooted
In us, thy friend. Give me thy hand, stand up.
[*Cranmer rises.*]
Prithee let's walk. Now by my holidame,
What manner of man are you? My lord, I look'd
You would have given me your petition that
I should have ta'en some pains to bring together
Yourself and your accusers and to have heard you
Without indurance further.

Cran. Most dread liege,
The good I stand on is my truth and honesty.
If they shall fail, I with mine enemies
Will triumph o'er my person, which I weigh not,
Being of those virtues vacant. I fear nothing
What can be said against me.

King. Know you not
How your state stands i' th' world, with the whole world?
Your enemies are many and not small; their practices
Must bear the same proportion; and not ever
The justice and the truth o' th' question carries
The due o' th' verdict with it. At what ease
Might corrupt minds procure knaves as corrupt
To swear against you! Such things have been done.
You are potently oppos'd, and with a malice
Of as great size. Ween you of better luck,
I mean in perjur'd witness, than your Master,
Whose minister you are, whiles here he liv'd
Upon this naughty earth? Go to, go to!
You take a precipice for no leap of danger
And woo your own destruction.

Cran. God and your Majesty
Protect mine innocence, or I fall into
The trap is laid for me!

King. Be of good cheer.
They shall no more prevail than we give way to.
Keep comfort to you, and this morning see
You do appear before them. If they shall chance,
In charging you with matters, to commit you,
The best persuasions to the contrary
Fail not to use, and with what vehemency
Th' occasion shall instruct you. If entreaties
Will render you no remedy, this ring
Deliver them and your appeal to us
There make before them. Look, the good man weeps!
He's honest, on mine honour. God's blest Mother!
I swear he is true-hearted, and a soul
None better in my kingdom. Get you gone
And do as I have bid you. (*Exit Cranmer.*) He has strangled
His language in his tears.

Enter *Old Lady.*

Gent. (*within*) Come back! What mean you?

Lady. I'll not come back. The tidings that I bring
Will make my boldness manners. Now good angels
Fly o'er thy royal head and shade thy person
Under their blessed wings!

King. Now by thy looks
I guess thy message. Is the Queen deliver'd?
Say ay, and of a boy.

Lady. Ay, ay, my liege!
And of a lovely boy. The God of heaven
Both now and ever bless her! 'Tis a girl
Promises boys hereafter. Sir, your queen
Desires your visitation, and to be
Acquainted with this stranger. 'Tis as like you
As cherry is to cherry.

King. Lovell!

[Enter *Lovell.*]

Lov. Sir?

King. Give her an hundred marks. I'll to the Queen. *Exit.*

Lady. An hundred marks? By this light, I'll ha' more!
An ordinary groom is for such payment.
I will have more or scold it out of him.
Said I for this the girl was like to him?
I will have more or else unsay 't, and now,
While it is hot, I'll put it to the issue.
Exeunt.

Scene II. [*Lobby before the Council Chamber.*]

[*Pursuivants and others in waiting.*]

Enter *Cranmer, Archbishop of Canterbury.*

Cran. I hope I am not too late; and yet the gentleman
That was sent to me from the Council pray'd me
To make great haste. All fast? What means this? Ho!
Who waits there? Sure you know me?

Enter *Keeper.*

Keep. Yes, my lord.
But yet I cannot help you.
Cran. Why?
Keep. Your Grace must wait till you be call'd for.

Enter *Doctor Butts.*

Cran. So.
Butts. [*aside*] This is a piece of malice. I am glad
I came this way so happily. The King
Shall understand it presently. *Exit.*
Cran. 'Tis Butts,
The King's physician. As he pass'd along,
How earnestly he cast his eyes upon me!
Pray heaven he sound not my disgrace! For certain,
This is of purpose laid by some that hate me
(God turn their hearts! I never sought their malice)
To quench mine honour. They would shame to make me
Wait else at door, a fellow councillor,
'Mong boys, grooms, and lackeys. But their pleasures
Must be fulfill'd, and I attend with patience.

Enter the *King* and *Butts* at a window above.

Butts. I'll show your Grace the strangest sight —
King. What's that, Butts?
Butts. I think your Highness saw this many a day.
King. Body o' me, where is it?
Butts. There, my lord:
The high promotion of his Grace of Canterbury,
Who holds his state at door 'mongst pursuivants,
Pages, and footboys.
King. Ha? 'Tis he indeed.
Is this the honour they do one another?
'Tis well there's one above 'em yet. I had thought
They had parted so much honesty among 'em —
At least, good manners — as not thus to suffer
A man of his place and so near our favour
To dance attendance on their lordships' pleasures,
And at the door too, like a post with packets.
By holy Mary, Butts, there's knavery!
Let 'em alone, and draw the curtain close.
We shall hear more anon. [*Exeunt.*]

[Scene III. *The Council Chamber.*]

A Council table brought in, with chairs and stools, and placed under the state. Enter *Lord Chancellor,* places himself at the upper end of the table on the left hand, a seat being left void above him, as for *Canterbury's* seat. *Duke of Suffolk, Duke of Norfolk, Surrey, Lord Chamberlain, Gardiner* seat themselves in order on each side; *Cromwell* at lower end, as Secretary. [*Keeper at the door.*]

Chan. Speak to the business, Master Secretary.
Why are we met in Council?
Crom. Please your Honours,
The chief cause concerns his Grace of Canterbury.
Gard. Has he had knowledge of it?
Crom. Yes.
Nor. Who waits there?
Keep. Without, my noble lords?
Gard. Yes.
Keep. My Lord Archbishop,
And has done half an hour to know your pleasures.
Chan. Let him come in.
Keep. Your Grace may enter now.
Cranmer approaches the Council table.
Chan. My good Lord Archbishop, I'm very sorry
To sit here at this present and behold
That chair stand empty; but we all are men,
In our own natures frail and capable
Of our flesh; few are angels; out of which frailty
And want of wisdom, you, that best should teach us,
Have misdemean'd yourself, and not a little:
Toward the King first, then his laws, in filling

The whole realm by your teaching and your chaplains
(For so we are inform'd) with new opinions,
Divers and dangerous; which are heresies,
And, not reform'd, may prove pernicious.
Gard. Which reformation must be sudden too,
My noble lords; for those that tame wild horses
Pace 'em not in their hands to make 'em gentle,
But stop their mouths with stubborn bits and spur 'em
Till they obey the manage. If we suffer,
Out of our easiness and childish pity
To one man's honour, this contagious sickness,
Farewell all physic! And what follows then?
Commotions, uproars, with a general taint
Of the whole state, as of late days our neighbours,
The upper Germany, can dearly witness,
Yet freshly pitied in our memories.
Cran. My good lords, hitherto, in all the progress
Both of my life and office, I have labour'd,
And with no little study, that my teaching
And the strong course of my authority
Might go one way, and safely; and the end
Was ever to do well; nor is there living
(I speak it with a single heart, my lords)
A man that more detests, more stirs against,
Both in his private conscience and his place,
Defacers of a public peace than I do.
Pray heaven the King may never find a heart
With less allegiance in it! Men that make
Envy and crooked malice nourishment
Dare bite the best. I do beseech your lordships
That in this case of justice my accusers,
Be what they will, may stand forth face to face
And freely urge against me.
Suf. Nay, my lord,
That cannot be. You are a Councillor,
And by that virtue no man dare accuse you.
Gard. My lord, because we have business of more moment,
We will be short with you. 'Tis his Highness' pleasure
And our consent, for better trial of you,
From hence you be committed to the Tower,
Where, being but a private man again,
You shall know many dare accuse you boldly,
More than, I fear, you are provided for.
Cran. Ah, my good Lord of Winchester, I thank you.
You are always my good friend. If your will pass,
I shall both find your lordship judge and juror,
You are so merciful. I see your end —
'Tis my undoing. Love and meekness, lord,
Become a churchman better than ambition;
Win straying souls with modesty again,
Cast none away. That I shall clear myself,
Lay all the weight ye can upon my patience,
I make as little doubt as you do conscience
In doing daily wrongs. I could say more,
But reverence to your calling makes me modest.
Gard. My lord, my lord, you are a sectary!
That's the plain truth. Your painted gloss discovers,
To men that understand you, words and weakness.
Crom. My Lord of Winchester, you are a little,
By your good favour, too sharp. Men so noble,
However faulty, yet should find respect
For what they have been. 'Tis a cruelty
To load a falling man.
Gard. Good Master Secretary,
I cry your Honour mercy. You may worst
Of all this table say so.
Crom. Why, my lord?
Gard. Do not I know you for a favourer
Of this new sect? Ye are not sound.
Crom. Not sound?
Gard. Not sound, I say.
Crom. Would you were half so honest!
Men's prayers then would seek you, not their fears.
Gard. I shall remember this bold language.
Crom. Do.
Remember your bold life too.
Chan. This is too much.
Forbear for shame, my lords.
Gard. I have done.
Crom. And I.
Chan. Then thus for you, my lord: it stands agreed,
I take it, by all voices, that forthwith
You be convey'd to th' Tower a prisoner,
There to remain till the King's further pleasure
Be known unto us. Are you all agreed, lords?
All. We are.
Cran. Is there no other way of mercy
But I must needs to th' Tower, my lords?
Gard. What other
Would you expect? You are strangely troublesome.
Let some o' th' guard be ready there!

Enter the *Guard*.

Cran. For me?
Must I go like a traitor thither?
Gard. Receive him
And see him safe i' th' Tower.
Cran. Stay, good my lords,
I have a little yet to say. Look there, my lords.
[*Shows ring.*]
By virtue of that ring I take my cause
Out of the gripes of cruel men and give it
To a most noble judge, the King my master.
Chan. This is the King's ring.
Sur. 'Tis no counterfeit.
Suf. 'Tis the right ring, by heav'n! I told ye all,
When we first put this dangerous stone a-rolling,
'Twould fall upon ourselves.
Nor. Do you think, my lords,
The King will suffer but the little finger
Of this man to be vex'd?
Chan. 'Tis now too certain.
How much more is his life in value with him!
Would I were fairly out on't!
Crom. My mind gave me,
In seeking tales and informations
Against this man — whose honesty the devil
And his disciples only envy at —
Ye blew the fire that burns ye. Now have at ye!

Enter *King*, frowning on them; *takes his seat.*

Gard. Dread sovereign, how much are we bound to heaven
In daily thanks, that gave us such a prince,
Not only good and wise but most religious;
One that in all obedience makes the Church
The chief aim of his honour, and, to strengthen
That holy duty, out of dear respect,
His royal self in judgment comes to hear
The cause betwixt her and this great offender.
King. You were ever good at sudden commendations,
Bishop of Winchester. But know I come not
To hear such flattery now, and in my presence.
They are too thin and bare to hide offences.
To me you cannot reach you play the spaniel
And think with wagging of your tongue to win me.
But whatsoe'er thou tak'st me for, I'm sure
Thou hast a cruel nature and a bloody.
[*To Cranmer*] Good man, sit down. Now let me see the proudest,
He that dares most, but wag his finger at thee.
By all that's holy, he had better starve
Than but once think this place becomes thee not.
Sur. May it please your Grace —
King. No, sir, it does not please me.
I had thought I had had men of some understanding
And wisdom of my Council; but I find none.
Was it discretion, lords, to let this man,
This good man (few of you deserve that title),
This honest man, wait like a lousy footboy
At chamber door? and one as great as you are?
Why, what a shame was this! Did my commission
Bid ye so far forget yourselves? I gave ye
Power as he was a Councillor to try him,
Not as a groom. There's some of ye, I see,
More out of malice than integrity,
Would try him to the utmost, had ye mean;
Which ye shall never have while I live.
Chan. Thus far,
My most dread sovereign, may it like your Grace
To let my tongue excuse all. What was purpos'd
Concerning his imprisonment was rather
(If there be faith in men) meant for his trial
And fair purgation to the world than malice,
I'm sure, in me.
King. Well, well, my lords, respect him.
Take him, and use him well; he's worthy of it.
I will say thus much for him — if a prince
May be beholding to a subject, I
Am for his love and service so to him.
Make me no more ado, but all embrace him.
Be friends for shame, my lords! My Lord of Canterbury,
I have a suit which you must not deny me.
That is, a fair young maid that yet wants baptism,
You must be godfather and answer for her.
Cran. The greatest monarch now alive may glory
In such an honour. How may I deserve it
That am a poor and humble subject to you?
King. Come, come, my lord, you'd spare your spoons! You shall have
Two noble partners with you, the old Duchess of Norfolk
And Lady Marquess Dorset. Will these please you?
Once more, my Lord of Winchester, I charge you
Embrace and love this man.
Gard. With a true heart
And brother's love I do it.
Cran. And let heaven
Witness how dear I hold this confirmation.

King. Good man, those joyful tears show thy true heart.
The common voice I see is verified
Of thee, which says thus: 'Do my Lord of Canterbury
A shrewd turn, and he's your friend for ever.'
Come, lords, we trifle time away. I long
To have this young one made a Christian.
As I have made ye one, lords, one remain;
So I grow stronger, you more honour gain.
Exeunt.

Scene [IV. *The Palace Yard.*]

Noise and tumult within. Enter *Porter* and his *Man.*

Port. You'll leave your noise anon, ye rascals! Do you take the court for Parish Garden? Ye rude slaves, leave your gaping!

(*Within*) Good Master Porter, I belong to th' larder.

Port. Belong to th' gallows and be hang'd, ye rogue! Is this a place to roar in? Fetch me a dozen crabtree staves, and strong ones. These are but switches to 'em. I'll scratch your heads. You must be seeing christenings! Do you look for ale and cakes here, you rude rascals?

Man. Pray, sir, be patient! 'Tis as much impossible,
Unless we sweep 'em from the door with cannons,
To scatter 'em as 'tis to make 'em sleep
On May Day morning, which will never be.
We may as well push against Powl's as stir 'em.

Port. How got they in, and be hang'd?

Man. Alas, I know not. How gets the tide in?
As much as one sound cudgel of four foot
(You see the poor remainder) could distribute,
I made no spare, sir.

Port. You did nothing, sir.

Man. I am not Samson, nor Sir Guy, nor Colebrand,
To mow 'em down before me; but if I spar'd any
That had a head to hit, either young or old,
He or she, cuckold or cuckold-maker,
Let me ne'er hope to see a chine again;
And that I would not for a cow, God save her!

(*Within*) Do you hear, Master Porter?

Port. I shall be with you presently, good Master Puppy!
Keep the door close, sirrah.

Man. What would you have me do?

Port. What should you do but knock 'em down by th' dozens? Is this Moorfields to muster in? Or have we some strange Indian with the great tool come to court, the women so besiege us? Bless me, what a fry of fornication is at door! On my Christian conscience, this one christening will beget a thousand; here will be father, godfather, and all together.

Man. The spoons will be the bigger, sir. There is a fellow somewhat near the door; he should be a brazier by his face, for, o' my conscience, twenty of the dogdays now reign in's nose. All that stand about him are under the Line; they need no other penance. That firedrake did I hit three times on the head, and three times was his nose discharged against me. He stands there like a mortar-piece to blow us. There was a haberdasher's wife of small wit near him, that rail'd upon me till her pink'd porringer fell off her head, for kindling such a combustion in the state. I miss'd the meteor once and hit that woman, who cried out 'Clubs!' when I might see from far some forty truncheoners draw to her succour, which were the hope o' th' Strond, where she was quartered. They fell on; I made good my place. At length they came to th' broomstaff to me. I defied 'em still; when suddenly a file of boys behind 'em, loose shot, deliver'd such a show'r of pebbles that I was fain to draw mine honour in and let 'em win the work. The devil was amongst 'em, I think surely.

Port. These are the youths that thunder at a playhouse and fight for bitten apples; that no audience but the tribulation of Tower Hill or the limbs of Limehouse, their dear brothers, are able to endure. I have some of 'em in Limbo Patrum, and there they are like to dance these three days, besides the running banquet of two beadles that is to come.

Enter *Lord Chamberlain.*

Cham. Mercy o' me, what a multitude are here!
They grow still too; from all parts they are coming
As if we kept a fair here! Where are these porters,
These lazy knaves? Y'have made a fine hand, fellows!
There's a trim rabble let in. Are all these
Your faithful friends o' th' suburbs? We shall have
Great store of room, no doubt, left for the ladies
When they pass back from the christening.

Port. An't please your Honour,
We are but men; and what so many may do,
Not being torn a-pieces, we have done.
An army cannot rule 'em.
Cham. As I live,
If the King blame me for't, I'll lay ye all
By th' heels, and suddenly, and on your heads
Clap round fines for neglect. Y'are lazy knaves,
And here ye lie baiting of bombards when
Ye should do service. Hark! the trumpets sound;
Th'are come already from the christening.
Go break among the press and find a way out
To let the troop pass fairly, or I'll find
A Marshalsea shall hold ye play these two months.
Port. Make way there for the Princess!
Man. You great fellow,
Stand close up, or I'll make your head ache!
Port. You i' th' chamblet,
Get up o' th' rail. I'll peck you o'er the pales else! *Exeunt.*

Scene V. [*The Palace.*]

Enter *Trumpets*, sounding; then two *Aldermen*, *Lord Mayor*, *Garter*, *Cranmer*, *Duke of Norfolk* with his Marshal's staff, *Duke of Suffolk*, two *Noblemen* bearing great standing bowls for the christening gifts; then four *Noblemen* bearing a canopy, under which the *Duchess of Norfolk*, godmother, bearing the child richly habited in a mantle, &c., train borne by a *Lady*; then follows the *Marchioness Dorset*, the other godmother, and *Ladies*. The troop pass once about the stage, and *Garter* speaks.

Gart. Heaven, from thy endless goodness send prosperous life, long, and ever happy, to the high and mighty Princess of England, Elizabeth!

Flourish. Enter *King* and *Guard*.

Cran. [*kneels*] And to your royal Grace and the good Queen!
My noble partners and myself thus pray
All comfort, joy, in this most gracious lady,
Heaven ever laid up to make parents happy,
May hourly fall upon ye!
King. Thank you, good Lord Archbishop:
What is her name?
Cran. Elizabeth.
King. Stand up, lord.
[*Cranmer rises. The King kisses the child.*]
With this kiss take my blessing. God protect thee!
Into whose hand I give thy life.
Cran. Amen.
King. My noble gossips, y'have been too prodigal.
I thank ye heartily. So shall this lady,
When she has so much English.
Cran. Let me speak, sir,
For heaven now bids me; and the words I utter
Let none think flattery, for they'll find 'em truth.
This royal infant — heaven still move about her! —
Though in her cradle, yet now promises
Upon this land a thousand thousand blessings,
Which time shall bring to ripeness. She shall be
(But few now living can behold that goodness)
A pattern to all princes living with her
And all that shall succeed. Saba was never
More covetous of wisdom and fair virtue
Than this pure soul shall be. All princely graces
That mould up such a mighty piece as this is,
With all the virtues that attend the good,
Shall still be doubled on her. Truth shall nurse her,
Holy and heavenly thoughts still counsel her.
She shall be lov'd and fear'd. Her own shall bless her;
Her foes shake like a field of beaten corn
And hang their heads with sorrow. Good grows with her.
In her days every man shall eat in safety
Under his own vine what he plants, and sing
The merry songs of peace to all his neighbours.
God shall be truly known, and those about her
From her shall read the perfect ways of honour
And by those claim their greatness, not by blood.
Nor shall this peace sleep with her; but as when
The bird of wonder dies, the maiden phœnix,
Her ashes new create another heir
As great in admiration as herself,
So shall she leave her blessedness to one
(When heaven shall call her from this cloud of darkness)
Who from the sacred ashes of her honour
Shall starlike rise, as great in fame as she was,
And so stand fix'd. Peace, plenty, love, truth, terror,
That were the servants to this chosen infant,
Shall then be his and like a vine grow to him.
Wherever the bright sun of heaven shall shine,
His honour and the greatness of his name

Shall be, and make new nations. He shall flourish
And like a mountain cedar reach his branches
To all the plains about him. Our children's children
Shall see this, and bless heaven.

King. Thou speakest wonders.

Cran. She shall be, to the happiness of England,
An aged princess; many days shall see her,
And yet no day without a deed to crown it.
Would I had known no more! But she must die —
She must, the saints must have her — yet a virgin,
A most unspotted lily, shall she pass
To th' ground, and all the world shall mourn her.

King. O Lord Archbishop,
Thou hast made me now a man! Never before
This happy child did I get anything.
This oracle of comfort has so pleas'd me
That when I am in heaven I shall desire
To see what this child does, and praise my Maker.
I thank ye all. To you, my good Lord Mayor,
And your good brethren I am much beholding.
I have receiv'd much honour by your presence,
And ye shall find me thankful. Lead the way, lords.
Ye must all see the Queen, and she must thank ye;
She will be sick else. This day no man think
'Has business at his house; for all shall stay.
This little one shall make it holiday.

Exeunt.

THE EPILOGUE.

'Tis ten to one this play can never please
All that are here. Some come to take their ease
And sleep an act or two; but those, we fear,
W'have frighted with our trumpets; so, 'tis clear,
They'll say 'tis naught; others, to hear the city
Abus'd extremely, and to cry 'That's witty!'
Which we have not done neither; that, I fear,
All the expected good w'are like to hear
For this play at this time, is only in
The merciful construction of good women;
For such a one we show'd 'em. If they smile
And say 'twill do, I know within a while
All the best men are ours; for 'tis ill hap,
If they hold when their ladies bid 'em clap.

Troilus and Cressida

Troilus and Cressida was entered in the Stationers' Register on February 7, 1603, but it was not printed until 1609. Of the Quarto of 1609 there were two issues. The second prefixes a curious address to the reader in praise of the play. 'A new play,' the anonymous writer calls it, 'neuer stal'd with the Stage, neuer clapper-clawd with the palmes of the vulger.' Yet, when first registered (in 1603), it is described as 'acted by my lord Chamberlen's Men.' Perhaps it had never been brought upon the public stage.

For the date of composition the hither limit is fixed by the entry of 1603. The earlier is 1601 if we can trust the evidence of the Prologue. In 1601 Ben Jonson's *Poetaster* was first acted. An 'armed Prologue' explains that he appears in this equipment to defend the play against 'base detractors and illiterate apes.' To this the Prologue of Troilus and Cressida seems to allude in lines 22–25. But this Prologue is not in the Quarto, and the allusion would have been timely in or about 1616, when *Poetaster* was republished with some parade in Jonson's *Workes*. However, 1602 is a reasonable date for Troilus and Cressida.

The relation between the text of the Quarto and that of the Folio is not clear, but the differences are unimportant. Each omits a few lines which the other supplies. Collation establishes the correct reading in almost every instance. When readings differ and both seem satisfactory, the preference is given to the Quarto.

The mediæval tale of Troilus had interested Shakespeare long before he dramatized it. The stage was actually set in the 'skilful painting' so elaborately described in *Lucrece* (lines 1366–1561). There stood Ajax, in whose 'eyes blunt rage and rigour roll'd,' and 'sly Ulysses,' and 'grave Nestor' with 'beard all silver white' that 'wagg'd up and down' when he charmed the Greeks with 'golden words.' Trojan mothers on the walls gazed at the fight when the red blood ran 'from the strond of Dardan to Simois' reedy banks.' 'Pale cowards' were not lacking in the picture. And Lucrece styles Helen 'the strumpet that began this stir.' Lorenzo's night-piece to Jessica (*Merchant of Venice*, v, 1, 1–6) recalls a beautiful passage in Chaucer (v, 645–679), but other references are of a different nature. Benedick styles Troilus 'the first employer of panders' (*Much Ado*, v, 2, 31). Rosalind, arguing that 'men have died and worms have eaten them, but not for love,' cites Troilus as an example: 'Troilus had his brains dash'd out with a Grecian club; yet he did what he could to die before, and he is one of the patterns of love' (*As You Like It*, iv, 1, 97 ff.). Feste, begging a second gratuity, declares that he 'would play Lord Pandarus of Phrygia, to bring a Cressida to this Troilus,' adding facetiously that 'Cressida was a beggar' (*Twelfth Night*, iii, 1, 54 ff.). And Pistol calls Doll a 'lazar kite of Cressid's kind' (*Henry V*, ii, 1, 80). The last two passages are highly significant. They show that Shakespeare knew and accepted the account of Cressida's fate given in Robert Henryson's poem *The Testament of Cresseid*, accessible in Thynne's edition of Chaucer (1532, 1542, *ca.* 1550), in Stow's (1561), and in Speght's (1598), in all of which it follows Chaucer's *Troilus*. This seems also to have been accepted by Chettle and Dekker in their *Troilus and Cressida* in 1599. The play is lost, but a manuscript outline or 'plot' doubtless represents it, and this contains the stage direction 'Enter Cressida, with Beggars.' Henryson's *Cresseid* — since his tale was commonly accepted as Chaucer's, or at least as of equal authority — worked powerfully in the seventy years that intervened between its publication and Shakespeare's play, until, when Shakespeare took pen in hand, Cressida's name had become a synonym for a strumpet, as the name of Pandarus had become a synonym for a base procurer. If we compare Shakespeare with Chaucer, we think that Shakespeare has debased Cressida. If we compare him with the general opinion of his time, we find that he has raised her out of the mire.

For the idea that Shakespeare has cynically degraded the heroes of the *Iliad*, Thersites is mainly responsible. But he is merely Homer's Thersites copiously dramatized. Nobody in the play takes him seriously. His satirical comments upon the Grecian and Trojan heroes do not express Shakespeare's opinion, nor would any Elizabethan audience have taken them in that sense. As a clownish servant in a great household might fill the office of the fool, so, in a military camp, a railing coward might fill the office of the clown. 'There is no slander in an allow'd fool,' Olivia reminds Malvolio, 'though he do nothing but rail.' To the Elizabethans Thersites was simply the comic chorus. Unless we identify Thersites with Shakespeare, we cannot say that Shakespeare has debased the Homeric heroes. He has merely translated them from the epic dialect into the dramatic; and in this rendition he has varied in no essential trait from his epic original. They are still heroic, both in speech and action; and in their human imperfections they are true to Homeric portrayal. The only exception is the treachery of Achilles (v, 7–8). That is, no doubt, a flaw; but it is a negligible detail. Like all Englishmen, Shakespeare took sides with the Trojans; he could not let Hector be vanquished in fair fight.

The play as we have it is doubtless all Shakespeare's, except perhaps Pandar's epilogue. The huddled appearance of the last six scenes need not shake one's faith. As presented on the curtainless Elizabethan stage these were merely the several events in one continuous action with no shifting of scenery.

Eight books of the *Iliad* (i, ii, vii–xi, xviii) were accessible to Shakespeare in Chapman's translation (1598) and the first ten books in that of Arthur Hall (1581). He probably consulted Lydgate's *Sege of Troye* and Caxton's *Recuyell of the Historyes of Troye*. Both are versions of Guido delle Colonne's *Historia Destructionis Troiae* (Caxton's through the French of Raoul le Fèvre). But everybody knew the classic tales in those days, and Homer is not hard reading even for one who has little Greek.

THE TRAGEDY OF

TROILUS AND CRESSIDA

[Dramatis Personæ.

Priam, King of Troy.
Hector, *Troilus*, *Paris*, *Deiphobus*, *Helenus*, his sons.
Margarelon, a bastard son of *Priam*.
Æneas, *Antenor*, Trojan commanders.
Calchas, a Trojan priest, taking part with the Greeks.
Pandarus, uncle to *Cressida*.
Agamemnon, the Grecian general.
Menelaus, his brother.
Achilles, *Ajax*, *Ulysses*, *Nestor*, *Diomedes*, *Patroclus*, Grecian commanders.
Thersites, a deformed and scurrilous Grecian.
Alexander, servant to *Cressida*.
Servant to *Troilus*.
Servant to *Paris*.
Servant *to Diomedes*.
Myrmidons, soldiers of the troop of *Achilles*.

Helen, wife to *Menelaus*.
Andromache, wife to *Hector*.
Cassandra, daughter of *Priam*, a prophetess.
Cressida, daughter of *Calchas*.

Trojan and Greek Soldiers, Attendants.

SCENE. — *Troy, and the Grecian camp before it.*]

THE PROLOGUE.

In Troy there lies the scene. From isles of Greece
The princes orgillous, their high blood chaf'd,
Have to the Port of Athens sent their ships
Fraught with the ministers and instruments
Of cruel war. Sixty-and-nine that wore
Their crownets regal, from th' Athenian bay
Put forth toward Phrygia; and their vow is made
To ransack Troy, within whose strong immures
The ravish'd Helen, Menelaus' queen,
With wanton Paris sleeps, and that's the quarrel.
To Tenedos they come,
And the deep-drawing barks do there disgorge
Their warlike fraughtage. Now on Dardan plains
The fresh and yet unbruised Greeks do pitch
Their brave pavilions. Priam's six-gated city,
Dardan and Timbria, Helias, Chetas, Troien,
And Antenorides, with massy staples
And corresponsive and fulfilling bolts
Sperr up the sons of Troy.
Now expectation, tickling skittish spirits
On one and other side, Troyan and Greek,
Sets all on hazard. And hither am I come,
A Prologue arm'd, but not in confidence
Of author's pen or actor's voice, but suited
In like conditions as our argument,
To tell you, fair beholders, that our play
Leaps o'er the vaunt and firstlings of those broils,
Beginning in the middle; starting thence away
To what may be digested in a play.
Like, or find fault; do as your pleasures are:
Now good or bad, 'tis but the chance of war.

Act I. Scene I. [*Troy. Before* Priam's *Palace.*]

Enter *Pandarus* and *Troilus.*

Tro. Call here my varlet; I'll unarm again.
Why should I war without the walls of Troy
That find such cruel battle here within?
Each Troyan that is master of his heart,
Let him to field: Troilus, alas, hath none!

Pan. Will this gear ne'er be mended?

Tro. The Greeks are strong, and skilful to their strength,
Fierce to their skill, and to their fierceness valiant;
But I am weaker than a woman's tear,
Tamer than sleep, fonder than ignorance,
Less valiant than the virgin in the night,
And skilless as unpractis'd infancy.

Pan. Well, I have told you enough of this. For my part, I'll not meddle nor make no farther. He that will have a cake out of the wheat must needs tarry the grinding.

Tro. Have I not tarried?

Pan. Ay, the grinding; but you must tarry the bolting.

Tro. Have I not tarried?

Pan. Ay, the bolting; but you must tarry the leavening.

Tro. Still have I tarried.

Pan. Ay, to the leavening; but here's yet in the word 'hereafter' the kneading, the making of the cake, the heating of the oven, and the baking. Nay, you must stay the cooling too, or you may chance to burn your lips.

Tro. Patience herself, what goddess e'er she be,
Doth lesser blench at suff'rance than I do.
At Priam's royal table do I sit,
And when fair Cressid comes into my thoughts—
So, traitor? 'when she comes'? When is she thence?

Pan. Well, she look'd yesternight fairer than ever I saw her look, or any woman else.

Tro. I was about to tell thee: when my heart,
As wedged with a sigh, would rive in twain—
Lest Hector or my father should perceive me,
I have (as when the sun doth light a storm)
Buried this sigh in wrinkle of a smile.
But sorrow that is couch'd in seeming gladness
Is like that mirth fate turns to sudden sadness.

Pan. An her hair were not somewhat darker than Helen's — well, go to! — there were no more comparison between the women. But, for my part, she is my kinswoman; I would not, as they term it, praise her, but I would somebody had heard her talk yesterday as I did. I will not dispraise your sister Cassandra's wit, but —

Tro. O Pandarus! I tell thee, Pandarus —
When I do tell thee there my hopes lie drown'd,
Reply not in how many fadoms deep
They lie indrench'd. I tell thee I am mad
In Cressid's love. Thou answer'st 'She is fair'!
Pour'st in the open ulcer of my heart
Her eyes, her hair, her cheek, her gait, her voice;
Handlest in thy discourse, O, that her hand,
In whose comparison all whites are ink
Writing their own reproach, to whose soft seizure
The cygnet's down is harsh and spirit of sense
Hard as the palm of ploughman! This thou tell'st me,
As true thou tell'st me, when I say I love her;
But saying thus, instead of oil and balm
Thou lay'st in every gash that love hath given me
The knife that made it.

Pan. I speak no more than truth.

Tro. Thou dost not speak so much.

Pan. Faith, I'll not meddle in't. Let her be as she is. If she be fair, 'tis the better for her; an she be not, she has the mends in her own hands.

Tro. Good Pandarus! How now, Pandarus?

Pan. I have had my labour for my travail, ill thought on of her and ill thought on of you! gone between and between, but small thanks for my labour!

Tro. What, art thou angry, Pandarus? What, with me?

Pan. Because she's kin to me, therefore she's not so fair as Helen. An she were not kin to me, she would be as fair a Friday as Helen is on Sunday. But what care I? I care not an she were a blackamoor! 'Tis all one to me.

Tro. Say I she is not fair?

Pan. I do not care whether you do or no. She's a fool to stay behind her father. Let her to the Greeks, and so I'll tell her the next time I see her. For my part, I'll meddle nor make no more i' th' matter.

Tro. Pandarus!

Pan. Not I.

Tro. Sweet Pandarus!

Pan. Pray you speak no more to me. I will leave all as I found it, and there an end.

Exit. Sound alarum.

Tro. Peace, you ungracious clamours! peace, rude sounds!
Fools on both sides, Helen must needs be fair
When with your blood you daily paint her thus!
I cannot fight upon this argument;
It is too starv'd a subject for my sword.
But Pandarus — O gods, how do you plague me!
I cannot come to Cressid but by Pandar,
And he's as tetchy to be woo'd to woo
As she is stubborn-chaste against all suit.
Tell me, Apollo, for thy Daphne's love,
What Cressid is, what Pandar, and what we.
Her bed is India; there she lies, a pearl;
Between our Ilium and where she resides,
Let it be call'd the wild and wand'ring flood,
Ourself the merchant, and this sailing Pandar
Our doubtful hope, our convoy, and our bark.

Alarum. Enter *Æneas.*

Æne. How now, Prince Troilus? Wherefore not afield?

Tro. Because not there. This woman's answer sorts,
For womanish it is to be from thence.
What news, Æneas, from the field to-day?

Æne. That Paris is returned home, and hurt.

Tro. By whom, Æneas?

Æne. Troilus, by Menelaus.

Tro. Let Paris bleed! 'Tis but a scar to scorn;
Paris is gor'd with Menelaus' horn. *Alarum.*

Æne. Hark what good sport is out of town to-day!

Tro. Better at home, if 'would I might' were 'may.'
But to the sport abroad! Are you bound thither?

Æne. In all swift haste.

Tro. Come, go we then togither.

Exeunt.

[Scene II. *Troy. A street.*]

Enter *Cressid* and her *Man* [*Alexander*].

Cres. Who were those went by?

Man. Queen Hecuba and Helen.

Cres. And whither go they?

Man. Up to the eastern tower,
Whose height commands as subject all the vale,
To see the battle. Hector, whose patience
Is as a virtue fix'd, to-day was mov'd.
He chid Andromache and struck his armourer;
And, like as there were husbandry in war,
Before the sun rose he was harness'd light,
And to the field goes he, where every flower
Did as a prophet weep what it foresaw
In Hector's wrath.

Cres. What was his cause of anger?

Man. The noise goes, this: there is among the Greeks
A lord of Troyan blood, nephew to Hector;
They call him Ajax.

Cres. Good; and what of him?

Man. They say he is a very man per se
And stands alone.

Cres. So do all men, unless they are drunk, sick, or have no legs.

Man. This man, lady, hath robb'd many beasts of their particular additions. He is as valiant as the lion, churlish as the bear, slow as the elephant; a man into whom nature hath so crowded humours that his valour is crush'd into folly, his folly sauced with discretion. There is no man hath a virtue that he hath not a glimpse of, nor any man an attaint but he carries some stain of it. He is melancholy without cause and merry against the hair. He hath the joints of everything, but everything so out of joint that he is a gouty Briareus, many hands and no use, or purblind Argus, all eyes and no sight.

Cres. But how should this man, that makes me smile, make Hector angry?

Man. They say he yesterday cop'd Hector in the battle and struck him down, the disdain and shame whereof hath ever since kept Hector fasting and waking.

Enter *Pandarus.*

Cres. Who comes here?

Man. Madam, your uncle Pandarus.

Cres. Hector's a gallant man.

Man. As may be in the world, lady.

Pan. What's that? What's that?

Cres. Good morrow, uncle Pandarus.

Pan. Good morrow, cousin Cressid. What do you talk of? Good morrow, Alexander. How do you, cousin? When were you at Ilium?

Cres. This morning, uncle.

Pan. What were you talking of when I came? Was Hector arm'd and gone ere ye came to Ilium? Helen was not up, was she?

Cres. Hector was gone, but Helen was not up.

Pan. E'en so. Hector was stirring early.

Cres. That were we talking of, and of his anger.

Pan. Was he angry?

Cres. So he says here.

Pan. True, he was so. I know the cause too. He'll lay about him to-day, I can tell them that; and there's Troilus will not come far behind him; let them take heed of Troilus. I can tell them that too.

Cres. What, is he angry too?

Pan. Who? Troilus? Troilus is the better man of the two.

Cres. O Jupiter! there's no comparison.

Pan. What, not between Troilus and Hector? Do you know a man if you see him?

Cres. Ay, if I ever saw him before and knew him.

Pan. Well, I say Troilus is Troilus.

Cres. Then you say as I say, for I am sure he is not Hector.

Pan. No, nor Hector is not Troilus in some degrees.

Cres. 'Tis just to each of them. He is himself.

Pan. Himself? Alas, poor Troilus! I would he were.

Cres. So he is.

Pan. Condition I had gone barefoot to India.

Cres. He is not Hector.

Pan. Himself? No, he's not himself. Would 'a were himself! Well, the gods are above; time must friend or end. Well, Troilus, well. I would my heart were in her body! No, Hector is not a better man than Troilus.

Cres. Excuse me.

Pan. He is elder.

Cres. Pardon me, pardon me!

Pan. Th' other's not come to't. You shall tell me another tale when th' other's come to't. Hector shall not have his wit this year.

Cres. He shall not need it, if he have his own.

Pan. Nor his qualities.

Cres. No matter.

Pan. Nor his beauty.

Cres. 'Twould not become him; his own's better.

Pan. You have no judgment, niece. Helen herself swore th' other day that Troilus, for a brown favour (for so 'tis, I must confess) — not brown neither —

Cres. No, but brown.

Pan. Faith, to say truth, brown and not brown.

Cres. To say the truth, true and not true.

Pan. She prais'd his complexion above Paris.

Cres. Why, Paris hath colour enough.

Pan. So he has.

Cres. Then Troilus should have too much. If she prais'd him above, his complexion is higher than his. He having colour enough, and the other higher, is too flaming a praise for a good complexion. I had as lieve Helen's golden tongue had commended Troilus for a copper nose.

Pan. I swear to you I think Helen loves him better than Paris.

Cres. Then she's a merry Greek indeed!

Pan. Nay, I am sure she does. She came to him th' other day into the compass'd window — and you know he has not past three or four hairs on his chin —

Cres. Indeed a tapster's arithmetic may soon bring his particulars therein to a total.

Pan. Why, he is very young; and yet will he within three pound lift as much as his brother Hector.

Cres. Is he so young a man and so old a lifter?

Pan. But to prove to you that Helen loves him: she came and puts me her white hand to his cloven chin —

Cres. Juno have mercy! How came it cloven?

Pan. Why, you know 'tis dimpled. I think his smiling becomes him better than any man in all Phrygia.

Cres. O, he smiles valiantly.

Pan. Does he not?

Cres. O yes, an 'twere a cloud in autumn.

Pan. Why, go to then! But to prove to you that Helen loves Troilus —

Cres. Troilus will stand to the proof, if you'll prove it so.

Pan. Troilus? Why, he esteems her no more than I esteem an addle egg.

Cres. If you love an addle egg as well as you love an idle head, you would eat chickens i' th' shell.

Pan. I cannot choose but laugh to think how she tickled his chin. Indeed she has a marvell's white hand, I must needs confess.

Cres. Without the rack.

Pan. And she takes upon her to spy a white hair on his chin.

Cres. Alas, poor chin! Many a wart is richer.

Pan. But there was such laughing! Queen Hecuba laugh'd that her eyes ran o'er.

Cres. With millstones.

Pan. And Cassandra laugh'd.

Cres. But there was a more temperate fire under the pot of her eyes. Did her eyes run o'er too?

Pan. And Hector laugh'd.

Cres. At what was all this laughing?

Pan. Marry, at the white hair that Helen spied on Troilus' chin.

Cres. An't had been a green hair, I should have laugh'd too.

Pan. They laugh'd not so much at the hair as at his pretty answer.

Cres. What was his answer?

Pan. Quoth she, 'Here's but two-and-fifty hairs on your chin, and one of them is white.'

Cres. This is her question.

Pan. That's true; make no question of that. 'Two-and-fifty hairs,' quoth he, 'and one white. That white hair is my father, and all the rest are his sons.' 'Jupiter!' quoth she, 'which of these hairs is Paris my husband?' 'The forked one,' quoth he. 'Pluck't out and give it him.' But there was such laughing! and Helen so blush'd, and Paris so chaf'd, and all the rest so laugh'd, that it pass'd!

Cres. So let it now, for it has been a great while going by.

Pan. Well, cousin, I told you a thing yesterday. Think on't.

Cres. So I do.

Pan. I'll be sworn 'tis true. He will weep you an 'twere a man born in April.

Cres. And I'll spring up in his tears an 'twere a nettle against May.

Sound a retreat.

Pan. Hark! they are coming from the field. Shall we stand up here and see them as they pass toward Ilium? Good niece, do, sweet niece Cressida!

Cres. At your pleasure.

Pan. Here, here, here's an excellent place; here we may see most bravely. I'll tell you them all by their names as they pass by; but mark Troilus above the rest.

Enter *Æneas* [and passes].

Cres. Speak not so loud.

Pan. That's Æneas. Is not that a brave man? He's one of the flowers of Troy, I can tell you. But mark Troilus; you shall see anon.

Cres. Who's that?

Enter *Antenor* [and passes].

Pan. That's Antenor. He has a shrowd wit, I can tell you, and he's a man good enough. He's one o' th' soundest judgments in Troy, whosoever, and a proper man of person. When comes Troilus? I'll show you Troilus anon. If he see me, you shall see him nod at me.

Cres. Will he give you the nod?

Pan. You shall see.

Cres. If he do, the rich shall have more.

Enter *Hector* [and passes].

Pan. That's Hector, that, that, look you, that! There's a fellow! Go thy way, Hector! There's a brave man, niece. O brave Hector! Look how he looks! There's a countenance! Is't not a brave man?

Cres. O, a brave man!

Pan. Is 'a not? It does a man's heart good. Look you what hacks are on his helmet! Look you yonder, do you see? Look you there. There's no jesting! There's laying on, take't off who will, as they say. There be hacks!

Cres. Be those with swords?

Enter *Paris* [and passes].

Pan. Swords? Anything, he cares not. An the devil come to him, it's all one. By God's lid, it does one's heart good. Yonder comes Paris, yonder comes Paris! Look ye yonder, niece. Is't not a gallant man too, is't not? Why, this is brave now. Who said he came hurt home to-day? He's not hurt. Why, this will do Helen's heart good now, ha! Would I could see Troilus now! You shall see Troilus anon.

Cres. Who's that?

Enter *Helenus* [and passes].

Pan. That's Helenus. I marvel where Troilus is. That's Helenus. I think he went not forth to-day. That's Helenus.

Cres. Can Helenus fight, uncle?

Pan. Helenus? No. Yes, he'll fight indifferent well. I marvel where Troilus is. Hark! do you not hear the people cry 'Troilus'? Helenus is a priest.

Cres. What sneaking fellow comes yonder?

Enter *Troilus* [and passes].

Pan. Where? yonder? That's Deiphobus. 'Tis Troilus! There's a man, niece! Hem! Brave Troilus, the prince of chivalry!

Cres. Peace, for shame, peace!

Pan. Mark him; note him. O brave Troilus! Look well upon him, niece. Look you how his sword is bloodied, and his helm more hack'd than Hector's, and how he looks, and how he goes! O admirable youth! He never saw three-and-twenty. Go thy way,

Troilus, go thy way! Had I a sister were a Grace or a daughter a goddess, he should take his choice. O admirable man! Paris? Paris is dirt to him, and I warrant Helen, to change, would give an eye to boot.

Enter *Common Soldiers* [and pass].

Cres. Here comes more.

Pan. Asses, fools, dolts! chaff and bran, chaff and bran! porridge after meat! I could live and die i' th' eyes of Troilus. Ne'er look, ne'er look! The eagles are gone. Crows and daws, crows and daws! I had rather be such a man as Troilus than Agamemnon and all Greece.

Cres. There is among the Greeks Achilles, a better man than Troilus.

Pan. Achilles? A drayman, a porter, a very camel!

Cres. Well, well.

Pan. Well, well? Why, have you any discretion? Have you any eyes? Do you know what a man is? Is not birth, beauty, good shape, discourse, manhood, learning, gentleness, virtue, youth, liberality, and such-like, the spice and salt that season a man?

Cres. Ay, a minc'd man! and then to be bak'd with no date in the pie, for then the man's date is out.

Pan. You are such another woman! A man knows not at what ward you lie.

Cres. Upon my back, to defend my belly; upon my wit, to defend my wiles; upon my secrecy, to defend mine honesty; my mask, to defend my beauty; and you, to defend all these; and at all these wards I lie at, at a thousand watches.

Pan. Say one of your watches.

Cres. Nay, I'll watch you for that! and that's one of the chiefest of them too. If I cannot ward what I would not have hit, I can watch you for telling how I took the blow, unless it swell past hiding, and then it's past watching.

Pan. You are such another!

Enter [*Troilus'*] *Boy.*

Boy. Sir, my lord would instantly speak with you.

Pan. Where?

Boy. At your own house; there he unarms him.

Pan. Good boy, tell him I come. [*Exit Boy.*] I doubt he be hurt. Fare ye well, good niece.

Cres. Adieu, uncle.

Pan. I'll be with you, niece, by-and-by.

Cres. To bring, uncle?

Pan. Ay, a token from Troilus.

Cres. By the same token, you are a bawd.

Exit Pandarus.

Words, vows, gifts, tears, and love's full sacrifice
He offers in another's enterprise.
But more in Troilus thousandfold I see
Than in the glass of Pandar's praise may be.
Yet hold I off. Women are angels, wooing:
Things won are done; joy's soul lies in the doing.
That she belov'd knows naught that knows not this:
Men prize the thing ungain'd more than it is.
That she was never yet that ever knew
Love got so sweet as when desire did sue.
Therefore this maxim out of love I teach:
Achievement is command; ungain'd, beseech.
Then, though my heart's content firm love doth bear,
Nothing of that shall from mine eyes appear.

Exeunt.

[Scene III. *The Grecian camp. Before Agamemnon's tent.*]

Sennet. Enter *Agamemnon, Nestor, Ulysses, Diomedes, Menelaus,* with others.

Agam. Princes,
What grief hath set these jaundies o'er your cheeks?
The ample proposition that hope makes
In all designs begun on earth below
Fails in the promis'd largeness. Checks and disasters
Grow in the veins of actions highest rear'd,
As knots, by the conflux of meeting sap,
Infects the sound pine, and diverts his grain
Tortive and errant from his course of growth.
Nor, princes, is it matter new to us
That we come short of our suppose so far
That after seven years' siege yet Troy walls stand;
Sith every action that hath gone before
Whereof we have record, trial did draw
Bias and thwart, not answering the aim
And that unbodied figure of the thought
That gave't surmised shape. Why then, you princes,
Do you with cheeks abash'd behold our works
And call them shames? which are, indeed, naught else

But the protractive trials of great Jove
To find persistive constancy in men;
The fineness of which metal is not found
In Fortune's love; for then the bold and coward,
The wise and fool, the artist and unread,
The hard and soft, seem all affin'd and kin.
But in the wind and tempest of her frown
Distinction, with a broad and pow'rful fan,
Puffing at all, winnows the light away,
And what hath mass or matter, by itself
Lies rich in virtue and unmingled.

Nest. With due observance of thy godlike seat,
Great Agamemnon, Nestor shall apply
Thy latest words. In the reproof of chance
Lies the true proof of men. The sea being smooth,
How many shallow bauble boats dare sail
Upon her patient breast, making their way
With those of nobler bulk!
But let the ruffian Boreas once enrage
The gentle Thetis, and anon behold
The strong-ribb'd bark through liquid mountains cut,
Bounding between the two moist elements
Like Perseus' horse. Where's then the saucy boat
Whose weak untimber'd sides but even now
Corrivall'd greatness? Either to harbour fled
Or made a toast for Neptune. Even so
Doth valour's show and valour's worth divide
In storms of fortune. For in her ray and brightness
The herd hath more annoyance by the brize
Than by the tiger; but when the splitting wind
Makes flexible the knees of knotted oaks
And flies fled under shade, why then the thing of courage,
As rous'd with rage, with rage doth sympathize,
And with an accent tun'd in selfsame key
Retorts to chiding fortune.

Ulyss. Agamemnon,
Thou great commander, nerve and bone of Greece,
Heart of our numbers, soul and only spirit
In whom the tempers and the minds of all
Should be shut up — hear what Ulysses speaks.
Besides th' applause and approbation
The which, [*to Agamemnon*] most mighty for thy place and sway,
[*To Nestor*] And thou most reverend for thy stretch'd-out life,
I give to both your speeches; which were such
As Agamemnon and the hand of Greece
Should hold up high in brass — and such again
As venerable Nestor, hatch'd in silver,
Should with a bond of air (strong as the axletree
On which heaven rides) knit all the Greekish ears
To his experienc'd tongue: yet let it please both,
Thou great, and wise, to hear Ulysses speak.

Agam. Speak, Prince of Ithaca; and be't of less expect
That matter needless, of importless burthen,
Divide thy lips than we are confident,
When rank Thersites opes his mastic jaws,
We shall hear music, wit, and oracle.

Ulyss. Troy, yet upon his basis, had been down,
And the great Hector's sword had lack'd a master,
But for these instances:
The specialty of rule hath been neglected;
And look, how many Grecian tents do stand
Hollow upon this plain, so many hollow factions.
When that the general is not like the hive,
To whom the foragers shall all repair,
What honey is expected? Degree being vizarded,
Th' unworthiest shows as fairly in the mask.
The heavens themselves, the planets, and this centre
Observe degree, priority, and place,
Insisture, course, proportion, season, form,
Office, and custom, in all line of order;
And therefore is the glorious planet Sol
In noble eminence enthron'd and spher'd
Amidst the other, whose med'cinable eye
Corrects the ill aspects of planets evil
And posts, like the commandment of a king,
Sans check, to good and bad. But when the planets
In evil mixture to disorder wander,
What plagues and what portents, what mutiny,
What raging of the sea, shaking of earth,
Commotion in the winds! Frights, changes, horrors
Divert and crack, rend and deracinate
The unity and married calm of states
Quite from their fixure! O, when degree is shak'd,
Which is the ladder to all high designs,
Then enterprise is sick! How could communities,
Degrees in schools and brotherhoods in cities,
Peaceful commerce from dividable shores,
The primogenity and due of birth,

Prerogative of age, crowns, sceptres, laurels,
But by degree, stand in authentic place?
Take but degree away, untune that string,
And hark what discord follows! Each thing meets
In mere oppugnancy. The bounded waters
Should lift their bosoms higher than the shores
And make a sop of all this solid globe;
Strength should be lord of imbecility,
And the rude son should strike his father dead;
Force should be right; or rather, right and wrong
(Between whose endless jar justice resides)
Should lose their names, and so should justice too.
Then everything includes itself in power,
Power into will, will into appetite;
And appetite, an universal wolf,
So doubly seconded with will and power,
Must make perforce an universal prey,
And last eat up himself. Great Agamemnon,
This chaos, when degree is suffocate,
Follows the choking.
And this neglection of degree it is
That by a pace goes backward with a purpose
It hath to climb. The general's disdain'd
By him one step below, he by the next;
That next by him beneath. So every step,
Exampled by the first pace that is sick
Of his superior, grows to an envious fever
Of pale and bloodless emulation.
And 'tis this fever that keeps Troy on foot,
Not her own sinews. To end a tale of length,
Troy in our weakness stands, not in her strength.

Nest. Most wisely hath Ulysses here discover'd
The fever whereof all our power is sick.

Agam. The nature of the sickness found, Ulysses,
What is the remedy?

Ulyss. The great Achilles, whom opinion crowns
The sinew and the forehand of our host,
Having his ear full of his airy fame,
Grows dainty of his worth and in his tent
Lies mocking our designs. With him Patroclus
Upon a lazy bed the livelong day
Breaks scurrile jests,
And with ridiculous and awkward action
(Which, slanderer, he imitation calls)
He pageants us. Sometime, great Agamemnon,
Thy topless deputation he puts on;
And, like a strutting player — whose conceit
Lies in his hamstring, and doth think it rich
To hear the wooden dialogue and sound
'Twixt his stretch'd footing and the scaffolage—
Such to-be-pitied and o'er-wrested seeming
He acts thy greatness in; and when he speaks,
'Tis like a chime a-mending, with terms unsquar'd,
Which, from the tongue of roaring Typhon dropp'd,
Would seem hyperboles. At this fusty stuff
The large Achilles, on his press'd bed lolling,
From his deep chest laughs out a loud applause;
Cries 'Excellent! 'Tis Agamemnon just.
Now play me Nestor. Hem, and stroke thy beard,
As he being dress'd to some oration.'
That's done, as near as the extremest ends
Of parallels, as like as Vulcan and his wife.
Yet god Achilles still cries 'Excellent!
'Tis Nestor right. Now play him me, Patroclus,
Arming to answer in a night alarm.'
And then, forsooth, the faint defects of age
Must be the scene of mirth: to cough and spit,
And, with a palsy fumbling on his gorget,
Shake in and out the rivet. And at this sport
Sir Valour dies, cries 'O, enough, Patroclus,
Or give me ribs of steel! I shall split all
In pleasure of my spleen.' And in this fashion
All our abilities, gifts, natures, shapes,
Severals and generals of grace exact,
Achievements, plots, orders, preventions,
Excitements to the field or speech for truce,
Success or loss, what is or is not, serves
As stuff for these two to make paradoxes.

Nest. And in the imitation of these twain—
Who, as Ulysses says, opinion crowns
With an imperial voice — many are infect:
Ajax is grown self-will'd and bears his head
In such a rein, in full as proud a place
As broad Achilles; keeps his tent like him;
Makes factious feasts; rails on our state of war,
Bold as an oracle, and sets Thersites,
A slave whose gall coins slanders like a mint,
To match us in comparisons with dirt,
To weaken and discredit our exposure,
How rank soever rounded in with danger.

Ulyss. They tax our policy and call it cowardice,
Count wisdom as no member of the war,
Forestall prescience, and esteem no act
But that of hand. The still and mental parts,
That do contrive how many hands shall strike
When fitness calls them on, and know by measure
Of their observant toil the enemies' weight —
Why, this hath not a finger's dignity!

They call this bedwork, mapp'ry, closet war;
So that the ram that batters down the wall,
For the great swinge and rudeness of his poise,
They place before his hand that made the engine
Or those that with the fineness of their souls
By reason guide his execution.

Nest. Let this be granted, and Achilles' horse
Makes many Thetis' sons. *Tucket.*

Agam. What trumpet? Look, Menelaus.

Men. From Troy.

Enter *Æneas.*

Agam. What would you fore our tent?

Æne. Is this great Agamemnon's tent, I pray you?

Agam. Even this.

Æne. May one that is a herald and a prince
Do a fair message to his kingly eyes?

Agam. With surety stronger than Achilles' arm
Fore all the Greekish heads, which with one voice
Call Agamemnon head and general.

Æne. Fair leave and large security. How may
A stranger to those most imperial looks
Know them from eyes of other mortals?

Agam. How?

Æne. Ay.
I ask that I might waken reverence
And bid the cheek be ready with a blush
Modest as Morning when she coldly eyes
The youthful Phœbus.
Which is that god in office, guiding men?
Which is the high and mighty Agamemnon?

Agam. This Troyan scorns us, or the men of Troy
Are ceremonious courtiers.

Æne. Courtiers as free, as debonair, unarm'd,
As bending angels. That's their fame in peace.
But when they would seem soldiers, they have galls,
Good arms, strong joints, true swords; and, Jove's accord,
Nothing so full of heart. But peace, Æneas;
Peace, Troyan! Lay thy finger on thy lips!
The worthiness of praise distains his worth
If that the prais'd himself bring the praise forth;
But what the repining enemy commends,
That breath fame blows; that praise, sole pure, transcends.

Agam. Sir, you of Troy, call you yourself Æneas?

Æne. Ay, Greek, that is my name.

Agam. What's your affair, I pray you?

Æne. Sir, pardon; 'tis for Agamemnon's ears.

Agam. He hears naught privately that comes from Troy.

Æne. Nor I from Troy come not to whisper him.
I bring a trumpet to awake his ear,
To set his sense on the attentive bent,
And then to speak.

Agam. Speak frankly as the wind.
It is not Agamemnon's sleeping hour.
That thou shalt know, Troyan, he is awake,
He tells thee so himself.

Æne. Trumpet, blow loud,
Send thy brass voice through all these lazy tents;
And every Greek of mettle, let him know
What Troy means fairly shall be spoke aloud.
Sound trumpet.
We have, great Agamemnon, here in Troy
A prince call'd Hector — Priam is his father —
Who in this dull and long-continu'd truce
Is resty grown. He bade me take a trumpet
And to this purpose speak: Kings, princes, lords!
If there be one among the fair'st of Greece
That holds his honour higher than his ease,
That seeks his praise more than he fears his peril,
That knows his valour and knows not his fear,
That loves his mistress more than in confession
With truant vows to her own lips he loves,
And dare avow her beauty and her worth
In other arms than hers—to him this challenge!
Hector, in view of Troyans and of Greeks,
Shall make it good or do his best to do it:
He hath a lady, wiser, fairer, truer,
Than ever Greek did compass in his arms;
And will to-morrow with his trumpet call
Midway between your tents and walls of Troy
To rouse a Grecian that is true in love.
If any come, Hector shall honour him;
If none, he'll say in Troy when he retires,
The Grecian dames are sunburnt and not worth
The splinter of a lance. Even so much.

Agam. This shall be told our lovers, Lord Æneas.
If none of them have soul in such a kind,
We left them all at home. But we are soldiers;
And may that soldier a mere recreant prove
That means not, hath not, or is not in love!

If then one is, or hath, or means to be,
That one meets Hector; if none else, I am he.

Nest. Tell him of Nestor, one that was a man
When Hector's grandsire suck'd. He is old now;
But if there be not in our Grecian host
One noble man that hath one spark of fire
To answer for his love, tell him from me
I'll hide my silver beard in a gold beaver,
And in my vantbrace put this withered brawn,
And, meeting him, will tell him that my lady
Was fairer than his grandam and as chaste
As may be in the world. His youth in flood,
I'll prove this truth with my three drops of blood.

Æne. Now heavens forfend such scarcity of youth!

Ulyss. Amen.

Agam. Fair Lord Æneas, let me touch your hand.
To our pavilion shall I lead you first.
Achilles shall have word of this intent;
So shall each lord of Greece from tent to tent.
Yourself shall feast with us before you go
And find the welcome of a noble foe.

Exeunt. Manent Ulysses and Nestor.

Ulyss. Nestor.

Nest. What says Ulysses?

Ulyss. I have a young conception in my brain.
Be you my time to bring it to some shape.

Nest. What is't?

Ulyss. This 'tis:
Blunt wedges rive hard knots. The seeded pride
That hath to this maturity blown up
In rank Achilles must or now be cropp'd,
Or, shedding, breed a nursery of like evil
To overbulk us all.

Nest. Well, and how?

Ulyss. This challenge that the gallant Hector sends,
However it is spread in general name,
Relates in purpose only to Achilles.

Nest. True.
The purpose is perspicuous even as substance,
Whose grossness little characters sum up;
And, in the publication, make no strain
But that Achilles, were his brain as barren
As banks of Libya (though, Apollo knows,
'Tis dry enough), will with great speed of judgment,
Ay, with celerity, find Hector's purpose
Pointing on him.

Ulyss. And wake him to the answer, think you?

Nest. Why, 'tis most meet. Who may you else oppose,
That can from Hector bring those honours off,
If not Achilles? Though't be a sportful combat,
Yet in the trial much opinion dwells;
For here the Troyans taste our dear'st repute
With their fin'st palate. And trust to me, Ulysses,
Our imputation shall be oddly pois'd
In this wild action; for the success,
Although particular, shall give a scantling
Of good or bad unto the general;
And in such indexes (although small pricks
To their subsequent volumes) there is seen
The baby figure of the giant mass
Of things to come at large. It is suppos'd
He that meets Hector issues from our choice;
And choice, being mutual act of all our souls,
Makes merit her election and doth boil,
As 'twere from forth us all, a man distill'd
Out of our virtues; who miscarrying,
What heart receives from hence the conquering part
To steel a strong opinion to themselves?
Which entertain'd, limbs are his instruments,
In no less working than are swords and bows
Directive by the limbs.

Ulyss. Give pardon to my speech.
Therefore 'tis meet Achilles meet not Hector.
Let us, like merchants, show our foulest wares,
And think perchance they'll sell; if not,
The lustre of the better yet to show,
Shall show the better. Do not consent
That ever Hector and Achilles meet;
For both our honour and our shame in this
Are dogg'd with two strange followers.

Nest. I see them not with my old eyes. What are they?

Ulyss. What glory our Achilles shares from Hector,
Were he not proud, we all should share with him.
But he already is too insolent;
And it were better parch in Afric sun
Than in the pride and salt scorn of his eyes
Should he scape Hector fair. If he were foil'd,
Why, then we did our main opinion crush
In taint of our best man. No, make a lot'try,
And by device let blockish Ajax draw
The sort to fight with Hector. Among ourselves
Give him allowance as the worthier man;
For that will physic the great Myrmidon,
Who broils in loud applause, and make him fall

His crest, that prouder than blue Iris bends.
If the dull brainless Ajax come safe off,
We'll dress him up in voices; if he fail,
Yet go we under our opinion still
That we have better men. But, hit or miss,
Our project's life this shape of sense assumes —
Ajax employ'd plucks down Achilles' plumes.

Nest. Now,
Ulysses, I begin to relish thy advice,
And I will give a taste of it forthwith
To Agamemnon. Go we to him straight.
Two curs shall tame each other. Pride alone
Must tarre the mastiffs on, as 'twere their bone.
Exeunt.

[ACT II. Scene I. *The Grecian camp.*]

Enter *Ajax* and *Thersites.*

Ajax. Thersites!

Ther. Agamemnon — how if he had biles — full, all over, generally?

Ajax. Thersites!

Ther. And those biles did run — say so? Did not the general run then? Were not that a botchy core?

Ajax. Dog!

Ther. Then would come some matter from him. I see none now.

Ajax. Thou bitch-wolf's son, canst thou not hear? Feel then. *Strikes him.*

Ther. The plague of Greece upon thee, thou mongrel beef-witted lord!

Ajax. Speak then, thou whinid'st leaven, speak! I will beat thee into handsomeness.

Ther. I shall sooner rail thee into wit and holiness; but I think thy horse will sooner con an oration than thou learn a prayer without book. Thou canst strike, canst thou? A red murrain o' thy jade's tricks!

Ajax. Toadstool, learn me the proclamation.

Ther. Dost thou think I have no sense, thou strik'st me thus?

Ajax. The proclamation!

Ther. Thou art proclaim'd fool, I think.

Ajax. Do not, porpentine, do not! My fingers itch.

Ther. I would thou didst itch from head to foot and I had the scratching of thee. I would make thee the loathsom'st scab in Greece. When thou art forth in the incursions, thou strikest as slow as another.

Ajax. I say, the proclamation!

Ther. Thou grumblest and railest every hour on Achilles; and thou art as full of envy at his greatness as Cerberus is at Proserpina's beauty — ay, that thou bark'st at him.

Ajax. Mistress Thersites!

Ther. Thou shouldst strike him.

Ajax. Cobloaf!

Ther. He would pun thee into shivers with his fist, as a sailor breaks a biscuit.

Ajax. You whoreson cur! [*Strikes him.*]

Ther. Do, do.

Ajax. Thou stool for a witch!

Ther. Ay, do, do. Thou sodden-witted lord! Thou hast no more brain than I have in mine elbows; an asinico may tutor thee. Thou scurvy valiant ass! Thou art here but to thrash Troyans, and thou art bought and sold among those of any wit like a barbarian slave. If thou use to beat me, I will begin at thy heel and tell what thou art by inches, thou thing of no bowels, thou!

Ajax. You dog!

Ther. You scurvy lord!

Ajax. You cur! [*Strikes him.*]

Ther. Mars his idiot! Do, rudeness! do, camel! do, do!

Enter *Achilles* and *Patroclus.*

Achil. Why, how now, Ajax? Wherefore do ye thus? How now, Thersites? What's the matter, man?

Ther. You see him there, do you?

Achil. Ay. What's the matter?

Ther. Nay, look upon him.

Achil. So I do. What's the matter?

Ther. Nay, but regard him well.

Achil. Well? Why, so I do.

Ther. But yet you look not well upon him; for, whosomever you take him to be, he is Ajax.

Achil. I know that, fool.

Ther. Ay, but that fool knows not himself.

Ajax. Therefore I beat thee.

Ther. Lo, lo, lo, lo, what modicums of wit he utters! His evasions have ears thus long. I have bobb'd his brain more than he has beat my bones. I will buy nine sparrows for a penny, and his pia mater is not worth the ninth part of a sparrow. This lord, Achilles, Ajax — who wears his wit in his belly and his guts in his head — I'll tell you what I say of him.

Achil. What?

Ther. I say, this Ajax —
[*Ajax offers to strike him.*]
Achil. Nay, good Ajax.
Ther. Has not so much wit —
Achil. Nay, I must hold you.
Ther. As will stop the eye of Helen's needle, for whom he comes to fight.
Achil. Peace, fool!
Ther. I would have peace and quietness, but the fool will not — he there! that he! Look you there!
Ajax. O thou damn'd cur! I shall —
Achil. Will you set your wit to a fool's?
Ther. No, I warrant you; for the fool's will shame it.
Patr. Good words, Thersites.
Achil. What's the quarrel?
Ajax. I bade the vile owl go learn me the tenour of the proclamation, and he rails upon me.
Ther. I serve thee not.
Ajax. Well, go to, go to.
Ther. I serve here voluntary.
Achil. Your last service was suff'rance; 'twas not voluntary. No man is beaten voluntary. Ajax was here the voluntary, and you as under an impress.
Ther. E'en so. A great deal of your wit too lies in your sinews, or else there be liars. Hector shall have a great catch an 'a knock out either of your brains! 'A were as good crack a fusty nut with no kernel.
Achil. What, with me too, Thersites?
Ther. There's Ulysses, and old Nestor — whose wit was mouldy ere your grandsires had nails on their toes — yoke you like draught oxen and make you plough up the wars.
Achil. What? what?
Ther. Yes, good sooth. To, Achilles! To, Ajax, to!
Ajax. I shall cut out your tongue.
Ther. 'Tis no matter. I shall speak as much as thou afterwards.
Patr. No more words, Thersites; peace!
Ther. I will hold my peace when Achilles' brach bids me, shall I?
Achil. There's for you, Patroclus.
Ther. I will see you hang'd like clotpolls ere I come any more to your tents. I will keep where there is wit stirring and leave the faction of fools. *Exit.*
Patr. A good riddance.
Achil. Marry, this, sir, is proclaim'd through all our host:
That Hector, by the first hour of the sun,
Will with a trumpet 'twixt our tents and Troy
To-morrow morning call some knight to arms
That hath a stomach, and such a one that dare
Maintain — I know not what. 'Tis trash. Farewell.
Ajax. Farewell. Who shall answer him?
Achil. I know not. 'Tis put to lott'ry. Otherwise
He knew his man.
[*Exeunt Achilles and Patroclus.*]
Ajax. O, meaning you? I will go learn more of it. *Exit.*

[Scene II. *Troy.* Priam's *Palace.*]

Enter *Priam, Hector, Troilus, Paris,* and *Helenus.*

Pri. After so many hours, lives, speeches spent,
Thus once again says Nestor from the Greeks:
'Deliver Helen, and all damage else
(As honour, loss of time, travail, expense,
Wounds, friends, and what else dear that is consum'd
In hot digestion of this cormorant war)
Shall be stroke off.' Hector, what say you to't?
Hect. Though no man lesser fears the Greeks than I,
As far as toucheth my particular,
Yet, dread Priam,
There is no lady of more softer bowels,
More spongy to suck in the sense of fear,
More ready to cry out 'Who knows what follows?'
Than Hector is. The wound of peace is surety,
Surety secure; but modest doubt is call'd
The beacon of the wise, the tent that searches
To th' bottom of the worst. Let Helen go.
Since the first sword was drawn about this question,
Every tithe soul 'mongst many thousand dismes
Hath been as dear as Helen. I mean, of ours.
If we have lost so many tenths of ours
To guard a thing not ours nor worth to us
(Had it our name) the value of one ten,
What merit's in that reason which denies
The yielding of her up?
Tro. Fie, fie, my brother!
Weigh you the worth and honour of a king
So great as our dread father in a scale
Of common ounces? Will you with counters sum
The past-proportion of his infinite?

And buckle in a waist most fathomless
With spans and inches so diminutive
As fears and reasons? Fie, for godly shame!
Hel. No marvel though you bite so sharp at reasons,
You are so empty of them. Should not our father
Bear the great sway of his affairs with reason,
Because your speech hath none that tell him so?
Tro. You are for dreams and slumbers, brother priest;
You fur your gloves with reason. Here are your reasons:
You know an enemy intends you harm,
You know a sword employ'd is perilous,
And reason flies the object of all harm.
Who marvels, then, when Helenus beholds
A Grecian and his sword, if he do set
The very wings of reason to his heels
And fly like chidden Mercury from Jove
Or like a star disorb'd? Nay, if we talk of reason,
Let's shut our gates and sleep. Manhood and honour
Should have hare hearts, would they but fat their thoughts
With this cramm'd reason. Reason and respect
Make livers pale and lustihood deject.
Hect. Brother, she is not worth what she doth cost
The holding.
Tro. What is aught but as 'tis valu'd?
Hect. But value dwells not in particular will:
It holds his estimate and dignity
As well wherein 'tis precious of itself
As in the prizer. 'Tis mad idolatry
To make the service greater than the god;
And the will dotes that is attributive
To what infectiously itself affects
Without some image of th' affected merit.
Tro. I take to-day a wife, and my election
Is led on in the conduct of my will,
My will enkindled by mine eyes and ears,
Two traded pilots 'twixt the dangerous shores
Of will and judgment. How may I avoid,
Although my will distaste what it elected,
The wife I chose? There can be no evasion
To blench from this and to stand firm by honour.
We turn not back the silks upon the merchant
When we have soil'd them, nor the remainder viands
We do not throw in unrespective sieve
Because we now are full. It was thought meet
Paris should do some vengeance on the Greeks.
Your breath of full consent bellied his sails;
The seas and winds, old wranglers, took a truce
And did him service. He touch'd the ports desir'd;
And for an old aunt whom the Greeks held captive
He brought a Grecian queen, whose youth and freshness
Wrinkles Apollo's and makes stale the morning.
Why keep we her? The Grecians keep our aunt.
Is she worth keeping? Why, she is a pearl
Whose price hath launch'd above a thousand ships
And turn'd crown'd kings to merchants.
If you'll avouch 'twas wisdom Paris went
(As you must needs, for you all cried 'Go, go!'),
If you'll confess he brought home worthy prize
(As you must needs, for you all clapp'd your hands
And cried 'Inestimable!'), why do you now
The issue of your proper wisdoms rate,
And do a deed that never fortune did,
Beggar the estimation which you priz'd
Richer than sea and land? O theft most base,
That we have stol'n what we do fear to keep!
But thieves unworthy of a thing so stol'n
That in their country did them that disgrace
We fear to warrant in our native place!
Cas. [*within*] Cry, Troyans, cry!
Pri. What noise, what shriek is this?
Tro. 'Tis our mad sister. I do know her voice.
Cas. [*within*] Cry, Troyans!
Hect. It is Cassandra.

Enter *Cassandra*, raving, with her hair about her ears.

Cas. Cry, Troyans, cry! Lend me ten thousand eyes,
And I will fill them with prophetic tears.
Hect. Peace, sister, peace!
Cas. Virgins and boys, mid-age and wrinkled eld,
Soft infancy, that nothing canst but cry,
Add to my clamours! Let us pay betimes
A moiety of that mass of moan to come.
Cry, Troyans, cry! Practise your eyes with tears!
Troy must not be, nor goodly Ilion stand;
Our firebrand brother Paris burns us all.
Cry, Troyans, cry! A Helen and a woe!
Cry, cry! Troy burns, or else let Helen go.
Exit.
Hect. Now, youthful Troilus, do not these high strains

Of divination in our sister work
Some touches of remorse? Or is your blood
So madly hot that no discourse of reason,
Nor fear of bad success in a bad cause,
Can qualify the same?

Tro. Why, brother Hector,
We may not think the justness of each act
Such and no other than event doth form it,
Nor once deject the courage of our minds
Because Cassandra's mad. Her brainsick raptures
Cannot distaste the goodness of a quarrel
Which hath our several honours all engag'd
To make it gracious. For my private part,
I am no more touch'd than all Priam's sons;
And Jove forbid there should be done amongst us
Such things as might offend the weakest spleen
To fight for and maintain!

Par. Else might the world convince of levity
As well my undertakings as your counsels;
But I attest the gods, your full consent
Gave wings to my propension and cut off
All fears attending on so dire a project.
For what, alas, can these my single arms?
What propugnation is in one man's valour
To stand the push and enmity of those
This quarrel would excite? Yet I protest,
Were I alone to pass the difficulties
And had as ample power as I have will,
Paris should ne'er retract what he hath done
Nor faint in the pursuit.

Pri. Paris, you speak
Like one besotted on your sweet delights.
You have the honey still, but these the gall;
So to be valiant is no praise at all.

Par. Sir, I propose not merely to myself
The pleasures such a beauty brings with it,
But I would have the soil of her fair rape
Wip'd off in honourable keeping her.
What treason were it to the ransack'd queen,
Disgrace to your great worths, and shame to me,
Now to deliver her possession up
On terms of base compulsion! Can it be
That so degenerate a strain as this
Should once set footing in your generous bosoms?
There's not the meanest spirit on our party
Without a heart to dare or sword to draw
When Helen is defended; nor none so noble
Whose life were ill bestow'd or death unfam'd
Where Helen is the subject. Then, I say,
Well may we fight for her whom we know well
The world's large spaces cannot parallel.

Hect. Paris and Troilus, you have both said well;
And on the cause and question now in hand
Have gloz'd, but superficially; not much
Unlike young men, whom Aristotle thought
Unfit to hear moral philosophy.
The reasons you allege do more conduce
To the hot passion of distemp'red blood
Than to make up a free determination
'Twixt right and wrong; for pleasure and revenge
Have ears more deaf than adders to the voice
Of any true decision. Nature craves
All dues be rend'red to their owners. Now
What nearer debt in all humanity
Than wife is to the husband? If this law
Of nature be corrupted through affection,
And that great minds, of partial indulgence
To their benumbed wills, resist the same,
There is a law in each well-ord'red nation
To curb those raging appetites that are
Most disobedient and refractory.
If Helen then be wife to Sparta's king
(As it is known she is), these moral laws
Of nature and of nations speak aloud
To have her back return'd. Thus to persist
In doing wrong extenuates not wrong,
But makes it much more heavy. Hector's opinion
Is this in way of truth. Yet ne'ertheless,
My sprightly brethren, I propend to you
In resolution to keep Helen still;
For 'tis a cause that hath no mean dependence
Upon our joint and several dignities.

Tro. Why, there you touch'd the life of our design.
Were it not glory that we more affected
Than the performance of our heaving spleens,
I would not wish a drop of Troyan blood
Spent more in her defence. But, worthy Hector,
She is a theme of honour and renown,
A spur to valiant and magnanimous deeds,
Whose present courage may beat down our foes,
And fame in time to come canonize us.
For I presume brave Hector would not lose
So rich advantage of a promis'd glory
As smiles upon the forehead of this action
For the wide world's revenue.

Hect. I am yours,
You valiant offspring of great Priamus.
I have a roisting challenge sent amongst
The dull and factious nobles of the Greeks
Will strike amazement to their drowsy spirits.
I was advertis'd their great general slept
Whilst emulation in the army crept.
This I presume will wake him. *Exeunt.*

[Scene III. *The Grecian camp. Before the tent of* Achilles.]

Enter *Thersites* solus.

Ther. How now, Thersites? What, lost in the labyrinth of thy fury? Shall the elephant Ajax carry it thus? He beats me, and I rail at him. O worthy satisfaction! Would it were otherwise: that I could beat him whilst he rail'd at me. 'Sfoot, I'll learn to conjure and raise devils but I'll see some issue of my spiteful execrations. Then there's Achilles, a rare enginer. If Troy be not taken till these two undermine it, the walls will stand till they fall of themselves. O thou great thunder-darter of Olympus, forget that thou art Jove, the king of gods, and, Mercury, lose all the serpentine craft of thy caduceus, if ye take not that little little less than little wit from them that they have! which short-arm'd ignorance itself knows is so abundant scarce it will not in circumvention deliver a fly from a spider without drawing their massy irons and cutting the web. After this, the vengeance on the whole camp! or rather the Neapolitan bone-ache! for that methinks is the curse dependent on those that war for a placket. I have said my prayers; and devil Envy say 'Amen!' What ho! my Lord Achilles!

Enter *Patroclus.*

Patr. Who's there? Thersites? Good Thersites, come in and rail.

Ther. If I could 'a' rememb'red a gilt counterfeit, thou wouldst not have slipp'd out of my contemplation; but it is no matter — thyself upon thyself! The common curse of mankind, folly and ignorance, be thine in great revenue! Heaven bless thee from a tutor, and discipline come not near thee! Let thy blood be thy direction till thy death! Then if she that lays thee out says thou art a fair corse, I'll be sworn and sworn upon't she never shrouded any but lazars. Amen. Where's Achilles?

Patr. What, art thou devout? Wast thou in prayer?

Ther. Ay. The heavens hear me!

Enter *Achilles.*

Achil. Who's there?

Patr. Thersites, my lord.

Achil. Where? where? O, where? Art thou come? Why, my cheese, my digestion, why hast thou not serv'd thyself in to my table so many meals? Come, what's Agamemnon?

Ther. Thy commander, Achilles. Then tell me, Patroclus, what's Achilles?

Patr. Thy lord, Thersites. Then tell me, I pray thee, what's thyself?

Ther. Thy knower, Patroclus. Then tell me, Patroclus, what art thou?

Patr. Thou mayst tell that knowest.

Achil. O, tell, tell!

Ther. I'll decline the whole question. Agamemnon commands Achilles; Achilles is my lord; I am Patroclus' knower; and Patroclus is a fool.

Patr. You rascal!

Ther. Peace, fool! I have not done.

Achil. He is a privileg'd man. Proceed, Thersites.

Ther. Agamemnon is a fool; Achilles is a fool; Thersites is a fool; and, as aforesaid, Patroclus is a fool.

Achil. Derive this, come.

Ther. Agamemnon is a fool to offer to command Achilles; Achilles is a fool to be commanded of Agamemnon; Thersites is a fool to serve such a fool; and Patroclus is a fool positive.

Patr. Why am I a fool?

Ther. Make that demand to the Creator. It suffices me thou art. Look you, who comes here?

Enter *Agamemnon, Ulysses, Nestor, Diomedes, Ajax,* and *Calchas.*

Achil. Patroclus, I'll speak with nobody. Come in with me, Thersites. *Exit.*

Ther. Here is such patchery, such juggling, and such knavery! All the argument is a whore and a cuckold — a good quarrel to draw emulous factions and bleed to death upon. Now, the dry suppeago on the subject, and war and lechery confound all! [*Exit.*]

Agam. Where is Achilles?

Patr. Within his tent; but ill-dispos'd, my lord.

Agam. Let it be known to him that we are here.
He shent our messengers, and we lay by
Our appertainments, visiting of him.
Let him be told so, lest perchance he think
We dare not move the question of our place
Or know not what we are.

Patr. I shall say so to him. [*Exit.*]

Ulyss. We saw him at the opening of his tent.
He is not sick.

Ajax. Yes, lion-sick, sick of proud heart. You may call it melancholy, if you will favour the man; but, by my head, 'tis pride. But why? why? Let him show us a cause. A word, my lord. [*Takes Agamemnon aside.*]

Nest. What moves Ajax thus to bay at him?

Ulyss. Achilles hath inveigled his fool from him.

Nest. Who? Thersites?

Ulyss. He.

Nest. Then will Ajax lack matter, if he have lost his argument.

Ulyss. No, you see he is his argument that has his argument — Achilles.

Nest. All the better. Their fraction is more our wish than their faction. But it was a strong composure a fool could disunite.

Ulyss. The amity that wisdom knits not, folly may easily untie.

Enter *Patroclus.*

Here comes Patroclus.

Nest. No Achilles with him?

Ulyss. The elephant hath joints, but none for courtesy; his legs are legs for necessity, not for flexure.

Patr. Achilles bids me say he is much sorry
If anything more than your sport and pleasure
Did move your greatness and this noble state
To call upon him. He hopes it is no other
But for your health and your digestion sake,
An after-dinner's breath.

Agam. Hear you, Patroclus.
We are too well acquainted with these answers;
But his evasion, wing'd thus swift with scorn,
Cannot outfly our apprehensions.
Much attribute he hath, and much the reason
Why we ascribe it to him. Yet all his virtues,
Not virtuously on his own part beheld,
Do in our eyes begin to lose their gloss;
Yea, like fair fruit in an unwholesome dish,
Are like to rot untasted. Go and tell him
We come to speak with him; and you shall not sin
If you do say we think him over-proud
And under-honest, in self-assumption greater
Than in the note of judgment; and worthier than himself
Here tend the savage strangeness he puts on,
Disguise the holy strength of their command,
And underwrite in an observing kind
His humorous predominance; yea, watch
His pettish lunes, his ebbs and flows, as if
The passage and whole carriage of this action
Rode on his ride. Go tell him this, and add
That if he overhold his price so much,
We'll none of him, but let him, like an engine
Not portable, lie under this report:
'Bring action hither; this cannot go to war.'
A stirring dwarf we do allowance give
Before a sleeping giant. Tell him so.

Patr. I shall, and bring his answer presently. [*Exit.*]

Agam. In second voice we'll not be satisfied;
We come to speak with him. Ulysses, enter you.
Exit Ulysses.

Ajax. What is he more than another?

Agam. No more than what he thinks he is.

Ajax. Is he so much? Do you not think he thinks himself a better man than I am?

Agam. No question.

Ajax. Will you subscribe his thought and say he is?

Agam. No, noble Ajax. You are as strong, as valiant, as wise, no less noble, much more gentle, and altogether more tractable.

Ajax. Why should a man be proud? How doth pride grow? I know not what pride is.

Agam. Your mind is the clearer, Ajax, and your virtues the fairer. He that is proud eats up himself. Pride is his own glass, his own trumpet, his own chronicle; and whatever praises itself but in the deed, devours the deed in the praise.

Enter *Ulysses.*

Ajax. I do hate a proud man as I hate the engend'ring of toads.

Nest. [*aside*] And yet he loves himself. Is't not strange?

Ulyss. Achilles will not to the field to-morrow.

Agam. What's his excuse?

Ulyss. He doth rely on none,
But carries on the stream of his dispose,
Without observance or respect of any,
In will peculiar and in self-admission.

Agam. Why will he not upon our fair request
Untent his person and share the air with us?

Ulyss. Things small as nothing, for request's sake only,
He makes important. Possess'd he is with greatness,
And speaks not to himself but with a pride
That quarrels at self-breath. Imagin'd worth
Holds in his blood such swol'n and hot discourse
That 'twixt his mental and his active parts
Kingdom'd Achilles in commotion rages
And batters down himself. What should I say?

He is so plaguy proud that the death tokens of it
Cry 'No recovery.'
Agam. Let Ajax go to him.
Dear lord, go you and greet him in his tent.
'Tis said he holds you well, and will be led
At your request a little from himself.
Ulyss. O Agamemnon, let it not be so!
We'll consecrate the steps that Ajax makes
When they go from Achilles. Shall the proud lord
That bastes his arrogance with his own seam
And never suffers matter of the world
Enter his thoughts, save such as doth revolve
And ruminate himself — shall he be worshipp'd
Of that we hold an idol more than he?
No, this thrice worthy and right valiant lord
Must not so stale his palm, nobly acquir'd,
Nor, by my will, assubjugate his merit,
As amply titled as Achilles is,
By going to Achilles.
That were to enlard his fat-already pride
And add more coals to Cancer when he burns
With entertaining great Hyperion.
This lord go to him? Jupiter forbid,
And say in thunder, 'Achilles go to him!'
Nest. [*aside*] O, this is well! He rubs the vein of him.
Dio. [*aside*] And how his silence drinks up this applause!
Ajax. If I go to him, with my armed fist
I'll pash him o'er the face.
Agam. O, no, you shall not go.
Ajax. An 'a be proud with me, I'll pheese his pride.
Let me go to him.
Ulyss. Not for the worth that hangs upon our quarrel.
Ajax. A paltry insolent fellow!
Nest. [*aside*] How he describes himself!
Ajax. Can he not be sociable?
Ulyss. [*aside*] The raven chides blackness.
Ajax. I'll let his humours blood.
Agam. [*aside*] He will be the physician that should be the patient.
Ajax. An all men were o' my mind —
Ulyss. [*aside*] Wit would be out of fashion.
Ajax. 'A should not bear it so, 'a should eat swords first.
Shall pride carry it?
Nest. [*aside*] An 'twould, you'ld carry half.
Ulyss. [*aside*] 'A would have ten shares.
Ajax. I will knead him; I'll make him supple.
Nest. [*aside*] He's not yet through warm.
Force him with praises. Pour in, pour in; his ambition is dry.
Ulyss. [*to Agamemnon*] My lord, you feed too much on this dislike.
Nest. Our noble general, do not do so.
Dio. You must prepare to fight without Achilles.
Ulyss. Why, 'tis this naming of him does him harm.
Here is a man — but 'tis before his face;
I will be silent.
Nest. Wherefore should you so?
He is not emulous, as Achilles is.
Ulyss. Know the whole world, he is as valiant.
Ajax. A whoreson dog, that shall palter with us thus!
Would he were a Troyan!
Nest. What a vice were it in Ajax now —
Ulyss. If he were proud.
Dio. Or covetous of praise.
Ulyss. Ay, or surly borne.
Dio. Or strange, or self-affected.
Ulyss. Thank the heavens, lord, thou art of sweet composure.
Praise him that got thee, she that gave thee suck;
Fam'd be thy tutor, and thy parts of nature
Thrice fam'd beyond, beyond all erudition!
But he that disciplin'd thine arms to fight —
Let Mars divide eternity in twain
And give him half; and for thy vigour,
Bull-bearing Milo his addition yield
To sinewy Ajax. I will not praise thy wisdom,
Which, like a bourn, a pale, a shore, confines
Thy spacious and dilated parts. Here's Nestor,
Instructed by the antiquary times:
He must, he is, he cannot but be wise;
But pardon, father Nestor, were your days
As green as Ajax and your brain so temper'd,
You should not have the eminence of him
But be as Ajax.
Ajax. Shall I call you father?
Nest. Ay, my good son.
Dio. Be rul'd by him, Lord Ajax.
Ulyss. There is no tarrying here; the hart Achilles
Keeps thicket. Please it our great general
To call together all his state of war.
Fresh kings are come to Troy; to-morrow
We must with all our main of power stand fast;
And here's a lord — come knights from East to West
And cull their flower, Ajax shall cope the best.
Agam. Go we to council. Let Achilles sleep.
Light boats sail swift, though greater hulks draw deep. *Exeunt.*

[Act III. Scene I. *Troy.* Priam's *Palace.*]

Music sounds within. Enter *Pandarus* and a *Servant.*

Pan. Friend, you — pray you a word. Do you not follow the young Lord Paris?

Serv. Ay, sir, when he goes before me.

Pan. You depend upon him, I mean.

Serv. Sir, I do depend upon the Lord.

Pan. You depend upon a notable gentleman; I must needs praise him.

Serv. The Lord be praised!

Pan. You know me, do you not?

Serv. Faith, sir, superficially.

Pan. Friend, know me better: I am the Lord Pandarus.

Serv. I hope I shall know your honour better.

Pan. I do desire it.

Serv. You are in the state of grace.

Pan. Grace? Not so, friend. Honour and Lordship are my titles. What music is this?

Serv. I do but partly know, sir. It is music in parts.

Pan. Know you the musicians?

Serv. Wholly, sir.

Pan. Who play they to?

Serv. To the hearers, sir.

Pan. At whose pleasure, friend?

Serv. At mine, sir, and theirs that love music.

Pan. Command, I mean, friend.

Serv. Who shall I command, sir?

Pan. Friend, we understand not one another. I am too courtly, and thou art too cunning. At whose request do these men play? 31

Serv. That's to't, indeed, sir. Marry, sir, at the request of Paris my lord, who is there in person; with him, the mortal Venus, the heart-blood of beauty, love's invisible soul.

Pan. Who? my cousin Cressida?

Serv. No, sir, Helen. Could not you find out that by her attributes?

Pan. It should seem, fellow, that thou hast not seen the Lady Cressida. I come to speak with Paris from the Prince Troilus. I will make a complimental assault upon him, for my business seethes.

Serv. Sodden business! There's a stew'd phrase indeed!

Enter *Paris* and *Helen,* [attended].

Pan. Fair be to you, my lord, and to all this fair company! Fair desires in all fair measure fairly guide them! Especially to you, fair queen! Fair thoughts be your fair pillow! 49

Helen. Dear lord, you are full of fair words.

Pan. You speak your fair pleasure, sweet queen. Fair prince, here is good broken music.

Par. You have broke it, cousin; and, by my life, you shall make it whole again; you shall piece it out with a piece of your performance. Nell, he is full of harmony. 56

Pan. Truly, lady, no.

Helen. O, sir —

Pan. Rude, in sooth; in good sooth, very rude.

Par. Well said, my lord! Well, you say so in fits.

Pan. I have business to my lord, dear queen. My lord, will you vouchsafe me a word?

Helen. Nay, this shall not hedge us out. We'll hear you sing, certainly. 66

Pan. Well, sweet queen, you are pleasant with me. But, marry, thus, my lord: my dear lord and most esteemed friend, your brother Troilus —

Helen. My lord Pandarus, honey-sweet lord!

Pan. Go to, sweet queen, go to! — commends himself most affectionately to you —

Helen. You shall not bob us out of our melody. If you do, our melancholy upon your head! 76

Pan. Sweet queen, sweet queen! That's a sweet queen, i' faith!

Helen. And to make a sweet lady sad is a sour offence.

Pan. Nay, that shall not serve your turn; that shall it not, in truth, la! Nay, I care not for such words; no, no. — And, my lord, he desires you that, if the King call for him at supper, you will make his excuse.

Helen. My Lord Pandarus!

Pan. What says my sweet queen, my very very sweet queen?

Par. What exploit's in hand? Where sups he to-night?

Helen. Nay, but, my lord —

Pan. What says my sweet queen? — My cousin will fall out with you. You must not know where he sups.

Par. I'll lay my life, with my disposer Cressida. 96

Pan. No, no, no such matter! you are wide. Come, your disposer is sick.

Par. Well, I'll make 's excuse.

Pan. Ay, good my lord. Why should you say Cressida? No, your poor disposer's sick.

Par. I spy!

Pan. You spy? What do you spy? — Come, give me an instrument. Now, sweet queen.

Helen. Why, this is kindly done.

Pan. My niece is horribly in love with a thing you have, sweet queen.

Helen. She shall have it, my lord, if it be not my Lord Paris.

Pan. He? No, she'll none of him. They two are twain.

Helen. Falling in, after falling out, may make them three.

Pan. Come, come, I'll hear no more of this. I'll sing you a song now.

Helen. Ay, ay, prithee now. By my troth, sweet lord, thou hast a fine forehead.

Pan. Ay, you may, you may.

Helen. Let thy song be love. This love will undo us all. O Cupid, Cupid, Cupid!

Pan. Love? Ay, that it shall, i' faith.

Par. Ay, good now, love, love, nothing but love.

Pan. In good troth, it begins so. [*Sings.*]

Love, love, nothing but love, still love, still more!
    For, O, love's bow
    Shoots buck and doe;
    The shaft confounds
    Not that it wounds,
But tickles still the sore.
These lovers cry, O ho! they die!
    Yet that which seems the wound to kill
Doth turn O ho! to ha! ha! he!
    So dying love lives still.
O ho! awhile, but ha! ha! ha!
O ho! groans out for ha! ha! ha! — hey ho!

Helen. In love, i' faith, to the very tip of the nose!

Par. He eats nothing but doves, love, and that breeds hot blood, and hot blood begets hot thoughts, and hot thoughts beget hot deeds, and hot deeds is love.

Pan. Is this the generation of love — hot blood, hot thoughts, and hot deeds? Why, they are vipers! Is love a generation of vipers? Sweet lord, who's afield to-day?

Par. Hector, Deiphobus, Helenus, Antenor, and all the gallantry of Troy. I would fain have arm'd to-day, but my Nell would not have it so. How chance my brother Troilus went not?

Helen. He hangs the lip at something. You know all, Lord Pandarus.

Pan. Not I, honey-sweet queen. I long to hear how they sped to-day. — You'll remember your brother's excuse?

Par. To a hair.

Pan. Farewell, sweet queen.

Helen. Commend me to your niece.

Pan. I will, sweet queen. [*Exit.*]

Sound a retreat.

Par. They're come from field. Let us to Priam's hall
To greet the warriors. Sweet Helen, I must woo you
To help unarm our Hector. His stubborn buckles,
With these your white enchanting fingers touch'd,
Shall more obey than to the edge of steel
Or force of Greekish sinews. You shall do more
Than all the island kings — disarm great Hector.

Helen. 'Twill make us proud to be his servant, Paris.
Yea, what he shall receive of us in duty
Gives us more palm in beauty than we have,
Yea, overshines ourself.

Par. Sweet, above thought I love thee!

Exeunt.

[Scene II. *Troy.* Pandarus' *orchard.*]

Enter *Pandarus* and *Troilus' Man.*

Pan. How now? Where's thy master? at my cousin Cressida's?

Man. No, sir; he stays for you to conduct him thither.

Enter *Troilus.*

Pan. O, here he comes. How now, how now?

Tro. Sirrah, walk off. [*Exit Man.*]

Pan. Have you seen my cousin?

Tro. No, Pandarus. I stalk about her door
Like a strange soul upon the Stygian banks
Staying for waftage. O, be thou my Charon,
And give me swift transportance to those fields
Where I may wallow in the lily beds
Propos'd for the deserver! O gentle Pandar,
From Cupid's shoulder pluck his painted wings.
And fly with me to Cressid!

Pan. Walk here i' th' orchard; I'll bring her straight. *Exit.*

Tro. I am giddy; expectation whirls me round.
Th' imaginary relish is so sweet

That it enchants my sense. What will it be
When that the wat'ry palates taste indeed
Love's thrice-repured nectar? Death, I fear me;
Sounding destruction; or some joy too fine,
Too subtile-potent, tun'd too sharp in sweetness
For the capacity of my ruder powers.
I fear it much; and I do fear besides
That I shall lose distinction in my joys,
As doth a battle when they charge on heaps
The enemy flying.

Enter *Pandarus.*

Pan. She's making her ready; she'll come straight. You must be witty now. She does so blush, and fetches her wind so short, as if she were fray'd with a sprite. I'll fetch her. It is the prettiest villain! She fetches her breath as short as a new-ta'en sparrow. *Exit.*

Tro. Even such a passion doth embrace my bosom.
My heart beats thicker than a feverous pulse,
And all my powers do their bestowing lose,
Like vassalage at unawares encount'ring
The eye of majesty.

Enter *Pandarus* and *Cressida.*

Pan. Come, come, what need you blush? Shame's a baby. — Here she is now. Swear the oaths now to her that you have sworn to me. — What, are you gone again? You must be watch'd ere you be made tame, must you? Come your ways, come your ways. An you draw backward, we'll put you i' th' fills. Why do you not speak to her? Come, draw this curtain and let's see your picture. Alas the day, how loath you are to offend daylight! An 'twere dark, you'ld close sooner. So, so; rub on, and kiss the mistress. How now? a kiss in fee-farm? Build there, carpenter; the air is sweet. Nay, you shall fight your hearts out ere I part you. The falcon as the tercel, for all the ducks i' th' river! Go to, go to.

Tro. You have bereft me of all words, lady.

Pan. Words pay no debts, give her deeds. But she'll bereave you o' th' deeds too, if she call your activity in question. What, billing again? Here's 'In witness whereof the parties interchangeably.'—Come in, come in! I'll go get a fire. [*Exit.*]

Cres. Will you walk in, my lord?

Tro. O Cressid, how often have I wish'd me thus!

Cres. Wish'd, my lord? The gods grant — O my lord!

Tro. What should they grant? What makes this pretty abruption? What too curious dreg espies my sweet lady in the fountain of our love?

Cres. More dregs than water, if my fears have eyes.

Tro. Fears make devils of cherubins; they never see truly.

Cres. Blind fear that seeing reason leads, finds safer footing than blind reason stumbling without fear. To fear the worst oft cures the worse.

Tro. O, let my lady apprehend no fear! In all Cupid's pageant there is presented no monster.

Cres. Nor nothing monstrous neither?

Tro. Nothing but our undertakings when we vow to weep seas, live in fire, eat rocks, tame tigers — thinking it harder for our mistress to devise imposition enough than for us to undergo any difficulty imposed. This is the monstruosity in love, lady, that the will is infinite and the execution confin'd, that the desire is boundless and the act a slave to limit.

Cres. They say all lovers swear more performance than they are able, and yet reserve an ability that they never perform, vowing more than the perfection of ten, and discharging less than the tenth part of one. They that have the voice of lions and the act of hares, are they not monsters?

Tro. Are there such? Such are not we! Praise us as we are tasted; allow us as we prove. Our head shall go bare till merit crown it. No perfection in reversion shall have a praise in present. We will not name desert before his birth, and, being born, his addition shall be humble. Few words to fair faith! Troilus shall be such to Cressid as what envy can say worst shall be a mock for his truth, and what truth can speak truest not truer than Troilus.

Cres. Will you walk in, my lord?

Enter *Pandarus.*

Pan. What, blushing still? Have you not done talking yet?

Cres. Well, uncle, what folly I commit I dedicate to you.

Pan. I thank you for that. If my lord get a boy of you, you'll give him me. Be true to my lord. If he flinch, chide me for it.

Tro. You know now your hostages — your uncle's word and my firm faith.

Pan. Nay, I'll give my word for her too. Our kindred, though they be long ere they be wooed, they are constant being won. They are burrs, I can tell you; they'll stick where they are thrown.

Cres. Boldness comes to me now and brings me heart.
Prince Troilus, I have lov'd you night and day
For many weary months.

Tro. Why was my Cressid then so hard to win?

Cres. Hard to seem won; but I was won, my lord,
With the first glance that ever — pardon me!
If I confess much, you will play the tyrant.
I love you now; but till now not so much
But I might master it. In faith, I lie!
My thoughts were like unbridled children, grown
Too headstrong for their mother. See, we fools!
Why have I blabb'd? Who shall be true to us
When we are so unsecret to ourselves?
But, though I lov'd you well, I woo'd you not;
And yet, good faith, I wish'd myself a man,
Or that we women had men's privilege
Of speaking first. Sweet, bid me hold my tongue,
For in this rapture I shall surely speak
The thing I shall repent. See, see, your silence,
Cunning in dumbness, from my weakness draws
My very soul of counsel! Stop my mouth.

Tro. And shall, albeit sweet music issues thence. [*Kisses her.*]

Pan. Pretty, i' faith.

Cres. My lord, I do beseech you pardon me.
'Twas not my purpose thus to beg a kiss.
I am asham'd. O heavens! what have I done?
For this time will I take my leave, my lord.

Tro. Your leave, sweet Cressid?

Pan. Leave? An you take leave till to-morrow morning —

Cres. Pray you content you.

Tro. What offends you, lady?

Cres. Sir, mine own company.

Tro. You cannot shun yourself.

Cres. Let me go and try.
I have a kind of self resides with you;
But an unkind self, that itself will leave
To be another's fool. I would be gone.
Where is my wit? I know not what I speak.

Tro. Well know they what they speak that speak so wisely.

Cres. Perchance, my lord, I show more craft than love;
And fell so roundly to a large confession
To angle for your thoughts. But you are wise,
Or else you love not; for to be wise and love
Exceeds man's might: that dwells with gods above.

Tro. O that I thought it could be in a woman
(As, if it can, I will presume in you)
To feed for aye her lamp and flames of love;
To keep her constancy in plight and youth,
Outliving beauties outward, with a mind
That doth renew swifter than blood decays!
Or that persuasion could but thus convince me,
That my integrity and truth to you
Might be affronted with the match and weight
Of such a winnowed purity in love!
How were I then uplifted! but, alas,
I am as true as truth's simplicity
And simpler than the infancy of truth.

Cres. In that I'll war with you.

Tro. O virtuous fight,
When right with right wars who shall be most right!
True swains in love shall in the world to come
Approve their truth by Troilus. When their rhymes,
Full of protest, of oath, and big compare,
Want similes, truth tir'd with iteration —
'As true as steel, as plantage to the moon,
As sun to day, as turtle to her mate,
As iron to adamant, as earth to th' centre' —
Yet, after all comparisons of truth,
As truth's authentic author to be cited,
'As true as Troilus' shall crown up the verse
And sanctify the numbers.

Cres. Prophet may you be!
If I be false, or swerve a hair from truth,
When time is old and hath forgot itself,
When water drops have worn the stones of Troy,
And blind oblivion swallow'd cities up,
And mighty states characterless are grated
To dusty nothing — yet let memory,
From false to false, among false maids in love,
Upbraid my falsehood! When th' have said 'as false
As air, as water, wind, or sandy earth,
As fox to lamb, or wolf to heifer's calf,
Pard to the hind, or stepdame to her son' —
'Yea,' let them say, to stick the heart of falsehood,
'As false as Cressid.'

Pan. Go to, a bargain made! Seal it, seal it; I'll be the witness. Here I hold your hand; here my cousin's. If ever you prove false one to another, since I have taken such pain to bring you together, let all pitiful goers-between be call'd to the world's end after my name; call them all Pandars. Let all constant men be Troiluses, all false women Cressids, and all brokers-between Pandars! Say 'Amen.'

Tro. Amen.

Cres. Amen.

Pan. Amen. Whereupon I will show you a chamber with a bed, which, because it shall not speak of your pretty encounters, press it to death. Away!

Exeunt [*Troilus and Cressida*].

And Cupid grant all tongue-tied maidens here
Bed, chamber, Pandar to provide this gear!

Exit.

[Scene III. *The Grecian camp.*]

Flourish. Enter *Ulysses, Diomedes, Nestor, Agamemnon,* [*Ajax,*] *Menelaus,* and *Calchas.*

Cal. Now, princes, for the service I have done you,
Th' advantage of the time prompts me aloud
To call for recompense. Appear it to your mind
That, through the sight I bear in things to love,
I have abandon'd Troy, left my possession,
Incurr'd a traitor's name, expos'd myself
From certain and possess'd conveniences
To doubtful fortunes, sequest'ring from me all
That time, acquaintance, custom, and condition
Made tame and most familiar to my nature,
And here, to do you service, am become
As new into the world, strange, unacquainted:
I do beseech you, as in way of taste,
To give me now a little benefit
Out of those many regist'red in promise
Which you say live to come in my behalf.

Agam. What wouldst thou of us, Troyan? Make demand.

Cal. You have a Troyan prisoner call'd Antenor,
Yesterday took. Troy holds him very dear.
Oft have you (often have you thanks therefore)
Desir'd my Cressid in right great exchange,
Whom Troy hath still denied; but this Antenor
I know is such a wrest in their affairs
That their negotiations all must slack,
Wanting his manage; and they will almost
Give us a prince of blood, a son of Priam,
In change of him. Let him be sent, great princes,
And he shall buy my daughter; and her presence
Shall quite strike off all service I have done,
In most accepted pain.

Agam. Let Diomedes bear him
And bring us Cressid hither. Calchas shall have
What he requests of us. Good Diomed,
Furnish you fairly for this interchange.
Withal bring word if Hector will to-morrow
Be answered in his challenge. Ajax is ready.

Dio. This shall I undertake, and 'tis a burthen
Which I am proud to bear.

Exeunt [*Diomedes and Calchas*].

Achilles and Patroclus stand in their tent.

Ulyss. Achilles stands i' th' entrance of his tent.
Please it our general pass strangely by him,
As if he were forgot; and, princes all,
Lay negligent and loose regard upon him.
I will come last. 'Tis like he'll question me
Why such unplausive eyes are bent, why turn'd on him.
If so, I have derision med'cinable
To use between your strangeness and his pride,
Which his own will shall have desire to drink.
It may do good. Pride hath no other glass
To show itself but pride; for supple knees
Feed arrogance and are the proud man's fees.

Agam. We'll execute your purpose and put on
A form of strangeness as we pass along.
So do each lord, and either greet him not,
Or else disdainfully, which shall shake him more
Than if not look'd on. I will lead the way.

Achil. What, comes the general to speak with me?
You know my mind; I'll fight no more 'gainst Troy.

Agam. What says Achilles? Would he aught with us?

Nest. Would you, my lord, aught with the general?

Achil. No.

Nest. Nothing, my lord.

Agam. The better.

[*Exeunt Agamemnon and Nestor.*]

Achil. Good day, good day.

Men. How do you? How do you? [*Exit.*]

Achil. What, does the cuckold scorn me?

Ajax. How now, Patroclus?

Achil. Good morrow, Ajax.

Ajax. Ha?

Achil. Good morrow.

Ajax. Ay, and good next day too. *Exit.*
Achil. What mean these fellows? Know they not Achilles?
Patr. They pass by strangely. They were us'd to bend,
To send their smiles before them to Achilles,
To come as humbly as they us'd to creep
To holy altars.
Achil. What, am I poor of late?
'Tis certain, greatness, once fall'n out with fortune,
Must fall out with men too. What the declin'd is
He shall as soon read in the eyes of others
As feel in his own fall; for men, like butterflies,
Show not their mealy wings but to the summer;
And not a man for being simply man
Hath any honour, but honour for those honours
That are without him, as place, riches, and favour,
Prizes of accident as oft as merit;
Which when they fall, as being slippery standers,
The love that lean'd on them as slippery too,
Doth one pluck down another, and together
Die in the fall. But 'tis not so with me.
Fortune and I are friends. I do enjoy
At ample point all that I did possess
Save these men's looks, who do methinks find out
Something not worth in me such rich beholding
As they have often given. Here is Ulysses.
I'll interrupt his reading.
How now, Ulysses?
Ulyss. Now, great Thetis' son!
Achil. What are you reading?
Ulyss. A strange fellow here
Writes me, that man — how dearly ever parted,
How much in having, or without or in —
Cannot make boast to have that which he hath,
Nor feels not what he owes, but by reflection;
As when his virtues, aiming upon others,
Heat them, and they retort that heat again
To the first giver.
Achil. This is not strange, Ulysses.
The beauty that is borne here in the face
The bearer knows not, but commends itself
To others' eyes; nor doth the eye itself,
That most pure spirit of sense, behold itself,
Not going from itself; but eye to eye oppos'd
Salutes each other with each other's form;
For speculation turns not to itself
Till it hath travell'd, and is mirror'd there
Where it may see itself. This is not strange at all.
Ulyss. I do not strain at the position,
It is familiar, but at the author's drift,
Who, in his circumstance, expressly proves
That no man is the lord of anything,
Though in and of him there be much consisting,
Till he communicate his parts to others;
Nor doth he of himself know them for aught
Till he behold them formed in th' applause
Where th' are extended, who, like an arch, reverb'rate
The voice again; or, like a gate of steel
Fronting the sun, receives and renders back
His figure and his heat. I was much rapt in this,
And apprehended here immediately
Th' unknown Ajax. Heavens, what a man is there!
A very horse, that has he knows not what.
Nature, what things there are
Most abject in regard and dear in use!
What things again most dear in the esteem
And poor in worth! Now shall we see to-morrow
(An act that very chance doth throw upon him)
Ajax renown'd. O heavens, what some men do
While some men leave to do!
How some men creep in skittish Fortune's hall
Whiles others play the idiots in her eyes!
How one man eats into another's pride
While pride is fasting in his wantonness!
To see these Grecian lords! Why, even already
They clap the lubber Ajax on the shoulder,
As if his foot were on brave Hector's breast
And great Troy shrieking.
Achil. I do believe it; for they pass'd by me
As misers do by beggars; neither gave to me
Good word nor look. What, are my deeds forgot?
Ulyss. Time hath, my lord, a wallet at his back,
Wherein he puts alms for oblivion,
A great-siz'd monster of ingratitudes.
Those scraps are good deeds past, which are devour'd
As fast as they are made, forgot as soon
As done. Perseverance, dear my lord,
Keeps honour bright. To have done is to hang
Quite out of fashion, like a rusty mail
In monumental mock'ry. Take the instant way;
For honour travels in a strait so narrow
Where one but goes abreast. Keep then the path,
For emulation hath a thousand sons
That one by one pursue. If you give way,
Or hedge aside from the direct forthright,

Like to an ent'red tide they all rush by
And leave you hindmost;
Or, like a gallant horse fall'n in first rank,
Lie there for pavement to the abject rear,
O'errun and trampled on. Then what they do in present,
Though less than yours in past, must o'ertop yours;
For Time is like a fashionable host,
That slightly shakes his parting guest by th' hand,
And with his arms outstretch'd as he would fly
Grasps in the comer. The welcome ever smiles,
And farewell goes out sighing. Let not virtue seek
Remuneration for the thing it was!
For beauty, wit,
High birth, vigour of bone, desert in service,
Love, friendship, charity, are subjects all
To envious and calumniating Time.
One touch of nature makes the whole world kin,
That all with one consent praise new-born gauds,
Though they are made and moulded of things past,
And give to dust that is a little gilt
More laud than gilt o'erdusted.
The present eye praises the present object.
Then marvel not, thou great and complete man,
That all the Greeks begin to worship Ajax,
Since things in motion sooner catch the eye
Than what not stirs. The cry went once on thee,
And still it might, and yet it may again,
If thou wouldst not entomb thyself alive
And case thy reputation in thy tent,
Whose glorious deeds, but in these fields of late,
Made emulous missions 'mongst the gods themselves
And drave great Mars to faction.

Achil. Of this my privacy
I have strong reasons.

Ulyss. But 'gainst your privacy
The reasons are more potent and heroical.
'Tis known, Achilles, that you are in love
With one of Priam's daughters.

Achil. Ha? known?

Ulyss. Is that a wonder?
The providence that's in a watchful state
Knows almost every grain of Pluto's gold;
Finds bottom in th' uncomprehensive depth;
Keeps place with thought, and almost, like the gods,
Does thoughts unveil in their dumb cradles.
There is a mystery (with whom relation
Durst never meddle) in the soul of state,
Which hath an operation more divine
Than breath or pen can give expressure to.
All the commerce that you have had with Troy
As perfectly is ours as yours, my lord;
And better would it fit Achilles much
To throw down Hector than Polyxena.
But it must grieve young Pyrrhus now at home
When fame shall in our islands sound her trump
And all the Greekish girls shall tripping sing
'Great Hector's sister did Achilles win,
But our great Ajax bravely beat down him.'
Farewell, my lord. I as your lover speak.
The fool slides o'er the ice that you should break. [*Exit.*]

Patr. To this effect, Achilles, have I mov'd you.
A woman impudent and mannish grown
Is not more loath'd than an effeminate man
In time of action. I stand condemn'd for this.
They think my little stomach to the war
And your great love to me restrains you thus.
Sweet, rouse yourself, and the weak wanton Cupid
Shall from your neck unloose his amorous fold,
And, like a dewdrop from the lion's mane,
Be shook to air.

Achil. Shall Ajax fight with Hector?

Patr. Ay, and perhaps receive much honour by him.

Achil. I see my reputation is at stake;
My fame is shrowdly gor'd.

Patr. O, then, beware!
Those wounds heal ill that men do give themselves.
Omission to do what is necessary
Seals a commission to a blank of danger,
And danger like an ague subtly taints
Even then when we sit idly in the sun.

Achil. Go call Thersites hither, sweet Patroclus.
I'll send the fool to Ajax and desire him
T' invite the Troyan lords after the combat
To see us here unarm'd. I have a woman's longing,
An appetite that I am sick withal,
To see great Hector in his weeds of peace;
To talk with him, and to behold his visage
Even to my full of view.

Enter *Thersites.*

A labour sav'd!

Ther. A wonder!

Achil. What?

Ther. Ajax goes up and down the field, asking for himself.

Achil. How so?

Ther. He must fight singly to-morrow with Hector, and is so prophetically proud of an heroical cudgelling that he raves in saying nothing.

Achil. How can that be?

Ther. Why, 'a stalks up and down like a peacock — a stride and a stand; ruminates like an hostess that hath no arithmetic but her brain to set down her reckoning; bites his lip with a politic regard, as who should say 'There were wit in this head, an 'twould out.' And so there is; but it lies as coldly in him as fire in a flint, which will not show without knocking. The man's undone for ever; for if Hector break not his neck i' th' combat, he'll break't himself in vainglory. He knows not me. I said 'Good morrow, Ajax,' and he replies 'Thanks, Agamemnon.' What think you of this man that takes me for the general? He's grown a very land-fish, languageless, a monster. A plague of opinion! A man may wear it on both sides like a leather jerkin.

Achil. Thou must be my ambassador to him, Thersites.

Ther. Who? I? Why, he'll answer nobody. He professes not answering. Speaking is for beggars; he wears his tongue in's arms. I will put on his presence. Let Patroclus make his demands to me, you shall see the pageant of Ajax.

Achil. To him, Patroclus. Tell him I humbly desire the valiant Ajax to invite the most valorous Hector to come unarm'd to my tent, and to procure safe-conduct for his person of the magnanimous and most illustrious six or seven times honour'd Captain General of the Grecian army, Agamemnon, et cetera. Do this.

Patr. Jove bless great Ajax!

Ther. Hum!

Patr. I come from the worthy Achilles —

Ther. Ha!

Patr. Who most humbly desires you to invite Hector to his tent —

Ther. Hum!

Patr. And to procure safe-conduct from Agamemnon.

Ther. Agamemnon?

Patr. Ay, my lord.

Ther. Ha!

Patr. What say you to't?

Ther. God b' wi' you with all my heart.

Patr. Your answer, sir.

Ther. If to-morrow be a fair day, by eleven of the clock it will go one way or other. Howsoever, he shall pay for me ere he has me.

Patr. Your answer, sir.

Ther. Fare ye well with all my heart.

Achil. Why, but he is not in this tune, is he?

Ther. No, but he's out o' tune thus. What music will be in him when Hector has knock'd out his brains I know not; but, I am sure, none, unless the fiddler Apollo get his sinews to make catlings on.

Achil. Come, thou shalt bear a letter to him straight.

Ther. Let me carry another to his horse; for that's the more capable creature.

Achil. My mind is troubled like a fountain stirr'd,
And I myself see not the bottom of it.

[*Exeunt Achilles and Patroclus.*]

Ther. Would the fountain of your mind were clear again, that I might water an ass at it! I had rather be a tick in a sheep than such a valiant ignorance. [*Exit.*]

[ACT IV. Scene I. *Troy. A street.*]

Enter, at one door, *Æneas,* [and *Servant*] with a torch; at another, *Paris, Deiphobus, Antenor, Diomedes the Grecian,* [and others,] with torches.

Par. See, ho! Who is that there?
Dei. It is the Lord Æneas.
Æne. Is the prince there in person?
Had I so good occasion to lie long
As you, Prince Paris, nothing but heavenly business
Should rob my bedmate of my company.
Dio. That's my mind too. Good morrow, Lord Æneas.
Par. A valiant Greek, Æneas — take his hand:
Witness the process of your speech, wherein
You told how Diomed, a whole week by days,
Did haunt you in the field.
Æne. Health to you, valiant sir,
During all question of the gentle truce;
But when I meet you arm'd, as black defiance
As heart can think or courage execute!

Dio. The one and other Diomed embraces.
Our bloods are now in calm, and so long, health!
But when contention and occasion meet,
By Jove, I'll play the hunter for thy life
With all my force, pursuit, and policy.

Æne. And thou shalt hunt a lion that will fly
With his face backward. In humane gentleness,
Welcome to Troy! now by Anchises' life,
Welcome indeed! By Venus' hand I swear,
No man alive can love in such a sort
The thing he means to kill more excellently.

Dio. We sympathize. Jove let Æneas live,
If to my sword his fate be not the glory,
A thousand complete courses of the sun!
But in mine emulous honour let him die,
With every joint a wound, and that to-morrow!

Æne. We know each other well.

Dio. We do, and long to know each other worse.

Par. This is the most despiteful gentle greeting,
The noblest hateful love, that e'er I heard of.
What business, lord, so early?

Æne. I was sent for to the King; but why, I know not.

Par. His purpose meets you. 'Twas to bring this Greek
To Calchas' house, and there to render him,
For the enfreed Antenor, the fair Cressid.
Let's have your company; or if you please,
Haste there before us. I constantly believe
(Or rather call my thought a certain knowledge)
My brother Troilus lodges there to-night.
Rouse him and give him note of our approach,
With the whole quality wherefore. I fear
We shall be much unwelcome.

Æne. That I assure you.
Troilus had rather Troy were borne to Greece
Than Cressid borne from Troy.

Par. There is no help.
The bitter disposition of the time
Will have it so. On, lord; we'll follow you.

Æne. Good morrow, all. *Exit [with Servant].*

Par. And tell me, noble Diomed — faith, tell me true,
Even in the soul of sound good-fellowship —
Who in your thoughts deserves fair Helen best,
Myself or Menelaus?

Dio. Both alike.
He merits well to have her that doth seek her,
Not making any scruple of her soilure,
With such a hell of pain and world of charge;
And you as well to keep her, that defend her,
Not palating the taste of her dishonour,
With such a costly loss of wealth and friends.
He like a puling cuckold would drink up
The lees and dregs of a flat tamed piece;
You, like a lecher, out of whorish loins
Are pleas'd to breed out your inheritors.
Both merits pois'd, each weighs nor less nor more;
But he as he, the heavier for a whore.

Par. You are too bitter to your countrywoman.

Dio. She's bitter to her country. Hear me, Paris:
For every false drop in her bawdy veins
A Grecian's life hath sunk; for every scruple
Of her contaminated carrion weight
A Troyan hath been slain. Since she could speak,
She hath not given so many good words breath
As for her Greeks and Troyans suff'red death.

Par. Fair Diomed, you do as chapmen do,
Dispraise the thing that you desire to buy;
But we in silence hold this virtue well,
We'll not commend what we intend to sell.
Here lies our way. *Exeunt.*

[Scene II. *Troy. Court of* Pandarus' *house.*]

Enter *Troilus* and *Cressida.*

Tro. Dear, trouble not yourself; the morn is cold.

Cres. Then, sweet my lord, I'll call mine uncle down;
He shall unbolt the gates.

Tro. Trouble him not.
To bed, to bed! Sleep kill those pretty eyes,
And give as soft attachment to thy senses
As infants empty of all thought!

Cres. Good morrow then.

Tro. I prithee now, to bed.

Cres. Are you aweary of me?

Tro. O Cressida! but that the busy day
Wak'd by the lark hath rous'd the ribald crows,
And dreaming night will hide our joys no longer,
I would not from thee.

Cres. Night hath been too brief.

Tro. Beshrew the witch! With venomous wights she stays
As tediously as hell, but flies the grasps of love
With wings more momentary-swift than thought.
You will catch cold, and curse me.

Cres. Prithee tarry.
You men will never tarry.
O foolish Cressid! I might have still held off,
And then you would have tarried. Hark! there's one up.

Pan. (*within*) What's all the doors open here?

Tro. It is your uncle.

Enter *Pandarus.*

Cres. A pestilence on him! Now will he be mocking.
I shall have such a life!

Pan. How now, how now? How go maidenheads? Here, you maid! where's my cousin Cressid?

Cres. Go hang yourself, you naughty mocking uncle!
You bring me to do — and then you flout me too.

Pan. To do what? to do what? Let her say what. What have I brought you to do?

Cres. Come, come, beshrew your heart! You'll ne'er be good
Nor suffer others.

Pan. Ha, ha! Alas, poor wretch! a poor chipochia! hast not slept to-night? Would he not (a naughty man) let it sleep? A bugbear take him!

Cres. Did not I tell you? Would he were knock'd i' th' head! *One knocks.*
Who's that at door? Good uncle, go and see.
My lord, come you again into my chamber.
You smile and mock me, as if I meant naughtily.

Tro. Ha, ha!

Cres. Come, you are deceiv'd, I think of no such thing. *Knock.*
How earnestly they knock! Pray you come in.
I would not for half Troy have you seen here.
Exeunt [*Troilus and Cressida*].

Pan. Who's there? What's the matter? Will you beat down the door? How now? What's the matter?

[Enter *Æneas.*]

Æne. Good morrow, lord, good morrow.

Pan. Who's there? My Lord Æneas! By my troth,
I knew you not. What news with you so early?

Æne. Is not Prince Troilus here?

Pan. Here? What should he do here?

Æne. Come, he is here, my lord; do not deny him.
It doth import him much to speak with me.

Pan. Is he here, say you? It's more than I know, I'll be sworn. For my own part, I came in late. What should he do here?

Æne. Who? Nay, then. Come, come, you'll do him wrong ere you are ware. You'll be so true to him to be false to him. Do not you know of him, but yet go fetch him hither, go.

Enter *Troilus.*

Tro. How now? What's the matter?

Æne. My lord, I scarce have leisure to salute you,
My matter is so rash. There is at hand
Paris your brother and Deiphobus,
The Grecian Diomed, and our Antenor
Deliver'd to us; and for him forthwith,
Ere the first sacrifice, within this hour,
We must give up to Diomedes' hand
The Lady Cressida.

Tro. Is it so concluded?

Æne. By Priam and the general state of Troy.
They are at hand and ready to effect it.

Tro. How my achievements mock me!
I will go meet them; and, my Lord Æneas,
We met by chance; you did not find me here.

Æne. Good, good, my lord. The secrets of nature
Have not more gift in taciturnity.
Exeunt [*Troilus and Æneas*].

Pan. Is't possible? No sooner got but lost. The devil take Antenor! The young prince will go mad. A plague upon Antenor! I would they had broke 's neck!

Enter *Cressida.*

Cres. How now? What's the matter? Who was here?

Pan. Ah, ah!

Cres. Why sigh you so profoundly? Where's my lord? gone? Tell me, sweet uncle, what's the matter?

Pan. Would I were as deep under the earth as I am above!

Cres. O the gods! What's the matter?

Pan. Prithee get thee in. Would thou hadst ne'er been born! I knew thou wouldst be his death. O, poor gentleman! A plague upon Antenor!

Cres. Good uncle, I beseech you, on my knees I beseech you, what's the matter?

Pan. Thou must be gone, wench; thou must be gone. Thou art chang'd for Antenor. Thou must to thy father and be gone from Troilus. 'Twill be his death; 'twill be his bane; he cannot bear it.

Cres. O you immortal gods! I will not go.

Pan. Thou must.

Cres. I will not, uncle. I have forgot my father;
I know no touch of consanguinity,
No kin, no love, no blood, no soul so near me
As the sweet Troilus. O you gods divine,
Make Cressid's name the very crown of falsehood
If ever she leave Troilus! Time, force, and death,
Do to this body what extremes you can,
But the strong base and building of my love
Is as the very centre of the earth,
Drawing all things to it. I'll go in and weep —

Pan. Do, do.

Cres. Tear my bright hair and scratch my praised cheeks,
Crack my clear voice with sobs, and break my heart
With sounding 'Troilus.' I will not go from Troy. *Exeunt.*

[Scene III. *Troy. Street before* Pandarus' *house.*]

Enter *Paris, Troilus, Æneas, Deiphobus, Antenor,* and *Diomedes.*

Par. It is great morning, and the hour prefix'd
For her delivery to this valiant Greek
Comes fast upon. Good my brother Troilus,
Tell you the lady what she is to do
And haste her to the purpose.

Tro. Walk into her house.
I'll bring her to the Grecian presently;
And to his hand when I deliver her,
Think it an altar, and thy brother Troilus
A priest, there off'ring to it his own heart. [*Exit.*]

Par. I know what 'tis to love,
And would, as I shall pity, I could help.
Please you walk in, my lords. *Exeunt.*

[Scene IV. *Troy.* Pandarus' *house.*]

Enter *Pandarus* and *Cressida.*

Pan. Be moderate, be moderate.

Cres. Why tell you me of moderation?
The grief is fine, full, perfect, that I taste,
And violenteth in a sense as strong
As that which causeth it. How can I moderate it?
If I could temporize with my affection
Or brew it to a weak and colder palate,
The like allayment could I give my grief.
My love admits no qualifying dross;
No more my grief in such a precious loss.

Enter *Troilus.*

Pan. Here, here, here he comes. Ah, sweet ducks!

Cres. O Troilus, Troilus!

Pan. What a pair of spectacles is here! Let me embrace too. 'O heart,' as the goodly saying is,

'O heart, heavy heart,
Why sigh'st thou without breaking?

where he answers again

'Because thou canst not ease thy smart
By friendship nor by speaking.'

There was never a truer rhyme. Let us cast away nothing, for we may live to have need of such a verse. We see it, we see it. How now, lambs?

Tro. Cressid, I love thee in so strain'd a purity
That the blest gods, as angry with my fancy,
More bright in zeal than the devotion which
Cold lips blow to their deities, take thee from me.

Cres. Have the gods envy?

Pan. Ay, ay, ay, ay! 'Tis too plain a case.

Cres. And is it true that I must go from Troy?

Tro. A hateful truth.

Cres. What, and from Troilus too?

Tro. From Troy and Troilus.

Cres. Is't possible?

Tro. And suddenly, where injury of chance
Puts back leave-taking, justles roughly by
All time of pause, rudely beguiles our lips
Of all rejoindure, forcibly prevents
Our lock'd embrasures, strangles our dear vows
Even in the birth of our own labouring breath.
We two that with so many thousand sighs
Did buy each other, must poorly sell ourselves
With the rude brevity and discharge of one.
Injurious Time now with a robber's haste
Crams his rich thiev'ry up, he knows not how.
As many farewells as be stars in heaven,
With distinct breath and consign'd kisses to them,
He fumbles up into a loose adieu,
And scants us with a single famish'd kiss,
Distasted with the salt of broken tears.

Æne. (*within*) My lord, is the lady ready?

TROILUS and CRESSIDA

Laurence Harvey as Prince Troilus, the constant lover of the fickle Cressida

Muriel Pavlow in the role of Cressida, the wanton daughter of a Trojan priest

PHOTOGRAPHS BY ANGUS MCBEAN
PRODUCED BY MEMORIAL THEATRE COMPANY, STRATFORD-UPON-AVON

Above left: The Trojan leaders return from battle. Cressida and Pandarus (Anthony Quayle) watch as Paris (Basil Hoskins) removes his armor *(Act I, Scene II)*. *Right:* Seeking to further Troilus' suit, Pandarus questions Cressida *(Act I, Scene II)*. *Center:* The council of war in the Greek camp. Ulysses (Leo McKern) warns Menelaus (Philip Morant), Agamemnon (William Devlin), and the aged Nestor (Mervyn Blade) of the danger of Achilles' inactivity *(Act I, Scene III)*

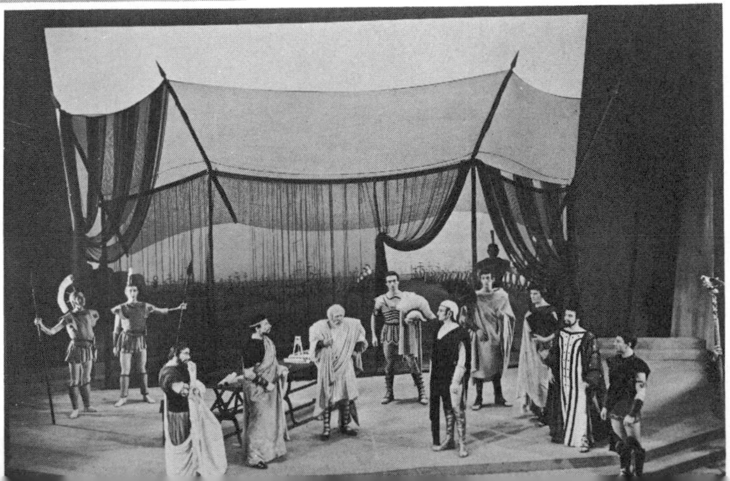

Right: The Trojan general Aeneas (Powys Thomas) enters with a challenge to the Greeks from the Trojan champion, Hector. Nestor assures Aeneas that he himself will splinter a lance with Hector if no one else accepts *(Act I, Scene III)*

Priam's palace. Pandarus brings Paris a message from Troilus and engages in banter with the fabulous Helen (Barbara Jefford), the Grecian beauty whose elopement with Paris brought about the Trojan war *(Act III, Scene I)*

An irrepressible extrovert, Pandarus entertains the Trojan court with an aria on the pangs of unfulfilled love: "Love, love, nothing but love" *(Act III, Scene I)*

Below left: Beaming triumphantly, Pandarus presides as the match he has been promoting is finally realized and Troilus and Cressida plight their troths *(Act III, Scene II)*. *Right:* Troilus pledges that his name shall live as an emblem of constancy: "True swains in love shall in the world to come approve their truths by Troilus" *(Act III, Scene I)*

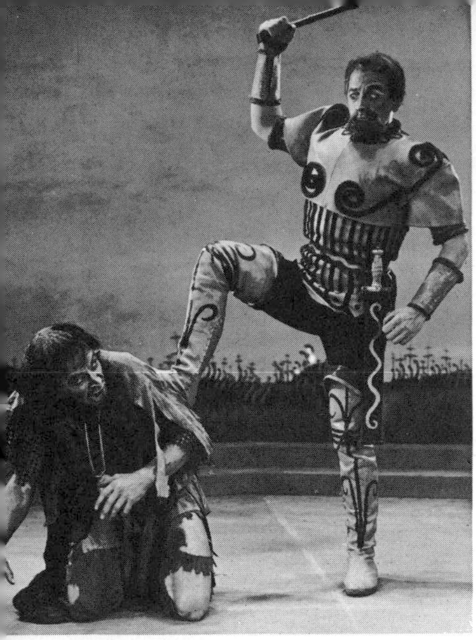

Above left: Ajax (James Grout) beats Thersites (Tony Britton), who provokes more blows with his savage raillery *(Act II, Scene I)*

Above right: Foul-mouthed Thersites baits the Greek heroes Achilles (Keith Mitchell) and Patroclus (Jerome Willis) in their tent *(Act II, Scene III)*

Above: The leaders of the Trojans debate on whether to surrender the wife of Menelaus, whose elopement with Paris led to the war with the Greeks. Enthroned at the right, King Priam (Geoffrey Bayldon) is presiding.

Below: Aeneas halts the fight of Hector (Raymond Westwell) and Ajax *(Act IV, Scene V)*

Above: "Time, my lord, hath a wallet at his back, wherein he puts alms for oblivion." While Achilles sits petulantly before his tent and broods on the way his glorious past has been forgotten, Ulysses strives to rouse him to return to battle *(Act III, Scene III)*

Below: "Cry, Trojans, cry!" Priam's mad daughter, Cassandra (Jean Wilson), prophesies doom to Troy and invites the people to join her in her lamentations on the destruction that is to come because of the passion of her firebrand brother *(Act II, Scene II)*

Brought to the Greek camp in exchange for a Trojan prisoner, Cressida is greeted with a kiss from all the generals, and the aged Nestor proposes to begin the series of embraces *(Act IV, Scene V)*

Concealed in the tent of Menelaus, Troilus and Ulysses spy on the amorous dalliance of Diomedes (Bernard Kay) and the unfaithful Cressida. "Sweet honey Greek, tempt me no more to folly," protests Cressida *(Act V, Scene II)*

Rivals for the affection of Cressida, Diomedes and Troilus meet in the battle on the plain outside the gates of Troy. Diomedes has attached Cressida's sleeve to his helmet as a gage *(Act V, Scene IV)*

"Now they are clapper-clawing one another; I'll go look on." Thersites appears on the field in a soliloquy that sets the scene for the bitter encounter between Diomedes and Troilus *(Act V, Scene IV)*

"I must not break my faith." Hector prepares to enter the battle in spite of the prophetic outbursts of Cassandra and the plea of his wife, Andromache (Jan Bashford) and his father, the king *(Act V, Scene III)*

"Come here about me, you my Myrmidons." Roused by the death of Patroclus, Achilles summons his wild tribesmen and tells them to be prepared to strike Hector *(Act V, Scene VII)*

"Strike, fellows, strike! this is the man I seek." Ignoring Hector's plea that he is unarmed, Achilles bids the Myrmidons murder him in cold blood *(Act V, Scene VIII)*

Troilus leaves the scene with a final lament for the great Trojan hero: "Hector is dead; there is no more to say" *(Act V, Scene X)*

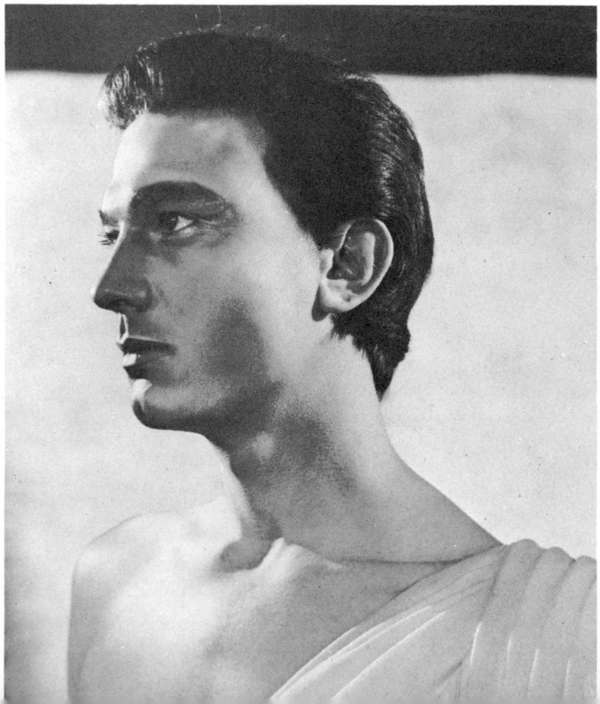

Tro. Hark! you are call'd. Some say the genius so
Cries 'Come!' to him that instantly must die.
Bid them have patience; she shall come anon.

Pan. Where are my tears? Rain, to lay this wind, or my heart will be blown up by the root. [*Exit.*]

Cres. I must then to the Grecians?

Tro. No remedy.

Cres. A woful Cressid 'mongst the merry Greeks!
When shall we see again?

Tro. Hear me, my love. Be thou but true of heart —

Cres. I true? How now? What wicked deem is this?

Tro. Nay, we must use expostulation kindly,
For it is parting from us.
I speak not 'Be thou true' as fearing thee,
For I will throw my glove to Death himself
That there's no maculation in thy heart;
But 'Be thou true' say I to fashion in
My sequent protestation: Be thou true,
And I will see thee.

Cres. O, you shall be expos'd, my lord, to dangers
As infinite as imminent! But I'll be true.

Tro. And I'll grow friend with danger. Wear this sleeve.

Cres. And you this glove. When shall I see you?

Tro. I will corrupt the Grecian sentinels
To give thee nightly visitation.
But yet be true.

Cres. O heavens! 'Be true' again?

Tro. Hear why I speak it, love.
The Grecian youths are full of quality;
They're loving, well compos'd with gifts of nature,
And flowing o'er with arts and exercise.
How novelty may move, and parts with person,
Alas, a kind of godly jealousy,
Which I beseech you call a virtuous sin,
Makes me afeard.

Cres. O heavens! you love me not.

Tro. Die I a villain then!
In this I do not call your faith in question
So mainly as my merit. I cannot sing,
Nor heel the high lavolt, nor sweeten talk,
Nor play at subtile games — fair virtues all
To which the Grecians are most prompt and pregnant;
But I can tell that in each grace of these
There lurks a still and dumb-discoursive devil
That tempts most cunningly — but be not tempted.

Cres. Do you think I will?

Tro. No.
But something may be done that we will not;
And sometimes we are devils to ourselves,
When we will tempt the frailty of our powers,
Presuming on their changeful potency.

Æne. (*within*) Nay, good my lord!

Tro. Come, kiss; and let us part.

Par. (*within*) Brother Troilus!

Tro. Good brother, come you hither,
And bring Æneas and the Grecian with you.

Cres. My lord, will you be true?

Tro. Who? I? Alas, it is my vice, my fault!
Whiles others fish with craft for great opinion,
I with great truth catch mere simplicity.
Whilst some with cunning gild their copper crowns,
With truth and plainness I do wear mine bare.

Enter [*Æneas, Paris, Antenor, Deiphobus,* and *Diomedes*].

Fear not my truth. The moral of my wit
Is 'plain and true'; there's all the reach of it.
Welcome, Sir Diomed! Here is the lady
Which for Antenor we deliver you.
At the port, lord, I'll give her to thy hand,
And by the way possess thee what she is.
Entreat her fair; and, by my soul, fair Greek,
If e'er thou stand at mercy of my sword,
Name Cressid, and thy life shall be as safe
As Priam is in Ilion.

Dio. Fair Lady Cressid,
So please you, save the thanks this prince expects.
The lustre in your eye, heaven in your cheek,
Pleads your fair usage; and to Diomed
You shall be mistress and command him wholly.

Tro. Grecian, thou dost not use me courteously
To shame the seal of my petition to thee
In praising her. I tell thee, lord of Greece,
She is as far high-soaring o'er thy praises
As thou unworthy to be call'd her servant.
I charge thee use her well, even for my charge;
For by the dreadful Pluto, if thou dost not,
Though the great bulk Achilles be thy guard,
I'll cut thy throat.

Dio. O, be not mov'd, Prince Troilus.
Let me be privileg'd by my place and message
To be a speaker free. When I am hence,
I'll answer to my lust; and know you, lord,
I'll nothing do on charge. To her own worth

She shall be priz'd; but that you say 'Be't so,'
I speak it in my spirit and honour, 'No.'

Tro. Come, to the port! I'll tell thee, Diomed,
This brave shall oft make thee to hide thy head.
Lady, give me your hand; and as we walk
To our own selves bend we our needful talk.

[*Exeunt Troilus, Cressida, and Diomedes.*]
Sound trumpet.

Par. Hark! Hector's trumpet.

Æne. How have we spent this morning!
The Prince must think me tardy and remiss,
That swore to ride before him to the field.

Par. 'Tis Troilus' fault. Come, come, to field with him!

Dei. Let us make ready straight.

Æne. Yea, with a bridegroom's fresh alacrity
Let us address to tend on Hector's heels.
The glory of our Troy doth this day lie
On his fair worth and single chivalry. *Exeunt.*

[Scene V. *The Grecian camp. Lists set out.*]

Enter *Ajax*, armed; *Achilles, Patroclus, Agamemnon, Menelaus, Ulysses, Nestor, Calchas,* &c.

Agam. Here art thou in appointment fresh and fair,
Anticipating time with starting courage.
Give with thy trumpet a loud note to Troy,
Thou dreadful Ajax, that the appalled air
May pierce the head of the great combatant
And hale him hither.

Ajax. Thou, trumpet, there's my purse.
Now crack thy lungs and split thy brazen pipe.
Blow, villain, till thy sphered bias cheek
Outswell the colic of puff'd Aquilon.
Come, stretch thy chest and let thy eyes spout blood.
Thou blowest for Hector.

[*Trumpet sounds.*]

Ulyss. No trumpet answers.

Achil. 'Tis but early days.

[Enter *Diomedes* and *Cressida.*]

Agam. Is not yond Diomed with Calchas' daughter?

Ulyss. 'Tis he, I ken the manner of his gait;
He rises on the toe. That spirit of his
In aspiration lifts him from the earth.

Agam. Is this the Lady Cressid?

Dio. Even she.

Agam. Most dearly welcome to the Greeks, sweet lady. [*Kisses her.*]

Nest. Our general doth salute you with a kiss.

Ulyss. Yet is the kindness but particular;
'Twere better she were kiss'd in general.

Nest. And very courtly counsel. I'll begin. [*Kisses her.*]
So much for Nestor.

Achil. I'll take that winter from your lips, fair lady.
Achilles bids you welcome. [*Kisses her.*]

Men. I had good argument for kissing once.

Patr. But that's no argument for kissing now;
For thus popp'd Paris in his hardiment,
And parted thus you and your argument.

[*Kisses her.*]

Ulyss. O deadly gall, and theme of all our scorns,
For which we lose our heads to gild his horns!

Patr. The first was Menelaus' kiss; this, mine:
Patroclus kisses you. [*Kisses her again.*]

Men. O, this is trim!

Patr. Paris and I kiss evermore for him.

Men. I'll have my kiss, sir. Lady, by your leave.

Cres. In kissing do you render or receive?

Men. Both take and give.

Cres. I'll make my match to live,
The kiss you take is better than you give.
Therefore no kiss.

Men. I'll give you boot; I'll give you three for one.

Cres. You are an odd man. Give even or give none.

Men. An odd man, lady? Every man is odd.

Cres. No, Paris is not; for you know 'tis true
That you are odd, and he is even with you.

Men. You fillip me o' th' head.

Cres. No, I'll be sworn.

Ulyss. It were no match, your nail against his horn.
May I, sweet lady, beg a kiss of you?

Cres. You may.

Ulyss. I do desire it.

Cres. Why, beg then.

Ulyss. Why then, for Venus' sake give me a kiss
When Helen is a maid again, and his.

Cres. I am your debtor; claim it when 'tis due.

Ulyss. Never's my day, and then a kiss of you.

Dio. Lady, a word. I'll bring you to your father. [*Exit with Cressida.*]

Nest. A woman of quick sense.

Ulyss. Fie, fie upon her!
There's language in her eye, her cheek, her lip;
Nay, her foot speaks. Her wanton spirits look out
At every joint and motive of her body.
O, these encounterers so glib of tongue,
That give accosting welcome ere it comes
And wide unclasp the tables of their thoughts
To every ticklish reader — set them down
For sluttish spoils of opportunity
And daughters of the game!

Flourish. Enter all of Troy: *Hector, Paris, Æneas, Helenus,* and *Attendants.*

All [*the Greeks*]. The Troyans' trumpet!
Agam. Yonder comes the troop.
Æne. Hail, all the state of Greece! What shall be done
To him that victory commands? Or do you purpose
A victor shall be known? Will you the knights
Shall to the edge of all extremity
Pursue each other, or shall they be divided
By any voice, or order of the field?
Hector bade ask.
Agam. Which way would Hector have it?
Æne. He cares not; he'll obey conditions.
Achil. 'Tis done like Hector; but securely done,
A little proudly, and great deal misprizing
The knight oppos'd.
Æne. If not Achilles, sir,
What is your name?
Achil. If not Achilles, nothing.
Æne. Therefore Achilles. But whate'er, know this:
In the extremity of great and little
Valour and pride excel themselves in Hector;
The one almost as infinite as all,
The other blank as nothing. Weigh him well,
And that which looks like pride is courtesy.
This Ajax is half made of Hector's blood;
In love whereof half Hector stays at home;
Half heart, half hand, half Hector comes to seek
This blended knight, half Troyan and half Greek.
Achil. A maiden battle then? O, I perceive you.

[Enter *Diomedes.*]

Agam. Here is Sir Diomed. Go, gentle knight,
Stand by our Ajax. As you and Lord Æneas
Consent upon the order of their fight,
So be it; either to the uttermost,
Or else a breath. The combatants being kin
Half stints their strife before their strokes begin.
[*Ajax and Hector enter the lists.*]
Ulyss. They are oppos'd already.
Agam. What Troyan is that same that looks so heavy?
Ulyss. The youngest son of Priam, a true knight;
Not yet mature, yet matchless; firm of word;
Speaking in deeds and deedless in his tongue;
Not soon provok'd, nor being provok'd soon calm'd;
His heart and hand both open and both free,
For what he has he gives, what thinks he shows,
Yet gives he not till judgment guide his bounty,
Nor dignifies an impair thought with breath;
Manly as Hector, but more dangerous;
For Hector in his blaze of wrath subscribes
To tender objects, but he in heat of action
Is more vindicative than jealous love.
They call him Troilus, and on him erect
A second hope as fairly built as Hector.
Thus says Æneas, one that knows the youth
Even to his inches, and with private soul
Did in great Ilion thus translate him to me.
Alarum. [*Hector and Ajax fight.*]
Agam. They are in action.
Nest. Now, Ajax, hold thine own!
Tro. Hector, thou sleep'st;
Awake thee!
Agam. His blows are well dispos'd. There, Ajax! *Trumpets cease.*
Dio. You must no more.
Æne. Princes, enough, so please you.
Ajax. I am not warm yet. Let us fight again.
Dio. As Hector pleases.
Hect. Why, then will I no more.
Thou art, great lord, my father's sister's son,
A cousin german to great Priam's seed.
The obligation of our blood forbids
A gory emulation 'twixt us twain.
Were thy commixtion Greek and Troyan so
That thou couldst say 'This hand is Grecian all,
And this is Troyan; the sinews of this leg
All Greek, and this all Troy; my mother's blood
Runs on the dexter cheek, and this sinister
Bounds in my father's,' by Jove multipotent,
Thou shouldst not bear from me a Greekish member
Wherein my sword had not impressure made
Of our rank feud; but the just gods gainsay
That any drop thou borrow'dst from thy mother,
My sacred aunt, should by my mortal sword
Be drained! Let me embrace thee, Ajax.

By him that thunders, thou hast lusty arms!
Hector would have them fall upon him thus.
Cousin, all honour to thee!
Ajax. I thank thee, Hector.
Thou art too gentle and too free a man.
I came to kill thee, cousin, and bear hence
A great addition earned in thy death.
Hect. Not Neoptolemus so mirable,
On whose bright crest Fame with her loud'st Oyes
Cries 'This is he!' could promise to himself
A thought of added honour torn from Hector.
Æne. There is expectance here from both the sides
What further you will do.
Hect. We'll answer it.
The issue is embracement. Ajax, farewell.
Ajax. If I might in entreaties find success,
As seld I have the chance, I would desire
My famous cousin to our Grecian tents.
Dio. 'Tis Agamemnon's wish, and great Achilles
Doth long to see unarm'd the valiant Hector.
Hect. Æneas, call my brother Troilus to me,
And signify this loving interview.
To the expecters of our Troyan part;
Desire them home. Give me thy hand, my cousin;
I will go eat with thee and see your knights.

Agamemnon and the rest [of the Greeks come forward].

Ajax. Great Agamemnon comes to meet us here.
Hect. The worthiest of them tell me name by name;
But for Achilles, my own searching eyes
Shall find him by his large and portly size.
Agam. Worthy all arms! as welcome as to one
That would be rid of such an enemy.
But that's no welcome. Understand more clear,
What's past and what's to come is strew'd with husks
And formless ruin of oblivion;
But in this extant moment, faith and troth,
Strain'd purely from all hollow bias-drawing,
Bids thee with most divine integrity
From heart of very heart, great Hector, welcome.
Hect. I thank thee, most imperious Agamemnon.
Agam. [*to Troilus*] My well-fam'd lord of Troy, no less to you.
Men. Let me confirm my princely brother's greeting.
You brace of warlike brothers, welcome hither.
Hect. Who must we answer?
Æne. The noble Menelaus.
Hect. O, you, my lord! By Mars his gauntlet, thanks!
Mock not that I affect th' untraded oath;
Your quondam wife swears still by Venus' glove.
She's well, but bade me not commend her to you.
Men. Name her not now, sir; she's a deadly theme.
Hect. O, pardon! I offend.
Nest. I have, thou gallant Troyan, seen thee oft,
Labouring for destiny, make cruel way
Through ranks of Greekish youth; and I have seen thee,
As hot as Perseus, spur thy Phrygian steed,
Despising many forfeits and subduements,
When thou hast hung thy advanced sword i' th' air,
Not letting it decline on the declined;
That I have said to some my standers-by,
'Lo, Jupiter is yonder, dealing life!'
And I have seen thee pause and take thy breath
When that a ring of Greeks have hemm'd thee in,
Like an Olympian wrestling. This have I seen;
But this thy countenance, still lock'd in steel,
I never saw till now. I knew thy grandsire
And once fought with him. He was a soldier good,
But by great Mars, the captain of us all,
Never like thee. Let an old man embrace thee,
And, worthy warrior, welcome to our tents.
Æne. 'Tis the old Nestor.
Hect. Let me embrace thee, good old chronicle,
That hast so long walk'd hand in hand with time.
Most reverend Nestor, I am glad to clasp thee.
Nest. I would my arms could match thee in contention
As they contend with thee in courtesy.
Hect. I would they could.
Nest. Ha!
By this white beard, I'ld fight with thee to-morrow.
Well, welcome, welcome! I have seen the time —
Ulyss. I wonder now how yonder city stands
When we have here her base and pillar by us.

Hect. I know your favour, Lord Ulysses, well.
Ah, sir, there's many a Greek and Troyan dead
Since first I saw yourself and Diomed
In Ilion on your Greekish embassy.
Ulyss. Sir, I foretold you then what would ensue.
My prophecy is but half his journey yet,
For yonder walls, that pertly front your town,
Yon towers, whose wanton tops do buss the clouds,
Must kiss their own feet.
Hect. I must not believe you.
There they stand yet; and modestly I think
The fall of every Phrygian stone will cost
A drop of Grecian blood. The end crowns all,
And that old common arbitrator, Time,
Will one day end it.
Ulyss. So to him we leave it.
Most gentle and most valiant Hector, welcome.
After the General, I beseech you next
To feast with me and see me at my tent.
Achil. I shall forestall thee, Lord Ulysses, thou!
Now, Hector, I have fed mine eyes on thee;
I have with exact view perus'd thee, Hector,
And quoted joint by joint.
Hect. Is this Achilles?
Achil. I am Achilles.
Hect. Stand fair, I pray thee; let me look on thee.
Achil. Behold thy fill.
Hect. Nay, I have done already.
Achil. Thou art too brief. I will the second time,
As I would buy thee, view thee limb by limb.
Hect. O, like a book of sport thou'lt read me o'er;
But there's more in me than thou understand'st.
Why dost thou so oppress me with thine eye?
Achil. Tell me, you heavens, in which part of his body
Shall I destroy him? whether there, or there, or there?
That I may give the local wound a name,
And make distinct the very breach whereout
Hector's great spirit flew. Answer me, heavens!
Hect. It would discredit the blest gods, proud man,
To answer such a question. Stand again.
Think'st thou to catch my life so pleasantly
As to prenominate in nice conjecture
Where thou wilt hit me dead?
Achil. I tell thee yea.
Hect. Wert thou an oracle to tell me so,
I'ld not believe thee. Henceforth guard thee well;
For I'll not kill thee there, nor there, nor there,
But, by the forge that stithied Mars his helm,
I'll kill thee everywhere, yea, o'er and o'er!
You wisest Grecians, pardon me this brag.
His insolence draws folly from my lips,
But I'll endeavour deeds to match these words
Or may I never —
Ajax. Do not chafe thee, cousin;
And you, Achilles, let these threats alone
Till accident or purpose bring you to't.
You may have every day enough of Hector
If you have stomach. The general state, I fear,
Can scarce entreat you to be odd with him.
Hect. I pray you let us see you in the field.
We have had pelting wars since you refus'd
The Grecians' cause.
Achil. Dost thou entreat me, Hector?
To-morrow do I meet thee, fell as death;
To-night all friends.
Hect. Thy hand upon that match.
Agam. First, all you peers of Greece, go to my tent;
There in the full convive we. Afterwards,
As Hector's leisure and your bounties shall
Concur together, severally entreat him.
Beat loud the tabourins, let the trumpets blow,
That this great soldier may his welcome know.
Exeunt [*all but Troilus and Ulysses*].
Tro. My Lord Ulysses, tell me, I beseech you,
In what place of the field doth Calchas keep?
Ulyss. At Menelaus' tent, most princely Troilus.
There Diomed doth feast with him to-night,
Who neither looks upon the heaven nor earth,
But gives all gaze and bent of amorous view
On the fair Cressid.
Tro. Shall I, sweet lord, be bound to you so much,
After we part from Agamemnon's tent,
To bring me thither?
Ulyss. You shall command me, sir.
As gentle tell me, of what honour was
This Cressida in Troy? Had she no lover there
That wails her absence?
Tro. O sir, to such as boasting show their scars
A mock is due. Will you walk on, my lord?
She was belov'd, she lov'd; she is, and doth;
But still sweet love is food for fortune's tooth.
Exeunt.

[Act V. Scene I. *The Grecian camp. Before the tent of* Achilles.]

Enter *Achilles* and *Patroclus*.

Achil. I'll heat his blood with Greekish wine to-night,
Which with my scimitar I'll cool to-morrow.
Patroclus, let us feast him to the height.

Patr. Here comes Thersites.

Enter *Thersites*.

Achil. How now, thou core of envy?
Thou crusty batch of nature, what's the news?

Ther. Why, thou picture of what thou seem'st, and idol of idiot-worshippers, here's a letter for thee. [*Gives letter.*]

Achil. From whence, fragment?

Ther. Why, thou full dish of fool, from Troy.

Patr. Who keeps the tent now?

Ther. The surgeon's box or the patient's wound.

Patr. Well said, adversity! and what needs these tricks?

Ther. Prithee be silent, boy; I profit not by thy talk. Thou art thought to be Achilles' male varlot.

Patr. Male varlot, you rogue? What's that?

Ther. Why, his masculine whore. Now the rotten diseases of the South, the guts-griping, ruptures, catarrhs, loads o' gravel i' th' back, lethargies, cold palsies, raw eyes, dirt-rotten livers, whissing lungs, bladders full of imposthume, sciaticas, limekilns i' th' palm, incurable boneache, and the rivelled fee simple of the tetter, take and take again such preposterous discoveries!

Patr. Why, thou damnable box of envy thou, what mean'st thou to curse thus?

Ther. Do I curse thee?

Patr. Why, no, you ruinous butt! you whoreson indistinguishable cur, no!

Ther. No? Why art thou then exasperate, thou idle immaterial skein of sleave silk, thou green sarcenet flap for a sore eye, thou tassel of a prodigal's purse, thou? Ah, how the poor world is pest'red with such waterflies — diminutives of nature!

Patr. Out, gall!

Ther. Finch egg!

Achil. My sweet Patroclus, I am thwarted quite
From my great purpose in to-morrow's battle.
Here is a letter from Queen Hecuba,
A token from her daughter, my fair love,
Both taxing me and gaging me to keep
An oath that I have sworn. I will not break it.
Fall Greeks, fail fame, honour or go or stay,
My major vow lies here, this I'll obey.
Come, come, Thersites, help to trim my tent.
This night in banqueting must all be spent.
Away, Patroclus. *Exit* [*with Patroclus*].

Ther. With too much blood and too little brain these two may run mad; but if with too much brain and too little blood they do, I'll be a curer of madmen. Here's Agamemnon, an honest fellow enough and one that loves quails, but he has not so much brain as earwax; and the goodly transformation of Jupiter there, his brother, the bull, the primitive statue and oblique memorial of cuckolds, a thrifty shoeing horn in a chain, hanging at his brother's leg — to what form but that he is should wit larded with malice, and malice forced with wit, turn him to? To an ass were nothing; he is both ass and ox: to an ox were nothing; he is both ox and ass. To be a dog, a mule, a cat, a fitchook, a toad, a lizard, an owl, a puttock, or a herring without a roe, I would not care; but to be Menelaus, I would conspire against destiny. Ask me not what I would be if I were not Thersites; for I care not to be the louse of a lazar, so I were not Menelaus. — Hoy-day! sprites and fires!

Enter *Hector*, [*Troilus*,] *Ajax*, *Agamemnon*, *Ulysses*, *Nestor*, [*Menelaus*,] and *Diomed*, with lights.

Agam. We go wrong, we go wrong.

Ajax. No, yonder 'tis,
There where we see the lights.

Hect. I trouble you.

Ajax. No, not a whit.

Enter *Achilles*.

Ulyss. Here comes himself to guide you.

Achil. Welcome, brave Hector; welcome, princes all.

Agam. So now, fair Prince of Troy, I bid good night.
Ajax commands the guard to tend on you.

Hect. Thanks and good night to the Greeks' general.

Men. Good night, my lord.

Hect. Good night, sweet Lord Menelaus.

Ther. Sweet draught! 'sweet,' quoth 'a? sweet sink, sweet sewer!

Achil. Good night and welcome, both at once, to those
That go or tarry.

Agam. Good night.

Exeunt Agamemnon, Menelaus.

Achil. Old Nestor tarries; and you too, Diomed,
Keep Hector company an hour or two.

Dio. I cannot, lord; I have important business,
The tide whereof is now. Good night, great Hector.

Hect. Give me your hand.

Ulyss. [*aside to Troilus*] Follow his torch; he goes to Calchas' tent.
I'll keep you company.

Tro. Sweet sir, you honour me.

Hect. And so good night.

[*Exit Diomedes; Ulysses and Troilus following.*]

Achil. Come, come, enter my tent.

Exeunt [*all but Thersites*].

Ther. That same Diomed's a false-hearted rogue, a most unjust knave. I will no more trust him when he leers than I will a serpent when he hisses. He will spend his mouth and promise, like Brabbler the hound; but when he performs, astronomers foretell it; it is prodigious, there will come some change. The sun borrows of the moon when Diomed keeps his word. I will rather leave to see Hector than not to dog him. They say he keeps a Troyan drab and uses the traitor Calchas' tent. I'll after. Nothing but lechery! All incontinent varlots!

Exit.

[Scene II. *The Grecian camp. Before* Calchas' *tent.*]

Enter *Diomed.*

Dio. What, are you up here, ho? Speak.

Cal. [*within*] Who calls?

Dio. Diomed. Calchas, I think. Where's your daughter?

Cal. [*within*] She comes to you.

Enter *Troilus* and *Ulysses,* [at some distance; after them *Thersites*].

Ulyss. Stand where the torch may not discover us.

Enter *Cressid.*

Tro. Cressid comes forth to him.

Dio. How now, my charge?

Cres. Now, my sweet guardian! Hark, a word with you. [*Whispers.*]

Tro. Yea, so familiar?

Ulyss. She will sing any man at first sight.

Ther. And any man may sing her, if he can take her cliff. She's noted.

Dio. Will you remember?

Cres. Remember? Yes.

Dio. Nay, but do then,
And let your mind be coupled with your words.

Tro. What shall she remember?

Ulyss. List.

Cres. Sweet honey Greek, tempt me no more to folly.

Ther. Roguery!

Dio. Nay then —

Cres. I'll tell you what —

Dio. Foh, foh! come, tell a pin! You are forsworn.

Cres. In faith, I cannot. What would you have me do?

Ther. A juggling trick — to be secretly open.

Dio. What did you swear you would bestow on me?

Cres. I prithee do not hold me to mine oath.
Bid me do anything but that, sweet Greek.

Dio. Good night.

Tro. Hold, patience!

Ulyss. How now, Troyan?

Cres. Diomed!

Dio. No, no, good night. I'll be your fool no more.

Tro. Thy better must.

Cres. Hark one word in your ear.

Tro. O plague and madness!

Ulyss. You are moved, Prince. Let us depart, I pray,
Lest your displeasure should enlarge itself
To wrathful terms. This place is dangerous,
The time right deadly. I beseech you go.

Tro. Behold, I pray you!

Ulyss. Nay, good my lord, go off.
You flow to great distraction. Come, my lord.

Tro. I prithee stay.

Ulyss. You have not patience. Come.

Tro. I pray you stay. By hell and all hell's torments,
I will not speak a word!

Dio. And so good night.

Cres. Nay, but you part in anger.

Tro. Doth that grieve thee?
O withered truth!
Ulyss. Why, how now, lord?
Tro. By Jove,
I will be patient.
Cres. Guardian! Why, Greek!
Dio. Foh, foh! adieu. You palter.
Cres. In faith, I do not. Come hither once again.
Ulyss. You shake, my lord, at something. Will you go?
You will break out.
Tro. She strokes his cheek!
Ulyss. Come, come.
Tro. Nay, stay. By Jove, I will not speak a word.
There is between my will and all offences
A guard of patience. Stay a little while.
Ther. How the devil luxury, with his fat rump and potato finger, tickles these together! Fry, lechery, fry!
Dio. But will you then?
Cres. In faith, I will, lo! Never trust me else.
Dio. Give me some token for the surety of it.
Cres. I'll fetch you one. *Exit.*
Ulyss. You have sworn patience.
Tro. Fear me not, sweet lord.
I will not be myself nor have cognition
Of what I feel. I am all patience.

Enter *Cressid.*

Ther. Now the pledge! now, now, now!
Cres. Here, Diomed, keep this sleeve.
Tro. O beauty, where is thy faith?
Ulyss. My lord!
Tro. I will be patient; outwardly I will.
Cres. You look upon that sleeve? Behold it well.
He lov'd me — O false wench! — Give't me again.
Dio. Whose was't?
Cres. It is no matter now I ha't again.
I will not meet with you to-morrow night.
I prithee, Diomed, visit me no more.
Ther. Now she sharpens. Well said, whetstone!
Dio. I shall have it.
Cres. What, this?
Dio. Ay, that.
Cres. O all you gods! O pretty, pretty pledge!
Thy master now lies thinking in his bed
Of thee and me, and sighs, and takes my glove,
And gives memorial dainty kisses to it,
As I kiss thee. Nay, do not snatch it from me!
He that takes that doth take my heart withal.
Dio. I had your heart before; this follows it.
Tro. I did swear patience.
Cres. You shall not have it, Diomed; faith, you shall not.
I'll give you something else.
Dio. I will have this. Whose was it?
Cres. It is no matter.
Dio. Come, tell me whose it was.
Cres. 'Twas one's that lov'd me better than you will.
But now you have it, take it.
Dio. Whose was it?
Cres. By all Diana's waiting women yond,
And by herself, I will not tell you whose.
Dio. To-morrow will I wear it on my helm
And grieve his spirit that dares not challenge it.
Tro. Wert thou the devil and wor'st it on thy horn,
It should be challeng'd.
Cres. Well, well, 'tis done, 'tis past; and yet it is not.
I will not keep my word.
Dio. Why then, farewell.
Thou never shalt mock Diomed again.
Cres. You shall not go. One cannot speak a word
But it straight starts you.
Dio. I do not like this fooling.
Ther. Nor I, by Pluto! but that that likes not you
Pleases me best.
Dio. What, shall I come? the hour —
Cres. Ay, come. O Jove! Do, come! I shall be plagu'd.
Dio. Farewell till then. *Exit.*
Cres. Good night. I prithee come.
Troilus, farewell! One eye yet looks on thee,
But with my heart the other eye doth see.
Ah, poor our sex! this fault in us I find,
The error of our eye directs our mind.
What error leads must err. O, then conclude
Minds sway'd by eyes are full of turpitude.
Exit.
Ther. A proof of strength she could not publish more
Unless she said 'My mind is now turn'd whore.'
Ulyss. All's done, my lord.
Tro. It is.
Ulyss. Why stay we then?
Tro. To make a recordation to my soul
Of every syllable that here was spoke.
But if I tell how these two did coact,
Shall I not lie in publishing a truth?

Sith yet there is a credence in my heart,
An esperance so obstinately strong,
That doth invert th' attest of eyes and ears,
As if those organs were deceptious functions,
Created only to calumniate.
Was Cressid here?

Ulyss. I cannot conjure, Troyan.

Tro. She was not, sure.

Ulyss. Most sure she was.

Tro. Why, my negation hath no taste of madness.

Ulyss. Nor mine, my lord. Cressid was here but now.

Tro. Let it not be believ'd for womanhood!
Think we had mothers. Do not give advantage
To stubborn critics, apt, without a theme
For depravation, to square the general sex
By Cressid's rule. Rather think this not Cressid.

Ulyss. What hath she done, Prince, that can soil our mothers?

Tro. Nothing at all, unless that this were she.

Ther. Will 'a swagger himself out on's own eyes?

Tro. This she? No, this is Diomed's Cressida!
If beauty have a soul, this is not she;
If souls guide vows, if vows be sanctimonies,
If sanctimony be the gods' delight,
If there be rule in unity itself —
This is not she. O madness of discourse,
That cause sets up with and against itself!
Bifold authority! where reason can revolt
Without perdition, and loss assume all reason
Without revolt: this is, and is not, Cressid!
Within my soul there doth conduce a fight
Of this strange nature, that a thing inseparate
Divides more wider than the sky and earth;
And yet the spacious breadth of this division
Admits no orifex for a point as subtle
As Ariachne's broken woof to enter.
Instance, O instance! strong as Pluto's gates:
Cressid is mine, tied with the bonds of heaven.
Instance, O instance! strong as heaven itself:
The bonds of heaven are slipp'd, dissolv'd, and loos'd;
And with another knot, five-finger-tied,
The fractions of her faith, orts of her love,
The fragments, scraps, the bits, and greasy relics
Of her o'ereaten faith, are given to Diomed.

Ulyss. May worthy Troilus be half attached
With that which here his passion doth express?

Tro. Ay, Greek; and that shall be divulged well
In characters as red as Mars his heart
Inflam'd with Venus. Never did young man fancy
With so eternal and so fix'd a soul.
Hark, Greek! As much as I do Cressid love,
So much by weight hate I her Diomed.
That sleeve is mine that he'll bear on his helm.
Were it a casque compos'd by Vulcan's skill,
My sword should bite it. Not the dreadful spout
Which shipmen do the hurricano call,
Constring'd in mass by the almighty sun,
Shall dizzy with more clamour Neptune's ear
In his descent than shall my prompted sword
Falling on Diomed.

Ther. He'll tickle it for his concupy.

Tro. O Cressid! O false Cressid! false, false, false!
Let all untruths stand by thy stained name
And they'll seem glorious.

Ulyss. O, contain yourself.
Your passion draws ears hither.

Enter *Æneas.*

Æne. I have been seeking you this hour, my lord.
Hector by this is arming him in Troy.
Ajax, your guard, stays to conduct you home.

Tro. Have with you, Prince. My courteous lord, adieu.
Farewell, revolted fair! and, Diomed,
Stand fast and wear a castle on thy head!

Ulyss. I'll bring you to the gates.

Tro. Accept distracted thanks.

Exeunt Troilus, Æneas, and Ulysses.

Ther. Would I could meet that rogue Diomed! I would croak like a raven; I would bode, I would bode. Patroclus will give me anything for the intelligence of this whore. The parrot will not do more for an almond than he for a commodious drab. Lechery, lechery! still wars and lechery! Nothing else holds fashion. A burning devil take them! *Exit.*

[Scene III. *Troy. Before* Priam's *Palace.*]

Enter *Hector* and *Andromache.*

And. When was my lord so much ungently temper'd
To stop his ears against admonishment?
Unarm, unarm, and do not fight to-day.

Hect. You train me to offend you. Get you in.
By all the everlasting gods, I'll go!

And. My dreams will, sure, prove ominous to the day.
Hect. No more, I say.

Enter *Cassandra.*

Cas. Where is my brother Hector?
And. Here, sister, arm'd, and bloody in intent.
Consort with me in loud and dear petition,
Pursue we him on knees; for I have dreamt
Of bloody turbulence, and this whole night
Hath nothing been but shapes and forms of slaughter.
Cas. O, 'tis true.
Hect. Ho! bid my trumpet sound!
Cas. No notes of sally, for the heavens, sweet brother!
Hect. Be gone, I say. The gods have heard me swear.
Cas. The gods are deaf to hot and peevish vows.
They are polluted off'rings, more abhorr'd
Than spotted livers in the sacrifice.
And. O, be persuaded! Do not count it holy
To hurt by being just. It is as lawful,
For we would give much, to use violent thefts
And rob in the behalf of charity.
Cas. It is the purpose that makes strong the vow;
But vows to every purpose must not hold.
Unarm, sweet Hector.
Hect. Hold you still, I say.
Mine honour keeps the weather of my fate.
Life every man holds dear, but the dear man
Holds honour far more precious-dear than life.

Enter *Troilus.*

How now, young man? Mean'st thou to fight to-day?
And. Cassandra, call my father to persuade.
Exit Cassandra.
Hect. No, faith, young Troilus. Doff thy harness, youth.
I am to-day i' th' vein of chivalry.
Let grow thy sinews till their knots be strong
And tempt not yet the brushes of the war.
Unarm thee, go; and doubt thou not, brave boy,
I'll stand to-day for thee and me and Troy.
Tro. Brother, you have a vice of mercy in you
Which better fits a lion than a man.
Hect. What vice is that? Good Troilus, chide me for it.
Tro. When many times the captive Grecian falls,
Even in the fan and wind of your fair sword,
You bid them rise and live.
Hect. O, 'tis fair play.
Tro. Fool's play, by heaven, Hector.
Hect. How now? how now?
Tro. For th' love of all the gods,
Let's leave the hermit Pity with our mother;
And when we have our armours buckled on,
The venom'd vengeance ride upon our swords,
Spur them to ruthful work, rein them from ruth!
Hect. Fie, savage, fie!
Tro. Hector, then 'tis wars.
Hect. Troilus, I would not have you fight to-day.
Tro. Who should withhold me?
Not fate, obedience, nor the hand of Mars
Beck'ning with fiery truncheon my retire;
Not Priamus and Hecuba on knees,
Their eyes o'ergalled with recourse of tears;
Nor you, my brother, with your true sword drawn,
Oppos'd to hinder me, should stop my way,
But by my ruin.

Enter *Priam* and *Cassandra.*

Cas. Lay hold upon him, Priam; hold him fast!
He is thy crutch. Now if thou lose thy stay,
Thou on him leaning, and all Troy on thee,
Fall all together.
Pri. Come, Hector, come, go back.
Thy wife hath dreamt; thy mother hath had visions;
Cassandra doth foresee; and I myself
Am like a prophet suddenly enrapt
To tell thee that this day is ominous.
Therefore come back.
Hect. Æneas is afield,
And I do stand engag'd to many Greeks,
Even in the faith of valour, to appear
This morning to them.
Pri. Ay, but thou shalt not go.
Hect. I must not break my faith.
You know me dutiful; therefore, dear sir,
Let me not shame respect, but give me leave
To take that course by your consent and voice
Which you do here forbid me, royal Priam.
Cas. O Priam, yield not to him!
And. Do not, dear father.
Hect. Andromache, I am offended with you.
Upon the love you bear me, get you in.
Exit Andromache.

Tro. This foolish, dreaming, superstitious girl
Makes all these bodements.
Cas. O, farewell, dear Hector!
Look how thou diest! look how thy eye turns pale!
Look how thy wounds do bleed at many vents!
Hark how Troy roars! how Hecuba cries out!
How poor Andromache shrills her dolours forth!
Behold, distraction, frenzy, and amazement,
Like witless antics, one another meet,
And all cry 'Hector! Hector's dead!' O Hector!
Tro. Away, away!
Cas. Farewell! — yet, soft! Hector, I take my leave.
Thou dost thyself and all our Troy deceive.
Exit.
Hect. You are amaz'd, my liege, at her exclaim.
Go in and cheer the town; we'll forth and fight,
Do deeds worth praise and tell you them at night.
Pri. Farewell. The gods with safety stand about thee!
[*Exeunt severally Priam and Hector.*]
Alarum.
Tro. They are at it, hark! Proud Diomed, believe
I come to lose my arm or win my sleeve.

Enter *Pandar.*

Pan. Do you hear, my lord? Do you hear?
Tro. What now?
Pan. Here's a letter come from yond poor girl. [*Gives letter.*]
Tro. Let me read.

Pan. A whoreson tisick, a whoreson rascally tisick, so troubles me, and the foolish fortune of this girl, and what one thing, what another, that I shall leave you one o' th's days. And I have a rheum in mine eyes too, and such an ache in my bones that, unless a man were curs'd, I cannot tell what to think on't. What says she there?

Tro. Words, words, mere words, no matter from the heart;
Th' effect doth operate another way.
[*Tears the letter.*]
Go, wind, to wind! there turn and change together.
My love with words and errors still she feeds,
But edifies another with her deeds.
Alarum. Exeunt [*severally*].

[Scene IV. *The field between Troy and the Grecian camp.*]

Enter *Thersites. Excursions.*

Ther. Now they are clapper-clawing one another; I'll go look on. That dissembling abominable varlet, Diomed, has got that same scurvy doting foolish young knave's sleeve of Troy there in his helm. I would fain see them meet, that that same young Troyan ass that loves the whore there, might send that Greekish whoremasterly villain with the sleeve back to the dissembling luxurious drab of a sleeveless errand. O' th' t'other side, the policy of those crafty swearing rascals — that stale old mouse-eaten dry cheese, Nestor, and that same dog-fox, Ulysses — is not prov'd worth a blackberry. They set me up, in policy, that mongrel cur Ajax against that dog of as bad a kind, Achilles; and now is the cur Ajax prouder than the cur Achilles and will not arm to-day; whereupon the Grecians began to proclaim barbarism, and policy grows into an ill opinion.

Enter *Diomed* and *Troilus.*

Soft! here comes sleeve and t'other.
Tro. Fly not; for shouldst thou take the river Styx,
I would swim after.
Dio. Thou dost miscall retire.
I do not fly, but advantageous care
Withdrew me from the odds of multitude.
Have at thee!

Ther. Hold thy whore, Grecian! Now for thy whore, Troyan! Now the sleeve! now the sleeve!

[*Exeunt Troilus and Diomedes, fighting.*]

Enter *Hector.*

Hect. What art thou, Greek? Art thou for Hector's match?
Art thou of blood and honour?

Ther. No, no! I am a rascal, a scurvy railing knave, a very filthy rogue.

Hect. I do believe thee. Live. [*Exit.*]

Ther. God-a-mercy that thou wilt believe me; but a plague break thy neck for frighting me! What's become of the wenching rogues? I think they have swallowed one another. I would laugh at that miracle; yet, in a sort, lechery eats itself. I'll seek them. *Exit.*

[Scene V. *Another Part of the field.*]

Enter *Diomed* and *Servant.*

Dio. Go, go, my servant, take thou Troilus' horse;
Present the fair steed to my lady Cressid.
Fellow, commend my service to her beauty;
Tell her I have chastis'd the amorous Troyan
And am her knight by proof.
Serv. I go, my lord.
[*Exit.*]

Enter *Agamemnon.*

Agam. Renew, renew! The fierce Polydamas
Hath beat down Menon; bastard Margarelon
Hath Doreus prisoner,
And stands Colossus-wise, waving his beam
Upon the pashed corses of the kings
Epistrophus and Cedius. Polyxenes is slain;
Amphimachus and Thoas deadly hurt;
Patroclus ta'en or slain, and Palamedes
Sore hurt and bruis'd. The dreadful Sagittary
Appals our numbers. Haste we, Diomed,
To reinforcement, or we perish all.

Enter *Nestor.*

Nest. Go bear Patroclus' body to Achilles,
And bid the snail-pac'd Ajax arm for shame.
There is a thousand Hectors in the field.
Now here he fights on Galathe his horse,
And there lacks work; anon he's there afoot,
And there they fly or die, like scaled sculls
Before the belching whale; then is he yonder,
And there the strawy Greeks, ripe for his edge,
Fall down before him like a mower's swath.
Here, there, and everywhere he leaves and takes;
Dexterity so obeying appetite
That what he will he does, and does so much
That proof is call'd impossibility.

Enter *Ulysses.*

Ulyss. O, courage, courage, princes! Great Achilles
Is arming, weeping, cursing, vowing vengeance.
Patroclus' wounds have rous'd his drowsy blood,
Together with his mangled Myrmidons,
That noseless, handless, hack'd and chipp'd, come to him,
Crying on Hector. Ajax hath lost a friend
And foams at mouth, and he is arm'd and at it,
Roaring for Troilus; who hath done to-day
Mad and fantastic execution,
Engaging and redeeming of himself
With such a careless force and forceless care
As if that luck, in very spite of cunning,
Bade him win all.

Enter *Ajax.*

Ajax. Troilus! thou coward Troilus! *Exit.*
Dio. Ay, there, there!
Nest. So, so, we draw together. *Exit.*

Enter *Achilles.*

Achil. Where is this Hector?
Come, come, thou boy-queller, show thy face.
Know what it is to meet Achilles angry.
Hector! where's Hector? I will none but Hector. *Exeunt.*

[Scene VI. *Another part of the field.*]

Enter *Ajax.*

Ajax. Troilus, thou coward Troilus, show thy head!

Enter *Diomed.*

Dio. Troilus, I say! Where's Troilus?
Ajax. What wouldst thou?
Dio. I would correct him.
Ajax. Were I the general, thou shouldst have my office
Ere that correction. Troilus, I say! What, Troilus!

Enter *Troilus.*

Tro. O traitor Diomed! Turn thy false face, thou traitor,
And pay thy life thou owest me for my horse!
Dio. Ha, art thou there?
Ajax. I'll fight with him alone. Stand, Diomed.
Dio. He is my prize! I will not look upon.
Tro. Come both, you cogging Greeks; have at you both!
Exeunt, [*fighting*].

Enter *Hector.*

Hect. Yea, Troilus? O, well fought, my youngest brother!

Enter *Achilles.*

Achil. Now do I see thee, ha! Have at thee, Hector!
Hect. Pause, if thou wilt.
Achil. I do disdain thy courtesy, proud Troyan.

Be happy that my arms are out of use;
My rest and negligence befriends thee now,
But thou anon shalt hear of me again;
Till when, go seek thy fortune. *Exit.*

Hect. Fare thee well.
I would have been much more a fresher man,
Had I expected thee.

Enter *Troilus.*

How now, my brother?

Tro. Ajax hath ta'en Æneas. Shall it be?
No, by the flame of yonder glorious heaven,
He shall not carry him! I'll be ta'en too
Or bring him off. Fate, hear me what I say!
I reck not though I end my life to-day. *Exit.*

Enter *one in armour.*

Hect. Stand, stand, thou Greek! Thou art a goodly mark.
No? Wilt thou not? I like thy armour well.
I'll frush it and unlock the rivets all
But I'll be master of it. Wilt thou not, beast, abide?
Why then, fly on; I'll hunt thee for thy hide.
Exeunt.

[Scene VII. *Another part of the field.*]

Enter *Achilles* with *Myrmidons.*

Achil. Come here about me, you my Myrmidons;
Mark what I say. Attend me where I wheel.
Strike not a stroke, but keep yourselves in breath;
And when I have the bloody Hector found,
Empale him with your weapons round about;
In fellest manner execute your arms.
Follow me, sirs, and my proceedings eye.
It is decreed Hector the great must die.
Exeunt.

Enter *Thersites*; *Menelaus* and *Paris* [fighting].

Ther. The cuckold and the cuckold-maker are at it. Now, bull! now, dog! 'Loo, Paris, 'loo! Now my double-henn'd sparrow! 'Loo, Paris, 'loo! The bull has the game. Ware horns, ho!

Exeunt Paris and Menelaus.

Enter *Bastard* [*Margarelon*].

Bast. Turn, slave, and fight!

Ther. What art thou?

Bast. A bastard son of Priam's.

Ther. I am a bastard too; I love bastards. I am bastard begot, bastard instructed, bastard in mind, bastard in valour, in everything illegitimate. One bear will not bite another, and wherefore should one bastard? Take heed, the quarrel's most ominous to us. If the son of a whore fight for a whore, he tempts judgment. Farewell, bastard. [*Exit.*]

Bast. The devil take thee, coward! *Exit.*

[Scene VIII. *Another part of the field.*]

Enter *Hector.*

Hect. Most putrefied core so fair without,
Thy goodly armour thus hath cost thy life.
Now is my day's work done; I'll take good breath.
Rest, sword; thou hast thy fill of blood and death. [*Disarms.*]

Enter *Achilles* and his *Myrmidons.*

Achil. Look, Hector, how the sun begins to set;
How ugly night comes breathing at his heels.
Even with the vail and dark'ning of the sun,
To close the day up, Hector's life is done.

Hect. I am unarm'd; forgo this vantage, Greek.

Achil. Strike, fellows, strike! This is the man I seek.
[*Hector falls.*]
So, Ilion, fall thou next! Now, Troy, sink down!
Here lies thy heart, thy sinews, and thy bone.
On, Myrmidons, and cry you all amain,
'Achilles hath the mighty Hector slain.'
Retreat [*sounded*].
Hark! a retire upon our Grecian part.

One. The Troyan trumpets sound the like, my lord.

Achil. The dragon wing of night o'erspreads the earth,
And, stickler-like, the armies separates.
My half-supp'd sword, that frankly would have fed,
Pleas'd with this dainty bait, thus goes to bed.
[*Sheathes his sword.*]
Come, tie his body to my horse's tail;
Along the field I will the Troyan trail.
Exeunt.

[Scene IX. *Another part of the field.*]

Sound retreat. Shout. Enter *Agamemnon, Ajax, Menelaus, Nestor, Diomedes,* and the rest, marching.

Agam. Hark! hark! what shout is that?
Nest. Peace, drums.
Soldiers. (*within*) Achilles! Achilles! Hector's slain! Achilles!
Dio. The bruit is Hector's slain, and by Achilles.
Ajax. If it be so, yet bragless let it be.
Great Hector was as good a man as he.
Agam. March patiently along. Let one be sent
To pray Achilles see us at our tent.
If in his death the gods have us befriended, 9
Great Troy is ours, and our sharp wars are ended. *Exeunt.*

[Scene X. *Another part of the field.*]

Enter *Æneas, Paris, Antenor,* and *Deiphobus.*

Æne. Stand, ho! yet are we masters of the field.
Never go home; here starve we out the night.

Enter *Troilus.*

Tro. Hector is slain.
All. Hector? The gods forbid!
Tro. He's dead, and at the murtherer's horse's tail
In beastly sort dragg'd through the shameful field.
Frown on, you heavens, effect your rage with speed!
Sit, gods, upon your thrones, and smite all Troy,
I say, at once! Let your brief plagues be mercy,
And linger not our sure destructions on!
Æne. My lord, you do discomfort all the host.
Tro. You understand me not that tell me so.
I do not speak of flight, of fear, of death,
But dare all imminence that gods and men
Address their dangers in. Hector is gone.
Who shall tell Priam so? or Hecuba?
Let him that will a screech owl aye be call'd
Go into Troy and say there 'Hector's dead':
There is a word will Priam turn to stone;
Make wells and Niobes of the maids and wives,
Cold statues of the youth, and in a word
Scare Troy out of itself. But march away.
Hector is dead; there is no more to say.
Stay yet. You vile abominable tents,
Thus proudly pight upon our Phrygian plains,
Let Titan rise as early as he dare,
I'll through and through you! And, thou great-siz'd coward,
No space of earth shall sunder our two hates;
I'll haunt thee like a wicked conscience still,
That mouldeth goblins swift as frenzy's thoughts.
Strike a free march to Troy! With comfort go.
Hope of revenge shall hide our inward woe. 31

Enter *Pandarus.*

Pan. But hear you! hear you!
Tro. Hence, broker, lackey! Ignomy and shame
Pursue thy life and live aye with thy name!
Exeunt all but Pandarus.
Pan. A goodly med'cine for my aching bones!
O world! world! world! thus is the poor agent despis'd! O traders and bawds, how earnestly are you set awork and how ill requited! Why should our endeavour be so lov'd and the performance so loath'd? What verse for it? What instance for it? Let me see: 41

Full merrily the humblebee doth sing
Till he hath lost his honey and his sting;
And being once subdu'd in armed tail,
Sweet honey and sweet notes together fail.

Good traders in the flesh, set this in your painted cloths.
As many as be here of Panders' Hall,
Your eyes, half out, weep out at Pandar's fall;
Or if you cannot weep, yet give some groans,
Though not for me, yet for your aching bones.
Brethren and sisters of the hold-door trade,
Some two months hence my will shall here be made.
It should be now, but that my fear is this,
Some galled goose of Winchester would hiss.
Till then I'll sweat and seek about for eases,
And at that time bequeath you my diseases.
Exit.

Coriolanus

Coriolanus was first printed in the Folio of 1623. The Folio text is in one sense good, for it goes back to an authentic copy; but there are abundant errata, and in many passages of verse the division into lines is incorrect. Mere misprints like 'Antients' for 'Antiates' (i, 6, 53), 'teach' for 'touch' (ii, 1, 271), 'tongue' for 'toge' (ii, 3, 122), 'God!' for 'good' (iii, 1, 91), 'heart' for 'herd' (iii, 2, 32), almost correct themselves. Theobald's change of the Folio 'things' to 'thwartings' ('thwarting' in this edition) is a stroke of editorial genius (iii, 2, 21). His 'our' for the Folio 'one' (iii, 1, 288) is equally convincing, though not always accepted. 'Cato's' for 'Calues' (i, 4, 57) is also Theobald's correction, from Plutarch: 'For he was euen such another, as *Cato* would haue a souldier and a captaine to be, not only terrible, and fierce to lay about him, but to make the enemie afearde with the sounde of his voyce, and grimnes of his countenance.'

In the late period to which the play obviously belongs, Shakespeare handled his verse with great freedom. When, therefore, a line seems hypermetrical, one cannot be sure that the printer has gone astray. When, on the other hand, a verse halts from the lack of an easily supplied syllable or two, the chances are that the poet is not responsible. See, for instance, i, 1, 255; i, 2, 31; i, 5, 29; i, 9, 17, 82; ii, 1, 216, 286; iii, 1, 139, 227; iii, 2, 87; iii, 3, 133; iv, 5, 109, 148; iv, 6, 104; v, 3, 192.

Mislineation is, in general, easy to adjust, even when verse is printed as prose or prose as verse. Now and then, however, the question arises whether Shakespeare intended a passage to be verse or prose. See, for instance, ii, 3, 69–90, where, in what seems to be a prose passage, some lines of verse appear to be imbedded.

There is a bad muddle in the Folio text of ii, 1, 180–183:

> Within Corioles Gates: where he hath wonne,
> With Fame, a Name to *Martius Caius:*
> These in honor followes *Martius Caius Coriolanus.*
> Welcome to Rome, renowned *Coriolanus.*

A curious instance of confusing omission occurs in ii, 3, 251–253, where the Folio reads:

> And Nobly nam'd, so twice being Censor,
> Was his great Ancestor.

Here North's Plutarch has led editors gradually to what must be in effect the right reading. The passage which Shakespeare was versifying runs as follows: 'Of the same house were *Publius & Quintus*, who brought to Rome their best water they had by conduites. *Censorinus* also came of that familie, that was so surnamed, because the people had chosen him *Censor* twise.'

As evidence for the date of composition, two supposed allusions to the play have been cited — one from Ben Jonson and one from Robert Armin.

Cominius the Consul, celebrating the exploits of Coriolanus (ii, 2, 86 ff.), says that at the age of sixteen he won the oaken garland in the battle against Tarquin, and that

> In the brunt of seventeen battles since
> He lurch'd all swords of the garland.

That is, 'he robbed all other warriors of the prize for valour.' Ben Jonson uses the same phrase figuratively in *Epicœne; or, The Silent Woman*: 'You have lurch'd your friends of the better half of the garland' (v, 4). *Epicœne* was first acted in 1609. If Jonson was echoing Shakespeare, this fixes one limit for the date of CORIOLANUS. But 'garland' in a figurative sense is not uncommon and 'lurch' for 'cheat' or 'rob' was a familiar colloquialism. The other supposed quotation, rather more striking, occurs in Robert Armin's preface to his poem *The Italian Taylor and his Boy*, printed in 1609: 'A strange time of taxation, wherein euery Pen and inck-horne Boy will throw vp his Cap at the hornes of the Moone in censure, although his wit hang there, not returning vnless monthly in the wane.' Compare i, 1, 216–217:

They threw their caps
As they would hang them on the horns o' th' moon.

Armin certainly acted in some of Shakespeare's plays, for his name stands in the list of 'the Principall Actors' in the First Folio. He joined the company about 1599 and still belonged to it in 1610, when he was one of 'the principall Comœdians' in Jonson's *Alchemist*. His special talent was for Clowns and Fools. There is good reason to believe that he played Dogberry in *Much Ado*. What part he took (if any) in CORIOLANUS is a matter of conjecture. Menenius has been suggested, but that is no clown's rôle. One of the comic Volscian servingmen seems more likely — perhaps the Third (iv, 5, 180 ff.). At all events, Armin's head was crammed with scraps of plays, as his pamphlets show, and such a wild hyperbole as this of caps on the moon's horns would doubtless take his fancy. Thus he is a better witness than usual. Yet all such evidence, however entertaining, is indecisive. Style and metre are far better tests, and these put CORIOLANUS beyond question in Shakespeare's latest period. Sometime in 1608, perhaps soon after *Antony and Cleopatra*, satisfies all the conditions.

For material Shakespeare went to the life of Coriolanus in Sir Thomas North's translation of Plutarch (1595). He uses North in the Roman plays as he uses Holinshed in the English 'histories' and tragedies: in some passages he merely turns North's eloquent prose into verse; in others he takes a suggestion and elaborates it. As to characters, Plutarch describes and Shakespeare creates.

His use of North may be illustrated by Menenius' fable (i, 1, 99 ff.) of the Belly and the Members. In North this runs as follows:

On a time all the members of mans body did rebell against the bellie, complaining of it, that it onely remained in the middest of the bodie, without doing any thing, neither did beare any labour to the maintenaunce of the rest: whereas all other partes and members did labour paynefully, & were very carefull to satisfie the appetites and desires of the bodie. And so the bellie, all this notwithstanding laughed at their follie, and sayed. It is true, I first receiue all meates that norish mans bodie: but afterwardes I send it againe to the norishment of other partes of the same. Euen so (quoth he) o you, my maisters, and citizens of ROME: the reason is alike betweene the Senate & you. For matters being wel digested, & their counsells throughly examined, touching the benefite of the common wealth: the Senatours are cause of the common commoditie that commeth vnto euery one of you.

The fable is of Oriental origin. It made its way somehow into Roman history of the legendary period and is attached to Menenius by Livy (ii, 32) and Plutarch. Camden tells it in his *Remaines* (1605). Of course Shakespeare could read Livy.

THE TRAGEDY OF CORIOLANUS

[Dramatis Personæ.

Caius Marcius, afterwards *Caius Marcius Coriolanus.*
Titus Lartius, / *Cominius,* — Generals against the Volscians.
Menenius Agrippa, friend to *Coriolanus.*
Sicinius Velutus, / *Junius Brutus,* — Tribunes of the People.
Young Marcius, son to *Coriolanus.*
A Roman Herald.
Nicanor, a Roman.
Tullus Aufidius, General of the Volscians.
Lieutenant to *Aufidius.*
Conspirators with *Aufidius.*
Adrian, a Volscian.
A Citizen of Antium.
Two Volscian Guards.

Volumnia, mother to *Coriolanus.*
Virgilia, wife to *Coriolanus.*
Valeria, friend to *Virgilia.*
Gentlewoman, attending on *Virgilia.*

Senators (Roman and Volscian), Patricians, Ædiles, Lictors, Soldiers, Citizens, Messengers, Servants to Aufidius, Attendants.

SCENE. — *Rome and the neighbourhood; Corioles (Corioli) and the neighbourhood; Antium.*]

ACT I. Scene I. [*Rome. A street.*]

Enter a company of mutinous *Citizens,* with staves, clubs, and other weapons.

1. Cit. Before we proceed any further, hear me speak.

All. Speak, speak!

1. Cit. You are all resolv'd rather to die than to famish?

All. Resolv'd, resolv'd!

1. Cit. First, you know Caius Marcius is chief enemy to the people.

All. We know't, we know't!

1. Cit. Let us kill him, and we'll have corn at our own price. Is't a verdict?

All. No more talking on't! Let it be done! Away, away!

2. Cit. One word, good citizens.

1. Cit. We are accounted poor citizens, the patricians good. What authority surfeits on would relieve us. If they would yield us but the superfluity while it were wholesome, we might guess they relieved us humanely; but they think we are too dear. The leanness that afflicts us, the object of our misery, is as an inventory to particularize their abundance; our sufferance is a gain to them. Let us revenge this with our pikes ere we become rakes; for the gods know I speak this in hunger for bread, not in thirst for revenge.

2. Cit. Would you proceed especially against Caius Marcius?

1. Cit. Against him first. He's a very dog to the commonalty.

2. Cit. Consider you what services he has done for his country?

1. Cit. Very well, and could be content to give him good report for't but that he pays himself with being proud.

2. Cit. Nay, but speak not maliciously.

1. Cit. I say unto you, what he hath done famously, he did it to that end. Though soft-conscienc'd men can be content to say it was for his country, he did it to please his mother and to be partly proud, which he is, even to the altitude of his virtue.

2. Cit. What he cannot help in his nature, you account a vice in him. You must in no way say he is covetous.

1. Cit. If I must not, I need not be barren of accusations. He hath faults (with surplus) to tire in repetition.

Shouts within.

What shouts are these? The other side o' th' city is risen. Why stay we prating here? To th' Capitol!

All. Come, come!

1. Cit. Soft! who comes here?

Enter *Menenius Agrippa.*

2. Cit. Worthy Menenius Agrippa, one that hath always lov'd the people.

1. Cit. He's one honest enough. Would all the rest were so!

Men. What work's, my countrymen, in hand? Where go you
With bats and clubs? The matter? Speak, I pray you.

2. Cit. Our business is not unknown to th' Senate. They have had inkling this fortnight what we intend to do, which now we'll show 'em in deeds. They say poor suitors have strong breaths; they shall know we have strong arms too.

Men. Why, masters, my good friends, mine honest neighbours,
Will you undo yourselves?

2. Cit. We cannot, sir; we are undone already.

Men. I tell you, friends, most charitable care
Have the patricians of you. For your wants,
Your suffering in this dearth, you may as well
Strike at the heaven with your staves as lift them
Against the Roman state; whose course will on
The way it takes, cracking ten thousand curbs
Of more strong link asunder than can ever
Appear in your impediment. For the dearth,
The gods, not the patricians, make it, and
Your knees to them (not arms) must help. Alack!
You are transported by calamity
Thither where more attends you; and you slander
The helms o' th' state, who care for you like fathers,
When you curse them as enemies.

2. Cit. Care for us? True indeed! They ne'er car'd for us yet: suffer us to famish, and their storehouses cramm'd with grain; make edicts for usury, to support usurers; repeal daily any wholesome act established against the rich, and provide more piercing statutes daily to chain up and restrain the poor. If the wars eat us not up, they will; and there's all the love they bear us.

Men. Either you must
Confess yourselves wondrous malicious
Or be accus'd of folly. I shall tell you
A pretty tale. It may be you have heard it;
But since it serves my purpose, I will venture
To stale't a little more.

2. Cit. Well, I'll hear it, sir; yet you must not think to fob off our disgrace with a tale. But, an't please you, deliver.

Men. There was a time when all the body's members
Rebell'd against the belly; thus accus'd it:
That only like a gulf it did remain
I' th' midst o' th' body, idle and unactive,
Still cupboarding the viand, never bearing
Like labour with the rest; where th' other instruments
Did see and hear, devise, instruct, walk, feel,
And, mutually participate, did minister
Unto the appetite and affection common
Of the whole body. The belly answer'd.

2. Cit. Well, sir, what answer made the belly?

Men. Sir, I shall tell you. With a kind of smile,
Which ne'er came from the lungs, but even thus —
For look you, I may make the belly smile
As well as speak — it tauntingly replied
To th' discontented members, the mutinous parts
That envied his receipt; even so most fitly
As you malign our senators for that
They are not such as you.

2. Cit. Your belly's answer? What?
The kingly crowned head, the vigilant eye,
The counsellor heart, the arm our soldier,
Our steed the leg, the tongue our trumpeter,
With other muniments and petty helps
In this our fabric, if that they —

Men. What then?
Fore me, this fellow speaks! What then? What then?

2. Cit. Should by the cormorant belly be restrain'd,
Who is the sink o' th' body —

Men. Well, what then?

2. Cit. The former agents, if they did complain,
What could the belly answer?

Men. I will tell you;
If you'll bestow a small (of what you have little)
Patience awhile, you'st hear the belly's answer.

2. Cit. Y'are long about it.

Men. Note me this, good friend:
Your most grave belly was deliberate,
Not rash like his accusers, and thus answer'd:
'True is it, my incorporate friends,' quoth he,
'That I receive the general food at first
Which you do live upon; and fit it is,
Because I am the storehouse and the shop
Of the whole body. But, if you do remember,
I send it through the rivers of your blood
Even to the court, the heart, to th' seat o' th' brain,
And, through the cranks and offices of man,
The strongest nerves and small inferior veins

From me receive that natural competency
Whereby they live. And though that all at once
You, my good friends' — This says the belly. Mark me.

2. Cit. Ay, sir, well, well.

Men. 'Though all at once cannot
See what I do deliver out to each,
Yet I can make my audit up, that all
From me do back receive the flour of all
And leave me but the bran.' What say you to't?

2. Cit. It was an answer. How apply you this?

Men. The senators of Rome are this good belly,
And you the mutinous members. For, examine
Their counsels and their cares, disgest things rightly
Touching the weal o' th' common, you shall find
No public benefit which you receive
But it proceeds or comes from them to you,
And no way from yourselves. What do you think,
You, the great toe of this assembly?

2. Cit. I the great toe? Why the great toe?

Men. For that, being one o' th' lowest, basest, poorest
Of this most wise rebellion, thou goest foremost.
Thou rascal, that art worst in blood to run,
Lead'st first to win some vantage.
But make you ready your stiff bats and clubs.
Rome and her rats are at the point of battle;
The one side must have bale.

Enter *Caius Marcius.*

Hail, noble Marcius!

Mar. Thanks. What's the matter, you dissentious rogues
That, rubbing the poor itch of your opinion,
Make yourselves scabs?

2. Cit. We have ever your good word.

Mar. He that will give good words to thee will flatter
Beneath abhorring. What would you have, you curs,
That like nor peace nor war? The one affrights you,
The other makes you proud. He that trusts to you,
Where he should find you lions, finds you hares;
Where foxes, geese. You are no surer, no,
Than is the coal of fire upon the ice
Or hailstone in the sun. Your virtue is
To make him worthy whose offence subdues him,
And curse that justice did it. Who deserves greatness
Deserves your hate; and your affections are
A sick man's appetite, who desires most that
Which would increase his evil. He that depends
Upon your favours swims with fins of lead
And hews down oaks with rushes. Hang ye! Trust ye?
With every minute you do change a mind
And call him noble that was now your hate,
Him vile that was your garland. What's the matter
That in these several places of the city
You cry against the noble Senate, who
(Under the gods) keep you in awe, which else
Would feed on one another? What's their seeking?

Men. For corn at their own rates, whereof they say
The city is well stor'd.

Mar. Hang 'em! They say?
They'll sit by th' fire and presume to know
What's done i' th' Capitol, who's like to rise,
Who thrives and who declines; side factions and give out
Conjectural marriages, making parties strong
And feebling such as stand not in their liking
Below their cobbled shoes. They say there's grain enough?
Would the nobility lay aside their ruth
And let me use my sword, I'd make a quarry
With thousands of these quarter'd slaves as high
As I could pick my lance.

Men. Nay, these are almost thoroughly persuaded;
For though abundantly they lack discretion,
Yet are they passing cowardly. But I beseech you,
What says the other troop?

Mar. They are dissolv'd. Hang 'em!
They said they were anhungry; sigh'd forth proverbs —
That hunger broke stone walls, that dogs must eat,
That meat was made for mouths, that the gods sent not
Corn for the rich men only. With these shreds
They vented their complainings; which being answer'd
And a petition granted them, a strange one,
To break the heart of generosity
And make bold power look pale, they threw their caps

As they would hang them on the horns o' th' moon,
Shouting their emulation.

Men. What is granted them?

Mar. Five tribunes to defend their vulgar wisdoms
Of their own choice. One's Junius Brutus,
Sicinius Velutus, and I know not — 'Sdeath!
The rabble should have first unroof'd the city
Ere so prevail'd with me. It will in time
Win upon power and throw forth greater themes
For insurrection's arguing.

Men. This is strange.

Mar. Go get you home, you fragments!

Enter a *Messenger* hastily.

Mess. Where's Caius Marcius?

Mar. Here. What's the matter?

Mess. The news is, sir, the Volsces are in arms.

Mar. I am glad on't. Then we shall ha' means to vent
Our musty superfluity. See, our best elders.

Enter *Cominius, Titus Lartius,* with other *Senators*; *Sicinius Velutus, Junius Brutus.*

1. Sen. Marcius, 'tis true that you have lately told us:
The Volsces are in arms.

Mar. They have a leader,
Tullus Aufidius, that will put you to't.
I sin in envying his nobility;
And were I anything but what I am,
I would wish me only he.

Com. You have fought together?

Mar. Were half to half the world by th' ears, and he
Upon my party, I'd revolt, to make
Only my wars with him. He is a lion
That I am proud to hunt.

1. Sen. Then, worthy Marcius,
Attend upon Cominius to these wars.

Com. It is your former promise.

Mar. Sir, it is,
And I am constant. Titus Lartius, thou
Shalt see me once more strike at Tullus' face.
What, art thou stiff? Stand'st out?

Tit. No, Caius Marcius.
I'll lean upon one crutch and fight with t'other
Ere stay behind this business.

Men. O, true-bred!

1. Sen. Your company to th' Capitol, where I know
Our greatest friends attend us.

Tit. [*to Cominius*] Lead you on.
[*To Marcius*] Follow Cominius. We must follow you;
Right worthy you priority.

Com. Noble Marcius!

1. Sen. [*to the Citizens*] Hence to your homes! be gone!

Mar. Nay, let them follow.
The Volsces have much corn. Take these rats thither
To gnaw their garners. Worshipful mutiners,
Your valour puts well forth. Pray follow.

Exeunt. Citizens steal away. Manent Sicinius and Brutus.

Sic. Was ever man so proud as is this Marcius?

Bru. He has no equal.

Sic. When we were chosen tribunes for the people —

Bru. Mark'd you his lip and eyes?

Sic. Nay, but his taunts!

Bru. Being mov'd, he will not spare to gird the gods.

Sic. Bemock the modest moon.

Bru. The present wars devour him! He is grown
Too proud to be so valiant.

Sic. Such a nature,
Tickled with good success, disdains the shadow
Which he treads on at noon. But I do wonder
His insolence can brook to be commanded
Under Cominius.

Bru. Fame, at the which he aims,
In whom already he's well grac'd, cannot
Better be held nor more attain'd than by
A place below the first; for what miscarries
Shall be the general's fault, though he perform
To th' utmost of a man, and giddy censure
Will then cry out of Marcius, 'O, if he
Had borne the business!'

Sic. Besides, if things go well,
Opinion, that so sticks on Marcius, shall
Of his demerits rob Cominius.

Bru. Come.
Half all Cominius' honours are to Marcius,
Though Marcius earn'd them not; and all his faults
To Marcius shall be honours, though indeed
In aught he merit not.

Sic. Let's hence and hear
How the dispatch is made and in what fashion,
More than his singularity, he goes
Upon this present action.

Bru. Let's along. *Exeunt.*

[Scene II. *Corioles. The Senate House.*]

Enter *Tullus Aufidius* with *Senators of Corioles.*

1. Sen. So, your opinion is, Aufidius,
That they of Rome are ent'red in our counsels
And know how we proceed.
Auf. Is it not yours?
What ever have been thought on in this state
That could be brought to bodily act ere Rome
Had circumvention? 'Tis not four days gone
Since I heard thence. These are the words. I think
I have the letter here. Yes, here it is:
'They have press'd a power, but it is not known
Whether for east or west. The dearth is great,
The people mutinous; and it is rumour'd,
Cominius, Marcius your old enemy
(Who is of Rome worse hated than of you),
And Titus Lartius, a most valiant Roman,
These three lead on this preparation
Whither 'tis bent. Most likely 'tis for you.
Consider of it.'
1. Sen. Our army 's in the field.
We never yet made doubt but Rome was ready
To answer us.
Auf. Nor did you think it folly
To keep your great pretences veil'd till when
They needs must show themselves, which in the hatching,
It seem'd, appear'd to Rome. By the discovery
We shall be short'ned in our aim, which was
To take in many towns ere (almost) Rome
Should know we were afoot.
2. Sen. Noble Aufidius,
Take your commission; hie you to your bands.
Let us alone to guard Corioles.
If they set down before 's, for the remove
Bring up your army; but, I think, you'll find
Th' have not prepar'd for us.
Auf. O, doubt not that!
I speak from certainties. Nay more,
Some parcels of their power are forth already
And only hitherward. I leave your honours.
If we and Caius Marcius chance to meet,
'Tis sworn between us we shall ever strike
Till one can do no more.
All. The gods assist you!
Auf. And keep your honours safe!
1. Sen. Farewell.
2. Sen. Farewell.
All. Farewell. *Exeunt omnes.*

[Scene III. *Rome. A room in the house of* Marcius.]

Enter *Volumnia* and *Virgilia,* mother and wife to *Marcius.* They set them down on two low stools and sew.

Vol. I pray you, daughter, sing, or express yourself in a more comfortable sort. If my son were my husband, I should freelier rejoice in that absence wherein he won honour than in the embracements of his bed where he would show most love. When yet he was but tender-bodied and the only son of my womb, when youth with comeliness pluck'd all gaze his way, when for a day of kings' entreaties a mother should not sell him an hour from her beholding, I (considering how honour would become such a person; that it was no better than picture-like to hang by th' wall, if renown made it not stir) was pleas'd to let him seek danger where he was like to find fame. To a cruel war I sent him, from whence he return'd, his brows bound with oak. I tell thee, daughter, I sprang not more in joy at first hearing he was a man-child than now in first seeing he had proved himself a man.

Vir. But had he died in the business, madam, how then?

Vol. Then his good report should have been my son; I therein would have found issue. Hear me profess sincerely, had I a dozen sons, each in my love alike, and none less dear than thine and my good Marcius, I had rather had eleven die nobly for their country than one voluptuously surfeit out of action.

Enter a *Gentlewoman.*

Gent. Madam, the Lady Valeria is come to visit you.

Vir. Beseech you give me leave to retire myself.

Vol. Indeed you shall not.
Methinks I hear hither your husband's drum;
See him pluck Aufidius down by th' hair;
As children from a bear, the Volsces shunning him.
Methinks I see him stamp thus, and call thus:
'Come on, you cowards! You were got in fear,
Though you were born in Rome.' His bloody brow
With his mail'd hand then wiping, forth he goes,
Like to a harvestman that's task'd to mow
Or all or lose his hire.
Vir. His bloody brow? O Jupiter, no blood!

Vol. Away, you fool! It more becomes a man
Than gilt his trophy. The breasts of Hecuba
When she did suckle Hector, look'd not lovelier
Than Hector's forehead when it spit forth blood
At Grecian sword, contemning. Tell Valeria
We are fit to bid her welcome.

Exit Gentlewoman.

Vir. Heavens bless my lord from fell Aufidius!

Vol. He'll beat Aufidius' head below his knee
And tread upon his neck.

Enter *Valeria* (with an *Usher*) and a *Gentlewoman.*

Val. My ladies both, good day to you.

Vol. Sweet madam!

Vir. I am glad to see your ladyship.

Val. How do you both? You are manifest housekeepers. What are you sewing here? A fine spot, in good faith. How does your little son?

Vir. I thank your ladyship; well, good madam.

Vol. He had rather see the swords and hear a drum than look upon his schoolmaster.

Val. O' my word, the father's son! I'll swear 'tis a very pretty boy. O' my troth, I look'd upon him a Wednesday half an hour together. Has such a confirm'd countenance! I saw him run after a gilded butterfly; and when he caught it, he let it go again, and after it again, and over and over he comes, and up again; catch'd it again; or whether his fall enrag'd him or how 'twas, he did so set his teeth and tear it! O, I warrant, how he mammock'd it!

Vol. One on 's father's moods.

Val. Indeed, la, 'tis a noble child.

Vir. A crack, madam.

Val. Come, lay aside your stitchery. I must have you play the idle housewife with me this afternoon.

Vir. No, good madam. I will not out of doors.

Val. Not out of doors?

Vol. She shall, she shall!

Vir. Indeed, no, by your patience. I'll not over the threshold till my lord return from the wars.

Val. Fie, you confine yourself most unreasonably. Come, you must go visit the good lady that lies in.

Vir. I will wish her speedy strength and visit her with my prayers, but I cannot go thither.

Vol. Why, I pray you?

Vir. 'Tis not to save labour nor that I want love.

Val. You would be another Penelope. Yet, they say, all the yarn she spun in Ulysses' absence did but fill Ithaca full of moths. Come, I would your cambric were sensible as your finger, that you might leave pricking it for pity. Come, you shall go with us.

Vir. No, good madam, pardon me. Indeed I will not forth.

Val. In truth, la, go with me, and I'll tell you excellent news of your husband.

Vir. O, good madam, there can be none yet.

Val. Verily I do not jest with you. There came news from him last night.

Vir. Indeed, madam?

Val. In earnest, it's true; I heard a senator speak it. Thus it is: the Volsces have an army forth; against whom Cominius the general is gone with one part of our Roman power. Your lord and Titus Lartius are set down before their city Corioles. They nothing doubt prevailing and to make it brief wars. This is true, on mine honour; and so I pray go with us.

Vir. Give me excuse, good madam. I will obey you in everything hereafter.

Vol. Let her alone, lady. As she is now, she will but disease our better mirth.

Val. In troth, I think she would. — Fare you well then. — Come, good sweet lady. — Prithee, Virgilia, turn thy solemness out o' door and go along with us.

Vir. No, at a word, madam. Indeed I must not. I wish you much mirth.

Val. Well then, farewell.

Exeunt Ladies.

[Scene IV. *Before Corioles.*]

Enter *Marcius, Titus Lartius,* with *Drum* and *Colours,* with *Captains* and *Soldiers,* as before the city Corioles: to them a *Messenger.*

Mar. Yonder comes news. A wager they have met.

Lart. My horse to yours, no.

Mar. 'Tis done.

Lart. Agreed.

Mar. Say, has our general met the enemy?

Mess. They lie in view, but have not spoke as yet.

Lart. So, the good horse is mine.

Mar. I'll buy him of you.

Lart. No, I'll nor sell nor give him. Lend you him I will
For half a hundred years. Summon the town.
Mar. How far off lie these armies?
Mess. Within this mile and half.
Mar. Then shall we hear their 'larum and they ours.
Now, Mars, I prithee make us quick in work,
That we with smoking swords may march from hence
To help our fielded friends! Come, blow thy blast.

They sound a parley. Enter two *Senators* with others on the walls of Corioles.

Tullus Aufidius, is he within your walls?
1. Sen. No, nor a man that fears you less than he.
That's lesser than a little. *Drum afar off.* Hark, our drums
Are bringing forth our youth! We'll break our walls
Rather than they shall pound us up. Our gates,
Which yet seem shut, we have but pinn'd with rushes;
They'll open of themselves. *Alarum far off.* Hark you, far off!
There is Aufidius. List what work he makes
Amongst your cloven army.
Mar. O, they are at it!
Lart. Their noise be our instruction. Ladders, ho!

Enter the *Army* of the *Volsces.*

Mar. They fear us not, but issue forth their city.
Now put your shields before your hearts, and fight
With hearts more proof than shields. Advance, brave Titus.
They do disdain us much beyond our thoughts,
Which makes me sweat with wrath. Come on, my fellows.
He that retires, I'll take him for a Volsce,
And he shall feel mine edge.

Alarum. The Romans are beat back to their trenches. Enter *Marcius,* cursing.

Mar. All the contagion of the South light on you,
You shames of Rome! you herd of — Biles and plagues
Plaster you o'er, that you may be abhorr'd
Farther than seen and one infect another
Against the wind a mile! You souls of geese
That bear the shapes of men, how have you run
From slaves that apes would beat! Pluto and hell!
All hurt behind! backs red, and faces pale
With flight and agued fear! Mend and charge home,
Or, by the fires of heaven, I'll leave the foe
And make my wars on you! Look to't. Come on!
If you'll stand fast, we'll beat them to their wives,
As they us to our trenches. Follow me!

Another alarum. [The Volsces retire,] and Marcius follows them to gates, and is shut in.

So, now the gates are ope. Now prove good seconds.
'Tis for the followers fortune widens them,
Not for the fliers. Mark me and do the like.

Enter the gates.

1. Sol. Foolhardiness! Not I.
2. Sol. Nor I.
1. Sol. See, they have shut him in.

Alarum continues.

All. To th' pot, I warrant him.

Enter *Titus Lartius.*

Lart. What is become of Marcius?
All. Slain, sir, doubtless.
1. Sol. Following the fliers at the very heels,
With them he enters; who upon the sudden
Clapp'd to their gates. He is himself alone,
To answer all the city.
Lart. O noble fellow!
Who sensibly outdares his senseless sword
And when it bows, stand'st up! Thou art lost, Marcius.
A carbuncle entire, as big as thou art,
Were not so rich a jewel. Thou wast a soldier
Even to Cato's wish, not fierce and terrible
Only in strokes, but with thy grim looks and
The thunder-like percussion of thy sounds
Thou mad'st thine enemies shake, as if the world
Were feverous and did tremble.

Enter *Marcius,* bleeding, assaulted by the *Enemy.*

1. Sol. Look, sir.
Lart. O, 'tis Marcius!
Let's fetch him off or make remain alike.

They fight, and all enter the city.

[Scene V. *Corioles. A street.*]

Enter certain *Romans* with spoils.

1. Rom. This will I carry to Rome.
2. Rom. And I this.
3. Rom. A murrain on't! I took this for silver.

Alarum continues still afar off.

Enter *Marcius* and *Titus* [*Lartius*] with a *Trumpet*.

Mar. See here these movers that do prize their honours
At a crack'd drachma! Cushions, leaden spoons,
Irons of a doit, doublets that hangmen would
Bury with those that wore them, these base slaves,
Ere yet the fight be done, pack up. Down with them!

Exeunt [*the Spoilers*].

And hark, what noise the general makes! To him!
There is the man of my soul's hate, Aufidius,
Piercing our Romans. Thou, valiant Titus, take
Convenient numbers to make good the city,
Whilst I, with those that have the spirit, will haste
To help Cominius.
Lart. Worthy sir, thou bleed'st.
Thy exercise hath been too violent for
A second course of fight.
Mar. Sir, praise me not.
My work hath yet not warm'd me. Fare you well.
The blood I drop is rather physical
Than dangerous to me. To Aufidius thus
I will appear and fight.
Lart. Now the fair goddess Fortune
Fall deep in love with thee, and her great charms
Misguide thy opposers' swords! Bold gentleman,
Prosperity be thy page!
Mar. Thy friend no less
Than those she placeth highest! So farewell.
Lart. Thou worthiest Marcius!

[*Exit Marcius.*]

Go sound thy trumpet in the market place.
Call thither all the officers o' th' town,
Where they shall know our mind. Away!

Exeunt.

[Scene VI. *Near the camp of* Cominius.]

Enter *Cominius* as it were in retire, with *Soldiers*.

Com. Breathe you, my friends. Well fought! We are come off
Like Romans, neither foolish in our stands
Nor cowardly in retire. Believe me, sirs,
We shall be charg'd again. Whiles we have struck,
By interims and conveying gusts we have heard
The charges of our friends. Ye Roman gods,
Lead their successes as we wish our own,
That both our powers, with smiling fronts encount'ring,
May give you thankful sacrifice!

Enter a *Messenger*.

Thy news?
Mess. The citizens of Corioles have issued
And given to Lartius and to Marcius battle.
I saw our party to their trenches driven,
And then I came away.
Com. Though thou speakest truth,
Methinks thou speak'st not well. How long is't since?
Mess. Above an hour, my lord.
Com. 'Tis not a mile; briefly we heard their drums.
How couldst thou in a mile confound an hour
And bring thy news so late?
Mess. Spies of the Volsces
Held me in chase, that I was forc'd to wheel
Three or four miles about. Else had I, sir,
Half an hour since brought my report.

Enter *Marcius*.

Com. Who's yonder
That does appear as he were flay'd? O gods!
He has the stamp of Marcius, and I have
Beforetime seen him thus.
Mar. Come I too late?
Com. The shepherd knows not thunder from a tabor
More than I know the sound of Marcius' tongue
From every meaner man.
Mar. Come I too late?
Com. Ay, if you come not in the blood of others,
But mantled in your own.
Mar. O, let me clip ye
In arms as sound as when I woo'd, in heart
As merry as when our nuptial day was done
And tapers burn'd to bedward!

Com. Flower of warriors!
How is't with Titus Lartius?
Mar. As with a man busied about decrees:
Condemning some to death, and some to exile;
Ransoming him or pitying, threat'ning th' other;
Holding Corioles in the name of Rome
Even like a fawning greyhound in the leash,
To let him slip at will.
Com. Where is that slave
Which told me they had beat you to your trenches?
Where is he? Call him hither.
Mar. Let him alone.
He did inform the truth. But for our gentlemen,
The common file (a plague! tribunes for them!),
The mouse ne'er shunn'd the cat as they did budge
From rascals worse than they.
Com. But how prevail'd you?
Mar. Will the time serve to tell? I do not think.
Where is the enemy? Are you lords o' th' field?
If not, why cease you till you are so?
Com. Marcius,
We have at disadvantage fought, and did
Retire to win our purpose.
Mar. How lies their battle? Know you on which side
They have plac'd their men of trust?
Com. As I guess, Marcius,
Their bands i' th' vaward are the Antiates,
Of their best trust; o'er them Aufidius,
Their very heart of hope.
Mar. I do beseech you,
By all the battles wherein we have fought,
By th' blood we have shed together, by th' vows
We have made to endure friends, that you directly
Set me against Aufidius and his Antiates;
And that you not delay the present, but,
Filling the air with swords advanc'd and darts,
We prove this very hour.
Com. Though I could wish
You were conducted to a gentle bath
And balms applied to you, yet dare I never
Deny your asking. Take your choice of those
That best can aid your action.
Mar. Those are they
That most are willing. If any such be here
(As it were sin to doubt) that love this painting
Wherein you see me smear'd; if any fear
Lesser his person than an ill report;
If any think brave death outweighs bad life
And that his country's dearer than himself,
Let him alone, or so many so minded,
Wave thus to express his disposition,
And follow Marcius.

They all shout and wave their swords, take him up in their arms and cast up their caps.

O, me alone? Make you a sword of me?
If these shows be not outward, which of you
But is four Volsces? None of you but is
Able to bear against the great Aufidius
A shield as hard as his. A certain number
(Though thanks to all) must I select. The rest
Shall bear the business in some other fight,
As cause will be obey'd. Please you to march;
And I shall quickly draw out my command,
Which men are best inclin'd.
Com. March on, my fellows.
Make good this ostentation, and you shall
Divide in all with us. *Exeunt.*

[Scene VII. *The gates of Corioles.*]

Titus Lartius, having set a guard upon Corioles, going with *Drum* and *Trumpet* toward *Cominius* and *Caius Marcius*, enters with a *Lieutenant*, other *Soldiers*, and a *Scout*.

Lart. So, let the ports be guarded. Keep your duties
As I have set them down. If I do send, dispatch
Those centuries to our aid; the rest will serve
For a short holding. If we lose the field,
We cannot keep the town.
Lieut. Fear not our care, sir.
Lart. Hence, and shut your gates upon's.
Our guider, come; to th' Roman camp conduct us. *Exeunt.*

[Scene VIII. *A field of battle between the Roman and the Volscian camp.*]

Alarum, as in battle. Enter *Marcius* and *Aufidius* at several doors.

Mar. I'll fight with none but thee, for I do hate thee
Worse than a promise-breaker.
Auf. We hate alike.
Not Afric owns a serpent I abhor
More than thy fame and envy. Fix thy foot.

Mar. Let the first budger die the other's slave,
And the gods doom him after!
Auf. If I fly, Marcius,
Holloa me like a hare.
Mar. Within these three hours, Tullus,
Alone I fought in your Corioles walls
And made what work I pleas'd. 'Tis not my blood
Wherein thou seest me mask'd. For thy revenge
Wrench up thy power to th' highest.
Auf. Wert thou the Hector
That was the whip of your bragg'd progeny,
Thou shouldst not scape me here.

Here they fight, and certain Volsces come in the aid of Aufidius. Marcius fights till they be driven in breathless.

Officious, and not valiant! you have sham'd me
In your condemned seconds. [*Exeunt.*]

[Scene IX. *The Roman camp.*]

Flourish. Alarum. A retreat is sounded. Enter, at one door, *Cominius* with the *Romans*; at another door, *Marcius*, with his arm in a scarf.

Com. If I should tell thee o'er this thy day's work,
Thou't not believe thy deeds; but I'll report it
Where senators shall mingle tears with smiles;
Where great patricians shall attend and shrug,
I' th' end admire; where ladies shall be frighted
And, gladly quak'd, hear more; where the dull tribunes,
That with the fusty plebeians hate thine honours,
Shall say, against their hearts, 'We thank the gods
Our Rome hath such a soldier!'
Yet cam'st thou to a morsel of this feast,
Having fully din'd before.

Enter *Titus* [*Lartius*] with his *Power*, from the pursuit.

Lart. O General,
Here is the steed, we the caparison.
Hadst thou beheld —
Mar. Pray now, no more. My mother,
Who has a charter to extol her blood,
When she does praise me grieves me. I have done
As you have done — that's what I can; induc'd
As you have been — that's for my country.
He that has but effected his good will
Hath overta'en mine act.
Com. You shall not be
The grave of your deserving. Rome must know
The value of her own. 'Twere a concealment
Worse than a theft, no less than a traducement,
To hide your doings and to silence that
Which, to the spire and top of praises vouch'd,
Would seem but modest. Therefore, I beseech you
(In sign of what you are, not to reward
What you have done) before our army hear me.
Mar. I have some wounds upon me, and they smart
To hear themselves rememb'red.
Com. Should they not,
Well might they fester 'gainst ingratitude
And tent themselves with death. Of all the horses
(Whereof we have ta'en good, and good store), of all
The treasure in this field achiev'd and city,
We render you the tenth, to be ta'en forth
Before the common distribution at
Your only choice.
Mar. I thank you, General,
But cannot make my heart consent to take
A bribe to pay my sword. I do refuse it
And stand upon my common part with those
That have beheld the doing.

A long flourish. They all cry, 'Marcius! Marcius!' *cast up their caps and lances. Cominius and Lartius stand bare.*

May these same instruments which you profane
Never sound more! When drums and trumpets shall
I' th' field prove flatterers, let courts and cities be
Made all of false-fac'd soothing! When steel grows
Soft as the parasite's silk, let him be made
A coverture for th' wars! No more, I say!
For that I have not wash'd my nose that bled
Or foil'd some debile wretch (which without note
Here's many else have done), you shout me forth
In acclamations hyperbolical,
As if I lov'd my little should be dieted
In praises sauc'd with lies.
Com. Too modest are you,
More cruel to your good report than grateful
To us that give you truly. By your patience,

If 'gainst yourself you be incens'd, we'll put you
(Like one that means his proper harm) in manacles,
Then reason safely with you. Therefore be it known,
As to us, to all the world, that Caius Marcius
Wears this war's garland; in token of the which,
My noble steed, known to the camp, I give him
With all his trim belonging; and from this time,
For what he did before Corioles, call him,
With all th' applause and clamour of the host,
Caius Marcius Coriolanus. Bear
Th' addition nobly ever!

Flourish. Trumpets sound and drums.

Omnes. Caius Marcius Coriolanus!

Mar. I will go wash;
And when my face is fair, you shall perceive
Whether I blush or no. Howbeit, I thank you.
I mean to stride your steed, and at all times
To undercrest your good addition
To th' fairness of my power.

Com. So, to our tent,
Where, ere we do repose us, we will write
To Rome of our success. You, Titus Lartius,
Must to Corioles back. Send us to Rome
The best, with whom we may articulate
For their own good and ours.

Lart. I shall, my lord.

Mar. The gods begin to mock me. I, that now
Refus'd most princely gifts, am bound to beg
Of my Lord General.

Com. Take't; 'tis yours. What is't?

Mar. I sometime lay here in Corioles
At a poor man's house; he us'd me kindly.
He cried to me; I saw him prisoner;
But then Aufidius was within my view,
And wrath o'erwhelm'd my pity. I request you
To give my poor host freedom.

Com. O, well begg'd!
Were he the butcher of my son, he should
Be free as is the wind. Deliver him, Titus.

Lart. Marcius, his name?

Mar. By Jupiter, forgot!
I am weary; yea, my memory is tir'd.
Have we no wine here?

Com. Go we to our tent.
The blood upon your visage dries; 'tis time
It should be look'd to. Come. *Exeunt.*

[Scene X. *The camp of the Volsces.*]

A flourish. Cornets. Enter *Tullus Aufidius* bloody, with two or three *Soldiers.*

Auf. The town is ta'en!

Soldier. 'Twill be deliver'd back on good condition.

Auf. Condition?
I would I were a Roman; for I cannot,
Being a Volsce, be that I am. Condition?
What good condition can a treaty find
I' th' part that is at mercy? Five times, Marcius,
I have fought with thee. So often hast thou beat me;
And wouldst do so, I think, should we encounter
As often as we eat. By th' elements,
If e'er again I meet him beard to beard,
He's mine, or I am his. Mine emulation
Hath not that honour in't it had; for where
I thought to crush him in an equal force,
True sword to sword, I'll potch at him some way.
Or wrath or craft may get him.

Soldier. He's the devil.

Auf. Bolder, though not so subtle. My valour's poison'd
With only suff'ring stain by him; for him
Shall fly out of itself. Nor sleep nor sanctuary,
Being naked, sick, nor fane nor Capitol,
The prayers of priests nor times of sacrifice,
Embargements all of fury, shall lift up
Their rotten privilege and custom 'gainst
My hate to Marcius. Where I find him, were it
At home, upon my brother's guard, even there,
Against the hospitable canon, would I
Wash my fierce hand in's heart. Go you to th' city.
Learn how 'tis held, and what they are that must
Be hostages for Rome.

Soldier. Will not you go?

Auf. I am attended at the cypress grove.
I pray you
('Tis south the city mills) bring me word thither
How the world goes, that to the pace of it
I may spur on my journey.

Soldier. I shall, sir. [*Exeunt.*]

ACT II. [Scene I. *Rome. A public place.*]

Enter *Menenius*, with the two *Tribunes of the People, Sicinius* and *Brutus.*

Men. The augurer tells me we shall have news to-night.

Bru. Good or bad?

Men. Not according to the prayer of the people, for they love not Marcius.

Sic. Nature teaches beasts to know their friends.

Men. Pray you, who does the wolf love?

Sic. The lamb.

Men. Ay, to devour him, as the hungry plebeians would the noble Marcius.

Bru. He's a lamb indeed, that baes like a bear.

Men. He's a bear indeed, that lives like a lamb. You two are old men. Tell me one thing I shall ask you.

Both. Well, sir.

Men. In what enormity is Marcius poor in that you two have not in abundance?

Bru. He's poor in no one fault, but stor'd with all.

Sic. Especially in pride.

Bru. And topping all others in boasting.

Men. This is strange now. Do you two know how you are censured here in the city, I mean of us o' th' right-hand file? Do you?

Both. Why, how are we censur'd?

Men. Because you talk of pride now — Will you not be angry?

Both. Well, well, sir, well.

Men. Why, 'tis no great matter, for a very little thief of occasion will rob you of a great deal of patience. Give your dispositions the reins and be angry at your pleasures — at the least, if you take it as a pleasure to you in being so. You blame Marcius for being proud.

Bru. We do it not alone, sir.

Men. I know you can do very little alone; for your helps are many, or else your actions would grow wondrous single. Your abilities are too infant-like for doing much alone. You talk of pride. O that you could turn your eyes toward the napes of your necks and make but an interior survey of your good selves! O that you could!

Both. What then, sir?

Men. Why, then you should discover a brace of unmeriting, proud, violent, testy magistrates (alias fools) as any in Rome.

Sic. Menenius, you are known well enough too.

Men. I am known to be a humorous patrician, and one that loves a cup of hot wine with not a drop of allaying Tiber in't; said to be something imperfect in favouring the first complaint, hasty and tinder-like upon too trivial motion; one that converses more with the buttock of the night than with the forehead of the morning. What I think, I utter, and spend my malice in my breath. Meeting two such wealsmen as you are (I cannot call you Lycurguses), if the drink you give me touch my palate adversely, I make a crooked face at it. I cannot say your worships have deliver'd the matter well when I find the ass in compound with the major part of your syllables; and though I must be content to bear with those that say you are reverend grave men, yet they lie deadly that tell you have good faces. If you see this in the map of my microcosm, follows it that I am known well enough too? What harm can your beesom conspectuities glean out of this character, if I be known well enough too?

Bru. Come, sir, come, we know you well enough.

Men. You know neither me, yourselves, nor anything. You are ambitious for poor knaves' caps and legs. You wear out a good wholesome forenoon in hearing a cause between an orange-wife and a forset-seller, and then rejourn the controversy of threepence to a second day of audience. When you are hearing a matter between party and party, if you chance to be pinch'd with the colic, you make faces like mummers, set up the bloody flag against all patience, and, in roaring for a chamber pot, dismiss the controversy bleeding, the more entangled by your hearing. All the peace you make in their cause is, calling both the parties knaves. You are a pair of strange ones.

Bru. Come, come, you are well understood to be a perfecter giber for the table than a necessary bencher in the Capitol.

Men. Our very priests must become mockers if they shall encounter such ridiculous subjects as you are. When you speak best unto the purpose, it is not worth the wagging of your beards; and your beards deserve not so honourable a grave as to stuff a botcher's cushion or to be entomb'd in an ass's packsaddle. Yet you must be saying Marcius is proud; who, in a cheap estimation, is worth all your predecessors since Deucalion, though peradventure some of the best of 'em were hereditary hangmen. God-den to your worships. More of your conversation would infect my brain, being the herdsmen of the beastly plebeians. I will be bold to take my leave of you.

Brutus and Sicinius aside.

Enter *Volumnia, Virgilia,* and *Valeria.*

How now, my as fair as noble ladies — and the moon, were she earthly, no nobler, whither do you follow your eyes so fast?

Vol. Honourable Menenius, my boy Marcius approaches. For the love of Juno, let's go.

Men. Ha? Marcius coming home?

Vol. Ay, worthy Menenius, and with most prosperous approbation.

Men. Take my cap, Jupiter, and I thank thee. Hoo! Marcius coming home?

2 Ladies. Nay, 'tis true.

Vol. Look, here's a letter from him. The state hath another, his wife another, and, I think, there's one at home for you.

Men. I will make my very house reel tonight. A letter for me?

Vir. Yes, certain, there's a letter for you. I saw't.

Men. A letter for me? It gives me an estate of seven years' health, in which time I will make a lip at the physician. The most sovereign prescription in Galen is but empiricutic and, to this preservative, of no better report than a horse-drench. Is he not wounded? He was wont to come home wounded.

Vir. O, no, no, no!

Vol. O, he is wounded! I thank the gods for't.

Men. So do I too, if it be not too much. Brings 'a victory in his pocket? The wounds become him.

Vol. On's brows. Menenius, he comes the third time home with the oaken garland.

Men. Has he disciplin'd Aufidius soundly?

Vol. Titus Lartius writes they fought together, but Aufidius got off.

Men. And 'twas time for him too, I'll warrant him that. An he had stay'd by him, I would not have been so fidius'd for all the chests in Corioles and the gold that's in them. Is the Senate possess'd of this?

Vol. Good ladies, let's go. Yes, yes, yes! The Senate has letters from the General, wherein he gives my son the whole name of the war. He hath in this action outdone his former deeds doubly.

Val. In troth, there's wondrous things spoke of him.

Men. Wondrous? Ay, I warrant you, and not without his true purchasing.

Vir. The gods grant them true!

Vol. True? Pow, waw!

Men. True? I'll be sworn they are true. Where is he wounded? [*To the Tribunes*] God save your good worships! Marcius is coming home. He has more cause to be proud. — Where is he wounded?

Vol. I' th' shoulder and i' th' left arm. There will be large cicatrices to show the people when he shall stand for his place. He received in the repulse of Tarquin seven hurts i' th' body.

Men. One i' th' neck, and two i' th' thigh. There's nine that I know.

Vol. He had before this last expedition twenty-five wounds upon him.

Men. Now it's twenty-seven. Every gash was an enemy's grave. (*A shout and flourish.*) Hark! the trumpets.

Vol. These are the ushers of Marcius. Before him he carries noise, and behind him he leaves tears.
Death, that dark spirit, in's nervy arm doth lie,
Which, being advanc'd, declines, and then men die.

A sennet. Trumpets sound. Enter *Cominius* the *General* and *Titus Lartius*; between them, *Coriolanus,* crown'd with an oaken garland; with *Captains* and *Soldiers* and a *Herald.*

Herald. Know, Rome, that all alone Marcius did fight
Within Corioles gates, where he hath won,
With fame, a name to Caius Marcius. These
In honour follows Coriolanus. Welcome,
Welcome to Rome, renowned Coriolanus!

Sound. Flourish.

All. Welcome to Rome, renowned Coriolanus!

Cor. No more of this; it does offend my heart.
Pray now, no more.

Com. Look, sir, your mother!

Cor. O,
You have, I know, petition'd all the gods
For my prosperity. *Kneels.*

Vol. Nay, my good soldier, up.
My gentle Marcius, worthy Caius, and
By deed-achieving honour newly nam'd —

What is it — Coriolanus — must I call thee?
But O, thy wife!
Cor. My gracious silence, hail!
Wouldst thou have laugh'd had I come coffin'd home
That weep'st to see me triumph? Ah, my dear,
Such eyes the widows in Corioles wear
And mothers that lack sons.
Men. Now the gods crown thee!
Cor. And live you yet? [*To Valeria*] O my sweet lady, pardon.
Vol. I know not where to turn. O, welcome home!
And welcome, General! and y'are welcome all!
Men. A hundred thousand welcomes! I could weep
And I could laugh; I am light and heavy. Welcome.
A curse begin at very root on's heart
That is not glad to see thee! You are three
That Rome should dote on; yet, by the faith of men,
We have some old crabtrees here at home that will not
Be grafted to your relish. Yet welcome, warriors!
We call a nettle but a nettle and
The faults of fools but folly.
Com. Ever right.
Cor. Menenius, ever, ever.
Herald. Give way there, and go on!
Cor. [*to Volumnia and Virgilia*] Your hand, and yours!
Ere in our own house I do shade my head,
The good patricians must be visited,
From whom I have receiv'd not only greetings,
But with them charge of honours.
Vol. I have liv'd
To see inherited my very wishes,
And the buildings of my fancy. Only
There's one thing wanting, which I doubt not but
Our Rome will cast upon thee.
Cor. Know, good mother,
I had rather be their servant in my way
Than sway with them in theirs.
Com. On, to the Capitol!
Flourish. Cornets. Exeunt in state, as before.

Brutus and Sicinius [*come forward*].

Bru. All tongues speak of him, and the bleared sights
Are spectacled to see him. Your prattling nurse
Into a rapture lets her baby cry
While she chats him. The kitchen Malkin pins
Her richest lockram 'bout her reechy neck,
Clamb'ring the walls to eye him. Stalls, bulks, windows
Are smother'd up, leads fill'd, and ridges hors'd
With variable complexions, all agreeing
In earnestness to see him. Seld-shown flamens
Do press among the popular throngs and puff
To win a vulgar station. Our veil'd dames
Commit the war of white and damask in
Their nicely gauded cheeks to th' wanton spoil
Of Phœbus' burning kisses. Such a poother
As if that whatsoever god who leads him
Were slily crept into his human powers
And gave him graceful posture.
Sic. On the sudden
I warrant him consul.
Bru. Then our office may
During his power go sleep.
Sic. He cannot temp'rately transport his honours
From where he should begin and end, but will
Lose those he hath won.
Bru. In that there's comfort.
Sic. Doubt not
The commoners, for whom we stand, but they
Upon their ancient malice will forget
With the least cause these his new honours; which
That he will give them make I as little question
As he is proud to do't.
Bru. I heard him swear,
Were he to stand for consul, never would he
Appear i' th' market place, nor on him put
The napless vesture of humility,
Nor, showing (as the manner is) his wounds
To th' people, beg their stinking breaths.
Sic. 'Tis right.
Bru. It was his word. O, he would miss it, rather
Than carry it but by the suit of the gentry to him
And the desire of the nobles.
Sic. I wish no better
Than have him hold that purpose and to put it
In execution.
Bru. 'Tis most like he will.
Sic. It shall be to him then, as our good wills,
A sure destruction.
Bru. So it must fall out
To him or our authorities for an end.
We must suggest the people in what hatred
He still hath held them; that to's power he would

Have made them mules, silenc'd their pleaders, and
Dispropertied their freedoms; holding them,
In human action and capacity,
Of no more soul nor fitness for the world
Than camels in the war, who have their provand
Only for bearing burthens, and sore blows
For sinking under them.

Sic. This, as you say, suggested
At some time when his soaring insolence
Shall touch the people — which time shall not want
If he be put upon't, and that's as easy
As to set dogs on sheep — will be his fire
To kindle their dry stubble; and their blaze
Shall darken him for ever.

Enter a *Messenger*.

Bru. What's the matter?

Mess. You are sent for to the Capitol. 'Tis thought
That Marcius shall be consul.
I have seen the dumb men throng to see him and
The blind to hear him speak. Matrons flung gloves,
Ladies and maids their scarfs and handkerchers,
Upon him as he pass'd; the nobles bended
As to Jove's statue, and the commons made
A shower and thunder with their caps and shouts.
I never saw the like.

Bru. Let's to the Capitol,
And carry with us ears and eyes for th' time,
But hearts for the event.

Sic. Have with you.

Exeunt.

[Scene II. *Rome. The Capitol.*]

Enter two *Officers*, to lay cushions, as it were in the Capitol.

1. Off. Come, come, they are almost here. How many stand for consulships?

2. Off. Three, they say; but 'tis thought of every one Coriolanus will carry it.

1. Off. That's a brave fellow; but he's vengeance proud and loves not the common people.

2. Off. Faith, here hath been many great men that have flatter'd the people, who ne'er loved them; and there be many that they have loved, they know not wherefore; so that, if they love they know not why, they hate upon no better a ground. Therefore, for Coriolanus neither to care whether they love or hate him manifests the true knowledge he has in their disposition, and out of his noble carelessness lets them plainly see't.

1. Off. If he did not care whether he had their love or no, he waved indifferently 'twixt doing them neither good nor harm; but he seeks their hate with greater devotion than they can render it him and leaves nothing undone that may fully discover him their opposite. Now to seem to affect the malice and displeasure of the people is as bad as that which he dislikes — to flatter them for their love.

2. Off. He hath deserved worthily of his country; and his ascent is not by such easy degrees as those who, having been supple and courteous to the people, bonneted, without any further deed to have them at all into their estimation and report; but he hath so planted his honours in their eyes and his actions in their hearts that for their tongues to be silent and not confess so much were a kind of ingrateful injury; to report otherwise were a malice that, giving itself the lie, would pluck reproof and rebuke from every ear that heard it.

1. Off. No more of him; he's a worthy man.
Make way; they are coming.

A sennet. Enter the *Patricians* and the *Tribunes of the People*, *Lictors* before them; *Coriolanus*, *Menenius*, *Cominius* the *Consul*. *Sicinius* and *Brutus* take their places by themselves. *Coriolanus* stands.

Men. Having determin'd of the Volsces and
To send for Titus Lartius, it remains,
As the main point of this our after-meeting,
To gratify his noble service that
Hath thus stood for his country. Therefore please you,
Most reverend and grave elders, to desire
The present consul and last general
In our well-found successes, to report
A little of that worthy work perform'd
By Caius Marcius Coriolanus, whom
We met here both to thank, and to remember
With honours like himself.

[*Coriolanus sits.*]

1. Sen. Speak, good Cominius.
Leave nothing out for length, and make us think
Rather our state 's defective for requital
Than we to stretch it out. [*To the Tribunes*]
Masters o' th' people,
We do request your kindest ears, and after,
Your loving motion toward the common body
To yield what passes here.

Sic. We are convented
Upon a pleasing treaty, and have hearts
Inclinable to honour and advance
The theme of our assembly.
Bru. Which the rather
We shall be blest to do, if he remember
A kinder value of the people than
He hath hereto priz'd them at.
Men. That's off, that's off!
I would you rather had been silent. Please you
To hear Cominius speak?
Bru. Most willingly;
But yet my caution was more pertinent
Than the rebuke you give it.
Men. He loves your people;
But tie him not to be their bedfellow.
Worthy Cominius, speak.
Coriolanus rises, and offers to go away.
Nay, keep your place.
1. Sen. Sit, Coriolanus. Never shame to hear
What you have nobly done.
Cor. Your Honours' pardon.
I had rather have my wounds to heal again
Than hear say how I got them.
Bru. Sir, I hope
My words disbench'd you not?
Cor. No, sir. Yet oft,
When blows have made me stay, I fled from words.
You sooth'd not, therefore hurt not; but your people,
I love them as they weigh —
Men. Pray now, sit down.
Cor. I had rather have one scratch my head i' th' sun
When the alarum were struck than idly sit
To hear my nothings monster'd. *Exit.*
Men. Masters of the people,
Your multiplying spawn how can he flatter
(That's thousand to one good one) when you now see
He had rather venture all his limbs for honour
Than one on's ears to hear it? Proceed, Cominius.
Com. I shall lack voice. The deeds of Coriolanus
Should not be utter'd feebly. It is held
That valour is the chiefest virtue and
Most dignifies the haver. If it be,
The man I speak of cannot in the world
Be singly counterpois'd. At sixteen years,
When Tarquin made a head for Rome, he fought
Beyond the mark of others. Our then Dictator,
Whom with all praise I point at, saw him fight
When with his Amazonian chin he drove
The bristled lips before him. He bestrid
An o'erpress'd Roman and i' th' consul's view
Slew three opposers. Tarquin's self he met
And struck him on his knee. In that day's feats,
When he might act the woman in the scene,
He prov'd best man i' th' field and for his meed
Was brow-bound with the oak. His pupil age
Man-ent'red thus, he waxed like a sea,
And in the brunt of seventeen battles since
He lurch'd all swords of the garland. For this last,
Before and in Corioles, let me say
I cannot speak him home. He stopp'd the fliers
And by his rare example made the coward
Turn terror into sport. As waves before
A vessel under sail, so men obey'd
And fell below his stem. His sword, death's stamp,
Where it did mark, it took. From face to foot
He was a thing of blood, whose every motion
Was tim'd with dying cries. Alone he ent'red
The mortal gate of th' city, which he painted
With shunless destiny; aidless came off,
And with a sudden reinforcement struck
Corioles like a planet. Now all's his,
When by-and-by the din of war gan pierce
His ready sense; then straight his doubled spirit
Requick'ned what in flesh was fatigate,
And to the battle came he, where he did
Run reeking o'er the lives of men, as if
'Twere a perpetual spoil; and till we call'd
Both field and city ours, he never stood
To ease his breast with panting.
Men. Worthy man!
1. Sen. He cannot but with measure fit the honours
Which we devise him.
Com. Our spoils he kick'd at
And look'd upon things precious as they were
The common muck of the world. He covets less
Than misery itself would give, rewards
His deeds with doing them, and is content
To spend the time to end it.
Men. He's right noble.
Let him be call'd for.
1. Sen. Call Coriolanus.
Officer. He doth appear.

Enter *Coriolanus.*

Men. The Senate, Coriolanus, are well pleas'd
To make thee consul.

CORIOLANUS

Richard Burton in the role of Coriolanus, a proud aristocrat whose enemies procure his banishment from Rome

PHOTOGRAPHS BY ANGUS MCBEAN
PRODUCED BY THE OLD VIC COMPANY

Volumnia (Fay Compton), Coriolanus' mother

Menenius (William Squire), Coriolanus' friend

"Too modest are you; more cruel to your good report than grateful to us that give you truly." Cominius (John Neville) praises Coriolanus' valor *(Act I, Scene IX)*

Coriolanus is acclaimed for his valor at Corioli *(Act I, Scene IX)*

"You know the cause, sir, of my standing here?" Following custom, Coriolanus stands in the forum humbly dressed and asks election as consul *(Act II, Scene III)*

"How does your little son?" Valeria (Gwen Cherrell) visits Virgilia (Claire Bloom), the wife of Coriolanus *(Act I, Scene III)*

The tribunes (Laurence Hardy and Edgar Wreford) rouse the Roman people to banish Coriolanus *(Act III, Scene I)*

Claire Bloom as Coriolanus' wife, Virgilia: an exemplar of Roman womanhood

"Hear me speak: as I do know the consul's worthiness, so can I name his faults." Menenius defends his friend Coriolanus *(Act III, Scene I)*

"I would the gods had nothing else to do but to confirm my curses!" Volumnia rails against the tribunes, who have stirred up the Roman people to oust her son, Coriolanus *(Act IV, Scene II)*

"You common cry of curs!" Coriolanus bitterly turns upon the people of Rome *(Act III, Scene III)*

"There is a world elsewhere." The rejected hero accepts his banishment and contemptuously turns his back on Rome *(Act III, Scene III)*

Coriolanus' wife and mother accompany him to the gates *(Act IV, Scene I)*

Banished from Rome, Coriolanus presents himself in the camp of the Volscians *(Act IV, Scene V)*

"My son! my son! thou art preparing fire for us." Menenius comes to the Volscian camp and pleads with his friend Coriolanus to spare Rome and his countrymen *(Act V, Scene II)*

"Down, ladies; let us shame him with our knees." Volumnia brings the family of Coriolanus to the Volscian camp and beseeches him to forego vengeance upon Rome *(Act V, Scene III)*

"He has betray'd your business, and given up, for certain drops of salt, your city Rome."
Aufidius (Paul Daneman) spurs the Volscians to the murder of Coriolanus *(Act V, Scene VI)*

Cor. I do owe them still
My life and services.
Men. It then remains
That you do speak to the people.
Cor. I do beseech you,
Let me o'erleap that custom; for I cannot
Put on the gown, stand naked, and entreat them
For my wounds' sake to give their suffrage. Please you
That I may pass this doing.
Sic. Sir, the people
Must have their voices; neither will they bate
One jot of ceremony.
Men. Put them not to't.
Pray you go fit you to the custom and
Take to you, as your predecessors have,
Your honour with the form.
Cor. It is a part
That I shall blush in acting, and might well
Be taken from the people.
Bru. [*to Sicinius*] Mark you that?
Cor. To brag unto them, 'Thus I did, and thus!'
Show them th' unaching scars which I should hide,
As if I had receiv'd them for the hire
Of their breath only!
Men. Do not stand upon't.
We recommend to you, Tribunes of the People,
Our purpose to them; and to our noble consul
Wish we all joy and honour.
1. Sen. To Coriolanus come all joy and honour!

Flourish. Cornets. Then exeunt. Manent Sicinius and Brutus.

Bru. You see how he intends to use the people.
Sic. May they perceive 's intent! He will require them
As if he did contemn what he requested
Should be in them to give.
Bru. Come, we'll inform them
Of our proceedings here. On th' market place
I know they do attend us. [*Exeunt.*]

[Scene III. *Rome. The Forum.*]

Enter seven or eight *Citizens.*

1. Cit. Once if he do require our voices, we ought not to deny him.

2. Cit. We may, sir, if we will.

3. Cit. We have power in ourselves to do it, but it is a power that we have no power to do; for if he show us his wounds and tell us his deeds, we are to put our tongues into those wounds and speak for them. So, if he tell us his noble deeds, we must also tell him our noble acceptance of them. Ingratitude is monstrous; and for the multitude to be ingrateful were to make a monster of the multitude, of the which we being members, should bring ourselves to be monstrous members.

1. Cit. And to make us no better thought of, a little help will serve; for once we stood up about the corn, he himself stuck not to call us the many-headed multitude.

3. Cit. We have been call'd so of many; not that our heads are some brown, some black, some abram, some bald, but that our wits are so diversely colour'd. And truly I think, if all our wits were to issue out of one skull, they would fly east, west, north, south, and their consent of one direct way should be at once to all the points o' th' compass.

2. Cit. Think you so? Which way do you judge my wit would fly?

3. Cit. Nay, your wit will not so soon out as another man's will. 'Tis strongly wedg'd up in a blockhead. But if it were at liberty, 'twould sure southward.

2. Cit. Why that way?

3. Cit. To lose itself in a fog; where being three parts melted away with rotten dews, the fourth would return for conscience sake, to help to get thee a wife.

2. Cit. You are never without your tricks. You may, you may!

3. Cit. Are you all resolv'd to give your voices? But that's no matter, the greater part carries it. I say, if he would incline to the people, there was never a worthier man.

Enter *Coriolanus* in a gown of humility, with *Menenius.*

Here he comes, and in the gown of humility. Mark his behaviour. We are not to stay all together, but to come by him where he stands, by ones, by twos, and by threes. He's to make his requests by particulars; wherein every one of us has a single honour, in giving him our own voices with our own tongues. Therefore follow me, and I'll direct you how you shall go by him.

All. Content, content!

[*Exeunt Citizens.*]

Men. O sir, you are not right. Have you not known
The worthiest men have done't?

Cor. What must I say?
'I pray, sir' — Plague upon't! I cannot bring
My tongue to such a pace. 'Look, sir, my wounds.
I got them in my country's service, when
Some certain of your brethren roar'd, and ran
From th' noise of our own drums.'

Men. O me, the gods!
You must not speak of that. You must desire them
To think upon you.

Cor. Think upon me? Hang 'em!
I would they would forget me, like the virtues
Which our divines lose by 'em.

Men. You'll mar all.
I'll leave you. Pray you speak to 'em. I pray you,
In wholesome manner. *Exit.*

Enter three of the *Citizens.*

Cor. Bid them wash their faces
And keep their teeth clean. So, here comes a brace.
You know the cause, sir, of my standing here.

3. Cit. We do, sir. Tell us what hath brought you to't.

Cor. Mine own desert.

2. Cit. Your own desert?

Cor. Ay, not mine own desire.

3. Cit. How? Not your own desire?

Cor. No, sir, 'twas never my desire yet to trouble the poor with begging.

3. Cit. You must think, if we give you anything, we hope to gain by you.

Cor. Well then, I pray, your price o' th' consulship?

1. Cit. The price is, to ask it kindly.

Cor. Kindly, sir, I pray let me ha't. I have wounds to show you, which shall be yours in private. Your good voice, sir. What say you?

2. Cit. You shall ha't, worthy sir.

Cor. A match, sir. There's in all two worthy voices begg'd. I have your alms. Adieu.

3. Cit. But this is something odd.

2. Cit. An 'twere to give again — but 'tis no matter.

Exeunt [the three Citizens].

Enter two other *Citizens.*

Cor. Pray you now, if it may stand with the tune of your voices that I may be consul, I have here the customary gown.

1. Cit. You have deserved nobly of your country, and you have not deserved nobly.

Cor. Your enigma?

1. Cit. You have been a scourge to her enemies; you have been a rod to her friends. You have not indeed loved the common people.

Cor. You should account me the more virtuous that I have not been common in my love. I will, sir, flatter my sworn brother, the people, to earn a dearer estimation of them. 'Tis a condition they account gentle; and since the wisdom of their choice is rather to have my hat than my heart, I will practise the insinuating nod and be off to them most counterfeitly: that is, sir, I will counterfeit the bewitchment of some popular man and give it bountiful to the desirers. Therefore, beseech you I may be consul.

2. Cit. We hope to find you our friend; and therefore give you our voices heartily.

1. Cit. You have received many wounds for your country.

Cor. I will not seal your knowledge with showing them. I will make much of your voices, and so trouble you no farther.

Both. The gods give you joy, sir, heartily!

[*Exeunt Citizens.*]

Cor. Most sweet voices!
Better it is to die, better to starve,
Than crave the hire which first we do deserve.
Why in this wolvish toge should I stand here
To beg of Hob and Dick that do appear
Their needless vouches? Custom calls me to't.
What custom wills, in all things should we do't,
The dust on antique time would lie unswept,
And mountainous error be too highly heapt
For truth to o'erpeer. Rather than fool it so,
Let the high office and the honour go
To one that would do thus. I am half through;
The one part suffer'd, the other will I do.

Enter three *Citizens* more.

Here come moe voices. —
Your voices! For your voices I have fought;
Watch'd for your voices; for your voices bear
Of wounds two dozen odd; battles thrice six
I have seen and heard of; for your voices have
Done many things, some less, some more. Your voices!
Indeed I would be consul.

1. Cit. He has done nobly and cannot go without any honest man's voice.

2. Cit. Therefore let him be consul. The gods give him joy and make him good friend to the people!

All. Amen, amen. God save thee, noble Consul!

Cor. Worthy voices!

[*Exeunt Citizens.*]

Enter *Menenius*, with *Brutus* and *Sicinius*.

Men. You have stood your limitation, and the tribunes
Endue you with the people's voice. Remains
That, in th' official marks invested, you
Anon do meet the Senate.
Cor. Is this done?
Sic. The custom of request you have discharg'd.
The people do admit you, and are summon'd
To meet anon upon your approbation.
Cor. Where? at the Senate House?
Sic. There, Coriolanus.
Cor. May I change these garments?
Sic. You may, sir.
Cor. That I'll straight do and, knowing myself again,
Repair to th' Senate House.
Men. I'll keep you company. — Will you along?
Bru. We stay here for the people.
Sic. Fare you well.
Exeunt Coriolanus and Menenius.
He has it now; and by his looks, methinks,
'Tis warm at's heart.
Bru. With a proud heart he wore
His humble weeds. Will you dismiss the people?

Enter the *Plebeians*.

Sic. How now, my masters? Have you chose this man?
1. Cit. He has our voices, sir.
Bru. We pray the gods he may deserve your loves.
2. Cit. Amen, sir. To my poor unworthy notice,
He mock'd us when he begg'd our voices.
3. Cit. Certainly
He flouted us downright.
1. Cit. No, 'tis his kind of speech; he did not mock us.
2. Cit. Not one amongst us, save yourself, but says
He us'd us scornfully. He should have show'd us
His marks of merit, wounds receiv'd for's country.
Sic. Why, so he did, I am sure.
All. No, no! No man saw 'em.
3. Cit. He said he had wounds which he could show in private,
And with his hat, thus waving it in scorn,
'I would be consul,' says he. 'Aged custom
But by your voices will not so permit me.
Your voices therefore!' When we granted that,
Here was 'I thank you for your voices, thank you!
Your most sweet voices! Now you have left your voices,
I have no further with you.' Was not this mockery?
Sic. Why either were you ignorant to see't,
Or, seeing it, of such childish friendliness
To yield your voices?
Bru. Could you not have told him
As you were lesson'd? When he had no power
But was a petty servant to the state,
He was your enemy; ever spake against
Your liberties and the charters that you bear
I' th' body of the weal; and now, arriving
A place of potency and sway o' th' state,
If he should still malignantly remain
Fast foe to th' plebeii, your voices might
Be curses to yourselves. You should have said
That, as his worthy deeds did claim no less
Than what he stood for, so his gracious nature
Would think upon you for your voices and
Translate his malice towards you into love,
Standing your friendly lord.
Sic. Thus to have said,
As you were fore-advis'd, had touch'd his spirit
And tried his inclination; from him pluck'd
Either his gracious promise, which you might,
As cause had call'd you up, have held him to;
Or else it would have gall'd his surly nature,
Which easily endures not article
Tying him to aught. So, putting him to rage,
You should have ta'en th' advantage of his choler
And pass'd him unelected.
Bru. Did you perceive
He did solicit you in free contempt
When he did need your loves, and do you think
That his contempt shall not be bruising to you
When he hath power to crush? Why, had your bodies
No heart among you? Or had you tongues to cry
Against the rectorship of judgment?
Sic. Have you,
Ere now, denied the asker, and now again,
Of him that did not ask but mock, bestow
Your su'd-for tongues?
3. Cit. He's not confirm'd; we may deny him yet.
2. Cit. And will deny him.
I'll have five hundred voices of that sound.
1. Cit. I twice five hundred, and their friends to piece 'em.

Bru. Get you hence instantly, and tell those friends
They have chose a consul that will from them take
Their liberties; make them of no more voice
Than dogs, that are as often beat for barking
As therefore kept to do so.
Sic. Let them assemble;
And, on a safer judgment, all revoke
Your ignorant election. Enforce his pride
And his old hate unto you. Besides, forget not
With what contempt he wore the humble weed;
How in his suit he scorn'd you; but your loves,
Thinking upon his services, took from you
The apprehension of his present portance,
Which most gibingly, ungravely, he did fashion
After the inveterate hate he bears you.
Bru. Lay
A fault on us, your tribunes, that we labour'd,
No impediment between, but that you must
Cast your election on him.
Sic. Say you chose him
More after our commandment than as guided
By your own true affections; and that your minds,
Preoccupied with what you rather must do
Than what you should, made you against the grain
To voice him consul. Lay the fault on us.
Bru. Ay, spare us not. Say we read lectures to you,
How youngly he began to serve his country,
How long continued; and what stock he springs of,
The noble house o' th' Marcians; from whence came
That Ancus Marcius, Numa's daughter's son,
Who after great Hostilius here was King;
Of the same house Publius and Quintus were,
That our best water brought by conduits hither;
And [Censorinus, who was] nobly nam'd so,
Twice being [by the people chosen] Censor,
Was his great ancestor.
Sic. One thus descended,
That hath beside well in his person wrought
To be set high in place, we did commend
To your remembrances; but you have found,
Scaling his present bearing with his past,
That he's your fixed enemy, and revoke
Your sudden approbation.
Bru. Say you ne'er had done't
(Harp on that still) but by our putting on;
And presently, when you have drawn your number,
Repair to th' Capitol.
All. We will so. Almost all
Repent in their election. *Exeunt Plebeians.*
Bru. Let them go on.
This mutiny were better put in hazard
Than stay, past doubt, for greater.
If, as his nature is, he fall in rage
With their refusal, both observe and answer
The vantage of his anger.
Sic. To th' Capitol, come.
We will be there before the stream o' th' people;
And this shall seem, as partly 'tis, their own,
Which we have goaded onward.
Exeunt.

ACT III. [Scene I. *Rome. A street.*]

Cornets. Enter *Coriolanus, Menenius,* all the *Gentry, Cominius, Titus Lartius,* and other *Senators.*

Cor. Tullus Aufidius, then, had made new head?
Lart. He had, my lord, and that it was which caus'd
Our swifter composition.
Cor. So then the Volsces stand but as at first,
Ready, when time shall prompt them, to make road
Upon's again.
Com. They are worn, Lord Consul, so
That we shall hardly in our ages see
Their banners wave again.
Cor. Saw you Aufidius?
Lart. On safeguard he came to me, and did curse
Against the Volsces for they had so vilely
Yielded the town. He is retir'd to Antium.
Cor. Spoke he of me?
Lart. He did, my lord.
Cor. How? what?
Lart. How often he had met you sword to sword;
That of all things upon the earth he hated
Your person most; that he would pawn his fortunes
To hopeless restitution, so he might
Be call'd your vanquisher.
Cor. At Antium lives he?

Lart. At Antium.
Cor. I wish I had a cause to seek him there,
To oppose his hatred fully. Welcome home.

Enter *Sicinius* and *Brutus.*

Behold, these are the tribunes of the people,
The tongues o' th' common mouth. I do despise them,
For they do prank them in authority
Against all noble sufferance.
Sic. Pass no further.
Cor. Ha! What is that?
Bru. It will be dangerous to go on. No further.
Cor. What makes this change?
Men. The matter?
Com. Hath he not pass'd the noble and the common?
Bru. Cominius, no.
Cor. Have I had children's voices?
1. Sen. Tribunes, give way. He shall to th' market place.
Bru. The people are incens'd against him.
Sic. Stop,
Or all will fall in broil.
Cor. Are these your herd?
Must these have voices, that can yield them now
And straight disclaim their tongues? What are your offices?
You being their mouths, why rule you not their teeth?
Have you not set them on?
Men. Be calm, be calm.
Cor. It is a purpos'd thing and grows by plot
To curb the will of the nobility.
Suffer't, and live with such as cannot rule
Nor ever will be rul'd.
Bru. Call't not a plot.
The people cry you mock'd them; and of late,
When corn was given them gratis, you repin'd;
Scandal'd the suppliants for the people, call'd them
Time-pleasers, flatterers, foes to nobleness.
Cor. Why, this was known before.
Bru. Not to them all.
Cor. Have you inform'd them sithence?
Bru. How? I inform them?
Cor. You are like to do such business.
Bru. Not unlike
Each way to better yours.
Cor. Why then should I be consul? By yond clouds,
Let me deserve so ill as you, and make me
Your fellow tribune.
Sic. You show too much of that
For which the people stir. If you will pass
To where you are bound, you must enquire your way,
Which you are out of, with a gentler spirit,
Or never be so noble as a consul
Nor yoke with him for tribune.
Men. Let's be calm.
Com. The people are abus'd, set on. This palt'ring
Becomes not Rome; nor has Coriolanus
Deserv'd this so dishonour'd rub, laid falsely
I' th' plain way of his merit.
Cor. Tell me of corn!
This was my speech, and I will speak't again —
Men. Not now! not now!
1. Sen. Not in this heat, sir, now.
Cor. Now, as I live, I will! My nobler friends,
I crave their pardons.
For the mutable, rank-scented meiny, let them
Regard me as I do not flatter, and
Therein behold themselves. I say again,
In soothing them we nourish 'gainst our Senate
The cockle of rebellion, insolence, sedition,
Which we ourselves have plough'd for, sow'd, and scatter'd
By mingling them with us, the honour'd number,
Who lack not virtue, no, nor power, but that
Which they have given to beggars.
Men. Well, no more.
1. Sen. No more words, we beseech you.
Cor. How? No more?
As for my country I have shed my blood,
Not fearing outward force, so shall my lungs
Coin words till their decay against those measles
Which we disdain should tetter us, yet sought
The very way to catch them.
Bru. You speak o' th' people
As if you were a god to punish, not
A man of their infirmity.
Sic. 'Twere well
We let the people know't.
Men. What, what? his choler?
Cor. Choler?
Were I as patient as the midnight sleep,
By Jove, 'twould be my mind!
Sic. It is a mind
That shall remain a poison where it is,
Not poison any further.
Cor. Shall remain?
Hear you this Triton of the minnows? Mark you
His absolute 'shall'?

Com. 'Twas from the canon.
Cor. 'Shall'?
O good but most unwise patricians! Why,
You grave but reckless senators, have you thus
Given Hydra here to choose an officer
That with his peremptory 'shall,' being but
The horn and noise o' th' monster's, wants not spirit
To say he'll turn your current in a ditch
And make your channel his? If he have power,
Then vail your ignorance; if none, awake
Your dangerous lenity. If you are learn'd,
Be not as common fools; if you are not,
Let them have cushions by you. You are plebeians
If they be senators; and they are no less
When, both your voices blended, the great'st taste
Most palates theirs. They choose their magistrate;
And such a one as he, who puts his 'shall,'
His popular 'shall,' against a graver bench
Than ever frown'd in Greece. By Jove himself,
It makes the consuls base! and my soul aches
To know, when two authorities are up,
Neither supreme, how soon confusion
May enter 'twixt the gap of both and take
The one by th' other.
Com. Well, on to th' market place.
Cor. Whoever gave that counsel to give forth
The corn o' th' storehouse gratis, as 'twas us'd
Sometime in Greece —
Men. Well, well, no more of that.
Cor. Though there the people had more absolute pow'r —
I say they nourish'd disobedience, fed
The ruin of the state.
Bru. Why, shall the people give
One that speaks thus their voice?
Cor. I'll give my reasons,
More worthier than their voices. They know the corn
Was not our recompense, resting well assur'd
They ne'er did service for't. Being press'd to th' war
Even when the navel of the state was touch'd,
They would not thread the gates. This kind of service
Did not deserve corn gratis. Being i' th' war,
Their mutinies and revolts, wherein they show'd
Most valour, spoke not for them. Th' accusation
Which they have often made against the Senate,
All cause unborn, could never be the motive
Of our so frank donation. Well, what then?
How shall this beesom multitude digest
The Senate's courtesy? Let deeds express
What's like to be their words: 'We did request it;
We are the greater poll, and in true fear
They gave us our demands.' Thus we debase
The nature of our seats and make the rabble
Call our cares fears; which will in time break ope
The locks o' th' Senate and bring in the crows
To peck the eagles.
Men. Come, enough.
Bru. Enough, with over-measure.
Cor. No, take more!
What may be sworn by, both divine and human,
Seal what I end withal! This double worship —
Where one part does disdain with cause, the other
Insult without all reason; where gentry, title, wisdom
Cannot conclude but by the yea and no
Of general ignorance — it must omit
Real necessities, and give way the while
To unstable slightness. Purpose so barr'd, it follows
Nothing is done to purpose. Therefore, beseech you —
You that will be less fearful than discreet;
That love the fundamental part of state
More than you doubt the change on't; that prefer
A noble life before a long, and wish
To jump a body with a dangerous physic
That's sure of death without it — at once pluck out
The multitudinous tongue; let them not lick
The sweet which is their poison. Your dishonour
Mangles true judgment, and bereaves the state
Of that integrity which should become't,
Not having the power to do the good it would
For th' ill which doth control't.
Bru. Has said enough.
Sic. Has spoken like a traitor and shall answer
As traitors do.
Cor. Thou wretch, despite o'erwhelm thee!
What should the people do with these bald tribunes?
On whom depending, their obedience fails
To th' greater bench. In a rebellion,
When what's not meet, but what must be, was law,
Then were they chosen. In a better hour,

Let what is meet be said it must be meet,
And throw their power i' th' dust.
Bru. Manifest treason!
Sic. This a consul? No.
Bru. The ædiles, ho!

Enter an *Ædile.*

Let him be apprehended.
Sic. Go call the people, [*exit Ædile*] in whose name myself
Attach thee as a traitorous innovator,
A foe to th' public weal. Obey, I charge thee,
And follow to thine answer.
Cor. Hence, old goat!
All [*Patricians*]. We'll surety him.
Com. Aged sir, hands off.
Cor. Hence, rotten thing! or I shall shake thy bones
Out of thy garments.
Sic. Help, ye citizens!

Enter a rabble of *Plebeians,* with the *Ædiles.*

Men. On both sides more respect.
Sic. Here's he that would take from you all your power.
Bru. Seize him, ædiles!
All [*Plebeians*]. Down with him! down with him!
2. Sen. Weapons, weapons, weapons!

They all bustle about Coriolanus, [*crying*]:

Tribunes! — Patricians! — Citizens! — What, ho! —
Sicinius! — Brutus! — Coriolanus! — Citizens!
All [*Patricians*]. Peace, peace, peace! Stay, hold, peace!
Men. What is about to be? I am out of breath.
Confusion's near. I cannot speak. You, Tribunes,
Speak to th' people. Coriolanus, patience.
Speak, good Sicinius.
Sic. Hear me, people. Peace!
All [*Plebeians*]. Let's hear our tribune. Peace! Speak, speak, speak!
Sic. You are at point to lose your liberties.
Marcius would have all from you, Marcius,
Whom late you have nam'd for consul.
Men. Fie, fie, fie!
This is the way to kindle, not to quench.
1. Sen. To unbuild the city and to lay all flat.
Sic. What is the city but the people?
All [*Plebeians*]. True!
The people are the city.
Bru. By the consent of all we were establish'd
The people's magistrates.
All [*Plebeians*]. You so remain.
Men. And so are like to do.
Com. That is the way to lay the city flat,
To bring the roof to the foundation,
And bury all which yet distinctly ranges
In heaps and piles of ruin.
Sic. This deserves death
Bru. Or let us stand to our authority
Or let us lose it. We do here pronounce
Upon the part o' th' people, in whose power
We were elected theirs, Marcius is worthy
Of present death.
Sic. Therefore lay hold of him.
Bear him to th' Rock Tarpeian and from thence
Into destruction cast him.
Bru. Ædiles, seize him!
All Plebeians. Yield, Marcius, yield!
Men. Hear me one word.
Beseech you, Tribunes, hear me but a word.
Ædiles. Peace, peace!
Men. [*to Brutus*] Be that you seem, truly your country's friend,
And temp'rately proceed to what you would
Thus violently redress.
Bru. Sir, those cold ways
That seem like prudent helps are very poisonous
Where the disease is violent. — Lay hands upon him
And bear him to the Rock.

Coriolanus draws his sword.

Cor. No, I'll die here.
There's some among you have beheld me fighting.
Come try upon yourselves what you have seen me.
Men. Down with that sword! Tribunes, withdraw awhile.
Bru. Lay hands upon him.
Men. Help Marcius, help!
You that be noble, help him, young and old!
All [*Plebeians*]. Down with him! down with him!

In this mutiny the Tribunes, the Ædiles, and the People are beat in.

Men. Go, get you to your house! Be gone, away!
All will be naught else.
2. Sen. Get you gone.
Cor. Stand fast!
We have as many friends as enemies.
Men. Shall it be put to that?

1. Sen. The gods forbid!
I prithee, noble friend, home to thy house.
Leave us to cure this cause.
Men. For 'tis a sore upon us
You cannot tent yourself. Be gone, beseech you.
Com. Come, sir, along with us.
Cor. I would they were barbarians, as they are,
Though in Rome litter'd; not Romans, as they are not,
Though calv'd i' th' porch o' th' Capitol.
Men. Be gone.
Put not your worthy rage into your tongue.
One time will owe another.
Cor. On fair ground
I could beat forty of them.
Men. I could myself
Take up a brace o' th' best of them; yea, the two tribunes.
Com. But now 'tis odds beyond arithmetic,
And manhood is call'd foolery when it stands
Against a falling fabric. Will you hence
Before the tag return? whose rage doth rend
Like interrupted waters, and o'erbear
What they are us'd to bear.
Men. Pray you be gone.
I'll try whether my old wit be in request
With those that have but little. This must be patch'd
With cloth of any colour.
Com. Nay, come away.
Exeunt Coriolanus and Cominius, [with others].
Patrician. This man has marr'd his fortune.
Men. His nature is too noble for the world.
He would not flatter Neptune for his trident
Or Jove for's power to thunder. His heart's his mouth;
What his breast forges, that his tongue must vent,
And being angry does forget that ever
He heard the name of death. *A noise within.*
Here's goodly work!
Patrician. I would they were abed!
Men. I would they were in Tiber! What the vengeance,
Could he not speak 'em fair?

Enter *Brutus* and *Sicinius* with the *Rabble* again.

Sic. Where is this viper
That would depopulate the city and
Be every man himself?
Men. You worthy Tribunes —
Sic. He shall be thrown down the Tarpeian Rock
With rigorous hands. He hath resisted law,
And therefore law shall scorn him further trial
Than the severity of the public power,
Which he so sets at naught.
1. Cit. He shall well know
The noble tribunes are the people's mouths,
And we their hands.
All [Plebeians]. He shall, sure on't!
Men. Sir, sir —
Sic. Peace!
Men. Do not cry havoc where you should but hunt
With modest warrant.
Sic. Sir, how comes't that you
Have holp to make this rescue?
Men. Hear me speak.
As I do know the consul's worthiness,
So can I name his faults.
Sic. Consul? What consul?
Men. The consul Coriolanus.
Bru. He consul?
All [Plebeians]. No, no, no, no, no!
Men. If, by the tribunes' leave, and yours, good people,
I may be heard, I would crave a word or two,
The which shall turn you to no further harm
Than so much loss of time.
Sic. Speak briefly then,
For we are peremptory to dispatch
This viperous traitor. To eject him hence
Were but our danger, and to keep him here
Our certain death. Therefore it is decreed
He dies to-night.
Men. Now the good gods forbid
That our renowned Rome, whose gratitude
Towards her deserved children is enroll'd
In Jove's own book, like an unnatural dam
Should now eat up her own!
Sic. He's a disease that must be cut away.
Men. O, he's a limb that has but a disease:
Mortal, to cut it off; to cure it, easy.
What has he done to Rome that's worthy death?
Killing our enemies, the blood he hath lost
(Which, I dare vouch, is more than that he hath,
By many an ounce) he dropp'd it for his country;
And what is left, to lose it by his country
Were to us all that do't and suffer it
A brand to th' end o' th' world.
Sic. This is clean kam.
Bru. Merely awry. When he did love his country,
It honour'd him.

Men. The service of the foot,
Being once gangren'd, is not then respected
For what before it was.
Bru. We'll hear no more.
Pursue him to his house and pluck him thence,
Lest his infection, being of catching nature,
Spread further.
Men. One word more, one word!
This tiger-footed rage, when it shall find
The harm of unscann'd swiftness, will (too late)
Tie leaden pounds to's heels. Proceed by process,
Lest parties (as he is belov'd) break out
And sack great Rome with Romans.
Bru. If it were so —
Sic. What do ye talk?
Have we not had a taste of his obedience —
Our ædiles smote? ourselves resisted? Come!
Men. Consider this: he has been bred i' th' wars
Since 'a could draw a sword, and is ill-school'd
In bolted language; meal and bran together
He throws without distinction. Give me leave,
I'll go to him and undertake to bring him
Where he shall answer by a lawful form
(In peace) to his utmost peril.
1. Sen. Noble Tribunes,
It is the humane way. The other course
Will prove too bloody, and the end of it
Unknown to the beginning.
Sic. Noble Menenius,
Be you then as the people's officer.
Masters, lay down your weapons.
Bru. Go not home.
Sic. Meet on the market place. We'll attend you there,
Where if you bring not Marcius, we'll proceed
In our first way.
Men. I'll bring him to you. [*To the Senators*] Let me
Desire your company. He must come, or what
Is worst will follow.
1. Sen. Pray you, let's to him.
Exeunt omnes.

[Scene II. *A room in the house of* Coriolanus.]

Enter *Coriolanus* with *Nobles.*

Cor. Let them pull all about mine ears; present me
Death on the wheel or at wild horses' heels;
Or pile ten hills on the Tarpeian Rock,
That the precipitation might down stretch
Below the beam of sight — yet will I still
Be thus to them.
Noble. You do the nobler.
Cor. I muse my mother
Does not approve me further, who was wont
To call them woollen vassals, things created
To buy and sell with groats, to show bare heads
In congregations, to yawn, be still, and wonder
When one but of my ordinance stood up
To speak of peace or war.

Enter *Volumnia.*

I talk of you.
Why did you wish me milder? Would you have me
False to my nature? Rather say, I play
The man I am.
Vol. O, sir, sir, sir!
I would have had you put your power well on
Before you had worn it out.
Cor. Let't go.
Vol. You might have been enough the man you are
With striving less to be so. Lesser had been
The thwarting of your dispositions, if
You had not show'd them how ye were dispos'd
Ere they lack'd power to cross you.
Cor. Let them hang.
Vol. Ay, and burn too!

Enter *Menenius* with the *Senators.*

Men. Come, come, you have been too rough, something too rough.
You must return and mend it.
Senator. There's no remedy,
Unless, by not so doing, our good city
Cleave in the midst and perish.
Vol. Pray be counsell'd.
I have a heart as little apt as yours,
But yet a brain that leads my use of anger
To better vantage.
Men. Well said, noble woman!
Before he should thus stoop to th' herd, but that
The violent fit o' th' time craves it as physic
For the whole state, I would put mine armour on,
Which I can scarcely bear.
Cor. What must I do?
Men. Return to th' tribunes.
Cor. Well, what then? what then?
Men. Repent what you have spoke.
Cor. For them? I cannot do it to the gods.
Must I then do't to them?

Vol. You are too absolute;
Though therein you can never be too noble,
But when extremities speak. I have heard you say,
Honour and policy, like unsever'd friends,
I' th' war do grow together. Grant that, and tell me,
In peace what each of them by th' other lose,
That they combine not there.
Cor. Tush, tush!
Men. A good demand.
Vol. If it be honour in your wars to seem
The same you are not, — which, for your best ends,
You adopt your policy, — how is it less or worse
That it shall hold companionship in peace
With honour, as in war; since that to both
It stands in like request?
Cor. Why force you this?
Vol. Because that now it lies you on to speak
To th' people, not by your own instruction,
Nor by th' matter which your heart prompts you,
But with such words that are but roted in
Your tongue, though but bastards and syllables
Of no allowance to your bosom's truth.
Now, this no more dishonours you at all
Than to take in a town with gentle words
Which else would put you to your fortune and
The hazard of much blood.
I would dissemble with my nature where
My fortunes and my friends at stake requir'd
I should do so in honour. I am in this
Your wife, your son, these senators, the nobles;
And you will rather show our general louts
How you can frown than spend a fawn upon 'em
For the inheritance of their loves and safeguard
Of what that want might ruin.
Men. Noble lady!
Come, go with us. Speak fair. You may salve so,
Not what is dangerous present, but the loss
Of what is past.
Vol. I prithee now, my son,
Go to them, with this bonnet in thy hand;
And thus far having stretch'd it (here be with them),
Thy knee bussing the stones (for in such business
Action is eloquence, and the eyes of th' ignorant
More learned than the ears), waving thy head,
Which often, thus, correcting thy stout heart,
Now humble as the ripest mulberry
That will not hold the handling — say to them
Thou art their soldier, and, being bred in broils,
Hast not the soft way which, thou dost confess,
Were fit for thee to use, as they to claim,
In asking their good loves; but thou wilt frame
Thyself (forsooth) hereafter theirs, so far
As thou hast power and person.
Men. This but done
Even as she speaks, why, their hearts were yours!
For they have pardons, being ask'd, as free
As words to little purpose.
Vol. Prithee now,
Go, and be rul'd; although I know thou hadst rather
Follow thine enemy in a fiery gulf
Than flatter him in a bower.

Enter *Cominius.*

Here is Cominius.
Com. I have been i' th' market place; and, sir, 'tis fit
You make strong party, or defend yourself
By calmness or by absence. All's in anger.
Men. Only fair speech.
Com. I think 'twill serve, if he
Can thereto frame his spirit.
Vol. He must and will.
Prithee now, say you will, and go about it.
Cor. Must I go show them my unbarb'd sconce? Must I
With my base tongue give to my noble heart
A lie that it must bear? Well, I will do't.
Yet, were there but this single plot to lose,
This mould of Marcius, they to dust should grind it
And throw't against the wind. To th' market place!
You have put me now to such a part which never
I shall discharge to th' life.
Com. Come, come, we'll prompt you.
Vol. I prithee now, sweet son, as thou hast said
My praises made thee first a soldier, so,
To have my praise for this, perform a part
Thou hast not done before.
Cor. Well, I must do't.
Away, my disposition, and possess me
Some harlot's spirit! My throat of war be turn'd,
Which quier'd with my drum, into a pipe
Small as an eunuch or the virgin voice
That babies lulls asleep! The smiles of knaves
Tent in my cheeks, and schoolboys' tears take up
The glasses of my sight! A beggar's tongue

Make motion through my lips, and my arm'd knees,
Who bow'd but in my stirrup, bend like his
That hath receiv'd an alms! I will not do't,
Lest I surcease to honour mine own truth
And by my body's action teach my mind
A most inherent baseness.

Vol. At thy choice then.
To beg of thee, it is my more dishonour
Than thou of them. Come all to ruin! Let
Thy mother rather feel thy pride than fear
Thy dangerous stoutness; for I mock at death
With as big heart as thou. Do as thou list.
Thy valiantness was mine, thou suck'st it from me;
But owe thy pride thyself.

Cor. Pray be content.
Mother, I am going to the market place.
Chide me no more. I'll mountebank their loves,
Cog their hearts from them, and come home belov'd
Of all the trades in Rome. Look, I am going.
Commend me to my wife. I'll return consul,
Or never trust to what my tongue can do
I' th' way of flattery further.

Vol. Do your will. *Exit.*

Com. Away! The tribunes do attend you. Arm yourself
To answer mildly, for they are prepar'd
With accusations, as I hear, more strong
Than are upon you yet.

Cor. The word is 'mildly.' Pray you let us go.
Let them accuse me by invention; I
Will answer in mine honour.

Men. Ay, but mildly.

Cor. Well, mildly be it then — mildly. *Exeunt.*

[Scene III. *Rome. The Forum.*]

Enter *Sicinius* and *Brutus.*

Bru. In this point charge him home, that he affects
Tyrannical power. If he evade us there,
Enforce him with his envy to the people,
And that the spoil got on the Antiates
Was ne'er distributed.

Enter an *Ædile.*

What, will he come?

Æd. He's coming.

Bru. How accompanied?

Æd. With old Menenius and those senators
That always favour'd him.

Sic. Have you a catalogue
Of all the voices that we have procur'd
Set down by th' poll?

Æd. I have; 'tis ready.

Sic. Have you collected them by tribes?

Æd. I have.

Sic. Assemble presently the people hither;
And when they hear me say 'It shall be so
I' th' right and strength o' th' commons,' be it either
For death, for fine, or banishment, then let them,
If I say fine, cry 'Fine!'—if death, cry 'Death!'
Insisting on the old prerogative
And power i' th' truth o' th' cause.

Æd. I shall inform them.

Bru. And when such time they have begun to cry,
Let them not cease, but with a din confus'd
Enforce the present execution
Of what we chance to sentence.

Æd. Very well.

Sic. Make them be strong, and ready for this hint
When we shall hap to give't them.

Bru. Go about it.
[*Exit Ædile.*]
Put him to choler straight. He hath been us'd
Ever to conquer, and to have his worth
Of contradiction. Being once chaf'd, he cannot
Be rein'd again to temperance; then he speaks
What's in his heart, and that is there which looks
With us to break his neck.

Enter *Coriolanus, Menenius,* and *Cominius,* with others [of their party].

Sic. Well, here he comes.

Men. Calmly, I do beseech you.

Cor. Ay, as an hostler, that for th' poorest piece
Will bear the knave by th' volume. Th' honour'd gods
Keep Rome in safety, and the chairs of justice
Supplied with worthy men! plant love among's!
Throng our large temples with the shows of peace
And not our streets with war!

1. Sen. Amen, amen.

Men. A noble wish.

Enter the *Ædile,* with the *Plebeians.*

Sic. Draw near, ye people.

Æd. List to your tribunes. Audience! Peace, I say!

Cor. First hear me speak.
Both Tribunes. Well, say. Peace, ho!
Cor. Shall I be charg'd no further than this present?
Must all determine here?
Sic. I do demand
If you submit you to the people's voices,
Allow their officers, and are content
To suffer lawful censure for such faults
As shall be prov'd upon you.
Cor. I am content.
Men. Lo, citizens, he says he is content.
The warlike service he has done, consider. Think
Upon the wounds his body bears, which show
Like graves i' th' holy churchyard.
Cor. Scratches with briers,
Scars to move laughter only.
Men. Consider further,
That when he speaks not like a citizen,
You find him like a soldier. Do not take
His rougher accents for malicious sounds,
But, as I say, such as become a soldier
Rather than envy you.
Com. [*to Coriolanus*] Well, well, no more.
Cor. What is the matter,
That, being pass'd for consul with full voice,
I am so dishonour'd that the very hour
You take it off again?
Sic. Answer to us.
Cor. Say then. 'Tis true, I ought so.
Sic. We charge you that you have contriv'd to take
From Rome all season'd office and to wind
Yourself into a power tyrannical,
For which you are a traitor to the people.
Cor. How? traitor?
Men. Nay, temperately! Your promise.
Cor. The fires i' th' lowest hell fold-in the people!
Call me their traitor, thou injurious tribune?
Within thine eyes sat twenty thousand deaths,
In thy hands clutch'd as many millions, in
Thy lying tongue both numbers, I would say
'Thou liest' unto thee with a voice as free
As I do pray the gods.
Sic. Mark you this, people?
All [*Plebeians*]. To th' Rock, to th' Rock with him!
Sic. Peace!
We need not put new matter to his charge.
What you have seen him do and heard him speak,
Beating your officers, cursing yourselves,
Opposing laws with strokes, and here defying
Those whose great power must try him — even this,
So criminal and in such capital kind,
Deserves th' extremest death.
Bru. But since he hath
Serv'd well for Rome —
Cor. What do you prate of service?
Bru. I talk of that that know it.
Cor. You?
Men. Is this the promise that you made your mother?
Com. Know, I pray you —
Cor. I'll know no further.
Let them pronounce the steep Tarpeian death,
Vagabond exile, flaying, pent to linger
But with a grain a day — I would not buy
Their mercy at the price of one fair word,
Nor check my courage for what they can give,
To have't with saying 'Good morrow.'
Sic. For that he has
(As much as in him lies) from time to time
Envied against the people, seeking means
To pluck away their power; as now at last
Given hostile strokes, and that not in the presence
Of dreaded justice but on the ministers
That do distribute it — in the name o' th' people
And in the power of us the tribunes, we
(Ev'n from this instant) banish him our city,
In peril of precipitation
From off the Rock Tarpeian, never more
To enter our Rome gates. I' th' people's name,
I say it shall be so.
All [*Plebeians*]. It shall be so! it shall be so! Let him away!
He's banish'd, and it shall be so!
Com. Hear me, my masters and my common friends!
Sic. He's sentenc'd. No more hearing.
Com. Let me speak.
I have been consul, and can show for Rome
Her enemies' marks upon me. I do love
My country's good with a respect more tender,
More holy and profound, than mine own life,
My dear wive's estimate, her womb's increase
And treasure of my loins. Then if I would
Speak that —
Sic. We know your drift. Speak what?
Bru. There's no more to be said, but he is banish'd,
As enemy to the people and his country.
It shall be so.

All [*Plebeians*]. It shall be so! it shall be so!

Cor. You common cry of curs, whose breath I hate
As reek o' th' rotten fens, whose loves I prize
As the dead carcasses of unburied men
That do corrupt my air, I banish you!
And here remain with your uncertainty.
Let every feeble rumour shake your hearts!
Your enemies with nodding of their plumes
Fan you into despair! Have the power still
To banish your defenders, till at length
Your ignorance (which finds not till it feels,
Making not reservation of yourselves,
Still your own foes) deliver you, as most
Abated captives, to some nation
That won you without blows! Despising
For you the city, thus I turn my back.
There is a world elsewhere.

Exeunt Coriolanus, Cominius, [*Menenius,*] *with* [*the other Patricians*].

Æd. The people's enemy is gone, is gone!

They all shout and throw up their caps.

All. Our enemy is banish'd! he is gone.
Hoo! hoo!

Sic. Go see him out at gates and follow him
As he hath follow'd you, with all despite;
Give him deserv'd vexation. Let a guard
Attend us through the city.

All. Come, come, let's see him out at gates! Come!
The gods preserve our noble tribunes! Come!

Exeunt.

ACT IV. [Scene I. *Rome. At a gate of the city.*]

Enter *Coriolanus, Volumnia, Virgilia, Menenius, Cominius,* with the young *Nobility* of Rome.

Cor. Come, leave your tears. A brief farewell. The beast
With many heads butts me away. Nay, mother,
Where is your ancient courage? You were us'd
To say extremity was the trier of spirits;
That common chances common men could bear;
That when the sea was calm, all boats alike
Show'd mastership in floating; fortune's blows
When most struck home, being gentle wounded craves
A noble cunning. You were us'd to load me
With precepts that would make invincible
The heart that conn'd them.

Vir. O heavens! O heavens!

Cor. Nay, I prithee, woman —

Vol. Now the red pestilence strike all trades in Rome,
And occupations perish!

Cor. What, what, what!
I shall be lov'd when I am lack'd. Nay, mother,
Resume that spirit when you were wont to say,
If you had been the wife of Hercules,
Six of his labours you'ld have done, and sav'd
Your husband so much sweat. Cominius,
Droop not; adieu. Farewell, my wife, my mother.
I'll do well yet. Thou old and true Menenius,
Thy tears are salter than a younger man's
And venomous to thine eyes. My (sometime) General,
I have seen thee stern, and thou hast oft beheld
Heart-hard'ning spectacles. Tell these sad women
'Tis fond to wail inevitable strokes,
As 'tis to laugh at 'em. My mother, you wot well
My hazards still have been your solace; and
Believe't not lightly — though I go alone,
Like to a lonely dragon, that his fen
Makes fear'd and talk'd of more than seen — your son
Will or exceed the common or be caught
With cautelous baits and practice.

Vol. My first son,
Whither wilt thou go? Take good Cominius
With thee awhile. Determine on some course
More than a wild exposture to each chance
That starts i' th' way before thee.

Vir. O the gods!

Com. I'll follow thee a month, devise with thee
Where thou shalt rest, that thou mayst hear of us,
And we of thee. So, if the time thrust forth
A cause for thy repeal, we shall not send
O'er the vast world to seek a single man
And lose advantage, which doth ever cool
I' th' absence of the needer.

Cor. Fare ye well.
Thou hast years upon thee, and thou art too full
Of the wars' surfeits to go rove with one

That's yet unbruis'd. Bring me but out at gate.
Come, my sweet wife, my dearest mother, and
My friends of noble touch. When I am forth,
Bid me farewell, and smile. I pray you come.
While I remain above the ground, you shall
Hear from me still, and never of me aught
But what is like me formerly.
Men. That's worthily
As any ear can hear. Come, let's not weep.
If I could shake off but one seven years
From these old arms and legs, by the good gods,
I'ld with thee, every foot.
Cor. Give me thy hand.
Come. *Exeunt.*

[Scene II. *Rome. A street near the gate.*]

Enter the two *Tribunes, Sicinius* and *Brutus*, with the *Ædile.*

Sic. Bid them all home. He's gone, and we'll no further.
The nobility are vex'd, whom we see have sided
In his behalf.
Bru. Now we have shown our power,
Let us seem humbler after it is done
Than when it was a-doing.
Sic. Bid them home.
Say their great enemy is gone, and they
Stand in their ancient strength.
Bru. Dismiss them home.
[*Exit Ædile.*]
Here comes his mother.

Enter *Volumnia, Virginia,* and *Menenius.*

Sic. Let's not meet her.
Bru. Why?
Sic. They say she's mad.
Bru. They have ta'en note of us. Keep on your way.
Vol. O, y'are well met. The hoarded plague o' th' gods
Requit your love!
Men. Peace, peace! Be not so loud.
Vol. If that I could for weeping, you should hear —
Nay, and you shall hear some. [*To Brutus*] Will you be gone?
Vir. [*to Sicinius*] You shall stay too. I would I had the power
To say so to my husband.
Sic. Are you mankind?
Vol. Ay, fool. Is that a shame? Note but this fool!
Was not a man my father? Hadst thou foxship
To banish him that struck more blows for Rome
Than thou hast spoken words?
Sic. O blessed heavens!
Vol. Moe noble blows than ever thou wise words,
And for Rome's good. I'll tell thee what — Yet go!
Nay, but thou shalt stay too. I would my son
Were in Arabia, and thy tribe before him,
His good sword in his hand.
Sic. What then?
Vir. What then?
He'ld make an end of thy posterity.
Vol. Bastards and all.
Good man, the wounds that he does bear for Rome!
Men. Come, come, peace.
Sic. I would he had continued to his country
As he began, and not unknit himself
The noble knot he made.
Bru. I would he had.
Vol. 'I would he had'? 'Twas you incens'd the rabble.
Cats, that can judge as fitly of his worth
As I can of those mysteries which heaven
Will not have earth to know!
Bru. Pray let us go.
Vol. Now, pray, sir, get you gone.
You have done a brave deed. Ere you go, hear this:
As far as doth the Capitol exceed
The meanest house in Rome, so far my son
(This lady's husband here, this! Do you see?)
Whom you have banish'd does exceed you all.
Bru. Well, well, we'll leave you.
Sic. Why stay we to be baited
With one that wants her wits?
Exeunt Tribunes.
Vol. Take my prayers with you.
I would the gods had nothing else to do
But to confirm my curses. Could I meet 'em
But once a day, it would unclog my heart
Of what lies heavy to't.
Men. You have told them home,
And, by my troth, you have cause. You'll sup with me?
Vol. Anger's my meat. I sup upon myself,
And so shall starve with feeding. — Come, let's go.
Leave this faint puling, and lament as I do,
In anger, Juno-like. Come, come, come!
Exeunt [*Volumnia and Virgilia*].
Men. Fie, fie, fie!
Exit.

[Scene III. *A highway between Rome and Antium.*]

Enter a *Roman* and a *Volsce* [meeting].

Rom. I know you well, sir, and you know me. Your name, I think, is Adrian.

Volsce. It is so, sir. Truly I have forgot you.

Rom. I am a Roman; and my services are, as you are, against 'em. Know you me yet?

Volsce. Nicanor? No?

Rom. The same, sir.

Volsce. You had more beard when I last saw you, but your favour is well approv'd by your tongue. What's the news in Rome? I have a note from the Volscian state to find you out there. You have well saved me a day's journey.

Rom. There hath been in Rome strange insurrections — the people against the senators, patricians, and nobles.

Volsce. Hath been? Is it ended then? Our state thinks not so. They are in a most warlike preparation and hope to come upon them in the heat of their division.

Rom. The main blaze of it is past, but a small thing would make it flame again; for the nobles receive so to heart the banishment of that worthy Coriolanus that they are in a ripe aptness to take all power from the people and to pluck from them their tribunes for ever. This lies glowing, I can tell you, and is almost mature for the violent breaking out.

Volsce. Coriolanus banish'd?

Rom. Banish'd, sir.

Volsce. You will be welcome with this intelligence, Nicanor.

Rom. The day serves well for them now. I have heard it said the fittest time to corrupt a man's wife is when she's fall'n out with her husband. Your noble Tullus Aufidius will appear well in these wars, his great opposer, Coriolanus, being now in no request of his country.

Volsce. He cannot choose. I am most fortunate thus accidentally to encounter you. You have ended my business, and I will merrily accompany you home.

Rom. I shall between this and supper tell you most strange things from Rome, all tending to the good of their adversaries. Have you an army ready, say you?

Volsce. A most royal one, — the centurions and their charges, distinctly billeted, already in th' entertainment and to be on foot at an hour's warning.

Rom. I am joyful to hear of their readiness and am the man, I think, that shall set them in present action. So, sir, heartily well met, and most glad of your company.

Volsce. You take my part from me, sir. I have the most cause to be glad of yours.

Rom. Well, let us go together. *Exeunt.*

[Scene IV. *Antium. Before* Aufidius's *house.*]

Enter *Coriolanus* in mean apparel, disguis'd and muffled.

Cor. A goodly city is this Antium. City,
'Tis I that made thy widows. Many an heir
Of these fair edifices fore my wars
Have I heard groan and drop. Then know me not,
Lest that thy wives with spits and boys with stones
In puny battle slay me.

Enter a *Citizen.*

Save you, sir.

Cit. And you.

Cor. Direct me, if it be your will,
Where great Aufidius lies. Is he in Antium?

Cit. He is, and feasts the nobles of the state
At his house this night.

Cor. Which is his house, beseech you?

Cit. This here before you.

Cor. Thank you, sir. Farewell.

Exit Citizen.

O world, thy slippery turns! Friends now fast sworn,
Whose double bosom seems to wear one heart,
Whose hours, whose bed, whose meal and exercise
Are still together, who twin (as 'twere) in love
Unseparable, shall within this hour,
On a dissension of a doit, break out
To bitterest enmity. So fellest foes,
Whose passions and whose plots have broke their sleep
To take the one the other, by some chance,
Some trick not worth an egg, shall grow dear friends
And interjoin their issues. So with me.
My birthplace hate I, and my love's upon
This enemy town. I'll enter. If he slay me,
He does fair justice; if he give me way,
I'll do his country service. *Exit.*

[Scene V. *Antium. A hall in* Aufidius's *house.*]

Music plays. Enter a *Servingman.*

1. Serv. Wine, wine, wine! What service is here! I think our fellows are asleep. [*Exit.*]

Enter another *Servingman.*

2. Serv. Where's Cotus? My master calls for him. Cotus! *Exit.*

Enter *Coriolanus.*

Cor. A goodly house. The feast smells well, but I
Appear not like a guest.

Enter the first *Servingman.*

1. Serv. What would you have, friend? Whence are you? Here's no place for you. Pray go to the door. *Exit.*

Cor. I have deserv'd no better entertainment
In being Coriolanus.

Enter second *Servant.*

2. Serv. Whence are you, sir? Has the porter his eyes in his head that he gives entrance to such companions? Pray get you out.

Cor. Away!

2. Serv. Away? Get you away!

Cor. Now th'art troublesome.

2. Serv. Are you so brave? I'll have you talk'd with anon.

Enter third *Servingman*; the first meets him.

3. Serv. What fellow's this?

1. Serv. A strange one as ever I look'd on. I cannot get him out o' th' house. Prithee call my master to him.

3. Serv. What have you to do here, fellow? Pray you avoid the house.

Cor. Let me but stand. I will not hurt your hearth.

3. Serv. What are you?

Cor. A gentleman.

3. Serv. A marv'llous poor one.

Cor. True, so I am.

3. Serv. Pray you, poor gentleman, take up some other station. Here's no place for you. Pray you avoid. Come.

Cor. Follow your function, go and batten on cold bits. *Pushes him away from him.*

3. Serv. What, you will not? Prithee tell my master what a strange guest he has here.

2. Serv. And I shall. *Exit.*

3. Serv. Where dwell'st thou?

Cor. Under the canopy.

3. Serv. Under the canopy?

Cor. Ay.

3. Serv. Where's that?

Cor. I' th' city of kites and crows.

3. Serv. I' th' city of kites and crows? What an ass it is! — Then thou dwell'st with daws too?

Cor. No, I serve not thy master.

3. Serv. How, sir? Do you meddle with my master?

Cor. Ay. 'Tis an honester service than to meddle with thy mistress.
Thou prat'st and prat'st. Serve with thy trencher. Hence! *Beats him away.*

Enter *Aufidius,* with the [second] *Servingman.*

Auf. Where is this fellow?

2. Serv. Here, sir. I'd have beaten him like a dog but for disturbing the lords within.

[*While Aufidius and Coriolanus converse, the first and second Servingmen stand back.*]

Auf. Whence com'st thou? What wouldst thou? Thy name?
Why speak'st not? Speak, man. What's thy name?

Cor. If, Tullus, [*Unmuffles.*]
Not yet thou know'st me, and, seeing me, dost not
Think me for the man I am, necessity
Commands me name myself.

Auf. What is thy name?

Cor. A name unmusical to the Volscians' ears
And harsh in sound to thine.

Auf. Say, what's thy name?
Thou hast a grim appearance, and thy face
Bears a command in't. Though thy tackle's torn,
Thou show'st a noble vessel. What's thy name?

Cor. Prepare thy brow to frown. Know'st thou me yet?

Auf. I know thee not. Thy name?

Cor. My name is Caius Marcius, who hath done
To thee particularly and to all the Volsces
Great hurt and mischief. Thereto witness may
My surname Coriolanus. The painful service,
The extreme dangers, and the drops of blood
Shed for my thankless country are requitted
But with that surname — a good memory
And witness of the malice and displeasure
Which thou shouldst bear me. Only that name remains.
The cruelty and envy of the people,

Permitted by our dastard nobles, who
Have all forsook me, hath devour'd the rest
And suffer'd me by th' voice of slaves to be
Whoop'd out of Rome. Now this extremity
Hath brought me to thy hearth; not out of hope
(Mistake me not) to save my life; for if
I had fear'd death, of all the men i' th' world
I would have 'voided thee; but in mere spite,
To be full quit of those my banishers,
Stand I before thee here. Then if thou hast
A heart of wreak in thee, that wilt revenge
Thine own particular wrongs and stop those maims
Of shame seen through thy country, speed thee straight
And make my misery serve thy turn. So use it
That my revengeful services may prove
As benefits to thee; for I will fight
Against my cank'red country with the spleen
Of all the under fiends. But if so be
Thou dar'st not this, and that to prove more fortunes
Th'art tir'd, then, in a word, I also am
Longer to live most weary, and present
My throat to thee and to thy ancient malice;
Which not to cut would show thee but a fool,
Since I have ever followed thee with hate,
Drawn tuns of blood out of thy country's breast,
And cannot live but to thy shame, unless
It be to do thee service.

Auf. O Marcius, Marcius!
Each word thou hast spoke hath weeded from my heart
A root of ancient envy. If Jupiter
Should from yond cloud speak divine things
And say ''Tis true,' I'd not believe them more
Than thee, all-noble Marcius. Let me twine
Mine arms about that body whereagainst
My grained ash an hundred times hath broke
And scarr'd the moon with splinters. Here I cleep
The anvil of my sword, and do contest
As hotly and as nobly with thy love
As ever in ambitious strength I did
Contend against thy valour. Know thou first,
I lov'd the maid I married; never man
Sigh'd truer breath. But that I see thee here,
Thou noble thing, more dances my rapt heart
Than when I first my wedded mistress saw
Bestride my threshold. Why, thou Mars, I tell thee
We have a power on foot, and I had purpose
Once more to hew thy target from thy brawn
Or lose mine arm for't. Thou hast beat me out
Twelve several times, and I have nightly since
Dreamt of encounters 'twixt thyself and me —
We have been down together in my sleep,
Unbuckling helms, fisting each other's throat —
And wak'd half dead with nothing. Worthy Marcius,
Had we no other quarrel else to Rome but that
Thou art thence banish'd, we would muster all
From twelve to seventy, and, pouring war
Into the bowels of ungrateful Rome,
Like a bold flood o'erbeat. O, come, go in,
And take our friendly senators by th' hands,
Who now are here, taking their leaves of me
Who am prepar'd against your territories,
Though not for Rome itself.

Cor. You bless me, gods!

Auf. Therefore, most absolute sir, if thou wilt have
The leading of thine own revenges, take
Th' one half of my commission, and set down —
As best thou art experienc'd, since thou know'st
Thy country's strength and weakness — thine own ways,
Whether to knock against the gates of Rome,
Or rudely visit them in parts remote
To fright them ere destroy. But come in.
Let me commend thee first to those that shall
Say yea to thy desires. A thousand welcomes!
And more a friend than e'er an enemy.
Yet, Marcius, that was much. Your hand. Most welcome!

Exeunt [*Coriolanus and Aufidius*].

Two of the *Servingmen*, [the first and second, come forward].

1. Serv. Here's a strange alteration!

2. Serv. By my hand, I had thought to have stroken him with a cudgel — and yet my mind gave me his clothes made a false report of him.

1. Serv. What an arm he has! He turn'd me about with his finger and his thumb as one would set up a top.

2. Serv. Nay, I knew by his face that there was something in him. He had, sir, a kind of face, methought — I cannot tell how to term it.

1. Serv. He had so, looking as it were — Would I were hang'd but I thought there was more in him than I could think.

2. Serv. So did I, I'll be sworn. He is simply the rarest man i' th' world.

1. Serv. I think he is; but a greater soldier than he you wot on.

2. Serv. Who? My master?

1. Serv. Nay, it's no matter for that.

2. Serv. Worth six on him.

1. Serv. Nay, not so neither. But I take him to be the greater soldier.

2. Serv. Faith, look you, one cannot tell how to say that. For the defence of a town our general is excellent.

1. Serv. Ay, and for an assault too.

Enter the third *Servingman.*

3. Serv. O slaves, I can tell you news! news, you rascals!

Both 1. and 2. Serv. What, what, what? Let's partake.

3. Serv. I would not be a Roman, of all nations. I had as live be a condemn'd man.

Both. Wherefore? wherefore?

3. Serv. Why, here's he that was wont to thwack our general — Caius Marcius.

1. Serv. Why do you say 'thwack our general'?

3. Serv. I do not say 'thwack our general,' but he was always good enough for him.

2. Serv. Come, we are fellows and friends. He was ever too hard for him. I have heard him say so himself.

1. Serv. He was too hard for him directly, to say the troth on't. Before Corioles he scotch'd him and notch'd him like a carbonado.

2. Serv. An he had been cannibally given, he might have broil'd and eaten him too.

1. Serv. But more of thy news!

3. Serv. Why, he is so made on here within as if he were son and heir to Mars; set at upper end o' th' table; no question ask'd him by any of the senators but they stand bald before him. Our general himself makes a mistress of him, sanctifies himself with's hand and turns up the white o' th' eye to his discourse. But the bottom of the news is, our general is cut i' th' middle and but one half of what he was yesterday, for the other has half by the entreaty and grant of the whole table. He'll go, he says, and sole the porter of Rome gates by th' ears. He will mow all down before him and leave his passage poll'd.

2. Serv. And he's as like to do't as any man I can imagine.

3. Serv. Do't? He will do't; for look you, sir, he has as many friends as enemies; which friends, sir, as it were, durst not (look you, sir) show themselves (as we term it) his friends whilst he's in directitude.

1. Serv. Directitude? What's that?

3. Serv. But when they shall see, sir, his crest up again and the man in blood, they will out of their burrows, like conies after rain, and revel all with him.

1. Serv. But when goes this forward?

3. Serv. To-morrow, to-day, presently. You shall have the drum struck up this afternoon. 'Tis as it were a parcel of their feast, and to be executed ere they wipe their lips.

2. Serv. Why, then we shall have a stirring world again. This peace is nothing but to rust iron, increase tailors, and breed ballad-makers.

1. Serv. Let me have war, say I. It exceeds peace as far as day does night. It's sprightly, waking, audible, and full of vent. Peace is a very apoplexy, lethargy; mull'd, deaf, sleepy, insensible; a getter of more bastard children than war's a destroyer of men.

2. Serv. 'Tis so; and as war in some sort may be said to be a ravisher, so it cannot be denied but peace is a great maker of cuckolds.

1. Serv. Ay, and it makes men hate one another.

3. Serv. Reason; because they then less need one another. The wars for my money! I hope to see Romans as cheap as Volscians. They are rising, they are rising.

Both [*1. and 2. Serv.*]. In, in, in, in!

Exeunt.

[Scene VI. *Rome. A public place.*]

Enter the two *Tribunes, Sicinius* and *Brutus.*

Sic. We hear not of him, neither need we fear him:
His remedies are tame. The present peace
And quietness of the people, which before
Were in wild hurry here, do make his friends
Blush that the world goes well; who rather had,
Though they themselves did suffer by't, behold
Dissentious numbers pest'ring streets than see
Our tradesmen singing in their shops and going
About their functions friendly.

Bru. We stood to't in good time.

Enter *Menenius.*

Is this Menenius?

Sic. 'Tis he, 'tis he! O, he is grown most kind
Of late. — Hail, sir!

Men. Hail to you both!

Sic. Your Coriolanus is not much miss'd
But with his friends. The commonwealth doth stand,
And so would do, were he more angry at it.

Men. All's well, and might have been much better if
He could have temporiz'd.

Sic. Where is he, hear you?

Men. Nay, I hear nothing. His mother and his wife
Hear nothing from him.

Enter three or four *Citizens.*

All [*Citizens*]. The gods preserve you both!
Sic. Good-en, our neighbours.
Bru. Good-en to you all, good-en to you all.
1. Cit. Ourselves, our wives, and children, on our knees
Are bound to pray for you both.
Sic. Live and thrive!
Bru. Farewell, kind neighbours. We wish'd Coriolanus
Had lov'd you as we did.
All [*Citizens*]. Now the gods keep you!
Both Trib. Farewell, farewell.
Exeunt Citizens.
Sic. This is a happier and more comely time
Than when these fellows ran about the streets
Crying confusion.
Bru. Caius Marcius was
A worthy officer i' th' war, but insolent,
O'ercome with pride, ambitious past all thinking,
Self-loving —
Sic. And affecting one sole throne
Without assistance.
Men. I think not so.
Sic. We should by this, to all our lamentation,
If he had gone forth consul, found it so.
Bru. The gods have well prevented it, and Rome
Sits safe and still without him.

Enter an *Ædile.*

Æd. Worthy tribunes,
There is a slave whom we have put in prison
Reports the Volsces with two several powers
Are ent'red in the Roman territories
And with the deepest malice of the war
Destroy what lies before 'em.
Men. 'Tis Aufidius,
Who, hearing of our Marcius' banishment,
Thrusts forth his horns again into the world,
Which were inshell'd when Marcius stood for Rome,
And durst not once peep out.
Sic. Come, what talk you of Marcius?
Bru. Go see this rumourer whipp'd. It cannot be
The Volsces dare break with us.
Men. Cannot be?
We have record that very well it can,
And three examples of the like hath been
Within my age. But reason with the fellow
Before you punish him, where he heard this,
Lest you shall chance to whip your information
And beat the messenger who bids beware
Of what is to be dreaded.
Sic. Tell not me.
I know this cannot be.
Bru. Not possible.

Enter a *Messenger.*

Mess. The nobles in great earnestness are going
All to the Senate House. Some news is come
That turns their countenances.
Sic. 'Tis this slave —
Go whip him fore the people's eyes! — his raising,
Nothing but his report.
Mess. Yes, worthy sir.
The slave's report is seconded, and more,
More fearful, is deliver'd.
Sic. What more fearful?
Mess. It is spoke freely out of many mouths
(How probable I do not know) that Marcius,
Join'd with Aufidius, leads a power 'gainst Rome
And vows revenge as spacious as between
The young'st and oldest thing.
Sic. This is most likely!
Bru. Rais'd only that the weaker sort may wish
Good Marcius home again.
Sic. The very trick on't.
Men. This is unlikely.
He and Aufidius can no more atone
Than violent'st contrariety.

Enter [another] *Messenger.*

Mess. You are sent for to the Senate.
A fearful army, led by Caius Marcius
Associated with Aufidius, rages
Upon our territories, and have already
O'erborne their way, consum'd with fire and took
What lay before them.

Enter *Cominius.*

Com. O, you have made good work!
Men. What news? What news?
Com. You have holp to ravish your own daughters and
To melt the city leads upon your pates,
To see your wives dishonour'd to your noses —
Men. What's the news? What's the news?

Com. Your temples burned in their cement, and
Your franchises, whereon you stood, confin'd
Into an auger's bore.
Men. Pray now, your news!
You have made fair work, I fear me. Pray, your news!
If Marcius should be join'd with Volscians —
Com. If?
He is their god. He leads them like a thing
Made by some other deity than Nature,
That shapes man better; and they follow him
Against us brats with no less confidence
Than boys pursuing summer butterflies
Or butchers killing flies.
Men. You have made good work,
You and your apron-men! you that stood so much
Upon the voice of occupation and
The breath of garlic-eaters!
Com. He will shake
Your Rome about your ears.
Men. As Hercules
Did shake down mellow fruit. You have made fair work!
Bru. But is this true, sir?
Com. Ay, and you'll look pale
Before you find it other. All the regions
Do smilingly revolt, and who resist
Are mock'd for valiant ignorance
And perish constant fools. Who is't can blame him?
Your enemies and his find something in him.
Men. We are all undone unless
The noble man have mercy.
Com. Who shall ask it?
The tribunes cannot do't for shame. The people
Deserve such pity of him as the wolf
Does of the shepherds. For his best friends, if they
Should say 'Be good to Rome,' they charg'd him even
As those should do that had deserv'd his hate,
And therein show'd like enemies.
Men. 'Tis true.
If he were putting to my house the brand
That should consume it, I have not the face
To say 'Beseech you cease.' You have made fair hands,
You and your crafts! You have crafted fair!
Com. You have brought
A trembling upon Rome, such as was never
S' incapable of help.
Tribunes. Say not we brought it.
Men. How? Was it we? We lov'd him, but, like beasts
And cowardly nobles, gave way unto your clusters,
Who did hoot him out o' th' city.
Com. But I fear
They'll roar him in again. Tullus Aufidius,
The second name of men, obeys his points
As if he were his officer. Desperation
Is all the policy, strength, and defence
That Rome can make against them.

Enter a troop of *Citizens.*

Men. Here come the clusters.
And is Aufidius with him? You are they
That made the air unwholesome when you cast
Your stinking greasy caps in hooting at
Coriolanus' exile. Now he's coming,
And not a hair upon a soldier's head
Which will not prove a whip. As many coxcombs
As you threw caps up will he tumble down
And pay you for your voices. 'Tis no matter.
If he could burn us all into one coal,
We have deserv'd it.
Omnes. Faith, we hear fearful news.
1. Cit. For mine own part,
When I said banish him, I said 'twas pity.
2. Cit. And so did I.
3. Cit. And so did I; and, to say the truth, so did very many of us. That we did, we did for the best; and though we willingly consented to his banishment, yet it was against our will.
Com. Y'are goodly things, you voices!
Men. You have made
Good work, you and your cry! Shall's to the Capitol?
Com. O, ay! What else? *Exeunt both.*
Sic. Go, masters, get you home. Be not dismay'd.
These are a side that would be glad to have
This true which they so seem to fear. Go home
And show no sign of fear.
1. Cit. The gods be good to us! Come, masters, let's home. I ever said we were i' th' wrong when we banish'd him.
2. Cit. So did we all. But come, let's home.
Exeunt Citizens.
Bru. I do not like this news.
Sic. Nor I.
Bru. Let's to the Capitol. Would half my wealth
Would buy this for a lie!
Sic. Pray let us go.
Exeunt Tribunes.

[Scene VII. *A camp, at a short distance from Rome.*]

Enter *Aufidius* with his *Lieutenant*.

Auf. Do they still fly to th' Roman?
Lieut. I do not know what witchcraft's in him, but
Your soldiers use him as the grace fore meat,
Their talk at table, and their thanks at end;
And you are dark'ned in this action, sir,
Even by your own.
Auf. I cannot help it now,
Unless by using means I lame the foot
Of our design. He bears himself more proudlier,
Even to my person, than I thought he would
When first I did embrace him. Yet his nature
In that's no changeling, and I must excuse
What cannot be amended.
Lieut. Yet I wish, sir
(I mean for your particular), you had not
Join'd in commission with him; but either
Had borne the action of yourself, or else
To him had left it solely.
Auf. I understand thee well; and be thou sure,
When he shall come to his account, he knows not
What I can urge against him. Although it seems,
And so he thinks, and is no less apparent
To th' vulgar eye, that he bears all things fairly
And shows good husbandry for the Volscian state,
Fights dragon-like, and does achieve as soon
As draw his sword; yet he hath left undone
That which shall break his neck or hazard mine
Whene'er we come to our account.
Lieut. Sir, I beseech you, think you he'll carry Rome?
Auf. All places yield to him ere he sits down,
And the nobility of Rome are his;
The senators and patricians love him too.
The tribunes are no soldiers, and their people
Will be as rash in the repeal as hasty
To expel him thence. I think he'll be to Rome
As is the osprey to the fish, who takes it
By sovereignty of nature. First he was
A noble servant to them, but he could not
Carry his honours even. Whether 'twas pride,
Which out of daily fortune ever taints
The happy man; whether defect of judgment,
To fail in the disposing of those chances
Which he was lord of; or whether nature,
Not to be other than one thing, not moving
From th' casque to th' cushion, but commanding peace
Even with the same austerity and garb
As he controll'd the war; but one of these
(As he hath spices of them all, not all,
For I dare so far free him) made him fear'd,
So hated, and so banish'd. But he has a merit
To choke it in the utt'rance. So our virtues
Lie in th' interpretation of the time;
And power, unto itself most commendable,
Hath not a tomb so evident as a chair
T' extol what it hath done.
One fire drives out one fire; one nail, one nail;
Rights by rights falter, strengths by strengths do fail.
Come, let's away. When, Caius, Rome is thine,
Thou art poor'st of all; then shortly art thou mine. *Exeunt.*

Act V. [Scene I. *Rome. A public place.*]

Enter *Menenius, Cominius*; *Sicinius, Brutus,* the two *Tribunes*; with others.

Men. No, I'll not go. You hear what he hath said
Which was sometime his general, who lov'd him
In a most dear particular. He call'd me father.
But what o' that? Go you that banish'd him;
A mile before his tent fall down, and knee
The way into his mercy. Nay, if he coy'd
To hear Cominius speak, I'll keep at home.
Com. He would not seem to know me.
Men. Do you hear?
Com. Yet one time he did call me by my name.
I urg'd our old acquaintance, and the drops
That we have bled together. Coriolanus
He would not answer to; forbade all names.
He was a kind of nothing, titleless,
Till he had forg'd himself a name i' th' fire
Of burning Rome.
Men. Why, so! You have made good work!
A pair of tribunes that have wrack'd fair Rome
To make coals cheap! A noble memory!
Com. I minded him how royal 'twas to pardon
When it was less expected. He replied,

It was a bare petition of a state
To one whom they had punish'd.
Men. Very well.
Could he say less?
Com. I offered to awaken his regard
For 's private friends. His answer to me was,
He could not stay to pick them in a pile
Of noisome musty chaff. He said 'twas folly,
For one poor grain or two, to leave unburnt
And still to nose th' offence.
Men. For one poor grain or two?
I am one of those! his mother, wife, his child,
And this brave fellow too — we are the grains;
You are the musty chaff, and you are smelt
Above the moon. We must be burnt for you!
Sic. Nay, pray be patient. If you refuse your aid
In this so never-needed help, yet do not
Upbraid 's with our distress. But sure, if you
Would be your country's pleader, your good tongue,
More than the instant army we can make,
Might stop our countryman.
Men. No, I'll not meddle.
Sic. Pray you go to him.
Men. What should I do?
Bru. Only make trial what your love can do
For Rome, towards Marcius.
Men. Well, and say that Marcius
Return me, as Cominius is return'd,
Unheard — what then?
But as a discontented friend, grief-shot
With his unkindness? Say't be so?
Sic. Yet your good will
Must have that thanks from Rome after the measure
As you intended well.
Men. I'll undertake't.
I think he'll hear me. Yet, to bite his lip
And hum at good Cominius much unhearts me.
He was not taken well; he had not din'd.
The veins unfill'd, our blood is cold, and then
We pout upon the morning, are unapt
To give or to forgive; but when we have stuff'd
These pipes and these conveyances of our blood
With wine and feeding, we have suppler souls
Than in our priest-like fasts. Therefore I'll watch him
Till he be dieted to my request,
And then I'll set upon him.
Bru. You know the very road into his kindness
And cannot lose your way.
Men. Good faith, I'll prove him,
Speed how it will. I shall ere long have knowledge
Of my success. *Exit.*
Com. He'll never hear him.
Sic. Not?
Com. I tell you he does sit in gold, his eye
Red as 'twould burn Rome, and his injury
The jailer to his pity. I kneel'd before him.
'Twas very faintly he said 'Rise'; dismiss'd me
Thus with his speechless hand. What he would do
He sent in writing after me, what he would not,
Bound with an oath to yield to his conditions;
So that all hope is vain
Unless in his noble mother and his wife,
Who, as I hear, mean to solicit him
For mercy to his country. Therefore let's hence
And with our fair entreaties haste them on.
Exeunt.

[Scene II. *The Volscian camp before Rome.*]

Enter *Menenius* to the *Watch* on guard.

1. Watch. Stay. Whence are you?
2. Watch. Stand, and go back.
Men. You guard like men; 'tis well. But, by your leave,
I am an officer of state and come
To speak with Coriolanus.
1. Watch. From whence?
Men. From Rome.
1. Watch. You may not pass; you must return. Our general
Will no more hear from thence.
2. Watch. You'll see your Rome embrac'd with fire before
You'll speak with Coriolanus.
Men. Good my friends,
If you have heard your general talk of Rome
And of his friends there, it is lots to blanks
My name hath touch'd your ears. It is Menenius.
1. Watch. Be it so! Go back. The virtue of your name
Is not here passable.
Men. I tell thee, fellow,
Thy general is my lover. I have been
The book of his good acts, whence men have read
His fame unparallel'd, haply amplified;
For I have ever verified my friends
(Of whom he's chief) with all the size that verity

Would without lapsing suffer. Nay, sometimes,
Like to a bowl upon a subtle ground,
I have tumbled past the throw, and in his praise
Have (almost) stamp'd the leasing. Therefore, fellow,
I must have leave to pass.

1. Watch. Faith, sir, if you had told as many lies in his behalf as you have uttered words in your own, you should not pass here. No, though it were as virtuous to lie as to live chastely. Therefore go back.

Men. Prithee, fellow, remember my name is Menenius, always factionary on the party of your general.

2. Watch. Howsoever you have been his liar, as you say you have, I am one that, telling true under him, must say you cannot pass. Therefore go back.

Men. Has he din'd, canst thou tell? For I would not speak with him till after dinner.

1. Watch. You are a Roman, are you?

Men. I am, as thy general is.

1. Watch. Then you should hate Rome, as he does. Can you, when you have push'd out your gates the very defender of them, and in a violent popular ignorance given your enemy your shield, think to front his revenges with the easy groans of old women, the virginal palms of your daughters, or with the palsied intercession of such a decay'd dotant as you seem to be? Can you think to blow out the intended fire your city is ready to flame in with such weak breath as this? No, you are deceiv'd. Therefore, back to Rome and prepare for your execution. You are condemn'd; our general has sworn you out of reprieve and pardon.

Men. Sirrah, if thy captain knew I were here, he would use me with estimation.

1. Watch. Come, my captain knows you not.

Men. I mean thy general.

1. Watch. My general cares not for you. Back, I say, go! lest I let forth your half-pint of blood. Back! That's the utmost of your having. Back!

Men. Nay, but, fellow, fellow —

Enter *Coriolanus* with *Aufidius*.

Cor. What's the matter?

Men. Now, you companion, I'll say an errand for you. You shall know now that I am in estimation. You shall perceive that a Jack guardant cannot office me from my son Coriolanus. Guess, but by my entertainment with him, if thou stand'st not i' th' state of hanging, or of some death more long in spectatorship and crueller in suffering. Behold now presently, and swoond for what's to come upon thee. [*To Coriolanus*] The glorious gods sit in hourly synod about thy particular prosperity and love thee no worse than thy old father Menenius does! O my son, my son! Thou art preparing fire for us. Look thee, here's water to quench it. I was hardly moved to come to thee; but being assured none but myself could move thee, I have been blown out of our gates with sighs, and conjure thee to pardon Rome and thy petitionary countrymen. The good gods assuage thy wrath, and turn the dregs of it upon this varlet here — this, who, like a block, hath denied my access to thee.

Cor. Away!

Men. How? Away?

Cor. Wife, mother, child I know not. My affairs
Are servanted to others. Though I owe
My revenge properly, my remission lies
In Volscian breasts. That we have been familiar,
Ingrate forgetfulness shall poison rather
Than pity note how much. Therefore be gone.
Mine ears against your suits are stronger than
Your gates against my force. Yet, for I lov'd thee,
Take this along. I writ it for thy sake
[*Gives a letter.*]
And would have sent it. Another word, Menenius,
I will not hear thee speak. This man, Aufidius,
Was my belov'd in Rome; yet thou behold'st.

Auf. You keep a constant temper.

Exeunt. Manent the Guard and Menenius.

1. Watch. Now, sir, is your name Menenius?

2. Watch. 'Tis a spell, you see, of much power. You know the way home again.

1. Watch. Do you hear how we are shent for keeping your greatness back?

2. Watch. What cause do you think I have to swoond?

Men. I neither care for th' world nor your general; for such things as you, I can scarce think there's any, y'are so slight. He that hath a will to die by himself fears it not from another. Let your general do his worst. For you, be that you are, long; and your misery increase with your age! I say to you, as I was said to, 'Away!' *Exit.*

1. Watch. A noble fellow, I warrant him.

2. Watch. The worthy fellow is our general.
He's the rock, the oak not to be wind-shaken.
Exit Watch.

[Scene III. *The tent of* Coriolanus.]

Enter *Coriolanus* and *Aufidius*, [with others].

Cor. We will before the walls of Rome to-morrow
Set down our host. My partner in this action,
You must report to th' Volscian lords how plainly
I have borne this business.
Auf. Only their ends
You have respected; stopp'd your ears against
The general suit of Rome; never admitted
A private whisper — no, not with such friends
That thought them sure of you.
Cor. This last old man,
Whom with a crack'd heart I have sent to Rome,
Lov'd me above the measure of a father;
Nay, godded me indeed. Their latest refuge
Was to send him; for whose old love I have
(Though I show'd sourly to him) once more offer'd
The first conditions, which they did refuse
And cannot now accept. To grace him only
That thought he could do more, a very little
I have yielded to. Fresh embassies and suits,
Nor from the state nor private friends, hereafter
Will I lend ear to. (*Shout within.*) Ha! What shout is this?
Shall I be tempted to infringe my vow
In the same time 'tis made? I will not.

Enter *Virgilia, Volumnia, Valeria, Young Marcius*, with *Attendants*.

My wife comes foremost; then the honour'd mould
Wherein this trunk was fram'd, and in her hand
The grandchild to her blood. But out, affection!
All bond and privilege of nature, break!
Let it be virtuous to be obstinate.
What is that curtsy worth? or those dove's eyes,
Which can make gods forsworn? I melt and am not
Of stronger earth than others. My mother bows,
As if Olympus to a molehill should
In supplication nod; and my young boy
Hath an aspect of intercession which
Great Nature cries 'Deny not.' — Let the Volsces
Plough Rome and harrow Italy! I'll never
Be such a gosling to obey instinct, but stand
As if a man were author of himself
And knew no other kin.
Vir. My lord and husband!
Cor. These eyes are not the same I wore in Rome.
Vir. The sorrow that delivers us thus chang'd
Makes you think so.
Cor. Like a dull actor now,
I have forgot my part and I am out,
Even to a full disgrace. Best of my flesh,
Forgive my tyranny; but do not say
For that, 'Forgive our Romans.' O, a kiss
Long as my exile, sweet as my revenge!
Now by the jealous queen of heaven, that kiss
I carried from thee, dear, and my true lip
Hath virgin'd it e'er since. You gods! I prate
And the most noble mother of the world
Leave unsaluted. Sink, my knee, i' th' earth; *Kneels.*
Of thy deep duty more impression show
Than that of common sons.
Vol. O, stand up bless'd! [*Raises him.*]
Whilst with no softer cushion than the flint
I kneel before thee, and unproperly
Show duty, as mistaken all this while
Between the child and parent. [*Kneels; he raises her.*]
Cor. What is this?
Your knees to me? to your corrected son?
Then let the pebbles on the hungry beach
Fillop the stars! Then let the mutinous winds
Strike the proud cedars 'gainst the fiery sun,
Murd'ring impossibility, to make
What cannot be, slight work!
Vol. Thou art my warrior;
I holp to frame thee. Do you know this lady?
Cor. The noble sister of Publicola,
The moon of Rome, chaste as the icicle
That's curded by the frost from purest snow
And hangs on Dian's temple! Dear Valeria!
Vol. This is a poor epitome of yours,
Which by th' interpretation of full time
May show like all yourself.
Cor. The god of soldiers,
With the consent of supreme Jove, inform
Thy thoughts with nobleness, that thou mayst prove
To shame unvulnerable, and stick i' th' wars
Like a great seamark, standing every flaw
And saving those that eye thee!
Vol. Your knee, sirrah.
Cor. That's my brave boy!
Vol. Even he, your wife, this lady, and myself
Are suitors to you.

Cor. I beseech you, peace!
Or, if you'ld ask, remember this before:
The thing I have forsworn to grant may never
Be held by you denials. Do not bid me
Dismiss my soldiers or capitulate
Again with Rome's mechanics. Tell me not
Wherein I seem unnatural. Desire not
T' allay my rages and revenges with
Your colder reasons.
Vol. O, no more, no more!
You have said you will not grant us anything;
For we have nothing else to ask but that
Which you deny already: yet we will ask,
That, if you fail in our request, the blame
May hang upon your hardness. Therefore hear us.
Cor. Aufidius, and you Volsces, mark; for we'll
Hear naught from Rome in private. — Your request?
Vol. Should we be silent and not speak, our raiment
And state of bodies would bewray what life
We have led since thy exile. Think with thyself
How more unfortunate than all living women
Are we come hither; since that thy sight, which should
Make our eyes flow with joy, hearts dance with comforts,
Constrains them weep and shake with fear and sorrow,
Making the mother, wife, and child to see
The son, the husband, and the father tearing
His country's bowels out. And to poor we
Thine enmity's most capital. Thou barr'st us
Our prayers to the gods, which is a comfort
That all but we enjoy. For how can we,
Alas, how can we for our country pray,
Whereto we are bound, together with thy victory,
Whereto we are bound? Alack, or we must lose
The country, our dear nurse, or else thy person,
Our comfort in the country. We must find
An evident calamity, though we had
Our wish, which side should win; for either thou
Must as a foreign recreant be led
With manacles thorough our streets, or else
Triumphantly tread on thy country's ruin
And bear the palm for having bravely shed
Thy wife and children's blood. For myself, son,
I purpose not to wait on fortune till
These wars determine. If I cannot persuade thee
Rather to show a noble grace to both parts
Than seek the end of one, thou shalt no sooner
March to assault thy country than to tread
(Trust to't, thou shalt not) on thy mother's womb
That brought thee to this world.
Vir. Ay, and on mine,
That brought you forth this boy to keep your name
Living to time.
Boy. 'A shall not tread on me!
I'll run away till I am bigger, but then I'll fight.
Cor. Not of a woman's tenderness to be
Requires nor child nor woman's face to see.
I have sat too long. [*Rises.*]
Vol. Nay, go not from us thus!
If it were so that our request did tend
To save the Romans, thereby to destroy
The Volsces whom you serve, you might condemn us
As poisonous of your honour. No! our suit
Is that you reconcile them while the Volsces
May say 'This mercy we have show'd,' the Romans,
'This we receiv'd,' and each in either side
Give the all-hail to thee and cry 'Be blest
For making up this peace!' Thou know'st, great son,
The end of war's uncertain, but this certain,
That, if thou conquer Rome, the benefit
Which thou shalt thereby reap is such a name
Whose repetition will be dogg'd with curses,
Whose chronicle thus writ, 'The man was noble,
But with his last attempt he wip'd it out,
Destroy'd his country, and his name remains
To th' ensuing age abhorr'd.' Speak to me, son.
Thou hast affected the fine strains of honour,
To imitate the graces of the gods,
To tear with thunder the wide cheeks o' th' air,
And yet to charge thy sulphur with a bolt
That should but rive an oak. Why dost not speak?
Think'st thou it honourable for a noble man
Still to remember wrongs? Daughter, speak you.
He cares not for your weeping. Speak thou, boy.
Perhaps thy childishness will move him more
Than can our reasons. There's no man in the world
More bound to's mother; yet here he lets me prate
Like one i' th' stocks. Thou hast never in thy life
Show'd thy dear mother any courtesy,

When she (poor hen), fond of no second brood,
Has cluck'd thee to the wars, and safely home
Loaden with honour. Say my request's unjust,
And spurn me back. But if it be not so,
Thou art not honest, and the gods will plague thee
That thou restrain'st from me the duty which
To a mother's part belongs. He turns away.
Down, ladies! Let us shame him with our knees.
To his surname Coriolanus 'longs more pride
Than pity to our prayers. Down! An end!
[*They kneel.*]
This is the last. So, we will home to Rome
And die among our neighbours. Nay, behold's!
This boy, that cannot tell what he would have
But kneels and holds up hands for fellowship,
Does reason our petition with more strength
Than thou hast to deny't. Come, let us go.
[*They rise.*]
This fellow had a Volscian to his mother;
His wife is in Corioles, and this child
Like him by chance. Yet give us our dispatch.
I am hush'd until our city be afire.
And then I'll speak a little.
He holds her by the hand, silent.

Cor. O mother, mother!
What have you done? Behold, the heavens do ope,
The gods look down, and this unnatural scene
They laugh at. O my mother, mother! O!
You have won a happy victory to Rome;
But for your son — believe it, O believe it! —
Most dangerously you have with him prevail'd,
If not most mortal to him. But let it come.
Aufidius, though I cannot make true wars,
I'll frame convenient peace. Now, good Aufidius,
Were you in my stead, would you have heard
A mother less? or granted less, Aufidius?

Auf. I was mov'd withal.

Cor. I dare be sworn you were!
And, sir, it is no little thing to make
Mine eyes to sweat compassion. But, good sir,
What peace you'll make, advise me. For my part,
I'll not to Rome, I'll back with you; and pray you
Stand to me in this cause. O mother! wife!

Auf. [*aside*] I am glad thou hast set thy mercy and thy honour
At difference in thee. Out of that I'll work
Myself a former fortune.

Cor. Ay, by-and-by.
But we will drink together; and you shall bear
A better witness back than words, which we,
On like conditions, will have counterseal'd.
Come, enter with us. Ladies, you deserve
To have a temple built you. All the swords
In Italy, and her confederate arms,
Could not have made this peace. *Exeunt.*

[Scene IV. *Rome. A public place.*]

Enter *Menenius* and *Sicinius*.

Men. See you yond coign o' th' Capitol, yond cornerstone?

Sic. Why, what of that?

Men. If it be possible for you to displace it with your little finger, there is some hope the ladies of Rome, especially his mother, may prevail with him. But I say there is no hope in't. Our throats are sentenc'd and stay upon execution.

Sic. Is't possible that so short a time can alter the condition of a man?

Men. There is differency between a grub and a butterfly; yet your butterfly was a grub. This Marcius is grown from man to dragon. He has wings; he's more than a creeping thing.

Sic. He lov'd his mother dearly.

Men. So did he me; and he no more remembers his mother now than an eight-year-old horse. The tartness of his face sours ripe grapes. When he walks, he moves like an engine, and the ground shrinks before his treading. He is able to pierce a corslet with his eye, talks like a knell, and his hum is a battery. He sits in his state, as a thing made for Alexander. What he bids be done is finish'd with his bidding. He wants nothing of a god but eternity and a heaven to throne in.

Sic. Yes, mercy, if you report him truly.

Men. I paint him in the character. Mark what mercy his mother shall bring from him. There is no more mercy in him than there is milk in a male tiger. That shall our poor city find; and all this is long of you.

Sic. The gods be good unto us!

Men. No, in such a case the gods will not be good unto us. When we banish'd him, we respected not them; and, he returning to break our necks, they respect not us.

Enter a *Messenger*.

Mess. Sir, if you'd save your life, fly to your house.
The plebeians have got your fellow tribune

And hale him up and down; all swearing, if
The Roman ladies bring not comfort home,
They'll give him death by inches.

Enter another *Messenger.*

Sic. What's the news?
Mess. Good news, good news! The ladies have prevail'd,
The Volscians are dislodg'd, and Marcius gone.
A merrier day did never yet greet Rome;
No, not th' expulsion of the Tarquins.
Sic. Friend,
Art thou certain this is true? Is it most certain?
Mess. As certain as I know the sun is fire.
Where have you lurk'd that you make doubt of it?
Ne'er through an arch so hurried the blown tide
As the recomforted through th' gates. Why, hark you!

Trumpets, hautboys; drums beat; all together.

The trumpets, sackbuts, psalteries, and fifes,
Tabors and cymbals and the shouting Romans
Make the sun dance. Hark you!

A shout within.

Men. This is good news.
I will go meet the ladies. This Volumnia
Is worth of consuls, senators, patricians,
A city full; of tribunes such as you,
A sea and land full. You have pray'd well to-day.
This morning for ten thousand of your throats
I'd not have given a doit. Hark, how they joy!

Sound still with the shouts.

Sic. First, the gods bless you for your tidings; next,
Accept my thankfulness.
Mess. Sir, we have all
Great cause to give great thanks.
Sic. They are near the city.
Mess. Almost at point to enter.
Sic. We will meet them
And help the joy. *Exeunt.*

[Scene V. *Rome. A street near the gate.*]

Enter two *Senators,* with *Ladies,* [*Volumnia, Virgilia, Valeria,*] passing over the stage, with other *Lords.*

Senator. Behold our patroness, the life of Rome!
Call all your tribes together, praise the gods,
And make triumphant fires; strew flowers before them.
Unshout the noise that banish'd Marcius;
Repeal him with the welcome of his mother.
Cry, 'Welcome, ladies, welcome!'
All. Welcome, ladies,
Welcome!

A flourish with drums and trumpets. [Exeunt.]

[Scene VI. *Corioles. A public place.*]

Enter *Tullus Aufidius,* with *Attendants.*

Auf. Go tell the lords o' th' city I am here.
Deliver them this paper. Having read it,
Bid them repair to th' market place, where I,
Even in theirs and in the commons' ears,
Will vouch the truth of it. Him I accuse
The city ports by this hath enter'd and
Intends t' appear before the people, hoping
To purge himself with words. Dispatch.

[*Exeunt Attendants.*]

Enter three or four *Conspirators* of *Aufidius'* faction.

Most welcome!
1. Con. How is it with our general?
Auf. Even so
As with a man by his own alms empoison'd
And with his charity slain.
2. Con. Most noble sir,
If you do hold the same intent wherein
You wish'd us parties, we'll deliver you
Of your great danger.
Auf. Sir, I cannot tell.
We must proceed as we do find the people.
3. Con. The people will remain uncertain whilst
'Twixt you there's difference; but the fall of either
Makes the survivor heir of all.
Auf. I know it;
And my pretext to strike at him admits
A good construction. I rais'd him, and I pawn'd
Mine honour for his truth; who being so heighten'd,
He watered his new plants with dews of flattery,
Seducing so my friends; and to this end
He bow'd his nature, never known before
But to be rough, unswayable, and free.
3. Con. Sir, his stoutness
When he did stand for consul, which he lost
By lack of stooping —
Auf. That I would have spoke of.
Being banish'd for't, he came unto my hearth,

Presented to my knife his throat. I took him;
Made him joint-servant with me; gave him way
In all his own desires; nay, let him choose
Out of my files, his projects to accomplish,
My best and freshest men; serv'd his designments
In mine own person; holp to reap the fame
Which he did end all his, and took some pride
To do myself this wrong; till at the last
I seem'd his follower, not partner, and
He wag'd me with his countenance as if
I had been mercenary.

1. Con. So he did, my lord.
The army marvell'd at it; and, in the last,
When he had carried Rome and that we look'd
For no less spoil than glory —

Auf. There was it!
For which my sinews shall be stretch'd upon him.
At a few drops of women's rheum, which are
As cheap as lies, he sold the blood and labour
Of our great action. Therefore shall he die,
And I'll renew me in his fall. But hark!

Drums and trumpets sound, with great shouts of the people.

1. Con. Your native town you enter'd like a post
And had no welcomes home; but he returns
Splitting the air with noise.

2. Con. And patient fools,
Whose children he hath slain, their base throats tear
With giving him glory.

3. Con. Therefore, at your vantage,
Ere he express himself or move the people
With what he would say, let him feel your sword,
Which we will second. When he lies along,
After your way his tale pronounc'd shall bury
His reasons with his body.

Auf. Say no more.
Here come the lords.

Enter the *Lords* of the city.

All Lords. You are most welcome home.

Auf. I have not deserv'd it.
But, worthy lords, have you with heed perus'd
What I have written to you?

All. We have.

1. Lord. And grieve to hear't.
What faults he made before the last, I think
Might have found easy fines; but there to end
Where he was to begin, and give away
The benefit of our levies, answering us
With our own charge, making a treaty where
There was a yielding — this admits no excuse.

Auf. He approaches. You shall hear him.

Enter *Coriolanus,* marching with *Drum* and *Colours,* the *Commoners* being with him.

Cor. Hail, lords! I am return'd your soldier;
No more infected with my country's love
Than when I parted hence, but still subsisting
Under your great command. You are to know
That prosperously I have attempted, and
With bloody passage led your wars even to
The gates of Rome. Our spoils we have brought home
Doth more than counterpoise a full third part
The charges of the action. We have made peace
With no less honour to the Antiates
Than shame to th' Romans; and we here deliver,
Subscrib'd by th' consuls and patricians,
Together with the seal o' th' Senate, what
We have compounded on.

Auf. Read it not, noble lords;
But tell the traitor in the highest degree
He hath abus'd your powers.

Cor. Traitor? How now?

Auf. Ay, traitor, Marcius.

Cor. Marcius?

Auf. Ay, Marcius, Caius Marcius! Dost thou think
I'll grace thee with that robbery, thy stol'n name
Coriolanus, in Corioles?
You lords and heads o' th' state, perfidiously
He has betray'd your business and given up,
For certain drops of salt, your city Rome
(I say 'your city') to his wife and mother;
Breaking his oath and resolution like
A twist of rotten silk; never admitting
Counsel o' th' war; but at his nurse's tears
He whin'd and roar'd away your victory,
That pages blush'd at him, and men of heart
Look'd wond'ring each at other.

Cor. Hear'st thou, Mars?

Auf. Name not the god, thou boy of tears!

Cor. Ha!

Auf. No more.

Cor. Measureless liar, thou hast made my heart
Too great for what contains it. Boy? O slave!
Pardon me, lords; 'tis the first time that ever
I was forc'd to scold. Your judgments, my grave lords,
Must give this cur the lie; and his own notion —

Who wears my stripes impress'd upon him, that
Must bear my beating to his grave — shall join
To thrust the lie unto him.

1. Lord. Peace both, and hear me speak.

Cor. Cut me to pieces, Volsces. Men and lads,
Stain all your edges on me. Boy? False hound!
If you have writ your annals true, 'tis there,
That, like an eagle in a dovecote, I
Flutter'd your Volscians in Corioles.
Alone I did it. Boy?

Auf. Why, noble lords,
Will you be put in mind of his blind fortune,
Which was your shame, by this unholy braggart?
Fore your own eyes and ears?

All Conspirators. Let him die for't!

All People. Tear him to pieces! — Do it presently! — He kill'd my son! — My daughter! — He kill'd my cousin Marcus! — He kill'd my father!

2. Lord. Peace, ho! No outrage! Peace!
The man is noble, and his fame folds in
This orb o' th' earth. His last offences to us
Shall have judicious hearing. Stand, Aufidius,
And trouble not the peace.

Cor. O that I had him,
With six Aufidiuses, or more — his tribe,
To use my lawful sword!

Auf. Insolent villain!

All Conspirators. Kill, kill, kill, kill, kill him!

Draw the Conspirators, and kill Marcius, who falls. Aufidius stands on him.

Lords. Hold, hold, hold, hold!

Auf. My noble masters, hear me speak.

1. Lord. O Tullus!

2. Lord. Thou hast done a deed whereat valour will weep.

3. Lord. Tread not upon him. Masters all, be quiet!
Put up your swords.

Auf. My lords, when you shall know (as in this rage
Provok'd by him you cannot) the great danger
Which this man's life did owe you, you'll rejoice
That he is thus cut off. Please it your Honours
To call me to your Senate, I'll deliver
Myself your loyal servant or endure
Your heaviest censure.

1. Lord. Bear from hence his body,
And mourn you for him. Let him be regarded
As the most noble corse that ever herald
Did follow to his urn.

2. Lord. His own impatience
Takes from Aufidius a great part of blame.
Let's make the best of it.

Auf. My rage is gone,
And I am struck with sorrow. Take him up.
Help three o' th' chiefest soldiers; I'll be one.
Beat thou the drum that it speak mournfully.
Trail your steel pikes. Though in this city he
Hath widowed and unchilded many a one,
Which to this hour bewail the injury,
Yet he shall have a noble memory.
Assist.

Exeunt, bearing the body of Marcius. A dead march sounded.

Titus Andronicus

On January 24, 1594, Henslowe's *Diary* records '*Titus & Ondronicous*' as a new play acted by the Earl of Sussex's men. On February 6th 'a Noble Roman Historye of Tytus Andronicus' was entered in the Stationers' Register by John Danter, who printed the First Quarto in the same year. The title-page professes to give the tragedy 'As it was Plaide by the . . . Earle of Darbie, Earle of Pembrooke, and Earle of Sussex their Seruants.' This identifies it with that recorded by Henslowe as 'new,' and would fix the date of composition as not later than 1593.

In the anonymous comedy *A Knack to Know a Knave*, a passage of eight lines refers unmistakably to Titus's 'conquest on the Goths' and to the offer of 'the imperiall Diademe' 'in requitall of his seruice done.' *A Knack*, though not printed until 1594, is recorded by Henslowe as a new play acted on June 10, 1592. This seems to put the composition of Titus Andronicus back to 1592, which is certainly a reasonable date, though it seems to conflict with Henslowe, whose record would indicate a first performance in January, 1594. The 'Tittus and Vespacia' (for 'Vespasian') acted on April 11, 1592, dealt in all probability with the fall of Jerusalem and had nothing to do with Titus Andronicus. In the Induction to Jonson's *Bartholomew Fair*, the Articles of Agreement between the spectators and the author (dated October 31, 1614) provide that 'he that will swear *Jeronimo* [i.e. Kyd's *Spanish Tragedy*] or *Andronicus* are the best plays yet, shall pass unexcepted at here, as a man whose judgment shows it is constant, and hath stood still these five-and-twenty or thirty years.' This would put *The Spanish Tragedy* back to 1584–1589; but twenty-five and thirty are obviously round numbers. It is certainly older than Titus Andronicus; and, if we date Kyd's play about 1589, we are at liberty to put Titus Andronicus anywhere in the first half of the next decade. On the whole, it is safe to settle upon 1592 or 1593, with preference for 1592.

For the text, the First Quarto (1594) is the authority. Two other quartos, which came out in 1600 and 1611, supply v, 3, 201–204. The second scene of Act iii appears for the first time in the Folio.

Shakespeare's connection with Titus Andronicus has been a moot question for two centuries and a half, ever since the irresponsible minor playwright Edward Ravenscroft, in the Address prefixed to his *Titus Andronicus, or the Rape of Lavinia* (acted in 1678, printed in 1687), acknowledged his indebtedness to Shakespeare's play and remarked, 'I have been told by some anciently conversant with the Stage, that it was not Originally his, but brought by a private Authour to be Acted, and he only gave some Master-touches to one or two of the Principal Parts or Characters.' The idle gossip which he reports (or invents) cannot weigh against the positive assertion of Meres — made in 1598, when the play was only five or six years old — that it is one of Shakespeare's 'excellent' tragedies. Nobody would have listened to Ravenscroft but for the feeling that Titus Andronicus is too horrible to be Shakespeare's. But Shakespeare was always prone to try experiments, and it would be strange if he had not written one out-and-out tragedy of blood when Kyd had shown how powerfully such things appealed to playgoers.

For his plot, the author has skilfully fused two famous classical stories of revenge, both involving the Thyestean banquet — the Revenge of Atreus, from Seneca's *Thyestes*, and the Rape of Philomela, from Ovid's *Metamorphoses*. With these he has combined the story of Virginius and his daughter (v, 3, 35–58), the revolt of Coriolanus (iv, 4, 62–68), and the sacrifice of a young and innocent captive to appease the restless shades of the dead (i, 1, 97 ff.). This is taken from Seneca's *Troades*. It becomes the moving cause of the whole drama of revenge and counter-revenge. Tamora, whose son is thus sacrificed, is bidden (i, 1, 136 ff.) to hope for aid from

> The selfsame gods that arm'd the Queen of Troy
> With opportunity of sharp revenge
> Upon the Thracian tyrant in his tent.

The rape of Philomela is made contributory to Tamora's vengeance,[1] which thus becomes more than the *lex talionis* could justify. The principle of excess is asserted by the raging Atreus in *Thyestes*, 195: 'Scelera non ulcisceris nisi vincis.' As applied by Shakespeare, it shifts our sympathies to the side of Titus. Additional savagery in the mutilation, beyond that in the Ovidian tale, increases the debit balance, and for the rest of the tragedy the revenger is Titus, on his daughter's behalf as well as his own.

In all these matters the author makes his sources clear by actual citation. Philomela is mentioned no less than six times, and Lavinia shows her father the story in a copy of 'Ovid's Metamorphoses' (iv, 1, 42). Scraps from Ovid (i, 150) and Seneca (*Phædra*, 1180, cf. *Hercules Furens*, 90; *Phædra*, 671–672, cf. 902, 1159) are quoted in Latin (iv, 3, 4; ii, 1, 135; iv, 1, 81–82). Coriolanus and Virginius are mentioned by name (iv, 4, 68; v, 3, 36). With these credits in mind, one recognizes the influence of Ovid and Seneca in many passages. Tamora's vivid description of the 'barren detested vale' (ii, 3, 93 ff.) is reminiscent both of Seneca's *Thyestes* (650 ff.) and of Ovid (vi, 521). 'Was never Scythia half so barbarous' (i, 1, 131) echoes the words of Andromache in the *Troades* (1104 ff.). 'Andronicus, stain not thy tomb with blood' comes from the same play (255–256):

> Quid caede dira nobiles clari ducis
> Aspergis umbras?

The fear of 'prodigies on earth' (i, 1, 100–101) is also from the *Troades* (168 ff.) and Tamora's supplication to Titus (i, 1, 104 ff.) recalls Hecuba's to Ulysses (691 ff.). Even the grotesque detail of Titus in cook's attire (v, 3, 25) is suggested by what Atreus tells of himself in *Thyestes* (1059–1066).

The classical sources, however, give us no hint of Aaron. For him the author had recourse to some story of a cruel Moor not unlike a tale in Bandello's *Novelle* (iii, 21). He developed the character as that of a Machiavellian villain, but in the episode of Aaron and his black baby he contrived to bring the Moor into vivid contact with normal human nature.

Distaste for horrors ought not to make one regardless of the skilful construction of the play, of its dramatic power, and of the magnificence of many poetical passages. With all its faults, it is far beyond the abilities of either Peele or Greene. Shakespeare must have the credit as well as the discredit of its authorship.

[1] This point is brought out distinctly in ii, 3, 39 ff., 120 ff., 161–167, 187–191.

THE TRAGEDY OF TITUS ANDRONICUS

PHOTOGRAPHS BY ANGUS MCBEAN
PRODUCED BY MEMORIAL THEATRE COMPANY
STRATFORD-UPON-AVON

Sir Laurence Olivier as the Roman general Titus Andronicus—a stern patrician type

Lavinia (Vivien Leigh), heroine of a drama of foul crimes and horrible vengeance

Anthony Quayle as the Moor, Aaron, one of the most evil characters conceived by Shakespeare

Maxine Audley as Tamora, Queen of the Goths, taken by young Saturninus as his Empress

"Thrice-noble Titus, spare my first-born son." Tamora pleads vainly with Titus for the life of her eldest son, who has been taken prisoner by the Romans *(Act I, Scene I)*

"Lavinia, live; outlive thy father's days." Titus greets his daughter on his return to Rome *(Act I, Scene I)*

"Behold, I choose thee, Tamora, for my bride." Saturninus (Frank Thring) passes over Lavinia and accepts the captive Tamora as his wife *(Act I, Scene I)*

"I'll find a day to massacre them all." Tamora tells Saturninus of her hatred for Titus and his family *(Act I, Scene I)*

Chaste and beautiful, Lavinia is the first victim of the vengeful Tamora

Aaron halts a duel between the sons of Tamora, Chiron (Kevin Miles) and Demetrius (Lee Montague), both of whom claim they love Lavinia *(Act II, Scene I)*

"Ah! my sweet Moor, sweeter to me than life." The ruthless Tamora and her unscrupulous lover, Aaron *(Act II, Scene III)*

Tamora threatens Lavinia as she weeps beside her dead lover, Bassianus (Ralph Michael), slain by the Queen's sons *(Act II, Scene III)*

Having ravished Lavinia, Chiron and Demetrius taunt their victim *(Act II, Scene IV)*

The mutilated Lavinia is helpless to testify against her ravishers, Tamora's sons

Titus beseeches Lavinia to name those who wronged her *(Act III, Scene I)*

In an effort to reveal her fate, Lavinia seeks in a book the story of Philomela, who suffered a similar experience *(Act IV, Scene I)*

Holding a staff in her maimed arms, Lavinia traces in the sand the names of her ravishers *(Act IV, Scene I)*

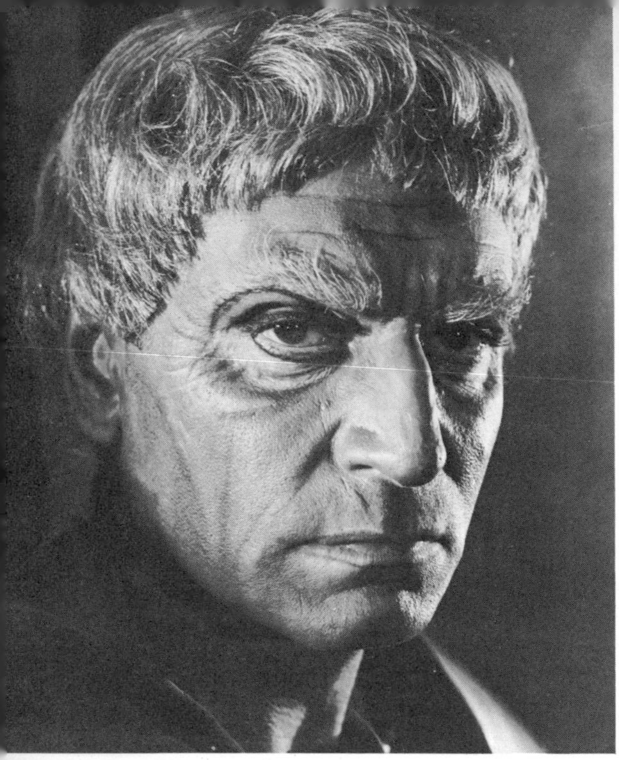

A stern observer of the ancient code, Titus slays his own daughter rather than let her live on in shame *(Act V, Scene III)*

Titus' son Lucius (Michael Denison) joins the Goths to avenge his family *(Act V, Scene I)*

THE TRAGEDY OF
TITUS ANDRONICUS

[Dramatis Personæ.

Saturninus, son to the late Emperor of Rome, and afterwards declared Emperor.
Bassianus, brother to *Saturninus*; in love with *Lavinia*.
Titus Andronicus, a Roman, General against the Goths.
Marcus Andronicus, Tribune of the People, brother to *Titus*.
Lucius, *Quintus*, *Martius*, *Mutius*, sons to *Titus Andronicus*.
Young Lucius, a boy, son to *Lucius*.
Publius, son to *Marcus Andronicus*.
Sempronius, *Caius*, *Valentine*, kinsmen to *Titus Andronicus*.
Æmilius, a noble Roman.
Alarbus, *Demetrius*, *Chiron*, sons to *Tamora*.
Aaron, a Moor, beloved by *Tamora*.
A Captain.
A Messenger.
A Clown.

Tamora, Queen of the Goths.
Lavinia, daughter to *Titus Andronicus*.
A Nurse, and a black Child.

Romans and Goths, Senators, Tribunes, Officers, Soldiers, Attendants.

SCENE. — *Rome and the neighbourhood*.]

ACT I. Scene I. [*Rome. Before the Capitol.*]

Flourish. Enter the *Tribunes* and *Senators* aloft. And then enter [below] *Saturninus* and his *Followers* at one door; and *Bassianus* and his *Followers* at the other, with *Drums* and *Trumpets*.

Sat. Noble patricians, patrons of my right,
Defend the justice of my cause with arms.
And, countrymen, my loving followers,
Plead my successive title with your swords.
I am his first-born son that was the last
That ware the imperial diadem of Rome.
Then let my father's honours live in me,
Nor wrong mine age with this indignity.

Bas. Romans, friends, followers, favourers of my right,
If ever Bassianus, Cæsar's son,
Were gracious in the eyes of royal Rome,
Keep then this passage to the Capitol;
And suffer not dishonour to approach
The imperial seat, to virtue consecrate,
To justice, continence, and nobility;
But let desert in pure election shine;
And, Romans, fight for freedom in your choice.

Enter *Marcus Andronicus*, aloft, with the crown.

Marc. Princes that strive by factions and by friends
Ambitiously for rule and empery,
Know that the people of Rome, for whom we stand
A special party, have by common voice
In election for the Roman empery
Chosen Andronicus, surnamed Pius
For many good and great deserts to Rome.
A nobler man, a braver warrior,
Lives not this day within the city walls.
He by the Senate is accited home
From weary wars against the barbarous Goths,
That with his sons (a terror to our foes)
Hath yok'd a nation strong, train'd up in arms.
Ten years are spent since first he undertook
This cause of Rome, and chastised with arms
Our enemies' pride. Five times he hath return'd

Bleeding to Rome, bearing his valiant sons
In coffins from the field;[1]
And now at last, laden with honour's spoils,
Returns the good Andronicus to Rome,
Renowned Titus, flourishing in arms.
Let us entreat by honour of his name
Whom (worthily) you would have now succeed,
And in the Capitol and Senate's right,
Whom you pretend to honour and adore,
That you withdraw you and abate your strength,
Dismiss your followers, and, as suitors should,
Plead your deserts in peace and humbleness.

Sat. How fair the Tribune speaks to calm my thoughts!

Bas. Marcus Andronicus, so I do affy
In thy uprightness and integrity,
And so I love and honour thee and thine,
Thy noble brother Titus and his sons,
And her to whom my thoughts are humbled all,
Gracious Lavinia, Rome's rich ornament,
That I will here dismiss my loving friends
And to my fortunes and the people's favour
Commit my cause in balance to be weigh'd.

Exeunt Soldiers [and other Followers of Bassianus].

Sat. Friends that have been thus forward in my right,
I thank you all and here dismiss you all,
And to the love and favour of my country
Commit myself, my person, and the cause.

[Exeunt the Followers of Saturninus.]

Rome, be as just and gracious unto me
As I am confident and kind to thee.
Open the gates and let me in.

Bas. Tribunes, and me, a poor competitor.

Flourish. They go up into the Senate House.

Enter a *Captain.*

Capt. Romans, make way. The good Andronicus,
Patron of virtue, Rome's best champion,
Successful in the battles that he fights,
With honour and with fortune is return'd
From where he circumscribed with his sword
And brought to yoke the enemies of Rome.

Sound drums and trumpets; and then enter two of *Titus'* sons, [*Martius* and *Mutius*;] and then two men bearing a coffin covered with black; then [*Lucius* and *Quintus,*] two other sons; then *Titus Andronicus*; and then *Tamora*, the Queen of Goths, and her two sons, *Chiron* and *Demetrius*, with *Aaron* the Moor and others, as many as can be, [including *Tamora's* son *Alarbus* and other Goths, prisoners]. Then set down the coffin, and *Titus* speaks.

Tit. Hail, Rome, victorious in thy mourning weeds!
Lo, as the bark that hath discharg'd her fraught
Returns with precious lading to the bay
From whence at first she weigh'd her anchorage,
Cometh Andronicus, bound with laurel boughs,
To resalute his country with his tears,
Tears of true joy for his return to Rome.
Thou great defender of this Capitol,
Stand gracious to the rites that we intend!
Romans, of five-and-twenty valiant sons,
Half of the number that King Priam had,
Behold the poor remains, alive and dead!
These that survive let Rome reward with love;
These that I bring unto their latest home,
With burial amongst their ancestors.
Here Goths have given me leave to sheathe my sword.
Titus unkind, and careless of thine own,
Why suffer'st thou thy sons, unburied yet,
To hover on the dreadful shore of Styx?
Make way to lay them by their bretheren.

They open the tomb.

There greet in silence, as the dead are wont,
And sleep in peace, slain in your country's wars.
O sacred receptacle of my joys,
Sweet cell of virtue and nobility,
How many sons hast thou of mine in store
That thou wilt never render to me more!

Luc. Give us the proudest prisoner of the Goths,
That we may hew his limbs and on a pile
Ad manes fratrum sacrifice his flesh
Before this earthy prison of their bones,
That so the shadows be not unappeas'd,
Nor we disturb'd with prodigies on earth.

Tit. I give him you — the noblest that survives,
The eldest son of this distressed queen.

Tam. Stay, Roman brethren! Gracious conqueror,
Victorious Titus, rue the tears I shed,
A mother's tears in passion for her son;
And if thy sons were ever dear to thee,

[1] Here, before line 36, the First Quarto inserts:

and at this day,
To the monument of that *Andronicy*
Done sacrifice of expiation,
And slaine the Noblest prisoner of the *Gothes.*

O, think my son to be as dear to me!
Sufficeth not that we are brought to Rome
To beautify thy triumphs, and return
Captive to thee and to thy Roman yoke;
But must my sons be slaughtered in the streets
For valiant doings in their country's cause?
O, if to fight for king and commonweal
Were piety in thine, it is in these!
Andronicus, stain not thy tomb with blood.
Wilt thou draw near the nature of the gods?
Draw near them then in being merciful.
Sweet mercy is nobility's true badge.
Thrice-noble Titus, spare my first-born son!

Tit. Patient yourself, madam, and pardon me.
These are their brethren, whom your Goths beheld
Alive and dead; and for their brethren slain
Religiously they ask a sacrifice.
To this your son is mark'd, and die he must
T' appease their groaning shadows that are gone.

Luc. Away with him, and make a fire straight,
And with our swords, upon a pile of wood,
Let's hew his limbs till they be clean consum'd.

Exeunt Titus' sons with Alarbus.

Tam. O cruel irreligious piety!

Chi. Was never Scythia half so barbarous.

Dem. Oppose not Scythia to ambitious Rome.
Alarbus goes to rest, and we survive
To tremble under Titus' threat'ning look.
Then, madam, stand resolv'd; but hope withal,
The selfsame gods that arm'd the Queen of Troy
With opportunity of sharp revenge
Upon the Thracian tyrant in his tent
May favour Tamora, the Queen of Goths
(When Goths were Goths, and Tamora was queen),
To quit the bloody wrongs upon her foes.

Enter [*Lucius, Quintus, Martius,* and *Mutius,*] the sons of *Andronicus,* again, [with their swords bloody].

Luc. See, lord and father, how we have perform'd
Our Roman rites. Alarbus' limbs are lopp'd
And entrails feed the sacrificing fire,
Whose smoke like incense doth perfume the sky.
Remaineth naught but to inter our brethren
And with loud 'larums welcome them to Rome.

Tit. Let it be so, and let Andronicus
Make this his latest farewell to their souls.

Sound trumpets, and lay the coffin in the tomb.

In peace and honour rest you here, my sons;
Rome's readiest champions, repose you here in rest,
Secure from worldly chances and mishaps!
Here lurks no treason, here no envy swells,
Here grow no damned drugs, here are no storms,
No noise, but silence and eternal sleep.
In peace and honour rest you here, my sons!

Enter *Lavinia.*

Lav. In peace and honour live Lord Titus long!
My noble lord and father, live in fame!
Lo, at this tomb my tributary tears
I render for my brethren's obsequies;
And at thy feet I kneel with tears of joy
Shed on this earth for thy return to Rome.
O, bless me here with thy victorious hand,
Whose fortunes Rome's best citizens applaud!

Tit. Kind Rome, that hast thus lovingly reserv'd
The cordial of mine age to glad my heart!
Lavinia, live; outlive thy father's days,
And fame's eternal date, for virtue's praise!

[Enter, below, *Marcus Andronicus* and *Tribunes.* Enter *Saturninus* and *Bassanius,* attended.]

Marc. Long live Lord Titus, my beloved brother,
Gracious triumpher in the eyes of Rome!

Tit. Thanks, gentle Tribune, noble brother Marcus.

Marc. And welcome, nephews, from successful wars,
You that survive, and you that sleep in fame!
Fair lords, your fortunes are alike in all
That in your country's service drew your swords;
But safer triumph is this funeral pomp
That hath aspir'd to Solon's happiness
And triumphs over chance in honour's bed.
Titus Andronicus, the people of Rome,
Whose friend in justice thou hast ever been,
Send thee by me, their Tribune and their trust,
This palliament of white and spotless hue;
And name thee in election for the empire
With these our late-deceased Emperor's sons.
Be candidatus then, and put it on,
And help to set a head on headless Rome.

Tit. A better head her glorious body fits
Than his that shakes for age and feebleness.
What should I don this robe, and trouble you?
Be chosen with proclamations to-day,
To-morrow yield up rule, resign my life,

And set abroach new business for you all?
Rome, I have been thy soldier forty years,
And led my country's strength successfully,
And buried one-and-twenty valiant sons,
Knighted in field, slain manfully in arms
In right and service of their noble country.
Give me a staff of honour for mine age,
But not a sceptre to control the world.
Upright he held it, lords, that held it last.

Marc. Titus, thou shalt obtain and ask the empery.

Sat. Proud and ambitious Tribune, canst thou tell?

Tit. Patience, Prince Saturnine.

Sat. Romans, do me right!
Patricians, draw your swords, and sheathe them not
Till Saturninus be Rome's Emperor.
Andronicus, would thou were shipp'd to hell
Rather than rob me of the people's hearts!

Luc. Proud Saturnine, interrupter of the good
That noble-minded Titus means to thee!

Tit. Content thee, prince. I will restore to thee
The people's hearts, and wean them from themselves.

Bas. Andronicus, I do not flatter thee,
But honour thee, and will do till I die.
My faction if thou strengthen with thy friends,
I will most thankful be; and thanks to men
Of noble minds is honourable meed.

Tit. People of Rome, and People's Tribunes here,
I ask your voices and your suffrages.
Will ye bestow them friendly on Andronicus?

Tribunes. To gratify the good Andronicus,
And gratulate his safe return to Rome,
The people will accept whom he admits.

Tit. Tribunes, I thank you; and this suit I make,
That you create our Emperor's eldest son,
Lord Saturnine; whose virtues will, I hope,
Reflect on Rome as Titan's rays on earth
And ripen justice in this commonweal.
Then, if you will elect by my advice,
Crown him and say 'Long live our Emperor!'

Marc. With voices and applause of every sort,
Patricians and plebeians, we create
Lord Saturninus Rome's great Emperor
And say 'Long live our Emperor Saturnine!'

A long flourish till they come down.

Sat. Titus Andronicus, for thy favours done
To us in our election this day
I give thee thanks in part of thy deserts,
And will with deeds requite thy gentleness;
And for an onset, Titus, to advance
Thy name and honourable family,
Lavinia will I make my emperess,
Rome's royal mistress, mistress of my heart,
And in the sacred Pantheon her espouse.
Tell me, Andronicus, doth this motion please thee?

Tit. It doth, my worthy lord, and in this match
I hold me highly honoured of your Grace;
And here in sight of Rome, to Saturnine,
King and commander of our commonweal,
The wide world's Emperor, do I consecrate
My sword, my chariot, and my prisoners,
Presents well worthy Rome's imperious lord.
Receive them then, the tribute that I owe,
Mine honour's ensigns humbled at thy feet.

Sat. Thanks, noble Titus, father of my life.
How proud I am of thee and of thy gifts
Rome shall record; and when I do forget
The least of these unspeakable deserts,
Romans, forget your fealty to me.

Tit. [*to Tamora*] Now, madam, are you prisoner to an emperor,
To him that, for your honour and your state,
Will use you nobly and your followers.

Sat. [*aside*] A goodly lady, trust me; of the hue
That I would choose, were I to choose anew.—
Clear up, fair Queen, that cloudy countenance.
Though chance of war hath wrought this change of cheer,
Thou com'st not to be made a scorn in Rome.
Princely shall be thy usage every way.
Rest on my word, and let not discontent
Daunt all your hopes. Madam, he comforts you
Can make you greater than the Queen of Goths.
Lavinia, you are not displeas'd with this?

Lav. Not I, my lord, sith true nobility
Warrants these words in princely courtesy.

Sat. Thanks, sweet Lavinia. Romans, let us go.
Ransomless here we set our prisoners free.
Proclaim our honours, lords, with trump and drum.

[*Flourish.*]

Bas. Lord Titus, by your leave, this maid is mine. [*Seizes Lavinia.*]

Tit. How, sir? Are you in earnest then, my lord?

Bas. Ay, noble Titus, and resolv'd withal
To do myself this reason and this right.

Marc. *Suum cuique* is our Roman justice.
This prince in justice seizeth but his own.

Luc. And that he will and shall, if Lucius live.
Tit. Traitors, avaunt! Where is the Emperor's guard?
Treason, my lord! Lavinia is surpris'd!
Sat. Surpris'd? By whom?
Bas. By him that justly may
Bear his betroth'd from all the world away.
[*Exeunt Bassianus and Marcus with Lavinia.*]
Mutius. Brothers, help to convey her hence away,
And with my sword I'll keep this door safe.
[*Exeunt Lucius, Quintus, and Martius.*]
Tit. Follow, my lord, and I'll soon bring her back.
Mutius. My lord, you pass not here.
Tit. What, villain boy?
Bar'st me my way in Rome?
Mutius. Help, Lucius, help!
[*Titus*] *kills him.*
[*During the fray, exeunt Saturninus, Tamora, Demetrius, Chiron, and Aaron.*]

[Enter *Lucius.*]

Luc. My lord, you are unjust, and more than so!
In wrongful quarrel you have slain your son.
Tit. Nor thou nor he are any sons of mine;
My sons would never so dishonour me.

Enter aloft the *Emperor* with *Tamora* and her two *Sons*, and *Aaron* the *Moor*.

Traitor, restore Lavinia to the Emperor.
Luc. Dead, if you will; but not to be his wife,
That is another's lawful promis'd love. [*Exit.*]
Sat. No, Titus, no. The Emperor needs her not —
Nor her, nor thee, nor any of thy stock.
I'll trust by leisure him that mocks me once;
Thee never, nor thy traitorous haughty sons,
Confederates all thus to dishonour me.
Was there none else in Rome to make a stale
But Saturnine? Full well, Andronicus,
Agree these deeds with that proud brag of thine
That saidst I begg'd the empire at thy hands.
Tit. O monstrous! What reproachful words are these?
Sat. But go thy ways! Go give that changing piece
To him that flourish'd for her with his sword!
A valiant son-in-law thou shalt enjoy;
One fit to bandy with thy lawless sons,
To ruffle in the commonwealth of Rome.
Tit. These words are razors to my wounded heart.
Sat. And therefore, lovely Tamora, Queen of Goths,
That, like the stately Phœbe 'mongst her nymphs,
Dost overshine the gallant'st dames of Rome,
If thou be pleas'd with this my sudden choice,
Behold, I choose thee, Tamora, for my bride
And will create thee Emperess of Rome.
Speak, Queen of Goths, dost thou applaud my choice?
And here I swear by all the Roman gods —
Sith priest and holy water are so near,
And tapers burn so bright, and everything
In readiness for Hymenæus stand —
I will not resalute the streets of Rome
Or climb my palace till from forth this place
I lead espous'd my bride along with me.
Tam. And here in sight of heaven to Rome I swear,
If Saturnine advance the Queen of Goths,
She will a handmaid be to his desires,
A loving nurse, a mother to his youth.
Sat. Ascend, fair Queen, Pantheon. Lords, accompany
Your noble Emperor and his lovely bride,
Sent by the heavens for Prince Saturnine,
Whose wisdom hath her fortune conquered.
There shall we consummate our spousal rites.
Exeunt [*all but Titus*].
Tit. I am not bid to wait upon this bride.
Titus, when wert thou wont to walk alone,
Dishonoured thus and challenged of wrongs?

Enter *Marcus* and *Titus' Sons* — [*Lucius*, *Quintus*, and *Martius*].

Marc. O Titus, see! O, see what thou hast done!
In a bad quarrel slain a virtuous son.
Tit. No, foolish Tribune, no! no son of mine —
Nor thou, nor these, confederates in the deed
That hath dishonoured all our family;
Unworthy brother, and unworthy sons!
Luc. But let us give him burial as becomes;
Give Mutius burial with our bretheren.
Tit. Traitors, away! He rests not in this tomb!
This monument five hundreth years hath stood,
Which I have sumptuously reëdified.
Here none but soldiers and Rome's servitors
Repose in fame; none basely slain in brawls.
Bury him where you can, he comes not here.

Marc. My lord, this is impiety in you.
My nephew Mutius' deeds do plead for him;
He must be buried with his bretheren.

Titus' two sons speak.

[*Quint.*, *Mart.*] And shall, or him we will accompany.

Tit. 'And shall'? What villain was it spake that word?

Titus' son speaks.

[*Quint.*] He that would vouch it in any place but here.

Tit. What, would you bury him in my despite?

Marc. No, noble Titus, but entreat of thee
To pardon Mutius and to bury him.

Tit. Marcus, even thou hast stroke upon my crest,
And with these boys mine honour thou hast wounded.
My foes I do repute you every one;
So trouble me no more, but get you gone.

3. Son [*Mart.*] He is not with himself. Let us withdraw.

2. Son [*Quint.*] Not I, till Mutius' bones be buried.

The Brother and the Sons kneel.

Marc. Brother, for in that name doth nature plead —

2. Son [*Quint.*] Father, and in that name doth nature speak —

Tit. Speak thou no more, if all the rest will speed.

Marc. Renowmed Titus, more than half my soul —

Luc. Dear father, soul and substance of us all —

Marc. Suffer thy brother Marcus to inter
His noble nephew here in virtue's nest,
That died in honour and Lavinia's cause.
Thou art a Roman; be not barbarous.
The Greeks upon advice did bury Ajax,
That slew himself; and wise Laertes' son
Did graciously plead for his funerals.
Let not young Mutius then, that was thy joy,
Be barr'd his entrance here.

Tit. Rise, Marcus, rise.

[*They rise.*]

The dismall'st day is this that e'er I saw,
To be dishonoured by my sons in Rome.
Well, bury him, and bury me the next.

They put him in the tomb.

Luc. There lie thy bones, sweet Mutius, with thy friends,
Till we with trophies do adorn thy tomb!

They all kneel and say:

No man shed tears for noble Mutius!
He lives in fame that died in virtue's cause.

[*They rise, and*] *all but Marcus and Titus* [*stand aside*].

Marc. My lord — to step out of these dreary dumps —
How comes it that the subtile Queen of Goths
Is of a sudden thus advanc'd in Rome?

Tit. I know not, Marcus; but I know it is —
Whether by device or no, the heavens can teli.
Is she not then beholding to the man
That brought her for this high good turn so far?
Yes, and will nobly him remunerate.

Flourish. Enter the *Emperor, Tamora* and her two *Sons*, with the *Moor*, at one door. Enter at the other door *Bassianus* and *Lavinia*, with others.

Sat. So, Bassianus, you have play'd your prize.
God give you joy, sir, of your gallant bride!

Bas. And you of yours, my lord! I say no more
Nor wish no less, and so I take my leave.

Sat. Traitor, if Rome have law or we have power,
Thou and thy faction shall repent this rape.

Bas. Rape call you it, my lord, to seize my own,
My true betrothed love, and now my wife?
But let the laws of Rome determine all;
Meanwhile am I possess'd of that is mine.

Sat. 'Tis good, sir. You are very short with us;
But if we live, we'll be as sharp with you.

Bas. My lord, what I have done, as best I may
Answer I must, and shall do with my life.
Only thus much I give your Grace to know:
By all the duties that I owe to Rome,
This noble gentleman, Lord Titus here,
Is in opinion and in honour wrong'd,
That, in the rescue of Lavinia,
With his own hand did slay his youngest son,
In zeal to you, and highly mov'd to wrath
To be controll'd in that he frankly gave.
Receive him then to favour, Saturnine,
That hath express'd himself in all his deeds
A father and a friend to thee and Rome.

Tit. Prince Bassianus, leave to plead my deeds.
'Tis thou, and those, that have dishonoured me.
Rome and the righteous heavens be my judge
How I have lov'd and honoured Saturnine!

Tam. My worthy lord, if ever Tamora
Were gracious in those princely eyes of thine,
Then hear me speak indifferently for all;
And at my suit, sweet, pardon what is past.
Sat. What, madam? be dishonoured openly
And basely put it up without revenge?
Tam. Not so, my lord. The gods of Rome forfend
I should be author to dishonour you!
But on mine honour dare I undertake
For good Lord Titus' innocence in all;
Whose fury not dissembled speaks his griefs.
Then at my suit look graciously on him:
Lose not so noble a friend on vain suppose,
Nor with sour looks afflict his gentle heart.
[*Aside to Sat.*] My lord, be rul'd by me, be won at last;
Dissemble all your griefs and discontents.
You are but newly planted in your throne;
Lest, then, the people, and patricians too,
Upon a just survey take Titus' part,
And so supplant you for ingratitude,
Which Rome reputes to be a heinous sin,
Yield at entreats; and then let me alone:
I'll find a day to massacre them all
And rase their faction and their family,
The cruel father and his traitorous sons,
To whom I sued for my dear son's life;
And make them know what 'tis to let a queen
Kneel in the streets and beg for grace in vain. —
Come, come, sweet Emperor. — Come, Andronicus. —
Take up this good old man, and cheer the heart
That dies in tempest of thy angry frown.
Sat. Rise, Titus, rise; my empress hath prevail'd.
Tit. I thank your Majesty, and her, my lord.
These words, these looks, infuse new life in me.
Tam. Titus, I am incorporate in Rome,
A Roman now adopted happily,
And must advise the Emperor for his good.
This day all quarrels die, Andronicus.
And let it be mine honour, good my lord,
That I have reconcil'd your friends and you.
For you, Prince Bassianus, I have pass'd
My word and promise to the Emperor
That you will be more mild and tractable.
And fear not, lords — and you, Lavinia.
By my advice, all humbled on your knees
You shall ask pardon of his Majesty.
[*Marcus, Lavinia, and the Sons of Titus kneel.*]
Son [*Luc.*] We do, and vow to heaven and to his Highness
That what we did was mildly as we might,
Tend'ring our sister's honour and our own.
Marc. That on mine honour here do I protest.
Sat. Away, and talk not. Trouble us no more.
Tam. Nay, nay, sweet Emperor, we must all be friends.
The Tribune and his nephews kneel for grace.
I will not be denied! Sweet heart, look back.
Sat. Marcus, for thy sake and thy brother's here,
And at my lovely Tamora's entreats,
I do remit these young men's heinous faults.
Stand up! [*They rise.*]
Lavinia, though you left me like a churl,
I found a friend; and sure as death I swore
I would not part a bachelor from the priest.
Come, if the Emperor's court can feast two brides,
You are my guest, Lavinia, and your friends.
This day shall be a love-day, Tamora.
Tit. To-morrow, an it please your Majesty
To hunt the panther and the hart with me,
With horn and hound we'll give your Grace bonjour.
Sat. Be it so, Titus, and gramercy too.
Exeunt. Sound trumpets.

ACT II. [Scene I. *Rome. Before the Palace.*]

Enter *Aaron* alone.

Aar. Now climbeth Tamora Olympus' top,
Safe out of Fortune's shot, and sits aloft,
Secure of thunder's crack or lightning flash,
Advanc'd above pale envy's threat'ning reach.
As when the golden sun salutes the morn
And, having gilt the ocean with his beams,
Gallops the zodiac in his glistering coach
And overlooks the highest-peering hills,
So Tamora.
Upon her wit doth earthly honour wait,
And virtue stoops and trembles at her frown.
Then, Aaron, arm thy heart and fit thy thoughts
To mount aloft with thy imperial mistress,
And mount her pitch whom thou in triumph long
Hast prisoner held, fett'red in amorous chains,
And faster bound to Aaron's charming eyes
Than is Prometheus tied to Caucasus.

Away with slavish weeds and servile thoughts!
I will be bright and shine in pearl and gold,
To wait upon this new-made emperess.
To wait, said I? To wanton with this queen,
This goddess, this Semiramis, this nymph,
This siren that will charm Rome's Saturnine
And see his shipwrack and his commonweal's.
Holloa! what storm is this?

Enter *Chiron* and *Demetrius*, braving.

Dem. Chiron, thy years wants wit, thy wit wants edge
And manners, to intrude where I am grac'd
And may, for aught thou knowest, affected be.
Chi. Demetrius, thou dost overween in all;
And so in this, to bear me down with braves.
'Tis not the difference of a year or two
Makes me less gracious, or thee more fortunate.
I am as able and as fit as thou
To serve, and to deserve my mistress' grace;
And that my sword upon thee shall approve,
And plead my passions for Lavinia's love.
Aar. [*aside*] Clubs, clubs! These lovers will not keep the peace.
Dem. Why, boy, although our mother (unadvis'd)
Gave you a dancing rapier by your side,
Are you so desperate grown to threat your friends?
Go to! Have your lath glued within your sheath
Till you know better how to handle it.
Chi. Meanwhile, sir, with the little skill I have,
Full well shalt thou perceive how much I dare.
Dem. Ay, boy, grow ye so brave?
They draw.
Aar. Why, how now, lords?
So near the Emperor's palace dare ye draw
And maintain such a quarrel openly?
Full well I wot the ground of all this grudge.
I would not for a million of gold
The cause were known to them it most concerns;
Nor would your noble mother for much more
Be so dishonoured in the court of Rome.
For shame, put up!
Dem. Not I, till I have sheath'd
My rapier in his bosom, and withal
Thrust those reproachful speeches down his throat
That he hath breath'd in my dishonour here.
Chi. For that I am prepar'd and full resolv'd,
Foul-spoken coward, that thund'rest with thy tongue
And with thy weapon nothing dar'st perform.
Aar. Away, I say!
Now, by the gods that warlike Goths adore,
This petty brabble will undo us all.
Why, lords, and think you not how dangerous
It is to jet upon a prince's right?
What, is Lavinia then become so loose,
Or Bassianus so degenerate,
That for her love such quarrels may be broach'd
Without controlment, justice, or revenge?
Young lords, beware! and should the Empress know
This discord's ground, the music would not please.
Chi. I care not, I, knew she and all the world.
I love Lavinia more than all the world.
Dem. Youngling, learn thou to make some meaner choice.
Lavinia is thine elder brother's hope.
Aar. Why, are ye mad? or know ye not, in Rome
How furious and impatient they be,
And cannot brook competitors in love?
I tell you, lords, you do but plot your deaths
By this device.
Chi. Aaron, a thousand deaths
Would I propose to achieve her whom I love.
Aar. To achieve her? How?
Dem. Why mak'st thou it so strange?
She is a woman, therefore may be woo'd;
She is a woman, therefore may be won;
She is Lavinia, therefore must be lov'd.
What, man! More water glideth by the mill
Than wots the miller of; and easy it is
Of a cut loaf to steal a shive, we know.
Though Bassianus be the Emperor's brother,
Better than he have worn Vulcan's badge.
Aar. [*aside*] Ay, and as good as Saturninus may.
Dem. Then why should he despair that knows to court it
With words, fair looks, and liberality?
What, hast not thou full often stroke a doe,
And borne her cleanly by the keeper's nose?
Aar. Why, then it seems some certain snatch or so
Would serve your turns.
Chi. Ay, so the turn were serv'd.
Dem. Aaron, thou hast hit it.
Aar. Would you had hit it too!
Then should not we be tir'd with this ado.
Why, hark ye, hark ye! and are you such fools
To square for this? Would it offend you then
That both should speed?
Chi. Faith, not me.
Dem. Nor me, so I were one.

Aar. For shame, be friends, and join for that you jar!
'Tis policy and stratagem must do
That you affect; and so must you resolve
That what you cannot as you would achieve
You must perforce accomplish as you may.
Take this of me: Lucrece was not more chaste
Than this Lavinia, Bassianus' love.
A speedier course than ling'ring languishment
Must we pursue, and I have found the path.
My lords, a solemn hunting is in hand;
There will the lovely Roman ladies troop.
The forest walks are wide and spacious,
And many unfrequented plots there are,
Fitted by kind for rape and villany.
Single you thither then this dainty doe,
And strike her home by force, if not by words.
This way, or not at all, stand you in hope.
Come, come, our Empress, with her sacred wit
To villany and vengeance consecrate,
Will we acquaint with all that we intend;
And she shall file our engines with advice,
That will not suffer you to square yourselves,
But to your wishes' height advance you both.
The Emperor's court is like the House of Fame,
The palace full of tongues, of eyes and ears;
The woods are ruthless, dreadful, deaf, and dull.
There speak and strike, brave boys, and take your turns.
There serve your lust, shadowed from heaven's eye,
And revel in Lavinia's treasury.

Chi. Thy counsel, lad, smells of no cowardice.

Dem. *Sit fas aut nefas*, till I find the stream
To cool this heat, a charm to calm these fits,
Per Styga, per manes vehor. *Exeunt.*

[Scene II. *A forest near Rome.*]

Enter *Titus Andronicus* and his three *Sons*, [*Martius, Lucius,* and *Quintus,*] making a noise with hounds and horns; and *Marcus.*

Tit. The hunt is up, the morn is bright and grey,
The fields are fragrant, and the woods are green.
Uncouple here, and let us make a bay,
And wake the Emperor and his lovely bride,
And rouse the Prince, and ring a hunter's peal,
That all the court may echo with the noise.
Sons, let it be your charge, as it is ours,
To attend the Emperor's person carefully.
I have been troubled in my sleep this night,
But dawning day new comfort hath inspir'd.

Here a cry of hounds, and wind horns in a peal. Then enter Saturninus, Tamora, Bassianus, Lavinia, Chiron, Demetrius, and their *Attendants.*

Many good morrows to your Majesty!
Madam, to you as many and as good!
I promised your Grace a hunter's peal.

Sat. And you have rung it lustily, my lords,
Somewhat too early for new-married ladies.

Bas. Lavinia, how say you?

Lav. I say no.
I have been broad awake two hours and more.

Sat. Come on then. Horse and chariots let us have,
And to our sport! [*To Tamora*] Madam, now shall ye see
Our Roman hunting.

Marc. I have dogs, my lord,
Will rouse the proudest panther in the chase
And climb the highest promontory top.

Tit. And I have horse will follow where the game
Makes way, and run like swallows o'er the plain.

Dem. Chiron, we hunt not, we, with horse nor hound,
But hope to pluck a dainty doe to ground.
Exeunt.

[Scene III. *A lonely part of the forest.*]

Enter *Aaron* alone, [with a bag of gold].

Aar. He that had wit would think that I had none
To bury so much gold under a tree
And never after to inherit it.
Let him that thinks of me so abjectly
Know that this gold must coin a stratagem,
Which, cunningly effected, will beget
A very excellent piece of villany.
And so repose, sweet gold, for their unrest [*Hides the gold.*]
That have their alms out of the Empress' chest.

Enter *Tamora* alone, to the *Moor.*

Tam. My lovely Aaron, wherefore look'st thou sad
When everything doth make a gleeful boast?
The birds chaunt melody on every bush;
The snake lies rolled in the cheerful sun;
The green leaves quiver with the cooling wind
And make a checker'd shadow on the ground.

Under their sweet shade, Aaron, let us sit,
And whilst the babbling echo mocks the hounds,
Replying shrilly to the well-tun'd horns,
As if a double hunt were heard at once,
Let us sit down and mark their yellowing noise;
And — after conflict such as was suppos'd
The wand'ring prince and Dido once enjoy'd,
When with a happy storm they were surpris'd,
And curtain'd with a counsel-keeping cave —
We may, each wreathed in the other's arms
(Our pastimes done), possess a golden slumber,
Whiles hounds and horns and sweet melodious birds
Be unto us as is a nurse's song
Of lullaby to bring her babe asleep.

Aar. Madam, though Venus govern your desires,
Saturn is dominator over mine.
What signifies my deadly-standing eye,
My silence, and my cloudy melancholy,
My fleece of woolly hair that now uncurls
Even as an adder when she doth unroll
To do some fatal execution?
No, madam, these are no Venereal signs.
Vengeance is in my heart, death in my hand,
Blood and revenge are hammering in my head.
Hark, Tamora, the empress of my soul,
Which never hopes more heaven than rests in thee —
This is the day of doom for Bassianus;
His Philomel must lose her tongue to-day,
Thy sons make pillage of her chastity
And wash their hands in Bassianus' blood.
Seest thou this letter? Take it up, I pray thee,
And give the King this fatal-plotted scroll.
Now question me no more. We are espied.
Here comes a parcel of our hopeful booty,
Which dreads not yet their lives' destruction.

Enter *Bassianus* and *Lavinia.*

Tam. Ah, my sweet Moor, sweeter to me than life!

Aar. No more, great Empress. Bassianus comes.
Be cross with him; and I'll go fetch thy sons
To back thy quarrels, whatsoe'er they be. [*Exit.*]

Bas. Who have we here? Rome's royal Emperess,
Unfurnish'd of her well-beseeming troop?
Or is it Dian, habited like her,
Who hath abandoned her holy groves
To see the general hunting in this forest?

Tam. Saucy controller of my private steps!
Had I the power that some say Dian had,
Thy temples should be planted presently
With horns, as was Actæon's, and the hounds
Should drive upon thy new-transformed limbs,
Unmannerly intruder as thou art!

Lav. Under your patience, gentle Empress,
'Tis thought you have a goodly gift in horning,
And to be doubted that your Moor and you
Are singled forth to try experiments.
Jove shield your husband from his hounds to-day!
'Tis pity they should take him for a stag.

Bas. Believe me, Queen, your swarth Cimmerian
Doth make your honour of his body's hue,
Spotted, detested, and abominable.
Why are you sequest'red from all your train,
Dismounted from your snow-white goodly steed,
And wand'red hither to an obscure plot,
Accompanied but with a barbarous Moor,
If foul desire had not conducted you?

Lav. And being intercepted in your sport,
Great reason that my noble lord be rated
For sauciness. — I pray you let us hence,
And let her joy her raven-coloured love.
This valley fits the purpose passing well.

Bas. The King my brother shall have note of this.

Lav. Ay, for these slips have made him noted long.
Good king, to be so mightily abus'd!

Tam. Why have I patience to endure all this?

Enter *Chiron* and *Demetrius.*

Dem. How now, dear sovereign and our gracious mother?
Why doth your Highness look so pale and wan?

Tam. Have I not reason, think you, to look pale?
These two have 'tic'd me hither to this place.
A barren detested vale you see it is;
The trees, though summer, yet forlorn and lean,
O'ercome with moss and baleful mistletoe.
Here never shines the sun; here nothing breeds,
Unless the nightly owl or fatal raven.
And when they show'd me this abhorred pit,
They told me, here, at dead time of the night,
A thousand fiends, a thousand hissing snakes,
Ten thousand swelling toads, as many urchins,
Would make such fearful and confused cries
As any mortal body hearing it
Should straight fall mad, or else die suddenly.
No sooner had they told this hellish tale
But straight they told me they would bind me here
Unto the body of a dismal yew

And leave me to this miserable death.
And then they call'd me foul adulteress,
Lascivious Goth, and all the bitterest terms
That ever ear did hear to such effect;
And had you not by wondrous fortune come,
This vengeance on me had they executed.
Revenge it, as you love your mother's life,
Or be ye not henceforth call'd my children.

Dem. This is a witness that I am thy son. *Stab* [*Bassianus*].

Chi. And this for me, struck home to show my strength. [*Stab him.*]

Lav. Ay, come, Semiramis — nay, barbarous Tamora!
For no name fits thy nature but thy own!

Tam. Give me the poniard. You shall know, my boys,
Your mother's hand shall right your mother's wrong.

Dem. Stay, madam! Here is more belongs to her.
First thrash the corn, then after burn the straw.
This minion stood upon her chastity,
Upon her nuptial vow, her loyalty,
And with that painted hope braves your mightiness;
And shall she carry this unto her grave?

Chi. An if she do, I would I were an eunuch.
Drag hence her husband to some secret hole,
And make his dead trunk pillow to our lust.

Tam. But when ye have the honey ye desire,
Let not this wasp outlive, us both to sting.

Chi. I warrant you, madam, we will make that sure.
Come, mistress, now perforce we will enjoy
That nice-preserved honesty of yours.

Lav. O Tamora! thou bearest a woman's face —

Tam. I will not hear her speak. Away with her!

Lav. Sweet lords, entreat her hear me but a word.

Dem. Listen, fair madam. Let it be your glory
To see her tears; but be your heart to them
As unrelenting flint to drops of rain.

Lav. When did the tiger's young ones teach the dam?
O, do not learn her wrath! She taught it thee;
The milk thou suck'dst from her did turn to marble;
Even at thy teat thou hadst thy tyranny.
Yet every mother breeds not sons alike.
[*To Chiron*] Do thou entreat her show a woman's pity.

Chi. What, wouldst thou have me prove myself a bastard?

Lav. 'Tis true — the raven doth not hatch a lark.
Yet have I heard (O, could I find it now!)
The lion, mov'd with pity, did endure
To have his princely paws par'd all away.
Some say that ravens foster forlorn children
The whilst their own birds famish in their nests.
O, be to me, though thy hard heart say no,
Nothing so kind, but something pitiful!

Tam. I know not what it means. Away with her!

Lav. O, let me teach thee! For my father's sake,
That gave thee life when well he might have slain thee,
Be not obdurate, open thy deaf ears.

Tam. Hadst thou in person ne'er offended me,
Even for his sake am I pitiless.
Remember, boys, I pour'd forth tears in vain
To save your brother from the sacrifice;
But fierce Andronicus would not relent.
Therefore away with her, and use her as you will;
The worse to her, the better lov'd of me.

Lav. O Tamora, be call'd a gentle queen
And with thine own hands kill me in this place!
For 'tis not life that I have begg'd so long.
Poor I was slain when Bassianus died.

Tam. What begg'st thou then? Fond woman, let me go.

Lav. 'Tis present death I beg; and one thing more
That womanhood denies my tongue to tell:
O, keep me from their worse than killing lust,
And tumble me into some loathsome pit,
Where never man's eye may behold my body.
Do this, and be a charitable murderer.

Tam. So should I rob my sweet sons of their fee.
No, let them satisfy their lust on thee.

Dem. Away! for thou hast stay'd us here too long.

Lav. No grace? no womanhood? Ah, beastly creature,
The blot and enemy to our general name!
Confusion fall —

Chi. Nay then, I'll stop your mouth. — Bring thou her husband.
This is the hole where Aaron bid us hide him.

[*Demetrius throws the body of Bassianus into the pit; then exeunt Demetrius and Chiron, dragging off Lavinia.*]

Tam. Farewell, my sons. See that you make her sure.
Ne'er let my heart know merry cheer indeed
Till all the Andronici be made away.
Now will I hence to seek my lovely Moor
And let my spleenful sons this trull deflow'r.
Exit.

Enter *Aaron,* with two of *Titus' Sons,* [*Quintus* and *Martius*].

Aar. Come on, my lords; the better foot before.
Straight will I bring you to the loathsome pit
Where I espied the panther fast asleep.
Quint. My sight is very dull, whate'er it bodes.
Mart. And mine, I promise you. Were it not for shame,
Well could I leave our sport to sleep awhile.
[*Falls into the pit.*]
Quint. What, art thou fallen? What subtile hole is this,
Whose mouth is covered with rude-growing briers,
Upon whose leaves are drops of new-shed blood
As fresh as morning dew distill'd on flowers?
A very fatal place it seems to me.
Speak, brother. Hast thou hurt thee with the fall?
Mart. O brother, with the dismall'st object hurt
That ever eye with sight made heart lament!
Aar. [*aside*] Now will I fetch the King to find them here,
That he thereby may have a likely guess
How these were they that made away his brother.
Exit.
Mart. Why dost not comfort me and help me out
From this unhallowed and blood-stained hole?
Quint. I am surprised with an uncouth fear;
A chilling sweat o'erruns my trembling joints;
My heart suspects more than mine eye can see.
Mart. To prove thou hast a true-divining heart,
Aaron and thou look down into this den
And see a fearful sight of blood and death.
Quint. Aaron is gone, and my compassionate heart
Will not permit mine eyes once to behold
The thing whereat it trembles by surmise.
O, tell me who it is! for ne'er till now
Was I a child to fear I know not what.
Mart. Lord Bassianus lies embrewed here,
All on a heap, like to a slaughtered lamb,
In this detested, dark, blood-drinking pit.
Quint. If it be dark, how dost thou know 'tis he?
Mart. Upon his bloody finger he doth wear
A precious ring that lightens all this hole,
Which, like a taper in some monument,
Doth shine upon the dead man's earthy cheeks
And shows the ragged entrails of the pit.
So pale did shine the moon on Pyramus
When he by night lay bath'd in maiden blood.
O brother, help me with thy fainting hand
(If fear hath made thee faint, as me it hath)
Out of this fell devouring receptacle,
As hateful as Cocytus' misty mouth.
Quint. Reach me thy hand, that I may help thee out,
Or, wanting strength to do thee so much good,
I may be pluck'd into the swallowing womb
Of this deep pit, poor Bassianus' grave.
I have no strength to pluck thee to the brink.
Mart. Nor I no strength to climb without thy help.
Quint. Thy hand once more! I will not loose again
Till thou art here aloft, or I below.
Thou canst not come to me — I come to thee.
Both fall in.

Enter the *Emperor* [*Saturninus*] and *Aaron* the Moor.

Sat. Along with me! I'll see what hole is here
And what he is that now is leapt into it.
Say, who art thou that lately didst descend
Into this gaping hollow of the earth?
Mart. The unhappy son of old Andronicus,
Brought hither in a most unlucky hour
To find thy brother Bassianus dead.
Sat. My brother dead? I know thou dost but jest.
He and his lady both are at the lodge
Upon the north side of this pleasant chase.
'Tis not an hour since I left them there.
Mart. We know not where you left them all alive;
But, out alas! here have we found him dead.

Enter *Tamora* [with *Attendants*; *Titus*] *Andronicus,* and *Lucius.*

Tam. Where is my lord the King?
Sat. Here, Tamora; though griev'd with killing grief.
Tam. Where is thy brother Bassianus?

Sat. Now to the bottom dost thou search my wound.
Poor Bassianus here lies murthered.
Tam. Then all too late I bring this fatal writ,
The complot of this timeless tragedy;
And wonder greatly that man's face can fold
In pleasing smiles such murderous tyranny.
She giveth Saturnine a letter.

Saturninus reads the letter.

'An if we miss to meet him handsomely,
Sweet huntsman — Bassianus 'tis we mean—
Do thou so much as dig the grave for him.
Thou know'st our meaning. Look for thy reward
Among the nettles at the elder tree
Which overshades the mouth of that same pit
Where we decreed to bury Bassianus.
Do this, and purchase us thy lasting friends.'

Sat. O Tamora! was ever heard the like?
This is the pit, and this the elder tree.
Look, sirs, if you can find the huntsman out
That should have murthered Bassianus here.
Aar. My gracious lord, here is the bag of gold.
Sat. [*to Titus*] Two of thy whelps, fell curs of bloody kind,
Have here bereft my brother of his life. —
Sirs, drag them from the pit unto the prison.
There let them bide until we have devis'd
Some never-heard-of torturing pain for them.
Tam. What, are they in this pit? O wondrous thing!
How easily murder is discovered!
Tit. High Emperor, upon my feeble knee
I beg this boon, with tears not lightly shed,
That this fell fault of my accursed sons —
Accursed if the fault be prov'd in them —
Sat. If it be prov'd? You see it is apparent.
Who found this letter? Tamora, was it you?
Tam. Andronicus himself did take it up.
Tit. I did, my lord. Yet let me be their bail;
For by my father's reverent tomb I vow
They shall be ready at your Highness' will
To answer their suspicion with their lives.
Sat. Thou shalt not bail them. See thou follow me.
Some bring the murthered body, some the murtherers.
Let them not speak a word — the guilt is plain;
For, by my soul, were there worse end than death,
That end upon them should be executed.
Tam. Andronicus, I will entreat the King.
Fear not thy sons; they shall do well enough.
Tit. Come, Lucius, come! Stay not to talk with them.
Exeunt.

[Scene IV. *Another part of the forest.*]

Enter the *Empress' Sons,* [*Demetrius* and *Chiron,*] with *Lavinia,* her hands cut off, and her tongue cut out, and ravish'd.

Dem. So, now go tell, an if thy tongue can speak,
Who 'twas that cut thy tongue and ravish'd thee.
Chi. Write down thy mind, bewray thy meaning so,
An if thy stumps will let thee play the scribe.
Dem. See how with signs and tokens she can scrowl.
Chi. Go home, call for sweet water, wash thy hands.
Dem. She hath no tongue to call, nor hands to wash;
And so let's leave her to her silent walks.
Chi. An 'twere my cause, I should go hang myself.
Dem. If thou hadst hands to help thee knit the cord.
Exeunt [*Demetrius and Chiron*].

Wind horns. Enter *Marcus,* from hunting.

Mar. Who is this? — my niece, that flies away so fast?
Cousin, a word. Where is your husband?
If I do dream, would all my wealth would wake me!
If I do wake, some planet strike me down,
That I may slumber an eternal sleep!
Speak, gentle niece. What stern ungentle hand
Hath lopp'd and hew'd and made thy body bare
Of her two branches — those sweet ornaments
Whose circling shadows kings have sought to sleep in
And might not gain so great a happiness
As half thy love? Why dost not speak to me?
Alas, a crimson river of warm blood,
Like to a bubbling fountain stirr'd with wind,
Doth rise and fall between thy rosed lips,
Coming and going with thy honey breath.
But sure some Tereus hath deflow'red thee,
And lest thou shouldst detect him, cut thy tongue.
Ah, now thou turn'st away thy face for shame!
And, notwithstanding all this loss of blood,
As from a conduit with three issuing spouts,

Yet do thy cheeks look red as Titan's face
Blushing to be encoun'tred with a cloud.
Shall I speak for thee? Shall I say 'tis so?
O that I knew thy heart! and knew the beast,
That I might rail at him to ease my mind!
Sorrow concealed, like an oven stopp'd,
Doth burn the heart to cinders where it is.
Fair Philomel — why, she but lost her tongue,
And in a tedious sampler sew'd her mind;
But, lovely niece, that mean is cut from thee.
A craftier Tereus, cousin, hast thou met,
And he hath cut those pretty fingers off
That could have better sew'd than Philomel.
O, had the monster seen those lily hands
Tremble like aspen leaves upon a lute
And make the silken strings delight to kiss them,
He would not then have touch'd them for his life!
Or had he heard the heavenly harmony
Which that sweet tongue hath made,
He would have dropp'd his knife, and fell asleep,
As Cerberus at the Thracian poet's feet.
Come, let us go and make thy father blind;
For such a sight will blind a father's eye.
One hour's storm will drown the fragrant meads;
What will whole months of tears thy father's eyes?
Do not draw back, for we will mourn with thee.
O, could our mourning ease thy misery!
Exeunt.

ACT III. [Scene I. *Rome. A street.*]

Enter the *Judges*, [*Tribunes*,] and *Senators*, with *Titus'* two *Sons*, [*Martius* and *Quintus*,] bound, passing on the stage to the place of execution, and *Titus* going before, pleading.

Tit. Hear me, grave fathers — noble Tribunes, stay,
For pity of mine age, whose youth was spent
In dangerous wars whilst you securely slept.
For all my blood in Rome's great quarrel shed,
For all the frosty nights that I have watch'd,
And for these bitter tears which now you see
Filling the aged wrinkles in my cheeks,
Be pitiful to my condemned sons,
Whose souls are not corrupted as 'tis thought.
For two-and-twenty sons I never wept,
Because they died in honour's lofty bed.

Andronicus lieth down, and the Judges [*etc.*] *pass by him* [*with the prisoners and exeunt*].

For these, Tribunes, in the dust I write
My heart's deep languor and my soul's sad tears.
Let my tears stanch the earth's dry appetite.
My sons' sweet blood will make it shame and blush.
O earth, I will befriend thee more with rain
That shall distil from these two ancient urns
Than youthful April shall with all his show'rs.
In summer's drought I'll drop upon thee still,
In winter with warm tears I'll melt the snow,
And keep eternal springtime on thy face,
So thou refuse to drink my dear sons' blood.

Enter *Lucius*, with his weapon drawn.

O reverent Tribunes, O gentle aged men,
Unbind my sons, reverse the doom of death;
And let me say (that never wept before)
My tears are now prevailing orators!

Luc. O noble father, you lament in vain.
The Tribunes hear you not; no man is by,
And you recount your sorrows to a stone.

Tit. Ah, Lucius, for thy brothers let me plead.
Grave Tribunes, once more I entreat of you —

Luc. My gracious lord, no tribune hears you speak.

Tit. Why, 'tis no matter, man. If they did hear,
They would not mark me; or if they did mark,
They would not pity me. Yet plead I must;
And bootless unto them.
Therefore I tell my sorrows to the stones;
Who, though they cannot answer my distress,
Yet in some sort they are better than the Tribunes,
For that they will not intercept my tale.
When I do weep, they humbly at my feet
Receive my tears and seem to weep with me;
And were they but attired in grave weeds,
Rome could afford no tribune like to these.
A stone is soft as wax, tribunes more hard than stones.
A stone is silent and offendeth not,
And tribunes with their tongues doom men to death. [*Rises.*]

But wherefore stand'st thou with thy weapon drawn?
Luc. To rescue my two brothers from their death;
For which attempt the judges have pronounc'd
My everlasting doom of banishment.
Tit. O happy man! they have befriended thee.
Why, foolish Lucius, dost thou not perceive
That Rome is but a wilderness of tigers?
Tigers must prey, and Rome affords no prey
But me and mine. How happy art thou then
From these devourers to be banished!
But who comes with our brother Marcus here?

Enter *Marcus* with *Lavinia.*

Marc. Titus, prepare thy aged eyes to weep,
Or if not so, thy noble heart to break.
I bring consuming sorrow to thine age.
Tit. Will it consume me? Let me see it then.
Marc. This was thy daughter.
Tit. Why, Marcus, so she is.
Luc. Ay me, this object kills me!
Tit. Faint-hearted boy, arise and look upon her.
Speak, Lavinia, what accursed hand
Hath made thee handless in thy father's sight?
What fool hath added water to the sea
Or brought a fagot to bright-burning Troy?
My grief was at the height before thou cam'st,
And now like Nilus it disdaineth bounds.
Give me a sword! I'll chop off my hands too;
For they have fought for Rome, and all in vain;
And they have nurs'd this woe in feeding life;
In bootless prayer have they been held up,
And they have serv'd me to effectless use.
Now all the service I require of them
Is that the one will help to cut the other.
'Tis well, Lavinia, that thou hast no hands;
For hands to do Rome service, is but vain.
Luc. Speak, gentle sister. Who hath martyr'd thee?
Marc. O, that delightful engine of her thoughts
That blabb'd them with such pleasing eloquence
Is torn from forth that pretty hollow cage
Where, like a sweet melodious bird, it sung
Sweet varied notes, enchanting every ear!
Luc. O, say thou for her! Who hath done this deed?
Marc. O, thus I found her straying in the park,
Seeking to hide herself as doth the deer
That hath receiv'd some unrecuring wound.
Tit. It was my dear, and he that wounded her
Hath hurt me more than had he kill'd me dead;
For now I stand as one upon a rock,
Environ'd with a wilderness of sea,
Who marks the waxing tide grow wave by wave,
Expecting ever when some envious surge
Will in his brinish bowels swallow him.
This way to death my wretched sons are gone;
Here stands my other son, a banish'd man,
And here my brother, weeping at my woes.
But that which gives my soul the greatest spurn
Is dear Lavinia, dearer than my soul.
Had I but seen thy picture in this plight,
It would have madded me. What shall I do
Now I behold thy lively body so?
Thou hast no hands to wipe away thy tears,
Nor tongue to tell me who hath martyr'd thee.
Thy husband he is dead, and for his death
Thy brothers are condemn'd, and dead by this.
Look, Marcus! Ah, son Lucius, look on her!
When I did name her brothers, then fresh tears
Stood on her cheeks, as doth the honeydew
Upon a gath'red lily almost withered.
Marc. Perchance she weeps because they kill'd her husband;
Perchance because she knows them innocent.
Tit. If they did kill thy husband, then be joyful,
Because the law hath ta'en revenge on them.
No, no! they would not do so foul a deed;
Witness the sorrow that their sister makes.
Gentle Lavinia, let me kiss thy lips,
Or make some sign how I may do thee ease.
Shall thy good uncle and thy brother Lucius
And thou and I sit round about some fountain,
Looking all downwards to behold our cheeks
How they are stain'd, like meadows yet not dry
With miry slime left on them by a flood?
And in the fountain shall we gaze so long
Till the fresh taste be taken from that clearness,
And made a brine-pit with our bitter tears?
Or shall we cut away our hands like thine?
Or shall we bite our tongues, and in dumb shows
Pass the remainder of our hateful days?
What shall we do? Let us that have our tongues
Plot some device of further misery,
To make us wond'red at in time to come.
Luc. Sweet father, cease your tears; for at your grief
See how my wretched sister sobs and weeps.
Marc. Patience, dear niece. Good Titus, dry thine eyes.

Tit. Ah, Marcus, Marcus! Brother, well I wot
Thy napkin cannot drink a tear of mine,
For thou, poor man, hast drown'd it with thine own.
Luc. Ah, my Lavinia, I will wipe thy cheeks.
Tit. Mark, Marcus, mark! I understand her signs.
Had she a tongue to speak, now would she say
That to her brother which I said to thee.
His napkin, with his true tears all bewet,
Can do no service on her sorrowful cheeks.
O, what a sympathy of woe is this —
As far from help as Limbo is from bliss!

Enter *Aaron* the *Moor.*

Aar. Titus Andronicus, my lord the Emperor
Sends thee this word, that, if thou love thy sons,
Let Marcus, Lucius, or thyself, old Titus,
Or any one of you, chop off your hand
And send it to the King: he for the same
Will send thee hither both thy sons alive;
And that shall be the ransom for their fault.
Tit. O gracious Emperor! O gentle Aaron!
Did ever raven sing so like a lark
That gives sweet tidings of the sun's uprise?
With all my heart I'll send the Emperor my hand.
Good Aaron, wilt thou help to chop it off?
Luc. Stay, father! for that noble hand of thine,
That hath thrown down so many enemies,
Shall not be sent. My hand will serve the turn.
My youth can better spare my blood than you,
And therefore mine shall save my brothers' lives.
Marc. Which of your hands hath not defended Rome
And rear'd aloft the bloody battleaxe,
Writing destruction on the enemy's castle?
O, none of both but are of high desert!
My hand hath been but idle; let it serve
To ransom my two nephews from their death.
Then have I kept it to a worthy end.
Aar. Nay, come, agree whose hand shall go along,
For fear they die before their pardon come.
Marc. My hand shall go.
Luc. By heaven, it shall not go!
Tit. Sirs, strive no more. Such with'red herbs as these
Are meet for plucking up, and therefore mine!
Luc. Sweet father, if I shall be thought thy son,
Let me redeem my brothers both from death.
Marc. And for our father's sake and mother's care,
Now let me show a brother's love to thee.
Tit. Agree between you. I will spare my hand.
Luc. Then I'll go fetch an axe.
Marc. But I will use the axe.
Exeunt [*Lucius and Marcus*].
Tit. Come hither, Aaron. I'll deceive them both.
Lend me thy hand, and I will give thee mine.
Aar. [*aside*] If that be call'd deceit, I will be honest
And never whilst I live deceive men so.
But I'll deceive you in another sort,
And that you'll say ere half an hour pass.
He cuts off Titus' hand.

Enter *Lucius* and *Marcus* again.

Tit. Now stay your strife. What shall be is dispatch'd.
Good Aaron, give his Majesty my hand.
Tell him it was a hand that warded him
From thousand dangers; bid him bury it.
More hath it merited — that let it have.
As for my sons, say I account of them
As jewels purchas'd at an easy price;
And yet dear too, because I bought mine own.
Aar. I go, Andronicus; and for thy hand
Look by-and-by to have thy sons with thee.
[*Aside*] Their heads, I mean. O, how this villany
Doth fat me with the very thoughts of it!
Let fools do good, and fair men call for grace,
Aaron will have his soul black like his face.
Exit.
Tit. O, here I lift this one hand up to heaven
And bow this feeble ruin to the earth.
If any power pities wretched tears,
To that I call! — [*To Lavinia*] What, wouldst thou kneel with me?
Do then, dear heart; for heaven shall hear our prayers,
Or with our sighs we'll breathe the welkin dim
And stain the sun with fog, as sometime clouds
When they do hug him in their melting bosoms.
Marc. O brother, speak with possibility,
And do not break into these deep extremes.
Tit. Is not my sorrow deep, having no bottom?
Then be my passions bottomless with them!
Marc. But yet let reason govern thy lament.

Tit. If there were reason for these miseries,
Then into limits could I bind my woes.
When heaven doth weep, doth not the earth o'erflow?
If the winds rage, doth not the sea wax mad,
Threat'ning the welkin with his big-swol'n face?
And wilt thou have a reason for this coil?
I am the sea; hark how her sighs do blow!
She is the weeping welkin, I the earth:
Then must my sea be moved with her sighs;
Then must my earth with her continual tears
Become a deluge, overflow'd and drown'd;
For why my bowels cannot hide her woes,
But like a drunkard must I vomit them.
Then give me leave; for losers will have leave
To ease their stomachs with their bitter tongues.

Enter a *Messenger*, with two heads and a hand.

Mess. Worthy Andronicus, ill art thou repaid
For that good hand thou sent'st the Emperor.
Here are the heads of thy two noble sons;
And here's thy hand, in scorn to thee sent back —
Thy grief their sports, thy resolution mock'd,
That woe is me to think upon thy woes
More than remembrance of my father's death. *Exit.*

Marc. Now let hot Ætna cool in Sicily,
And be my heart an ever-burning hell!
These miseries are more than may be borne.
To weep with them that weep doth ease some deal;
But sorrow flouted at is double death.

Luc. Ah, that this sight should make so deep a wound
And yet detested life not shrink thereat!
That ever death should let life bear his name
Where life hath no more interest but to breathe!
[*Lavinia kisses Titus.*]

Marc. Alas, poor heart! that kiss is comfortless
As frozen water to a starved snake.

Tit. When will this fearful slumber have an end?

Marc. Now farewell, flatt'ry; die, Andronicus.
Thou dost not slumber. See thy two sons' heads,
Thy warlike hand, thy mangled daughter here,
Thy other banish'd son with this dear sight
Struck pale and bloodless, and thy brother, I,
Even like a stony image, cold and numb.
Ah, now no more will I control thy griefs!
Rent off thy silver hair, thy other hand
Gnawing with thy teeth; and be this dismal sight
The closing up of our most wretched eyes.
Now is a time to storm. Why art thou still?

Tit. Ha, ha, ha!

Marc. Why dost thou laugh? It fits not with this hour.

Tit. Why, I have not another tear to shed.
Besides, this sorrow is an enemy,
And would usurp upon my wat'ry eyes
And make them blind with tributary tears.
Then which way shall I find Revenge's cave?
For these two heads do seem to speak to me,
And threat me I shall never come to bliss
Till all these mischiefs be return'd again
Even in their throats that have committed them.
Come, let me see what task I have to do.
You heavy people, circle me about,
That I may turn me to each one of you
And swear unto my soul to right your wrongs.
The vow is made. Come, brother, take a head;
And in this hand the other will I bear.
Lavinia, thou shalt be employ'd in these things.
Bear thou my hand, sweet wench, between thy teeth.
As for thee, boy, go get thee from my sight!
Thou art an exile, and thou must not stay.
Hie to the Goths and raise an army there;
And if ye love me, as I think you do,
Let's kiss and part, for we have much to do.
Exeunt. Manet Lucius.

Luc. Farewell, Andronicus, my noble father,
The wofull'st man that ever liv'd in Rome.
Farewell, proud Rome, till Lucius come again!
He leaves his pledges dearer than his life.
Farewell, Lavinia, my noble sister.
O, would thou wert as thou tofore hast been!
But now nor Lucius nor Lavinia lives
But in oblivion and hateful griefs.
If Lucius live, he will requite your wrongs
And make proud Saturnine and his emperess
Beg at the gates like Tarquin and his queen.
Now will I to the Goths and raise a pow'r,
To be reveng'd on Rome and Saturnine. *Exit.*

[Scene II. *A room in the house of Titus.*]

A banquet. Enter [*Titus*] *Andronicus, Marcus, Lavinia,* and the *Boy* [*Lucius*].

Tit. So, so, now sit; and look you eat no more
Than will preserve just so much strength in us
As will revenge these bitter woes of ours.

Marcus, unknit that sorrow-wreathen knot.
Thy niece and I (poor creatures) want our hands
And cannot passionate our tenfold grief
With folded arms. This poor right hand of mine
Is left to tyrannize upon my breast;
Who, when my heart, all mad with misery,
Beats in this hollow prison of my flesh,
Then thus I thump it down.
[*To Lavinia*] Thou map of woe, that thus dost talk in signs!
When thy poor heart beats with outrageous beating,
Thou canst not strike it thus to make it still.
Wound it with sighing, girl, kill it with groans;
Or get some little knife between thy teeth
And just against thy heart make thou a hole,
That all the tears that thy poor eyes let fall
May run into that sink, and soaking in,
Drown the lamenting fool in sea-salt tears.
Marc. Fie, brother, fie! Teach her not thus to lay
Such violent hands upon her tender life.
Tit. How now? Has sorrow made thee dote already?
Why, Marcus, no man should be mad but I.
What violent hands can she lay on her life?
Ah, wherefore dost thou urge the name of hands,
To bid Æneas tell the tale twice o'er
How Troy was burnt and he made miserable?
O, handle not the theme, to talk of hands,
Lest we remember still that we have none.
Fie, fie, how franticly I square my talk,
As if we should forget we had no hands
If Marcus did not name the word of hands!
Come, let's fall to; and, gentle girl, eat this.
Here is no drink! Hark, Marcus, what she says.
I can interpret all her martyr'd signs.
She says she drinks no other drink but tears,
Brew'd with her sorrow, mesh'd upon her cheeks.
Speechless complainer, I will learn thy thought.
In thy dumb action will I be as perfect
As begging hermits in their holy prayers.
Thou shalt not sigh, nor hold thy stumps to heaven,
Nor wink, nor nod, nor kneel, nor make a sign,
But I (of these) will wrest an alphabet
And by still practice learn to know thy meaning.
Boy. Good grandsire, leave these bitter deep laments.
Make my aunt merry with some pleasing tale.
Marc. Alas, the tender boy, in passion mov'd,
Doth weep to see his grandsire's heaviness!
Tit. Peace, tender sapling! Thou art made of tears,
And tears will quickly melt thy life away.
Marcus strikes the dish with a knife.
What dost thou strike at, Marcus, with thy knife?
Marc. At that that I have kill'd, my lord — a fly.
Tit. Out on thee, murderer! Thou kill'st my heart.
Mine eyes are cloy'd with view of tyranny.
A deed of death done on the innocent
Becomes not Titus' brother. Get thee gone!
I see thou art not for my company.
Marc. Alas, my lord, I have but kill'd a fly.
Tit. But? How if that fly had a father and mother?
How would he hang his slender gilded wings
And buzz lamenting doings in the air!
Poor harmless fly,
That, with his pretty buzzing melody,
Came here to make us merry — and thou hast kill'd him.
Marc. Pardon me, sir. It was a black ill-favour'd fly,
Like to the Empress' Moor. Therefore I kill'd him.
Tit. O, O, O!
Then pardon me for reprehending thee,
For thou hast done a charitable deed.
Give me thy knife, I will insult on him,
Flattering myself, as if it were the Moor
Come hither purposely to poison me.
There's for thyself! and that's for Tamora!
Ah, sirrah!
Yet, I think, we are not brought so low
But that between us we can kill a fly
That comes in likeness of a coal-black Moor.
Marc. Alas, poor man! Grief has so wrought on him
He takes false shadows for true substances.
Tit. Come, take away. Lavinia, go with me.
I'll to thy closet and go read with thee
Sad stories chanced in the times of old.
Come, boy, and go with me. Thy sight is young,
And thou shalt read when mine begin to dazzle.
Exeunt.

Act IV. [Scene I. *Rome.* Titus' *garden.*]

Enter *Lucius' Son* and *Lavinia* running after him, and the *Boy* flies from her with his books under his arm. Enter *Titus* and *Marcus.*

Boy. Help, grandsire, help! My aunt Lavinia
Follows me everywhere, I know not why.
Good uncle Marcus, see how swift she comes!
Alas, sweet aunt, I know not what you mean.
Marc. Stand by me, Lucius. Do not fear thine aunt.
Tit. She loves thee, boy, too well to do thee harm.
Boy. Ay, when my father was in Rome she did.
Marc. What means my niece Lavinia by these signs?
Tit. Fear her not, Lucius. Somewhat doth she mean.
See, Lucius, see, how much she makes of thee!
Somewhither would she have thee go with her.
Ah, boy, Cornelia never with more care
Read to her sons than she hath read to thee
Sweet poetry and Tully's Orator.
Marc. Canst thou not guess wherefore she plies thee thus?
Boy. My lord, I know not, I, nor can I guess,
Unless some fit or frenzy do possess her;
For I have heard my grandsire say full oft,
Extremity of griefs would make men mad;
And I have read that Hecuba of Troy
Ran mad for sorrow. That made me to fear;
Although, my lord, I know my noble aunt
Loves me as dear as e'er my mother did,
And would not, but in fury, fright my youth;
Which made me down to throw my books, and fly —
Causeless, perhaps. But pardon me, sweet aunt;
And, madam, if my uncle Marcus go,
I will most willingly attend your ladyship.
Marc. Lucius, I will.
[*Lavinia turns over with her stumps the books which Lucius has let fall.*]
Tit. How now, Lavinia? Marcus, what means this?
Some book there is that she desires to see. —
Which is it, girl, of these? — Open them, boy. —
But thou art deeper read and better skill'd.
Come and take choice of all my library,
And so beguile thy sorrow, till the heavens
Reveal the damn'd contriver of this deed.
Why lifts she up her arms in sequence thus?
Marc. I think she means that there were more than one
Confederate in the fact. Ay, more there was;
Or else to heaven she heaves them for revenge.
Tit. Lucius, what book is that she tosseth so?
Boy. Grandsire, 'tis Ovid's Metamorphoses.
My mother gave it me.
Marc. For love of her that's gone
Perhaps she cull'd it from among the rest.
Tit. Soft! So busily she turns the leaves!
Help her! What would she find? Lavinia, shall I read?
This is the tragic tale of Philomel
And treats of Tereus' treason and his rape;
And rape, I fear, was root of thine annoy.
Marc. See, brother, see! Note how she quotes the leaves.
Tit. Lavinia, wert thou thus surpris'd, sweet girl,
Ravish'd and wrong'd as Philomela was,
Forc'd in the ruthless, vast, and gloomy woods?
See, see!
Ay, such a place there is where we did hunt
(O had we never, never hunted there!)
Pattern'd by that the poet here describes,
By nature made for murthers and for rapes.
Marc. O, why should nature build so foul a den,
Unless the gods delight in tragedies?
Tit. Give signs, sweet girl, for here are none but friends,
What Roman lord it was durst do the deed.
Or slunk not Saturnine, as Tarquin erst,
That left the camp to sin in Lucrece' bed?
Marc. Sit down, sweet niece. Brother, sit down by me.
Apollo, Pallas, Jove, or Mercury,
Inspire me, that I may this treason find.
My lord, look here! Look here, Lavinia!
He writes his name with his staff, and guides it with feet and mouth.
This sandy plot is plain. Guide, if thou canst,
This after me. I have writ my name
Without the help of any hand at all.
Curs'd be that heart that forc'd us to this shift!
Write thou, good niece, and here display at last
What God will have discovered for revenge.

Heaven guide thy pen to print thy sorrows plain,
That we may know the traitors and the truth!
She takes the staff in her mouth and guides it with her stumps and writes.

Tit. O, do ye read, my lord, what she hath writ?
'Stuprum — Chiron — Demetrius.'

Marc. What, what? the lustful sons of Tamora
Performers of this heinous bloody deed?

Tit. *Magni dominator poli,*
Tam lentus audis scelera? tam lentus vides?

Marc. O, calm thee, gentle lord! although I know
There is enough written upon this earth
To stir a mutiny in the mildest thoughts
And arm the minds of infants to exclaims.
My lord, kneel down with me; Lavinia, kneel;
And kneel, sweet boy, the Roman Hector's hope;
And swear with me — as with the woful feere
And father of that chaste dishonoured dame
Lord Junius Brutus sware for Lucrece' rape —
That we will prosecute by good advice
Mortal revenge upon these traitorous Goths,
And see their blood or die with this reproach.

Tit. 'Tis sure enough, an you knew how.
But if you hunt these bear-whelps, then beware.
The dam will wake; and if she wind ye once,
She's with the lion deeply still in league,
And lulls him whilst she playeth on her back,
And when he sleeps will she do what she list.
You are a young huntsman, Marcus; let't alone;
And come, I will go get a leaf of brass,
And with a gad of steel will write these words,
And lay it by. The angry northen wind
Will blow these sands like Sibyl's leaves abroad,
And where's our lesson then? Boy, what say you?

Boy. I say, my lord, that if I were a man,
Their mother's bedchamber should not be safe
For these base bondmen to the yoke of Rome.

Marc. Ay, that's my boy! Thy father hath full oft
For his ungrateful country done the like.

Boy. And, uncle, so will I, an if I live.

Tit. Come go with me into mine armory.
Lucius, I'll fit thee; and withal my boy
Shall carry from me to the Empress' sons
Presents that I intend to send them both.
Come, come! Thou'lt do my message, wilt thou not?

Boy. Ay, with my dagger in their bosoms, grandsire.

Tit. No, boy, not so. I'll teach thee another course.
Lavinia, come. Marcus, look to my house.
Lucius and I'll go brave it at the court.
Ay, marry, will we, sir! and we'll be waited on.
Exeunt [*Titus, Lavinia, and Young Lucius*].

Marc. O heavens, can you hear a good man groan
And not relent, or not compassion him?
Marcus, attend him in his ecstasy,
That hath more scars of sorrow in his heart
Than foemen's marks upon his batt'red shield,
But yet so just that he will not revenge.
Revenge the heavens for old Andronicus!
Exit.

[Scene II. *Rome. The Palace.*]

Enter *Aaron, Chiron,* and *Demetrius* at one door; and at the other door *Young Lucius* and *another,* with a bundle of weapons, and verses writ upon them.

Chi. Demetrius, here's the son of Lucius.
He hath some message to deliver us.

Aar. Ay, some mad message from his mad grandfather.

Boy. My lords, with all the humbleness I may,
I greet your Honours from Andronicus —
[*Aside*] And pray the Roman gods confound you both!

Dem. Gramercy, lovely Lucius. What's the news?

Boy. [*aside*] That you are both decipher'd, that's the news,
For villains mark'd with rape. — May it please you,
My grandsire, well advis'd, hath sent by me
The goodliest weapons of his armory
To gratify your honourable youth,
The hope of Rome; for so he bid me say;
And so I do, and with his gifts present
Your lordships, that, whenever you have need,
You may be armed and appointed well.
And so I leave you both — [*aside*] like bloody villains.
Exit [*with Attendant*].

Dem. What's here? A scroll, and written round about?
Let's see.
[*Reads*] *Integer vitae scelerisque purus*
Non eget Mauri iaculis nec arcu.

Chi. O, 'tis a verse in Horace. I know it well.
I read it in the grammar long ago.

Aar. Ay, just — a verse in Horace. Right, you have it!
[*Aside*] Now what a thing it is to be an ass!
Here's no sound jest! The old man hath found their guilt,
And sends them weapons wrapp'd about with lines
That wound (beyond their feeling) to the quick.
But were our witty Empress well afoot,
She would applaud Andronicus' conceit.
But let her rest in her unrest awhile. —
And now, young lords, was't not a happy star
Led us to Rome, strangers, and more than so,
Captives, to be advanced to this height?
It did me good, before the palace gate
To brave the Tribune in his brother's hearing.
Dem. But me more good to see so great a lord
Basely insinuate, and send us gifts.
Aar. Had he not reason, Lord Demetrius?
Did you not use his daughter very friendly?
Dem. I would we had a thousand Roman dames
At such a bay, by turn to serve our lust.
Chi. A charitable wish and full of love!
Aar. Here lacks but your mother for to say amen.
Chi. And that would she for twenty thousand more.
Dem. Come, let us go and pray to all the gods
For our beloved mother in her pains.
Aar. [*aside*] Pray to the devils. The gods have given us over. *Trumpets sound.*
Dem. Why do the Emperor's trumpets flourish thus?
Chi. Belike for joy the Emperor hath a son.
Dem. Soft! Who comes here?

Enter *Nurse*, with a blackamoor *Child*.

Nurse. Good morrow, lords.
O, tell me, did you see Aaron the Moor?
Aar. Well, more or less, or ne'er a whit at all!
Here Aaron is; and what with Aaron now?
Nurse. O gentle Aaron, we are all undone!
Now help, or woe betide thee evermore!
Aar. Why, what a caterwauling dost thou keep!
What dost thou wrap and fumble in thine arms?
Nurse. O, that which I would hide from heaven's eye —
Our Empress' shame and stately Rome's disgrace!
She is delivered, lords; she is delivered.
Aar. To whom?
Nurse. I mean she is brought abed.
Aar. Well, God give her good rest! What hath he sent her?
Nurse. A devil.
Aar. Why, then she is the devil's dam —
A joyful issue!
Nurse. A joyless, dismal, black, and sorrowful issue!
Here is the babe, as loathsome as a toad
Amongst the fairest breeders of our clime.
The Empress sends it thee, thy stamp, thy seal,
And bids thee christen it with thy dagger's point.
Aar. Zounds, ye whore! is black so base a hue?
Sweet blowse, you are a beauteous blossom sure.
Dem. Villain, what hast thou done?
Aar. That which thou canst not undo.
Chi. Thou hast undone our mother.
Aar. Villain, I have done thy mother.
Dem. And therein, hellish dog, thou hast undone her.
Woe to her chance, and damn'd her loathed choice!
Accurs'd the offspring of so foul a fiend!
Chi. It shall not live.
Aar. It shall not die.
Nurse. Aaron, it must. The mother wills it so.
Aar. What, must it, nurse? Then let no man but I
Do execution on my flesh and blood.
Dem. I'll broach the tadpole on my rapier's point.
Nurse, give it me! My sword shall soon dispatch it.
Aar. Sooner this sword shall plough thy bowels up.
[*Takes the Child from the Nurse, and draws.*]
Stay, murtherous villains! Will you kill your brother?
Now by the burning tapers of the sky,
That shone so brightly when this boy was got,
He dies upon my scimitar's sharp point
That touches this my first-born son and heir!
I tell you, younglings, not Enceladus,
With all his threat'ning band of Typhon's brood,
Nor great Alcides, nor the god of war,
Shall seize this prey out of his father's hands.
What, what, ye sanguine, shallow-hearted boys!
Ye white-lim'd walls! ye alehouse painted signs!
Coal-black is better than another hue
In that it scorns to bear another hue;

For all the water in the ocean
Can never turn the swan's black legs to white,
Although she lave them hourly in the flood.
Tell the Empress from me I am of age
To keep mine own — excuse it how she can.

Dem. Wilt thou betray thy noble mistress thus?

Aar. My mistress is my mistress; this myself,
The vigour and the picture of my youth.
This before all the world do I prefer;
This maugre all the world will I keep safe,
Or some of you shall smoke for it in Rome!

Dem. By this our mother is for ever sham'd.

Chi. Rome will despise her for this foul escape.

Nurse. The Emperor in his rage will doom her death.

Chi. I blush to think upon this ignomy.

Aar. Why, there's the privilege your beauty bears.
Fie, treacherous hue, that will betray with blushing
The close enacts and counsels of thy heart!
Here's a young lad fram'd of another leer.
Look how the black slave smiles upon the father,
As who should say 'Old lad, I am thine own.'
He is your brother, lords, sensibly fed
Of that self blood that first gave life to you;
And from that womb where you imprisoned were
He is enfranchised and come to light.
Nay, he is your brother by the surer side,
Although my seal be stamped in his face.

Nurse. Aaron, what shall I say unto the Empress?

Dem. Advise thee, Aaron, what is to be done,
And we will all subscribe to thy advice.
Save thou the child, so we may all be safe.

Aar. Then sit we down and let us all consult.
My son and I will have the wind of you.
Keep there. Now talk at pleasure of your safety.

Dem. How many women saw this child of his?

Aar. Why, so, brave lords! When we join in league,
I am a lamb; but if you brave the Moor,
The chafed boar, the mountain lioness,
The ocean swells not so as Aaron storms.
But say again, how many saw the child?

Nurse. Cornelia the midwife and myself;
And no one else but the delivered Empress.

Aar. The Empress, the midwife, and yourself —
Two may keep counsel when the third's away.
Go to the Empress; tell her this I said!

He kills her.

Weeke, weeke! — So cries a pig prepared to the spit.

Dem. What mean'st thou, Aaron? Wherefore didst thou this?

Aar. O Lord, sir, 'tis a deed of policy!
Shall she live to betray this guilt of ours —
A long-tongu'd babbling gossip? No, lords, no.
And now be it known to you my full intent.
Not far one Muli lives, my countryman,
His wife but yesternight was brought to bed;
His child is like to her, fair as you are.
Go pack with him, and give the mother gold,
And tell them both the circumstance of all;
And how by this their child shall be advanc'd,
And be received for the Emperor's heir
And substituted in the place of mine,
To calm this tempest whirling in the court;
And let the Emperor dandle him for his own.
Hark ye, lords. You see I have given her physic,
And you must needs bestow her funeral.
The fields are near, and you are gallant grooms.
This done, see that you take no longer days,
But send the midwife presently to me.
The midwife and the nurse well made away,
Then let the ladies tattle what they please.

Chi. Aaron, I see thou wilt not trust the air
With secrets.

Dem. For this care of Tamora,
Herself and hers are highly bound to thee.

Exeunt [Demetrius and Chiron, bearing off the dead Nurse].

Aar. Now to the Goths, as swift as swallow flies,
There to dispose this treasure in mine arms
And secretly to greet the Empress' friends.
Come on, you thick-lipp'd slave, I'll bear you hence;
For it is you that puts us to our shifts.
I'll make you feed on berries and on roots,
And feed on curds and whey, and suck the goat,
And cabin in a cave, and bring you up
To be a warrior and command a camp. *Exit.*

[Scene III. *Rome. A public place.*]

Enter *Titus, Old Marcus, Young Lucius,* and other *Gentlemen,* [*Publius, Sempronius,* and *Caius,*] with bows, and *Titus* bears the arrows with letters on the ends of them.

Tit. Come, Marcus, come. Kinsmen, this is the way.
Sir boy, let me see your archery:
Look ye draw home enough, and 'tis there straight.
Terras Astraea reliquit,
Be you rememb'red, Marcus: she's gone, she's fled.
Sirs, take you to your tools. You, cousins, shall
Go sound the ocean, and cast your nets;
Happily you may catch her in the sea.
Yet there's as little justice as at land.
No! Publius and Sempronius, you must do it.
'Tis you must dig with mattock and with spade
And pierce the inmost centre of the earth;
Then, when you come to Pluto's region,
I pray you deliver him this petition.
Tell him it is for justice and for aid,
And that it comes from old Andronicus,
Shaken with sorrows in ungrateful Rome.
Ah, Rome! Well, well, I made thee miserable
What time I threw the people's suffrages
On him that thus doth tyrannize o'er me.
Go get you gone; and pray be careful all,
And leave you not a man-of-war unsearch'd.
This wicked emperor may have shipp'd her hence;
And, kinsmen, then we may go pipe for justice.

Marc. O Publius, is not this a heavy case,
To see thy noble uncle thus distract?

Pub. Therefore, my lords, it highly us concerns
By day and night t' attend him carefully,
And feed his humour kindly as we may
Till time beget some careful remedy.

Marc. Kinsmen, his sorrows are past remedy.
Join with the Goths, and with revengeful war
Take wreak on Rome for this ingratitude,
And vengeance on the traitor Saturnine.

Tit. Publius, how now? How now, my masters?
What, have you met with her?

Pub. No, my good lord; but Pluto sends you word,
If you will have Revenge from hell, you shall.
Marry, for Justice, she is so employ'd,
He thinks, with Jove in heaven, or somewhere else,
So that perforce you must needs stay a time.

Tit. He doth me wrong to feed me with delays.
I'll dive into the burning lake below
And pull her out of Acheron by the heels.
Marcus, we are but shrubs, no cedars we,
No big-bon'd men fram'd of the Cyclops' size;
But metal, Marcus, steel to the very back,
Yet wrung with wrongs more than our backs can bear;
And, sith there is no justice in earth nor hell,
We will solicit heaven, and move the gods
To send down Justice for to wreak our wrongs.
Come, to this gear. You are a good archer, Marcus. *He gives them the arrows.*
Ad Jovem, that's for you. Here, *Ad Apollinem.*
Ad Martem, that's for myself.
Here, boy, *To Pallas.* Here, *To Mercury.*
To Saturn, Caius — not to Saturnine!
You were as good to shoot against the wind.
To it, boy! Marcus, loose when I bid.
Of my word, I have written to effect;
There's not a god left unsolicited.

Marc. Kinsmen, shoot all your shafts into the court.
We will afflict the Emperor in his pride.

Tit. Now, masters, draw. [*They shoot.*] O, well said, Lucius!
Good boy, in Virgo's lap! Give it Pallas.

Marc. My lord, I aim a mile beyond the moon.
Your letter is with Jupiter by this.

Tit. Ha, ha!
Publius, Publius, what hast thou done?
See, see, thou hast shot off one of Taurus' horns!

Marc. This was the sport, my lord. When Publius shot,
The Bull, being gall'd, gave Aries such a knock
That down fell both the Ram's horns in the court;
And who should find them but the Empress' villain?
She laugh'd, and told the Moor he should not choose
But give them to his master for a present.

Tit. Why, there it goes! God give his lordship joy!

Enter the *Clown,* with a basket, and two pigeons in it.

News, news from heaven! Marcus, the post is come.
Sirrah, what tidings? Have you any letters?
Shall I have justice? What says Jupiter?

Clown. Who? the gibbet-maker? He says that he hath taken them down again, for the man must not be hang'd till the next week.

Tit. But what says Jupiter I ask thee?

Clown. Alas, sir, I know not Jupiter. I never drank with him in all my life.

Tit. Why, villain, art not thou the carrier?

Clown. Ay, of my pigeons, sir; nothing else.

Tit. Why, didst thou not come from heaven?

Clown. From heaven? Alas, sir, I never came there. God forbid I should be so bold to press to heaven in my young days. Why, I am going with my pigeons to the Tribunal Plebs, to take up a matter of brawl betwixt my uncle and one of the Emperial's men.

Marc. Why, sir, that is as fit as can be to serve for your oration; and let him deliver the pigeons to the Emperor from you.

Tit. Tell me, can you deliver an oration to the Emperor with a grace?

Clown. Nay, truly, sir, I could never say grace in all my life.

Tit. Sirrah, come hither. Make no more ado,
But give your pigeons to the Emperor.
By me thou shalt have justice at his hands.
Hold, hold! Meanwhile here's money for thy charges.
Give me pen and ink. Sirrah, can you with a grace deliver a supplication?

Clown. Ay, sir.

Tit. Then here is a supplication for you. And when you come to him, at the first approach you must kneel; then kiss his foot; then deliver up your pigeons; and then look for your reward. I'll be at hand, sir. See you do it bravely.

Clown. I warrant you, sir. Let me alone.

Tit. Sirrah, hast thou a knife? Come, let me see it.
Here, Marcus, fold it in the oration;
For thou hast made it like an humble suppliant.
And when thou hast given it to the Emperor,
Knock at my door and tell me what he says.

Clown. God be with you, sir; I will. *Exit.*

Tit. Come, Marcus, let us go. Publius, follow me. *Exeunt.*

[Scene IV. *Rome. Before the Palace.*]

Enter *Emperor* and *Empress*, and her two *Sons*, [*Demetrius* and *Chiron*; *Lords*, and others]. The *Emperor* brings the arrows in his hand that *Titus* shot at him.

Sat. Why, lords, what wrongs are these! Was ever seen
An emperor in Rome thus overborne,
Troubled, confronted thus; and, for the extent
Of egal justice, us'd in such contempt?
My lords, you know, as know the mightful gods,
However these disturbers of our peace
Buzz in the people's ears, there naught hath pass'd,
But even with law, against the wilful sons
Of old Andronicus. And what an if
His sorrows have so overwhelm'd his wits?
Shall we be thus afflicted in his wreaks,
His fits, his frenzy, and his bitterness?
And now he writes to heaven for his redress.
See, here's *To Jove*, and this *To Mercury*;
This *To Apollo*; this *To the god of war.*
Sweet scrolls to fly about the streets of Rome!
What's this but libelling against the Senate
And blazoning our unjustice everywhere?
A goodly humour, is it not, my lords?
As who would say, in Rome no justice were.
But if I live, his feigned ecstasies
Shall be no shelter to these outrages;
But he and his shall know that justice lives
In Saturninus' health; whom, if he sleep,
He'll so awake as he in fury shall
Cut off the proud'st conspirator that lives.

Tam. My gracious lord, my lovely Saturnine,
Lord of my life, commander of my thoughts,
Calm thee, and bear the faults of Titus' age,
Th' effects of sorrow for his valiant sons,
Whose loss hath pierc'd him deep and scarr'd his heart;
And rather comfort his distressed plight
Than prosecute the meanest or the best
For these contempts. (*Aside*) Why, thus it shall become
High-witted Tamora to gloze with all.
But, Titus, I have touch'd thee to the quick,
Thy lifeblood out. If Aaron now be wise,
Then is all safe, the anchor in the port.

Enter *Clown.*

How now, good fellow? Wouldst thou speak with us?

Clown. Yea, forsooth, an your mistriship be Emperial.

Tam. Empress I am, but yonder sits the Emperor.

Clown. 'Tis he. — God and Saint Stephen give you god-den. I have brought you a letter and a couple of pigeons here.

[*Saturninus*] *reads the letter.*

Sat. Go take him away, and hang him presently.

Clown. How much money must I have?

Tam. Come, sirrah, you must be hang'd.
Clown. Hang'd? By'r Lady, then I have brought up a neck to a fair end.
Exit [*guarded*].
Sat. Despiteful and intolerable wrongs!
Shall I endure this monstrous villany?
I know from whence this same device proceeds.
May this be borne? As if his traitorous sons,
That died by law for murther of our brother,
Have by my means been butchered wrongfully!
Go drag the villain hither by the hair!
Nor age nor honour shall shape privilege.
For this proud mock I'll be thy slaughterman,
Sly frantic wretch, that holp'st to make me great
In hope thyself should govern Rome and me!

Enter *Nuntius Æmilius.*

What news with thee, Æmilius?
Æmil. Arm, my lords! Rome never had more cause!
The Goths have gathered head; and with a power
Of high-resolved men, bent to the spoil,
They hither march amain, under conduct
Of Lucius, son to old Andronicus;
Who threats in course of this revenge to do
As much as ever Coriolanus did.
Sat. Is warlike Lucius general of the Goths?
These tidings nip me; and I hang the head
As flowers with frost or grass beat down with storms.
Ay, now begins our sorrows to approach.
'Tis he the common people love so much;
Myself hath often overheard them say,
When I have walked like a private man,
That Lucius' banishment was wrongfully,
And they have wish'd that Lucius were their emperor.
Tam. Why should you fear? Is not your city strong?
Sat. Ay, but the citizens favour Lucius
And will revolt from me to succour him.
Tam. King, be thy thoughts imperious like thy name.
Is the sun dimm'd that gnats do fly in it?
The eagle suffers little birds to sing,
And is not careful what they mean thereby,
Knowing that with the shadow of his wings
He can at pleasure stint their melody.
Even so mayest thou the giddy men of Rome.
Then cheer thy spirit; for know thou, Emperor,
I will enchant the old Andronicus
With words more sweet, and yet more dangerous,
Than baits to fish or honey stalks to sheep,
When as the one is wounded with the bait,
The other rotted with delicious feed.
Sat. But he will not entreat his son for us.
Tam. If Tamora entreat him, then he will;
For I can smooth, and fill his aged ears
With golden promises, that, were his heart
Almost impregnable, his old ears deaf,
Yet should both ear and heart obey my tongue.
[*To Æmilius*] Go thou before to be our ambassador;
Say that the Emperor requests a parley
Of warlike Lucius, and appoint the meeting
Even at his father's house, the old Andronicus.
Sat. Æmilius, do this message honourably;
And if he stand on hostage for his safety,
Bid him demand what pledge will please him best.
Æmil. Your bidding shall I do effectually.
Exit.
Tam. Now will I to that old Andronicus
And temper him with all the art I have
To pluck proud Lucius from the warlike Goths.
And now, sweet Emperor, be blithe again
And bury all thy fear in my devices.
Sat. Then go successantly, and plead to him.
Exeunt.

ACT V. [Scene I. *Plains near Rome.*]

Flourish. Enter *Lucius*, with an army of *Goths*, with *Drum* and *Soldiers*.

Luc. Approved warriors and my faithful friends,
I have received letters from great Rome
Which signifies what hate they bear their Emperor
And how desirous of our sight they are.
Therefore, great lords, be as your titles witness,
Imperious, and impatient of your wrongs;
And wherein Rome hath done you any scath,
Let him make treble satisfaction.
Goth. Brave slip sprung from the great Andronicus,
Whose name was once our terror, now our comfort,
Whose high exploits and honourable deeds
Ingrateful Rome requites with foul contempt,
Be bold in us. We'll follow where thou lead'st,

Like stinging bees in hottest summer's day,
Led by their master to the flow'red fields,
And be aveng'd on cursed Tamora.

Omnes. And as he saith, so say we all with him.

Luc. I humbly thank him, and I thank you all.
But who comes here, led by a lusty Goth?

Enter a *Goth,* leading of *Aaron* with his *Child* in his arms.

Goth. Renowmed Lucius, from our troops I stray'd
To gaze upon a ruinous monastery;
And as I earnestly did fix mine eye
Upon the wasted building, suddenly
I heard a child cry underneath a wall.
I made unto the noise, when soon I heard
The crying babe controll'd with this discourse:
'Peace, tawny slave, half me and half thy dam!
Did not thy hue bewray whose brat thou art,
Had nature lent thee but thy mother's look,
Villain, thou mightst have been an emperor.
But where the bull and cow are both milk-white,
They never do beget a coal-black calf.
Peace, villain, peace!'— even thus he rates the babe —
'For I must bear thee to a trusty Goth,
Who, when he knows thou art the Empress' babe,
Will hold thee dearly for thy mother's sake.'
With this, my weapon drawn, I rush'd upon him,
Surpris'd him suddenly, and brought him hither
To use as you think needful of the man.

Luc. O worthy Goth, this is the incarnate devil
That robb'd Andronicus of his good hand.
This is the pearl that pleas'd your Empress' eye;
And here's the base fruit of her burning lust.
Say, wall-ey'd slave, whither wouldst thou convey
This growing image of thy fiendlike face?
Why dost not speak? What, deaf? not a word?
A halter, soldiers! Hang him on this tree,
And by his side his fruit of bastardy.

Aar. Touch not the boy! He is of royal blood.

Luc. Too like the sire for ever being good.
First hang the child, that he may see it sprawl—
A sight to vex the father's soul withal.
Get me a ladder.

[*A ladder brought, which Aaron is made to climb.*]

Aar. Lucius, save the child
And bear it from me to the Emperess.
If thou do this, I'll show thee wondrous things
That highly may advantage thee to hear;
If thou wilt not, befall what may befall,
I'll speak no more — but vengeance rot you all!

Luc. Say on; and if it please me which thou speak'st,
Thy child shall live, and I will see it nourish'd.

Aar. And if it please thee? Why, assure thee, Lucius,
'Twill vex thy soul to hear what I shall speak;
For I must talk of murthers, rapes, and massacres,
Acts of black night, abominable deeds,
Complots of mischief, treason, villanies
Ruthful to hear, yet piteously perform'd;
And this shall all be buried in my death
Unless thou swear to me my child shall live.

Luc. Tell on thy mind. I say thy child shall live.

Aar. Swear that he shall, and then I will begin.

Luc. Who should I swear by? Thou believest no god.
That granted, how canst thou believe an oath?

Aar. What if I do not? as indeed I do not.
Yet, for I know thou art religious
And hast a thing within thee called conscience,
With twenty popish tricks and ceremonies
Which I have seen thee careful to observe,
Therefore I urge thy oath. For that I know
An idiot holds his bauble for a god
And keeps the oath which by that god he swears,
To that I'll urge him. Therefore thou shalt vow
By that same god, what god soe'er it be,
That thou adorest and hast in reverence,
To save my boy, to nourish and bring him up,
Or else I will discover naught to thee.

Luc. Even by my god I swear to thee I will.

Aar. First know thou, I begot him on the Empress.

Luc. O most insatiate and luxurious woman!

Aar. Tut, Lucius, this was but a deed of charity
To that which thou shalt hear of me anon.
'Twas her two sons that murdered Bassianus;
They cut thy sister's tongue, and ravish'd her,
And cut her hands, and trimm'd her as thou sawest.

Luc. O detestable villain! call'st thou that trimming?

Aar. Why, she was wash'd and cut and trimm'd, and 'twas
Trim sport for them which had the doing of it.
Luc. O barbarous beastly villains like thyself!
Aar. Indeed I was their tutor to instruct them.
That codding spirit had they from their mother,
As sure a card as ever won the set.
That bloody mind I think they learn'd of me,
As true a dog as ever fought at head.
Well, let my deeds be witness of my worth.
I train'd thy brethren to that guileful hole
Where the dead corpse of Bassianus lay.
I wrote the letter that thy father found
And hid the gold within that letter mention'd,
Confederate with the Queen and her two sons;
And what not done, that thou hast cause to rue,
Wherein I had no stroke of mischief in it?
I play'd the cheater for thy father's hand,
And when I had it, drew myself apart
And almost broke my heart with extreme laughter.
I pried me through the crevice of a wall
When for his hand he had his two sons' heads,
Beheld his tears, and laugh'd so heartily
That both mine eyes were rainy like to his;
And when I told the Empress of this sport,
She sounded almost at my pleasing tale
And for my tidings gave me twenty kisses.
Goth. What, canst thou say all this and never blush?
Aar. Ay, like a black dog, as the saying is.
Luc. Art thou not sorry for these heinous deeds?
Aar. Ay, that I had not done a thousand more.
Even now I curse the day (and yet I think
Few come within the compass of my curse)
Wherein I did not some notorious ill:
As kill a man, or else devise his death;
Ravish a maid, or plot the way to do it;
Accuse some innocent, and forswear myself;
Set deadly enmity between two friends;
Make poor men's cattle break their necks;
Set fire on barns and haystacks in the night
And bid the owners quench them with their tears.
Oft have I digg'd up dead men from their graves
And set them upright at their dear friends' door
Even when their sorrow almost was forgot,
And on their skins, as on the bark of trees,
Have with my knife carved in Roman letters
'Let not your sorrow die, though I am dead.'
Tut, I have done a thousand dreadful things
As willingly as one would kill a fly;
And nothing grieves me heartily indeed
But that I cannot do ten thousand more.
Luc. Bring down the devil, for he must not die
So sweet a death as hanging presently.

[*Aaron is brought down from the ladder.*]

Aar. If there be devils, would I were a devil,
To live and burn in everlasting fire,
So I might have your company in hell
But to torment you with my bitter tongue!
Luc. Sirs, stop his mouth and let him speak no more.

Enter *Æmilius.*

Goth. My lord, there is a messenger from Rome
Desires to be admitted to your presence.
Luc. Let him come near.
Welcome, Æmilius. What's the news from Rome?
Æmil. Lord Lucius, and you princes of the Goths,
The Roman Emperor greets you all by me;
And, for he understands you are in arms,
He craves a parley at your father's house,
Willing you to demand your hostages,
And they shall be immediately deliver'd.
Goth. What says our general?
Luc. Æmilius, let the Emperor give his pledges
Unto my father and my uncle Marcus,
And we will come. — March, away!

Flourish. Exeunt.

[Scene II. *Rome. Before the house of* Titus.]

Enter *Tamora* and her two *Sons*, [*Demetrius* and *Chiron*,] disguised.

Tam. Thus, in this strange and sad habiliament,
I will encounter with Andronicus
And say I am Revenge, sent from below
To join with him and right his heinous wrongs.
Knock at his study, where they say he keeps
To ruminate strange plots of dire revenge.
Tell him Revenge is come to join with him
And work confusion on his enemies.

They knock, and Titus opens his study door [*above*].

Tit. Who doth molest my contemplation?
Is it your trick to make me ope the door,
That so my sad decrees may fly away

And all my study be to no effect?
You are deceiv'd; for what I mean to do
See here in bloody lines I have set down;
And what is written shall be executed.

Tam. Titus, I am come to talk with thee.

Tit. No, not a word! How can I grace my talk,
Wanting a hand to give it that accord?
Thou hast the odds of me; therefore no more!

Tam. If thou didst know me, thou wouldst talk with me.

Tit. I am not mad; I know thee well enough.
Witness this wretched stump, witness these crimson lines,
Witness these trenches made by grief and care,
Witness the tiring day and heavy night,
Witness all sorrow, that I know thee well
For our proud Empress, mighty Tamora!
Is not thy coming for my other hand?

Tam. Know, thou sad man, I am not Tamora;
She is thy enemy, and I thy friend.
I am Revenge, sent from th' infernal kingdom
To ease the gnawing vulture of thy mind
By working wreakful vengeance on thy foes.
Come down and welcome me to this world's light;
Confer with me of murder and of death.
There's not a hollow cave or lurking place,
No vast obscurity or misty vale,
Where bloody murther or detested rape
Can couch for fear, but I will find them out
And in their ears tell them my dreadful name —
Revenge, which makes the foul offender quake.

Tit. Art thou Revenge? and art thou sent to me
To be a torment to mine enemies?

Tam. I am; therefore come down and welcome me.

Tit. Do me some service ere I come to thee.
Lo, by thy side where Rape and Murder stands,
Now give some surance that thou art Revenge—
Stab them, or tear them on thy chariot wheels;
And then I'll come and be thy wagoner
And whirl along with thee about the globe.
Provide thee two proper palfreys, black as jet,
To hale thy vengeful wagon swift away
And find out murderers in their guilty caves;
And when thy car is loaden with their heads,
I will dismount, and by thy wagon wheel
Trot like a servile footman all day long,
Even from Hyperion's rising in the East
Until his very downfall in the sea;
And day by day I'll do this heavy task,
So thou destroy Rapine and Murder there.

Tam. These are my ministers and come with me.

Tit. Are these thy ministers? What are they call'd?

Tam. Rapine and Murder; therefore called so
'Cause they take vengeance of such kind of men.

Tit. Good Lord, how like the Empress' sons they are!
And you the Empress! But we worldly men
Have miserable, mad, mistaking eyes.
O sweet Revenge, now do I come to thee;
And, if one arm's embracement will content thee,
I will embrace thee in it by-and-by.
[*Exit above.*]

Tam. This closing with him fits his lunacy.
Whate'er I forge to feed his brainsick humours
Do you uphold and maintain in your speeches,
For now he firmly takes me for Revenge;
And, being credulous in this mad thought,
I'll make him send for Lucius his son,
And whilst I at a banquet hold him sure,
I'll find some cunning practice out of hand
To scatter and disperse the giddy Goths,
Or at the least make them his enemies.
See, here he comes, and I must ply my theme.

[Enter *Titus*, below.]

Tit. Long have I been forlorn, and all for thee.
Welcome, dread Fury, to my woful house.
Rapine and Murther, you are welcome too.
How like the Empress and her sons you are!
Well are you fitted, had you but a Moor.
Could not all hell afford you such a devil?
For well I wot the Empress never wags
But in her company there is a Moor;
And, would you represent our queen aright,
It were convenient you had such a devil.
But welcome as you are. What shall we do?

Tam. What wouldst thou have us do, Andronicus?

Dem. Show me a murtherer, I'll deal with him.

Chi. Show me a villain that hath done a rape,
And I am sent to be reveng'd on him.

Tam. Show me a thousand that have done thee wrong,
And I will be revenged on them all.

Tit. Look round about the wicked streets of Rome,
And when thou find'st a man that's like thyself,
Good Murther, stab him; he's a murtherer.
Go thou with him, and when it is thy hap
To find another that is like to thee.

Good Rapine, stab him; he's a ravisher.
Go thou with them; and in the Emperor's court
There is a queen, attended by a Moor.
Well shalt thou know her by thine own proportion,
For up and down she doth resemble thee.
I pray thee do on them some violent death;
They have been violent to me and mine.

Tam. Well hast thou lesson'd us; this shall we do.
But would it please thee, good Andronicus,
To send for Lucius, thy thrice-valiant son,
Who leads towards Rome a band of warlike Goths,
And bid him come and banquet at thy house —
When he is here, even at thy solemn feast,
I will bring in the Empress and her sons,
The Emperor himself, and all thy foes;
And at thy mercy shall they stoop and kneel,
And on them shalt thou ease thy angry heart.
What says Andronicus to this device?

Tit. Marcus, my brother! 'Tis sad Titus calls.

Enter *Marcus*.

Go, gentle Marcus, to thy nephew Lucius;
Thou shalt enquire him out among the Goths.
Bid him repair to me and bring with him
Some of the chiefest princes of the Goths.
Bid him encamp his soldiers where they are.
Tell him the Emperor and the Empress too
Feast at my house, and he shall feast with them.
This do thou for my love; and so let him,
As he regards his aged father's life.

Marc. This will I do and soon return again. [*Exit.*]

Tam. Now will I hence about thy business
And take my ministers along with me.

Tit. Nay, nay! Let Rape and Murder stay with me;
Or else I'll call my brother back again
And cleave to no revenge but Lucius.

Tam. [*aside to her sons*] What say you, boys? Will you abide with him
Whiles I go tell my lord the Emperor
How I have govern'd our determin'd jest?
Yield to his humour, smooth and speak him fair,
And tarry with him till I turn again.

Tit. [*aside*] I knew them all, though they suppos'd me mad,
And will o'erreach them in their own devices —
A pair of cursed hellhounds and their dam!

Dem. Madam, depart at pleasure; leave us here.

Tam. Farewell, Andronicus. Revenge now goes
To lay a complot to betray thy foes.

Tit. I know thou dost; and, sweet Revenge, farewell. [*Exit Tamora.*]

Chi. Tell us, old man, how shall we be employ'd?

Tit. Tut, I have work enough for you to do.
Publius, come hither! Caius and Valentine!

[Enter *Publius, Caius,* and *Valentine.*]

Pub. What is your will?

Tit. Know you these two?

Pub. The Empress' sons
I take them — Chiron and Demetrius.

Tit. Fie, Publius, fie! thou art too much deceiv'd.
The one is Murder, Rape is the other's name;
And therefore bind them, gentle Publius —
Caius and Valentine, lay hands on them.
Oft have you heard me wish for such an hour,
And now I find it. Therefore bind them sure,
And stop their mouths if they begin to cry. [*Exit.*]

[*They lay hold on Chiron and Demetrius.*]

Chi. Villains, forbear! We are the Empress' sons.

Pub. And therefore do we what we are commanded.
Stop close their mouths; let them not speak a word.
Is he sure bound? Look that you bind them fast.

Enter *Titus Andronicus* with a knife, and *Lavinia* with a basin.

Tit. Come, come, Lavinia! Look, thy foes are bound.
Sirs, stop their mouths, let them not speak to me;
But let them hear what fearful words I utter.
O villains, Chiron and Demetrius!
Here stands the spring whom you have stain'd with mud,
This goodly summer with your winter mix'd.
You kill'd her husband; and for that vile fault
Two of her brothers were condemn'd to death,
My hand cut off and made a merry jest;
Both her sweet hands, her tongue — and that more dear
Than hands or tongue, her spotless chastity,
Inhuman traitors, you constrain'd and forc'd.
What would you say if I should let you speak?
Villains, for shame you could not beg for grace.

Hark, wretches, how I mean to martyr you.
This one hand yet is left to cut your throats
Whiles that Lavinia 'tween her stumps doth hold
The basin that receives your guilty blood.
You know your mother means to feast with me,
And calls herself Revenge, and thinks me mad.
Hark, villains! I will grind your bones to dust,
And with your blood and it I'll make a paste;
And of the paste a coffin I will rear,
And make two pasties of your shameful heads,
And bid that strumpet, your unhallowed dam,
Like to the earth, swallow her own increase.
This is the feast that I have bid her to,
And this the banquet she shall surfeit on;
For worse than Philomel you us'd my daughter,
And worse than Progne I will be reveng'd.
And now prepare your throats. Lavinia, come,
Receive the blood; and when that they are dead,
Let me go grind their bones to powder small
And with this hateful liquor temper it;
And in that paste let their vile heads be bak'd.
Come, come, be every one officious
To make this banquet, which I wish may prove
More stern and bloody than the Centaurs' feast. *He cuts their throats.*
So!
Now bring them in, for I will play the cook
And see them ready against their mother comes.
Exeunt [*with the dead bodies*].

[Scene III. *Court of* Titus' *house.*]

Enter *Lucius*, *Marcus*, and the *Goths*, [with *Aaron* prisoner, and his *Child* in the arms of an *Attendant*].

Luc. Uncle Marcus, since it is my father's mind
That I repair to Rome, I am content.
Goth. And ours with thine, befall what fortune will.
Luc. Good uncle, take you in this barbarous Moor,
This ravenous tiger, this accursed devil.
Let him receive no sust'nance, fetter him,
Till he be brought unto the Empress' face
For testimony of her foul proceedings.
And see the ambush of our friends be strong;
I fear the Emperor means no good to us.
Aar. Some devil whisper curses in mine ear
And prompt me that my tongue may utter forth
The venomous malice of my swelling heart!
Luc. Away, inhuman dog, unhallowed slave!
Sirs, help our uncle to convey him in.
[*Exeunt some Goths, with Aaron.*] *Flourish.*
The trumpets show the Emperor is at hand.

Sound trumpets. Enter *Emperor* and *Empress*, with [*Æmilius*,] *Tribunes*, [*Senators*,] and others.

Sat. What, hath the firmament moe suns than one?
Luc. What boots it thee to call thyself a sun?
Marc. Rome's Emperor, and nephew, break the parle;
These quarrels must be quietly debated.
The feast is ready which the careful Titus
Hath ordain'd to an honourable end —
For peace, for love, for league, and good to Rome.
Please you therefore draw nigh and take your places.
Sat. Marcus, we will.
A table brought in. [*The company sit.*]

Trumpets sounding, enter *Titus* like a Cook, placing the dishes, and *Lavinia* with a veil over her face; [also *Young Lucius* and others].

Tit. Welcome, my gracious lord; welcome, dread Queen;
Welcome, ye warlike Goths; welcome, Lucius;
And welcome all. Although the cheer be poor,
'Twill fill your stomachs. Please you eat of it.
Sat. Why art thou thus attir'd, Andronicus?
Tit. Because I would be sure to have all well
To entertain your Highness and your Empress.
Tam. We are beholding to you, good Andronicus.
Tit. An if your Highness knew my heart, you were.
My lord the Emperor, resolve me this:
Was it well done of rash Virginius
To slay his daughter with his own right hand,
Because she was enforc'd, stain'd, and deflow'r'd?
Sat. It was, Andronicus.
Tit. Your reason, mighty lord?
Sat. Because the girl should not survive her shame,
And by her presence still renew his sorrows.
Tit. A reason mighty, strong, and effectual;
A pattern, precedent, and lively warrant
For me (most wretched) to perform the like.
Die, die, Lavinia, and thy shame with thee!
And with thy shame thy father's sorrow die!
He kills her.
Sat. What hast thou done, unnatural and unkind?

Tit. Kill'd her for whom my tears have made me blind.
I am as woful as Virginius was,
And have a thousand times more cause than he
To do this outrage; and it now is done.

Sat. What, was she ravish'd? Tell who did the deed.

Tit. Will 't please you eat? Will 't please your Highness feed?

Tam. Why hast thou slain thine only daughter thus?

Tit. Not I! 'Twas Chiron and Demetrius.
They ravish'd her and cut away her tongue;
And they, 'twas they, that did her all this wrong.

Sat. Go fetch them hither to us presently.

Tit. Why, there they are both, baked in that pie,
Whereof their mother daintily hath fed,
Eating the flesh that she herself hath bred.
'Tis true, 'tis true! Witness my knive's sharp point! *He stabs the Empress.*

Sat. Die, frantic wretch, for this accursed deed! [*He stabs Titus.*]

Luc. Can the son's eye behold his father bleed?
There's meed for meed, death for a deadly deed!

[*He stabs Saturninus. A great tumult. Lucius, Marcus, and their Friends go up into a gallery.*]

Marc. You sad-fac'd men, people and sons of Rome,
By uproar sever'd, as a flight of fowl
Scatt'red by winds and high tempestuous gusts,
O, let me teach you how to knit again
This scattered corn into one mutual sheaf,
These broken limbs again into one body;
Lest Rome herself be bane unto herself,
And she whom mighty kingdoms cursy to,
Like a forlorn and desperate castaway,
Do shameful execution on herself.
But if my frosty signs and chaps of age,
Grave witnesses of true experience,
Cannot induce you to attend my words,
[*To Lucius*] Speak, Rome's dear friend, as erst our ancestor,
When with his solemn tongue he did discourse
To lovesick Dido's sad-attending ear
The story of that baleful-burning night
When subtile Greeks surpris'd King Priam's Troy.
Tell us what Sinon hath bewitch'd our ears,
Or who hath brought the fatal engine in
That gives our Troy, our Rome, the civil wound.
My heart is not compact of flint nor steel;
Nor can I utter all our bitter grief,
But floods of tears will drown my oratory
And break my utt'rance, even in the time
When it should move ye to attend me most,
And force you to commiseration.
Here's Rome's young captain; let him tell the tale,
While I stand by and weep to hear him speak.

Luc. Then, gracious auditory, be it known to you
That Chiron and the damn'd Demetrius
Were they that murdered our Emperor's brother,
And they it were that ravished our sister.
For their fell faults our brothers were beheaded,
Our father's tears despis'd, and basely cozen'd
Of that true hand that fought Rome's quarrel out
And sent her enemies unto the grave.
Lastly, myself unkindly banished,
The gates shut on me, and turn'd weeping out
To beg relief among Rome's enemies;
Who drown'd their enmity in my true tears
And op'd their arms to embrace me as a friend.
I am the turned forth, be it known to you,
That have preserv'd her welfare in my blood
And from her bosom took the enemy's point,
Sheathing the steel in my advent'rous body.
Alas, you know I am no vaunter, I!
My scars can witness, dumb although they are,
That my report is just and full of truth.
But soft! methinks I do digress too much,
Citing my worthless praise. O, pardon me!
For when no friends are by, men praise themselves.

Marc. Now is my turn to speak. Behold the child.

[*Points to the Child in the arms of an Attendant.*]

Of this was Tamora delivered,
The issue of an irreligious Moor,
Chief architect and plotter of these woes.
The villain is alive in Titus' house,
Damn'd as he is, to witness this is true.
Now judge what cause had Titus to revenge
These wrongs unspeakable, past patience,
Or more than any living man could bear.
Now you have heard the truth, what say you, Romans?
Have we done aught amiss? Show us wherein,
And, from the place where you behold us pleading,
The poor remainder of Andronici
Will hand in hand all headlong hurl ourselves

And on the ragged stones beat forth our brains
And make a mutual closure of our house.
Speak, Romans, speak! and if you say we shall,
Lo, hand in hand, Lucius and I will fall.

Æmil. Come, come, thou reverent man of Rome,
And bring our Emperor gently in thy hand —
Lucius our Emperor; for well I know
The common voice do cry it shall be so.

All. Lucius, all hail, Rome's royal Emperor!

Marc. Go, go into old Titus' sorrowful house,
And hither hale that misbelieving Moor
To be adjudg'd some direful slaught'ring death,
As punishment for his most wicked life.

[*Exeunt some Attendants.*]

[*Lucius, Marcus, and the others descend.*]

All. Lucius, all hail, Rome's gracious governor!

Luc. Thanks, gentle Romans. May I govern so
To heal Rome's harms and wipe away her woe!
But, gentle people, give me aim awhile,
For nature puts me to a heavy task.
Stand all aloof. But, uncle, draw you near
To shed obsequious tears upon this trunk.
O, take this warm kiss on thy pale cold lips,
These sorrowful drops upon thy bloodstain'd face,
The last true duties of thy noble son!

Marc. Tear for tear, and loving kiss for kiss,
Thy brother Marcus tenders on thy lips.
O, were the sum of these that I should pay
Countless and infinite, yet would I pay them!

Luc. Come hither, boy; come, come, and learn of us
To melt in showers. Thy grandsire lov'd thee well.
Many a time he danc'd thee on his knee,
Sung thee asleep, his loving breast thy pillow.
Many a story hath he told to thee,
And bid thee bear his pretty tales in mind
And talk of them when he was dead and gone.

Marc. How many thousand times have these poor lips,
When they were living, warm'd themselves on thine!
O, now, sweet boy, give them their latest kiss![1]
Bid him farewell; commit him to the grave;
Do him that kindness, and take leave of him.

Boy. O grandsire, grandsire! ev'n with all my heart
Would I were dead, so you did live again!
O Lord, I cannot speak to him for weeping;
My tears will choke me if I ope my mouth.

[Enter *Attendants* with *Aaron.*]

Roman. You sad Andronici, have done with woes.
Give sentence on this execrable wretch
That hath been breeder of these dire events.

Luc. Set him breast-deep in earth, and famish him.
There let him stand and rave and cry for food.
If any one relieves or pities him,
For the offence he dies. This is our doom.
Some stay to see him fast'ned in the earth.

Aar. Ah, why should wrath be mute and fury dumb?
I am no baby, I, that with base prayers
I should repent the evils I have done.
Ten thousand worse than ever yet I did
Would I perform if I might have my will.
If one good deed in all my life I did,
I do repent it from my very soul.

Luc. Some loving friends convey the Emperor hence
And give him burial in his father's grave.
My father and Lavinia shall forthwith
Be closed in our household's monument.
As for that ravenous tiger, Tamora,
No funeral rite, nor man in mourning weeds,
No mournful bell shall ring her burial;
But throw her forth to beasts and birds of prey.
Her life was beastly and devoid of pity,
And being dead, let birds on her take pity!
See justice done on Aaron, that damn'd Moor,
By whom our heavy haps had their beginning.
Then, afterwards, to order well the state,
That like events may ne'er it ruinate!

Exeunt.

[1] The text follows the First Quarto. For 165–169 the Second Quarto and the Folios have:

Meet and agreeing with thine infancy:
In that respect then, like a loving child,
Shed yet some small drops from thy tender spring,
Because kind nature doth require it so:
Friends should associate friends in grief and woe

Romeo and Juliet

The First Quarto of Romeo and Juliet (1597) prints the play in a curtailed and corrupt form. The Second Quarto (1599) is our authority for the text; but it is carelessly printed, and the First Quarto very often provides the correct reading where the Second has gone astray. The Third Quarto appeared in 1609; the Fourth is undated. These are of no textual authority, though they sometimes supply a good reading The First Folio (1623) used the Third Quarto as printer's copy.

The date of composition is uncertain. On April 6, 1580, there was an earthquake which frightened the audiences in the London theatres. Anthony Munday reports that 'the people came running foorth, supprised with great astonishment.' Two days later a ballad was registered 'intituled comme from the plaie, comme from the playe: . . . the earth quakes, lett us hast awaye.' The Nurse, recalling an incident of Juliet's childhood, dates it by remarking ''Tis since the earthquake now eleven years' and 'Since that time it is eleven years' (i, 3, 23, 35). Thus, some think, she fixes the date of the play as 1591. Doubtless Shakespeare thought of the London earthquake when he wrote the Nurse's speech, but his concern, like hers, was to determine Juliet's birthday ('Come Lammas Eve at night shall she be fourteen'), not to hand down to posterity the date of his drama.

For the play in its present form, 1591 is manifestly too early a date; and there is no good reason for thinking that this form is Shakespeare's revision of an earlier drama, whether his own or another's. Differences in style and metre of course appear, but these accord with mood and circumstances in every case. The so-called 'lyrical period' (about 1595) fits all the conditions. This brings Romeo and Juliet into close relation with *A Midsummer Night's Dream*. Which of the two is earlier is an open question — probably *A Midsummer Night's Dream*, though some scholars (oddly enough) maintain that *Pyramus and Thisbe*, as acted by Bottom and his friends, is a parody of the theme of Romeo and Juliet and, in particular, that Romeo's leaping the orchard wall in Act II is burlesqued by the business of Wall in that comic interlude.

For his plot Shakespeare used a poem by Arthur Broke (or Brooke), printed in 1562, 'The Tragicall Historye of Romeus and Iuliet, written first in Italian by Bandell, and nowe in Englishe by Ar. Br.' Broke's source was the ninth story in Part II of Matteo Bandello's *Novelle* (1554). This he knew in the French version in Boaistuau's *Histoires Tragiques* (1559), which adds some details and modifies others. Broke's *Romeus and Juliet*, though he follows the narrative faithfully, is by no means a mere versification of Boaistuau. He touches up many details and adds many reflections. He develops the character of the Nurse with genuine humour; he inserts a long conversation between Romeo and the Friar, in which Romeo rages in despair and the Friar sternly counsels self-control; he describes Romeo's sorrows during his sojourn at Mantua. There is a prose translation of Boaistuau's text in Painter's *Palace of Pleasure*, Vol. II, No. 25 (1567), but Shakespeare does not seem to have taken anything from it.

Shakespeare's use of Broke's poem resembles his use of Holinshed in his

English plays and of North's Plutarch in his Roman tragedies. It gave him the whole plot, and he does not hesitate to borrow such turns of phrase as take his fancy. The character of the Nurse owes much to Broke, and now and then he makes a suggestion which Shakespeare has developed in the case of the other *dramatis personæ*; but Mercutio, one of the most original of all Shakespeare's characters, is barely foreshadowed in Boaistuau and Broke.

The romantic history of ROMEO AND JULIET was more or less familiar to Elizabethans before Shakespeare wrote. Broke, in his preface, speaks of a drama on the subject which he had seen acted: 'Though I saw the same argument lately set foorth on stage with more commendation then I can look for: (being there much better set forth then I haue or can dooe) yet the same matter penned as it is, may serue to lyke good effect.' The performance which Broke commends may have been a Christmas show at the Inner Temple. It is just possible that Jacob Struijs's Dutch play *Romeo en Juliette* (1630) was founded on it. Perhaps some of Broke's changes in Boaistuau's tale were suggested by the play he mentions; but there is no reason to suppose that Shakespeare was influenced by it. Broke's poem is the only source from which he appears to have drawn.

The plot of ROMEO AND JULIET has a long and complicated history. In a Greek romance of the third or fourth century, the *Ephesiaca* of one Xenophon of Ephesus (perhaps a pseudonym), the heroine, Anthia — separated by miscellaneous adventures from her husband Habrocomes, and anxious to avoid an adulterous second marriage — begs a physician to provide her with a deadly poison. He substitutes a sleeping draught, and she awakes in the tomb. She resolves to die of starvation, but robbers find her and carry her off. After many perils, Anthia and her husband are reunited (Books iii-iv). There is a rather similar episode in another Greek romance, the *Babyloniaca* of Iamblichus Syrus, which dates from the middle of the second century. Some form of this ancient tale, combined with a tragic story of star-crossed lovers, forms the substance of Shakespeare's plot. Such a combination is found in the 33d story in *Il Novellino* of Masuccio Salernitano (1476) and in Luigi da Porto's *Hystoria di due nobili Amanti* (printed *ca.* 1525). Da Porto may have drawn from Masuccio, but he says he heard the story from a Veronese comrade. In Masuccio the scene is Siena; in Da Porto it is Verona. Da Porto was the first to call the hero and heroine Romeo and Giulietta and to associate them with the Montecchi and the Cappelletti. Bandello's novel is derived from Da Porto, but may owe something to a previous derivative — 'L'infelice amore de i due fedelissimi amanti Giulia e Romeo, scritto in ottava rima da Clitia nobile Veronese ad Ardeo suo' (1553), usually ascribed to Gherardo Bolderi, *alias* Boldiero.

A few points of resemblance between ROMEO AND JULIET and Luigi Groto's tragedy *La Hadriana* (1578), if not fortuitous, require an elaborate theory to account for them: namely, that both the *Hadriana* and the lost play which Broke had seen, drew from some Italian version that has not survived, and that Shakespeare made use of the lost play. Coincidence seems more probable; but thought is free.

THE TRAGEDY OF
ROMEO AND JULIET

[Dramatis Personæ.

Chorus.

Escalus, Prince of Verona.
Paris, a young Count, kinsman to the *Prince*.
Montague, } heads of two houses at variance with
Capulet, } each other.
An old Man, of the Capulet family.
Romeo, son to *Montague*.
Mercutio, kinsman to the *Prince*, and friend to *Romeo*.
Benvolio, nephew to *Montague*, and friend to *Romeo*.
Tybalt, nephew to *Lady Capulet*.
Friar Laurence, } Franciscans.
Friar John, }
Balthasar, servant to *Romeo*.
Abram, servant to *Montague*.
Sampson, } servants to *Capulet*.
Gregory, }
Peter, servant to *Juliet's* nurse.
An Apothecary.
Three Musicians.
An Officer.

Lady Montague, wife to *Montague*.
Lady Capulet, wife to Capulet.
Juliet, daughter to *Capulet*.
Nurse to *Juliet*.

Citizens of Verona; Gentlemen and Gentlewomen of both houses; Maskers, Torchbearers, Pages, Guards, Watchmen, Servants, and Attendants.

SCENE. — *Verona; Mantua.*]

THE PROLOGUE.

[Enter *Chorus*.]

Chor. Two households, both alike in dignity,
In fair Verona, where we lay our scene,
From ancient grudge break to new mutiny,
Where civil blood makes civil hands unclean.
From forth the fatal loins of these two foes
A pair of star-cross'd lovers take their life;
Whose misadventur'd piteous overthrows
Doth with their death bury their parents' strife.
The fearful passage of their death-mark'd love,
And the continuance of their parents' rage,
Which, but their children's end, naught could remove,
Is now the two hours' traffic of our stage;
The which if you with patient ears attend,
What here shall miss, our toil shall strive to mend. [*Exit*.]

ACT I. Scene I. [*Verona. A public place.*]

Enter *Sampson* and *Gregory* (with swords and bucklers) of the house of *Capulet*.

Samp. Gregory, on my word, we'll not carry coals.

Greg. No, for then we should be colliers.

Samp. I mean, an we be in choler, we'll draw.

Greg. Ay, while you live, draw your neck out of collar.

Samp. I strike quickly, being moved.

Greg. But thou art not quickly moved to strike.

Samp. A dog of the house of Montague moves me.

Greg. To move is to stir, and to be valiant is to stand. Therefore, if thou art moved, thou runn'st away.

Samp. A dog of that house shall move me to stand. I will take the wall of any man or maid of Montague's.

Greg. That shows thee a weak slave; for the weakest goes to the wall.

Samp. 'Tis true; and therefore women, being the weaker vessels, are ever thrust to the wall. Therefore I will push Montague's men from the wall and thrust his maids to the wall.

Greg. The quarrel is between our masters and us their men.

Samp. 'Tis all one. I will show myself a

tyrant. When I have fought with the men, I will be cruel with the maids — I will cut off their heads.

Greg. The heads of the maids?

Samp. Ay, the heads of the maids, or their maidenheads. Take it in what sense thou wilt.

Greg. They must take it in sense that feel it.

Samp. Me they shall feel while I am able to stand; and 'tis known I am a pretty piece of flesh.

Greg. 'Tis well thou art not fish; if thou hadst, thou hadst been poor-John. Draw thy tool! Here comes two of the house of Montagues.

Enter two other *Servingmen* [*Abram* and *Balthasar*].

Samp. My naked weapon is out. Quarrel! I will back thee.

Greg. How? turn thy back and run?

Samp. Fear me not.

Greg. No, marry. I fear thee!

Samp. Let us take the law of our sides; let them begin.

Greg. I will frown as I pass by, and let them take it as they list.

Samp. Nay, as they dare. I will bite my thumb at them; which is disgrace to them, if they bear it.

Abr. Do you bite your thumb at us, sir?

Samp. I do bite my thumb, sir.

Abr. Do you bite your thumb at us, sir?

Samp. [*aside to Gregory*] Is the law of our side if I say ay?

Greg. [*aside to Sampson*] No.

Samp. No, sir, I do not bite my thumb at you, sir; but I bite my thumb, sir.

Greg. Do you quarrel, sir?

Abr. Quarrel, sir? No, sir.

Samp. But if you do, sir, I am for you. I serve as good a man as you.

Abr. No better.

Samp. Well, sir.

Enter *Benvolio.*

Greg. [*aside to Sampson*] Say 'better.' Here comes one of my master's kinsmen.

Samp. Yes, better, sir.

Abr. You lie.

Samp. Draw, if you be men. Gregory, remember thy swashing blow. *They fight.*

Ben. Part, fools! [*Beats down their swords.*]
Put up your swords. You know not what you do.

Enter *Tybalt.*

Tyb. What, art thou drawn among these heartless hinds?
Turn thee, Benvolio! look upon thy death.

Ben. I do but keep the peace. Put up thy sword,
Or manage it to part these men with me.

Tyb. What, drawn, and talk of peace? I hate the word
As I hate hell, all Montagues, and thee.
Have at thee, coward! [*They*] *fight.*

Enter [an *Officer*, and] three or four *Citizens* with clubs or partisans.

Officer. Clubs, bills, and partisans! Strike! beat them down!

Citizens. Down with the Capulets! down with the Montagues!

Enter *Old Capulet* in his gown, and his *Wife.*

Cap. What noise is this? Give me my long sword, ho!

Wife. A crutch, a crutch! Why call you for a sword?

Cap. My sword, I say! Old Montague is come
And flourishes his blade in spite of me.

Enter *Old Montague* and his *Wife.*

Mon. Thou villain Capulet! — Hold me not, let me go.

M. Wife. Thou shalt not stir one foot to seek a foe.

Enter *Prince Escalus,* with his *Train.*

Prince. Rebellious subjects, enemies to peace,
Profaners of this neighbour-stained steel —
Will they not hear? What, ho! you men, you beasts,
That quench the fire of your pernicious rage
With purple fountains issuing from your veins!
On pain of torture, from those bloody hands
Throw your mistempered weapons to the ground
And hear the sentence of your moved prince.
Three civil brawls, bred of an airy word
By thee, old Capulet, and Montague,
Have thrice disturb'd the quiet of our streets
And made Verona's ancient citizens
Cast by their grave beseeming ornaments
To wield old partisans, in hands as old,
Cank'red with peace, to part your cank'red hate.
If ever you disturb our streets again,

Your lives shall pay the forfeit of the peace.
For this time all the rest depart away.
You, Capulet, shall go along with me;
And, Montague, come you this afternoon,
To know our farther pleasure in this case,
To old Freetown, our common judgment place.
Once more, on pain of death, all men depart.
Exeunt [*all but Montague, his Wife, and Benvolio*].

Mon. Who set this ancient quarrel new abroach?
Speak, nephew, were you by when it began?

Ben. Here were the servants of your adversary
And yours, close fighting ere I did approach.
I drew to part them. In the instant came
The fiery Tybalt, with his sword prepar'd;
Which, as he breath'd defiance to my ears,
He swung about his head and cut the winds,
Who, nothing hurt withal, hiss'd him in scorn.
While we were interchanging thrusts and blows,
Came more and more, and fought on part and part,
Till the Prince came, who parted either part.

M. Wife. O, where is Romeo? Saw you him to-day?
Right glad I am he was not at this fray.

Ben. Madam, an hour before the worshipp'd sun
Peer'd forth the golden window of the East,
A troubled mind drave me to walk abroad;
Where, underneath the grove of sycamore
That westward rooteth from the city's side,
So early walking did I see your son.
Towards him I made; but he was ware of me
And stole into the covert of the wood.
I — measuring his affections by my own,
Which then most sought where most might not be found,
Being one too many by my weary self —
Pursu'd my humour, not pursuing his,
And gladly shunn'd who gladly fled from me.

Mon. Many a morning hath he there been seen,
With tears augmenting the fresh morning's dew,
Adding to clouds more clouds with his deep sighs;
But all so soon as the all-cheering sun
Should in the farthest East begin to draw
The shady curtains from Aurora's bed,
Away from light steals home my heavy son
And private in his chamber pens himself,
Shuts up his windows, locks fair daylight out,
And makes himself an artificial night.
Black and portentous must this humour prove
Unless good counsel may the cause remove.

Ben. My noble uncle, do you know the cause?

Mon. I neither know it nor can learn of him.

Ben. Have you importun'd him by any means?

Mon. Both by myself and many other friends;
But he, his own affections' counsellor,
Is to himself — I will not say how true —
But to himself so secret and so close,
So far from sounding and discovery,
As is the bud bit with an envious worm
Ere he can spread his sweet leaves to the air
Or dedicate his beauty to the sun.
Could we but learn from whence his sorrows grow,
We would as willingly give cure as know.

Enter *Romeo.*

Ben. See, where he comes. So please you step aside,
I'll know his grievance, or be much denied.

Mon. I would thou wert so happy by thy stay
To hear true shrift. Come, madam, let's away.
Exeunt [*Montague and Wife*].

Ben. Good morrow, cousin.

Rom. Is the day so young?

Ben. But new struck nine.

Rom. Ay me! sad hours seem long.
Was that my father that went hence so fast?

Ben. It was. What sadness lengthens Romeo's hours?

Rom. Not having that which having makes them short.

Ben. In love?

Rom. Out —

Ben. Of love?

Rom. Out of her favour where I am in love.

Ben. Alas that love, so gentle in his view,
Should be so tyrannous and rough in proof!

Rom. Alas that love, whose view is muffled still,
Should without eyes see pathways to his will!
Where shall we dine? O me! What fray was here?
Yet tell me not, for I have heard it all.
Here's much to do with hate, but more with love.
Why then, O brawling love! O loving hate!
O anything, of nothing first create!
O heavy lightness! serious vanity!
Misshapen chaos of well-seeming forms!

Feather of lead, bright smoke, cold fire, sick health!
Still-waking sleep, that is not what it is!
This love feel I, that feel no love in this.
Dost thou not laugh?

Ben. No, coz, I rather weep.

Rom. Good heart, at what?

Ben. At thy good heart's oppression.

Rom. Why, such is love's transgression.
Griefs of mine own lie heavy in my breast,
Which thou wilt propagate, to have it prest
With more of thine. This love that thou hast shown
Doth add more grief to too much of mine own.
Love is a smoke rais'd with the fume of sighs;
Being purg'd, a fire sparkling in lovers' eyes;
Being vex'd, a sea nourish'd with lovers' tears.
What is it else? A madness most discreet,
A choking gall, and a preserving sweet.
Farewell, my coz.

Ben. Soft! I will go along.
An if you leave me so, you do me wrong.

Rom. Tut! I have lost myself; I am not here:
This is not Romeo, he's some other where.

Ben. Tell me in sadness, who is that you love?

Rom. What, shall I groan and tell thee?

Ben. Groan? Why, no;
But sadly tell me who.

Rom. Bid a sick man in sadness make his will.
Ah, word ill urg'd to one that is so ill!
In sadness, cousin, I do love a woman.

Ben. I aim'd so near when I suppos'd you lov'd.

Rom. A right good markman! And she's fair I love.

Ben. A right fair mark, fair coz, is soonest hit.

Rom. Well, in that hit you miss. She'll not be hit
With Cupid's arrow. She hath Dian's wit,
And, in strong proof of chastity well arm'd,
From Love's weak childish bow she lives unharm'd.
She will not stay the siege of loving terms,
Nor bide th' encounter of assailing eyes,
Nor ope her lap to saint-seducing gold.
O, she is rich in beauty; only poor
That, when she dies, with beauty dies her store.

Ben. Then she hath sworn that she will still live chaste?

Rom. She hath, and in that sparing makes huge waste;
For beauty, starv'd with her severity,
Cuts beauty off from all posterity.
She is too fair, too wise, wisely too fair,
To merit bliss by making me despair.
She hath forsworn to love, and in that vow
Do I live dead that live to tell it now.

Ben. Be rul'd by me: forget to think of her.

Rom. O, teach me how I should forget to think!

Ben. By giving liberty unto thine eyes.
Examine other beauties.

Rom. 'Tis the way
To call hers (exquisite) in question more.
These happy masks that kiss fair ladies' brows,
Being black puts us in mind they hide the fair.
He that is strucken blind cannot forget
The precious treasure of his eyesight lost.
Show me a mistress that is passing fair,
What doth her beauty serve but as a note
Where I may read who pass'd that passing fair?
Farewell. Thou canst not teach me to forget.

Ben. I'll pay that doctrine, or else die in debt. *Exeunt.*

[Scene II. *A street.*]

Enter *Capulet*, *County Paris*, and [*Servant*]—the *Clown*.

Cap. But Montague is bound as well as I,
In penalty alike; and 'tis not hard, I think,
For men so old as we to keep the peace.

Par. Of honourable reckoning are you both,
And pity 'tis you liv'd at odds so long.
But now, my lord, what say you to my suit?

Cap. But saying o'er what I have said before:
My child is yet a stranger in the world,
She hath not seen the change of fourteen years;
Let two more summers wither in their pride
Ere we may think her ripe to be a bride.

Par. Younger than she are happy mothers made.

Cap. And too soon marr'd are those so early made.
The earth hath swallowed all my hopes but she;
She is the hopeful lady of my earth.
But woo her, gentle Paris, get her heart;
My will to her consent is but a part.
An she agree, within her scope of choice
Lies my consent and fair according voice.
This night I hold an old accustom'd feast,
Whereto I have invited many a guest,
Such as I love; and you among the store,
One more, most welcome, makes my number more.

At my poor house look to behold this night
Earth-treading stars that make dark heaven light.
Such comfort as do lusty young men feel
When well-apparell'd April on the heel
Of limping Winter treads, even such delight
Among fresh female buds shall you this night
Inherit at my house. Hear all, all see,
And like her most whose merit most shall be;
Which, on more view of many, mine, being one,
May stand in number, though in reck'ning none.
Come, go with me. [*To Servant, giving him a paper*] Go, sirrah, trudge about
Through fair Verona; find those persons out
Whose names are written there, and to them say,
My house and welcome on their pleasure stay.

Exeunt [*Capulet and Paris*].

Serv. Find them out whose names are written here? It is written that the shoemaker should meddle with his yard and the tailor with his last, the fisher with his pencil and the painter with his nets; but I am sent to find those persons whose names are here writ, and can never find what names the writing person hath here writ. I must to the learned. In good time!

Enter *Benvolio* and *Romeo*.

Ben. Tut, man, one fire burns out another's burning;
One pain is less'ned by another's anguish;
Turn giddy, and be holp by backward turning;
One desperate grief cures with another's languish.
Take thou some new infection to thy eye,
And the rank poison of the old will die.

Rom. Your plantain leaf is excellent for that.

Ben. For what, I pray thee?

Rom. For your broken shin.

Ben. Why, Romeo, art thou mad?

Rom. Not mad, but bound more than a madman is;
Shut up in prison, kept without my food,
Whipp'd and tormented and — God-den, good fellow.

Serv. God gi' go-den. I pray, sir, can you read?

Rom. Ay, mine own fortune in my misery.

Serv. Perhaps you have learned it without book. But I pray, can you read anything you see?

Rom. Ay, if I know the letters and the language.

Serv. Ye say honestly. Rest you merry!

Rom. Stay, fellow; I can read. *He reads.*

'Signior Martino and his wife and daughters;
County Anselmo and his beauteous sisters;
The lady widow of Vitruvio;
Signior Placentio and his lovely nieces;
Mercutio and his brother Valentine;
Mine uncle Capulet, his wife, and daughters;
My fair niece Rosaline and Livia;
Signior Valentio and his cousin Tybalt;
Lucio and the lively Helena.'

[*Gives back the paper.*] A fair assembly. Whither should they come?

Serv. Up.

Rom. Whither?

Serv. To supper, to our house.

Rom. Whose house?

Serv. My master's.

Rom. Indeed I should have ask'd you that before.

Serv. Now I'll tell you without asking. My master is the great rich Capulet; and if you be not of the house of Montagues, I pray come and crush a cup of wine. Rest you merry! *Exit.*

Ben. At this same ancient feast of Capulet's
Sups the fair Rosaline whom thou so lov'st;
With all the admired beauties of Verona.
Go thither, and with unattainted eye
Compare her face with some that I shall show,
And I will make thee think thy swan a crow.

Rom. When the devout religion of mine eye
Maintains such falsehood, then turn tears to fires;
And these, who, often drown'd, could never die,
Transparent heretics, be burnt for liars!
One fairer than my love? The all-seeing sun
Ne'er saw her match since first the world begun.

Ben. Tut! you saw her fair, none else being by,
Herself pois'd with herself in either eye;
But in that crystal scales let there be weigh'd
Your lady's love against some other maid
That I will show you shining at this feast,
And she shall scant show well that now seems best.

Rom. I'll go along, no such sight to be shown,
But to rejoice in splendour of mine own.

[*Exeunt.*]

[Scene III. Capulet's *house*.]

Enter *Capulet's Wife*, and *Nurse*.

Wife. Nurse, where's my daughter? Call her forth to me.

Nurse. Now, by my maidenhead at twelve year old,

I bade her come. What, lamb! what, ladybird!
God forbid! Where's this girl? What, Juliet!

Enter *Juliet*.

Jul. How now? Who calls?
Nurse. Your mother.
Jul. Madam, I am here.
What is your will?
Wife. This is the matter — Nurse, give leave awhile,
We must talk in secret. Nurse, come back again;
I have remembr'red me, thou's hear our counsel.
Thou knowest my daughter's of a pretty age.
Nurse. Faith, I can tell her age unto an hour.
Wife. She's not fourteen.
Nurse. I'll lay fourteen of my teeth —
And yet, to my teen be it spoken, I have but four —
She is not fourteen. How long is it now
To Lammastide?
Wife. A fortnight and odd days.
Nurse. Even or odd, of all days in the year,
Come Lammas Eve at night shall she be fourteen.
Susan and she (God rest all Christian souls!)
Were of an age. Well, Susan is with God;
She was too good for me. But, as I said,
On Lammas Eve at night shall she be fourteen;
That shall she, marry; I remember it well.
'Tis since the earthquake now eleven years;
And she was wean'd (I never shall forget it),
Of all the days of the year, upon that day;
For I had then laid wormwood to my dug,
Sitting in the sun under the dovehouse wall.
My lord and you were then at Mantua.
Nay, I do bear a brain. But, as I said,
When it did taste the wormwood on the nipple
Of my dug and felt it bitter, pretty fool,
To see it tetchy and fall out with the dug!
Shake, quoth the dovehouse! 'Twas no need, I trow,
To bid me trudge.
And since that time it is eleven years,
For then she could stand high-lone; nay, by th' rood,
She could have run and waddled all about;
For even the day before, she broke her brow;
And then my husband (God be with his soul!
'A was a merry man) took up the child.
'Yea,' quoth he, 'dost thou fall upon thy face?
Thou wilt fall backward when thou hast more wit;
Wilt thou not, Jule?' and, by my holidam,
Tbe pretty wretch left crying, and said 'Ay.'
To see now how a jest shall come about!
I warrant, an I should live a thousand years,
I never should forget it. 'Wilt thou not, Jule?' quoth he,
And, pretty fool, it stinted, and said 'Ay.'
Wife. Enough of this. I pray thee hold thy peace.
Nurse. Yes, madam. Yet I cannot choose but laugh
To think it should leave crying and say 'Ay.'
And yet, I warrant, it had upon it brow
A bump as big as a young cock'rel's stone;
A perilous knock; and it cried bitterly.
'Yea,' quoth my husband, 'fall'st upon thy face?
Thou wilt fall backward when thou comest to age;
Wilt thou not, Jule?' It stinted, and said 'Ay.'
Jul. And stint thou too, I pray thee, nurse, say I.
Nurse. Peace, I have done. God mark thee to his grace!
Thou wast the prettiest babe that e'er I nurs'd.
An I might live to see thee married once,
I have my wish.
Wife. Marry, that 'marry' is the very theme
I came to talk of. Tell me, daughter Juliet,
How stands your disposition to be married?
Jul. It is an honour that I dream not of.
Nurse. An honour? Were not I thine only nurse,
I would say thou hadst suck'd wisdom from thy teat.
Wife. Well, think of marriage now. Younger than you,
Here in Verona, ladies of esteem,
Are made already mothers. By my count,
I was your mother much upon these years
That you are now a maid. Thus then in brief:
The valiant Paris seeks you for his love.
Nurse. A man, young lady! lady, such a man
As all the world — why, he's a man of wax.
Wife. Verona's summer hath not such a flower.
Nurse. Nay, he's a flower, in faith — a very flower.
Wife. What say you? Can you love the gentleman?
This night you shall behold him at our feast.
Read o'er the volume of young Paris' face,
And find delight writ there with beauty's pen;
Examine every married lineament,
And see how one another lends content;
And what obscur'd in this fair volume lies

Find written in the margent of his eyes.
This precious book of love, this unbound lover,
To beautify him only lacks a cover.
The fish lives in the sea, and 'tis much pride
For fair without the fair within to hide.
That book in many's eyes doth share the glory,
That in gold clasps locks in the golden story;
So shall you share all that he doth possess,
By having him making yourself no less.

Nurse. No less? Nay, bigger! Women grow by men.

Wife. Speak briefly, can you like of Paris' love?

Jul. I'll look to like, if looking liking move;
But no more deep will I endart mine eye
Than your consent gives strength to make it fly.

Enter *Servingman.*

Serv. Madam, the guests are come, supper serv'd up, you call'd, my young lady ask'd for, the nurse curs'd in the pantry, and everything in extremity. I must hence to wait. I beseech you follow straight.

Wife. We follow thee. *Exit [Servingman].*
Juliet, the County stays.

Nurse. Go, girl, seek happy nights to happy days. *Exeunt.*

[Scene IV. *A street.*]

Enter *Romeo, Mercutio, Benvolio,* with five or six other *Maskers*; *Torchbearers.*

Rom. What, shall this speech be spoke for our excuse?
Or shall we on without apology?

Ben. The date is out of such prolixity.
We'll have no Cupid hoodwink'd with a scarf,
Bearing a Tartar's painted bow of lath,
Scaring the ladies like a crowkeeper;
Nor no without-book prologue, faintly spoke
After the prompter, for our entrance;
But, let them measure us by what they will,
We'll measure them a measure, and be gone.

Rom. Give me a torch. I am not for this ambling.
Being but heavy, I will bear the light.

Mer. Nay, gentle Romeo, we must have you dance.

Rom. Not I, believe me. You have dancing shoes
With nimble soles; I have a soul of lead
So stakes me to the ground I cannot move.

Mer. You are a lover. Borrow Cupid's wings
And soar with them above a common bound.

Rom. I am too sore enpierced with his shaft
To soar with his light feathers; and so bound
I cannot bound a pitch above dull woe.
Under love's heavy burthen do I sink.

Mer. And, to sink in it, should you burthen love —
Too great oppression for a tender thing.

Rom. Is love a tender thing? It is too rough,
Too rude, too boist'rous, and it pricks like thorn.

Mer. If love be rough with you, be rough with love.
Prick love for pricking, and you beat love down.
Give me a case to put my visage in.
A visor for a visor! What care I
What curious eye doth quote deformities?
Here are the beetle brows shall blush for me.

Ben. Come, knock and enter; and no sooner in
But every man betake him to his legs.

Rom. A torch for me! Let wantons light of heart
Tickle the senseless rushes with their heels;
For I am proverb'd with a grandsire phrase,
I'll be a candle-holder and look on;
The game was ne'er so fair, and I am done.

Mer. Tut! dun's the mouse, the constable's own word!
If thou art Dun, we'll draw thee from the mire
Of this sir-reverence love, wherein thou stick'st
Up to the ears. Come, we burn daylight, ho!

Rom. Nay, that's not so.

Mer. I mean, sir, in delay
We waste our lights in vain, like lamps by day.
Take our good meaning, for our judgment sits
Five times in that ere once in our five wits.

Rom. And we mean well, in going to this masque;
But 'tis no wit to go.

Mer. Why, may one ask?

Rom. I dreamt a dream to-night.

Mer. And so did I.

Rom. Well, what was yours?

Mer. That dreamers often lie.

Rom. In bed asleep, while they do dream things true.

Mer. O, then I see Queen Mab hath been with you.
She is the fairies' midwife, and she comes
In shape no bigger than an agate stone
On the forefinger of an alderman,
Drawn with a team of little atomies
Athwart men's noses as they lie asleep;
Her wagon spokes made of long spinners' legs;
The cover, of the wings of grasshoppers;

Her traces, of the smallest spider's web;
Her collars, of the moonshine's wat'ry beams;
Her whip, of cricket's bone; the lash, of film;
Her wagoner, a small grey-coated gnat,
Not half so big as a round little worm
Prick'd from the lazy finger of a maid;
Her chariot is an empty hazelnut,
Made by the joiner squirrel or old grub,
Time out o' mind the fairies' coachmakers.
And in this state she gallops night by night
Through lovers' brains, and then they dream of love;
O'er courtiers' knees, that dream on cursies straight;
O'er lawyers' fingers, who straight dream on fees;
O'er ladies' lips, who straight on kisses dream,
Which oft the angry Mab with blisters plagues,
Because their breaths with sweetmeats tainted are.
Sometime she gallops o'er a courtier's nose,
And then dreams he of smelling out a suit;
And sometime comes she with a tithe-pig's tail
Tickling a parson's nose as 'a lies asleep,
Then dreams he of another benefice.
Sometime she driveth o'er a soldier's neck,
And then dreams he of cutting foreign throats,
Of breaches, ambuscadoes, Spanish blades,
Of healths five fadom deep; and then anon
Drums in his ear, at which he starts and wakes,
And being thus frighted, swears a prayer or two
And sleeps again. This is that very Mab
That plats the manes of horses in the night
And bakes the elflocks in foul sluttish hairs,
Which once untangled much misfortune bodes.
This is the hag, when maids lie on their backs,
That presses them and learns them first to bear,
Making them women of good carriage.
This is she —

Rom. Peace, peace, Mercutio, peace!
Thou talk'st of nothing.

Mer. True, I talk of dreams;
Which are the children of an idle brain,
Begot of nothing but vain fantasy;
Which is as thin of substance as the air,
And more inconstant than the wind, who wooes
Even now the frozen bosom of the North
And, being anger'd, puffs away from thence,
Turning his face to the dew-dropping South.

Ben. This wind you talk of blows us from ourselves.
Supper is done, and we shall come too late.

Rom. I fear, too early; for my mind misgives
Some consequence, yet hanging in the stars,
Shall bitterly begin his fearful date
With this night's revels and expire the term
Of a despised life, clos'd in my breast,
By some vile forfeit of untimely death.
But he that hath the steerage of my course
Direct my sail! On, lusty gentlemen!

Ben. Strike, drum.

They march about the stage. [*Exeunt.*]

[Scene V. Capulet's *house.*]

Servingmen come forth with napkins.

1. Serv. Where's Potpan, that he helps not to take away? He shift a trencher! he scrape a trencher!

2. Serv. When good manners shall lie all in one or two men's hands, and they unwash'd too, 'tis a foul thing.

1. Serv. Away with the join-stools, remove the court-cubbert, look to the plate. Good thou, save me a piece of marchpane and, as thou loves me, let the porter let in Susan Grindstone and Nell. Anthony, and Potpan!

2. Serv. Ay, boy, ready.

1. Serv. You are look'd for and call'd for, ask'd for and sought for, in the great chamber.

3. Serv. We cannot be here and there too. Cheerly, boys! Be brisk awhile, and the longer liver take all. *Exeunt.*

[Enter the *Maskers.*] Enter, [with *Servants*, *Capulet*, his *Wife*, *Juliet*, *Tybalt*, and] all the *Guests* and *Gentlewomen* to the *Maskers.*

Cap. Welcome, gentlemen! Ladies that have their toes
Unplagu'd with corns will have a bout with you.
Ah ha, my mistresses! which of you all
Will now deny to dance? She that makes dainty,
She I'll swear hath corns. Am I come near ye now?
Welcome, gentlemen! I have seen the day
That I have worn a visor and could tell
A whispering tale in a fair lady's ear,
Such as would please. 'Tis gone, 'tis gone, 'tis gone!
You are welcome, gentlemen! Come, musicians, play.
A hall, a hall! give room! and foot it, girls.

Music plays, and they dance.

More light, you knaves! and turn the tables up,
And quench the fire, the room is grown too hot.
Ah, sirrah, this unlook'd-for sport comes well.

Nay, sit, nay, sit, good cousin Capulet,
For you and I are past our dancing days.
How long is't now since last yourself and I
Were in a mask?

2. Cap. By'r Lady, thirty years.

Cap. What, man? 'Tis not so much, 'tis not so much!
'Tis since the nuptial of Lucentio,
Come Pentecost as quickly as it will,
Some five-and-twenty years, and then we mask'd.

2. Cap. 'Tis more, 'tis more! His son is elder, sir;
His son is thirty.

Cap. Will you tell me that?
His son was but a ward two years ago.

Rom. [*to a Servingman*] What lady's that, which doth enrich the hand
Of yonder knight?

Serv. I know not, sir.

Rom. O, she doth teach the torches to burn bright!
It seems she hangs upon the cheek of night
Like a rich jewel in an Ethiop's ear —
Beauty too rich for use, for earth too dear!
So shows a snowy dove trooping with crows
As yonder lady o'er her fellows shows.
The measure done, I'll watch her place of stand
And, touching hers, make blessed my rude hand.
Did my heart love till now? Forswear it, sight!
For I ne'er saw true beauty till this night.

Tyb. This, by his voice, should be a Montague.
Fetch me my rapier, boy. What, dares the slave
Come hither, cover'd with an antic face,
To fleer and scorn at our solemnity?
Now, by the stock and honour of my kin,
To strike him dead I hold it not a sin.

Cap. Why, how now, kinsman? Wherefore storm you so?

Tyb. Uncle, this is a Montague, our foe;
A villain, that is hither come in spite
To scorn at our solemnity this night.

Cap. Young Romeo is it?

Tyb. 'Tis he, that villain Romeo.

Cap. Content thee, gentle coz, let him alone.
'A bears him like a portly gentleman,
And, to say truth, Verona brags of him
To be a virtuous and well-govern'd youth.
I would not for the wealth of all this town
Here in my house do him disparagement.
Therefore be patient, take no note of him.
It is my will; the which if thou respect, 74
Show a fair presence and put off these frowns,
An ill-beseeming semblance for a feast.

Tyb. It fits when such a villain is a guest.
I'll not endure him.

Cap. He shall be endur'd.
What, goodman boy? I say he shall. Go to!
Am I the master here, or you? Go to!
You'll not endure him? God shall mend my soul!
You'll make a mutiny among my guests!
You will set cock-a-hoop! you'll be the man!

Tyb. Why, uncle, 'tis a shame.

Cap. Go to, go to!
You are a saucy boy. Is't so, indeed?
This trick may chance to scathe you. I know what.
You must contrary me! Marry, 'tis time. —
Well said, my hearts! — You are a princox — go!
Be quiet, or — More light, more light! — For shame!
I'll make you quiet; what! — Cheerly, my hearts!

Tyb. Patience perforce with wilful choler meeting
Makes my flesh tremble in their different greeting.
I will withdraw; but this intrusion shall,
Now seeming sweet, convert to bitt'rest gall.
Exit.

Rom. If I profane with my unworthiest hand
This holy shrine, the gentle fine is this:
My lips, two blushing pilgrims, ready stand
To smooth that rough touch with a tender kiss.

Jul. Good pilgrim, you do wrong your hand too much,
Which mannerly devotion shows in this;
For saints have hands that pilgrims' hands do touch,
And palm to palm is holy palmers' kiss.

Rom. Have not saints lips, and holy palmers too?

Jul. Ay, pilgrim, lips that they must use in pray'r.

Rom. O, then, dear saint, let lips do what hands do!
They pray; grant thou, lest faith turn to despair.

Jul. Saints do not move, though grant for prayers' sake.

Rom. Then move not while my prayer's effect I take.
Thus from my lips, by thine my sin is purg'd.
[*Kisses her.*]

Jul. Then have my lips the sin that they have took.
Rom. Sin from my lips? O trespass sweetly urg'd!
Give me my sin again. [*Kisses her.*]
Jul. You kiss by th' book.
Nurse. Madam, your mother craves a word with you.
Rom. What is her mother?
Nurse. Marry, bachelor,
Her mother is the lady of the house.
And a good lady, and a wise and virtuous.
I nurs'd her daughter that you talk'd withal.
I tell you, he that can lay hold of her
Shall have the chinks.
Rom. Is she a Capulet?
O dear account! my life is my foe's debt.
Ben. Away, be gone; the sport is at the best.
Rom. Ay, so I fear; the more is my unrest.
Cap. Nay, gentlemen, prepare not to be gone;
We have a trifling foolish banquet towards.
Is it e'en so? Why then, I thank you all.
I thank you, honest gentlemen. Good night.
More torches here! [*Exeunt Maskers.*] Come on then, let's to bed.
Ah, sirrah, by my fay, it waxes late;
I'll to my rest.
Exeunt [*all but Juliet and Nurse*].
Jul. Come hither, nurse. What is yond gentleman?
Nurse. The son and heir of old Tiberio.
Jul. What's he that now is going out of door?
Nurse. Marry, that, I think, be young Petruchio.
Jul. What's he that follows there, that would not dance?
Nurse. I know not.
Jul. Go ask his name. — If he be married,
My grave is like to be my wedding bed.
Nurse. His name is Romeo, and a Montague,
The only son of your great enemy.
Jul. My only love, sprung from my only hate!
Too early seen unknown, and known too late!
Prodigious birth of love it is to me
That I must love a loathed enemy.
Nurse. What's this? what's this?
Jul. A rhyme I learnt even now
Of one I danc'd withal.
One calls within, 'Juliet.'
Nurse. Anon, anon!
Come, let's away; the strangers all are gone.
Exeunt.

[ACT II.]

[PROLOGUE.]

[Enter *Chorus.*]

Chor. Now old desire doth in his deathbed lie,
And young affection gapes to be his heir;
That fair for which love groan'd for and would die,
With tender Juliet match'd, is now not fair.
Now Romeo is belov'd, and loves again,
Alike bewitched by the charm of looks;
But to his foe suppos'd he must complain,
And she steal love's sweet bait from fearful hooks.
Being held a foe, he may not have access
To breathe such vows as lovers use to swear,
And she as much in love, her means much less
To meet her new beloved anywhere;
But passion lends them power, time means, to meet,
Temp'ring extremities with extreme sweet.
[*Exit.*]

[Scene I. *A lane by the wall of* Capulet's *orchard.*]

Enter *Romeo* alone.

Rom. Can I go forward when my heart is here?
Turn back, dull earth, and find thy centre out.
[*Climbs the wall and leaps down within it.*]

Enter *Benvolio* with *Mercutio.*

Ben. Romeo! my cousin Romeo! Romeo!
Mer. He is wise,
And, on my life, hath stol'n him home to bed.
Ben. He ran this way, and leapt this orchard wall.
Call, good Mercutio.
Mer. Nay, I'll conjure too.
Romeo! humours! madman! passion! lover!
Appear thou in the likeness of a sigh;
Speak but one rhyme, and I am satisfied!
Cry but 'Ay me!' pronounce but 'love' and 'dove';

Speak to my gossip Venus one fair word,
One nickname for her purblind son and heir,
Young Adam Cupid, he that shot so trim
When King Cophetua lov'd the beggar maid!
He heareth not, he stirreth not, he moveth not;
The ape is dead, and I must conjure him.
I conjure thee by Rosaline's bright eyes,
By her high forehead and her scarlet lip,
By her fine foot, straight leg, and quivering thigh,
And the demesnes that there adjacent lie,
That in thy likeness thou appear to us!

Ben. An if he hear thee, thou wilt anger him.

Mer. This cannot anger him. 'Twould anger him
To raise a spirit in his mistress' circle
Of some strange nature, letting it there stand
Till she had laid it and conjur'd it down.
That were some spite; my invocation
Is fair and honest: in his mistress' name,
I conjure only but to raise up him.

Ben. Come, he hath hid himself among these trees
To be consorted with the humorous night.
Blind is his love and best befits the dark.

Mer. If love be blind, love cannot hit the mark.
Now will he sit under a medlar tree
And wish his mistress were that kind of fruit
As maids call medlars when they laugh alone.
O, Romeo, that she were, O that she were
An open et cetera, thou a pop'rin pear!
Romeo, good night. I'll to my truckle-bed;
This field-bed is too cold for me to sleep.
Come, shall we go?

Ben. Go then, for 'tis in vain
To seek him here that means not to be found.
Exeunt.

[Scene II. Capulet's *orchard.*]

[Enter *Romeo.*]

Rom. He jests at scars that never felt a wound.

[Enter *Juliet* above at a window.]

But soft! What light through yonder window breaks?
It is the East, and Juliet is the sun!
Arise, fair sun, and kill the envious moon,
Who is already sick and pale with grief
That thou her maid art far more fair than she.
Be not her maid, since she is envious.
Her vestal livery is but sick and green,
And none but fools do wear it. Cast it off.
It is my lady; O, it is my love!
O that she knew she were!
She speaks, yet she says nothing. What of that?
Her eye discourses; I will answer it.
I am too bold; 'tis not to me she speaks.
Two of the fairest stars in all the heaven,
Having some business, do entreat her eyes
To twinkle in their spheres till they return.
What if her eyes were there, they in her head?
The brightness of her cheek would shame those stars
As daylight doth a lamp; her eyes in heaven
Would through the airy region stream so bright
That birds would sing and think it were not night.
See how she leans her cheek upon her hand!
O that I were a glove upon that hand,
That I might touch that cheek!

Jul. Ay me!

Rom. She speaks.
O, speak again, bright angel! for thou art
As glorious to this night, being o'er my head,
As is a winged messenger of heaven
Unto the white-upturned wond'ring eyes
Of mortals that fall back to gaze on him
When he bestrides the lazy-pacing clouds
And sails upon the bosom of the air.

Jul. O Romeo, Romeo! wherefore art thou Romeo?
Deny thy father and refuse thy name!
Or, if thou wilt not, be but sworn my love,
And I'll no longer be a Capulet.

Rom. [*aside*] Shall I hear more, or shall I speak at this?

Jul. 'Tis but thy name that is my enemy.
Thou art thyself, though not a Montague.
What's Montague? It is nor hand, nor foot,
Nor arm, nor face, nor any other part
Belonging to a man. O, be some other name!
What's in a name? That which we call a rose
By any other name would smell as sweet.
So Romeo would, were he not Romeo call'd,
Retain that dear perfection which he owes
Without that title. Romeo, doff thy name;
And for that name, which is no part of thee,
Take all myself.

Rom. I take thee at thy word.
Call me but love, and I'll be new baptiz'd;
Henceforth I never will be Romeo.

Jul. What man art thou that, thus bescreen'd in night,
So stumblest on my counsel?

Rom. By a name
I know not how to tell thee who I am.
My name, dear saint, is hateful to myself,
Because it is an enemy to thee.
Had I it written, I would tear the word.

Jul. My ears have yet not drunk a hundred words
Of that tongue's utterance, yet I know the sound.
Art thou not Romeo, and a Montague?

Rom. Neither, fair saint, if either thee dislike.

Jul. How cam'st thou hither, tell me, and wherefore?
The orchard walls are high and hard to climb,
And the place death, considering who thou art,
If any of my kinsmen find thee here.

Rom. With love's light wings did I o'erperch these walls;
For stony limits cannot hold love out,
And what love can do, that dares love attempt.
Therefore thy kinsmen are no let to me.

Jul. If they do see thee, they will murther thee.

Rom. Alack, there lies more peril in thine eye
Than twenty of their swords! Look thou but sweet,
And I am proof against their enmity.

Jul. I would not for the world they saw thee here.

Rom. I have night's cloak to hide me from their sight;
And but thou love me, let them find me here.
My life were better ended by their hate
Than death prorogued, wanting of thy love.

Jul. By whose direction found'st thou out this place?

Rom. By love, that first did prompt me to enquire.
He lent me counsel, and I lent him eyes.
I am no pilot; yet, wert thou as far
As that vast shore wash'd with the farthest sea,
I would adventure for such merchandise.

Jul. Thou knowest the mask of night is on my face;
Else would a maiden blush bepaint my cheek
For that which thou hast heard me speak to-night.
Fain would I dwell on form — fain, fain deny
What I have spoke; but farewell compliment!
Dost thou love me? I know thou wilt say 'Ay';
And I will take thy word. Yet, if thou swear'st,
Thou mayst prove false. At lovers' perjuries,
They say Jove laughs. O gentle Romeo,
If thou dost love, pronounce it faithfully.
Or if thou thinkest I am too quickly won,
I'll frown, and be perverse, and say thee nay,
So thou wilt woo; but else, not for the world.
In truth, fair Montague, I am too fond,
And therefore thou mayst think my haviour light;
But trust me, gentleman, I'll prove more true
Than those that have more cunning to be strange.
I should have been more strange, I must confess,
But that thou overheard'st, ere I was ware,
My true-love passion. Therefore pardon me,
And not impute this yielding to light love,
Which the dark night hath so discovered.

Rom. Lady, by yonder blessed moon I swear,
That tips with silver all these fruit-tree tops —

Jul. O, swear not by the moon, th' inconstant moon,
That monthly changes in her circled orb,
Lest that thy love prove likewise variable.

Rom. What shall I swear by?

Jul. Do not swear at all;
Or if thou wilt, swear by thy gracious self,
Which is the god of my idolatry,
And I'll believe thee.

Rom. If my heart's dear love —

Jul. Well, do not swear. Although I joy in thee,
I have no joy of this contract to-night.
It is too rash, too unadvis'd, too sudden;
Too like the lightning, which doth cease to be
Ere one can say 'It lightens.' Sweet, good night!
This bud of love, by summer's ripening breath,
May prove a beauteous flow'r when next we meet.
Good night, good night! As sweet repose and rest
Come to thy heart as that within my breast!

Rom. O, wilt thou leave me so unsatisfied?

Jul. What satisfaction canst thou have to-night?

Rom. Th' exchange of thy love's faithful vow for mine.

Jul. I gave thee mine before thou didst request it;
And yet I would it were to give again.

Rom. Wouldst thou withdraw it? For what purpose, love?

Jul. But to be frank and give it thee again.
And yet I wish but for the thing I have.
My bounty is as boundless as the sea,
My love as deep; the more I give to thee,
The more I have, for both are infinite.

I hear some noise within. Dear love, adieu!
[*Nurse*] *calls within.*
Anon, good nurse! Sweet Montague, be true.
Stay but a little, I will come again. [*Exit.*]
Rom. O blessed, blessed night! I am afeard,
Being in night, all this is but a dream,
Too flattering-sweet to be substantial.

[Enter *Juliet* above.]

Jul. Three words, dear Romeo, and good night indeed.
If that thy bent of love be honourable,
Thy purpose marriage, send me word to-morrow,
By one that I'll procure to come to thee,
Where and what time thou wilt perform the rite;
And all my fortunes at thy foot I'll lay
And follow thee my lord throughout the world.
Nurse. (*within*) Madam!
Jul. I come, anon. — But if thou meanest not well,
I do beseech thee —
Nurse. (*within*) Madam!
Jul. By-and-by I come. —
To cease thy suit and leave me to my grief.
To-morrow will I send.
Rom. So thrive my soul —
Jul. A thousand times good night! *Exit.*
Rom. A thousand times the worse, to want thy light!
Love goes toward love as schoolboys from their books;
But love from love, toward school with heavy looks.

Enter *Juliet* again, [above].

Jul. Hist! Romeo, hist! O for a falc'ner's voice
To lure this tassel-gentle back again!
Bondage is hoarse and may not speak aloud;
Else would I tear the cave where Echo lies,
And make her airy tongue more hoarse than mine
With repetition of my Romeo's name.
Romeo!
Rom. It is my soul that calls upon my name.
How silver-sweet sound lovers' tongues by night,
Like softest music to attending ears!
Jul. Romeo!
Rom. My dear?
Jul. At what o'clock to-morrow
Shall I send to thee?
Rom. By the hour of nine.
Jul. I will not fail. 'Tis twenty years till then.
I have forgot why I did call thee back.
Rom. Let me stand here till thou remember it.
Jul. I shall forget, to have thee still stand there,
Rememb'ring how I love thy company.
Rom. And I'll still stay, to have thee still forget,
Forgetting any other home but this.
Jul. 'Tis almost morning. I would have thee gone
And yet no farther than a wanton's bird,
That lets it hop a little from her hand,
Like a poor prisoner in his twisted gyves,
And with a silk thread plucks it back again,
So loving-jealous of his liberty.
Rom. I would I were thy bird.
Jul. Sweet, so would I.
Yet I should kill thee with much cherishing.
Good night, good night! Parting is such sweet sorrow,
That I shall say good night till it be morrow.
[*Exit.*]
Rom. Sleep dwell upon thine eyes, peace in thy breast!
Would I were sleep and peace, so sweet to rest!
Hence will I to my ghostly father's cell,
His help to crave and my dear hap to tell.
Exit.

[Scene III. Friar Laurence's *cell.*]

Enter *Friar* [*Laurence*] alone, with a basket.

Friar. The grey-ey'd morn smiles on the frowning night,
Check'ring the Eastern clouds with streaks of light;
And flecked darkness like a drunkard reels
From forth day's path and Titan's fiery wheels.
Now, ere the sun advance his burning eye
The day to cheer and night's dank dew to dry,
I must up-fill this osier cage of ours
With baleful weeds and precious-juiced flowers.
The earth that's nature's mother is her tomb.
What is her burying grave, that is her womb;
And from her womb children of divers kind
We sucking on her natural bosom find;
Many for many virtues excellent,
None but for some, and yet all different.
O, mickle is the powerful grace that lies
In plants, herbs, stones, and their true qualities;

For naught so vile that on the earth doth live
But to the earth some special good doth give;
Nor aught so good but, strain'd from that fair use,
Revolts from true birth, stumbling on abuse.
Virtue itself turns vice, being misapplied,
And vice sometime's by action dignified.
Within tne infant rind of this small flower
Poison hath residence, and medicine power;
For this, being smelt, with that part cheers each part;
Being tasted, slays all senses with the heart.
Two such opposed kings encamp them still
In man as well as herbs — grace and rude will;
And where the worser is predominant,
Full soon the canker death eats up that plant.

Enter *Romeo.*

Rom. Good morrow, father.
Friar. Benedicite!
What early tongue so sweet saluteth me?
Young son, it argues a distempered head
So soon to bid good morrow to thy bed.
Care keeps his watch in every old man's eye,
And where care lodges sleep will never lie;
But where unbruised youth with unstuff'd brain
Doth couch his limbs, there golden sleep doth reign.
Therefore thy earliness doth me assure
Thou art uprous'd with some distemp'rature;
Or if not so, then here I hit it right —
Our Romeo hath not been in bed to-night.
Rom. That last is true — the sweeter rest was mine.
Friar. God pardon sin! Wast thou with Rosaline?
Rom. With Rosaline, my ghostly father? No.
I have forgot that name, and that name's woe.
Friar. That's my good son! But where hast thou been then?
Rom. I'll tell thee ere thou ask it me again.
I have been feasting with mine enemy,
Where on a sudden one hath wounded me
That's by me wounded. Both our remedies
Within thy help and holy physic lies.
I bear no hatred, blessed man, for, lo,
My intercession likewise steads my foe.
Friar. Be plain, good son, and homely in thy drift.
Riddling confession finds but riddling shrift.
Rom. Then plainly know my heart's dear love is set
On the fair daughter of rich Capulet;
As mine on hers, so hers is set on mine,
And all combin'd, save what thou must combine
By holy marriage. When, and where, and how
We met, we woo'd, and made exchange of vow,
I'll tell thee as we pass; but this I pray,
That thou consent to marry us to-day.
Friar. Holy Saint Francis! What a change is here!
Is Rosaline, that thou didst love so dear,
So soon forsaken? Young men's love then lies
Not truly in their hearts, but in their eyes.
Jesu Maria! What a deal of brine
Hath wash'd thy sallow cheeks for Rosaline!
How much salt water thrown away in waste,
To season love, that of it doth not taste!
The sun not yet thy sighs from heaven clears,
Thy old groans ring yet in mine ancient ears.
Lo, here upon thy cheek the stain doth sit
Of an old tear that is not wash'd off yet.
If e'er thou wast thyself, and these woes thine,
Thou and these woes were all for Rosaline.
And art thou chang'd? Pronounce this sentence then:
Women may fall when there's no strength in men.
Rom. Thou chid'st me oft for loving Rosaline.
Friar. For doting, not for loving, pupil mine.
Rom. And bad'st me bury love.
Friar. Not in a grave
To lay one in, another out to have.
Rom. I pray thee chide not. She whom I love now
Doth grace for grace and love for love allow.
The other did not so.
Friar. O, she knew well
Thy love did read by rote, that could not spell.
But come, young waverer, come go with me.
In one respect I'll thy assistant be;
For this alliance may so happy prove
To turn your households' rancour to pure love.
Rom. O, let us hence! I stand on sudden haste.
Friar. Wisely, and slow. They stumble that run fast. *Exeunt.*

[Scene IV. *A street.*]

Enter *Benvolio* and *Mercutio.*

Mer. Where the devil should this Romeo be?
Came he not home to-night?
Ben. Not to his father's. I spoke with his man.
Mer. Why, that same pale hard-hearted wench, that Rosaline,
Torments him so that he will sure run mad.

Ben. Tybalt, the kinsman to old Capulet, Hath sent a letter to his father's house.

Mer. A challenge, on my life.

Ben. Romeo will answer it.

Mer. Any man that can write may answer a letter.

Ben. Nay, he will answer the letter's master, how he dares, being dared.

Mer. Alas, poor Romeo, he is already dead! stabb'd with a white wench's black eye; shot through the ear with a love song; the very pin of his heart cleft with the blind bow-boy's butt-shaft; and is he a man to encounter Tybalt?

Ben. Why, what is Tybalt?

Mer. More than Prince of Cats, I can tell you. O, he's the courageous captain of compliments. He fights as you sing pricksong — keeps time, distance, and proportion; rests me his minim rest, one, two, and the third in your bosom! the very butcher of a silk button, a duellist, a duellist! a gentleman of the very first house, of the first and second cause. Ah, the immortal passado! the punto reverso! the hay!

Ben. The what?

Mer. The pox of such antic, lisping, affecting fantasticoes — these new tuners of accent! 'By Jesu, a very good blade! a very tall man! a very good whore!' Why, is not this a lamentable thing, grandsir, that we should be thus afflicted with these strange flies, these fashion-mongers, these pardona-mi's, who stand so much on the new form that they cannot sit at ease on the old bench? O, their bones, their bones!

Enter *Romeo.*

Ben. Here comes Romeo! here comes Romeo!

Mer. Without his roe, like a dried herring. O flesh, flesh, how art thou fishified! Now is he for the numbers that Petrarch flowed in. Laura, to his lady, was but a kitchen wench (marry, she had a better love to berhyme her), Dido a dowdy, Cleopatra a gypsy, Helen and Hero hildings and harlots, Thisbe a gray eye or so, but not to the purpose. Signior Romeo, bon jour! There's a French salutation to your French slop. You gave us the counterfeit fairly last night.

Rom. Good morrow to you both. What counterfeit did I give you?

Mer. The slip, sir, the slip. Can you not conceive?

Rom. Pardon, good Mercutio. My business was great, and in such a case as mine a man may strain courtesy.

Mer. That's as much as to say, such a case as yours constrains a man to bow in the hams.

Rom. Meaning, to cursy.

Mer. Thou hast most kindly hit it.

Rom. A most courteous exposition.

Mer. Nay, I am the very pink of courtesy.

Rom. Pink for flower.

Mer. Right.

Rom. Why, then is my pump well-flower'd.

Mer. Well said! Follow me this jest now till thou hast worn out thy pump, that, when the single sole of it is worn, the jest may remain, after the wearing, solely singular.

Rom. O single-sol'd jest, solely singular for the singleness!

Mer. Come between us, good Benvolio! My wits faint.

Rom. Swits and spurs, swits and spurs! or I'll cry a match.

Mer. Nay, if our wits run the wild-goose chase, I am done; for thou hast more of the wild goose in one of thy wits than, I am sure, I have in my whole five. Was I with you there for the goose?

Rom. Thou wast never with me for anything when thou wast not there for the goose.

Mer. I will bite thee by the ear for that jest.

Rom. Nay, good goose, bite not!

Mer. Thy wit is a very bitter sweeting; it is a most sharp sauce.

Rom. And is it not, then, well serv'd in to a sweet goose?

Mer. O, here's a wit of cheveril, that stretches from an inch narrow to an ell broad!

Rom. I stretch it out for that word 'broad,' which, added to the goose, proves thee far and wide a broad goose.

Mer. Why, is not this better now than groaning for love? Now art thou sociable, now art thou Romeo; now art thou what thou art, by art as well as by nature. For this drivelling love is like a great natural that runs lolling up and down to hide his bauble in a hole.

Ben. Stop there, stop there!

Mer. Thou desirest me to stop in my tale against the hair.

Ben. Thou wouldst else have made thy tale large.

Mer. O, thou art deceiv'd! I would have made it short; for I was come to the whole depth of my tale, and meant indeed to occupy the argument no longer.

Rom. Here's goodly gear!

Enter *Nurse* and her *Man* [*Peter*].

Mer. A sail, a sail!

Ben. Two, two! a shirt and a smock.

Nurse. Peter!

Peter. Anon.

Nurse. My fan, Peter.

Mer. Good Peter, to hide her face; for her fan's the fairer face of the two.

Nurse. God ye good morrow, gentlemen.

Mer. God ye good-den, fair gentlewoman.

Nurse. Is it good-den?

Mer. 'Tis no less, I tell ye; for the bawdy hand of the dial is now upon the prick of noon.

Nurse. Out upon you! What a man are you!

Rom. One, gentlewoman, that God hath made for himself to mar.

Nurse. By my troth, it is well said. 'For himself to mar,' quoth 'a? Gentlemen, can any of you tell me where I may find the young Romeo?

Rom. I can tell you; but young Romeo will be older when you have found him than he was when you sought him. I am the youngest of that name, for fault of a worse.

Nurse. You say well.

Mer. Yea, is the worst well? Very well took, i' faith! wisely, wisely.

Nurse. If you be he, sir, I desire some confidence with you.

Ben. She will endite him to some supper.

Mer. A bawd, a bawd, a bawd! So ho!

Rom. What hast thou found?

Mer. No hare, sir; unless a hare, sir, in a lenten pie, that is something stale and hoar ere it be spent.

He walks by them and sings.

An old hare hoar,
And an old hare hoar,
Is very good meat in Lent;
But a hare that is hoar
Is too much for a score
When it hoars ere it be spent.

Romeo, will you come to your father's? We'll to dinner thither.

Rom. I will follow you.

Mer. Farewell, ancient lady. Farewell, [*sings*] lady, lady, lady.

Exeunt Mercutio, Benvolio.

Nurse. Marry, farewell! I pray you, sir, what saucy merchant was this that was so full of his ropery?

Rom. A gentleman, nurse, that loves to hear himself talk and will speak more in a minute than he will stand to in a month.

Nurse. An 'a speak anything against me, I'll take him down, an 'a were lustier than he is, and twenty such Jacks; and if I cannot, I'll find those that shall. Scurvy knave! I am none of his flirt-gills; I am none of his skains-mates. And thou must stand by too, and suffer every knave to use me at his pleasure!

Peter. I saw no man use you at his pleasure. If I had, my weapon should quickly have been out, I warrant you. I dare draw as soon as another man, if I see occasion in a good quarrel, and the law on my side.

Nurse. Now, afore God, I am so vex'd that every part about me quivers. Scurvy knave! Pray you, sir, a word; and, as I told you, my young lady bid me enquire you out. What she bid me say, I will keep to myself; but first let me tell ye, if ye should lead her into a fool's paradise, as they say, it were a very gross kind of behaviour, as they say; for the gentlewoman is young; and therefore, if you should deal double with her, truly it were an ill thing to be off'red to any gentlewoman, and very weak dealing.

Rom. Nurse, commend me to thy lady and mistress. I protest unto thee —

Nurse. Good heart, and i' faith I will tell her as much. Lord, Lord! she will be a joyful woman.

Rom. What wilt thou tell her, nurse? Thou dost not mark me.

Nurse. I will tell her, sir, that you do protest, which, as I take it, is a gentlemanlike offer.

Rom. Bid her devise
Some means to come to shrift this afternoon;
And there she shall at Friar Laurence' cell
Be shriv'd and married. Here is for thy pains.

Nurse. No, truly, sir; not a penny.

Rom. Go to! I say you shall.

Nurse. This afternoon, sir? Well, she shall be there.

Rom. And stay, good nurse, behind the abbey wall.
Within this hour my man shall be with thee
And bring thee cords made like a tackled stair,
Which to the high topgallant of my joy
Must be my convoy in the secret night.
Farewell. Be trusty, and I'll quit thy pains.
Farewell. Commend me to thy mistress.

Nurse. Now God in heaven bless thee! Hark you, sir.

Rom. What say'st thou, my dear nurse?

Nurse. Is your man secret? Did you ne'er hear say,
Two may keep counsel, putting one away?

Rom. I warrant thee my man's as true as steel.

Nurse. Well, sir, my mistress is the sweetest lady. Lord, Lord! when 'twas a little prating thing — O, there is a nobleman in town, one Paris, that would fain lay knife aboard; but she, good soul, had as lieve see a toad, a very toad, as see him. I anger her sometimes, and tell her that Paris is the properer man; but I'll warrant you, when I say so, she looks as pale as any clout in the versal world. Doth not rosemary and Romeo begin both with a letter?

Rom. Ay, nurse; what of that? Both with an R.

Nurse. Ah, mocker! that's the dog's name. R is for the — No; I know it begins with some other letter; and she hath the prettiest sententious of it, of you and rosemary, that it would do you good to hear it.

Rom. Commend me to thy lady.

Nurse. Ay, a thousand times. [*Exit Romeo.*] Peter!

Peter. Anon.

Nurse. Peter, take my fan, and go before, and apace. *Exeunt.*

[Scene V. Capulet's *orchard.*]

Enter *Juliet.*

Jul. The clock struck nine when I did send the nurse;
In half an hour she promis'd to return.
Perchance she cannot meet him. That's not so.
O, she is lame! Love's heralds should be thoughts,
Which ten times faster glide than the sun's beams
Driving back shadows over low'ring hills.
Therefore do nimble-pinion'd doves draw Love,
And therefore hath the wind-swift Cupid wings.
Now is the sun upon the highmost hill
Of this day's journey, and from nine till twelve
Is three long hours; yet she is not come.
Had she affections and warm youthful blood,
She would be as swift in motion as a ball;
My words would bandy her to my sweet love,
And his to me.
But old folks, many feign as they were dead —
Unwieldy, slow, heavy and pale as lead.

Enter *Nurse* [and *Peter*].

O God, she comes! O honey nurse, what news?
Hast thou met with him? Send thy man away.

Nurse. Peter, stay at the gate.
[*Exit Peter.*]

Jul. Now, good sweet nurse — O Lord, why look'st thou sad?
Though news be sad, yet tell them merrily;
If good, thou shamest the music of sweet news
By playing it to me with so sour a face.

Nurse. I am aweary, give me leave awhile.
Fie, how my bones ache! What a jaunce have I had!

Jul. I would thou hadst my bones, and I thy news.
Nay, come, I pray thee speak. Good, good nurse, speak.

Nurse. Jesu, what haste! Can you not stay awhile?
Do you not see that I am out of breath?

Jul. How art thou out of breath when thou hast breath
To say to me that thou art out of breath?
The excuse that thou dost make in this delay
Is longer than the tale thou dost excuse.
Is thy news good or bad? Answer to that.
Say either, and I'll stay the circumstance.
Let me be satisfied, is't good or bad?

Nurse. Well, you have made a simple choice; you know not how to choose a man. Romeo? No, not he. Though his face be better than any man's, yet his leg excels all men's; and for a hand and a foot, and a body, though they be not to be talk'd on, yet they are past compare. He is not the flower of courtesy, but, I'll warrant him, as gentle as a lamb. Go thy ways, wench; serve God. What, have you din'd at home?

Jul. No, no. But all this did I know before.
What says he of our marriage? What of that?

Nurse. Lord, how my head aches! What a head have I!
It beats as it would fall in twenty pieces.
My back o' t' other side — ah, my back, my back!
Beshrew your heart for sending me about
To catch my death with jauncing up and down!

Jul. I' faith, I am sorry that thou art not well.
Sweet, sweet, sweet nurse, tell me, what says my love?

Nurse. Your love says, like an honest gentleman, and a courteous, and a kind, and a handsome, and, I warrant, a virtuous — Where is your mother?

Jul. Where is my mother? Why, she is within.
Where should she be? How oddly thou repliest!

'Your love says, like an honest gentleman,
"Where is your mother?"'

Nurse. O God's Lady dear!
Are you so hot? Marry come up, I trow.
Is this the poultice for my aching bones?
Henceforward do your messages yourself.

Jul. Here's such a coil! Come, what says Romeo?

Nurse. Have you got leave to go to shrift to-day?

Jul. I have.

Nurse. Then hie you hence to Friar Laurence' cell;
There stays a husband to make you a wife.
Now comes the wanton blood up in your cheeks:
They'll be in scarlet straight at any news.
Hie you to church; I must another way,
To fetch a ladder, by the which your love
Must climb a bird's nest soon when it is dark.
I am the drudge, and toil in your delight;
But you shall bear the burthen soon at night.
Go; I'll to dinner; hie you to the cell.

Jul. Hie to high fortune! Honest nurse, farewell. *Exeunt.*

[Scene VI. Friar Laurence's *cell*.]

Enter *Friar* [*Laurence*] and *Romeo*.

Friar. So smile the heavens upon this holy act
That after-hours with sorrow chide us not!

Rom. Amen, amen! But come what sorrow can,
It cannot countervail the exchange of joy
That one short minute gives me in her sight.
Do thou but close our hands with holy words,
Then love-devouring death do what he dare —
It is enough I may but call her mine.

Friar. These violent delights have violent ends
And in their triumph die, like fire and powder,
Which, as they kiss, consume. The sweetest honey
Is loathsome in his own deliciousness
And in the taste confounds the appetite.
Therefore love moderately: long love doth so;
Too swift arrives as tardy as too slow.

Enter *Juliet*.

Here comes the lady. O, so light a foot
Will ne'er wear out the everlasting flint.
A lover may bestride the gossamer
That idles in the wanton summer air,
And yet not fall; so light is vanity.

Jul. Good even to my ghostly confessor.

Friar. Romeo shall thank thee, daughter, for us both.

Jul. As much to him, else is his thanks too much.

Rom. Ah, Juliet, if the measure of thy joy
Be heap'd like mine, and that thy skill be more
To blazon it, then sweeten with thy breath
This neighbour air, and let rich music's tongue
Unfold the imagin'd happiness that both
Receive in either by this dear encounter.

Jul. Conceit, more rich in matter than in words,
Brags of his substance, not of ornament.
They are but beggars that can count their worth;
But my true love is grown to such excess
I cannot sum up sum of half my wealth.

Friar. Come, come with me, and we will make short work;
For, by your leaves, you shall not stay alone
Till Holy Church incorporate two in one.
[*Exeunt.*]

[ACT III. Scene I. *A public place.*]

Enter *Mercutio, Benvolio,* and *Men.*

Ben. I pray thee, good Mercutio, let's retire.
The day is hot, the Capulets abroad,
And if we meet, we shall not scape a brawl,
For now, these hot days, is the mad blood stirring.

Mer. Thou art like one of these fellows that, when he enters the confines of a tavern, claps me his sword upon the table and says 'God send me no need of thee!' and by the operation of the second cup draws him on the drawer, when indeed there is no need.

Ben. Am I like such a fellow?

Mer. Come, come, thou art as hot a Jack in thy mood as any in Italy; and as soon moved to be moody, and as soon moody to be moved.

Ben. And what to?

Mer. Nay, an there were two such, we should have none shortly, for one would kill the other. Thou! why, thou wilt quarrel with a man that hath a hair more or a hair less in his beard than thou hast. Thou wilt quarrel with a man for cracking nuts, having no other reason but because thou hast hazel eyes. What eye but such an eye would spy out such a quarrel? Thy head is as full of quarrels as an egg is full of meat; and yet thy head hath been beaten as addle as an egg for quarrelling. Thou hast quarrell'd with a man for coughing in the street, because he hath wakened thy dog that hath lain asleep in the sun. Didst thou not fall out with a tailor for wearing his new doublet before Easter? with another for tying his new shoes with old riband? And yet thou wilt tutor me from quarrelling!

Ben. An I were so apt to quarrel as thou art, any man should buy the fee simple of my life for an hour and a quarter.

Mer. The fee simple? O simple!

Enter *Tybalt* and others.

Ben. By my head, here come the Capulets.

Mer. By my heel, I care not.

Tyb. Follow me close, for I will speak to them.
Gentlemen, good den. A word with one of you.

Mer. And but one word with one of us? Couple it with something; make it a word and a blow.

Tyb. You shall find me apt enough to that, sir, an you will give me occasion.

Mer. Could you not take some occasion without giving?

Tyb. Mercutio, thou consortest with Romeo.

Mer. Consort? What, dost thou make us minstrels? An thou make minstrels of us, look to hear nothing but discords. Here's my fiddlestick; here's that shall make you dance. Zounds, consort!

Ben. We talk here in the public haunt of men.
Either withdraw unto some private place
And reason coldly of your grievances,
Or else depart. Here all eyes gaze on us.

Mer. Men's eyes were made to look, and let them gaze.
I will not budge for no man's pleasure, I.

Enter *Romeo.*

Tyb. Well, peace be with you, sir. Here comes my man.

Mer. But I'll be hang'd, sir, if he wear your livery.
Marry, go before to field, he'll be your follower!
Your worship in that sense may call him man.

Tyb. Romeo, the love I bear thee can afford
No better term than this: thou art a villain.

Rom. Tybalt, the reason that I have to love thee
Doth much excuse the appertaining rage
To such a greeting. Villain am I none.
Therefore farewell. I see thou knowest me not.

Tyb. Boy, this shall not excuse the injuries
That thou hast done me; therefore turn and draw.

Rom. I do protest I never injur'd thee,
But love thee better than thou canst devise
Till thou shalt know the reason of my love;
And so, good Capulet, which name I tender
As dearly as mine own, be satisfied.

Mer. O calm, dishonourable, vile submission!
Alla stoccata carries it away. [*Draws.*]
Tybalt, you ratcatcher, will you walk?

Tyb. What wouldst thou have with me?

Mer. Good King of Cats, nothing but one of your nine lives. That I mean to make bold withal, and, as you shall use me hereafter, dry-beat the rest of the eight. Will you pluck your sword out of his pilcher by the ears? Make haste, lest mine be about your ears ere it be out.

Tyb. I am for you. [*Draws.*]

Rom. Gentle Mercutio, put thy rapier up.

Mer. Come, sir, your passado! [*They fight.*]

Rom. Draw, Benvolio; beat down their weapons.
Gentlemen, for shame! forbear this outrage!
Tybalt, Mercutio, the Prince expressly hath
Forbid this bandying in Verona streets.
Hold, Tybalt! Good Mercutio!

Tybalt under Romeo's arm thrusts Mercutio in, and flies [*with his Followers*].

Mer. I am hurt.
A plague o' both your houses! I am sped.
Is he gone and hath nothing?

Ben. What, art thou hurt?

Mer. Ay, ay, a scratch, a scratch. Marry, 'tis enough.
Where is my page? Go, villain, fetch a surgeon. [*Exit Page.*]

Rom. Courage, man. The hurt cannot be much.

Mer. No, 'tis not so deep as a well, nor so wide as a church door; but 'tis enough, 'twill serve. Ask for me to-morrow, and you shall find me a grave man. I am peppered, I warrant, for this world. A plague o' both your houses! Zounds, a dog, a rat, a mouse, a cat, to scratch a man to death! a braggart, a rogue, a villain, that fights by the book of arithmetic! Why the devil came you between us? I was hurt under your arm.

Rom. I thought all for the best.

Mer. Help me into some house, Benvolio,
Or I shall faint. A plague o' both your houses!
They have made worms' meat of me. I have it,
And soundly too. Your houses!

Exit, [supported by Benvolio].

Rom. This gentleman, the Prince's near ally,
My very friend, hath got this mortal hurt
In my behalf — my reputation stain'd
With Tybalt's slander — Tybalt, that an hour
Hath been my kinsman. O sweet Juliet,
Thy beauty hath made me effeminate
And in my temper soft'ned valour's steel!

Enter *Benvolio.*

Ben. O Romeo, Romeo, brave Mercutio's dead!
That gallant spirit hath aspir'd the clouds,
Which too untimely here did scorn the earth.

Rom. This day's black fate on moe days doth depend;
This but begins the woe others must end.

Enter *Tybalt.*

Ben. Here comes the furious Tybalt back again.

Rom. Alive in triumph, and Mercutio slain?
Away to heaven respective lenity,
And fire-ey'd fury be my conduct now!
Now, Tybalt, take the 'villain' back again
That late thou gavest me; for Mercutio's soul
Is but a little way above our heads,
Staying for thine to keep him company.
Either thou or I, or both, must go with him.

Tyb. Thou, wretched boy, that didst consort him here,
Shalt with him hence.

Rom. This shall determine that.

They fight. Tybalt falls.

Ben. Romeo, away, be gone!
The citizens are up, and Tybalt slain.
Stand not amaz'd. The Prince will doom thee death
If thou art taken. Hence, be gone, away!

Rom. O, I am fortune's fool!

Ben. Why dost thou stay?

Exit Romeo.

Enter *Citizens.*

Citizen. Which way ran he that kill'd Mercutio?
Tybalt, that murtherer, which way ran he?

Ben. There lies that Tybalt.

Citizen. Up, sir, go with me.
I charge thee in the Prince's name obey.

Enter *Prince* [attended], *Old Montague, Capulet,* their *Wives,* and [others].

Prince. Where are the vile beginners of this fray?

Ben. O noble Prince, I can discover all
The unlucky manage of this fatal brawl.
There lies the man, slain by young Romeo,
That slew thy kinsman, brave Mercutio.

Cap. Wife. Tybalt, my cousin! O my brother's child!
O Prince! O husband! O, the blood is spill'd
Of my dear kinsman! Prince, as thou art true,
For blood of ours shed blood of Montague.
O cousin, cousin!

Prince. Benvolio, who began this bloody fray?

Ben. Tybalt, here slain, whom Romeo's hand did slay.
Romeo, that spoke him fair, bid him bethink
How nice the quarrel was, and urg'd withal
Your high displeasure. All this — uttered
With gentle breath, calm look, knees humbly bow'd —
Could not take truce with the unruly spleen
Of Tybalt deaf to peace, but that he tilts
With piercing steel at bold Mercutio's breast;
Who, all as hot, turns deadly point to point,
And, with a martial scorn, with one hand beats
Cold death aside and with the other sends
It back to Tybalt, whose dexterity
Retorts it. Romeo he cries aloud,
'Hold, friends! friends, part!' and swifter than his tongue,
His agile arm beats down their fatal points,
And 'twixt them rushes; underneath whose arm
An envious thrust from Tybalt hit the life
Of stout Mercutio, and then Tybalt fled;
But by-and-by comes back to Romeo,
Who had but newly entertain'd revenge,
And to't they go like lightning; for, ere I
Could draw to part them, was stout Tybalt slain;
And, as he fell, did Romeo turn and fly.
This is the truth, or let Benvolio die.

Cap. Wife. He is a kinsman to the Montague;
Affection makes him false, he speaks not true.
Some twenty of them fought in this black strife,
And all those twenty could but kill one life.
I beg for justice, which thou, Prince, must give.
Romeo slew Tybalt; Romeo must not live.

Prince. Romeo slew him; he slew Mercutio.
Who now the price of his dear blood doth owe?
Mon. Not Romeo, Prince; he was Mercutio's friend;
His fault concludes but what the law should end,
The life of Tybalt.
Prince. And for that offence
Immediately we do exile him hence.
I have an interest in your hate's proceeding,
My blood for your rude brawls doth lie a-bleeding;
But I'll amerce you with so strong a fine
That you shall all repent the loss of mine.
I will be deaf to pleading and excuses;
Nor tears nor prayers shall purchase out abuses.
Therefore use none. Let Romeo hence in haste,
Else, when he is found, that hour is his last.
Bear hence this body, and attend our will.
Mercy but murders, pardoning those that kill.
Exeunt.

[Scene II. Capulet's *orchard.*]

Enter *Juliet* alone.

Jul. Gallop apace, you fiery-footed steeds,
Towards Phœbus' lodging! Such a wagoner
As Phaëton would whip you to the West
And bring in cloudy night immediately.
Spread thy close curtain, love-performing night,
That runaway eyes may wink, and Romeo
Leap to these arms untalk'd of and unseen.
Lovers can see to do their amorous rites
By their own beauties; or, if love be blind,
It best agrees with night. Come, civil night,
Thou sober-suited matron, all in black,
And learn me how to lose a winning match,
Play'd for a pair of stainless maidenhoods.
Hood my unmann'd blood, bating in my cheeks,
With thy black mantle till strange love, grown bold,
Think true love acted simple modesty.
Come, night; come, Romeo; come, thou day in night;
For thou wilt lie upon the wings of night
Whiter than new snow upon a raven's back.
Come, gentle night; come, loving, black-brow'd night;
Give me my Romeo; and, when he shall die,
Take him and cut him out in little stars,
And he will make the face of heaven so fine
That all the world will be in love with night
And pay no worship to the garish sun.
O, I have bought the mansion of a love,
But not possess'd it; and though I am sold,
Not yet enjoy'd. So tedious is this day
As is the night before some festival
To an impatient child that hath new robes
And may not wear them. O, here comes my nurse,

Enter *Nurse,* with cords.

And she brings news; and every tongue that speaks
But Romeo's name speaks heavenly eloquence.
Now, nurse, what news? What hast thou there? the cords
That Romeo bid thee fetch?
Nurse. Ay, ay, the cords.
[*Throws them down.*]
Jul. Ay me! what news? Why dost thou wring thy hands?
Nurse. Ah, weraday! he's dead, he's dead, he's dead!
We are undone, lady, we are undone!
Alack the day! he's gone, he's kill'd, he's dead!
Jul. Can heaven be so envious?
Nurse. Romeo can,
Though heaven cannot. O Romeo, Romeo!
Who ever would have thought it? Romeo!
Jul. What devil art thou that dost torment me thus?
This torture should be roar'd in dismal hell.
Hath Romeo slain himself? Say thou but 'I,'
And that bare vowel 'I' shall poison more
Than the death-darting eye of cockatrice.
I am not I, if there be such an 'I';
Or those eyes shut that make thee answer 'I.'
If he be slain, say 'I'; or if not, 'no.'
Brief sounds determine of my weal or woe.
Nurse. I saw the wound, I saw it with mine eyes,
(God save the mark!) here on his manly breast.
A piteous corse, a bloody piteous corse;
Pale, pale as ashes, all bedaub'd in blood,
All in gore-blood. I swounded at the sight.
Jul. O, break, my heart! poor bankrout, break at once!
To prison, eyes; ne'er look on liberty!
Vile earth, to earth resign; end motion here,
And thou and Romeo press one heavy bier!
Nurse. O Tybalt, Tybalt, the best friend I had!
O courteous Tybalt! honest gentleman!
That ever I should live to see thee dead!
Jul. What storm is this that blows so contrary?
Is Romeo slaught'red, and is Tybalt dead?
My dear-lov'd cousin, and my dearer lord?

Then, dreadful trumpet, sound the general doom!
For who is living, if those two are gone?
Nurse. Tybalt is gone, and Romeo banished;
Romeo that kill'd him, he is banished.
Jul. O God! Did Romeo's hand shed Tybalt's blood?
Nurse. It did, it did! alas the day, it did!
Jul. O serpent heart, hid with a flow'ring face!
Did ever dragon keep so fair a cave?
Beautiful tyrant! fiend angelical!
Dove-feather'd raven! wolvish-ravening lamb!
Despised substance of divinest show!
Just opposite to what thou justly seem'st —
A damned saint, an honourable villain!
O nature, what hadst thou to do in hell
When thou didst bower the spirit of a fiend
In mortal paradise of such sweet flesh?
Was ever book containing such vile matter
So fairly bound? O, that deceit should dwell
In such a gorgeous palace!
Nurse. There's no trust,
No faith, no honesty in men; all perjur'd,
All forsworn, all naught, all dissemblers.
Ah, where's my man? Give me some aqua-vitæ.
These griefs, these woes, these sorrows make me old.
Shame come to Romeo!
Jul. Blister'd be thy tongue
For such a wish! He was not born to shame.
Upon his brow shame is asham'd to sit;
For 'tis a throne where honour may be crown'd
Sole monarch of the universal earth.
O, what a beast was I to chide at him!
Nurse. Will you speak well of him that kill'd your cousin?
Jul. Shall I speak ill of him that is my husband?
Ah, poor my lord, what tongue shall smooth thy name
When I, thy three-hours wife, have mangled it?
But wherefore, villain, didst thou kill my cousin?
That villain cousin would have kill'd my husband.
Back, foolish tears, back to your native spring!
Your tributary drops belong to woe,
Which you, mistaking, offer up to joy.
My husband lives, that Tybalt would have slain;
And Tybalt's dead, that would have slain my husband.
All this is comfort; wherefore weep I then?
Some word there was, worser than Tybalt's death,
That murd'red me. I would forget it fain;
But O, it presses to my memory
Like damned guilty deeds to sinners' minds!
'Tybalt is dead, and Romeo — banished.'
That 'banished,' that one word 'banished,'
Hath slain ten thousand Tybalts. Tybalt's death
Was woe enough, if it had ended there;
Or, if sour woe delights in fellowship
And needly will be rank'd with other griefs,
Why followed not, when she said 'Tybalt's dead,'
Thy father, or thy mother, nay, or both,
Which modern lamentation might have mov'd?
But with a rearward following Tybalt's death,
'Romeo is banished' — to speak that word
Is father, mother, Tybalt, Romeo, Juliet,
All slain, all dead. 'Romeo is banished' —
There is no end, no limit, measure, bound,
In that word's death; no words can that woe sound.
Where is my father and my mother, nurse?
Nurse. Weeping and wailing over Tybalt's corse.
Will you go to them? I will bring you thither.
Jul. Wash they his wounds with tears? Mine shall be spent,
When theirs are dry, for Romeo's banishment.
Take up those cords. Poor ropes, you are beguil'd,
Both you and I, for Romeo is exil'd.
He made you for a highway to my bed;
But I, a maid, die maiden-widowed.
Come, cords; come, nurse. I'll to my wedding bed;
And death, not Romeo, take my maidenhead!
Nurse. Hie to your chamber. I'll find Romeo
To comfort you. I wot well where he is.
Hark ye, your Romeo will be here at night.
I'll to him; he is hid at Laurence' cell.
Jul. O, find him! give this ring to my true knight
And bid him come to take his last farewell.
Exeunt.

[Scene III. Friar Laurence's *cell.*]

Enter *Friar* [*Laurence*].

Friar. Romeo, come forth; come forth, thou fearful man.
Affliction is enamour'd of thy parts,
And thou art wedded to calamity.

Enter *Romeo.*

Rom. Father, what news? What is the Prince's doom?
What sorrow craves acquaintance at my hand
That I yet know not?
Friar. Too familiar
Is my dear son with such sour company.
I bring thee tidings of the Prince's doom.
Rom. What less than doomsday is the Prince's doom?
Friar. A gentler judgment vanish'd from his lips —
Not body's death, but body's banishment.
Rom. Ha, banishment? Be merciful, say 'death';
For exile hath more terror in his look,
Much more than death. Do not say 'banishment.'
Friar. Hence from Verona art thou banished.
Be patient, for the world is broad and wide.
Rom. There is no world without Verona walls,
But purgatory, torture, hell itself.
Hence banished is banish'd from the world,
And world's exile is death. Then 'banishment'
Is death misterm'd. Calling death 'banishment,'
Thou cut'st my head off with a golden axe
And smilest upon the stroke that murders me.
Friar. O deadly sin! O rude unthankfulness!
Thy fault our law calls death; but the kind Prince,
Taking thy part, hath rush'd aside the law,
And turn'd that black word death to banishment.
This is dear mercy, and thou seest it not.
Rom. 'Tis torture, and not mercy. Heaven is here,
Where Juliet lives; and every cat and dog
And little mouse, every unworthy thing,
Live here in heaven and may look on her;
But Romeo may not. More validity,
More honourable state, more courtship lives
In carrion flies than Romeo. They may seize
On the white wonder of dear Juliet's hand
And steal immortal blessing from her lips,
Who, even in pure and vestal modesty,
Still blush, as thinking their own kisses sin;
But Romeo may not — he is banished.
This may flies do, when I from this must fly;
They are free men, but I am banished.
And sayest thou yet that exile is not death?
Hadst thou no poison mix'd, no sharp-ground knife,
No sudden mean of death, though ne'er so mean,
But 'banished' to kill me — 'banished'?
O friar, the damned use that word in hell;
Howling attends it! How hast thou the heart,
Being a divine, a ghostly confessor,
A sin-absolver, and my friend profess'd,
To mangle me with that word 'banished'?
Friar. Thou fond mad man, hear me a little speak.
Rom. O, thou wilt speak again of banishment.
Friar. I'll give thee armour to keep off that word;
Adversity's sweet milk, philosophy,
To comfort thee, though thou art banished.
Rom. Yet 'banished'? Hang up philosophy!
Unless philosophy can make a Juliet,
Displant a town, reverse a prince's doom,
It helps not, it prevails not. Talk no more.
Friar. O, then I see that madmen have no ears.
Rom. How should they, when that wise men have no eyes?
Friar. Let me dispute with thee of thy estate.
Rom. Thou canst not speak of that thou dost not feel.
Wert thou as young as I, Juliet thy love,
An hour but married, Tybalt murdered,
Doting like me, and like me banished,
Then mightst thou speak, then mightst thou tear thy hair,
And fall upon the ground, as I do now,
Taking the measure of an unmade grave.
Knock [*within*].
Friar. Arise; one knocks. Good Romeo, hide thyself.
Rom. Not I; unless the breath of heartsick groans,
Mist-like infold me from the search of eyes.
Knock.
Friar. Hark, how they knock! Who's there? Romeo, arise;
Thou wilt be taken. — Stay awhile! — Stand up; *Knock.*
Run to my study. — By-and-by! — God's will,
What simpleness is this! — I come, I come!
Knock.
Who knocks so hard? Whence come you? What's your will?
Nurse. [*within*] Let me come in, and you shall know my errand.
I come from Lady Juliet.
Friar. Welcome then.

Enter *Nurse.*

Nurse. O holy friar, O, tell me, holy friar,
Where is my lady's lord, where's Romeo?
Friar. There on the ground, with his own tears made drunk.
Nurse. O, he is even in my mistress' case,
Just in her case!
Friar. O woful sympathy!
Piteous predicament!
Nurse. Even so lies she,
Blubb'ring and weeping, weeping and blubbering.
Stand up, stand up! Stand, an you be a man.
For Juliet's sake, for her sake, rise and stand!
Why should you fall into so deep an O?
Rom. (*rises*) Nurse —
Nurse. Ah sir! ah sir! Well, death 's the end of all.
Rom. Spakest thou of Juliet? How is it with her?
Doth not she think me an old murtherer,
Now I have stain'd the childhood of our joy
With blood remov'd but little from her own?
Where is she? and how doth she? and what says
My conceal'd lady to our cancell'd love?
Nurse. O, she says nothing, sir, but weeps and weeps;
And now falls on her bed, and then starts up,
And Tybalt calls; and then on Romeo cries,
And then down falls again.
Rom. As if that name,
Shot from the deadly level of a gun,
Did murther her; as that name's cursed hand
Murder'd her kinsman. O, tell me, friar, tell me,
In what vile part of this anatomy
Doth my name lodge? Tell me, that I may sack
The hateful mansion. [*Draws his dagger.*]
Friar. Hold thy desperate hand.
Art thou a man? Thy form cries out thou art;
Thy tears are womanish, thy wild acts denote
The unreasonable fury of a beast.
Unseemly woman in a seeming man!
Or ill-beseeming beast in seeming both!
Thou hast amaz'd me. By my holy order,
I thought thy disposition better temper'd.
Hast thou slain Tybalt? Wilt thou slay thyself?
And slay thy lady that in thy life lives,
By doing damned hate upon thyself?
Why railest thou on thy birth, the heaven, and earth?
Since birth and heaven and earth, all three do meet
In thee at once; which thou at once wouldst lose.
Fie, fie, thou shamest thy shape, thy love, thy wit,
Which, like a usurer, abound'st in all,
And usest none in that true use indeed
Which should bedeck thy shape, thy love, thy wit.
Thy noble shape is but a form of wax,
Digressing from the valour of a man;
Thy dear love sworn but hollow perjury,
Killing that love which thou hast vow'd to cherish;
Thy wit, that ornament to shape and love,
Misshapen in the conduct of them both,
Like powder in a skilless soldier's flask,
Is set afire by thine own ignorance,
And thou dismem'bred with thine own defence.
What, rouse thee, man! Thy Juliet is alive,
For whose dear sake thou wast but lately dead.
There art thou happy. Tybalt would kill thee,
But thou slewest Tybalt. There art thou happy too.
The law, that threat'ned death, becomes thy friend
And turns it to exile. There art thou happy.
A pack of blessings light upon thy back;
Happiness courts thee in her best array;
But, like a misbehav'd and sullen wench,
Thou pout'st upon thy fortune and thy love.
Take heed, take heed, for such die miserable.
Go get thee to thy love, as was decreed,
Ascend her chamber, hence and comfort her.
But look thou stay not till the watch be set,
For then thou canst not pass to Mantua,
Where thou shalt live till we can find a time
To blaze your marriage, reconcile your friends,
Beg pardon of the Prince, and call thee back
With twenty hundred thousand times more joy
Than thou went'st forth in lamentation.
Go before, nurse. Commend me to thy lady,
And bid her hasten all the house to bed,
Which heavy sorrow makes them apt unto.
Romeo is coming.
Nurse. O Lord, I could have stay'd here all the night
To hear good counsel. O, what learning is!
My lord, I'll tell my lady you will come.
Rom. Do so, and bid my sweet prepare to chide.
Nurse. Here is a ring she bid me give you, sir.
Hie you, make haste, for it grows very late.
Exit.

Rom. How well my comfort is reviv'd by this!

Friar. Go hence; good night; and here stands all your state:
Either be gone before the watch be set,
Or by the break of day disguis'd from hence.
Sojourn in Mantua. I'll find out your man,
And he shall signify from time to time
Every good hap to you that chances here.
Give me thy hand. 'Tis late. Farewell; good night.

Rom. But that a joy past joy calls out on me,
It were a grief so brief to part with thee.
Farewell. *Exeunt.*

[Scene IV. Capulet's *house.*]

Enter *Old Capulet,* his *Wife,* and *Paris.*

Cap. Things have fall'n out, sir, so unluckily
That we have had no time to move our daughter.
Look you, she lov'd her kinsman Tybalt dearly,
And so did I. Well, we were born to die.
'Tis very late; she'll not come down to-night.
I promise you, but for your company,
I would have been abed an hour ago.

Par. These times of woe afford no time to woo.
Madam, good night. Commend me to your daughter.

Lady. I will, and know her mind early to-morrow;
To-night she's mew'd up to her heaviness.

Cap. Sir Paris, I will make a desperate tender
Of my child's love. I think she will be rul'd
In all respects by me; nay more, I doubt it not.
Wife, go you to her ere you go to bed;
Acquaint her here of my son Paris' love
And bid her (mark you me?) on Wednesday next —
But, soft! what day is this?

Par. Monday, my lord.

Cap. Monday! ha, ha! Well, Wednesday is too soon.
A Thursday let it be — a Thursday, tell her,
She shall be married to this noble earl.
Will you be ready? Do you like this haste?
We'll keep no great ado — a friend or two;
For hark you, Tybalt being slain so late,
It may be thought we held him carelessly,
Being our kinsman, if we revel much.
Therefore we'll have some half a dozen friends,
And there an end. But what say you to Thursday?

Par. My lord, I would that Thursday were to-morrow.

Cap. Well, get you gone. A Thursday be it then.
Go you to Juliet ere you go to bed;
Prepare her, wife, against this wedding day.
Farewell, my lord. — Light to my chamber, ho!
Afore me, it is so very very late
That we may call it early by-and-by.
Good night. *Exeunt.*

[Scene V. Capulet's *orchard.*]

Enter *Romeo* and *Juliet* aloft, at the window.

Jul. Wilt thou be gone? It is not yet near day.
It was the nightingale, and not the lark,
That pierc'd the fearful hollow of thine ear.
Nightly she sings on yond pomegranate tree.
Believe me, love, it was the nightingale.

Rom. It was the lark, the herald of the morn;
No nightingale. Look, love, what envious streaks
Do lace the severing clouds in yonder East.
Night's candles are burnt out, and jocund day
Stands tiptoe on the misty mountain tops.
I must be gone and live, or stay and die.

Jul. Yond light is not daylight; I know it, I.
It is some meteor that the sun exhales
To be to thee this night a torchbearer
And light thee on thy way to Mantua.
Therefore stay yet; thou need'st not to be gone.

Rom. Let me be ta'en, let me be put to death.
I am content, so thou wilt have it so.
I'll say yon grey is not the morning's eye,
'Tis but the pale reflex of Cynthia's brow;
Nor that is not the lark whose notes do beat
The vaulty heaven so high above our heads.
I have more care to stay than will to go.
Come, death, and welcome! Juliet wills it so.
How is't, my soul? Let's talk; it is not day.

Jul. It is, it is! Hie hence, be gone, away!
It is the lark that sings so out of tune,
Straining harsh discords and unpleasing sharps.
Some say the lark makes sweet division;
This doth not so, for she divideth us.
Some say the lark and loathed toad chang'd eyes;
O, now I would they had chang'd voices too,
Since arm from arm that voice doth us affray,
Hunting thee hence with hunt's-up to the day!
O, now be gone! More light and light it grows.

Rom. More light and light — more dark and dark our woes!

Enter *Nurse.*

Nurse. Madam!
Jul. Nurse?
Nurse. Your lady mother is coming to your chamber.
The day is broke; be wary, look about. [*Exit.*]
Jul. Then, window, let day in, and let life out.
Rom. Farewell, farewell! One kiss, and I'll descend. *He goeth down.*
Jul. Art thou gone so, my lord, my love, my friend?
I must hear from thee every day in the hour,
For in a minute there are many days.
O, by this count I shall be much in years
Ere I again behold my Romeo!
Rom. Farewell!
I will omit no opportunity
That may convey my greetings, love, to thee.
Jul. O, think'st thou we shall ever meet again?
Rom. I doubt it not; and all these woes shall serve
For sweet discourses in our time to come.
Jul. O God, I have an ill-divining soul!
Methinks I see thee, now thou art below,
As one dead in the bottom of a tomb.
Either my eyesight fails, or thou look'st pale.
Rom. And trust me, love, in my eye so do you.
Dry sorrow drinks our blood. Adieu, adieu! *Exit.*
Jul. O Fortune, Fortune! all men call thee fickle.
If thou art fickle, what dost thou with him
That is renowm'd for faith? Be fickle, Fortune,
For then I hope thou wilt not keep him long
But send him back.
Lady. [*within*] Ho, daughter! are you up?
Jul. Who is't that calls? It is my lady mother.
Is she not down so late, or up so early?
What unaccustom'd cause procures her hither?

Enter *Mother.*

Lady. Why, how now, Juliet?
Jul. Madam, I am not well.
Lady. Evermore weeping for your cousin's death?
What, wilt thou wash him from his grave with tears?
An if thou couldst, thou couldst not make him live.
Therefore have done. Some grief shows much of love;
But much of grief shows still some want of wit.
Jul. Yet let me weep for such a feeling loss.
Lady. So shall you feel the loss, but not the friend
Which you weep for.
Jul. Feeling so the loss,
I cannot choose but ever weep the friend.
Lady. Well, girl, thou weep'st not so much for his death
As that the villain lives which slaughter'd him.
Jul. What villain, madam?
Lady. That same villain Romeo.
Jul. [*aside*] Villain and he be many miles asunder. —
God pardon him! I do, with all my heart;
And yet no man like he doth grieve my heart.
Lady. That is because the traitor murderer lives.
Jul. Ay, madam, from the reach of these my hands.
Would none but I might venge my cousin's death!
Lady. We will have vengeance for it, fear thou not.
Then weep no more. I'll send to one in Mantua,
Where that same banish'd runagate doth live,
Shall give him such an unaccustom'd dram
That he shall soon keep Tybalt company;
And then I hope thou wilt be satisfied.
Jul. Indeed I never shall be satisfied
With Romeo till I behold him — dead —
Is my poor heart so for a kinsman vex'd.
Madam, if you could find out but a man
To bear a poison, I would temper it;
That Romeo should, upon receipt thereof,
Soon sleep in quiet. O, how my heart abhors
To hear him nam'd and cannot come to him,
To wreak the love I bore my cousin Tybalt
Upon his body that hath slaughter'd him!
Lady. Find thou the means, and I'll find such a man.
But now I'll tell thee joyful tidings, girl.
Jul. And joy comes well in such a needy time.
What are they, I beseech your ladyship?
Lady. Well, well, thou hast a careful father, child;
One who, to put thee from thy heaviness,
Hath sorted out a sudden day of joy
That thou expects not nor I look'd not for.

Jul. Madam, in happy time! What day is that?
Lady. Marry, my child, early next Thursday morn
The gallant, young, and noble gentleman,
The County Paris, at Saint Peter's Church,
Shall happily make thee there a joyful bride.
Jul. Now by Saint Peter's Church, and Peter too,
He shall not make me there a joyful bride!
I wonder at this haste, that I must wed
Ere he that should be husband comes to woo.
I pray you tell my lord and father, madam,
I will not marry yet; and when I do, I swear
It shall be Romeo, whom you know I hate,
Rather than Paris. These are news indeed!
Lady. Here comes your father. Tell him so yourself,
And see how he will take it at your hands.

Enter *Capulet* and *Nurse.*

Cap. When the sun sets the air doth drizzle dew,
But for the sunset of my brother's son
It rains downright.
How now? a conduit, girl? What, still in tears?
Evermore show'ring? In one little body
Thou counterfeit'st a bark, a sea, a wind:
For still thy eyes, which I may call the sea,
Do ebb and flow with tears; the bark thy body is,
Sailing in this salt flood; the winds, thy sighs,
Who, raging with thy tears and they with them,
Without a sudden calm will overset
Thy tempest-tossed body. How now, wife?
Have you delivered to her our decree?
Lady. Ay, sir; but she will none, she gives you thanks.
I would the fool were married to her grave!
Cap. Soft! take me with you, take me with you, wife.
How? Will she none? Doth she not give us thanks?
Is she not proud? Doth she not count her blest,
Unworthy as she is, that we have wrought
So worthy a gentleman to be her bridegroom?
Jul. Not proud you have, but thankful that you have.
Proud can I never be of what I hate,
But thankful even for hate that is meant love.
Cap. How, how, how, how, choplogic? What is this?
'Proud' — and 'I thank you' — and 'I thank you not' —
And yet 'not proud'? Mistress minion you,
Thank me no thankings, nor proud me no prouds,
But fettle your fine joints 'gainst Thursday next
To go with Paris to Saint Peter's Church,
Or I will drag thee on a hurdle thither.
Out, you green-sickness carrion! out, you baggage!
You tallow-face!
Lady. Fie, fie! what, are you mad?
Jul. Good father, I beseech you on my knees,
Hear me with patience but to speak a word.
Cap. Hang thee, young baggage! disobedient wretch!
I tell thee what — get thee to church a Thursday
Or never after look me in the face.
Speak not, reply not, do not answer me!
My fingers itch. Wife, we scarce thought us blest
That God had lent us but this only child;
But now I see this one is one too much,
And that we have a curse in having her.
Out on her, hilding!
Nurse. God in heaven bless her!
You are to blame, my lord, to rate her so.
Cap. And why, my Lady Wisdom? Hold your tongue,
Good Prudence. Smatter with your gossips, go!
Nurse. I speak no treason.
Cap. O, God-i-god-en!
Nurse. May not one speak?
Cap. Peace, you mumbling fool!
Utter your gravity o'er a gossip's bowl,
For here we need it not.
Lady. You are too hot.
Cap. God's bread! it makes me mad. Day, night, late, early,
At home, abroad, alone, in company,
Waking or sleeping, still my care hath been
To have her match'd; and having now provided
A gentleman of princely parentage,
Of fair demesnes, youthful, and nobly train'd,
Stuff'd, as they say, with honourable parts,
Proportion'd as one's thought would wish a man —
And then to have a wretched puling fool,
A whining mammet, in her fortune's tender,
To answer 'I'll not wed, I cannot love;
I am too young, I pray you pardon me'!
But, an you will not wed, I'll pardon you.
Graze where you will, you shall not house with me.
Look to't, think on't; I do not use to jest.

Thursday is near; lay hand on heart, advise:
An you be mine, I'll give you to my friend;
An you be not, hang, beg, starve, die in the streets,
For, by my soul, I'll ne'er acknowledge thee,
Nor what is mine shall never do thee good.
Trust to't. Bethink you. I'll not be forsworn. *Exit.*

Jul. Is there no pity sitting in the clouds
That sees into the bottom of my grief?
O sweet my mother, cast me not away!
Delay this marriage for a month, a week;
Or if you do not, make the bridal bed
In that dim monument where Tybalt lies.

Lady. Talk not to me, for I'll not speak a word.
Do as thou wilt, for I have done with thee. *Exit.*

Jul. O God! — O nurse, how shall this be prevented?
My husband is on earth, my faith in heaven.
How shall that faith return again to earth
Unless that husband send it me from heaven
By leaving earth? Comfort me, counsel me.
Alack, alack, that heaven should practise stratagems
Upon so soft a subject as myself!
What say'st thou? Hast thou not a word of joy?
Some comfort, nurse.

Nurse. Faith, here it is.
Romeo is banish'd; and all the world to nothing
That he dares ne'er come back to challenge you;
Or if he do, it needs must be by stealth.
Then, since the case so stands as now it doth,
I think it best you married with the County.
O, he's a lovely gentleman!
Romeo's a dishclout to him. An eagle, madam,
Hath not so green, so quick, so fair an eye
As Paris hath. Beshrew my very heart,
I think you are happy in this second match,
For it excels your first; or if it did not,
Your first is dead — or 'twere as good he were
As living here and you no use of him.

Jul. Speak'st thou this from thy heart?

Nurse. And from my soul too; else beshrew them both.

Jul. Amen!

Nurse. What?

Jul. Well, thou hast comforted me marvellous much.
Go in; and tell my lady I am gone,
Having displeas'd my father, to Laurence' cell,
To make confession and to be absolv'd.

Nurse. Marry, I will; and this is wisely done. *Exit.*

Jul. Ancient damnation! O most wicked fiend!
Is it more sin to wish me thus forsworn,
Or to dispraise my lord with that same tongue
Which she hath prais'd him with above compare
So many thousand times? Go, counsellor!
Thou and my bosom henceforth shall be twain.
I'll to the friar to know his remedy.
If all else fail, myself have power to die. *Exit.*

[ACT IV. Scene I. Friar Laurence's *cell.*]

Enter *Friar* [*Laurence*] and *County Paris.*

Friar. On Thursday, sir? The time is very short.

Par. My father Capulet will have it so,
And I am nothing slow to slack his haste.

Friar. You say you do not know the lady's mind.
Uneven is the course; I like it not.

Par. Immoderately she weeps for Tybalt's death,
And therefore have I little talk'd of love;
For Venus smiles not in a house of tears.
Now, sir, her father counts it dangerous
That she do give her sorrow so much sway,
And in his wisdom hastes our marriage
To stop the inundation of her tears,
Which, too much minded by herself alone,
May be put from her by society.
Now do you know the reason of this haste.

Friar. [*aside*] I would I knew not why it should be slow'd. —
Look, sir, here comes the lady toward my cell.

Enter *Juliet.*

Par. Happily met, my lady and my wife!

Jul. That may be, sir, when I may be a wife.

Par. That may be must be, love, on Thursday next.

Jul. What must be shall be.

Friar. That's a certain text.

Par. Come you to make confession to this father?

Jul. To answer that, I should confess to you.

Par. Do not deny to him that you love me.

Jul. I will confess to you that I love him.

Par. So will ye, I am sure, that you love me.
Jul. If I do so, it will be of more price,
Being spoke behind your back, than to your face.
Par. Poor soul, thy face is much abus'd with tears.
Jul. The tears have got small victory by that,
For it was bad enough before their spite.
Par. Thou wrong'st it more than tears with that report.
Jul. That is no slander, sir, which is a truth;
And what I spake, I spake it to my face.
Par. Thy face is mine, and thou hast slan-d'red it.
Jul. It may be so, for it is not mine own.
Are you at leisure, holy father, now,
Or shall I come to you at evening mass?
Friar. My leisure serves me, pensive daugh-ter, now.
My lord, we must entreat the time alone.
Par. God shield I should disturb devotion!
Juliet, on Thursday early will I rouse ye.
Till then, adieu, and keep this holy kiss. *Exit.*
Jul. O, shut the door! and when thou hast done so,
Come weep with me — past hope, past cure, past help!
Friar. Ah, Juliet, I already know thy grief;
It strains me past the compass of my wits.
I hear thou must, and nothing may prorogue it,
On Thursday next be married to this County.
Jul. Tell me not, friar, that thou hear'st of this,
Unless thou tell me how I may prevent it.
If in thy wisdom thou canst give no help,
Do thou but call my resolution wise
And with this knife I'll help it presently.
God join'd my heart and Romeo's, thou our hands;
And ere this hand, by thee to Romeo's seal'd,
Shall be the label to another deed,
Or my true heart with treacherous revolt
Turn to another, this shall slay them both.
Therefore, out of thy long-experienc'd time,
Give me some present counsel; or, behold,
'Twixt my extremes and me this bloody knife
Shall play the umpire, arbitrating that
Which the commission of thy years and art
Could to no issue of true honour bring.
Be not so long to speak. I long to die
If what thou speak'st speak not of remedy.
Friar. Hold, daughter. I do spy a kind of hope,
Which craves as desperate an execution
As that is desperate which we would prevent.
If, rather than to marry County Paris,
Thou hast the strength of will to slay thyself,
Then is it likely thou wilt undertake
A thing like death to chide away this shame,
That cop'st with death himself to scape from it;
And, if thou dar'st, I'll give thee remedy.
Jul. O, bid me leap, rather than marry Paris,
From off the battlements of yonder tower,
Or walk in thievish ways, or bid me lurk
Where serpents are; chain me with roaring bears,
Or shut me nightly in a charnel house,
O'ercover'd quite with dead men's rattling bones,
With reeky shanks and yellow chapless skulls;
Or bid me go into a new-made grave
And hide me with a dead man in his shroud —
Things that, to hear them told, have made me tremble —
And I will do it without fear or doubt,
To live an unstain'd wife to my sweet love.
Friar. Hold, then. Go home, be merry, give consent
To marry Paris. Wednesday is to-morrow.
To-morrow night look that thou lie alone;
Let not the nurse lie with thee in thy chamber.
Take thou this vial, being then in bed,
And this distilled liquor drink thou off;
When presently through all thy veins shall run
A cold and drowsy humour; for no pulse
Shall keep his native progress, but surcease;
No warmth, no breath, shall testify thou livest;
The roses in thy lips and cheeks shall fade
To paly ashes, thy eyes' windows fall
Like death when he shuts up the day of life;
Each part, depriv'd of supple government,
Shall, stiff and stark and cold, appear like death;
And in this borrowed likeness of shrunk death
Thou shalt continue two-and-forty hours,
And then awake as from a pleasant sleep.
Now, when the bridegroom in the morning comes
To rouse thee from thy bed, there art thou dead.
Then, as the manner of our country is,
In thy best robes uncovered on the bier
Thou shalt be borne to that same ancient vault
Where all the kindred of the Capulets lie.
In the mean time, against thou shalt awake,
Shall Romeo by my letters know our drift;
And hither shall he come; and he and I
Will watch thy waking, and that very night
Shall Romeo bear thee hence to Mantua.
And this shall free thee from this present shame,

If no inconstant toy nor womanish fear
Abate thy valour in the acting it.
Jul. Give me, give me! O, tell not me of fear!
Friar. Hold! Get you gone, be strong and prosperous
In this resolve. I'll send a friar with speed
To Mantua, with my letters to thy lord.
Jul. Love give me strength! and strength shall help afford.
Farewell, dear father. *Exeunt.*

[Scene II. Capulet's *house.*]

Enter *Father Capulet, Mother, Nurse,* and *Servingmen,* two or three.

Cap. So many guests invite as here are writ. [*Exit a Servingman.*]
Sirrah, go hire me twenty cunning cooks.

Serv. You shall have none ill, sir; for I'll try if they can lick their fingers.

Cap. How canst thou try them so?

Serv. Marry, sir, 'tis an ill cook that cannot lick his own fingers. Therefore he that cannot lick his fingers goes not with me.

Cap. Go, be gone. *Exit Servingman.*
We shall be much unfurnish'd for this time.
What, is my daughter gone to Friar Laurence?
Nurse. Ay, forsooth.
Cap. Well, he may chance to do some good on her.
A peevish self-will'd harlotry it is.

Enter *Juliet.*

Nurse. See where she comes from shrift with merry look.
Cap. How now, my headstrong? Where have you been gadding?
Jul. Where I have learnt me to repent the sin
Of disobedient opposition
To you and your behests, and am enjoin'd
By holy Laurence to fall prostrate here
To beg your pardon. Pardon, I beseech you!
Henceforward I am ever rul'd by you.
Cap. Send for the County. Go tell him of this.
I'll have this knot knit up to-morrow morning.
Jul. I met the youthful lord at Laurence' cell
And gave him what becomed love I might,
Not stepping o'er the bounds of modesty.
Cap. Why, I am glad on't. This is well. Stand up.
This is as't should be. Let me see the County.
Ay, marry, go, I say, and fetch him hither.
Now, afore God, this reverend holy friar,
All our whole city is much bound to him.
Jul. Nurse, will you go with me into my closet
To help me sort such needful ornaments
As you think fit to furnish me to-morrow?
Mother. No, not till Thursday. There is time enough.
Cap. Go, nurse, go with her. We'll to church to-morrow.
Exeunt Juliet and Nurse.
Mother. We shall be short in our provision.
'Tis now near night.
Cap. Tush, I will stir about,
And all things shall be well, I warrant thee, wife.
Go thou to Juliet, help to deck up her.
I'll not to bed to-night; let me alone.
I'll play the housewife for this once. What, ho!
They are all forth; well, I will walk myself
To County Paris, to prepare him up
Against to-morrow. My heart is wondrous light,
Since this same wayward girl is so reclaim'd.
Exeunt.

[Scene III. Juliet's *chamber.*]

Enter *Juliet* and *Nurse.*

Jul. Ay, those attires are best; but, gentle nurse,
I pray thee leave me to myself to-night;
For I have need of many orisons
To move the heavens to smile upon my state,
Which, well thou knowest, is cross and full of sin.

Enter *Mother.*

Mother. What, are you busy, ho? Need you my help?
Jul. No, madam; we have cull'd such necessaries
As are behooffull for our state to-morrow.
So please you, let me now be left alone,
And let the nurse this night sit up with you;
For I am sure you have your hands full all
In this so sudden business.
Mother. Good night.
Get thee to bed, and rest; for thou hast need.
Exeunt [*Mother and Nurse*].

ROMEO AND JULIET

Claire Bloom as Juliet, exquisite heroine of Shakespeare's immortal tragedy of star-crossed lovers

Alan Badel as Romeo, Juliet's passionate, impetuous suitor

PHOTOGRAPHS BY HOUSTON ROGERS
PRODUCED BY THE OLD VIC COMPANY

Romeo, disguised as a masker, meets Juliet for the first time at a revel at the Capulet house *(Act I, Scene V)*

Juliet with the Capulets' nurse (Athene Seyler), who shares the secret of her love for Romeo and carries her messages to her lover

From a balcony overlooking the Capulet orchard, Juliet listens to her lover's impassioned wooing *(Act II, Scene II)*

"Good-night, good-night! parting is such sweet sorrow
That I shall say good-night till it be morrow" *(Act II, Scene II)*

Peter Finch as the madcap Mercutio, a friend and confidant of Romeo

In search of Romeo, the nurse is baited by Mercutio and his friends. Embarrassed, she asks her comic attendant, Peter (Newton Blick), to hand her her fan
(Act II, Scene IV)

The nurse plays an acid-tongued termagant in her encounter with Romeo and his friends

Lewis Casson in the role of Friar Laurence, who attempts to aid the unfortunate lovers

Friar Laurence counsels Romeo and Juliet on the eve of their marriage
(Act II, Scene VI)

Furious with Juliet, who refuses to marry Paris and dares not admit her secret marriage with Romeo, her father orders her to accept his choice or leave his house. Lady Capulet, played by Yvonne Coulette, is equally chagrined. She looks on coldly as Juliet cowers in the nurse's arms *(Act III, Scene V)*

Tybalt *(right)*, played by Laurence Payne, having failed to provoke Romeo to a duel, is suddenly engaged by the firebrand Mercutio, who draws his sword in defense of his friend's honor *(Act III, Scene I)*

Mortally wounded by Tybalt, Mercutio regrets having intervened in the feud of the Capulets and the Montagues: "A plague o' both your houses! They have made worms' meat of me" *(Act III, Scene I)*

"Where are the vile beginners of this fray?" Coming on the body of Tybalt, just slain by Romeo, the Prince of Verona (William Devlin) asks for an explanation *(Act III, Scene I)*

The great hall of the Capulet house becomes a scene of comic confusion as the servants make frantic attempts to prepare for the approaching marriage of Juliet and Paris *(Act IV, Scene IV)*

Banished from Verona for his fatal duel with Tybalt, Romeo bids Juliet farewell, embracing her for the last time *(Act III, Scene V)*

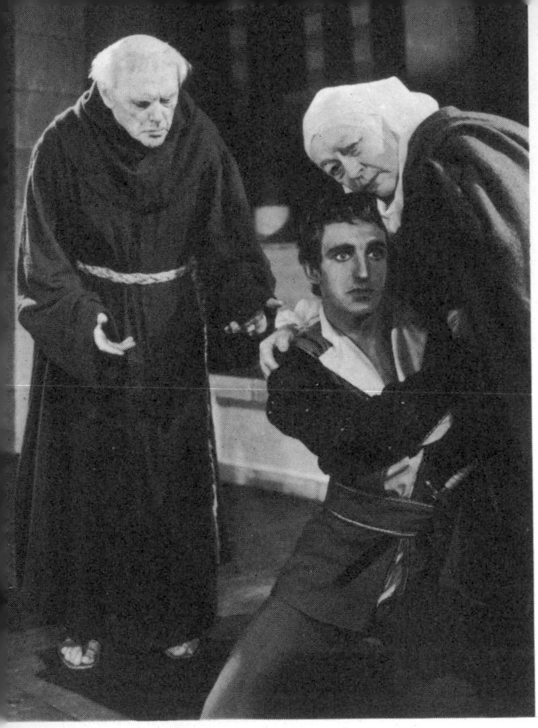

Hiding in Friar Laurence's cell after his duel with Tybalt, the despairing Romeo is visited by Juliet's nurse with a message from her mistress. "Rouse thee, man," says the friar. "Thy Juliet is alive" *(Act III, Scene III)*

Believing that his beloved Juliet is dead, Romeo buys a dram of poison from an apothecary, deciding to take his own life *(Act IV, Scene I)*

Awakening from her drugged sleep, Juliet finds Romeo lying dead beside her *(Act V, Scene III)*

Jul. Farewell! God knows when we shall meet again.
I have a faint cold fear thrills through my veins
That almost freezes up the heat of life.
I'll call them back again to comfort me.
Nurse! — What should she do here?
My dismal scene I needs must act alone.
Come, vial.
What if this mixture do not work at all?
Shall I be married then to-morrow morning?
No, no! This shall forbid it. Lie thou there.
[*Lays down a dagger.*]
What if it be a poison which the friar
Subtilly hath minist'red to have me dead,
Lest in this marriage he should be dishonour'd
Because he married me before to Romeo?
I fear it is; and yet methinks it should not,
For he hath still been tried a holy man.
I will not entertain so bad a thought.
How if, when I am laid into the tomb,
I wake before the time that Romeo
Come to redeem me? There's a fearful point!
Shall I not then be stifled in the vault,
To whose foul mouth no healthsome air breathes in,
And there die strangled ere my Romeo comes?
Or, if I live, is it not very like
The horrible conceit of death and night,
Together with the terror of the place —
As in a vault, an ancient receptacle
Where for this many hundred years the bones
Of all my buried ancestors are pack'd;
Where bloody Tybalt, yet but green in earth,
Lies fest'ring in his shroud; where, as they say,
At some hours in the night spirits resort —
Alack, alack, is it not like that I,
So early waking — what with loathsome smells,
And shrieks like mandrakes torn out of the earth,
That living mortals, hearing them, run mad —
O, if I wake, shall I not be distraught,
Environed with all these hideous fears,
And madly play with my forefathers' joints,
And pluck the mangled Tybalt from his shroud,
And, in this rage, with some great kinsman's bone
As with a club dash out my desp'rate brains?
O, look! methinks I see my cousin's ghost
Seeking out Romeo, that did spit his body
Upon a rapier's point. Stay, Tybalt, stay!
Romeo, I come! this do I drink to thee.

She [*drinks and*] *falls upon her bed within the curtains.*

[Scene IV. Capulet's *house.*]

Enter *Lady of the House* and *Nurse*

Lady. Hold, take these keys and fetch more spices, nurse.
Nurse. They call for dates and quinces in the pastry.

Enter *Old Capulet.*

Cap. Come, stir, stir, stir! The second cock hath crow'd,
The curfew bell hath rung, 'tis three o'clock.
Look to the bak'd meats, good Angelica;
Spare not for cost.
Nurse. Go, you cot-quean, go,
Get you to bed! Faith, you'll be sick to-morrow
For this night's watching.
Cap. No, not a whit. What, I have watch'd ere now
All night for lesser cause, and ne'er been sick.
Lady. Ay, you have been a mouse-hunt in your time;
But I will watch you from such watching now.
Exeunt Lady and Nurse.
Cap. A jealous hood, a jealous hood!

Enter three or four [*Fellows*], with spits and logs and baskets.

Now, fellow,
What is there?
Fellow. Things for the cook, sir; but I know not what.
Cap. Make haste, make haste. [*Exit Fellow.*] Sirrah, fetch drier logs.
Call Peter; he will show thee where they are.
Fellow. I have a head, sir, that will find out logs
And never trouble Peter for the matter.
Cap. Mass, and well said; a merry whoreson, ha!
Thou shalt be loggerhead. [*Exit Fellow.*] Good faith, 'tis day.
The County will be here with music straight,
For so he said he would. *Play music.*
I hear him near.
Nurse! Wife! What, ho! What, nurse, I say!

Enter *Nurse.*

Go waken Juliet; go and trim her up.
I'll go and chat with Paris. Hie, make haste,
Make haste! The bridegroom he is come already:
Make haste, I say. [*Exeunt.*]

[Scene V. Juliet's *chamber*.]

[Enter *Nurse*.]

Nurse. Mistress! what, mistress! Juliet! Fast, I warrant her, she.
Why, lamb! why, lady! Fie, you slug-abed!
Why, love, I say! madam! sweetheart! Why, bride!
What, not a word? You take your pennyworths now!
Sleep for a week; for the next night, I warrant,
The County Paris hath set up his rest
That you shall rest but little. God forgive me!
Marry, and amen. How sound is she asleep!
I needs must wake her. Madam, madam, madam!
Ay, let the County take you in your bed!
He'll fright you up, i' faith. Will it not be?

[*Draws aside the curtains.*]

What, dress'd, and in your clothes, and down again?
I must needs wake you. Lady! lady! lady!
Alas, alas! Help, help! my lady's dead!
O weraday that ever I was born!
Some aqua-vitæ, ho! My lord! my lady!

Enter *Mother*.

Mother. What noise is here?

Nurse. O lamentable day!

Mother. What is the matter?

Nurse. Look, look! O heavy day!

Mother. O me, O me! My child, my only life!
Revive, look up, or I will die with thee!
Help, help! Call help.

Enter *Father*.

Father. For shame, bring Juliet forth; her lord is come.

Nurse. She's dead, deceas'd; she's dead! Alack the day!

Mother. Alack the day, she's dead, she's dead, she's dead!

Cap. Ha! let me see her. Out alas! she's cold,
Her blood is settled, and her joints are stiff;
Life and these lips have long been separated.
Death lies on her like an untimely frost
Upon the sweetest flower of all the field.

Nurse. O lamentable day!

Mother. O woful time!

Cap. Death, that hath ta'en her hence to make me wail,
Ties up my tongue and will not let me speak.

Enter *Friar* [*Laurence*] and the *County* [*Paris*], with *Musicians*.

Friar. Come, is the bride ready to go to church?

Cap. Ready to go, but never to return.
O son, the night before thy wedding day
Hath Death lain with thy wife. See, there she lies,
Flower as she was, deflowered by him.
Death is my son-in-law, Death is my heir;
My daughter he hath wedded. I will die
And leave him all. Life, living, all is Death's.

Par. Have I thought long to see this morning's face,
And doth it give me such a sight as this?

Mother. Accurs'd, unhappy, wretched, hateful day!
Most miserable hour that e'er time saw
In lasting labour of his pilgrimage!
But one, poor one, one poor and loving child,
But one thing to rejoice and solace in,
And cruel Death hath catch'd it from my sight!

Nurse. O woe! O woful, woful, woful day!
Most lamentable day, most woful day
That ever ever I did yet behold!
O day! O day! O day! O hateful day!
Never was seen so black a day as this.
O woful day! O woful day!

Par. Beguil'd, divorced, wronged, spited, slain!
Most detestable Death, by thee beguil'd,
By cruel cruel thee quite overthrown!
O love! O life! not life, but love in death!

Cap. Despis'd, distressed, hated, martyr'd, kill'd!
Uncomfortable time, why cam'st thou now
To murther, murther our solemnity?
O child! O child! my soul, and not my child!
Dead art thou, dead! alack, my child is dead,
And with my child my joys are buried!

Friar. Peace, ho, for shame! Confusion's cure lives not
In these confusions. Heaven and yourself
Had part in this fair maid; now heaven hath all,
And all the better is it for the maid.
Your part in her you could not keep from death,
But heaven keeps his part in eternal life.
The most you sought was her promotion,
For 'twas your heaven she should be advanc'd;
And weep ye now, seeing she is advanc'd
Above the clouds, as high as heaven itself?
O, in this love, you love your child so ill
That you run mad, seeing that she is well.

She's not well married that lives married long,
But she's best married that dies married young.
Dry up your tears and stick your rosemary
On this fair corse, and, as the custom is,
In all her best array bear her to church;
For though fond nature bids us all lament,
Yet nature's tears are reason's merriment.

Cap. All things that we ordained festival
Turn from their office to black funeral —
Our instruments to melancholy bells,
Our wedding cheer to a sad burial feast;
Our solemn hymns to sullen dirges change;
Our bridal flowers serve for a buried corse;
And all things change them to the contrary.

Friar. Sir, go you in; and, madam, go with him;
And go, Sir Paris. Every one prepare
To follow this fair corse unto her grave.
The heavens do low'r upon you for some ill;
Move them no more by crossing their high will.

Exeunt. Manent Musicians [and Nurse].

1. Mus. Faith, we may put up our pipes and be gone.

Nurse. Honest good fellows, ah, put up, put up!
For well you know this is a pitiful case. [*Exit.*]

1. Mus. Ay, by my troth, the case may be amended.

Enter *Peter.*

Pet. Musicians, O, musicians, 'Heart's ease,' 'Heart's ease!' O, an you will have me live, play 'Heart's ease.'

1. Mus. Why 'Heart's ease'?

Pet. O, musicians, because my heart itself plays 'My heart is full of woe.' O, play me some merry dump to comfort me.

1. Mus. Not a dump we! 'Tis no time to play now.

Pet. You will not then?

1. Mus. No.

Pet. I will then give it you soundly.

1. Mus. What will you give us?

Pet. No money, on my faith, but the gleek. I will give you the minstrel.

1. Mus. Then will I give you the serving-creature.

Pet. Then will I lay the serving-creature's dagger on your pate. I will carry no crotchets. I'll re you, I'll fa you. Do you note me?

1. Mus. An you re us and fa us, you note us.

2. Mus. Pray you put up your dagger, and put out your wit.

Pet. Then have at you with my wit! I will dry-beat you with an iron wit, and put up my iron dagger. Answer me like men.

'When griping grief the heart doth wound,
And doleful dumps the mind oppress,
Then music with her silver sound' —

Why 'silver sound'? Why 'music with her silver sound'? What say you, Simon Catling?

1. Mus. Marry, sir, because silver hath a sweet sound.

Pet. Pretty! What say you, Hugh Rebeck?

2. Mus. I say, 'silver sound' because musicians sound for silver.

Pet. Pretty too! What say you, James Soundpost?

3. Mus. Faith, I know not what to say.

Pet. O, I cry you mercy! you are the singer. I will say for you. It is 'music with her silver sound' because musicians have no gold for sounding.

'Then music with her silver sound
With speedy help doth lend redress.' *Exit.*

1. Mus. What a pestilent knave is this same!

2. Mus. Hang him, Jack! Come, we'll in here, tarry for the mourners, and stay dinner.

Exeunt.

[ACT V. Scene I. *Mantua. A street.*]

Enter *Romeo.*

Rom. If I may trust the flattering truth of sleep,
My dreams presage some joyful news at hand.
My bosom's lord sits lightly in his throne,
And all this day an unaccustom'd spirit
Lifts me above the ground with cheerful thoughts.
I dreamt my lady came and found me dead
(Strange dream that gives a dead man leave to think!)
And breath'd such life with kisses in my lips
That I reviv'd and was an emperor.
Ah me! how sweet is love itself possess'd,
When but love's shadows are so rich in joy!

Enter *Romeo's Man Balthasar*, booted.

News from Verona! How now, Balthasar?
Dost thou not bring me letters from the friar?

How doth my lady? Is my father well?
How fares my Juliet? That I ask again,
For nothing can be ill if she be well.
Man. Then she is well, and nothing can be ill.
Her body sleeps in Capel's monument,
And her immortal part with angels lives.
I saw her laid low in her kindred's vault
And presently took post to tell it you.
O, pardon me for bringing these ill news,
Since you did leave it for my office, sir.
Rom. Is it e'en so? Then I defy you, stars!
Thou knowest my lodging. Get me ink and paper
And hire posthorses. I will hence to-night.
Man. I do beseech you, sir, have patience.
Your looks are pale and wild and do import
Some misadventure.
Rom. Tush, thou art deceiv'd.
Leave me and do the thing I bid thee do.
Hast thou no letters to me from the friar?
Man. No, my good lord.
Rom. No matter. Get thee gone
And hire those horses. I'll be with thee straight.
Exit [Balthasar].
Well, Juliet, I will lie with thee to-night.
Let's see for means. O mischief, thou art swift
To enter in the thoughts of desperate men!
I do remember an apothecary,
And hereabouts 'a dwells, which late I noted
In tatt'red weeds, with overwhelming brows,
Culling of simples. Meagre were his looks,
Sharp misery had worn him to the bones;
And in his needy shop a tortoise hung,
An alligator stuff'd, and other skins
Of ill-shap'd fishes; and about his shelves
A beggarly account of empty boxes,
Green earthen pots, bladders, and musty seeds,
Remnants of packthread, and old cakes of roses
Were thinly scattered, to make up a show.
Noting this penury, to myself I said,
'An if a man did need a poison now
Whose sale is present death in Mantua,
Here lives a caitiff wretch would sell it him.'
O, this same thought did but forerun my need,
And this same needy man must sell it me.
As I remember, this should be the house.
Being holiday, the beggar's shop is shut.
What, ho! apothecary!

Enter *Apothecary.*

Apoth. Who calls so loud?
Rom. Come hither, man. I see that thou art poor.
Hold, there is forty ducats. Let me have
A dram of poison, such soon-speeding gear
As will disperse itself through all the veins
That the life-weary taker may fall dead,
And that the trunk may be discharg'd of breath
As violently as hasty powder fir'd
Doth hurry from the fatal cannon's womb.
Apoth. Such mortal drugs I have; but Mantua's law
Is death to any he that utters them.
Rom. Art thou so bare and full of wretchedness
And fearest to die? Famine is in thy cheeks,
Need and oppression starveth in thine eyes,
Contempt and beggary hangs upon thy back:
The world is not thy friend, nor the world's law;
The world affords no law to make thee rich;
Then be not poor, but break it and take this.
Apoth. My poverty but not my will consents.
Rom. I pay thy poverty and not thy will.
Apoth. Put this in any liquid thing you will
And drink it off, and if you had the strength
Of twenty men, it would dispatch you straight.
Rom. There is thy gold — worse poison to men's souls,
Doing more murther in this loathsome world,
Than these poor compounds that thou mayst not sell.
I sell thee poison; thou hast sold me none.
Farewell. Buy food and get thyself in flesh.
Come, cordial and not poison, go with me
To Juliet's grave; for there must I use thee.
Exeunt.

[Scene II. *Verona.* Friar Laurence's *cell.*]

Enter *Friar John* to *Friar Laurence.*

John. Holy Franciscan friar, brother, ho!

Enter *Friar Laurence.*

Laur. This same should be the voice of Friar John.
Welcome from Mantua. What says Romeo?
Or, if his mind be writ, give me his letter.
John. Going to find a barefoot brother out,
One of our order, to associate me
Here in this city visiting the sick,
And finding him, the searchers of the town,
Suspecting that we both were in a house
Where the infectious pestilence did reign,
Seal'd up the doors, and would not let us forth,
So that my speed to Mantua there was stay'd.
Laur. Who bare my letter, then, to Romeo?
John. I could not send it — here it is again —

Nor get a messenger to bring it thee,
So fearful were they of infection.
Laur. Unhappy fortune! By my brotherhood,
The letter was not nice, but full of charge,
Of dear import; and the neglecting it
May do much danger. Friar John, go hence,
Get me an iron crow and bring it straight
Unto my cell.
John. Brother, I'll go and bring it thee.
Exit.
Laur. Now must I to the monument alone.
Within this three hours will fair Juliet wake.
She will beshrew me much that Romeo
Hath had no notice of these accidents;
But I will write again to Mantua,
And keep her at my cell till Romeo come —
Poor living corse, clos'd in a dead man's tomb!
Exit.

[Scene III. *Verona. A churchyard; in it the monument of the* Capulets.]

Enter *Paris* and his *Page* with flowers and [a torch].

Par. Give me thy torch, boy. Hence, and stand aloof.
Yet put it out, for I would not be seen.
Under yond yew tree lay thee all along,
Holding thine ear close to the hollow ground.
So shall no foot upon the churchyard tread
(Being loose, unfirm, with digging up of graves)
But thou shalt hear it. Whistle then to me,
As signal that thou hear'st something approach.
Give me those flowers. Do as I bid thee, go.
Page. [*aside*] I am almost afraid to stand alone
Here in the churchyard; yet I will adventure.
[*Retires.*]
Par. Sweet flower, with flowers thy bridal bed I strew
(O woe! thy canopy is dust and stones)
Which with sweet water nightly I will dew;
Or, wanting that, with tears distill'd by moans.
The obsequies that I for thee will keep
Nightly shall be to strew thy grave and weep.
Whistle Boy.
The boy gives warning something doth approach.
What cursed foot wanders this way to-night
To cross my obsequies and true love's rite?
What, with a torch? Muffle me, night, awhile.
[*Retires.*]

Enter *Romeo*, and *Balthasar* with a torch, a mattock, and a crow of iron.

Rom. Give me that mattock and the wrenching iron.
Hold, take this letter. Early in the morning
See thou deliver it to my lord and father.
Give me the light. Upon thy life I charge thee,
Whate'er thou hearest or seest, stand all aloof
And do not interrupt me in my course.
Why I descend into this bed of death
Is partly to behold my lady's face,
But chiefly to take thence from her dead finger
A precious ring — a ring that I must use
In dear employment. Therefore hence, be gone.
But if thou, jealous, dost return to pry
In what I farther shall intend to do,
By heaven, I will tear thee joint by joint
And strew this hungry churchyard with thy limbs.
The time and my intents are savage-wild,
More fierce and more inexorable far
Than empty tigers or the roaring sea.
Bal. I will be gone, sir, and not trouble you.
Rom. So shalt thou show me friendship. Take thou that.
Live, and be prosperous; and farewell, good fellow.
Bal. [*aside*] For all this same, I'll hide me hereabout.
His looks I fear, and his intents I doubt.
[*Retires.*]
Rom. Thou detestable maw, thou womb of death,
Gorg'd with the dearest morsel of the earth,
Thus I enforce thy rotten jaws to open,
And in despite I'll cram thee with more food.
Romeo opens the tomb.
Par. This is that banish'd haughty Montague
That murd'red my love's cousin — with which grief
It is supposed the fair creature died —
And here is come to do some villanous shame
To the dead bodies. I will apprehend him.
Stop thy unhallowed toil, vile Montague!
Can vengeance be pursu'd further than death?
Condemned villain, I do apprehend thee.
Obey, and go with me; for thou must die.
Rom. I must indeed; and therefore came I hither.
Good gentle youth, tempt not a desp'rate man.
Fly hence and leave me. Think upon these gone;
Let them affright thee. I beseech thee, youth,

Put not another sin upon my head
By urging me to fury. O, be gone!
By heaven, I love thee better than myself,
For I come hither arm'd against myself.
Stay not, be gone. Live, and hereafter say
A madman's mercy bid thee run away.

Par. I do defy thy conjuration
And apprehend thee for a felon here.

Rom. Wilt thou provoke me? Then have at thee, boy! *They fight.*

Page. O Lord, they fight! I will go call the watch.
[*Exit. Paris falls.*]

Par. O, I am slain! If thou be merciful,
Open the tomb, lay me with Juliet. [*Dies.*]

Rom. In faith, I will. Let me peruse this face.
Mercutio's kinsman, noble County Paris!
What said my man when my betossed soul
Did not attend him as we rode? I think
He told me Paris should have married Juliet.
Said he not so? or did I dream it so?
Or am I mad, hearing him talk of Juliet,
To think it was so? O, give me thy hand,
One writ with me in sour misfortune's book!
I'll bury thee in a triumphant grave.
A grave? O, no, a lanthorn, slaught'red youth,
For here lies Juliet, and her beauty makes
This vault a feasting presence full of light.
Death, lie thou there, by a dead man interr'd.
[*Lays him in the tomb.*]
How oft when men are at the point of death
Have they been merry! which their keepers call
A lightning before death. O, how may I
Call this a lightning? O my love! my wife!
Death, that hath suck'd the honey of thy breath,
Hath had no power yet upon thy beauty.
Thou art not conquer'd. Beauty's ensign yet
Is crimson in thy lips and in thy cheeks,
And death's pale flag is not advanced there.
Tybalt, liest thou there in thy bloody sheet?
O, what more favour can I do to thee
Than with that hand that cut thy youth in twain
To sunder his that was thine enemy?
Forgive me, cousin! Ah, dear Juliet,
Why art thou yet so fair? Shall I believe
That unsubstantial Death is amorous,
And that the lean abhorred monster keeps
Thee here in dark to be his paramour?
For fear of that I still will stay with thee
And never from this palace of dim night
Depart again. Here, here will I remain
With worms that are thy chambermaids. O, here
Will I set up my everlasting rest
And shake the yoke of inauspicious stars
From this world-wearied flesh. Eyes, look your last!
Arms, take your last embrace! and, lips, O you
The doors of breath, seal with a righteous kiss
A dateless bargain to engrossing death!
Come, bitter conduct; come, unsavoury guide!
Thou desperate pilot, now at once run on
The dashing rocks thy seasick weary bark!
Here's to my love! [*Drinks.*] O true apothecary!
Thy drugs are quick. Thus with a kiss I die.
Falls.

Enter *Friar* [*Laurence*], with lanthorn, crow, and spade.

Friar. Saint Francis be my speed! how oft to-night
Have my old feet stumbled at graves! Who's there?

Bal. Here's one, a friend, and one that knows you well.

Friar. Bliss be upon you! Tell me, good my friend,
What torch is yond that vainly lends his light
To grubs and eyeless skulls? As I discern,
It burneth in the Capels' monument.

Bal. It doth so, holy sir; and there's my master,
One that you love.

Friar. Who is it?

Bal. Romeo.

Friar. How long hath he been there?

Bal. Full half an hour.

Friar. Go with me to the vault.

Bal. I dare not, sir.
My master knows not but I am gone hence,
And fearfully did menace me with death
If I did stay to look on his intents.

Friar. Stay then; I'll go alone. Fear comes upon me.
O, much I fear some ill unthrifty thing.

Bal. As I did sleep under this yew tree here,
I dreamt my master and another fought,
And that my master slew him.

Friar. Romeo!
Alack, alack, what blood is this which stains
The stony entrance of this sepulchre?
What mean these masterless and gory swords
To lie discolour'd by this place of peace?
[*Enters the tomb.*]
Romeo! O, pale! Who else? What, Paris too?
And steep'd in blood? Ah, what an unkind hour
Is guilty of this lamentable chance!
The lady stirs.

Juliet rises.

Jul. O comfortable friar! where is my lord?
I do remember well where I should be,
And there I am. Where is my Romeo?
Friar. I hear some noise. Lady, come from that nest
Of death, contagion, and unnatural sleep.
A greater power than we can contradict
Hath thwarted our intents. Come, come away.
Thy husband in thy bosom there lies dead;
And Paris too. Come, I'll dispose of thee
Among a sisterhood of holy nuns.
Stay not to question, for the watch is coming.
Come, go, good Juliet. I dare no longer stay.
Jul. Go, get thee hence, for I will not away.
Exit [*Friar*].
What's here? A cup, clos'd in my true love's hand?
Poison, I see, hath been his timeless end.
O churl! drunk all, and left no friendly drop
To help me after? I will kiss thy lips.
Haply some poison yet doth hang on them
To make me die with a restorative.
[*Kisses him.*]
Thy lips are warm!
Chief Watch. [*within*] Lead, boy. Which way?
Jul. Yea, noise? Then I'll be brief. O happy dagger! [*Snatches Romeo's dagger.*]
This is thy sheath; there rest, and let me die.
She stabs herself and falls [*on Romeo's body*].

Enter [*Paris's*] *Boy* and *Watch.*

Boy. This is the place. There, where the torch doth burn.
Chief Watch. The ground is bloody. Search about the churchyard.
Go, some of you; whoe'er you find attach.
[*Exeunt some of the Watch.*]
Pitiful sight! here lies the County slain;
And Juliet bleeding, warm, and newly dead,
Who here hath lain this two days buried.
Go, tell the Prince; run to the Capulets;
Raise up the Montagues; some others search.
[*Exeunt others of the Watch.*]
We see the ground whereon these woes do lie,
But the true ground of all these piteous woes
We cannot without circumstance descry.

Enter [some of the *Watch,*] with *Romeo's Man* [*Balthasar*].

2. Watch. Here's Romeo's man. We found him in the churchyard.
Chief Watch. Hold him in safety till the Prince come hither.

Enter *Friar* [*Laurence*] and another *Watchman.*

3. Watch. Here is a friar that trembles, sighs, and weeps.
We took this mattock and this spade from him
As he was coming from this churchyard side.
Chief Watch. A great suspicion! Stay the friar too.

Enter the *Prince* [and *Attendants*].

Prince. What misadventure is so early up,
That calls our person from our morning rest?

Enter *Capulet* and his *Wife* [with others].

Cap. What should it be, that they so shriek abroad?
Wife. The people in the street cry 'Romeo,'
Some 'Juliet,' and some 'Paris'; and all run,
With open outcry, toward our monument.
Prince. What fear is this which startles in our ears?
Chief Watch. Sovereign, here lies the County Paris slain;
And Romeo dead; and Juliet, dead before,
Warm and new kill'd.
Prince. Search, seek, and know how this foul murder comes.
Chief Watch. Here is a friar, and slaughter'd Romeo's man,
With instruments upon them fit to open
These dead men's tombs.
Cap. O heavens! O wife, look how our daughter bleeds!
This dagger hath mista'en, for, lo, his house
Is empty on the back of Montague,
And it missheathed in my daughter's bosom!
Wife. O me! this sight of death is as a bell
That warns my old age to a sepulchre.

Enter *Montague* [and others].

Prince. Come, Montague; for thou art early up
To see thy son and heir more early down.
Mon. Alas, my liege, my wife is dead to-night!
Grief of my son's exile hath stopp'd her breath.
What further woe conspires against mine age?
Prince. Look, and thou shalt see.
Mon. O thou untaught! what manners is in this,
To press before thy father to a grave?
Prince. Seal up the mouth of outrage for a while,
Till we can clear these ambiguities
And know their spring, their head, their true descent;

And then will I be general of your woes
And lead you even to death. Meantime forbear,
And let mischance be slave to patience.
Bring forth the parties of suspicion.

Friar. I am the greatest, able to do least,
Yet most suspected, as the time and place
Doth make against me, of this direful murther;
And here I stand, both to impeach and purge
Myself condemned and myself excus'd.

Prince. Then say at once what thou dost know in this.

Friar. I will be brief, for my short date of breath
Is not so long as is a tedious tale.
Romeo, there dead, was husband to that Juliet;
And she, there dead, that Romeo's faithful wife.
I married them; and their stol'n marriage day
Was Tybalt's doomsday, whose untimely death
Banish'd the new-made bridegroom from this city;
For whom, and not for Tybalt, Juliet pin'd.
You, to remove that siege of grief from her,
Betroth'd and would have married her perforce
To County Paris. Then comes she to me
And with wild looks bid me devise some mean
To rid her from this second marriage,
Or in my cell there would she kill herself.
Then gave I her (so tutor'd by my art)
A sleeping potion; which so took effect
As I intended, for it wrought on her
The form of death. Meantime I writ to Romeo
That he should hither come as this dire night
To help to take her from her borrowed grave,
Being the time the potion's force should cease.
But he which bore my letter, Friar John,
Was stay'd by accident, and yesternight
Return'd my letter back. Then all alone
At the prefixed hour of her waking
Came I to take her from her kindred's vault;
Meaning to keep her closely at my cell
Till I conveniently could send to Romeo.
But when I came, some minute ere the time
Of her awaking, here untimely lay
The noble Paris and true Romeo dead.
She wakes; and I entreated her come forth
And bear this work of heaven with patience;
But then a noise did scare me from the tomb,
And she, too desperate, would not go with me,
But, as it seems, did violence on herself.
All this I know, and to the marriage
Her nurse is privy; and if aught in this
Miscarried by my fault, let my old life
Be sacrific'd, some hour before his time,
Unto the rigour of severest law.

Prince. We still have known thee for a holy man.
Where's Romeo's man? What can he say in this?

Bal. I brought my master news of Juliet's death;
And then in post he came from Mantua
To this same place, to this same monument.
This letter he early bid me give his father,
And threat'ned me with death, going in the vault,
If I departed not and left him there.

Prince. Give me the letter. I will look on it.
Where is the County's page that rais'd the watch?
Sirrah, what made your master in this place?

Boy. He came with flowers to strew his lady's grave;
And bid me stand aloof, and so I did.
Anon comes one with light to ope the tomb;
And by-and-by my master drew on him;
And then I ran away to call the watch.

Prince. This letter doth make good the friar's words,
Their course of love, the tidings of her death;
And here he writes that he did buy a poison
Of a poor pothecary, and therewithal
Came to this vault to die, and lie with Juliet.
Where be these enemies? Capulet, Montague,
See what a scourge is laid upon your hate,
That heaven finds means to kill your joys with love!
And I, for winking at your discords too,
Have lost a brace of kinsmen. All are punish'd.

Cap. O brother Montague, give me thy hand.
This is my daughter's jointure, for no more
Can I demand.

Mon. But I can give thee more;
For I will raise her statue in pure gold,
That whiles Verona by that name is known,
There shall no figure at such rate be set
As that of true and faithful Juliet.

Cap. As rich shall Romeo's by his lady's lie —
Poor sacrifices of our enmity!

Prince. A glooming peace this morning with it brings.
The sun for sorrow will not show his head.
Go hence, to have more talk of these sad things;
Some shall be pardon'd, and some punished;
For never was a story of more woe
Than this of Juliet and her Romeo.

Exeunt omnes.

Timon of Athens

Timon of Athens was first printed in the Folio of 1623. The Folio text, our sole authority, is badly mislined. In several scenes there is a strange jumble of good verse, limping metre, and out-and-out prose.

The structure of the play is rather loose. The interlude of Apemantus and the Fool (ii, 2, 47–131), for example, seems intrusive. In fact, however, something is needed to occupy the time between line 45 (when Timon goes in with his guests to dinner) and line 133 (when he enters after bidding his guests adieu). There is real confusion as to Timon's interview with the Poet and the Painter (v, 1) and his encounter with the Banditti. In iv, 3, 356, Apemantus tells Timon that a poet and a painter are in sight; but it is the Banditti who come up (399). Both Poet and Painter have vanished; they do not enter until the beginning of Act V.

Such flaws and irregularities — as well as the defective interweaving of the two main strands of the plot, the Timon story and the Alcibiades story — are adequately explained by the obvious fact that Shakespeare never really finished the play. This theory is practically proved by Timon's epitaph (v, 4, 70–73). It consists of two inconsistent couplets. Shakespeare found them both in North's Plutarch, where they are quite distinct; he copied them both and never decided which to keep.

When Shakespeare undertook the tragedy of Timon, he had long been acquainted with the classical story, which, indeed, was a commonplace in his time. In *Love's Labour's Lost* 'critic Timon,' forgetting his misanthropy so far as to 'laugh at idle toys,' is equated, for absurdity, with Hercules whipping a top and Nestor 'playing at push-pin' (iv, 3, 163 ff.).

For material Shakespeare went to the life of Mark Antony in North's Plutarch and to Lucian's *Timon*, perhaps the best of his dialogues. Plutarch gives most of the significant facts. He supplies the anecdote of the fig tree (v, 1, 208 ff.) and explains, without specific instances, that Timon's hatred of mankind was caused by 'the unthankfulnes of those he had done good vnto, and whom he tooke to be his friends.' Two instances are furnished by Lucian — the freeing of a friend from prison by paying his debt (i, 1, 94 ff.) and the gift which makes a marriage possible (i, 1, 109 ff.). The conclusion weaves Plutarch and Lucian together. From Lucian come Timon's discovery of gold and the return of the parasites, whom Timon drives away with blows; also the visit of the Senators, with their promise of 'special dignities.' From Plutarch are taken Timon's death, his burial (v, 1, 219 ff.), and the epitaphs. He 'was buried vpon the sea side' and 'it chanced so, that the sea getting in, it compassed his tombe round about, that no man could come to it.'

If Shakespeare read any Greek at all, he could hardly escape contact with Lucian, who was a favourite author with all educated men. Anyhow, his *Timon* was accessible in Latin and in French. A few doubtful echoes of Lucian's phrases have been discovered in Shakespeare's Timon. Some of them are rather striking, but, even in the aggregate, they are not decisive. When Shakespeare had once made Lucian's acquaintance, he could not have been satisfied with a single dialogue. Perhaps he also read the *Symposium*, which tells of a riotous feast. Certainly Timon's remark in announcing Apemantus

—'Look who comes here. Will you be chid?' (i, 1, 175) — and their exchange of civilities at the banquet (i, 2), where Apemantus behaves as if he were an uninvited guest, are curiously like the situation in Lucian's *Symposium*, where Lucinus tells how Alcidamas the Cynic 'burst in, unsent for' and jocosely quoted the common saying, 'Menelaus has come of his own accord.' The guests, we are told, stood in fear of Alcidamas, for he 'was absolutely good at the battle cry and the noisiest of all dogs.'

Alcibiades is not mentioned in Lucian's *Timon*. In combining his career with the story of Timon, Shakespeare develops a mere hint in Plutarch's life of Antony. Timon, Plutarch says, 'made much of' young Alcibiades, 'a bold and insolent youth, whom he would greatly feast.' When Apemantus asked the reason, Timon replied, 'I doe it because I know that one day he shall doe great mischief vnto the Athenians' (cf. iv, 3, 102 ff.). The anecdote is repeated, in a different form, in Plutarch's life of Alcibiades.

A bare suggestion for the cynical Apemantus and his wit combats with Timon and others is given in the life of Antony: Once when 'they two feasted together by themselues, Apemantus sayed vnto the other: O heere is a trim banquet Timon. Timon answered againe, yea sayd he, so thou wert not heer' (cf. iv, 3, 282 f.). In developing his character, Shakespeare remembered the philosopher Thrasycles (who comes in at the end of Lucian's dialogue like Apemantus in Act IV) and perhaps also Diogenes in Lyly's *Campaspe*. But Apemantus is much like Thersites, and the wit combats in TIMON are not essentially different from those in *The Two Gentlemen*, in *Love's Labour's Lost*, in *As You Like It*, and even in *Antony and Cleopatra*.

Most of the Alcibiades material is fictitious, but suggestions are taken from Plutarch's life of Alcibiades. There Shakespeare found a full account of his character, the name of his last mistress, Timandra, and the fact that he was banished and recalled. The banishment, however, is made by Shakespeare an almost personal matter and, in the address of Alcibiades to the Senate (iii, 5), seems to be brought into an oddly unhistorical connection with the murder of Phrynichus.

For the date of TIMON we have no direct evidence. Tests of mood, style, and metre might put it anywhere from 1605 to 1608. Timon's frantic misanthropy reminds one of Lear's delirium. Coriolanus and Alcibiades are parallel lives in Plutarch. The subject of TIMON may have impressed itself on Shakespeare's mind when he was reading Plutarch with a view to his *Antony and Cleopatra*. Doubtless he worked on the play at different times and, as we have seen, he never actually finished it.

There is nothing in TIMON that may not well be Shakespeare's own. Dual authorship has, as a matter of course, been suggested. Some scholars maintain that Shakespeare revised an older play and let some of it stand without alteration; others, that a play of Shakespeare's has been remade by an inferior hand. As for the second author, critics are quite at variance.

An anonymous comedy, *Timon*, founded on Lucian and intended for an academic audience, is preserved in manuscript. It is older than Shakespeare's tragedy. *A priori* there is little probability that he ever saw it; but two points in common — the devoted steward and the mock feast — are not found in any of his sources. Perhaps he knew it after all. This, at any rate, is an easier hypothesis than to infer that both the anonymous author and Shakespeare drew from a lost play of which no record exists.

THE LIFE OF
TIMON OF ATHENS

The Actors' Names.

Timon of Athens.
Lucius, *Lucullus*, *Sempronius*, flattering Lords.
Ventidius, one of *Timon's* false friends.
Apemantus, a churlish philosopher.
Alcibiades, an Athenian Captain.
[*Flavius*, Steward to *Timon*.]
Poet, Painter, Jeweller, Merchant, [Mercer].
[An old Athenian.]
Flaminius, [*Lucilius*,] *Servilius*, *Timon's* Servants.
Caphis, *Philotus*, *Titus*, *Hortensius*, [And others,] several servants to [*Timon's* creditors].
[A Page.]
[A Fool.]
[Three Strangers.]
[*Phrynia*, [*Timandra*, mistresses to *Alcibiades*.]
Certain Maskers [as] *Cupid* [and *Amazons*].
[Lords,] Senators, [Officers, Soldiers,] Thieves, Servants, and Attendants.

[SCENE. — *Athens and the woods near by*.]

ACT I. Scene I. [*Athens*. Timon's *house*.]

Enter *Poet*, *Painter*, *Jeweller*, *Merchant*, and *Mercer*, at several doors.

Poet. Good day, sir.
Paint. I am glad y'are well.
Poet. I have not seen you long. How goes the world?
Paint. It wears, sir, as it grows.
Poet. Ay, that's well known.
But what particular rarity? What strange,
Which manifold record not matches? See,
Magic of bounty, all these spirits thy power
Hath conjur'd to attend! I know the merchant.
Paint. I know them both. Th' other's a jeweller.
Merch. O, 'tis a worthy lord!
Jew. Nay, that's most fix'd.
Merch. A most incomparable man; breath'd, as it were,
To an untirable and continuate goodness.
He passes.
Jew. I have a jewel here —
Merch. O, pray let's see't. For the Lord Timon, sir?
Jew. If he will touch the estimate; but for that —
Poet. [*recites*] 'When we for recompense have prais'd the vile,
It stains the glory in that happy verse
Which aptly sings the good.'
Merch. [*looks at the jewel*] 'Tis a good form.
Jew. And rich. Here is a water, look ye.
Paint. You are rapt, sir, in some work, some dedication
To the great lord.
Poet. A thing slipp'd idly from me.
Our poesy is as a gum, which oozes
From whence 'tis nourish'd. The fire i' th' flint
Shows not till it be struck. Our gentle flame
Provokes itself and like the current flies
Each bound it chafes. What have you there?
Paint. A picture, sir. When comes your book forth?
Poet. Upon the heels of my presentment, sir.
Let's see your piece.
Paint. 'Tis a good piece.
Poet. So 'tis. This comes off well and excellent.
Paint. Indifferent.
Poet. Admirable! How this grace
Speaks his own standing! What a mental power
This eye shoots forth! How big imagination
Moves in this lip! To th' dumbness of the gesture
One might interpret.

Paint. It is a pretty mocking of the life.
Here is a touch. Is't good?
Poet. I will say of it,
It tutors nature. Artificial strife
Lives in these touches, livelier than life.

Enter certain *Senators* [and pass over].

Paint. How this lord is followed!
Poet. The senators of Athens. Happy man!
Paint. Look, moe!
Poet. You see this confluence, this great flood of visitors.
I have in this rough work shap'd out a man
Whom this beneath world doth embrace and hug
With amplest entertainment. My free drift
Halts not particularly, but moves itself
In a wide sea of wax. No levell'd malice
Infects one comma in the course I hold,
But flies an eagle flight, bold and forth on
Leaving no tract behind.
Paint. How shall I understand you?
Poet. I will unbolt to you.
You see how all conditions, how all minds,
As well of glib and slipp'ry creatures as
Of grave and austere quality, tender down
Their services to Lord Timon. His large fortune,
Upon his good and gracious nature hanging,
Subdues and properties to his love and tendance
All sorts of hearts; yea, from the glass-fac'd flatterer
To Apemantus, that few things loves better
Than to abhor himself. Even he drops down
The knee before him and returns in peace
Most rich in Timon's nod.
Paint. I saw them speak together.
Poet. Sir, I have upon a high and pleasant hill
Feign'd Fortune to be thron'd. The base o' th' mount
Is rank'd with all deserts, all kind of natures
That labour on the bosom of this sphere
To propagate their states. Amongst them all
Whose eyes are on this sovereign lady fix'd
One do I personate of Lord Timon's frame,
Whom Fortune with her ivory hand wafts to her,
Whose present grace to present slaves and servants
Translates his rivals.
Paint. 'Tis conceiv'd to scope.
This throne, this Fortune, and this hill, methinks,
With one man beckon'd from the rest below,
Bowing his head against the steepy mount
To climb his happiness, would be well express'd
In our condition.
Poet. Nay, sir, but hear me on.
All those which were his fellows but of late
(Some better than his value) on the moment
Follow his strides, his lobbies fill with tendance,
Rain sacrificial whisperings in his ear,
Make sacred even his stirrup, and through him
Drink the free air.
Paint. Ay, marry, what of these?
Poet. When Fortune in her shift and change of mood
Spurns down her late beloved, all his dependants,
Which labour'd after him to the mountain's top
Even on their knees and hands, let him slip down,
Not one accompanying his declining foot.
Paint. 'Tis common.
A thousand moral paintings I can show
That shall demonstrate these quick blows of Fortune's
More pregnantly than words. Yet you do well
To show Lord Timon that mean eyes have seen
The foot above the head.

Trumpets sound. Enter *Lord Timon,* addressing himself courteously to every suitor, [a *Messenger* from *Ventidius* talking with him; *Lucilius* and other *Servants* following].

Tim. Imprison'd is he, say you?
Mess. Ay, my good lord. Five talents is his debt,
His means most short, his creditors most strait.
Your honourable letter he desires
To those have shut him up, which failing
Periods his comfort.
Tim. Noble Ventidius! Well.
I am not of that feather to shake off
My friend when he most needs me. I do know him
A gentleman that well deserves a help,
Which he shall have. I'll pay the debt and free him.
Mess. Your lordship ever binds him.
Tim. Commend me to him. I will send his ransom;
And being enfranchis'd, bid him come to me.
'Tis not enough to help the feeble up,
But to support him after. Fare you well.
Mess. All happiness to your honour! *Exit.*

Enter an *Old Athenian.*

Old Man. Lord Timon, hear me speak.
Tim. Freely, good father.

Old Man. Thou hast a servant nam'd Lucilius.
Tim. I have so. What of him?
Old Man. Most noble Timon, call the man before thee.
Tim. Attends he here, or no? Lucilius!
Lucil. Here, at your lordship's service.
Old Man. This fellow here, Lord Timon, this thy creature,
By night frequents my house. I am a man
That from my first have been inclin'd to thrift,
And my estate deserves an heir more rais'd
Than one which holds a trencher.
Tim. Well. What further?
Old Man. One only daughter have I, no kin else
On whom I may confer what I have got.
The maid is fair, o' th' youngest for a bride,
And I have bred her at my dearest cost
In qualities of the best. This man of thine
Attempts her love. I prithee, noble lord,
Join with me to forbid him her resort.
Myself have spoke in vain.
Tim. The man is honest.
Old Man. Therefore he will be, Timon.
His honesty rewards him in itself;
It must not bear my daughter.
Tim. Does she love him?
Old Man. She is young and apt.
Our own precedent passions do instruct us
What levity's in youth.
Tim. Love you the maid?
Lucil. Ay, my good lord, and she accepts of it.
Old Man. If in her marriage my consent be missing,
I call the gods to witness I will choose
Mine heir from forth the beggars of the world
And dispossess her all.
Tim. How shall she be endow'd
If she be mated with an equal husband?
Old Man. Three talents on the present; in future, all.
Tim. This gentleman of mine hath serv'd me long.
To build his fortune I will strain a little,
For 'tis a bond in men. Give him thy daughter.
What you bestow, in him I'll counterpoise
And make him weigh with her.
Old Man. Most noble lord,
Pawn me to this your honour, she is his.
Tim. My hand to thee; mine honour on my promise.
Lucil. Humbly I thank your lordship. Never may
That state or fortune fall into my keeping
Which is not owed to you!
Exeunt [Lucilius and Old Athenian].
Poet. [*presents his poem*] Vouchsafe my labour, and long live your lordship!
Tim. I thank you. You shall hear from me anon.
Go not away. — What have you there, my friend?
Paint. A piece of painting, which I do beseech
Your lordship to accept.
Tim. Painting is welcome.
The painting is almost the natural man;
For since dishonour traffics with man's nature,
He is but outside; these pencill'd figures are
Even such as they give out. I like your work,
And you shall find I like it. Wait attendance
Till you hear further from me.
Paint. The gods preserve ye!
Tim. Well fare you, gentleman. Give me your hand;
We must needs dine together. — Sir, your jewel
Hath suffered under praise.
Jew. What, my lord? Dispraise?
Tim. A mere satiety of commendations.
If I should pay you for't as 'tis extoll'd,
It would unclew me quite.
Jew. My lord, 'tis rated
As those which sell would give; but you well know
Things of like value, differing in the owners,
Are prized by their masters. Believe't, dear lord,
You mend the jewel by the wearing it.
Tim. Well mock'd.

Enter *Apemantus.*

Merch. No, my good lord. He speaks the common tongue
Which all men speak with him.
Tim. Look who comes here.
Will you be chid?
Jew. We'll bear, with your lordship.
Merch. He'll spare none.
Tim. Good morrow to thee, gentle Apemantus.
Apem. Till I be gentle stay thou for thy good morrow;
When thou art Timon's dog, and these knaves honest.
Tim. Why dost thou call them knaves? Thou know'st them not.
Apem. Are they not Athenians?
Tim. Yes.

Apem. Then I repent not.

Jew. You know me, Apemantus?

Apem. Thou know'st I do; I call'd thee by thy name.

Tim. Thou art proud, Apemantus.

Apem. Of nothing so much as that I am not like Timon.

Tim. Whither art going?

Apem. To knock out an honest Athenian's brains.

Tim. That's a deed thou't die for.

Apem. Right, if doing nothing be death by th' law.

Tim. How lik'st thou this picture, Apemantus?

Apem. The best for the innocence.

Tim. Wrought he not well that painted it?

Apem. He wrought better that made the painter; and yet he's but a filthy piece of work.

Paint. Y'are a dog.

Apem. Thy mother's of my generation. What's she, if I be a dog?

Tim. Wilt dine with me, Apemantus?

Apem. No, I eat not lords.

Tim. An thou shouldst, thou'dst anger ladies.

Apem. O, they eat lords. So they come by great bellies.

Tim. That's a lascivious apprehension.

Apem. So thou apprehend'st it. Take it for thy labour.

Tim. How dost thou like this jewel, Apemantus?

Apem. Not so well as plain-dealing, which will not cost a man a doit.

Tim. What dost thou think 'tis worth?

Apem. Not worth my thinking. How now, poet?

Poet. How now, philosopher?

Apem. Thou liest.

Poet. Art not one?

Apem. Yes.

Poet. Then I lie not.

Apem. Art not a poet?

Poet. Yes.

Apem. Then thou liest. Look in thy last work, where thou hast feign'd him a worthy fellow.

Poet. That's not feign'd; he is so.

Apem. Yes, he is worthy of thee, and to pay thee for thy labour. He that loves to be flattered is worthy o' th' flatterer. Heavens, that I were a lord!

Tim. What wouldst do then, Apemantus?

Apem. E'en as Apemantus does now — hate a lord with my heart.

Tim. What, thyself?

Apem. Ay.

Tim. Wherefore?

Apem. That I had no angry wit to be a lord. Art not thou a merchant?

Merch. Ay, Apemantus.

Apem. Traffic confound thee, if the gods will not!

Merch. If traffic do it, the gods do it.

Apem. Traffic's thy god; and thy god confound thee!

Trumpet sounds. Enter a *Messenger.*

Tim. What trumpet's that?

Mess. 'Tis Alcibiades and some twenty horse,
All of companionship.

Tim. Pray entertain them; give them guide to us.
[*Exeunt some Attendants.*]
You must needs dine with me. Go not you hence
Till I have thank'd you. When dinner's done,
Show me this piece. — I am joyful of your sights.

Enter *Alcibiades* with the rest.

Most welcome, sir! [*They salute.*]

Apem. So, so, there!
Aches contract and starve your supple joints!
That there should be small love amongst these sweet knaves,
And all this courtesy! The strain of man's bred out
Into baboon and monkey.

Alcib. Sir, you have sav'd my longing, and I feed
Most hungerly on your sight.

Tim. Right welcome, sir!
Ere we depart we'll share a bounteous time
In different pleasures. Pray you, let us in.
Exeunt [*all but Apemantus*].

Enter two *Lords.*

1. Lord. What time o' day is't, Apemantus?

Apem. Time to be honest.

1. Lord. That time serves still.

Apem. The more accursed thou that still omit'st it.

2. Lord. Thou art going to Lord Timon's feast?

Apem. Ay, to see meat fill knaves and wine heat fools.

2. Lord. Fare thee well, fare thee well.

Apem. Thou art a fool to bid me farewell twice.

2. Lord. Why, Apemantus?

Apem. Shouldst have kept one to thyself, for I mean to give thee none.

1. Lord. Hang thyself!

Apem. No, I will do nothing at thy bidding. Make thy requests to thy friend.

2. Lord. Away, unpeaceable dog, or I'll spurn thee hence!

Apem. I will fly, like a dog, the heels o' th' ass. [*Exit.*]

1. Lord. He's opposite to humanity. Come, shall we in
And taste Lord Timon's bounty? He outgoes
The very heart of kindness.

2. Lord. He pours it out. Plutus, the god of gold,
Is but his steward. No meed but he repays
Sevenfold above itself. No gift to him
But breeds the giver a return exceeding
All use of quittance.

1. Lord. The noblest mind he carries
That ever govern'd man.

2. Lord. Long may he live
In fortunes! Shall we in?

1. Lord. I'll keep you company. *Exeunt.*

[Scene II. *A room of state in* Timon's *house.*]

Hautboys playing loud music. A great banquet serv'd in, [*Flavius* the *Steward* and others attending]; and then enter *Lord Timon,* the *States,* the *Athenian Lords, Ventidius* (which *Timon* redeem'd from prison). Then comes, dropping after all, *Apemantus,* discontentedly, *like himself.*

Ven. Most honoured Timon,
It hath pleas'd the gods to remember my father's age
And call him to long peace.
He is gone happy and has left me rich.
Then, as in grateful virtue I am bound
To your free heart, I do return those talents,
Doubled with thanks and service, from whose help
I deriv'd liberty.

Tim. O, by no means,
Honest Ventidius! You mistake my love.
I gave it freely ever; and there's none
Can truly say he gives, if he receives.
If our betters play at that game, we must not dare
To imitate them. Faults that are rich are fair.

Ven. A noble spirit!

Tim. Nay, my lords, ceremony was but devis'd at first
To set a gloss on faint deeds, hollow welcomes,
Recanting goodness, sorry ere 'tis shown;
But where there is true friendship, there needs none.
Pray sit. More welcome are ye to my fortunes
Than my fortunes to me. [*They sit.*]

1. Lord. My lord, we always have confess'd it.

Apem. Ho, ho, confess'd it? Hang'd it, have you not?

Tim. O, Apemantus, you are welcome.

Apem. No,
You shall not make me welcome.
I come to have thee thrust me out of doors.

Tim. Fie, th'art a churl; y'have got a humour there
Does not become a man; 'tis much to blame.
They say, my lords, *Ira furor brevis est*; but yond man is ever angry. Go, let him have a table by himself; for he does neither affect company nor is he fit for't indeed.

Apem. Let me stay at thine apperil, Timon. I come to observe; I give thee warning on't.

Tim. I take no heed of thee. Th'art an Athenian, therefore welcome. I myself would have no power; prithee let my meat make thee silent.

Apem. I scorn thy meat. 'Twould choke me, for I should ne'er flatter thee. O you gods, what a number of men eats Timon, and he sees 'em not! It grieves me to see so many dip their meat in one man's blood; and all the madness is, he cheers them up too.
I wonder men dare trust themselves with men.
Methinks they should invite them without knives:
Good for their meat, and safer for their lives.
There's much example for't. The fellow that sits next him now, parts bread with him, pledges the breath of him in a divided draught, is the readiest man to kill him. 'T has been proved. If I were a huge man, I should fear to drink at meals,
Lest they should spy my windpipe's dangerous notes.
Great men should drink with harness on their throats.

Tim. [*to a Lord who drinks to him*] My lord, in heart! and let the health go round.

2. Lord. Let it flow this way, my good lord.

Apem. Flow this way? A brave fellow! He keeps his tides well. Those healths will make

thee and thy state look ill, Timon. Here's that which is too weak to be a sinner, honest water, which ne'er left man i' th' mire.
This and my food are equals; there's no odds.
Feasts are too proud to give thanks to the gods.

Apemantus' Grace.

Immortal gods, I crave no pelf.
I pray for no man but myself.
Grant I may never prove so fond
To trust man on his oath or bond,
Or a harlot for her weeping,
Or a dog that seems a-sleeping,
Or a keeper with my freedom,
Or my friends, if I should need 'em.
Amen. So fall to't.
Rich men sin, and I eat root.

[*Eats and drinks.*]

Much good dich thy good heart, Apemantus!

Tim. Captain Alcibiades, your heart 's in the field now.

Alcib. My heart is ever at your service, my lord.

Tim. You had rather be at a breakfast of enemies than a dinner of friends.

Alcib. So they were bleeding new, my lord, there's no meat like 'em. I could wish my best friend at such a feast.

Apem. Would all those flatterers were thine enemies then, that then thou mightst kill 'em — and bid me to 'em!

1. Lord. Might we but have that happiness, my lord, that you would once use our hearts, whereby we might express some part of our zeals, we should think ourselves for ever perfect.

Tim. O, no doubt, my good friends, but the gods themselves have provided that I shall have much help from you. How had you been my friends else? Why have you that charitable title from thousands, did not you chiefly belong to my heart? I have told more of you to myself than you can with modesty speak in your own behalf; and thus far I confirm you. O you gods, think I, what need we have any friends if we should ne'er have need of 'em? They were the most needless creatures living, should we ne'er have use for 'em; and would most resemble sweet instruments hung up in cases, that keep their sounds to themselves. Why, I have often wish'd myself poorer, that I might come nearer to you. We are born to do benefits; and what better or properer can we call our own than the riches of our friends? O, what a precious comfort 'tis to have so many like brothers commanding one another's fortunes! O, joy 's e'en made away ere 't can be born! Mine eyes cannot hold out water, methinks. To forget their faults, I drink to you.

Apem. Thou weep'st to make them drink, Timon.

2. Lord. Joy had the like conception in our eyes
And at that instant like a babe sprung up.

Apem. Ho, ho! I laugh to think that babe a bastard.

3. Lord. I promise you, my lord, you mov'd me much.

Apem. Much! *Sound tucket.*

Tim. What means that trump?

Enter *Servant.*

How now?

Serv. Please you, my lord, there are certain ladies most desirous of admittance.

Tim. Ladies? What are their wills?

Serv. There comes with them a forerunner, my lord, which bears that office to signify their pleasures.

Tim. I pray let them be admitted. [*Exit Servant.*]

Enter *Cupid.*

Cup. Hail to thee, worthy Timon! and to all
That of his bounties taste! The five best Senses
Acknowledge thee their patron, and come freely
To gratulate thy plenteous bosom. Th' Ear,
Taste, Touch, and Smell, pleas'd from thy table rise;
They only now come but to feast thine eyes.

Tim. They're welcome all; let 'em have kind admittance.
Music, make their welcome! [*Exit Cupid.*]

1. Lord. You see, my lord, how ample y'are belov'd.

[*Music.*] Enter *Cupid,* with the *Masque of Ladies* [as] *Amazons* with lutes in their hands, dancing and playing.

Apem. Hoy-day! What a sweep of vanity comes this way!
They dance? They are mad women.
Like madness is the glory of this life,
As this pomp shows to a little oil and root.
We make ourselves fools to disport ourselves,
And spend our flatteries to drink those men
Upon whose age we void it up again
With poisonous spite and envy.
Who lives that's not depraved or depraves?
Who dies that bears not one spurn to their graves

Of their friends' gift?
I should fear those that dance before me now
Would one day stamp upon me. 'T has been done.
Men shut their doors against a setting sun.

The Lords rise from table, with much adoring of Timon; and to show their loves, each single out an Amazon, and all dance, men with women, a lofty strain or two to the hautboys, and cease.

Tim. You have done our pleasures much grace, fair ladies,
Set a fair fashion on our entertainment,
Which was not half so beautiful and kind.
You have added worth unto't and lustre
And entertain'd me with mine own device.
I am to thank you for't.

1. Lady. My lord, you take us even at the best.

Apem. Faith, for the worst is filthy, and would not hold taking, I doubt me.

Tim. Ladies, there is an idle banquet attends you.
Please you to dispose yourselves.

All Ladies. Most thankfully, my lord.

Exeunt [*Cupid and Ladies*].

Tim. Flavius.

Flav. My lord?

Tim. The little casket bring me hither.

Flav. Yes, my lord. [*Aside*] More jewels yet?
There is no crossing him in's humour;
Else I should tell him well (i' faith, I should),
When all's spent, he'ld be cross'd then, an he could.
'Tis pity bounty had not eyes behind,
That man might ne'er be wretched for his mind.

Exit.

1. Lord. Where be our men?

Serv. Here, my lord, in readiness.

2. Lord. Our horses!

[Enter *Flavius* with the casket.]

Tim. O my friends,
I have one word to say to you. Look you, my good lord,
I must entreat you honour me so much
As to advance this jewel. Accept and wear it,
Kind my lord.

1. Lord. I am so far already in your gifts —

All. So are we all.

Enter a *Servant.*

Serv. My lord, there are certain nobles of the Senate
Newly alighted and come to visit you.

Tim. They are fairly welcome.

[*Exit Servant.*]

Flav. I beseech your honour,
Vouchsafe me a word. It does concern you near.

Tim. Near? Why then, another time I'll hear thee. I prithee
Let's be provided to show them entertainment.

Flav. [*aside*] I scarce know how.

Enter another *Servant.*

Serv. May it please your honour, Lord Lucius,
Out of his free love, hath presented to you
Four milk-white horses, trapp'd in silver.

Tim. I shall accept them fairly. Let the presents
Be worthily entertain'd.

[*Exit Servant.*]

Enter a third *Servant.*

How now? What news?

Serv. Please you, my lord, that honourable gentleman, Lord Lucullus, entreats your company to-morrow to hunt with him and has sent your honour two brace of greyhounds.

Tim. I'll hunt with him; and let them be receiv'd,
Not without fair reward.

[*Exit Servant.*]

Flav. [*aside*] What will this come to?
He commands us to provide and give great gifts,
And all out of an empty coffer;
Nor will he know his purse, or yield me this,
To show him what a beggar his heart is,
Being of no power to make his wishes good.
His promises fly so beyond his state
That what he speaks is all in debt; he owes
For ev'ry word. He is so kind that he now
Pays interest for't; his land's put to their books.
Well, would I were gently put out of office
Before I were forc'd out!
Happier is he that has no friend to feed
Than such that do e'en enemies exceed.
I bleed inwardly for my lord.

Exit.

Tim. You do yourselves
Much wrong; you bate too much of your own merits.
Here, my lord — a trifle of our love.

2. Lord. With more than common thanks I will receive it.

3. Lord. O, he's the very soul of bounty!

Tim. And now I remember, my lord, you gave
Good words the other day of a bay courser
I rode on. It is yours because you lik'd it.
3. Lord. O, I beseech you pardon me, my lord, in that!
Tim. You may take my word, my lord. I know, no man
Can justly praise but what he does affect.
I weigh my friend's affection with mine own.
I'll tell you true. I'll call to you.
All Lords. O, none so welcome!
Tim. I take all and your several visitations
So kind to heart 'tis not enough to give.
Methinks I could deal kingdoms to my friends
And ne'er be weary. Alcibiades,
Thou art a soldier, therefore seldom rich.
It comes in charity to thee; for all thy living
Is 'mongst the dead, and all the lands thou hast
Lie in a pitch'd field.
Alcib. Ay, defil'd land, my lord.
1. Lord. We are so virtuously bound —
Tim. And so
Am I to you.
2. Lord. So infinitely endear'd —
Tim. All to you. Lights, more lights!
1. Lord. The best of happiness,
Honour, and fortunes keep with you, Lord Timon!
Tim. Ready for his friends.
Exeunt Lords [*and others. Manent Apemantus and Timon*].
Apem. What a coil's here!
Serving of becks and jutting-out of bums!
I doubt whether their legs be worth the sums
That are given for 'em. Friendship's full of dregs.
Methinks false hearts should never have sound legs.
Thus honest fools lay out their wealth on curtsies.
Tim. Now, Apemantus, if thou wert not sullen,
I would be good to thee.
Apem. No, I'll nothing; for if I should be brib'd too, there would be none left to rail upon thee, and then thou wouldst sin the faster. Thou giv'st so long, Timon, I fear me thou wilt give away thyself in paper shortly. What needs these feasts, pomps, and vainglories?
Tim. Nay, an you begin to rail on society once, I am sworn not to give regard to you. Farewell, and come with better music. *Exit.*
Apem. So.
Thou wilt not hear me now; thou shalt not then.
I'll lock thy heaven from thee.
O that men's ears should be
To counsel deaf but not to flattery! *Exit.*

[ACT II. Scene I. *A* Senator's *house*.]

Enter a *Senator*, [with papers in his hand].

Sen. And late five thousand. To Varro and to Isidore
He owes nine thousand; besides my former sum,
Which makes it five-and-twenty. Still in motion
Of raging waste? It cannot hold; it will not.
If I want gold, steal but a beggar's dog
And give it Timon — why, the dog coins gold.
If I would sell my horse and buy twenty moe
Better than he — why, give my horse to Timon.
Ask nothing, give it him — it foals me straight,
And able horses. No porter at his gate,
But rather one that smiles and still invites
All that pass by. It cannot hold; no reason
Can sound his state in safety. Caphis, ho!
Caphis, I say!

Enter *Caphis.*

Caph. Here, sir. What is your pleasure?
Sen. Get on your cloak and haste you to Lord Timon.
Importune him for my moneys. Be not ceas'd
With slight denial, nor then silenc'd when
'Commend me to your master' and the cap
Plays in the right hand, thus; but tell him
My uses cry to me, I must serve my turn
Out of mine own; his days and times are past,
And my reliances on his fracted dates
Have smit my credit. I love and honour him,
But must not break my back to heal his finger.
Immediate are my needs, and my relief
Must not be toss'd and turn'd to me in words
But find supply immediate. Get you gone.
Put on a most importunate aspect,
A visage of demand; for I do fear,
When every feather sticks in his own wing,

Lord Timon will be left a naked gull,
Which flashes now a phœnix. Get you gone.
Caph. I go, sir.
Sen. Take the bonds along with you
And have the dates in compt.
Caph. I will, sir.
Sen. Go. *Exeunt.*

[Scene II. *Before* Timon's *house.*]

Enter [*Flavius, Timon's*] *Steward*, with many bills in his hand.

Stew. No care, no stop! So senseless of expense
That he will neither know how to maintain it
Nor cease his flow of riot; takes no accompt
How things go from him nor resumes no care
Of what is to continue. Never mind
Was to be so unwise, to be so kind.
What shall be done? He will not hear till feel.
I must be round with him. Now he comes from hunting.
Fie, fie, fie, fie!

Enter *Caphis* [and the *Servants* of] *Isidore* and *Varro.*

Caph. Good even, Varro. What, you come for money?
Var. Serv. Is't not your business too?
Caph. It is; and yours too, Isidore?
Isid. Serv. It is so.
Caph. Would we were all discharg'd!
Var. Serv. I fear it.
Caph. Here comes the lord.

Enter *Timon* and his *Train*, [with *Alcibiades*].

Tim. So soon as dinner's done we'll forth again,
My Alcibiades. — With me? What is your will?
Caph. My lord, here is a note of certain dues.
Tim. Dues? Whence are you?
Caph. Of Athens here, my lord.
Tim. Go to my steward.
Caph. Please it your lordship, he hath put me off
To the succession of new days this month.
My master is awak'd by great occasion
To call upon his own, and humbly prays you
That with your other noble parts you'll suit
In giving him his right.
Tim. Mine honest friend,
I prithee but repair to me next morning.
Caph. Nay, good my lord —
Tim. Contain thyself, good friend.
Var. Serv. One Varro's servant, my good lord.
Isid. Serv. From Isidore.
He humbly prays your speedy payment.
Caph. If you did know, my lord, my master's wants —
Var. Serv. 'Twas due on forfeiture, my lord, six weeks
And past.
Isid. Serv. Your steward puts me off, my lord,
And I am sent expressly to your lordship.
Tim. Give me breath.
I do beseech you, good my lords, keep on;
I'll wait upon you instantly.
[*Exeunt Alcibiades, Lords, &c.*]
[*To Flavius*] Come hither. Pray you,
How goes the world that I am thus encount'red
With clamorous demands of date-broke bonds
And the detention of long-since-due debts,
Against my honour?
Stew. Please you, gentlemen,
The time is unagreeable to this business.
Your importunacy cease till after dinner,
That I may make his lordship understand
Wherefore you are not paid.
Tim. Do so, my friends. See them well entertain'd. [*Exit.*]
Stew. Pray draw near. *Exit.*

Enter *Apemantus* and *Fool.*

Caph. Stay, stay, here comes the fool with Apemantus.
Let's ha' some sport with 'em.
Var. Serv. Hang him, he'll abuse us!
Isid. Serv. A plague upon him, dog!
Var. Serv. How dost, fool?
Apem. Dost dialogue with thy shadow?
Var. Serv. I speak not to thee.
Apem. No, 'tis to thyself. — [*To the Fool*] Come away.
Isid. Serv. [*to Var. Serv.*] There's the fool hangs on your back already.
Apem. No, thou stand'st single; th'art not on him yet.
Caph. Where's the fool now?
Apem. He last ask'd the question. Poor rogues, and usurers' men! bawds between gold and want!
All Serv. What are we, Apemantus?
Apem. Asses.
All Serv. Why?
Apem. That you ask me what you are, and do not know yourselves. Speak to 'em, fool.

Fool. How do you, gentlemen?

All Serv. Gramercies, good fool. How does your mistress?

Fool. She's e'en setting on water to scald such chickens as you are. Would we could see you at Corinth!

Apem. Good! gramercy.

Enter *Page.*

Fool. Look you, here comes my mistress' page.

Page. [*to the Fool*] Why, how now, captain? What do you in this wise company? How dost thou, Apemantus?

Apem. Would I had a rod in my mouth, that I might answer thee profitably!

Page. Prithee, Apemantus, read me the superscription of these letters. I know not which is which.

Apem. Canst not read?

Page. No.

Apem. There will little learning die, then, that day thou art hang'd. This is to Lord Timon; this to Alcibiades. Go; thou wast born a bastard and thou't die a bawd.

Page. Thou wast whelp'd a dog and thou shalt famish a dog's death. Answer not; I am gone. *Exit.*

Apem. E'en so thou outrun'st grace. Fool, I will go with you to Lord Timon's.

Fool. Will you leave me there?

Apem. If Timon stay at home. You three serve three usurers?

All Serv. Ay. Would they serv'd us!

Apem. So would I — as good a trick as ever hangman serv'd thief.

Fool. Are you three usurers' men?

All Serv. Ay, fool.

Fool. I think no usurer but has a fool to his servant. My mistress is one, and I am her fool. When men come to borrow of your masters, they approach sadly and go away merry; but they enter my mistress' house merrily and go away sadly. The reason of this?

Var. Serv. I could render one.

Apem. Do it then, that we may account thee a whoremaster and a knave; which notwithstanding, thou shalt be no less esteemed.

Var. Serv. What is a whoremaster, fool?

Fool. A fool in good clothes, and something like thee. 'Tis a spirit. Sometime 't appears like a lord; sometime like a lawyer; sometime like a philosopher, with two stones moe than 's artificial one. He is very often like a knight; and, generally, in all shapes that man goes up and down in from fourscore to thirteen, this spirit walks in.

Var. Serv. Thou art not altogether a fool.

Fool. Nor thou altogether a wise man. As much foolery as I have, so much wit thou lack'st.

Apem. That answer might have become Apemantus.

All Serv. Aside, aside! Here comes Lord Timon.

Enter *Timon* and [*Flavius,* his] *Steward.*

Apem. Come with me, fool, come.

Fool. I do not always follow lover, elder brother, and woman; sometime the philosopher.

[*Exeunt Apemantus and Fool.*]

Stew. Pray you walk near; I'll speak with you anon.

Exeunt [*Servants*].

Tim. You make me marvel. Wherefore ere this time
Had you not fully laid my state before me,
That I might so have rated my expense
As I had leave of means?

Stew. You would not hear me
At many leisures I propos'd.

Tim. Go to!
Perchance some single vantages you took,
When my indisposition put you back,
And that unaptness made your minister
Thus to excuse yourself.

Stew. O my good lord,
At many times I brought in my accompts,
Laid them before you. You would throw them off
And say you found them in mine honesty.
When for some trifling present you have bid me
Return so much, I have shook my head and wept;
Yea, 'gainst th' authority of manners pray'd you
To hold your hand more close. I did endure
Not seldom, nor no slight checks, when I have
Prompted you in the ebb of your estate
And your great flow of debts. My lov'd lord,
Though you hear now (too late), yet now's a time:
The greatest of your having lacks a half
To pay your present debts.

Tim. Let all my land be sold.

Stew. 'Tis all engag'd, some forfeited and gone;
And what remains will hardly stop the mouth
Of present dues. The future comes apace.

What shall defend the interim? and at length
How goes our reck'ning?
Tim. To Lacedæmon did my land extend.
Stew. O my good lord, the world is but a word.
Were it all yours to give it in a breath,
How quickly were it gone!
Tim. You tell me true.
Stew. If you suspect my husbandry or falsehood,
Call me before th' exactest auditors
And set me on the proof. So the gods bless me,
When all our offices have been oppress'd
With riotous feeders, when our vaults have wept
With drunken spilth of wine, when every room
Hath blaz'd with lights and bray'd with minstrelsy,
I have retir'd me to a wasteful cock
And set mine eyes at flow.
Tim. Prithee no more.
Stew. Heavens, have I said, the bounty of this lord!
How many prodigal bits have slaves and peasants
This night englutted! Who is not Lord Timon's?
What heart, head, sword, force, means, but is Lord Timon's?
Great Timon! noble, worthy, royal Timon!
Ah, when the means are gone that buy this praise,
The breath is gone whereof this praise is made.
Feast-won, fast-lost. One cloud of winter show'rs,
These flies are couch'd.
Tim. Come, sermon me no further.
No villanous bounty yet hath pass'd my heart;
Unwisely, not ignobly, have I given.
Why dost thou weep? Canst thou the conscience lack
To think I shall lack friends? Secure thy heart.
If I would broach the vessels of my love
And try the argument of hearts by borrowing,
Men and men's fortunes could I frankly use
As I can bid thee speak.
Stew. Assurance bless your thoughts!
Tim. And in some sort these wants of mine are crown'd,
That I account them blessings; for by these
Shall I try friends. You shall perceive how you
Mistake my fortunes; I am wealthy in my friends.
Within there! Flaminius! Servilius!

Enter three *Servants* [*Flaminius, Servilius,* and another].

Servants. My lord? My lord?
Tim. I will dispatch you severally: — [*to Servilius*] you to Lord Lucius; [*to Flaminius*] to Lord Lucullus you; I hunted with his honour to-day; [*to the other*] you to Sempronius. Commend me to their loves; and I am proud, say, that my occasions have found time to use 'em toward a supply of money. Let the request be fifty talents.
Flam. As you have said, my lord.
[*Exeunt Servants.*]
Stew. [*aside*] Lord Lucius and Lucullus? Humh?
Tim. Go you, sir, to the senators,
Of whom, even to the state's best health, I have
Deserv'd this hearing. Bid 'em send o' th' instant
A thousand talents to me.
Stew. I have been bold
(For that I knew it the most general way)
To them to use your signet and your name;
But they do shake their heads, and I am here
No richer in return.
Tim. Is't true? Can't be?
Stew. They answer in a joint and corporate voice,
That now they are at fall, want treasure, cannot
Do what they would, are sorry: you are honourable;
But yet they could have wish'd — they know not what —
Something hath been amiss — a noble nature
May catch a wrench — would all were well! 'tis pity —
And so, intending other serious matters,
After distasteful looks and these hard fractions,
With certain half-caps and cold-moving nods
They froze me into silence.
Tim. You gods, reward them!
Prithee, man, look cheerily. These old fellows
Have their ingratitude in them hereditary.
Their blood is cak'd, 'tis cold, it seldom flows.
'Tis lack of kindly warmth they are not kind;
And nature, as it grows again toward earth,
Is fashion'd for the journey, dull and heavy.
Go to Ventidius. Prithee be not sad,
Thou art true and honest. Ingeniously I speak,
No blame belongs to thee. Ventidius lately
Buried his father, by whose death he's stepp'd
Into a great estate. When he was poor,
Imprison'd, and in scarcity of friends,

I clear'd him with five talents. Greet him from me.
Bid him suppose some good necessity
Touches his friend, which craves to be remem-b'red
With those five talents. That had, give't these fellows
To whom 'tis instant due. Nev'r speak or think
That Timon's fortunes 'mong his friends can sink.

Stew. I would I could not think it. That thought is bounty's foe.
Being free itself, it thinks all others so.
Exeunt.

[ACT III. Scene I. *The house of* Lucullus.]

Flaminius waiting to speak with a *Lord*, [*Lucullus*,] from his Master, enters a *Servant* to him.

Serv. I have told my lord of you. He is coming down to you.

Flam. I thank you, sir.

Enter *Lucullus.*

Serv. Here's my lord.

Lucul. [*aside*] One of Lord Timon's men? A gift, I warrant. Why, this hits right; I dreamt of a silver basin and ewer to-night. — Flaminius, honest Flaminius, you are very respectively welcome, sir. Fill me some wine. [*Exit Servant.*] And how does that honourable, complete, free-hearted gentleman of Athens, thy very bountiful good lord and master?

Flam. His health is well, sir.

Lucul. I am right glad that his health is well, sir. And what hast thou there under thy cloak, pretty Flaminius?

Flam. Faith, nothing but an empty box, sir, which in my lord's behalf I come to entreat your honour to supply; who, having great and instant occasion to use fifty talents, hath sent to your lordship to furnish him, nothing doubting your present assistance therein.

Lucul. La, la, la, la! 'Nothing doubting,' says he? Alas, good lord! a noble gentleman 'tis, if he would not keep so good a house. Many a time and often I ha' din'd with him and told him on't, and come again to supper to him of purpose to have him spend less; and yet he would embrace no counsel, take no warning by my coming. Every man has his fault, and honesty is his. I ha' told him on't, but I could ne'er get him from't.

Enter *Servant* with wine.

Serv. Please your lordship, here is the wine.

Lucul. Flaminius, I have noted thee always wise. Here's to thee.

Flam. Your lordship speaks your pleasure.

Lucul. I have observed thee always for a towardly prompt spirit (give thee thy due) and one that knows what belongs to reason, and canst use the time well if the time use thee well. Good parts in thee! — [*To Servant*] Get you gone, sirrah. [*Exit Servant.*] Draw nearer, honest Flaminius. Thy lord's a bountiful gentleman; but thou art wise, and thou know'st well enough, although thou com'st to me, that this is no time to lend money, especially upon bare friendship without security. Here's three solidares for thee. Good boy, wink at me and say thou saw'st me not. Fare thee well.

Flam. Is't possible the world should so much differ,
And we alive that liv'd? Fly, damned baseness,
To him that worships thee!
[*Throws the money back.*]

Lucul. Ha! Now I see thou art a fool, and fit for thy master. *Exit.*

Flam. May these add to the number that may scald thee!
Let molten coin be thy damnation,
Thou disease of a friend, and not himself!
Has friendship such a faint and milky heart
It turns in less than two nights? O you gods!
I feel my master's passion. This slave,
Unto his honour, has my lord's meat in him.
Why should it thrive and turn to nutriment
When he is turn'd to poison?
O, may diseases only work upon't!
And when he's sick to death, let not that part of nature
Which my lord paid for, be of any power
To expel sickness, but prolong his hour! *Exit.*

[Scene II. *A public place.*]

Enter *Lucius* with three *Strangers.*

Luc. Who? the Lord Timon? He is my very good friend and an honourable gentleman.

1. Stran. We know him for no less, though we are but strangers to him. But I can tell you one thing, my lord, and which I hear from common rumours: now Lord Timon's happy hours are done and past, and his estate shrinks from him.

Luc. Fie, no! Do not believe it. He cannot want for money.

2. Stran. But believe you this, my lord, that not long ago one of his men was with the Lord Lucullus to borrow so many talents; nay, urg'd extremely for't, and showed what necessity belong'd to't, and yet was denied.

Luc. How?

2. Stran. I tell you, denied, my lord.

Luc. What a strange case was that! Now, before the gods, I am asham'd on't. Denied that honourable man? There was very little honour show'd in't. For my own part, I must needs confess, I have received some small kindnesses from him, as money, plate, jewels, and such-like trifles, nothing comparing to his; yet, had he mistook him and sent to me, I should ne'er have denied his occasion so many talents.

Enter *Servilius.*

Servil. See, by good hap, yonder's my lord. I have sweat to see his honour. — My honour'd lord!

Luc. Servilius? You are kindly met, sir. Fare thee well. Commend me to thy honourable virtuous lord, my very exquisite friend.

Servil. May it please your honour, my lord hath sent —

Luc. Ha! What has he sent? I am so much endeared to that lord! He's ever sending. How shall I thank him, think'st thou? And what has he sent now?

Servil. Has only sent his present occasion now, my lord, requesting your lordship to supply his instant use with so many talents.

Luc. I know his lordship is but merry with me.
He cannot want fifty-five hundred talents.

Servil. But in the mean time he wants less, my lord.
If his occasion were not virtuous,
I should not urge it half so faithfully.

Luc. Dost thou speak seriously, Servilius?

Servil. Upon my soul, 'tis true, sir.

Luc. What a wicked beast was I to disfurnish myself against such a good time, when I might ha' shown myself honourable! How unluckily it happ'ned that I should purchase the day before for a little part and undo a great deal of honour! Servilius, now before the gods, I am not able to do — the more beast, I say! I was sending to use Lord Timon myself, these gentlemen can witness; but I would not for the wealth of Athens I had done't now. Commend me bountifully to his good lordship; and I hope his honour will conceive the fairest of me, because I have no power to be kind. And tell him this from me, I count it one of my greatest afflictions, say, that I cannot pleasure such an honourable gentleman. Good Servilius, will you befriend me so far as to use mine own words to him?

Servil. Yes, sir, I shall.

Luc. I'll look you out a good turn, Servilius. *Exit Servilius.*
True, as you said, Timon is shrunk indeed;
And he that's once denied will hardly speed.
Exit.

1. Stran. Do you observe this, Hostilius?

2. Stran. Ay, too well.

1. Stran. Why, this is the world's soul, and just of the same piece
Is every flatterer's spirit. Who can call him
His friend that dips in the same dish? For in
My knowing Timon has been this lord's father
And kept his credit with his purse,
Supported his estate. Nay, Timon's money
Has paid his men their wages. He ne'er drinks
But Timon's silver treads upon his lip;
And yet — O, see the monstrousness of man
When he looks out in an ungrateful shape! —
He does deny him (in respect of his)
What charitable men afford to beggars.

3. Stran. Religion groans at it.

1. Stran. For mine own part,
I never tasted Timon in my life,
Nor came any of his bounties over me
To mark me for his friend; yet I protest,
For his right noble mind, illustrious virtue,
And honourable carriage,
Had his necessity made use of me,
I would have put my wealth into donation
And the best half should have return'd to him,
So much I love his heart. But I perceive
Men must learn now with pity to dispense;
For policy sits above conscience. *Exeunt.*

[Scene III. Sempronius' *house.*]

Enter a third *Servant* [of *Timon's*] with *Sempronius,* another of *Timon's Friends.*

Sem. Must he needs trouble me in't? Hum! 'Bove all others?
He might have tried Lord Lucius or Lucullus;

And now Ventidius is wealthy too,
Whom he redeem'd from prison. All these
Owe their estates unto him.

Serv. My lord, they
Have all been touch'd and found base metal, for
They have all denied him.

Sem. How? Have they denied him?
Has Ventidius and Lucullus denied him,
And does he send to me? Three? Humh!
It shows but little love or judgment in him.
Must I be his last refuge? His friends, like physicians,
Thrice give him over. Must I take th' cure upon me?
Has much disgrac'd me in't; I'm angry at him,
That might have known my place. I see no sense for't,
But his occasions might have woo'd me first;
For, in my conscience, I was the first man
That e'er received gift from him;
And does he think so backwardly of me now
That I'll requite it last? No.
So it may prove an argument of laughter
To th' rest, and I 'mongst lords be thought a fool.
I'd rather than the worth of thrice the sum
Had sent to me first, but for my mind's sake;
I'd such a courage to do him good. But now return,
And with their faint reply this answer join:
Who bates mine honour shall not know my coin.
Exit.

Serv. Excellent! Your lordship's a goodly villain. The devil knew not what he did when he made man politic. He crossed himself by't; and I cannot think but, in the end, the villanies of man will set him clear. How fairly this lord strives to appear foul! takes virtuous copies to be wicked, like those that under hot ardent zeal would set whole realms on fire.
Of such a nature is his politic love.
This was my lord's best hope. Now all are fled
Save the gods only. Now his friends are dead.
Doors that were ne'er acquainted with their wards
Many a bounteous year, must be employ'd
Now to guard sure their master.
And this is all a liberal course allows;
Who cannot keep his wealth must keep his house. *Exit.*

[Scene IV. *A hall in* Timon's *house.*]

Enter [two of] *Varro's Men,* meeting [*Lucius's Servant* and] others, all [being *Servants* of] *Timon's* creditors, to wait for his coming out. Then enter *Titus* and *Hortensius.*

1. Var. Man. Well met! Good morrow, Titus and Hortensius.

Tit. The like to you, kind Varro.

Hor. Lucius!
What, do we meet together?

Luc. Serv. Ay, and I think
One business does command us all, for mine
Is money.

Tit. So is theirs and ours.

Enter *Philotus.*

Luc. Serv. And Sir Philotus too!

Phi. Good day at once.

Luc. Serv. Welcome, good brother.
What do you think the hour?

Phi. Labouring for nine.

Luc. Serv. So much?

Phi. Is not my lord seen yet?

Luc. Serv. Not yet.

Phi. I wonder on't. He was wont to shine at seven.

Luc. Serv. Ay, but the days are wax'd shorter with him.
You must consider that a prodigal course
Is like the sun's, but not like his recoverable.
I fear
'Tis deepest winter in Lord Timon's purse.
That is, one may reach deep enough and yet
Find little.

Phi. I am of your fear for that.

Tit. I'll show you how t' observe a strange event.
Your lord sends now for money.

Hor. Most true, he does.

Tit. And he wears jewels now of Timon's gift,
For which I wait for money.

Hor. It is against my heart.

Luc. Serv. Mark how strange it shows
Timon in this should pay more than he owes;
And e'en as if your lord should wear rich jewels
And send for money for 'em.

Hor. I'm weary of this charge, the gods can witness.
I know my lord hath spent of Timon's wealth,
And now ingratitude makes it worse than stealth.

1. Var. Man. Yes, mine's three thousand crowns. What's yours?
Luc. Serv. Five thousand mine.
1. Var. Man. 'Tis much deep; and it should seem by th' sum
Your master's confidence was above mine;
Else surely his had equall'd.

Enter *Flaminius.*

Tit. One of Lord Timon's men.

Luc. Serv. Flaminius? Sir, a word. Pray, is my lord ready to come forth?

Flam. No, indeed he is not.

Tit. We attend his lordship. Pray signify so much.

Flam. I need not tell him that. He knows you are too diligent. [*Exit.*]

Enter [*Timon's*] *Steward,* [*Flavius,*] in a cloak, muffled.

Luc. Serv. Ha! Is not that his steward muffled so?
He goes away in a cloud. Call him, call him!
Tit. Do you hear, sir?
2. Var. Man. By your leave, sir —
Stew. What do ye ask of me, my friend?
Tit. We wait for certain money here, sir.
Stew. Ay,
If money were as certain as your waiting,
'Twere sure enough.
Why then preferr'd you not your sums and bills
When your false masters eat of my lord's meat?
Then they could smile, and fawn upon his debts,
And take down th' int'rest into their glutt'nous maws.
You do yourselves but wrong to stir me up.
Let me pass quietly.
Believe't, my lord and I have made an end;
I have no more to reckon, he to spend.
Luc. Serv. Ay, but this answer will not serve.
Stew. If 'twill not serve, 'tis not so base as you;
For you serve knaves. [*Exit.*]

1. Var. Man. How? What does his cashier'd worship mutter?

2. Var. Man. No matter what. He's poor, and that's revenge enough. Who can speak broader than he that has no house to put his head in? Such may rail against great buildings.

Enter *Servilius.*

Tit. O, here's Servilius. Now we shall know some answer.

Servil. If I might beseech you, gentlemen, to repair some other hour, I should derive much from't. For take 't of my soul, my lord leans wondrously to discontent. His comfortable temper has forsook him; he's much out of health and keeps his chamber.

Luc. Serv. Many do keep their chambers are not sick;
And if it be so far beyond his health,
Methinks he should the sooner pay his debts
And make a clear way to the gods.
Servil. Good gods!

Tit. We cannot take this for an answer, sir.

Flam. (*within*) Servilius, help! My lord! my lord!

Enter *Timon,* in a rage, [*Flaminius* following].

Tim. What, are my doors oppos'd against my passage?
Have I been ever free, and must my house
Be my retentive enemy, my jail?
The place which I have feasted, does it now,
Like all mankind, show me an iron heart?
Luc. Serv. Put in now, Titus.
Tit. My lord, here is my bill.
Luc. Serv. Here's mine.
Hor. And mine, my lord.
Both Var. Men. And ours, my lord.
Phi. All our bills.
Tim. Knock me down with 'em! Cleave me to the girdle!
Luc. Serv. Alas, my lord —
Tim. Cut my heart in sums!
Tit. Mine, fifty talents.
Tim. Tell out my blood!
Luc. Serv. Five thousand crowns, my lord.
Tim. Five thousand drops pays that. What yours? and yours?
1. Var. Man. My lord —
2. Var. Man. My lord —
Tim. Tear me, take me, and the gods fall upon you! *Exit.*

Hor. Faith, I perceive our masters may throw their caps at their money. These debts may well be call'd desperate ones, for a madman owes 'em. *Exeunt.*

Enter *Timon* [and *Flavius,* his *Steward*].

Tim. They have e'en put my breath from me, the slaves!
Creditors? Devils!
Stew. My dear lord -
Tim. What if it should be so?
Stew. My lord —
Tim. I'll have it so. My steward?
Stew. Here, my lord.

Tim. So fitly? Go, bid all my friends again,
Lucius, Lucullus, and Sempronius — all.
I'll once more feast the rascals.
Stew. O my lord,
You only speak from your distracted soul.
There is not so much left to furnish out
A moderate table.
Tim. Be it not in thy care. Go,
I charge thee, invite them all; let in the tide
Of knaves once more. My cook and I'll provide.
Exeunt.

[Scene V. *The Senate House.*]

Enter three *Senators* at one door, *Alcibiades* meeting them, with *Attendants.*

1. Sen. My lord, you have my voice to't. The fault's bloody.
'Tis necessary he should die.
Nothing emboldens sin so much as mercy.
2. Sen. Most true! The law shall bruise him.
Alcib. Honour, health, and compassion to the Senate!
1. Sen. Now, Captain?
Alcib. I am an humble suitor to your virtues;
For pity is the virtue of the law,
And none but tyrants use it cruelly.
It pleases time and fortune to lie heavy
Upon a friend of mine, who in hot blood
Hath stepp'd into the law, which is past depth
To those that (without heed) do plunge into't.
He is a man (setting his fault aside)
Of comely virtues;
Nor did he soil the fact with cowardice
(An honour in him which buys out his fault)
But with a noble fury and fair spirit,
Seeing his reputation touch'd to death,
He did oppose his foe;
And with such sober and unnoted passion
He did behave his anger, ere 'twas spent,
As if he had but prov'd an argument.
1. Sen. You undergo too strict a paradox,
Striving to make an ugly deed look fair.
Your words have took such pains as if they labour'd
To bring manslaughter into form and set
Quarrelling upon the head of valour; which indeed
Is valour misbegot, and came into the world
When sects and factions were newly born.
He's truly valiant that can wisely suffer
The worst that man can breathe, and make his wrongs
His outsides, to wear them like his raiment, carelessly,
And ne'er prefer his injuries to his heart,
To bring it into danger.
If wrongs be evils, and enforce us kill,
What folly 'tis to hazard life for ill!
Alcib. My lords —
1. Sen. You cannot make gross sins look clear.
To revenge is no valour, but to bear.
Alcib. My lords, then, under favour, pardon me
If I speak like a captain.
Why do fond men expose themselves to battle
And not endure all threats? sleep upon't,
And let the foes quietly cut their throats
Without repugnancy? If there be
Such valour in the bearing, what make we
Abroad? Why then, women are more valiant
That stay at home, if bearing carry it;
And the ass more captain than the lion; the felon
Loaden with irons wiser than the judge,
If wisdom be in suffering. O my lords,
As you are great, be pitifully good.
Who cannot condemn rashness in cold blood?
To kill, I grant, is sin's extremest gust;
But, in defence, by mercy, 'tis most just.
To be in anger is impiety;
But who is man that is not angry?
Weigh but the crime with this.
2. Sen. You breathe in vain.
Alcib. In vain? His service done
At Lacedæmon and Byzantium
Were a sufficient briber for his life.
1. Sen. What's that?
Alcib. Why, I say, my lords, has done fair service
And slain in fight many of your enemies.
How full of valour did he bear himself
In the last conflict, and made plenteous wounds!
2. Sen. He has made too much plenty with 'em.
He's a sworn rioter; he has a sin that often
Drowns him and takes his valour prisoner.
If there were no more foes, that were enough
To overcome him. In that beastly fury
He has been known to commit outrages
And cherish factions. 'Tis inferr'd to us
His days are foul and his drink dangerous.
1. Sen. He dies.
Alcib. Hard fate! He might have died in war.
My lords, if not for any parts in him —

Though his right arm might purchase his own time,
And be in debt to none — yet, more to move you,
Take my deserts to his and join 'em both;
And, for I know your reverend ages love
Security, I'll pawn my victories, all
My honours to you, upon his good returns.
If by this crime he owes the law his life,
Why, let the war receive't in valiant gore;
For law is strict, and war is nothing more.

1. Sen. We are for law. He dies. Urge it no more
On height of our displeasure. Friend or brother,
He forfeits his own blood that spills another.

Alcib. Must it be so? It must not be. My lords,
I do beseech you know me.

2. Sen. How?

Alcib. Call me to your remembrances.

3. Sen. What!

Alcib. I cannot think but your age has forgot me.
It could not else be I should prove so base
To sue, and be denied such common grace.
My wounds ache at you.

1. Sen. Do you dare our anger?
'Tis in few words, but spacious in effect:
We banish thee for ever.

Alcib. Banish me?
Banish your dotage! Banish usury,
That makes the Senate ugly!

1. Sen. If after two days' shine Athens contain thee,
Attend our weightier judgment. And, not to swell our spirit,
He shall be executed presently.

Exeunt [*Senators*].

Alcib. Now the gods keep you old enough that you may live
Only in bone, that none may look on you!
I'm worse than mad. I have kept back their foes
While they have told their money and let out
Their coin upon large interest, I myself
Rich only in large hurts. All those for this?
Is this the balsam that the usuring Senate
Pours into captains' wounds? Banishment!
It comes not ill. I hate not to be banish'd.
It is a cause worthy my spleen and fury,
That I may strike at Athens. I'll cheer up
My discontented troops and lay for hearts.
'Tis honour with most lands to be at odds.
Soldiers should brook as little wrongs as gods.

Exit.

[Scene VI. *A banqueting hall in* Timon's *house.*]

[*Music. Tables set out: Servants attending.*] Enter divers *Friends* [of *Timon*, being *Senators* and *Lords*,] at several doors.

1. Friend. The good time of day to you, sir.

2. Friend. I also wish it to you. I think this honourable lord did but try us this other day.

1. Friend. Upon that were my thoughts tiring when we encount'red. I hope it is not so low with him as he made it seem in the trial of his several friends.

2. Friend. It should not be, by the persuasion of his new feasting.

1. Friend. I should think so. He hath sent me an earnest inviting, which many my near occasions did urge me to put off; but he hath conjur'd me beyond them, and I must needs appear.

2. Friend. In like manner was I in debt to my importunate business, but he would not hear my excuse. I am sorry, when he sent to borrow of me, that my provision was out.

1. Friend. I am sick of that grief too, as I understand how all things go.

2. Friend. Every man here's so. What would he have borrowed of you?

1. Friend. A thousand pieces.

2. Friend. A thousand pieces?

1. Friend. What of you?

2. Friend. He sent to me, sir — Here he comes.

Enter *Timon* and *Attendants.*

Tim. With all my heart, gentlemen both! And how fare you?

1. Friend. Ever at the best, hearing well of your lordship.

2. Friend. The swallow follows not summer more willing than we your lordship.

Tim. [*aside*] Nor more willingly leaves winter; such summer birds are men. — Gentlemen, our dinner will not recompense this long stay. Feast your ears with the music awhile, if they will fare so harshly. O, th' trumpets sound. We shall to't presently.

1. Friend. I hope it remains not unkindly with your lordship that I return'd you an empty messenger.

Tim. O sir, let it not trouble you.

2. Friend. My noble lord —

Tim. Ah, my good friend, what cheer?

2. Friend. My most honourable lord, I am e'en sick of shame that, when your lordship this other day sent to me, I was so unfortunate a beggar.

Tim. Think not on't, sir.

2. Friend. If you had sent but two hours before —

Tim. Let it not cumber your better remembrance. (*The banquet brought in.*) Come, bring in all together.

2. Friend. All cover'd dishes!

1. Friend. Royal cheer, I warrant you.

3. Friend. Doubt not that, if money and the season can yield it.

1. Friend. How do you? What's the news?

3. Friend. Alcibiades is banish'd. Hear you of it?

Both. Alcibiades banish'd?

3. Friend. 'Tis so; be sure of it.

1. Friend. How? how?

2. Friend. I pray you, upon what?

Tim. My worthy friends, will you draw near?

3. Friend. I'll tell you more anon. Here's a noble feast toward.

2. Friend. This is the old man still.

3. Friend. Will't hold? Will't hold?

2. Friend. It does; but time will — and so —

3. Friend. I do conceive.

Tim. Each man to his stool, with that spur as he would to the lip of his mistress. Your diet shall be in all places alike. Make not a city feast of it, to let the meat cool ere we can agree upon the first place. Sit, sit. The gods require our thanks.

You great benefactors, sprinkle our society with thankfulness. For your own gifts, make yourselves prais'd; but reserve still to give, lest your deities be despised. Lend to each man enough, that one need not lend to another; for, were your godheads to borrow of men, men would forsake the gods. Make the meat be beloved more than the man that gives it. Let no assembly of twenty be without a score of villains. If there sit twelve women at the table, let a dozen of them be — as they are. The rest of your foes, O gods, the senators of Athens, together with the common lag of people, what is amiss in them, you gods, make suitable for destruction. For these my present friends, as they are to me nothing, so in nothing bless them, and to nothing are they welcome.

Uncover, dogs, and lap.

[*The dishes are uncovered, and seen to be full of warm water.*]

Some speak. What does his lordship mean?

Some other. I know not.

Tim. May you a better feast never behold,
You knot of mouth-friends! Smoke and lukewarm water
Is your perfection. This is Timon's last!
Who, stuck and spangled with your flatteries,
Washes it off and sprinkles in your faces
[*Throws the water in their faces.*]
Your reeking villany. Live loath'd, and long,
Most smiling, smooth, detested parasites,
Courteous destroyers, affable wolves, meek bears,
You fools of fortune, trencher friends, time's flies,
Cap-and-knee slaves, vapours, and minute-jacks!
Of man and beast the infinite malady
Crust you quite o'er! What, dost thou go?
Soft! take thy physic first! thou too! and thou!
Stay, I will lend thee money, borrow none.
[*Drives them out.*]
What, all in motion? Henceforth be no feast
Whereat a villain's not a welcome guest.
Burn house! Sink Athens! Henceforth hated be
Of Timon man and all humanity! *Exit.*

Enter [the *Friends* —] the *Senators* with other *Lords,* [returning].

1. Friend. How now, my lords?

2. Friend. Know you the quality of Lord Timon's fury?

3. Friend. Push! Did you see my cap?

4. Friend. I have lost my gown

1. Friend. He's but a mad lord and naught but humours sways him. He gave me a jewel th' other day, and now he has beat it out of my hat. Did you see my jewel?

3. Friend. Did you see my cap?

2. Friend. Here 'tis.

4. Friend. Here lies my gown.

1. Friend. Let's make no stay.

2. Friend. Lord Timon's mad.

3. Friend. I feel't upon my bones.

4. Friend. One day he gives us diamonds, next day stones. *Exeunt.*

[Act IV. Scene I. *Without the walls of Athens.*]

Enter *Timon.*

Tim. Let me look back upon thee. O thou wall
That girdles in those wolves, dive in the earth
And fence not Athens! Matrons, turn incontinent!
Obedience fail in children! Slaves and fools,
Pluck the grave wrinkled Senate from the bench
And minister in their steads! To general filths
Convert o' th' instant, green virginity!
Do't in your parents' eyes! Bankrupts, hold fast!
Rather than render back, out with your knives
And cut your trusters' throats! Bound servants, steal!
Large-handed robbers your grave masters are
And pill by law. Maid, to thy master's bed!
Thy mistress is o' th' brothel. Son of sixteen,
Pluck the lin'd crutch from thy old limping sire;
With it beat out his brains! Piety and fear,
Religion to the gods, peace, justice, truth,
Domestic awe, night-rest and neighbourhood,
Instruction, manners, mysteries and trades,
Degrees, observances, customs and laws,
Decline to your confounding contraries
And let confusion live! Plagues incident to men,
Your potent and infectious fevers heap
On Athens, ripe for stroke! Thou cold sciatica,
Cripple our senators, that their limbs may halt
As lamely as their manners! Lust and liberty
Creep in the minds and marrows of our youth,
That 'gainst the stream of virtue they may strive
And drown themselves in riot! Itches, blains,
Sow all th' Athenian bosoms, and their crop
Be general leprosy! Breath infect breath,
That their society (as their friendship) may
Be merely poison! Nothing I'll bear from thee
But nakedness, thou detestable town!
Take thou that too, with multiplying bans!
Timon will to the woods, where he shall find
Th' unkindest beast more kinder than mankind.
The gods confound (hear me, you good gods all)
Th' Athenians both within and out that wall!
And grant, as Timon grows, his hate may grow
To the whole race of mankind, high and low!
Amen. *Exit.*

[Scene II. *Athens.* Timon's *house.*]

Enter [*Flavius* the] *Steward* with two or three *Servants.*

1. Serv. Hear you, Master Steward. Where's our master?
Are we undone? cast off? nothing remaining?
Stew. Alack, my fellows, what should I say to you?
Let me be recorded by the righteous gods,
I am as poor as you.
1. Serv. Such a house broke?
So noble a master fall'n? All gone? and not
One friend to take his fortune by the arm
And go along with him?
2. Serv. As we do turn our backs
From our companion, thrown into his grave,
So his familiars to his buried fortunes —
Slink all away; leave their false vows with him,
Like empty purses pick'd; and his poor self,
A dedicated beggar to the air,
With his disease of all-shunn'd poverty,
Walks, like contempt, alone. More of our fellows.

Enter other *Servants.*

Stew. All broken implements of a ruin'd house.
3. Serv. Yet do our hearts wear Timon's livery.
That see I by our faces. We are fellows still,
Serving alike in sorrow. Leak'd is our bark;
And we, poor mates, stand on the dying deck,
Hearing the surges threat. We must all part
Into this sea of air.
Stew. Good fellows all,
The latest of my wealth I'll share amongst you.
Wherever we shall meet, for Timon's sake
Let's yet be fellows; let's shake our heads and say,
As 'twere a knell unto our master's fortunes,
'We have seen better days.' Let each take some. [*Gives money.*]
Nay, put out all your hands. Not one word more!
Thus part we rich in sorrow, parting poor.
Embrace, and part several ways.
O the fierce wretchedness that glory brings us!
Who would not wish to be from wealth exempt,
Since riches point to misery and contempt?

Who would be so mock'd with glory, or to live
But in a dream of friendship,
To have his pomp, and all what state compounds,
But only painted, like his varnish'd friends?
Poor honest lord, brought low by his own heart,
Undone by goodness! Strange, unusual blood,
When man's worst sin is he does too much good!
Who then dares to be half so kind again?
For bounty, that makes gods, does still mar men.
My dearest lord — blest, to be most accurst,
Rich, only to be wretched — thy great fortunes
Are made thy chief afflictions. Alas, kind lord!
He's flung in rage from this ingrateful seat
Of monstrous friends; nor has he with him to
Supply his life, or that which can command it.
I'll follow and enquire him out.
I'll ever serve his mind with my best will;
Whilst I have gold, I'll be his steward still.
Exit.

[Scene III. *The woods, near the seashore. Before* Timon's *cave.*]

Enter *Timon* in the woods.

Tim. O blessed breeding sun, draw from the earth
Rotten humidity; below thy sister's orb
Infect the air! Twinn'd brothers of one womb—
Whose procreation, residence, and birth
Scarce is dividant — touch them with several fortunes,
The greater scorns the lesser. Not nature
(To whom all sores lay siege) can bear great fortune
But by contempt of nature.
Raise me this beggar and deny't that lord:
The senator shall bear contempt hereditary,
The beggar native honour.
It is the pasture lards the rother's sides,
The want that makes him lean. Who dares, who dares
In purity of manhood stand upright
And say 'This man's a flatterer'? If one be,
So are they all; for every grize of fortune
Is smooth'd by that below. The learned pate
Ducks to the golden fool. All's obliquy;
There's nothing level in our cursed natures
But direct villany. Therefore be abhorr'd
All feasts, societies, and throngs of men!
His semblable, yea, himself, Timon disdains.
Destruction fang mankind! Earth, yield me roots! [*Digs.*]
Who seeks for better of thee, sauce his palate
With thy most operant poison! What is here?
Gold? Yellow, glittering, precious gold? No, gods,
I am no idle votarist. Roots, you clear heavens!
Thus much of this will make black white, foul fair,
Wrong right, base noble, old young, coward valiant.
Ha, you gods! why this? What, this, you gods? Why, this
Will lug your priests and servants from your sides,
Pluck sick men's pillows from below their heads:
This yellow slave
Will knit and break religions, bless th' accurs'd,
Make the hoar leprosy ador'd, place thieves
And give them title, knee, and approbation
With senators on the bench. This is it
That makes the wappen'd widow wed again;
She whom the spital-house and ulcerous sores
Would cast the gorge at, this embalms and spices
To th' April day again. Come, damned earth,
Thou common whore of mankind, that puts odds
Among the rout of nations, I will make thee
Do thy right nature. *March afar off.*
Ha! a drum? Th'art quick,
But yet I'll bury thee. Thou't go, strong thief,
When gouty keepers of thee cannot stand.
Nay, stay thou out for earnest.
[*Keeps some gold.*]

Enter *Alcibiades*, with *Drum* and *Fife*, in warlike manner; and *Phrynia* and *Timandra*.

Alcib. What art thou there?
Speak.
Tim. A beast, as thou art. The canker gnaw thy heart,
For showing me again the eyes of man!
Alcib. What is thy name? Is man so hateful to thee
That art thyself a man?
Tim. I am Misanthropos and hate mankind.
For thy part, I do wish thou wert a dog,
That I might love thee something.
Alcib. I know thee well;
But in thy fortunes am unlearn'd and strange.
Tim. I know thee too; and more than that I know thee,
I not desire to know. Follow thy drum;
With man's blood paint the ground gules, gules!

Religious canons, civil laws are cruel;
Then what should war be? This fell whore of thine
Hath in her more destruction than thy sword
For all her cherubin look.

Phry. Thy lips rot off!

Tim. I will not kiss thee; then the rot returns
To thine own lips again.

Alcib. How came the noble Timon to this change?

Tim. As the moon does, by wanting light to give.
But then renew I could not, like the moon;
There were no suns to borrow of.

Alcib. Noble Timon,
What friendship may I do thee?

Tim. None, but to
Maintain my opinion.

Alcib. What is it, Timon?

Tim. Promise me friendship, but perform none. If thou wilt not promise, the gods plague thee, for thou art a man! if thou dost perform, confound thee, for thou art a man!

Alcib. I have heard in some sort of thy miseries.

Tim. Thou saw'st them when I had prosperity.

Alcib. I see them now; then was a blessed time.

Tim. As thine is now, held with a brace of harlots.

Timan. Is this th' Athenian minion whom the world
Voic'd so regardfully?

Tim. Art thou Timandra?

Timan. Yes.

Tim. Be a whore still. They love thee not that use thee.
Give them diseases, leaving with thee their lust.
Make use of thy salt hours. Season the slaves
For tubs and baths; bring down rose-cheeked youth
To the tub-fast and the diet.

Timan. Hang thee, monster!

Alcib. Pardon him, sweet Timandra; for his wits
Are drown'd and lost in his calamities.
I have but little gold of late, brave Timon,
The want whereof doth daily make revolt
In my penurious band. I have heard, and griev'd,
How cursed Athens, mindless of thy worth,
Forgetting thy great deeds when neighbour states,
But for thy sword and fortune, trod upon them —

Tim. I prithee beat thy drum and get thee gone.

Alcib. I am thy friend and pity thee, dear Timon.

Tim. How dost thou pity him whom thou dost trouble?
I had rather be alone.

Alcib. Why, fare thee well.
Here is some gold for thee.

Tim. Keep it. I cannot eat it.

Alcib. When I have laid proud Athens on a heap —

Tim. Warr'st thou 'gainst Athens?

Alcib. Ay, Timon, and have cause.

Tim. The gods confound them all in thy conquest,
And thee after, when thou hast conquered!

Alcib. Why me, Timon?

Tim. That by killing of villains
Thou wast born to conquer my country.
Put up thy gold. Go on. Here's gold. Go on.
Be as a planetary plague when Jove
Will o'er some high-vic'd city hang his poison
In the sick air. Let not thy sword skip one.
Pity not honour'd age for his white beard;
He is an usurer. Strike me the counterfeit matron;
It is her habit only that is honest,
Herself's a bawd. Let not the virgin's cheek
Make soft thy trenchant sword; for those milk paps
That through the window bars bore at men's eyes
Are not within the leaf of pity writ,
But set them down horrible traitors. Spare not the babe
Whose dimpled smiles from fools exhaust their mercy.
Think it a bastard whom the oracle
Hath doubtfully pronounc'd thy throat shall cut,
And mince it sans remorse. Swear against objects.
Put armour on thine ears and on thine eyes
Whose proof nor yells of mothers, maids, nor babes,
Nor sight of priests in holy vestments bleeding,
Shall pierce a jot. There's gold to pay thy soldiers.
Make large confusion; and, thy fury spent,
Confounded be thyself! Speak not, be gone.

Alcib. Hast thou gold yet? I'll take the gold thou givest me,
Not all thy counsel.

Tim. Dost thou, or dost thou not, heaven's curse upon thee!
Both [*Women*]. Give us some gold, good Timon. Hast thou more?
Tim. Enough to make a whore forswear her trade,
And to make whores, a bawd. Hold up, you sluts,
Your aprons mountant. You are not oathable,
Although I know you'll swear, terribly swear
Into strong shudders and to heavenly agues
Th' immortal gods that hear you. Spare your oaths;
I'll trust to your conditions. Be whores still;
And he whose pious breath seeks to convert you —
Be strong in whore, allure him, burn him up,
Let your close fire predominate his smoke,
And be no turncoats. Yet may your pains six months
Be quite contrary! And thatch your poor thin roofs
With burthens of the dead — some that were hang'd.
No matter! Wear them, betray with them. Whore still.
Paint till a horse may mire upon your face.
A pox of wrinkles!
Both. Well, more gold! What then?
Believe't that we'll do anything for gold.
Tim. Consumptions sow
In hollow bones of man; strike their sharp shins,
And mar men's spurring. Crack the lawyer's voice,
That he may never more false title plead
Nor sound his quillets shrilly. Hoar the flamen,
That scolds against the quality of flesh
And not believes himself. Down with the nose —
Down with it flat; take the bridge quite away —
Of him that, his particular to foresee,
Smells from the general weal. Make curl'd-pate ruffians bald,
And let the unscarr'd braggarts of the war
Derive some pain from you. Plague all;
That your activity may defeat and quell
The source of all erection. There's more gold.
Do you damn others, and let this damn you,
And ditches grave you all!
Both. More counsel with more money, bounteous Timon.
Tim. More whore, more mischief first. I have given you earnest.
Alcib. Strike up the drum towards Athens! Farewell, Timon.
If I thrive well, I'll visit thee again.
Tim. If I hope well, I'll never see thee more.
Alcib. I never did thee harm.
Tim. Yes, thou spok'st well of me.
Alcib. Call'st thou that harm?
Tim. Men daily find it. Get thee away and take
Thy beagles with thee.
Alcib. We but offend him. Strike!
[*Drum beats.*] *Exeunt.* [*Manet Timon.*]
Tim. That nature, being sick of man's unkindness,
Should yet be hungry! Common mother, thou [*Digs.*]
Whose womb unmeasurable and infinite breast
Teems and feeds all, whose selfsame mettle
Whereof thy proud child, arrogant man, is puff'd
Engenders the black toad and adder blue,
The gilded newt and eyeless venom'd worm,
With all th' abhorred births below crisp heaven
Whereon Hyperion's quick'ning fire doth shine —
Yield him who all thy human sons doth hate,
From forth thy plenteous bosom, one poor root!
Ensear thy fertile and conceptious womb;
Let it no more bring out ingrateful man!
Go great with tigers, dragons, wolves, and bears;
Teem with new monsters whom thy upward face
Hath to the marbled mansion all above
Never presented! — O, a root! Dear thanks! —
Dry up thy marrows, vines, and plough-torn leas,
Whereof ingrateful man with licourish draughts
And morsels unctious greases his pure mind,
That from it all consideration slips —

Enter *Apemantus.*

More man? Plague, plague!
Apem. I was directed hither. Men report
Thou dost affect my manners and dost use them.
Tim. 'Tis then because thou dost not keep a dog,
Whom I would imitate. Consumption catch thee!
Apem. This is in thee a nature but infected,
A poor unmanly melancholy sprung
From change of fortune. Why this spade? this place?
This slave-like habit and these looks of care?

André Morell as Timon, an altruist who learns to hate his fellowmen

TIMON OF ATHENS

PHOTOGRAPHS BY JOHN VICKERS
PRODUCED BY THE OLD VIC COMPANY

"My heart is ever at your service, my lord." The great general, Alcibiades (Peter Coke), is one of those who accept the hospitality of Timon *(Act I, Scene II)*

"Methinks, I could deal kingdoms to my friends, and ne'er be weary, Alcibiades." Timon explains to Alcibiades the happiness which he gets from offering pleasure to his friends *(Act I, Scene II)*

David Waller as Lucius and John Phillips as Lucullus, two of the elegant parasites who live on the bounty of Timon of Athens

"It grieves me to see so many dip their meat in one man's blood." The philosopher Apemantus (Leo McKern) warns Timon that those who batten at his board are not his friends
(Act I, Scene II)

Apemantus rails at Lucullus and Lucius, the two stupid nobles who fawn upon Timon
(Act I, Scene II)

" 'Tis in few words, but spacious in effect; we banish thee for ever." For asking the Senate to have mercy on a friend guilty of murder, Alcibiades is banished from Athens *(Act III, Scene V)*

Alcibiades consoles his two mistresses, Phrynia (Joan Poulter) and Timandra (Yvonne Bonnamy), who are shocked by Timon's vituperation *(Act IV, Scene III)*

"Here's that which is too weak to be a sinner, honest water, which ne'er left man in the mire." The cynical philosopher, Apemantus, scorns wine at the banquet given by Timon
(Act I, Scene II)

The warrior Alcibiades is the only one of Timon's acquaintances who shows any compassion for him in his misfortune

"My lord, here is a note of certain dues." Caphis and the other servants of Timon's creditors gather at his house to demand the money he owes their masters *(Act II, Scene II)*

The leader of the Athenian Senators (Ernest Hare) sends out his man Caphis (Peter Sallis) to dun the unfortunate Timon, his former host (*Act II, Scene I*)

Having lost all his riches, Timon invites his sycophant friends to a last feast and serves them dishes filled with warm water. Here he invokes the blessing at the "feast" *(Act III, Scene VI)*

"May you a better feast never behold, you knot of mouth-friends! smoke and lukewarm water are your perfection." The climax of the mock feast Timon offers his friends *(Act III, Scene VI)*

"Destruction fang mankind! Earth, yield me roots." Left bitter and penniless by his one-time friends, Timon digs for roots in the ground by his cave *(Act IV, Scene III)*

"Dead is noble Timon: of whose memory hereafter more." Alcibiades, Timon's avenger and his only friend, delivers the epilogue *(Act V, Scene IV)*

Thy flatterers yet wear silk, drink wine, lie soft,
Hug their diseas'd perfumes, and have forgot
That ever Timon was. Shame not these woods
By putting on the cunning of a carper.
Be thou a flatterer now, and seek to thrive
By that which has undone thee. Hinge thy knee,
And let his very breath whom thou'lt observe
Blow off thy cap. Praise his most vicious strain
And call it excellent. Thou wast told thus.
Thou gav'st thine ears (like tapsters that bade welcome)
To knaves and all approachers. 'Tis most just
That thou turn rascal; hadst thou wealth again,
Rascals should have't. Do not assume my likeness.

Tim. Were I like thee, I'd throw away myself.

Apem. Thou hast cast away thyself, being like thyself;
A madman so long, now a fool. What, think'st
That the bleak air, thy boisterous chamberlain,
Will put thy shirt on warm? Will these moss'd trees,
That have outliv'd the eagle, page thy heels
And skip when thou point'st out? Will the cold brook,
Candied with ice, caudle thy morning taste
To cure thy o'er-night's surfeit? Call the creatures
Whose naked natures live in all the spite
Of wreakful heaven, whose bare unhoused trunks,
To the conflicting elements expos'd,
Answer mere nature — bid them flatter thee.
O, thou shalt find —

Tim. A fool of thee. Depart.

Apem. I love thee better now than e'er I did.

Tim. I hate thee worse.

Apem. Why?

Tim. Thou flatter'st misery.

Apem. I flatter not, but say thou art a caitiff.

Tim. Why dost thou seek me out?

Apem. To vex thee.

Tim. Always a villain's office or a fool's.
Dost please thyself in't?

Apem. Ay.

Tim. What, a knave too?

Apem. If thou didst put this sour cold habit on
To castigate thy pride, 'twere well; but thou
Dost it enforcedly. Thou'dst courtier be again,
Wert thou not beggar. Willing misery
Outlives incertain pomp, is crown'd before.
The one is filling still, never complete;
The other, at high wish. Best state, contentless,
Hath a distracted and most wretched being,
Worse than the worst, content.
Thou shouldst desire to die, being miserable.

Tim. Not by his breath that is more miserable.
Thou art a slave whom Fortune's tender arm
With favour never clasp'd, but bred a dog.
Hadst thou, like us from our first swath, proceeded
The sweet degrees that this brief world affords
To such as may the passive drugs of it
Freely command, thou wouldst have plung'd thyself
In general riot, melted down thy youth
In different beds of lust, and never learn'd
The icy precepts of respect, but followed
The sug'red game before thee. But myself,
Who had the world as my confectionary;
The mouths, the tongues, the eyes, and hearts of men
At duty, more than I could frame employment;
That numberless upon me stuck, as leaves
Do on the oak, have with one winter's brush
Fell from their boughs and left me open, bare
For every storm that blows — I to bear this,
That never knew but better, is some burthen.
Thy nature did commence in sufferance; time
Hath made thee hard in't. Why shouldst thou hate men?
They never flatter'd thee. What hast thou given?
If thou wilt curse, thy father (that poor rag)
Must be thy subject, who in spite put stuff
To some she-beggar and compounded thee
Poor rogue hereditary. Hence, be gone!
If thou hadst not been born the worst of men,
Thou hadst been a knave and flatterer.

Apem. Art thou proud yet?

Tim. Ay, that I am not thee.

Apem. I, that I was
No prodigal.

Tim. I, that I am one now.
Were all the wealth I have shut up in thee,
I'ld give thee leave to hang it. Get thee gone.
That the whole life of Athens were in this!
Thus would I eat it. [*Gnaws a root.*]

Apem. Here! I will mend thy feast. [*Offers him food.*]

Tim. First mend my company; take away thyself.

Apem. So I shall mend mine own, by th' lack of thine.

Tim. 'Tis not well mended so; it is but botch'd.
If not, I would it were.

Apem. What wouldst thou have to Athens?

Tim. Thee thither in a whirlwind. If thou wilt,
Tell them there I have gold. Look, so I have.

Apem. Here is no use for gold.

Tim. The best and truest;
For here it sleeps, and does no hired harm.

Apem. Where liest a-nights, Timon?

Tim. Under that's above me.
Where feed'st thou a-days, Apemantus?

Apem. Where my stomach finds meat; or rather, where I eat it.

Tim. Would poison were obedient and knew my mind!

Apem. Where wouldst thou send it?

Tim. To sauce thy dishes.

Apem. The middle of humanity thou never knewest, but the extremity of both ends. When thou wast in thy gilt and thy perfume, they mock'd thee for too much curiosity; in thy rags thou know'st none, but art despis'd for the contrary. There's a medlar for thee. Eat it.

Tim. On what I hate I feed not.

Apem. Dost hate a medlar?

Tim. Ay, though it look like thee.

Apem. An th' hadst hated meddlers sooner, thou shouldst have loved thyself better now. What man didst thou ever know unthrift that was beloved after his means?

Tim. Who, without those means thou talk'st of, didst thou ever know belov'd?

Apem. Myself.

Tim. I understand thee. Thou hadst some means to keep a dog.

Apem. What things in the world canst thou nearest compare to thy flatterers?

Tim. Women nearest; but men — men are the things themselves. What wouldst thou do with the world, Apemantus, if it lay in thy power?

Apem. Give it the beasts, to be rid of the men.

Tim. Wouldst thou have thyself fall in the confusion of men, and remain a beast with the beasts?

Apem. Ay, Timon.

Tim. A beastly ambition, which the gods grant thee t' attain to! If thou wert the lion, the fox would beguile thee. If thou wert the lamb, the fox would eat thee. If thou wert the fox, the lion would suspect thee when peradventure thou wert accus'd by the ass. If thou wert the ass, thy dulness would torment thee, and still thou liv'dst but as a breakfast to the wolf. If thou wert the wolf, thy greediness would afflict thee, and oft thou shouldst hazard thy life for thy dinner. Wert thou the unicorn, pride and wrath would confound thee and make thine own self the conquest of thy fury. Wert thou a bear, thou wouldst be kill'd by the horse; wert thou a horse, thou wouldst be seiz'd by the leopard; wert thou a leopard, thou wert germane to the lion, and the spots of thy kindred were jurors on thy life. All thy safety were remotion, and thy defence absence. What beast couldst thou be that were not subject to a beast? And what a beast art thou already, that seest not thy loss in transformation!

Apem. If thou couldst please me with speaking to me, thou mightst have hit upon it here. The commonwealth of Athens is become a forest of beasts.

Tim. How has the ass broke the wall, that thou art out of the city?

Apem. Yonder comes a poet and a painter. The plague of company light upon thee! I will fear to catch it, and give way. When I know not what else to do, I'll see thee again.

Tim. When there is nothing living but thee, thou shalt be welcome. I had rather be a beggar's dog than Apemantus.

Apem. Thou art the cap of all the fools alive.

Tim. Would thou wert clean enough to spit upon!

Apem. A plague on thee! thou art too bad to curse.

Tim. All villains that do stand by thee are pure.

Apem. There is no leprosy but what thou speak'st.

Tim. If I name thee.
I'll beat thee — but I should infect my hands.

Apem. I would my tongue could rot them off!

Tim. Away, thou issue of a mangy dog!
Choler does kill me that thou art alive;
I swoond to see thee.

Apem. Would thou wouldst burst!

Tim. Away,
Thou tedious rogue! I am sorry I shall lose
A stone by thee. [*Throws a stone at him.*]

Apem. Beast!

Tim. Slave!

Apem. Toad!

Tim. Rogue, rogue, rogue!
I am sick of this false world, and will love naught
But even the mere necessities upon't.

Then, Timon, presently prepare thy grave.
Lie where the light foam of the sea may beat
Thy gravestone daily. Make thine epitaph,
That death in me at others' lives may laugh.
[*To the gold*] O thou sweet king-killer, and dear divorce
'Twixt natural son and sire! thou bright defiler
Of Hymen's purest bed! thou valiant Mars!
Thou ever young, fresh, lov'd, and delicate wooer,
Whose blush doth thaw the consecrated snow
That lies on Dian's lap! thou visible god,
That sold'rest close impossibilities
And mak'st them kiss! that speak'st with every tongue
To every purpose! O thou touch of hearts!
Think thy slave man rebels, and by thy virtue
Set them into confounding odds, that beasts
May have the world in empire!

Apem. Would 'twere so!
But not till I am dead. I'll say th' hast gold.
Thou wilt be throng'd to shortly.

Tim. Throng'd to?

Apem. Ay.

Tim. Thy back, I prithee.

Apem. Live, and love thy misery!

Tim. Long live so, and so die!

Exit Apemantus.

I am quit.
Moe things like men! Eat, Timon, and abhor them.

Enter the *Banditti*.

1. Ban. Where should he have this gold? It is some poor fragment, some slender ort of his remainder. The mere want of gold and the falling-from of his friends drove him into this melancholy.

2. Ban. It is nois'd he hath a mass of treasure.

3. Ban. Let us make the assay upon him. If he care not for't, he will supply us easily; if he covetously reserve it, how shall 's get it?

2. Ban. True; for he bears it not about him; 'tis hid.

1. Ban. Is not this he?

All. Where?

2. Ban. 'Tis his description.

3. Ban. He! I know him.

All. Save thee, Timon!

Tim. Now, thieves?

All. Soldiers, not thieves.

Tim. Both too, and women's sons.

All. We are not thieves, but men that much do want.

Tim. Your greatest want is, you want much of meat.
Why should you want? Behold, the earth hath roots;
Within this mile break forth a hundred springs;
The oaks bear mast, the briers scarlet heps;
The bounteous housewife Nature on each bush
Lays her full mess before you. Want? Why want?

1. Ban. We cannot live on grass, on berries, water,
As beasts and birds and fishes.

Tim. Nor on the beasts themselves, the birds and fishes;
You must eat men. Yet thanks I must you con
That you are thieves profess'd, that you work not
In holier shapes; for there is boundless theft
In limited professions. Rascal thieves,
Here's gold. Go, suck the subtle blood o' th' grape
Till the high fever seethe your blood to froth,
And so scape hanging. Trust not the physician;
His antidotes are poison, and he slays
Moe than you rob. Take wealth and lives together.
Do villany, do, since you protest to do't,
Like workmen. I'll example you with thievery.
The sun 's a thief, and with his great attraction
Robs the vast sea. The moon 's an arrant thief,
And her pale fire she snatches from the sun.
The sea's a thief, whose liquid surge resolves
The moon into salt tears. The earth 's a thief,
That feeds and breeds by a composture stol'n
From gen'ral excrement. Each thing 's a thief.
The laws, your curb and whip, in their rough power
Have uncheck'd theft. Love not yourselves; away,
Rob one another. There's more gold. Cut throats.
All that you meet are thieves. To Athens go,
Break open shops; nothing can you steal
But thieves do lose it. Steal no less for this
I give you; and gold confound you howsoe'er!
Amen.

3. Ban. Has almost charm'd me from my profession, by persuading me to it.

1. Ban. 'Tis in the malice of mankind that he thus advises us; not to have us thrive in our mystery.

2. Ban. I'll believe him as an enemy and give over my trade.

1. Ban. Let us first see peace in Athens. There is no time so miserable but a man may be true.

Exeunt Thieves.

Enter [*Flavius*] the *Steward*, to *Timon.*

Stew. O you gods!
Is yond despis'd and ruinous man my lord?
Full of decay and failing? O monument
And wonder of good deeds evilly bestow'd!
What an alteration of honour
Has desp'rate want made!
What viler thing upon the earth than friends,
Who can bring noblest minds to basest ends!
How rarely does it meet with this time's guise
When man was wish'd to love his enemies!
Grant I may ever love, and rather woo
Those that would mischief me than those that do!
Has caught me in his eye; I will present
My honest grief unto him, and as my lord
Still serve him with my life. My dearest master!
Tim. Away! What art thou?
Stew. Have you forgot me, sir?
Tim. Why dost ask that? I have forgot all men;
Then, if thou grant'st th'art a man, I have forgot thee.
Stew. An honest poor servant of yours.
Tim. Then I know thee not.
I never had honest man about me, I.
All I kept were knaves, to serve-in meat to villains.
Stew. The gods are witness,
Nev'r did poor steward wear a truer grief
For his undone lord than mine eyes for you.
Tim. What, dost thou weep? Come nearer. Then I love thee
Because thou art a woman and disclaim'st
Flinty mankind, whose eyes do never give
But thorough lust and laughter. Pity's sleeping.
Strange times, that weep with laughing, not with weeping!
Stew. I beg of you to know me, good my lord,
T' accept my grief, and whilst this poor wealth lasts
To entertain me as your steward still.
Tim. Had I a steward
So true, so just, and now so comfortable?
It almost turns my dangerous nature mild.
Let me behold thy face. Surely, this man
Was born of woman.
Forgive my general and exceptless rashness,
You perpetual-sober gods! I do proclaim
One honest man. Mistake me not — but one!
No more, I pray — and he's a steward.
How fain would I have hated all mankind,
And thou redeem'st thyself! But all save thee
I fell with curses.
Methinks thou art more honest now than wise;
For, by oppressing and betraying me,
Thou mightst have sooner got another service;
For many so arrive at second masters,
Upon their first lord's neck. But tell me true
(For I must ever doubt, though ne'er so sure),
Is not thy kindness subtle, covetous,
If not a usuring kindness, and as rich men deal gifts,
Expecting in return twenty for one?
Stew. No, my most worthy master, in whose breast
Doubt and suspect, alas, are plac'd too late!
You should have fear'd false times when you did feast.
Suspect still comes where an estate is least.
That which I show, heaven knows, is merely love,
Duty, and zeal to your unmatched mind,
Care of your food and living; and believe it,
My most honour'd lord,
For any benefit that points to me,
Either in hope or present, I'd exchange
For this one wish, that you had power and wealth
To requite me by making rich yourself.
Tim. Look thee, 'tis so! Thou singly honest man,
Here, take! The gods out of my misery
Have sent thee treasure. Go, live rich and happy,
But thus condition'd: thou shalt build from men;
Hate all, curse all, show charity to none,
But let the famish'd flesh slide from the bone
Ere thou relieve the beggar. Give to dogs
What thou deniest to men. Let prisons swallow 'em,
Debts wither 'em to nothing. Be men like blasted woods,
And may diseases lick up their false bloods!
And so farewell, and thrive.
Stew. O, let me stay
And comfort you, my master.
Tim. If thou hat'st
Curses, stay not. Fly whilst thou art blest and free.
Ne'er see thou man, and let me ne'er see thee.

Exeunt [*severally*].

[Act V. Scene I. *The woods. Before* Timon's *cave.*]

Enter *Poet* and *Painter*. [*Timon* watches them from his cave.]

Paint. As I took note of the place, it cannot be far where he abides.

Poet. What's to be thought of him? Does the rumour hold for true, that he's so full of gold?

Paint. Certain. Alcibiades reports it. Phrynia and Timandra had gold of him. He likewise enrich'd poor straggling soldiers with great quantity. 'Tis said he gave unto his steward a mighty sum.

Poet. Then this breaking of his has been but a try for his friends?

Paint. Nothing else. You shall see him a palm in Athens again, and flourish with the highest. Therefore 'tis not amiss we tender our loves to him in this suppos'd distress of his. It will show honestly in us and is very likely to load our purposes with what they travail for, if it be a just and true report that goes of his having.

Poet. What have you now to present unto him?

Paint. Nothing at this time but my visitation. Only I will promise him an excellent piece.

Poet. I must serve him so too, tell him of an intent that's coming toward him.

Paint. Good as the best. Promising is the very air o' th' time; it opens the eyes of expectation. Performance is ever the duller for his act; and, but in the plainer and simpler kind of people, the deed of saying is quite out of use. To promise is most courtly and fashionable; performance is a kind of will or testament which argues a great sickness in his judgment that makes it.

Enter *Timon* from his cave.

Tim. [*aside*] Excellent workman! Thou canst not paint a man so bad as is thyself.

Poet. I am thinking what I shall say I have provided for him. It must be a personating of himself; a satire against the softness of prosperity, with a discovery of the infinite flatteries that follow youth and opulency.

Tim. [*aside*] Must thou needs stand for a villain in thine own work? Wilt thou whip thine own faults in other men? Do so, I have gold for thee.

Poet. Nay, let's seek him.
Then do we sin against our own estate
When we may profit meet, and come too late.

Paint. True.
When the day serves, before black-corner'd night,
Find what thou want'st by free and offer'd light.
Come.

Tim. [*aside*] I'll meet you at the turn. What a god's gold
That he is worshipp'd in a baser temple
Than where swine feed!
'Tis thou that rig'st the bark and plough'st the foam,
Settlest admired reverence in a slave.
To thee be worship! and thy saints for aye
Be crown'd with plagues, that thee alone obey!
Fit I meet them. [*Comes forward.*]

Poet. Hail, worthy Timon!

Paint. Our late noble master!

Tim. Have I once liv'd to see two honest men?

Poet. Sir,
Having often of your open bounty tasted,
Hearing you were retir'd, your friends fall'n off,
Whose thankless natures (O abhorred spirits!)
Not all the whips of heaven are large enough —
What, to you,
Whose starlike nobleness gave life and influence
To their whole being? I am rapt, and cannot cover
The monstrous bulk of this ingratitude
With any size of words.

Tim. Let it go naked; men may see't the better.
You that are honest, by being what you are,
Make them best seen and known.

Paint. He and myself
Have travail'd in the great show'r of your gifts,
And sweetly felt it.

Tim. Ay, you are honest men.

Paint. We are hither come to offer you our service.

Tim. Most honest men! Why, how shall I requite you?
Can you eat roots and drink cold water? No?

Both. What we can do, we'll do, to do you service.

Tim. Y'are honest men. Y'have heard that I have gold.

I am sure you have. Speak truth; y'are honest men.
Paint. So it is said, my noble lord; but therefore
Came not my friend, nor I.
Tim. Good honest men! Thou draw'st a counterfeit
Best in all Athens. Th'art indeed the best;
Thou counterfeit'st most lively.
Paint. So so, my lord.
Tim. E'en so, sir, as I say. — [*To the Poet*] And for thy fiction,
Why, thy verse swells with stuff so fine and smooth
That thou art even natural in thine art.
But for all this, my honest-natur'd friends,
I must needs say you have a little fault.
Marry, 'tis not monstrous in you; neither wish I
You take much pains to mend.
Both. Beseech your honour
To make it known to us.
Tim. You'll take it ill.
Both. Most thankfully, my lord.
Tim. Will you, indeed?
Both. Doubt it not, worthy lord.
Tim. There's never a one of you but trusts a knave
That mightily deceives you.
Both. Do we, my lord?
Tim. Ay, and you hear him cog, see him dissemble,
Know his gross patchery, love him, feed him,
Keep in your bosom; yet remain assur'd
That he's a made-up villain.
Paint. I know none such, my lord.
Poet. Nor I.
Tim. Look you, I love you well; I'll give you gold,
Rid me these villains from your companies.
Hang them or stab them, drown them in a draught,
Confound them by some course, and come to me,
I'll give you gold enough.
Both. Name them, my lord; let's know them.
Tim. You that way, and you this — but two in company;
Each man apart, all single and alone,
Yet an arch-villain keeps him company.
[*To Painter*] If, where thou art, two villains shall not be,
Come not near him. — [*To Poet*] If thou wouldst not reside
But where one villain is, then him abandon. —
Hence, pack! There's gold. You came for gold, ye slaves!
[*To Painter*] You have work for me; there's payment. Hence!
[*To Poet*] You are an alchemist; make gold of that. —
Out, rascal dogs!
Exeunt [*both, beaten out by Timon, who retires to his cave*].

Enter [*Flavius* the] *Steward* [and two *Senators.*

Stew. It is in vain that you would speak with Timon;
For he is set so only to himself
That nothing but himself which looks like man
Is friendly with him.
1. Sen. Bring us to his cave.
It is our part and promise to th' Athenians
To speak with Timon.
2. Sen. At all times alike
Men are not still the same. 'Twas time and griefs
That fram'd him thus. Time, with his fairer hand
Offering the fortunes of his former days,
The former man may make him. Bring us to him,
And chance it as it may.
Stew. Here is his cave.
Peace and content be here! Lord Timon! Timon!
Look out, and speak to friends. Th' Athenians
By two of their most reverend Senate greet thee.
Speak to them, noble Timon.

Enter *Timon* out of his cave.

Tim. Thou sun that comforts, burn! Speak and be hang'd!
For each true word a blister, and each false
Be as a cauterizing to the root o' th' tongue,
Consuming it with speaking!
1. Sen. Worthy Timon —
Tim. Of none but such as you, and you of Timon.
1. Sen. The senators of Athens greet thee, Timon.
Tim. I thank them; and would send them back the plague,
Could I but catch it for them.
1. Sen. O, forget
What we are sorry for ourselves in thee.
The senators with one consent of love
Entreat thee back to Athens, who have thought
On special dignities, which vacant lie
For thy best use and wearing.

2. Sen. They confess
Toward thee forgetfulness too general, gross;
And now the public body, which doth seldom
Play the recanter, feeling in itself
A lack of Timon's aid, hath sense withal
Of it own fail, restraining aid to Timon,
And send forth us to make their sorrowed render,
Together with a recompense more fruitful
Than their offence can weigh down by the dram;
Ay, even such heaps and sums of love and wealth
As shall to thee blot out what wrongs were theirs
And write in thee the figures of their love,
Ever to read them thine.
Tim. You witch me in it;
Surprise me to the very brink of tears.
Lend me a fool's heart and a woman's eyes,
And I'll beweep these comforts, worthy senators.
1. Sen. Therefore so please thee to return with us
And of our Athens, thine and ours, to take
The captainship, thou shalt be met with thanks,
Allow'd with absolute power, and thy good name
Live with authority. So soon we shall drive back
Of Alcibiades th' approaches wild,
Who, like a boar too savage, doth root up
His country's peace.
2. Sen. And shakes his threat'ning sword
Against the walls of Athens.
1. Sen. Therefore, Timon —
Tim. Well, sir, I will. Therefore I will, sir, thus:
If Alcibiades kill my countrymen,
Let Alcibiades know this of Timon,
That Timon cares not. But if he sack fair Athens
And take our goodly aged men by th' beards,
Giving our holy virgins to the stain
Of contumelious, beastly, mad-brain'd war,
Then let him know (and tell him Timon speaks it
In pity of our aged and our youth)
I cannot choose but tell him that I care not,
And let him take't at worst; for their knives care not,
While you have throats to answer. For myself,
There's not a whittle in th' unruly camp
But I do prize it at my love, before
The reverend'st throat in Athens. So I leave you
To the protection of the prosperous gods,
As thieves to keepers.
Stew. Stay not. All's in vain.
Tim. Why, I was writing of my epitaph.
It will be seen to-morrow. My long sickness
Of health and living now begins to mend,
And nothing brings me all things. Go, live still.
Be Alcibiades your plague, you his,
And last so long enough!
1. Sen. We speak in vain.
Tim. But yet I love my country and am not
One that rejoices in the common wrack,
As common bruit doth put it.
1. Sen. That's well spoke.
Tim. Commend me to my loving countrymen —
1. Sen. These words become your lips as they pass thorough them.
2. Sen. And enter in our ears like great triumphers
In their applauding gates.
Tim. Commend me to them,
And tell them that, to ease them of their griefs,
Their fears of hostile strokes, their achës, losses,
Their pangs of love, with other incident throes
That nature's fragile vessel doth sustain
In life's uncertain voyage, I will some kindness do them.
I'll teach them to prevent wild Alcibiades' wrath.
1. Sen. I like this well. He will return again.
Tim. I have a tree which grows here in my close
That mine own use invites me to cut down,
And shortly must I fell it. Tell my friends,
Tell Athens, in the sequence of degree
From high to low throughout, that whoso please
To stop affliction, let him take his haste,
Come hither ere my tree hath felt the axe,
And hang himself. I pray you do my greeting.
Stew. Trouble him no further. Thus you still shall find him.
Tim. Come not to me again; but say to Athens,
Timon hath made his everlasting mansion
Upon the beached verge of the salt flood,
Who once a day with his embossed froth
The turbulent surge shall cover. Thither come,
And let my gravestone be your oracle.
Lips, let sour words go by and language end.
What is amiss, plague and infection mend!
Graves only be men's works, and death their gain.

Sun, hide thy beams! Timon hath done his reign. *Exit Timon [into his cave].*
1. Sen. His discontents are unremovably
Coupled to nature.
2. Sen. Our hope in him is dead. Let us return
And strain what other means is left unto us
In our dear peril.
1. Sen. It requires swift foot. *Exeunt.*

[Scene II. *Before the walls of Athens.*]

Enter two other *Senators* with a *Messenger.*

1. Sen. Thou hast painfully discover'd. Are his files
As full as thy report?
Mess. I have spoke the least.
Besides, his expedition promises
Present approach.
2. Sen. We stand much hazard if they bring not Timon.
Mess. I met a courier, one mine ancient friend;
Whom, though in general part we were oppos'd,
Yet our old love had a particular force
And made us speak like friends. This man was riding
From Alcibiades to Timon's cave
With letters of entreaty, which imported
His fellowship i' th' cause against your city,
In part for his sake mov'd.

Enter the other *Senators* [from *Timon*].

1. Sen. Here come our brothers.
3. Sen. No talk of Timon! Nothing of him expect.
The enemies' drum is heard, and fearful scouring
Doth choke the air with dust. In, and prepare!
Ours is the fall, I fear; our foes the snare.
Exeunt.

[Scene III. *The woods.* Timon's *cave and a rude tomb seen.*]

Enter a *Soldier* in the woods, seeking *Timon.*

Sold. By all description this should be the place.
Who's here? Speak, ho! No answer? What is this?
Timon is dead, who hath outstretch'd his span.
Some beast rear'd this; here does not live a man.
Dead, sure; and this his grave. What's on this tomb
I cannot read. The character I'll take with wax.
Our captain hath in every figure skill,
An ag'd interpreter, though young in days.
Before proud Athens he's set down by this,
Whose fall the mark of his ambition is. *Exit.*

[Scene IV. *Before the walls of Athens.*]

Trumpets sound. Enter *Alcibiades* with his *Powers* before Athens.

Alcib. Sound to this coward and lascivious town
Our terrible approach.

Sound a parley. The *Senators* appear upon the walls.

Till now you have gone on and fill'd the time
With all licentious measure, making your wills
The scope of justice. Till now myself and such
As slept within the shadow of your power,
Have wander'd with our travers'd arms and breath'd
Our sufferance vainly. Now the time is flush,
When crouching marrow in the bearer strong
Cries, of itself 'No more!' Now breathless wrong
Shall sit and pant in your great chairs of ease,
And pursy insolence shall break his wind
With fear and horrid flight.
1. Sen. Noble and young,
When thy first griefs were but a mere conceit,
Ere thou hadst power or we had cause of fear,
We sent to thee, to give thy rages balm,
To wipe out our ingratitude with loves
Above their quantity.
2. Sen. So did we woo
Transformed Timon to our city's love
By humble message and by promis'd means.
We were not all unkind, nor all deserve
The common stroke of war.
1. Sen. These walls of ours
Were not erected by their hands from whom
You have receiv'd your griefs; nor are they such
That these great tow'rs, trophies, and schools should fall
For private faults in them.

2. Sen. Nor are they living
Who were the motives that you first went out.
Shame, that they wanted cunning, in excess
Hath broke their hearts. March, noble lord,
Into our city with thy banners spread.
By decimation, and a tithed death,
If thy revenges hunger for that food
Which nature loathes, take thou the destin'd tenth,
And by the hazard of the spotted die
Let die the spotted.

1. Sen. All have not offended.
For those that were, it is not square to take
On those that are, revenges. Crimes, like lands,
Are not inherited. Then, dear countryman,
Bring in thy ranks, but leave without thy rage.
Spare thy Athenian cradle, and those kin
Which in the bluster of thy wrath must fall
With those that have offended. Like a shepherd,
Approach the fold and cull th' infected forth,
But kill not all together.

2. Sen. What thou wilt,
Thou rather shalt enforce it with thy smile
Than hew to't with thy sword.

1. Sen. Set but thy foot
Against our rampir'd gates, and they shall ope,
So thou wilt send thy gentle heart before
To say thou't enter friendly.

2. Sen. Throw thy glove,
Or any token of thine honour else,
That thou wilt use the wars as thy redress
And not as our confusion, all thy powers
Shall make their harbour in our town till we
Have seal'd thy full desire.

Alcib. Then there's my glove;
Descend, and open your uncharged ports.
Those enemies of Timon's and mine own
Whom you yourselves shall set out for reproof
Fall, and no more. And, to atone your fears
With my more noble meaning, not a man
Shall pass his quarter or offend the stream
Of regular justice in your city's bounds
But shall be render'd to your public laws
At heaviest answer.

Both. 'Tis most nobly spoken.

Alcib. Descend, and keep your words.
[*The Senators descend and open the gates.*]

Enter [*Soldier* as] a *Messenger.*

Mess. My noble general, Timon is dead,
Entomb'd upon the very hem o' th' sea,
And on his gravestone this insculpture, which
With wax I brought away, whose soft impression
Interprets for my poor ignorance.

Alcibiades reads the Epitaph.

'Here lies a wretched corse, of wretched soul bereft.
Seek not my name. A plague consume you wicked caitiffs left!
Here lie I, Timon, who alive all living men did hate.
Pass by, and curse thy fill; but pass, and stay not here thy gait.'

These well express in thee thy latter spirits.
Though thou abhorr'dst in us our human griefs,
Scorn'dst our brine's flow and those our droplets which
From niggard nature fall, yet rich conceit
Taught thee to make vast Neptune weep for aye
On thy low grave, on faults forgiven. Dead
Is noble Timon, of whose memory
Hereafter more. Bring me into your city,
And I will use the olive, with my sword,
Make war breed peace, make peace stint war, make each
Prescribe to other, as each other's leech.
Let our drums strike. *Exeunt.*

Julius Cæsar

For the text of Julius Cæsar the First Folio is the sole authority. The play is exceptionally well printed, and there are few passages where one need hesitate as to the correct reading. One such is in 1, 3, 21, where the Folio reads 'glaz'd.' Rowe's emendation, 'glar'd,' is adopted in the present edition (cf. Macbeth, iii, 4, 96), though 'her gay glasying eyen' occurs in *Calisto and Melebea*, and 'that glazing star' in *Sir Clyomon and Sir Clamydes* (xxii, 295), and 'glaze-worm' for glowworm in Lyly's *Euphues*.

John Weever, who in his *Epigrammes* (1599) addressed a complimentary poem to 'honie-tong'd Shakespeare,' refers to Julius Cæsar in *The Mirror of Martyrs; or, The Life and Death of Sir John Oldcastle*, printed in 1601, but ready for the press, he tells us, 'some two yeares agoe':

> The many-headed multitude were drawne
> By *Brutus* speach, that *Cæsar* was ambitious,
> When cloquent *Mark Antonie* had showne
> His vertues, who but *Brutus* then was vicious?

This would give 1599, at the latest, as the probable date for Julius Cæsar. On September 21, 1599, Thomas Platter, a German visitor, attended a performance of some 'Tragedy vom ersten Keyser Julio Caesarc' in a theatre on the south side of the Thames. This was in all probability Shakespeare's play, and 1599 may be confidently accepted as the date of composition. It is not mentioned in Meres's list of 1598 (see p. 33, above).

Shakespeare found his materials in North's translation of Plutarch, in the lives of Julius Cæsar, Marcus Brutus, and Marcus Antonius. He has often merely turned North's eloquent prose into his own splendid verse. Phrase after phrase comes straight from North. Several dramas on Cæsar, in Latin, French, or English, were written before Shakespeare took up the subject.

Cæsar's character, as represented by Shakespeare, has evoked much hostile criticism. How can we accept this pompous, strutting figure, who stalks blindly to his doom, as 'the foremost man of all this world'?

> Cæsar shall forth. The things that threaten'd me
> Ne'er look'd but on my back. When they shall see
> The face of Cæsar, they are vanished.

Is this the conqueror, the wit, the scholar, the mighty organizer whose plans have changed all history — the dead but sceptred sovereign who still rules our spirits from his urn? Was the historical Cæsar so antipathetic to Shakespeare that he either could not or would not portray him adequately? To answer such questions is not difficult. Cæsar's lordly style, his pompous habit of speaking of himself in the third person, has been adequately explained by reference to the Latin tragedy of *Julius Cæsar*, by Muretus, first published in 1553. Muretus invested Cæsar with the style and manner of Seneca's braggart Hercules, and this device had established a fashion: the audience expected the Cæsarian dialect. And, quite apart from the mere question of language, Shakespeare is representing Cæsar, not in complete biography, but at the very end of his triumphant career. He has risen so high that he has become the victim of infatuation; he has lost that sense of values which alone could maintain him in equilibrium. This is the self-deification that Cassius finds intolerable (i, 2, 115ff.). It is not Cæsar in his best estate, then, that Shakespeare has to bring upon the stage, but Cæsar drunk with dominion, forgetful of his own mortality — careless, therefore, of the ordinary rules of prudence and self-protection. Whether or not this conception is historical need not concern us. It is easy to find evidence in Plutarch to justify it; and, in any case, it accords with the ancient doctrine of infatuation — that blindness which the gods send upon those who profanely aspire to divinity. The principle was familiar to Shakespeare. Nowhere has it been better expressed than in *Antony and Cleopatra* (iii, 13, 111 ff.):

But when we in our viciousness grow hard
(O misery on't!) the wise gods seel our eyes,
In our own filth drop our clear judgments, make us
Adore our errors, laugh at's while we strut
To our confusion.

The structure of the play has often been questioned and the correctness of the title has been challenged accordingly. It is rather the tragedy of Brutus, we are told, or of Brutus and Cassius, than the tragedy of Cæsar; and the plot is not unified, for Cæsar disappears in the middle of the drama: thus there are two catastrophes — the murder of Cæsar and the disaster at Philippi. It has even been suggested that Shakespeare reworked and combined two distinct lost plays — a *Death of Cæsar* and a *Revenge for Cæsar*. These strictures and this ingenious reconstruction come from ignoring the supernatural, which is as important an element in JULIUS CÆSAR as in *Macbeth* and *Hamlet*. There is no lack of unity in the plot. Cæsar vanquishes Brutus and Cassius at Philippi as truly as he vanquished Pompey at Pharsalus. Antony and Octavius are not Cæsar's avengers: they are merely Cæsar's agents; he avenges himself. These points are all brought out in significant speeches. In iii, 1, 270 ff., Antony prophesies that

Cæsar's spirit, ranging for revenge,
With Ate by his side come hot from hell,
Shall in these confines with a monarch's voice
Cry 'Havoc!' and let slip the dogs of war.

And, as Cæsar was warned to beware the ides of March, so Brutus, in a speech full of tragic irony, warns Cassius: 'Remember March; the ides of March remember.' This is at Sardis, in the fourth act, when the real crisis is imminent, and that night the ghost of Cæsar appears to Brutus and warns him of what is to come: 'Thou shalt see me at Philippi.' It was no idle threat. Nor is it an accident that Cassius takes leave of life with the words

Cæsar, thou art reveng'd
Even with the sword that kill'd thee,

and that Brutus, finding Cassius and Titinius dead, cries out

O Julius Cæsar, thou art mighty yet!
Thy spirit walks abroad and turns our swords
In our own proper entrails.

Cæsar, alive or dead, pervades and operates the drama — and not less after his death than in his life.

THE TRAGEDY OF
JULIUS CÆSAR

[Dramatis Personæ.

Julius Cæsar.
Octavius Cæsar, *Marcus Antonius*, *M. Æmilius Lepidus*, — Triumvirs after the death of *Julius Cæsar*.
Cicero, *Publius*, *Popilius Lena*, — Senators.
Marcus Brutus, *Cassius*, *Casca*, *Trebonius*, *Ligarius*, *Decius Brutus*, *Metellus Cimber*, *Cinna*, — Conspirators against *Julius Cæsar*.
Flavius and *Marullus*, Tribunes of the People.
Artemidorus, a Sophist.
A Soothsayer.
Cinna, a poet.
Another Poet.
Lucilius, *Titinius*, *Messala*, *Young Cato*, *Volumnius*, — friends to *Brutus* and *Cassius*.
Varro, *Clitus*, *Claudius*, *Strato*, *Lucius*, *Dardanius*, — servants to *Brutus*.
Pindarus, servant to *Cassius*.
A Servant to *Cæsar*; to *Antony*; to *Octavius*.

Calphurnia, wife to *Cæsar*.
Portia, wife to *Brutus*.

The Ghost of *Cæsar*.

Senators, Citizens, Guards, Attendants, &c.

Scene. — *Rome; near Sardis; near Philippi.*]

Act I. Scene I. [*Rome. A street.*]

Enter *Flavius*, *Marullus*, and certain *Commoners* over the stage.

Flav. Hence! home, you idle creatures, get you home!
Is this a holiday? What, know you not,
Being mechanical, you ought not walk
Upon a labouring day without the sign
Of your profession? Speak, what trade art thou?

Carpenter. Why, sir, a carpenter.

Mar. Where is thy leather apron and thy rule?
What dost thou with thy best apparel on?
You, sir, what trade are you?

Cobbler. Truly, sir, in respect of a fine workman I am but, as you would say, a cobbler.

Mar. But what trade art thou? Answer me directly.

Cob. A trade, sir, that I hope I may use with a safe conscience, which is indeed, sir, a mender of bad soles.

Mar. What trade, thou knave? Thou naughty knave, what trade?

Cob. Nay, I beseech you, sir, be not out with me. Yet if you be out, sir, I can mend you.

Mar. What mean'st thou by that? Mend me, thou saucy fellow?

Cob. Why, sir, cobble you.

Flav. Thou art a cobbler, art thou?

Cob. Truly, sir, all that I live by is with the awl. I meddle with no tradesman's matters nor women's matters, but with all. I am indeed, sir, a surgeon to old shoes. When they are in great danger, I recover them. As proper men as ever trod upon neat's leather have gone upon my handiwork.

Flav. But wherefore art not in thy shop to-day?
Why dost thou lead these men about the streets?

Cob. Truly, sir, to wear out their shoes, to get myself into more work. But indeed, sir, we make holiday to see Cæsar and to rejoice in his triumph.

Mar. Wherefore rejoice? What conquest brings he home?
What tributaries follow him to Rome
To grace in captive bonds his chariot wheels?
You blocks, you stones, you worse than senseless things!
O you hard hearts, you cruel men of Rome!
Knew you not Pompey? Many a time and oft
Have you climb'd up to walls and battlements,
To tow'rs and windows, yea, to chimney tops,
Your infants in your arms, and there have sat
The livelong day, with patient expectation,
To see great Pompey pass the streets of Rome.
And when you saw his chariot but appear,
Have you not made an universal shout,
That Tiber trembled underneath her banks
To hear the replication of your sounds
Made in her concave shores?
And do you now put on your best attire?
And do you now cull out a holiday?
And do you now strew flowers in his way
That comes in triumph over Pompey's blood?
Be gone!
Run to your houses, fall upon your knees,
Pray to the gods to intermit the plague
That needs must light on this ingratitude.

Flav. Go, go, good countrymen, and for this fault
Assemble all the poor men of your sort;
Draw them to Tiber banks, and weep your tears
Into the channel, till the lowest stream
Do kiss the most exalted shores of all.
Exeunt all the Commoners.
See, whe'r their basest metal be not mov'd.
They vanish tongue-tied in their guiltiness.
Go you down that way towards the Capitol;
This way will I. Disrobe the images
If you do find them deck'd with ceremonies.

Mar. May we do so?
You know it is the feast of Lupercal.

Flav. It is no matter. Let no images
Be hung with Cæsar's trophies. I'll about
And drive away the vulgar from the streets.
So do you too, where you perceive them thick.
These growing feathers pluck'd from Cæsar's wing
Will make him fly an ordinary pitch,
Who else would soar above the view of men
And keep us all in servile fearfulness. *Exeunt.*

[Scene II. *Rome. A public place.*]

[*Music.*] Enter *Cæsar, Antony* (for the course), *Calphurnia, Portia, Decius, Cicero, Brutus, Cassius, Casca,* [a great crowd following, among them,] a *Soothsayer*; after them, *Marullus* and *Flavius.*

Cæs. Calphurnia.

Casca. Peace, ho! Cæsar speaks.
[*Music ceases.*]

Cæs. Calphurnia.

Cal. Here, my lord.

Cæs. Stand you directly in Antonius' way
When he doth run his course. Antonius.

Ant. Cæsar, my lord?

Cæs. Forget not in your speed, Antonius,
To touch Calphurnia; for our elders say
The barren, touched in this holy chase,
Shake off their sterile curse.

Ant. I shall remember.
When Cæsar says 'Do this,' it is perform'd.

Cæs. Set on, and leave no ceremony out.
[*Music.*]

Sooth. Cæsar!

Cæs. Ha! Who calls?

Casca. Bid every noise be still. Peace yet again! [*Music ceases.*]

Cæs. Who is it in the press that calls on me?
I hear a tongue shriller than all the music
Cry 'Cæsar!' Speak. Cæsar is turn'd to hear.

Sooth. Beware the ides of March.

Cæs. What man is that?

Bru. A soothsayer bids you beware the ides of March.

Cæs. Set him before me; let me see his face.

Cass. Fellow, come from the throng; look upon Cæsar.

Cæs. What say'st thou to me now? Speak once again.

Sooth. Beware the ides of March.

Cæs. He is a dreamer. Let us leave him. Pass.

Sennet. Exeunt. Manent Brutus and Cassius.

Cass. Will you go see the order of the course?

Bru. Not I.

Cass. I pray you do.

Bru. I am not gamesome. I do lack some part
Of that quick spirit that is in Antony.
Let me not hinder, Cassius, your desires.
I'll leave you.

Cass. Brutus, I do observe you now of late;
I have not from your eyes that gentleness
And show of love as I was wont to have.

You bear too stubborn and too strange a hand
Over your friend that loves you.
Bru. Cassius,
Be not deceiv'd. If I have veil'd my look,
I turn the trouble of my countenance
Merely upon myself. Vexed I am
Of late with passions of some difference,
Conceptions only proper to myself,
Which give some soil, perhaps, to my behaviours;
But let not therefore my good friends be griev'd
(Among which number, Cassius, be you one)
Nor construe any further my neglect
Than that poor Brutus, with himself at war,
Forgets the shows of love to other men.
Cass. Then, Brutus, I have much mistook your passion;
By means whereof this breast of mine hath buried
Thoughts of great value, worthy cogitations.
Tell me, good Brutus, can you see your face?
Bru. No, Cassius; for the eye sees not itself
But by reflection, by some other things.
Cass. 'Tis just.
And it is very much lamented, Brutus,
That you have no such mirrors as will turn
Your hidden worthiness into your eye,
That you might see your shadow. I have heard
Where many of the best respect in Rome
(Except immortal Cæsar), speaking of Brutus
And groaning underneath this age's yoke,
Have wish'd that noble Brutus had his eyes.
Bru. Into what dangers would you lead me, Cassius,
That you would have me seek into myself
For that which is not in me?
Cass. Therefore, good Brutus, be prepar'd to hear;
And since you know you cannot see yourself
So well as by reflection, I, your glass,
Will modestly discover to yourself
That of yourself which you yet know not of.
And be not jealous on me, gentle Brutus.
Were I a common laugher, or did use
To stale with ordinary oaths my love
To every new protester; if you know
That I do fawn on men and hug them hard,
And after scandal them; or if you know
That I profess myself in banqueting
To all the rout, then hold me dangerous.

Flourish and shout.

Bru. What means this shouting? I do fear the people
Choose Cæsar for their king.
Cass. Ay, do you fear it?
Then must I think you would not have it so.
Bru. I would not, Cassius; yet I love him well.
But wherefore do you hold me here so long?
What is it that you would impart to me?
If it be aught toward the general good,
Set honour in one eye and death i' th' other,
And I will look on both indifferently;
For let the gods so speed me as I love
The name of honour more than I fear death.
Cass. I know that virtue to be in you, Brutus,
As well as I do know your outward favour.
Well, honour is the subject of my story.
I cannot tell what you and other men
Think of this life; but for my single self,
I had as lief not be as live to be
In awe of such a thing as I myself.
I was born free as Cæsar; so were you.
We both have fed as well, and we can both
Endure the winter's cold as well as he.
For once, upon a raw and gusty day,
The troubled Tiber chafing with her shores,
Cæsar said to me, 'Dar'st thou, Cassius, now
Leap in with me into this angry flood
And swim to yonder point?' Upon the word,
Accoutred as I was, I plunged in
And bade him follow. So indeed he did.
The torrent roar'd, and we did buffet it
With lusty sinews, throwing it aside
And stemming it with hearts of controversy.
But ere we could arrive the point propos'd,
Cæsar cried, 'Help me, Cassius, or I sink!'
I, as Æneas, our great ancestor,
Did from the flames of Troy upon his shoulder
The old Anchises bear, so from the waves of Tiber
Did I the tired Cæsar. And this man
Is now become a god, and Cassius is
A wretched creature and must bend his body
If Cæsar carelessly but nod on him.
He had a fever when he was in Spain,
And when the fit was on him, I did mark
How he did shake. 'Tis true, this god did shake.
His coward lips did from their colour fly,
And that same eye whose bend doth awe the world
Did lose his lustre. I did hear him groan.
Ay, and that tongue of his that bade the Romans
Mark him and write his speeches in their books,
Alas, it cried, 'Give me some drink, Titinius,'
As a sick girl! Ye gods, it doth amaze me
A man of such a feeble temper should

So get the start of the majestic world
And bear the palm alone.

Shout. Flourish.

Bru. Another general shout?
I do believe that these applauses are
For some new honours that are heap'd on Cæsar.
Cass. Why, man, he doth bestride the narrow world
Like a Colossus, and we petty men
Walk under his huge legs and peep about
To find ourselves dishonourable graves.
Men at some time are masters of their fates.
The fault, dear Brutus, is not in our stars,
But in ourselves, that we are underlings.
'Brutus,' and 'Cæsar.' What should be in that 'Cæsar'?
Why should that name be sounded more than yours?
Write them together: yours is as fair a name.
Sound them: it doth become the mouth as well.
Weigh them: it is as heavy. Conjure with 'em:
'Brutus' will start a spirit as soon as 'Cæsar.'
Now in the names of all the gods at once,
Upon what meat doth this our Cæsar feed
That he is grown so great? Age, thou art sham'd!
Rome, thou hast lost the breed of noble bloods!
When went there by an age since the great Flood
But it was fam'd with more than with one man?
When could they say (till now) that talk'd of Rome
That her wide walls encompass'd but one man?
Now is it Rome indeed, and room enough,
When there is in it but one only man!
O, you and I have heard our fathers say
There was a Brutus once that would have brook'd
Th' eternal devil to keep his state in Rome
As easily as a king.
Bru. That you do love me I am nothing jealous.
What you would work me to, I have some aim.
How I have thought of this, and of these times,
I shall recount hereafter. For this present,
I would not (so with love I might entreat you)
Be any further mov'd. What you have said
I will consider; what you have to say
I will with patience hear, and find a time
Both meet to hear and answer such high things.
Till then, my noble friend, chew upon this:
Brutus had rather be a villager
Than to repute himself a son of Rome
Under these hard conditions as this time
Is like to lay upon us.
Cass. I am glad
That my weak words have struck but thus much show
Of fire from Brutus.

Enter *Cæsar* and his *Train.*

Bru. The games are done, and Cæsar is returning.
Cass. As they pass by, pluck Casca by the sleeve,
And he will (after his sour fashion) tell you
What hath proceeded worthy note to-day.
Bru. I will do so. But look you, Cassius!
The angry spot doth glow on Cæsar's brow,
And all the rest look like a chidden train.
Calphurnia's cheek is pale, and Cicero
Looks with such ferret and such fiery eyes
As we have seen him in the Capitol,
Being cross'd in conference by some senators.
Cass. Casca will tell us what the matter is.
Cæs. Antonius.
Ant. Cæsar?
Cæs. Let me have men about me that are fat,
Sleek-headed men, and such as sleep a-nights.
Yond Cassius has a lean and hungry look.
He thinks too much. Such men are dangerous.
Ant. Fear him not, Cæsar; he's not dangerous.
He is a noble Roman, and well given.
Cæs. Would he were fatter! But I fear him not.
Yet if my name were liable to fear,
I do not know the man I should avoid
So soon as that spare Cassius. He reads much,
He is a great observer, and he looks
Quite through the deeds of men. He loves no plays
As thou dost, Antony; he hears no music.
Seldom he smiles, and smiles in such a sort
As if he mock'd himself and scorn'd his spirit
That could be mov'd to smile at anything.
Such men as he be never at heart's ease
Whiles they behold a greater than themselves,
And therefore are they very dangerous.
I rather tell thee what is to be fear'd
Than what I fear; for always I am Cæsar.
Come on my right hand, for this ear is deaf,
And tell me truly what thou think'st of him.

Sennet. Exeunt Cæsar and his Train.
[*Manet Casca.*]

Casca. You pull'd me by the cloak. Would you speak with me?

Bru. Ay, Casca. Tell us what hath chanc'd to-day
That Cæsar looks so sad.

Casca. Why, you were with him, were you not?

Bru. I should not then ask Casca what had chanc'd.

Casca. Why, there was a crown offer'd him; and being offer'd him, he put it by with the back of his hand thus; and then the people fell a-shouting.

Bru. What was the second noise for?

Casca. Why, for that too.

Cass. They shouted thrice. What was the last cry for?

Casca. Why, for that too.

Bru. Was the crown offer'd him thrice?

Casca. Ay, marry, was't! and he put it by thrice, every time gentler than other; and at every putting-by mine honest neighbours shouted.

Cass. Who offer'd him the crown?

Casca. Why, Antony.

Bru. Tell us the manner of it, gentle Casca.

Casca. I can as well be hang'd as tell the manner of it. It was mere foolery; I did not mark it. I saw Mark Antony offer him a crown — yet 'twas not a crown neither, 'twas one of these coronets — and, as I told you, he put it by once; but for all that, to my thinking, he would fain have had it. Then he offered it to him again; then he put it by again; but to my thinking, he was very loath to lay his fingers off it. And then he offered it the third time. He put it the third time by; and still as he refus'd it, the rabblement hooted, and clapp'd their chopt hands, and threw up their sweaty night-caps, and uttered such a deal of stinking breath because Cæsar refus'd the crown that it had, almost, chok'd Cæsar; for he swoonded and fell down at it. And for mine own part, I durst not laugh, for fear of opening my lips and receiving the bad air.

Cass. But soft, I pray you. What, did Cæsar swound?

Casca. He fell down in the market place and foam'd at mouth and was speechless.

Bru. 'Tis very like. He hath the falling sickness.

Cass. No, Cæsar hath it not; but you, and I,
And honest Casca, we have the falling sickness.

Casca. I know not what you mean by that, but I am sure Cæsar fell down. If the tag-rag people did not clap him and hiss him, according as he pleas'd and displeas'd them, as they use to do the players in the theatre, I am no true man.

Bru. What said he when he came unto himself?

Casca. Marry, before he fell down, when he perceiv'd the common herd was glad he refus'd the crown, he pluck'd me ope his doublet and offer'd them his throat to cut. An I had been a man of any occupation, if I would not have taken him at a word I would I might go to hell among the rogues. And so he fell. When he came to himself again, he said, if he had done or said anything amiss, he desir'd their worships to think it was his infirmity. Three or four wenches where I stood cried 'Alas, good soul!' and forgave him with all their hearts. But there's no heed to be taken of them. If Cæsar had stabb'd their mothers, they would have done no less.

Bru. And after that, he came thus sad away?

Casca. Ay.

Cass. Did Cicero say anything?

Casca. Ay, he spoke Greek.

Cass. To what effect?

Casca. Nay, an I tell you that, I'll ne'er look you i' th' face again. But those that understood him smil'd at one another and shook their heads; but for mine own part, it was Greek to me. I could tell you more news too. Marullus and Flavius, for pulling scarfs off Cæsar's images, are put to silence. Fare you well. There was more foolery yet, if I could remember it.

Cass. Will you sup with me to-night, Casca?

Casca. No, I am promis'd forth.

Cass. Will you dine with me to-morrow?

Casca. Ay, if I be alive, and your mind hold, and your dinner worth the eating.

Cass. Good. I will expect you.

Casca. Do so. Farewell both. *Exit.*

Bru. What a blunt fellow is this grown to be!
He was quick mettle when he went to school.

Cass. So is he now in execution
Of any bold or noble enterprise,
However he puts on this tardy form.
This rudeness is a sauce to his good wit,
Which gives men stomach to disgest his words
With better appetite.

Bru. And so it is. For this time I will leave you.
To-morrow, if you please to speak with me,
I will come home to you; or if you will,
Come home to me, and I will wait for you.

Cass. I will do so. Till then, think of the world. *Exit Brutus.*

Well, Brutus, thou art noble; yet I see
Thy honourable mettle may be wrought
From that it is dispos'd. Therefore it is meet
That noble minds keep ever with their likes;
For who so firm that cannot be seduc'd?
Cæsar doth bear me hard; but he loves Brutus.
If I were Brutus now and he were Cassius,
He should not humour me. I will this night,
In several hands, in at his windows throw,
As if they came from several citizens,
Writings, all tending to the great opinion
That Rome holds of his name; wherein obscurely
Cæsar's ambition shall be glanced at.
And after this let Cæsar seat him sure,
For we will shake him, or worse days endure.
Exit.

[Scene III. *Rome. A street.*]

Thunder and lightning. Enter, [from opposite sides,] *Casca,* [with his sword drawn,] and *Cicero.*

Cic. Good even, Casca. Brought you Cæsar home?
Why are you breathless? and why stare you so?
Casca. Are not you mov'd when all the sway of earth
Shakes like a thing unfirm? O Cicero,
I have seen tempests when the scolding winds
Have riv'd the knotty oaks, and I have seen
Th' ambitious ocean swell and rage and foam
To be exalted with the threat'ning clouds;
But never till to-night, never till now,
Did I go through a tempest dropping fire.
Either there is a civil strife in heaven,
Or else the world, too saucy with the gods,
Incenses them to send destruction.
Cic. Why, saw you any thing more wonderful?
Casca. A common slave (you know him well by sight)
Held up his left hand, which did flame and burn
Like twenty torches join'd; and yet his hand,
Not sensible of fire, remain'd unscorch'd.
Besides (I ha' not since put up my sword),
Against the Capitol I met a lion,
Who glar'd upon me, and went surly by
Without annoying me. And there were drawn
Upon a heap a hundred ghastly women,
Transformed with their fear, who swore they saw
Men, all in fire, walk up and down the streets.
And yesterday the bird of night did sit
Even at noonday upon the market place,
Hooting and shrieking. When these prodigies
Do so conjointly meet, let not men say
'These are their reasons — they are natural,'
For I believe they are portentous things
Unto the climate that they point upon.
Cic. Indeed it is a strange-disposed time.
But men may construe things after their fashion,
Clean from the purpose of the things themselves.
Comes Cæsar to the Capitol to-morrow?
Casca. He doth; for he did bid Antonius
Send word to you he would be there to-morrow.
Cic. Good night then, Casca. This disturbed sky
Is not to walk in.
Casca. Farewell, Cicero.
Exit Cicero.

Enter *Cassius.*

Cass. Who's there?
Casca. A Roman.
Cass. Casca, by your voice.
Casca. Your ear is good. Cassius, what night is this!
Cass. A very pleasing night to honest men.
Casca. Who ever knew the heavens menace so?
Cass. Those that have known the earth so full of faults.
For my part, I have walk'd about the streets,
Submitting me unto the perilous night,
And, thus unbraced, Casca, as you see,
Have bar'd my bosom to the thunder-stone;
And when the cross blue lightning seem'd to open
The breast of heaven, I did present myself
Even in the aim and very flash of it.
Casca. But wherefore did you so much tempt the heavens?
It is the part of men to fear and tremble
When the most mighty gods by tokens send
Such dreadful heralds to astonish us.
Cass. You are dull, Casca, and those sparks of life
That should be in a Roman you do want,
Or else you use not. You look pale, and gaze,
And put on fear, and cast yourself in wonder,
To see the strange impatience of the heavens;
But if you would consider the true cause —
Why all these fires, why all these gliding ghosts,
Why birds and beasts, from quality and kind;
Why old men fool and children calculate;

Why all these things change from their ordinance,
Their natures, and preformed faculties,
To monstrous quality — why, you shall find
That heaven hath infus'd them with these spirits
To make them instruments of fear and warning
Unto some monstrous state.
Now could I, Casca, name to thee a man
Most like this dreadful night
That thunders, lightens, opens graves, and roars
As doth the lion in the Capitol;
A man no mightier than thyself or me
In personal action, yet prodigious grown
And fearful, as these strange eruptions are.

Casca. 'Tis Cæsar that you mean. Is it not, Cassius?

Cass. Let it be who it is. For Romans now
Have thews and limbs like to their ancestors;
But woe the while! our fathers' minds are dead,
And we are govern'd with our mothers' spirits;
Our yoke and sufferance show us womanish.

Casca. Indeed, they say the senators tomorrow
Mean to establish Cæsar as a king,
And he shall wear his crown by sea and land
In every place save here in Italy.

Cass. I know where I will wear this dagger then;
Cassius from bondage will deliver Cassius.
Therein, ye gods, you make the weak most strong;
Therein, ye gods, you tyrants do defeat.
Nor stony tower, nor walls of beaten brass,
Nor airless dungeon, nor strong links of iron,
Can be retentive to the strength of spirit;
But life, being weary of these worldly bars,
Never lacks power to dismiss itself.
If I know this, know all the world besides,
That part of tyranny that I do bear
I can shake off at pleasure. *Thunder still.*

Casca. So can I.
So every bondman in his own hand bears
The power to cancel his captivity.

Cass. And why should Cæsar be a tyrant then?
Poor man! I know he would not be a wolf
But that he sees the Romans are but sheep;
He were no lion, were not Romans hinds.
Those that with haste will make a mighty fire
Begin it with weak straws. What trash is Rome,
What rubbish and what offal, when it serves
For the base matter to illuminate
So vile a thing as Cæsar! But, O grief,
Where hast thou led me? I, perhaps, speak this
Before a willing bondman. Then I know
My answer must be made. But I am arm'd,
And dangers are to me indifferent.

Casca. You speak to Casca, and to such a man
That is no fleering telltale. Hold, my hand.
Be factious for redress of all these griefs,
And I will set this foot of mine as far
As who goes farthest.

Cass. There's a bargain made.
Now know you, Casca, I have mov'd already
Some certain of the noblest-minded Romans
To undergo with me an enterprise
Of honourable-dangerous consequence;
And I do know, by this they stay for me
In Pompey's Porch; for now, this fearful night,
There is no stir or walking in the streets,
And the complexion of the element
In favour 's like the work we have in hand,
Most bloody, fiery, and most terrible.

Enter *Cinna.*

Casca. Stand close awhile, for here comes one in haste.

Cass. 'Tis Cinna. I do know him by his gait.
He is a friend. Cinna, where haste you so?

Cin. To find out you. Who's that? Metellus Cimber?

Cass. No, it is Casca, one incorporate
To our attempts. Am I not stay'd for, Cinna?

Cin. I am glad on't. What a fearful night is this!
There's two or three of us have seen strange sights.

Cass. Am I not stay'd for? Tell me.

Cin. Yes, you are.
O Cassius, if you could
But win the noble Brutus to our party —

Cass. Be you content. Good Cinna, take this paper
And look you lay it in the prætor's chair,
Where Brutus may but find it. And throw this
In at his window. Set this up with wax
Upon old Brutus' statue. All this done,
Repair to Pompey's Porch, where you shall find us.
Is Decius Brutus and Trebonius there?

Cin. All but Metellus Cimber, and he's gone
To seek you at your house. Well, I will hie
And so bestow these papers as you bade me.

Cass. That done, repair to Pompey's Theatre.
Exit Cinna.
Come, Casca, you and I will yet ere day
See Brutus at his house. Three parts of him

Is ours already, and the man entire
Upon the next encounter yields him ours.

Casca. O, he sits high in all the people's hearts;
And that which would appear offence in us,
His countenance, like richest alchemy,
Will change to virtue and to worthiness.

Cass. Him and his worth and our great need of him
You have right well conceited. Let us go,
For it is after midnight; and ere day
We will awake him and be sure of him.
Exeunt.

ACT II. [Scene I. *Rome.*]

Enter *Brutus* in his orchard.

Bru. What, Lucius, ho!
I cannot by the progress of the stars
Give guess how near to day. Lucius, I say!
I would it were my fault to sleep so soundly.
When, Lucius, when? Awake, I say! What, Lucius!

Enter *Lucius.*

Luc. Call'd you, my lord?

Bru. Get me a taper in my study, Lucius.
When it is lighted, come and call me here.

Luc. I will, my lord. *Exit.*

Bru. It must be by his death; and for my part,
I know no personal cause to spurn at him,
But for the general. He would be crown'd.
How that might change his nature, there's the question.
It is the bright day that brings forth the adder,
And that craves wary walking. Crown him — that!
And then I grant we put a sting in him
That at his will he may do danger with.
Th' abuse of greatness is, when it disjoins
Remorse from power. And to speak truth of Cæsar,
I have not known when his affections sway'd
More than his reason. But 'tis a common proof
That lowliness is young ambition's ladder,
Whereto the climber-upward turns his face;
But when he once attains the upmost round,
He then unto the ladder turns his back,
Looks in the clouds, scorning the base degrees
By which he did ascend. So Cæsar may.
Then lest he may, prevent. And since the quarrel
Will bear no colour for the thing he is,
Fashion it thus: that what he is, augmented,
Would run to these and these extremities;
And therefore think him as a serpent's egg,
Which, hatch'd, would as his kind grow mischievous,
And kill him in the shell.

Enter *Lucius.*

Luc. The taper burneth in your closet, sir.
Searching the window for a flint, I found
This paper, thus seal'd up; and I am sure
It did not lie there when I went to bed.
Gives him the letter.

Bru. Get you to bed again; it is not day.
Is not to-morrow, boy, the ides of March?

Luc. I know not, sir.

Bru. Look in the calendar and bring me word.

Luc. I will, sir. *Exit.*

Bru. The exhalations, whizzing in the air,
Give so much light that I may read by them.
Opens the letter and reads.

'Brutus, thou sleep'st. Awake, and see thyself!
Shall Rome, &c. Speak, strike, redress!'

'Brutus, thou sleep'st. Awake!'
Such instigations have been often dropp'd
Where I have took them up.
'Shall Rome, &c.' Thus must I piece it out:
Shall Rome stand under one man's awe? What, Rome?
My ancestors did from the streets of Rome
The Tarquin drive when he was call'd a king.
'Speak, strike, redress!' Am I entreated
To speak and strike? O Rome, I make thee promise,
If the redress will follow, thou receivest
Thy full petition at the hand of Brutus!

Enter *Lucius.*

Luc. Sir, March is wasted fifteen days.
Knock within.

Bru. 'Tis good. Go to the gate; somebody knocks.
[*Exit Lucius.*]
Since Cassius first did whet me against Cæsar,
I have not slept.
Between the acting of a dreadful thing
And the first motion, all the interim is
Like a phantasma or a hideous dream.

The genius and the mortal instruments
Are then in council, and the state of man,
Like to a little kingdom, suffers then
The nature of an insurrection.

Enter *Lucius.*

Luc. Sir, 'tis your brother Cassius at the door,
Who doth desire to see you.

Bru. Is he alone?

Luc. No, sir, there are moe with him.

Bru. Do you know them?

Luc. No, sir. Their hats are pluck'd about their ears
And half their faces buried in their cloaks,
That by no means I may discover them
By any mark of favour.

Bru. Let 'em enter.

[*Exit Lucius.*]

They are the faction. O conspiracy,
Sham'st thou to show thy dang'rous brow by night,
When evils are most free? O, then by day
Where wilt thou find a cavern dark enough
To mask thy monstrous visage? Seek none, conspiracy.
Hide it in smiles and affability!
For if thou path, thy native semblance on,
Not Erebus itself were dim enough
To hide thee from prevention.

Enter the *Conspirators, Cassius, Casca, Decius, Cinna, Metellus* [*Cimber*], and *Trebonius.*

Cass. I think we are too bold upon your rest.
Good morrow, Brutus. Do we trouble you?

Bru. I have been up this hour, awake all night.
Know I these men that come along with you?

Cass. Yes, every man of them; and no man here
But honours you; and every one doth wish
You had but that opinion of yourself
Which every noble Roman bears of you.
This is Trebonius.

Bru. He is welcome hither.

Cass. This, Decius Brutus.

Bru. He is welcome too.

Cass. This, Casca; this, Cinna; and this, Metellus Cimber.

Bru. They are all welcome.
What watchful cares do interpose themselves
Betwixt your eyes and night?

Cass. Shall I entreat a word?

They whisper.

Dec. Here lies the east. Doth not the day break here?

Casca. No.

Cin. O, pardon, sir, it doth; and yon grey lines
That fret the clouds are messengers of day.

Casca. You shall confess that you are both deceiv'd.
Here, as I point my sword, the sun arises,
Which is a great way growing on the south,
Weighing the youthful season of the year.
Some two months hence, up higher toward the north
He first presents his fire; and the high east
Stands as the Capitol, directly here.

Bru. Give me your hands all over, one by one.

Cass. And let us swear our resolution.

Bru. No, not an oath. If not the face of men,
The sufferance of our souls, the time's abuse —
If these be motives weak, break off betimes,
And every man hence to his idle bed.
So let high-sighted tyranny range on
Till each man drop by lottery. But if these
(As I am sure they do) bear fire enough
To kindle cowards and to steel with valour
The melting spirits of women, then, countrymen,
What need we any spur but our own cause
To prick us to redress? what other bond
Than secret Romans that have spoke the word
And will not palter? and what other oath
Than honesty to honesty engag'd
That this shall be, or we will fall for it?
Swear priests and cowards and men cautelous,
Old feeble carrions and such suffering souls
That welcome wrongs; unto bad causes swear
Such creatures as men doubt; but do not stain
The even virtue of our enterprise,
Nor th' insuppressive mettle of our spirits,
To think that or our cause or our performance
Did need an oath; when every drop of blood
That every Roman bears, and nobly bears,
Is guilty of a several bastardy
If he do break the smallest particle
Of any promise that hath pass'd from him.

Cass. But what of Cicero? Shall we sound him?
I think he will stand very strong with us.

Casca. Let us not leave him out.

Cin. No, by no means.

Met. O, let us have him! for his silver hairs
Will purchase us a good opinion
And buy men's voices to commend our deeds.

It shall be said his judgment rul'd our hands.
Our youths and wildness shall no whit appear,
But all be buried in his gravity.
Bru. O, name him not! Let us not break with him;
For he will never follow anything
That other men begin.
Cass. Then leave him out.
Casca. Indeed he is not fit.
Dec. Shall no man else be touch'd but only Cæsar?
Cass. Decius, well urg'd. I think it is not meet
Mark Antony, so well belov'd of Cæsar,
Should outlive Cæsar. We shall find of him
A shrewd contriver; and you know, his means,
If he improve them, may well stretch so far
As to annoy us all; which to prevent,
Let Antony and Cæsar fall together.
Bru. Our course will seem too bloody, Caius Cassius,
To cut the head off and then hack the limbs,
Like wrath in death and envy afterwards;
For Antony is but a limb of Cæsar.
Let us be sacrificers, but not butchers, Caius.
We all stand up against the spirit of Cæsar,
And in the spirit of men there is no blood.
O that we then could come by Cæsar's spirit
And not dismember Cæsar! But, alas,
Cæsar must bleed for it! And, gentle friends,
Let's kill him boldly, but not wrathfully;
Let's carve him as a dish fit for the gods,
Not hew him as a carcass fit for hounds.
And let our hearts, as subtle masters do,
Stir up their servants to an act of rage
And after seem to chide 'em. This shall make
Our purpose necessary, and not envious;
Which so appearing to the common eyes,
We shall be call'd purgers, not murderers.
And for Mark Antony, think not of him;
For he can do no more than Cæsar's arm
When Cæsar's head is off.
Cass. Yet I fear him;
For in the ingrafted love he bears to Cæsar —
Bru. Alas, good Cassius, do not think of him!
If he love Cæsar, all that he can do
Is to himself — take thought, and die for Cæsar.
And that were much he should; for he is given
To sports, to wildness, and much company.
Treb. There is no fear in him. Let him not die;
For he will live, and laugh at this hereafter.
Clock strikes.
Bru. Peace! Count the clock.
Cass. The clock hath stricken three.
Treb. 'Tis time to part.
Cass. But it is doubtful yet
Whether Cæsar will come forth to-day or no;
For he is superstitious grown of late,
Quite from the main opinion he held once
Of fantasy, of dreams, and ceremonies.
It may be these apparent prodigies,
The unaccustom'd terror of this night,
And the persuasion of his augurers
May hold him from the Capitol to-day.
Dec. Never fear that. If he be so resolv'd,
I can o'ersway him; for he loves to hear
That unicorns may be betray'd with trees
And bears with glasses, elephants with holes,
Lions with toils, and men with flatterers;
But when I tell him he hates flatterers,
He says he does, being then most flattered.
Let me work;
For I can give his humour the true bent
And I will bring him to the Capitol.
Cass. Nay, we will all of us be there to fetch him.
Bru. By the eighth hour. Is that the uttermost?
Cin. Be that the uttermost, and fail not then.
Met. Caius Ligarius doth bear Cæsar hard,
Who rated him for speaking well of Pompey.
I wonder none of you have thought of him.
Bru. Now, good Metellus, go along by him.
He loves me well, and I have given him reasons.
Send him but hither, and I'll fashion him.
Cass. The morning comes upon's. We'll leave you, Brutus.
And, friends, disperse yourselves; but all remember
What you have said and show yourselves true Romans.
Bru. Good gentlemen, look fresh and merrily.
Let not our looks put on our purposes,
But bear it as our Roman actors do,
With untir'd spirits and formal constancy.
And so good morrow to you every one.
Exeunt. Manet Brutus.
Boy! Lucius! Fast asleep? It is no matter.
Enjoy the honey-heavy dew of slumber.
Thou hast no figures nor no fantasies
Which busy care draws in the brains of men;
Therefore thou sleep'st so sound.

Enter *Portia.*

Por. Brutus, my lord!
Bru. Portia! What mean you? Wherefore rise you now?
It is not for your health thus to commit
Your weak condition to the raw cold morning.

Por. Nor for yours neither. Y' have ungently, Brutus,
Stole from my bed. And yesternight at supper
You suddenly arose and walk'd about,
Musing and sighing with your arms across;
And when I ask'd you what the matter was,
You star'd upon me with ungentle looks.
I urg'd you further; then you scratch'd your head
And too impatiently stamp'd with your foot.
Yet I insisted; yet you answer'd not,
But with an angry wafture of your hand
Gave sign for me to leave you. So I did,
Fearing to strengthen that impatience
Which seem'd too much enkindled, and withal
Hoping it was but an effect of humour,
Which sometime hath his hour with every man.
It will not let you eat nor talk nor sleep,
And could it work so much upon your shape
As it hath much prevail'd on your condition,
I should not know you Brutus. Dear my lord,
Make me acquainted with your cause of grief.
Bru. I am not well in health, and that is all.
Por. Brutus is wise and, were he not in health,
He would embrace the means to come by it.
Bru. Why, so I do. Good Portia, go to bed.
Por. Is Brutus sick, and is it physical
To walk unbraced and suck up the humours
Of the dank morning? What, is Brutus sick,
And will he steal out of his wholesome bed
To dare the vile contagion of the night,
And tempt the rheumy and unpurged air,
To add unto his sickness? No, my Brutus.
You have some sick offence within your mind,
Which by the right and virtue of my place
I ought to know of; and upon my knees
I charm you, by my once commended beauty,
By all your vows of love, and that great vow
Which did incorporate and make us one,
That you unfold to me, yourself, your half,
Why you are heavy — and what men to-night
Have had resort to you; for here have been
Some six or seven, who did hide their faces
Even from darkness.
Bru. Kneel not, gentle Portia.
Por. I should not need if you were gentle Brutus.
Within the bond of marriage, tell me, Brutus,
Is it excepted I should know no secrets
That appertain to you? Am I yourself
But, as it were, in sort or limitation?
To keep with you at meals, comfort your bed,
And talk to you sometimes? Dwell I but in the suburbs
Of your good pleasure? If it be no more,
Portia is Brutus' harlot, not his wife.
Bru. You are my true and honourable wife,
As dear to me as are the ruddy drops
That visit my sad heart.
Por. If this were true, then should I know this secret.
I grant I am a woman; but withal
A woman that Lord Brutus took to wife.
I grant I am a woman; but withal
A woman well-reputed, Cato's daughter.
Think you I am no stronger than my sex,
Being so father'd and so husbanded?
Tell me your counsels; I will not disclose 'em.
I have made strong proof of my constancy,
Giving myself a voluntary wound
Here, in the thigh. Can I bear that with patience,
And not my husband's secrets?
Bru. O ye gods,
Render me worthy of this noble wife! *Knock.*
Hark, hark! One knocks. Portia, go in awhile,
And by-and-by thy bosom shall partake
The secrets of my heart.
All my engagements I will construe to thee,
All the charactery of my sad brows.
Leave me with haste.

Exit Portia.

Lucius, who's that knocks?

Enter *Lucius* and [*Caius*] *Ligarius.*

Luc. Here is a sick man that would speak with you.
Bru. Caius Ligarius, that Metellus spake of.
Boy, stand aside. Caius Ligarius, how?
Caius. Vouchsafe good-morrow from a feeble tongue.
Bru. O, what a time have you chose out, brave Caius,
To wear a kerchief! Would you were not sick!
Caius. I am not sick if Brutus have in hand
Any exploit worthy the name of honour.
Bru. Such an exploit have I in hand, Ligarius,
Had you a healthful ear to hear of it.
Caius. By all the gods that Romans bow before,
I here discard my sickness! [*Throws off his kerchief.*] Soul of Rome!
Brave son, deriv'd from honourable loins!
Thou like an exorcist hast conjur'd up
My mortified spirit. Now bid me run,
And I will strive with things impossible;
Yea, get the better of them. What's to do?

Bru. A piece of work that will make sick men whole.
Caius. But are not some whole that we must make sick?
Bru. That must we also. What it is, my Caius,
I shall unfold to thee as we are going
To whom it must be done.
Caius. Set on your foot,
And with a heart new-fir'd I follow you,
To do I know not what; but it sufficeth
That Brutus leads me on. *Thunder.*
Bru. Follow me then. *Exeunt.*

[Scene II. *Rome.* Cæsar's *house.*]

Thunder and lightning. Enter *Julius Cæsar,* in his nightgown.

Cæs. Nor heaven nor earth have been at peace to-night.
Thrice hath Calphurnia in her sleep cried out
'Help, ho! They murther Cæsar!' Who's within?

Enter a *Servant.*

Serv. My lord?
Cæs. Go bid the priests do present sacrifice,
And bring me their opinions of success.
Serv. I will, my lord. *Exit.*

Enter *Calphurnia.*

Cal. What mean you, Cæsar? Think you to walk forth?
You shall not stir out of your house to-day.
Cæs. Cæsar shall forth. The things that threaten'd me
Ne'er look'd but on my back. When they shall see
The face of Cæsar, they are vanished.
Cal. Cæsar, I never stood on ceremonies,
Yet now they fright me. There is one within,
Besides the things that we have heard and seen,
Recounts most horrid sights seen by the watch.
A lioness hath whelped in the streets,
And graves have yawn'd and yielded up their dead.
Fierce fiery warriors fought upon the clouds
In ranks and squadrons and right form of war,
Which drizzled blood upon the Capitol.
The noise of battle hurtled in the air,
Horses did neigh, and dying men did groan,
And ghosts did shriek and squeal about the streets.
O Cæsar, these things are beyond all use,
And I do fear them!
Cæs. What can be avoided
Whose end is purpos'd by the mighty gods?
Yet Cæsar shall go forth; for these predictions
Are to the world in general as to Cæsar.
Cal. When beggars die there are no comets seen;
The heavens themselves blaze forth the death of princes.
Cæs. Cowards die many times before their deaths;
The valiant never taste of death but once.
Of all the wonders that I yet have heard,
It seems to me most strange that men should fear,
Seeing that death, a necessary end,
Will come when it will come.

Enter a *Servant.*

What say the augurers?
Serv. They would not have you to stir forth to-day.
Plucking the entrails of an offering forth,
They could not find a heart within the beast.
Cæs. The gods do this in shame of cowardice.
Cæsar should be a beast without a heart
If he should stay at home to-day for fear.
No, Cæsar shall not. Danger knows full well
That Cæsar is more dangerous than he.
We are two lions litter'd in one day,
And I the elder and more terrible,
And Cæsar shall go forth.
Cal. Alas, my lord!
Your wisdom is consum'd in confidence.
Do not go forth to-day. Call it my fear
That keeps you in the house and not your own.
We'll send Mark Antony to the Senate House,
And he shall say you are not well to-day.
Let me upon my knee prevail in this.
Cæs. Mark Antony shall say I am not well,
And for thy humour I will stay at home.

Enter *Decius.*

Here's Decius Brutus; he shall tell them so.
Dec. Cæsar, all hail! Good morrow, worthy Cæsar!
I come to fetch you to the Senate House.
Cæs. And you are come in very happy time
To bear my greeting to the senators
And tell them that I will not come to-day.
Cannot, is false; and that I dare not, falser:
I will not come to-day. Tell them so, Decius.
Cal. Say he is sick.
Cæs. Shall Cæsar send a lie?

Have I in conquest stretch'd mine arm so far
To be afeard to tell greybeards the truth?
Decius, go tell them Cæsar will not come.
Dec. Most mighty Cæsar, let me know some cause,
Lest I be laugh'd at when I tell them so.
Cæs. The cause is in my will: I will not come.
That is enough to satisfy the Senate;
But for your private satisfaction,
Because I love you, I will let you know.
Calphurnia here, my wife, stays me at home.
She dreamt to-night she saw my statuë,
Which, like a fountain with an hundred spouts,
Did run pure blood; and many lusty Romans
Came smiling and did bathe their hands in it.
And these does she apply for warnings and portents
And evils imminent, and on her knee
Hath begg'd that I will stay at home to-day.
Dec. This dream is all amiss interpreted;
It was a vision fair and fortunate.
Your statue spouting blood in many pipes,
In which so many smiling Romans bath'd,
Signifies that from you great Rome shall suck
Reviving blood, and that great men shall press
For tinctures, stains, relics, and cognizance.
This by Calphurnia's dream is signified.
Cæs. And this way have you well expounded it.
Dec. I have, when you have heard what I can say;
And know it now. The Senate have concluded
To give this day a crown to mighty Cæsar.
If you shall send them word you will not come,
Their minds may change. Besides, it were a mock
Apt to be render'd, for some one to say
'Break up the Senate till another time,
When Cæsar's wife shall meet with better dreams.'
If Cæsar hide himself, shall they not whisper
'Lo, Cæsar is afraid'?
Pardon me, Cæsar; for my dear dear love
To your proceeding bids me tell you this,
And reason to my love is liable.
Cæs. How foolish do your fears seem now, Calphurnia!
I am ashamed I did yield to them.
Give me my robe, for I will go.

Enter *Brutus, Ligarius, Metellus, Casca, Trebonius, Cinna,* and *Publius.*

And look where Publius is come to fetch me.
Pub. Good morrow, Cæsar.
Cæs. Welcome, Publius.
What, Brutus, are you stirr'd so early too?
Good morrow, Casca. Caius Ligarius,
Cæsar was ne'er so much your enemy
As that same ague which hath made you lean.
What is't o'clock?
Bru. Cæsar, 'tis strucken eight.
Cæs. I thank you for your pains and courtesy.

Enter *Antony.*

See! Antony, that revels long a-nights,
Is notwithstanding up. Good morrow, Antony.
Ant. So to most noble Cæsar.
Cæs. Bid them prepare within.
I am to blame to be thus waited for.
Now, Cinna. Now, Metellus. What, Trebonius;
I have an hour's talk in store for you;
Remember that you call on me to-day;
Be near me, that I may remember you.
Treb. Cæsar, I will. [*Aside*] And so near will I be
That your best friends shall wish I had been further.
Cæs. Good friends, go in and taste some wine with me,
And we (like friends) will straightway go together.
Bru. [*aside*] That every like is not the same, O Cæsar,
The heart of Brutus erns to think upon.
Exeunt.

[Scene III. *Rome. A street near the Capitol.*]

Enter *Artemidorus,* [reading a paper].

Art. 'Cæsar, beware of Brutus; take heed of Cassius; come not near Casca; have an eye to Cinna; trust not Trebonius; mark well Metellus Cimber; Decius Brutus loves thee not; thou hast wrong'd Caius Ligarius. There is but one mind in all these men, and it is bent against Cæsar. If thou beest not immortal, look about you. Security gives way to conspiracy. The mighty gods defend thee!
'Thy lover,
'ARTEMIDORUS.'

Here will I stand till Cæsar pass along
And as a suitor will I give him this.
My heart laments that virtue cannot live
Out of the teeth of emulation.
If thou read this, O Cæsar, thou mayst live;
If not, the Fates with traitors do contrive.
Exit.

[Scene IV. *Before the house of* Brutus.]

Enter *Portia* and *Lucius*.

Por. I prithee, boy, run to the Senate House.
Stay not to answer me, but get thee gone!
Why dost thou stay?
Luc. To know my errand, madam.
Por. I would have had thee there and here again
Ere I can tell thee what thou shouldst do there.
[*Aside*] O constancy, be strong upon my side,
Set a huge mountain 'tween my heart and tongue!
I have a man's mind, but a woman's might.
How hard it is for women to keep counsel!
Art thou here yet?
Luc. Madam, what should I do?
Run to the Capitol and nothing else?
And so return to you and nothing else?
Por. Yes, bring me word, boy, if thy lord look well,
For he went sickly forth; and take good note
What Cæsar doth, what suitors press to him.
Hark, boy! What noise is that?
Luc. I hear none, madam.
Por. Prithee listen well.
I heard a bustling rumour like a fray,
And the wind brings it from the Capitol.
Luc. Sooth, madam, I hear nothing.

Enter the *Soothsayer*.

Por. Come hither, fellow. Which way hast thou been?
Sooth. At mine own house, good lady.
Por. What is't o'clock?
Sooth. About the ninth hour, lady.
Por. Is Cæsar yet gone to the Capitol?
Sooth. Madam, not yet. I go to take my stand,
To see him pass on to the Capitol.
Por. Thou hast some suit to Cæsar, hast thou not?
Sooth. That I have, lady, if it will please Cæsar
To be so good to Cæsar as to hear me:
I shall beseech him to befriend himself.
Por. Why, know'st thou any harm's intended towards him?
Sooth. None that I know will be, much that I fear may chance.
Good morrow to you. Here the street is narrow.
The throng that follows Cæsar at the heels,
Of senators, of prætors, common suitors,
Will crowd a feeble man almost to death.
I'll get me to a place more void and there
Speak to great Cæsar as he comes along.
Exit.
Por. I must go in. Ay me, how weak a thing
The heart of woman is! O Brutus,
The heavens speed thee in thine enterprise!
Sure the boy heard me. — Brutus hath a suit
That Cæsar will not grant. — O, I grow faint. —
Run, Lucius, and commend me to my lord;
Say I am merry. Come to me again
And bring me word what he doth say to thee.
Exeunt [*severally*].

ACT III. [Scene I. *Rome. A street before the Capitol.*]

Flourish. Enter *Cæsar, Brutus, Cassius, Casca, Decius, Metellus, Trebonius, Cinna, Antony, Lepidus, Artemidorus,* [*Popilius,*] *Publius,* and the *Soothsayer*.

Cæs. The ides of March are come.
Sooth. Ay, Cæsar, but not gone.
Art. Hail, Cæsar! Read this schedule.
Dec. Trebonius doth desire you to o'erread
(At your best leisure) this his humble suit.
Art. O Cæsar, read mine first; for mine's a suit
That touches Cæsar nearer. Read it, great Cæsar!
Cæs. What touches us ourself shall be last serv'd.
Art. Delay not, Cæsar! Read it instantly!
Cæs. What, is the fellow mad?
Pub. Sirrah, give place.
Cass. What, urge you your petitions in the street?
Come to the Capitol.

[*Cæsar enters the Capitol, the rest following.*]

Pop. I wish your enterprise to-day may thrive.
Cass. What enterprise, Popilius?
Pop. Fare you well. [*Advances to Cæsar.*]
Bru. What said Popilius Lena?
Cass. He wish'd to-day our enterprise might thrive.
I fear our purpose is discovered.
Bru. Look how he makes to Cæsar. Mark him.

Cass. Casca, be sudden, for we fear prevention.
Brutus, what shall be done? If this be known,
Cassius or Cæsar never shall turn back,
For I will slay myself.
Bru. Cassius, be constant.
Popilius Lena speaks not of our purposes;
For look, he smiles, and Cæsar doth not change.
Cass. Trebonius knows his time; for look you, Brutus,
He draws Mark Antony out of the way.
[*Exeunt Antony and Trebonius.*]
Dec. Where is Metellus Cimber? Let him go
And presently prefer his suit to Cæsar.
Bru. He is address'd. Press near and second him.
Cin. Casca, you are the first that rears your hand.
Cæs. Are we all ready? What is now amiss
That Cæsar and his Senate must redress?
Met. Most high, most mighty, and most puissant Cæsar,
Metellus Cimber throws before thy seat
An humble heart. [*Kneels.*]
Cæs. I must prevent thee, Cimber.
These couchings and these lowly courtesies
Might fire the blood of ordinary men
And turn preordinance and first decree
Into the law of children. Be not fond
To think that Cæsar bears such rebel blood
That will be thaw'd from the true quality
With that which melteth fools — I mean, sweet words,
Low-crooked curtsies, and base spaniel fawning.
Thy brother by decree is banished.
If thou dost bend and pray and fawn for him,
I spurn thee like a cur out of my way.
Know, Cæsar doth not wrong, nor without cause
Will he be satisfied.
Met. Is there no voice more worthy than my own,
To sound more sweetly in great Cæsar's ear
For the repealing of my banish'd brother?
Bru. I kiss thy hand, but not in flattery, Cæsar,
Desiring thee that Publius Cimber may
Have an immediate freedom of repeal.
Cæs. What, Brutus?
Cass. Pardon, Cæsar! Cæsar, pardon!
As low as to thy foot doth Cassius fall
To beg enfranchisement for Publius Cimber.
Cæs. I could be well mov'd, if I were as you;
If I could pray to move, prayers would move me:
But I am constant as the Northern Star,
Of whose true-fix'd and resting quality
There is no fellow in the firmament.
The skies are painted with unnumb'red sparks,
They are all fire, and every one doth shine;
But there's but one in all doth hold his place.
So in the world: 'Tis furnish'd well with men,
And men are flesh and blood, and apprehensive;
Yet in the number I do know but one
That unassailable holds on his rank,
Unshak'd of motion; and that I am he,
Let me a little show it, even in this —
That I was constant Cimber should be banish'd
And constant do remain to keep him so.
Cin. O Cæsar!
Cæs. Hence! Wilt thou lift up Olympus?
Dec. Great Cæsar!
Cæs. Doth not Brutus bootless kneel?
Casca. Speak hands for me!
They stab Cæsar [— *Casca first, Brutus last*].
Cæs. Et tu, Brute? — Then fall Cæsar!
Dies.
Cin. Liberty! Freedom! Tyranny is dead!
Run hence, proclaim, cry it about the streets!
Cass. Some to the common pulpits and cry out
'Liberty, freedom, and enfranchisement!'
Bru. People and Senators, be not affrighted.
Fly not; stand still. Ambition's debt is paid.
Casca. Go to the pulpit, Brutus.
Dec. And Cassius too.
Bru. Where's Publius?
Cin. Here, quite confounded with this mutiny.
Met. Stand fast together, lest some friend of Cæsar's
Should chance —
Bru. Talk not of standing! Publius, good cheer.
There is no harm intended to your person
Nor to no Roman else. So tell them, Publius.
Cass. And leave us, Publius, lest that the people,
Rushing on us, should do your age some mischief.
Bru. Do so; and let no man abide this deed
But we the doers.

Enter *Trebonius.*

Cass. Where is Antony?
Treb. Fled to his house amaz'd.
Men, wives, and children stare, cry out, and run,
As it were doomsday.

Bru. Fates, we will know your pleasures.
That we shall die, we know; 'tis but the time,
And drawing days out, that men stand upon.
Cass. Why, he that cuts off twenty years of life
Cuts off so many years of fearing death.
Bru. Grant that, and then is death a benefit.
So are we Cæsar's friends, that have abridg'd
His time of fearing death. Stoop, Romans, stoop,
And let us bathe our hands in Cæsar's blood
Up to the elbows and besmear our swords.
Then walk we forth, even to the market place,
And waving our red weapons o'er our heads,
Let's all cry 'Peace, freedom, and liberty!'
Cass. Stoop then and wash. How many ages hence
Shall this our lofty scene be acted over
In states unborn and accents yet unknown!
Bru. How many times shall Cæsar bleed in sport,
That now on Pompey's basis lies along
No worthier than the dust!
Cass. So oft as that shall be,
So often shall the knot of us be call'd
The men that gave their country liberty.
Dec. What, shall we forth?
Cass. Ay, every man away.
Brutus shall lead, and we will grace his heels
With the most boldest and best hearts of Rome.

Enter a *Servant.*

Bru. Soft! who comes here? A friend of Antony's.
Serv. Thus, Brutus, did my master bid me kneel;
Thus did Mark Antony bid me fall down;
And being prostrate, thus he bade me say:
Brutus is noble, wise, valiant, and honest;
Cæsar was mighty, bold, royal, and loving.
Say I love Brutus and I honour him;
Say I fear'd Cæsar, honour'd him, and lov'd him.
If Brutus will vouchsafe that Antony
May safely come to him and be resolv'd
How Cæsar hath deserv'd to lie in death,
Mark Antony shall not love Cæsar dead
So well as Brutus living; but will follow
The fortunes and affairs of noble Brutus
Thorough the hazards of this untrod state
With all true faith. So says my master Antony.
Bru. Thy master is a wise and valiant Roman.
I never thought him worse.
Tell him, so please him come unto this place,
He shall be satisfied and, by my honour,
Depart untouch'd.
Serv. I'll fetch him presently. *Exit.*
Bru. I know that we shall have him well to friend.
Cass. I wish we may. But yet have I a mind
That fears him much; and my misgiving still
Falls shrewdly to the purpose.

Enter *Antony.*

Bru. But here comes Antony. Welcome, Mark Antony.
Ant. O mighty Cæsar! dost thou lie so low?
Are all thy conquests, glories, triumphs, spoils,
Shrunk to this little measure? Fare thee well.
I know not, gentlemen, what you intend,
Who else must be let blood, who else is rank.
If I myself, there is no hour so fit
As Cæsar's death's hour; nor no instrument
Of half that worth as those your swords, made rich
With the most noble blood of all this world.
I do beseech ye, if you bear me hard,
Now, whilst your purpled hands do reek and smoke,
Fulfil your pleasure. Live a thousand years,
I shall not find myself so apt to die;
No place will please me so, no mean of death,
As here by Cæsar, and by you cut off,
The choice and master spirits of this age.
Bru. O Antony, beg not your death of us!
Though now we must appear bloody and cruel,
As by our hands and this our present act
You see we do, yet see you but our hands
And this the bleeding business they have done.
Our hearts you see not. They are pitiful;
And pity to the general wrong of Rome
(As fire drives out fire, so pity pity)
Hath done this deed on Cæsar. For your part,
To you our swords have leaden points, Mark Antony.
Our arms in strength of malice, and our hearts
Of brothers' temper, do receive you in
With all kind love, good thoughts, and reverence.
Cass. Your voice shall be as strong as any man's
In the disposing of new dignities.
Bru. Only be patient till we have appeas'd
The multitude, beside themselves with fear,
And then we will deliver you the cause
Why I, that did love Cæsar when I struck him,
Have thus proceeded.
Ant. I doubt not of your wisdom.
Let each man render me his bloody hand.

First, Marcus Brutus, will I shake with you;
Next, Caius Cassius, do I take your hand;
Now, Decius Brutus, yours; now yours, Metellus;
Yours, Cinna; and, my valiant Casca, yours.
Though last, not least in love, yours, good Trebonius.
Gentlemen all — Alas, what shall I say?
My credit now stands on such slippery ground
That one of two bad ways you must conceit me,
Either a coward or a flatterer.
That I did love thee, Cæsar, O, 'tis true!
If then thy spirit look upon us now,
Shall it not grieve thee dearer than thy death
To see thy Antony making his peace,
Shaking the bloody fingers of thy foes,
Most noble! in the presence of thy corse?
Had I as many eyes as thou hast wounds,
Weeping as fast as they stream forth thy blood,
It would become me better than to close
In terms of friendship with thine enemies.
Pardon me, Julius! Here wast thou bay'd, brave hart;
Here didst thou fall; and here thy hunters stand,
Sign'd in thy spoil, and crimson'd in thy lethe.
O world, thou wast the forest to this hart;
And this indeed, O world, the heart of thee!
How like a deer, stroken by many princes,
Dost thou here lie!

Cass. Mark Antony —

Ant. Pardon me, Caius Cassius.
The enemies of Cæsar shall say this;
Then, in a friend, it is cold modesty.

Cass. I blame you not for praising Cæsar so;
But what compact mean you to have with us?
Will you be prick'd in number of our friends,
Or shall we on, and not depend on you?

Ant. Therefore I took your hands; but was indeed
Sway'd from the point by looking down on Cæsar.
Friends am I with you all, and love you all,
Upon this hope, that you shall give me reasons
Why and wherein Cæsar was dangerous.

Bru. Or else were this a savage spectacle.
Our reasons are so full of good regard
That were you, Antony, the son of Cæsar,
You should be satisfied.

Ant. That's all I seek;
And am moreover suitor that I may
Produce his body to the market place
And in the pulpit, as becomes a friend,
Speak in the order of his funeral.

Bru. You shall, Mark Antony.

Cass. Brutus, a word with you.
[*Aside to Brutus*] You know not what you do. Do not consent
That Antony speak in his funeral.
Know you how much the people may be mov'd
By that which he will utter?

Bru. [*aside to Cassius*] By your pardon —
I will myself into the pulpit first
And show the reason of our Cæsar's death.
What Antony shall speak, I will protest
He speaks by leave and by permission;
And that we are contented Cæsar shall
Have all true rites and lawful ceremonies.
It shall advantage more than do us wrong.

Cass. [*aside to Brutus*] I know not what may fall. I like it not.

Bru. Mark Antony, here, take you Cæsar's body.
You shall not in your funeral speech blame us,
But speak all good you can devise of Cæsar;
And say you do't by our permission.
Else shall you not have any hand at all
About his funeral. And you shall speak
In the same pulpit whereto I am going,
After my speech is ended.

Ant. Be it so.
I do desire no more.

Bru. Prepare the body then, and follow us.

Exeunt. Manet Antony.

Ant. O, pardon me, thou bleeding piece of earth,
That I am meek and gentle with these butchers!
Thou art the ruins of the noblest man
That ever lived in the tide of times.
Woe to the hand that shed this costly blood!
Over thy wounds now do I prophesy
(Which, like dumb mouths, do ope their ruby lips
To beg the voice and utterance of my tongue),
A curse shall light upon the limbs of men;
Domestic fury and fierce civil strife
Shall cumber all the parts of Italy;
Blood and destruction shall be so in use
And dreadful objects so familiar
That mothers shall but smile when they behold
Their infants quartered with the hands of war,
All pity chok'd with custom of fell deeds;
And Cæsar's spirit, ranging for revenge,
With Ate by his side come hot from hell,
Shall in these confines with a monarch's voice
Cry 'Havoc!' and let slip the dogs of war,
That this foul deed shall smell above the earth
With carrion men, groaning for burial.

Enter *Octavius' Servant.*

You serve Octavius Cæsar, do you not?

Serv. I do, Mark Antony.

Ant. Cæsar did write for him to come to Rome.

Serv. He did receive his letters and is coming,
And bid me say to you by word of mouth —
O Cæsar!

Ant. Thy heart is big. Get thee apart and weep.
Passion, I see, is catching; for mine eyes,
Seeing those beads of sorrow stand in thine,
Began to water. Is thy master coming?

Serv. He lies to-night within seven leagues of Rome.

Ant. Post back with speed and tell him what hath chanc'd.
Here is a mourning Rome, a dangerous Rome,
No Rome of safety for Octavius yet.
Hie hence and tell him so. Yet stay awhile.
Thou shalt not back till I have borne this corse
Into the market place. There shall I try
In my oration how the people take
The cruel issue of these bloody men;
According to the which thou shalt discourse
To young Octavius of the state of things.
Lend me your hand.

Exeunt [with Cæsar's body].

[Scene II. *Rome. The Forum.*]

Enter *Brutus* and *Cassius,* with the *Plebeians.*

Plebeians. We will be satisfied! Let us be satisfied!

Bru. Then follow me and give me audience, friends.
Cassius, go you into the other street
And part the numbers.
Those that will hear me speak, let 'em stay here;
Those that will follow Cassius, go with him;
And public reasons shall be rendered
Of Cæsar's death.

1. Pleb. I will hear Brutus speak.

2. Pleb. I will hear Cassius, and compare their reasons
When severally we hear them rendered.

[*Exit Cassius, with some of the Plebeians.*]
Brutus goes into the pulpit.

3. Pleb. The noble Brutus is ascended. Silence!

Bru. Be patient till the last.
Romans, countrymen, and lovers, hear me for my cause, and be silent, that you may hear. Believe me for mine honour, and have respect to mine honour, that you may believe. Censure me in your wisdom, and awake your senses, that you may the better judge. If there be any in this assembly, any dear friend of Cæsar's, to him I say that Brutus' love to Cæsar was no less than his. If then that friend demand why Brutus rose against Cæsar, this is my answer: Not that I lov'd Cæsar less, but that I lov'd Rome more. Had you rather Cæsar were living, and die all slaves, than that Cæsar were dead, to live all freemen? As Cæsar lov'd me, I weep for him; as he was fortunate, I rejoice at it; as he was valiant, I honour him; but — as he was ambitious, I slew him. There is tears for his love; joy for his fortune; honour for his valour; and death for his ambition. Who is here so base that would be a bondman? If any, speak; for him have I offended. Who is here so rude that would not be a Roman? If any, speak; for him have I offended. Who is here so vile that will not love his country? If any, speak; for him have I offended. I pause for a reply.

All. None, Brutus, none!

Bru. Then none have I offended. I have done no more to Cæsar than you shall do to Brutus. The question of his death is enroll'd in the Capitol; his glory not extenuated, wherein he was worthy; nor his offences enforc'd, for which he suffered death.

Enter *Mark Antony* [and others], with *Cæsar's* body.

Here comes his body, mourn'd by Mark Antony, who, though he had no hand in his death, shall receive the benefit of his dying, a place in the commonwealth, as which of you shall not? With this I depart, that, as I slew my best lover for the good of Rome, I have the same dagger for myself when it shall please my country to need my death.

All. Live, Brutus! live, live!

1. Pleb. Bring him with triumph home unto his house.

2. Pleb. Give him a statue with his ancestors.

3. Pleb. Let him be Cæsar.

4. Pleb. Cæsar's better parts
Shall be crown'd in Brutus.

1. Pleb. We'll bring him to his house with shouts and clamours.

Bru. My countrymen —

2. Pleb. Peace! silence! Brutus speaks.

1. Pleb. Peace, ho!

Bru. Good countrymen, let me depart alone,
And, for my sake, stay here with Antony.
Do grace to Cæsar's corpse, and grace his speech
Tending to Cæsar's glories which Mark Antony,
By our permission, is allow'd to make.
I do entreat you, not a man depart,
Save I alone, till Antony have spoke. *Exit.*
1. Pleb. Stay, ho! and let us hear Mark Antony.
3. Pleb. Let him go up into the public chair.
We'll hear him. Noble Antony, go up.
Ant. For Brutus' sake I am beholding to you. [*Goes up.*]
4. Pleb. What does he say of Brutus?
3. Pleb. He says for Brutus' sake
He finds himself beholding to us all.
4. Pleb. 'Twere best he speak no harm of Brutus here!
1. Pleb. This Cæsar was a tyrant.
3. Pleb. Nay, that's certain.
We are blest that Rome is rid of him.
2. Pleb. Peace! Let us hear what Antony can say.
Ant. You gentle Romans —
All. Peace, ho! Let us hear him.
Ant. Friends, Romans, countrymen, lend me your ears;
I come to bury Cæsar, not to praise him.
The evil that men do lives after them;
The good is oft interred with their bones.
So let it be with Cæsar. The noble Brutus
Hath told you Cæsar was ambitious.
If it were so, it was a grievous fault,
And grievously hath Cæsar answer'd it.
Here, under leave of Brutus and the rest
(For Brutus is an honourable man;
So are they all, all honourable men),
Come I to speak in Cæsar's funeral.
He was my friend, faithful and just to me;
But Brutus says he was ambitious,
And Brutus is an honourable man.
He hath brought many captives home to Rome,
Whose ransoms did the general coffers fill.
Did this in Cæsar seem ambitious?
When that the poor have cried, Cæsar hath wept;
Ambition should be made of sterner stuff.
Yet Brutus says he was ambitious;
And Brutus is an honourable man.
You all did see that on the Lupercal
I thrice presented him a kingly crown,
Which he did thrice refuse. Was this ambition?
Yet Brutus says he was ambitious;
And sure he is an honourable man.
I speak not to disprove what Brutus spoke,
But here I am to speak what I do know.
You all did love him once, not without cause.
What cause withholds you then to mourn for him?
O judgment, thou art fled to brutish beasts,
And men have lost their reason! Bear with me.
My heart is in the coffin there with Cæsar,
And I must pause till it come back to me.
1. Pleb. Methinks there is much reason in his sayings.
2. Pleb. If thou consider rightly of the matter,
Cæsar has had great wrong.
3. Pleb. Has he not, masters?
I fear there will a worse come in his place.
4. Pleb. Mark'd ye his words? He would not take the crown;
Therefore 'tis certain he was not ambitious.
1. Pleb. If it be found so, some will dear abide it.
2. Pleb. Poor soul! his eyes are red as fire with weeping.
3. Pleb. There's not a nobler man in Rome than Antony.
4. Pleb. Now mark him. He begins again to speak.
Ant. But yesterday the word of Cæsar might
Have stood against the world. Now lies he there,
And none so poor to do him reverence.
O masters! If I were dispos'd to stir
Your hearts and minds to mutiny and rage,
I should do Brutus wrong, and Cassius wrong,
Who, you all know, are honourable men.
I will not do them wrong. I rather choose
To wrong the dead, to wrong myself and you,
Than I will wrong such honourable men.
But here's a parchment with the seal of Cæsar.
I found it in his closet; 'tis his will.
Let but the commons hear this testament,
Which (pardon me) I do not mean to read,
And they would go and kiss dead Cæsar's wounds
And dip their napkins in his sacred blood;
Yea, beg a hair of him for memory,
And dying, mention it within their wills,
Bequeathing it as a rich legacy
Unto their issue.
4. Pleb. We'll hear the will! Read it, Mark Antony.
All. The will, the will! We will hear Cæsar's will!
Ant. Have patience, gentle friends; I must not read it.
It is not meet you know how Cæsar lov'd you.
You are not wood, you are not stones, but men;

And being men, hearing the will of Cæsar,
It will inflame you, it will make you mad.
'Tis good you know not that you are his heirs;
For if you should, O, what would come of it?

4. Pleb. Read the will! We'll hear it, Antony!
You shall read us the will, Cæsar's will!

Ant. Will you be patient? Will you stay awhile?
I have o'ershot myself to tell you of it.
I fear I wrong the honourable men
Whose daggers have stabb'd Cæsar; I do fear it.

4. Pleb. They were traitors. Honourable men!

All. The will! the testament!

2. Pleb. They were villains, murderers! The will! Read the will!

Ant. You will compel me then to read the will?
Then make a ring about the corpse of Cæsar
And let me show you him that made the will.
Shall I descend? and will you give me leave?

All. Come down.

2. Pleb. Descend.

3. Pleb. You shall have leave.

[*Antony comes down.*]

4. Pleb. A ring! Stand round.

1. Pleb. Stand from the hearse! Stand from the body!

2. Pleb. Room for Antony, most noble Antony!

Ant. Nay, press not so upon me. Stand far off.

All. Stand back! Room! Bear back!

Ant. If you have tears, prepare to shed them now.
You all do know this mantle. I remember
The first time ever Cæsar put it on.
'Twas on a summer's evening in his tent,
That day he overcame the Nervii.
Look, in this place ran Cassius' dagger through.
See what a rent the envious Casca made.
Through this the well-beloved Brutus stabb'd;
And as he pluck'd his cursed steel away,
Mark how the blood of Cæsar followed it,
As rushing out of doors to be resolv'd
If Brutus so unkindly knock'd or no;
For Brutus, as you know, was Cæsar's angel.
Judge, O you gods, how dearly Cæsar lov'd him!
This was the most unkindest cut of all;
For when the noble Cæsar saw him stab,
Ingratitude, more strong than traitors' arms,
Quite vanquish'd him. Then burst his mighty heart;
And in his mantle muffling up his face,
Even at the base of Pompey's statuë
(Which all the while ran blood) great Cæsar fell.
O, what a fall was there, my countrymen!
Then I, and you, and all of us fell down,
Whilst bloody treason flourish'd over us.
O, now you weep, and I perceive you feel
The dint of pity. These are gracious drops.
Kind souls, what weep you when you but behold
Our Cæsar's vesture wounded? Look you here!
Here is himself, marr'd as you see with traitors.

1. Pleb. O piteous spectacle!

2. Pleb. O noble Cæsar!

3. Pleb. O woful day!

4. Pleb. O traitors, villains!

1. Pleb. O most bloody sight!

2. Pleb. We will be reveng'd.

All. Revenge! About! Seek! Burn! Fire! Kill! Slay! Let not a traitor live!

Ant. Stay, countrymen.

1. Pleb. Peace there! Hear the noble Antony.

2. Pleb. We'll hear him, we'll follow him, we'll die with him!

Ant. Good friends, sweet friends, let me not stir you up
To such a sudden flood of mutiny.
They that have done this deed are honourable.
What private griefs they have, alas, I know not,
That made them do it. They are wise and honourable,
And will no doubt with reasons answer you.
I come not, friends, to steal away your hearts.
I am no orator, as Brutus is,
But (as you know me all) a plain blunt man
That love my friend; and that they know full well
That gave me public leave to speak of him.
For I have neither wit, nor words, nor worth,
Action, nor utterance, nor the power of speech
To stir men's blood. I only speak right on.
I tell you that which you yourselves do know,
Show you sweet Cæsar's wounds, poor poor dumb mouths,
And bid them speak for me. But were I Brutus,
And Brutus Antony, there were an Antony
Would ruffle up your spirits, and put a tongue
In every wound of Cæsar that should move
The stones of Rome to rise and mutiny.

All. We'll mutiny.

JULIUS CAESAR

Robin Bailey as the subtle and eloquent Mark Antony

Douglas Campbell as mighty Caesar, cut down by conspirators at the height of his triumph

William Devlin as Brutus, "noblest Roman of them all"

PHOTOGRAPHS BY DESMOND TRIPP
PRODUCED BY THE OLD VIC COMPANY

Paul Rogers as the insidious Cassius

As Caesar and his retinue cross a public square, a soothsayer (Wolfe Morris) comes to him with the mysterious warning: "Beware the Ides of March" *(Act I, Scene II)*

Portia (Helen Cherry), the anxious and devoted wife of Brutus, asks him to let her share his problems *(Act II, Scene I)*

Cassius, Brutus, and Casca (William Squire) linger behind to discuss the events of the day *(Act I, Scene II)*

The conspirators meet in an orchard outside Brutus' house to discuss strategy. Casca, Trebonius (Patrick Wymark), Cassius, Brutus, Decius Brutus (John Warner), Metellus Cimber (Daniel Thorndike), and Cinna (James Maxwell) are included *(Act II, Scene I)*

The night before her husband's death, Calphurnia (Yvonne Coulette), full of premonitions, beseeches Caesar to avoid the Senate *(Act II, Scene II)*

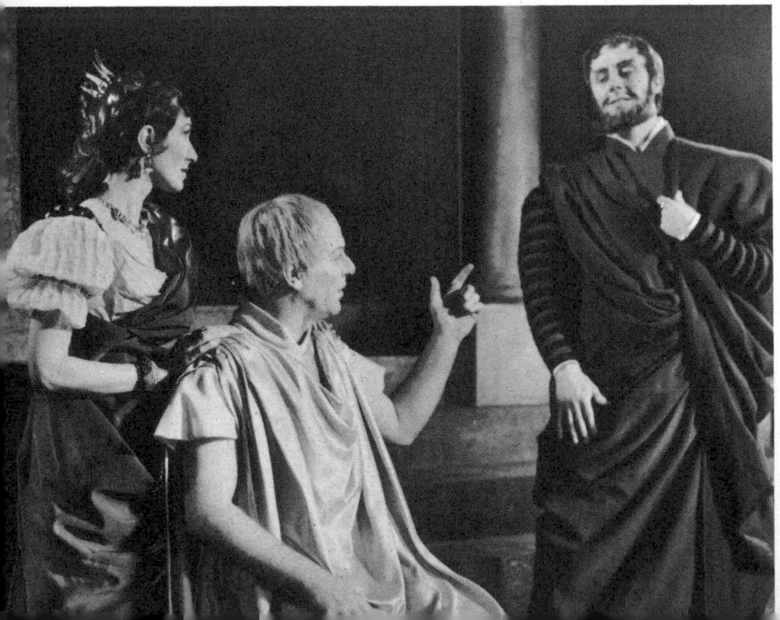

Persuaded by Decius Brutus that all augurs well, Caesar agrees to go to the Senate *(Act II, Scene II)*

Seated in the Senate, Caesar hears the specious plea of Metellus Cimber in behalf of his brother, Publius, requesting immediate repeal of his banishment *(Act III, Scene I)*

As Caesar refuses the petition, the conspirators stab him. With a pathetic rebuke to the trusted Brutus, the great man dies *(Act III, Scene I)*

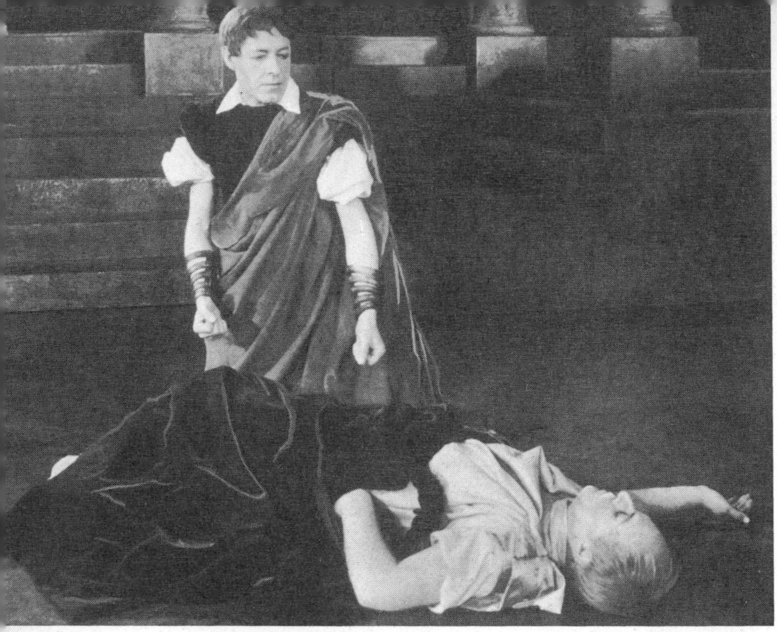

Mark Antony mourns over the murdered monarch's body: "O mighty Caesar, dost thou lie so low?" *(Act III, Scene I)*

Mark Antony stirs the people by revealing that Caesar's will includes a generous bequest for every citizen *(Act III, Scene II)*

Infuriated against the murderers of their benefactor, the mob kills the poet Cinna (John Warner), mistaking him for the conspirator *(Act III, Scene III)*

Douglas Campbell in his role as Octavius, Caesar's avenger

Brutus in his tent near Sardis. While his henchmen Claudius (James Maxwell) and Varro (Bernard Kilby) rest, he asks the youth Lucius (Terry Whale) to provide music *(Act IV, Scene III)*

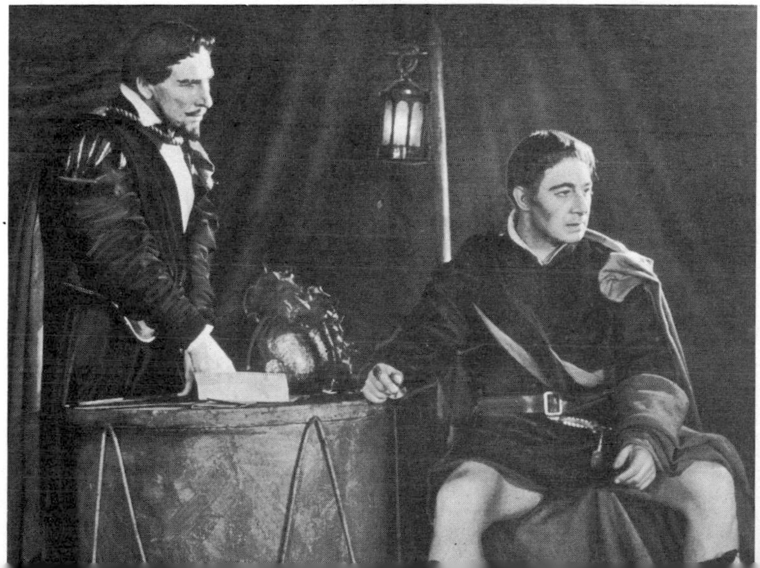

A quarrel breaks out as Brutus accuses Cassius of corrupting Sardis *(Act IV, Scene III)*

Cassius despairs as his servant Pindarus (Wolfe Morris), standing on an eminence, reports the loss of their forces at the battlefield of Philippi *(Act V, Scene III)*

Antony's funeral elegy over the body of Brutus: "His life was gentle, and the elements so mix'd in him that Nature might stand up and say to all the world, 'This was a man' " *(Act V, Scene V)*

1. Pleb. We'll burn the house of Brutus.
3. Pleb. Away then! Come, seek the conspirators.
Ant. Yet hear me, countrymen. Yet hear me speak.
All. Peace, ho! Hear Antony, most noble Antony!
Ant. Why, friends, you go to do you know not what.
Wherein hath Cæsar thus deserv'd your loves?
Alas, you know not! I must tell you then.
You have forgot the will I told you of.
All. Most true! The will! Let's stay and hear the will.
Ant. Here is the will, and under Cæsar's seal.
To every Roman citizen he gives,
To every several man, seventy-five drachmas.
2. Pleb. Most noble Cæsar! We'll revenge his death!
3. Pleb. O royal Cæsar!
Ant. Hear me with patience.
All. Peace, ho!
Ant. Moreover, he hath left you all his walks,
His private arbours, and new-planted orchards,
On this side Tiber; he hath left them you,
And to your heirs for ever — common pleasures,
To walk abroad and recreate yourselves.
Here was a Cæsar! When comes such another?
1. Pleb. Never, never! Come, away, away!
We'll burn his body in the holy place
And with the brands fire the traitors' houses.
Take up the body.
2. Pleb. Go fetch fire!
3. Pleb. Pluck down benches!
4. Pleb. Pluck down forms, windows, anything!

Exeunt Plebeians [*with the body*].

Ant. Now let it work. Mischief, thou art afoot,
Take thou what course thou wilt.

Enter *Servant*.

How now, fellow?
Serv. Sir, Octavius is already come to Rome.
Ant. Where is he?
Serv. He and Lepidus are at Cæsar's house.
Ant. And thither will I straight to visit him.
He comes upon a wish. Fortune is merry,
And in this mood will give us anything.
Serv. I heard him say Brutus and Cassius
Are rid like madmen through the gates of Rome.
Ant. Belike they had some notice of the people
How I had mov'd them. Bring me to Octavius.

Exeunt.

[Scene III. *Rome. A street.*]

Enter *Cinna* the *Poet*, and after him the *Plebeians*.

Cin. I dreamt to-night that I did feast with Cæsar,
And things unluckily charge my fantasy.
I have no will to wander forth of doors,
Yet something leads me forth.
1. Pleb. What is your name?
2. Pleb. Whither are you going?
3. Pleb. Where do you dwell?
4. Pleb. Are you a married man or a bachelor?
2. Pleb. Answer every man directly.
1. Pleb. Ay, and briefly.
4. Pleb. Ay, and wisely.
3. Pleb. Ay, and truly, you were best.

Cin. What is my name? Whither am I going? Where do I dwell? Am I a married man or a bachelor? Then, to answer every man directly and briefly, wisely and truly: wisely I say, I am a bachelor.

2. Pleb. That's as much as to say they are fools that marry. You'll bear me a bang for that, I fear. Proceed — directly.

Cin. Directly I am going to Cæsar's funeral.
1. Pleb. As a friend or an enemy?
Cin. As a friend.
2. Pleb. That matter is answered directly.
4. Pleb. For your dwelling — briefly.
Cin. Briefly, I dwell by the Capitol.
3. Pleb. Your name, sir, truly.
Cin. Truly, my name is Cinna.

1. Pleb. Tear him to pieces! He's a conspirator.

Cin. I am Cinna the poet! I am Cinna the poet!

4. Pleb. Tear him for his bad verses! Tear him for his bad verses!

Cin. I am not Cinna the conspirator.

4. Pleb. It is no matter; his name's Cinna! Pluck but his name out of his heart, and turn him going.

3. Pleb. Tear him, tear him! Come, brands, ho! firebrands! To Brutus', to Cassius'! Burn all! Some to Decius' house and some to Casca's; some to Ligarius'! Away, go!

Exeunt all the Plebeians [*with Cinna*].

Act IV. [Scene I. *Rome.* Antony's *house.*]

Enter *Antony, Octavius,* and *Lepidus.*

Ant. These many, then, shall die; their names are prick'd.
Oct. Your brother too must die. Consent you, Lepidus?
Lep. I do consent —
Oct. Prick him down, Antony.
Lep. Upon condition Publius shall not live,
Who is your sister's son, Mark Antony.
Ant. He shall not live. Look, with a spot I damn him.
But, Lepidus, go you to Cæsar's house.
Fetch the will hither, and we shall determine
How to cut off some charge in legacies.
Lep. What? shall I find you here?
Oct. Or here or at the Capitol.
Exit Lepidus.
Ant. This is a slight unmeritable man,
Meet to be sent on errands. Is it fit,
The threefold world divided, he should stand
One of the three to share it?
Oct. So you thought him,
And took his voice who should be prick'd to die
In our black sentence and proscription.
Ant. Octavius, I have seen more days than you;
And though we lay these honours on this man
To ease ourselves of divers sland'rous loads,
He shall but bear them as the ass bears gold,
To groan and sweat under the business,
Either led or driven as we point the way;
And having brought our treasure where we will,
Then take we down his load, and turn him off
(Like to the empty ass) to shake his ears
And graze in commons.
Oct. You may do your will;
But he's a tried and valiant soldier.
Ant. So is my horse, Octavius, and for that
I do appoint him store of provender.
It is a creature that I teach to fight,
To wind, to stop, to run directly on,
His corporal motion govern'd by my spirit.
And, in some taste, is Lepidus but so.
He must be taught, and train'd, and bid go forth:
A barren-spirited fellow; one that feeds
On objects, arts, and imitations
Which, out of use and stal'd by other men
Begin his fashion. Do not talk of him,
But as a property. And now, Octavius,
Listen great things. Brutus and Cassius
Are levying powers. We must straight make head.
Therefore let our alliance be combin'd,
Our best friends made, and our best means stretch'd out;
And let us presently go sit in council
How covert matters may be best disclos'd
And open perils surest answered.
Oct. Let us do so; for we are at the stake
And bay'd about with many enemies;
And some that smile have in their hearts, I fear,
Millions of mischiefs. *Exeunt.*

[Scene II. *The camp near Sardis. Before the tent of* Brutus.]

Drum. Enter *Brutus, Lucilius,* [*Lucius,*] and the *Army. Titinius* and *Pindarus* meet them.

Bru. Stand ho!
Lucil. Give the word, ho! and stand!
Bru. What now, Lucilius? Is Cassius near?
Lucil. He is at hand, and Pindarus is come
To do you salutation from his master.
Bru. He greets me well. Your master, Pindarus,
In his own change, or by ill officers,
Hath given me some worthy cause to wish
Things done undone; but if he be at hand,
I shall be satisfied.
Pin. I do not doubt
But that my noble master will appear
Such as he is, full of regard and honour.
Bru. He is not doubted. A word, Lucilius,
How he receiv'd you. Let me be resolv'd.
Lucil. With courtesy and with respect enough,
But not with such familiar instances
Nor with such free and friendly conference
As he hath us'd of old.
Bru. Thou hast describ'd
A hot friend cooling. Ever note, Lucilius,
When love begins to sicken and decay
It useth an enforced ceremony.
There are no tricks in plain and simple faith;
But hollow men, like horses hot at hand,
Make gallant show and promise of their mettle;
Low march within.
But when they should endure the bloody spur,

They fall their crests, and like deceitful jades
Sink in the trial. Comes his army on?
Lucil. They mean this night in Sardis to be quarter'd.
The greater part, the horse in general,
Are come with Cassius.
Bru. Hark! He is arriv'd.
March gently on to meet him.

Enter *Cassius* and his *Powers*.

Cass. Stand, ho!
Bru. Stand, ho! Speak the word along.
1. Sold. Stand!
2. Sold. Stand!
3. Sold. Stand!
Cass. Most noble brother, you have done me wrong.
Bru. Judge me, you gods! wrong I mine enemies?
And if not so, how should I wrong a brother?
Cass. Brutus, this sober form of yours hides wrongs;
And when you do them —
Bru. Cassius, be content.
Speak your griefs softly. I do know you well.
Before the eyes of both our armies here
(Which should perceive nothing but love from us)
Let us not wrangle. Bid them move away.
Then in my tent, Cassius, enlarge your griefs,
And I will give you audience.
Cass. Pindarus,
Bid our commanders lead their charges off
A little from this ground.
Bru. Lucilius, do you the like; and let no man
Come to our tent till we have done our conference.
Let Lucius and Titinius guard our door.
Exeunt.

[Scene III. *The camp near Sardis. Within the tent of* Brutus.]

Enter *Brutus* and *Cassius*.

Cass. That you have wrong'd me doth appear in this:
You have condemn'd and noted Lucius Pella
For taking bribes here of the Sardians;
Wherein my letters, praying on his side,
Because I knew the man, were slighted off.
Bru. You wrong'd yourself to write in such a case.
Cass. In such a time as this it is not meet
That every nice offence should bear his comment.
Bru. Let me tell you, Cassius, you yourself
Are much condemn'd to have an itching palm,
To sell and mart your offices for gold
To undeservers.
Cass. I an itching palm?
You know that you are Brutus that speaks this,
Or, by the gods, this speech were else your last!
Bru. The name of Cassius honours this corruption,
And chastisement doth therefore hide his head.
Cass. Chastisement?
Bru. Remember March; the ides of March remember.
Did not great Julius bleed for justice sake?
What villain touch'd his body that did stab
And not for justice? What, shall one of us,
That struck the foremost man of all this world
But for supporting robbers — shall we now
Contaminate our fingers with base bribes,
And sell the mighty space of our large honours
For so much trash as may be grasped thus?
I had rather be a dog and bay the moon
Than such a Roman.
Cass. Brutus, bait not me!
I'll not endure it. You forget yourself
To hedge me in. I am a soldier, I,
Older in practice, abler than yourself
To make conditions.
Bru. Go to! You are not, Cassius.
Cass. I am.
Bru. I say you are not.
Cass. Urge me no more! I shall forget myself.
Have mind upon your health. Tempt me no farther.
Bru. Away, slight man!
Cass. Is't possible?
Bru. Hear me, for I will speak.
Must I give way and room to your rash choler?
Shall I be frighted when a madman stares?
Cass. O ye gods, ye gods! Must I endure all this?
Bru. All this? Ay, more! Fret till your proud heart break.
Go show your slaves how choleric you are
And make your bondmen tremble. Must I budge?
Must I observe you? Must I stand and crouch
Under your testy humour? By the gods,
You shall digest the venom of your spleen,
Though it do split you; for from this day forth

I'll use you for my mirth, yea, for my laughter,
When you are waspish.
Cass. Is it come to this?
Bru. You say you are a better soldier.
Let it appear so; make your vaunting true,
And it shall please me well. For mine own part,
I shall be glad to learn of noble men.
Cass. You wrong me every way! You wrong me, Brutus!
I said an elder soldier, not a better.
Did I say 'better'?
Bru. If you did, I care not.
Cass. When Cæsar liv'd he durst not thus have mov'd me.
Bru. Peace, peace! You durst not so have tempted him.
Cass. I durst not?
Bru. No.
Cass. What, durst not tempt him?
Bru. For your life you durst not.
Cass. Do not presume too much upon my love.
I may do that I shall be sorry for.
Bru. You have done that you should be sorry for.
There is no terror, Cassius, in your threats;
For I am arm'd so strong in honesty
That they pass by me as the idle wind,
Which I respect not. I did send to you
For certain sums of gold, which you denied me;
For I can raise no money by vile means.
By heaven, I had rather coin my heart
And drop my blood for drachmas than to wring
From the hard hands of peasants their vile trash
By any indirection. I did send
To you for gold to pay my legions,
Which you denied me. Was that done like Cassius?
Should I have answer'd Caius Cassius so?
When Marcus Brutus grows so covetous
To lock such rascal counters from his friends,
Be ready, gods, with all your thunderbolts,
Dash him to pieces!
Cass. I denied you not.
Bru. You did.
Cass. I did not. He was but a fool that brought
My answer back. Brutus hath riv'd my heart.
A friend should bear his friend's infirmities,
But Brutus makes mine greater than they are.
Bru. I do not, till you practise them on me.
Cass. You love me not.
Bru. I do not like your faults.
Cass. A friendly eye could never see such faults.
Bru. A flatterer's would not, though they do appear
As huge as high Olympus.
Cass. Come, Antony, and young Octavius, come!
Revenge yourselves alone on Cassius.
For Cassius is aweary of the world:
Hated by one he loves; brav'd by his brother;
Check'd like a bondman; all his faults observ'd,
Set in a notebook, learn'd and conn'd by rote
To cast into my teeth. O, I could weep
My spirit from mine eyes! There is my dagger,
And here my naked breast; within, a heart
Dearer than Pluto's mine, richer than gold.
If that thou be'st a Roman, take it forth.
I, that denied thee gold, will give my heart.
Strike as thou didst at Cæsar; for I know,
When thou didst hate him worst, thou lov'dst him better
Than ever thou lov'dst Cassius.
Bru. Sheathe your dagger.
Be angry when you will; it shall have scope.
Do what you will; dishonour shall be humour.
O Cassius, you are yoked with a lamb
That carries anger as the flint bears fire;
Who, much enforced, shows a hasty spark,
And straight is cold again.
Cass. Hath Cassius liv'd
To be but mirth and laughter to his Brutus
When grief and blood ill-temper'd vexeth him?
Bru. When I spoke that, I was ill-temper'd too.
Cass. Do you confess so much? Give me your hand.
Bru. And my heart too.
Cass. O Brutus!
Bru. What's the matter?
Cass. Have not you love enough to bear with me
When that rash humour which my mother gave me
Makes me forgetful?
Bru. Yes, Cassius; and from henceforth,
When you are over-earnest with your Brutus,
He'll think your mother chides, and leave you so.

Enter a *Poet* [followed by *Lucilius*, *Titinius*, and *Lucius*].

Poet. Let me go in to see the generals!
There is some grudge between 'em. 'Tis not meet
They be alone.

Lucil. You shall not come to them.
Poet. Nothing but death shall stay me.
Cass. How now? What's the matter?
Poet. For shame, you generals! What do you mean?
Love and be friends, as two such men should be;
For I have seen more years, I'm sure, than ye.
Cass. Ha, ha! How vilely doth this cynic rhyme!
Bru. Get you hence, sirrah! Saucy fellow, hence!
Cass. Bear with him, Brutus. 'Tis his fashion.
Bru. I'll know his humour when he knows his time.
What should the wars do with these jigging fools?
Companion, hence!
Cass. Away, away, be gone! *Exit Poet.*
Bru. Lucilius and Titinius, bid the commanders
Prepare to lodge their companies to-night.
Cass. And come yourselves, and bring Messala with you
Immediately to us.
[*Exeunt Lucilius and Titinius.*]
Bru. Lucius, a bowl of wine.
[*Exit Lucius.*]
Cass. I did not think you could have been so angry.
Bru. O Cassius, I am sick of many griefs.
Cass. Of your philosophy you make no use
If you give place to accidental evils.
Bru. No man bears sorrow better. Portia is dead.
Cass. Ha! Portia?
Bru. She is dead.
Cass. How scap'd I killing when I cross'd you so?
O insupportable and touching loss!
Upon what sickness?
Bru. Impatient of my absence,
And grief that young Octavius with Mark Antony
Have made themselves so strong; for with her death
That tidings came. With this she fell distract,
And (her attendants absent) swallow'd fire.
Cass. And died so?
Bru. Even so.
Cass. O ye immortal gods!

Enter *Boy* [*Lucius*], with wine and tapers.

Bru. Speak no more of her. Give me a bowl of wine.
In this I bury all unkindness, Cassius.
Drinks.
Cass. My heart is thirsty for that noble pledge.
Fill, Lucius, till the wine o'erswell the cup.
I cannot drink too much of Brutus' love.
[*Drinks. Exit Lucius.*]

Enter *Titinius* and *Messala.*

Bru. Come in, Titinius! Welcome, good Messala.
Now sit we close about this taper here
And call in question our necessities.
Cass. Portia, art thou gone?
Bru. No more, I pray you.
Messala, I have here received letters
That young Octavius and Mark Antony
Come down upon us with a mighty power,
Bending their expedition toward Philippi.
Mes. Myself have letters of the selfsame tenure.
Bru. With what addition?
Mes. That by proscription and bills of outlawry
Octavius, Antony, and Lepidus
Have put to death an hundred senators.
Bru. Therein our letters do not well agree.
Mine speak of seventy senators that died
By their proscriptions, Cicero being one.
Cass. Cicero one?
Mes. Cicero is dead,
And by that order of proscription.
Had you your letters from your wife, my lord?
Bru. No, Messala.
Mes. Nor nothing in your letters writ of her?
Bru. Nothing, Messala.
Mes. That methinks is strange.
Bru. Why ask you? Hear you aught of her in yours?
Mes. No, my lord.
Bru. Now as you are a Roman, tell me true.
Mes. Then like a Roman bear the truth I tell;
For certain she is dead, and by strange manner.
Bru. Why, farewell, Portia. We must die, Messala.
With meditating that she must die once,
I have the patience to endure it now.
Mes. Even so great men great losses should endure.

Cass. I have as much of this in art as you,
But yet my nature could not bear it so.

Bru. Well, to our work alive. What do you think
Of marching to Philippi presently?

Cass. I do not think it good.

Bru. Your reason?

Cass. This it is:
'Tis better that the enemy seek us.
So shall he waste his means, weary his soldiers,
Doing himself offence, whilst we, lying still,
Are full of rest, defence, and nimbleness.

Bru. Good reasons must of force give place to better.
The people 'twixt Philippi and this ground
Do stand but in a forc'd affection;
For they have grudg'd us contribution.
The enemy, marching along by them,
By them shall make a fuller number up,
Come on refresh'd, new-added, and encourag'd;
From which advantage shall we cut him off
If at Philippi we do face him there,
These people at our back.

Cass. Hear me, good brother.

Bru. Under your pardon. You must note beside
That we have tried the utmost of our friends,
Our legions are brimful, our cause is ripe.
The enemy increaseth every day;
We, at the height, are ready to decline.
There is a tide in the affairs of men
Which, taken at the flood, leads on to fortune;
Omitted, all the voyage of their life
Is bound in shallows and in miseries.
On such a full sea are we now afloat,
And we must take the current when it serves
Or lose our ventures.

Cass. Then, with your will, go on.
We'll along ourselves and meet them at Philippi.

Bru. The deep of night is crept upon our talk
And nature must obey necessity,
Which we will niggard with a little rest.
There is no more to say?

Cass. No more. Good night.
Early to-morrow will we rise and hence.

Bru. Lucius! (*Enter Lucius.*) My gown.
[*Exit Lucius.*] Farewell, good Messala.
Good night, Titinius. Noble, noble Cassius,
Good night and good repose!

Cass. O my dear brother,
This was an ill beginning of the night!
Never come such division 'tween our souls!
Let it not, Brutus.

Enter *Lucius*, with the gown.

Bru. Everything is well.

Cass. Good night, my lord.

Bru. Good night, good brother.

Tit., Mes. Good night, Lord Brutus.

Bru. Farewell every one.

Exeunt [*Cassius, Titinius, and Messala*].

Give me the gown. Where is thy instrument?

Luc. Here in the tent.

Bru. What, thou speak'st drowsily?
Poor knave, I blame thee not; thou art o'er-watch'd.
Call Claudius and some other of my men;
I'll have them sleep on cushions in my tent.

Luc. Varro and Claudius!

Enter *Varro* and *Claudius*.

Var. Calls my lord?

Bru. I pray you, sirs, lie in my tent and sleep.
It may be I shall raise you by-and-by]
On business to my brother Cassius.

Var. So please you, we will stand and watch your pleasure.

Bru. I will not have it so. Lie down, good sirs.
It may be I shall otherwise bethink me.
[*Varro and Claudius lie down.*]
Look, Lucius, here's the book I sought for so;
I put it in the pocket of my gown.

Luc. I was sure your lordship did not give it me.

Bru. Bear with me, good boy, I am much forgetful.
Canst thou hold up thy heavy eyes awhile,
And touch thy instrument a strain or two?

Luc. Ay, my lord, an't please you.

Bru. It does, my boy.
I trouble thee too much, but thou art willing.

Luc. It is my duty, sir.

Bru. I should not urge thy duty past thy might.
I know young bloods look for a time of rest.

Luc. I have slept, my lord, already.

Bru. It was well done; and thou shalt sleep again;
I will not hold thee long. If I do live,
I will be good to thee.

Music, and a song. [*Lucius falls asleep.*]

This is a sleepy tune. O murd'rous slumber!
Layest thou thy leaden mace upon my boy,
That plays thee music? Gentle knave, good night.
I will not do thee so much wrong to wake thee.

If thou dost nod, thou break'st thy instrument;
I'll take it from thee; and, good boy, good night.
Let me see, let me see. Is not the leaf turn'd down
Where I left reading? Here it is, I think.
[*Sits.*]

Enter the *Ghost of Cæsar.*

How ill this taper burns! Ha! who comes here?
I think it is the weakness of mine eyes
That shapes this monstrous apparition.
It comes upon me. Art thou anything?
Art thou some god, some angel, or some devil,
That mak'st my blood cold and my hair to stare?
Speak to me what thou art.

Ghost. Thy evil spirit, Brutus.

Bru. Why com'st thou?

Ghost. To tell thee thou shalt see me at Philippi.

Bru. Well; then I shall see thee again?

Ghost. Ay, at Philippi.

Bru. Why, I will see thee at Philippi then.
[*Exit Ghost.*]
Now I have taken heart thou vanishest.
Ill spirit, I would hold more talk with thee.
Boy! Lucius! Varro! Claudius! Sirs! Awake!
Claudius!

Luc. The strings, my lord, are false.

Bru. He thinks he still is at his instrument.
Lucius, awake!

Luc. My lord?

Bru. Didst thou dream, Lucius, that thou so criedst out?

Luc. My lord, I do not know that I did cry.

Bru. Yes, that thou didst. Didst thou see anything?

Luc. Nothing, my lord.

Bru. Sleep again, Lucius. Sirrah Claudius!
[*To Varro*] Fellow thou, awake!

Var. My lord?

Clau. My lord?

Bru. Why did you so cry out, sirs, in your sleep?

Both. Did we, my lord?

Bru. Ay. Saw you anything?

Var. No, my lord, I saw nothing.

Clau. Nor I, my lord.

Bru. Go and commend me to my brother Cassius.
Bid him set on his pow'rs betimes before,
And we will follow.

Both. It shall be done, my lord. *Exeunt.*

ACT V. [Scene I. *Near Philippi.*]

Enter *Octavius, Antony,* and their *Army.*

Oct. Now, Antony, our hopes are answered.
You said the enemy would not come down
But keep the hills and upper regions.
It proves not so. Their battles are at hand;
They mean to warn us at Philippi here,
Answering before we do demand of them.

Ant. Tut! I am in their bosoms and I know
Wherefore they do it. They could be content
To visit other places, and come down
With fearful bravery, thinking by this face
To fasten in our thoughts that they have courage.
But 'tis not so.

Enter a *Messenger.*

Mess. Prepare you, generals.
The enemy comes on in gallant show;
Their bloody sign of battle is hung out,
And something to be done immediately.

Ant. Octavius, lead your battle softly on
Upon the left hand of the even field.

Oct. Upon the right hand I. Keep thou the left.

Ant. Why do you cross me in this exigent?

Oct. I do not cross you; but I will do so.
March.

Drum. Enter *Brutus, Cassius,* and their *Army*; [*Lucilius, Titinius, Messala,* and others].

Bru. They stand and would have parley.

Cass. Stand fast, Titinius. We must out and talk.

Oct. Mark Antony, shall we give sign of battle?

Ant. No, Cæsar, we will answer on their charge.
Make forth. The generals would have some words.

Oct. Stir not until the signal.

Bru. Words before blows. Is it so, countrymen?

Oct. Not that we love words better, as you do.

Bru. Good words are better than bad strokes, Octavius.

Ant. In your bad strokes, Brutus, you give good words;

Witness the hole you made in Cæsar's heart,
Crying 'Long live! Hail, Cæsar!'

Cass. Antony,
The posture of your blows are yet unknown;
But for your words, they rob the Hybla bees,
And leave them honeyless.

Ant. Not stingless too.

Bru. O yes, and soundless too!
For you have stol'n their buzzing, Antony,
And very wisely threat before you sting.

Ant. Villains! you did not so when your vile daggers
Hack'd one another in the sides of Cæsar.
You show'd your teeth like apes, and fawn'd like hounds,
And bow'd like bondmen, kissing Cæsar's feet;
Whilst damned Casca, like a cur, behind
Struck Cæsar on the neck. O you flatterers!

Cass. Flatterers? Now, Brutus, thank yourself!
This tongue had not offended so to-day
If Cassius might have rul'd.

Oct. Come, come, the cause! If arguing make us sweat,
The proof of it will turn to redder drops.
Look,
I draw a sword against conspirators.
When think you that the sword goes up again?
Never, till Cæsar's three-and-thirty wounds
Be well aveng'd, or till another Cæsar
Have added slaughter to the sword of traitors.

Bru. Cæsar, thou canst not die by traitors' hands
Unless thou bring'st them with thee.

Oct. So I hope.
I was not born to die on Brutus' sword.

Bru. O, if thou wert the noblest of thy strain,
Young man, thou couldst not die more honourable.

Cass. A peevish schoolboy, worthless of such honour,
Join'd with a masker and a reveller!

Ant. Old Cassius still.

Oct. Come, Antony. Away!
Defiance, traitors, hurl we in your teeth.
If you dare fight to-day, come to the field;
If not, when you have stomachs.

Exeunt Octavius, Antony, and Army.

Cass. Why, now blow wind, swell billow, and swim bark!
The storm is up, and all is on the hazard.

Bru. Ho, Lucilius! Hark, a word with you.

Lucilius stands forth.

Lucil. My lord?

[*Brutus and Lucilius converse apart.*]

Cass. Messala. *Messala stands forth.*

Mes. What says my general?

Cass. Messala,
This is my birthday; as this very day
Was Cassius born. Give me thy hand, Messala
Be thou my witness that against my will
(As Pompey was) am I compell'd to set
Upon one battle all our liberties.
You know that I held Epicurus strong
And his opinion. Now I change my mind
And partly credit things that do presage.
Coming from Sardis, on our former ensign
Two mighty eagles fell; and there they perch'd,
Gorging and feeding from our soldiers' hands,
Who to Philippi here consorted us.
This morning are they fled away and gone,
And in their steads do ravens, crows, and kites
Fly o'er our heads and downward look on us
As we were sickly prey. Their shadows seem
A canopy most fatal, under which
Our army lies, ready to give up the ghost.

Mes. Believe not so.

Cass. I but believe it partly;
For I am fresh of spirit and resolv'd
To meet all perils very constantly.

Bru. Even so, Lucilius.

Cass. Now, most noble Brutus,
The gods to-day stand friendly, that we may,
Lovers in peace, lead on our days to age!
But since the affairs of men rest still incertain,
Let's reason with the worst that may befall.
If we do lose this battle, then is this
The very last time we shall speak together.
What are you then determined to do?

Bru. Even by the rule of that philosophy
By which I did blame Cato for the death
Which he did give himself — I know not how,
But I do find it cowardly and vile,
For fear of what might fall, so to prevent
The time of life — arming myself with patience
To stay the providence of some high powers
That govern us below.

Cass. Then, if we lose this battle,
You are contented to be led in triumph
Thorough the streets of Rome.

Bru. No, Cassius, no. Think not, thou noble Roman,
That ever Brutus will go bound to Rome.
He bears too great a mind. But this same day
Must end that work the ides of March begun,
And whether we shall meet again I know not.
Therefore our everlasting farewell take.
For ever and for ever farewell, Cassius!

If we do meet again, why, we shall smile;
If not, why then this parting was well made.
Cass. For ever and for ever farewell, Brutus!
If we do meet again, we'll smile indeed;
If not, 'tis true this parting was well made.
Bru. Why then, lead on. O that a man might know
The end of this day's business ere it come!
But it sufficeth that the day will end,
And then the end is known. Come, ho! Away!
Exeunt.

[Scene II. *Near Philippi. The field of battle.*]

Alarum. Enter *Brutus* and *Messala.*

Bru. Ride, ride, Messala, ride, and give these bills
Unto the legions on the other side.
Loud alarum.
Let them set on at once; for I perceive
But cold demeanour in Octavius' wing,
And sudden push gives them the overthrow.
Ride, ride, Messala! Let them all come down.
Exeunt.

[Scene III. *Another part of the field.*]

Alarums. Enter *Cassius* and *Titinius.*

Cass. O, look, Titinius, look! The villains fly!
Myself have to mine own turn'd enemy.
This ensign here of mine was turning back;
I slew the coward and did take it from him.
Tit. O Cassius, Brutus gave the word too early,
Who, having some advantage on Octavius,
Took it too eagerly. His soldiers fell to spoil,
Whilst we by Antony are all enclos'd.

Enter *Pindarus.*

Pin. Fly further off, my lord! fly further off!
Mark Antony is in your tents, my lord.
Fly, therefore, noble Cassius, fly far off!
Cass. This hill is far enough. Look, look, Titinius!
Are those my tents where I perceive the fire?
Tit. They are, my lord.
Cass. Titinius, if thou lovest me,
Mount thou my horse and hide thy spurs in him
Till he have brought thee up to yonder troops
And here again, that I may rest assur'd
Whether yond troops are friend or enemy.
Tit. I will be here again even with a thought.
Exit.
Cass. Go, Pindarus, get higher on that hill.
My sight was ever thick. Regard Titinius,
And tell me what thou not'st about the field.
[*Pindarus goes up.*]
This day I breathed first. Time is come round,
And where I did begin, there shall I end.
My life is run his compass. Sirrah, what news?
Pin. (*above*) O my lord!
Cass. What news?
Pin. [*above*] Titinius is enclosed round about
With horsemen that make to him on the spur.
Yet he spurs on. Now they are almost on him.
Now, Titinius!
Now some light. O, he lights too! He's ta'en.
(*Shout.*) And hark!
They shout for joy.
Cass. Come down; behold no more.
O coward that I am to live so long
To see my best friend ta'en before my face!

Enter *Pindarus* [from above].

Come hither, sirrah.
In Parthia did I take thee prisoner;
And then I swore thee, saving of thy life,
That whatsoever I did bid thee do,
Thou shouldst attempt it. Come now, keep thine oath.
Now be a freeman, and with this good sword,
That ran through Cæsar's bowels, search this bosom.
Stand not to answer. Here, take thou the hilts;
And when my face is cover'd, as 'tis now,
Guide thou the sword. [*Pindarus stabs him.*]
— Cæsar, thou art reveng'd
Even with the sword that kill'd thee. [*Dies.*]
Pin. So, I am free; yet would not so have been,
Durst I have done my will. O Cassius!
Far from this country Pindarus shall run,
Where never Roman shall take note of him.
[*Exit.*]

Enter *Titinius* and *Messala.*

Mes. It is but change, Titinius; for Octavius
Is overthrown by noble Brutus' power,
As Cassius' legions are by Antony.
Tit. These tidings will well comfort Cassius.
Mes. Where did you leave him?
Tit. All disconsolate,
With Pindarus his bondman, on this hill.

Mes. Is not that he that lies upon the ground?
Tit. He lies not like the living. O my heart!
Mes. Is not that he?
Tit. No, this was he, Messala,
But Cassius is no more. O setting sun,
As in thy red rays thou dost sink to night,
So in his red blood Cassius' day is set!
The sun of Rome is set. Our day is gone;
Clouds, dews, and dangers come; our deeds are done!
Mistrust of my success hath done this deed.
Mes. Mistrust of good success hath done this deed.
O hateful Error, Melancholy's child,
Why dost thou show to the apt thoughts of men
The things that are not? O Error, soon conceiv'd,
Thou never com'st unto a happy birth,
But kill'st the mother that engend'red thee!
Tit. What, Pindarus! Where art thou, Pindarus?
Mes. Seek him, Titinius, whilst I go to meet
The noble Brutus, thrusting this report
Into his ears. I may say 'thrusting' it;
For piercing steel and darts envenomed
Shall be as welcome to the ears of Brutus
As tidings of this sight.
Tit. Hie you, Messala,
And I will seek for Pindarus the while.
[*Exit Messala.*]
Why didst thou send me forth, brave Cassius?
Did I not meet thy friends, and did not they
Put on my brows this wreath of victory
And bid me give it thee? Didst thou not hear their shouts?
Alas, thou hast misconstrued everything!
But hold thee, take this garland on thy brow.
Thy Brutus bid me give it thee, and I
Will do his bidding. Brutus, come apace
And see how I regarded Caius Cassius.
By your leave, gods. This is a Roman's part.
Come, Cassius' sword, and find Titinius' heart.
Dies.

Alarum. Enter *Brutus, Messala, Young Cato, Strato, Volumnius,* and *Lucilius.*

Bru. Where, where, Messala, doth his body lie?
Mes. Lo, yonder, and Titinius mourning it.
Bru. Titinius' face is upward.
Cato. He is slain.
Bru. O Julius Cæsar, thou art mighty yet!
Thy spirit walks abroad and turns our swords
In our own proper entrails. *Low alarums.*
Cato. Brave Titinius!
Look whe'r he have not crown'd dead Cassius.
Bru. Are yet two Romans living such as these?
The last of all the Romans, fare thee well!
It is impossible that ever Rome
Should breed thy fellow. Friends, I owe moe tears
To this dead man than you shall see me pay.
I shall find time, Cassius; I shall find time.
Come therefore, and to Thasos send his body.
His funerals shall not be in our camp,
Lest it discomfort us. Lucilius, come;
And come, young Cato. Let us to the field.
Labeo and Flavius set our battles on.
'Tis three o'clock; and, Romans, yet ere night
We shall try fortune in a second fight.
Exeunt.

[Scene IV. *Another part of the field.*]

Alarum. Enter *Brutus, Messala,* [*Young*] *Cato, Lucilius,* and *Flavius.*

Bru. Yet, countrymen, O, yet hold up your heads!
Cato. What bastard doth not? Who will go with me?
I will proclaim my name about the field.
I am the son of Marcus Cato, ho!
A foe to tyrants, and my country's friend.
I am the son of Marcus Cato, ho!

Enter *Soldiers* and fight.

Bru. And I am Brutus, Marcus Brutus I!
Brutus, my country's friend! Know me for Brutus! [*Exit.*]
[*Young Cato falls.*]
Lucil. O young and noble Cato, art thou down?
Why, now thou diest as bravely as Titinius,
And mayst be honour'd, being Cato's son.
1. Sold. Yield, or thou diest.
Lucil. Only I yield to die.
[*Offers money.*] There is so much that thou wilt kill me straight.
Kill Brutus, and be honour'd in his death.
1. Sold. We must not. A noble prisoner!

Enter *Antony.*

2. Sold. Room ho! Tell Antony Brutus is ta'en.
1. Sold. I'll tell the news. Here comes the general.
Brutus is ta'en! Brutus is ta'en, my lord!

Ant. Where is he?
Lucil. Safe, Antony; Brutus is safe enough.
I dare assure thee that no enemy
Shall ever take alive the noble Brutus.
The gods defend him from so great a shame!
When you do find him, or alive or dead,
He will be found like Brutus, like himself.
Ant. This is not Brutus, friend; but, I assure you,
A prize no less in worth. Keep this man safe;
Give him all kindness. I had rather have
Such men my friends than enemies. Go on,
And see whe'r Brutus be alive or dead;
And bring us word unto Octavius' tent
How every thing is chanc'd. *Exeunt.*

[Scene V. *Another part of the field.*]

Enter *Brutus, Dardanius, Clitus, Strato,* and *Volumnius.*

Bru. Come, poor remains of friends, rest on this rock.
Cli. Statilius show'd the torchlight; but, my lord,
He came not back. He is or ta'en or slain.
Bru. Sit thee down, Clitus. Slaying is the word.
It is a deed in fashion. Hark thee, Clitus. [*Whispers.*]
Cli. What, I, my lord? No, not for all the world!
Bru. Peace then. No words.
Cli. I'll rather kill myself.
Bru. Hark thee, Dardanius. [*Whispers.*]
Dar. Shall I do such a deed?
Cli. O Dardanius!
Dar. O Clitus!
Cli. What ill request did Brutus make to thee?
Dar. To kill him, Clitus. Look, he meditates.
Cli. Now is that noble vessel full of grief,
That it runs over even at his eyes.
Bru. Come hither, good Volumnius. List a word.
Vol. What says my lord?
Bru. Why this, Volumnius.
The ghost of Cæsar hath appear'd to me
Two several times by night — at Sardis once,
And this last night here in Philippi fields.
I know my hour is come.
Vol. Not so, my lord.
Bru. Nay, I am sure it is, Volumnius.
Thou seest the world, Volumnius, how it goes.
Our enemies have beat us to the pit. *Low alarums.*
It is more worthy to leap in ourselves
Than tarry till they push us. Good Volumnius,
Thou know'st that we two went to school together.
Even for that our love of old, I prithee
Hold thou my sword-hilts whilst I run on it.
Vol. That's not an office for a friend, my lord. *Alarum still.*
Cli. Fly, fly, my lord! There is no tarrying here.
Bru. Farewell to you; and you; and you, Volumnius.
Strato, thou hast been all this while asleep.
Farewell to thee too, Strato. Countrymen,
My heart doth joy that yet in all my life
I found no man but he was true to me.
I shall have glory by this losing day
More than Octavius and Mark Antony
By this vile conquest shall attain unto.
So fare you well at once; for Brutus' tongue
Hath almost ended his live's history.
Night hangs upon mine eyes; my bones would rest,
That have but labour'd to attain this hour.
Alarum. Cry within: Fly, fly, fly!
Cli. Fly, my lord, fly!
Bru. Hence! I will follow.
[*Exeunt Clitus, Dardanius, and Volumnius.*]
I prithee, Strato, stay thou by thy lord.
Thou art a fellow of a good respect;
Thy life hath had some smatch of honour in it.
Hold then my sword, and turn away thy face
While I do run upon it. Wilt thou, Strato?
Stra. Give me your hand first. Fare you well, my lord.
Bru. Farewell, good Strato. Cæsar, now be still.
I kill'd not thee with half so good a will.
[*He runs on his sword and*] *dies.*

Alarum. Retreat. Enter *Octavius, Antony, Messala, Lucilius,* and the *Army.*

Oct. What man is that?
Mes. My master's man. Strato, where is thy master?
Stra. Free from the bondage you are in, Messala.
The conquerors can but make a fire of him;

For Brutus only overcame himself,
And no man else hath honour by his death.
Lucil. So Brutus should be found. I thank thee, Brutus,
That thou hast prov'd Lucilius' saying true.
Oct. All that serv'd Brutus, I will entertain them.
Fellow, wilt thou bestow thy time with me?
Stra. Ay, if Messala will prefer me to you.
Oct. Do so, good Messala.
Mes. How died my master, Strato?
Stra. I held the sword, and he did run on it.
Mes. Octavius, then take him to follow thee,
That did the latest service to my master.
Ant. This was the noblest Roman of them all.
All the conspirators save only he
Did that they did in envy of great Cæsar;
He, only in a general honest thought
And common good to all, made one of them.
His life was gentle, and the elements
So mix'd in him that Nature might stand up
And say to all the world, 'This was a man!'
Oct. According to his virtue let us use him,
With all respect and rites of burial.
Within my tent his bones to-night shall lie,
Most like a soldier, ordered honourably.
So call the field to rest, and let's away
To part the glories of this happy day.
Exeunt omnes.

MACBETH

For the text of MACBETH the only authority is the First Folio. This prints what is obviously an acting version of the play, somewhat changed from its original form. Hecate is an intrusive character, quite foreign to Shakespeare's conception of the powers and attributes of the Weird Sisters: the whole of the fifth scene in Act iii is a manifest interpolation; and the same is true of iv, 1, 39–43, 125–132, which must stand or fall with that scene. Two stage directions in the Folio (iii, 5, 33; iv, 1, 43) call for songs that are preserved in Middleton's tragicomedy *The Witch*. This fact, as well as the character of Hecate in Middleton, suggests that he may have been the playwright employed to revise Shakespeare's MACBETH in an operatic spirit, out of harmony with the original design. Two other bits of the Folio text seem to be spurious ('Whiles . . . gives,' ii, 1, 60–61; and 'Before . . . shield,' v, 8, 32–33), but they do not sound like Middleton. Probably the reviser made some cuts, for the play is very short; but nothing essential has been lost.

Several passages besides the Hecate material have been thought to be interpolated, but without good reason. Coleridge rejected the Porter's soliloquy (ii, 3), oblivious of its dramatic irony and of the need for something of the kind to separate the exit of Macbeth and his wife from their reëntrance. The speeches of the wounded Sergeant (i, 2) have been attacked on the ground that their bombastic phraseology is not like Shakespeare's language; but their mixture of bombast and grotesque bluntness accords perfectly with what was expected of a stage soldier.

There is no decisive evidence for date. Many supposed criteria have been cited — all of them interesting, but none of them decisive. For the Weird Sisters Shakespeare needed no hint from Matthew Gwinne's 'Tres Sibyllae' (1605); they are central figures of the Macbeth legend as told by Holinshed. The farmer (or other speculator in wheat) 'that hang'd himself on th' expectation of plenty' was a stock figure as early as the thirteenth century and is not to be connected especially with the price of wheat in 1606. The Porter's 'equivocator' need not involve an allusion to Garnet, who was tried on March 28, 1606. Possible echoes of MACBETH in almost contemporary plays are interesting but by no means conclusive. The most striking is in *The Knight of the Burning Pestle* (v, 1, 20–30) — itself a play of uncertain date but probably assignable to 1607. Everything considered, however, Malone's date for MACBETH, 1606, has stood all tests for more than a century. Style and metre fit this date, but 1605 is also possible (cf. p. 1195).

For the plot Shakespeare had recourse to Holinshed's *Chronicle*. Since he was writing a tragedy and not a 'history,' he did not hesitate to take liberties. The rebellion of Macdonwald and the invasion of 'Sweno the Norways' king' are brought together. For the murder of Duncan, he has used Holinshed's account of the murder of King Duff by Donwald, which includes the drugging of the chamberlains and the prodigies described in ii, 4. The voice that cried 'Sleep no more!' was apparently suggested by what Holinshed tells of the dream of King Kenneth III. The Weird Sisters disappear from history immediately after their meeting with Macbeth upon the blasted heath. The warning to 'beware Macduff' (iv, 1, 71) is given by 'certeine wizzards, in whose words [Macbeth] put great confidence'; the prophecies concerning 'none of woman born' and Birnam Wood (80, 92–93) are made by 'a certeine witch, whome hee had in great trust.' Holinshed's authority for Macbeth's history was Hector Boece's *Scotorum Historiae*, which goes back to Fordun's *Scotichronicon* and Wyntown's *Cronykil*. The material combines sober history (A.D. 1040–1057) with much ancient legend and some out-and-out fiction.

The Weird Sisters are the Norns of Scandinavian mythology. The Norns were goddesses who shaped beforehand the life of every man. Sometimes they came in the night and stood by the cradle of the new-born child, uttering their decrees; for their office was not to prophesy only, but to determine. Sometimes they were met in wild places and at unexpected moments. Once they were seen in a remote lodge in the woods, weaving the visible web of doom on the eve of a great battle in which many perished. Now they appear as the guardians of a favourite hero; again, they are hostile, and bent only on a man's destruction: but always and everywhere they are great and terrible powers, from whose mandate there is no appeal. The Scandinavian Norns are present and operative in Holinshed's history of Macbeth under the name of 'the weird sisters, that is, the goddesses of destinie.' In all probability, their attachment to the story goes back to the time of Macbeth himself. Their presence is due to the large infusion of Norse blood in the Scottish race, and their function is in full accord with the doctrines of Norse heathendom. That function, then, was an essential element in the history of Macbeth as it came into Shakespeare's hands. These were not ordinary witches or seeresses. They were great powers of destiny, great ministers of fate. They had determined the past; they governed the present; they not only foresaw the future, but decreed it. All this was manifest to Shakespeare as he read the chronicle. He assimilated the conception in its entirety by a single act of sympathetic imagination; and he reproduced it in his tragedy, not in any literal or dogmatic shape, but coloured and intensified by his creative genius, and modified by his trained sense of what it is possible to represent upon the actual stage. The Weird Sisters, then, are not hags in the service of the devil; they are not mere personifications of a man's evil desires or his ruthless craving for power. They are as actual and objective as the Furies that lie snoring in bloodthirsty dreams round about the fugitive Orestes as he clings affrighted to the altar of Apollo.

Thus the tragedy of MACBETH is inevitably fatalistic, but Shakespeare attempts no solution of the problem of free will and predestination. It is not his office to make a contribution to philosophy or theology. He never gives us the impression that a man is not responsible for his own acts. 'It will have blood, they say; blood will have blood.'

Obviously, however, Shakespeare could not produce the goddesses of fate *in propria persona* upon the stage in a Scottish tragedy. He had to bring them within the range of the spectators' beliefs and experiences. And this he accomplished by giving them several attributes of a class of women with whom the audience had perfect familiarity — the witch. They kill swine, they brew hell-broth, they have familiar spirits, they dig up the dead to use fragments of mortality in their charms. Yet they remain indisputably supernatural. They are not amenable to the halter or the stake. If they choose to wear the garb of witches for a time, that is their own affair. Their empire is as wide as the world, and their power extends to the last syllable of recorded time.

THE TRAGEDY OF
MACBETH

[Dramatis Personæ.

Duncan, King of Scotland.
Malcolm, *Donalbain*, his sons.
Macbeth, *Banquo*, Generals of the Scottish Army.
Macduff, *Lennox*, *Ross*, *Menteith*, *Angus*, *Caithness*, Noblemen of Scotland.
Fleance, Son to Banquo.
Siward, Earl of Northumberland, General of the English forces.
Young Siward, his son.
Seyton, an Officer attending on *Macbeth*.
Boy, son to *Macduff*.

A Sergeant.
A Porter.
An Old Man.
An English Doctor.
A Scottish Doctor.

Lady Macbeth.
Lady Macduff.
A Gentlewoman, attending on *Lady Macbeth*.

The *Weird Sisters*.
Hecate.
The Ghost of *Banquo*.
Apparitions.

Lords, Gentlemen, Officers, Soldiers, Murderers, Messengers, Attendants.

SCENE. — *Scotland; England*.]

ACT I. Scene I. [*Scotland. An open place.*]

Thunder and lightning. Enter three *Witches*.

1. Witch. When shall we three meet again
In thunder, lightning, or in rain?
2. Witch. When thc hurlyburly's done,
When the battle's lost and won.
3. Witch. That will be ere the set of sun.
1. Witch. Where the place?
2. Witch. Upon the heath.
3. Witch. There to meet with Macbeth.
1. Witch. I come, Graymalkin!
2. Witch. Paddock calls.
3. Witch. Anon!
All. Fair is foul, and foul is fair.
Hover through the fog and filthy air. *Exeunt.*

Scene II. [*A camp near Forres.*]

Alarum within. Enter *King* [*Duncan*], *Malcolm*, *Donalbain*, *Lennox*, with *Attendants*, meeting a bleeding *Sergeant*.

King. What bloody man is that? He can report,
As seemeth by his plight, of the revolt
The newest state.
Mal. This is the sergeant
Who like a good and hardy soldier fought
'Gainst my captivity. Hail, brave friend!
Say to the King the knowledge of the broil
As thou didst leave it.
Serg. Doubtful it stood,
As two spent swimmers that do cling together
And choke their art. The merciless Macdonwald
(Worthy to be a rebel, for to that
The multiplying villanies of nature
Do swarm upon him) from the Western Isles
Of kerns and gallowglasses is supplied;
And Fortune, on his damned quarrel smiling,
Show'd like a rebel's whore. But all's too weak;
For brave Macbeth (well he deserves that name),
Disdaining Fortune, with his brandish'd steel,
Which smok'd with bloody execution
(Like valour's minion), carv'd out his passage
Till he fac'd the slave;
Which ne'er shook hands nor bade farewell to him
Till he unseam'd him from the nave to th' chaps
And fix'd his head upon our battlements.

King. O valiant cousin! worthy gentleman!
Serg. As whence the sun gins his reflection
Shipwracking storms and direful thunders break,
So from that spring whence comfort seem'd to come
Discomfort swells. Mark, King of Scotland, mark.
No sooner justice had, with valour arm'd,
Compell'd these skipping kerns to trust their heels
But the Norweyan lord, surveying vantage,
With furbish'd arms and new supplies of men,
Began a fresh assault.
King. Dismay'd not this
Our captains, Macbeth and Banquo?
Serg. Yes,
As sparrows eagles, or the hare the lion.
If I say sooth, I must report they were
As cannons overcharg'd with double cracks, so they
Doubly redoubled strokes upon the foe.
Except they meant to bathe in reeking wounds,
Or memorize another Golgotha,
I cannot tell —
But I am faint; my gashes cry for help.
King. So well thy words become thee as thy wounds;
They smack of honour both. Go get him surgeons.
[*Exit Sergeant, attended.*]

Enter *Ross.*

Who comes here?
Mal. The worthy Thane of Ross.
Len. What a haste looks through his eyes! So should he look
That seems to speak things strange.
Ross. God save the King!
King. Whence cam'st thou, worthy thane?
Ross. From Fife, great King,
Where the Norweyan banners flout the sky
And fan our people cold. Norway himself,
With terrible numbers,
Assisted by that most disloyal traitor
The Thane of Cawdor, began a dismal conflict,
Till that Bellona's bridegroom, lapp'd in proof,
Confronted him with self-comparisons,
Point against point, rebellious arm 'gainst arm,
Curbing his lavish spirit; and to conclude,
The victory fell on us.
King. Great happiness!
Ross. That now
Sweno, the Norways' king, craves composition;
Nor would we deign him burial of his men
Till he disbursed, at Saint Colme's Inch,
Ten thousand dollars to our general use.
King. No more that Thane of Cawdor shall deceive
Our bosom interest. Go pronounce his present death
And with his former title greet Macbeth.
Ross. I'll see it done.
Dun. What he hath lost noble Macbeth hath won. *Exeunt.*

Scene III. [*A blasted heath.*]

Thunder. Enter the three *Witches.*

1. Witch. Where hast thou been, sister?
2. Witch. Killing swine.
3. Witch. Sister, where thou?
1. Witch. A sailor's wife had chestnuts in her lap
And mounch'd and mounch'd and mounch'd. 'Give me,' quoth I.
'Aroint thee, witch!' the rump-fed ronyon cries.
Her husband's to Aleppo gone, master o' th' Tiger;
But in a sieve I'll thither sail
And, like a rat without a tail,
I'll do, I'll do, and I'll do.
2. Witch. I'll give thee a wind.
1. Witch. Th' art kind.
3. Witch. And I another.
1. Witch. I myself have all the other,
And the very ports they blow,
All the quarters that they know
I' th' shipman's card.
I will drain him dry as hay.
Sleep shall neither night nor day
Hang upon his penthouse lid.
He shall live a man forbid.
Weary sev'nights, nine times nine,
Shall he dwindle, peak, and pine.
Though his bark cannot be lost,
Yet it shall be tempest-tost.
Look what I have.
2. Witch. Show me! show me!
1. Witch. Here I have a pilot's thumb,
Wrack'd as homeward he did come.
Drum within.
3. Witch. A drum, a drum!
Macbeth doth come.
All. The Weird Sisters, hand in hand,
Posters of the sea and land,
Thus do go about, about,
Thrice to thine, and thrice to mine,

And thrice again, to make up nine.
Peace! The charm's wound up.

Enter *Macbeth* and *Banquo*.

Macb. So foul and fair a day I have not seen.
Ban. How far is't call'd to Forres? What are these,
So wither'd, and so wild in their attire,
That look not like th' inhabitants o' th' earth,
And yet are on't? Live you? or are you aught
That man may question? You seem to understand me,
By each at once her choppy finger laying
Upon her skinny lips. You should be women,
And yet your beards forbid me to interpret
That you are so.
Macb. Speak, if you can. What are you?
1. Witch. All hail, Macbeth! Hail to thee, Thane of Glamis!
2. Witch. All hail, Macbeth! Hail to thee, Thane of Cawdor!
3. Witch. All hail, Macbeth, that shalt be King hereafter!
Ban. Good sir, why do you start and seem to fear
Things that do sound so fair? I' th' name of truth,
Are ye fantastical, or that indeed
Which outwardly ye show? My noble partner
You greet with present grace and great prediction
Of noble having and of royal hope,
That he seems rapt withal. To me you speak not.
If you can look into the seeds of time
And say which grain will grow and which will not,
Speak then to me, who neither beg nor fear
Your favours nor your hate.
1. Witch. Hail!
2. Witch. Hail!
3. Witch. Hail!
1. Witch. Lesser than Macbeth, and greater.
2. Witch. Not so happy, yet much happier.
3. Witch. Thou shalt get kings, though thou be none.
So all hail, Macbeth and Banquo!
1. Witch. Banquo and Macbeth, all hail!
Macb. Stay, you imperfect speakers, tell me more!
By Sinel's death I know I am Thane of Glamis;
But how of Cawdor? The Thane of Cawdor lives,
A prosperous gentleman; and to be King
Stands not within the prospect of belief,
No more than to be Cawdor. Say from whence
You owe this strange intelligence, or why
Upon this blasted heath you stop our way
With such prophetic greeting. Speak, I charge you. *Witches vanish.*
Ban. The earth hath bubbles, as the water has,
And these are of them. Whither are they vanish'd?
Macb. Into the air, and what seem'd corporal melted
As breath into the wind. Would they had stay'd!
Ban. Were such things here as we do speak about?
Or have we eaten on the insane root
That takes the reason prisoner?
Macb. Your children shall be kings.
Ban. You shall be King.
Macb. And Thane of Cawdor too. Went it not so?
Ban. To th' selfsame tune and words. Who's here?

Enter *Ross* and *Angus*.

Ross. The King hath happily receiv'd, Macbeth,
The news of thy success; and when he reads
Thy personal venture in the rebels' fight,
His wonders and his praises do contend
Which should be thine or his. Silenc'd with that,
In viewing o'er the rest o' th' selfsame day,
He finds thee in the stout Norweyan ranks,
Nothing afeard of what thyself didst make,
Strange images of death. As thick as tale
Came post with post, and every one did bear
Thy praises in his kingdom's great defence
And pour'd them down before him.
Ang. We are sent
To give thee from our royal master thanks;
Only to herald thee into his sight,
Not pay thee.
Ross. And for an earnest of a greater honour,
He bade me, from him, call thee Thane of Cawdor;
In which addition, hail, most worthy Thane!
For it is thine.
Ban. What, can the devil speak true?
Macb. The Thane of Cawdor lives. Why do you dress me
In borrowed robes?
Ang. Who was the Thane lives yet,
But under heavy judgment bears that life
Which he deserves to lose. Whether he was combin'd

With those of Norway, or did line the rebel
With hidden help and vantage, or that with both
He labour'd in his country's wrack, I know not;
But treasons capital, confess'd and prov'd,
Have overthrown him.

Macb. [*aside*] Glamis, and Thane of Cawdor!
The greatest is behind. — [*To Ross and Angus.*] Thanks for your pains.
[*Aside to Banquo*] Do you not hope your children shall be kings,
When those that gave the Thane of Cawdor to me
Promis'd no less to them?

Ban. [*aside to Macbeth*] That, trusted home,
Might yet enkindle you unto the crown,
Besides the Thane of Cawdor. But 'tis strange!
And oftentimes, to win us to our harm,
The instruments of darkness tell us truths,
Win us with honest trifles, to betray's
In deepest consequence. —
Cousins, a word, I pray you.

Macb. [*aside*] Two truths are told,
As happy prologues to the swelling act
Of the imperial theme. — I thank you, gentlemen. —
[*Aside*] This supernatural soliciting
Cannot be ill; cannot be good. If ill,
Why hath it given me earnest of success,
Commencing in a truth? I am Thane of Cawdor.
If good, why do I yield to that suggestion
Whose horrid image doth unfix my hair
And make my seated heart knock at my ribs
Against the use of nature? Present fears
Are less than horrible imaginings.
My thought, whose murther yet is but fantastical,
Shakes so my single state of man that function
Is smother'd in surmise and nothing is
But what is not.

Ban. Look how our partner's rapt.

Macb. [*aside*] If chance will have me King, why, chance may crown me,
Without my stir.

Ban. New honours come upon him,
Like our strange garments, cleave not to their mould
But with the aid of use.

Macb. [*aside*] Come what come may,
Time and the hour runs through the roughest day.

Ban. Worthy Macbeth, we stay upon your leisure.

Macb. Give me your favour. My dull brain was wrought
With things forgotten. Kind gentlemen, your pains
Are regist'red where every day I turn
The leaf to read them. Let us toward the King.
[*Aside to Banquo*] Think upon what hath chanc'd; and, at more time,
The interim having weigh'd it, let us speak
Our free hearts each to other.

Ban. [*aside to Macbeth*] Very gladly.

Macb. [*aside to Banquo*] Till then, enough. — Come, friends. *Exeunt.*

Scene IV. [*Forres. The Palace.*]

Flourish. Enter *King* [*Duncan*], *Lennox, Malcolm, Donalbain,* and *Attendants.*

King. Is execution done on Cawdor? Are not
Those in commission yet return'd?

Mal. My liege,
They are not yet come back. But I have spoke
With one that saw him die; who did report
That very frankly he confess'd his treasons,
Implor'd your Highness' pardon, and set forth
A deep repentance. Nothing in his life
Became him like the leaving it. He died
As one that had been studied in his death
To throw away the dearest thing he ow'd
As 'twere a careless trifle.

King. There's no art
To find the mind's construction in the face.
He was a gentleman on whom I built
An absolute trust.

Enter *Macbeth, Banquo, Ross,* and *Angus.*

O worthiest cousin,
The sin of my ingratitude even now
Was heavy on me! Thou art so far before
That swiftest wing of recompense is slow
To overtake thee. Would thou hadst less deserv'd,
That the proportion both of thanks and payment
Might have been mine! Only I have left to say,
More is thy due than more than all can pay.

Macb. The service and the loyalty I owe,
In doing it pays itself. Your Highness' part
Is to receive our duties; and our duties
Are to your throne and state children and servants,
Which do but what they should by doing everything
Safe toward your love and honour.

King. Welcome hither.
I have begun to plant thee and will labour
To make thee full of growing. Noble Banquo,
That hast no less deserv'd, nor must be known
No less to have done so, let me infold thee
And hold thee to my heart.

Ban. There if I grow,
The harvest is your own.

King. My plenteous joys,
Wanton in fulness, seek to hide themselves
In drops of sorrow. Sons, kinsmen, thanes,
And you whose places are the nearest, know
We will establish our estate upon
Our eldest, Malcolm, whom we name hereafter
The Prince of Cumberland; which honour must
Not unaccompanied invest him only,
But signs of nobleness, like stars, shall shine
On all deservers. From hence to Inverness,
And bind us further to you.

Macb. The rest is labour, which is not us'd for you!
I'll be myself the harbinger, and make joyful
The hearing of my wife with your approach;
So, humbly take my leave.

King. My worthy Cawdor!

Macb. [*aside*] The Prince of Cumberland! That is a step
On which I must fall down, or else o'erleap,
For in my way it lies. Stars, hide your fires!
Let not light see my black and deep desires.
The eye wink at the hand; yet let that be,
Which the eye fears, when it is done, to see.
Exit.

King. True, worthy Banquo: he is full so valiant,
And in his commendations I am fed;
It is a banquet to me. Let's after him,
Whose care is gone before to bid us welcome.
It is a peerless kinsman. *Flourish. Exeunt.*

Scene V. [*Inverness. Macbeth's Castle.*]

Enter *Macbeth's Wife*, alone, with a letter.

Lady. [*reads*] 'They met me in the day of success; and I have learn'd by the perfect'st report they have more in them than mortal knowledge. When I burn'd in desire to question them further, they made themselves air, into which they vanish'd. Whiles I stood rapt in the wonder of it, came missives from the King, who all-hail'd me Thane of Cawdor, by which title, before, these Weird Sisters saluted me, and referr'd me to the coming on of time with "Hail, King that shalt be!" This have I thought good to deliver thee, my dearest partner of greatness, that thou mightst not lose the dues of rejoicing by being ignorant of what greatness is promis'd thee. Lay it to thy heart, and farewell.'
Glamis thou art, and Cawdor, and shalt be—
What thou art promis'd. Yet do I fear thy nature.
It is too full o' th' milk of human kindness
To catch the nearest way. Thou wouldst be great;
Art not without ambition, but without
The illness should attend it. What thou wouldst highly,
That wouldst thou holily; wouldst not play false,
And yet wouldst wrongly win. Thou'ldst have, great Glamis,
That which cries 'Thus thou must do,' if thou have it;
And that which rather thou dost fear to do
Than wishest should be undone. Hie thee hither,
That I may pour my spirits in thine ear
And chastise with the valour of my tongue
All that impedes thee from the golden round
Which fate and metaphysical aid doth seem
To have thee crown'd withal.

Enter *Messenger.*

What is your tidings?

Mess. The King comes here to-night.

Lady. Thou'rt mad to say it!
Is not thy master with him? who, were't so,
Would have inform'd for preparation.

Mess. So please you, it is true. Our Thane is coming.
One of my fellows had the speed of him,
Who, almost dead for breath, had scarcely more
Than would make up his message.

Lady. Give him tending;
He brings great news.
Exit Messenger.
The raven himself is hoarse
That croaks the fatal entrance of Duncan
Under my battlements. Come, you spirits
That tend on mortal thoughts, unsex me here,
And fill me, from the crown to the toe, top-full
Of direst cruelty! Make thick my blood;
Stop up th' access and passage to remorse,
That no compunctious visitings of nature
Shake my fell purpose nor keep peace between
Th' effect and it! Come to my woman's breasts
And take my milk for gall, you murth'ring ministers,
Wherever in your sightless substances

You wait on nature's mischief! Come, thick night,
And pall thee in the dunnest smoke of hell,
That my keen knife see not the wound it makes,
Nor heaven peep through the blanket of the dark
To cry 'Hold, hold!'

Enter *Macbeth*

Great Glamis! worthy Cawdor!
Greater than both, by the all-hail hereafter!
Thy letters have transported me beyond
This ignorant present, and I feel now
The future in the instant.

Macb. My dearest love,
Duncan comes here to-night.

Lady. And when goes hence?

Macb. To-morrow, as he purposes.

Lady. O, never
Shall sun that morrow see!
Your face, my Thane, is as a book where men
May read strange matters. To beguile the time,
Look like the time; bear welcome in your eye,
Your hand, your tongue; look like the innocent flower,
But be the serpent under't. He that's coming
Must be provided for; and you shall put
This night's great business into my dispatch,
Which shall to all our nights and days to come
Give solely sovereign sway and masterdom.

Macb. We will speak further.

Lady. Only look up clear.
To alter favour ever is to fear.
Leave all the rest to me. *Exeunt.*

Scene VI. [*Inverness. Before* Macbeth's *castle.*]

Hautboys and torches. Enter *King* [*Duncan*], *Malcolm, Donalbain, Banquo, Lennox, Macduff, Ross, Angus,* and *Attendants.*

King. This castle hath a pleasant seat. The air
Nimbly and sweetly recommends itself
Unto our gentle senses.

Ban. This guest of summer,
The temple-haunting martlet, does approve
By his lov'd mansionry that the heaven's breath
Smells wooingly here. No jutty, frieze,
Buttress, nor coign of vantage, but this bird
Hath made his pendent bed and procreant cradle.
Where they most breed and haunt, I have observ'd
The air is delicate.

Enter *Lady* [*Macbeth*].

King. See, see, our honour'd hostess!
The love that follows us sometime is our trouble,
Which still we thank as love. Herein I teach you
How you shall bid God 'ield us for your pains
And thank us for your trouble.

Lady. All our service
In every point twice done, and then done double,
Were poor and single business to contend
Against those honours deep and broad wherewith
Your Majesty loads our house. For those of old,
And the late dignities heap'd up to them,
We rest your hermits.

King. Where's the Thane of Cawdor?
We cours'd him at the heels and had a purpose
To be his purveyor; but he rides well,
And his great love, sharp as his spur, hath holp him
To his home before us. Fair and noble hostess,
We are your guest to-night.

Lady. Your servants ever
Have theirs, themselves, and what is theirs, in compt,
To make their audit at your Highness' pleasure,
Still to return your own.

King. Give me your hand;
Conduct me to mine host. We love him highly
And shall continue our graces towards him.
By your leave, hostess. *Exeunt.*

Scene VII. [*Inverness.* Macbeth's *Castle.*]

Hautboys. Torches. Enter a *Sewer,* and divers *Servants* with dishes and service over the stage. Then enter *Macbeth.*

Macb. If it were done when 'tis done, then 'twere well
It were done quickly. If th' assassination
Could trammel up the consequence, and catch,
With his surcease, success; that but this blow
Might be the be-all and the end-all here,
But here, upon this bank and shoal of time,
We'd jump the life to come. But in these cases
We still have judgment here, that we but teach

Bloody instructions, which, being taught, return
To plague th' inventor. This even-handed justice
Commends th' ingredience of our poison'd chalice
To our own lips. He's here in double trust:
First, as I am his kinsman and his subject —
Strong both against the deed; then, as his host,
Who should against his murtherer shut the door,
Not bear the knife myself. Besides, this Duncan
Hath borne his faculties so meek, hath been
So clear in his great office, that his virtues
Will plead like angels, trumpet-tongu'd, against
The deep damnation of his taking-off;
And pity, like a naked new-born babe,
Striding the blast, or heaven's cherubin, hors'd
Upon the sightless couriers of the air,
Shall blow the horrid deed in every eye,
That tears shall drown the wind. I have no spur
To prick the sides of my intent, but only
Vaulting ambition, which o'erleaps itself
And falls on th' other side.

Enter *Lady* [*Macbeth*].

How now? What news?

Lady. He has almost supp'd. Why have you left the chamber?

Macb. Hath he ask'd for me?

Lady. Know you not he has?

Macb. We will proceed no further in this business.
He hath honour'd me of late, and I have bought
Golden opinions from all sorts of people,
Which would be worn now in their newest gloss,
Not cast aside so soon.

Lady. Was the hope drunk
Wherein you dress'd yourself? Hath it slept since?
And wakes it now to look so green and pale
At what it did so freely? From this time
Such I account thy love. Art thou afeard
To be the same in thine own act and valour
As thou art in desire? Wouldst thou have that
Which thou esteem'st the ornament of life,
And live a coward in thine own esteem,
Letting 'I dare not' wait upon 'I would,'
Like the poor cat i' th' adage?

Macb. Prithee peace!
I dare do all that may become a man.
Who dares do more is none.

Lady. What beast was't then
That made you break this enterprise to me?
When you durst do it, then you were a man;
And to be more than what you were, you would
Be so much more the man. Nor time nor place
Did then adhere, and yet you would make both.
They have made themselves, and that their fitness now
Does unmake you. I have given suck, and know
How tender 'tis to love the babe that milks me.
I would, while it was smiling in my face,
Have pluck'd my nipple from his boneless gums
And dash'd the brains out, had I so sworn as you
Have done to this.

Macb. If we should fail?

Lady. We fail?
But screw your courage to the sticking place,
And we'll not fail. When Duncan is asleep
(Whereto the rather shall his day's hard journey
Soundly invite him), his two chamberlains
Will I with wine and wassail so convince
That memory, the warder of the brain,
Shall be a fume, and the receipt of reason
A limbeck only. When in swinish sleep
Their drenched natures lie as in a death,
What cannot you and I perform upon
Th' unguarded Duncan? what not put upon
His spongy officers, who shall bear the guilt
Of our great quell?

Macb. Bring forth men-children only;
For thy undaunted mettle should compose
Nothing but males. Will it not be receiv'd,
When we have mark'd with blood those sleepy two
Of his own chamber and us'd their very daggers,
That they have done't?

Lady. Who dares receive it other,
As we shall make our griefs and clamour roar
Upon his death?

Macb. I am settled and bend up
Each corporal agent to this terrible feat.
Away, and mock the time with fairest show;
False face must hide what the false heart doth know.
Exeunt.

Act II. Scene I. [*Inverness. Court of* Macbeth's *Castle.*]

Enter *Banquo*, and *Fleance* with a torch before him.

Ban. How goes the night, boy?
Fle. The moon is down; I have not heard the clock.
Ban. And she goes down at twelve.
Fle. I take't, 'tis later, sir.
Ban. Hold, take my sword. There's husbandry in heaven;
Their candles are all out. Take thee that too.
A heavy summons lies like lead upon me,
And yet I would not sleep. Merciful powers,
Restrain in me the cursed thoughts that nature
Gives way to in repose!

Enter *Macbeth*, and a *Servant* with a torch.

Give me my sword.
Who's there?
Macb. A friend.
Ban. What, sir, not yet at rest? The King's abed.
He hath been in unusual pleasure and
Sent forth great largess to your offices.
This diamond he greets your wife withal
By the name of most kind hostess, and shut up
In measureless content.
Macb. Being unprepar'd,
Our will became the servant to defect,
Which else should free have wrought.
Ban. All's well. 19
I dreamt last night of the three Weird Sisters.
To you they have show'd some truth.
Macb. I think not of them.
Yet when we can entreat an hour to serve,
We would spend it in some words upon that business,
If you would grant the time.
Ban. At your kind'st leisure.
Macb. If you shall cleave to my consent, when 'tis,
It shall make honour for you.
Ban. So I lose none
In seeking to augment it but still keep
My bosom franchis'd and allegiance clear,
I shall be counsell'd.
Macb. Good repose the while!
Ban. Thanks, sir. The like to you!
Exeunt Banquo [and Fleance].
Macb. Go bid thy mistress, when my drink is ready,
She strike upon the bell. Get thee to bed.
Exit [Servant].
Is this a dagger which I see before me,
The handle toward my hand? Come, let me clutch thee!
I have thee not, and yet I see thee still.
Art thou not, fatal vision, sensible
To feeling as to sight? or art thou but
A dagger of the mind, a false creation,
Proceeding from the heat-oppressed brain?
I see thee yet, in form as palpable
As this which now I draw.
Thou marshall'st me the way that I was going,
And such an instrument I was to use.
Mine eyes are made the fools o' th' other senses,
Or else worth all the rest. I see thee still;
And on thy blade and dudgeon gouts of blood,
Which was not so before. There's no such thing.
It is the bloody business which informs
Thus to mine eyes. Now o'er the one half-world
Nature seems dead, and wicked dreams abuse
The curtain'd sleep. Now witchcraft celebrates
Pale Hecate's offerings; and wither'd murther,
Alarum'd by his sentinel, the wolf,
Whose howl's his watch, thus with his stealthy pace,
With Tarquin's ravishing strides, towards his design
Moves like a ghost. Thou sure and firm-set earth,
Hear not my steps which way they walk, for fear
Thy very stones prate of my whereabout
And take the present horror from the time,
Which now suits with it. Whiles I threat, he lives;
Words to the heat of deeds too cold breath gives.
A bell rings.
I go, and it is done. The bell invites me.
Hear it not, Duncan, for it is a knell
That summons thee to heaven, or to hell. *Exit.*

Scene II. [*Inverness.* Macbeth's *Castle.*]

Enter *Lady* [*Macbeth*].

Lady. That which hath made them drunk hath made me bold;
What hath quench'd them hath given me fire.
Hark! Peace!

It was the owl that shriek'd, the fatal bellman
Which gives the stern'st good-night. He is about it.
The doors are open, and the surfeited grooms
Do mock their charge with snores. I have drugg'd their possets,
That death and nature do contend about them
Whether they live or die.

Macb. [*within*] Who's there? What, ho?

Lady. Alack, I am afraid they have awak'd,
And 'tis not done! Th' attempt, and not the deed,
Confounds us. Hark! I laid their daggers ready;
He could not miss 'em. Had he not resembled
My father as he slept, I had done't.

Enter *Macbeth*.

My husband!

Macb. I have done the deed. Didst thou not hear a noise?

Lady. I heard the owl scream and the crickets cry.
Did not you speak?

Macb. When?

Lady. Now.

Macb. As I descended?

Lady. Ay.

Macb. Hark!
Who lies i' th' second chamber?

Lady. Donalbain.

Macb. This is a sorry sight. [*Looks on his hands.*]

Lady. A foolish thought, to say a sorry sight.

Macb. There's one did laugh in's sleep, and one cried 'Murther!'
That they did wake each other. I stood and heard them.
But they did say their prayers and address'd them
Again to sleep.

Lady. There are two lodg'd together.

Macb. One cried 'God bless us!' and 'Amen!' the other,
As they had seen me with these hangman's hands,
List'ning their fear. I could not say 'Amen!'
When they did say 'God bless us!'

Lady. Consider it not so deeply.

Macb. But wherefore could not I pronounce 'Amen'?
I had most need of blessing, and 'Amen'
Stuck in my throat.

Lady. These deeds must not be thought
After these ways. So, it will make us mad.

Macb. Methought I heard a voice cry 'Sleep no more!
Macbeth does murther sleep.' — the innocent sleep,
Sleep that knits up the ravell'd sleave of care,
The death of each day's life, sore labour's bath,
Balm of hurt minds, great nature's second course,
Chief nourisher in life's feast.

Lady. What do you mean?

Macb. Still it cried 'Sleep no more!' to all the house;
'Glamis hath murther'd sleep, and therefore Cawdor
Shall sleep no more! Macbeth shall sleep no more!'

Lady. Who was it that thus cried? Why, worthy Thane,
You do unbend your noble strength to think
So brainsickly of things. Go get some water
And wash this filthy witness from your hand.
Why did you bring these daggers from the place?
They must lie there. Go carry them and smear
The sleepy grooms with blood.

Macb. I'll go no more.
I am afraid to think what I have done;
Look on't again I dare not.

Lady. Infirm of purpose!
Give me the daggers. The sleeping and the dead
Are but as pictures. 'Tis the eye of childhood
That fears a painted devil. If he do bleed,
I'll gild the faces of the grooms withal,
For it must seem their guilt. *Exit. Knocking within.*

Macb. Whence is that knocking?
How is't with me when every noise appals me?
What hands are here? Ha! they pluck out mine eyes!
Will all great Neptune's ocean wash this blood
Clean from my hand? No. This my hand will rather
The multitudinous seas incarnadine,
Making the green one red.

Enter *Lady* [*Macbeth*].

Lady. My hands are of your colour, but I shame
To wear a heart so white. (*Knock.*) I hear a knocking
At the south entry. Retire we to our chamber.
A little water clears us of this deed.
How easy is it then! Your constancy
Hath left you unattended. (*Knock.*) Hark! more knocking.

Get on your nightgown, lest occasion call us
And show us to be watchers. Be not lost
So poorly in your thoughts.

Macb. To know my deed, 'twere best not know myself. *Knock.*
Wake Duncan with thy knocking! I would thou couldst! *Exeunt.*

Scene III. [*Inverness.* Macbeth's *Castle.*]

Enter a *Porter*. Knocking within.

Porter. Here's a knocking indeed! If a man were porter of hell gate, he should have old turning the key. (*Knock.*) Knock, knock, knock! Who's there, i' th' name of Belzebub? Here's a farmer that hang'd himself on th' expectation of plenty. Come in time! Have napkins enow about you; here you'll sweat for't. (*Knock.*) Knock, knock! Who's there, in th' other devil's name? Faith, here's an equivocator, that could swear in both the scales against either scale; who committed treason enough for God's sake, yet could not equivocate to heaven. O, come in, equivocator! (*Knock.*) Knock, knock, knock! Who's there? Faith, here's an English tailor come hither for stealing out of a French hose. Come in, tailor. Here you may roast your goose. (*Knock.*) Knock, knock! Never at quiet! What are you? But this place is too cold for hell. I'll devil-porter it no further. I had thought to have let in some of all professions that go the primrose way to th' everlasting bonfire. (*Knock.*) Anon, anon! [*Opens the gate.*] I pray you remember the porter.

Enter *Macduff* and *Lennox*.

Macd. Was it so late, friend, ere you went to bed,
That you do lie so late?

Port. Faith, sir, we were carousing till the second cock; and drink, sir, is a great provoker of three things.

Macd. What three things does drink especially provoke?

Port. Marry, sir, nose-painting, sleep, and urine. Lechery, sir, it provokes, and unprovokes: it provokes the desire, but it takes away the performance. Therefore much drink may be said to be an equivocator with lechery: it makes him, and it mars him; it sets him on, and it takes him off; it persuades him, and disheartens him; makes him stand to, and not stand to; in conclusion, equivocates him in a sleep, and, giving him the lie, leaves him.

Macd. I believe drink gave thee the lie last night.

Port. That it did, sir, i' the very throat on me; but I requited him for his lie; and, I think, being too strong for him, though he took up my legs sometime, yet I made a shift to cast him.

Macd. Is thy master stirring?

Enter *Macbeth.*

Our knocking has awak'd him; here he comes.

Len. Good morrow, noble sir.

Macb. Good morrow, both.

Macd. Is the King stirring, worthy Thane?

Macb. Not yet.

Macd. He did command me to call timely on him;
I have almost slipp'd the hour.

Macb. I'll bring you to him.

Macd. I know this is a joyful trouble to you;
But yet 'tis one.

Macb. The labour we delight in physics pain.
This is the door.

Macd. I'll make so bold to call,
For 'tis my limited service. *Exit.*

Len. Goes the King hence to-day?

Macb. He does; he did appoint so.

Len. The night has been unruly. Where we lay,
Our chimneys were blown down; and, as they say,
Lamentings heard i' th' air, strange screams of death,
And prophesying, with accents terrible,
Of dire combustion and confus'd events
New hatch'd to th' woful time. The obscure bird
Clamour'd the livelong night. Some say the earth
Was feverous and did shake.

Macb. 'Twas a rough night.

Len. My young remembrance cannot parallel
A fellow to it.

Enter *Macduff*.

Macd. O horror, horror, horror! Tongue nor heart
Cannot conceive nor name thee!

Macb. and Len. What's the matter?

Macd. Confusion now hath made his masterpiece!
Most sacrilegious murther hath broke ope
The Lord's anointed temple and stole thence
The life o' th' building!

Macb. What is't you say? the life?

Len. Mean you his Majesty?
Macd. Approach the chamber, and destroy your sight
With a new Gorgon. Do not bid me speak.
See, and then speak yourselves.
Exeunt Macbeth and Lennox.
Awake, awake!
Ring the alarum bell. Murther and treason!
Banquo and Donalbain! Malcolm! awake!
Shake off this downy sleep, death's counterfeit,
And look on death itself! Up, up, and see
The great doom's image! Malcolm! Banquo!
As from your graves rise up and walk like sprites
To countenance this horror! Ring the bell!
Bell rings.

Enter *Lady* [*Macbeth*].

Lady. What's the business,
That such a hideous trumpet calls to parley
The sleepers of the house? Speak, speak!
Macd. O gentle lady,
'Tis not for you to hear what I can speak!
The repetition in a woman's ear
Would murther as it fell.

Enter *Banquo.*

O Banquo, Banquo,
Our royal master's murther'd!
Lady. Woe, alas!
What, in our house?
Ban. Too cruel anywhere.
Dear Duff, I prithee contradict thyself
And say it is not so.

Enter *Macbeth, Lennox,* and *Ross.*

Macb. Had I but died an hour before this chance,
I had liv'd a blessed time; for from this instant
There's nothing serious in mortality;
All is but toys; renown and grace is dead;
The wine of life is drawn, and the mere lees
Is left this vault to brag of.

Enter *Malcolm* and *Donalbain.*

Don. What is amiss?
Macb. You are, and do not know't.
The spring, the head, the fountain of your blood
Is stopp'd, the very source of it is stopp'd.
Macd. Your royal father's murther'd.
Mal. O, by whom?
Len. Those of his chamber, as it seem'd, had done't.
Their hands and faces were all badg'd with blood;
So were their daggers, which unwip'd we found
Upon their pillows.
They star'd and were distracted. No man's life
Was to be trusted with them.
Macb. O, yet I do repent me of my fury
That I did kill them.
Macd. Wherefore did you so?
Macb. Who can be wise, amaz'd, temp'rate and furious,
Loyal and neutral, in a moment? No man.
The expedition of my violent love
Outrun the pauser, reason. Here lay Duncan,
His silver skin lac'd with his golden blood,
And his gash'd stabs look'd like a breach in nature
For ruin's wasteful entrance; there, the murtherers,
Steep'd in the colours of their trade, their daggers
Unmannerly breech'd with gore. Who could refrain
That had a heart to love and in that heart
Courage to make 's love known?
Lady. Help me hence, ho!
Macd. Look to the lady.
Mal. [*aside to Donalbain*] Why do we hold our tongues,
That most may claim this argument for ours?
Don. [*aside to Malcolm*] What should be spoken here, where our fate,
Hid in an auger hole, may rush and seize us?
Let's away.
Our tears are not yet brew'd.
Mal. [*aside to Donalbain*] Nor our strong sorrow
Upon the foot of motion.
Ban. Look to the lady.
[*Lady Macbeth is carried out.*]
And when we have our naked frailties hid,
That suffer in exposure, let us meet
And question this most bloody piece of work,
To know it further. Fears and scruples shake us.
In the great hand of God I stand, and thence
Against the undivulg'd pretence I fight
Of treasonous malice.
Macd. And so do I.
All. So all.
Macb. Let's briefly put on manly readiness
And meet i' th' hall together.
All. Well contented.
Exeunt [*all but Malcolm and Donalbain*].
Mal. What will you do? Let's not consort with them.
To show an unfelt sorrow is an office
Which the false man does easy. I'll to England.
Don. To Ireland I. Our separated fortune

Shall keep us both the safer. Where we are,
There's daggers in men's smiles; the near in blood,
The nearer bloody.

Mal. This murtherous shaft that's shot
Hath not yet lighted, and our safest way
Is to avoid the aim. Therefore to horse!
And let us not be dainty of leave-taking
But shift away. There's warrant in that theft
Which steals itself when there's no mercy left.
Exeunt.

Scene IV. [*Inverness. Without* Macbeth's *Castle.*]

Enter *Ross* with an *Old Man.*

Old Man. Threescore and ten I can remember well;
Within the volume of which time I have seen
Hours dreadful and things strange; but this sore night
Hath trifled former knowings.

Ross. Ah, good father,
Thou seest the heavens, as troubled with man's act,
Threaten his bloody stage. By th' clock 'tis day,
And yet dark night strangles the travelling lamp.
Is't night's predominance, or the day's shame,
That darkness does the face of earth entomb
When living light should kiss it?

Old Man. 'Tis unnatural,
Even like the deed that's done. On Tuesday last
A falcon, tow'ring in her pride of place,
Was by a mousing owl hawk'd at and kill'd.

Ross. And Duncan's horses (a thing most strange and certain),
Beauteous and swift, the minions of their race,
Turn'd wild in nature, broke their stalls, flung out,
Contending 'gainst obedience, as they would make
War with mankind.

Old Man. 'Tis said they eat each other.

Ross. They did so, to th' amazement of mine eyes
That look'd upon't.

Enter *Macduff.*

Here comes the good Macduff.
How goes the world, sir, now?

Macd. Why, see you not?

Ross. Is't known who did this more than bloody deed?

Macd. Those that Macbeth hath slain.

Ross. Alas, the day!
What good could they pretend?

Macd. They were suborn'd.
Malcolm and Donalbain, the King's two sons,
Are stol'n away and fled, which puts upon them
Suspicion of the deed.

Ross. 'Gainst nature still!
Thriftless ambition, that wilt raven up
Thine own live's means! Then 'tis most like
The sovereignty will fall upon Macbeth.

Macd. He is already nam'd, and gone to Scone
To be invested.

Ross. Where is Duncan's body?

Macd. Carried to Colmekill,
The sacred storehouse of his predecessors
And guardian of their bones.

Ross. Will you to Scone?

Macd. No, cousin, I'll to Fife.

Ross. Well, I will thither.

Macd. Well, may you see things well done there. Adieu,
Lest our old robes sit easier than our new!

Ross. Farewell, father.

Old Man. God's benison go with you, and with those
That would make good of bad, and friends of foes!
Exeunt omnes.

ACT III. Scene I. [*Forres. The Palace.*]

Enter *Banquo.*

Ban. Thou hast it now — King, Cawdor, Glamis, all,
As the Weird Women promis'd; and I fear
Thou play'dst most foully for't. Yet it was said
It should not stand in thy posterity,
But that myself should be the root and father
Of many kings. If there come truth from them,
(As upon thee, Macbeth, their speeches shine),
Why, by the verities on thee made good,
May they not be my oracles as well
And set me up in hope? But, hush, no more!

Sennet sounded. Enter *Macbeth*, as *King*; *Lady* [*Macbeth*, as *Queen*]; *Lennox, Ross, Lords*, and *Attendants*.

Macb. Here's our chief guest.
Lady. If he had been forgotten,
It had been as a gap in our great feast,
And all-thing unbecoming.
Macb. To-night we hold a solemn supper, sir,
And I'll request your presence.
Ban. Let your Highness
Command upon me, to the which my duties
Are with a most indissoluble tie
For ever knit.
Macb. Ride you this afternoon?
Ban. Ay, my good lord.
Macb. We should have else desir'd your good advice
(Which still hath been both grave and prosperous)
In this day's council; but we'll take to-morrow.
Is't far you ride?
Ban. As far, my lord, as will fill up the time
'Twixt this and supper. Go not my horse the better,
I must become a borrower of the night
For a dark hour or twain.
Macb. Fail not our feast.
Ban. My lord, I will not.
Macb. We hear our bloody cousins are bestow'd
In England and in Ireland, not confessing
Their cruel parricide, filling their hearers
With strange invention. But of that to-morrow,
When therewithal we shall have cause of state
Craving us jointly. Hie you to horse. Adieu,
Till you return at night. Goes Fleance with you?
Ban. Ay, my good lord. Our time does call upon's.
Macb. I wish your horses swift and sure of foot,
And so I do commend you to their backs.
Farewell. *Exit Banquo.*
Let every man be master of his time
Till seven at night. To make society
The sweeter welcome, we will keep ourself
Till supper time alone. While then, God be with you!
Exeunt Lords [*and others. Manent Macbeth and a Servant*].
Sirrah, a word with you. Attend those men
Our pleasure?
Serv. They are, my lord, without the palace gate.
Macb. Bring them before us. *Exit Servant.*
To be thus is nothing,
But to be safely thus. Our fears in Banquo
Stick deep; and in his royalty of nature
Reigns that which would be fear'd. 'Tis much he dares,
And to that dauntless temper of his mind
He hath a wisdom that doth guide his valour
To act in safety. There is none but he
Whose being I do fear; and under him
My Genius is rebuk'd, as it is said
Mark Antony's was by Cæsar. He chid the Sisters
When first they put the name of King upon me,
And bade them speak to him. Then, prophet-like,
They hail'd him father to a line of kings.
Upon my head they plac'd a fruitless crown
And put a barren sceptre in my gripe,
Thence to be wrench'd with an unlineal hand,
No son of mine succeeding. If't be so,
For Banquo's issue have I fil'd my mind;
For them the gracious Duncan have I murther'd;
Put rancours in the vessel of my peace
Only for them, and mine eternal jewel
Given to the common enemy of man
To make them kings, the seed of Banquo kings!
Rather than so, come, Fate, into the list,
And champion me to th' utterance! Who's there?

Enter *Servant* and two *Murtherers.*

Now go to the door and stay there till we call.
Exit Servant.
Was it not yesterday we spoke together?
Murtherers. It was, so please your Highness.
Macb. Well then, now
Have you consider'd of my speeches? Know
That it was he, in the times past, which held you
So under fortune, which you thought had been
Our innocent self. This I made good to you
In our last conference, pass'd in probation with you
How you were borne in hand, how cross'd; the instruments;
Who wrought with them; and all things else that might
To half a soul and to a notion craz'd
Say 'Thus did Banquo.'
1. Mur. You made it known to us.
Macb. I did so; and went further, which is now
Our point of second meeting. Do you find
Your patience so predominant in your nature

That you can let this go? Are you so gospell'd
To pray for this good man and for his issue,
Whose heavy hand hath bow'd you to the grave
And beggar'd yours for ever?
1. Mur. We are men, my liege.
Macb. Ay, in the catalogue ye go for men,
As hounds and greyhounds, mongrels, spaniels, curs,
Shoughs, water-rugs, and demi-wolves are clipt
All by the name of dogs. The valued file
Distinguishes the swift, the slow, the subtle,
The housekeeper, the hunter, every one
According to the gift which bounteous nature
Hath in him clos'd; whereby he does receive
Particular addition, from the bill
That writes them all alike; and so of men.
Now, if you have a station in the file,
Not i' th' worst rank of manhood, say't;
And I will put that business in your bosoms
Whose execution takes your enemy off,
Grapples you to the heart and love of us,
Who wear our health but sickly in his life,
Which in his death were perfect.
2. Mur. I am one, my liege,
Whom the vile blows and buffets of the world
Have so incens'd that I am reckless what
I do to spite the world.
1. Mur. And I another,
So weary with disasters, tugg'd with fortune,
That I would set my life on any chance,
To mend it or be rid on't.
Macb. Both of you
Know Banquo was your enemy.
Murtherers. True, my lord.
Macb. So is he mine; and in such bloody distance
That every minute of his being thrusts
Against my near'st of life; and though I could
With barefac'd power sweep him from my sight
And bid my will avouch it, yet I must not,
For certain friends that are both his and mine,
Whose loves I may not drop, but wail his fall
Who I myself struck down. And thence it is
That I to your assistance do make love,
Masking the business from the common eye
For sundry weighty reasons.
2. Mur. We shall, my lord,
Perform what you command us.
1. Mur. Though our lives —
Macb. Your spirits shine through you. Within this hour at most
I will advise you where to plant yourselves,
Acquaint you with the perfect spy o' th' time,
The moment on't; for't must be done to-night,
And something from the palace; always thought
That I require a clearness; and with him,
To leave no rubs nor botches in the work,
Fleance his son, that keeps him company,
Whose absence is no less material to me
Than is his father's, must embrace the fate
Of that dark hour. Resolve yourselves apart;
I'll come to you anon.
Murtherers. We are resolv'd, my lord.
Macb. I'll call upon you straight. Abide within.
[*Exeunt Murtherers.*]
It is concluded. Banquo, thy soul's flight,
If it find heaven, must find it out to-night.
Exit.

Scene II. [*Forres. The Palace.*]

Enter *Macbeth's Lady* and a *Servant.*

Lady. Is Banquo gone from court?
Serv. Ay, madam, but returns again to-night.
Lady. Say to the King I would attend his leisure
For a few words.
Serv. Madam, I will. *Exit.*
Lady. Naught's had, all's spent,
Where our desire is got without content.
'Tis safer to be that which we destroy
Than by destruction dwell in doubtful joy.

Enter *Macbeth.*

How now, my lord? Why do you keep alone,
Of sorriest fancies your companions making,
Using those thoughts which should indeed have died
With them they think on? Things without all remedy
Should be without regard. What's done is done.
Macb. We have scotch'd the snake, not kill'd it.
She'll close, and be herself, whilst our poor malice
Remains in danger of her former tooth.
But let the frame of things disjoint, both the worlds suffer,
Ere we will eat our meal in fear and sleep
In the affliction of these terrible dreams
That shake us nightly. Better be with the dead,
Whom we, to gain our peace, have sent to peace,

Than on the torture of the mind to lie
In restless ecstasy. Duncan is in his grave;
After life's fitful fever he sleeps well.
Treason has done his worst. Nor steel nor poison,
Malice domestic, foreign levy, nothing,
Can touch him further.

Lady. Come on.
Gentle my lord, sleek o'er your rugged looks;
Be bright and jovial among your guests to-night.

Macb. So shall I, love; and so, I pray, be you.
Let your remembrance apply to Banquo;
Present him eminence both with eye and tongue —
Unsafe the while, that we
Must lave our honours in these flattering streams
And make our faces vizards to our hearts,
Disguising what they are.

Lady. You must leave this.

Macb. O, full of scorpions is my mind, dear wife!
Thou know'st that Banquo, and his Fleance, lives.

Lady. But in them Nature's copy's not eterne.

Macb. There's comfort yet! They are assailable.
Then be thou jocund. Ere the bat hath flown
His cloister'd flight, ere to black Hecate's summons
The shard-borne beetle with his drowsy hums
Hath rung night's yawning peal, there shall be done
A deed of dreadful note.

Lady. What's to be done?

Macb. Be innocent of the knowledge, dearest chuck,
Till thou applaud the deed. Come, seeling night,
Scarf up the tender eye of pitiful day,
And with thy bloody and invisible hand
Cancel and tear to pieces that great bond
Which keeps me pale! Light thickens, and the crow
Makes wing to th' rooky wood.
Good things of day begin to droop and drowse,
Whiles night's black agents to their preys do rouse.
Thou marvell'st at my words; but hold thee still:
Things bad begun make strong themselves by ill.
So prithee go with me. *Exeunt.*

Scene III. [*Forres. A park near the Palace.*]

Enter three *Murtherers.*

1. Mur. But who did bid thee join with us?

3. Mur. Macbeth.

2. Mur. He needs not our mistrust, since he delivers
Our offices, and what we have to do,
To the direction just.

1. Mur. Then stand with us.
The west yet glimmers with some streaks of day.
Now spurs the lated traveller apace
To gain the timely inn, and near approaches
The subject of our watch.

3. Mur. Hark! I hear horses.

Ban. (*within*) Give us a light there, ho!

2. Mur. Then 'tis he! The rest
That are within the note of expectation
Already are i' th' court.

1. Mur. His horses go about.

3. Mur. Almost a mile; but he does usually,
So all men do, from hence to th' palace gate
Make it their walk.

Enter *Banquo,* and *Fleance* with a torch.

2. Mur. A light, a light!

3. Mur. 'Tis he.

1. Mur. Stand to't.

Ban. It will be rain to-night.

1. Mur. Let it come down!
[*They fall upon Banquo.*]

Ban. O, treachery! Fly, good Fleance, fly, fly, fly!
Thou mayst revenge. O slave!
[*Dies. Fleance escapes.*]

3. Mur. Who did strike out the light?

1. Mur. Was't not the way?

3. Mur. There's but one down; the son is fled.

2. Mur. We have lost
Best half of our affair.

1. Mur. Well, let's away, and say how much is done. *Exeunt.*

Scene IV. [*Forres. Hall in the Palace.*]

Banquet prepar'd. Enter *Macbeth, Lady* [*Macbeth*], *Ross, Lennox, Lords,* and *Attendants.*

Macb. You know your own degrees, sit down. At first
And last the hearty welcome.

Lords. Thanks to your Majesty.

Macb. Ourself will mingle with society
And play the humble host.
Our hostess keeps her state, but in best time
We will require her welcome.

Lady. Pronounce it for me, sir, to all our friends,
For my heart speaks they are welcome.

Enter *First Murtherer* [to the door].

Macb. See, they encounter thee with their hearts' thanks.
Both sides are even. Here I'll sit i' th' midst.
Be large in mirth; anon we'll drink a measure
The table round. [*Goes to the door.*] There's blood upon thy face.

Mur. 'Tis Banquo's then.

Macb. 'Tis better thee without than he within.
Is he dispatch'd?

Mur. My lord, his throat is cut. That I did for him.

Macb. Thou art the best o' th' cutthroats! Yet he's good
That did the like for Fleance. If thou didst it,
Thou art the nonpareil.

Mur. Most royal sir,
Fleance is scap'd.

Macb. [*aside*] Then comes my fit again. I had else been perfect;
Whole as the marble, founded as the rock,
As broad and general as the casing air.
But now I am cabin'd, cribb'd, confin'd, bound in
To saucy doubts and fears. — But Banquo's safe?

Mur. Ay, my good lord. Safe in a ditch he bides,
With twenty trenched gashes on his head,
The least a death to nature.

Macb. Thanks for that!
There the grown serpent lies; the worm that's fled
Hath nature that in time will venom breed,
No teeth for th' present. Get thee gone. To-morrow
We'll hear ourselves again.

Exit Murderer.

Lady. My royal lord,
You do not give the cheer. The feast is sold
That is not often vouch'd, while 'tis a-making,
'Tis given with welcome. To feed were best at home.
From thence, the sauce to meat is ceremony;
Meeting were bare without it.

Enter the *Ghost of Banquo,* and sits in *Macbeth's* place.

Macb. Sweet remembrancer!
Now good digestion wait on appetite,
And health on both!

Len. May't please your Highness sit.

Macb. Here had we now our country's honour, roof'd,
Were the grac'd person of our Banquo present;
Who may I rather challenge for unkindness
Than pity for mischance!

Ross. His absence, sir,
Lays blame upon his promise. Please't your Highness
To grace us with your royal company?

Macb. The table's full.

Len. Here is a place reserv'd, sir.

Macb. Where?

Len. Here, my good lord. What is't that moves your Highness?

Macb. Which of you have done this?

Lords. What, my good lord?

Macb. Thou canst not say I did it. Never shake
Thy gory locks at me.

Ross. Gentlemen, rise. His Highness is not well.

Lady. Sit, worthy friends. My lord is often thus,
And hath been from his youth. Pray you keep seat.
The fit is momentary; upon a thought
He will again be well. If much you note him,
You shall offend him and extend his passion.
Feed, and regard him not. — Are you a man?

Macb. Ay, and a bold one, that dare look on that
Which might appal the devil.

Lady. O proper stuff!
This is the very painting of your fear.
This is the air-drawn dagger which you said
Led you to Duncan. O, these flaws and starts
(Impostors to true fear) would well become
A woman's story at a winter's fire,
Authoriz'd by her grandam. Shame itself!
Why do you make such faces? When all's done,
You look but on a stool.

Macb. Prithee see there! behold! look! lo! How say you?
Why, what care I? If thou canst nod, speak too.
If charnel houses and our graves must send

Those that we bury back, our monuments
Shall be the maws of kites.

[*Exit Ghost.*]

Lady. What, quite unmann'd in folly?
Macb. If I stand here, I saw him.
Lady. Fie, for shame!
Macb. Blood hath been shed ere now, i' th' olden time,
Ere humane statute purg'd the gentle weal;
Ay, and since too, murthers have been perform'd
Too terrible for the ear. The time has been
That, when the brains were out, the man would die,
And there an end! But now they rise again,
With twenty mortal murthers on their crowns,
And push us from our stools. This is more strange
Than such a murther is.
Lady. My worthy lord,
Your noble friends do lack you.
Macb. I do forget.
Do not muse at me, my most worthy friends.
I have a strange infirmity, which is nothing
To those that know me. Come, love and health to all!
Then I'll sit down. Give me some wine, fill full.

Enter *Ghost.*

I drink to th' general joy o' th' whole table,
And to our dear friend Banquo, whom we miss.
Would he were here! To all, and him, we thirst,
And all to all.
Lords. Our duties, and the pledge.
Macb. Avaunt, and quit my sight! Let the earth hide thee!
Thy bones are marrowless, thy blood is cold;
Thou hast no speculation in those eyes
Which thou dost glare with!
Lady. Think of this, good peers,
But as a thing of custom. 'Tis no other.
Only it spoils the pleasure of the time.
Macb. What man dare, I dare.
Approach thou like the rugged Russian bear,
The arm'd rhinoceros, or th' Hyrcan tiger;
Take any shape but that, and my firm nerves
Shall never tremble. Or be alive again
And dare me to the desert with thy sword.
If trembling I inhabit then, protest me
The baby of a girl. Hence, horrible shadow!
Unreal mock'ry, hence!

[*Exit Ghost.*]

Why, so! Being gone,
I am a man again. Pray you sit still.
Lady. You have displac'd the mirth, broke the good meeting
With most admir'd disorder.
Macb. Can such things be,
And overcome us like a summer's cloud
Without our special wonder? You make me strange
Even to the disposition that I owe,
When now I think you can behold such sights
And keep the natural ruby of your cheeks
When mine is blanch'd with fear.
Ross. What sights, my lord?
Lady. I pray you speak not. He grows worse and worse;
Question enrages him. At once, good night.
Stand not upon the order of your going,
But go at once.
Len. Good night, and better health
Attend his Majesty!
Lady. A kind good night to all!

Exeunt Lords [*and Attendants*].

Macb. It will have blood, they say; blood will have blood.
Stones have been known to move and trees to speak;
Augures and understood relations have
By maggot-pies and choughs and rooks brought forth
The secret'st man of blood. What is the night?
Lady. Almost at odds with morning, which is which.
Macb. How say'st thou that Macduff denies his person
At our great bidding?
Lady. Did you send to him, sir?
Macb. I hear it by the way; but I will send.
There's not a one of them but in his house
I keep a servant fee'd. I will to-morrow
(And betimes I will) unto the Weird Sisters.
More shall they speak; for now I am bent to know
By the worst means the worst. For mine own good
All causes shall give way. I am in blood
Stepp'd in so far that, should I wade no more,
Returning were as tedious as go o'er.
Strange things I have in head, that will to hand,
Which must be acted ere they may be scann'd.
Lady. You lack the season of all natures, sleep.

Macb. Come, we'll to sleep. My strange and self-abuse
Is the initiate fear that wants hard use.
We are yet but young in deed.
Exeunt.

Scene V. [*A heath.*]

Thunder. Enter the three *Witches*, meeting *Hecate.*

1. Witch. Why, how now, Hecate? You look angerly.
Hec. Have I not reason, beldams as you are,
Saucy and overbold? How did you dare
To trade and traffic with Macbeth
In riddles and affairs of death;
And I, the mistress of your charms,
The close contriver of all harms,
Was never call'd to bear my part
Or show the glory of our art?
And, which is worse, all you have done
Hath been but for a wayward son,
Spiteful and wrathful, who, as others do,
Loves for his own ends, not for you.
But make amends now. Get you gone
And at the pit of Acheron
Meet me i' th' morning. Thither he
Will come to know his destiny.
Your vessels and your spells provide,
Your charms and everything beside.
I am for th' air. This night I'll spend
Unto a dismal and a fatal end.
Great business must be wrought ere noon.
Upon the corner of the moon
There hangs a vap'rous drop profound.
I'll catch it ere it come to ground;
And that, distill'd by magic sleights,
Shall raise such artificial sprites
As by the strength of their illusion
Shall draw him on to his confusion.
He shall spurn fate, scorn death, and bear
His hopes 'bove wisdom, grace, and fear;
And you all know security
Is mortals' chiefest enemy.
Music and a song within. 'Come away, come away,' &c.
Hark! I am call'd. My little spirit, see,
Sits in a foggy cloud and stays for me.
[*Exit.*]
1. Witch. Come, let's make haste. She'll soon be back again.
Exeunt.

Scene VI. [*Forres. The Palace.*]

Enter *Lennox* and another *Lord.*

Len. My former speeches have but hit your thoughts,
Which can interpret farther. Only I say
Things have been strangely borne. The gracious Duncan
Was pitied of Macbeth. Marry, he was dead!
And the right valiant Banquo walk'd too late;
Whom, you may say (if't please you) Fleance kill'd,
For Fleance fled. Men must not walk too late.
Who cannot want the thought how monstrous
It was for Malcolm and for Donalbain
To kill their gracious father? Damned fact!
How it did grieve Macbeth! Did he not straight,
In pious rage, the two delinquents tear,
That were the slaves of drink and thralls of sleep?
Was not that nobly done? Ay, and wisely too!
For 'twould have anger'd any heart alive
To hear the men deny't. So that I say
He has borne all things well; and I do think
That, had he Duncan's sons under his key
(As, an't please heaven, he shall not), they should find
What 'twere to kill a father. So should Fleance.
But peace! for from broad words, and 'cause he fail'd
His presence at the tyrant's feast, I hear
Macduff lives in disgrace. Sir, can you tell
Where he bestows himself?
Lord. The son of Duncan,
From whom this tyrant holds the due of birth,
Lives in the English court, and is receiv'd
Of the most pious Edward with such grace
That the malevolence of fortune nothing
Takes from his high respect. Thither Macduff
Is gone to pray the holy King upon his aid
To wake Northumberland and warlike Siward;
That by the help of these (with Him above
To ratify the work) we may again
Give to our tables meat, sleep to our nights,
Free from our feasts and banquets bloody knives,
Do faithful homage and receive free honours —
All which we pine for now. And this report
Hath so exasperate the King that he
Prepares for some attempt of war.

MACBETH

Macbeth, the bloody thane of
Glamis, played by Paul Rogers

PHOTOGRAPHS BY HOUSTON ROGERS
PRODUCED BY THE OLD VIC COMPANY

Ann Todd as the ruthless Lady Macbeth

Macduff (John Neville), Macbeth's nemesis

Macbeth, accompanied by his friend Banquo, meets three witches on a lonely moor and is accosted by one with the mysterious words: "All hail, Macbeth, that shall be king hereafter" *(Act I, Scene III)*

King Duncan (Robert Hardy) honors Macbeth and promises advancement: "I have begun to plant thee, and will labour to make thee full of growing" *(Act I, Scene IV)*

Macbeth's friend, Banquo (Eric Porter), is the first victim of his drive for royal power

"We will establish our estate upon our eldest." King Duncan names his son Malcolm (Paul Daneman) to succeed him, thus thwarting Macbeth's ambition *(Act I, Scene IV)*

"Give me your hand; conduct me to mine host." King Duncan greets his treacherous hostess, Lady Macbeth as he arrives at the Macbeth castle at Inverness during a procession through his realm *(Act I, Scene VI)*

"Screw your courage to the sticking-place, and we'll not fail." The baleful Lady Macbeth urges her irresolute husband to murder King Duncan *(Act I, Scene VII)*

Having murdered the king, Macbeth is afraid to return the daggers of the drugged grooms who will be accused of the crime. "Infirm of purpose!" cries his wife, "give me the daggers" *(Act II, Scene II)*

Macduff descends from the king's chamber and tells Macbeth and Lennox (John Wood) that Duncan is murdered *(Act II, Scene III)*

During a banquet, Macbeth is confronted by Banquo's ghost. Regarding the apparition as an accusation of his guilt, he cries: "Thou canst not say I did it: never shake thy gory locks at me" *(Act III, Scene IV)*

Lady Macduff (Gwen Cherrell) and her son (Bunny May) are comforted by the thane of Ross, played by Meredith Edwards *(Act IV, Scene II)*

Haunted by her crimes, Lady Macbeth knows no rest. With open but unseeing eyes, she wanders through the castle in the dead of night *(Act V, Scene I)*

Malcolm seeks to console Macduff, who has just been informed by the thane of Ross (right) that Macbeth has murdered his wife and children *(Act IV, Scene III)*

"Canst thou not cure a mind diseas'd." Himself half-mad, Macbeth vainly seeks a remedy for his wife's tormented conscience *(Act V, Scene III)*

"Out, damned spot!" Mad with horror, Lady Macbeth shrieks at imagined blood stains on her hand *(Act V, Scene I)*

Though convinced he is to die at the hands of Macduff, Macbeth bids him continue the fight: "Lay on, Macduff, and damn'd be him that first cries, 'Hold, enough' " *(Act V, Scene VII)*

Brought to bay, the haggard villain is challenged by Macduff: "Turn, hell-hound, turn" *(Act V, Scene VII)*

Len. Sent he to Macduff?
Lord. He did; and with an absolute 'Sir, not I!'
The cloudy messenger turns me his back
And hums, as who should say, 'You'll rue the time
That clogs me with this answer.'
Len. And that well might
Advise him to a caution t' hold what distance
His wisdom can provide. Some holy angel
Fly to the court of England and unfold
His message ere he come, that a swift blessing
May soon return to this our suffering country
Under a hand accurs'd!
Lord. I'll send my prayers with him.
Exeunt.

ACT IV. Scene I. [*A cavern. In the middle, a cauldron boiling.*]

Thunder. Enter the three *Witches.*

1. Witch. Thrice the brinded cat hath mew'd.
2. Witch. Thrice and once the hedge-pig whin'd.
3. Witch. Harpier cries; 'tis time, 'tis time.
1. Witch. Round about the cauldron go;
In the poison'd entrails throw.
Toad, that under cold stone
Days and nights has thirty-one
Swelt'red venom sleeping got,
Boil thou first i' th' charmed pot.
All. Double, double, toil and trouble;
Fire burn, and cauldron bubble.
2. Witch. Fillet of a fenny snake,
In the cauldron boil and bake;
Eye of newt, and toe of frog,
Wool of bat, and tongue of dog,
Adder's fork, and blindworm's sting,
Lizard's leg, and howlet's wing;
For a charm of pow'rful trouble
Like a hell-broth boil and bubble.
All. Double, double, toil and trouble;
Fire burn, and cauldron bubble.
3. Witch. Scale of dragon, tooth of wolf
Witch's mummy, maw and gulf
Of the ravin'd salt-sea shark,
Root of hemlock, digg'd i' th' dark;
Liver of blaspheming Jew,
Gall of goat, and slips of yew
Sliver'd in the moon's eclipse;
Nose of Turk and Tartar's lips;
Finger of birth-strangled babe
Ditch-deliver'd by a drab:
Make the gruel thick and slab.
Add thereto a tiger's chaudron
For th' ingredience of our cauldron.
All. Double, double, toil and trouble;
Fire burn, and cauldron bubble.
2. Witch. Cool it with a baboon's blood,
Then the charm is firm and good.

Enter *Hecate* to the other three *Witches.*

Hec. O, well done! I commend your pains,
And every one shall share i' th' gains.
And now about the cauldron sing
Like elves and fairies in a ring,
Enchanting all that you put in.
Music and a song, 'Black spirits,' &c.
[*Exit Hecate.*]
2. Witch. By the pricking of my thumbs,
Something wicked this way comes.
Open locks,
Whoever knocks!

Enter *Macbeth.*

Macb. How now, you secret, black, and midnight hags?
What is't you do?
All. A deed without a name.
Macb. I conjure you by that which you profess
(Howe'er you come to know it), answer me.
Though you untie the winds and let them fight
Against the churches; though the yesty waves
Confound and swallow navigation up;
Though bladed corn be lodg'd and trees blown down;
Though castles topple on their warders' heads;
Though palaces and pyramids do slope
Their heads to their foundations; though the treasure
Of nature's germens tumble all together,
Even till destruction sicken — answer me
To what I ask you.
1. Witch. Speak.
2. Witch. Demand.
3. Witch. We'll answer.
1. Witch. Say, if th' hadst rather hear it from our mouths
Or from our masters.
Macb. Call 'em! Let me see 'em.
1. Witch. Pour in sow's blood, that hath eaten

Her nine farrow; grease that's sweaten
From the murderer's gibbet throw
Into the flame.
All. Come, high or low;
Thyself and office deftly show!

Thunder. First Apparition, an Armed Head.

Macb. Tell me, thou unknown power —
1. Witch. He knows thy thought.
Hear his speech, but say thou naught.
1. Appar. Macbeth! Macbeth! Macbeth! Beware Macduff;
Beware the Thane of Fife. Dismiss me. Enough. *He descends.*
Macb. Whate'er thou art, for thy good caution thanks!
Thou hast harp'd my fear aright. But one word more —
1. Witch. He will not be commanded. Here's another,
More potent than the first.

Thunder. Second Apparition, a Bloody Child.

2. Appar. Macbeth! Macbeth! Macbeth!
Macb. Had I three ears, I'ld hear thee.
2. Appar. Be bloody, bold, and resolute; laugh to scorn
The pow'r of man, for none of woman born
Shall harm Macbeth. *Descends.*
Macb. Then live, Macduff. What need I fear of thee?
But yet I'll make assurance double sure
And take a bond of fate. Thou shalt not live!
That I may tell pale-hearted fear it lies
And sleep in spite of thunder.

Thunder. Third Apparition, a Child Crowned, with a tree in his hand.

What is this
That rises like the issue of a king
And wears upon his baby-brow the round
And top of sovereignty?
All. Listen, but speak not to't.
3. Appar. Be lion-mettled, proud, and take no care
Who chafes, who frets, or where conspirers are.
Macbeth shall never vanquish'd be until
Great Birnam Wood to high Dunsinane Hill
Shall come against him. *Descends.*
Macb. That will never be.
Who can impress the forest, bid the tree
Unfix his earth-bound root? Sweet bodements, good!
Rebellion's head rise never till the Wood
Of Birnam rise, and our high-plac'd Macbeth
Shall live the lease of nature, pay his breath
To time and mortal custom. Yet my heart
Throbs to know one thing. Tell me, if your art
Can tell so much — shall Banquo's issue ever
Reign in this kingdom?
All. Seek to know no more.
Macb. I will be satisfied. Deny me this,
And an eternal curse fall on you! Let me know.
Why sinks that cauldron? and what noise is this?
Hautboys.
1. Witch. Show!
2. Witch. Show!
3. Witch. Show!
All. Show his eyes, and grieve his heart!
Come like shadows, so depart!

A show of eight Kings, [the eighth] with a glass in his hand, and Banquo last.

Macb. Thou art too like the spirit of Banquo. Down!
Thy crown does sear mine eyeballs. And thy hair,
Thou other gold-bound brow, is like the first.
A third is like the former. Filthy hags!
Why do you show me this? A fourth? Start, eyes!
What, will the line stretch out to th' crack of doom?
Another yet? A seventh? I'll see no more.
And yet the eighth appears, who bears a glass
Which shows me many more; and some I see
That twofold balls and treble sceptres carry.
Horrible sight! Now I see 'tis true;
For the blood-bolter'd Banquo smiles upon me
And points at them for his. [*Apparitions vanish.*] What? Is this so?
1. Witch. Ay, sir, all this is so. But why
Stands Macbeth thus amazedly?
Come, sisters, cheer we up his sprites
And show the best of our delights.
I'll charm the air to give a sound
While you perform your antic round,
That this great king may kindly say
Our duties did his welcome pay.

Music. The Witches dance, and vanish.

Macb. Where are they? Gone? Let this pernicious hour
Stand aye accursed in the calendar!
Come in, without there!

Enter *Lennox.*

Len. What's your Grace's will?
Macb. Saw you the Weird Sisters?
Len. No, my lord.
Macb. Came they not by you?

Len. No indeed, my lord.
Macb. Infected be the air whereon they ride,
And damn'd all those that trust them! I did hear
The galloping of horse. Who was't came by?
Len. 'Tis two or three, my lord, that bring you word
Macduff is fled to England.
Macb. Fled to England?
Len. Ay, my good lord.
Macb. [*aside*] Time, thou anticipat'st my dread exploits.
The flighty purpose never is o'ertook
Unless the deed go with it. From this moment
The very firstlings of my heart shall be
The firstlings of my hand. And even now,
To crown my thoughts with acts, be it thought and done!
The castle of Macduff I will surprise,
Seize upon Fife, give to the edge o' th' sword
His wife, his babes, and all unfortunate souls
That trace him in his line. No boasting like a fool!
This deed I'll do before this purpose cool.
But no more sights! — Where are these gentlemen?
Come, bring me where they are. *Exeunt.*

Scene II. [*Fife.* Macduff's *Castle.*]

Enter *Macduff's Wife*, her *Son*, and *Ross.*

Wife. What had he done to make him fly the land?
Ross. You must have patience, madam.
Wife. He had none.
His flight was madness. When our actions do not,
Our fears do make us traitors.
Ross. You know not
Whether it was his wisdom or his fear.
Wife. Wisdom? To leave his wife, to leave his babes,
His mansion, and his titles, in a place
From whence himself does fly? He loves us not,
He wants the natural touch. For the poor wren,
(The most diminitive of birds) will fight,
Her young ones in her nest, against the owl.
All is the fear, and nothing is the love,
As little is the wisdom, where the flight
So runs against all reason.
Ross. My dearest coz,
I pray you school yourself. But for your husband,
He is noble, wise, judicious, and best knows
The fits o' th' season. I dare not speak much further;
But cruel are the times, when we are traitors
And do not know ourselves; when we hold rumour
From what we fear, yet know not what we fear,
But float upon a wild and violent sea
Each way and none. I take my leave of you.
Shall not be long but I'll be here again.
Things at the worst will cease, or else climb upward
To what they were before. — My pretty cousin,
Blessing upon you!
Wife. Father'd he is, and yet he's fatherless.
Ross. I am so much a fool, should I stay longer,
It would be my disgrace and your discomfort.
I take my leave at once. *Exit.*
Wife. Sirrah, your father's dead;
And what will you do now? How will you live?
Son. As birds do, mother.
Wife. What, with worms and flies?
Son. With what I get, I mean; and so do they.
Wife. Poor bird! thou'dst never fear the net nor lime,
The pitfall nor the gin.
Son. Why should I, mother? Poor birds they are not set for.
My father is not dead, for all your saying.
Wife. Yes, he is dead. How wilt thou do for a father?
Son. Nay, how will you do for a husband?
Wife. Why, I can buy me twenty at any market.
Son. Then you'll buy 'em to sell again.
Wife. Thou speak'st with all thy wit; and yet, i' faith,
With wit enough for thee.
Son. Was my father a traitor, mother?
Wife. Ay, that he was!
Son. What is a traitor?
Wife. Why, one that swears, and lies.
Son. And be all traitors that do so?
Wife. Every one that does so is a traitor and must be hang'd.
Son. And must they all be hang'd that swear and lie?
Wife. Every one.
Son. Who must hang them?
Wife. Why, the honest men.
Son. Then the liars and swearers are fools; for there are liars and swearers enow to beat the honest men and hang up them.

Wife. Now God help thee, poor monkey!
But how wilt thou do for a father?

Son. If he were dead, you'ld weep for him. If you would not, it were a good sign that I should quickly have a new father.

Wife. Poor prattler, how thou talk'st!

Enter a *Messenger*.

Mess. Bless you, fair dame! I am not to you known,
Though in your state of honour I am perfect.
I doubt some danger does approach you nearly.
If you will take a homely man's advice,
Be not found here. Hence with your little ones!
To fright you thus methinks I am too savage;
To do worse to you were fell cruelty,
Which is too nigh your person. Heaven preserve you!
I dare abide no longer. *Exit.*

Wife. Whither should I fly?
I have done no harm. But I remember now
I am in this earthly world, where to do harm
Is often laudable, to do good sometime
Accounted dangerous folly. Why then, alas,
Do I put up that womanly defence
To say I have done no harm? — What are these faces?

Enter *Murtherers*.

Mur. Where is your husband?

Wife. I hope, in no place so unsanctified
Where such as thou mayst find him.

Mur. He's a traitor.

Son. Thou liest, thou shag-ear'd villain!

Mur. What, you egg! [*Stabs him.*]
Young fry of treachery!

Son. He has kill'd me, mother.
Run away, I pray you! [*Dies.*]

Exit [*Wife*], *crying* 'Murther!' [*and pursued by the Murtherers*].

Scene III. [*England. Before* King Edward's *Palace.*]

Enter *Malcolm* and *Macduff*.

Mal. Let us seek out some desolate shade, and there
Weep our sad bosoms empty.

Macd. Let us rather
Hold fast the mortal sword and, like good men,
Bestride our downfall'n birthdom. Each new morn
New widows howl, new orphans cry, new sorrows
Strike heaven on the face, that it resounds
As if it felt with Scotland and yell'd out
Like syllable of dolour.

Mal. What I believe, I'll wail;
What know, believe; and what I can redress,
As I shall find the time to friend, I will.
What you have spoke, it may be so perchance.
This tyrant, whose sole name blisters our tongues,
Was once thought honest; you have lov'd him well;
He hath not touch'd you yet. I am young; but something
You may deserve of him through me, and wisdom
To offer up a weak, poor, innocent lamb
T' appease an angry god.

Macd. I am not treacherous.

Mal. But Macbeth is.
A good and virtuous nature may recoil
In an imperial charge. But I shall crave your pardon.
That which you are, my thoughts cannot transpose.
Angels are bright still, though the brightest fell.
Though all things foul would wear the brows of grace,
Yet grace must still look so.

Macd. I have lost my hopes.

Mal. Perchance even there where I did find my doubts.
Why in that rawness left you wife and child,
Those precious motives, those strong knots of love,
Without leave-taking? I pray you,
Let not my jealousies be your dishonours,
But mine own safeties. You may be rightly just,
Whatever I shall think.

Macd. Bleed, bleed, poor country!
Great tyranny, lay thou thy basis sure,
For goodness dare not check thee! Wear thou thy wrongs;
The title is affeer'd! Fare thee well, lord.
I would not be the villain that thou think'st
For the whole space that's in the tyrant's grasp
And the rich East to boot.

Mal. Be not offended.
I speak not as in absolute fear of you.
I think our country sinks beneath the yoke,
It weeps, it bleeds, and each new day a gash
Is added to her wounds. I think withal
There would be hands uplifted in my right;

And here from gracious England have I offer
Of goodly thousands. But, for all this,
When I shall tread upon the tyrant's head
Or wear it on my sword, yet my poor country
Shall have more vices than it had before,
More suffer and more sundry ways than ever,
By him that shall succeed.

Macd. What should he be?

Mal. It is myself I mean; in whom I know
All the particulars of vice so grafted
That, when they shall be open'd, black Macbeth
Will seem as pure as snow, and the poor state
Esteem him as a lamb, being compar'd
With my confineless harms.

Macd. Not in the legions
Of horrid hell can come a devil more damn'd
In evils to top Macbeth.

Mal. I grant him bloody,
Luxurious, avaricious, false, deceitful,
Sudden, malicious, smacking of every sin
That has a name. But there's no bottom, none,
In my voluptuousness. Your wives, your daughters,
Your matrons, and your maids could not fill up
The cistern of my lust; and my desire
All continent impediments would o'erbear
That did oppose my will. Better Macbeth
Than such an one to reign.

Macd. Boundless intemperance
In nature is a tyranny. It hath been
Th' untimely emptying of the happy throne
And fall of many kings. But fear not yet
To take upon you what is yours. You may
Convey your pleasures in a spacious plenty,
And yet seem cold — the time you may so hoodwink.
We have willing dames enough. There cannot be
That vulture in you to devour so many
As will to greatness dedicate themselves,
Finding it so inclin'd.

Mal. With this there grows
In my most ill-compos'd affection such
A stanchless avarice that, were I King,
I should cut off the nobles for their lands,
Desire his jewels, and this other's house,
And my more-having would be as a sauce
To make me hunger more, that I should forge
Quarrels unjust against the good and loyal,
Destroying them for wealth.

Macd. This avarice
Sticks deeper, grows with more pernicious root
Than summer-seeming lust; and it hath been
The sword of our slain kings. Yet do not fear.
Scotland hath foisons to fill up your will
Of your mere own. All these are portable,
With other graces weigh'd.

Mal. But I have none. The king-becoming graces,
As justice, verity, temp'rance, stableness,
Bounty, perseverance, mercy, lowliness,
Devotion, patience, courage, fortitude,
I have no relish of them, but abound
In the division of each several crime,
Acting it many ways. Nay, had I pow'r, I should
Pour the sweet milk of concord into hell,
Uproar the universal peace, confound
All unity on earth.

Macd. O Scotland, Scotland!

Mal. If such a one be fit to govern, speak.
I am as I have spoken.

Macd. Fit to govern?
No, not to live. O nation miserable,
With an untitled tyrant bloody-scept'red,
When shalt thou see thy wholesome days again,
Since that the truest issue of thy throne
By his own interdiction stands accurs'd
And does blaspheme his breed? Thy royal father
Was a most sainted king; the queen that bore thee,
Oft'ner upon her knees than on her feet,
Died every day she liv'd. Fare thee well!
These evils thou repeat'st upon thyself
Have banish'd me from Scotland. O my breast,
Thy hope ends here!

Mal. Macduff, this noble passion,
Child of integrity, hath from my soul
Wip'd the black scruples, reconcil'd my thoughts
To thy good truth and honour. Devilish Macbeth
By many of these trains hath sought to win me
Into his power; and modest wisdom plucks me
From over-credulous haste; but God above
Deal between thee and me! for even now
I put myself to thy direction and
Unspeak mine own detraction, here abjure
The taints and blames I laid upon myself
For strangers to my nature. I am yet
Unknown to woman, never was forsworn,
Scarcely have coveted what was mine own,
At no time broke my faith, would not betray
The devil to his fellow, and delight
No less in truth than life. My first false speaking
Was this upon myself. What I am truly,
Is thine and my poor country's to command:

Whither indeed, before thy here-approach,
Old Siward with ten thousand warlike men
Already at a point was setting forth.
Now we'll together; and the chance of goodness
Be like our warranted quarrel! Why are you silent?

Macd. Such welcome and unwelcome things at once
'Tis hard to reconcile.

Enter a *Doctor*.

Mal. Well, more anon. Comes the King forth, I pray you?

Doct. Ay, sir. There are a crew of wretched souls
That stay his cure. Their malady convinces
The great assay of art; but at his touch,
Such sanctity hath heaven given his hand,
They presently amend.

Mal. I thank you, doctor.

Exit [*Doctor*].

Macd. What's the disease he means?

Mal. 'Tis call'd the evil:
A most miraculous work in this good king,
Which often since my here-remain in England
I have seen him do. How he solicits heaven
Himself best knows; but strangely-visited people,
All swol'n and ulcerous, pitiful to the eye,
The mere despair of surgery, he cures,
Hanging a golden stamp about their necks,
Put on with holy prayers; and 'tis spoken,
To the succeeding royalty he leaves
The healing benediction. With this strange virtue,
He hath a heavenly gift of prophecy,
And sundry blessings hang about his throne
That speak him full of grace.

Enter *Ross*.

Macd. See who comes here.

Mal. My countryman; but yet I know him not.

Macd. My ever gentle cousin, welcome hither.

Mal. I know him now. Good God betimes remove
The means that makes us strangers!

Ross. Sir, amen.

Macd. Stands Scotland where it did?

Ross. Alas, poor country,
Almost afraid to know itself! It cannot
Be call'd our mother, but our grave; where nothing,
But who knows nothing, is once seen to smile;
Where sighs and groans, and shrieks that rent the air,
Are made, not mark'd; where violent sorrow seems
A modern ecstasy. The dead man's knell
Is there scarce ask'd for who; and good men's lives
Expire before the flowers in their caps,
Dying or ere they sicken.

Macd. O, relation
Too nice, and yet too true!

Mal. What's the newest grief?

Ross. That of an hour's age doth hiss the speaker;
Each minute teems a new one.

Macd. How does my wife?

Ross. Why, well.

Macd. And all my children?

Ross. Well too.

Macd. The tyrant has not batter'd at their peace?

Ross. No; they were well at peace when I did leave 'em.

Macd. Be not a niggard of your speech. How goes't?

Ross. When I came hither to transport the tidings
Which I have heavily borne, there ran a rumour
Of many worthy fellows that were out;
Which was to my belief witness'd the rather
For that I saw the tyrant's power afoot.
Now is the time of help. Your eye in Scotland
Would create soldiers, make our women fight
To doff their dire distresses.

Mal. Be't their comfort
We are coming thither. Gracious England hath
Lent us good Siward and ten thousand men.
An older and a better soldier none
That Christendom gives out.

Ross. Would I could answer
This comfort with the like! But I have words
That would be howl'd out in the desert air,
Where hearing should not latch them.

Macd. What concern they?
The general cause? or is it a fee-grief
Due to some single breast?

Ross. No mind that's honest
But in it shares some woe, though the main part
Pertains to you alone.

Macd. If it be mine,
Keep it not from me, quickly let me have it.

Ross. Let not your ears despise my tongue for ever,

Which shall possess them with the heaviest sound
That ever yet they heard.
Macd. Humh! I guess at it.
Ross. Your castle is surpris'd; your wife and babes
Savagely slaughter'd. To relate the manner,
Were, on the quarry of these murther'd deer,
To add the death of you.
Mal. Merciful heaven!
What, man! Ne'er pull your hat upon your brows.
Give sorrow words. The grief that does not speak
Whispers the o'erfraught heart and bids it break.
Macd. My children too?
Ross. Wife, children, servants, all
That could be found.
Macd. And I must be from thence?
My wife kill'd too?
Ross. I have said.
Mal. Be comforted.
Let's make us med'cines of our great revenge
To cure this deadly grief.
Macd. He has no children. All my pretty ones?
Did you say all? O hell-kite! All?
What, all my pretty chickens and their dam
At one fell swoop?
Mal. Dispute it like a man.
Macd. I shall do so;
But I must also feel it as a man.
I cannot but remember such things were
That were most precious to me. Did heaven look on
And would not take their part? Sinful Macduff,
They were all struck for thee! Naught that I am,
Not for their own demerits, but for mine,
Fell slaughter on their souls. Heaven rest them now!
Mal. Be this the whetstone of your sword. Let grief
Convert to anger; blunt not the heart, enrage it.
Macd. O, I could play the woman with mine eyes
And braggart with my tongue! But, gentle heavens,
Cut short all intermission. Front to front
Bring thou this fiend of Scotland and myself.
Within my sword's length set him. If he scape,
Heaven forgive him too!
Mal. This tune goes manly.
Come, go we to the King. Our power is ready;
Our lack is nothing but our leave. Macbeth
Is ripe for shaking, and the pow'rs above
Put on their instruments. Receive what cheer you may.
The night is long that never finds the day.
Exeunt.

ACT V. SCENE I. [*Dunsinane.* Macbeth's *Castle.*]

Enter a *Doctor of Physic* and a *Waiting Gentlewoman.*

Doct. I have two nights watch'd with you, but can perceive no truth in your report. When was it she last walk'd?

Gent. Since his Majesty went into the field I have seen her rise from her bed, throw her nightgown upon her, unlock her closet, take forth paper, fold it, write upon't, read it, afterwards seal it, and again return to bed; yet all this while in a most fast sleep.

Doct. A great perturbation in nature, to receive at once the benefit of sleep and do the effects of watching! In this slumb'ry agitation, besides her walking and other actual performances, what (at any time) have you heard her say?

Gent. That, sir, which I will not report after her.

Doct. You may to me, and 'tis most meet you should.

Gent. Neither to you nor any one, having no witness to confirm my speech.

Enter *Lady* [*Macbeth*], with a taper.

Lo you, here she comes! This is her very guise, and, upon my life, fast asleep! Observe her; stand close.

Doct. How came she by that light?

Gent. Why, it stood by her. She has light by her continually. 'Tis her command.

Doct. You see her eyes are open.

Gent. Ay; but their sense is shut.

Doct. What is it she does now? Look how she rubs her hands.

Gent. It is an accustom'd action with her, to seem thus washing her hands. I have known her continue in this a quarter of an hour.

Lady. Yet here's a spot.

Doct. Hark, she speaks! I will set down what comes from her, to satisfy my remembrance the more strongly.

Lady. Out, damned spot! out, I say! One; two. Why then 'tis time to do't. Hell is murky. Fie, my lord, fie! a soldier, and afeard? What need we fear who knows it, when none can call our pow'r to accompt? Yet who would have thought the old man to have had so much blood in him?

Doct. Do you mark that?

Lady. The Thane of Fife had a wife. Where is she now? What, will these hands ne'er be clean? No more o' that, my lord, no more o' that! You mar all with this starting.

Doct. Go to, go to! You have known what you should not.

Gent. She has spoke what she should not, I am sure of that. Heaven knows what she has known.

Lady. Here's the smell of the blood still. All the perfumes of Arabia will not sweeten this little hand. Oh, oh, oh!

Doct. What a sigh is there! The heart is sorely charg'd.

Gent. I would not have such a heart in my bosom for the dignity of the whole body.

Doct. Well, well, well.

Gent. Pray God it be, sir.

Doct. This disease is beyond my practice. Yet I have known those which have walk'd in their sleep who have died holily in their beds.

Lady. Wash your hands, put on your nightgown, look not so pale! I tell you yet again, Banquo's buried. He can not come out on's grave.

Doct. Even so?

Lady. To bed, to bed! There's knocking at the gate. Come, come, come, come, give me your hand! What's done cannot be undone. To bed, to bed, to bed! *Exit.*

Doct. Will she go now to bed?

Gent. Directly.

Doct. Foul whisp'rings are abroad. Unnatural deeds
Do breed unnatural troubles. Infected minds
To their deaf pillows will discharge their secrets.
More needs she the divine than the physician.
God, God forgive us all! Look after her;
Remove from her the means of all annoyance,
And still keep eyes upon her. So good night.
My mind she has mated, and amaz'd my sight.
I think, but dare not speak.

Gent. Good night, good doctor.

Exeunt.

Scene II. [*The country near Dunsinane.*]

Drum and Colours. Enter *Menteith, Caithness, Angus, Lennox, Soldiers.*

Ment. The English pow'r is near, led on by Malcolm,
His uncle Siward, and the good Macduff.
Revenges burn in them; for their dear causes
Would to the bleeding and the grim alarm
Excite the mortified man.

Ang. Near Birnam Wood
Shall we well meet them; that way are they coming.

Caith. Who knows if Donalbain be with his brother?

Len. For certain, sir, he is not. I have a file
Of all the gentry. There is Siward's son
And many unrough youths that even now
Protest their first of manhood.

Ment. What does the tyrant?

Caith. Great Dunsinane he strongly fortifies.
Some say he's mad; others, that lesser hate him,
Do call it valiant fury; but for certain
He cannot buckle his distemper'd cause
Within the belt of rule.

Ang. Now does he feel
His secret murthers sticking on his hands.
Now minutely revolts upbraid his faith-breach.
Those he commands move only in command,
Nothing in love. Now does he feel his title
Hang loose about him, like a giant's robe
Upon a dwarfish thief.

Ment. Who then shall blame
His pester'd senses to recoil and start,
When all that is within him does condemn
Itself for being there?

Caith. Well, march we on
To give obedience where 'tis truly ow'd.
Meet we the med'cine of the sickly weal;
And with him pour we in our country's purge
Each drop of us.

Len. Or so much as it needs
To dew the sovereign flower and drown the weeds.
Make we our march towards Birnam.

Exeunt, marching.

Scene III. [*Dunsinane. A room in the Castle.*]

Enter *Macbeth, Doctor,* and *Attendants.*

Macb. Bring me no more reports. Let them fly all!
Till Birnam Wood remove to Dunsinane,
I cannot taint with fear. What's the boy Malcolm?
Was he not born of woman? The spirits that know
All mortal consequences have pronounc'd me thus:
'Fear not, Macbeth. No man that's born of woman
Shall e'er have power upon thee.' Then fly, false thanes,
And mingle with the English epicures.
The mind I sway by and the heart I bear
Shall never sag with doubt nor shake with fear.

Enter *Servant.*

The devil damn thee black, thou cream-fac'd loon!
Where got'st thou that goose look?
Serv. There is ten thousand —
Macb. Geese, villain?
Serv. Soldiers, sir.
Macb. Go prick thy face and over-red thy fear,
Thou lily-liver'd boy. What soldiers, patch?
Death of thy soul! Those linen cheeks of thine
Are counsellors to fear. What soldiers, whey-face?
Serv. The English force, so please you.
Macb. Take thy face hence.

[*Exit Servant.*]

Seyton! — I am sick at heart,
When I behold — Seyton, I say! — This push
Will cheer me ever, or disseat me now.
I have liv'd long enough. My way of life
Is fall'n into the sere, the yellow leaf;
And that which should accompany old age,
As honour, love, obedience, troops of friends,
I must not look to have; but, in their stead,
Curses not loud but deep, mouth-honour, breath,
Which the poor heart would fain deny, and dare not.
Seyton!

Enter *Seyton.*

Sey. What's your gracious pleasure?
Macb. What news more?
Sey. All is confirm'd, my lord, which was reported.
Macb. I'll fight, till from my bones my flesh be hack'd.
Give me my armour.
Sey. 'Tis not needed yet.
Macb. I'll put it on.
Send out moe horses, skirr the country round;
Hang those that talk of fear. Give me mine armour.
How does your patient, doctor?
Doct. Not so sick, my lord,
As she is troubled with thick-coming fancies
That keep her from her rest.
Macb. Cure her of that!
Canst thou not minister to a mind diseas'd,
Pluck from the memory a rooted sorrow,
Raze out the written troubles of the brain,
And with some sweet oblivious antidote
Cleanse the stuff'd bosom of that perilous stuff
Which weighs upon the heart?
Doct. Therein the patient
Must minister to himself.
Macb. Throw physic to the dogs, I'll none of it! —
Come, put mine armour on. Give me my staff. —
Seyton, send out. — Doctor, the thanes fly from me. —
Come, sir, dispatch. — If thou couldst, doctor, cast
The water of my land, find her disease,
And purge it to a sound and pristine health,
I would applaud thee to the very echo,
That should applaud again. — Pull't off, I say. —
What rhubarb, senna, or what purgative drug,
Would scour these English hence? Hear'st thou of them?
Doct. Ay, my good lord. Your royal preparation
Makes us hear something.
Macb. Bring it after me!
I will not be afraid of death and bane
Till Birnam Forest come to Dunsinane.

[*Exeunt all but the Doctor.*]

Doct. Were I from Dunsinane away and clear,
Profit again should hardly draw me here.

Exit.

Scene IV. [*Country near Birnam Wood.*]

Drum and Colours. Enter *Malcolm, Siward, Macduff, Siward's Son, Menteith, Caithness, Angus,* [*Lennox, Ross,*] and *Soldiers,* marching.

Mal. Cousins, I hope the days are near at hand
That chambers will be safe.
Ment. We doubt it nothing.
Siw. What wood is this before us?
Ment. The Wood of Birnam.
Mal. Let every soldier hew him down a bough
And bear't before him. Thereby shall we shadow
The numbers of our host and make discovery
Err in report of us.
Soldiers. It shall be done.
Siw. We learn no other but the confident tyrant
Keeps still in Dunsinane and will endure
Our setting down before't.
Mal. 'Tis his main hope;
For where there is advantage to be given,
Both more and less have given him the revolt;
And none serve with him but constrained things,
Whose hearts are absent too.
Macd. Let our just censures
Attend the true event, and put we on
Industrious soldiership.
Siw. The time approaches
That will with due decision make us know
What we shall say we have, and what we owe.
Thoughts speculative their unsure hopes relate,
But certain issue strokes must arbitrate;
Towards which advance the war.
Exeunt, marching.

Scene V. [*Dunsinane. Within the Castle.*]

Enter *Macbeth, Seyton,* and *Soldiers,* with *Drum* and *Colours.*

Macb. Hang out our banners on the outward walls.
The cry is still, 'They come!' Our castle's strength
Will laugh a siege to scorn. Here let them lie
Till famine and the ague eat them up.
Were they not forc'd with those that should be ours,
We might have met them dareful, beard to beard,
And beat them backward home.
A cry within of women.
What is that noise?
Sey. It is the cry of women, my good lord.
[*Exit.*]
Macb. I have almost forgot the taste of fears.
The time has been, my senses would have cool'd
To hear a night-shriek, and my fell of hair
Would at a dismal treatise rouse and stir
As life were in't. I have supp'd full with horrors.
Direness, familiar to my slaughterous thoughts,
Cannot once start me.

[Enter *Seyton.*]

Wherefore was that cry?
Sey. The Queen, my lord, is dead.
Macb. She should have died hereafter;
There would have been a time for such a word.
To-morrow, and to-morrow, and to-morrow
Creeps in this petty pace from day to day
To the last syllable of recorded time;
And all our yesterdays have lighted fools
The way to dusty death. Out, out, brief candle!
Life's but a walking shadow, a poor player,
That struts and frets his hour upon the stage
And then is heard no more. It is a tale
Told by an idiot, full of sound and fury,
Signifying nothing.

Enter a *Messenger.*

Thou com'st to use thy tongue. Thy story quickly!
Mess. Gracious my lord,
I should report that which I say I saw,
But know not how to do't.
Macb. Well, say, sir!
Mess. As I did stand my watch upon the hill,
I look'd toward Birnam, and anon methought
The wood began to move.
Macb. Liar and slave!
Mess. Let me endure your wrath if't be not so.
Within this three mile may you see it coming;
I say, a moving grove.
Macb. If thou speak'st false,
Upon the next tree shalt thou hang alive,
Till famine cling thee. If thy speech be sooth,
I care not if thou dost for me as much.
I pull in resolution, and begin
To doubt th' equivocation of the fiend,
That lies like truth. 'Fear not, till Birnam wood
Do come to Dunsinane!' and now a wood

Comes toward Dunsinane. Arm, arm, and out!
If this which he avouches does appear,
There is nor flying hence nor tarrying here.
I gin to be aweary of the sun,
And wish th' estate o' th' world were now undone.
Ring the alarum bell! Blow wind, come wrack,
At least we'll die with harness on our back!
Exeunt.

SCENE VI. [*Dunsinane. Before the Castle.*]

Drum and Colours. Enter *Malcolm, Siward, Macduff,* and their *Army,* with boughs.

Mal. Now near enough. Your leavy screens throw down
And show like those you are. You, worthy uncle,
Shall with my cousin, your right noble son,
Lead our first battle. Worthy Macduff and we
Shall take upon's what else remains to do,
According to our order.

Siw. Fare you well.
Do we but find the tyrant's power to-night,
Let us be beaten if we cannot fight.

Macd. Make all our trumpets speak, give them all breath,
Those clamorous harbingers of blood and death.
Exeunt. Alarums continued.

Scene VII. [*Another part of the field.*]

Enter *Macbeth.*

Macb. They have tied me to a stake. I cannot fly,
But bear-like I must fight the course. What's he
That was not born of woman? Such a one
Am I to fear, or none.

Enter *Young Siward.*

Y. Siw. What is thy name?

Macb. Thou'lt be afraid to hear it.

Y. Siw. No; though thou call'st thyself a hotter name
Than any is in hell.

Macb. My name's Macbeth.

Y. Siw. The devil himself could not pronounce a title
More hateful to mine ear.

Macb. No, nor more fearful.

Y. Siw. Thou liest, abhorred tyrant! With my sword
I'll prove the lie thou speak'st.
Fight, and Young Siward slain.

Macb. Thou wast born of woman.
But swords I smile at, weapons laugh to scorn,
Brandish'd by man that's of a woman born.
Exit.

Alarums. Enter *Macduff.*

Macd. That way the noise is. Tyrant, show thy face!
If thou beest slain and with no stroke of mine,
My wife and children's ghosts will haunt me still.
I cannot strike at wretched kerns, whose arms
Are hir'd to bear their staves. Either thou, Macbeth,
Or else my sword with an unbattered edge
I sheathe again undeeded. There thou shouldst be.
By this great clatter one of greatest note
Seems bruited. Let me find him, Fortune!
And more I beg not. *Exit. Alarums.*

Enter *Malcolm* and *Siward.*

Siw. This way, my lord. The castle's gently rend'red:
The tyrant's people on both sides do fight;
The noble thanes do bravely in the war;
The day almost itself professes yours,
And little is to do.

Mal. We have met with foes
That strike beside us.

Siw. Enter, sir, the castle.
Exeunt. Alarum.

[Scene VIII. *Another part of the field.*]

Enter *Macbeth.*

Macb. Why should I play the Roman fool and die
On mine own sword? Whiles I see lives, the gashes
Do better upon them.

Enter *Macduff.*

Macd. Turn, hellhound, turn!

Macb. Of all men else I have avoided thee.
But get thee back! My soul is too much charg'd
With blood of thine already.

Macd. I have no words;
My voice is in my sword, thou bloodier villain
Than terms can give thee out!

Fight. Alarum.

Macb. Thou losest labour.
As easy mayst thou the intrenchant air
With thy keen sword impress as make me bleed.
Let fall thy blade on vulnerable crests.
I bear a charmed life, which must not yield
To one of woman born.

Macd. Despair thy charm!
And let the angel whom thou still hast serv'd
Tell thee, Macduff was from his mother's womb
Untimely ripp'd.

Macb. Accursed be that tongue that tells me so,
For it hath cow'd my better part of man!
And be these juggling fiends no more believ'd,
That palter with us in a double sense,
That keep the word of promise to our ear
And break it to our hope! I'll not fight with thee!

Macd. Then yield thee, coward,
And live to be the show and gaze o' th' time!
We'll have thee, as our rarer monsters are,
Painted upon a pole, and underwrit
'Here may you see the tyrant.'

Macb. I will not yield,
To kiss the ground before young Malcolm's feet
And to be baited with the rabble's curse.
Though Birnam Wood be come to Dunsinane,
And thou oppos'd, being of no woman born,
Yet I will try the last. Before my body
I throw my warlike shield. Lay on, Macduff,
And damn'd be him that first cries 'Hold, enough!'

Exeunt fighting. Alarums.

Retreat and flourish. Enter, with *Drum* and *Colours, Malcolm, Siward, Ross, Thanes,* and *Soldiers.*

Mal. I would the friends we miss were safe arriv'd.

Siw. Some must go off; and yet, by these I see,
So great a day as this is cheaply bought.

Mal. Macduff is missing, and your noble son.

Ross. Your son, my lord, has paid a soldier's debt.
He only liv'd but till he was a man,
The which no sooner had his prowess confirm'd
In the unshrinking station where he fought
But like a man he died.

Siw. Then he is dead?

Ross. Ay, and brought off the field. Your cause of sorrow
Must not be measur'd by his worth, for then
It hath no end.

Siw. Had he his hurts before?

Ross. Ay, on the front.

Siw. Why then, God's soldier be he!
Had I as many sons as I have hairs,
I would not wish them to a fairer death.
And so his knell is knoll'd.

Mal. He's worth more sorrow,
And that I'll spend for him.

Siw. He's worth no more.
They say he parted well and paid his score,
And so, God be with him! Here comes newer comfort.

Enter *Macduff*, with *Macbeth's* head.

Macd. Hail, King! for so thou art. Behold where stands
Th' usurper's cursed head. The time is free.
I see thee compass'd with thy kingdom's pearl,
That speak my salutation in their minds;
Whose voices I desire aloud with mine —
Hail, King of Scotland!

All. Hail, King of Scotland! *Flourish.*

Mal. We shall not spend a large expense of time
Before we reckon with your several loves
And make us even with you. My Thanes and kinsmen,
Henceforth be Earls, the first that ever Scotland
In such an honour nam'd. What's more to do
Which would be planted newly with the time —
As calling home our exil'd friends abroad
That fled the snares of watchful tyranny,
Producing forth the cruel ministers
Of this dead butcher and his fiendlike queen,
Who (as 'tis thought) by self and violent hands
Took off her life — this, and what needful else
That calls upon us, by the grace of Grace
We will perform in measure, time, and place.
So thanks to all at once and to each one,
Whom we invite to see us crown'd at Scone.

Flourish. Exeunt omnes.

Hamlet

On July 26, 1602, 'The Revenge of Hamlett Prince Denmarke as yt was latelie Acted by the Lord Chamberleyne his servantes' (Shakespeare's company) was entered in the Stationers' Register. In 1603 the First Quarto appeared: 'The Tragicall Historie of Hamlet Prince of Denmarke By William Shake-speare. As it hath beene diuerse times acted by his Highnesse seruants in the Cittie of London: as also in the two Vniuersities of Cambridge and Oxford, and else-where.' The Second Quarto was issued in 1604: 'Newly imprinted and enlarged to almost as much againe as it was, according to the true and perfect Coppie.' This is the authority for the text. The Third Quarto (1611) and the Fourth (undated) are of no textual consequence. The First Folio (1623) omits some two hundred lines that are undoubtedly Shakespeare's; but it supplies (besides a line or so here and there) five genuine passages which the Quarto omits — ii, 2, 244–276 ('Let . . . attended'); 352–379; iv, 5, 161–163; v, 1, 38–41 ('Why . . . without arms'); v, 2, 68–80 — and it often corrects a manifest error or affords a superior reading.

External evidence for the date of Hamlet is scanty. Meres, writing in 1598, does not mention it. 'The humorous man shall end his part in peace' (ii, 2, 335) may or may not allude to Jonson's *Every Man Out of his Humour*, which seems to have been acted late in 1599. Gabriel Harvey's manuscript note in his copy of Speght's 1598 edition of Chaucer is indecisive: 'The younger sort takes much delight in Shakespeare's Venus, & Adonis: but his Lucrece, & his tragedie of Hamlet, Prince of Denmarke, haue it in them, to please the wiser sort.' It has been argued that the note must have been written before the death of the second Earl of Essex (February 25, 1601) because Harvey remarks, 'The Earle of Essex much commendes Albions England'; but that is forcing the present tense rather hard. However, 1600 or 1601 is a reasonable date for the play (cf. p. 63, above).

For the plot Shakespeare went to Volume V of Belleforest's *Histoires Tragiques* (1576). Belleforest worked up his *histoire* from the *Historica Danica* of Saxo Grammaticus (*ca.* 1200; first printed in 1514), expanding and moralizing *more suo*. An English translation of the tale was printed in 1608.

In Belleforest there is no mystery about the king's death. His brother kills him at a banquet and justifies the act by alleging that it was done to rescue the Queen from a murderous attack by her husband. Hamlet is a mere stripling, absolutely in his uncle's power. He feigns madness to protect himself until there shall come an opportunity for revenge. The ancient idea that madmen are sacred is implied, though not expressed. His uncle is suspicious, and resolves to put him to death at once if he can satisfy himself that the boy is not mad indeed. He attempts to entrap him by means of a young woman, and also by the agency of a spy who hides in the Queen's chamber; but in vain. The repentant Queen becomes her son's confidante in his plan of revenge. After a riotous feast, Hamlet sets fire to the hall and burns the drunken courtiers to death. His uncle, who has retired to his chamber, he decapitates. Then he delivers an oration to the people, explaining all the facts, and is crowned as king. His further history does not concern us. He is finally killed in battle with another uncle.

Between Belleforest's story and Shakespeare's Hamlet an old play on the subject intervenes. Henslowe records a performance of it on June 11, 1594, and Thomas Lodge quotes it in his *Wits Miserie, and the Worlds Madnesse* (1596): 'As pale as the Visard of ye ghost which cried so miserally at ye

Theator, like an oister wife, *Hamlet, reuenge*' (p. 56). Nashe alludes to it in his epistle prefixed to Greene's *Menaphon* (1589): 'English *Seneca* read by Candle light yeelds many good sentences . . .; and if you intreate him faire in a frostie morning, hee will afford you whole *Hamlets*, I should say handfuls of Tragicall speeches.' The author is unknown. Nashe seems to glance at Thomas Kyd in the context of the passage just quoted, but his language does not even hint at Kyd's authorship of the old *Hamlet*. The old play was evidently of the Senecan sort, like *The Spanish Tragedy*, and one of the characters was a pale-faced ghost (presumably of the murdered king) who cried 'Hamlet, revenge!' Further than this, we have no knowledge of its contents. The First Quarto seems to be merely a bad copy of an abridged version of Shakespeare's HAMLET — perhaps of a version cobbled up for provincial acting; but some passages may possibly be remnants of the old play. The Queen's vow to assist Hamlet agrees with Belleforest in a point in which Shakespeare differs.

Both in Shakespeare and in Belleforest we have a story of necessarily deferred revenge, but the situation at the outset is not the same, and the ground of the necessity differs accordingly. In the old tale the murder is no secret, but the avenger is helpless, a mere boy in his uncle's hands. In the drama, on the other hand, the murder is suspected by no one until the ghost reveals it. But this is 'spectral evidence.' Hamlet believes that the apparition is indeed the ghost of his father and that it has told the truth. Yet it may be a demon in his father's shape, tempting him to kill an innocent man. This doubt as to the ambiguous apparition accords with ancient doctrine and was perfectly intelligible to any Elizabethan audience. Disregard of Hamlet's dilemma has led to misinterpretation of his character, as if he were a procrastinator, a vain dreamer, an impulsive creature of feeble will. But Shakespeare has done his best to enforce the imperative scruple as to the apparition. It inspires and dictates Horatio's challenge (i, 1, 46 ff.); it is implicit in Bernardo's assent (109); it is manifest in Hamlet's declared resolution (i, 2, 244), and it finds solemn utterance when he adjures the ghost to speak (i, 4, 40 ff.). Nothing could be clearer, in this regard, than Horatio's warning (i, 4, 69 ff.):

What if it tempt you toward the flood, my lord,
Or to the dreadful summit of the cliff
That beetles o'er his base into the sea,
And there assume some other, horrible form
Which might deprive your sovereignty of reason
And draw you into madness?[1]

All this leads up to Hamlet's soliloquy at the end of Act II:

The spirit that I have seen
May be a devil; and the devil hath power
T' assume a pleasing shape; yea, and perhaps
Out of my weakness and my melancholy,
As he is very potent with such spirits,
Abuses me to damn me. I'll have grounds
More relative than this.

He cannot act upon mere spectral evidence. The testimony of the ghost must somehow be corroborated. The murderer must be forced to testify against himself. Then, and not till then, will action be possible for a reasonable man. 'The play's the thing!'

[1] Cf. *King Lear*, iv, 6, 67 ff.

THE TRAGEDY OF
HAMLET, PRINCE OF DENMARK

[Dramatis Personæ.

Claudius, King of Denmark.
Hamlet, son to the former, and nephew to the present King.
Polonius, Lord Chamberlain.
Horatio, friend to *Hamlet*.
Laertes, son to *Polonius*.
Voltemand, *Cornelius*, *Rosencrantz*, *Guildenstern*, *Osric*, A Gentleman, } courtiers.
A Priest.
Marcellus, *Bernardo*, } officers.

Francisco, a soldier.
Reynaldo, servant to *Polonius*.
Players.
Two Clowns, gravediggers.
Fortinbras, Prince of Norway.
A Norwegian Captain.
English Ambassadors.

Gertrude, Queen of Denmark, mother to *Hamlet*.
Ophelia, daughter to *Polonius*.

Ghost of *Hamlet's* Father.

Lords, Ladies, Officers, Soldiers, Sailors, Messengers, Attendants.

SCENE. — *Elsinore*.]

ACT I. Scene I. [*Elsinore. A platform before the Castle.*]

Enter two *Sentinels* — [first,] *Francisco*, [who paces up and down at his post; then] *Bernardo*, [who approaches him].

Ber. Who's there?
Fran. Nay, answer me. Stand and unfold yourself.
Ber. Long live the King!
Fran. Bernardo?
Ber. He.
Fran. You come most carefully upon your hour.
Ber. 'Tis now struck twelve. Get thee to bed, Francisco.
Fran. For this relief much thanks. 'Tis bitter cold,
And I am sick at heart.
Ber. Have you had quiet guard?
Fran. Not a mouse stirring.
Ber. Well, good night.
If you do meet Horatio and Marcellus,
The rivals of my watch, bid them make haste.

Enter *Horatio* and *Marcellus*.

Fran. I think I hear them. Stand, ho! Who is there?
Hor. Friends to this ground.
Mar. And liegemen to the Dane.
Fran. Give you good night.
Mar. O, farewell, honest soldier.
Who hath reliev'd you?
Fran. Bernardo hath my place.
Give you good night. *Exit*.
Mar. Holla, Bernardo!
Ber. Say —
What, is Horatio there?
Hor. A piece of him.
Ber. Welcome, Horatio. Welcome, good Marcellus.
Mar. What, has this thing appear'd again to-night?
Ber. I have seen nothing.
Mar. Horatio says 'tis but our fantasy,
And will not let belief take hold of him
Touching this dreaded sight, twice seen of us.
Therefore I have entreated him along,
With us to watch the minutes of this night,
That, if again this apparition come,
He may approve our eyes and speak to it.
Hor. Tush, tush, 'twill not appear.
Ber. Sit down awhile,
And let us once again assail your ears,
That are so fortified against our story,
What we two nights have seen.

Hor. Well, sit we down,
And let us hear Bernardo speak of this.
Ber. Last night of all,
When yond same star that's westward from the pole
Had made his course t' illume that part of heaven
Where now it burns, Marcellus and myself,
The bell then beating one —

Enter *Ghost.*

Mar. Peace! break thee off! Look where it comes again!
Ber. In the same figure, like the King that's dead.
Mar. Thou art a scholar; speak to it, Horatio.
Ber. Looks it not like the King? Mark it, Horatio.
Hor. Most like. It harrows me with fear and wonder.
Ber. It would be spoke to.
Mar. Question it, Horatio.
Hor. What art thou that usurp'st this time of night
Together with that fair and warlike form
In which the majesty of buried Denmark
Did sometimes march? By heaven I charge thee speak!
Mar. It is offended.
Ber. See, it stalks away!
Hor. Stay! Speak, speak! I charge thee speak!

Exit Ghost.

Mar. 'Tis gone and will not answer.
Ber. How now, Horatio? You tremble and look pale.
Is not this something more than fantasy?
What think you on't?
Hor. Before my God, I might not this believe
Without the sensible and true avouch
Of mine own eyes.
Mar. Is it not like the King?
Hor. As thou art to thyself.
Such was the very armour he had on
When he th' ambitious Norway combated.
So frown'd he once when, in an angry parle,
He smote the sledded Polacks on the ice.
'Tis strange.
Mar. Thus twice before, and jump at this dead hour,
With martial stalk hath he gone by our watch.
Hor. In what particular thought to work I know not;
But, in the gross and scope of my opinion,
This bodes some strange eruption to our state.
Mar. Good now, sit down, and tell me he that knows,
Why this same strict and most observant watch
So nightly toils the subject of the land,
And why such daily cast of brazen cannon
And foreign mart for implements of war;
Why such impress of shipwrights, whose sore task
Does not divide the Sunday from the week.
What might be toward, that this sweaty haste
Doth make the night joint-labourer with the day?
Who is't that can inform me?
Hor. That can I.
At least, the whisper goes so. Our last king,
Whose image even but now appear'd to us,
Was, as you know, by Fortinbras of Norway,
Thereto prick'd on by a most emulate pride,
Dar'd to the combat; in which our valiant Hamlet
(For so this side of our known world esteem'd him)
Did slay this Fortinbras; who, by a seal'd compact,
Well ratified by law and heraldry,
Did forfeit, with his life, all those his lands
Which he stood seiz'd of, to the conqueror;
Against the which a moiety competent
Was gaged by our king; which had return'd
To the inheritance of Fortinbras,
Had he been vanquisher, as, by the same comart
And carriage of the article design'd,
His fell to Hamlet. Now, sir, young Fortinbras,
Of unimproved mettle hot and full,
Hath in the skirts of Norway, here and there,
Shark'd up a list of lawless resolutes,
For food and diet, to some enterprise
That hath a stomach in't; which is no other,
As it doth well appear unto our state,
But to recover of us, by strong hand
And terms compulsatory, those foresaid lands
So by his father lost; and this, I take it,
Is the main motive of our preparations,
The source of this our watch, and the chief head
Of this post-haste and romage in the land.
Ber. I think it be no other but e'en so.
Well may it sort that this portentous figure
Comes armed through our watch, so like the King
That was and is the question of these wars.
Hor. A mote it is to trouble the mind's eye.
In the most high and palmy state of Rome,

A little ere the mightiest Julius fell,
The graves stood tenantless, and the sheeted dead
Did squeak and gibber in the Roman streets;
As stars with trains of fire, and dews of blood,
Disasters in the sun; and the moist star
Upon whose influence Neptune's empire stands
Was sick almost to doomsday with eclipse.
And even the like precurse of fierce events,
As harbingers preceding still the fates
And prologue to the omen coming on,
Have heaven and earth together demonstrated
Unto our climature and countrymen.

Enter *Ghost* again.

But soft! behold! Lo, where it comes again!
I'll cross it, though it blast me. — Stay, illusion!
Spreads his arms.
If thou hast any sound, or use of voice,
Speak to me.
If there be any good thing to be done,
That may to thee do ease, and grace to me,
Speak to me.
If thou art privy to thy country's fate,
Which happily foreknowing may avoid,
O, speak!
Or if thou hast uphoarded in thy life
Extorted treasure in the womb of earth
(For which, they say, you spirits oft walk in death),
The cock crows.
Speak of it! Stay, and speak! — Stop it, Marcellus!
Mar. Shall I strike at it with my partisan?
Hor. Do, if it will not stand.
Ber. 'Tis here!
Hor. 'Tis here!
Mar. 'Tis gone!
Exit Ghost.
We do it wrong, being so majestical,
To offer it the show of violence;
For it is as the air, invulnerable,
And our vain blows malicious mockery.
Ber. It was about to speak, when the cock crew.
Hor. And then it started, like a guilty thing
Upon a fearful summons. I have heard
The cock, that is the trumpet to the morn,
Doth with his lofty and shrill-sounding throat
Awake the god of day; and at his warning,
Whether in sea or fire, in earth or air,
Th' extravagant and erring spirit hies
To his confine; and of the truth herein
This present object made probation.
Mar. It faded on the crowing of the cock.
Some say that ever, 'gainst that season comes
Wherein our Saviour's birth is celebrated,
The bird of dawning singeth all night long;
And then, they say, no spirit dare stir abroad,
The nights are wholesome, then no planets strike,
No fairy takes, nor witch hath power to charm,
So hallow'd and so gracious is the time.
Hor. So have I heard and do in part believe it.
But look, the morn, in russet mantle clad,
Walks o'er the dew of yon high eastward hill.
Break we our watch up; and by my advice
Let us impart what we have seen to-night
Unto young Hamlet; for, upon my life,
This spirit, dumb to us, will speak to him.
Do you consent we shall acquaint him with it,
As needful in our loves, fitting our duty?
Mar. Let's do't, I pray; and I this morning know
Where we shall find him most conveniently.
Exeunt.

Scene II. [*Elsinore. A room of state in the Castle.*]

Flourish. Enter *Claudius, King of Denmark, Gertrude the Queen, Hamlet, Polonius, Laertes* and his sister *Ophelia,* [*Voltemand, Cornelius,*] *Lords Attendant.*

King. Though yet of Hamlet our dear brother's death
The memory be green, and that it us befitted
To bear our hearts in grief, and our whole kingdom
To be contracted in one brow of woe,
Yet so far hath discretion fought with nature
That we with wisest sorrow think on him
Together with remembrance of ourselves.
Therefore our sometime sister, now our queen,
Th' imperial jointress to this warlike state,
Have we, as 'twere with a defeated joy,
With an auspicious, and a dropping eye,
With mirth in funeral, and with dirge in marriage,
In equal scale weighing delight and dole,
Taken to wife; nor have we herein barr'd
Your better wisdoms, which have freely gone
With this affair along. For all, our thanks.
Now follows, that you know, young Fortinbras,
Holding a weak supposal of our worth,
Or thinking by our late dear brother's death
Our state to be disjoint and out of frame,

Colleagued with this dream of his advantage,
He hath not fail'd to pester us with message
Importing the surrender of those lands
Lost by his father, with all bands of law,
To our most valiant brother. So much for him.
Now for ourself and for this time of meeting.
Thus much the business is: we have here writ
To Norway, uncle of young Fortinbras,
Who, impotent and bedrid, scarcely hears
Of this his nephew's purpose, to suppress
His further gait herein, in that the levies,
The lists, and full proportions are all made
Out of his subject; and we here dispatch
You, good Cornelius, and you, Voltemand,
For bearers of this greeting to old Norway,
Giving to you no further personal power
To business with the King, more than the scope
Of these dilated articles allow. [*Gives a paper.*]
Farewell, and let your haste commend your duty.

Cor., Volt. In that, and all things, will we show our duty.

King. We doubt it nothing. Heartily farewell.

Exeunt Voltemand and Cornelius.

And now, Laertes, what's the news with you?
You told us of some suit. What is't, Laertes?
You cannot speak of reason to the Dane
And lose your voice. What wouldst thou beg, Laertes,
That shall not be my offer, not thy asking?
The head is not more native to the heart,
The hand more instrumental to the mouth,
Than is the throne of Denmark to thy father.
What wouldst thou have, Laertes?

Laer. My dread lord,
Your leave and favour to return to France;
From whence though willingly I came to Denmark
To show my duty in your coronation,
Yet now I must confess, that duty done,
My thoughts and wishes bend again toward France
And bow them to your gracious leave and pardon.

King. Have you your father's leave? What says Polonius?

Pol. He hath, my lord, wrung from me my slow leave
By laboursome petition, and at last
Upon his will I seal'd my hard consent.
I do beseech you give him leave to go.

King. Take thy fair hour, Laertes. Time be thine,
And thy best graces spend it at thy will!
But now, my cousin Hamlet, and my son —

Ham. [*aside*] A little more than kin, and less than kind!

King. How is it that the clouds still hang on you?

Ham. Not so, my lord. I am too much i' th' sun.

Queen. Good Hamlet, cast thy nighted colour off,
And let thine eye look like a friend on Denmark.
Do not for ever with thy vailed lids
Seek for thy noble father in the dust.
Thou know'st 'tis common. All that lives must die,
Passing through nature to eternity.

Ham. Ay, madam, it is common.

Queen. If it be,
Why seems it so particular with thee?

Ham. Seems, madam? Nay, it is. I know not 'seems.'
'Tis not alone my inky cloak, good mother,
Nor customary suits of solemn black,
Nor windy suspiration of forc'd breath,
No, nor the fruitful river in the eye,
Nor the dejected haviour of the visage,
Together with all forms, moods, shapes of grief,
That can denote me truly. These indeed seem,
For they are actions that a man might play;
But I have that within which passeth show —
These but the trappings and the suits of woe.

King. 'Tis sweet and commendable in your nature, Hamlet,
To give these mourning duties to your father;
But you must know, your father lost a father;
That father lost, lost his, and the survivor bound
In filial obligation for some term
To do obsequious sorrow. But to persever
In obstinate condolement is a course
Of impious stubbornness. 'Tis unmanly grief;
It shows a will most incorrect to heaven,
A heart unfortified, a mind impatient,
An understanding simple and unschool'd;
For what we know must be, and is as common
As any the most vulgar thing to sense,
Why should we in our peevish opposition
Take it to heart? Fie! 'tis a fault to heaven,
A fault against the dead, a fault to nature,
To reason most absurd, whose common theme
Is death of fathers, and who still hath cried,
From the first corse till he that died to-day,
'This must be so.' We pray you throw to earth
This unprevailing woe, and think of us
As of a father; for let the world take note

You are the most immediate to our throne,
And with no less nobility of love
Than that which dearest father bears his son
Do I impart toward you. For your intent
In going back to school in Wittenberg,
It is most retrograde to our desire;
And we beseech you, bend you to remain
Here in the cheer and comfort of our eye,
Our chiefest courtier, cousin, and our son.

Queen. Let not thy mother lose her prayers, Hamlet.
I pray thee stay with us, go not to Wittenberg.

Ham. I shall in all my best obey you, madam.

King. Why, 'tis a loving and a fair reply.
Be as ourself in Denmark. Madam, come.
This gentle and unforc'd accord of Hamlet
Sits smiling to my heart; in grace whereof,
No jocund health that Denmark drinks to-day
But the great cannon to the clouds shall tell,
And the King's rouse the heaven shall bruit again,
Respeaking earthly thunder. Come away.

Flourish. Exeunt all but Hamlet.

Ham. O that this too too solid flesh would melt,
Thaw, and resolve itself into a dew!
Or that the Everlasting had not fix'd
His canon 'gainst self-slaughter! O God! God!
How weary, stale, flat, and unprofitable
Seem to me all the uses of this world!
Fie on't! ah, fie! 'Tis an unweeded garden
That grows to seed; things rank and gross in nature
Possess it merely. That it should come to this!
But two months dead! Nay, not so much, not two.
So excellent a king, that was to this
Hyperion to a satyr; so loving to my mother
That he might not beteem the winds of heaven
Visit her face too roughly. Heaven and earth!
Must I remember? Why, she would hang on him
As if increase of appetite had grown
By what it fed on; and yet, within a month —
Let me not think on't! Frailty, thy name is woman! —
A little month, or ere those shoes were old
With which she followed my poor father's body
Like Niobe, all tears — why she, even she
(O God! a beast that wants discourse of reason
Would have mourn'd longer) married with my uncle;
My father's brother, but no more like my father
Than I to Hercules. Within a month,
Ere yet the salt of most unrighteous tears
Had left the flushing in her galled eyes,
She married. O, most wicked speed, to post
With such dexterity to incestuous sheets!
It is not, nor it cannot come to good.
But break my heart, for I must hold my tongue!

Enter *Horatio, Marcellus,* and *Bernardo.*

Hor. Hail to your lordship!

Ham. I am glad to see you well.
Horatio! — or I do forget myself.

Hor. The same, my lord, and your poor servant ever.

Ham. Sir, my good friend — I'll change that name with you.
And what make you from Wittenberg, Horatio?
Marcellus?

Mar. My good lord!

Ham. I am very glad to see you. — [*To Bernardo*] Good even, sir. —
But what, in faith, make you from Wittenberg?

Hor. A truant disposition, good my lord.

Ham. I would not hear your enemy say so,
Nor shall you do my ear that violence
To make it truster of your own report
Against yourself. I know you are no truant.
But what is your affair in Elsinore?
We'll teach you to drink deep ere you depart.

Hor. My lord, I came to see your father's funeral.

Ham. I prithee do not mock me, fellow student.
I think it was to see my mother's wedding.

Hor. Indeed, my lord, it followed hard upon.

Ham. Thrift, thrift, Horatio! The funeral bak'd meats
Did coldly furnish forth the marriage tables.
Would I had met my dearest foe in heaven
Or ever I had seen that day, Horatio!
My father — methinks I see my father.

Hor. O, where, my lord?

Ham. In my mind's eye, Horatio.

Hor. I saw him once. He was a goodly king.

Ham. He was a man, take him for all in all.
I shall not look upon his like again.

Hor. My lord, I think I saw him yesternight.

Ham. Saw? who?

Hor. My lord, the King your father.

Ham. The King my father?

Hor. Season your admiration for a while
With an attent ear, till I may deliver,
Upon the witness of these gentlemen,
This marvel to you.

Ham. For God's love let me hear!

Hor. Two nights together had these gentlemen
(Marcellus and Bernardo) on their watch
In the dead vast and middle of the night
Been thus encount'red. A figure like your father,
Armed at point exactly, cap-a-pe,
Appears before them and with solemn march
Goes slow and stately by them. Thrice he walk'd
By their oppress'd and fear-surprised eyes,
Within his truncheon's length; whilst they distill'd
Almost to jelly with the act of fear,
Stand dumb and speak not to him. This to me
In dreadful secrecy impart they did,
And I with them the third night kept the watch;
Where, as they had deliver'd, both in time,
Form of the thing, each word made true and good,
The apparition comes. I knew your father.
These hands are not more like.
Ham. But where was this?
Mar. My lord, upon the platform where we watch'd.
Ham. Did you not speak to it?
Hor. My lord, I did;
But answer made it none. Yet once methought
It lifted up it head and did address
Itself to motion, like as it would speak;
But even then the morning cock crew loud,
And at the sound it shrunk in haste away
And vanish'd from our sight.
Ham. 'Tis very strange.
Hor. As I do live, my honour'd lord, 'tis true;
And we did think it writ down in our duty
To let you know of it.
Ham. Indeed, indeed, sirs. But this troubles me.
Hold you the watch to-night?
Both [*Mar. and Ber.*] We do, my lord.
Ham. Arm'd, say you?
Both. Arm'd, my lord.
Ham. From top to toe?
Both. My lord, from head to foot.
Ham. Then saw you not his face?
Hor. O, yes, my lord! He wore his beaver up.
Ham. What, look'd he frowningly?
Hor. A countenance more in sorrow than in anger.
Ham. Pale or red?
Hor. Nay, very pale.
Ham. And fix'd his eyes upon you?
Hor. Most constantly.
Ham. I would I had been there.
Hor. It would have much amaz'd you.
Ham. Very like, very like. Stay'd it long?
Hor. While one with moderate haste might tell a hundred.
Both. Longer, longer.
Hor. Not when I saw't.
Ham. His beard was grizzled — no?
Hor. It was, as I have seen it in his life,
A sable silver'd.
Ham. I will watch to-night.
Perchance 'twill walk again.
Hor. I warr'nt it will.
Ham. If it assume my noble father's person,
I'll speak to it, though hell itself should gape
And bid me hold my peace. I pray you all,
If you have hitherto conceal'd this sight,
Let it be tenable in your silence still;
And whatsoever else shall hap to-night,
Give it an understanding but no tongue.
I will requite your loves. So, fare you well.
Upon the platform, 'twixt eleven and twelve,
I'll visit you.
All. Our duty to your honour.
Ham. Your loves, as mine to you. Farewell.
Exeunt [*all but Hamlet*].
My father's spirit — in arms? All is not well.
I doubt some foul play. Would the night were come!
Till then sit still, my soul. Foul deeds will rise,
Though all the earth o'erwhelm them, to men's eyes. *Exit.*

Scene III. [*Elsinore. A room in the house of* Polonius.]

Enter *Laertes* and *Ophelia.*

Laer. My necessaries are embark'd. Farewell.
And, sister, as the winds give benefit
And convoy is assistant, do not sleep,
But let me hear from you.
Oph. Do you doubt that?
Laer. For Hamlet, and the trifling of his favour,
Hold it a fashion, and a toy in blood;
A violet in the youth of primy nature,
Forward, not permanent — sweet, not lasting;
The perfume and suppliance of a minute;
No more.
Oph. No more but so?
Laer. Think it no more.
For nature crescent does not grow alone
In thews and bulk: but as this temple waxes.

The inward service of the mind and soul
Grows wide withal. Perhaps he loves you now,
And now no soil nor cautel doth besmirch
The virtue of his will; but you must fear,
His greatness weigh'd, his will is not his own;
For he himself is subject to his birth.
He may not, as unvalued persons do,
Carve for himself, for on his choice depends
The safety and health of this whole state,
And therefore must his choice be circumscrib'd
Unto the voice and yielding of that body
Whereof he is the head. Then if he says he loves you,
It fits your wisdom so far to believe it
As he in his particular act and place
May give his saying deed; which is no further
Than the main voice of Denmark goes withal.
Then weigh what loss your honour may sustain
If with too credent ear you list his songs,
Or lose your heart, or your chaste treasure open
To his unmast'red importunity.
Fear it, Ophelia, fear it, my dear sister,
And keep you in the rear of your affection,
Out of the shot and danger of desire.
The chariest maid is prodigal enough
If she unmask her beauty to the moon.
Virtue itself scapes not calumnious strokes.
The canker galls the infants of the spring
Too oft before their buttons be disclos'd,
And in the morn and liquid dew of youth
Contagious blastments are most imminent.
Be wary then; best safety lies in fear.
Youth to itself rebels, though none else near.

Oph I shall th' effect of this good lesson keep
As watchman to my heart. But, good my brother,
Do not as some ungracious pastors do,
Show me the steep and thorny way to heaven,
Whiles, like a puff'd and reckless libertine,
Himself the primrose path of dalliance treads
And recks not his own rede.

Laer. O, fear me not!

Enter *Polonius.*

I stay too long. But here my father comes.
A double blessing is a double grace;
Occasion smiles upon a second leave.

Pol. Yet here, Laertes? Aboard, aboard, for shame!
The wind sits in the shoulder of your sail,
And you are stay'd for. There — my blessing with thee!
And these few precepts in thy memory
Look thou character. Give thy thoughts no tongue,
Nor any unproportion'd thought his act.
Be thou familiar, but by no means vulgar:
Those friends thou hast, and their adoption tried,
Grapple them unto thy soul with hoops of steel;
But do not dull thy palm with entertainment
Of each new-hatch'd, unfledg'd comrade. Beware
Of entrance to a quarrel; but being in,
Bear't that th' opposed may beware of thee.
Give every man thine ear, but few thy voice;
Take each man's censure, but reserve thy judgment.
Costly thy habit as thy purse can buy,
But not express'd in fancy; rich, not gaudy;
For the apparel oft proclaims the man,
And they in France of the best rank and station
Are most select and generous, chief in that.
Neither a borrower nor a lender be;
For loan oft loses both itself and friend,
And borrowing dulls the edge of husbandry.
This above all — to thine own self be true,
And it must follow, as the night the day,
Thou canst not then be false to any man.
Farewell. My blessing season this in thee!

Laer. Most humbly do I take my leave, my lord.

Pol. The time invites you. Go, your servants tend.

Laer. Farewell, Ophelia, and remember well
What I have said to you.

Oph. 'Tis in my memory lock'd,
And you yourself shall keep the key of it.

Laer. Farewell. *Exit.*

Pol. What is't, Ophelia, he hath said to you?

Oph. So please you, something touching the Lord Hamlet.

Pol. Marry, well bethought!
'Tis told me he hath very oft of late
Given private time to you, and you yourself
Have of your audience been most free and bounteous.
If it be so — as so 'tis put on me,
And that in way of caution — I must tell you
You do not understand yourself so clearly
As it behooves my daughter and your honour.
What is between you? Give me up the truth.

Oph. He hath, my lord, of late made many tenders
Of his affection to me.

Pol. Affection? Pooh! You speak like a green girl,
Unsifted in such perilous circumstance.
Do you believe his tenders, as you call them?

Oph. I do not know, my lord, what I should think.
Pol. Marry, I will teach you! Think yourself a baby
That you have ta'en these tenders for true pay,
Which are not sterling. Tender yourself more dearly,
Or (not to crack the wind of the poor phrase,
Running it thus) you'll tender me a fool.
Oph. My lord, he hath importun'd me with love
In honourable fashion.
Pol. Ay, fashion you may call it. Go to, go to!
Oph. And hath given countenance to his speech, my lord,
With almost all the holy vows of heaven.
Pol. Ay, springes to catch woodcocks! I do know,
When the blood burns, how prodigal the soul
Lends the tongue vows. These blazes, daughter,
Giving more light than heat, extinct in both
Even in their promise, as it is a-making,
You must not take for fire. From this time
Be something scanter of your maiden presence.
Set your entreatments at a higher rate
Than a command to parley. For Lord Hamlet,
Believe so much in him, that he is young,
And with a larger tether may he walk
Than may be given you. In few, Ophelia,
Do not believe his vows; for they are brokers,
Not of that dye which their investments show,
But mere implorators of unholy suits,
Breathing like sanctified and pious bawds,
The better to beguile. This is for all:
I would not, in plain terms, from this time forth
Have you so slander any moment leisure
As to give words or talk with the Lord Hamlet.
Look to't, I charge you. Come your ways.
Oph. I shall obey, my lord. *Exeunt.*

[Scene IV. *Elsinore. The platform before the Castle.*]

Enter *Hamlet, Horatio,* and *Marcellus.*

Ham. The air bites shrewdly; it is very cold.
Hor. It is a nipping and an eager air.
Ham. What hour now?
Hor. I think it lacks of twelve.
Mar. No, it is struck.
Hor. Indeed? I heard it not. It then draws near the season
Wherein the spirit held his wont to walk.
A flourish of trumpets, and two pieces go off.
What does this mean, my lord?
Ham. The King doth wake to-night and takes his rouse,
Keeps wassail, and the swagg'ring upspring reels,
And, as he drains his draughts of Rhenish down,
The kettledrum and trumpet thus bray out
The triumph of his pledge.
Hor. Is it a custom?
Ham. Ay, marry, is't;
But to my mind, though I am native here
And to the manner born, it is a custom
More honour'd in the breach than the observance.
This heavy-headed revel east and west
Makes us traduc'd and tax'd of other nations;
They clip us drunkards and with swinish phrase
Soil our addition; and indeed it takes
From our achievements, though perform'd at height,
The pith and marrow of our attribute.
So oft it chances in particular men
That, for some vicious mole of nature in them,
As in their birth, — wherein they are not guilty,
Since nature cannot choose his origin, —
By the o'ergrowth of some complexion,
Oft breaking down the pales and forts of reason,
Or by some habit that too much o'erleavens
The form of plausive manners, that these men
Carrying, I say, the stamp of one defect,
Being nature's livery, or fortune's star,
Their virtues else — be they as pure as grace,
As infinite as man may undergo —
Shall in the general censure take corruption
From that particular fault. The dram of e'il
Doth all the noble substance often dout
To his own scandal.

Enter *Ghost.*

Hor. Look, my lord, it comes!
Ham. Angels and ministers of grace defend us!
Be thou a spirit of health or goblin damn'd,
Bring with thee airs from heaven or blasts from hell,
Be thy intents wicked or charitable,
Thou com'st in such a questionable shape
That I will speak to thee. I'll call thee Hamlet,
King, father, royal Dane. O, answer me!
Let me not burst in ignorance, but tell
Why thy canoniz'd bones, hearsed in death,
Have burst their cerements; why the sepulchre

Wherein we saw thee quietly inurn'd,
Hath op'd his ponderous and marble jaws
To cast thee up again. What may this mean
That thou, dead corse, again in complete steel,
Revisits thus the glimpses of the moon,
Making night hideous, and we fools of nature
So horridly to shake our disposition
With thoughts beyond the reaches of our souls?
Say, why is this? wherefore? What should we do?

Ghost beckons Hamlet.

Hor. It beckons you to go away with it,
As if it some impartment did desire
To you alone.

Mar. Look with what courteous action
It waves you to a more removed ground.
But do not go with it!

Hor. No, by no means!

Ham. It will not speak. Then will I follow it.

Hor. Do not, my lord!

Ham. Why, what should be the fear?
I do not set my life at a pin's fee;
And for my soul, what can it do to that,
Being a thing immortal as itself?
It waves me forth again. I'll follow it.

Hor. What if it tempt you toward the flood, my lord,
Or to the dreadful summit of the cliff
That beetles o'er his base into the sea,
And there assume some other, horrible form
Which might deprive your sovereignty of reason
And draw you into madness? Think of it.
The very place puts toys of desperation,
Without more motive, into every brain
That looks so many fadoms to the sea
And hears it roar beneath.

Ham. It waves me still.
Go on. I'll follow thee.

Mar. You shall not go, my lord.

Ham. Hold off your hands!

Hor. Be rul'd. You shall not go.

Ham. My fate cries out
And makes each petty artire in this body
As hardy as the Nemean lion's nerve.

[*Ghost beckons.*]

Still am I call'd. Unhand me, gentlemen.
By heaven, I'll make a ghost of him that lets me! —
I say, away! — Go on. I'll follow thee.

Exeunt Ghost and Hamlet.

Hor. He waxes desperate with imagination.

Mar. Let's follow. 'Tis not fit thus to obey him.

Hor. Have after. To what issue will this come?

Mar. Something is rotten in the state of Denmark.

Hor. Heaven will direct it.

Mar. Nay, let's follow him. *Exeunt.*

[Scene V. *Elsinore. The Castle. Another part of the fortifications.*]

Enter *Ghost* and *Hamlet.*

Ham. Whither wilt thou lead me? Speak! I'll go no further.

Ghost. Mark me.

Ham. I will.

Ghost. My hour is almost come,
When I to sulph'rous and tormenting flames
Must render up myself.

Ham. Alas, poor ghost!

Ghost. Pity me not, but lend thy serious hearing
To what I shall unfold.

Ham. Speak. I am bound to hear.

Ghost. So art thou to revenge, when thou shalt hear.

Ham. What?

Ghost. I am thy father's spirit,
Doom'd for a certain term to walk the night,
And for the day confin'd to fast in fires,
Till the foul crimes done in my days of nature
Are burnt and purg'd away. But that I am forbid
To tell the secrets of my prison house,
I could a tale unfold whose lightest word
Would harrow up thy soul, freeze thy young blood,
Make thy two eyes, like stars, start from their spheres,
Thy knotted and combined locks to part,
And each particular hair to stand an end
Like quills upon the fretful porpentine.
But this eternal blazon must not be
To ears of flesh and blood. List, list, O, list!
If thou didst ever thy dear father love —

Ham. O God!

Ghost. Revenge his foul and most unnatural murther.

Ham. Murther?

Ghost. Murther most foul, as in the best it is;
But this most foul, strange, and unnatural.

Ham. Haste me to know't, that I, with wings as swift
As meditation or the thoughts of love,
May sweep to my revenge.

Ghost. I find thee apt;
And duller shouldst thou be than the fat weed
That rots itself in ease on Lethe wharf,
Wouldst thou not stir in this. Now, Hamlet, hear.
'Tis given out that, sleeping in my orchard,
A serpent stung me. So the whole ear of Denmark
Is by a forged process of my death
Rankly abus'd. But know, thou noble youth,
The serpent that did sting thy father's life
Now wears his crown.

Ham. O my prophetic soul!
My uncle?

Ghost. Ay, that incestuous, that adulterate beast,
With witchcraft of his wit, with traitorous gifts —
O wicked wit and gifts, that have the power
So to seduce! — won to his shameful lust
The will of my most seeming-virtuous queen.
O Hamlet, what a falling-off was there,
From me, whose love was of that dignity
That it went hand in hand even with the vow
I made to her in marriage, and to decline
Upon a wretch whose natural gifts were poor
To those of mine!
But virtue, as it never will be mov'd,
Though lewdness court it in a shape of heaven,
So lust, though to a radiant angel link'd,
Will sate itself in a celestial bed
And prey on garbage.
But soft! methinks I scent the morning air.
Brief let me be. Sleeping within my orchard,
My custom always of the afternoon,
Upon my secure hour thy uncle stole,
With juice of cursed hebona in a vial,
And in the porches of my ears did pour
The leperous distilment; whose effect
Holds such an enmity with blood of man
That swift as quicksilver it courses through
The natural gates and alleys of the body,
And with a sudden vigour it doth posset
And curd, like eager droppings into milk,
The thin and wholesome blood. So did it mine;
And a most instant tetter bark'd about,
Most lazar-like, with vile and loathsome crust
All my smooth body.
Thus was I, sleeping, by a brother's hand
Of life, of crown, of queen, at once dispatch'd;
Cut off even in the blossoms of my sin,
Unhous'led, disappointed, unanel'd,
No reck'ning made, but sent to my account
With all my imperfections on my head.

Ham. O, horrible! O, horrible! most horrible!

Ghost. If thou hast nature in thee, bear it not.
Let not the royal bed of Denmark be
A couch for luxury and damned incest.
But, howsoever thou pursuest this act,
Taint not thy mind, nor let thy soul contrive
Against thy mother aught. Leave her to heaven,
And to those thorns that in her bosom lodge
To prick and sting her. Fare thee well at once.
The glowworm shows the matin to be near
And gins to pale his uneffectual fire.
Adieu, adieu, adieu! Remember me. *Exit*

Ham. O all you host of heaven! O earth! What else?
And shall I couple hell? Hold, hold, my heart!
And you, my sinews, grow not instant old,
But bear me stiffly up. Remember thee?
Ay, thou poor ghost, while memory holds a seat
In this distracted globe. Remember thee?
Yea, from the table of my memory
I'll wipe away all trivial fond records,
All saws of books, all forms, all pressures past
That youth and observation copied there,
And thy commandment all alone shall live
Within the book and volume of my brain,
Unmix'd with baser matter. Yes, by heaven!
O most pernicious woman!
O villain, villain, smiling, damned villain!
My tables! Meet it is I set it down
That one may smile, and smile, and be a villain;
At least I am sure it may be so in Denmark.
[*Writes.*]
So, uncle, there you are. Now to my word:
It is 'Adieu, adieu! Remember me.'
I have sworn't.

Hor. (*within*) My lord, my lord!

Enter *Horatio* and *Marcellus.*

Mar. Lord Hamlet!

Hor. Heaven secure him!

Ham. So be it!

Mar. Illo, ho, ho, my lord!

Ham. Hillo, ho, ho, boy! Come, bird, come.

Mar. How is't, my noble lord?

Hor. What news, my lord?

Ham. O, wonderful!
Hor. Good my lord, tell it.
Ham. No, you will reveal it.
Hor. Not I, my lord, by heaven!
Mar. Nor I, my lord.
Ham. How say you then? Would heart of man once think it?
But you'll be secret?
Both. Ay, by heaven, my lord.
Ham. There's ne'er a villain dwelling in all Denmark
But he's an arrant knave.
Hor. There needs no ghost, my lord, come from the grave
To tell us this.
Ham. Why, right! You are in the right!
And so, without more circumstance at all,
I hold it fit that we shake hands and part;
You, as your business and desire shall point you,
For every man hath business and desire,
Such as it is; and for my own poor part,
Look you, I'll go pray.
Hor. These are but wild and whirling words, my lord.
Ham. I am sorry they offend you, heartily;
Yes, faith, heartily.
Hor. There's no offence, my lord.
Ham. Yes, by Saint Patrick, but there is, Horatio,
And much offence too. Touching this vision here,
It is an honest ghost, that let me tell you.
For your desire to know what is between us,
O'ermaster't as you may. And now, good friends,
As you are friends, scholars, and soldiers,
Give me one poor request.
Hor. What is't, my lord? We will.
Ham. Never make known what you have seen to-night.
Both. My lord, we will not.
Ham. Nay, but swear't.
Hor. In faith,
My lord, not I.
Mar. Nor I, my lord — in faith.
Ham. Upon my sword.
Mar. We have sworn, my lord, already.
Ham. Indeed, upon my sword, indeed.

Ghost cries under the stage.

Ghost. Swear.
Ham. Aha boy, say'st thou so? Art thou there, truepenny?
Come on! You hear this fellow in the cellarage.
Consent to swear.
Hor. Propose the oath, my lord.
Ham. Never to speak of this that you have seen.
Swear by my sword.
Ghost. [*beneath*] Swear.
Ham. Hic et ubique? Then we'll shift our ground.
Come hither, gentlemen,
And lay your hands again upon my sword.
Never to speak of this that you have heard:
Swear by my sword.
Ghost. [*beneath*] Swear by his sword.
Ham. Well said, old mole! Canst work i' th' earth so fast?
A worthy pioner! Once more remove, good friends.
Hor. O day and night, but this is wondrous strange!
Ham. And therefore as a stranger give it welcome.
There are more things in heaven and earth, Horatio,
Than are dreamt of in your philosophy.
But come!
Here, as before, never, so help you mercy,
How strange or odd soe'er I bear myself
(As I perchance hereafter shall think meet
To put an antic disposition on),
That you, at such times seeing me, never shall,
With arms encumb'red thus, or this head-shake,
Or by pronouncing of some doubtful phrase,
As 'Well, well, we know,' or 'We could, an if we would,'
Or 'If we list to speak,' or 'There be, an if they might,'
Or such ambiguous giving out, to note
That you know aught of me — this not to do,
So grace and mercy at your most need help you,
Swear.
Ghost. [*beneath*] Swear.
[*They swear.*]
Ham. Rest, rest, perturbed spirit! So, gentlemen,
With all my love I do commend me to you;
And what so poor a man as Hamlet is
May do t' express his love and friending to you,
God willing, shall not lack. Let us go in together;
And still your fingers on your lips, I pray.
The time is out of joint. O cursed spite
That ever I was born to set it right!
Nay, come, let's go together. *Exeunt.*

Act II. [Scene I. *Elsinore. A room in the house of* Polonius.]

Enter *Polonius* and *Reynaldo.*

Pol. Give him this money and these notes, Reynaldo.
Rey. I will, my lord.
Pol. You shall do marvell's wisely, good Reynaldo,
Before you visit him, to make inquire
Of his behaviour.
Rey. My lord, I did intend it.
Pol. Marry, well said, very well said. Look you, sir,
Enquire me first what Danskers are in Paris;
And how, and who, what means, and where they keep,
What company, at what expense; and finding
By this encompassment and drift of question
That they do know my son, come you more nearer
Than your particular demands will touch it.
Take you, as 'twere, some distant knowledge of him;
As thus, 'I know his father and his friends,
And in part him.' Do you mark this, Reynaldo?
Rey. Ay, very well, my lord.
Pol. 'And in part him, but,' you may say, 'not well.
But if't be he I mean, he's very wild
Addicted so and so'; and there put on him
What forgeries you please; marry, none so rank
As may dishonour him — take heed of that;
But, sir, such wanton, wild, and usual slips
As are companions noted and most known
To youth and liberty.
Rey. As gaming, my lord.
Pol. Ay, or drinking, fencing, swearing, quarrelling,
Drabbing. You may go so far.
Rey. My lord, that would dishonour him.
Pol. Faith, no, as you may season it in the charge.
You must not put another scandal on him,
That he is open to incontinency.
That's not my meaning. But breathe his faults so quaintly
That they may seem the taints of liberty,
The flash and outbreak of a fiery mind,
A savageness in unreclaimed blood,
Of general assault.
Rey. But, my good lord —
Pol. Wherefore should you do this?
Rey. Ay, my lord,
I would know that.
Pol. Marry, sir, here's my drift,
And I believe it is a fetch of warrant.
You laying these slight sullies on my son
As 'twere a thing a little soil'd i' th' working,
Mark you,
Your party in converse, him you would sound,
Having ever seen in the prenominate crimes
The youth you breathe of guilty, be assur'd
He closes with you in this consequence:
'Good sir,' or so, or 'friend,' or 'gentleman' —
According to the phrase or the addition
Of man and country —
Rey. Very good, my lord.
Pol. And then, sir, does 'a this — 'a does —
What was I about to say? By the mass, I was about to say something! Where did I leave?
Rey. At 'closes in the consequence,' at 'friend or so,' and 'gentleman.'
Pol. At 'closes in the consequence' — Ay, marry!
He closes thus: 'I know the gentleman.
I saw him yesterday, or t'other day,
Or then, or then, with such or such; and, as you say,
There was 'a gaming; there o'ertook in's rouse;
There falling out at tennis'; or perchance,
'I saw him enter such a house of sale,'
Videlicet, a brothel, or so forth.
See you now —
Your bait of falsehood takes this carp of truth;
And thus do we of wisdom and of reach,
With windlasses and with assays of bias,
By indirections find directions out.
So, by my former lecture and advice,
Shall you my son. You have me, have you not?
Rey. My lord, I have.
Pol. God b' wi' ye, fare ye well!
Rey. Good my lord! [*Going.*]
Pol. Observe his inclination in yourself.
Rey. I shall, my lord.
Pol. And let him ply his music.
Rey. Well, my lord.
Pol. Farewell! *Exit Reynaldo.*

Enter *Ophelia.*

How now, Ophelia? What's the matter?
Oph. O my lord, my lord, I have been so affrighted!

Pol. With what, i' th' name of God?
Oph. My lord, as I was sewing in my closet,
Lord Hamlet, with his doublet all unbrac'd,
No hat upon his head, his stockings foul'd,
Ungart'red, and down-gyved to his ankle;
Pale as his shirt, his knees knocking each other,
And with a look so piteous in purport
As if he had been loosed out of hell
To speak of horrors — he comes before me.
Pol. Mad for thy love?
Oph. My lord, I do not know,
But truly I do fear it.
Pol. What said he?
Oph. He took me by the wrist and held me hard;
Then goes he to the length of all his arm,
And, with his other hand thus o'er his brow,
He falls to such perusal of my face
As he would draw it. Long stay'd he so.
At last, a little shaking of mine arm,
And thrice his head thus waving up and down,
He rais'd a sigh so piteous and profound
As it did seem to shatter all his bulk
And end his being. That done, he lets me go,
And with his head over his shoulder turn'd
He seem'd to find his way without his eyes,
For out o' doors he went without their help
And to the last bended their light on me.
Pol. Come, go with me. I will go seek the King.
This is the very ecstasy of love,
Whose violent property fordoes itself
And leads the will to desperate undertakings
As oft as any passion under heaven
That does afflict our natures. I am sorry.
What, have you given him any hard words of late?
Oph. No, my good lord; but, as you did command,
I did repel his letters and denied
His access to me.
Pol. That hath made him mad.
I am sorry that with better heed and judgment
I had not quoted him. I fear'd he did but trifle
And meant to wrack thee; but beshrew my jealousy!
By heaven, it is as proper to our age
To cast beyond ourselves in our opinions
As it is common for the younger sort
To lack discretion. Come, go we to the King.
This must be known; which, being kept close, might move
More grief to hide than hate to utter love.
Come. *Exeunt.*

Scene II. [*Elsinore. A room in the Castle.*]

Flourish. Enter *King* and *Queen, Rosencrantz,* and *Guildenstern,* cum aliis.

King. Welcome, dear Rosencrantz and Guildenstern.
Moreover that we much did long to see you,
The need we have to use you did provoke
Our hasty sending. Something have you heard
Of Hamlet's transformation. So I call it,
Sith nor th' exterior nor the inward man
Resembles that it was. What it should be,
More than his father's death, that thus hath put him
So much from th' understanding of himself,
I cannot dream of. I entreat you both
That, being of so young days brought up with him,
And since so neighbour'd to his youth and haviour,
That you vouchsafe your rest here in our court
Some little time; so by your companies
To draw him on to pleasures, and to gather
So much as from occasion you may glean,
Whether aught to us unknown afflicts him thus
That, open'd, lies within our remedy.
Queen. Good gentlemen, he hath much talk'd of you,
And sure I am two men there are not living
To whom he more adheres. If it will please you
To show us so much gentry and good will
As to expend your time with us awhile
For the supply and profit of our hope,
Your visitation shall receive such thanks
As fits a king's remembrance.
Ros. Both your Majesties
Might, by the sovereign power you have of us,
Put your dread pleasures more into command
Than to entreaty.
Guil. But we both obey,
And here give up ourselves, in the full bent,
To lay our service freely at your feet,
To be commanded.
King. Thanks, Rosencrantz and gentle Guildenstern.
Queen. Thanks, Guildenstern and gentle Rosencrantz.
And I beseech you instantly to visit

My too much changed son. — Go, some of you,
And bring these gentlemen where Hamlet is.

Guil. Heavens make our presence and our practices
Pleasant and helpful to him!

Queen. Ay, amen!

Exeunt Rosencrantz and Guildenstern, [*with some Attendants*].

Enter *Polonius.*

Pol. Th' ambassadors from Norway, my good lord,
Are joyfully return'd.

King. Thou still hast been the father of good news.

Pol. Have I, my lord? Assure you, my good liege,
I hold my duty as I hold my soul,
Both to my God and to my gracious king;
And I do think — or else this brain of mine
Hunts not the trail of policy so sure
As it hath us'd to do — that I have found
The very cause of Hamlet's lunacy.

King. O, speak of that! That do I long to hear.

Pol. Give first admittance to th' ambassadors.
My news shall be the fruit to that great feast.

King. Thyself do grace to them, and bring them in.

[*Exit Polonius.*]

He tells me, my dear Gertrude, he hath found
The head and source of all your son's distemper.

Queen. I doubt it is no other but the main,
His father's death and our o'erhasty marriage.

King. Well, we shall sift him.

Enter *Polonius, Voltemand,* and *Cornelius.*

Welcome, my good friends.
Say, Voltemand, what from our brother Norway?

Volt. Most fair return of greetings and desires.
Upon our first, he sent out to suppress
His nephew's levies; which to him appear'd
To be a preparation 'gainst the Polack,
But better look'd into, he truly found
It was against your Highness; whereat griev'd,
That so his sickness, age, and impotence
Was falsely borne in hand, sends out arrests
On Fortinbras; which he, in brief, obeys,
Receives rebuke from Norway, and, in fine,
Makes vow before his uncle never more
To give th' assay of arms against your Majesty.
Whereon old Norway, overcome with joy,
Gives him three thousand crowns in annual fee
And his commission to employ those soldiers,
So levied as before, against the Polack;
With an entreaty, herein further shown,

[*Gives a paper.*]

That it might please you to give quiet pass
Through your dominions for this enterprise,
On such regards of safety and allowance
As therein are set down.

King. It likes us well;
And at our more consider'd time we'll read,
Answer, and think upon this business.
Meantime we thank you for your well-took labour.
Go to your rest; at night we'll feast together.
Most welcome home! *Exeunt Ambassadors.*

Pol. This business is well ended.
My liege, and madam, to expostulate
What majesty should be, what duty is,
Why day is day, night night, and time is time,
Were nothing but to waste night, day, and time.
Therefore, since brevity is the soul of wit,
And tediousness the limbs and outward flourishes,
I will be brief. Your noble son is mad.
Mad call I it; for, to define true madness,
What is't but to be nothing else but mad?
But let that go.

Queen. More matter, with less art.

Pol. Madam, I swear I use no art at all.
That he is mad, 'tis true: 'tis true 'tis pity;
And pity 'tis 'tis true. A foolish figure!
But farewell it, for I will use no art.
Mad let us grant him then. And now remains
That we find out the cause of this effect —
Or rather say, the cause of this defect,
For this effect defective comes by cause.
Thus it remains, and the remainder thus.
Perpend.
I have a daughter (have while she is mine),
Who in her duty and obedience, mark,
Hath given me this. Now gather, and surmise.

[*Reads*] *the letter.*

'To the celestial, and my soul's idol, the most beautified Ophelia,' —

That's an ill phrase, a vile phrase; 'beautified' is a vile phrase. But you shall hear. Thus:

[*Reads.*]

'In her excellent white bosom, these, &c.'

Queen. Came this from Hamlet to her?

Pol. Good madam, stay awhile. I will be faithful. [*Reads.*]

'Doubt thou the stars are fire;
Doubt that the sun doth move;
Doubt truth to be a liar;
But never doubt I love.

'O dear Ophelia, I am ill at these numbers; I have not art to reckon my groans; but that I love thee best, O most best, believe it. Adieu.

'Thine evermore, most dear lady, whilst this machine is to him, HAMLET.'

This, in obedience, hath my daughter shown me;
And more above, hath his solicitings,
As they fell out by time, by means, and place,
All given to mine ear.

King. But how hath she
Receiv'd his love?

Pol. What do you think of me?

King. As of a man faithful and honourable.

Pol. I would fain prove so. But what might you think,
When I had seen this hot love on the wing
(As I perceiv'd it, I must tell you that,
Before my daughter told me), what might you,
Or my dear Majesty your queen here, think,
If I had play'd the desk or table book,
Or given my heart a winking, mute and dumb,
Or look'd upon this love with idle sight?
What might you think? No, I went round to work
And my young mistress thus I did bespeak:
'Lord Hamlet is a prince, out of thy star.
This must not be.' And then I prescripts gave her,
That she should lock herself from his resort,
Admit no messengers, receive no tokens.
Which done, she took the fruits of my advice,
And he, repulsed, a short tale to make,
Fell into a sadness, then into a fast,
Thence to a watch, thence into a weakness,
Thence to a lightness, and, by this declension,
Into the madness wherein now he raves,
And all we mourn for.

King. Do you think 'tis this?

Queen. It may be, very like.

Pol. Hath there been such a time — I would fain know that —
That I have positively said ''Tis so,'
When it prov'd otherwise?

King. Not that I know.

Pol. [*points to his head and shoulder*] Take this from this, if this be otherwise.
If circumstances lead me, I will find
Where truth is hid, though it were hid indeed
Within the centre.

King. How may we try it further?

Pol. You know sometimes he walks four hours together
Here in the lobby.

Queen. So he does indeed.

Pol. At such a time I'll loose my daughter to him.
Be you and I behind an arras then.
Mark the encounter. If he love her not,
And be not from his reason fall'n thereon,
Let me be no assistant for a state,
But keep a farm and carters.

King. We will try it.

Enter *Hamlet*, reading on a book.

Queen. But look where sadly the poor wretch comes reading.

Pol. Away, I do beseech you, both away!
I'll board him presently. O, give me leave.

Exeunt King and Queen, [*with Attendants*].

How does my good Lord Hamlet?

Ham. Well, God-a-mercy.

Pol. Do you know me, my lord?

Ham. Excellent well. You are a fishmonger.

Pol. Not I, my lord.

Ham. Then I would you were so honest a man.

Pol. Honest, my lord?

Ham. Ay, sir. To be honest, as this world goes, is to be one man pick'd out of ten thousand.

Pol. That's very true, my lord.

Ham. For if the sun breed maggots in a dead dog, being a god kissing carrion — Have you a daughter?

Pol. I have, my lord.

Ham. Let her not walk i' th' sun. Conception is a blessing, but not as your daughter may conceive. Friend, look to't.

Pol. [*aside*] How say you by that? Still harping on my daughter. Yet he knew me not at first. He said I was a fishmonger. He is far gone, far gone! And truly in my youth I suff'red much extremity for love — very near this. I'll speak to him again. — What do you read, my lord?

Ham. Words, words, words.

Pol. What is the matter, my lord?

Ham. Between who?

Pol. I mean, the matter that you read, my lord.

Ham. Slanders, sir; for the satirical rogue says here that old men have grey beards; that their faces are wrinkled; their eyes purging thick amber and plum-tree gum: and that they have a plentiful lack of wit, together with most weak hams. All which, sir, though I most powerfully and potently believe, yet I hold it not honesty to have it thus set down; for you yourself, sir, should be old as I am if, like a crab, you could go backward.

Pol. [*aside*] Though this be madness, yet there is method in't. — Will you walk out of the air, my lord?

Ham. Into my grave?

Pol. Indeed, that is out o' th' air. [*Aside*] How pregnant sometimes his replies are! a happiness that often madness hits on, which reason and sanity could not so prosperously be delivered of. I will leave him and suddenly contrive the means of meeting between him and my daughter. — My honourable lord, I will most humbly take my leave of you.

Ham. You cannot, sir, take from me anything that I will more willingly part withal — except my life, except my life, except my life.

Enter *Rosencrantz* and *Guildenstern*.

Pol. Fare you well, my lord.

Ham. These tedious old fools!

Pol. You go to seek the Lord Hamlet. There he is.

Ros. [*to Polonius*] God save you, sir!

Exit [*Polonius*].

Guil. My honour'd lord!

Ros. My most dear lord!

Ham. My excellent good friends! How dost thou, Guildenstern? Ah, Rosencrantz! Good lads, how do ye both?

Ros. As the indifferent children of the earth.

Guil. Happy in that we are not over-happy. On Fortune's cap we are not the very button.

Ham. Nor the soles of her shoe?

Ros. Neither, my lord.

Ham. Then you live about her waist, or in the middle of her favours?

Guil. Faith, her privates we.

Ham. In the secret parts of Fortune? O, most true! she is a strumpet. What news?

Ros. None, my lord, but that the world 's grown honest.

Ham. Then is doomsday near! But your news is not true. Let me question more in particular. What have you, my good friends, deserved at the hands of Fortune that she sends you to prison hither?

Guil. Prison, my lord?

Ham. Denmark 's a prison.

Ros. Then is the world one.

Ham. A goodly one; in which there are many confines, wards, and dungeons, Denmark being one o' th' worst.

Ros. We think not so, my lord.

Ham. Why, then 'tis none to you; for there is nothing either good or bad but thinking makes it so. To me it is a prison.

Ros. Why, then your ambition makes it one. 'Tis too narrow for your mind.

Ham. O God, I could be bounded in a nutshell and count myself a king of infinite space, were it not that I have bad dreams.

Guil. Which dreams indeed are ambition; for the very substance of the ambitious is merely the shadow of a dream.

Ham. A dream itself is but a shadow.

Ros. Truly, and I hold ambition of so airy and light a quality that it is but a shadow's shadow.

Ham. Then are our beggars bodies, and our monarchs and outstretch'd heroes the beggars' shadows. Shall we to th' court? for, by my fay, I cannot reason.

Both. We'll wait upon you.

Ham. No such matter! I will not sort you with the rest of my servants; for, to speak to you like an honest man, I am most dreadfully attended. But in the beaten way of friendship, what make you at Elsinore?

Ros. To visit you, my lord; no other occasion.

Ham. Beggar that I am, I am even poor in thanks; but I thank you; and sure, dear friends, my thanks are too dear a halfpenny. Were you not sent for? Is it your own inclining? Is it a free visitation? Come, deal justly with me. Come, come! Nay, speak.

Guil. What should we say, my lord?

Ham. Why, anything — but to th' purpose. You were sent for; and there is a kind of confession in your looks, which your modesties have not craft enough to colour. I know the good King and Queen have sent for you.

Ros. To what end, my lord?

Ham. That you must teach me. But let me conjure you by the rights of our fellowship, by the consonancy of our youth, by the obligation of our ever-preserved love, and by what more dear a better proposer could charge you withal, be even and direct with me, whether you were sent for or no.

Ros. [*aside to Guildenstern*] What say you?

Ham. [*aside*] Nay then, I have an eye of you. — If you love me, hold not off.

Guil. My lord, we were sent for.

Ham. I will tell you why. So shall my anticipation prevent your discovery, and your secrecy to the King and Queen moult no feather. I have of late — but wherefore I know not — lost all my mirth, forgone all custom of exercises; and indeed, it goes so heavily with my disposition that this goodly frame, the earth, seems to me a sterile promontory; this most excellent canopy, the air, look you, this brave o'erhanging firmament, this majestical roof fretted with golden fire — why, it appeareth no other thing to me than a foul and pestilent congregation of vapours. What a piece of work is a man! how noble in reason! how infinite in faculties! in form and moving how express and admirable! in action how like an angel! in apprehension how like a god! the beauty of the world, the paragon of animals! And yet to me what is this quintessence of dust? Man delights not me — no, nor woman neither, though by your smiling you seem to say so.

Ros. My lord, there was no such stuff in my thoughts.

Ham. Why did you laugh then, when I said 'Man delights not me'?

Ros. To think, my lord, if you delight not in man, what lenten entertainment the players shall receive from you. We coted them on the way, and hither are they coming to offer you service.

Ham. He that plays the king shall be welcome — his Majesty shall have tribute of me; the adventurous knight shall use his foil and target; the lover shall not sigh gratis; the humorous man shall end his part in peace; the clown shall make those laugh whose lungs are tickle o' th' sere; and the lady shall say her mind freely, or the blank verse shall halt for't. What players are they?

Ros. Even those you were wont to take such delight in, the tragedians of the city.

Ham. How chances it they travel? Their residence, both in reputation and profit, was better both ways.

Ros. I think their inhibition comes by the means of the late innovation.

Ham. Do they hold the same estimation they did when I was in the city? Are they so follow'd?

Ros. No indeed are they not.

Ham. How comes it? Do they grow rusty?

Ros. Nay, their endeavour keeps in the wonted pace; but there is, sir, an eyrie of children, little eyases, that cry out on the top of question and are most tyrannically clapp'd for't. These are now the fashion, and so berattle the common stages (so they call them) that many wearing rapiers are afraid of goose-quills and dare scarce come thither.

Ham. What, are they children? Who maintains 'em? How are they escoted? Will they pursue the quality no longer than they can sing? Will they not say afterwards, if they should grow themselves to common players (as it is most like, if their means are no better), their writers do them wrong to make them exclaim against their own succession.

Ros. Faith, there has been much to do on both sides; and the nation holds it no sin to tarre them to controversy. There was, for a while, no money bid for argument unless the poet and the player went to cuffs in the question.

Ham. Is't possible?

Guil. O, there has been much throwing about of brains.

Ham. Do the boys carry it away?

Ros. Ay, that they do, my lord — Hercules and his load too.

Ham. It is not very strange; for my uncle is King of Denmark, and those that would make mows at him while my father lived give twenty, forty, fifty, a hundred ducats apiece for his picture in little. 'Sblood, there is something in this more than natural, if philosophy could find it out.

Flourish for the Players.

Guil. There are the players.

Ham. Gentlemen, you are welcome to Elsinore. Your hands, come! Th' appurtenance of welcome is fashion and ceremony. Let me comply with you in this garb, lest my extent to the players (which I tell you must show fairly outwards) should more appear like entertainment than yours. You are welcome. But my uncle-father and aunt-mother are deceiv'd.

Guil. In what, my dear lord?

Ham. I am but mad north-north-west. When the wind is southerly I know a hawk from a handsaw.

Enter *Polonius.*

Pol. Well be with you, gentlemen!

Ham. Hark you, Guildenstern — and you too — at each ear a hearer! That great baby you see there is not yet out of his swaddling clouts.

Ros. Happily he's the second time come to them; for they say an old man is twice a child.

Ham. I will prophesy he comes to tell me of the players. Mark it. — You say right, sir; a Monday morning; 'twas so indeed.

Pol. My lord, I have news to tell you.

Ham. My lord, I have news to tell you. When Roscius was an actor in Rome —

Pol. The actors are come hither, my lord.

Ham. Buzz, buzz!

Pol. Upon my honour —

Ham. Then came each actor on his ass —

Pol. The best actors in the world, either for tragedy, comedy, history, pastoral, pastoral-comical, historical-pastoral, tragical-historical, tragical-comical-historical-pastoral; scene individable, or poem unlimited. Seneca cannot be too heavy, nor Plautus too light. For the law of writ and the liberty, these are the only men.

Ham. O Jephthah, judge of Israel, what a treasure hadst thou!

Pol. What treasure had he, my lord?

Ham. Why,

'One fair daughter, and no more,
The which he loved passing well.'

Pol. [*aside*] Still on my daughter.

Ham. Am I not i' th' right, old Jephthah?

Pol. If you call me Jephthah, my lord, I have a daughter that I love passing well.

Ham. Nay, that follows not.

Pol. What follows then, my lord?

Ham. Why,

'As by lot, God wot,'

and then, you know,

'It came to pass, as most like it was.'

The first row of the pious chanson will show you more; for look where my abridgment comes

Enter four or five *Players*.

You are welcome, masters; welcome, all. — I am glad to see thee well. —Welcome, good friends. — O, my old friend? Why, thy face is valanc'd since I saw thee last. Com'st thou to beard me in Denmark? — What, my young lady and mistress? By'r Lady, your ladyship is nearer to heaven than when I saw you last by the altitude of a chopine. Pray God your voice, like a piece of uncurrent gold, be not crack'd within the ring. — Masters, you are all welcome. We'll e'en to't like French falconers, fly at anything we see. We'll have a speech straight. Come, give us a taste of your quality. Come, a passionate speech.

1. Play. What speech, my good lord?

Ham. I heard thee speak me a speech once, but it was never acted; or if it was, not above once; for the play, I remember, pleas'd not the million, 'twas caviary to the general; but it was (as I receiv'd it, and others, whose judgments in such matters cried in the top of mine) an excellent play, well digested in the scenes, set down with as much modesty as cunning. I remember one said there were no sallets in the lines to make the matter savoury, nor no matter in the phrase that might indict the author of affectation; but call'd it an honest method, as wholesome as sweet, and by very much more handsome than fine. One speech in't I chiefly lov'd. 'Twas Æneas' tale to Dido, and thereabout of it especially where he speaks of Priam's slaughter. If it live in your memory, begin at this line — let me see, let me see:

'The rugged Pyrrhus, like th' Hyrcanian beast —'

'Tis not so; it begins with Pyrrhus:

'The rugged Pyrrhus, he whose sable arms,
Black as his purpose, did the night resemble
When he lay couched in the ominous horse,
Hath now this dread and black complexion smear'd
With heraldry more dismal. Head to foot
Now is he total gules, horridly trick'd
With blood of fathers, mothers, daughters, sons,
Bak'd and impasted with the parching streets,
That lend a tyrannous and a damned light
To their lord's murther. Roasted in wrath and fire,
And thus o'ersized with coagulate gore,
With eyes like carbuncles, the hellish Pyrrhus
Old grandsire Priam seeks.'

So, proceed you.

Pol. Fore God, my lord, well spoken, with good accent and good discretion.

1. Play. 'Anon he finds him,
Striking too short at Greeks. His antique sword,
Rebellious to his arm, lies where it falls,
Repugnant to command. Unequal match'd,
Pyrrhus at Priam drives, in rage strikes wide;
But with the whiff and wind of his fell sword
Th' unnerved father falls. Then senseless Ilium,
Seeming to feel this blow, with flaming top
Stoops to his base, and with a hideous crash
Takes prisoner Pyrrhus' ear. For lo! his sword,
Which was declining on the milky head
Of reverend Priam, seem'd i' th' air to stick.
So, as a painted tyrant, Pyrrhus stood,
And, like a neutral to his will and matter,
Did nothing.
But, as we often see, against some storm,
A silence in the heavens, the rack stand still,
The bold winds speechless, and the orb below
As hush as death — anon the dreadful thunder

"Alas! poor Yorick. I knew Him . . . a fellow of infinite jest." In the graveyard scene *(Act V, Scene I)*, the melancholy Hamlet (Richard Burton) broods over a grisly relic of wit, the skull of a former jester

HAMLET

PHOTOGRAPHS BY ANGUS MCBEAN
PRODUCED BY THE OLD VIC COMPANY

Above left: Michael Hordern as Polonius, the sententious lord chamberlain, the father of Ophelia and Laertes

Above right: Fay Compton in the role of Hamlet's mother, Gertrude

Center right: Claire Bloom, the lovelorn victim of Hamlet's obsession with the death of his father

Below: the hall of the royal Danish castle at Elsinore. Surrounded by the members of his court, King Claudius (Laurence Hardy) questions Hamlet on the reasons for his prolonged mourning for his father, the late king: "How is it that the clouds still hang on you?" *(Act I, Scene II)*

Polonius advises Laertes (Robert Hardy), his son *(Act I, Scene III)*

Right: Viewing all things darkly, Hamlet sees no place for the romantic Ophelia in the somber drama in which he finds himself cast. He affects ignorance as she tries to stir him by returning the jewels he gave her as tokens of his love *(Act III, Scene I)*

Below: "Out, out, thou strumpet, Fortune! All you gods, in general synod, take away her power." Hamlet directs the First Player (Edgar Wreford) as he recites Aeneas' tale to Dido. Polonius and the courtiers Guildenstern (John Dearth) and Rosencrantz (David Williams) stand listening beside Hamlet *(Act II, Scene II)*

The presentation of the "play within the play," Hamlet's device for revealing the guilt of King Claudius, the murderer of his father *(Act III, Scene II)*

"Do you see yonder cloud that's almost in shape of a camel?" Hamlet leads Polonius to think him mad *(Act III, Scene II)*

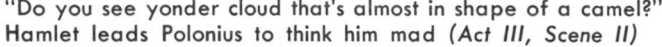

"O Hamlet! thou hast cleft my heart in twain." The queen is distraught as Hamlet upbraids her for her marriage with King Claudius, the murderer of his father *(Act III, Scene IV)*

"How all occasions do inform against me." Hamlet laments his indecision in avenging his father *(Act IV, Scene IV)*

"Now might I do it pat, now he is praying." Finding Claudius praying, unattended, Hamlet is tempted to kill him *(Act III, Scene III)*

"Once more, good-night: and when you are desirous to be bless'd, I'll blessing beg of you." The prince consoles his anguished mother *(Act III, Scene IV)*

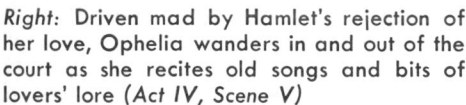

Right: Driven mad by Hamlet's rejection of her love, Ophelia wanders in and out of the court as she recites old songs and bits of lovers' lore *(Act IV, Scene V)*

Left: "I would give you some violets, but they withered all when my father died." The mad Ophelia clings desperately to the queen as she appears for the last time before her tragic death *(Act IV, Scene V)*

Above: "O thou vile king, give me my father." Returning to Elsinore to seek revenge for the death of Polonius, Laertes accuses Claudius, whom he presumes to be guilty *(Act IV, Scene V)*

Right: "Her garments, heavy with their drink, pull'd the poor wretch from her melodious lay to muddy death." The stunned Laertes kneels as the queen relates how Ophelia died *(Act IV, Scene VII)*

"I knew him, Horatio; a fellow of infinite jest." Hamlet and Horatio (William Squire) in the macabre interlude in the graveyard
(Act V, Scene I)

Hamlet engages in a fencing match with Laertes, unaware that Claudius has poisoned the tip of his antagonist's foil *(Act V, Scene II)*

"Let four captains bear Hamlet, like a soldier, to the stage; for he was likely, had he been put on, to have prov'd most royally: and, for his passage, the soldiers' music and the rites of war speak loudly for him." The Prince of Norway, Fortinbras (John Neville), orders military exequies for Hamlet *(Act V, Scene II)*

Doth rend the region; so, after Pyrrhus' pause,
Aroused vengeance sets him new awork;
And never did the Cyclops' hammers fall
On Mars's armour, forg'd for proof eterne,
With less remorse than Pyrrhus' bleeding sword
Now falls on Priam.
Out, out, thou strumpet Fortune! All you gods,
In general synod take away her power;
Break all the spokes and fellies from her wheel,
And bowl the round nave down the hill of heaven,
As low as to the fiends!'

Pol. This is too long.

Ham. It shall to the barber's, with your beard. — Prithee say on. He's for a jig or a tale of bawdry, or he sleeps. Say on; come to Hecuba.

1. Play. 'But who, O who, had seen the mobled queen —'

Ham. 'The mobled queen'?

Pol. That's good! 'Mobled queen' is good.

1. Play. 'Run barefoot up and down, threat'ning the flames
With bisson rheum; a clout upon that head
Where late the diadem stood, and for a robe,
About her lank and all o'erteemed loins,
A blanket, in the alarm of fear caught up —
Who this had seen, with tongue in venom steep'd
'Gainst Fortune's state would treason have pronounc'd.
But if the gods themselves did see her then,
When she saw Pyrrhus make malicious sport
In mincing with his sword her husband's limbs,
The instant burst of clamour that she made
(Unless things mortal move them not at all)
Would have made milch the burning eyes of heaven
And passion in the gods.'

Pol. Look, whe'r he has not turn'd his colour, and has tears in's eyes. Prithee no more!

Ham. 'Tis well. I'll have thee speak out the rest of this soon. — Good my lord, will you see the players well bestow'd? Do you hear? Let them be well us'd; for they are the abstract and brief chronicles of the time. After your death you were better have a bad epitaph than their ill report while you live.

Pol. My lord, I will use them according to their desert.

Ham. God's bodykins, man, much better! Use every man after his desert, and who should scape whipping? Use them after your own honour and dignity. The less they deserve, the more merit is in your bounty. Take them in.

Pol. Come, sirs.

Ham. Follow him, friends. We'll hear a play to-morrow.

Exeunt Polonius and Players [*except the First*].

Dost thou hear me, old friend? Can you play 'The Murther of Gonzago'?

1. Play. Ay, my lord.

Ham. We'll ha't to-morrow night. You could, for a need, study a speech of some dozen or sixteen lines which I would set down and insert in't, could you not?

1. Play. Ay, my lord.

Ham. Very well. Follow that lord — and look you mock him not. [*Exit First Player.*] My good friends, I'll leave you till night. You are welcome to Elsinore.

Ros. Good my lord!

Ham. Ay, so, God b' wi' ye!

Exeunt [*Rosencrantz and Guildenstern*].

Now I am alone.
O, what a rogue and peasant slave am I!
Is it not monstrous that this player here,
But in a fiction, in a dream of passion,
Could force his soul so to his own conceit
That, from her working, all his visage wann'd,
Tears in his eyes, distraction in's aspect,
A broken voice, and his whole function suiting
With forms to his conceit? And all for nothing!
For Hecuba!
What's Hecuba to him, or he to Hecuba,
That he should weep for her? What would he do,
Had he the motive and the cue for passion
That I have? He would drown the stage with tears
And cleave the general ear with horrid speech;
Make mad the guilty and appal the free,
Confound the ignorant, and amaze indeed
The very faculties of eyes and ears.
Yet I,
A dull and muddy-mettled rascal, peak
Like John-a-dreams, unpregnant of my cause,
And can say nothing! No, not for a king,
Upon whose property and most dear life
A damn'd defeat was made. Am I a coward?
Who calls me villain? breaks my pate across?
Plucks off my beard and blows it in my face?
Tweaks me by th' nose? gives me the lie i' th' throat
As deep as to the lungs? Who does me this, ha?
'Swounds, I should take it! for it cannot be
But I am pigeon-liver'd and lack gall
To make oppression bitter, or ere this
I should have fatted all the region kites,
With this slave's offal. Bloody, bawdy villain!

Remorseless, treacherous, lecherous, kindless villain!
O, vengeance!
Why, what an ass am I! This is most brave,
That I, the son of a dear father murther'd,
Prompted to my revenge by heaven and hell,
Must (like a whore) unpack my heart with words
And fall a-cursing like a very drab,
A scullion!
Fie upon't! foh! About, my brain! Hum, I have heard
That guilty creatures, sitting at a play,
Have by the very cunning of the scene
Been struck so to the soul that presently
They have proclaim'd their malefactions;
For murther, though it have no tongue, will speak
With most miraculous organ. I'll have these players
Play something like the murther of my father
Before mine uncle. I'll observe his looks;
I'll tent him to the quick. If he but blench,
I know my course. The spirit that I have seen
May be a devil; and the devil hath power
T' assume a pleasing shape; yea, and perhaps
Out of my weakness and my melancholy,
As he is very potent with such spirits,
Abuses me to damn me. I'll have grounds
More relative than this. The play's the thing
Wherein I'll catch the conscience of the King.
Exit.

[ACT III. Scene I. *Elsinore. A room in the Castle.*]

Enter *King, Queen, Polonius, Ophelia, Rosencrantz, Guildenstern,* and *Lords.*

King. And can you by no drift of circumstance
Get from him why he puts on this confusion,
Grating so harshly all his days of quiet
With turbulent and dangerous lunacy?

Ros. He does confess he feels himself distracted,
But from what cause he will by no means speak.

Guil. Nor do we find him forward to be sounded,
But with a crafty madness keeps aloof
When we would bring him on to some confession
Of his true state.

Queen. Did he receive you well?

Ros. Most like a gentleman.

Guil. But with much forcing of his disposition.

Ros. Niggard of question, but of our demands
Most free in his reply.

Queen. Did you assay him
To any pastime?

Ros. Madam, it so fell out that certain players
We o'erraught on the way. Of these we told him,
And there did seem in him a kind of joy
To hear of it. They are here about the court,
And, as I think, they have already order
This night to play before him.

Pol. 'Tis most true;
And he beseech'd me to entreat your Majesties
To hear and see the matter.

King. With all my heart, and it doth much content me
To hear him so inclin'd.
Good gentlemen, give him a further edge
And drive his purpose on to these delights.

Ros. We shall, my lord.

Exeunt Rosencrantz and Guildenstern.

King. Sweet Gertrude, leave us too;
For we have closely sent for Hamlet hither,
That he, as 'twere by accident, may here
Affront Ophelia.
Her father and myself (lawful espials)
Will so bestow ourselves that, seeing unseen,
We may of their encounter frankly judge
And gather by him, as he is behav'd,
If't be th' affliction of his love, or no,
That thus he suffers for.

Queen. I shall obey you;
And for your part, Ophelia, I do wish
That your good beauties be the happy cause
Of Hamlet's wildness. So shall I hope your virtues
Will bring him to his wonted way again,
To both your honours.

Oph. Madam, I wish it may.
[*Exit Queen.*]

Pol. Ophelia, walk you here. — Gracious, so please you,
We will bestow ourselves. — [*To Ophelia*] Read on this book,
That show of such an exercise may colour
Your loneliness. — We are oft to blame in this,

'Tis too much prov'd, that with devotion's visage
And pious action we do sugar o'er
The devil himself.
King. [*aside*] O, 'tis too true!
How smart a lash that speech doth give my conscience!
The harlot's cheek, beautied with plast'ring art,
Is not more ugly to the thing that helps it
Than is my deed to my most painted word.
O heavy burthen!
Pol. I hear him coming. Let's withdraw, my lord.
Exeunt [*King and Polonius*].

Enter *Hamlet.*

Ham. To be, or not to be — that is the question:
Whether 'tis nobler in the mind to suffer
The slings and arrows of outrageous fortune
Or to take arms against a sea of troubles,
And by opposing end them. To die — to sleep —
No more; and by a sleep to say we end
The heartache, and the thousand natural shocks
That flesh is heir to. 'Tis a consummation
Devoutly to be wish'd. To die — to sleep.
To sleep — perchance to dream: ay, there's the rub!
For in that sleep of death what dreams may come
When we have shuffled off this mortal coil,
Must give us pause. There's the respect
That makes calamity of so long life.
For who would bear the whips and scorns of time,
Th' oppressor's wrong, the proud man's contumely,
The pangs of despis'd love, the law's delay,
The insolence of office, and the spurns
That patient merit of th' unworthy takes,
When he himself might his quietus make
With a bare bodkin? Who would these fardels bear,
To grunt and sweat under a weary life,
But that the dread of something after death —
The undiscover'd country, from whose bourn
No traveller returns — puzzles the will,
And makes us rather bear those ills we have
Than fly to others that we know not of?
Thus conscience does make cowards of us all,
And thus the native hue of resolution
Is sicklied o'er with the pale cast of thought,
And enterprises of great pith and moment
With this regard their currents turn awry
And lose the name of action. — Soft you now!
The fair Ophelia! — Nymph, in thy orisons
Be all my sins rememb'red.
Oph. Good my lord,
How does your honour for this many a day?
Ham. I humbly thank you; well, well, well.
Oph. My lord, I have remembrances of yours
That I have longed long to re-deliver.
I pray you, now receive them.
Ham. No, not I!
I never gave you aught.
Oph. My honour'd lord, you know right well you did,
And with them words of so sweet breath compos'd
As made the things more rich. Their perfume lost,
Take these again; for to the noble mind
Rich gifts wax poor when givers prove unkind.
There, my lord.
Ham. Ha, ha! Are you honest?
Oph. My lord?
Ham. Are you fair?
Oph. What means your lordship?
Ham. That if you be honest and fair, your honesty should admit no discourse to your beauty.
Oph. Could beauty, my lord, have better commerce than with honesty?
Ham. Ay, truly; for the power of beauty will sooner transform honesty from what it is to a bawd than the force of honesty can translate beauty into his likeness. This was sometime a paradox, but now the time gives it proof. I did love you once.
Oph. Indeed, my lord, you made me believe so.
Ham. You should not have believ'd me; for virtue cannot so inoculate our old stock but we shall relish of it. I loved you not.
Oph. I was the more deceived.
Ham. Get thee to a nunnery! Why wouldst thou be a breeder of sinners? I am myself indifferent honest, but yet I could accuse me of such things that it were better my mother had not borne me. I am very proud, revengeful, ambitious; with more offences at my beck than I have thoughts to put them in, imagination to give them shape, or time to act them in. What should such fellows as I do, crawling between earth and heaven? We are arrant knaves all; believe none of us. Go thy ways to a nunnery. Where's your father?
Oph. At home, my lord.

Ham. Let the doors be shut upon him, that he may play the fool nowhere but in's own house. Farewell.

Oph. O, help him, you sweet heavens!

Ham. If thou dost marry, I'll give thee this plague for thy dowry: be thou as chaste as ice, as pure as snow, thou shalt not escape calumny. Get thee to a nunnery. Go, farewell. Or if thou wilt needs marry, marry a fool; for wise men know well enough what monsters you make of them. To a nunnery, go; and quickly too. Farewell.

Oph. O heavenly powers, restore him!

Ham. I have heard of your paintings too, well enough. God hath given you one face, and you make yourselves another. You jig, you amble, and you lisp; you nickname God's creatures and make your wantonness your ignorance. Go to, I'll no more on't! it hath made me mad. I say, we will have no moe marriages. Those that are married already — all but one — shall live; the rest shall keep as they are. To a nunnery, go. *Exit.*

Oph. O, what a noble mind is here o'erthrown!
The courtier's, scholar's, soldier's, eye, tongue, sword,
Th' expectancy and rose of the fair state,
The glass of fashion and the mould of form,
Th' observ'd of all observers — quite, quite down!
And I, of ladies most deject and wretched,
That suck'd the honey of his music vows,
Now see that noble and most sovereign reason,
Like sweet bells jangled, out of tune and harsh;
That unmatch'd form and feature of blown youth
Blasted with ecstasy. O, woe is me
T' have seen what I have seen, see what I see!

Enter *King* and *Polonius.*

King. Love? his affections do not that way tend;
Nor what he spake, though it lack'd form a little,
Was not like madness. There's something in his soul
O'er which his melancholy sits on brood;
And I do doubt the hatch and the disclose
Will be some danger; which for to prevent,
I have in quick determination
Thus set it down: he shall with speed to England
For the demand of our neglected tribute.
Haply the seas, and countries different,
With variable objects, shall expel
This something-settled matter in his heart,
Whereon his brains still beating puts him thus
From fashion of himself. What think you on't?

Pol. It shall do well. But yet do I believe
The origin and commencement of his grief
Sprung from neglected love. — How now, Ophelia?
You need not tell us what Lord Hamlet said.
We heard it all. — My lord, do as you please;
But if you hold it fit, after the play
Let his queen mother all alone entreat him
To show his grief. Let her be round with him;
And I'll be plac'd, so please you, in the ear
Of all their conference. If she find him not,
To England send him; or confine him where
Your wisdom best shall think.

King. It shall be so.
Madness in great ones must not unwatch'd go.
Exeunt.

[Scene II. *Elsinore. A hall in the Castle.*]

Enter *Hamlet* and three of the *Players.*

Ham. Speak the speech, I pray you, as I pronounc'd it to you, trippingly on the tongue. But if you mouth it, as many of our players do, I had as live the town crier spoke my lines. Nor do not saw the air too much with your hand, thus, but use all gently; for in the very torrent, tempest, and (as I may say) whirlwind of your passion, you must acquire and beget a temperance that may give it smoothness. O, it offends me to the soul to hear a robustious periwig-pated fellow tear a passion to tatters, to very rags, to split the ears of the groundlings, who (for the most part) are capable of nothing but inexplicable dumb shows and noise. I would have such a fellow whipp'd for o'erdoing Termagant. It out-herods Herod. Pray you avoid it.

Player. I warrant your honour.

Ham. Be not too tame neither; but let your own discretion be your tutor. Suit the action to the word, the word to the action; with this special observance, that you o'erstep not the modesty of nature: for anything so overdone is from the purpose of playing, whose end, both at the first and now, was and is, to hold, as 'twere, the mirror up to nature; to show virtue her own feature, scorn her own image, and the very age and body of the time his form and pressure. Now this overdone, or come tardy off, though it make the unskilful laugh, cannot but make the judicious grieve; the censure of the which one must in your allowance o'erweigh a whole theatre of others. O, there be players that I have seen play, and heard others praise, and that highly (not to speak it profanely), that, neither having the accent of Christians, nor the gait of Christian, pagan, nor man, have so strutted and bellowed that I have thought some of Nature's journeymen had made men, and not made them well, they imitated humanity so abominably.

Player. I hope we have reform'd that indifferently with us, sir.

Ham. O, reform it altogether! And let those that play your clowns speak no more than is set down for them. For there be of them that will themselves laugh, to set on some quantity of barren spectators to laugh too, though in the mean time some necessary question of the play be then to be considered. That's villanous and shows a most pitiful ambition in the fool that uses it. Go make you ready.

Exeunt Players.

Enter *Polonius, Rosencrantz,* and *Guildenstern.*

How now, my lord? Will the King hear this piece of work?

Pol. And the Queen too, and that presently.

Ham. Bid the players make haste. (*Exit Polonius.*) Will you two help to hasten them?

Both. We will, my lord. *Exeunt they two.*

Ham. What, ho, Horatio!

Enter *Horatio.*

Hor. Here, sweet lord, at your service.

Ham. Horatio, thou art e'en as just a man
As e'er my conversation cop'd withal.

Hor. O, my dear lord!

Ham. Nay, do not think I flatter;
For what advancement may I hope from thee,
That no revenue hast but thy good spirits
To feed and clothe thee? Why should the poor be flatter'd?
No, let the candied tongue lick absurd pomp,
And crook the pregnant hinges of the knee
Where thrift may follow fawning. Dost thou hear?
Since my dear soul was mistress of her choice
And could of men distinguish, her election
Hath seal'd thee for herself. For thou hast been
As one, in suff'ring all, that suffers nothing;
A man that Fortune's buffets and rewards
Hast ta'en with equal thanks; and blest are those
Whose blood and judgment are so well commingled
That they are not a pipe for Fortune's finger
To sound what stop she please. Give me that man
That is not passion's slave, and I will wear him
In my heart's core, ay, in my heart of heart,
As I do thee. Something too much of this!
There is a play to-night before the King.
One scene of it comes near the circumstance,
Which I have told thee, of my father's death
I prithee, when thou seest that act afoot,
Even with the very comment of thy soul
Observe my uncle. If his occulted guilt
Do not itself unkennel in one speech,
It is a damned ghost that we have seen,
And my imaginations are as foul
As Vulcan's stithy. Give him heedful note;
For I mine eyes will rivet to his face,
And after we will both our judgments join
In censure of his seeming.

Hor. Well, my lord.
If he steal aught the whilst this play is playing,
And scape detecting, I will pay the theft.

Sound a flourish. Enter *Trumpets* and *Kettle-drums.* Danish march. Enter *King, Queen, Polonius, Ophelia, Rosencrantz, Guildenstern,* and other *Lords* attendant, with the *Guard* carrying torches.

Ham. They are coming to the play. I must be idle.
Get you a place.

King. How fares our cousin Hamlet?

Ham. Excellent, i' faith; of the chameleon's dish. I eat the air, promise-cramm'd. You cannot feed capons so.

King. I have nothing with this answer, Hamlet. These words are not mine.

Ham. No, nor mine now. [*To Polonius*] My lord, you play'd once i' th' university, you say?

Pol. That did I, my lord, and was accounted a good actor.

Ham. What did you enact?

Pol. I did enact Julius Cæsar; I was kill'd i' th' Capitol; Brutus kill'd me.

Ham. It was a brute part of him to kill so capital a calf there. Be the players ready?

Ros. Ay, my lord. They stay upon your patience.

Queen. Come hither, my dear Hamlet, sit by me.

Ham. No, good mother. Here's metal more attractive.

Pol. [*to the King*] O, ho! do you mark that?

Ham. Lady, shall I lie in your lap?

[*Sits down at Ophelia's feet.*]

Oph. No, my lord.

Ham. I mean, my head upon your lap?

Oph. Ay, my lord.

Ham. Do you think I meant country matters?

Oph. I think nothing, my lord.

Ham. That's a fair thought to lie between maids' legs.

Oph. What is, my lord?

Ham. Nothing.

Oph. You are merry, my lord.

Ham. Who, I?

Oph. Ay, my lord.

Ham. O God, your only jig-maker! What should a man do but be merry? For look you how cheerfully my mother looks, and my father died within 's two hours.

Oph. Nay, 'tis twice two months, my lord.

Ham. So long? Nay then, let the devil wear black, for I'll have a suit of sables. O heavens! die two months ago, and not forgotten yet? Then there's hope a great man's memory may outlive his life half a year. But, by 'r Lady, he must build churches then; or else shall he suffer not thinking on, with the hobby-horse, whose epitaph is 'For O, for O, the hobby-horse is forgot!'

Hautboys play. The dumb show enters.

Enter a *King* and a *Queen* very lovingly; the *Queen* embracing him, and he her. She kneels, and makes show of protestation unto him. He takes her up, and declines his head upon her neck. He lays him down upon a bank of flowers. She, seeing him asleep, leaves him. Anon comes in a fellow, takes off his crown, kisses it, pours poison in the sleeper's ears, and leaves him. The *Queen* returns, finds the *King* dead, and makes passionate action. The *Poisoner* with some three or four *Mutes*, come in again, seem to condole with her. The dead body is carried away. The *Poisoner* wooes the *Queen* with gifts; she seems harsh and unwilling awhile, but in the end accepts his love.

Exeunt.

Oph. What means this, my lord?

Ham. Marry, this is miching malhecho; it means mischief.

Oph. Belike this show imports the argument of the play.

Enter *Prologue.*

Ham. We shall know by this fellow. The players cannot keep counsel; they'll tell all.

Oph. Will he tell us what this show meant?

Ham. Ay, or any show that you'll show him. Be not you asham'd to show, he'll not shame to tell you what it means.

Oph. You are naught, you are naught! I'll mark the play.

Pro. For us, and for our tragedy,
Here stooping to your clemency,
We beg your hearing patiently.

[*Exit.*]

Ham. Is this a prologue, or the posy of a ring?

Oph. 'Tis brief, my lord.

Ham. As woman's love.

Enter [two *Players* as] *King* and *Queen.*

King. Full thirty times hath Phœbus' cart gone round
Neptune's salt wash and Tellus' orbed ground,
And thirty dozen moons with borrowed sheen
About the world have times twelve thirties been,
Since love our hearts, and Hymen did our hands,
Unite comutual in most sacred bands.

Queen. So many journeys may the sun and moon
Make us again count o'er ere love be done!
But woe is me! you are so sick of late,
So far from cheer and from your former state,
That I distrust you. Yet, though I distrust,
Discomfort you, my lord, it nothing must;
For women's fear and love holds quantity,
In neither aught, or in extremity.
Now what my love is, proof hath made you know;
And as my love is siz'd, my fear is so.
Where love is great, the littlest doubts are fear;
Where little fears grow great, great love grows there.

King. Faith, I must leave thee, love, and shortly too;
My operant powers their functions leave to do.
And thou shalt live in this fair world behind,
Honour'd, belov'd, and haply one as kind
For husband shalt thou —

Queen. O, confound the rest!
Such love must needs be treason in my breast.
In second husband let me be accurst!
None wed the second but who kill'd the first.

Ham. [*aside*] Wormwood, wormwood!

Queen. The instances that second marriage move
Are base respects of thrift, but none of love.
A second time I kill my husband dead
When second husband kisses me in bed.

King. I do believe you think what now you speak;
But what we do determine oft we break.
Purpose is but the slave to memory,
Of violent birth, but poor validity;

Which now, like fruit unripe, sticks on the tree,
But fall unshaken when they mellow be.
Most necessary 'tis that we forget
To pay ourselves what to ourselves is debt.
What to ourselves in passion we propose,
The passion ending, doth the purpose lose.
The violence of either grief or joy
Their own enactures with themselves destroy.
Where joy most revels, grief doth most lament;
Grief joys, joy grieves, on slender accident.
This world is not for aye, nor 'tis not strange
That even our loves should with our fortunes change;
For 'tis a question left us yet to prove,
Whether love lead fortune, or else fortune love.
The great man down, you mark his favourite flies,
The poor advanc'd makes friends of enemies;
And hitherto doth love on fortune tend,
For who not needs shall never lack a friend,
And who in want a hollow friend doth try,
Directly seasons him his enemy.
But, orderly to end where I begun,
Our wills and fates do so contrary run
That our devices still are overthrown;
Our thoughts are ours, their ends none of our own.
So think thou wilt no second husband wed;
But die thy thoughts when thy first lord is dead.

Queen. Nor earth to me give food, nor heaven light,
Sport and repose lock from me day and night,
To desperation turn my trust and hope,
An anchor's cheer in prison be my scope,
Each opposite that blanks the face of joy
Meet what I would have well, and it destroy,
Both here and hence pursue me lasting strife,
If, once a widow, ever I be wife!

Ham. If she should break it now!

King. 'Tis deeply sworn. Sweet, leave me here awhile.
My spirits grow dull, and fain I would beguile
The tedious day with sleep.

Queen. Sleep rock thy brain, *[He] sleeps.*
And never come mischance between us twain!
Exit.

Ham. Madam, how like you this play?

Queen. The lady doth protest too much, methinks.

Ham. O, but she'll keep her word.

King. Have you heard the argument? Is there no offence in't?

Ham. No, no! They do but jest, poison in jest; no offence i' th' world.

King. What do you call the play?

Ham. 'The Mousetrap.' Marry, how? Tropically. This play is the image of a murther done in Vienna. Gonzago is the duke's name; his wife, Baptista. You shall see anon. 'Tis a knavish piece of work; but what o' that? Your Majesty, and we that have free souls, it touches us not. Let the gall'd jade winch; our withers are unwrung.

Enter *Lucianus.*

This is one Lucianus, nephew to the King.

Oph. You are as good as a chorus, my lord.

Ham. I could interpret between you and your love, if I could see the puppets dallying.

Oph. You are keen, my lord, you are keen.

Ham. It would cost you a groaning to take off my edge.

Oph. Still better, and worse.

Ham. So you must take your husbands. — Begin, murtherer. Pox, leave thy damnable faces, and begin! Come, the croaking raven doth bellow for revenge.

Luc. Thoughts black, hands apt, drugs fit, and time agreeing;
Confederate season, else no creature seeing;
Thou mixture rank, of midnight weeds collected,
With Hecate's ban thrice blasted, thrice infected,
Thy natural magic and dire property
On wholesome life usurp immediately.
Pours the poison in his ears.

Ham. He poisons him i' th' garden for's estate. His name's Gonzago. The story is extant, and written in very choice Italian. You shall see anon how the murtherer gets the love of Gonzago's wife.

Oph. The King rises.

Ham. What, frighted with false fire?

Queen. How fares my lord?

Pol. Give o'er the play.

King. Give me some light! Away!

All. Lights, lights, lights!

Exeunt all but Hamlet and Horatio.

Ham. Why, let the strucken deer go weep,
The hart ungalled play;
For some must watch, while some must sleep:
Thus runs the world away.
Would not this, sir, and a forest of feathers — if the rest of my fortunes turn Turk with me — with two Provincial roses on my raz'd shoes, get me a fellowship in a cry of players, sir?

Hor. Half a share.

Ham. A whole one I!
For thou dost know, O Damon dear,
This realm dismantled was
Of Jove himself; and now reigns here
A very, very — pajock.

Hor. You might have rhym'd.

Ham. O good Horatio, I'll take the ghost's word for a thousand pound! Didst perceive?

Hor. Very well, my lord.

Ham. Upon the talk of the poisoning?

Hor. I did very well note him.

Ham. Aha! Come, some music! Come, the recorders!

For if the King like not the comedy,
Why then, belike he likes it not, perdy.

Come, some music!

Enter *Rosencrantz* and *Guildenstern*.

Guil. Good my lord, vouchsafe me a word with you.

Ham. Sir, a whole history.

Guil. The King, sir —

Ham. Ay, sir, what of him?

Guil. Is in his retirement, marvellous distemper'd.

Ham. With drink, sir?

Guil. No, my lord; rather with choler.

Ham. Your wisdom should show itself more richer to signify this to the doctor; for for me to put him to his purgation would perhaps plunge him into far more choler.

Guil. Good my lord, put your discourse into some frame, and start not so wildly from my affair.

Ham. I am tame, sir; pronounce.

Guil. The Queen, your mother, in most great affliction of spirit hath sent me to you.

Ham. You are welcome.

Guil. Nay, good my lord, this courtesy is not of the right breed. If it shall please you to make me a wholesome answer, I will do your mother's commandment; if not, your pardon and my return shall be the end of my business.

Ham. Sir, I cannot.

Guil. What, my lord?

Ham. Make you a wholesome answer; my wit's diseas'd. But, sir, such answer as I can make, you shall command; or rather, as you say, my mother. Therefore no more, but to the matter! My mother, you say —

Ros. Then thus she says: your behaviour hath struck her into amazement and admiration.

Ham. O wonderful son, that can so stonish a mother! But is there no sequel at the heels of this mother's admiration? Impart.

Ros. She desires to speak with you in her closet ere you go to bed.

Ham. We shall obey, were she ten times our mother. Have you any further trade with us?

Ros. My lord, you once did love me.

Ham. And do still, by these pickers and stealers!

Ros. Good my lord, what is your cause of distemper? You do surely bar the door upon your own liberty, if you deny your griefs to your friend.

Ham. Sir, I lack advancement.

Ros. How can that be, when you have the voice of the King himself for your succession in Denmark?

Ham. Ay, sir, but 'while the grass grows' — the proverb is something musty.

Enter the *Players* with recorders.

O, the recorders! Let me see one. To withdraw with you — why do you go about to recover the wind of me, as if you would drive me into a toil?

Guil. O my lord, if my duty be too bold, my love is too unmannerly.

Ham. I do not well understand that. Will you play upon this pipe?

Guil. My lord, I cannot.

Ham. I pray you.

Guil. Believe me, I cannot.

Ham. I do beseech you.

Guil. I know no touch of it, my lord.

Ham. It is as easy as lying. Govern these ventages with your fingers and thumbs, give it breath with your mouth, and it will discourse most eloquent music. Look you, these are the stops.

Guil. But these cannot I command to any utt'rance of harmony. I have not the skill.

Ham. Why, look you now, how unworthy a thing you make of me! You would play upon me; you would seem to know my stops; you would pluck out the heart of my mystery; you would sound me from my lowest note to the top of my compass; and there is much music, excellent voice, in this little organ, yet cannot you make it speak. 'Sblood, do you think I am easier to be play'd on than a pipe? Call me what instrument you will, though you can fret me, you cannot play upon me.

Enter *Polonius*.

God bless you, sir!

Pol. My lord, the Queen would speak with you, and presently.

Ham. Do you see yonder cloud that's almost in shape of a camel?

Pol. By th' mass, and 'tis like a camel indeed.

Ham. Methinks it is like a weasel.

Pol. It is back'd like a weasel.

Ham. Or like a whale.

Pol. Very like a whale.

Ham. Then will I come to my mother by-

and-by. — They fool me to the top of my bent. — I will come by-and-by.

Pol. I will say so. *Exit.*

Ham. 'By-and-by' is easily said. — Leave me, friends.

[*Exeunt all but Hamlet.*]

'Tis now the very witching time of night,
When churchyards yawn, and hell itself breathes out
Contagion to this world. Now could I drink hot blood
And do such bitter business as the day
Would quake to look on. Soft! now to my mother!
O heart, lose not thy nature; let not ever
The soul of Nero enter this firm bosom.
Let me be cruel, not unnatural;
I will speak daggers to her, but use none.
My tongue and soul in this be hypocrites —
How in my words somever she be shent,
To give them seals never, my soul, consent!

Exit.

[Scene III. *A room in the Castle.*]

Enter *King*, *Rosencrantz*, and *Guildenstern.*

King. I like him not, nor stands it safe with us
To let his madness range. Therefore prepare you;
I your commission will forthwith dispatch,
And he to England shall along with you.
The terms of our estate may not endure
Hazard so near us as doth hourly grow
Out of his lunacies.

Guil. We will ourselves provide.
Most holy and religious fear it is
To keep those many many bodies safe
That live and feed upon your Majesty.

Ros. The single and peculiar life is bound
With all the strength and armour of the mind
To keep itself from noyance; but much more
That spirit upon whose weal depends and rests
The lives of many. The cesse of majesty
Dies not alone, but like a gulf doth draw
What's near it with it. It is a massy wheel,
Fix'd on the summit of the highest mount,
To whose huge spokes ten thousand lesser things
Are mortis'd and adjoin'd; which when it falls,
Each small annexment, petty consequence,
Attends the boist'rous ruin. Never alone
Did the king sigh, but with a general groan.

King. Arm you, I pray you, to this speedy voyage;
For we will fetters put upon this fear,
Which now goes too free-footed.

Both. We will haste us.

Exeunt Gentlemen.

Enter *Polonius.*

Pol. My lord, he's going to his mother's closet.
Behind the arras I'll convey myself
To hear the process. I'll warrant she'll tax him home;
And, as you said, and wisely was it said,
'Tis meet that some more audience than a mother,
Since nature makes them partial, should o'er-hear
The speech, of vantage. Fare you well, my liege.
I'll call upon you ere you go to bed
And tell you what I know.

King. Thanks, dear my lord.

Exit [*Polonius*].

O, my offence is rank, it smells to heaven;
It hath the primal eldest curse upon't,
A brother's murther! Pray can I not,
Though inclination be as sharp as will.
My stronger guilt defeats my strong intent,
And, like a man to double business bound,
I stand in pause where I shall first begin,
And both neglect. What if this cursed hand
Were thicker than itself with brother's blood,
Is there not rain enough in the sweet heavens
To wash it white as snow? Whereto serves mercy
But to confront the visage of offence?
And what's in prayer but this twofold force,
To be forestalled ere we come to fall,
Or pardon'd being down? Then I'll look up;
My fault is past. But, O, what form of prayer
Can serve my turn? 'Forgive me my foul murther'?
That cannot be; since I am still possess'd
Of those effects for which I did the murther —
My crown, mine own ambition, and my queen.
May one be pardon'd and retain th' offence?
In the corrupted currents of this world
Offence's gilded hand may shove by justice,
And oft 'tis seen the wicked prize itself
Buys out the law; but 'tis not so above.
There is no shuffling; there the action lies
In his true nature, and we ourselves compell'd,
Even to the teeth and forehead of our faults,
To give in evidence. What then? What rests?
Try what repentance can. What can it not?
Yet what can it when one cannot repent?
O wretched state! O bosom black as death!

O limed soul, that, struggling to be free,
Art more engag'd! Help, angels! Make assay.
Bow, stubborn knees; and heart with strings of steel,
Be soft as sinews of the new-born babe!
All may be well. *He kneels.*

Enter *Hamlet.*

Ham. Now might I do it pat, now he is praying;
And now I'll do't. And so he goes to heaven,
And so am I reveng'd. That would be scann'd.
A villain kills my father; and for that,
I, his sole son, do this same villain send
To heaven.
Why, this is hire and salary, not revenge!
He took my father grossly, full of bread,
With all his crimes broad blown, as flush as May;
And how his audit stands, who knows save heaven?
But in our circumstance and course of thought,
'Tis heavy with him; and am I then reveng'd,
To take him in the purging of his soul,
When he is fit and season'd for his passage?
No.
Up, sword, and know thou a more horrid hent.
When he is drunk asleep; or in his rage;
Or in th' incestuous pleasure of his bed;
At gaming, swearing, or about some act
That has no relish of salvation in't —
Then trip him, that his heels may kick at heaven,
And that his soul may be as damn'd and black
As hell, whereto it goes. My mother stays.
This physic but prolongs thy sickly days. *Exit.*

King. [*rises*] My words fly up, my thoughts remain below.
Words without thoughts never to heaven go. *Exit.*

[Scene IV. *The* Queen's *closet.*]

Enter *Queen* and *Polonius.*

Pol. He will come straight. Look you lay home to him.
Tell him his pranks have been too broad to bear with,
And that your Grace hath screen'd and stood between
Much heat and him. I'll silence me even here.
Pray you be round with him.

Ham. (*within*) Mother, mother, mother!

Queen. I'll warrant you; fear me not. Withdraw; I hear him coming.
[*Polonius hides behind the arras.*]

Enter *Hamlet.*

Ham. Now, mother, what's the matter?

Queen. Hamlet, thou hast thy father much offended.

Ham. Mother, you have my father much offended.

Queen. Come, come, you answer with an idle tongue.

Ham. Go, go, you question with a wicked tongue.

Queen. Why, how now, Hamlet?

Ham. What's the matter now?

Queen. Have you forgot me?

Ham. No, by the rood, not so!
You are the Queen, your husband's brother's wife,
And (would it were not so!) you are my mother.

Queen. Nay, then I'll set those to you that can speak.

Ham. Come, come, and sit you down. You shall not budge!
You go not till I set you up a glass
Where you may see the inmost part of you.

Queen. What wilt thou do? Thou wilt not murther me?
Help, help, ho!

Pol. [*behind*] What, ho! help, help, help!

Ham. [*draws*] How now? a rat? Dead for a ducat, dead!
[*Makes a pass through the arras and*] *kills Polonius.*

Pol. [*behind*] O, I am slain!

Queen. O me, what hast thou done?

Ham. Nay, I know not. Is it the King?

Queen. O, what a rash and bloody deed is this!

Ham. A bloody deed — almost as bad, good mother,
As kill a king, and marry with his brother.

Queen. As kill a king?

Ham. Ay, lady, it was my word.
[*Lifts up the arras and sees Polonius.*]
Thou wretched, rash, intruding fool, farewell!
I took thee for thy better. Take thy fortune.
Thou find'st to be too busy is some danger.
Leave wringing of your hands. Peace! sit you down
And let me wring your heart; for so I shall
If it be made of penetrable stuff;
If damned custom have not braz'd it so
That it is proof and bulwark against sense.

Queen. What have I done that thou dar'st wag thy tongue
In noise so rude against me?
Ham. Such an act
That blurs the grace and blush of modesty;
Calls virtue hypocrite; takes off the rose
From the fair forehead of an innocent love,
And sets a blister there; makes marriage vows
As false as dicers' oaths. O, such a deed
As from the body of contraction plucks
The very soul, and sweet religion makes
A rhapsody of words! Heaven's face doth glow;
Yea, this solidity and compound mass,
With tristful visage, as against the doom,
Is thought-sick at the act.
Queen. Ay me, what act,
That roars so loud and thunders in the index?
Ham. Look here upon this picture, and on this,
The counterfeit presentment of two brothers.
See what a grace was seated on this brow;
Hyperion's curls; the front of Jove himself;
An eye like Mars, to threaten and command;
A station like the herald Mercury
New lighted on a heaven-kissing hill:
A combination and a form indeed
Where every god did seem to set his seal
To give the world assurance of a man.
This was your husband. Look you now what follows.
Here is your husband, like a mildew'd ear
Blasting his wholesome brother. Have you eyes?
Could you on this fair mountain leave to feed,
And batten on this moor? Ha! have you eyes?
You cannot call it love; for at your age
The heyday in the blood is tame, it's humble,
And waits upon the judgment; and what judgment
Would step from this to this? Sense sure you have,
Else could you not have motion; but sure that sense
Is apoplex'd; for madness would not err,
Nor sense to ecstasy was ne'er so thrall'd
But it reserv'd some quantity of choice
To serve in such a difference. What devil was't
That thus hath cozen'd you at hoodman-blind?
Eyes without feeling, feeling without sight,
Ears without hands or eyes, smelling sans all,
Or but a sickly part of one true sense
Could not so mope.
O shame! where is thy blush? Rebellious hell,
If thou canst mutine in a matron's bones,
To flaming youth let virtue be as wax
And melt in her own fire. Proclaim no shame
When the compulsive ardour gives the charge,
Since frost itself as actively doth burn,
And reason panders will.
Queen. O Hamlet, speak no more!
Thou turn'st mine eyes into my very soul,
And there I see such black and grained spots
As will not leave their tinct.
Ham. Nay, but to live
In the rank sweat of an enseamed bed,
Stew'd in corruption, honeying and making love
Over the nasty sty!
Queen. O, speak to me no more!
These words like daggers enter in mine ears.
No more, sweet Hamlet!
Ham. A murtherer and a villain!
A slave that is not twentieth part the tithe
Of your precedent lord; a vice of kings;
A cutpurse of the empire and the rule,
That from a shelf the precious diadem stole
And put it in his pocket!
Queen. No more!

Enter the *Ghost* in his nightgown.

Ham. A king of shreds and patches! —
Save me and hover o'er me with your wings,
You heavenly guards! What would your gracious figure?
Queen. Alas, he's mad!
Ham. Do you not come your tardy son to chide,
That, laps'd in time and passion, lets go by
Th' important acting of your dread command?
O, say!
Ghost. Do not forget. This visitation
Is but to whet thy almost blunted purpose.
But look, amazement on thy mother sits.
O, step between her and her fighting soul!
Conceit in weakest bodies strongest works.
Speak to her, Hamlet.
Ham. How is it with you, lady?
Queen. Alas, how is't with you,
That you do bend your eye on vacancy,
And with th' incorporal air do hold discourse?
Forth at your eyes your spirits wildly peep;
And, as the sleeping soldiers in th' alarm,
Your bedded hairs, like life in excrements,
Start up and stand an end. O gentle son,
Upon the heat and flame of thy distemper
Sprinkle cool patience! Whereon do you look?
Ham. On him, on him! Look you how pale he glares!
His form and cause conjoin'd, preaching to stones,
Would make them capable. — Do not look upon me,

Lest with this piteous action you convert
My stern effects. Then what I have to do
Will want true colour — tears perchance for blood.

Queen. To whom do you speak this?

Ham. Do you see nothing there?

Queen. Nothing at all; yet all that is I see.

Ham. Nor did you nothing hear?

Queen. No, nothing but ourselves.

Ham. Why, look you there! Look how it steals away!
My father, in his habit as he liv'd!
Look where he goes even now out at the portal!

Exit Ghost.

Queen. This is the very coinage of your brain.
This bodiless creation ecstasy
Is very cunning in.

Ham. Ecstasy?
My pulse as yours doth temperately keep time
And makes as healthful music. It is not madness
That I have utt'red. Bring me to the test,
And I the matter will reword; which madness
Would gambol from. Mother, for love of grace,
Lay not that flattering unction to your soul,
That not your trespass but my madness speaks.
It will but skin and film the ulcerous place,
Whiles rank corruption, mining all within,
Infects unseen. Confess yourself to heaven;
Repent what's past; avoid what is to come;
And do not spread the compost on the weeds
To make them ranker. Forgive me this my virtue;
For in the fatness of these pursy times
Virtue itself of vice must pardon beg —
Yea, curb and woo for leave to do him good.

Queen. O Hamlet, thou hast cleft my heart in twain.

Ham. O, throw away the worser part of it,
And live the purer with the other half.
Good night — but go not to my uncle's bed.
Assume a virtue, if you have it not.
That monster, custom, who all sense doth eat
Of habits evil, is angel yet in this,
That to the use of actions fair and good
He likewise gives a frock or livery,
That aptly is put on. Refrain to-night,
And that shall lend a kind of easiness
To the next abstinence; the next more easy;
For use almost can change the stamp of nature,
And either [master] the devil, or throw him out
With wondrous potency. Once more, good night;
And when you are desirous to be blest,
I'll blessing beg of you. — For this same lord,
I do repent; but heaven hath pleas'd it so,
To punish me with this, and this with me,
That I must be their scourge and minister.
I will bestow him, and will answer well
The death I gave him. So again, good night.
I must be cruel, only to be kind;
Thus bad begins, and worse remains behind.
One word more, good lady.

Queen. What shall I do?

Ham. Not this, by no means, that I bid you do:
Let the bloat King tempt you again to bed;
Pinch wanton on your cheek; call you his mouse;
And let him, for a pair of reechy kisses,
Or paddling in your neck with his damn'd fingers,
Make you to ravel all this matter out,
That I essentially am not in madness,
But mad in craft. 'Twere good you let him know;
For who that's but a queen, fair, sober, wise,
Would from a paddock, from a bat, a gib,
Such dear concernings hide? Who would do so?
No, in despite of sense and secrecy,
Unpeg the basket on the house's top,
Let the birds fly, and like the famous ape,
To try conclusions, in the basket creep
And break your own neck down.

Queen. Be thou assur'd, if words be made of breath,
And breath of life, I have no life to breathe
What thou hast said to me.

Ham. I must to England; you know that?

Queen. Alack,
I had forgot! 'Tis so concluded on.

Ham. There's letters seal'd; and my two schoolfellows,
Whom I will trust as I will adders fang'd,
They bear the mandate; they must sweep my way
And marshal me to knavery. Let it work;
For 'tis the sport to have the enginer
Hoist with his own petar; and 't shall go hard
But I will delve one yard below their mines
And blow them at the moon. O, 'tis most sweet
When in one line two crafts directly meet.
This man shall set me packing.
I'll lug the guts into the neighbour room. —
Mother, good night. — Indeed, this counsellor
Is now most still, most secret, and most grave,
Who was in life a foolish prating knave.
Come, sir, to draw toward an end with you.
Good night, mother.

[Exit the Queen. Then] exit Hamlet, tugging in Polonius.

[Act IV. Scene I. *Elsinore. A room in the Castle.*]

Enter *King* and *Queen*, with *Rosencrantz* and *Guildenstern.*

King. There's matter in these sighs. These profound heaves
You must translate; 'tis fit we understand them.
Where is your son?
Queen. Bestow this place on us a little while.
[*Exeunt Rosencrantz and Guildenstern.*]
Ah, mine own lord, what have I seen to-night!
King. What, Gertrude? How does Hamlet?
Queen. Mad as the sea and wind when both contend
Which is the mightier. In his lawless fit,
Behind the arras hearing something stir,
Whips out his rapier, cries 'A rat, a rat!'
And in this brainish apprehension kills
The unseen good old man.
King. O heavy deed!
It had been so with us, had we been there.
His liberty is full of threats to all —
To you yourself, to us, to every one.
Alas, how shall this bloody deed be answer'd?
It will be laid to us, whose providence
Should have kept short, restrain'd, and out of haunt
This mad young man. But so much was our love
We would not understand what was most fit,
But, like the owner of a foul disease,
To keep it from divulging, let it feed
Even on the pith of life. Where is he gone?
Queen. To draw apart the body he hath kill'd;
O'er whom his very madness, like some ore
Among a mineral of metals base,
Shows itself pure. He weeps for what is done.
King. O Gertrude, come away!
The sun no sooner shall the mountains touch
But we will ship him hence; and this vile deed
We must with all our majesty and skill
Both countenance and excuse. Ho, Guildenstern!

Enter *Rosencrantz* and *Guildenstern.*

Friends both, go join you with some further aid.
Hamlet in madness hath Polonius slain,
And from his mother's closet hath he dragg'd him.
Go seek him out; speak fair, and bring the body
Into the chapel. I pray you haste in this.
Exeunt [*Rosencrantz and Guildenstern*].
Come, Gertrude, we'll call up our wisest friends
And let them know both what we mean to do
And what's untimely done. [So haply slander —]
Whose whisper o'er the world's diameter,
As level as the cannon to his blank,
Transports his pois'ned shot — may miss our name
And hit the woundless air. — O, come away!
My soul is full of discord and dismay.
Exeunt.

[Scene II. *Elsinore. A passage in the Castle.*]

Enter *Hamlet.*

Ham. Safely stow'd.

Gentlemen. (*within*) Hamlet! Lord Hamlet!

Ham. But soft! What noise? Who calls on Hamlet? O, here they come.

Enter *Rosencrantz* and *Guildenstern.*

Ros. What have you done, my lord, with the dead body?

Ham. Compounded it with dust, whereto 'tis kin.

Ros. Tell us where 'tis, that we may take it thence
And bear it to the chapel.

Ham. Do not believe it.

Ros. Believe what?

Ham. That I can keep your counsel, and not mine own. Besides, to be demanded of a sponge, what replication should be made by the son of a king?

Ros. Take you me for a sponge, my lord?

Ham. Ay, sir; that soaks up the King's countenance, his rewards, his authorities. But such officers do the King best service in the end. He keeps them, like an ape, in the corner of his jaw; first mouth'd, to be last swallowed. When he needs what you have glean'd, it is but squeezing you and, sponge, you shall be dry again.

Ros. I understand you not, my lord.

Ham. I am glad of it. A knavish speech sleeps in a foolish ear.

Ros. My lord, you must tell us where the body is and go with us to the King.

Ham. The body is with the King, but the King is not with the body. The King is a thing —

Guil. A thing, my lord?

Ham. Of nothing. Bring me to him. Hide fox, and all after. *Exeunt.*

[Scene III. *Elsinore. A room in the Castle.*]

Enter *King.*

King. I have sent to seek him and to find the body.
How dangerous is it that this man goes loose!
Yet must not we put the strong law on him.
He's lov'd of the distracted multitude,
Who like not in their judgment, but their eyes;
And where 'tis so, th' offender's scourge is weigh'd,
But never the offence. To bear all smooth and even,
This sudden sending him away must seem
Deliberate pause. Diseases desperate grown
By desperate appliance are reliev'd,
Or not at all.

Enter *Rosencrantz.*

How now? What hath befall'n?

Ros. Where the dead body is bestow'd, my lord,
We cannot get from him.

King. But where is he?

Ros. Without, my lord; guarded, to know your pleasure.

King. Bring him before us.

Ros. Ho, Guildenstern! Bring in my lord.

Enter *Hamlet* and *Guildenstern* [with *Attendants*].

King. Now, Hamlet, where's Polonius?

Ham. At supper.

King. At supper? Where?

Ham. Not where he eats, but where he is eaten. A certain convocation of politic worms are e'en at him. Your worm is your only emperor for diet. We fat all creatures else to fat us, and we fat ourselves for maggots. Your fat king and your lean beggar is but variable service — two dishes, but to one table. That's the end.

King. Alas, alas!

Ham. A man may fish with the worm that hath eat of a king, and eat of the fish that hath fed of that worm.

King. What dost thou mean by this?

Ham. Nothing but to show you how a king may go a progress through the guts of a beggar.

King. Where is Polonius?

Ham. In heaven. Send thither to see. If your messenger find him not there, seek him i' th' other place yourself. But indeed, if you find him not within this month, you shall nose him as you go up the stairs into the lobby.

King. Go seek him there. [*To Attendants.*]

Ham. He will stay till you come.

[*Exeunt Attendants.*]

King. Hamlet, this deed, for thine especial safety, —
Which we do tender as we dearly grieve
For that which thou hast done, — must send thee hence
With fiery quickness. Therefore prepare thyself.
The bark is ready and the wind at help,
Th' associates tend, and everything is bent
For England.

Ham. For England?

King. Ay, Hamlet.

Ham. Good.

King. So is it, if thou knew'st our purposes.

Ham. I see a cherub that sees them. But come, for England! Farewell, dear mother.

King. Thy loving father, Hamlet.

Ham. My mother! Father and mother is man and wife; man and wife is one flesh; and so, my mother. Come, for England! *Exit.*

King. Follow him at foot; tempt him with speed aboard.
Delay it not; I'll have him hence to-night.
Away! for everything is seal'd and done
That else leans on th' affair. Pray you make haste.

[*Exeunt Rosencrantz and Guildenstern.*]

And, England, if my love thou hold'st at aught, —
As my great power thereof may give thee sense,
Since yet thy cicatrice looks raw and red
After the Danish sword, and thy free awe
Pays homage to us, — thou mayst not coldly set
Our sovereign process, which imports at full,
By letters congruing to that effect,
The present death of Hamlet. Do it, England;
For like the hectic in my blood he rages,
And thou must cure me. Till I know 'tis done,
Howe'er my haps, my joys were ne'er begun.

Exit

[Scene IV. *Near Elsinore.*]

Enter *Fortinbras* with his *Army* over the stage.

For. Go, Captain, from me greet the Danish king.
Tell him that by his license Fortinbras
Craves the conveyance of a promis'd march
Over his kingdom. You know the rendezvous.
If that his Majesty would aught with us,
We shall express our duty in his eye;
And let him know so.

Capt. I will do't, my lord.

For. Go softly on.

Exeunt [*all but the Captain*].

Enter *Hamlet, Rosencrantz,* [*Guildenstern,*] and others.

Ham. Good sir, whose powers are these?

Capt. They are of Norway, sir.

Ham. How purpos'd, sir, I pray you?

Capt. Against some part of Poland.

Ham. Who commands them, sir?

Capt. The nephew to old Norway, Fortinbras.

Ham. Goes it against the main of Poland, sir,
Or for some frontier?

Capt. Truly to speak, and with no addition,
We go to gain a little patch of ground
That hath in it no profit but the name.
To pay five ducats, five, I would not farm it;
Nor will it yield to Norway or the Pole
A ranker rate, should it be sold in fee.

Ham. Why, then the Polack never will defend it.

Capt. Yes, it is already garrison'd.

Ham. Two thousand souls and twenty thousand ducats
Will not debate the question of this straw.
This is th' imposthume of much wealth and peace,
That inward breaks, and shows no cause without
Why the man dies. — I humbly thank you, sir.

Capt. God b' wi' you, sir. [*Exit.*]

Ros. Will't please you go, my lord?

Ham. I'll be with you straight. Go a little before.

[*Exeunt all but Hamlet.*]

How all occasions do inform against me
And spur my dull revenge! What is a man,
If his chief good and market of his time
Be but to sleep and feed? A beast, no more.
Sure he that made us with such large discourse,
Looking before and after, gave us not
That capability and godlike reason
To fust in us unus'd. Now, whether it be
Bestial oblivion, or some craven scruple
Of thinking too precisely on th' event, —
A thought which, quarter'd, hath but one part wisdom
And ever three parts coward, — I do not know
Why yet I live to say 'This thing's to do,'
Sith I have cause, and will, and strength, and means
To do't. Examples gross as earth exhort me.
Witness this army of such mass and charge,
Led by a delicate and tender prince,
Whose spirit, with divine ambition puff'd,
Makes mouths at the invisible event,
Exposing what is mortal and unsure
To all that fortune, death, and danger dare,
Even for an eggshell. Rightly to be great
Is not to stir without great argument,
But greatly to find quarrel in a straw
When honour's at the stake. How stand I then,
That have a father kill'd, a mother stain'd,
Excitements of my reason and my blood,
And let all sleep, while to my shame I see
The imminent death of twenty thousand men
That for a fantasy and trick of fame
Go to their graves like beds, fight for a plot
Whereon the numbers cannot try the cause,
Which is not tomb enough and continent
To hide the slain? O, from this time forth,
My thoughts be bloody, or be nothing worth!

Exit.

[Scene V. *Elsinore. A room in the Castle.*]

Enter *Horatio, Queen,* and a *Gentleman.*

Queen. I will not speak with her.

Gent. She is importunate, indeed distract.
Her mood will needs be pitied.

Queen. What would she have?

Gent. She speaks much of her father; says she hears
There's tricks i' th' world, and hems, and beats her heart;
Spurns enviously at straws; speaks things in doubt,
That carry but half sense. Her speech is nothing,
Yet the unshaped use of it doth move
The hearers to collection; they aim at it,
And botch the words up fit to their own thoughts;
Which, as her winks and nods and gestures yield them,

Indeed would make one think there might be thought,
Though nothing sure, yet much unhappily.

Hor. 'Twere good she were spoken with; for she may strew
Dangerous conjectures in ill-breeding minds.

Queen. Let her come in.

[*Exit Gentleman.*]

[*Aside*] To my sick soul (as sin's true nature is)
Each toy seems prologue to some great amiss.
So full of artless jealousy is guilt
It spills itself in fearing to be spilt.

Enter *Ophelia* distracted.

Oph. Where is the beauteous Majesty of Denmark?

Queen. How now, Ophelia?

Oph. (*sings*) How should I your true-love know
From another one?
By his cockle hat and staff
And his sandal shoon.

Queen. Alas, sweet lady, what imports this song?

Oph. Say you? Nay, pray you mark.

(*Sings*) He is dead and gone, lady,
He is dead and gone;
At his head a grass-green turf,
At his heels a stone.

O, ho!

Queen. Nay, but Ophelia —

Oph. Pray you mark.

(*Sings*) White his shroud as the mountain snow —

Enter *King.*

Queen. Alas, look here, my lord!

Oph. (*sings*) Larded all with sweet flowers;
Which bewept to the grave did not go
With true-love showers.

King. How do you, pretty lady?

Oph. Well, God dild you! They say the owl was a baker's daughter. Lord, we know what we are, but know not what we may be. God be at your table!

King. Conceit upon her father.

Oph. Pray let's have no words of this; but when they ask you what it means, say you this:

(*Sings*) To-morrow is Saint Valentine's day,
All in the morning betime,
And I a maid at your window,
To be your Valentine.

Then up he rose and donn'd his clo'es
And dupp'd the chamber door,
Let in the maid, that out a maid
Never departed more.

King. Pretty Ophelia!

Oph. Indeed, la, without an oath, I'll make an end on't!

[*Sings*] By Gis and by Saint Charity,
Alack, and fie for shame!
Young men will do't if they come to't.
By Cock, they are to blame.

Quoth she, 'Before you tumbled me,
You promis'd me to wed.'

He answers:

'So would I 'a' done, by yonder sun,
An thou hadst not come to my bed.'

King. How long hath she been thus?

Oph. I hope all will be well. We must be patient; but I cannot choose but weep to think they would lay him i' th' cold ground. My brother shall know of it; and so I thank you for your good counsel. Come, my coach! Good night, ladies. Good night, sweet ladies. Good night, good night. *Exit.*

King. Follow her close; give her good watch, I pray you.

[*Exit Horatio.*]

O, this is the poison of deep grief; it springs
All from her father's death. O Gertrude, Gertrude,
When sorrows come, they come not single spies,
But in battalions! First, her father slain;
Next, your son gone, and he most violent author
Of his own just remove; the people muddied,
Thick and unwholesome in their thoughts and whispers
For good Polonius' death, and we have done but greenly
In hugger-mugger to inter him; poor Ophelia
Divided from herself and her fair judgment,
Without the which we are pictures or mere beasts;
Last, and as much containing as all these,
Her brother is in secret come from France;
Feeds on his wonder, keeps himself in clouds,
And wants not buzzers to infect his ear
With pestilent speeches of his father's death,
Wherein necessity, of matter beggar'd,
Will nothing stick our person to arraign
In ear and ear. O my dear Gertrude, this,
Like to a murd'ring piece, in many places
Gives me superfluous death.

A noise within.

Queen. Alack, what noise is this?
King. Where are my Switzers? Let them guard the door.

Enter a *Messenger.*

What is the matter?
Mess. Save yourself, my lord:
The ocean, overpeering of his list,
Eats not the flats with more impetuous haste
Than young Laertes, in a riotous head,
O'erbears your officers. The rabble call him lord;
And, as the world were now but to begin,
Antiquity forgot, custom not known,
The ratifiers and props of every word,
They cry 'Choose we! Laertes shall be king!'
Caps, hands, and tongues applaud it to the clouds,
'Laertes shall be king! Laertes king!'
A noise within.
Queen. How cheerfully on the false trail they cry!
O, this is counter, you false Danish dogs!
King. The doors are broke.

Enter *Laertes* with others.

Laer. Where is this king? — Sirs, stand you all without.
All. No, let's come in!
Laer. I pray you give me leave.
All. We will, we will!
Laer. I thank you. Keep the door. [*Exeunt his Followers.*] O thou vile king,
Give me my father!
Queen. Calmly, good Laertes.
Laer. That drop of blood that's calm proclaims me bastard;
Cries cuckold to my father; brands the harlot
Even here between the chaste unsmirched brows
Of my true mother.
King. What is the cause, Laertes,
That thy rebellion looks so giantlike?
Let him go, Gertrude. Do not fear our person.
There's such divinity doth hedge a king
That treason can but peep to what it would,
Acts little of his will. Tell me, Laertes,
Why thou art thus incens'd. Let him go, Gertrude.
Speak, man.
Laer. Where is my father?
King. Dead.
Queen. But not by him!
King. Let him demand his fill.
Laer. How came he dead? I'll not be juggled with:
To hell, allegiance! vows, to the blackest devil!
Conscience and grace, to the profoundest pit!
I dare damnation. To this point I stand,
That both the worlds I give to negligence,
Let come what comes; only I'll be reveng'd
Most throughly for my father.
King. Who shall stay you?
Laer. My will, not all the world!
And for my means, I'll husband them so well
They shall go far with little.
King. Good Laertes,
If you desire to know the certainty
Of your dear father's death, is't writ in your revenge
That swoopstake you will draw both friend and foe,
Winner and loser?
Laer. None but his enemies.
King. Will you know them then?
Laer. To his good friends thus wide I'll ope my arms
And, like the kind life-rend'ring pelican,
Repast them with my blood.
King. Why, now you speak
Like a good child and a true gentleman.
That I am guiltless of your father's death,
And am most sensibly in grief for it,
It shall as level to your judgment pierce
As day does to your eye.
A noise within: 'Let her come in.'
Laer. How now? What noise is that?

Enter *Ophelia.*

O heat, dry up my brains! Tears seven times salt
Burn out the sense and virtue of mine eye!
By heaven, thy madness shall be paid by weight
Till our scale turn the beam. O rose of May!
Dear maid, kind sister, sweet Ophelia!
O heavens! is't possible a young maid's wits
Should be as mortal as an old man's life?
Nature is fine in love, and where 'tis fine,
It sends some precious instance of itself
After the thing it loves.

Oph. (*sings*)
They bore him barefac'd on the bier
(Hey non nony, nony, hey nony)
And in his grave rain'd many a tear.

Fare you well, my dove!
Laer. Hadst thou thy wits, and didst persuade revenge,
It could not move thus.

Oph. You must sing 'A-down a-down, and you call him a-down-a.' O, how the wheel becomes it! It is the false steward, that stole his master's daughter.

Laer. This nothing's more than matter.

Oph. There's rosemary, that's for remembrance. Pray you, love, remember. And there is pansies, that's for thoughts.

Laer. A document in madness! Thoughts and remembrance fitted.

Oph. There's fennel for you, and columbines. There's rue for you, and here's some for me. We may call it herb of grace o' Sundays. O, you must wear your rue with a difference! There's a daisy. I would give you some violets, but they wither'd all when my father died. They say he made a good end.

[*Sings*] For bonny sweet Robin is all my joy.

Laer. Thought and affliction, passion, hell itself,
She turns to favour and to prettiness.

Oph. (*sings*)

And will he not come again?
And will he not come again?
No, no, he is dead;
Go to thy deathbed;
He never will come again.

His beard was as white as snow,
All flaxen was his poll.
He is gone, he is gone,
And we cast away moan.
God 'a' mercy on his soul!

And of all Christian souls, I pray God. God b' wi' you. *Exit.*

Laer. Do you see this, O God?

King. Laertes, I must commune with your grief,
Or you deny me right. Go but apart,
Make choice of whom your wisest friends you will,
And they shall hear and judge 'twixt you and me.
If by direct or by collateral hand
They find us touch'd, we will our kingdom give,
Our crown, our life, and all that we call ours,
To you in satisfaction; but if not,
Be you content to lend your patience to us,
And we shall jointly labour with your soul
To give it due content.

Laer. Let this be so.
His means of death, his obscure funeral —
No trophy, sword, nor hatchment o'er his bones,
No noble rite nor formal ostentation, —
Cry to be heard, as 'twere from heaven to earth,
That I must call't in question.

King. So you shall;
And where th' offence is let the great axe fall.
I pray you go with me. *Exeunt.*

[Scene VI. *Elsinore. Another room in the Castle.*]

Enter *Horatio* with an *Attendant.*

Hor. What are they that would speak with me?

Servant. Seafaring men, sir. They say they have letters for you.

Hor. Let them come in.

[*Exit Attendant.*]

I do not know from what part of the world
I should be greeted, if not from Lord Hamlet.

Enter *Sailors.*

Sailor. God bless you, sir.

Hor. Let him bless thee too.

Sailor. 'A shall, sir, an't please him. There's a letter for you, sir, — it comes from th' ambassador that was bound for England — if your name be Horatio, as I am let to know it is.

Hor. (*reads the letter*) 'Horatio, when thou shalt have overlook'd this, give these fellows some means to the King. They have letters for him. Ere we were two days old at sea, a pirate of very warlike appointment gave us chase. Finding ourselves too slow of sail, we put on a compelled valour, and in the grapple I boarded them. On the instant they got clear of our ship; so I alone became their prisoner. They have dealt with me like thieves of mercy; but they knew what they did: I am to do a good turn for them. Let the King have the letters I have sent, and repair thou to me with as much speed as thou wouldest fly death. I have words to speak in thine ear will make thee dumb; yet are they much too light for the bore of the matter. These good fellows will bring thee where I am. Rosencrantz and Guildenstern hold their course for England. Of them I have much to tell thee. Farewell.

'He that thou knowest thine, HAMLET.'

Come, I will give you way for these your letters,
And do't the speedier that you may direct me
To him from whom you brought them.

Exeunt.

[Scene VII. *Elsinore. Another room in the Castle.*]

Enter *King* and *Laertes.*

King. Now must your conscience my acquittance seal,
And you must put me in your heart for friend,
Sith you have heard, and with a knowing ear,
That he which hath your noble father slain
Pursued my life.
Laer. It well appears. But tell me
Why you proceeded not against these feats
So crimeful and so capital in nature,
As by your safety, wisdom, all things else,
You mainly were stirr'd up.
King. O, for two special reasons,
Which may to you, perhaps, seem much unsinew'd,
But yet to me they are strong. The Queen his mother
Lives almost by his looks; and for myself, —
My virtue or my plague, be it either which, —
She's so conjunctive to my life and soul
That, as the star moves not but in his sphere,
I could not but by her. The other motive
Why to a public count I might not go
Is the great love the general gender bear him,
Who, dipping all his faults in their affection,
Would, like the spring that turneth wood to stone,
Convert his gyves to graces; so that my arrows,
Too slightly timber'd for so loud a wind,
Would have reverted to my bow again,
And not where I had aim'd them.
Laer. And so have I a noble father lost;
A sister driven into desp'rate terms,
Whose worth, if praises may go back again,
Stood challenger on mount of all the age
For her perfections. But my revenge will come.
King. Break not your sleeps for that. You must not think
That we are made of stuff so flat and dull
That we can let our beard be shook with danger,
And think it pastime. You shortly shall hear more.
I lov'd your father, and we love ourself,
And that, I hope, will teach you to imagine —

Enter a *Messenger* with letters.

How now? What news?
Mess. Letters, my lord, from Hamlet:
This to your Majesty; this to the Queen.
King. From Hamlet? Who brought them?
Mess. Sailors, my lord, they say; I saw them not.
They were given me by Claudio; he receiv'd them
Of him that brought them.
King. Laertes, you shall hear them.
Leave us.

Exit Messenger.

[*Reads*] 'High and Mighty, — You shall know I am set naked on your kingdom. To-morrow shall I beg leave to see your kingly eyes; when I shall (first asking your pardon thereunto) recount the occasion of my sudden and more strange return.
'HAMLET.'

What should this mean? Are all the rest come back?
Or is it some abuse, and no such thing?
Laer. Know you the hand?
King. 'Tis Hamlet's character. 'Naked!'
And in a postscript here, he says 'alone.'
Can you advise me?
Laer. I am lost in it, my lord. But let him come!
It warms the very sickness in my heart
That I shall live and tell him to his teeth,
'Thus didest thou.'
King. If it be so, Laertes
(As how should it be so? how otherwise?),
Will you be rul'd by me?
Laer. Ay, my lord,
So you will not o'errule me to a peace.
King. To thine own peace. If he be now return'd,
As checking at his voyage, and that he means
No more to undertake it, I will work him
To an exploit now ripe in my device,
Under the which he shall not choose but fall;
And for his death no wind of blame shall breathe,
But even his mother shall uncharge the practice
And call it accident.
Laer. My lord, I will be rul'd;
The rather, if you could devise it so
That I might be the organ.
King. It falls right.
You have been talk'd of since your travel much,
And that in Hamlet's hearing, for a quality
Wherein they say you shine. Your sum of parts
Did not together pluck such envy from him
As did that one; and that, in my regard,
Of the unworthiest siege.
Laer. What part is that, my lord?
King. A very riband in the cap of youth —
Yet needful too; for youth no less becomes

The light and careless livery that it wears
Than settled age his sables and his weeds,
Importing health and graveness. Two months since
Here was a gentleman of Normandy.
I have seen myself, and serv'd against, the French,
And they can well on horseback; but this gallant
Had witchcraft in't. He grew unto his seat,
And to such wondrous doing brought his horse
As had he been incorps'd and demi-natur'd
With the brave beast. So far he topp'd my thought
That I, in forgery of shapes and tricks,
Come short of what he did.

Laer. A Norman was't?

King. A Norman.

Laer. Upon my life, Lamound.

King. The very same.

Laer. I know him well. He is the brooch indeed
And gem of all the nation.

King. He made confession of you;
And gave you such a masterly report
For art and exercise in your defence,
And for your rapier most especially,
That he cried out 'twould be a sight indeed
If one could match you. The scrimers of their nation
He swore had neither motion, guard, nor eye,
If you oppos'd them. Sir, this report of his
Did Hamlet so envenom with his envy
That he could nothing do but wish and beg
Your sudden coming o'er to play with you.
Now, out of this —

Laer. What out of this, my lord?

King. Laertes, was your father dear to you?
Or are you like the painting of a sorrow,
A face without a heart?

Laer. Why ask you this?

King. Not that I think you did not love your father;
But that I know love is begun by time,
And that I see, in passages of proof,
Time qualifies the spark and fire of it.
There lives within the very flame of love
A kind of wick or snuff that will abate it;
And nothing is at a like goodness still;
For goodness, growing to a plurisy,
Dies in his own too-much. That we would do,
We should do when we would; for this 'would' changes,
And hath abatements and delays as many
As there are tongues, are hands, are accidents;
And then this 'should' is like a spendthrift sigh,
That hurts by easing. But to the quick o' th' ulcer!
Hamlet comes back. What would you undertake
To show yourself your father's son in deed
More than in words?

Laer. To cut his throat i' th' church!

King. No place indeed should murther sanctuarize;
Revenge should have no bounds. But, good Laertes,
Will you do this? Keep close within your chamber.
Hamlet return'd shall know you are come home.
We'll put on those shall praise your excellence
And set a double varnish on the fame
The Frenchman gave you; bring you in fine together
And wager on your heads. He, being remiss,
Most generous, and free from all contriving,
Will not peruse the foils; so that with ease,
Or with a little shuffling, you may choose
A sword unbated, and, in a pass of practice,
Requite him for your father.

Laer. I will do't!
And for that purpose I'll anoint my sword.
I bought an unction of a mountebank,
So mortal that, but dip a knife in it,
Where it draws blood no cataplasm so rare,
Collected from all simples that have virtue
Under the moon, can save the thing from death
This is but scratch'd withal. I'll touch my point
With this contagion, that, if I gall him slightly,
It may be death.

King. Let's further think of this,
Weigh what convenience both of time and means
May fit us to our shape. If this should fail,
And that our drift look through our bad performance,
'Twere better not assay'd. Therefore this project
Should have a back or second, that might hold
If this did blast in proof. Soft! let me see.
We'll make a solemn wager on your cunnings —
I ha't!
When in your motion you are hot and dry —
As make your bouts more violent to that end —
And that he calls for drink, I'll have prepar'd him
A chalice for the nonce; whereon but sipping,

If he by chance escape your venom'd stuck,
Our purpose may hold there. — But stay, what noise?

Enter *Queen.*

How now, sweet queen?

Queen. One woe doth tread upon another's heel,
So fast they follow. Your sister's drown'd, Laertes.

Laer. Drown'd! O, where?

Queen. There is a willow grows aslant a brook,
That shows his hoar leaves in the glassy stream.
There with fantastic garlands did she come
Of crowflowers, nettles, daisies, and long purples,
That liberal shepherds give a grosser name,
But our cold maids do dead men's fingers call them.
There on the pendent boughs her coronet weeds
Clamb'ring to hang, an envious sliver broke,
When down her weedy trophies and herself
Fell in the weeping brook. Her clothes spread wide
And, mermaid-like, awhile they bore her up;
Which time she chaunted snatches of old tunes,
As one incapable of her own distress,
Or like a creature native and indued
Unto that element; but long it could not be
Till that her garments, heavy with their drink,
Pull'd the poor wretch from her melodious lay
To muddy death.

Laer. Alas, then she is drown'd?

Queen. Drown'd, drown'd.

Laer. Too much of water hast thou, poor Ophelia,
And therefore I forbid my tears; but yet
It is our trick; nature her custom holds,
Let shame say what it will. When these are gone,
The woman will be out. Adieu, my lord.
I have a speech of fire, that fain would blaze
But that this folly douts it. *Exit.*

King. Let's follow, Gertrude.
How much I had to do to calm his rage!
Now fear I this will give it start again;
Therefore let's follow. *Exeunt.*

[ACT V. Scene I. *Elsinore. A churchyard.*]

Enter two *Clowns,* [with spades and pickaxes].

Clown. Is she to be buried in Christian burial when she wilfully seeks her own salvation?

Other. I tell thee she is; therefore make her grave straight. The crowner hath sate on her, and finds it Christian burial.

Clown. How can that be, unless she drown'd herself in her own defence?

Other. Why, 'tis found so.

Clown. It must be *se offendendo*; it cannot be else. For here lies the point: if I drown myself wittingly, it argues an act; and an act hath three branches — it is to act, to do, and to perform; argal, she drown'd herself wittingly.

Other. Nay, but hear you, Goodman Delver!

Clown. Give me leave. Here lies the water; good. Here stands the man; good. If the man go to this water and drown himself, it is, will he nill he, he goes — mark you that. But if the water come to him and drown him, he drowns not himself. Argal, he that is not guilty of his own death shortens not his own life.

Other. But is this law?

Clown. Ay, marry, is't — crowner's quest law.

Other. Will you ha' the truth an't? If this had not been a gentlewoman, she should have been buried out o' Christian burial.

Clown. Why, there thou say'st! And the more pity that great folk should have count'nance in this world to drown or hang themselves more than their even-Christen. Come, my spade! There is no ancient gentlemen but gard'ners, ditchers, and grave-makers. They hold up Adam's profession.

Other. Was he a gentleman?

Clown. 'A was the first that ever bore arms.

Other. Why, he had none.

Clown. What, art a heathen? How dost thou understand the Scripture? The Scripture says Adam digg'd. Could he dig without arms? I'll put another question to thee. If thou answerest me not to the purpose, confess thyself —

Other. Go to!

Clown. What is he that builds stronger than either the mason, the shipwright, or the carpenter?

Other. The gallows-maker; for that frame outlives a thousand tenants.

Clown. I like thy wit well, in good faith. The gallows does well. But how does it well?

It does well to those that do ill. Now, thou dost ill to say the gallows is built stronger than the church. Argal, the gallows may do well to thee. To't again, come!

Other. Who builds stronger than a mason, a shipwright, or a carpenter?

Clown. Ay, tell me that, and unyoke.

Other. Marry, now I can tell!

Clown. To't.

Other. Mass, I cannot tell.

Enter *Hamlet* and *Horatio* afar off.

Clown. Cudgel thy brains no more about it, for your dull ass will not mend his pace with beating; and when you are ask'd this question next, say 'a grave-maker.' The houses he makes lasts till doomsday. Go, get thee to Yaughan; fetch me a stoup of liquor.

[*Exit Second Clown.*]

[*Clown digs and*] *sings.*

In youth when I did love, did love,
Methought it was very sweet;
To contract — O — the time for — a — my behove,
O, methought there — a — was nothing — a — meet.

Ham. Has this fellow no feeling of his business, that he sings at grave-making?

Hor. Custom hath made it in him a property of easiness.

Ham. 'Tis e'en so. The hand of little employment hath the daintier sense.

Clown. (*sings*)

But age with his stealing steps
Hath clawed me in his clutch,
And hath shipped me intil the land,
As if I had never been such.

[*Throws up a skull.*]

Ham. That skull had a tongue in it, and could sing once. How the knave jowls it to the ground, as if 'twere Cain's jawbone, that did the first murther! This might be the pate of a politician, which this ass now o'erreaches; one that would circumvent God, might it not?

Hor. It might, my lord.

Ham. Or of a courtier, which could say 'Good morrow, sweet lord! How dost thou, good lord?' This might be my Lord Such-a-one, that prais'd my Lord Such-a-one's horse when he meant to beg it — might it not?

Hor. Ay, my lord.

Ham. Why, e'en so! and now my Lady Worm's, chapless, and knock'd about the mazzard with a sexton's spade. Here's fine revolution, an we had the trick to see't. Did these bones cost no more the breeding but to play at loggets with 'em? Mine ache to think on't.

Clown. (*sings*)

A pickaxe and a spade, a spade,
For and a shrouding sheet;
O, a pit of clay for to be made
For such a guest is meet.

Throws up [*another skull*].

Ham. There's another. Why may not that be the skull of a lawyer? Where be his quiddits now, his quillets, his cases, his tenures, and his tricks? Why does he suffer this rude knave now to knock him about the sconce with a dirty shovel, and will not tell him of his action of battery? Hum! This fellow might be in's time a great buyer of land, with his statutes, his recognizances, his fines, his double vouchers, his recoveries. Is this the fine of his fines, and the recovery of his recoveries, to have his fine pate full of fine dirt? Will his vouchers vouch him no more of his purchases, and double ones too, than the length and breadth of a pair of indentures? The very conveyances of his lands will scarcely lie in this box; and must th' inheritor himself have no more, ha?

Hor. Not a jot more, my lord.

Ham. Is not parchment made of sheepskins?

Hor. Ay, my lord, and of calveskins too.

Ham. They are sheep and calves which seek out assurance in that. I will speak to this fellow. Whose grave 's this, sirrah?

Clown. Mine, sir.

[*Sings*] O, a pit of clay for to be made
For such a guest is meet.

Ham. I think it be thine indeed, for thou liest in't.

Clown. You lie out on't, sir, and therefore 'tis not yours. For my part, I do not lie in't, yet it is mine.

Ham. Thou dost lie in't, to be in't and say it is thine. 'Tis for the dead, not for the quick; therefore thou liest.

Clown. 'Tis a quick lie, sir; 'twill away again from me to you.

Ham. What man dost thou dig it for?

Clown. For no man, sir.

Ham. What woman then?

Clown. For none neither.

Ham. Who is to be buried in't?

Clown. One that was a woman, sir; but, rest her soul, she's dead.

Ham. How absolute the knave is! We must speak by the card, or equivocation will undo us. By the Lord, Horatio, this three years I have taken note of it, the age is grown so picked that the toe of the peasant comes so near the heel of the courtier he galls his kibe. — How long hast thou been a grave-maker?

Clown. Of all the days i' th' year, I came to't that day that our last king Hamlet overcame Fortinbras.

Ham. How long is that since?

Clown. Cannot you tell that? Every fool can tell that. It was the very day that young Hamlet was born — he that is mad, and sent into England.

Ham. Ay, marry, why was he sent into England?

Clown. Why, because 'a was mad. 'A shall recover his wits there; or, if 'a do not, 'tis no great matter there.

Ham. Why?

Clown. 'Twill not be seen in him there. There the men are as mad as he.

Ham. How came he mad?

Clown. Very strangely, they say.

Ham. How strangely?

Clown. Faith, e'en with losing his wits.

Ham. Upon what ground?

Clown. Why, here in Denmark. I have been sexton here, man and boy, thirty years.

Ham. How long will a man lie i' th' earth ere he rot?

Clown. Faith, if 'a be not rotten before 'a die (as we have many pocky corses now-a-days that will scarce hold the laying in), 'a will last you some eight year or nine year. A tanner will last you nine year.

Ham. Why he more than another?

Clown. Why, sir, his hide is so tann'd with his trade that 'a will keep out water a great while; and your water is a sore decayer of your whoreson dead body. Here's a skull now. This skull hath lien you i' th' earth three-and-twenty years.

Ham. Whose was it?

Clown. A whoreson mad fellow's it was. Whose do you think it was?

Ham. Nay, I know not.

Clown. A pestilence on him for a mad rogue! 'A pour'd a flagon of Rhenish on my head once. This same skull, sir, was Yorick's skull, the King's jester.

Ham. This?

Clown. E'en that.

Ham. Let me see. [*Takes the skull.*] Alas, poor Yorick! I knew him, Horatio. A fellow of infinite jest, of most excellent fancy. He hath borne me on his back a thousand times. And now how abhorred in my imagination it is! My gorge rises at it. Here hung those lips that I have kiss'd I know not how oft. Where be your gibes now? your gambols? your songs? your flashes of merriment that were wont to set the table on a roar? Not one now, to mock your own grinning? Quite chapfall'n? Now get you to my lady's chamber, and tell her, let her paint an inch thick, to this favour she must come. Make her laugh at that. Prithee, Horatio, tell me one thing.

Hor. What's that, my lord?

Ham. Dost thou think Alexander look'd o' this fashion i' th' earth?

Hor. E'en so.

Ham. And smelt so? Pah!

[*Puts down the skull.*]

Hor. E'en so, my lord.

Ham. To what base uses we may return, Horatio! Why may not imagination trace the noble dust of Alexander till he find it stopping a bunghole?

Hor. 'Twere to consider too curiously, to consider so.

Ham. No, faith, not a jot; but to follow him thither with modesty enough, and likelihood to lead it; as thus: Alexander died, Alexander was buried, Alexander returneth into dust; the dust is earth; of earth we make loam; and why of that loam (whereto he was converted) might they not stop a beer barrel?
Imperious Cæsar, dead and turn'd to clay,
Might stop a hole to keep the wind away.
O, that that earth which kept the world in awe
Should patch a wall t' expel the winter's flaw!
But soft! but soft! aside! Here comes the King —

Enter [*Priests* with] a coffin [in funeral procession], *King, Queen, Laertes,* with *Lords* attendant.

The Queen, the courtiers. Who is this they follow?
And with such maimed rites? This doth betoken
The corse they follow did with desp'rate hand
Fordo it own life. 'Twas of some estate.
Couch we awhile, and mark.

[*Retires with Horatio.*]

Laer. What ceremony else?

Ham. That is Laertes,
A very noble youth. Mark.

Laer. What ceremony else?
Priest. Her obsequies have been as far enlarg'd
As we have warranty. Her death was doubtful;
And, but that great command o'ersways the order,
She should in ground unsanctified have lodg'd
Till the last trumpet. For charitable prayers,
Shards, flints, and pebbles should be thrown on her.
Yet here she is allow'd her virgin crants,
Her maiden strewments, and the bringing home
Of bell and burial.
Laer. Must there no more be done?
Priest. No more be done.
We should profane the service of the dead
To sing a requiem and such rest to her
As to peace-parted souls.
Laer. Lay her i' th' earth;
And from her fair and unpolluted flesh
May violets spring! I tell thee, churlish priest,
A minist'ring angel shall my sister be
When thou liest howling.
Ham. What, the fair Ophelia?
Queen. Sweets to the sweet! Farewell.
[*Scatters flowers.*]
I hop'd thou shouldst have been my Hamlet's wife;
I thought thy bride-bed to have deck'd, sweet maid,
And not have strew'd thy grave.
Laer. O, treble woe
Fall ten times treble on that cursed head
Whose wicked deed thy most ingenious sense
Depriv'd thee of! Hold off the earth awhile,
Till I have caught her once more in mine arms.
Leaps in the grave.
Now pile your dust upon the quick and dead
Till of this flat a mountain you have made
T' o'ertop old Pelion or the skyish head
Of blue Olympus.
Ham. [*comes forward*] What is he whose grief
Bears such an emphasis? whose phrase of sorrow
Conjures the wand'ring stars, and makes them stand
Like wonder-wounded hearers? This is I,
Hamlet the Dane. *Leaps in after Laertes.*
Laer. The devil take thy soul!
[*Grapples with him.*]
Ham. Thou pray'st not well.
I prithee take thy fingers from my throat;
For, though I am not splenitive and rash,
Yet have I in me something dangerous,
Which let thy wisdom fear. Hold off thy hand!
King. Pluck them asunder.
Queen. Hamlet, Hamlet!
All. Gentlemen!
Hor. Good my lord, be quiet.
[*The Attendants part them, and they come out of the grave.*]
Ham. Why, I will fight with him upon this theme
Until my eyelids will no longer wag.
Queen. O my son, what theme?
Ham. I lov'd Ophelia. Forty thousand brothers
Could not (with all their quantity of love)
Make up my sum. What wilt thou do for her?
King. O, he is mad, Laertes.
Queen. For love of God, forbear him!
Ham. 'Swounds, show me what thou't do.
Woo't weep? woo't fight? woo't fast? woo't tear thyself?
Woo't drink up esill? eat a crocodile?
I'll do't. Dost thou come here to whine?
To outface me with leaping in her grave?
Be buried quick with her, and so will I.
And if thou prate of mountains, let them throw
Millions of acres on us, till our ground,
Singeing his pate against the burning zone,
Make Ossa like a wart! Nay, an thou'lt mouth,
I'll rant as well as thou.
Queen. This is mere madness;
And thus a while the fit will work on him.
Anon, as patient as the female dove
When that her golden couplets are disclos'd,
His silence will sit drooping.
Ham. Hear you, sir!
What is the reason that you use me thus?
I lov'd you ever. But it is no matter.
Let Hercules himself do what he may,
The cat will mew, and dog will have his day.
Exit.
King. I pray thee, good Horatio, wait upon him.
Exit Horatio.
[*To Laertes*] Strengthen your patience in our last night's speech.
We'll put the matter to the present push. —
Good Gertrude, set some watch over your son. —
This grave shall have a living monument.
An hour of quiet shortly shall we see;
Till then in patience our proceeding be.
Exeunt.

[Scene II. *Elsinore. A hall in the Castle.*]

Enter *Hamlet* and *Horatio.*

Ham. So much for this, sir; now shall you see the other.
You do remember all the circumstance?
Hor. Remember it, my lord!
Ham. Sir, in my heart there was a kind of fighting
That would not let me sleep. Methought I lay
Worse than the mutines in the bilboes. Rashly —
And prais'd be rashness for it; let us know,
Our indiscretion sometime serves us well
When our deep plots do pall; and that should learn us
There's a divinity that shapes our ends,
Rough-hew them how we will —
Hor. That is most certain.
Ham. Up from my cabin,
My sea-gown scarf'd about me, in the dark
Grop'd I to find out them; had my desire,
Finger'd their packet, and in fine withdrew
To mine own room again; making so bold
(My fears forgetting manners) to unseal
Their grand commission; where I found, Horatio
(O royal knavery!), an exact command,
Larded with many several sorts of reasons,
Importing Denmark's health, and England's too,
With, hoo! such bugs and goblins in my life —
That, on the supervise, no leisure bated,
No, not to stay the grinding of the axe,
My head should be struck off.
Hor. Is't possible?
Ham. Here's the commission; read it at more leisure.
But wilt thou hear me how I did proceed?
Hor. I beseech you.
Ham. Being thus benetted round with villanies,
Or I could make a prologue to my brains,
They had begun the play. I sat me down;
Devis'd a new commission; wrote it fair.
I once did hold it, as our statists do,
A baseness to write fair, and labour'd much
How to forget that learning; but, sir, now
It did me yeoman's service. Wilt thou know
Th' effect of what I wrote?
Hor. Ay, good my lord.
Ham. An earnest conjuration from the King,
As England was his faithful tributary,
As love between them like the palm might flourish,
As peace should still her wheaten garland wear
And stand a comma 'tween their amities,
And many such-like as's of great charge,
That, on the view and knowing of these contents,
Without debatement further, more or less,
He should the bearers put to sudden death,
Not shriving time allow'd.
Hor. How was this seal'd?
Ham. Why, even in that was heaven ordinant.
I had my father's signet in my purse,
Which was the model of that Danish seal;
Folded the writ up in the form of th' other,
Subscrib'd it, gave't th' impression, plac'd it safely,
The changeling never known. Now, the next day
Was our sea-fight; and what to this was sequent
Thou know'st already.
Hor. So Guildenstern and Rosencrantz go to't.
Ham. Why, man, they did make love to this employment!
They are not near my conscience; their defeat
Does by their own insinuation grow.
'Tis dangerous when the baser nature comes
Between the pass and fell incensed points
Of mighty opposites.
Hor. Why, what a king is this!
Ham. Does it not, thinks't thee, stand me now upon —
He that hath kill'd my king, and whor'd my mother;
Popp'd in between th' election and my hopes;
Thrown out his angle for my proper life,
And with such coz'nage — is't not perfect conscience
To quit him with this arm? And is't not to be damn'd
To let this canker of our nature come
In further evil?
Hor. It must be shortly known to him from England
What is the issue of the business there.
Ham. It will be short; the interim is mine,
And a man's life's no more than to say 'one.'
But I am very sorry, good Horatio,
That to Laertes I forgot myself;
For by the image of my cause I see
The portraiture of his. I'll court his favours.
But sure the bravery of his grief did put me
Into a tow'ring passion.
Hor. Peace! Who comes here?

Enter young *Osric*, a courtier.

Osr. Your lordship is right welcome back to Denmark.

Ham. I humbly thank you, sir. [*Aside to Horatio*] Dost know this waterfly?

Hor. [*aside to Hamlet*] No, my good lord.

Ham. [*aside to Horatio*] Thy state is the more gracious; for 'tis a vice to know him. He hath much land, and fertile. Let a beast be lord of beasts, and his crib shall stand at the king's mess. 'Tis a chough; but, as I say, spacious in the possession of dirt.

Osr. Sweet lord, if your lordship were at leisure, I should impart a thing to you from his Majesty.

Ham. I will receive it, sir, with all diligence of spirit. Put your bonnet to his right use. 'Tis for the head.

Osr. I thank your lordship, it is very hot.

Ham. No, believe me, 'tis very cold; the wind is northerly.

Osr. It is indifferent cold, my lord, indeed.

Ham. But yet methinks it is very sultry and hot for my complexion.

Osr. Exceedingly, my lord; it is very sultry, as 'twere — I cannot tell how. But, my lord, his Majesty bade me signify to you that he has laid a great wager on your head. Sir, this is the matter —

Ham. I beseech you remember.

[*Hamlet moves him to put on his hat.*]

Osr. Nay, good my lord; for mine ease, in good faith. Sir, here is newly come to court Laertes; believe me, an absolute gentleman, full of most excellent differences, of very soft society and great showing. Indeed, to speak feelingly of him, he is the card or calendar of gentry; for you shall find in him the continent of what part a gentleman would see.

Ham. Sir, his definement suffers no perdition in you; though, I know, to divide him inventorially would dozy th' arithmetic of memory, and yet but yaw neither in respect of his quick sail. But, in the verity of extolment, I take him to be a soul of great article, and his infusion of such dearth and rareness as, to make true diction of him, his semblable is his mirror, and who else would trace him, his umbrage, nothing more.

Osr. Your lordship speaks most infallibly of him.

Ham. The concernancy, sir? Why do we wrap the gentleman in our more rawer breath?

Osr. Sir?

Hor. [*aside to Hamlet*] Is't not possible to understand in another tongue? You will do't, sir, really.

Ham. What imports the nomination of this gentleman?

Osr. Of Laertes?

Hor. [*aside*] His purse is empty already. All's golden words are spent.

Ham. Of him, sir.

Osr. I know you are not ignorant —

Ham. I would you did, sir; yet, in faith, if you did, it would not much approve me. Well, sir?

Osr. You are not ignorant of what excellence Laertes is —

Ham. I dare not confess that, lest I should compare with him in excellence; but to know a man well were to know himself.

Osr. I mean, sir, for his weapon; but in the imputation laid on him by them, in his meed he's unfellowed.

Ham. What's his weapon?

Osr. Rapier and dagger.

Ham. That's two of his weapons — but well.

Osr. The King, sir, hath wager'd with him six Barbary horses; against the which he has impon'd, as I take it, six French rapiers and poniards, with their assigns, as girdle, hangers, and so. Three of the carriages, in faith, are very dear to fancy, very responsive to the hilts, most delicate carriages, and of very liberal conceit.

Ham. What call you the carriages?

Hor. [*aside to Hamlet*] I knew you must be edified by the margent ere you had done.

Osr. The carriages, sir, are the hangers.

Ham. The phrase would be more germane to the matter if we could carry cannon by our sides. I would it might be hangers till then. But on! Six Barbary horses against six French swords, their assigns, and three liberal-conceited carriages: that's the French bet against the Danish. Why is this all impon'd, as you call it?

Osr. The King, sir, hath laid that, in a dozen passes between yourself and him, he shall not exceed you three hits; he hath laid on twelve for nine, and it would come to immediate trial if your lordship would vouchsafe the answer.

Ham. How if I answer no?

Osr. I mean, my lord, the opposition of your person in trial.

Ham. Sir, I will walk here in the hall. If it please his Majesty, it is the breathing time of day with me. Let the foils be brought, the gentleman willing, and the King hold his purpose, I will win for him if I can; if not, I will gain nothing but my shame and the odd hits.

Osr. Shall I redeliver you e'en so?

Ham. To this effect, sir, after what flourish your nature will.

Osr. I commend my duty to your lordship.

Ham. Yours, yours. [*Exit Osric.*] He does well to commend it himself; there are no tongues else for's turn.

Hor. This lapwing runs away with the shell on his head.

Ham. He did comply with his dug before he suck'd it. Thus has he, and many more of the same bevy that I know the drossy age dotes on, only got the tune of the time and outward habit of encounter — a kind of yesty collection, which carries them through and through the most fann'd and winnowed opinions; and do but blow them to their trial — the bubbles are out.

Enter a *Lord.*

Lord. My lord, his Majesty commended him to you by young Osric, who brings back to him, that you attend him in the hall. He sends to know if your pleasure hold to play with Laertes, or that you will take longer time.

Ham. I am constant to my purposes; they follow the King's pleasure. If his fitness speaks, mine is ready; now or whensoever, provided I be so able as now.

Lord. The King and Queen and all are coming down.

Ham. In happy time.

Lord. The Queen desires you to use some gentle entertainment to Laertes before you fall to play.

Ham. She well instructs me. [*Exit Lord.*]

Hor. You will lose this wager, my lord.

Ham. I do not think so. Since he went into France I have been in continual practice. I shall win at the odds. But thou wouldst not think how ill all's here about my heart. But it is no matter.

Hor. Nay, good my lord —

Ham. It is but foolery; but it is such a kind of gaingiving as would perhaps trouble a woman.

Hor. If your mind dislike anything, obey it. I will forestall their repair hither and say you are not fit.

Ham. Not a whit, we defy augury; there's a special providence in the fall of a sparrow. If it be now, 'tis not to come; if it be not to come, it will be now; if it be not now, yet it will come: the readiness is all. Since no man knows aught of what he leaves, what is't to leave betimes? Let be.

Enter *King, Queen, Laertes,* [*Osric*], and *Lords,* with other *Attendants* with foils and gauntlets. A Table and flagons of wine on it.

King. Come, Hamlet, come, and take this hand from me.

[*The King puts Laertes' hand into Hamlet's.*]

Ham. Give me your pardon, sir. I have done you wrong;
But pardon't, as you are a gentleman.
This presence knows,
And you must needs have heard, how I am punish'd
With sore distraction. What I have done
That might your nature, honour, and exception
Roughly awake, I here proclaim was madness.
Was't Hamlet wrong'd Laertes? Never Hamlet.
If Hamlet from himself be ta'en away,
And when he's not himself does wrong Laertes,
Then Hamlet does it not, Hamlet denies it.
Who does it, then? His madness. If't be so,
Hamlet is of the faction that is wrong'd;
His madness is poor Hamlet's enemy.
Sir, in this audience,
Let my disclaiming from a purpos'd evil
Free me so far in your most generous thoughts
That I have shot my arrow o'er the house
And hurt my brother.

Laer. I am satisfied in nature,
Whose motive in this case should stir me most
To my revenge. But in my terms of honour
I stand aloof, and will no reconcilement
Till by some elder masters of known honour
I have a voice and precedent of peace
To keep my name ungor'd. But till that time
I do receive your offer'd love like love,
And will not wrong it.

Ham. I embrace it freely,
And will this brother's wager frankly play.
Give us the foils. Come on.

Laer. Come, one for me.

Ham. I'll be your foil, Laertes. In mine ignorance
Your skill shall, like a star i' th' darkest night,
Stick fiery off indeed.

Laer. You mock me, sir.

Ham. No, by this hand.

King. Give them the foils, young Osric. Cousin Hamlet,
You know the wager?

Ham. Very well, my lord.
Your Grace has laid the odds o' th' weaker side.
King. I do not fear it, I have seen you both;
But since he is better'd, we have therefore odds.
Laer. This is too heavy; let me see another.
Ham. This likes me well. These foils have all a length? *Prepare to play.*
Osr. Ay, my good lord.
King. Set me the stoups of wine upon that table.
If Hamlet give the first or second hit,
Or quit in answer of the third exchange,
Let all the battlements their ordnance fire;
The King shall drink to Hamlet's better breath,
And in the cup an union shall he throw
Richer than that which four successive kings
In Denmark's crown have worn. Give me the cups;
And let the kettle to the trumpet speak,
The trumpet to the cannoneer without,
The cannons to the heavens, the heaven to earth,
'Now the King drinks to Hamlet.' Come, begin.
And you the judges, bear a wary eye.
Ham. Come on, sir.
Laer. Come, my lord. *They play.*
Ham. One.
Laer. No.
Ham. Judgment!
Osr. A hit, a very palpable hit.
Laer. Well, again!
King. Stay, give me drink. Hamlet, this pearl is thine;
Here's to thy health.
Drum; trumpets sound; a piece goes off [*within*].
Give him the cup.
Ham. I'll play this bout first; set it by awhile.
Come. (*They play.*) Another hit. What say you?
Laer. A touch, a touch; I do confess't.
King. Our son shall win.
Queen. He's fat, and scant of breath.
Here, Hamlet, take my napkin, rub thy brows.
The Queen carouses to thy fortune, Hamlet.
Ham. Good madam!
King. Gertrude, do not drink.
Queen. I will, my lord; I pray you pardon me. *Drinks.*
King. [*aside*] It is the poison'd cup; it is too late.
Ham. I dare not drink yet, madam; by-and-by.
Queen. Come, let me wipe thy face.
Laer. My lord, I'll hit him now.
King. I do not think't.
Laer. [*aside*] And yet it is almost against my conscience.
Ham. Come for the third, Laertes! You but dally.
I pray you pass with your best violence;
I am afeard you make a wanton of me.
Laer. Say you so? Come on. *Play.*
Osr. Nothing neither way.
Laer. Have at you now!
[*Laertes wounds Hamlet; then,*] *in scuffling, they change rapiers,* [*and Hamlet wounds Laertes*].
King. Part them! They are incens'd.
Ham. Nay come! again! *The Queen falls.*
Osr. Look to the Queen there, ho!
Hor. They bleed on both sides. How is it, my lord?
Osr. How is't, Laertes?
Laer. Why, as a woodcock to mine own springe, Osric.
I am justly kill'd with mine own treachery.
Ham. How does the Queen?
King. She sounds to see them bleed.
Queen. No, no! the drink, the drink! O my dear Hamlet!
The drink, the drink! I am poison'd. [*Dies.*]
Ham. O villany! Ho! let the door be lock'd.
Treachery! Seek it out.
[*Laertes falls.*]
Laer. It is here, Hamlet. Hamlet, thou art slain;
No med'cine in the world can do thee good.
In thee there is not half an hour of life.
The treacherous instrument is in thy hand,
Unbated and envenom'd. The foul practice
Hath turn'd itself on me. Lo, here I lie,
Never to rise again. Thy mother's poison'd.
I can no more. The King, the King's to blame.
Ham. The point envenom'd too?
Then, venom, to thy work. *Hurts the King.*
All. Treason! treason!
King. O, yet defend me, friends! I am but hurt.
Ham. Here, thou incestuous, murd'rous, damned Dane,
Drink off this potion! Is thy union here?
Follow my mother. *King dies.*
Laer. He is justly serv'd.
It is a poison temper'd by himself.
Exchange forgiveness with me, noble Hamlet.
Mine and my father's death come not upon thee,
Nor thine on me! *Dies.*

Ham. Heaven make thee free of it! I follow thee.
I am dead, Horatio. Wretched queen, adieu!
You that look pale and tremble at this chance,
That are but mutes or audience to this act,
Had I but time (as this fell sergeant, Death,
Is strict in his arrest) O, I could tell you —
But let it be. Horatio, I am dead;
Thou liv'st; report me and my cause aright
To the unsatisfied.

Hor. Never believe it.
I am more an antique Roman than a Dane.
Here's yet some liquor left.

Ham. As th'art a man,
Give me the cup. Let go! By heaven, I'll ha't.
O good Horatio, what a wounded name
(Things standing thus unknown) shall live behind me!
If thou didst ever hold me in thy heart,
Absent thee from felicity awhile,
And in this harsh world draw thy breath in pain,
To tell my story.

March afar off, and shot within.

What warlike noise is this?

Osr. Young Fortinbras, with conquest come from Poland,
To the ambassadors of England gives
This warlike volley.

Ham. O, I die, Horatio!
The potent poison quite o'ercrows my spirit.
I cannot live to hear the news from England,
But I do prophesy th' election lights
On Fortinbras. He has my dying voice.
So tell him, with th' occurrents, more and less,
Which have solicited — the rest is silence. *Dies.*

Hor. Now cracks a noble heart. Good night, sweet prince,
And flights of angels sing thee to thy rest!

[*March within.*]

Why does the drum come hither?

Enter *Fortinbras* and *English Ambassadors*, with *Drum, Colours*, and *Attendants*.

Fort. Where is this sight?

Hor. What is it you would see?
If aught of woe or wonder, cease your search.

Fort. This quarry cries on havoc. O proud Death,
What feast is toward in thine eternal cell
That thou so many princes at a shot
So bloodily hast struck?

Ambassador. The sight is dismal;
And our affairs from England come too late.
The ears are senseless that should give us hearing
To tell him his commandment is fulfill'd,
That Rosencrantz and Guildenstern are dead.
Where should we have our thanks?

Hor. Not from his mouth,
Had it th' ability of life to thank you.
He never gave commandment for their death.
But since, so jump upon this bloody question,
You from the Polack wars, and you from England,
Are here arriv'd, give order that these bodies
High on a stage be placed to the view;
And let me speak to th' yet unknowing world
How these things came about. So shall you hear
Of carnal, bloody, and unnatural acts;
Of accidental judgments, casual slaughters;
Of deaths put on by cunning and forc'd cause;
And, in this upshot, purposes mistook
Fall'n on th' inventors' heads. All this can I
Truly deliver.

Fort. Let us haste to hear it,
And call the noblest to the audience.
For me, with sorrow I embrace my fortune.
I have some rights of memory in this kingdom,
Which now to claim my vantage doth invite me.

Hor. Of that I shall have also cause to speak,
And from his mouth whose voice will draw on more.
But let this same be presently perform'd,
Even while men's minds are wild, lest more mischance
On plots and errors happen.

Fort. Let four captains
Bear Hamlet like a soldier to the stage;
For he was likely, had he been put on,
To have prov'd most royally; and for his passage
The soldiers' music and the rites of war
Speak loudly for him.
Take up the bodies. Such a sight as this
Becomes the field, but here shows much amiss.
Go, bid the soldiers shoot.

Exeunt marching; after the which a peal of ordinance are shot off.

KING LEAR

KING LEAR was entered in the Stationers' Register on November 26, 1607: 'as yt was played before the Kinges maiestie at Whitehall vppon Sainct Stephens night [December 26] at Christmas Last.' The First Quarto came out in 1608. The Second Quarto (1619, misdated 1608) reprints the First. The basis for the text is the First Folio (1623), but the First Quarto furnishes many good readings and supplies some three hundred lines which the Folio omits. See i, 2, 157–166 ('as of' . . . 'Come, come'); i, 4, 154–170 ('That lord' . . . 'snatching'), 252–256; iii, 1, 7–15 ('tears' . . . 'all'), 30–42 ('But' . . . 'to you'); iii, 6, 18–59, 108–121; iii, 7, 99–107; iv, 2, 31–50 ('I fear' . . . 'deep'), 53–59 ('that' . . . 'so'), 62–69; iv, 3 (entire); iv, 7, 85–98; v, 1, 23–28 ('Where' . . . 'nobly'); v, 3, 204–221 ('This' . . . 'slave'). The Fool's burlesque prophecy (iii, 2, 79–96) in the Folio (omitted in the Quarto) is commonly regarded as a spurious insertion.

All the evidence for date would fit either 1605 or 1606. One limit is fixed by the performance at court on December 26, 1606; the other by 'these late eclipses in the sun and moon' (i, 2, 112), which occurred in September and October, 1605. The situation and dialogue when the disguised Kent seeks service with the king (i, 4, 9–42) seem to be imitated by Edward Sharpham in his comedy *The Fleire* (sig. C3), where Sir Antifront, likewise disguised, talks in the same vein. *The Fleire* was not printed until 1607, but it was registered on May 13, 1606.

To Lear (Llyr, Ler), a divine but shadowy figure in the mythology of the ancient Britons, of whose children wild tales are told in Irish and Welsh, Geoffrey of Monmouth in his twelfth-century *Historia Regum Britanniae* (ii, 11–15) attached the old folk-tale of the three daughters. From Geoffrey the legend was taken over by Holinshed in his *Chronicle*, by Spenser in *The Faerie Queene* (ii, 10, 27–32), and by John Higgins (1574) in *A Mirrour for Magistrates*. All these books were familiar to every Elizabethan who read anything. The tale had also been dramatized in *The True Chronicle History of King Leir*, printed in 1605. This was entered in the Stationers' Register on May 14, 1594, and performances are recorded by Henslowe in April of that year. In the pre-Shakespearean narratives the story is substantially identical. The catastrophe is quite different from that with which we are familiar. Cordelia is victorious; Lear is restored to the throne, reigns two or three years, and dies peacefully. Cordelia succeeds and reigns for five years. Then her two nephews, the sons of Goneril and Regan, rebel, dethrone her, and shut her up in prison, where she kills herself. The old play ends happily with the triumph of Cordelia and the reinstatement of Lear.

Shakespeare owes little to the old play except the impulse to write a new one. Now and then a phrase reminds us of something in KING LEAR, but these resemblances are trifling. Kent may be foreshadowed by Perillus, but the likeness is shadowy indeed. Perillus is an old man, his protests are very mild, and he is not banished; therefore he does not, like Kent, disguise himself to enter the service of his master. The Messenger whom Regan employs to murder her father may have given a hint for Oswald. The business of the letter (iv, 5) is rather like a scene between Goneril and the Messenger in the old play. In various matters Shakespeare abandons the novel devices of his predecessor: as in i, 1, where the old play complicates the plot by bringing in a scheme of Cordelia's sisters to ensure her giving an unacceptable answer. To Spenser Shakespeare owes nothing except, perhaps, the form 'Cordelia' (for 'Cordeilla' or 'Cordella'). Two lines in Higgins's poem may have suggested Cordelia's remark (i, 1, 102 ff.) about love for some future husband (which is in none of the other sources):

> Yet shortly I may chance, if Fortune will,
> To find in heart to beare another more good will.

But this is a very natural reflection (cf. *Othello* i, 3, 180 ff.). In Lear's intent to show his 'largest bounty' to the most deserving (i, 1, 53–54), Shakespeare is close to Geoffrey ('ut sciat quae illarum maiore regni parte dignior esset') where Holinshed goes astray, and here too the *Mirrour* coincides: 'He thought to guerdon most where fauour most he fand.' In the old play Lear means to divide his kingdom equally, and the test of affection is merely to 'resolue a doubt which much molests [his] mind.'

Gloucester and his two sons do not appear in the ancient legend. Their story Shakespeare adapted from the episode of the King of Paphlagonia in Sidney's *Arcadia* (ii, 10). This he has so dexterously interwoven with the legend that Edmund's villany becomes the determining factor in the tragic catastrophe. Edgar's description of the fiend that led his father to the edge of the cliff (iv, 6, 69 ff.) recalls Horatio's warning to Hamlet (i, 4, 69 ff.).

Eminent critics have found difficulty in reconciling Cordelia's character with her refusal to compete with her sisters' lies by speaking the truth her father longs to hear. The inconsistency was of course obvious to Shakespeare, who has done everything possible to conceal it by introducing the vehement Kent as Cordelia's advocate and by letting France explain her offishness as

> a tardiness in nature
> Which often leaves the history unspoke
> That it intends to do.

But Cordelia finds no difficulty in expressing herself fluently, either in this scene or elsewhere. The inconsistency, however, is not chargeable to Shakespeare. It is the essential point in the ancient story and goes back to a time long anterior to any ideal of probability in narrative. If Shakespeare had changed the tale here, his tragedy would have come to a happy ending in the first act.

Lear's madness has no place in the old story; it is Shakespeare's own invention. Eminent alienists have diagnosed it as senile dementia. His mind was failing, they contend, at the beginning of the play. To the Elizabethans, however, irascibility was not insanity. Nothing can be clearer than that Shakespeare intended Lear's madness to be simply an attack of feverous delirium, brought on by exposure to the storm and superinduced by the terrible strain to which his emotions had been subjected. The physician actually cures him. Even the dreadful events that follow do not overthrow his restored reason, for, when he enters with the murdered Cordelia in his arms, he is not mad. At the moment of death, when his powers fail utterly, so that he cannot recognize his nearest friends, it is not madness but dissolution.

KING LEAR

PHOTOGRAPHS BY JOHN VICKERS
PRODUCED BY THE OLD VIC COMPANY

Laurence Olivier as King Lear

Joyce Redman playing the role of Cordelia

Pamela Brown as the cruel, ungrateful Goneril

Margaret Leighton as the equally evil Regan

Alec Guinness as the fool of King Lear, the retainer most loyal to him in his adversity

Edgar (Michael Warre), Gloucester's loyal son

Above: George Relph as the Earl of Gloucester

Right: Gloucester's son, Edmund (Peter Copley)

King Lear hears the suitors for Cordelia's hand (*Act I, Scene I*)

Lear is offended by Cordelia's refusal to flatter (*Act I, Scene I*)

Lear threatens Kent (Nicholas Hannen) for intervening in behalf of young Cordelia (*Act I, Scene I*)

Left: "You see how full of changes his age is." Goneril and Regan discuss their plans for ridding themselves of their mad father (*Act I, Scene I*)

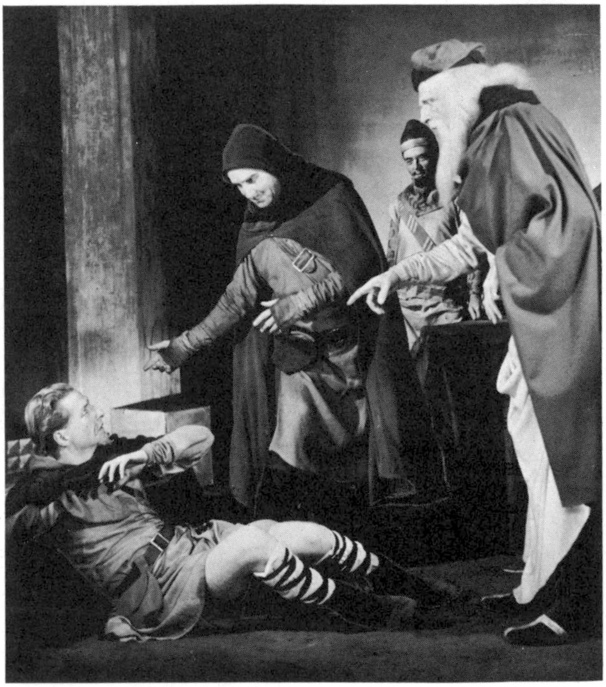

Lear rebukes Oswald (Frank Duncan) as impertinent (*Act I, Scene IV*)

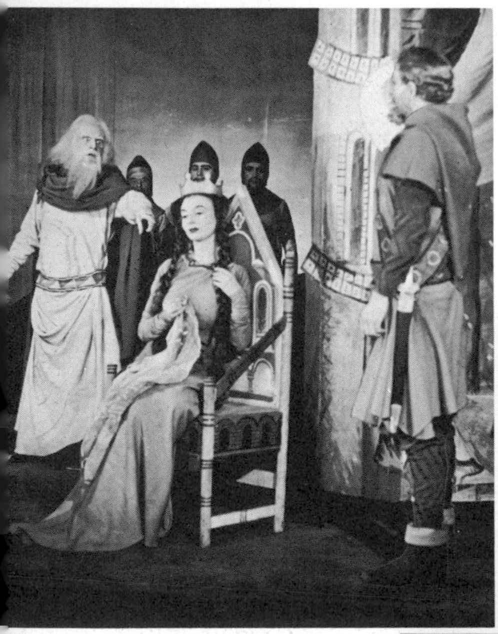

Lear rails against his daughter Goneril for her ingratitude to him (*Act I, Scene IV*)

Lear curses his daughter Regan (*Act II Scene IV*)

"When came this to you? Who brought it?" Edmund shows his father a letter he has forged, supposedly telling of Edgar's plans to murder his father (*Act I, Scene II*)

"Bethink yourself wherein you may have offended him." Edmund affects ignorance of the reason for their father's terrible rage against Edgar (*Act I, Scene II*)

"Look sir, I bleed." Edmund sees his father's sympathy (*Act II, Scene I*)

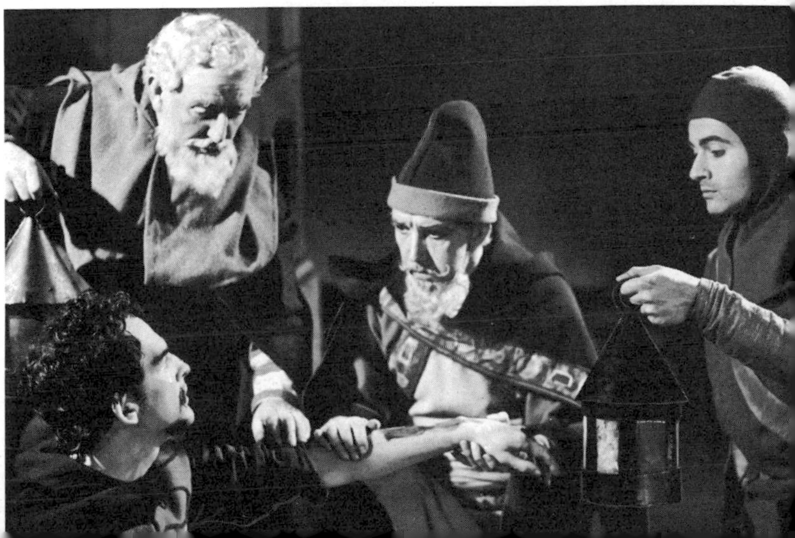

"I'll pray, and then I'll sleep." Lear on the heath (*Act III, Scene IV*)

"Blow, winds, and crack your cheeks!" The king's exasperation reaches its climax (*Act III, Scene II*)

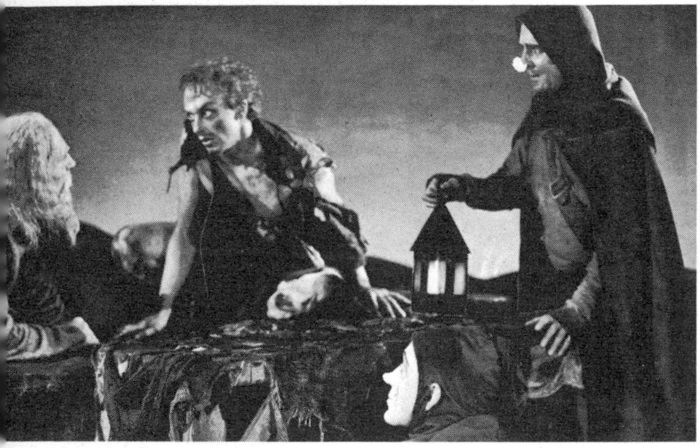

"Do poor Tom some charity." Edgar pretends to be mad in order to escape his father (*Act III, Scene IV*)

"Arraign her first; 'tis Goneril." In his madness, Lear imagines his daughters brought before him for judgment (*Act III, Scene VI*)

"You are not worth the dust which the rude wind blows in your face." Albany (Cecil Winter) is horrified by the cruelty of his wife, Goneril, to her father (*Act IV, Scene II*)

Lear and the blinded Gloucester meet on the heath and lament together (*Act IV, Scene VI*)

Above: "Sir, do you know me?" Cordelia seeks to recall her father from his insane meandering (*Act IV, Scene VII*)

Left: "I think this lady to be my child Cordelia." Lear united with his daughter (*Act IV, Scene VII*)

"Howl, howl, howl, howl! O! you are men of stones." Lear brings in the body of Cordelia (*Act V, Scene III*)

Below: "Vex not his ghost: O! let him pass" (*Act V, Scene III*)

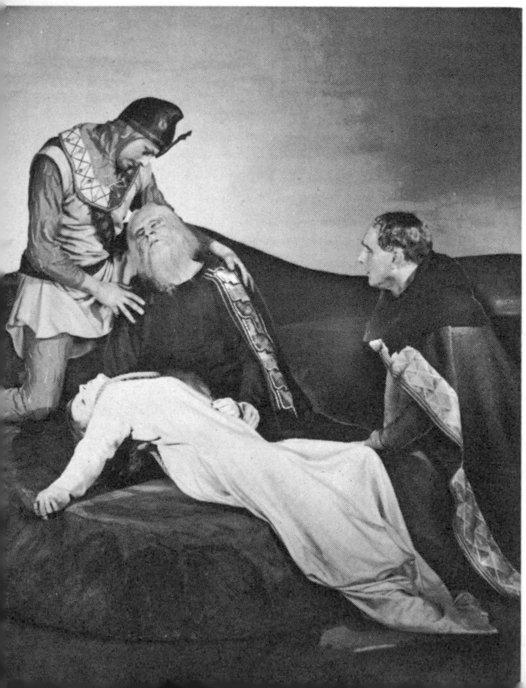

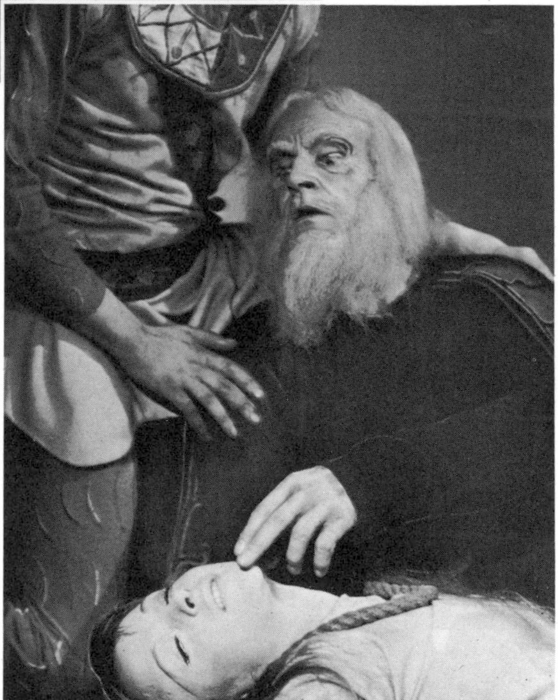

"Why should a dog, a horse, a rat, have life, and thou no breath at all?" King Lear mourns over Cordelia's body (*Act V, Scene III*)

THE TRAGEDY OF KING LEAR

[Dramatis Personæ.

Lear, King of Britain.
King of France.
Duke of Burgundy.
Duke of Cornwall.
Duke of Albany.
Earl of Kent.
Earl of Gloucester.
Edgar, son to *Gloucester.*
Edmund, bastard son to *Gloucester.*
Curan, a courtier.
Old Man, tenant to *Gloucester.*
Doctor.
Lear's Fool.
Oswald, Steward to *Goneril.*
A Captain under *Edmund's* command.
Gentleman, attendant on *Cordelia.*
A Herald.
Servants to *Cornwall.*

Goneril, *Regan*, *Cordelia*, } daughters to *Lear.*

Knights attending on *Lear*, Officers, Messengers, Soldiers, Attendants.

SCENE. — *Britain.*]

ACT I. Scene I. [King Lear's *Palace.*]

Enter *Kent, Gloucester*, and *Edmund.* [*Kent* and *Gloucester* converse. *Edmund* stands back.]

Kent. I thought the King had more affected the Duke of Albany than Cornwall.

Glou. It did always seem so to us; but now, in the division of the kingdom, it appears not which of the Dukes he values most, for equalities are so weigh'd that curiosity in neither can make choice of either's moiety.

Kent. Is not this your son, my lord?

Glou. His breeding, sir, hath been at my charge. I have so often blush'd to acknowledge him that now I am braz'd to't.

Kent. I cannot conceive you.

Glou. Sir, this young fellow's mother could; whereupon she grew round-womb'd, and had indeed, sir, a son for her cradle ere she had a husband for her bed. Do you smell a fault?

Kent. I cannot wish the fault undone, the issue of it being so proper.

Glou. But I have, sir, a son by order of law, some year elder than this, who yet is no dearer in my account. Though this knave came something saucily into the world before he was sent for, yet was his mother fair, there was good sport at his making, and the whoreson must be acknowledged. — Do you know this noble gentleman, Edmund?

Edm. [*comes forward*] No, my lord.

Glou. My Lord of Kent. Remember him hereafter as my honourable friend.

Edm. My services to your lordship.

Kent. I must love you, and sue to know you better.

Edm. Sir, I shall study deserving.

Glou. He hath been out nine years, and away he shall again. *Sound a sennet.* The King is coming.

Enter *one bearing a coronet*; then *Lear*; then the *Dukes of Albany* and *Cornwall*; next, *Goneril, Regan, Cordelia*, with *Followers.*

Lear. Attend the lords of France and Burgundy, Gloucester.

Glou. I shall, my liege.

Exeunt [*Gloucester and Edmund*].

Lear. Meantime we shall express our darker purpose.
Give me the map there. Know we have divided
In three our kingdom; and 'tis our fast intent
To shake all cares and business from our age,
Conferring them on younger strengths while we
Unburthen'd crawl toward death. Our son of Cornwall,
And you, our no less loving son of Albany,
We have this hour a constant will to publish
Our daughters' several dowers, that future strife
May be prevented now. The princes, France and Burgundy,
Great rivals in our youngest daughter's love,
Long in our court have made their amorous sojourn,

And here are to be answer'd. Tell me, my daughters
(Since now we will divest us both of rule,
Interest of territory, cares of state),
Which of you shall we say doth love us most?
That we our largest bounty may extend
Where nature doth with merit challenge. Goneril,
Our eldest-born, speak first.

Gon. Sir, I love you more than words can wield the matter;
Dearer than eyesight, space, and liberty;
Beyond what can be valued, rich or rare;
No less than life, with grace, health, beauty, honour;
As much as child e'er lov'd, or father found;
A love that makes breath poor, and speech unable.
Beyond all manner of so much I love you.

Cor. [*aside*] What shall Cordelia speak? Love, and be silent.

Lear. Of all these bounds, even from this line to this,
With shadowy forests and with champains rich'd,
With plenteous rivers and wide-skirted meads,
We make thee lady. To thine and Albany's issue
Be this perpetual. — What says our second daughter,
Our dearest Regan, wife to Cornwall? Speak.

Reg. Sir, I am made
Of the selfsame metal that my sister is,
And prize me at her worth. In my true heart
I find she names my very deed of love;
Only she comes too short, that I profess
Myself an enemy to all other joys
Which the most precious square of sense possesses,
And find I am alone felicitate
In your dear Highness' love.

Cor. [*aside*] Then poor Cordelia!
And yet not so; since I am sure my love's
More richer than my tongue.

Lear. To thee and thine hereditary ever
Remain this ample third of our fair kingdom,
No less in space, validity, and pleasure
Than that conferr'd on Goneril. — Now, our joy,
Although the last, not least; to whose young love
The vines of France and milk of Burgundy
Strive to be interest; what can you say to draw
A third more opulent than your sisters? Speak.

Cor. Nothing, my lord.

Lear. Nothing?

Cor. Nothing.

Lear. Nothing can come of nothing. Speak again.

Cor. Unhappy that I am, I cannot heave
My heart into my mouth. I love your Majesty
According to my bond; no more nor less.

Lear. How, how, Cordelia? Mend your speech a little,
Lest it may mar your fortunes.

Cor. Good my lord,
You have begot me, bred me, lov'd me; I
Return those duties back as are right fit,
Obey you, love you, and most honour you.
Why have my sisters husbands, if they say
They love you all? Haply, when I shall wed,
That lord whose hand must take my plight shall carry
Half my love with him, half my care and duty.
Sure I shall never marry like my sisters,
To love my father all.

Lear. But goes thy heart with this?

Cor. Ay, good my lord.

Lear. So young, and so untender?

Cor. So young, my lord, and true.

Lear. Let it be so! thy truth then be thy dower!
For, by the sacred radiance of the sun,
The mysteries of Hecate and the night;
By all the operation of the orbs
From whom we do exist and cease to be;
Here I disclaim all my paternal care,
Propinquity and property of blood,
And as a stranger to my heart and me
Hold thee from this for ever. The barbarous Scythian,
Or he that makes his generation messes
To gorge his appetite, shall to my bosom
Be as well neighbour'd, pitied, and reliev'd,
As thou my sometime daughter.

Kent. Good my liege —

Lear. Peace, Kent!
Come not between the dragon and his wrath.
I lov'd her most, and thought to set my rest
On her kind nursery. — Hence and avoid my sight! —
So be my grave my peace as here I give
Her father's heart from her! Call France! Who stirs?
Call Burgundy! Cornwall and Albany,
With my two daughters' dowers digest this third;
Let pride, which she calls plainness, marry her.
I do invest you jointly in my power,
Preëminence, and all the large effects

That troop with majesty. Ourself, by monthly course,
With reservation of an hundred knights,
By you to be sustain'd, shall our abode
Make with you by due turns. Only we still retain
The name, and all th' additions to a king. The sway,
Revenue, execution of the rest,
Beloved sons, be yours; which to confirm,
This coronet part betwixt you.
Kent. Royal Lear,
Whom I have ever honour'd as my king,
Lov'd as my father, as my master follow'd,
As my great patron thought on in my prayers —
Lear. The bow is bent and drawn; make from the shaft.
Kent. Let it fall rather, though the fork invade
The region of my heart! Be Kent unmannerly
When Lear is mad. What wouldst thou do, old man?
Think'st thou that duty shall have dread to speak
When power to flattery bows? To plainness honour's bound
When majesty falls to folly. Reverse thy doom;
And in thy best consideration check
This hideous rashness. Answer my life my judgment,
Thy youngest daughter does not love thee least,
Nor are those empty-hearted whose low sound
Reverbs no hollowness.
Lear. Kent, on thy life, no more!
Kent. My life I never held but as a pawn
To wage against thine enemies; nor fear to lose it,
Thy safety being the motive.
Lear. Out of my sight!
Kent. See better, Lear, and let me still remain
The true blank of thine eye.
Lear. Now by Apollo —
Kent. Now by Apollo, King,
Thou swear'st thy gods in vain.
Lear. O vassal! miscreant!
[*Lays his hand on his sword.*]
Alb., Corn. Dear sir, forbear!
Kent. Do!
Kill thy physician, and the fee bestow
Upon the foul disease. Revoke thy gift,
Or, whilst I can vent clamour from my throat,
I'll tell thee thou dost evil.
Lear. Hear me, recreant!
On thine allegiance, hear me!
Since thou hast sought to make us break our vow —
Which we durst never yet — and with strain'd pride
To come between our sentence and our power, —
Which nor our nature nor our place can bear, —
Our potency made good, take thy reward.
Five days we do allot thee for provision
To shield thee from diseases of the world,
And on the sixth to turn thy hated back
Upon our kingdom. If, on the tenth day following,
Thy banish'd trunk be found in our dominions,
The moment is thy death. Away! By Jupiter,
This shall not be revok'd.
Kent. Fare thee well, King. Since thus thou wilt appear,
Freedom lives hence, and banishment is here.
[*To Cordelia*] The gods to their dear shelter take thee, maid,
That justly think'st and hast most rightly said!
[*To Regan and Goneril*] And your large speeches may your deeds approve,
That good effects may spring from words of love.
Thus Kent, O princes, bids you all adieu;
He'll shape his old course in a country new.
Exit.

Flourish. Enter *Gloucester*, with *France* and *Burgundy*; *Attendants*.

Glou. Here's France and Burgundy, my noble lord.
Lear. My Lord of Burgundy,
We first address toward you, who with this king
Hath rivall'd for our daughter. What in the least
Will you require in present dower with her,
Or cease your quest of love?
Bur. Most royal Majesty,
I crave no more than hath your Highness offer'd,
Nor will you tender less.
Lear. Right noble Burgundy,
When she was dear to us, we did hold her so;
But now her price is fall'n. Sir, there she stands.
If aught within that little seeming substance,
Or all of it, with our displeasure piec'd,
And nothing more, may fitly like your Grace,
She's there, and she is yours.
Bur. I know no answer.
Lear. Will you, with those infirmities she owes,

Unfriended, new adopted to our hate,
Dow'r'd with our curse, and stranger'd with our oath,
Take her, or leave her?

Bur. Pardon me, royal sir.
Election makes not up on such conditions.

Lear. Then leave her, sir; for, by the pow'r that made me,
I tell you all her wealth. [*To France*] For you, great King,
I would not from your love make such a stray
To match you where I hate; therefore beseech you
T' avert your liking a more worthier way
Than on a wretch whom nature is asham'd
Almost t' acknowledge hers.

France. This is most strange,
That she that even but now was your best object,
The argument of your praise, balm of your age,
Most best, most dearest, should in this trice of time
Commit a thing so monstrous to dismantle
So many folds of favour. Sure her offence
Must be of such unnatural degree
That monsters it, or your fore-vouch'd affection
Fall'n into taint; which to believe of her
Must be a faith that reason without miracle
Should never plant in me.

Cor. I yet beseech your Majesty,
If for I want that glib and oily art
To speak and purpose not, since what I well intend,
I'll do't before I speak — that you make known
It is no vicious blot, murther, or foulness,
No unchaste action or dishonoured step,
That hath depriv'd me of your grace and favour;
But even for want of that for which I am richer —
A still-soliciting eye, and such a tongue
As I am glad I have not, though not to have it
Hath lost me in your liking.

Lear. Better thou
Hadst not been born than not t' have pleas'd me better.

France. Is it but this — a tardiness in nature
Which often leaves the history unspoke
That it intends to do? My Lord of Burgundy,
What say you to the lady? Love 's not love
When it is mingled with regards that stands
Aloof from th' entire point. Will you have her?
She is herself a dowry.

Bur. Royal Lear,
Give but that portion which yourself propos'd,
And here I take Cordelia by the hand,
Duchess of Burgundy.

Lear. Nothing! I have sworn; I am firm.

Bur. I am sorry then you have so lost a father
That you must lose a husband.

Cor. Peace be with Burgundy!
Since that respects of fortune are his love,
I shall not be his wife.

France. Fairest Cordelia, that art most rich, being poor;
Most choice, forsaken; and most lov'd, despis'd!
Thee and thy virtues here I seize upon.
Be it lawful I take up what's cast away.
Gods, gods! 'tis strange that from their cold'st neglect
My love should kindle to inflam'd respect.
Thy dow'rless daughter, King, thrown to my chance,
Is queen of us, of ours, and our fair France.
Not all the dukes in wat'rish Burgundy
Can buy this unpriz'd precious maid of me.
Bid them farewell, Cordelia, though unkind.
Thou losest here, a better where to find.

Lear. Thou hast her, France; let her be thine; for we
Have no such daughter, nor shall ever see
That face of hers again. Therefore be gone
Without our grace, our love, our benison.
Come, noble Burgundy.

Flourish. Exeunt Lear, Burgundy, [*Cornwall, Albany, Gloucester, and Attendants*].

France. Bid farewell to your sisters.

Cor. The jewels of our father, with wash'd eyes
Cordelia leaves you. I know you what you are;
And, like a sister, am most loath to call
Your faults as they are nam'd. Use well our father.
To your professed bosoms I commit him;
But yet, alas, stood I within his grace,
I would prefer him to a better place!
So farewell to you both.

Gon. Prescribe not us our duties.

Reg. Let your study
Be to content your lord, who hath receiv'd you
At fortune's alms. You have obedience scanted,
And well are worth the want that you have wanted.

Cor. Time shall unfold what plighted cunning hides.
Who cover faults, at last shame them derides.
Well may you prosper!

France. Come, my fair Cordelia.

Exeunt France and Cordelia.

Gon. Sister, it is not little I have to say of what most nearly appertains to us both. I think our father will hence to-night.

Reg. That's most certain, and with you; next month with us.

Gon. You see how full of changes his age is. The observation we have made of it hath not been little. He always lov'd our sister most, and with what poor judgment he hath now cast her off appears too grossly.

Reg. 'Tis the infirmity of his age; yet he hath ever but slenderly known himself.

Gon. The best and soundest of his time hath been but rash; then must we look to receive from his age, not alone the imperfections of long-ingraffed condition, but therewithal the unruly waywardness that infirm and choleric years bring with them.

Reg. Such unconstant starts are we like to have from him as this of Kent's banishment.

Gon. There is further compliment of leave-taking between France and him. Pray you let's hit together. If our father carry authority with such dispositions as he bears, this last surrender of his will but offend us.

Reg. We shall further think on't.

Gon. We must do something, and i' th' heat.

Exeunt.

Scene II. [The Earl of Gloucester's *Castle.*]

Enter [*Edmund* the] *Bastard* solus, [with a letter].

Edm. Thou, Nature, art my goddess; to thy law
My services are bound. Wherefore should I
Stand in the plague of custom, and permit
The curiosity of nations to deprive me,
For that I am some twelve or fourteen moonshines
Lag of a brother? Why bastard? wherefore base?
When my dimensions are as well compact,
My mind as generous, and my shape as true,
As honest madam's issue? Why brand they us
With base? with baseness? bastardy? base, base?
Who, in the lusty stealth of nature, take
More composition and fierce quality
Than doth, within a dull, stale, tired bed,
Go to th' creating a whole tribe of fops
Got 'tween asleep and wake? Well then,
Legitimate Edgar, I must have your land.
Our father's love is to the bastard Edmund
As to th' legitimate. Fine word — 'legitimate'!
Well, my legitimate, if this letter speed,
And my invention thrive, Edmund the base
Shall top th' legitimate. I grow; I prosper.
Now, gods, stand up for bastards!

Enter *Gloucester.*

Glou. Kent banish'd thus? and France in choler parted?
And the King gone to-night? subscrib'd his pow'r?
Confin'd to exhibition? All this done
Upon the gad? Edmund, how now? What news?

Edm. So please your lordship, none.

[*Puts up the letter.*]

Glou. Why so earnestly seek you to put up that letter?

Edm. I know no news, my lord.

Glou. What paper were you reading?

Edm. Nothing, my lord.

Glou. No? What needed then that terrible dispatch of it into your pocket? The quality of nothing hath not such need to hide itself. Let's see. Come, if it be nothing, I shall not need spectacles.

Edm. I beseech you, sir, pardon me. It is a letter from my brother that I have not all o'er-read; and for so much as I have perus'd, I find it not fit for your o'erlooking.

Glou. Give me the letter, sir.

Edm. I shall offend, either to detain or give it. The contents, as in part I understand them, are to blame.

Glou. Let's see, let's see!

Edm. I hope, for my brother's justification, he wrote this but as an essay or taste of my virtue.

Glou. (*reads*) 'This policy and reverence of age makes the world bitter to the best of our times; keeps our fortunes from us till our oldness cannot relish them. I begin to find an idle and fond bondage in the oppression of aged tyranny, who sways, not as it hath power, but as it is suffer'd. Come to me, that of this I may speak more. If our father would sleep till I wak'd him, you should enjoy half his revenue for ever, and live the beloved of your brother,

'EDGAR.'

Hum! Conspiracy? 'Sleep till I wak'd him, you should enjoy half his revenue.' My son Edgar! Had he a hand to write this? a heart and brain to breed it in? When came this to you? Who brought it?

Edm. It was not brought me, my lord: there's the cunning of it. I found it thrown in at the casement of my closet.

Glou. You know the character to be your brother's?

Edm. If the matter were good, my lord, I durst swear it were his; but in respect of that, I would fain think it were not.

Glou. It is his.

Edm. It is his hand, my lord; but I hope his heart is not in the contents.

Glou. Hath he never before sounded you in this business?

Edm. Never, my lord. But I have heard him oft maintain it to be fit that, sons at perfect age, and fathers declining, the father should be as ward to the son, and the son manage his revenue.

Glou. O villain, villain! His very opinion in the letter! Abhorred villain! Unnatural, detested, brutish villain! worse than brutish! Go, sirrah, seek him. I'll apprehend him. Abominable villain! Where is he?

Edm. I do not well know, my lord. If it shall please you to suspend your indignation against my brother till you can derive from him better testimony of his intent, you should run a certain course; where, if you violently proceed against him, mistaking his purpose, it would make a great gap in your own honour and shake in pieces the heart of his obedience. I dare pawn down my life for him that he hath writ this to feel my affection to your honour, and to no other pretence of danger.

Glou. Think you so?

Edm. If your honour judge it meet, I will place you where you shall hear us confer of this and by an auricular assurance have your satisfaction, and that without any further delay than this very evening.

Glou. He cannot be such a monster.

Edm. Nor is not, sure.

Glou. To his father, that so tenderly and entirely loves him. Heaven and earth! Edmund, seek him out; wind me into him, I pray you; frame the business after your own wisdom. I would unstate myself to be in a due resolution.

Edm. I will seek him, sir, presently; convey the business as I shall find means, and acquaint you withal.

Glou. These late eclipses in the sun and moon portend no good to us. Though the wisdom of nature can reason it thus and thus, yet nature finds itself scourg'd by the sequent effects. Love cools, friendship falls off, brothers divide. In cities, mutinies; in countries, discord; in palaces, treason; and the bond crack'd 'twixt son and father. This villain of mine comes under the prediction; there's son against father: the King falls from bias of nature; there's father against child. We have seen the best of our time. Machinations, hollowness, treachery, and all ruinous disorders follow us disquietly to our graves. Find out this villain, Edmund; it shall lose thee nothing; do it carefully. And the noble and true-hearted Kent banish'd! his offence, honesty! 'Tis strange. *Exit.*

Edm. This is the excellent foppery of the world, that, when we are sick in fortune, often the surfeit of our own behaviour, we make guilty of our disasters the sun, the moon, and the stars; as if we were villains on necessity; fools by heavenly compulsion; knaves, thieves, and treachers by spherical predominance; drunkards, liars, and adulterers by an enforc'd obedience of planetary influence; and all that we are evil in, by a divine thrusting on. An admirable evasion of whoremaster man, to lay his goatish disposition to the charge of a star! My father compounded with my mother under the Dragon's Tail, and my nativity was under Ursa Major, so that it follows I am rough and lecherous. Fut! I should have been that I am, had the maidenliest star in the firmament twinkled on my bastardizing. Edgar —

Enter *Edgar.*

and pat! he comes, like the catastrophe of the old comedy. My cue is villanous melancholy, with a sigh like Tom o' Bedlam. O, these eclipses do portend these divisions! Fa, sol, la, mi.

Edg. How now, brother Edmund? What serious contemplation are you in?

Edm. I am thinking, brother, of a prediction I read this other day, what should follow these eclipses.

Edg. Do you busy yourself with that?

Edm. I promise you, the effects he writes of succeed unhappily: as of unnaturalness between the child and the parent; death, dearth, dissolutions of ancient amities; divisions in state, menaces and maledictions against king and nobles; needless diffidences, banishment of friends, dissipation of cohorts, nuptial breaches, and I know not what.

Edg. How long have you been a sectary astronomical?

Edm. Come, come! When saw you my father last?

Edg. The night gone by.

Edm. Spake you with him?

Edg. Ay, two hours together.

Edm. Parted you in good terms? Found you no displeasure in him by word or countenance?

Edg. None at all.

Edm. Bethink yourself wherein you may have offended him; and at my entreaty forbear his presence until some little time hath qualified the heat of his displeasure, which at this instant so rageth in him that with the mischief of your person it would scarcely allay.

Edg. Some villain hath done me wrong.

Edm. That's my fear. I pray you have a continent forbearance till the speed of his rage goes slower; and, as I say, retire with me to my lodging, from whence I will fitly bring you to hear my lord speak. Pray ye, go! There's my key. If you do stir abroad, go arm'd.

Edg. Arm'd, brother?

Edm. Brother, I advise you to the best. Go arm'd. I am no honest man if there be any good meaning toward you. I have told you what I have seen and heard; but faintly, nothing like the image and horror of it. Pray you, away!

Edg. Shall I hear from you anon?

Edm. I do serve you in this business.

Exit Edgar.

A credulous father! and a brother noble,
Whose nature is so far from doing harms
That he suspects none; on whose foolish honesty
My practices ride easy! I see the business.
Let me, if not by birth, have lands by wit;
All with me's meet that I can fashion fit.

Exit.

Scene III. [The Duke of Albany's *Palace.*]

Enter *Goneril* and [her] *Steward* [*Oswald*].

Gon. Did my father strike my gentleman for chiding of his fool?

Osw. Ay, madam.

Gon. By day and night, he wrongs me! Every hour
He flashes into one gross crime or other
That sets us all at odds. I'll not endure it.
His knights grow riotous, and himself upbraids us
On every trifle. When he returns from hunting,
I will not speak with him. Say I am sick.
If you come slack of former services,
You shall do well; the fault of it I'll answer.

[*Horns within.*]

Osw. He's coming, madam; I hear him.

Gon. Put on what weary negligence you please,
You and your fellows. I'd have it come to question.
If he distaste it, let him to our sister,
Whose mind and mine I know in that are one,
Not to be overrul'd. Idle old man,
That still would manage those authorities
That he hath given away! Now, by my life,
Old fools are babes again, and must be us'd
With checks as flatteries, when they are seen abus'd.
Remember what I have said.

Osw. Very well, madam.

Gon. And let his knights have colder looks among you.
What grows of it, no matter. Advise your fellows so.
I would breed from hence occasions, and I shall.
That I may speak. I'll write straight to my sister
To hold my very course. Prepare for dinner.

Exeunt.

Scene IV. [The Duke of Albany's *Palace.*]

Enter *Kent*, [disguised].

Kent. If but as well I other accents borrow,
That can my speech defuse, my good intent
May carry through itself to that full issue
For which I raz'd my likeness. Now, banish'd Kent,
If thou canst serve where thou dost stand condemn'd,
So may it come, thy master, whom thou lov'st,
Shall find thee full of labours.

Horns within. Enter *Lear*, [*Knights*,] and *Attendants*.

Lear. Let me not stay a jot for dinner; go get it ready. [*Exit an Attendant.*] How now? What art thou?

Kent. A man, sir.

Lear. What dost thou profess? What wouldst thou with us?

Kent. I do profess to be no less than I seem, to serve him truly that will put me in trust, to love him that is honest, to converse with him that is wise and says little, to fear judgment, to fight when I cannot choose, and to eat no fish.

Lear. What art thou?

Kent. A very honest-hearted fellow, and as poor as the King.

Lear. If thou be'st as poor for a subject as he's for a king, thou art poor enough. What wouldst thou?

Kent. Service.

Lear. Who wouldst thou serve?

Kent. You.

Lear. Dost thou know me, fellow?

Kent. No, sir; but you have that in your countenance which I would fain call master.

Lear. What's that?

Kent. Authority.

Lear. What services canst thou do?

Kent. I can keep honest counsel, ride, run, mar a curious tale in telling it and deliver a plain message bluntly. That which ordinary men are fit for, I am qualified in, and the best of me is diligence.

Lear. How old art thou?

Kent. Not so young, sir, to love a woman for singing, nor so old to dote on her for anything. I have years on my back forty-eight.

Lear. Follow me; thou shalt serve me. If I like thee no worse after dinner, I will not part from thee yet. Dinner, ho, dinner! Where's my knave? my fool? Go you and call my fool hither.

[*Exit an Attendant.*]

Enter [*Oswald* the] *Steward.*

You, you, sirrah, where's my daughter?

Osw. So please you — *Exit.*

Lear. What says the fellow there? Call the clotpoll back. [*Exit a Knight.*] Where's my fool, ho? I think the world's asleep.

[Enter *Knight.*]

How now? Where's that mongrel?

Knight. He says, my lord, your daughter is not well.

Lear. Why came not the slave back to me when I call'd him?

Knight. Sir, he answered me in the roundest manner, he would not.

Lear. He would not?

Knight. My lord, I know not what the matter is; but to my judgment your Highness is not entertain'd with that ceremonious affection as you were wont. There's a great abatement of kindness appears as well in the general dependants as in the Duke himself also and your daughter.

Lear. Ha! say'st thou so?

Knight. I beseech you pardon me, my lord, if I be mistaken; for my duty cannot be silent when I think your Highness wrong'd.

Lear. Thou but remember'st me of mine own conception. I have perceived a most faint neglect of late, which I have rather blamed as mine own jealous curiosity than as a very pretence and purpose of unkindness. I will look further into't. But where's my fool? I have not seen him this two days.

Knight. Since my young lady's going into France, sir, the fool hath much pined away.

Lear. No more of that; I have noted it well. Go you and tell my daughter I would speak with her. [*Exit Knight.*] Go you, call hither my fool.

[*Exit an Attendant.*]

Enter [*Oswald* the] *Steward.*

O, you, sir, you! Come you hither, sir. Who am I, sir?

Osw. My lady's father.

Lear. 'My lady's father'? My lord's knave! You whoreson dog! you slave! you cur!

Osw. I am none of these, my lord; I beseech your pardon.

Lear. Do you bandy looks with me, you rascal? [*Strikes him.*]

Osw. I'll not be strucken, my lord.

Kent. Nor tripp'd neither, you base football player? [*Trips up his heels.*]

Lear. I thank thee, fellow. Thou serv'st me, and I'll love thee.

Kent. Come, sir, arise, away! I'll teach you differences. Away, away! If you will measure your lubber's length again, tarry; but away! Go to! Have you wisdom? So.

[*Pushes him out.*]

Lear. Now, my friendly knave, I thank thee. There's earnest of thy service.

[*Gives money.*]

Enter *Fool.*

Fool. Let me hire him too. Here's my coxcomb. [*Offers Kent his cap.*]

Lear. How now, my pretty knave? How dost thou?

Fool. Sirrah, you were best take my coxcomb.

Kent. Why, fool?

Fool. Why? For taking one's part that's out of favour. Nay, an thou canst not smile as the wind sits, thou'lt catch cold shortly. There, take my coxcomb! Why, this fellow hath banish'd two on's daughters, and did the third a blessing against his will. If thou follow him, thou must needs wear my coxcomb. — How now, nuncle? Would I had two coxcombs and two daughters!

Lear. Why, my boy?

Fool. If I gave them all my living, I'ld keep my coxcombs myself. There's mine! beg another of thy daughters.

Lear. Take heed, sirrah — the whip.

Fool. Truth's a dog must to kennel; he must be whipp'd out, when Lady the brach may stand by th' fire and stink.

Lear. A pestilent gall to me!

Fool. Sirrah, I'll teach thee a speech.

Lear. Do.

Fool. Mark it, nuncle.

Have more than thou showest,
Speak less than thou knowest,
Lend less than thou owest,
Ride more than thou goest,
Learn more than thou trowest,
Set less than thou throwest;
Leave thy drink and thy whore,
And keep in-a-door,
And thou shalt have more
Than two tens to a score.

Kent. This is nothing, fool.

Fool. Then 'tis like the breath of an unfeed lawyer — you gave me nothing for't. Can you make no use of nothing, nuncle?

Lear. Why, no, boy. Nothing can be made out of nothing.

Fool. [*to Kent*] Prithee tell him, so much the rent of his land comes to. He will not believe a fool.

Lear. A bitter fool!

Fool. Dost thou know the difference, my boy, between a bitter fool and a sweet fool?

Lear. No, lad; teach me.

Fool. That lord that counsell'd thee
To give away thy land,
Come place him here by me —
Do thou for him stand.
The sweet and bitter fool
Will presently appear;
The one in motley here,
The other found out there.

Lear. Dost thou call me fool, boy?

Fool. All thy other titles thou hast given away; that thou wast born with.

Kent. This is not altogether fool, my lord.

Fool. No, faith; lords and great men will not let me. If I had a monopoly out, they would have part on't. And ladies too, they will not let me have all the fool to myself; they'll be snatching. Give me an egg, nuncle, and I'll give thee two crowns.

Lear. What two crowns shall they be?

Fool. Why, after I have cut the egg i' th' middle and eat up the meat, the two crowns of the egg. When thou clovest thy crown i' th' middle and gav'st away both parts, thou bor'st thine ass on thy back o'er the dirt. Thou hadst little wit in thy bald crown when thou gav'st thy golden one away. If I speak like myself in this, let him be whipp'd that first finds it so.

[*Sings*] Fools had ne'er less grace in a year,
For wise men are grown foppish;
They know not how their wits to wear,
Their manners are so apish.

Lear. When were you wont to be so full of songs, sirrah?

Fool. I have us'd it, nuncle, ever since thou mad'st thy daughters thy mother; for when thou gav'st them the rod, and put'st down thine own breeches,

[*Sings*] Then they for sudden joy did weep,
And I for sorrow sung,
That such a king should play bo-peep
And go the fools among.

Prithee, nuncle, keep a schoolmaster that can teach thy fool to lie. I would fain learn to lie.

Lear. An you lie, sirrah, we'll have you whipp'd.

Fool. I marvel what kin thou and thy daughters are. They'll have me whipp'd for speaking true; thou'lt have me whipp'd for lying; and sometimes I am whipp'd for holding my peace. I had rather be any kind o' thing than a fool! And yet I would not be thee, nuncle. Thou hast pared thy wit o' both sides and left nothing i' th' middle. Here comes one o' the parings.

Enter *Goneril.*

Lear. How now, daughter? What makes that frontlet on? Methinks you are too much o' late i' th' frown.

Fool. Thou wast a pretty fellow when thou hadst no need to care for her frowning. Now thou art an O without a figure. I am better than thou art now: I am a fool, thou art nothing. [*To Goneril*] Yes, forsooth, I will hold my tongue. So your face bids me, though you say nothing. Mum, mum!

He that keeps nor crust nor crum,
Weary of all, shall want some. —

[*Points at Lear*] That's a sheal'd peascod.

Gon. Not only, sir, this your all-licens'd fool,
But other of your insolent retinue
Do hourly carp and quarrel, breaking forth
In rank and not-to-be-endured riots. Sir,
I had thought, by making this well known unto you,
To have found a safe redress, but now grow fearful,
By what yourself, too, late have spoke and done,
That you protect this course, and put it on
By your allowance; which if you should, the fault
Would not scape censure, nor the redresses sleep,
Which, in the tender of a wholesome weal,
Might in their working do you that offence
Which else were shame, that then necessity
Must call discreet proceeding.
Fool. For you know, nuncle,

The hedge-sparrow fed the cuckoo so long
That it had it head bit off by it young.

So out went the candle, and we were left darkling.
Lear. Are you our daughter?
Gon. Come, sir,
I would you would make use of that good wisdom
Whereof I know you are fraught, and put away
These dispositions that of late transform you
From what you rightly are.
Fool. May not an ass know when the cart draws the horse?
Whoop, Jug, I love thee!
Lear. Doth any here know me? This is not Lear.
Doth Lear walk thus? speak thus? Where are his eyes?
Either his notion weakens, his discernings
Are lethargied — Ha! waking? 'Tis not so!
Who is it that can tell me who I am?
Fool. Lear's shadow.
Lear. I would learn that; for, by the marks of sovereignty,
Knowledge, and reason, I should be false persuaded
I had daughters.
Fool. Which they will make an obedient father.
Lear. Your name, fair gentlewoman?
Gon. This admiration, sir, is much o' th' savour
Of other your new pranks. I do beseech you
To understand my purposes aright.
As you are old and reverend, you should be wise.
Here do you keep a hundred knights and squires;
Men so disorder'd, so debosh'd, and bold
That this our court, infected with their manners,
Shows like a riotous inn. Epicurism and lust
Make it more like a tavern or a brothel
Than a grac'd palace. The shame itself doth speak
For instant remedy. Be then desir'd
By her that else will take the thing she begs
A little to disquantity your train,
And the remainder that shall still depend
To be such men as may besort your age,
Which know themselves, and you.
Lear. Darkness and devils!
Saddle my horses! Call my train together!
Degenerate bastard, I'll not trouble thee;
Yet have I left a daughter.
Gon. You strike my people, and your disorder'd rabble
Make servants of their betters.

Enter *Albany*.

Lear. Woe that too late repents! — O, sir, are you come?
Is it your will? Speak, sir! — Prepare my horses.
Ingratitude, thou marble-hearted fiend,
More hideous when thou show'st thee in a child
Than the sea-monster!
Alb. Pray, sir, be patient.
Lear. [*to Goneril*] Detested kite, thou liest!
My train are men of choice and rarest parts,
That all particulars of duty know
And in the most exact regard support
The worships of their name. — O most small fault,
How ugly didst thou in Cordelia show!
Which, like an engine, wrench'd my frame of nature
From the fix'd place; drew from my heart all love
And added to the gall. O Lear, Lear, Lear!
Beat at this gate that let thy folly in [*Strikes his head.*]
And thy dear judgment out! Go, go, my people.
Alb. My lord, I am guiltless, as I am ignorant
Of what hath mov'd you.
Lear. It may be so, my lord
Hear, Nature, hear! dear goddess, hear!
Suspend thy purpose, if thou didst intend
To make this creature fruitful.

Into her womb convey sterility;
Dry up in her the organs of increase;
And from her derogate body never spring
A babe to honour her! If she must teem,
Create her child of spleen, that it may live
And be a thwart disnatur'd torment to her.
Let it stamp wrinkles in her brow of youth,
With cadent tears fret channels in her cheeks,
Turn all her mother's pains and benefits
To laughter and contempt, that she may feel
How sharper than a serpent's tooth it is
To have a thankless child! Away, away! *Exit.*

Alb. Now, gods that we adore, whereof comes this?

Gon. Never afflict yourself to know the cause;
But let his disposition have that scope
That dotage gives it.

Enter *Lear.*

Lear. What, fifty of my followers at a clap?
Within a fortnight?

Alb. What's the matter, sir?

Lear. I'll tell thee. [*To Goneril*] Life and death! I am asham'd
That thou hast power to shake my manhood thus;
That these hot tears, which break from me perforce,
Should make thee worth them. Blasts and fogs upon thee!
Th' untented woundings of a father's curse
Pierce every sense about thee! — Old fond eyes,
Beweep this cause again, I'll pluck ye out,
And cast you, with the waters that you lose,
To temper clay. Yea, is it come to this?
Let it be so. Yet have I left a daughter,
Who I am sure is kind and comfortable.
When she shall hear this of thee, with her nails
She'll flay thy wolvish visage. Thou shalt find
That I'll resume the shape which thou dost think
I have cast off for ever; thou shalt, I warrant thee.

Exeunt [*Lear, Kent, and Attendants*].

Gon. Do you mark that, my lord?

Alb. I cannot be so partial, Goneril,
To the great love I bear you —

Gon. Pray you, content.—What, Oswald, ho!
[*To the Fool*] You, sir, more knave than fool, after your master!

Fool. Nuncle Lear, nuncle Lear, tarry! Take the fool with thee.

A fox, when one has caught her,
And such a daughter,
Should sure to the slaughter,
If my cap would buy a halter.
So the fool follows after. *Exit.*

Gon. This man hath had good counsel! A hundred knights?
'Tis politic and safe to let him keep
At point a hundred knights; yes, that on every dream,
Each buzz, each fancy, each complaint, dislike,
He may enguard his dotage with their pow'rs
And hold our lives in mercy. — Oswald, I say!

Alb. Well, you may fear too far.

Gon. Safer than trust too far.
Let me still take away the harms I fear,
Not fear still to be taken. I know his heart.
What he hath utter'd I have writ my sister.
If she sustain him and his hundred knights,
When I have show'd th' unfitness —

Enter [*Oswald* the] *Steward.*

How now, Oswald?
What, have you writ that letter to my sister?

Osw. Yes, madam.

Gon. Take you some company, and away to horse!
Inform her full of my particular fear,
And thereto add such reasons of your own
As may compact it more. Get you gone,
And hasten your return. [*Exit Oswald.*] No, no, my lord!
This milky gentleness and course of yours,
Though I condemn it not, yet, under pardon,
You are much more at task for want of wisdom
Than prais'd for harmful mildness.

Alb. How far your eyes may pierce I cannot tell.
Striving to better, oft we mar what's well.

Gon. Nay then —

Alb. Well, well; th' event. *Exeunt.*

Scene V. [*Court before the* Duke of Albany's *Palace.*]

Enter *Lear, Kent,* and *Fool.*

Lear. Go you before to Gloucester with these letters. Acquaint my daughter no further with anything you know than comes from her demand out of the letter. If your diligence be not speedy, I shall be there afore you.

Kent. I will not sleep, my lord, till I have delivered your letter. *Exit.*

Fool. If a man's brains were in's heels, were't not in danger of kibes?

Lear. Ay, boy.

Fool. Then I prithee be merry. Thy wit shall ne'er go slipshod.

Lear. Ha, ha, ha!

Fool. Shalt see thy other daughter will use thee kindly; for though she's as like this as a crab's like an apple, yet I can tell what I can tell.

Lear. What canst tell, boy?

Fool. She'll taste as like this as a crab does to a crab. Thou canst tell why one's nose stands i' th' middle on's face?

Lear. No.

Fool. Why, to keep one's eyes of either side's nose, that what a man cannot smell out, 'a may spy into.

Lear. I did her wrong.

Fool. Canst tell how an oyster makes his shell?

Lear. No.

Fool. Nor I neither; but I can tell why a snail has a house.

Lear. Why?

Fool. Why, to put's head in; not to give it away to his daughters, and leave his horns without a case.

Lear. I will forget my nature. So kind a father! — Be my horses ready?

Fool. Thy asses are gone about 'em. The reason why the seven stars are no moe than seven is a pretty reason.

Lear. Because they are not eight?

Fool. Yes indeed. Thou wouldst make a good fool.

Lear. To take't again perforce! Monster ingratitude!

Fool. If thou wert my fool, nuncle, I'ld have thee beaten for being old before thy time.

Lear. How's that?

Fool. Thou shouldst not have been old till thou hadst been wise.

Lear. O, let me not be mad, not mad, sweet heaven!
Keep me in temper; I would not be mad!

[Enter a *Gentleman.*]

How now? Are the horses ready?

Gent. Ready, my lord.

Lear. Come, boy.

Fool. She that's a maid now, and laughs at my departure,
Shall not be a maid long, unless things be cut shorter. *Exeunt.*

ACT II. Scene I. [*A court within the Castle of the* Earl of Gloucester.]

Enter [*Edmund* the] *Bastard* and *Curan,* meeting.

Edm. Save thee, Curan.

Cur. And you, sir. I have been with your father, and given him notice that the Duke of Cornwall and Regan his Duchess will be here with him this night.

Edm. How comes that?

Cur. Nay, I know not. You have heard of the news abroad — I mean the whisper'd ones, for they are yet but ear-kissing arguments?

Edm. Not I. Pray you, what are they?

Cur. Have you heard of no likely wars toward 'twixt the two Dukes of Cornwall and Albany?

Edm. Not a word.

Cur. You may do, then, in time. Fare you well, sir. *Exit.*

Edm. The Duke be here to-night? The better! best!
This weaves itself perforce into my business.
My father hath set guard to take my brother:
And I have one thing, of a queasy question,
Which I must act. Briefness and fortune, work!
Brother, a word! Descend! Brother, I say!

Enter *Edgar.*

My father watches. O sir, fly this place!
Intelligence is given where you are hid.
You have now the good advantage of the night.
Have you not spoken 'gainst the Duke of Cornwall?
He's coming hither; now, i' th' night, i' th' haste,
And Regan with him. Have you nothing said
Upon his party 'gainst the Duke of Albany?
Advise yourself.

Edg. I am sure on't, not a word.

Edm. I hear my father coming. Pardon me!
In cunning I must draw my sword upon you.
Draw, seem to defend yourself; now quit you well. —
Yield! Come before my father. Light, ho, here!

Fly, brother. — Torches, torches! — So farewell.

Exit Edgar.

Some blood drawn on me would beget opinion
Of my more fierce endeavour. [*Stabs his arm.*] I have seen drunkards
Do more than this in sport. — Father, father! —
Stop, stop! No help?

Enter *Gloucester*, and *Servants* with torches.

Glou. Now, Edmund, where's the villain?
Edm. Here stood he in the dark, his sharp sword out,
Mumbling of wicked charms, conjuring the moon
To stand 's auspicious mistress.
Glou. But where is he?
Edm. Look, sir, I bleed.
Glou. Where is the villain, Edmund?
Edm. Fled this way, sir. When by no means he could —
Glou. Pursue him, ho! Go after. [*Exeunt some Servants.*] By no means what?
Edm. Persuade me to the murther of your lordship;
But that I told him the revenging gods
'Gainst parricides did all their thunders bend;
Spoke with how manifold and strong a bond
The child was bound to th' father sir, in fine,
Seeing how loathly opposite I stood
To his unnatural purpose, in fell motion
With his prepared sword he charges home
My unprovided body, lanch'd mine arm;
But when he saw my best alarum'd spirits,
Bold in the quarrel's right, rous'd to th' encounter,
Or whether gasted by the noise I made,
Full suddenly he fled.
Glou. Let him fly far.
Not in this land shall he remain uncaught;
And found — dispatch. The noble Duke my master,
My worthy arch and patron, comes to-night.
By his authority I will proclaim it,
That he which finds him shall deserve our thanks,
Bringing the murderous caitiff to the stake;
He that conceals him, death.
Edm. When I dissuaded him from his intent
And found him pight to do it, with curst speech
I threaten'd to discover him. He replied,
'Thou unpossessing bastard, dost thou think,
If I would stand against thee, would the reposal
Of any trust, virtue, or worth in thee
Make thy words faith'd? No. What I should deny
(As this I would; ay, though thou didst produce
My very character), I'ld turn it all
To thy suggestion, plot, and damned practice;
And thou must make a dullard of the world,
If they not thought the profits of my death
Were very pregnant and potential spurs
To make thee seek it.'
Glou. Strong and fast'ned villain!
Would he deny his letter? I never got him.

Tucket within.

Hark, the Duke's trumpets! I know not why he comes.
All ports I'll bar; the villain shall not scape;
The Duke must grant me that. Besides, his picture
I will send far and near, that all the kingdom
May have due note of him, and of my land,
Loyal and natural boy, I'll work the means
To make thee capable.

Enter *Cornwall*, *Regan*, and *Attendants*.

Corn. How now, my noble friend? Since I came hither
(Which I can call but now) I have heard strange news.
Reg. If it be true, all vengeance comes too short
Which can pursue th' offender. How dost, my lord?
Glou. O madam, my old heart is crack'd, it's crack'd!
Reg. What, did my father's godson seek your life?
He whom my father nam'd? your Edgar?
Glou. O lady, lady, shame would have it hid!
Reg. Was he not companion with the riotous knights
That tend upon my father?
Glou. I know not, madam. 'Tis too bad, too bad!
Edm. Yes, madam, he was of that consort.
Reg. No marvel then though he were ill affected.
'Tis they have put him on the old man's death,
To have th' expense and waste of his revenues.
I have this present evening from my sister
Been well inform'd of them, and with such cautions
That, if they come to sojourn at my house,
I'll not be there.
Corn. Nor I, assure thee, Regan.

Edmund, I hear that you have shown your father
A childlike office.
Edm. 'Twas my duty, sir.
Glou. He did bewray his practice, and receiv'd
This hurt you see, striving to apprehend him.
Corn. Is he pursued?
Glou. Ay, my good lord.
Corn. If he be taken, he shall never more
Be fear'd of doing harm. Make your own purpose,
How in my strength you please. For you, Edmund,
Whose virtue and obedience doth this instant
So much commend itself, you shall be ours.
Natures of such deep trust we shall much need;
You we first seize on.
Edm. I shall serve you, sir,
Truly, however else.
Glou. For him I thank your Grace.
Corn. You know not why we came to visit you —
Reg. Thus out of season, threading dark-ey'd night.
Occasions, noble Gloucester, of some poise,
Wherein we must have use of your advice.
Our father he hath writ, so hath our sister,
Of differences, which I best thought it fit
To answer from our home. The several messengers
From hence attend dispatch. Our good old friend,
Lay comforts to your bosom, and bestow
Your needful counsel to our business,
Which craves the instant use.
Glou. I serve you, madam.
Your Graces are right welcome.
Exeunt. Flourish.

Scene II. [*Before* Gloucester's *Castle.*]

Enter *Kent* and [*Oswald* the] *Steward,* severally.

Osw. Good dawning to thee, friend. Art of this house?

Kent. Ay.

Osw. Where may we set our horses?

Kent. I' th' mire.

Osw. Prithee, if thou lov'st me, tell me.

Kent. I love thee not.

Osw. Why then, I care not for thee.

Kent. If I had thee in Lipsbury Pinfold, I would make thee care for me.

Osw. Why dost thou use me thus? I know thee not.

Kent. Fellow, I know thee.

Osw. What dost thou know me for?

Kent. A knave; a rascal; an eater of broken meats; a base, proud, shallow, beggarly, three-suited, hundred-pound, filthy, worsted-stocking knave; a lily-liver'd, action-taking, whoreson, glass-gazing, superserviceable, finical rogue; one-trunk-inheriting slave; one that wouldst be a bawd in way of good service, and art nothing but the composition of a knave, beggar, coward, pander, and the son and heir of a mongrel bitch; one whom I will beat into clamorous whining, if thou deny the least syllable of thy addition.

Osw. Why, what a monstrous fellow art thou, thus to rail on one that's neither known of thee nor knows thee!

Kent. What a brazen-fac'd varlet art thou, to deny thou knowest me! Is it two days ago since I beat thee and tripp'd up thy heels before the King? [*Draws his sword.*] Draw, you rogue! for, though it be night, yet the moon shines. I'll make a sop o' th' moonshine o' you. Draw, you whoreson cullionly barbermonger! draw!

Osw. Away! I have nothing to do with thee.

Kent. Draw, you rascal! You come with letters against the King, and take Vanity the puppet's part against the royalty of her father. Draw, you rogue, or I'll so carbonado your shanks! Draw, you rascal! Come your ways!

Osw. Help, ho! murther! help!

Kent. Strike, you slave! Stand, rogue! Stand, you neat slave! Strike! [*Beats him.*]

Osw. Help, ho! murther! murther!

Enter *Edmund,* with his rapier drawn, *Gloucester, Cornwall, Regan, Servants.*

Edm. How now? What's the matter? *Parts* [*them*].

Kent. With you, goodman boy, an you please! Come, I'll flesh ye! Come on, young master!

Glou. Weapons? arms? What's the matter here?

Corn. Keep peace, upon your lives!
He dies that strikes again. What is the matter?

Reg. The messengers from our sister and the King.

Corn. What is your difference? Speak.

Osw. I am scarce in breath, my lord.

Kent. No marvel, you have so bestirr'd your valour. You cowardly rascal, nature disclaims in thee; a tailor made thee.

Corn. Thou art a strange fellow. A tailor make a man?

Kent. Ay, a tailor, sir. A stonecutter or a painter could not have made him so ill, though he had been but two hours at the trade.

Corn. Speak yet, how grew your quarrel?

Osw. This ancient ruffian, sir, whose life I have spar'd
At suit of his grey beard —

Kent. Thou whoreson zed! thou unnecessary letter! My lord, if you'll give me leave, I will tread this unbolted villain into mortar and daub the walls of a jakes with him. 'Spare my grey beard,' you wagtail?

Corn. Peace, sirrah!
You beastly knave, know you no reverence?

Kent. Yes, sir, but anger hath a privilege.

Corn. Why art thou angry?

Kent. That such a slave as this should wear a sword,
Who wears no honesty. Such smiling rogues as these,
Like rats, oft bite the holy cords atwain
Which are too intrinse t' unloose; smooth every passion
That in the natures of their lords rebel,
Bring oil to fire, snow to their colder moods;
Renege, affirm, and turn their halcyon beaks
With every gale and vary of their masters,
Knowing naught (like dogs) but following.
A plague upon your epileptic visage!
Smile you my speeches, as I were a fool?
Goose, an I had you upon Sarum Plain,
I'ld drive ye cackling home to Camelot.

Corn. What, art thou mad, old fellow?

Glou. How fell you out? Say that.

Kent. No contraries hold more antipathy
Than I and such a knave.

Corn. Why dost thou call him knave? What is his fault?

Kent. His countenance likes me not.

Corn. No more perchance does mine, or his, or hers.

Kent. Sir, 'tis my occupation to be plain.
I have seen better faces in my time
Than stands on any shoulder that I see
Before me at this instant.

Corn. This is some fellow
Who, having been prais'd for bluntness, doth affect
A saucy roughness, and constrains the garb
Quite from his nature. He cannot flatter, he!
An honest mind and plain — he must speak truth!
An they will take it, so; if not, he's plain.
These kind of knaves I know which in this plainness
Harbour more craft and more corrupter ends
Than twenty silly-ducking observants
That stretch their duties nicely.

Kent. Sir, in good faith, in sincere verity,
Under th' allowance of your great aspect,
Whose influence, like the wreath of radiant fire
On flickering Phœbus' front —

Corn. What mean'st by this?

Kent. To go out of my dialect, which you discommend so much. I know, sir, I am no flatterer. He that beguil'd you in a plain accent was a plain knave, which, for my part, I will not be, though I should win your displeasure to entreat me to't.

Corn. What was th' offence you gave him?

Osw. I never gave him any.
It pleas'd the King his master very late
To strike at me, upon his misconstruction;
When he, conjunct, and flattering his displeasure,
Tripp'd me behind; being down, insulted, rail'd
And put upon him such a deal of man
That worthied him, got praises of the King
For him attempting who was self-subdu'd;
And, in the fleshment of this dread exploit,
Drew on me here again.

Kent. None of these rogues and cowards
But Ajax is their fool.

Corn. Fetch forth the stocks!
You stubborn ancient knave, you reverent braggart,
We'll teach you —

Kent. Sir, I am too old to learn.
Call not your stocks for me. I serve the King;
On whose employment I was sent to you.
You shall do small respect, show too bold malice
Against the grace and person of my master,
Stocking his messenger.

Corn. Fetch forth the stocks! As I have life and honour,
There shall he sit till noon.

Reg. Till noon? Till night, my lord, and all night too!

Kent. Why, madam, if I were your father's dog,
You should not use me so.

Reg. Sir, being his knave, I will.

Corn. This is a fellow of the selfsame colour
Our sister speaks of. Come, bring away the stocks!

Stocks brought out.

Glou. Let me beseech your Grace not to do so.

His fault is much, and the good King his master
Will check him for't. Your purpos'd low correction
Is such as basest and contemn'dest wretches
For pilf'rings and most common trespasses
Are punish'd with. The King must take it ill
That he, so slightly valued in his messenger,
Should have him thus restrain'd.

Corn. I'll answer that.

Reg. My sister may receive it much more worse,
To have her gentleman abus'd, assaulted,
For following her affairs. Put in his legs. —

[*Kent is put in the stocks.*]

Come, my good lord, away.

Exeunt [*all but Gloucester and Kent*].

Glou. I am sorry for thee, friend. 'Tis the Duke's pleasure,
Whose disposition, all the world well knows,
Will not be rubb'd nor stopp'd. I'll entreat for thee.

Kent. Pray do not, sir. I have watch'd and travell'd hard.
Some time I shall sleep out, the rest I'll whistle.
A good man's fortune may grow out at heels.
Give you good morrow!

Glou. The Duke's to blame in this; 'twill be ill taken. *Exit.*

Kent. Good King, that must approve the common saw,
Thou out of heaven's benediction com'st
To the warm sun!
Approach, thou beacon to this under globe,
That by thy comfortable beams I may
Peruse this letter. Nothing almost sees miracles
But misery. I know 'tis from Cordelia,
Who hath most fortunately been inform'd
Of my obscured course — and [*reads*] 'shall find time
From this enormous state, seeking to give
Losses their remedies'—All weary and o'erwatch'd,
Take vantage, heavy eyes, not to behold
This shameful lodging.
Fortune, good night; smile once more, turn thy wheel. *Sleeps.*

[Scene III. *The open country.*]

Enter *Edgar.*

Edg. I heard myself proclaim'd,
And by the happy hollow of a tree
Escap'd the hunt. No port is free, no place
That guard and most unusual vigilance
Does not attend my taking. Whiles I may scape,
I will preserve myself; and am bethought
To take the basest and most poorest shape
That ever penury, in contempt of man,
Brought near to beast. My face I'll grime with filth,
Blanket my loins, elf all my hair in knots,
And with presented nakedness outface
The winds and persecutions of the sky.
The country gives me proof and precedent
Of Bedlam beggars, who, with roaring voices,
Strike in their numb'd and mortified bare arms
Pins, wooden pricks, nails, sprigs of rosemary;
And with this horrible object, from low farms,
Poor pelting villages, sheepcotes, and mills,
Sometime with lunatic bans, sometime with prayers,
Enforce their charity. 'Poor Turlygod! poor Tom!'
That's something yet! Edgar I nothing am.

Exit.

[Scene IV. *Before* Gloucester's *Castle*; Kent *in the stocks.*]

Enter *Lear, Fool,* and *Gentleman.*

Lear. 'Tis strange that they should so depart from home,
And not send back my messenger.

Gent. As I learn'd,
The night before there was no purpose in them
Of this remove.

Kent. Hail to thee, noble master!

Lear. Ha!
Mak'st thou this shame thy pastime?

Kent. No, my lord.

Fool. Ha, ha! look! he wears cruel garters. Horses are tied by the head, dogs and bears by th' neck, monkeys by th' loins, and men by th' legs. When a man's over-lusty at legs, then he wears wooden nether-stocks.

Lear. What's he that hath so much thy place mistook
To set thee here?

Kent. It is both he and she —
Your son and daughter.

Lear. No.

Kent. Yes.

Lear. No, I say.

Kent. I say yea.

Lear. No, no, they would not!

Kent. Yes, they have.
Lear. By Jupiter, I swear no!
Kent. By Juno, I swear ay!
Lear. They durst not do't;
They would not, could not do't. 'Tis worse than murther
To do upon respect such violent outrage.
Resolve me with all modest haste which way
Thou mightst deserve or they impose this usage,
Coming from us.
Kent. My lord, when at their home
I did commend your Highness' letters to them,
Ere I was risen from the place that show'd
My duty kneeling, came there a reeking post,
Stew'd in his haste, half breathless, panting forth
From Goneril his mistress salutations;
Deliver'd letters, spite of intermission,
Which presently they read; on whose contents,
They summon'd up their meiny, straight took horse,
Commanded me to follow and attend
The leisure of their answer, gave me cold looks,
And meeting here the other messenger,
Whose welcome I perceiv'd had poison'd mine—
Being the very fellow which of late
Display'd so saucily against your Highness—
Having more man than wit about me, drew.
He rais'd the house with loud and coward cries.
Your son and daughter found this trespass worth
The shame which here it suffers.

Fool. Winter's not gone yet, if the wild geese fly that way.

Fathers that wear rags
Do make their children blind;
But fathers that bear bags
Shall see their children kind.
Fortune, that arrant whore,
Ne'er turns the key to th' poor.

But for all this, thou shalt have as many dolours for thy daughters as thou canst tell in a year.

Lear. O, how this mother swells up toward my heart!
Hysterica passio! Down, thou climbing sorrow!
Thy element's below! Where is this daughter?
Kent. With the Earl, sir, here within.
Lear. Follow me not;
Stay here. *Exit.*
Gent. Made you no more offence but what you speak of?
Kent. None.
How chance the King comes with so small a number?

Fool. An thou hadst been set i' th' stocks for that question, thou'dst well deserv'd it.

Kent. Why, fool?

Fool. We'll set thee to school to an ant, to teach thee there's no labouring i' th' winter. All that follow their noses are led by their eyes but blind men, and there's not a nose among twenty but can smell him that's stinking. Let go thy hold when a great wheel runs down a hill, lest it break thy neck with following it; but the great one that goes upward, let him draw thee after. When a wise man gives thee better counsel, give me mine again. I would have none but knaves follow it, since a fool gives it.

That sir which serves and seeks for gain,
And follows but for form,
Will pack when it begins to rain
And leave thee in the storm.
But I will tarry; the fool will stay,
And let the wise man fly.
The knave turns fool that runs away;
The fool no knave, perdy.

Kent. Where learn'd you this, fool?
Fool. Not i' th' stocks, fool.

Enter *Lear* and *Gloucester*.

Lear. Deny to speak with me? They are sick? they are weary?
They have travell'd all the night? Mere fetches—
The images of revolt and flying off!
Fetch me a better answer.
Glou. My dear lord,
You know the fiery quality of the Duke,
How unremovable and fix'd he is
In his own course.
Lear. Vengeance! plague! death! confusion!
Fiery? What quality? Why, Gloucester, Gloucester,
I'ld speak with the Duke of Cornwall and his wife.
Glou. Well, my good lord, I have inform'd them so.
Lear. Inform'd them? Dost thou understand me, man?
Glou. Ay, my good lord.
Lear. The King would speak with Cornwall; the dear father
Would with his daughter speak, commands her service.
Are they inform'd of this? My breath and blood!
Fiery? the fiery Duke? Tell the hot Duke that—

No, but not yet! May be he is not well.
Infirmity doth still neglect all office
Whereto our health is bound. We are not ourselves
When nature, being oppress'd, commands the mind
To suffer with the body. I'll forbear;
And am fallen out with my more headier will,
To take the indispos'd and sickly fit
For the sound man. — Death on my state! Wherefore
Should he sit here? This act persuades me
That this remotion of the Duke and her
Is practice only. Give me my servant forth.
Go tell the Duke and 's wife I'ld speak with them —
Now, presently. Bid them come forth and hear me,
Or at their chamber door I'll beat the drum
Till it cry sleep to death.

Glou. I would have all well betwixt you. *Exit.*

Lear. O me, my heart, my rising heart! But down!

Fool. Cry to it, nuncle, as the cockney did to the eels when she put 'em i' th' paste alive. She knapp'd 'em o' th' coxcombs with a stick and cried 'Down, wantons, down!' 'Twas her brother that, in pure kindness to his horse, buttered his hay.

Enter *Cornwall, Regan, Gloucester, Servants.*

Lear. Good morrow to you both.

Corn. Hail to your Grace!
Kent here set at liberty.

Reg. I am glad to see your Highness.

Lear. Regan, I think you are; I know what reason
I have to think so. If thou shouldst not be glad,
I would divorce me from thy mother's tomb,
Sepulchring an adultress. [*To Kent*] O, are you free?
Some other time for that. — Beloved Regan,
Thy sister's naught. O Regan, she hath tied
Sharp-tooth'd unkindness, like a vulture, here!
[*Lays his hand on his heart.*]
I can scarce speak to thee. Thou'lt not believe
With how deprav'd a quality — O Regan!

Reg. I pray you, sir, take patience. I have hope
You less know how to value her desert
Than she to scant her duty.

Lear. Say, how is that?

Reg. I cannot think my sister in the least
Would fail her obligation. If, sir, perchance
She have restrain'd the riots of your followers,
'Tis on such ground, and to such wholesome end,
As clears her from all blame.

Lear. My curses on her!

Reg. O, sir, you are old!
Nature in you stands on the very verge
Of her confine. You should be rul'd, and led
By some discretion that discerns your state
Better than you yourself. Therefore I pray you
That to our sister you do make return;
Say you have wrong'd her, sir.

Lear. Ask her forgiveness?
Do you but mark how this becomes the house:
'Dear daughter, I confess that I am old.
[*Kneels.*]
Age is unnecessary. On my knees I beg
That you'll vouchsafe me raiment, bed, and food.'

Reg. Good sir, no more! These are unsightly tricks.
Return you to my sister.

Lear. [*rises*] Never, Regan!
She hath abated me of half my train;
Look'd black upon me; struck me with her tongue,
Most serpent-like, upon the very heart.
All the stor'd vengeances of heaven fall
On her ingrateful top! Strike her young bones,
You taking airs, with lameness!

Corn. Fie, sir, fie!

Lear. You nimble lightnings, dart your blinding flames
Into her scornful eyes! Infect her beauty,
You fen-suck'd fogs, drawn by the pow'rful sun,
To fall and blast her pride!

Reg. O the blest gods! so will you wish on me
When the rash mood is on.

Lear. No, Regan, thou shalt never have my curse.
Thy tender-hefted nature shall not give
Thee o'er to harshness. Her eyes are fierce; but thine
Do comfort, and not burn. 'Tis not in thee
To grudge my pleasures, to cut off my train,
To bandy hasty words, to scant my sizes,
And, in conclusion, to oppose the bolt
Against my coming in. Thou better know'st
The offices of nature, bond of childhood,
Effects of courtesy, dues of gratitude.
Thy half o' th' kingdom hast thou not forgot,
Wherein I thee endow'd.

Reg. Good sir, to th' purpose.
Tucket within.

Lear. Who put my man i' th' stocks?

Corn. What trumpet's that?
Reg. I know't — my sister's. This approves her letter,
That she would soon be here.

Enter [*Oswald* the] *Steward.*

Is your lady come?
Lear. This is a slave, whose easy-borrowed pride
Dwells in the fickle grace of her he follows.
Out, varlet, from my sight!
Corn. What means your Grace?

Enter *Goneril.*

Lear. Who stock'd my servant? Regan, I have good hope
Thou didst not know on't. — Who comes here? O heavens!
If you do love old men, if your sweet sway
Allow obedience — if yourselves are old,
Make it your cause! Send down, and take my part!
[*To Goneril*] Art not asham'd to look upon this beard? —
O Regan, wilt thou take her by the hand?
Gon. Why not by th' hand, sir? How have I offended?
All's not offence that indiscretion finds
And dotage terms so.
Lear. O sides, you are too tough!
Will you yet hold? How came my man i' th' stocks?
Corn. I set him there, sir; but his own disorders
Deserv'd much less advancement.
Lear. You? Did you?
Reg. I pray you, father, being weak, seem so.
If, till the expiration of your month,
You will return and sojourn with my sister,
Dismissing half your train, come then to me.
I am now from home, and out of that provision
Which shall be needful for your entertainment.
Lear. Return to her, and fifty men dismiss'd?
No, rather I abjure all roofs, and choose
To wage against the enmity o' th' air,
To be a comrade with the wolf and owl —
Necessity's sharp pinch! Return with her?
Why, the hot-blooded France, that dowerless took
Our youngest born, I could as well be brought
To knee his throne, and, squire-like, pension beg
To keep base life afoot. Return with her?
Persuade me rather to be slave and sumpter
To this detested groom. [*Points at Oswald.*]
Gon. At your choice, sir.
Lear. I prithee, daughter, do not make me mad.
I will not trouble thee, my child; farewell.
We'll no more meet, no more see one another.
But yet thou art my flesh, my blood, my daughter;
Or rather a disease that's in my flesh,
Which I must needs call mine. Thou art a boil,
A plague sore, an embossed carbuncle
In my corrupted blood. But I'll not chide thee.
Let shame come when it will, I do not call it.
I do not bid the Thunder-bearer shoot
Nor tell tales of thee to high-judging Jove.
Mend when thou canst; be better at thy leisure;
I can be patient, I can stay with Regan,
I and my hundred knights.
Reg. Not altogether so.
I look'd not for you yet, nor am provided
For your fit welcome. Give ear, sir, to my sister;
For those that mingle reason with your passion
Must be content to think you old, and so —
But she knows what she does.
Lear. Is this well spoken?
Reg. I dare avouch it, sir. What, fifty followers?
Is it not well? What should you need of more?
Yea, or so many, sith that both charge and danger
Speak 'gainst so great a number? How in one house
Should many people, under two commands,
Hold amity? 'Tis hard; almost impossible.
Gon. Why might not you, my lord, receive attendance
From those that she calls servants, or from mine?
Reg. Why not, my lord? If then they chanc'd to slack ye,
We could control them. If you will come to me
(For now I spy a danger), I entreat you
To bring but five-and-twenty. To no more
Will I give place or notice.
Lear. I gave you all —
Reg. And in good time you gave it!
Lear. Made you my guardians, my depositaries;
But kept a reservation to be followed
With such a number. What, must I come to you
With five-and-twenty, Regan? Said you so?
Reg. And speak't again, my lord. No more with me.

Lear. Those wicked creatures yet do look well-favour'd
When others are more wicked; not being the worst
Stands in some rank of praise. [*To Goneril*] I'll go with thee.
Thy fifty yet doth double five-and-twenty,
And thou art twice her love.
Gon. Hear me, my lord.
What need you five-and-twenty, ten, or five,
To follow in a house where twice so many
Have a command to tend you?
Reg. What need one?
Lear. O, reason not the need! Our basest beggars
Are in the poorest thing superfluous.
Allow not nature more than nature needs,
Man's life is cheap as beast's. Thou art a lady:
If only to go warm were gorgeous,
Why, nature needs not what thou gorgeous wear'st,
Which scarcely keeps thee warm. But, for true need —
You heavens, give me that patience, patience I need!
You see me here, you gods, a poor old man,
As full of grief as age; wretched in both.
If it be you that stirs these daughters' hearts
Against their father, fool me not so much
To bear it tamely; touch me with noble anger,
And let not women's weapons, water drops,
Stain my man's cheeks! No, you unnatural hags!
I will have such revenges on you both
That all the world shall — I will do such things —
What they are yet, I know not; but they shall be
The terrors of the earth! You think I'll weep.
No, I'll not weep.
I have full cause of weeping, but this heart
Shall break into a hundred thousand flaws
Or ere I'll weep. O fool, I shall go mad!
Exeunt Lear, Gloucester, Kent, and Fool.
Storm and tempest.
Corn. Let us withdraw; 'twill be a storm.
Reg. This house is little; the old man and 's people
Cannot be well bestow'd.
Gon. 'Tis his own blame; hath put himself from rest
And must needs taste his folly.
Reg. For his particular, I'll receive him gladly,
But not one follower.
Gon. So am I purpos'd.
Where is my Lord of Gloucester?
Corn. Followed the old man forth.

Enter *Gloucester*.

He is return'd.
Glou. The King is in high rage.
Corn. Whither is he going?
Glou. He calls to horse, but will I know not whither.
Corn. 'Tis best to give him way; he leads himself.
Gon. My lord, entreat him by no means to stay.
Glou. Alack, the night comes on, and the bleak winds
Do sorely ruffle. For many miles about
There's scarce a bush.
Reg. O, sir, to wilful men
The injuries that they themselves procure
Must be their schoolmasters. Shut up your doors.
He is attended with a desperate train,
And what they may incense him to, being apt
To have his ear abus'd, wisdom bids fear.
Corn. Shut up your doors, my lord; 'tis a wild night.
My Regan counsels well. Come out o' th' storm. *Exeunt.*

ACT III. Scene I. [*A heath.*]

Storm still. Enter *Kent* and a *Gentleman* at several doors.

Kent. Who's there, besides foul weather?
Gent. One minded like the weather, most unquietly.
Kent. I know you. Where's the King?
Gent. Contending with the fretful elements;
Bids the wind blow the earth into the sea,
Or swell the curled waters 'bove the main,
That things might change or cease; tears his white hair,
Which the impetuous blasts, with eyeless rage,
Catch in their fury and make nothing of;
Strives in his little world of man to outscorn
The to-and-fro-conflicting wind and rain.

This night, wherein the cub-drawn bear would couch,
The lion and the belly-pinched wolf
Keep their fur dry, unbonneted he runs,
And bids what will take all.

Kent. But who is with him?

Gent. None but the fool, who labours to outjest
His heart-struck injuries.

Kent. Sir, I do know you,
And dare upon the warrant of my note
Commend a dear thing to you. There is division
(Although as yet the face of it be cover'd
With mutual cunning) 'twixt Albany and Cornwall;
Who have (as who have not, that their great stars
Thron'd and set high?) servants, who seem no less,
Which are to France the spies and speculations
Intelligent of our state. What hath been seen,
Either in snuffs and packings of the Dukes,
Or the hard rein which both of them have borne
Against the old kind King, or something deeper,
Whereof, perchance, these are but furnishings—
But, true it is, from France there comes a power
Into this scattered kingdom, who already,
Wise in our negligence, have secret feet
In some of our best ports and are at point
To show their open banner. Now to you:
If on my credit you dare build so far
To make your speed to Dover, you shall find
Some that will thank you, making just report
Of how unnatural and bemadding sorrow
The King hath cause to plain.
I am a gentleman of blood and breeding,
And from some knowledge and assurance offer
This office to you.

Gent. I will talk further with you.

Kent. No, do not.
For confirmation that I am much more
Than my out-wall, open this purse and take
What it contains. If you shall see Cordelia
(As fear not but you shall), show her this ring,
And she will tell you who your fellow is
That yet you do not know. Fie on this storm!
I will go seek the King.

Gent. Give me your hand. Have you no more to say?

Kent. Few words, but, to effect, more than all yet:
That, when we have found the King (in which your pain
That way, I'll this), he that first lights on him
Holla the other. *Exeunt* [*severally*].

Scene II. [*Another part of the heath.*]

Storm still. Enter *Lear* and *Fool.*

Lear. Blow, winds, and crack your cheeks! rage! blow!
You cataracts and hurricanoes, spout
Till you have drench'd our steeples, drown'd the cocks!
You sulph'rous and thought-executing fires,
Vaunt-couriers to oak-cleaving thunderbolts,
Singe my white head! And thou, all-shaking thunder,
Strike flat the thick rotundity o' th' world,
Crack Nature's moulds, all germains spill at once,
That make ingrateful man!

Fool. O nuncle, court holy water in a dry house is better than this rain water out o' door. Good nuncle, in, and ask thy daughters blessing! Here's a night pities neither wise men nor fools.

Lear. Rumble thy bellyful! Spit, fire! spout, rain!
Nor rain, wind, thunder, fire are my daughters.
I tax not you, you elements, with unkindness.
I never gave you kingdom, call'd you children,
You owe me no subscription. Then let fall
Your horrible pleasure. Here I stand your slave,
A poor, infirm, weak, and despis'd old man.
But yet I call you servile ministers,
That will with two pernicious daughters join
Your high-engender'd battles 'gainst a head
So old and white as this! O! O! 'tis foul!

Fool. He that has a house to put 's head in has a good headpiece.

The codpiece that will house
Before the head has any,
The head and he shall louse:
So beggars marry many.
The man that makes his toe
What he his heart should make
Shall of a corn cry woe,
And turn his sleep to wake.

For there was never yet fair woman but she made mouths in a glass.

Enter *Kent.*

Lear. No, I will be the pattern of all patience; I will say nothing.

Kent. Who's there?

Fool. Marry, here's grace and a codpiece; that's a wise man and a fool.

Kent. Alas, sir, are you here? Things that love night

Love not such nights as these. The wrathful skies
Gallow the very wanderers of the dark
And make them keep their caves. Since I was man,
Such sheets of fire, such bursts of horrid thunder,
Such groans of roaring wind and rain, I never
Remember to have heard. Man's nature cannot carry
Th' affliction nor the fear.

Lear. Let the great gods,
That keep this dreadful pudder o'er our heads,
Find out their enemies now. Tremble, thou wretch,
That hast within thee undivulged crimes
Unwhipp'd of justice. Hide thee, thou bloody hand;
Thou perjur'd, and thou simular man of virtue
That art incestuous. Caitiff, in pieces shake
That under covert and convenient seeming
Hast practis'd on man's life. Close pent-up guilts,
Rive your concealing continents, and cry
These dreadful summoners grace. I am a man
More sinn'd against than sinning.

Kent. Alack, bareheaded?
Gracious my lord, hard by here is a hovel;
Some friendship will it lend you 'gainst the tempest.
Repose you there, whilst I to this hard house
(More harder than the stones whereof 'tis rais'd,
Which even but now, demanding after you,
Denied me to come in) return, and force
Their scanted courtesy.

Lear. My wits begin to turn.
Come on, my boy. How dost, my boy? Art cold?
I am cold myself. Where is this straw, my fellow?
The art of our necessities is strange,
That can make vile things precious. Come, your hovel.
Poor fool and knave, I have one part in my heart
That's sorry yet for thee.

Fool. [*sings*]

He that has and a little tiny wit —
With hey, ho, the wind and the rain —
Must make content with his fortunes fit,
For the rain it raineth every day.

Lear. True, my good boy. Come, bring us to this hovel. *Exeunt* [*Lear and Kent*].

Fool. This is a brave night to cool a courtesan. I'll speak a prophecy ere I go:

When priests are more in word than matter;
When brewers mar their malt with water;
When nobles are their tailors' tutors,
No heretics burn'd, but wenches' suitors;
When every case in law is right,
No squire in debt nor no poor knight;
When slanders do not live in tongues,
Nor cutpurses come not to throngs;
When usurers tell their gold i' th' field,
And bawds and whores do churches build:
Then shall the realm of Albion
Come to great confusion.
Then comes the time, who lives to see't,
That going shall be us'd with feet.

This prophecy Merlin shall make, for I live before his time. *Exit.*

Scene III. [Gloucester's *Castle.*]

Enter *Gloucester* and *Edmund.*

Glou. Alack, alack, Edmund, I like not this unnatural dealing! When I desir'd their leave that I might pity him, they took from me the use of mine own house, charg'd me on pain of perpetual displeasure neither to speak of him, entreat for him, nor any way sustain him.

Edm. Most savage and unnatural!

Glou. Go to; say you nothing. There is division betwixt the Dukes, and a worse matter than that. I have received a letter this night — 'tis dangerous to be spoken — I have lock'd the letter in my closet. These injuries the King now bears will be revenged home; there's part of a power already footed; we must incline to the King. I will seek him and privily relieve him. Go you and maintain talk with the Duke, that my charity be not of him perceived. If he ask for me, I am ill and gone to bed. Though I die for't, as no less is threat'ned me, the King my old master must be relieved. There is some strange thing toward, Edmund. Pray you be careful. *Exit.*

Edm. This courtesy, forbid thee, shall the Duke
Instantly know, and of that letter too.
This seems a fair deserving, and must draw me
That which my father loses — no less than all.
The younger rises when the old doth fall. *Exit.*

Scene IV. [*The heath. Before a hovel.*]

Storm still. Enter *Lear, Kent,* and *Fool.*

Kent. Here is the place, my lord. Good my lord, enter.
The tyranny of the open night's too rough
For nature to endure.

Lear. Let me alone.

Kent. Good my lord, enter here.

Lear. Wilt break my heart?

Kent. I had rather break mine own. Good my lord, enter.

Lear. Thou think'st 'tis much that this contentious storm
Invades us to the skin. So 'tis to thee;
But where the greater malady is fix'd,
The lesser is scarce felt. Thou'dst shun a bear;
But if thy flight lay toward the raging sea,
Thou'dst meet the bear i' th' mouth. When the mind's free,
The body's delicate. The tempest in my mind
Doth from my senses take all feeling else
Save what beats there. Filial ingratitude!
Is it not as this mouth should tear this hand
For lifting food to't? But I will punish home!
No, I will weep no more. In such a night
To shut me out! Pour on; I will endure.
In such a night as this! O Regan, Goneril!
Your old kind father, whose frank heart gave all!
O, that way madness lies; let me shun that!
No more of that.

Kent. Good my lord, enter here.

Lear. Prithee go in thyself; seek thine own ease.
This tempest will not give me leave to ponder
On things would hurt me more. But I'll go in.
[*To the Fool*] In, boy; go first. — You houseless poverty —
Nay, get thee in. I'll pray, and then I'll sleep.

Exit [*Fool*].

Poor naked wretches, wheresoe'er you are,
That bide the pelting of this pitiless storm,
How shall your houseless heads and unfed sides,
Your loop'd and window'd raggedness, defend you
From seasons such as these? O, I have ta'en
Too little care of this! Take physic, pomp;
Expose thyself to feel what wretches feel,
That thou mayst shake the superflux to them
And show the heavens more just.

Edg. [*within*] Fathom and half, fathom and half! Poor Tom!

Enter *Fool* [from the hovel].

Fool. Come not in here, nuncle, here's a spirit. Help me, help me!

Kent. Give me thy hand. Who's there?

Fool. A spirit, a spirit! He says his name's poor Tom.

Kent. What art thou that dost grumble there i' th' straw? Come forth.

Enter *Edgar* [disguised as a madman].

Edg. Away! the foul fiend follows me! Through the sharp hawthorn blows the cold wind. Humh! go to thy cold bed, and warm thee.

Lear. Hast thou given all to thy two daughters, and art thou come to this?

Edg. Who gives anything to poor Tom? whom the foul fiend hath led through fire and through flame, through ford and whirlpool, o'er bog and quagmire; that hath laid knives under his pillow and halters in his pew, set ratsbane by his porridge, made him proud of heart, to ride on a bay trotting horse over four-inch'd bridges, to course his own shadow for a traitor. Bless thy five wits! Tom's acold. O, do de, do de, do de. Bless thee from whirlwinds, star-blasting, and taking! Do poor Tom some charity, whom the foul fiend vexes. There could I have him now — and there — and there again — and there! *Storm still.*

Lear. What, have his daughters brought him to this pass?
Couldst thou save nothing? Didst thou give 'em all?

Fool. Nay, he reserv'd a blanket, else we had been all sham'd.

Lear. Now all the plagues that in the pendulous air
Hang fated o'er men's faults light on thy daughters!

Kent. He hath no daughters, sir.

Lear. Death, traitor! nothing could have subdu'd nature
To such a lowness but his unkind daughters.
Is it the fashion that discarded fathers
Should have thus little mercy on their flesh?
Judicious punishment! 'Twas this flesh begot
Those pelican daughters.

Edg. Pillicock sat on Pillicock's Hill. 'Allow, 'allow, loo, loo!

Fool. This cold night will turn us all to fools and madmen.

Edg. Take heed o' th' foul fiend; obey thy parents; keep thy word justly; swear not;

commit not with man's sworn spouse; set not thy sweet heart on proud array. Tom's acold.

Lear. What hast thou been?

Edg. A servingman, proud in heart and mind; that curl'd my hair, wore gloves in my cap; serv'd the lust of my mistress' heart and did the act of darkness with her; swore as many oaths as I spake words, and broke them in the sweet face of heaven; one that slept in the contriving of lust, and wak'd to do it. Wine lov'd I deeply, dice dearly; and in woman out-paramour'd the Turk. False of heart, light of ear, bloody of hand; hog in sloth, fox in stealth, wolf in greediness, dog in madness, lion in prey. Let not the creaking of shoes nor the rustling of silks betray thy poor heart to woman. Keep thy foot out of brothel, thy hand out of placket, thy pen from lender's book, and defy the foul fiend. Still through the hawthorn blows the cold wind; says suum, mun, hey, no, nonny. Dolphin my boy, my boy, sessa! let him trot by.

Storm still.

Lear. Why, thou wert better in thy grave than to answer with thy uncover'd body this extremity of the skies. Is man no more than this? Consider him well. Thou ow'st the worm no silk, the beast no hide, the sheep no wool, the cat no perfume. Ha! Here's three on's are sophisticated! Thou art the thing itself; unaccommodated man is no more but such a poor, bare, forked animal as thou art. Off, off, you lendings! Come, unbutton here.

[*Tears at his clothes.*]

Fool. Prithee, nuncle, be contented! 'Tis a naughty night to swim in. Now a little fire in a wild field were like an old lecher's heart — a small spark, all the rest on's body cold. Look, here comes a walking fire.

Enter *Gloucester* with a torch.

Edg. This is the foul fiend Flibbertigibbet. He begins at curfew, and walks till the first cock. He gives the web and the pin, squints the eye, and makes the harelip; mildews the white wheat, and hurts the poor creature of earth.

Saint Withold footed thrice the 'old;
He met the nightmare, and her nine fold;
Bid her alight
And her troth plight,
And aroint thee, witch, aroint thee!

Kent. How fares your Grace?

Lear. What's he?

Kent. Who's there? What is't you seek?

Glou. What are you there? Your names?

Edg. Poor Tom, that eats the swimming frog, the toad, the todpole, the wall-newt and the water; that in the fury of his heart, when the foul fiend rages, eats cow-dung for sallets, swallows the old rat and the ditch-dog, drinks the green mantle of the standing pool; who is whipp'd from tithing to tithing, and stock-punish'd and imprison'd; who hath had three suits to his back, six shirts to his body, horse to ride, and weapon to wear;

But mice and rats, and such small deer,
Have been Tom's food for seven long year

Beware my follower. Peace, Smulkin! peace, thou fiend!

Glou. What, hath your Grace no better company?

Edg. The prince of darkness is a gentleman!
Modo he's call'd, and Mahu.

Glou. Our flesh and blood is grown so vile, my lord,
That it doth hate what gets it.

Edg. Poor Tom's acold.

Glou. Go in with me. My duty cannot suffer
T' obey in all your daughters' hard commands.
Though their injunction be to bar my doors
And let this tyrannous night take hold upon you,
Yet have I ventur'd to come seek you out
And bring you where both fire and food is ready.

Lear. First let me talk with this philosopher.
What is the cause of thunder?

Kent. Good my lord, take his offer; go into th' house.

Lear. I'll talk a word with this same learned Theban.
What is your study?

Edg. How to prevent the fiend and to kill vermin.

Lear. Let me ask you one word in private.

Kent. Importune him once more to go, my lord.
His wits begin t' unsettle.

Glou. Canst thou blame him?

Storm still.

His daughters seek his death. Ah, that good Kent!
He said it would be thus — poor banish'd man!
Thou say'st the King grows mad: I'll tell thee, friend,
I am almost mad myself. I had a son,
Now outlaw'd from my blood. He sought my life
But lately, very late. I lov'd him, friend —
No father his son dearer. True to tell thee,

The grief hath craz'd my wits. What a night's this!
I do beseech your Grace —

Lear. O, cry you mercy, sir.
Noble philosopher, your company.

Edg. Tom's acold.

Glou. In, fellow, there, into th' hovel; keep thee warm.

Lear. Come, let's in all.

Kent. This way, my lord.

Lear. With him!
I will keep still with my philosopher.

Kent. Good my lord, soothe him; let him take the fellow.

Glou. Take him you on.

Kent. Sirrah, come on; go along with us.

Lear. Come, good Athenian.

Glou. No words, no words! hush.

Edg. Child Rowland to the dark tower came;
His word was still

Fie, foh, and fum!
I smell the blood of a British man. *Exeunt.*

Scene V. [Gloucester's *Castle.*]

Enter *Cornwall* and *Edmund.*

Corn. I will have my revenge ere I depart his house.

Edm. How, my lord, I may be censured, that nature thus gives way to loyalty, something fears me to think of.

Corn. I now perceive it was not altogether your brother's evil disposition made him seek his death; but a provoking merit, set awork by a reproveable badness in himself.

Edm. How malicious is my fortune that I must repent to be just! This is the letter he spoke of, which approves him an intelligent party to the advantages of France. O heavens! that this treason were not — or not I the detector!

Corn. Go with me to the Duchess.

Edm. If the matter of this paper be certain, you have mighty business in hand.

Corn. True or false, it hath made thee Earl of Gloucester. Seek out where thy father is, that he may be ready for our apprehension.

Edm. [*aside*] If I find him comforting the King, it will stuff his suspicion more fully. — I will persever in my course of loyalty, though the conflict be sore between that and my blood.

Corn. I will lay trust upon thee, and thou shalt find a dearer father in my love. *Exeunt.*

Scene VI. [*A farmhouse near* Gloucester's *Castle.*]

Enter *Gloucester, Lear, Kent, Fool,* and *Edgar.*

Glou. Here is better than the open air; take it thankfully. I will piece out the comfort with what addition I can. I will not be long from you.

Kent. All the power of his wits have given way to his impatience. The gods reward your kindness!

Exit [*Gloucester*].

Edg. Frateretto calls me, and tells me Nero is an angler in the lake of darkness. Pray, innocent, and beware the foul fiend.

Fool. Prithee, nuncle, tell me whether a madman be a gentleman or a yeoman.

Lear. A king, a king!

Fool. No, he's a yeoman that has a gentleman to his son; for he's a mad yeoman that sees his son a gentleman before him.

Lear. To have a thousand with red burning spits
Come hizzing in upon 'em —

Edg. The foul fiend bites my back.

Fool. He's mad that trusts in the tameness of a wolf, a horse's health, a boy's love, or a whore's oath.

Lear. It shall be done; I will arraign them straight.
[*To Edgar*] Come, sit thou here, most learned justicer.
[*To the Fool*] Thou, sapient sir, sit here. Now, you she-foxes!

Edg. Look, where he stands and glares!
Want'st thou eyes at trial, madam?

Come o'er the bourn, Bessy, to me.

Fool. Her boat hath a leak,
And she must not speak
Why she dares not come over to thee.

Edg. The foul fiend haunts poor Tom in the voice of a nightingale. Hoppedance cries in Tom's belly for two white herring. Croak not, black angel; I have no food for thee.

Kent. How do you, sir? Stand you not so amaz'd.
Will you lie down and rest upon the cushions?

Lear. I'll see their trial first. Bring in their evidence.
[*To Edgar*] Thou, robed man of justice, take thy place.
[*To the Fool*] And thou, his yokefellow of equity,

Bench by his side. [*To Kent*] You are o' th' commission,
Sit you too.

Edg. Let us deal justly.

Sleepest or wakest thou, jolly shepherd?
Thy sheep be in the corn;
And for one blast of thy minikin mouth
Thy sheep shall take no harm.

Purr! the cat is gray.

Lear. Arraign her first. 'Tis Goneril. I here take my oath before this honourable assembly, she kick'd the poor King her father.

Fool. Come hither, mistress. Is your name Goneril?

Lear. She cannot deny it.

Fool. Cry you mercy, I took you for a joint-stool.

Lear. And here's another, whose warp'd looks proclaim
What store her heart is made on. Stop her there!
Arms, arms! sword! fire! Corruption in the place!
False justicer, why hast thou let her scape?

Edg. Bless thy five wits!

Kent. O pity! Sir, where is the patience now
That you so oft have boasted to retain?

Edg. [*aside*] My tears begin to take his part so much
They'll mar my counterfeiting.

Lear. The little dogs and all,
Tray, Blanch, and Sweetheart, see, they bark at me.

Edg. Tom will throw his head at them. Avaunt, you curs!

Be thy mouth or black or white,
Tooth that poisons if it bite;
Mastiff, greyhound, mongrel grim,
Hound or spaniel, brach or lym,
Bobtail tyke or trundle-tail —
Tom will make them weep and wail;
For, with throwing thus my head,
Dogs leap the hatch, and all are fled.

Do de, de, de. Sessa! Come, march to wakes and fairs and market towns. Poor Tom, thy horn is dry.

Lear. Then let them anatomize Regan. See what breeds about her heart. Is there any cause in nature that makes these hard hearts? [*To Edgar*] You, sir — I entertain you for one of my hundred; only I do not like the fashion of your garments. You'll say they are Persian attire; but let them be chang'd.

Kent. Now, good my lord, lie here and rest awhile.

Lear. Make no noise, make no noise; draw the curtains. So, so, so. We'll go to supper i' th' morning. So, so, so.

Fool. And I'll go to bed at noon.

Enter *Gloucester*.

Glou. Come hither, friend. Where is the King my master?

Kent. Here, sir; but trouble him not; his wits are gone.

Glou. Good friend, I prithee take him in thy arms.
I have o'erheard a plot of death upon him.
There is a litter ready; lay him in't
And drive towards Dover, friend, where thou shalt meet
Both welcome and protection. Take up thy master.
If thou shouldst dally half an hour, his life,
With thine, and all that offer to defend him,
Stand in assured loss. Take up, take up!
And follow me, that will to some provision
Give thee quick conduct.

Kent. Oppressed nature sleeps.
This rest might yet have balm'd thy broken senses,
Which, if convenience will not allow,
Stand in hard cure. [*To the Fool*] Come, help to bear thy master.
Thou must not stay behind.

Glou. Come, come, away!

Exeunt [*all but Edgar*].

Edg. When we our betters see bearing our woes,
We scarcely think our miseries our foes.
Who alone suffers suffers most i' th' mind,
Leaving free things and happy shows behind;
But then the mind much sufferance doth o'erskip
When grief hath mates, and bearing fellowship.
How light and portable my pain seems now,
When that which makes me bend makes the King bow,
He childed as I fathered! Tom, away!
Mark the high noises, and thyself bewray
When false opinion, whose wrong thought defiles thee,
In thy just proof repeals and reconciles thee.
What will hap more to-night, safe scape the King!
Lurk, lurk. [*Exit.*]

Scene VII. [Gloucester's *Castle*.]

Enter *Cornwall, Regan, Goneril,* [*Edmund* the] *Bastard*, and *Servants*.

Corn. [*to Goneril*] Post speedily to my lord your husband, show him this letter. The army of France is landed. — Seek out the traitor Gloucester.

[*Exeunt some of the Servants.*]

Reg. Hang him instantly.
Gon. Pluck out his eyes.

Corn. Leave him to my displeasure. Edmund, keep you our sister company. The revenges we are bound to take upon your traitorous father are not fit for your beholding. Advise the Duke where you are going, to a most festinate preparation. We are bound to the like. Our posts shall be swift and intelligent betwixt us. Farewell, dear sister; farewell, my Lord of Gloucester.

Enter [*Oswald* the] *Steward*.

How now? Where's the King?

Osw. My Lord of Gloucester hath convey'd him hence.
Some five or six and thirty of his knights,
Hot questrists after him, met him at gate;
Who, with some other of the lord's dependants,
Are gone with him towards Dover, where they boast
To have well-armed friends.

Corn. Get horses for your mistress.
Gon. Farewell, sweet lord, and sister.
Corn. Edmund, farewell.

Exeunt Goneril, [*Edmund, and Oswald*].

Go seek the traitor Gloucester,
Pinion him like a thief, bring him before us.

[*Exeunt other Servants.*]

Though well we may not pass upon his life
Without the form of justice, yet our power
Shall do a court'sy to our wrath, which men
May blame, but not control.

Enter *Gloucester*, brought in by two or three.

Who's there? the traitor?
Reg. Ingrateful fox! 'tis he.
Corn. Bind fast his corky arms.
Glou. What mean your Graces? Good my friends, consider
You are my guests. Do me no foul play, friends.
Corn. Bind him, I say.

[*Servants bind him.*]

Reg. Hard, hard. O filthy traitor!
Glou. Unmerciful lady as you are, I am none.
Corn. To this chair bind him. Villain, thou shalt find — [*Regan plucks his beard.*]
Glou. By the kind gods, 'tis most ignobly done
To pluck me by the beard.
Reg. So white, and such a traitor!
Glou. Naughty lady,
These hairs which thou dost ravish from my chin
Will quicken, and accuse thee. I am your host.
With robber's hands my hospitable favours
You should not ruffle thus. What will you do?
Corn. Come, sir, what letters had you late from France?
Reg. Be simple-answer'd, for we know the truth.
Corn. And what confederacy have you with the traitors
Late footed in the kingdom?
Reg. To whose hands have you sent the lunatic King?
Speak.
Glou. I have a letter guessingly set down,
Which came from one that's of a neutral heart,
And not from one oppos'd.
Corn. Cunning.
Reg. And false.
Corn. Where hast thou sent the King?
Glou. To Dover.
Reg. Wherefore to Dover? Wast thou not charg'd at peril —
Corn. Wherefore to Dover? Let him first answer that.
Glou. I am tied to th' stake, and I must stand the course.
Reg. Wherefore to Dover, sir?
Glou. Because I would not see thy cruel nails
Pluck out his poor old eyes; nor thy fierce sister
In his anointed flesh stick boarish fangs.
The sea, with such a storm as his bare head
In hell-black night endur'd, would have buoy'd up
And quench'd the stelled fires.
Yet, poor old heart, he holp the heavens to rain.
If wolves had at thy gate howl'd that stern time,
Thou shouldst have said, 'Good porter, turn the key.'
All cruels else subscrib'd. But I shall see
The winged vengeance overtake such children.
Corn. See't shalt thou never. Fellows, hold the chair.
Upon these eyes of thine I'll set my foot.
Glou. He that will think to live till he be old,
Give me some help! — O cruel! O ye gods!

Reg. One side will mock another. Th' other too!
Corn. If you see vengeance —
1. Serv. Hold your hand, my lord!
I have serv'd you ever since I was a child;
But better service have I never done you
Than now to bid you hold.
Reg. How now, you dog?
1. Serv. If you did wear a beard upon your chin,
I'ld shake it on this quarrel.
Reg. What do you mean?
Corn. My villain! *Draw and fight.*
1. Serv. Nay, then, come on, and take the chance of anger.
Reg. Give me thy sword. A peasant stand up thus?
She takes a sword and runs at him behind.
1. Serv. O, I am slain! My lord, you have one eye left
To see some mischief on him. O!
He dies.
Corn. Lest it see more, prevent it. Out, vile jelly!
Where is thy lustre now?
Glou. All dark and comfortless! Where's my son Edmund?
Edmund, enkindle all the sparks of nature
To quit this horrid act.
Reg. Out, treacherous villain!
Thou call'st on him that hates thee. It was he
That made the overture of thy treasons to us;
Who is too good to pity thee.
Glou. O my follies! Then Edgar was abus'd.
Kind gods, forgive me that, and prosper him!
Reg. Go thrust him out at gates, and let him smell
His way to Dover.
Exit [one] with Gloucester.
How is't, my lord? How look you?
Corn. I have receiv'd a hurt. Follow me, lady.
Turn out that eyeless villain. Throw this slave
Upon the dunghill. Regan, I bleed apace.
Untimely comes this hurt. Give me your arm.
Exit [Cornwall, led by Regan].
2. Serv. I'll never care what wickedness I do,
If this man come to good.
3. Serv. If she live long,
And in the end meet the old course of death,
Women will all turn monsters.
2. Serv. Let's follow the old Earl, and get the bedlam
To lead him where he would. His roguish madness
Allows itself to anything.
3. Serv. Go thou. I'll fetch some flax and whites of eggs
To apply to his bleeding face. Now heaven help him!
Exeunt.

ACT IV. Scene I. [*The heath.*]

Enter *Edgar*.

Edg. Yet better thus, and known to be contemn'd,
Than still contemn'd and flatter'd. To be worst,
The lowest and most dejected thing of fortune,
Stands still in esperance, lives not in fear.
The lamentable change is from the best;
The worst returns to laughter. Welcome then,
Thou unsubstantial air that I embrace!
The wretch that thou hast blown unto the worst
Owes nothing to thy blasts.

Enter *Gloucester*, led by an *Old Man.*

But who comes here?
My father, poorly led? World, world, O world!
But that thy strange mutations make us hate thee,
Life would not yield to age.
Old Man. O my good lord,
I have been your tenant, and your father's tenant,
These fourscore years.
Glou. Away, get thee away! Good friend, be gone.
Thy comforts can do me no good at all;
Thee they may hurt.
Old Man. You cannot see your way.
Glou. I have no way, and therefore want no eyes;
I stumbled when I saw. Full oft 'tis seen
Our means secure us, and our mere defects
Prove our commodities. Ah dear son Edgar,
The food of thy abused father's wrath!
Might I but live to see thee in my touch,
I'ld say I had eyes again!
Old Man. How now? Who's there?
Edg. [*aside*] O gods! Who is't can say 'I am at the worst'?
I am worse than e'er I was.

Old Man. 'Tis poor mad Tom.
Edg. [*aside*] And worse I may be yet. The worst is not
So long as we can say 'This is the worst.'
Old Man. Fellow, where goest?
Glou. Is it a beggarman?
Old Man. Madman and beggar too.
Glou. He has some reason, else he could not beg.
I' th' last night's storm I such a fellow saw,
Which made me think a man a worm. My son
Came then into my mind, and yet my mind
Was then scarce friends with him. I have heard more since.
As flies to wanton boys are we to th' gods.
They kill us for their sport.
Edg. [*aside*] How should this be?
Bad is the trade that must play fool to sorrow,
Ang'ring itself and others. — Bless thee, master!
Glou. Is that the naked fellow?
Old Man. Ay, my lord.
Glou. Then prithee get thee gone. If for my sake
Thou wilt o'ertake us hence a mile or twain
I' th' way toward Dover, do it for ancient love;
And bring some covering for this naked soul,
Who I'll entreat to lead me.
Old Man. Alack, sir, he is mad!
Glou. 'Tis the time's plague when madmen lead the blind.
Do as I bid thee, or rather do thy pleasure.
Above the rest, be gone.
Old Man. I'll bring him the best 'parel that I have,
Come on't what will. *Exit.*
Glou. Sirrah naked fellow —
Edg. Poor Tom's acold. [*Aside*] I cannot daub it further.
Glou. Come hither, fellow.
Edg. [*aside*] And yet I must. — Bless thy sweet eyes, they bleed.
Glou. Know'st thou the way to Dover?
Edg. Both stile and gate, horseway and footpath. Poor Tom hath been scar'd out of his good wits. Bless thee, good man's son, from the foul fiend! Five fiends have been in poor Tom at once: of lust, as Obidicut; Hobbididence, prince of dumbness; Mahu, of stealing; Modo, of murder; Flibbertigibbet, of mopping and mowing, who since possesses chambermaids and waiting women. So, bless thee, master!
Glou. Here, take this purse, thou whom the heavens' plagues
Have humbled to all strokes. That I am wretched
Makes thee the happier. Heavens, deal so still!
Let the superfluous and lust-dieted man,
That slaves your ordinance, that will not see
Because he does not feel, feel your pow'r quickly;
So distribution should undo excess,
And each man have enough. Dost thou know Dover?
Edg. Ay, master.
Glou. There is a cliff, whose high and bending head
Looks fearfully in the confined deep.
Bring me but to the very brim of it,
And I'll repair the misery thou dost bear
With something rich about me. From that place
I shall no leading need.
Edg. Give me thy arm.
Poor Tom shall lead thee. *Exeunt.*

Scene II. [*Before the* Duke of Albany's *Palace.*]

Enter *Goneril* and [*Edmund* the] *Bastard.*

Gon. Welcome, my lord. I marvel our mild husband
Not met us on the way.

Enter [*Oswald* the] *Steward.*

Now, where's your master?
Osw. Madam, within, but never man so chang'd.
I told him of the army that was landed:
He smil'd at it. I told him you were coming:
His answer was, 'The worse.' Of Gloucester's treachery
And of the loyal service of his son
When I inform'd him, then he call'd me sot
And told me I had turn'd the wrong side out.
What most he should dislike seems pleasant to him;
What like, offensive.
Gon. [*to Edmund*] Then shall you go no further.
It is the cowish terror of his spirit,
That dares not undertake. He'll not feel wrongs
Which tie him to an answer. Our wishes on the way
May prove effects. Back, Edmund, to my brother.
Hasten his musters and conduct his pow'rs.

I must change arms at home and give the distaff
Into my husband's hands. This trusty servant
Shall pass between us. Ere long you are like to hear
(If you dare venture in your own behalf)
A mistress's command. Wear this.
[*Gives a favour.*]
Spare speech.
Decline your head. This kiss, if it durst speak,
Would stretch thy spirits up into the air.
Conceive, and fare thee well.

Edm. Yours in the ranks of death! *Exit.*

Gon. My most dear Gloucester!
O, the difference of man and man!
To thee a woman's services are due;
My fool usurps my body.

Osw. Madam, here comes my lord. *Exit.*

Enter *Albany.*

Gon. I have been worth the whistle.

Alb. O Goneril,
You are not worth the dust which the rude wind
Blows in your face! I fear your disposition.
That nature which contemns it origin
Cannot be bordered certain in itself.
She that herself will sliver and disbranch
From her material sap, perforce must wither
And come to deadly use.

Gon. No more! The text is foolish.

Alb. Wisdom and goodness to the vile seem vile;
Filths savour but themselves. What have you done?
Tigers, not daughters, what have you perform'd?
A father, and a gracious aged man,
Whose reverence even the head-lugg'd bear would lick,
Most barbarous, most degenerate, have you madded.
Could my good brother suffer you to do it?
A man, a prince, by him so benefited!
If that the heavens do not their visible spirits
Send quickly down to tame these vile offences,
It will come,
Humanity must perforce prey on itself,
Like monsters of the deep.

Gon. Milk-liver'd man!
That bear'st a cheek for blows, a head for wrongs;
Who hast not in thy brows an eye discerning
Thine honour from thy suffering; that not know'st
Fools do those villains pity who are punish'd
Ere they have done their mischief. Where's thy drum?
France spreads his banners in our noiseless land,
With plumed helm thy state begins to threat,
Whiles thou, a moral fool, sit'st still, and criest
'Alack, why does he so?'

Alb. See thyself, devil!
Proper deformity seems not in the fiend
So horrid as in woman.

Gon. O vain fool!

Alb. Thou changed and self-cover'd thing, for shame!
Bemonster not thy feature! Were't my fitness
To let these hands obey my blood,
They are apt enough to dislocate and tear
Thy flesh and bones. Howe'er thou art a fiend,
A woman's shape doth shield thee.

Gon. Marry, your manhood mew!

Enter a *Gentleman.*

Alb. What news?

Gent. O, my good lord, the Duke of Cornwall's dead,
Slain by his servant, going to put out
The other eye of Gloucester.

Alb. Gloucester's eyes?

Gent. A servant that he bred, thrill'd with remorse,
Oppos'd against the act, bending his sword
To his great master; who, thereat enrag'd,
Flew on him, and amongst them fell'd him dead;
But not without that harmful stroke which since
Hath pluck'd him after.

Alb. This shows you are above,
You justicers, that these our nether crimes
So speedily can venge! But O poor Gloucester!
Lost he his other eye?

Gent. Both, both, my lord.
This letter, madam, craves a speedy answer.
'Tis from your sister.

Gon. [*aside*] One way I like this well;
But being widow, and my Gloucester with her,
May all the building in my fancy pluck
Upon my hateful life. Another way
The news is not so tart. — I'll read, and answer.
Exit.

Alb. Where was his son when they did take his eyes?

Gent. Come with my lady hither.

Alb. He is not here.

Gent. No, my good lord; I met him back again.

Alb. Knows he the wickedness?

Gent. Ay, my good lord. 'Twas he inform'd against him,
And quit the house on purpose, that their punishment
Might have the freer course.
Alb. Gloucester, I live
To thank thee for the love thou show'dst the King,
And to revenge thine eyes. Come hither, friend.
Tell me what more thou know'st. *Exeunt.*

[Scene III. *The French camp near Dover.*]

Enter *Kent* and a *Gentleman.*

Kent. Why the King of France is so suddenly gone back know you the reason?

Gent. Something he left imperfect in the state, which since his coming forth is thought of, which imports to the kingdom so much fear and danger that his personal return was most required and necessary.

Kent. Who hath he left behind him general?

Gent. The Marshal of France, Monsieur La Far.

Kent. Did your letters pierce the Queen to any demonstration of grief?

Gent. Ay, sir. She took them, read them in my presence,
And now and then an ample tear trill'd down
Her delicate cheek. It seem'd she was a queen
Over her passion, who, most rebel-like,
Sought to be king o'er her.
Kent. O, then it mov'd her?
Gent. Not to a rage. Patience and sorrow strove
Who should express her goodliest. You have seen
Sunshine and rain at once: her smiles and tears
Were like, a better way. Those happy smilets
That play'd on her ripe lip seem'd not to know
What guests were in her eyes, which parted thence
As pearls from diamonds dropp'd. In brief,
Sorrow would be a rarity most belov'd,
If all could so become it.
Kent. Made she no verbal question?
Gent. Faith, once or twice she heav'd the name of father
Pantingly forth, as if it press'd her heart;
Cried 'Sisters, sisters! Shame of ladies! Sisters!
Kent! father! sisters! What, i' th' storm? i' th' night?
Let pity not be believ'd!' There she shook
The holy water from her heavenly eyes,
And clamour moisten'd. Then away she started
To deal with grief alone.
Kent. It is the stars,
The stars above us, govern our conditions;
Else one self mate and mate could not beget
Such different issues. You spoke not with her since?
Gent. No.
Kent. Was this before the King return'd?
Gent. No, since.
Kent. Well, sir, the poor distressed Lear's i' th' town;
Who sometime, in his better tune, remembers
What we are come about, and by no means
Will yield to see his daughter.
Gent. Why, good sir?
Kent. A sovereign shame so elbows him; his own unkindness,
That stripp'd her from his benediction, turn'd her
To foreign casualties, gave her dear rights
To his dog-hearted daughters — these things sting
His mind so venomously that burning shame
Detains him from Cordelia.
Gent. Alack, poor gentleman!
Kent. Of Albany's and Cornwall's powers you heard not?
Gent. 'Tis so; they are afoot.
Kent. Well, sir, I'll bring you to our master Lear
And leave you to attend him. Some dear cause
Will in concealment wrap me up awhile.
When I am known aright, you shall not grieve
Lending me this acquaintance. I pray you go
Along with me. *Exeunt.*

Scene [IV. *The French camp.*]

Enter, with *Drum* and *Colours, Cordelia, Doctor,* and *Soldiers.*

Cor. Alack, 'tis he! Why, he was met even now
As mad as the vex'd sea, singing aloud,
Crown'd with rank fumiter and furrow weeds,
With hardocks, hemlock, nettles, cuckoo flow'rs,
Darnel, and all the idle weeds that grow
In our sustaining corn. A century send forth.
Search every acre in the high-grown field
And bring him to our eye. [*Exit an Officer.*]
What can man's wisdom
In the restoring his bereaved sense?
He that helps him take all my outward worth

Doct. There is means, madam.
Our foster nurse of nature is repose,
The which he lacks. That to provoke in him
Are many simples operative, whose power
Will close the eye of anguish.
Cor. All blest secrets,
All you unpublish'd virtues of the earth,
Spring with my tears! be aidant and remediate
In the good man's distress! Seek, seek for him!
Lest his ungovern'd rage dissolve the life
That wants the means to lead it.

Enter *Messenger.*

Mess. News, madam.
The British pow'rs are marching hitherward.
Cor. 'Tis known before. Our preparation stands
In expectation of them. O dear father,
It is thy business that I go about.
Therefore great France
My mourning and important tears hath pitied.
No blown ambition doth our arms incite,
But love, dear love, and our ag'd father's right.
Soon may I hear and see him! *Exeunt.*

Scene [V. Gloucester's *Castle.*]

Enter *Regan* and [*Oswald* the] *Steward.*

Reg. But are my brother's pow'rs set forth?
Osw. Ay, madam.
Reg. Himself in person there?
Osw. Madam, with much ado
Your sister is the better soldier.
Reg. Lord Edmund spake not with your lord at home?
Osw. No, madam.
Reg. What might import my sister's letter to him?
Osw. I know not, lady.
Reg. Faith, he is posted hence on serious matter.
It was great ignorance, Gloucester's eyes being out,
To let him live. Where he arrives he moves
All hearts against us. Edmund, I think, is gone,
In pity of his misery, to dispatch
His nighted life; moreover, to descry
The strength o' th' enemy.
Osw. I must needs after him, madam, with my letter.
Reg. Our troops set forth to-morrow. Stay with us.
The ways are dangerous.
Osw. I may not, madam.
My lady charg'd my duty in this business.
Reg. Why should she write to Edmund? Might not you
Transport her purposes by word? Belike,
Something — I know not what — I'll love thee much —
Let me unseal the letter.
Osw. Madam, I had rather —
Reg. I know your lady does not love her husband;
I am sure of that; and at her late being here
She gave strange eliads and most speaking looks
To noble Edmund. I know you are of her bosom.
Osw. I, madam?
Reg. I speak in understanding. Y'are! I know't.
Therefore I do advise you take this note.
My lord is dead; Edmund and I have talk'd,
And more convenient is he for my hand
Than for your lady's. You may gather more.
If you do find him, pray you give him this;
And when your mistress hears thus much from you,
I pray desire her call her wisdom to her.
So farewell.
If you do chance to hear of that blind traitor,
Preferment falls on him that cuts him off.
Osw. Would I could meet him, madam! I should show
What party I do follow.
Reg. Fare thee well. *Exeunt.*

Scene [VI. *The country near Dover.*]

Enter *Gloucester,* and *Edgar* [like a *Peasant*].

Glou. When shall I come to th' top of that same hill?
Edg. You do climb up it now. Look how we labour.
Glou. Methinks the ground is even.
Edg. Horrible steep.
Hark, do you hear the sea?
Glou. No, truly.
Edg. Why then, your other senses grow imperfect
By your eyes' anguish.
Glou. So may it be indeed.
Methinks thy voice is alter'd, and thou speak'st
In better phrase and matter than thou didst.

Edg. Y'are much deceiv'd. In nothing am I chang'd
But in my garments.
Glou. Methinks y'are better spoken.
Edg. Come on, sir; here's the place. Stand still. How fearful
And dizzy 'tis to cast one's eyes so low!
The crows and choughs that wing the midway air
Show scarce so gross as beetles. Halfway down
Hangs one that gathers sampire — dreadful trade!
Methinks he seems no bigger than his head.
The fishermen that walk upon the beach
Appear like mice; and yond tall anchoring bark,
Diminish'd to her cock; her cock, a buoy
Almost too small for sight. The murmuring surge
That on th' unnumb'red idle pebble chafes
Cannot be heard so high. I'll look no more,
Lest my brain turn, and the deficient sight
Topple down headlong.
Glou. Set me where you stand.
Edg. Give me your hand. You are now within a foot
Of th' extreme verge. For all beneath the moon
Would I not leap upright.
Glou. Let go my hand.
Here, friend, 's another purse; in it a jewel
Well worth a poor man's taking. Fairies and gods
Prosper it with thee! Go thou further off;
Bid me farewell, and let me hear thee going.
Edg. Now fare ye well, good sir.
Glou. With all my heart.
Edg. [*aside*]. Why I do trifle thus with his despair
Is done to cure it.
Glou. O you mighty gods! *He kneels.*
This world I do renounce, and, in your sights
Shake patiently my great affliction off.
If I could bear it longer and not fall
To quarrel with your great opposeless wills,
My snuff and loathed part of nature should
Burn itself out. If Edgar live, O, bless him!
Now, fellow, fare thee well.
He falls [*forward and swoons*].
Edg. Gone, sir, farewell. —
And yet I know not how conceit may rob
The treasury of life when life itself
Yields to the theft. Had he been where he thought,
By this had thought been past. — Alive or dead?
Ho you, sir! friend! Hear you, sir? Speak! —
Thus might he pass indeed. Yet he revives.
What are you, sir?
Glou. Away, and let me die.
Edg. Hadst thou been aught but gossamer, feathers, air,
So many fadom down precipitating,
Thou'dst shiver'd like an egg; but thou dost breathe;
Hast heavy substance; bleed'st not; speak'st; art sound.
Ten masts at each make not the altitude
Which thou hast perpendicularly fell.
Thy life's a miracle. Speak yet again.
Glou. But have I fall'n, or no?
Edg. From the dread summit of this chalky bourn.
Look up a-height. The shrill-gorg'd lark so far
Cannot be seen or heard. Do but look up.
Glou. Alack, I have no eyes!
Is wretchedness depriv'd that benefit
To end itself by death? 'Twas yet some comfort
When misery could beguile the tyrant's rage
And frustrate his proud will.
Edg. Give me your arm.
Up — so. How is't? Feel you your legs? You stand.
Glou. Too well, too well.
Edg. This is above all strangeness.
Upon the crown o' th' cliff what thing was that
Which parted from you?
Glou. A poor unfortunate beggar.
Edg. As I stood here below, methought his eyes
Were two full moons; he had a thousand noses,
Horns whelk'd and wav'd like the enridged sea.
It was some fiend. Therefore, thou happy father,
Think that the clearest gods, who make them honours
Of men's impossibilities, have preserv'd thee.
Glou. I do remember now. Henceforth I'll bear
Affliction till it do cry out itself
'Enough, enough,' and die. That thing you speak of,
I took it for a man. Often 'twould say
'The fiend, the fiend' — he led me to that place.
Edg. Bear free and patient thoughts.

Enter *Lear*, mad, [fantastically dressed with weeds].

But who comes here?
The safer sense will ne'er accommodate
His master thus.

Lear. No, they cannot touch me for coining; I am the King himself.

Edg. O thou side-piercing sight!

Lear. Nature's above art in that respect. There's your press money. That fellow handles his bow like a crow-keeper. Draw me a clothier's yard. Look, look, a mouse! Peace, peace; this piece of toasted cheese will do't. There's my gauntlet; I'll prove it on a giant. Bring up the brown bills. O, well flown, bird! i' th' clout, i' th' clout! Hewgh! Give the word.

Edg. Sweet marjoram.

Lear. Pass.

Glou. I know that voice.

Lear. Ha! Goneril with a white beard? They flatter'd me like a dog, and told me I had white hairs in my beard ere the black ones were there. To say 'ay' and 'no' to everything I said! 'Ay' and 'no' too was no good divinity. When the rain came to wet me once, and the wind to make me chatter; when the thunder would not peace at my bidding; there I found 'em, there I smelt 'em out. Go to, they are not men o' their words! They told me I was everything. 'Tis a lie — I am not ague-proof.

Glou. The trick of that voice I do well remember.
Is't not the King?

Lear. Ay, every inch a king!
When I do stare, see how the subject quakes.
I pardon that man's life. What was thy cause?
Adultery?
Thou shalt not die. Die for adultery? No.
The wren goes to't, and the small gilded fly
Does lecher in my sight.
Let copulation thrive; for Gloucester's bastard son
Was kinder to his father than my daughters
Got 'tween the lawful sheets.
To't, luxury, pell-mell! for I lack soldiers.
Behold yond simp'ring dame,
Whose face between her forks presageth snow,
That minces virtue, and does shake the head
To hear of pleasure's name.
The fitchew nor the soiled horse goes to't
With a more riotous appetite.
Down from the waist they are Centaurs,
Though women all above.
But to the girdle do the gods inherit,
Beneath is all the fiend's.
There's hell, there's darkness, there's the sulphurous pit; burning, scalding, stench, consumption. Fie, fie, fie! pah, pah! Give me an ounce of civet, good apothecary, to sweeten my imagination. There's money for thee.

Glou. O, let me kiss that hand!

Lear. Let me wipe it first; it smells of mortality.

Glou. O ruin'd piece of nature! This great world
Shall so wear out to naught. Dost thou know me?

Lear. I remember thine eyes well enough. Dost thou squiny at me? No, do thy worst, blind Cupid! I'll not love. Read thou this challenge; mark but the penning of it.

Glou. Were all the letters suns, I could not see one.

Edg. [*aside*] I would not take this from report. It is,
And my heart breaks at it.

Lear. Read.

Glou. What, with the case of eyes?

Lear. O, ho, are you there with me? No eyes in your head, nor no money in your purse? Your eyes are in a heavy case, your purse in a light. Yet you see how this world goes.

Glou. I see it feelingly.

Lear. What, art mad? A man may see how the world goes with no eyes. Look with thine ears. See how yond justice rails upon yond simple thief. Hark in thine ear. Change places and, handy-dandy, which is the justice, which is the thief? Thou hast seen a farmer's dog bark at a beggar?

Glou. Ay, sir.

Lear. And the creature run from the cur? There thou mightst behold the great image of authority: a dog 's obey'd in office.
Thou rascal beadle, hold thy bloody hand!
Why dost thou lash that whore? Strip thine own back.
Thou hotly lusts to use her in that kind
For which thou whip'st her. The usurer hangs the cozener.
Through tatter'd clothes small vices do appear;
Robes and furr'd gowns hide all. Plate sin with gold,
And the strong lance of justice hurtless breaks;
Arm it in rags, a pygmy's straw does pierce it.
None does offend, none — I say none! I'll able 'em.
Take that of me, my friend, who have the power
To seal th' accuser's lips. Get thee glass eyes
And, like a scurvy politician, seem
To see the things thou dost not. Now, now, now, now!
Pull off my boots. Harder, harder! So.

Edg. O, matter and impertinency mix'd!
Reason in madness!

Lear. If thou wilt weep my fortunes, take my eyes.
I know thee well enough; thy name is Gloucester.
Thou must be patient. We came crying hither;
Thou know'st, the first time that we smell the air
We wawl and cry. I will preach to thee. Mark.
Glou. Alack, alack the day!
Lear. When we are born, we cry that we are come
To this great stage of fools. This' a good block.
It were a delicate stratagem to shoe
A troop of horse with felt. I'll put't in proof,
And when I have stol'n upon these sons-in-law,
Then kill, kill, kill, kill, kill, kill!

Enter a *Gentleman* [with *Attendants*].

Gent. O, here he is! Lay hand upon him. — Sir,
Your most dear daughter —
Lear. No rescue? What, a prisoner? I am even
The natural fool of fortune. Use me well;
You shall have ransom. Let me have a surgeon;
I am cut to th' brains.
Gent. You shall have anything.
Lear. No seconds? All myself?
Why, this would make a man a man of salt,
To use his eyes for garden waterpots,
Ay, and laying autumn's dust.
Gent. Good sir —
Lear. I will die bravely, like a smug bridegroom. What!
I will be jovial. Come, come, I am a king;
My masters, know you that?
Gent. You are a royal one, and we obey you.
Lear. Then there's life in't. Nay, an you get it, you shall get it by running. Sa, sa, sa, sa!

Exit running. [*Attendants follow*.]

Gent. A sight most pitiful in the meanest wretch,
Past speaking of in a king! Thou hast one daughter
Who redeems nature from the general curse
Which twain have brought her to.
Edg. Hail, gentle sir.
Gent. Sir, speed you. What's your will?
Edg. Do you hear aught, sir, of a battle toward?
Gent. Most sure and vulgar. Every one hears that
Which can distinguish sound.
Edg. But, by your favour,
How near's the other army?
Gent. Near and on speedy foot. The main descry
Stands on the hourly thought.
Edg. I thank you, sir. That's all.
Gent. Though that the Queen on special cause is here,
Her army is mov'd on.
Edg. I thank you, sir.

Exit [*Gentleman*].

Glou. You ever-gentle gods, take my breath from me;
Let not my worser spirit tempt me again
To die before you please!
Edg. Well pray you, father.
Glou. Now, good sir, what are you?
Edg. A most poor man, made tame to fortune's blows,
Who, by the art of known and feeling sorrows,
Am pregnant to good pity. Give me your hand;
I'll lead you to some biding.
Glou. Hearty thanks.
The bounty and the benison of heaven
To boot, and boot!

Enter [*Oswald* the] *Steward*.

Osw. A proclaim'd prize! Most happy!
That eyeless head of thine was first fram'd flesh
To raise my fortunes. Thou old unhappy traitor,
Briefly thyself remember. The sword is out
That must destroy thee.
Glou. Now let thy friendly hand
Put strength enough to't.

[*Edgar interposes*.]

Osw. Wherefore, bold peasant,
Dar'st thou support a publish'd traitor? Hence!
Lest that th' infection of his fortune take
Like hold on thee. Let go his arm.
Edg. Chill not let go, zir, without vurther 'cagion.
Osw. Let go, slave, or thou diest!
Edg. Good gentleman, go your gait, and let poor voke pass. An chud ha' bin zwagger'd out of my life, 'twould not ha' bin zo long as 'tis by a vortnight. Nay, come not near th' old man. Keep out, che vore ye, or Ise try whether your costard or my ballow be the harder. Chill be plain with you.
Osw. Out, dunghill! *They fight*.
Edg. Chill pick your teeth, zir. Come! No matter vor your foins.

[*Oswald falls*.]

Osw. Slave, thou hast slain me. Villain, take my purse.
If ever thou wilt thrive, bury my body,

And give the letters which thou find'st about me
To Edmund Earl of Gloucester. Seek him out
Upon the British party. O, untimely death!
Death! *He dies.*

Edg. I know thee well. A serviceable villain,
As duteous to the vices of thy mistress
As badness would desire.

Glou. What, is he dead?

Edg. Sit you down, father; rest you.
Let's see his pockets; these letters that he speaks of
May be my friends. He's dead. I am only sorry
He had no other deathsman. Let us see.
Leave, gentle wax; and, manners, blame us not.
To know our enemies' minds, we'ld rip their hearts;
Their papers, is more lawful. *Reads the letter.*

'Let our reciprocal vows be rememb'red. You have many opportunities to cut him off. If your will want not, time and place will be fruitfully offer'd. There is nothing done, if he return the conqueror. Then am I the prisoner, and his bed my jail; from the loathed warmth whereof deliver me, and supply the place for your labour.

'Your (wife, so I would say) affectionate servant,
'GONERIL.'

O indistinguish'd space of woman's will!
A plot upon her virtuous husband's life,
And the exchange my brother! Here in the sands
Thee I'll rake up, the post unsanctified
Of murtherous lechers; and in the mature time
With this ungracious paper strike the sight
Of the death-practis'd Duke. For him 'tis well
That of thy death and business I can tell.

Glou. The King is mad. How stiff is my vile sense,
That I stand up, and have ingenious feeling
Of my huge sorrows! Better I were distract.
So should my thoughts be sever'd from my griefs,
And woes by wrong imaginations lose
The knowledge of themselves.
A drum afar off.

Edg. Give me your hand.
Far off methinks I hear the beaten drum.
Come, father, I'll bestow you with a friend.
Exeunt.

Scene VII. [*A tent in the French camp.*]

Enter *Cordelia, Kent, Doctor,* and *Gentleman.*

Cor. O thou good Kent, how shall I live and work
To match thy goodness? My life will be too short
And every measure fail me.

Kent. To be acknowledg'd, madam, is o'erpaid.
All my reports go with the modest truth;
Nor more nor clipp'd, but so.

Cor. Be better suited.
These weeds are memories of those worser hours.
I prithee put them off.

Kent. Pardon, dear madam.
Yet to be known shortens my made intent.
My boon I make it that you know me not
Till time and I think meet.

Cor. Then be't so, my good lord. [*To the Doctor*] How does the King?

Doct. Madam, sleeps still.

Cor. O you kind gods,
Cure this great breach in his abused nature!
Th' untun'd and jarring senses, O, wind up
Of this child-changed father!

Doct. So please your Majesty
That we may wake the King? He hath slept long.

Cor. Be govern'd by your knowledge, and proceed
I' th' sway of your own will. Is he array'd?

Enter *Lear* in a chair carried by *Servants.*

Gent. Ay, madam. In the heaviness of sleep
We put fresh garments on him.

Doct. Be by, good madam, when we do awake him.
I doubt not of his temperance.

Cor. Very well.
[*Music.*]

Doct. Please you draw near. Louder the music there!

Cor. O my dear father, restoration hang
Thy medicine on my lips, and let this kiss
Repair those violent harms that my two sisters
Have in thy reverence made!

Kent. Kind and dear princess!

Cor. Had you not been their father, these white flakes
Had challeng'd pity of them. Was this a face
To be oppos'd against the warring winds?
To stand against the deep dread-bolted thunder?
In the most terrible and nimble stroke
Of quick cross lightning? to watch — poor perdu! —
With this thin helm? Mine enemy's dog,
Though he had bit me, should have stood that night

Against my fire; and wast thou fain, poor father,
To hovel thee with swine and rogues forlorn,
In short and musty straw? Alack, alack!
'Tis wonder that thy life and wits at once
Had not concluded all. — He wakes. Speak to him.

Doct. Madam, do you; 'tis fittest.

Cor. How does my royal lord? How fares your Majesty?

Lear. You do me wrong to take me out o' th' grave.
Thou art a soul in bliss; but I am bound
Upon a wheel of fire, that mine own tears
Do scald like molten lead.

Cor. Sir, do you know me?

Lear. You are a spirit, I know. When did you die?

Cor. Still, still, far wide!

Doct. He's scarce awake. Let him alone awhile.

Lear. Where have I been? Where am I? Fair daylight?
I am mightily abus'd. I should e'en die with pity,
To see another thus. I know not what to say.
I will not swear these are my hands. Let's see.
I feel this pin prick. Would I were assur'd
Of my condition!

Cor. O, look upon me, sir,
And hold your hands in benediction o'er me.
No, sir, you must not kneel.

Lear. Pray, do not mock me.
I am a very foolish fond old man,
Fourscore and upward, not an hour more nor less;
And, to deal plainly,
I fear I am not in my perfect mind.
Methinks I should know you, and know this man;
Yet I am doubtful; for I am mainly ignorant
What place this is; and all the skill I have
Remembers not these garments; nor I know not
Where I did lodge last night. Do not laugh at me;
For (as I am a man) I think this lady
To be my child Cordelia.

Cor. And so I am! I am!

Lear. Be your tears wet? Yes, faith. I pray weep not.
If you have poison for me, I will drink it.
I know you do not love me; for your sisters
Have, as I do remember, done me wrong.
You have some cause, they have not.

Cor. No cause, no cause.

Lear. Am I in France?

Kent. In your own kingdom, sir.

Lear. Do not abuse me.

Doct. Be comforted, good madam. The great rage
You see is kill'd in him; and yet it is danger
To make him even o'er the time he has lost.
Desire him to go in. Trouble him no more
Till further settling.

Cor. Will't please your Highness walk?

Lear. You must bear with me.
Pray you now, forget and forgive. I am old and foolish.

Exeunt. Manent Kent and Gentleman.

Gent. Holds it true, sir, that the Duke of Cornwall was so slain?

Kent. Most certain, sir.

Gent. Who is conductor of his people?

Kent. As 'tis said, the bastard son of Gloucester.

Gent. They say Edgar, his banish'd son, is with the Earl of Kent in Germany.

Kent. Report is changeable. 'Tis time to look about; the powers of the kingdom approach apace.

Gent. The arbitrement is like to be bloody. Fare you well, sir. [*Exit.*]

Kent. My point and period will be throughly wrought,
Or well or ill, as this day's battle 's fought. *Exit.*

ACT V. Scene I. [*The British camp near Dover.*]

Enter, with *Drum* and *Colours, Edmund, Regan, Gentlemen,* and *Soldiers.*

Edm. Know of the Duke if his last purpose hold,
Or whether since he is advis'd by aught
To change the course. He's full of alteration
And self-reproving. Bring his constant pleasure.

[*Exit an Officer.*]

Reg. Our sister's man is certainly miscarried.

Edm. 'Tis to be doubted, madam.

Reg. Now, sweet lord.
You know the goodness I intend upon you.

Tell me — but truly — but then speak the truth —
Do you not love my sister?

Edm. In honour'd love.

Reg. But have you never found my brother's way
To the forfended place?

Edm. That thought abuses you.

Reg. I am doubtful that you have been conjunct
And bosom'd with her, as far as we call hers.

Edm. No, by mine honour, madam.

Reg. I never shall endure her. Dear my lord,
Be not familiar with her.

Edm. Fear me not.
She and the Duke her husband!

Enter, with *Drum* and *Colours, Albany, Goneril, Soldiers.*

Gon. [*aside*] I had rather lose the battle than that sister
Should loosen him and me.

Alb. Our very loving sister, well bemet.
Sir, this I hear: the King is come to his daughter,
With others whom the rigour of our state
Forc'd to cry out. Where I could not be honest,
I never yet was valiant. For this business,
It toucheth us as France invades our land,
Not bolds the King, with others whom, I fear,
Most just and heavy causes make oppose.

Edm. Sir, you speak nobly.

Reg. Why is this reason'd?

Gon. Combine together 'gainst the enemy;
For these domestic and particular broils
Are not the question here.

Alb. Let's then determine
With th' ancient of war on our proceeding.

Edm. I shall attend you presently at your tent.

Reg. Sister, you'll go with us?

Gon. No.

Reg. 'Tis most convenient. Pray you go with us.

Gon. [*aside*] O, ho, I know the riddle. — I will go.

[As they are going out,] enter *Edgar* [disguised].

Edg. If e'er your Grace had speech with man so poor,
Hear me one word.

Alb. I'll overtake you. — Speak.

Exeunt [*all but Albany and Edgar*].

Edg. Before you fight the battle, ope this letter.
If you have victory, let the trumpet sound
For him that brought it. Wretched though I seem,
I can produce a champion that will prove
What is avouched there. If you miscarry,
Your business of the world hath so an end,
And machination ceases. Fortune love you!

Alb. Stay till I have read the letter.

Edg. I was forbid it.
When time shall serve, let but the herald cry,
And I'll appear again.

Alb. Why, fare thee well. I will o'erlook thy paper.

Exit [*Edgar*].

Enter *Edmund.*

Edm. The enemy's in view; draw up your powers.
Here is the guess of their true strength and forces
By diligent discovery; but your haste
Is now urg'd on you.

Alb. We will greet the time. *Exit.*

Edm. To both these sisters have I sworn my love;
Each jealous of the other, as the stung
Are of the adder. Which of them shall I take?
Both? one? or neither? Neither can be enjoy'd,
If both remain alive. To take the widow
Exasperates, makes mad her sister Goneril;
And hardly shall I carry out my side,
Her husband being alive. Now then, we'll use
His countenance for the battle, which being done,
Let her who would be rid of him devise
His speedy taking off. As for the mercy
Which he intends to Lear and to Cordelia —
The battle done, and they within our power,
Shall never see his pardon; for my state
Stands on me to defend, not to debate. *Exit.*

Scene II. [*A field between the two camps.*]

Alarum within. Enter, with *Drum* and *Colours,* the *Powers of France* over the stage, *Cordelia* with her *Father* in her hand, and exeunt.

Enter *Edgar* and *Gloucester.*

Edg. Here, father, take the shadow of this tree
For your good host. Pray that the right may thrive.

If ever I return to you again,
I'll bring you comfort.
Glou. Grace go with you, sir!
Exit [Edgar].

Alarum and retreat within. Enter *Edgar.*

Edg. Away, old man! give me thy hand! away!
King Lear hath lost, he and his daughter ta'en.
Give me thy hand! come on!
Glou. No further, sir. A man may rot even here.
Edg. What, in ill thoughts again? Men must endure
Their going hence, even as their coming hither;
Ripeness is all. Come on.
Glou. And that's true too. *Exeunt.*

Scene III. [*The British camp, near Dover.*]

Enter, in conquest, with *Drum* and *Colours, Edmund*; *Lear* and *Cordelia* as prisoners; *Soldiers, Captain.*

Edm. Some officers take them away. Good guard
Until their greater pleasures first be known
That are to censure them.
Cor. We are not the first
Who with best meaning have incurr'd the worst.
For thee, oppressed king, am I cast down;
Myself could else outfrown false Fortune's frown.
Shall we not see these daughters and these sisters?
Lear. No, no, no, no! Come, let's away to prison.
We two alone will sing like birds i' th' cage.
When thou dost ask me blessing, I'll kneel down
And ask of thee forgiveness. So we'll live,
And pray, and sing, and tell old tales, and laugh
At gilded butterflies, and hear poor rogues
Talk of court news; and we'll talk with them too —
Who loses and who wins; who's in, who's out —
And take upon 's the mystery of things,
As if we were God's spies; and we'll wear out,
In a wall'd prison, packs and sects of great ones
That ebb and flow by th' moon.
Edm. Take them away.
Lear. Upon such sacrifices, my Cordelia,
The gods themselves throw incense. Have I caught thee?
He that parts us shall bring a brand from heaven
And fire us hence like foxes. Wipe thine eyes.
The goodyears shall devour 'em, flesh and fell,
Ere they shall make us weep! We'll see 'em starv'd first.
Come.
Exeunt [Lear and Cordelia, guarded].
Edm. Come hither, Captain; hark.
Take thou this note [*gives a paper*]. Go follow them to prison.
One step I have advanc'd thee. If thou dost
As this instructs thee, thou dost make thy way
To noble fortunes. Know thou this, that men
Are as the time is. To be tender-minded
Does not become a sword. Thy great employment
Will not bear question. Either say thou'lt do't,
Or thrive by other means.
Capt. I'll do't, my lord.
Edm. About it! and write happy when th' hast done.
Mark — I say, instantly; and carry it so
As I have set it down.
Capt. I cannot draw a cart, nor eat dried oats;
If it be man's work, I'll do't. *Exit.*

Flourish. Enter *Albany, Goneril, Regan, Soldiers.*

Alb. Sir, you have show'd to-day your valiant strain,
And fortune led you well. You have the captives
Who were the opposites of this day's strife.
We do require them of you, so to use them
As we shall find their merits and our safety
May equally determine.
Edm. Sir, I thought it fit
To send the old and miserable King
To some retention and appointed guard;
Whose age has charms in it, whose title more,
To pluck the common bosom on his side
And turn our impress'd lances in our eyes
Which do command them. With him I sent the Queen,
My reason all the same; and they are ready
To-morrow, or at further space, t' appear
Where you shall hold your session. At this time
We sweat and bleed: the friend hath lost his friend;
And the best quarrels, in the heat, are curs'd
By those that feel their sharpness.
The question of Cordelia and her father
Requires a fitter place.
Alb. Sir, by your patience,
I hold you but a subject of this war,
Not as a brother.

Reg. That's as we list to grace him.
Methinks our pleasure might have been demanded
Ere you had spoke so far. He led our powers,
Bore the commission of my place and person,
The which immediacy may well stand up
And call itself your brother.
Gon. Not so hot!
In his own grace he doth exalt himself
More than in your addition.
Reg. In my rights
By me invested, he compeers the best.
Gon. That were the most if he should husband you.
Reg. Jesters do oft prove prophets.
Gon. Holla, holla!
That eye that told you so look'd but asquint.
Reg. Lady, I am not well; else I should answer
From a full-flowing stomach. General,
Take thou my soldiers, prisoners, patrimony;
Dispose of them, of me; the walls are thine.
Witness the world that I create thee here
My lord and master.
Gon. Mean you to enjoy him?
Alb. The let-alone lies not in your good will.
Edm. Nor in thine, lord.
Alb. Half-blooded fellow, yes.
Reg. [*to Edmund*] Let the drum strike, and prove my title thine.
Alb. Stay yet; hear reason. Edmund, I arrest thee
On capital treason; and, in thine attaint,
This gilded serpent [*points to Goneril*]. For your claim, fair sister,
I bar it in the interest of my wife.
'Tis she is subcontracted to this lord,
And I, her husband, contradict your banes.
If you will marry, make your loves to me;
My lady is bespoke.
Gon. An interlude!
Alb. Thou art arm'd, Gloucester. Let the trumpet sound.
If none appear to prove upon thy person
Thy heinous, manifest, and many treasons,
There is my pledge [*throws down a glove*]! I'll prove it on thy heart,
Ere I taste bread, thou art in nothing less
Than I have here proclaim'd thee.
Reg. Sick, O, sick!
Gon. [*aside*] If not, I'll ne'er trust medicine.
Edm. There's my exchange [*throws down a glove*]. What in the world he is
That names me traitor, villain-like he lies.
Call by thy trumpet. He that dares approach,
On him, on you, who not? I will maintain
My truth and honour firmly.
Alb. A herald, ho!
Edm. A herald, ho, a herald!
Alb. Trust to thy single virtue; for thy soldiers,
All levied in my name, have in my name
Took their discharge.
Reg. My sickness grows upon me.
Alb. She is not well. Convey her to my tent.
[*Exit Regan, led.*]

Enter a *Herald.*

Come hither, herald. Let the trumpet sound,
And read out this.
Capt. Sound, trumpet! *A trumpet sounds.*

Her. (*reads*) 'If any man of quality or degree within the lists of the army will maintain upon Edmund, supposed Earl of Gloucester, that he is a manifold traitor, let him appear by the third sound of the trumpet. He is bold in his defence.'

Edm. Sound! *First trumpet.*
Her. Again! *Second trumpet.*
Her. Again! *Third trumpet.*
Trumpet answers within.

Enter *Edgar*, armed, at the third sound, a *Trumpet* before him.

Alb. Ask him his purposes, why he appears
Upon this call o' th' trumpet.
Her. What are you?
Your name, your quality? and why you answer
This present summons?
Edg. Know my name is lost;
By treason's tooth bare-gnawn and canker-bit.
Yet am I noble as the adversary
I come to cope.
Alb. Which is that adversary?
Edg. What's he that speaks for Edmund Earl of Gloucester?
Edm. Himself. What say'st thou to him?
Edg. Draw thy sword,
That, if my speech offend a noble heart,
Thy arm may do thee justice. Here is mine.
Behold, it is the privilege of mine honours,
My oath, and my profession. I protest —
Maugre thy strength, youth, place, and eminence,
Despite thy victor sword and fire-new fortune,
Thy valour and thy heart — thou art a traitor;
False to thy gods, thy brother, and thy father;
Conspirant 'gainst this high illustrious prince;
And from th' extremest upward of thy head
To the descent and dust beneath thy foot,

A most toad-spotted traitor. Say thou 'no,'
This sword, this arm, and my best spirits are bent
To prove upon thy heart, whereto I speak,
Thou liest.

Edm. In wisdom I should ask thy name;
But since thy outside looks so fair and warlike,
And that thy tongue some say of breeding breathes,
What safe and nicely I might well delay
By rule of knighthood, I disdain and spurn.
Back do I toss those treasons to thy head;
With the hell-hated lie o'erwhelm thy heart;
Which — for they yet glance by and scarcely bruise —
This sword of mine shall give them instant way
Where they shall rest for ever. Trumpets, speak!

Alarums. Fight. [*Edmund falls.*]

Alb. Save him, save him!

Gon. This is mere practice, Gloucester.
By th' law of arms thou wast not bound to answer
An unknown opposite. Thou art not vanquish'd,
But cozen'd and beguil'd.

Alb. Shut your mouth, dame,
Or with this paper shall I stop it. [*Shows her her letter to Edmund.*] — [*To Edmund*]. Hold, sir.
[*To Goneril*] Thou worse than any name, read thine own evil.
No tearing, lady! I perceive you know it.

Gon. Say if I do — the laws are mine, not thine.
Who can arraign me for't?

Alb. Most monstrous!
Know'st thou this paper?

Gon. Ask me not what I know. *Exit.*

Alb. Go after her. She's desperate; govern her.

[*Exit an Officer.*]

Edm. What you have charg'd me with, that have I done,
And more, much more. The time will bring it out.
'Tis past, and so am I. — But what art thou
That hast this fortune on me? If thou'rt noble,
I do forgive thee.

Edg. Let's exchange charity.
I am no less in blood than thou art, Edmund;
If more, the more th' hast wrong'd me.
My name is Edgar and thy father's son.
The gods are just, and of our pleasant vices
Make instruments to scourge us.
The dark and vicious place where thee he got
Cost him his eyes.

Edm. Th' hast spoken right; 'tis true.
The wheel is come full circle; I am here.

Alb. Methought thy very gait did prophesy
A royal nobleness. I must embrace thee.
Let sorrow split my heart if ever I
Did hate thee, or thy father!

Edg. Worthy prince, I know't.

Alb. Where have you hid yourself?
How have you known the miseries of your father?

Edg. By nursing them, my lord. List a brief tale;
And when 'tis told, O that my heart would burst!
The bloody proclamation to escape
That follow'd me so near (O, our lives' sweetness!
That with the pain of death would hourly die
Rather than die at once!) taught me to shift
Into a madman's rags, t' assume a semblance
That very dogs disdain'd; and in this habit
Met I my father with his bleeding rings,
Their precious stones new lost; became his guide,
Led him, begg'd for him, sav'd him from despair;
Never (O fault!) reveal'd myself unto him
Until some half hour past, when I was arm'd,
Not sure, though hoping of this good success,
I ask'd his blessing, and from first to last
Told him my pilgrimage. But his flaw'd heart
(Alack, too weak the conflict to support!)
'Twixt two extremes of passion, joy and grief,
Burst smilingly.

Edm. This speech of yours hath mov'd me,
And shall perchance do good; but speak you on;
You look as you had something more to say.

Alb. If there be more, more woful, hold it in;
For I am almost ready to dissolve,
Hearing of this.

Edg. This would have seem'd a period
To such as love not sorrow; but another,
To amplify too much, would make much more,
And top extremity.
Whilst I was big in clamour, came there a man,
Who, having seen me in my worst estate,
Shunn'd my abhorr'd society; but then, finding
Who 'twas that so endur'd, with his strong arms
He fastened on my neck, and bellowed out
As he'd burst heaven; threw him on my father;
Told the most piteous tale of Lear and him
That ever ear receiv'd; which in recounting

His grief grew puissant, and the strings of life
Began to crack. Twice then the trumpets sounded,
And there I left him tranc'd.

Alb. But who was this?

Edg. Kent, sir, the banish'd Kent; who in disguise
Followed his enemy king and did him service
Improper for a slave.

Enter a *Gentleman* with a bloody knife.

Gent. Help, help! O, help!

Edg. What kind of help?

Alb. Speak, man.

Edg. What means that bloody knife?

Gent. 'Tis hot, it smokes.
It came even from the heart of — O, she's dead!

Alb. Who dead? Speak, man.

Gent. Your lady, sir, your lady! and her sister
By her is poisoned; she hath confess'd it.

Edm. I was contracted to them both. All three
Now marry in an instant.

Enter *Kent.*

Edg. Here comes Kent.

Alb. Produce their bodies, be they alive or dead.

[*Exit Gentleman.*]

This judgment of the heavens, that makes us tremble,
Touches us not with pity. O, is this he?
The time will not allow the compliment
That very manners urges.

Kent. I am come
To bid my king and master aye good night.
Is he not here?

Alb. Great things of us forgot!
Speak, Edmund, where's the King? and where's Cordelia?

The bodies of Goneril and Regan are brought in.

Seest thou this object, Kent?

Kent. Alack, why thus?

Edm. Yet Edmund was belov'd.
The one the other poisoned for my sake,
And after slew herself.

Alb. Even so. Cover their faces.

Edm. I pant for life. Some good I mean to do,
Despite of mine own nature. Quickly send
(Be brief in't) to the castle; for my writ
Is on the life of Lear and on Cordelia.
Nay, send in time.

Alb. Run, run, O, run!

Edg. To who, my lord? Who has the office? Send
Thy token of reprieve.

Edm. Well thought on. Take my sword;
Give it the Captain.

Alb. Haste thee for thy life.

[*Exit Edgar.*]

Edm. He hath commission from thy wife and me
To hang Cordelia in the prison and
To lay the blame upon her own despair
That she fordid herself.

Alb. The gods defend her! Bear him hence awhile.

[*Edmund is borne off.*]

Enter *Lear,* with *Cordelia* [dead] in his arms, [*Edgar, Captain,* and others following].

Lear. Howl, howl, howl, howl! O, you are men of stone.
Had I your tongues and eyes, I'ld use them so
That heaven's vault should crack. She's gone for ever!
I know when one is dead, and when one lives.
She's dead as earth. Lend me a looking glass.
If that her breath will mist or stain the stone,
Why, then she lives.

Kent. Is this the promis'd end?

Edg. Or image of that horror?

Alb. Fall and cease!

Lear. This feather stirs; she lives! If it be so,
It is a chance which does redeem all sorrows
That ever I have felt.

Kent. O my good master!

Lear. Prithee away!

Edg. 'Tis noble Kent, your friend.

Lear. A plague upon you, murderers, traitors all!
I might have sav'd her; now she's gone for ever!
Cordelia, Cordelia! stay a little. Ha!
What is't thou say'st? Her voice was ever soft,
Gentle, and low — an excellent thing in woman.
I kill'd the slave that was a-hanging thee.

Capt. 'Tis true, my lords, he did.

Lear. Did I not, fellow?
I have seen the day, with my good biting falchion
I would have made them skip. I am old now,
And these same crosses spoil me. Who are you?
Mine eyes are not o' th' best. I'll tell you straight.

Kent. If fortune brag of two she lov'd and hated,
One of them we behold.

Lear. This' a dull sight. Are you not Kent?
Kent. The same —
Your servant Kent. Where is your servant Caius?
Lear. He's a good fellow, I can tell you that.
He'll strike, and quickly too. He's dead and rotten.
Kent. No, my good lord; I am the very man —
Lear. I'll see that straight.
Kent. That from your first of difference and decay
Have followed your sad steps.
Lear. You're welcome hither.
Kent. Nor no man else! All's cheerless, dark, and deadly.
Your eldest daughters have fordone themselves,
And desperately are dead.
Lear. Ay, so I think.
Alb. He knows not what he says; and vain is it
That we present us to him.
Edg. Very bootless.

Enter a *Captain.*

Capt. Edmund is dead, my lord.
Alb. That's but a trifle here.
You lords and noble friends, know our intent.
What comfort to this great decay may come
Shall be applied. For us, we will resign,
During the life of this old Majesty,
To him our absolute power; [*to Edgar and Kent*] you to your rights;
With boot, and such addition as your honours
Have more than merited. — All friends shall taste
The wages of their virtue, and all foes
The cup of their deservings. — O, see, see!
Lear. And my poor fool is hang'd! No, no, no life!
Why should a dog, a horse, a rat, have life,
And thou no breath at all? Thou'lt come no more,
Never, never, never, never, never!
Pray you undo this button. Thank you, sir.
Do you see this? Look on her! look! her lips!
Look there, look there! *He dies.*
Edg. He faints! My lord, my lord!
Kent. Break, heart; I prithee break!
Edg. Look up, my lord.
Kent. Vex not his ghost. O, let him pass! He hates him
That would upon the rack of this tough world
Stretch him out longer.
Edg. He is gone indeed.
Kent. The wonder is, he hath endur'd so long.
He but usurp'd his life.
Alb. Bear them from hence. Our present business
Is general woe. [*To Kent and Edgar*] Friends of my soul, you twain
Rule in this realm, and the gor'd state sustain.
Kent. I have a journey, sir, shortly to go.
My master calls me; I must not say no.
Alb. The weight of this sad time we must obey,
Speak what we feel, not what we ought to say.
The oldest have borne most; we that are young
Shall never see so much, nor live so long.
Exeunt with a dead march.

OTHELLO

OTHELLO was entered in the Stationers' Register on October 6, 1621, and the First Quarto came out in 1622: 'The Tragœdy of Othello, The Moore of Venice. As it hath beene diuerse times acted at the Globe, and at the Black Friers, by his Maiesties Seruants. Written by William Shakespeare.' The Quarto and the Folio are both of service in constituting a text. Many slight omissions in the Folio are supplied by the Quarto. The Quarto omits the following important passages, all of which are in the Folio: i, 1, 122–138; i, 2, 65, 72–77; i, 3, 24–30; ii, 3, 280 ff. ('Drunk' . . . 'shadow'); iii, 3, 383–390 ('By the world' . . . 'satisfied'), 453–460 ('Iago' . . . 'heaven'); iv, 1, 38–44 ('To confess' . . . 'devil'); iv, 2, 151–164 ('Here' . . . 'make me'); iv, 3, 31–53 ('I have' . . . 'next'), 55–57, 60–63, 89–106; v, 2, 151–154, 185–193, 246–248 ('What' . . . 'willow'), 266–272.

OTHELLO was performed at court on November 1, 1604. Probably it was written in that year. The supposed allusion in Dekker and Middleton's *Honest Whore*, i, 1, 37, accords with this date.

The plot of OTHELLO comes from the seventh *novella* of the third decade in the *Hecatommithi* of Giovanni Battista Giraldi (surnamed Cinthio or Cintio), first printed in 1565 (see p. 97, above). All the chief characters are represented in the novel except the Duke, Gratiano and the other Venetian nobles, Montano, and Roderigo; but only Desdemona has a name (*Disdemona*). Shakespeare's Iago is called simply the ensign (*alfiero*); Cassio is the captain of a company (*capo di squadra*); Emilia is the beautiful and virtuous wife of the ensign. Roderigo is barely suggested by the soldier whom we are told the *capo* struck (cf. ii, 3, 150 ff.). Act i is new.

In the novel we are told briefly that the Moor is highly regarded by the lords of Venice for his valour and his military genius, and that they appoint him commander of the troops they are sending to Cyprus. He has married a Venetian lady who had fallen in love with him because of his *virtù*, but no account is given of his wonderful adventures. Nothing is said of any objection on the part of the lady's family. The ensign is not a disappointed candidate for Cassio's place. He has conceived a violent passion for Disdemona and thinks that her coldness is due to her love for the *capo di squadra*, with whom he believes she is carrying on an intrigue. His love turns to hatred. The *capo di squadra* is cashiered by the Moor for disorderly conduct on guard and for beating a soldier, and Disdemona urges her husband to reinstate him. The ensign, to convince the Moor of Disdemona's guilt, declares that the *capo* has boasted to him of his success. The handkerchief is stolen by the ensign's little child, acting under his orders, and is dropped by him in the *capo's* lodging. The Moor and the ensign agree that Disdemona and her supposed lover must die. The ensign attacks the *capo*, but does not succeed in killing him. The Moor asks the ensign's advice. 'Shall Disdemona be poisoned, or shall she be killed with a knife?' He replies that he has thought of a better way. 'The ceiling of your chamber is badly cracked. Let us beat her to death with a stocking filled with sand, so that no bruises may show. Then we will pull down the ceiling and pretend that a beam has fallen upon her head. Everybody will think her death an accident.' The plan is successfully carried out; but the Moor, who loved Disdemona 'more than his eyes,' runs mad with grief and rushes about, searching for her everywhere in the house. He deprives the ensign of his office and they become bitter enemies. The Moor, whom the ensign accuses of the murder, is tortured by the Venetian authorities, but will not confess. He is condemned to lifelong exile and is finally killed by Disdemona's relatives. The ensign is not suspected. Later, however, he dies under torture to which he has been subjected in connection with another affair. After his death his wife reveals the whole truth about the murder.

No subtlety of characterization is to be expected or justly demanded of Cinthio's tale. His *alfiero* is a mere villain of the strictest Italian school. Iago is completely Shakespeare's. In *King Lear*, which perhaps came next in order of time, he is matched by Edmund, equally an individual, but comparable with Iago in many ways. The essential difference is that Iago is a passionate and revengeful Italian, whereas the almost cynically dispassionate Edmund is actuated by self-interest alone (i, 2, 199–200). Coleridge describes Iago's soliloquy in i, 3, 392 ff., as 'the motive-hunting of a motiveless malignity.' This reduces Iago to the level of Aaron in *Titus Andronicus*; or, indeed, to something even less human, for Aaron is in league with Tamora, who has savage cause for vindictive passion. In Iago's case, it is the initial impulse that we have to determine — the prime incentive. That is something which Shakespeare usually defines with perfect clearness. In Macbeth, it is the ambition of a fatalist; in Brutus, it is love of country; in Cassius, it is fierce impatience of servitude; in Antony, it is unreasoning passion for Cleopatra. It would be strange indeed if Iago, of all men, were left without a motive, since OTHELLO is, in plan and structure, that rare phenomenon in literature — a tragedy in which the hero is passive (or acted upon) and the force that opposes him (the villain of the piece) is the power that sways him until the turning point. In fact, Iago's initial motive is set forth with passionate vigour. He is actuated by resentment for injustice, and there are few motives to which men so instantly respond. Cassio has the place which Iago expected and to which, so far as we can weigh their merits, he seems to have had the better claim. At all events, Cassio's behaviour in his office is far from meritorious, and Iago's military record is unassailable. Iago feels all the practical soldier's contempt for the technical theorist. There is further ground for resentment in the fact that Cassio is a foreigner — 'one Michael Cassio, a Florentine,' one of a tribe of bankers and bookkeepers, whose very princes were merchants. There is no difficulty, then, in finding a motive for Iago, and (what is vital in every tragic action) this motive is not only human (that is, neither monstrous nor maniacal), but has a kind of foundation in reason and justice. In Iago's cankered nature, resentment for real or fancied injury brought with it boundless possibilities of crime. But Shakespeare has combined with this the motive that he found in Cinthio — lust (ii, 1, 300); and to this he has added the suspicion that Othello is Emilia's lover. This last is not a mere pretence; it is a raging torment —

> the thought whereof
> Doth, like a poisonous mineral, gnaw my inwards.

It is a common error to assume that Iago's whole course of villany is deliberate. Until the end of the first act he has no definite scheme in mind — only a general desire to be revenged. His plans take shape gradually, and their progress is carefully indicated. He is a deliberate opportunist and he modifies them to fit each emergency. His wish is to ruin Cassio and to torment Othello, but he contemplates no tragic issue; nor is it clear to him until the third scene of Act iii that both Cassio and Desdemona must die. Nothing else can prevent the exposure of his perfidy.

Othello, 'not easily jealous' (for we are bound to accept what Shakespeare makes him say of himself) is helpless in the hands of a man like Iago, as Gloucester is helpless in the hands of Edmund. So his words to Emilia bear witness, at the very acme of the tragic climax, when revelation is at hand: 'My friend, thy husband; honest, honest Iago.'

THE TRAGEDY OF OTHELLO, THE MOOR OF VENICE

The Names of the Actors.

Duke of Venice.
Brabantio, [a Senator,] father to *Desdemona.*
Senators.
Gratiano, [brother to *Brabantio,*] } two noble Venetians.
Lodovico, [kinsman to *Brabantio,*] }
Othello, the Moor, [in the service of Venice].
Cassio, [his] honourable Lieutenant.
Iago, [his Ancient,] a villain.
Roderigo, a gull'd [Venetian] gentleman.
Montano, [former] Governor of Cyprus.
Clown, [servant to *Othello*].
Desdemona, [daughter to *Brabantio* and] wife to *Othello.*
Emilia, wife to *Iago.*
Bianca, a courtesan, [in love with *Cassio*].
Sailor, [Messenger, Herald, Officers, Gentlemen, Musicians, Attendants].

[Scene. — *Venice; Cyprus.*]

Act I. Scene I. [*Venice. A street.*]

Enter *Roderigo* and *Iago.*

Rod. Tush, never tell me! I take it much unkindly
That thou, Iago, who hast had my purse
As if the strings were thine, shouldst know of this.
Iago. 'Sblood, but you will not hear me!
If ever I did dream of such a matter,
Abhor me.
Rod. Thou told'st me thou didst hold him in thy hate.
Iago. Despise me if I do not. Three great ones of the city,
In personal suit to make me his lieutenant,
Off-capp'd to him; and, by the faith of man,
I know my price, I am worth no worse a place.
But he, as loving his own pride and purposes,
Evades them with a bombast circumstance,
Horribly stuff'd with epithets of war;
And, in conclusion,
Nonsuits my mediators; for, 'Certes,' says he,
'I have already chose my officer.'
And what was he?
Forsooth, a great arithmetician,
One Michael Cassio, a Florentine
(A fellow almost damn'd in a fair wife),
That never set a squadron in the field,
Nor the division of a battle knows
More than a spinster; unless the bookish theoric,
Wherein the toged consuls can propose
As masterly as he. Mere prattle, without practice,
Is all his soldiership. But he, sir, had th' election;
And I (of whom his eyes had seen the proof
At Rhodes, at Cyprus, and on other grounds
Christian and heathen) must be belee'd and calm'd
By debitor and creditor, this counter-caster.
He (in good time!) must his lieutenant be,
And I (God bless the mark!) his Moorship's ancient.
Rod. By heaven, I rather would have been his hangman.
Iago. Why, there's no remedy; 'tis the curse of service.
Preferment goes by letter and affection,
And not by old gradation, where each second
Stood heir to th' first. Now, sir, be judge yourself,
Whether I in any just term am affin'd
To love the Moor.
Rod. I would not follow him then.
Iago. O, sir, content you.
I follow him to serve my turn upon him.
We cannot all be masters, nor all masters
Cannot be truly follow'd. You shall mark
Many a duteous and knee-crooking knave
That, doting on his own obsequious bondage,
Wears out his time, much like his master's ass,
For naught but provender; and when he's old, cashier'd.

Whip me such honest knaves! Others there are
Who, trimm'd in forms and visages of duty,
Keep yet their hearts attending on themselves;
And, throwing but shows of service on their lords,
Do well thrive by them, and when they have lin'd their coats,
Do themselves homage. These fellows have some soul;
And such a one do I profess myself. For, sir,
It is as sure as you are Roderigo,
Were I the Moor, I would not be Iago.
In following him, I follow but myself;
Heaven is my judge, not I for love and duty,
But seeming so, for my peculiar end;
For when my outward action doth demonstrate
The native act and figure of my heart
In compliment extern, 'tis not long after
But I will wear my heart upon my sleeve
For daws to peck at. I am not what I am.

Rod. What a full fortune does the thick-lips owe
If he can carry't thus!

Iago. Call up her father,
Rouse him. — Make after him, poison his delight,
Proclaim him in the streets. Incense her kinsmen,
And though he in a fertile climate dwell,
Plague him with flies; though that his joy be joy,
Yet throw such changes of vexation on't
As it may lose some colour.

Rod. Here is her father's house. I'll call aloud.

Iago. Do, with like timorous accent and dire yell
As when, by night and negligence, the fire
Is spied in populous cities.

Rod. What, ho, Brabantio! Signior Brabantio, ho!

Iago. Awake! What, ho, Brabantio! Thieves! thieves! thieves!
Look to your house, your daughter, and your bags!
Thieves! thieves!

[Enter] *Brabantio* above, at a window.

Bra. What is the reason of this terrible summons?
What is the matter there?

Rod. Signior, is all your family within?

Iago. Are your doors lock'd?

Bra. Why, wherefore ask you this?

Iago. Zounds, sir, y'are robb'd! For shame put on your gown!
Your heart is burst; you have lost half your soul.
Even now, now, very now, an old black ram
Is tupping your white ewe. Arise, arise!
Awake the snorting citizens with the bell,
Or else the devil will make a grandsire of you.
Arise, I say!

Bra. What, have you lost your wits?

Rod. Most reverend signior, do you know my voice?

Bra. Not I. What are you?

Rod. My name is Roderigo.

Bra. The worser welcome!
I have charg'd thee not to haunt about my doors.
In honest plainness thou hast heard me say
My daughter is not for thee; and now, in madness,
Being full of supper and distemp'ring draughts,
Upon malicious bravery dost thou come
To start my quiet.

Rod. Sir, sir, sir —

Bra. But thou must needs be sure
My spirit and my place have in them power
To make this bitter to thee.

Rod. Patience, good sir.

Bra. What tell'st thou me of robbing? This is Venice;
My house is not a grange.

Rod. Most grave Brabantio,
In simple and pure soul I come to you.

Iago. Zounds, sir, you are one of those that will not serve God if the devil bid you. Because we come to do you service, and you think we are ruffians, you'll have your daughter cover'd with a Barbary horse; you'll have your nephews neigh to you; you'll have coursers for cousins, and gennets for germans.

Bra. What profane wretch art thou?

Iago. I am one, sir, that come to tell you your daughter and the Moor are now making the beast with two backs.

Bra. Thou art a villain.

Iago. You are — a senator.

Bra. This thou shalt answer. I know thee, Roderigo.

Rod. Sir, I will answer anything. But I beseech you,
If't be your pleasure and most wise consent
(As partly I find it is) that your fair daughter,
At this odd-even and dull watch o' th' night,
Transported, with no worse nor better guard
But with a knave of common hire, a gondolier,

To the gross clasps of a lascivious Moor —
If this be known to you, and your allowance,
We then have done you bold and saucy wrongs;
But if you know not this, my manners tell me
We have your wrong rebuke. Do not believe
That, from the sense of all civility,
I thus would play and trifle with your reverence.
Your daughter, if you have not given her leave,
I say again, hath made a gross revolt,
Tying her duty, beauty, wit, and fortunes
In an extravagant and wheeling stranger
Of here and everywhere. Straight satisfy yourself.
If she be in her chamber, or your house,
Let loose on me the justice of the state
For thus deluding you.

Bra. Strike on the tinder, ho!
Give me a taper! Call up all my people!
This accident is not unlike my dream.
Belief of it oppresses me already.
Light, I say! light! *Exit [above].*

Iago. Farewell, for I must leave you.
It seems not meet, nor wholesome to my place,
To be produc'd (as, if I stay, I shall)
Against the Moor. For I do know the state,
However this may gall him with some check,
Cannot with safety cast him; for he's embark'd
With such loud reason to the Cyprus wars,
Which even now stand in act, that for their souls
Another of his fathom they have none
To lead their business; in which regard,
Though I do hate him as I do hell pains,
Yet, for necessity of present life,
I must show out a flag and sign of love,
Which is indeed but sign. That you shall surely find him,
Lead to the Sagittary the raised search;
And there will I be with him. So farewell.
Exit.

Enter, [below,] *Brabantio,* in his nightgown, and *Servants* with torches.

Bra. It is too true an evil. Gone she is;
And what's to come of my despised time
Is naught but bitterness. Now, Roderigo,
Where didst thou see her? — O unhappy girl! —
With the Moor, say'st thou? — Who would be a father? —
How didst thou know 'twas she? — O, she deceives me
Past thought! — What said she to you? — Get moe tapers!
Raise all my kindred! — Are they married, think you?

Rod. Truly I think they are.

Bra. O heaven! How got she out? O treason of the blood!
Fathers, from hence trust not your daughters' minds
By what you see them act. Is there not charms
By which the property of youth and maidhood
May be abus'd? Have you not read, Roderigo,
Of some such thing?

Rod. Yes, sir, I have indeed.

Bra. Call up my brother. — O, would you had had her! —
Some one way, some another. — Do you know
Where we may apprehend her and the Moor?

Rod. I think I can discover him, if you please
To get good guard and go along with me.

Bra. Pray you lead on. At every house I'll call;
I may command at most. — Get weapons, ho!
And raise some special officers of night. —
On, good Roderigo. I'll deserve your pains.
Exeunt.

Scene II. [*Venice. Another street.*]

Enter *Othello, Iago,* and *Attendants* with torches.

Iago. Though in the trade of war I have slain men,
Yet do I hold it very stuff o' th' conscience
To do no contriv'd murther. I lack iniquity
Sometimes to do me service. Nine or ten times
I had thought t' have yerk'd him here under the ribs.

Oth. 'Tis better as it is.

Iago. Nay, but he prated,
And spoke such scurvy and provoking terms
Against your honour
That with the little godliness I have
I did full hard forbear him. But I pray you, sir,
Are you fast married? Be assur'd of this,
That the magnifico is much belov'd,
And hath in his effect a voice potential —
As double as the Duke's. He will divorce you,
Or put upon you what restraint and grievance
The law, with all his might to enforce it on,
Will give him cable.

Oth. Let him do his spite.
My services which I have done the signiory
Shall outtongue his complaints. 'Tis yet to know —

Which, when I know that boasting is an honour,
I shall promulgate — I fetch my life and being
From men of royal siege; and my demerits
May speak (unbonneted) to as proud a fortune
As this that I have reach'd. For know, Iago,
But that I love the gentle Desdemona,
I would not my unhoused free condition
Put into circumscription and confine
For the sea's worth.

Enter *Cassio*, and *Officers* with torches.

But look what lights come yond.

Iago. Those are the raised father and his friends.
You were best go in.

Oth. Not I. I must be found.
My parts, my title, and my perfect soul
Shall manifest me rightly. Is it they?

Iago. By Janus, I think no.

Oth. The servants of the Duke? and my lieutenant?
The goodness of the night upon you, friends!
What is the news?

Cas. The Duke does greet you, General;
And he requires your haste-post-haste appearance
Even on the instant.

Oth. What's the matter, think you?

Cas. Something from Cyprus, as I may divine.
It is a business of some heat. The galleys
Have sent a dozen sequent messengers
This very night at one another's heels;
And many of the consuls, rais'd and met,
Are at the Duke's already. You have been hotly call'd for;
When, being not at your lodging to be found,
The Senate hath sent about three several quests
To search you out.

Oth. 'Tis well I am found by you.
I will but spend a word here in the house,
And go with you. [*Exit.*]

Cas. Ancient, what makes he here?

Iago. Faith, he to-night hath boarded a land carack.
If it prove lawful prize, he's made for ever.

Cas. I do not understand.

Iago. He's married.

Cas. To who?

[Enter *Othello.*]

Iago. Marry, to — Come, Captain, will you go?

Oth. Have with you.

Cas. Here comes another troop to seek for you.

Enter *Brabantio, Roderigo,* and *Officers* with torches and weapons.

Iago. It is Brabantio. General, be advis'd.
He comes to bad intent.

Oth. Holla! stand there!

Rod. Signior, it is the Moor.

Bra. Down with him, thief!

[*They draw on both sides.*]

Iago. You, Roderigo! Come, sir, I am for you.

Oth. Keep up your bright swords, for the dew will rust them.
Good signior, you shall more command with years
Than with your weapons.

Bra. O thou foul thief, where hast thou stow'd my daughter?
Damn'd as thou art, thou hast enchanted her!
For I'll refer me to all things of sense,
If she in chains of magic were not bound,
Whether a maid so tender, fair, and happy,
So opposite to marriage that she shunn'd
The wealthy curled darlings of our nation,
Would ever have (t' incur a general mock)
Run from her guardage to the sooty bosom
Of such a thing as thou — to fear, not to delight.
Judge me the world if 'tis not gross in sense
That thou hast practis'd on her with foul charms,
Abus'd her delicate youth with drugs or minerals
That weaken motion. I'll have't disputed on.
'Tis probable, and palpable to thinking.
I therefore apprehend and do attach thee
For an abuser of the world, a practiser
Of arts inhibited and out of warrant.
Lay hold upon him. If he do resist,
Subdue him at his peril.

Oth. Hold your hands,
Both you of my inclining and the rest.
Were it my cue to fight, I should have known it
Without a prompter. Where will you that I go
To answer this your charge?

Bra. To prison, till fit time
Of law and course of direct session
Call thee to answer.

Oth. What if I do obey?
How may the Duke be therewith satisfied,
Whose messengers are here about my side
Upon some present business of the state
To bring me to him?

Officer. 'Tis true, most worthy signior.

The Duke's in council, and your noble self
I am sure is sent for.
Bra. How? The Duke in council?
In this time of the night? Bring him away!
Mine's not an idle cause. The Duke himself,
Or any of my brothers of the state,
Cannot but feel this wrong as 'twere their own;
For if such actions may have passage free,
Bondslaves and pagans shall our statesmen be.
Exeunt.

Scene III. [*Venice. A council chamber.*]

Enter *Duke* and *Senators,* set at a table, with lights and *Attendants.*

Duke. There is no composition in these news
That gives them credit.
1. Sen. Indeed they are disproportion'd.
My letters say a hundred and seven galleys.
Duke. And mine a hundred forty.
2. Sen. And mine two hundred.
But though they jump not on a just account
(As in these cases where the aim reports
'Tis oft with difference), yet do they all confirm
A Turkish fleet, and bearing up to Cyprus.
Duke. Nay, it is possible enough to judgment.
I do not so secure me in the error
But the main article I do approve
In fearful sense.
Sailor. (*within*) What, ho! what, ho! what, ho!

Enter *Sailor.*

Officer. A messenger from the galleys.
Duke. Now, what's the business?
Sailor. The Turkish preparation makes for Rhodes.
So was I bid report here to the state
By Signior Angelo.
Duke. How say you by this change?
1. Sen. This cannot be
By no assay of reason. 'Tis a pageant
To keep us in false gaze. When we consider
Th' importancy of Cyprus to the Turk,
And let ourselves again but understand
That, as it more concerns the Turk than Rhodes,
So may he with more facile question bear it,
For that it stands not in such warlike brace,
But altogether lacks th' abilities
That Rhodes is dress'd in — if we make thought of this,
We must not think the Turk is so unskilful
To leave that latest which concerns him first,
Neglecting an attempt of ease and gain
To wake and wage a danger profitless.
Duke. Nay, in all confidence he's not for Rhodes.
Officer. Here is more news.

Enter a *Messenger.*

Mess. The Ottomites, reverend and gracious.
Steering with due course toward the isle of Rhodes,
Have there injointed them with an after fleet.
1. Sen. Ay, so I thought. How many, as you guess?
Mess. Of thirty sail; and now they do restem
Their backward course, bearing with frank appearance
Their purposes toward Cyprus. Signior Montano,
Your trusty and most valiant servitor,
With his free duty recommends you thus,
And prays you to believe him.
Duke. 'Tis certain then for Cyprus.
Marcus Luccicos, is not he in town?
1. Sen. He's now in Florence.
Duke. Write from us to him; post-post-haste dispatch.

Enter *Brabantio, Othello, Cassio, Iago, Roderigo,* and *Officers.*

1. Sen. Here comes Brabantio and the valiant Moor.
Duke. Valiant Othello, we must straight employ you
Against the general enemy Ottoman.
[*To Brabantio*] I did not see you. Welcome, gentle signior.
We lack'd your counsel and your help to-night.
Bra. So did I yours. Good your Grace, pardon me.
Neither my place, nor aught I heard of business,
Hath rais'd me from my bed; nor doth the general care
Take hold on me; for my particular grief
Is of so floodgate and o'erbearing nature
That it engluts and swallows other sorrows,
And it is still itself.
Duke. Why, what's the matter?
Bra. My daughter! O, my daughter!
All. Dead?
Bra. Ay, to me!
She is abus'd, stol'n from me, and corrupted
By spells and medicines bought of mountebanks;
For nature so prepost'rously to err.

Being not deficient, blind, or lame of sense,
Sans witchcraft could not.

Duke. Whoe'er he be that in this foul proceeding
Hath thus beguil'd your daughter of herself,
And you of her, the bloody book of law
You shall yourself read in the bitter letter
After your own sense; yea, though our proper son
Stood in your action.

Bra. Humbly I thank your Grace.
Here is the man — this Moor, whom now, it seems,
Your special mandate, for the state affairs,
Hath hither brought.

All. We are very sorry for't.

Duke. [*to Othello*] What, in your own part, can you say to this?

Bra. Nothing, but this is so.

Oth. Most potent, grave, and reverend signiors,
My very noble, and approv'd good masters,
That I have ta'en away this old man's daughter,
It is most true; true I have married her.
The very head and front of my offending
Hath this extent, no more. Rude am I in my speech,
And little bless'd with the soft phrase of peace;
For since these arms of mine had seven years' pith
Till now some nine moons wasted, they have us'd
Their dearest action in the tented field;
And little of this great world can I speak
More than pertains to feats of broil and battle;
And therefore little shall I grace my cause
In speaking for myself. Yet, by your gracious patience,
I will a round unvarnish'd tale deliver
Of my whole course of love — what drugs, what charms,
What conjuration, and what mighty magic
(For such proceeding am I charg'd withal)
I won his daughter.

Bra. A maiden never bold;
Of spirit so still and quiet that her motion
Blush'd at herself; and she — in spite of nature,
Of years, of country, credit, everything —
To fall in love with what she fear'd to look on!
It is a judgment maim'd and most imperfect
That will confess perfection so could err
Against all rules of nature, and must be driven
To find out practices of cunning hell
Why this should be. I therefore vouch again
That with some mixtures pow'rful o'er the blood,
Or with some dram, conjur'd to this effect,
He wrought upon her.

Duke. To vouch this is no proof,
Without more certain and more overt test
Than these thin habits and poor likelihoods
Of modern seeming do prefer against him.

1. Sen. But, Othello, speak.
Did you by indirect and forced courses
Subdue and poison this young maid's affections?
Or came it by request, and such fair question
As soul to soul affordeth?

Oth. I do beseech you,
Send for the lady to the Sagittary
And let her speak of me before her father.
If you do find me foul in her report,
The trust, the office, I do hold of you
Not only take away, but let your sentence
Even fall upon my life.

Duke. Fetch Desdemona hither.

Oth. Ancient, conduct them; you best know the place.

Exeunt [*Iago and*] *two or three* [*Attendants*].

And till she come, as truly as to heaven
I do confess the vices of my blood,
So justly to your grave ears I'll present
How I did thrive in this fair lady's love,
And she in mine.

Duke. Say it, Othello.

Oth. Her father lov'd me, oft invited me;
Still question'd me the story of my life
From year to year — the battles, sieges, fortunes
That I have pass'd.
I ran it through, even from my boyish days
To th' very moment that he bade me tell it.
Wherein I spake of most disastrous chances,
Of moving accidents by flood and field;
Of hairbreadth scapes i' th' imminent deadly breach;
Of being taken by the insolent foe
And sold to slavery; of my redemption thence
And portance in my travel's history;
Wherein of anters vast and deserts idle,
Rough quarries, rocks, and hills whose heads touch heaven,
It was my hint to speak — such was the process;
And of the Cannibals that each other eat,
The Anthropophagi, and men whose heads
Do grow beneath their shoulders. This to hear
Would Desdemona seriously incline;
But still the house affairs would draw her thence;
Which ever as she could with haste dispatch,

She'ld come again, and with a greedy ear
Devour up my discourse. Which I observing,
Took once a pliant hour, and found good means
To draw from her a prayer of earnest heart
That I would all my pilgrimage dilate,
Whereof by parcels she had something heard,
But not intentively. I did consent,
And often did beguile her of her tears
When I did speak of some distressful stroke
That my youth suffer'd. My story being done,
She gave me for my pains a world of sighs.
She swore, in faith, 'twas strange, 'twas passing strange;
'Twas pitiful, 'twas wondrous pitiful.
She wish'd she had not heard it; yet she wish'd
That heaven had made her such a man. She thank'd me;
And bade me, if I had a friend that lov'd her,
I should but teach him how to tell my story,
And that would woo her. Upon this hint I spake.
She lov'd me for the dangers I had pass'd,
And I lov'd her that she did pity them.
This only is the witchcraft I have us'd.
Here comes the lady. Let her witness it.

Enter *Desdemona, Iago, Attendants.*

Duke. I think this tale would win my daughter too.
Good Brabantio,
Take up this mangled matter at the best.
Men do their broken weapons rather use
Than their bare hands.

Bra. I pray you hear her speak.
If she confess that she was half the wooer,
Destruction on my head if my bad blame
Light on the man! Come hither, gentle mistress.
Do you perceive in all this noble company
Where most you owe obedience?

Des. My noble father,
I do perceive here a divided duty.
To you I am bound for life and education;
My life and education both do learn me
How to respect you: you are the lord of duty;
I am hitherto your daughter. But here's my husband;
And so much duty as my mother show'd
To you, preferring you before her father,
So much I challenge that I may profess
Due to the Moor my lord.

Bra. God b' wi' ye! I have done.
Please it your Grace, on to the state affairs.
I had rather to adopt a child than get it.
Come hither, Moor.
I here do give thee that with all my heart
Which, but thou hast already, with all my heart
I would keep from thee. For your sake, jewel,
I am glad at soul I have no other child;
For thy escape would teach me tyranny,
To hang clogs on them. I have done, my lord.

Duke. Let me speak like yourself and lay a sentence
Which, as a grise or step, may help these lovers
Into your favour.
When remedies are past, the griefs are ended
By seeing the worst, which late on hopes depended.
To mourn a mischief that is past and gone
Is the next way to draw new mischief on.
What cannot be preserv'd when fortune takes,
Patience her injury a mock'ry makes.
The robb'd that smiles steals something from the thief;
He robs himself that spends a bootless grief.

Bra. So let the Turk of Cyprus us beguile:
We lose it not, so long as we can smile.
He bears the sentence well that nothing bears
But the free comfort which from thence he hears;
But he bears both the sentence and the sorrow
That to pay grief must of poor patience borrow.
These sentences, to sugar, or to gall,
Being strong on both sides, are equivocal.
But words are words. I never yet did hear
That the bruis'd heart was pieced through the ear.
Beseech you, now to the affairs of state.

Duke. The Turk with a most mighty preparation makes for Cyprus. Othello, the fortitude of the place is best known to you; and though we have there a substitute of most allowed sufficiency, yet opinion, a sovereign mistress of effects, throws a more safer voice on you. You must therefore be content to slubber the gloss of your new fortunes with this more stubborn and boist'rous expedition.

Oth. The tyrant custom, most grave senators,
Hath made the flinty and steel couch of war
My thrice-driven bed of down. I do agnize
A natural and prompt alacrity
I find in hardness; and do undertake
These present wars against the Ottomites.
Most humbly, therefore, bending to your state,
I crave fit disposition for my wife;
Due reference of place, and exhibition,
With such accommodation and besort
As levels with her breeding.

Duke. If you please,
Be't at her father's.

Bra. I'll not have it so.
Oth. Nor I.
Des. Nor I. I would not there reside,
To put my father in impatient thoughts
By being in his eye. Most gracious Duke,
To my unfolding lend your prosperous ear,
And let me find a charter in your voice,
T' assist my simpleness.
Duke. What would you, Desdemona?
Des. That I did love the Moor to live with him,
My downright violence, and storm of fortunes,
May trumpet to the world. My heart's subdu'd
Even to the very quality of my lord.
I saw Othello's visage in his mind,
And to his honours and his valiant parts
Did I my soul and fortunes consecrate.
So that, dear lords, if I be left behind,
A moth of peace, and he go to the war,
The rights for which I love him are bereft me,
And I a heavy interim shall support
By his dear absence. Let me go with him.
Oth. Let her have your voices.
Vouch with me heaven, I therefore beg it not
To please the palate of my appetite,
Nor to comply with heat — the young affects
In me defunct — and proper satisfaction;
But to be free and bounteous to her mind.
And heaven defend your good souls that you think
I will your serious and great business scant
For she is with me. No, when light-wing'd toys
Of feather'd Cupid seel with wanton dullness
My speculative and offic'd instruments,
That my disports corrupt and taint my business,
Let housewives make a skillet of my helm,
And all indign and base adversities
Make head against my estimation!
Duke. Be it as you shall privately determine,
Either for her stay or going. Th' affair cries haste,
And speed must answer it. You must hence to-night.
Des. To-night, my lord?
Duke. This night.
Oth. With all my heart.
Duke. At nine i' th' morning here we'll meet again.
Othello, leave some officer behind,
And he shall our commission bring to you;
With such things else of quality and respect
As doth import you.
Oth. So please your Grace, my ancient.
A man he is of honesty and trust.
To his conveyance I assign my wife,
With what else needful your good Grace shall think
To be sent after me.
Duke. Let it be so.
Good night to every one. [*To Brabantio*] And, noble signior,
If virtue no delighted beauty lack,
Your son-in-law is far more fair than black.
1. Sen. Adieu, brave Moor. Use Desdemona well.
Bra. Look to her, Moor, if thou hast eyes to see.
She has deceiv'd her father, and may thee.
Exeunt [Duke, Senators, Officers, &c.].
Oth. My life upon her faith! — Honest Iago,
My Desdemona must I leave to thee.
I prithee let thy wife attend on her,
And bring them after in the best advantage.
Come, Desdemona. I have but an hour
Of love, of worldly matters and direction,
To spend with thee. We must obey the time.
Exeunt Moor and Desdemona.
Rod. Iago.
Iago. What say'st thou, noble heart?
Rod. What will I do, think'st thou?
Iago. Why, go to bed and sleep.
Rod. I will incontinently drown myself.

Iago. If thou dost, I shall never love thee after. Why, thou silly gentleman!

Rod. It is silliness to live when to live is torment; and then have we a prescription to die when death is our physician.

Iago. O villanous! I have look'd upon the world for four times seven years; and since I could distinguish betwixt a benefit and an injury, I never found man that knew how to love himself. Ere I would say I would drown myself for the love of a guinea hen, I would change my humanity with a baboon.

Rod. What should I do? I confess it is my shame to be so fond, but it is not in my virtue to amend it.

Iago. Virtue? a fig! 'Tis in ourselves that we are thus or thus. Our bodies are our gardens, to the which our wills are gardeners; so that if we will plant nettles or sow lettuce, set hyssop and weed up thyme, supply it with one gender of herbs or distract it with many — either to have it sterile with idleness or manured with industry — why, the power and corrigible authority of this lies in our wills. If the balance of our lives had not one scale of reason to poise another of sensuality, the blood and baseness of our natures would conduct us to most prepost'rous conclusions. But we have reason to cool our raging motions, our carnal stings, our unbitted lusts; whereof I take this that you call love to be a sect or scion.

Rod. It cannot be.

Iago. It is merely a lust of the blood and a permission of the will. Come, be a man! Drown thyself? Drown cats and blind puppies! I have profess'd me thy friend, and I confess me knit to thy deserving with cables of perdurable toughness. I could never better stead thee than now. Put money in thy purse. Follow these wars; defeat thy favour with an usurp'd beard. I say, put money in thy purse. It cannot be that Desdemona should long continue her love to the Moor — put money in thy purse — nor he his to her. It was a violent commencement, and thou shalt see an answerable sequestration. Put but money in thy purse. These Moors are changeable in their wills. Fill thy purse with money. The food that to him now is as luscious as locusts shall be to him shortly as bitter as coloquintida. She must change for youth. When she is sated with his body, she will find the error of her choice. She must have change, she must. Therefore put money in thy purse. If thou wilt needs damn thyself, do it a more delicate way than drowning. Make all the money thou canst. If sanctimony and a frail vow betwixt an erring barbarian and a supersubtle Venetian be not too hard for my wits and all the tribe of hell, thou shalt enjoy her. Therefore make money. A pox of drowning thyself! It is clean out of the way. Seek thou rather to be hang'd in compassing thy joy than to be drown'd and go without her.

Rod. Wilt thou be fast to my hopes, if I depend on the issue?

Iago. Thou art sure of me. Go, make money. I have told thee often, and I retell thee again and again, I hate the Moor. My cause is hearted; thine hath no less reason. Let us be conjunctive in our revenge against him. If thou canst cuckold him, thou dost thyself a pleasure, me a sport. There are many events in the womb of time, which will be delivered. Traverse! go! provide thy money! We will have more of this to-morrow. Adieu.

Rod. Where shall we meet i' th' morning?

Iago. At my lodging.

Rod. I'll be with thee betimes.

Iago. Go to, farewell. — Do you hear, Roderigo?

Rod. What say you?

Iago. No more of drowning, do you hear?

Rod. I am chang'd. I'll go sell all my land.
Exit.

Iago. Thus do I ever make my fool my purse;
For I mine own gain'd knowledge should profane
If I would time expend with such a snipe
But for my sport and profit. I hate the Moor;
And it is thought abroad that 'twixt my sheets
'Has done my office. I know not if't be true;
Yet I, for mere suspicion in that kind,
Will do as if for surety. He holds me well;
The better shall my purpose work on him.
Cassio's a proper man. Let me see now:
To get his place, and to plume up my will
In double knavery — How, how? Let's see.
After some time, to abuse Othello's ear
That he is too familiar with his wife.
He hath a person and a smooth dispose
To be suspected — fram'd to make women false.
The Moor is of a free and open nature
That thinks men honest that but seem to be so;
And will as tenderly be led by th' nose
As asses are.
I have't! It is engend'red! Hell and night
Must bring this monstrous birth to the world's light.
Exit.

ACT II. Scene I. [*A seaport in Cyprus. An open place.*]

Enter *Montano* and two *Gentlemen.*

Mon. What from the cape can you discern at sea?

1. Gent. Nothing at all. It is a high-wrought flood.
I cannot 'twixt the heaven and the main
Descry a sail.

Mon. Methinks the wind hath spoke aloud at land;
A fuller blast ne'er shook our battlements.
If it hath ruffian'd so upon the sea,
What ribs of oak, when mountains melt on them,
Can hold the mortise? What shall we hear of this?

2. Gent. A segregation of the Turkish fleet.
For do but stand upon the foaming shore,
The chidden billow seems to pelt the clouds;

The wind-shak'd surge, with high and monstrous mane,
Seems to cast water on the burning Bear
And quench the Guards of th' ever-fixed pole.
I never did like molestation view
On the enchafed flood.

Mon. If that the Turkish fleet
Be not enshelter'd and embay'd, they are drown'd.
It is impossible they bear it out.

Enter a third *Gentleman*.

3. Gent. News, lads! Our wars are done.
The desperate tempest hath so bang'd the Turks
That their designment halts. A noble ship of Venice
Hath seen a grievous wrack and sufferance
On most part of their fleet.

Mon. How? Is this true?

3. Gent. The ship is here put in,
A Veronesa; Michael Cassio,
Lieutenant to the warlike Moor Othello,
Is come on shore; the Moor himself at sea,
And is in full commission here for Cyprus.

Mon. I am glad on't. 'Tis a worthy governor.

3. Gent. But this same Cassio, though he speak of comfort
Touching the Turkish loss, yet he looks sadly
And prays the Moor be safe, for they were parted
With foul and violent tempest.

Mon. Pray heaven he be;
For I have serv'd him, and the man commands
Like a full soldier. Let's to the seaside, ho!
As well to see the vessel that's come in
As to throw out our eyes for brave Othello,
Even till we make the main and th' aerial blue
An indistinct regard.

3. Gent. Come, let's do so;
For every minute is expectancy
Of more arrivance.

Enter *Cassio*.

Cas. Thanks you, the valiant of this warlike isle,
That so approve the Moor! O, let the heavens
Give him defence against the elements,
For I have lost him on a dangerous sea!

Mon. Is he well shipp'd?

Cas. His bark is stoutly timber'd, and his pilot
Of very expert and approv'd allowance.
Therefore my hopes (not surfeited to death)
Stand in bold cure.

(*Within*) 'A sail, a sail, a sail!'

Enter a *Messenger*.

Cas. What noise?

Mess. The town is empty; on the brow o' th' sea
Stand ranks of people, and they cry 'A sail!'

Cas. My hopes do shape him for the Governor.

A shot.

2. Gent. They do discharge their shot of courtesy.
Our friends at least.

Cas. I pray you, sir, go forth
And give us truth who 'tis that is arriv'd.

2. Gent. I shall. *Exit.*

Mon. But, good Lieutenant, is your general wiv'd?

Cas. Most fortunately. He hath achiev'd a maid
That paragons description and wild fame;
One that excels the quirks of blazoning pens,
And in th' essential vesture of creation
Does tire the ingener.

Enter *Second Gentleman*.

How now? Who has put in?

2. Gent. 'Tis one Iago, ancient to the General.

Cas. Has had most favourable and happy speed.
Tempests themselves, high seas, and howling winds,
The gutter'd rocks and congregated sands,
Traitors ensteep'd to clog the guiltless keel,
As having sense of beauty, do omit
Their mortal natures, letting go safely by
The divine Desdemona.

Mon. What is she?

Cas. She that I spake of, our great captain's captain,
Left in the conduct of the bold Iago,
Whose footing here anticipates our thoughts
A se'nnight's speed. Great Jove, Othello guard,
And swell his sail with thine own pow'rful breath,
That he may bless this bay with his tall ship,
Make love's quick pants in Desdemona's arms,
Give renew'd fire to our extincted spirits,
And bring all Cyprus comfort!

Enter *Desdemona, Iago, Emilia,* and *Roderigo,* [with *Attendants*].

O, behold!
The riches of the ship is come on shore!
Ye men of Cyprus, let her have your knees.
Hail to thee, lady! and the grace of heaven,
Before, behind thee, and on every hand,
Enwheel thee round!

Des. I thank you, valiant Cassio.
What tidings can you tell me of my lord?

Cas. He is not yet arriv'd; nor know I aught
But that he's well and will be shortly here.

Des. O, but I fear! How lost you company?

Cas. The great contention of the sea and skies
Parted our fellowship.
(*Within*) 'A sail, a sail!' [*A shot.*]
But hark. A sail!

2. Gent. They give their greeting to the citadel.
This likewise is a friend.

Cas. See for the news.
[*Exit Gentleman.*]
Good ancient, you are welcome. [*To Emilia*] Welcome, mistress. —
Let it not gall your patience, good Iago,
That I extend my manners. 'Tis my breeding
That gives me this bold show of courtesy.
[*Kisses her.*]

Iago. Sir, would she give you so much of her lips
As of her tongue she oft bestows on me,
You would have enough.

Des. Alas, she has no speech!

Iago. In faith, too much.
I find it still when I have list to sleep.
Marry, before your ladyship, I grant,
She puts her tongue a little in her heart
And chides with thinking.

Emil. You have little cause to say so.

Iago. Come on, come on! You are pictures out of doors,
Bells in your parlours, wildcats in your kitchens,
Saints in your injuries, devils being offended,
Players in your housewifery, and housewives in your beds.

Des. O, fie upon thee, slanderer!

Iago. Nay, it is true, or else I am a Turk.
You rise to play, and go to bed to work.

Emil. You shall not write my praise.

Iago. No, let me not.

Des. What wouldst thou write of me, if thou shouldst praise me?

Iago. O gentle lady, do not put me to't,
For I am nothing if not critical.

Des. Come on, assay. — There's one gone to the harbour?

Iago. Ay, madam.

Des. I am not merry; but I do beguile
The thing I am by seeming otherwise.
Come, how wouldst thou praise me?

Iago. I am about it; but indeed my invention
Comes from my pate as birdlime does from frieze —
It plucks out brains and all. But my Muse labours,
And thus she is deliver'd:

If she be fair and wise, fairness and wit —
The one's for use, the other useth it.

Des. Well prais'd! How if she be black and witty?

Iago. If she be black, and thereto have a wit,
She'll find a white that shall her blackness fit.

Des. Worse and worse!

Emil. How if fair and foolish?

Iago. She never yet was foolish that was fair,
For even her folly help'd her to an heir.

Des. These are old fond paradoxes to make fools laugh i' th' alehouse. What miserable praise hast thou for her that's foul and foolish?

Iago. There's none so foul, and foolish thereunto,
But does foul pranks which fair and wise ones do.

Des. O heavy ignorance! Thou praisest the worst best. But what praise couldst thou bestow on a deserving woman indeed — one that, in the authority of her merit, did justly put on the vouch of very malice itself?

Iago. She that was ever fair, and never proud;
Had tongue at will, and yet was never loud;
Never lack'd gold, and yet went never gay;
Fled from her wish, and yet said 'Now I may';
She that, being ang'red, her revenge being nigh,
Bade her wrong stay, and her displeasure fly;
She that in wisdom never was so frail
To change the cod's head for the salmon's tail;
She that could think, and ne'er disclose her mind;
See suitors following, and not look behind:
She was a wight (if ever such wight were) —

Des. To do what?

Iago. To suckle fools and chronicle small beer.

Des. O most lame and impotent conclusion! Do not learn of him, Emilia, though he be thy husband. How say you, Cassio? Is he not a most profane and liberal counsellor?

Cas. He speaks home, madam. You may relish him more in the soldier than in the scholar.

Iago. [*aside*] He takes her by the palm. Ay, well said, whisper! With as little a web as this will I ensnare as great a fly as Cassio. Ay, smile upon her, do! I will gyve thee in thine own courtship. You say true; 'tis so, indeed! If such tricks as these strip you out of your lieutenantry, it had been better you had not kiss'd your three fingers so oft — which now again you are most apt to play the sir in. Very good! well kiss'd! an excellent curtsy! 'Tis so, indeed. Yet again your fingers to your lips? Would they were clyster pipes for your sake! (*Trumpet within.*) The Moor! I know his trumpet.

Cas. 'Tis truly so.

Des. Let's meet him and receive him.

Cas. Lo, where he comes!

Enter *Othello* and *Attendants.*

Oth. O my fair warrior!

Des. My dear Othello!

Oth. It gives me wonder great as my content
To see you here before me. O my soul's joy!
If after every tempest come such calms,
May the winds blow till they have waken'd death!
And let the labouring bark climb hills of seas
Olympus-high, and duck again as low
As hell's from heaven! If it were now to die,
'Twere now to be most happy; for I fear
My soul hath her content so absolute
That not another comfort like to this
Succeeds in unknown fate.

Des. The heavens forbid
But that our loves and comforts should increase
Even as our days do grow!

Oth. Amen to that, sweet powers!
I cannot speak enough of this content;
It stops me here; it is too much of joy.
And this, and this, the greatest discords be
They kiss.
That e'er our hearts shall make!

Iago. [*aside*] O, you are well tun'd now!
But I'll set down the pegs that make this music,
As honest as I am.

Oth. Come, let us to the castle.
News, friends! Our wars are done; the Turks are drown'd.
How does my old acquaintance of this isle? —
Honey, you shall be well desir'd in Cyprus;
I have found great love amongst them. O my sweet,
I prattle out of fashion, and I dote
In mine own comforts. I prithee, good Iago,
Go to the bay and disembark my coffers.
Bring thou the master to the citadel.
He is a good one, and his worthiness
Does challenge much respect. — Come, Desdemona,
Once more well met at Cyprus.

Exeunt [*all but Iago and Roderigo*].

Iago. [*To an Attendant, who goes out*] Do thou meet me presently at the harbour. [*To Roderigo*] Come hither. If thou be'st valiant (as they say base men being in love have then a nobility in their natures more than is native to them), list me. The Lieutenant to-night watches on the court of guard. First, I must tell thee this: Desdemona is directly in love with him.

Rod. With him? Why, 'tis not possible.

Iago. Lay thy finger thus, and let thy soul be instructed. Mark me with what violence she first lov'd the Moor, but for bragging and telling her fantastical lies; and will she love him still for prating? Let not thy discreet heart think it. Her eye must be fed; and what delight shall she have to look on the devil? When the blood is made dull with the act of sport, there should be, again to inflame it and to give satiety a fresh appetite, loveliness in favour, sympathy in years, manners, and beauties; all which the Moor is defective in. Now for want of these requir'd conveniences, her delicate tenderness will find itself abus'd, begin to heave the gorge, disrelish and abhor the Moor. Very nature will instruct her in it and compel her to some second choice. Now, sir, this granted (as it is a most pregnant and unforc'd position), who stands so eminent in the degree of this fortune as Cassio does? A knave very voluble; no further conscionable than in putting on the mere form of civil and humane seeming for the better compassing of his salt and most hidden loose affection? Why, none! why, none! A slipper and subtle knave; a finder-out of occasions; that has an eye can stamp and counterfeit advantages, though true advantage never present itself; a devilish knave! Besides, the knave is handsome, young, and hath all those requisites in him that folly and green minds look after. A pestilent complete knave! and the woman hath found him already.

Rod. I cannot believe that in her. She's full of most blessed condition.

Iago. Blessed fig's-end! The wine she drinks is made of grapes. If she had been blessed, she would never have lov'd the Moor. Blessed pudding! Didst thou not see her paddle with the palm of his hand? Didst not mark that?

Rod. Yes, that I did; but that was but courtesy.

Iago. Lechery, by this hand! an index and obscure prologue to the history of lust and foul thoughts. They met so near with their lips that their breaths embrac'd together. Villanous thoughts, Roderigo! When these mutualities so marshal the way, hard at hand comes the master and main exercise, th' incorporate conclusion. Pish! But, sir, be you rul'd by me. I have brought you from Venice. Watch you to-night; for the command, I'll lay't upon you. Cassio knows you not. I'll not be far from you. Do you find some occasion to anger Cassio, either by speaking too loud, or tainting his discipline, or from what other course you please which the time shall more favourably minister.

Rod. Well.

Iago. Sir, he is rash and very sudden in choler, and haply with his truncheon may strike at you. Provoke him that he may; for even out of that will I cause these of Cyprus to mutiny; whose qualification shall come into no true taste again but by the displanting of Cassio. So shall you have a shorter journey to your desires by the means I shall then have to prefer them; and the impediment most profitably removed without the which there were no expectation of our prosperity.

Rod. I will do this if I can bring it to any opportunity.

Iago. I warrant thee. Meet me by-and-by at the citadel. I must fetch his necessaries ashore. Farewell.

Rod. Adieu. *Exit.*

Iago. That Cassio loves her, I do well believe it;
That she loves him, 'tis apt and of great credit.
The Moor (howbeit that I endure him not)
Is of a constant, loving, noble nature,
And I dare think he'll prove to Desdemona
A most dear husband. Now I do love her too;
Not out of absolute lust (though peradventure
I stand accountant for as great a sin)
But partly led to diet my revenge,
For that I do suspect the lusty Moor
Hath leap'd into my seat; the thought whereof
Doth, like a poisonous mineral, gnaw my inwards;
And nothing can or shall content my soul
Till I am even'd with him, wife for wife;
Or failing so, yet that I put the Moor
At least into a jealousy so strong
That judgment cannot cure. Which thing to do,
If this poor trash of Venice, whom I trash
For his quick hunting, stand the putting on,
I'll have our Michael Cassio on the hip,
Abuse him to the Moor in the rank garb
(For I fear Cassio with my nightcap too),
Make the Moor thank me, love me, and reward me
For making him egregiously an ass
And practising upon his peace and quiet
Even to madness. 'Tis here, but yet confus'd.
Knavery's plain face is never seen till us'd.
Exit.

Scene II. [*Cyprus. A street.*]

Enter *Othello's Herald*, reading a proclamation; [people following].

Her. It is Othello's pleasure, our noble and valiant general, that, upon certain tidings now arriv'd, importing the mere perdition of the Turkish fleet, every man put himself into triumph; some to dance, some to make bonfires, each man to what sport and revels his addiction leads him. For, besides these beneficial news, it is the celebration of his nuptial. So much was his pleasure should be proclaimed. All offices are open, and there is full liberty of feasting from this present hour of five till the bell have told eleven. Heaven bless the isle of Cyprus and our noble general Othello! *Exeunt.*

[Scene III. *Cyprus. A hall in the Castle.*]

Enter *Othello, Desdemona, Cassio,* and *Attendants.*

Oth. Good Michael, look you to the guard to-night.
Let's teach ourselves that honourable stop,
Not to outsport discretion.

Cas. Iago hath direction what to do;
But notwithstanding, with my personal eye
Will I look to't.

Oth. Iago is most honest.
Michael, good night. To-morrow with your earliest

Let me have speech with you. — Come, my dear love.
The purchase made, the fruits are to ensue;
That profit 's yet to come 'tween me and you. —
Good night.

Exeunt Othello and Desdemona [*with Attendants*].

Enter *Iago*.

Cas. Welcome, Iago. We must to the watch.

Iago. Not this hour, Lieutenant; 'tis not yet ten o' th' clock. Our general cast us thus early for the love of his Desdemona; who let us not therefore blame. He hath not yet made wanton the night with her, and she is sport for Jove.

Cas. She's a most exquisite lady.

Iago. And I'll warrant her, full of game.

Cas. Indeed, she's a most fresh and delicate creature.

Iago. What an eye she has! Methinks it sounds a parley to provocation.

Cas. An inviting eye; and yet methinks right modest.

Iago. And when she speaks, is it not an alarum to love?

Cas. She is indeed perfection.

Iago. Well, happiness to their sheets! Come, Lieutenant, I have a stope of wine, and here without are a brace of Cyprus gallants that would fain have a measure to the health of black Othello.

Cas. Not to-night, good Iago. I have very poor and unhappy brains for drinking. I could well wish courtesy would invent some other custom of entertainment.

Iago. O, they are our friends. But one cup! I'll drink for you.

Cas. I have drunk but one cup to-night, and that was craftily qualified too; and behold what innovation it makes here. I am unfortunate in the infirmity and dare not task my weakness with any more.

Iago. What, man! 'Tis a night of revels. The gallants desire it.

Cas. Where are they?

Iago. Here at the door. I pray you call them in.

Cas. I'll do't, but it dislikes me. *Exit.*

Iago. If I can fasten but one cup upon him
With that which he hath drunk to-night already,
He'll be as full of quarrel and offence
As my young mistress' dog. Now my sick fool Roderigo,
Whom love hath turn'd almost the wrong side out,
To Desdemona hath to-night carous'd
Potations pottle-deep; and he's to watch.
Three lads of Cyprus — noble swelling spirits,
That hold their honours in a wary distance,
The very elements of this warlike isle —
Have I to-night fluster'd with flowing cups,
And they watch too. Now, 'mongst this flock of drunkards
Am I to put our Cassio in some action
That may offend the isle.

Enter *Cassio, Montano,* and *Gentlemen*; [*Servant* with wine].

But here they come.
If consequence do but approve my dream,
My boat sails freely, both with wind and stream.

Cas. Fore God, they have given me a rouse already.

Mon. Good faith, a little one; not past a pint, as I am a soldier.

Iago. Some wine, ho!

[*Sings*]

And let me the canakin clink, clink;
And let me the canakin clink.
A soldier 's a man;
O, man's life's but a span,
Why then, let a soldier drink.

Some wine, boys!

Cas. Fore God, an excellent song!

Iago. I learn'd it in England, where indeed they are most potent in potting. Your Dane, your German, and your swag-bellied Hollander — Drink, ho! — are nothing to your English.

Cas. Is your Englishman so expert in his drinking?

Iago. Why, he drinks you with facility your Dane dead drunk; he sweats not to overthrow your Almain; he gives your Hollander a vomit ere the next pottle can be fill'd.

Cas. To the health of our General!

Mon. I am for it, Lieutenant, and I'll do you justice.

Iago. O sweet England!

[*Sings*]

King Stephen was and a worthy peer;
His breeches cost him but a crown;
He held 'em sixpence all too dear,
With that he call'd the tailor lown.

He was a wight of high renown,
And thou art but of low degree.
'Tis pride that pulls the country down;
Then take thine auld cloak about thee.

Some wine, ho!

Cas. Fore God, this is a more exquisite song than the other.

Iago. Will you hear't again?

Cas. No, for I hold him to be unworthy of his place that does those things. Well, God's above all; and there be souls must be saved, and there be souls must not be saved.

Iago. It's true, good Lieutenant.

Cas. For mine own part — no offence to the General, nor any man of quality — I hope to be saved.

Iago. And so do I too, Lieutenant.

Cas. Ay, but, by your leave, not before me. The lieutenant is to be saved before the ancient. Let's have no more of this; let's to our affairs. God forgive us our sins! Gentlemen, let's look to our business. Do not think, gentlemen, I am drunk. This is my ancient. This is my right hand, and this is my left. I am not drunk now. I can stand well enough, and speak well enough.

All. Excellent well!

Cas. Why, very well then. You must not think then that I am drunk. *Exit.*

Mon. To th' platform, masters. Come, let's set the watch.

Iago. You see this fellow that is gone before.
He is a soldier fit to stand by Cæsar
And give direction; and do but see his vice.
'Tis to his virtue a just equinox,
The one as long as th' other. 'Tis pity of him.
I fear the trust Othello puts him in,
On some odd time of his infirmity,
Will shake this island.

Mon. But is he often thus?

Iago. 'Tis evermore the prologue to his sleep.
He'll watch the horologe a double set
If drink rock not his cradle.

Mon. It were well
The General were put in mind of it.
Perhaps he sees it not, or his good nature
Prizes the virtue that appears in Cassio
And looks not on his evils. Is not this true?

Enter *Roderigo.*

Iago. [*aside to him*] How now, Roderigo?
I pray you after the Lieutenant, go!
Exit Roderigo.

Mon. And 'tis great pity that the noble Moor
Should hazard such a place as his own second
With one of an ingraft infirmity.
It were an honest action to say
So to the Moor.

Iago. Not I, for this fair island!
I do love Cassio well and would do much
To cure him of this evil.
(*Within*) 'Help! help!'
But hark! What noise?

Enter *Cassio,* driving in *Roderigo.*

Cas. Zounds, you rogue! you rascal!

Mon. What's the matter, Lieutenant?

Cas. A knave teach me my duty?
I'll beat the knave into a twiggen bottle.

Rod. Beat me?

Cas. Dost thou prate, rogue?
[*Strikes him.*]

Mon. Nay, good Lieutenant!
[*Stays him.*]
I pray you, sir, hold your hand.

Cas. Let me go, sir,
Or I'll knock you o'er the mazzard.

Mon. Come, come, you're drunk!

Cas. Drunk?

Iago. [*aside to Roderigo*] Away, I say! Go out and cry a mutiny! *They fight.*
Exit Roderigo.
Nay, good Lieutenant. God's will, gentlemen!
Help, ho! — Lieutenant — sir — Montano — sir —
Help, masters! — Here's a goodly watch indeed!
A bell rung.
Who's that which rings the bell? Diablo, ho!
The town will rise. God's will, Lieutenant, hold!
You will be sham'd for ever.

Enter *Othello* and *Gentlemen* with weapons.

Oth. What is the matter here?

Mon. Zounds, I bleed still. I am hurt to the death. *He faints.*

Oth. Hold for your lives!

Iago. Hold, hold! Lieutenant — sir — Montano — gentlemen!
Have you forgot all sense of place and duty?
Hold! The General speaks to you. Hold, hold, for shame!

Oth. Why, how now, ho? From whence ariseth this?
Are we turn'd Turks, and to ourselves do that
Which heaven hath forbid the Ottomites?
For Christian shame put by this barbarous brawl!
He that stirs next to carve for his own rage
Holds his soul light; he dies upon his motion.

Silence that dreadful bell! It frights the isle
From her propriety. What's the matter, masters?
Honest Iago, that looks dead with grieving,
Speak. Who began this? On thy love, I charge thee.

Iago. I do not know. Friends all but now, even now,
In quarter, and in terms like bride and groom
Devesting them for bed; and then, but now
(As if some planet had unwitted men)
Swords out, and tilting one at other's breast
In opposition bloody. I cannot speak
Any beginning to this peevish odds,
And would in action glorious I had lost
Those legs that brought me to a part of it!

Oth. How comes it, Michael, you are thus forgot?

Cas. I pray you pardon me. I cannot speak.

Oth. Worthy Montano, you were wont be civil;
The gravity and stillness of your youth
The world hath noted, and your name is great
In mouths of wisest censure. What's the matter
That you unlace your reputation thus
And spend your rich opinion for the name
Of a night-brawler? Give me answer to't.

Mon. Worthy Othello, I am hurt to danger.
Your officer, Iago, can inform you,
While I spare speech, which something now offends me,
Of all that I do know; nor know I aught
By me that's said or done amiss this night,
Unless self-charity be sometimes a vice,
And to defend ourselves it be a sin
When violence assails us.

Oth. Now, by heaven,
My blood begins my safer guides to rule,
And passion, having my best judgment collied,
Assays to lead the way. If I once stir
Or do but lift this arm, the best of you
Shall sink in my rebuke. Give me to know
How this foul rout began, who set it on;
And he that is approv'd in this offence,
Though he had twinn'd with me, both at a birth,
Shall lose me. What! in a town of war,
Yet wild, the people's hearts brimful of fear,
To manage private and domestic quarrel?
In night, and on the court and guard of safety?
'Tis monstrous. Iago, who began 't?

Mon. If partially affin'd, or leagu'd in office,
Thou dost deliver more or less than truth,
Thou art no soldier.

Iago. Touch me not so near.
I had rather have this tongue cut from my mouth
Than it should do offence to Michael Cassio.
Yet I persuade myself, to speak the truth
Shall nothing wrong him. Thus it is, General.
Montano and myself being in speech,
There comes a fellow crying out for help,
And Cassio following him with determin'd sword
To execute upon him. Sir, this gentleman
Steps in to Cassio and entreats his pause.
Myself the crying fellow did pursue,
Lest by his clamour (as it so fell out)
The town might fall in fright. He, swift of foot,
Outran my purpose; and I return'd the rather
For that I heard the clink and fall of swords,
And Cassio high in oath; which till to-night
I ne'er might say before. When I came back
(For this was brief) I found them close together
At blow and thrust, even as again they were
When you yourself did part them.
More of this matter cannot I report;
But men are men; the best sometimes forget.
Though Cassio did some little wrong to him,
As men in rage strike those that wish them best,
Yet surely Cassio I believe receiv'd
From him that fled some strange indignity,
Which patience could not pass.

Oth. I know, Iago,
Thy honesty and love doth mince this matter,
Making it light to Cassio. Cassio, I love thee;
But never more be officer of mine.

Enter *Desdemona*, attended.

Look if my gentle love be not rais'd up!
I'll make thee an example.

Des. What's the matter?

Oth. All's well now, sweeting; come away to bed.
[*To Montano*] Sir, for your hurts, myself will be your surgeon.
Lead him off.

[*Montano is led off.*]

Iago, look with care about the town
And silence those whom this vile brawl distracted.
Come, Desdemona. 'Tis the soldiers' life
To have their balmy slumbers wak'd with strife.

Exeunt [*all but Iago and Cassio*].

Iago. What, are you hurt, Lieutenant?

Cas. Ay, past all surgery.

Iago. Marry, God forbid!

Cas. Reputation, reputation, reputation! O, I have lost my reputation! I have lost the immortal part of myself, and what remains is bestial. My reputation, Iago, my reputation!

Iago. As I am an honest man, I thought you had receiv'd some bodily wound. There is more sense in that than in reputation. Reputation is an idle and most false imposition; oft got without merit and lost without deserving. You have lost no reputation at all unless you repute yourself such a loser. What, man! there are ways to recover the General again. You are but now cast in his mood — a punishment more in policy than in malice, even so as one would beat his offenceless dog to affright an imperious lion. Sue to him again, and he's yours.

Cas. I will rather sue to be despis'd than to deceive so good a commander with so slight, so drunken, and so indiscreet an officer. Drunk? and speak parrot? and squabble? swagger? swear? and discourse fustian with one's own shadow? O thou invisible spirit of wine, if thou hast no name to be known by, let us call thee devil!

Iago. What was he that you follow'd with your sword? What had he done to you?

Cas. I know not.

Iago. Is't possible?

Cas. I remember a mass of things, but nothing distinctly; a quarrel, but nothing wherefore. O God, that men should put an enemy in their mouths to steal away their brains! that we should with joy, pleasance, revel, and applause transform ourselves into beasts!

Iago. Why, but you are now well enough. How came you thus recovered?

Cas. It hath pleas'd the devil drunkenness to give place to the devil wrath. One unperfectness shows me another, to make me frankly despise myself.

Iago. Come, you are too severe a moraler. As the time, the place, and the condition of this country stands, I could heartily wish this had not so befall'n; but since it is as it is, mend it for your own good.

Cas. I will ask him for my place again: he shall tell me I am a drunkard! Had I as many mouths as Hydra, such an answer would stop them all. To be now a sensible man, by-and-by a fool, and presently a beast! O strange! Every inordinate cup is unblest, and the ingredience is a devil.

Iago. Come, come, good wine is a good familiar creature if it be well us'd. Exclaim no more against it. And, good Lieutenant, I think you think I love you.

Cas. I have well approv'd it, sir. I drunk?

Iago. You or any man living may be drunk at a time, man. I'll tell you what you shall do. Our General's wife is now the General. I may say so in this respect, for that he hath devoted and given up himself to the contemplation, mark, and denotement of her parts and graces. Confess yourself freely to her. Importune her help to put you in your place again. She is of so free, so kind, so apt, so blessed a disposition she holds it a vice in her goodness not to do more than she is requested. This broken joint between you and her husband entreat her to splinter; and my fortunes against any lay worth naming, this crack of your love shall grow stronger than 'twas before.

Cas. You advise me well.

Iago. I protest, in the sincerity of love and honest kindness.

Cas. I think it freely; and betimes in the morning will I beseech the virtuous Desdemona to undertake for me. I am desperate of my fortunes if they check me here.

Iago. You are in the right. Good night, Lieutenant. I must to the watch.

Cas. Good night, honest Iago. *Exit.*

Iago. And what's he then that says I play the villain,
When this advice is free I give and honest,
Probal to thinking, and indeed the course
To win the Moor again? For 'tis most easy
Th' inclining Desdemona to subdue
In any honest suit. She's fram'd as fruitful
As the free elements. And then for her
To win the Moor — were't to renounce his baptism —
All seals and symbols of redeemed sin —
His soul is so enfetter'd to her love
That she may make, unmake, do what she list,
Even as her appetite shall play the god
With his weak function. How am I then a villain
To counsel Cassio to this parallel course,
Directly to his good? Divinity of hell!
When devils will the blackest sins put on,
They do suggest at first with heavenly shows,
As I do now. For whiles this honest fool
Plies Desdemona to repair his fortunes,
And she for him pleads strongly to the Moor,
I'll pour this pestilence into his ear —
That she repeals him for her body's lust;
And by how much she strives to do him good,
She shall undo her credit with the Moor.
So will I turn her virtue into pitch,
And out of her own goodness make the net
That shall enmesh them all.

Enter *Roderigo.*

How now, Roderigo?

Rod. I do follow here in the chase, not like a hound that hunts, but one that fills up the cry. My money is almost spent; I have been to-night exceedingly well cudgell'd; and I think the issue will be — I shall have so much experience for my pains; and so, with no money at all, and a little more wit, return again to Venice.

Iago. How poor are they that have not patience!
What wound did ever heal but by degrees?
Thou know'st we work by wit, and not by witchcraft;
And wit depends on dilatory time.
Does't not go well? Cassio hath beaten thee,
And thou by that small hurt hast cashier'd Cassio.
Though other things grow fair against the sun,
Yet fruits that blossom first will first be ripe.
Content thyself awhile. By th' mass, 'tis morning!
Pleasure and action make the hours seem short.
Retire thee; go where thou art billeted.
Away, I say! Thou shalt know more hereafter.
Nay, get thee gone!

Exit Roderigo.

Two things are to be done:
My wife must move for Cassio to her mistress;
I'll set her on;
Myself the while to draw the Moor apart
And bring him jump when he may Cassio find
Soliciting his wife. Ay, that's the way!
Dull not device by coldness and delay. *Exit.*

ACT III. Scene I. [*Cyprus. Before the Castle.*]

Enter *Cassio,* with *Musicians.*

Cas. Masters, play here, I will content your pains:
Something that's brief; and bid 'Good morrow, General.' *They play.*

Enter the *Clown.*

Clown. Why, masters, have your instruments been at Naples, that they speak i' th' nose thus?

Mus. How, sir, how?

Clown. Are these, I pray, call'd wind instruments?

Mus. Ay, marry, are they, sir.

Clown. O, thereby hangs a tail.

Mus. Whereby hangs a tale, sir?

Clown. Marry, sir, by many a wind instrument that I know. But, masters, here's money for you; and the General so likes your music that he desires you, of all loves, to make no more noise with it.

Mus. Well, sir, we will not.

Clown. If you have any music that may not be heard, to't again. But, as they say, to hear music the General does not greatly care.

Mus. We have none such, sir.

Clown. Then put up your pipes in your bag, for I'll away.
Go, vanish into air, away!

Exeunt Musicians.

Cas. Dost thou hear, my honest friend?

Clown. No, I hear not your honest friend. I hear you.

Cas. Prithee keep up thy quillets. There's a poor piece of gold for thee. If the gentlewoman that attends the General's wife be stirring, tell her there's one Cassio entreats her a little favour of speech. Wilt thou do this?

Clown. She is stirring, sir. If she will stir hither, I shall seem to notify unto her.

Cas. Do, good my friend.

Exit Clown.

Enter *Iago.*

In happy time, Iago.

Iago. You have not been abed then?

Cas. Why, no. The day had broke
Before we parted. I have made bold, Iago,
To send in to your wife. My suit to her
Is that she will to virtuous Desdemona
Procure me some access.

Iago. I'll send her to you presently;
And I'll devise a mean to draw the Moor
Out of the way, that your converse and business
May be more free.

Cas. I humbly thank you for't.

Exit [*Iago*].

I never knew
A Florentine more kind and honest.

Enter *Emilia.*

Emil. Good morrow, good Lieutenant. I am sorry
For your displeasure; but all will sure be well.

Douglas Campbell in the title role

OTHELLO

PHOTOGRAPHS BY JOHN VICKERS
PRODUCED BY THE OLD VIC COMPANY

Above: Nicholas Hannen as the Senator Brabantio. *Right:* Irene Worth as Desdemona, Brabantio's daughter and the wife of Othello

Left: Coral Browne as Desdemona's attendant Emilia, wife of Iago. *Below:* Ernest Milton as Lodovico, Brabantio's kinsman

The night scene *(Act I, Scene I)* in which Iago (Paul Rogers) and Roderigo (Douglas Wilmer) waken Brabantio to tell him that his daughter has been married to Othello

As Othello is on his way to the Senate, he is intercepted by Brabantio and the officers. He agrees to a hearing before the Senate *(Act I, Scene II)*

Learning that his daughter loves the Moor, the heartbroken Brabantio reluctantly accepts the marriage and joins their hands *(Act I, Scene III)*

Desdemona and Emilia, the unwitting tool of Iago in his intrigue against the happiness of Othello and his wife

"Receive it from me; I speak not yet of proof. Look to your wife, observe her well with Cassio." Iago plants the seed of jealousy in Othello's mind, suggesting Desdemona and Cassio are lovers *(Act III, Scene III)*

"They met so near with their lips that their breaths embraced together. Villainous thoughts, Roderigo!" Working on the passions of another one of his foils, Iago informs him that Desdemona accepts the love of Cassio *(Act II, Scene I)*

Ninka Dolega as Bianca and Robert Shaw as her lover, Cassio, pathetic dupe of Iago

Othello defies Iago to prove his charges against Desdemona *(Act III, Scene III)*

Othello receives the order to return to Venice *(Act IV, Scene I)*

"O! banish me, my lord, but kill me not!" Desdemona pleads desperately for her life, but Othello, mad with jealousy, smothers her and learns too late of Iago's deception *(Act V, Scene II)*

"Sweet Desdemona! O! sweet mistress, speak" Emilia finds Desdemona as she lies dying *(Act V, Scene II)*

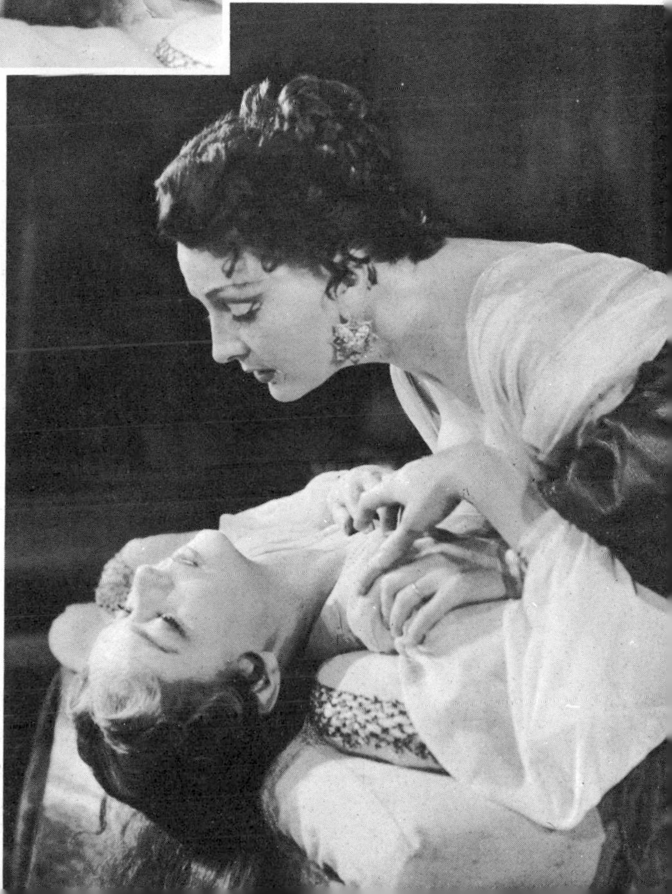

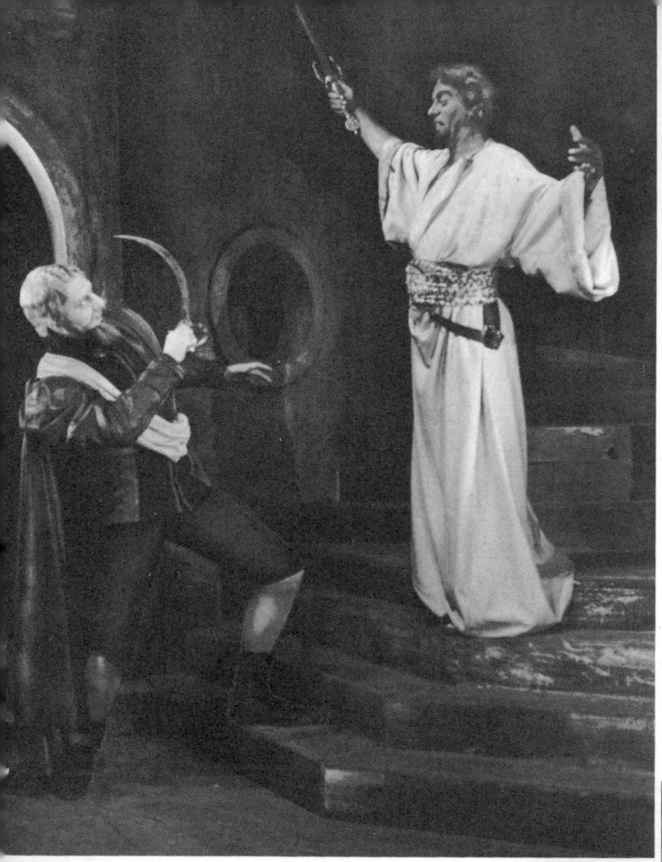

"What is the matter? How now, general!" Montano (Anthony van Bridge) interrupts the mad attack of Othello upon Emilia *(Act V, Scene II)*

"Speak of me as I am; nothing extenuate, nor set down aught in malice: then, must you speak of one that lov'd not wisely but too well." Othello's final speech to the legates *(Act V, Scene II)*

The General and his wife are talking of it,
And she speaks for you stoutly. The Moor replies
That he you hurt is of great fame in Cyprus
And great affinity, and that in wholesome wisdom
He might not but refuse you. But he protests he loves you,
And needs no other suitor but his likings
To take the safest occasion by the front
To bring you in again.

Cas. Yet I beseech you,
If you think fit, or that it may be done,
Give me advantage of some brief discourse
With Desdemon alone.

Emil. Pray you come in.
I will bestow you where you shall have time
To speak your bosom freely.

Cas. I am much bound to you. *Exeunt.*

Scene II. [*Cyprus. A room in the Castle.*]

Enter *Othello, Iago,* and *Gentlemen.*

Oth. These letters give, Iago, to the pilot
And by him do my duties to the state.
That done, I will be walking on the works.
Repair there to me.

Iago. Well, my good lord, I'll do't.

Oth. This fortification, gentlemen, shall we see't?

Gent. We'll wait upon your lordship.
Exeunt.

Scene III. [*Cyprus. The garden of the Castle.*]

Enter *Desdemona, Cassio,* and *Emilia.*

Des. Be thou assur'd, good Cassio, I will do
All my abilities in thy behalf.

Emil. Good madam, do. I warrant it grieves my husband
As if the cause were his.

Des. O, that's an honest fellow. Do not doubt, Cassio,
But I will have my lord and you again
As friendly as you were.

Cas. Bounteous madam,
Whatever shall become of Michael Cassio,
He's never anything but your true servant.

Des. I know't; I thank you. You do love my lord;
You have known him long; and be you well assur'd
He shall in strangeness stand no farther off
Than in a politic distance.

Cas. Ay, but, lady,
That policy may either last so long,
Or feed upon such nice and waterish diet,
Or breed itself so out of circumstance,
That, I being absent, and my place supplied,
My general will forget my love and service.

Des. Do not doubt that. Before Emilia here
I give thee warrant of thy place. Assure thee,
If I do vow a friendship, I'll perform it
To the last article. My lord shall never rest;
I'll watch him tame and talk him out of patience;
His bed shall seem a school, his board a shrift;
I'll intermingle everything he does
With Cassio's suit. Therefore be merry, Cassio,
For thy solicitor shall rather die
Than give thy cause away.

Enter *Othello* and *Iago.*

Emil. Madam, here comes my lord.

Cas. Madam, I'll take my leave.

Des. Why, stay, and hear me speak.

Cas. Madam, not now. I am very ill at ease.
Unfit for mine own purposes.

Des. Well, do your discretion.
Exit Cassio.

Iago. Ha! I like not that.

Oth. What dost thou say?

Iago. Nothing, my lord; or if — I know not what.

Oth. Was not that Cassio parted from my wife?

Iago. Cassio, my lord? No, sure, I cannot think it,
That he would steal away so guilty-like,
Seeing you coming.

Oth. I do believe 'twas he.

Des. How now, my lord?
I have been talking with a suitor here,
A man that languishes in your displeasure.

Oth. Who is't you mean?

Des. Why, your lieutenant, Cassio. Good my lord,
If I have any grace or power to move you,
His present reconciliation take;
For if he be not one that truly loves you,
That errs in ignorance, and not in cunning,
I have no judgment in an honest face.
I prithee call him back.

Oth. Went he hence now?

Des. Yes, faith; so humbled
That he hath left part of his grief with me
To suffer with him. Good love, call him back.

Oth. Not now, sweet Desdemon; some other time.
Des. But shall't be shortly?
Oth. The sooner, sweet, for you.
Des. Shall't be to-night at supper?
Oth. No, not to-night.
Des. To-morrow dinner then?
Oth. I shall not dine at home.
I meet the captains at the citadel.
Des. Why then, to-morrow night, or Tuesday morn,
Or Tuesday noon or night, or Wednesday morn.
I prithee name the time, but let it not
Exceed three days. I' faith, he's penitent;
And yet his trespass, in our common reason
(Save that, they say, the wars must make examples
Out of their best) is not almost a fault
T' incur a private check. When shall he come?
Tell me, Othello. I wonder in my soul
What you could ask me that I should deny
Or stand so mamm'ring on. What? Michael Cassio,
That came a-wooing with you, and so many a time,
When I have spoke of you dispraisingly,
Hath ta'en your part — to have so much to do
To bring him in? Trust me, I could do much —
Oth. Prithee no more. Let him come when he will!
I will deny thee nothing.
Des. Why, this is not a boon.
'Tis as I should entreat you wear your gloves,
Or feed on nourishing dishes, or keep you warm,
Or sue to you to do a peculiar profit
To your own person. Nay, when I have a suit
Wherein I mean to touch your love indeed,
It shall be full of poise and difficult weight,
And fearful to be granted.
Oth. I will deny thee nothing!
Whereon I do beseech thee grant me this,
To leave me but a little to myself.
Des. Shall I deny you? No. Farewell, my lord.
Oth. Farewell, my Desdemon. I'll come to thee straight.
Des. Emilia, come. — Be as your fancies teach you.
Whate'er you be, I am obedient.
Exeunt Desdemona and Emilia.
Oth. Excellent wretch! Perdition catch my soul
But I do love thee! and when I love thee not,
Chaos is come again.
Iago. My noble lord —
Oth. What dost thou say, Iago?
Iago. Did Michael Cassio, when you woo'd my lady,
Know of your love?
Oth. He did, from first to last. Why dost thou ask?
Iago. But for a satisfaction of my thought;
No further harm.
Oth. Why of thy thought, Iago?
Iago. I did not think he had been acquainted with her.
Oth. O, yes, and went between us very oft.
Iago. Indeed?
Oth. Indeed? Ay, indeed! Discern'st thou aught in that?
Is he not honest?
Iago. Honest, my lord?
Oth. Honest? Ay, honest.
Iago. My lord, for aught I know.
Oth. What dost thou think?
Iago. Think, my lord?
Oth. Think, my lord?
By heaven, he echoes me,
As if there were some monster in his thought
Too hideous to be shown. Thou dost mean something.
I heard thee say even now, thou lik'st not that,
When Cassio left my wife. What didst not like?
And when I told thee he was of my counsel
In my whole course of wooing, thou cried'st 'Indeed?'
And didst contract and purse thy brow together,
As if thou then hadst shut up in thy brain
Some horrible conceit. If thou dost love me,
Show me thy thought.
Iago. My lord, you know I love you.
Oth. I think thou dost;
And, for I know thou'rt full of love and honesty
And weigh'st thy words before thou giv'st them breath,
Therefore these stops of thine fright me the more;
For such things in a false disloyal knave
Are tricks of custom; but in a man that's just
They are close dilations, working from the heart
That passion cannot rule.
Iago. For Michael Cassio,
I dare be sworn I think that he is honest.
Oth. I think so too.
Iago. Men should be what they seem;
Or those that be not, would they might seem none!
Oth. Certain, men should be what they seem.
Iago. Why then, I think Cassio's an honest man.

Oth. Nay, yet there's more in this.
I prithee speak to me, as to thy thinkings,
As thou dost ruminate, and give thy worst of thoughts
The worst of words.
Iago. Good my lord, pardon me.
Though I am bound to every act of duty,
I am not bound to that all slaves are free to.
Utter my thoughts? Why, say they are vile and false,
As where's that palace whereinto foul things
Sometimes intrude not? Who has a breast so pure
But some uncleanly apprehensions
Keep leets and law days, and in session sit
With meditations lawful?
Oth. Thou dost conspire against thy friend, Iago,
If thou but think'st him wrong'd, and mak'st his ear
A stranger to thy thoughts.
Iago. I do beseech you —
Though I perchance am vicious in my guess
(As I confess it is my nature's plague
To spy into abuses, and oft my jealousy
Shapes faults that are not), that your wisdom yet
From one that so imperfectly conceits
Would take no notice, nor build yourself a trouble
Out of his scattering and unsure observance.
It were not for your quiet nor your good,
Nor for my manhood, honesty, or wisdom,
To let you know my thoughts.
Oth. What dost thou mean?
Iago. Good name in man and woman, dear my lord,
Is the immediate jewel of their souls.
Who steals my purse steals trash; 'tis something, nothing;
'Twas mine, 'tis his, and has been slave to thousands;
But he that filches from me my good name
Robs me of that which not enriches him
And makes me poor indeed.
Oth. By heaven, I'll know thy thoughts!
Iago. You cannot, if my heart were in your hand;
Nor shall not whilst 'tis in my custody.
Oth. Ha!
Iago. O, beware, my lord, of jealousy!
It is the green-ey'd monster, which doth mock
The meat it feeds on. That cuckold lives in bliss
Who, certain of his fate, loves not his wronger;
But O, what damned minutes tells he o'er
Who dotes, yet doubts — suspects, yet strongly loves!
Oth. O misery!
Iago. Poor and content is rich, and rich enough;
But riches fineless is as poor as winter
To him that ever fears he shall be poor.
Good heaven, the souls of all my tribe defend
From jealousy!
Oth. Why, why is this?
Think'st thou I'ld make a life of jealousy,
To follow still the changes of the moon
With fresh suspicions? No! To be once in doubt
Is once to be resolv'd. Exchange me for a goat
When I shall turn the business of my soul
To such exsufflicate and blown surmises,
Matching thy inference. 'Tis not to make me jealous
To say my wife is fair, feeds well, loves company,
Is free of speech, sings, plays, and dances well.
Where virtue is, these are more virtuous.
Nor from mine own weak merits will I draw
The smallest fear or doubt of her revolt,
For she had eyes, and chose me. No, Iago;
I'll see before I doubt; when I doubt, prove;
And on the proof there is no more but this —
Away at once with love or jealousy!
Iago. I am glad of it; for now I shall have reason
To show the love and duty that I bear you
With franker spirit. Therefore, as I am bound,
Receive it from me. I speak not yet of proof.
Look to your wife; observe her well with Cassio;
Wear your eye thus, not jealous nor secure.
I would not have your free and noble nature,
Out of self-bounty, be abus'd. Look to't.
I know our country disposition well:
In Venice they do let heaven see the pranks
They dare not show their husbands; their best conscience
Is not to leave't undone, but keep't unknown.
Oth. Dost thou say so?
Iago. She did deceive her father, marrying you;
And when she seem'd to shake and fear your looks,
She lov'd them most.
Oth. And so she did.
Iago. Why, go to then!
She that, so young, could give out such a seeming
To seel her father's eyes up close as oak —

He thought 'twas witchcraft — but I am much to blame.
I humbly do beseech you of your pardon
For too much loving you.
Oth. I am bound to thee for ever.
Iago. I see this hath a little dash'd your spirits.
Oth. Not a jot, not a jot.
Iago. I' faith, I fear it has.
I hope you will consider what is spoke
Comes from my love. But I do see y'are mov'd.
I am to pray you not to strain my speech
To grosser issues nor to larger reach
Than to suspicion.
Oth. I will not.
Iago. Should you do so, my lord,
My speech should fall into such vile success
As my thoughts aim not at. Cassio's my worthy friend —
My lord, I see y'are mov'd.
Oth. No, not much mov'd.
I do not think but Desdemona's honest.
Iago. Long live she so! and long live you to think so!
Oth. And yet, how nature erring from itself —
Iago. Ay, there's the point! as (to be bold with you)
Not to affect many proposed matches
Of her own clime, complexion, and degree,
Whereto we see in all things nature tends —
Foh! one may smell in such a will most rank,
Foul disproportion, thoughts unnatural —
But pardon me — I do not in position
Distinctly speak of her; though I may fear
Her will, recoiling to her better judgment,
May fall to match you with her country forms,
And happily repent.
Oth. Farewell, farewell!
If more thou dost perceive, let me know more.
Set on thy wife to observe. Leave me, Iago.
Iago. My lord, I take my leave. [*Going.*]
Oth. Why did I marry? This honest creature doubtless
Sees and knows more, much more, than he unfolds.
Iago. [*returns*] My lord, I would I might entreat your Honour
To scan this thing no further. Leave it to time.
Though it be fit that Cassio have his place,
For sure he fills it up with great ability,
Yet, if you please to hold him off awhile,
You shall by that perceive him and his means.
Note if your lady strain his entertainment
With any strong or vehement importunity.
Much will be seen in that. In the mean time
Let me be thought too busy in my fears
(As worthy cause I have to fear I am)
And hold her free, I do beseech your Honour.
Oth. Fear not my government.
Iago. I once more take my leave. *Exit.*
Oth. This fellow's of exceeding honesty,
And knows all qualities, with a learned spirit
Of human dealings. If I do prove her haggard,
Though that her jesses were my dear heart-strings,
I'ld whistle her off and let her down the wind
To prey at fortune. Haply, for I am black
And have not those soft parts of conversation
That chamberers have, or for I am declin'd
Into the vale of years (yet that's not much),
She's gone. I am abus'd, and my relief
Must be to loathe her. O curse of marriage,
That we can call these delicate creatures ours,
And not their appetites! I had rather be a toad
And live upon the vapour of a dungeon
Than keep a corner in the thing I love
For others' uses. Yet 'tis the plague of great ones;
Prerogativ'd are they less than the base.
'Tis destiny unshunnable, like death.
Even then this forked plague is fated to us
When we do quicken. Desdemona comes.

Enter *Desdemona* and *Emilia*.

If she be false, O, then heaven mocks itself!
I'll not believe't.
Des. How now, my dear Othello?
Your dinner, and the generous islanders
By you invited, do attend your presence.
Oth. I am to blame.
Des. Why do you speak so faintly?
Are you not well?
Oth. I have a pain upon my forehead, here.
Des. Faith, that's with watching; 'twill away again.
Let me but bind it hard, within this hour
It will be well.
Oth. Your napkin is too little.
[*He puts the handkerchief from him, and she drops it.*]
Let it alone. Come, I'll go in with you.
Des. I am very sorry that you are not well.
Exeunt Othello and Desdemona.
Emil. I am glad I have found this napkin.
This was her first remembrance from the Moor.
My wayward husband hath a hundred times
Woo'd me to steal it; but she so loves the token
(For he conjur'd her she should ever keep it)
That she reserves it evermore about her

To kiss and talk to. I'll have the work ta'en out
And give't Iago.
What he will do with it heaven knows, not I;
I nothing but to please his fantasy.

Enter *Iago*.

Iago. How now? What do you here alone?
Emil. Do not you chide; I have a thing for you.
Iago. A thing for me? It is a common thing—
Emil. Ha?
Iago. To have a foolish wife.
Emil. O, is that all? What will you give me now
For that same handkerchief?
Iago. What handkerchief?
Emil. What handkerchief?
Why, that the Moor first gave to Desdemona;
That which so often you did bid me steal.
Iago. Hast stol'n it from her?
Emil. No, faith; she let it drop by negligence,
And to th' advantage, I, being here, took't up.
Look, here it is.
Iago. A good wench! Give it me.
Emil. What will you do with't, that you have been so earnest
To have me filch it?
Iago. Why, what's that to you?
[*Snatches it.*]
Emil. If it be not for some purpose of import,
Give't me again. Poor lady, she'll run mad
When she shall lack it.
Iago. Be not you acknown on't; I have use for it.
Go, leave me.
Exit Emilia.
I will in Cassio's lodging lose this napkin
And let him find it. Trifles light as air
Are to the jealous confirmations strong
As proofs of holy writ. This may do something.
The Moor already changes with my poison.
Dangerous conceits are in their natures poisons
Which at the first are scarce found to distaste,
But with a little act upon the blood
Burn like the mines of sulphur.

Enter *Othello*.

I did say so.
Look where he comes! Not poppy nor mandragora,
Nor all the drowsy syrups of the world,
Shall ever medicine thee to that sweet sleep
Which thou ow'dst yesterday.
Oth. Ha! ha! false to me?
Iago. Why, how now, General? No more of that!
Oth. Avaunt! be gone! Thou hast set me on the rack.
I swear 'tis better to be much abus'd
Than but to know't a little.
Iago. How now, my lord?
Oth. What sense had I of her stol'n hours of lust?
I saw't not, thought it not, it harm'd not me.
I slept the next night well, was free and merry;
I found not Cassio's kisses on her lips.
He that is robb'd, not wanting what is stol'n,
Let him not know't, and he's not robb'd at all.
Iago. I am sorry to hear this.
Oth. I had been happy if the general camp,
Pioners and all, had tasted her sweet body,
So I had nothing known. O, now for ever
Farewell the tranquil mind! farewell content!
Farewell the plumed troop, and the big wars
That make ambition virtue! O, farewell!
Farewell the neighing steed and the shrill trump,
The spirit-stirring drum, th' ear-piercing fife,
The royal banner, and all quality,
Pride, pomp, and circumstance of glorious war!
And O ye mortal engines whose rude throats
Th' immortal Jove's dread clamours counterfeit,
Farewell! Othello's occupation's gone!
Iago. Is't possible, my lord?
Oth. Villain, be sure thou prove my love a whore!
Be sure of it; give me the ocular proof;
Or, by the worth of man's eternal soul,
Thou hadst been better have been born a dog
Than answer my wak'd wrath!
Iago. Is't come to this?
Oth. Make me to see't; or at the least so prove it
That the probation bear no hinge nor loop
To hang a doubt on — or woe upon thy life!
Iago. My noble lord —
Oth. If thou dost slander her and torture me,
Never pray more; abandon all remorse;
On horror's head horrors accumulate;
Do deeds to make heaven weep, all earth amaz'd;
For nothing canst thou to damnation add
Greater than that.
Iago. O grace! O heaven forgive me!
Are you a man? Have you a soul or sense? —
God b' wi' you! take mine office. O wretched fool,
That liv'st to make thine honesty a vice!

O monstrous world! Take note, take note, O world,
To be direct and honest is not safe.
I thank you for this profit; and from hence
I'll love no friend, sith love breeds such offence.
Oth. Nay, stay. Thou shouldst be honest.
Iago. I should be wise; for honesty 's a fool
And loses that it works for.
Oth. By the world,
I think my wife be honest, and think she is not;
I think that thou art just, and think thou art not.
I'll have some proof. Her name, that was as fresh
As Dian's visage, is now begrim'd and black
As mine own face. If there be cords, or knives,
Poison, or fire, or suffocating streams,
I'll not endure it. Would I were satisfied!
Iago. I see, sir, you are eaten up with passion.
I do repent me that I put it to you.
You would be satisfied?
Oth. Would? Nay, I will.
Iago. And may. But how? how satisfied, my lord?
Would you, the supervisor, grossly gape on?
Behold her topp'd?
Oth. Death and damnation! O!
Iago. It were a tedious difficulty, I think,
To bring them to that prospect. Damn them then,
If ever mortal eyes do see them bolster
More than their own! What then? How then?
What shall I say? Where's satisfaction?
It is impossible you should see this,
Were they as prime as goats, as hot as monkeys,
As salt as wolves in pride, and fools as gross
As ignorance made drunk. But yet, I say,
If imputation and strong circumstances
Which lead directly to the door of truth
Will give you satisfaction, you may have't.
Oth. Give me a living reason she's disloyal.
Iago. I do not like the office.
But sith I am enter'd in this cause so far,
Prick'd to't by foolish honesty and love,
I will go on. I lay with Cassio lately,
And being troubled with a raging tooth,
I could not sleep.
There are a kind of men so loose of soul
That in their sleeps will mutter their affairs.
One of this kind is Cassio.
In sleep I heard him say, 'Sweet Desdemona,
Let us be wary, let us hide our loves!'
And then, sir, would he gripe and wring my hand,
Cry 'O sweet creature!' and then kiss me hard,
As if he pluck'd up kisses by the roots
That grew upon my lips; then laid his leg
Over my thigh, and sigh'd, and kiss'd, and then
Cried 'Cursed fate that gave thee to the Moor!'
Oth. O monstrous! monstrous!
Iago. Nay, this was but his dream.
Oth. But this denoted a foregone conclusion.
'Tis a shrewd doubt, though it be but a dream.
Iago. And this may help to thicken other proofs
That do demonstrate thinly.
Oth. I'll tear her all to pieces!
Iago. Nay, but be wise. Yet we see nothing done;
She may be honest yet. Tell me but this —
Have you not sometimes seen a handkerchief
Spotted with strawberries in your wive's hand?
Oth. I gave her such a one; 'twas my first gift.
Iago. I know not that; but such a handkerchief
(I am sure it was your wive's) did I to-day
See Cassio wipe his beard with.
Oth. If't be that —
Iago. If it be that, or any that was hers,
It speaks against her, with the other proofs.
Oth. O, that the slave had forty thousand lives!
One is too poor, too weak for my revenge.
Now do I see 'tis true. Look here, Iago:
All my fond love thus do I blow to heaven.
'Tis gone.
Arise, black vengeance, from the hollow hell!
Yield up, O love, thy crown and hearted throne
To tyrannous hate! Swell, bosom, with thy fraught,
For 'tis of aspics' tongues!
Iago. Yet be content.
Oth. O, blood, blood, blood!
Iago. Patience, I say. Your mind perhaps may change.
Oth. Never, Iago. Like to the Pontic sea,
Whose icy current and compulsive course
Ne'er feels retiring ebb, but keeps due on
To the Propontic and the Hellespont;
Even so my bloody thoughts, with violent pace,
Shall ne'er look back, ne'er ebb to humble love,
Till that a capable and wide revenge
Swallow them up. (*He kneels.*) Now, by yond marble heaven,
In the due reverence of a sacred vow
I here engage my words.
Iago. Do not rise yet.
Iago kneels.

Witness, you ever-burning lights above,
You elements that clip us round about,
Witness that here Iago doth give up
The execution of his wit, hands, heart
To wrong'd Othello's service! Let him command,
And to obey shall be in me remorse,
What bloody business ever. [*They rise.*]

Oth. I greet thy love,
Not with vain thanks but with acceptance bounteous,
And will upon the instant put thee to't.
Within these three days let me hear thee say
That Cassio 's not alive.

Iago. My friend is dead; 'tis done at your request.
But let her live.

Oth. Damn her, lewd minx! O, damn her!
Come, go with me apart. I will withdraw
To furnish me with some swift means of death
For the fair devil. Now art thou my lieutenant.

Iago. I am your own for ever. *Exeunt.*

Scene IV. [*Cyprus. Before the Castle.*]

Enter *Desdemona, Emilia,* and *Clown.*

Des. Do you know, sirrah, where Lieutenant Cassio lies?

Clown. I dare not say he lies anywhere.

Des. Why, man?

Clown. He's a soldier; and for one to say a soldier lies is stabbing.

Des. Go to. Where lodges he?

Clown. To tell you where he lodges is to tell you where I lie.

Des. Can anything be made of this?

Clown. I know not where he lodges; and for me to devise a lodging, and say he lies here or he lies there, were to lie in mine own throat.

Des. Can you enquire him out, and be edified by report?

Clown. I will catechize the world for him; that is, make questions, and by them answer.

Des. Seek him, bid him come hither. Tell him I have mov'd my lord on his behalf and hope all will be well.

Clown. To do this is within the compass of man's wit, and therefore I'll attempt the doing of it. *Exit.*

Des. Where should I lose that handkerchief, Emilia?

Emil. I know not, madam.

Des. Believe me, I had rather have lost my purse
Full of crusadoes; and but my noble Moor
Is true of mind, and made of no such baseness
As jealous creatures are, it were enough
To put him to ill thinking.

Emil. Is he not jealous?

Des. Who? he? I think the sun where he was born
Drew all such humours from him.

Enter *Othello.*

Emil. Look where he comes.

Des. I will not leave him now till Cassio
Be call'd to him. — How is't with you, my lord?

Oth. Well, my good lady. [*Aside*] O, hardness to dissemble! —
How do you, Desdemona?

Des. Well, my good lord.

Oth. Give me your hand. This hand is moist, my lady.

Des. It yet hath felt no age nor known no sorrow.

Oth. This argues fruitfulness and liberal heart.
Hot, hot, and moist. This hand of yours requires
A sequester from liberty, fasting and prayer,
Much castigation, exercise devout;
For here's a young and sweating devil here
That commonly rebels. 'Tis a good hand,
A frank one.

Des. You may, indeed, say so;
For 'twas that hand that gave away my heart.

Oth. A liberal hand! The hearts of old gave hands;
But our new heraldry is hands, not hearts.

Des. I cannot speak of this. Come now, your promise!

Oth. What promise, chuck?

Des. I have sent to bid Cassio come speak with you.

Oth. I have a salt and sorry rheum offends me.
Lend me thy handkerchief.

Des. Here, my lord.

Oth. That which I gave you.

Des. I have it not about me.

Oth. Not?

Des. No indeed, my lord.

Oth. That is a fault.
That handkerchief
Did an Egyptian to my mother give.
She was a charmer, and could almost read

The thoughts of people. She told her, while she kept it,
'Twould make her amiable and subdue my father
Entirely to her love; but if she lost it
Or made a gift of it, my father's eye
Should hold her loathly, and his spirits should hunt
After new fancies. She, dying, gave it me,
And bid me, when my fate would have me wive,
To give it her. I did so; and take heed on't;
Make it a darling like your precious eye. 66
To lose't or give't away were such perdition
As nothing else could match.

Des. Is't possible?

Oth. 'Tis true. There's magic in the web of it.
A sibyl that had numb'red in the world
The sun to course two hundred compasses,
In her prophetic fury sew'd the work;
The worms were hallowed that did breed the silk;
And it was dy'd in mummy which the skilful
Conserv'd of maiden's hearts.

Des. I' faith? Is't true?

Oth. Most veritable. Therefore look to't well.

Des. Then would to God that I had never seen't!

Oth. Ha! Wherefore?

Des. Why do you speak so startingly and rash?

Oth. Is't lost? Is't gone? Speak, is it out o' th' way?

Des. Heaven bless us!

Oth. Say you?

Des. It is not lost. But what an if it were?

Oth. How?

Des. I say it is not lost.

Oth. Fetch't, let me see't!

Des. Why, so I can, sir; but I will not now.
This is a trick to put me from my suit.
Pray you let Cassio be receiv'd again.

Oth. Fetch me the handkerchief! My mind misgives.

Des. Come, come!
You'll never meet a more sufficient man.

Oth. The handkerchief!

Des. I pray talk me of Cassio.

Oth. The handkerchief!

Des. A man that all his time
Hath founded his good fortunes on your love,
Shar'd dangers with you —

Oth. The handkerchief!

Des. In sooth, you are to blame.

Oth. Away! *Exit.*

Emil. Is not this man jealous?

Des. I ne'er saw this before.
Sure there's some wonder in this handkerchief.
I am most unhappy in the loss of it.

Emil. 'Tis not a year or two shows us a man.
They are all but stomachs, and we all but food;
They eat us hungerly, and when they are full,
They belch us.

Enter *Iago* and *Cassio.*

Look you — Cassio and my husband!

Iago. There is no other way; 'tis she must do't.
And lo the happiness! Go and importune her.

Des. How now, good Cassio? What's the news with you?

Cas. Madam, my former suit. I do beseech you
That by your virtuous means I may again
Exist, and be a member of his love
Whom I with all the office of my heart
Entirely honour. I would not be delay'd.
If my offence be of such mortal kind
That neither service past, nor present sorrows,
Nor purpos'd merit in futurity,
Can ransom me into his love again,
But to know so must be my benefit.
So shall I clothe me in a forc'd content,
And shut myself up in some other course,
To fortune's alms.

Des. Alas, thrice-gentle Cassio!
My advocation is not now in tune.
My lord is not my lord; nor should I know him,
Were he in favour as in humour alter'd.
So help me every spirit sanctified
As I have spoken for you all my best
And stood within the blank of his displeasure
For my free speech! You must awhile be patient.
What I can do I will; and more I will
Than for myself I dare. Let that suffice you.

Iago. Is my lord angry?

Emil. He went hence but now,
And certainly in strange unquietness.

Iago. Can he be angry? I have seen the cannon
When it hath blown his ranks into the air
And, like the devil, from his very arm
Puff'd his own brother — and can he be angry?
Something of moment then. I will go meet him.
There's matter in't indeed if he be angry.

Des. I prithee do so.

Exit [*Iago*].

Something sure of state,
Either from Venice or some unhatch'd practice
Made demonstrable here in Cyprus to him,

Hath puddled his clear spirit; and in such cases
Men's natures wrangle with inferior things,
Though great ones are their object. 'Tis even so.
For let our finger ache, and it endues
Our other, healthful, members even to that sense
Of pain. Nay, we must think men are not gods,
Nor of them look for such observancy
As fits the bridal. Beshrew me much, Emilia,
I was (unhandsome warrior as I am!)
Arraigning his unkindness with my soul;
But now I find I had suborn'd the witness,
And he's indicted falsely.

Emil. Pray heaven it be state matters, as you think,
And no conception nor no jealous toy
Concerning you.

Des. Alas the day! I never gave him cause.

Emil. But jealous souls will not be answer'd so.
They are not ever jealous for the cause,
But jealous for they are jealous. 'Tis a monster
Begot upon itself, born on itself.

Des. Heaven keep that monster from Othello's mind!

Emil. Lady, amen.

Des. I will go seek him. Cassio, walk here about.
If I do find him fit, I'll move your suit
And seek to effect it to my uttermost.

Cas. I humbly thank your ladyship.

Exeunt Desdemona and Emilia.

Enter *Bianca.*

Bian. Save you, friend Cassio!

Cas. What make you from home?
How is it with you, my most fair Bianca?
I' faith, sweet love, I was coming to your house.

Bian. And I was going to your lodging, Cassio.
What, keep a week away? seven days and nights?
Eightscore eight hours? and lovers' absent hours,
More tedious than the dial eightscore times?
O weary reck'ning!

Cas. Pardon me, Bianca.
I have this while with leaden thoughts been press'd;
But I shall in a more continuate time
Strike off this score of absence. Sweet Bianca,
[*Gives her Desdemona's handkerchief.*]
Take me this work out.

Bian. O Cassio, whence came this?
This is some token from a newer friend.
To the felt absence now I feel a cause.
Is't come to this? Well, well.

Cas. Go to, woman!
Throw your vile guesses in the devil's teeth,
From whence you have them. You are jealous now
That this is from some mistress, some remembrance.
No, by my faith, Bianca.

Bian. Why, whose is it?

Cas. I know not, sweet. I found it in my chamber.
I like the work well. Ere it be demanded,
As like enough it will, I would have it copied.
Take it and do't, and leave me for this time.

Bian. Leave you? Wherefore?

Cas. I do attend here on the General
And think it no addition, nor my wish,
To have him see me woman'd.

Bian. Why, I pray you?

Cas. Not that I love you not.

Bian. But that you do not love me!
I pray you bring me on the way a little,
And say if I shall see you soon at night.

Cas. 'Tis but a little way that I can bring you,
For I attend here; but I'll see you soon.

Bian. 'Tis very good. I must be circumstanc'd.

Exeunt.

ACT IV. Scene I. [*Cyprus. Before the Castle.*]

Enter *Othello* and *Iago.*

Iago. Will you think so?

Oth. Think so, Iago?

Iago. What,
To kiss in private?

Oth. An unauthoriz'd kiss.

Iago. Or to be naked with her friend in bed
An hour, or more, not meaning any harm?

Oth. Naked in bed, Iago, and not mean harm?
It is hypocrisy against the devil.
They that mean virtuously, and yet do so,
The devil their virtue tempts, and they tempt heaven.

Iago. So they do nothing, 'tis a venial slip.
But if I give my wife a handkerchief —

Oth. What then?

Iago. Why, then 'tis hers, my lord; and being hers,
She may, I think, bestow't on any man.
Oth. She is protectress of her honour too.
May she give that?
Iago. Her honour is an essence that's not seen;
They have it very oft that have it not.
But for the handkerchief —
Oth. By heaven, I would most gladly have forgot it!
Thou said'st (O, it comes o'er my memory
As doth the raven o'er the infected house,
Boding to all!) he had my handkerchief.
Iago. Ay, what of that?
Oth. That's not so good now.
Iago. What
If I had said I had seen him do you wrong?
Or heard him say — as knaves be such abroad
Who having, by their own importunate suit,
Or voluntary dotage of some mistress,
Convinced or supplied them, cannot choose
But they must blab —
Oth. Hath he said anything?
Iago. He hath, my lord; but be you well assur'd,
No more than he'll unswear.
Oth. What hath he said?
Iago. Faith, that he did — I know not what he did.
Oth. What? what?
Iago. Lie —
Oth. With her?
Iago. With her, on her; what you will.

Oth. Lie with her? lie on her? — We say lie on her when they belie her. — Lie with her! Zounds, that's fulsome. — Handkerchief — confessions — handkerchief! — To confess, and be hang'd for his labour — first to be hang'd, and then to confess! I tremble at it. Nature would not invest herself in such shadowing passion without some instruction. It is not words that shakes me thus. — Pish! Noses, ears, and lips? Is't possible? — Confess? — handkerchief? — O devil! *Falls in a trance.*

Iago. Work on,
My medicine, work! Thus credulous fools are caught,
And many worthy and chaste dames even thus,
All guiltless, meet reproach. — What, ho! my lord!
My lord, I say! Othello!

Enter Cassio.

How now, Cassio?
Cas. What's the matter?
Iago. My lord is fall'n into an epilepsy.
This is his second fit; he had one yesterday.
Cas. Rub him about the temples.
Iago. No, forbear.
The lethargy must have his quiet course.
If not, he foams at mouth, and by-and-by
Breaks out to savage madness. Look, he stirs.
Do you withdraw yourself a little while.
He will recover straight. When he is gone,
I would on great occasion speak with you.
Exit Cassio.
How is it, General? Have you not hurt your head?
Oth. Dost thou mock me?
Iago. I mock you? No, by heaven.
Would you would bear your fortune like a man!
Oth. A horned man's a monster and a beast.
Iago. There's many a beast then in a populous city,
And many a civil monster.
Oth. Did he confess it?
Iago. Good sir, be a man.
Think every bearded fellow that's but yok'd
May draw with you. There's millions now alive
That nightly lie in those unproper beds
Which they dare swear peculiar. Your case is better.
O, 'tis the spite of hell, the fiend's arch-mock,
To lip a wanton in a secure couch,
And to suppose her chaste! No, let me know;
And knowing what I am, I know what she shall be.
Oth. O, thou art wise! 'Tis certain.
Iago. Stand you awhile apart;
Confine yourself but in a patient list.
Whilst you were here, o'erwhelmed with your grief
(A passion most unfitting such a man),
Cassio came hither. I shifted him away
And laid good 'scuse upon your ecstasy;
Bade him anon return, and here speak with me;
The which he promis'd. Do but encave yourself
And mark the fleers, the gibes, and notable scorns
That dwell in every region of his face;
For I will make him tell the tale anew —
Where, how, how oft, how long ago, and when
He hath, and is again to cope your wife.
I say, but mark his gesture. Marry, patience!
Or I shall say you are all in all in spleen,
And nothing of a man.

Oth. Dost thou hear, Iago?
I will be found most cunning in my patience;
But (dost thou hear?) most bloody.

Iago. That's not amiss;
But yet keep time in all. Will you withdraw?
[*Othello retires.*]
Now will I question Cassio of Bianca,
A huswife that by selling her desires
Buys herself bread and clothes. It is a creature
That dotes on Cassio, as 'tis the strumpet's plague
To beguile many and be beguil'd by one.
He, when he hears of her, cannot refrain
From the excess of laughter. Here he comes.

Enter *Cassio.*

As he shall smile, Othello shall go mad;
And his unbookish jealousy must conster
Poor Cassio's smiles, gestures, and light behaviour
Quite in the wrong. How do you now, Lieutenant?

Cas. The worser that you give me the addition
Whose want even kills me.

Iago. Ply Desdemona well, and you are sure on't.
Now, if this suit lay in Bianca's power,
How quickly should you speed!

Cas. Alas, poor caitiff!

Oth. Look how he laughs already!

Iago. I never knew a woman love man so.

Cas. Alas, poor rogue! I think, i' faith, she loves me.

Oth. Now he denies it faintly, and laughs it out.

Iago. Do you hear, Cassio?

Oth. Now he importunes him
To tell it o'er. Go to! Well said, well said!

Iago. She gives it out that you shall marry her.
Do you intend it?

Cas. Ha, ha, ha!

Oth. Do you triumph, Roman? Do you triumph?

Cas. I marry her? What, a customer? Prithee bear some charity to my wit; do not think it so unwholesome. Ha, ha, ha!

Oth. So, so, so, so! Laugh that wins!

Iago. Faith, the cry goes that you shall marry her.

Cas. Prithee say true.

Iago. I am a very villain else.

Oth. Have you scor'd me? Well.

Cas. This is the monkey's own giving out. She is persuaded I will marry her out of her own love and flattery, not out of my promise.

Oth. Iago beckons me. Now he begins the story.

Cas. She was here even now; she haunts me in every place. I was t'other day talking on the sea bank with certain Venetians, and thither comes the bauble, and, by this hand, she falls me thus about my neck —

Oth. Crying 'O dear Cassio!' as it were. His gesture imports it.

Cas. So hangs, and lolls, and weeps upon me; so hales and pulls me! Ha, ha, ha!

Oth. Now he tells how she pluck'd him to my chamber. O, I see that nose of yours, but not that dog I shall throw't to.

Cas. Well, I must leave her company.

Enter *Bianca.*

Iago. Before me! Look where she comes.

Cas. 'Tis such another fitchew! marry, a perfum'd one. What do you mean by this haunting of me?

Bian. Let the devil and his dam haunt you! What did you mean by that same handkerchief you gave me even now? I was a fine fool to take it. I must take out the whole work? A likely piece of work that you should find it in your chamber and know not who left it there! This is some minx's token, and I must take out the work? There! give it your hobby-horse. Wheresoever you had it, I'll take out no work on't.

Cas. How now, my sweet Bianca? How now? how now?

Oth. By heaven, that should be my handkerchief!

Bian. An you'll come to supper to-night, you may; an you will not, come when you are next prepar'd for. *Exit.*

Iago. After her, after her!

Cas. Faith, I must; she'll rail i' th' street else.

Iago. Will you sup there?

Cas. Yes, I intend so.

Iago. Well, I may chance to see you; for I would very fain speak with you.

Cas. Prithee come. Will you?

Iago. Go to! say no more.
Exit Cassio.

Oth. [*comes forward*] How shall I murther him, Iago?

Iago. Did you perceive how he laugh'd at his vice?

Oth. O Iago!

Iago. And did you see the handkerchief?

Oth. Was that mine?

Iago. Yours, by this hand! And to see how he prizes the foolish woman your wife! She gave it him, and he hath giv'n it his whore.

Oth. I would have him nine years a-killing! — A fine woman! a fair woman! a sweet woman!

Iago. Nay, you must forget that.

Oth. Ay, let her rot, and perish, and be damn'd to-night; for she shall not live. No, my heart is turn'd to stone. I strike it, and it hurts my hand. O, the world hath not a sweeter creature! She might lie by an emperor's side and command him tasks.

Iago. Nay, that's not your way.

Oth. Hang her! I do but say what she is. So delicate with her needle! an admirable musician! O, she will sing the savageness out of a bear! Of so high and plenteous wit and invention!

Iago. She's the worse for all this.

Oth. O, a thousand thousand times! And then, of so gentle a condition!

Iago. Ay, too gentle.

Oth. Nay, that's certain. But yet the pity of it, Iago! O Iago, the pity of it, Iago!

Iago. If you are so fond over her iniquity, give her patent to offend; for if it touch not you, it comes near nobody.

Oth. I will chop her into messes! Cuckold me!

Iago. O, 'tis foul in her.

Oth. With mine officer!

Iago. That's fouler.

Oth. Get me some poison, Iago, this night. I'll not expostulate with her, lest her body and beauty unprovide my mind again. This night, Iago!

Iago. Do it not with poison. Strangle her in her bed, even the bed she hath contaminated.

Oth. Good, good! The justice of it pleases. Very good!

Iago. And for Cassio, let me be his undertaker. You shall hear more by midnight.

Oth. Excellent good! *A trumpet.*
What trumpet is that same?

Iago. Something from Venice, sure.

Enter *Lodovico, Desdemona,* and *Attendants.*

'Tis Lodovico,
Come from the Duke; and see, your wife is with him.

Lod. God save you, worthy General!

Oth. With all my heart, sir.

Lod. The Duke and Senators of Venice greet you. [*Gives him a letter.*]

Oth. I kiss the instrument of their pleasures. [*Opens the letter and reads.*]

Des. And what's the news, good cousin Lodovico?

Iago. I am very glad to see you, signior.
Welcome to Cyprus.

Lod. I thank you. How does Lieutenant Cassio?

Iago. Lives, sir.

Des. Cousin, there's fall'n between him and my lord
An unkind breach; but you shall make all well.

Oth. Are you sure of that?

Des. My lord?

Oth. [*reads*] 'This fail you not to do, as you will —'

Lod. He did not call; he's busy in the paper.
Is there division 'twixt thy lord and Cassio?

Des. A most unhappy one. I would do much
T' atone them, for the love I bear to Cassio.

Oth. Fire and brimstone!

Des. My lord?

Oth. Are you wise?

Des. What, is he angry?

Lod. May be the letter mov'd him;
For, as I think, they do command him home,
Deputing Cassio in his government.

Des. By my troth, I am glad on't.

Oth. Indeed?

Des. My lord?

Oth. I am glad to see you mad.

Des. Why, sweet Othello!

Oth. Devil! [*Strikes her.*]

Des. I have not deserv'd this.

Lod. My lord, this would not be believ'd in Venice,
Though I should swear I saw't. 'Tis very much.
Make her amends; she weeps.

Oth. O devil, devil!
If that the earth could teem with woman's tears,
Each drop she falls would prove a crocodile.
Out of my sight!

Des. I will not stay to offend you. [*Going.*]

Lod. Truly, an obedient lady.
I do beseech your lordship call her back.

Oth. Mistress!

Des. My lord?

Oth. What would you with her, sir?

Lod. Who? I, my lord?

Oth. Ay! You did wish that I would make her turn.

Sir, she can turn, and turn, and yet go on,
And turn again; and she can weep, sir, weep;
And she's obedient; as you say, obedient,
Very obedient. — Proceed you in your tears. —
Concerning this, sir (O well-painted passion!),
I am commanded home. — Get you away;
I'll send for you anon. — Sir, I obey the mandate
And will return to Venice. — Hence, avaunt!
[*Exit Desdemona.*]
Cassio shall have my place. And, sir, to-night
I do entreat that we may sup together.
You are welcome, sir, to Cyprus. — Goats and monkeys! *Exit.*

Lod. Is this the noble Moor whom our full Senate
Call all in all sufficient? Is this the nature
Whom passion could not shake? whose solid virtue
The shot of accident nor dart of chance
Could neither graze nor pierce?

Iago. He is much chang'd.

Lod. Are his wits safe? Is he not light of brain?

Iago. He's that he is. I may not breathe my censure.
What he might be — if what he might he is not —
I would to heaven he were!

Lod. What, strike his wife?

Iago. Faith, that was not so well; yet would I knew
That stroke would prove the worst!

Lod. Is it his use?
Or did the letters work upon his blood
And new-create this fault?

Iago. Alas, alas!
It is not honesty in me to speak
What I have seen and known. You shall observe him,
And his own courses will denote him so
That I may save my speech. Do but go after
And mark how he continues.

Lod. I am sorry that I am deceiv'd in him.
Exeunt.

Scene II. [*Cyprus. A room in the Castle.*]

Enter *Othello* and *Emilia.*

Oth. You have seen nothing then?

Emil. Nor ever heard, nor ever did suspect.

Oth. Yes, you have seen Cassio and she together.

Emil. But then I saw no harm, and then I heard
Each syllable that breath made up between them.

Oth. What, did they never whisper?

Emil. Never, my lord.

Oth. Nor send you out o' th' way?

Emil. Never.

Oth. To fetch her fan, her gloves, her mask, nor nothing?

Emil. Never, my lord.

Oth. That's strange.

Emil. I durst, my lord, to wager she is honest,
Lay down my soul at stake. If you think other,
Remove your thought; it doth abuse your bosom.
If any wretch have put this in your head,
Let heaven requite it with the serpent's curse!
For if she be not honest, chaste, and true,
There's no man happy; the purest of their wives
Is foul as slander.

Oth. Bid her come hither. Go.
Exit Emilia.
She says enough; yet she's a simple bawd
That cannot say as much. This is a subtle whore,
A closet lock and key of villanous secrets;
And yet she'll kneel and pray; I have seen her do't.

Enter *Desdemona* and *Emilia.*

Des. My lord, what is your will?

Oth. Pray, chuck, come hither.

Des. What is your pleasure?

Oth. Let me see your eyes.
Look in my face.

Des. What horrible fancy 's this?

Oth. [*to Emilia*] Some of your function, mistress.
Leave procreants alone and shut the door;
Cough or cry hem if anybody come.
Your mystery, your mystery! Nay, dispatch!
Exit Emilia.

Des. Upon my knees, what doth your speech import?
I understand a fury in your words,
But not the words.

Oth. Why, what art thou?

Des. Your wife, my lord; your true
And loyal wife.

Oth. Come, swear it, damn thyself;
Lest, being like one of heaven, the devils themselves

Should fear to seize thee. Therefore be double-damn'd —
Swear thou art honest.

Des. Heaven doth truly know it.

Oth. Heaven truly knows that thou art false as hell.

Des. To whom, my lord? With whom? How am I false?

Oth. O, Desdemon! away! away! away!

Des. Alas the heavy day! Why do you weep?
Am I the motive of these tears, my lord?
If haply you my father do suspect
An instrument of this your calling back,
Lay not your blame on me. If you have lost him,
Why, I have lost him too.

Oth. Had it pleas'd heaven
To try me with affliction, had they rain'd
All kinds of sores and shames on my bare head,
Steep'd me in poverty to the very lips,
Given to captivity me and my utmost hopes,
I should have found in some place of my soul
A drop of patience. But, alas, to make me
A fixed figure for the time of scorn
To point his slow unmoving finger at!
Yet could I bear that too; well, very well.
But there where I have garner'd up my heart,
Where either I must live or bear no life,
The fountain from the which my current runs
Or else dries up — to be discarded thence,
Or keep it as a cistern for foul toads
To knot and gender in — turn thy complexion there,
Patience, thou young and rose-lipp'd cherubin!
Ay, there look grim as hell!

Des. I hope my noble lord esteems me honest.

Oth. O, ay! as summer flies are in the shambles,
That quicken even with blowing. O thou weed,
Who art so lovely fair, and smell'st so sweet,
That the sense aches at thee, would thou hadst ne'er been born!

Des. Alas, what ignorant sin have I committed?

Oth. Was this fair paper, this most goodly book,
Made to write 'whore' upon? What committed?
Committed? O thou public commoner!
I should make very forges of my cheeks
That would to cinders burn up modesty,
Did I but speak thy deeds. What committed?
Heaven stops the nose at it, and the moon winks;
The bawdy wind, that kisses all it meets,
Is hush'd within the hollow mine of earth
And will not hear it. What committed?
Impudent strumpet!

Des. By heaven, you do me wrong!

Oth. Are not you a strumpet?

Des. No, as I am a Christian!
If to preserve this vessel for my lord
From any other foul unlawful touch
Be not to be a strumpet, I am none.

Oth. What, not a whore?

Des. No, as I shall be sav'd!

Oth. Is't possible?

Des. O, heaven forgive us!

Oth. I cry you mercy then.
I took you for that cunning whore of Venice
That married with Othello. — You, mistress,
That have the office opposite to Saint Peter
And keep the gate of hell!

Enter *Emilia.*

You, you, ay, you!
We have done our course. There's money for your pains.
I pray you turn the key, and keep our counsel.
Exit.

Emil. Alas, what does this gentleman conceive?
How do you, madam? How do you, my good lady?

Des. Faith, half asleep.

Emil. Good madam, what's the matter with my lord?

Des. With who?

Emil. Why, with my lord, madam.

Des. Who is thy lord?

Emil. He that is yours, sweet lady.

Des. I have none. Do not talk to me, Emilia.
I cannot weep; nor answer have I none
But what should go by water. Prithee to-night
Lay on my bed my wedding sheets, remember;
And call thy husband hither.

Emil. Here's a change indeed! *Exit.*

Des. 'Tis meet I should be us'd so, very meet.
How have I been behav'd, that he might stick
The small'st opinion on my least misuse?

Enter *Iago* and *Emilia.*

Iago. What is your pleasure, madam? How is't with you?

Des. I cannot tell. Those that do teach young babes
Do it with gentle means and easy tasks.

He might have chid me so; for, in good faith,
I am a child to chiding.

Iago. What is the matter, lady?

Emil. Alas, Iago, my lord hath so bewhor'd her,
Thrown such despite and heavy terms upon her
As true hearts cannot bear.

Des. Am I that name, Iago?

Iago. What name, fair lady?

Des. Such as she says my lord did say I was.

Emil. He call'd her whore. A beggar in his drink
Could not have laid such terms upon his callet.

Iago. Why did he so?

Des. I do not know. I am sure I am none such.

Iago. Do not weep, do not weep. Alas the day!

Emil. Hath she forsook so many noble matches,
Her father and her country, all her friends,
To be call'd whore? Would it not make one weep?

Des. It is my wretched fortune.

Iago. Beshrew him for't!
How comes this trick upon him?

Des. Nay, heaven doth know.

Emil. I will be hang'd if some eternal villain,
Some busy and insinuating rogue,
Some cogging, cozening slave, to get some office,
Have not devis'd this slander. I'll be hang'd else.

Iago. Fie, there is no such man! It is impossible.

Des. If any such there be, heaven pardon him!

Emil. A halter pardon him! and hell gnaw his bones!
Why should he call her whore? Who keeps her company?
What place? what time? what form? what likelihood?
The Moor's abus'd by some most villanous knave,
Some base notorious knave, some scurvy fellow.
O heaven, that such companions thou'dst unfold,
And put in every honest hand a whip
To lash the rascals naked through the world
Even from the East to th' West!

Iago. Speak within door.

Emil. O, fie upon them! Some such squire he was
That turn'd your wit the seamy side without
And made you to suspect me with the Moor.

Iago. You are a fool. Go to.

Des. O good Iago,
What shall I do to win my lord again?
Good friend, go to him; for, by this light of heaven,
I know not how I lost him. Here I kneel.
If e'er my will did trespass 'gainst his love,
Either in discourse of thought or actual deed,
Or that mine eyes, mine ears, or any sense
Delighted them in any other form,
Or that I do not yet, and ever did,
And ever will (though he do shake me off
To beggarly divorcement) love him dearly,
Comfort forswear me! Unkindness may do much;
And his unkindness may defeat my life,
But never taint my love. I cannot say 'whore.'
It doth abhor me now I speak the word;
To do the act that might th' addition earn
Not the world's mass of vanity could make me.

Iago. I pray you be content. 'Tis but his humour.
The business of the state does him offence,
And he does chide with you.

Des. If 'twere no other —

Iago. 'Tis but so, I warrant.

[*Trumpets within.*]

Hark how these instruments summon you to supper.
The messengers of Venice stay the meat.
Go in, and weep not. All things shall be well.

Exeunt Desdemona and Emilia.

Enter *Roderigo.*

How now, Roderigo?

Rod. I do not find that thou deal'st justly with me.

Iago. What in the contrary?

Rod. Every day thou daff'st me with some device, Iago, and rather, as it seems to me now, keep'st from me all conveniency than suppliest me with the least advantage of hope. I will indeed no longer endure it; nor am I yet persuaded to put up in peace what already I have foolishly suffer'd.

Iago. Will you hear me, Roderigo?

Rod. Faith, I have heard too much; for your words and performance are no kin together.

Iago. You charge me most unjustly.

Rod. With naught but truth. I have wasted myself out of means. The jewels you have had from me to deliver to Desdemona would half have corrupted a votarist. You have told me she hath receiv'd them, and return'd me expectations and comforts of sudden respect and acquaintance; but I find none.

Iago. Well, go to; very well.

Rod. Very well! go to! I cannot go to, man; nor 'tis not very well. Nay, I think it is scurvy, and begin to find myself fopp'd in it.

Iago. Very well.

Rod. I tell you 'tis not very well. I will make myself known to Desdemona. If she will return me my jewels, I will give over my suit and repent my unlawful solicitation. If not, assure yourself I will seek satisfaction of you.

Iago. You have said now.

Rod. Ay, and said nothing but what I protest intendment of doing.

Iago. Why, now I see there's mettle in thee; and even from this instant do build on thee a better opinion than ever before. Give me thy hand, Roderigo. Thou hast taken against me a most just exception; but yet I protest I have dealt most directly in thy affair.

Rod. It hath not appear'd.

Iago. I grant indeed it hath not appear'd; and your suspicion is not without wit and judgment. But, Roderigo, if thou hast that in thee indeed which I have greater reason to believe now than ever (I mean purpose, courage, and valour), this night show it. If thou the next night following enjoy not Desdemona, take me from this world with treachery and devise engines for my life.

Rod. Well, what is it? Is it within reason and compass?

Iago. Sir, there is especial commission come from Venice to depute Cassio in Othello's place.

Rod. Is that true? Why, then Othello and Desdemona return again to Venice.

Iago. O, no. He goes into Mauritania and takes away with him the fair Desdemona, unless his abode be linger'd here by some accident; wherein none can be so determinate as the removing of Cassio.

Rod. How do you mean removing of him?

Iago. Why, by making him uncapable of Othello's place — knocking out his brains.

Rod. And that you would have me to do?

Iago. Ay, if you dare do yourself a profit and a right. He sups to-night with a harlotry, and thither will I go to him. He knows not yet of his honourable fortune. If you will watch his going thence, which I will fashion to fall out between twelve and one, you may take him at your pleasure. I will be near to second your attempt, and he shall fall between us. Come, stand not amaz'd at it, but go along with me. I will show you such a necessity in his death that you shall think yourself bound to put it on him. It is now high supper time, and the night grows to waste. About it!

Rod. I will hear further reason for this.

Iago. And you shall be satisfied. *Exeunt.*

Scene III. [*Cyprus. Another room in the Castle.*]

Enter *Othello, Lodovico, Desdemona, Emilia,* and *Attendants.*

Lod. I do beseech you, sir, trouble yourself no further.

Oth. O, pardon me; 'twill do me good to walk.

Lod. Madam, good night. I humbly thank your ladyship.

Des. Your Honour is most welcome.

Oth. Will you walk, sir?
O, Desdemona —

Des. My lord?

Oth. Get you to bed on th' instant. I will be return'd forthwith. Dispatch your attendant there. Look't be done.

Des. I will, my lord.

Exeunt [*Othello, Lodovico, and Attendants*].

Emil. How goes it now? He looks gentler than he did.

Des. He says he will return incontinent.
He hath commanded me to go to bed,
And bid me to dismiss you.

Emil. Dismiss me?

Des. It was his bidding. Therefore, good Emilia,
Give me my nightly wearing, and adieu.
We must not now displease him.

Emil. I would you had never seen him!

Des. So would not I. My love doth so approve him
That even his stubbornness, his checks, his frowns
(Prithee unpin me) have grace and favour in them.

Emil. I have laid those sheets you bade me on the bed.

Des. All's one. Good faith, how foolish are our minds!
If I do die before thee, prithee shroud me
In one of those same sheets.

Emil. Come, come! You talk.

Des. My mother had a maid call'd Barbary.
She was in love; and he she lov'd prov'd mad
And did forsake her. She had a song of 'Willow.'

An old thing 'twas; but it express'd her fortune,
And she died singing it. That song to-night
Will not go from my mind. I have much to do
But to go hang my head all at one side
And sing it like poor Barbary. Prithee dispatch.

Emil. Shall I go fetch your nightgown?

Des. No, unpin me here.
This Lodovico is a proper man.

Emil. A very handsome man.

Des. He speaks well.

Emil. I know a lady in Venice would have walk'd barefoot to Palestine for a touch of his nether lip.

Des. (*sings*)

The poor soul sat sighing by a sycamore tree,
Sing all a green willow:
Her hand on her bosom, her head on her knee,
Sing willow, willow, willow.
The fresh streams ran by her and murmur'd her moans;
Sing willow, willow, willow;
Her salt tears fell from her, and soft'ned the stones.
Sing willow —

Lay by these.

willow, willow;

Prithee hie thee; he'll come anon.

Sing all a green willow must be my garland.
Let nobody blame him; his scorn I approve —

Nay, that's not next. Hark! who is't that knocks?

Emil. It is the wind.

Des. I call'd my love false love; but what said he then?
Sing willow, willow, willow:
If I court moe women, you'll couch with moe men.'

So, get thee gone; good night. Mine eyes do itch.
Doth that bode weeping?

Emil. 'Tis neither here nor there.

Des. I have heard it said so. O, these men, these men!
Dost thou in conscience think — tell me, Emilia —
That there be women do abuse their husbands
In such gross kind?

Emil. There be some such, no question.

Des. Wouldst thou do such a deed for all the world?

Emil. Why, would not you?

Des. No, by this heavenly light!

Emil. Nor I neither by this heavenly light. I might do't as well i' th' dark.

Des. Wouldst thou do such a deed for all the world?

Emil. The world's a huge thing. It is a great price for a small vice.

Des. Good troth, I think thou wouldst not.

Emil. By my troth, I think I should; and undo't when I had done it. Marry, I would not do such a thing for a joint-ring, nor for measures of lawn, nor for gowns, petticoats, nor caps, nor any petty exhibition; but, for all the whole world — 'Ud's pity! who would not make her husband a cuckold to make him a monarch? I should venture purgatory for't.

Des. Beshrew me if I would do such a wrong
For the whole world.

Emil. Why, the wrong is but a wrong i' th' world; and having the world for your labour, 'tis a wrong in your own world, and you might quickly make it right.

Des. I do not think there is any such woman.

Emil. Yes, a dozen; and as many to th' vantage as would store the world they play'd for.
But I do think it is their husbands' faults
If wives do fall. Say that they slack their duties
And pour our treasures into foreign laps;
Or else break out in peevish jealousies,
Throwing restraint upon us; or say they strike us,
Or scant our former having in despite —
Why, we have galls; and though we have some grace,
Yet have we some revenge. Let husbands know
Their wives have sense like them. They see, and smell,
And have their palates both for sweet and sour,
As husbands have. What is it that they do
When they change us for others? Is it sport?
I think it is. And doth affection breed it?
I think it doth. Is't frailty that thus errs?
It is so too. And have not we affections,
Desires for sport, and frailty, as men have?
Then let them use us well; else let them know,
The ills we do, their ills instruct us so.

Des. Good night, good night. Heaven me such uses send,
Not to pick bad from bad, but by bad mend!

Exeunt.

ACT V. Scene I. [*Cyprus. A street.*]

Enter *Iago* and *Roderigo*.

Iago. Here, stand behind this bulk; straight will he come.
Wear thy good rapier bare, and put it home.
Quick, quick! Fear nothing; I'll be at thy elbow.
It makes us, or it mars us — think on that,
And fix most firm thy resolution.

Rod. Be near at hand. I may miscarry in't.

Iago. Here, at thy hand. Be bold, and take thy stand. [*Stands aside.*]

Rod. I have no great devotion to the deed,
And yet he hath given me satisfying reasons.
'Tis but a man gone. Forth my sword! He dies!

Iago. I have rubb'd this young quat almost to the sense,
And he grows angry. Now whether he kill Cassio,
Or Cassio him, or each do kill the other,
Every way makes my game. Live Roderigo,
He calls me to a restitution large
Of gold and jewels that I bobb'd from him
As gifts to Desdemona.
It must not be. If Cassio do remain,
He hath a daily beauty in his life
That makes me ugly; and besides, the Moor
May unfold me to him; there stand I in much peril.
No, he must die. But so! I hear him coming.

Enter *Cassio*.

Rod. I know his gait. 'Tis he. Villain, thou diest! [*Makes a pass at Cassio.*]

Cas. That thrust had been mine enemy indeed
But that my coat is better than thou know'st.
I will make proof of thine.
[*Draws, and wounds Roderigo.*]

Rod. O, I am slain!

[*Iago rushes from his post, wounds Cassio in the leg, and exit.*]

Cas. I am maim'd for ever. Help, ho! Murther! murther! [*Falls.*]

Enter *Othello*.

Oth. The voice of Cassio. Iago keeps his word.

Rod. O, villain that I am!

Oth. It is even so.

Cas. O, help, ho! light! a surgeon!

Oth. 'Tis he. O brave Iago, honest and just,
That hast such noble sense of thy friend's wrong!
Thou teachest me. Minion, your dear lies dead,
And your unblest fate hies. Strumpet, I come.
Forth of my heart those charms, thine eyes, are blotted.
Thy bed, lust-stain'd, shall with lust's blood be spotted. *Exit.*

Enter *Lodovico* and *Gratiano*.

Cas. What, ho? No watch? No passage? Murther! murther!

Gra. 'Tis some mischance. The cry is very direful.

Cas. O, help!

Lod. Hark!

Rod. O wretched villain!

Lod. Two or three groan. It is a heavy night.
These may be counterfeits. Let's think't unsafe
To come in to the cry without more help.

Rod. Nobody come? Then shall I bleed to death.

Lod. Hark!

Enter *Iago*, with a light.

Gra. Here's one comes in his shirt, with light and weapons.

Iago. Who's there? Whose noise is this that cries on murther?

Lod. We do not know.

Iago. Did not you hear a cry?

Cas. Here, here! For heaven's sake, help me!

Iago. What's the matter?

Gra. This is Othello's ancient, as I take it.

Lod. The same indeed, a very valiant fellow.

Iago. What are you here that cry so grievously?

Cas. Iago? O, I am spoil'd, undone by villains!
Give me some help.

Iago. O me, Lieutenant! What villains have done this?

Cas. I think that one of them is hereabout
And cannot make away.

Iago. O treacherous villains!
What are you there? Come in, and give some help. [*To Lodovico and Gratiano.*]

Rod. O, help me here!

Cas. That's one of them

Iago. O murd'rous slave! O villain!
[*Stabs Roderigo.*]

Rod. O damn'd Iago! O inhuman dog!

Iago. Kill men i' th' dark? Where be these bloody thieves?
How silent is this town! Ho! murther! murther!
What may you be? Are you of good or evil?

Lod. As you shall prove us, praise us.

Iago. Signior Lodovico?

Lod. He, sir.

Iago. I cry you mercy. Here's Cassio hurt by villains.

Gra. Cassio?

Iago. How is it, brother?

Cas. My leg is cut in two.

Iago. Marry, heaven forbid!
Light, gentlemen. I'll bind it with my shirt.

Enter *Bianca.*

Bian. What is the matter, ho? Who is't that cried?

Iago. Who is't that cried?

Bian. O my dear Cassio! my sweet Cassio!
O Cassio, Cassio, Cassio!

Iago. O notable strumpet! — Cassio, may you suspect
Who they should be that thus have mangled you?

Cas. No.

Gra. I am sorry to find you thus. I have been to seek you.

Iago. Lend me a garter. So. O for a chair
To bear him easily hence!

Bian. Alas, he faints! O Cassio, Cassio, Cassio!

Iago. Gentlemen all, I do suspect this trash
To be a party in this injury. —
Patience awhile, good Cassio. — Come, come!
Lend me a light. Know we this face or no?
Alas, my friend and my dear countryman
Roderigo? No. Yes, sure. O heaven! Roderigo.

Gra. What, of Venice?

Iago. Even he, sir. Did you know him?

Gra. Know him? Ay.

Iago. Signior Gratiano? I cry you gentle pardon.
These bloody accidents must excuse my manners
That so neglected you.

Gra. I am glad to see you.

Iago. How do you, Cassio? — O, a chair, a chair!

Gra. Roderigo?

Iago. He, he, 'tis he! [*A chair brought in.*]
O, that's well said! the chair.
Some good man bear him carefully from hence.
I'll fetch the General's surgeon. [*To Bianca*]
For you, mistress,
Save you your labour. — He that lies slain here, Cassio,
Was my dear friend. What malice was between you?

Cas. None in the world; nor do I know the man.

Iago. [*to Bianca*] What, look you pale? —
O, bear him out o' th' air.

[*Cassio and Roderigo are borne off.*]

Stay you, good gentlemen. — Look you pale, mistress? —
Do you perceive the gastness of her eye? —
Nay, an you stare, we shall hear more anon.
Behold her well; I pray you look upon her.
Do you see, gentlemen? Nay, guiltiness will speak,
Though tongues were out of use.

Enter *Emilia.*

Emil. 'Las, what's the matter? What's the matter, husband?

Iago. Cassio hath here been set on in the dark
By Roderigo, and fellows that are scap'd.
He's almost slain, and Roderigo dead.

Emil. Alas, good gentleman! alas, good Cassio!

Iago. This is the fruit of whoring. Prithee, Emilia,
Go know of Cassio where he supp'd to-night.
[*To Bianca*] What, do you shake at that?

Bian. He supp'd at my house; but I therefore shake not.

Iago. O, did he so? I charge you go with me.

Emil. Fie, fie upon thee, strumpet!

Bian. I am no strumpet, but of life as honest
As you that thus abuse me.

Emil. As I? Foh! fie upon thee!

Iago. Kind gentlemen, let's go see poor Cassio dress'd.
[*To Bianca*] Come, mistress, you must tell's another tale. —
Emilia, run you to the citadel
And tell my lord and lady what hath happ'd. —
Will you go on afore? [*Aside*] This is the night
That either makes me or fordoes me quite.

Exeunt.

Scene II. [*Cyprus. A bedchamber in the Castle.*]

Desdemona in her bed. Enter *Othello* with a light.

Oth. It is the cause, it is the cause, my soul.
Let me not name it to you, you chaste stars!
It is the cause. Yet I'll not shed her blood,
Nor scar that whiter skin of hers than snow,
And smooth as monumental alablaster.
Yet she must die, else she'll betray more men.
Put out the light, and then put out the light.
If I quench thee, thou flaming minister,
I can again thy former light restore,
Should I repent me; but once put out thy light,
Thou cunning'st pattern of excelling nature,
I know not where is that Promethean heat
That can thy light relume. When I have pluck'd the rose,
I cannot give it vital growth again;
It needs must wither. I'll smell it on the tree.
He kisses her.
O balmy breath, that dost almost persuade
Justice to break her sword! One more, one more!
Be thus when thou art dead, and I will kill thee,
And love thee after. One more, and this the last!
So sweet was ne'er so fatal. I must weep,
But they are cruel tears. This sorrow's heavenly;
It strikes where it doth love. She wakes.
Des. Who's there? Othello?
Oth. Ay, Desdemona.
Des. Will you come to bed, my lord?
Oth. Have you pray'd to-night, Desdemon?
Des. Ay, my lord.
Oth. If you bethink yourself of any crime
Unreconcil'd as yet to heaven and grace,
Solicit for it straight.
Des. Alack, my lord, what may you mean by that?
Oth. Well, do it, and be brief; I will walk by.
I would not kill thy unprepared spirit.
No, heaven forfend! I would not kill thy soul.
Des. Talk you of killing?
Oth. Ay, I do.
Des. Then heaven
Have mercy on me!
Oth. Amen, with all my heart!
Des. If you say so, I hope you will not kill me.
Oth. Humh!
Des. And yet I fear you; for you are fatal then
When your eyes roll so. Why I should fear I know not,
Since guiltiness I know not; but yet I feel I fear.
Oth. Think on thy sins.
Des. They are loves I bear to you.
Oth. Ay, and for that thou diest.
Des. That death's unnatural that kills for loving.
Alas, why gnaw you so your nether lip?
Some bloody passion shakes your very frame.
These are portents; but yet I hope, I hope,
They do not point on me.
Oth. Peace and be still!
Des. I will so. What's the matter?
Oth. That handkerchief which I so lov'd and gave thee
Thou gav'st to Cassio.
Des. No, by my life and soul!
Send for the man and ask him.
Oth. Sweet soul, take heed,
Take heed of perjury; thou art on thy deathbed.
Des. Ay, but not yet to die.
Oth. Yes, presently.
Therefore confess thee freely of thy sin;
For to deny each article with oath
Cannot remove nor choke the strong conception
That I do groan withal. Thou art to die.
Des. Then Lord have mercy on me!
Oth. I say amen.
Des. And have you mercy too! I never did
Offend you in my life; never lov'd Cassio
But with such general warranty of heaven
As I might love. I never gave him token.
Oth. By heaven, I saw my handkerchief in's hand!
O perjur'd woman! thou dost stone my heart,
And mak'st me call what I intend to do
A murther, which I thought a sacrifice.
I saw the handkerchief.
Des. He found it then.
I never gave it him. Send for him hither.
Let him confess a truth.
Oth. He hath confess'd.
Des. What, my lord?
Oth. That he hath us'd thee.
Des. How? unlawfully?
Oth. Ay.
Des. He will not say so.
Oth. No, his mouth is stopp'd.
Honest Iago hath ta'en order for't.
Des. O, my fear interprets. What, is he dead?

Oth. Had all his hairs been lives, my great revenge
Had stomach for them all.
Des. Alas, he is betray'd, and I undone!
Oth. Out, strumpet! Weep'st thou for him to my face?
Des. O, banish me, my lord, but kill me not!
Oth. Down, strumpet!
Des. Kill me to-morrow; let me live to-night!
Oth. Nay, an you strive —
Des. But half an hour!
Oth. Being done, there is no pause.
Des. But while I say one prayer!
Oth. It is too late. *He smothers her.*

Emilia at the door.

Emil. (*calls within*) My lord, my lord! What, ho! my lord, my lord!
Oth. What noise is this? Not dead? not yet quite dead?
I that am cruel am yet merciful;
I would not have thee linger in thy pain.
So, so.
Emil. (*within*) What, ho! my lord, my lord!
Oth. Who's there?
Emil. [*within*] O, good my lord, I would speak a word with you!
Oth. Yes, 'tis Emilia. — By-and-by. — She's dead. —
'Tis like she comes to speak of Cassio's death.
The noise was here. Ha! no more moving?
Still as the grave. — Shall she come in? Were't good? —
I think she stirs again. No. — What's the best?
If she come in, she'll sure speak to my wife.
My wife! my wife! what wife? I have no wife.
O, insupportable! O heavy hour!
Methinks it should be now a huge eclipse
Of sun and moon, and that th' affrighted globe
Should yawn at alteration.
Emil. [*within*] I do beseech you
That I may speak with you, O good my lord!
Oth. I had forgot thee. O, come in, Emilia.
Soft, by-and-by. — Let me the curtains draw. —
Where art thou? [*Opens the door.*]

Enter *Emilia.*

What's the matter with thee now?
Emil. O my good lord, yonder's foul murther done!
Oth. What? now?
Emil. But now, my lord.
Oth. It is the very error of the moon.
She comes more near the earth than she was wont
And makes men mad.
Emil. Cassio, my lord, hath kill'd a young Venetian
Call'd Roderigo.
Oth. Roderigo kill'd?
And Cassio kill'd?
Emil. No, Cassio is not kill'd.
Oth. Not Cassio kill'd? Then murther's out of tune,
And sweet revenge grows harsh.
Des. O, falsely, falsely murder'd!
Emil. O Lord! what cry is that?
Oth. That? What?
Emil. Out and alas! that was my lady's voice.
Help! help, ho! help! O lady, speak again!
Sweet Desdemona! O sweet mistress, speak!
Des. A guiltless death I die.
Emil. O, who hath done this deed?
Des. Nobody — I myself. Farewell.
Commend me to my kind lord. O, farewell!
She dies.
Oth. Why, how should she be murd'red?
Emil. Alas, who knows?
Oth. You heard her say herself, it was not I.
Emil. She said so. I must needs report a truth.
Oth. She's like a liar gone to burning hell!
'Twas I that kill'd her.
Emil. O, the more angel she,
And you the blacker devil!
Oth. She turn'd to folly, and she was a whore.
Emil. Thou dost belie her, and thou art a devil.
Oth. She was false as water.
Emil. Thou art rash as fire to say
That she was false. O, she was heavenly true!
Oth. Cassio did top her. Ask thy husband else.
O, I were damn'd beneath all depth in hell
But that I did proceed upon just grounds
To this extremity. Thy husband knew it all.
Emil. My husband?
Oth. Thy husband.
Emil. That she was false to wedlock?
Oth. Ay, with Cassio. Nay, had she been true,
If heaven would make me such another world
Of one entire and perfect chrysolite,
I'ld not have sold her for it.
Emil. My husband?
Oth. Ay, 'twas he that told me first.

An honest man he is, and hates the slime
That sticks on filthy deeds.

Emil. My husband?

Oth. What needs this iterance, woman? I say, thy husband.

Emil. O mistress, villany hath made mocks with love!
My husband say that she was false?

Oth. He, woman.
I say, thy husband. Dost understand the word?
My friend, thy husband; honest, honest Iago.

Emil. If he say so, may his pernicious soul
Rot half a grain a day! he lies to th' heart.
She was too fond of her most filthy bargain.

Oth. Ha!

Emil. Do thy worst.
This deed of thine is no more worthy heaven
Than thou wast worthy her.

Oth. Peace, you were best.

Emil. Thou hast not half the power to do me harm
As I have to be hurt. O gull! O dolt!
As ignorant as dirt! thou hast done a deed —
I care not for thy sword; I'll make thee known,
Though I lost twenty lives. Help! help! O, help!
The Moor hath kill'd my mistress! Murther! murther!

Enter *Montano, Gratiano, Iago,* and others.

Mon. What is the matter? How now, General?

Emil. O, are you come, Iago? You have done well,
That men must lay their murthers on your neck.

Gra. What is the matter?

Emil. Disprove this villain, if thou be'st a man.
He says thou told'st him that his wife was false.
I know thou didst not; thou'rt not such a villain.
Speak, for my heart is full.

Iago. I told him what I thought, and told no more
Than what he found himself was apt and true.

Emil. But did you ever tell him she was false?

Iago. I did.

Emil. You told a lie, an odious damned lie!
Upon my soul, a lie! a wicked lie!
She false with Cassio? Did you say with Cassio?

Iago. With Cassio, mistress. Go to, charm your tongue.

Emil. I will not charm my tongue; I am bound to speak:
My mistress here lies murthered in her bed —

All. O heavens forfend!

Emil. And your reports have set the murther on.

Oth. Nay, stare not, masters. It is true indeed.

Gra. 'Tis a strange truth.

Mon. O monstrous act!

Emil. Villany, villany, villany!
I think upon't, I think! I smell't! O villany!
I thought so then. I'll kill myself for grief.
O villany, villany!

Iago. What, are you mad? I charge you get you home.

Emil. Good gentlemen, let me have leave to speak.
'Tis proper I obey him, but not now.
Perchance, Iago, I will ne'er go home.

Oth. O! O! O! *Falls on the bed.*

Emil. Nay, lay thee down and roar!
For thou hast kill'd the sweetest innocent
That e'er did lift up eye.

Oth. O, she was foul! [*Rises.*]
I scarce did know you, uncle. There lies your niece,
Whose breath, indeed, these hands have newly stopp'd.
I know this act shows horrible and grim.

Gra. Poor Desdemon! I am glad thy father's dead.
Thy match was mortal to him, and pure grief
Shore his old thread atwain. Did he live now,
This sight would make him do a desperate turn;
Yea, curse his better angel from his side,
And fall to reprobance.

Oth. 'Tis pitiful; but yet Iago knows
That she with Cassio hath the act of shame
A thousand times committed. Cassio confess'd it;
And she did gratify his amorous works
With that recognizance and pledge of love
Which I first gave her. I saw it in his hand.
It was a handkerchief, an antique token
My father gave my mother.

Emil. O God! O heavenly pow'rs!

Iago. Zounds, hold your peace!

Emil. 'Twill out, 'twill out! I peace?
No, I will speak as liberal as the North.
Let heaven and men and devils, let them all,
All, all, cry shame against me, yet I'll speak.

Iago. Be wise, and get you home.

Emil. I will not.

[*Iago draws and threatens Emilia.*]

Gra. Fie!
Your sword upon a woman?

Emil. O thou dull Moor, that handkerchief thou speak'st of
I found by fortune, and did give my husband;
For often with a solemn earnestness
(More than indeed belong'd to such a trifle)
He begg'd of me to steal't.

Iago. Villanous whore!

Emil. She give it Cassio? No, alas, I found it,
And I did give't my husband.

Iago. Filth, thou liest!

Emil. By heaven, I do not, I do not, gentlemen.
O murd'rous coxcomb! what should such a fool
Do with so good a wife?

Oth. Are there no stones in heaven
But what serves for the thunder? Precious villain!

The Moor runs at Iago, [but is disarmed by Montano]. Iago kills his wife.

Gra. The woman falls. Sure he hath kill'd his wife.

Emil. Ay, ay. O, lay me by my mistress' side.

Exit Iago.

Gra. He's gone, but his wife's kill'd.

Mon. 'Tis a notorious villain. Take you this weapon,
Which I have here recover'd from the Moor.
Come, guard the door without. Let him not pass,
But kill him rather. I'll after that same villain,
For 'tis a damned slave.

Exeunt Montano and Gratiano [with others. Manent Othello and Emilia].

Oth. I am not valiant neither;
But every puny whipster gets my sword.
But why should honour outlive honesty?
Let it go all.

Emil. What did thy song bode, lady?
Hark, canst thou hear me? I will play the swan,
And die in music. [*Sings*] 'Willow, willow, willow.'
Moor, she was chaste; she lov'd thee, cruel Moor.
So come my soul to bliss as I speak true.
So speaking as I think, I die, I die.

She dies.

Oth. I have another weapon in this chamber:
It is a sword of Spain, the ice-brook's temper.
O, here it is. — Uncle, I must come forth.

Gra. (*within*) If thou attempt it, it will cost thee dear.
Thou hast no weapon, and perforce must suffer.

Oth. Look in upon me then and speak with me,
Or, naked as I am, I will assault thee.

[Enter *Gratiano.*]

Gra. What is the matter?

Oth. Behold, I have a weapon.
A better never did itself sustain
Upon a soldier's thigh. I have seen the day
That with this little arm and this good sword
I have made my way through more impediments
Than twenty times your stop. But O vain boast!
Who can control his fate? 'Tis not so now.
Be not afraid, though you do see me weapon'd.
Here is my journey's end, here is my butt,
And very seamark of my utmost sail.
Do you go back dismay'd? 'Tis a lost fear.
Man but a rush against Othello's breast,
And he retires. Where should Othello go?
Now, how dost thou look now? O ill-starr'd wench!
Pale as thy smock! When we shall meet at compt,
This look of thine will hurl my soul from heaven,
And fiends will snatch at it. Cold, cold, my girl?
Even like thy chastity. — O cursed slave!
Whip me, ye devils,
From the possession of this heavenly sight!
Blow me about in winds! roast me in sulphur!
Wash me in steep-down gulfs of liquid fire!
O Desdemona, Desdemona! dead!
O! O! O!

Enter *Lodovico, Montano, Iago* [as prisoner,] and *Officers*; *Cassio* in a chair.

Lod. Where is this rash and most unfortunate man?

Oth. That's he that was Othello. Here I am.

Lod. Where is that viper? Bring the villain forth.

Oth. I look down towards his feet — but that's a fable.
If that thou be'st a devil, I cannot kill thee.

[*Wounds Iago.*]

Lod. Wrench his sword from him.

[*Othello is disarmed.*]

Iago. I bleed, sir, but not kill'd.

Oth. I am not sorry neither. I'ld have thee live;
For in my sense, 'tis happiness to die.
Lod. O thou Othello that wert once so good,
Fall'n in the practice of a damned slave,
What shall be said to thee?
Oth. Why, anything:
An honourable murderer, if you will;
For naught did I in hate, but all in honour.
Lod. This wretch hath part confess'd his villany.
Did you and he consent in Cassio's death?
Oth. Ay.
Cas. Dear General, I never gave you cause.
Oth. I do believe it, and I ask your pardon.
Will you, I pray, demand that demi-devil
Why he hath thus ensnar'd my soul and body?
Iago. Demand me nothing. What you know, you know.
From this time forth I never will speak word.
Lod. What, not to pray?
Gra. Torments will ope your lips.
Oth. Well, thou dost best.
Lod. Sir, you shall understand what hath befall'n,
Which, as I think, you know not. Here is a letter
Found in the pocket of the slain Roderigo;
And here another. The one of them imports
The death of Cassio to be undertook
By Roderigo.
Oth. O villain!
Cas. Most heathenish and most gross!
Lod. Now here's another discontented paper
Found in his pocket too; and this, it seems,
Roderigo meant t' have sent this damned villain;
But that, belike, Iago in the interim
Came in and satisfied him.
Oth. O thou pernicious caitiff! —
How came you, Cassio, by that handkerchief
That was my wife's?
Cas. I found it in my chamber;
And he himself confess'd but even now
That there he dropp'd it for a special purpose
Which wrought to his desire.
Oth. O fool! fool! fool!
Cas. There is besides in Roderigo's letter,
How he upbraids Iago that he made him
Brave me upon the watch; whereon it came
That I was cast; and even but now he spake,
After long seeming dead — Iago hurt him,
Iago set him on.
Lod. You must forsake this room and go with us.
Your power and your command is taken off,
And Cassio rules in Cyprus. For this slave,
If there be any cunning cruelty
That can torment him much and hold him long,
It shall be his. You shall close prisoner rest
Till that the nature of your fault be known
To the Venetian state. Come, bring away.
Oth. Soft you! a word or two before you go.
I have done the state some service, and they know't —
No more of that. I pray you, in your letters,
When you shall these unlucky deeds relate,
Speak of me as I am. Nothing extenuate,
Nor set down aught in malice. Then must you speak
Of one that lov'd not wisely, but too well;
Of one not easily jealous, but, being wrought,
Perplex'd in the extreme; of one whose hand
(Like the base Indian) threw a pearl away
Richer than all his tribe; of one whose subdu'd eyes,
Albeit unused to the melting mood,
Drop tears as fast as the Arabian trees
Their med'cinable gum. Set you down this;
And say besides that in Aleppo once,
Where a malignant and a turban'd Turk
Beat a Venetian and traduc'd the state,
I took by th' throat the circumcised dog
And smote him — thus. *He stabs himself.*
Lod. O bloody period!
Gra. All that's spoke is marr'd.
Oth. I kiss'd thee ere I kill'd thee. No way but this —
Killing myself, to die upon a kiss.
He [falls upon the bed and] dies.
Cas. This did I fear, but thought he had no weapon;
For he was great of heart.
Lod. O Spartan dog,
More fell than anguish, hunger, or the sea!
Look on the tragic loading of this bed.
This is thy work. The object poisons sight;
Let it be hid. Gratiano, keep the house,
And seize upon the fortunes of the Moor,
For they succeed on you. To you, Lord Governor,
Remains the censure of this hellish villain.
The time, the place, the torture — O, enforce it!
Myself will straight aboard, and to the state
This heavy act with heavy heart relate.
Exeunt omnes.

ANTONY AND CLEOPATRA

ANTONY AND CLEOPATRA was entered in the Stationers' Register on May 20, 1608, but it was not published, so far as we know, until it was included in the First Folio (1623). A date as early as 1607 is suggested by certain changes which Samuel Daniel's tragedy of *Cleopatra*, as reissued in that year and described as 'newly altered,' shows from the editions of 1594–1605. These are thought to prove that Daniel had seen ANTONY AND CLEOPATRA on the stage. Such evidence is very elusive, but late in 1606 or early in 1607 is a reasonable date for Shakespeare's play. This date, however, can hardly be said to be in any degree confirmed by the asps used by a poisoner — and styled 'Cleopatra's birds' — in *The Devil's Charter*, a tragedy by Barnabe Barnes, which was acted before King James on Candlemas night (February 2), 1607. Everybody knew the story of Cleopatra.

For the text the only authority is the First Folio. Misprints are plentiful, but they are usually easy to correct and many of them are set right in the Second Folio (1632). 'Lackeying' for the Folio 'lacking' (i, 4, 46), 'charge' for 'change' (i, 2, 5), 'dear'd' for 'fear'd' (i, 4, 44), and 'Tawny-finn'd' for 'Tawny fine' (ii, 5, 12) are corrections made in Theobald's edition (1733). 'Wassails' for 'Vassailes' (i, 4, 56) is due to Pope; 'spaniel'd' for 'pannelled' (iv, 12, 21) to Hanmer; 'doits' for 'Dolts' (iv, 12, 37) to Thirlby; 'tower'd' for 'toward' (iv, 14, 4) and 'awry' for 'away' (v, 2, 321) to Rowe. In i, 4, 24, 'foyles' (i.e. 'foils,' 'disgraces') should not be changed to 'soils.' In ii, 2, 44, 'was Theame [theme] for you' needs no correction; the sense is clear: 'was something that concerned you,' 'was your affair' (as the next line goes on to interpret). In ii, 2, 213, 'and made their bends adornings' affords excellent sense: 'The graceful inclinations of the attendants were in their effect adornments to the mistress whom they tended, adding beauty to the picture.' 'That art not what th'art sure of' (ii, 5, 103) is quite as clear as many another place in Shakespeare: 'Thou art not identical with the message which thou dost so insist on, and yet thy message makes thee my enemy.' 'Abstract' (iii, 6, 61) should not be emended to 'obstruct': the meaning is 'To let you return gave him an opportunity to hasten away to his mistress.' 'The meered question' (iii, 13, 10) seems to mean 'the definite matter in question'; that is, 'the person that was the centre or main business of the whole war.'

Two readings are still matters of debate. One is 'ribaudred' (iii, 10, 10), where 'ribald-rid' (Steevens's conjecture) seems best. The other is 'arme-gaunt' (i, 5, 48), for which every conceivable substitute has been proposed — from 'arrogant' or 'termagant' or 'rampant' to 'armigerent.' The difficulty vanishes when one remembers that 'gaunt' did not necessarily mean 'wasted' in Shakespeare's time, but was consistent with that degree of thinness which is proper to a finely trained man or animal.

Shakespeare's material comes from Plutarch's life of Antony in Sir Thomas North's translation. In this case, as in *Julius Cæsar* and *Coriolanus*, many passages are suggested, not only in thought but in language, by the source from which Shakespeare was drawing (cf. pp. 924, 1079, above).

The gorgeous passage in which Enobarbus describes Cleopatra and her barge to the entranced Agrippa (ii, 2, 196 ff.) appears in North as follows:

She disdained to set forward otherwise, but to take her barge in the riuer of Cydnus, the poope whereof was of gold, the sailes of purple, and the owers of siluer, which kept stroke in rowing after the sound of the musicke of flutes, howboyes, cytherns, vyolls, and such other instruments as they played vpon in the barge. And now for the person of her selfe: she was laide vnder a pauillion of cloth of golde of tissue, apparelled and attired like the goddesse *Venus*, commonly drawen in picture: and hard by her, on either hand of her, pretie faire boyes apparelled as painters doe set foorth god *Cupide*, with litle fans in their hands, with the which they fanned winde vpon her. Her Ladies and gentlewomen also, the fairest of them were apparelled like the nymphes *Nereides* (which are the myrmaides of the waters) and like the *Graces*, some stearing the helme, others tending the tackle and ropes of the barge, out of the which there came a wonderfull passing sweete sauor of perfumes, that perfumed the wharfes side, pestered with innumerable multitudes of people. Some of them followed the barge all alongst the riuers side: others also ranne out of the citie to see her comming in. So that in the end, there ranne such multitudes of people one after an other to see her, that *Antonius* was left post alone in the market place, in his Imperiall seate to giue audience: and there went a rumour in the peoples mouthes, that the goddesse *Venus* was come to play with the god *Bacchus*, for the generall good of all Asia. When *Cleopatra* landed, *Antonius* sent to inuite her to supper to him. But she sent him worde againe, he should doe better rather to come and suppe with her. *Antonius* therefore to shew himselfe curteous vnto her at her arriuall, was contented to obey her, and went to supper to her: where he found such passing sumptuous fare, that no tongue can expresse it.

A fine example of the dramatizing of narrative is the little episode of the protesting soldier (iii, 7, 61 ff.). In North:

As he was setting his men in order of battel, there was a Captaine, and a valiant man, that had serued *Antonius* in many battels & conflicts, & had all his body hacked and cut: who as *Antonius* passed by him, cryed out vnto him & said: O noble Emperor, how commeth it to passe that you trust to these vile brittle shippes? what, doe you mistrust these wounds of mine and this sword? Let the Egyptians and Phenicians fight by sea, and set vs on the main land, where we vse to conquer, or to be slaine on our feete.

Most wonderful of all is the transmutation (in v, 2, 321 ff.) of North's admirable description of the closing scene:

But when they had opened the doores, they found *Cleopatra* starke dead, layed vpon a bed of gold, attired & arayed in her royall robes, and one of her two women, which was called *Iras*, dead at her feete: and her other woman called *Charmion* halfe dead, and trembling, trimming the Diademe which *Cleopatra* ware vpon her head. One of the souldiers seeing her, angrily sayd vnto her: is that well done *Charmion*? Very well sayd she againe, and meete for a Princesse discended from the race of so many noble kings. She sayd no more, but fell downe dead hard by the bed.

THE TRAGEDY OF ANTONY AND CLEOPATRA

[Dramatis Personæ.

Mark Antony, *Octavius Cæsar*, *M. Æmilius Lepidus*, — Triumvirs.
Sextus Pompeius.
Domitius Enobarbus, *Ventidius*, *Eros*, *Scarus*, *Dercetas*, *Demetrius*, *Philo*, — friends to *Antony*.
Canidius, Lieutenant-General to *Antony*.
Mæcenas, *Agrippa*, *Dolabella*, *Proculeius*, *Thyreus*, *Gallus*, — friends to *Cæsar*.
Taurus, Lieutenant-General to *Cæsar*.
Menas, *Menecrates*, *Varrius*, — friends to *Pompey*.
Silius, an Officer in the army of *Ventidius*.
Euphronius, an Ambassador from *Antony* to *Cæsar*.
Alexas, *Mardian*, *Seleucus*, *Diomedes*, — attendants on *Cleopatra*.
A Soothsayer.
A Clown.

Cleopatra, Queen of Egypt.
Octavia, sister to *Cæsar* and wife to *Antony*.
Charmian, *Iras*, — ladies attending on *Cleopatra*.

Officers, Soldiers, Messengers, Attendants.

SCENE. — *In several parts of the Roman empire.*]

ACT I. Scene I. [*Alexandria. A room in* Cleopatra's *Palace.*]

Enter *Demetrius* and *Philo*.

Phi. Nay, but this dotage of our general's
O'erflows the measure. Those his goodly eyes
That o'er the files and musters of the war
Have glow'd like plated Mars, now bend, now turn
The office and devotion of their view
Upon a tawny front. His captain's heart,
Which in the scuffles of great fights hath burst
The buckles on his breast, reneges all temper
And is become the bellows and the fan
To cool a gypsy's lust.

Flourish. Enter *Antony*, *Cleopatra*, her *Ladies*, the *Train*, with *Eunuchs* fanning her.

Look where they come!
Take but good note, and you shall see in him
The triple pillar of the world transform'd
Into a strumpet's fool. Behold and see.

Cleo. If it be love indeed, tell me how much.

Ant. There's beggary in the love that can be reckon'd.

Cleo. I'll set a bourn how far to be belov'd.

Ant. Then must thou needs find out new heaven, new earth.

Enter a *Messenger*.

Mess. News, my good lord, from Rome.

Ant. Grates me! The sum.

Cleo. Nay, hear them, Antony.
Fulvia perchance is angry; or who knows
If the scarce-bearded Cæsar have not sent
His pow'rful mandate to you: 'Do this, or this;
Take in that kingdom, and enfranchise that.
Perform't, or else we damn thee.'

Ant. How, my love?

Cleo. Perchance? Nay, and most like:
You must not stay here longer; your dismission
Is come from Cæsar; therefore hear it, Antony.
Where's Fulvia's process? Cæsar's I would say — both?
Call in the messengers. As I am Egypt's Queen,
Thou blushest, Antony, and that blood of thine
Is Cæsar's homager! Else so thy cheek pays shame

When shrill-tongu'd Fulvia scolds. The messengers!
Ant. Let Rome in Tiber melt and the wide arch
Of the rang'd empire fall! Here is my space.
Kingdoms are clay; our dungy earth alike
Feeds beast as man. The nobleness of life
Is to do thus [*embracing*]; when such a mutual pair
And such a twain can do't, in which I bind,
On pain of punishment, the world to weet
We stand up peerless.
Cleo. Excellent falsehood!
Why did he marry Fulvia, and not love her?
I'll seem the fool I am not. Antony
Will be himself.
Ant. But stirr'd by Cleopatra.
Now for the love of Love and her soft hours,
Let's not confound the time with conference harsh.
There's not a minute of our lives should stretch
Without some pleasure now. What sport to-night?
Cleo. Hear the ambassadors.
Ant. Fie, wrangling queen!
Whom every thing becomes — to chide, to laugh,
To weep; whose every passion fully strives
To make itself, in thee, fair and admir'd!
No messenger but thine, and all alone
To-night we'll wander through the streets and note
The qualities of people. Come, my queen;
Last night you did desire it. — Speak not to us.
Exeunt [*Antony and Cleopatra*] *with the Train.*
Dem. Is Cæsar with Antonius priz'd so slight?
Phi. Sir, sometimes when he is not Antony
He comes too short of that great property
Which still should go with Antony.
Dem. I am full sorry
That he approves the common liar, who
Thus speaks of him at Rome; but I will hope
Of better deeds to-morrow. Rest you happy!
Exeunt.

[Scene II. *Alexandria. Another room in* Cleopatra's *Palace.*]

Enter a *Soothsayer, Charmian, Iras,* and *Alexas.*

Char. Lord Alexas, sweet Alexas, most any-thing Alexas, almost most absolute Alexas, where's the soothsayer that you prais'd so to th' Queen? O that I knew this husband which, you say, must charge his horns with garlands!

Alex. Soothsayer!
Sooth. Your will?
Char. Is this the man? Is't you, sir, that know things?
Sooth. In nature's infinite book of secrecy
A little I can read.
Alex. Show him your hand.

[Enter *Enobarbus.*]

Eno. Bring in the banquet quickly; wine enough
Cleopatra's health to drink.
Char. Good sir, give me good fortune.
Sooth. I make not, but foresee.
Char. Pray then, foresee me one.
Sooth. You shall be yet far fairer than you are.
Char. He means in flesh.
Iras. No, you shall paint when you are old.
Char. Wrinkles forbid!
Alex. Vex not his prescience; be attentive.
Char. Hush!
Sooth. You shall be more beloving than beloved.

Char. I had rather heat my liver with drinking.

Alex. Nay, hear him.

Char. Good now, some excellent fortune! Let me be married to three kings in a forenoon and widow them all. Let me have a child at fifty, to whom Herod of Jewry may do homage. Find me to marry me with Octavius Cæsar, and companion me with my mistress.

Sooth. You shall outlive the lady whom you serve.

Char. O excellent! I love long life better than figs.

Sooth. You have seen and prov'd a fairer former fortune
Than that which is to approach.

Char. Then belike my children shall have no names. Prithee, how many boys and wenches must I have?

Sooth. If every of your wishes had a womb,
And fertile every wish, a million.

Char. Out, fool! I forgive thee for a witch.

Alex. You think none but your sheets are privy to your wishes.

Char. Nay, come, tell Iras hers.

Alex. We'll know all our fortunes.

Eno. Mine, and most of our fortunes, to-night, shall be — drunk to bed.

Iras. There's a palm presages chastity, if nothing else.

Char. E'en as the o'erflowing Nilus presageth famine.

Iras. Go, you wild bedfellow, you cannot soothsay.

Char. Nay, if an oily palm be not a fruitful prognostication, I cannot scratch mine ear. Prithee tell her but a workyday fortune.

Sooth. Your fortunes are alike.

Iras. But how, but how? Give me particulars.

Sooth. I have said.

Iras. Am I not an inch of fortune better than she?

Char. Well, if you were but an inch of fortune better than I, where would you choose it?

Iras. Not in my husband's nose.

Char. Our worser thoughts heavens mend! Alexas — come, his fortune, his fortune! O, let him marry a woman that cannot go, sweet Isis, I beseech thee! and let her die too, and give him a worse! and let worse follow worse till the worst of all follow him laughing to his grave, fiftyfold a cuckold! Good Isis, hear me this prayer, though thou deny me a matter of more weight; good Isis, I beseech thee!

Iras. Amen. Dear goddess, hear that prayer of the people! For, as it is a heartbreaking to see a handsome man loose-wiv'd, so it is a deadly sorrow to behold a foul knave uncuckolded. Therefore, dear Isis, keep decorum, and fortune him accordingly!

Char. Amen.

Alex. Lo now, if it lay in their hands to make me a cuckold, they would make themselves whores but they'ld do't!

Eno. Hush! Here comes Antony.

Enter *Cleopatra.*

Char. Not he! the Queen.
Cleo. Saw you my lord?
Eno. No, lady.
Cleo. Was he not here?
Char. No, madam.
Cleo. He was dispos'd to mirth; but on the sudden
A Roman thought hath struck him. Enobarbus!
Eno. Madam?
Cleo. Seek him, and bring him hither. Where's Alexas?
Alex. Here at your service. My lord approaches.

Enter *Antony* with a *Messenger* [and *Attendants*].

Cleo. We will not look upon him. Go with us.
Exeunt [*Cleopatra, Enobarbus and the rest*].
Mess. Fulvia thy wife first came into the field.
Ant. Against my brother Lucius?
Mess. Ay.
But soon that war had end, and the time's state
Made friends of them, jointing their force 'gainst Cæsar,
Whose better issue in the war from Italy
Upon the first encounter drave them.
Ant. Well, what worst?
Mess. The nature of bad news infects the teller.
Ant. When it concerns the fool or coward On!
Things that are past are done with me. 'Tis thus:
Who tells me true, though in his tale lie death,
I hear him as he flatter'd.
Mess. Labienus
(This is stiff news) hath with his Parthian force
Extended Asia from Euphrates,
His conquering banner shook from Syria
To Lydia and to Ionia,
Whilst —
Ant. Antony, thou wouldst say.
Mess. O, my lord!
Ant. Speak to me home. Mince not the general tongue.
Name Cleopatra as she is call'd in Rome.
Rail thou in Fulvia's phrase, and taunt my faults
With such full license as both truth and malice
Have power to utter. O, then we bring forth weeds
When our quick minds lie still, and our ills told us
Is as our earing. Fare thee well awhile.
Mess. At your noble pleasure. *Exit.*
Ant. From Sicyon, ho, the news! Speak there!
1. Att. The man from Sicyon — is there such an one?
2. Att. He stays upon your will.
Ant. Let him appear.
These strong Egyptian fetters I must break
Or lose myself in dotage.

Enter another *Messenger*, with a letter.

What are you?

Mess. Fulvia thy wife is dead.

Ant. Where died she?

Mess. In Sicyon.
Her length of sickness, with what else more serious
Importeth thee to know, this bears.

[*Gives the letter.*]

Ant. Forbear me.

[*Exit Messenger.*]

There's a great spirit gone! Thus did I desire it.
What our contempts do often hurl from us,
We wish it ours again. The present pleasure,
By revolution low'ring, does become
The opposite of itself. She's good, being gone;
The hand could pluck her back that shov'd her on.
I must from this enchanting queen break off.
Ten thousand harms more than the ills I know
My idleness doth hatch. How now, Enobarbus!

Enter *Enobarbus*.

Eno. What's your pleasure, sir?

Ant. I must with haste from hence.

Eno. Why, then we kill all our women. We see how mortal an unkindness is to them. If they suffer our departure, death's the word.

Ant. I must be gone.

Eno. Under a compelling occasion let women die. It were pity to cast them away for nothing, though, between them and a great cause, they should be esteemed nothing. Cleopatra, catching but the least noise of this, dies instantly. I have seen her die twenty times upon far poorer moment. I do think there is mettle in death, which commits some loving act upon her, she hath such a celerity in dying.

Ant. She is cunning past man's thought.

Eno. Alack, sir, no! Her passions are made of nothing but the finest part of pure love. We cannot call her winds and waters sighs and tears. They are greater storms and tempests than almanacs can report. This cannot be cunning in her; if it be, she makes a show'r of rain as well as Jove.

Ant. Would I had never seen her!

Eno. O, sir, you had then left unseen a wonderful piece of work, which not to have been blest withal would have discredited your travel.

Ant. Fulvia is dead.

Eno. Sir?

Ant. Fulvia is dead.

Eno. Fulvia?

Ant. Dead.

Eno. Why, sir, give the gods a thankful sacrifice. When it pleaseth their deities to take the wife of a man from him, it shows to man the tailors of the earth; comforting therein, that when old robes are worn out, there are members to make new. If there were no more women but Fulvia, then had you indeed a cut, and the case to be lamented. This grief is crown'd with consolation; your old smock brings forth a new petticoat; and indeed the tears live in an onion that should water this sorrow.

Ant. The business she hath broached in the state
Cannot endure my absence.

Eno. And the business you have broach'd here cannot be without you; especially that of Cleopatra's, which wholly depends on your abode.

Ant. No more light answers. Let our officers
Have notice what we purpose. I shall break
The cause of our expedience to the Queen
And get her leave to part. For not alone
The death of Fulvia, with more urgent touches,
Do strongly speak to us, but the letters too
Of many our contriving friends in Rome
Petition us at home. Sextus Pompeius
Hath given the dare to Cæsar and commands
The empire of the sea. Our slippery people,
Whose love is never link'd to the deserver
Till his deserts are past, begin to throw
Pompey the Great and all his dignities
Upon his son; who, high in name and power,
Higher than both in blood and life, stands up
For the main soldier; whose quality, going on,
The sides o' th' world may danger. Much is breeding
Which, like the courser's hair, hath yet but life
And not a serpent's poison. Say, our pleasure,
To such whose place is under us, requires
Our quick remove from hence.

Eno. I shall do't. [*Exeunt.*]

[Scene III. *Alexandria. Another room in* Cleopatra's *Palace.*]

Enter *Cleopatra, Charmian, Alexas,* and *Iras.*

Cleo. Where is he?

Char. I did not see him since.

Cleo. See where he is, who's with him, what he does.
I did not send you. If you find him sad,

Say I am dancing; if in mirth, report
That I am sudden sick. Quick, and return!
[*Exit Alexas.*]

Char. Madam, methinks, if you did love him dearly,
You do not hold the method to enforce
The like from him.

Cleo. What should I do, I do not?

Char. In each thing give him way, cross him in nothing.

Cleo. Thou teachest like a fool. The way to lose him!

Char. Tempt him not so too far; I wish, forbear.
In time we hate that which we often fear.

Enter *Antony.*

But here comes Antony.

Cleo. I am sick and sullen.

Ant. I am sorry to give breathing to my purpose —

Cleo. Help me away, dear Charmian! I shall fall.
It cannot be thus long; the sides of nature
Will not sustain it.

Ant. Now, my dearest queen —

Cleo. Pray you stand farther from me.

Ant. What's the matter?

Cleo. I know by that same eye there's some good news.
What says the married woman? You may go.
Would she had never given you leave to come!
Let her not say 'tis I that keep you here.
I have no power upon you; hers you are.

Ant. The gods best know —

Cleo. O, never was there queen
So mightily betray'd! Yet at the first
I saw the treasons planted.

Ant. Cleopatra —

Cleo. Why should I think you can be mine, and true,
Though you in swearing shake the throned gods,
Who have been false to Fulvia? Riotous madness,
To be entangled with those mouth-made vows
Which break themselves in swearing!

Ant. Most sweet queen —

Cleo. Nay, pray you seek no colour for your going,
But bid farewell, and go. When you su'd staying,
Then was the time for words. No going then!
Eternity was in our lips and eyes,
Bliss in our brows' bent, none our parts so poor
But was a race of heaven. They are so still,
Or thou, the greatest soldier of the world,
Art turn'd the greatest liar.

Ant. How now, lady?

Cleo. I would I had thy inches! Thou shouldst know
There were a heart in Egypt.

Ant. Hear me, Queen.
The strong necessity of time commands
Our services awhile; but my full heart
Remains in use with you. Our Italy
Shines o'er with civil swords. Sextus Pompeius
Makes his approaches to the port of Rome.
Equality of two domestic powers
Breed scrupulous faction. The hated, grown to strength,
Are newly grown to love. The condemn'd Pompey,
Rich in his father's honour, creeps apace
Into the hearts of such as have not thriv'd
Upon the present state, whose numbers threaten;
And quietness, grown sick of rest, would purge
By any desperate change. My more particular,
And that which most with you should safe my going,
Is Fulvia's death.

Cleo. Though age from folly could not give me freedom,
It does from childishness. Can Fulvia die?

Ant. She's dead, my queen.
Look here, and at thy sovereign leisure read
The garboils she awak'd. At the last, best,
See when and where she died.

Cleo. O most false love!
Where be the sacred vials thou shouldst fill
With sorrowful water? Now I see, I see,
In Fulvia's death, how mine receiv'd shall be.

Ant. Quarrel no more, but be prepar'd to know
The purposes I bear; which are, or cease,
As you shall give the advice. By the fire
That quickens Nilus' slime, I go from hence
Thy soldier, servant, making peace or war
As thou affect'st.

Cleo. Cut my lace, Charmian, come!
But let it be. I am quickly ill, and well —
So Antony loves.

Ant. My precious queen, forbear,
And give true evidence to his love, which stands
An honourable trial.

Cleo. So Fulvia told me.
I prithee turn aside and weep for her;
Then bid adieu to me, and say the tears
Belong to Egypt. Good now, play one scene

Of excellent dissembling, and let it look
Like perfect honour.

Ant. You'll heat my blood. No more!

Cleo. You can do better yet; but this is meetly.

Ant. Now by my sword —

Cleo. And target. Still he mends;
But this is not the best. Look, prithee, Charmian,
How this Herculean Roman does become
The carriage of his chafe.

Ant. I'll leave you, lady.

Cleo. Courteous lord, one word.
Sir, you and I must part — but that's not it.
Sir, you and I have lov'd — but there's not it.
That you know well. Something it is I would —
O, my oblivion is a very Antony,
And I am all forgotten!

Ant. But that your royalty
Holds idleness your subject, I should take you
For idleness itself.

Cleo. 'Tis sweating labour
To bear such idleness so near the heart
As Cleopatra this. But, sir, forgive me;
Since my becomings kill me when they do not
Eye well to you. Your honour calls you hence;
Therefore be deaf to my unpitied folly,
And all the gods go with you! Upon your sword
Sit laurel victory, and smooth success
Be strew'd before your feet!

Ant. Let us go. Come.
Our separation so abides and flies
That thou, residing here, go'st yet with me,
And I, hence fleeting, here remain with thee.
Away! *Exeunt.*

[Scene IV. *Rome.* Cæsar's *house.*]

Enter *Octavius* [*Cæsar*], reading a letter, *Lepidus*, and their *Train*.

Cæs. You may see, Lepidus, and henceforth know
It is not Cæsar's natural vice to hate
Our great competitor. From Alexandria
This is the news: he fishes, drinks, and wastes
The lamps of night in revel; is not more manlike
Than Cleopatra, nor the queen of Ptolemy
More womanly than he; hardly gave audience, or
Vouchsaf'd to think he had partners. You shall find there
A man who is the abstract of all faults
That all men follow.

Lep. I must not think there are
Evils enow to darken all his goodness.
His faults, in him, seem as the spots of heaven,
More fiery by night's blackness; hereditary
Rather than purchas'd; what he cannot change
Than what he chooses.

Cæs. You are too indulgent. Let us grant it is not
Amiss to tumble on the bed of Ptolemy,
To give a kingdom for a mirth, to sit
And keep the turn of tippling with a slave,
To reel the streets at noon, and stand the buffet
With knaves that smell of sweat. Say this becomes him
(As his composure must be rare indeed
Whom these things cannot blemish), yet must Antony
No way excuse his foils when we do bear
So great weight in his lightness. If he fill'd
His vacancy with his voluptuousness,
Full surfeits and the dryness of his bones
Call on him for't! But to confound such time
That drums him from his sport and speaks as loud
As his own state and ours — 'tis to be chid
As we rate boys who, being mature in knowledge,
Pawn their experience to their present pleasure
And so rebel to judgment.

Enter a *Messenger*.

Lep. Here's more news.

Mess. Thy biddings have been done, and every hour,
Most noble Cæsar, shalt thou have report
How 'tis abroad. Pompey is strong at sea,
And it appears he is belov'd of those
That only have fear'd Cæsar. To the ports
The discontents repair, and men's reports
Give him much wrong'd.

Cæs. I should have known no less.
It hath been taught us from the primal state
That he which is was wish'd until he were;
And the ebb'd man, ne'er lov'd till ne'er worth love,
Comes dear'd by being lack'd. This common body,
Like to a vagabond flag upon the stream,

ANTONY AND CLEOPATRA

Michael Redgrave as Antony, a strong man weakened by drink and indolence

Peggy Ashcroft as Cleopatra of Egypt, the enchantment and mystery of the Orient incarnate

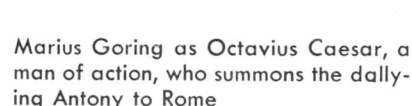

Marius Goring as Octavius Caesar, a man of action, who summons the dallying Antony to Rome

PHOTOGRAPHS BY ANGUS MCBEAN
PRODUCED BY THE MEMORIAL THEATRE COMPANY
STRATFORD-UPON-AVON

"Now, for the love of Love and her soft hours, let's not confound the time with conference harsh." Absorbed in romance with Cleopatra, Antony refuses to see the courier from Rome *(Act I, Scene I)*

Left: "If it be love indeed, tell me how much." The daughter of the Pharaohs invites a romantic rhapsody from her lover *(Act I, Scene I)*

Below: "Let me be married to three kings in a forenoon, and widow them all." A soothsayer (Philip Morant) tells the fortunes of Charmian (Jean Wilson) and Iras (Mary Watson), attendants of Cleopatra *(Act I, Scene II)*

"Welcome to Rome." Antony is greeted coldly by Caesar in returning to Rome *(Act II, Scene II)*

"I had rather fast from all four days than drink so much in one." A guest with Antony on the galley of Pompey, Caesar does not relish the levity and drinking there *(Act II, Scene VII)*

"O Charmian, where think'st thou he is now?" Reclining in her palace at Alexandria, Cleopatra dreams of Antony, her absent lover *(Act I, Scene V)*

Above: "You take from me a great part of myself; use me well in't." The farewell of Caesar to his sister, Octavia (Rachel Kempson), whom Antony has married for reasons of policy *(Act III, Scene II)*

"Horrible villain! or I'll spurn thine eyes like balls before me." Cleopatra attacks the messenger who brings the news of Antony's marriage *(Act II, Scene V)*

"Where is the fellow?" Cleopatra questions her servant, Alexas (Alan Townsend), regarding the Roman messenger *(Act III, Scene III)*

"Such as I am, I come from Antony." Antony's ambassador, Euphronius (Peter Norris), comes to the camp of Caesar on a mission of peace *(Act III, Scene XII)*

Left: "He calls me boy, and chides as he had power to beat me out of Egypt." Caesar is incensed at the overbearing tone of Antony's letter *(Act IV, Scene I)*

Above: Harry Andrews as Enobarbus, a close friend of Antony who deserted him in his need and then perished of sheer remorse

Left: "Give me grace to lay my duty on your hand." Thyreus (William Peacock), ambassador from Rome, tries to persuade Cleopatra to leave Antony for Caesar *(Act III, Scene XIII)*

"My nightingale, we have beat them to their beds." Antony greets Cleopatra jubilantly on his return from battle *(Act IV, Scene VIII)*

"Come, then; for with a wound I must be cur'd." Despairing of victory and believing Cleopatra is dead, Antony begs his page Eros (David O'Brien) to kill him *(Act IV, Scene XIV)*

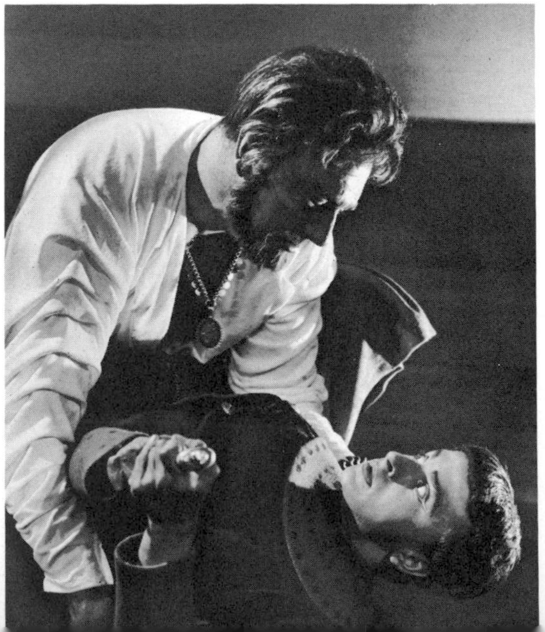

"Thus do I escape the sorrow of Antony's death." Disobeying Antony's plea to kill him, Eros stabs himself *(Act IV, Scene XIV)*

"Help, friends below! let's draw him hither." The dying Antony is carried by his guard to the monument where Cleopatra has taken refuge *(Act IV, Scene XV)*

"I am dying, Egypt, dying. Give me some wine, and let me speak a little." Antony dies after bidding his love to put her trust in Caesar alone *(Act IV, Scene XV)*

Right: The queen's lamentation *(Act IV, Scene XV)*

Below: Cleopatra's women attend her as she swoons after the death of her lover *(Act IV, Scene XV)*

The dead Cleopatra sits enthroned in her robes of state, with her two waiting women, Charmian and Iras, dead at her feet *(Act V, Scene II)*

"She shall be buried by her Antony: no grave upon earth shall clip in it a pair so famous." Octavius Caesar gives directions for the burial of Antony and Cleopatra *(Act V, Scene II)*

Goes to and back, lackeying the varying tide,
To rot itself with motion.
Mess. Cæsar, I bring thee word
Menecrates and Menas, famous pirates,
Make the sea serve them, which they ear and wound
With keels of every kind. Many hot inroads
They make in Italy; the borders maritime
Lack blood to think on't, and flush youth revolt.
No vessel can peep forth but 'tis as soon
Taken as seen; for Pompey's name strikes more
Than could his war resisted.
Cæs. Antony,
Leave thy lascivious wassails. When thou once
Wast beaten from Modena, where thou slew'st
Hirtius and Pansa, consuls, at thy heel
Did famine follow; whom thou fought'st against
(Though daintily brought up) with patience more
Than savages could suffer. Thou didst drink
The stale of horses and the gilded puddle
Which beasts would cough at. Thy palate then did deign
The roughest berry on the rudest hedge.
Yea, like the stag when snow the pasture sheets,
The barks of trees thou browsed'st. On the Alps
It is reported thou didst eat strange flesh,
Which some did die to look on. And all this
(It wounds thine honour that I speak it now)
Was borne so like a soldier that thy cheek
So much as lank'd not.
Lep. It is pity of him.
Cæs. Let his shames quickly
Drive him to Rome. 'Tis time we twain
Did show ourselves i' th' field; and to that end
Assemble we immediate council. Pompey
Thrives in our idleness.
Lep. To-morrow, Cæsar,
I shall be furnish'd to inform you rightly
Both what by sea and land I can be able
To front this present time.
Cæs. Till which encounter,
It is my business too. Farewell.
Lep. Farewell, my lord. What you shall know meantime
Of stirs abroad, I shall beseech you, sir,
To let me be partaker.
Cæs. Doubt not, sir;
I knew it for my bond. *Exeunt.*

[Scene V. *Alexandria. A room in* Cleopatra's *Palace.*]

Enter *Cleopatra, Charmian, Iras,* and *Mardian.*

Cleo. Charmian!
Char. Madam?
Cleo. Ha, ha!
Give me to drink mandragora.
Char. Why, madam?
Cleo. That I might sleep out this great gap of time
My Antony is away.
Char. You think of him too much.
Cleo. O, 'tis treason!
Char. Madam, I trust, not so.
Cleo. Thou, eunuch Mardian!
Mar. What's your Highness' pleasure?
Cleo. Not now to hear thee sing. I take no pleasure
In aught an eunuch has. 'Tis well for thee
That, being unseminar'd, thy freer thoughts
May not fly forth of Egypt. Hast thou affections?
Mar. Yes, gracious madam.
Cleo. Indeed?
Mar. Not in deed, madam; for I can do nothing
But what indeed is honest to be done.
Yet have I fierce affections, and think
What Venus did with Mars.
Cleo. O Charmian!
Where think'st thou he is now? Stands he, or sits he?
Or does he walk? or is he on his horse?
O happy horse, to bear the weight of Antony!
Do bravely, horse! for wot'st thou whom thou mov'st?
The demi-Atlas of this earth, the arm
And burgonet of men. He's speaking now,
Or murmuring 'Where's my serpent of old Nile?'
For so he calls me. Now I feed myself
With most delicious poison. Think on me,
That am with Phœbus' amorous pinches black
And wrinkled deep in time? Broad-fronted Cæsar,
When thou wast here above the ground, I was
A morsel for a monarch; and great Pompey
Would stand and make his eyes grow in my brow;
There would he anchor his aspect, and die
With looking on his life.

Enter *Alexas.*

Alex. Sovereign of Egypt, hail!
Cleo. How much unlike art thou Mark Antony!
Yet, coming from him, that great med'cine hath
With his tinct gilded thee.
How goes it with my brave Mark Antony?
Alex. Last thing he did, dear Queen,
He kiss'd — the last of many doubled kisses —
This orient pearl. His speech sticks in my heart.
Cleo. Mine ear must pluck it thence.
Alex. 'Good friend,' quoth he,
'Say the firm Roman to great Egypt sends
This treasure of an oyster; at whose foot,
To mend the petty present, I will piece
Her opulent throne with kingdoms. All the East,
Say thou, shall call her mistress.' So he nodded,
And soberly did mount an arm-gaunt steed,
Who neigh'd so high that what I would have spoke
Was beastly dumb'd by him.
Cleo. What, was he sad or merry?
Alex. Like to the time o' th' year between the extremes
Of hot and cold. He was nor sad nor merry.
Cleo. O well-divided disposition! Note him,
Note him, good Charmian; 'tis the man; but note him!
He was not sad, for he would shine on those
That make their looks by his; he was not merry,
Which seem'd to tell them his remembrance lay
In Egypt with his joy; but between both.
O heavenly mingle! Be'st thou sad or merry,
The violence of either thee becomes,
So does it no man else. — Met'st thou my posts?
Alex. Ay, madam, twenty several messengers.
Why do you send so thick?
Cleo. Who's born that day
When I forget to send to Antony
Shall die a beggar. Ink and paper, Charmian.
Welcome, my good Alexas. Did I, Charmian,
Ever love Cæsar so?
Char. O that brave Cæsar!
Cleo. Be chok'd with such another emphasis!
Say 'the brave Antony.'
Char. The valiant Cæsar!
Cleo. By Isis, I will give thee bloody teeth
If thou with Cæsar paragon again
My man of men!
Char. By your most gracious pardon,
I sing but after you.
Cleo. My salad days,
When I was green in judgment, cold in blood,
To say as I said then. But come, away!
Get me ink and paper.
He shall have every day a several greeting,
Or I'll unpeople Egypt. *Exeunt.*

[ACT II. Scene I. *Messina.* Pompey's *house.*]

Enter *Pompey, Menecrates,* and *Menas,* in warlike manner.

Pom. If the great gods be just, they shall assist
The deeds of justest men.
Menec. Know, worthy Pompey,
That what they do delay, they not deny.
Pom. Whiles we are suitors to their throne, decays
The thing we sue for.
Menec. We, ignorant of ourselves,
Beg often our own harms, which the wise pow'rs
Deny us for our good. So find we profit
By losing of our prayers.
Pom. I shall do well.
The people love me, and the sea is mine;
My powers are crescent, and my auguring hope
Says it will come to th' full. Mark Antony
In Egypt sits at dinner, and will make
No wars without doors. Cæsar gets money where
He loses hearts. Lepidus flatters both,
Of both is flatter'd; but he neither loves,
Nor either cares for him.
Menas. Cæsar and Lepidus
Are in the field; a mighty strength they carry.
Pom. Where have you this? 'Tis false.
Menas. From Silvius, sir.
Pom. He dreams. I know they are in Rome together,
Looking for Antony. But all the charms of love,
Salt Cleopatra, soften thy wan'd lip!
Let witchcraft join with beauty, lust with both!
Tie up the libertine in a field of feasts,
Keep his brain fuming. Epicurean cooks
Sharpen with cloyless sauce his appetite,
That sleep and feeding may prorogue his honour
Even till a Lethe'd dulness!

Enter *Varrius.*

How now, Varrius?

Var. This is most certain that I shall deliver:
Mark Antony is every hour in Rome
Expected. Since he went from Egypt 'tis
A space for farther travel.

Pom. I could have given less matter
A better ear. Menas, I did not think
This amorous surfeiter would have donn'd his helm
For such a petty war. His soldiership
Is twice the other twain. But let us rear
The higher our opinion, that our stirring
Can from the lap of Egypt's widow pluck
The ne'er-lust-wearied Antony.

Menas. I cannot hope
Cæsar and Antony shall well greet together.
His wife that's dead did trespasses to Cæsar;
His brother warr'd upon him; although, I think,
Not mov'd by Antony.

Pom. I know not, Menas,
How lesser enmities may give way to greater.
Were't not that we stand up against them all,
'Twere pregnant they should square between themselves,
For they have entertained cause enough
To draw their swords; but how the fear of us
May cement their divisions and bind up
The petty difference we yet not know.
Be't as our gods will have't! It only stands
Our lives upon to use our strongest hands.
Come, Menas. *Exeunt.*

[Scene II. *Rome. The house of* Lepidus.]

Enter *Enobarbus* and *Lepidus.*

Lep. Good Enobarbus, 'tis a worthy deed,
And shall become you well, to entreat your captain
To soft and gentle speech.

Eno. I shall entreat him
To answer like himself. If Cæsar move him,
Let Antony look over Cæsar's head
And speak as loud as Mars. By Jupiter,
Were I the wearer of Antonius' beard,
I would not shave't to-day!

Lep. 'Tis not a time
For private stomaching.

Eno. Every time
Serves for the matter that is then born in't.

Lep. But small to greater matters must give way.

Eno. Not if the small come first.

Lep. Your speech is passion;
But pray you stir no embers up. Here comes
The noble Antony.

Enter *Antony* and *Ventidius.*

Eno. And yonder, Cæsar.

Enter *Cæsar, Mæcenas,* and *Agrippa.*

Ant. If we compose well here, to Parthia.
Hark, Ventidius.

Cæs. I do not know,
Mæcenas. Ask Agrippa.

Lep. Noble friends,
That which combin'd us was most great, and let not
A leaner action rend us. What's amiss,
May it be gently heard. When we debate
Our trivial difference loud, we do commit
Murther in healing wounds. Then, noble partners,
The rather for I earnestly beseech,
Touch you the sourest points with sweetest terms,
Nor curstness grow to th' matter.

Ant. 'Tis spoken well.
Were we before our armies, and to fight,
I should do thus. *Flourish.*

Cæs. Welcome to Rome.

Ant. Thank you.

Cæs. Sit.

Ant. Sit, sir.

Cæs. Nay then.
[*They sit.*]

Ant. I learn you take things ill which are not so,
Or being, concern you not.

Cæs. I must be laugh'd at
If, or for nothing or a little, I
Should say myself offended, and with you
Chiefly i' th' world; more laugh'd at that I should
Once name you derogately when to sound your name
It not concern'd me.

Ant. My being in Egypt, Cæsar,
What was't to you?

Cæs. No more than my residing here at Rome
Might be to you in Egypt. Yet if you there
Did practise on my state, your being in Egypt
Might be my question.

Ant. How intend you? practis'd?

Cæs. You may be pleas'd to catch at mine intent

By what did here befall me. Your wife and brother
Made wars upon me, and their contestation
Was theme for you; you were the word of war.

Ant. You do mistake your business. My brother never
Did urge me in his act. I did inquire it
And have my learning from some true reports
That drew their swords with you. Did he not rather
Discredit my authority with yours,
And make the wars alike against my stomach,
Having alike your cause? Of this my letters
Before did satisfy you. If you'll patch a quarrel,
As matter whole you have not to make it with,
It must not be with this.

Cæs. You praise yourself
By laying defects of judgment to me; but
You patch'd up your excuses.

Ant. Not so, not so!
I know you could not lack, I am certain on't,
Very necessity of this thought, that I,
Your partner in the cause 'gainst which he fought,
Could not with graceful eyes attend those wars
Which fronted mine own peace. As for my wife,
I would you had her spirit in such another!
The third o' th' world is yours, which with a snaffle
You may pace easy, but not such a wife.

Eno. Would we had all such wives, that the men might go to wars with the women!

Ant. So much uncurbable, her garboils, Cæsar,
Made out of her impatience, — which not wanted
Shrewdness of policy too, — I grieving grant
Did you too much disquiet. For that you must
But say I could not help it.

Cæs. I wrote to you
When rioting in Alexandria. You
Did pocket up my letters, and with taunts
Did gibe my missive out of audience.

Ant. Sir,
He fell upon me ere admitted. Then
Three kings I had newly feasted, and did want
Of what I was i' th' morning; but next day
I told him of myself, which was as much
As to have ask'd him pardon. Let this fellow
Be nothing of our strife. If we contend,
Out of our question wipe him.

Cæs. You have broken
The article of your oath, which you shall never
Have tongue to charge me with.

Lep. Soft. Cæsar!

Ant. No,
Lepidus; let him speak.
The honour is sacred which he talks on now,
Supposing that I lack'd it. But on, Cæsar.
The article of my oath —

Cæs. To lend me arms and aid when I requir'd them,
The which you both denied.

Ant. Neglected rather;
And then when poisoned hours had bound me up
From mine own knowledge. As nearly as I may,
I'll play the penitent to you; but mine honesty
Shall not make poor my greatness, nor my power
Work without it. Truth is, that Fulvia,
To have me out of Egypt, made wars here,
For which myself, the ignorant motive, do
So far ask pardon as befits mine honour
To stoop in such a case.

Lep. 'Tis noble spoken.

Mæc. If it might please you to enforce no further
The griefs between ye — to forget them quite
Were to remember that the present need
Speaks to atone you.

Lep. Worthily spoken, Mæcenas.

Eno. Or, if you borrow one another's love for the instant, you may, when you hear no more words of Pompey, return it again. You shall have time to wrangle in when you have nothing else to do.

Ant. Thou art a soldier only. Speak no more.

Eno. That truth should be silent I had almost forgot.

Ant. You wrong this presence; therefore speak no more.

Eno. Go to, then! your considerate stone.

Cæs. I do not much dislike the matter, but
The manner of his speech; for 't cannot be
We shall remain in friendship, our conditions
So diff'ring in their acts. Yet if I knew
What hoop should hold us staunch, from edge to edge
O' th' world I would pursue it.

Agr. Give me leave, Cæsar.

Cæs. Speak, Agrippa.

Agr. Thou hast a sister by the mother's side,
Admir'd Octavia. Great Mark Antony
Is now a widower.

Cæs. Say not so, Agrippa.
If Cleopatra heard you, your reproof
Were well deserv'd of rashness.

Ant. I am not married, Cæsar. Let me hear
Agrippa further speak.

Agr. To hold you in perpetual amity,
To make you brothers, and to knit your hearts
With an unslipping knot, take Antony
Octavia to his wife; whose beauty claims
No worse a husband than the best of men;
Whose virtue and whose general graces speak
That which none else can utter. By this marriage
All little jealousies, which now seem great,
And all great fears, which now import their dangers,
Would then be nothing. Truths would be tales,
Where now half-tales be truths. Her love to both
Would each to other, and all loves to both,
Draw after her. Pardon what I have spoke;
For 'tis a studied, not a present thought,
By duty ruminated.

Ant. Will Cæsar speak?

Cæs. Not till he hears how Antony is touch'd
With what is spoke already.

Ant. What power is in Agrippa,
If I would say 'Agrippa, be it so,'
To make this good?

Cæs. The power of Cæsar, and
His power unto Octavia.

Ant. May I never
To this good purpose, that so fairly shows,
Dream of impediment! Let me have thy hand.
Further this act of grace; and from this hour
The heart of brothers govern in our loves
And sway our great designs!

Cæs. There is my hand.
A sister I bequeath you, whom no brother
Did ever love so dearly. Let her live
To join our kingdoms and our hearts; and never
Fly off our loves again!

Lep. Happily, amen!

Ant. I did not think to draw my sword 'gainst Pompey;
For he hath laid strange courtesies and great
Of late upon me. I must thank him only,
Lest my remembrance suffer ill report;
At heel of that, defy him.

Lep. Time calls upon's.
Of us must Pompey presently be sought,
Or else he seeks out us.

Ant. Where lies he?

Cæs. About the Mount Misenum.

Ant. What is his strength by land?

Cæs. Great and increasing; but by sea
He is an absolute master.

Ant. So is the fame.
Would we had spoke together! Haste we for it.
Yet, ere we put ourselves in arms, dispatch we
The business we have talk'd of.

Cæs. With most gladness;
And do invite you to my sister's view,
Whither straight I'll lead you.

Ant. Let us, Lepidus,
Not lack your company.

Lep. Noble Antony,
Not sickness should detain me.

Flourish. Exeunt. Manent Enobarbus, Agrippa, Mæcenas.

Mæc. Welcome from Egypt, sir.

Eno. Half the heart of Cæsar, worthy Mæcenas! My honourable friend, Agrippa!

Agr. Good Enobarbus!

Mæc. We have cause to be glad that matters are so well disgested. You stay'd well by't in Egypt.

Eno. Ay, sir; we did sleep day out of countenance and made the night light with drinking.

Mæc. Eight wild boars roasted whole at a breakfast, and but twelve persons there. Is this true?

Eno. This was but as a fly by an eagle. We had much more monstrous matter of feast, which worthily deserved noting.

Mæc. She's a most triumphant lady, if report be square to her.

Eno. When she first met Mark Antony, she purs'd up his heart, upon the river of Cydnus.

Agr. There she appear'd indeed; or my reporter devis'd well for her.

Eno. I will tell you.
The barge she sat in, like a burnish'd throne,
Burn'd on the water. The poop was beaten gold;
Purple the sails, and so perfumed that
The winds were lovesick with them; the oars were silver,
Which to the tune of flutes kept stroke, and made
The water which they beat to follow faster,
As amorous of their strokes. For her own person,
It beggar'd all description. She did lie
In her pavilion, cloth-of-gold of tissue,
O'erpicturing that Venus where we see
The fancy outwork nature. On each side her
Stood pretty dimpled boys, like smiling Cupids,
With divers-colour'd fans, whose wind did seem
To glow the delicate cheeks which they did cool,
And what they undid did.

Agr. O, rare for Antony!

Eno. Her gentlewomen, like the Nereides,
So many mermaids, tended her i' th' eyes,

And made their bends adornings. At the helm
A seeming mermaid steers. The silken tackle
Swell with the touches of those flower-soft hands
That yarely frame the office. From the barge
A strange invisible perfume hits the sense
Of the adjacent wharfs. The city cast
Her people out upon her; and Antony,
Enthron'd i' th' market place, did sit alone,
Whistling to th' air; which, but for vacancy,
Had gone to gaze on Cleopatra too,
And made a gap in nature.
Agr. Rare Egyptian!
Eno. Upon her landing, Antony sent to her,
Invited her to supper. She replied,
It should be better he became her guest;
Which she entreated. Our courteous Antony,
Whom ne'er the word of 'no' woman heard speak,
Being barber'd ten times o'er, goes to the feast,
And for his ordinary pays his heart
For what his eyes eat only.
Agr. Royal wench!
She made great Cæsar lay his sword to bed.
He plough'd her, and she cropp'd.
Eno. I saw her once
Hop forty paces through the public street;
And having lost her breath, she spoke, and panted,
That she did make defect perfection
And, breathless, pow'r breathe forth.
Mæc. Now Antony must leave her utterly.
Eno. Never! He will not.
Age cannot wither her nor custom stale
Her infinite variety. Other women cloy
The appetites they feed, but she makes hungry
Where most she satisfies; for vilest things
Become themselves in her, that the holy priests
Bless her when she is riggish.
Mæc. If beauty, wisdom, modesty, can settle
The heart of Antony, Octavia is
A blessed lottery to him.
Agr. Let us go.
Good Enobarbus, make yourself my guest
Whilst you abide here.
Eno. Humbly, sir, I thank you. *Exeunt.*

[Scene III. *Rome.* Cæsar's *house.*]

Enter *Antony, Cæsar, Octavia* between them.

Ant. The world and my great office will sometimes
Divide me from your bosom.
Octa. All which time
Before the gods my knee shall bow my prayers
To them for you.
Ant. Good night, sir. My Octavia,
Read not my blemishes in the world's report.
I have not kept my square; but that to come
Shall all be done by th' rule. Good night, dear lady.
Octa. Good night, sir.
Cæs. Good night.
Exit [*with Octavia*].

Enter *Soothsayer.*

Ant. Now, sirrah, you do wish yourself in Egypt?
Sooth. Would I had never come from thence, nor you thither!
Ant. If you can, your reason!
Sooth. I see it in my motion, have it not in my tongue.
But yet hie you to Egypt again.
Ant. Say to me,
Whose fortunes shall rise higher, Cæsar's or mine?
Sooth. Cæsar's.
Therefore, O Antony, stay not by his side!
Thy dæmon, that thy spirit which keeps thee, is
Noble, courageous, high, unmatchable,
Where Cæsar's is not; but near him thy angel
Becomes a fear, as being o'erpow'r'd. Therefore
Make space enough between you.
Ant. Speak this no more.
Sooth. To none but thee; no more but when to thee.
If thou dost play with him at any game,
Thou art sure to lose; and of that natural luck
He beats thee 'gainst the odds. Thy lustre thickens
When he shines by. I say again, thy spirit
Is all afraid to govern thee near him;
But he away, 'tis noble.
Ant. Get thee gone.
Say to Ventidius I would speak with him.
Exit [*Soothsayer*].
He shall to Parthia. — Be it art or hap,
He hath spoken true. The very dice obey him,
And in our sports my better cunning faints
Under his chance. If we draw lots, he speeds;
His cocks do win the battle still of mine
When it is all to naught, and his quails ever
Beat mine, inhoop'd, at odds. I will to Egypt;
And though I make this marriage for my peace,
I' th' East my pleasure lies.

Enter *Ventidius.*

O, come, Ventidius,
You must to Parthia. Your commission's ready;
Follow me, and receive't. *Exeunt.*

[Scene IV. *Rome. A street.*]

Enter *Lepidus, Mæcenas,* and *Agrippa.*

Lep. Trouble yourselves no further. Pray you, hasten
Your generals after.
Agr. Sir, Mark Antony
Will e'en but kiss Octavia, and we'll follow.
Lep. Till I shall see you in your soldier's dress,
Which will become you both, farewell.
Mæc. We shall,
As I conceive the journey, be at th' Mount
Before you, Lepidus.
Lep. Your way is shorter;
My purposes do draw me much about.
You'll win two days upon me.
Both. Sir, good success!
Lep. Farewell. *Exeunt.*

[Scene V. *Alexandria.* Cleopatra's *Palace.*]

Enter *Cleopatra, Charmian, Iras,* and *Alexas.*

Cleo. Give me some music! music, moody food
Of us that trade in love.
Omnes. The music, ho!

Enter *Mardian* the *Eunuch.*

Cleo. Let it alone! Let's to billiards. Come, Charmian.
Char. My arm is sore; best play with Mardian.
Cleo. As well a woman with an eunuch play'd
As with a woman. Come, you'll play with me, sir?
Mar. As well as I can, madam.
Cleo. And when good will is show'd, though 't come too short,
The actor may plead pardon. I'll none now.
Give me mine angle! we'll to th' river. There,
My music playing far off, I will betray
Tawny-finn'd fishes. My bended hook shall pierce
Their slimy jaws; and as I draw them up,
I'll think them every one an Antony,
And say, 'Ah, ha! y'are caught!'
Char. 'Twas merry when
You wager'd on your angling, when your diver
Did hang a salt fish on his hook, which he
With fervency drew up.
Cleo. That time? O times!
I laugh'd him out of patience; and that night
I laugh'd him into patience; and next morn
Ere the ninth hour I drunk him to his bed,
Then put my tires and mantles on him, whilst
I wore his sword Philippan.

Enter a *Messenger.*

O, from Italy!
Ram thou thy fruitful tidings in mine ears,
That long time have been barren.
Mess. Madam, madam —
Cleo. Antony's dead! If thou say so, villain,
Thou kill'st thy mistress; but well and free,
If thou so yield him, there is gold, and here
My bluest veins to kiss — a hand that kings
Have lipp'd, and trembled kissing.
Mess. First, madam, he is well.
Cleo. Why, there's more gold.
But, sirrah, mark, we use
To say the dead are well. Bring it to that,
The gold I give thee will I melt and pour
Down thy ill-uttering throat.
Mess. Good madam, hear me.
Cleo. Well, go to, I will.
But there's no goodness in thy face. If Antony
Be free and healthful, why so tart a favour
To trumpet such good tidings? If not well,
Thou shouldst come like a Fury crown'd with snakes,
Not like a formal man.
Mess. Will't please you hear me?
Cleo. I have a mind to strike thee ere thou speak'st.
Yet, if thou say Antony lives, is well,
Or friends with Cæsar or not captive to him,
I'll set thee in a shower of gold and hail
Rich pearls upon thee.
Mess. Madam, he's well.
Cleo. Well said.
Mess. And friends with Cæsar.
Cleo. Th'art an honest man.
Mess. Cæsar and he are greater friends than ever.
Cleo. Make thee a fortune from me!
Mess. But yet, madam —

Cleo. I do not like 'but yet.' It does allay
The good precedence. Fie upon 'but yet'!
'But yet' is as a jailer to bring forth
Some monstrous malefactor. Prithee, friend,
Pour out the pack of matter to mine ear,
The good and bad together. He's friends with Cæsar;
In state of health thou say'st; and thou say'st free.
Mess. Free, madam? No; I made no such report.
He's bound unto Octavia.
Cleo. For what good turn?
Mess. For the best turn i' th' bed.
Cleo. I am pale, Charmian.
Mess. Madam, he's married to Octavia.
Cleo. The most infectious pestilence upon thee! *Strikes him down.*
Mess. Good madam, patience.
Cleo. What say you? *Strikes him.*
Hence,
Horrible villain! or I'll spurn thine eyes
Like balls before me. I'll unhair thy head!
She hales him up and down.
Thou shalt be whipp'd with wire and stew'd in brine,
Smarting in ling'ring pickle.
Mess. Gracious madam,
I that do bring the news made not the match.
Cleo. Say 'tis not so, a province I will give thee
And make thy fortunes proud. The blow thou hadst
Shall make thy peace for moving me to rage;
And I will boot thee with what gift beside
Thy modesty can beg.
Mess. He's married, madam.
Cleo. Rogue, thou hast liv'd too long.
Draw a knife.
Mess. Nay, then I'll run.
What mean you, madam? I have made no fault. *Exit.*
Char. Good madam, keep yourself within yourself.
The man is innocent.
Cleo. Some innocents scape not the thunderbolt.
Melt Egypt into Nile! and kindly creatures
Turn all to serpents! Call the slave again.
Though I am mad, I will not bite him. Call!
Char. He is afeard to come.
Cleo. I will not hurt him.
These hands do lack nobility, that they strike
A meaner than myself; since I myself
Have given myself the cause.

Enter the *Messenger* again.

Come hither, sir.
Though it be honest, it is never good
To bring bad news. Give to a gracious message
An host of tongues, but let ill tidings tell
Themselves when they be felt.
Mess. I have done my duty.
Cleo. Is he married?
I cannot hate thee worser than I do
If thou again say yes.
Mess. He's married, madam.
Cleo. The gods confound thee! Dost thou hold there still?
Mess. Should I lie, madam?
Cleo. O, I would thou didst,
So half my Egypt were submerg'd and made
A cistern for scal'd snakes! Go get thee hence!
Hadst thou Narcissus in thy face, to me
Thou wouldst appear most ugly. He is married?
Mess. I crave your Highness' pardon.
Cleo. He is married?
Mess. Take no offence that I would not offend you.
To punish me for what you make me do
Seems much unequal. He's married to Octavia.
Cleo. O, that his fault should make a knave of thee,
That art not what th' art sure of! Get thee hence.
The merchandise which thou hast brought from Rome
Are all too dear for me. Lie they upon thy hand,
And be undone by 'em!
[*Exit Messenger.*]
Char. Good your Highness, patience.
Cleo. In praising Antony I have disprais'd Cæsar.
Char. Many times, madam.
Cleo. I am paid for't now.
Lead me from hence,
I faint. O Iras, Charmian! 'Tis no matter.
Go to the fellow, good Alexas. Bid him
Report the feature of Octavia, her years,
Her inclination; let him not leave out
The colour of her hair. Bring me word quickly.
[*Exit Alexas.*]
Let him for ever go! — let him not! — Charmian,
Though he be painted one way like a Gorgon,
The other way's a Mars. — [*To Mardian*] Bid you Alexas

Bring me word how tall she is.—Pity me, Charmian,
But do not speak to me. Lead me to my chamber. *Exeunt.*

[Scene VI. *Near Misenum.*]

Flourish. Enter *Pompey* [and] *Menas* at one door, with *Drum* and *Trumpet*: at another, *Cæsar, Lepidus, Antony, Enobarbus, Mæcenas, Agrippa,* with *Soldiers* marching.

Pom. Your hostages I have, so have you mine;
And we shall talk before we fight.
Cæs. Most meet
That first we come to words; and therefore have we
Our written purposes before us sent;
Which if thou hast considered, let us know
If 'twill tie up thy discontented sword
And carry back to Sicily much tall youth
That else must perish here.
Pom. To you all three,
The senators alone of this great world,
Chief factors for the gods: I do not know
Wherefore my father should revengers want,
Having a son and friends, since Julius Cæsar,
Who at Philippi the good Brutus ghosted,
There saw you labouring for him. What was't
That mov'd pale Cassius to conspire? and what
Made the all-honour'd honest Roman, Brutus,
With the arm'd rest, courtiers of beauteous freedom,
To drench the Capitol, but that they would
Have one man but a man? And that is it
Hath made me rig my navy, at whose burthen
The anger'd ocean foams; with which I meant
To scourge th' ingratitude that despiteful Rome
Cast on my noble father.
Cæs. Take your time.
Ant. Thou canst not fear us, Pompey, with thy sails.
We'll speak with thee at sea. At land thou know'st
How much we do o'ercount thee.
Pom. At land indeed
Thou dost o'ercount me of my father's house!
But since the cuckoo builds not for himself,
Remain in't as thou mayst.
Lep. Be pleas'd to tell us
(For this is from the present) how you take
The offers we have sent you.
Cæs. There's the point.
Ant. Which do not be entreated to, but weigh
What it is worth embrac'd.
Cæs. And what may follow,
To try a larger fortune.
Pom. You have made me offer
Of Sicily, Sardinia; and I must
Rid all the sea of pirates; then, to send
Measures of wheat to Rome; this 'greed upon,
To part with unhack'd edges and bear back
Our targes undinted.
Omnes. That's our offer.
Pom. Know then
I came before you here a man prepar'd
To take this offer; but Mark Antony
Put me to some impatience. Though I lose
The praise of it by telling, you must know,
When Cæsar and your brother were at blows,
Your mother came to Sicily and did find
Her welcome friendly.
Ant. I have heard it, Pompey,
And am well studied for a liberal thanks,
Which I do owe you.
Pom. Let me have your hand.
I did not think, sir, to have met you here.
Ant. The beds i' th' East are soft; and thanks to you,
That call'd me timelier than my purpose hither;
For I have gain'd by't.
Cæs. Since I saw you last
There is a change upon you.
Pom. Well, I know not
What counts harsh fortune casts upon my face;
But in my bosom shall she never come
To make my heart her vassal.
Lep. Well met here.
Pom. I hope so, Lepidus. Thus we are agreed.
I crave our composition may be written,
And seal'd between us.
Cæs. That's the next to do.
Pom. We'll feast each other ere we part, and let's
Draw lots who shall begin.
Ant. That will I, Pompey.
Pom. No, Antony, take the lot;
But, first or last, your fine Egyptian cookery
Shall have the fame. I have heard that Julius Cæsar
Grew fat with feasting there.
Ant. You have heard much.
Pom. I have fair meanings, sir.
Ant. And fair words to them.
Pom. Then so much have I heard;
And I have heard Apollodorus carried—

Eno. No more of that! He did so.
Pom. What, I pray you?
Eno. A certain queen to Cæsar in a mattress.
Pom. I know thee now. How far'st thou, soldier?
Eno. Well;
And well am like to do, for I perceive
Four feasts are toward.
Pom. Let me shake thy hand.
I never hated thee. I have seen thee fight
When I have envied thy behaviour.
Eno. Sir,
I never lov'd you much; but I ha' prais'd ye
When you have well deserv'd ten times as much
As I have said you did.
Pom. Enjoy thy plainness;
It nothing ill becomes thee.
Aboard my galley I invite you all.
Will you lead, lords?
All. Show us the way, sir.
Pom. Come.

Exeunt. Manent Enobarbus and Menas.

Menas. [*aside*] Thy father, Pompey, would ne'er have made this treaty. — You and I have known, sir.

Eno. At sea, I think.

Menas. We have, sir.

Eno. You have done well by water.

Menas. And you by land.

Eno. I will praise any man that will praise me; though it cannot be denied what I have done by land.

Menas. Nor what I have done by water.

Eno. Yes, something you can deny for your own safety. You have been a great thief by sea.

Menas. And you by land.

Eno. There I deny my land service. But give me your hand, Menas. If our eyes had authority, here they might take two thieves kissing.

Menas. All men's faces are true, whatsome'er their hands are.

Eno. But there is never a fair woman has a true face.

Menas. No slander. They steal hearts.

Eno. We came hither to fight with you.

Menas. For my part, I am sorry it is turn'd to a drinking. Pompey doth this day laugh away his fortune.

Eno. If he do, sure he cannot weep't back again.

Menas. Y'have said, sir. We look'd not for Mark Antony here. Pray you, is he married to Cleopatra?

Eno. Cæsar's sister is call'd Octavia.

Menas. True, sir. She was the wife of Caius Marcellus.

Eno. But she is now the wife of Marcus Antonius.

Menas. Pray ye, sir?

Eno. 'Tis true.

Menas. Then is Cæsar and he for ever knit together.

Eno. If I were bound to divine of this unity, I would not prophesy so.

Menas. I think the policy of that purpose made more in the marriage than the love of the parties.

Eno. I think so too. But you shall find the band that seems to tie their friendship together will be the very strangler of their amity. Octavia is of a holy, cold, and still conversation.

Menas. Who would not have his wife so?

Eno. Not he that himself is not so; which is Mark Antony. He will to his Egyptian dish again. Then shall the sighs of Octavia blow the fire up in Cæsar, and, as I said before, that which is the strength of their amity shall prove the immediate author of their variance. Antony will use his affection where it is. He married but his occasion here.

Menas. And thus it may be. Come, sir, will you aboard? I have a health for you.

Eno. I shall take it, sir. We have us'd our throats in Egypt.

Menas. Come, let's away. *Exeunt.*

[Scene VII. *On board* Pompey's *galley, off Misenum.*]

Music plays. Enter two or three *Servants*, with a banquet.

1. Serv. Here they'll be, man. Some o' their plants are ill-rooted already; the least wind i' th' world will blow them down.

2. Serv. Lepidus is high-colour'd.

1. Serv. They have made him drink alms-drink.

2. Serv. As they pinch one another by the disposition, he cries out 'No more!' reconciles them to his entreaty and himself to th' drink.

1. Serv. But it raises the greater war between him and his discretion.

2. Serv. Why, this it is to have a name in great men's fellowship. I had as live have a reed that will do me no service as a partisan I could not heave.

1. Serv. To be call'd into a huge sphere and not to be seen to move in't, are the holes where eyes should be, which pitifully disaster the cheeks.

A sennet sounded. Enter *Cæsar, Antony, Pompey, Lepidus, Agrippa, Mæcenas, Enobarbus, Menas,* with other *Captains.*

Ant. [*to Cæsar*] Thus do they, sir: they take the flow o' th' Nile
By certain scales i' th' pyramid. They know
By th' height, the lowness, or the mean, if dearth
Or foison follow. The higher Nilus swells,
The more it promises. As it ebbs, the seedsman
Upon the slime and ooze scatters his grain,
And shortly comes to harvest.

Lep. Y'have strange serpents there.

Ant. Ay, Lepidus.

Lep. Your serpent of Egypt is bred now of your mud by the operation of your sun; so is your crocodile.

Ant. They are so.

Pom. Sit — and some wine! A health to Lepidus!

Lep. I am not so well as I should be, but I'll ne'er out.

Eno. Not till you have slept. I fear me you'll be in till then.

Lep. Nay, certainly, I have heard the Ptolemies' pyramises are very goodly things. Without contradiction I have heard that.

Menas. [*aside to Pompey*] Pompey, a word.

Pom. [*aside to Menas*] Say in mine ear. What is't?

Menas. [*aside to Pompey*] Forsake thy seat, I do beseech thee, Captain,
And hear me speak a word.

Pom. [*aside to Menas*] Forbear me till anon. *Whispers in's ear.*
This wine for Lepidus!

Lep. What manner o' thing is your crocodile?

Ant. It is shap'd, sir, like itself, and it is as broad as it hath breadth. It is just so high as it is, and moves with it own organs. It lives by that which nourisheth it, and the elements once out of it, it transmigrates.

Lep. What colour is it of?

Ant. Of it own colour too.

Lep. 'Tis a strange serpent.

Ant. 'Tis so. And the tears of it are wet.

Cæs. Will this description satisfy him?

Ant. With the health that Pompey gives him; else he is a very epicure.

Pom. [*aside to Menas*] Go hang, sir, hang! Tell me of that? Away!
Do as I bid you. — Where's this cup I call'd for?

Menas. [*aside to Pompey*] If for the sake of merit thou wilt hear me,
Rise from thy stool.

Pom. [*aside to Menas*] I think th'art mad. [*Rises and walks aside.*]
The matter?

Menas. I have ever held my cap off to thy fortunes.

Pom. Thou hast serv'd me with much faith. What's else to say? —
Be jolly, lords.

Ant. These quicksands, Lepidus,
Keep off them, for you sink.

Menas. Wilt thou be lord of all the world?

Pom. What say'st thou?

Menas. Wilt thou be lord of the whole world? That's twice.

Pom. How should that be?

Menas. But entertain it,
And though thou think me poor, I am the man
Will give thee all the world.

Pom. Hast thou drunk well?

Menas. No, Pompey, I have kept me from the cup.
Thou art, if thou dar'st be, the earthly Jove.
Whate'er the ocean pales, or sky inclips,
Is thine, if thou wilt ha't.

Pom. Show me which way.

Menas. These three world-sharers, these competitors,
Are in thy vessel. Let me cut the cable;
And when we are put off, fall to their throats.
All there is thine.

Pom. Ah, this thou shouldst have done,
And not have spoke on't! In me 'tis villany;
In thee 't had been good service. Thou must know,
'Tis not my profit that does lead mine honour;
Mine honour, it. Repent that e'er thy tongue
Hath so betray'd thine act. Being done unknown,
I should have found it afterwards well done,
But must condemn it now. Desist, and drink.

Menas. [*aside*] For this,
I'll never follow thy pall'd fortunes more.
Who seeks, and will not take when once 'tis offer'd,
Shall never find it more.

Pom. This health to Lepidus!

Ant. Bear him ashore. I'll pledge it for him, Pompey.

Eno. Here's to thee, Menas!

Menas. Enobarbus, welcome!

Pom. Fill till the cup be hid.
Eno. There's a strong fellow, Menas.
[*Points to the Servant who carries off Lepidus.*]
Menas. Why?
Eno. 'A bears the third part of the world, man; see'st not?
Menas. The third part, then, is drunk. Would it were all,
That it might go on wheels!
Eno. Drink thou. Increase the reels.
Menas. Come.
Pom. This is not yet an Alexandrian feast.
Ant. It ripens towards it. Strike the vessels, ho!
Here's to Cæsar!
Cæs. I could well forbear't.
It's monstrous labour when I wash my brain
And it grows fouler.
Ant. Be a child o' th' time.
Cæs. Possess it; I'll make answer.
But I had rather fast from all four days
Than drink so much in one.
Eno. [*to Antony*] Ha, my brave emperor!
Shall we dance now the Egyptian Bacchanals
And celebrate our drink?
Pom. Let's ha't, good soldier.
Ant. Come, let's all take hands
Till that the conquering wine hath steep'd our sense
In soft and delicate Lethe.
Eno. All take hands.
Make battery to our ears with the loud music.
The while I'll place you; then the boy shall sing.
The holding every man shall bear as loud
As his strong sides can volley.
Music plays. Enobarbus places them hand in hand.

The Song.

Come, thou monarch of the vine,
Plumpy Bacchus with pink eyne!
In thy fats our cares be drown'd,
With thy grapes our hairs be crown'd.
Cup us till the world go round,
Cup us till the world go round!

Cæs. What would you more? Pompey, good night. Good brother,
Let me request you off. Our graver business
Frowns at this levity. Gentle lords, let's part;
You see we have burnt our cheeks. Strong Enobarb
Is weaker than the wine, and mine own tongue
Splits what it speaks. The wild disguise hath almost
Antick'd us all. What needs more words? Good night.
Good Antony, your hand.
Pom. I'll try you on the shore.
Ant. And shall, sir.—Give 's your hand.
Pom. O Antony,
You have my father's house — but what? We are friends!
Come, down into the boat.
Eno. Take heed you fall not.
[*Exeunt all but Enobarbus and Menas.*]
Menas, I'll not on shore.
Menas. No, to my cabin.
These drums! these trumpets, flutes! what!
Let Neptune hear we bid a loud farewell
To these great fellows. Sound and be hang'd, sound out!
Sound a flourish, with drums.
Eno. Hoo! says 'a. There's my cap.
Menas. Hoo! Noble Captain, come.
Exeunt.

[ACT III. Scene I. *A plain in Syria.*]

Enter *Ventidius* as it were in triumph, [with *Silius* and other *Romans*, *Officers*, and *Soldiers*;] the dead body of *Pacorus* borne before him.

Ven. Now, darting Parthia, art thou stroke, and now
Pleas'd fortune does of Marcus Crassus' death
Make me revenger. Bear the King's son's body
Before our army. Thy Pacorus, Orodes,
Pays this for Marcus Crassus.
Sil. Noble Ventidius.
Whilst yet with Parthian blood thy sword is warm,
The fugitive Parthians follow. Spur through Media,
Mesopotamia, and the shelters whither
The routed fly. So thy grand captain, Antony,
Shall set thee on triumphant chariots and
Put garlands on thy head.
Ven. O Silius, Silius,
I have done enough. A lower place, note well,
May make too great an act. For learn this, Silius:

Better to leave undone than by our deed
Acquire too high a fame when him we serve's away.
Cæsar and Antony have ever won
More in their officer than person. Sossius,
One of my place in Syria, his lieutenant,
For quick accumulation of renown,
Which he achiev'd by th' minute, lost his favour.
Who does i' th' wars more than his captain can
Becomes his captain's captain; and ambition,
The soldier's virtue, rather makes choice of loss
Than gain which darkens him.
I could do more to do Antonius good,
But 'twould offend him; and in his offence
Should my performance perish.

Sil. Thou hast, Ventidius, that
Without the which a soldier and his sword
Grants scarce distinction. Thou wilt write to Antony?

Ven. I'll humbly signify what in his name,
That magical word of war, we have effected;
How with his banners and his well-paid ranks
The ne'er-yet-beaten horse of Parthia
We have jaded out o' th' field.

Sil. Where is he now?

Ven. He purposeth to Athens; whither, with what haste
The weight we must convey with 's will permit,
We shall appear before him. — On, there! Pass along! *Exeunt.*

[Scene II. *Rome.* Cæsar's *house.*]

Enter *Agrippa* at one door, *Enobarbus* at another.

Agr. What, are the brothers parted?

Eno. They have dispatch'd with Pompey; he is gone;
The other three are sealing. Octavia weeps
To part from Rome; Cæsar is sad; and Lepidus
Since Pompey's feast, as Menas says, is troubled
With the green sickness.

Agr. 'Tis a noble Lepidus.

Eno. A very fine one. O, how he loves Cæsar!

Agr. Nay, but how dearly he adores Mark Antony!

Eno. Cæsar? Why, he's the Jupiter of men.

Agr. What's Antony? The god of Jupiter.

Eno. Spake you of Cæsar? Hoo! the nonpareil!

Agr. O Antony! O thou Arabian bird!

Eno. Would you praise Cæsar, say 'Cæsar'— go no further.

Agr. Indeed he plied them both with excellent praises.

Eno. But he loves Cæsar best. Yet he loves Antony!
Hoo! hearts, tongues, figures, scribes, bards, poets, cannot
Think, speak, cast, write, sing, number—hoo!—
His love to Antony. But as for Cæsar,
Kneel down, kneel down, and wonder!

Agr. Both he loves.

Eno. They are his shards, and he their beetle. [*Trumpet within.*] So —
This is to horse. Adieu, noble Agrippa.

Agr. Good fortune, worthy soldier, and farewell!

Enter *Cæsar, Antony, Lepidus,* and *Octavia.*

Ant. No further, sir.

Cæs. You take from me a great part of myself;
Use me well in't. Sister, prove such a wife
As my thoughts make thee, and as my farthest band
Shall pass on thy approof. Most noble Antony,
Let not the piece of virtue which is set
Betwixt us as the cement of our love
To keep it builded, be the ram to batter
The fortress of it; for better might we
Have lov'd without this mean, if on both parts
This be not cherish'd.

Ant. Make me not offended
In your distrust.

Cæs. I have said.

Ant. You shall not find,
Though you be therein curious, the least cause
For what you seem to fear. So the gods keep you
And make the hearts of Romans serve your ends!
We will here part.

Cæs. Farewell, my dearest sister, fare thee well.
The elements be kind to thee and make
Thy spirits all of comfort! Fare thee well.

Octa. My noble brother!

Ant. The April's in her eyes. It is love's spring,
And these the showers to bring it on. Be cheerful.

Octa. Sir, look well to my husband's house; and —

Cæs. What,
Octavia?

Octa. I'll tell you in your ear.

Ant. Her tongue will not obey her heart, nor can
Her heart inform her tongue — the swan's down-feather
That stands upon the swell at full of tide,
And neither way inclines.

Eno. [*aside to Agrippa*] Will Cæsar weep?

Agr. [*aside to Enobarbus*] He has a cloud in's face.

Eno. [*aside to Agrippa*] He were the worse for that, were he a horse;
So is he, being a man.

Agr. [*aside to Enobarbus*] Why, Enobarbus,
When Antony found Julius Cæsar dead,
He cried almost to roaring; and he wept
When at Philippi he found Brutus slain.

Eno. [*aside to Agrippa*] That year indeed he was troubled with a rheum.
What willingly he did confound he wail'd,
Believe 't, till I wept too.

Cæs. No, sweet Octavia,
You shall hear from me still. The time shall not
Outgo my thinking on you.

Ant. Come, sir, come.
I'll wrestle with you in my strength of love.
Look, here I have you; thus I let you go,
And give you to the gods.

Cæs. Adieu, be happy!

Lep. Let all the number of the stars give light
To thy fair way!

Cæs. Farewell, farewell!
Kisses Octavia.

Ant. Farewell!
Trumpets sound. Exeunt.

[Scene III. *Alexandria.* Cleopatra's *Palace.*]

Enter *Cleopatra, Charmian, Iras,* and *Alexas.*

Cleo. Where is the fellow?

Alex. Half afeard to come.

Cleo. Go to, go to!

Enter the *Messenger,* as before.

Come hither, sir.

Alex. Good Majesty,
Herod of Jewry dare not look upon you
But when you are well pleas'd.

Cleo. That Herod's head
I'll have! But how, when Antony is gone
Through whom I might command it? Come thou near.

Mess. Most gracious Majesty!

Cleo. Didst thou behold Octavia?

Mess. Ay, dread Queen.

Cleo. Where?

Mess. Madam, in Rome.
I look'd her in the face, and saw her led
Between her brother and Mark Antony.

Cleo. Is she as tall as me?

Mess. She is not, madam.

Cleo. Didst hear her speak? Is she shrill-tongu'd or low?

Mess. Madam, I heard her speak. She is low-voic'd.

Cleo. That's not so good! He cannot like her long.

Char. Like her? O Isis! 'tis impossible.

Cleo. I think so, Charmian. Dull of tongue, and dwarfish!
What majesty is in her gait? Remember,
If e'er thou look'dst on majesty.

Mess. She creeps!
Her motion and her station are as one.
She shows a body rather than a life,
A statue than a breather.

Cleo. Is this certain?

Mess. Or I have no observance.

Char. Three in Egypt
Cannot make better note.

Cleo. He's very knowing;
I do perceive't. There's nothing in her yet.
The fellow has good judgment.

Char. Excellent.

Cleo. Guess at her years, I prithee.

Mess. Madam,
She was a widow —

Cleo. Widow? Charmian, hark!

Mess. And I do think she's thirty.

Cleo. Bear'st thou her face in mind? Is't long or round?

Mess. Round even to faultiness.

Cleo. For the most part, too, they are foolish that are so.
Her hair, what colour?

Mess. Brown, madam; and her forehead
As low as she would wish it.

Cleo. There's gold for thee.
Thou must not take my former sharpness ill.
I will employ thee back again; I find thee
Most fit for business. Go, make thee ready;
Our letters are prepar'd.

[*Exit Messenger.*]

Char. A proper man.

Cleo. Indeed he is so. I repent me much

That so I harried him. Why, methinks, by him,
This creature 's no such thing.
Char. Nothing, madam.
Cleo. The man hath seen some majesty, and should know.
Char. Hath he seen majesty? Isis else defend,
And serving you so long!
Cleo. I have one thing more to ask him yet, good Charmian.
But 'tis no matter. Thou shalt bring him to me
Where I will write. All may be well enough.
Char. I warrant you, madam. *Exeunt.*

[Scene IV. *Athens.* Antony's *house.*]

Enter *Antony* and *Octavia.*

Ant. Nay, nay, Octavia; not only that —
That were excusable, that and thousands more
Of semblable import — but he hath wag'd
New wars 'gainst Pompey; made his will, and read it
To public ear;
Spoke scantly of me: when perforce he could not
But pay me terms of honour, cold and sickly
He vented them, most narrow measure lent me;
When the best hint was given him, he not took't,
Or did it from his teeth.
Octa. O, my good lord,
Believe not all; or if you must believe,
Stomach not all. A more unhappy lady,
If this division chance, ne'er stood between,
Praying for both parts.
The good gods will mock me presently
When I shall pray 'O, bless my lord and husband!'
Undo that prayer by crying out as loud
'O, bless my brother!' Husband win, win brother,
Prays, and destroys the prayer; no midway
'Twixt these extremes at all.
Ant. Gentle Octavia,
Let your best love draw to that point which seeks
Best to preserve it. If I lose mine honour,
I lose myself. Better I were not yours
Than yours so branchless. But, as you requested,
Yourself shall go between 's. The mean time, lady,
I'll raise the preparation of a war
Shall stain your brother. Make your soonest haste;
So your desires are yours.
Octa. Thanks to my lord.
The Jove of power make me most weak, most weak,
Your reconciler! Wars 'twixt you twain would be
As if the world should cleave, and that slain men
Should solder up the rift.
Ant. When it appears to you where this begins,
Turn your displeasure that way, for our faults
Can never be so equal that your love
Can equally move with them. Provide your going;
Choose your own company, and command what cost
Your heart has mind to. *Exeunt.*

[Scene V. *Athens. Another room in* Antony's *house.*]

Enter *Enobarbus* and *Eros,* [meeting].

Eno. How now, friend Eros?
Eros. There's strange news come, sir.
Eno. What, man?
Eros. Cæsar and Lepidus have made wars upon Pompey.
Eno. This is old. What is the success?
Eros. Cæsar, having made use of him in the wars 'gainst Pompey, presently denied him rivality, would not let him partake in the glory of the action; and not resting here, accuses him of letters he had formerly wrote to Pompey; upon his own appeal, seizes him. So the poor third is up till death enlarge his confine.
Eno. Then, world, thou hast a pair of chaps, no more;
And throw between them all the food thou hast,
They'll grind the one the other. Where's Antony?
Eros. He's walking in the garden thus, and spurns
The rush that lies before him; cries 'Fool Lepidus!'
And threats the throat of that his officer
That murd'red Pompey.
Eno. Our great navy 's rigg'd.
Eros. For Italy and Cæsar. More, Domitius:
My lord desires you presently. My news
I might have told hereafter.

Eno. 'Twill be naught;
But let it be. Bring me to Antony.
Eros. Come, sir. *Exeunt.*

[Scene VI. *Rome.* Cæsar's *house.*]

Enter *Agrippa, Mæcenas,* and *Cæsar.*

Cæs. Contemning Rome, he has done all this and more
In Alexandria. Here's the manner of't:
I' th' market place on a tribunal silver'd
Cleopatra and himself in chairs of gold
Were publicly enthron'd. At the feet sat
Cæsarion, whom they call my father's son,
And all the unlawful issue that their lust
Since then hath made between them. Unto her
He gave the stablishment of Egypt; made her
Of lower Syria, Cyprus, Lydia,
Absolute queen.
Mæc. This in the public eye?
Cæs. I' th' common show-place, where they exercise.
His sons he there proclaim'd the kings of kings:
Great Media, Parthia, and Armenia
He gave to Alexander; to Ptolemy he assign'd
Syria, Cilicia, and Phœnicia. She
In th' habiliments of the goddess Isis
That day appear'd; and oft before gave audience,
As 'tis reported, so.
Mæc. Let Rome be thus
Inform'd.
Agr. Who, queasy with his insolence
Already, will their good thoughts call from him.
Cæs. The people know it, and have now receiv'd
His accusations.
Agr. Who does he accuse?
Cæs. Cæsar; and that, having in Sicily
Sextus Pompeius spoil'd, we had not rated him
His part o' th' isle. Then does he say he lent me
Some shipping unrestor'd. Lastly, he frets
That Lepidus of the triumvirate
Should be depos'd; and, being, that we detain
All his revenue.
Agr. Sir, this should be answer'd.
Cæs. 'Tis done already, and the messenger gone.
I have told him Lepidus was grown too cruel,
That he his high authority abus'd
And did deserve his change. For what I have conquer'd,
I grant him part; but then in his Armenia,
And other of his conquer'd kingdoms, I
Demand the like.
Mæc. He'll never yield to that.
Cæs. Nor must not then be yielded to in this.

Enter *Octavia* with her *Train.*

Octa. Hail, Cæsar, and my lord! hail, most dear Cæsar!
Cæs. That ever I should call thee castaway!
Octa. You have not call'd me so, nor have you cause.
Cæs. Why have you stol'n upon us thus? You come not
Like Cæsar's sister. The wife of Antony
Should have an army for an usher, and
The neighs of horse to tell of her approach
Long ere she did appear. The trees by th' way
Should have borne men, and expectation fainted,
Longing for what it had not. Nay, the dust
Should have ascended to the roof of heaven,
Rais'd by your populous troops. But you are come
A market-maid to Rome, and have prevented
The ostentation of our love, which, left unshown,
Is often left unlov'd. We should have met you
By sea and land, supplying every stage
With an augmented greeting.
Octa. Good my lord,
To come thus was I not constrain'd, but did it
On my free will. My lord, Mark Antony,
Hearing that you prepar'd for war, acquainted
My grieved ear withal; whereon I begg'd
His pardon for return.
Cæs. Which soon he granted,
Being an abstract 'tween his lust and him.
Octa. Do not say so, my lord.
Cæs. I have eyes upon him,
And his affairs come to me on the wind.
Where is he now?
Octa. My lord, in Athens.
Cæs. No, my most wronged sister. Cleopatra
Hath nodded him to her. He hath given his empire
Up to a whore, who now are levying
The kings o' th' earth for war. He hath assembled
Bocchus, the king of Libya; Archelaus,
Of Cappadocia; Philadelphos, king
Of Paphlagonia; the Thracian king, Adallas;
King Malchus of Arabia; King of Pont;
Herod of Jewry; Mithridates, king

Of Comagene; Polemon and Amyntas,
The kings of Mede and Lycaonia, with a
More larger list of sceptres.
Octa. Ay me most wretched,
That have my heart parted betwixt two friends
That do afflict each other!
Cæs. Welcome hither.
Your letters did withhold our breaking forth,
Till we perceived both how you were wrong'd
And we in negligent danger. Cheer your heart!
Be you not troubled with the time, which drives
O'er your content these strong necessities;
But let determin'd things to destiny
Hold unbewail'd their way. Welcome to Rome,
Nothing more dear to me! You are abus'd
Beyond the mark of thought; and the high gods,
To do you justice, make them ministers
Of us and those that love you. Best of comfort,
And ever welcome to us!
Agr. Welcome, lady.
Mæc. Welcome, dear madam.
Each heart in Rome does love and pity you.
Only th' adulterous Antony, most large
In his abominations, turns you off
And gives his potent regiment to a trull
That noises it against us.
Octa. Is it so, sir?
Cæs. Most certain. Sister, welcome. Pray you
Be ever known to patience. My dear'st sister!
Exeunt.

[Scene VII. Antony's *camp, near Actium.*]

Enter *Cleopatra* and *Enobarbus.*

Cleo. I will be even with thee, doubt it not.
Eno. But why, why, why?
Cleo. Thou hast forspoke my being in these wars,
And say'st it is not fit.
Eno. Well, is it, is it?
Cleo. Is't not denounc'd against us? Why should not we
Be there in person?
Eno. [*aside*] Well, I could reply:
If we should serve with horse and mares together,
The horse were merely lost; the mares would bear
A soldier and his horse.
Cleo. What is't you say?
Eno. Your presence needs must puzzle Antony;
Take from his heart, take from his brain, from 's time,
What should not then be spar'd. He is already
Traduc'd for levity; and 'tis said in Rome
That Photinus an eunuch and your maids
Manage this war.
Cleo. Sink Rome, and their tongues rot
That speak against us! A charge we bear i' th' war
And, as the president of my kingdom, will
Appear there for a man. Speak not against it.
I will not stay behind!

Enter *Antony* and *Canidius.*

Eno. Nay, I have done.
Here comes the Emperor.
Ant. Is it not strange, Canidius,
That from Tarentum and Brundusium
He could so quickly cut the Ionian sea
And take in Toryne? — You have heard on't, sweet?
Cleo. Celerity is never more admir'd
Than by the negligent.
Ant. A good rebuke,
Which might have well becom'd the best of men
To taunt at slackness. Canidius, we
Will fight with him by sea.
Cleo. By sea? What else?
Can. Why will my lord do so?
Ant. For that he dares us to't.
Eno. So hath my lord dar'd him to single fight.
Can. Ay, and to wage this battle at Pharsalia,
Where Cæsar fought with Pompey. But these offers,
Which serve not for his vantage, he shakes off;
And so should you.
Eno. Your ships are not well mann'd;
Your mariners are muleters, reapers, people
Ingross'd by swift impress. In Cæsar's fleet
Are those that often have 'gainst Pompey fought;
Their ships are yare; yours, heavy. No disgrace
Shall fall you for refusing him at sea,
Being prepar'd for land.
Ant. By sea, by sea!
Eno. Most worthy sir, you therein throw away
The absolute soldiership you have by land;
Distract your army, which doth most consist
Of war-mark'd footmen; leave unexecuted
Your own renowned knowledge; quite forgo
The way which promises assurance, and

Give up yourself merely to chance and hazard
From firm security.

Ant. I'll fight at sea.

Cleo. I have sixty sails, Cæsar none better.

Ant. Our overplus of shipping will we burn,
And with the rest full-mann'd, from th' head of Actium
Beat the approaching Cæsar. But if we fail,
We then can do't at land.

Enter a *Messenger*.

Thy business?

Mess. The news is true, my lord. He is descried;
Cæsar has taken Toryne.

Ant. Can he be there in person? 'Tis impossible;
Strange that his power should be! Canidius,
Our nineteen legions thou shalt hold by land
And our twelve thousand horse. We'll to our ship.
Away, my Thetis!

Enter a *Soldier*.

How now, worthy soldier?

Sold. O noble Emperor, do not fight by sea!
Trust not to rotten planks. Do you misdoubt
This sword and these my wounds? Let the Egyptians
And the Phœnicians go a-ducking. We
Have us'd to conquer standing on the earth
And fighting foot to foot.

Ant. Well, well. Away!

Exeunt Antony, Cleopatra, and Enobarbus.

Sold. By Hercules, I think I am i' th' right.

Can. Soldier, thou art; but his whole action grows
Not in the power on't. So our leader's led,
And we are women's men.

Sold. You keep by land
The legions and the horse whole, do you not?

Can. Marcus Octavius, Marcus Justeius,
Publicola, and Cælius are for sea;
But we keep whole by land. This speed of Cæsar's
Carries beyond belief.

Sold. While he was yet in Rome,
His power went out in such distractions as
Beguil'd all spies.

Can. Who's his lieutenant, hear you?

Sold. They say, one Taurus.

Can. Well I know the man.

Enter a *Messenger*.

Mess. The Emperor calls Canidius.

Can. With news the time's with labour and throes forth
Each minute some. *Exeunt.*

[Scene VIII. *A plain near Actium.*]

Enter *Cæsar*, with his *Army*, marching.

Cæs. Taurus!

Taur. My lord?

Cæs. Strike not by land; keep whole: provoke not battle
Till we have done at sea. Do not exceed
The prescript of this scroll. Our fortune lies
Upon this jump. *Exeunt.*

[Scene IX. *Another part of the plain.*]

Enter *Antony* and *Enobarbus*.

Ant. Set we our squadrons on yond side o' th' hill
In eye of Cæsar's battle; from which place
We may the number of the ships behold,
And so proceed accordingly. *Exeunt.*

[Scene X. *Another part of the plain.*]

Canidius marcheth with his land army one way over the stage, and *Taurus*, the *Lieutenant* of *Cæsar*, the other way. After their going in, is heard the noise of a sea-fight.

Alarum. Enter *Enobarbus*.

Eno. Naught, naught, all naught! I can behold no longer.
Th' Antoniad, the Egyptian admiral,
With all their sixty, fly and turn the rudder.
To see't mine eyes are blasted.

Enter *Scarus*.

Scar. Gods and goddesses,
All the whole synod of them!

Eno. What's thy passion?

Scar. The greater cantle of the world is lost
With very ignorance. We have kiss'd away
Kingdoms and provinces.

Eno. How appears the fight?

Scar. On our side like the token'd pestilence
Where death is sure. Yon ribald-rid nag of Egypt
(Whom leprosy o'ertake!) i' th' midst o' th' fight,
When vantage like a pair of twins appear'd,
Both as the same, or rather ours the elder, —
The breese upon her, like a cow in June, —
Hoists sails, and flies.

Eno. That I beheld.
Mine eyes did sicken at the sight and could not
Endure a further view.

Scar. She once being loof'd,
The noble ruin of her magic, Antony,
Claps on his sea-wing, and (like a doting mallard)
Leaving the fight in heighth, flies after her.
I never saw an action of such shame.
Experience, manhood, honour, ne'er before
Did violate so itself.

Eno. Alack, alack!

Enter *Canidius.*

Can. Our fortune on the sea is out of breath
And sinks most lamentably. Had our general
Been what he knew himself, it had gone well.
O, he has given example for our flight
Most grossly by his own!

Eno. Ay, are you thereabouts?
Why then, good night indeed.

Can. Toward Peloponnesus are they fled.

Scar. 'Tis easy to't; and there I will attend
What further comes.

Can. To Cæsar will I render
My legions and my horse. Six kings already
Show me the way of yielding.

Eno. I'll yet follow
The wounded chance of Antony, though my reason
Sits in the wind against me. [*Exeunt.*]

[Scene XI. *Alexandria.* Cleopatra's *Palace.*]

Enter *Antony* with *Attendants.*

Ant. Hark! the land bids me tread no more upon't!
It is asham'd to bear me! Friends, come hither.
I am so lated in the world that I
Have lost my way for ever. I have a ship
Laden with gold. Take that; divide it. Fly,
And make your peace with Cæsar.

Omnes. Fly? Not we!

Ant. I have fled myself, and have instructed cowards
To run and show their shoulders. Friends, be gone.
I have myself resolv'd upon a course
Which has no need of you. Be gone.
My treasure's in the harbour. Take it! O,
I follow'd that I blush to look upon.
My very hairs do mutiny; for the white
Reprove the brown for rashness, and they them
For fear and doting. Friends, be gone. You shall
Have letters from me to some friends that will
Sweep your way for you. Pray you look not sad
Nor make replies of loathness. Take the hint
Which my despair proclaims. Let that be left
Which leaves itself. To the seaside straightway!
I will possess you of that ship and treasure.
Leave me, I pray, a little; pray you now!
Nay, do so; for indeed I have lost command;
Therefore I pray you. I'll see you by and by.
Sits down.

Enter *Cleopatra* led by *Charmian* and *Iras,* [*Eros* following].

Eros. Nay, gentle madam, to him! comfort him!

Iras. Do, most dear Queen.

Char. Do? Why, what else?

Cleo. Let me sit down. O Juno!

Ant. No, no, no, no, no!

Eros. See you here, sir?

Ant. O fie, fie, fie!

Char. Madam!

Iras. Madam, O good Empress!

Eros. Sir, sir!

Ant. Yes, my lord, yes! He at Philippi kept
His sword e'en like a dancer, while I struck
The lean and wrinkled Cassius; and 'twas I
That the mad Brutus ended. He alone
Dealt on lieutenantry and no practice had
In the brave squares of war. Yet now — No matter.

Cleo. Ah, stand by!

Eros. The Queen, my lord, the Queen!

Iras. Go to him, madam, speak to him.
He is unqualitied with very shame.

Cleo. Well then, sustain me. O!

Eros. Most noble sir, arise. The Queen approaches.
Her head's declin'd, and death will seize her, but
Your comfort makes the rescue.

Ant. I have offended reputation —
A most unnoble swerving.

Eros. Sir, the Queen.

Ant. O, whither hast thou led me, Egypt? See
How I convey my shame out of thine eyes
By looking back what I have left behind
Stroy'd in dishonour.

Cleo. O my lord, my lord,
Forgive my fearful sails! I little thought
You would have followed.

Ant. Egypt, thou knew'st too well
My heart was to thy rudder tied by th' strings,
And thou shouldst tow me after. O'er my spirit
Thy full supremacy thou knew'st, and that
Thy beck might from the bidding of the gods
Command me.

Cleo. O, my pardon!

Ant. Now I must
To the young man send humble treaties, dodge
And palter in the shifts of lowness, who
With half the bulk o' th' world play'd as I pleas'd,
Making and marring fortunes. You did know
How much you were my conqueror, and that
My sword, made weak by my affection, would
Obey it on all cause.

Cleo. Pardon, pardon!

Ant. Fall not a tear, I say. One of them rates
All that is won and lost. Give me a kiss.
Even this repays me. We sent our schoolmaster.
Is 'a come back? Love, I am full of lead.
Some wine, within there, and our viands! Fortune knows
We scorn her most when most she offers blows.

Exeunt.

[Scene XII. Cæsar's *camp in Egypt.*]

Enter *Cæsar, Agrippa, Dolabella,* [*Thyreus,*] with others.

Cæs. Let him appear that's come from Antony.
Know you him?

Dol. Cæsar, 'tis his schoolmaster.
An argument that he is pluck'd, when hither
He sends so poor a pinion of his wing,
Which had superfluous kings for messengers
Not many moons gone by.

Enter [*Euphronius,*] *Ambassador* from *Antony.*

Cæs. Approach and speak.

Amb. Such as I am, I come from Antony.
I was of late as petty to his ends
As is the morn-dew on the myrtle leaf
To his grand sea.

Cæs. Be't so. Declare thine office.

Amb. Lord of his fortunes he salutes thee, and
Requires to live in Egypt; which not granted,
He lessens his requests and to thee sues
To let him breathe between the heavens and earth,
A private man in Athens. This for him.
Next, Cleopatra does confess thy greatness,
Submits her to thy might, and of thee craves
The circle of the Ptolemies for her heirs,
Now hazarded to thy grace.

Cæs. For Antony,
I have no ears to his request. The Queen
Of audience nor desire shall fail, so she
From Egypt drive her all-disgraced friend
Or take his life there. This if she perform,
She shall not sue unheard. So to them both.

Amb. Fortune pursue thee!

Cæs. Bring him through the bands.

[*Exit Ambassador.*]

[*To Thyreus*] To try thy eloquence now 'tis time. Dispatch.
From Antony win Cleopatra. Promise,
And in our name, what she requires; add more,
From thine invention, offers. Women are not
In their best fortunes strong, but want will perjure
The ne'er-touch'd Vestal. Try thy cunning, Thyreus.
Make thine own edict for thy pains, which we
Will answer as a law.

Thyr. Cæsar, I go.

Cæs. Observe how Antony becomes his flaw,
And what thou think'st his very action speaks
In every power that moves.

Thyr. Cæsar, I shall.

Exeunt.

[Scene XIII. *Alexandria.* Cleopatra's *Palace.*]

Enter *Cleopatra, Enobarbus, Charmian,* and *Iras.*

Cleo. What shall we do, Enobarbus?

Eno. Think, and die.

Cleo. Is Antony or we in fault for this?

Eno. Antony only, that would make his will
Lord of his reason. What though you fled
From that great face of war whose several ranges
Frighted each other? Why should he follow?
The itch of his affection should not then

Have nick'd his captainship, at such a point,
When half to half the world oppos'd, he being
The meered question. 'Twas a shame no less
Than was his loss, to course your flying flags
And leave his navy gazing.
Cleo. Prithee peace!

Enter the *Ambassador* [*Euphronius*] with *Antony*.

Ant. Is that his answer?
Amb. Ay, my lord.
Ant. The Queen shall then have courtesy, so she
Will yield us up.
Amb. He says so.
Ant. Let her know't.
To the boy Cæsar send this grizzled head,
And he will fill thy wishes to the brim
With principalities.
Cleo. That head, my lord?
Ant. To him again! Tell him he wears the rose
Of youth upon him; from which the world should note
Something particular. His coin, ships, legions
May be a coward's, whose ministers would prevail
Under the service of a child as soon
As i' th' command of Cæsar. I dare him therefore
To lay his gay comparisons apart
And answer me declin'd, sword against sword,
Ourselves alone. I'll write it. Follow me.
[*Exeunt Antony and Ambassador.*]
Eno. [*aside*] Yes, like enough high-battled Cæsar will
Unstate his happiness and be stag'd to th' show
Against a sworder! I see men's judgments are
A parcel of their fortunes, and things outward
Do draw the inward quality after them
To suffer all alike. That he should dream,
Knowing all measures, the full Cæsar will
Answer his emptiness! Cæsar, thou hast subdu'd
His judgment too.

Enter a *Servant*.

Serv. A messenger from Cæsar.
Cleo. What, no more ceremony? See, my women!
Against the blown rose may they stop their nose
That kneel'd unto the buds. Admit him, sir.
[*Exit Servant.*]
Eno. [*aside*] Mine honesty and I begin to square.
The loyalty well held to fools does make
Our faith mere folly. Yet he that can endure
To follow with allegiance a fall'n lord
Does conquer him that did his master conquer
And earns a place i' th' story.

Enter *Thyreus*.

Cleo. Cæsar's will?
Thyr. Hear it apart.
Cleo. None but friends. Say boldly.
Thyr. So haply are they friends to Antony.
Eno. He needs as many, sir, as Cæsar has,
Or needs not us. If Cæsar please, our master
Will leap to be his friend. For us, you know
Whose he is we are, and that is Cæsar's.
Thyr. So.
Thus then, thou most renown'd: Cæsar entreats
Not to consider in what case thou stand'st
Further than he is Cæsar.
Cleo. Go on. Right royal!
Thyr. He knows that you embrace not Antony
As you did love, but as you fear'd him.
Cleo. O!
Thyr. The scars upon your honour, therefore, he
Does pity, as constrained blemishes,
Not as deserv'd.
Cleo. He is a god, and knows
What is most right. Mine honour was not yielded,
But conquer'd merely.
Eno. [*aside*] To be sure of that,
I will ask Antony. Sir, sir, thou art so leaky
That we must leave thee to thy sinking, for
Thy dearest quit thee. *Exit.*
Thyr. Shall I say to Cæsar
What you require of him? For he partly begs
To be desir'd to give. It much would please him
That of his fortunes you should make a staff
To lean upon. But it would warm his spirits
To hear from me you had left Antony
And put yourself under his shrowd,
The universal landlord.
Cleo. What's your name?
Thyr. My name is Thyreus.
Cleo. Most kind messenger,
Say to great Cæsar this: in deputation
I kiss his conqu'ring hand. Tell him I am prompt
To lay my crown at's feet, and there to kneel.
Tell him, from his all-obeying breath I hear
The doom of Egypt.
Thyr. 'Tis your noblest course.

Wisdom and fortune combating together,
If that the former dare but what it can,
No chance may shake it. Give me grace to lay
My duty on your hand.

Cleo. Your Cæsar's father oft,
When he hath mus'd of taking kingdoms in,
Bestow'd his lips on that unworthy place
As it rain'd kisses.

Enter *Antony* and *Enobarbus*.

Ant. Favours, by Jove that thunders!
What art thou, fellow?

Thyr. One that but performs
The bidding of the fullest man, and worthiest
To have command obey'd.

Eno. [*aside*] You will be whipp'd.

Ant. Approach there! — Ah, you kite! — Now, gods and devils!
Authority melts from me. Of late, when I cried 'Ho!'
Like boys unto a muss, kings would start forth
And cry 'Your will?' Have you no ears? I am
Antony yet.

Enter *Servants*.

Take hence this Jack and whip him.

Eno. [*aside*] 'Tis better playing with a lion's whelp
Than with an old one dying.

Ant. Moon and stars!
Whip him. Were't twenty of the greatest tributaries
That do acknowledge Cæsar, should I find them
So saucy with the hand of she here — what's her name
Since she was Cleopatra? Whip him, fellows,
Till like a boy you see him cringe his face
And whine aloud for mercy. Take him hence.

Thyr. Mark Antony —

Ant. Tug him away. Being whipp'd,
Bring him again. This Jack of Cæsar's shall
Bear us an errand to him.

Exeunt [*Servants*] *with Thyreus.*

You were half blasted ere I knew you. Ha!
Have I my pillow left unpress'd in Rome,
Forborne the getting of a lawful race,
And by a gem of women, to be abus'd
By one that looks on feeders?

Cleo. Good my lord —

Ant. You have been a boggler ever.
But when we in our viciousness grow hard
(O misery on't!) the wise gods seel our eyes,
In our own filth drop our clear judgments, make us
Adore our errors, laugh at's while we strut
To our confusion.

Cleo. O, is't come to this?

Ant. I found you as a morsel cold upon
Dead Cæsar's trencher. Nay, you were a fragment
Of Gneius Pompey's, besides what hotter hours,
Unregist'red in vulgar fame, you have
Luxuriously pick'd out: for I am sure,
Though you can guess what temperance should be,
You know not what it is.

Cleo. Wherefore is this?

Ant. To let a fellow that will take rewards,
And say 'God quit you!' be familiar with
My playfellow, your hand, this kingly seal
And plighter of high hearts! O that I were
Upon the hill of Basan to outroar
The horned herd! for I have savage cause,
And to proclaim it civilly were like
A halter'd neck which does the hangman thank
For being yare about him.

Enter a *Servant* with *Thyreus*.

Is he whipp'd?

Serv. Soundly, my lord.

Ant. Cried he? and begg'd 'a pardon?

Serv. He did ask favour.

Ant. If that thy father live, let him repent
Thou wast not made his daughter; and be thou sorry
To follow Cæsar in his triumph, since
Thou hast been whipp'd for following him. Henceforth
The white hand of a lady fever thee!
Shake thou to look on't! Get thee back to Cæsar;
Tell him thy entertainment. Look thou say
He makes me angry with him; for he seems
Proud and disdainful, harping on what I am,
Not what he knew I was. He makes me angry;
And at this time most easy 'tis to do't,
When my good stars that were my former guides
Have empty left their orbs and shot their fires
Into th' abysm of hell. If he mislike
My speech and what is done, tell him he has
Hipparchus, my enfranched bondman, whom
He may at pleasure whip or hang or torture,
As he shall like, to quit me. Urge it thou.
Hence with thy stripes, be gone!

Exit Thyreus.

Cleo. Have you done yet?

Ant. Alack, our terrene moon
Is now eclips'd, and it portends alone
The fall of Antony!

Cleo. I must stay his time.

Ant. To flatter Cæsar, would you mingle eyes
With one that ties his points?
Cleo. Not know me yet?
Ant. Cold-hearted toward me?
Cleo. Ah, dear, if I be so,
From my cold heart let heaven engender hail,
And poison it in the source, and the first stone
Drop in my neck; as it determines, so
Dissolve my life! The next Cæsarion smite!
Till by degrees the memory of my womb,
Together with my brave Egyptians all,
By the discandying of this pelleted storm,
Lie graveless, till the flies and gnats of Nile
Have buried them for prey!
Ant. I am satisfied.
Cæsar sits down in Alexandria, where
I will oppose his fate. Our force by land
Hath nobly held; our sever'd navy too
Have knit again, and fleet, threat'ning most sea-like.
Where hast thou been, my heart? Dost thou hear, lady?
If from the field I shall return once more
To kiss these lips, I will appear in blood.
I and my sword will earn our chronicle.
There's hope in't yet.
Cleo. That's my brave lord!
Ant. I will be treble-sinewed, hearted, breath'd,
And fight maliciously. For when mine hours
Were nice and lucky, men did ransom lives
Of me for jests; but now I'll set my teeth
And send to darkness all that stop me. Come,
Let's have one other gaudy night. Call to me
All my sad captains; fill our bowls once more.
Let's mock the midnight bell.
Cleo. It is my birthday.
I had thought t' have held it poor; but since my lord
Is Antony again, I will be Cleopatra.
Ant. We will yet do well.
Cleo. Call all his noble captains to my lord.
Ant. Do so, we'll speak to them; and to-night I'll force
The wine peep through their scars. Come on, my queen,
There's sap in't yet! The next time I do fight,
I'll make Death love me; for I will contend
Even with his pestilent scythe.
Exeunt [*all but Enobarbus*].
Eno. Now he'll outstare the lightning. To be furious
Is to be frighted out of fear, and in that mood
The dove will peck the estridge. I see still
A diminution in our captain's brain
Restores his heart. When valour preys on reason,
It eats the sword it fights with. I will seek
Some way to leave him. *Exit.*

[ACT IV. Scene I. Cæsar's *camp before Alexandria.*]

Enter *Cæsar, Agrippa,* and *Mæcenas,* with his *Army*; *Cæsar* reading a letter.

Cæs. He calls me boy, and chides as he had power
To beat me out of Egypt. My messenger
He hath whipp'd with rods; dares me to personal combat,
Cæsar to Antony. Let the old ruffian know
I have many other ways to die, meantime
Laugh at his challenge.
Mæc. Cæsar must think,
When one so great begins to rage, he's hunted
Even to falling. Give him no breath, but now
Make boot of his distraction. Never anger
Made good guard for itself.
Cæs. Let our best heads
Know that to-morrow the last of many battles
We mean to fight. Within our files there are,
Of those that serv'd Mark Antony but late,
Enough to fetch him in. See it done;
And feast the army. We have store to do't,
And they have earn'd the waste. Poor Antony!
Exeunt.

[Scene II. *Alexandria.* Cleopatra's *Palace.*]

Enter *Antony, Cleopatra, Enobarbus, Charmian, Iras, Alexas,* with others.

Ant. He will not fight with me, Domitius?
Eno. No.
Ant. Why should he not?
Eno. He thinks, being twenty times of better fortune,
He is twenty men to one.
Ant. To-morrow, soldier,
By sea and land I'll fight. Or I will live,
Or bathe my dying honour in the blood
Shall make it live again. Woo't thou fight well?

Eno. I'll strike, and cry 'Take all!'

Ant. Well said. Come on.
Call forth my household servants. Let's to-night
Be bounteous at our meal.

Enter three or four *Servitors.*

Give me thy hand,
Thou hast been rightly honest. So hast thou;
And thou, and thou, and thou. You have serv'd me well,
And kings have been your fellows.

Cleo. [*aside to Enobarbus*] What means this?

Eno. [*aside to Cleopatra*] 'Tis one of those odd tricks which sorrow shoots
Out of the mind.

Ant. And thou art honest too.
I wish I could be made so many men,
And all of you clapp'd up together in
An Antony, that I might do you service
So good as you have done.

Omnes. The gods forbid!

Ant. Well, my good fellows, wait on me to-night.
Scant not my cups, and make as much of me
As when mine empire was your fellow too
And suffer'd my command.

Cleo. [*aside to Enobarbus*] What does he mean?

Eno. [*aside to Cleopatra*] To make his followers weep.

Ant. Tend me to-night.
May be it is the period of your duty.
Haply you shall not see me more; or if,
A mangled shadow. Perchance to-morrow
You'll serve another master. I look on you
As one that takes his leave. Mine honest friends,
I turn you not away; but, like a master
Married to your good service, stay till death.
Tend me to-night two hours, I ask no more,
And the gods yield you for't!

Eno. What mean you, sir,
To give them this discomfort? Look, they weep,
And I, an ass, am onion-ey'd. For shame!
Transform us not to women.

Ant. Ho, ho, ho!
Now the witch take me if I meant it thus!
Grace grow where those drops fall! My hearty friends,
You take me in too dolorous a sense;
For I spake to you for your comfort, did desire you
To burn this night with torches. Know, my hearts,
I hope well of to-morrow, and will lead you
Where rather I'll expect victorious life
Than death and honour. Let's to supper, come,
And drown consideration. *Exeunt.*

[Scene III. *Alexandria. Before* Cleopatra's *Palace.*]

Enter a *Company of Soldiers.*

1. Sold. Brother, good night. To-morrow is the day.

2. Sold. It will determine one way. Fare you well.
Heard you of nothing strange about the streets?

1. Sold. Nothing. What news?

2. Sold. Belike 'tis but a rumour. Good night to you.

1. Sold. Well, sir, good night.

They meet other Soldiers.

2. Sold. Soldiers, have careful watch.

3. Sold. And you. Good night, good night.

They place themselves in every corner of the stage.

4. Sold. Here we. And if to-morrow
Our navy thrive, I have an absolute hope
Our landmen will stand up.

3. Sold. 'Tis a brave army,
And full of purpose.

Music of the hautboys is under the stage.

2. Sold. Peace! What noise?

1. Sold. List, list!

2. Sold. Hark!

1. Sold. Music i' th' air.

3. Sold. Under the earth.

4. Sold. It signs well, does it not?

3. Sold. No.

1. Sold. Peace, I say!
What should this mean?

2. Sold. 'Tis the god Hercules, whom Antony lov'd,
Now leaves him.

1. Sold. Walk. Let's see if other watchmen
Do hear what we do.

2. Sold. How now, masters?

Omnes. (*speak together*) How now?
How now? Do you hear this?

1. Sold. Ay. Is't not strange?

3. Sold. Do you hear, masters? Do you hear?

1. Sold. Follow the noise so far as we have quarter.
Let's see how it will give off.
Omnes. Content. 'Tis strange. *Exeunt.*

[Scene IV. *Alexandria.* Cleopatra's *Palace.*]

Enter *Antony* and *Cleopatra,* [*Charmian, Iras,*] with others.

Ant. Eros! mine armour, Eros!
Cleo. Sleep a little.
Ant. No, my chuck. Eros! Come, mine armour, Eros!

Enter *Eros* [with armour].

Come, good fellow, put mine iron on.
If fortune be not ours to-day, it is
Because we brave her. Come.
Cleo. Nay, I'll help too.
What's this for?
Ant. Ah, let be, let be! Thou art
The armourer of my heart. False, false! This, this!
Cleo. Sooth, la, I'll help. Thus it must be.
Ant. Well, well.
We shall thrive now. Seest thou, my good fellow?
Go put on thy defences.
Eros. Briefly, sir.
Cleo. Is not this buckled well?
Ant. Rarely, rarely!
He that unbuckles this, till we do please
To daff't for our repose, shall hear a storm.
Thou fumblest, Eros, and my queen's a squire
More tight at this than thou. Dispatch. O love,
That thou couldst see my wars to-day, and knew'st
The royal occupation! Thou shouldst see
A workman in't.

Enter an armed *Soldier.*

Good morrow to thee! Welcome.
Thou look'st like him that knows a warlike charge.
To business that we love we rise betime
And go to't with delight.
Sold. A thousand, sir,
Early though't be, have on their riveted trim
And at the port expect you.

[*Shout. Trumpets. Flourish.* Enter *Captains* and *Soldiers.*

Capt. The morn is fair. Good morrow, General.
All. Good morrow, General.
Ant. 'Tis well blown, lads.
This morning, like the spirit of a youth
That means to be of note, begins betimes.
So, so. Come, give me that! This way. Well said.
Fare thee well, dame, whate'er becomes of me.
This is a soldier's kiss. Rebukable
And worthy shameful check it were to stand
On more mechanic compliment. I'll leave thee
Now like a man of steel. You that will fight,
Follow me close; I'll bring you to't. Adieu.
Exeunt [*Antony, Eros, Captains, and Soldiers*].
Char. Please you retire to your chamber?
Cleo. Lead me.
He goes forth gallantly. That he and Cæsar might
Determine this great war in single fight!
Then Antony — but now — Well, on! *Exeunt.*

[Scene V. *Alexandria.* Antony's *camp.*]

Trumpets sound. Enter *Antony* and *Eros.* [a *Soldier* meeting them].

Sold. The gods make this a happy day to Antony!
Ant. Would thou and those thy scars had once prevail'd
To make me fight at land!
Sold. Hadst thou done so,
The kings that have revolted and the soldier
That has this morning left thee would have still
Followed thy heels.
Ant. Who's gone this morning?
Sold. Who?
One ever near thee. Call for Enobarbus,
He shall not hear thee, or from Cæsar's camp
Say 'I am none of thine.'
Ant. What sayest thou?
Sold. Sir,
He is with Cæsar.
Eros. Sir, his chests and treasure
He has not with him.
Ant. Is he gone?
Sold. Most certain.
Ant. Go, Eros, send his treasure after. Do it;
Detain no jot, I charge thee. Write to him

(I will subscribe) gentle adieus and greetings.
Say that I wish he never find more cause
To change a master. O, my fortunes have
Corrupted honest men! Dispatch. Enobarbus!
Exeunt.

[Scene VI. *Alexandria.* Cæsar's *camp.*]

Flourish. Enter *Agrippa, Cæsar,* with *Enobarbus,* and *Dolabella.*

Cæs. Go forth, Agrippa, and begin the fight.
Our will is Antony be took alive.
Make it so known.
Agr. Cæsar, I shall. [*Exit.*]
Cæs. The time of universal peace is near.
Prove this a prosp'rous day, the three-nook'd world
Shall bear the olive freely.

Enter a *Messenger.*

Mess. Antony
Is come into the field.
Cæs. Go charge Agrippa
Plant those that have revolted in the van,
That Antony may seem to spend his fury
Upon himself.
Exeunt [*all but Enobarbus*].
Eno. Alexas did revolt and went to Jewry on
Affairs of Antony; there did dissuade
Great Herod to incline himself to Cæsar
And leave his master Antony. For this pains
Cæsar hath hang'd him. Canidius and the rest
That fell away have entertainment, but
No honourable trust. I have done ill,
Of which I do accuse myself so sorely,
That I will joy no more.

Enter a *Soldier* of *Cæsar's.*

Sold. Enobarbus, Antony
Hath after thee sent all thy treasure, with
His bounty overplus. The messenger
Came on my guard and at thy tent is now
Unloading of his mules.
Eno. I give it you!
Sold. Mock not, Enobarbus.
I tell you true. Best you saf'd the bringer
Out of the host. I must attend mine office
Or would have done't myself. Your emperor
Continues still a Jove. *Exit.*
Eno. I am alone the villain of the earth,
And feel I am so most. O Antony,
Thou mine of bounty, how wouldst thou have paid
My better service, when my turpitude
Thou dost so crown with gold! This blows my heart.
If swift thought break it not, a swifter mean
Shall outstrike thought; but thought will do't, I feel.
I fight against thee? No! I will go seek
Some ditch wherein to die; the foul'st best fits
My latter part of life. *Exit.*

[Scene VII. *Field of battle between the camps.*]

Alarum. Drums and trumpets. Enter *Agrippa* [and others].

Agr. Retire. We have engag'd ourselves too far.
Cæsar himself has work, and our oppression
Exceeds what we expected. *Exeunt.*

Alarums. Enter *Antony,* and *Scarus* wounded.

Scar. O my brave Emperor, this is fought indeed!
Had we done so at first, we had droven them home
With clouts about their heads.
Ant. Thou bleed'st apace.
Scar. I had a wound here that was like a T,
But now 'tis made an H.
[*Sound retreat*] *far off.*
Ant. They do retire.
Scar. We'll beat 'em into bench-holes. I have yet
Room for six scotches more.

Enter *Eros.*

Eros. They are beaten, sir, and our advantage serves
For a fair victory.
Scar. Let us score their backs
And snatch 'em up, as we take hares, behind!
'Tis sport to maul a runner.
Ant. I will reward thee
Once for thy sprightly comfort, and tenfold
For thy good valour. Come thee on!
Scar. I'll halt after.
Exeunt.

[Scene VIII. *Under the walls of Alexandria.*]

Alarum. Enter *Antony* again in a march; *Scarus,* with others.

Ant. We have beat him to his camp. Run one before
And let the Queen know of our gests. To-morrow,
Before the sun shall see 's, we'll spill the blood
That has to-day escap'd. I thank you all;
For doughty-handed are you, and have fought
Not as you serv'd the cause, but as 't had been
Each man's like mine. You have shown all Hectors.
Enter the city, clip your wives, your friends,
Tell them your feats, whilst they with joyful tears
Wash the congealment from your wounds and kiss
The honour'd gashes whole.

Enter *Cleopatra* [attended].

[*To Scarus*] Give me thy hand. —
To this great fairy I'll commend thy acts,
Make her thanks bless thee. [*To Cleopatra*] O thou day o' th' world,
Chain mine arm'd neck! Leap thou, attire and all,
Through proof of harness to my heart, and there
Ride on the pants triumphing!

Cleo. Lord of lords!
O infinite virtue, com'st thou smiling from
The world's great snare uncaught?

Ant. My nightingale,
We have beat them to their beds. What, girl! though grey
Do something mingle with our younger brown, yet ha' we
A brain that nourishes our nerves, and can
Get goal for goal of youth. Behold this man.
Commend unto his lips thy favouring hand. —
Kiss it, my warrior! — He hath fought to-day
As if a god in hate of mankind had
Destroyed in such a shape.

Cleo. I'll give thee, friend,
An armour all of gold. It was a king's.

Ant. He has deserv'd it, were it carbuncled
Like holy Phœbus' car. Give me thy hand.
Through Alexandria make a jolly march;
Bear our hack'd targets like the men that owe them.
Had our great palace the capacity
To camp this host, we all would sup together
And drink carouses to the next day's fate,
Which promises royal peril. Trumpeters,
With brazen din blast you the city's ear;
Make mingle with our rattling tabourines,
That heaven and earth may strike their sounds together,
Applauding our approach. *Exeunt.*

[Scene IX. Cæsar's *camp.*]

Enter a *Sentry* and his *Company. Enobarbus* follows.

Sent. If we be not reliev'd within this hour,
We must return to th' court of guard. The night
Is shiny, and they say we shall embattle
By th' second hour i' th' morn.

1. Watch. This last day was
A shrewd one to's.

Eno. O, bear me witness, night —

2. Watch. What man is this?

1. Watch. Stand close, and list him.

Eno. Be witness to me, O thou blessed moon,
When men revolted shall upon record
Bear hateful memory, poor Enobarbus did
Before thy face repent!

Sent. Enobarbus?

2. Watch. Peace!
Hark further.

Eno. O sovereign mistress of true melancholy,
The poisonous damp of night disponge upon me,
That life, a very rebel to my will,
May hang no longer on me! Throw my heart
Against the flint and hardness of my fault,
Which, being dried with grief, will break to powder,
And finish all foul thoughts. O Antony,
Nobler than my revolt is infamous,
Forgive me in thine own particular,
But let the world rank me in register
A master-leaver and a fugitive!
O Antony! O Antony! [*Dies.*]

1. Watch. Let's speak
To him.

Sent. Let's hear him, for the things he speaks
May concern Cæsar.

2. Watch. Let's do so. But he sleeps.

Sent. Swoonds rather; for so bad a prayer as his
Was never yet for sleep.

1. Watch. Go we to him.

2. Watch. Awake, sir, awake! Speak to us!
1. Watch. Hear you, sir?
Sent. The hand of death hath raught him. (*Drums afar off.*) Hark! The drums
Demurely wake the sleepers. Let us bear him
To th' court of guard. He is of note. Our hour
Is fully out.
2. Watch. Come on then.
He may recover yet. *Exeunt* [*with the body*].

[Scene X. *Between the two camps.*]

Enter *Antony* and *Scarus*, with their *Army*.

Ant. Their preparation is to-day by sea;
We please them not by land.
Scar. For both, my lord.
Ant. I would they'ld fight i' th' fire or i' th' air;
We'ld fight there too. But this it is, our foot
Upon the hills adjoining to the city
Shall stay with us. Order for sea is given;
They have put forth the haven. [Go we up]
Where their appointment we may best discover
And look on their endeavour. *Exeunt.*

[Scene XI. *Between the camps.*]

Enter *Cæsar* and his *Army*.

Cæs. But being charg'd, we will be still by land,
Which, as I take't, we shall; for his best force
Is forth to man his galleys. To the vales,
And hold our best advantage. *Exeunt.*

[Scene XII. *Hill adjoining Alexandria.*]

Enter *Antony* and *Scarus*.

Ant. Yet they are not join'd. Where yond pine does stand
I shall discover all. I'll bring thee word
Straight how 'tis like to go. *Exit.*
Scar. Swallows have built
In Cleopatra's sails their nests. The augurers
Say they know not, they cannot tell; look grimly
And dare not speak their knowledge. Antony
Is valiant, and dejected; and by starts
His fretted fortunes give him hope and fear
Of what he has and has not.
Alarum afar off, as at a sea-fight.

Enter *Antony*.

Ant. All is lost!
This foul Egyptian hath betrayed me!
My fleet hath yielded to the foe, and yonder
They cast their caps up and carouse together
Like friends long lost. Triple-turn'd whore! 'tis thou
Hast sold me to this novice, and my heart
Makes only wars on thee. Bid them all fly!
For when I am reveng'd upon my charm,
I have done all. Bid them all fly; begone!
[*Exit Scarus.*]
O sun, thy uprise shall I see no more.
Fortune and Antony part here; even here
Do we shake hands. All come to this? The hearts
That spaniel'd me at heels, to whom I gave
Their wishes, do discandy, melt their sweets
On blossoming Cæsar; and this pine is bark'd,
That overtopp'd them all. Betray'd I am.
O this false soul of Egypt! this grave charm —
Whose eye beck'd forth my wars and call'd them home,
Whose bosom was my crownet, my chief end —
Like a right gypsy hath at fast and loose
Beguil'd me to the very heart of loss!
What, Eros, Eros!

Enter *Cleopatra*.

Ah, thou spell! Avaunt!
Cleo. Why is my lord enrag'd against his love?
Ant. Vanish, or I shall give thee thy deserving
And blemish Cæsar's triumph. Let him take thee
And hoist thee up to the shouting plebeians.
Follow his chariot, like the greatest spot
Of all thy sex. Most monster-like be shown
For poor'st diminitives, for doits, and let
Patient Octavia plough thy visage up
With her prepared nails.
Exit Cleopatra.
'Tis well th'art gone,
If it be well to live; but better 'twere
Thou fell'st into my fury, for one death
Might have prevented many. Eros, ho!
The shirt of Nessus is upon me. Teach me,
Alcides, thou mine ancestor, thy rage.
Let me lodge Lichas on the horns o' th' moon
And with those hands that grasp'd the heaviest club
Subdue my worthiest self. The witch shall die.

To the young Roman boy she hath sold me, and I fall
Under this plot. She dies for't. Eros, ho! *Exit.*

[Scene XIII. *Alexandria.* Cleopatra's *Palace.*]

Enter *Cleopatra, Charmian, Iras, Mardian.*

Cleo. Help me, my women! O, he is more mad
Than Telamon for his shield. The boar of Thessaly
Was never so emboss'd.
Char. To th' monument!
There lock yourself, and send him word you are dead.
The soul and body rive not more in parting
Than greatness going off.
Cleo. To th' monument!
Mardian, go tell him I have slain myself.
Say that the last I spoke was 'Antony'
And word it, prithee, piteously. Hence, Mardian,
And bring me how he takes my death. To th' monument! *Exeunt.*

[Scene XIV. Cleopatra's *Palace. Another room.*]

Enter *Antony* and *Eros.*

Ant. Eros, thou yet behold'st me?
Eros. Ay, noble lord.
Ant. Sometime we see a cloud that's dragonish;
A vapour sometime like a bear or lion,
A tower'd citadel, a pendent rock,
A forked mountain, or blue promontory
With trees upon't that nod unto the world
And mock our eyes with air. Thou hast seen these signs;
They are black Vesper's pageants.
Eros. Ay, my lord.
Ant. That which is now a horse, even with a thought
The rack dislimns, and makes it indistinct
As water is in water.
Eros. It does, my lord.
Ant. My good knave Eros, now thy captain is
Even such a body. Here I am Antony;
Yet cannot hold this visible shape, my knave.
I made these wars for Egypt; and the Queen —
Whose heart I thought I had, for she had mine,
Which, whilst it was mine, had annex'd unto't
A million moe, now lost — she, Eros, has
Pack'd cards with Cæsar and false-play'd my glory
Unto an enemy's triumph.
Nay, weep not, gentle Eros. There is left us
Ourselves to end ourselves.

Enter *Mardian.*

O, thy vile lady!
She has robb'd me of my sword.
Mar. No, Antony.
My mistress lov'd thee and her fortunes mingled
With thine entirely.
Ant. Hence, saucy eunuch! Peace!
She hath betray'd me and shall die the death.
Mar. Death of one person can be paid but once,
And that she has discharg'd. What thou wouldst do
Is done unto thy hand. The last she spake
Was, 'Antony! most noble Antony!'
Then in the midst a tearing groan did break
The name of Antony; it was divided
Between her heart and lips. She rend'red life,
Thy name so buried in her.
Ant. Dead, then?
Mar. Dead.
Ant. Unarm me, Eros. The long day's task is done,
And we must sleep. [*To Mardian*] That thou depart'st hence safe
Does pay thy labour richly. Go.
Exit Mardian.
Off, pluck off!
The sevenfold shield of Ajax cannot keep
The battery from my heart. O, cleave, my sides!
Heart, once be stronger than thy continent,
Crack thy frail case! Apace, Eros, apace. —
No more a soldier. Bruised pieces, go;
You have been nobly borne. — From me awhile.
Exit Eros.
I will o'ertake thee, Cleopatra, and
Weep for my pardon. So it must be, for now
All length is torture. Since the torch is out,
Lie down, and stray no farther. Now all labour
Mars what it does; yea, very force entangles
Itself with strength. Seal then, and all is done.
Eros! — I come, my queen. — Eros! — Stay for me.
Where souls do couch on flowers, we'll hand in hand

And with our sprightly port make the ghosts gaze.
Dido and her Æneas shall want troops,
And all the haunt be ours. — Come, Eros, Eros!

Enter *Eros.*

Eros. What would my lord?
Ant. Since Cleopatra died
I have liv'd in such dishonour that the gods
Detest my baseness. I, that with my sword
Quarter'd the world and o'er green Neptune's back
With ships made cities, condemn myself to lack
The courage of a woman — less noble mind
Than she which by her death our Cæsar tells
'I am conqueror of myself.' Thou art sworn, Eros,
That, when the exigent should come (which now
Is come indeed) when I should see behind me
Th' inevitable prosecution of
Disgrace and horror, that, on my command,
Thou then wouldst kill me. Do't; the time is come.
Thou strik'st not me; 'tis Cæsar thou defeat'st.
Put colour in thy cheek.
Eros. The gods withhold me!
Shall I do that which all the Parthian darts,
Though enemy, lost aim and could not?
Ant. Eros,
Wouldst thou be window'd in great Rome and see
Thy master thus with pleach'd arms, bending down
His corrigible neck, his face subdu'd
To penetrative shame, whilst the wheel'd seat
Of fortunate Cæsar, drawn before him, branded
His baseness that ensu'd?
Eros. I would not see't.
Ant. Come then; for with a wound I must be cur'd.
Draw that thy honest sword, which thou hast worn
Most useful for thy country.
Eros. O sir, pardon me!
Ant. When I did make thee free, swor'st thou not then
To do this when I bade thee? Do it at once,
Or thy precedent services are all
But accidents unpurpos'd. Draw, and come.
Eros. Turn from me then that noble countenance
Wherein the worship of the whole world lies.
Ant. Lo thee! [*Turns from him.*]
Eros. My sword is drawn.
Ant. Then let it do at once
The thing why thou hast drawn it.
Eros. My dear master,
My captain, and my emperor, let me say,
Before I strike this bloody stroke, farewell.
Ant. 'Tis said, man; and farewell.
Eros. Farewell, great chief. Shall I strike now?
Ant. Now, Eros.
Eros. Why, there then! Thus I do escape the sorrow
Of Antony's death. *Kills himself.*
Ant. Thrice nobler than myself!
Thou teachest me, O valiant Eros, what
I should, and thou couldst not. My queen and Eros
Have by their brave instruction got upon me
A nobleness in record. But I will be
A bridegroom in my death and run into't
As to a lover's bed. Come then; and, Eros,
Thy master dies thy scholar. To do thus [*Falls on his sword.*]
I learn'd of thee. How? not dead? not dead?—
The guard, ho! O, dispatch me!

Enter [*Dercetas* and] a *Guard.*

1. Guard. What's the noise?
Ant. I have done my work ill, friends. O, make an end
Of what I have begun.
2. Guard. The star is fall'n.
1. Guard. And time is at his period.
All. Alas, and woe!
Ant. Let him that loves me strike me dead.
1. Guard. Not I.
2. Guard. Nor I.
3. Guard. Nor any one. *Exeunt* [*Guard*].
Der. Thy death and fortunes bid thy followers fly.
This sword but shown to Cæsar, with this tidings,
Shall enter me with him.

Enter *Diomedes.*

Dio. Where's Antony?
Der. There, Diomed, there.
Dio. Lives he?
Wilt thou not answer, man? [*Exit Dercetas.*]
Ant. Art thou there, Diomed? Draw thy sword and give me
Sufficing strokes for death.
Dio. Most absolute lord,
My mistress Cleopatra sent me to thee.
Ant. When did she send thee?

Dio. Now, my lord.
Ant. Where is she?
Dio. Lock'd in her monument. She had a prophesying fear
Of what hath come to pass; for when she saw
(Which never shall be found) you did suspect
She had dispos'd with Cæsar, and that your rage
Would not be purg'd, she sent you word she was dead;
But, fearing since how it might work, hath sent
Me to proclaim the truth; and I am come,
I dread, too late.
Ant. Too late, good Diomed. Call my guard, I prithee.
Dio. What ho! the Emperor's guard! the guard, what ho!
Come, your lord calls!

Enter four or five of the *Guard* of *Antony*.

Ant. Bear me, good friends, where Cleopatra bides.
'Tis the last service that I shall command you.
1. Guard. Woe, woe are we, sir, you may not live to wear
All your true followers out.
All. Most heavy day!
Ant. Nay, good my fellows, do not please sharp fate
To grace it with your sorrows. Bid that welcome
Which comes to punish us, and we punish it,
Seeming to bear it lightly. Take me up.
I have led you oft; carry me now, good friends,
And have my thanks for all.
Exeunt, bearing Antony.

[Scene XV. *Alexandria. A monument.*]

Enter *Cleopatra* and her *Maids* aloft, with *Charmian* and *Iras*.

Cleo. O Charmian, I will never go from hence.
Char. Be comforted, dear madam.
Cleo. No, I will not.
All strange and terrible events are welcome,
But comforts we despise. Our size of sorrow,
Proportion'd to our cause, must be as great
As that which makes it.

Enter *Diomed* [below].

How now? Is he dead?
Dio. His death's upon him, but not dead.
Look out o' th' other side your monument.
His guard have brought him thither.

Enter, [below,] *Antony* and the *Guard* [bearing him].

Cleo. O sun,
Burn the great sphere thou mov'st in! Darkling stand
The varying shore o' th' world! O Antony,
Antony, Antony! Help, Charmian; help, Iras; help!
Help, friends below! Let's draw him hither.
Ant. Peace!
Not Cæsar's valour hath o'erthrown Antony,
But Antony's hath triumph'd on itself.
Cleo. So it should be, that none but Antony
Should conquer Antony; but woe 'tis so!
Ant. I am dying, Egypt, dying; only
I here importune death awhile, until
Of many thousand kisses the poor last
I lay upon thy lips.
Cleo. I dare not, dear.
Dear my lord, pardon! I dare not,
Lest I be taken. Not th' imperious show
Of the full-fortun'd Cæsar ever shall
Be brooch'd with me! If knife, drugs, serpents have
Edge, sting, or operation, I am safe.
Your wife Octavia, with her modest eyes
And still conclusion, shall acquire no honour
Demuring upon me. But come, come, Antony!
Help me, my women. We must draw thee up.
Assist, good friends.
Ant. O, quick, or I am gone.
Cleo. Here's sport indeed! How heavy weighs my lord!
Our strength is all gone into heaviness:
That makes the weight. Had I great Juno's power,
The strong-wing'd Mercury should fetch thee up
And set thee by Jove's side. Yet come a little!
Wishers were ever fools. O, come, come, come!
They heave Antony aloft to Cleopatra.
And welcome, welcome! Die where thou hast liv'd!
Quicken with kissing. Had my lips that power,
Thus would I wear them out.
All. A heavy sight!
Ant. I am dying, Egypt, dying.
Give me some wine, and let me speak a little.
Cleo. No, let me speak; and let me rail so high
That the false huswife Fortune break her wheel,
Provok'd by my offence.
Ant. One word, sweet queen.

Of Cæsar seek your honour, with your safety. O!
Cleo. They do not go together.
Ant. Gentle, hear me.
None about Cæsar trust but Proculeius.
Cleo. My resolution and my hands I'll trust;
None about Cæsar.
Ant. The miserable change now at my end
Lament nor sorrow at; but please your thoughts
In feeding them with those my former fortunes,
Wherein I liv'd the greatest prince o' th' world,
The noblest; and do now not basely die,
Not cowardly put off my helmet to
My countryman — a Roman by a Roman
Valiantly vanquish'd. Now my spirit is going.
I can no more.
Cleo. Noblest of men, woo't die?
Hast thou no care of me? Shall I abide
In this dull world, which in thy absence is
No better than a sty? O, see, my women,
[*Antony dies.*]
The crown o' th' earth doth melt. My lord!
O, wither'd is the garland of the war,
The soldier's pole is fall'n! Young boys and girls
Are level now with men. The odds is gone,
And there is nothing left remarkable
Beneath the visiting moon. [*Swoons.*]
Char. O, quietness, lady!
Iras. She's dead too, our sovereign.
Char. Lady!
Iras. Madam!
Char. O madam, madam, madam!
Iras. Royal Egypt!
Empress!
Char. Peace, peace, Iras!
Cleo. No more but e'en a woman, and commanded
By such poor passion as the maid that milks
And does the meanest chares. It were for me
To throw my sceptre at the injurious gods,
To tell them that this world did equal theirs
Till they had stol'n our jewel. All's but naught.
Patience is sottish, and impatience does
Become a dog that's mad. Then is it sin
To rush into the secret house of death
Ere death dare come to us? How do you, women?
What, what! good cheer! Why, how now, Charmian?
My noble girls! Ah, women, women, look!
Our lamp is spent, it's out! Good sirs, take heart.
We'll bury him; and then, what's brave, what's noble,
Let's do it after the high Roman fashion
And make death proud to take us. Come, away!
This case of that huge spirit now is cold.
Ah, women, women! Come; we have no friend
But resolution and the briefest end.
Exeunt; [*those above*] *bearing off Antony's body.*

[ACT V. Scene I. *Alexandria.* Cæsar's *camp.*]

Enter *Cæsar, Agrippa, Dolabella, Mæcenas,* [*Gallus, Proculeius,* and others], his *Council of War.*

Cæs. Go to him, Dolabella; bid him yield.
Being so frustrate, tell him he mocks
The pauses that he makes.
Dol. Cæsar, I shall. [*Exit.*]

Enter *Dercetas,* with the sword of *Antony.*

Cæs. Wherefore is that? And what art thou that dar'st
Appear thus to us?
Der. I am call'd Dercetas.
Mark Antony I serv'd, who best was worthy
Best to be serv'd. Whilst he stood up and spoke,
He was my master, and I wore my life
To spend upon his haters. If thou please
To take me to thee, as I was to him
I'll be to Cæsar; if thou pleasest not,
I yield thee up my life.
Cæs. What is't thou say'st?
Der. I say, O Cæsar, Antony is dead.
Cæs. The breaking of so great a thing should make
A greater crack. The round world
Should have shook lions into civil streets
And citizens to their dens. The death of Antony
Is not a single doom; in the name lay
A moiety of the world.
Der. He is dead, Cæsar,
Not by a public minister of justice
Nor by a hired knife; but that self hand
Which writ his honour in the acts it did
Hath, with the courage which the heart did lend it,
Splitted the heart. This is his sword.
I robb'd his wound of it. Behold it stain'd
With his most noble blood.

Cæs. Look you sad, friends?
The gods rebuke me but it is tidings
To wash the eyes of kings!
Agr. And strange it is
That nature must compel us to lament
Our most persisted deeds.
Mæc. His taints and honours
Wag'd equal with him.
Agr. A rarer spirit never
Did steer humanity; but you gods will give us
Some faults to make us men. Cæsar is touch'd.
Mæc. When such a spacious mirror's set before him,
He needs must see himself.
Cæs. O Antony,
I have followed thee to this! But we do lanch
Diseases in our bodies. I must perforce
Have shown to thee such a declining day
Or look on thine: we could not stall together
In the whole world. But yet let me lament
With tears as sovereign as the blood of hearts
That thou, my brother, my competitor
In top of all design, my mate in empire,
Friend and companion in the front of war,
The arm of mine own body, and the heart
Where mine his thoughts did kindle — that our stars,
Unreconciliable, should divide
Our equalness to this. Hear me, good friends —

Enter an *Egyptian.*

But I will tell you at some meeter season.
The business of this man looks out of him;
We'll hear him what he says. Whence are you?
Egyp. A poor Egyptian yet. The Queen my mistress,
Confin'd in all she has, her monument,
Of thy intents desires instruction,
That she preparedly may frame herself
To th' way she's forc'd to.
Cæs. Bid her have good heart.
She soon shall know of us, by some of ours,
How honourable and how kindly we
Determine for her; for Cæsar cannot live
To be ungentle.
Egyp. So the gods preserve thee! *Exit.*
Cæs. Come hither, Proculeius. Go and say
We purpose her no shame. Give her what comforts
The quality of her passion shall require,
Lest, in her greatness, by some mortal stroke
She do defeat us; for her life in Rome
Would be eternal in our triumph. Go,
And with your speediest bring us what she says
And how you find of her.
Pro. Cæsar, I shall. *Exit.*
Cæs. Gallus, go you along. [*Exit Gallus.*] Where's Dolabella,
To second Proculeius?
All. Dolabella!
Cæs. Let him alone, for I remember now
How he's employ'd. He shall in time be ready.
Go with me to my tent; where you shall see
How hardly I was drawn into this war,
How calm and gentle I proceeded still
In all my writings. Go with me and see
What I can show in this. *Exeunt.*

[Scene II. *Alexandria. The monument.*]

Enter *Cleopatra, Charmian, Iras,* and *Mardian.*

Cleo. My desolation does begin to make
A better life. 'Tis paltry to be Cæsar.
Not being Fortune, he's but Fortune's knave,
A minister of her will. And it is great
To do that thing that ends all other deeds,
Which shackles accidents and bolts up change,
Which sleeps, and never palates more the dung,
The beggar's nurse and Cæsar's.

Enter, [to the gates of the monument,] *Proculeius,* [*Gallus,* and *Soldiers*].

Pro. Cæsar sends greeting to the Queen of Egypt,
And bids thee study on what fair demands
Thou mean'st to have him grant thee.
Cleo. What's thy name?
Pro. My name is Proculeius.
Cleo. Antony
Did tell me of you, bade me trust you; but
I do not greatly care to be deceiv'd,
That have no use for trusting. If your master
Would have a queen his beggar, you must tell him
That majesty, to keep decorum, must
No less beg than a kingdom. If he please
To give me conquer'd Egypt for my son,
He gives me so much of mine own as I
Will kneel to him with thanks.
Pro. Be of good cheer.
Y'are fall'n into a princely hand; fear nothing.
Make your full reference freely to my lord,
Who is so full of grace that it flows over
On all that need. Let me report to him
Your sweet dependency, and you shall find
A conqueror that will pray in aid for kindness,
Where he for grace is kneel'd to.

Cleo. Pray you tell him
I am his fortune's vassal and I send him
The greatness he has got. I hourly learn
A doctrine of obedience, and would gladly
Look him i' th' face.
Pro. This I'll report, dear lady.
Have comfort, for I know your plight is pitied
Of him that caus'd it.
Gal. You see how easily she may be surpris'd.
[*Here Proculeius and two of the Guard ascend the monument by a ladder placed against a window, and come behind Cleopatra. Some of the Guard unbar and open the gates.*]
Guard her till Cæsar come. [*Exit.*]
Iras. Royal Queen!
Char. O Cleopatra! thou art taken, Queen!
Cleo. Quick, quick, good hands!
[*Draws a dagger.*]
Pro. Hold, worthy lady, hold!
[*Disarms her.*]
Do not yourself such wrong, who are in this
Reliev'd, but not betray'd.
Cleo. What, of death too,
That rids our dogs of languish?
Pro. Cleopatra,
Do not abuse my master's bounty by
Th' undoing of yourself. Let the world see
His nobleness well acted, which your death
Will never let come forth.
Cleo. Where art thou, death?
Come hither, come! Come, come, and take a queen
Worth many babes and beggars!
Pro. O, temperance, lady!
Cleo. Sir, I will eat no meat; I'll not drink, sir;
If idle talk will once be necessary,
I'll not sleep neither. This mortal house I'll ruin,
Do Cæsar what he can. Know, sir, that I
Will not wait pinion'd at your master's court
Nor once be chastis'd with the sober eye
Of dull Octavia. Shall they hoist me up
And show me to the shouting varlotry
Of censuring Rome? Rather a ditch in Egypt
Be gentle grave unto me! Rather on Nilus' mud
Lay me stark-nak'd and let the waterflies
Blow me into abhorring! Rather make
My country's high pyramides my gibbet
And hang me up in chains!
Pro. You do extend
These thoughts of horror further than you shall
Find cause in Cæsar.

Enter *Dolabella.*

Dol. Proculeius,
What thou hast done thy master Cæsar knows,
And he hath sent me for thee. For the Queen,
I'll take her to my guard.
Pro. So, Dolabella,
It shall content me best. Be gentle to her.
[*To Cleopatra*] To Cæsar I will speak what you shall please,
If you'll employ me to him.
Cleo. Say, I would die.
Exeunt Proculeius [*and Soldiers*].
Dol. Most noble Empress, you have heard of me?
Cleo. I cannot tell.
Dol. Assuredly you know me.
Cleo. No matter, sir, what I have heard or known.
You laugh when boys or women tell their dreams;
Is't not your trick?
Dol. I understand not, madam.
Cleo. I dreamt there was an Emperor Antony —
O, such another sleep, that I might see
But such another man!
Dol. If it might please ye —
Cleo. His face was as the heav'ns, and therein stuck
A sun and moon, which kept their course and lighted
The little O, the earth.
Dol. Most sovereign creature —
Cleo. His legs bestrid the ocean: his rear'd arm
Crested the world. His voice was propertied
As all the tuned spheres, and that to friends;
But when he meant to quail and shake the orb,
He was as rattling thunder. For his bounty,
There was no winter in't; an autumn 'twas
That grew the more by reaping. His delights
Were dolphin-like: they show'd his back above
The element they liv'd in. In his livery
Walk'd crowns and crownets. Realms and islands were
As plates dropp'd from his pocket.
Dol. Cleopatra —
Cleo. Think you there was or might be such a man
As this I dreamt of?
Dol. Gentle madam, no.
Cleo. You lie, up to the hearing of the gods!
But, if there be or ever were one such,

It's past the size of dreaming. Nature wants stuff
To vie strange forms with fancy; yet, t' imagine
An Antony were nature's piece 'gainst fancy,
Condemning shadows quite.
Dol. Hear me, good madam.
Your loss is as yourself, great; and you bear it
As answering to the weight. Would I might never
O'ertake pursu'd success but I do feel,
By the rebound of yours, a grief that smites
My very heart at root.
Cleo. I thank you, sir.
Know you what Cæsar means to do with me?
Dol. I am loth to tell you what I would you knew.
Cleo. Nay, pray you, sir.
Dol. Though he be honourable —
Cleo. He'll lead me, then, in triumph?
Dol. Madam, he will. I know't. *Flourish.*
[*Shout within.*] 'Make way there! Cæsar!'

Enter *Cæsar*; *Proculeius, Gallus, Mæcenas,* [*Seleucus,*] and others of his *Train.*

Cæs. Which is the Queen of Egypt?
Dol. It is the Emperor, madam.
Cleopatra kneels.
Cæs. Arise! You shall not kneel.
I pray you rise. Rise, Egypt.
Cleo. Sir, the gods
Will have it thus. My master and my lord
I must obey.
Cæs. Take to you no hard thoughts.
The record of what injuries you did us,
Though written in our flesh, we shall remember
As things but done by chance.
Cleo. Sole sir o' th' world,
I cannot project mine own cause so well
To make it clear; but do confess I have
Been laden with like frailties which before
Have often sham'd our sex.
Cæs. Cleopatra, know
We will extenuate rather than enforce.
If you apply yourself to our intents,
Which towards you are most gentle, you shall find
A benefit in this change; but if you seek
To lay on me a cruelty by taking
Antony's course, you shall bereave yourself
Of my good purposes, and put your children
To that destruction which I'll guard them from
If thereon you rely. I'll take my leave.
Cleo. And may, through all the world! 'Tis yours, and we,
Your scutcheons and your signs of conquest, shall
Hang in what place you please. Here, my good lord.
Cæs. You shall advise me in all for Cleopatra.
Cleo. This is the brief of money, plate, and jewels
I am possess'd of. 'Tis exactly valued,
Not petty things admitted. Where's Seleucus?
Sel. Here, madam.
Cleo. This is my treasurer. Let him speak, my lord,
Upon his peril, that I have reserv'd
To myself nothing. Speak the truth, Seleucus.
Sel. Madam,
I had rather seel my lips than to my peril
Speak that which is not.
Cleo. What have I kept back?
Sel. Enough to purchase what you have made known.
Cæs. Nay, blush not, Cleopatra. I approve
Your wisdom in the deed.
Cleo. See, Cæsar! O, behold,
How pomp is followed! Mine will now be yours;
And should we shift estates, yours would be mine.
The ingratitude of this Seleucus does
Even make me wild. O slave, of no more trust
Than love that's hir'd! What, goest thou back? Thou shalt
Go back, I warrant thee; but I'll catch thine eyes,
Though they had wings. Slave, soulless villain, dog!
O rarely base!
Cæs. Good Queen, let us entreat you.
Cleo. O Cæsar, what a wounding shame is this,
That thou vouchsafing here to visit me,
Doing the honour of thy lordliness
To one so meek, that mine own servant should
Parcel the sum of my disgraces by
Addition of his envy! Say, good Cæsar,
That I some lady trifles have reserv'd,
Immoment toys, things of such dignity
As we greet modern friends withal; and say
Some nobler token I have kept apart
For Livia and Octavia, to induce
Their mediation — must I be unfolded
With one that I have bred? The gods! It smites me
Beneath the fall I have. [*To Seleucus*] Prithee go hence!

Or I shall show the cinders of my spirits
Through th' ashes of my chance. Wert thou a man,
Thou wouldst have mercy on me.
Cæs. Forbear, Seleucus.
[*Exit Seleucus.*]
Cleo. Be it known that we, the greatest, are misthought
For things that others do; and, when we fall,
We answer others' merits in our name,
Are therefore to be pitied.
Cæs. Cleopatra,
Not what you have reserv'd, nor what acknowledg'd,
Put we i' th' roll of conquest. Still be't yours,
Bestow it at your pleasure; and believe
Cæsar's no merchant, to make prize with you
Of things that merchants sold. Therefore be cheer'd;
Make not your thoughts your prisons. No, dear Queen;
For we intend so to dispose you as
Yourself shall give us counsel. Feed and sleep.
Our care and pity is so much upon you
That we remain your friend; and so adieu.
Cleo. My master and my lord!
Cæs. Not so. Adieu.
Flourish. Exeunt Cæsar and his Train.
Cleo. He words me, girls, he words me, that I should not
Be noble to myself! But hark thee, Charmian.
[*Whispers Charmian.*]
Iras. Finish, good lady. The bright day is done,
And we are for the dark.
Cleo. Hie thee again.
I have spoke already, and it is provided.
Go put it to the haste.
Char. Madam, I will.

Enter *Dolabella.*

Dol. Where is the Queen?
Char. Behold, sir. [*Exit.*]
Cleo. Dolabella!
Dol. Madam, as thereto sworn, by your command
(Which my love makes religion to obey)
I tell you this: Cæsar through Syria
Intends his journey, and within three days
You with your children will he send before.
Make your best use of this. I have perform'd
Your pleasure and my promise.
Cleo. Dolabella,
I shall remain your debtor.
Dol. I your servant.
Adieu, good Queen; I must attend on Cæsar.
Cleo. Farewell, and thanks.
Exit [*Dolabella*].
Now, Iras, what think'st thou?
Thou, an Egyptian puppet, shalt be shown
In Rome as well as I. Mechanic slaves,
With greasy aprons, rules, and hammers, shall
Uplift us to the view. In their thick breaths,
Rank of gross diet, shall we be enclouded,
And forc'd to drink their vapour.
Iras. The gods forbid!
Cleo. Nay, 'tis most certain, Iras. Saucy lictors
Will catch at us like strumpets, and scald rhymers
Ballad us out o' tune. The quick comedians
Extemporally will stage us and present
Our Alexandrian revels. Antony
Shall be brought drunken forth, and I shall see
Some squeaking Cleopatra boy my greatness
I' th' posture of a whore.
Iras. O the good gods!
Cleo. Nay, that's certain.
Iras. I'll never see't; for I am sure my nails
Are stronger than mine eyes.
Cleo. Why, that's the way
To fool their preparation and to conquer
Their most absurd intents.

Enter *Charmian.*

Now, Charmian!
Show me, my women, like a queen. Go fetch
My best attires. I am again for Cydnus,
To meet Mark Antony. Sirrah Iras, go.
Now, noble Charmian, we'll dispatch indeed;
And when thou hast done this chare, I'll give thee leave
To play till doomsday. — Bring our crown and all.
A noise within.
[*Exit Iras.*]
Wherefore's this noise?

Enter a *Guardsman.*

Guard. Here is a rural fellow
That will not be denied your Highness' presence.
He brings you figs.
Cleo. Let him come in.
Exit Guardsman.
What poor an instrument
May do a noble deed! He brings me liberty.
My resolution's plac'd, and I have nothing
Of woman in me. Now from head to foot

I am marble-constant. Now the fleeting moon
No planet is of mine.

Enter *Guardsman* and *Clown* [with basket].

Guard. This is the man.
Cleo. Avoid, and leave him.
Exit Guardsman.
Hast thou the pretty worm of Nilus there
That kills and pains not?

Clown. Truly I have him. But I would not be the party that should desire you to touch him, for his biting is immortal. Those that do die of it do seldom or never recover.

Cleo. Remember'st thou any that have died on't?

Clown. Very many, men and women too. I heard of one of them no longer than yesterday; a very honest woman, but something given to lie, as a woman should not do but in the way of honesty — how she died of the biting of it, what pain she felt. Truly, she makes a very good report o' th' worm; but he that will believe all that they say shall never be saved by half that they do. But this is most falliable, the worm's an odd worm.

Cleo. Get thee hence; farewell.

Clown. I wish you all joy of the worm.
[*Sets down his basket.*]

Cleo. Farewell.

Clown. You must think this, look you, that the worm will do his kind.

Cleo. Ay, ay; farewell.

Clown. Look you, the worm is not to be trusted but in the keeping of wise people; for indeed there is no goodness in the worm.

Cleo. Take thou no care; it shall be heeded.

Clown. Very good. Give it nothing, I pray you, for it is not worth the feeding.

Cleo. Will it eat me?

Clown. You must not think I am so simple but I know the devil himself will not eat a woman. I know that a woman is a dish for the gods, if the devil dress her not. But truly, these same whoreson devils do the gods great harm in their women; for in every ten that they make, the devils mar five.

Cleo. Well, get thee gone; farewell.

Clown. Yes, forsooth. I wish you joy o' th' worm. *Exit.*

[Enter *Iras* with a robe, crown, etc.]

Cleo. Give me my robe, put on my crown. I have
Immortal longings in me. Now no more
The juice of Egypt's grape shall moist this lip.
Yare, yare, good Iras; quick. Methinks I hear
Antony call. I see him rouse himself
To praise my noble act. I hear him mock
The luck of Cæsar, which the gods give men
To excuse their after wrath. Husband, I come!
Now to that name my courage prove my title!
I am fire and air; my other elements
I give to baser life. So, have you done?
Come then and take the last warmth of my lips.
Farewell, kind Charmian. Iras, long farewell.
[*Kisses them. Iras falls and dies.*]
Have I the aspic in my lips? Dost fall?
If thou and nature can so gently part,
The stroke of death is as a lover's pinch,
Which hurts, and is desir'd. Dost thou lie still?
If thus thou vanishest, thou tell'st the world
It is not worth leave-taking.

Char. Dissolve, thick cloud, and rain, that I may say
The gods themselves do weep!

Cleo. This proves me base.
If she first meet the curled Antony,
He'll make demand of her, and spend that kiss
Which is my heaven to have. Come, thou mortal wretch,
[*To an asp, which she applies to her breast.*]
With thy sharp teeth this knot intrinsicate
Of life at once untie. Poor venomous fool,
Be angry, and dispatch. O, couldst thou speak.
That I might hear thee call great Cæsar ass
Unpolicied!

Char. O Eastern star!

Cleo. Peace, peace!
Dost thou not see my baby at my breast,
That sucks the nurse asleep?

Char. O, break! O, break!

Cleo. As sweet as balm, as soft as air, as gentle —
O Antony! Nay, I will take thee too:
[*Applies another asp to her arm.*]
What should I stay — *Dies.*

Char. In this wild world? So fare thee well.
Now boast thee, death, in thy possession lies
A lass unparallel'd. Downy windows, close;
And golden Phœbus never be beheld
Of eyes again so royal! Your crown's awry.
I'll mend it, and then play —

Enter the *Guard*, rustling in.

1. Guard. Where is the Queen?

Char. Speak softly, wake her not.

1. Guard. Cæsar hath sent —

Char. Too slow a messenger.
[*Applies an asp.*]
O, come apace, dispatch. I partly feel thee.

1. Guard. Approach, ho! All's not well. Cæsar's beguil'd.
2. Guard. There's Dolabella sent from Cæsar. Call him.
1. Guard. What work is here! Charmian, is this well done?
Char. It is well done, and fitting for a princess
Descended of so many royal kings.
Ah, soldier! *Charmian dies.*

Enter *Dolabella.*

Dol. How goes it here?
2. Guard. All dead.
Dol. Cæsar, thy thoughts
Touch their effects in this. Thyself art coming
To see perform'd the dreaded act which thou
So sought'st to hinder.
[*Shout within.*] A way there, a way for Cæsar!

Enter *Cæsar* and all his *Train.*

Dol. O sir, you are too sure an augurer:
That you did fear is done.
Cæs. Bravest at the last!
She levell'd at our purposes, and being royal,
Took her own way. The manner of their deaths?
I do not see them bleed.
Dol. Who was last with them?
1. Guard. A simple countryman, that brought her figs.
This was his basket.
Cæs. Poison'd, then.
1. Guard. O Cæsar,
This Charmian liv'd but now; she stood and spake.
I found her trimming up the diadem
On her dead mistress. Tremblingly she stood,
And on the sudden dropp'd.
Cæs. O noble weakness!
If they had swallow'd poison, 'twould appear
By external swelling; but she looks like sleep,
As she would catch another Antony
In her strong toil of grace.
Dol. Here on her breast
There is a vent of blood, and something blown;
The like is on her arm.
1. Guard. This is an aspic's trail; and these fig leaves
Have slime upon them, such as th' aspic leaves
Upon the caves of Nile.
Cæs. Most probable
That so she died; for her physician tells me
She hath pursu'd conclusions infinite
Of easy ways to die. Take up her bed,
And bear her women from the monument.
She shall be buried by her Antony.
No grave upon the earth shall clip in it
A pair so famous. High events as these
Strike those that make them; and their story is
No less in pity than his glory which
Brought them to be lamented. Our army shall
In solemn show attend this funeral,
And then to Rome. Come, Dolabella, see
High order in this great solemnity.
Exeunt omnes.

Cymbeline

For the text of Cymbeline the First Folio (1623) is the only authority. The Second Folio (1632) corrects a good many misprints. 'Rocks' for 'Oakes' is Seward's emendation (iii, 1, 20); 'bribe' for 'Babe' is Hanmer's (iii, 3, 23); 'afore't' for 'a-foot' is Rowe's (iii, 4, 81); 'crare' for 'care' is Sympson's (iv, 2, 205). 'Th' unnumber'd beach,' Theobald's correction for 'the number'd beach' (i, 6, 36), seems compulsive: cf. 'th' unnumb'red idle pebble' (*King Lear*, iv, 6, 21). The Folio 'illustrious' (i, 6, 109) in the sense of 'not lustrous' is probably right. So is 'foil' (ii, 3, 126) in the sense of 'debase,' 'disgrace': cf. *Antony and Cleopatra*, i, 4, 24. 'Wing-led' (ii, 4, 24) is apparently a bold metaphor for 'swept on, as with strong pinions.' Now and then a line limps (as i, 1, 132) from the loss of a word or two which cannot be supplied with any confidence.

The vision in v, 4, is usually regarded as spurious, in whole or in part. The rhyming speeches in lines 30–92 can hardly be Shakespeare's, but the rest may well be genuine. Verses such as 114–122 were certainly not written by the interpolator.

One limit for the date of composition is fixed by Simon Forman's memorandum (see p. 431, above). He saw Cymbeline acted (undoubtedly at the Globe) sometime in 1611, apparently between the 20th and the 30th of April. He died on September 12 in that year. Forman does not say that it was a new play, but style and metre justify referring it to *ca.* 1610.

The relation of Cymbeline to Beaumont and Fletcher's *Philaster* has been much discussed. The resemblance between the plots is slight and gives no indication of borrowing either way. There is no Roman-British frame in *Philaster*; no wager; no concealment in a trunk; no sleeping potion; no stealing of a king's sons. As to characters, Philaster is not much like Leonatus, nor is Pharamond much like Cloten; and there is no wicked queen and no Iachimo. Even if there were significant resemblances, that would not help to fix the date of Cymbeline, since the date of *Philaster* is uncertain.

In constructing the plot Shakespeare fitted the story of Iachimo's wager into an ancient British frame. The story of the wager he found in Boccaccio's *Decameron* (ii, 9). It is a wide-spread folk-tale and ballad and is extant in several mediæval versions: in the thirteenth-century *Roman de la Violette* and *Roman du Comte de Poitiers* and *Li Contes du Roi Flore et de la Bielle Jehane*, in the miracle play of *Ostes Roy d'Espaingne*, and in an episode in the romance of *Perceforest*. Bandello tells it in his twenty-first *novella*. A similar tale is in the Welsh *Mabinogion*. See also the ballad of *The Twa Knights* (Child, No. 268). Wild life in a cave and other points of resemblance to Cymbeline have been discovered in the old play *The Rare Triumphs of Love and Fortune* (printed in 1589, but probably as old as 1582), in which the heroine is named Fidelia and her lover is Hermione (cf. *The Winter's Tale*). Cave-dwellers are common in romantic fiction, but the names look significant.

The ancient British frame comes from Geoffrey of Monmouth's *Historia Regum Britanniae* (see p. 1195, above), as adapted and interwoven with passages from other authors in Holinshed's *Chronicle*. Geoffrey's Kymbelinus is the historical British king Cunobelinus, mentioned by Suetonius and Dio

Cassius. He lived in the first half of the first century and his capital was Camulodunum (Colchester). Geoffrey tells little about Cymbeline except that he was a sturdy warrior (*miles strenuus*) whom Augustus had trained (*nutriverat*) and that he was so friendly to the Romans that, although he could have withheld tribute, he paid it of his own accord. He adds that he had two sons, Guiderius and Arviragus, and that Guiderius, his successor, refused the tribute. War followed; Guiderius was killed and Arviragus became king. The episode of Belarius and the stolen princes is Shakespeare's invention. Cloten is a new character, whose name is taken from that of a Cornish king in Geoffrey (ii, 17) and Holinshed. The queen and her plots are also fictitious, as well as the whole history of Posthumus. The change of costume by Posthumus and his fighting 'against the part he comes with' (v, 1, 22 ff.) may have been suggested by the curious stratagem of Hamo in Geoffrey (iv, 13).

The rout changed to victory by the 'strange chance' of 'a narrow lane, an old man, and two boys' (v, 3) was probably suggested by Holinshed's account of a similar incident in the Battle of Loncart between the Scots and the Danes. An old husbandman named Hay, 'strong and stiffe in making and shape of bodie,' was at work with his two sons in a field near by. At a crisis in the battle, seeing the Scottish king and his nobles in danger, Hay and his sons 'placed themselues ouerthwart the lane' where the fleeing Scots 'were beaten downe by the enemies on heaps.' The Danes were 'staied in the lane by the great valiancie of the father and the sonnes,' and thus 'by his meanes chieflie was the victoire atchiued.'

Tantalizing are the recollections of *Titus Andronicus* in CYMBELINE. As the son of Titus demands the sacrifice of 'the proudest prisoner of the Goths' *ad manes fratrum* (i, 1, 96 ff.), so, in CYMBELINE (v, 5, 69 ff.), the king tells Lucius, kinsmen of the Britons who fell in battle with the Romans

have made suit
That their good souls may be appeas'd with slaughter
Of you their captives, which ourself have granted.

The wicked queen and her abominable son Cloten recall Tamora and her sons Chiron and Demetrius. She hoodwinks the uxorious Cymbeline as Tamora deludes Saturninus. Cloten's hideous plan of murder and rape set forth in soliloquy (iii, 5, 125–150; cf. iv, 1) is an elaboration of Chiron's words in *Titus* (ii, 3, 129–130). When Imogen went to sleep (ii, 2), she had been reading 'the tale of Tereus,' and Iachimo found the leaf turned down 'where Philomel gave up.' One is tempted to believe that Shakespeare himself had been reading his own old-fashioned tragedy, and that he was determined to forestall modern objections to his authorship.

CYMBELINE

[Dramatis Personæ.

Cymbeline, King of Britain.
Cloten, son to the *Queen* by a former husband.
Posthumus Leonatus, a gentleman, husband to *Imogen.*
Belarius, a banished lord, disguised under the name of *Morgan.*
Guiderius, / *Arviragus,* — sons to *Cymbeline,* disguised under the names of *Polydore* and *Cadwal,* supposed sons of *Morgan.*
Philario, friend to *Posthumus,* / *Iachimo,* friend to *Philario,* — Italians.
A French Gentleman, friend to *Philario.*
Caius Lucius, General of the Roman forces.
A Roman Captain.
Two British Captains.
Pisanio, servant to *Posthumus.*
Cornelius, a physician.
Two Lords of *Cymbeline's* court.
Two Gentlemen of the same.
Two Jailers.

Queen, wife to *Cymbeline.*
Imogen, daughter to *Cymbeline* by a former queen.
Helen, a lady attending on *Imogen.*

Apparitions.

Lords, Ladies, Roman Senators, Tribunes, a Soothsayer, a Dutch Gentleman, a Spanish Gentleman, Musicians, Officers, Captains, Soldiers, Messengers, Attendants.

SCENE. — *Britain; Italy.*]

ACT I. Scene I. [*Britain. The garden of* Cymbeline's *Palace.*]

Enter two *Gentlemen.*

1. Gent. You do not meet a man but frowns. Our bloods
No more obey the heavens than our courtiers
Still seem as does the King.
2. Gent. But what's the matter?
1. Gent. His daughter, and the heir of's kingdom, whom
He purpos'd to his wive's sole son (a widow
That late he married), hath referr'd herself
Unto a poor but worthy gentleman. She's wedded;
Her husband banish'd; she imprison'd. All
Is outward sorrow, though I think the King
Be touch'd at very heart.
2. Gent. None but the King?
1. Gent. He that hath lost her too. So is the Queen,
That most desir'd the match. But not a courtier,
Although they wear their faces to the bent
Of the King's looks, hath a heart that is not
Glad at the thing they scowl at.
2. Gent. And why so?
1. Gent. He that hath miss'd the Princess is a thing
Too bad for bad report; and he that hath her
(I mean, that married her, alack, good man!
And therefore banish'd) is a creature such
As, to seek through the regions of the earth
For one his like, there would be something failing
In him that should compare. I do not think
So fair an outward and such stuff within
Endows a man but he.
2. Gent. You speak him far.
1. Gent. I do extend him, sir, within himself;
Crush him together rather than unfold
His measure duly.
2. Gent. What's his name and birth?
1. Gent. I cannot delve him to the root. His father
Was call'd Sicilius, who did join his honour
Against the Romans with Cassibelan,
But had his titles by Tenantius, whom
He serv'd with glory and admir'd success,
So gain'd the sur-addition Leonatus;
And had, besides this gentleman in question,
Two other sons, who, in the wars o' th' time,
Died with their swords in hand; for which their father,
Then old and fond of issue, took such sorrow
That he quit being; and his gentle lady,
Big of this gentleman, our theme, deceas'd
As he was born. The King he takes the babe
To his protection, calls him Posthumus Leonatus,

Breeds him and makes him of his bedchamber,
Puts to him all the learnings that his time
Could make him the receiver of; which he took,
As we do air, fast as 'twas minist'red
And in's spring became a harvest, liv'd in court
(Which rare it is to do) most prais'd, most lov'd,
A sample to the youngest, to th' more mature
A glass that feated them, and to the graver
A child that guided dotards. To his mistress,
For whom he now is banish'd — her own price
Proclaims how she esteem'd him and his virtue.
By her election may be truly read
What kind of man he is.

2. Gent. I honour him
Even out of your report. But pray you tell me,
Is she sole child to th' King?

1. Gent. His only child.
He had two sons (if this be worth your hearing,
Mark it), the eldest of them at three years old,
I' th' swathing clothes the other, from their nursery
Were stol'n, and to this hour no guess in knowledge
Which way they went.

2. Gent. How long is this ago?

1. Gent. Some twenty years.

2. Gent. That a king's children should be so convey'd,
So slackly guarded, and the search so slow
That could not trace them!

1. Gent. Howsoe'er 'tis strange,
Or that the negligence may well be laugh'd at,
Yet is it true, sir.

2. Gent. I do well believe you.

1. Gent. We must forbear. Here comes the gentleman,
The Queen, and Princess. *Exeunt.*

Enter the *Queen, Posthumus,* and *Imogen.*

Queen. No, be assur'd you shall not find me, daughter,
After the slander of most stepmothers,
Evil-ey'd unto you. You're my prisoner, but
Your jailer shall deliver you the keys
That lock up your restraint. For you, Posthumus,
So soon as I can win th' offended King,
I will be known your advocate. Marry, yet
The fire of rage is in him, and 'twere good
You lean'd unto his sentence with what patience
Your wisdom may inform you.

Post. Please your Highness,
I will from hence to-day.

Queen. You know the peril.
I'll fetch a turn about the garden, pitying
The pangs of barr'd affections, though the King
Hath charg'd you should not speak together. *Exit.*

Imo.
Dissembling courtesy! How fine this tyrant
Can tickle where she wounds! My dearest husband,
I something fear my father's wrath, but nothing
(Always reserv'd my holy duty) what
His rage can do on me. You must be gone;
And I shall here abide the hourly shot
Of angry eyes, not comforted to live
But that there is this jewel in the world
That I may see again.

Post. My queen! my mistress!
O lady, weep no more, lest I give cause
To be suspected of more tenderness
Than doth become a man. I will remain
The loyal'st husband that did e'er plight troth;
My residence in Rome at one Philario's,
Who to my father was a friend, to me
Known but by letter. Thither write, my queen,
And with mine eyes I'll drink the words you send,
Though ink be made of gall.

Enter *Queen.*

Queen. Be brief, I pray you.
If the King come, I shall incur I know not
How much of his displeasure. — [*Aside*] Yet I'll move him
To walk this way. I never do him wrong
But he does buy my injuries, to be friends;
Pays dear for my offences. [*Exit.*]

Post. Should we be taking leave
As long a term as yet we have to live,
The loathness to depart would grow. Adieu!

Imo. Nay, stay a little.
Were you but riding forth to air yourself,
Such parting were too petty. Look here, love.
This diamond was my mother's. Take it, heart,
But keep it till you woo another wife
When Imogen is dead.

Post. How, how? another?
You gentle gods, give me but this I have,
And cere up my embracements from a next
With bonds of death! [*Puts on the ring.*] Remain, remain thou here
While sense can keep it on! And, sweetest, fairest,
As I my poor self did exchange for you
To your so infinite loss, so in our trifles

I still win of you. For my sake wear this.
It is a manacle of love; I'll place it
Upon this fairest prisoner.
[*Puts a bracelet on her arm.*]
Imo. O the gods!
When shall we see again?

Enter *Cymbeline* and *Lords*.

Post. Alack, the King!
Cym. Thou basest thing, avoid! hence, from my sight!
If after this command thou fraught the court
With thy unworthiness, thou diest. Away!
Thou'rt poison to my blood.
Post. The gods protect you,
And bless the good remainders of the court!
I am gone. *Exit.*
Imo. There cannot be a pinch in death
More sharp than this is.
Cym. O disloyal thing
That shouldst repair my youth, thou heap'st
A year's age on me!
Imo. I beseech you, sir,
Harm not yourself with your vexation.
I am senseless of your wrath; a touch more rare
Subdues all pangs, all fears.
Cym. Past grace? obedience?
Imo. Past hope, and in despair; that way, past grace.
Cym. That mightst have had the sole son of my queen!
Imo. O blessed that I might not! I chose an eagle
And did avoid a puttock.
Cym. Thou took'st a beggar, wouldst have made my throne
A seat for baseness.
Imo. No; I rather added
A lustre to it.
Cym. O thou vile one!
Imo. Sir,
It is your fault that I have lov'd Posthumus.
You bred him as my playfellow, and he is
A man worth any woman; overbuys me
Almost the sum he pays.
Cym. What, art thou mad?
Imo. Almost, sir. Heaven restore me! Would I were
A neatherd's daughter, and my Leonatus
Our neighbour shepherd's son!

Enter *Queen*.

Cym. Thou foolish thing!
[*To Queen*] They were again together. You have done
Not after our command. Away with her
And pen her up.
Queen. Beseech your patience. — Peace,
Dear lady daughter, peace! — Sweet sovereign,
Leave us to ourselves, and make yourself some comfort
Out of your best advice.
Cym. Nay, let her languish
A drop of blood a day and, being aged,
Die of this folly! *Exit* [*with Lords*].

Enter *Pisanio*.

Queen. Fie! you must give way.
Here is your servant. How now, sir? What news?
Pis. My lord your son drew on my master.
Queen. Ha!
No harm, I trust, is done?
Pis. There might have been
But that my master rather play'd than fought
And had no help of anger. They were parted
By gentlemen at hand.
Queen. I am very glad on't.
Imo. Your son's my father's friend; he takes his part
To draw upon an exile. O brave sir!
I would they were in Afric both together;
Myself by with a needle, that I might prick
The goer-back. Why came you from your master?
Pis. On his command. He would not suffer me
To bring him to the haven; left these notes
Of what commands I should be subject to
When't pleas'd you to employ me.
Queen. This hath been
Your faithful servant. I dare lay mine honour
He will remain so.
Pis. I humbly thank your Highness.
Queen. Pray walk awhile.
Imo. About some half-hour hence
I pray you speak with me. You shall, at least,
Go see my lord aboard. For this time leave me.
Exeunt.

Scene [II. *Britain. A public place*].

Enter *Cloten* and two *Lords*.

1. Lord. Sir, I would advise you to shift a shirt. The violence of action hath made you reek as a sacrifice. Where air comes out, air comes in. There's none abroad so wholesome as that you vent.

Clo. If my shirt were bloody, then to shift it. Have I hurt him?

2. Lord. [*aside*] No, faith; not so much as his patience.

1. Lord. Hurt him? His body's a passable carcass if he be not hurt. It is a throughfare for steel if it be not hurt.

2. Lord. [*aside*] His steel was in debt. It went o' th' backside the town.

Clo. The villain would not stand me.

2. Lord. [*aside*] No; but he fled forward still, toward your face.

1. Lord. Stand you? You have land enough of your own; but he added to your having, gave you some ground.

2. Lord. [*aside*] As many inches as you have oceans. Puppies!

Clo. I would they had not come between us.

2. Lord. [*aside*] So would I, till you had measur'd how long a fool you were upon the ground.

Clo. And that she should love this fellow and refuse me!

2. Lord. [*aside*] If it be a sin to make a true election, she is damn'd.

1. Lord. Sir, as I told you always, her beauty and her brain go not together. She's a good sign, but I have seen small reflection of her wit.

2. Lord. [*aside*] She shines not upon fools, lest the reflection should hurt her.

Clo. Come, I'll to my chamber. Would there had been some hurt done!

2. Lord. [*aside*] I wish not so, unless it had been the fall of an ass, which is no great hurt.

Clo. You'll go with us?

1. Lord. I'll attend your lordship.

Clo. Nay, come, let's go together.

2. Lord. Well, my lord. *Exeunt.*

Scene [III. *Britain.* Cymbeline's *Palace*].

Enter *Imogen* and *Pisanio.*

Imo. I would thou grew'st unto the shores o' th' haven
And questionedst every sail. If he should write
And I not have it, 'twere a paper lost
As offer'd mercy is. What was the last
That he spake to thee?
Pis. It was 'his queen, his queen!'
Imo. Then wav'd his handkerchief?
Pis. And kiss'd it, madam.
Imo. Senseless linen, happier therein than I!
And that was all?
Pis. No, madam; for so long
As he could make me with this eye or ear
Distinguish him from others, he did keep
The deck, with glove or hat or handkerchief
Still waving, as the fits and stirs of's mind
Could best express how slow his soul sail'd on,
How swift his ship.
Imo. Thou shouldst have made him
As little as a crow, or less, ere left
To after-eye him.
Pis. Madam, so I did.
Imo. I would have broke mine eyestrings, crack'd them but
To look upon him, till the diminution
Of space had pointed him sharp as my needle;
Nay, followed him till he had melted from
The smallness of a gnat to air, and then
Have turn'd mine eye and wept. But, good Pisanio,
When shall we hear from him?
Pis. Be assur'd, madam,
With his next vantage.
Imo. I did not take my leave of him, but had
Most pretty things to say. Ere I could tell him
How I would think on him at certain hours
Such thoughts and such; or I could make him swear
The shes of Italy should not betray
Mine interest and his honour; or have charg'd him,
At the sixth hour of morn, at noon, at midnight,
T' encounter me with orisons, for then
I am in heaven for him; or ere I could
Give him that parting kiss which I had set
Betwixt two charming words — comes in my father,
And, like the tyrannous breathing of the North,
Shakes all our buds from growing.

Enter a *Lady.*

Lady. The Queen, madam,
Desires your Highness' company.
Imo. Those things I bid you do, get them dispatch'd.
I will attend the Queen.
Pis. Madam, I shall. *Exeunt.*

Scene [IV. *Rome.* Philario's *house*].

Enter *Philario, Iachimo,* a *Frenchman,* a *Dutchman,* and a *Spaniard.*

Iach. Believe it, sir, I have seen him in Britain. He was then of a crescent note, expected to prove so worthy as since he hath been allowed the name of. But I could then have look'd on him without the help of admiration, though the catalogue of his endowments had been tabled by his side and I to peruse him by items.

Phil. You speak of him when he was less furnish'd than now he is with that which makes him both without and within.

French. I have seen him in France. We had very many there could behold the sun with as firm eyes as he.

Iach. This matter of marrying his king's daughter, wherein he must be weighed rather by her value than his own, words him, I doubt not, a great deal from the matter.

French. And then his banishment.

Iach. Ay, and the approbation of those that weep this lamentable divorce under her colours are wonderfully to extend him, be it but to fortify her judgment, which else an easy battery might lay flat for taking a beggar without less quality. But how comes it he is to sojourn with you? How creeps acquaintance?

Phil. His father and I were soldiers together, to whom I have been often bound for no less than my life.

Enter *Posthumus.*

Here comes the Briton. Let him be so entertained amongst you as suits, with gentlemen of your knowing, to a stranger of his quality. — I beseech you all be better known to this gentleman, whom I commend to you as a noble friend of mine. How worthy he is I will leave to appear hereafter, rather than story him in his own hearing.

French. Sir, we have known together in Orleans.

Post. Since when I have been debtor to you for courtesies, which I will be ever to pay, and yet pay still.

French. Sir, you o'errate my poor kindness. I was glad I did atone my countryman and you. It had been pity you should have been put together with so mortal a purpose as then each bore, upon importance of so slight and trivial a nature.

Post. By your pardon, sir, I was then a young traveller; rather shunn'd to go even with what I heard than in my every action to be guided by others' experiences; but upon my mended judgment (if I offend not to say it is mended) my quarrel was not altogether slight.

French. Faith, yes, to be put to the arbitrement of swords, and by such two that would by all likelihood have confounded one the other or have fall'n both.

Iach. Can we, with manners, ask what was the difference?

French. Safely, I think. 'Twas a contention in public, which may (without contradiction) suffer the report. It was much like an argument that fell out last night, where each of us fell in praise of our country mistresses; this gentleman at that time vouching (and upon warrant of bloody affirmation) his to be more fair, virtuous, wise, chaste, constant, qualified, and less attemptable, than any the rarest of our ladies in France.

Iach. That lady is not now living, or this gentleman's opinion, by this, worn out.

Post. She holds her virtue still, and I my mind.

Iach. You must not so far prefer her fore ours of Italy.

Post. Being so far provok'd as I was in France, I would abate her nothing, though I profess myself her adorer, not her friend.

Iach. As fair and as good — a kind of hand-in-hand comparison — had been something too fair and too good for any lady in Brittany. If she went before others I have seen as that diamond of yours outlustres many I have beheld, I could not but believe she excelled many; but I have not seen the most precious diamond that is, nor you the lady.

Post. I prais'd her as I rated her. So do I my stone.

Iach. What do you esteem it at?

Post. More than the world enjoys.

Iach. Either your unparagon'd mistress is dead, or she's outpriz'd by a trifle.

Post. You are mistaken. The one may be sold or given, if there were wealth enough for the purchase or merit for the gift; the other is not a thing for sale, and only the gift of the gods.

Iach. Which the gods have given you?

Post. Which by their graces I will keep.

Iach. You may wear her in title yours; but you know strange fowl light upon neighbouring ponds. Your ring may be stol'n too. So your brace of unprizable estimations, the one is but frail and the other casual. A cunning thief, or a that-way-accomplish'd courtier, would hazard the winning both of first and last.

Post. Your Italy contains none so accomplish'd a courtier to convince the honour of my mistress, if, in the holding or loss of that, you term her frail. I do nothing doubt you have store of thieves; notwithstanding, I fear not my ring.

Phil. Let us leave here, gentlemen.

Post. Sir, with all my heart. This worthy signior, I thank him, makes no stranger of me; we are familiar at first.

Iach. With five times so much conversation I should get ground of your fair mistress, make her go back, even to the yielding, had I admittance, and opportunity to friend.

Post. No, no!

Iach. I dare thereupon pawn the moiety of my estate to your ring, which in my opinion o'ervalues it something. But I make my wager rather against your confidence than her reputation; and, to bar your offence herein too, I durst attempt it against any lady in the world.

Post. You are a great deal abus'd in too bold a persuasion, and I doubt not you sustain what y'are worthy of by your attempt.

Iach. What's that?

Post. A repulse; though your attempt, as you call it, deserve more — a punishment too.

Phil. Gentlemen, enough of this. It came in too suddenly. Let it die as it was born, and I pray you be better acquainted.

Iach. Would I had put my estate and my neighbour's on th' approbation of what I have spoke!

Post. What lady would you choose to assail?

Iach. Yours, whom in constancy you think stands so safe. I will lay you ten thousand ducats to your ring that, commend me to the court where your lady is, with no more advantage than the opportunity of a second conference, and I will bring from thence that honour of hers which you imagine so reserv'd.

Post. I will wage against your gold, gold to it. My ring I hold dear as my finger; 'tis part of it.

Iach. You are afraid, and therein the wiser. If you buy ladies' flesh at a million a dram, you cannot preserve it from tainting. But I see you have some religion in you, that you fear.

Post. This is but a custom in your tongue. You bear a graver purpose, I hope.

Iach. I am the master of my speeches, and would undergo what's spoken, I swear.

Post. Will you? I shall but lend my diamond till your return. Let there be covenants drawn between's. My mistress exceeds in goodness the hugeness of your unworthy thinking. I dare you to this match. Here's my ring.

Phil. I will have it no lay.

Iach. By the gods, it is one! If I bring you no sufficient testimony that I have enjoy'd the dearest bodily part of your mistress, my ten thousand ducats are yours; so is your diamond too. If I come off and leave her in such honour as you have trust in, she your jewel, this your jewel, and my gold are yours — provided I have your commendation for my more free entertainment.

Post. I embrace these conditions. Let us have articles betwixt us. Only, thus far you shall answer: if you make your voyage upon her and give me directly to understand you have prevail'd, I am no further your enemy; she is not worth our debate. If she remain unseduc'd, you not making it appear otherwise, for your ill opinion and th' assault you have made to her chastity you shall answer me with your sword.

Iach. Your hand — a covenant! We will have these things set down by lawful counsel, and straight away for Britain, lest the bargain should catch cold and starve. I will fetch my gold and have our two wagers recorded.

Post. Agreed.

[*Exeunt Posthumus and Iachimo.*]

French. Will this hold, think you?

Phil. Signior Iachimo will not from it. Pray let us follow 'em. *Exeunt.*

Scene [V. *Britain.* Cymbeline's *Palace*].

Enter *Queen, Ladies,* and *Cornelius.*

Queen. Whiles yet the dew's on ground, gather those flowers.
Make haste. Who has the note of them?
Lady. I, madam.
Queen. Dispatch. *Exeunt Ladies.*
Now, Master Doctor, have you brought those drugs?
Cor. Pleaseth your Highness, ay. Here they are, madam. [*Presents a box.*]
But I beseech your Grace, without offence
(My conscience bids me ask), wherefore you have
Commanded of me these most poisonous compounds,
Which are the movers of a languishing death,
But though slow, deadly.
Queen. I wonder, Doctor,
Thou ask'st me such a question. Have I not been
Thy pupil long? Hast thou not learn'd me how
To make perfumes? distil? preserve? yea, so
That our great king himself doth woo me oft
For my confections? Having thus far proceeded
(Unless thou think'st me devilish), is't not meet
That I did amplify my judgment in

Other conclusions? I will try the forces
Of these thy compounds on such creatures as
We count not worth the hanging (but none human)
To try the vigour of them and apply
Allayments to their act, and by them gather
Their several virtues and effects.

Cor. Your Highness
Shall from this practice but make hard your heart.
Besides, the seeing these effects will be
But noisome and infectious.

Queen. O, content thee.

Enter *Pisanio.*

[*Aside*] Here comes a flattering rascal. Upon him
Will I first work. He's for his master,
And enemy to my son. — How now, Pisanio?
Doctor, your service for this time is ended;
Take your own way.

Cor. [*aside*] I do suspect you, madam;
But you shall do no harm.

Queen. [*to Pisanio*] Hark thee, a word.

Cor. [*aside*] I do not like her. She doth think she has
Strange ling'ring poisons. I do know her spirit
And will not trust one of her malice with
A drug of such damn'd nature. Those she has
Will stupefy and dull the sense awhile;
Which first, perchance, she'll prove on cats and dogs,
Then afterward up higher; but there is
No danger in what show of death it makes,
More than the locking up the spirits a time,
To be more fresh, reviving. She is fool'd
With a most false effect; and I the truer
So to be false with her.

Queen. No further service, Doctor,
Until I send for thee.

Cor. I humbly take my leave. *Exit.*

Queen. Weeps she still, say'st thou? Dost thou think in time
She will not quench and let instructions enter
Where folly now possesses? Do thou work.
When thou shalt bring me word she loves my son,
I'll tell thee on the instant thou art then
As great as is thy master; greater, for
His fortunes all lie speechless and his name
Is at last gasp. Return he cannot nor
Continue where he is. To shift his being
Is to exchange one misery with another,
And every day that comes comes to decay
A day's work in him. What shalt thou expect
To be depender on a thing that leans,
Who cannot be new built, nor has no friends
So much as but to prop him?
[*Drops the box. Pisanio takes it up.*]
Thou tak'st up
Thou know'st not what. But take it for thy labour.
It is a thing I made which hath the King
Five times redeem'd from death. I do not know
What is more cordial. Nay, I prithee take it.
It is an earnest of a farther good
That I mean to thee. Tell thy mistress how
The case stands with her. Do't as from thyself.
Think what a chance thou changest on; but think
Thou hast thy mistress still; to boot, my son,
Who shall take notice of thee. I'll move the King
To any shape of thy preferment, such
As thou'lt desire; and then myself, I chiefly,
That set thee on to this desert, am bound
To load thy merit richly. Call my women.
Think on my words.
Exit Pisanio.
A sly and constant knave,
Not to be shak'd; the agent for his master,
And the remembrancer of her to hold
The handfast to her lord. I have given him that
Which, if he take, shall quite unpeople her
Of leigers for her sweet, and which she after,
Except she bend her humour, shall be assur'd
To taste of too.

Enter *Pisanio* and *Ladies.*

So, so. Well done, well done.
The violets, cowslips, and the primroses
Bear to my closet. Fare thee well, Pisanio.
Think on my words.
Exeunt Queen and Ladies.

Pis. And shall do.
But when to my good lord I prove untrue,
I'll choke myself. There's all I'll do for you!
Exit.

Scene [VI. *Britain. Another room in the Palace*].

Enter *Imogen* alone.

Imo. A father cruel, and a stepdame false;
A foolish suitor to a wedded lady
That hath her husband banish'd. O, that husband!
My supreme crown of grief! and those repeated

Vexations of it! Had I been thief-stol'n,
As my two brothers, happy! but most miserable
Is the desire that's glorious. Blessed be those,
How mean soe'er, that have their honest wills,
Which seasons comfort. Who may this be? Fie!

Enter *Pisanio* and *Iachimo*.

Pis. Madam, a noble gentleman of Rome
Comes from my lord with letters.
Iach. Change you, madam?
The worthy Leonatus is in safety
And greets your Highness dearly. [*Presents a letter.*]
Imo. Thanks, good sir.
You're kindly welcome.
Iach. [*aside*] All of her that is out of door most rich!
If she be furnish'd with a mind so rare,
She is alone th' Arabian bird, and I
Have lost the wager. Boldness be my friend!
Arm me, audacity, from head to foot!
Or, like the Parthian, I shall flying fight;
Rather, directly fly.

Imo. (*reads*) 'He is one of the noblest note, to whose kindnesses I am most infinitely tied. Reflect upon him accordingly, as you value your trust.
'LEONATUS.'

So far I read aloud;
But even the very middle of my heart
Is warm'd by th' rest and takes it thankfully.
You are as welcome, worthy sir, as I
Have words to bid you, and shall find it so
In all that I can do.
Iach. Thanks, fairest lady.
What, are men mad? Hath nature given them eyes
To see this vaulted arch and the rich crop
Of sea and land, which can distinguish 'twixt
The fiery orbs above, and the twinn'd stones
Upon th' unnumber'd beach, and can we not
Partition make with spectacles so precious
Twixt fair and foul?
Imo. What makes your admiration?
Iach. It cannot be i' th' eye, for apes and monkeys,
'Twixt two such shes, would chatter this way and
Contemn with mows the other; nor i' th' judgment,
For idiots, in this case of favour, would
Be wisely definite; nor i' th' appetite:
Sluttery, to such neat excellence oppos'd,
Should make desire vomit emptiness,
Not so allur'd to feed.
Imo. What is the matter, trow?
Iach. The cloyed will —
That satiate yet unsatisfied desire, that tub
Both fill'd and running — ravening first the lamb,
Longs after for the garbage.
Imo. What, dear sir,
Thus raps you? Are you well?
Iach. Thanks, madam; well. — Beseech you, sir, desire
My man's abode where I did leave him.
He's strange and peevish.
Pis. I was going, sir,
To give him welcome. *Exit.*
Imo. Continues well my lord? His health, beseech you?
Iach. Well, madam.
Imo. Is he dispos'd to mirth? I hope he is.
Iach. Exceeding pleasant; none a stranger there
So merry and so gamesome. He is call'd
The Britain reveller.
Imo. When he was here
He did incline to sadness, and ofttimes
Not knowing why.
Iach. I never saw him sad.
There is a Frenchman his companion, one
An eminent monsieur that, it seems, much loves
A Gallian girl at home. He furnaces
The thick sighs from him; whiles the jolly Briton
(Your lord, I mean) laughs from's free lungs, cries 'O,
Can my sides hold to think that man who knows
By history, report, or his own proof
What woman is, yea, what she cannot choose
But must be, will 's free hours languish for
Assured bondage?'
Imo. Will my lord say so?
Iach. Ay, madam, with his eyes in flood with laughter.
It is a recreation to be by
And hear him mock the Frenchman. But heavens know
Some men are much to blame.
Imo. Not he, I hope.
Iach. Not he; but yet heaven's bounty towards him might
Be us'd more thankfully. In himself, 'tis much;
In you, which I account his, beyond all talents.

Whilst I am bound to wonder, I am bound
To pity too.
Imo. What do you pity, sir?
Iach. Two creatures heartily.
Imo. Am I one, sir?
You look on me. What wrack discern you in me
Deserves your pity?
Iach. Lamentable! What,
To hide me from the radiant sun and solace
I' th' dungeon by a snuff?
Imo. I pray you, sir,
Deliver with more openness your answers
To my demands. Why do you pity me?
Iach. That others do
(I was about to say) enjoy your — But
It is an office of the gods to venge it,
Not mine to speak on't.
Imo. You do seem to know
Something of me, or what concerns me. Pray you —
Since doubting things go ill often hurts more
Than to be sure they do; for certainties
Either are past remedies, or, timely knowing,
The remedy then born — discover to me
What both you spur and stop.
Iach. Had I this cheek
To bathe my lips upon; this hand, whose touch,
Whose every touch, would force the feeler's soul
To th' oath of loyalty; this object, which
Takes prisoner the wild motion of mine eye,
Fixing it only here; should I (damn'd then)
Slaver with lips as common as the stairs
That mount the Capitol; join gripes with hands
Made hard with hourly falsehood — falsehood, as
With labour; then lie peeping in an eye
Base and illustrious as the smoky light
That's fed with stinking tallow: it were fit
That all the plagues of hell should at one time
Encounter such revolt.
Imo. My lord, I fear,
Has forgot Britain.
Iach. And himself. Not I,
Inclin'd to this intelligence, pronounce
The beggary of his change, but 'tis your graces
That from my mutest conscience to my tongue
Charms this report out.
Imo. Let me hear no more.
Iach. O dearest soul, your cause doth strike my heart
With pity that doth make me sick! A lady
So fair, and fasten'd to an empery
Would make the great'st king double, to be partner'd
With tomboys hir'd with that self exhibition
Which your own coffers yield! with diseas'd ventures
That play with all infirmities for gold
Which rottenness can lend nature! such boil'd stuff
As well might poison poison! Be reveng'd!
Or she that bore you was no queen and you
Recoil from your great stock.
Imo. Reveng'd?
How should I be reveng'd? If this be true
(As I have such a heart that both mine ears
Must not in haste abuse) — if it be true,
How should I be reveng'd?
Iach. Should he make me
Live like Diana's priest, betwixt cold sheets,
Whiles he is vaulting variable ramps,
In your despite, upon your purse? Revenge it!
I dedicate myself to your sweet pleasure,
More noble than that runagate to your bed,
And will continue fast to your affection,
Still close as sure.
Imo. What, ho, Pisanio!
Iach. Let me my service tender on your lips.
Imo. Away! I do condemn mine ears that have
So long attended thee. If thou wert honourable,
Thou wouldst have told this tale for virtue, not
For such an end thou seek'st, as base as strange.
Thou wrong'st a gentleman who is as far
From thy report as thou from honour, and
Solicit'st here a lady that disdains
Thee and the devil alike.—What ho, Pisanio!—
The King my father shall be made acquainted
Of thy assault. If he shall think it fit
A saucy stranger in his court to mart
As in a Romish stew and to expound
His beastly mind to us, he hath a court
He little cares for and a daughter who
He not respects at all. — What, ho, Pisanio!
Iach. O happy Leonatus! I may say
The credit that thy lady hath of thee
Deserves thy trust, and thy most perfect goodness
Her assur'd credit. Blessed live you long,
A lady to the worthiest sir that ever
Country call'd his! and you his mistress, only
For the most worthiest fit! Give me your pardon.
I have spoke this to know if your affiance
Were deeply rooted, and shall make your lord
That which he is, new o'er! And he is one
The truest manner'd, such a holy witch
That he enchants societies into him,
Half all men's hearts are his.
Imo. You make amends.

Iach. He sits 'mongst men like a descended god.
He hath a kind of honour sets him off
More than a mortal seeming. Be not angry,
Most mighty Princess, that I have adventur'd
To try your taking of a false report, which hath
Honour'd with confirmation your great judgment
In the election of a sir so rare,
Which you know cannot err. The love I bear him
Made me to fan you thus; but the gods made you,
Unlike all others, chaffless. Pray your pardon.
Imo. All's well, sir. Take my pow'r i' th' court for yours.
Iach. My humble thanks. I had almost forgot
T' entreat your Grace but in a small request,
And yet of moment too, for it concerns
Your lord. Myself and other noble friends
Are partners in the business.
Imo. Pray, what is't?
Iach. Some dozen Romans of us, and your lord
(The best feather of our wing) have mingled sums
To buy a present for the Emperor;
Which I (the factor for the rest) have done
In France. 'Tis plate of rare device and jewels
Of rich and exquisite form, their values great;
And I am something curious, being strange,
To have them in safe stowage. May it please you
To take them in protection?
Imo. Willingly;
And pawn mine honour for their safety. Since
My lord hath interest in them, I will keep them
In my bedchamber.
Iach. They are in a trunk
Attended by my men. I will make bold
To send them to you, only for this night.
I must aboard to-morrow.
Imo. O, no, no!
Iach. Yes, I beseech; or I shall short my word
By length'ning my return. From Gallia
I cross'd the seas on purpose and on promise
To see your Grace.
Imo. I thank you for your pains.
But not away to-morrow!
Iach. O, I must, madam.
Therefore I shall beseech you, if you please
To greet your lord with writing, do't to-night.
I have outstood my time, which is material
To th' tender of our present.
Imo. I will write.
Send your trunk to me; it shall safe be kept
And truly yielded you. You're very welcome.
Exeunt.

ACT II. Scene I. [*Britain. Before* Cymbeline's *Palace.*]

Enter *Cloten* and the two *Lords.*

Clo. Was there ever man had such luck? When I kiss'd the jack, upon an upcast to be hit away! I had a hundred pound on't. And then a whoreson jackanapes must take me up for swearing, as if I borrowed mine oaths of him and might not spend them at my pleasure.

1. Lord. What got he by that? You have broke his pate with your bowl.

2. Lord. [*aside*] If his wit had been like him that broke it, it would have run all out.

Clo. When a gentleman is dispos'd to swear, it is not for any standers-by to curtal his oaths. Ha?

2. Lord. No, my lord; [*aside*] nor crop the ears of them.

Clo. Whoreson dog! I give him satisfaction? Would he had been one of my rank!

2. Lord. [*aside*] To have smell'd like a fool.

Clo. I am not vex'd more at anything in th' earth. A pox on't! I had rather not be so noble as I am. They dare not fight with me, because of the Queen my mother. Every Jack-slave hath his belly full of fighting, and I must go up and down like a cock that nobody can match.

2. Lord. [*aside*] You are cock and capon too, and you crow, cock, with your comb on.

Clo. Sayest thou?

2. Lord. It is not fit your lordship should undertake every companion that you give offence to.

Clo. No, I know that; but it is fit I should commit offence to my inferiors.

2. Lord. Ay, it is fit for your lordship only.

Clo. Why, so I say.

1. Lord. Did you hear of a stranger that's come to court to-night?

Clo. A stranger, and I not know on't?

2. Lord. [*aside*] He's a strange fellow himself, and knows it not.

1. Lord. There's an Italian come, and, 'tis thought, one of Leonatus' friends.

Clo. Leonatus? A banish'd rascal! and he's another, whatsoever he be. Who told you of this stranger?

1. Lord. One of your lordship's pages.

Clo. Is it fit I went to look upon him? Is there no derogation in't?

2. Lord You cannot derogate, my lord.

Clo. Not easily, I think.

2. Lord. [*aside*] You are a fool granted; therefore your issues, being foolish, do not derogate.

Clo. Come, I'll go see this Italian. What I have lost to-day at bowls I'll win to-night of him. Come, go.

2. Lord. I'll attend your lordship.

Exeunt [*Cloten and First Lord*].

That such a crafty devil as is his mother
Should yield the world this ass! a woman that
Bears all down with her brain; and this her son
Cannot take two from twenty, for his heart,
And leave eighteen. Alas, poor princess,
Thou divine Imogen, what thou endur'st,
Betwixt a father by thy stepdame govern'd,
A mother hourly coining plots, a wooer
More hateful than the foul expulsion is
Of thy dear husband, than that horrid act
Of the divorce he'ld make! The heavens hold firm
The walls of thy dear honour, keep unshak'd
That temple, thy fair mind, that thou mayst stand,
T' enjoy thy banish'd lord and this great land!

Exit.

Scene II. [*Britain.* Imogen's *bedchamber in* Cymbeline's *Palace*; *a trunk in one corner.*]

Enter *Imogen* in her bed, and a *Lady* [attending].

Imo. Who's there? My woman? Helen!
Lady. Please you, madam.
Imo. What hour is it?
Lady. Almost midnight, madam.
Imo. I have read three hours then. Mine eyes are weak.
Fold down the leaf where I have left. To bed!
Take not away the taper, leave it burning;
And if thou canst awake by four o' th' clock,
I prithee call me. Sleep hath seiz'd me wholly.

[*Exit Lady.*]

To your protection I commend me, gods.
From fairies and the tempters of the night
Guard me, beseech ye!

Sleeps. Iachimo [*comes*] *from the trunk.*

Iach. The crickets sing and man's o'er-labour'd sense
Repairs itself by rest. Our Tarquin thus
Did softly press the rushes ere he waken'd
The chastity he wounded. Cytherea,
How bravely thou becom'st thy bed! fresh lily,
And whiter than the sheets! That I might touch!
But kiss; one kiss! Rubies unparagon'd,
How dearly they do't! 'Tis her breathing that
Perfumes the chamber thus. The flame o' th' taper
Bows toward her and would underpeep her lids
To see th' enclosed lights, now canopied
Under these windows white and azure, lac'd
With blue of heaven's own tinct. But my design —
To note the chamber. I will write all down:
Such and such pictures; there the window; such
Th' adornment of her bed; the arras, figures —
Why, such and such; and the contents o' th' story.
Ah, but some natural notes about her body,
Above ten thousand meaner moveables
Would testify, t' enrich mine inventory.
O sleep, thou ape of death, lie dull upon her!
And be her sense but as a monument,
Thus in a chapel lying! Come off, come off!

[*Takes off her bracelet.*]

As slippery as the Gordian knot was hard!
'Tis mine! and this will witness outwardly
As strongly as the conscience does within,
To th' madding of her lord. On her left breast
A mole cinque-spotted, like the crimson drops
I' th' bottom of a cowslip. Here's a voucher
Stronger than ever law could make. This secret
Will force him think I have pick'd the lock and ta'en
The treasure of her honour. No more. To what end?
Why should I write this down that's riveted,
Screw'd to my memory? She hath been reading late
The tale of Tereus. Here the leaf 's turn'd down
Where Philomel gave up. I have enough.
To th' trunk again, and shut the spring of it.
Swift, swift, you dragons of the night, that dawning

May bare the raven's eye! I lodge in fear.
Though this a heavenly angel, hell is here.
Clock strikes.
One, two, three. Time, time!
Exit [*into the trunk*].

Scene III. [Cymbeline's *Palace. An ante-chamber adjoining* Imogen's *apartments.*]

Enter *Cloten* and *Lords.*

1. Lord. Your lordship is the most patient man in loss, the most coldest that ever turn'd up ace.

Clo. It would make any man cold to lose.

1. Lord. But not every man patient after the noble temper of your lordship. You are most hot and furious when you win.

Clo. Winning will put any man into courage. If I could get this foolish Imogen, I should have gold enough. It's almost morning, is't not?

1. Lord. Day, my lord.

Clo. I would this music would come. I am advised to give her music a-mornings; they say it will penetrate.

Enter *Musicians.*

Come on, tune! If you can penetrate her with your fingering, so. We'll try with tongue too. If none will do, let her remain; but I'll never give o'er. First, a very excellent good conceited thing; after, a wonderful sweet air with admirable rich words to it — and then let her consider.

Song.

Hark, hark! the lark at heaven's gate sings,
And Phœbus gins arise,
His steeds to water at those springs
On chalic'd flowers that lies;
And winking Mary-buds begin
To ope their golden eyes.
With every thing that pretty is,
My lady sweet, arise;
Arise, arise!

Clo. So, get you gone. If this penetrate, I will consider your music the better; if it do not, it is a vice in her ears which horsehairs and calves' guts, nor the voice of unpaved eunuch to boot, can never amend.
[*Exeunt Musicians.*]

Enter *Cymbeline* and *Queen.*

2. Lord. Here comes the King.

Clo. I am glad I was up so late, for that's the reason I was up so early. He cannot choose but take this service I have done fatherly. — Good morrow to your Majesty and to my gracious mother.

Cym. Attend you here the door of our stern daughter?
Will she not forth?

Clo. I have assail'd her with musics, but she vouchsafes no notice.

Cym. The exile of her minion is too new;
She hath not yet forgot him. Some more time
Must wear the print of his remembrance out,
And then she's yours.

Queen. You are most bound to th' King,
Who lets go by no vantages that may
Prefer you to his daughter. Frame yourself
To orderly soliciting, and be friended
With aptness of the season. Make denials
Increase your services. So seem as if
You were inspir'd to do those duties which
You tender to her; that you in all obey her,
Save when command to your dismission tends,
And therein you are senseless.

Clo. Senseless? Not so.

[Enter a *Messenger.*]

Mess. So like you, sir, ambassadors from Rome.
The one is Caius Lucius.

Cym. A worthy fellow,
Albeit he comes on angry purpose now.
But that's no fault of his. We must receive him
According to the honour of his sender;
And towards himself, his goodness forespent on us,
We must extend our notice. Our dear son,
When you have given good morning to your mistress,
Attend the Queen and us. We shall have need
T' employ you towards this Roman. Come, our queen.
Exeunt [*all but Cloten*].

Clo. If she be up, I'll speak with her; if not,
Let her lie still and dream. By your leave, ho!
[*Knocks.*]
I know her women are about her. What
If I do line one of their hands? 'Tis gold
Which buys admittance; oft it doth — yea, and makes
Diana's rangers false themselves, yield up
Their deer to th' stand o' th' stealer; and 'tis gold
Which makes the true man kill'd and saves the thief;
Nay, sometime hangs both thief and true man. What

Can it not do and undo? I will make
One of her women lawyer to me, for
I yet not understand the case myself.
By your leave. *Knocks.*

Enter a *Lady.*

Lady. Who's there that knocks?
Clo. A gentleman.
Lady. No more?
Clo. Yes, and a gentlewoman's son.
Lady. That's more
Than some whose tailors are as dear as yours
Can justly boast of. What's your lordship's pleasure?
Clo. Your lady's person. Is she ready?
Lady. Ay,
To keep her chamber.
Clo. There is gold for you.
Sell me your good report.
Lady. How? My good name? or to report of you
What I shall think is good? The Princess!

Enter *Imogen.*

Clo. Good morrow, fairest sister. Your sweet hand.
[*Exit Lady.*]
Imo. Good morrow, sir. You lay out too much pains
For purchasing but trouble. The thanks I give
Is telling you that I am poor of thanks
And scarce can spare them.
Clo. Still I swear I love you.
Imo. If you but said so, 'twere as deep with me.
If you swear still, your recompense is still
That I regard it not.
Clo. This is no answer.
Imo. But that you shall not say I yield being silent,
I would not speak. I pray you spare me. Faith,
I shall unfold equal discourtesy
To your best kindness. One of your great knowing
Should learn, being taught, forbearance.
Clo. To leave you in your madness, 'twere my sin.
I will not.
Imo. Fools are not mad folks.
Clo. Do you call me fool?
Imo. As I am mad, I do.
If you'll be patient, I'll no more be mad:
That cures us both. I am much sorry, sir,
You put me to forget a lady's manners
By being so verbal; and learn now, for all,
That I, which know my heart, do here pronounce,
By th' very truth of it, I care not for you,
And am so near the lack of charity
To accuse myself I hate you; which I had rather
You felt than make't my boast.
Clo. You sin against
Obedience, which you owe your father. For
The contract you pretend with that base wretch,
One bred of alms and foster'd with cold dishes,
With scraps o' th' court — it is no contract, none;
And though it be allow'd in meaner parties
(Yet who than he more mean?) to knit their souls
(On whom there is no more dependency
But brats and beggary) in self-figur'd knot,
Yet you are curb'd from that enlargement by
The consequence o' th' crown, and must not foil
The precious note of it with a base slave,
A hilding for a livery, a squire's cloth,
A pantler — not so eminent!
Imo. Profane fellow!
Wert thou the son of Jupiter, and no more
But what thou art besides, thou wert too base
To be his groom. Thou wert dignified enough,
Even to the point of envy, if 'twere made
Comparative for your virtues to be styl'd
The under-hangman of his kingdom, and hated
For being preferr'd so well.
Clo. The south-fog rot him!
Imo. He never can meet more mischance than come
To be but nam'd of thee. His meanest garment
That ever hath but clipp'd his body is dearer
In my respect than all the hairs above thee,
Were they all made such men. — How now, Pisanio?

Enter *Pisanio.*

Clo. 'His garment'? Now the devil —
Imo. To Dorothy my woman hie thee presently.
Clo. 'His garment'?
Imo. I am sprited with a fool;
Frighted, and ang'red worse. Go bid my woman
Search for a jewel that too casually
Hath left mine arm. It was thy master's. Shrew me
If I would lose it for a revenue
Of any king's in Europe. I do think
I saw't this morning; confident I am

Last night 'twas on mine arm; I kiss'd it.
I hope it be not gone to tell my lord
That I kiss aught but he.
Pis. 'Twill not be lost.
Imo. I hope so. Go and search.
[*Exit Pisanio.*]
Clo. You have abus'd me.
'His meanest garment'?
Imo. Ay, I said so, sir.
If you will make't an action, call witness to't.
Clo. I will inform your father.
Imo. Your mother too.
She's my good lady and will conceive, I hope,
But the worst of me. So I leave you, sir,
To th' worst of discontent. *Exit.*
Clo. I'll be reveng'd.
'His meanest garment'? Well. *Exit.*

Scene IV. [*Rome.* Philario's *house.*]

Enter *Posthumus* and *Philario.*

Post. Fear it not, sir. I would I were so sure
To win the King as I am bold her honour
Will remain hers.
Phil. What means do you make to him?
Post. Not any; but abide the change of time,
Quake in the present winter's state, and wish
That warmer days would come. In these fear'd hopes
I barely gratify your love; they failing,
I must die much your debtor.
Phil. Your very goodness and your company
O'erpays all I can do. By this, your king
Hath heard of great Augustus. Caius Lucius
Will do's commission throughly; and I think
He'll grant the tribute, send th' arrearages,
Or look upon our Romans, whose remembrance
Is yet fresh in their grief.
Post. I do believe
(Statist though I am none, nor like to be)
That this will prove a war; and you shall hear
The legions now in Gallia sooner landed
In our not-fearing Britain than have tidings
Of any penny tribute paid. Our countrymen
Are men more order'd than when Julius Cæsar
Smil'd at their lack of skill but found their courage
Worthy his frowning at. Their discipline
(Now wing-led with their courages) will make known
To their approvers they are people such
That mend upon the world.

Enter *Iachimo.*

Phil. See! Iachimo!
Post. The swiftest harts have posted you by land,
And winds of all the corners kiss'd your sails
To make your vessel nimble.
Phil. Welcome, sir.
Post. I hope the briefness of your answer made
The speediness of your return.
Iach. Your lady
Is one of the fairest that I have look'd upon.
Post. And therewithal the best; or let her beauty
Look through a casement to allure false hearts,
And be false with them.
Iach. Here are letters for you.
Post. Their tenure good, I trust.
Iach. 'Tis very like.
Phil. Was Caius Lucius in the Britain court
When you were there?
Iach. He was expected then
But not approach'd.
Post. All is well yet.
Sparkles this stone as it was wont, or is't not
Too dull for your good wearing?
Iach. If I had lost it,
I should have lost the worth of it in gold.
I'll make a journey twice as far t' enjoy
A second night of such sweet shortness which
Was mine in Britain; for the ring is won.
Post. The stone's too hard to come by.
Iach. Not a whit,
Your lady being so easy.
Post. Make not, sir,
Your loss your sport. I hope you know that we
Must not continue friends.
Iach. Good sir, we must,
If you keep covenant. Had I not brought
The knowledge of your mistress home, I grant
We were to question farther; but I now
Profess myself the winner of her honour,
Together with your ring, and not the wronger
Of her or you, having proceeded but
By both your wills.
Post. If you can make't apparent
That you have tasted her in bed, my hand
And ring is yours; if not, the foul opinion
You had of her pure honour gains, or loses,
Your sword, or mine; or masterless leave both
To who shall find them.
Iach. Sir, my circumstances,
Being so near the truth as I will make them,

Must first induce you to believe; whose strength
I will confirm with oath, which I doubt not
You'll give me leave to spare when you shall find
You need it not.

Post. Proceed.

Iach. First, her bedchamber
(Where I confess I slept not, but profess
Had that was well worth watching) — it was hang'd
With tapesty of silk and silver; the story
Proud Cleopatra, when she met her Roman
And Cydnus swell'd above the banks, or for
The press of boats or pride: a piece of work
So bravely done, so rich, that it did strive
In workmanship and value; which I wonder'd
Could be so rarely and exactly wrought,
Since the true life on't was —

Post. This is true;
And this you might have heard of here, by me
Or by some other.

Iach. More particulars
Must justify my knowledge.

Post. So they must,
Or do your honour injury.

Iach. The chimney
Is south the chamber, and the chimney piece
Chaste Dian bathing. Never saw I figures
So likely to report themselves. The cutter
Was as another nature, dumb; outwent her,
Motion and breath left out.

Post. This is a thing
Which you might from relation likewise reap,
Being, as it is, much spoke of.

Iach. The roof o' th' chamber
With golden cherubins is fretted. Her andirons
(I had forgot them) were two winking Cupids
Of silver, each on one foot standing, nicely
Depending on their brands.

Post. This is her honour!
Let it be granted you have seen all this (and praise
Be given to your remembrance), the description
Of what is in her chamber nothing saves
The wager you have laid.

Iach. Then, if you can,
[*Shows the bracelet.*]
Be pale. I beg but leave to air this jewel. See!
And now 'tis up again. It must be married
To that your diamond. I'll keep them.

Post. Jove!
Once more let me behold it Is it that
Which I left with her?

Iach. Sir (I thank her), that.
She stripp'd it from her arm. I see her yet.
Her pretty action did outsell her gift,
And yet enrich'd it too. She gave it me, and said
She priz'd it once.

Post. May be she pluck'd it off
To send it me.

Iach. She writes so to you? doth she?

Post. O, no, no, no! 'tis true. Here, take this too! [*Gives the ring.*]
It is a basilisk unto mine eye,
Kills me to look on't. Let there be no honour
Where there is beauty; truth, where semblance; love,
Where there's another man! The vows of women
Of no more bondage be to where they are made
Than they are to their virtues, which is nothing!
O, above measure false!

Phil. Have patience, sir,
And take your ring again; 'tis not yet won.
It may be probable she lost it; or
Who knows if one of her women, being corrupted,
Hath stol'n it from her?

Post. Very true;
And so I hope he came by't. Back my ring!
Render to me some corporal sign about her
More evident than this; for this was stol'n.

Iach. By Jupiter, I had it from her arm!

Post. Hark you, he swears; by Jupiter he swears.
'Tis true — nay, keep the ring! 'tis true. I am sure
She would not lose it. Her attendants are
All sworn and honourable. They induc'd to steal it?
And by a stranger? No, he hath enjoy'd her.
The cognizance of her incontinency
Is this. She hath bought the name of whore thus dearly.
There, take thy hire! and all the fiends of hell
Divide themselves between you!

Phil. Sir, be patient.
This is not strong enough to be believ'd
Of one persuaded well of.

Post. Never talk on't.
She hath been colted by him.

Iach. If you seek
For further satisfying, under her breast
(Worthy the pressing) lies a mole, right proud
Of that most delicate lodging. By my life,
I kiss'd it and it gave me present hunger
To feed again, though full. You do remember
This stain upon her?

Post. Ay, and it doth confirm
Another stain, as big as hell can hold,
Were there no more but it.
Iach. Will you hear more?
Post. Spare your arithmetic; never count the turns.
Once, and a million!
Iach. I'll be sworn —
Post. No swearing.
If you will swear you have not done't, you lie;
And I will kill thee if thou dost deny
Thou'st made me cuckold.
Iach. I'll deny nothing.
Post. O that I had her here, to tear her limbmeal!
I will go there and do't, i' th' court, before
Her father. I'll do something — *Exit.*
Phil. Quite besides
The government of patience! You have won.
Let's follow him and pervert the present wrath
He hath against himself.
Iach. With all my heart. *Exeunt.*

[Scene V. *Rome. Another room in* Philario's *house.*]

Enter *Posthumus.*

Post. Is there no way for men to be, but women
Must be half-workers? We are all bastards,
And that most venerable man which I
Did call my father was I know not where
When I was stamp'd. Some coiner with his tools
Made me a counterfeit. Yet my mother seem'd
The Dian of that time. So doth my wife
The nonpareil of this. O, vengeance, vengeance!
Me of my lawful pleasure she restrain'd
And pray'd me oft forbearance; did it with
A pudency so rosy, the sweet view on't
Might well have warm'd old Saturn; that I thought her
As chaste as unsunn'd snow. O, all the devils!
This yellow Iachimo in an hour — was't not?
Or less! — at first? Perchance he spoke not, but,
Like a full-acorn'd boar, a German one,
Cried 'O!' and mounted; found no opposition
But what he look'd for should oppose and she
Should from encounter guard. Could I find out
The woman's part in me! For there's no motion
That tends to vice in man but I affirm
It is the woman's part. Be it lying, note it,
The woman's; flattering, hers; deceiving, hers;
Lust and rank thoughts, hers, hers; revenges, hers;
Ambitions, covetings, change of prides, disdain,
Nice longing, slanders, mutability —
All faults that may be nam'd, nay, that hell knows,
Why, hers, in part or all; but rather all!
For even to vice
They are not constant, but are changing still
One vice but of a minute old for one
Not half so old as that. I'll write against them,
Detest them, curse them. Yet 'tis greater skill
In a true hate to pray they have their will:
The very devils cannot plague them better.
Exit.

ACT III. Scene I. [*Britain. A hall in* Cymbeline's *Palace.*]

Enter, in state, *Cymbeline, Queen, Cloten,* and *Lords* at one door; and at another, *Caius Lucius* and *Attendants.*

Cym. Now say, what would Augustus Cæsar with us?
Luc. When Julius Cæsar (whose remembrance yet
Lives in men's eyes and will to ears and tongues
Be theme and hearing ever) was in this Britain
And conquer'd it, Cassibelan thine uncle
(Famous in Cæsar's praises, no whit less
Than in his feats deserving it) for him
And his succession granted Rome a tribute,
Yearly three thousand pounds, which by thee lately
Is left untender'd.
Queen. And, to kill the marvel,
Shall be so ever.
Clo. There be many Cæsars,
Ere such another Julius. Britain is
A world by itself, and we will nothing pay
For wearing our own noses.
Queen. That opportunity
Which then they had to take from's, to resume
We have again. Remember, sir, my liege,
The kings your ancestors, together with
The natural bravery of your isle, which stands
As Neptune's park, ribbed and paled in
With rocks unscalable and roaring waters,
With sands that will not bear your enemies' boats
But suck them up to th' topmast. A kind of conquest

Cæsar made here; but made not here his brag
Of 'came, and saw, and overcame.' With shame
(The first that ever touch'd him) he was carried
From off our coast, twice beaten; and his shipping,
Poor ignorant baubles, on our terrible seas,
Like eggshells mov'd upon their surges, crack'd
As easily 'gainst our rocks; for joy whereof
The fam'd Cassibelan, who was once at point
(O giglet Fortune!) to master Cæsar's sword,
Made Lud's Town with rejoicing fires bright
And Britons strut with courage.

Clo. Come, there's no more tribute to be paid. Our kingdom is stronger than it was at that time, and, as I said, there is no moe such Cæsars. Other of them may have crook'd noses, but to owe such straight arms, none.

Cym. Son, let your mother end.

Clo. We have yet many among us can gripe as hard as Cassibelan. I do not say I am one; but I have a hand. Why tribute? Why should we pay tribute? If Cæsar can hide the sun from us with a blanket or put the moon in his pocket, we will pay him tribute for light; else, sir, no more tribute, pray you now.

Cym. You must know,
Till the injurious Romans did extort
This tribute from us, we were free. Cæsar's ambition,
Which swell'd so much that it did almost stretch
The sides o' th' world, against all colour here
Did put the yoke upon's; which to shake off
Becomes a warlike people, whom we reckon
Ourselves to be.

Clo. We do.

Cym. Say then to Cæsar,
Our ancestor was that Mulmutius which
Ordain'd our laws, whose use the sword of Cæsar
Hath too much mangled, whose repair and franchise
Shall, by the power we hold, be our good deed,
Though Rome be therefore angry. Mulmutius made our laws,
Who was the first of Britain which did put
His brows within a golden crown and call'd
Himself a king.

Luc. I am sorry, Cymbeline,
That I am to pronounce Augustus Cæsar
(Cæsar, that hath moe kings his servants than
Thyself domestic officers) thine enemy.
Receive it from me then: war and confusion
In Cæsar's name pronounce I 'gainst thee. Look
For fury not to be resisted. Thus defied,
I thank thee for myself.

Cym. Thou art welcome, Caius.
Thy Cæsar knighted me; my youth I spent
Much under him; of him I gather'd honour,
Which he to seek of me again, perforce,
Behooves me keep at utterance. I am perfect
That the Pannonians and Dalmatians for
Their liberties are now in arms — a precedent
Which not to read would show the Britons cold.
So Cæsar shall not find them.

Luc. Let proof speak.

Clo. His Majesty bids you welcome. Make pastime with us a day or two, or longer. If you seek us afterwards in other terms, you shall find us in our salt-water girdle. If you beat us out of it, it is yours; if you fall in the adventure, our crows shall fare the better for you; and there's an end.

Luc. So, sir.

Cym. I know your master's pleasure, and he mine.
All the remain is, welcome. *Exeunt.*

Scene II. [*Britain. Another room in* Cymbeline's *Palace.*]

Enter *Pisanio*, reading of a letter.

Pis. How? of adultery? Wherefore write you not
What monster's her accuser? Leonatus!
O master! what a strange infection
Is fall'n into thy ear! What false Italian,
As poisonous-tongu'd as handed, hath prevail'd
On thy too ready hearing? Disloyal? No!
She's punish'd for her truth and undergoes,
More goddess-like than wife-like, such assaults
As would take in some virtue. O my master!
Thy mind to her is now as low as were
Thy fortunes. How? that I should murther her,
Upon the love and truth and vows which I
Have made to thy command? I her? Her blood?
If it be so to do good service, never
Let me be counted serviceable. How look I
That I should seem to lack humanity
So much as this fact comes to? [*Reads.*] 'Do't! The letter
That I have sent her, by her own command
Shall give thee opportunity.' O damn'd paper,
Black as the ink that's on thee! Senseless bauble,

Art thou a feodary for this act, and look'st
So virgin-like without? Lo, here she comes.

Enter *Imogen.*

I am ignorant in what I am commanded.
Imo. How now, Pisanio?
Pis. Madam, here is a letter from my lord.
Imo. Who? thy lord? That is my lord — Leonatus.
O, learn'd indeed were that astronomer
That knew the stars as I his characters!
He'ld lay the future open. You good gods,
Let what is here contain'd relish of love,
Of my lord's health, of his content! yet not
That we two are asunder; let that grieve him!
Some griefs are med'cinable; that is one of them,
For it doth physic love — of his content
All but in that! Good wax, thy leave. Blest be
You bees that make these locks of counsel! Lovers
And men in dangerous bonds pray not alike.
Though forfeiters you cast in prison, yet
You clasp young Cupid's tables. Good news, gods! [*Reads.*]

'Justice and your father's wrath, should he take me in his dominion, could not be so cruel to me as you, O the dearest of creatures, would even renew me with your eyes. Take notice that I am in Cambria at Milford Haven. What your own love will out of this advise you, follow. So he wishes you all happiness that remains loyal to his vow, and your increasing in love

'LEONATUS POSTHUMUS.'

O, for a horse with wings! Hear'st thou, Pisanio?
He is at Milford Haven. Read, and tell me
How far 'tis thither. If one of mean affairs
May plod it in a week, why may not I
Glide thither in a day? Then, true Pisanio,
Who long'st, like me, to see thy lord — who long'st
(O, let me bate!) but not like me, yet long'st,
But in a fainter kind — O, not like me!
For mine's beyond beyond — say, and speak thick
(Love's counsellor should fill the bores of hearing,
To th' smothering of the sense), how far it is
To this same blessed Milford. And by th' way
Tell me how Wales was made so happy as
T' inherit such a haven. But first of all,
How we may steal from hence; and for the gap
That we shall make in time from our hence-going
And our return, to excuse. But first, how get hence.
Why should excuse be born or ere begot?
We'll talk of that hereafter. Prithee speak,
How many score of miles may we well rid
'Twixt hour and hour?
Pis. One score 'twixt sun and sun,
Madam, 's enough for you; and too much too.
Imo. Why, one that rode to's execution, man,
Could never go so slow! I have heard of riding wagers
Where horses have been nimbler than the sands
That run i' th' clock's behalf. But this is fool'ry.
Go bid my woman feign a sickness, say
She'll home to her father; and provide me presently
A riding suit, no costlier than would fit
A franklin's housewife.
Pis. Madam, you're best consider.
Imo. I see before me, man. Nor here, nor here,
Nor what ensues, but have a fog in them
That I cannot look through. Away, I prithee.
Do as I bid thee. There's no more to say.
Accessible is none but Milford way. *Exeunt.*

Scene III. [*Wales. A mountainous country with a cave.*]

Enter [from the cave] *Belarius, Guiderius,* and *Arviragus.*

Bel. A goodly day not to keep house with such
Whose roof 's as low as ours! Stoop, boys. This gate
Instructs you how t' adore the heavens and bows you
To a morning's holy office. The gates of monarchs
Are arch'd so high that giants may jet through
And keep their impious turbands on without
Good morrow to the sun. Hail, thou fair heaven!
We house i' th' rock, yet use thee not so hardly
As prouder livers do.
Gui. Hail, heaven!
Arv. Hail, heaven!
Bel. Now for our mountain sport. Up to yond hill!
Your legs are young; I'll tread these flats. Consider,

When you above perceive me like a crow,
That it is place which lessens and sets off;
And you may then revolve what tales I have told you
Of courts, of princes, of the tricks in war.
This service is not service, so being done,
But being so allow'd. To apprehend thus
Draws us a profit from all things we see;
And often, to our comfort, shall we find
The sharded beetle in a safer hold
Than is the full-wing'd eagle. O, this life
Is nobler than attending for a check,
Richer than doing nothing for a bribe,
Prouder than rustling in unpaid-for silk:
Such gain the cap of him that makes 'em fine
Yet keeps his book uncross'd. No life to ours!

Gui. Out of your proof you speak. We poor unfledg'd
Have never wing'd from view o' th' nest, nor know not
What air's from home. Haply this life is best
If quiet life be best, sweeter to you
That have a sharper known, well corresponding
With your stiff age; but unto us it is
A cell of ignorance, traveling abed,
A prison for a debtor that not dares
To stride a limit.

Arv. What should we speak of
When we are old as you? When we shall hear
The rain and wind beat dark December, how
In this our pinching cave shall we discourse
The freezing hours away? We have seen nothing.
We are beastly: subtle as the fox for prey,
Like warlike as the wolf for what we eat.
Our valour is to chase what flies; our cage
We make a choir, as doth the prison'd bird,
And sing our bondage freely.

Bel. How you speak!
Did you but know the city's usuries
And felt them knowingly; the art o' th' court,
As hard to leave as keep, whose top to climb
Is certain falling, or so slipp'ry that
The fear's as bad as falling; the toil o' th' war,
A pain that only seems to seek out danger
I' th' name of fame and honour, which dies i' th' search
And hath as oft a sland'rous epitaph
As record of fair act; nay, many times
Doth ill deserve by doing well; what's worse,
Must curtsy at the censure! O boys, this story
The world may read in me. My body's mark'd
With Roman swords, and my report was once
First with the best of note. Cymbeline lov'd me;
And when a soldier was the theme, my name
Was not far off. Then was I as a tree
Whose boughs did bend with fruit. But in one night,
A storm or robbery (call it what you will)
Shook down my mellow hangings, nay, my leaves,
And left me bare to weather.

Gui. Uncertain favour!

Bel. My fault being nothing (as I have told you oft)
But that two villains, whose false oaths prevail'd
Before my perfect honour, swore to Cymbeline
I was confederate with the Romans. So
Followed my banishment; and this twenty years
This rock and these demesnes have been my world,
Where I have liv'd at honest freedom, paid
More pious debts to heaven than in all
The fore-end of my time. But up to th' mountains!
This is not hunters' language. He that strikes
The venison first shall be the lord o' th' feast;
To him the other two shall minister;
And we will fear no poison, which attends
In place of greater state. I'll meet you in the valleys.

Exeunt [*Guiderius and Arviragus*].

How hard it is to hide the sparks of nature!
These boys know little they are sons to th' King;
Nor Cymbeline dreams that they are alive.
They think they are mine; and though train'd up thus meanly
I' th' cave wherein they bow, their thoughts do hit
The roofs of palaces, and nature prompts them
In simple and low things to prince it much
Beyond the trick of others. This Polydore, —
The heir of Cymbeline and Britain, who
The King his father call'd Guiderius — Jove!
When on my three-foot stool I sit and tell
The warlike feats I have done, his spirits fly out
Into my story; say 'Thus mine enemy fell,
And thus I set my foot on's neck!' — even then
The princely blood flows in his cheek, he sweats,
Strains his young nerves, and puts himself in posture
That acts my words. The younger brother Cadwal,
Once Arviragus, in as like a figure
Strikes life into my speech and shows much more

His own conceiving. — Hark, the game is rous'd! —
O Cymbeline! heaven and my conscience knows
Thou didst unjustly banish me; whereon,
At three and two years old, I stole these babes,
Thinking to bar thee of succession as
Thou reft'st me of my lands. Euriphile,
Thou wast their nurse. They took thee for their mother,
And every day do honour to her grave.
Myself, Belarius, that am Morgan call'd,
They take for natural father. — The game is up. *Exit.*

Scene IV. [*Britain. Near Milford Haven.*]

Enter *Pisanio* and *Imogen.*

Imo. Thou told'st me, when we came from horse, the place
Was near at hand. Ne'er long'd my mother so
To see me first as I have now. Pisanio! man!
Where is Posthumus? What is in thy mind
That makes thee stare thus? Wherefore breaks that sigh
From th' inward of thee? One but painted thus
Would be interpreted a thing perplex'd
Beyond self-explication. Put thyself
Into a haviour of less fear, ere wildness
Vanquish my staider senses. What's the matter?
Why tender'st thou that paper to me with
A look untender? If't be summer news,
Smile to't before; if winterly, thou need'st
But keep that count'nance still. My husband's hand?
That drug-damn'd Italy hath outcrafted him,
And he's at some hard point. Speak, man! Thy tongue
May take off some extremity which to read
Would be even mortal to me.

Pis. Please you read,
And you shall find me, wretched man, a thing
The most disdain'd of fortune.

Imo. (*reads*) 'Thy mistress, Pisanio, hath play'd the strumpet in my bed, the testimonies whereof lie bleeding in me. I speak not out of weak surmises, but from proof as strong as my grief and as certain as I expect my revenge. That part thou, Pisanio, must act for me, if thy faith be not tainted with the breach of hers. Let thine own hands take away her life. I shall give thee opportunity at Milford Haven; she hath my letter for the purpose; where, if thou fear to strike and to make me certain it is done, thou art the pander to her dishonour and equally to me disloyal.'

Pis. What shall I need to draw my sword? The paper
Hath cut her throat already. No, 'tis slander,
Whose edge is sharper than the sword, whose tongue
Outvenoms all the worms of Nile, whose breath
Rides on the posting winds and doth belie
All corners of the world. Kings, queens, and states,
Maids, matrons, nay, the secrets of the grave
This viperous slander enters. What cheer, madam?

Imo. False to his bed? What is it to be false?
To lie in watch there and to think on him?
To weep 'twixt clock and clock? if sleep charge nature,
To break it with a fearful dream of him
And cry myself awake? That's false to's bed, is it?

Pis. Alas, good lady!

Imo. I false? Thy conscience witness! Iachimo,
Thou didst accuse him of incontinency.
Thou then look'dst like a villain; now, methinks,
Thy favour's good enough. Some jay of Italy,
Whose mother was her painting, hath betray'd him.
Poor I am stale, a garment out of fashion;
And, for I am richer than to hang by th' walls,
I must be ripp'd. To pieces with me! O,
Men's vows are women's traitors! All good seeming,
By thy revolt, O husband, shall be thought
Put on for villany; not born where't grows,
But worn a bait for ladies.

Pis. Good madam, hear me.

Imo. True honest men being heard like false Æneas,
Were in his time thought false; and Sinon's weeping
Did scandal many a holy tear, took pity
From most true wretchedness. So thou, Posthumus,
Wilt lay the leaven on all proper men;
Goodly and gallant shall be false and perjur'd
From thy great fail. Come, fellow, be thou honest;
Do thou thy master's bidding. When thou seest him,
A little witness my obedience. Look!
I draw the sword myself. Take it, and hit
The innocent mansion of my love, my heart.
Fear not! 'Tis empty of all things but grief.

Thy master is not there, who was indeed
The riches of it. Do his bidding, strike!
Thou mayst be valiant in a better cause,
But now thou seem'st a coward.
Pis. Hence, vile instrument!
Thou shalt not damn my hand.
Imo. Why, I must die;
And if I do not by thy hand, thou art
No servant of thy master's. Against self-slaughter
There is a prohibition so divine
That cravens my weak hand. Come, here's my heart —
Something's afore't. Soft, soft! we'll no defence! —
Obedient as the scabbard. What is here?
The scriptures of the loyal Leonatus
All turn'd to heresy? Away, away,
Corrupters of my faith! You shall no more
Be stomachers to my heart. [*Takes his letters out of her bosom.*] Thus may poor fools
Believe false teachers. Though those that are betray'd
Do feel the treason sharply, yet the traitor
Stands in worse case of woe.
And thou, Posthumus, thou that didst set up
My disobedience 'gainst the King my father
And make me put into contempt the suits
Of princely fellows, shalt hereafter find
It is no act of common passage, but
A strain of rareness; and I grieve myself
To think, when thou shalt be disedg'd by her
That now thou tirest on, how thy memory
Will then be pang'd by me. Prithee dispatch!
The lamb entreats the butcher. Where's thy knife?
Thou art too slow to do thy master's bidding
When I desire it too.
Pis. O gracious lady,
Since I receiv'd command to do this business
I have not slept one wink.
Imo. Do't, and to bed then!
Pis. I'll wake mine eyeballs out first.
Imo. Wherefore then
Didst undertake it? Why hast thou abus'd
So many miles with a pretence? this place?
Mine action? and thine own? our horses' labour?
The time inviting thee? the perturb'd court
For my being absent? whereunto I never
Purpose return. Why hast thou gone so far
To be unbent when thou hast ta'en thy stand,
Th' elected deer before thee?
Pis. But to win time
To lose so bad employment: in the which
I have consider'd of a course. Good lady,
Hear me with patience.
Imo. Talk thy tongue weary, speak!
I have heard I am a strumpet; and mine ear,
Therein false struck, can take no greater wound,
Nor tent to bottom that. But speak!
Pis. Then, madam,
I thought you would not back again.
Imo. Most like,
Bringing me here to kill me.
Pis. Not so, neither.
But if I were as wise as honest, then
My purpose would prove well. It cannot be
But that my master is abus'd. Some villain,
Ay, and singular in his art, hath done you both
This cursed injury.
Imo. Some Roman courtesan!
Pis. No, on my life!
I'll give but notice you are dead, and send him
Some bloody sign of it; for 'tis commanded
I should do so. You shall be miss'd at court,
And that will well confirm it.
Imo. Why, good fellow,
What shall I do the while? where bide? how live?
Or in my life what comfort, when I am
Dead to my husband?
Pis. If you'll back to th' court —
Imo. No court, no father! nor no more ado
With that harsh, noble, simple nothing — Cloten!
That Cloten whose love suit hath been to me
As fearful as a siege.
Pis. If not at court,
Then not in Britain must you bide.
Imo. Where then?
Hath Britain all the sun that shines? Day? night?
Are they not but in Britain? I' th' world's volume
Our Britain seems as of it, but not in't;
In a great pool a swan's nest. Prithee think
There's livers out of Britain.
Pis. I am most glad
You think of other place. Th' ambassador,
Lucius the Roman, comes to Milford Haven
To-morrow. Now if you could wear a mind
Dark as your fortune is, and but disguise
That which, t' appear itself, must not yet be
But by self-danger, you should tread a course
Pretty and full of view; yea, happily, near
The residence of Posthumus; so nigh, at least,
That though his actions were not visible, yet
Report should render him hourly to your ear
As truly as he moves.

Imo. O, for such means,
Though peril to my modesty, not death on't
I would adventure!
Pis. Well then, here's the point:
You must forget to be a woman; change
Command into obedience; fear and niceness
(The handmaids of all women, or more truly
Woman it pretty self) into a waggish courage,
Ready in gibes, quick-answer'd, saucy, and
As quarrelous as the weasel. Nay, you must
Forget that rarest treasure of your cheek,
Exposing it (but O, the harder heart!
Alack, no remedy!) to the greedy touch
Of common-kissing Titan, and forget
Your laboursome and dainty trims, wherein
You made great Juno angry.
Imo. Nay, be brief.
I see into thy end and am almost
A man already.
Pis. First, make yourself but like one.
Forethinking this, I have already fit
('Tis in my cloak-bag) doublet, hat, hose, all
That answer to them. Would you, in their serving,
And with what imitation you can borrow
From youth of such a season, fore noble Lucius
Present yourself, desire his service, tell him
Wherein you're happy, — which will make him know,
If that his head have ear in music, — doubtless
With joy he will embrace you; for he's honourable,
And, doubling that, most holy. Your means abroad —
You have me, rich; and I will never fail
Beginning nor supplyment.
Imo. Thou art all the comfort
The gods will diet me with. Prithee away!
There's more to be consider'd; but we'll even
All that good time will give us. This attempt
I am soldier to, and will abide it with
A prince's courage. Away, I prithee.
Pis. Well, madam, we must take a short farewell,
Lest, being miss'd, I be suspected of
Your carriage from the court. My noble mistress,
Here is a box; I had it from the Queen.
What's in't is precious. If you are sick at sea
Or stomach-qualm'd at land, a dram of this
Will drive away distemper. To some shade,
And fit you to your manhood. May the gods
Direct you to the best!
Imo. Amen. I thank thee.
Exeunt [severally].

Scene V. [*Britain.* Cymbeline's *Palace.*]

Enter *Cymbeline*, [attended,] *Queen, Cloten, Lucius*, and *Lords.*

Cym. Thus far; and so farewell.
Luc. Thanks, royal sir.
My emperor hath wrote; I must from hence,
And am right sorry that I must report ye
My master's enemy.
Cym. Our subjects, sir,
Will not endure his yoke; and for ourself
To show less sovereignty than they, must needs
Appear unkinglike.
Luc. So, sir. I desire of you
A conduct overland to Milford Haven.
Madam, all joy befall your Grace, and you!
Cym. My lords, you are appointed for that office.
The due of honour in no point omit.
So farewell, noble Lucius.
Luc. Your hand, my lord.
Clo. Receive it friendly; but from this time forth
I wear it as your enemy.
Luc. Sir, the event
Is yet to name the winner. Fare you well.
Cym. Leave not the worthy Lucius, good my lords,
Till he have cross'd the Severn. Happiness!
Exeunt Lucius and [*Lords*].
Queen. He goes hence frowning; but it honours us
That we have given him cause.
Clo. 'Tis all the better;
Your valiant Britons have their wishes in it.
Cym. Lucius hath wrote already to the Emperor
How it goes here. It fits us therefore ripely
Our chariots and our horsemen be in readiness.
The pow'rs that he already hath in Gallia
Will soon be drawn to head, from whence he moves
His war for Britain.
Queen. 'Tis not sleepy business,
But must be look'd to speedily and strongly.
Cym. Our expectation that it would be thus
Hath made us forward. But, my gentle queen,
Where is our daughter? She hath not appear'd
Before the Roman, nor to us hath tender'd
The duty of the day. She looks us like
A thing more made of malice than of duty.
We have noted it. Call her before us, for
We have been too slight in sufferance.
[*Exit a Messenger.*]

Queen. Royal sir,
Since the exile of Posthumus, most retir'd
Hath her life been; the cure whereof, my lord,
'Tis time must do. Beseech your Majesty,
Forbear sharp speeches to her. She's a lady
So tender of rebukes that words are strokes,
And strokes death to her.

Enter a *Messenger*.

Cym. Where is she, sir? How
Can her contempt be answer'd?
Mess. Please you, sir,
Her chambers are all lock'd, and there's no answer
That will be given to th' loudest noise we make.
Queen. My lord, when last I went to visit her,
She pray'd me to excuse her keeping close;
Whereto constrain'd by her infirmity,
She should that duty leave unpaid to you
Which daily she was bound to proffer. This
She wish'd me to make known; but our great court
Made me to blame in memory.
Cym. Her doors lock'd?
Not seen of late? Grant, heavens, that which I fear
Prove false! *Exit.*
Queen. Son, I say, follow the King.
Clo. That man of hers, Pisanio, her old servant,
I have not seen these two days.
Queen. Go, look after.
Exit [*Cloten*].
Pisanio, thou that stand'st so for Posthumus!
He hath a drug of mine. I pray his absence
Proceed by swallowing that; for he believes
It is a thing most precious. But for her,
Where is she gone? Haply despair hath seiz'd her;
Or, wing'd with fervour of her love, she's flown
To her desir'd Posthumus. Gone she is
To death or to dishonour, and my end
Can make good use of either. She being down,
I have the placing of the British crown.

Enter *Cloten*.

How now, my son?
Clo. 'Tis certain she is fled.
Go in and cheer the King. He rages; none
Dare come about him.
Queen. [*aside*] All the better. May
This night forestall him of the coming day!
Exit.
Clo. I love and hate her; for she's fair and royal,
And that she hath all courtly parts more exquisite
Than lady, ladies, woman. From every one
The best she hath, and she, of all compounded,
Outsells them all. I love her therefore; but
Disdaining me and throwing favours on
The low Posthumus slanders so her judgment
That what's else rare is chok'd; and in that point
I will conclude to hate her, nay, indeed,
To be reveng'd upon her. For, when fools
Shall —

Enter *Pisanio*.

Who is here? What, are you packing, sirrah?
Come hither. Ah, you precious pander! Villain,
Where is thy lady? In a word! or else
Thou art straightway with the fiends.
Pis. O good my lord!
Clo. Where is thy lady? or, by Jupiter —
I will not ask again. Close villain,
I'll have this secret from thy heart, or rip
Thy heart to find it. Is she with Posthumus?
From whose so many weights of baseness cannot
A dram of worth be drawn.
Pis. Alas, my lord,
How can she be with him? When was she miss'd?
He is in Rome.
Clo. Where is she, sir? Come nearer.
No farther halting! Satisfy me home
What is become of her.
Pis. O my all-worthy lord!
Clo. All-worthy villain!
Discover where thy mistress is at once,
At the next word. No more of 'worthy lord'!
Speak, or thy silence on the instant is
Thy condemnation and thy death.
Pis. Then, sir,
This paper is the history of my knowledge
Touching her flight. [*Presents a letter.*]
Clo. Let's see't. I will pursue her
Even to Augustus' throne.
Pis. [*aside*] Or this, or perish.
She's far enough; and what he learns by this
May prove his travel, not her danger.
Clo. Humh!
Pis. [*aside*] I'll write to my lord she's dead. O Imogen,
Safe mayst thou wander, safe return again!
Clo. Sirrah, is this letter true?
Pis. Sir, as I think.
Clo. It is Posthumus' hand; I know't.

Sirrah, if thou wouldst not be a villain, but do me true service, undergo those employments wherein I should have cause to use thee with a serious industry, — that is, what villany soe'er I bid thee do, to perform it directly and truly, — I would think thee an honest man; thou shouldst neither want my means for thy relief nor my voice for thy preferment.

Pis. Well, my good lord.

Clo. Wilt thou serve me? For since patiently and constantly thou hast stuck to the bare fortune of that beggar Posthumus, thou canst not, in the course of gratitude, but be a diligent follower of mine. Wilt thou serve me?

Pis. Sir, I will.

Clo. Give me thy hand. Here's my purse. Hast any of thy late master's garments in thy possession?

Pis. I have, my lord, at my lodging, the same suit he wore when he took leave of my lady and mistress.

Clo. The first service thou dost me, fetch that suit hither. Let it be thy first service. Go.

Pis. I shall, my lord. *Exit.*

Clo. Meet thee at Milford Haven! I forgot to ask him one thing; I'll remember't anon. Even there, thou villain Posthumus, will I kill thee. I would these garments were come. She said upon a time (the bitterness of it I now belch from my heart) that she held the very garment of Posthumus in more respect than my noble and natural person, together with the adornment of my qualities. With that suit upon my back will I ravish her; first kill him, and in her eyes. There shall she see my valour, which will then be a torment to her contempt. He on the ground, my speech of insultment ended on his dead body, and when my lust hath dined (which, as I say, to vex her I will execute in the clothes that she so prais'd), to the court I'll knock her back, foot her home again. She hath despis'd me rejoicingly, and I'll be merry in my revenge.

Enter *Pisanio* [with the clothes].

Be those the garments?

Pis. Ay, my noble lord.

Clo. How long is't since she went to Milford Haven?

Pis. She can scarce be there yet.

Clo. Bring this apparel to my chamber. That is the second thing that I have commanded thee. The third is that thou wilt be a voluntary mute to my design. Be but duteous and true, preferment shall tender itself to thee. My revenge is now at Milford. Would I had wings to follow it! Come, and be true.

Exit.

Pis. Thou bid'st me to my loss; for true to thee
Were to prove false, which I will never be,
To him that is most true. To Milford go,
And find not her whom thou pursuest. Flow, flow,
You heavenly blessings, on her! This fool's speed
Be cross'd with slowness! Labour be his meed!

Exit.

Scene VI. [*Wales. Before the cave of* Belarius.]

Enter *Imogen* alone, [in boy's clothes].

Imo. I see a man's life is a tedious one.
I have tir'd myself, and for two nights together
Have made the ground my bed. I should be sick
But that my resolution helps me. Milford,
When from the mountain top Pisanio show'd thee,
Thou wast within a ken. O Jove! I think
Foundations fly the wretched; such, I mean,
Where they should be reliev'd. Two beggars told me
I could not miss my way. Will poor folks lie,
That have afflictions on them, knowing 'tis
A punishment or trial? Yes; no wonder,
When rich ones scarce tell true. To lapse in fulness
Is sorer than to lie for need; and falsehood
Is worse in kings than beggars. My dear lord!
Thou art one o' th' false ones. Now I think on thee
My hunger's gone; but even before, I was
At point to sink for food. But what is this?
Here is a path to't. 'Tis some savage hold.
I were best not call; I dare not call. Yet famine,
Ere clean it o'erthrow nature, makes it valiant.
Plenty and peace breeds cowards; hardness ever
Of hardiness is mother. Ho! who's here?
If anything that's civil, speak; if savage,

Leon Quartermaine as Cymbeline, King of Britain

CYMBELINE

PHOTOGRAPHS BY ANGUS MCBEAN
PRODUCED BY MEMORIAL THEATRE COMPANY,
STRATFORD-UPON-AVON

Banished for having married the king's daughter, Posthumus (Clement McCallin) says farewell to his wife, Imogen (Kathleen Michael), as the evil queen (Wynne Clark) looks on *(Act I, Scene I)*

"For my sake wear this; it is a manacle of love." Posthumus presents the bracelet later stolen by Iachimo and flaunted as a trophy of his triumph over Imogen's virtue *(Act I, Scene I)*

Iachimo (John Slater) wagers with Posthumus, staking a thousand ducats against a gold ring that he can prove Imogen unfaithful *(Act II, Scene IV)*

"Frame yourself to orderly soliciting, and be friended with aptness of the season." The queen advises her ill-favored son, Cloten (William Squire), to be more ardent in his wooing of his half sister, Imogen. The court fool cowers in the foreground *(Act II, Scene III)*

"Do you call me fool?" Discouraged in his avowal of love, Cloten turns angrily on Imogen *(Act II, Scene III)*

"I have assail'd her with musics but she vouchsafes no answer." Cloten complains to his mother that Imogen is resisting *(Act II, Scene III)*

Above: "Now, Master doctor, have you brought those drugs?" The queen welcomes Cornelius (Julian Amyes), a physician from whom she has ordered poison which she intends for the followers of Posthumus *(Act I, Scene V)*

Left: Imogen prepares for sleep on the fateful night of Iachimo's sly intrusion *(Act II, Scene II)*

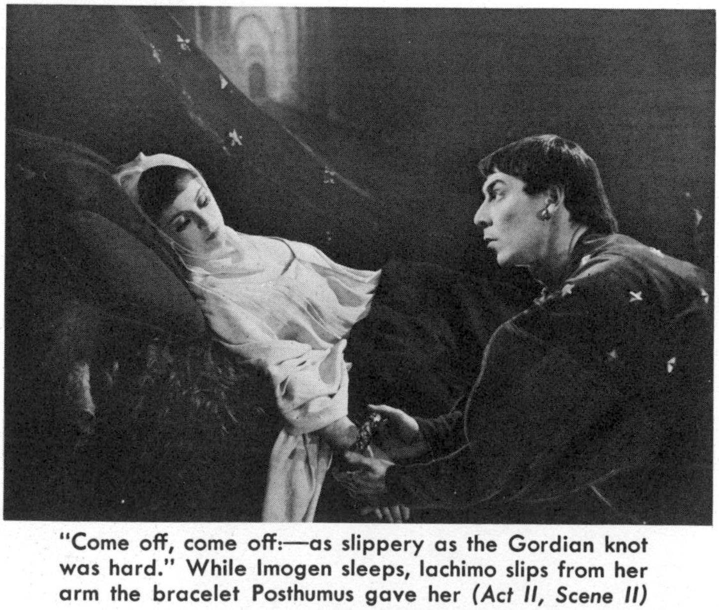

"Come off, come off:—as slippery as the Gordian knot was hard." While Imogen sleeps, Iachimo slips from her arm the bracelet Posthumus gave her *(Act II, Scene II)*

"Why tribute? why should we pay tribute?" Cloten challenges Caius Lucius (Michael Gwynn), the general of the Roman forces, who has come to the court of Cymbeline to demand the tribute to Rome *(Act III, Scene I)*

Below: Convinced of Imogen's innocence, Pisanio advises her to escape *(Act III, Scene IV)*

Above: Having learned from Pisanio (Harry Andrews) that Posthumus believes her unfaithful, Imogen begs him to do his master's bidding and slay her at once: "Prithee, dispatch; the lamb entreats the butcher" *(Act III, Scene IV)*

"Cymbeline lov'd me, and wnen a soldier was the theme, my name was not far off." The outlawed noble, Belarius boasts to his two adopted sons (actually the sons of Cymbeline) of his former greatness and his favor at the court *(Act III, Scene III)*

"I'll have this secret from thy heart, or rip thy heart to find it." Cloten threatens Pisanio, who is reluctant to tell him the whereabouts of Imogen *(Act III, Scene V)*

"Be sprightly, for you fall 'mongst friends." Belarius and his sons welcome Imogen, disguised as a youth *(Act III, Scene VI)*

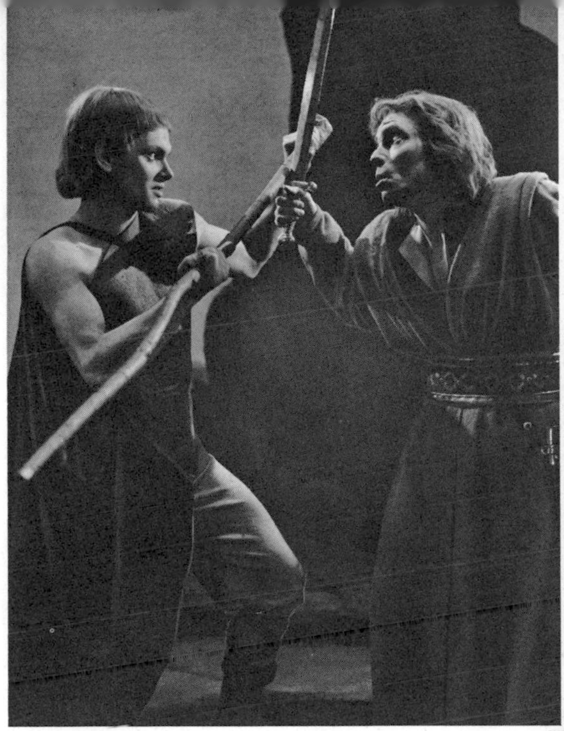

Guiderius (Paul Hansard), Belarius' son, intercepts Cloten, who is pursuing Imogen to Milford Haven *(Act IV, Scene II)*

Right: Heartsick, Imogen has taken the drug from Pisanio's box and fallen into a deathlike sleep. Believing her dead, the sons of Belarius mourn over her *(Act IV, Scene II)*

Below: "This was my master, a very valiant Briton and a good, that here by mountaineers lies slain." Imogen weeps over the headless body of Cloten, which she thinks is that of her husband, Posthumus *(Act IV, Scene II)*

"That diamond upon your finger, say how came it to be yours?" Cymbeline recognizes the ring on Iachimo's finger as belonging to Imogen *(Act V, Scene V)*

"Pardon's the word to all." Cymbeline is reconciled with his son-in-law and Belarius and all misunderstandings are finally resolved *(Act V, Scene V)*

Take or lend. Ho! No answer? Then I'll enter.
Best draw my sword; and if mine enemy
But fear the sword like me, he'll scarcely look on't.
Such a foe, good heavens! *Exit [into the cave].*

Enter *Belarius, Guiderius,* and *Arviragus.*

Bel. You, Polydore, have prov'd best woodman and
Are master of the feast; Cadwal and I
Will play the cook and servant. 'Tis our match.
The sweat of industry would dry and die,
But for the end it works to. Come! Our stomachs
Will make what's homely savoury. Weariness
Can snore upon the flint when resty sloth
Finds the down pillow hard. Now peace be here,
Poor house, that keep'st thyself!
Gui. I am throughly weary.
Arv. I am weak with toil, yet strong in appetite.
Gui. There is cold meat i' th' cave. We'll browse on that
Whilst what we have kill'd be cook'd.
Bel. [*looks into the cave*] Stay, come not in!
But that it eats our victuals, I should think
Here were a fairy.
Gui. What's the matter, sir?
Bel. By Jupiter, an angel! or, if not,
An earthly paragon! Behold divineness
No elder than a boy!

Enter *Imogen.*

Imo. Good masters, harm me not.
Before I enter'd here, I call'd, and thought
To have begg'd or bought what I have took. Good troth,
I have stol'n naught; nor would not, though I had found
Gold strew'd i' th' floor. Here's money for my meat.
I would have left it on the board, so soon
As I had made my meal, and parted
With pray'rs for the provider.
Gui. Money, youth?
Arv. All gold and silver rather turn to dirt!
And 'tis no better reckon'd, but of those
Who worship dirty gods.
Imo. I see you're angry.
Know, if you kill me for my fault, I should
Have died had I not made it.
Bel. Whither bound?
Imo. To Milford Haven.
Bel. What's your name?
Imo. Fidele, sir. I have a kinsman who
Is bound for Italy; he embark'd at Milford;
To whom being going, almost spent with hunger,
I am fall'n in this offence.
Bel. Prithee, fair youth,
Think us no churls, nor measure our good minds
By this rude place we live in. Well encounter'd!
'Tis almost night. You shall have better cheer
Ere you depart, and thanks to stay and eat it.
Boys, bid him welcome.
Gui. Were you a woman, youth,
I should woo hard but be your groom. In honesty,
I bid for you as I'ld buy.
Arv. I'll make't my comfort
He is a man. I'll love him as my brother;
And such a welcome as I'ld give to him
After long absence, such is yours. Most welcome!
Be sprightly, for you fall 'mongst friends.
Imo. 'Mongst friends,
If brothers. [*Aside*] Would it had been so that they
Had been my father's sons! Then had my prize
Been less, and so more equal ballasting
To thee, Posthumus.
Bel. He wrings at some distress.
Gui. Would I could free't!
Arv. Or I, whate'er it be,
What pain it cost, what danger! Gods!
Bel. Hark, boys. [*Whispers.*]
Imo. Great men,
That had a court no bigger than this cave,
That did attend themselves, and had the virtue
Which their own conscience seal'd them, laying by
That nothing-gift of differing multitudes,
Could not outpeer these twain. Pardon me, gods!
I'ld change my sex to be companion with them,
Since Leonatus' false.
Bel. It shall be so.

Boys, we'll go dress our hunt. Fair youth, come in.
Discourse is heavy, fasting. When we have supp'd,
We'll mannerly demand thee of thy story,
So far as thou wilt speak it.

Gui. Pray draw near.

Arv. The night to th' owl and morn to th' lark less welcome!

Imo. Thanks, sir.

Arv. I pray draw near. *Exeunt.*

Scene [VII. *Rome. A public place*].

Enter two *Roman Senators*, and *Tribunes*.

1. Sen. This is the tenour of the Emperor's writ:
That since the common men are now in action
'Gainst the Pannonians and Dalmatians,
And that the legions now in Gallia are
Full weak to undertake our wars against
The fall'n-off Britons, that we do incite
The gentry to this business. He creates
Lucius proconsul; and to you the tribunes,
For this immediate levy, he commands
His absolute commission. Long live Cæsar!

Tribune. Is Lucius general of the forces?

2. Sen. Ay.

Tribune. Remaining now in Gallia?

1. Sen. With those legions
Which I have spoke of, whereunto your levy
Must be supplyant. The words of your commission
Will tie you to the numbers and the time
Of their dispatch.

Tribune. We will discharge our duty. *Exeunt.*

ACT IV. Scene I. [*Wales. Near the cave of* Belarius.]

Enter *Cloten* alone.

Clo. I am near to th' place where they should meet, if Pisanio have mapp'd it truly. How fit his garments serve me! Why should his mistress, who was made by him that made the tailor, not be fit too? the rather (saving reverence of the word) for 'tis said a woman's fitness comes by fits. Therein I must play the workman. I dare speak it to myself (for it is not vainglory for a man and his glass to confer in his own chamber) — I mean, the lines of my body are as well drawn as his; no less young, more strong, not beneath him in fortunes, beyond him in the advantage of the time, above him in birth, alike conversant in general services, and more remarkable in single oppositions. Yet this imperceiverant thing loves him in my despite. What mortality is! Posthumus, thy head, which now is growing upon thy shoulders, shall within this hour be off; thy mistress enforced; thy garments cut to pieces before her face; and all this done, spurn her home to her father; who may (happily) be a little angry for my so rough usage; but my mother, having power of his testiness, shall turn all into my commendations. My horse is tied up safe. Out, sword, and to a sore purpose! Fortune, put them into my hand! This is the very description of their meeting place; and the fellow dares not deceive me. *Exit.*

Scene II. [*Wales. Before the cave of* Belarius.]

Enter *Belarius, Guiderius, Arviragus,* and *Imogen*, from the cave.

Bel. [*to Imogen*] You are not well. Remain here in the cave;
We'll come to you after hunting.

Arv. [*to Imogen*] Brother, stay here.
Are we not brothers?

Imo. So man and man should be;
But clay and clay differs in dignity,
Whose dust is both alike. I am very sick.

Gui. Go you to hunting; I'll abide with him.

Imo. So sick I am not, yet I am not well;
But not so citizen a wanton as
To seem to die ere sick. So please you, leave me;
Stick to your journal course. The breach of custom
Is breach of all. I am ill, but your being by me
Cannot amend me; society is no comfort
To one not sociable. I am not very sick,
Since I can reason of it. Pray you trust me here.
I'll rob none but myself; and let me die,
Stealing so poorly.

Gui. I love thee. I have spoke it,
How much the quantity, the weight as much
As I do love my father.

Bel. What? how? how?

Arv. If it be sin to say so, sir, I yoke me
In my good brother's fault. I know not why
I love this youth, and I have heard you say
Love's reason's without reason. The bier at door,
And a demand who is't shall die, I'ld say
'My father, not this youth.'
Bel. [*aside*] O noble strain!
O worthiness of nature! breed of greatness!
Cowards father cowards and base things sire base.
Nature hath meal and bran, contempt and grace.
I'm not their father; yet who this should be,
Doth miracle itself, lov'd before me. —
'Tis the ninth hour o' th' morn.
Arv. Brother, farewell.
Imo. I wish ye sport.
Arv. You health. — [*To Belarius*] So please you, sir.
Imo. [*aside*] These are kind creatures. Gods, what lies I have heard!
Our courtiers say all's savage but at court.
Experience, O, thou disprov'st report!
Th' imperious seas breed monsters; for the dish
Poor tributary rivers as sweet fish.
I am sick still; heartsick. Pisanio,
I'll now taste of thy drug. [*Swallows some.*]
Gui. I could not stir him.
He said he was gentle, but unfortunate;
Dishonestly afflicted, but yet honest.
Arv. Thus did he answer me; yet said hereafter
I might know more.
Bel. To th' field, to th' field!
We'll leave you for this time; go in and rest.
Arv. We'll not be long away.
Bel. Pray be not sick,
For you must be our housewife.
Imo. Well or ill,
I am bound to you. *Exit* [*into the cave*].
Bel. And shalt be ever.
This youth, howe'er distress'd, appears he hath had
Good ancestors.
Arv. How angel-like he sings!
Gui. But his neat cookery! He cut our roots in characters,
And sauc'd our broths as Juno had been sick
And he her dieter.
Arv. Nobly he yokes
A smiling with a sigh; as if the sigh
Was that it was for not being such a smile;
The smile mocking the sigh, that it would fly
From so divine a temple to commix
With winds that sailors rail at.
Gui. I do note
That grief and patience, rooted in him both,
Mingle their spurs together.
Arv. Grow patience!
And let the stinking elder, grief, untwine
His perishing root with the increasing vine!
Bel. It is great morning. Come, away!
Who's there?

Enter *Cloten.*

Clo. I cannot find those runagates. That villain
Hath mock'd me. I am faint.
Bel. 'Those runagates'!
Means he not us? I partly know him. 'Tis
Cloten, the son o' th' Queen. I fear some ambush.
I saw him not these many years, and yet
I know 'tis he. — We are held as outlaws. Hence!
Gui. He is but one. You and my brother search
What companies are near. Pray you, away!
Let me alone with him.
[*Exeunt Belarius and Arviragus.*]
Clo. Soft! What are you
That fly me thus? Some villain mountainers?
I have heard of such. What slave art thou?
Gui. A thing
More slavish did I ne'er than answering
A 'slave' without a knock.
Clo. Thou art a robber,
A lawbreaker, a villain. Yield thee, thief!
Gui. To who? To thee? What art thou? Have not I
An arm as big as thine? a heart as big?
Thy words, I grant, are bigger; for I wear not
My dagger in my mouth. Say what thou art;
Why I should yield to thee.
Clo. Thou villain base,
Know'st me not by my clothes?
Gui. No, nor thy tailor, rascal,
Who is thy grandfather. He made those clothes,
Which, as it seems, make thee.
Clo. Thou precious varlet,
My tailor made them not.
Gui. Hence then, and thank
The man that gave them thee. Thou art some fool.
I am loath to beat thee.
Clo. Thou injurious thief,
Hear but my name and tremble.

Gui. What's thy name?
Clo. Cloten, thou villain.
Gui. Cloten, thou double villain, be thy name,
I cannot tremble at it. Were it Toad, or Adder, Spider,
'Twould move me sooner.
Clo. To thy further fear,
Nay, to thy mere confusion, thou shalt know
I am son to th' Queen.
Gui. I am sorry for't; not seeming
So worthy as thy birth.
Clo. Art not afeard?
Gui. Those that I reverence, those I fear — the wise;
At fools I laugh, not fear them.
Clo. Die the death!
When I have slain thee with my proper hand,
I'll follow those that even now fled hence
And on the gates of Lud's Town set your heads.
Yield, rustic mountaineer! *Fight and exeunt.*

Enter *Belarius* and *Arviragus.*

Bel. No company's abroad?
Arv. None in the world. You did mistake him sure.
Bel. I cannot tell. Long is it since I saw him,
But time hath nothing blurr'd those lines of favour
Which then he wore. The snatches in his voice,
And burst of speaking, were as his. I am absolute
'Twas very Cloten.
Arv. In this place we left them.
I wish my brother make good time with him,
You say he is so fell.
Bel. Being scarce made up
(I mean, to man), he had not apprehension
Of roaring terrors; for defect of judgment
Is oft the cause of fear.

Enter *Guiderius* [with *Cloten's* head].

But, see, thy brother.
Gui. This Cloten was a fool, an empty purse;
There was no money in't. Not Hercules
Could have knock'd out his brains, for he had none.
Yet I not doing this, the fool had borne
My head as I do his.
Bel. What hast thou done?
Gui. I am perfect what: cut off one Cloten's head,
Son to the Queen, after his own report;
Who call'd me traitor, mountaineer, and swore
With his own single hand he'ld take us in,
Displace our heads where (thank the gods!) they grow,
And set them on Lud's Town.
Bel. We are all undone.
Gui. Why, worthy father, what have we to lose
But that he swore to take, our lives? The law
Protects not us. Then why should we be tender
To let an arrogant piece of flesh threat us
Play judge and executioner all himself,
For we do fear the law? What company
Discover you abroad?
Bel. No single soul
Can we set eye on, but in all safe reason
He must have some attendants. Though his humour
Was nothing but mutation, — ay, and that
From one bad thing to worse, — not frenzy, not
Absolute madness could so far have rav'd
To bring him here alone. Although perhaps
It may be heard at court that such as we
Cave here, hunt here, are outlaws, and in time
May make some stronger head; the which he hearing
(As it is like him) might break out and swear
He'ld fetch us in; yet is't not probable
To come alone, either he so undertaking,
Or they so suffering. Then on good ground we fear,
If we do fear this body hath a tail
More perilous than the head.
Arv. Let ordinance
Come as the gods foresay it. Howsoe'er,
My brother hath done well.
Bel. I had no mind
To hunt this day. The boy Fidele's sickness
Did make my way long forth.
Gui. With his own sword,
Which he did wave against my throat, I have ta'en
His head from him. I'll throw't into the creek
Behind our rock; and let it to the sea
And tell the fishes he's the Queen's son, Cloten.
That's all I reck. *Exit.*
Bel. I fear 'twill be reveng'd.
Would, Polydore, thou hadst not done't! though valour
Becomes thee well enough.
Arv. Would I had done't,
So the revenge alone pursu'd me! Polydore,
I love thee brotherly, but envy much
Thou hast robb'd me of this deed. I would revenges

That possible strength might meet, would seek us through
And put us to our answer.
Bel. Well, 'tis done.
We'll hunt no more to-day, nor seek for danger
Where there's no profit. I prithee, to our rock.
You and Fidele play the cooks. I'll stay
Till hasty Polydore return, and bring him
To dinner presently.
Arv. Poor sick Fidele!
I'll willingly to him. To gain his colour
I'ld let a parish of such Clotens blood
And praise myself for charity. *Exit.*
Bel. O thou goddess,
Thou divine Nature, how thyself thou blazon'st
In these two princely boys! They are as gentle
As zephyrs blowing below the violet,
Not wagging his sweet head; and yet as rough
(Their royal blood enchaf'd) as the rud'st wind
That by the top doth take the mountain pine
And make him stoop to th' vale. 'Tis wonder
That an invisible instinct should frame them
To royalty unlearn'd, honour untaught,
Civility not seen from other, valour
That wildly grows in them but yields a crop
As if it had been sow'd. Yet still it's strange
What Cloten's being here to us portends,
Or what his death will bring us.

Enter *Guiderius.*

Gui. Where's my brother?
I have sent Cloten's clotpoll down the stream
In embassy to his mother; his body's hostage
For his return. *Solemn music.*
Bel. My ingenious instrument!
Hark, Polydore, it sounds! But what occasion
Hath Cadwal now to give it motion? Hark!
Gui. Is he at home?
Bel. He went hence even now.
Gui. What does he mean? Since death of my dear'st mother
It did not speak before. All solemn things
Should answer solemn accidents. The matter?
Triumphs for nothing and lamenting toys
Is jollity for apes and grief for boys.
Is Cadwal mad?

Enter *Arviragus,* with *Imogen,* [as] dead, bearing her in his arms.

Bel. Look, here he comes,
And brings the dire occasion in his arms
Of what we blame him for!
Arv. The bird is dead
That we have made so much on. I had rather
Have skipp'd from sixteen years of age to sixty,
To have turn'd my leaping time into a crutch,
Than have seen this.
Gui. O sweetest, fairest lily!
My brother wears thee not the one half so well
As when thou grew'st thyself.
Bel. O melancholy,
Who ever yet could sound thy bottom? find
The ooze, to show what coast thy sluggish crare
Might easilest harbour in? Thou blessed thing!
Jove knows what man thou mightst have made; but I,
Thou diedst, a most rare boy, of melancholy.
How found you him?
Arv. Stark, as you see;
Thus smiling, as some fly had tickled slumber,
Not as death's dart, being laugh'd at; his right cheek
Reposing on a cushion.
Gui. Where?
Arv. O' th' floor;
His arms thus leagu'd. I thought he slept, and put
My clouted brogues from off my feet, whose rudeness
Answer'd my steps too loud.
Gui. Why, he but sleeps!
If he be gone, he'll make his grave a bed;
With female fairies will his tomb be haunted,
And worms will not come to thee.
Arv. With fairest flowers.
Whilst summer lasts and I live here, Fidele,
I'll sweeten thy sad grave. Thou shalt not lack
The flower that's like thy face, pale primrose; nor
The azur'd harebell, like thy veins; no, nor
The leaf of eglantine, whom not to slander,
Outsweet'ned not thy breath. The raddock would
With charitable bill (O bill, sore shaming
Those rich-left heirs that let their fathers lie
Without a monument!) bring thee all this;
Yea, and furr'd moss besides, when flowers are none,
To winter-ground thy corse.
Gui. Prithee have done,
And do not play in wench-like words with that
Which is so serious. Let us bury him,
And not protract with admiration what
Is now due debt. To th' grave!
Arv. Say, where shall's lay him?
Gui. By good Euriphile, our mother.
Arv. Be't so;
And let us, Polydore, though now our voices

Have got the mannish crack, sing him to th' ground,
As once our mother; use like note and words,
Save that 'Euriphile' must be 'Fidele.'

Gui. Cadwal,
I cannot sing. I'll weep, and word it with thee;
For notes of sorrow out of tune are worse
Than priests and fanes that lie.

Arv. We'll speak it then.

Bel. Great griefs, I see, med'cine the less; for Cloten
Is quite forgot. He was a queen's son, boys;
And though he came our enemy, remember
He was paid for that. Though mean and mighty rotting
Together have one dust, yet reverence
(That angel of the world) doth make distinction
Of place 'tween high and low. Our foe was princely;
And though you took his life as being our foe,
Yet bury him as a prince.

Gui. Pray you fetch him hither.
Thersites' body is as good as Ajax'
When neither are alive.

Arv. If you'll go fetch him,
We'll say our song the whilst. Brother, begin.
[*Exit Belarius.*]

Gui. Nay, Cadwal, we must lay his head to th' east.
My father hath a reason for't.

Arv. 'Tis true.

Gui. Come on then and remove him.

Arv. So. Begin.

Song.

Gui. Fear no more the heat o' th' sun
Nor the furious winter's rages;
Thou thy worldly task hast done,
Home art gone, and ta'en thy wages.
Golden lads and girls all must,
As chimney-sweepers, come to dust.

Arv. Fear no more the frown o' th' great;
Thou art past the tyrant's stroke.
Care no more to clothe and eat;
To thee the reed is as the oak.
The sceptre, learning, physic, must
All follow this and come to dust.

Gui. Fear no more the lightning flash —
Arv. Nor th' all-dreaded thunder-stone;
Gui. Fear not slander, censure rash;
Arv. Thou hast finish'd joy and moan.
Both. All lovers young, all lovers must
Consign to thee and come to dust.

Gui. No exorciser harm thee!
Arv. Nor no witchcraft charm thee!
Gui. Ghost unlaid forbear thee!
Arv. Nothing ill come near thee!
Both. Quiet consummation have,
And renowned be thy grave!

Enter *Belarius* with the body of *Cloten.*

Gui. We have done our obsequies. Come, lay him down.

Bel. Here's a few flowers; but 'bout midnight, more.
The herbs that have on them cold dew o' th' night
Are strewings fitt'st for graves. Upon their faces.
You were as flow'rs, now wither'd. Even so
These herblets shall which we upon you strew.
Come on, away! Apart upon our knees.
The ground that gave them first has them again.
Their pleasures here are past, so is their pain.
Exeunt [*Belarius, Guiderius, and Arviragus*].

Imo. (*awakes*) Yes, sir, to Milford Haven. Which is the way?
I thank you. — By yond bush? — Pray, how far thither?
'Ods pittikins! can it be six mile yet?
I have gone all night. Faith, I'll lie down and sleep. [*Sees the body of Cloten.*]
But, soft! no bedfellow! O gods and goddesses!
These flow'rs are like the pleasures of the world;
This bloody man, the care on't. I hope I dream;
For so I thought I was a cave-keeper
And cook to honest creatures. But 'tis not so;
'Twas but a bolt of nothing, shot at nothing,
Which the brain makes of fumes. Our very eyes
Are sometimes like our judgments, blind. Good faith,
I tremble still with fear; but if there be
Yet left in heaven as small a drop of pity
As a wren's eye, fear'd gods, a part of it!
The dream 's here still. Even when I wake it is
Without me, as within me; not imagin'd, felt.
A headless man? The garments of Posthumus?
I know the shape of's leg; this is his hand,
His foot Mercurial, his Martial thigh,
The brawns of Hercules; but his Jovial face —
Murther in heaven? How? 'Tis gone. Pisanio,
All curses madded Hecuba gave the Greeks,
And mine to boot, be darted on thee! Thou,
Conspir'd with that irregulous devil Cloten,
Hast here cut off my lord. To write and read

Be henceforth treacherous! Damn'd Pisanio
Hath with his forged letters (damn'd Pisanio!)
From this most bravest vessel of the world
Struck the maintop! O Posthumus! alas,
Where is thy head? Where's that? Ay me! where's that?
Pisanio might have kill'd thee at the heart
And left this head on. How should this be? Pisanio?
'Tis he and Cloten. Malice and lucre in them
Have laid this woe here. O, 'tis pregnant, pregnant!
The drug he gave me, which he said was precious
And cordial to me, have I not found it
Murd'rous to th' senses? That confirms it home.
This is Pisanio's deed, and Cloten. O!
Give colour to my pale cheek with thy blood,
That we the horrider may seem to those
Which chance to find us. O my lord, my lord!
[*Falls fainting on the body.*]

Enter *Lucius*, *Captains*, and a *Soothsayer*.

Capt. To them the legions garrison'd in Gallia,
After your will, have cross'd the sea, attending
You here at Milford Haven with your ships.
They are here in readiness.
Luc. But what from Rome?
Capt. The Senate hath stirr'd up the confiners
And gentlemen of Italy, most willing spirits
That promise noble service; and they come
Under the conduct of bold Iachimo.
Syenna's brother.
Luc. When expect you them?
Capt. With the next benefit o' th' wind.
Luc. This forwardness
Makes our hopes fair. Command our present numbers
Be muster'd; bid the captains look to't. — Now, sir,
What have you dream'd of late of this war's purpose?
Sooth. Last night the very gods show'd me a vision
(I fast and pray'd for their intelligence) thus:
I saw Jove's bird, the Roman eagle, wing'd
From the spongy South to this part of the West,
There vanish'd in the sunbeams; which portends
(Unless my sins abuse my divination)
Success to th' Roman host.
Luc. Dream often so,
And never false. Soft, ho! What trunk is here?
Without his top? The ruin speaks that sometime
It was a worthy building. How? a page?
Or dead, or sleeping on him? But dead rather;
For nature doth abhor to make his bed
With the defunct or sleep upon the dead.
Let's see the boy's face.
Capt. He's alive, my lord.
Luc. He'll, then, instruct us of this body. Young one,
Inform us of thy fortunes; for it seems
They crave to be demanded. Who is this
Thou mak'st thy bloody pillow? Or who was he
That, otherwise than noble nature did,
Hath alter'd that good picture? What's thy interest
In this sad wrack? How came't? Who is't? What art thou?
Imo. I am nothing; or if not,
Nothing to be were better. This was my master,
A very valiant Briton and a good,
That here by mountaineers lies slain. Alas,
There is no more such masters! I may wander
From East to Occident, cry out for service,
Try many, all good, serve truly, never
Find such another master.
Luc. 'Lack, good youth!
Thou mov'st no less with thy complaining than
Thy master in bleeding. Say his name, good friend.
Imo. Richard du Champ. [*Aside*] If I do lie and do
No harm by it, though the gods hear, I hope
They'll pardon it. Say you, sir?
Luc. Thy name?
Imo. Fidele, sir.
Luc. Thou dost approve thyself the very same:
Thy name well fits thy faith, thy faith thy name.
Wilt take thy chance with me? I will not say
Thou shalt be so well master'd; but be sure
No less belov'd. The Roman Emperor's letters
Sent by a consul to me should not sooner
Than thine own worth prefer thee. Go with me.
Imo. I'll follow, sir. But first, an't please the gods,
I'll hide my master from the flies, as deep
As these poor pickaxes can dig; and when
With wild wood-leaves and weeds I ha' strew'd his grave
And on it said a century of prayers
(Such as I can) twice o'er, I'll weep and sigh,

And leaving so his service, follow you,
So please you entertain me.
Luc. Ay, good youth,
And rather father thee than master thee.
My friends,
The boy hath taught us manly duties. Let us
Find out the prettiest daisied plot we can
And make him with our pikes and partisans
A grave. Come, arm him. Boy, he's preferr'd
By thee to us, and he shall be interr'd
As soldiers can. Be cheerful; wipe thine eyes.
Some falls are means the happier to arise.
Exeunt.

Scene III. [*Britain.* Cymbeline's *Palace.*]

Enter *Cymbeline, Lords,* and *Pisanio,* [with *Attendants*].

Cym. Again; and bring me word how 'tis with her.
[*Exit an Attendant.*]
A fever with the absence of her son;
A madness, of which her life's in danger. Heavens,
How deeply you at once do touch me! Imogen,
The great part of my comfort, gone; my queen
Upon a desperate bed, and in a time
When fearful wars point at me; her son gone,
So needful for this present! It strikes me past
The hope of comfort. But for thee, fellow,
Who needs must know of her departure and
Dost seem so ignorant, we'll enforce it from thee
By a sharp torture.
Pis. Sir, my life is yours,
I humbly set it at your will; but for my mistress,
I nothing know where she remains, why gone,
Nor when she purposes return. Beseech your Highness,
Hold me your loyal servant.
Lord. Good my liege,
The day that she was missing he was here.
I dare be bound he's true and shall perform
All parts of his subjection loyally. For Cloten,
There wants no diligence in seeking him,
And will no doubt be found.
Cym. The time is troublesome.
[*To Pisanio*] We'll slip you for a season, but our jealousy
Does yet depend.
Lord. So please your Majesty,
The Roman legions, all from Gallia drawn,
Are landed on your coast, with a supply
Of Roman gentlemen by the Senate sent.
Cym. Now for the counsel of my son and queen!
I am amaz'd with matter.
Lord. Good my liege,
Your preparation can affront no less
Than what you hear of. Come more, for more you're ready.
The want is but to put those pow'rs in motion
That long to move.
Cym. I thank you. Let's withdraw,
And meet the time as it seeks us. We fear not
What can from Italy annoy us, but
We grieve at chances here. Away!
Exeunt [*all but Pisanio*].
Pis. I heard no letter from my master since
I wrote him Imogen was slain. 'Tis strange!
Nor hear I from my mistress, who did promise
To yield me often tidings. Neither know I
What is betid to Cloten; but remain
Perplex'd in all. The heavens still must work.
Wherein I am false I am honest; not true, to be true.
These present wars shall find I love my country,
Even to the note o' th' King, or I'll fall in them.
All other doubts, by time let them be clear'd:
Fortune brings in some boats that are not steer'd. *Exit.*

Scene IV. [*Wales. Before the cave of* Belarius.]

Enter *Belarius, Guiderius,* and *Arviragus.*

Gui. The noise is round about us.
Bel. Let us from it.
Arv. What pleasure, sir, find we in life, to lock it
From action and adventure?
Gui. Nay, what hope
Have we in hiding us? This way, the Romans
Must or for Britons slay us, or receive us
For barbarous and unnatural revolts
During their use, and slay us after.
Bel. Sons,
We'll higher to the mountains; there secure us.
To the King's party there's no going. Newness
Of Cloten's death (we being not known, not muster'd
Among the bands) may drive us to a render
Where we have liv'd, and so extort from's that
Which we have done, whose answer would be death
Drawn on with torture.

Gui. This is, sir, a doubt
In such a time nothing becoming you
Nor satisfying us.
Arv. It is not likely
That when they hear the Roman horses neigh,
Behold their quarter'd fires, have both their eyes
And ears so cloy'd importantly as now,
That they will waste their time upon our note,
To know from whence we are.
Bel. O, I am known
Of many in the army. Many years,
Though Cloten then but young, you see, not wore him
From my remembrance. And besides, the King
Hath not deserv'd my service nor your loves,
Who find in my exile the want of breeding,
The certainty of this hard life; aye hopeless
To have the courtesy your cradle promis'd,
But to be still hot summer's tanlings and
The shrinking slaves of winter.
Gui. Than be so
Better to cease to be. Pray, sir, to th' army.
I and my brother are not known; yourself
So out of thought, and thereto so o'ergrown,
Cannot be question'd.
Arv. By this sun that shines,
I'll thither! What thing is it that I never
Did see man die! scarce ever look'd on blood,
But that of coward hares, hot goats, and venison!
Never bestrid a horse, save one that had
A rider like myself, who ne'er wore rowel
Nor iron on his heel! I am asham'd
To look upon the holy sun, to have
The benefit of his blest beams, remaining
So long a poor unknown.
Gui. By heavens, I'll go!
If you will bless me, sir, and give me leave,
I'll take the better care; but if you will not,
The hazard therefore due fall on me by
The hands of Romans!
Arv. So say I. Amen.
Bel. No reason I, since of your lives you set
So slight a valuation, should reserve
My crack'd one to more care. Have with you, boys!
If in your country wars you chance to die,
That is my bed too, lads, and there I'll lie.
Lead, lead. [*Aside*] The time seems long; their blood thinks scorn
Till it fly out and show them princes born.
Exeunt.

ACT V. Scene I. [*Britain. The Roman camp.*]

Enter *Posthumus* alone, [with a bloody handkerchief].

Post. Yea, bloody cloth, I'll keep thee; for I wish'd
Thou shouldst be colour'd thus. You married ones,
If each of you should take this course, how many
Must murther wives much better than themselves
For wrying but a little! O Pisanio,
Every good servant does not all commands!
No bond but to do just ones. Gods, if you
Should have ta'en vengeance on my faults, I never
Had liv'd to put on this; so had you sav'd
The noble Imogen to repent, and struck
Me (wretch!) more worth your vengeance. But alack,
You snatch some hence for little faults; that's love,
To have them fall no more: you some permit
To second ills with ills, each elder worse,
And make them dread it, to the doers' thrift.
But Imogen is your own. Do your best wills,
And make me blest to obey! I am brought hither
Among th' Italian gentry, and to fight
Against my lady's kingdom. 'Tis enough
That, Britain, I have kill'd thy mistress. Peace!
I'll give no wound to thee. Therefore, good heavens,
Hear patiently my purpose. I'll disrobe me
Of these Italian weeds and suit myself
As does a Britain peasant. So I'll fight
Against the part I come with; so I'll die
For thee, O Imogen, even for whom my life
Is, every breath, a death; and thus, unknown,
Pitied nor hated, to the face of peril
Myself I'll dedicate. Let me make men know
More valour in me than my habits show.
Gods, put the strength o' th' Leonati in me!
To shame the guise o' th' world, I will begin
The fashion, less without and more within.
Exit.

Scene II. [*Britain. A field of battle between the British and Roman camps.*]

Enter *Lucius, Iachimo,* and the *Roman Army* at one door, and the *Britain Army* at another, *Leonatus Posthumus* following like a poor soldier. They march over and go out. [Alarums.] Then enter again, in skirmish, *Iachimo* and *Posthumus.* He vanquisheth and disarmeth *Iachimo* and then leaves him.

Iach. The heaviness and guilt within my bosom
Takes off my manhood. I have belied a lady,
The Princess of this country, and the air on't
Revengingly enfeebles me; or could this carl,
A very drudge of Nature's, have subdu'd me
In my profession? Knighthoods and honours, borne
As I wear mine, are titles but of scorn.
If that thy gentry, Britain, go before
This lout as he exceeds our lords, the odds
Is that we scarce are men and you are gods.
Exit.

The battle continues. The Britons fly; Cymbeline is taken. Then enter, to his rescue, *Belarius, Guiderius,* and *Arviragus.*

Bel. Stand, stand! We have th' advantage of the ground.
The lane is guarded. Nothing routs us but
The villany of our fears.
Gui., Arv. Stand, stand, and fight!

Enter *Posthumus,* and seconds the *Britons.* They rescue *Cymbeline,* and exeunt. Then enter *Lucius, Iachimo,* and *Imogen.*

Luc. Away, boy, from the troops, and save thyself;
For friends kill friends, and the disorder's such
As war were hoodwink'd.
Iach. 'Tis their fresh supplies.
Luc. It is a day turn'd strangely. Or betimes
Let's reinforce or fly. *Exeunt.*

Scene III. [*Another part of the field.*]

Enter *Posthumus* and a *Britain Lord.*

Lord. Cam'st thou from where they made the stand?
Post. I did;
Though you, it seems, come from the fliers.
Lord. I did.
Post. No blame be to you, sir, for all was lost,
But that the heavens fought. The King himself
Of his wings destitute, the army broken,
And but the backs of Britons seen, all flying
Through a strait lane — the enemy, full-hearted,
Lolling the tongue with slaught'ring, having work
More plentiful than tools to do't, struck down
Some mortally, some slightly touch'd, some falling
Merely through fear, that the strait pass was damm'd
With dead men hurt behind, and cowards living
To die with length'ned shame.
Lord. Where was this lane?
Post. Close by the battle, ditch'd, and wall'd with turf;
Which gave advantage to an ancient soldier
(An honest one, I warrant), who deserv'd
So long a breeding as his white beard came to,
In doing this for's country. Athwart the lane
He with two striplings (lads more like to run
The country base than to commit such slaughter;
With faces fit for masks, or rather fairer
Than those for preservation cas'd or shame)
Made good the passage, cried to those that fled,
'Our Britain's harts die flying, not our men.
To darkness fleet souls that fly backwards! Stand!
Or we are Romans and will give you that,
Like beasts, which you shun beastly, and may save
But to look back in frown. Stand, stand!' These three,
Three thousand confident, in act as many
(For three performers are the file when all
The rest do nothing), with this word 'Stand, stand!'
Accommodated by the place, more charming
With their own nobleness, which could have turn'd
A distaff to a lance, gilded pale looks,
Part shame, part spirit renew'd; that some, turn'd coward
But by example (O, a sin in war,
Damn'd in the first beginners!) gan to look
The way that they did and to grin like lions
Upon the pikes o' th' hunters. Then began
A stop i' th' chaser, a retire; anon
A rout, confusion thick. Forthwith they fly
Chickens, the way which they stoop'd eagles; slaves,
The strides they victors made; and now our cowards,

Like fragments in hard voyages, became
The life o' th' need. Having found the back-door open
Of the unguarded hearts, heavens, how they wound!
Some slain before, some dying, some their friends
O'erborne i' th' former wave. Ten chas'd by one
Are now each one the slaughterman of twenty.
Those that would die or ere resist are grown
The mortal bugs o' th' field.

Lord. This was strange chance —
A narrow lane, an old man, and two boys!

Post. Nay, do not wonder at it. You are made
Rather to wonder at the things you hear
Than to work any. Will you rhyme upon't
And vent it for a mock'ry? Here is one:
'Two boys, an old man (twice a boy), a lane,
Preserv'd the Britons, was the Romans' bane.'

Lord. Nay, be not angry, sir.

Post. 'Lack, to what end?
Who dares not stand his foe, I'll be his friend;
For if he'll do as he is made to do,
I know he'll quickly fly my friendship too.
You have put me into rhyme.

Lord. Farewell. You're angry. *Exit.*

Post. Still going? This is a lord! O noble misery,
To be i' th' field, and ask 'What news?' of me!
To-day how many would have given their honours
To have sav'd their carcasses! took heel to do't,
And yet died too! I, in mine own woe charm'd,
Could not find Death where I did hear him groan
Nor feel him where he struck. Being an ugly monster,
'Tis strange he hides him in fresh cups, soft beds,
Sweet words; or hath moe ministers than we
That draw his knives i' th' war. Well, I will find him;
For being now a favourer to the Briton,
No more a Briton, I have resum'd again
The part I came in. Fight I will no more,
But yield me to the veriest hind that shall
Once touch my shoulder. Great the slaughter is
Here made by th' Roman; great the answer be
Britons must take. For me, my ransom's death.
On either side I come to spend my breath,
Which neither here I'll keep nor bear again,
But end it by some means for Imogen.

Enter two [*Britain*] *Captains* and *Soldiers.*

1. Capt. Great Jupiter be prais'd! Lucius is taken.
'Tis thought the old man and his sons were angels.

2. Capt. There was a fourth man, in a silly habit,
That gave th' affront with them.

1. Capt. So 'tis reported;
But none of 'em can be found. Stand! Who's there?

Post. A Roman;
Who had not now been drooping here if seconds
Had answer'd him.

2. Capt. Lay hands on him. A dog!
A leg of Rome shall not return to tell
What crows have peck'd them here. He brags his service
As if he were of note. Bring him to th' King.

Enter *Cymbeline, Belarius, Guiderius, Arviragus, Pisanio,* and *Roman Captives.* The *Captains* present *Posthumus* to *Cymbeline,* who delivers him over to a *Jailer.*

[*Exeunt omnes.*]

Scene IV. [*Britain. A prison.*]

Enter *Posthumus* and [two] *Jailer*[*s*].

1. Jail. You shall not now be stol'n; you have locks upon you.
So graze as you find pasture.

2. Jail. Ay, or a stomach.

[*Exeunt Jailers.*]

Post. Most welcome, bondage! for thou art a way,
I think, to liberty. Yet am I better
Than one that's sick o' th' gout, since he had rather
Groan so in perpetuity than be cur'd
By th' sure physician, Death, who is the key
T' unbar these locks. My conscience, thou art fetter'd
More than my shanks and wrists. You good gods, give me
The penitent instrument to pick that bolt,
Then free for ever! Is't enough I am sorry?
So children temporal fathers do appease;
Gods are more full of mercy. Must I repent,
I cannot do it better than in gyves,
Desir'd more than constrain'd. To satisfy,

If of my freedom 'tis the main part, take
No stricter render of me than my all.
I know you are more clement than vile men,
Who of their broken debtors take a third,
A sixth, a tenth, letting them thrive again
On their abatement. That's not my desire.
For Imogen's dear life take mine; and though
'Tis not so dear, yet 'tis a life; you coin'd it.
'Tween man and man they weigh not every stamp —
Though light, take pieces for the figure's sake;
You rather mine, being yours: and so, great pow'rs,
If you will take this audit, take this life
And cancel these cold bonds. O Imogen,
I'll speak to thee in silence. [*Sleeps*.]

Solemn music. Enter (as in an apparition) *Sicilius Leonatus*, father to *Posthumus*, an old man, attired like a warrior; leading in his hand an ancient *Matron* (his wife, and mother to *Posthumus*), with *Music* before them. Then, after other *Music*, follow the two young *Leonati* (brothers to *Posthumus*), with wounds as they died in the wars. *They circle Posthumus round as he lies sleeping.*

Sicil. No more, thou Thunder-master, show
Thy spite on mortal flies.
With Mars fall out, with Juno chide,
That thy adulteries
Rates and revenges.
Hath my poor boy done aught but well,
Whose face I never saw?
I died whilst in the womb he stay'd
Attending nature's law;
Whose father then, as men report
Thou orphans' father art,
Thou shouldst have been, and shielded him
From this earth-vexing smart.

Mother. Lucina lent not me her aid,
But took me in my throes,
That from me was Posthumus ripp'd,
Came crying 'mongst his foes,
A thing of pity.

Sicil. Great Nature like his ancestry
Moulded the stuff so fair
That he deserv'd the praise o' th' world,
As great Sicilius' heir.

1. Bro. When once he was mature for man,
In Britain where was he
That could stand up his parallel,
Or fruitful object be
In eye of Imogen, that best
Could deem his dignity?

Mother. With marriage wherefore was he mock'd,
To be exil'd and thrown
From Leonati seat and cast
From her his dearest one,
Sweet Imogen?

Sicil. Why did you suffer Iachimo,
Slight thing of Italy,
To taint his nobler heart and brain
With needless jealousy,
And to become the geek and scorn
O' th' other's villany?

2. Bro. For this, from stiller seats we came,
Our parents and us twain,
That, striking in our country's cause,
Fell bravely and were slain,
Our fealty and Tenantius' right
With honour to maintain.

1. Bro. Like hardiment Posthumus hath
To Cymbeline perform'd.
Then, Jupiter, thou king of gods,
Why hast thou thus adjourn'd
The graces for his merits due,
Being all to dolours turn'd?

Sicil. Thy crystal window ope; look out.
No longer exercise
Upon a valiant race thy harsh
And potent injuries.

Mother. Since, Jupiter, our son is good,
Take off his miseries.

Sicil. Peep through thy marble mansion. Help!
Or we poor ghosts will cry
To th' shining synod of the rest
Against thy deity.

Brothers. Help, Jupiter! or we appeal
And from thy justice fly.

Jupiter descends in thunder and lightning, sitting upon an eagle. He throws a thunderbolt. The Ghosts fall on their knees.

Jup. No more, you petty spirits of region low,
Offend our hearing. Hush! How dare you ghosts
Accuse the Thunderer, whose bolt, you know,
Sky-planted, batters all rebelling coasts?

Poor shadows of Elysium, hence, and rest
Upon your never-withering banks of flow'rs.
Be not with mortal accidents opprest.
No care of yours it is; you know 'tis ours.
Whom best I love I cross; to make my gift,
The more delay'd, delighted. Be content.
Your low-laid son our godhead will uplift;
His comforts thrive, his trials well are spent.
Our Jovial star reign'd at his birth, and in
Our temple was he married. Rise, and fade!
He shall be lord of Lady Imogen,
And happier much by his affliction made.
This tablet lay upon his breast, wherein
Our pleasure his full fortune doth confine;
And so, away! No farther with your din
Express impatience, lest you stir up mine.
Mount, eagle, to my palace crystalline.
Ascends.

Sicil. He came in thunder; his celestial breath
Was sulphurous to smell; the holy eagle
Stoop'd, as to foot us. His ascension is
More sweet than our blest fields; his royal bird
Prunes the immortal wing and cloys his beak,
As when his god is pleas'd.

All. Thanks, Jupiter!

Sicil. The marble pavement closes; he is enter'd
His radiant roof. Away! and, to be blest,
Let us with care perform his great behest.
[*The Ghosts*] *vanish.*

Post. [*wakes*] Sleep, thou hast been a grandsire and begot
A father to me, and thou hast created
A mother and two brothers; but (O scorn!)
Gone! They went hence so soon as they were born.
And so I am awake. Poor wretches that depend
On greatness' favour, dream as I have done;
Wake, and find nothing. But, alas, I swerve!
Many dream not to find, neither deserve,
And yet are steep'd in favours. So am I,
That have this golden chance and know not why.
What fairies haunt this ground? A book? O rare one!
Be not, as is our fangled world, a garment
Nobler than that it covers. Let thy effects
So follow to be most unlike our courtiers,
As good as promise.

(*Reads*) 'When as a lion's whelp shall, to himself unknown, without seeking find, and be embrac'd by a piece of tender air; and when from a stately cedar shall be lopp'd branches which, being dead many years, shall after revive, be jointed to the old stock, and freshly grow; then shall Posthumus end his miseries, Britain be fortunate and flourish in peace and plenty.'

'Tis still a dream, or else such stuff as madmen
Tongue, and brain not: either both, or nothing;
Or senseless speaking, or a speaking such
As sense cannot untie. Be what it is,
The action of my life is like it, which
I'll keep, if but for sympathy.

Enter *Jailer.*

Jail. Come, sir, are you ready for death?

Post. Over-roasted rather; ready long ago.

Jail. Hanging is the word, sir. If you be ready for that, you are well cook'd.

Post. So, if I prove a good repast to the spectators, the dish pays the shot.

Jail. A heavy reckoning for you, sir. But the comfort is, you shall be called to no more payments, fear no more tavern bills, which are often the sadness of parting, as the procuring of mirth. You come in faint for want of meat, depart reeling with too much drink; sorry that you have paid too much, and sorry that you are paid too much; purse and brain both empty; the brain the heavier for being too light, the purse too light being drawn of heaviness. Of this contradiction you shall now be quit. O, the charity of a penny cord! It sums up thousands in a trice. You have no true debitor and creditor but it; of what's past, is, and to come, the discharge. Your neck, sir, is pen, book, and counters; so the acquittance follows.

Post. I am merrier to die than thou art to live.

Jail. Indeed, sir, he that sleeps feels not the toothache; but a man that were to sleep your sleep, and a hangman to help him to bed, I think he would change places with his officer; for look you, sir, you know not which way you shall go.

Post. Yes indeed do I, fellow.

Jail. Your death has eyes in's head then. I have not seen him so pictur'd. You must either be directed by some that take upon them to know, or take upon yourself that which I am sure you do not know, or jump the after-enquiry on your own peril. And how you shall speed in your journey's end, I think you'll never return to tell one.

Post. I tell thee, fellow, there are none want eyes to direct them the way I am going but such as wink and will not use them.

Jail. What an infinite mock is this, that a man should have the best use of eyes to see the way of blindness! I am sure hanging's the way of winking.

Enter a *Messenger.*

Mess. Knock off his manacles. Bring your prisoner to the King.

Post. Thou bring'st good news. I am call'd to be made free.

Jail. I'll be hanged then.

Post. Thou shalt be then freer than a jailer.
No bolts for the dead.

Exeunt [*Posthumus and Messenger*].

Jail. Unless a man would marry a gallows and beget young gibbets, I never saw one so prone. Yet, on my conscience, there are verier knaves desire to live, for all he be a Roman; and there be some of them too that die against their wills. So should I, if I were one. I would we were all of one mind, and one mind good. O, there were desolation of jailers and gallowses! I speak against my present profit; but my wish hath a preferment in't. *Exit.*

Scene V. [*Britain.* Cymbeline's *tent.*]

Enter *Cymbeline, Belarius, Guiderius, Arviragus, Pisanio,* and *Lords,* [*Officers,* and *Attendants*].

Cym. Stand by my side, you whom the gods have made
Preservers of my throne. Woe is my heart
That the poor soldier that so richly fought,
Whose rags sham'd gilded arms, whose naked breast
Stepp'd before targes of proof, cannot be found.
He shall be happy that can find him, if
Our grace can make him so.

Bel. I never saw
Such noble fury in so poor a thing;
Such precious deeds in one that promis'd naught
But beggary and poor looks.

Cym. No tidings of him?

Pis. He hath been search'd among the dead and living,
But no trace of him.

Cym. To my grief, I am
The heir of his reward; [*to Belarius, Guiderius, and Arviragus*] which I will add
To you, the liver, heart, and brain of Britain,
By whom (I grant) she lives. 'Tis now the time
To ask of whence you are. Report it.

Bel. Sir,
In Cambria are we born, and gentlemen.
Further to boast were neither true nor modest,
Unless I add we are honest.

Cym. Bow your knees.
Arise my knights o' th' battle. I create you
Companions to our person and will fit you
With dignities becoming your estates.

Enter *Cornelius* and *Ladies.*

There's business in these faces. Why so sadly
Greet you our victory? You look like Romans
And not o' th' court of Britain.

Cor. Hail, great King!
To sour your happiness I must report
The Queen is dead.

Cym. Who worse than a physician
Would this report become? But I consider
By med'cine life may be prolong'd, yet death
Will seize the doctor too. How ended she?

Cor. With horror, madly dying, like her life,
Which (being cruel to the world) concluded
Most cruel to herself. What she confess'd
I will report, so please you. These her women
Can trip me if I err, who with wet cheeks
Were present when she finish'd.

Cym. Prithee say.

Cor. First, she confess'd she never lov'd you, only
Affected greatness got by you, not you;
Married your royalty, was wife to your place;
Abhorr'd your person.

Cym. She alone knew this;
And, but she spoke it dying, I would not
Believe her lips in opening it. Proceed.

Cor. Your daughter, whom she bore in hand to love
With such integrity, she did confess
Was as a scorpion to her sight, whose life,
But that her flight prevented it, she had
Ta'en off by poison.

Cym. O most delicate fiend!
Who is't can read a woman? Is there more?

Cor. More, sir, and worse. She did confess she had
For you a mortal mineral, which, being took,
Should by the minute feed on life, and ling'ring,
By inches waste you. In which time she purpos'd,
By watching, weeping, tendance, kissing, to
O'ercome you with her show; and in time,
When she had fitted you with her craft, to work
Her son into th' adoption of the crown;
But failing of her end by his strange absence,
Grew shameless desperate, open'd (in despite

Of heaven and men) her purposes, repented
The evils she hatch'd were not effected; so
Despairing died.

Cym. Heard you all this, her women?

Lady. We did, so please your Highness.

Cym. Mine eyes
Were not in fault, for she was beautiful;
Mine ears, that heard her flattery; nor my heart,
That thought her like her seeming. It had been vicious
To have mistrusted her. Yet (O my daughter!)
That it was folly in me thou mayst say,
And prove it in thy feeling. Heaven mend all!

Enter *Lucius, Iachimo,* [the *Soothsayer,*] and other *Roman Prisoners,* [guarded]; *Leonatus* behind, and *Imogen.*

Thou com'st not, Caius, now for tribute. That
The Britons have ras'd out, though with the loss
Of many a bold one; whose kinsmen have made suit
That their good souls may be appeas'd with slaughter
Of you their captives, which ourself have granted.
So think of your estate.

Luc. Consider, sir, the chance of war. The day
Was yours by accident. Had it gone with us,
We should not, when the blood was cool, have threaten'd
Our prisoners with the sword. But since the gods
Will have it thus, that nothing but our lives
May be call'd ransom, let it come. Sufficeth
A Roman with a Roman's heart can suffer.
Augustus lives to think on't — and so much
For my peculiar care. This one thing only
I will entreat: my boy, a Briton born,
Let him be ransom'd. Never master had
A page so kind, so duteous, diligent,
So tender over his occasions, true,
So feat, so nurse-like. Let his virtue join
With my request, which I'll make bold your Highness
Cannot deny. He hath done no Briton harm,
Though he have serv'd a Roman. Save him, sir,
And spare no blood beside.

Cym. I have surely seen him;
His favour is familiar to me. Boy,
Thou hast look'd thyself into my grace
And art mine own. I know not why, wherefore,
To say 'Live, boy!' Ne'er thank thy master. Live;
And ask of Cymbeline what boon thou wilt,
Fitting my bounty and thy state, I'll give it;
Yea, though thou do demand a prisoner,
The noblest ta'en.

Imo. I humbly thank your Highness.

Luc. I do not bid thee beg my life, good lad;
And yet I know thou wilt.

Imo. No, no! Alack,
There's other work in hand! I see a thing
Bitter to me as death. Your life, good master,
Must shuffle for itself.

Luc. The boy disdains me;
He leaves me, scorns me. Briefly die their joys
That place them on the truth of girls and boys.
Why stands he so perplex'd?

Cym. What wouldst thou, boy?
I love thee more and more. Think more and more
What's best to ask. Know'st him thou look'st on? Speak.
Wilt have him live? Is he thy kin? thy friend?

Imo. He is a Roman; no more kin to me
Than I to your Highness, who, being born your vassal,
Am something nearer.

Cym. Wherefore ey'st him so?

Imo. I'll tell you, sir, in private, if you please
To give me hearing.

Cym. Ay, with all my heart,
And lend my best attention. What's thy name?

Imo. Fidele, sir.

Cym. Thou'rt my good youth, my page.
I'll be thy master. Walk with me. Speak freely.

[*Cymbeline and Imogen converse apart.*]

Bel. Is not this boy reviv'd from death?

Arv. One sand another
Not more resembles. — That sweet rosy lad
Who died, and was Fidele? What think you?

Gui. The same dead thing alive.

Bel. Peace, peace! See further. He eyes us not. Forbear.
Creatures may be alike. Were't he, I am sure
He would have spoke to us.

Gui. But we saw him dead.

Bel. Be silent. Let's see further.

Pis. [*aside*] It is my mistress.
Since she is living, let the time run on
To good or bad.

[*Cymbeline and Imogen advance.*]

Cym. Come, stand thou by our side.
Make thy demand aloud. [*To Iachimo*] Sir, step you forth
Give answer to this boy, and do it freely;
Or, by our greatness and the grace of it,
Which is our honour, bitter torture shall
Winnow the truth from falsehood. — On, speak to him.

Imo. My boon is that this gentleman may render
Of whom he had this ring.

Post. [*aside*] What's that to him?

Cym. That diamond upon your finger, say
How came it yours.

Iach. Thou'lt torture me to leave unspoken that
Which to be spoke would torture thee.

Cym. How? me?

Iach. I am glad to be constrain'd to utter that
Which torments me to conceal. By villany
I got this ring. 'Twas Leonatus' jewel,
Whom thou didst banish; and (which more may grieve thee,
As it doth me) a nobler sir ne'er liv'd
'Twixt sky and ground. Wilt thou hear more, my lord?

Cym. All that belongs to this.

Iach. That paragon, thy daughter,
For whom my heart drops blood and my false spirits
Quail to remember — Give me leave! I faint.

Cym. My daughter? What of her? Renew thy strength.
I had rather thou shouldst live while nature will
Than die ere I hear more. Strive, man, and speak.

Iach. Upon a time (unhappy was the clock
That struck the hour!); it was in Rome (accurs'd
The mansion where!); 'twas at a feast (O, would
Our viands had been poison'd, or at least
Those which I heav'd to head!); the good Posthumus
(What should I say? He was too good to be
Where ill men were, and was the best of all
Amongst the rar'st of good ones), sitting sadly,
Hearing us praise our loves of Italy
For beauty that made barren the swell'd boast
Of him that best could speak; for feature, laming
The shrine of Venus or straight-pight Minerva,
Postures beyond brief nature; for condition,
A shop of all the qualities that man
Loves woman for; besides that hook of wiving,
Fairness which strikes the eye —

Cym. I stand on fire.
Come to the matter.

Iach. All too soon I shall,
Unless thou wouldst grieve quickly. This Posthumus,
Most like a noble lord in love and one
That had a royal lover, took his hint;
And (not dispraising whom we prais'd; therein
He was as calm as virtue) he began
His mistress' picture; which by his tongue being made,
And then a mind put in't, either our brags
Were crack'd of kitchen trulls, or his description
Prov'd us unspeaking sots.

Cym. Nay, nay, to th' purpose!

Iach. Your daughter's chastity — there it begins.
He spake of her, as Dian had hot dreams
And she alone were cold; whereat I, wretch,
Made scruple of his praise, and wager'd with him
Pieces of gold 'gainst this which then he wore
Upon his honour'd finger, to attain
In suit the place of's bed and win this ring
By hers and mine adultery. He, true knight,
No lesser of her honour confident
Than I did truly find her, stakes this ring;
And would so, had it been a carbuncle
Of Phœbus' wheel; and might so safely, had it
Been all the worth of's car. Away to Britain
Post I in this design. Well may you, sir,
Remember me at court, where I was taught
Of your chaste daughter the wide difference
'Twixt amorous and villanous. Being thus quench'd
Of hope, not longing, mine Italian brain
Gan in your duller Britain operate
Most vilely; for my vantage, excellent;
And, to be brief, my practice so prevail'd
That I return'd with simular proof enough
To make the noble Leonatus mad
By wounding his belief in her renown
With tokens thus and thus; averring notes
Of chamber hanging, pictures, this her bracelet
(O cunning, how I got it!) — nay, some marks
Of secret on her person, that he could not
But think her bond of chastity quite crack'd,
I having ta'en the forfeit. Whereupon —
Methinks I see him now —

Post. [*advances*] Ay, so thou dost,
Italian fiend! Ay me, most credulous fool,
Egregious murtherer, thief, anything
That's due to all the villains past, in being,

To come! O, give me cord or knife or poison,
Some upright justicer! Thou, King, send out
For torturers ingenious. It is I
That all th' abhorred things o' th' earth amend
By being worse than they. I am Posthumus,
That kill'd thy daughter — villain-like, I lie! —
That caus'd a lesser villain than myself,
A sacrilegious thief, to do't. The temple
Of virtue was she; yea, and she herself!
Spit, and throw stones, cast mire upon me, set
The dogs o' th' street to bay me! Every villain
Be call'd Posthumus Leonatus, and
Be villany less than 'twas! O Imogen!
My queen, my life, my wife! O Imogen,
Imogen, Imogen!

Imo. Peace, my lord. Hear, hear!

Post. Shall's have a play of this? Thou scornful page,
There lie thy part! [*Strikes her. She falls.*]

Pis. O gentlemen, help!
Mine and your mistress! O my lord Posthumus!
You ne'er kill'd Imogen till now. Help, help!
Mine honour'd lady!

Cym. Does the world go round?

Post. How comes these staggers on me?

Pis. Wake, my mistress!

Cym. If this be so, the gods do mean to strike me
To death with mortal joy.

Pis. How fares my mistress?

Imo. O, get thee from my sight!
Thou gav'st me poison. Dangerous fellow, hence!
Breathe not where princes are.

Cym. The tune of Imogen!

Pis. Lady,
The gods throw stones of sulphur on me if
That box I gave you was not thought by me
A precious thing. I had it from the Queen.

Cym. New matter still?

Imo. It poison'd me.

Cor. O gods!
I left out one thing which the Queen confess'd,
Which must approve thee honest. 'If Pisanio
Have,' said she, 'given his mistress that confection
Which I gave him for cordial, she is serv'd
As I would serve a rat.'

Cym. What's this, Cornelius?

Cor. The Queen, sir, very oft importun'd me
To temper poisons for her; still pretending
The satisfaction of her knowledge, only
In killing creatures vile, as cats and dogs
Of no esteem. I, dreading that her purpose
Was of more danger, did compound for her
A certain stuff which, being ta'en, would cease
The present pow'r of life, but in short time
All offices of nature should again
Do their due functions. Have you ta'en of it?

Imo. Most like I did, for I was dead.

Bel. My boys,
There was our error.

Gui. This is sure Fidele.

Imo. Why did you throw your wedded lady from you?
Think that you are upon a rock, and now
Throw me again. [*Embraces him.*]

Post. Hang there like fruit, my soul,
Till the tree die!

Cym. How now, my flesh? my child?
What, mak'st thou me a dullard in this act?
Wilt thou not speak to me?

Imo. [*kneels*] Your blessing, sir.

Bel. [*to Guiderius and Arviragus*] Though you did love this youth, I blame ye not;
You had a motive for't.

Cym. My tears that fall
Prove holy water on thee! Imogen,
Thy mother's dead.

Imo. I am sorry for't, my lord.

Cym. O, she was naught, and long of her it was
That we meet here so strangely; but her son
Is gone, we know not how nor where.

Pis. My lord,
Now fear is from me, I'll speak troth. Lord Cloten,
Upon my lady's missing, came to me
With his sword drawn, foam'd at the mouth, and swore,
If I discover'd not which way she was gone,
It was my instant death. By accident
I had a feigned letter of my master's
Then in my pocket, which directed him
To seek her on the mountains near to Milford;
Where, in a frenzy, in my master's garments
(Which he enforc'd from me) away he posts
With unchaste purpose, and with oath to violate
My lady's honour. What became of him
I further know not.

Gui. Let me end the story.
I slew him there.

Cym. Marry, the gods forfend!
I would not thy good deeds should from my lips
Pluck a hard sentence. Prithee, valiant youth,
Deny't again.

Gui. I have spoke it, and I did it.

Cym. He was a prince.

Gui. A most incivil one. The wrongs he did me
Were nothing princelike; for he did provoke me
With language that would make me spurn the sea,
If it could so roar to me. I cut off's head,
And am right glad he is not standing here
To tell this tale of mine.
Cym. I am sorry for thee.
By thine own tongue thou art condemn'd, and must
Endure our law. Thou'rt dead.
Imo. That headless man
I thought had been my lord.
Cym. Bind the offender
And take him from our presence.
Bel. Stay, Sir King.
This man is better than the man he slew,
As well descended as thyself, and hath
More of thee merited than a band of Clotens
Had ever scar for. [*To the Guard*] Let his arms alone;
They were not born for bondage.
Cym. Why, old soldier,
Wilt thou undo the worth thou art unpaid for
By tasting of our wrath? How of descent
As good as we?
Arv. In that he spake too far.
Cym. And thou shalt die for't.
Bel. We will die all three
But I will prove that two on's are as good
As I have given out him. My sons, I must
For mine own part unfold a dangerous speech,
Though haply well for you.
Arv. Your danger's ours.
Gui. And our good his.
Bel. Have at it then by leave!
Thou hadst, great king, a subject who
Was call'd Belarius.
Cym. What of him? He is
A banish'd traitor.
Bel. He it is that hath
Assum'd this age; indeed a banish'd man;
I know not how a traitor.
Cym. Take him hence.
The whole world shall not save him.
Bel. Not too hot!
First pay me for the nursing of thy sons,
And let it be confiscate all, so soon
As I have receiv'd it.
Cym. Nursing of my sons?
Bel. I am too blunt and saucy. Here's my knee.
Ere I arise I will prefer my sons;
Then spare not the old father. Mighty sir,
These two young gentlemen that call me father
And think they are my sons are none of mine;
They are the issue of your loins, my liege,
And blood of your begetting.
Cym. How? my issue?
Bel. So sure as you your father's. I, old Morgan,
Am that Belarius whom you sometime banish'd.
Your pleasure was my mere offence, my punishment
Itself, and all my treason. That I suffer'd
Was all the harm I did. These gentle princes
(For such and so they are) these twenty years
Have I train'd up. Those arts they have as I
Could put into them. My breeding was, sir, as
Your Highness knows. Their nurse, Euriphile
(Whom for the theft I wedded), stole these children
Upon my banishment. I mov'd her to't,
Having receiv'd the punishment before
For that which I did then. Beaten for loyalty
Excited me to treason. Their dear loss,
The more of you 'twas felt, the more it shap'd
Unto my end of stealing them. But, gracious sir,
Here are your sons again; and I must lose
Two of the sweet'st companions in the world.
The benediction of these covering heavens
Fall on their heads like dew! for they are worthy
To inlay heaven with stars.
Cym. Thou weep'st and speak'st.
The service that you three have done is more
Unlike than this thou tell'st. I lost my children.
If these be they, I know not how to wish
A pair of worthier sons.
Bel. Be pleas'd awhile.
This gentleman whom I call Polydore,
Most worthy prince, as yours, is true Guiderius;
This gentleman, my Cadwal, Arviragus,
Your younger princely son. He, sir, was lapp'd
In a most curious mantle, wrought by th' hand
Of his queen mother, which for more probation
I can with ease produce.
Cym. Guiderius had
Upon his neck a mole, a sanguine star.
It was a mark of wonder.
Bel. This is he,
Who hath upon him still that natural stamp.
It was wise Nature's end in the donation
To be his evidence now.
Cym. O, what am I?
A mother to the birth of three? Ne'er mother
Rejoic'd deliverance more. Blest pray you be,

That, after this strange starting from your orbs,
You may reign in them now! O Imogen,
Thou hast lost by this a kingdom.

Imo. No, my lord;
I have got two worlds by't. O my gentle brothers,
Have we thus met? O, never say hereafter
But I am truest speaker! You call'd me brother
When I was but your sister, I you brothers
When we were so indeed.

Cym. Did you e'er meet?

Arv. Ay, my good lord.

Gui. And at first meeting lov'd,
Continu'd so until we thought he died.

Cor. By the Queen's dram she swallow'd.

Cym. O rare instinct!
When shall I hear all through? This fierce abridgment
Hath to it circumstantial branches, which
Distinction should be rich in. Where? how liv'd you?
And when came you to serve our Roman captive?
How parted with your brothers? how first met them?
Why fled you from the court? and whither? These,
And your three motives to the battle, with
I know not how much more, should be demanded,
And all the other by-dependences
From chance to chance; but nor the time nor place
Will serve our long inter'gatories. See,
Posthumus anchors upon Imogen;
And she (like harmless lightning) throws her eye
On him, her brothers, me, her master, hitting
Each object with a joy; the counterchange
Is severally in all. Let's quit this ground
And smoke the temple with our sacrifices.
[*To Belarius*] Thou art my brother; so we'll hold thee ever.

Imo. You are my father too, and did relieve me
To see this gracious season.

Cym. All o'erjoy'd
Save these in bonds. Let them be joyful too,
For they shall taste our comfort.

Imo. My good master,
I will yet do you service.

Luc. Happy be you!

Cym. The forlorn soldier, that so nobly fought,
He would have well becom'd this place and grac'd
The thankings of a king.

Post. I am, sir,
The soldier that did company these three
In poor beseeming. 'Twas a fitment for
The purpose I then follow'd. That I was he
Speak, Iachimo. I had you down and might
Have made you finish.

Iach. [*kneels*] I am down again;
But now my heavy conscience sinks my knee,
As then your force did. Take that life, beseech you,
Which I so often owe; but your ring first,
And here the bracelet of the truest princess
That ever swore her faith.

Post. Kneel not to me.
The pow'r that I have on you is to spare you;
The malice towards you to forgive you. Live,
And deal with others better.

Cym. Nobly doom'd!
We'll learn our freeness of a son-in-law.
Pardon's the word to all.

Arv. You holp us, sir,
As you did mean indeed to be our brother.
Joy'd are we that you are.

Post. Your servant, Princes. Good my lord of Rome,
Call forth your soothsayer. As I slept, methought
Great Jupiter, upon his eagle back'd,
Appear'd to me, with other spritely shows
Of mine own kindred. When I wak'd, I found
This label on my bosom; whose containing
Is so from sense in hardness that I can
Make no collection of it. Let him show
His skill in the construction.

Luc. Philarmonus!

Sooth. Here, my good lord.

Luc. Read, and declare the meaning.

Sooth. (*reads*) 'When as a lion's whelp shall, to himself unknown, without seeking find, and be embrac'd by a piece of tender air; and when from a stately cedar shall be lopp'd branches which, being dead many years, shall after revive, be jointed to the old stock, and freshly grow; then shall Posthumus end his miseries, Britain be fortunate and flourish in peace and plenty.'

Thou, Leonatus, art the lion's whelp.
The fit and apt construction of thy name,
Being *Leo-natus*, doth import so much;
[*To Cymbeline*] The piece of tender air, thy virtuous daughter,
Which we call *mollis aer*, and *mollis aer*

We term it *mulier*; which *mulier* I divine
Is this most constant wife, who even now
Answering the letter of the oracle,
[*To Posthumus*] Unknown to you, unsought, you were clipp'd about
With this most tender air.

Cym. This hath some seeming.

Sooth. The lofty cedar, royal Cymbeline,
Personates thee; and thy lopp'd branches point
Thy two sons forth; who, by Belarius stol'n
For many years thought dead, are now reviv'd,
To the majestic cedar join'd, whose issue
Promises Britain peace and plenty.

Cym. Well,
My peace we will begin. And, Caius Lucius,
Although the victor, we submit to Cæsar
And to the Roman empire, promising
To pay our wonted tribute, from the which
We were dissuaded by our wicked queen,
Whom heavens in justice, both on her and hers,
Have laid most heavy hand.

Sooth. The fingers of the pow'rs above do tune
The harmony of this peace. The vision
Which I made known to Lucius ere the stroke
Of yet this scarce-cold battle, at this instant
Is full accomplish'd; for the Roman eagle,
From South to West on wing soaring aloft,
Lessen'd herself and in the beams o' th' sun
So vanish'd; which foreshow'd our princely eagle,
Th' imperial Cæsar, should again unite
His favour with the radiant Cymbeline,
Which shines here in the West.

Cym. Laud we the gods;
And let our crooked smokes climb to their nostrils
From our blest altars. Publish we this peace
To all our subjects. Set we forward. Let
A Roman and a British ensign wave
Friendly together. So through Lud's Town march;
And in the temple of great Jupiter
Our peace we'll ratify; seal it with feasts.
Set on there! Never was a war did cease,
Ere bloody hands were wash'd, with such a peace. *Exeunt.*

Pericles

Pericles was included in neither the First Folio (1623) nor the Second (1632), but it was taken into the second edition of the Third Folio (1664), along with six other plays (*Locrine*, *Sir John Oldcastle*, *Thomas Lord Cromwell*, *The London Prodigal*, *The Puritan*, and *A Yorkshire Tragedy*). None of the six has any claim to be regarded as Shakespeare's. There are six earlier quarto editions of Pericles: 1609 (two issues), 1611, 1619, 1630, 1635. The only authority for the text, however, is the First Quarto of 1609: 'The Late, And much admired Play, Called Pericles, Prince of Tyre. With the true Relation of the whole Historie, aduentures, and fortunes of the said Prince: As also, The no lesse strange, and worthy accidents, in the Birth and Life, of his Daughter Mariana. As it hath been diuers and sundry times acted by his Maiesties Seruants, at the Globe on the Banck-side. By William Shakespeare.' On May 20, 1608, Edward Blount had registered for publication 'the book of Pericles prynce of Tyre.' On some day between January 5, 1606, and November 23, 1608, Giustinian, ambassador from Venice, attended a performance of Pericles. In 1608 appeared a novel by George Wilkins entitled 'The Painfull Aduentures of *Pericles* Prince of Tyre. *Being* The true History of the Play of *Pericles*, as it was lately presented by the worthy and ancient Poet *Iohn Gower*.' The 'argument' enjoins upon the reader 'to receiue this Historie in the same maner as it was vnder the habite of ancient *Gower* the famous English Poet, by the Kings Maiesties Players excellently presented.'

That Pericles is not all Shakespeare's is an obvious and undisputed fact. In style and metre it falls into two strongly contrasted parts: (1) Acts i-ii and (2) Acts iii-v. Most of the second part is certainly Shakespeare's work in his latest period. The first part cannot be his, except perhaps for an occasional touch. Whether the completed play is the result of active personal collaboration, or whether some minor playwright completed a work which Shakespeare had not finished, is a problem that defies solution. It is even possible that Shakespeare remade an old play, allowing the first two acts to stand without much change. The brothel scenes, though occurring in the Shakespearean Act iv, are so disagreeable that his authorship is often denied; but they are an essential element in the old story and are certainly not the work of the unknown author of Acts i-ii. The hypothesis of a third playwright is a desperate expedient. It is safe to ascribe them to the author of like scenes in *Measure for Measure*, that is, to Shakespeare himself. The octosyllabic Gower choruses should be judged, not in and for themselves, but as imitations of Gower's style and archaic language. As such, they serve their purpose well enough. There is no visible reason for insisting that they are all the work of the collaborator. The octosyllabic verse-letter read aloud by Cerimon in iii, 2, 68–75, is a necessary part of the text, which would be unintelligible without it. The lines are a close paraphrase of Gower (1122–1130). They must be Shakespeare's; and, if so, it seems arbitrary to reject the other octosyllabic verses in iii-v. To Shakespeare, at all events, are assignable the decasyllabic Gower passages in the second part. With iv, 4, 17–19, may be compared the Prologue to *Henry V*, Act iii: 'Grapple your minds to sternage of this navy.' Emphasis on thought is the burden of every chorus in *Henry V*.

For divers reasons of chronology it would be convenient to date PERICLES late in 1608, but that involves the reference of the entry of May, 1608, to a lost play and not to the PERICLES printed in the next year. Metrical tests must not be worked too hard. Early in 1608 is a good enough date for PERICLES complete; but just when — within a few months — Shakespeare wrote his part of it cannot be determined.

The avowed source of PERICLES is the Latin *Historia Apollonii Regis Tyri* as retold by Gower in his *Confessio Amantis* (viii, 271–2008) on the authority of the *Pantheon* of Godfrey of Viterbo, a poetical chronicle of the late twelfth century. Apart from the chorus passages (in which of course the language of the *Confessio* is much used) there are occasional echoes of Gower's phrases throughout the play. The most striking is in iii, 2, 106, where Shakespeare has preserved Gower's very words (1206–1207), which, indeed, he could not improve:

Where am I?
Where is my lord? What world is this?

With Gower's tale both authors of PERICLES have combined the version 'gathered into English' by Laurence Twine in *The Patterne of Painefull Aduentures*, registered in 1576 and extant in two editions — one undated, the other of 1607. Twine follows his immediate source (the *Gesta Romanorum*) closely; but now and then he adds or varies a detail, and he sometimes indulges in flamboyant description. The version in the *Gesta* is not materially different from the original *Historia* or from that in the *Pantheon* as retold by Gower. When Gower and Twine disagree with each other, the authors of PERICLES usually prefer Gower, but now and then they follow Twine. In some scenes these two sources are worked together, and there is much original matter in both parts of the play (for example, in i, 2; ii, 1–2; ii, 5; iv, 1–2; iv, 6), but nothing is added that changes the plot to any extent.

The Latin *Historia Regis Apollonii* is doubtless based upon some lost Greek romance. In several episodes it closely resembles the *Ephesiaca* of the so-called Xenophon, which is a remote ancestor of *Romeo and Juliet* (see p. 1006 above). The popularity of the *Historia* was enormous. It is found in unnumbered manuscripts, and mediæval versions are extant in a great variety of languages. There is a fragmentary Anglo-Saxon translation dating from about the year 1000. Copland's *Kynge Appolyn of Thyre* was printed by Wynkyn de Worde in 1510.

Wilkins must have written his *Painfull Adventures* with both Twine's romance and the play at his elbow. He takes whole pages from Twine and he repeats the language of PERICLES in scores of instances. These bits of quotation come from almost every scene. The text of PERICLES that he used was probably a manuscript, borrowed perhaps from the King's players, for whom we know he wrote *The Miseries of Enforced Marriage* (1607). A few passages in his book that fall into verse may belong in PERICLES, the text of which is obviously more or less cut. So, possibly, Thaisa's letter, which would fit well in ii, 5 — a scene that has been somewhat mangled in the reporting. That Wilkins was the author of Acts i-ii is not very likely.

The name 'Pericles,' substituted by the authors of the play for the traditional 'Apollonius,' may or may not be a perversion of the name of Pyrocles, a much-shipwrecked hero in Sidney's *Arcadia*.

PERICLES, PRINCE OF TYRE

[Dramatis Personæ.

Gower, as Chorus.

Antiochus, King of Antioch.
Pericles, Prince of Tyre.
Helicanus, } two lords of Tyre.
Escanes, }
Simonides, King of Pentapolis.
Cleon, Governor of Tharsus.
Lysimachus, Governor of Mytilene.
Cerimon, a lord of Ephesus.
Thaliard, a lord of Antioch.
Philemon, servant to *Cerimon.*
Leonine, servant to *Dionyza.*
Marshal.
A Pander.
Boult, his servant.

The Daughter of *Antiochus.*
Dionyza, wife to *Cleon.*
Thaisa, daughter to *Simonides.*
Marina, daughter to *Pericles* and *Thaisa.*
Lychorida, nurse to *Marina.*
A Bawd.

Diana.

Lords, Ladies, Knights, Gentlemen, Sailors, Pirates, Fishermen, Messengers.

SCENE. — *In various countries.*]

ACT I.

Enter *Gower.*

[*Antioch. Before the Palace of Antiochus.*]

To sing a song that old was sung,
From ashes ancient Gower is come,
Assuming man's infirmities
To glad your ear and please your eyes.
It hath been sung at festivals,
On ember-eves and holy-ales;
And lords and ladies in their lives
Have read it for restoratives.
The purchase is to make men glorious,
Et bonum quo antiquius, eo melius.
If you, born in these latter times
When wit's more ripe, accept my rhymes,
And that to hear an old man sing
May to your wishes pleasure bring,
I life would wish, and that I might
Waste it for you, like taper light.
This Antioch, then, Antiochus the Great
Built up, this city, for his chiefest seat,
The fairest in all Syria —
I tell you what mine authors say.
This king unto him took a feere,
Who died and left a female heir,
So buxom, blithe, and full of face
As heaven had lent her all his grace;
With whom the father liking took
And her to incest did provoke.
Bad child; worse father! to entice his own
To evil should be done by none.
By custom what they did begin
Was with long use account'd no sin.
The beauty of this sinful dame
Made many princes thither frame,
To seek her as a bedfellow,
In marriage pleasures playfellow;
Which to prevent he made a law —
To keep her still, and men in awe —
That whoso ask'd her for his wife,
His riddle told not, lost his life.
So for her many a wight did die,
As yon grim looks do testify.
What now ensues, to the judgment of your eye
I give, my cause who best can justify. *Exit.*

Scene I. [*Antioch. A room in the Palace.*]

Enter *Antiochus, Prince Pericles,* and *Followers.*

Ant. Young Prince of Tyre, you have at large receiv'd
The danger of the task you undertake.

Per. I have, Antiochus, and, with a soul
Embold'ned with the glory of her praise,
Think death no hazard in this enterprise.
Music.

Ant. Bring in our daughter, clothed like a bride
For the embracements even of Jove himself;

At whose conception, till Lucina reign'd,
Nature this dowry gave to glad her presence,
The senate house of planets all did sit
To knit in her their best perfections.

Enter *Antiochus' Daughter.*

Per. See where she comes, apparell'd like the spring,
Graces her subjects, and her thoughts the king
Of every virtue gives renown to men!
Her face the book of praises, where is read
Nothing but curious pleasures, as from thence
Sorrow were ever ras'd, and testy wrath
Could never be her mild companion.
You gods that made me man, and sway in love,
That have inflam'd desire in my breast
To taste the fruit of yon celestial tree
Or die in the adventure, be my helps,
As I am son and servant to your will,
To compass such a boundless happiness!

Ant. Prince Pericles —

Per. That would be son to great Antiochus.

Ant. Before thee stands this fair Hesperides,
With golden fruit, but dangerous to be touch'd;
For death, like dragons, here affright the hoard.
Her face, like heaven, enticeth thee to view
Her countless glory, which desert must gain;
And which, without desert because their eye
Presumes to reach, all this whole heap must die.
Yon sometime famous princes, like thyself,
Drawn by report, advent'rous by desire,
Tell thee, with speechless tongues and semblance pale,
That, without covering, save yon field of stars,
Here they stand martyrs slain in Cupid's wars;
And with dead cheeks advise thee to desist
For going on death's net, whom none resist.

Per. Antiochus, I thank thee, who hast taught
My frail mortality to know itself,
And by those fearful objects to prepare
This body, like to them, to what I must;
For death remembered should be like a mirror,
Who tells us life's but breath, to trust it error.
I'll make my will then, and, as sick men do,
Who know the world, see heaven, but, feeling woe,
Gripe not at earthly joys as erst they did,
So I bequeath a happy peace to you
And all good men, as every prince should do;
My riches to the earth, from whence they came;
But my unspotted fire of love to you. [*To the Princess.*]
Thus ready for the way of life or death,
I wait the sharpest blow, Antiochus.

Ant. Scorning advice, read the conclusion then;
Which read and not expounded, 'tis decreed,
As these before thee, thou thyself shalt bleed.

Daugh. Of all 'say'd yet, mayst thou prove prosperous!
Of all 'say'd yet, I wish thee happiness!

Per. Like a bold champion I assume the lists,
Nor ask advice of any other thought
But faithfulness and courage. [*Reads.*]

The Riddle.

'I am no viper, yet I feed
On mother's flesh which did me breed.
I sought a husband, in which labour
I found that kindness in a father.
He's father, son, and husband mild;
I mother, wife, and yet his child.
How they may be, and yet in two,
As you will live, resolve it you.'

Sharp physic is the last! but, O you powers
That give heaven countless eyes to view men's acts,
Why cloud they not their sights perpetually
If this be true which makes me pale to read it?
Fair glass of light, I lov'd you, and could still,
Were not this glorious casket stor'd with ill.
But I must tell you, now my thoughts revolt;
For he's no man on whom perfections wait
That, knowing sin within, will touch the gate.
Y'are a fair viol, and your sense the strings;
Who, finger'd to make man his lawful music,
Would draw heaven down, and all the gods, to hearken;
But being play'd upon before your time,
Hell only danceth at so harsh a chime.
Good sooth, I care not for you.

Ant. Prince Pericles, touch not, upon thy life,
For that's an article within our law,
As dangerous as the rest. Your time 's expir'd.
Either expound now, or receive your sentence.

Per. Great king,
Few love to hear the sins they love to act.
'Twould braid yourself too near for me to tell it.
Who has a book of all that monarchs do,
He's more secure to keep it shut than shown;
For vice repeated is like the wand'ring wind,
Blows dust in others' eyes, to spread itself;
And yet the end of all is bought thus dear,
The breath is gone, and the sore eyes see clear
To stop the air would hurt them. The blind mole casts
Copp'd hills towards heaven, to tell the earth is throng'd

By man's oppression, and the poor worm doth die for't.
Kings are earth's gods; in vice their law's their will;
And if Jove stray, who dares say Jove doth ill?
It is enough you know; and it is fit,
What being more known grows worse, to smother it.
All love the womb that their first being bred,
Then give my tongue like leave to love my head.

Ant. [*aside*] Heaven, that I had thy head! He has found the meaning.
But I will gloze with him. — Young Prince of Tyre,
Though by the tenour of our strict edict,
Your exposition misinterpreting,
We might proceed to cancel off your days,
Yet hope, succeeding from so fair a tree
As your fair self, doth tune us otherwise.
Forty days longer we do respite you;
If by which time our secret be undone,
This mercy shows we'll joy in such a son;
And until then your entertain shall be
As doth befit our honour and your worth.
Exeunt. Manet Pericles solus.

Per. How courtesy would seem to cover sin,
When what is done is like an hypocrite,
The which is good in nothing but in sight!
If it be true that I interpret false,
Then were it certain you were not so bad
As with foul incest to abuse your soul;
Where now you're both a father and a son
By your untimely claspings with your child
(Which pleasures fit a husband, not a father),
And she an eater of her mother's flesh
By the defiling of her parents' bed;
And both like serpents are, who though they feed
On sweetest flowers, yet they poison breed.
Antioch, farewell! for wisdom sees, those men
Blush not in actions blacker than the night,
Will shun no course to keep them from the light.
One sin, I know, another doth provoke;
Murther's as near to lust as flame to smoke.
Poison and treason are the hands of sin;
Ay, and the targets to put off the shame.
Then, lest my life be cropp'd to keep you clear,
By flight I'll shun the danger which I fear. *Exit.*

Enter *Antiochus.*

Ant. He hath found the meaning, for the which we mean
To have his head.
He must not live to trumpet forth my infamy,
Nor tell the world Antiochus doth sin
In such a loathed manner;
And therefore instantly this prince must die;
For by his fall my honour must keep high.
Who attends us there?

Enter *Thaliard.*

Thal. Doth your Highness call?
Ant. Thaliard,
You are of our chamber, Thaliard, and our mind partakes
Her private actions to your secrecy;
And for your faithfulness we will advance you.
Thaliard, behold, here's poison, and here's gold.
We hate the Prince of Tyre, and thou must kill him.
It fits thee not to ask the reason why.
Because we bid it. Say, is it done?
Thal. My lord,
'Tis done.

Enter a *Messenger.*

Ant. Enough. —
Let your breath cool yourself, telling your haste.
Mess. My lord, Prince Pericles is fled. [*Exit.*]
Ant. As thou
Wilt live, fly after; and, like an arrow shot
From a well-experienc'd archer hits the mark
His eye doth level at, so thou ne'er return
Unless thou say Prince Pericles is dead.
Thal. My lord,
If I can get him within my pistol's length,
I'll make him sure enough. So farewell to your Highness.
Ant. Thaliard, adieu! [*Exit Thaliard.*] Till Pericles be dead
My heart can lend no succour to my head. *Exit.*

[Scene II. *Tyre. The Palace.*]

Enter *Pericles* with his *Lords.*

Per. Let none disturb us. [*Exeunt Lords.*] Why should this charge of thought,
The sad companion, dull-ey'd melancholy,
Be my so us'd a guest as not an hour
In the day's glorious walk or peaceful night,
The tomb where grief should sleep, can breed me quiet?
Here pleasures court mine eyes, and mine eyes shun them,
And danger, which I feared, is at Antioch,
Whose arm seems far too short to hit me here,
Yet neither pleasure's art can joy my spirits,
Nor yet the other's distance comfort me.

Then it is thus: the passions of the mind,
That have their first conception by misdread,
Have after-nourishment and life by care;
And what was first but fear what might be done,
Grows elder now, and cares it be not done.
And so with me. The great Antiochus —
'Gainst whom I am too little to contend,
Since he's so great can make his will his act,
Will think me speaking, though I swear to silence;
Nor boots it me to say I honour him
If he suspect I may dishonour him.
And what may make him blush in being known,
He'll stop the course by which it might be known.
With hostile forces he'll o'erspread the land,
And with th' ostent of war will look so huge
Amazement shall drive courage from the state,
Our men be vanquish'd ere they do resist,
And subjects punish'd that ne'er thought offence;
Which care of them, not pity of myself —
Who am no more but as the tops of trees,
Which fence the roots they grow by and defend them —
Makes both my body pine and soul to languish,
And punish that before that he would punish.

Enter [*Helicanus* and] all the *Lords* to *Pericles.*

1. Lord. Joy and all comfort in your sacred breast!

2. Lord. And keep your mind, till you return to us,
Peaceful and comfortable!

Hel. Peace, peace, and give experience tongue!
They do abuse the king that flatter him.
For flattery is the bellows blows up sin;
The thing the which is flattered, but a spark
To which that blast gives heat and stronger glowing;
Whereas reproof, obedient and in order,
Fits kings as they are men, for they may err.
When Signior Sooth here does proclaim a peace,
He flatters you, makes war upon your life.
Prince, pardon me; or strike me, if you please.
I cannot be much lower than my knees. [*Kneels.*]

Per. All leave us else; but let your cares o'erlook
What shipping and what lading's in our haven,
And then return to us. [*Exeunt Lords.*] Helicanus, thou
Hast moved us. What seest thou in our looks?

Hel. An angry brow, dread lord.

Per. If there be such a dart in princes' frowns,
How durst thy tongue move anger to our face?

Hel. How dare the plants look up to heaven, from whence
They have their nourishment?

Per. Thou know'st I have power
To take thy life from thee.

Hel. I have ground the axe myself.
Do but you strike the blow.

Per. Rise, prithee, rise. [*He rises.*]
Sit down. Thou art no flatterer.
I thank thee for't; and heaven forbid
That kings should let their ears hear their faults hid!
Fit counsellor and servant for a prince,
Who by thy wisdom makes a prince thy servant,
What wouldst thou have me do?

Hel. To bear with patience
Such griefs as you yourself do lay upon yourself.

Per. Thou speak'st like a physician, Helicanus,
That ministers a potion unto me
That thou wouldst tremble to receive thyself.
Attend me then. I went to Antioch,
Where, as thou know'st, against the face of death
I sought the purchase of a glorious beauty,
From whence an issue I might propagate
Are arms to princes and bring joys to subjects.
Her face was to mine eye beyond all wonder;
The rest (hark in thine ear) as black as incest;
Which by my knowledge found, the sinful father
Seem'd not to strike, but smooth. But thou know'st this,
'Tis time to fear when tyrants seem to kiss.
Which fear so grew in me I hither fled
Under the covering of a careful night,
Who seem'd my good protector; and being here,
Bethought me what was past, what might succeed.
I knew him tyrannous; and tyrants' fears
Decrease not, but grow faster than the years;
And should he doubt it, as no doubt he doth,
That I should open to the list'ning air
How many worthy princes' bloods were shed
To keep his bed of blackness unlaid ope,
To lop that doubt, he'll fill this land with arms
And make pretence of wrong that I have done him;
When all, for mine, if I may call offence,
Must feel war's blow, who spares not innocence;

Which love to all, of which thyself art one,
Who now reprov'd'st me for't —

Hel. Alas, sir!

Per. Drew sleep out of mine eyes, blood from my cheeks,
Musings into my mind, with thousand doubts
How I might stop this tempest ere it came;
And finding little comfort to relieve them,
I thought it princely charity to grieve them.

Hel. Well, my lord, since you have given me leave to speak,
Freely will I speak. Antiochus you fear,
And justly too I think you fear the tyrant,
Who either by public war or private treason
Will take away your life.
Therefore, my lord, go travel for a while,
Till that his rage and anger be forgot,
Or till the Destinies do cut his thread of life.
Your rule direct to any; if to me,
Day serves not light more faithful than I'll be.

Per. I do not doubt thy faith;
But should he wrong my liberties in my absence?

Hel. We'll mingle our bloods together in the earth,
From whence we had our being and our birth.

Per. Tyre, I now look from thee then and to Tharsus
Intend my travel, where I'll hear from thee;
And by whose letters I'll dispose myself.
The care I had and have of subjects' good
On thee I lay, whose wisdom's strength can bear it.
I'll take thy word for faith, not ask thine oath.
Who shuns not to break one will sure crack both:
But in our orbs we'll live so round and safe
That time of both this truth shall ne'er convince,
Thou show'dst a subject's shine, I a true prince.

Exeunt.

[Scene III. *Tyre. The Palace.*]

Enter *Thaliard* solus.

Thal. So, this is Tyre, and this the court. Here must I kill King Pericles; and if I do it not, I am sure to be hang'd at home. 'Tis dangerous. Well, I perceive he was a wise fellow and had good discretion that, being bid to ask what he would of the king, desired he might know none of his secrets. Now do I see he had some reason for't; for if a king bid a man be a villain, he's bound by the indenture of his oath to be one. Husht! here comes the lords of Tyre.

Enter *Helicanus, Escanes,* with other *Lords.*

Hel. You shall not need, my fellow peers of Tyre,
Further to question me of your king's departure.
His seal'd commission, left in trust with me,
Does speak sufficiently he's gone to travel.

Thal. [*aside*] How? the King gone?

Hel. If further yet you will be satisfied
Why (as it were unlicens'd of your loves)
He would depart, I'll give some light unto you.
Being at Antioch —

Thal. [*aside*] What from Antioch?

Hel. Royal Antiochus, on what cause I know not,
Took some displeasure at him; at least he judg'd so;
And doubting lest that he had err'd or sinn'd,
To show his sorrow, he'd correct himself;
So puts himself unto the shipman's toil,
With whom each minute threatens life or death.

Thal. [*aside*] Well, I perceive
I shall not be hang'd now, although I would;
But since he's gone, the King's ears it must please
He scap'd the land to perish on the seas.
I'll present myself. — Peace to the lords of Tyre!

Hel. Lord Thaliard from Antiochus is welcome.

Thal. From him I come
With message unto princely Pericles;
But since my landing I have understood
Your lord has betook himself to unknown travels.
Now message must return from whence it came.

Hel. We have no reason to desire it,
Commended to our master, not to us.
Yet, ere you shall depart, this we desire —
As friends to Antioch, we may feast in Tyre.

Exeunt.

[Scene IV. *Tharsus. The* Governor's *house.*]

Enter *Cleon,* the Governor of Tharsus, with his wife [*Dionyza*] and *Others.*

Cleon. My Dionyza, shall we rest us here,
And by relating tales of others' griefs,
See if 'twill teach us to forget our own?

Dio. That were to blow at fire in hope to quench it;

For who digs hills because they do aspire
Throws down one mountain to cast up a higher.
O my distressed lord, even such our griefs are!
Here they are but felt and seen with mischief's size,
But like to groves, being topp'd, they higher rise.

Cleon. O Dionyza,
Who wanteth food, and will not say he wants it,
Or can conceal his hunger till he famish?
Our tongues and sorrows do sound deep
Our woes into the air; our eyes do weep
Till tongues fetch breath that may proclaim them louder;
That, if heaven slumber while their creatures want,
They may awake their helps to comfort them.
I'll then discourse our woes, felt several years,
And, wanting breath to speak, help me with tears.

Dio. I'll do my best, sir.

Cleon. This Tharsus, o'er which I have the government,
A city on whom Plenty held full hand,
For Riches strew'd herself even in the streets;
Whose towers bore heads so high they kiss'd the clouds,
And strangers ne'er beheld but wond'red at;
Whose men and dames so jetted and adorn'd,
Like one another's glass to trim them by;
Their tables were stor'd full, to glad the sight,
And not so much to feed on as delight;
All poverty was scorn'd, and pride so great
The name of help grew odious to repeat.

Dio. O, 'tis too true!

Cleon. But see what heaven can do! By this our change
Those mouths who, but of late, earth, sea, and air
Were all too little to content and please,
Although they gave their creatures in abundance,
As houses are defil'd for want of use,
They are now starv'd for want of exercise.
Those palates who, not yet two savours younger,
Must have inventions to delight the taste,
Would now be glad of bread, and beg for it.
Those mothers who to nouzle up their babes
Thought naught too curious, are ready now
To eat those little darlings whom they lov'd.
So sharp are hunger's teeth that man and wife
Draw lots who first shall die to lengthen life.
Here stands a lord, and there a lady weeping;
Here many sink, yet those which see them fall
Have scarce strength left to give them burial.
Is not this true?

Dio. Our cheeks and hollow eyes do witness it.

Cleon. O, let those cities that of Plenty's cup
And her prosperities so largely taste
With their superfluous riots, hear these tears!
The misery of Tharsus may be theirs.

Enter a *Lord.*

Lord. Where's the Lord Governor?

Cleon. Here.
Speak out thy sorrows which thou bring'st in haste,
For comfort is too far for us to expect.

Lord. We have descried, upon our neighbouring shore,
A portly sail of ships make hitherward.

Cleon. I thought as much.
One sorrow never comes but brings an heir
That may succeed as his inheritor;
And so in ours, some neighbouring nation,
Taking advantage of our misery,
Hath stuff'd these hollow vessels with their power,
To beat us down, the which are down already;
And make a conquest of unhappy me,
Whereas no glory 's got to overcome.

Lord. That's the least fear; for, by the semblance
Of their white flags display'd, they bring us peace
And come to us as favourers, not as foes.

Cleon. Thou speak'st like him's untutor'd to repeat:
Who makes the fairest show means most deceit.
But bring they what they will and what they can,
What need we fear?
The ground 's the lowest, and we are half-way there.
Go tell their general we attend him here,
To know for what he comes, and whence he comes,
And what he craves.

Lord. I go, my lord. [*Exit.*]

Cleon. Welcome is peace, if he on peace consist;
If wars, we are unable to resist.

Enter *Pericles* with *Attendants.*

Per. Lord Governor, for so we hear you are,
Let not our ships and number of our men
Be like a beacon fir'd t' amaze your eyes.
We have heard your miseries as far as Tyre,

And seen the desolation of your streets;
Nor come we to add sorrow to your tears,
But to relieve them of their heavy load;
And these our ships you happily may think
Are like the Troyan horse was stuff'd within
With bloody veins, expecting overthrow,
Are stor'd with corn to make your needy bread
And give them life whom hunger starv'd half dead.

Omnes. The gods of Greece protect you!
And we'll pray for you. [*They kneel.*]

Per. Arise, I pray you, rise.
We do not look for reverence, but for love,
And harbourage for ourself, our ships, and men.

Cleon. The which when any shall not gratify,
Or pay you with unthankfulness in thought —
Be it our wives, our children, or ourselves —
The curse of heaven and men succeed their evils!
Till when (the which, I hope, shall ne'er be seen)
Your Grace is welcome to our town and us.

Per. Which welcome we'll accept, feast here awhile,
Until our stars that frown lend us a smile.
Exeunt.

ACT II.

Enter *Gower.*

Gow. Here have you seen a mighty king
His child i-wis to incest bring;
A better prince and benign lord,
That will prove awful both in deed and word.
Be quiet then, as men should be,
Till he hath pass'd necessity.
I'll show you those in troubles reign,
Losing a mite, a mountain gain.
The good in conversation,
To whom I give my benison,
Is still at Tharsus, where each man
Thinks all is writ he speken can;
And, to remember what he does,
Build his statue to make him glorious.
But tidings to the contrary
Are brought your eyes. What need speak I?

Dumb Show.

Enter, at one door, *Pericles,* talking with *Cleon*; all the *Train* with them. Enter, at another door, a *Gentleman* with a letter to *Pericles. Pericles* shows the letter to *Cleon. Pericles* gives the *Messenger* a reward and knights him. Exit *Pericles* at one door and *Cleon* at another, [with their *Trains*].

Good Helicane, that stay'd at home —
Not to eat honey like a drone
From others' labours, though he strive
To killen bad, keep good alive,
And to fulfil his prince' desire —
Sends word of all that haps in Tyre:
How Thaliard came full bent with sin
And had intent to murder him;
And that in Tharsus was not best
Longer for him to make his rest.
He, doing so, put forth to seas,
Where when men been, there's seldom ease;
For now the wind begins to blow;
Thunder above, and deeps below,
Makes such unquiet that the ship
Should house him safe is wrack'd and split,
And he, good prince, having all lost,
By waves from coast to coast is tost.
All perishen of man, of pelf,
Ne aught escapen but himself;
Till fortune, tir'd with doing bad,
Threw him ashore, to give him glad.
And here he comes. What shall be next
Pardon old Gower; this longs the text. [*Exit.*]

[Scene I. *Pentapolis. An open place by the seaside.*]

Enter *Pericles,* wet.

Per. Yet cease your ire, you angry stars of heaven!
Wind, rain, and thunder, remember earthly man
Is but a substance that must yield to you;
And I, as fits my nature, do obey you.
Alas! the sea hath cast me on the rocks,
Wash'd me from shore to shore, and left me breath
Nothing to think on but ensuing death.
Let it suffice the greatness of your powers
To have bereft a prince of all his fortunes,
And having thrown him from your wat'ry grave,
Here to have death in peace is all he'll crave.

Enter three *Fishermen.*

1. Fish. What ho, Pilch!

2. Fish. Ha, come and bring away the nets!

1. Fish. What, Patchbreech, I say!

3. Fish. What say you, master?

1. Fish. Look how thou stirr'st now! Come away, or I'll fetch thee with a wanion.

3. Fish. Faith, master, I am thinking of the poor men that were cast away before us even now.

1. Fish. Alas, poor souls! It grieved my heart to hear what pitiful cries they made to us to help them, when (well-a-day!) we could scarce help ourselves.

3. Fish. Nay, master, said not I as much when I saw the porpas, how he bounc'd and tumbled? They say they're half fish, half flesh. A plague on them! They ne'er come but I look to be wash'd. Master, I marvel how the fishes live in the sea.

1. Fish. Why, as men do aland — the great ones eat up the little ones. I can compare our rich misers to nothing so fitly as to a whale. 'A plays and tumbles, driving the poor fry before him, and at last devours them all at a mouthful. Such whales have I heard on o' th' land, who never leave gaping till they've swallow'd the whole parish — church, steeple, bells, and all.

Per. [*aside*] A pretty moral.

3. Fish. But, master, if I had been the sexton, I would have been that day in the belfry.

2. Fish. Why, man?

3. Fish. Because he should have swallowed me too; and when I had been in his belly, I would have kept such a jangling of the bells that he should never have left till he cast bells, steeple, church, and parish up again. But if the good King Simonides were of my mind —

Per. [*aside*] Simonides?

3. Fish. He would purge the land of these drones that rob the bee of her honey.

Per. [*aside*] How from the finny subject of the sea
These fishers tell the infirmities of men,
And from their wat'ry empire recollect
All that may men approve or men detect! —
Peace be at your labour, honest fishermen.

2. Fish. Honest, good fellow? What's that? If it be a day fits you, scratch't out of the calendar, and nobody look after it.

Per. May see the sea hath cast upon your coast —

2. Fish. What a drunken knave was the sea to cast thee in our way!

Per. A man whom both the waters and the wind,
In that vast tennis court, have made the ball
For them to play upon, entreats you pity him.
He asks of you that never us'd to beg.

1. Fish. No, friend? Cannot you beg? Here's them in our country of Greece gets more with begging than we can do with working.

2. Fish. Canst thou catch any fishes then?

Per. I never practis'd it.

2. Fish. Nay, then thou wilt starve sure; for here's nothing to be got now-a-days unless thou canst fish for't.

Per. What I have been I have forgot to know;
But what I am, want teaches me to think on:
A man throng'd up with cold; my veins are chill,
And have no more of life than may suffice
To give my tongue that heat to ask your help;
Which if you shall refuse, when I am dead,
For that I am a man, pray you see me buried.

1. Fish. Die koth-a? Now gods forbid't! And I have a gown here; come put it on; keep thee warm. Now, afore me, a handsome fellow! Come, thou shalt go home, and we'll have flesh for holidays, fish for fasting days, and moreo'er puddings and flapjacks; and thou shalt be welcome.

Per. I thank you, sir.

2. Fish. Hark you, my friend. You said you could not beg?

Per. I did but crave.

2. Fish. But crave? Then I'll turn craver too, and so I shall scape whipping.

Per. Why, are all your beggars whipp'd then?

2. Fish. O, not all, my friend, not all! For if all your beggars were whipp'd, I would wish no better office than to be beadle. But, master, I'll go draw up the net.

[*Exit with Third Fisherman.*]

Per. [*aside*] How well this honest mirth becomes their labour!

1. Fish. Hark you, sir. Do you know where ye are?

Per. Not well.

1. Fish. Why, I'll tell you. This is call'd Pentapolis, and our king the good Simonides.

Per. The good Simonides do you call him?

1. Fish. Ay, sir; and he deserves so to be call'd for his peaceable reign and good government.

Per. He is a happy king, since he gains from his subjects the name of good by his government. How far is his court distant from this shore?

1. Fish. Marry, sir, half a day's journey. And I'll tell you, he hath a fair daughter, and to-morrow is her birthday, and there are princes and knights come from all parts of the world to just and tourney for her love.

Per. Were my fortunes equal to my desires, I could wish to make one there.

1. Fish. O, sir, things must be as they may; and what a man cannot get, he may lawfully deal for — his wive's soul.

Enter the two [other] *Fishermen*, drawing up a net.

2. Fish. Help, master, help! Here's a fish hangs in the net like a poor man's right in the law. 'Twill hardly come out. Ha! bots on't! 'tis come at last, and 'tis turn'd to a rusty armour.

Per. An armour, friends? I pray you let me see it.
Thanks, Fortune, yet, that, after all thy crosses,
Thou givest me somewhat to repair myself!
And though it was mine own, part of my heritage
Which my dead father did bequeath to me,
With this strict charge, even as he left his life,
'Keep it, my Pericles. It hath been a shield
'Twixt me and death' — and pointed to this brace;
'For that it sav'd me, keep it. In like necessity —
(The which the gods protect thee from!) may defend thee.'
It kept where I kept, I so dearly lov'd it;
Till the rough seas, that spare not any man,
Took it in rage — though, calm'd, have given't again —
I thank thee for't. My shipwrack now's no ill,
Since I have here my father's gift in his will.

1. Fish. What mean you, sir?

Per. To beg of you, kind friends, this coat of worth,
For it was sometime target to a king.
I know it by this mark. He lov'd me dearly,
And for his sake I wish the having of it;
And that you'd guide me to your sovereign's court,
Where with it I may appear a gentleman;
And if that ever my low fortune's better,
I'll pay your bounties; till then rest your debtor.

1. Fish. Why, wilt thou tourney for the lady?

Per. I'll show the virtue I have borne in arms.

1. Fish. Why, do'ee take it, and the gods give thee good on't!

2. Fish. Ay, but hark you, my friend! 'Twas we that made up this garment through the rough seams of the waters. There are certain condolements, certain vails. I hope, sir, if you thrive, you'll remember from whence you had it.

Per. Believe't, I will.
By your furtherance I am cloth'd in steel;
And, spite of all the rapture of the sea,
This jewel holds his building on my arm.
Unto thy value I will mount myself
Upon a courser whose delighted steps
Shall make the gazer joy to see him tread.
Only, my friend, I yet am unprovided
Of a pair of bases.

2. Fish. We'll sure provide. Thou shalt have my best gown to make thee a pair; and I'll bring thee to the court myself.

Per. Then honour be but a goal to my will,
This day I'll rise, or else add ill to ill. [*Exeunt.*]

[Scene II. *Pentapolis. A public way or platform leading to the lists. A pavilion by the side of it for the reception of the* King, Princess, Lords, *&c.*]

Enter [*King*] *Simonides*, with attendance, and *Thaisa*.

King. Are the knights ready to begin the triumph?

1. Lord. They are, my liege,
And stay your coming to present themselves.

King. Return them, we are ready; and our daughter,
In honour of whose birth these triumphs are,
Sits here like beauty's child, whom nature gat
For men to see, and seeing wonder at.
[*Exit a Lord.*]

Thai. It pleaseth you, my royal father, to express
My commendations great, whose merit's less.

King. It's fit it should be so, for princes are
A model which heaven makes like to itself.
As jewels lose their glory if neglected,
So princes their renowns if not respected.
'Tis now your honour, daughter, to entertain
The labour of each knight in his device.

Thai. Which, to preserve mine honour, I'll perform.

The First Knight passes by, [and his Squire shows his shield to the Princess].

King. Who is the first that doth prefer himself?

Thai. A knight of Sparta, my renowned father;
And the device he bears upon his shield
Is a black Ethiope reaching at the sun;
The word, 'Lux tua vita mihi.'

King. He loves you well that holds his life of you.

The Second Knight.

Who is the second that presents himself?

Thai. A prince of Macedon, my royal father;
And the device he bears upon his shield
Is an armed knight that's conquered by a lady;
The motto thus in Spanish, 'Piu por dulzura que por fuerza.'

Third Knight.

King. And what's the third?

Thai. The third of Antioch;
And his device, a wreath of chivalry;
The word, 'Me pompae provexit apex.'

Fourth Knight.

King. What is the fourth?

Thai. A burning torch that's turned upside down;
The word, 'Quod me alit, me extinguit.'

King. Which shows that beauty hath his power and will,
Which can as well inflame as it can kill.

Fifth Knight.

Thai. The fifth, an hand environed with clouds,
Holding out gold that's by the touchstone tried;
The motto thus, 'Sic spectanda fides.'

Sixth Knight [Pericles].

King. And what's
The sixth and last, the which the knight himself
With such a graceful courtesy deliver'd?

Thai. He seems to be a stranger; but his present is
A withered branch that's only green at top;
The motto, 'In hac spe vivo.'

King. A pretty moral.
From the dejected state wherein he is
He hopes by you his fortunes yet may flourish.

1. Lord. He had need mean better than his outward show
Can any way speak in his just commend;
For by his rusty outside he appears
To have practis'd more the whipstock than the lance.

2. Lord. He well may be a stranger, for he comes
To an honour'd triumph strangely furnished.

3. Lord. And on set purpose let his armour rust
Until this day, to scour it in the dust.

King. Opinion's but a fool, that makes us scan
The outward habit by the inward man.
But stay, the knights are coming. We will withdraw
Into the gallery. *[Exeunt.]*

Great shouts [within,] and all cry 'The mean knight!'

[Scene III. *Pentapolis. A hall of state; a banquet prepared.*]

Enter the *King* [*Simonides, Thaisa, Ladies, Lords,*] and *Knights*, from tilting.

King. Knights,
To say you're welcome were superfluous.
To place upon the volume of your deeds,
As in a title-page, your worth in arms
Were more than you expect, or more than's fit,
Since every worth in show commends itself.
Prepare for mirth, for mirth becomes a feast.
You are princes and my guests.

Thai. But you, my knight and guest;
To whom this wreath of victory I give,
And crown you king of this day's happiness.

Per. 'Tis more by fortune, lady, than my merit.

King. Call it by what you will, the day is yours;
And here, I hope, is none that envies it.
In framing an artist, art hath thus decreed,
To make some good, but others to exceed;
And you are her labour'd scholar. Come, queen o' th' feast,
For, daughter, so you are; here take your place.
Marshal the rest as they deserve their grace.

Knights. We are honour'd much by good Simonides.

"Cease your ire, you angry stars of heaven!" Shipwrecked on the shores of Pentapolis, Pericles (Paul Scofield) challenges the elements as he emerges half-drowned from the sea (*Act II, Scene I*)

PERICLES

PHOTOGRAPHS BY ANGUS MC BEAN
PRODUCED BY MEMORIAL THEATRE COMPANY
STRATFORD-UPON-AVON

Above: "It was mine own, part of mine heritage, which my dead father did bequeath to me." Pericles claims his armour, which has been discovered by fishermen on the shore *(Act II, Scene I)*

"Good madam, make me blessed in your care in bringing up my child." Believing his wife Thaisa dead, Pericles leaves his infant daughter Marina in the care of Dionyza (Muriel Davidson) and her husband, Cleon (Paul Stephenson) *(Act III, Scene III)*

"Madam, this letter, and some certain jewels, lay with you in your coffer." The physician Cerimon (Douglas Seale) tells Thaisa (Irene Sutcliffe) how she was found on the seashore *(Act III, Scene IV)*

"Come, Leonine, take her by the arm, walk with her." Hating Marina (Daphne Slater) because she is so beautiful, Dionyza orders Leonine (Duncan Ross) to murder her *(Act IV, Scene I)*

"You will not do 't for all the world, I hope." Marina makes a pathetic plea for her life *(Act IV, Scene I)*

"She has a good face, speaks well, and has excellent good clothes." Boult (John Blatchley) and the Bawd (Margaret Courtenay) discuss the qualities of Marina, who has been installed in a vile brothel *(Act IV, Scene II)*

"Come, we will leave his honour and her together." Boult and the Bawd leave Marina with Lysimachus (Myles Eason), the governor of Mitylene, hoping he will destroy the virtue which they themselves could not tarnish *(Act IV, Scene VI)*

"Here is the lady that I sent for. Welcome, fair one!" Lying ill aboard his ship in the harbor of Mitylene, Pericles has Marina brought to sing for him, not knowing that she is his daughter *(Act V, Scene I)*

"Thou lookest like one I lov'd." Pericles suspects that Marina is his daughter *(Act V, Scene I)*

"I embrace you. Give me my robes. I am wild in my beholding." The prince is overwhelmed at recovering his daughter Marina, whom he thought dead *(Act V, Scene I)*

"Hail, Dian!" Pericles appears with Marina at the temple of Diana in Ephesus *(Act V, Scene III)*

"Look, who kneels here! Flesh of thy flesh, Thaisa." Pericles presents Marina to her mother, whom he has found serving in the temple *(Act V, Scene III)*

"This prince, the fair-betrothed of your daughter, shall marry her at Pentapolis." Pericles tells of the betrothal of Marina and Lysimachus, who protected her at Mitylene *(Act V, Scene III)*

King. Your presence glads our days. Honour we love;
For who hates honour hates the gods above.
Marshal. Sir, yonder is your place.
Per. Some other is more fit.
1. Knight. Contend not, sir; for we are gentlemen
That neither in our hearts nor outward eyes
Envy the great nor shall the low despise.
Per. You are right courteous knights.
King. Sit, sir, sit.
[*Aside*] By Jove, I wonder, that is king of thoughts,
These cates resist me, he not thought upon.
Thai. [*aside*] By Juno, that is queen of marriage,
All viands that I eat do seem unsavoury,
Wishing him my meat. — Sure he's a gallant gentleman.
King. [*aside*] He's but a country gentleman.
Has done no more than other knights have done;
Has broken a staff or so; so let it pass.
Thai. [*aside*] To me he seems like diamond to glass.
Per. [*aside*] Yon king's to me like to my father's picture,
Which tells me in that glory once he was;
Had princes sit like stars about his throne,
And he the sun for them to reverence;
None that beheld him but, like lesser lights,
Did vail their crowns to his supremacy;
Where now his son's like a glowworm in the night,
The which hath fire in darkness, none in light.
Whereby I see that Time's the king of men;
He's both their parent, and he is their grave,
And gives them what he will, not what they crave.
King. What, are you merry, knights?
Knights. Who can be other in this royal presence?
King. Here, with a cup that's stor'd unto the brim —
As you do love, fill to your mistress' lips —
We drink this health to you.
Knights. We thank your Grace.
King. Yet pause awhile.
Yon knight doth sit too melancholy,
As if the entertainment in our court
Had not a show might countervail his worth.
Note it not you, Thaisa?
Thai. What is't to me, my father?
King. O, attend, my daughter.
Princes, in this, should live like gods above,
Who freely give to every one that comes
To honour them;
And princes not doing so are like to gnats,
Which make a sound, but kill'd are wond'red at.
Therefore to make his entertain more sweet,
Here, say we drink this standing bowl of wine to him.
Thai. Alas, my father, it befits not me
Unto a stranger knight to be so bold!
He may my proffer take for an offence,
Since men take women's gifts for impudence.
King. How?
Do as I bid you, or you'll move me else.
Thai. [*aside*] Now, by the gods, he could not please me better.
King. And furthermore tell him we desire to know of him
Of whence he is, his name and parentage.
Thai. The King my father, sir, has drunk to you —
Per. I thank him.
Thai. Wishing it so much blood unto your life.
Per. I thank both him and you, and pledge him freely.
Thai. And further, he desires to know of you
Of whence you are, your name and parentage.
Per. A gentleman of Tyre; my name, Pericles;
My education been in arts and arms;
Who, looking for adventures in the world,
Was by the rough seas reft of ships and men
And, after shipwrack, driven upon this shore.
Thai. He thanks your Grace; names himself Pericles,
A gentleman of Tyre,
Who only by misfortune of the seas
Bereft of ships and men, cast on this shore.
King. Now, by the gods, I pity his misfortune
And will awake him from his melancholy.
Come, gentlemen, we sit too long on trifles
And waste the time which looks for other revels.
Even in your armours, as you are address'd,
Will very well become a soldier's dance.
I will not have excuse, with saying this
Loud music is too harsh for ladies' heads,
Since they love men in arms as well as beds.
They dance.
So, this was well ask'd, 'twas so well perform'd.
Come, sir.
Here is a lady that wants breathing too;

And I have heard, you knights of Tyre
Are excellent in making ladies trip,
And that their measures are as excellent.
Per. In those that practise them they are, my lord.
King. O, that's as much as you would be denied
Of your fair courtesy.
[*The Knights and Ladies*] *dance.*
Unclasp, unclasp!
Thanks, gentlemen, to all; all have done well,
[*To Pericles*] But you the best. — Pages and lights, to conduct
These knights unto their several lodgings! — Yours, sir,
We have given order to be next our own.
Per. I am at your Grace's pleasure.
King. Princes, it is too late to talk of love;
And that's the mark I know you level at.
Therefore each one betake him to his rest;
To-morrow all for speeding do their best.
[*Exeunt.*]

[Scene IV. *Tyre. The house of* Helicanus, *the Governor.*]

Enter *Helicanus* and *Escanes.*

Hel. No, Escanes; know this of me —
Antiochus from incest liv'd not free;
For which, the most high gods not minding longer
To withhold the vengeance that they had in store,
Due to this heinous capital offence,
Even in the height and pride of all his glory,
When he was seated in a chariot
Of an inestimable value, and his daughter with him,
A fire from heaven came and shrivell'd up
Their bodies, even to loathing; for they so stunk
That all those eyes ador'd them ere their fall
Scorn now their hand should give them burial.
Esca. 'Twas very strange.
Hel. And yet but justice; for though
This king were great, his greatness was no guard
To bar heaven's shaft, but sin had his reward.
Esca. 'Tis very true.

Enter two or three *Lords.*

1. Lord. See, not a man in private conference
Or council has respect with him but he.
2. Lord. It shall no longer grieve without reproof.
3. Lord. And curs'd be he that will not second it!
1. Lord. Follow me then. Lord Helicane, a word.
Hel. With me? and welcome. Happy day, my lords.
1. Lord. Know that our griefs are risen to the top
And now at length they overflow their banks.
Hel. Your griefs? for what? Wrong not your prince you love.
1. Lord. Wrong not yourself then, noble Helicane;
But if the prince do live, let us salute him,
Or know what ground's made happy by his breath.
If in the world he live, we'll seek him out;
If in his grave he rest, we'll find him there
And be resolv'd he lives to govern us,
Or, dead, give 's cause to mourn his funeral,
And leave us to our free election.
2. Lord. Whose death's indeed the strongest in our censure;
And knowing this kingdom, if without a head,
Like goodly buildings left without a roof,
Soon fall to ruin, your noble self,
That best know how to rule and how to reign,
We thus submit unto — our sovereign.
Omnes. Live, noble Helicane!
Hel. For honour's cause forbear your suffrages.
If that you love Prince Pericles, forbear.
Take I your wish, I leap into the seas,
Where's hourly trouble for a minute's ease.
A twelvemonth longer let me entreat you
To forbear the absence of your king;
If in which time expir'd he not return,
I shall with aged patience bear your yoke.
But if I cannot win you to this love,
Go search like nobles, like noble subjects,
And in your search spend your adventurous worth;
Whom if you find and win unto return,
You shall like diamonds sit about his crown.
1. Lord. To wisdom he's a fool that will not yield;
And since Lord Helicane enjoineth us,
We with our travels will endeavour it.
Hel. Then you love us, we you, and we'll clasp hands.
When peers thus knit, a kingdom ever stands.
Exeunt.

[Scene V. *Pentapolis. The Palace of* King Simonides.]

Enter the *King* [*Simonides*], reading of a letter at one door. The *Knights* meet him.

1. Knight. Good morrow to the good Simonides.

King. Knights, from my daughter this I let you know,
That for this twelvemonth she'll not undertake
A married life.
Her reason to herself is only known,
Which from her by no means can I get.

2. Knight. May we not get access to her, my lord?

King. Faith, by no means. She hath so strictly tied her
To her chamber that it is impossible.
One twelve moons more she'll wear Diana's livery.
This by the eye of Cynthia hath she vow'd,
And on her virgin honour will not break it.

3. Knight. Loath to bid farewell, we take our leaves. *Exeunt* [*Knights*].

King. So,
They are well dispatch'd. Now to my daughter's letter.
She tells me here, she'll wed the stranger knight,
Or never more to view nor day nor light.
'Tis well, mistress; your choice agrees with mine;
I like that well. Nay, how absolute she's in't,
Not minding whether I dislike or no!
Well, I do commend her choice;
And will no longer have it be delay'd.
Soft! here he comes; I must dissemble it.

Enter *Pericles*.

Per. All fortune to the good Simonides!

King. To you as much, sir! I am beholding to you
For your sweet music this last night. I do
Protest my ears were never better fed
With such delightful pleasing harmony.

Per. It is your Grace's pleasure to commend;
Not my desert.

King. Sir, you are music's master.

Per. The worst of all her scholars, my good lord.

King. Let me ask you one thing:
What do you think of my daughter, sir?

Per. A most virtuous princess.

King. And she is fair too, is she not?

Per. As a fair day in summer—wondrous fair.

King. Sir, my daughter thinks very well of you;
Ay, so well that you must be her master
And she will be your scholar. Therefore look to it.

Per. I am unworthy for her schoolmaster.

King. She thinks not so. Peruse this writing else.

Per. [*aside*] What's here?
A letter, that she loves the knight of Tyre?
'Tis the King's subtilty to have my life.—
O, seek not to entrap me, gracious lord,
A stranger and distressed gentleman,
That never aim'd so high to love your daughter,
But bent all offices to honour her.

King. Thou hast bewitch'd my daughter, and thou art
A villain.

Per. By the gods, I have not!
Never did thought of mine levy offence;
Nor never did my actions yet commence
A deed might gain her love or your displeasure.

King. Traitor, thou liest!

Per. Traitor?

King. Ay, traitor.

Per. Even in his throat—unless it be the King—
That calls me traitor, I return the lie.

King. [*aside*] Now, by the gods, I do applaud his courage.

Per. My actions are as noble as my thoughts,
That never relish'd of a base descent.
I came unto your court for honour's cause,
And not to be a rebel to her state;
And he that otherwise accounts of me,
This sword shall prove he's honour's enemy.

King. No?
Here comes my daughter, she can witness it.

Enter *Thaisa*.

Per. Then, as you are as virtuous as fair,
Resolve your angry father if my tongue
Did e'er solicit, or my hand subscribe
To any syllable that made love to you.

Thai. Why, sir, say if you had,
Who takes offence at that would make me glad?

King. Yea, mistress, are you so peremptory?
(*Aside*) I am glad on't with all my heart.—
I'll tame you; I'll bring you in subjection!
Will you, not having my consent,
Bestow your love and your affections
Upon a stranger?—(*aside*) who, for aught I know,
May be (nor can I think the contrary)
As great in blood as I myself.—

Therefore hear you, mistress: either frame
Your will to mine — and you, sir, hear you,
Either be rul'd by me, or I'll make you —
Man and wife.
Nay, come, your hands and lips must seal it too;
And being join'd, I'll thus your hopes destroy,
And for a further grief — God give you joy!
What, are you both pleas'd?

Thai. Yes, if you love me, sir.

Per. Even as my life my blood that fosters it!

King. What, are you both agreed?

Ambo. Yes, if't please your Majesty.

King. It pleaseth me so well that I will see you wed;
And then, with what haste you can, get you to bed. *Exeunt.*

[ACT III.]

Enter *Gower.*

Gow. Now sleep yslacked hath the rout;
No din but snores the house about,
Made louder by the o'erfed breast
Of this most pompous marriage feast.
The cat, with eyne of burning coal,
Now couches fore the mouse's hole;
And crickets sing at the oven's mouth,
E'er the blither for their drouth.
Hymen hath brought the bride to bed,
Where, by the loss of maidenhead,
A babe is moulded. Be attent,
And time that is so briefly spent
With your fine fancies quaintly eche.
What's dumb in show I'll plain with speech.

Dumb Show.

Enter *Pericles* and *Simonides* at one door, with *Attendants*; a *Messenger* meets them, kneels, and gives *Pericles* a letter. *Pericles* shows it *Simonides*. The *Lords* kneel to him, [*Pericles*]. Then enter *Thaisa* with child, with *Lychorida*, a nurse. The *King* shows her the letter; she rejoices. She and *Pericles* take leave of her father, and depart [with *Lychorida* and their *Attendants*. Then exeunt *Simonides* and the rest].

By many a dern and painful perch
Of Pericles the careful search,
By the four opposing coigns
Which the world together joins,
Is made with all due diligence
That horse and sail and high expense
Can stead the quest. At last from Tyre,
Fame answering the most strange enquire,
To th' court of King Simonides
Are letters brought, the tenour these:
Antiochus and his daughter dead,
The men of Tyrus on the head
Of Helicanus would set on
The crown of Tyre, but he will none.
The mutiny he there hastes t' oppress;
Says to 'em, if King Pericles
Come not home in twice six moons,
He, obedient to their dooms,
Will take the crown. The sum of this,
Brought hither to Pentapolis,
Yravished the regions round,
And every one with claps can sound,
'Our heir apparent is a king!
Who dreamt, who thought of such a thing?'
Brief, he must hence depart to Tyre.
His queen with child makes her desire
(Which who shall cross?) along to go.
Omit we all their dole and woe.
Lychorida her nurse she takes,
And so to sea. Their vessel shakes
On Neptune's billow; half the flood
Hath their keel cut: but fortune's mood
Varies again; the grisled North
Disgorges such a tempest forth
That, as a duck for life that dives,
So up and down the poor ship drives.
The lady shrieks, and, well-a-near,
Does fall in travail with her fear;
And what ensues in this fell storm
Shall for itself itself perform.
I nill relate, action may
Conveniently the rest convey,
Which might not what by me is told.
In your imagination hold
This stage the ship, upon whose deck
The sea-tost Pericles appears to speak. *Exit.*

[Scene I.]

Enter *Pericles* a-shipboard.

Per. Thou god of this great vast, rebuke these surges,
Which wash both heaven and hell; and thou that hast

Upon the winds command, bind them in brass,
Having recall'd them from the deep! O, still
Thy deaf'ning dreadful thunders; gently quench
Thy nimble sulphurous flashes! — O, how, Lychorida,
How does my queen? — Thou stormest venomously;
Wilt thou spet all thyself? The seaman's whistle
Is as a whisper in the ears of death,
Unheard. — Lychorida! — Lucina, O
Divinest patroness and midwife gentle
To those that cry by night, convey thy deity
Aboard our dancing boat; make swift the pangs
Of my queen's travails!

Enter *Lychorida* [with an *Infant*].

Now, Lychorida!

Lyc. Here is a thing too young for such a place,
Who, if it had conceit, would die, as I
Am like to do. Take in your arms this piece
Of your dead queen.

Per. How? how, Lychorida?

Lyc. Patience, good sir; do not assist the storm.
Here's all that is left living of your queen —
A little daughter. For the sake of it,
Be manly and take comfort.

Per. O you gods!
Why do you make us love your goodly gifts
And snatch them straight away? We here below
Recall not what we give, and therein may
Vie honour with you.

Lyc. Patience, good sir,
Even for this charge.

Per. Now mild may be thy life!
For a more blusterous birth had never babe;
Quiet and gentle thy conditions! for
Thou art the rudeliest welcome to this world
That ever was prince's child. Happy what follows!
Thou hast as chiding a nativity
As fire, air, water, earth, and heaven can make,
To herald thee from the womb. Even at the first
Thy loss is more than can thy portage quit
With all thou canst find here. Now the good gods
Throw their best eyes upon't!

Enter two *Sailors.*

1. Sail. What courage, sir? God save you!

Per. Courage enough. I do not fear the flaw;
It hath done to me the worst. Yet for the love
Of this poor infant, this fresh new seafarer,
I would it would be quiet.

1. Sail. Slack the bolins there! Thou wilt not, wilt thou? Blow, and split thyself.

2. Sail. But searoom, an the brine and cloudy billow kiss the moon, I care not.

1. Sail. Sir, your queen must overboard. The sea works high, the wind is loud, and will not lie till the ship be clear'd of the dead.

Per. That's your superstition.

1. Sail. Pardon us, sir. With us at sea it hath been still observed, and we are strong in custom. Therefore briefly yield 'er; for she must overboard straight.

Per. As you think meet. Most wretched queen!

Lyc. Here she lies, sir.

Per. A terrible childbed hast thou had, my dear;
No light, no fire. Th' unfriendly elements
Forgot thee utterly; nor have I time
To give thee hallow'd to thy grave, but straight
Must cast thee, scarcely coffin'd, in the ooze;
Where, for a monument upon thy bones,
And e'er-remaining lamps, the belching whale
And humming water must o'erwhelm thy corpse
Lying with simple shells. O Lychorida,
Bid Nestor bring me spices, ink and paper,
My casket and my jewels; and bid Nicander
Bring me the satin coffer. Lay the babe
Upon the pillow. Hie thee, whiles I say
A priestly farewell to her. Suddenly, woman.
[*Exit Lychorida.*]

2. Sail. Sir, we have a chest beneath the hatches, caulk'd and bitumed ready.

Per. I thank thee. Mariner, say, what coast is this?

2. Sail. We are near Tharsus.

Per. Thither, gentle mariner,
Alter thy course for Tyre. When canst thou reach it?

2. Sail. By break of day, if the wind cease.

Per. O, make for Tharsus!
There will I visit Cleon, for the babe
Cannot hold out to Tyrus. There I'll leave it
At careful nursing. Go thy ways, good mariner;
I'll bring the body presently. *Exeunt.*

[Scene **II.** ***Ephesus.*** Cerimon's *house*].

Enter ***Lord Cerimon,*** with a *Servant* [and some *Persons* who have been shipwrecked].

Cer. Philemon, ho!

Enter *Philemon.*

Phil. Doth my lord call?
Cer. Get fire and meat for these poor men.
'T 'as been a turbulent and stormy night.
Serv. I have been in many; but such a night as this
Till now I ne'er endured.
Cer. Your master will be dead ere you return.
There's nothing can be minist'red to nature
That can recover him. [*To Philemon*] Give this to the pothecary,
And tell me how it works.

[*Exeunt all but Cerimon.*]

Enter two *Gentlemen.*

1. Gent. Good morrow.
2. Gent. Good morrow to your lordship.
Cer. Gentlemen,
Why do you stir so early?
1. Gent. Sir,
Our lodgings, standing bleak upon the sea,
Shook as the earth did quake.
The very principals did seem to rend,
And all to topple. Pure surprise and fear
Made me to quit the house.
2. Gent. That is the cause we trouble you so early;
'Tis not our husbandry.
Cer. O, you say well.
1. Gent. But I much marvel that your lordship, having
Rich tire about you, should at these early hours
Shake off the golden slumber of repose.
'Tis most strange
Nature should be so conversant with pain,
Being thereto not compell'd.
Cer. I held it ever
Virtue and cunning were endowments greater
Than nobleness and riches. Careless heirs
May the two latter darken and expend;
But immortality attends the former,
Making a man a god. 'Tis known, I ever
Have studied physic, through which secret art,
By turning o'er authorities, I have,
Together with my practice, made familiar
To me and to my aid the blest infusions
That dwell in vegetives, in metals, stones;
And I can speak of the disturbances
That nature works, and of her cures; which doth give me
A more content in course of true delight
Than to be thirsty after tottering honour,
Or tie my treasure up in silken bags,
To please the fool and death.
2. Gent. Your honour has through Ephesus pour'd forth
Your charity, and hundreds call themselves
Your creatures, who by you have been restor'd;
And not your knowledge, your personal pain, but even
Your purse, still open, hath built Lord Cerimon
Such strong renown as time shall never raze.

Enter two or three [*Servants*] with a chest.

Serv. So, lift there.
Cer. What is that?
Serv. Sir, even now
Did the sea toss up upon our shore this chest.
'Tis of some wrack.
Cer. Set 't down; let's look upon't.
2. Gent. 'Tis like a coffin, sir.
Cer. Whate'er it be,
'Tis wondrous heavy. Wrench it open straight.
If the sea's stomach be o'ercharg'd with gold,
'Tis a good constraint of fortune it belches upon us.
2. Gent. 'Tis so, my lord.
Cer. How close 'tis caulk'd and bitumed!
Did the sea cast it up?
Serv. I never saw so huge a billow, sir,
As toss'd it upon shore.
Cer. Wrench it open.
Soft! It smells most sweetly in my sense.
2. Gent. A delicate odour.
Cer. As ever hit my nostril. So, up with it!
O you most potent gods! what's here? a corse!
1. Gent. Most strange!
Cer. Shrouded in cloth of state; balm'd and entreasur'd
With full bags of spices! A passport too!
Apollo, perfect me in the characters!

[*Reads from a scroll.*]

'Here I give to understand —
If e'er this coffin drives aland —
I, King Pericles, have lost
This queen, worth all our mundane cost.
Who finds her, give her burying;
She was the daughter of a king.
Besides this treasure for a fee,
The gods requit his charity!'

If thou livest, Pericles, thou hast a heart
That even cracks for woe! This chanc'd to-night.

2. Gent. Most likely, sir.

Cer. Nay, certainly to-night;
For look how fresh she looks! They were too rough
That threw her in the sea. Make a fire within.
Fetch hither all my boxes in my closet.

[*Exit a Servant.*]

Death may usurp on nature many hours,
And yet the fire of life kindle again
The o'erpress'd spirits. I heard of an Egyptian
That had nine hours lien dead,
Who was by good appliance recovered.

Enter *one* with [boxes,] napkins, and fire.

Well said, well said! the fire and cloths.
The rough and woful music that we have,
Cause it to sound, beseech you.
The viol once more. How thou stirr'st, thou block!
The music there! I pray you give her air.
Gentlemen,
This queen will live; nature awakes; a warmth
Breathes out of her. She hath not been entranc'd
Above five hours. See how she gins to blow
Into life's flower again!

1. Gent. The heavens,
Through you, increase our wonder, and set up
Your fame for ever.

Cer. She is alive! Behold,
Her eyelids, cases to those heavenly jewels
Which Pericles hath lost, begin to part
Their fringes of bright gold. The diamonds
Of a most praised water do appear
To make the world twice rich. Live, and make
Us weep to hear your fate, fair creature,
Rare as you seem to be! *She moves.*

Thai. O dear Diana,
Where am I? Where's my lord? What world is this?

2. Gent. Is not this strange?

1. Gent. Most rare.

Cer. Hush, my gentle neighbours!
Lend me your hands; to the next chamber bear her.
Get linen. Now this matter must be look'd to,
For her relapse is mortal. Come, come!
And Æsculapius guide us!

They carry her away. Exeunt omnes.

[Scene III. *Tharsus.* Cleon's *house.*]

Enter *Pericles* at Tharsus, with *Cleon* and *Dionyza,* [and *Lychorida* with *Marina* in her arms].

Per. Most honour'd Cleon, I must needs be gone.
My twelve months are expir'd, and Tyrus stands
In a litigious peace. You and your lady
Take from my heart all thankfulness! The gods
Make up the rest upon you!

Cleon. Your shafts of fortune, though they hurt you mortally,
Yet glance full wand'ringly on us.

Dion. O your sweet queen!
That the strict Fates had pleas'd you had brought her hither
To have bless'd mine eyes with her!

Per. We cannot but obey
The powers above us. Could I rage and roar
As doth the sea she lies in, yet the end
Must be as 'tis. My gentle babe Marina — whom,
For she was born at sea, I have nam'd so — here
I charge your charity withal, leaving her
The infant of your care; beseeching you
To give her princely training, that she may be
Manner'd as she is born.

Cleon. Fear not, my lord, but think
Your Grace, that fed my country with your corn,
For which the people's prayers still fall upon you,
Must in your child be thought on. If neglection
Should therein make me vile, the common body,
By you reliev'd, would force me to my duty.
But if to that my nature need a spur,
The gods revenge it upon me and mine
To the end of generation!

Per. I believe you.
Your honour and your goodness teach me to't
Without your vows. Till she be married, madam,
By bright Diana, whom we honour all,
Unscissor'd shall this hair of mine remain,
Though I show ill in't. So I take my leave.
Good madam, make me blessed in your care
In bringing up my child.

Dion. I have one myself,
Who shall not be more dear to my respect
Than yours, my lord.

Per. Madam, my thanks and prayers.

Cleon. We'll bring your Grace e'en to the edge o' th' shore,

Then give you up to the mask'd Neptune and
The gentlest winds of heaven.

Per. I will embrace
Your offer. Come, dearest madam. O, no tears,
Lychorida, no tears!
Look to your little mistress, on whose grace
You may depend hereafter. Come, my lord.
[*Exeunt.*]

[Scene IV. *Ephesus.* Cerimon's *house.*]

Enter *Cerimon* and *Thaisa.*

Cer. Madam, this letter, and some certain jewels,
Lay with you in your coffer; which are here
At your command. Know you the character?

Thai. It is my lord's.
That I was shipp'd at sea I well remember,
Even on my eaning time; but whether there
Delivered, by the holy gods,
I cannot rightly say. But since King Pericles,
My wedded lord, I ne'er shall see again,
A vestal livery will I take me to,
And never more have joy.

Cer. Madam, if this you purpose as ye speak,
Diana's temple is not distant far,
Where you may abide until your date expire.
Moreover, if you please, a niece of mine
Shall there attend you.

Thai. My recompense is thanks, that's all;
Yet my good will is great, though the gift small.
Exeunt.

[ACT IV.]

Enter *Gower.*

Gow. Imagine Pericles arriv'd at Tyre,
Welcom'd and settled to his own desire.
His woful queen we leave at Ephesus,
Unto Diana there's a votaress.
Now to Marina bend your mind,
Whom our fast-growing scene must find
At Tharsus, and by Cleon train'd
In music, letters; who hath gain'd
Of education all the grace,
Which makes her both the heart and place
Of general wonder. But, alack,
That monster, Envy, oft the wrack
Of earned praise, Marina's life
Seeks to take off by treason's knife.
And in this kind hath our Cleon
One daughter, and a wench full grown,
Even ripe for marriage rite. This maid
Hight Philoten; and it is said
For certain in our story, she
Would ever with Marina be.
Be't when she weav'd the sleided silk
With fingers long, small, white as milk;
Or when she would with sharp needle wound
The cambric, which she made more sound
By hurting it; or when to th' lute
She sung, and made the night-bird mute
That still records with moan; or when
She would with rich and constant pen
Vail to her mistress Dian; still
This Philoten contends in skill
With absolute Marina. So
With the dove of Paphos might the crow
Vie feathers white. Marina gets
All praises, which are paid as debts,
And not as given. This so darks
In Philoten all graceful marks
That Cleon's wife, with envy rare,
A present murder does prepare
For good Marina, that her daughter
Might stand peerless by this slaughter.
The sooner her vile thoughts to stead,
Lychorida, our nurse, is dead;
And cursed Dionyza hath
The pregnant instrument of wrath
Prest for this blow. The unborn event
I do commend to your content:
Only I carry winged time
Post on the lame feet of my rhyme;
Which never could I so convey
Unless your thoughts went on my way.
Dionyza does appear,
With Leonine, a murtherer. *Exit.*

[Scene I. *Tharsus. An open place near the seashore.*]

Enter *Dionyza* with *Leonine.*

Dion. Thy oath remember; thou hast sworn to do't.
'Tis but a blow, which never shall be known.
Thou canst not do a thing in the world so soon

To yield thee so much profit. Let not conscience,
Which is but cold, inflaming love in thy bosom,
Inflame too nicely; nor let pity, which
Even women have cast off, melt thee, but be
A soldier to thy purpose.

Leon. I will do't.
But yet she is a goodly creature.

Dion. The fitter then the gods should have her. Here
She comes weeping for her only mistress' death.
Thou art resolv'd?

Leon. I am resolv'd.

Enter *Marina*, with a basket of flowers.

Mar. No, I will rob Tellus of her weed,
To strow thy green with flowers. The yellows, blues,
The purple violets, and marigolds,
Shall, as a carpet, hang upon thy grave
While summer days do last. Ay me, poor maid,
Born in a tempest when my mother died!
This world to me is like a lasting storm,
Whirring me from my friends.

Dion. How now, Marina? Why do you keep alone?
How chance my daughter is not with you? Do not
Consume your blood with sorrowing. You have
A nurse of me. Lord, how your favour's chang'd
With this unprofitable woe! Come, come!
Give me your flowers. On the sea margent
Walk with Leonine. The air is quick there,
And it pierces and sharpens the stomach. Come,
Leonine, take her by the arm, walk with her.

Mar. No, I pray you.
I'll not bereave you of your servant.

Dion. Come, come!
I love the King your father, and yourself,
With more than foreign heart. We every day
Expect him here. When he shall come and find
Our paragon to all reports thus blasted,
He will repent the breadth of his great voyage;
Blame both my lord and me, that we have taken
No care to your best courses. Go, I pray you.
Walk, and be cheerful once again. Reserve
That excellent complexion which did steal
The eyes of young and old. Care not for me;
I can go home alone.

Mar. Well, I will go;
But yet I have no desire to it.

Dion. Come, come!
I know 'tis good for you.
Walk half an hour, Leonine, at the least.
Remember what I have said.

Leon. I warrant you, madam.

Dion. I'll leave you, my sweet lady, for a while.
Pray walk softly; do not heat your blood.
What, I must have care of you.

Mar. My thanks, sweet madam.
[*Exit Dionyza.*]
Is this wind westerly that blows?

Leon. Southwest.

Mar. When I was born the wind was north.

Leon. Was't so?

Mar. My father, as nurse says, did never fear,
But cried 'Good seamen!' to the sailors, galling
His kingly hands haling ropes;
And, clasping to the mast, endur'd a sea
That almost burst the deck.

Leon. When was this?

Mar. When I was born.
Never was waves nor wind more violent;
And from the ladder tackle washes off
A canvas climber. 'Ha!' says one, 'wolt out?'
And with a dropping industry they skip
From stem to stern. The boatswain whistles, and
The master calls and trebles their confusion.

Leon. Come, say your prayers.

Mar. What mean you?

Leon. If you require a little space for prayer,
I grant it. Pray; but be not tedious, for
The gods are quick of ear, and I am sworn
To do my work with haste.

Mar. Why will you kill me?

Leon. To satisfy my lady.

Mar. Why would she have me kill'd?
Now, as I can remember, by my troth,
I never did her hurt in all my life.
I never spake bad word nor did ill turn
To any living creature. Believe me, la,
I never kill'd a mouse, nor hurt a fly.
I trod upon a worm against my will,
But I wept for it. How have I offended
Wherein my death might yield her any profit
Or my life imply her any danger?

Leon. My commission
Is not to reason of the deed, but do't.

Mar. You will not do't for all the world, I hope.
You are well-favoured, and your looks foreshow
You have a gentle heart. I saw you lately
When you caught hurt in parting two that fought.
Good sooth, it show'd well in you. Do so now.

Your lady seeks my life; come you between,
And save poor me, the weaker.

Leon. I am sworn,
And will dispatch. [*Seizes her.*]

Enter *Pirates.*

1. Pirate. Hold, villain! [*Leonine runs away.*]

2. Pirate. A prize! a prize!

3. Pirate. Half part, mates, half part! Come, let's have her aboard suddenly.

Exeunt [*Pirates with Marina*].

Enter *Leonine.*

Leon. These roguing thieves serve the great pirate Valdes,
And they have seiz'd Marina. Let her go.
There's no hope she will return. I'll swear she's dead
And thrown into the sea. But I'll see further.
Perhaps they will but please themselves upon her,
Not carry her aboard. If she remain,
Whom they have ravish'd must by me be slain.

Exit.

[Scene II. *Mytilene. A brothel.*]

Enter *Pander, Bawd,* and *Boult.*

Pand. Boult!

Boult. Sir?

Pand. Search the market narrowly. Mytilene is full of gallants. We lost too much money this mart by being too wenchless.

Bawd. We were never so much out of creatures. We have but poor three, and they can do no more than they can do; and they with continual action are even as good as rotten.

Pand. Therefore let's have fresh ones, whate'er we pay for them. If there be not a conscience to be us'd in every trade, we shall never prosper.

Bawd. Thou say'st true. 'Tis not our bringing up of poor bastards, as, I think, I have brought up some eleven —

Boult. Ay, to eleven; and brought them down again. But shall I search the market?

Bawd. What else, man? The stuff we have, a strong wind will blow it to pieces, they are so pitifully sodden.

Pand. Thou sayest true; they're too unwholesome, o' conscience. The poor Transylvanian is dead that lay with the little baggage.

Boult. Ay, she quickly poop'd him; she made him roast meat for worms. But I'll go search the market. *Exit.*

Pand. Three or four thousand checkins were as pretty a proportion to live quietly, and so give over.

Bawd. Why to give over, I pray you? Is it a shame to get when we are old?

Pand. O, our credit comes not in like the commodity, nor the commodity wages not with the danger. Therefore, if in our youths we could pick up some pretty estate, 'twere not amiss to keep our door hatch'd. Besides, the sore terms we stand upon with the gods will be strong with us for giving o'er.

Bawd. Come, other sorts offend as well as we.

Pand. As well as we? Ay, and better too. We offend worse. Neither is our profession any trade; it's no calling. But here comes Boult.

Enter *Boult,* with the *Pirates* and *Marina.*

Boult. [*to Marina*] Come your ways.— My masters, you say she's a virgin?

Sailor. O, sir, we doubt it not.

Boult. Master, I have gone through for this piece you see. If you like her, so; if not, I have lost my earnest.

Bawd. Boult, has she any qualities?

Boult. She has a good face, speaks well, and has excellent good clothes. There's no farther necessity of qualities can make her be refus'd.

Bawd. What's her price, Boult?

Boult. I cannot be bated one doit of a thousand pieces.

Pand. Well, follow me, my masters; you shall have your money presently. Wife, take her in; instruct her what she has to do, that she may not be raw in her entertainment.

[*Exeunt Pander and Pirates.*]

Bawd. Boult, take you the marks of her — the colour of her hair, complexion, height, her age, with warrant of her virginity; and cry, 'He that will give most shall have her first.' Such a maidenhead were no cheap thing, if men were as they have been. Get this done as I command you.

Boult. Performance shall follow. *Exit.*

Mar. Alack that Leonine was so slack, so slow!
He should have struck, not spoke; or that these pirates,
Not enough barbarous, had not o'erboard thrown me
For to seek my mother!

Bawd. Why lament you, pretty one?

Mar. That I am pretty.

Bawd. Come, the gods have done their part in you.

Mar. I accuse them not.

Bawd. You are light into my hands, where you are like to live.

Mar. The more my fault
To scape his hands where I was like to die.

Bawd. Ay, and you shall live in pleasure.

Mar. No.

Bawd. Yes, indeed shall you, and taste gentlemen of all fashions. You shall fare well; you shall have the difference of all complexions. What, do you stop your ears?

Mar. Are you a woman?

Bawd. What would you have me be, an I be not a woman?

Mar. An honest woman, or not a woman.

Bawd. Marry whip thee, gosling! I think I shall have something to do with you. Come, you're a young foolish sapling, and must be bowed as I would have you.

Mar. The gods defend me!

Bawd. If it please the gods to defend you by men, then men must comfort you, men must feed you, men must stir you up. Boult's return'd.

Enter *Boult.*

Now, sir, hast thou cried her through the market?

Boult. I have cried her almost to the number of her hairs; I have drawn her picture with my voice.

Bawd. And I prithee tell me, how dost thou find the inclination of the people, especially of the younger sort?

Boult. Faith, they listened to me as they would have hearkened to their father's testament. There was a Spaniard's mouth so wat'red! and he went to bed to her very description.

Bawd. We shall have him here to-morrow with his best ruff on.

Boult. To-night, to-night! But, mistress, do you know the French knight that cow'rs i' the hams?

Bawd. Who, Monsieur Verollus?

Boult. Ay, he. He offered to cut a caper at the proclamation; but he made a groan at it, and swore he would see her to-morrow.

Bawd. Well, well; as for him, he brought his disease hither: here he does but repair it. I know he will come in our shadow, to scatter his crowns in the sun.

Boult. Well, if we had of every nation a traveller, we should lodge them with this sign.

Bawd. [*to Marina*] Pray you come hither awhile. You have fortunes coming upon you. Mark me: you must seem to do that fearfully which you commit willingly, despise profit where you have most gain. To weep that you live as ye do makes pity in your lovers. Seldom but that pity begets you a good opinion, and that opinion a mere profit.

Mar. I understand you not.

Boult. O, take her home, mistress, take her home! These blushes of hers must be quench'd with some present practice.

Bawd. Thou sayest true, i'faith; so they must; for your bride goes to that with shame which is her way to go with warrant.

Boult. Faith, some do, and some do not. But, mistress, if I have bargain'd for the joint —

Bawd. Thou mayst cut a morsel off the spit?

Boult. I may so.

Bawd. Who should deny it? Come, young one, I like the manner of your garments well.

Boult. Ay, by my faith, they shall not be chang'd yet.

Bawd. Boult, spend thou that in the town. Report what a sojourner we have; you'll lose nothing by custom. When Nature fram'd this piece, she meant thee a good turn. Therefore say what a paragon she is, and thou hast the harvest out of thine own report.

Boult. I warrant you, mistress, thunder shall not so awake the beds of eels as my giving out her beauty stirs up the lewdly inclined. I'll bring home some to-night.

Bawd. Come your ways, follow me.

Mar. If fires be hot, knives sharp, or waters deep,
Untied I still my virgin knot will keep.
Diana aid my purpose!

Bawd. What have we to do with Diana? Pray you, will you go with us? *Exeunt.*

[Scene III. *Tharsus.* Cleon's *house.*]

Enter *Cleon* and *Dionyza.*

Dion. Why are you foolish? Can it be undone?

Cleon. O Dionyza, such a piece of slaughter
The sun and moon ne'er look'd upon!

Dion. I think
You'll turn a child again.

Cleon. Were I chief lord of all this spacious world,

I'd give it to undo the deed. O lady,
Much less in blood than virtue, yet a princess
To equal any single crown o' th' earth
I' th' justice of compare! O villain Leonine!
Whom thou hast pois'ned too.
If thou hadst drunk to him, 't had been a kindness
Becoming well thy fact. What canst thou say
When noble Pericles shall demand his child?

Dion. That she is dead. Nurses are not the Fates,
To foster it, nor ever to preserve.
She died at night; I'll say so. Who can cross it?
Unless you play the pious innocent
And for an honest attribute cry out
'She died by foul play.'

Cleon. O, go to! Well, well,
Of all the faults beneath the heavens, the gods
Do like this worst.

Dion. Be one of those that think
The petty wrens of Tharsus will fly hence
And open this to Pericles. I do shame
To think of what a noble strain you are,
And of how coward a spirit.

Cleon. To such proceeding
Who ever but his approbation added,
Though not his prime consent, he did not flow
From honourable sources.

Dion. Be it so, then.
Yet none does know but you how she came dead,
Nor none can know, Leonine being gone.
She did distain my child and stood between
Her and her fortunes. None would look on her,
But cast their gazes on Marina's face,
Whilst ours was blurted at, and held a mawkin,
Not worth the time of day. It pierc'd me thorough;
And though you call my course unnatural,
You not your child well loving, yet I find
It greets me as an enterprise of kindness
Perform'd to your sole daughter.

Cleon. Heavens forgive it!

Dion. And as for Pericles,
What should he say? We wept after her hearse,
And yet we mourn. Her monument
Is almost finish'd, and her epitaphs
In glitt'ring golden characters express
A general praise to her, and care in us
At whose expense 'tis done.

Cleon. Thou art like the harpy,
Which, to betray, dost, with thine angel's face,
Seize with thine eagle's talents.

Dion. You are like one that superstitiously
Doth swear to th' gods that winter kills the flies;
But yet I know you'll do as I advise. *Exeunt.*

[Scene IV. *Before the monument of* Marina *at Tharsus.*]

Enter *Gower.*

Gow. Thus time we waste and longest leagues make short;
Sail seas in cockles, have and wish but for't;
Making, to take your imagination,
From bourn to bourn, region to region.
By you being pardoned, we commit no crime
To use one language in each several clime
Where our scenes seem to live. I do beseech you
To learn of me, who stand i' th' gaps to teach you,
The stages of our story. Pericles
Is now again thwarting the wayward seas,
Attended on by many a lord and knight,
To see his daughter, all his live's delight.
Old Helicanus goes along. Behind
Is left to govern it, you bear in mind,
Old Escanes, whom Helicanus late
Advanc'd in time to great and high estate.
Well-sailing ships and bounteous winds have brought
This king to Tharsus — think his pilot thought;
So with his steerage shall your thoughts grow on —
To fetch his daughter home, who first is gone.
Like motes and shadows see them move awhile.
Your ears unto your eyes I'll reconcile.

[*Dumb Show.*]

Enter *Pericles*, at one door, with all his *Train*; *Cleon* and *Dionyza* at the other. *Cleon* shows *Pericles* the tomb [of *Marina*], whereat *Pericles* makes lamentation, puts on sackcloth, and in a mighty passion departs. [Then exeunt *Cleon*, *Dionyza*, and the rest.]

See how belief may suffer by foul show!
This borrowed passion stands for true old woe;
And Pericles, in sorrow all devour'd,
With sighs shot through and biggest tears o'ershow'r'd,
Leaves Tharsus and again embarks. He swears
Never to wash his face nor cut his hairs.

He puts on sackcloth, and to sea. He bears
A tempest which his mortal vessel tears,
And yet he rides it out. Now please you wit
The epitaph is for Marina writ
By wicked Dionyza. [*Reads the inscription.*]

'The fairest, sweet'st, and best lies here,
Who withered in her spring of year.
She was of Tyrus the King's daughter,
On whom foul death hath made this slaughter;
Marina was she call'd, and at her birth,
Thetis, being proud, swallowed some part o' th' earth.
Therefore the earth, fearing to be o'erflowed,
Hath Thetis' birth-child on the heavens bestowed;
Wherefore she does (and swears she'll never stint)
Make raging battery upon shores of flint.'

No visor does become black villany
So well as soft and tender flattery.
Let Pericles believe his daughter's dead
And bear his courses to be ordered
By Lady Fortune, while our scene must play
His daughter's woe and heavy well-a-day
In her unholy service. Patience then,
And think you now are all in Mytilen. *Exit.*

[Scene V. *Mytilene. A street before the brothel.*]

Enter two *Gentlemen* [from the brothel].

1. Gent. Did you ever hear the like?

2. Gent. No, nor never shall do in such a place as this, she being once gone.

1. Gent. But to have divinity preach'd there! Did you ever dream of such a thing?

2. Gent. No, no. Come, I am for no more bawdy houses. Shall's go hear the Vestals sing?

1. Gent. I'll do anything now that is virtuous, but I am out of the road of rutting for ever. *Exeunt.*

[Scene VI. *Mytilene. A room in the brothel.*]

Enter [*Pander, Bawd,* and *Boult*].

Pand. Well, I had rather than twice the worth of her she had ne'er come here.

Bawd. Fie, fie upon her! she's able to freeze the god Priapus and undo a whole generation. We must either get her ravished or be rid of her. When she should do for clients her fitment, and do me the kindness of our profession, she has me her quirks, her reasons, her master reasons, her prayers, her knees, that she would make a Puritan of the devil if he should cheapen a kiss of her.

Boult. Faith, I must ravish her, or she'll disfurnish us of all our cavaliers and make our swearers priests.

Pand. Now the pox upon her greensickness for me!

Bawd. Faith, there's no way to be rid on't but by the way to the pox. Here comes the Lord Lysimachus disguised.

Boult. We should have both lord and lown if the peevish baggage would but give way to customers.

Enter *Lysimachus.*

Lys. How now? How a dozen of virginities?

Bawd. Now the gods to bless your Honour!

Boult. I am glad to see your Honour in good health.

Lys. You may so; 'tis the better for you that your resorters stand upon sound legs. How now, wholesome iniquity? Have you that a man may deal withal and defy the surgeon?

Bawd. We have here one, sir, if she would — but there never came her like in Mytilene.

Lys. If she'd do the deed of darkness, thou wouldst say.

Bawd. Your Honour knows what 'tis to say well enough.

Lys. Well, call forth, call forth.

Boult. For flesh and blood, sir, white and red, you shall see a rose; and she were a rose indeed, if she had but —

Lys. What, prithee?

Boult. O, sir, I can be modest.

Lys. That dignifies the renown of a bawd, no less than it gives a good report to a number to be chaste.

[*Exit Boult.*]

Bawd. Here comes that which grows to the stalk — never pluck'd yet, I can assure you.

Enter [*Boult* with] *Marina.*

Is she not a fair creature?

Lys. Faith, she would serve after a long voyage at sea. Well, there's for you. Leave us.

Bawd. I beseech your Honour give me leave a word, and I'll have done presently.

Lys. I beseech you do.

Bawd. [*to Marina*] First, I would have you note this is an honourable man.

Mar. I desire to find him so, that I may worthily note him.

Bawd. Next, he's the governor of this country, and a man whom I am bound to.

Mar. If he govern the country, you are bound to him indeed; but how honourable he is in that, I know not.

Bawd. Pray you, without any more virginal fencing, will you use him kindly? He will line your apron with gold.

Mar. What he will do graciously, I will thankfully receive.

Lys. Ha' you done?

Bawd. My lord, she's not pac'd yet; you must take some pains to work her to your manage. — Come, we will leave his honour and her together. — Go thy ways.

Exeunt Bawd, [Pander, and Boult].

Lys. Now, pretty one, how long have you been at this trade?

Mar. What trade, sir?

Lys. Why, I cannot name't but I shall offend.

Mar. I cannot be offended with my trade. Please you to name it.

Lys. How long have you been of this profession?

Mar. E'er since I can remember.

Lys. Did you go to't so young? Were you a gamester at five, or at seven?

Mar. Earlier too, sir, if now I be one.

Lys. Why, the house you dwell in proclaims you to be a creature of sale.

Mar. Do you know this house to be a place of such resort, and will come into't? I hear say you're of honourable parts, and are the governor of this place.

Lys. Why, hath your principal made known unto you who I am?

Mar. Who is my principal?

Lys. Why, your herb-woman, she that sets seeds and roots of shame and iniquity. O, you have heard something of my power, and so stand aloof for more serious wooing. But I protest to thee, pretty one, my authority shall not see thee, or else look friendly upon thee. Come, bring me to some private place. Come, come!

Mar. If you were born to honour, show it now;
If put upon you, make the judgment good
That thought you worthy of it.

Lys. How's this? how's this? Some more; be sage.

Mar. For me,
That am a maid, though most ungentle fortune
Have plac'd me in this sty, where, since I came,
Diseases have been sold dearer than physic —
O that the gods
Would set me free from this unhallowed place,
Though they did change me to the meanest bird
That flies i' th' purer air!

Lys. I did not think
Thou couldst have spoke so well; ne'er dreamt thou couldst.
Had I brought hither a corrupted mind,
Thy speech had altered it. Hold, here's gold for thee.
Persever in that clear way thou goest,
And the gods strengthen thee!

Mar. The good gods preserve you!

Lys. For me, be you thoughten
That I came with no ill intent; for to me
The very doors and windows savour vilely.
Fare thee well. Thou art a piece of virtue, and
I doubt not but thy training hath been noble.
Hold, here's more gold for thee.
A curse upon him, die he like a thief,
That robs thee of thy goodness! If thou dost
Hear from me, it shall be for thy good.

[Enter *Boult.*]

Boult. I beseech your Honour, one piece for me.

Lys. Avaunt thou damned doorkeeper!
Your house, but for this virgin that doth prop it,
Would sink, and overwhelm you. Away! [*Exit.*]

Boult. How's this? We must take another course with you! If your peevish chastity, which is not worth a breakfast in the cheapest country under the cope, shall undo a whole household, let me be gelded like a spaniel. Come your ways.

Mar. Whither would you have me?

Boult. I must have your maidenhead taken off, or the common hangman shall execute it. Come your ways. We'll have no more gentlemen driven away. Come your ways, I say.

Enter *Bawd.*

Bawd. How now? What's the matter?

Boult. Worse and worse, mistress. She has here spoken holy words to the Lord Lysimachus.

Bawd. O abominable!

Boult. She makes our profession as it were to stink afore the face of the gods.

Bawd. Marry hang her up for ever!

Boult. The nobleman would have dealt with her like a nobleman, and she sent him away as cold as a snowball; saying his prayers too.

Bawd. Boult, take her away; use her at thy

pleasure. Crack the glass of her virginity and make the rest malleable.

Boult. An if she were a thornier piece of ground than she is, she shall be ploughed.

Mar. Hark, hark, you gods!

Bawd. She conjures. Away with her! Would she had never come within my doors! — Marry hang you! — She's born to undo us. — Will you not go the way of womenkind? Marry come up, my dish of chastity with rosemary and bays! *Exit.*

Boult. Come, mistress; come your ways with me.

Mar. Whither wilt thou have me?

Boult. To take from you the jewel you hold so dear.

Mar. Prithee tell me one thing first.

Boult. Come now, your one thing.

Mar. What canst thou wish thine enemy to be?

Boult. Why, I could wish him to be my master, or rather my mistress.

Mar. Neither of these are so bad as thou art,
Since they do better thee in their command.
Thou hold'st a place for which the pained'st fiend
Of hell would not in reputation change.
Thou art the damned doorkeeper to every
Custrel that comes enquiring for his Tib.
To the choleric fisting of every rogue
Thy ear is liable. Thy food is such
As hath been belch'd on by infected lungs.

Boult. What would you have me do? go to the wars, would you? where a man may serve seven years for the loss of a leg, and have not money enough in the end to buy him a wooden one?

Mar. Do anything but this thou doest. Empty
Old receptacles, or common shores, of filth;
Serve by indenture to the common hangman.
Any of these ways are yet better than this;
For what thou professest, a baboon, could he speak,
Would own a name too dear. O that the gods
Would safely deliver me from this place!
Here, here's gold for thee.
If that thy master would gain by me,
Proclaim that I can sing, weave, sew, and dance,
With other virtues, which I'll keep from boast;
And I will undertake all these to teach.
I doubt not but this populous city will
Yield many scholars.

Boult. But can you teach all this you speak of?

Mar. Prove that I cannot, take me home again
And prostitute me to the basest groom
That doth frequent your house.

Boult. Well, I will see what I can do for thee.
If I can place thee, I will.

Mar. But amongst honest women.

Boult. Faith, my acquaintance lies little amongst them. But since my master and mistress have bought you, there's no going but by their consent. Therefore I will make them acquainted with your purpose, and I doubt not but I shall find them tractable enough. Come, I'll do for thee what I can. Come your ways. *Exeunt.*

[ACT V.]

Enter *Gower.*

Gow. Marina thus the brothel scapes and chances
Into an honest house, our story says.
She sings like one immortal, and she dances
As goddess-like to her admired lays;
Deep clerks she dumbs; and with her neele composes
Nature's own shape of bud, bird, branch, or berry,
That even her art sisters the natural roses;
Her inkle, silk, twin with the rubied cherry;
That pupils lacks she none of noble race,
Who pour their bounty on her; and her gain
She gives the cursed bawd. Here we her place;
And to her father turn our thoughts again.
Where we left him on the sea, we there him lost;
Whence, driven before the winds, he is arriv'd
Here where his daughter dwells; and on this coast
Suppose him now at anchor. The city striv'd
God Neptune's annual feast to keep; from whence
Lysimachus our Tyrian ship espies,
His banners sable, trimm'd with rich expense,
And to him in his barge with fervour hies.
In your supposing once more put your sight
Of heavy Pericles. Think this his bark,
Where what is done in action (more, if might)
Shall be discover'd — please you sit and hark.
Exit

[Scene I. *On board* Pericles' *ship, off Mytilene. A pavilion on deck, with a curtain before it;* Pericles *within it, on a couch. A barge lying beside the Tyrian vessel.*]

Enter *Helicanus*; to him two *Sailors*, [one belonging to the Tyrian vessel, the other to the barge].

1. Sail. [*to the Sailor of Mytilene*] Where is Lord Helicane? He can resolve you.
O, here he is.
Sir, there is a barge put off from Mytilene,
And in it is Lysimachus the Governor,
Who craves to come aboard. What is your will?

Hel. That he have his. Call up some gentlemen.

1. Sail. Ho, gentlemen! my lord calls.

Enter two or three *Gentlemen.*

1. Gent. Doth your lordship call?

Hel. Gentlemen, there is some of worth would come aboard.
I pray ye greet them fairly.

[*Exeunt Gentlemen and the two Sailors.*]

Enter [from the barge] *Lysimachus* [and *Lords*, with the *Gentlemen* and the two *Sailors*].

1. Sail. Sir,
This is the man that can, in aught you would,
Resolve you.

Lys. Hail, reverent sir! the gods preserve you!

Hel. And you, sir, to outlive the age I am,
And die as I would do.

Lys. You wish me well.
Being on shore, honouring of Neptune's triumphs,
Seeing this goodly vessel ride before us,
I made to it, to know of whence you are.

Hel. First, what is your place?

Lys. I am the Governor
Of this place you lie before.

Hel. Sir,
Our vessel is of Tyre, in it the King;
A man who for this three months hath not spoken
To any one, nor taken sustenance
But to prorogue his grief.

Lys. Upon what ground is his distemperature?

Hel. 'Twould be too tedious to repeat;
But the main grief springs from the loss
Of a beloved daughter and a wife.

Lys. May we not see him?

Hel. You may;
But bootless is your sight. He will not speak
To any.

Lys. Yet let me obtain my wish.

Hel. Behold him. [*Draws the curtain and discovers Pericles.*] This was a goodly person
Till the disaster that, one mortal night,
Drove him to this.

Lys. Sir King, all hail! The gods preserve you!
Hail, royal sir!

Hel. It is in vain; he will not speak to you.

Lord. Sir,
We have a maid in Mytilene; I durst wager
Would win some words of him.

Lys. 'Tis well bethought.
She, questionless, with her sweet harmony
And other chosen attractions, would allure,
And make a batt'ry through his deafen'd parts,
Which now are midway stopp'd.
She is all happy as the fairest of all,
And, with her fellow maids, is now upon
The leavy shelter that abuts against
The island's side.

[*Gives an order to a Lord, who exit.*]

Hel. Sure, all effectless! yet nothing we'll omit
That bears recovery's name. But since your kindness
We have stretch'd thus far, let us beseech you
That for our gold we may provision have,
Wherein we are not destitute for want,
But weary for the staleness.

Lys. O, sir, a courtesy
Which if we should deny, the most just gods
For every graff would send a caterpillar,
And so inflict our province. Yet once more
Let me entreat to know at large the cause
Of your king's sorrow.

Hel. Sit, sir; I will recount it to you.
But see, I am prevented.

Enter [*Lord*, with] *Marina* [and a young *Lady*].

Lys. O, here is
The lady that I sent for. Welcome, fair one!
Is't not a goodly presence?

Hel. She's a gallant lady.

Lys. She's such a one that, were I well assur'd
Came of a gentle kind and noble stock,
I'd wish no better choice, and think me rarely wed.
Fair one, all goodness that consists in bounty
Expect even here, where is a kingly patient.
If that thy prosperous and artificial feat
Can draw him but to answer thee in aught,

Thy sacred physic shall receive such pay
As thy desires can wish.
Mar. Sir, I will use
My utmost skill in his recovery,
Provided
That none but I and my companion maid
Be suffered to come near him.
Lys. Come, let us leave her;
And the gods make her prosperous!
The song.
Lys. Mark'd he your music?
Mar. No, nor look'd on us.
Lys. See, she will speak to him.
Mar. Hail, sir! my lord, lend ear.
Per. Hum, ha!
Mar. I am a maid,
My lord, that ne'er before invited eyes,
But have been gaz'd on like a comet. She speaks,
My lord, that, may be, hath endur'd a grief
Might equal yours, if both were justly weigh'd.
Though wayward fortune did malign my state,
My derivation was from ancestors
Who stood equivalent with mighty kings;
But time hath rooted out my parentage,
And to the world and awkward casualties
Bound me in servitude. [*Aside*] I will desist;
But there is something glows upon my cheek,
And whispers in mine ear 'Go not till he speak.'
Per. My fortunes — parentage — good parentage —
To equal mine — Was it not thus? What say you?
Mar. I said, my lord, if you did know my parentage,
You would not do me violence.
Per. I do think so. Pray you turn your eyes upon me.
You are like something that — What countrywoman?
Here of these shores?
Mar. No, nor of any shores.
Yet I was mortally brought forth, and am
No other than I appear.
Per. I am great with woe, and shall deliver weeping.
My dearest wife was like this maid, and such a one
My daughter might have been. My queen's square brows;
Her stature to an inch; as wand-like straight;
As silver-voic'd; her eyes as jewel-like,
And cas'd as richly; in pace another Juno;
Who starves the ears she feeds, and makes them hungry,
The more she gives them speech. Where do you live?
Mar. Where I am but a stranger. From the deck
You may discern the place.
Per. Where were you bred?
And how achiev'd you these endowments which
You make more rich to owe?
Mar. If I should tell my history, it would seem
Like lies disdain'd in the reporting.
Per. Prithee speak!
Falseness cannot come from thee; for thou lookest
Modest as Justice, and thou seem'st a palace
For the crown'd truth to dwell in. I will believe thee,
And make my senses credit thy relation
To points that seem impossible; for thou lookest
Like one I lov'd indeed. What were thy friends?
Didst thou not say, when I did push thee back
(Which was when I perceiv'd thee) that thou cam'st
From good descending?
Mar. So indeed I did.
Per. Report thy parentage. I think thou said'st
Thou hadst been toss'd from wrong to injury,
And that thou thought'st thy griefs might equal mine,
If both were opened.
Mar. Some such thing
I said, and said no more but what my thoughts
Did warrant me was likely.
Per. Tell thy story.
If thine considered prove the thousand part
Of my endurance, thou art a man, and I
Have suffered like a girl. Yet thou dost look
Like Patience gazing on kings' graves and smiling
Extremity out of act. What were thy friends?
How lost thou them? Thy name, my most kind virgin?
Recount, I do beseech thee. Come, sit by me.
Mar. My name is Marina.
Per. O, I am mock'd,
And thou by some incensed god sent hither
To make the world to laugh at me.
Mar. Patience, good sir,
Or here I'll cease.
Per. Nay, I'll be patient.
Thou little know'st how thou dost startle me
To call thyself Marina.
Mar. The name

Was given me by one that had some power —
My father, and a king.
Per. How? a king's daughter?
And call'd Marina?
Mar. You said you would believe me;
But, not to be a troubler of your peace,
I will end here.
Per. But are you flesh and blood?
Have you a working pulse? and are no fairy?
No motion? Well, speak on. Where were you born?
And wherefore call'd Marina?
Mar. Call'd Marina
For I was born at sea.
Per. At sea? What mother?
Mar. My mother was the daughter of a king;
Who died the very minute I was born,
As my good nurse Lychorida hath oft
Delivered weeping.
Per. O, stop there a little!
[*Aside*] This is the rarest dream that e'er dull sleep
Did mock sad fools withal. This cannot be.
My daughter's buried. — Well, where were you bred?
I'll hear you more, to th' bottom of your story,
And never interrupt you.
Mar. You'll scarce believe me;
'Twere best I did give o'er.
Per. I will believe you by the syllable
Of what you shall deliver. Yet give me leave:
How came you in these parts? Where were you bred?
Mar. The King my father did in Tharsus leave me,
Till cruel Cleon, with his wicked wife,
Did seek to murther me; and having woo'd
A villain to attempt it, who having drawn to do't,
A crew of pirates came and rescued me;
Brought me to Mytilene. But, good sir,
Whither will you have me? Why do you weep? It may be,
You think me an imposture. No, good faith!
I am the daughter to King Pericles,
If good King Pericles be.
Per. Ho, Helicanus!
Hel. Calls my lord?
Per. Thou art a grave and noble counsellor,
Most wise in general. Tell me, if thou canst,
What this maid is, or what is like to be,
That thus hath made me weep?
Hel. I know not; but
Here is the regent, sir, of Mytilene
Speaks nobly of her.
Lys. She would never tell
Her parentage. Being demanded that,
She would sit still and weep.
Per. O Helicanus, strike me, honour'd sir,
Give me a gash, put me to present pain,
Lest this great sea of joys rushing upon me
O'erbear the shores of my mortality
And drown me with their sweetness. O, come hither,
Thou that beget'st him that did thee beget;
Thou that wast born at sea, buried at Tharsus,
And found at sea again! O Helicanus,
Down on thy knees, thank the holy gods as loud
As thunder threatens us. This is Marina.
What was thy mother's name? Tell me but that,
For truth can never be confirm'd enough,
Though doubts did ever sleep.
Mar. First, sir, I pray,
What is your title?
Per. I am Pericles of Tyre. But tell me now
My drown'd queen's name, as in the rest you said
Thou hast been godlike perfect . . .
The heir of kingdoms, and another life
To Pericles thy father.
Mar. Is it no more to be your daughter than
To say my mother's name was Thaisa?
Thaisa was my mother, who did end
The minute I began.
Per. Now blessing on thee! Rise; thou art my child.
Give me fresh garments. Mine own, Helicanus!
She is not dead at Tharsus, as she should have been,
By savage Cleon. She shall tell thee all;
When thou shalt kneel, and justify in knowledge
She is thy very princess. — Who is this?
Hel. Sir, 'tis the Governor of Mytilene,
Who, hearing of your melancholy state,
Did come to see you.
Per. I embrace you.
Give me my robes. I am wild in my beholding.
O heavens bless my girl! But hark, what music?
Tell Helicanus, my Marina, tell him
O'er, point by point, for yet he seems to doubt,
How sure you are my daughter. But what music?
Hel. My lord, I hear none.
Per. None?
The music of the spheres! List, my Marina.
Lys. It is not good to cross him. Give him way.
Per. Rarest sounds! Do ye not hear?

Lys. Music, my lord? I hear.
Per. Most heavenly music!
It nips me unto list'ning, and thick slumber
Hangs upon mine eyes. Let me rest. [*Sleeps.*]
Lys. A pillow for his head!
So, leave him all. Well, my companion friends,
If this but answer to my just belief,
I'll well remember you.
[*Exeunt all but Pericles.*]

Diana [appears].

Diana. My temple stands in Ephesus. Hie thee thither
And do upon mine altar sacrifice.
There, when my maiden priests are met together,
Before the people all
Reveal how thou at sea didst lose thy wife.
To mourn thy crosses, with thy daughter's, call,
And give them repetition to the life.
Or perform my bidding, or thou livest in woe;
Do it, and happy — by my silver bow!
Awake, and tell thy dream. [*Vanishes.*]
Per. Celestial Dian, goddess argentine,
I will obey thee. Helicanus!

[Enter *Helicanus, Lysimachus,* and *Marina.*]

Hel. Sir?
Per. My purpose was for Tharsus, there to strike
The inhospitable Cleon; but I am
For other service first. Toward Ephesus
Turn our blown sails; eftsoons I'll tell thee why.
[*To Lysimachus*] Shall we refresh us, sir, upon your shore,
And give you gold for such provision
As our intents will need?
Lys. Sir,
With all my heart; and, when you come ashore,
I have another suit.
Per. You shall prevail,
Were it to woo my daughter; for it seems
You have been noble towards her.
Lys. Sir, lend me your arm.
Per. Come, my Marina. *Exeunt.*

[Scene II. *Before the Temple of* Diana *at Ephesus.*]

Enter *Gower.*

Gow. Now our sands are almost run;
More a little, and then dumb.
This, my last boon, give me,
For such kindness must relieve me:
That you aptly will suppose
What pageantry, what feats, what shows,
What minstrelsy and pretty din
The regent made in Mytilin
To greet the King. So he thrived
That he is promis'd to be wived
To fair Marina; but in no wise
Till he had done his sacrifice,
As Dian bade; whereto being bound,
The interim, pray you, all confound.
In feather'd briefness sails are fill'd,
And wishes fall out as they're will'd.
At Ephesus the temple see,
Our king, and all his company.
That he can hither come so soon
Is by your fancies' thankful doom. *Exit.*

[Scene III.]

[*The Temple of* Diana *at Ephesus;* Thaisa *standing near the altar, as High Priestess; a number of* Virgins *on each side;* Cerimon *and other* Ephesians *attending.*]

Enter *Pericles, Lysimachus, Helicanus, Marina,* and others.

Per. Hail, Dian! To perform thy just command,
I here confess myself the King of Tyre;
Who, frighted from my country, did wed
At Pentapolis the fair Thaisa.
At sea in childbed died she, but brought forth
A maid child call'd Marina; who, O goddess,
Wears yet thy silver livery. She at Tharsus
Was nurs'd with Cleon; who at fourteen years
He sought to murder; but her better stars
Brought her to Mytilene; 'gainst whose shore
Riding, her fortunes brought the maid aboard us,
Where, by her own most clear remembrance, she
Made known herself my daughter.
Thai. Voice and favour!
You are, you are — O royal Pericles! [*Swoons.*]
Per. What means the nun? She dies! Help, gentlemen!
Cer. Noble sir,
If you have told Diana's altar true,
This is your wife.
Per. Reverent appearer, no.
I threw her overboard with these very arms.
Cer. Upon this coast, I warrant you.
Per. 'Tis most certain.
Cer. Look to the lady. O, she's but overjoy'd.

Early in blustering morn this lady was
Thrown upon this shore. I op'd the coffin,
Found there rich jewels; recovered her, and plac'd her
Here in Diana's temple.

Per. May we see them?

Cer. Great sir, they shall be brought you to my house,
Whither I invite you. Look, Thaisa is
Recovered.

Thai. O, let me look!
If he be none of mine, my sanctity
Will to my sense bend no licentious ear,
But curb it, spite of seeing. O my lord,
Are you not Pericles? Like him you spake;
Like him you are. Did you not name a tempest,
A birth, and death?

Per. The voice of dead Thaisa!

Thai. That Thaisa am I, supposed dead
And drown'd.

Per. Immortal Dian!

Thai. Now I know you better.
When we with tears parted Pentapolis,
The King my father gave you such a ring.
[*Shows a ring.*]

Per. This, this! No more, you gods! your present kindness
Makes my past miseries sports. You shall do well
That on the touching of her lips I may
Melt and no more be seen. O, come, be buried
A second time within these arms!

Mar. My heart
Leaps to be gone into my mother's bosom.
[*Kneels to Thaisa.*]

Per. Look who kneels here! Flesh of thy flesh, Thaisa;
Thy burden at the sea, and call'd Marina
For she was yielded there.

Thai. Blest, and mine own!

Hel. Hail, madam, and my queen!

Thai. I know you not.

Per. You have heard me say, when I did fly from Tyre,
I left behind an ancient substitute.
Can you remember what I call'd the man?
I have nam'd him oft.

Thai. 'Twas Helicanus then.

Per. Still confirmation!
Embrace him, dear Thaisa; this is he.
Now do I long to hear how you were found;
How possibly preserv'd; and who to thank,
Besides the gods, for this great miracle.

Thai. Lord Cerimon, my lord. This is the man,
Through whom the gods have shown their power, that can
From first to last resolve you.

Per. Reverent sir,
The gods can have no mortal officer
More like a god than you. Will you deliver
How this dead queen relives?

Cer. I will, my lord.
Beseech you first, go with me to my house,
Where shall be shown you all was found with her;
How she came placed here in the temple;
No needful thing omitted.

Per. Pure Dian, bless thee for thy vision! I
Will offer night oblations to thee. Thaisa,
This prince, the fair betrothed of your daughter,
Shall marry her at Pentapolis. And now
This ornament
Makes me look dismal will I clip to form;
And what this fourteen years no razor touch'd,
To grace thy marriage day I'll beautify.

Thai. Lord Cerimon hath letters of good credit, sir,
My father's dead.

Per. Heavens make a star of him! Yet there, my queen,
We'll celebrate their nuptials, and ourselves
Will in that kingdom spend our following days.
Our son and daughter shall in Tyrus reign.
Lord Cerimon, we do our longing stay
To hear the rest untold. Sir, lead 's the way.
Exeunt.

Enter *Gower.*

Gow. In Antiochus and his daughter you have heard
Of monstrous lust the due and just reward;
In Pericles, his queen, and daughter, seen,
Although assail'd with fortune fierce and keen,
Virtue preserv'd from fell destruction's blast,
Led on by heaven, and crown'd with joy at last.
In Helicanus may you well descry
A figure of truth, of faith, of loyalty.
In reverend Cerimon there well appears
The worth that learned charity aye wears.
For wicked Cleon and his wife, when fame
Had spread their cursed deed, the honour'd name
Of Pericles, to rage the city turn,
That him and his they in his palace burn.
The gods for murder seemed so content
To punish them — although not done, but meant.
So, on your patience evermore attending,
New joy wait on you! Here our play has ending.
[*Exit.*]

The Two Noble Kinsmen

The Two Noble Kinsmen was entered in the Stationers' Register on April 8, 1634, as 'by John Fletcher and William Shakespeare,' and the Quarto came out in the same year: 'The Two Noble Kinsmen: Presented at the Blackfriers by the Kings Maiesties servants, with great applause: Written by the memorable Worthies of their time; Mr. John Fletcher, and Mr. William Shakspeare.' In an entry of 1646 'The Noble Kinsman' is described as 'by Mr. Flesher.' The play was included in the 1679 Folio of 'Fifty Comedies and Tragedies. Written by Francis Beaumont and John Fletcher, Gentlemen.' The authority for the text is the Quarto of 1634, which is printed with unusual accuracy. The ascription to Fletcher and Shakespeare in the title page is undoubtedly correct. Probably they worked in active collaboration, as was perhaps also the case in *King Henry VIII* (see p. 838, above).

For the date of composition 1613 is acceptable. The play may be put immediately after *Henry VIII*. Style and metre accord with this period in the work of both authors. One limit is fixed by the morris dance in iii, 5, which brings in several characters (122–132) from the Second Antimasque in Beaumont's *Masque of the Inner Temple and Gray's Inn*, presented at Whitehall on February 20, 1613, in honour of the marriage of the Princess Elizabeth and Frederick the Elector Palatine (see p. 3, above). In the edition of the *Masque* printed in 1613, this antimasque is described as follows: 'The second Antimasque rush in, dance their measure, and as rudely depart; consisting of a Pedant, May Lord, May Lady; Servingman, Chambermaid; a Country Clown or Shepherd, Country Wench; an Host, Hostess; a He-Baboon, She-Baboon; a He-Fool, She-Fool, ushering them in. All these persons apparelled to the life. . . . The music was extremely well fitted, having such a spirit of country jollity as can hardly be imagined; but the perpetual laughter and applause was above the music.'

Antimasques were usually performed by hired actors, and the reproduction on a public stage of a piece of buffooning that had so much amused royalty would doubtless come soon after its success at Whitehall. Beaumont's permission would, for Fletcher, be a matter of course; but nothing indicates that Beaumont had any share in the text of the drama. If we like, however, we may beguile an idle moment by detecting his hand in the Schoolmaster's long speech as Presenter of the dance (iii, 5, 100 ff.).

In allotting shares in The Two Noble Kinsmen to Shakespeare and Fletcher, critics are in substantial agreement. Certainly Shakespeare's are i, 1–3; iii, 1; v, 1; v, 3–4. Certainly Fletcher's are ii, 2–6; iii, 3–6; iv, 1–2; v, 2. Probably Shakespeare's is i, 4. This leaves debatable i, 5 (very doubtful, but perhaps Fletcher's); ii, 1 (perhaps Shakespeare's); iii, 2 (probably Fletcher's); iv, 3 (perhaps Shakespeare's). Some of the Shakespearean scenes may have been touched up by Fletcher, and possibly Fletcher's work includes a bit of Shakespeare here and there. Exact details are beyond the scope of sane criticism. The Prologue and Epilogue are of quite uncertain authorship. They are surely not Shakespeare's, and they may not be Fletcher's either. The only interesting matter they contain is the tribute to Chaucer ('of all admir'd') in the Prologue.

The main plot follows Chaucer's *Knight's Tale* closely, but time is much condensed. In *The Knight's Tale* (which is founded on Boccaccio's *Teseide*) Palamon languishes in prison for seven years, and then, 'by helping of a friend,' he drugs the jailer, makes his escape, and encounters Arcite in the woods. In the play, his escape is managed by the jailer's daughter, who has fallen in love with him. Thus the underplot, of which there is no trace in Chaucer, is brought into connection with the main story. The details of the underplot are certainly Fletcher's, but, if there was actual collaboration, the general idea may have been Shakespeare's, and at all events he must share Fletcher's responsibility. If Shakespeare, as seems likely, wrote the first scene of Act ii, he must have had the main point of the underplot in mind — that is, the love of the jailer's daughter for Palamon. Apart from one or two characteristic Fletcherian touches, there is nothing in the underplot to justify the heroics with which some critics have assailed it. With the Theseus legend in general Shakespeare was well acquainted when he wrote *A Midsummer Night's Dream*, for which he used the life of Theseus in North's Plutarch (see p. 229, above).

The fragments sung by the mad girl in iii, 5, 59 ff., are bits of two old songs. The first is somehow related to the ballad of 'the George Aloo and the Swiftestake' (i.e. Sweepstake), registered on March 19, 1611 (cf. Child, No. 285). The second is the earliest record of a ditty still in oral circulation in England and America. It is found in a seventeenth-century broadside in the Rawlinson collection (I, 32). With the first two lines that she sings in iii, 4, cf. the ballad of *Child Waters* in the Percy MS. (Child, No. 63A, sts. 9–10).

Two lost dramas on the same subject as The Two Noble Kinsmen are recorded: *Palamon* (or *Palæmon*) *and Arcite*, by Richard Edwardes, was performed at Christ Church, Oxford, before Queen Elizabeth in 1566; and Henslowe's diary registers (in various spellings) a *Palamon and Arsett*, performed, as a new play, in 1594. Neither of these is likely to have been used by Shakespeare or Fletcher.

THE TWO NOBLE KINSMEN

[Dramatis Personæ.

Theseus, Duke of Athens.
Pirithous, an Athenian general.
Artesius, an Athenian captain.
Palamon, *Arcite*, } nephews to *Creon*, King of Thebes.
Valerius, a Theban nobleman.
Six Knights.
Herald.
Jailer (also called *Keeper*).
Wooer to the Jailer's Daughter.
Doctor.
Brother *Friends* } to the Jailer.

Gentleman.
Gerrold, a schoolmaster.

Hymen.

Hippolyta, an Amazon, bride to *Theseus*.
Emilia, her sister.
Three Queens.
Jailer's Daughter.
Waiting woman to *Emilia*.
Nymphs.

Countrymen, Country Girls, Messengers, Tabourer, Boy, Executioner, Guard, Servant, Attendants.

SCENE. — *Athens and the neighbourhood; Thebes and the neighbourhood.*]

PROLOGUE.

Flourish.

New plays and maidenheads are near akin —
Much follow'd both, for both much money gi'n,
If they stand sound and well; and a good play
(Whose modest scenes blush on his marriage day
And shake to lose his honour) is like her
That, after holy tie and first night's stir,
Yet still is modesty, and still retains
More of the maid to sight than husband's pains.
We pray our play may be so; for I am sure
It has a noble breeder and a pure,
A learned, and a poet never went
More famous yet 'twixt Po and silver Trent.
Chaucer, of all admir'd, the story gives;
There constant to eternity it lives.
If we let fall the nobleness of this,
And the first sound this child hear be a hiss,
How will it shake the bones of that good man
And make him cry from under ground, 'O, fan
From me the witless chaff of such a writer
That blasts my bays and my fam'd works makes lighter
Than Robin Hood!' This is the fear we bring;
For, to say truth, it were an endless thing,
And too ambitious, to aspire to him.
Weak as we are, and almost breathless swim
In this deep water, do but you hold out
Your helping hands, and we shall tack about
And something do to save us. You shall hear
Scenes, though below his art, may yet appear
Worth two hours' travail. To his bones sweet sleep!
Content to you! If this play do not keep
A little dull time from us, we perceive
Our losses fall so thick we must needs leave.

Flourish.

ACT I. [Scene I. *Athens. Before the Temple.*]

Enter *Hymen* with a torch burning; a *Boy*, in a white robe, before, singing and strewing flowers; after *Hymen*, a *Nymph*, encompass'd in her tresses, bearing a wheaten garland; then *Theseus*, between two other *Nymphs* with wheaten chaplets on their heads; then *Hippolyta*, the bride, led by *Pirithous*, and another holding a garland over her head (her tresses likewise hanging); after her, *Emilia*, holding up her train; [*Artesius* and *Attendants*].

Music.

The Song [*by the Boy*].

Roses, their sharp spines being gone,
Not royal in their smells alone,
But in their hue;
Maiden pinks, of odour faint,
Daisies smell-less, yet most quaint,
And sweet thyme true;

Primrose, first-born child of Ver,
Merry springtime's harbinger,
With her bells dim;

Oxlips in their cradles growing,
Marigolds on deathbeds blowing,
Larks'-heels trim;

All dear Nature's children sweet,
Lie fore bride and bridegroom's feet,
Blessing their sense! *Strew flowers.*
Not an angel of the air,
Bird melodious or bird fair,
Be absent hence!

The crow, the sland'rous cuckoo, nor
The boding raven, nor chough hoar,
Nor chatt'ring pie
May on our bridehouse perch or sing,
Or with them any discord bring,
But from it fly!

Enter three *Queens*, in black, with veils stain'd, with imperial crowns. The first *Queen* falls down at the foot of *Theseus*; the second falls down at the foot of *Hippolyta*; the third before *Emilia*.

1. Queen. For pity's sake and true gentility's,
Hear and respect me!
2. Queen. For your mother's sake,
And as you wish your womb may thrive with fair ones,
Hear and respect me!
3. Queen. Now for the love of him whom Jove hath mark'd
The honour of your bed, and for the sake
Of clear virginity, be advocate
For us and our distresses! This good deed
Shall raze you out o' th' book of trespasses
All you are set down there.
Thes. Sad lady, rise.
Hip. Stand up.
Emil. No knees to me!
What woman I may stead that is distress'd
Does bind me to her.
Thes. What's your request? Deliver you for all.
1. Queen. We are three queens, whose sovereigns fell before
The wrath of cruel Creon; who endure
The beaks of ravens, talents of the kites,
And pecks of crows in the foul fields of Thebes.
He will not suffer us to burn their bones,
To urn their ashes, nor to take th' offence
Of mortal loathsomeness from the blest eye
Of holy Phœbus, but infects the winds
With stench of our slain lords. O, pity, Duke!
Thou purger of the earth, draw thy fear'd sword
That does good turns to th' world; give us the bones
Of our dead kings, that we may chapel them;
And, of thy boundless goodness, take some note
That for our crowned heads we have no roof
Save this, which is the lion's and the bear's,
And vault to every thing!
Thes. Pray you kneel not.
I was transported with your speech, and suffer'd
Your knees to wrong themselves. I have heard the fortunes
Of your dead lords, which gives me sucn lamenting
As wakes my vengeance and revenge for 'em.
King Capaneus was your lord. The day
That he should marry you, at such a season
As now it is with me, I met your groom
By Mars's altar. You were that time fair;
Not Juno's mantle fairer than your tresses,
Nor in more bounty spread. Your wheaten wreath
Was then nor thresh'd nor blasted; Fortune at you
Dimpled her cheek with smiles. Hercules our kinsman
(Then weaker than your eyes) laid by his club;
He tumbled down upon his Nemean hide,
And swore his sinews thaw'd. O grief and time,
Fearful consumers, you will all devour!
1. Queen. O, I hope some god,
Some god hath put his mercy in your manhood,
Whereto he'll infuse pow'r and press you forth
Our undertaker!
Thes. O, no knees, none, widow!
Unto the helmeted Bellona use them
And pray for me, your soldier.
Troubled I am. *Turns away.*
2. Queen. Honoured Hippolyta,
Most dreaded Amazonian, that hast slain
The scythe-tusk'd boar; that with thy arm, as strong
As it is white, wast near to make the male
To thy sex captive, but that this thy lord —
Born to uphold creation in that honour
First Nature styl'd it in — shrunk thee into
The bound thou wast o'erflowing, at once subduing
Thy force and thy affection; soldieress
That equally canst poise sternness with pity;
Who now, I know, hast much more power on him
Than ever he had on thee; who ow'st his strength,
And his love too, who is a servant for

The tenour of thy speech; dear glass of ladies,
Bid him that we, whom flaming War doth scorch,
Under the shadow of his sword may cool us;
Require him he advance it o'er our heads;
Speak't in a woman's key, like such a woman
As any of us three; weep ere you fail;
Lend us a knee;
But touch the ground for us no longer time
Than a dove's motion when the head's pluck'd off;
Tell him, if he i' th' blood-siz'd field lay swol'n,
Showing the sun his teeth, grinning at the moon,
What you would do!

Hip. Poor lady, say no more.
I had as lief trace this good action with you
As that whereto I am going, and never yet
Went I so willing way. My lord is taken
Heart-deep with your distress. Let him consider.
I'll speak anon.

3. Queen. O, my petition was
Kneel to Emilia.
Set down in ice, which, by hot grief uncandied,
Melts into drops; so sorrow, wanting form,
Is press'd with deeper matter.

Emil. Pray stand up.
Your grief is written in your cheek.

3. Queen. O, woe!
You cannot read it there. There, through my tears,
Like wrinkled pebbles in a glassy stream,
You may behold 'em. Lady, lady, alack!
He that will all the treasure know o' th' earth
Must know the centre too; he that will fish
For my least minnow, let him lead his line
To catch one at my heart. O, pardon me!
Extremity, that sharpens sundry wits,
Makes me a fool.

Emil. Pray you say nothing; pray you.
Who cannot feel nor see the rain, being in't,
Knows neither wet nor dry. If that you were
The ground-piece of some painter, I would buy you
T'instruct me 'gainst a capital grief indeed
Such heart-pierc'd demonstration; but, alas,
Being a natural sister of our sex,
Your sorrow beats so ardently upon me
That it shall make a counter-reflect 'gainst
My brother's heart, and warm it to some pity,
Though it were made of stone. Pray have good comfort.

Thes. Forward to th' temple! Leave not out a jot
O' th' sacred ceremony.

1. Queen. O, this celebration
Will longer last and be more costly than
Your suppliants' war! Remember that your fame
Knolls in the ear o' th' world. What you do quickly
Is not done rashly; your first thought is more
Than others' laboured meditance; your premeditating
More than their actions; but — O Jove! — your actions,
Soon as they move, as ospreys do the fish,
Subdue before they touch. Think, dear Duke, think
What beds our slain kings have!

2. Queen. What griefs our beds,
That our dear lords have none!

3. Queen. None fit for th' dead!
Those that with cords, knives, drams, precipitance,
Weary of this world's light, have to themselves
Been death's most horrid agents, humane grace
Affords them dust and shadow.

1. Queen. But our lords
Lie blist'ring fore the visitating sun,
And were good kings when living.

Thes. It is true;
And I will give you comfort
To give your dead lords graves; the which to do
Must make some work with Creon.

1. Queen. And that work
Presents itself to th' doing.
Now 'twill take form; the heats are gone to-morrow.
Then bootless toil must recompense itself
With its own sweat; now he is secure,
Not dreams we stand before your puissance,
Wrinching our holy begging in our eyes
To make petition clear.

2. Queen. Now you may take him
Drunk with his victory.

3. Queen. And his army full
Of bread and sloth.

Thes. Artesius, that best knowest
How to draw out, fit to this enterprise,
The prim'st for this proceeding, and the number
To carry such a business, forth and levy
Our worthiest instruments; whilst we dispatch
This grand act of our life, this daring deed
Of fate in wedlock.

1. Queen. Dowagers, take hands.
Let us be widows to our woes; delay
Commends us to a famishing hope.

All Queens. Farewell!

2. Queen. We come unseasonably; but when could grief
Cull forth, as unpang'd judgment can, fitt'st time
For best solicitation?
Thes. Why, good ladies,
This is a service, whereto I am going,
Greater than any war. It more imports me
Than all the actions that I have foregone
Or futurely can cope.
1. Queen. The more proclaiming
Our suit shall be neglected. When her arms,
Able to lock Jove from a synod, shall
By warranting moonlight corslet thee — O, when
Her twinning cherries shall their sweetness fall
Upon thy tasteful lips, what wilt thou think
Of rotten kings or blubber'd queens? what care
For what thou feel'st not? what thou feel'st being able
To make Mars spurn his drum. O, if thou couch
But one night with her, every hour in't will
Take hostage of thee for a hundred, and
Thou shalt remember nothing more than what
That banquet bids thee to!
Hip. Though much unlike
You should be so transported, as much sorry
I should be such a suitor; yet I think,
Did I not by th' abstaining of my joy,
Which breeds a deeper longing, cure their surfeit
That craves a present med'cine, I should pluck
All ladies' scandal on me. Therefore, sir, [*Kneels.*]
As I shall here make trial of my pray'rs,
Either presuming them to have some force,
Or sentencing for aye their vigour dumb,
Prorogue this business we are going about, and hang
Your shield afore your heart, about that neck
Which is my fee, and which I freely lend
To do these poor queens service.
All Queens. [*to Emilia*] O, help now!
Our cause cries for your knee.
Emil. [*kneels*] If you grant not
My sister her petition, in that force,
With that celerity and nature, which
She makes it in, from henceforth I'll not dare
To ask you anything, nor be so hardy
Ever to take a husband.
Thes. Pray stand up. [*They rise.*]
I am entreating of myself to do
That which you kneel to have me. — Pirithous,
Lead on the bride. Get you and pray the gods
For success and return; omit not any thing
In the pretended celebration. — Queens,
Follow your soldier. — [*To Artesius*] As before, hence you,
And at the banks of Aulis meet us with
The forces you can raise, where we shall find
The moiety of a number, for a business
More bigger-look'd. — [*To Hippolyta*] Since that our theme is haste,
I stamp this kiss upon thy currant lip.
Sweet, keep it as my token. — [*To Artesius*] Set you forward;
For I will see you gone. [*Exit Artesius.*]
Farewell, my beauteous sister. — Pirithous,
Keep the feast full; bate not an hour on't.
Pir. Sir,
I'll follow you at heels; the feast's solemnity
Shall want till your return.
Thes. Cousin, I charge you
Budge not from Athens. We shall be returning
Ere you can end this feast, of which I pray you
Make no abatement. Once more, farewell all.
Exeunt towards the Temple [*all but Theseus and the Queens*].
1. Queen. Thus dost thou still make good
The tongue o' th' world.
2. Queen. And earn'st a deity
Equal with Mars.
3. Queen. If not above him; for
Thou, being but mortal, makest affections bend
To godlike honours; they themselves, some say,
Groan under such a mast'ry.
Thes. As we are men,
Thus should we do. Being sensually subdu'd,
We lose our human title. Good cheer, ladies!
Now turn we towards your comforts.
Flourish. Exeunt.

Scene II. [*Thebes. The court of the Palace.*]

Enter *Palamon* and *Arcite.*

Arc. Dear Palamon, dearer in love than blood,
And our prime cousin, yet unhard'ned in
The crimes of nature — let us leave the city
Thebes and the temptings in't before we further
Sully our gloss of youth.
And here to keep in abstinence we shame
As in incontinence; for not to swim
I' th' aid o' th' current were almost to sink,
At least to frustrate striving; and to follow

The common stream, 'twould bring us to an eddy
Where we should turn or drown; if labour through,
Our gain but life and weakness.
Pal. Your advice
Is cried up with example. What strange ruins,
Since first we went to school, may we perceive
Walking in Thebes! scars and bare weeds
The gain o' th' Martialist, who did propound
To his bold ends honour and golden ingots,
Which, though he won, he had not; and now flurted
By peace, for whom he fought! Who then shall offer
To Mars's so scorn'd altar? I do bleed
When such I meet, and wish great Juno would
Resume her ancient fit of jealousy,
To get the soldier work, that peace might purge
For her repletion, and retain anew
Her charitable heart, now hard, and harsher
Than strife or war could be.
Arc. Are you not out?
Meet you no ruin but the soldier in
The cranks and turns of Thebes? You did begin
As if you met decays of many kinds.
Perceive you none that do arouse your pity,
But th' unconsider'd soldier?
Pal. Yes, I pity
Decays where'er I find them; but such most
That, sweating in an honourable toil,
Are paid with ice to cool 'em.
Arc. 'Tis not this
I did begin to speak of. This is virtue
Of no respect in Thebes. I spake of Thebes,
How dangerous, if we will keep our honours,
It is for our residing; where every evil
Hath a good colour; where ev'ry seeming good 's
A certain evil; where not to be ev'n jump
As they are here, were to be strangers, and
Such things to be, mere monsters.
Pal. 'Tis in our power
(Unless we fear that apes can tutor 's) to
Be masters of our manners. What need I
Affect another's gait, which is not catching
Where there is faith? or to be fond upon
Another's way of speech, when by mine own
I may be reasonably conceiv'd, sav'd too,
Speaking it truly? Why am I bound
By any generous bond to follow him
Follows his tailor, haply so long until
The follow'd make pursuit? Or let me know
Why mine own barber is unblest, with him
My poor chin too, for 'tis not scissor'd just
To such a favourite's glass? What canon is there
That does command my rapier from my hip,
To dangle't in my hand, or to go tiptoe
Before the street be foul? Either I am
The fore-horse in the team, or I am none
That draw i' th' sequent trace. These poor slight sores
Need not a plaintain; that which rips my bosom
Almost to th' heart's —
Arc. Our uncle Creon.
Pal. He,
A most unbounded tyrant, whose successes
Makes heaven unfear'd, and villany assur'd
Beyond its power there's nothing; almost puts
Faith in a fever, and deifies alone
Voluble chance; who only attributes
The faculties of other instruments
To his own nerves and act; commands men service,
And what they win in't, boot and glory on't;
That fears not to do harm, good dares not. Let
The blood of mine that's sib to him be suck'd
From me with leeches! Let them break and fall
Off me with that corruption!
Arc. Clear-spirited cousin,
Let's leave his court, that we may nothing share
Of his loud infamy; for our milk
Will relish of the pasture, and we must
Be vile or disobedient — not his kinsmen
In blood unless in quality.
Pal. Nothing truer.
I think the echoes of his shames have deaf'd
The ears of heav'nly justice. Widows' cries
Descend again into their throats and have not
Due audience of the gods.

Enter *Valerius.*

Valerius!
Val. The King calls for you; yet be leaden-footed
Till his great rage be off him. Phœbus, when
He broke his whipstock and exclaim'd against
The horses of the sun, but whisper'd, to
The loudness of his fury.
Pal. Small winds shake him.
But what's the matter?
Val. Theseus (who where he threats appals) hath sent
Deadly defiance to him, and pronounces
Ruin to Thebes; who is at hand to seal
The promise of his wrath.
Arc. Let him approach.
But that we fear the gods in him, he brings not

A jot of terror to us. Yet what man
Thirds his own worth (the case is each of ours)
When that his action's dregg'd with mind assur'd
'Tis bad he goes about?
Pal. Leave that unreason'd.
Our services stand now for Thebes, not Creon.
Yet to be neutral to him were dishonour,
Rebellious to oppose; therefore we must
With him stand to the mercy of our fate,
Who hath bounded our last minute.
Arc. So we must.
Is't said this war's afoot? or it shall be,
On fail of some condition?
Val. 'Tis in motion;
The intelligence of state came in the instant
With the defier.
Pal. Let's to the King; who, were he
A quarter carrier of that honour which
His enemy comes in, the blood we venture
Should be as for our health; which were not spent,
Rather laid out for purchase. But, alas,
Our hands advanc'd before our hearts, what will
The fall o' th' stroke do damage?
Arc. Let th' event,
That never-erring arbitrator, tell us
When we know all ourselves, and let us follow
The becking of our chance. *Exeunt.*

Scene III. [*At the gates of Athens.*]

Enter *Pirithous, Hippolyta, Emilia.*

Pir. No further!
Hip. Sir, farewell. Repeat my wishes
To our great lord, of whose success I dare not
Make any timorous question; yet I wish him
Excess and overflow of power, an't might be,
To dure ill-dealing fortune. Speed to him;
Store never hurts good governors.
Pir. Though I know
His ocean needs not my poor drops, yet they
Must yield their tribute there. My precious maid,
Those best affections that the heavens infuse
In their best-temper'd pieces, keep enthron'd
In your dear heart!
Emil. Thanks, sir. Remember me
To our all-royal brother; for whose speed
The great Bellona I'll solicit; and
Since in our terrene state petitions are not
Without gifts understood, I'll offer to her
What I shall be advis'd she likes. Our hearts
Are in his army, in his tent.
Hip. In's bosom.
We have been soldiers, and we cannot weep
When our friends don their helms, or put to sea,
Or tell of babes broach'd on the lance, or women
That have sod their infants in (and after eat them)
The brine they wept at killing 'em. Then, if
You stay to see of us such spinsters, we
Should hold you here for ever.
Pir. Peace be to you
As I pursue this war! which shall be then
Beyond further requiring. *Exit.*
Emil. How his longing
Follows his friend! Since his depart, his sports,
Though craving seriousness and skill, pass'd slightly
His careless execution, where nor gain
Made him regard, or loss consider; but
Playing one business in his hand, another
Directing in his head, his mind nurse equal
To these so diff'ring twins. Have you observ'd him
Since our great lord departed?
Hip. With much labour;
And I did love him for't. They two have cabin'd
In many as dangerous as poor a corner,
Peril and want contending; they have skiff'd
Torrents whose roaring tyranny and power
I' th' least of these was dreadful; and they have
Fought out together where death's self was lodg'd;
Yet fate hath brought them off. Their knot of love
Tied, weav'd, entangled, with so true, so long,
And with a finger of so deep a cunning,
May be outworn, never undone. I think
Theseus cannot be umpire to himself,
Cleaving his conscience into twain and doing
Each side like justice, which he loves best.
Emil. Doubtless
There is a best, and reason has no manners
To say it is not you. I was acquainted
Once with a time when I enjoy'd a playfellow.
You were at wars when she the grave enrich'd
Who made too proud the bed, took leave o' th' moon
(Which then look'd pale at parting) when our count
Was each eleven.
Hip. 'Twas Flavina.
Emil. Yes.
You talk of Pirithous' and Theseus' love.
Theirs has more ground, is more maturely season'd,

More buckled with strong judgment, and their needs
The one of th' other may be said to water
Their intertangled roots of love; but I
And she I sigh and spoke of, were things innocent,
Lov'd for we did, and like the elements
That know not what nor why, yet do effect
Rare issues by their operance, our souls
Did so to one another. What she lik'd
Was then of me approv'd; what not, condemn'd,
No more arraignment. The flow'r that I would pluck
And put between my breasts (then but beginning
To swell about the blossom) she would long
Till she had such another, and commit it
To the like innocent cradle, where, phœnix-like,
They died in perfume. On my head no toy
But was her pattern; her affections (pretty,
Though happily her careless wear) I followed
For my most serious decking. Had mine ear
Stol'n some new air, or at adventure humm'd one
From musical coinage, why, it was a note
Whereon her spirits would sojourn (rather dwell on)
And sing it in her slumbers. This rehearsal
(Which, ev'ry innocent wots well, comes in
Like old importment's bastard) has this end,
That the true love 'tween maid and maid may be
More than in sex dividual.

Hip. Y'are out of breath;
And this high-speeded pace is but to say
That you shall never, like the maid Flavina,
Love any that's call'd man.

Emil. I am sure I shall not.

Hip. Now, alack! weak sister,
I must no more believe thee in this point
(Though in't I know thou dost believe thyself)
Than I will trust a sickly appetite,
That loathes even as it longs. But sure, my sister,
If I were ripe for your persuasion, you
Have said enough to shake me from the arm
Of the all-noble Theseus; for whose fortunes
I will now in and kneel, with great assurance
That we, more than his Pirithous, possess
The high throne in his heart.

Emil. I am not
Against your faith; yet I continue mine.

Exeunt.

Scene IV. [*A field before Thebes. Dead bodies lying on the ground; among them* Palamon *and* Arcite.]

A battle struck within; then a retreat; flourish. Then enter Theseus (victor), [Herald, and Attendants]. The three Queens meet him and fall on their faces before him.

1. Queen. To thee no star be dark!

2. Queen. Both heaven and earth
Friend thee for ever!

3. Queen. All the good that may
Be wish'd upon thy head, I cry amen to't!

Thes. Th' impartial gods, who from the mounted heavens
View us their mortal herd, behold who err,
And in their time chastise. Go and find out
The bones of your dead lords, and honour them
With treble ceremony. Rather than a gap
Should be in their dear rites, we would supply't.
But those we will depute which shall invest
You in your dignities, and even each thing
Our haste does leave imperfect. So, adieu,
And heaven's good eyes look on you!

Exeunt Queens.

What are those?

Herald. Men of great quality, as may be judg'd
By their appointment. Some of Thebes have told 's
They are sisters' children, nephews to the King.

Thes. By th' helm of Mars, I saw them in the war,
Like to a pair of lions smear'd with prey,
Make lanes in troops aghast. I fix'd my note
Constantly on them; for they were a mark
Worth a god's view. What was't that prisoner told me
When I enquir'd their names?

Herald. We learn they're call'd
Arcite and Palamon.

Thes. 'Tis right — those, those.
They are not dead?

Herald. Nor in a state of life. Had they been taken
When their last hurts were given, 'twas possible
They might have been recovered. Yet they breathe
And have the name of men.

Thes. Then like men use 'em.
The very lees of such, millions of rates,
Exceed the wine of others. All our surgeons
Convent in their behoof; our richest balms

Rather than niggard, waste. Their lives concern us
Much more than Thebes is worth. Rather than have 'em
Freed of this plight, and in their morning state,
Sound and at liberty, I would 'em dead;
But forty thousand fold we had rather have 'em
Prisoners to us than death. Bear 'em speedily
From our kind air, to them unkind, and minister
What man to man may do; for our sake, more.
Since I have known fight's fury, friends' behests,
Love's provocations, zeal in a mistress' task,
Desire of liberty, a fever, madness,
'Have set a mark which nature could not reach to
Without some imposition, sickness in will,
Or wrestling strength in reason. For our love,
And great Apollo's mercy, all our best
Their best skill tender! — Lead into the city;
Where, having bound things scatter'd, we will post
To Athens fore our army.

Flourish. Exeunt; [*Attendants carrying Palamon and Arcite*].

Scene V. [*Another part of the Theban field, more remote from Thebes.*]

Music. Enter the *Queens* with the hearses of their *Knights* in a funeral solemnity, &c.

Urns and odours bring away.
Vapours, sighs, darken the day.
Our dole more deadly looks than dying;
Balms, and gums, and heavy cheers,
Sacred vials fill'd with tears,
And clamours through the wild air flying!

Come all sad and solemn shows
That are quick-ey'd pleasure's foes!
We convent naught else but woes:
We convent, &c.

3. Queen. This funeral path brings to your household's grave.
Joy seize on you again! Peace sleep with him!
2. Queen. And this to yours.
1. Queen. Yours this way. Heavens lend
A thousand differing ways to one sure end.
3. Queen. This world 's a city full of straying streets,
And death 's the market place, where each one meets.

Exeunt severally.

ACT II. Scene I. [*Athens. A garden, with a castle in the background.*]

Enter *Jailer* and *Wooer.*

Jailer. I may depart with little, while I live; something I may cast to you, not much. Alas! the prison I keep, though it be for great ones, yet they seldom come: before one salmon, you shall take a number of minnows. I am given out to be better lin'd than it can appear to me report is a true speaker. I would I were really that I am deliver'd to be. Marry, what I have (be it what it will) I will assure upon my daughter at the day of my death.

Wooer. Sir, I demand no more than your own offer; and I will estate your daughter in what I have promised.

Jailer. Well, we will talk more of this when the solemnity is past. But have you a full promise of her?

Enter [*Jailer's*] *Daughter* [with strewings].

When that shall be seen, I tender my consent.

Wooer. I have, sir. Here she comes.

Jailer. Your friend and I have chanced to name you here, upon the old business; but no more of that now. So soon as the court hurry is over, we will have an end of it. I' th' meantime, look tenderly to the two prisoners. I can tell you they are princes.

Daugh. These strewings are for their chamber. 'Tis pity they are in prison, and 'twere pity they should be out. I do think they have patience to make any adversity asham'd. The prison itself is proud of 'em; and they have all the world in their chamber.

Jailer. They are fam'd to be a pair of absolute men.

Daugh. By my troth, I think fame but stammers 'em; they stand a grise above the reach of report.

Jailer. I heard them reported in the battle to be the only doers.

Daugh. Nay, most likely, for they are noble suff'rers. I marvel how they would have look'd had they been victors, that with such a constant nobility enforce a freedom out of bondage, making misery their mirth ana affliction a toy to jest at.

Jailer. Do they so?

Daugh. It seems to me they have no more sense of their captivity than I of ruling Athens.

They eat well, look merrily, discourse of many things, but nothing of their own restraint and disasters. Yet sometime a divided sigh, martyr'd as 'twere i' th' deliverance, will break from one of them; when the other presently gives it so sweet a rebuke that I could wish myself a sigh to be so chid, or at least a sigher to be comforted.

Wooer. I never saw 'em.

Jailer. The Duke himself came privately in the night, and so did they. What the reason of it is, I know not.

Enter *Palamon* and *Arcite* above, [as at a window].

Look, yonder they are! That's Arcite looks out.

Daugh. No, sir, no; that's Palamon. Arcite is the lower of the twain; you may perceive a part of him.

Jailer. Go to, leave your pointing. They would not make us their object. Out of their sight!

Daugh. It is a holiday to look on them. Lord, the diff'rence of men! *Exeunt.*

Scene II. [*The same.*]

Enter *Palamon* and *Arcite* in prison.

Pal. How do you, noble cousin?
Arc. How do you, sir?
Pal. Why, strong enough to laugh at misery
And bear the chance of war yet. We are prisoners
I fear for ever, cousin.
Arc. I believe it,
And to that destiny have patiently
Laid up my hour to come.
Pal. O cousin Arcite,
Where is Thebes now? where is our noble country?
Where are our friends and kindreds? Never more
Must we behold those comforts; never see
The hardy youths strive for the games of honour,
Hung with the painted favours of their ladies,
Like tall ships under sail; then start amongst 'em
And, as an east wind, leave 'em all behind us
Like lazy clouds, whilst Palamon and Arcite,
Even in the wagging of a wanton leg,
Outstripp'd the people's praises, won the garlands,
Ere they have time to wish 'em ours. O, never
Shall we two exercise, like twins of honour,
Our arms again, and feel our fiery horses
Like proud seas under us! Our good swords now
(Better the red-ey'd god of war nev'r wore),
Ravish'd our sides, like age, must run to rust
And deck the temples of those gods that hate us.
These hands shall never draw 'em out like lightning,
To blast whole armies, more!
Arc. No, Palamon;
Those hopes are prisoners with us. Here we are,
And here the graces of our youths must wither
Like a too-timely spring. Here age must find us,
And, which is heaviest, Palamon, unmarried.
The sweet embraces of a loving wife,
Loaden with kisses, arm'd with thousand Cupids,
Shall never clasp our necks; no issue know us;
No figures of ourselves shall we ev'r see
To glad our age, and like young eagles teach 'em
Boldly to gaze against bright arms, and say
'Remember what your fathers were, and conquer!'
The fair-ey'd maids shall weep our banishments
And in their songs curse ever-blinded Fortune
Till she for shame see what a wrong she has done
To youth and nature. This is all our world:
We shall know nothing here but one another;
Hear nothing but the clock that tells our woes;
The vine shall grow, but we shall never see it;
Summer shall come, and with her all delights,
But dead-cold winter must inhabit here still.
Pal. 'Tis too true, Arcite. To our Theban hounds,
That shook the aged forest with their echoes,
No more now must we halloa; no more shake
Our pointed javelins whilst the angry swine
Flies like a Parthian quiver from our rages,
Stuck with our well-steel'd darts. All valiant uses
(The food and nourishment of noble minds)
In us two here shall perish; we shall die
(Which is the curse of honour) lastly
Children of grief and ignorance.
Arc. Yet, cousin,
Even from the bottom of these miseries,
From all that fortune can inflict upon us,
I see two comforts rising, two mere blessings,
If the gods please — to hold here a brave patience,
And the enjoying of our griefs together.
Whilst Palamon is with me, let me perish
If I think this our prison!

Pal. Certainly
'Tis a main goodness, cousin, that our fortunes
Were twin'd together. 'Tis most true, two souls
Put in two noble bodies, let 'em suffer
The gall of hazard, so they grow together,
Will never sink; they must not; say they could,
A willing man dies sleeping, and all's done.
Arc. Shall we make worthy uses of this place
That all men hate so much?
Pal. How, gentle cousin?
Arc. Let's think this prison holy sanctuary
To keep us from corruption of worse men.
We are young and yet desire the ways of honour,
That liberty and common conversation,
The poison of pure spirits, might, like women,
Woo us to wander from. What worthy blessing
Can be, but our imaginations
May make it ours? And here being thus together,
We are an endless mine to one another;
We are one another's wife, ever begetting
New births of love; we are father, friends, acquaintance;
We are, in one another, families.
I am your heir, and you are mine. This place
Is our inheritance. No hard oppressor
Dare take this from us. Here, with a little patience,
We shall live long, and loving. No surfeits seek us;
The hand of war hurts none here, nor the seas
Swallow their youth. Were we at liberty,
A wife might part us lawfully, or business;
Quarrels consume us; envy of ill men
Crave our acquaintance; I might sicken, cousin,
Where you should never know it, and so perish
Without your noble hand to close mine eyes,
Or prayers to the gods. A thousand chances,
Were we from hence, would sever us.
Pal. You have made me
(I thank you, cousin Arcite) almost wanton
With my captivity. What a misery
It is to live abroad, and everywhere!
'Tis like a beast, methinks. I find the court here —
I am sure, a more content; and all those pleasures
That woo the wills of men to vanity
I see through now, and am sufficient
To tell the world 'tis but a gaudy shadow
That old Time, as he passes by, takes with him.
What had we been, old in the court of Creon,
Where sin is justice, lust and ignorance
The virtues of the great ones? Cousin Arcite,
Had not the loving gods found this place for us,
We had died as they do, ill old men, unwept,
And had their epitaphs, the people's curses.
Shall I say more?
Arc. I would hear you still.
Pal. Ye shall.
Is there record of any two that lov'd
Better than we do, Arcite?
Arc. Sure, there cannot.
Pal. I do not think it possible our friendship
Should ever leave us.
Arc. Till our deaths it cannot,

Enter *Emilia* and her *Woman* [below].

And after death our spirits shall be led
To those that love eternally. Speak on, sir.
Emil. This garden has a world of pleasures in't.
What flower is this?
Woman. 'Tis call'd narcissus, madam.
Emil. That was a fair boy certain, but a fool
To love himself. Were there not maids enough?
Arc. Pray, forward.
Pal. Yes.
Emil. Or were they all hard-hearted?
Woman. They could not be to one so fair.
Emil. Thou wouldst not.
Woman. I think I should not, madam.
Emil. That's a good wench!
But take heed to your kindness though!
Woman. Why, madam?
Emil. Men are mad things.
Arc. Will ye go forward, cousin?
Emil. Canst not thou work such flowers in silk, wench?
Woman. Yes.
Emil. I'll have a gown full of 'em — and of these:
This is a pretty colour; will't not do
Rarely upon a skirt, wench?
Woman. Dainty, madam.
Arc. Cousin, cousin! how do you, sir? why, Palamon!
Pal. Never till now I was in prison, Arcite.
Arc. Why, what's the matter, man?
Pal. Behold, and wonder!
By heaven, she is a goddess!
Arc. Ha!
Pal. Do reverence;
She is a goddess, Arcite!
Emil. Of all flow'rs
Methinks a rose is best.

Woman. Why, gentle madam?
Emil. It is the very emblem of a maid;
For when the west wind courts her gently,
How modestly she blows, and paints the sun
With her chaste blushes! When the north comes near her,
Rude and impatient, then, like chastity,
She locks her beauties in her bud again
And leaves him to base briers.
Woman. Yet, good madam,
Sometimes her modesty will blow so far she falls for't.
A maid, if she have any honour, would be loath
To take example by her.
Emil. Thou art wanton.
Arc. She is wondrous fair!
Pal. She is all the beauty extant!
Emil. The sun grows high; let's walk in. Keep these flowers;
We'll see how near art can come near their colours.
I am wondrous merry-hearted; I could laugh now.
Woman. I could lie down, I am sure.
Emil. And take one with you?
Woman. That's as we bargain, madam.
Emil. Well, agree then.
Exeunt Emilia and Woman.
Pal. What think you of this beauty?
Arc. 'Tis a rare one.
Pal. Is't but a rare one?
Arc. Yes, a matchless beauty.
Pal. Might not a man well lose himself and love her?
Arc. I cannot tell what you have done; I have —
Beshrew mine eyes for't! Now I feel my shackles.
Pal. You love her then?
Arc. Who would not?
Pal. And desire her?
Arc. Before my liberty.
Pal. I saw her first.
Arc. That's nothing.
Pal. But it shall be.
Arc. I saw her too.
Pal. Yes, but you must not love her.
Arc. I will not, as you do, to worship her
As she is heavenly and a blessed goddess.
I love her as a woman, to enjoy her.
So both may love.
Pal. You shall not love at all.
Arc. Not love at all! who shall deny me?
Pal. I, that first saw her; I, that took possession
First with mine eye of all those beauties in her
Reveal'd to mankind. If thou lovest her,
Or entertain'st a hope to blast my wishes,
Thou art a traitor, Arcite, and a fellow
False as thy title to her. Friendship, blood,
And all the ties between us, I disclaim
If thou once think upon her!
Arc. Yes, I love her;
And if the lives of all my name lay on it,
I must do so; I love her with my soul.
If that will lose ye, farewell, Palamon!
I say again, I love; and, in loving her, maintain
I am as worthy and as free a lover,
And have as just a title to her beauty,
As any Palamon or any living
That is a man's son.
Pal. Have I call'd thee friend?
Arc. Yes, and have found me so. Why are you mov'd thus?
Let me deal coldly with you. Am not I
Part of your blood, part of your soul? You have told me
That I was Palamon, and you were Arcite.
Pal. Yes.
Arc. Am not I liable to those affections,
Those joys, griefs, angers, fears, my friend shall suffer?
Pal. Ye may be.
Arc. Why then would you deal so cunningly,
So strangely, so unlike a noble kinsman,
To love alone? Speak truly: do you think me
Unworthy of her sight?
Pal. No; but unjust
If thou pursue that sight.
Arc. Because another
First sees the enemy, shall I stand still, 194
And let mine honour down, and never charge?
Pal. Yes, if he be but one.
Arc. But say that one
Had rather combat me?
Pal. Let that one say so,
And use thy freedom: else, if thou pursu'st her,
Be as that cursed man that hates his country,
A branded villain!
Arc. You are mad.
Pal. I must be,
Till thou art worthy, Arcite — it concerns me;
And in this madness if I hazard thee
And take thy life, I deal but truly.
Arc. Fie, sir!
You play the child extremely. I will love her,

I must, I ought to do so, and I dare —
And all this justly.

Pal. O, that now, that now
Thy false self and thy friend had but this fortune,
To be one hour at liberty and grasp
Our good swords in our hands! I would quickly teach thee
What 'twere to filch affection from another!
Thou art baser in it than a cutpurse.
Put but thy head out of this window more,
And, as I have a soul, I'll nail thy life to't!

Arc. Thou dar'st not, fool; thou canst not; thou art feeble.
Put my head out? I'll throw my body out,
And leap the garden, when I see her next,

Enter *Keeper*.

And pitch between her arms to anger thee.

Pal. No more! the keeper's coming. I shall live
To knock thy brains out with my shackles.

Arc. Do!

Keeper. By your leave, gentlemen.

Pal. Now, honest keeper?

Keeper. Lord Arcite, you must presently to th' Duke.
The cause I know not yet.

Arc. I am ready, keeper.

Keeper. Prince Palamon, I must awhile bereave you
Of your fair cousin's company.

Exeunt Arcite and Keeper.

Pal. And me too,
Even when you please, of life. Why is he sent for?
It may be he shall marry her; he's goodly,
And like enough the Duke hath taken notice
Both of his blood and body. But his falsehood!
Why should a friend be treacherous? If that
Get him a wife so noble and so fair,
Let honest men ne'er love again. Once more
I would but see this fair one. Blessed garden,
And fruit and flowers more blessed, that still blossom
As her bright eyes shine on ye! Would I were,
For all the fortune of my life hereafter,
Yon little tree, yon blooming apricock!
How I would spread, and fling my wanton arms
In at her window! I would bring her fruit
Fit for the gods to feed on; youth and pleasure,
Still as she tasted, should be doubled on her;
And if she be not heavenly, I would make her
So near the gods in nature, they should fear her;
And then I am sure she would love me.

Enter *Keeper*.

How now, keeper!
Where's Arcite?

Keeper. Banish'd. Prince Pirithous
Obtain'd his liberty; but never more,
Upon his oath and life, must he set foot
Upon this kingdom.

Pal. [*aside*] He's a blessed man!
He shall see Thebes again and call to arms
The bold young men that, when he bids 'em charge,
Fall on like fire. Arcite shall have a fortune,
If he dare make himself a worthy lover,
Yet in the field to strike a battle for her;
And if he lose her then, he's a cold coward.
How bravely may he bear himself to win her,
If he be noble Arcite — thousand ways!
Were I at liberty, I would do things
Of such a virtuous greatness that this lady,
This blushing virgin, should take manhood to her
And seek to ravish me.

Keeper. My lord, for you
I have this charge too —

Pal. To discharge my life?

Keeper. No; but from this place to remove your lordship.
The windows are too open.

Pal. Devils take 'em
That are so envious to me! Prithee kill me.

Keeper. And hang for't afterward!

Pal. By this good light,
Had I a sword, I would kill thee.

Keeper. Why, my lord?

Pal. Thou bring'st such pelting scurvy news continually
Thou art not worthy life. I will not go.

Keeper. Indeed you must, my lord.

Pal. May I see the garden?

Keeper. No.

Pal. Then I am resolv'd I will not go.

Keeper. I must
Constrain you then; and, for you are dangerous,
I'll clap more irons on you.

Pal. Do, good keeper.
I'll shake 'em so ye shall not sleep;
I'll make ye a new morris. Must I go?

Keeper. There is no remedy.

Pal. [*aside*] Farewell, kind window.
May rude wind never hurt thee! O my lady,
If ever thou hast felt what sorrow was,
Dream how I suffer! — Come, now bury me.

Exeunt.

Scene III. [*The country near Athens.*]

Enter *Arcite.*

Arc. Banish'd the kingdom? 'Tis a benefit,
A mercy I must thank 'em for; but banish'd
The free enjoying of that face I die for —
O, 'twas a studied punishment, a death
Beyond imagination! such a vengeance
That, were I old and wicked, all my sins
Could never pluck upon me. Palamon,
Thou hast the start now; thou shalt stay and see
Her bright eyes break each morning 'gainst thy window
And let in life into thee; thou shalt feed
Upon the sweetness of a noble beauty,
That nature nev'r exceeded nor nev'r shall.
Good gods, what happiness has Palamon!
Twenty to one, he'll come to speak to her,
And, if she be as gentle as she's fair,
I know she's his; he has a tongue will tame
Tempests and make the wild rocks wanton. Come what can come,
The worst is death. I will not leave the kingdom.
I know mine own is but a heap of ruins,
And no redress there. If I go, he has her.
I am resolv'd: another shape shall make me,
Or end my fortunes; either way, I am happy.
I'll see her and be near her, or no more.
[*Retires.*]

Enter four *Country People*, and one with a garland before them.

1. My masters, I'll be there, that's certain.
2. And I'll be there.
3. And I.
4. Why then, have with ye, boys! 'Tis but a chiding.
Let the plough play to-day; I'll tickle't out
Of the jades' tails to-morrow.
1. I am sure
To have my wife as jealous as a turkey.
But that's all one: I'll go through, let her mumble.
2. Clap her aboard to-morrow night and stow her,
And all's made up again.
3. Ay, do but put
A fescue in her fist, and you shall see her
Take a new lesson out and be a good wench.
Do we all hold against the Maying?
4. Hold?
What should ail us?
3. Arcas will be there.
2. And Sennois,
And Rycas; and three better lads nev'r danc'd
Under green tree; and ye know what wenches, ha?
But will the dainty domine, the schoolmaster,
Keep touch, do you think? for he does all, ye know.
3. He'll eat a hornbook ere he fail. Go to!
The matter is too far driven between
Him and the tanner's daughter to let slip now;
And she must see the Duke and she must dance too.
4. Shall we be lusty?
2. All the boys in Athens
Blow wind i' th' breech on us; and here I'll be,
And there I'll be, for our town, and here again,
And there again. Ha, boys, heigh for the weavers!
1. This must be done i' th' woods.
4. O, pardon me!
2. By any means; our thing of learning says so —
Where he himself will edify the Duke
Most parlously in our behalfs. He's excellent i' th' woods;
Bring him to th' plains, his learning makes no cry.
3. We'll see the sports; then every man to's tackle!
And, sweet companions, let's rehearse by any means
Before the ladies see us, and do sweetly,
And God knows what may come on't.
4. Content. The sports
Once ended, we'll perform. Away, boys, and hold!
Arc. [*comes forward*] By your leaves, honest friends. Pray you, whither go you?
4. Whither? Why, what a question 's that!
Arc. Yes, 'tis a question
To me that know not.
3. To the games, my friend.
2. Where were you bred you know it not?
Arc. Not far, sir.
Are there such games to-day?
1. Yes, marry, are there;
And such as you never saw. The Duke himself
Will be in person there.
Arc. What pastimes are they?
2. Wrestling and running. — 'Tis a pretty fellow.
3. Thou wilt not go along?
Arc. Not yet, sir.

4. Well, sir,
Take your own time. Come, boys.
1. My mind misgives me
This fellow has a vengeance trick o' th' hip.
Mark how his body 's made for't.
2. I'll be hang'd though,
If he dare venture. Hang him, plum porridge!
He wrestle? He roast eggs! Come, let's be gone, lads.
Exeunt four.
Arc. This is an offer'd opportunity
I durst not wish for. Well I could have wrestled,
The best men call'd it excellent; and run
Swifter than wind upon a field of corn,
Curling the wealthy ears, never flew. I'll venture
And in some poor disguise be there. Who knows
Whether my brows may not be girt with garlands,
And happiness prefer me to a place
Where I may ever dwell in sight of her? *Exit.*

Scene IV. [*Athens. The prison.*]

Enter *Jailer's Daughter* alone.

Daugh. Why should I love this gentleman? 'Tis odds
He never will affect me. I am base,
My father the mean keeper of his prison,
And he a prince. To marry him is hopeless,
To be his whore is witless. Out upon't!
What pushes are we wenches driven to
When fifteen once has found us! First, I saw him:
I, seeing, thought he was a goodly man;
He has as much to please a woman in him
(If he please to bestow it so) as ever
These eyes yet look'd on. Next I pitied him;
And so would any young wench, o' my conscience,
That ever dream'd, or vow'd her maidenhead
To a young handsome man. Then I lov'd him,
Extremely lov'd him, infinitely lov'd him;
And yet he had a cousin, fair as he too;
But in my heart was Palamon, and there,
Lord, what a coil he keeps! To hear him
Sing in an evening, what a heaven it is!
And yet his songs are sad ones. Fairer spoken
Was never gentleman. When I come in
To bring him water in a morning, first
He bows his noble body, then salutes me thus:
'Fair gentle maid, good morrow. May thy goodness
Get thee a happy husband!' Once he kiss'd me.
I lov'd my lips the better ten days after.
Would he would do so ev'ry day! He grieves much,
And me as much to see his misery.
What should I do to make him know I love him?
For I would fain enjoy him. Say I ventur'd
To set him free? What says the law then?
Thus much for law or kindred! I will do it;
And this night or to-morrow he shall love me.
Exit.

Scene V. [*An open place in Athens.*]

A short flourish of cornets, and shouts within. Enter *Theseus, Hippolyta, Pirithous, Emilia*; *Arcite* [disguised,] with a garland; and [*Countrymen*].

Thes. You have done worthily. I have not seen,
Since Hercules, a man of tougher sinews.
Whate'er you are, you run the best, and wrestle,
That these times can allow.
Arc. I am proud to please you.
Thes. What country bred you?
Arc. This; but far off, prince.
Thes. Are you a gentleman?
Arc. My father said so;
And to those gentle uses gave me life.
Thes. Are you his heir?
Arc. His youngest, sir.
Thes. Your father
Sure is a happy sire then. What proves you?
Arc. A little of all noble qualities.
I could have kept a hawk, and well have holloa'd
To a deep cry of dogs. I dare not praise
My feat in horsemanship; yet they that knew me
Would say it was my best piece. Last and greatest,
I would be thought a soldier.
Thes. You are perfect.
Pir. Upon my soul, a proper man!
Emil. He is so.
Pir. How do you like him, lady?
Hip. I admire him.
I have not seen so young a man so noble,
If he say true, of his sort.
Emil. Believe
His mother was a wondrous handsome woman;
His face methinks goes that way.

Hip. But his body
And fiery mind illustrate a brave father.

Pir. Mark how his virtue, like a hidden sun,
Breaks through his baser garments.

Hip. He's well got, sure.

Thes. What made you seek this place, sir?

Arc. Noble Theseus,
To purchase name, and do my ablest service
To such a well-found wonder as thy worth;
For only in thy court, of all the world,
Dwells fair-ey'd Honour.

Pir. All his words are worthy.

Thes. Sir, we are much indebted to your travel,
Nor shall you lose your wish. Pirithous,
Dispose of this fair gentleman.

Pir. Thanks, Theseus. —
Whate'er you are, y'are mine; and I shall give you
To a most noble service — to this lady,
This bright young virgin. Pray observe her goodness.
You have honour'd her fair birthday with your virtues,
And, as your due, y'are hers. Kiss her fair hand, sir.

Arc. Sir, y'are a noble giver. — [*To Emilia*] Dearest beauty,
Thus let me seal my vow'd faith. [*Kisses her hand.*] When your servant —
Your most unworthy creature — but offends you,
Command him die, he shall.

Emil. That were too cruel.
If you deserve well, sir, I shall soon see't.
Y'are mine, and somewhat better than your rank I'll use you.

Pir. I'll see you furnish'd; and because you say
You are a horseman, I must needs entreat you
This afternoon to ride; but 'tis a rough one. 46

Arc. I like him better, prince. I shall not then
Freeze in my saddle.

Thes. Sweet, you must be ready —
And you, Emilia — and you, friend — and all—
To-morrow, by the sun, to do observance
To flow'ry May, in Dian's wood. —Wait well, sir,
Upon your mistress. — Emily, I hope
He shall not go afoot.

Emil. That were a shame, sir,
While I have horses. — Take your choice; and what
You want at any time, let me but know it.
If you serve faithfully, I dare assure you
You'll find a loving mistress.

Arc. If I do not,
Let me find that my father ever hated —
Disgrace and blows.

Thes. Go lead the way; you have won it.
It shall be so; you shall receive all dues
Fit for the honour you have won; 'twere wrong else.
Sister, beshrew my heart, you have a servant
That, if I were a woman, would be master;
But you are wise.

Emil. I hope too wise for that, sir.
Flourish. Exeunt omnes.

Scene VI. [*Athens. Before the Prison.*]

Enter *Jailer's Daughter*, alone.

Daugh. Let all the dukes and all the devils roar,
He is at liberty! I have ventur'd for him;
And out I have brought him to a little wood
A mile hence. I have sent him where a cedar, 4
Higher than all the rest, spreads like a plane
Fast by a brook; and there he shall keep close
Till I provide him files and food; for yet
His iron bracelets are not off. O Love,
What a stout-hearted child thou art! My father
Durst better have endur'd cold iron than done it.
I love him beyond love and beyond reason,
Or wit, or safety. I have made him know it.
I care not; I am desperate. If the law
Find me, and then condemn me for't, some wenches,
Some honest-hearted maids, will sing my dirge
And tell to memory my death was noble, 16
Dying almost a martyr. That way he takes
I purpose is my way too. Sure he cannot
Be so unmanly as to leave me here.
If he do, maids will not so easily
Trust men again. And yet he has not thank'd me
For what I have done; no, not so much as kiss'd me;
And that, methinks, is not so well; nor scarcely
Could I persuade him to become a freeman,
He made such scruples of the wrong he did
To me and to my father. Yet I hope,
When he considers more, this love of mine

Will take more root within him. Let him do
What he will with me, so he use me kindly;
For use me so he shall, or I'll proclaim him,
And to his face, no man. I'll presently
Provide him necessaries and pack my clothes up,
And where there is a patch of ground I'll venture,
So he be with me. By him, like a shadow,
I'll ever dwell. Within this hour the whoobub
Will be all o'er the prison. I am then
Kissing the man they look for. Farewell, father!
Get many more such prisoners and such daughters,
And shortly you may keep yourself. Now to him! [*Exit.*]

ACT III. Scene I. [*A Forest near Athens.*]

Cornets in sundry places. Noise and halloaing, as people a-Maying. Enter *Arcite*, alone.

Arc. The Duke has lost Hippolyta; each took
A several land. This is a solemn rite
They owe bloom'd May, and the Athenians pay it
To th' heart of ceremony. O queen Emilia,
Fresher than May, sweeter
Than her gold buttons on the boughs or all
Th' enamell'd knacks o' th' mead or garden! Yea,
We challenge too the bank of any nymph,
That makes the stream seem flowers! Thou, O jewel
O' th' wood, o' th' world, hast likewise bless'd a place
With thy sole presence. In thy rumination
That I, poor man, might eftsoons come between
And chop on some cold thought! Thrice-blessed chance,
To drop on such a mistress, expectation
Most guiltless on't. Tell me, O Lady Fortune
(Next after Emily my sovereign), how far
I may be proud. She takes strong note of me,
Hath made me near her, and this beauteous morn,
The prim'st of all the year, presents me with
A brace of horses; two such steeds might well
Be by a pair of kings back'd in a field
That their crowns' titles tried. Alas, alas,
Poor cousin Palamon, poor prisoner! thou
So little dream'st upon my fortune that
Thou think'st thyself the happier thing to be
So near Emilia. Me thou deem'st at Thebes,
And therein wretched, although free. But if
Thou knew'st my mistress breath'd on me and that
I ear'd her language, liv'd in her eye, O coz,
What passion would enclose thee!

Enter *Palamon*, as out of a bush, with his shackles; bends his fist at *Arcite*.

Pal. Traitor kinsman,
Thou shouldst perceive my passion if these signs
Of prisonment were off me and this hand
But owner of a sword! By all oaths in one,
I, and the justice of my love, would make thee
A confess'd traitor! O thou most perfidious
That ever gently look'd! the void'st of honour
That ev'r bore gentle token! falsest cousin
That ever blood made kin! call'st thou her thine?
I'll prove it in my shackles, with these hands
Void of appointment, that thou li'st, and art
A very thief in love, a chaffy lord,
Nor worth the name of villain! Had I a sword,
And these house-clogs away —

Arc. Dear cousin Palamon —

Pal. Cozener Arcite — give me language such
As thou hast show'd me feat!

Arc. Not finding in
The circuit of my breast any gross stuff
To form me like your blazon, holds me to
This gentleness of answer. 'Tis your passion
That thus mistakes; the which, to you being enemy,
Cannot to me be kind. Honour and honesty
I cherish and depend on, howsoev'r
You skip them in me; and with them, fair coz,
I'll maintain my proceedings. Pray be pleas'd
To show in generous terms your griefs, since that
Your question's with your equal, who professes
To clear his own way with the mind and sword
Of a true gentleman.

Pal. That thou durst, Arcite!

Arc. My coz, my coz, you have been well advertis'd
How much I dare. Y'ave seen me use my sword
Against th' advice of fear. Sure, of another

You would not hear me doubted, but your silence
Should break out, though i' th' sanctuary.
Pal. Sir,
I have seen you move in such a place which well
Might justify your manhood; you were call'd
A good knight and a bold. But the whole week's not fair
If any day it rain. Their valiant temper
Men lose when they incline to treachery;
And then they fight like compell'd bears, would fly
Were they not tied.
Arc. Kinsman, you might as well
Speak this and act it in your glass as to
His ear which now disdains you.
Pal. Come up to me!
Quit me of these cold gyves, give me a sword,
Though it be rusty, and the charity
Of one meal lend me — come before me then,
A good sword in thy hand, and do but say
That Emily is thine, I will forgive
The trespass thou hast done me, yea, my life,
If then thou carry't; and brave souls in shades,
That have died manly, which will seek of me
Some news from earth, they shall get none but this —
That thou art brave and noble.
Arc. Be content;
Again betake you to your hawthorn house.
With counsel of the night, I will be here
With wholesome viands. These impediments
Will I file off; you shall have garments, and
Perfumes to kill the smell o' th' prison; after,
When you shall stretch yourself, and say but, 'Arcite,
I am in plight,' there shall be at your choice
Both sword and armour.
Pal. O you heavens, dares any
So noble bear a guilty business? None
But only Arcite; therefore none but Arcite
In this kind is so bold.
Arc. Sweet Palamon —
Pal. I do embrace you and your offer. For
Your offer do't I only, sir; your person
Without hypocrisy I may not wish
More than my sword's edge on't.
Wind horns [*within*].
Arc. You hear the horns:
Enter your musit, lest this match between's
Be cross'd ere met. Give me your hand; farewell.
I'll bring you every needful thing. I pray you
Take comfort and be strong.
Pal. Pray hold your promise,
And do the deed with a bent brow. Most certain
You love me not. Be rough with me and pour
This oil out of your language. By this air,
I could for each word give a cuff, my stomach
Not reconcil'd by reason.
Arc. Plainly spoken!
Yet pardon me hard language. When I spur
My horse, I chide him not. Content and anger
In me have but one face. *Wind horns.*
Hark, sir! they call
The scatter'd to the banquet. You must guess
I have an office there.
Pal. Sir, your attendance
Cannot please heaven; and I know your office
Unjustly is achiev'd.
Arc. I've a good title.
I am persuaded this question sick between's
By bleeding must be cur'd. I am a suitor
That to your sword you will bequeath this plea
And talk of it no more.
Pal. But this one word:
You are going now to gaze upon my mistress;
For note you, mine she is —
Arc. Nay then —
Pal. Nay, pray you —
You talk of feeding me to breed me strength;
You are going now to look upon a sun
That strengthens what it looks on. There you have
A vantage o'er me; but enjoy it till
I may enforce my remedy. Farewell.
Exeunt [*severally*].

Scene II. [*Another part of the Forest.*]

Enter *Jailer's Daughter* alone.

Daugh. He has mistook the brake I meant; is gone
After his fancy. 'Tis now well-nigh morning.
No matter. Would it were perpetual night,
And darkness lord o' th' world! Hark! 'tis a wolf.
In me hath grief slain fear, and, but for one thing,
I care for nothing, and that's Palamon.
I reck not if the wolves would jaw me, so
He had this file. What if I halloa'd for him?
I cannot halloa. If I whoop'd, what then?
If he not answer'd, I should call a wolf,
And do him but that service. I have heard
Strange howls this livelong night. Why may't not be

They have made prey of him? He has no weapons;
He cannot run; the jingling of his gyves
Might call fell things to listen, who have in them
A sense to know a man unarm'd and can
Smell where resistance is. I'll set it down
He's torn to pieces. They howl'd many together,
And then they fed on him. So much for that!
Be bold to ring the bell. How stand I then?
All's char'd when he is gone. No, no, I lie!
My father's to be hang'd for his escape;
Myself to beg, if I priz'd life so much
As to deny my act; but that I would not,
Should I try death by dozens. I am mop'd:
Food took I none these two days; [once, indeed,
I] sipp'd some water. I have not clos'd mine eyes
Save when my lids scour'd off their brine. Alas,
Dissolve, my life! Let not my sense unsettle,
Lest I should drown or stab or hang myself!
O state of nature, fail together in me,
Since thy best props are warp'd! So, which way now?
The best way is, the next way to a grave.
Each errant step beside is torment. Lo,
The moon is down, the crickets chirp, the screech owl
Calls in the dawn! All offices are done
Save what I fail in. But the point is this —
An end, and that is all. *Exit.*

Scene III. [*The same part of the Forest as in Scene I.*]

Enter *Arcite*, with meat, wine, and files.

Arc. I should be near the place. Ho, cousin Palamon!

Enter *Palamon.*

Pal. Arcite?
Arc. The same. I have brought you food and files.
Come forth and fear not; here's no Theseus.
Pal. Nor none so honest, Arcite.
Arc. That's no matter.
We'll argue that hereafter. Come, take courage;
You shall not die thus beastly. Here, sir, drink.
I know you are faint. Then I'll talk further with you.
Pal. Arcite, thou mightst now poison me.
Arc. I might;
But I must fear you first. Sit down; and, good now,
No more of these vain parleys. Let us not,
Having our ancient reputation with us,
Make talk for fools and cowards. To your health! [*Drinks.*]
Pal. Do.
Arc. Pray, sit down then; and let me entreat you
By all the honesty and honour in you,
No mention of this woman! 'Twill disturb us;
We shall have time enough.
Pal. Well, sir, I'll pledge you. [*Drinks.*]
Arc. Drink a good hearty draught; it breeds good blood, man.
Do not you feel it thaw you?
Pal. Stay; I'll tell you
After a draught or two more.
Arc. Spare it not;
The Duke has more, coz. Eat now.
Pal. Yes. [*Eats.*]
Arc. I am glad
You have so good a stomach.
Pal. I am gladder
I have so good meat to't.
Arc. Is't not mad lodging
Here in the wild woods, cousin?
Pal. Yes, for them
That have wild consciences.
Arc. How tastes your victuals?
Your hunger needs no sauce, I see.
Pal. Not much.
But if it did, yours is too tart, sweet cousin.
What is this?
Arc. Venison.
Pal. 'Tis a lusty meat.
Give me more wine. Here, Arcite, to the wenches
We have known in our days! The Lord Steward's daughter —
Do you remember her?
Arc. After you, coz.
Pal. She lov'd a black-hair'd man.
Arc. She did so. Well, sir?
Pal. And I have heard some call him Arcite, and —
Arc. Out with it, faith!
Pal. She met him in an arbour.
What did she there, coz? play o' th' virginals?
Arc. Something she did, sir.
Pal. Made her groan a month for't;
Or two, or three, or ten.
Arc. The Marshal's sister
Had her share too, as I remember, cousin;
Else there be tales abroad. You'll pledge her?

Pal. Yes.
Arc. A pretty brown wench 'tis. There was a time
When young men went a-hunting, and a wood,
And a broad beech; and thereby hangs a tale.
Heigh-ho!
Pal. For Emily, upon my life! Fool,
Away with this strain'd mirth! I say again,
That sigh was breath'd for Emily. Base cousin,
Dar'st thou break first?
Arc. You are wide.
Pal. By heaven and earth,
There's nothing in thee honest.
Arc. Then I'll leave you.
You are a beast now.
Pal. As thou mak'st me, traitor!
Arc. There's all things needful — files and shirts and perfumes.
I'll come again some two hours hence and bring
That that shall quiet all.
Pal. A sword and armour.
Arc. Fear me not. You are now too foul; farewell.
Get off your trinkets; you shall want nought.
Pal. Sirrah —
Arc. I'll hear no more. *Exit.*
Pal. If he keep touch, he dies for't. *Exit.*

Scene IV. [*Another part of the Forest.*]

Enter *Jailer's Daughter.*

Daugh. I am very cold; and all the stars are out too,
The little stars and all, that look like aglets.
The sun has seen my folly. Palamon!
Alas, no! he's in heaven. Where am I now?
Yonder's the sea, and there's a ship. How't tumbles!
And there's a rock lies watching under water.
Now, now, it beats upon it — now, now, now!
There's a leak sprung, a sound one. How they cry!
Spoon her before the wind! you'll lose all else.
Up with a course or two and tack about, boys!
Good night, good night; y'are gone. I am very hungry:
Would I could find a fine frog! He would tell me
News from all parts o' th' world. Then would I make
A careck of a cockleshell, and sail
By east and north-east to the King of Pygmies,
For he tells fortunes rarely. Now my father,
Twenty to one, is truss'd up in a trice
To-morrow morning. I'll say never a word.
Sing.

For I'll cut my green coat a foot above my knee,
And I'll clip my yellow locks an inch below mine e'e.
Hey, nonny, nonny, nonny.

He's buy me a white cut, forth for to ride,
And I'll go seek him through the world that is so wide.
Hey, nonny, nonny, nonny.

O for a prick now, like a nightingale,
To put my breast against! I shall sleep like a top else. *Exit.*

Scene V. [*Another part of the Forest.*]

Enter [*Gerrold*] a *Schoolmaster*, four *Countrymen* [as Morris-dancers] and [another as] *Bavian*, [five] *Wenches*, with a *Tabourer*.

School. Fie, fie!
What tediosity and disensanity
Is here among ye! Have my rudiments
Been labour'd so long with ye, milk'd unto ye,
And, by a figure, even the very plum-broth
And marrow of my understanding laid upon ye,
And do you still cry 'Where?' and 'How?' and 'Wherefore?'
You most coarse frieze capacities, ye jane judgments,
Have I said 'Thus let be,' and 'There let be,'
And 'Then let be,' and no man understand me?
Proh Deum, medius fidius, ye are all dunces!
For-why here stand I; here the Duke comes; there are you,
Close in the thicket. The Duke appears; I meet him
And unto him I utter learned things
And many figures; he hears, and nods, and hums,
And then cries 'Rare!' and I go forward. At length
I fling my cap up. Mark there! Then do you,
As once did Meleager and the boar,
Break comely out before him, like true lovers,
Cast yourselves in a body decently,
And sweetly, by a figure, trace and turn, boys.
1. Man. And sweetly we will do it, Master Gerrold.
2. Draw up the company. Where's the tabourer?
3. Why, Timothy!
Tabourer. Here, my mad boys! have at ye!

School. But I say, where's their women?
4. Here's Friz and Maudline.
2. And little Luce with the white legs, and bouncing Barbary.
1. And freckled Nell, that never fail'd her master.
School. Where be your ribands, maids? Swim with your bodies,
And carry it sweetly and deliverly;
And now and then a favour and a frisk.
Nell. Let us alone, sir.
School. Where's the rest o' th' music?
3. Dispers'd as you commanded.
School. Couple then,
And see what's wanting. Where's the Bavian?
My friend, carry your tail without offence
Or scandal to the ladies; and be sure
You tumble with audacity and manhood;
And when you bark, do it with judgment.
Bavian. Yes, sir.
School. Quo usque tandem? Here is a woman wanting.
4. We may go whistle; all the fat's i' th' fire.
School. We have, as learned authors utter, wash'd a tile;
We have been fatuus, and laboured vainly.
2. This is that scornful piece, that scurvy hilding,
That gave her promise faithfully she would
Be here, Cicely the sempster's daughter.
The next gloves that I give her shall be dogskin.
Nay, an she fail me once — You can tell, Arcas,
She swore by wine and bread she would not break.
School. An eel and woman,
A learned poet says, unless by th' tail
And with thy teeth thou hold, will either fail.
In manners this was false position.
1. A fire ill take her! Does she flinch now?
3. What
Shall we determine, sir?
School. Nothing.
Our business is become a nullity,
Yea, and a woful and a piteous nullity.
4. Now, when the credit of our town lay on it,
Now to be frampal, now to piss o' th' nettle!
Go thy ways. I'll remember thee, I'll fit thee!

Enter *Jailer's Daughter* [and sings].

The George Alow came from the south,
From the coast of Barbary-a;
And there he met with brave gallants of war,
By one, by two, by three-a.

Well hail'd, well hail'd, you jolly gallants!
And whither now are you bound-a?
O, let me have your company
Till I come to the Sound-a!

There was three fools fell out about an howlet:
The one said it was an owl;
The other he said nay;
The third he said it was a hawk,
And her bells were cut away.

3. There's a dainty mad woman, master,
Comes i' th' nick; as mad as a March hare.
If we can get her dance, we are made again.
I warrant her she'll do the rarest gambols.
1. A mad woman? We are made, boys!
School. And are you mad, good woman?
Daugh. I would be sorry else.
Give me your hand.
School. Why?
Daugh. I can tell your fortune.
You are a fool. Tell ten. I have pos'd him. Buzz!
Friend, you must eat no white bread; if you do,
Your teeth will bleed extremely. Shall we dance, ho?
I know you; y'are a tinker. Sirrah tinker,
Stop no more holes but what you should.
School. Dii boni!
A tinker, damsel?
Daugh. Or a conjurer.
Raise me a devil now, and let him play
Qui passa o' th' bells and bones.
School. Go, take her,
And fluently persuade her to a peace.
'Et opus exegi quod nec Iovis ira nec ignis'—
Strike up, and lead her in.
2. Come, lass, let's trip it.
Daugh. I'll lead. *Wind horns.*
3. Do, do.
School. Persuasively and cunningly. Away, boys!
I hear the horns. Give me some meditation,
And mark your cue.
Exeunt all but Schoolmaster.
Pallas inspire me!

Enter *Theseus, Pirithous, Hippolyta, Emilia, Arcite,* and *Train.*

Thes. This way the stag took.
School. Stay and edify.
Thes. What have we here?
Pir. Some country sport, upon my life, sir.
Thes. Well, sir, go forward; we will edify.
Ladies, sit down; we'll stay it.
School. Thou doughty Duke, all hail! All hail, sweet ladies!

Thes. This is a cold beginning.
School. If you but favour, our country pastime made is.
We are a few of those collected here
That ruder tongues distinguish villager;
And, to say verity and not to fable,
We are a merry rout, or else a rable,
Or company, or by a figure, choris,
That fore thy dignity will dance a morris.
And I, that am the rectifier of all,
By title paedagogus, that let fall
The birch upon the breeches of the small ones
And humble with a ferula the tall ones,
Do here present this machine, or this frame.
And, dainty Duke, whose doughty dismal fame
From Dis to Dædalus, from post to pillar,
Is blown abroad, help me, thy poor well-willer,
And with thy twinkling eyes look right and straight
Upon this mighty *morr* — of mickle weight —
Is — now comes in, which being glu'd together
Makes *morris*, and the cause that we came hether.
The body of our sport, of no small study.
I first appear, though rude and raw and muddy,
To speak, before thy noble grace, this tenner;
At whose great feet I offer up my penner. 124
The next, the Lord of May and Lady bright,
The Chambermaid and Servingman, by night
That seek out silent hanging. Then mine Host
And his fat spouse, that welcomes to their cost
The galled traveller, and with a beck'ning 129
Informs the tapster to inflame the reck'ning.
Then the beast-eating Clown, and next the Fool,
The Bavian, with long tail and eke long tool;
Cum multis aliis that make a dance.
Say 'Ay,' and all shall presently advance.
Thes. Ay, ay, by any means, dear Domine.
Pir. Produce. *Music.* 136
School. Intrate, filii; come forth, and foot it.

Enter the *Dance.* [A morris is danced.]

Ladies, if we have been merry,
And have pleas'd ye with a derry
And a derry and a down,
Say the schoolmaster's no clown.
Duke, if we have pleas'd thee too
And have done as good boys should do,
Give us but a tree or twain
For a Maypole, and again,
Ere another year run out,
We'll make thee laugh and all this rout.
Thes. Take twenty, Domine. — How does my sweetheart?
Hip. Never so pleas'd, sir.
Emil. 'Twas an excellent dance; and for a preface,
I never heard a better.
Thes. Schoolmaster, I thank you.
One see 'em all rewarded.
Pir. And here's something [*Gives money.*]
To paint your pole withal.
Thes. Now to our sports again.
School.
May the stag thou hunt'st stand long
And thy dogs be swift and strong!
May they kill him without lets,
And the ladies eat his doucets!
[*Exeunt Theseus and his company.*] *Wind horns.*
Come, we are all made. Dii deaeque omnes!
Ye have danc'd rarely, wenches. *Exeunt.*

Scene VI. [*The same part of the Forest as in Scene III.*]

Enter *Palamon* from the bush.

Pal. About this hour my cousin gave his faith
To visit me again and with him bring
Two swords and two good armours. If he fail,
He's neither man nor soldier. When he left me,
I did not think a week could have restor'd
My lost strength to me, I was grown so low
And crestfall'n with my wants. I thank thee, Arcite.
Thou art yet a fair foe; and I feel myself,
With this refreshing, able once again
To outdure danger. To delay it longer
Would make the world think, when it comes to hearing,
That I lay fatting like a swine, to fight,
And not a soldier. Therefore this blest morning
Shall be the last; and that sword he refuses,
If it but hold, I kill him with. 'Tis justice.
So, love and fortune for me!

Enter *Arcite* with armours and swords.

O, good morrow.
Arc. Good morrow, noble kinsman.
Pal. I have put you
To too much pains, sir.
Arc. That too much, fair cousin,
Is but a debt to honour and my duty.
Pal. Would you were so in all, sir! I could wish ye
As kind a kinsman as you force me find
A beneficial foe, that my embraces
Might thank ye, not my blows.

Arc. I shall think either,
Well done, a noble recompense.
Pal. Then I shall quit you.
Arc. Defy me in these fair terms, and you show
More than a mistress to me. No more anger,
As you love any thing that's honourable.
We were not bred to talk, man. When we are arm'd
And both upon our guards, then let our fury,
Like meeting of two tides, fly strongly from us;
And then to whom the birthright of this beauty
Truly pertains (without upbraidings, scorns,
Despisings of our persons, and such poutings,
Fitter for girls and schoolboys) will be seen,
And quickly, yours or mine. Will't please you arm, sir?
Or, if you feel yourself not fitting yet
And furnish'd with your old strength, I'll stay, cousin,
And ev'ry day discourse you into health,
As I am spar'd. Your person I am friends with;
And I could wish I had not said I lov'd her,
Though I had died; but, loving such a lady,
And justifying my love, I must not fly from't.
Pal. Arcite, thou art so brave an enemy
That no man but thy cousin's fit to kill thee.
I am well and lusty; choose your arms.
Arc. Choose you, sir.
Pal. Wilt thou exceed in all, or dost thou do it
To make me spare thee?
Arc. If you think so, cousin,
You are deceiv'd; for, as I am a soldier,
I will not spare you.
Pal. That's well said.
Arc. You'll find it.
Pal. Then, as I am an honest man, and love
With all the justice of affection,
I'll pay thee soundly. This I'll take.
Arc. That's mine then.
I'll arm you first.
Pal. Do. Pray thee tell me, cousin,
Where got'st thou this good armour?
Arc. 'Tis the Duke's;
And, to say true, I stole it. Do I pinch you?
Pal. No.
Arc. Is't not too heavy?
Pal. I have worn a lighter,
But I shall make it serve.
Arc. I'll buckle't close.
Pal. By any means.
Arc. You care not for a grand-guard?
Pal. No, no! we'll use no horses. I perceive
You would be fain at that fight.
Arc. I am indifferent.
Pal. Faith, so am I. Good cousin, thrust the buckle
Through far enough.
Arc. I warrant you.
Pal. My casque now.
Arc. Will you fight bare-arm'd?
Pal. We shall be the nimbler.
Arc. But use your gauntlets though. Those are o' th' least.
Prithee take mine, good cousin.
Pal. Thank you, Arcite.
How do I look? Am I fall'n much away?
Arc. Faith, very little. Love has us'd you kindly.
Pal. I'll warrant thee I'll strike home.
Arc. Do, and spare not.
I'll give you cause, sweet cousin.
Pal. Now to you, sir.
Methinks this armour's very like that, Arcite,
Thou wor'st that day the three kings fell, but lighter.
Arc. That was a very good one; and that day,
I well remember, you outdid me, cousin.
I never saw such valour. When you charg'd
Upon the left wing of the enemy,
I spurr'd hard to come up, and under me
I had a right good horse.
Pal. You had indeed —
A bright bay, I remember.
Arc. Yes. But all
Was vainly labour'd in me. You outwent me,
Nor could my wishes reach you. Yet a little
I did by imitation.
Pal. More by virtue.
You are modest, cousin.
Arc. When I saw you charge first,
Methought I heard a dreadful clap of thunder
Break from the troop.
Pal. But still before that flew
The lightning of your valour. Stay a little.
Is not this piece too strait?
Arc. No, no; 'tis well.
Pal. I would have nothing hurt thee but my sword.
A bruise would be dishonour.
Arc. Now I am perfect.
Pal. Stand off then.
Arc. Take my sword; I hold it better.
Pal. I thank ye, no. Keep it; your life lies on it.
Here's one, if it but hold, I ask no more
For all my hopes. My cause and honour guard me!

Arc. And me my love!

They bow several ways; then advance and stand.

Is there aught else to say?

Pal. This only, and no more: thou art mine aunt's son,
And that blood we desire to shed is mutual —
In me thine, and in thee mine. My sword
Is in my hand, and, if thou killest me,
The gods and I forgive thee. If there be
A place prepar'd for those that sleep in honour,
I wish his weary soul that falls may win it.
Fight bravely, cousin. Give me thy noble hand.

Arc. Here, Palamon. This hand shall never more
Come near thee with such friendship.

Pal. I commend thee.

Arc. If I fall, curse me and say I was a coward;
For none but such dare die in these just trials.
Once more farewell, my cousin.

Pal. Farewell, Arcite.

Fight. Horns within. They stand.

Arc. Lo, cousin, lo! our folly has undone us.

Pal. Why?

Arc. This is the Duke, a-hunting as I told you.
If we be found, we are wretched. O, retire,
For honour's sake and safety, presently
Into your bush again. Sir, we shall find
Too many hours to die in. Gentle cousin,
If you be seen, you perish instantly
For breaking prison; and I, if you reveal me,
For my contempt. Then all the world will scorn us,
And say we had a noble difference,
But base disposers of it.

Pal. No, no, cousin!
I will no more be hidden, nor put off
This great adventure to a second trial.
I know your cunning and I know your cause.
He that faints now, shame take him! Put thyself
Upon thy present guard —

Arc. You are not mad?

Pal. Or I will make th' advantage of this hour
Mine own; and what to come shall threaten me
I fear less than my fortune. Know, weak cousin,
I love Emilia, and in that I'll bury
Thee and all crosses else.

Arc. Then come what can come
Thou shalt know, Palamon, I dare as well
Die as discourse or sleep. Only this fears me,
The law will have the honour of our ends.
Have at thy life!

Pal. Look to thine own well, Arcite.

Fight again. Horns [within].

Enter *Theseus, Hippolyta, Emilia, Pirithous,* and *Train.*

Thes. What ignorant and mad-malicious traitors
Are you that, 'gainst the tenour of my laws,
Are making battle, thus like knights appointed
Without my leave and officers of arms?
By Castor, both shall die.

Pal. Hold thy word, Theseus.
We are certainly both traitors, both despisers
Of thee and of thy goodness. I am Palamon,
That cannot love thee, he that broke thy prison —
Think well what that deserves; and this is Arcite;
A bolder traitor never trod thy ground,
A falser nev'r seem'd friend. This is the man
Was begg'd and banish'd. This is he contemns thee
And what thou dar'st do; and in this disguise,
Against thine own edict, follows thy sister,
That fortunate bright star, the fair Emilia;
Whose servant (if there be a right in seeing
And first bequeathing of the soul to) justly
I am; and, which is more, dares think her his.
This treachery, like a most trusty lover,
I call'd him now to answer. If thou be'st,
As thou art spoken, great and virtuous,
The true decider of all injuries,
Say 'Fight again!' and thou shalt see me, Theseus,
Do such a justice thou thyself wilt envy.
Then take my life; I'll woo thee to't.

Pir. O heaven,
What more than man is this!

Thes. I have sworn.

Arc. We seek not
Thy breath of mercy, Theseus. 'Tis to me
A thing as soon to die as thee to say it,
And no more mov'd. Where this man calls me traitor,
Let me say thus much: if in love be treason
In service of so excellent a beauty,
As I love most, and in that faith will perish,
As I have brought my life here to confirm it,
As I have serv'd her truest, worthiest,
As I dare kill this cousin that denies it,
So let me be most traitor, and ye please me.
For scorning thy edict, Duke, ask that lady
Why she is fair, and why her eyes command me

Stay here to love her; and if she say 'traitor,'
I am a villain fit to lie unburied.

Pal. Thou shalt have pity of us both, O Theseus,
If unto neither thou show mercy. Stop,
As thou art just, thy noble ear against us;
As thou art valiant, for thy cousin's soul,
Whose twelve strong labours crown his memory,
Let's die together, at one instant, Duke.
Only a little let him fall before me,
That I may tell my soul he shall not have her.

Thes. I grant your wish; for, to say true, your cousin
Has ten times more offended, for I gave him
More mercy than you found, sir, your offences
Being no more than his. None here speak for 'em;
For, ere the sun set, both shall sleep for ever.

Hip. Alas, the pity! Now or never, sister,
Speak, not to be denied. That face of yours
Will bear the curses else of after-ages
For these lost cousins.

Emil. In my face, dear sister,
I find no anger to 'em, nor no ruin:
The misadventure of their own eyes kill 'em.
Yet that I will be woman and have pity,
My knees shall grow to th' ground but I'll get mercy.
Help me, dear sister. In a deed so virtuous
The powers of all women will be with us.
Most royal brother — [*They kneel.*]

Hip. Sir, by our tie of marriage —

Emil. By your own spotless honour —

Hip. By that faith,
That fair hand, and that honest heart you gave me —

Emil. By that you would have pity in another,
By your own virtues infinite —

Hip. By valour,
By all the chaste nights I have ever pleas'd you —

Thes. These are strange conjurings.

Pir. Nay, then, I'll in too. [*Kneels.*]
By all our friendship, sir, by all our dangers,
By all you love most — wars, and this sweet lady —

Emil. By that you would have trembled to deny
A blushing maid —

Hip. By your own eyes; by strength,
In which you swore I went beyond all women,
Almost all men, and yet I yielded, Theseus —

Pir. To crown all this, by your most noble soul,
Which cannot want due mercy, I beg first.

Hip. Next hear my prayers.

Emil. Last let me entreat, sir.

Pir. For mercy.

Hip. Mercy.

Emil. Mercy on these princes.

Thes. Ye make my faith reel. Say I felt
Compassion to 'em both, how would you place it?

Emil. Upon their lives; but with their banishments.

Thes. You are a right woman, sister; you have pity,
But want the understanding where to use it.
If you desire their lives, invent a way
Safer than banishment. Can these two live,
And have the agony of love about 'em,
And not kill one another? Every day
They'ld fight about you; hourly bring your honour
In public question with their swords. Be wise then
And here forget 'em. It concerns your credit
And my oath equally. I have said they die.
Better they fall by th' law than one another.
Bow not my honour.

Emil. O my noble brother,
That oath was rashly made and in your anger;
Your reason will not hold it. If such vows
Stand for express will, all the world must perish.
Beside, I have another oath 'gainst yours,
Of more authority, I am sure more love;
Not made in passion neither, but good heed.

Thes. What is it, sister?

Pir. Urge it home, brave lady.

Emil. That you would nev'r deny me anything
Fit for my modest suit and your free granting.
I tie you to your word now. If ye fall in't,
Think how you maim your honour
(For now I am set a-begging, sir, I am deaf
To all but your compassion), how their lives
Might breed the ruin of my name, opinion!
Shall anything that loves me perish for me?
That were a cruel wisdom! Do men proin
The straight young boughs that blush with thousand blossoms,
Because they may be rotten? O Duke Theseus,
The goodly mothers that have groan'd for these,
And all the longing maids that ever lov'd 'em,
If your vow stand, shall curse me and my beauty,
And in their funeral songs for these two cousins

Despise my cruelty and cry woe worth me,
Till I am nothing but the scorn of women.
For heaven's sake save their lives, and banish 'em.

Thes. On what conditions?

Emil. Swear 'em never more
To make me their contention or to know me,
To tread upon thy dukedom, and to be,
Wherever they shall travel, ever strangers
To one another.

Pal. I'll be cut a-pieces
Before I take this oath. Forget I love her?
O all ye gods, despise me then. Thy banishment
I not mislike, so we may fairly carry
Our swords and cause along; else, never trifle,
But take our lives, Duke. I must love, and will;
And for that love must and dare kill this cousin,
On any piece the earth has.

Thes. Will you, Arcite,
Take these conditions?

Pal. He's a villain then.

Pir. These are men!

Arc. No, never, Duke. 'Tis worse to me than begging
To take my life so basely. Though I think
I never shall enjoy her, yet I'll preserve
The honour of affection and die for her,
Make death a devil.

Thes. What may be done? for now I feel compassion.

Pir. Let it not fall again, sir.

Thes. Say, Emilia,
If one of them were dead, as one must, are you
Content to take the other to your husband?
They cannot both enjoy you. They are princes
As goodly as your own eyes, and as noble
As ever fame yet spoke of. Look upon 'em
And, if you can love, end this difference.
I give consent. Are you content too, princes?

Both. With all our souls.

Thes. He that she refuses
Must die then.

Both. Any death thou canst invent, Duke.

Pal. If I fall from that mouth, I fall with favour,
And lovers yet unborn shall bless my ashes.

Arc. If she refuse me, yet my grave will wed me
And soldiers sing my epitaph.

Thes. Make choice then.

Emil. I cannot, sir; they are both too excellent.
For me, a hair shall never fall of these men.

Hip. What will become of 'em?

Thes. Thus I ordain it;
And, by mine honour, once again it stands,
Or both shall die: you shall both to your country,
And each within this month, accompanied
With three fair knights, appear again in this place,
In which I'll plant a pyramid; and whether,
Before us that are here, can force his cousin
By fair and knightly strength to touch the pillar,
He shall enjoy her; the other lose his head,
And all his friends; nor shall he grudge to fall,
Nor think he dies with interest in this lady.
Will this content ye?

Pal. Yes. Here, cousin Arcite,
I am friends again till that hour.

Arc. I embrace ye.

Thes. Are you content, sister?

Emil. Yes; I must, sir;
Else both miscarry.

Thes. Come, shake hands again then;
And take heed, as you are gentlemen, this quarrel
Sleep till the hour prefix'd, and hold your course.

Pal. We dare not fail thee, Theseus.

Thes. Come, I'll give ye
Now usage like to princes and to friends.
When ye return, who wins I'll settle here;
Who loses, yet I'll weep upon his bier. *Exeunt.*

ACT IV. Scene I. [*Athens. The Prison.*]

Enter *Jailer* and his *Friend.*

Jailer. Hear you no more? Was nothing said of me
Concerning the escape of Palamon?
Good sir, remember.

Friend. Nothing that I heard;
For I came home before the business
Was fully ended. Yet I might perceive,
Ere I departed, a great likelihood
Of both their pardons; for Hippolyta
And fair-ey'd Emily upon their knees
Begg'd with such handsome pity that the Duke
Methought stood staggering whether he should follow
His rash oath or the sweet compassion
Of those two ladies; and to second them,
That truly noble prince Pirithous,

Half his own heart, set in too, that I hope
All shall be well. Neither heard I one question
Of your name or his scape.

Jailer. Pray heaven it hold so!

Enter *Second Friend.*

2. Friend. Be of good comfort, man. I bring you news,
Good news.

Jailer. They are welcome.

2. Friend. Palamon has clear'd you,
And got your pardon, and discover'd how
And by whose means he escap'd, which was your daughter's,
Whose pardon is procur'd too; and the prisoner —
Not to be held ungrateful to her goodness —
Has given a sum of money to her marriage,
A large one, I'll assure you.

Jailer. Ye are a good man
And ever bring good news.

1. Friend. How was it ended?

2. Friend. Why, as it should be. They that never begg'd
But they prevail'd, had their suits fairly granted.
The prisoners have their lives.

1. Friend. I knew 'twould be so.

2. Friend. But there be new conditions, which you'll hear of
At better time.

Jailer. I hope they are good.

2. Friend. They are honourable.
How good they'll prove I know not.

1. Friend. 'Twill be known.

Enter *Wooer.*

Wooer. Alas, sir, where's your daughter?

Jailer. Why do you ask?

Wooer. O sir, when did you see her?

2. Friend. How he looks!

Jailer. This morning.

Wooer. Was she well? was she in health, sir?
When did she sleep?

1. Friend. These are strange questions.

Jailer. I do not think she was very well; for, now
You make me mind her, but this very day
I ask'd her questions, and she answered me
So far from what she was, so childishly,
So sillily, as if she were a fool,
An innocent; and I was very angry.
But what of her, sir?

Wooer. Nothing but my pity.
But you must know it, and as good by me
As by another that less loves her.

Jailer. Well, sir?

1. Friend. Not right?

2. Friend. Not well?

Wooer. No, sir; not well:
'Tis too true, she is mad.

1. Friend. It cannot be.

Wooer. Believe you'll find it so.

Jailer. I half suspected
What you have told me. The gods comfort her!
Either this was her love to Palamon,
Or fear of my miscarrying on his scape,
Or both.

Wooer. 'Tis likely.

Jailer. But why all this haste, sir?

Wooer. I'll tell you quickly. As I late was angling
In the great lake that lies behind the palace,
From the far shore, thick set with reeds and sedges,
As patiently I was attending sport,
I heard a voice, a shrill one; and attentive
I gave my ear; when I might well perceive
'Twas one that sung, and, by the smallness of it,
A boy or woman. I then left my angle
To his own skill, came near, but yet perceiv'd not
Who made the sound, the rushes and the reeds
Had so encompass'd it. I laid me down
And list'ned to the words she sung; for then,
Through a small glade cut by the fishermen,
I saw it was your daughter.

Jailer. Pray go on, sir.

Wooer. She sung much, but no sense; only I heard her
Repeat this often, 'Palamon is gone,
Is gone to th' wood to gather mulberries.
I'll find him out to-morrow.'

1. Friend. Pretty soul!

Wooer. 'His shackles will betray him, he'll be taken;
And what shall I do then? I'll bring a bevy,
A hundred black-ey'd maids that love as I do,
With chaplets on their heads of daffadillies,
With cherry lips and cheeks of damask roses,
And all we'll dance an antic fore the Duke
And beg his pardon.' Then she talk'd of you, sir —
That you must lose your head to-morrow morning,
And she must gather flowers to bury you
And see the house made handsome. Then she sung

Nothing but 'Willow, willow, willow'; and between
Ever was 'Palamon, fair Palamon,'
And 'Palamon was a tall young man.' The place
Was knee-deep where she sat; her careless tresses
A wreath of bulrush rounded; about her stuck
Thousand fresh water-flowers of several colours;
That methought she appear'd like the fair nymph
That feeds the lake with waters, or as Iris
Newly dropt down from heaven. Rings she made
Of rushes that grew by, and to 'em spoke
The prettiest posies — 'Thus our true love's tied,'
'This you may loose, not me,' and many a one;
And then she wept, and sung again, and sigh'd,
And with the same breath smil'd and kiss'd her hand.

2. Friend. Alas, what pity it is!

Wooer. I made in to her.
She saw me and straight sought the flood. I sav'd her
And set her safe to land; when presently
She slipt away, and to the city made
With such a cry and swiftness that, believe me,
She left me far behind her. Three or four
I saw from far off cross her — one of 'em
I knew to be your brother; where she stay'd,
And fell, scarce to be got away. I left them with her
And hither came to tell you.

Enter *Brother, Daughter,* and others.

Here they are.

Daugh. [*sings*]

May you never more enjoy the light, &c.

Is not this a fine song?

Broth. O, a very fine one!

Daugh. I can sing twenty more.

Broth. I think you can.

Daugh. Yes, truly, can I. I can sing 'The Broom'
And 'Bonny Robin.' Are not you a tailor?

Broth. Yes.

Daugh. Where's my wedding gown?

Broth. I'll bring it to-morrow.

Daugh. Do, very rearly; I must be abroad else,
To call the maids and pay the minstrels;
For I must lose my maidenhead by cocklight;
'Twill never thrive else. *Sings.*

O fair, O sweet, &c.

Broth. You must ev'n take it patiently.

Jailer. 'Tis true.

Daugh. Good ev'n, good men. Pray did you ever hear
Of one young Palamon?

Jailer. Yes, wench, we know him.

Daugh. Is't not a fine young gentleman?

Jailer. 'Tis love!

Broth. By no mean cross her; she is then distemper'd
Far worse than now she shows.

1. Friend. Yes, he's a fine man.

Daugh. O, is he so? You have a sister?

1. Friend. Yes.

Daugh. But she shall never have him, tell her so,
For a trick that I know. Y'had best look to her,
For, if she see him once, she's gone — she's done
And undone in an hour. All the young maids
Of our town are in love with him; but I laugh at 'em
And let 'em all alone. Is't not a wise course?

1. Friend. Yes.

Daugh. There is at least two hundred now with child by him —
There must be four. Yet I keep close for all this,
Close as a cockle. And all these must be boys —
He has the trick on't; and at ten years old
They must be all gelt for musicians
And sing the wars of Theseus.

2. Friend. This is strange.

Daugh. As ever you heard; but say nothing.

1. Friend. No.

Daugh. They come from all parts of the dukedom to him.
I'll warrant ye he had not so few last night
As twenty to dispatch. He'll tickle't up
In two hours, if his hand be in.

Jailer. She's lost,
Past all cure.

Broth. Heaven forbid, man!

Daugh. Come hither; you are a wise man.

1. Friend. Does she know him?

2. Friend. No; would she did!

Daugh. You are master of a ship?

Jailer. Yes.

Daugh. Where's your compass?

Jailer. Here.

Daugh. Set it to th' north.

And now direct your course to th' wood, where Palamon
Lies longing for me. For the tackling
Let me alone. Come, weigh, my hearts, cheerly!
All. Owgh, owgh, owgh! 'Tis up! The wind is fair.
Top the bowling! Out with the mainsail!
Where's your whistle, master?
Broth. Let's get her in.
Jailer. Up to the top, boy!
Broth. Where's the pilot?
1. Friend. Here.
Daugh. What kenn'st thou?
2. Friend. A fair wood.
Daugh. Bear for it, master.
Tack about! *Sings.*

When Cynthia with her borrowed light, &c.

Exeunt.

Scene II. [*Athens. The Palace.*]

Enter *Emilia* alone, with two pictures.

Emil. Yet I may bind those wounds up, that must open
And bleed to death for my sake else. I'll choose
And end their strife. Two such young handsome men
Shall never fall for me; their weeping mothers
Following the dead-cold ashes of their sons,
Shall never curse my cruelty. Good heaven,
What a sweet face has Arcite! If wise Nature,
With all her best endowments, all those beauties
She sows into the births of noble bodies,
Were here a mortal woman and had in her
The coy denials of young maids, yet doubtless
She would run mad for this man. What an eye,
Of what a fiery sparkle and quick sweetness,
Has this young prince! Here Love himself sits smiling.
Just such another wanton Ganymede
Set Jove afire with, and enforc'd the god
Snatch up the goodly boy and set him by him,
A shining constellation. What a brow,
Of what a spacious majesty, he carries,
Arch'd like the great-ey'd Juno's, but far sweeter,
Smoother than Pelops' shoulder! Fame and Honour,
Methinks, from hence, as from a promontory
Pointed in heaven, should clap their wings and sing
To all the under-world the loves and fights
Of gods and such men near 'em. Palamon
Is but his foil; to him, a mere dull shadow.
He's swarth and meagre, of an eye as heavy
As if he had lost his mother; a still temper,
No stirring in him, no alacrity;
Of all this sprightly sharpness, not a smile.
Yet these that we count errors may become him:
Narcissus was a sad boy, but a heavenly.
O, who can find the bent of woman's fancy?
I am a fool, my reason is lost in me;
I have no choice, and I have lied so lewdly
That women ought to beat me. On my knees
I ask thy pardon, Palamon. Thou art alone
And only beautiful; and these the eyes,
These the bright lamps of beauty, that command
And threaten Love; and what young maid dare cross 'em?
What a bold gravity, and yet inviting,
Has this brown manly face! O Love, this only
From this hour is complexion. Lie there, Arcite!
Thou art a changeling to him, a mere gypsy,
And this the noble body. I am sotted,
Utterly lost. My virgin's faith has fled me,
For, if my brother but even now had ask'd me
Whether I lov'd, I had run mad for Arcite;
Now if my sister, more for Palamon.
Stand both together. Now come ask me, brother.
Alas, I know not! Ask me now, sweet sister.
I may go look! — What a mere child is fancy,
That, having two fair gauds of equal sweetness,
Cannot distinguish, but must cry for both!

Enter *Gentleman.*

How now, sir?
Gent. From the noble Duke your brother,
Madam, I bring you news. The knights are come.
Emil. To end the quarrel?
Gent. Yes.
Emil. Would I might end first!
What sins have I committed, chaste Diana,
That my unspotted youth must now be soil'd
With blood of princes, and my chastity
Be made the altar where the lives of lovers —
Two greater and two better never yet
Made mothers joy — must be the sacrifice
To my unhappy beauty?

Enter *Theseus, Hippolyta, Pirithous,* and *Attendants.*

Thes. Bring 'em in
Quickly by any means; I long to see 'em.
Your two contending lovers are return'd,

And with them their six knights. Now, my fair sister,
You must love one of them.
Emil. I had rather both;
So neither for my sake should fall untimely.
Thes. Who saw 'em?
Pir. I a while.
Gent. And I.

Enter *Messenger*.

Thes. From whence come you, sir?
Mess. From the knights.
Thes. Pray speak,
You that have seen them, what they are.
Mess. I will, sir,
And truly what I think. Six braver spirits
Than these they have brought (if we judge by the outside)
I never saw nor read of. He that stands
In the first place with Arcite, by his seeming
Should be a stout man, by his face a prince —
His very looks so say him; his complexion
Nearer a brown than black; stern, and yet noble,
Which shows him hardy, fearless, proud of dangers.
The circles of his eyes show fire within him,
And as a heated lion so he looks.
His hair hangs long behind him, black and shining
Like ravens' wings; his shoulders broad and strong;
Arm'd long and round; and on his thigh a sword
Hung by a curious baldrick, when he frowns
To seal his will with. Better, o' my conscience,
Was never soldier's friend.
Thes. Thou hast well describ'd him.
Pir. Yet a great deal short,
Methinks, of him that's first with Palamon.
Thes. Pray speak him, friend.
Pir. I guess he is a prince too,
And, if it may be, greater; for his show
Has all the ornament of honour in't.
He's somewhat bigger than the knight he spoke of,
But of a face far sweeter; his complexion
Is, as a ripe grape, ruddy. He has felt
Without doubt what he fights for, and so apter
To make this cause his own. In's face appears
All the fair hopes of what he undertakes;
And when he's angry, then a settled valour,
Not tainted with extremes, runs through his body
And guides his arm to brave things. Fear he cannot;
He shows no such soft temper. His head's yellow,
Hard-hair'd, and curl'd, thick-twin'd like ivy-tods,
Not to undo with thunder. In his face
The livery of the warlike maid appears,
Pure red and white, for yet no beard has blest him;
And in his rolling eyes sits Victory,
As if she ever meant to crown his valour.
His nose stands high, a character of honour;
His red lips, after fights, are fit for ladies.
Emil. Must these men die too?
Pir. When he speaks, his tongue
Sounds like a trumpet. All his lineaments
Are as a man would wish 'em, strong and clean.
He wears a well-steel'd axe, the staff of gold;
His age some five-and-twenty.
Mess. There's another,
A little man, but of a tough soul, seeming
As great as any. Fairer promises
In such a body yet I never look'd on.
Pir. O, he that's freckle-fac'd?
Mess. The same, my lord.
Are they not sweet ones?
Pir. Yes, they are well.
Mess. Methinks,
Being so few and well-dispos'd, they show
Great and fine art in nature. He's white-hair'd,
Not wanton white, but such a manly colour
Next to an aborn; tough and nimble-set,
Which shows an active soul; his arms are brawny,
Lin'd with strong sinews; to the shoulder-piece
Gently they swell, like women new-conceiv'd,
Which speaks him prone to labour, never fainting
Under the weight of arms; stout-hearted, still,
But, when he stirs, a tiger. He's grey-ey'd,
Which yields compassion where he conquers; sharp
To spy advantages, and where he finds 'em,
He's swift to make 'em his. He does no wrongs,
Nor takes none. He's round-fac'd, and when he smiles
He shows a lover, when he frowns, a soldier.
About his head he wears the winner's oak,
And in it stuck the favour of his lady.
His age some six-and-thirty. In his hand
He bears a charging staff emboss'd with silver.
Thes. Are they all thus?
Pir. They are all the sons of honour.

Thes. Now, as I have a soul, I long to see 'em.
Lady, you shall see men fight now.
Hip. I wish it,
But not the cause, my lord. They would show
Bravely about the titles of two kingdoms.
'Tis pity Love should be so tyrannous.
O my soft-hearted sister, what think you?
Weep not, till they weep blood, wench. It must be.
Thes. You have steel'd 'em with your beauty. —Honour'd friend,
To you I give the field; pray order it
Fitting the persons that must use it.
Pir. Yes, sir.
Thes. Come, I'll go visit 'em. I cannot stay—
Their fame has fir'd me so — till they appear.
Good friend, be royal.
Pir. There shall want no bravery.
Emil. Poor wench, go weep; for whosoever wins
Loses a noble cousin for thy sins. *Exeunt.*

Scene III. [*Athens. The Prison.*]

Enter *Jailer, Wooer, Doctor.*

Doctor. Her distraction is more at some time of the moon than at other some, is it not?

Jailer. She is continually in a harmless distemper; sleeps little; altogether without appetite, save often drinking; dreaming of another world and a better; and what broken piece of matter soe'er she's about, the name Palamon lards it, that she farces ev'ry business withal, fits it to every question.

Enter *Daughter.*

Look where she comes. You shall perceive her behaviour.

Daugh. I have forgot it quite; the burden on't was 'Down-a, down-a'; and penn'd by no worse man than Giraldo, Emilia's schoolmaster. He's as fantastical, too, as ever he may go upon's legs; for in the next world will Dido see Palamon, and then will she be out of love with Æneas.

Doctor. What stuff's here! Poor soul!

Jailer. Ev'n thus all day long.

Daugh. Now for this charm that I told you of. You must bring a piece of silver on the tip of your tongue, or no ferry. Then, if it be your chance to come where the blessed spirits — as there's a sight now! We maids that have our livers perish'd, crack'd to pieces with love, we shall come there, and do nothing all day long but pick flowers with Proserpine. Then will I make Palamon a nosegay; then let him — mark me — then —

Doctor. How prettily she's amiss! Note her a little further.

Daugh. Faith, I'll tell you. Sometime we go to barley-break, we of the blessed. Alas, 'tis a sore life they have i' th' other place, such burning, frying, boiling, hissing, howling, chatt'ring, cursing! O, they have shrowd measure! Take heed: if one be mad, or hang or drown themselves, thither they go — Jupiter bless us! — and there shall we be put in a caldron of lead and usurers' grease, amongst a whole million of cutpurses, and there boil like a gammon of bacon that will never be enough.

Doctor. How her brain coins!

Daugh. Lords and courtiers that have got maids with child, they are in this place. They shall stand in fire up to the navel, and in ice up to th' heart, and there th' offending part burns, and the deceiving part freezes: in troth, a very grievous punishment, as one would think, for such a trifle. Believe me, one would marry a leprous witch to be rid on't, I'll assure you.

Doctor. How she continues this fancy! 'Tis not an engraffed madness, but a most thick and profound melancholy.

Daugh. To hear there a proud lady and a proud city-wife howl together! I were a beast an I'ld call it good sport. One cries 'O, this smoke!' th' other, 'This fire!' One cries 'O, that ever I did it behind the arras!' and then howls; th' other curses a suing fellow and her garden house. *Sings.*

I will be true, my stars, my fate, &c.

Exit.

Jailer. What think you of her, sir?

Doctor. I think she has a perturbed mind which I cannot minister to.

Jailer. Alas, what then?

Doctor. Understand you she ever affected any man ere she beheld Palamon?

Jailer. I was once, sir, in great hope she had fix'd her liking on this gentleman, my friend.

Wooer. I did think so too; and would account I had a great pen'worth on't to give half my state that both she and I at this present stood unfeignedly on the same terms.

Doctor. That intemp'rate surfeit of her eye hath distemper'd the other senses. They may return and settle again to execute their preordain'd faculties; but they are now in a most extravagant vagary. This you must do: confine her to a place where the light may rather seem to steal in than be permitted. Take upon you, young sir her friend, the name of Palamon; say you come to eat with her and to commune of love. This will catch her attention, for this her mind beats upon; other objects that are inserted 'tween her mind and eye become the pranks and friskings of her madness. Sing to her such green songs of love as she says Palamon hath sung in prison. Come to her, stuck in as sweet flowers as the season is mistress of, and thereto make an addition of some other compounded odours which are grateful to the sense. All this shall become Palamon, for Palamon can sing, and Palamon is sweet, and ev'ry good thing. Desire to eat with her, carve her, drink to her, and still among intermingle your petition of grace and acceptance into her favour. Learn what maids have been her companions and playfeeres; and let them repair to her with Palamon in their mouths and appear with tokens, as if they suggested for him. It is a falsehood she is in, which is with falsehoods to be combated. This may bring her to eat, to sleep, and reduce what's now out of square in her into their former law and regiment. I have seen it approved, how many times I know not; but to make the number more I have great hope in this. I will, between the passages of this project, come in with my appliance. Let us put it in execution; and hasten the success, which doubt not will bring forth comfort.

Exeunt.

ACT V. Scene I. [*Athens. An open place. Three altars — to Mars, Venus, and Diana.*]

Flourish. Enter *Theseus, Pirithous, Hippolyta, Attendants.*

Thes. Now let 'em enter and before the gods
Tender their holy prayers. Let the temples
Burn bright with sacred fires, and the altars
In hallowed clouds commend their swelling incense
To those above us. Let no due be wanting.
They have a noble work in hand will honour
The very powers that love 'em.

Flourish of cornets. Enter *Palamon* and *Arcite* and their *Knights.*

Pir. Sir, they enter.
Thes. You valiant and strong-hearted enemies,
You royal germane foes, that this day come
To blow that nearness out that flames between ye,
Lay by your anger for an hour, and dove-like,
Before the holy altars of your helpers,
The all-fear'd gods, bow down your stubborn bodies.
Your ire is more than mortal; so your help be!
And, as the gods regard ye, fight with justice.
I'll leave you to your prayers, and betwixt ye
I part my wishes.
Pir. Honour crown the worthiest!

Exeunt Theseus and his Train.

Pal. The glass is running now that cannot finish
Till one of us expire. Think you but thus,
That, were there aught in me which strove to show
Mine enemy in this business, were 't one eye
Against another, arm oppress'd by arm,
I would destroy th' offender; coz, I would,
Though parcel of myself. Then from this gather
How I should tender you.
Arc. I am in labour
To push your name, your ancient love, our kindred,
Out of my memory; and i' th' selfsame place
To seat something I would confound. So hoist we
The sails that must these vessels port even where
The heavenly limiter pleases.
Pal. You speak well.
Before I turn, let me embrace thee, cousin.
This I shall never do again.
Arc. One farewell!
Pal. Why, let it be so. Farewell, coz!
Arc. Farewell, sir!

[*They embrace.*] *Exeunt Palamon and his Knights.*

Knights, kinsmen, lovers, yea, my sacrifices,
True worshippers of Mars, whose spirit in you
Expels the seeds of fear and th' apprehension
Which still is father of it, go with me
Before the god of our profession. There
Require of him the hearts of lions and
The breath of tigers; yea, the fierceness too;
Yea, the speed also — to go on, I mean;
Else wish we to be snails. You know my prize

Must be dragg'd out of blood; force and great feat
Must put my garland on, where she sticks
The queen of flowers. Our intercession then
Must be to him that makes the camp a cestron
Brimm'd with the blood of men. Give me your aid
And bend your spirits towards him.

They [advance to the altar of Mars and fall on their faces; then] kneel.

Thou mighty one that with thy power hast turn'd
Green Neptune into purple; [whose approach]
Comets prewarn; whose havoc in vast field
Unearthed skulls proclaim; whose breath blows down
The teeming Ceres' foison; who dost pluck
With hand armipotent from forth blue clouds
The mason'd turrets; that both mak'st and break'st
The stony girths of cities: me thy pupil,
Youngest follower of thy drum, instruct this day
With military skill, that to thy laud
I may advance my streamer, and by thee
Be styl'd the lord o' th' day. Give me, great Mars,
Some token of thy pleasure.

Here they fall on their faces as formerly, and there is heard clanging of armour, with a short thunder, as the burst of a battle, whereupon they all rise and bow to the altar.

O great corrector of enormous times,
Shaker of o'er-rank states, thou grand decider
Of dusty and old titles, that heal'st with blood
The earth when it is sick, and cur'st the world
O' th' plurisy of people! I do take
Thy signs auspiciously, and in thy name
To my design march boldly. — Let us go.

Exeunt.

Enter *Palamon* and his *Knights*, with the former observance.

Pal. Our stars must glister with new fire or be
To-day extinct. Our argument is love,
Which if the goddess of it grant, she gives
Victory too. Then blend your spirits with mine,
You whose free nobleness do make my cause
Your personal hazard. To the goddess Venus
Commend we our proceeding and implore
Her power unto our party.

Here they [advance to the altar of Venus, and fall on their faces; then] kneel, as formerly.

Hail, sovereign queen of secrets, who hast power
To call the fiercest tyrant from his rage,
And weep unto a girl; that hast the might,
Even with an eye-glance, to choke Mars's drum
And turn th' alarm to whispers; that canst make
A cripple flourish with his crutch, and cure him
Before Apollo; that mayst force the king
To be his subject's vassal, and induce
Stale gravity to dance; the polled bachelor —
Whose youth, like wanton boys through bonfires,
Have skipp'd thy flame — at seventy thou canst catch,
And make him, to the scorn of his hoarse throat,
Abuse young lays of love. What godlike power
Hast thou not power upon? To Phœbus thou
Add'st flames, hotter than his: the heavenly fires
Did scorch his mortal son, thine him. The huntress
All moist and cold, some say, began to throw
Her bow away, and sigh. Take to thy grace
Me thy vow'd soldier, who do bear thy yoke
As 'twere a wreath of roses, yet is heavier
Than lead itself, stings more than nettles. I
Have never been foul-mouth'd against thy law;
Nev'r reveal'd secret, for I knew none — would not,
Had I kenn'd all that were. I never practis'd
Upon man's wife, nor would the libels read
Of liberal wits. I never at great feasts
Sought to betray a beauty, but have blush'd
At simp'ring sirs that did. I have been harsh
To large confessors, and have hotly ask'd them
If they had mothers. I had one, a woman,
And women 'twere they wrong'd. I knew a man
Of eighty winters — this I told them — who
A lass of fourteen brided. 'Twas thy power
To put life into dust. The aged cramp
Had screw'd his square foot round,
The gout had knit his fingers into knots,
Torturing convulsions from his globy eyes
Had almost drawn their spheres, that what was life
In him seem'd torture. This anatomy
Had by his young fair feere a boy, and I
Believ'd it was his, for she swore it was,
And who would not believe her? Brief, I am
To those that prate and have done, no companion;
To those that boast and have not, a defier;
To those that would and cannot, a rejoicer.

Yea, him I do not love that tells close offices
The foulest way, nor names concealments in
The boldest language. Such a one I am,
And vow that lover never yet made sigh
Truer than I. O, then, most soft-sweet goddess,
Give me the victory of this question, which
Is true love's merit, and bless me with a sign
Of thy great pleasure.

Here music is heard, and doves are seen to flutter. They fall again upon their faces, then on their knees.

O thou that from eleven to ninety reign'st
In mortal bosoms, whose chase is this world,
And we in herds thy game, I give thee thanks
For this fair token; which being laid unto
Mine innocent true heart, arms in assurance
My body to this business. — Let us rise
And bow before the goddess. Time comes on.

They bow [and] exeunt.

Still music of records. Enter *Emilia* in white, her hair about her shoulders, [and wearing] a wheaten wreath; one in white holding up her train, her hair stuck with flowers; one before her carrying a silver hind, in which is convey'd incense and sweet odours, which being set upon the altar [of *Diana*], her *Maids* standing aloof, she sets fire to it; then they curtsy and kneel.

Emil. O sacred, shadowy, cold, and constant queen,
Abandoner of revels, mute, contemplative,
Sweet, solitary, white as chaste, and pure
As wind-fann'd snow, who to thy female knights
Allow'st no more blood than will make a blush,
Which is their order's robe: I here, thy priest,
Am humbled fore thine altar. O, vouchsafe,
With that thy rare green eye — which never yet
Beheld thing maculate — look on thy virgin;
And, sacred silver mistress, lend thine ear
(Which nev'r heard scurril term, into whose port
Ne'er ent'red wanton sound) to my petition,
Season'd with holy fear. This is my last
Of vestal office; I am bride-habited,
But maiden-hearted. A husband I have 'pointed,
But do not know him. Out of two I should
Choose one and pray for his success; but I
Am guiltless of election. Of mine eyes
Were I to lose one, they are equal precious —
I could doom neither; that which perish'd should
Go to't unsentenc'd. Therefore, most modest queen,
He of the two pretenders that best loves me
And has the truest title in't, let him
Take off my wheaten garland, or else grant
The file and quality I hold I may
Continue in thy band.

Here the hind vanishes under the altar, and in the place ascends a rose tree, having one rose upon it.

See what our general of ebbs and flows
Out from the bowels of her holy altar
With sacred act advances: but one rose!
If well inspir'd, this battle shall confound
Both these brave knights, and I, a virgin flow'r,
Must grow alone, unpluck'd.

Here is heard a sudden twang of instruments, and the rose falls from the tree, [which vanishes under the altar].

The flow'r is fall'n, the tree descends. O mistress,
Thou here dischargest me. I shall be gather'd,
I think so; but I know not thine own will.
Unclasp thy mystery. — I hope she's pleas'd;
Her signs were gracious.

They curtsy and exeunt.

Scene II. [*Athens. The Prison.*]

Enter *Doctor, Jailer,* and *Wooer* in habit of *Palamon.*

Doctor. Has this advice I told you done any good upon her?

Wooer. O, very much! The maids that kept her company
Have half persuaded her that I am Palamon.
Within this half-hour she came smiling to me
And ask'd me what I would eat, and when I would kiss her.
I told her, presently, and kiss'd her twice.

Doctor. 'Twas well done. Twenty times had been far better;
For there the cure lies mainly.

Wooer. Then she told me
She would watch with me to-night, for well she knew
What hour my fit would take me.

Doctor. Let her do so;
And when your fit comes, fit her home, and presently.

Wooer. She would have me sing.

Doctor. You did so?

Wooer. No.

Doctor. 'Twas very ill done then.
You should observe her ev'ry way

Wooer. Alas,
I have no voice, sir, to confirm her that way!
Doctor. That's all one, if ye make a noise.
If she entreat again, do anything;
Lie with her, if she ask you.
Jailer. Ho there, doctor!
Doctor. Yes, in the way of cure.
Jailer. But first, by your leave,
I' th' way of honesty.
Doctor. That's but a niceness.
Nev'r cast your child away for honesty.
Cure her first this way; then, if she will be honest,
She has the path before her.
Jailer. Thank ye, doctor.
Doctor. Pray bring her in
And let's see how she is.
Jailer. I will, and tell her
Her Palamon stays for her; but, doctor,
Methinks you are i' th' wrong still. *Exit.*
Doctor. Go, go!
You fathers are fine fools. Her honesty!
An we should give her physic till we find that —
Wooer. Why, do you think she is not honest, sir?
Doctor. How old is she?
Wooer. She's eighteen.
Doctor. She may be;
But that's all one, 'tis nothing to our purpose.
Whate'er her father says, if you perceive
Her mood inclining that way that I spoke of,
Videlicet, the way of flesh — you have me?
Wooer. Yes, very well, sir.
Doctor. Please her appetite,
And do it home; it cures her ipso facto
The melancholy humour that infects her.
Wooer. I am of your mind, doctor.

Enter *Jailer, Daughter, Maid.*

Doctor. You'll find it so. She comes. Pray humour her.
Jailer. Come, your love Palamon stays for you, child,
And has done this long hour, to visit you.
Daugh. I thank him for his gentle patience.
He's a kind gentleman, and I am much bound to him.
Did you nev'r see the horse he gave me?
Jailer. Yes.
Daugh. How do you like him?
Jailer. He's a very fair one.
Daugh. You never saw him dance?
Jailer. No.
Daugh. I have often.
He dances very finely, very comely;
And, for a jig, come cut and long-tail to him!
He turns ye like a top.
Jailer. That's fine indeed.
Daugh. He'll dance the morris twenty mile an hour,
And that will founder the best hobby-horse,
If I have any skill, in all the parish;
And gallops to the tune of 'Light o' Love.'
What think you of this horse?
Jailer. Having these virtues,
I think he might be brought to play at tennis.
Daugh. Alas, that's nothing.
Jailer. Can he write and read too?
Daugh. A very fair hand, and casts himself th' accounts
Of all his hay and provender. That hostler
Must rise betime that cozens him. You know
The chestnut mare the Duke has?
Jailer. Very well.
Daugh. She is horribly in love with him, poor beast!
But he is like his master, coy and scornful.
Jailer. What dowry has she?
Daugh. Some two hundred bottles,
And twenty strike of oats; but he'll ne'er have her.
He lisps in's neighing able to entice
A miller's mare; he'll be the death of her.
Doctor. What stuff she utters!
Jailer. Make curtsy; here your love comes.
Wooer. Pretty soul,
How do ye? That's a fine maid! There's a curtsy!
Daugh. Yours to command i' th' way of honesty.
How far is't now to th' end o' th' world, my masters?
Doctor. Why, a day's journey, wench.
Daugh. Will you go with me?
Wooer. What shall we do there, wench?
Daugh. Why, play at stoolball:
What is there else to do?
Wooer. I am content,
If we shall keep our wedding there.
Daugh. 'Tis true;
For there, I will assure you, we shall find
Some blind priest for the purpose that will venture
To marry us, for here they are nice and foolish.
Besides, my father must be hang'd to-morrow,
And that would be a blot i' th' business.
Are not you Palamon?
Wooer. Do not you know me?

Daugh. Yes; but you care not for me. I have nothing
But this poor petticoat and two coarse smocks.
Wooer. That's all one; I will have you.
Daugh. Will you surely?
Wooer. Yes, by this fair hand, will I.
Daugh. We'll to bed, then.
Wooer. Ev'n when you will. [*Kisses her.*]
Daugh. O, sir, you would fain be nibbling.
Wooer. Why do you rub my kiss off?
Daugh. 'Tis a sweet one
And will perfume me finely against the wedding.
Is not this your cousin Arcite?
Doctor. Yes, sweetheart;
And I am glad my cousin Palamon
Has made so fair a choice.
Daugh. Do you think he'll have me?
Doctor. Yes, without doubt.
Daugh. Do you think so too?
Jailer. Yes.
Daugh. We shall have many children. — Lord, how y'are grown!
My Palamon I hope will grow, too, finely,
Now he's at liberty. Alas, poor chicken!
He was kept down with hard meat and ill lodging;
But I'll kiss him up again.

Enter a *Messenger.*

Mess. What do you here? You'll lose the noblest sight
That ev'r was seen.
Jailer. Are they i' th' field?
Mess. They are.
You bear a charge there too.
Jailer. I'll away straight.
I must ev'n leave you here.
Doctor. Nay, we'll go with you.
I will not lose the sight.
Jailer. How did you like her?
Doctor. I'll warrant you within these three or four days
I'll make her right again. You must not from her,
But still preserve her in this way.
Wooer. I will.
Doctor. Let's get her in.
Wooer. Come, sweet, we'll go to dinner,
And then we'll play at cards.
Daugh. And shall we kiss too?
Wooer. A hundred times.
Daugh. And twenty?
Wooer. Ay, and twenty.
Daugh. And then we'll sleep together?
Doctor. Take her offer.
Wooer. Yes, marry, will we.
Daugh. But you shall not hurt me.
Wooer. I will not, sweet.
Daugh. If you do, love, I'll cry. *Exeunt.*

Scene III. [*A part of the Forest near Athens, and near the place appointed for the combat.*]

Flourish. Enter *Theseus, Hippolyta, Emilia, Pirithous,* and some *Attendants.*

Emil. I'll no step further.
Pir. Will you lose this sight?
Emil. I had rather see a wren hawk at a fly
Than this decision. Ev'ry blow that falls
Threats a brave life; each stroke laments
The place whereon it falls, and sounds more like
A bell than blade. I will stay here.
It is enough, my hearing shall be punish'd
With what shall happen — 'gainst the which there is
No deafing — but to hear, not taint mine eye
With dread sights it may shun.
Pir. Sir, my good lord,
Your sister will no further.
Thes. O, she must.
She shall see deeds of honour in their kind
Which sometime show well, pencill'd. Nature now
Shall make and act the story, the belief
Both seal'd with eye and ear. You must be present;
You are the victor's meed, the price and garland
To crown the questant's title.
Emil. Pardon me.
If I were there, I'ld wink.
Thes. You must be there.
This trial is as 'twere i' th' night, and you
The only star to shine.
Emil. I am extinct.
There is but envy in that light which shows
The one the other. Darkness, which ever was
The dam of Horror, who does stand accurs'd
Of many mortal millions, may even now,
By casting her black mantle over both,
That neither could find other, get herself
Some part of a good name, and many a murther
Set off whereto she's guilty.
Hip. You must go.
Emil. In faith, I will not.
Thes. Why, the knights must kindle
Their valour at your eye. Know, of this war

You are the treasure, and must needs be by
To give the service pay.
Emil. Sir, pardon me.
The title of a kingdom may be tried
Out of itself.
Thes. Well, well, then, at your pleasure.
Those that remain with you could wish their office
To any of their enemies.
Hip. Farewell, sister.
I am like to know your husband fore yourself
By some small start of time. He whom the gods
Do of the two know best, I pray them he
Be made your lot.
Exeunt [all except Emilia and some Attendants].
Emil. Arcite is gently visag'd; yet his eye
Is like an engine bent, or a sharp weapon
In a soft sheath; mercy and manly courage
Are bedfellows in his visage. Palamon
Has a most menacing aspect; his brow
Is grav'd and seems to bury what it frowns on:
Yet sometime 'tis not so, but alters to
The quality of his thoughts; long time his eye
Will dwell upon his object; melancholy
Becomes him nobly. So does Arcite's mirth;
But Palamon's sadness is a kind of mirth,
So mingled as if mirth did make him sad,
And sadness merry. Those darker humours that
Stick misbecomingly on others, on him
Live in fair dwelling.
Cornets. Trumpets sound as to a charge.
Hark, how yon spurs to spirit do incite
The princes to their proof! Arcite may win me;
And yet may Palamon wound Arcite to
The spoiling of his figure. O, what pity
Enough for such a chance! If I were by,
I might do hurt; for they would glance their eyes
Toward my seat, and in that motion might
Omit a ward, or forfeit an offence,
Which crav'd that very time. It is much better
I am not there. O, better never born
Than minister to such harm!

Enter a *Servant.*

What is the chance?
Serv. The cry's 'A Palamon!'
Emil. Then he has won. 'Twas ever likely:
He look'd all grace and success, and he is
Doubtless the prim'st of men. I prithee run
And tell me how it goes.
Shout and cornets. Crying 'A Palamon!' [*within*].
Serv. Still 'Palamon!'
Emil. Run and enquire.
[*Exit Servant.*]
Poor servant, thou hast lost.
Upon my right side still I wore thy picture,
Palamon's on the left. Why so, I know not.
I had no end in't else; chance would have it so.
On the sinister side the heart lies; Palamon
Had the best-boding chance.
Another cry, and shout within, and cornets.
This burst of clamour
Is sure the end o' th' combat.

Enter *Servant.*

Serv. They said that Palamon had Arcite's body
Within an inch o' th' pyramid, that the cry
Was general 'A Palamon!' but anon
Th' assistants made a brave redemption, and
The two bold titlers at this instant are
Hand to hand at it.
Emil. Were they metamorphis'd
Both into one — O, why? there were no woman
Worth so compos'd a man! Their single share,
Their nobleness peculiar to them, gives
The prejudice of disparity, value's shortness,
To any lady breathing.
Cornets. Cry within, 'Arcite, Arcite!'
More exulting?
'Palamon' still?
Serv. Nay, now the sound is 'Arcite.'
Emil. I prithee lay attention to the cry;
Set both thine ears to th' business.
Cornets. A great shout and cry, 'Arcite! victory!'
Serv. The cry is
'Arcite!' and 'victory!' Hark: 'Arcite! victory!'
The combat's consummation is proclaim'd
By the wind instruments.
Emil. Half-sights saw
That Arcite was no babe. God's lid! his richness
And costliness of spirit look'd through him; it could
No more be hid in him than fire in flax,
Than humble banks can go to law with waters
That drift-winds force to raging. I did think
Good Palamon would miscarry; yet I knew not
Why I did think so. Our reasons are not prophets
When oft our fancies are. They are coming off.
Alas, poor Palamon! *Cornets.*

Enter *Theseus, Hippolyta, Pirithous, Arcite* as victor, and *Attendants*, &c.

Thes. Lo where our sister is in expectation,
Yet quaking and unsettled. Fairest Emily,
The gods by their divine arbitrement
Have given you this knight: he is a good one
As ever struck at head. Give me your hands.
Receive you her, you him; be plighted with
A love that grows as you decay.
Arc. Emily,
To buy you I have lost what's dearest to me
Save what is bought; and yet I purchase cheaply,
As I do rate your value.
Thes. O loved sister,
He speaks now of as brave a knight as e'er
Did spur a noble steed. Surely the gods
Would have him die a bachelor, lest his race
Should show i' th' world too godlike. His behaviour
So charm'd me that methought Alcides was
To him a sow of lead. If I could praise
Each part of him to th' all I have spoke, your Arcite
Did not lose by't; for he that was thus good
Encount'red yet his better. I have heard
Two emulous Philomels beat the ear o' th' night
With their contentious throats, now one the higher,
Anon the other, then again the first,
And by-and-by outbreasted, that the sense
Could not be judge between 'em. So it far'd
Good space between these kinsmen; till heavens did
Make hardly one the winner. — Wear the garland
With joy that you have won. — For the subdu'd,
Give them our present justice, since I know
Their lives but pinch 'em. Let it here be done.
The scene's not for our seeing; go we hence,
Right joyful, with some sorrow. — Arm your prize;
I know you will not lose her. — Hippolyta,
I see one eye of yours conceives a tear,
The which it will deliver.
Emil. Is this winning?
O all you heavenly powers, where is your mercy?
But that your wills have said it must be so,
And charge me live to comfort this unfriended,
This miserable prince, that cuts away
A life more worthy from him than all women,
I should and would die too.
Hip. Infinite pity
That four such eyes should be so fix'd on one
That two must needs be blind for't!
Thes. So it is.
Flourish. Exeunt.

Scene IV. [*The same. A block ready.*]

Enter *Palamon* and his *Knights* pinion'd, *Jailer, Executioner, &c., Guard.*

Pal. There's many a man alive that hath outliv'd
The love o' th' people; yea, i' th' selfsame state
Stands many a father with his child. Some comfort
We have by so considering: we expire,
And not without men's pity; to live still
Have their good wishes; we prevent
The loathsome misery of age, beguile
The gout and rheum, that in lag hours attend
For grey approachers; we come towards the gods,
Young and unwapper'd, not halting under crimes
Many and stale. That sure shall please the gods
Sooner than such, to give us nectar with 'em,
For we are more clear spirits. My dear kinsmen,
Whose lives for this poor comfort are laid down,
You have sold 'em too too cheap.
1. Knight. What ending could be
Of more content? O'er us the victors have
Fortune, whose title is as momentary
As to us death is certain. A grain of honour
They not o'erweigh us.
2. Knight. Let us bid farewell;
And with our patience anger tott'ring Fortune,
Who, at her certain'st, reels.
3. Knight. Come. Who begins?
Pal. Ev'n he that led you to this banquet shall
Taste to you all. Ah, ha, my friend, my friend!
Your gentle daughter gave me freedom once;
You'll see't done now for ever. Pray, how does she?
I heard she was not well; her kind of ill
Gave me some sorrow.
Jailer. Sir, she's well restor'd,
And to be married shortly.
Pal. By my short life,
I am most glad on't. 'Tis the latest thing

I shall be glad of. Prithee tell her so;
Commend me to her, and, to piece her portion,
Tender her this. [*Gives purse.*]
1. Knight. Nay, let's be offerers all.
2. Knight. Is it a maid?
Pal. Verily I think so;
A right good creature, more to me deserving
Than I can quite or speak of.
All Knights. Commend us to her.
They give their purses.
Jailer. The gods requite you all, and make her thankful!
Pal. Adieu; and let my life be now as short
As my leave-taking. *Lies on the block.*
1. Knight. Lead, courageous cousin.
All Knights. We'll follow cheerfully.
A great noise within crying 'Run! Save! Hold!'

Enter in haste a *Messenger.*

Mess. Hold, hold! O, hold, hold, hold!

Enter *Pirithous* in haste.

Pir. Hold, ho! It is a cursed haste you made
If you have done so quickly. — Noble Palamon,
The gods will show their glory in a life
That thou art yet to lead.
Pal. Can that be when
Venus I have said is false? How do things fare?
Pir. Arise, great sir, and give the tidings ear [*Palamon rises.*]
That are most dearly sweet and bitter.
Pal. What
Hath wak'd us from our dream?
Pir. List then. Your cousin,
Mounted upon a steed that Emily
Did first bestow on him — a black one, owing
Not a hair-worth of white, which some will say
Weakens his price, and many will not buy
His goodness with this note; which superstition
Here finds allowance — on this horse is Arcite
Trotting the stones of Athens, which the calkins
Did rather tell than trample; for the horse
Would make his length a mile, if't pleas'd his rider
To put pride in him. As he thus went counting
The flinty pavement, dancing as 'twere to th' music
His own hoofs made (for, as they say, from iron
Came music's origin), what envious flint,
Cold as old Saturn, and like him possess'd
With fire malevolent, darted a spark,
Or what fierce sulphur else, to this end made,
I comment not — the hot horse, hot as fire,
Took toy at this, and fell to what disorder
His power could give his will, bounds, comes on end,
Forgets school-doing, being therein train'd
And of kind manage; pig-like he whines
At the sharp rowel, which he frets at rather
Than any jot obeys; seeks all foul means
Of boist'rous and rough jad'ry, to disseat
His lord that kept it bravely. When naught serv'd,
When neither curb would crack, girth break, nor diff'ring plunges
Disroot his rider whence he grew, but that
He kept him 'tween his legs, on his hind hoofs
On end he stands,
That Arcite's legs, being higher than his head,
Seem'd with strange art to hang. His victor's wreath
Even then fell off his head; and presently
Backward the jade comes o'er, and his full poise
Becomes the rider's load. Yet is he living;
But such a vessel 'tis that floats but for
The surge that next approaches. He much desires
To have some speech with you. Lo, he appears.

Enter *Theseus, Hippolyta, Emilia, Arcite* in a chair.

Pal. O miserable end of our alliance!
The gods are mighty. Arcite, if thy heart,
Thy worthy, manly heart, be yet unbroken,
Give me thy last words. I am Palamon,
One that yet loves thee dying.
Arc. Take Emilia,
And with her all the world's joy. Reach thy hand.
Farewell; I have told my last hour. I was false,
Yet never treacherous. Forgive me, cousin.
One kiss from fair Emilia. — 'Tis done.
Take her. I die. [*Dies.*]
Pal. Thy brave soul seek Elysium!
Emil. I'll close thine eyes, prince; blessed souls be with thee!
Thou art a right good man; and while I live,
This day I give to tears.
Pal. And I to honour.
Thes. In this place first you fought; ev'n very here
I sund'red you. Acknowledge to the gods
Your thanks that you are living.
His part is play'd, and, though it were too short,
He did it well; your day is length'ned, and
The blissful dew of heaven does arrose you.

The powerful Venus well hath grac'd her altar,
And given you your love. Our master Mars
Hath vouch'd his oracle, and to Arcite gave
The grace of the contention. So the deities
Have show'd due justice. — Bear this hence.
[*Arcite is carried out.*]

Pal. O cousin,
That we should things desire which do cost us
The loss of our desire! that naught could buy
Dear love but loss of dear love!

Thes. Never fortune
Did play a subtler game. The conquer'd triumphs,
The victor has the loss; yet in the passage
The gods have been most equal. Palamon,
Your kinsman hath confess'd the right o' th' lady
Did lie in you; for you first saw her, and
Even then proclaim'd your fancy. He restor'd her
As your stol'n jewel, and desir'd your spirit
To send him hence forgiven. The gods my justice
Take from my hand, and they themselves become
The executioners. Lead your lady off;
And call your lovers from the stage of death,
Whom I adopt my friends. A day or two
Let us look sadly and give grace unto
The funeral of Arcite; in whose end
The visages of bridegrooms we'll put on
And smile with Palamon; for whom an hour,
But one hour since, I was as dearly sorry
As glad of Arcite, and am now as glad
As for him sorry. O you heavenly charmers,
What things you make of us! For what we lack
We laugh, for what we have are sorry; still
Are children in some kind. Let us be thankful
For that which is, and with you leave dispute
That are above our question. Let's go off,
And bear us like the time. *Flourish. Exeunt.*

EPILOGUE.

I would now ask ye how ye like the play;
But, as it is with schoolboys, cannot say.
I am cruel fearful. Pray yet stay a while,
And let me look upon ye. No man smile?
Then it goes hard, I see. He that has
Lov'd a young handsome wench, then, show his face —
'Tis strange if none be here — and, if he will
Against his conscience, let him hiss, and kill
Our market. 'Tis in vain, I see, to stay ye.
Have at the worst can come, then! Now what say ye?
And yet mistake me not. I am not bold;
We have no such cause. If the tale we have told
(For 'tis no other) any way content ye
(For to that honest purpose it was meant ye),
We have our end; and ye shall have ere long,
I dare say, many a better, to prolong
Your old loves to us. We and all our might
Rest at your service. Gentlemen, good night.
Flourish.

VENUS AND ADONIS AND LUCRECE

VENUS AND ADONIS was entered in the Stationers' Register by Richard Field on April 18, 1593, and the First Quarto was printed by him in the same year. This is the authority for the text. Nine other editions appeared before Shakespeare's death in 1616 and several others came out during the first half of the seventeenth century.

The poem was much admired. Meres who, in his *Palladis Tamia* (1598), praises Shakespeare for his comedies and tragedies (see p. 33, above), declares that 'the sweete wittie soule of *Ouid* liues in mellifluous & hony-tongued *Shakespeare*, witness his *Venus and Adonis*, his *Lucrece*, his sugred Sonnets among his priuate friends.' John Weever celebrates it (along with *Lucrece*, *Romeo and Juliet*, and '*Richard*') in an address to 'honie-tong'd Shakespeare' in his *Epigrammes* (1599). Gabriel Harvey testifies that 'the younger sort takes much delight in Shakespeares Venus, & Adonis: but his Lucrece, & his tragedie of Hamlet . . . haue it in them, to please the wiser sort' (see p. 1145, above). 'I'le worshipp sweet Mr. Shakspeare,' says Gullio in the Cambridge play *The Return from Parnassus*, 'and to honoure him will lay his Venus and Adonis under my pillowe' (Part I: *ca.* 1599).

When the poem was written we do not know. In the dedication Shakespeare calls it 'the first heir of my invention,' but these words by no means imply that it was the first thing he had ever written. Before 1593 he had certainly done a good deal of dramatic composition (see p. 746). None of his work, however, had been published when VENUS AND ADONIS appeared. That the poem abounds in rural imagery is no proof that he wrote it before he left Stratford, for the scene is laid in the woods and fields. Probably it was written not long before the date of publication, perhaps in 1592.

Shakespeare undoubtedly read the story of Adonis at school, for Ovid's *Metamorphoses*, which tells it (x, 520–559, 705–739), was in every schoolboy's hand (cf. *Titus Andronicus*, iv, 1, 41–42). It is not necessary to appeal to Golding's English translation of the *Metamorphoses* (1567). The Latin motto in the title page of VENUS AND ADONIS comes from Ovid's *Amores* (i, 15, 35–36). The reluctance of Adonis is taken from Ovid's story of Hermaphroditus (iv, 316 ff.) and from that of Narcissus and Echo (iii, 356 ff.). In this feature perhaps Shakespeare was also influenced by Lodge's *Scilla's Metamorphosis* (1589), which has the same form of stanza as VENUS AND ADONIS. This stanza, however, was common at the time. Shakespeare uses it in *Love's Labour's Lost*, i, 1, 150–162. The story of Narcissus is mentioned in LUCRECE, 265–266.

The Quarto of LUCRECE, as the title page styles the poem, though the title heading is THE RAPE OF LUCRECE, came out in 1594. It had been registered on May 9 of that year. Four other editions appeared before 1616. The text of the Quarto is authoritative.

In the dedication to VENUS AND ADONIS, Shakespeare had 'vowed to take advantage of all idle hours' for 'some graver labour.' LUCRECE was the fulfilment of his pledge. It was probably written in 1593 or 1594. That it was regarded by contemporaries as indeed a graver and more solid piece of work is shown by Harvey's note (quoted above).

The seven-line stanza (known as 'rhyme royal') had long been a favourite form with English poets. Chaucer had used it in four of his *Canterbury Tales* and with extraordinary skill and variety in his *Troilus*, with which Shakespeare was familiar. Lydgate had adopted it for his *Falls of Princes*, once a highly esteemed performance. Sixteenth-century critics regarded this stanza as peculiarly fit 'for grave discourses.' Spenser adopted it for *The Ruines of Time* (1590) and Daniel for *The Complaint of Rosamond* (1592). There are some echoes of Daniel's phraseology in Shakespeare's poem, and Lucrece's study of the painting which figures the Trojan war (1366 ff.) may have been suggested by a similar incident in the *Rosamond*. In describing the picture Shakespeare doubtless had in mind the paintings on the walls of Dido's temple (Æneid, ii, 453 ff.).

The sources of LUCRECE were naturally Livy (i, 57–60) and Ovid (*Fasti*, ii, 721–852). Painter, in *The Palace of Pleasure* (1566) had published a rather close translation of Livy's story, but Shakespeare owes nothing to Painter. He could read Livy for himself. His version, indeed, serves to correct a mistake in Painter, whose 'from whence he [Brutus] should conceive that determination' is a blundering rendition of 'unde novum in Bruti pectore ingenium.' Shakespeare's words about Brutus's assumed idiocy (1807–1820) show that he understood the passage. It is possible that he had read the story in Belleforest's *Histoires Tragiques*, or in Bandello, whom Belleforest translated, but Livy (i, 56) and Ovid (ii, 717) gave him all information about Brutus's stratagem that he needed. Livy's description of Brutus as 'ludibrium verius quam comes' to the Tarquins is expanded in verses 1811–1813 of LUCRECE.

Livy's 'addit ad metum dedecus' appears in verse 516 as 'To kill thine honour with thy live's decay.' His 'Nec ulla deinde inpudica Lucretiae exemplo vivet' is rendered in verses 1714–1715 by

> 'No, no!' quoth she. 'No dame hereafter living
> By my excuse shall claim excuse's giving.'

Cf. also with verses 1619–1621 Livy's 'Vestigia viri alieni, Conlatine, in lecto sunt tuo.' Many suggestions are also taken from Ovid. The first stanza reflects one of his elegiac couplets (761–762):

> Interea iuvenis furiales regius ignis
> Concipit et caeco raptus amore furit.

Brutus's oath 'by chaste Lucrece' soul' (1839) is Ovid's 'per tuos manes' (842). His 'Ter conata loqui, ter destitit' (823) appears in verses 1604–1605. The metaphor of the wolf and the lamb (677) comes from Ovid (799–800). The long and eloquent passage describing Tarquin's revulsion of feeling (689 ff.) may have been suggested by Ovid (811–812):

> Quid, victor, gaudes? Haec te victoria perdet.
> Heu quanto regnis nox stetit una tuis!

It is altogether probable that Shakespeare knew Chaucer's *Legend of Good Women*, in which the story of Lucretia is told in strict accordance with Ovid's *Fasti*; but LUCRECE owes nothing to Chaucer.

VENUS AND ADONIS

Vilia miretur vulgus: mihi flavus Apollo
Pocula Castalia plena ministret aqua.

TO THE

RIGHT HONOURABLE HENRY WRIOTHESLEY,

EARL OF SOUTHAMPTON, AND BARON OF TITCHFIELD.

RIGHT HONOURABLE,

I know not how I shall offend in dedicating my unpolish'd lines to your Lordship, nor how the world will censure me for choosing so strong a prop to support so weak a burthen; only, if your Honour seem but pleased, I account myself highly praised, and vow to take advantage of all idle hours till I have honoured you with some graver labour. But if the first heir of my invention prove deformed, I shall be sorry it had so noble a godfather, and never after ear so barren a land, for fear it yield me still so bad a harvest. I leave it to your honourable survey, and your Honour to your heart's content; which I wish may always answer your own wish and the world's hopeful expectation.

Your Honour's in all duty,

WILLIAM SHAKESPEARE.

Even as the sun with purple-colour'd face
Had ta'en his last leave of the weeping morn,
Rose-cheek'd Adonis hied him to the chase.
Hunting he lov'd, but love he laugh'd to scorn.
Sick-thoughted Venus makes amain unto him
And like a bold-fac'd suitor gins to woo him.

'Thrice fairer than myself,' thus she began,
'The field's chief flower, sweet above compare,
Stain to all nymphs, more lovely than a man,
More white and red than doves or roses are,
Nature that made thee, with herself at strife,
Saith that the world hath ending with thy life.

'Vouchsafe, thou wonder, to alight thy steed
And rein his proud head to the saddlebow.
If thou wilt deign this favour, for thy meed
A thousand honey secrets shalt thou know.
Here come and sit, where never serpent hisses,
And being set, I'll smother thee with kisses,

'And yet not cloy thy lips with loath'd satiety,
But rather famish them amid their plenty,
Making them red and pale with fresh variety —
Ten kisses short as one, one long as twenty.
A summer's day will seem an hour but short,
Being wasted in such time-beguiling sport.'

With this she seizeth on his sweating palm,
The precedent of pith and livelihood,
And, trembling in her passion, calls it balm,
Earth's sovereign salve to do a goddess good.
Being so enrag'd, desire doth lend her force
Courageously to pluck him from his horse.

Over one arm the lusty courser's rein,
Under her other was the tender boy,
Who blush'd and pouted in a dull disdain,
With leaden appetite, unapt to toy;
She red and hot as coals of glowing fire,
He red for shame, but frosty in desire.

The studded bridle on a ragged bough
Nimbly she fastens. O, how quick is love!
The steed is stalled up, and even now
To tie the rider she begins to prove.
Backward she push'd him, as she would be thrust,
And govern'd him in strength, though not in lust.

So soon was she along as he was down,
Each leaning on their elbows and their hips.
Now doth she stroke his cheek, now doth he frown
And gins to chide; but soon she stops his lips
And kissing speaks, with lustful language broken:
'If thou wilt chide, thy lips shall never open.'

He burns with bashful shame; she with her tears
Doth quench the maiden burning of his cheeks.
Then with her windy sighs and golden hairs
To fan and blow them dry again she seeks.
He saith she is immodest, blames her miss;
What follows more she murthers with a kiss.

Even as an empty eagle, sharp by fast,
Tires with her beak on feathers, flesh, and bone,
Shaking her wings, devouring all in haste,
Till either gorge be stuff'd or prey be gone —

Even so she kiss'd his brow, his cheek, his chin,
And where she ends she doth anew begin.

Forc'd to content, but never to obey,
Panting he lies and breatheth in her face.
She feedeth on the steam as on a prey
And calls it heavenly moisture, air of grace;
Wishing her cheeks were gardens full of flowers,
So they were dew'd with such distilling showers.

Look how a bird lies tangled in a net,
So fast'ned in her arms Adonis lies.
Pure shame and aw'd resistance made him fret,
Which bred more beauty in his angry eyes.
Rain added to a river that is rank
Perforce will force it overflow the bank.

Still she entreats, and prettily entreats,
For to a pretty ear she tunes her tale.
Still is he sullen, still he low'rs and frets,
'Twixt crimson shame and anger ashy-pale.
Being red, she loves him best; and being white,
Her best is better'd with a more delight.

Look how he can, she cannot choose but love;
And by her fair immortal hand she swears
From his soft bosom never to remove
Till he take truce with her contending tears,
Which long have rain'd, making her cheeks all wet;
And one sweet kiss shall pay this comptless debt.

Upon this promise did he raise his chin,
Like a divedapper peering through a wave,
Who, being look'd on, ducks as quickly in.
So offers he to give what she did crave;
But when her lips were ready for his pay,
He winks and turns his lips another way.

Never did passenger in summer's heat
More thirst for drink than she for this good turn.
Her help she sees, but help she cannot get;
She bathes in water, yet her fire must burn.
'O, pity,' gan she cry, 'flint-hearted boy!
'Tis but a kiss I beg. Why art thou coy?

'I have been wooed, as I entreat thee now,
Even by the stern and direful god of war,
Whose sinewy neck in battle ne'er did bow,
Who conquers where he comes in every jar;
Yet hath he been my captive and my slave
And begg'd for that which thou unask'd shalt have.

'Over my altars hath he hung his lance,
His batt'red shield, his uncontrolled crest,
And for my sake hath learn'd to sport and dance,
To toy, to wanton, dally, smile, and jest,
Scorning his churlish drum and ensign red,
Making my arms his field, his tent my bed.

'Thus he that overrul'd I overswayed,
Leading him prisoner in a red-rose chain.
Strong-temper'd steel his stronger strength obeyed;
Yet was he servile to my coy disdain.
O, be not proud, nor brag not of thy might,
For mast'ring her that foil'd the god of fight!

'Touch but my lips with those fair lips of thine—
Though mine be not so fair, yet are they red—
The kiss shall be thine own as well as mine.
What see'st thou in the ground? Hold up thy head.
Look in mine eyeballs; there thy beauty lies.
Then why not lips on lips, since eyes in eyes?

'Art thou asham'd to kiss? Then wink again,
And I will wink. So shall the day seem night.
Love keeps his revels where there are but twain.
Be bold to play; our sport is not in sight.
These blue-vein'd violets whereon we lean
Never can blab, nor know not what we mean.

'The tender spring upon thy tempting lip
Shows thee unripe; yet mayst thou well be tasted.
Make use of time, let not advantage slip;
Beauty within itself should not be wasted.
Fair flowers that are not gath'red in their prime
Rot and consume themselves in little time.

'Were I hard-favour'd, foul, or wrinkled old,
Ill-nurtur'd, crooked, churlish, harsh in voice,
O'erworn, despised, rheumatic, and cold,
Thick-sighted, barren, lean and lacking juice,
Then mightst thou pause, for then I were not for thee;
But having no defects, why dost abhor me?

'Thou canst not see one wrinkle in my brow;
Mine eyes are grey and bright and quick in turning;

My beauty as the spring doth yearly grow,
My flesh is soft and plump, my marrow burning;
My smooth moist hand, were it with thy hand felt,
Would in thy palm dissolve or seem to melt.

'Bid me discourse, I will enchant thine ear,
Or, like a fairy, trip upon the green,
Or, like a nymph, with long dishevelled hair,
Dance on the sands, and yet no footing seen.
Love is a spirit all compact of fire,
Not gross to sink, but light, and will aspire.

'Witness this primrose bank whereon I lie;
These forceless flowers like sturdy trees support me.
Two strengthless doves will draw me through the sky
From morn till night, even where I list to sport me.
Is love so light, sweet boy, and may it be
That thou should think it heavy unto thee?

'Is thine own heart to thine own face affected?
Can thy right hand seize love upon thy left?
Then woo thyself, be of thyself rejected;
Steal thine own freedom, and complain on theft.
Narcissus so himself himself forsook,
And died to kiss his shadow in the brook.

'Torches are made to light, jewels to wear,
Dainties to taste, fresh beauty for the use,
Herbs for their smell, and sappy plants to bear.
Things growing to themselves are growth's abuse.
Seeds spring from seeds, and beauty breedeth beauty.
Thou wast begot; to get it is thy duty.

'Upon the earth's increase why shouldst thou feed
Unless the earth with thy increase be fed?
By law of nature thou art bound to breed,
That thine may live when thou thyself art dead;
And so, in spite of death, thou dost survive,
In that thy likeness still is left alive.'

By this, the lovesick queen began to sweat,
For where they lay the shadow had forsook them,
And Titan, tired in the midday heat,
With burning eye did hotly overlook them,
Wishing Adonis had his team to guide,
So he were like him, and by Venus' side.

And now Adonis, with a lazy sprite,
And with a heavy, dark, disliking eye,
His low'ring brows o'erwhelming his fair sight,
Like misty vapours when they blot the sky,
Souring his cheeks, cries, 'Fie, no more of love!
The sun doth burn my face. I must remove.'

'Ay me!' quoth Venus, 'young, and so unkind?
What bare excuses mak'st thou to be gone!
I'll sigh celestial breath, whose gentle wind
Shall cool the heat of this descending sun.
I'll make a shadow for thee of my hairs.
If they burn too, I'll quench them with my tears.

'The sun that shines from heaven shines but warm;
And, lo, I lie between that sun and thee.
The heat I have from thence doth little harm;
Thine eye darts forth the fire that burneth me,
And were I not immortal, life were done
Between this heavenly and earthly sun.

'Art thou obdurate, flinty, hard as steel?
Nay, more than flint, for stone at rain relenteth.
Art thou a woman's son, and canst not feel
What 'tis to love? how want of love tormenteth?
O, had thy mother borne so hard a mind,
She had not brought forth thee, but died unkind!

'What am I that thou shouldst contemn me this?
Or what great danger dwells upon my suit?
What were thy lips the worse for one poor kiss?
Speak, fair! but speak fair words, or else be mute.
Give me one kiss, I'll give it thee again,
And one for int'rest, if thou wilt have twain.

'Fie, liveless picture, cold and senseless stone,
Well-painted idol, image dull and dead,
Statue contenting but the eye alone,
Thing like a man, but of no woman bred!
Thou art no man, though of a man's complexion,
For men will kiss even by their own direction.'

This said, impatience chokes her pleading tongue,
And swelling passion doth provoke a pause;
Red cheeks and fiery eyes blaze forth her wrong;
Being judge in love, she cannot right her cause.

And now she weeps, and now she fain would speak,
And now her sobs do her intendments break.

Sometime she shakes her head, and then his hand;
Now gazeth she on him, now on the ground;
Sometime her arms infold him like a band —
She would, he will not in her arms be bound;
And when from thence he struggles to be gone,
She locks her lily fingers one in one.

'Fondling,' she saith, 'since I have hemm'd thee here
Within the circuit of this ivory pale,
I'll be a park, and thou shalt be my deer;
Feed where thou wilt, on mountain or in dale;
Graze on my lips; and if those hills be dry,
Stray lower, where the pleasant fountains lie.

'Within this limit is relief enough,
Sweet bottom-grass, and high delightful plain,
Round rising hillocks, brakes obscure and rough,
To shelter thee from tempest and from rain.
Then be my deer, since I am such a park.
No dog shall rouse thee, though a thousand bark.'

At this Adonis smiles as in disdain,
That in each cheek appears a pretty dimple.
Love made those hollows, if himself were slain,
He might be buried in a tomb so simple,
Foreknowing well, if there he came to lie,
Why, there Love liv'd, and there he could not die.

These lovely caves, these round enchanting pits,
Open'd their mouths to swallow Venus' liking.
Being mad before, how doth she now for wits?
Struck dead at first, what needs a second striking?
Poor queen of love, in thine own law forlorn,
To love a cheek that smiles at thee in scorn!

Now which way shall she turn? what shall she say?
Her words are done, her woes the more increasing;
The time is spent, her object will away,
And from her twining arms doth urge releasing.
'Pity!' she cries, 'some favour, some remorse!'
Away he springs and hasteth to his horse.

But, lo, from forth a copse that neighbours by
A breeding jennet, lusty, young, and proud,
Adonis' trampling courser doth espy,
And forth she rushes, snorts, and neighs aloud.
The strong-neck'd steed, being tied unto a tree,
Breaketh his rein, and to her straight goes he.

Imperiously he leaps, he neighs, he bounds,
And now his woven girths he breaks asunder;
The bearing earth with his hard hoof he wounds,
Whose hollow womb resounds like heaven's thunder;
The iron bit he crusheth 'tween his teeth,
Controlling what he was controlled with.

His ears up-prick'd; his braided hanging mane
Upon his compass'd crest now stand on end;
His nostrils drink the air, and forth again,
As from a furnace, vapours doth he send;
His eye, which scornfully glisters like fire,
Shows his hot courage and his high desire.

Sometime he trots, as if he told the steps,
With gentle majesty and modest pride;
Anon he rears upright, curvets, and leaps,
As who should say, 'Lo, thus my strength is tried,
And this I do to captivate the eye
Of the fair breeder that is standing by.'

What recketh he his rider's angry stir,
His flattering 'Holla' or his 'Stand, I say'?
What cares he now for curb or pricking spur?
For rich caparisons or trappings gay?
He sees his love, and nothing else he sees,
For nothing else with his proud sight agrees.

Look, when a painter would surpass the life
In limning out a well-proportioned steed,
His art with nature's workmanship at strife,
As if the dead the living should exceed —
So did this horse excel a common one
In shape, in courage, colour, pace, and bone.

Round-hoof'd, short-jointed, fetlocks shag and long,
Broad breast, full eye, small head, and nostril wide,
High crest, short ears, straight legs and passing strong,
Thin mane, thick tail, broad buttock, tender hide:
Look, what a horse should have he did not lack,
Save a proud rider on so proud a back.

Sometime he scuds far off, and there he stares;
Anon he starts at stirring of a feather;

To bid the wind a base he now prepares,
And whe'r he run or fly they know not whether,
For through his mane and tail the high wind sings,
Fanning the hairs, who wave like feath'red wings.

He looks upon his love and neighs unto her;
She answers him, as if she knew his mind.
Being proud, as females are, to see him woo her,
She puts on outward strangeness, seems unkind,
Spurns at his love and scorns the heat he feels,
Beating his kind embracements with her heels.

Then, like a melancholy malcontent,
He vails his tail, that, like a falling plume,
Cool shadow to his melting buttock lent;
He stamps, and bites the poor flies in his fume.
His love, perceiving how he is enrag'd,
Grew kinder, and his fury was assuag'd.

His testy master goeth about to take him,
When, lo, the unback'd breeder, full of fear,
Jealous of catching, swiftly doth forsake him,
With her the horse, and left Adonis there.
As they were mad, unto the wood they hie them,
Outstripping crows that strive to overfly them.

All swol'n with chafing, down Adonis sits,
Banning his boist'rous and unruly beast;
And now the happy season once more fits
That lovesick Love by pleading may be blest;
For lovers say the heart hath treble wrong
When it is barr'd the aidance of the tongue.

An oven that is stopp'd, or river stay'd,
Burneth more hotly, swelleth with more rage;
So of concealed sorrow may be said:
Free vent of words love's fire doth assuage;
But when the heart's attorney once is mute,
The client breaks, as desperate in his suit.

He sees her coming and begins to glow,
Even as a dying coal revives with wind,
And with his bonnet hides his angry brow,
Looks on the dull earth with disturbed mind,
Taking no notice that she is so nigh,
For all askance he holds her in his eye.

O, what a sight it was, wistly to view
How she came stealing to the wayward boy!
To note the fighting conflict of her hue,
How white and red each other did destroy!
But now her cheek was pale, and by-and-by
It flash'd forth fire, as lightning from the sky.

Now was she just before him as he sat,
And like a lowly lover down she kneels;
With one fair hand she heaveth up his hat,
Her other tender hand his fair cheek feels.
His tend'rer cheek receives her soft hand's print
As apt as new-fall'n snow takes any dint.

O, what a war of looks was then between them,
Her eyes petitioners to his eyes suing!
His eyes saw her eyes as they had not seen them;
Her eyes wooed still, his eyes disdain'd the wooing;
And all this dumb play had his acts made plain
With tears which chorus-like her eyes did rain.

Full gently now she takes him by the hand,
A lily prison'd in a jail of snow,
Or ivory in an alablaster band —
So white a friend engirts so white a foe.
This beauteous combat, wilful and unwilling,
Showed like two silver doves that sit a-billing.

Once more the engine of her thoughts began:
'O fairest mover on this mortal round,
Would thou wert as I am, and I a man,
My heart all whole as thine, thy heart my wound!
For one sweet look thy help I would assure thee,
Though nothing but my body's bane would cure thee.'

'Give me my hand!' saith he. 'Why dost thou feel it?'
'Give me my heart,' saith she, 'and thou shalt have it.
O, give it me, lest thy hard heart do steel it,
And being steel'd, soft sighs can never grave it.
Then love's deep groans I never shall regard,
Because Adonis' heart hath made mine hard.'

'For shame!' he cries. 'Let go, and let me go!
My day's delight is past, my horse is gone,
And 'tis your fault I am bereft him so.
I pray you hence, and leave me here alone;
For all my mind, my thought, my busy care
Is how to get my palfrey from the mare.'

Thus she replies: 'Thy palfrey, as he should,
Welcomes the warm approach of sweet desire.

Affection is a coal that must be cool'd;
Else, suffer'd, it will set the heart on fire.
The sea hath bounds, but deep desire hath none;
Therefore no marvel though thy horse be gone.

'How like a jade he stood, tied to the tree,
Servilely master'd with a leathern rein!
But when he saw his love, his youth's fair fee,
He held such petty bondage in disdain,
Throwing the base thong from his bending crest,
Enfranchising his mouth, his back, his breast.

'Who sees his true-love in her naked bed,
Teaching the sheets a whiter hue than white,
But, when his glutton eye so full hath fed,
His other agents aim at like delight?
Who is so faint that dares not be so bold
To touch the fire, the weather being cold?

'Let me excuse thy courser, gentle boy;
And learn of him, I heartily beseech thee,
To take advantage on presented joy.
Though I were dumb, yet his proceedings teach thee.
O, learn to love! The lesson is but plain,
And once made perfect, never lost again.'

'I know not love,' quoth he, 'nor will not know it,
Unless it be a boar, and then I chase it.
'Tis much to borrow, and I will not owe it.
My love to love is love but to disgrace it;
For I have heard it is a life in death,
That laughs, and weeps, and all but with a breath.

'Who wears a garment shapeless and unfinish'd?
Who plucks the bud before one leaf put forth?
If springing things be any jot diminish'd,
They wither in their prime, prove nothing worth.
The colt that's back'd and burthen'd being young
Loseth his pride and never waxeth strong.

'You hurt my hand with wringing. Let us part,
And leave this idle theme, this bootless chat.
Remove your siege from my unyielding heart;
To love's alarms it will not ope the gate.
Dismiss your vows, your feigned tears, your flatt'ry;
For where a heart is hard they make no batt'ry.'

'What! canst thou talk?' quoth she. 'Hast thou a tongue?
O, would thou hadst not, or I had no hearing!
Thy mermaid's voice hath done me double wrong;
I had my load before, now press'd with bearing:
Melodious discord, heavenly tune harsh sounding,
Ear's deep-sweet music, and heart's deep-sore wounding.

'Had I no eyes but ears, my ears would love
That inward beauty and invisible;
Or were I deaf, thy outward parts would move
Each part in me that were but sensible.
Though neither eyes nor ears, to hear nor see,
Yet should I be in love by touching thee.

'Say that the sense of feeling were bereft me,
And that I could not see, nor hear, nor touch,
And nothing but the very smell were left me,
Yet would my love to thee be still as much;
For from the stillitory of thy face excelling
Comes breath perfum'd that breedeth love by smelling.

'But, O, what banquet wert thou to the taste,
Being nurse and feeder of the other four!
Would they not wish the feast might ever last
And bid Suspicion double-lock the door,
Lest Jealousy, that sour unwelcome guest,
Should by his stealing in disturb the feast?'

Once more the ruby-colour'd portal open'd
Which to his speech did honey passage yield;
Like a red morn, that ever yet betoken'd
Wrack to the seaman, tempest to the field,
Sorrow to shepherds, woe unto the birds,
Gusts and foul flaws to herdmen and to herds.

This ill presage advisedly she marketh.
Even as the wind is hush'd before it raineth,
Or as the wolf doth grin before he barketh,
Or as the berry breaks before it staineth,
Or like the deadly bullet of a gun,
His meaning struck her ere his words begun.

And at his look she flatly falleth down,
For looks kill love, and love by looks reviveth;
A smile recures the wounding of a frown.
But blessed bankrout that by love so thriveth!
The silly boy, believing she is dead,
Claps her pale cheek till clapping makes it red,

And all amaz'd brake off his late intent,
For sharply he did think to reprehend her,
Which cunning love did wittily prevent.
Fair fall the wit that can so well defend her!
For on the grass she lies as she were slain
Till his breath breatheth life in her again.

He wrings her nose, he strikes her on the cheeks,
He bends her fingers, holds her pulses hard,
He chafes her lips; a thousand ways he seeks
To mend the hurt that his unkindness marr'd.
He kisses her; and she, by her good will,
Will never rise, so he will kiss her still.

The night of sorrow now is turn'd to day:
Her two blue windows faintly she upheaveth,
Like the fair sun when in his fresh array
He cheers the morn and all the earth relieveth;
And as the bright sun glorifies the sky,
So is her face illumin'd with her eye;

Whose beams upon his hairless face are fix'd,
As if from thence they borrowed all their shine.
Were never four such lamps together mix'd,
Had not his clouded with his brow's repine;
But hers, which through the crystal tears gave light,
Shone like the moon in water seen by night.

'O, where am I?' quoth she, 'in earth or heaven,
Or in the ocean drench'd, or in the fire?
What hour is this? or morn or weary even?
Do I delight to die, or life desire?
But now I liv'd, and life was death's annoy;
But now I died, and death was lively joy.

'O, thou didst kill me! Kill me once again!
Thy eyes' shrowd tutor, that hard heart of thine,
Hath taught them scornful tricks, and such disdain
That they have mur'dred this poor heart of mine;
And these mine eyes, true leaders to their queen,
But for thy piteous lips no more had seen.

'Long may they kiss each other, for this cure!
O, never let their crimson liveries wear!
And as they last, their verdure still endure,
To drive infection from the dangerous year!
That the stargazers, having writ on death,
May say the plague is banish'd by thy breath.

'Pure lips, sweet seals in my soft lips imprinted,
What bargains may I make, still to be sealing?
To sell myself I can be well contented,
So thou wilt buy, and pay, and use good dealing;
Which purchase if thou make, for fear of slips
Set thy seal manual on my wax-red lips.

'A thousand kisses buys my heart from me;
And pay them at thy leisure, one by one.
What is ten hundred touches unto thee?
Are they not quickly told and quickly gone?
Say for nonpayment that the debt should double,
Is twenty hundred kisses such a trouble?'

'Fair queen,' quoth he, 'if any love you owe me,
Measure my strangeness with my unripe years.
Before I know myself, seek not to know me.
No fisher but the ungrown fry forbears.
The mellow plum doth fall, the green sticks fast,
Or being early pluck'd is sour to taste.

'Look, the world's comforter, with weary gait,
His day's hot task hath ended in the West;
The owl, night's herald, shrieks; 'tis very late;
The sheep are gone to fold, birds to their nest,
And coal-black clouds that shadow heaven's light
Do summon us to part and bid good night.

'Now let me say "Good night," and so say you.
If you will say so, you shall have a kiss.'
'Good night,' quoth she; and, ere he says 'Adieu,'
The honey fee of parting tend'red is:
Her arms do lend his neck a sweet embrace;
Incorporate then they seem; face grows to face;

Till breathless he disjoin'd, and backward drew
The heavenly moisture, that sweet coral mouth,
Whose precious taste her thirsty lips well knew,
Whereon they surfeit, yet complain on drouth.
He with her plenty press'd, she faint with dearth,
Their lips together glu'd, fall to the earth.

Now quick desire hath caught the yielding prey,
And glutton-like she feeds, yet never filleth.
Her lips are conquerors, his lips obey,
Paying what ransom the insulter willeth;
Whose vulture thought doth pitch the price so high
That she will draw his lips' rich treasure dry.

And having felt the sweetness of the spoil,
With blindfold fury she begins to forage.
Her face doth reek and smoke, her blood doth boil,
And careless lust stirs up a desperate courage,
Planting oblivion, beating reason back,
Forgetting shame's pure blush and honour's wrack.

Hot, faint, and weary with her hard embracing,
Like a wild bird being tam'd with too much handling,
Or as the fleet-foot roe that's tir'd with chasing,
Or like the froward infant still'd with dandling,
He now obeys and now no more resisteth,
While she takes all she can, not all she listeth.

What wax so frozen but dissolves with temp'ring
And yields at last to every light impression?
Things out of hope are compass'd oft with vent'ring,
Chiefly in love, whose leave exceeds commission.
Affection faints not like a pale-fac'd coward,
But then wooes best when most his choice is froward.

When he did frown, O, had she then gave over,
Such nectar from his lips she had not suck'd.
Foul words and frowns must not repel a lover.
What though the rose have prickles, yet 'tis pluck'd.
Were beauty under twenty locks kept fast,
Yet love breaks through and picks them all at last.

For pity now she can no more detain him.
The poor fool prays her that he may depart.
She is resolv'd no longer to restrain him;
Bids him farewell, and look well to her heart,
The which, by Cupid's bow she doth protest,
He carries thence incaged in his breast.

'Sweet boy,' she says, 'this night I'll waste in sorrow,
For my sick heart commands mine eyes to watch.
Tell me, love's master, shall we meet to-morrow?
Say, shall we? shall we? wilt thou make the match?'
He tells her no; to-morrow he intends
To hunt the boar with certain of his friends.

'The boar!' quoth she; whereat a sudden pale,
Like lawn being spread upon the blushing rose,
Usurps her cheek; she trembles at his tale,
And on his neck her yoking arms she throws;
She sinketh down, still hanging by his neck,
He on her belly falls, she on her back.

Now is she in the very lists of love,
Her champion mounted for the hot encounter.
All is imaginary she doth prove,
He will not manage her, although he mount her;
That worse than Tantalus' is her annoy,
To clip Elysium and to lack her joy.

Even so poor birds, deceiv'd with painted grapes,
Do surfeit by the eye and pine the maw;
Even so she languisheth in her mishaps
As those poor birds that helpless berries saw.
The warm effects which she in him finds missing
She seeks to kindle with continual kissing.

But all in vain. Good queen, it will not be!
She hath assay'd as much as may be prov'd.
Her pleading hath deserv'd a greater fee:
She's Love, she loves, and yet she is not lov'd.
'Fie, fie!' he says. 'You crush me; let me go!
You have no reason to withhold me so.'

'Thou hadst been gone,' quoth she, 'sweet boy, ere this,
But that thou told'st me thou wouldst hunt the boar.
O, be advis'd! Thou know'st not what it is
With javelin's point a churlish swine to gore,
Whose tushes never sheath'd he whetteth still,
Like to a mortal butcher bent to kill.

'On his bow-back he hath a battle set
Of bristly pikes that ever threat his foes;
His eyes like glowworms shine when he doth fret;
His snout digs sepulchres where'er he goes;
Being mov'd, he strikes whate'er is in his way,
And whom he strikes his crooked tushes slay.

'His brawny sides, with hairy bristles armed,
Are better proof than thy spear's point can enter;
His short thick neck cannot be easily harmed;
Being ireful, on the lion he will venter.
The thorny brambles and embracing bushes,
As fearful of him, part; through whom he rushes.

'Alas, he naught esteems that face of thine,
To which Love's eyes pays tributary gazes;

Nor thy soft hands, sweet lips, and crystal eyne,
Whose full perfection all the world amazes;
But having thee at vantage (wondrous dread!),
Would root these beauties as he roots the mead.

'O, let him keep his loathsome cabin still!
Beauty hath naught to do with such foul fiends.
Come not within his danger by thy will.
They that thrive well take counsel of their friends.
When thou didst name the boar, not to dissemble,
I fear'd thy fortune, and my joints did tremble.

'Didst thou not mark my face? Was it not white?
Sawest thou not signs of fear lurk in mine eye?
Grew I not faint? and fell I not downright?
Within my bosom, whereon thou dost lie,
My boding heart pants, beats, and takes no rest,
But, like an earthquake, shakes thee on my breast.

'For where Love reigns, disturbing Jealousy
Doth call himself Affection's sentinel,
Gives false alarms, suggesteth mutiny,
And in a peaceful hour doth cry "Kill, kill!"
Distemp'ring gentle Love in his desire,
As air and water do abate the fire.

'This sour informer, this bate-breeding spy,
This canker that eats up Love's tender spring,
This carry-tale, dissentious Jealousy,
That sometime true news, sometime false doth bring,
Knocks at my heart, and whispers in mine ear
That if I love thee, I thy death should fear;

'And more than so, presenteth to mine eye
The picture of an angry chafing boar,
Under whose sharp fangs on his back doth lie
An image like thyself, all stain'd with gore;
Whose blood upon the fresh flowers being shed
Doth make them droop with grief and hang the head.

'What should I do, seeing thee so indeed,
That tremble at th' imagination?
The thought of it doth make my faint heart bleed,
And fear doth teach it divination.
I prophesy thy death, my living sorrow,
If thou encounter with the boar to-morrow.

'But if thou needs wilt hunt, be rul'd by me;
Uncouple at the timorous flying hare,
Or at the fox which lives by subtlety,
Or at the roe which no encounter dare.
Pursue these fearful creatures o'er the downs,
And on thy well-breath'd horse keep with thy hounds.

'And when thou hast on foot the purblind hare,
Mark the poor wretch, to overshoot his troubles,
How he outruns the wind, and with what care
He cranks and crosses with a thousand doubles.
The many musits through the which he goes
Are like a labyrinth to amaze his foes.

'Sometime he runs among a flock of sheep,
To make the cunning hounds mistake their smell,
And sometime where earth-delving conies keep,
To stop the loud pursuers in their yell;
And sometime sorteth with a herd of deer.
Danger deviseth shifts; wit waits on fear;

'For there his smell with others being mingled,
The hot scent-snuffing hounds are driven to doubt,
Ceasing their clamorous cry till they have singled
With much ado the cold fault cleanly out.
Then do they spend their mouths; echo replies,
As if another chase were in the skies.

'By this, poor Wat, far off upon a hill,
Stands on his hinder legs with list'ning ear,
To hearken if his foes pursue him still.
Anon their loud alarums he doth hear,
And now his grief may be compared well
To one sore sick that hears the passing bell.

'Then shalt thou see the dew-bedabbled wretch
Turn and return, indenting with the way.
Each envious brier his weary legs do scratch;
Each shadow makes him stop, each murmur stay;
For misery is trodden on by many
And, being low, never reliev'd by any.

'Lie quietly and hear a little more.
Nay, do not struggle, for thou shalt not rise.
To make thee hate the hunting of the boar,
Unlike myself thou hear'st me moralize,

Applying this to that, and so to so;
For love can comment upon every woe.

'Where did I leave?' 'No matter where,' quoth he.
'Leave me, and then the story aptly ends.
The night is spent.' 'Why, what of that?' quoth she.
'I am,' quoth he, 'expected of my friends;
And now 'tis dark, and going I shall fall.'
'In night,' quoth she, 'desire sees best of all.

'But if thou fall, O, then imagine this:
The earth, in love with thee, thy footing trips,
And all is but to rob thee of a kiss.
Rich preys make true men thieves. So do thy lips
Make modest Dian cloudy and forlorn,
Lest she should steal a kiss and die forsworn.

'Now of this dark night I perceive the reason:
Cynthia for shame obscures her silver shine,
Till forging Nature be condemn'd of treason
For stealing moulds from heaven that were divine;
Wherein she fram'd thee, in high heaven's despite,
To shame the sun by day, and her by night.

'And therefore hath she brib'd the Destinies
To cross the curious workmanship of Nature,
To mingle beauty with infirmities
And pure perfection with impure defeature,
Making it subject to the tyranny
Of mad mischances and much misery;

'As burning fevers, agues pale and faint,
Life-poisoning pestilence, and frenzies wood,
The marrow-eating sickness whose attaint
Disorder breeds by heating of the blood,
Surfeits, imposthumes, grief, and damn'd despair
Swear Nature's death for framing thee so fair.

'And not the least of all these maladies
But in one minute's fight brings beauty under.
Both favour, savour, hue, and qualities,
Whereat th' impartial gazer late did wonder,
Are on the sudden wasted, thaw'd, and done,
As mountain snow melts with the midday sun.

'Therefore, despite of fruitless chastity,
Love-lacking vestals, and self-loving nuns,
That on the earth would breed a scarcity
And barren dearth of daughters and of sons,
Be prodigal. The lamp that burns by night
Dries up his oil to lend the world his light.

'What is thy body but a swallowing grave,
Seeming to bury that posterity
Which by the rights of time thou needs must have
If thou destroy them not in dark obscurity?
If so, the world will hold thee in disdain,
Sith in thy pride so fair a hope is slain.

'So in thyself thyself art made away —
A mischief worse than civil home-bred strife,
Or theirs whose desperate hands themselves do slay,
Or butcher sire that reaves his son of life.
Foul cank'ring rust the hidden treasure frets,
But gold that's put to use more gold begets.'

'Nay, then,' quoth Adon, 'you will fall again
Into your idle over-handled theme.
The kiss I gave you is bestow'd in vain,
And all in vain you strive against the stream;
For, by this black-fac'd night, desire's foul nurse,
Your treatise makes me like you worse and worse.

'If love have lent you twenty thousand tongues,
And every tongue more moving than your own,
Bewitching like the wanton mermaid's songs,
Yet from mine ear the tempting tune is blown;
For know, my heart stands armed in mine ear
And will not let a false sound enter there,

'Lest the deceiving harmony should run
Into the quiet closure of my breast;
And then my little heart were quite undone,
In his bedchamber to be barr'd of rest.
No, lady, no! My heart longs not to groan,
But soundly sleeps while now it sleeps alone.

'What have you urg'd that I cannot reprove?
The path is smooth that leadeth on to danger.
I hate not love, but your device in love,
That lends embracements unto every stranger.
You do it for increase. O strange excuse,
When reason is the bawd to lust's abuse!

'Call it not love, for Love to heaven is fled
Since sweating Lust on earth usurp'd his name;
Under whose simple semblance he hath fed
Upon fresh beauty, blotting it with blame;
Which the hot tyrant stains and soon bereaves,
As caterpillars do the tender leaves.

'Love comforteth like sunshine after rain,
But Lust's effect is tempest after sun.
Love's gentle spring doth always fresh remain;
Lust's winter comes ere summer half be done.
  Love surfeits not, Lust like a glutton dies;
  Love is all truth, Lust full of forged lies.

'More I could tell, but more I dare not say:
The text is old, the orator too green.
Therefore in sadness now I will away.
My face is full of shame, my heart of teen;
  Mine ears, that to your wanton talk attended,
  Do burn themselves for having so offended.'

With this he breaketh from the sweet embrace
Of those fair arms which bound him to her breast
And homeward through the dark laund runs apace;
Leaves Love upon her back, deeply distress'd.
  Look how a bright star shooteth from the sky —
  So glides he in the night from Venus' eye;

Which after him she darts, as one on shore
Gazing upon a late-embarked friend
Till the wild waves will have him seen no more,
Whose ridges with the meeting clouds contend.
  So did the merciless and pitchy night
  Fold in the object that did feed her sight.

Whereat amaz'd, as one that unaware
Hath dropp'd a precious jewel in the flood,
Or stonish'd as night-wand'rers often are,
Their light blown out in some mistrustful wood —
  Even so confounded in the dark she lay,
  Having lost the fair discovery of her way.

And now she beats her heart, whereat it groans,
That all the neighbour caves, as seeming troubled,
Make verbal repetition of her moans.
Passion on passion deeply is redoubled:
  'Ay me!' she cries, and twenty times, 'Woe, woe!'
  And twenty echoes twenty times cry so.

She, marking them, begins a wailing note
And sings extemporally a woful ditty —
How love makes young men thrall, and old men dote;
How love is wise in folly, foolish-witty.
  Her heavy anthem still concludes in woe,
  And still the choir of echoes answer so.

Her song was tedious and outwore the night,
For lovers' hours are long, though seeming short.
If pleas'd themselves, others, they think, delight
In such-like circumstance, with such-like sport.
  Their copious stories, oftentimes begun,
  End without audience and are never done.

For who hath she to spend the night withal
But idle sounds resembling parasits,
Like shrill-tongu'd tapsters answering every call,
Soothing the humour of fantastic wits?
  She says ''Tis so.' They answer all, ''Tis so!'
  And would say after her if she said 'No.'

Lo, here the gentle lark, weary of rest,
From his moist cabinet mounts up on high
And wakes the morning, from whose silver breast
The sun ariseth in his majesty;
  Who doth the world so gloriously behold
  That cedar tops and hills seem burnish'd gold.

Venus salutes him with this fair good-morrow:
'O thou clear god, and patron of all light,
From whom each lamp and shining star doth borrow
The beauteous influence that makes him bright,
  There lives a son that suck'd an earthly mother
  May lend thee light, as thou dost lend to other.'

This said, she hasteth to a myrtle grove,
Musing the morning is so much o'erworn
And yet she hears no tidings of her love.
She hearkens for his hounds and for his horn.
  Anon she hears them chant it lustily,
  And all in haste she coasteth to the cry;

And as she runs, the bushes in the way
Some catch her by the neck, some kiss her face,
Some twine about her thigh to make her stay.
She wildly breaketh from their strict embrace,
  Like a milch doe whose swelling dugs do ache
  Hasting to feed her fawn hid in some brake.

By this, she hears the hounds are at a bay;
Whereat she starts, like one that spies an adder
Wreath'd up in fatal folds just in his way,
The fear whereof doth make him shake and shudder.
  Even so the timorous yelping of the hounds
  Appals her senses and her spirit confounds.

For now she knows it is no gentle chase,
But the blunt boar, rough bear, or lion proud,
Because the cry remaineth in one place,
Where fearfully the dogs exclaim aloud.
  Finding their enemy to be so curst,
  They all strain court'sy who shall cope him first.

This dismal cry rings sadly in her ear,
Through which it enters to surprise her heart,
Who, overcome by doubt and bloodless fear,
With cold-pale weakness numbs each feeling part:
  Like soldiers when their captain once doth yield,
  They basely fly and dare not stay the field.

Thus stands she in a trembling ecstasy;
Till, cheering up her senses all dismay'd,
She tells them 'tis a causeless fantasy,
And childish error that they are afraid;
  Bids them leave quaking, bids them fear no more;
  And with that word she spied the hunted boar,

Whose frothy mouth, bepainted all with red,
Like milk and blood being mingled both togither,
A second fear through all her sinews spread,
Which madly hurries her she knows not whither.
  This way she runs, and now she will no further,
  But back retires to rate the boar for murther.

A thousand spleens bear her a thousand ways;
She treads the path that she untreads again;
Her more than haste is mated with delays,
Like the proceedings of a drunken brain,
  Full of respects, yet naught at all respecting,
  In hand with all things, naught at all effecting.

Here kennell'd in a brake she finds a hound
And asks the weary caitiff for his master;
And there another licking of his wound,
'Gainst venom'd sores the only sovereign plaster;
  And here she meets another sadly scowling,
  To whom she speaks, and he replies with howling.

When he hath ceas'd his ill-resounding noise,
Another flap-mouth'd mourner, black and grim,
Against the welkin volleys out his voice.
Another and another answer him,
  Clapping their proud tails to the ground below,
  Shaking their scratch'd ears, bleeding as they go.

Look how the world's poor people are amazed
At apparitions, signs, and prodigies,
Whereon with fearful eyes they long have gazed,
Infusing them with dreadful prophecies:
  So she at these sad signs draws up her breath
  And, sighing it again, exclaims on Death.

'Hard-favour'd tyrant, ugly, meagre, lean,
Hateful divorce of love!' (thus chides she Death) —
'Grim-grinning ghost, earth's worm, what dost thou mean
To stifle beauty and to steal his breath
  Who, when he liv'd, his breath and beauty set
  Gloss on the rose, smell to the violet?

'If he be dead — O no, it cannot be,
Seeing his beauty, thou shouldst strike at it!
O yes, it may! Thou hast no eyes to see,
But hatefully at randon dost thou hit.
  Thy mark is feeble age; but thy false dart
  Mistakes that aim and cleaves an infant's heart.

'Hadst thou but bid beware, then he had spoke,
And, hearing him, thy power had lost his power.
The Destinies will curse thee for this stroke.
They bid thee crop a weed; thou pluck'st a flower.
  Love's golden arrow at him should have fled,
  And not Death's ebon dart to strike him dead.

'Dost thou drink tears, that thou provok'st such weeping?
What may a heavy groan advantage thee?
Why hast thou cast into eternal sleeping
Those eyes that taught all other eyes to see?
  Now Nature cares not for thy mortal vigour,
  Since her best work is ruin'd with thy rigour.'

Here overcome, as one full of despair,
She vail'd her eyelids, who, like sluices, stopp'd
The crystal tide that from her two cheeks fair
In the sweet channel of her bosom dropp'd;
  But through the floodgates breaks the silver rain
  And with his strong course opens them again.

O, how her eyes and tears did lend and borrow,
Her eyes seen in the tears, tears in her eye!

Both crystals, where they view'd each other's sorrow —
Sorrow that friendly sighs sought still to dry;
But like a stormy day, now wind, now rain,
Sighs dry her cheeks, tears make them wet again.

Variable passions throng her constant woe,
As striving who should best become her grief.
All entertain'd, each passion labours so
That every present sorrow seemeth chief,
But none is best. Then join they all together,
Like many clouds consulting for foul weather.

By this, far off she hears some hunstman halloa.
A nurse's song ne'er pleas'd her babe so well.
The dire imagination she did follow
This sound of hope doth labour to expel;
For now reviving joy bids her rejoice
And flatters her it is Adonis' voice.

Whereat her tears began to turn their tide,
Being prison'd in her eye like pearls in glass;
Yet sometimes falls an orient drop beside,
Which her cheek melts, as scorning it should pass
To wash the foul face of the sluttish ground,
Who is but drunken when she seemeth drown'd.

O hard-believing love, how strange it seems
Not to believe, and yet too credulous!
Thy weal and woe are both of them extremes;
Despair and hope makes thee ridiculous:
The one doth flatter thee in thoughts unlikely,
In likely thoughts the other kills thee quickly.

Now she unweaves the web that she hath wrought:
Adonis lives, and Death is not to blame;
It was not she that call'd him all to naught.
Now she adds honours to his hateful name:
She clepes him king of graves, and grave for kings,
Imperious supreme of all mortal things.

'No, no!' quoth she. 'Sweet Death, I did but jest.
Yet pardon me I felt a kind of fear
When as I met the boar, that bloody beast
Which knows no pity but is still severe.
Then, gentle shadow (truth I must confess),
I rail'd on thee, fearing my love's decesse.

''Tis not my fault. The boar provok'd my tongue.
Be wreak'd on him, invisible commander.
'Tis he, foul creature, that hath done thee wrong.
I did but act; he's author of thy slander.
Grief hath two tongues, and never woman yet
Could rule them both without ten women's wit.'

Thus hoping that Adonis is alive,
Her rash suspect she doth extenuate;
And that his beauty may the better thrive,
With Death she humbly doth insinuate;
Tells him of trophies, statues, tombs, and stories,
His victories, his triumphs, and his glories.

'O Jove,' quoth she, 'how much a fool was I
To be of such a weak and silly mind
To wail his death who lives, and must not die
Till mutual overthrow of mortal kind!
For he being dead, with him is beauty slain,
And, beauty dead, black chaos comes again.

'Fie, fie, fond love, thou art so full of fear
As one with treasure laden hemm'd with thieves.
Trifles, unwitnessed with eye or ear,
Thy coward heart with false bethinking grieves.'
Even at this word she hears a merry horn,
Whereat she leaps that was but late forlorn.

As falcons to the lure, away she flies.
The grass stoops not, she treads on it so light;
And in her haste unfortunately spies
The foul boar's conquest on her fair delight;
Which seen, her eyes, as murd'red with the view,
Like stars asham'd of day, themselves withdrew;

Or as the snail, whose tender horns being hit,
Shrinks backward in his shelly cave with pain,
And there, all smooth'red up, in shade doth sit,
Long after fearing to creep forth again;
So at his bloody view her eyes are fled
Into the deep-dark cabins of her head;

Where they resign their office and their light
To the disposing of her troubled brain;
Who bids them still consort with ugly night
And never wound the heart with looks again;
Who, like a king perplexed in his throne,
By their suggestion gives a deadly groan,

Whereat each tributary subject quakes,
As when the wind, imprison'd in the ground,
Struggling for passage, earth's foundation shakes,
Which with cold terror doth men's minds confound.
This mutiny each part doth so surprise
That from their dark beds once more leap her eyes,

And, being open'd, threw unwilling light
Upon the wide wound that the boar had trench'd
In his soft flank; whose wonted lily white
With purple tears that his wound wept was drench'd.
No flow'r was nigh, no grass, herb, leaf, or weed,
But stole his blood and seem'd with him to bleed.

This solemn sympathy poor Venus noteth.
Over one shoulder doth she hang her head.
Dumbly she passions, franticly she doteth:
She thinks he could not die, he is not dead;
Her voice is stopp'd, her joints forget to bow;
Her eyes are mad that they have wept till now.

Upon his hurt she looks so steadfastly
That her sight dazzling makes the wound seem three;
And then she reprehends her mangling eye,
That makes more gashes where no breach should be.
His face seems twain, each several limb is doubled;
For oft the eye mistakes, the brain being troubled.

'My tongue cannot express my grief for one,
And yet,' quoth she, 'behold two Adons dead!
My sighs are blown away, my salt tears gone,
Mine eyes are turn'd to fire, my heart to lead.
Heavy heart's lead, melt at mine eyes' red fire!
So shall I die by drops of hot desire.

'Alas, poor world, what treasure hast thou lost!
What face remains alive that's worth the viewing?
Whose tongue is music now? What canst thou boast
Of things long since, or any thing ensuing?
The flowers are sweet, their colours fresh and trim;
But true-sweet beauty liv'd and died with him.

'Bonnet nor veil henceforth no creature wear!
Nor sun nor wind will ever strive to kiss you.
Having no fair to lose, you need not fear.
The sun doth scorn you, and the wind doth hiss you;
But when Adonis liv'd, sun and sharp air
Lurk'd like two thieves, to rob him of his fair;

'And therefore would he put his bonnet on,
Under whose brim the gaudy sun would peep;
The wind would blow it off, and, being gone,
Play with his locks. Then would Adonis weep,
And straight, in pity of his tender years,
They both would strive who first should dry his tears.

'To see his face the lion walk'd along
Behind some hedge, because he would not fear him.
To recreate himself when he hath song,
The tiger would be tame, and gently hear him.
If he had spoke, the wolf would leave his prey
And never fright the silly lamb that day.

'When he beheld his shadow in the brook,
The fishes spread on it their golden gills.
When he was by, the birds such pleasure took
That some would sing, some other in their bills
Would bring him mulberries and ripe-red cherries:
He fed them with his sight, they him with berries.

'But this foul, grim, and urchin-snouted boar,
Whose downward eye still looketh for a grave,
Ne'er saw the beauteous livery that he wore:
Witness the entertainment that he gave.
If he did see his face, why then I know
He thought to kiss him, and hath kill'd him so.

''Tis true, 'tis true! thus was Adonis slain:
He ran upon the boar with his sharp spear,
Who did not whet his teeth at him again,
But by a kiss thought to persuade him there;
And nuzzling in his flank, the loving swine
Sheath'd unaware the tusk in his soft groin.

'Had I been tooth'd like him, I must confess,
With kissing him I should have kill'd him first;
But he is dead, and never did he bless
My youth with his — the more am I accurst.'
With this, she falleth in the place she stood
And stains her face with his congealed blood.

She looks upon his lips, and they are pale;
She takes him by the hand, and that is cold;
She whispers in his ears a heavy tale,
As if they heard the woful words she told;
She lifts the coffer-lids that close his eyes,
Where, lo, two lamps burnt out in darkness lies;

Two glasses, where herself herself beheld
A thousand times, and now no more reflect,
Their virtue lost wherein they late excell'd,
And every beauty robb'd of his effect.
'Wonder of time,' quoth she, 'this is my spite,
That, thou being dead, the day should yet be light.

'Since thou art dead, lo, here I prophesy
Sorrow on love hereafter shall attend.
It shall be waited on with jealousy,
Find sweet beginning, but unsavoury end,
Ne'er settled equally, but high or low,
That all love's pleasure shall not match his woe.

'It shall be fickle, false, and full of fraud,
Bud and be blasted in a breathing while,
The bottom poison, and the top o'erstraw'd
With sweets that shall the truest sight beguile.
The strongest body shall it make most weak,
Strike the wise dumb, and teach the fool to speak.

'It shall be sparing, and too full of riot,
Teaching decrepit age to tread the measures;
The staring ruffian shall it keep in quiet,
Pluck down the rich, enrich the poor with treasures;
It shall be raging mad and silly mild,
Make the young old, the old become a child.

'It shall suspect where is no cause of fear;
It shall not fear where it should most mistrust;
It shall be merciful, and too severe,
And most deceiving when it seems most just;
Perverse it shall be where it shows most toward,
Put fear to valour, courage to the coward.

'It shall be cause of war and dire events
And set dissension 'twixt the son and sire,
Subject and servile to all discontents,
As dry combustious matter is to fire.
Sith in his prime death doth my love destroy,
They that love best their loves shall not enjoy.'

By this, the boy that by her side lay kill'd
Was melted like a vapour from her sight,
And in his blood, that on the ground lay spill'd,
A purple flower sprung up, check'red with white,
Resembling well his pale cheeks and the blood
Which in round drops upon their whiteness stood.

She bows her head the new-sprung flower to smell,
Comparing it to her Adonis' breath,
And says within her bosom it shall dwell,
Since he himself is reft from her by death;
She crops the stalk, and in the breach appears
Green-dropping sap, which she compares to tears.

'Poor flow'r,' quoth she, 'this was thy father's guise —
Sweet issue of a more sweet-smelling sire —
For every little grief to wet his eyes.
To grow unto himself was his desire,
And so 'tis thine; but know, it is as good
To wither in my breast as in his blood.

'Here was thy father's bed, here in my breast;
Thou art the next of blood, and 'tis thy right.
Lo, in this hollow cradle take thy rest;
My throbbing heart shall rock thee day and night.
There shall not be one minute in an hour
Wherein I will not kiss my sweet love's flow'r.'

Thus weary of the world, away she hies
And yokes her silver doves, by whose swift aid
Their mistress, mounted, through the empty skies
In her light chariot quickly is convey'd,
Holding their course to Paphos, where their queen
Means to immure herself and not be seen.

THE RAPE OF LUCRECE

TO THE

RIGHT HONOURABLE HENRY WRIOTHESLEY,

EARL OF SOUTHAMPTON, AND BARON OF TITCHFIELD.

The love I dedicate to your Lordship is without end; whereof this pamphlet without beginning is but a superfluous moiety. The warrant I have of your honourable disposition, not the worth of my untutor'd lines, makes it assured of acceptance. What I have done is yours; what I have to do is yours; being part in all I have, devoted yours. Were my worth greater, my duty would show greater; meantime, as it is, it is bound to your Lordship, to whom I wish long life still length'ned with all happiness.

Your Lordship's in all duty,

WILLIAM SHAKESPEARE.

THE ARGUMENT.

Lucius Tarquinius (for his excessive pride surnamed Superbus), after he had caused his own father-in-law Servius Tullius to be cruelly murd'red, and, contrary to the Roman laws and customs, not requiring or staying for the people's suffrages, had possessed himself of the kingdom, went, accompanied with his sons and other noblemen of Rome, to besiege Ardea; during which siege the principal men of the army meeting one evening at the tent of Sextus Tarquinius, the King's son, in their discourses after supper every one commended the virtues of his own wife; among whom Collatinus extolled the incomparable chastity of his wife Lucretia. In that pleasant humour they all posted to Rome; and intending by their secret and sudden arrival to make trial of that which every one had before avouched, only Collatinus finds his wife (though it were late in the night) spinning amongst her maids; the other ladies were all found dancing and revelling, or in several disports. Whereupon the noblemen yielded Collatinus the victory, and his wife the fame. At that time Sextus Tarquinius being inflamed with Lucrece' beauty, yet smoothering his passions for the present, departed with the rest back to the camp; from whence he shortly after privily withdrew himself, and was (according to his estate) royally entertained and lodged by Lucrece at Collatium. The same night he treacherously stealeth into her chamber, violently ravish'd her, and early in the morning speedeth away. Lucrece, in this lamentable plight, hastily dispatcheth messengers, one to Rome for her father, another to the camp for Collatine. They came, the one accompanied with Junius Brutus, the other with Publius Valerius; and finding Lucrece attired in mourning habit, demanded the cause of her sorrow. She, first taking an oath of them for her revenge, revealed the actor and whole manner of his dealing, and withal suddenly stabbed herself. Which done, with one consent they all vowed to root out the whole hated family of the Tarquins; and bearing the dead body to Rome, Brutus acquainted the people with the doer and manner of the vile deed, with a bitter invective against the tyranny of the King; wherewith the people were so moved that with one consent and a general acclamation the Tarquins were all exiled, and the state government changed from kings to consuls.

From the besieged Ardea all in post,
Borne by the trustless wings of false desire,
Lust-breathed Tarquin leaves the Roman host
And to Collatium bears the lightless fire
Which, in pale embers hid, lurks to aspire
  And girdle with embracing flames the waist
  Of Collatine's fair love, Lucrece the chaste.

Haply that name of 'chaste' unhap'ly set
This bateless edge on his keen appetite;
When Collatine unwisely did not let
To praise the clear unmatched red and white
Which triumph'd in that sky of his delight,
  Where mortal stars, as bright as heaven's beauties,
  With pure aspects did him peculiar duties.

For he the night before, in Tarquin's tent,
Unlock'd the treasure of his happy state:
What priceless wealth the heavens had him lent
In the possession of his beauteous mate;
Reck'ning his fortune at such high proud rate
  That kings might be espoused to more fame,
  But king nor peer to such a peerless dame.

O happiness enjoy'd but of a few,
And, if possess'd, as soon decay'd and done
As is the morning's silver-melting dew
Against the golden splendour of the sun!
An expir'd date, cancell'd ere well begun.
  Honour and beauty, in the owner's arms,
  Are weakly fortress'd from a world of harms.

Beauty itself doth of itself persuade
The eyes of men without an orator.
What needeth then apology be made
To set forth that which is so singular?
Or why is Collatine the publisher
Of that rich jewel he should keep unknown
From thievish ears, because it is his own?

Perchance his boast of Lucrece' sov'reignty
Suggested this proud issue of a king;
For by our ears our hearts oft tainted be.
Perchance that envy of so rich a thing
Braving compare, disdainfully did sting
His high-pitch'd thoughts that meaner men should vaunt
That golden hap which their superiors want.

But some untimely thought did instigate
His all too timeless speed, if none of those.
His honour, his affairs, his friends, his state,
Neglected all, with swift intent he goes
To quench the coal which in his liver glows.
O rash false heat, wrapp'd in repentant cold,
Thy hasty spring still blasts and ne'er grows old!

When at Collatium this false lord arrived,
Well was he welcom'd by the Roman dame,
Within whose face Beauty and Virtue strived
Which of them both should underprop her fame.
When Virtue bragg'd, Beauty would blush for shame;
When Beauty boasted blushes, in despite
Virtue would stain that o'er with silver white.

But Beauty, in that white entituled,
From Venus' doves doth challenge that fair field.
Then Virtue claims from Beauty Beauty's red,
Which Virtue gave the Golden Age to gild
Their silver cheeks, and call'd it then their shield,
Teaching them thus to use it in the fight,
When shame assail'd, the red should fence the white.

This heraldry in Lucrece' face was seen,
Argued by Beauty's red and Virtue's white.
Of either's colour was the other queen,
Proving from world's minority their right.
Yet their ambition makes them still to fight,
The sovereignty of either being so great
That oft they interchange each other's seat.

This silent war of lilies and of roses
Which Tarquin view'd in her fair face's field,
In their pure ranks his traitor eye encloses;
Where, lest between them both it should be kill'd,
The coward captive vanquished doth yield
To those two armies that would let him go
Rather than triumph in so false a foe.

Now thinks he that her husband's shallow tongue,
The niggard prodigal that prais'd her so,
In that high task hath done her beauty wrong,
Which far exceeds his barren skill to show.
Therefore that praise which Collatine doth owe
Enchanted Tarquin answers with surmise,
In silent wonder of still-gazing eyes.

This earthly saint, adored by this devil,
Little suspecteth the false worshipper;
For unstain'd thoughts do seldom dream on evil;
Birds never lim'd no secret bushes fear.
So guiltless she securely gives good cheer
And reverend welcome to her princely guest,
Whose inward ill no outward harm express'd;

For that he colour'd with his high estate,
Hiding base sin in pleats of majesty;
That nothing in him seem'd inordinate,
Save sometime too much wonder of his eye,
Which, having all, all could not satisfy;
But, poorly rich, so wanteth in his store
That, cloy'd with much, he pineth still for more.

But she, that never cop'd with stranger eyes,
Could pick no meaning from their parling looks,
Nor read the subtle-shining secrecies
Writ in the glassy margents of such books.
She touch'd no unknown baits, nor fear'd no hooks;
Nor could she moralize his wanton sight,
More than his eyes were open'd to the light.

He stories to her ears her husband's fame,
Won in the fields of fruitful Italy;
And decks with praises Collatine's high name,
Made glorious by his manly chivalry,
With bruised arms and wreaths of victory.
Her joy with heav'd-up hand she doth express,
And wordless so greets heaven for his success.

Far from the purpose of his coming thither
He makes excuses for his being there.
No cloudy show of stormy blust'ring weather

Doth yet in his fair welkin once appear,
Till sable Night, mother of dread and fear,
Upon the world dim darkness doth display
And in her vaulty prison stows the day.

For then is Tarquin brought unto his bed,
Intending weariness with heavy sprite;
For, after supper, long he questioned
With modest Lucrece, and wore out the night.
Now leaden slumber with live's strength doth fight,
And every one to rest themselves betake,
Save thieves, and cares, and troubled minds that wake.

As one of which doth Tarquin lie revolving
The sundry dangers of his will's obtaining;
Yet ever to obtain his will resolving,
Though weak-built hopes persuade him to abstaining.
Despair to gain doth traffic oft for gaining;
And when great treasure is the meed proposed,
Though death be adjunct, there's no death supposed.

Those that much covet are with gain so fond
For what they have not, that which they possess,
They scatter and unloose it from their bond,
And so, by hoping more, they have but less;
Or, gaining more, the profit of excess
Is but to surfeit, and such griefs sustain
That they prove bankrout in this poor rich gain.

The aim of all is but to nurse the life
With honour, wealth, and ease in waning age;
And in this aim there is such thwarting strife
That one for all, or all for one we gage:
As life for honour in fell battle's rage;
Honour for wealth; and oft that wealth doth cost
The death of all, and all together lost;

So that in vent'ring ill we leave to be
The things we are for that which we expect;
And this ambitious foul infirmity,
In having much, torments us with defect
Of that we have: so then we do neglect
The thing we have; and, all for want of wit,
Make something nothing by augmenting it.

Such hazard now must doting Tarquin make,
Pawning his honour to obtain his lust;
And for himself himself he must forsake.
Then where is truth, if there be no self-trust?
When shall he think to find a stranger just
When he himself himself confounds, betrays
To sland'rous tongues and wretched hateful days?

Now stole upon the time the dead of night,
When heavy sleep had clos'd up mortal eyes.
No comfortable star did lend his light,
No noise but owls' and wolves' death-boding cries.
Now serves the season that they may surprise
The silly lambs. Pure thoughts are dead and still,
While lust and murder wakes to stain and kill.

And now this lustful lord leapt from his bed,
Throwing his mantle rudely o'er his arm;
Is madly toss'd between desire and dread:
Th' one sweetly flatters, th' other feareth harm;
But honest fear, bewitch'd with lust's foul charm,
Doth too too oft betake him to retire,
Beaten away by brainsick rude desire,

His falchion on a flint he softly smiteth,
That from the cold stone sparks of fire do fly;
Whereat a waxen torch forthwith he lighteth,
Which must be lodestar to his lustful eye;
And to the flame thus speaks advisedly:
'As from this cold flint I enforc'd this fire,
So Lucrece must I force to my desire.'

Here pale with fear he doth premeditate
The dangers of his loathsome enterprise,
And in his inward mind he doth debate
What following sorrow may on this arise;
Then looking scornfully, he doth despise
His naked armour of still-slaughtered lust
And justly thus controls his thoughts unjust:

'Fair torch, burn out thy light, and lend it not
To darken her whose light excelleth thine!
And die, unhallowed thoughts, before you blot
With your uncleanness that which is divine!
Offer pure incense to so pure a shrine.
Let fair humanity abhor the deed
That spots and stains love's modest snow-white weed.

'O shame to knighthood and to shining arms!
O foul dishonour to my household's grave!
O impious act including all foul harms!
A martial man to be soft fancy's slave!

True valour still a true respect should have;
Then my digression is so vile, so base,
That it will live engraven in my face.

'Yea, though I die, the scandal will survive
And be an eyesore in my golden coat.
Some loathsome dash the herald will contrive
To cipher me how fondly I did dote;
That my posterity, sham'd with the note,
Shall curse my bones, and hold it for no sin
To wish that I their father had not been.

'What win I if I gain the thing I seek?
A dream, a breath, a froth of fleeting joy.
Who buys a minute's mirth to wail a week?
Or sells eternity to get a toy?
For one sweet grape who will the vine destroy?
Or what fond beggar, but to touch the crown,
Would with the sceptre straight be stroken down?

'If Collatinus dream of my intent,
Will he not wake, and in a desp'rate rage
Post hither this vile purpose to prevent —
This siege that hath engirt his marriage,
This blur to youth, this sorrow to the sage,
This dying virtue, this surviving shame,
Whose crime will bear an ever-during blame?

'O, what excuse can my invention make
When thou shalt charge me with so black a deed?
Will not my tongue be mute, my frail joints shake,
Mine eyes forgo their light, my false heart bleed?
The guilt being great, the fear doth still exceed;
And extreme fear can neither fight nor fly,
But coward-like with trembling terror die.

'Had Collatinus kill'd my son or sire,
Or lain in ambush to betray my life,
Or were he not my dear friend, this desire
Might have excuse to work upon his wife,
As in revenge or quittal of such strife;
But as he is my kinsman, my dear friend,
The shame and fault finds no excuse nor end.

'Shameful it is. Ay, if the fact be known.
Hateful it is. There is no hate in loving.
I'll beg her love. But she is not her own.
The worst is but denial and reproving.
My will is strong, past reason's weak removing.
Who fears a sentence or an old man's saw
Shall by a painted cloth be kept in awe.'

Thus graceless holds he disputation
'Tween frozen conscience and hot-burning will,
And with good thoughts makes dispensation,
Urging the worser sense for vantage still;
Which in a moment doth confound and kill
All pure effects, and doth so far proceed
That what is vile shows like a virtuous deed.

Quoth he, 'She took me kindly by the hand
And gaz'd for tidings in my eager eyes,
Fearing some hard news from the warlike band
Where her beloved Collatinus lies.
O, how her fear did make her colour rise!
First red as roses that on lawn we lay,
Then white as lawn, the roses took away.

'And how her hand, in my hand being lock'd,
Forc'd it to tremble with her loyal fear!
Which struck her sad, and then it faster rock'd
Until her husband's welfare she did hear;
Whereat she smiled with so sweet a cheer
That, had Narcissus seen her as she stood,
Self-love had never drown'd him in the flood.

'Why hunt I then for colour or excuses?
All orators are dumb when beauty pleadeth;
Poor wretches have remorse in poor abuses;
Love thrives not in the heart that shadows dreadeth.
Affection is my captain, and he leadeth;
And when his gaudy banner is display'd,
The coward fights and will not be dismay'd.

'Then childish fear avaunt! debating die!
Respect and reason wait on wrinkled age!
My heart shall never countermand mine eye.
Sad pause and deep regard beseems the sage;
My part is youth, and beats these from the stage.
Desire my pilot is, beauty my prize;
Then who fears sinking where such treasure lies?'

As corn o'ergrown by weeds, so heedful fear
Is almost chok'd by unresisted lust.
Away he steals with open list'ning ear,
Full of foul hope and full of fond mistrust;
Both which, as servitors to the unjust,
So cross him with their opposite persuasion
That now he vows a league, and now invasion.

Within his thought her heavenly image sits,
And in the selfsame seat sits Collatine.
That eye which looks on her confounds his wits;

That eye which him beholds, as more divine,
Unto a view so false will not incline;
But with a pure appeal seeks to the heart,
Which once corrupted takes the worser part;

And therein heartens up his servile powers,
Who, flatt'red by their leader's jocund show,
Stuff up his lust, as minutes fill up hours;
And as their captain, so their pride doth grow,
Paying more slavish tribute than they owe.
By reprobate desire thus madly led,
The Roman lord marcheth to Lucrece' bed.

The locks between her chamber and his will,
Each one by him enforc'd retires his ward;
But, as they open, they all rate his ill,
Which drives the creeping thief to some regard.
The threshold grates the door to have him heard;
Night-wand'ring weasels shriek to see him there;
They fright him, yet he still pursues his fear.

As each unwilling portal yields him way,
Through little vents and crannies of the place
The wind wars with his torch to make him stay,
And blows the smoke of it into his face,
Extinguishing his conduct in this case;
But his hot heart, which fond desire doth scorch,
Puffs forth another wind that fires the torch;

And being lighted, by the light he spies
Lucretia's glove, wherein her needle sticks.
He takes it from the rushes where it lies,
And griping it, the needle his finger pricks,
As who should say, 'This glove to wanton tricks
Is not inur'd. Return again in haste!
Thou see'st our mistress' ornaments are chaste.'

But all these poor forbiddings could not stay him;
He in the worst sense consters their denial:
The doors, the wind, the glove, that did delay him,
He takes for accidental things of trial;
Or as those bars which stop the hourly dial,
Who with a ling'ring stay his course doth let
Till every minute pays the hour his debt.

'So, so,' quoth he, 'these lets attend the time,
Like little frosts that sometime threat the spring
To add a more rejoicing to the prime
And give the sneaped birds more cause to sing.
Pain pays the income of each precious thing:
Huge rocks, high winds, strong pirates, shelves and sands,
The merchant fears ere rich at home he lands.'

Now is he come unto the chamber door
That shuts him from the heaven of his thought,
Which with a yielding latch, and with no more,
Hath barr'd him from the blessed thing he sought.
So from himself impiety hath wrought
That for his prey to pray he doth begin,
As if the heavens should countenance his sin.

But in the midst of his unfruitful prayer,
Having solicited th' eternal power
That his foul thoughts might compass his fair fair,
And they would stand auspicious to the hour,
Even there he starts. Quoth he, 'I must deflow'r.
The powers to whom I pray abhor this fact;
How can they then assist me in the act?

'Then Love and Fortune be my gods, my guide!
My will is back'd with resolution.
Thoughts are but dreams till their effects be tried;
The blackest sin is clear'd with absolution;
Against love's fire fear's frost hath dissolution.
The eye of heaven is out, and misty night
Covers the shame that follows sweet delight.'

This said, his guilty hand pluck'd up the latch,
And with his knee the door he opens wide.
The dove sleeps fast that this night owl will catch.
Thus treason works ere traitors be espied.
Who sees the lurking serpent steps aside;
But she, sound sleeping, fearing no such thing,
Lies at the mercy of his mortal sting.

Into the chamber wickedly he stalks
And gazeth on her yet unstained bed.
The curtains being close, about he walks,
Rolling his greedy eyeballs in his head.
By their high treason is his heart misled,
Which gives the watchword to his hand full soon
To draw the cloud that hides the silver moon.

Look, as the fair and fiery-pointed sun,
Rushing from forth a cloud, bereaves our sight,
Even so, the curtain drawn, his eyes begun

To wink, being blinded with a greater light;
Whether it is that she reflects so bright
That dazzleth them, or else some shame supposed —
But blind they are, and keep themselves enclosed.

O, had they in that darksome prison died,
Then had they seen the period of their ill!
Then Collatine again, by Lucrece' side,
In his clear bed might have reposed still!
But they must ope, this blessed league to kill,
And holy-thoughted Lucrece to their sight
Must sell her joy, her life, her world's delight.

Her lily hand her rosy cheek lies under,
Coz'ning the pillow of a lawful kiss;
Who, therefore angry, seems to part in sunder,
Swelling on either side to want his bliss;
Between whose hills her head entombed is;
Where like a virtuous monument she lies,
To be admir'd of lewd unhallowed eyes.

Without the bed her other fair hand was,
On the green coverlet; whose perfect white
Show'd like an April daisy on the grass,
With pearly sweat resembling dew of night.
Her eyes, like marigolds, had sheath'd their light,
And canopied in darkness sweetly lay
Till they might open to adorn the day.

Her hair like golden threads play'd with her breath —
O modest wantons! wanton modesty!
Showing life's triumph in the map of death,
And death's dim look in life's mortality.
Each in her sleep themselves so beautify
As if between them twain there were no strife,
But that life liv'd in death, and death in life.

Her breasts like ivory globes circled with blue,
A pair of maiden worlds unconquered,
Save of their lord no bearing yoke they knew,
And him by oath they truly honoured.
These worlds in Tarquin new ambition bred,
Who like a foul usurper went about
From this fair throne to heave the owner out.

What could he see but mightily he noted?
What did he note but strongly he desired?
What he beheld, on that he firmly doted,
And in his will his wilful eye he tired.
With more than admiration he admired
Her azure veins, her alablaster skin,
Her coral lips, her snow-white dimpled chin.

As the grim lion fawneth o'er his prey,
Sharp hunger by the conquest satisfied,
So o'er this sleeping soul doth Tarquin stay,
His rage of lust by gazing qualified;
Slack'd, not suppress'd; for, standing by her side,
His eye, which late this mutiny restrains,
Unto a greater uproar tempts his veins;

And they, like straggling slaves for pillage fighting,
Obdurate vassals fell exploits effecting,
In bloody death and ravishment delighting,
Nor children's tears nor mothers' groans respecting,
Swell in their pride, the onset still expecting.
Anon his beating heart, alarum striking,
Gives the hot charge and bids them do their liking.

His drumming heart cheers up his burning eye,
His eye commends the leading to his hand;
His hand, as proud of such a dignity,
Smoking with pride, march'd on to make his stand
On her bare breast, the heart of all her land;
Whose ranks of blue veins, as his hand did scale,
Left their round turrets destitute and pale.

They, must'ring to the quiet cabinet
Where their dear governess and lady lies,
Do tell her she is dreadfully beset
And fright her with confusion of their cries.
She, much amaz'd, breaks ope her lock'd-up eyes,
Who, peeping forth this tumult to behold,
Are by his flaming torch dimm'd and controll'd.

Imagine her as one in dead of night,
From forth dull sleep by dreadful fancy waking,
That thinks she hath beheld some ghastly sprite,
Whose grim aspect sets every joint a-shaking.
What terror 'tis! but she, in worser taking,
From sleep disturbed, heedfully doth view
The sight which makes supposed terror true.

Wrapp'd and confounded in a thousand fears,
Like to a new-kill'd bird she trembling lies.
She dares not look; yet, winking, there appears

Quick-shifting antics ugly in her eyes.
Such shadows are the weak brain's forgeries,
Who, angry that the eyes fly from their lights,
In darkness daunts them with more dreadful sights.

His hand, that yet remains upon her breast
(Rude ram, to batter such an ivory wall!)
May feel her heart (poor citizen!) distress'd,
Wounding itself to death, rise up and fall,
Beating her bulk, that his hand shakes withal.
This moves in him more rage and lesser pity,
To make the breach and enter this sweet city.

First like a trumpet doth his tongue begin
To sound a parley to his heartless foe;
Who o'er the white sheet peers her whiter chin,
The reason of this rash alarm to know,
Which he by dumb demeanour seeks to show;
But she with vehement prayers urgeth still
Under what colour he commits this ill.

Thus he replies: 'The colour in thy face,
That even for anger makes the lily pale
And the red rose blush at her own disgrace,
Shall plead for me and tell my loving tale.
Under that colour am I come to scale
Thy never-conquered fort. The fault is thine,
For those thine eyes betray thee unto mine.

'Thus I forestall thee, if thou mean to chide:
Thy beauty hath ensnar'd thee to this night,
Where thou with patience must my will abide—
My will, that marks thee for my earth's delight,
Which I to conquer sought with all my might;
But as reproof and reason beat it dead,
By thy bright beauty was it newly bred.

'I see what crosses my attempt will bring;
I know what thorns the growing rose defends;
I think the honey guarded with a sting:
All this beforehand counsel comprehends;
But Will is deaf and hears no heedful friends;
Only he hath an eye to gaze on Beauty,
And dotes on what he looks, 'gainst law or duty.

'I have debated even in my soul
What wrong, what shame, what sorrow I shall breed;
But nothing can affection's course control
Or stop the headlong fury of his speed.
I know repentant tears ensue the deed
Reproach, disdain, and deadly enmity;
Yet strive I to embrace mine infamy.'

This said, he shakes aloft his Roman blade,
Which, like a falcon tow'ring in the skies,
Coucheth the fowl below with his wings' shade,
Whose crooked beak threats if he mount he dies.
So under his insulting falchion lies
Harmless Lucretia, marking what he tells
With trembling fear, as fowl hear falcons' bells.

'Lucrece,' quoth he, 'this night I must enjoy thee.
If thou deny, then force must work my way;
For in thy bed I purpose to destroy thee.
That done, some worthless slave of thine I'll slay,
To kill thine honour with thy live's decay;
And in thy dead arms do I mean to place him,
Swearing I slew him, seeing thee embrace him.

'So thy surviving husband shall remain
The scornful mark of every open eye;
Thy kinsmen hang their heads at this disdain,
Thy issue blurr'd with nameless bastardy;
And thou, the author of their obloquy,
Shalt have thy trespass cited up in rhymes
And sung by children in succeeding times.

'But if thou yield, I rest thy secret friend:
The fault unknown is as a thought unacted.
A little harm done to a great good end
For lawful policy remains enacted.
The poisonous simple sometime is compacted
In a pure compound; being so applied,
His venom in effect is purified.

'Then, for thy husband and thy children's sake,
Tender my suit. Bequeath not to their lot
The shame that from them no device can take,
The blemish that will never be forgot;
Worse than a slavish wipe or birth-hour's blot;
For marks descried in men's nativity
Are nature's faults, not their own infamy.'

Here with a cockatrice' dead-killing eye
He rouseth up himself and makes a pause;
While she, the picture of pure piety,
Like a white hind under the gripe's sharp claws,
Pleads, in a wilderness where are no laws,
To the rough beast that knows no gentle right
Nor aught obeys but his foul appetite.

But when a black-fac'd cloud the world doth threat,
In his dim mist th' aspiring mountains hiding,

From earth's dark womb some gentle gust doth get,
Which blows these pitchy vapours from their biding,
Hind'ring their present fall by this dividing —
So his unhallowed haste her words delays,
And moody Pluto winks while Orpheus plays.

Yet, foul night-waking cat, he doth but dally,
While in his hold-fast foot the weak mouse panteth.
Her sad behaviour feeds his vulture folly,
A swallowing gulf that even in plenty wanteth.
His ear her prayers admits, but his heart granteth
No penetrable entrance to her plaining.
Tears harden lust, though marble wear with raining.

Her pity-pleading eyes are sadly fixed
In the remorseless wrinkles of his face.
Her modest eloquence with sighs is mixed,
Which to her oratory adds more grace.
She puts the period often from his place,
And midst the sentence so her accent breaks
That twice she doth begin ere once she speaks.

She conjures him by high almighty Jove,
By knighthood, gentry, and sweet friendship's oath,
By her untimely tears, her husband's love,
By holy human law and common troth,
By heaven and earth, and all the power of both,
That to his borrowed bed he make retire
And stoop to honour, not to foul desire.

Quoth she, 'Reward not hospitality
With such black payment as thou hast pretended;
Mud not the fountain that gave drink to thee;
Mar not the thing that cannot be amended.
End thy ill aim before thy shoot be ended.
He is no woodman that doth bend his bow
To strike a poor unseasonable doe.

'My husband is thy friend — for his sake spare me;
Thyself art mighty — for thine own sake leave me;
Myself a weakling — do not then ensnare me;
Thou look'st not like deceit — do not deceive me.
My sighs like whirlwinds labour hence to heave thee.
If ever man were mov'd with woman's moans,
Be moved with my tears, my sighs, my groans;

'All which together, like a troubled ocean,
Beat at thy rocky and wrack-threat'ning heart,
To soften it with their continual motion;
For stones dissolv'd to water do convert.
O, if no harder than a stone thou art,
Melt at my tears and be compassionate!
Soft pity enters at an iron gate.

'In Tarquin's likeness I did entertain thee:
Hast thou put on his shape to do him shame?
To all the host of heaven I complain me:
Thou wrong'st his honour, wound'st his princely name.
Thou art not what thou seem'st; and if the same,
Thou seem'st not what thou art, a god, a king;
For kings like gods should govern everything.

'How will thy shame be seeded in thine age
When thus thy vices bud before thy spring?
If in thy hope thou dar'st do such outrage,
What dar'st thou not when once thou art a king?
O, be remember'd, no outrageous thing
From vassal actors can be wip'd away:
Then kings' misdeeds cannot be hid in clay.

'This deed will make thee only lov'd for fear;
But happy monarchs still are fear'd for love.
With foul offenders thou perforce must bear
When they in thee the like offences prove.
If but for fear of this, thy will remove;
For princes are the glass, the school, the book,
Where subjects' eyes do learn, do read, do look.

'And wilt thou be the school where Lust shall learn?
Must he in thee read lectures of such shame?
Wilt thou be glass wherein it shall discern
Authority for sin, warrant for blame,
To privilege dishonour in thy name?
Thou back'st reproach against long-living laud
And mak'st fair reputation but a bawd.

'Hast thou command? By him that gave it thee,
From a pure heart command thy rebel will!
Draw not thy sword to guard iniquity,
For it was lent thee all that brood to kill.
Thy princely office how canst thou fulfil
When, pattern'd by thy fault, foul Sin may say,
He learn'd to sin, and thou didst teach the way?

'Think but how vile a spectacle it were
To view thy present trespass in another.
Men's faults do seldom to themselves appear;
Their own transgressions partially they smother:
This guilt would seem death-worthy in thy brother.
O, how are they wrapp'd in with infamies
That from their own misdeeds askaunce their eyes!

'To thee, to thee, my heav'd-up hands appeal,
Not to seducing lust, thy rash relier!
I sue for exil'd majesty's repeal;
Let him return, and flatt'ring thoughts retire.
His true respect will prison false desire
And wipe the dim mist from thy doting eyne,
That thou shalt see thy state, and pity mine.'

'Have done,' quoth he. 'My uncontrolled tide
Turns not, but swells the higher by this let.
Small lights are soon blown out; huge fires abide
And with the wind in greater fury fret.
The petty streams that pay a daily debt
To their salt sovereign with their fresh falls' haste,
Add to his flow, but alter not his taste.'

'Thou art,' quoth she, 'a sea, a sovereign king;
And, lo, there falls into thy boundless flood
Black lust, dishonour, shame, misgoverning,
Who seek to stain the ocean of thy blood.
If all these petty ills shall change thy good,
Thy sea within a puddle's womb is hearsed,
And not the puddle in thy sea dispersed.

'So shall these slaves be king, and thou their slave;
Thou nobly base, they basely dignified;
Thou their fair life, and they thy fouler grave;
Thou loathed in their shame, they in thy pride.
The lesser thing should not the greater hide.
The cedar stoops not to the base shrub's foot,
But low shrubs wither at the cedar's root.

'So let thy thoughts, low vassals to thy state'—
'No more,' quoth he. 'By heaven, I will not hear thee!
Yield to my love; if not, enforced hate,
Instead of love's coy touch, shall rudely tear thee.
That done, despitefully I mean to bear thee
Unto the base bed of some rascal groom,
To be thy partner in this shameful doom.'

This said, he sets his foot upon the light,
For light and lust are deadly enemies;
Shame folded up in blind concealing night,
When most unseen, then most doth tyrannize.
The wolf hath seiz'd his prey; the poor lamb cries,
Till with her own white fleece her voice controll'd
Entombs her outcry in her lips' sweet fold;

For with the nightly linen that she wears
He pens her piteous clamours in her head,
Cooling his hot face in the chastest tears
That ever modest eyes with sorrow shed.
O, that prone lust should stain so pure a bed!
The spots whereof could weeping purify,
Her tears should drop on them perpetually.

But she hath lost a dearer thing than life,
And he hath won what he would lose again.
This forced league doth force a further strife;
This momentary joy breeds months of pain;
This hot desire converts to cold disdain;
Pure Chastity is rifled of her store,
And Lust, the thief, far poorer than before.

Look, as the full-fed hound or gorged hawk,
Unapt for tender smell or speedy flight,
Make slow pursuit, or altogether balk
The prey wherein by nature they delight,
So surfeit-taking Tarquin fares this night:
His taste delicious, in digestion souring,
Devours his will, that liv'd by foul devouring.

O, deeper sin than bottomless conceit
Can comprehend in still imagination!
Drunken Desire must vomit his receipt
Ere he can see his own abomination.
While Lust is in his pride, no exclamation
Can curb his heat or rein his rash desire
Till, like a jade, Self-will himself doth tire.

And then with lank and lean discolour'd cheek,
With heavy eye, knit brow, and strengthless pace,
Feeble Desire, all recreant, poor, and meek,
Like to a bankrout beggar wails his case.
The flesh being proud, Desire doth fight with Grace,
For there it revels; and when that decays,
The guilty rebel for remission prays.

So fares it with this fault-full lord of Rome,
Who this accomplishment so hotly chased;
For now against himself he sounds this doom

That through the length of times he stands disgraced.
Besides, his soul's fair temple is defaced;
To whose weak ruins muster troops of cares,
To ask the spotted princess how she fares.

She says her subjects with foul insurrection
Have batter'd down her consecrated wall,
And by their mortal fault brought in subjection
Her immortality and made her thrall
To living death and pain perpetual;
Which in her prescience she controlled still,
But her foresight could not forestall their will.

Ev'n in this thought through the dark night he stealeth,
A captive victor that hath lost in gain;
Bearing away the wound that nothing healeth,
The scar that will despite of cure remain;
Leaving his spoil perplex'd in greater pain.
She bears the load of lust he left behind,
And he the burthen of a guilty mind.

He like a thievish dog creeps sadly thence;
She like a wearied lamb lies panting there.
He scowls, and hates himself for his offence;
She desperate with her nails her flesh doth tear.
He faintly flies, sweating with guilty fear;
She stays, exclaiming on the direful night;
He runs, and chides his vanish'd loath'd delight.

He thence departs a heavy convertite;
She there remains a hopeless castaway.
He in his speed looks for the morning light;
She prays she never may behold the day,
'For day,' quoth she, 'night's scapes doth open lay,
And my true eyes have never practis'd how
To cloak offences with a cunning brow.

'They think not but that every eye can see
The same disgrace which they themselves behold;
And therefore would they still in darkness be,
To have their unseen sin remain untold;
For they their guilt with weeping will unfold
And grave, like water that doth eat in steel,
Upon my cheeks what helpless shame I feel.'

Here she exclaims against repose and rest
And bids her eyes hereafter still be blind.
She wakes her heart by beating on her breast
And bids it leap from thence, where it may find
Some purer chest to close so pure a mind.
Frantic with grief thus breathes she forth her spite
Against the unseen secrecy of night:

'O comfort-killing Night, image of hell!
Dim register and notary of shame!
Black stage for tragedies and murthers fell!
Vast sin-concealing chaos! nurse of blame!
Blind muffled bawd! dark harbour for defame!
Grim cave of death! whisp'ring conspirator
With close-tongu'd treason and the ravisher!

'O hateful, vaporous, and foggy Night!
Since thou art guilty of my cureless crime,
Muster thy mists to meet the Eastern light,
Make war against proportion'd course of time;
Or if thou wilt permit the sun to climb
His wonted height, yet ere he go to bed,
Knit poisonous clouds about his golden head.

'With rotten damps ravish the morning air;
Let their exhal'd unwholesome breaths make sick
The life of purity, the supreme fair,
Ere he arrive his weary noontide prick;
And let thy musty vapours march so thick
That in their smoky ranks his smoth'red light
May set at noon and make perpetual night.

'Were Tarquin Night, as he is but Night's child,
The silver-shining queen he would distain;
Her twinkling handmaids too, by him defil'd,
Through Night's black bosom should not peep again.
So should I have copartners in my pain;
And fellowship in woe doth woe assuage,
As palmers' chat makes short their pilgrimage;

'Where now I have no one to blush with me,
To cross their arms and hang their heads with mine,
To mask their brows and hide their infamy;
But I alone, alone must sit and pine,
Seasoning the earth with show'rs of silver brine,
Mingling my talk with tears, my grief with groans,
Poor wasting monuments of lasting moans.

'O Night, thou furnace of foul reeking smoke,
Let not the jealous Day behold that face
Which underneath thy black all-hiding cloak
Immodestly lies martyr'd with disgrace!
Keep still possession of thy gloomy place,

That all the faults which in thy reign are made
May likewise be sepulcher'd in thy shade!

'Make me not object to the telltale Day!
The light will show, character'd in my brow,
The story of sweet chastity's decay,
The impious breach of holy wedlock vow.
Yea, the illiterate, that know not how
To cipher what is writ in learned books,
Will quote my loathsome trespass in my looks.

'The nurse, to still her child, will tell my story
And fright her crying babe with Tarquin's name.
The orator, to deck his oratory,
Will couple my reproach to Tarquin's shame.
Feast-finding minstrels, tuning my defame,
Will tie the hearers to attend each line,
How Tarquin wronged me, I Collatine.

'Let my good name, that senseless reputation,
For Collatine's dear love be kept unspotted.
If that be made a theme for disputation,
The branches of another root are rotted,
And undeserv'd reproach to him allotted
That is as clear from this attaint of mine
As I ere this was pure to Collatine.

'O unseen shame! invisible disgrace!
O unfelt sore! crest-wounding private scar!
Reproach is stamp'd in Collatinus' face,
And Tarquin's eye may read the mot afar,
How he in peace is wounded, not in war.
Alas, how many bear such shameful blows
Which not themselves, but he that gives them knows!

'If, Collatine, thine honour lay in me,
From me by strong assault it is bereft;
My honey lost, and I, a drone-like bee,
Have no perfection of my summer left,
But robb'd and ransack'd by injurious theft.
In thy weak hive a wand'ring wasp hath crept
And suck'd the honey which thy chaste bee kept.

'Yet am I guilty of thy honour's wrack;
Yet for thy honour did I entertain him.
Coming from thee, I could not put him back,
For it had been dishonour to disdain him.
Besides, of weariness he did complain him
And talk'd of virtue — O unlook'd-for evil
When virtue is profan'd in such a devil!

'Why should the worm intrude the maiden bud?
Or hateful cuckoos hatch in sparrows' nests?
Or toads infect fair founts with venom mud?
Or tyrant folly lurk in gentle breasts?
Or kings be breakers of their own behests?
But no perfection is so absolute
That some impurity doth not pollute.

'The aged man that coffers up his gold
Is plagu'd with cramps and gouts and painful fits,
And scarce hath eyes his treasure to behold,
But like still-pining Tantalus he sits
And useless barns the harvest of his wits,
Having no other pleasure of his gain
But torment that it cannot cure his pain.

'So then he hath it when he cannot use it,
And leaves it to be mast'red by his young,
Who in their pride do presently abuse it.
Their father was too weak, and they too strong,
To hold their cursed-blessed fortune long.
The sweets we wish for turn to loathed sours
Even in the moment that we call them ours.

'Unruly blasts wait on the tender spring;
Unwholesome weeds take root with precious flow'rs;
The adder hisses where the sweet birds sing;
What virtue breeds iniquity devours.
We have no good that we can say is ours,
But ill-annexed opportunity
Or kills his life or else his quality.

'O Opportunity, thy guilt is great!
'Tis thou that execut'st the traitor's treason;
Thou sets the wolf where he the lamb may get;
Whoever plots the sin, thou point'st the season.
'Tis thou that spurn'st at right, at law, at reason;
And in thy shady cell, where none may spy him,
Sits Sin, to seize the souls that wander by him.

'Thou makest the vestal violate her oath;
Thou blowest the fire when temperance is thaw'd;
Thou smother'st honesty, thou murth'rest troth,
Thou foul abettor! thou notorious bawd!
Thou plantest scandal and displacest laud.
Thou ravisher, thou traitor, thou false thief!
Thy honey turns to gall, thy joy to grief.

'Thy secret pleasure turns to open shame,
Thy private feasting to a public fast,
Thy smoothing titles to a ragged name,
Thy sug'red tongue to bitter wormwood taste:
Thy violent vanities can never last.
How comes it then, vile Opportunity,
Being so bad, such numbers seek for thee?

'When wilt thou be the humble suppliant's friend
And bring him where his suit may be obtained?
When wilt thou sort an hour great strifes to end?
Or free that soul which wretchedness hath chained?
Give physic to the sick, ease to the pained?
The poor, lame, blind, halt, creep, cry out for thee;
But they ne'er meet with Opportunity.

'The patient dies while the physician sleeps;
The orphan pines while the oppressor feeds;
Justice is feasting while the widow weeps;
Advice is sporting while infection breeds.
Thou grant'st no time for charitable deeds:
Wrath, envy, treason, rape, and murther's rages,
Thy heinous hours wait on them as their pages.

'When Truth and Virtue have to do with thee,
A thousand crosses keep them from thy aid.
They buy thy help; but Sin ne'er gives a fee,
He gratis comes; and thou art well apaid
As well to hear as grant what he hath said.
My Collatine would else have come to me
When Tarquin did, but he was stay'd by thee.

'Guilty thou art of murther and of theft,
Guilty of perjury and subornation,
Guilty of treason, forgery, and shift,
Guilty of incest, that abomination —
An accessary by thine inclination
To all sins past and all that are to come,
From the creation to the general doom.

'Misshapen Time, copesmate of ugly Night,
Swift subtle post, carrier of grisly care,
Eater of youth, false slave to false delight,
Base watch of woes, sin's packhorse, virtue's snare!
Thou nursest all, and murth'rest all that are.
O, hear me then, injurious, shifting Time!
Be guilty of my death, since of my crime.

'Why hath thy servant Opportunity
Betray'd the hours thou gav'st me to repose?
Cancell'd my fortunes, and enchained me
To endless date of never-ending woes?
Time's office is to fine the hate of foes,
To eat up errors by opinion bred,
Not spend the dowry of a lawful bed.

'Time's glory is to calm contending kings,
To unmask falsehood and bring truth to light,
To stamp the seal of time in aged things,
To wake the morn and sentinel the night,
To wrong the wronger till he render right,
To ruinate proud buildings with thy hours,
And smear with dust their glitt'ring golden tow'rs;

'To fill with wormholes stately monuments,
To feed oblivion with decay of things,
To blot old books and alter their contents,
To pluck the quills from ancient ravens' wings
To dry the old oak's sap and cherish springs,
To spoil antiquities of hammer'd steel
And turn the giddy round of Fortune's wheel;

'To show the beldame daughters of her daughter,
To make the child a man, the man a child,
To slay the tiger that doth live by slaughter,
To tame the unicorn and lion wild,
To mock the subtle in themselves beguil'd,
To cheer the ploughman with increaseful crops
And waste huge stones with little water-drops.

'Why work'st thou mischief in thy pilgrimage,
Unless thou couldst return to make amends?
One poor retiring minute in an age
Would purchase thee a thousand thousand friends,
Lending him wit that to bad debtors lends.
O this dread night, wouldst thou one hour come back,
I could prevent this storm and shun thy wrack!

'Thou ceaseless lackey to Eternity,
With some mischance cross Tarquin in his flight.
Devise extremes beyond extremity
To make him curse this cursed crimeful night.
Let ghastly shadows his lewd eyes affright,
And the dire thought of his committed evil
Shape every bush a hideous shapeless devil.

'Disturb his hours of rest with restless trances;
Afflict him in his bed with bedrid groans;
Let there bechance him pitiful mischances
To make him moan, but pity not his moans.
Stone him with hard'ned hearts harder than stones,
And let mild women to him lose their mildness,
Wilder to him than tigers in their wildness.

'Let him have time to tear his curled hair,
Let him have time against himself to rave,
Let him have time of Time's help to despair,
Let him have time to live a loathed slave,
Let him have time a beggar's orts to crave,
And time to see one that by alms doth live
Disdain to him disdained scraps to give.

'Let him have time to see his friends his foes
And merry fools to mock at him resort;
Let him have time to mark how slow time goes
In time of sorrow, and how swift and short
His time of folly and his time of sport;
And ever let his unrecalling crime
Have time to wail th' abusing of his time.

'O Time, thou tutor both to good and bad,
Teach me to curse him that thou taught'st this ill!
At his own shadow let the thief run mad,
Himself himself seek every hour to kill!
Such wretched hands such wretched blood should spill;
For who so base would such an office have
As sland'rous deathsman to so base a slave?

'The baser is he, coming from a king,
To shame his hope with deeds degenerate.
The mightier man, the mightier is the thing
That makes him honour'd or begets him hate;
For greatest scandal waits on greatest state.
The moon being clouded presently is miss'd,
But little stars may hide them when they list.

'The crow may bathe his coal-black wings in mire
And unperceiv'd fly with the filth away;
But if the like the snow-white swan desire,
The stain upon his silver down will stay.
Poor grooms are sightless night, kings glorious day:
Gnats are unnoted wheresoe'er they fly,
But eagles gaz'd upon with every eye.

'Out, idle words, servants to shallow fools!
Unprofitable sounds, weak arbitrators!
Busy yourselves in skill-contending schools;
Debate where leisure serves with dull debaters;
To trembling clients be you mediators:
For me, I force not argument a straw,
Since that my case is past the help of law.

'In vain I rail at Opportunity,
At Time, at Tarquin, and uncheerful Night;
In vain I cavil with mine infamy;
In vain I spurn at my confirm'd despite:
This helpless smoke of words doth me no right.
The remedy indeed to do me good
Is to let forth my foul defiled blood.

'Poor hand, why quiver'st thou at this decree?
Honour thyself to rid me of this shame;
For if I die, my honour lives in thee;
But if I live, thou liv'st in my defame.
Since thou couldst not defend thy loyal dame
And wast afeard to scratch her wicked foe,
Kill both thyself and her for yielding so.'

This said, from her betumbled couch she starteth
To find some desp'rate instrument of death;
But this no slaughterhouse no tool imparteth
To make more vent for passage of her breath;
Which, thronging through her lips, so vanisheth
As smoke from Ætna that in air consumes
Or that which from discharged cannon fumes.

'In vain,' quoth she, 'I live, and seek in vain
Some happy mean to end a hapless life.
I fear'd by Tarquin's falchion to be slain,
Yet for the selfsame purpose seek a knife;
But when I fear'd I was a loyal wife.
So am I now. — O no, that cannot be!
Of that true type hath Tarquin rifled me.

'O, that is gone for which I sought to live,
And therefore now I need not fear to die.
To clear this spot by death, at least I give
A badge of fame to slander's livery,
A dying life to living infamy.
Poor helpless help, the treasure stol'n away,
To burn the guiltless casket where it lay!

'Well, well, dear Collatine, thou shalt not know
The stained taste of violated troth.
I will not wrong thy true affection so,
To flatter thee with an infringed oath.
This bastard graff shall never come to growth:
He shall not boast who did thy stock pollute
That thou art doting father of his fruit.

'Nor shall he smile at thee in secret thought,
Nor laugh with his companions at thy state;
But thou shalt know thy int'rest was not bought
Basely with gold, but stol'n from forth thy gate.
For me, I am the mistress of my fate,
And with my trespass never will dispense
Till life to death acquit my forc'd offence.

'I will not poison thee with my attaint
Nor fold my fault in cleanly coin'd excuses;
My sable ground of sin I will not paint
To hide the truth of this false night's abuses.
My tongue shall utter all; mine eyes, like sluices,
As from a mountain spring that feeds a dale,
Shall gush pure streams to purge my impure tale.'

By this, lamenting Philomele had ended
The well-tun'd warble of her nightly sorrow,
And solemn night with slow sad gait descended
To ugly hell; when, lo, the blushing morrow
Lends light to all fair eyes that light will borrow;
But cloudy Lucrece shames herself to see
And therefore still in night would cloist'red be.

Revealing day through every cranny spies
And seems to point her out where she sits weeping;
To whom she sobbing speaks: 'O eye of eyes,
Why pry'st thou through my window? Leave thy peeping.
Mock with thy tickling beams eyes that are sleeping.
Brand not my forehead with thy piercing light,
For day hath naught to do what's done by night.'

Thus cavils she with everything she sees.
True grief is fond and testy as a child,
Who wayward once, his mood with naught agrees.
Old woes, not infant sorrows, bear them mild:
Continuance tames the one; the other wild,
Like an unpractis'd swimmer plunging still,
With too much labour drowns for want of skill.

So she, deep drenched in a sea of care,
Holds disputation with each thing she views
And to herself all sorrow doth compare;
No object but her passion's strength renews;
And as one shifts, another straight ensues.
Sometime her grief is dumb and hath no words;
Sometime 'tis mad and too much talk affords.

The little birds that tune their morning's joy
Make her moans mad with their sweet melody:
For mirth doth search the bottom of annoy;
Sad souls are slain in merry company;
Grief best is pleas'd with grief's society;
True sorrow then is feelingly suffic'd
When with like semblance it is sympathiz'd.

'Tis double death to drown in ken of shore;
He ten times pines that pines beholding food;
To see the salve doth make the wound ache more;
Great grief grieves most at that would do it good;
Deep woes roll forward like a gentle flood,
Who, being stopp'd, the bounding banks o'erflows;
Grief dallied with nor law nor limit knows.

'You mocking birds,' quoth she, 'your tunes entomb
Within your hollow-swelling feathered breasts,
And in my hearing be you mute and dumb;
My restless discord loves no stops nor rests —
A woful hostess brooks not merry guests.
Relish your nimble notes to pleasing ears;
Distress likes dumps when time is kept with tears.

'Come, Philomele, that sing'st of ravishment,
Make thy sad grove in my dishevell'd hair.
As the dank earth weeps at thy languishment,
So I at each sad strain will strain a tear
And with deep groans the diapason bear;
For burthen-wise I'll hum on Tarquin still,
While thou on Tereus descants better skill;

'And whiles against a thorn thou bear'st thy part
To keep thy sharp woes waking, wretched I,
To imitate thee well, against my heart
Will fix a sharp knife to affright mine eye;
Who, if it wink, shall thereon fall and die.
These means, as frets upon an instrument,
Shall tune our heartstrings to true languishment.

'And for, poor bird, thou sing'st not in the day.
As shaming any eye should thee behold,
Some dark deep desert, seated from the way,

That knows not parching heat nor freezing cold,
Will we find out; and there we will unfold
To creatures stern sad tunes, to change their kinds.
Since men prove beasts, let beasts bear gentle minds.'

As the poor frighted deer that stands at gaze,
Wildly determining which way to fly,
Or one encompass'd with a winding maze
That cannot tread the way out readily,
So with herself is she in mutiny,
To live or die which of the twain were better
When life is sham'd and death reproach's debtor.

'To kill myself,' quoth she, 'alack, what were it
But with my body my poor soul's pollution?
They that lose half with greater patience bear it
Than they whose whole is swallowed in confusion.
That mother tries a merciless conclusion
Who, having two sweet babes, when death takes one,
Will slay the other and be nurse to none.

'My body or my soul, which was the dearer
When the one pure, the other made divine?
Whose love of either to myself was nearer
When both were kept for heaven and Collatine?
Ay me! the bark pil'd from the lofty pine,
His leaves will wither and his sap decay.
So must my soul, her bark being pil'd away.

'Her house is sack'd, her quiet interrupted,
Her mansion batter'd by the enemy;
Her sacred temple spotted, spoil'd, corrupted,
Grossly engirt with daring infamy.
Then let it not be call'd impiety
If in this blemish'd fort I make some hole
Through which I may convey this troubled soul.

'Yet die I will not till my Collatine
Have heard the cause of my untimely death;
That he may vow, in that sad hour of mine,
Revenge on him that made me stop my breath.
My stained blood to Tarquin I'll bequeath,
Which, by him tainted, shall for him be spent
And as his due writ in my testament.

'My honour I'll bequeath unto the knife
That wounds my body so dishonoured.
'Tis honour to deprive dishonour'd life:
The one will live, the other being dead.
So of shame's ashes shall my fame be bred,
For in my death I murther shameful scorn;
My shame so dead, mine honour is new born.

'Dear lord of that dear jewel I have lost,
What legacy shall I bequeath to thee?
My resolution, love, shall be thy boast,
By whose example thou reveng'd mayst be.
How Tarquin must be us'd, read it in me:
Myself thy friend will kill myself thy foe,
And for my sake serve thou false Tarquin so.

'This brief abridgment of my will I make:
My soul and body to the skies and ground;
My resolution, husband, do thou take;
Mine honour be the knife's that makes my wound;
My shame be his that did my fame confound;
And all my fame that lives disbursed be
To those that live and think no shame of me.

'Thou, Collatine, shalt oversee this will.
How was I overseen that thou shalt see it!
My blood shall wash the slander of mine ill;
My live's foul deed, my life's fair end shall free it.
Faint not, faint heart, but stoutly say, "So be it."
Yield to my hand; my hand shall conquer thee:
Thou dead, both die, and both shall victors be.'

This plot of death when sadly she had laid
And wip'd the brinish pearl from her bright eyes,
With untun'd tongue she hoarsely calls her maid,
Whose swift obedience to her mistress hies;
For swift-wing'd duty with thought's feathers flies.
Poor Lucrece' cheeks unto her maid seem so
As winter meads when sun doth melt their snow.

Her mistress she doth give demure good-morrow
With soft-slow tongue, true mark of modesty,
And sorts a sad look to her lady's sorrow,
For-why her face wore sorrow's livery;
But durst not ask of her audaciously
Why her two suns were cloud-eclipsed so,
Nor why her fair cheeks overwash'd with woe.

But as the earth doth weep, the sun being set,
Each flower moist'ned like a melting eye,

Even so the maid with swelling drops gan wet
Her circled eyne, enforc'd by sympathy
Of those fair suns set in her mistress' sky,
Who in a salt-wav'd ocean quench their light,
Which makes the maid weep like the dewy night.

A pretty while these pretty creatures stand,
Like ivory conduits coral cisterns filling.
One justly weeps; the other takes in hand
No cause, but company, of her drops spilling.
Their gentle sex to weep are often willing,
Grieving themselves to guess at others' smarts,
And then they drown their eyes or break their hearts.

For men have marble, women waxen minds,
And therefore are they form'd as marble will.
The weak oppress'd, th' impression of strange kinds
Is form'd in them by force, by fraud, or skill.
Then call them not the authors of their ill,
No more than wax shall be accounted evil
Wherein is stamp'd the semblance of a devil.

Their smoothness, like a goodly champain plain,
Lays open all the little worms that creep;
In men, as in a rough-grown grove, remain
Cave-keeping evils that obscurely sleep.
Through crystal walls each little mote will peep.
Though men can cover crimes with bold stern looks,
Poor women's faces are their own faults' books.

No man inveigh against the withered flow'r,
But chide rough winter that the flow'r hath kill'd.
Not that devour'd, but that which doth devour,
Is worthy blame. O, let it not be hild
Poor women's faults that they are so fulfill'd
With men's abuses: those proud lords to blame
Make weak-made women tenants to their shame.

The precedent whereof in Lucrece view,
Assail'd by night with circumstances strong
Of present death, and shame that might ensue
By that her death, to do her husband wrong.
Such danger to resistance did belong
That dying fear through all her body spread;
And who cannot abuse a body dead?

By this, mild patience bid fair Lucrece speak
To the poor counterfeit of her complaining.
'My girl,' quoth she, 'on what occasion break
Those tears from thee that down thy cheeks are raining?
If thou dost weep for grief of my sustaining,
Know, gentle wench, it small avails my mood.
If tears could help, mine own would do me good.

'But tell me, girl, when went' (and there she stay'd
Till after a deep groan) 'Tarquin from hence?'
'Madam, ere I was up,' replied the maid,
'The more to blame my sluggard negligence.
Yet with the fault I thus far can dispense:
Myself was stirring ere the break of day,
And ere I rose was Tarquin gone away.

'But, lady, if your maid may be so bold,
She would request to know your heaviness.'
'O, peace!' quoth Lucrece. 'If it should be told,
The repetition cannot make it less;
For more it is than I can well express,
And that deep torture may be call'd a hell
When more is felt than one hath power to tell.

'Go get me hither paper, ink, and pen.
Yet save that labour, for I have them here.
What should I say? One of my husband's men
Bid thou be ready, by-and-by, to bear
A letter to my lord, my love, my dear.
Bid him with speed prepare to carry it;
The cause craves haste, and it will soon be writ.'

Her maid is gone, and she prepares to write,
First hovering o'er the paper with her quill.
Conceit and grief an eager combat fight;
What wit sets down is blotted straight with will.
This is too curious good, this blunt and ill:
Much like a press of people at a door,
Throng her inventions, which shall go before.

At last she thus begins: 'Thou worthy lord
Of that unworthy wife that greeteth thee,
Health to thy person! Next vouchsafe t' afford
(If ever, love, thy Lucrece thou wilt see)
Some present speed to come and visit me.
So I commend me, from our house in grief.
My woes are tedious, though my words are brief.'

Here folds she up the tenure of her woe,
Her certain sorrow writ uncertainly.
By this short schedule Collatine may know
Her grief, but not her grief's true quality.
She dares not thereof make discovery,
Lest he should hold it her own gross abuse
Ere she with blood had stain'd her stain'd excuse.

Besides, the life and feeling of her passion
She hoards, to spend when he is by to hear her,
When sighs and groans and tears may grace the fashion
Of her disgrace, the better so to clear her
From that suspicion which the world might bear her.
To shun this blot, she would not blot the letter
With words till action might become them better.

To see sad sights moves more than hear them told;
For then the eye interprets to the ear
The heavy motion that it doth behold,
When every part a part of woe doth bear.
'Tis but a part of sorrow that we hear:
Deep sounds make lesser noise than shallow fords,
And sorrow ebbs, being blown with wind of words.

Her letter now is seal'd, and on it writ,
'At Ardea to my lord with more than haste.'
The post attends, and she delivers it,
Charging the sour-fac'd groom to hie as fast
As lagging fowls before the Northern blast.
Speed more than speed but dull and slow she deems:
Extremity still urgeth such extremes.

The homely villain cursies to her low;
And, blushing on her, with a steadfast eye
Receives the scroll without or yea or no
And forth with bashful innocence doth hie.
But they whose guilt within their bosoms lie
Imagine every eye beholds their blame;
For Lucrece thought he blush'd to see her shame,

When, seely groom! God wot, it was defect
Of spirit, life, and bold audacity.
Such harmless creatures have a true respect
To talk in deeds, while others saucily
Promise more speed, but do it leisurely.
Even so this pattern of the worn-out age
Pawn'd honest looks, but laid no words to gage.

His kindled duty kindled her mistrust,
That two red fires in both their faces blazed.
She thought he blush'd as knowing Tarquin's lust,
And, blushing with him, wistly on him gazed;
Her earnest eye did make him more amazed.
The more she saw the blood his cheeks replenish,
The more she thought he spied in her some blemish.

But long she thinks till he return again,
And yet the duteous vassal scarce is gone.
The weary time she cannot entertain,
For now 'tis stale to sigh, to weep and groan.
So woe hath wearied woe, moan tired moan,
That she her plaints a little while doth stay,
Pausing for means to mourn some newer way.

At last she calls to mind where hangs a piece
Of skilful painting, made for Priam's Troy,
Before the which is drawn the power of Greece,
For Helen's rape the city to destroy,
Threat'ning cloud-kissing Ilion with annoy;
Which the conceited painter drew so proud
As heaven, it seem'd, to kiss the turrets bow'd.

A thousand lamentable objects there,
In scorn of nature, art gave liveless life.
Many a dry drop seem'd a weeping tear
Shed for the slaught'red husband by the wife.
The red blood reek'd, to show the painter's strife;
And dying eyes gleam'd forth their ashy lights,
Like dying coals burnt out in tedious nights.

There might you see the labouring pioner
Begrim'd with sweat, and smeared all with dust;
And from the tow'rs of Troy there would appear
The very eyes of men through loopholes thrust,
Gazing upon the Greeks with little lust.
Such sweet observance in this work was had
That one might see those far-off eyes look sad.

In great commanders grace and majesty
You might behold triumphing in their faces;
In youth, quick bearing and dexterity;
And here and there the painter interlaces
Pale cowards marching on with trembling paces,

Which heartless peasants did so well resemble
That one would swear he saw them quake and tremble.

In Ajax and Ulysses, O, what art
Of physiognomy might one behold!
The face of either cipher'd either's heart;
Their face their manners most expressly told:
In Ajax' eyes blunt rage and rigour roll'd;
But the mild glance that sly Ulysses lent
Show'd deep regard and smiling government.

There pleading might you see grave Nestor stand,
As 'twere encouraging the Greeks to fight,
Making such sober action with his hand
That it beguil'd attention, charm'd the sight.
In speech it seem'd his beard, all silver white,
Wagg'd up and down, and from his lips did fly
Thin winding breath, which purl'd up to the sky.

About him were a press of gaping faces
Which seem'd to swallow up his sound advice,
All jointly list'ning, but with several graces,
As if some mermaid did their ears entice,
Some high, some low — the painter was so nice.
The scalps of many, almost hid behind,
To jump up higher seem'd, to mock the mind.

Here one man's hand lean'd on another's head,
His nose being shadowed by his neighbour's ear;
Here one, being throng'd, bears back, all boll'n and red;
Another, smother'd, seems to pelt and swear;
And in their rage such signs of rage they bear
As, but for loss of Nestor's golden words,
It seem'd they would debate with angry swords.

For much imaginary work was there;
Conceit deceitful, so compact, so kind,
That for Achilles' image stood his spear,
Grip'd in an armed hand; himself behind
Was left unseen, save to the eye of mind:
A hand, a foot, a face, a leg, a head
Stood for the whole to be imagined.

And from the walls of strong-besieged Troy
When their brave hope, bold Hector, march'd to field,
Stood many Troyan mothers, sharing joy
To see their youthful sons bright weapons wield;
And to their hope they such odd action yield
That through their light joy seemed to appear
(Like bright things stain'd) a kind of heavy fear.

And from the strond of Dardan, where they fought,
To Simois' reedy banks the red blood ran,
Whose waves to imitate the battle sought
With swelling ridges; and their ranks began
To break upon the galled shore, and than
Retire again, till, meeting greater ranks,
They join, and shoot their foam at Simois' banks.

To this well-painted piece is Lucrece come,
To find a face where all distress is stell'd.
Many she sees where cares have carved some,
But none where all distress and dolour dwell'd
Till she despairing Hecuba beheld,
Staring on Priam's wounds with her old eyes,
Which bleeding under Pyrrhus' proud foot lies.

In her the painter had anatomiz'd
Time's ruin, beauty's wrack, and grim care's reign;
Her cheeks with chops and wrinkles were disguis'd;
Of what she was no semblance did remain.
Her blue blood, chang'd to black in every vein,
Wanting the spring that those shrunk pipes had fed,
Show'd life imprison'd in a body dead.

On this sad shadow Lucrece spends her eyes
And shapes her sorrow to the beldame's woes,
Who nothing wants to answer her but cries
And bitter words to ban her cruel foes.
The painter was no god to lend her those;
And therefore Lucrece swears he did her wrong
To give her so much grief and not a tongue.

'Poor instrument,' quoth she, 'without a sound!
I'll tune thy woes with my lamenting tongue,
And drop sweet balm in Priam's painted wound,
And rail on Pyrrhus that hath done him wrong,
And with my tears quench Troy that burns so long,
And with my knife scratch out the angry eyes
Of all the Greeks that are thine enemies.

'Show me the strumpet that began this stir,
That with my nails her beauty I may tear.
Thy heat of lust, fond Paris, did incur
This load of wrath that burning Troy doth bear.
Thy eye kindled the fire that burneth here,
And here in Troy, for trespass of thine eye,
The sire, the son, the dame and daughter die.

'Why should the private pleasure of some one
Become the public plague of many moe?
Let sin, alone committed, light alone
Upon his head that hath transgressed so;
Let guiltless souls be freed from guilty woe.
For one's offence why should so many fall,
To plague a private sin in general?

'Lo, here weeps Hecuba, here Priam dies,
Here manly Hector faints, here Troilus sounds,
Here friend by friend in bloody channel lies,
And friend to friend gives unadvised wounds,
And one man's lust these many lives confounds.
Had doting Priam check'd his son's desire,
Troy had been bright with fame, and not with fire.'

Here feelingly she weeps Troy's painted woes:
For sorrow, like a heavy hanging bell,
Once set on ringing, with his own weight goes;
Then little strength rings out the doleful knell.
So Lucrece, set awork, sad tales doth tell
To pencill'd pensiveness and colour'd sorrow:
She lends them words, and she their looks doth borrow.

She throws her eyes about the painting round,
And who she finds forlorn she doth lament.
At last she sees a wretched image bound
That piteous looks to Phrygian shepherds lent.
His face, though full of cares, yet show'd content;
Onward to Troy with the blunt swains he goes,
So mild that Patience seem'd to scorn his woes.

In him the painter labour'd with his skill
To hide deceit, and give the harmless show
An humble gait, calm looks, eyes wailing still,
A brow unbent that seem'd to welcome woe,
Cheeks neither red nor pale, but mingled so
That blushing red no guilty instance gave
Nor ashy pale the fear that false hearts have;

But, like a constant and confirmed devil,
He entertain'd a show so seeming just,
And therein so ensconc'd his secret evil,
That jealousy itself could not mistrust
False creeping craft and perjury should thrust
Into so bright a day such black-fac'd storms
Or blot with hell-born sin such saintlike forms.

The well-skill'd workman this mild image drew
For perjur'd Sinon, whose enchanting story
The credulous old Priam after slew;
Whose words like wildfire burnt the shining glory
Of rich-built Ilion, that the skies were sorry,
And little stars shot from their fixed places
When their glass fell wherein they view'd their faces.

This picture she advisedly perus'd
And chid the painter for his wondrous skill,
Saying, some shape in Sinon's was abus'd;
So fair a form lodg'd not a mind so ill.
And still on him she gaz'd, and gazing still,
Such signs of truth in his plain face she spied
That she concludes the picture was belied.

'It cannot be,' quoth she, 'that so much guile'—
She would have said 'can lurk in such a look';
But Tarquin's shape came in her mind the while
And from her tongue 'can lurk' from 'cannot' took.
'It cannot be' she in that sense forsook
And turn'd it thus: 'It cannot be, I find,
But such a face should bear a wicked mind;

'For even as subtile Sinon here is painted,
So sober-sad, so weary, and so mild—
As if with grief or travail he had fainted—
To me came Tarquin armed; so beguil'd
With outward honesty, but yet defil'd
With inward vice. As Priam him did cherish,
So did I Tarquin; so my Troy did perish.

'Look, look, how list'ning Priam wets his eyes
To see those borrowed tears that Sinon sheeds!
Priam, why art thou old, and yet not wise?
For every tear he falls a Troyan bleeds.
His eye drops fire, no water thence proceeds.
Those round clear pearls of his that move thy pity
Are balls of quenchless fire to burn thy city.

'Such devils steal effects from lightless hell;
For Sinon in his fire doth quake with cold
And in that cold hot burning fire doth dwell.
These contraries such unity do hold

Only to flatter fools and make them bold.
So Priam's trust false Sinon's tears doth flatter
That he finds means to burn his Troy with water.'

Here, all enrag'd, such passion her assails
That patience is quite beaten from her breast.
She tears the senseless Sinon with her nails,
Comparing him to that unhappy guest
Whose deed hath made herself herself detest.
At last she smilingly with this gives o'er:
'Fool, fool!' quoth she, 'His wounds will not be sore.'

Thus ebbs and flows the current of her sorrow,
And time doth weary time with her complaining.
She looks for night, and then she longs for morrow,
And both she thinks too long with her remaining.
Short time seems long in sorrow's sharp sustaining;
Though woe be heavy, yet it seldom sleeps,
And they that watch see time how slow it creeps;

Which all this time hath overslipp'd her thought
That she with painted images hath spent,
Being from the feeling of her own grief brought
By deep surmise of others' detriment,
Losing her woes in shows of discontent.
It easeth some, though none it ever cured,
To think their dolour others have endured.

But now the mindful messenger, come back,
Brings home his lord and other company;
Who finds his Lucrece clad in mourning black,
And round about her tear-distained eye
Blue circles stream'd, like rainbows in the sky.
These water-galls in her dim element
Foretell new storms to those already spent.

Which when her sad-beholding husband saw,
Amazedly in her sad face he stares.
Her eyes, though sod in tears, look'd red and raw,
Her lively colour kill'd with deadly cares.
He hath no power to ask her how she fares;
But stood, like old acquaintance in a trance,
Met far from home, wond'ring each other's chance.

At last he takes her by the bloodless hand
And thus begins: 'What uncouth ill event
Hath thee befall'n, that thou dost trembling stand?
Sweet love, what spite hath thy fair colour spent?
Why art thou thus attir'd in discontent?
Unmask, dear dear, this moody heaviness
And tell thy grief, that we may give redress.'

Three times with sighs she gives her sorrow fire
Ere once she can discharge one word of woe.
At length address'd to answer his desire,
She modestly prepares to let them know
Her honour is ta'en prisoner by the foe,
While Collatine and his consorted lords
With sad attention long to hear her words.

And now this pale swan in her wat'ry nest
Begins the sad dirge of her certain ending:
'Few words,' quoth she, 'shall fit the trespass best
Where no excuse can give the fault amending.
In me moe woes than words are now depending,
And my laments would be drawn out too long
To tell them all with one poor tired tongue.

'Then be this all the task it hath to say:
Dear husband, in the interest of thy bed
A stranger came and on that pillow lay
Where thou wast wont to rest thy weary head;
And what wrong else may be imagined
By foul enforcement might be done to me,
From that, alas, thy Lucrece is not free.

'For in the dreadful dead of dark midnight
With shining falchion in my chamber came
A creeping creature with a flaming light
And softly cried, "Awake, thou Roman dame,
And entertain my love; else lasting shame
On thee and thine this night I will inflict,
If thou my love's desire do contradict.

'"For some hard-favour'd groom of thine," quoth he,
"Unless thou yoke thy liking to my will,
I'll murther straight, and then I'll slaughter thee
And swear I found you where you did fulfil
The loathsome act of lust, and so did kill
The lechers in their deed. This act will be
My fame and thy perpetual infamy."

'With this I did begin to start and cry;
And then against my heart he set his sword,

Swearing, unless I took all patiently,
I should not live to speak another word.
So should my shame still rest upon record,
And never be forgot in mighty Rome
Th' adulterate death of Lucrece and her groom.

'Mine enemy was strong, my poor self weak —
And far the weaker with so strong a fear.
My bloody judge forbode my tongue to speak;
No rightful plea might plead for justice there.
His scarlet lust came evidence to swear
That my poor beauty had purloin'd his eyes;
And when the judge is robb'd, the prisoner dies.

'O, teach me how to make mine own excuse!
Or (at the least) this refuge let me find:
Though my gross blood be stain'd with this abuse,
Immaculate and spotless is my mind;
That was not forc'd; that never was inclin'd
To accessary yieldings, but still pure
Doth in her poison'd closet yet endure.'

Lo, here, the hopeless merchant of this loss,
With head declin'd and voice damm'd up with woe,
With sad-set eyes and wreathed arms across,
From lips new waxen pale begins to blow
The grief away that stops his answer so.
But, wretched as he is, he strives in vain;
What he breathes out his breath drinks up again.

As through an arch the violent roaring tide
Outruns the eye that doth behold his haste,
Yet in the eddy boundeth in his pride
Back to the strait that forc'd him on so fast;
In rage sent out, recall'd in rage being past:
Even so his sighs, his sorrows, make a saw,
To push grief on, and back the same grief draw.

Which speechless woe of his poor she attendeth
And his untimely frenzy thus awaketh:
'Dear lord, thy sorrow to my sorrow lendeth
Another power. No flood by raining slaketh.
My woe too sensible thy passion maketh
More feeling-painful. Let it then suffice
To drown one woe, one pair of weeping eyes.

'And for my sake when I might charm thee so,
For she that was thy Lucrece — now attend me.
Be suddenly revenged on my foe,
Thine, mine, his own. Suppose thou dost defend me
From what is past. The help that thou shalt lend me
Comes all too late, yet let the traitor die;
For sparing justice feeds iniquity.

'But ere I name him, you fair lords,' quoth she,
Speaking to those that came with Collatine,
'Shall plight your honourable faiths to me
With swift pursuit to venge this wrong of mine;
For 'tis a meritorious fair design
To chase injustice with revengeful arms.
Knights by their oaths should right poor ladies' harms.'

At this request, with noble disposition
Each present lord began to promise aid,
As bound in knighthood to her imposition,
Longing to hear the hateful foe bewray'd.
But she, that yet her sad task hath not said,
The protestation stops. 'O, speak!' quoth she,
'How may this forced stain be wip'd from me?

'What is the quality of my offence,
Being constrain'd with dreadful circumstance?
May my pure mind with the foul act dispense,
My low-declined honour to advance?
May any terms acquit me from this chance?
The poisoned fountain clears itself again;
And why not I from this compelled stain?'

With this they all at once began to say,
Her body's stain her mind untainted clears;
While with a joyless smile she turns away
The face, that map which deep impression bears
Of hard misfortune, carv'd in it with tears.
'No, no!' quoth she, 'No dame hereafter living
By my excuse shall claim excuse's giving.'

Here with a sigh as if her heart would break
She throws forth Tarquin's name: 'He, he!' she says,
But more than 'he' her poor tongue could not speak,
Till after many accents and delays,
Untimely breathings, sick and short assays,
She utters this: 'He, he! fair lords, 'tis he
That guides this hand to give this wound to me.'

Even here she sheathed in her harmless breast
A harmful knife, that thence her soul unsheathed.
That blow did bail it from the deep unrest
Of that polluted prison where it breathed.
Her contrite sighs unto the clouds bequeathed
  Her winged sprite, and through her wounds doth fly
  Live's lasting date from cancell'd destiny.

Stone-still, astonish'd with this deadly deed,
Stood Collatine and all his lordly crew,
Till Lucrece' father, that beholds her bleed,
Himself on her self-slaught'red body threw,
And from the purple fountain Brutus drew
  The murd'rous knife, and, as it left the place,
  Her blood, in poor revenge, held it in chase;

And bubbling from her breast, it doth divide
In two slow rivers, that the crimson blood
Circles her body in on every side,
Who, like a late-sack'd island, vastly stood
Bare and unpeopled in this fearful flood.
  Some of her blood still pure and red remain'd,
  And some look'd black, and that false Tarquin stain'd.

About the mourning and congealed face
Of that black blood a wat'ry rigoll goes,
Which seems to weep upon the tainted place;
And ever since, as pitying Lucrece' woes,
Corrupted blood some watery token shows,
  And blood untainted still doth red abide,
  Blushing at that which is so putrefied.

'Daughter, dear daughter!' old Lucretius cries,
'That life was mine which thou hast here deprived.
If in the child the father's image lies,
Where shall I live now Lucrece is unlived?
Thou wast not to this end from me derived.
  If children predecease progenitors,
  We are their offspring, and they none of ours.

'Poor broken glass, I often did behold
In thy sweet semblance my old age new born;
But now that fresh fair mirror, dim and old,
Shows me a bare-bon'd death by time outworn.
O, from thy cheeks my image thou hast torn
  And shiver'd all the beauty of my glass,
  That I no more can see what once I was.

'O time, cease thou thy course, and last no longer,
If they surcease to be that should survive.
Shall rotten death make conquest of the stronger
And leave the falt'ring feeble souls alive?
The old bees die, the young possess their hive.
  Then live, sweet Lucrece, live again and see
  Thy father die, and not thy father thee.'

By this, starts Collatine as from a dream
And bids Lucretius give his sorrow place;
And then in key-cold Lucrece' bleeding stream
He falls, and bathes the pale fear in his face,
And counterfeits to die with her a space;
  Till manly shame bids him possess his breath
  And live to be revenged on her death.

The deep vexation of his inward soul
Hath serv'd a dumb arrest upon his tongue;
Who, mad that sorrow should his use control,
Or keep him from heart-easing words so long,
Begins to talk; but through his lips do throng
  Weak words, so thick come in his poor heart's aid
  That no man could distinguish what he said.

Yet sometime 'Tarquin' was pronounced plain,
But through his teeth, as if the name he tore.
This windy tempest, till it blow up rain,
Held back his sorrow's tide, to make it more.
At last it rains, and busy winds give o'er;
  Then son and father weep with equal strife
  Who should weep most, for daughter or for wife.

The one doth call her his, the other his;
Yet neither may possess the claim they lay.
The father says 'She's mine.' 'O, mine she is!'
Replies her husband. 'Do not take away
My sorrow's interest. Let no mourner say
  He weeps for her; for she was only mine,
  And only must be wail'd by Collatine.'

'O,' quoth Lucretius, 'I did give that life
Which she too early and too late hath spill'd.'
'Woe, woe!' quoth Collatine. 'She was my wife,
I owed her, and 'tis mine that she hath kill'd.'
'My daughter' and 'my wife' with clamours fill'd
  The dispers'd air, who, holding Lucrece' life,
  Answer'd their cries, 'my daughter' and 'my wife.'

Brutus, who pluck'd the knife from Lucrece' side,
Seeing such emulation in their woe,

Began to clothe his wit in state and pride,
Burying in Lucrece' wound his folly's show.
He with the Romans was esteemed so
As seely jeering idiots are with kings,
For sportive words and utt'ring foolish things;

But now he throws that shallow habit by
Wherein deep policy did him disguise,
And arm'd his long-hid wits advisedly
To check the tears in Collatinus' eyes.
'Thou wronged lord of Rome,' quoth he, 'arise!
Let my unsounded self, suppos'd a fool,
Now set thy long-experienc'd wit to school.

'Why, Collatine, is woe the cure for woe?
Do wounds help wounds, or grief help grievous deeds?
Is it revenge to give thyself a blow
For his foul act by whom thy fair wife bleeds?
Such childish humour from weak minds proceeds.
Thy wretched wife mistook the matter so,
To slay herself that should have slain her foe.

'Courageous Roman, do not steep thy heart
In such relenting dew of lamentations;
But kneel with me, and help to bear thy part
To rouse our Roman gods with invocations
That they will suffer these abominations
(Since Rome herself in them doth stand disgraced)
By our strong arms from forth her fair streets chased.

'Now, by the Capitol that we adore,
And by this chaste blood so unjustly stained,
By heaven's fair sun that breeds the fat earth's store,
By all our country rights in Rome maintained,
And by chaste Lucrece' soul that late complained
Her wrongs to us, and by this bloody knife,
We will revenge the death of this true wife.'

This said, he struck his hand upon his breast
And kiss'd the fatal knife to end his vow;
And to his protestation urg'd the rest,
Who, wond'ring at him, did his words allow.
Then jointly to the ground their knees they bow;
And that deep vow which Brutus made before
He doth again repeat, and that they swore.

When they had sworn to this advised doom,
They did conclude to bear dead Lucrece thence,
To show her bleeding body thorough Rome,
And so to publish Tarquin's foul offence;
Which being done with speedy diligence,
The Romans plausibly did give consent
To Tarquin's everlasting banishment.

On May 20, 1609, Thomas Thorpe registered 'A Booke called Shakespeares sonnettes.' This came out in quarto in that same year: 'Shake-speares Sonnets. Neuer before Imprinted.' The same Quarto contains A Lover's Complaint, which follows the Sonnets and is ascribed to 'William Shake-speare' in the title heading. His authorship of this curious poem is very doubtful. Two of the sonnets in Thorpe's collection (cxxxviii, cxliv) had already been published in The Passionate Pilgrim (1599); cvii seems to refer to the death of Elizabeth and the accession of James I in 1603. The dates of the rest are not to be determined. They must have been written at different times and on miscellaneous occasions throughout Shakespeare's literary life from *ca.* 1592 to 1609. Though the Quarto was not, apparently, an authorized edition, and although it was carelessly printed, the text of the Sonnets is reasonably good. Numerous misprints have proved easy to correct. About a score of passages are still doubtful, but in most of these the sense is clear enough.

It is customary to regard Sonnets i-cxxvi as a continuous series and to assume that they are all addressed to the same person — some young man of noble birth. This idea takes it for granted that Thorpe's arrangement is Shakespeare's. That, however, is a pure assumption. Nor does it follow, even if the arrangement is admitted to be canonical, that the same person is addressed in all the hundred and twenty-six. *A priori* such unity of dedication is not very likely, and unprepossessed reading confirms the antecedent improbability. The first seventeen sonnets form a group by themselves. They sound like merely fanciful variations on the theme of *Venus and Adonis*, verses 129–132, 163–174, 751–768 (cf. *Romeo and Juliet*, i, 1, 215–231; *All's Well*, i, 1, 137–162; *Twelfth Night*, i, 5, 259–261). Nos. xxv, xxvi, xxxviii, might have been sent to a noble and friendly patron; in tone and manner they are very like the dedication to *Lucrece*. Nos. xxx-xxxii might be addressed to the same patron or to some friend of more nearly the poet's own rank. No. cviii can hardly have been sent to that patron or friend. In any case, this sonnet, if compared with lxx, is enough to destroy the theory of a continuous and orderly series (i-cxxvi); for cviii calls the recipient 'sweet boy,' and lxx is addressed to some one who has 'pass'd by the ambush of young days.' Several sonnets of the supposed series are manifestly addressed to a woman; and several of the others (e.g., xx, xxi, xlviii, lvi, lxvi, lxix, lxxiii-lxxv, cxviii, cxix, cxxvi) cannot reasonably be supposed to have been offered to a great nobleman. The young man thought to be addressed in i-cxxvi has been identified with the Earl of Southampton and the Earl of Pembroke. These interpretations are more or less mixed up with Thorpe's mysterious 'Mr. W. H.,' to whom he dedicated the book. 'W. H.' would fit Pembroke, whose name was William Herbert; he became Earl in 1601. 'W. H.' (reversed) would fit Southampton (Henry Wriothesley), to whom Shakespeare dedicated both *Venus and Adonis* and *Lucrece*. Southampton is the favourite claimant; but his title is no stronger than Pembroke's, perhaps not so strong. Neither case is at all demonstrated or demonstrable. Nos. lxxviii, lxxx, lxxxii-lxxxvi raise the vexed question of the Rival Poet. He has been identified with more than a dozen poets of the time — including Spenser, Marlowe, Barnabe Barnes, Ben Jonson, John Davies, Chapman, and Daniel. Chapman is the most popular candidate, but his popularity is waning.

Whatever one may think of the continuity of i-cxxvi, it is quite clear that the remaining sonnets (cxxvii-cliv) do not make an orderly sequence. The Dark Lady who haunts them may be a real person who played a sinister rôle in Shakespeare's life, but she is somehow connected with the dark Rosaline of *Love's Labour's Lost*. Some of the sonnets that concern her are not more serious in autobiographical significance than Berowne's paradox (iv, 3, 248–265; cf. v, 2, 32 ff.). If she is to be identified with the stolen mistress of xl-xlii, that is further disproof of the continuity and completeness of the supposed first cycle. To identify her with Mary Fitton is impossible. She must remain a mystery.

In treating the SONNETS as material for Shakespeare's biography, we should not forget that we are dealing with the supreme dramatist — with that extraordinary genius who, beyond all others, could put himself in the place of any human being, man or woman, and then could make that person express thoughts and feelings and passions as he or she would have uttered them if endowed with superhuman power of expression. In a sonnet, both from its very nature and from the conventions that attend it, the author must seem to 'unlock his heart.' He must either refrain or run the risk of a literal (that is, a personal) interpretation. Nothing, therefore, can prove that Shakespeare's sonnets are, or are not, autobiographical except the discovery of outside evidence that they accord, or do not accord, with facts of his life; and no such evidence is forthcoming. It is idle to talk of 'sincerity' in this regard. Hamlet's soliloquies are sincere, and Iago's cynical revelations of his code, and Macbeth's poetic imaginings that visualize to the brink of delirium. The testimony of the SONNETS must remain ambiguous.

'THE PASSIONATE PILGRIME. *By W. Shakespeare*,' a tiny octavo, was printed for William Jaggard in 1599. The title is simply the publisher's fancy. The book contains twenty short poems. Nos. xv-xx, however, have a separate title page ('Sonnets To sundry notes of Musicke'), which does not claim the poems for Shakespeare. Nos. i and ii are Sonnets cxxxviii and cxliv (see pp. 1516, 1517); iii, v, and xvi are from *Love's Labour's Lost* (iv, 3, 60–73; iv, 2, 109–122; iv, 3, 101–120 (see pp. 209, 211)); xii is usually accepted as Shakespeare's. None of the other poems can be ascribed to Shakespeare with any confidence. Nos. xv and xix are certainly not his, and are therefore omitted in the present edition. Nos. iv, vi, ix, and xi may be by Bartholomew Griffin. They resemble each other strongly, and No. xi is contained in his *Fidessa* (1596). Nos. viii and xx are found in Richard Barnfield's *Poems: in Divers Humours* (1598), and xvii may also be his, though part of it is printed in Thomas Weelkes's *Madrigals* (1597). Probably Weelkes wrote the music only. This leaves vii, x, xiii, xiv, and xviii. Their right to be regarded as Shakespeare's is far from strong, but no other poet claims them.

THE PHŒNIX AND TURTLE is unquestionably genuine. It is printed, with Shakespeare's signature (as one of 'some new compositions of seuerall moderne Writers whose names are subscribed'), in Robert Chester's 'Loves Martyr: Or, Rosalins Complaint. Allegorically shadowing the truth of Loue, in the constant Fate of the Phoenix and Turtle' (1601). The volume also contains signed poems by Jonson, Chapman, and Marston.

SONNETS

TO. THE. ONLIE. BEGETTER. OF.
THESE. INSVING. SONNETS.
MR. W. H. ALL. HAPPINESSE.
AND. THAT. ETERNITIE.
PROMISED.
BY.
OVR. EVER-LIVING. POET.
WISHETH.
THE. WELL-WISHING.
ADVENTVRER. IN.
SETTING.
FORTH.

T. T.

I

From fairest creatures we desire increase,
That thereby beauty's rose might never die,
But as the riper should by time decease,
His tender heir might bear his memory;
But thou, contracted to thine own bright eyes,
Feed'st thy light's flame with self-substantial fuel,
Making a famine where abundance lies,
Thyself thy foe, to thy sweet self too cruel.
Thou that art now the world's fresh ornament
And only herald to the gaudy spring,
Within thine own bud buriest thy content
And, tender churl, mak'st waste in niggarding.
  Pity the world, or else this glutton be,
  To eat the world's due, by the grave and thee.

II

When forty winters shall besiege thy brow
And dig deep trenches in thy beauty's field,
Thy youth's proud livery, so gaz'd on now,
Will be a tatter'd weed of small worth held.
Then being ask'd where all thy beauty lies,
Where all the treasure of thy lusty days,
To say, within thine own deep-sunken eyes
Were an all-eating shame and thriftless praise.
How much more praise deserv'd thy beauty's use
If thou couldst answer, 'This fair child of mine
Shall sum my count and make my old excuse,'
Proving his beauty by succession thine!
  This were to be new made when thou art old
  And see thy blood warm when thou feel'st it cold.

III

Look in thy glass and tell the face thou viewest
Now is the time that face should form another,
Whose fresh repair if now thou not renewest,
Thou dost beguile the world, unbless some mother.
For where is she so fair whose unear'd womb
Disdains the tillage of thy husbandry?
Or who is he so fond will be the tomb
Of his self-love, to stop posterity?
Thou art thy mother's glass, and she in thee
Calls back the lovely April of her prime.
So thou through windows of thine age shalt see,
Despite of wrinkles, this thy golden time.
  But if thou live remem'bred not to be,
  Die single, and thine image dies with thee.

IV

Unthrifty loveliness, why dost thou spend
Upon thyself thy beauty's legacy?
Nature's bequest gives nothing, but doth lend,
And, being frank, she lends to those are free.
Then, beauteous niggard, why dost thou abuse
The bounteous largess given thee to give?
Profitless usurer, why dost thou use
So great a sum of sums, yet canst not live?
For, having traffic with thyself alone,
Thou of thyself thy sweet self dost deceive.
Then how, when nature calls thee to be gone,
What acceptable audit canst thou leave?
  Thy unus'd beauty must be tomb'd with thee,
  Which, used, lives th' executor to be.

V

Those hours that with gentle work did frame
The lovely gaze where every eye doth dwell,
Will play the tyrants to the very same
And that unfair which fairly doth excel;
For never-resting time leads summer on
To hideous winter and confounds him there,
Sap check'd with frost and lusty leaves quite gone,
Beauty o'ersnow'd and bareness everywhere.
Then, were not summer's distillation left
A liquid prisoner pent in walls of glass,
Beauty's effect with beauty were bereft —
Nor it, nor no remembrance what it was;

But flowers distill'd, though they with winter meet,
Leese but their show — their substance still lives sweet.

VI

Then let not winter's ragged hand deface
In thee thy summer ere thou be distill'd.
Make sweet some vial; treasure thou some place
With beauty's treasure ere it be self-kill'd.
That use is not forbidden usury
Which happies those that pay the willing loan:
That's for thyself to breed another thee,
Or ten times happier, be it ten for one.
Ten times thyself were happier than thou art,
If ten of thine ten times refigur'd thee.
Then what could death do if thou shouldst depart,
Leaving thee living in posterity?
Be not self-will'd, for thou art much too fair
To be death's conquest and make worms thine heir.

VII

Lo, in the Orient when the gracious light
Lifts up his burning head, each under eye
Doth homage to his new-appearing sight,
Serving with looks his sacred majesty;
And having climb'd the steep-up heavenly hill,
Resembling strong youth in his middle age,
Yet mortal looks adore his beauty still,
Attending on his golden pilgrimage;
But when from highmost pitch, with weary car,
Like feeble age he reeleth from the day,
The eyes (fore duteous) now converted are
From his low tract and look another way.
So thou, thyself outgoing in thy noon,
Unlook'd on diest unless thou get a son.

VIII

Music to hear, why hear'st thou music sadly?
Sweets with sweets war not, joy delights in joy.
Why lov'st thou that which thou receiv'st not gladly,
Or else receiv'st with pleasure thine annoy?
If the true concord of well-tuned sounds,
By unions married, do offend thine ear,
They do but sweetly chide thee, who confounds
In singleness the parts that thou shouldst bear.
Mark how one string, sweet husband to another,
Strikes each in each by mutual ordering;
Resembling sire and child and happy mother,
Who. all in one, one pleasing note do sing;
Whose speechless song, being many, seeming one,
Sings this to thee: 'Thou single wilt prove none.'

IX

Is it for fear to wet a widow's eye
That thou consum'st thyself in single life?
Ah! if thou issueless shalt hap to die,
The world will wail thee like a makeless wife;
The world will be thy widow, and still weep
That thou no form of thee hast left behind
When every private widow well may keep,
By children's eyes, her husband's shape in mind.
Look, what an unthrift in the world doth spend
Shifts but his place, for still the world enjoys it;
But beauty's waste hath in the world an end,
And kept unus'd, the user so destroys it.
No love toward others in that bosom sits
That on himself such murd'rous shame commits.

X

For shame! Deny that thou bear'st love to any,
Who for thyself art so unprovident.
Grant, if thou wilt, thou art belov'd of many,
But that thou none lov'st is most evident;
For thou art so possess'd with murd'rous hate
That 'gainst thyself thou stick'st not to conspire,
Seeking that beauteous roof to ruinate
Which to repair should be thy chief desire.
O, change thy thought, that I may change my mind!
Shall hate be fairer lodg'd than gentle love?
Be as thy presence is, gracious and kind,
Or to thyself at least kind-hearted prove.
Make thee another self for love of me,
That beauty still may live in thine or thee.

XI

As fast as thou shalt wane, so fast thou grow'st
In one of thine, from that which thou departest;
And that fresh blood which youngly thou bestow'st
Thou mayst call thine when thou from youth convertest.
Herein lives wisdom, beauty, and increase;
Without this, folly, age, and cold decay.
If all were minded so, the times should cease,
And threescore year would make the world away.

Let those whom Nature hath not made for store,
Harsh, featureless, and rude, barrenly perish.
Look, whom she best endow'd she gave the more,
Which bounteous gift thou shouldst in bounty cherish.
  She carv'd thee for her seal, and meant thereby
  Thou shouldst print more, not let that copy die.

XII

When I do count the clock that tells the time
And see the brave day sunk in hideous night,
When I behold the violet past prime
And sable curls all silver'd o'er with white,
When lofty trees I see barren of leaves,
Which erst from heat did canopy the herd,
And summer's green all girded up in sheaves
Borne on the bier with white and bristly beard—
Then of thy beauty do I question make
That thou among the wastes of time must go,
Since sweets and beauties do themselves forsake
And die as fast as they see others grow,
  And nothing 'gainst Time's scythe can make defence
  Save breed, to brave him when he takes thee hence.

XIII

O, that you were yourself! but, love, you are
No longer yours than you yourself here live.
Against this coming end you should prepare
And your sweet semblance to some other give.
So should that beauty which you hold in lease
Find no determination; then you were
Yourself again after yourself's decease
When your sweet issue your sweet form should bear.
Who lets so fair a house fall to decay,
Which husbandry in honour might uphold
Against the stormy gusts of winter's day
And barren rage of death's eternal cold?
  O, none but unthrifts! Dear my love, you know
  You had a father — let your son say so.

XIV

Not from the stars do I my judgment pluck,
And yet methinks I have astronomy;
But not to tell of good or evil luck,
Of plagues, of dearths, or seasons' quality;
Nor can I fortune to brief minutes tell,
Pointing to each his thunder, rain, and wind,
Or say with princes if it shall go well
By oft predict that I in heaven find;
But from thine eyes my knowledge I derive,
And, constant stars, in them I read such art
As truth and beauty shall together thrive
If from thyself to store thou wouldst convert;
  Or else of thee this I prognosticate:
  Thy end is truth's and beauty's doom and date.

XV

When I consider every thing that grows
Holds in perfection but a little moment,
That this huge stage presenteth naught but shows
Whereon the stars in secret influence comment;
When I perceive that men as plants increase,
Cheered and check'd even by the selfsame sky,
Vaunt in their youthful sap, at height decrease,
And wear their brave state out of memory:
Then the conceit of this inconstant stay,
Sets you most rich in youth before my sight,
Where wasteful Time debateth with Decay
To change your day of youth to sullied night
  And, all in war with Time for love of you,
  As he takes from you, I ingraft you new.

XVI

But wherefore do not you a mightier way
Make war upon this bloody tyrant, Time?
And fortify yourself in your decay
With means more blessed than my barren rhyme?
Now stand you on the top of happy hours;
And many maiden gardens, yet unset,
With virtuous wish would bear your living flowers,
Much liker than your painted counterfeit.
So should the lines of life that life repair
Which this time's pencil, or my pupil pen,
Neither in inward worth nor outward fair
Can make you live yourself in eyes of men.
  To give away yourself keeps yourself still,
  And you must live, drawn by your own sweet skill.

XVII

Who will believe my verse in time to come
If it were fill'd with your most high deserts?
Though yet, heaven knows, it is but as a tomb
Which hides your life and shows not half your parts.

If I could write the beauty of your eyes
And in fresh numbers number all your graces,
The age to come would say, 'This poet lies!
Such heavenly touches ne'er touch'd earthly faces.'
So should my papers (yellowed with their age)
Be scorn'd, like old men of less truth than tongue,
And your true rights be term'd a poet's rage
And stretched metre of an antique song.
But were some child of yours alive that time,
You should live twice — in it, and in my rhyme.

XVIII

Shall I compare thee to a summer's day?
Thou art more lovely and more temperate.
Rough winds do shake the darling buds of May,
And summer's lease hath all too short a date.
Sometime too hot the eye of heaven shines,
And often is his gold complexion dimm'd;
And every fair from fair sometime declines,
By chance, or nature's changing course, untrimm'd;
But thy eternal summer shall not fade
Nor lose possession of that fair thou ow'st,
Nor shall Death brag thou wand'rest in his shade
When in eternal lines to time thou grow'st.
So long as men can breathe or eyes can see,
So long lives this, and this gives life to thee.

XIX

Devouring Time, blunt thou the lion's paws
And make the earth devour her own sweet brood;
Pluck the keen teeth from the fierce tiger's jaws
And burn the long-liv'd phœnix in her blood;
Make glad and sorry seasons as thou fleets,
And do whate'er thou wilt, swift-footed Time,
To the wide world and all her fading sweets;
But I forbid thee one most heinous crime:
O, carve not with thy hours my love's fair brow,
Nor draw no lines there with thine antique pen!
Him in thy course untainted do allow
For beauty's pattern to succeeding men.
Yet do thy worst, old Time! Despite thy wrong,
My love shall in my verse ever live young.

XX

A woman's face, with Nature's own hand painted,
Hast thou, the master mistress of my passion;
A woman's gentle heart, but not acquainted
With shifting change, as is false women's fashion;
An eye more bright than theirs, less false in rolling,
Gilding the object whereupon it gazeth;
A man in hue all hues in his controlling,
Which steals men's eyes and women's souls amazeth.
And for a woman wert thou first created,
Till Nature as she wrought thee fell a-doting
And by addition me of thee defeated
By adding one thing to my purpose nothing.
But since she prick'd thee out for women's pleasure,
Mine be thy love, and thy love's use their treasure.

XXI

So is it not with me as with that Muse
Stirr'd by a painted beauty to his verse,
Who heaven itself for ornament doth use
And every fair with his fair doth rehearse;
Making a couplement of proud compare
With sun and moon, with earth and sea's rich gems,
With April's first-born flowers, and all things rare
That heaven's air in this huge rondure hems.
O, let me, true in love, but truly write,
And then believe me, my love is as fair
As any mother's child, though not so bright
As those gold candles fix'd in heaven's air.
Let them say more that like of hearsay well;
I will not praise that purpose not to sell.

XXII

My glass shall not persuade me I am old
So long as youth and thou are of one date;
But when in thee time's furrows I behold,
Then look I death my days should expiate.
For all that beauty that doth cover thee
Is but the seemly raiment of my heart,
Which in thy breast doth live, as thine in me.
How can I then be elder than thou art?
O, therefore, love, be of thyself so wary
As I, not for myself, but for thee will,
Bearing thy heart, which I will keep so chary
As tender nurse her babe from faring ill.

Presume not on thy heart when mine is slain:
Thou gav'st me thine, not to give back again.

XXIII

As an unperfect actor on the stage
Who with his fear is put besides his part,
Or some fierce thing replete with too much rage,
Whose strength's abundance weakens his own heart;
So I, for fear of trust, forget to say
The perfect ceremony of love's rite,
And in mine own love's strength seem to decay,
O'ercharg'd with burthen of mine own love's might.
O, let my looks be then the eloquence
And dumb presagers of my speaking breast,
Who plead for love, and look for recompense,
More than that tongue that more hath more express'd.
O, learn to read what silent love hath writ!
To hear with eyes belongs to love's fine wit.

XXIV

Mine eye hath play'd the painter and hath stell'd
Thy beauty's form in table of my heart;
My body is the frame wherein 'tis held,
And perspective it is best painter's art.
For through the painter must you see his skill
To find where your true image pictur'd lies,
Which in my bosom's shop is hanging still,
That hath his windows glazed with thine eyes.
Now see what good turns eyes for eyes have done:
Mine eyes have drawn thy shape, and thine for me
Are windows to my breast, wherethrough the sun
Delights to peep, to gaze therein on thee.
Yet eyes this cunning want to grace their art —
They draw but what they see, know not the heart.

XXV

Let those who are in favour with their stars
Of public honour and proud titles boast,
Whilst I, whom fortune of such triumph bars,
Unlook'd for joy in that I honour most.
Great princes' favourites their fair leaves spread
But as the marigold at the sun's eye;
And in themselves their pride lies buried,
For at a frown they in their glory die.
The painful warrior famoused for fight,
After a thousand victories once foil'd,
Is from the book of honour rased quite,
And all the rest forgot for which he toil'd.
Then happy I, that love and am beloved
Where I may not remove nor be removed.

XXVI

Lord of my love, to whom in vassalage
Thy merit hath my duty strongly knit,
To thee I send this written embassage,
To witness duty, not to show my wit:
Duty so great, which wit so poor as mine
May make seem bare, in wanting words to show it,
But that I hope some good conceit of thine
In thy soul's thought (all naked) will bestow it;
Till whatsoever star that guides my moving
Points on me graciously with fair aspect,
And puts apparel on my tattered loving
To show me worthy of thy sweet respect.
Then may I dare to boast how I do love thee;
Till then not show my head where thou mayst prove me.

XXVII

Weary with toil, I haste me to my bed,
The dear repose for limbs with travel tired;
But then begins a journey in my head
To work my mind when body's work's expired.
For then my thoughts, from far where I abide,
Intend a zealous pilgrimage to thee,
And keep my drooping eyelids open wide,
Looking on darkness which the blind do see;
Save that my soul's imaginary sight
Presents thy shadow to my sightless view,
Which, like a jewel hung in ghastly night,
Makes black night beauteous and her old face new.
Lo, thus, by day my limbs, by night my mind,
For thee, and for myself, no quiet find.

XXVIII

How can I then return in happy plight
That am debarr'd the benefit of rest,
When day's oppression is not eas'd by night,
But day by night and night by day oppress'd,
And each, though enemies to either's reign,
Do in consent shake hands to torture me,
The one by toil, the other to complain
How far I toil, still farther off from thee?

I tell the day, to please him, thou art bright
And dost him grace when clouds do blot the heaven;
So flatter I the swart-complexion'd night,
When sparkling stars twire not, thou gild'st the even.
But day doth daily draw my sorrows longer,
And night doth nightly make grief's strength seem stronger.

XXIX

When, in disgrace with Fortune and men's eyes,
I all alone beweep my outcast state,
And trouble deaf heaven with my bootless cries,
And look upon myself and curse my fate,
Wishing me like to one more rich in hope,
Featur'd like him, like him with friends possess'd,
Desiring this man's art, and that man's scope,
With what I most enjoy contented least;
Yet in these thoughts myself almost despising,
Haply I think on thee, and then my state,
Like to the lark at break of day arising
From sullen earth, sings hymns at heaven's gate;
For thy sweet love rememb'red such wealth brings
That then I scorn to change my state with kings.

XXX

When to the sessions of sweet silent thought
I summon up remembrance of things past,
I sigh the lack of many a thing I sought
And with old woes new wail my dear time's waste.
Then can I drown an eye (unus'd to flow)
For precious friends hid in death's dateless night,
And weep afresh love's long since cancell'd woe,
And moan th' expense of many a vanish'd sight.
Then can I grieve at grievances foregone,
And heavily from woe to woe tell o'er
The sad account of fore-bemoaned moan,
Which I new pay as if not paid before.
But if the while I think on thee, dear friend,
All losses are restor'd and sorrows end.

XXXI

Thy bosom is endeared with all hearts
Which I by lacking have supposed dead;
And there reigns love, and all love's loving parts,
And all those friends which I thought buried.
How many a holy and obsequious tear
Hath dear religious love stol'n from mine eye,
As interest of the dead, which now appear
But things remov'd that hidden in thee lie!
Thou art the grave where buried love doth live,
Hung with the trophies of my lovers gone,
Who all their parts of me to thee did give:
That due of many now is thine alone.
Their images I lov'd I view in thee,
And thou (all they) hast all the all of me.

XXXII

If thou survive my well-contented day
When that churl Death my bones with dust shall cover,
And shalt by fortune once more resurvey
These poor rude lines of thy deceased lover,
Compare them with the bett'ring of the time,
And though they be outstripp'd by every pen,
Reserve them for my love not for their rhyme,
Exceeded by the height of happier men.
O, then vouchsafe me but this loving thought:
'Had my friend's Muse grown with this growing age,
A dearer birth than this his love had brought,
To march in ranks of better equipage;
But since he died, and poets better prove,
Theirs for their style I'll read, his for his love.'

XXXIII

Full many a glorious morning have I seen
Flatter the mountain tops with sovereign eye,
Kissing with golden face the meadows green,
Gilding pale streams with heavenly alchemy;
Anon permit the basest clouds to ride
With ugly rack on his celestial face
And from the forlorn world his visage hide,
Stealing unseen to West with this disgrace.
Even so my sun one early morn did shine
With all triumphant splendour on my brow;
But, out alack! he was but one hour mine,
The region cloud hath mask'd him from me now.
Yet him for this my love no whit disdaineth;
Suns of the world may stain when heaven's sun staineth.

XXXIV

Why didst thou promise such a beauteous day
And make me travel forth without my cloak,
To let base clouds o'ertake me in my way,
Hiding thy brav'ry in their rotten smoke?

'Tis not enough that through the cloud thou break
To dry the rain on my storm-beaten face,
For no man well of such a salve can speak
That heals the wound, and cures not the disgrace:
Nor can thy shame give physic to my grief;
Though thou repent, yet I have still the loss.
Th' offender's sorrow lends but weak relief
To him that bears the strong offence's cross.
Ah, but those tears are pearl which thy love sheeds,
And they are rich and ransom all ill deeds.

XXXV

No more be griev'd at that which thou hast done:
Roses have thorns, and silver fountains mud;
Clouds and eclipses stain both moon and sun,
And loathsome canker lives in sweetest bud.
All men make faults, and even I in this,
Authorizing thy trespass with compare,
Myself corrupting, salving thy amiss,
Excusing thy sins more than thy sins are;
For to thy sensual fault I bring in sense —
Thy adverse party is thy advocate —
And 'gainst myself a lawful plea commence.
Such civil war is in my love and hate
That I an accessary needs must be
To that sweet thief which sourly robs from me.

XXXVI

Let me confess that we two must be twain,
Although our undivided loves are one.
So shall those blots that do with me remain,
Without thy help by me be borne alone.
In our two loves there is but one respect,
Though in our lives a separable spite,
Which though it alter not love's sole effect,
Yet doth it steal sweet hours from love's delight.
I may not evermore acknowledge thee,
Lest my bewailed guilt should do thee shame;
Nor thou with public kindness honour me,
Unless thou take that honour from thy name.
But do not so. I love thee in such sort
As, thou being mine, mine is thy good report.

XXXVII

As a decrepit father takes delight
To see his active child do deeds of youth,
So I, made lame by Fortune's dearest spite,
Take all my comfort of thy worth and truth;
For whether beauty, birth, or wealth, or wit,
Or any of these all, or all, or more,
Entitled in thy parts do crowned sit,
I make my love engrafted to this store.
So then I am not lame, poor, nor despis'd
Whilst that this shadow doth such substance give
That I in thy abundance am suffic'd
And by a part of all thy glory live.
Look what is best — that best I wish in thee.
This wish I have; then ten times happy me!

XXXVIII

How can my Muse want subject to invent
While thou dost breathe, that pour'st into my verse
Thine own sweet argument, too excellent
For every vulgar paper to rehearse?
O, give thyself the thanks if aught in me
Worthy perusal stand against thy sight;
For who's so dumb that cannot write to thee,
When thou thyself dost give invention light?
Be thou the tenth Muse, ten times more in worth
Than those old nine which rhymers invocate;
And he that calls on thee, let him bring forth
Eternal numbers to outlive long date.
If my slight Muse do please these curious days,
The pain be mine, but thine shall be the praise.

XXXIX

O, how thy worth with manners may I sing
When thou art all the better part of me?
What can mine own praise to mine own self bring?
And what is't but mine own when I praise thee?
Even for this let us divided live
And our dear love lose name of single one,
That by this separation I may give
That due to thee which thou deserv'st alone.
O absence, what a torment wouldst thou prove,
Were it not thy sour leisure gave sweet leave
To entertain the time with thoughts of love,
Which time and thoughts so sweetly doth deceive,
And that thou teachest how to make one twain —
By praising him here who doth hence remain!

XL

Take all my loves, my love, yea, take them all!
What hast thou then more than thou hadst before?
No love, my love, that thou mayst true love call;
All mine was thine before thou hadst this more.
Then, if for my love thou my love receivest,
I cannot blame thee for my love thou usest;
But yet be blam'd if thou thyself deceivest
By wilful taste of what thyself refusest.
I do forgive thy robb'ry, gentle thief,
Although thou steal thee all my poverty;
And yet love knows it is a greater grief
To bear love's wrong than hate's known injury.
Lascivious grace, in whom all ill well shows,
Kill me with spites; yet we must not be foes.

XLI

Those pretty wrongs that liberty commits
When I am sometime absent from thy heart,
Thy beauty and thy years full well befits,
For still temptation follows where thou art.
Gentle thou art, and therefore to be won;
Beauteous thou art, therefore to be assailed;
And when a woman wooes, what woman's son
Will sourly leave her till she have prevailed?
Ay me! but yet thou mightst my seat forbear,
And chide thy beauty and thy straying youth,
Who lead thee in their riot even there
Where thou art forc'd to break a twofold truth —
Hers, by thy beauty tempting her to thee,
Thine, by thy beauty being false to me.

XLII

That thou hast her, it is not all my grief,
And yet it may be said I lov'd her dearly;
That she hath thee is of my wailing chief,
A loss in love that touches me more nearly.
Loving offenders, thus I will excuse ye:
Thou dost love her because thou know'st I love her,
And for my sake even so doth she abuse me,
Suff'ring my friend for my sake to approve her.
If I lose thee, my loss is my love's gain,
And losing her, my friend hath found that loss:
Both find each other, and I lose both twain,
And both for my sake lay on me this cross.
But here's the joy — my friend and I are one.
Sweet flattery! then she loves but me alone.

XLIII

When most I wink, then do mine eyes best see,
For all the day they view things unrespected,
But when I sleep, in dreams they look on thee
And, darkly bright, are bright in dark directed.
Then thou, whose shadow shadows doth make bright,
How would thy shadow's form form happy show
To the clear day with thy much clearer light
When to unseeing eyes thy shade shines so!
How would, I say, mine eyes be blessed made
By looking on thee in the living day,
When in dead night thy fair imperfect shade
Through heavy sleep on sightless eyes doth stay!
All days are nights to see till I see thee,
And nights bright days when dreams do show thee me.

XLIV

If the dull substance of my flesh were thought,
Injurious distance should not stop my way;
For then, despite of space, I would be brought,
From limits far remote, where thou dost stay.
No matter then although my foot did stand
Upon the farthest earth remov'd from thee;
For nimble thought can jump both sea and land
As soon as think the place where he would be.
But, ah, thought kills me that I am not thought,
To leap large lengths of miles when thou art gone,
But that, so much of earth and water wrought,
I must attend time's leisure with my moan,
Receiving naught by elements so slow
But heavy tears, badges of either's woe.

XLV

The other two, slight air and purging fire,
Are both with thee, wherever I abide;
The first my thought, the other my desire,
These present-absent with swift motion slide.
For when these quicker elements are gone
In tender embassy of love to thee,
My life, being made of four, with two alone
Sinks down to death, oppress'd with melancholy;
Until live's composition be recured
By those swift messengers return'd from thee,
Who even but now come back again, assured
Of thy fair health, recounting it to me.
This told, I joy; but then no longer glad,
I send them back again and straight grow sad.

XLVI

Mine eye and heart are at a mortal war
How to divide the conquest of thy sight;
Mine eye my heart thy picture's sight would bar,
My heart mine eye the freedom of that right.
My heart doth plead that thou in him dost lie
(A closet never pierc'd with crystal eyes);
But the defendant doth that plea deny
And says in him thy fair appearance lies.
To 'cide this title is impanneled
A quest of thoughts, all tenants to the heart,
And by their verdict is determined
The clear eye's moiety and the dear heart's part:
  As thus — mine eye's due is thy outward part,
  And my heart's right thy inward love of heart.

XLVII

Betwixt mine eye and heart a league is took,
And each doth good turns now unto the other.
When that mine eye is famish'd for a look,
Or heart in love with sighs himself doth smother,
With my love's picture then my eye doth feast
And to the painted banquet bids my heart.
Another time mine eye is my heart's guest
And in his thoughts of love doth share a part.
So, either by thy picture or my love,
Thyself away art present still with me;
For thou not farther than my thoughts canst move,
And I am still with them, and they with thee;
  Or, if they sleep, thy picture in my sight
  Awakes my heart to heart's and eye's delight.

XLVIII

How careful was I, when I took my way,
Each trifle under truest bars to thrust,
That to my use it might unused stay
From hands of falsehood, in sure wards of trust!
But thou, to whom my jewels trifles are,
Most worthy comfort, now my greatest grief,
Thou, best of dearest, and mine only care,
Art left the prey of every vulgar thief.
Thee have I not lock'd up in any chest,
Save where thou art not, though I feel thou art,
Within the gentle closure of my breast,
From whence at pleasure thou mayst come and part;
  And even thence thou wilt be stol'n, I fear,
  For truth proves thievish for a prize so dear.

XLIX

Against that time (if ever that time come)
When I shall see thee frown on my defects,
When as thy love hath cast his utmost sum,
Call'd to that audit by advis'd respects;
Against that time when thou shalt strangely pass
And scarcely greet me with that sun, thine eye,
When love, converted from the thing it was,
Shall reasons find of settled gravity —
Against that time do I ensconce me here
Within the knowledge of mine own desart,
And this my hand against myself uprear,
To guard the lawful reasons on thy part.
  To leave poor me thou hast the strength of laws,
  Since why to love I can allege no cause.

L

How heavy do I journey on the way
When what I seek (my weary travel's end)
Doth teach that ease and that repose to say,
'Thus far the miles are measur'd from thy friend!'
The beast that bears me, tired with my woe,
Plods dully on, to bear that weight in me,
As if by some instinct the wretch did know
His rider lov'd not speed, being made from thee.
The bloody spur cannot provoke him on
That sometimes anger thrusts into his hide;
Which heavily he answers with a groan,
More sharp to me than spurring to his side;
  For that same groan doth put this in my mind —
  My grief lies onward and my joy behind.

LI

Thus can my love excuse the slow offence
Of my dull bearer when from thee I speed:
From where thou art, why should I haste me thence?
Till I return, of posting is no need.
O, what excuse will my poor beast then find
When swift extremity can seem but slow?
Then should I spur, though mounted on the wind,
In winged speed no motion shall I know.
Then can no horse with my desire keep pace;
Therefore desire, of perfect'st love being made,
Shall neigh (no dull flesh) in his fiery race;
But love, for love, thus shall excuse my jade —
  Since from thee going he went wilful slow,
  Towards thee I'll run and give him leave to go.

LII

So am I as the rich whose blessed key
Can bring him to his sweet up-locked treasure,
The which he will not ev'ry hour survey,
For blunting the fine point of seldom pleasure.
Therefore are feasts so solemn and so rare,
Since, seldom coming, in the long year set,
Like stones of worth they thinly placed are,
Or captain jewels in the carcanet.
So is the time that keeps you as my chest,
Or as the wardrobe which the robe doth hide,
To make some special instant special blest
By new unfolding his imprison'd pride.
Blessed are you, whose worthiness gives scope,
Being had, to triumph, being lack'd, to hope.

LIII

What is your substance, whereof are you made,
That millions of strange shadows on you tend?
Since every one hath, every one, one shade,
And you, but one, can every shadow lend.
Describe Adonis, and the counterfeit
Is poorly imitated after you.
On Helen's cheek all art of beauty set,
And you in Grecian tires are painted new.
Speak of the spring, and foison of the year:
The one doth shadow of your beauty show,
The other as your bounty doth appear,
And you in every blessed shape we know.
In all external grace you have some part,
But you like none, none you, for constant heart.

LIV

O, how much more doth beauty beauteous seem
By that sweet ornament which truth doth give!
The rose looks fair, but fairer we it deem
For that sweet odour which doth in it live.
The canker blooms have full as deep a dye
As the perfumed tincture of the roses,
Hang on such thorns, and play as wantonly
When summer's breath their masked buds discloses;
But, for their virtue only is their show,
They live unwoo'd and unrespected fade,
Die to themselves. Sweet roses do not so:
Of their sweet deaths are sweetest odours made.
And so of you, beauteous and lovely youth,
When that shall vade, by verse distills your truth.

LV

Not marble nor the gilded monuments
Of princes shall outlive this pow'rful rhyme;
But you shall shine more bright in these contents
Than unswept stone, besmear'd with sluttish time.
When wasteful war shall statues overturn,
And broils root out the work of masonry,
Nor Mars his sword nor war's quick fire shall burn
The living record of your memory.
'Gainst death and all-oblivious enmity
Shall you pace forth; your praise shall still find room
Even in the eyes of all posterity
That wear this world out to the ending doom.
So, till the judgment that yourself arise,
You live in this, and dwell in lovers' eyes.

LVI

Sweet love, renew thy force; be it not said
Thy edge should blunter be than appetite,
Which but to-day by feeding is allay'd,
To-morrow sharp'ned in his former might.
So, love, be thou: although to-day thou fill
Thy hungry eyes even till they wink with fulness,
To-morrow see again, and do not kill
The spirit of love with a perpetual dulness.
Let this sad int'rim like the ocean be
Which parts the shore where two contracted new
Come daily to the banks, that, when they see
Return of love, more blest may be the view;
Or call it winter, which, being full of care,
Makes summer's welcome thrice more wish'd, more rare.

LVII

Being your slave, what should I do but tend
Upon the hours and times of your desire?
I have no precious time at all to spend,
Nor services to do, till you require.
Nor dare I chide the world-without-end hour
Whilst I, my sovereign, watch the clock for you,
Nor think the bitterness of absence sour
When you have bid your servant once adieu.
Nor dare I question with my jealious thought
Where you may be, or your affairs suppose,
But, like a sad slave, stay and think of nought
Save where you are how happy you make those.
So true a fool is love that in your will,
Though you do anything, he thinks no ill.

LVIII

That god forbid that made me first your slave
I should in thought control your times of pleasure,
Or at your hand th' account of hours to crave,
Being your vassal bound to stay your leisure!
O, let me suffer (being at your beck)
Th' imprison'd absence of your liberty;
And patience, tame to sufferance, bide each check
Without accusing you of injury.
Be where you list; your charter is so strong
That you yourself may privilege your time
To what you will; to you it doth belong
Yourself to pardon of self-doing crime.
I am to wait, though waiting so be hell;
Not blame your pleasure, be it ill or well.

LIX

If there be nothing new, but that which is
Hath been before, how are our brains beguil'd,
Which, labouring for invention, bear amiss
The second burthen of a former child!
O that record could with a backward look,
Even of five hundreth courses of the sun,
Show me your image in some antique book,
Since mind at first in character was done!
That I might see what the old world could say
To this composed wonder of your frame;
Whether we are mended, or whe'r better they,
Or whether revolution be the same.
O, sure I am the wits of former days
To subjects worse have given admiring praise.

LX

Like as the waves make towards the pebbled shore,
So do our minutes hasten to their end;
Each changing place with that which goes before,
In sequent toil all forwards do contend.
Nativity, once in the main of light,
Crawls to maturity, wherewith being crown'd,
Crooked eclipses 'gainst his glory fight,
And Time that gave doth now his gift confound.
Time doth transfix the flourish set on youth
And delves the parallels in beauty's brow,
Feeds on the rarities of nature's truth,
And nothing stands but for his scythe to mow;
And yet to times in hope my verse shall stand,
Praising thy worth, despite his cruel hand.

LXI

Is it thy will thy image should keep open
My heavy eyelids to the weary night?
Dost thou desire my slumbers should be broken
While shadows like to thee do mock my sight?
Is it thy spirit that thou send'st from thee
So far from home into my deeds to pry,
To find out shames and idle hours in me,
The scope and tenure of thy jealousy?
O, no! thy love, though much, is not so great.
It is my love that keeps mine eye awake;
Mine own true love that doth my rest defeat,
To play the watchman ever for thy sake.
For thee watch I whilst thou dost wake elsewhere,
From me far off, with others all too near.

LXII

Sin of self-love possesseth all mine eye
And all my soul and all my every part;
And for this sin there is no remedy,
It is so grounded inward in my heart.
Methinks no face so gracious is as mine,
No shape so true, no truth of such account,
And for myself mine own worth do define
As I all other in all worths surmount.
But when my glass shows me myself indeed,
Beated and chopt with tann'd antiquity,
Mine own self-love quite contrary I read;
Self so self-loving were iniquity.
'Tis thee (myself) that for myself I praise,
Painting my age with beauty of thy days.

LXIII

Against my love shall be as I am now,
With Time's injurious hand crush'd and o'erworn;
When hours have drain'd his blood, and fill'd his brow
With lines and wrinkles; when his youthful morn
Hath travell'd on to age's steepy night,
And all those beauties whereof now he's king
Are vanishing, or vanish'd out of sight,
Stealing away the treasure of his spring —
For such a time do I now fortify
Against confounding age's cruel knife,
That he shall never cut from memory
My sweet love's beauty, though my lover's life.
His beauty shall in these black lines be seen,
And they shall live, and he in them still green.

LXIV

When I have seen by Time's fell hand defaced
The rich proud cost of outworn buried age;
When sometime lofty towers I see down rased,
And brass eternal slave to mortal rage;
When I have seen the hungry ocean gain
Advantage on the kingdom of the shore,
And the firm soil win of the wat'ry main,
Increasing store with loss, and loss with store;
When I have seen such interchange of state,
Or state itself confounded, to decay;
Ruin hath taught me thus to ruminate,
That Time will come and take my love away.
  This thought is as a death, which cannot choose
  But weep to have that which it fears to lose.

LXV

Since brass, nor stone, nor earth, nor boundless sea,
But sad mortality o'ersways their power,
How with this rage shall beauty hold a plea,
Whose action is no stronger than a flower?
O, how shall summer's honey breath hold out
Against the wrackful siege of batt'ring days,
When rocks impregnable are not so stout,
Nor gates of steel so strong, but Time decays?
O fearful meditation! Where, alack,
Shall Time's best jewel from Time's chest lie hid?
Or what strong hand can hold his swift foot back?
Or who his spoil of beauty can forbid?
  O, none! unless this miracle have might,
  That in black ink my love may still shine bright.

LXVI

Tir'd with all these, for restful death I cry:
As, to behold desert a beggar born,
And needy nothing trimm'd in jollity,
And purest faith unhappily forsworn,
And gilded honour shamefully misplac'd,
And maiden virtue rudely strumpeted,
And right perfection wrongfully disgrac'd,
And strength by limping sway disabled,
And art made tongue-tied by authority,
And folly (doctor-like) controlling skill,
And simple truth miscall'd simplicity,
And captive good attending captain ill.
  Tir'd with all these, from these would I be gone,
  Save that, to die, I leave my love alone.

LXVII

Ah, wherefore with infection should he live
And with his presence grace impiety,
That sin by him advantage should achieve
And lace itself with his society?
Why should false painting imitate his cheek
And steal dead seeing of his living hue?
Why should poor beauty indirectly seek
Roses of shadow, since his rose is true?
Why should he live, now Nature bankrout is,
Beggar'd of blood to blush through lively veins?
For she hath no exchequer now but his,
And, proud of many, lives upon his gains.
  O, him she stores, to show what wealth she had
  In days long since, before these last so bad.

LXVIII

Thus is his cheek the map of days outworn,
When beauty liv'd and died as flowers do now,
Before these bastard signs of fair were born
Or durst inhabit on a living brow;
Before the golden tresses of the dead,
The right of sepulchres, were shorn away
To live a second life on second head;
Ere beauty's dead fleece made another gay.
In him those holy antique hours are seen,
Without all ornament, itself and true,
Making no summer of another's green,
Robbing no old to dress his beauty new;
  And him as for a map doth Nature store,
  To show false Art what beauty was of yore.

LXIX

Those parts of thee that the world's eye doth view
Want nothing that the thought of hearts can mend.
All tongues (the voice of souls) give thee that due,
Utt'ring bare truth, even so as foes commend.
Thy outward thus with outward praise is crown'd;
But those same tongues that give thee so thine own
In other accents do this praise confound
By seeing farther than the eye hath shown.
They look into the beauty of thy mind,
And that in guess they measure by thy deeds;
Then, churls, their thoughts (although their eyes were kind)
To thy fair flower add the rank smell of weeds;

But why thy odour matcheth not thy show,
The soil is this — that thou dost common grow.

LXX

That thou art blam'd shall not be thy defect,
For slander's mark was ever yet the fair;
The ornament of beauty is suspect,
A crow that flies in heaven's sweetest air.
So thou be good, slander doth but approve
Thy worth the greater, being woo'd of time;
For canker vice the sweetest buds doth love,
And thou present'st a pure unstained prime.
Thou hast pass'd by the ambush of young days,
Either not assail'd, or victor being charg'd;
Yet this thy praise cannot be so thy praise
To tie up envy, evermore enlarg'd.
If some suspect of ill mask'd not thy show,
Then thou alone kingdoms of hearts shouldst owe.

LXXI

No longer mourn for me when I am dead
Than you shall hear the surly sullen bell
Give warning to the world that I am fled
From this vile world, with vilest worms to dwell.
Nay, if you read this line, remember not
The hand that writ it; for I love you so
That I in your sweet thoughts would be forgot
If thinking on me then should make you woe.
O, if, I say, you look upon this verse
When I, perhaps, compounded am with clay,
Do not so much as my poor name rehearse,
But let your love even with my life decay,
Lest the wise world should look into your moan
And mock you with me after I am gone.

LXXII

O, lest the world should task you to recite
What merit liv'd in me, that you should love
After my death, dear love, forget me quite,
For you in me can nothing worthy prove;
Unless you would devise some virtuous lie,
To do more for me than mine own desert
And hang more praise upon deceased I
Than niggard truth would willingly impart.
O, lest your true love may seem false in this,
That you for love speak well of me untrue,
My name be buried where my body is,
And live no more to shame nor me nor you!
For I am sham'd by that which I bring forth,
And so should you, to love things nothing worth.

LXXIII

That time of year thou mayst in me behold
When yellow leaves, or none, or few, do hang
Upon those boughs which shake against the cold,
Bare ruin'd choirs where late the sweet birds sang.
In me thou see'st the twilight of such day
As after sunset fadeth in the West,
Which by-and-by black night doth take away,
Death's second self, that seals up all in rest.
In me thou see'st the glowing of such fire
That on the ashes of his youth doth lie,
As the deathbed whereon it must expire,
Consum'd with that which it was nourish'd by.
This thou perceiv'st, which makes thy love more strong,
To love that well which thou must leave ere long.

LXXIV

But be contented. When that fell arrest
Without all bail shall carry me away,
My life hath in this line some interest,
Which for memorial still with thee shall stay.
When thou reviewest this, thou dost review
The very part was consecrate to thee.
The earth can have but earth, which is his due;
My spirit is thine, the better part of me.
So then thou hast but lost the dregs of life,
The prey of worms, my body being dead —
The coward conquest of a wretch's knife,
Too base of thee to be remembered.
The worth of that is that which it contains,
And that is this, and this with thee remains.

LXXV

So are you to my thoughts as food to life,
Or as sweet-season'd showers are to the ground;
And for the peace of you I hold such strife
As 'twixt a miser and his wealth is found:
Now proud as an enjoyer, and anon
Doubting the filching age will steal his treasure;
Now counting best to be with you alone,
Then better'd that the world may see my pleasure;
Sometime all full with feasting on your sight,
And by-and-by clean starved for a look;
Possessing or pursuing no delight
Save what is had or must from you be took.
Thus do I pine and surfeit day by day,
Or gluttoning on all, or all away.

LXXVI

Why is my verse so barren of new pride?
So far from variation or quick change?
Why, with the time, do I not glance aside
To new-found methods and to compounds strange?
Why write I still all one, ever the same,
And keep invention in a noted weed,
That every word doth almost tell my name,
Showing their birth, and where they did proceed?
O, know, sweet love, I always write of you,
And you and love are still my argument:
So all my best is dressing old words new,
Spending again what is already spent;
  For as the sun is daily new and old,
  So is my love still telling what is told.

LXXVII

Thy glass will show thee how thy beauties wear,
Thy dial how thy precious minutes waste.
The vacant leaves thy mind's imprint will bear,
And of this book this learning mayst thou taste.
The wrinkles which thy glass will truly show,
Of mouthed graves will give thee memory.
Thou by thy dial's shady stealth mayst know
Time's thievish progress to eternity.
Look, what thy memory cannot contain,
Commit to these waste blanks, and thou shalt find
Those children nurs'd, deliver'd from thy brain,
To take a new acquaintance of thy mind.
  These offices, so oft as thou wilt look,
  Shall profit thee and much enrich thy book.

LXXVIII

So oft have I invok'd thee for my Muse
And found such fair assistance in my verse
As every alien pen hath got my use
And under thee their poesy disperse.
Thine eyes, that taught the dumb on high to sing
And heavy ignorance aloft to fly,
Have added feathers to the learned's wing
And given grace a double majesty.
Yet be most proud of that which I compile,
Whose influence is thine, and born of thee.
In others' works thou dost but mend the style,
And arts with thy sweet graces graced be;
  But thou art all my art and dost advance
  As high as learning my rude ignorance.

LXXIX

Whilst I alone did call upon thy aid,
My verse alone had all thy gentle grace;
But now my gracious numbers are decay'd,
And my sick Muse doth give another place.
I grant, sweet love, thy lovely argument
Deserves the travail of a worthier pen;
Yet what of thee thy poet doth invent
He robs thee of, and pays it thee again.
He lends thee virtue, and he stole that word
From thy behaviour. Beauty doth he give,
And found it in thy cheek. He can afford
No praise to thee but what in thee doth live.
  Then thank him not for that which he doth say,
  Since what he owes thee thou thyself dost pay.

LXXX

O, how I faint when I of you do write,
Knowing a better spirit doth use your name
And in the praise thereof spends all his might
To make me tongue-tied, speaking of your fame!
But since your worth, wide as the ocean is,
The humble as the proudest sail doth bear,
My saucy bark, inferior far to his,
On your broad main doth wilfully appear.
Your shallowest help will hold me up afloat
Whilst he upon your soundless deep doth ride;
Or, being wrack'd, I am a worthless boat, 11
He of tall building and of goodly pride.
  Then if he thrive, and I be cast away,
  The worst was this: my love was my decay.

LXXXI

Or I shall live your epitaph to make,
Or you survive when I in earth am rotten.
From hence your memory death cannot take,
Although in me each part will be forgotten. 4
Your name from hence immortal life shall have,
Though I, once gone, to all the world must die.
The earth can yield me but a common grave
When you entombed in men's eyes shall lie.
Your monument shall be my gentle verse,
Which eyes not yet created shall o'erread;
And tongues to be your being shall rehearse
When all the breathers of this world are dead.
  You still shall live (such virtue hath my pen)
  Where breath most breathes, even in the mouths of men.

LXXXII

I grant thou wert not married to my Muse
And therefore mayst without attaint o'erlook
The dedicated words which writers use
Of their fair subject, blessing every book.
Thou art as fair in knowledge as in hue,
Finding thy worth a limit past my praise;
And therefore art enforc'd to seek anew
Some fresher stamp of the time-bettering days.
And do so, love; yet when they have devis'd
What strained touches rhetoric can lend,
Thou, truly fair, wert truly sympathiz'd
In true plain words by thy true-telling friend;
And their gross painting might be better us'd
Where cheeks need blood; in thee it is abus'd.

LXXXIII

I never saw that you did painting need,
And therefore to your fair no painting set;
I found (or thought I found) you did exceed
The barren tender of a poet's debt;
And therefore have I slept in your report,
That you yourself, being extant, well might show
How far a modern quill doth come too short,
Speaking of worth, what worth in you doth grow.
This silence for my sin you did impute,
Which shall be most my glory, being dumb;
For I impair not beauty, being mute,
When others would give life, and bring a tomb.
There lives more life in one of your fair eyes
Than both your poets can in praise devise.

LXXXIV

Who is it that says most which can say more
Than this rich praise — that you alone are you?
In whose confine immured is the store
Which should example where your equal grew.
Lean penury within that pen doth dwell
That to his subject lends not some small glory;
But he that writes of you, if he can tell
That you are you, so dignifies his story.
Let him but copy what in you is writ,
Not making worse what nature made so clear,
And such a counterpart shall fame his wit,
Making his style admired everywhere.
You to your beauteous blessings add a curse,
Being fond on praise, which makes your praises worse.

LXXXV

My tongue-tied Muse in manners holds her still
While comments of your praise, richly compil'd,
Reserve their character with golden quill
And precious phrase by all the Muses fil'd.
I think good thoughts whilst other write good words,
And, like unlettered clerk, still cry 'Amen'
To every hymn that able spirit affords
In polish'd form of well-refined pen.
Hearing you prais'd, I say ''Tis so, 'tis true!'
And to the most of praise add something more;
But that is in my thought, whose love to you,
Though words come hindmost, holds his rank before.
Then others for the breath of words respect;
Me for my dumb thoughts, speaking in effect.

LXXXVI

Was it the proud full sail of his great verse,
Bound for the prize of all-too-precious you,
That did my ripe thoughts in my brain inhearse,
Making their tomb the womb wherein they grew?
Was it his spirit, by spirits taught to write
Above a mortal pitch, that struck me dead?
No, neither he, nor his compeers by night
Giving him aid, my verse astonished.
He, nor that affable familiar ghost
Which nightly gulls him with intelligence,
As victors, of my silence cannot boast —
I was not sick of any fear from thence;
But when your countenance fill'd up his line,
Then lack'd I matter; that enfeebled mine.

LXXXVII

Farewell! thou art too dear for my possessing,
And like enough thou know'st thy estimate.
The charter of thy worth gives thee releasing;
My bonds in thee are all determinate.
For how do I hold thee but by thy granting,
And for that riches where is my deserving?
The cause of this fair gift in me is wanting,
And so my patent back again is swerving.
Thyself thou gav'st, thy own worth then not knowing,
Or me, to whom thou gav'st it, else mistaking:
So thy great gift, upon misprision growing,
Comes home again, on better judgment making.
Thus have I had thee as a dream doth flatter —
In sleep a king, but waking no such matter.

LXXXVIII

When thou shalt be dispos'd to set me light
And place my merit in the eye of scorn,
Upon thy side against myself I'll fight
And prove thee virtuous, though thou art forsworn.
With mine own weakness being best acquainted,
Upon thy part I can set down a story
Of faults conceal'd wherein I am attainted,
That thou, in losing me, shalt win much glory.
And I by this will be a gainer too;
For, bending all my loving thoughts on thee,
The injuries that to myself I do,
Doing thee vantage, double vantage me.
  Such is my love, to thee I so belong,
  That for thy right myself will bear all wrong.

LXXXIX

Say that thou didst forsake me for some fault,
And I will comment upon that offence.
Speak of my lameness, and I straight will halt,
Against thy reasons making no defence.
Thou canst not, love, disgrace me half so ill,
To set a form upon desired change,
As I'll myself disgrace, knowing thy will.
I will acquaintance strangle and look strange,
Be absent from thy walks, and in my tongue
Thy sweet beloved name no more shall dwell,
Lest I (too much profane) should do it wrong
And haply of our old acquaintance tell.
  For thee, against myself I'll vow debate,
  For I must ne'er love him whom thou dost hate.

XC

Then hate me when thou wilt! if ever, now!
Now, while the world is bent my deeds to cross,
Join with the spite of fortune, make me bow,
And do not drop in for an after-loss.
Ah, do not, when my heart hath scap'd this sorrow,
Come in the rearward of a conquer'd woe;
Give not a windy night a rainy morrow,
To linger out a purpos'd overthrow.
If thou wilt leave me, do not leave me last,
When other petty griefs have done their spite,
But in the onset come. So shall I taste
At first the very worst of fortune's might;
  And other strains of woe, which now seem woe,
  Compar'd with loss of thee will not seem so.

XCI

Some glory in their birth, some in their skill,
Some in their wealth, some in their body's force;
Some in their garments, though newfangled ill;
Some in their hawks and hounds, some in their horse;
And every humour hath his adjunct pleasure,
Wherein it finds a joy above the rest;
But these particulars are not my measure:
All these I better in one general best.
Thy love is better than high birth to me,
Richer than wealth, prouder than garments' cost,
Of more delight than hawks or horses be,
And having thee, of all men's pride I boast —
  Wretched in this alone, that thou mayst take
  All this away and me most wretched make.

XCII

But do thy worst to steal thyself away,
For term of life thou art assured mine;
And life no longer than thy love will stay,
For it depends upon that love of thine.
Then need I not to fear the worst of wrongs
When in the least of them my life hath end.
I see a better state to me belongs
Than that which on thy humour doth depend.
Thou canst not vex me with inconstant mind,
Since that my life on thy revolt doth lie.
O, what a happy title do I find,
Happy to have thy love, happy to die!
  But what's so blessed-fair that fears no blot?
  Thou mayst be false, and yet I know it not.

XCIII

So shall I live, supposing thou art true,
Like a deceived husband; so love's face
May still seem love to me, though alter'd new —
Thy looks with me, thy heart in other place.
For there can live no hatred in thine eye;
Therefore in that I cannot know thy change.
In many's looks the false heart's history
Is writ in moods and frowns and wrinkles strange;
But heaven in thy creation did decree
That in thy face sweet love should ever dwell;
Whate'er thy thoughts or thy heart's workings be,
Thy looks should nothing thence but sweetness tell.
  How like Eve's apple doth thy beauty grow
  If thy sweet virtue answer not thy show!

XCIV

They that have pow'r to hurt and will do none,
That do not do the thing they most do show,
Who, moving others, are themselves as stone,
Unmoved, cold, and to temptation slow —
They rightly do inherit heaven's graces
And husband nature's riches from expense;
They are the lords and owners of their faces,
Others but stewards of their excellence.
The summer's flow'r is to the summer sweet,
Though to itself it only live and die;
But if that flow'r with base infection meet,
The basest weed outbraves his dignity:
For sweetest things turn sourest by their deeds;
Lilies that fester smell far worse than weeds.

XCV

How sweet and lovely dost thou make the shame
Which, like a canker in the fragrant rose,
Doth spot the beauty of thy budding name!
O, in what sweets dost thou thy sins enclose!
That tongue that tells the story of thy days
(Making lascivious comments on thy sport)
Cannot dispraise but in a kind of praise:
Naming thy name blesses an ill report.
O, what a mansion have those vices got
Which for their habitation chose out thee,
Where beauty's veil doth cover every blot
And all things turns to fair that eyes can see!
Take heed, dear heart, of this large privilege.
The hardest knife ill us'd doth lose his edge.

XCVI

Some say thy fault is youth, some wantonness;
Some say thy grace is youth and gentle sport.
Both grace and faults are lov'd of more and less;
Thou mak'st faults graces that to thee resort.
As on the finger of a throned queen
The basest jewel will be well esteem'd,
So are those errors that in thee are seen
To truths translated and for true things deem'd.
How many lambs might the stern wolf betray
If like a lamb he could his looks translate!
How many gazers mightst thou lead away
If thou wouldst use the strength of all thy state!
But do not so. I love thee in such sort
As, thou being mine, mine is thy good report.

XCVII

How like a winter hath my absence been
From thee, the pleasure of the fleeting year!
What freezings have I felt, what dark days seen!
What old December's bareness everywhere!
And yet this time remov'd was summer's time,
The teeming autumn, big with rich increase,
Bearing the wanton burthen of the prime,
Like widowed wombs after their lords' decease;
Yet this abundant issue seem'd to me
But hope of orphans and unfathered fruit;
For summer and his pleasures wait on thee,
And, thou away, the very birds are mute;
Or, if they sing, 'tis with so dull a cheer
That leaves look pale, dreading the winter's near.

XCVIII

From you have I been absent in the spring,
When proud-pied April, dress'd in all his trim,
Hath put a spirit of youth in everything,
That heavy Saturn laugh'd and leapt with him,
Yet nor the lays of birds, nor the sweet smell
Of different flowers in odour and in hue,
Could make me any summer's story tell,
Or from their proud lap pluck them where they grew;
Nor did I wonder at the lily's white,
Nor praise the deep vermilion in the rose:
They were but sweet, but figures of delight,
Drawn after you, you pattern of all those.
Yet seem'd it winter still, and, you away,
As with your shadow I with these did play.

XCIX

The forward violet thus did I chide:
Sweet thief, whence didst thou steal thy sweet that smells,
If not from my love's breath? The purple pride
Which on thy soft cheek for complexion dwells
In my love's veins thou hast too grossly dy'd.
The lily I condemned for thy hand;
And buds of marjoram had stol'n thy hair.
The roses fearfully on thorns did stand,
One blushing shame, another white despair;
A third, nor red nor white, had stol'n of both,
And to his robb'ry had annex'd thy breath;
But, for his theft, in pride of all his growth
A vengeful canker eat him up to death.
More flowers I noted, yet I none could see
But sweet or colour it had stol'n from thee.

C

Where art thou, Muse, that thou forget'st so long
To speak of that which gives thee all thy might?
Spend'st thou thy fury on some worthless song,
Dark'ning thy pow'r to lend base subjects light?
Return, forgetful Muse, and straight redeem
In gentle numbers time so idly spent.
Sing to the ear that doth thy lays esteem
And gives thy pen both skill and argument.
Rise, resty Muse, my love's sweet face survey,
If Time have any wrinkle graven there.
If any, be a satire to decay
And make Time's spoils despised everywhere.
  Give my love fame faster than Time wastes life:
  So thou prevent'st his scythe and crooked knife.

CI

O truant Muse, what shall be thy amends
For thy neglect of truth in beauty dy'd?
Both truth and beauty on my love depends;
So dost thou too, and therein dignified.
Make answer, Muse. Wilt thou not haply say,
'Truth needs no colour, with his colour fix'd;
Beauty no pencil, beauty's truth to lay;
But best is best, if never intermix'd'?
Because he needs no praise, wilt thou be dumb?
Excuse not silence so; for't lies in thee
To make him much outlive a gilded tomb
And to be prais'd of ages yet to be.
  Then do thy office, Muse. I teach thee how
  To make him seem, long hence, as he shows now.

CII

My love is strength'ned, though more weak in seeming;
I love not less, though less the show appear.
That love is merchandiz'd whose rich esteeming
The owner's tongue doth publish everywhere.
Our love was new, and then but in the spring,
When I was wont to greet it with my lays,
As Philomel in summer's front doth sing
And stops her pipe in growth of riper days;
Not that the summer is less pleasant now
Than when her mournful hymns did hush the night,
But that wild music burthens every bough,
And sweets grown common lose their dear delight.
  Therefore, like her, I sometime hold my tongue,
  Because I would not dull you with my song.

CIII

Alack, what poverty my Muse brings forth,
That, having such a scope to show her pride,
The argument all bare is of more worth
Than when it hath my added praise beside!
O, blame me not if I no more can write!
Look in your glass, and there appears a face
That overgoes my blunt invention quite,
Dulling my lines and doing me disgrace.
Were it not sinful then, striving to mend,
To mar the subject that before was well?
For to no other pass my verses tend
Than of your graces and your gifts to tell;
  And more, much more, than in my verse can sit
  Your own glass shows you when you look in it.

CIV

To me, fair friend, you never can be old,
For as you were when first your eye I ey'd,
Such seems your beauty still. Three winters cold
Have from the forests shook three summers' pride,
Three beauteous springs to yellow autumn turn'd
In process of the seasons have I seen,
Three April perfumes in three hot Junes burn'd,
Since first I saw you fresh, which yet are green.
Ah, yet doth beauty, like a dial hand,
Steal from his figure, and no pace perceiv'd!
So your sweet hue, which methinks still doth stand,
Hath motion, and mine eye may be deceiv'd;
  For fear of which, hear this, thou age unbred:
  Ere you were born was beauty's summer dead.

CV

Let not my love be call'd idolatry
Nor my beloved as an idol show,
Since all alike my songs and praises be
To one, of one, still such, and ever so.
Kind is my love to-day, to-morrow kind,
Still constant in a wondrous excellence;
Therefore my verse, to constancy confin'd,
One thing expressing, leaves out difference.
'Fair, kind, and true,' is all my argument,
'Fair, kind, and true,' varying to other words;
And in this change is my invention spent,
Three themes in one, which wondrous scope affords.
  Fair, kind, and true have often liv'd alone,
  Which three till now never kept seat in one.

CVI

When in the chronicle of wasted time
I see descriptions of the fairest wights,
And beauty making beautiful old rhyme
In praise of ladies dead and lovely knights,
Then, in the blazon of sweet beauty's best,
Of hand, of foot, of lip, of eye, of brow,
I see their antique pen would have express'd
Even such a beauty as you master now.
So all their praises are but prophecies
Of this our time, all you prefiguring;
And, for they look'd but with divining eyes,
They had not skill enough your worth to sing;
For we, which now behold these present days,
Have eyes to wonder, but lack tongues to praise.

CVII

Not mine own fears, nor the prophetic soul
Of the wide world, dreaming on things to come,
Can yet the lease of my true love control,
Suppos'd as forfeit to a confin'd doom.
The mortal moon hath her eclipse endur'd,
And the sad augurs mock their own presage;
Incertainties now crown themselves assur'd,
And peace proclaims olives of endless age.
Now with the drops of this most balmy time
My love looks fresh, and Death to me subscribes,
Since, spite of him, I'll live in this poor rhyme
While he insults o'er dull and speechless tribes;
And thou in this shalt find thy monument
When tyrants' crests and tombs of brass are spent.

CVIII

What's in the brain that ink may character
Which hath not figur'd to thee my true spirit?
What's new to speak, what new to register,
That may express my love or thy dear merit?
Nothing, sweet boy; but yet, like prayers divine,
I must each day say o'er the very same;
Counting no old thing old, thou mine, I thine,
Even as when first I hallowed thy fair name.
So that eternal love in love's fresh case
Weighs not the dust and injury of age,
Nor gives to necessary wrinkles place,
But makes antiquity for aye his page,
Finding the first conceit of love there bred
Where time and outward form would show it dead.

CIX

O, never say that I was false of heart,
Though absence seem'd my flame to qualify!
As easy might I from myself depart
As from my soul, which in thy breast doth lie.
That is my home of love. If I have rang'd,
Like him that travels I return again,
Just to the time, not with the time exchang'd,
So that myself bring water for my stain.
Never believe, though in my nature reign'd
All frailties that besiege all kinds of blood,
That it could so preposterously be stain'd
To leave for nothing all thy sum of good;
For nothing this wide universe I call
Save thou, my rose; in it thou art my all.

CX

Alas, 'tis true I have gone here and there
And made myself a motley to the view,
Gor'd mine own thoughts, sold cheap what is most dear,
Made old offences of affections new.
Most true it is that I have look'd on truth
Askance and strangely; but, by all above,
These blenches gave my heart another youth,
And worse essays prov'd thee my best of love.
Now all is done, have what shall have no end!
Mine appetite I never more will grind
On newer proof, to try an older friend,
A god in love, to whom I am confin'd.
Then give me welcome, next my heaven the best,
Even to thy pure and most most loving breast.

CXI

O, for my sake do you with Fortune chide,
The guilty goddess of my harmful deeds,
That did not better for my life provide
Than public means which public manners breeds.
Thence comes it that my name receives a brand;
And almost thence my nature is subdu'd
To what it works in, like the dyer's hand.
Pity me then, and wish I were renew'd,
Whilst, like a willing patient, I will drink
Potions of eysell 'gainst my strong infection;
No bitterness that I will bitter think,
Nor double penance, to correct correction.
Pity me, then, dear friend, and I assure ye
Even that your pity is enough to cure me.

CXII

Your love and pity doth th' impression fill
Which vulgar scandal stamp'd upon my brow;
For what care I who calls me well or ill,
So you o'er-green my bad, my good allow?
You are my all the world, and I must strive
To know my shames and praises from your tongue —
None else to me, nor I to none alive,
That my steel'd sense or changes right or wrong.
In so profound abysm I throw all care
Of others' voices that my adder's sense
To critic and to flatterer stopped are.
Mark how with my neglect I do dispense:
  You are so strongly in my purpose bred
  That all the world besides methinks are dead.

CXIII

Since I left you, mine eye is in my mind;
And that which governs me to go about
Doth part his function and is partly blind,
Seems seeing, but effectually is out;
For it no form delivers to the heart
Of bird, of flow'r, or shape which it doth latch;
Of his quick objects hath the mind no part,
Nor his own vision holds what it doth catch;
For if it see the rud'st or gentlest sight,
The most sweet favour or deformed'st creature,
The mountain or the sea, the day or night,
The crow or dove, it shapes them to your feature.
  Incapable of more, replete with you,
  My most true mind thus mak'th mine eye untrue.

CXIV

Or whether doth my mind, being crown'd with you,
Drink up the monarch's plague, this flattery?
Or whether shall I say mine eye saith true,
And that your love taught it this alchemy,
To make of monsters and things indigest
Such cherubins as your sweet self resemble,
Creating every bad a perfect best
As fast as objects to his beams assemble?
O, 'tis the first! 'Tis flatt'ry in my seeing,
And my great mind most kingly drinks it up.
Mine eye well knows what with his gust is greeing,
And to his palate doth prepare the cup.
  If it be poison'd, 'tis the lesser sin
  That mine eye loves it and doth first begin.

CXV

Those lines that I before have writ do lie,
Even those that said I could not love you dearer.
Yet then my judgment knew no reason why
My most full flame should afterwards burn clearer.
But reckoning Time, whose million'd accidents
Creep in 'twixt vows and change decrees of kings,
Tan sacred beauty, blunt the sharp'st intents,
Divert strong minds to th' course of alt'ring things —
Alas, why, fearing of Time's tyranny,
Might I not then say 'Now I love you best'
When I was certain o'er incertainty,
Crowning the present, doubting of the rest?
  Love is a babe. Then might I not say so,
  To give full growth to that which still doth grow.

CXVI

Let me not to the marriage of true minds
Admit impediments. Love is not love
Which alters when it alteration finds
Or bends with the remover to remove.
O, no! it is an ever-fixed mark
That looks on tempests and is never shaken;
It is the star to every wand'ring bark,
Whose worth's unknown, although his highth be taken.
Love's not Time's fool, though rosy lips and cheeks
Within his bending sickle's compass come.
Love alters not with his brief hours and weeks,
But bears it out even to the edge of doom.
  If this be error, and upon me proved,
  I never writ, nor no man ever loved.

CXVII

Accuse me thus: that I have scanted all
Wherein I should your great deserts repay;
Forgot upon your dearest love to call,
Whereto all bonds do tie me day by day;
That I have frequent been with unknown minds
And given to time your own dear-purchas'd right;
That I have hoisted sail to all the winds
Which should transport me farthest from your sight.

Book both my wilfulness and errors down,
And on just proof surmise accumulate;
Bring me within the level of your frown,
But shoot not at me in your wakened hate;
Since my appeal says I did strive to prove
The constancy and virtue of your love.

CXVIII

Like as, to make our appetites more keen,
With eager compounds we our palate urge;
As, to prevent our maladies unseen,
We sicken to shun sickness when we purge:
Even so, being full of your ne'er-cloying sweetness,
To bitter sauces did I frame my feeding;
And, sick of welfare, found a kind of meetness
To be diseas'd ere that there was true needing.
Thus policy in love, t' anticipate
The ills that were not, grew to faults assured,
And brought to medicine a healthful state,
Which, rank of goodness, would by ill be cured.
But thence I learn, and find the lesson true,
Drugs poison him that so fell sick of you.

CXIX

What potions have I drunk of Siren tears,
Distill'd from limbecks foul as hell within,
Applying fears to hopes and hopes to fears,
Still losing when I saw myself to win!
What wretched errors hath my heart committed
Whilst it hath thought itself so blessed never!
How have mine eyes out of their spheres been fitted
In the distraction of this madding fever!
O benefit of ill! Now I find true
That better is by evil still made better;
And ruin'd love, when it is built anew,
Grows fairer than at first, more strong, far greater.
So I return rebuk'd to my content,
And gain by ills thrice more than I have spent.

CXX

That you were once unkind befriends me now,
And for that sorrow which I then did feel
Needs must I under my transgression bow,
Unless my nerves were brass or hammered steel.
For if you were by my unkindness shaken,
As I by yours, y'have pass'd a hell of time,
And I, a tyrant, have no leisure taken
To weigh how once I suffered in your crime.
O that our night of woe might have rememb'red
My deepest sense how hard true sorrow hits,
And soon to you, as you to me then, tend'red
The humble salve which wounded bosoms fits!
But that your trespass now becomes a fee;
Mine ransoms yours, and yours must ransom me.

CXXI

'Tis better to be vile than vile esteemed
When not to be receives reproach of being,
And the just pleasure lost, which is so deemed
Not by our feeling but by others' seeing.
For why should others' false adulterate eyes
Give salutation to my sportive blood?
Or on my frailties why are frailer spies,
Which in their wills count bad what I think good?
No, I am that I am; and they that level
At my abuses reckon up their own.
I may be straight though they themselves be bevel;
By their rank thoughts my deeds must not be shown,
Unless this general evil they maintain —
All men are bad and in their badness reign.

CXXII

Thy gift, thy tables, are within my brain
Full character'd with lasting memory,
Which shall above that idle rank remain
Beyond all date, even to eternity;
Or, at the least, so long as brain and heart
Have faculty by nature to subsist,
Till each to raz'd oblivion yield his part
Of thee, thy record never can be miss'd.
That poor retention could not so much hold,
Nor need I tallies thy dear love to score.
Therefore to give them from me was I bold,
To trust those tables that receive thee more.
To keep an adjunct to remember thee
Were to import forgetfulness in me.

CXXIII

No, Time, thou shalt not boast that I do change!
Thy pyramids built up with newer might
To me are nothing novel, nothing strange;
They are but dressings of a former sight.

Our dates are brief, and therefore we admire
What thou dost foist upon us that is old,
And rather make them born to our desire
Than think that we before have heard them told.
Thy registers and thee I both defy,
Not wond'ring at the present nor the past;
For thy records and what we see doth lie,
Made more or less by thy continual haste.
This I do vow, and this shall ever be —
I will be true, despite thy scythe and thee.

CXXIV

If my dear love were but the child of state,
It might for Fortune's bastard be unfather'd,
As subject to Time's love or to Time's hate,
Weeds among weeds, or flowers with flowers gather'd.
No, it was builded far from accident;
It suffers not in smiling pomp, nor falls
Under the blow of thralled discontent,
Whereto th' inviting time our fashion calls.
It fears not Policy, that heretic
Which works on leases of short-numb'red hours,
But all alone stands hugely politic, 11
That it nor grows with heat nor drowns with show'rs.
To this I witness call the fools of time,
Which die for goodness, who have liv'd for crime.

CXXV

Were't aught to me I bore the canopy,
With my extern the outward honouring,
Or laid great bases for eternity,
Which prove more short than waste or ruining?
Have I not seen dwellers on form and favour
Lose all, and more, by paying too much rent,
For compound sweet forgoing simple savour —
Pitiful thrivers, in their gazing spent?
No, let me be obsequious in thy heart,
And take thou my oblation, poor but free,
Which is not mix'd with seconds, knows no art
But mutual render, only me for thee.
Hence, thou suborn'd informer! A true soul
When most impeach'd stands least in thy control.

CXXVI

O thou, my lovely boy, who in thy power
Dost hold Time's fickle glass, his sickle hour;
Who hast by waning grown, and therein show'st
Thy lovers withering as thy sweet self grow'st—
If Nature (sovereign mistress over wrack),
As thou goest onwards, still will pluck thee back,
She keeps thee to this purpose, that her skill
May time disgrace, and wretched minutes kill.
Yet fear her, O thou minion of her pleasure!
She may detain, but not still keep, her treasure;
Her audit, though delay'd, answer'd must be,
And her quietus is to render thee.

CXXVII

In the old age black was not counted fair,
Or if it were, it bore not beauty's name;
But now is black beauty's successive heir,
And beauty slander'd with a bastard shame;
For since each hand hath put on nature's power,
Fairing the foul with art's false borrow'd face,
Sweet beauty hath no name, no holy bower,
But is profan'd, if not lives in disgrace.
Therefore my mistress' brows are raven black,
Her eyes so suited, and they mourners seem
At such who, not born fair, no beauty lack,
Sland'ring creation with a false esteem.
Yet so they mourn, becoming of their woe,
That every tongue says beauty should look so.

CXXVIII

How oft, when thou, my music, music play'st
Upon that blessed wood whose motion sounds
With thy sweet fingers when thou gently sway'st
The wiry concord that mine ear confounds,
Do I envy those jacks that nimble leap
To kiss the tender inward of thy hand,
Whilst my poor lips, which should that harvest reap,
At the wood's boldness by thee blushing stand!
To be so tickled, they would change their state
And situation with those dancing chips
O'er whom thy fingers walk with gentle gait,
Making dead wood more blest than living lips.
Since saucy jacks so happy are in this,
Give them thy fingers, me thy lips to kiss.

CXXIX

Th' expense of spirit in a waste of shame
Is lust in action; and till action, lust
Is perjur'd, murd'rous, bloody, full of blame,
Savage, extreme, rude, cruel, not to trust;

Enjoy'd no sooner but despised straight;
Past reason hunted, and no sooner had,
Past reason hated, as a swallowed bait
On purpose laid to make the taker mad;
Mad in pursuit, and in possession so;
Had, having, and in quest to have, extreme;
A bliss in proof — and prov'd, a very woe;
Before, a joy propos'd; behind, a dream.
All this the world well knows; yet none knows well
To shun the heaven that leads men to this hell.

CXXX

My mistress' eyes are nothing like the sun;
Coral is far more red than her lips' red;
If snow be white, why then her breasts are dun;
If hairs be wires, black wires grow on her head.
I have seen roses damask'd, red and white,
But no such roses see I in her cheeks;
And in some perfumes is there more delight
Than in the breath that from my mistress reeks.
I love to hear her speak; yet well I know
That music hath a far more pleasing sound.
I grant I never saw a goddess go:
My mistress, when she walks, treads on the ground.
And yet, by heaven, I think my love as rare
As any she belied with false compare.

CXXXI

Thou art as tyrannous, so as thou art,
As those whose beauties proudly make them cruel;
For well thou know'st to my dear-doting heart
Thou art the fairest and most precious jewel.
Yet, in good faith, some say that thee behold,
Thy face hath not the power to make love groan.
To say they err I dare not be so bold,
Although I swear it to myself alone.
And, to be sure that is not false I swear,
A thousand groans, but thinking on thy face,
One on another's neck, do witness bear
Thy black is fairest in my judgment's place.
In nothing art thou black save in thy deeds,
And thence this slander, as I think, proceeds.

CXXXII

Thine eyes I love, and they, as pitying me,
Knowing thy heart torments me with disdain,
Have put on black and loving mourners be,
Looking with pretty ruth upon my pain.
And truly not the morning sun of heaven
Better becomes the grey cheeks of the East,
Nor that full star that ushers in the even
Doth half that glory to the sober West,
As those two mourning eyes become thy face.
O, let it then as well beseem thy heart
To mourn for me, since mourning doth thee grace,
And suit thy pity like in every part.
Then will I swear beauty herself is black
And all they foul that thy complexion lack.

CXXXIII

Beshrew that heart that makes my heart to groan
For that deep wound it gives my friend and me!
Is't not enough to torture me alone
But slave to slavery my sweet'st friend must be?
Me from myself thy cruel eye hath taken,
And my next self thou harder hast engrossed.
Of him, myself, and thee I am forsaken —
A torment thrice threefold thus to be crossed.
Prison my heart in thy steel bosom's ward;
But then my friend's heart let my poor heart bail;
Whoe'er keeps me, let my heart be his guard:
Thou canst not then use rigour in my jail.
And yet thou wilt: for I, being pent in thee,
Perforce am thine, and all that is in me.

CXXXIV

So, now I have confess'd that he is thine
And I myself am mortgag'd to thy will,
Myself I'll forfeit, so that other mine
Thou wilt restore to be my comfort still.
But thou wilt not, nor he will not be free,
For thou art covetous, and he is kind;
He learn'd but surety-like to write for me
Under that bond that him as fast doth bind.
The statute of thy beauty thou wilt take,
Thou usurer that put'st forth all to use,
And sue a friend came debtor for my sake:
So him I lose through my unkind abuse.
Him have I lost, thou hast both him and me:
He pays the whole, and yet am I not free.

CXXXV

Whoever hath her wish, thou hast thy Will,
And Will to boot, and Will in overplus.
More than enough am I that vex thee still,
To thy sweet will making addition thus.

Wilt thou, whose will is large and spacious,
Not once vouchsafe to hide my will in thine?
Shall will in others seem right gracious
And in my will no fair acceptance shine?
The sea, all water, yet receives rain still
And in abundance addeth to his store;
So thou, being rich in Will, add to thy Will
One will of mine to make thy large Will more.
  Let no unkind no fair beseechers kill;
  Think all but one, and me in that one Will.

CXXXVI

If thy soul check thee that I come so near,
Swear to thy blind soul that I was thy Will,
And will, thy soul knows, is admitted there:
Thus far for love my love-suit, sweet, fulfil.
Will will fulfil the treasure of thy love,
Ay, fill it full with wills, and my will one.
In things of great receipt with ease we prove
Among a number one is reckon'd none.
Then in the number let me pass untold,
Though in thy store's account I one must be;
For nothing hold me, so it please thee hold
That nothing me, a something, sweet, to thee.
  Make but my name thy love, and love that still,
  And then thou lovest me, for my name is Will.

CXXXVII

Thou blind fool, Love, what dost thou to mine eyes
That they behold, and see not what they see?
They know what beauty is, see where it lies,
Yet what the best is take the worst to be.
If eyes, corrupt by over-partial looks,
Be anchor'd in the bay where all men ride,
Why of eyes' falsehood hast thou forged hooks,
Whereto the judgment of my heart is tied?
Why should my heart think that a several plot
Which my heart knows the wide world's common place?
Or mine eyes seeing this, say this is not,
To put fair truth upon so foul a face?
  In things right true my heart and eyes have erred,
  And to this false plague are they now transferred.

CXXXVIII

When my love swears that she is made of truth
I do believe her, though I know she lies,
That she might think me some untutor'd youth,
Unlearned in the world's false subtilties.
Thus vainly thinking that she thinks me young,
Although she knows my days are past the best,
Simply I credit her false-speaking tongue:
On both sides thus is simple truth suppress'd.
But wherefore says she not she is unjust?
And wherefore say not I that I am old?
O, love's best habit is in seeming trust,
And age in love loves not to have years told.
  Therefore I lie with her and she with me,
  And in our faults by lies we flattered be.

CXXXIX

O, call not me to justify the wrong
That thy unkindness lays upon my heart!
Wound me not with thine eye, but with thy tongue;
Use power with power, and slay me not by art!
Tell me thou lov'st elsewhere; but in my sight,
Dear heart, forbear to glance thine eye aside.
What need'st thou wound with cunning when thy might
Is more than my o'erpress'd defence can bide?
Let me excuse thee: — Ah, my love well knows
Her pretty looks have been mine enemies;
And therefore from my face she turns my foes,
That they elsewhere might dart their injuries.
  Yet do not so; but since I am near slain,
  Kill me outright with looks and rid my pain.

CXL

Be wise as thou art cruel; do not press
My tongue-tied patience with too much disdain;
Lest sorrow lend me words, and words express
The manner of my pity-wanting pain.
If I might teach thee wit, better it were,
Though not to love, yet, love, to tell me so;
As testy sick men, when their deaths be near,
No news but health from their physicians know.
For if I should despair, I should grow mad,
And in my madness might speak ill of thee.
Now this ill-wresting world is grown so bad
Mad slanderers by mad ears believed be.
  That I may not be so, nor thou belied,
  Bear thine eyes straight, though thy proud heart go wide.

CXLI

In faith, I do not love thee with mine eyes,
For they in thee a thousand errors note;
But 'tis my heart that loves what they despise,
Who in despite of view is pleas'd to dote.
Nor are mine ears with thy tongue's tune delighted;
Nor tender feeling to base touches prone,
Nor taste, nor smell, desire to be invited
To any sensual feast with thee alone;
But my five wits nor my five senses can
Dissuade one foolish heart from serving thee,
Who leaves unsway'd the likeness of a man,
Thy proud heart's slave and vassal wretch to be.
  Only my plague thus far I count my gain,
  That she that makes me sin awards me pain.

CXLII

Love is my sin, and thy dear virtue hate,
Hate of my sin, grounded on sinful loving.
O, but with mine compare thou thine own state,
And thou shalt find it merits not reproving!
Or if it do, not from those lips of thine,
That have profan'd their scarlet ornaments
And seal'd false bonds of love as oft as mine,
Robb'd others' beds' revenues of their rents.
Be it lawful I love thee as thou lov'st those
Whom thine eyes woo as mine importune thee.
Root pity in thy heart, that, when it grows,
Thy pity may deserve to pitied be.
  If thou dost seek to have what thou dost hide,
  By self-example mayst thou be denied!

CXLIII

Lo, as a careful housewife runs to catch
One of her feathered creatures broke away,
Sets down her babe, and makes all swift dispatch
In pursuit of the thing she would have stay;
Whilst her neglected child holds her in chase,
Cries to catch her whose busy care is bent
To follow that which flies before her face,
Not prizing her poor infant's discontent —
So runn'st thou after that which flies from thee,
Whilst I thy babe chase thee afar behind;
But if thou catch thy hope, turn back to me
And play the mother's part, kiss me, be kind.
  So will I pray that thou mayst have thy Will,
  If thou turn back and my loud crying still.

CXLIV

Two loves I have, of comfort and despair,
Which like two spirits do suggest me still.
The better angel is a man right fair,
The worser spirit a woman colour'd ill.
To win me soon to hell, my female evil
Tempteth my better angel from my side,
And would corrupt my saint to be a devil,
Wooing his purity with her foul pride.
And whether that my angel be turn'd fiend
Suspect I may, yet not directly tell;
But being both from me, both to each friend,
I guess one angel in another's hell.
  Yet this shall I ne'er know, but live in doubt,
  Till my bad angel fire my good one out.

CXLV

Those lips that Love's own hand did make
Breath'd forth the sound that said 'I hate'
To me that languish'd for her sake;
But when she saw my woful state,
Straight in her heart did mercy come,
Chiding that tongue that ever sweet
Was us'd in giving gentle doom,
And taught it thus anew to greet:
'I hate' she alter'd with an end
That follow'd it as gentle day
Doth follow night, who, like a fiend,
From heaven to hell is flown away.
  'I hate' from hate away she threw,
  And sav'd my life, saying 'not you.'

CXLVI

Poor soul, the centre of my sinful earth,
. . . these rebel pow'rs that thee array,
Why dost thou pine within and suffer dearth,
Painting thy outward walls so costly gay?
Why so large cost, having so short a lease,
Dost thou upon thy fading mansion spend?
Shall worms, inheritors of this excess,
Eat up thy charge? Is this thy body's end?
Then, soul, live thou upon thy servant's loss,
And let that pine to aggravate thy store;
Buy terms divine in selling hours of dross;
Within be fed, without be rich no more.
  So shalt thou feed on Death, that feeds on men,
  And Death once dead, there's no more dying then.

CXLVII

My love is as a fever, longing still
For that which longer nurseth the disease;
Feeding on that which doth preserve the ill,
Th' uncertain sickly appetite to please.
My Reason, the physician to my Love,
Angry that his prescriptions are not kept,
Hath left me, and I desperate now approve
Desire is death, which physic did except.
Past cure I am, now reason is past care,
And frantic-mad with evermore unrest;
My thoughts and my discourse as madmen's are,
At randon from the truth vainly express'd;
  For I have sworn thee fair, and thought thee bright,
  Who art as black as hell, as dark as night.

CXLVIII

O me, what eyes hath Love put in my head,
Which have no correspondence with true sight!
Or, if they have, where is my judgment fled,
That censures falsely what they see aright?
If that be fair whereon my false eyes dote,
What means the world to say it is not so?
If it be not, then love doth well denote
Love's eye is not so true as all men's no.
How can it? O, how can Love's eye be true,
That is so vex'd with watching and with tears?
No marvel then though I mistake my view:
The sun itself sees not till heaven clears.
  O cunning Love! with tears thou keep'st me blind,
  Lest eyes well-seeing thy foul faults should find.

CXLIX

Canst thou, O cruel! say I love thee not
When I against myself with thee partake?
Do I not think on thee when I forgot
Am of myself, all tyrant for thy sake?
Who hateth thee that I do call my friend?
On whom frown'st thou that I do fawn upon?
Nay, if thou low'r'st on me, do I not spend
Revenge upon myself with present moan?
What merit do I in myself respect
That is so proud thy service to despise,
When all my best doth worship thy defect,
Commanded by the motion of thine eyes?
  But, love, hate on, for now I know thy mind:
  Those that can see thou lov'st, and I am blind.

CL

O, from what pow'r hast thou this pow'rful might
With insufficiency my heart to sway?
To make me give the lie to my true sight
And swear that brightness doth not grace the day?
Whence hast thou this becoming of things ill,
That in the very refuse of thy deeds
There is such strength and warrantise of skill
That in my mind thy worst all best exceeds?
Who taught thee how to make me love thee more,
The more I hear and see just cause of hate?
O, though I love what others do abhor,
With others thou shouldst not abhor my state!
  If thy unworthiness rais'd love in me,
  More worthy I to be belov'd of thee.

CLI

Love is too young to know what conscience is;
Yet who knows not conscience is born of love?
Then, gentle cheater, urge not my amiss,
Lest guilty of my faults thy sweet self prove.
For, thou betraying me, I do betray
My nobler part to my gross body's treason;
My soul doth tell my body that he may
Triumph in love; flesh stays no farther reason,
But, rising at thy name, doth point out thee
As his triumphant prize. Proud of this pride,
He is contented thy poor drudge to be,
To stand in thy affairs, fall by thy side.
  No want of conscience hold it that I call
  Her 'love' for whose dear love I rise and fall.

CLII

In loving thee thou know'st I am forsworn,
But thou art twice forsworn, to me love swearing;
In act thy bed-vow broke, and new faith torn
In vowing new hate after new love bearing.
But why of two oaths' breach do I accuse thee
When I break twenty? I am perjur'd most;
For all my vows are oaths but to misuse thee,
And all my honest faith in thee is lost;
For I have sworn deep oaths of thy deep kindness,
Oaths of thy love, thy truth, thy constancy;
And, to enlighten thee, gave eyes to blindness,
Or made them swear against the thing they see;
  For I have sworn thee fair — more perjur'd I,
  To swear against the truth so foul a lie!

CLIII

Cupid laid by his brand and fell asleep.
A maid of Dian's this advantage found
And his love-kindling fire did quickly steep
In a cold valley-fountain of that ground;
Which borrow'd from this holy fire of Love
A dateless lively heat, still to endure,
And grew a seething bath, which yet men prove
Against strange maladies a sovereign cure.
But at my mistress' eye Love's brand new fired,
The boy for trial needs would touch my breast.
I, sick withal, the help of bath desired
And thither hied, a sad distemper'd guest,
But found no cure. The bath for my help lies
Where Cupid got new fire — my mistress' eyes.

CLIV

The little Love-god, lying once asleep,
Laid by his side his heart-inflaming brand,
Whilst many nymphs that vow'd chaste life to keep
Came tripping by; but in her maiden hand
The fairest votary took up that fire
Which many legions of true hearts had warm'd;
And so the general of hot desire
Was sleeping by a virgin hand disarm'd.
This brand she quenched in a cool well by,
Which from Love's fire took heat perpetual,
Growing a bath and healthful remedy
For men diseas'd; but I, my mistress' thrall,
Came there for cure, and this by that I prove —
Love's fire heats water, water cools not love.

A LOVER'S COMPLAINT

From off a hill whose concave womb reworded
A plaintful story from a sist'ring vale,
My spirits t' attend this double voice accorded,
And down I laid to list the sad-tun'd tale;
Ere long espied a fickle maid full pale,
Tearing of papers, breaking rings atwain,
Storming her world with sorrow's wind and rain.

Upon her head a platted hive of straw,
Which fortified her visage from the sun,
Whereon the thought might think sometime it saw
The carcass of a beauty spent and done.
Time had not scythed all that youth begun,
Nor youth all quit; but, spite of heaven's fell rage,
Some beauty peep'd through lattice of sear'd age.

Oft did she heave her napkin to her eyne,
Which on it had conceited characters,
Laund'ring the silken figures in the brine
That seasoned woe had pelleted in tears,
And often reading what contents it bears;
As often shrieking undistinguish'd woe
In clamours of all size, both high and low.

Sometimes her levell'd eyes their carriage ride,
As they did batt'ry to the spheres intend;
Sometime diverted their poor balls are tied
To th' orbed earth; sometimes they do extend
Their view right on; anon their gazes lend
To every place at once, and, nowhere fix'd,
The mind and sight distractedly commix'd.

Her hair, nor loose nor tied in formal plat,
Proclaim'd in her a careless hand of pride;
For some, untuck'd, descended her sheav'd hat,
Hanging her pale and pined cheek beside;
Some in her threaden fillet still did bide
And, true to bondage, would not break from thence,
Though slackly braided in loose negligence.

A thousand favours from a maund she drew
Of amber, crystal, and of beaded jet,
Which one by one she in a river threw,
Upon whose weeping margent she was set;
Like usury, applying wet to wet,
Or monarch's hands that lets not bounty fall
Where want cries some but where excess begs all.

Of folded schedules had she many a one,
Which she perus'd, sigh'd, tore, and gave the flood;
Crack'd many a ring of posied gold and bone,
Bidding them find their sepulchres in mud;
Found yet moe letters sadly penn'd in blood,
With sleided silk feat and affectedly
Enswath'd and seal'd to curious secrecy.

These often bath'd she in her fluxive eyes,
And often kiss'd, and often gan to tear;
Cried, 'O false blood, thou register of lies,
What unapproved witness dost thou bear!
Ink would have seem'd more black and damned here!'
This said, in top of rage the lines she rents,
Big discontent so breaking their contents.

A reverend man that graz'd his cattle nigh —
Sometime a blusterer that the ruffle knew
Of court, of city, and had let go by
The swiftest hours, observed as they flew —
Towards this afflicted fancy fastly drew,
And, privileg'd by age, desires to know
In brief the grounds and motives of her woe.

So slides he down upon his grained bat,
And comely distant sits he by her side;
When he again desires her, being sat,
Her grievance with his hearing to divide.
If that from him there may be aught applied
Which may her suffering ecstasy assuage,
'Tis promis'd in the charity of age.

'Father,' she says, 'though in me you behold
The injury of many a blasting hour,
Let it not tell your judgment I am old.
Not age, but sorrow, over me hath power.
I might as yet have been a spreading flower,
Fresh to myself, if I had self-applied
Love to myself, and to no love beside.

'But woe is me! too early I attended
A youthful suit — it was to gain my grace —
Of one by nature's outwards so commended
That maidens' eyes stuck over all his face.
Love lack'd a dwelling and made him her place;
And when in his fair parts she did abide,
She was new lodg'd and newly deified.

'His browny locks did hang in crooked curls,
And every light occasion of the wind
Upon his lips their silken parcels hurls.
What's sweet to do, to do will aptly find:
Each eye that saw him did enchant the mind;
For on his visage was in little drawn
What largeness thinks in Paradise was sawn.

'Small show of man was yet upon his chin;
His phœnix down began but to appear,
Like unshorn velvet, on that termless skin,
Whose bare out-bragg'd the web it seem'd to wear.
Yet show'd his visage by that cost more dear;
And nice affections wavering stood in doubt
If best were as it was, or best without.

'His qualities were beauteous as his form,
For maiden-tongu'd he was, and thereof free;
Yet, if men mov'd him, was he such a storm
As oft 'twixt May and April is to see,
When winds breathe sweet, unruly though they be.
His rudeness so with his authoriz'd youth
Did livery falseness in a pride of truth.

'Well could he ride, and often men would say,
"That horse his mettle from his rider takes.
Proud of subjection, noble by the sway,
What rounds, what bounds, what course, what stop he makes!"
And controversy hence a question takes,
Whether the horse by him became his deed,
Or he his manage by th' well-doing steed.

'But quickly on this side the verdict went:
His real habitude gave life and grace
To appertainings and to ornament,
Accomplish'd in himself, not in his case.
All aids, themselves made fairer by their place,
Came for additions; yet their purpos'd trim
Piec'd not his grace but were all grac'd by him.

'So on the tip of his subduing tongue
All kind of arguments and question deep,
All replication prompt and reason strong,
For his advantage still did wake and sleep.
To make the weeper laugh, the laugher weep,
He had the dialect and different skill,
Catching all passions in his craft of will;

'That he did in the general bosom reign
Of young, of old, and sexes both enchanted,
To dwell with him in thoughts, or to remain
In personal duty, following where he haunted.
Consents bewitch'd, ere he desire, have granted,
And dialogu'd for him what he would say,
Ask'd their own wills and made their wills obey.

'Many there were that did his picture get,
To serve their eyes, and in it put their mind;
Like fools that in th' imagination set
The goodly objects which abroad they find
Of lands and mansions, theirs in thought assign'd,
And labouring in moe pleasures to bestow them
Than the true gouty landlord which doth owe them.

'So many have, that never touch'd his hand,
Sweetly suppos'd them mistress of his heart.
My woful self, that did in freedom stand
And was my own fee-simple, not in part,
What with his art in youth and youth in art,
Threw my affections in his charmed power,
Reserv'd the stalk and gave him all my flower.

'Yet did I not, as some my equals did,
Demand of him, nor being desired yielded.
Finding myself in honour so forbid,
With safest distance I mine honour shielded.
Experience for me many bulwarks builded
Of proofs new-bleeding, which remain'd the foil
Of this false jewel, and his amorous spoil.

'But, ah, who ever shunn'd by precedent
The destin'd ill she must herself assay?
Or forc'd examples, 'gainst her own content,
To put the by-past perils in her way?
Counsel may stop awhile what will not stay;
For when we rage, advice is often seen
By blunting us to make our wits more keen.

'Nor gives it satisfaction to our blood
That we must curb it upon others' proof,
To be forbod the sweets that seem so good
For fear of harms that preach in our behoof.
O appetite, from judgment stand aloof!
The one a palate hath that needs will taste,
Though Reason weep and cry "It is thy last."

'For further I could say, "This man's untrue,"
And knew the patterns of his foul beguiling;
Heard where his plants in others' orchards grew;
Saw how deceits were gilded in his smiling;
Knew vows were ever brokers to defiling;
Thought characters and words merely but art,
And bastards of his foul adulterate heart.

'And long upon these terms I held my city,
Till thus he gan besiege me: "Gentle maid,
Have of my suffering youth some feeling pity
And be not of my holy vows afraid.
That's to ye sworn to none was ever said;
For feasts of love I have been call'd unto,
Till now did ne'er invite nor never woo.

'"All my offences that abroad you see
Are errors of the blood, none of the mind.
Love made them not. With acture they may be,
Where neither party is nor true nor kind.
They sought their shame that so their shame did find;
And so much less of shame in me remains
By how much of me their reproach contains.

'"Among the many that mine eyes have seen,
Not one whose flame my heart so much as warmed,
Or my affection put to th' smallest teen,
Or any of my leisures ever charmed.
Harm have I done to them, but ne'er was harmed;
Kept hearts in liveries, but mine own was free
And reign'd commanding in his monarchy.

'"Look here what tributes wounded fancies sent me
Of pallid pearls and rubies red as blood,
Figuring that they their passions likewise lent me
Of grief and blushes, aptly understood
In bloodless white and the encrimson'd mood—
Effects of terror and dear modesty,
Encamp'd in hearts, but fighting outwardly.

'"And, lo, behold these talents of their hair,
With twisted metal amorously empleach'd,
I have receiv'd from many a several fair,
Their kind acceptance weepingly beseech'd,
With the annexions of fair gems enrich'd,
And deep-brain'd sonnets that did amplify
Each stone's dear nature, worth, and quality.

'"The diamond—why, 'twas beautiful and hard,
Whereto his invis'd properties did tend;
The deep-green em'rald, in whose fresh regard
Weak sights their sickly radiance do amend;
The heaven-hu'd sapphire, and the opal blend
With objects manifold: each several stone,
With wit well blazon'd, smil'd or made some moan.

'"Lo, all these trophies of affections hot,
Of pensiv'd and subdu'd desires the tender,
Nature hath charg'd me that I hoard them not,
But yield them up where I myself must render:
That is, to you, my origin and ender;
For these of force must your oblations be,
Since I their altar, you enpatron me.

'"O, then, advance of yours that phraseless hand
Whose white weighs down the airy scale of praise!
Take all these similes to your own command,
Hallowed with sighs that burning lungs did raise.
What me, your minister, for you obeys,
Works under you; and to your audit comes
Their distract parcels in combined sums.

'"Lo, this device was sent me from a nun,
Or sister sanctified, of holiest note,
Which late her noble suit in court did shun,
Whose rarest havings made the blossoms dote;
For she was sought by spirits of richest coat,
But kept cold distance, and did thence remove
To spend her living in eternal love.

'"But, O my sweet, what labour is't to leave
The thing we have not, mast'ring what not strives,
Paling the place which did no form receive,
Playing patient sports in unconstrained gyves?
She that her fame so to herself contrives,
The scars of battle scapeth by the flight
And makes her absence valiant, not her might.

'"O, pardon me, in that my boast is true!
The accident which brought me to her eye
Upon the moment did her force subdue,
And now she would the caged cloister fly.
Religious love put out religion's eye.
Not to be tempted, would she be immur'd,
And now, to tempt all, liberty procur'd.

'"How mighty then you are, O, hear me tell!
The broken bosoms that to me belong
Have emptied all their fountains in my well,
And mine I pour your ocean all among.
I strong o'er them, and you o'er me being strong,
Must for your victory us all congest,
As compound love to physic your cold breast.

"'My parts had pow'r to charm a sacred nun,
Who, disciplin'd, ay, dieted in grace,
Believ'd her eyes when they t' assail begun,
All vows and consecrations giving place.
O most potential love! vow, bond, nor space
In thee hath neither sting, knot, nor confine,
For thou art all, and all things else are thine.

"'When thou impressest, what are precepts worth
Of stale example? When thou wilt inflame,
How coldly those impediments stand forth
Of wealth, of filial fear, law, kindred, fame!
Love's arms are peace, 'gainst rule, 'gainst sense, 'gainst shame;
And sweetens, in the suff'ring pangs it bears,
The aloes of all forces, shocks, and fears.

"'Now all these hearts that do on mine depend,
Feeling it break, with bleeding groans they pine;
And supplicant their sighs to you extend,
To leave the batt'ry that you make 'gainst mine,
Lending soft audience to my sweet design,
And credent soul to that strong-bonded oath
That shall prefer and undertake my troth."

'This said, his wat'ry eyes he did dismount,
Whose sights till then were levell'd on my face;
Each cheek a river running from a fount
With brinish current downward flow'd apace.
O, how the channel to the stream gave grace!
Who glaz'd with crystal gate the glowing roses
That flame through water which their hue encloses.

'O father, what a hell of witchcraft lies
In the small orb of one particular tear!
But with the inundation of the eyes
What rocky heart to water will not wear?
What breast so cold that is not warmed here?
O cleft effect! cold modesty, hot wrath,
Both fire from hence and chill extincture hath.

'For, lo, his passion, but an art of craft,
Even there resolv'd my reason into tears;
There my white stole of chastity I daff'd,
Shook off my sober guards and civil fears;
Appear to him as he to me appears,
All melting; though our drops this diff'rence bore —
His poison'd me, and mine did him restore.

'In him a plenitude of subtle matter,
Applied to cautels, all strange forms receives,
Of burning blushes, or of weeping water,
Or sounding paleness; and he takes and leaves,
In either's aptness, as it best deceives —
To blush at speeches rank, to weep at woes,
Or to turn white and sound at tragic shows;

'That not a heart which in his level came
Could scape the hail of his all-hurting aim,
Showing fair nature is both kind and tame;
And, veil'd in them, did win whom he would maim.
Against the thing he sought he would exclaim:
When he most burn'd in heart-wish'd luxury,
He preach'd pure maid and prais'd cold chastity.

'Thus merely with the garment of a Grace
The naked and concealed fiend he cover'd;
That th' unexperient gave the tempter place,
Which, like a cherubin, above them hover'd.
Who, young and simple, would not be so lover'd?
Ay me! I fell; and yet do question make
What I should do again for such a sake.

'O, that infected moisture of his eye,
O, that false fire which in his cheek so glow'd,
O, that forc'd thunder from his heart did fly,
O, that sad breath his spongy lungs bestow'd,
O, all that borrowed motion seeming ow'd,
Would yet again betray the fore-betray'd
And new pervert a reconciled maid!'

THE PASSIONATE PILGRIM

IV

Sweet Cytherea, sitting by a brook
With young Adonis, lovely, fresh, and green,
Did court the lad with many a lovely look,
Such looks as none could look but beauty's queen.
She told him stories to delight his ear;
She show'd him favours to allure his eye;
To win his heart she touch'd him here and there —
Touches so soft still conquer chastity.
But whether unripe years did want conceit,
Or he refus'd to take her figured proffer,
The tender nibbler would not touch the bait,
But smile and jest at every gentle offer.
Then fell she on her back, fair queen, and toward.
He rose and ran away. Ah, fool too froward!

VI

Scarce had the sun dried up the dewy morn,
And scarce the herd gone to the hedge for shade,
When Cytherea, all in love forlorn,
A longing tarriance for Adonis made
Under an osier growing by a brook,
A brook where Adon us'd to cool his spleen.
Hot was the day; she hotter that did look
For his approach that often there had been.
Anon he comes, and throws his mantle by,
And stood stark naked on the brook's green brim.
The sun look'd on the world with glorious eye,
Yet not so wistly as this queen on him.
He, spying her, bounc'd in whereas he stood.
'O Jove,' quoth she, 'why was not I a flood?'

VII

Fair is my love, but not so fair as fickle;
Mild as a dove, but neither true nor trusty;
Brighter than glass, and yet as glass is brittle;
Softer than wax, and yet as iron rusty;
A lily pale, with damask dye to grace her:
None fairer, nor none falser to deface her.

Her lips to mine how often hath she joined,
Between each kiss her oaths of true love swearing!
How many tales to please me hath she coined,
Dreading my love, the loss whereof still fearing!
Yet, in the midst of all her pure protestings,
Her faith, her oaths, her tears, and all were jestings.

She burnt with love, as straw with fire flameth;
She burnt out love, as soon as straw outburneth;
She fram'd the love, and yet she foil'd the framing;
She bade love last, and yet she fell a-turning.
Was this a lover, or a lecher whether?
Bad in the best, though excellent in neither.

VIII

If music and sweet poetry agree,
As they must needs (the sister and the brother),
Then must the love be great 'twixt thee and me,
Because thou lov'st the one, and I the other.
Dowland to thee is dear, whose heavenly touch
Upon the lute doth ravish human sense;
Spenser to me, whose deep conceit is such
As, passing all conceit, needs no defence.
Thou lov'st to hear the sweet melodious sound
That Phœbus' lute (the queen of music) makes;
And I in deep delight am chiefly drown'd
When as himself to singing he betakes.
One god is god of both, as poets feign;
One knight loves both, and both in thee remain.

IX

Fair was the morn when the fair queen of love,

* * * * * * * * *

Paler for sorrow than her milk-white dove,
For Adon's sake, a youngster proud and wild,
Her stand she takes upon a steep-up hill.
Anon Adonis comes with horn and hounds.
She, silly queen, with more than love's good will,
Forbade the boy he should not pass those grounds.
'Once,' quoth she, 'did I see a fair sweet youth
Here in these brakes deep wounded with a boar,
Deep in the thigh, a spectacle of ruth!
See, in my thigh,' quoth she, 'here was the sore.'
She showed hers; he saw more wounds than one,
And blushing fled and left her all alone.

X

Sweet rose, fair flower, untimely pluck'd, soon vaded,
Pluck'd in the bud, and vaded in the spring!
Bright orient pearl, alack, too timely shaded!
Fair creature, kill'd too soon by death's sharp sting!
Like a green plum that hangs upon a tree,
And falls, through wind, before the fall should be.

I weep for thee, and yet no cause I have;
For why, thou lefts me nothing in thy will:
And yet thou lefts me more than I did crave;
For why, I craved nothing of thee still.
O yes, dear friend, I pardon crave of thee!
Thy discontent thou didst bequeath to me.

XI

Venus, with young Adonis sitting by her
Under a myrtle shade, began to woo him.
She told the youngling how god Mars did try her,
And as he fell to her, so fell she to him.
'Even thus,' quoth she, 'the warlike god embrac'd me,'
And then she clipp'd Adonis in her arms.
'Even thus,' quoth she, 'the warlike god unlac'd me,'
As if the boy should use like loving charms.
'Even thus,' quoth she, 'he seized on my lips,'
And with her lips on his did act the seizure;
And as she fetched breath, away he skips,
And would not take her meaning nor her pleasure.
Ah, that I had my lady at this bay,
To kiss and clip me till I run away!

XII

Crabbed age and youth cannot live together:
Youth is full of pleasance, age is full of care;
Youth like summer morn, age like winter weather;
Youth like summer brave, age like winter bare.
Youth is full of sport, age's breath is short;
Youth is nimble, age is lame;
Youth is hot and bold, age is weak and cold;
Youth is wild, and age is tame.
Age, I do abhor thee; youth, I do adore thee.
O, my love, my love is young!
Age, I do defy thee.
O sweet shepherd, hie thee,
For methinks thou stays too long.

XIII

Beauty is but a vain and doubtful good;
A shining gloss that vadeth suddenly;
A flower that dies when first it gins to bud;
A brittle glass that's broken presently;
A doubtful good, a gloss, a glass, a flower,
Lost, vaded, broken, dead within an hour.

And as goods lost are seld or never found,
As vaded gloss no rubbing will refresh,
As flowers dead lie withered on the ground,
As broken glass no cement can redress:
So beauty blemish'd once, for ever lost,
In spite of physic, painting, pain, and cost.

XIV

Good night, good rest. Ah, neither be my share!
She bade good night that kept my rest away,
And daff'd me to a cabin hang'd with care
To descant on the doubts of my decay.
'Farewell,' quoth she, 'and come again tomorrow.'
Fare well I could not, for I supp'd with sorrow.

Yet at my parting sweetly did she smile,
In scorn or friendship, nill I conster whether.
'T may be she joy'd to jest at my exile;
'T may be again, to make me wander thither:
'Wander'— a word for shadows like myself
As take the pain but cannot pluck the pelf.

Lord, how mine eyes throw gazes to the East![1]
My heart doth charge the watch; the morning rise
Doth cite each moving sense from idle rest,
Not daring trust the office of mine eyes.
While Philomela sits and sings, I sit and mark,
And wish her lays were tuned like the lark;

For she doth welcome daylight with her ditty
And drives away dark dreaming night.
The night so pack'd, I post unto my pretty;
Heart hath his hope, and eyes their wished sight;
Sorrow chang'd to solace and solace mix'd with sorrow;
For why, she sigh'd and bade me come tomorrow.

[1] The next three stanzas are in many editions printed as a separate poem.

Were I with her, the night would post too soon,
But now are minutes added to the hours;
To spite me now, each minute seems a moon;
Yet not for me, shine sun to succour flowers!
Pack night, peep day! Good day, of night now borrow.
Short, night, to-night, and length thyself to-morrow.

XVII

My flocks feed not,
My ewes breed not,
My rams speed not,
All is amiss:
Love's denying,
Faith's defying,
Heart's renying,
Causer of this.
All my merry jigs are quite forgot,
All my lady's love is lost, God wot.
Where her faith was firmly fix'd in love,
There a nay is plac'd without remove.
One silly cross
Wrought all my loss.
O frowning Fortune, cursed fickle dame!
For now I see
Inconstancy
More in women than in men remain.

In black mourn I,
All fears scorn I,
Love hath forlorn me,
Living in thrall.
Heart is bleeding,
All help needing —
O cruel speeding,
Fraughted with gall!
My shepherd's pipe can sound no deal;
My wether's bell rings doleful knell;
My curtail dog, that wont to have play'd,
Plays not at all, but seems afraid.
My sighs so deep
Procure to weep,
In howling wise, to see my doleful plight.
How sighs resound
Through heartless ground,
Like a thousand vanquish'd men in bloody fight!

Clear wells spring not,
Sweet birds sing not,
Green plants bring not
Forth their dye.
Herds stand weeping,
Flocks all sleeping,
Nymphs back peeping
Fearfully.
All our pleasure known to us poor swains,
All our merry meetings on the plains,
All our evening sport from us is fled,
All our love is lost, for Love is dead.
Farewell, sweet lass!
Thy like ne'er was
For a sweet content, the cause of all my moan.
Poor Corydon
Must live alone.
Other help for him I see that there is none.

XVIII

When as thine eye hath chose the dame
And stall'd the deer that thou shouldst strike,
Let reason rule things worthy blame,
As well as fancy, partial might;
Take counsel of some wiser head,
Neither too young nor yet unwed.

And when thou com'st thy tale to tell,
Smooth not thy tongue with filed talk,
Lest she some subtile practice smell —
A cripple soon can find a halt;
But plainly say thou lov'st her well,
And set thy person forth to sell.

What though her frowning brows be bent,
Her cloudy looks will calm ere night;
And then too late she will repent
That thus dissembled her delight,
And twice desire, ere it be day,
That which with scorn she put away.

What though she strive to try her strength,
And ban and brawl and say thee nay?
Her feeble force will yield at length,
When craft hath taught her thus to say:
'Had women been so strong as men,
In faith, you had not had it then.'

And to her will frame all thy ways.
Spare not to spend, and chiefly there
Where thy desert may merit praise
By ringing in thy lady's ear.
The strongest castle, tower, and town,
The golden bullet beats it down.

Serve always with assured trust
And in thy suit be humble-true.

Unless thy lady prove unjust,
Press never thou to choose a new.
When time shall serve, be thou not slack
To proffer, though she put thee back.

The wiles and guiles that women work,
Dissembled with an outward show,
The tricks and toys that in them lurk,
The cock that treads them shall not know.
Have you not heard it said full oft,
A woman's nay doth stand for naught?

Think women still to strive with men
To sin, and never for to saint.
There is no heaven: be holy then
When time with age shall them attaint.
Were kisses all the joys in bed,
One woman would another wed.

But, soft! enough! — too much, I fear;
Lest that my mistress hear my song.
She will not stick to round me on th' ear,
To teach my tongue to be so long.
Yet will she blush, here be it said,
To hear her secrets so bewray'd.

XX

As it fell upon a day
In the merry month of May,
Sitting in a pleasant shade
Which a grove of myrtles made,
Beasts did leap and birds did sing,
Trees did grow and plants did spring;
Everything did banish moan,
Save the nightingale alone.
She, poor bird, as all forlorn,
Lean'd her breast up-till a thorn
And there sung the dolefull'st ditty,
That to hear it was great pity.
'Fie, fie, fie!' now would she cry;
'Tereu, tereu!' by-and-by;
That to hear her so complain
Scarce I could from tears refrain;
For her griefs, so lively shown,
Made me think upon mine own.
'Ah,' thought I, 'thou mourn'st in vain!
None takes pity on thy pain.
Senseless trees they cannot hear thee;
Ruthless beasts they will not cheer thee.
King Pandion, he is dead;
All thy friends are lapp'd in lead;
All thy fellow birds do sing,
Careless of thy sorrowing.
Even so, poor bird, like thee,
None alive will pity me.
Whilst as fickle Fortune smil'd,
Thou and I were both beguil'd.'
Every one that flatters thee
Is no friend in misery.
Words are easy, like the wind;
Faithful friends are hard to find.
Every man will be thy friend
Whilst thou hast wherewith to spend;
But if store of crowns be scant,
No man will supply thy want.
If that one be prodigal,
Bountiful they will him call,
And with such-like flattering,
'Pity but he were a king.'
If he be addict to vice,
Quickly him they will entice.
If to women he be bent,
They have at commandëment.
But if Fortune once do frown,
Then farewell his great renown!
They that fawn'd on him before
Use his company no more.
He that is thy friend indeed,
He will help thee in thy need.
If thou sorrow, he will weep;
If thou wake, he cannot sleep.
Thus of every grief in heart
He with thee doth bear a part.
These are certain signs to know
Faithful friend from flatt'ring foe.

THE PHŒNIX AND TURTLE

Let the bird of loudest lay,
On the sole Arabian tree,
Herald sad and trumpet be,
To whose sound chaste wings obey.

But thou shrieking harbinger,
Foul precurrer of the fiend,
Augur of the fever's end,
To this troop come thou not near!

From this session interdict
Every fowl of tyrant wing,
Save the eagle, feath'red king:
Keep the obsequy so strict.

Let the priest in surplice white,
That defunctive music can,
Be the death-divining swan,
Lest the requiem lack his right.

And thou treble-dated crow,
That thy sable gender mak'st
With the breath thou giv'st and tak'st,
'Mongst our mourners shalt thou go.

Here the anthem doth commence:
Love and constancy is dead,
Phœnix and the turtle fled
In a mutual flame from hence.

So they lov'd as love in twain
Had the essence but in one;
Two distincts, division none:
Number there in love was slain.

Hearts remote, yet not asunder;
Distance, and no space was seen
'Twixt this turtle and his queen;
But in them it were a wonder.

So between them love did shine
That the turtle saw his right
Flaming in the phœnix' sight:
Either was the other's mine.

Property was thus appalled,
That the self was not the same;
Single nature's double name
Neither two nor one was called.

Reason, in itself confounded,
Saw division grow together,
To themselves yet either neither,
Simple were so well compounded;

That it cried, 'How true a twain
Seemeth this concordant one!
Love hath reason, reason none,
If what parts can so remain.'

Whereupon it made this threne
To the phœnix and the dove,
Co-supremes and stars of love,
As chorus to their tragic scene.

THRENOS.

Beauty, truth, and rarity,
Grace in all simplicity,
Here enclos'd in cinders lie.

Death is now the phœnix' nest;
And the turtle's loyal breast
To eternity doth rest,

Leaving no posterity:
'Twas not their infirmity,
It was married chastity.

Truth may seem, but cannot be;
Beauty brag, but 'tis not she:
Truth and Beauty buried be.

To this urn let those repair
That are either true or fair;
For these dead birds sigh a prayer.

GLOSSARY

a, in, on
'a, he
'a', have
abate, to humble; shorten; dull; reduce the estimate of; omit; cut off
abide, *see* aby
abject, a servile creature (*Rich. III*, i, 1, 106)
able, to authorize (*Lear*, iv, 6, 172)
abode, to bode, forebode
abodement, bad omen
aborn, auburn
abortive, an unnatural thing, abnormality (*K. John*, iii, 4, 158)
abram, auburn
Abram, Abraham (*M. of V.*, i, 3, 73)
abridgment, pastime; that which cuts short
abroad, away from here; outside one's house; on foot; here and there; in the world; current
abrogate, avoid (*L. L. L.*, iv, 2, 55)
abrook, to brook, endure (*2 Hen. VI*, ii, 4, 10)
abruption, a breaking off
absey book, A B C book, primer
absolute, perfect; accomplished; precise, finical
abstract, a summary, epitome; condensation; a short cut, a means of shortening one's way
abuse, to deceive
abuse, deception; fault
abuser, deceiver
aby (abide), pay for, answer for
abysm, abyss
academe, academy
accept, decision (*Hen. V*, v, 2, 82)
accepted, acceptable
accidence, that part of grammar that treats of inflectional forms
accident, a chance occurrence (good or bad), incident
accite, to summon; incite, prompt (*2 Hen. IV*, ii, 2, 64)
accommodate, to equip, furnish; attire
accomplice, an associate (*1 Hen. VI*, v, 2, 9)
accomplish, to finish off; furnish; obtain, win
accompt, *n.*, account, reckoning
accord, harmony; consent, assent
according, accordingly
accountant, accountable
accoustrement, accoutrement
accuse, accusation
ace, the number one (in dice)
achieve, to obtain, acquire
achievement, acquisition
acknown on (to be), to admit knowledge of
acold, cold, chilly
aconitum, aconite, monkshood
acquit, to pay for (in full); free, absolve; *p.p.*, rid
acquittance, *n.*, a receipt in full; acquittal; *v.*, to acquit, clear
act, action, operation
action-taking, prone to go to law instead of fighting
acture, action (*Compl.*, 185)
adamant, magnet
addiction, inclination
addition, name; title; honour
address, to direct; prepare, make ready
adhere, to be consistent or appropriate; be connected; be attached (in friendship)
admirable, wonderful, strange
admiral, the admiral's ship
admiration, wonder; object of wonder
admire, to wonder, wonder at
admired, admirable; wonderful, strange
admit, to accept, favour; include
admittance, accepted fashion; social prestige
adoor, *see* in-a-door
adoptious Christendoms, fond nicknames (*All's W.*, i, 1, 188)
adulterate, *v.*, to commit adultery; *adj.*, adulterous
advance, to raise, lift up; display
advantage, *n.*, interest, usury; *v.*, to benefit; increase (by interest)
adventure, *n.*, chance; *v.*, to take the risk
advertise, inform, instruct
advertisement, information; advice, counsel
advice, consideration
advise, to consider; inform
advised, wise, discreet, considerate; carefully considered; (be), consider, take care
advisedly, with due consideration
aery, the nest of a bird of prey, eyrie; brood
affect, *n.*, inclination, liking; *v.*, to care for, love, like; strive for
affected, disposed; in love
affectedly, fancifully (*Compl.*, 48)
affection, disposition, inclination; fancy, thing fancied for the moment; passion; affectation
affectioned, *adj.*, affected
affeered, confirmed, established by authority (*Macb.*, iv, 3, 34)
affiance, trust; loyalty
affined, *adj.*, related; under obligation
affinity, relationship, kindred
affliction, the beating of the storm (*Lear*, iii, 2, 49)
affray, to frighten
affright, to surround with fear (*Per.*, i, 1, 29)
affront, *n.*, an encounter face to face; *v.*, to meet, encounter
affy, to confide, trust; betroth
afoot, in infantry (*All's W.*, iv, 3, 181)
afore, before
Afric, Africa, African
afront, face to face with one
after, according to; at the rate of; afterwards
after-debts, indebtedness for a service already performed (*All's W.*, iv, 3, 255)
after-eye, *v.*, to follow with one's eyes (*Cymb.*, i, 3, 16)
against, in preparation for or expectation of; just before; in anticipation of the time when
agazed, gazing, with their eyes fixed (*1 Hen. VI*, i, 1, 126)
aged, befitting or characteristic of old age
agent, the doer
aglet, the metal tag of a lace
aglet-baby, a girl as small as an aglet (*T. of S.*, i, 2, 79)
agnize, to recognize as one's own (*Oth.*, i, 3, 232)
agued, *adj.*, quaking as with ague
a-height (a-high), on high, aloft
ahold, close to the wind (*Temp.*, i, 1, 52)
ahungry (anhungry), hungry
aidance, aid, help
aidant, helpful
aim, *n.*, *v.*, guess, conjecture. *See* cry aim
air, the style, fashion
air-drawn, imaginary
alablaster, alabaster
aland, on land, to land
alarm, a call to arms; assault
alarum, *n.*, a call to arms, combat; *v.*, to call to arms or to the combat
albeit, although
alderliefest, dearest of all, very dear (*2 Hen. VI*, i, 1, 28)
ale, ale-drinking
a-life, as much as life (*W. T.*, iv, 4, 264)
alight, to dismount from (*Ven.*, 13)
allay, relief
allayment, mitigation
allegiant, loyal
All-hallond eve, the eve of All Saints' Day
Allhallowmas, All Saints' Day (November 1)
All-hallown summer, summer weather in late autumn, Indian summer (*1 Hen. IV*, i, 2, 178)
all hid, hide and seek
allied, related, kindred
alligant, *for* elegant (*M. W.*, ii, 2, 69)
allottery, allotted portion
allow, to approve
allowance, acknowledgement, approval
all-thing, *adv.*, altogether, in every way (*Macb.* iii, 1, 13)
all-watched, passed without sleep
ally, kinsman
allycholly (allicholly), *for* melancholy
Almain, a German
alms-drink, more than his share (*A. and C.*, ii, 7, 5)
aloft, *prep.*, above
alone, unparalleled, superior to all
along, at one's full length
alter, to exchange
alway, always
amain, strongly, aloud, swiftly
amaze, *v.*, to bring into a maze, confound, confuse utterly; *n.*, confusion
amazedly, with utter confusion, as one in a maze
amazedness, bewilderment; panic
amazement, utter perplexity; panic
ambuscado, ambuscade, ambush
amerce, to punish (with a fine)
ames-ace, two aces (in dice)
amiss, offence, misfortune; astray (in one's mind)

among, *see* ever among
amort, dispirited, in dejection
ample, amply, fully
an, on
an, if; if only; even if, though; as if; (an if), if
anatomize, dissect
anatomy, skeleton
anchor, anchorite, hermit
ancient, *n.*, ensign (flag *or* officer); *adj.*, aged; old, former, bygone
ancientry, the old, aged people; old-fashioned ceremony
an end, on end, upright. *See* still an end
angel, a gold coin, half a pound
angerly, angrily
anguish, excruciating pain (of body or mind)
anhungry, *see* ahungry
annexion, addition
annothanize, to anatomize, interpret (*L. L. L.*, iv, 1, 69)
annoy, *n.*, pain, grief; harm, injury; *v.*, to hurt, molest
annoyance, harm, injury
anon, soon, presently; and then; (ever and), now and then
answer, *n.*, response in action, retaliation; acceptance of a challenge; return attack, return blow or thrust; *v.*, to meet in combat; answer for; atone for
an't, on it, of it
anter, cavern
Anthropophagi, cannibals
Anthropophaginian, cannibal, man-eater
Antiates, the people of Antium
antic, *adj.*, quaint, queer, fantastic; *n.*, odd person, buffoon; a fantastic dance; *v.*, to turn one to a buffoon
ap (*Welsh*), son of (*Rich. III*, iv, 5, 15)
apaid, satisfied, contented
apish, imitative (*Rich II*, ii, 1, 22)
apology, an explanatory address in defence
apoplexed, paralyzed
apostropha, omission of a letter or letters (*L. L. L.*, iv. 2, 123)
appalled, pale, pallid; annulled (*Phœn.*, 37)
apparent, heir apparent (i.e., one whose right is indefeasible)
apparitions, appearances
appeach, inform against, impeach
appeal, *n.*, impeachment, accusation; *v.*, to accuse, impeach
appellant, accuser
apperil, peril, risk
apple-John, a late apple (which shrinks when it ripens)
appliance, medicine, medical treatment, remedy
apply, administer (a medicine or potion); devote one's self
appoint, equip
appointment, equipment, attire
apprehensive, quick-witted, perceptive
approbation, proof
approof, approval; proof, testing
appropriation, special credit (*M. of V.*, i, 2, 46)
approve, test, prove; confirm, justify
approver, one who tests
apricock, apricot
apron-man, mechanic, craftsman
apt, ready; probable
aqua-vitæ, distilled liquor
Aquilon, the north wind
Arabian bird, phœnix
araise, raise from the dead
arbitrement, decision, legal inquiry
arch, *n.*, *adj.*, chief
argal (argo), *for* ergo, therefore
argentine, silver-bright
Argier, Algiers
argosy, a merchant ship of the largest size
argument, theme, subject matter, plot (of a play)
arm, furnish, prepare; embrace
arm-gaunt, slender and spirited in his armour (*A. and C.*, i, 5, 48)
armigero, esquire
armipotent, powerful in war
aroint thee, avaunt, get thee gone
arras, tapestry hangings
arrivance, persons arriving
arrive, arrive at, reach
arrose, besprinkle (*T. N. K.*, v, 4, 104)
Arthur's Show, a company of London archers who called themselves by the names of King Arthur's knights
article (of great), consisting of many items of excellence
articulate, negotiate; itemize
artificial, made by art
artire, sinew, muscle (*Haml.*, i, 4, 82)
artist, learned and skilful man; physician
artless, lacking skill or wisdom
arts-man, scholarly person
asinico, little ass; fool
askaunce, to turn aside (*Lucr.*, 637)
aspect, the action of the planets (by virtue of their astrological positions) upon human affairs; influence
aspersion, sprinkling (as of dew), shower
aspic, asp
aspire, mount up, rise; soar to
assay, *n.*, a trial, test; an attempt; criterion; raid; *v.*, to try, test, make trial of; attempt; tempt; make an attempt upon
assemblance, semblance, appearance
assigns, appurtenances
assist, accompany, attend
assubjugate, degrade, debase
assured, betrothed
astonish, stun, stupefy
a-tilt (run), to tilt, to just
atomy, atom; tiny creature
atone, reconcile; accord with one another
attach, take hold of, seize, attack, arrest
attainder, dishonour, stain, disgrace
attaint, *n.*, stain, disgrace; infection; worn and fatigued appearance; *v.*, to stain, dishonour; convict; deprive of civil rights
attainture, conviction and disgrace
at task, blamed
attent, attentive
attest, testimony, evidence
attribute, good reputation, credit
atwain, in two, asunder
audible, quick of ear
augure, augury
augurer, augur
auld, old (*Oth.*, ii, 3, 99)
aunt, old dame; prostitute
avised, sensible, considerate; informed
avoid, leave; get rid of
aweless, fearless; inspiring no awe
awful, reverential; awe-inspiring
awkward, back-handed; adverse, contrary; irregular or contrary to right

baccare, stand back!
back friend, false friend
backsword man, a single-stick fencer
back-trick, a caper backward in a dance
baffle, degrade from knighthood; treat with contempt
bait, to set dogs upon; attack, harass
baked meats, pies, pasties
balk, to neglect, pass by, overlook
balked, heaped up in ridges
ball, the globe used at coronation, the orb (*Hen. V*, iv, 1, 277)
ballow, cudgel
ban, *n.*, *v.*, curse
band, bond
bandog, dog kept chained, mastiff
bandy, knock to and fro; contend
bane, poison; destruction, ruin
banes, the bans (notice of intended marriage given in church)
bank, to coast along by (*K. John*, v, 2, 104)
bankrout, bankrupt
banquet, a service of fruit and sweetmeats
barbed, armed with a barb (a covering for the breast of a warhorse)
barely, in a bare condition
barful, much impeded
barley-break, a rustic game
barnacle, a kind of wild goose
barne, child
Bartholomew, served at Bartholomew Fair (*2 Hen. IV*, ii, 4, 250)
base, the game of prisoner's base. *See* bid
base court, the lower court of a castle
bases, a skirt attached to an armed horseman's doublet
Basilisco-like, like Basilisco (a braggart knight in the old play of *Soliman and Perseda*)
basilisk, a cockatrice, a fabulous reptile whose eyes were deadly; a large cannon
basta, enough
bastard, a sweet Spanish wine
batch, a baking of bread
bate, *n.*, contention, dispute; *v.*, to flap the wings
bate, abate, diminish, weaken; deduct, remit
bate-breeding, causing strife
bateless, not to be dulled
bat-fowling, bird-catching by night
batlet, a bat used to beat clothes in washing
battalia, army
batten, feed coarsely
battle, battalion, army, troop
bauble, a worthless thing or person; a trifle or toy; a fool's sceptre
bavian, baboon
bavin, *adj.*, like brushwood (*1 Hen. IV*, iii, 2, 61)
bawcock, fine fellow
beadsman, one who prays for another
be-all, all there is to the matter (*Macb.*, i, 7, 5)
bear (a brain), to have a good mind; (hard), bear a grudge against; (in hand), deceive by a course of false pretences, cajole; (it, it away), win, get the victory

bearing cloth, mantle in which an infant is carried to the font to be christened
beaver, lower moveable part of a helmet; visor; helmet
becking, *n.*, beckoning
becomed, fitting, becoming
bedlam, *n.*, Bethlehem hospital for lunatics; madhouse; madman; *adj.*, insane
bed-swerver, adulteress
been, are (*Per.*, ii, Gow., 28)
beesom (bisson), blind, purblind
beg us, sue for and obtain guardianship of us as idiotic (*L. L. L.*, v, 2, 490)
begnaw, gnaw at, eat away
beholding, beholden, under obligation
being, *n.*, life, existence; residence; *adv.*, while, since
beldam(e), grandmother; old woman; hag
belee'd, forced into the lee (away from the wind)
belied, falsified (*Lucr.*, 1533)
bellman, watchman (with a bell)
bemadding, maddening
bemet, *p.p.*, met
bemoiled, besmeared with mud
bench, sit on the bench (as judge); raise to a high seat or station
bend, *n.*, look, glance; direction; bow, graceful and reverential attitude; *v.*, to aim, direct; make tense or ready for action
benevolence, a forced loan (as if in gift)
bent, force and direction (as from a bent bow); inclination; look
ben venuto, welcome
berard (berod), bearward
berattle, berate, decry
Bergomask dance, a grotesque dance imitating the natives of Bergamo in Italy
Bermoothes, Bermudas
berod (berard), bearward
beseeming, appearance, guise
beshrew, curse (*a light word*)
besides, out of (*Sonn.*, 23)
beslubber, smear
besonian (bezonian), a miserable creature, low fellow
besort, *v.*, suit; *n.*, suitability
bespeak, speak to, address
bestead (worse), in a worse plight
bestow, stow, place, dispose of; use, employ; behave
bestraught, distracted (*T. of S.*, Ind., ii, 27)
bestride, defend (a fallen soldier)
beteem, allow
betime, betimes, early
bewray, reveal, disclose
bezonian, *see* besonian
bias, *n.*, a weight on a bowl which gives it an oblique course; the oblique course; tendency, inclination, propensity; indirect means; *adv.*, awry; *adj.*, swollen, puffed out
bid a (*or* the) base, to challenge to a race
biddy, chicken
bide, abide, endure, undergo
biding, place of abode
bigamy, marriage with a widow (*Rich. III*, iii, 7, 189)
biggen, nightcap
big-looked, menacing (*T. N. K.*, i, 1, 215)
bilbo, sword (made at Bilboa, Spain), swordsman
bilboes, a shackled bar
bile, a boil
bill, halberd, pike
bill, written paper, document, order
bird, young bird, nestling
bird-bolt, blunt-headed arrow for shooting birds
birding, fowling
birth-child (Thetis'), child belonging to Thetis because born at sea (*Per.*, iv, 4, 41)
birthdom, native land
bisson, *see* beesom
bite the thumb, an insulting and contemptuous gesture
bitumed, daubed with bitumen
black, of dark complexion
black-cornered, that darkens corners (hiding places)
Black Monday, Easter Monday
blacks, black or mourning garments
blank, *n.*, the white spot at the centre of a target; line of aim; *v.*, to blanch, make pale
blanks, grants or charters with blank spaces left to be filled in; lottery tickets that win nothing; blank pages
blaze, make public
blazon, *n.*, description; *v.*, to describe
blench, *v.*, to start, flinch; start away, show inconstancy; *n.*, an inconstant action
blend, blended (*Compl.*, 215)
blistered, adorned with puffs
blood-boltered, having the hair matted with blood
blood-sized, daubed with clotted blood
blow, make flyblown
blown, windy, inflated, unsubstantial
blowse, a ruddy, fat-cheeked girl
blue-cap, a Scot
blue eye, one having a dark circle round it
blue-eyed, with eyes surrounded by blue circles
blunt, stupid
blurted at, greeted with scornful 'pooh's'
board, accost, address, woo
bob, *v.*, beat, thrash; cheat, trick; *n.*, a taunting jest
bodkin, stiletto
bodykins (God's bodykins), an oath (by God's body)
boggle, to shy, equivocate
boggler, an inconstant person
boldened, made bold
bolin, bowline
bollen, swollen
bolting hutch, a box or chest into which anything is bolted or sifted
bombard, a big leather bottle
bombast, *n.*, cotton wool; padding; *adj.*, bombastic
bona roba, a showy wanton
bonnet, to doff the hat
bonny, handsome; stalwart
boot, *n.*, booty; profit, gain; avail; (to), for our help; *v.*, to avail; to present (one) over and above
boothose, a heavy stocking to be worn instead of a boot
bore, to cheat, gull
boresprit, bowsprit
bosky, bushy
botch, to patch, mend clumsily
bots, a disease of horses, caused by worms
bottle, a bundle of hay
bottled, swollen unwholesomely
bottom, *n.*, skein or ball (of thread); *v.*, to wind
bottom, a ship; low land by a river
bound, to make to leap (*Hen. V*, v, 2, 146); *p.p.*, confined, circumscribed (*J. C.*, iv, 3, 221)
bounty, goodness
bourn, boundary; brook
bowels, offspring; compassion, feeling
bow-hand, the (left) hand which holds the bow
bowling, bowline (*T. N. K.*, iv, 1, 148)
boy-queller, boy-killer
brabble, brawl, quarrel
brace, a piece of armour; posture or condition of defence
brach, a bitch-hound
braid, *adj.*, deceitful, tricky
braid, to upbraid (*Per.* i, 1, 93)
brain, *v.*, comprehend
brainish, insane
brainpan, skull
brainsick, insane
brake, underbrush
brave, *adj.*, fine, splendid, grand (in appearance or character); *v.*, to make fine, adorn; challenge, defy (especially in a swaggering manner); show off, make a display
bravery, splendour, display; finery; ostentation; bravado
brawl, a kind of dance
brawn, muscle; mass of flesh
breach of the sea, breaking waves, surf
breast, voice (in singing)
breath, mild exercise
breathe, speak softly; utter, reveal; take exercise
breathed, well exercised, in good condition as to wind
breed-bate, a stirrer-up of quarrels
breeder, a mare
breese (brize), gadfly
bribed buck, a stolen deer (*M. W.*, v, 5, 27)
bride, to marry
brief, a letter; a short document; a summary; a brief account
briefly, a little while ago; soon; without delay
brinded, brindled, marked with dark streaks
bring out, confuse, put out
Britain, *n.*, Brittany; *adj.*, British Breton
Briton, native of Brittany
Brittany, Britain
brize (breese), gadfly
broach, to stick upon and pierce, spit; tap; bleed; set going, start
brock, badger
brogue, a coarse heavy shoe
broke, act as go-between or agent
broken (music), arranged for various instruments, concerted
broker, one who brokes
brooch, adorn (as with a brooch)
brooded, watchful (as a hen over her brood) (*K. John*, iii, 3, 52)
Brownist, member of the non-conformist sect founded by Robert Brown about 1581
bubble, worthless fellow
bubukles, red swellings, great pimples

buck, a lot of soiled clothes for the wash
buck-basket, a basket for soiled clothes
buckle, bend, give way; join in hand-to-hand fight, grapple
buckler, to shield, defend
Bucklersbury, a London street in which were many grocers and apothecaries
bug, bugbear
bulk, trunk; huge body; a projecting stall
bully, fine fellow (common as a friendly form of address: as, 'bully doctor')
bully rook, jovial fellow
bum-baily, a sheriff's officer
bung, cutpurse, pickpocket
burgonet, a kind of helmet
busky, bushy
buss, *n.*, *v.*, kiss
buttery, storeroom for liquor and food
button, a bud
buttons (in his), within his grasp (*M. W.*, iii, 2, 71)
butt-shaft, unbarbed arrow
buzzer, whisperer (of scandal)
by-and-by, immediately
by-dependences, incidental circumstances (*Cymb.*, v, 5, 390)
by-drinkings, drinks between meals
by'r, by our

cabin, to shut up in a cabin; to be confined
cacodemon, evil spirit, devil
cade, a 'barrel' of herrings (720 in number)
cadent, ever-falling
cage, a lock-up
'cagion, occasion, cause
Cain-coloured, of the same colour as Cain's, red, (*M. W.*, i, 4, 23)
caitiff, *n.*, wretch, miserable creature; *adj.*, miserable
caliver, a light musket
calkins, calks on a horseshoe (*T. N. K.*, v, 4, 55)
callet (callot), low woman
calm, *for* qualm (*2 Hen. IV*, ii, 4, 40)
Cambyses' vein, bombastic style (as in Thomas Preston's tragedy of *Cambyses*)
can (*for* gan), did
can, can do or accomplish, has skill or ability; knows
canakin, little can
canary, a sweet wine from the Canary Islands; a lively Spanish dance; quandary (*M. W.*, ii, 2, 61)
candidatus, clad in white, as a candidate for the consulship
candle mine, vast deposit of tallow
canker, a sore, an ulcer; a worm that eats rosebuds; a wild rose
cankered, ulcerated, malignant; tarnished
canon, rule; law, divine law
canstick, candlestick
cantle, piece cut out, segment
canton, song
canvass, to toss (as in a canvas sheet)
canzonet, a short song
capable, ready to take, to feel, or to understand; ample; susceptible; intelligent; legally qualified as inheritor (*Lear*, ii, 1, 87)
capitulate, draw up an agreement, come to terms
capriccio, caprice, notion
captain, chief commander, general
captious, ready to take (*All's W.*, i, 3, 208)
captivate, to take or keep captive
captive, take captive
car, chariot
carack (careck, carrect), galleon
carbonado, *n.*, piece of meat slashed for broiling; *v.*, to slash
carcanet, jewelled necklace
card, *n.*, the compass card marked with the points of the compass; chart; (by the), with precision, accurately; *v.*, to mix, adulterate
cardecue, quart d'écu, a French coin worth a quarter of a French gold crown
cardinally, *for* carnally (*M. for M.*, ii, 1, 81)
career, a short gallop; a headstrong action or whim
careful, anxious, care-burdened
care-tuned, sorrowful in sound
carl, a rustic, peasant
carnal, flesh-eating, ravenous (*Rich. III*, iv, 4, 56)
carouse, *n.*, a full cup drunk at a draught; *v.*, to drink a toast
carpet consideration, grounds of mere gallantry and courtly service (*T. N.*, iii, 4, 258)
carpet-monger, one who frequents carpeted rooms, a gallant
carrect, *see* carack
carriage, load, burden, purport, tenour
carry, to manage; (out my side), win my game, achieve my object
cart, *n.*, chariot; *v.*, to expose to disgrace by carrying (one) about the streets in a cart
carve, to serve in carving at table; to act and speak with attentive courtesy; (for), to serve (one) in carving; to indulge; (to), to serve (one) at table
case, *n.*, body; skin; socket (of the eye); setting; a full set; *v.*, to mask; skin, flay
cashier, dismiss; slang for 'cleaned out' (by a pickpocket)
cast, *v.*, cashier, dismiss (from office); inspect (for diagnosis); *adj.*, thrown aside, discarded
Cataian, native of Cathay, Chinaman
cataract, waterspout
catastrophe, rump
cater-cousins, intimate friends
catlings, fiddlestrings of catgut
caudle, a warm spiced drink
cautel, deceit, crafty scheme
cautelous, deceitful, deceptive
cavaleiro, cavalier, gallant
cavalery, cavalier
caviary, caviare
cease, *n.*, decease
censure, *n.*, judgment, opinion; *v.*, to judge, pass judgment on
centre, the earth (as the centre of the universe)
cerecloth, waxed cloth for wrapping a corpse
'cern, to concern (*T. of S.*, v, 1, 77)
certes, certainly, assuredly
cess (out of all), beyond all measure
cesse, *n.*, cessation, death; *v.*, to cease, come to an end
cestron, cistern
chafe, *n.*, anger; *v.*, to show anger; make angry
chaffy, worthless (*T. N. K.*, iii, 1, 41)
challenger, claimant
cham, khan (ruler of Tartary)
chamber, a small piece of ordnance
chamber councils, private councils
chamberer, a gallant
chamberlain, a servant in charge of the chambers at an inn
chamblet, a garment made of camlet (a light fabric)
champain (champian), a fertile plain; level country
champion, *v.*, meet in single combat
chance, *v.*, chances
change, to deal in exchange
changeable, of varying colours
changeling, a fickle person
channel, a gutter
chanson, song
chape, metal tip of a sheath
chapel, bury with due rites (*T. N. K.*, i, 1, 50)
chapeless, without a chape
chapfallen, lacking the lower jaw (*with a pun*) (*Haml.*, v, 1, 212)
chapless, without a (lower) jaw,
chaps, jaws
character, *n.*, handwriting; a mark, sign; *v.*, to write, inscribe
charactery, writing; what is written or inscribed
chare, *n.*, chore, small job; *v.*, to do (a task)
charect, carat
charge, *n.*, load, burden; importance; expense, cost, value; military command; troop; *v.*, to load
chargeful, costly, expensive
charge house, a boarding school
Charles' wain, the Great Bear
charneco, a kind of Portuguese wine
chase, the first bound of an unreturned tennis ball; a hunting preserve
chaudron, entrails
che, I
cheapen, to bargain for
cheater, escheator
check, *n.*, *v.*, rebuke; check at
checkin, a sequin (an Italian coin)
cherry-pit, a children's game (throwing cherry stones into a small hole or pit)
cheveril (chev'ril, chiverel), kid leather (soft and easily stretched); made of cheveril; yielding, elastic
chewet, a small mince pie; *fig.*, a fat fellow
child, a girl baby
childing, *adj.*, fruitful, fertile
chill, I will (*Lear*, iv, 6, 240)
chipochia (*Ital.* capocchia), simpleton (*T. and C.*, iv, 2, 33)
chirurgeonly, like a surgeon
chiverel, *see* cheveril
choler, bile; anger
chop, to exchange, make an exchange
chopine, a shoe with a thick sole of cork
choplogic, one who argues contentiously
chops, *n.*, fissures, deep lines (*Lucr.*, 1452)
chops, a fat-cheeked fellow
chopt, seamed, wrinkled (*Sonn.*, 62)
choris, *for* chorus (*T. N. K.*, iii, 5 107)
chough, a kind of crow
christen, christened
christom child, infant wearing the chrisom, a white robe put on when

he was christened; innocent (*Hen. V*, ii, 3, 12)
chuck, chick (a term of affection)
chud, I would (*Lear*, iv, 6, 243)
chuff, a boor; a miser
Ciciter, Cirencester
'cide, decide
Cimmerian, native of the Land of Darkness, blackamoor
cinque-pace (sink-a-pace), a lively dance, galliard
cipher, decipher
circummured, walled round
circumstance, circumlocution, elaborate style or phraseology; talk
cital, mention
cite, summon, urge
citizen, *adj*., city-bred, delicate
cittern, an instrument somewhat like a guitar
civil, civilized, decorous, well-behaved; (doctor), a doctor of civil (Roman) law
clack-dish, a beggar's dish with a cover which he clacked to attract notice
clap hands, to clasp hands (in a bargain or agreement); *hence*, clap, to pledge
clap i' th' clout, hit the bull's eye
clapperclaw, scratch and beat
clean, shapely, well-moulded
clear, pure
clearness, freedom from being suspected (*Mach*., iii, 1, 133)
cleep (clip), embrace
clepe (clip) to call, style
clerk, a scholar
cliff, clef, key (in music)
climate, *n*., region, clime; quarter of the sky; *v*., to sojourn
climature, clime, region
cling, cause (one) to shrivel up
clinquant, glittering (with gold)
clip (cleep), to embrace
clip (clepe), to call, style
clipper, one who clips coins
cloistress, nun
close, *adj*., secret; secretive
close, enclose; join closely; come together; come to an agreement, agree; come to grips, grapple
closet, private room
closure, enclosure; close, end
clotpoll (i. e., sod-head), blockhead
clothier's yard, an arrow a cloth yard long
cloudy, sad, sullen, gloomy
clout, a piece of cloth; the mark, the bull's eye
clouted, having the soles set with nails or strips of metal
clown, a rustic, boor, clumsy fellow; clownish servant; jester
cloy, to claw (*Cymb*., v, 4, 118)
coast, to move in a sly or circuitous course (*Hen. VIII*, iii, 2, 38)
clyster pipe, syringe
cobloaf, a small loaf with a round head
cock, cockboat
Cock, a corrupt form of 'God'
cock-a-hoop (set), to carry all before you
cocklight, morning twilight
cockney, one reared in the city and ignorant of all but town life
cockshut time, evening twilight
cod, a peapod
codding, lustful
codling, small unripe apple
codpiece, part of the hose
coffin, a pastry mould for a pie
cog, to cheat; beguile
cognizance, heraldic badge or sign; token; distinguishing mark
cohere, agree
coif (quoif), a close-fitting cap
coign, corner, corner stone, projection
coil, tumult, disturbance (in *Haml*., iii, 1, 67, with a play on the sense 'entanglement')
Colbrand, a Danish giant slain by Guy of Warwick
cold fault, cold or lost scent (in hunting)
collect, gather (mentally), infer
collection, putting together (mentally), inference
collied, darkened; black
collop, slice of meat, piece of flesh
collusion, *for* allusion (*L. L. L*., iv, 2, 43)
colour, pretext, excuse
colourable, plausible, specious
colt, to trick
comart, a bargain, agreement (*Haml*., i, 1, 93)
combinate, betrothed (*M. for M*., iii, 1, 231)
combustion, tumult, riotous disturbance
come (near), to touch, to hit; (tardy off), not satisfactorily performed
comely, becomingly
comely-distant, at a proper distance
comfect, comfit, sweetmeat
comfort, *n*., support, assistance; *v*., to take comfort, cheer up; support, assist
comfortable, helpful, comforting
comfortless, unhelpful
coming-in, income, revenue
coming-on, complaisant, forward
command, to issue with authority; require of
commandment, command, orders
commend, *n*., recommendation; *pl*., regards
commend, *v*., recommend; deliver, present; (me), give my regards
comment, power in observing or scrutinizing (*Haml*., iii, 2, 84)
commerce, intercourse
commixtion, mixture, composition
commodity, advantage, expediency; convenient opportunity, convenience of intercourse; a lot or quantity (of goods or persons)
commoner, prostitute
comonty, *for* comedy (*T. of S*., Ind., ii, 140)
compact, composed (of)
companion, bad fellow, knave
comparative, *adj*., clever in making satirical comparisons; *n*., one who is or tries to be thus clever (*1 Hen. IV*, iii, 2, 67)
compare, comparison
compassed, rounded
compassed window, bay window
compassionate (to be), to show passionate grief
compeer, to be a peer of, to rank with
competitor, partner, associate
compile, to compose, write
complement, fulness of accomplishments and good qualities (*Hen. V*, ii, 2, 134); *pl*., abundant accomplishments; accomplishments; stores
complexion, temperament, disposition; appearance
complice, accomplice, associate
compliment, ceremony, courtesy, civility; manners, bearing; appearance
complimental, courteous
comply, use courteous ceremony
compose well, come to an agreement
composture, compost, manure
composure, constitution, temperament; combination, union
compt, account; the last accounting, the Day of Judgment (*Oth*., v, 2, 273); (in), computed; on deposit
compter, *see* counter
comptible to, sensitive to
comptless, past counting
con (thanks), feel (gratitude)
concealments, secrets; secret arts
conceit, *n*., conception, idea; thought, imagination; clever or fanciful idea or device; *v*., to conceive, estimate, judge
conceited, having an idea or opinion (about one); fanciful, imaginative, clever
conceitless, witless
conceptious, prolific
concern, to be of importance, signify; matter to (one)
concernancy, purport, import
concernings, important matters
conclusion, an experiment; a riddle
conclusions passed the careers, the affairs proceeded in due course to the end (*M. W*., i, 1, 184)
condition, rank, station; character, nature, quality
condole, mourn for
condolement, mourning; *pl*., *for* doles (*Per*., ii, 1, 156)
confidence, private conference
confiner, inhabitant
confirmity, *for* infirmity (*2 Hen. IV*, ii, 4, 64)
confound, destroy; (*of time*), spend, waste
confusion, destruction, ruin
congest, bring together, compound
congree, harmonize
congreet, meet and greet
congrue, agree
congruent, appropriate, fitting
congy, to congee, take formal leave
conjunct, joined, intimate; in conjunction
conscience, consciousness, inmost thought, honest opinion
conscionable, conscientious
consequence, what follows, the future, future events
consider, to reward, remunerate
considered, affording leisure for deliberation
consign, agree
consist, stand firm, insist
consort, company; band of musicians; concert
conspectuity, sense of sight (*Cor*., ii, 1, 71)
constancy, consistent probability
constant, rational, logical
constringed, drawn together
contemptible, contemptuous
contemptuous, contemptible
contend, to contend with
content, *n*., happiness; *v*., to please; *adj*., calm
continent, container; bank (of a river); sum and substance

continue, retain
contraction, the act of making a contract
contrive, wear away, spend (time)
control, refute; rebuke; overpower
convenience, propriety
convent, call together, summon
conversation, intercourse; behaviour
convertite, a convert
convey, bring or carry or manage secretly; palm off as; steal
conveyance, fraud, trickery
conveyer, robber, trickster
convicted, defeated, vanquished
convince, overcome, convict, disprove
convive, feast in company
convoy, means of conveyance
cony, rabbit
cony-catch, to cheat
cooling card, something that disconcerts one
copatain, high in the crown (*T. of S.*, v, 1, 70)
cope, the sky
cope, have to do with, encounter, repay
copesmate, associate, companion
copped, with rounded top
copulative, one wishing to be married (*A. Y. L.*, v, 4, 58)
copy, copyhold tenure (*cf.* 'lease of life')
coram, *for* quorum, certain specially designated justices of the peace (*M. W.*, i, 1, 6)
coranto, a running dance
Corinthian, a sporting character, a sport
corn, wheat
cornuto, cuckold
corollary (a), more than enough
corporal, corporeal, material
correspondent, submissive
corresponsive, well fitted (*T. and C.*, Prol., 18)
corrigible, corrective
corrival, associate
corroborate, *adj.*, *Pistol's word for* broken to pieces (*Hen. V*, ii, 1, 130)
corrosive, irritant; a caustic remedy
corslet, to embrace, clasp
cost, attack, assail (*3 Hen. VI*, i, 1, 268)
costard, an apple; the head
cote, to pass
cot-quean, a man who interferes in housewifely matters
Cotshall (Cotsall, Cotsole), Cotswold
couch, to lie in bed
counsel, secret
countenance, authority, favour
counter (compter), a round piece of metal or bone used in computation; a worthless coin
counter, *adv.*, in a reverse direction
Counter, a prison for debtors
counter-caster, accountant
counterfeit, likeness, portrait
counterpoint, counterpane, bedquilt
counter-reflect, a corresponding reflection (*T. N. K.*, i, 1, 127)
countervail, to equal
county, a count
couplet, a couple, pair; *pl.*, twins
courage, disposition; desire
course, one attack in bear-baiting; a sail
court-cubbert (cupboard), a sideboard for plate
court-hand, style of penmanship used in legal documents
court holy water, flattering words
cousin, a collateral kinsman more distant than brother; nephew, etc.
covent, a convent
cover, to prepare the table for a meal
cowish, cowardly
cowl-staff, a stout pole to which is attached a basket or other burden which two persons carry between them
Cox, *for* God's
coy, to scorn; to stroke
coystrill (custrel), a low fellow
coz, cousin
cozen, to cheat
cozier, a cobbler
crack, *n.*, a lively youngster; *v.*, to brag
crackhemp, one likely to be hanged
crank, *n.*, winding passage; *v.*, to wind
crants, wreaths, garlands (*Haml.*, v, 2, 255)
crare, a small trading vessel
credent, credulous; credible
creek, a narrow passage
crescive, growing, increasing
cresset, an iron fire-basket; a torch
crime, an offence (serious or trivial)
cringe, shrink up, distort
crisp, curly; rippled
Crispin Crispian, the day sacred to Saints Crispinus and Crispianus (Crispinianus), October 25 (*Hen. V*, iv, 3, 57)
cross, *n.*, a coin stamped with a cross; any coin; trouble; *adj.*, perverse; *adv.*, *prep.*, across
cross-row, the alphabet
crow-keeper, a guard against crows; a scarecrow
crowner, coroner
crownet, coronet
crudy, thick and heavy
crusado, a Portuguese coin marked with a cross
crush, quaff (*literally*, squeeze)
cry, a report, rumour; a pack; a troop
cry aim, to encourage, abet
cry on, to cry out, shout
cubiculo, bedroom
cullion, a low fellow
culverin, a long cannon
curiosity, nice care, fussy particularity, scrupulosity, fastidiousness
curious, careful, particular, scrupulous; elegant, choice; elaborate
currance, flow
cursorary, cursory
curst, ill-tempered, cross, shrewish
cursy, *n.*, *v.*, curtsy
curtal, *adj.*, with a docked tail; *v.*, to curtail
curtleaxe, cutlass
cushes, cuisses
Custalorum, Custos Rotulorum, Keeper of the Rolls
custard coffin, *see* coffin
customer, a prostitute
custrel, *see* coystrill
cut, a gelding; a horse; a dock-tailed dog or horse
cuttle, cutpurse, pickpocket
cypress, crape, lawn

daff, doff, put aside or off
Daintry, Daventry (Northamptonshire)
dainty (to make), to object, be reluctant
damask, of a damask-rose colour
Dan Cupid, Sir Cupid
danger, uncompliance; (within his), in his power
Dansker, a Dane
Dardan, Troy, Trojan
dare, to daze, terrify
dareful, in bold defiance
darkling, in the dark
darraign, draw up, array
dash, mark of infamy
date, time, length of time
dateless, everlasting
daub'ry, coarse imposture
day-bed, sofa, lounge
day-woman, dairy-woman
deaf, to deafen
dear (*used to emphasize the sense of a noun*), important, intensive, heartfelt, bitter, grievous, hateful
dearly, intensely
death-practised, whose death is plotted
death tokens, spots on the body of a plague-stricken patient forewarning him of death
debate, *n.*, quarrel, combat, fight; *v.*, to settle by combat
debile, weak, feeble
deboshed, debauched; disgraced
decay, one in misfortune, a wreck
decern, *for* concern (*M. Ado*, iii, 5, 4)
decesse, *n.*, decease (*Ven.*, 1002)
decking, adornment
decline, recite in order
decoct, to heat
deem, idea, notion
deep-fet, deep-fetched (groan)
deer, animals, creatures
deface, destroy; lay waste
defeat, *n.*, destruction; *v.*, to unmake, destroy, mar, disfigure
defeature, damage, disfigurement
defence, fencing
defend, forbid
defensible, able to defend
deformed, deforming
defunct, deadened
defunction, decease
defunctive, funereal
defuse, confuse, make unrecognizable
defused, disordered; deformed, misshapen
delighted, delightful; sensitive to pleasure
deliver, to report
deliverance, utterance
deliverly, skilfully
demand, ask
demerits, deserts, merits, services
demonstrable, apparent, clear
demure, look demurely
denay, *n.*, refusal; *v.*, to deny
denier, a small copper coin
denounce, proclaim, declare
denunciation, announcement
depart, *n.*, departure; *v.*, to part company
depend, to lean; impend; be a dependant
depravation, detraction
deprave, to slander
deprive, take away
deputation, the office of a substitute
deracinate, uproot
dern, *adj.*, secret (*Per.*, iii, Prol., 15)
derogate, *v.*, to fail in honour and dignity; *adj.*, degenerate

descant, *n.*, musical variations; a comment (with variations, as in music); *v.*, to dwell (upon)
deserved, meritorious
design, to draw up (a document); mark
designment, an undertaking
despised, contemptible, despicable
detect, uncover, reveal; accuse, discredit
determinate, to terminate, bring to a close
determination, ending
determine, come to an end
detest, *for* protest (*M. W.*, i, 4, 160)
devest, to undress
devoted, devout
dexteriously, dexterously
dexterity, agile speed
diablo, the devil
diaper, a linen napkin
dibble, a tool for making holes for planting
dich, may it do (*Tim.*, i, 2, 73)
diet, to limit, restrict
dieted, fed
difference, a decline in fortune; distinction as to rank; a variation in a coat of arms
diffidence, distrust, suspicion
diffused, confused, uncouth
digress, stray from the right, err
digression, error, transgression
dig-you-den, give you good e'en (*L. L. L.*, iv, 1, 42)
dilated, expressed in full, detailed
dilation, swelling (*or for* delation, information) (*Oth.*, iii, 3, 123)
dildo, burden of a song
diluculo surgere (saluberrimum est), early to rise (to rise at dawn) makes a man healthy (*T. N.*, ii, 3, 2)
dimensions, parts of the frame, limbs
diminitive, *adj.*, diminutive, tiny; *n.*, any very small coin
direct, to assign, depute
directions, truths, facts (*Haml.*, ii, 1, 66)
directitude (in), in a discredited position, under a cloud (*Cor.*, iv, 5, 222)
directive, fit to be managed
Dis, Pluto
disable, belittle, disparage
disanimate, dishearten
disappointed, not fitted out, unprepared
disaster, *n.*, evil astrological sign, portentous appearance; *v.*, to disfigure, mar
disbenched you, made you leave your seat
discandy, melt
discase (one's self), take off the outer garment(s)
discharge, perform (a task), play (a part); pay
disclaims in thee, disowns every part of thee (*Lear*, ii, 2, 59)
disclose, *v.*, to open; hatch; *n.* what is hatched
discontenting, *adj.*, feeling displeasure
discourse, the reason; the reasoning process; (of reason), the process of reasoning; the reasoning faculty; (of thought), the process of thought
discover, lay open, reveal, show; recognize; scout
discoverer, a scout
discovery, disclosure; scouting; that which is discovered (*Temp.*, ii, 1, 243)
disdained, disdainful
disease, discomfort, trouble; *v.*, to disturb
disedge, to have the appetite dulled
disensanity, stupidity (*T. N. K.*, iii, 5, 2)
disfurnish myself, i.e., of ready money
disgest, to digest
disgracious, displeasing, out of favour
disguise, a revel. drinking bout (*A. and C.*, ii, 7, 129)
dishabit, dislodge
dishonest, dishonourable, unchaste
dislike, displease
dislimn, obliterate, blur
dismal, ill-omened, ominous
disme, tenth man
dismount, to lower, let fall, cast down (*Compl.*, 281)
disnatured, unnatural
disorbed, unsphered
dispark, throw open
dispatch, deprive, bereave
dispiteous, pitiless, merciless
disponge, pour out
dispose, *n.*, disposal; disposition, temperament; *v.*, to make or come to terms
disposer (my), one who rules me as she will (*T. and C.*, iii, 1, 95)
disposition, mood, state of mind or feeling; mental constitution
disproperty, dispossess (one) of
dispurse, disburse
disputable, fond of discussion, argumentative
disputation, discussion, conference
dispute, argue, discuss
disquantity, reduce in number
disroot, uproot, unseat
disseat, unseat
dissemble, to disguise
dissembly, *for* assembly (*M. Ado*, iv, 2, 1)
dissolve, undo, loose
distain, to stain, defile, pollute
distance, enmity
distaste, to be or make distasteful; dislike
distemper, *n.*, any disorder of body or mind; *v.*, to derange, disorder
distemperature, ailment, disorder, derangement
distilled, dissolved
distinctly, separately; in particular; intelligibly
distinguish, describe as, designate
distract, divide; diversify
distractions, separate and distinct parts
distrain, seize, confiscate
distressful, earned by severe toil
disvouch, disavow, contradict
dive-dapper, didapper, grebe
dividable, separate, different
dividant, separate, distinguishable
dividual, different, distinct
division, modulation
divulged (well), favourably reported, of good reputation
do, *see* withal
document, piece of instruction
dogged, surly, savage, fierce
doit, a coin worth half a farthing
dole, sorrow, lamentation
dole, dealing out, distribution; portion, lot
domine, schoolmaster
doom, *n.*, judgment; *v.*, to judge, decide
dotant, dotard
doubt, *n.*, *v.*, fear
doubtless, without fear or anxiety
doucets, a deer's testes
dout, to put out; abolish
dowlas, a coarse kind of linen
dowle, bit of down
dowln, down (of a feather)
dowlny, downy
down, *prep.*, down along (*M. Ado*, iii, 4, 20)
down-gyved, down and round the ankles like fetters
down-roping, hanging in viscous strings
doxy, mistress, sweetheart
dozy, confuse (*Haml.*, v, 2, 119)
draff, swill
draught, privy
draw, assemble, muster; withdraw; track (in hunting)
drawer, waiter who draws and serves wine
drawn, emptied
dreg, to clog, as with dregs (*T. N. K.*, i, 2, 97)
drench, a dose (for horses)
dress, make ready
dribbling, feeble (of an arrow ill shot)
drift, purpose, intention
drift-winds, strong steady winds
drollery, puppet show; comic picture
dropping, dripping wet (*Per.*, iv, 1, 63)
drouth, drought
drovier, drover
drugs, dull sluggish masses (*Tim.*, iv, 3, 254)
drum, drummer
Drum, *see* John Drum
drumble, move slowly
dry, thirsty; stupid, dull
dry-beat, thrash soundly
dry-foot (draw), to track by the scent of the foot
ducdame, purposely unintelligible formula of invitation (*A. Y. L.*, ii, 5, 56)
dudgeon, hilt of a dagger
due, *n.*, fit ceremony; *v.*, to endow
duello, duelling and its rules
duke, leader (*Hen. V*, iii, 2, 23)
dumb, to silence
dumb show, a dramatic action without words
dump, a doleful song or tune; any song or tune
dun, dark, mouse-coloured; *n.*, a dun horse; (dun's the mouse), *proverbial for* keep quiet or the like; (Dun is in the mire), a Christmas sport in which a heavy log (called by the horse's name) is lifted and carried
dup, do up, open
durance, imprisonment; a kind of stout cloth
duty, homage, respectful ceremony; tribute of respect

each (at), joined in succession
eager, sour, acid; biting, bitter cold
ean, to bring forth offspring
eaning time, time of giving birth
eanling, lamb just born
ear, to plough, till
ear, to give ear to
earl, a count

earnest, a sum paid in advance to bind the bargain
earth, bury, inter
easedropper, eavesdropper
easy, trivial, slight, insignificant
ebon, black as ebony
eche, eke out; draw out, lengthen
ecstasy, state of being beside one's self; passion of joy, terror, sorrow, etc.; fit of excitement; swoon; madness
edify, instruct; be instructed
effect, fulfilment, accomplishment; manifestation, sign; act, action
effectually, to all intents and purposes (*Sonn.*, 113)
effigies, image, likeness
effuse, *n.*, effusion
eftest, most fitting (*M. Ado*, iv, 2, 38)
eftsoons, soon, presently
egal, equal
egally, equally
eggs for money (take), suffer imposition tamely (*W. T.*, i, 2, 161)
egma, *for* enigma (*L. L. L.*, iii, 1, 73)
e'il, *n.*, evil (*Haml.*, i, 4, 36)
'eild, *see* God-dild
elbow, to prod with the elbow; *fig.*, to torment roughly and continually
eld, old age; old times
element, the sky; the air
elf, to tie in tangled knots
elflocks, locks of hair matted by the fairies
eliad (illiad), œillade, languishing look
elvish-marked, marked by elves; ugly and misshapen (*Rich. III*, i, 3, 228)
emballing, the investing with the ball at coronation (*Hen. VIII*, ii, 3, 47). *See* ball
embargement, embargo, hindrance, restraint
embayed, sheltered in a bay or harbour
ember-eve, the eve (vigil) of a fast-day (ember-day) (*Per.*, i, Prol., 6)
emboss, to drive (a hunted creature) into a thicket or ambush; to drive to an extremity
embossed, infuriated (like a boar at bay); exhausted
embossed, swollen; corpulent; rising in knobs
embounded, enclosed
embowelled, eviscerated, emptied
embrace, submit to, accept
embrasure, embrace
embrewed, stained with blood (*T. A.*, ii, 3, 222). *See* imbrue
empale (impale), hem in, surround, encircle
emperial, emperor (*T. A.*, iv, 3, 94; iv, 4, 40)
empery, imperial dominion; empire
empiricutic, empirical, quackish (*Cor.*, ii, 1, 128)
emulate pride, pride of rivalry
emulation, envy
emulous, envious
enact, action
enacture, action
encave, hide, conceal
enchantingly, as if by magic
encompassment, roundabout method
encounter, behaviour; social intercourse; assault
encounterer, one ready to meet another halfway; coquette
encumbered, (arms) folded
end, to get in, as a crop at harvest (*Cor.*, v, 6, 36)
end-all, conclusion of the whole matter
endeared, bound, obliged
endite, *see* indite
endue, *see* indue
enew, drive into the water; pursue, chase, prosecute (*M. for M.*, iii, 1, 91)
enfeoff, deliver (as a fief), give up entirely, devote
enforce, to force; attack vigorously; urge
enfranch, enfranchise, set free (*A. and C.*, iii, 13, 149)
enfreedom, set free (*L. L. L.*, iii, 1, 125)
engage, to pledge; pledge as a hostage; hold as prisoner; entangle; involve (in a conflict)
engine, machine, apparatus; instrument; implement of war; contrivance; plot
englut, engulf, swallow
engraffed to, intimately associated with, attached to. *See* ingraffed
engross, fatten; take or purchase in gross (at wholesale or entire); accumulate; monopolize
engrossments, accumulations, store of wealth
enjail, imprison
enlard, fatten grossly
enlarge, set free, liberate
enlargement, liberation, release; liberty; freedom of action
enlighten, make bright or brilliant
enormous, abnormal
enow, enough
enpatron me, are my patron saint (*Compl.*, 224)
enridged, with a surface rising in ridges (*Lear*, iv, 6, 71)
ensconce (one's self into), take refuge in. *See* insconce
enseamed, defiled with sweat
ensear, dry up
enshield, to cover (as with a shield), conceal
ensinewed, closely knit
ensteeped, immersed, lying under water
entertain, *v.*, to receive (as a guest or in general); take into service; treat; spend (time); *n.*, reception, entertainment
entertainment, reception; treatment; polite attention; service
entitled, having a claim
entranced, in a swoon, unconscious
entreat, *v.*, treat; negotiate: *n.*, entreaty, petition
entreatments, negotiations
envious, malicious, ill-willed, malevolent
envy, *n.*, malice, spite, ill will; *v.*, to show ill will
enwheel, encircle
Ephesian, jovial fellow, boon companion
Epicurian, Epicurean
epithet, phrase, term
epitheton, phrase, term
equal, *n.*, one of the same age; *adj.*, impartial; *v.*, to match
equivocation, ambiguity
Ercles, Hercules
erection, *for* direction (*M. W.*, iii, 5, 41)
erewhile, a little while ago, just now
eringo, the candied root of the sea-holly
ern (yearn), grieve
errant, wandering; deviating
erring, *adj.*, wandering
error, a defect
erst, formerly
escape, flight; escapade; (of wit), sally, clever and whimsical idea (*M. for M.*, iv, 1, 63)
escapen, escape (*Per.*, ii, Gow., 36)
escoted, supported, maintained
esill, *see* eysell
esperance, hope
espial, a spy
essay, a trial, test. *See* assay
estate, *n.*, state or condition; rank, position; one's affairs; situation; the state (commonweal); *v.*, to settle or bestow (on); (in), settle one in the possession of
estimable, valuable; (wonder), admiring judgment
estimation, opinion, conjecture
estridge, ostrich
eterne, eternal, everlasting
eternize, immortalize
even, *v.*, act on a par with, match by our actions (*Cymb.*, iii, 4, 184)
even-Christen, even-Christian, fellow Christian
evened (I am), I am made even, I have squared accounts (*Oth.*, ii, 1, 308)
even-pleached, smoothly plaited
event, the outcome
ever among, ever and always (*2 Hen. IV*, v, 3, 23)
evil, disease; the king's evil, scrofula
evitate, avoid
examine, call in question
exceed, be preëminent
except, take exception
except before excepted, including all previous exceptions
exception, objection, disapproval, dissatisfaction
exchange, transformation
excite, incite
excitement, incentive; exhortation
exclaim, *n.*, outcry; *pl.*, cries (of grief, anger, etc.)
excrement, outgrowth, hair, beard
executor, executioner
exempt, separated, removed, expelled; remote; estranged
exercise, devout practice, act of devotion; preaching; penance
exhalation, meteor
exhale, breathe out; breathe your last (*Hen. V*, ii, 1, 66); draw out (blood, tears, a meteor)
exhaust, draw forth
exhibition, an allowance (of money)
exigent, exigence, emergency, crisis; end
exion, *for* action (*2 Hen. IV*, ii, 1, 33)
exorciser (exorcist), conjurer
exorcism, conjuration
expect, await
expectancy, hope (*Haml.*, iii, 1, 160)
expedience, speed; expedition
expedient, speedy
expend, spend, waste
expense, the spending; waste; loss
expiate, bring to a close (*Sonn.*, 22); fully come (*Rich. III*, iii, 3, 23)
exploit, a combat
expostulate, discuss, argue
exposture, exposure (*Cor.*, iv, 1, 36)
express, *v.*, to show, manifest; *adj.*,

exactly fitted to its purpose and function
expressive, frank and cordial (*All's W.*, ii, 1, 54)
expressly, clearly
expressure, expression; figure or inscription
expulse, expel, banish
exsufflicate, inflated, unsubstantial (*Oth.*, iii, 3, 182)
extant, *adj.*, present
extend, prolong, increase, magnify; seize upon; show, display
extent, seizure (by legal process); assault; manifestation; courteous greeting
extenuate, diminish; mitigate; palliate; belittle
extermine, banish; put an end to
extern, *adj.*, outward; *n.*, outward appearance
extinct (extincted), extinguished
extincture, extinction
extinguish, to eclipse
extirp, extirpate, clear away
extracting, distracting
extraught, extracted, derived (by birth)
extravagancy, random travel
extravagant, straying from home or out of bounds
eyas, a hawk still in the eyrie (nest), a falcon nestling
eyas-musket, a male sparrow hawk nestling; a lively youngster
eye, *n.*, tinge or slight shade (of colour); immediate presence; *v.*, to look, appear
eye-glass, the crystalline lens of the eye
eyestrings, muscles and tendons of the eye
eyne, eyes
eysell (esill), vinegar

face, *n.*, appearance; bold appearance, effrontery; *v.*, to brave; outface; play the hypocrite; patch, trim
face it with a card of ten, to bluff when one's highest card is a ten; to put a good face on it (*T. of S.*, ii, 1, 407)
facinerious, facinorous, wicked
fact, evil deed, crime
faction, a party, union as a party, party spirit
factionary, strongly partisan
factious, active as a partisan; (be), form a party
factor, agent, representative
faculty, power, authority; strength, vigour; potency; natural quality
fadge, succeed, come off
fading, burden of a song
fadom, fathom
fail, failure
fain, glad, content; forced, obliged; gladly
faint, languid; neglectful
fair, *n.*, fairness, beauty; beautiful person or thing; *v.*, to make beautiful
fairing, gift bought at a fair
faithed, credited, believed
faithless, unbelieving
faitor, rogue, vagabond
fall, *n.*, ebb, low tide; cadence; *v.*, to shrink, grow thin; let fall; give birth to; be born; befall; fail, prove false
fall (a-bleeding, etc.), begin to; (away), desert; shrink, grow thin; (in with), join, become intimate; (out), quarrel; happen, turn out; (over), desert, revolt
falliable, *for* infallible
falling-from, desertion (*Tim.*, iv, 3, 402)
falling sickness, epilepsy
fallow, of a brownish colour
false, *n.*, falsehood, lying; (fire), a flash in the pan
falsing, deceptive, fallacious
fame, *n.*, rumour, report; reputation; *v.*, to make famous
famed, *p.p.*, reported (by common fame)
familiar, *adj.*, serviceable; *n.*, intimate friend; familiar (serviceable) spirit
famoused, made famous, renowned
fan, to winnow
fancies, song tunes (in impromptu style)
fancy, *n.*, *v.*, love
fang, seize as with fangs
fangled, fantastically minded, given to showy follies (*Cymb.*, v, 4, 134)
fantastic, imaginary; prodigious
fantastical, imaginary; imaginative; fantastic
fantastico, a fantastic coxcomb
fantasy, love
fap, drunk (*M. W.*, i, 1, 183)
far (farre), farther
farborough, thirdborough, constable (*L. L. L.*, i, 1, 185)
farce, to stuff
farced, stuffed; bombastic
fardel (farthel), bundle, parcel, burden
fardingale, *see* farthingale
far-fet, far-fetched, devious
farm, to let (on lease); to hire
farrow, young pigs (a litter)
farthel, *see* fardel
farthingale (fardingale), a hooped petticoat
fartuous, *for* virtuous (*M. W.*, ii, 2, 101)
fashion-monger, follower of every new fashion
fashion-monging, *adj.*, following the fashion
fashions, the farcy (a disease of horses similar to glanders)
fastened, confirmed
fat, vat
fat, *adj.*, gross, stupid; nauseating
fated, invested with the control of men's fate (*All's W.*, i, 1, 232)
fatigate, fatigued
fat-room, vat-room
fatuus, foolish
fault, *n.*, default, lack, want; mistake, loss of scent (in hunting). *See* cold fault
favour, feature, face, countenance; form; likeness; appearance; a posture in dancing
fay, faith
fear, an object of fear, person or thing feared; *v.*, to make (one) afraid, frighten; (for), be anxious about
feared by, an object of anxiety to (one)
fearful, full of fear, afraid; terrible
fear-surprised, seized upon by fear
feast, feast-day, festival; celebration; fête
feasted, *adj.*, fêted (*W. T.*, iv, 4, 63)
feat, deed; wicked deed, crime; skill
feat, *adj.*, neat; clever, dexterous
feated them, showed them how they should look, gave them a model for behaviour (*Cymb.*, i, 1, 49)
feathered, swiftly passing (*Per.*, v, 2, 15)
featly, gracefully and with skill; nimbly
feature, shape, form; likeness, make-up
featured, formed, shaped
featureless, shapeless, misshapen, ugly
fedary (feodary, federary), confederate, accomplice
fee, possession; income; rate, value
feeder, a menial; a parasite
feeding, pasturage
fee-farm (in), in perpetuity (an estate in fee-farm being granted for ever, with reservation of a certain rent)
fee grief, a personal grief
fee simple, absolute ownership
feere, *see* fere
felicitate, made happy
fell, *n.*, skin; (of hair), skin with the hair on it
fell, *adj.*, fierce, cruel, savage
fellies, felloes, segments of the rim of a wheel
fellow, *n.*, associate, comrade, companion; an equal, one's peer, match, like; *v.*, to pair or couple with
fellowly, *adj.*, companionable, sympathetic
fellowship, company, association, partnership, friendly relations, companionship
fence, to protect
feodary, *see* fedary
fere (feere), companion, spouse
ferret, *adj.*, inflamed (like a ferret's eyes); *v.*, to worry, tear, mangle
ferula, ferule
fescue, twig
festinate, speedy
festinately, speedily
fet, fetched
fetch, *n.*, trick, device, stratagem; pretence, pretext
fetch in, take captive, dupe
fettle, settle, make ready, adjust
few (in), in few words, in short
fico (figo), fig. *See* fig
fidiused, trounced (*Cor.*, ii, 1, 144)
fielded, in the battlefield (*Cor.* i, 4, 12)
fifteenth, tax amounting to a fifteenth of one's personal property
fig, *n.*, an insulting gesture made with the thumb between the first and the second finger; *v.*, to insult with this gesture
fights, canvas screens to hide the crew in a sea-fight
figo (fico), *see* fig
figure, *n.*, statue, model, image; a form in the mind or imagination; idea; *v.*, to imagine; symbolize; prefigure
file, *n.*, list, catalogue; number (of persons); position, rank; *v.*, to smooth, polish; perfect; keep pace with
fill, thill, shaft (of cart)
fill-horse, cart-horse
fillip (fillop), to snap (one) with the finger; buffet; send up into the air by a blow on a tilted board (*2 Hen. IV*, i, 2, 255)

filth, a vile person
find, find out, detect; furnish, provide, fit out. *See* well-found
fine, *n.*, *v.*, end; *v.*, to make fine or specious, adorn; (for), to fix as the price
fineless, endless, infinite
firago, *for* virago, fury (*T. N.*, iii, 4, 302)
fire, to drive out or away by fire
fire-drake, fiery dragon
fire-new, fresh from the forge, brand new
firk, to drub, thrash
fisnomy, physiognomy
fit, canto
fitchew (fitchook), polecat; harlot
fitment, what befits, proper service
fitted, forced by a spasm
five for one, a method of travellers' insurance by which the person insured received five times his stake
fives, a glandular disease of horses
fixure, fixed or stable position
flake, a strand (or lock) of hair
flapdragon, a raisin floating in flaming brandy and to be caught up and swallowed; *v.*, to swallow
flap-mouthed, with broad hanging lips (*Ven.*, 920)
flat, a plain or level region; low marshy ground; a shoal, a shallow
flatlong, with the flat side
flatness, absoluteness
flatter up, indulge, soothe
flaunts, showy attire, finery
flaw, *n.*, crack, breach; fragment; gust of wind, storm; passionate impulse; outbreak, outburst; disaster, ruin; *v.*, to crack, break
flecked, dappled (with light)
fleer, *n.*, *v.*, mock, sneer, gibe (in look or speech)
fleet, float; fade, dissolve; fly away, pass swiftly; while away (time)
fleeting, inconstant
flesh, to give one a first taste of flesh, initiate; to make fierce (as by feeding on raw meat); to satiate, glut
fleshment, stimulation (by a first success)
flewed, having flews (the hanging chaps of a deep-mouthed dog)
flexure, bending, obeisance
flight, a light arrow for long-distance shooting
flighty, flying (away) quickly
flirt-gill, flighty woman (*R. and J.*, ii, 4, 162)
flote, flood, sea (*Temp.*, i, 2, 234)
flourish, *n.*, adornment, ornamentation; flowery language; fanfare (of trumpets); *v.*, to embellish; brandish; show off, swagger; blossom gorgeously; sound a flourish
flower-de-luce (fleur-de-luce), iris; fleur-de-lis
fluent, abundant, copious
flurt, to scoff at, scout
flush, in full bloom or vigour
flushing, redness (*Haml.*, i, 2, 155)
fluxive, flowing (with tears)
fly, to cause a hawk to fly after the game
fob, to cheat, trick; (off), put off with an excuse
foil, *n.*, rapier; swordsman; defeat, discomfiture, disgrace; shortcoming; leaf of metal placed under a gem to set it off; setting; *v.*, to defeat; soil, disgrace
foin, *n.*, *v.*, thrust (with a sword)
foison, abundance, harvest
fold, offspring (*Lear*, iii, 4, 126)
folly, unchastity
folly-fallen, fallen into dotage (*T. N.*, iii, 1, 75)
fond, *adj.*, foolish, trifling; (upon), foolishly partial to; *adv.*, foolishly; *v.*, to dote
fool, *n.*, a term of endearment or compassion; *v.*, to make foolish
fool-begged, so foolish as to deserve a petition for guardianship as an idiot; idiotic (*C. of E.*, ii, 1, 41)
foot, to kick, spurn; seize with the talons (*Cymb.*, v, 4, 116)
footcloth, an ornamented robe on a horse's back hanging down to the ground on both sides
footed, landed
fop, *n.*, a fool; *v.*, to dupe, cheat
foppery, foolishness; deceit
foppish, foolish
for, because; as for
forage, *n.*, preying; *v.*, to glut one's self, to raven
forbid, under a ban (*Macb.*, i, 3, 21)
forbod, *p.p.*, forbidden (*Compl.*, 164)
forbode, forbade (*Lucr.*, 1648)
force (of), of necessity, perforce; of weight
force, to reinforce; enforce; ravish, violate; urge, insist on; value, care for, regard; (not), do not hesitate or scruple
force, to farce, stuff
force perforce, by strong constraint
fordo, undo, destroy
fordone, tired out, exhausted
fore, before
forego, to go through with previously
forehand, *n.*, superior position, the better; the mainstay; *adj.*, anticipatory; (shaft), for straightforward long-distance shooting
forehorse, leading horse in a team; usher
foresay, to decree (for the future)
forespent, past; previously spent
forestall, prevent by anticipation; deprive
forestalled, refused in advance (*2 Hen. IV*, v, 2, 38)
foreward, vanguard
forfend, forbid
forgery, invention, imagination
forgetive, quick and fertile in ideas, inventive
forked, horned (as a cuckold)
forlorn, lost
formal, in proper form, regular; rational, sane
former, forward
forsake, to refuse, deny
forset-seller, dealer in faucets (taps for casks)
forslow, to delay, linger
forspeak, speak against, oppose
forspent, tired out, exhausted
forted, fortified
forthcoming, ready to appear
forthright, straight course or path
fortune, *v.*, happen, chance; determine one's fortune
forwearied, tired out
foul, not fair, ill-looking, ugly; dirty
fouled, soiled
foulness, ugliness
founder, to exhaust, cause to break down
fox, a sword
foxship, craft, guile
fracted, broken
fraction, separation, dissension
frame, structure, edifice; device, invention
frampold (frampal), ill-tempered, perverse; turbulent
franchise, liberation, restoration; *pl.*, rights and privileges
franchised, free from offence or guilt
frank, free; liberal, free-handed
frank, *n.*, a sty for hogs; *v.*, to shut up in a sty
franklin, freeholder (of rank just below the gentry)
fraught, *n.*, cargo; load; *v.*, to load, burden; *p.p.*, laden, loaded; burdened; freighted; filled
fraughtage, cargo, freight
fraughting souls, persons on board a ship
fray, frighten, terrify
free, *adj.*, free from care, happy; innocent, free from guile; generous, noble-minded; *v.*, to acquit, absolve; *adv.*, freely
freeness, generosity
frequent, intimate; addicted, devoted
fresh, *adj.*, blooming, fair; *n.*, spring of fresh water
freshness, youthful bloom
fret, eat or wear away; variegate; ornament with carving etc.
fretful, gnawing, irritating
frets, bars under the strings of a musical instrument
friend, to befriend, help
frippery, a shop for old clothes
frize, frieze
from, out of accord with, alien to, contrary to; absent from
front, *n.*, forehead, face; forelock; first part; *v.*, to face, confront, oppose; march in front; defend
frontier, outwork
frontlet, a forehead cloth (or band)
froward, refractory, perverse, rebellious
fruitful, bounteous, bountiful
fruitfully, fully, abundantly
fruitless, barren
frush, break up
frutify, explain in full (*M. of V.*, ii, 2, 143)
fub off, put off with excuses
fulfil, fill full; fit close (*T. and C.*, Prol., 18)
fullam, false dice (*M. W.*, i, 3, 94)
fulsome, lustful
fumiter, fumitory
fust, grow musty
fustian, gibberish, especially if bombastic
fustilarian, musty old creature
futurely, in the future

gaberdine, a smock frock
gad, a sharp spike; a stylus; (upon the), on the spur of the moment
gage, *n.*, a pledge (*especially*, a glove as pledge of combat); *v.*, to pledge, risk; entangle, involve
gaingiving, misgiving
gait, act of going, way; going on, proceeding
gall, *v.*, excoriate, scratch, chafe, gnaw; vex, annoy; scoff (at); make bitter; *n.*, an irritant or annoyance; distress; bitterness, resentment

Gallia, France
Gallian, French
galliard, a kind of lively dance
gallias, a large heavy galley
gallimaufry, a hotchpotch, all sorts
gallow, frighten, terrify
gallowglass, a kind of Irish soldier
gallows, gallows bird, scamp
gambol, *adj.*, sportive; *v.*, to wander incoherently
gamester, a frolicksome fellow; a prostitute
gan, began
garb, fashion, manner
garboil, disturbance, brawl
garden house, arbour, summer house
garnish, attire, equipment
gaskins, loose breeches
gasted, frightened
gastness, terrified expression
gaud, gewgaw, toy
Gawlia, Wales
gaze, object gazed at
gear, attire; stuff; business, state of affairs
geck (geek), a butt, object of ridicule; dupe
geminy, a pair (of twins)
gender, *n.*, kind, species; sort (of people); *v.*, to breed
general, *n.*, the general run of people, the multitude; *adj.*, universal
generally, universally, without exception
generation, offspring, progeny
generative, born of woman, human (*M. for M.*, iii, 2, 119)
generosity, nobility
generous, of noble or gentle birth; of noble nature; gentlemanlike, refined
genius, attendant spirit (good or evil); personification (*2 Hen. IV*, iii, 2, 337)
gennet (jennet), a small Spanish horse
gentility, gentle or noble birth; polite manners
gentle, *n.*, of gentle birth; gentlemanly; *pl.*, gentlefolk; *v.*, to ennoble
gentry, gentle birth; polite accomplishments; courtesy
George, a jewel representing Saint George and the Dragon (in the insignia of the Order of the Garter)
germains, *see* germens
german, a kinsman, a near relation
germane, related by blood
germens (germains), seeds
gest, end of the time allotted for a visit (in a royal progress)
gests, exploits in war
gesture, bearing, demeanour
ghost, to appear to one as a ghost
gi', give
gib (gib-cat), a tomcat
gibbet, to hang
giddily, carelessly
giddiness, precipitancy (*A. Y. L.*, v, 2, 6)
gig, a top
giglot (giglet), trollop
gild, to smear, colour; make drunk
gill, *see* flirt-gill *and* Jill
gillyvor, gillyflower, clove pink
gilt, gold
gimmaled, jointed
gimmors, jointed machinery
gin, a snare, trap
gin, begin
gi'n, given
ging, a gang, a pack
Ginn, Jenny
gird, *n.*, gibe, reproof; *v.*, to gibe, taunt
girdle (turn his), to shift his girdle (so as to make it easy to draw his dagger), *with a pun*—to change his temper or mood (*M. Ado*, v, 1, 142)
girt, to gird
Gis, Jesu
give, to give as a name, apply as an epithet; to display in one's coat of arms
give out, to show, report, publish
glad, gladness, joy (*Per.*, ii, Gow., 38)
glance, *n.*, indirect hit, hint, allusion; (at), *v.*, to hint at, allude to
glass, mirror
gleek (glike), jest, jeer, gibe
glib, geld, castrate
glike, *see* gleek
glimpse, the lustre; the glamour (of novelty); a tinge or touch
globy, swollen, protuberant (*T. N. K.*, v, 1, 113)
glorious, eager for glory
gloze (glose), *n.*, a subtlety; *v.*, to comment, interpret; talk cleverly or speciously; use flattering words
glut, to swallow
gnarl, to snarl
go, to walk; (through), to make a bargain; (go to), go away — used as an exclamation of protest, impatience, etc.
goatish, lecherous
gobbet, piece of raw flesh
god, to deify, idolize
god-a-mercy, God have mercy; gramercy, thank you
god-den (good-den, good-en), good e'en (evening)
God-dild (God 'ild, God 'eild), may God reward
God gi' go-den (God ye good-den, God-i-god-en, God dig-you-den), God give you good evening!
Gogs-woons (by), by God's wounds
Golgotha, Calvary
gondilo (gundello), gondola
good, *adj.*, of sufficient means; *n.*, my good friend (*vocative*); (a), a good deal, heartily (*Two G.*, iv, 4, 170)
good cheap, *adv.*, cheap
good-deed, in deed, in very deed
good life (with), in a lifelike manner (*Temp.*, iii, 3, 86); (of), moral, edifying (*T. N.*, ii, 3, 37)
good-nights, good-night songs, farewells (*2 Hen. IV*, iii, 2, 343)
goodyear, goodyears, goodyere, pox
gorbellied, fat-paunched
gorge, throat, stomach; (cast or heave the), to be nauseated, vomit
gorget, armour for the throat
gospelled, converted to gospel teachings
gossamer, filmy thread of cobweb
gosse, gorse
gossip, *n.*, a sponsor, a godfather or godmother; *fem.*, familiar friend; busybody; *v.*, to stand sponsor for; make merry at a christening
gourd, a kind of false dice
gout, a drop
government, behaviour; conduct; self-control
governor, tutor; manager
grace, *n.*, any pleasing quality; favour, honour; virtue; *v.*, to honour; gratify; beautify
graced, honourable
graceful, favouring; holy
gracious, well-pleasing; virtuous, holy; lovely
graciously, persuasively, eloquently; virtuously
graff, *n.*, *v.*, graft
graft, *p.p.*, grafted
grafter, the tree from which the scion was taken
grain, cochineal dye; (in), dyed in a fast colour, grained
grained, dyed in grain; discoloured by age; tough-grained (*Cor.*, iv, 5, 113); forked (*Compl.*, 64)
gramercy (gramercies), much thanks, many thanks, thank you
grand-guard, a piece of armour for the left side
grandsir, grandsire
grange, farmhouse, country house
grate, vex, annoy; disturb; (on), pester, harass
gratify, reward, repay
gratillity, small gratuity (*T. N.*, ii, 3, 27)
gratulate, *v.*, greet, congratulate, wish joy; *adj.*, gratifying
grave, dignified, reverend
grave, bury; engrave
graved, furrowed, frowning
greaves, armour for the leg below the knee
'gree, agree
Greek, lively fellow, featherbrain
green, fresh, young; immature, un sophisticated; foolish; sallow
greenly, like a novice, foolishly
grievance, trouble, distress
grisled, grisly, fierce (*Per.*, iii, Gower, 47)
gripe, griffin
grize (grise), a step or stair
grizzle (a), a crop of grey hair
grizzled, grey-haired; dark with some white hairs
groat, a fourpenny piece
groom, a menial; a fellow; bridegroom
gross, *adj.*, large; coarse; stupid; manifest, obvious; *n.*, full amount; *adv.*, plainly
grossly, stupidly, foolishly; obviously; in a gross (unpurified, unabsolved) condition
grossness, absurdity
ground, plain-song, melody
groundling, a spectator in the pit
ground-piece, a model
grow, to accrue
grunt, to groan
guard, trimming
guardage, protection, guardianship
guardant, *n.*, protector; *adj.*, on guard
guess, *n.*, opinion; *v.*, to think, believe
guidon, a small flag
guiled, full of guile, treacherous
guinea hen, loose woman
gules, red colour (in heraldry)
gulf, abyss; whirlpool; belly
gull, *n.*, young bird, nestling; dupe, simpleton; imposture; *v.*, to dupe
gundello, *see* gondilo
gunstone, cannon ball
gurnet, a gurnard (fish)
gust, appetite; indulgence; *v.*, to taste, perceive
gyve, *n.*, *v.*, fetter

habit, fashion; behaviour, demeanour
habitude, one's nature, natural qualities
hack, *see* hick
hackneyed, made too familiar
haggard, *n.*, a wild hawk; *adj.*, unchaste
haggle, to hack, gash
hag-seed, witch's offspring
hair, nature, character
hair-worth, the worth of a hair, a jot
halcyon, kingfisher
hale, *v.*, pull, draw, drag, haul; maltreat
half-achieved, half-won
half-blooded, of good blood on one side only
half-caps, slight salutes with one's cap
half-cheek, profile
half-cheeked, having but one side-piece
half-face, thin face
half-faced, showing only half the face; thin-faced; miserable
half-kirtle, a short kirtle or gown
half-sights, purblind persons
half-sword (at), in close combat
halidome (holidam, holidame), holiness, all that one holds sacred
hall (a), make room (for dancing) (*R. and J.*, i, 5, 28)
Hallowmas, All Saints' Day (November 1)
halt, to limp
hand (at), when checked; (at any), by all means, at any rate, in any case; (in), by the hand; (out of), immediately; (to make a fair), to do a good job
handfast, close custody; contract of marriage
handkercher, handkerchief
hands (of all), in any event, at any rate; (of his), in action, in fight
handy-dandy, the formula in a childish game of choosing which of two closed hands holds an object
hanger, a strap or loop by which a rapier hangs from the belt
hanging, arras
hangman, *n.*, executioner; *adj.*, rascally
happily, haply, perchance, perhaps
happiness, felicity (of phrase); comeliness
happy, *adj.*, well-expressed, felicitous; cultivated, accomplished; *v.*, to make happy
hard-haired, with a heavy crop of hair
hardiment, prowess
hardly, with difficulty
hardness, hardship
hardock, hardhack, a kind of wild flower (*Lear*, iv, 4, 4)
Harflew, Harfleur
Har'ford, Haverford
harlot, *n.*, base man, rascal; *adj.*, lewd
harlotry, *n.*, harlot; wayward creature; *adj.*, rascally
harp, to sound, give expression to
Harpier, the name of a demon (perhaps suggested by 'harpy') (*Macb.*, iv, 1, 3)
Harry ten-shillings, pieces coined by King Harry (really by Henry VII) (*2 Hen. IV*, iii, 2, 236)
hatch, *n.*, half-door, the lower half of a door that opens in two segments
hatch, *v.*, to ornament with plates of metal (*fig.*, *T. and C.*, i, 3, 65)
hatched, closed with a half-door
hatchment, a tablet with coat of arms set up on the house of a deceased person
hateful, full of hate, malignant
haught, haughty
haunch, the latter end
have, catch one's meaning (*Haml.*, ii, 1, 68)
have-at-him, an attack, assault
have at you, let me get at you (as a notice of attack etc.). *Similarly*, have to it (let's get at it), have after, amongst, through, with
having, possession, estate, allowance
haviour, behaviour, demeanour, bearing
havoc, the cry 'No quarter!' 'Spare none!'; *v.*, to rend in pieces
hawking (eye), quick and bright, like a falcon's
hay, a country dance like a reel
hay, home thrust (*R. and J.*, ii, 4, 27)
hazard, a game at dice; one's stake; a winning opening in a tennis court
head, an armed force
headland, a strip left unploughed at the end of a field and ploughed afterwards in cross furrows (*2 Hen. IV*, v, 1, 16)
heap, a crowd, throng, band
hearse, bier, coffin
hearsed, coffined
heart, an oath 'by God's heart'
hearted, deep-seated in the heart
heartlings, little heart (*M. W.*, iii, 4, 59)
heat, to run across (*W. T.*, i, 2, 96)
heave, a sigh
heavily, mournfully
heaviness, drowsiness; sadness
heaving, a sigh
heavy, sad; sleepy
hebona, ebony
hectic, a continual fever
hedge, to turn aside; use shifts; sneak along
hedge-pig, hedgehog
hefts, retchings (*W. T.*, ii, 1, 45)
heighth, height
hell, a prison for debtors (*C. of E.*, iv, 2, 40)
helm, to steer, manage
helpless, unavailing; irremediable
hempen caudle, the hangman's noose
hempseed, one worthy to be hanged (*2 Hen. IV*, ii, 1, 64)
hence, not here, absent; henceforth
hent, *v.*, to seize, take; *n.*, time for being grasped (*Haml.*, iii, 3, 88)
heraldry, warrant (*All's W.*, ii, 3, 280)
herb of grace, rue
Herculean, descended from Hercules
hereby, near at hand; (that's), that depends, that's as may be
hereto, hitherto
hermit, beadsman, one bound to pray for a benefactor
hest, command; exploit
hether, hither
heyday, liveliness, youthful ardour
hick and hack, to cut and slash (*M. W.*, iv, 1, 68)
hide fox and all after, a game in which one hides and the rest try to find him
high and low, false dice
high-battled, commanding victorious armies
high-blown, puffed up, inflated
high-lone, on one's own feet (*R. and J.*, i, 3, 36)
high-sighted, arrogant
high-stomached, of haughty and irascible temper
hight, is named
highth, height
high-witted, quick-witted and ingenious
hild, held (*Lucr.*, 1257)
hilding, *n.*, a worthless creature; *adj.*, worthless, insignificant
hind, farm labourer; servant, menial; low fellow
hint, occasion, opportunity
hip (on *or* upon the), at one's mercy, in one's power
hipped, lamed in the hip
his, its
history, *n.*, story; historical drama; *v.*, to tell the story of
hit, to succeed; to interpret; (together), coöperate
hitherto, until now, up to the present
hizzing, whizzing (*Lear*, iii, 6, 17)
ho, *interj.*, stop, whoa (*T. N. K.*, v, 2, 18)
hoar, *adj.*, ghastly white; *v.*, to grow stale; to smite with leprosy
hobby-horse, simpleton; prostitute
hob nob, give or take (*T. N.*, iii, 4, 263)
hodge-pudding, a big sausage; a mishmash
hoise, to hoist; *p.p.*, blown up
hold, to interpret; wager; hold back, refrain; hold out; profit; hold good, prove true; (in), keep a secret
holding, burden (of a song); consistency
holidame, *see* halidome
Holland, linen
holp, helped
holy-ale, holiday celebration (*Per.*, Prol., 6)
home, *adv.*, to the destination intended (as by a home thrust), to a finish, thoroughly; to the point
honest, honourable, chaste
honesty, honour, decency, chastity
honeyseed, *for* homicide, homicidal (*2 Hen. IV.*, ii, 1, 57, 58)
honeysuckle, *for* homicidal (*2 Hen. IV*, ii, 1, 56)
honoured, honourable
honour-owing, honourable
hoodman, the blindfolded player in blindman's buff
hoodman-blind, blindman's buff
hoodwink, to blindfold; make invisible
hook of, that which tempts to (*Cymb.*, v, 5, 167)
hoop, to cry out, whoop
hope, *n.*, expectation (good or ill); *v.*, to expect
hopeful, hoped for, expected
horn, the mark of a cuckold
hornbook, a primer
horned man, a cuckold
horning (in), in making cuckolds
horn-mad, mad enough to gore one; mad because of being a cuckold
horn-maker, maker of cuckolds
horologe, clock
horse-drench, a dose for a horse
horse-leech, a large leech or bloodsucker

hose, breeches
host, to lodge
hothouse, a house for hot baths; a brothel
hourly, marking the hours
house-clogs, fetters
housekeeper, a dog that guards the house
hovel-post, a post supporting an open shed or a stack
howlet, owlet, owl
howsoever (howsoe'er), although; in any case, anyhow
hox, to hamstring
hoy, a small vessel
hugger-mugger (in), in secrecy
hulk, a large ship of burden
hull, to drift about
humane, civilized, civilizing
humorous, damp; capricious; governed by a humour, eccentric
humour, *n.*, one of the four liquids in the body (blood, phlegm, bile, and black bile or melancholy); dominant humour, temperament, disposition; disordered humour; caprice, fancy, idea; *v.*, to indulge; influence; flatter
hundreth, hundred
hungerly, *adj.*, sparse, thin; *adv.*, hungrily, with appetite
hunt, game
hunt's-up, a song to awake one early
hurly, tumult, noise
hurricano, a waterspout
hurtle, to sound confusedly
hurtling, disturbance, tumult
husband, *n.*, the master of a house; careful manager; husbandman; *v.*, to manage
husbandry, management, care; economy
hush, silent, still
husht, *interj.*, hush (*Per.*, i, 3, 10)
huswife, hussy
hyen, hyena
Hyperion, the sun god
Hyrcan, of Hyrcania (in Asia on the Caspian Sea)
hysterica passio, hysteria

I, ay (*R. and J.*, iii, 2, 45)
ice brook's temper, of steel tempered by immersing it in an ice-cold stream
Iceland dog, a sharp-eared dog
idea, exact image, likeness; mental image
idle, empty, useless, vain; waste; absurd, silly, trifling; meaningless, mad, incoherent
idle-headed, empty-headed, silly
idleness, want of cultivation; folly, absurdity
idly, madly, absurdly, heedlessly
i' fecks, in faith
ignis fatuus, will-o'-the-wisp
ignomy, ignominy
ignorant, causing ignorance, stupefying; unknown to one's self
'ild, *see* God-dild
Ilion, Troy
Ilion (Ilium), Priam's palace
ill-composed, composed of evil qualities
ill-disposed, poorly arranged
ill-favoured, ugly
ill-favouredly, unbecomingly
illiad; *see* eliad
ill-inhabited, poorly lodged
illness, evil quality, fault
ill-ta'en, mistaken
ill-tempered, distempered
illustrate, *v.*, to indicate brilliantly; *adj.*, illustrious
illustrious, without lustre (*Cymb.*, i, 6, 109)
ill-wresting, twisting everything awry (*Sonn.*, 140)
image, idea, thought; likeness, form, exact copy
imaginary, imaginative
imagined, of the imagination
imbare, to uncover, expose (*Hen. V*, i, 2, 94)
imbecility, weakness
imbrue (embrew), stain with blood; stain one's sword with blood, shed blood (*2 Hen. IV*, ii, 4, 210)
immanity, ferocity
immediacy, condition of an immediate representative
immediate jewel, the very jewel (*Oth.*, iii, 3, 156)
immediately, expressly
imminent deadly, threatening death
immodest, immoderate, unrestrained
immoment, of no account, of slight value
immures, surrounding walls
imp, *n.*, scion, youngster; *v.*, to graft; to mend (a wing) by grafting
impair, *v.*, to weaken; *adj.*, unbalanced, unfit (*T. and C.*, iv, 5, 103)
impale (empale), to hem in, surround, encircle
impart, make the gift (of heirship), *or* express my feelings (*Haml.*, i, 2, 112)
impartment, communication
impawn, to pledge as security
impeach, *v.*, to discredit, impugn; *n.*, accusation; discredit
impeachment, discredit; hindrance, opposition
imperator, commander
imperceiverant, undiscerning (*Cymb.*, iv, 1, 16)
imperial, emperor (*Two G.*, ii, 3, 5)
imperious, imperial
impeticos, pocket up (*T. N.*, ii, 3, 27)
impleached, interwoven
implorator, solicitor
impone, to wager
import, bring with them (*A. and C.*, ii, 2, 135)
importance, business; import; importunity
importancy, importance
important, importunate
importing, important, of import
importless, without significance
importment, signification, meaning
impose, *n.*, injunction; *v.*, to enjoin (one)
imposition, something laid upon or ascribed to (one); charge, imputation of guilt; penalty
imposthume, abscess
impotence, weakness, feeble health
impotent, infirm
imprese, one's emblematic device and motto
impress, *n.*, impression; impressment, conscription; *v.*, to enlist by conscription
improve, utilize
impudency, impudence
impudent, shameless, immodest
impugn, withstand
imputation, reputation; inference
in, into; on; in custody or prison
in-a-door, indoors
incapable, unable to take in, hold, or realize
incardinate, incarnate (*T. N.*, v, 1, 185)
incarnadine, to stain blood-red (*Macb.*, ii, 2, 62)
incarnation, *for* incarnate (*M. of V.*, ii, 2, 28)
incense, to incite, instigate; inflame with the idea (*Hen. VIII*, v, 1, 43)
inchmeal (by), inch by inch
incidency, act of falling upon, incidence
incision, bloodletting; surgical cutting
incivil, boorish, rude
incivility, boisterously rude behaviour
inclining, *adj.*, disposed to grant requests, obliging; *n.*, one's party, side; partiality
inclip, to embrace
include, bring to harmonious conclusion (*Two G.*, v, 4, 160)
income, the coming in, safe arrival (*Lucr.*, 334)
incontinent(-ly), immediately, forthwith
incony, dainty, delicate (*L. L. L.*, iii, 1, 136)
incorporal, bodiless
incorpsed, made one body
incorrect, undisciplined, rebellious
increaseful, abundant (*Lucr.*, 958)
incredulous, incredible
Inde, India, the Indies
indent, make an indenture (contract)
index, table of contents, prefatory summary; introduction, prologue
indifferency, moderate bulk; impartiality
indifferent, *adj.*, impartial; ordinary; average; *adv.*, rather, tolerably
indifferently, impartially; tolerably
indigest, *adj.*, shapeless; *n.*, chaos
indigested, shapeless
indign, disgraceful
indirect, wrong, unjust, irregular
indirection, devious ways; crooked or dishonest means
indirectly, wrongfully
indisposition, disinclination
indistinguishable, of inextricably mixed breed, mongrel (*T. and C.*, v, 1, 33)
indistinguished, past the limit of vision, boundless (*Lear*, iv, 6, 278)
indite (endite), invite, engage
individable, observing the unities of time and place (*Haml.*, ii, 2, 418)
indubitate, undoubted, notorious
induction, beginning, outset; preparatory scheme; introductory play (as in *T. of S.*)
indue (endue), to provide, furnish, endow; (to, unto), to furnish with qualities that adapt one to; to bring into sympathetic agreement with (*Oth.*, iii, 4, 146)
indurance, submission, long suffering (*Hen. VIII*, v, 1, 121)
industrious, skilful, ingenious; zealous
industriously, on purpose, deliberately
inequality, incongruity (*M. for M.*, v, 1, 65)
infamonize, brand with infamy (*L. L. L.*, v, 2, 684)
infection, *for* affection (*M. W.*, ii, 2, 120); desire (*M. of V.*, ii, 2, 133)

infer, to bring about, procure; allege, adduce; imply
infest, to harass
infinitive, infinite (*2 Hen. IV*, ii, 1, 26)
inflame, set on fire, make excessive (*T. N. K.*, iii, 5, 130)
inflict, afflict
influence, the inflowing of power from (*or* as from) the stars
inform (thus), to give this (false) information (*Macb.*, ii, 1, 48); (with nobleness), imbue, inspire (*Cor.*, v, 3, 71)
informal, distracted
infusion, nature, character; medicinal quality
ingenious, clever, naturally able; intellectual; conscious
ingeniously, ingenuously, sincerely (*Tim.*, ii, 2, 230)
ingraffed (ingraft, engraffed), ingrafted
ingredience, ingredients (collectively), contents
inhabit, abide
inhabitable, uninhabitable
inhearse, to entomb
inherit, to possess; (of), to make one entertain (*Rich. II*, i, 1, 85)
inheritor, owner
inhibition, what hinders
inhooped, surrounded with the hoop within which quails or cocks were set to fight
initiate, *adj.*, of a novice (*Macb.*, iii, 4, 143)
injoint, unite, combine
injurious, unjust, unrighteous; insulting
injury, *n.*, insult; *pl.*, things whose loss is an injury
inkhorn mate, one of these writing fellows
inkle, a sort of tape
inland, internal; (bred), in refined society (not in the wild outskirts of the land); (man), cultivated
inly, *adj.*, inward; *adv.*, inwardly
inn, *v.*, to get in, harvest (*All's W.*, i, 3, 48)
innocent, *n.*, fool, idiot
inoculate, to graft
inprimis, imprimis, first in order
inordinate, beyond moderation (*Oth.*, ii, 3, 311)
inquire, *n.*, inquiry
insane, causing insanity
insanie, insanity (*L. L. L.*, v, 1, 28)
insconce (ensconce), to hide. *See* ensconce
inscroll, enter on a scroll
insculp, engrave
insculpture, inscription
inseparate, inseparable
inshelled, drawn into the shell
insinuate, ingratiate one's self; remind, make (one) think (*L. L. L.*, v, 1, 28)
insinuation, *n.*, worming one's way in
insisture, steady motion onward (*T. and C.*, i, 3, 87)
insociable, remote from society; eccentric
instalment, seat of installation (*M. W.*, v, 5, 67)
instance, example, illustration; proof; motive, cause; adage
instant, instantly
instantly, at the same time
instate, invest
instrumental, naturally serviceable
insult, to exult insolently
insultment, arrogant triumph
intellect, purport, signification (*L. L. L.*, iv, 2, 136)
intelligence, spying
intelligencer, secret agent; interpreter
intelligencing, *adj.*, acting as secret agent
intelligent, carrying information
intemperance, unruly conduct; incontinence
intend, tend; pretend; mean
intended, understood, implied
intendment, intention; design
intenible, unable to retain (*All's W.*, i, 3, 208)
intention, intentness; intensity
intentively, with continuous attention
intercept, interrupt
interest, a claim
inter'gatory, interrogatory
interlude, a short play; a farce
intermission, interruption
intermissive, discontinued for a time
intertissued, interwoven
intervallum, interval
intil, into
intituled, entitled
intrenchant, not to be cut, invulnerable
intrinse (intrinsicate), intricately tied
intrude, force one's way into
inurned, entombed (*Haml.*, i, 4, 49)
invectively, with abusive language
investments, attire
invincible, not to be taken by the eye, invisible (*2 Hen. IV*, iii, 2, 337)
invised, unseen (*Compl.*, 212)
inward, *adj.*, inmost; secret; (with), in one's confidence; *n.*, inside; an intimate
inwardness, intimacy
irregulous, unprincipled, lawless
Ise, I shall (*Lear*, iv, 6, 246)
issue, result, product; action, deed
issued, descended
it, its
iterance, iteration, repetition
iwis, certainly

Jack (jack), fellow, chap, rogue; a man's figure which strikes the bell on a clock; a drinking vessel (*with a pun*); a small bowl aimed at by the players; a key in a virginal
jack-a-Lent, a man's figure pelted in sport during Lent; a butt; a little fellow
jackanapes, an ape or monkey
Jacksauce, impudent fellow
Jack-slave, a low fellow (*Cymb.*, ii, 1, 22)
jade, *n.*, a poor or worn-out horse, a nag; a worthless woman (*or* man); *v.*, to trick, befool; drive away exhausted
jaded, contemptible (*2 Hen. VI*, iv, 1, 52)
jadery, a nag's tricks
jakes, a privy
jane, a kind of fustian; *adj.*, coarse, untaught
jar, *n.*, *v.*, tick
jaunce, *v.*, to prance; to trudge; *n.*, a hard jaunt
jaundies, jaundice
jay, a showy woman (*Cymb.*, iii, 4, 51)
jealous (-ious), suspicious; (hood), a jealous dame (*R. and J.*, iv, 4, 13)
jealousy, suspicion
jennet, *see* gennet
jerkin, a close-fitting jacket
jesses, straps attached to a falcon's legs and connecting with the leash
jest, to sport
jet, to strut, swagger; parade; encroach
jig, *n.*, a comic song (and dance) in dialogue; *v.*, to perform a jig; to sing merrily; to walk with a dancing gait
Jill, Gillian; girl
John-a-dreams, a dreamy fellow
John Drum's entertainment (i.e., treatment), dismissal with a beating (*All's W.*, iii, 6, 41)
joinder, clasping
joined-stool, *see* joint-stool
jointress, dowager
joint-ring, a ring of separable halves
joint-stool (joined-, join-), stool made by a joiner
jordan, a chamber pot
journal, diurnal, daily
journey-bated, exhausted by travel
jowl, to dash
judicious, judicial
jump, *n.*, chance, hazard; *v.*, to risk, hazard; agree; coincide; *adv.*, exactly
junkets, sweetmeats, delicacies
justicer, a judge
justle, to jostle, elbow, push, force, shock
justling, turbulent
justly, rightly, exactly, precisely
jutty, *n.*, projection; *v.*, to overhang
juvenal, a youth

kam, cam, crooked, askew
kecksy, dry stalk
keech, a round lump of fat
keel, to skim
keep, *n.*, keeping, charge; *v.*, to guard; reside, stay; stay in or with; keep up, maintain; (touch), stand the test, come to time, fail not
keeper, guarding angel or spirit; doorkeeper
keeping, maintenance
Keiser, the Emperor (Kaiser)
ken, *v.*, to know; recognize; descry; *n.*, sight, range of eyesight
kennel, gutter; pack
kern, a light-armed Irish or Highland foot-soldier
kersey, coarse woolen cloth
kettle, kettledrum
kibe, chilblain
kickshaws, dainty dishes
kickshawses, fanciful amusements
kicy-wicky, pet, darling wife
kid-fox, a young fox
kidney, constitution (*M. W.*, iii, 5, 117)
killen, kill (*Per.*, ii, Prol., 20)
Killingworth, Kenilworth
kiln-hole, the fire-hole of a kiln or oven
kind, *n.*, nature; *adj.*, natural
kindle, to bring forth, bear
kindless, unnatural
kindly, *adj.*, natural; *adv.*, according to one's nature
kingdomed, *adj.*, like a (tumultuous) kingdom (*T. and C.*, ii, 3, 185)

kirtle, a gown
kissing comfits, perfumed sweetmeats
kitchen, to serve one as cook (*C. of E.*, v, 1, 415)
knack, gewgaw, knicknack; plaything (*W. T.*, iv, 4, 439)
knap, to snap off bit by bit; rap
knave, boy, youth; servant
knit, knitted texture
knoll, to ring, toll; sound, resound; call by a bell
knot, garden plot
knotty pated, with a head as dense as a knot in wood
koth-a, *see* quoth

label, an attached slip carrying the seal; a slip with writing on it
laboursome, elaborate
labras, lips (*M. W.*, i, 1, 166)
lace, to adorn
laced mutton, a strumpet
lade, to bail (*3 Hen. VI*, iii, 2, 139)
lag, *n.*, dregs, lowest sort; *adj.*, of old age; *adv.*, late; (of), behind, later than
lag-end, fag-end
Lakin (by'r) by our Lady (the Virgin)
lamentable, sorrowful
lamp, torch
lampass, a congestion of the mucous membrane in horses
lanch, to lance
land (laund), a forest glade
land-damn, *meaning unknown* (*W. T.*, ii, 1, 143)
land-rakers (foot), vagrant footpads
languish, *n.*, pining
lank, to grow thin
lanthorn, lantern; a turret with windows on every side
lap, to wrap
lapse, *n.*, slipping, loss of one's footing; *v.*, to fall into sin, to err
lapsed (if I be), if I do not heed my steps, walk circumspectly (*T. N.*, iii, 3, 36)
lapsed in, having proved dilatory and inconstant (*Haml.*, iii, 4, 107)
lard, to fatten; deck or strew (with); garnish
large, liberal; broad, loose; licentious
lark's-heel, larkspur
'larum: *see* alarum
'las, alas
latch, to catch; catch or bind as with a spell, enchant (*M. N. D.*, iii, 2, 36)
late, recent; lately, of late, once
lated, belated; overtaken by darkness
latten, made of latten (tin plate)
latter, last; (spring), coming late in the year, like Indian summer
laund (land), open space in the woods, glade
lavish, unrestrained, lawless, loose; wasteful
lavolt (lavolta), a high-capering dance
law of writ, drama that observes the classical rules (*Haml.*, ii, 2, 420)
lay, *n.*, stake, wager; *v.*, to stake, wager; beset; (by), lay down (one's pack); (for), set traps for, waylay; (up), fold up and lay in store
layer-up, preserver
lazar, leper
lead, to weight with lead
leading, command; military skill, generalship
leaguer, camp
leap, to leap into
learn, teach
learned, well educated
learning, an acquirement; information
leash, a set of three
leasing, lying; a falsehood
leather-coats, russet apples
leathren, leathern
leave, *n.*, permission to depart; liberty in excess, license; *v.*, leave off, cease, refrain from; give up; go out of business
leavened, matured, well-considered
leavy, leafy
lecture, instruction
leech, physician
leer, complexion, hue
leese, lose (*Sonn.*, 5)
leet, a manorial court; its day of session
leg, an elaborate bow, an obeisance
legatine, of a legate (an ecclesiastic representing the Pope)
'lege, allege
legerity, lightness, nimbleness
leiger, a resident ambassador or agent
leisure (by), hardly ever, never (*T. A.*, i, 1, 301); (by my good), having a favourable opportunity (*M. for M.*, iii, 2, 261)
leman, lover, sweetheart
lend, give
lendings, unessential furnishings (lent to one) (*Lear*, iii, 4, 114)
length, *n.*, delay (*A. and C.*, iv, 14, 46); stride (*T. N. K.*, v, 4, 57); range (*Per.*, i, 1, 168)
lengthen, to defer, delay
lenten, befitting Lent; scanty, meagre
l'envoy, epilogue, addendum
leperous, producing leprosy or the like
lesson, to teach
let, *n.*, impediment, hindrance; *v.*, to hinder; forbear, refrain
let-alone, prohibition
lethe, death (*J. C.*, iii, 1, 206)
letters, a letter, an epistle
level, *n.*, line of aim, range; *adj.*, on an equality; just, fair; *v.*, to guess
lewd, mean, low, given to low society
lewdly, basely; (bent), with base designs
lewdster, licentious fellow
Lewis, Louis
liable, subject (to); fit
libbard, leopard
liberal, free; outspoken; refined, cultivated; licentious
liberal-conceited (of liberal conceit), elegantly designed
liberty, license; drama that does not observe the classical rules (*Haml.*, ii, 2, 421); (of sin), wicked transgressor (*C. of E.*, i, 2, 102)
licourish, lickerish, delicious
lie, to lodge, dwell; be in prison; stand in a defensive posture; (on), depend on
lief, dear, beloved
lien, *p.p.*, lain
lieutenantry (deal on), to act by means of one's lieutenants or substitutes (*A. and C.*, iii, 11, 39)
lieve (live), lief, dear
lifelings, little life (*T. N.*, v, 1, 187)
lifter, a thief
liggens (God's), an oath
light, *p.p.*, alighted, arrived (*Per.*, iv, 2, 77)
lighten, enlighten
lightly, easily, readily, heedlessly; usually
like, to liken; to please, suit; (well), to be in good condition, to be fat
likelihood, probable indication; comparison
liking, bodily condition; (in some), not thin
limbeck, alembic; the cap of a still
limbmeal, limb from limb
limbo, a region on the border of hell; prison, captivity
Limbo Patrum (in), in prison (*lit.*, in the limbo reserved for the souls of the just who died before Christ's coming)
lime, *n.*, birdlime; *v.*, to smear with birdlime; to catch with (*or* as with) birdlime; to cement; to put lime into sack
lime-twig, a twig smeared with birdlime
limit, *n.*, appointed time; (strength of), strength gained during the period of lying-in (confinement); *v.*, to appoint
limiter, he who determines one's course
line, to delineate; to make strong, fortify
line, *n.*, lime tree, linden
linger, to protract, draw out
link, a torch
linsey-woolsey, a material of mixed linen and woollen; gibberish
linstock, the staff that holds the gunner's match
lip, to kiss
Lipsbury Pinfold (in), in the pound of Liptown, i.e. between my teeth, in my grip (*Lear*, ii, 2, 9)
liquor, to grease (boots)
list, boundary, limit; goal
list, *n.*, desire; *v.*, to desire, please
lither, pliant, yielding
live (lieve), lief
liveless, lifeless
livelihood, liveliness, life, vigour
lively, *adj.*, living, alive; lifelike; *adv.*, to the life
liver vein, the amatory style (the liver being regarded as the seat of the passion of love)
livery, *n.*, delivery of an estate to the heir; *v.*, to attire
live's, life's
loach, a small fish
lob, *n.*, bumpkin; *v.*, to lop, hang (the head), droop
lock, to restrain by embracing
lockram, a kind of linen
lodestar, guiding star, the polestar
loggets, a game like quoits but played with small logs
loggerhead, a blockhead
'long, to belong
longly, for a long while, intently
long of, on account of
'loo, halloo
loofed (being), having sailed off
look, to seek, search, search for, look up

loon (lown), rogue, rascal, lout; man of low rank, peasant
loop, loophole
looped, full of holes or slits
loose, *n.*, the discharge (of an arrow); *v.*, to discharge, shoot
loosely studied, given to low ways
loose shot, marksmen not attached to a company
lop, trimmings of trees (*Hen. VIII*, i, 2, 96)
lord, husband
lording, a little lord, a fine youngster
Lord's sake (for the), in prison (from the cry of poor prisoners begging for alms)
Lord's tokens, spots indicating the final stage of the plague (*L. L. L.*, v, 2, 423)
lose, to let slip, forget; to cast away, ruin, destroy
loss, ruin, disaster; casting away (*W. T.*, ii, 3, 191)
lots, lottery tickets that draw a prize; lots (to blanks), everything to nothing, practically certain
lottery, prize, allotment
lout, to mock, flout
love-broker, a go-between
love-day, a day appointed for the friendly settlement of quarrels, a day of reconciliation
lover, sweetheart; friend
lovered, provided with a lover (*Compl.*, 320)
loves (of all), for love's sake, if you love him, by all means (*Oth.*, iii, 1, 13)
love-springs, young shoots of love (as of a plant)
lown, *see* loon
lozel, scoundrel, wretch
lubber, *for* leopard (*2 Hen. IV*, ii, 1, 31)
luce, pike (fish)
lucre, covetousness
Lud's town, London
lull, loll (*Rich. III*, iii, 7, 72)
Lumbert Street, Lombard Street
lumpish, out of spirits, dull
lunes, mad fits or notions, lunacy
lurch, to pilfer, filch; (of), rob of, win from
lure, a kind of decoy for a falcon
lush, luxuriant
lust, delight, pleasure (*Lucr.*, 1384)
lust-breathed, urged on by lust (*Lucr.*, 3)
lust-dieted man, one whose every desire is fed (*Lear*, iv, 1, 68)
lustihood, vigour of body
lusty, merry
luxurious, lustful
luxuriously, lasciviously
luxury, lust
lym, bloodhound

Machiavel (Machivel), Macchiavelli
machine, contrivance, device, invention
maculate, stained, impure, unclean
maculation, stain, impurity
made-up, perfect, complete
maggot-pie, magpie
magnanimity, heroism
magnanimous, heroic
magnifico, a Venetian nobleman
maidenhead, virginity
Maid Marian, a character in May games and rustic dances
mail, *n.*, wallet, budget (*L. L. L.*, iii, 1, 74); *v.*, to cover, wrap (*2 Hen. VI*, ii, 4, 31)
main, *n.*, full strength; mainland; main part; stake (in diceplay)
main, *v.*, to maim (*2 Hen. VI*, iv, 2, 172)
main-course, mainsail
mainly, strongly; very (*Lear*, iv, 7, 65)
maintenance, bearing, behaviour
major, major premise in a syllogism (*1 Hen. IV.*, ii, 4, 544)
majority, superiority
make, to do; shut and bar (a door); collect, get together; make the fortune of; go; (dainty), to act coyly; (nice of), to reject fastidiously
makeless, mateless (*Sonn.*, 9)
malapert, saucy
malhecho, mischief, evil (*Haml.*, iii, 2, 147)
malkin (mawkin), a slattern, kitchen maid
mallard, drake
malmsey, a strong sweet wine
malthorse, a maltster's horse
maltworm, an ale-drinker
mammer on, to hesitate about
mammet, a doll; a babyish girl
mammock, to tear in pieces
man, to tame (a falcon); to provide with a manservant; to handle as a weapon (*Oth.*, v, 2, 270)
manage, *n.*, manège, art and practise of horsemanship; training; control; management; a course or short gallop; *v.*, to train; handle, wield; carry on
mandragora, mandrake
man-entered, initiated into manhood
mankind, *adj.*, masculine, mannish
manner (with the), in the act, in flagrante delicto
man-queller, man-killer
mantle, *n.*, scum; *v.*, to form scum
manure, to till, cultivate
mappery, map-making (*T. and C.*, i, 3, 205)
marches, border lands, frontier
marchpane, cake made of almonds, sugar, etc.
mare, the nightmare (a demon)
mare (the wild), a seesaw
margent, margin
marish, marsh
mark, two-thirds of a pound sterling
mark (God bless *or* save the), a phrase of unknown origin used to avert evil (like 'absit omen') or in apology
marmoset, a small monkey
marry, *an oath* 'by the Virgin Mary,' *but used as a light interjection*; indeed, to be sure, why
mart, *n.*, market, market place; market time; trading; bargain; *v.*, to bargain, traffic; to market
Martialist, follower of Mars, warrior
Martin, *see* Saint Martin
Martlemas, beef salted at Martinmas (St. Martin's day, November 11) — jocose nickname for Falstaff (*2 Hen. IV*, ii, 2, 110)
martlet, the martin
marvell's, marvellous
masked, *adj.*, with surface as unruffled as a mask is unchanging, calm (*Per.*, iii, 3, 36)
masoned, of masonry
Mary-buds, buds of the marigold
mastic, snarling (*T. and C.*, i, 3, 73)
match, appointment; bargain, agreement; plan, scheme
mate, *n.*, low fellow
mate, *v.*, to daze, stupefy
material, full of matter and sense (*A. Y. L.*, iii, 3, 32); that produces one's life and substance, elemental (*Lear*, iv, 2, 35)
matin, morning
matter, cause of complaint or quarrel, dispute
maugre, in spite of
maund, a hand basket
maw, stomach
mawkin, *see* malkin
maze, to daze, confound
mazzard, head, pate
meacock, cowardly, mean-spirited (*T. of S.*, ii, 1, 315)
mealed, spotted, stained (*M. for M.*, iv, 2, 86)
mean, *n.*, means; a part between treble and bass
mean, *v.*, to lament (*M. N. D.*, v, 1, 330)
measurable, fit, appropriate
measure, *n.*, a stately dance; tune; *v.*, to dance (a measure)
meat, food
meddler, trafficker, general agent (*W. T.*, iv, 4, 329)
medicinable (med'cinable), medicinal, curative
medicine, *n.*, drug, magic potion; the alchemist's tincture, the philosopher's stone; physician; *v.*, to restore
meditance, meditation
meditation, thought, a thought
medlar, a kind of pear
meed, *n.*, reward, pay; deserts, merit; excellence
meered, limited, sole and entire (*A. and C.*, iii, 13, 10)
meet, *adj.*, even, quits; *adv.*, fitly, successfully; *v.*, to meet with; acquire, gain
meeting, meeting place
meiny, household troop, retinue; multitude, common people
mell, to have to do, deal
memorize, make memorable or glorious
memory, a memorial, memento
mends, remedy (*T. and C.*, i, 1, 68)
mercatante, merchant (*T. of S.*, iv, 2, 63)
merchant, fellow; merchant ship
mercy (by), by a merciful interpretation (*Tim.*, iii, 5, 55); (cry one), to beg one's pardon
mere, absolute, entire, utter
merely, absolutely, utterly
merit, reward, recompense
mervailous, extraordinary (*Hen. V*, ii, 1, 50)
mesh, to brew (*T. A.*, iii, 2, 38)
mess, a portion of food; a group of four; (lower), less intelligent persons (*W. T.*, i, 2, 227)
metal, substance; character, nature; (good), a man of vigour and courage (*All's W.*, ii, 1, 42)
metamorphise, metamorphose
metaphysical, supernatural
mete, to measure; aim
mete-yard, a measuring rod
metheglin, a kind of spiced mead
mettle, spirit, high spirit
mew, to shut up (as a hawk in a mew or cage), to coop up

mewl, to mew like a cat (*A. Y. L.*, ii, 7, 144)
micher, a truant
miching, sneaking
mickle, great, much
middest, midst
middle earth, this earth
milch, *adj.*, giving milk; tearful (*Haml.*, ii, 2, 540)
milk-livered, white-livered, cowardly
mill-sixpence, a milled sixpence
mince, to walk with short steps; talk with affected elegance; affect, counterfeit with a prudish air
mincing, affectation, prudishness
mind, *n.*, intention; disposition; opinion; memory; *v.*, to conceive; mean, intend; notice, attend to; remind; remember
minded, *adj.*, disposed
mindless, without a mind; forgetful
mine, to undermine, sap
mineral, a mine
mingle, *n.*, mixture; *v.*, to compound, unite
minikin, *adj.*, pretty little
minim rest, a rest equal to a half-note
minime, not at all, by no means
minimus, smallest of human beings
minion, *n.*, darling, favourite; paramour, mistress; hussy; saucy creature
minister, servant, attendant; agent, deputy
ministration, service
minstrelsy, entertainment in story-telling
minute-jack, fickle-minded creature
minutely, every minute
mirable, wonderful, admirable
mirth, joy, rejoicing; a sport or entertainment
miscarry, to come to harm; be lost, perish; fail
misconster, misconstrue
miscreate, illegitimate, spurious
misdread, fear of evil, anxiety
miser, miserable creature
misgoverned, unruly
misgoverning (misgovernment), misconduct
misgraffed, grafted amiss, ill-matched
misprise (misprize), to undervalue, disdain
misprised, *adj.*, mistaken
misprision, mistake, misconception; contempt
misprize, *see* misprise
misproud, arrogant
miss, *n.*, misbehaviour; loss, deprivation; *v.*, to do without
missingly, because I have missed him (*W. T.*, iv, 2, 35)
missive, messenger
mistake, to misjudge
mistempered, tempered for a bad use, misused (*R. and J.*, i, 1, 94)
mistreadings, transgressions
mistress, lady love; madam; the jack in bowling, a small bowl at which the players aim
mistress court, the chief court
mistrustful, that makes one suspicious (*V. and A.*, 826)
misuse, *n.*, misbehaviour; *v.*, to abuse (in speech); delude; misrepresent (*Sonn.*, 152)
mobled, with the head wrapped up
Mock-water, tricky diagnostician (*M. W.*, ii, 3, 60)
model, copy (on a small scale); likeness; the very image; a small figure or shape
modern, commonplace, trite; ordinary, everyday
modest, moderate; decorous; mild
modestly, moderately, without exaggeration
modesty, moderation; sense of decency; restraint (in style)
module, mere image
moe, more
moiety, a part
moldwarp, the mole
mome, simpleton
momentany, momentary
Monarcho, a fantastical Italian well known at Elizabeth's court, famous for high-flown discourse (*L. L. L.*, iv, 1, 101)
monster, to make monstrous
monstruosity, monstrous inconsistency (*T. and C.*, iii, 2, 87)
montant, a swashing stroke from above (*M. W.*, ii, 3, 27)
month's mind, a strong inclination
monument, a memorial; a stately family tomb
monumental, memorial; handed down as an heirloom
mood, the mode (form of the scale) in music; *fig.*, the tune, style (*2 Hen. IV*, iv, 5, 200)
mood, anger, angry fit; bitter grief
moody, sullen, angry, irascible
moody-mad, mad with rage
moon, month
mooncalf, a monstrosity
moonish, fickle, capricious
mop, a grimace
mopping, *n.*, making affected faces
mope, to be in a daze; be stupefied; wander heedlessly
moped, out of sorts
moral, *n.*, a maxim, an adage; an emblem; the meaning; *v.*, to moralize; *adj.*, emblematical
moraler, moralizer
morality, moral instruction
moralize, to interpret, expound
Morisco, morris dance
Morning (the), Aurora
morris-pike, a pike invented by the Moors
morrow, morning
morsel, a trivial creature
mort, the notes on the horn to announce the deer's death
mortal, deadly, death-dealing
mortality, death; deadliness
mortified, deadened; withered and insensible to pain; paralyzed; moribund; dead to the world
mortifying, *adj.*, deadly; exhausting the vitality
mose in the chine, to suffer ulceration from glanders
mot, motto, emblematic device
mother, hysteria
motion, *n.*, proposal, suggestion; impulse, incitement; emotion, strong feeling, passion; mental action, perception; idea, notion; puppet show, puppet; *v.*, to propose
motive, moving cause; active force; incentive; occasion; limb or organ that moves
motley, the parti-coloured attire of a fool; a fool
motley-minded, foolish, fantastic
mought, *v.*, might
mould, earth
moulten, *adj.*, that has shed its feathers
mounch, to munch
mountainer, mountaineer
mountant, rising, raised
mountebank, *v.*, to win by artful speeches
mounted, *adj.*, high, on high
mouse, to bite and tear (like a cat)
mouse-hunt, a night-prowler (*R. and J.*, iv, 4, 11)
mouth, to declaim pompously
mouthed, *adj.*, gaping
move, *v.*, to propose, bring forward; anger; approach one with a suggestion or proposal
mow, a grimace
moy, Pistol's misunderstanding of the French pronoun *moi*, which he takes to be the name of a coin (*Hen. V*, iv, 4, 14, 23)
muddy, confused in mind
muddied, confused and suspicious
muddy-mettled, stupid, without sense or spirit
muleter, muleteer, mule-driver
mulled, stupefied, lethargic (*Cor.*, iv, 5, 239)
multiplying medicine, the philosopher's stone
multipotent, very powerful
multitude, the common herd
multitudinous, of the multitude (*Cor.*, iii, 1, 156); with its multitude of tossing waves (*Macb.*, ii, 2, 62)
mumble-news, a gossiping fellow
mummer, an actor in a dumb show or in a rustic play
mummy, human flesh dried and embalmed, used as a medicine or for magical purposes
muniments, furnishings
mural, wall
murdering piece, a cannon charged with many slugs
mure, wall
murk, darkness
murmur, rumour, gossip
murrion, *adj.*, killed by the murrain
Muse, poet
muse, to wonder, be surprised; wonder at
musit, a hole or gap in a hedge or thicket
Musko, a Muscovite, Russian (*All 's W.*, iv, 1, 76)
muss, a game in which the players scramble for some object
mute, an actor who has no speaking part
mutine, *n.*, mutineer, rebel; *v.*, to mutiny
mutiner, *n.*, mutineer; insurgent
mutiny, strife, uproar, tumult
mutton, a sheep; a harlot
mystery, trade, profession, art; skill

nail, the sixteenth of a yard
naked, unarmed
napkin, handkerchief
napless, threadbare
native, natural, genuine; related by birth, kindred; naturally adapted; by nature; at home
natural, *n.*, a born fool, an idiot; *adj.*, idiotic
nature, vitality; life
naught, good for nothing; wicked; naughty; come to naught, ruined; (a thing of), a wicked thing; (be naught awhile), efface yourself! get out!

naughty, good for nothing; bad; wicked
nave, navel; the hub of a wheel
nayward (to the), in the negative direction
nay-word, a watchword, a word for identification; a byword
ne, nor
neaf, fist
near, nearer
near-legged, knock-kneed
nearness, near kinship
neat, trimly dressed; foppish; elegant
neb, a bird's bill; the mouth
necessitied to, in pressing need of
needful, urgent; in need of troops
needless, not in want (*A. Y. L.*, ii, 1, 46)
needly, of necessity
needy, necessary, much needed
neele, needle (*Per.*, v, Prol., 5)
neeze, to sneeze
neglect, to let slip; do without; disregard; overlook
neglection, *n.*, neglect, disregard
neighbourhood, friendly relations
neither, not so either (denying an alternative)
nephew, cousin; grandchild
nerve, sinew, tendon
nervy, sinewy
nether, lower; on earth
nether-stocks, stockings
neuter, neutral
next way, the nearest (shortest) way
nice, precise; over precise, finical; squeamish; prudish; trivial, unsubstantial; foolish, silly
nicely, subtilely; punctiliously; foolishly
niceness (nicety), prudery; an over-precise scruple
nick, *n.*, a notch in a tally; (out of all), beyond reckoning, out of measure; (in the), in the nick of time; *v.*, to cut one's hair in a notched pattern as was done to fools; to mark with folly, to disgrace
niece, granddaughter
nighted, black as night; blinded
night-rule, actions by night (*M. N. D.*, iii, 2, 5)
nill, will not
nimble-set, agile (*T. N. K.*, iv, 2, 127)
nine men's morris, a game (not unlike hopscotch) played with nine 'men' (pebbles or discs)
nip, to force (as if by a rapture) (*Per.*, v, 1, 235)
nit, a louse's egg, a young louse
noble, a gold coin (one third of a pound)
noblesse, nobility
noddy, simpleton
noise, *n.*, rumour; music; band of musicians; *v.*, to rumour
nole, head
nonage, minority
non-come, the state of one *non compos mentis* (out of one's mind), utter confusion, a nonplus (*M. Ado*, iii, 5, 67)
nook-shotten, shot into a corner of the earth, remote
northen, from the north (*T. A.*, iv, 1, 104)
not, not only
note, *n.*, a mark, sign; brand of infamy, stigma; mark of inferiority; a letter, memorandum, bill; distinguished position or quality; knowledge; remark; *v.*, to mark with infamy, disgrace; show, indicate
notedly, exactly
nothing, not at all
nothing-gift, worthless gift or distinction
notify, to take notice (*M. W.*, ii, 2, 85)
notion, mind
notorious, well-known; notable
notoriously, notably
not-pated, *adj.*, having the hair notted (cut short)
nouzle up, to pamper
no-verbs, mispronounced words (*M. W.*, iii, 1, 107)
novum, a game at dice of which the best throws were nine and five
noyance, harm, injury
number, versify
numbers, rhythm, metre; verses, poetry
nuncio, messenger
nuncle, mine uncle (a fool's term in addressing his master)
nursery, nursing, fostering care
nurture, culture, good breeding; moral training
nuthook, a catchpole, sheriff's officer, beadle

O, a cipher, zero
o', of, on
oak, wreath of oak leaves
oathable, fit to take an oath
ob., abbreviation for *obolus*, halfpenny
object, a sight; object of attention or love
obliged, bound by a legal obligation
obliquy, obliquity (*Tim.*, iv, 3, 18)
oblivion, forgetfulness, loss of memory
oblivious, causing forgetfulness
obscene, abominable
obscenely, Costard's word for 'becomingly' (*L. L. L.*, iv, 1, 145); Bottom's word for 'conveniently' (*M. N. D.*, i, 2, 111)
obsequious, befitting a funeral, funereal; passionately mournful
observance, observation; attention; care; devotion; obligatory rule
observancy, devotion, homage
observant, obsequious attendant, sycophant
observation, ceremonial rites
observe, to be attentive or show respect to; indulge
observing, deferential
obstacle, obstinate (*1 Hen. VI*, v, 4, 17)
obstruction, stagnation, stagnancy (*M. for M.*, iii, 1, 119)
occasion, favourable opportunity
occulted, closely hidden
occupation, handicraft, trade
occupy, to cohabit with
occurrents, occurrences, incidents
odd, at odds, at enmity (*T. and C.*, iv, 5, 265)
odd-even, a time about midnight when one cannot tell whether it is P.M. or A.M. (*Oth.*, i, 1, 124)
odds, a quarrel, enmity; advantage (in a wager or match)
odorous, *for* odious (*M. Ado*, iii, 5, 18)
Od's, God's (in oaths)
o'erbeat, to overflow with dashing waves (*Cor.*, iv, 5, 136)
o'erblow, to blow away
o'ercount, to outnumber; (me of), to win from me by getting an advantage in the accounting
o'ercrow, to triumph over, overpower
o'ereaten, *adj.*, that has served for two meals and of which only scraps are left (*T. and C.*, v, 2, 160)
o'erflourished, painted over with ornamental designs
o'erfraught, overladen (with grief)
o'ergalled, much inflamed
o'ergreen, to deck with verdure, to give a good appearance to (*Sonn.*, 112)
o'ergrown, hairy; enfeebled by age
o'erleaven, to pervade and modify
o'erlook, to bewitch with the evil eye
o'erparted, having too difficult a part to play
o'erperch, to fly over
o'erposting, getting quickly over
o'erraught, overtook and passed; (of), cheated out of
o'ersized, smeared over
o'erstrawed, overstrewed
o'erteemed, exhausted by bearing children
o'erwatched, exhausted by lack of sleep
o'erweigh, outweigh
o'erwhelm (overwhelm), to jut out over, overhang
o'erwrested, over-strained, exaggerated
of, from; by; in, during; on
off, off the mark, all wrong (*Cor.*, ii, 2, 64)
offal, what falls off, chips and shavings, rubbish
offer, to threaten; be on the offensive; undertake, attempt
office, *n.*, duty, service; *v.*, to act as servants in; officiously keep one away (*Cor.*, v, 2, 68); *pl.*, rooms where the servants perform their several duties (kitchen, buttery, etc.)
officed, *adj.*, having their required duties
officer, agent; attendant
officious, zealous in service
'old, wold, upland (*Lear*, iii, 4, 125)
old (*a general intensive*), plentiful, hard, much, etc.
omen, disaster (which omens portend)
omit, to pass or lay by; neglect
on, of; because of, on account of
once, once for all
oneyers (great), great ones (*1 Hen. IV*, ii, 1, 84)
open, to give tongue
opener, interpreter
operance, operation
operant, active; potent
opinion, public opinion; reputation; self-opinion, self-conceit
opinioned, *for* pinioned (*M. Ado*, iv, 2, 69)
oppress, put down, suppress
oppugnancy, opposition, antagonism
or (or ere), before
or . . . or, either . . . or
orb, circle, round; the sphere (of a star); this earth
orchard, garden
order (take), make arrangements

ordinance, rank in society; ordnance
ordinant, decisively operative
ordinary, a meal at fixed price
ore, precious metal
orgillous, proud, haughty
orient, pearly
orifex, orifice
orphan, without parents (*M. W.*, v, 5, 43)
ort, a scrap; *pl.*, bits of food left after a meal, leavings
ostent, show, appearance; display
ostentation, show, display; a spectacle
ostridge, ostrich
other, others
othergates, otherwise, in another fashion
otherwhere, elsewhere
Ottomite, Turk
ouch, a brooch or jewelled buckle
ought, owed
ounce, lynx
ouph, elf, goblin
ousel, *see* woosel
out, abroad; in the field (as a soldier); out of one's part, at a loss, embarrassed; off the track, wrong, mistaken; ended, finished; expired; at variance, vexed; fully, quite; with a hole in one's shoe; out of
outbreast, to surpass in singing
outbrave, defy; outshine
outcraft, outwit
outlook, to outstare
outpeer, excel, outvie
outprized by, less valued than
outrage, violence in speech or action; violent outbreak; frantic behaviour
outdure, hold out against
outspeaks, manifestly (as it were, outspokenly) exceeds (*Hen. VIII*, iii, 2, 127)
outvied, beaten by a higher bid
outward man, an outsider
overcome, to come or pass over
overgo, surpass; exceed; overwhelm
overhold, overrate
overscutched, worn-out, stale (*2 Hen. IV*, iii, 2, 340)
overseen, deluded, discomfited (*Lucr.*, 1206)
overshot, beaten in shooting, discomfited
overture, disclosure
overwhelm, *see* o'erwhelm
overture, revealing, disclosure
owe, to own, possess, have
oxlip, a variety of the cowslip
oyes, proclamation ('Oyes,' i.e., 'Hear,' being the crier's opening call)

paced, trained, broken in
pack, to be off; conspire, make arrangements
packed, *p.p.*, engaged in a conspiracy; implicated
packing, conspiracy, secret doings
paction, agreement
paddock, toad
page, to attend like a page
pageant, to mimic (as in a show)
pain, *n.*, pains, effort, toil; penalty; *v.*, to cause toil or trouble to
painted, falsified, unreal; (cloth), a cheap substitute for tapestry hangings
pajock, peacock
palabras, words
palate, to taste; to get (the taste); to have the flavour of
pale, pallor
palisado, a palisade, fence of stakes
pall, to wrap as in a cloak or pall
pall, to grow weak, fail
palliament, the white gown of a candidate (*T. A.*, i, 1, 182)
palmer, pilgrim
palter, to prevaricate, equivocate; shuffle
pantaloon, a feeble silly old man
pantler, a servant who manages the pantry
paper, to summon by letter (*Hen. VIII*, i, 1, 80)
paragon, *v.*, to set up as a model; compare; excel
parasits, parasites (*Ven.*, 848)
parcel, *n.*, part, an item; party, group; *v.*, to increase by an item (*A. and C.*, v, 2, 163)
parcel-bawd, partly a procurer
parcel-gilt, partly gilt, gilded on the inside
parcelled, *adj.*, distributed, particular, separate
pard, leopard
pardon, *n.*, leave, permission; *v.*, to excuse
parfect, to enact, perform (a part)
Parish Garden, Paris Garden
parish top, a large top spun in parish sports
paritor, apparitor, an officer of an ecclesiastical court
parle (parley), *n.*, talk, conversation; conference (*esp.* as to truce or surrender); *v.*, to speak; confer, negotiate
parlous, perilous, hazardous; pert and clever
parmacity, spermaceti
part, *n.*, party; deed; quality; *v.*, to depart; depart from
partake, to take sides, side; impart, communicate
partaker, confederate, accomplice; sharer
parted, *adj.*, gifted, accomplished (*T and C.*, iii, 3, 96)
partialize, to make partial, unfair
partial slander, a slanderous censure for partiality (*Rich. II*, i, 3, 241)
participate, *adj.*, coöperative
particular, *n.*, one's own special case; special or personal part; personal relation; personal interests or concerns
particularly, with my individual self (*Tim.*, i, 1, 46)
partisan, a long-handled weapon with a piercing and cutting blade
Partlet, a name for the hen (Chaucer's 'Pertelote')
party, part, side
party-verdict, one's own part in a collective verdict
pash, *n.*, the head; *v.*, to strike with a smashing blow; mangle
pass, to pass by, disregard; manage; play the part of; decide, pass sentence; thrust (in fencing); die; happen; care; go beyond bounds or belief; *n.*, license; transgression; thrust, bout (in fencing); predicament; (of pate), an intellectual thrust, a witty speech (*Temp.*, iv, 1, 244); (of practice), a plotted thrust (*Haml.*, iv, 7, 139)
passable, enough to serve as a password (*Cor.*, v, 2, 13); that admits free passage (*Cymb.*, i, 2, 10)
passado, a forward thrust
passage, *n.*, course; procedure; wandering; act, action; occurrence; fact; passing away, death; time when the streets are thronged with people; (no) nobody passing
passant (*in heraldry*), walking
passenger, wayfarer
passing, *adj.*, exceeding, transcendent; *adv.*, exceedingly
passing bell, a bell rung to call for prayers for one who is dying
passion, any stormy emotion or its expression in words or action; grief, suffering; the sufferings and death of Christ; frenzy; mental disorder, insanity; a passionate speech in a play; *v.*, to grieve passionately
passionate, *adj.*, sorrowing; expressive of strong feeling; *v.*, to express with adequate emotion
passive, submissive
passport, a paper certifying a soldier's discharge and licensing his journey
passy measures pavin, a stately Italian dance; a solemn humbug (*T. N.*, v, 1, 206)
past-proportion, an amount too vast for computation
pastry, the room where pastry is made
patch, a fool
patched, *adj.*, motley
patchery, roguery, chicanery
patens, metal plates
path, *v.*, to walk abroad (*J. C.*, ii, 1, 83)
pathetical, *adj.*, touching
patience, calmness, fortitude; kind permission
patient, *adj.*, calm; *v.*, to compose (one's self)
patronage, *v.*, to protect; maintain, avouch
pattern, *n.*, a precedent; supreme exemplar; specimen of one's handiwork or skill; *v.*, to prefigure; match
pauca (pauca verba, paucas pallabris), few words
paunch, to stab in the belly
paved, covered with a slab of stone (*M. for M.*, v, 1, 440)
pax, a sacred tablet passed to the congregation to be kissed at mass
peach, to denounce (one) as; to become an informer
peak, to waste away; to move about feebly and dazedly; to sneak
pearl, *pl.*, pearls
peascod, peapod
peascod time, the season of early peas
peat, a pet, little girl
pebble, *pl.*, pebbles (*Lear*, iv, 6, 21)
peck, to pitch (*Hen. VIII*, v, 4, 94)
peculiar, personal; private; one's own
pedant, schoolmaster
pedascule, schoolmate, tutor
peeled, *adj.*, shaven, tonsured
peep, a pip, a spot on a die or playing card; (a peep out), not quite up to the mark
peer, to appear, show one's self; show
peevish, childish, silly; trivial
peevish-fond, childishly foolish

Peg-a-Ramsey, an old song and dance
peise (peize), to poise, balance; weigh down; (the time), to weight it so that it may not pass so quickly (*M. of V.*, iii, 2, 22)
pelf, goods, property, riches
pellet, to form into round drops (*Compl.*, 18)
pelt, to scold, rail (*Lucr.*, 1418)
pelting, paltry, insignificant
pencilled, painted, depicted
pendulous, overhanging (*Lear*, iii, 4, 69)
penitent, *adj.*, doing penance; *n.*, one who is doing penance
penner, pen case
pennorth, pennyworth, bargain
pensioner, one of the royal bodyguard
pensived, made pensive (*Compl.*, 219)
penthouse, a lean-to (with a single-pitched roof)
penurious, needy
pen'worth, pennyworth, bargain
perch, resting place, station (*Per.*, iii, Prol., 15)
perdie (perdy), pardieu (a trivial oath)
perdition, loss, destruction
perdu, a soldier set to watch at a dangerous post
perdurable, never-ending, lifelong
perdurably, eternally
perdy, *see* perdie
peregrinate, foreign in one's ways, affected
peremptory, imperious, domineering; resolved, determined
perfect, *adj.*, fully informed; fully equipped, ready; trustworthy; very proficient; *v.*, to finish, accomplish; instruct fully
perfection, achievement; accomplishment; acquisition
perforce, forcibly, by force; of necessity
perge, proceed, go on
periapt, a magic girdle
period, *n.*, end, close; goal; peroration; *v.*, to bring to a close, put an end to
perish, to destroy
perishen, perish (*Per.*, ii, Prol., 35)
perjure, *n.*, perjurer; *v.*, to make false to one's oath
peroration, elaborate oration
perpend, consider; pay attention
per se, all by himself, unique, peerless
persever, persevere
persistive, persistent, enduring
person, parson (*L. L. L.*, iv, 2, 84, 85)
personage, figure, personal appearance
perspective, a glass or optical instrument which distorts objects
perspectively, as seen in or through a perspective
persuade, to urge; win over
persuaded well of, having a favourable opinion of
pert, brisk, lively, animated
pertly, promptly; boldly, defiantly
pervert, turn aside
pester, to crowd, throng; infest
pestilent, plaguy
petar, petard, a small bomb
pettitoes, toes (*lit.*, pig's feet) (*W. T.*, iv, 4, 619)
pew-fellow, an associate, sharer
phantasime, a fantastic fellow
phantasma, an illusion
Pheazar, a comic name (*from* pheeze) (*M. W.*, i, 3, 10)
pheeze (pheese), to settle, fix (in a hostile sense); take down by a flogging
Philip, a proverbial name for a sparrow
Philip and Jacob (i.e., James), the day sacred to those saints, May 1
Philippan, wielded at the Battle of Philippi
Philomela (Philomel), the nightingale
philosopher, man of science
philosophical, scientific
Phœbus, the sun god, the sun
phrase, a word, a term
phraseless, of indescribable beauty (*Compl.*, 225)
physic, *n*, medicine; curative treatment, remedy; medical art or knowledge; *v.*, to cure, heal; restore
physical, curative, remedial; good for one's health
pia mater, the delicate membrane that envelops the brain; the brain
pick, to pitch
picked, refined, fastidious; carefully chosen
pickers (i.e., pilferers) and stealers, the fingers
picking, trivial
pickthank, a sycophantic talebearer
Pickt-hatch, a low quarter of London
piece, a work of art; masterpiece; accomplishment; creature
piety, devotion, patriotism
pight, pitched; determined
pilcher, pilchard, a kind of fish; scabbard
piled, stripped of hair (*with a pun on* furnished with a pile or velvet nap) (*M. for M.*, i, 2, 35)
pill, to pillage; take by robbery
pin, a peg at the centre of a target
pin and web, a disease of the eye, cataract
pinch, to pinch away (*Two G.*, iv, 4, 160)
pinched thing, a dupe (*W. T.*, ii, 1, 51)
pinfold, a pound
pink, half-closed, drowsy (*A. and C.*, ii, 7, 119)
pinked, perforated (for ornament)
pioned, *adj.*, trenched (*Temp.*, iv, 1, 64)
pioner, pioneer, a soldier who digs trenches, makes roads, etc.
pip, *see* peep
pipe-wine, wine from the pipe (from the wood) *with a pun on* musical pipe (*M. W.*, iii, 2, 90)
pitch, *n.*, height; the highest point reached by a soaring falcon; *v.*, to throw one's self, fall
pittikins (*diminutive*), pity (*Cymb.*, iv, 2, 293)
place, mansion; pitch (of a falcon)
placket, the slit at the top of a skirt
plain, *adj.*, smooth and level; out-and-out; simple; *v.*, to make plain, interpret
plain, to complain, lament
plain-song, simple melody
plaintful, lamenting, doleful (*Compl.*, 2)
planched, made of boards
plant, sole of the foot
plantage, vegetation, herbage
plantation, colonizing
plash, a shallow pool or puddle
plat, *n.*, a plait, braid; *v.*, to plait, braid
plate, *n.*, a coin; *v.*, to cover (with armour)
plated, *adj.*, wearing plate armour
platform, a paved level in a fortification; a careful plan
plausibly, with enthusiastic applause
plausive, pleasing, agreeable; plausible
play, to gamble for
playfeere, playfellow
pleached, interlaced; folded
pleasance, merriment
please-man, a sycophant, flatterer
pleat, a plait
pliant, susceptible to request (*Oth.*, i, 3, 151)
plight (in), in condition, ready, prepared
plighted, folded (so as to conceal); pledged, betrothed
pluck, to pull
plume up, to adorn (as with plumes); accomplish brilliantly
plurisy, excess, plethora
pocket up, to accept without resentment
poem, a drama in verse
point, a tagged lace; a trumpet signal (*2 Hen. IV*, iv, 1, 52); *pl.*, orders (*Cor.*, iv, 6, 125); (at), on the point of, ready; (at) completely; (at a), fully prepared; (at ample), amply
point-devise (-device), precise, exact in every detail; finical
'pointed, *p.p.*, appointed
pointing stock, an object of scorn
poise, *n.*, weight, importance; *v.*, weigh
poke, pocket, wallet
poking stick, a rod for adjusting the plaits of a ruff
Polack, Pole
pole, standard (*A. and C.*, iv, 15, 65)
pole-clipt, *adj.*, whose poles are embraced by vines (*Temp.*, iv, 1, 68)
policy, statecraft; diplomacy; strategy; politics; cunning
politic, treating of statecraft
polled, bald; stripped bare, cleared (*Cor.*, iv, 5, 215)
polusion, *for* allusion (*L. L. L.*, iv, 2, 47)
pomander, a ball of aromatic substances
Pomgarnet, Pomegranate (name of a room) (*1 Hen. IV*, ii, 4, 42)
pomp, procession; festal ceremony
Pompion (i.e., pumpkin), Costard's slip of the tongue (or joke) for Pompey (*L. L. L.*, v, 2, 503)
pompous, magnificent, glorious
pomwater, a large sweet apple
Pont, Pontus in Asia Minor
Pontic, the Black Sea, the Euxine
poop, to play (one) a foul trick
poor-John, dry salt hake
poother (pudder), turmoil
popingay, popinjay, parrot
pop'rin, a Flemish pear
popular, vulgar; ordinary
popularity, low company
populous, containing many men
porpas, porpoise
porpentine, porcupine
porringer, a cap shaped like a porridge bowl
port, *n.*, a gate, portal; mien, bear-

ing; style of living; *v.*, to bring to harbour
portable, easy to bear, tolerable
portage, portholes; cargo
portance, conduct
portly, stately, imposing; dignified and courteous
posied, inscribed with a posy (motto)
position, proposition
possess, to inform
possession, state of being possessed by an evil spirit; madness
posset, *v.*, to curdle
possitable, *for* positively (*M. W.*, i, 1, 244)
post (off), to put off, defer
poster of, one who courses over
posture, style, fashion (*J. C.*, v, 1, 33)
posy, motto (especially in verse)
pot (to the), to certain death (*Cor.*, i, 4, 47)
potable, drinkable (of gold in the form of *aurum potabile*) (*2 Hen. IV*, iv, 5, 163)
potch, to make a stab
potent, potentate
potential, powerful
pother, *see* poother
potting, *n.*, drinking
pottle, a two-quart tankard
poulter, a poulterer, dealer in poultry
pouncet box, a small box (with perforated top) for carrying perfume
pound, to shut up as in a pound
powder, to salt, pickle
powdering tub, a tub for pickling; sweating tub for the treatment of disease
power, an armed force, army
Powl's, Saint Paul's Church
pow, waw, *interj.*, pooh, pooh
practice, *n.*, plot, artifice, treason; treachery
practisant, partner in stratagem
practise, to plot, scheme, work craftily; (on, upon), work craftily upon or against, plot against
præmunire, the act of asserting or maintaining the authority of the Pope in England
praise, *n.*, merit, virtue; *v.*, to appraise
pray in aid, to ask for assistance
precedence, that which precedes
precedent, former
precedent, the original; indicative sign
precept, a written order, mandate, summons (as from a court or magistrate)
preceptial, in the form of precepts
precipitance, the act of casting one's self down from a height
precurrer, forerunner
precurse, a foretokening (by omens)
predicament, category, class; situation
predict, prediction
predominance, controlling astrological influence
preface, prologue
prefer, to present; advance, promote; recommend (for service)
prefixed, previously appointed
pregnancy, quick wit
pregnant, ready; quick-witted, clever; evident, obvious
pregnantly, readily and clearly
premised, sent before the appointed time
prenominate, *v.*, to name in advance; *adj.*, foresaid
prenzie, *an unknown word, probably a misreading* (*M. for M.*, iii, 1, 94, 97)
prepare, preparation
preposterous, extraordinary (*W. T.*, v, 2, 159)
prescript, *n.*, an order, mandate, instructions; *adj.*, prescriptive, regular and proper
presence, assembly, noble company; person; presence chamber
present, *adj.*, immediate, instant; *n.*, present time (moment) or occasion or business; ready money
present, to show, figure, represent; personate; bring a charge against
presentation, semblance
presently, immediately, instantly
presentment, presentation; representation (in portraiture)
press, *n.*, crowd, throng; conscription, impressment; *v.*, to crowd; force to enlist
press money, money paid to one on enlistment
pressure, shape, figure; impression on the mind, idea
prest, ready
Prester (i.e., priest) John, a fabulous Eastern ruler (both priest and king)
presupposed (upon), ascribed to (one) beforehand
pretence, purpose, intention
pretend, to intend, purpose; indicate; allege, lay claim to
pretender, claimant
prevail, avail
prevailment, persuasive force
prevent, anticipate; forestall
price, prize
prick, *n.*, a point on the dial; the bull's-eye; a dot in writing, a slight thing (*T. and C.*, i, 3, 343); a skewer; a spine (of a hedgehog); *pl.*, archery; *v.*, to spur, incite; to indicate or check by a puncture or dot; to stick, insert
pricket, a buck in the second year
pricksong, song with written notes
pride, display (in dress, etc.), fine attire, pomp; glory; height, highest pitch, prime; heat (*Oth.*, iii, 3, 404)
prig, thief
prime, *adj.*, first; chief; lustful; *n.*, the spring
primer, more pressing or immediate
primero, a kind of card game
primerose, primrose
primest, first; best
primy nature, the springtime of life
prince it, to act like a prince
principality, an angel of high rank
principals, the main timbers or posts (*Per.*, iii, 2, 16)
princox, a saucy youngster
print (in), by rule, methodically
prisonment, imprisonment
private, privacy; private (unofficial) communication
prize, *n.*, a match for a prize, an athletic contest; (war's), the rule in the game of war (*3 Hen. VI*, i, 4, 59); *v.*, to appraise, rate
prizer, a professional athlete; an appraiser, valuer
probal, *adj.*, such as to win assent, probable
probation, proof, demonstration; examination
process, the course of events; a story, an account; legal method; summons; mandate
process-server, a sheriff's officer, bailiff
procreant cradle, cradle for offspring
procurator, agent, proxy
procure, to bring (one); carry on the trade of procuress
prodigiously, by monstrous births
proditor, traitor
proface, may it do you good! your health!
professed, full of professions of love (*Lear*, i, 1, 275)
profession, occupation, trade
professor, a teacher or professor of religion
progeny, ancestry; lineage
progress, a formal journey by a sovereign
proin, to prune
project, to set forth, expound
projection, planning
prolixious, long drawn out
prolong, postpone
prompture, incitement, instigation
prone, eager, headlong
proof, *n.*, tested armour; impenetrability; experience; *adj.*, invulnerable, impregnable
propagate, to hand down; increase
propagation (for), in order to procure the handing down (due payment) (*M. for M.*, i, 2, 154)
propend, incline
propension, inclination
proper, one's own, peculiar; appropriate; (to), characteristic (of), appropriate (to); handsome; fine
properly, peculiarly
propertied, endowed with qualities
property, *n.*, identity; essential or characteristic quality; a thing to make use of, a tool; *v.*, to make subsidiary; to make (one) a mere agent or tool or chattel
proportion, portion, fortune; preponderance (*Macb.*, i, 4, 19); *pl.*, levies
propose, *v.*, to imagine; contemplate (as in the future); appoint; talk; *n.*, conversation
proposer, talker, speaker
propriety, one's self, own identity
propugnation, defensive strength
prorogue, to put off, postpone; prolong; make torpid by procrastination
prosperous, favourable, propitious
protest, *v.*, to proclaim, declare; *n.*, protestation, asseveration
protractive, long drawn out
proud, gorgeous (*esp.* of attire); high-mettled
provand, provender
provincial (here), belonging to this province or division of my order (*M. for M.*, v, 1, 318)
provoke, incite
prune, to trim and adjust the feathers, preen; trim and deck out
pudder, *see* poother
pudding, sausage
pudency, modesty
pugging, thievish
puisny (puny), raw, untrained
puissance, power; strength; armed forces
puissant, powerful, mighty
puke-stocking, wearing dark woollen stockings (*1 Hen. IV*, ii, 4, 78)

pullet-sperm, eggs
pulsidge, *for* pulse (*2 Hen. IV*, ii, 4, 26)
pumpion, pumpkin
pun, to pound
punk, a strumpet
punto, a thrust; (reverso *for* riverso), a back-handed thrust
puny, *see* puisne
purchase, *n.*, acquisition, gain; booty, loot; *v.*, to acquire, get; get by robbery
purgation, a cleansing of the system by cathartics; a cleansing of the conscience by confession
purge, to take physic
purl, rise in a spiral (*Lucr.*, 1407)
purple, the purple orchis
pursuivant, heraldic officer; a king's messenger
purveyor, an officer who arranges for the supplies on a royal progress
push, *interj.*, pshaw, pish; *n.*, a scoff (*M. Ado*, v, 1, 38)
pushes, straits, difficulties
push-pin, a children's game with pins
pussel, a harlot
put (*with inf.*), to cause, make; (forth), to emerge, appear; venture, hazard; show one's self; utter; (in), to interpose, intercede; present one's claim; (o'er), to refer; (on), to urge on, prompt, instigate, encourage; (to't), to put to the test, put to straits; (up), to pocket; tamely submit to, endure without resenting; (upon, on), to report, bring to one's attention; address (words) to one; force or inflict on, apply to; lay to one's charge
putter-on, inciter, instigator
putter-out, one who puts out or deposits money as a stake
puttock, a kite (the bird)
pyramis, pyramid

quail, *n.*, a wanton
quail, *v.*, to intimidate; destroy
quaint, ingenious, elaborate; fine, elegant; skilful; dainty, delicate
quaintly, ingeniously, skilfully; delicately
quaked, *p.p.*, made to shiver
qualification, pacification
qualify, to moderate; mitigate; calm, pacify; dilute
quality, the essential and characteristic quality, nature; an accomplishment; profession (*esp.*, that of an actor); ability, professional skill; rank
quantity, a small amount; small piece, bit; diminutive creature
quarrel, complaint; cause or ground of complaint or of dispute, cause; case
quarrelous, quarrelsome
quarry, all the deer killed in a hunt; heap of slain
quarter, a division of an army; range or limit; post; point of the compass; friendly relations, concord; (good) order
quartered, *adj.*, in the different quarters of the camp (*Cymb.*, iv, 4, 18)
quat, pimple
quatch, broad and fat
quean, wench, hussy
queasiness, nausea, loathing
queasy, inclined to nausea, qualmish; fastidious; nauseated, disgusted; ticklish (*Lear*, ii, 1, 19)
quell, *v.*, to kill, destroy; *n.*, slaughter
queller, killer
quench, become calm
quern, hand mill
quest, inquest
questant, seeker after honour, aspirant
question, *n.*, talk, conversation, dialogue; converse; subject of talk or dispute; *v.*, to discuss; talk, converse; speak to
questionable, demanding to be spoken to
questrist, seeker, one in quest of
quick, living, alive; lively, sprightly, quick-witted; with child
quicken, bring to life; revive; refresh; come to life
quiddity (quiddit), a subtle definition or distinction (*esp.* in law), quibble
quid for quo, tit for tat
quietus, receipt in full, final settlement
quill (in the), in concert, all together (*2 Hen. VI*, i, 3, 4)
quillet, a legal subtlety, quibble
quintain, a post or block set up to tilt at
qui passa, a certain tune (*T. N. K.*, iii, 5, 86)
quire, *n.*, company
quire (quier), *v.*, to sing in harmony; harmonize
quirk, a flourish (with the pen); evasion; eccentricity; odd variety; quip
quit, to release; remit; acquit; repay, reward, requite; avenge
quite, to repay in kind (*Rich. II*, v, 1, 43); requite
quittal, requital (*Lucr.*, 236)
quittance, *n.*, discharge (from debt); recompense; *v.*, to repay
quiver, nimble (*2 Hen. IV*, iii, 2, 301)
quoif, *see* coif
quote, to note, observe; scrutinize; set down, designate; mark (by contrast); show, exhibit; interpret, understand
quoth 'a? (koth-a?), did he say? (used to express or suggest dissent or irony)
quotidian, a fever that recurs daily

rabbit-sucket, a sucking rabbit
rable, rabble (*T. N. K.*, iii, 5, 106)
race (raze), a root
race, herd; native disposition, temper
rack, *n.*, floating cloud or mist; *v.*, to drive before the wind
rack, *v.*, to stretch, strain; raise unduly, exaggerate
racker, one who tortures and distorts
raddock, the ruddock, robin
rage, to enrage
ragged, rough; harsh
rag-of-muffin, ragamuffin
rake up, to cover lightly (*Lear*, iv, 6, 281)
ramp, a strumpet (*Cymb.*, i, 6, 134)
rampallian, rampant creature
rampired, barred and barricaded
randon, random
range, *n.*, a rank; *v.*, to rank, take rank; stand in order
ranged, *adj.*, arranged in order
rank, *n.*, a line, row; *adj.*, too luxuriant, overgrown; full, great; insolent; coarse, foul; fetid; in heat
rankle, to cause a festering wound
rankness, exuberance; arrogance
ransacked, *adj.*, carried away as booty
rap, to carry away (with emotion), transport; *p.p.*, enraptured; in a trance; beside one's self
rapture, delirious fit; paroxysm; violent robbery (*Per.*, ii, 1, 161)
rascal, a deer in poor condition
rase (raze), to erase; wipe out, destroy; pull (off)
rash, quick, sudden, hasty; operating quickly; urgent
rashly, hastily
rate, *n.*, estimate; estimation; number; price, value; rank; scale (of living); degree
ratified, duly observed, kept (*L. L. L.*, iv, 2, 125)
ratolorum, *for* rotulorum (of the rolls) (*M. W.*, i, 1, 8)
raught, reached
ravel, to become tangled; (out), unravel, disentangle
ravelled, *adj.*, tangled
ravin, *adj.*, ravening, raging with hunger
ravin (raven), to swallow or devour greedily
ravined, ravenous
ravished, *p.p.*, torn or snatched away from (*T. N. K.*, ii, 2, 22)
rawly, in an unprovided condition
rawness, inconsiderate haste
rayed, befouled; bedraggled
raze (race), *n.*, a root
raze, *v.*, *see* rase
razed, with ornamental slashes or openwork
razure, erasure
reach, far-reaching mental powers
read, to lecture, give instruction, teach
reading, *n.*, learning, erudition; interpretation
ready, dressed
re-answer, compensate, balance
rearward, the rear guard, rear
reason, *n.*, talk; a remark; (do), to give one satisfaction; *v.*, to talk, converse; discuss; explain
reave, bereave, deprive
rebate, to dull
rebato, a kind of high collar (*M. Ado*, iii, 4, 6)
rebellious, fighting against, meeting blow with blow (*Macb.*, i, 2, 56)
rebuke, *n.*, a shameful defeat, discomfiture; chastisement; *v.*, to check, repress; discomfit; cow, overawe
rebused, *for* abused (*T. of S.*, i, 2, 7)
receipt, what is received; size, capacity; reception; receptacle
receive, to accept as true, believe
received, *adj.*, accepted, approved
receiving, *n.*, receptivity, apprehension
recheat, a set of notes on the horn to call back the dogs
reck, to care
reclaim, to restrain, check
reclusive, retired (as a recluse)
recognizance, a token, keepsake; a bond given (to appear, pay a debt, etc.)
recoil, to go back, revert; give way; degenerate
recollect, to collect, gather

recollected, *adj.*, studied and elaborate (*T. N.*, ii, 4, 5)
recomforted, restored to happiness
recomforture, consolation
recompt, to recount
record, *n.*, a witness; *v.*, to bear witness; vouch for; sing. *See* recorder
recordation, memorial; repetition from memory (*T. and C.*, v, 2, 116)
recorder (record) a kind of musical pipe
recountment, narrative, story
recourse, repeated flowing
recover, to revive, restore, cure; get, obtain, win; reach
rectorship, authority as ruler
recure, to cure, restore to health
rede, advice, counsel
redeliver, to report in reply
redemption, ransom; rescue
red lattice, a mark of an alehouse
reduce, bring back; bring
reechy, smoke-begrimed; reeking, filthy
reed, *adj.*, piping (*M. of V.*, iii, 4, 67)
reeky, malodorous
reeling ripe, ready to stagger
refel, refute
refer (one's self), to appeal; stipulate for; take up with
reference, assignment; appeal; (have . . . to), to centre in
reflect, to shine
reflection, shining
reflex, *n.*, reflected light; *v.*, to shed, direct
reform, *for* inform (*M. Ado*, v, 1, 262)
refrain, hold back
refuge, plead in excuse of
refuse, renounce, disown
regard, *n.*, a look; view, sight; consideration, attention; respect; *pl.*, conditions, terms; *v.*, to look at; notice; honour; consider
regent, ruler, governor
regiment, authority as a ruler; regularity, order
region, the sky, upper air, heavens; station, rank
regreet, *n.*, greeting; *v.*, to greet again; greet; return to; address; send greetings
reguerdon, *n.*, *v.*, reward
rehearse, relate, recite; pronounce
reinforce, to rally (*Hen. V*, iv, 6, 36); bring up reinforcements (*Cymb.*, v, 2, 18)
reinforcement, a fresh assault (*Cor.*, ii, 2, 117)
rejoindure, reunion
rejourn, adjourn
relapse, a rebounding, recoil
relation, story, report, account, discourse
relative, going back to the fact, decisive, conclusive (*Haml.*, ii, 2, 632)
religion, religious devotion or obligation
religious, devoted; conscientious (*Hen. VIII*, iv, 2, 74)
relish, *n.*, a taste, smack; quality; meaning; *v.*, to taste; recognize; enjoy; have the taste of
relume, rekindle
remain, *n.*, stay; residue
remediate, curative
remember, to remind; mention
remonstrance, manifestation
remorse, compassion, pity
remorseful, compassionate
remote, distant
remotion, keeping away, aloofness
remove, a stage (of a progress); the raising of a siege; removal (by death)
removed, sequestered, recluse; remote, solitary
removedness, frequent absence
render, *v.*, to report, repeat; surrender; *n.*, an account, statement; payment
renegado, apostate (*T. N.*, iii, 2, 74)
renege, deny; renounce
renew, rally, renew the fight
renouncement, withdrawal from a worldly life
renowmed, renowned
rent, to rend, tear
reny, to deny
repair, *n.*, amendment, restoration; coming, arrival; *v.*, to revive, restore; come, go
repast, to feed, nourish
repasture, sustenance
repeal, *n.*, *v.*, recall
replenished, *adj.*, complete, perfect; well-stored
replication, echo; reply, answer
report, *n.*, a reporter, informant; *v.*, (themselves), to speak and tell what they were (*Cymb.*, ii, 4, 83)
reportingly, by report, on hearsay evidence
reprehend, *for* represent (*L. L. L.*, i, 1, 184)
reprisal, prize
reprobance, reprobation
reproof, disproof, refutation
reprove, disprove
repugn, contend against
repugnancy, active resistance
repugnant, refractory
repured, *see* thrice-repured
reputing of, making much of, vaunting (*2 Hen. VI*, iii, 1, 48)
requicken, revivify
require, to request, ask for; call for, deserve
required, *adj.*, requisite, due
requiring, *n.*, asking, requesting, petition
requit, requite
reremice, bats
reserve, preserve, keep safe, keep
resist, to be distasteful to (*Per.*, ii, 3, 29)
resolute, a stout-hearted fellow (*Haml.*, i, 1, 98)
resolution, a state of freedom from doubt (*Lear*, i, 2, 108)
resolve, to explain to (one), clear up one's doubts, satisfy, inform; solve, clear up; dissolve; (one's self), make up one's mind; *n.*, resolution
resolvedly, with detailed explanation (*All's W.*, v, 3, 332)
resorters, regular visitors
respect, *n.*, attention; regard, esteem; reputation; propriety; *v.*, to regard; consider; care for; hold in honour or regard
respected, *for* suspected (*M. for M.*, ii, 1, 170)
respective, considerate, scrupulous; worthy of regard
respectively, respectfully
respite, end of the period of respite (*Rich. III*, v, 1, 19)
responsive, accordant, well-suited (*Haml.*, v, 2, 159)
rest, *n.*, abode, stay; final stake, firm resolution; *v.*, to remain
rest (to set up one's), to risk one's final stake, to be resolved (at all hazards), make up one's mind; make one's abode.
'rest, to arrest
restem, to hold (their course) in the opposite direction (*Oth.*, i, 3, 37)
restrain, to pull back tightly; withhold
resty, torpid, sluggish, slothful
resume, take (*Tim.*, ii, 2, 4)
retail, hand down by retelling, recount, relate
retain, take into service; recover
retention, limitation; capacity; detention; (poor), thing of slight capacity (*Sonn.*, 122)
retentive, *adj.*, detaining, imprisoning; (to), strong enough to restrain
retire, *n.*, retreat, falling back; withdrawal; repair, resort
retort, to repay (*M. W.*, ii, 2, 1)
retrograde, moving backward, i.e., in a direction from east to west, contrary to the order of the signs of the zodiac
return, send or make answer
revenge, *n.*, vengeance, retribution; *v.*, to avenge
revengement, retribution, condign punishment
reverb, reverberate
reverberate, *adj.*, re-echoing
reverent, reverend
reverse, a backhanded stroke
revolt, *n.*, a rebel; *v.*, to draw back (from a wrong course) (*2 Hen. VI*, iv, 2, 133)
revolted, unfaithful
reword, to repeat by echoing
rheum, a watery discharge (tears, saliva, mucus); cold in the head, catarrh; rheumatic disorder
rheumatic, affected with catarrh; damp and misty; irritable; delirious (*Hen. V*, ii, 3, 40)
rheumy, damp
rib, to enclose
ribald-rid, ridden by ribalds
riband, ribbon
rid, to dispatch, destroy; get over, put behind one; (way), make quick progress (*3 Hen. VI*, v, 3, 21)
riggish, wanton
right, regular, thoroughgoing
rigoll, circle; ring
rim, midriff
ripe, ready
ripely, fully, decidedly
ripeness, *n.*, being prepared, a state of preparation
rivage, shore
rival, partner, associate
rivality, copartnership
rivelled, dry and furrowed
rivo, a reveller's interjection of no definite meaning, apparently an incentive to drink and be merry
road, a place where ships ride at anchor, harbour or roadstead; stage of a journey; inroad, raid; strumpet
Roan, Rouen
roast, *see* rule
robustious, violent; boisterous, noisy
rod, a staff carried as a symbol of office; sceptre

roguing, *adj.*, wandering
roguing thieves, roving pirates
roguish, vagrant
roisting, *adj.*, blustering, rousing
romage, turmoil of labour
Romish, Roman
rondure (roundure), circle
ronyon (runnion), a mangy creature, hag
roofed, under one roof (*Macb.*, iii, 4, 40)
rook, to perch in huddled fashion
rooky, frequented by rooks
ropery, knavish talk (*R. and J.*, ii, 4, 154)
rope-tricks, knavish tricks and talk (*T. of S.*, i, 2, 112)
roping, *adj.*, hanging in ropes
Rossillion, Rousillon
roted, learned by heart (*Cor.*, iii, 2, 55)
rother, ox
round, *n.*, a dance in a circle; *adj.*, plain, honest; outspoken, blunt; *adv.*, without mincing matters; *v.*, to surround, encircle
round, to whisper
roundel, a dance in a circle
roundly, outspokenly; without ceremony; in thoroughgoing fashion
roundure, *see* rondure
rouse, a bumper; (takes his), carouses
rout, company; gang; rabble; brawl
row, line, verse (*Haml.*, ii, 2, 438)
Rowland, Roland, the most famous of Charlemagne's Twelve Peers
royal, a gold coin worth half a pound
roynish, scurvy, paltry
rub, *n.*, impediment (in bowling), obstacle; annoyance; a rough place (not well finished); *v.*, to hinder; (on), to go on in spite of difficulties
rubied (rubious), ruby-red
rudesby, insolent fellow
ruffle, *n.*, bustle, noisy life (*Compl.*, 58); *v.*, to swagger; bluster; maltreat; outrage; (up), rouse to anger
ruffling, *adj.*, rich and showy (*T. of S.*, iv, 3, 60)
rug-headed, shaggy-haired
ruinate, to ruin, bring to destruction
rule, behaviour, conduct; manner of proceeding
rule the roast, to be master of the feast, carry all before one
rumour, noise, din, uproar
rump-fed, fat-rumped (*Macb.*, i, 3, 6)
runagate, renegade, traitor; runaway, fugitive
running, *adj.*, hasty, hurried, slight (*Hen. VIII*, i, 4, 12)
runnion, *see* ronyon
rush aside, to force or push aside
rushle, to rustle (*M. W.*, ii, 2, 68)
rustle, to rush noisily
ruttish, lecherous

'S, God's
's, us; she is (*Per.*, iv, Gow., 4)
s', so (*Cor.*, iv, 6, 120)
Saba, the Queen of Sheba
sack, a general term for sherry and similar wines
sackbut, a kind of trumpet or trombone
Sackerson, a famous Paris Garden bear
sacrificial, expressing devotion (*Tim.*, i, 1, 81)
sacring bell, a bell rung at mass at the elevation of the host
sad, grave, serious; glum, morose
sadness, seriousness; (in, in good), in earnest, in very truth
safe, *adj.*, sound; *v.*, to conduct in safety; make safe, obviate anxiety about (anything)
safety, safe custody
Sagittary, a Centaur; a house in Venice with the sign of the Centaur
sain, *p.p.*, said (*L. L. L.*, iii, 1, 83)
Saint Martin's summer, Indian summer
Saint Nicholas' clerks, robbers
salamander, a fabulous animal that lives in the element of fire
sale-work, wares made for sale (not for one's own use), hence of inferior quality
sallet, salad; a kind of helmet; spicy passage (*Haml.*, ii, 2, 462)
salt, *adj.*, stinging, mordant; lustful
saltiers, jumpers, *for* satyrs (*W. T.*, iv, 4, 334)
salute, to affect, stir (*Hen. VIII*, ii, 3, 103)
salvage, a savage
Samingo, *for* San (Saint) Domingo (*2 Hen. IV*, v, 3, 79)
sampire, samphire
sanctimonious, sacred, holy
sanctimony, a sacred obligation; faithfulness to such obligations
sanctuarize, to afford the protection of a sanctuary
sand-blind, dim of sight, purblind
sanded, of a sandy colour
sanguine, blood-red; ruddy; of a sanguine temperament physically
sans, without
sarcenet, a fine soft silk fabric; flimsy
Sarum, Salisbury
satire, satirist (*Sonn.*, 100)
saucy, insolently insistent; lascivious
savage, growing wild (*Hen. V*, iii, 5, 7)
savagery, wild vegetation, weeds
savour, get the taste of (*Lear*, iv, 2, 39)
sawn, sown (*Compl.*, 91)
say, *n.*, touch, trace
say, a kind of cloth resembling serge
'say, to assay, to make trial (*Per.*, i, 1, 59)
'Sblood, God's blood (an oath)
scaffolage, scaffoldage, wooden platform, stage
scald, scabby; scurvy, miserable
scale, to weigh in the balance
scall, *for* scald (*M. W.*, iii, 1, 123)
scamble, to scramble; struggle confusedly; fight
scamel, some kind of sea bird (*Temp.*, ii, 2, 176)
scandal, *n.*, censure; *v.*, to defame; cause to be defamed
scandaled, scandalous
scandalized, defamed; held in ill repute
scant, *adv.*, hardly, scarcely
scantling, a small pattern or specimen
scantly, grudgingly, with slight appreciation
scape, escape; escapade, prank; *pl.*, doings (*with a pun on* escape) (*M. of V.*, ii, 2, 174); *v.*, to escape
scarf, to wrap; (up), muffle, blindfold
scarfed, *adj.*, adorned with pennants and flags
scarre, a rock, precipice (*All's W.*, iv, 2, 38: *probably a misprint*)
scath (scathe), harm, injury
scathful, harmful, damaging
school, schooling, learning
school-doing, the actions and behaviour in which one has been schooled (*T. N. K.*, v, 4, 68)
science, knowledge, learning
sconce, a small fort, an earthwork; head, pate
scornful, disdained, bemocked (*Lucr.*, 520)
scot and lot, a municipal tax; payment in full
scotch, *n.*, a gash; *v.*, to gash, slash
scour, to run fast; purge
scrimer, fencer
scrip, a written list; a wallet or satchel; (and scrippage), a wallet and its contents (*A. Y. L.*, iii, 2, 171)
scripture, a sacred writing
scrowl, to scrawl, write clumsily; signify one's meaning (*T. A.*, ii, 4, 5)
scroyle, a scurvy wretch
scrubbed, stunted
scuffle, to fight or fence hand to hand or at close quarters
scull, a school of fish (*T. and C.*, v, 5, 22)
'scuse, an excuse
scut, tail (of a deer)
'Sdeath, God's death
seal, *n.*, confirmation, fulfilment; *v.*, to confirm, ratify
sea-like, in naval array (*A. and C.*, iii, 13, 171)
seam, fat, grease
seamy side without, wrong side out
search, *n.*, band of searchers; *v.*, to probe
season, a preservative; soundness; *v.*, to ripen; make ready; pickle, preserve; to control, moderate
seconds, inferior flour, second-rate matter (*Sonn.*, 125)
sect, class; party, faction; cutting; sex
secure, *adj.*, free from care; overconfident, careless, heedless; unsuspecting; *v.*, to make confident or careless
securely, without foreboding; heedlessly, without caution
security, lack of care or caution
seeded, run to seed, full-grown
seedness, the state of being just sown
seel, to sew up the eyes of (a falcon); *fig.*, to blind
seely, *see* silly
seeming, *n.*, appearance; false appearance; likelihood; *adv.*, becomingly
seen (well), well-skilled
segregation, dispersion
seignory, older rank, seniority (*Rich. III*, iv, 4, 36)
seized of, legally possessed of
seld, seldom
seldom, infrequent
seld-shown, rarely appearing in public
self, one's own; same
self-abuse, self-deception
self-admission, personal preference (*T. and C.*, ii, 3, 176)
self-affected, partial to one's self

self-assumption, self-conceit
self-bounty, natural goodness of heart
self-breath, one's own speech
self-comparisons (with), in actions that matched his own (*Macb.*, i, 2, 55)
self-covered, whose (woman's) self is covered (by a monstrous appearance) (*Lear*, iv, 2, 62)
self-figured, planned by one's self
self-gracious, spontaneously kind
self-substantial, consisting of one's own substance
self-unable, inadequate in itself (*All's W.*, iii, 1, 13)
semblable, *adj.*, similar; in seeming; *n.*, one's like
semblably, in appearance
semblative, in appearance (*T. N.*, i, 4, 34)
sempster, tailor (*T. N. K.*, iii, 5, 44)
sennet, a trumpet signal
se'nnight (sev'nnight, sevennight), a week
Senoys, Sienese, inhabitants of Siena
sense, sensuous perception; mental perception; sensual passion; (to the), to the quick
senses, good sense (*Hen. V*, ii, 3, 51)
sensible, capable of feeling, sensitive; keenly or deeply felt; of the senses or one of them (*Haml.*, i, 1, 57)
sensibly, intensely, acutely; in conscious being (*T. A.*, iv, 2, 122)
sentence, axiom, sententious remark
separable, *adj.*, that separates (*Sonn.*, 36)
Septentrion, the North
sequent, following; follower
sequester, sequestration
sere, a part of a gun-lock between the hammer and the trigger
sergeant, a sheriff's officer
serpigo (suppeago), a skin disease
servant, lover, suitor
servanted to, in the service of
sessa, *interj.*, come! away!
set, to value, appraise; wager, stake, risk; (down), encamp or lay siege; (off), compensate, atone for
Setebos, the chief deity of Sycorax (in fact, of the Patagonians) (*Temp.*, i, 2, 373)
setter, one who arranges opportunities for highwaymen (*1 Hen. IV*, ii, 2, 53)
sevennight (sev'nnight), *see* se'nnight
several, different, distinct; distinctive; privately owned
severals, individual persons or things; details, particulars
sewer, an attendant in charge of the service (at a feast)
'Sfoot, God's foot
shades, Hades, the world below
shadow, *n.*, protecting shade, shelter; shady spot; *v.*, to shelter
shadowing, *adj.*, darkening, obscuring one's consciousness
shadowy, frequenting the shady woods
shag, shaggy
shag-eared, with shaggy hair hanging about the ears (*Macb.*, iv, 2, 83)
shale, shell (of a nut)
shall, inevitably will
shall 's, shall we
shard, a potsherd, fragment of pottery
shard-borne, borne up by wings (or wing cases) like shards or bits of pottery (*Macb.*, iii, 2, 42)
sharded, having shard-like wing cases
shark up, to gather up hastily and indiscriminately
sharp-looking, lean-faced
shealed, *adj.*, shelled
shearman, one whose trade is to shear woollen cloth
sheaved, made of plaited straw (*Compl.*, 31)
sheed, to shed (*Sonn.*, 34)
sheep-biter, a dog that bites sheep, a malicious fellow
sheep-biting, *adj.*, snarling, ill-tempered
sheer, clear, pure; mere
shent, *p.p.*, scolded, taken to task
sheriff's post, a post at a sheriff's door (for notices, etc.)
sherris (sherris sack), sherry
shield, to forfend, forbid
ship-tire, a headdress like a ship
shive, a slice
shock, to meet in clash of arms
shog, to jog, walk
shoon, shoes
shore, sewer, cesspool
short, to shorten; come short of (*Cymb.*, i, 6, 200)
shot, tavern reckoning; expenditure
shot-free, without paying one's reckoning
shotten, *adj.*, that has cast the roe
shough, a rough-haired lapdog
shoulder in, to push aside into
shouldering, *n.*, jostling, insolent crowding
shoulder-shotten, with lame or dislocated shoulder
shovegroat, a game like shuffleboard played with coins
shovelboard, a shilling used in a game like shuffleboard (*M. W.*, i, 1, 159)
show, a pictured representation (*Lucr.*, 1507)
shrew, to curse (a light word), beshrew
shrewd (shrowd), shrewish, petulant; biting, mordant; harsh, hard; mischievous; bad, ill
shrewdly, sharply, keenly; badly; confoundedly, deucedly
shrieve, sheriff
shrift, confession, whether followed by absolution or not; confessional
shrill-gorged, shrill-throated (in its song)
shrive, to hear confession and absolve
shriver, confessor
shrow, shrew
shrowd, *see* shrewd
shut up, to conclude (*Macb.*, ii, 1, 16)
sib, related, kin
Sicil, Sicily
sick, to fall ill
sicken, to fall ill; impair
sicle, shekel (*M. for M.*, ii, 2, 149)
side, to take sides with (*Cor.*, i, 1, 197)
side-sleeve, a wide, open, hanging sleeve (*M. Ado*, iii, 4, 21)
siege, seat; rank; excrement
sightless, invisible; unsightly, repulsive
sights, the eyeholes in a helmet
sign, *n.*, outward appearance, image; signal flag; *v.*, to mark, designate
significant, sign, significant action; a letter that explains a story (*L. L. L.*, iii, 1, 131)
signiory, the Venetian government
signory, domain of a nobleman, dukedom, etc.; authority as a noble, lordship
silly (seely), innocent, harmless, inoffensive; plain and simple; poor, wretched
silverly, like drops of silver
simple, *adj.*, uncompounded; *n.*, medicinal herb (used in compounding remedies); ingredient
simple-answered, truthful in reply (*Lear*, iii, 7, 43)
simular, *adj.*, counterfeit, specious; (of virtue), simulating goodness
simulation, enigmatical expression
since, when in the past (once upon a time)
single, weak, feeble; sincere
singleness, simplicity
single-soled, thin, miserable
singly, uniquely; by any one man (*Cor.*, ii, 2, 91)
singularity, personality; an artistic rarity
singuled, segregated, separated
sinister, left; illegitimate
sink, to cause to fall or bend
sinking-ripe, all ready to sink
sir, lord; gentleman; dignitary; title of a priest or a university graduate
sirrah, sir (used in anger, insult, or familiarity, or as a title for a servant or an inferior)
sir-reverence (*for* save reverence, *salva reverentia*), with all due respect; *adj.*, not to be mentioned without apology (*R. and J.*, i, 4, 42)
sister, to match, equal (*Per.*, v, Prol., 7)
sistering, *adj.*, close-neighbouring (*Compl.*, 2)
sith, since
sithence, since
sizes, allowances (*Lear*, ii, 4, 178)
skains-mates, swaggering fellows (*R. and J.*, ii, 4, 162)
skiff, to cross in a skiff (*T. N. K.*, i, 3, 37)
skill, reasonable cause, reason
skilless, ignorant
skillet, a kind of saucepan
skills not, makes no difference, matters not
skimble-skamble, incoherent, nonsensical
skipper, saucy youngster (*T. of S.*, ii, 1, 341)
skirr, to scurry, scour; ride rapidly about
slab, viscous
slack, to neglect; be remiss in serving one
slander, *n.*, disgrace; *v.*, to calumniate; disgrace; denounce, upbraid
slanderous, disgraceful, bringing shame (to)
slave, to make a slave of, make subservient to one's own will
sleave, a skein
sleave silk, floss silk
sledded, *adj.*, that ride in sledges (*Haml.*, i, 1, 63)
sleeve-hand, wrist-band, cuff
sleeveless, futile, bootless
sleided, divided into threads
'Slid, God's lid
'Slight, God's light
slight, inattentive, negligent; *v.*, tc

throw contemptuously; (off), to put aside with contempt
slightly, carelessly, inconsiderately, without serious attention
slip, a counterfeit coin; a kind of leash
slipper, slippery, shifty
slipshod, wearing slippers
slobbery, dank and muddy
slops (slop), loose breeches or trousers; loose jacket
slow, to retard, check
slubber, to soil; to do hurriedly, huddle up
sluggardized, made sluggish
sluttery, sluttishness
sly-slow, passing with an imperceptible motion (*Rich. II*, i, 3, 150)
small, the slender part of the leg
smallness, shrill and high quality (of voice)
smatch, *n.*, smack, taste
smatter, to chatter, jabber
smile, to smile at
smilet, little smile
smoke, to torment (as with smoke), baste, thrash; to smell out, detect
smooth, to flatter; foster, encourage; talk insinuatingly
smoother, to smother
smother, stifling smoke
smug, neat and trim, spruce
sneak-cup, one who avoids drinking his share
sneap, *n.*, a snub, a sharp rebuke; *v.*, to nip with cold
sneck up, be hanged, go hang
snipe, insignificant creature
snort, to snore
snuff, open resentment; (to take in), to resent
so, very well, well and good
sod (sodden), *p.p.*, boiled
soft, hold! wait a moment!
soil, explanation (*Sonn.*, 69)
soiled, full-fed with green fodder (*Lear*, iv, 6, 124)
soilure, defilement
sola (sowla), *interj.*, halloo
solace, *n.*, happiness; *v.*, to entertain; take pleasure
soldieress, female warrior
sole, to pull by the ears, pull the ears of
solely, alone
solemn, ceremonial, formal, in due form; stately, state
solemnity, festival, festivity, celebration; solemnizing; dignity, stateliness
solicit, move; allure; prevail with
soliciting, *n.*, prompting, instigation
solidare, a gold coin
something, *adv.*, somewhat
sometime, sometimes; formerly, once
sometimes, formerly
somewhither, to some place or other
sonance, sound, signal
sonties (by God's), an oath of doubtful meaning, perhaps 'sanctity'
soon at night, to-night, this coming night
sooth, *n.*, truth; bland compliance (*Rich. II*, iii, 3, 136); *adj.*, true
soothe, to humour, indulge; flatter
soother, flatterer
sop, anything thoroughly saturated with a liquid
Sophy, the Shah of Persia
sore, a buck in the fourth year
sorel, a sorrel, a buck in the third year
sorrow-wreathen knot, the arms folded in sorrow (*T. A.*, iii, 2, 4)
sort, *n.*, rank; company; manner, way, fashion; lot (to be drawn); *v.*, to sort out, select; ordain; fit, adapt; keep company; be fit, suit, accord; come to pass, come out, result
sortance (hold), to accord
sot, fool, idiot
sotted, besotted, become utterly foolish
sottish, befitting an idiot
soul-fearing, striking terror to the soul
sound, *n.*, *v.*, swoon
soundless, unfathomable
sour (one's cheek), to scowl
souse, swoop down upon
soused, *adj.*, pickled
south, south wind
sovereign, efficacious (as a remedy)
sovereignly, supremely
sovereignty, efficacy
sow (of lead), a large mass
sowla, *see* sola
space, time, interval
span, *n.*, a measure of length, the distance from the tip of the thumb to that of the little finger when both are extended, about nine inches; a short time; *v.*, to limit, measure, bring to an end
span-counter, a game in which the player tries to throw his counter (a small disc) within a span's distance of his opponent's
spaniel, to follow like a spaniel
spare, to be scrupulous about offending (*M. for M.*, ii, 3, 33)
specialty, the essential quality; a particular document; a special contract or bond
speciously, *for* specially (*M. W.*, iii, 4, 113)
speculation, looking on, gazing; the act or faculty of sight; intelligent sight; a scout
speculative, having the faculty of sight
sped (to be), to be finished, done for
speed, *n.*, success, welfare; helper, patron saint, help to success; *v.*, to prosper, succeed; help, cause to prosper
speken, speak (*Per.*, ii, Prol., 12)
spent, used up
sperr, to bar (*T. and C.*, Prol., 19)
spet, to spit
sphere, one of the concentric hollow spheres in which (according to the Ptolemaic astronomy) each planet is fixed; eye socket
sphered, set in a sphere
spherical, planetary
sphery, starry
spill, destroy
spilth, spilling, pouring out
spinner, spider
spinster, spinner; unheroic emotional creature (*T. N. K.*, i, 3, 23)
spirit, vital power, vitality; *pl.*, certain subtle fluids supposed to permeate the blood and organs (classified as 'natural,' 'animal,' and 'vital'); vital powers
spital, hospital
splay, castrate
spleen, impetuosity; impetuous force or fury; passion; malevolence; irascible temper; grudge, ill will; capricious temper or impulse; restlessness; laughter, a fit of laughter, hysterics; a sudden action, flash
spleenful, impetuous, eager; angry
spleeny, ardent, headstrong
splenitive, irascible
splinter, to join and bind up in splints
spoil, to despoil; lay waste, ruin, destroy; seize as prey
spoon, to let (a ship) run before the wind
sportive, wanton
spot, figure in embroidery (*Cor.*, i, 3, 56)
sprag (*for* sprack), quick (*M. W.*, iv, 1, 84)
sprightful, spirited
spring, earliest part, beginning; a shoot
springe, a snare
springhalt, a kind of lameness in horses
sprite, spirit
sprited, haunted
spritely, ghostly, in the form of spirits
spurs, the main roots of a tree
spy, *n.*, note, observation (*Macb.*, iii, 1, 130)
squandered, *p.p.*, scattered
squandering, *adj.*, straggling, random
square, *adj.*, fair, just; *n.*, rule, regularity; a body of troops in square formation; troop; the bosom or breast-piece of a garment; *v.*, to rule, regulate; judge; quarrel, fall out
squarer, a quarrelsome fellow
squash, an unripe peapod; youngster
squier, *see* squire
squiny, peep, look with half-open eyes
squire (squier), a carpenter's square
stablish, establish
stablishment, confirmed possession
staff, stanza
stage, to exhibit publicly; bring on the stage
stagger, to assault, fell; hesitate, be in doubt
staggers, a disease of horses; dizziness; staggering condition, perplexed and ill-regulated life
stain, *n.*, tinge; a nonpareil that puts all others to shame; *v.*, to darken, eclipse; be darkened
stale, *n.*, decoy; laughingstock, butt; prostitute; urine; *v.*, to make stale, cheapen
stall, shut up, keep close; install
stammer, to report or describe imperfectly
stamp, *n.*, a coin; *v.*, to coin; vouch for, mark as true
stanch, satisfy
stanchless, insatiable
stand (on, upon), insist on; make much of; plume one's self on; depend on; concern
standing, *n.*, duration; high rank; *adj.*, stagnant
standing bed, a bed with a bedstead
standing tuck, a rapier standing upright
staniel, a kind of hawk, kestrel
stanze (stanzo), stanza
staple, fibre
star, lodestar; sphere, rank; *pl.*, fortunes

star-blasting, malign influence of the stars
star-crossed, thwarted by evil stars, ill-fated
stare, stand on end
stargazer, astrologer
starting hole, hole in which to take refuge, evasion
start-up, upstart
starve, benumb or kill with cold; paralyze; perish with cold; (out), outwatch
starved, shrunken, mean
state, *n.*, attitude in standing; estate; rank; high rank, majesty; appearance in state; a person of high rank or authority; chair of state
station, attitude when standing
statist, statesman, politician
statute, a special kind of bond
statute cap, a plain woollen cap prescribed by statute for persons below a certain rank
stead, to be of use, assist, oblige; (up), supply
stealth, theft; imperceptible movement; stealing away
steely, made of steel; unbending, inflexible
steepy, steep; precipitous
steerage, steering
stell, to fix, place
stelled, starry (*Lear*, iii, 7, 61)
sternage, the sterns
stick, to place, set; scruple, hesitate
sticking place, the place where it will remain fixed
stickler-like, like one who separates combatants
stiff, formidable, harsh (*A. and C.*, i, 2, 104)
stigmatic, one marked with deformity as with a brand of infamy
stigmatical, marked with deformity, misshapen
still, ever, always, constantly
still an end, without ceasing (*Two G.*, iv, 4, 67)
stillatory, a still
still-piecing, always closing again (*All's W.*, iii, 2, 113)
still-vexed, constantly buffeted by storms
sting, instinctive impulse
stitchery, needlework
stithy, *n.*, smithy; *v.*, to fashion at the anvil
stoccado (stoccata), a thrust
stock, stoccado, thrust; stocking
stockfish, dried codfish
stockish, stupid, insensible
stomach, *n.*, appetite; anger, resentment; arrogance; high spirit, courage; *v.*, to resent
stomaching, *n.*, quarrelling
stone, *n.*, *see* thunder-stone; *v.*, to make as hard as stone
stone-bow, a bow used for shooting stones
stonish, to confuse, astonish, disconcert
stoolball, a game resembling cricket (stool = wicket)
stope, *see* stoup
store, abundance, plenty; stuff, material; progeny
story, *n.*, history; *v.*, to recount, relate
stoup (stope), a large glass or tankard
stout, brave, bold; haughty
stoutness, arrogance
stover, winter food for cattle
straight, straightway, immediately
straight-pight, erect in carriage (*Cymb.*, v, 5, 164)
strain, *n.*, lineage, race; inherited or native character; trait of character; sort, kind; tendency; difficulty in believing, doubt; *v.*, to force; exaggerate; do violence to one's nature (*W. T.*, iii, 2, 51); (at), make a difficulty about, object to
strained, *adj.*, forced, artificial, exaggerated
strait, stingy; strict; pressing, rigorous
straited, *adj.*, in straits, at a loss
straitness, strictness, rigour
strange, foreign, alien; distant (in manner); extraordinary, remarkable
strange-achieved, acquired by extraordinary efforts or in foreign lands (*2 Hen. IV*, iv, 5, 72)
strangely, extraordinarily, surprisingly; like a stranger, as a foreigner (*W. T.*, ii, 3, 181)
strangeness, coldness of manner, aloofness
strangered, cast off as an alien
strappado, a torture in which the victim was hoisted by a pulley attached to his hands (which were strapped together behind him) and was let part way down with a jerk
stratagem, a frightful deed
stray, *n.*, straggler; *v.*, to lead astray
streamer, banner
strength, forces, army
strewments, flowers strewed
stricture, strict self-restraint
stride, to step over
strike, *n.*, a measure, a bushel; to strike (lower, take in) sail; smite with malign influence; broach (a cask)
striker, footpad
strond, strand
strossers, trousers
strow, strew
stroy, destroy
stubborn, rough, harsh, rude
stubbornness, roughness
stuck (stuck-in), a thrust, stoccado
studied, inclined, disposed
study, commit to memory
subdue to, to bring into conformity with
subduement, subdual
subject, subjects (collectively)
suborn, corruptly or by underhand means to procure or induce one to commit an unlawful or unworthy deed
subscribe, to sign away, renounce; to yield, submit, give way; declare, publish; assent to; (for), vouch for
subscription, deference, submission
substractor, caluminator, detractor
subtile (subtle), fine, delicate; crafty, artful, deceitful; deceptive
subtilly (subtly), artfully, craftily, deceitfully
subtilty (subtlety), craft; artful plan; illusion
succeeding, sequel, consequence
success, succession; what ensues, the course of time; the outcome (good or ill), the issue
successantly, immediately (*T. A.*, iv, 4, 113)
successive, hereditary, next in succession
successively, by hereditary succession
sudden, speedy, prompt; impromptu; hasty
suddenly, immediately, without delay
suffer, to suffer death, be executed
suffered, *p.p.*, let alone, allowed, permitted
sufferance, suffering; damage; forbearance, indulgence, acquiescence
suffering, submissive, tame
sufficiency, ability
sufficient, able; of adequate means
suffigance, *for* sufficience (*M. Ado*, iii, 5, 56)
suggest, tempt; insinuate to; woo
suggestion, temptation; wily insinuation (*Hen. VIII*, iv, 2, 35)
suit, *n.*, obligatory attendance; *v.*, to dress, attire; agree, accord
suited, adapted, nicely adjusted
suits (out of), out of favour
sullen, dismal, dark
sullens, moroseness, the dumps (*Rich. II*, ii, 1, 139)
sumless, countless, inestimable
summer-seeming, befitting the summer of life (*Macb.*, iv, 3, 86)
summoner, a sheriff's officer
sumpter, packhorse
sup, provide supper for, feed
superfluous, having more than one needs
superflux, superfluity
superpraise, to praise in excess
superscript, superscription, address (on a letter)
superserviceable, officious (*Lear*, ii, 2, 19)
superstitiously, with punctilious exactness (*W. T.*, iii, 3, 40)
supervise (on the), immediately after reading it over (*Haml.*, v, 2, 23)
supervisor, looker-on
suppeago, *see* serpigo
supplant, uproot, get rid of; knock out (*Temp.*, iii, 2, 55)
suppliance, what fills up, pastime
supply, to satisfy one's desire
supplyant, supplementary (*Cymb.*, iii, 7, 14)
supplyment, continued supply
supposal, opinion
suppose, supposition; expectation
supposed, *for* deposed (*M. for M.*, ii, 1, 163)
sur-addition, surname
surance, assurance
surcease, *n.*, coming to an end; *v.* to cease
surety, *n.*, confidence in one's safety; *v.*, to be surety or bail for
surprise, seize, capture; overpower
sur-reined, exhausted by hard riding, overridden
survey, to note, perceive (*Macb.*, i, 2, 31)
surveyor, supervisor, overseer; official in charge of the lands of an estate
suspect, *n.*, suspicion; *v.*, *for* respect (*M. Ado*, iv, 2, 77)
Sutton Co'fil', Sutton Coldfield in Warwickshire
swabber, a petty officer in charge of keeping the decks clean
swaddling, *see* swathling
swag-bellied, with hanging paunch
swarth (swart), swarthy, black, dark
swarth (swath), what is cut by one sweeping of the scythe

swasher, swaggerer, bully
swashing, *adj.*, swaggering
swath, *see* swarth
swath, swaddling clothes
swathling (swathing) clothes (swaddling clouts), clothes in which one is swaddled or wrapped
sway, *n.*, balanced motion; drawing or controlling force; *v.*, to turn aside; move
swayed, having a depression because of strain (*T. of S.*, iii, 2, 56)
swear, to invoke in swearing (*Lear*, i, 1, 163)
sweep, pompous motion, procession (*Tim.*, i, 2, 137)
sweet, fond of sweets (*Two G.*, iii, 1, 330)
sweet and twenty, one twenty times sweet, superlatively sweet (*T. N.*, ii, 3, 52)
sweeting, a sweet apple; sweet one
sweet-suggesting, sweetly seductive (*Two G.*, ii, 6, 7)
swelling, rising in clouds
swilled, washed (by dashing waves)
swinge, impetus, sway
swinge-buckler, one who strikes a buckler with dashing blows, swash-buckler, dashing fighter, roisterer
Switzers, Swiss bodyguard
swoond, to swoon
swoopstake, sweeping up all the stakes at one swoop, without discrimination
sword-and-buckler, *adj.*, using the weapons of the common people, swaggering in low company (*1 Hen. IV*, i, 3, 230)
'Swounds (Zounds), God's wounds
sympathize, agree, accord; sympathize with
sympathized, harmoniously arranged, consistent; harmoniously associated; described or expressed in one's veritable likeness
sympathy, agreement, conformity, equality

ta, thou (*2 Hen. IV*, ii, 1, 63)
table, *n.*, tablet; palm of the hand; *v.*, to set down in a list or catalogue
table book, memorandum book
tables, tablets for memoranda; backgammon
tabour, a small drum
tabourer, drummer on the tabour
tabourin, a kind of drum
tackled stair, rope ladder
taffeta, *n.*, a kind of silk; *adj.*, fine as silk
taffety, finely dressed in silk
tag, the rabble
taincture, defilement
taint, *n.*, loss of reputation, discredit; *v.*, to find fault with, discredit, disparage; hold culpable
take, to charm, enchant, please; strike with malignant power (by witchcraft or demonic influence), blast, infect; (to), betake one's self to; leap over; give (a blow, etc.); (air), come out, become known; (head), move violently away; (in), take, capture, subdue; (me with you), let me understand you; (off), kill; (on), pretend; (order), make arrangements; (out), copy; (peace, truce), come to terms; (scorn), disdain; (thought), become melancholy, grieve; (up), make up, settle, reconcile; purchase on credit; levy, enlist; rebuke; cope with
taking, infectious, blasting
tale (as thick as), in succession as rapidly as could be counted (*Macb.*, i, 3, 97)
talent, talon
talents, treasures, precious locks (*Compl.*, 204)
tall, lusty, valiant
tallow-catch, a tub for tallow (*1 Hen. IV*, ii, 4, 253)
tame, to repress, put down
tamed, *adj.*, gone stale, vapid (*T. and C.*, iv, 1, 62)
tang, *n.*, a sharp note (*Temp.*, ii, 2, 52); *v.*, to sound, ring; ring out
tanling, sun-tanned child (*Cymb.*, iv, 4, 29)
tardily, slowly
tardy, to hold in check
targe (target), a light shield, buckler
tarre, to set on, incite
tarriance, tarrying, waiting
Tartar, Tartarus, hell
task, to challenge, put to the test; call to account; tax
task (at), taken to task (*Lear*, i, 4, 366)
tasking, challenge
tassel-gentle, tercel-gentle, a male falcon
taste, *n.*, test; specimen; (in some), in some measure; *v.*, to try, test; taste (to), to be a taster for one (to guard against poison, *hence* taste to you all, die first) (*T. N. K.*, v, 4, 23)
tasteful, full of sweet taste
tawdry-lace, a kind of necktie
tax, *n.*, reproach, accusations; *v.*, to blame, reprove, reproach; (with), accuse of
taxation, demand, claim; satirical talk
tediosity, tediousness (*T. N. K.*, iii, 5, 2)
teem, to bring forth; bear children
teen, grief, sorrow
teeth (from his), grudgingly
tell, to count
temper, *n.*, temperament, disposition; *v.*, to mix, compound; mould, fashion; soften; dispose; bring to the proper state of mind for anything
temperality, *for* temper, i.e., physical condition (*2 Hen. IV*, ii, 4, 25)
temperance, climate; calmness, self-control; continence, chastity
temperate, chaste
tempered, *adj.*, disposed, in the right temper; (ill-), distempered
temporary meddler, one who meddles with worldly matters
tenable, held (*Haml.*, i, 2, 248)
tend, to attend, be ready; pay attention
tendance, service; attention; attentive visitors
tender, *n.*, *v.*, regard; *adj.*, dear
tender-hefted, stirred by tender feelings only (*Lear*, ii, 4, 174)
tenner, tenour, purport of a speech (*T. N. K.*, iii, 5, 123)
tent, *n.*, a roll of lint used in cleaning a wound or keeping it open; a probe; *v.*, to treat with a tent; to probe
tenure, purport, tenour
tercel, male falcon
Termagant, *n.*, a supposed god of the Saracens (of violent nature); *adj.*, furious, raging
terminations, the sharp points of her words (*M. Ado*, ii, 1, 257)
termless, fair beyond words (*Compl.*, 94)
terrene, terrestrial, earthly
tertian, a fever recurring every other day
tester, a sixpence
testern, to present with a sixpence
testimonied, *p.p.*, evidenced
testril, a sixpence
tetchy, irritable, touchy, fretful
tetter, to affect with a tetter or rash
than, then
thane, a Scottish title, earl
that, that which, what
that, so that; *for* if, since, etc.
thence, away, absent
theoric, theory
thereabout, at about that place (*Haml.*, ii, 2, 468)
thereabouts, something like that (*W. T.*, i, 2, 378)
thereafter, according (*2 Hen. IV*, iii, 2, 56)
thereto, in addition to that
thews, muscles and sinews
thick, hurriedly (*2 Hen. IV*, ii, 3, 24)
thicken, to grow dim
thick-eyed, dim-sighted
thick-pleached, *see* pleached
thick-skin, stupid fellow
thief, robber, highwayman
thievery, plunder, booty
think, to be melancholy, despond; seem
thirdborough, town constable
this, thus (*V. and A.*, 205)
this' (this), this is
thorough, through
thought, melancholy, despondency, sorrow
thoughten (be), consider (*Per.*, iv, 6, 115)
thought-executing, acting with the speed of thought (*Lear*, iii, 2, 4)
thoughtful, solicitous
thought-sick, sick at heart
thou's, thou shalt
thousand, thousandth
thrasonical, worthy of Thraso (the braggart soldier in Terence's *Eunuchus*)
three-farthings, an Elizabethan coin (thin, with an image of the Queen and the figure of a rose) (*K. John*, i, 1, 143)
three-man beetle, a heavy ramming implement worked by three men
three-pile, the heaviest velvet
three-piled, superlative
three-suited, having an allowance of three suits a year
threne, a funeral song, dirge
thrice-repured, thrice purified and refined
thrift, economy, frugality
thriftless, unprofitable, unavailing
thrifty, well-husbanded
throe, to agonize; (forth), give birth with throes
thronged, shrunk (*Per.*, ii, 1, 77)
through, *adj.*, thoroughgoing; *adv.*, thoroughly
throughly, thoroughly
throw, *n.*, the right distance (in bowling), the limit; (at this), at this cast of dice, this time; *v.*, to win at a throw of the dice

thrum, end of the warp
thrummed, ornamented with thrums or tufts
thunder-stone, thunderbolt
thwart, *adj.*, perverse; *v.*, to cross, traverse
'tice, to entice, lure
tickle, *adj.*, insecure; delicate, precarious; (of the sere), discharged at a touch (*see* sere); *v.*, (up), to finish up summarily
tickle-brain, dispenser of potent drink
ticklish, wanton
tick-tack, a kind of backgammon
tide, *n.*, time; a festival of the Church; course; *v.*, to betide
tidy, plump
tight, skilful
tightly, promptly; soundly
tile (to wash a), to labour in vain
tilly-vally (-fally), *interj.*, fiddlesticks
tilt, *see* a-tilt
tilth, tillage, agriculture; husbandry
time, the times, the age; the people of the time, the world
timeless, unseasonable, ill-timed; untimely
timely, early; in good season
timely-parted ghost, the body of one who had died at his appointed hour (a natural death) (*2 Hen. VI*, iii, 2, 161)
tinct, colour; the elixir that turns base metals to gold, the philosopher's stone; its transmuting potency
tincture, colour; blood-stained relics (*J. C.*, ii, 2, 89)
tire, *n.*, headdress; equipment, furnishings; *v.*, to attire
tire, to tear and feed ravenously; exercise one's self; glut
tire-valiant, a showy headdress
tiring house, dressing room (in a theatre)
tirrits, *for* terrors (*2 Hen. IV*, ii, 4, 219)
tisick, disease of the lungs
Titan, the sun god, the sun
tithe, *n.*, tenth part; *adj.*, tenth
tithe-pig, a pig due to the parson as a tithe
tithing, a district of a county
titler, claimant (*T. N. K.*, v, 3, 83)
tittles, very small things; poverty and obscurity (*L. L. L.*, iv, 1, 84)
to, in comparison with; according to; in addition to, besides
toaze (touse), to tear roughly, worry
tod, *n.*, twenty-eight pounds of wool; *v.*, to yield a tod
todpole, tadpole
tofore, before
toge, toga, gown
toged, wearing the toga, in the garb of peace
togither, together
token, a plague spot
tokened, marked with plague spots
tolerable, *for* intolerable (*M. Ado*, iii, 3, 37)
toll, to take toll; gather; (for), to pay toll and enter in the toll book at a fair in order to have the right to sell
tomboy, a strumpet
tongue, *n.*, voice, vote; *v.*, to speak; denounce
to-night, last night
top, *n.*, height; *v.*, to surpass, rise above, outdo; to poll, cut off the top; haul up
topless, supreme (*T. and C.*, i, 3, 152)
torcher, torchbearer (*All's W.*, ii, 1, 165)
tortive, twisted aside
touch, *n.*, test (by *or* as by the touchstone); the touchstone; a trait of countenance or of character; feeling; *v.*, to test, try
touse, *see* toaze
toward, promising, tractable, docile; forward, bold; at hand, coming, in preparation
towardly, ready to be influenced, docile
tower, to mount up, soar aloft
toy, *n.*, a trifle; an idle fancy, whim; (take), to take fright, be startled, shy (*T. N. K.*, v, 4, 66), *v.*, to dally amorously
trace, to follow, keep pace with; tread, walk along or through; move forward; carry out, perform
tract, visible track, trail, course
trade, resort; business, dealings; way, path
traded, *adj.*, practised, experienced
trade-fallen, bankrupt, ruined
traducement, slander, calumny
traffic, business
train, *n.*, allurement (*lit.*, line of bait); *v.*, to allure, entice
trammel up, to catch as in a trammel or net
Tranect, the Venetian ferry (*M. of V.*, iii, 4, 53)
transfix, remove, take away (*Sonn.*, 60)
translate, transform
transparent, bright
transport, to remove from this world to the next
transpose, to change, transform
trash, to hold back (a dog by a clog tied to the collar)
travail, *n.*, toil and trouble; *v.*, to toil
traverse, *v.*, to march; move from side to side, dodge; cross, fold; *adv.*, across
tray-trip, a game at dice
treacher, traitor
treasury, treasure
treatise, speech, discourse, story, tale
treaty, negotiation, conference; proposal; entreaty
treble-dated, living for three generations of men
trench, to turn aside by digging a trench
trenchant, cutting, keen-edged
trencher, a wooden plate
trencher friend (trencher knight), a parasite
trencherman, eater, feeder
Tribunal Plebs, *for* tribunus plebis (*T. A.*, iv, 3, 92)
trick, *n.*, knack; characteristic, one's way; touch; peculiarity; trifle; caprice; *v.*, to dress
tricking, *n.*, costumes
tricksy, sportive; fine, ornate
trifle, to make a trifle of, reduce to insignificance (*Macb.*, ii, 4, 4); waste
trigon (fiery), a triplicity, the three fiery signs of the Zodiac (Aries, Leo, and Sagittarius) in the form of an equilateral triangle
trill, to trickle
trim, *adj.*, fine; *adv.*, accurately; *v.*, to fit out (a ship); dress up
tripe-visaged, pale, sallow
triple, *adj.*, third
triple-turned, three times faithless
triplex, triple measure
tristful, sorrowful
triumph, splendid show or festival; trump, winning card (*with a pun*) (*A. and C.*, iv, 14, 20)
triumviry, triumvirate
troll-my-dames, a game like bagatelle
tropically, metaphorically
trot, old woman, hag
troth, truth; faith
trow, to believe, think; (I trow *or* trow *after a question*), pray, I wonder
Troyan, Trojan; fellow
truant, to play truant
truckle bed, trundle-bed
true, honest; trustworthy, faithful
true-love, a betrothed lover; sweetheart; (knot), a double bowknot
truepenny, honest fellow
truest mannered, most trustworthy in character
trumpet, trumpeter
truncheon, to cudgel
truncheoner, a man carrying a club
trundle-tail, a dog with a long draggly tail
trunk sleeve, a full puffed sleeve
try, *n.*, a test; (bring to try), bring (a ship) into the position of lying-to, as close to the wind as practicable
tub, sweating tub
tub-fast, the fast prescribed for a patient in the tub
tuck, rapier
tucket, a flourish or marching signal on the trumpet
tug, to contend in a hand-to-hand struggle
tuition, protection
tumble, perform a tumbler's feats
tun-dish, a kind of funnel
turband, turban
Turk (the), the Sultan; (turn), to become a Mohammedan, apostatize, prove utterly false, play the traitor
Turlygod, a name by which mad beggars called themselves (*Lear*, ii, 3, 20)
turn, to change; return; tune (*A. Y. L.*, ii, 5, 3)
Turnbull Street, Turnmill Street, a disreputable neighbourhood in London
turtle, turtledove
tush, tusk
twelf, twelfth (*T. N.*, ii, 3, 91)
twelve score, twelve-score yards
twiggen, covered with wickerwork
twilled, ridged (*Temp.*, iv, 1, 64)
twink, twinkling of an eye
twire, to peer, peep out (*Sonn.*, 28)
tyke, dog, cur
type, sign, mark, indication
tyrannically, boisterously
tyrannous, cruel, savage, fierce
tyranny, fury, rage
tyrant, usurper

umber, a brown pigment
umbered, coloured like umber
umbrage, shadow
unaccommodated, not furnished with artificial fittings, naked
unadvised, unintended; carelessly,

heedlessly; without due consideration, precipitate; inconsiderate
unadvisedly, inconsiderately
unaneled, not having received extreme unction
unapproved, unsupported by evidence
unapt, unfit; not prompt or quick; disinclined
unaptness, unreadiness, disinclination
unattainted, not infected by love; unprejudiced
unavoided, inevitable
unbaked, raw, unsophisticated
unbarbed, with bare (unarmed) head (*Cor.*, iii, 2, 99)
unbated, unblunted
unbent, smooth, unwrinkled (*Lucr.*, 1509)
unbid, uninvited, unwelcome, disconcerting (*3 Hen. VI*, v, 1, 18)
unbolted, unsifted, out-and-out (*Lear*, ii, 2, 71)
unbonneted, bareheaded (*Lear*, iii, 1, 14); cap in hand, with all due modesty, without boasting (*Oth.*, i, 2, 23)
unbookish, uninstructed
unbraced, unfastened, unbuttoned; with doublet open at the neck
unbraided wares, honest goods, not counterfeit or adulterated
unbreathed, unpractised
uncandy, to melt
uncape, off with your mantle, come out of your hiding-place (*M. W.*, iii, 3, 176)
uncase, to undress
uncharge, exonerate, acquit
uncharged, unassailed (*Tim.*, v, 4, 55)
unchary, unsparingly
unchecked, uncontradicted
unchild, to make childless
uncivil, uncivilized
unclew, to undo, ruin
unclog, to unburden
uncoined, not counterfeit, sound, genuine
uncomprehensive, beyond comprehension
unconfirmed, untrained, inexperienced
uncontrolled, unconquered; unsubdued; beyond control
uncouple, to let loose (hounds)
uncouth, unknown, strange; pathless, wild
uncrossed, uncancelled, with the account not crossed out as being settled (*Cymb.*, iii, 3, 26)
unction, salve, ointment
unctious, unctuous, oily, fat
uncurrent, improper, objectionable
undeeded, without having performed any action
under, under the sun, earthly; underground, of hell
underbear, to submit to, endure; trim on the lower edge
undercrest, to wear as an honour and justify (*Cor.*, i, 9, 71)
undergo, to be subjected to, endure; sustain; undertake
under-skinker, subordinate wine-server
undertake, to assume; take in charge; engage in combat with; accept a challenge; have to do with; vouch, warrant; (for), act or intercede in one's favour
undertaker, a contractor, one who takes charge; one who accepts a challenge or is ready to fight; champion
undervalued, inferior in value or reputation
underwrite, to confirm, as by signature (*T. and C.*, ii, 3, 137)
underwrought, undermined (*K. John*, ii, 1, 95)
undistinguished, extending beyond the limits of vision (*Lear*, iv, 6, 278)
undoubted, dauntless (*3 Hen. VI*, v, 7, 6)
undressed, rude, unrefined (*L. L. L.*, iv, 2, 17)
uneared, unploughed
uneath, hardly (*2 Hen. VI*, ii, 4, 8)
unequal, unjust
uneven, disturbing (*1 Hen. IV*, i, 1, 50)
unexperient, inexperienced (*Compl.*, 318)
unexpressive, inexpressible (*A. Y. L.*, iii, 2, 10)
unfair, to deprive of beauty (*Sonn.*, 5)
unfashionable, in misshapen wise (*Rich. III*, i, 1, 22)
unfolding, announcing the time to release the sheep from the sheepfold (*M. for M.*, iv, 2, 219)
unfool, to relieve of the imputation of folly (*M. W.*, iv, 2, 120)
unforced, self-evident (*Oth.*, ii, 1, 240)
unfurnish, to deprive
unfurnished, unprovided with a mate (*M. of V.*, iii, 2, 126)
ungalled, unhurt, without a scratch
ungenitured, impotent (*M. for M.*, iii, 2, 184)
ungird, to put off, lay aside (*T. N.*, iv, 1, 16)
ungracious, displeasing; graceless, wicked
unhaired, beardless (*K. John*, v, 2, 133)
unhandled, untrained, unbroken
unhandsome, inappropriate, unfitting; unfair
unhap'ly, unhappily, unfortunately (*Lucr.*, 8)
unhappily, with unpleasant accuracy; to one's disadvantage or discredit
unhappiness, evil nature; mischief (in speech or action); something amusing (*M. Ado*, ii, 1, 361)
unhappy, ill-omened; mischievous; sharp-tongued, satirical; sharp, ill-tempered
unhatched, not yet come to action; unhacked
unheart, to dishearten, discourage
unhopeful, unpromising
unhoused, unconfined by domesticity
unhouseled, not having received the Eucharist
unimproved, unused, not put to use
unintelligent of, not perceiving
union, a fine large pearl
unity, consistency
universal, constant, unrelieved, unvaried (*L. L. L.*, iv, 3, 305)
unjust, dishonest; false, faithless
unjustice, injustice
unkept, uncared-for
unkind, unnatural; childless
unlace, divest one's self of, cast off (*Oth.*, ii, 3, 194)
unlike, unlikely, improbable
unlimited, not observing the unities of time and place (*Haml.*, ii, 2, 419)
unlived, deprived of life (*Lucr.*, 1754)
unmanned, not trained (of a hawk), unruly
unnerved, weak in sinews, enfeebled (*Haml.*, ii, 2, 496)
unowed, having no recognized owner
unpack, to relieve
unpanged, suffering no pangs of grief
unparagoned, unmatched, matchless
unpaved, castrated
unpay, to undo, make good (*2 Hen. IV*, ii, 1, 130)
unpeaceable, incurably quarrelsome
unpinked, not furnished with scallops
unpitied, pitiless, unmerciful
unplausive, not expressing approbation, neglectful
unpolicied, lacking sagacity, senseless
unpossessing, having no right of inheritance
unpregnant, unready; (of), without due sense of
unprevailing, unavailing
unprizable, priceless, inestimable; contemptible
unprized, unvalued (*Lear*, i, 1, 262)
unprofited, profitless
unproper, not exclusively one's own
unproportioned, unsymmetrical, out of accord with a consistent plan of conduct
unprovide, to render irresolute
unqualitied, deprived of one's natural qualities
unquestionable, disinclined to conversation
unraised, uninspired
unraked, not raked together and covered with ashes
unready, not dressed
unrecalling, past recall (*Lucr.*, 993)
unreclaimed, untamed, undisciplined
unreconciliable, irrevocably at odds (*A. and C.*, v, 1, 47)
unrecuring, incurable
unresisted, irresistible
unrespected, not noticed, unheeded, uncared-for
unrespective, unthinking; indiscriminate
unreverent *and* unreverend, used indiscriminately in both senses
unrolled, struck off the official register
unrough, beardless
unsatisfied, uninformed
unscanned, heedless
unseam, to rip up
unseasoned, unripe, immature
unseen, invisible
unseminared, emasculated
unshape, to derange, disorder
unshaped, incoherent
unshunned, inevitable
unsisting, shaken, made to vibrate (*M. for M.*, iv, 2, 92)
unskilful, undiscriminating, uncritical
unsorted, unfit
unsought, unsearched (*C. of E.*, i, 1, 135)
unsquared, shapeless, uncouth (*T. and C.*, i, 3, 159)
unstanched, unquenchable; leaky
unstate, to deprive of rank and fortune; resign one's superiority in
untempering, not ingratiating
untented, too deep for the probe
unthrift, unthrifty, prodigal
unthrifty, prodigal; heedless; misbehaving; unfortunate

untoward, perverse, unmannerly
untowardly, to ill fortune, disastrously (*M. Ado*, iii, 2, 134)
untraded, unhackneyed, novel
untried, untouched in presentation (*W. T.*, iv, 1, 6)
untrimmed, divested of bridal array (*K. John*, iii, 1, 209)
untrussing, *n.*, undoing one's breeches
untucked, dishevelled (*Compl.*, 31)
unvalued, of ordinary rank; priceless
unwappered, not worn out (*T. N. K.*, v, 4, 10)
unwares, without knowing what one does
unwarily, when off one's guard
unwit, to deprive of one's wits, drive mad
unworthy, undeserved, unmerited
unyoke, call it a day's work
up, in the field, in arms; in confinement; in power; (and down), exactly, out and out
upcast, a cast in bowling (*Cymb.*, ii, 1, 2)
upon (on), because of, as a result of
uprighteously, uprightly, righteously (*M. for M.*, iii, 1, 206)
upshoot, the final shot
upspring, a wild kind of dance
upswarm, to raise in large numbers
up-till, up against
upward, *n.*, the top (*Lear*, v, 3, 136)
urchin, hedgehog; imp in hedgehog's shape
urchin-shows, visions of imps
urchin-snouted, with a snout like an urchin imp
urge, to mention, speak of; allege; propose
urn, a grave
usance, interest on money
use, *n.*, interest; advantage; profit; usufruct, possession for one's use; habit, custom; (*pl.*), ways, practices; *v.*, to make a practice of, practise; (one's self), conduct one's self, behave
usurer, one who lends money at interest
usuring, usurious
usurp, to exercise power without right; use unrighteously or without right or by imitation; be a usurper
usury, the taking of interest
utis, noisy merry-making, high jinks
utter, to sell, bring to market
utterance (at), at all hazards; (to the), in a duel to the death (*Macb.*, iii, 1, 72)

vacancy, leisure time; intermission
vade, to fade
vagrom, *for* vagrant (*M. Ado.*, iii, 3, 26)
vail, *n.*, setting; *v.*, to lower, let fall, bow; do homage
vails, gratuities
vain, empty-headed; deceitful (*C. of E.*, iii, 2, 27)
vainly, mistakenly
valance, drapery, especially on a bed canopy
valanced, draped (with a beard)
validity, strength; value
valued, furnished with notes of the several qualities (*Macb.*, iii, 1, 95)
vanity, worthlessness; frivolity in character or conduct, triviality; foolishness; a matter of no importance; a frivolous person
vantage, *n.*, advantage, favourable situation or opportunity; profit; superiority, overplus; (at), (of), advantageous, convenient; from an advantageous position; (to the), to boot, in addition
vantbrace, defensive armour for the forearm
vara, very (*L. L. L.*, v, 2, 487)
varlet (varlot), a knight's attendant; fellow, rascal, knave
varletto, varlet, fellow (*M. W.*, iv, 5, 66)
varlotry, rabble (*A. and C.*, v, 2, 56)
vassal, *n.*, fellow, wretch; *adj.*, low, servile
vassalage, vassals, subjects (collectively)
vast, an immense space, an expanse; waste, abysmal region
vastidity, vastitude (*M. for M.*, iii, 1, 69)
vastly, in a desolate condition
vaultages, vaulted or cavernous places
vaulty, arched like a vault; cavernous
vaunt, outset, beginning (*T. and C.*, Prol., 27)
vaunt-courier, forerunner, precursor
vaward, vanguard; early part
vegetives, plants (*Per.*, iii, 2, 36)
veins (bloody), bloody-minded men (*Per.*, i, 4, 94)
velure, velvet
velvet guards, velvet trimmings
veney (venew), a hit (in fencing or in a witty contest); a bout
vengeance, harm; God's vengeance (as a curse); *adj.*, cursed, confounded; *adv.*, cursedly (*Cor.*, ii, 2, 5)
venom, venomous
vent, a discharge (of blood); utterance, talk; energy, energetic action (*Cor.*, iv, 5, 238)
ventages, air holes (*Haml.*, iii, 2, 373)
ventricle, a cavity in the brain
Ver, the Spring
verbal, oral; outspoken, blunt (*Cymb.*, ii, 3, 111)
verge, circle, circlet
verify, to speak the truth in commendation of; affirm, maintain
verity, fidelity
Veronesa, a Veronese ship (*Oth.*, ii, 1, 26)
versal, universal (*R. and J.*, ii, 4, 218)
via, *interj.*, forward! away! come!
vice, a fault; a comic character (personifying iniquity in general or some fault) in the moral plays (moralities)
vice, to force (as by vice, screw, or winch)
vicious, faulty, erroneous
victoress, victress
vie, to wager, stake (at card play); make play with; compete with one in regard to (something)
viewless, invisible
vigil, the eve of (i.e., preceding) a holy day or festival
vigitant, *for* vigilant (*M. Ado*, iii, 3, 100)
vile, low in rank; poor, mean; worthless, contemptible
villager, countryman, rustic (*T. N. K.*, iii, 5, 104)
villain, bondman; fellow; rascal (as a term of endearment)
villiago, base peasant (*2 Hen. VI*, iv, 8, 48)
vindicative, vindictive, revengeful
viol-de-gamboys, a viol held between the legs
violent, to be violent, rage (*T. and C.*, iv, 4, 4)
virgin, to be a virgin
virginal, *n.*, an instrument like a spinet; *v.*, to tap the fingers (as upon the keys of a virginal)
virtue, excellence of any kind; an accomplishment; power; essence, essential quality
virtuous, medically powerful
visit, to attack, assail; punish (by divine judgment)
visitate, to visit
visitation, a visit
visited, attacked by the plague; afflicted with disease
visitings of nature, natural feelings or impulses (*Macb.*, i, 5, 46)
visitor, an ecclesiastical inspector or examiner; a spiritual adviser (*Temp.*, ii, 1, 11)
visor, a mask; a masked person; visage
vizaments, *for* advisements, i.e., thoughtful consideration (*M. W.*, i, 1, 39)
vizard, a mask
vizarded, masked
voice, *n.*, vote, suffrage, expressed choice or approval; *v.*, to elect by oral voting; acclaim
void, to leave, abandon
'void, to avoid, shun
voiding lobby, anteroom, waiting room
Volquessen, a district in France, formerly the country of the Velocasses (a Gallic tribe)
Volsce, Volscian
voluble, fickle, changeable
voluntary, a volunteer
voucher, the process of summoning one into court to vouch for the title to property
vouchsafe, to deign to receive (*J. C.*, ii, 1, 313)
vulgar, *adj.*, common, ordinary; public; *n.*, the common people; the vernacular
vulgarly, publicly

waft, to beckon; turn; transport by sea
waftage, passage by water, transportation
wafture, a waving motion
wag, *n.*, rogue; *v.*, to stir; be gone
wage, to wager; risk; carry on; pay wages to; (with), balance, be in proportion with
waggish, sportive, roguish
wagon, chariot, carriage, coach
wagoner, charioteer
wailful, doleful, lamenting
wain, wagon
waist, a waistband, girdle, belt
wait, to watch; be in attendance; (on, upon), attend; be on the watch for; be subservient to, tend
wake, *n.*, a festival on the vigil (eve) of a holiday; *v.*, to be awake; to sit up late; to revel at night
wall-eyed, with staring light-coloured eyes
Wallon, the borderland between France and the Netherlands
Walloon, a native of Wallon

waned, diminished; past its prime (*A. and C.*, ii, 1, 21)
wanion (with a), with a vengeance (*Per.*, ii, 1, 17)
wanton, *n.*, a spoiled child; cockered creature; a sportive person, playful creature; *adj.*, unrestrained, untamed; self-willed; lawless; perverse; sportive, playful; fanciful; effeminate; luxurious, self-indulgent; *v.*, to play, sport; dally
wantonly, sportively, in lively fashion
wantonness, sportiveness; self-indulgence, luxury; whimsicality, affectation
wappened, faded and worn out (*Tim.*, iv, 3, 38)
ward, *n.*, guard; posture of defence; cell; *pl.*, the projections in a lock, locks; *v.*, to guard, protect
warden, a kind of pear
warder, a kind of truncheon
wardrop, wardrobe
warn, to notify; summon officially or formally; defy, meet in combat (*J. C.*, v, 1, 5)
warp, to distort; deviate; change
warped, distorted; perverse
warrant, to guard, protect; assure; make good, stand to
warranted need (upon a), if ever the occasion justifies such a requirement or demand (*M. for M.*, iii, 2, 151)
warrantise, guaranty; assurance; one who serves as a surety
warrener, the keeper of a rabbit warren
waste, *n.*, ruin, destruction
Wat, Walter (nickname for the hare)
watch, *n.*, state of being awake; wakeful condition, insomnia; fixed interval; timepiece; circle of figures on a dial; *v.*, to tame by depriving of sleep
watcher, one who is awake
water-gall, a kind of feeble rainbow, supposed to foretell rain
water-rug, a kind of shaggy water-dog
waters (for all), fit to play any part, ready for anything (*T. N.*, iv, 2, 68)
waterwork (in), painted in water colours
wawl, to howl, squall
wax (a man of), as finely moulded as a wax figure
waxen, *v.*, increase
waxen, *adj.*, engraved in wax, and thus not permanent (*Hen. V*, i, 2, 233)
way, persuasion, faith (*Hen. VIII*, v, 1, 28)
waylay, to dog the steps of
weal, the commonwealth, the body politic
wealsman, statesman (*Cor.*, ii, 1, 59)
wealth, welfare, prosperity
wear, *n.*, fashion, style; *v.*, to be worn, be in fashion; become adapted; wear out, wear or waste away
weather, the windward
web and pin, cataract (of the eye)
weed, garment, attire
weeding, the weeds (*L. L. L.*, i, 1, 96)
week (in by the), thoroughly caught (*L. L. L.*, v, 2, 61)
ween, to expect
weet, to wit, know
weigh out, to weigh fully and accurately in order to repay in full (*Hen. VIII*, iii, 1, 88)
Weird Sisters, the Fatal Sisters, the Fates
welkin, the sky; blue as the sky
well, in a blessed state (euphemism for 'dead')
well-a-near, wellaway (*Per.*, iii, Prol., 51)
well-breathed, sound of wind (*Ven.*, 678)
well desired, made heartily welcome (*Oth.*, ii, 1, 206)
well-found, thoroughly versed; approved, sound
well-governed, well-behaved
well-graced, *adj.*, very popular, favourite
well-liking, plump, fat (*L. L. L.*, v, 2, 268)
well-respected, well-considered (*1 Hen. IV*, iv, 3, 10)
well said, well done
well seen, skilful, expert
Welsh hook, a weapon with a hooked cutting point and blade, like a billhook
wench-like, womanish
weraday, well-a-day, alas
wesand, windpipe, gullet
what, whatsoever
what . . . for, what kind of
wheel, *n.*, spinning wheel
wheeling, *adj.*, wandering, having no settled abode
Wheeson, Whitsun, Whitsunday
whelk, a knob, swelling, pustule
whelked, knobbed, knobby (*Lear*, iv, 6, 71)
when, an exclamation of impatience, much like 'make haste!' 'quick!'
when as, when
whe'r, whether
where, whereas; *n.*, a place elsewhere
whereagainst, against which
where as, where
wherein, in what attire
whereon, because of which
whereout, out of which
wherewithal, by means of which
whether, which of the two
whiffler, an officer who goes ahead to clear the way
while, until
whilere, a little while ago
whiles, while; until
whinid'st, very mouldy (*T. and C.*, ii, 1, 15)
whipping cheer (have), to be regaled with whipping (*2 Hen. IV*, v, 4, 5)
whipster, youngster (*Oth.*, v, 2, 244)
whissing, wheezing
whist, silent, quiet
white, the white circle at the centre of the target round the pin or bull's-eye; a fair pet or darling (*Oth.*, ii, 1, 134)
whitely, pale-faced (*L. L. L.*, iii, 1, 198)
whiting time, bleaching time (*M. W.*, iii, 3, 140)
whitster, bleacher (*M. W.*, iii, 3, 14)
whittle, a large knife
whole, sound, in good health, cured
whoobub, hubbub
whoreson, bastard; fellow, rascal
wide, far from the mark; much mistaken; astray; wildly; (of), far from
widow, *v.*, to endow with a widow's right to property; to survive as a widow
widowhood, widow's right to property (*T. of S.*, ii, 1, 125)
wight, person
wild, precipitate, headlong; without plan or forethought, at random
Wild, *n.*, the Weald (a tract of country, formerly a forest) in Kent
wilderness, wild growth (*M. for M.*, iii, 1, 142)
wild mare (ride the), to play at seesaw
wilful, willing; on purpose
wilful-blame, blameworthy for wilfulness (*1 Hen. IV*, iii, 1, 177)
will, sexual desire
wimpled, blindfolded (*L. L. L.*, iii, 1, 181)
Winchester goose, syphilitic person
wind, to blow (on a horn); to scent
wind, to insinuate, work one's way by subtlety
windgalls, soft tumours above the fetlock
windlasses, roundabout methods
window bars, openwork in a dress
windowed, full of great holes
windy, windward
wing-led, swept on, as with strong pinions (*Cymb.*, ii, 4, 24)
wink, *v.*, to shut the eye; *n.*, eye-shut, death
winter-ground, to protect from the cold by covering (*Cymb.*, iv, 2, 229)
wipe, a welt, wale, scar from the lash (*Lucr.*, 537)
wish, to recommend for service (*T. S.*, i, 1, 113)
wishtly, wistfully, eagerly (*Rich. II*, v, 4, 7)
wist, knew
wistly, intently
wit, *n.*, mind, intellect; good sense; cleverness; *v.*, to know
witch, a sorcerer or sorceress, wizard or witch
with, by (*of the agent*); (to be), to attend to, settle one's case, see to one; (himself), in his right mind (*T. A.*, i, 1, 368)
withal, with this, with it; at the same time; with (*at the end of a sentence*); (do), help it (*M. of V.*, iii, 4, 72)
within him (get), to close with him so that he cannot use his sword (*C. of E.*, v, 1, 34)
Withold (Saint), Saint Vitalis (*Lear*, iii, 4, 125)
without, beyond the limit of; unless
without-door, external
witness (with a), with a vengeance, and no mistake (*T. of S.*, v, 1, 122)
wittol, a contented cuckold
witty, clever, keen-witted; artful
wive's, wife's
woe, *adj.*, sorry
wolt, wilt
wolvish, wolfish; like a wolf in sheep's clothing (*Cor.*, ii, 3, 122)
woman, to make one womanish
womaned, accompanied by a woman
woman-queller, woman-killer
woman-tired, torn by a woman as by a bird of prey, henpecked
womb, *n.*, belly; *v.*, to enclose
womby, cavernous
wonder, to wonder at
wondered, having wonderful (magical) powers
wonder-wounded, amazed, astounded
wood, mad, insane
woodbine, honeysuckle; bindweed

woollen, with a woollen bag (*M. of V.*, iv, 1, 56); (in the), between woollen blankets, without sheets (*M. Ado*, ii, 1, 33)
woolward, with woollen next the skin, as a penance (*L. L. L.*, v, 2, 717)
woosel, ousel, blackbird
woo't, (wo't), wolt, wilt thou
word, *n.*, watchword, motto, the right word; order, command; the word of God, the Scripture; *v.*, to utter; express or represent in words; address persuasively, cajole
word (to be at a), to speak no more than one means, briefly and to the point
work, a fortification
working, any operation of the mind or emotions
workyday, everyday, ordinary
world, a wonder, a marvel, a great sight; (to go to the), to abandon the celibate life, marry; (a woman of the), a married woman
worm, serpent; feeble creature
worship, *n.*, reverence, honour; *v.*, to honour
wort, a vegetable; unfermented beer
worth, wealth; (to have one's worth of), to have one's way against or in spite of (*Cor.*, iii, 3, 26)
worth, befall
worthy, *adj.*, honourable; *v.*, to make one highly esteemed
wot, know
wo't (woo't), wolt, wilt
woundless, invulnerable
wrack, *n.*, *v.*, wreck
wrackful, destructive, ruinous (*Sonn.*, 65)
wrangler, opponent
wrastle, wrestle
wrath, wroth, angry (*M. N. D.*, ii, 1, 20)
wreak, *n.*, vengeance, revenge; *v.*, to avenge, revenge
wreakful, avenging, revengeful
wrest, a tuning key, a person indispensable for the regulation of affairs (*T. and C.*, iii, 3, 23)
wretch, a term of endearment (*Oth.*, iii, 3, 90)
wretched, abominable
wrinch, rinse (*T. N. K.*, i, 1, 156)
wring, to writhe, suffer extremely
wringing, torturing pain
writ, Holy Writ, Scripture; a writing; (law of), the classical rules, the unities (*Haml.*, ii, 2, 421)
write, to subscribe, entitle, use the style of; certify (*All's W.*, iii, 5, 69)
writhled, wizened, shrivelled
wroth, discomfiture (*M. of V.*, ii, 9, 78)
wrying, *n.*, leaving the straight path, going astray

yare, ready, prompt, quick
yarely, actively, nimbly
yaw, to follow a zigzag course. be unsteady
yclad, *p.p.*, clad, clothed
ycliped, *p.p.*, named, called
Yead, Ed, Edward (*M. W.*, i, 1, 160)
yea-forsooth, *adj.*, obsequious and hypocritical
yearn (ern), to grieve
yeast, foam
Yedward, Edward
yellowing, yelping, baying (*T. A.*, ii, 3, 20)
yellowness, jealousy (*M. W.*, i, 3, 111)
yellows, jaundice in horses
yeoman, a bailiff's man
yerk, to jerk, kick; give a quick thrust
yesty, foaming; frothy
yield, to report; reward (*A. and C.*, iv, 2, 33)
yielded, born
yokes, branching horns (*M. W.*, v, 5, 111)
youngling, a youth, youngster
youngly, in youth
younker, youngster; greenhorn
yravish, to ravish, delight (*Per.*, iii, Prol., 35)
yslacked, *p.p.*, quieted, relaxed (*Per.*, iii, Prol., 1)

zany, a clown's subordinate jester; a buffoon, a foolish fellow
zeal, devotion
zealous, devout
zed, the letter *z*
zone, the sphere of the sun
Zounds, *see* 'Swounds

PQRSTUV 069
PRINTED IN THE UNITED STATES OF AMERICA